Baseball America

2023 ALMANAC

BASEBALL AMERICA INC. · DURHAM, N.C.

Baseball America

ESTABLISHED 1981

P.O. BOX 12877, DURHAM, NC 27709 • PHONE (800) 845-2726

BASEBALL AMERICA (ISSN 0745-5372/USPS 591-210) December 2022, Volume 42, Issue 12 is published monthly, 12 issues per year, by Baseball America Enterprises, LLC, 4319 South Alston Ave, Suite 103, Durham, NC 27713. Subscription rate is $99.99 for one year; Canada $112.99 (U.S. funds); all other foreign $125.99 per year (U.S. funds). Periodicals postage paid at Durham, NC, & additional mailing offices. Occasionally our subscriber list is made available to reputable firms offering goods and services we believe would be of interest to our readers. If you prefer to be excluded, please send your current address label and a note requesting to be excluded from these promotions to Baseball America Enterprises, LLC, 4319 South Alston Ave, Suite 103, Durham, NC 27713, Attn: Privacy Coordinator. POSTMASTER: Send all UAA to CFS (See DMM 707.4.12.5); NON-POSTAL & MILITARY FACILITIES: send address corrections to Baseball America, P.O. Box 420235, Palm Coast, FL 32142-0235. CANADA POST: Return undeliverable Canadian addresses to IMEX Global Solutions, P.O. Box 25542, London, ON N6C 6B2. Please contact 1-800-381-1288 to start carrying Baseball America in your store.

Baseball America
2023 ALMANAC

Editors
J.J. Cooper, Chris Hilburn-Trenkle

Contributing Editors
Ben Badler, Teddy Cahill, Carlos Collazo, Matt Eddy, Joe Healy, Josh Norris, Geoff Pontes

Database and Application Development
Brent Lewis

Design & Production
Seth Mates, Neville Harvey

Cover Photo
MAIN PHOTO: Aaron Judge.
PHOTO BY: Jim McIsaac/Getty Images

For additional copies, visit our Website at BaseballAmerica.com or call 1-800-845-2726 to order.

US $22.95 / CAN $30.95, plus shipping and handling per order. Expedited shipping available.

Distributed by Simon & Schuster.
ISBN-13: 979-8-9869573-0-2

Statistics provided by Major League Baseball Advanced Media and Compiled by Baseball America.

EDITOR'S NOTE: Major league statistics are based on final, unofficial 2022 averages.

» The organization statistics, which begin on page 43, include all players who participated in at least one game during the 2022 season.

» Pitchers' batting statistics are not included, nor are the pitching statistics of field players who pitched in less than two games.

» For players who played with more than one team in the same league, the player's cumulative statistics appear on the line immediately after the player's statistics with each team.

TABLE OF CONTENTS

MAJOR LEAGUES 6

ORGANIZATION STATISTICS 42

MINOR LEAGUES 372

INDEPENDENT LEAGUES 419

INTERNATIONAL 437

COLLEGE 448

HIGH SCHOOL 505

DRAFT 512

APPENDIX 525

MAJOR LEAGUES

Tough Start, Solid Finish

THEARON W. HENDERSON/GETTY IMAGES

Astros closer Ryan Pressly recorded the final out of World Series Game 6 versus the Phillies.

BY KYLE GLASER

After two straight seasons affected by the coronavirus pandemic, Major League Baseball hoped for a return to normal in 2022.

Instead, normalcy was delayed once again. This time, the culprit was an old-fashioned labor dispute.

The owners locked out the players for 99 days following the expiration of the Collective Bargaining Agreement on Dec. 2, 2021, baseball's first work stoppage since the 1994-95 player strike.

Tensions between players and owners had been simmering for nearly a decade over an array of issues, including how little players are paid early in their careers and the proliferation of tanking throughout the sport. Those issues were only exacerbated by the financial difficulties brought about by the pandemic, including the lost revenues from two years of restrictions that either banned or limited fans from attending games.

The ramifications from the lockout were instant as soon as the deal expired. Transactions for all 40-man players were frozen, meaning the hot stove season was extinguished with trades, free-agent signings and other roster moves expressly forbidden. The Winter Meetings in Orlando, Fla., were canceled and the Major League Rule 5 draft was postponed (and eventually canceled). Players on 40-man rosters were barred from using team facilities or communicating with team personnel in any way, including trainers and medical staff.

In a move that further inflamed tensions, the league scrubbed player images from the league's website and removed all references to 40-man roster players from league-owned platforms, including MLB Network. The replacement of players' faces with silhouettes became a rallying point for the MLB Players Association, who saw it as a symbol of how teams had increasingly come to view players as disposable and replaceable with the rise of analytics.

In anticipation of the lockout, and knowing any roster moves would be prohibited once it began, teams engaged in a free-agent signing frenzy with little precedent. Teams committed more than \$1.9 billion to players before the lockout started, including a single-day record of \$1.4 billion on Dec. 1—the final day before the CBA expired. The Rangers agreed to deals worth \$500 million for shortstop Corey Seager (10 years, \$325 million) and second baseman Marcus Semien (seven years, $175 million).

The Mets signed righthander Max Scherzer for three years and $130 million, a new record for highest average annual salary ($43.3 million). That came after they'd already signed outfielder Starling Marte, third baseman Eduardo Escobar and outfielder Mark Canha to deals worth a combined $124.5 million. The Tigers signed shortstop Javier Baez (six years, $140 million) and lefthander Eduardo Rodriguez (five years, $77 million) in November to try and jump the market.

The Blue Jays signed righthander Kevin Gausman for five years and $110 million and the Mariners promptly signed reigning American League Cy Young Award winner Robbie Ray away from Toronto for five years and $115 million.

The free flow of cash did little to generate any lasting goodwill, however. Once the lockout began, the two sides dug in for a battle that lasted more than three months, and led to spring training being shortened and the start of the 2022 season being delayed.

"THE BEST MECHANISM"

As soon as midnight struck on Dec. 2 and the lockout officially began, Commissioner Rob Manfred released a letter addressed to fans.

"Simply put, we believe that an offseason lockout is the best mechanism to protect the 2022 season," Manfred wrote. "We hope that the lockout will jumpstart the negotiations and get us to an agreement that will allow the season to start on time. This defensive lockout was necessary because the players' association's vision for Major League Baseball would threaten the ability of most teams to be competitive. "

As it played out, the lockout neither allowed the 2022 season to start on time nor enhanced the competitiveness of teams.

For more than three months, the league and players' union gained little traction as they exchanged proposals in search of a deal. The union's primary goals were to get players paid more money earlier in their careers and to end anti-competitive tanking practices that had permeated the sport. The league's main goals were to expand the postseason and keep the game's economic model in place as much as possible—gross league revenues rose more than 30% over the life of the previous CBA while total payrolls declined 5% and the median player salary fell 30%, contributing to a financial windfall for owners.

Slowly but surely, the sides moved closer. The union dropped its initial demands for players to be eligible for arbitration after two years and free agency after five. The league agreed to raise minimum salaries and establish a bonus pool for pre-arbitration eligible players. The sides also agreed to institute a draft lottery, make the DH universal and eliminate draft pick compensation for free agents.

But after nine days of meetings at Roger Dean Chevrolet Stadium in Jupiter, Fla.—which featured the spectacle of each side walking across the parking lot to speak to the other side—no agreement was reached by March 1, the deadline set by MLB to reach a deal. The sides broke off negotiations and returned home. With no agreement, Manfred announced the first six games of the season would be canceled, the first loss of games since the 1994-95 strike.

"I had hoped against hope that I would not have to have this particular press conference in which I am going to cancel some regular-season games," Manfred wrote in a second statement addressed to

ALL-ROOKIE TEAM 2022

Pos	Player, Team	Age	AB	AVG	OBP	SLG	2B	HR	RBI	SB	Rundown
C	Adley Rutschman, Orioles	24	398	.254	.362	.445	35	13	42	9	Facing massive expectations, Rutschman met all of them
1B	Jose Miranda, Twins	24	444	.268	.325	.426	25	19	64	1	Provided a needed anchor in Twins lineup
2B	Brendan Donovan, Cardinals	25	391	.281	.394	.379	21	5	45	2	The Cardinals keep producing well-rounded infielders
3B	Bobby Witt Jr., Royals	22	591	.254	.294	.428	31	20	80	30	Showed power, speed and defense in Royals' debut
SS	Jeremy Peña, Astros	24	521	.253	.289	.426	20	22	63	11	Glove and power were steadying factors for Astros
OF	Michael Harris II, Braves	21	414	.297	.339	.514	27	19	64	20	Harris' defense in center field is as good as his bat
OF	Steven Kwan, Guardians	24	563	.298	.373	.400	25	6	52	19	Immediately became one of the tougher outs in the AL
OF	Julio Rodriguez, Mariners	21	511	.284	.345	.509	25	28	75	25	Rookie of the Year and face of the franchise went 25-25
DH	Seiya Suzuki, Cubs	27	397	.262	.336	.433	22	14	46	9	Looked comfortable while jump from NPB

Pos	Pitcher, Team	Age	W	L	SV	ERA	IP	BB	SO	Rundown
SP	Reid Detmers, Angels	22	7	6	0	3.77	129	46	122	Threw a no-hitter in just his 11th MLB start
SP	George Kirby, Mariners	24	8	5	0	3.39	130	22	133	Earned a spot in Mariners' postseason rotation
SP	Nick Lodolo, Reds	24	4	7	0	3.66	103	39	131	Lodolo made it easy to forget that he's a rookie
SP	Joe Ryan, Twins	26	13	8	0	3.55	147	47	151	His see-it-but-can't-hit-it fastball played in the majors
SP	Spencer Strider, Braves	23	11	5	0	2.67	132	45	202	Strider's 100 mph fastball may be his second-best pitch
RP	Felix Bautista, Orioles	27	4	4	30	2.19	66	23	88	Bautista stepped into Baltimore's closer role and thrived

JULIO AGUILAR/GETTY IMAGES

Commissioner Rob Manfred added a week to the schedule to allow for 162 games.

fans. "We worked hard to avoid an outcome that's bad for our fans, bad for our players and bad for our clubs."

The cancellation of games marked a low point for baseball, especially following the ugly disputes leading up to the shortened 2020 season and a 2021 season in which attendance was sharply limited during the early months. Given the opportunity for its first "normal" season in three years, MLB appeared to have struck out.

It was a scenario that would have been disastrous for the game. Luckily, both sides realized it before it was too late.

A WHOLE NEW BALLGAME

Spurred by the cancellation of games, and the resulting fan backlash, the two sides feverishly began working to strike a deal. Chief union negotiator Bruce Meyer and deputy commissioner Dan Halem met for a one-on-one meeting two days after negotiations were broken off in Jupiter.

The league put forth another proposal that moved closer to the players' stated desires. Three more days of exhausting negotiations continued.

Finally, on March 10, nine days after Manfred announced the cancellation of games, the players' executive subcommittee voted 26-12 to accept the league's latest proposal. Owners ratified the deal later that night, officially ending the lockout.

"Our union endured the second-longest work stoppage in its history to achieve significant progress in key areas that will improve not just current players' rights and benefits, but those of generations to come," MLBPA executive president Tony Clark said in a statement. "Players remain engaged and unified from beginning to end, and in the process re-energized in our fraternity."

MLB rescheduled the canceled games to ensure a full, 162-game season. Spring training was shortened from six to three weeks and Opening Day was pushed back from March 30 to April 7.

But the schedule changes for the 2022 season paled in comparison to the enormity of the financial and structural changes in the new CBA. With the deal, the league and players' union fundamentally altered how the league operated.

The changes touched on nearly every aspect of the game:

■ The postseason was expanded from 10 to 12 teams, with the top two teams in each league receiving a bye and the remaining four teams in each league playing in a new, best-of-three Wild Card Series to open the playoffs.

■ The DH was made universal, ending 48 years of the American and National leagues playing under different rules (except for the shortened 2020 season).

■ A draft lottery was implemented beginning with the 2023 draft, with the top six picks to be determined via lottery in an effort to discourage tanking. The 18 teams who missed the postseason would all be eligible for the lottery, with their odds of winning assigned in reverse order of winning percentage.

■ The minimum salary increased from $570,500 to $700,000, with guaranteed increases each year through the life of the CBA. Additionally, a $50 million bonus pool was created for pre-arbitration eligible players who reached certain award or statistical benchmarks, including in MVP and Rookie of the Year voting, guaranteeing higher pay for players earlier in their careers.

■ Extra draft picks, known as Prospect Promotion Incentive (PPI) selections, were made available to clubs that placed top prospects on Opening Day rosters, a mechanism designed to discourage service-time manipulation.

■ The competitive balance tax threshold was raised from $210 million to $230 million, with guaranteed increases each year through the life of the CBA.

■ Finally, the draft was formally cut from 40 to 20 rounds, though the draft had already been shortened each of the previous two seasons due to

PLAYER OF THE YEAR

Judge Homers His Way Into History

BY KYLE GLASER

Throughout the summer and fall of 1998, Aaron Boone had a front-row seat to history being made.

Boone was a rookie third baseman on the Reds that season. He was often on the opposing side as Mark McGwire and Sammy Sosa chased Roger Maris' record of 61 home runs in a season.

Boone started at third base the day McGwire hit home run No. 60 against the Reds. Boone was at the hot corner when Sosa hit Nos. 52 and 55 against Cincinnati.

Boone never forgot that season, and never dreamed he'd be so close to something like it again.

Twenty-four years later, as the Yankees manager watched Aaron Judge every day, he was.

"It's been remarkable," Boone said during a late-season series in Anaheim. "I was a young player in '98 playing in the National League Central when Sammy and McGwire were doing their thing down the stretch . . . I got to see that kind of a circus and the excitement that went with that, how big that was at the time for baseball.

"I think what Aaron's doing is certainly in line with that."

Judge hit 62 home runs this season, breaking Maris' American League record. He finished just shy of winning the Triple Crown and led the majors in runs, home runs, on-base percentage, slugging percentage, OPS, extra-base hits and total bases, all while taking over as the Yankees' everyday center fielder. He did it all while propping up a Yankees team that slumped badly down the stretch and carried them to the American League East title.

ELSA/GETTY IMAGES

Aaron Judge hit 16 more home runs than anyone else in the major leagues.

For his historic season, Judge is the 2022 Baseball America Major League Player of the Year.

"For me this goes back to the team we got here," Judge said. "We got a good group of guys in here who continue to show up every single day putting the work in. I'm just trying to do my part and be a part of this team and do anything I need to do to put ourselves in a good position going into the postseason."

Judge's season was remarkable in many ways. He became the first player to hit 60 home runs in a season since Sosa and Barry Bonds did it in 2001.

Judge hit 16 more home runs than Phillies outfielder Kyle Schwarber's second-best 46 else in MLB—the largest gap between the home run leader and runner-up since Jimmie Foxx in 1932.

He hit 51 home runs before September even began, in a season where Opening Day was delayed one week by a lockout, no less.

And when his team needed it most, he delivered again and again. ■

PREVIOUS POY WINNERS

2012: Mike Trout, OF, Angels
2013: Mike Trout, OF, Angels
2014: Clayton Kershaw, LHP, Dodgers
2015: Bryce Harper, OF, Nationals
2016: Mike Trout, OF, Angels
2017: Jose Altuve, 2B, Astros
2018: Mike Trout, OF, Angels
2019: Justin Verlander, RHP, Astros
2020: Freddie Freeman, 1B, Braves
2021: Shohei Ohtani, DH/RHP, Angels

Full list: search "Baseball America awards"

the coronavirus pandemic.

It was an all-encompassing agreement that touched on every concern the players had, while the owners got their greatest wish of an expanded postseason.

The lockout lasted 99 days, the second-longest work stoppage in MLB history behind only the 1994-95 players strike. But for all the acrimony, in the end, no games were lost.

"This negotiation started a long way apart—and in case anyone missed the memo—(the union) did come with a very, very broad agenda for change," Manfred said. "They're entitled to that. That's what the process is about."

PLAY BALL

Once the lockout ended, players had just three weeks of spring training to get ready for the regular season, as opposed to the usual six.

The lack of preparation time became apparent as soon as the season started.

The league-wide batting average was just .231 in April, the lowest ever for an opening month of the season. The league-wide OPS was .675, the lowest in any April since 1968, the year before the mound was lowered. Those numbers occurred despite the fact pitchers were no longer batting in the National League, a move that was supposed to boost offense.

With spring training cut in half, hitters simply never got a chance to get their timing back, and the effects spilled over into the regular season.

"We all think spring training might be a little long as it is, so I think we're all of the mindset that we can go with fewer at-bats or games than we've had in the past, but also at the same time this one felt pretty quick," Dodgers shortstop Trea Turner said. "I think a lot of guys felt like it was over almost too quick."

The other factor that led to a league-wide offensive freeze was the ball.

After home runs increased rapidly toward the end of the 2010s—capped by a record 6,776 home runs hit during the 2019 season—MLB deadened the ball by loosening its wool windings ahead of the 2021 season. In 2022, all 30 teams began using a humidor to store their baseballs for the first time, standardizing the amount of water in the air around the ball.

The compound effect of those two changes was a sharp and sudden decrease in home runs. For the first time since 2015, teams averaged less than one home run per game in April. Overall, the number of home runs per game dropped 20% compared to April 2021.

"The ball ain't the same as it used to be. I used to be 165 pounds soaking wet here flicking balls out," Brewers outfielder Andrew McCutchen told ESPN. "I've hit some that don't continue to keep going. Then we're having conversations like, 'How did this guy have an exit velo of 96 with a launch angle of 31, and his ball went out, and I had an exit velo of 100 and 28 launch angle and mine didn't go out?' . . . Baseball players aren't getting any weaker."

"Something is different, because we look at the metrics. We see how hard it's hit then we see the ball get caught," Cubs infielder Patrick Wisdom added. "It starts raising some eyebrows, raising some questions."

Hitters' frustrations, of course, meant joy for

AMERICAN LEAGUE STANDINGS

East	W	L	PCT	GB	Manager	General Manager	Attendance	Average	Last Penn.
New York Yankees	99	63	.611	—	Aaron Boone	Brian Cashman	1,621,316	29,478	2009
Toronto Blue Jays	92	70	.568	7	C. Montoyo/ J. Schneider	Ross Atkins	1,589,560	28,901	1993
Tampa Bay Rays	86	76	.531	13	Kevin Cash	Peter Bendix	943,862	16,559	2020
Baltimore Orioles	83	79	.512	16	Brandon Hyde	Mike Elias	1,202,314	21,093	1983
Boston Red Sox	78	84	.481	21	Alex Cora	Brian O'Halloran	1,595,920	27,516	2018
Central	**W**	**L**	**PCT**	**GB**	**Manager**	**General Manager**	**Attendance**	**Average**	**Last Penn.**
Cleveland Guardians	92	70	.568	—	Terry Francona	Mike Chernoff	915,982	18,694	2016
Chicago White Sox	81	81	.500	11	Tony La Russa	Rick Hahn	1,181,928	22,301	2005
Minnesota Twins	78	84	.481	14	Rocco Baldelli	Thad Levine	1,061,677	18,305	1991
Detroit Tigers	66	96	.407	26	A.J. Hinch	Al Avila	1,169,723	21,662	2012
Kansas City Royals	65	97	.401	27	Mike Matheny	J.J. Picollo	998,982	18,163	2015
West	**W**	**L**	**PCT**	**GB**	**Manager**	**General Manager**	**Attendance**	**Average**	**Last Penn.**
Houston Astros	106	56	.654	—	Dusty Baker	James Click	1,552,819	27,729	2022
Seattle Mariners	90	72	.556	16	Scott Servais	Jerry Dipoto	1,309,654	22,976	Never
Los Angeles Angels	73	89	.451	33	Joe Maddon/ Phil Nevin	Perry Minasian	1,702,540	28,857	2002
Texas Rangers	68	94	.420	38	C. Woodward/ T. Beasley	Chris Young	1,225,255	22,690	2011
Oakland Athletics	60	102	.370	46	Mark Kotsay	David Forst	921,139	15,882	1990

Wild Card Series: Guardians defeated Rays 2-0 and Mariners defeated Blue Jays 2-0 in best-of-3 series. **Division Series:** Yankees defeated Guardians 3-2 and Astros defeated Mariners 3-0 in best-of-5 series. **Championship Series:** Astros defeated Yankees 4-0 in a best-of-7 series.

ROOKIE OF THE YEAR

Rodriguez Takes Center Stage

BY KYLE GLASER

As baseball's best players descended on Los Angeles for All-Star Game festivities in July, one burgeoning young standout had their attention most of all.

Julio Rodriguez, the Mariners' exhilarating, ebullient 21-year-old center fielder, had powered Seattle to a 14-game win streak through the break, vaulting the Mariners from a sub-.500 record to wild card position in the American League.

The young Dominican shook off a slow start to earn an all-star selection as a rookie, showcasing a remarkable blend of power, speed and personality to captivate the city of Seattle and make the Mariners appointment-viewing television from coast to coast.

Rodriguez had been a major leaguer for barely three months by the time the All-Star Game rolled around. That was all the time he needed to earn the highest compliment possible from the game's most decorated player.

"He plays the game the right way," said Angels center fielder Mike Trout, the three-time American League MVP. "He's always having fun on the bench. He reminds of myself kind of when I first came up."

Rodriguez made that comparison look remarkably plausible in his major league debut this year. He became the fastest rookie to reach 25 home runs and 25 stolen bases, beating Trout's record by three games, and finished the year with 28 homers and 25 steals.

He became a staple of nightly highlight reels with his play in center field, showing speed and agility that exceeded even the most bullish projections held for him.

And, most importantly, he carried the Mariners to the postseason for the first time in 21 years, leading the team in batting average, runs, stolen bases, on-base percentage, slugging percentage and total bases to help end the longest playoff drought in North American professional sports.

For his transcendent season, Rodriguez is the 2022 Baseball America Rookie of the Year.

STEPH CHAMBERS/GETTY IMAGES

Julio Rodriguez hit 28 home runs and stole 25 bases in his Rookie of the Year season.

"I just trusted myself," Rodriguez said during a late-season series in Anaheim. "I trusted myself throughout the year. And I trusted the work that I put in through the offseason and basically just let everything play out."

In a matter of months, the Mariners took on Rodriguez's personality. They became baseball's most energetic team, holding on-field dance parties to celebrate wild wins. They surged back from their early-season hole with the 14-game winning streak that carried them into the all-star break. They won 24 games in their final at-bat, many of them fueled by Rodriguez.

At only 21 years old, Rodriguez became the team's leader not just statistically, but emotionally.

"The guy is special," Mariners second baseman Adam Frazier said. "It's not just his ability on the field, but the intangibles off the field too. ■

LAST 10 WINNERS

2012: Mike Trout, OF, Angels
2013: Jose Fernandez, RHP, Marlins
2014: Jose Abreu, 1B, White Sox
2015: Kris Bryant, 3B, Cubs
2016: Corey Seager, SS, Dodgers
2017: Aaron Judge, OF, Yankees
2018: Shohei Ohtani, RHP/DH, Angels
2019: Pete Alonso, 1B, Mets
2020: Tony Gonsolin, RHP, Dodgers
2021: Jonathan India, 2B, Reds
Full list: search "Baseball America awards"

pitchers. The first no-hitter of the year came just over three weeks into the season when Mets pitchers Tylor Megill, Drew Smith, Edwin Diaz, Seth Lugo and Joely Rodriguez combined to no-hit the Phillies on April 29. Less than two weeks later, Angels rookie lefthander Reid Detmers pitched a no-hitter against the Rays on May 10 despite having only two strikeouts, the fewest strikeouts in a no-hitter in 11 years.

Even as the weather warmed up and hitters adjusted, offense remained historically low throughout the 2022 season.

Teams hit just .243 over the course of the season, the lowest league-wide batting average since 1968. The league-wide strikeout rate was 22.4%, fourth-highest in history. Teams averaged 4.28 runs per game, a 5% decrease from 2021. They hit 729 fewer home runs, a 12% decrease from 2021.

While the game as a whole cratered offensively, a few individual hitters stepped up to deliver the performances of a lifetime.

CHASING MARIS

When Aaron Judge entered the 2022 season, he placed an enormous bet on himself.

The Yankees offered their star slugger a seven-year, $213.5 million contract extension just before Opening Day. Judge, entering his final season before free agency, declined.

The 6-foot-7 behemoth finished fourth in American League MVP voting the year before, but he had also failed to ever replicate his historic rookie numbers and was entering his age-30 season.

Given teams' increasing wariness of awarding massive contracts to position players in their 30s, it appeared to be a risky move for Judge to turn down such a lucrative offer.

Within a matter of weeks, it became clear that Judge had made the right choice.

Judge bashed 18 home runs in the first two months of the season, creating intrigue that he might have a chance to reach the American League record of 61 home runs still held by Roger Maris.

When Judge crushed another 11 home runs in June, the race was on.

Judge became a one-man wrecking crew the more pressure mounted. He hit 13 home runs in July, his highest total in any month, to give him 42 home runs by August 1. Powered by Judge, the Yankees got out to a 61-23 start, the fourth-best start through that many games in history.

The Bronx Bombers weren't all the way back, but one Bronx Bomber was carrying the team.

"It's been remarkable," Yankees manager Aaron Boone said during a late-August series. "I was a young player in '98 playing in the National League Central when Sammy (Sosa) and (Mark) McGwire were doing their thing down the stretch . . . I got to see that kind of a circus and the excitement that went with that, how big that was at the time for baseball.

"I think what Aaron's doing is certainly in line with that."

Even as the Yankees cooled, Judge never did.

Judge hit his 50th home run on Aug. 29 and added another the next day, giving him 51 home runs before September began.

He homered in four straight games from Sept. 3-7 and added a pair of two-home run games in

NATIONAL LEAGUE STANDINGS

East	W	L	PCT	GB	Manager	General Manager	Attendance	Average	Last Penn.
Atlanta Braves	101	61	.623	—	Brian Snitker	Alex Anthopoulos	1,954,270	34,285	2021
New York Mets	101	61	.623	—	Buck Showalter	Billy Eppler	1,699,210	30,895	2015
Philadelphia Phillies	87	75	.537	14	Joe Girardi/ Rob Thomson	Sam Fuld	1,640,034	29,286	2022
Miami Marlins	69	93	.426	32	Don Mattingly	Kim Ng	1,006,256	18,634	2003
Washington Nationals	55	107	.340	46	Dave Martinez	Mike Rizzo	1,283,657	21,757	2019
Central	**W**	**L**	**PCT**	**GB**	**Manager**	**General Manager**	**Attendance**	**Average**	**Last Penn.**
St. Louis Cardinals	93	69	.574	—	Oliver Marmol	Mike Girsch	1,756,609	30,818	2013
Milwaukee Brewers	86	76	.531	7	Craig Counsell	Matt Arnold	1,617,200	27,410	1982 (AL)
Chicago Cubs	74	88	.457	19	David Ross	Carter Hawkins	1,673,949	29,892	2016
Cincinnati Reds	62	100	.383	31	David Bell	Nick Krall	1,316,634	23,099	1990
Pittsburgh Pirates	62	100	.383	31	Derek Shelton	Ben Cherington	1,154,056	21,371	1979
West	**W**	**L**	**PCT**	**GB**	**Manager**	**General Manager**	**Attendance**	**Average**	**Last Penn.**
Los Angeles Dodgers	111	51	.685	—	Dave Roberts	Brandon Gomes	2,125,054	37,282	2020
San Diego Padres	89	73	.549	22	Bob Melvin	A.J. Preller	1,748,450	31,222	1998
San Francisco Giants	81	81	.500	30	Gabe Kapler	Scott Harris	1,523,249	27,695	2014
Arizona Diamondbacks	74	88	.457	37	Torey Lovullo	Mike Hazen	1,306,857	22,150	2001
Colorado Rockies	68	94	.420	43	Bud Black	Bill Schmidt	1,509,768	26,960	2007

Wild Card Series: Phillies beat Cardinals 2-0 and Padres defeated Mets 2-1 in best-of-3 series. **Division Series:** Phillies defeated Braves 3-1 and Padres defeated Dodgers 3-1 in best-of-5 series. **Championship Series:** Phillies defeated Padres 4-1 in best-of-7 series.

the ensuing days, drawing closer to Maris' record.

After hitting No. 60 against the Pirates on Sept. 20, teams began pitching around Judge. No one wanted to be the pitcher to give up the record-tying home run, and with the Yankees offense mired in a late-season slump, pitching around Judge was simply the prudent move.

Judge went seven games without a homer following his 60th, his longest homerless stretch in over a month. With the clock ticking down on the season, doubts began to creep in whether he would have a shot to break Maris' AL record.

But on Sept. 28, the Blue Jays decided to pitch to Judge in the seventh inning of a tie game. Judge got a 91 mph sinker from Blue Jays lefthanded reliever Tim Mayza and didn't miss it, sending a missile over the left-field wall at Rogers Centre for his AL record-tying 61st home run of the season.

"It's definitely some relief, getting to 61," Judge said. "It's a chance to tie Roger Maris. It's the stuff you dream about. It's not even real."

Five days later, on Oct. 4, the dream got even better. In the second game of a doubleheader against the Rangers, Judge led off with a towering home run to left field off righthander Jesus Tinoco, giving him his 62nd home run of the year and breaking Maris' record.

As Judge circled the bases, his teammates excitedly streamed out of the dugout. Yankees third base coach Luis Rojas tipped his cap as Judge rounded third base. When Judge finally got back to the dugout, he allowed himself a smile, knowing he'd accomplished something historic.

"Getting the chance to do this with the team we got, the guys surrounding me, the constant support from my family that has been with me through this whole thing, it's been a great honor," Judge said that night. "Getting a chance to have my name next to someone as great as Roger Maris, Babe Ruth, those guys, it's incredible."

STARS YOUNG AND OLD

Judge's season towered over all others. He led the major leagues in runs, home runs, RBIs, on-base percentage, slugging percentage, OPS, OPS+ and total bases. He hit .311, finishing four points shy of winning the American League triple crown while setting a new AL home run record. He did it all while moving to center field and stabilizing what had been a problem spot defensively for the Yankees for years.

But he was hardly the only one to deliver a memorable performance in 2022.

Angels two-way star Shohei Ohtani, the reigning AL MVP, delivered another spectacular season and challenged Judge for the title of best player in the game. He continued to be one of the game's best sluggers, with a .273 batting average, 34 home runs and 95 RBIs. Simultaneously, took a step forward to become a true ace on the mound. Ohtani, who had battled injuries and command issues as a pitcher, went 15-9, 2.33 with 219 strikeouts and 44 walks in 166 innings.

RONALD MARTINEZ/GETTY IMAGES

Lefthander Reid Detmers threw the Angels' 12th no-hitter in just his 11th career start.

He finished fifth in the majors in ERA and 10th in OPS, a demonstration of two-way excellence beyond what even he had previously shown.

"I definitely feel like this season is better overall," Ohtani said after his final home start of the season. "My pitching numbers are better. I'm just playing with more confidence after experiencing last year. I know that I won MVP last year, but I feel like I'm having a better season this year, which is leading to a lot of confidence."

While Judge and Ohtani were established stars, a new one emerged in Seattle.

Prized prospect Julio Rodriguez won the Mariners' Opening Day center field job with an electric performance in spring training. After a 6-for-44 start, he quickly ascended into one of the game's most visible and dynamic superstars.

With an incandescent smile and a remarkable blend of speed, strength and ability, Rodriguez rapidly became the face of baseball in Seattle and powered the Mariners toward the postseason. He made his first all-star team as a rookie and stole the show at the Home Run Derby at Dodger Stadium, bashing a rookie-record 32 home runs in the opening round and sending them a combined 2.54 miles, the longest combined distance of any competitor in the derby. He then proceeded to beat two-time defending champion Pete Alonso in the semifinals, becoming the first player to ever beat Alonso in a home run derby, and made it to the finals where he fell to fellow Dominican Juan Soto.

"I feel like it was a dream I had as a kid and I was able to fulfill it," Rodriguez said. "I just had a great time. Having all those players around there, being able to meet a lot of the players I looked up to throughout my whole career, my whole childhood and everything, it was amazing. It was a surreal experience and I feel like it couldn't have been any better."

Rodriguez's derby performance was far from the peak of his season. He became the fastest rookie to reach 25 home runs and 25 stolen bases, breaking a record previously held by three-time MVP Mike Trout, and finished top-10 in the AL in slugging percentage, OPS and stolen bases. He became a staple of nightly highlight reels with his defense in center field, where he showcased some of the best range and one of the strongest arms in the league. The Mariners signed him to one of the largest and most complex contract extensions in baseball history, a deal whose bonuses and clauses could keep him in Seattle for 18 years and pay him $470 million.

Most significantly of all, Rodriguez led the Mariners back to the playoffs for the first time in 21 years, ending the longest playoff drought in North American professional sports.

"I just trusted myself," Rodriguez said. "I trusted myself throughout the year. And I trusted the work that I put in through the offseason and basically just let everything play out."

While Judge, Ohtani and Rodriguez cemented themselves as among the current best players in the game, the former best player in the game experienced a historic resurgence in his final season.

Albert Pujols, 42, had fallen far from his peak days as baseball's most fearsome hitter. The Angels designated him for an assignment in 2021 and he finished the year as a part-time bench player for the Dodgers. He signed a one-year deal with the Cardinals before the 2022 season, stating it would be his final year before retirement.

The deal, for all intents and purposes, was a sentimental one. It was a chance for Pujols to take a victory lap in the city where he became a star, with little expectation he would play a major role.

At first, that was exactly what happened. Pujols hit .215 with six home runs in the first half of the season and later said he considered retiring in June. He was selected for the Home Run Derby and the All-Star Game solely as a final sendoff, essentially a chance for him to be celebrated on a national stage once more.

Then, Pujols suddenly and unexpectedly found the Fountain of Youth. He went 7-for-14 out of

AMERICAN LEAGUE BEST TOOLS

A Baseball America survey of American League managers, conducted at midseason 2022, ranked players with the best tools.

Best Hitter
1. Yordan Alvarez, Astros
2. Luis Arraez, Twins
3. Rafael Devers, Red Sox

Best Power
1. Aaron Judge, Yankees
2. Yordan Alvarez, Astros
3. Shohei Ohtani, Angels

Best Bunter
1. Cedric Mullins, Orioles
2. Nicky Lopez, Royals
3. Andres Gimenez, Guardians

Best Strike-Zone Judgment
1. Yandy Diaz, Rays
2. Alex Bregman, Astros
3. Yordan Alvarez, Astros

Best Hit-And-Run Artist
1. David Fletcher, Angels
2. Elvis Andrus, Athletics
3. Luis Arraez, Twins

Best Baserunner
1. Jose Ramirez, Guardians
2. Shohei Ohtani, Angels
3. Marcus Semien, Rangers

Fastest Baserunner
1. Bobby Witt Jr., Royals
2. Byron Buxton, Twins
3. Jorge Mateo, Orioles

Most Exciting Player
1. Shohei Ohtani, Angels
2. Byron Buxton, Twins
3. Julio Rodriguez, Mariners

Best Pitcher
1. Justin Verlander, Astros
2. Shane McClanahan, Rays
3. Dylan Cease, White Sox

Best Fastball
1. Justin Verlander, Astros
2. Emmanuel Clase, Guardians
3. Clay Holmes, Yankees

Best Curveball
1. Justin Verlander, Astros
2. Shane McClanahan, Rays
3. Gerrit Cole, Yankees

Best Slider
1. Andres Muñoz, Mariners
2. Dylan Cease, White Sox
3. Alek Manoah, Blue Jays

Best Changeup
1. Shohei Ohtani*, Angels
2. Kevin Gausman*, Blue Jays
3. Kendall Graveman, White Sox

* Splitter instead of changeup

Best Control
1. Justin Verlander, Astros
2. Corey Kluber, Rays
3. Shane McClanahan, Rays

Best Pickoff Move
1. Robbie Ray, Mariners
2. Zach Plesac, Guardians
3. Tarik Skubal, Tigers

Best Reliever
1. Emmanuel Clase, Guardians
2. Jorge Lopez, Twins
3. Clay Holmes, Yankees

Best Defensive Catcher
1. Jose Trevino, Yankees
2. Christian Vazquez, Astros
3. Austin Hedges, Guardians

Best Defensive 1B
1. Vladimir Guerrero Jr., Blue Jays
2. Ty France, Mariners
3. Ryan Mountcastle, Orioles

Best Defensive 2B
1. Jonathan Schoop, Tigers
2. Andres Gimenez, Guardians
3. Trevor Story, Red Sox

Best Defensive 3B
1. Matt Chapman, Blue Jays
2. Josh Donaldson, Yankees
3. Jose Ramirez, Guardians

Best Defensive SS
1. Andrew Velazquez, Angels
2. Carlos Correa, Twins
3. Jorge Mateo, Orioles

Best Infield Arm
1. Matt Chapman, Blue Jays
2. Carlos Correa, Twins
3. Jonathan Schoop, Tigers

Best Defensive OF
1. Byron Buxton, Twins
2. Michael A. Taylor, Royals
3. Kevin Kiermaier, Rays

Best Outfield Arm
1. Aaron Hicks, Yankees
2. Ramon Laureano, Athletics
3. Adolis Garcia, Rangers

Best Manager
1. Dusty Baker, Astros
2. Kevin Cash, Rays
3. Brandon Hyde, Orioles

ORGANIZATION OF THE YEAR

Mariners' Step Back Leads To Big Leap

BY RYAN DIVISH

Late in the 2018 season, as the dog days of August turned into the stretch run, the Mariners were clinging to fading hope. A possible surge in the final weeks might allow Seattle to sneak into the postseason as the second American League wild card and end an embarrassing postseason drought that dated back to 2001.

It was during those August days four years ago, when a veteran-laden Mariners team would continue to fizzle, that general manager Jerry Dipoto and manager Scott Servais were faced with the realization of what they had as a team—and what it could never be in its existing form.

Even with established players like Felix Hernandez, Kyle Seager, Jean Segura, Robinson Cano, James Paxton, Mike Zunino and a young Edwin Diaz on the roster, both Dipoto and Servais understood that they were farther away from being a winner than the people who wrote their paychecks realized.

The Mariners' roster was aging and the farm system was barren, having ranked last in Baseball America organization talent rankings heading into 2018. The reality was that a big-money free agent would not fix those issues.

So in a September meeting with then-president and CEO Kevin Mather and chairmen John Stanton and Chris Larson, Dipoto and Servais made their feelings known. They outlined a modified rebuilding plan, later referred to as a "step back," that would lead to consistent future success within three to four years, instead of the typical five to seven years that is typical for baseball rebuilds.

LAST 10 WINNERS

2012: Cincinnati Reds
2013: St. Louis Cardinals
2014: Kansas City Royals
2015: Pittsburgh Pirates
2016: Chicago Cubs
2017: Los Angeles Dodgers
2018: Milwaukee Brewers
2019: Tampa Bay Rays
2020: Los Angeles Dodgers
2021: Tampa Bay Rays
Full list: search "Baseball America awards"

JIM MCISAAC/GETTY IMAGES

The Mariners acquired Reds righthander Luis Castillo at the trade deadline.

Four years later, Dipoto watched as products of that "step back," including 2018 first-round righthander Logan Gilbert, hard-throwing reliever Matt Brash, acquired in a 2020 trade with the Padres; and 2018 third-round catcher Cal Raleigh, clinched the Mariners' first postseason berth in 21 years.

Gilbert and Brash combined to toss nine shutout innings, and Raleigh crushed a walk-off homer for a 1-0 victory. The Mariners not only made the postseason but defeated the Blue Jays in the American League Wild Card Series before eventually being swept in three games by the Astros in the AL Division Series they could have easily won.

The realized results of that "step back" rebuilding plan—Seattle entered 2022 with the top farm system in baseball—and a talented homegrown nucleus led by No. 1 prospect turned-Rookie of the Year Julio Rodriguez should lead to future success.

Mix in a continued investment in amateur scouting and player development, and the Mariners are the Baseball America Organization of the Year.

It is Seattle's first win in the 41st iteration of the award. ■

the all-star break and hit seven home runs in a 10-game stretch in August. Once seen as a longshot to reach 700 career homers, he kept hitting homer after homer until suddenly the milestone was in reach. With homers on back-to-back days in Pittsburgh on Sept. 10-11 and another shot in Cincinnati on Sept. 16, Pujols suddenly found himself just two away from the milestone.

On Sept. 23, Pujols and the Cardinals opened a three-game series at Dodger Stadium. In the third inning, he cracked a two-out, two-run homer off lefty Andrew Heaney to give the Cardinals their first lead and notch No. 699.

One inning later, facing reliever Phil Bickford, he got a hanging breaking ball on the inner half and pounded it into the left-field bleachers for his second homer of the game and No. 700 in his illustrious career.

"It's pretty special," Pujols said after the game. "When it's really going to hit me is when I'm done, at the end of the season, when I'm retired, and probably a moment or two after that I can look at the numbers."

Pujols became just the fourth player to hit 700 career home runs, joining Barry Bonds, Hank Aaron and Babe Ruth. He added three more homers in the season's final five days, giving him 703 to place fourth all-time.

With his second-half surge, Pujols hit .270 with 24 home runs and an .895 OPS on the season. It was his highest batting average in eight years, his most home runs in six years and his highest OPS in 11 years.

At age 42, Pujols once again thrilled fans the way he did in his prime, and finished his career on a high note.

RISING POWERS

A staple of great teams is the ability to reload no matter how much talent they lose. The Astros and Dodgers, baseball's reigning powers in the American and National Leagues, showed once again in 2022 that they were immune to seemingly any loss of talent.

The Dodgers lost shortstop Corey Seager and righthander Max Scherzer in free agency to the Rangers and Mets, respectively, and the Astros saw star shortstop Carlos Correa bolt for Minnesota.

Despite those losses, both teams remained the class of their leagues.

The Dodgers won 19 of their first 26 games and never slowed down, steamrolling all comers on their way to a franchise-record 111 wins. That happened even with Seager and Scherzer leaving, righthander Walker Buehler making just 12 starts before suffering a season-ending elbow injury and sluggers Cody Bellinger and Max Muncy slogging through miserable seasons.

The addition of first baseman Freddie Freeman and emergence of righthander Tony Gonsolin as a Cy Young Award contender helped make up for

NATIONAL LEAGUE BEST TOOLS

A Baseball America survey of National League managers, conducted at midseason 2022, ranked players with the best tools.

Best Hitter
1. Freddie Freeman, Dodgers
2. Paul Goldschmidt, Cardinals
3. Mookie Betts, Dodgers

Best Power
1. Pete Alonso, Mets
2. Austin Riley, Braves
3. Kyle Schwarber, Phillies

Best Bunter
1. Victor Robles, Nationals
2. Trent Grisham, Padres
3. Daulton Varsho, D-backs

Best Strike-Zone Judgment
1. Juan Soto, Padres
2. Kyle Schwarber, Phillies
3. Max Muncy, Dodgers

Best Hit-And-Run Artist
1. Jose Iglesias, Rockies
2. Miguel Rojas, Marlins
3. Yadier Molina, Cardinals

Best Baserunner
1. Mookie Betts, Dodgers
2. Tommy Edman, Cardinals
3. Jazz Chisholm Jr., Marlins

Fastest Baserunner
1. Trea Turner, Dodgers
2. Oneil Cruz, Pirates
3. Tyler O'Neill, Cardinals

Most Exciting Player
1. Trea Turner, Dodgers
2. Mookie Betts, Dodgers
3. Ronald Acuña Jr., Braves

Best Pitcher
1. Sandy Alcantara, Marlins
2. Max Fried, Braves
3. Corbin Burnes, Brewers

Best Fastball
1. Zack Wheeler, Phillies
2. Carlos Rodon, Giants
3. Ryan Helsley, Cardinals

Best Curveball
1. Max Fried, Braves
2. Aaron Nola, Phillies
3. David Robertson, Phillies

Best Slider
1. Sandy Alcantara, Marlins
2. Max Scherzer, Mets
3. Zack Wheeler, Phillies

Best Changeup
1. Devin Williams, Brewers
2. Sandy Alcantara, Marlins
3. Pablo Lopez, Marlins

Best Control
1. Aaron Nola, Phillies
2. Clayton Kershaw, Dodgers
3. Miles Mikolas, Cardinals

Best Pickoff Move
1. Max Fried, Braves
2. Clayton Kershaw, Dodgers
3. Patrick Corbin, Nationals

Best Reliever
1. Josh Hader, Padres
2. Edwin Diaz, Mets
3. Ryan Helsley, Cardinals

Best Defensive Catcher
1. JT Realmuto, Phillies
2. Yadier Molina, Cardinals
3. Will Smith, Dodgers

Best Defensive 1B
1. Freddie Freeman, Dodgers
2. Paul Goldschmidt, Cardinals
3. Christian Walker, D-backs

Best Defensive 2B
1. Tommy Edman, Cardinals
2. Jake Cronenworth, Padres
3. Brendan Rodgers, Rockies

Best Defensive 3B
1. Nolan Arenado, Cardinals
2. Ke'Bryan Hayes, Pirates
3. Manny Machado, Padres

Best Defensive SS
1. Dansby Swanson, Braves
2. Miguel Rojas, Marlins
3. Willy Adames, Brewers

Best Infield Arm
1. Manny Machado, Padres
2. Oneil Cruz, Pirates
3. Nolan Arenado, Cardinals

Best Defensive OF
1. Mookie Betts, Dodgers
2. Harrison Bader*, Cardinals
3. Michael Harris II, Braves
* Traded to Yankees, Aug. 2

Best Outfield Arm
1. Mookie Betts, Dodgers
2. Ronald Acuña Jr., Braves
3. Hunter Renfroe, Brewers

Best Manager
1. Buck Showalter, Mets
2. Craig Counsell, Brewers
3. Dave Roberts, Dodgers

MAJOR LEAGUE ALL-STARS

SELECTED BY BASEBALL AMERICA

THEARON W. HENDERSON/GETTY IMAGES

Shohei Ohtani earned first-team nods as both a DH and as a starting pitcher.

ELSA/GETTY IMAGES

In his return from Tommy John surgery, Justin Verlander went 18-4, 1.75.

FIRST TEAM

Pos.	Player, Team	AVG	OBP	SLG	AB	R	H	2B	3B	HR	RBI	BB	SO	SB	CS
C	J.T. Realmuto, Phillies	.276	.342	.478	504	75	139	26	5	22	84	41	119	21	1
1B	Paul Goldschmidt, Cardinals	.317	.404	.578	561	106	178	41	0	35	115	79	141	7	0
2B	Jose Altuve, Astros	.300	.387	.533	527	103	158	39	0	28	57	66	87	18	1
3B	Manny Machado, Padres	.298	.366	.531	578	100	172	37	1	32	102	63	133	9	1
SS	Trea Turner, Dodgers	.298	.343	.466	652	101	194	39	4	21	100	45	131	27	3
OF	Yordan Alvarez, Astros	.306	.406	.613	470	95	144	29	2	37	97	78	106	1	1
OF	Aaron Judge, Yankees	.311	.425	.686	570	133	177	28	0	62	131	111	175	16	3
OF	Mike Trout, Angels	.283	.369	.630	438	85	124	28	2	40	80	54	139	1	0
DH	Shohei Ohtani, Angels	.273	.356	.519	586	90	160	30	6	34	95	72	161	11	9

Pos.	Player, Team	W	L	ERA	G	GS	SV	IP	H	R	ER	HR	BB	SO	WHIP
SP	Sandy Alcantara, Marlins	14	9	2.28	32	32	0	229	174	67	58	16	50	207	0.98
SP	Dylan Cease, White Sox	14	8	2.20	32	32	0	184	126	55	45	16	78	227	1.11
SP	Shohei Ohtani, Angels	15	9	2.33	28	28	0	166	124	45	43	14	44	219	1.01
SP	Julio Urias, Dodgers	17	7	2.16	31	31	0	175	127	51	42	23	41	166	0.96
SP	Justin Verlander, Astros	18	4	1.75	28	28	0	175	116	43	34	12	29	185	0.83
RP	Edwin Diaz, Mets	3	1	1.31	61	0	32	62	34	9	9	3	18	118	0.84

SECOND TEAM

Pos.	Player, Team	AVG	OBP	SLG	AB	R	H	2B	3B	HR	RBI	BB	SO	SB	CS
C	Will Smith, Dodgers	.260	.343	.465	508	68	132	26	3	24	87	56	96	1	0
1B	Freddie Freeman, Dodgers	.325	.407	.511	612	117	199	47	2	21	100	84	102	13	3
2B	Andres Gimenez, Guardians	.297	.371	.466	491	66	146	26	3	17	69	34	112	20	3
3B	Nolan Arenado, Cardinals	.293	.358	.533	557	73	163	42	1	30	103	52	72	5	3
SS	Dansby Swanson, Braves	.277	.329	.447	640	99	177	32	1	25	96	49	182	18	7
OF	Mookie Betts, Dodgers	.269	.340	.533	572	117	154	40	3	35	82	55	104	12	2
OF	Jeff McNeil, Mets	.326	.382	.454	533	73	174	39	1	9	62	40	61	4	0
OF	Julio Rodriguez, Mariners	.284	.345	.509	511	84	145	25	3	28	75	40	145	25	7
DH	Austin Riley, Braves	.273	.349	.528	615	90	168	39	2	38	93	57	168	2	0

Pos.	Player, Team	W	L	ERA	G	GS	SV	IP	H	R	ER	HR	BB	SO	WHIP
SP	Max Fried, Braves	14	7	2.48	30	30	0	185	156	55	51	12	32	170	1.01
SP	Zac Gallen, D-backs	12	4	2.54	31	31	0	184	121	56	52	15	47	192	0.91
SP	Alek Manoah, Blue Jays	16	7	2.24	31	31	0	197	144	55	49	16	51	180	0.99
SP	Shane McClanahan, Rays	12	8	2.54	28	28	0	166	116	52	47	19	38	194	0.93
SP	Framber Valdez, Astros	17	6	2.82	31	31	0	201	166	71	63	11	67	194	1.16
RP	Emmanuel Clase, Guardians	3	4	1.36	77	0	42	73	43	18	11	3	10	77	0.73

EXECUTIVE OF THE YEAR

TODD KIRKLAND/GETTY IMAGES

Alex Anthopoulos

The Braves hired Alex Anthopoulos as general manager in November 2017. The club has done nothing but win ever since.

Since Anthopoulos took the reins, the Braves have finished first in the National League East for five consecutive seasons and won the 2021 World Series. Atlanta's .581 winning percentage since 2018 is fifth-best in MLB and second only to the Dodgers in the NL.

For his role in turning the Braves into one of baseball's most well-run machines, Anthopoulos is the Baseball America Major League Executive of the Year.

While the Braves weren't able to defend their 2021 title, they won 101 games, introduced impact rookies Michael Harris II and Spencer Strider and locked in a young core that ensures success in the years ahead. ■

LAST 10 WINNERS

2012: Billy Beane, Athletics
2013: Dan Duquette, Orioles
2014: Dan Duquette, Orioles
2015: Sandy Alderson, Mets
2016: Chris Antonetti, Indians
2017: Brian Cashman, Yankees
2018: Dave Dombrowski, Red Sox
2019: Mike Rizzo, Nationals
2020: Andrew Friedman, Dodgers
2021: Farhan Zaidi, Giants

Full list: search "Baseball America awards"

MANAGER OF THE YEAR

LACHLAN CUNNINGHAM/MLB PHOTOS VIA GETTY IMAGES

Brandon Hyde

When the 2022 season began, the Orioles were coming off their fifth consecutive losing season. In fact, it was one of the worst stretches for any team of the expansion era.

While Baltimore didn't make the playoffs in 2022, it managed to stay in the wild card hunt for much of the season. The Orioles' 83-79 record indicates that brighter days are ahead. Manager Brandon Hyde and his staff managed to turn the team around despite a lack of significant veteran additions. Baltimore's return to respectability relied heavily on young talent, led by catcher Adley Rutschman, but also an impressive ability to help established big leaguers reach new levels of success.

For that, Brandon Hyde is the Baseball America Major League Manager of the Year. ■

LAST 10 WINNERS

2012: Buck Showalter, Orioles
2013: Clint Hurdle, Pirates
2014: Buck Showalter, Orioles
2015: Joe Maddon, Cubs
2016: Terry Francona, Indians
2017: A.J. Hinch, Astros
2018: Bob Melvin, Athletics
2019: Craig Counsell, Brewers
2020: Brian Snitker, Braves
2021: Dusty Baker, Astros

Full list: search "Baseball America awards"

their losses, but even so, the Dodgers' ability to dominate no matter who they lost was remarkable. They led the majors in runs scored, allowed the fewest runs in the majors and outscored opponents by 334 runs, the largest run differential of any team since the 1939 Yankees.

The Astros, meanwhile, seamlessly replaced Correa with shortstop Jeremy Peña, a third-round pick from Maine in 2018. With a slick glove and power that would yield 22 home runs as a rookie, Peña kept the Astros humming along.

Houston won an American League-best 106 games as Justin Verlander returned from Tommy John surgery to go 18-4 with a major league-leading 1.75 ERA and DH Yordan Alvarez blossomed into one of the sport's most feared sluggers. The Astros spent 139 out of 158 possible days in first place in the AL West and repeatedly flexed their muscle against the AL's other powers, going 5-2 against the Yankees to leave no doubt who was the best team in the league.

The Yankees made it easy to determine that. After starting 61-23, the team crashed back to earth as injuries and defensive mistakes began to pile up. The Yankees went just 38-40 the rest of the season and saw their AL East division lead shrivel from 15 ½ to 3 ½ games at one point. Judge finished strong to save them, but it reinforced the fact that the Yankees remained second-fiddle to the Astros in the AL.

New York's other team also failed to retain its big early lead. Led by new manager Buck Showalter—who was honored after the season as the NL's Manager of the Year—the Mets stormed out of the gates by winning 15 of their first 21 games to take early control of the National League East. Scherzer and Jacob deGrom combined to give the Mets the most fearsome 1-2 rotation punch in MLB, and strong offensive seasons from Francisco Lindor and Pete Alonso made the Mets an early juggernaut.

All the while, the defending World Series champion Braves slumped. Their record stood at 23-27 entering June 1 following a walkoff loss to the lowly D-backs, with an offense that struck out too much and a rotation critically short on depth.

But just as they had in years past, the Braves turned around their fortunes with critical in-season roster moves. On May 28, the Braves called up rookie Michael Harris II from Triple-A to take over in center field. On May 30, they moved rookie righthander Spencer Strider from the bullpen to the rotation permanently. The two rookies would go on to deliver historically strong performances—Harris II won the NL's Rookie of the Year award and Strider was the runner-up—and helped the Braves overcome a 10 ½ game deficit and chase down the Mets.

Harris hit a rookie-best .297 with 19 homers and 20 steals in only 114 games while solidifying the Braves' center field defense and adding dynamism they were critically missing, especially with Freeman's departure and Ronald Acuña Jr.'s struggles to reclaim his prior form in his first season back from a torn ACL. Strider became the fastest pitcher to reach 200 strikeouts in a season—breaking a record held by Randy Johnson—and set a Braves record with 16 strikeouts in a game against the Rockies on Sept. 1.

With Harris and Strider energizing the team and shortstop Dansby Swanson and third baseman Austin Riley putting up MVP-caliber seasons, the Braves caught fire and chipped away at the Mets' lead. They cut the deficit from 10 ½ games on June 1 to 3 ½ games by July 1. The Mets held tough, but the Braves still pulled into a tie for first place by Sept. 6.

In the last week of the season, the Braves and Mets met for a decisive clash. The Mets went into Atlanta on Sept. 30 clutching to a one-game lead. The Braves' only realistic chance at taking the NL East was if they swept the Mets, a tough task given the Mets had deGrom and Scherzer lined up to pitch the first two games with talented righthander Chris Bassitt behind them.

Even that couldn't stop the Braves. Riley, Swanson and Matt Olson homered off deGrom as the Braves took the first game, 5-2. Swanson and Olson homered again the next night off of Scherzer in a 4-2 win that elevated the Braves all alone into first place. In the finale, Swanson and Olson homered yet again to lead the Braves to a 5-3 victory.

ELSA/GETTY IMAGES

Bryce Harper's season was hampered by an elbow injury, but he starred in the playoffs.

The Braves officially clinched the NL East two days later with a win over the Marlins, but for all intents and purposes, the division was decided with their sweep of the Mets.

"Everyone understood what was at stake during the series," Swanson said, "and we definitely rose to the occasion."

While the West divisions were won easily and the Easts were full of drama, the Central divisions were filled with subtle tension. The White Sox, expected to cruise to the AL Central title, instead became a daily melodrama of questionable coaching decisions, bad defense and underperforming players under manager Tony La Russa. The low point came when La Russa ordered an intentional walk of Dodgers shortstop Trea Turner with a 1-2 count on June 10. The next batter, Max Muncy, promptly homered. Bafflingly, La Russa called for another intentional walk on a 1-2 count against Guardians outfielder Oscar Gonzalez in August. La Russa left the team on medical leave in late August due to a heart condition and announced after the season he would not return as manager.

With the White Sox spiraling, the Guardians took advantage of the dysfunction to roll to a surprising AL Central title. Led by another standout pitching staff and a contact-heavy offense, Cleveland cruised to the division title by 11 games and was the only team in the AL Central to post a winning record.

The NL Central featured its own drama brought about by questionable decision-making. On Aug. 1, with the Brewers leading the division by three games, the club traded all-star closer Josh Hader to the Padres for struggling relievers Taylor Rogers and Dinelson Lamet and two prospects—the type

Stanton's Blast Leads AL to 3-2 Win

BY KYLE GLASER

Slowly but surely, Giancarlo Stanton is building a legacy.

He has won a MVP award and two home run titles. He's been selected to five All-Star Games and won two Silver Sluggers. He won a Home Run Derby with one of the greatest power displays of all time. He has 371 home runs at 32 years old, putting him well within reach of 500 for his career.

Now, the Yankees slugger can add an All-Star Game MVP award—in his hometown of Los Angeles, no less—to his list of accolades.

Stanton hit a mammoth game-tying, two-run home run in the fourth inning to help lead the American League to a 3-2 win against the National League in the All-Star Game. His blast off Dodgers righthander Tony Gonsolin traveled 457 feet into the left field stands, the same seats that Stanton used to sit in as a kid cheering on the Dodgers.

"I can't really explain how special this is," said Stanton, who estimated he had about 50 family and friends in attendance. "It's hard to put into words that this is reality right now."

Stanton grew up about 30 minutes away from Chavez Ravine and attended Notre Dame High in nearby Sherman Oaks. He grew up rooting for Raul Mondesi, Mike Piazza and Hideo Nomo with the Dodgers and always tried to come to games when Mark McGwire, Sammy Sosa, Barry Bonds and the game's other great sluggers came to town.

Stanton often arrived early for batting practice and even caught a few BP home run balls. Other times, he would buy tickets from scalpers in front of Dodger Stadium and come just to see even two at-bats from the game's greatest sluggers.

This year, starting an All-Star Game in left field, not far from where he used to sit, and hitting a home run into those same left field stands, it all came full circle.

"Me playing there—me playing in left as well—(I) always tried to get a ball thrown to me from whoever was playing left field when I was a kid," Stanton said. "Just to be out there is so fun, so cool." ■

ALL-STAR GAME

Giancarlo Stanton

KEVOR▪ DJANSEZIAN/GETTY IMAGES

2022 ALL-STAR GAME

JULY 19, 2022
AL 3, NL 2

AL All-Stars	AB	R	H	RBI	NL All-Stars	AB	R	H	RBI
Ohtani, DH	1	0	1	0	Acuña Jr., RF	3	1	1	0
Cabrera, M, PH-DH	1	0	0	0	Happ, CF	0	0	0	0
Martinez, PH-DH	2	0	0	0	Betts, CF	1	0	1	1
Judge, RF	2	0	0	0	Soto, J, PH-CF-RF	3	0	0	0
Tucker, RF	2	0	0	0	Machado, M, 3B	2	0	0	0
Devers, 3B	0	0	0	0	Riley, 3B	2	0	1	0
Ramirez, Jo, 3B	2	1	2	0	Goldschmidt, 1B	1	1	1	1
France, PH-1B	1	0	0	0	Freeman, F, PH	1	0	0	0
Guerrero, 1B	2	0	0	0	Alonso, 1B	0	0	0	0
Arraez, 1B-3B	2	0	1	0	Cron, 1B	1	0	0	0
Stanton, LF	2	1	1	2	Turner, SS	2	0	1	0
Benintendi, LF	2	0	0	0	Swanson, SS	2	0	0	0
Buxton, CF	2	1	1	1	Contreras, C	2	0	0	0
Rodriguez, J, CF	2	0	0	0	d'Arnaud, C	1	0	0	0
Anderson, Tim, SS	2	0	1	0	Contreras, Wm, DH	1	0	0	0
Bogaerts, SS	1	0	0	0	Pujols, PH-DH	1	0	0	0
Seager, SS	1	0	0	0	Cooper, PH-DH	2	0	0	0
Gimenez, 2B	2	0	0	0	Pederson, LF	2	0	0	0
Espinal, 2B	1	0	0	0	Schwarber, LF	2	0	0	0
Kirk, C	2	0	0	0	McNeil, 2B	1	0	0	0
Trevino, C	2	0	1	0	Cronenworth, 2B	2	0	0	0
Totals	**34**	**3**	**8**	**3**	**Totals**	**32**	**2**	**5**	**2**

2B: Acuña Jr. (1, McClanahan). **HR** : Goldschmidt (1, 1st inning off McClanahan, 0 on, 2 out); Stanton (1, 4th inning off Gonsolin, 1 on, 1 out); Buxton (1, 4th inning off Gonsolin, 0 on, 1 out). **TB**: Acuña Jr. 2; Betts; Goldschmidt 4; Riley; Turner; Anderson, Ti; Arraez; Buxton 4; Ohtani; Ramirez, Jo 2; Stanton 4; Trevino. **2-out RBI**: Goldschmidt. GIDP : Machado, M. **PO** : Ohtani (1st base by Kershaw). **E**: Ramirez, Jo (1, fielding). **DP**: (Gimenez-Anderson, Tim-Guerrero). **Pickoffs** : Kershaw (Ohtani at 1st base).

Time of Game: 3:11 Attendance: 52,518.

American	IP	H	R	SO	National	IP	H	R	SO
McClanahan	1	4	2	1	Kershaw	1	1	0	1
Manoah	1	0	0	3	Alcantara, S	1	0	0	2
Valdez, F (W)	1	0	0	0	Musgrove	1	0	0	2
Blackburn	1	0	0	1	Gonsolin (L)	1	4	3	1
Perez	1	0	0	0	Castillo, L	1	1	0	2
Cortes	1	0	0	2	Mantiply	1	0	0	1
Lopez, Jo	0.2	0	0	0	Williams, D	1	1	0	1
Soto, G	0.1	0	0	0	Helsley	1	1	0	2
Holmes	0.2	1	0	0	Bednar	1	0	0	0
Hendriks	0.1	0	0	0					
Clase (S)	1	0	0	3					

of move usually reserved for a selling team, not one in first place.

"It didn't send us the right message from the upstairs people trying to say, like, 'We're doing this and we're trying to put you guys in the best position and we're trying to win right now with you guys,' " Brewers lefthander Eric Lauer would later say. "It seemed like more of a, 'We're trying to develop for the future.' "

The Cardinals were happy to take advantage.

The Brewers lost five of six after the trade to surrender first place and never held it again. Fueled by Pujols' resurgence and MVP-caliber campaigns from first baseman Paul Goldschmidt and third baseman Nolan Arenado, the Cardinals stormed into first in the NL Central within a week of the deal and pulled away. Up three games on Aug. 1, the Brewers finished seven games back of the division and out of the wild card, missing the playoffs for the first time in five years.

"(The trade) had a more pronounced impact than I thought it would at the time," Brewers president of baseball operations David Stearns said after the season, "and the surrounding moves didn't adequately fortify the team in Josh's absence."

While the traditional powers won the division titles, surging powers took advantage of the wild card spots, helped by the addition of a third wild card to each league.

The Padres, seeking their first playoff berth in a full season since 2006, fueled up at the trade deadline by acquiring star outfielder Juan Soto and first baseman Josh Bell in a massive trade deadline deal with the Nationals that supplemented a roster which lacked star shortstop Fernando Tatis Jr., who missed the entire season due to injuries and a suspension after a positive test for performance-enhancing substances.

The Padres also added Hader from the Brewers and all-star Brandon Drury from the Reds to complete their massive deadline haul, and were rewarded with the second wild card spot in the NL behind the Mets.

After firing manager Joe Girardi in June and replacing him with interim manager Rob Thomson, the Phillies went on a 65-46 run to overcome a sub-.500 start and hold off the Brewers for the NL's final wild card spot.

In the AL, the Blue Jays and Mariners took the first and second wild card spots, led by their young, talented cores. The Rays, plucky as ever, did just enough to take the third wild-card spot in a weakened AL field. ■

ACTIVE LEADERS

Career leaders among those who played in at least one game in 2022. Batters require 3,000 plate appearances and pitchers 1,000 innings to qualify for percentage titles.

BATTERS			PITCHERS		
AVG	Miguel Cabrera	.308	**ERA**	Clayton Kershaw	2.48
OBP	Mike Trout	.415	**SO/9**	Chris Sale	11.1
SLG	Mike Trout	.587	**BB/9**	Corey Kluber	1.97
OPS	Mike Trout	1.002	**HR/9**	Clayton Kershaw	0.72
R	Albert Pujols	1,914	**W**	Justin Verlander	244
H	Albert Pujols	3,384	**L**	Zack Greinke	141
2B	Albert Pujols	686	**SV**	Craig Kimbrel	394
3B	Dexter Fowler	82	**IP**	Zack Greinke	3,247
HR	Albert Pujols	703	**SO**	Justin Verlander	3,198
RBI	Albert Pujols	2,218	**BB**	Justin Verlander	880
BB	Albert Pujols	1,373	**AVG**	Clayton Kershaw	.209
SO	Miguel Cabrera	2,031	**G**	Joe Smith	866
XBH	Albert Pujols	1,405	**GS**	Zack Greinke	514
SB	Dee Strange-Gordon	336	**HR**	Zack Greinke	342

MAJOR LEAGUE DEBUTS

ARIZONA DIAMONDBACKS
Cooper Hummel ..... Apr 7
Jose Herrera............ Apr 9
Tyler Holton.......... Apr 28
Alek Thomas.......... May 8
Buddy Kennedy.....Jun 17
Tommy Henry.........Aug 3
Stone Garrett........Aug 17
Corbin Carroll........Aug 29
Ryne Nelson .... Sep 5
Drey Jameson....... Sep 15

ATLANTA BRAVES
Bryce Elder........... Apr 12
William Woods..... Apr 27
Michael Harris..... May 28
Vaughn Grissom...Aug 10
Freddy Tarnok.......Aug 17

BALTIMORE ORIOLES
Félix Bautista........ Apr 10
Kyle Bradish.......... Apr 29
Rylan Bannon...... May 12
Denyi Reyes......... May 13
Logan Gillaspie.... May 17
Nick Vespi............ May 20
Adley Rutschman May 21
Cody Sedlock....... May 29
Kyle Stowers..........Jun 13
Terrin Vavra.............Jul 29
Yusniel Diaz............Aug 2
DL Hall..................Aug 13
Gunnar HendersonAug 31

BOSTON RED SOX
Josh Winckowski.. May 28
Jeter Downs..........Jun 22
Brayan Bello ....Jul 6
Zack Kelly ....Aug 29
Triston Casas........... Sep 4
Franklin German... Sep 17

CHICAGO CUBS
Seiya Suzuki .... Apr 7
Ethan Roberts......... Apr 9
Brandon Hughes.. May 17
Christopher Morel May 17
Anderson EspinozaMay 30
Matt Swarmer..... May 30
Nelson Velázquez. May 30
Caleb Kilian .... Jun 4
Narciso Crook.........Jun 30
Erich Uelmen..........Jul 22
Javier Assad..........Aug 23
Nicholas Padilla....Aug 23
Jeremiah Estrada..Aug 30
Brendon Little ......Aug 30
Hayden Wesneski.... Sep 6
Jared Young.......... Sep 16
Esteban Quiroz ..... Sep 17

CHICAGO WHITE SOX
Bennett Sousa........ Apr 8
Tanner Banks........ Apr 10
Anderson Severino Apr 14
Davis Martin........ May 17
Lenyn Sosa ....Jun 23
Carlos Perez..........Aug 26

MAJOR LEAGUE DEBUTS

CINCINNATI REDS

Alexis Diaz .... Apr 8
Daniel Duarte .... Apr 8
Hunter Greene .... Apr 10
Nick Lodolo .... Apr 13
Mark Kolozsvary .... Apr 20
Jared Solomon .... May 7
Graham Ashcraft .... May 22
Chris Okey .... Jun 10
Chuckie Robinson .... Aug 24
Fernando Cruz .... Sep 2
Spencer Steer .... Sep 2
Michael Siani .... Sep 22

CLEVELAND GUARDIANS

Steven Kwan .... Apr 7
Bryan Lavastida .... Apr 10
Konnor Pilkington .... Apr 15
Gabriel Arias .... Apr 20
Tanner Tully .... Apr 22
Kirk McCarty .... Apr 24
Richie Palacios .... Apr 25
Oscar Gonzalez .... May 26
Nolan Jones .... Jul 8
Alex Call .... Jul 11
Will Benson .... Aug 1
Tyler Freeman .... Aug 3
Hunter Gaddis .... Aug 5
Xzavion Curry .... Aug 15
Cody Morris .... Sep 2
Will Brennan .... Sep 21
Bo Naylor .... Oct 1

COLORADO ROCKIES

Elehuris Montero .... May 1
Brian Serven .... May 18
Chad Smith .... May 29
Jake Bird .... Jun 16
Sean Bouchard .... Jun 19
Wynton Bernard .... Aug 12
Michael Toglia .... Aug 30
Gavin Hollowell .... Sep 19
Ezequiel Tovar .... Sep 23
Noah Davis .... Oct 5

DETROIT TIGERS

Spencer Torkelson .... Apr 8
Elvin Rodriguez .... Apr 10
Beau Brieske .... Apr 23
Angel De Jesus .... Apr 23
Alex Faedo .... May 4
Joey Wentz .... May 11
Kody Clemens .... May 31
Riley Greene .... Jun 18
Garrett Hill .... Jul 4
Luis Castillo .... Aug 6
Kerry Carpenter .... Aug 10
Ryan Kreidler .... Sep 2
Josh Lester .... Sep 5
Brendon Davis .... Oct 1

HOUSTON ASTROS

Jeremy Pena .... Apr 7
Ronel Blanco .... Apr 8
Joe Perez .... Apr 8
Parker Mushinski .... Apr 17
J.J. Matijevic .... Apr 22
Korey Lee .... Jul 1
David Hensley .... Aug 27
Yainer Diaz .... Sep 2
Hunter Brown .... Sep 5

KANSAS CITY ROYALS

Bobby Witt .... Apr 7
Collin Snider .... Apr 9
MJ Melendez .... May 3
Dairon Blanco .... May 20
Brewer Hicklen .... May 26
Jose Cuas .... May 31
Vinnie Pasquantino .... Jun 28
Nate Eaton .... Jul 14
Nick Pratto .... Jul 14
Freddy Fermin .... Jul 15
Maikel Garcia .... Jul 15
Michael Massey .... Jul 15
Drew Waters .... Aug 22

LOS ANGELES ANGELS

Kenny Rosenberg .... Apr 18
Chase Silseth .... May 13
David MacKinnon .... Jun 18
Michael Stefanic .... Jul 3
Ryan Aguilar .... Aug 26
Livan Soto .... Sep 17
Logan O'Hoppe .... Sep 28
Nash Walters .... Oct 5

LOS ANGELES DODGERS

Ryan Pepiot .... May 11
Michael Grove .... May 15
James Outman .... Jul 31
Miguel Vargas .... Aug 3

MIAMI MARLINS

Joe Dunand .... May 7
Aneurys Zabala .... Jun 12
Jerar Encarnacion .... Jun 19
Max Meyer .... Jul 16
JJ Bleday .... Jul 23
Huascar Brazoban .... Jul 24
Charles Leblanc .... Jul 30
Jake Fishman .... Jul 31
Peyton Burdick .... Aug 5
A.J. Ladwig .... Aug 13
Andrew Nardi .... Aug 16
Bryan Hoeing .... Aug 20
Jordan Groshans .... Sep 13

MILWAUKEE BREWERS

Ethan Small .... May 30
Jason Alexander .... Jun 1
Peter Strzelecki .... Jun 2
Luke Barker .... Jun 3
Garrett Mitchell .... Aug 27

MINNESOTA TWINS

Jhoan Duran .... Apr 8
Josh Winder .... Apr 12
Cole Sands .... May 1
Jose Miranda .... May 2
Royce Lewis .... May 6
Yennier Cano .... May 11
Mark Contreras .... May 11
Jermaine Palacios .... May 31
Caleb Hamilton .... Jul 17
Louie Varland .... Sep 7
Matt Wallner .... Sep 17
Ronny Henriquez .... Sep 19
S.Woods Richardson .... Oct 2

NEW YORK METS

Nick Plummer .... Apr 15
Colin Holderman .... May 15
Brett Baty .... Aug 17
José Butto .... Aug 21
Nate Fisher .... Aug 21
Bryce Montes de Oca .... Sep 3
Mark Vientos .... Sep 11
Francisco Álvarez .... Sep 30

NEW YORK YANKEES

Ron Marinaccio .... Apr 9
JP Sears .... Apr 13
Oswaldo Cabrera .... Aug 17
Greg Weissert .... Aug 25
Oswald Peraza .... Sep 2

OAKLAND ATHLETICS

Jacob Lemoine .... Apr 8
Zach Jackson .... Apr 9
Adam Oller .... Apr 12
Nick Allen .... Apr 19
Zach Logue .... Apr 19
Christian Lopes .... Apr 20
Mickey McDonald .... Apr 20
Adrian Martinez .... May 10
Jared Koenig .... Jun 8
Jonah Bride .... Jun 14
Dermis Garcia .... Jul 12
Cal Stevenson .... Aug 10
Shea Langeliers .... Aug 16
Norge Ruíz .... Aug 19
Cody Thomas .... Sep 1
Ken Waldichuk .... Sep 1
Collin Wiles .... Sep 14
Jordan Diaz .... Sep 18
Nate Mondou .... Oct 4

PHILADELPHIA PHILLIES

Bryson Stott .... Apr 8
Simon Muzziotti .... Apr 11
Francisco Morales .... May 9
Michael Kelly .... Jun 16
Mark Appel .... Jun 29
Darick Hall .... Jun 29
Nick Duron .... Jul 13
Bubby Rossman .... Jul 13
Tyler Cyr .... Aug 21
Michael Plassmeyer .... Aug 23
Donny Sands .... Sep 2
Dalton Guthrie .... Sep 6

PITTSBURGH PIRATES

Diego Castillo .... Apr 7
Beau Sulser .... Apr 26
Jack Suwinski .... Apr 26
Cam Alldred .... May 12
Calvin Mitchell .... May 24
Y. De Los Santos .... May 25
Travis Swaggerty .... Jun 7
Jason Delay .... Jun 14
C. Smith-Njigba .... Jun 14
Cam Vieaux .... Jun 17
Liover Peguero .... Jun 18
Bligh Madris .... Jun 20
Luis Ortiz .... Sep 13
Ji Hwan Bae .... Sep 23

ST. LOUIS CARDINALS

Andre Pallante .... Apr 10
Brendan Donovan .... Apr 25
Juan Yepez .... May 4
Kramer Robertson .... May 10
Jake Walsh .... May 11
Nolan Gorman .... May 20
Matthew Liberatore .... May 21
Ivan Herrera .... May 24
Zack Thompson .... Jun 3
Conner Capel .... Jun 27
James Naile .... Jun 27
Ben DeLuzio .... Sep 2
Alec Burleson .... Sep 8

SAN DIEGO PADRES

Jose Azocar .... Apr 7
Robert Suarez .... Apr 7
CJ Abrams .... Apr 8
Steven Wilson .... Apr 9
MacKenzie Gore .... Apr 15
Ray Kerr .... Apr 24
Matthew Batten .... Jun 30
Esteury Ruiz .... Jul 12
Eguy Rosario .... Aug 26
Luis Liberato .... Sep 10

SAN FRANCISCO GIANTS

Heliot Ramos .... Apr 10
Yunior Marte .... Apr 12
Jason Krizan .... Apr 29
Sean Hjelle .... May 6
Michael Papierski .... May 21
David Villar .... Jul 4
Bryce Johnson .... Aug 3
Cole Waites .... Sep 13
Ford Proctor .... Sep 24

SEATTLE MARINERS

Julio Rodriguez .... Apr 8
Matt Brash .... Apr 12
Penn Murfee .... Apr 29
George Kirby .... May 8
Danny Young .... May 9
Marcus Wilson .... Jun 29
Brennan Bernardino .... Jul 31
Jack Larsen .... Jul 31
Brian O'Keefe .... Oct 1

TAMPA BAY RAYS

Tommy Romero .... Apr 12
Phoenix Sanders .... Apr 14
Rene Pinto .... Apr 26
Calvin Faucher .... May 9
Jonathan Aranda .... Jun 24
Cristofer Ogando .... Jul 3
Kevin Herget .... Sep 13
Miles Mastrobuoni .... Sep 22
Easton McGee .... Oct 2

TEXAS RANGERS

Josh Smith .... May 30
Ezequiel Duran .... Jun 4
Steele Walker .... Jun 5
Elier Hernandez .... Jul 14
Cole Ragans .... Aug 4
Bubba Thompson .... Aug 4
Josh Jung .... Sep 9
Yerry Rodriguez .... Oct 5

TORONTO BLUE JAYS

Gosuke Katoh .... Apr 9
Bowden Francis .... Apr 27
Vinny Capra .... May 1
Matt Gage .... Jun 6
Gabriel Moreno .... Jun 11
Max Castillo .... Jun 19

WASHINGTON NATIONALS

Lucius Fox .... Apr 10
Evan Lee .... Jun 1
Jackson Tetreault .... Jun 14
Joey Meneses .... Aug 2
Cade Cavalli .... Aug 26
Israel Pineda .... Sep 11

AMERICAN LEAGUE

2022 STATISTICS

CLUB BATTING

	AVG	G	AB	R	H	2B	3B	HR	RBI	BB	SO	SB	OBP	SLG
Houston	.267	162	5593	863	1496	299	14	221	834	569	1222	53	.339	.444
Toronto	.266	162	5476	846	1455	285	13	262	816	496	1218	81	.330	.466
Boston	.261	162	5495	829	1434	330	23	219	783	512	1386	40	.328	.449
Chicago	.256	162	5357	796	1373	275	22	190	757	586	1389	57	.336	.422
Kansas City	.249	162	5427	686	1349	251	29	163	647	421	1258	124	.306	.396
Los Angeles	.245	162	5437	723	1331	265	23	190	691	464	1394	79	.310	.407
Tampa Bay	.243	162	5507	857	1336	288	36	222	810	585	1542	88	.321	.429
Detroit	.242	162	5376	697	1299	236	37	179	675	490	1514	88	.308	.399
Minnesota	.241	162	5431	729	1311	271	17	228	690	525	1405	54	.314	.423
Baltimore	.239	162	5420	659	1296	266	15	195	632	451	1454	54	.304	.402
Oakland	.238	162	5395	743	1284	271	19	199	698	545	1349	88	.317	.406
Cleveland	.238	162	5332	717	1269	248	22	203	686	453	1387	109	.303	.407
New York	.237	162	5331	711	1266	213	12	222	666	621	1482	63	.322	.407
Texas	.232	162	5405	625	1254	225	24	167	598	433	1381	106	.294	.375
Seattle	.226	162	5355	697	1209	233	11	199	673	535	1492	64	.303	.385

CLUB PITCHING

	ERA	G	CG	SHO	SV	IP	H	R	ER	HR	BB	SO	AVG
Tampa Bay	3.67	162	1	13	42	1456	1264	651	593	184	436	1478	.232
Chicago	3.73	162	4	13	43	1403	1205	636	581	182	485	1588	.229
New York	3.74	162	3	13	47	1435	1243	669	596	196	492	1569	.231
Houston	3.78	162	2	8	34	1445	1231	658	607	187	549	1456	.228
Toronto	3.91	162	1	14	34	1405	1257	663	610	209	473	1468	.236
Oakland	4.02	162	3	11	39	1433	1362	687	640	191	439	1332	.247
Boston	4.26	162	0	7	49	1419	1409	749	671	176	546	1527	.258
Seattle	4.30	162	1	10	51	1440	1356	748	688	197	485	1328	.247
Detroit	4.32	162	2	7	42	1420	1370	756	681	199	571	1259	.252
Cleveland	4.34	162	0	9	39	1408	1281	727	679	216	522	1391	.240
Kansas City	4.64	162	1	7	37	1417	1375	788	731	189	591	1344	.254
Los Angeles	4.69	162	1	4	39	1422	1373	804	741	188	592	1453	.251
Texas	4.79	162	0	3	31	1424	1402	815	758	232	513	1239	.256
Minnesota	4.83	162	1	9	42	1419	1392	834	762	239	484	1317	.255
Baltimore	5.84	162	1	5	26	1402	1518	956	910	258	563	1234	.273

CLUB FIELDING

	PCT	PO	A	E	DP
Houston	.988	4335	1432	69	126
Oakland	.987	4299	1320	72	116
Baltimore	.987	4206	1359	74	101
Seattle	.986	4321	1384	79	135
Tampa Bay	.986	4367	1358	80	130
Detroit	.986	4259	1492	83	136
Texas	.986	4273	1462	83	146
Kansas City	.985	4252	1422	84	152
Cleveland	.985	4224	1400	86	138
Los Angeles	.985	4265	1419	88	131
Toronto	.984	4216	1371	90	122
New York	.983	4306	1318	98	112
Chicago	.982	4210	1210	97	112
Minnesota	.982	4258	1420	107	138
Boston	.981	4257	1421	108	143

INDIVIDUAL BATTING LEADERS

	AVG	G	AB	R	H	2B	3B	HR	RBI	BB	SO	SB
Luis Arraez, Minnesota	.316	144	547	88	173	31	1	8	49	50	43	4
Aaron Judge, New York	.311	157	570	133	177	28	0	62	131	111	175	16
Xander Bogaerts, Boston	.307	150	557	84	171	38	0	15	73	57	118	8
Yordan Alvarez, Houston	.306	135	470	95	144	29	2	37	97	78	106	1
Jose Abreu, Chicago	.304	157	601	85	183	40	0	15	75	62	110	0
Andrew Benintendi, New York	.304	126	461	54	140	23	3	5	51	52	77	8
Nate Lowe, Texas	.302	157	593	74	179	26	3	27	76	48	147	2
Jose Altuve, Houston	.300	141	527	103	158	39	0	28	57	66	87	18
Steven Kwan, Cleveland	.298	147	563	89	168	25	7	6	52	62	60	19
Andres Giménez, Cleveland	.297	146	491	66	146	26	3	17	69	34	112	20

INDIVIDUAL PITCHING LEADERS

	W	L	ERA	G	GS	CG	SV	IP	H	R	ER	BB	SO
Justin Verlander, Houston	18	4	1.75	28	28	0	0	175	116	43	34	29	185
Dylan Cease, Chicago	14	8	2.20	32	32	1	0	184	126	55	45	78	227
Alek Manoah, Toronto	16	7	2.24	31	31	0	0	197	144	55	49	51	180
Shohei Ohtani, Los Angeles	15	9	2.33	28	28	0	0	166	124	45	43	44	219
Shane McClanahan, Tampa Bay	12	8	2.54	28	28	0	0	166	116	52	47	38	194
Framber Valdez, Houston	17	6	2.82	31	31	3	0	201	166	71	63	67	194
Shane Bieber, Cleveland	13	8	2.88	31	31	1	0	200	172	70	64	36	198
Martin Perez, Texas	12	8	2.89	32	32	1	0	196	178	70	63	69	169
Triston McKenzie, Cleveland	11	11	2.96	31	30	0	0	191	138	65	63	44	190
Logan Gilbert, Seattle	13	6	3.20	32	32	0	0	186	170	71	66	49	174

AWARD WINNERS

Selected by Baseball Writers Association of America

MOST VALUABLE PLAYER

Player	1st	2nd	3rd	Total
Aaron Judge, Yankees	28	2		410
Shohei Ohtani, Angels	2	28		280
Yordan Alvarez, Astros			22	232
Jose Ramirez, Guardians			6	186
Jose Altuve, Astros				142
Andres Gimenez, Guardians			2	141
Julio Rodriguez, Mariners				108
Mike Trout, Angels				90
Xander Bogaerts, Red Sox				50
Justin Verlander, Astros				44
Bo Bichette, Blue Jays				16
Adley Rutschman, Orioles				14
Luis Arraez, Twins				12
Rafael Devers, Red Sox				10
Kyle Tucker, Astros				8
Vladimir Guerrero Jr., Blue Jays				7
José Abreu, White Sox				5
Alek Manoah, Blue Jays				5
Alex Bregman, Astros				4
Yandy Diaz, Rays				2
Framber Valdez, Astros				2
Sean Murphy, Athletics				1
Dylan Cease, White Sox				1

CY YOUNG AWARD

Player	1st	2nd	3rd	Total
Justin Verlander, Astros	30			210
Dylan Cease, White Sox		14	10	97
Alek Manoah, Blue Jays		7	13	87
Shohei Ohtani, Angels		9	7	82
Framber Valdez, Astros				14
Shane McClanahan, Rays				10
Shane Bieber, Guardians				5
Nestor Cortes, Yankees				3
Gerrit Cole, Yankees				1
Kevin Gausman, Blue Jays				1

ROOKIE OF THE YEAR

Player	1st	2nd	3rd	Total
Julio Rodriguez, Mariners	29	1		148
Adley Rutschman, Orioles	1	18	9	68
Steven Kwan, Guardians		10	14	44
Bobby Witt Jr., Royals		1	4	7
Jeremy Peña, Astros			2	2
George Kirby, Mariners			1	1

MANAGER OF THE YEAR

Player	1st	2nd	3rd	Total
Terry Francona, Guardians	17	9		112
Brandon Hyde, Orioles	9	9	7	79
Scott Servais, Mariners	1	8	14	43
Dusty Baker, Astros	3	3	7	31
Aaron Boone, Yankees		1	1	4
Kevin Cash, Rays			1	1

GOLD GLOVE WINNERS

Selected by AL managers and coaches

P—Shane Bieber, Guardians. **C**—Jose Trevino, Yankees. **1B**—Vladimir Guerrero Jr., Blue Jays. **2B**—Andres Gimenez, Guardians. **3B**—Ramon Urias, Orioles. **SS**—Jeremy Peña, Astros. **LF**—Steven Kwan, Guardians. **CF**—Myles Straw, Guardians. **RF**—Kyle Tucker, Astros. **UT**—DJ LeMahieu, Yankees.

AMERICAN LEAGUE DEPARTMENT LEADERS

BATTING

GAMES

Marcus Semien, Texas	161
Vladimir Guerrero, Toronto	160
Bo Bichette, Toronto	159
Jose Abreu, Chicago	157
4 others	157

AT-BATS

Marcus Semien, Texas	657
Bo Bichette, Toronto	652
Vladimir Guerrero, Toronto	638
Amed Rosario, Cleveland	637
Cedric Mullins, Baltimore	608

PLATE APPEARANCES

Marcus Semien, Texas	724
Vladimir Guerrero, Toronto	706
Bo Bichette, Toronto	697
Aaron Judge, New York	696
Jose Ramirez, Cleveland	685

RUNS

Aaron Judge, New York	133
Jose Altuve, Houston	103
Marcus Semien, Texas	101
Yordan Alvarez, Houston	95
Alex Bregman, Houston	93

HITS

Bo Bichette, Toronto	189
Jose Abreu, Chicago	183
Amed Rosario, Cleveland	180
Nathaniel Lowe, Texas	179
Aaron Judge, New York	177

TOTAL BASES

Aaron Judge, New York	391
Jose Ramirez, Cleveland	309
Bo Bichette, Toronto	306
Vladimir Guerrero, Toronto	306
Shohei Ohtani, Los Angeles	304

DOUBLES

Jose Ramirez, Cleveland	44
Bo Bichette, Toronto	43
J.D. Martinez, Boston	43
Rafael Devers, Boston	42
Randy Arozarena, Tampa Bay	41

TRIPLES

Amed Rosario, Cleveland	9
Steven Kwan, Cleveland	7
Jorge Mateo, Baltimore	7
Shohei Ohtani, Los Angeles	6
Bobby Witt Jr., Kansas City	6

EXTRA-BASE HITS

Aaron Judge, New York	90
Jose Ramirez, Cleveland	78
Rafael Devers, Boston	70
Shohei Ohtani, Los Angeles	70
Mike Trout, Los Angeles	70

HOME RUNS

Aaron Judge, New York	62
Mike Trout, Los Angeles	40
Yordan Alvarez, Houston	37
Shohei Ohtani, Los Angeles	34
2 tied	33

RUNS BATTED IN

Aaron Judge, New York	131
Jose Ramirez, Cleveland	126
Kyle Tucker, Houston	107
Adolis Garcia, Texas	101
2 tied	97

Jose Ramirez

SACRIFICES

Austin Hedges, Cleveland	10
Nicky Lopez, Kansas City	10
Nick Allen, Oakland	6
Reese McGuire, Boston	6
Andrew Velazquez, Los Angeles	6

SACRIFICE FLIES

Alex Bregman, Houston	10
Marcus Semien, Texas	10
Owen Miller, Cleveland	9
Jose Ramirez, Cleveland	9
Whit Merrifield, Toronto	8

HIT BY PITCHES

Andres Gimenez, Cleveland	25
Anthony Rizzo, New York	23
Ty France, Seattle	21
Josh Harrison, Chicago	14
2 tied	13

WALKS

Aaron Judge, New York	111
Alex Bregman, Houston	87
Jesse Winker, Seattle	84
Yordan Alvarez, Houston	78
Yandy Diaz, Tampa Bay	78

STOLEN BASES

Jorge Mateo, Baltimore	35
Cedric Mullins, Baltimore	34
Randy Arozarena, Tampa Bay	32
Bobby Witt Jr., Kansas City	30
4 tied	25

STOLEN BASE PERCENTAGE

Yuli Gurriel, Houston	1.000
Sean Murphy, Oakland	1.000
Jonathan Schoop, Detroit	1.000
Corey Seager, Texas	1.000
Gio Urshela, Minnesota	1.000

STRIKEOUTS

Eugenio Suarez, Seattle	196
Adolis Garcia, Texas	183
Aaron Judge, New York	175
Matt Chapman, Toronto	170
Shohei Ohtani, Los Angeles	161

AT-BATS PER STRIKEOUT

Luis Arraez, Minnesota	12.7
Steven Kwan, Cleveland	9.4
Alejandro Kirk, Toronto	8.1
Yandy Diaz, Tampa Bay	7.9
Yuli Gurriel, Houston	7.5

Yordan Alvarez

DOUBLE PLAYS

Vladimir Guerrero, Toronto	26
Bo Bichette, Toronto	21
Gio Urshela, Minnesota	21
J.D. Martinez, Boston	20
Jose Abreu, Chicago	19
2 others	19

MULTI-HIT GAMES

Bo Bichette, Toronto	56
Nathaniel Lowe, Texas	54
José Abreu, Chicago	53
Aaron Judge, New York	52
3 tied	49

ON-BASE PERCENTAGE

Aaron Judge, New York	.425
Yordan Alvarez, Houston	.406
Yandy Diaz, Tampa Bay	.401
Jose Altuve, Houston	.387
Jose Abreu, Chicago	.378

ON-BASE PLUS SLUGGING

Aaron Judge, New York	1.111
Yordan Alvarez, Houston	1.019
Jose Altuve, Houston	.920
Rafael Devers, Boston	.879
Shohei Ohtani, Los Angeles	.875

PITCHING

WINS

Justin Verlander, Houston	18
Framber Valdez, Houston	17
Alek Manoah, Toronto	16
Luis Garcia, Houston	15
Shohei Ohtani, Los Angeles	15
Cal Quantrill, Cleveland	15

LOSSES

Marco Gonzales, Seattle	15
Brad Keller, Kansas City	14
Kris Bubic, Kansas City	13
Cole Irvin, Oakland	13
Daniel Lynch, Kansas City	13
4 others	12

GAMES

Adam Cimber, Toronto	77
Emmanuel Clase, Cleveland	77
Alex Lange, Detroit	71
Rafael Montero, Houston	71
3 tied	70

GAMES STARTED

Gerrit Cole, New York	33
Nick Pivetta, Boston	33
Jose Berrios, Toronto	32
Dylan Cease, Chicago	32
7 others	32

GAMES FINISHED

Emmanuel Clase, Cleveland	67
Gregory Soto, Detroit	54
Jordan Romano, Toronto	52
Liam Hendriks, Chicago	51
Scott Barlow, Kansas City	47
Jorge Lopez, Minnesota	47

COMPLETE GAMES

Framber Valdez, Houston	3
Nathan Eovaldi, Boston	2
Brayan Bello, Boston	1
Shane Bieber, Cleveland	1
10 others	1

CHRISTIAN PETERSEN/GETTY IMAGES(RAMIREZ), HARRY HOW/GETTY IMAGES (ALVAREZ)

AMERICAN LEAGUE DEPARTMENT LEADERS

SHUTOUTS

Dylan Cease, Chicago	1
Nestor Cortes, New York	1
Reid Detmers, Los Angeles	1
Nathan Eovaldi, Boston	1
5 others	1

SAVES

Emmanuel Clase, Cleveland	42
Liam Hendriks, Chicago	37
Jordan Romano, Toronto	36
Ryan Pressly, Houston	33
Gregory Soto, Detroit	30
Scott Barlow, Kansas City	24

INNINGS PITCHED

Framber Valdez, Houston	201
Gerrit Cole, New York	201
Shane Bieber, Cleveland	200
Alek Manoah, Toronto	197
Martin Perez, Texas	196

HITS ALLOWED

Jose Berrios, Toronto	199
Jordan Lyles, Baltimore	196
Marco Gonzales, Seattle	194
Kevin Gausman, Toronto	188
Corey Kluber, Tampa	178
Martin Perez, Texas	178
Cal Quantrill, Cleveland	178

RUNS ALLOWED

Jose Berrios, Toronto	103
Marco Gonzales, Seattle	97
Jordan Lyles, Baltimore	94
Lucas Giolito, Chicago	92
Nick Pivetta, Boston	91

HOME RUNS ALLOWED

Gerrit Cole, New York	33
Robbie Ray, Seattle	32
Marco Gonzales, Seattle	30
Jose Berrios, Toronto	29
Jose Urquidy, Houston	29

WALKS ALLOWED

Dylan Cease, Chicago	78
Nick Pivetta, Boston	73
Martin Perez, Texas	69
Framber Valdez, Houston	67
Kris Bubic, Kansas City	63

Shane McClanahan

LOWEST WALKS PER NINE

Corey Kluber, Tampa Bay	1.2
Kevin Gausman, Toronto	1.4
Justin Verlander, Houston	1.5
Shane Bieber, Cleveland	1.6
Jameson Taillon, New York	1.6

HIT BATTERS

Alek Manoah, Toronto	15
Glenn Otto, Texas	13
Jose Berrios, Toronto	11
Dane Dunning, Texas	11
3 others	11

STRIKEOUTS

Gerrit Cole, New York	257
Dylan Cease, Chicago	227
Shohei Ohtani, Los Angeles	219
Robbie Ray, Seattle	212
Kevin Gausman, Toronto	205

STRIKEOUTS PER NINE

Shohei Ohtani, Los Angeles	11.9
Gerrit Cole, New York	11.5
Dylan Cease, Chicago	11.1
Kevin Gausman, Toronto	10.6
Shane McClanahan, Tampa Bay	10.5

STRIKEOUTS PER NINE
(Relievers)

Andres Muñoz, Seattle	13.3
Liam Hendriks, Chicago	13.3
Bryan Abreu, Houston	13.1
Jake Diekman, Chicago	12.3
Joe Jimenez, Detroit	12.2

DOUBLE PLAYS

Framber Valdez, Houston	25
Johnny Cueto, Chicago	20
Martin Perez, Texas	20
Kris Bubic, Kansas City	19
Lucas Giolito, Chicago	18
Jordan Lyles, Baltimore	18

PICKOFFS

Robbie Ray, Seattle	6
Aroldis Chapman, New York	3
Jeffrey Springs, Tampa Bay	3
Jose Berrios, Toronto	2
14 others	2

WILD PITCHES

Alex Lange, Detroit	15
Shohei Ohtani, Los Angeles	14
Brad Keller, Kansas City	11
Framber Valdez, Houston	11
Nick Pivetta, Boston	10
Drew Rasmussen, Tampa Bay	10

WALKS PLUS HITS PER INNING

Justin Verlander, Houston	0.83
Shane McClanahan, Tampa Bay	0.93
Triston McKenzie, Cleveland	0.95
Alek Manoah, Toronto	0.99
Shohei Ohtani, Los Angeles	1.01

OPPONENT AVERAGE

Justin Verlander, Houston	.186
Dylan Cease, Chicago	.190
Shane McClanahan, Tampa Bay	.194
Triston McKenzie, Cleveland	.201
Alek Manoah, Toronto	.202

WORST ERA
(min. 120 IP)

Kris Bubic, Kansas City	5.58
Jose Berrios, Toronto	5.23
Daniel Lynch, Kansas City	5.13
Brad Keller, Kansas City	5.09
Lucas Giolito, Chicago	4.90

FIELDING

PITCHER

PCT	7 players	1.000
PO	Zack Greinke, Kansas City	20
A	Framber Valdez, Houston	23
DP	Davis Martin, Chicago	3
E	4 tied	3

CATCHER

PCT	Martin Maldonado, Houston	.998
PO	Martin Maldonado, Houston	1,025
A	Martin Maldonado, Houston	49
DP	Max Stassi, Los Angeles	7
	Alejandro Kirk, Toronto	7
E	3 tied	8
CS	Cal Raleigh, Seattle	25
PB	Martin Maldonado, Houston	9

FIRST BASE

PCT	Spencer Torkelson, Detroit	.998
PO	Nathaniel Lowe, Texas	1,252
A	Ryan Mountcastle, Baltimore	74
DP	Nathaniel Lowe, Texas	125
E	Jose Abreu, Chicago	11

SECOND BASE

PCT	Jonathan Schoop, Detroit	.994
PO	Marcus Semien, Texas	252
A	Marcus Semien, Texas	398
DP	Marcus Semien, Texas	89
E	Rougned Odor, Baltimore	16

THIRD BASE

PCT	Matt Chapman, Toronto	.988
PO	Matt Chapman, Toronto	164
A	Matt Chapman, Toronto	263
	Alex Bregman, Houston	263
DP	Matt Chapman, Toronto	41
E	Rafael Devers, Boston	14

SHORTSTOP

PCT	Carlos Correa, Minnesota	.983
PO	Javier Baez, Detroit	187
A	Jorge Mateo, Baltimore	417
DP	Jorge Mateo, Baltimore	91
	Corey Seager, Texas	91
E	Javier Baez, Detroit	26

OUTFIELD

PCT	3 players	1.000
PO	Myles Straw, Cleveland	371
A	Myles Straw, Cleveland	12
DP	Cedric Mullins, Baltimore	4
E	Oscar Gonzalez, Cleveland	6
	Julio Rodriguez, Seattle	6

BEN JACKSON/MLB PHOTOS VIA GETTY IMAGES

NATIONAL LEAGUE 2022 STATISTICS

CLUB BATTING

	AVG	G	AB	R	H	2B	3B	HR	RBI	BB	SO	SB	OBP	SLG
Washington	.258	162	5385	724	1388	272	20	182	686	573	1303	56	.337	.417
Cincinnati	.249	162	5423	786	1352	295	13	222	756	553	1425	36	.328	.431
San Francisco	.249	162	5462	804	1360	271	25	241	768	602	1461	66	.329	.440
Colorado	.249	161	5374	739	1338	275	34	182	709	491	1356	76	.317	.414
Los Angeles	.244	162	5445	830	1330	247	24	237	799	613	1408	65	.330	.429
Atlanta	.244	161	5363	790	1307	269	20	239	762	549	1453	59	.319	.435
St. Louis	.244	162	5351	706	1303	261	22	198	678	478	1341	89	.313	.412
San Diego	.242	162	5384	729	1305	273	21	180	695	586	1324	110	.321	.401
Philadelphia	.240	162	5366	734	1288	262	24	198	700	564	1402	77	.318	.408
New York	.239	162	5210	636	1243	228	18	176	604	495	1392	54	.315	.391
Chicago	.237	162	5306	705	1255	225	26	210	672	502	1596	86	.312	.407
Pittsburgh	.236	162	5336	609	1261	240	35	124	570	529	1328	60	.309	.364
Arizona	.236	162	5489	679	1297	308	31	144	644	537	1465	43	.309	.382
Milwaukee	.233	162	5362	738	1251	255	18	101	700	586	1465	82	.317	.396
Miami	.233	162	5348	623	1244	226	23	158	594	450	1553	106	.298	.372

CLUB PITCHING

	ERA	G	CG	SHO	SV	IP	H	R	ER	HR	BB	SO	AVG
Los Angeles	3.01	162	1	17	56	1452	1107	561	486	161	486	1599	.207
San Francisco	3.24	162	2	18	56	1455	1254	594	524	151	416	1425	.230
Milwaukee	3.50	162	2	19	44	1436	1156	623	558	168	537	1618	.218
Atlanta	3.88	161	2	18	40	1411	1237	656	608	183	516	1417	.234
New York	3.90	162	2	8	41	1379	1221	668	597	190	475	1453	.236
Miami	3.96	162	1	8	33	1415	1282	701	622	162	529	1381	.241
St. Louis	3.98	162	3	15	50	1417	1234	672	626	152	608	1225	.234
San Diego	4.10	162	2	11	43	1430	1277	708	651	205	516	1517	.237
Philadelphia	4.39	162	5	12	36	1419	1321	745	692	200	509	1480	.244
Cincinnati	4.40	162	1	8	41	1434	1330	760	702	206	617	1524	.244
Washington	4.80	162	1	8	36	1394	1364	820	744	247	548	1346	.254
Colorado	4.82	161	3	6	33	1397	1397	796	748	196	539	1269	.260
Chicago	4.87	162	1	8	40	1413	1386	839	765	235	596	1358	.255
Pittsburgh	5.08	162	0	6	25	1396	1400	833	788	213	606	1312	.260
Arizona	5.11	162	3	4	22	1417	1480	893	804	232	555	1238	.267

CLUB FIELDING

	PCT	PO	A	E	DP
Atlanta	.988	4232	1483	71	104
Pittsburgh	.988	4189	1378	70	139
Colorado	.987	4191	1516	73	140
San Francisco	.986	4365	1471	80	122
San Diego	.986	4290	1399	82	139
St. Louis	.986	4251	1514	84	137
Chicago	.985	4238	1554	87	149

	PCT	PO	A	E	DP
Los Angeles	.985	4356	1303	89	94
Cincinnati	.984	4303	1422	91	124
Philadelphia	.984	4256	1439	94	142
Milwaukee	.984	4308	1331	94	102
Washington	.983	4186	1365	96	116
New York	.983	4138	1312	95	121
Arizona	.983	4252	1374	100	113
Miami	.979	4245	1444	122	146

INDIVIDUAL BATTING LEADERS

	AVG	G	AB	R	H	2B	3B	HR	RBI	BB	SO	SB
Jeff McNeil, New York	.326	148	533	73	174	39	1	9	62	40	61	4
Freddie Freeman, Los Angeles	.325	159	612	117	199	47	2	21	100	84	102	13
Paul Goldschmidt, St. Louis	.317	151	561	106	178	41	0	35	115	79	141	7
Manny Machado, San Diego	.298	150	578	100	172	37	1	32	102	63	133	9
Trea Turner, Los Angeles	.298	160	652	101	194	39	4	21	100	45	131	27
Nolan Arenado, St. Louis	.293	148	557	73	163	42	1	30	103	52	72	5
Starling Marte, New York	.292	118	466	76	136	24	5	16	63	26	97	18
Nico Hoerner, Chicago	.281	135	481	60	135	22	5	10	55	28	57	20
Alec Bohm, Philadelphia	.280	152	586	79	164	24	3	13	72	31	110	2
Justin Turner, Los Angeles	.278	128	468	61	130	36	0	13	81	50	89	3

INDIVIDUAL PITCHING LEADERS

	W	L	ERA	G	GS	CG	SV	IP	H	R	ER	BB	SO
Julio Urias, Los Angeles	17	7	2.16	31	31	0	0	175	127	51	42	41	166
Sandy Alcantara, Miami	14	9	2.28	32	32	6	0	229	174	67	58	50	207
Max Fried, Atlanta	14	7	2.48	30	30	0	0	185	156	55	51	32	170
Zac Gallen, Arizona	12	4	2.54	31	31	0	0	184	121	56	52	47	192
Tyler Anderson, Los Angeles	15	5	2.57	30	28	0	0	179	145	57	51	34	138
Carlos Rodon, San Francisco	14	8	2.88	31	31	1	0	178	131	59	57	52	237
Logan Webb, San Francisco	15	9	2.90	32	32	0	0	192	174	76	62	49	163
Jose Quintana, St. Louis	6	7	2.93	32	32	0	0	166	154	61	54	47	137
Joe Musgrove, San Diego	10	7	2.93	30	30	0	0	181	154	67	59	42	184
Corbin Burnes, Milwaukee	12	8	2.94	33	33	0	0	202	144	73	66	51	243

AWARD WINNERS

Selected by Baseball Writers Association of America

MOST VALUABLE PLAYER

Player	1st	2nd	3rd	Total
Paul Goldschmidt, Cardinals	22	8		380
Manny Machado, Padres	7	13	7	291
Nolan Arenado, Cardinals	1	2	15	232
Freddie Freeman, Dodgers		6	6	220
Mookie Betts, Dodgers			1	154
Austin Riley, Braves				116
J.T. Realmuto, Phillies				98
Pete Alonso, Mets		1		81
Francisco Lindor, Mets				77
Sandy Alcantara, Marlins				39
Trea Turner, Dodgers				29
Dansby Swanson, Braves				23
Michael Harris II, Braves				9
Julio Urias, Dodgers			1	8
Jeff McNeil, Mets				6
Daniel Bard, Rockies				2
Kyle Schwarber, Phillies				2
Edwin Diaz, Mets				2
Starling Marte, Mets				1

CY YOUNG AWARD

Player	1st	2nd	3rd	Total
Sandy Alcantara, Marlins	30			210
Max Fried, Braves		10	7	72
Julio Urias, Dodgers		7	9	66
Aaron Nola, Phillies		5	6	48
Zac Gallen, D-backs		3	5	45
Carlos Rodon, Giants		3	1	30
Corbin Burnes, Brewers		1	2	20
Yu Darvish, Padres				7
Edwin Diaz, Mets		1		6
Kyle Wright, Braves				3
Logan Webb, Giants				2
Ryan Helsley, Cardinals				1

ROOKIE OF THE YEAR

Player	1st	2nd	3rd	Total
Michael Harris II, Braves	22	8		134
Spencer Strider, Braves	8	21		103
Brendan Donovan, Cardinals			22	22
Jake McCarthy, D-backs			4	4
Alexis Diaz, Reds		1		3
Nick Lodolo, Reds			2	2
Oneil Cruz, Pirates			2	2

MANAGER OF THE YEAR

Player	1st	2nd	3rd	Total
Buck Showalter, Mets	8	10	7	77
Dave Roberts, Dodgers	8	4	5	57
Brian Snitker, Braves	7	5	5	55
Oliver Marmol, Cardinals	5	4	7	44
Rob Thomson, Phillies	2	7	5	36
Bob Melvin, Padres			1	1

GOLD GLOVE WINNERS

Selected by NL managers and coaches

P—Max Fried, Braves. **C**—J.T. Realmuto, Phillies. **1B**—Christian Walker, D-backs. **2B**—Brendan Rodgers, Rockies. **3B**—Nolan Arenado, Cardinals. **SS**—Dansby Swanson, Braves. **LF**—Ian Happ, Cubs. **CF**—Trent Grisham, Padres. **RF**—Mookie Betts, Dodgers. **UT**—Brendan Donovan, Cardinals.

NATIONAL LEAGUE DEPARTMENT LEADERS

BATTING

GAMES	
Matt Olson, Atlanta	162
Dansby Swanson, Atlanta	161
Trea Turner, Los Angeles	160
Freddie Freeman, Los Angeles	159
2 others	159

AT-BATS	
Trea Turner, Los Angeles	652
Dansby Swanson, Atlanta	640
Francisco Lindor, New York	630
Matt Olson, Atlanta	616
Austin Riley, Atlanta	615

PLATE APPEARANCES	
Freddie Freeman, Los Angeles	708
Trea Turner, Los Angeles	708
Francisco Lindor, New York	706
Matt Olson, Atlanta	699
Dansby Swanson, Atlanta	696

RUNS	
Mookie Betts, Los Angeles	117
Freddie Freeman, Los Angeles	117
Paul Goldschmidt, St. Louis	106
Brandon Nimmo, New York	102
Trea Turner, Los Angeles	101

HITS	
Freddie Freeman, Los Angeles	199
Trea Turner, Los Angeles	194
Paul Goldschmidt, St. Louis	178
Dansby Swanson, Atlanta	177
Jeff McNeil, New York	174

TOTAL BASES	
Austin Riley, Atlanta	325
Paul Goldschmidt, St. Louis	324
Freddie Freeman, Los Angeles	313
Pete Alonso, New York	309
Manny Machado, San Diego	307

DOUBLES	
Freddie Freeman, Los Angeles	47
Matt Olson, Atlanta	44
Nolan Arenado, St. Louis	42
Ian Happ, Chicago	42
Ketel Marte, Arizona	42
Paul Goldschmidt, St. Louis	41

TRIPLES	
Gavin Lux, Los Angeles	7
Brandon Nimmo, New York	7
Charlie Blackmon, Colorado	6
TJ Friedl, Cincinnati	5
4 others	5

EXTRA-BASE HITS	
Austin Riley, Atlanta	79
Mookie Betts, Los Angeles	78
Matt Olson, Atlanta	78
Paul Goldschmidt, St. Louis	76
Nolan Arenado, St. Louis	73

HOME RUNS	
Kyle Schwarber, Philadelphia	46
Pete Alonso, New York	40
Austin Riley, Atlanta	38
Christian Walker, Arizona	36
Mookie Betts, Los Angeles	35
Paul Goldschmidt, St. Louis	35
Rowdy Tellez, Milwaukee	35

Kyle Schwarber

RUNS BATTED IN	
Pete Alonso, New York	131
Paul Goldschmidt, St. Louis	115
Francisco Lindor, New York	107
Nolan Arenado, St. Louis	103
Matt Olson, Atlanta	103

SACRIFICES	
Tomas Nido, New York	12
Geraldo Perdomo, Arizona	12
Victor Robles, Washington	11
Trent Grisham, San Diego	7
2 tied	5

SACRIFICE FLIES	
Alec Bohm, Philadelphia	10
Pete Alonso, New York	9
Austin Nola, San Diego	9
Jake Cronenworth, San Diego	8
Justin Turner, Los Angeles	8

HIT BY PITCHES	
Mark Canha, New York	28
Willson Contreras, Chicago	24
Austin Riley, Atlanta	17
Jake Cronenworth, San Diego	16
2 tied	16

WALKS	
Juan Soto, San Diego	135
Max Muncy, Los Angeles	90
Christian Yelich, Milwaukee	88
Kyle Schwarber, Philadelphia	86
Freddie Freeman, Los Angeles	84

STOLEN BASES	
Jon Berti, Miami	41
Tommy Edman, St. Louis	32
Ronald Acuna Jr., Atlanta	29
Trea Turner, Los Angeles	27
2 tied	23

STOLEN BASE PERCENTAGE	
Jake Cronenworth, San Diego	1.000
Nelson Cruz, Washington	1.000
Paul Goldschmidt, St. Louis	1.000
Randal Grichuk, Colorado	1.000
5 others	1.000

STRIKEOUTS	
Kyle Schwarber, Philadelphia	200
Patrick Wisdom, Chicago	183
Dansby Swanson, Atlanta	182
Luke Voit, Washington	179
Matt Olson, Atlanta	170

Pete Alonso

AT-BATS PER STRIKEOUT	
Jeff McNeil, New York	8.7
Nico Hoerner, Chicago	8.4
Nolan Arenado, St. Louis	7.7
Miguel Rojas, Miami	7.7
Freddie Freeman, Los Angeles	6.0

DOUBLE PLAYS	
Brendan Rodgers, Colorado	25
Josh Bell, San Diego	22
Kyle Farmer, Cincinnati	20
Rowdy Tellez, Milwaukee	20
3 tied	18

MULTI-HIT GAMES	
Freddie Freeman, Los Angeles	57
Jeff McNeil, New York	53
Manny Machado, San Diego	50
Austin Riley, Atlanta	50
2 others	50

ON-BASE PERCENTAGE	
Freddie Freeman, Los Angeles	.407
Paul Goldschmidt, St. Louis	.404
Juan Soto, San Diego	.401
Jeff McNeil, New York	.382
Brandon Nimmo, New York	.367

ON-BASE PLUS SLUGGING	
Paul Goldschmidt, St. Louis	.982
Freddie Freeman, Los Angeles	.918
Manny Machado, San Diego	.897
Nolan Arenado, St. Louis	.891
Austin Riley, Atlanta	.877

PITCHING

WINS	
Kyle Wright, Atlanta	21
Julio Urias, Los Angeles	17
Yu Darvish, San Diego	16
Tony Gonsolin, Los Angeles	16
4 tied	15

LOSSES	
Patrick Corbin, Washington	19
Madison Bumgarner, Arizona	15
Erick Fedde, Washington	13
Hunter Greene, Cincinnati	13
3 others	13

GAMES	
John Brebbia, San Francisco	76
A.J. Minter, Atlanta	75
Brad Boxberger, Milwaukee	70
Steve Cishek, Washington	69
Joe Mantiply, Arizona	69

GAMES STARTED	
Corbin Burnes, Milwaukee	33
Merrill Kelly, Arizona	33
Sandy Alcantara, Miami	32
Pablo Lopez, Miami	32
5 others	32

GAMES FINISHED	
Kenley Jansen, Atlanta	54
Camilo Doval, San Francisco	51
Edwin Diaz, New York	49
Daniel Bard, Colorado	48
Mark Melancon, Arizona	48

COMPLETE GAMES	
Sandy Alcantara, Miami	6
Aaron Nola, Philadelphia	2
Walker Buehler, Los Angeles	1
Patrick Corbin, Washington	1
9 others	1

TIM NWACHUKWU/GETTY IMAGES (SCHWARBER), ELSA/GETTY IMAGES(ALONSO)

NATIONAL LEAGUE DEPARTMENT LEADERS

Sandy Alcantara

SHUTOUTS

Sandy Alcantara, Miami	1
Walker Buehler, Los Angeles	1
Bryce Elder, Atlanta	1
Hunter Greene, Cincinnati	1
3 others	1

SAVES

Kenley Jansen, Atlanta	41
Josh Hader, San Diego	36
Daniel Bard, Colorado	34
Edwin Diaz, New York	32
Taylor Rogers, Milwaukee	31

INNINGS PITCHED

Sandy Alcantara, Miami	229
Aaron Nola, Philadelphia	205
Miles Mikolas, St. Louis	202
Corbin Burnes, Milwaukee	202
Merrill Kelly, Arizona	200

HITS ALLOWED

Patrick Corbin, Washington	210
Kyle Freeland, Colorado	193
Adam Wainwright, St. Louis	192
German Marquez, Colorado	185
Madison Bumgarner, Arizona	179

RUNS ALLOWED

Patrick Corbin, Washington	119
German Marquez, Colorado	109
Kyle Gibson, Philadelphia	98
Madison Bumgarner, Arizona	97
Kyle Freeland, Colorado	96

HOME RUNS ALLOWED

Josiah Gray, Washington	38
German Marquez, Colorado	30
Sean Manaea, San Diego	29
Charlie Morton, Atlanta	28
2 tied	27

WALKS ALLOWED

Josiah Gray, Washington	66
German Marquez, Colorado	63
Charlie Morton, Atlanta	63
Dakota Hudson, St. Louis	61
Merrill Kelly, Arizona	61

LOWEST WALKS PER NINE

Aaron Nola, Philadelphia	1.3
Max Fried, Atlanta	1.6
Yu Darvish, San Diego	1.7
Tyler Anderson, Los Angeles	1.7
Miles Mikolas, St. Louis	1.7

HIT BATTERS

Nick Lodolo, Cincinnati	19
Charlie Morton, Atlanta	18
Kyle Freeland, Colorado	16
Joe Musgrove, San Diego	14
3 tied	13

STRIKEOUTS

Corbin Burnes, Milwaukee	243
Carlos Rodon, San Francisco	237
Aaron Nola, Philadelphia	235
Sandy Alcantara, Miami	207
Charlie Morton, Atlanta	205

STRIKEOUTS PER NINE

Carlos Rodon, San Francisco	12.0
Corbin Burnes, Milwaukee	10.8
Charlie Morton, Atlanta	10.7
Aaron Nola, Philadelphia	10.3
Zac Gallen, Arizona	9.4

STRIKEOUTS PER NINE

(Relievers)

Edwin Diaz, New York	17.1
Josh Hader, San Diego	14.6
Jose Alvarado, Philadelphia	14.3
Devin Williams, Milwaukee	14.2
Alex Vesia, Los Angeles	13.1

DOUBLE PLAYS

Dakota Hudson, St. Louis	25
Kyle Wright, Atlanta	25
Jose Quintana, St. Louis	23
Chris Bassitt, New York	22
2 others	22

PICKOFFS

Taijuan Walker, New York	5
Merrill Kelly, Arizona	4
Patrick Corbin, Washington	3
Max Fried, Atlanta	3
3 others	3

WILD PITCHES

Nick Nelson, Philadelphia	13
Roansy Contreras, Pittsburgh	11
Corbin Burnes, Milwaukee	10
Carlos Rodon, San Francisco	10
2 tied	9

WALKS PLUS HITS PER INNING

Zac Gallen, Arizona	0.91
Yu Darvish, San Diego	0.95
Julio Urias, Los Angeles	0.96
Aaron Nola, Philadelphia	0.96
Corbin Burnes, Milwaukee	0.97

OPPONENT AVERAGE

Zac Gallen, Arizona	.186
Corbin Burnes, Milwaukee	.197
Julio Urias, Los Angeles	.199
Carlos Rodon, San Francisco	.202
Yu Darvish, San Diego	.207

WORST ERA

(min. 120 IP)

Patrick Corbin, Washington	6.31
Erick Fedde, Washington	5.81
Chad Kuhl, Colorado	5.72
Austin Gomber, Colorado	5.56
Zach Thompson, Pittsburgh	5.18

FIELDING

PITCHER

PCT	9 players	1.000
PO	Corbin Burnes, Milwaukee	32
A	Tyler Anderson, Los Angeles	31
	Ranger Suarez, Philadelphia	31
DP	Alex Cobb, San Francisco	4
E	Luis Garcia, San Diego	4

CATCHER

PCT	Carson Kelly, Arizona	1.000
PO	JT Realmuto, Philadelphia	1,151
A	Elias Diaz, Colorado	52
DP	JT Realmuto, Philadelphia	11
E	Elias Diaz, Colorado	11
CS	JT Realmuto, Philadelphia	30
PB	Jorge Alfaro, San Diego	7
	Willson Contreras, Chicago	7

FIRST BASE

PCT	Paul Goldschmidt, St. Louis	.999
PO	Matt Olson, Atlanta	1,209
A	Rhys Hoskins, Philadelphia	103
DP	Paul Goldschmidt, St. Louis	118
E	Rhys Hoskins, Philadelphia	12

SECOND BASE

PCT	Jake Cronenworth, San Diego	.992
PO	Brendan Rodgers, Colorado	218
A	Brendan Rodgers, Colorado	411
DP	Brendan Rodgers, Colorado	99
E	Kolten Wong, Milwaukee	17

THIRD BASE

PCT	Ke'Bryan Hayes, Pittsburgh	.972
PO	Ke'Bryan Hayes, Pittsburgh	109
A	Ke'Bryan Hayes, Pittsburgh	307
DP	Nolan Arenado, St. Louis	42
E	Ryan McMahon, Colorado	17

SHORTSTOP

PCT	Miguel Rojas, Miami	.987
PO	Francisco Lindor, New York	198
A	Dansby Swanson, Atlanta	391
DP	Geraldo Perdomo, Arizona	83
E	Oneil Cruz, Pittsburgh	17

OUTFIELD

PCT	4 players	1.000
PO	Trent Grisham, San Diego	341
A	Aristides Aquino, Cincinnati	12
DP	3 players	4
E	Victor Robles, Washington	6
	Yonathan Daza, Colorado	6

PATRICK MCDERMOTT/GETTY IMAGES

TIM BRADBURY/GETTY IMAGES

Just five of the 26 Astros on the World Series roster were members of Houston's 2017 title team.

Astros Claim An Asterisk-Free World Series Championship

BY KYLE GLASER

When the Astros came into the 2022 season, the question that faced them was the same one as always: Could they win a World Series cleanly?

The Astros World Series title in 2017 was later revealed to have been aided by an elaborate sign-stealing scheme that made them pariahs of Major League Baseball and led to the suspensions—and eventual firings—of manager A.J. Hinch and general manager Jeff Luhnow. They reached the World Series again in 2019 and 2021, but lost both times.

As dominant as the Astros had been during the five-season span from 2017-21, including reaching five straight American League Championship Series, the fact remained their only championship came when they were proved to have been cheating. After losing franchise icon Carlos Correa to the Twins in free agency before the season, it appeared possible their window to win a World Series without a "but" attached might have closed.

Instead, the Astros reloaded and stormed their way through the AL playoff field and on to the second championship in franchise history.

The Astros left little doubt they were the best team in the AL once again, winning a league-high 106 games and leading the league with a 2.90 ERA. Justin Verlander, 39, returned from Tommy John surgery to go 18-4 with an MLB-best 1.75 ERA and won his third Cy Young Award. Lefthander Framber Valdez went 17-6, 2.82 while emerging as an ace. Righthander Lance McCullers returned from a forearm strain late in the year to go 4-2, 2.27 in eight starts. Young righthanders Cristian Javier (11-9, 2.54), Luis Garcia (15-8,

3.72) and Jose Urquidy (13-8, 3.94) all delivered excellent performances, giving the Astros the best and deepest starting staff in the league.

The offense, meanwhile, didn't miss a beat with Correa's departure. Old standbys Jose Altuve (.300, 28 HR) and Alex Bregman (23 HR, .820) had bounceback seasons and young lefthanded sluggers Yordan Alvarez (.306, 37 HR) and Kyle Tucker (30 HR, 107 RBI) blossomed into fearsome forces in the middle of the lineup. Jeremy Peña replaced Correa at shortstop and ably handled the job, becoming the first rookie shortstop to win a Gold Glove and hitting 22 home runs.

The Astros added further reinforcements at the trade deadline, acquiring catcher Christian Vazquez from the Red Sox and first baseman Trey Mancini from the Orioles.

The total sum was a juggernaut. The Astros clinched the AL West with more than two weeks remaining in the season and secured home field-advantage with nearly a week left. Once they got to the postseason, they continued to dominate while baseball's other titans fell.

DANIEL SHIREY/MLB PHOTOS VIA GETTY

The Astros' Dusty Baker earned his first World Series ring in his 25th year as a manager.

THE ROAD TO THE WORLD SERIES

MLB expanded the postseason in 2022, adding an additional wild card spot to each league and altering the format to include an additional, best-of-three Wild Card Round.

The top two teams in each league received a bye through the Wild Card Round. The bye was designed to be a reward for the best teams in the regular season and afford them extra rest. Instead, the bye appeared to have a chilling effect on those teams' momentum and led to upsets throughout.

The inaugural Wild Card Series thrilled. The Guardians outlasted the Rays and clinched the series with a 1-0 win on a walkoff home run by Oscar Gonzalez in the 15th inning of Game 2. The Mariners swept the Blue Jays by storming back from a seven-run deficit in Game 2 to win 10-9 after trailing 8-1 in the fifth inning. The Phillies scored six runs in the ninth inning to come back and beat the Cardinals in Game 1 of their series and beat the shell-shocked Cards 2-0 in Game 2 for a stunning upset. The Padres and Mets went the full three games and ended with the 89-win Padres eliminating the 101-win Mets after Joe Musgrove pitched seven scoreless innings of one-hit ball in the decisive Game 3.

The Dodgers, Braves, Astros and Yankees all had six days between the end of their regular seasons and the start of the Division Series. The layoff, intended to be a blessing, instead turned out to be a curse for all but the Astros.

The defending champion Braves, winners of 101 games, came out cold and were promptly eliminated by the 87-win Phillies in four games, with the Phillies scoring at least seven runs in each of their wins.

The Dodgers went 14-5 against the Padres during the regular season to continue their decade-long dominance against their rivals to the south, but after holding on to beat the Padres in Game 1 of their NLDS matchup, the Dodgers lost the next three to see their 111-win season come to a premature end. The Padres finished it with a five-run rally in the seventh inning of Game 4, turning a late 3-0 deficit into a 5-3 win.

The Yankees meanwhile struggled to put away the Guardians, needing all five games to emerge victorious. The Guardians jumped out to a 2-1 series lead after Gonzalez struck again with a walkoff single to cap a three-run rally in the bottom of the ninth in Game 3, but the Yankees recovered to win Game 4 on the strength of a dominant start by Gerrit Cole and took advantage of Cleveland's decision to start Aaron Civale instead of ace Shane Bieber in Game 5, jumping out to an early lead and holding on for a 5-1 win.

Only the Astros recorded a sweep, but even they didn't have it easy against the Mariners. The Astros trailed most of Game 1 before Alvarez's walkoff three-run homer in the ninth saved them and trailed again in Game 2 until Alvarez hit a go-ahead two-run homer in the sixth. In Game 3, the first playoff game in Seattle since 2001, the Astros and Mariners battled for 17 scoreless innings before Peña homered to lead off the 18th, sending the Astros a 1-0 victory in a battle that tied for the longest playoff game in postseason history.

With their initial scare behind them, the Astros had little trouble with the Yankees. The battle of the top two seeds in the AL was hardly an even fight, with the Astros cruising to an easy sweep. Home runs by Yuli Gurriel and Chas McCormick in the sixth inning broke an early tie in Game 1 to send the Astros to a 4-2 victory, Alex Bregman's early three-run homer and seven dominant innings from Framber Valdez led the Astros to a 3-2 victory in Game 2 and Cristian Javier combined with five relievers on a three-hit shutout in a 5-0 win in Game 3. With a chance to finish off the sweep at Yankee Stadium, the Astros erased deficits of 4-0 and 5-4 to pull out a 6-5 win and clinch the sweep. A throwing error by Yankees second baseman Gleyber Torres on a potential inning-ending double play ball in the seventh opened the door for the Astros, and Alvarez and Bregman followed with back-to-back RBI singles to give the Astros the lead and send them to the World Series.

While the AL's top two seeds met in the ALCS, the NL's bottom two seeds met in the NLCS as the fifth-seeded Padres met the sixth-seeded Phillies. The Phillies won Game 1 on the strength of a Bryce Harper solo homer and Kyle Schwarber's massive, 488-foot home run to second deck in right field, but the Padres staged a five-run, fifth-inning rally in Game 2 to overcome an early deficit and even the series with an 8-5 win.

Back home, the Phillies completed their unlikely run to the World Series. Schwarber set the tone with a leadoff home run off Musgrove to send the Phillies to a 4-2 win in Game 3. The Phillies overcame deficits of 4-0 in the first inning and 6-4 in the fifth inning to rally for a 10-6 win in Game 4, highlighted by two homers from Rhys Hoskins and Harper's go-ahead double in the fifth. In Game 5, the Phillies blew a late lead, but Harper saved them with an epic go-ahead, two-run homer in the bottom of the eighth to give them a 5-4 win and send them to the World Series for the first time since 2009.

ASTRO BALL

The 2022 World Series featured two teams who were polar opposites. The Astros won 106 games and were the top seed in the AL. The Phillies won 87 games and were the last team to get into the postseason. The Astros were a well-oiled machine with a dominant starting rotation, an explosive offense, squeaky-clean defense and an airtight bullpen. The Phillies were a flawed but entertaining bunch with a shaky bullpen, a comically bad defense, a starting rotation short on depth and an

AMERICAN LEAGUE CHAMPIONS, 1995-2022

American League postseason results in Wild Card Era, 1995-present, where (*) denotes wild card playoff entrant.

YEAR	CHAMPIONSHIP SERIES	ALCS MVP	DIVISION SERIES	DIVISION SERIES
2022	Houston 4, New York 0	Jeremy Peña, SS, Houston	Houston 3, Seattle* 0	New York 3, Cleveland 2
2021	Houston 4, Boston 2	Yordan Alvarez, OF, Houston	Houston 3, Chicago 1	Boston* 3, Tampa Bay 1
2020	Tampa Bay 4, Houston 3	Randy Arozarena, OF, Tampa Bay	Tampa Bay 3, New York* 2	Houston* 3, Oakland 1
2019	Houston 4, New York 2	Jose Altuve, 2B, Houston	Houston 3, Tampa Bay* 2	New York 3, Minnesota 0
2018	Boston 4, Houston 1	Jackie Bradley Jr., OF, Boston	Boston 3, New York* 1	Houston 3, Cleveland 0
2017	Houston 4, New York 3	Justin Verlander, RHP, Houston	New York* 3, Cleveland 2	Houston 3, Boston 1
2016	Cleveland 4, Toronto 1	Andrew Miller, LHP, Cleveland	Toronto* 3, Texas 0	Cleveland 3, Boston 0
2015	Kansas City 4, Toronto 2	Alcides Escobar, SS, Kansas City	Kansas City 3, Houston* 2	Baltimore 3, Texas 2
2014	Kansas City 4, Baltimore 0	Lorenzo Cain, OF, Kansas City	Kansas City* 3, Los Angeles 0	Baltimore 3, Detroit 0
2013	Boston 4, Detroit 2	Koji Uehara, RHP, Boston	Boston 3, Tampa Bay* 1	Detroit, 3, Oakland 2
2012	Detroit 4, New York 0	Delmon Young, OF, Detroit	New York 3, Baltimore* 2	Detroit 3, Oakland 2
2011	Texas 4, Detroit 2	Nelson Cruz, OF, Texas	Detroit 3, New York 2	Texas 3, Tampa Bay* 1
2010	Texas 4, New York 2	Josh Hamilton, OF, Texas	Texas 3, Tampa Bay 2	New York* 3, Minnesota 0
2009	New York 4, Los Angeles 2	CC Sabathia, LHP, New York	New York 3, Minnesota 0	Los Angeles 3, Boston* 0
2008	Tampa Bay 4, Boston 3	Matt Garza, RHP, Tampa Bay	Boston* 3, Los Angeles 1	Tampa Bay 3, Chicago 1
2007	Boston 4, Cleveland 3	Josh Beckett, RHP, Boston	Boston 3, Los Angeles 0	Cleveland 3, New York* 1
2006	Detroit 4, Oakland 0	Placido Polanco, 2B, Detroit	Detroit* 3, New York 1	Oakland 3, Minnesota 0
2005	Chicago 4, Los Angeles 1	Paul Konerko, 1B, Chicago	Chicago 3, Boston* 0	Los Angeles 3, New York 2
2004	Boston 4, New York 3	David Ortiz, DH, Boston	Boston* 3, Anaheim 0	New York 3, Minnesota 1
2003	New York 4, Boston 3	Mariano Rivera, RHP, New York	New York 3, Minnesota 1	Boston* 3, Oakland 2
2002	Anaheim 4, Minnesota 1	Adam Kennedy, 2B, Anaheim	Anaheim* 3, New York 1	Minnesota 3, Oakland 2
2001	New York 4, Seattle 1	Andy Pettitte, LHP, New York	Seattle 3, Cleveland 2	New York 3, Oakland* 2
2000	New York 4, Seattle 2	David Justice, OF, New York	New York 3, Oakland 2	Seattle* 3, Chicago 0
1999	New York 4, Boston 1	Orlando Hernandez, RHP, New York	Boston* 3, Cleveland 2	New York 3, Texas 0
1998	New York 4, Cleveland 2	David Wells, LHP, New York	Cleveland 3, Boston* 1	New York 3, Texas 0
1997	Cleveland 4, Baltimore 2	Marquis Grissom, OF, Cleveland	Cleveland 3, New York* 2	Baltimore 3, Seattle 1
1996	New York 4, Baltimore 1	Bernie Williams, OF, New York	Baltimore* 3, Cleveland 1	New York 3, Texas 1
1995	Cleveland 4, Seattle 2	Orel Hershiser, RHP, Cleveland	Cleveland 3, Boston 0	Seattle 3, New York* 2

offense that simply tried to outmash opponents to make up for the team's shortcomings.

The Phillies, red-hot and full of confidence after beating the higher-seeded Cardinals, Braves and Padres to get to the World Series, appeared primed for another upset early. They stormed back from a 5-0 deficit in Game 1 against Verlander and completed the rally on J.T. Realmuto's home run in the top of the 10th inning to steal a 6-5 win in Houston. The Astros jumped out to another early lead in Game 2 and Valdez held it for a 5-2, but the Phillies bashed five home runs off Lance McCullers in Game 3 back in Philadelphia in a 7-0 rout to take a 2-1 series lead.

The Astros, facing another World Series upset to an NL East team after losing to the Nationals in 2019 and Braves in 2021, turned the series with a historic performance in Game 4. Cristian Javier, Bryan Abreu, Rafael Montero, Ryan Pressly combined to throw the second no-hitter in World Series history and lead the Astros to a 5-0 win. The quartet's effort joined Don Larsen's 1956 perfect game as the only World Series no-hitters.

Energized by the no-hitter, the Astros dominant pitching staff finished the job. Verlander won his first career World Series start in a 3-2 win in Game 5. Back in Houston, the Astros fell behind early before Yordan Alvarez's monstrous, 450-foot, three-run homer over the batter's eye at Minute Maid Park gave them the lead for good and sent them on their way to a 4-1 win to secure the title.

After falling behind in the series 2-1, the Astros pitching staff allowed three runs combined in the next three games. They limited the Phillies to a .163 average over the course of the series and recorded a World Series-record 71 strikeouts.

Manager Dusty Baker was the biggest beneficiary of all. After 25 years of managing, he finally won his first World Series as a skipper, adding the final check on his Hall of Fame resume.

"I thought about it a lot," Baker said. "I tried not to dwell on it, but tried to have faith and perseverance and knowing that with the right team and the right personnel and right everything that this is going to happen.

Peña, the rookie shortstop who replaced Correa, won both ALCS MVP and World Series MVP. He became the first rookie position player to win World Series MVP after batting .400 (10-for-25) with a home run and three RBIs while making numerous highlight-reel defensive plays.

The Astros won with 21 of the 26 players on their World Series roster having not been a part of the sign-stealing 2017 team. They won 106 games in the regular season and went 11-2 in the postseason, showing the ability to win with a new general manager, new manager and a largely new group of players. In doing so, they cemented their place as a championship team worth remembering for more than just their sordid past. ■

NATIONAL LEAGUE CHAMPIONS, 1995-2022

National League postseason results in Wild Card Era, 1995-present, where (*) denotes wild card playoff entrant.

YEAR	CHAMPIONSHIP SERIES	NLCS MVP	DIVISION SERIES	DIVISION SERIES
2022	Philadelphia 4, San Diego 1	Bryce Harper, OF, Philadelphia	Philadelphia* 3, Atlanta 1	San Diego* 3, Los Angeles 1
2021	Atlanta 4, Los Angeles 2	Eddie Rosario, OF, Atlanta	Atlanta 3, Milwaukee 1	Los Angeles* 3, San Francisco 2
2020	Los Angeles 4, Atlanta 3	Corey Seager, SS, Los Angeles	Los Angeles 3, San Diego* 0	Atlanta 3, Miami* 0
2019	Washington 4, St. Louis 0	Howie Kendrick, 2B, Washington	Washington* 3, Los Angeles 2	St. Louis 3, Atlanta 2
2018	Los Angeles 4, Milwaukee 3	Cody Bellinger, 1B/OF, Los Angeles	Los Angeles 3, Atlanta 1	Milwaukee 3, Colorado 0*
2017	Los Angeles 4, Chicago 1	Justin Turner, 3B/Chris Taylor, CF, L.A.	Los Angeles 3, Arizona* 0	Chicago 3, Washington 2
2016	Chicago 4, Los Angeles 2	Javier Baez, 2B/Jon Lester, LHP, Chicago	Chicago 3, San Francisco* 1	Los Angeles 3, Washington 2
2015	New York 4, Chicago 0	Daniel Murphy, 2B, New York	New York 3, Los Angeles 2	Chicago* 3, St. Louis 1
2014	San Francisco 4, St. Louis 1	Madison Bumgarner, LHP, San Francisco	San Francisco* 3, Washington 1	St. Louis 3, Los Angeles 1
2013	St. Louis 4, Los Angeles 2	Michael Wacha, RHP, St. Louis	St. Louis 3, Pittsburgh* 2	Los Angeles 3, Atlanta 1
2012	San Francisco 4, St. Louis 3	Marco Scutaro, 2B, San Francisco	St. Louis* 3, Washington 2	San Francisco 3, Cincinnati 2
2011	St. Louis 4, Milwaukee 2	David Freese, 3B, St. Louis	St. Louis* 3, Philadelphia 2	Milwaukee 3, Arizona 2
2010	San Francisco 4, Philadelphia 2	Cody Ross, OF, San Francisco	Philadelphia 3, Cincinnati 0	San Francisco 3, Atlanta* 1
2009	Philadelphia 4, Los Angeles 1	Ryan Howard, 1B, Philadelphia	Los Angeles 3, St. Louis 0	Philadelphia 3, Colorado* 1
2008	Philadelphia 4, Los Angeles 1	Cole Hamels, LHP, Philadelphia	Los Angeles 3, Chicago 0	Philadelphia 3, Milwaukee* 1
2007	Colorado 4, Arizona 0	Matt Holliday, OF, Colorado	Arizona 3, Chicago 0	Colorado* 3, Philadelphia 0
2006	St. Louis 4, New York 3	Jeff Suppan, RHP, St. Louis	New York 3, Los Angeles* 0	St. Louis 3, San Diego 1
2005	Houston 4, St. Louis 2	Roy Oswalt, RHP, Houston	St. Louis 3, San Diego 0	Houston* 3, Atlanta 1
2004	St. Louis 4, Houston 3	Albert Pujols, 1B, St. Louis	St. Louis 3, Los Angeles 1	Houston* 3, Atlanta 2
2003	Florida 4, Chicago 3	Ivan Rodriguez, C, Florida	Florida* 3, San Francisco 1	Chicago 3, Atlanta 2
2002	San Francisco 4, St. Louis 1	Benito Santiago, C, San Francisco	San Francisco* 3, Atlanta 2	St. Louis 3, Arizona 0
2001	Arizona 4, Atlanta 1	Craig Counsell, SS, Arizona	Atlanta 3, Houston 0	Arizona 3, St. Louis* 2
2000	New York 4, St. Louis 1	Mike Hampton, LHP, New York	St. Louis 3, Atlanta 0	New York* 3, San Francisco 1
1999	Atlanta 4, New York 2	Eddie Perez, C, Atlanta	Atlanta 3, Houston 1	New York* 3, Arizona 1
1998	San Diego 4, Atlanta 2	Sterling Hitchcock, LHP, San Diego	Atlanta 3, Chicago* 0	San Diego 3, Houston 1
1997	Florida 4, Atlanta 2	Livan Hernandez, RHP, Florida	Florida* 3, San Francisco 0	Atlanta 3, Houston 0
1996	Atlanta 4, St. Louis 3	Javy Lopez, C, Atlanta	St. Louis 3, San Diego 0	Atlanta 3, Los Angeles* 0
1995	Atlanta 4, Cincinnati 0	Mike Devereaux, OF, Atlanta	Atlanta 3, Colorado* 1	Cincinnati 3, Los Angeles 0

THE WORLD SERIES YEAR-BY-YEAR

Jeremy Peña

ROB TRINGALI/MLB PHOTOS VIA GETTY IMAGES

Year	Winner	Loser	Result
1903	Boston (AL)	Pittsburgh (NL)	5-3
1904	NO SERIES		
1905	New York (NL)	Philadelphia (AL)	4-1
1906	Chicago (AL)	Chicago (NL)	4-2
1907	Chicago (NL)	Detroit (AL)	4-0
1908	Chicago (NL)	Detroit (AL)	4-1
1909	Pittsburgh (NL)	Detroit (AL)	4-3
1910	Philadelphia (AL)	Chicago (NL)	4-1
1911	Philadelphia (AL)	New York (NL)	4-2
1912	Boston (AL)	New York (NL)	4-3-1
1913	Philadelphia (AL)	New York (NL)	4-1
1914	Boston (NL)	Philadelphia (AL)	4-0
1915	Boston (AL)	Philadelphia (NL)	4-1
1916	Boston (AL)	Brooklyn (NL)	4-1
1917	Chicago (AL)	New York (NL)	4-2
1918	Boston (AL)	Chicago (NL)	4-2
1919	Cincinnati (NL)	Chicago (AL)	5-3
1920	Cleveland (AL)	Brooklyn (NL)	5-2
1921	New York (NL)	New York (AL)	5-3
1922	New York (NL)	New York (AL)	4-0
1923	New York (AL)	New York (NL)	4-2
1924	Washington (AL)	New York (NL)	4-3
1925	Pittsburgh (NL)	Washington (AL)	4-3
1926	St. Louis (NL)	New York (AL)	4-3
1927	New York (AL)	Pittsburgh (NL)	4-0
1928	New York (AL)	St. Louis (NL)	4-0
1929	Philadelphia (AL)	Chicago (NL)	4-1
1930	Philadelphia (AL)	St. Louis (NL)	4-2
1931	St. Louis (NL)	Philadelphia (AL)	4-3
1932	New York (AL)	Chicago (NL)	4-0
1933	New York (NL)	Washington (AL)	4-1
1934	St. Louis (NL)	Detroit (AL)	4-3
1935	Detroit (AL)	Chicago (NL)	4-2
1936	New York (AL)	New York (NL)	4-2
1937	New York (AL)	New York (NL)	4-1
1938	New York (AL)	Chicago (NL)	4-0
1939	New York (AL)	Cincinnati (NL)	4-0
1940	Cincinnati (NL)	Detroit (AL)	4-3
1941	New York (AL)	Brooklyn (NL)	4-1
1942	St. Louis (NL)	New York (AL)	4-1
1943	New York (AL)	St. Louis (NL)	4-1
1944	St. Louis (NL)	St. Louis (AL)	4-2
1945	Detroit (AL)	Chicago (NL)	4-3
1946	St. Louis (NL)	Boston (AL)	4-3
1947	New York (AL)	Brooklyn (NL)	4-3
1948	Cleveland (AL)	Boston (NL)	4-2
1949	New York (AL)	Brooklyn (NL)	4-1
1950	New York (AL)	Philadelphia (NL)	4-0
1951	New York (AL)	New York (NL)	4-2
1952	New York (AL)	Brooklyn (NL)	4-3
1953	New York (AL)	Brooklyn (NL)	4-2
1954	New York (NL)	Cleveland (AL)	4-0
1955	Brooklyn (NL)	New York (AL)	4-3
1956	New York (AL)	Brooklyn (NL)	4-3
1957	Milwaukee (NL)	New York (AL)	4-3
1958	New York (AL)	Milwaukee (NL)	4-3
1959	Los Angeles (NL)	Chicago (AL)	4-2
1960	Pittsburgh (NL)	New York (AL)	4-3
1961	New York (AL)	Cincinnati (NL)	4-1
1962	New York (AL)	San Francisco (NL)	4-3
1963	Los Angeles (NL)	New York (AL)	4-0
1964	St. Louis (NL)	New York (AL)	4-3
1965	Los Angeles (NL)	Minnesota (AL)	4-3
1966	Baltimore (AL)	Los Angeles (NL)	4-0
1967	St. Louis (NL)	Boston (AL)	4-3
1968	Detroit (AL)	St. Louis (NL)	4-3
1969	New York (NL)	Baltimore (AL)	4-1
1970	Baltimore (AL)	Cincinnati (NL)	4-1
1971	Pittsburgh (NL)	Baltimore (AL)	4-3
1972	Oakland (AL)	Cincinnati (NL)	4-3
1973	Oakland (AL)	New York (NL)	4-3
1974	Oakland (AL)	Los Angeles (NL)	4-1
1975	Cincinnati (NL)	Boston (AL)	4-3
1976	Cincinnati (NL)	New York (AL)	4-0
1977	New York (AL)	Los Angeles (NL)	4-2
1978	New York (AL)	Los Angeles (NL)	4-2
1979	Pittsburgh (NL)	Baltimore (AL)	4-3
1980	Philadelphia (NL)	Kansas City (AL)	4-2
1981	Los Angeles (NL)	New York (AL)	4-2
1982	St. Louis (NL)	Milwaukee (AL)	4-3
1983	Baltimore (AL)	Philadelphia (NL)	4-1
1984	Detroit (AL)	San Diego (NL)	4-1
1985	Kansas City (AL)	St. Louis (NL)	4-3
1986	New York (NL)	Boston (AL)	4-3
1987	Minnesota (AL)	St. Louis (NL)	4-3
1988	Los Angeles (NL)	Oakland (AL)	4-1
1989	Oakland (AL)	San Francisco (NL)	4-0
1990	Cincinnati (NL)	Oakland (AL)	4-0
1991	Minnesota (AL)	Atlanta (NL)	4-3
1992	Toronto (AL)	Atlanta (NL)	4-2
1993	Toronto (AL)	Philadelphia (NL)	4-2
1994	NO SERIES		
1995	Atlanta (NL)	Cleveland (AL)	4-2
1996	New York (AL)	Atlanta (NL)	4-2
1997	Florida (NL)	Cleveland (AL)	4-3
1998	New York (AL)	San Diego (NL)	4-0
1999	New York (AL)	Atlanta (NL)	4-0
2000	New York (AL)	New York (NL)	4-1
2001	Arizona (NL)	New York (AL)	4-3
2002	Anaheim (AL)	San Francisco (NL)	4-3
2003	Florida (NL)	New York (AL)	4-2
2004	Boston (AL)	St. Louis (NL)	4-0
2005	Chicago (AL)	Houston (NL)	4-0
2006	St. Louis (NL)	Detroit (AL)	4-1
2007	Boston (AL)	Colorado (NL)	4-0
2008	Philadelphia (NL)	Tampa Bay (AL)	4-1
2009	New York (AL)	Philadelphia (NL)	4-2
2010	San Francisco (NL)	Texas (AL)	4-1
2011	St. Louis (NL)	Texas (AL)	4-3
2012	San Francisco (NL)	Detroit (AL)	4-0
2013	Boston (AL)	St. Louis (NL)	4-2
2014	San Francisco (NL)	Kansas City (AL)	4-3
2015	Kansas City (AL)	New York (NL)	4-1
2016	Chicago (NL)	Cleveland (AL)	4-3
2017	Houston (AL)	Los Angeles (NL)	4-3
2018	Boston (AL)	Los Angeles (NL)	4-1
2019	Washington (NL)	Houston (AL)	4-3
2020	**Los Angeles (NL)**	Tampa Bay (AL)	4-2
2021	**Atlanta (NL)**	Houston (AL)	4-2
2022	**Houston (AL)**	Philadelphia (NL)	4-2

WORLD SERIES BOX SCORES

GAME ONE

October 28, 2022

PHILADELPHIA PHILLIES 6, HOUSTON ASTROS 5 (10)

	1	2	3	4	5	6	7	8	9	10	R	H	E
PHILADELPHIA	0	0	0	3	2	0	0	0	0	1	6	9	0
HOUSTON	0	2	3	0	0	0	0	0	0	0	5	10	0

PHILADELPHIA	AB	R	H	RBI	BB	SO	LOB	AVG
Schwarber, LF	4	1	1	0	1	2	0	.205
Hoskins, 1B	5	1	1	0	0	1	3	.184
Realmuto, C	4	1	2	3	1	0	1	.267
Harper, DH	4	1	2	0	1	1	1	.426
Castellanos, N, RF	5	1	1	1	0	2	5	.217
Bohm, 3B	5	0	1	2	0	1	1	.190
Sosa, E, 3B	0	0	0	0	0	0	0	.500
Stott, SS	3	0	0	0	2	2	0	.182
Segura, 2B	5	0	0	0	0	1	4	.225
Marsh, CF	4	1	1	0	0	1	0	.167
Nola, Aa, P	0	0	0	0	0	0	0	.000
Alvarado, P	0	0	0	0	0	0	0	.000
Eflin, P	0	0	0	0	0	0	0	.000
Suárez, R, P	0	0	0	0	0	0	0	.000
Domínguez, P	0	0	0	0	0	0	0	.000
Robertson, P	0	0	0	0	0	0	0	.000
TOTALS	**39**	**6**	**9**	**6**	**5**	**11**	**15**	**.231**

2B: Bohm (4, Verlander); Marsh (3, Verlander); Realmuto (1, Verlander). **HR:** Realmuto (3, 10th inning off Garcia, L, 0 on, 0 out). **TB:** Bohm 2; Castellanos, N; Harper 2; Hoskins; Marsh 2; Realmuto 6; Schwarber. **RBI:** Bohm 2 (7); Castellanos, N (7); Realmuto 3 (6). **2-out RBI:** Bohm 2; Castellanos, N. Runners left in scoring position, 2 ou**T:** Segura 2; Castellanos, N 3. **Team RISP:** 4-for-10. Team **LOB:** 8. **SB:** Schwarber (3, 2nd base off Abreu, B/Maldonado). **DP:** (Stott-Segura-Hoskins).

HOUSTON	AB	R	H	RBI	BB	SO	LOB	AVG
Altuve, 2B	5	0	1	0	0	1	2	.108
Peña, SS	5	1	1	0	0	2	1	.289
Alvarez, Y, LF	4	0	0	0	1	2	1	.212
Bregman, 3B	4	1	1	0	1	1	1	.324
Tucker, RF	5	2	3	4	0	1	1	.273
Gurriel, 1B	4	1	2	0	1	0	1	.382
Mancini, DH	4	0	0	0	0	2	3	.000
b-Diaz, PH	1	0	0	0	0	0	2	.067
McCormick, CF	3	0	1	0	1	2	0	.261
Maldonado, C	3	0	1	1	0	0	2	.235
a-Vazquez, PH-C	1	0	0	0	0	1	0	.182
Verlander, P	0	0	0	0	0	0	0	.000
Abreu, B, P	0	0	0	0	0	0	0	.000
Neris, P	0	0	0	0	0	0	0	.000
Montero, P	0	0	0	0	0	0	0	.000
Pressly, P	0	0	0	0	0	0	0	.000
Garcia, L, P	0	0	0	0	0	0	0	.000
Stanek, P	0	0	0	0	0	0	0	.000
TOTALS	**37**	**4**	**10**	**4**	**5**	**12**	**25**	**.270**

a-Struck out for Maldonado in the 9th. b-Grounded out for Mancini in the 10th. **2B:** Peña (4, Nola, Aa); Bregman (3, Robertson). **HR:** Tucker 2 (3, 2nd inning off Nola, Aa, 0 on, 0 out, 3rd inning off Nola, Aa, 2 on, 1 out). **TB:** Altuve; Bregman 2; Gurriel 2; Maldonado; McCormick; Peña 2; Tucker 9. **RBI:** Maldonado (2); Tucker 4 (5). **Runners left in scoring position, 2 out:** Peña; Maldonado; Diaz 2. **GIDP:** Altuve. Team **RISP:** 2-for-8. Team **LOB:** 8. **SB:** Altuve (1, 2nd base off Domínguez/Realmuto).

PHILADELPHIA	IP	H	R	ER	BB	SO	HR	ERA
Nola, Aa	4.1	6	5	5	2	5	2	4.57
Alvarado	1.0	0	0	0	0	1	0	3.00
Eflin	1.1	1	0	0	1	0	0	4.70
Suárez, R	0.2	1	0	0	0	1	0	1.86
Domínguez (W, 2-0)	1.2	1	0	0	0	3	0	0.96
Robertson (S, 1)	1.0	1	0	0	1	2	0	1.93
TOTALS	**10.0**	**10**	**5**	**5**	**4**	**12**	**2**	**4.50**

HOUSTON	IP	H	R	ER	BB	SO	HR	ERA
Verlander	5.0	6	5	5	2	5	0	7.20
Abreu, B	1.2	1	0	0	2	3	0	0.00
Neris	0.1	0	0	0	0	1	0	2.08
Montero	1.0	0	0	0	0	1	0	1.42
Pressly	1.0	0	0	0	0	1	0	0.00
Garcia, L (L, 1-1)	0.2	2	1	1	0	0	1	1.59
Stanek	0.1	0	0	0	1	0	0	0.00
TOTALS	**10.0**	**9**	**6**	**6**	**5**	**11**	**1**	**5.40**

WP: Robertson. **Pitches-strikes:** Nola, Aa 81-52; Alvarado 7-5; Eflin 20-11; Suárez, R 11-7; Domínguez 24-17; Robertson 25-14; Verlander 90-66; Abreu, B 32-17; Neris 5-3; Montero 8-7; Pressly 15-9; Garcia, L 16-11; Stanek 11-7. **Groundouts-flyouts:** Nola, Aa 5-1; Alvarado 0-1; Eflin 3-1; Suárez, R 1-0; Domínguez 1-1; Robertson 1-0; Verlander 3-2; Abreu, B 0-1; Neris 0-0; Montero 0-1; Pressly 1-0; Garcia, L 2-0; Stanek 0-0. **Batters faced:** Nola, Aa 20; Alvarado 3; Eflin 6; Suárez, R 3; Domínguez 6; Robertson 5; Verlander 23; Abreu, B 8; Neris 1; Montero 3; Pressly 3; Garcia, L 4; Stanek 2. **Inherited runners-scored:** Domínguez 1-0; Neris 3-0; Stanek 1-0.

Umpires: HP: James Hoye. **1B:** Dan Iassogna. **2B:** Tripp Gibson. **3B:** Jordan Baker. **LF:** Lance Barksdale. **RF:** Alan Porter. **Official scorer:** Rick Blount **Weather:** 73 degrees, Roof Closed **Wind:** 0 mph, None **First pitch:** 7:04 PM **T:** 4:34 **Att:** 42,903 **Venue:** Minute Maid Park

GAME TWO

October 29, 2022

HOUSTON ASTROS 5, PHILADELPHIA PHILLIES 2

	1	2	3	4	5	6	7	8	9	R	H	E
PHILADELPHIA	0	0	0	0	0	0	1	0	1	2	6	1
HOUSTON	3	0	0	0	2	0	0	0	X	5	7	2

PHILADELPHIA	AB	R	H	RBI	BB	SO	LOB	AVG
Schwarber, LF	3	0	1	0	1	0	1	.214
Hoskins, 1B	3	0	1	0	1	2	2	.192
Realmuto, C	4	0	1	0	0	2	4	.265
Harper, DH	4	0	0	0	0	1	5	.392
Castellanos, N, RF	4	1	1	0	0	2	0	.220
Bohm, 3B	3	1	1	0	1	1	1	.200
Segura, 2B	3	0	1	1	0	1	2	.233
Vierling, CF	2	0	0	0	0	0	2	.167
a-Maton, N, PH	1	0	0	0	0	0	0	.000
Marsh, CF	1	0	0	0	0	0	0	.161
Sosa, E, SS	2	0	0	0	0	2	0	.333
b-Stott, PH-SS	1	0	0	0	1	0	1	.176
Wheeler, P	0	0	0	0	0	0	0	.000
Bellatti, P	0	0	0	0	0	0	0	.000
Brogdon, P	0	0	0	0	0	0	0	.000
Hand, P	0	0	0	0	0	0	0	.000
TOTALS	**31**	**2**	**6**	**1**	**4**	**11**	**18**	**.214**

a-Lined out for Vierling in the 7th. b-Walked for Sosa, E in the 8th. **2B:** Castellanos, N (4, Valdez, F); Bohm (5, Pressly). **TB:** Bohm 2; Castellanos, N 2; Hoskins; Realmuto; Schwarber; Segura. **RBI:** Segura (6). Runners left in scoring position, 2 out : Stott; Harper. SF : Segura. **GIDP:** Harper; Vierling. **Team RISP:** 0-for-7. Team LOB : 7. E : Sosa, E (1, throw). **DP:** (Sosa, E-Segura-Hoskins).

HOUSTON	AB	R	H	RBI	BB	SO	LOB	AVG
Altuve, 2B	4	1	3	0	0	0	1	.171
Peña, SS	4	1	1	1	0	1	2	.286
Alvarez, Y, DH	3	2	1	1	1	1	1	.222
Bregman, 3B	4	1	1	2	0	1	2	.316
Tucker, RF	3	0	0	0	1	0	1	.250
Gurriel, 1B	4	0	0	0	0	0	1	.342
Díaz, LF	3	0	0	0	0	1	1	.056
Dubón, CF	0	0	0	0	0	0	0	.000
McCormick, CF-LF	2	0	1	0	1	0	0	.280
Maldonado, C	3	0	0	0	0	2	2	.200
Valdez, F, P	0	0	0	0	0	0	0	.000
Montero, P	0	0	0	0	0	0	0	.000
Pressly, P	0	0	0	0	0	0	0	.000
TOTALS	**30**	**5**	**7**	**4**	**3**	**6**	**11**	**.246**

2B: Altuve (2, Wheeler); Peña (5, Wheeler); Alvarez, Y (3, Wheeler). **HR:** Bregman

(3, 5th inning off Wheeler, 1 on, 2 out). **TB:** Altuve 4; Alvarez, Y 2; Bregman 4; McCormick; Peña 2. **RBI:** Alvarez, Y (9); Bregman 2 (9); Peña (6). **2-out RBI:** Bregman 2. **GIDP:** Bregman. **Team RISP:** 2-for-5. Team LOB : 4. CS : Altuve (1, 2nd base by Brogdon/Realmuto). E : Peña (1, throw); Gurriel (1, fielding). **DP:** 2 (Peña-Altuve-Gurriel; Altuve-Peña-Gurriel.

PHILADELPHIA	IP	H	R	ER	BB	SO	HR	ERA
Wheeler (L, 1-2)	5.0	6	5	4	3	3	1	2.67
Bellatti	1.0	0	0	0	0	1	0	1.80
Brogdon	1.0	1	0	0	0	1	0	3.18
Hand	1.0	0	0	0	0	1	0	5.79
TOTALS	**8.0**	**7**	**5**	**4**	**3**	**6**	**1**	**4.50**

HOUSTON	IP	H	R	ER	BB	SO	HR	ERA
VValdez, F (W, 2-0)	6.1	4	1	1	3	9	0	1.42
Montero	1.2	1	0	0	1	1	0	1.13
Pressly	1.0	1	1	0	0	1	0	0.00
TOTALS	**9.0**	**6**	**2**	**1**	**4**	**11**	**0**	**3.32**

Pitches-strikes: Wheeler 69-41; Bellatti 11-7; Brogdon 14-10; Hand 12-9; Valdez, F 104-70; Montero 33-23; Pressly 18-12. **Groundouts-flyouts:** Wheeler 7-2; Bellatti 1-0; Brogdon 0-1; Hand 1-1; Valdez, F 7-0; Montero 0-3; Pressly 2-1. **Batters faced:** Wheeler 24; Bellatti 3; Brogdon 3, Hand 3; Valdez, F 24; Montero 7; Pressly 5. **Inherited runners-scored:** Montero 1-1.

Umpires: HP: Pat Hoberg. **1B:** Tripp Gibson. **2B:** Jordan Baker. **3B:** Lance Barksdale. **LF:** Alan Porter. **RF:** James Hoye. **Official scorer:** Trey Wilkinson **Weather:** 73 degrees, Roof Closed **Wind:** 0 mph, None **First pitch:** 7:04 PM **T:** 3:18 **Att:** 42,926 **Venue:** Minute Maid Park.

GAME 3

November 1, 2022

PHILADELPHIA PHILLIES 7, HOUSTON ASTROS 0

	1	2	3	4	5	6	7	8	9	R	H	E
HOUSTON	0	0	0	0	0	0	0	0	0	0	5	0
PHILADELPHIA	2	2	0	0	3	0	0	0	x	7	7	0

HOUSTON	AB	R	H	RBI	BB	SO	LOB	AVG
Altuve, 2B	4	0	0	0	0	0	2	.156
Peña, SS	3	0	1	0	1	0	0	.289
Alvarez, Y, LF	4	0	0	0	0	1	2	.200
Bregman, 3B	3	0	0	0	1	0	1	.293
Tucker, RF	4	0	0	0	0	1	3	.225
Gurriel, 1B	4	0	1	0	0	0	0	.333
Hensley, DH	3	0	1	0	0	2	0	.250
a-Mancini, PH	1	0	0	0	0	0	0	.000
McCormick, CF	3	0	1	0	1	2	2	.286
Maldonado, C	3	0	1	0	0	1	1	.217
McCullers Jr., P	0	0	0	0	0	0	0	.000
Stanek, P	0	0	0	0	0	0	0	.000
Urquidy, P	0	0	0	0	0	0	0	.000
TOTALS	**32**	**0**	**5**	**0**	**3**	**7**	**11**	**.218**

a-Flied out for Hensley in the 9th. **TB:** Gurriel; Hensley; Maldonado; McCormick; Peña. **Runners left in scoring position, 2 ouT:** Tucker; McCormick; Altuve. **Team RISP:** 0-for-3. **Team LOB:** 8.

PHILADELPHIA	AB	R	H	RBI	BB	SO	LOB	AVG
Schwarber, LF	3	2	1	2	1	1	0	.222
Hoskins, 1B	4	1	1	1	0	2	1	.196
Realmuto, C	4	0	0	0	0	3	1	.245
Harper, DH	4	1	1	2	0	1	0	.382
Castellanos, N, RF	4	0	1	0	0	1	0	.222
Vierling, RF	0	0	0	0	0	0	0	.167
Bohm, 3B	3	1	1	1	1	0	0	.208
Sosa, E, 3B	0	0	0	0	0	0	0	.333
Stott, SS	3	0	0	0	0	2	2	.162
Segura, 2B	3	0	0	0	0	1	2	.217
Marsh, CF	3	2	2	1	0	0	2	.206
Suárez, R, P	0	0	0	0	0	0	0	.000
Brogdon, P	0	0	0	0	0	0	0	.000
Gibson, P	0	0	0	0	0	0	0	.000
Nelson, N, P	0	0	0	0	0	0	0	.000
Bellatti, P	0	0	0	0	0	0	0	.000
TOTALS	**31**	**7**	**7**	**7**	**2**	**11**	**8**	**.218**

HR: Harper (6, 1st inning off McCullers Jr., 1 on, 2 out); Bohm (1, 2nd inning off McCullers Jr., 0 on, 0 out); Marsh (2, 2nd inning off McCullers Jr., 0 on, 2 out); Schwarber (4, 5th inning off McCullers Jr., 1 on, 1 out); Hoskins (6, 5th inning off McCullers Jr., 0 on, 1 out). **TB:** Bohm 4; Castellanos, N; Harper 4; Hoskins 4; Marsh 5; Schwarber 4. **RBI:** Bohm (8); Harper 2 (13); Hoskins (12); Marsh (5); Schwarber 2 (8). **2-out RBI:** Marsh; Harper 2. Runners left in scoring position, 2 ou**T:** Marsh 2. Team **RISP:** 0-for-3. Team **LOB:** 2.

HOUSTON	IP	H	R	ER	BB	SO	HR	ERA
McCullers Jr. (L, 0-1)	4.1	6	7	7	1	5	5	5.87
Stanek	0.2	0	0	0	0	2	0	0.00
Urquidy	3.0	1	0	0	1	4	0	0.00
TOTALS	**8.0**	**7**	**7**	**7**	**2**	**11**	**5**	**4.67**

PHILADELPHIA	IP	H	R	ER	BB	SO	HR	ERA
Suárez, R (W, 2-0)	5.0	3	0	0	1	4	0	1.23
Brogdon	1.0	1	0	0	0	1	0	2.70
Gibson	1.0	1	0	0	0	1	0	0.00
Nelson, N	1.0	0	0	0	2	0	0	0.00
Bellatti	1.0	0	0	0	0	1	0	1.50
TOTALS	**9.0**	**5**	**0**	**0**	**3**	**7**	**0**	**3.00**

WP: Urquidy. **Pitches-strikes:** McCullers Jr. 78-52; Stanek 7-6; Urquidy 45-31; Suárez, R 76-48; Brogdon 13-12; Gibson 15-9; Nelson, N 30-16; Bellatti 14-8. **Groundouts-flyouts:** McCullers Jr. 6-1; Stanek 0-0; Urquidy 0-3; Suárez, R 7-1; Brogdon 0-0; Gibson 1-1; Nelson, N 1-2; Bellatti 0-1. **Batters faced:** McCullers Jr. 20; Stanek 2; Urquidy 11; Suárez, R 19; Brogdon 4; Gibson 4; Nelson, N 5; Bellatti 3.

Umpires: HP: Dan Iassogna. **1B:** Jordan Baker. **2B:** Lance Barksdale. **3B:** Alan Porter. **LF:** James Hoye. **RF:** Pat Hoberg. **Official scorer:** Dick Shute **Weather:** 65 degrees, Clear **Wind:** 5 mph, L To R **First pitch:** 8:05 PM **T:** 3:08 **Att:** 45,712 **Venue:** Citizens Bank Park.

GAME 4

November 2, 2022

HOUSTON ASTROS 5, WASHINGTON NATIONALS 0

	1	2	3	4	5	6	7	8	9	R	H	E
HOUSTON	0	0	0	0	5	0	0	0	0	5	10	0
PHILADELPHIA	0	0	0	0	0	0	0	0	0	0	0	0

HOUSTON	AB	R	H	RBI	BB	SO	LOB	AVG
Altuve, 2B	5	1	1	0	0	0	0	.160
Peña, SS	5	1	2	0	0	2	0	.300
Alvarez, Y, DH	4	1	1	1	0	1	1	.205
Bregman, 3B	5	1	1	2	0	0	2	.283
Tucker, RF	2	0	1	1	1	0	0	.238
Gurriel, 1B	4	0	2	1	0	0	2	.348
Vazquez, C	3	0	1	0	0	2	1	.214
Diaz, LF	4	0	0	0	0	3	5	.045
Dubón, CF	0	0	0	0	0	0	0	.000
McCormick, CF-LF	4	1	1	0	0	3	2	.281
Javier, P	0	0	0	0	0	0	0	.000
Abreu, B, P	0	0	0	0	0	0	0	.000
Montero, P	0	0	0	0	0	0	0	.000
Pressly, P	0	0	0	0	0	0	0	.000
TOTALS	**36**	**5**	**10**	**5**	**1**	**11**	**13**	**.234**

2B: Tucker (1, Nola, Aa); Bregman (4, Alvarado). **TB:** Altuve; Alvarez, Y; Bregman 2; Gurriel 2; McCormick; Peña 2; Tucker 2; Vazquez. **RBI:** Alvarez, Y (10); Bregman 2 (11); Gurriel (4); Tucker (6). **Runners left in scoring position, 2 out:** McCormick; Diaz 2. SF : Tucker. **Team RISP:** 3-for-8. **Team LOB:** 8. **SB:** Gurriel (2, 2nd base off Alvarado/Realmuto).

PHILADELPHIA	AB	R	H	RBI	BB	SO	LOB	AVG
Schwarber, LF	3	0	0	0	1	1	1	.208
Hoskins, 1B	4	0	0	0	0	0	2	.183
Realmuto, C	4	0	0	0	0	3	1	.228
Harper, DH	2	0	0	0	1	2	0	.368

Castellanos, N, RF	3	0	0	0	0	3	1	.211
Bohm, 3B	3	0	0	0	0	3	1	.196
Stott, SS	3	0	0	0	0	1	1	.150
Segura, 2B	3	0	0	0	0	0	0	.204
Marsh, CF	2	0	0	0	1	1	0	.194
Nola, Aa, P	0	0	0	0	0	0	0	.000
Alvarado, P	0	0	0	0	0	0	0	.000
Bellatti, P	0	0	0	0	0	0	0	.000
Robertson, P	0	0	0	0	0	0	0	.000
Eflin, P	0	0	0	0	0	0	0	.000
Hand, P	0	0	0	0	0	0	0	.00
TOTALS	**27**	**0**	**0**	**0**	**3**	**14**	**7**	**.172**

Runners left in scoring position, 2 out: Stott; Hoskins. Team **RISP:** 0-for-2. Team **LOB:** 3. **SB:** Harper (1, 2nd base off Javier/Vazquez); Marsh (1, 2nd base off Javier/Vazquez).

HOUSTON	IP	H	R	ER	BB	SO	HR	ERA
Javier (W, 2-0)	6.0	0	0	0	2	9	0	0.71
Abreu, B	1.0	0	0	0	0	3	0	0.00
Montero	1.0	0	0	0	0	1	0	1.00
Pressly	1.0	0	0	0	1	1	0	0.00
TOTALS	**9.0**	**0**	**0**	**0**	**3**	**14**	**0**	**3.50**

PHILADELPHIA	IP	H	R	ER	BB	SO	HR	ERA
Nola, Aa (L, 2-2)	4.0	7	3	3	0	4	0	4.91
Alvarado	1.0	2	2	2	0	2	0	4.50
Bellatti	1.0	0	0	0	0	1	0	1.29
Robertson	1.0	0	0	0	1	1	0	1.59
Eflin	1.0	0	0	0	0	3	0	4.15
Hand	1.0	1	0	0	0	0	0	4.76
TOTALS	**9.0**	**10**	**5**	**5**	**1**	**11**	**0**	**3.50**

Nola, Aa pitched to 3 batters in the 5th. **HBP:** Vazquez (by Nola, Aa); Alvarez, Y (by Alvarado). **Pitches-strikes:** Javier 97-63; Abreu, B 15-10; Montero 10-7; Pressly 19-11; Nola, Aa 67-48; Alvarado 22-16; Bellatti 9-7; Robertson 11-6; Eflin 12-9; Hand 16-11. **Groundouts-flyouts:** Javier 3-3; Abreu, B 0-0; Montero 0-1; Pressly 1-1; Nola, Aa 4-0; Alvarado 0-0; Bellatti 0-2; Robertson 0-1; Eflin 0-0; Hand 1-2. **Batters faced:** Javier 20; Abreu, B 3; Montero 3; Pressly 4; Nola, Aa 20; Alvarado 6; Bellatti 3; Robertson 4; Eflin 3; Hand 4. **Inherited runners-scored:** Alvarado 3-3.

Umpires: HP: Tripp Gibson. **1B:** Lance Barksdale. **2B:** Alan Porter. **3B:** James Hoye. **LF:** Pat Hoberg. **RF:** Dan Iassogna. **Official scorer:** Mark Gola **Weather:** 62 degrees, Partly Cloudy **Wind:** 2 mph, Out To CF **First pitch:** 8:03 PM **T:** 3:25 **Att:** 45,693 **Venue:** Citizens Bank Park.

GAME 5

November 3, 2022

HOUSTON ASTROS 3, PHILADELPHIA PHILLIES 2

	1	2	3	4	5	6	7	8	9	R	H	E
HOUSTON	1	0	0	1	0	0	0	1	0	3	9	0
PHILADELPHIA	1	0	0	0	0	0	0	1	0	2	6	1

HOUSTON	AB	R	H	RBI	BB	SO	LOB	AVG
Altuve, 2B	4	2	2	0	1	0	2	.185
Peña, SS	4	1	3	2	0	1	1	.333
Alvarez, Y, LF	4	0	0	1	0	2	3	.188
Bregman, 3B	2	0	1	0	1	1	0	.292
Tucker, RF	4	0	0	0	0	2	5	.217
Gurriel, 1B	3	0	1	0	0	1	1	.347
a-Mancini, PH-1B	1	0	0	0	0	1	2	.000
Hensley, DH	4	0	1	0	0	2	1	.250
McCormick, CF	4	0	0	0	0	1	2	.250
Maldonado, C	4	0	1	0	0	1	1	.222
Verlander, P	0	0	0	0	0	0	0	.000
Neris, P	0	0	0	0	0	0	0	.000
Abreu, B, P	0	0	0	0	0	0	0	.000
Montero, P	0	0	0	0	0	0	0	.000
Pressly, P	0	0	0	0	0	0	0	.000
TOTALS	**34**	**3**	**9**	**3**	**2**	**12**	**18**	**.240**

a-Struck out for Gurriel in the 8th. **2B:** Altuve (3, Syndergaard); Bregman (5, Brogdon); Gurriel (1, Domínguez). **HR:** Peña (4, 4th inning off Syndergaard, 0 on, 0 out). **TB:** Altuve 3; Bregman 2; Gurriel 2; Hensley; Maldonado; Peña 6. **RBI:** Alvarez, Y (11); Peña 2 (8). **Runners left in scoring position, 2 out:** Tucker; Mancini 2; Gurriel; Maldonado. **GIDP:** Altuve. Team **RISP:** 1-for-11. **Team LOB:** 7. **SB:** Bregman (1, 2nd base off Robertson/Realmuto). CS : Peña (1, 2nd base by Syndergaard/Realmuto).

PHILADELPHIA	AB	R	H	RBI	BB	SO	LOB	AVG
Schwarber, LF	4	1	1	1	1	1	4	.212
Hoskins, 1B	5	0	0	0	0	4	3	.169
Realmuto, C	5	0	0	0	0	3	0	.210
Harper, DH	2	0	1	0	2	0	0	.373
Castellanos, N, RF	4	1	0	0	1	0	4	.197
Bohm, 3B	4	0	2	0	0	1	1	.218
Stott, SS	3	0	0	0	1	0	3	.140
Segura, 2B	4	0	2	1	0	1	1	.226
Marsh, CF	2	0	0	0	1	2	2	.184
Syndergaard, P	0	0	0	0	0	0	0	.000
Brogdon, P	0	0	0	0	0	0	0	.000
Alvarado, P	0	0	0	0	0	0	0	.000
Domínguez, P	0	0	0	0	0	0	0	.000
Robertson, P	0	0	0	0	0	0	0	.000
Eflin, P	0	0	0	0	0	0	0	.000
TOTALS	**33**	**2**	**6**	**2**	**6**	**12**	**18**	**.174**

2B: Harper (7, Verlander). **HR:** Schwarber (5, 1st inning off Verlander, 0 on, 0 out). **TB:** Bohm 2; Harper 2; Schwarber 4; Segura 2. **RBI:** Schwarber (9); Segura (7). **Runners left in scoring position, 2 out:** Stott; Hoskins 2; Castellanos, N; Schwarber 2. Team **RISP:** 1-for-7. Team **LOB:** 12. E : Marsh (1, fielding). **DP:** 2 (Realmuto-Stott; Bohm-Hoskins).

HOUSTON	IP	H	R	ER	BB	SO	HR	ERA
Verlander (W, 2-0)	5.0	4	1	1	4	6	1	5.85
Neris (H, 2)	0.2	1	0	0	0	1	0	1.80
Abreu, B (H, 4)	1.1	0	0	0	0	2	0	0.00
Montero (H, 4)	0.1	1	1	1	2	1	0	1.93
Pressly (S, 5)	1.2	0	0	0	0	2	0	0.00
TOTALS	**9.0**	**6**	**2**	**2**	**6**	**12**	**1**	**3.20**

PHILADELPHIA	IP	H	R	ER	BB	SO	HR	ERA
Syndergaard (L, 0-1)	3.0	3	2	2	0	4	1	3.24
Brogdon	2.0	1	0	0	0	5	0	2.08
Alvarado	1.0	1	0	0	0	1	0	4.09
Domínguez	1.0	2	1	1	1	0	0	1.74
Robertson	1.0	0	0	0	1	1	0	1.35
Eflin	1.0	2	0	0	0	1	0	3.72
TOTALS	**9.0**	**9**	**3**	**3**	**2**	**12**	**1**	**3.40**

Syndergaard pitched to 1 batter in the 4th. Domínguez pitched to 2 batters in the 8th. **WP:** Domínguez. **HBP:** Bregman (by Alvarado); Marsh (by Abreu, B); Harper (by Pressly). **Pitches-strikes:** Verlander 94-58; Neris 11-7; Abreu, B 17-12; Montero 17-8; Pressly 26-17; Syndergaard 44-31; Brogdon 26-18; Alvarado 20-14; Domínguez 26-16; Robertson 20-11; Eflin 13-10. **Groundouts-flyouts:** Verlander 1-3; Neris 0-1; Abreu, B 1-0; Montero 0-0; Pressly 2-1; Syndergaard 1-2; Brogdon 1-0; Alvarado 1-0; Domínguez 3-0; Robertson 1-1; Eflin 1-0. **Batters faced:** Verlander 23; Neris 3; Abreu, B 5; Montero 4; Pressly 6; Syndergaard 11; Brogdon 7; Alvarado 5; Domínguez 6; Robertson 4; Eflin 4. **Inherited runners-scored:** Abreu, B 1-0; Pressly 2-0; Robertson 2-1.

Umpires: HP: Jordan Baker. **1B:** Alan Porter. **2B:** James Hoye. **3B:** Pat Hoberg. **LF:** Dan Iassogna. **RF:** Tripp Gibson. **Official scorer:** Mike Maconi **Weather:** 59 degrees, Clear **Wind:** 2 mph, Out To CF **First pitch:** 8:06 PM **T:** 3:57 **Att:** 45,693 **Venue:** Citizens Bank Park.

GAME 6

November 5, 2022

HOUSTON ASTROS 4, PHILADELPHIA PHILLIES 1

	1	2	3	4	5	6	7	8	9	R	H	E
PHILADELPHIA	0	0	0	0	0	1	0	0	0	1	3	1
HOUSTON	0	0	0	0	0	4	0	0	X	4	7	0

PHILADELPHIA	AB	R	H	RBI	BB	SO	LOB	AVG
Schwarber, LF	3	1	1	1	1	2	0	.218
Hoskins, 1B	4	0	0	0	0	1	1	.159
Realmuto, C	3	0	1	0	0	1	0	.215
Harper, DH	4	0	0	0	0	2	2	.349

Castellanos, N, RF	4	0	0	0	0	2	1	.185
Bohm, 3B	3	0	1	0	0	1	0	.224
Segura, 2B	3	0	0	0	0	2	1	.214
Vierling, CF	1	0	0	0	1	0	0	.154
a-Stott, PH-SS	1	0	0	0	0	0	0	.136
Sosa, E, SS	2	0	0	0	0	1	2	.250
b-Marsh, PH-CF	1	0	0	0	0	0	0	.179
Wheeler, P	0	0	0	0	0	0	0	.000
Alvarado, P	0	0	0	0	0	0	0	.000
Domínguez, P	0	0	0	0	0	0	0	.000
Eflin, P	0	0	0	0	0	0	0	.000
Robertson, P	0	0	0	0	0	0	0	.000
TOTALS	**29**	**1**	**3**	**1**	**2**	**12**	**7**	**.163**

a-Lined out for Vierling in the 8th. b-Flied out for Sosa, E in the 8th. **HR:** Schwarber (6, 6th inning off Valdez, F, 0 on, 0 out). **TB:** Bohm; Realmuto; Schwarber 4. **RBI:** Schwarber (10). **Runners left in scoring position, 2 ouT:** Sosa, E. **GIDP:** Hoskins. **Team RISP:** 0-for-1. **Team LOB:** 4. E : Schwarber (1, fielding). **Outfield assists:** Schwarber (Bregman at 2nd base). **DP:** (Sosa, E-Segura-Hoskins).

HOUSTON	AB	R	H	RBI	BB	SO	LOB	AVG
Altuve, 2B	4	1	1	0	0	2	2	.190
Peña, SS	4	1	2	0	0	1	1	.345
Alvarez, Y, LF	4	1	1	3	0	1	1	.192
Bregman, 3B	3	1	1	0	1	1	1	.294
Tucker, RF	3	0	0	0	1	1	2	.204
Vazquez, DH	3	0	1	1	0	0	1	.235
Mancini, 1B	3	0	1	0	0	1	1	.048
McCormick, CF	3	0	0	0	0	2	1	.231
Maldonado, C	2	0	0	0	0	0	1	.207
Valdez, F, P	0	0	0	0	0	0	0	.000
Neris, P	0	0	0	0	0	0	0	.000
Abreu, B, P	0	0	0	0	0	0	0	.000
Pressly, P	0	0	0	0	0	0	0	.000
TOTALS	**29**	**4**	**7**	**4**	**2**	**9**	**11**	**.240**

HR: Alvarez, Y (3, 6th inning off Alvarado, 2 on, 1 out).**TB:** Altuve; Alvarez, Y 4; Bregman; Mancini; Peña 2; Vazquez. **RBI:** Alvarez, Y 3 (14); Vazquez (3). **2-out RBI:** Vazquez. **Runners left in scoring position, 2 out:** Peña; Altuve. **GIDP:** Vazquez. **Team RISP:** 2-for-5. **Team LOB:** 4. **DP:** (Bregman-Altuve-Mancini).

PHILADELPHIA	IP	H	R	ER	BB	SO	HR	ERA
Wheeler (L, 1-3)	5.1	3	2	2	1	5	0	2.78
Alvarado (BS, 1)	0.1	1	2	2	1	1	1	5.56
Domínguez	0.1	1	0	0	0	0	0	1.69
Eflin	1.0	1	0	0	0	2	0	3.38
Robertson	1.0	1	0	0	0	1	0	1.17
TOTALS	**8.0**	**7**	**4**	**4**	**2**	**9**	**1**	**3.57**

HOUSTON	IP	H	R	ER	BB	SO	HR	ERA
Valdez, F (W, 3-0)	6.0	2	1	1	2	9	1	1.44
Neris (H, 3)	1.0	0	0	0	0	2	0	1.50
Abreu, B (H, 5)	1.0	0	0	0	0	1	0	0.00
Pressly (S, 6)	1.0	1	0	0	0	0	0	0.00
TOTALS	**9.0**	**3**	**1**	**1**	**2**	**12**	**1**	**2.83**

WP: Alvarado. **HBP:** Realmuto (by Valdez, F); Maldonado (by Wheeler). **Pitches-strikes:** Wheeler 70-49; Alvarado 18-9; Domínguez 9-6; Eflin 18-13; Robertson 15-10; Valdez, F 93-57; Neris 10-9, Abreu, B 10-7; Pressly 7-6. **Groundouts-flyouts:** Wheeler 8-2; Alvarado 0-0; Domínguez 1-0; Eflin 0-1; Robertson 0-1; Valdez, F 6-2; Neris 0-1; Abreu, B 0-1; Pressly 0-3. **Batters faced:** Wheeler 20; Alvarado 3; Domínguez 2; Eflin 4; Robertson 3; Valdez, F 22; Neris 3; Abreu, B 3; Pressly 4. **Inherited runners-scored:** Alvarado 2-2; Domínguez 1-1.

Umpires: HP: Lance Barksdale. **1B:** James Hoye. **2B:** Pat Hoberg. **3B:** Dan Iassogna. **LF:** Tripp Gibson. **RF:** Jordan Baker. **Official scorer:** Rick Blount **Weather:** 73 degrees, Roof Closed **Wind:** 0 mph, None **First pitch:** 7:04 PM T: 3:13 **Att:** 42,958 **Venue:** Minute Maid Park.

AMERICAN LEAGUE WILD CARD SERIES

CLEVELAND GUARDIANS VS. TAMPA BAY RAYS

CLEVELAND	AVG	G	AB	R	H	2B	3B	HR	RBI	BB	SO	SB
Will Brennan, DH	.200	1	5	0	1	0	0	0	0	0	2	0
Andres Gimenez, 2B	.125	2	8	0	1	0	0	0	0	0	6	0
Oscar Gonzalez, RF	.333	2	9	1	3	0	0	1	1	0	3	0
Austin Hedges, C	.000	2	6	0	0	0	0	0	0	0	3	0
Steven Kwan, LF	.000	2	9	0	0	0	0	0	0	1	1	0
Luke Maile, C	--	1	0	0	0	0	0	0	0	1	0	0
Owen Miller, DH	.000	2	4	0	0	0	0	0	0	0	1	0
Josh Naylor, 1B	.222	2	9	0	2	0	0	0	0	0	2	0
Jose Ramirez, 3B	.200	2	10	1	2	0	0	1	2	0	3	0
Amed Rosario, SS	.222	2	9	1	2	0	0	0	0	0	4	0
Myles Straw, CF	.286	2	7	0	2	0	0	0	0	1	1	1
Totals	**.171**	**30**	**76**	**3**	**13**	**0**	**0**	**2**	**3**	**3**	**26**	**1**

CLEVELAND	W	L	ERA	G	GS	SV	IP	H	R	ER	BB	SO
Shane Bieber	1	0	1.17	1	1	0	7.2	3	1	1	1	8
Emmanuel Clase	0	0	0.00	2	0	1	2.1	0	0	0	0	2
Enyel De Los Santos	0	0	0.00	1	0	0	1	1	0	0	1	0
Sam Hentges	1	0	0.00	1	0	0	3	3	0	0	0	6
James Karinchak	0	0	0.00	1	0	0	1	0	0	0	1	0
Triston McKenzie	0	0	0.00	1	1	0	6	2	0	0	2	8
Eli Morgan	0	0	0.00	1	0	0	1.1	0	0	0	0	2
Nick Sandlin	0	0	0.00	1	0	0	0.2	0	0	0	1	1
Trevor Stephan	0	0	0.00	1	0	0	1	0	0	0	0	2
Totals	**2**	**0**	**0.38**	**10**	**2**	**1**	**24**	**9**	**1**	**1**	**6**	**29**

TAMPA BAY	AVG	G	AB	R	H	2B	3B	HR	RBI	BB	SO	SB
Randy Arozarena, LF	.111	2	9	0	1	0	0	0	0	1	5	0
Christian Bethancourt, C	.000	2	5	0	0	0	0	0	0	0	3	0
Vidal Brujan, 2B	.500	2	2	0	1	0	0	0	0	0	0	2
Ji-Man Choi, 1B	.000	2	5	0	0	0	0	0	0	2	1	0
Yandy Díaz, 1B-3B	.000	2	10	0	0	0	0	0	0	0	4	0
Wander Franco, SS	.111	2	9	0	1	0	0	0	0	1	2	0
Manuel Margot, RF	.125	2	8	0	1	0	0	0	0	1	1	0
Francisco Mejia, C	.000	1	3	0	0	0	0	0	0	0	2	0
Isaac Paredes, 2B	.667	2	3	0	2	0	0	0	0	1	0	0
David Peralta, PH	.000	1	1	0	0	0	0	0	0	0	1	0
Harold Ramirez, DH	.111	2	9	0	1	0	0	0	0	0	3	0
Jose Siri, CF	.111	2	9	1	1	0	0	1	1	0	5	0
Taylor Walls, 2B-3B	.200	2	5	0	1	0	0	0	0	0	2	0
Totals	**.115**	**34**	**78**	**1**	**9**	**0**	**0**	**1**	**1**	**6**	**29**	**2**

TAMPA BAY	W	L	ERA	G	GS	SV	IP	H	R	ER	BB	SO
Jason Adam	0	0	0.00	1	0	0	2	1	0	0	0	2
Shawn Armstrong	0	0	0.00	1	0	0	1.1	1	0	0	0	3
Garrett Cleavinger	0	0	0.00	2	0	0	2.1	1	0	0	0	6
Pete Fairbanks	0	0		1	0	0	0	0	0	0	2	0
Tyler Glasnow	0	0	0.00	1	1	0	5	2	0	0	0	5
Corey Kluber	0	1	5.40	1	0	0	1.2	1	1	1	0	1
Shane McClanahan	0	1	2.57	1	1	0	7	7	2	2	0	5
Brooks Raley	0	0	0.00	1	0	0	1	0	0	0	1	2
Drew Rasmussen	0	0	0.00	1	0	0	1.2	0	0	0	0	2
Totals	**0**	**2**	**1.23**	**10**	**2**	**0**	**22**	**13**	**3**	**3**	**3**	**26**

SCORE BY INNING

TAMPA BAY	0	0	0	0	0	1	0	0	0	0	0	0	0	0	0	1
CLEVELAND	0	0	0	0	0	2	0	0	0	0	0	0	0	0	0	2

SEATTLE MARINERS VS. TORONTO BLUE JAYS

SEATTLE	AVG	G	AB	R	H	2B	3B	HR	RBI	BB	SO	SB
J.P. Crawford, SS	.143	2	7	0	1	1	0	0	3	2	1	0
Ty France, 1B	.200	2	10	1	2	0	0	0	0	0	1	0
Adam Frazier, 2B	.444	2	9	2	4	1	0	0	1	0	0	0
Mitch Haniger, RF	.222	2	9	1	2	1	0	0	0	0	2	0
Jarred Kelenic, LF	.000	2	5	0	0	0	0	0	1	0	2	0
Dylan Moore, LF	.000	1	2	0	0	0	0	0	0	1	2	0

	AVG	G	AB	R	H	2B	3B	HR	RBI	BB	SO	SB
Cal Raleigh, C	.500	2	8	4	4	1	0	1	3	1	3	0
Julio Rodriguez, CF	.143	2	7	2	1	0	0	0	0	1	2	0
Carlos Santana, DH	.250	2	8	1	2	1	0	1	3	1	4	0
Eugenio Suarez, 3B	.444	2	9	3	4	2	0	0	2	0	3	0
Taylor Trammell, DH		1	0	0	0	0	0	0	0	0	0	0
Totals	**.270**	**30**	**74**	**14**	**20**	**7**	**0**	**2**	**13**	**6**	**20**	**0**

SEATTLE	W	L	ERA	G	GS	SV	IP	H	R	ER	BB	SO
Matt Brash	0	0	0.00	1	0	0	1	0	0	0	0	1
Diego Castillo	0	0	0.00	1	0	0	0.1	0	0	0	0	0
Luis Castillo	1	0	0.00	1	1	0	7.1	6	0	0	0	5
Matthew Festa	0	0	6.75	1	0	0	1.1	1	1	1	0	0
George Kirby	0	0	0.00	1	0	1	1	0	0	0	1	1
Andres Munoz	1	0	0.00	2	0	0	2.2	1	0	0	1	3
Penn Murfee	0	0	0.00	1	0	0	0.2	2	0	0	0	0
Robbie Ray	0	0	12.00	1	1	0	3	6	4	4	0	4
Paul Sewald	0	0	54.00	1	0	0	0.2	3	4	4	2	1
Totals	**2**	**0**	**4.50**	**10**	**2**	**1**	**18**	**19**	**9**	**9**	**4**	**15**

TORONTO	AVG	G	AB	R	H	2B	3B	HR	RBI	BB	SO	SB
Bo Bichette, SS	.250	2	8	1	2	1	0	0	0	1	1	1
Jackie Bradley Jr., CF	.000	1	1	0	0	0	0	0	0	0	1	0
Matt Chapman, 3B	.429	2	7	0	3	1	0	0	1	1	2	0
Santiago Espinal, 2B	.500	1	4	2	2	1	0	0	0	0	0	0
Vladimir Guerrero Jr., 1B	.125	2	8	1	1	0	0	0	1	1	1	0
Teoscar Hernandez, RF	.250	2	8	3	2	0	0	2	4	0	1	1
Danny Jansen, C-DH	.375	2	8	0	3	1	0	0	2	0	4	0
Alejandro Kirk, C-DH	.375	2	8	2	3	1	0	0	0	1	1	0
Whit Merrifield, 2B-LF	.200	2	5	0	1	0	0	0	0	0	0	0
George Springer, CF	.286	2	7	0	2	0	0	0	0	0	3	0
Raimel Tapia, LF	.000	2	6	0	0	0	0	0	0	0	1	0
Totals	**.271**	**32**	**70**	**9**	**19**	**5**	**0**	**2**	**8**	**4**	**15**	**2**

TORONTO	W	L	ERA	G	GS	SV	IP	H	R	ER	BB	SO
Anthony Bass	0	0	inf	1	0	0	0	3	3	3	0	0
Adam Cimber	0	0	0.00	2	0	0	1	0	0	0	2	0
Yimi Garcia	0	0	0.00	2	0	0	1	1	0	0	0	1
Kevin Gausman	0	0	6.35	1	1	0	5.2	5	4	4	1	7
Alek Manoah	0	1	6.35	1	1	0	5.2	4	4	4	1	4
Tim Mayza	0	0	5.40	2	0	0	1.2	1	1	1	0	2
Zach Pop	0	0	0.00	1	0	0	0.1	2	0	0	0	1
Trevor Richards	0	0	0.00	1	0	0	1	0	0	0	1	1
Jordan Romano	0	1	10.80	1	0	0	1.2	4	2	2	1	4
Totals	**0**	**2**	**7.00**	**12**	**2**	**0**	**18**	**20**	**14**	**14**	**6**	**20**

SCORE BY INNING

SEATTLE	3	0	0	0	2	4	0	4	1	14
TORONTO	0	2	1	1	4	0	1	0	0	9

AMERICAN LEAGUE DIVISION SERIES

SEATTLE MARINERS VS. HOUSTON ASTROS

HOUSTON	AVG	G	AB	R	H	2B	3B	HR	RBI	BB	SO	SB
Jose Altuve, 2B	.000	3	16	1	0	0	0	0	0	1	6	0
Yordan Alvarez, LF	.267	3	15	3	4	1	0	2	7	1	2	0
Alex Bregman, 3B	.333	3	15	1	5	1	0	1	3	1	2	0
Aledmys Díaz, DH	.143	3	7	0	1	1	0	0	0	0	1	0
Mauricio Dubon, CF		3	0	0	0	0	0	0	0	0	0	0
Yuli Gurriel, 1B	.400	3	15	1	6	0	0	1	1	0	0	1
David Hensley, PH	.000	2	1	0	0	0	0	0	0	0	0	0
Martin Maldonado, C	.143	3	7	0	1	0	0	0	0	0	5	0
Trey Mancini, DH	.000	2	6	0	0	0	0	0	0	0	2	0
Chas McCormick, CF-LF	.286	2	7	1	2	0	0	0	0	0	2	0
Jake Meyers, CF	.000	2	2	1	0	0	0	0	0	0	2	0
Jeremy Pena, SS	.250	3	16	4	4	1	0	1	1	1	4	0
Kyle Tucker, RF	.267	3	15	1	4	0	0	1	1	1	7	1
Christian Vazquez, C	.143	2	7	0	1	0	0	0	0	0	3	0
Totals	**.217**	**55**	**129**	**13**	**28**	**4**	**0**	**6**	**13**	**5**	**36**	**2**

HOUSTON	W	L	ERA	G	GS	SV	IP	H	R	ER	BB	SO
Bryan Abreu	0	0	0.00	3	0	0	3	1	0	0	1	6
Hunter Brown	0	0	0.00	2	0	0	3	2	0	0	1	1
Luis Garcia	1	0	0.00	1	0	0	5	2	0	0	0	6
Cristian Javier	0	0	6.75	1	0	0	1	1	1	1	0	2
Lance McCullers Jr.	0	0	0.00	1	1	0	6	2	0	0	2	7
Rafael Montero	1	0	0.00	3	0	0	3	1	0	0	2	3
Hector Neris	1	0	0.00	2	0	0	1	0	0	0	0	2
Ryan Pressly	0	0	0.00	3	0	1	2	2	0	0	1	2
Ryne Stanek	0	0	0.00	1	0	0	1	0	0	0	0	1
Framber Valdez	0	0	3.18	1	1	0	5	4	2	2	3	6
Justin Verlander	0	0	13.50	1	1	0	4	10	6	6	1	3
Totals	**3**	**0**	**2.25**	**18**	**3**	**1**	**36**	**25**	**9**	**9**	**11**	**39**

SEATTLE	AVG	G	AB	R	H	2B	3B	HR	RBI	BB	SO	SB
J.P. Crawford, SS	.214	3	14	1	3	1	0	1	1	1	3	0
Ty France, 1B	.250	3	16	0	4	1	0	0	2	1	5	0
Adam Frazier, 2B	.071	3	14	1	1	0	0	0	0	1	5	0
Mitch Haniger, RF	.250	3	12	1	3	1	0	0	0	2	3	0
Jarred Kelenic, LF	.167	3	12	1	2	0	0	0	0	0	5	0
Dylan Moore, LF-3B	.200	2	5	0	1	0	0	0	1	1	2	0
Cal Raleigh, C	.071	3	14	0	1	0	0	0	1	1	5	0
Julio Rodriguez, CF	.250	3	16	3	4	3	1	0	2	2	5	1
Carlos Santana, DH	.214	3	14	0	3	1	0	0	1	1	4	0
Eugenio Suarez, 3B	.273	3	11	2	3	0	0	1	1	1	2	0
Taylor Trammell, DH		2	0	0	0	0	0	0	0	0	0	0
Totals	**.195**	**49**	**128**	**9**	**25**	**7**	**1**	**2**	**9**	**11**	**39**	**1**

SEATTLE	W	L	ERA	G	GS	SV	IP	H	R	ER	BB	SO
Matthew Boyd	0	0	0.00	1	0	0	0	1	0	0	1	0
Matt Brash	0	0	0.00	2	0	0	2	0	0	0	0	3
Diego Castillo	0	0	0.00	2	0	0	1	2	0	0	0	0
Luis Castillo	0	1	3.86	1	1	0	7	5	3	3	0	7
Matthew Festa	0	0	0.00	1	0	0	2	0	0	0	0	2
Logan Gilbert	0	0	5.06	1	1	0	5	5	3	3	2	5
George Kirby	0	0	0.00	1	1	0	7	6	0	0	0	5
Andres Munoz	0	0	9.00	3	0	0	3	5	3	3	2	6
Penn Murfee	0	1	4.50	1	0	0	2	2	1	1	0	1
Robbie Ray	0	1	13.50	2	0	0	0	1	1	1	0	1
Paul Sewald	0	0	6.75	2	0	0	2	1	2	2	0	5
Erik Swanson	0	0	0.00	1	0	0	1	0	0	0	0	1
Totals	**0**	**3**	**3.38**	**18**	**3**	**0**	**34**	**28**	**13**	**13**	**5**	**36**

SCORE BY INNING

HOUSTON	0	1	2	1	0	2	0	3	3	0	0
	0	0	0	0	0	0	12				
SEATTLE	1	3	0	4	0	0	1	0	0	0	0
	0	0	0	0	0	1	10				

CLEVELAND GUARDIANS VS. NEW YORK YANKEES

NEW YORK	AVG	G	AB	R	H	2B	3B	HR	RBI	BB	SO	SB
Harrison Bader, CF	.267	5	15	4	4	0	0	3	4	2	2	0
Oswaldo Cabrera, SS-LF	.105	5	19	2	2	1	0	1	2	0	10	0
Matt Carpenter, PH	.000	2	2	0	0	0	0	0	0	0	2	0
Josh Donaldson, 3B	.250	5	16	1	4	0	0	0	0	4	6	0
Marwin Gonzalez, LF	.000	1	1	0	0	0	0	0	0	0	1	0
Aaron Hicks, LF	.000	2	3	0	0	0	0	0	0	1	0	0
Kyle Higashioka, C	.000	2	3	0	0	0	0	0	0	1	2	0
Aaron Judge, RF	.200	5	20	4	4	0	0	2	3	1	11	1
Isiah Kiner-Falefa, SS	.273	4	11	1	3	0	0	0	0	1	1	1
Tim Locastro, DH	.000	1	1	0	0	0	0	0	0	0	0	1
Anthony Rizzo, 1B	.294	5	17	2	5	1	0	1	4	3	5	0
Giancarlo Stanton, DH	.125	5	16	2	2	0	0	2	6	2	6	0
Gleyber Torres, 2B	.158	5	19	4	3	0	0	0	0	2	3	2
Jose Trevino, C	.091	4	11	0	1	0	0	0	1	0	4	0
Totals	**.182**	**74**	**154**	**20**	**28**	**2**	**0**	**9**	**20**	**17**	**53**	**5**

NEW YORK	W	L	ERA	G	GS	SV	IP	H	R	ER	BB	SO
Gerrit Cole	2	0	2.03	2	2	0	13	10	3	3	2	16
Nestor Cortes	1	0	2.70	2	2	0	10	9	3	3	4	5
Clay Holmes	0	0	0.00	4	0	0	3	0	0	0	2	5

	W	L	ERA	G	GS	SV	IP	H	R	ER	BB	SO
Jonathan Loaisiga	0	0	0.00	4	0	0	5	6	0	0	0	3
Wandy Peralta	0	0	3.00	5	0	1	6	4	2	2	0	7
Clarke Schmidt	0	1	6.75	2	0	0	1	3	1	1	0	1
Luis Severino	0	0	4.76	1	1	0	5	8	3	3	0	6
Jameson Taillon	0	1	inf	1	0	0	0	3	2	2	0	0
Lou Trivino	0	0	0.00	2	0	0	1	1	0	0	1	2
Totals	**3**	**2**	**2.76**	**23**	**5**	**1**	**45**	**44**	**14**	**14**	**9**	**45**

CLEVELAND	AVG	G	AB	R	H	2B	3B	HR	RBI	BB	SO	SB
Gabriel Arias, 1B	.273	3	11	1	3	1	0	0	0	0	5	0
Will Benson, PH	.000	1	1	0	0	0	0	0	0	0	0	0
Will Brennan, DH	.167	4	6	0	1	0	0	0	1	0	4	0
Andres Gimenez, 2B	.200	5	20	1	4	1	0	0	1	1	8	1
Oscar Gonzalez, RF	.182	5	22	1	4	0	0	0	3	0	6	0
Austin Hedges, C	.222	5	9	1	2	0	0	0	0	3	2	0
Steven Kwan, LF	.429	5	21	4	9	1	0	1	2	1	1	1
Luke Maile, C	.333	4	3	0	1	0	0	0	0	0	0	0
Owen Miller, DH	.200	3	5	0	1	0	0	0	0	1	3	0
Josh Naylor, 1B-DH	.182	5	22	2	4	1	0	1	3	0	4	0
Jose Ramirez, 3B	.400	5	20	1	8	2	0	0	2	1	4	0
Amed Rosario, SS	.250	5	20	2	5	0	0	1	2	1	6	1
Myles Straw, CF	.111	5	18	1	2	1	0	0	0	1	2	0
Totals	**.247**	**76**	**178**	**14**	**44**	**7**	**0**	**3**	**14**	**9**	**45**	**3**

CLEVELAND	W	L	ERA	G	GS	SV	IP	H	R	ER	BB	SO
Shane Bieber		0	03.18	1	1	0	5	5	2	2	3	7
Aaron Civale	0	1	81.00	1	1	0	0	2	3	3	1	1
Emmanuel Clase		1	00.00	2	0	0	3	1	0	0	2	4
Enyel De Los Santos	0	0	0.00	2	0	0	2	1	0	0	0	1
Sam Hentges		0	05.40	2	0	0	3	2	2	2	2	4
James Karinchak	0	0	0.00	3	0	0	4	3	0	0	3	6
Triston McKenzie		0	07.20	1	1	0	5	4	4	4	1	5
Eli Morgan	1	0	4.50	2	0	0	2	2	1	1	0	3
Cody Morris		0	00.00	1	0	0	2	0	0	0	0	3
Zach Plesac	0	0	0.00	1	0	0	1	0	0	0	0	2
Cal Quantrill		0	25.40	2	2	0	10	8	7	6	4	8
Trevor Stephan	0	0	1.93	3	0	0	4	0	1	1	1	9
Totals	**2**	**3**	**3.89**	**21**	**5**	**0**	**44**	**28**	**20**	**19**	**17**	**53**

SCORE BY INNINGS

CLEVELAND	1	1	3	2	1	1	0	0	3	2	14
NY YANKEES	6	3	3	0	4	3	1	0	0	0	20

AMERICAN LEAGUE CHAMPIONSHIP SERIES

NEW YORK YANKEES VS. HOUSTON ASTROS

HOUSTON	AVG	G	AB	R	H	2B	3B	HR	RBI	BB	SO	SB
Jose Altuve, 2B	.188	4	16	2	3	1	0	0	0	2	5	0
Yordan Alvarez, LF-DH	.214	4	14	2	3	1	0	0	1	3	6	0
Alex Bregman, 3B	.333	4	15	2	5	1	0	1	4	1	0	0
Aledmys Díaz, LF-DH	.000	2	7	0	0	0	0	0	0	0	1	0
Mauricio Dubon, CF		1	0	0	0	0	0	0	0	0	0	0
Yuli Gurriel, 1B	.333	4	15	2	5	0	0	1	2	0	0	0
Martin Maldonado, C	.286	3	7	2	2	1	0	0	1	2	2	0
Trey Mancini, DH	.000	2	6	0	0	0	0	0	1	1	2	0
Chas McCormick, CF	.231	4	13	3	3	0	0	2	3	2	3	0
Jeremy Pena, SS	.353	4	17	3	6	2	0	2	4	0	4	0
Kyle Tucker, RF	.154	4	13	1	2	0	0	0	0	3	2	0
Christian Vazquez, C	.333	1	3	1	1	0	0	0	2	1	0	0
Totals	**.238**	**55**	**126**	**18**	**30**	**6**	**0**	**6**	**18**	**15**	**25**	**0**

HOUSTON	W	L	ERA	G	GS	SV	IP	H	R	ER	BB	SO
Bryan Abreu	0	0	0.00	3	0	0	3	2	0	0	1	4
Hunter Brown	0	0	0.00	1	0	0	0.2	0	0	0	2	0
Cristian Javier	1	0	0.00	1	1	0	5.1	1	0	0	3	5
Lance McCullers Jr.	0	0	5.40	1	1	0	5	8	4	3	1	6
Rafael Montero	0	0	4.50	3	0	0	2	2	1	1	1	3
Hector Neris	1	0	3.38	3	0	0	2.2	1	1	1	0	3
Ryan Pressly	0	0	0.00	3	0	3	3.1	0	0	0	1	6
Ryne Stanek	0	0	0.00	1	0	0	1	0	0	0	0	3
Framber Valdez	1	0	0.00	1	1	0	7	4	2	0	0	9
Justin Verlander	1	0	1.50	1	1	0	6	3	1	1	1	11
Totals	**4**	**0**	**1.50**	**18**	**4**	**3**	**36**	**21**	**9**	**6**	**10**	**50**

NEW YORK	AVG	G	AB	R	H	2B	3B	HR	RBI	BB	SO	SB
Harrison Bader, CF	.400	4	15	4	6	0	0	2	2	2	4	0
Oswaldo Cabrera, SS-LF	.000	3	9	0	0	0	0	0	0	1	2	0
Matt Carpenter, DH	.100	4	10	0	1	0	0	0	0	0	7	0
Josh Donaldson, 3B	.077	4	13	0	1	1	0	0	0	3	10	0
Kyle Higashioka, C	.000	1	3	0	0	0	0	0	0	0	3	0
Aaron Judge, RF	.063	4	16	1	1	0	0	0	0	1	4	0
Isiah Kiner-Falefa, 3B-SS	.286	2	7	1	2	1	0	0	0	0	3	0
Tim Locastro, PR	--	1	0	0	0	0	0	0	0	0	0	0
Oswald Peraza, SS	.000	3	3	0	0	0	0	0	0	0	2	0
Anthony Rizzo, 1B	.250	4	12	2	3	1	0	1	4	2	3	0
Giancarlo Stanton, LF-DH	.250	4	16	1	4	2	0	0	1	0	3	0
Gleyber Torres, 2B	.200	4	15	0	3	0	0	0	2	1	7	0
Jose Trevino, C	.000	3	11	0	0	0	0	0	0	0	2	0
Totals	**.162**	**57**	**130**	**9**	**21**	**5**	**0**	**3**	**9**	**10**	**50**	**0**

NEW YORK	W	L	ERA	G	GS	SV	IP	H	R	ER	BB	SO
Miguel Castro	0	0	0.00	2	0	0	2	0	0	0	0	2
Gerrit Cole	0	1	5.40	1	1	0	5	5	5	3	2	7
Nestor Cortes	0	0	13.50	1	1	0	2	2	3	3	3	2
Domingo German	0	0	0.00	1	0	0	1	0	0	0	2	1
Clay Holmes	0	0	0.00	1	0	0	2.2	2	0	0	0	2
Jonathan Loaisiga	0	1	2.08	2	0	0	4.1	3	2	1	1	1
Frankie Montas	0	0	9.00	1	0	0	1	1	1	1	0	1
Wandy Peralta	0	0	3.38	2	0	0	2.2	5	1	1	1	1
Clarke Schmidt	0	1	18.00	1	0	0	1	2	2	2	2	0
Luis Severino	0	1	5.06	1	1	0	5.1	5	3	3	1	6
Jameson Taillon	0	0	2.08	1	1	0	4.1	4	1	1	3	0
Lou Trivino	0	0	0.00	2	0	0	2.2	1	0	0	0	2
Totals	**0**	**4**	**3.97**	**16**	**4**	**0**	**34**	**30**	**18**	**15**	**15**	**254**

SCORE BY INNINGS

NEW YORK	0	0	4	0	4	2	1	4	0	0		21
HOUSTON	5	2	3	0	1	4	2	1	3	0	1	22

NATIONAL LEAGUE WILD CARD SERIES

SAN DIEGO PADRES VS. NEW YORK METS

SAN DIEGO	AVG	G	AB	R	H	2B	3B	HR	RBI	BB	SO	SB
Josh Bell, DH	.231	3	13	2	3	0	0	1	2	1	4	0
Jake Cronenworth, 2B	.000	3	13	0	0	0	0	0	0	0	6	0
Brandon Drury, 1B	.000	1	4	0	0	0	0	0	0	0	1	0
Trent Grisham, CF	.500	3	8	5	4	0	0	2	3	2	0	0
Ha-Seong Kim, SS	.250	3	8	4	2	1	0	0	0	4	4	1
Manny Machado, 3B	.231	3	13	1	3	1	0	1	3	1	6	0
Wil Myers, 1B	.000	2	8	0	0	0	0	0	0	0	4	0
Austin Nola, C	.444	3	9	1	4	1	0	0	2	1	3	0
Jurickson Profar, LF	.333	3	12	3	4	0	0	1	4	2	1	0
Juan Soto, RF	.333	3	12	0	4	0	0	0	2	1	2	0
Totals	**.240**	**38**	**100**	**16**	**24**	**3**	**0**	**5**	**16**	**12**	**31**	**1**

SAN DIEGO	W	L	ERA	G	GS	SV	IP	H	R	ER	BB	SO
Yu Darvish	1	0	1.29	1	1	0	7	6	1	1	0	4
Luis Garcia	0	0	0.00	1	0	0	1	1	0	0	1	1
Josh Hader	0	0	0.00	1	0	0	1	0	0	0	0	1
Pierce Johnson	0	0	0.00	1	0	0	1	2	0	0	0	2
Nick Martinez	0	1	3.38	1	0	0	2.2	1	1	1	1	0
Adrián Morejón	0	0	inf	1	0	0	0	2	4	4	2	0
Joe Musgrove	1	0	0.00	1	1	0	7	1	0	0	1	5
Blake Snell	0	0	5.40	1	1	0	3.1	4	2	2	6	5
Robert Suarez	0	0	0.00	2	0	0	2	0	0	0	0	2
Steven Wilson	0	0	0.00	1	0	0	1	0	0	0	0	2
Totals	**2**	**1**	**2.77**	**11**	**3**	**0**	**26**	**17**	**8**	**8**	**11**	**22**

NEW YORK	AVG	G	AB	R	H	2B	3B	HR	RBI	BB	SO	SB
Pete Alonso, 1B	.300	3	10	2	3	0	0	1	1	2	4	0
Francisco Álvarez, PH	.000	1	1	0	0	0	0	0	0	0	1	0
Mark Canha, LF	.000	3	10	1	0	0	0	0	0	2	2	0
Eduardo Escobar, 3B	.333	3	9	2	3	1	0	1	2	2	3	0
Terrance Gore, DH		1	0	0	0	0	0	0	0	0	0	0
Luis Guillorme, PH	.000	1	1	0	0	0	0	0	0	0	1	0
Francisco Lindor, SS	.200	3	10	2	2	0	0	1	1	1	2	1
Starling Marte, RF	.167	3	12	0	2	0	0	0	0	1	1	2
James McCann, C		1	0	0	0	0	0	0	0	0	0	0
Jeff McNeil, 2B	.182	3	11	1	2	1	0	0	2	0	1	0
Tomás Nido, C	.125	3	8	0	1	0	0	0	0	1	4	0
Brandon Nimmo, CF	.333	3	12	0	4	0	1	0	1	1	1	0
Darin Ruf, DH	.000	1	1	0	0	0	0	0	0	1	1	0
Daniel Vogelbach, DH	.000	3	7	0	0	0	0	0	1	0	1	0
Totals	**.185**	**48**	**92**	**8**	**17**	**2**	**1**	**3**	**8**	**11**	**22**	**3**

NEW YORK	W	L	ERA	G	GS	SV	IP	H	R	ER	BB	SO
Chris Bassitt	0	1	6.75	1	1	0	4	3	3	3	3	2
Jacob deGrom	1	0	3.00	1	1	0	6	5	2	2	2	8
Edwin Díaz	0	0	0.00	2	0	0	2.2	2	0	0	1	2
Mychal Givens	0	0	13.50	2	0	0	1.1	2	2	2	1	3
Seth Lugo	0	0	0.00	3	0	1	2	2	0	0	1	3
Trevor May	0	0	0.00	2	0	0	2.1	0	0	0	1	4
Adam Ottavino	0	0	9.00	1	0	0	1	0	1	1	3	2
David Peterson	0	0	4.50	2	0	0	2	2	1	1	0	2
Max Scherzer	0	1	13.50	1	1	0	4.2	7	7	7	0	4
Drew Smith	0	0	0.00	1	0	0	1	1	0	0	0	1
Totals	**1**	**2**	**5.33**	**16**	**3**	**1**	**27**	**24**	**16**	**16**	**12**	**31**

SCORE BY INNINGS

NY METS	1	0	0	1	2	0	4	0	0	8
SAN DIEGO	2	3	1	1	6	0	0	2	1	16

PHILADELPHIA PHILLIES VS. ST. LOUIS CARDINALS

PHILADELPHIA	AVG	G	AB	R	H	2B	3B	HR	RBI	BB	SO	SB
Alec Bohm, 3B	.400	2	5	1	2	2	0	0	1	2	0	0
Nick Castellanos, RF	.000	2	7	1	0	0	0	0	0	1	2	0
Bryce Harper, DH	.286	2	7	2	2	0	0	1	1	1	2	0
Rhys Hoskins, 1B	.000	2	9	0	0	0	0	0	0	0	3	0
Brandon Marsh, CF	.400	2	5	0	2	1	0	0	1	0	2	0
J.T. Realmuto, C	.167	2	6	1	1	0	0	0	0	2	0	0
Kyle Schwarber, LF	.000	2	7	0	0	0	0	0	2	0	4	0
Jean Segura, 2B	.200	2	5	1	1	0	0	0	2	0	0	0
Edmundo Sosa, 3B	--	2	0	1	0	0	0	0	0	0	0	0
Bryson Stott, SS	.000	2	4	1	0	0	0	0	1	3	1	0
Matt Vierling, CF	.500	1	2	0	1	0	0	0	0	0	0	0
Totals	**.158**	**29**	**57**	**8**	**9**	**3**	**0**	**1**	**8**	**9**	**14**	**0**

PHILADELPHIA	W	L	ERA	G	GS	SV	IP	H	R	ER	BB	SO
Jose Alvarado	0	0	13.50	2	0	0	1.1	1	2	2	2	0
Seranthony Dominguez	0	0	0.00	1	0	0	0.2	1	0	0	0	2
Zach Eflin	0	0	4.50	2	0	1	2	4	1	1	1	1
Aaron Nola	1	0	0.00	1	1	0	6.2	4	0	0	1	6
David Robertson	1	0	0.00	1	0	0	1	0	0	0	0	2
Zack Wheeler	0	0	0.00	1	1	0	6.1	2	0	0	1	4
Totals	**2**	**0**	**1.50**	**8**	**2**	**1**	**18**	**12**	**3**	**3**	**5**	**15**

ST. LOUIS	AVG	G	AB	R	H	2B	3B	HR	RBI	BB	SO	SB
Nolan Arenado, 3B	.125	2	8	1	1	0	0	0	0	0	2	0
Dylan Carlson, CF-RF	.000	2	2	1	0	0	0	0	0	2	0	0
Paul DeJong, SS	.000	1	1	0	0	0	0	0	0	0	0	0
Ben DeLuzio, CF-DH	--	2	0	0	0	0	0	0	0	0	0	0
Corey Dickerson, LF	.333	2	6	0	2	0	0	0	0	0	1	0
Brendan Donovan, 2B	.000	2	7	0	0	0	0	0	0	0	2	0
Tommy Edman, SS-2B	.167	2	6	0	1	0	0	0	0	1	1	0
Paul Goldschmidt, 1B	.000	2	7	0	0	0	0	0	0	0	4	0
Nolan Gorman, PH	1.000	1	1	0	1	0	0	0	1	0	0	0
Yadier Molina, C	.125	2	8	0	1	0	0	0	0	0	2	0
Lars Nootbaar, LF-CF-RF	.333	2	6	0	2	1	0	0	0	2	2	0
Albert Pujols, DH	.250	2	8	0	2	0	0	0	0	0	1	0
Juan Yepez, RF	.400	2	5	1	2	0	0	1	2	0	0	0
Totals	**.185**	**33**	**65**	**3**	**12**	**1**	**0**	**1**	**3**	**5**	**15**	**0**

ST. LOUIS	W	L	ERA	G	GS	SV	IP	H	R	ER	BB	SO
Giovanny Gallegos	0	0	0.00	2	0	0	2.1	0	0	0	1	1
Ryan Helsley	0	1	36.00	1	0	0	1	1	4	4	2	2
Jordan Hicks	0	0	0.00	2	0	0	1.2	0	0	0	1	1
Miles Mikolas	0	1	4.15	1	1	0	4.1	2	2	2	1	3
Jordan Montgomery	0	0	0.00	1	0	0	2.2	2	0	0	3	3
Andre Pallante	0	0	27.00	1	0	0	0.2	2	2	2	0	1
Jose Quintana	0	0	0.00	1	1	0	5.1	2	0	0	1	3
Totals	**0**	**2**	**4.00**	**9**	**2**	**0**	**18**	**9**	**8**	**8**	**9**	**14**

SCORE BY INNINGS

PHILADELPHIA	0	1	0	0	1	0	0	0	6	8
ST. LOUIS	0	0	0	0	0	0	2	0	1	3

NATIONAL LEAGUE DIVISION SERIES

PHILADELPHIA PHILLIES VS. ATLANTA BRAVES

PHILADELPHIA	AVG	G	AB	R	H	2B	3B	HR	RBI	BB	SO	SB
Alec Bohm, 3B	.133	4	15	1	2	0	0	0	2	0	2	0
Nick Castellanos, RF	.313	4	16	1	5	1	0	0	5	1	2	0
Dalton Guthrie, RF	--	1	0	0	0	0	0	0	0	0	0	0
Bryce Harper, DH	.500	4	16	4	8	3	0	2	5	1	4	0
Rhys Hoskins, 1B	.235	4	17	3	4	1	0	1	4	1	6	0
Brandon Marsh, CF	.250	4	8	2	2	1	0	1	3	2	4	0
J.T. Realmuto, C	.278	4	18	5	5	0	0	1	2	0	7	0
Kyle Schwarber, LF	.077	4	13	2	1	0	0	0	0	3	4	0
Jean Segura, 2B	.462	4	13	3	6	2	0	0	1	2	3	1
Edmundo Sosa, 3B-SS	.500	2	2	1	1	1	0	0	1	1	0	0
Bryson Stott, SS	.182	3	11	1	2	1	0	0	1	0	2	0
Matt Vierling, CF-LF	.000	4	4	1	0	0	0	0	0	0	1	0
Totals	**.271**	**62**	**133**	**24**	**36**	**10**	**0**	**5**	**24**	**11**	**35**	**1**

PHILADELPHIA	W	L	ERA	G	GS	SV	IP	H	R	ER	BB	SO
Jose Alvarado	0	0	2.45	3	0	0	3	1	1	1	0	5
Andrew Bellatti	0	0	3.38	3	0	0	2	2	1	1	0	3
Connor Brogdon	0	0	13.50	2	0	0	1	2	2	2	2	2
Seranthony Dominguez	1	0	0.00	2	0	0	3	0	0	0	0	6
Zach Eflin	0	0	11.57	2	0	0	2	3	3	3	0	4
Brad Hand	1	0	0.00	3	0	0	2	2	0	0	0	3
Aaron Nola	1	0	0.00	1	1	0	6	5	1	0	2	6
Ranger Suarez	0	0	2.70	1	1	0	3	3	1	1	5	5
Noah Syndergaard	0	0	2.25	2	1	0	4	1	1	1	1	4
Zack Wheeler	0	1	4.50	1	1	0	6	4	3	3	1	5
Totals	**3**	**1**	**3.09**	**20**	**4**	**0**	**35**	**23**	**13**	**12**	**11**	**43**

ATLANTA	AVG	G	AB	R	H	2B	3B	HR	RBI	BB	SO	SB
Ronald Acuna Jr., RF	.333	4	15	2	5	1	0	0	0	1	5	0
Orlando Arcia, 2B	.300	4	10	1	3	0	0	1	1	2	2	0
William Contreras, DH	.125	3	8	1	1	1	0	0	0	1	4	0
Travis d'Arnaud, C	.375	4	16	2	6	3	0	2	5	0	4	0
Vaughn Grissom, 2B	.000	2	3	0	0	0	0	0	0	0	3	0
Robbie Grossman, LF	.000	2	3	0	0	0	0	0	0	0	2	0
Michael Harris, CF	.071	4	14	0	1	0	0	0	1	0	2	1
Matt Olson, 1B	.333	4	12	4	4	0	0	2	5	5	4	0
Marcell Ozuna, LF-DH	.000	3	8	0	0	0	0	0	0	0	4	0
Austin Riley, 3B	.067	4	15	0	1	0	0	0	1	1	5	0
Eddie Rosario, LF	.000	4	8	0	0	0	0	0	0	0	1	0
Dansby Swanson, SS	.125	4	16	3	2	1	0	0	0	1	7	0
Totals	**.180**	**61**	**128**	**13**	**23**	**6**	**0**	**5**	**13**	**11**	**43**	**1**

ATLANTA	W	L	ERA	G	GS	SV	IP	H	R	ER	BB	SO
Jesse Chavez	0	0	5.40	2	0	0	3	4	2	2	1	3
Max Fried	0	1	10.80	1	1	0	3	8	6	4	1	2
Raisel Iglesias	0	0	6.75	2	0	0	1	4	1	1	1	1
Kenley Jansen	0	0	4.50	2	0	1	2	1	1	1	0	2
Dylan Lee	0	0	3.38	3	0	0	2	4	1	1	0	2
Collin McHugh	0	0	2.70	2	0	0	3	3	1	1	1	4

	W	L	ERA	G	GS	SV	IP	H	R	ER	BB	SO
A.J. Minter	0	0	6.75	2	0	0	2	1	2	2	0	4
Charlie Morton	0	1	13.50	1	1	0	2	4	3	3	1	3
Jake Odorizzi	0	0	6.00	1	0	0	3	1	2	2	3	2
Jackson Stephens	0	0	0.00	1	0	0	2	1	0	0	0	2
Spencer Strider	0	1	19.29	1	1	0	2	3	5	5	2	4
Kyle Wright	1	0	0.00	1	1	0	6	2	0	0	1	6
Totals	**1**	**3**	**5.82**	**19**	**4**	**1**	**34**	**36**	**24**	**22**	**11**	**35**

SCORE BY INNINGS

ATLANTA	0	1	1	1	2	4	1	0	3	13
PHILADELPHIA	2	3	9	2	1	3	3	1	0	24

SAN DIEGO PADRES VS. LOS ANGELES DODGERS

SAN DIEGO	AVG	G	AB	R	H	2B	3B	HR	RBI	BB	SO	SB
Jose Azocar, LF	--	2	0	0	0	0	0	0	0	0	0	1
Josh Bell, DH	.000	2	6	0	0	0	0	0	0	0	3	0
Jake Cronenworth, 2B	.438	4	16	3	7	0	0	1	5	0	4	0
Brandon Drury, DH	.091	3	11	0	1	0	0	0	0	0	5	0
Trent Grisham, CF	.308	4	13	2	4	0	0	1	2	2	6	0
Ha-Seong Kim, SS	.167	4	18	3	3	2	0	0	1	0	7	0
Manny Machado, 3B	.357	4	14	1	5	1	0	1	2	3	5	0
Wil Myers, 1B	.133	4	15	1	2	0	0	1	1	1	6	0
Austin Nola, C	.333	4	12	1	4	1	0	0	2	2	3	0
Jurickson Profar, LF	.231	4	13	1	3	0	0	0	1	3	3	0
Juan Soto, RF	.188	4	16	3	3	1	0	0	1	1	3	1
Totals	**.239**	**58**	**134**	**15**	**32**	**5**	**0**	**4**	**15**	**12**	**45**	**2**

SAN DIEGO	W	L	ERA	G	GS	SV	IP	H	R	ER	BB	SO
Mike Clevinger	0	1	13.50	1	1	0	2	6	5	4	2	3
Yu Darvish	1	0	5.40	1	1	0	5	7	3	3	2	7
Luis Garcia	0	0	0.00	1	0	0	1	0	0	0	0	2
Josh Hader	0	0	0.00	3	0	3	3	1	0	0	1	6
Tim Hill	1	0	0.00	2	0	0	1	0	0	0	0	2
Pierce Johnson	0	0	0.00	1	0	0	2	0	0	0	0	2
Nick Martinez	0	0	0.00	3	0	0	2	1	0	0	0	3
Joe Musgrove	0	0	3.00	1	1	0	6	6	2	2	3	8
Blake Snell	1	0	1.69	1	1	0	5	5	1	1	2	6
Robert Suarez	0	0	0.00	3	0	0	4	3	0	0	1	3
Steven Wilson	0	0	5.40	2	0	0	1	1	1	1	3	2
Totals	**3**	**1**	**2.83**	**19**	**4**	**3**	**35**	**30**	**12**	**11**	**14**	**44**

LOS ANGELES	AVG	G	AB	R	H	2B	3B	HR	RBI	BB	SO	SB
Austin Barnes, C	.667	2	3	0	2	1	0	0	0	0	0	0
Cody Bellinger, CF	.143	3	7	0	1	0	0	0	0	0	4	0
Mookie Betts, RF	.143	4	14	2	2	1	0	0	1	3	4	0
Freddie Freeman, 1B	.357	4	14	1	5	3	0	1	3	3	4	1
Joey Gallo, LF	--	1	0	0	0	0	0	0	0	0	0	0
Gavin Lux, 2B	.231	4	13	0	3	1	0	0	1	0	5	0
Max Muncy, 2B-3B	.286	4	14	2	4	1	0	1	2	2	6	0
Will Smith, C-DH	.188	4	16	2	3	2	0	0	2	0	2	0
Chris Taylor, LF	.000	2	7	0	0	0	0	0	0	0	5	0
Trayce Thompson, LF-CF	.154	4	13	1	2	0	0	0	0	3	6	0
Justin Turner, 3B-DH	.154	4	13	0	2	0	0	0	0	3	3	0
Trea Turner, SS	.333	4	18	4	6	2	0	2	2	0	5	1
Totals	**.227**	**62**	**132**	**12**	**30**	**11**	**0**	**4**	**11**	**14**	**44**	**2**

LOS ANGELES	W	L	ERA	G	GS	SV	IP	H	R	ER	BB	SO
Yency Almonte	0	1	7.71	3	0	0	2	2	2	2	0	6
Tyler Anderson	0	0	0.00	1	1	0	5	2	0	0	2	6
Tony Gonsolin	0	1	6.75	1	1	0	1	4	1	1	1	1
Brusdar Graterol	0	1	0.00	2	0	0	1	2	1	0	0	0
Andrew Heaney	0	0	3.00	1	0	0	3	3	1	1	2	4
Tommy Kahnle	0	0	13.50	3	0	0	2	2	3	3	1	4
Clayton Kershaw	0	0	5.40	1	1	0	5	6	3	3	0	6
Chris Martin	0	0	0.00	2	0	1	2	3	0	0	0	1
Evan Phillips	0	0	0.00	3	0	0	3	1	0	0	1	6
Blake Treinen	0	0	9.00	1	0	0	1	1	1	1	2	1
Julio Urias	1	0	5.40	1	1	0	5	4	3	3	0	6
Alex Vesia	0	0	0.00	3	0	0	2	2	0	0	3	4
Totals	**1**	**3**	**3.71**	**22**	**4**	**1**	**34**	**32**	**15**	**14**	**12**	**45**

SCORE BY INNINGS

LA DODGERS	3	1	6	0	1	0	1	0	0	12
SAN DIEGO	2	0	2	1	3	1	5	1	0	15

NATIONAL LEAGUE CHAMPIONSHIP SERIES

PHILADELPHIA PHILLIES VS. SAN DIEGO PADRES

PHILADELPHIA	AVG	G	AB	R	H	2B	3B	HR	RBI	BB	SO	SB
Alec Bohm, 3B	.176	5	17	2	3	1	0	0	2	0	7	0
Nick Castellanos, RF	.222	5	18	3	4	2	0	0	1	0	4	0
Bryce Harper, DH	.400	5	20	4	8	3	0	2	5	0	1	0
Rhys Hoskins, 1B	.222	5	18	4	4	0	0	4	7	2	5	0
Brandon Marsh, CF	.000	4	13	0	0	0	0	0	0	0	7	0
J.T. Realmuto, C	.235	5	17	4	4	0	0	1	1	3	5	0
Kyle Schwarber, LF	.400	5	15	6	6	0	0	3	4	6	3	2
Jean Segura, 2B	.118	5	17	0	2	0	0	0	2	0	5	0
Edmundo Sosa, SS-3B	.500	4	2	0	1	0	0	0	1	0	1	0
Bryson Stott, SS	.267	5	15	1	4	3	0	0	1	0	4	0
Matt Vierling, LF-CF	.250	4	4	1	1	1	0	0	1	0	3	0
TOTALS	**.237**	**77**	**156**	**25**	**37**	**10**	**0**	**10**	**25**	**11**	**45**	**2**

PHILADELPHIA	W	L	ERA	G	GS	SV	IP	H	R	ER	BB	SO
Jose Alvarado	1	0	0.00	3	0	1	3	3	0	0	2	4
Andrew Bellatti	0	0	0.00	2	0	0	1.1	0	0	0	1	3
Connor Brogdon	0	0	0.00	2	0	0	3.1	1	0	0	0	4
Seranthony Dominguez	0	0	2.25	3	0	1	4	2	1	1	0	7
Zach Eflin	0	0	0.00	2	0	0	2	2	0	0	0	1
Bailey Falter	0	0	54.00	1	1	0	0.2	3	4	4	1	0
Kyle Gibson	0	0	0.00	1	0	0	1.1	1	0	0	1	1
Brad Hand	1	0	27.00	2	0	0	1	3	3	3	1	0
Aaron Nola	0	1	11.57	1	1	0	4.2	7	6	6	0	6
David Robertson	0	0	3.38	3	0	0	2.2	4	1	1	2	4
Ranger Suarez	1	0	1.59	2	1	1	5.2	2	2	1	0	3
Noah Syndergaard	0	0	0.00	1	0	0	1.1	2	0	0	0	0
Zack Wheeler	1	0	1.38	2	2	0	13	4	2	2	1	16
Totals	**4**	**1**	**3.68**	**25**	**5**	**3**	**44**	**34**	**19**	**18**	**9**	**49**

SAN DIEGO	AVG	G	AB	R	H	2B	3B	HR	RBI	BB	SO	
Jose Azocar, DH	--	1	0	1	0	0	0	0	0	0	0	0
Josh Bell, 1B-DH	.353	5	17	2	6	1	0	1	3	0	5	0
Jake Cronenworth, 2B	.235	5	17	3	4	0	0	0	1	1	5	0
Brandon Drury, 1B-DH	.400	4	15	2	6	1	0	1	5	1	5	0
Trent Grisham, CF	.000	5	19	1	0	0	0	0	0	0	9	0
Ha-Seong Kim, SS	.176	5	17	1	3	0	0	0	2	2	3	0
Manny Machado, 3B	.238	5	21	2	5	1	0	2	2	0	6	0
Wil Myers, 1B	.167	4	6	0	1	0	0	0	0	0	3	0
Austin Nola, C	.053	5	19	1	1	0	0	0	1	0	4	0
Jurickson Profar, LF	.211	5	19	2	4	0	0	0	0	3	4	0
Juan Soto, RF	.222	5	18	4	4	1	0	2	4	2	5	0
TOTALS	**.202**	**67**	**168**	**19**	**34**	**4**	**0**	**6**	**18**	**949**	**2**	**0**

SAN DIEGO	W	L	ERA	G	GS	SV	IP	H	R	ER	BB	SO
Mike Clevinger	0	0	inf	1	1	0	0	3	3	3	1	0
Yu Darvish	0	1	2.77	2	2	0	13	7	4	4	4	12
Luis Garcia	0	0	3.38	2	0	0	2.2	2	1	1	0	2
Josh Hader	0	0	0.00	1	0	1	1	0	0	0	0	3
Tim Hill	0	0	0.00	1	0	0	1	1	0	0	0	0
Pierce Johnson	0	0	0.00	1	0	0	1.1	0	0	0	0	2
Sean Manaea	0	1	33.75	1	0	0	1.1	4	5	5	2	2
Nick Martinez	0	0	0.00	3	0	0	6	1	0	0	0	8
Adrián Morejón	0	0	0.00	1	0	0	1	1	0	0	0	1
Joe Musgrove	0	1	6.35	1	1	0	5.2	8	4	4	2	5
Blake Snell	1	0	7.20	1	1	0	5	5	4	4	1	6
Robert Suarez	0	1	9.00	2	0	0	3	4	3	3	1	4
Steven Wilson	0	0	9.00	1	0	0	1	1	1	1	0	0
Totals	**1**	**4**	**5.36**	**18**	**5**	**1**	**42**	**37**	**25**	**25**		**11454**

SCORE BY INNINGS

PHILADELPHIA	4	4	2	4	4	3	1	3	0	25
SAN DIEGO	4	2	0	2	8	0	3	0	0	19

ORGANIZATION STATISTICS

Arizona Diamondbacks

SEASON IN A SENTENCE: In the tough neighborhood that is the National League West, the D-backs improved by 22 games over their 2021 performance. While that still left them 74-88, Arizona was frisky, flirting with the .500 mark into September, and broke in some exciting new talent, lending hope for the near future.

HIGH POINT: Arizona got off to a surprisingly strong start, staying around the .500 mark through most of May. The D-backs swept the host White Sox in a three-game series, then took two of three from Kansas City to improve to 23-22 on May 24. The 8-6 comeback win included a game-tying three-run homer by pinch-hitter Jordan Luplow before Pavin Smith provided the final margin with a two-run homer.

LOW POINT: Arizona couldn't hang with the NL West's top clubs, going 5-14 against both the Dodgers and Padres. The Dodgers thumped the D-backs 26-8 at Chase Field May 25-28 in a four-game set, sending them below .500 permanently, while San Diego won five of seven from Arizona in September. The worst blow from the Padres came on Jorge Alfaro two-run walk-off single Sept. 6, after Arizona has closed within four games of .500.

NOTABLE ROOKIES: Geraldo Perdomo manned shortstop capably with the glove but hit just .195 in 500 at-bats. Arizona broke in a new lefthanded-hitting outfield to join catcher/outfielder Daulton Varsho. Alek Thomas, 22, had his struggles with the bat but showed speed and defense, as did Jake McCarthy (.283/.342/.427), who tied for the club lead with 23 steals. Top prospect Corbin Carroll retained his rookie eligibility in a 30-game cup of coffee and slugged .500 while showing top-shelf speed. Prospect pitchers Drey Jamison and Ryne Nelson also made their debuts in September but like Carroll remain rookie-eligible for 2023.

KEY TRANSACTIONS: The D-backs needed new outfielders to help replace veteran David Peralta, dealt to Tampa Bay in July, and got another with Druw Jones—son of Andruw Jones—with the second overall pick of the draft. The building blocks to the franchise likely will come from within.

ON THE FARM: Outfielder Corbin Carroll and shortstop Jordan Lawlar both impressed in their return from season-ending injuries in 2021. Righthander Brandon Pfaadt led the minors with 167 innings pitched and 218 strikeouts.

OPENING DAY PAYROLL: $93,254,795 (24th)

PLAYERS OF THE YEAR

MAJOR LEAGUE

Zac Gallen
RHP
12-4, 2.54 ERA
192 SO, 47 BB, 184 IP
0.91 WHIP led NL

MINOR LEAGUE

Corbin Carroll
OF
(AA/AAA)
.307/.425/.611
24 HR, 31 SB in 93 G

ORGANIZATION LEADERS

Batting — ***Minimum 250 AB**

MAJORS		
*AVG	Jake McCarthy	.283
*OPS	Christian Walker	.804
HR	Christian Walker	36
RBI	Christian Walker	94
MINORS		
*AVG	Jancarlos Cintron, Reno,Amarillo	.338
*OBP	Corbin Carroll, Amarillo, Reno, ACL D-backs Red	.425
*SLG	Corbin Carroll, Amarillo, Reno, ACL D-backs Red	.611
*OPS	Corbin Carroll, Amarillo, Reno, ACL D-backs Red	1.036
R	Jordan Lawlar, Amarillo, Hillsboro, Visalia, ACL D-backs Red	98
R	Dominic Fletcher, Reno, Amarillo	98
H	Dominic Fletcher, Reno, Amarillo	163
TB	Leandro Cedeno, Amarillo, Reno	264
2B	Dominic Fletcher, Reno, Amarillo	35
3B	Dominic Fletcher, Reno, Amarillo	10
HR	Leandro Cedeno, Amarillo, Reno	32
RBI	Deyvison De Los Santos, Visalia, Hillsboro, Amarillo	106
BB	Corbin Carroll, Amarillo, Reno, ACL D-backs Red	67
SO	Deyvison De Los Santos, Visalia, Hillsboro, Amarillo	147
SB	Wilderd Patino, Visalia, Hillsboro	67

Pitching — **#Minimum 75 IP**

MAJORS		
W	Merrill Kelly	13
#ERA	Zac Gallen	2.54
SO	Zac Gallen	192
SV	Mark Melancon	18
MINORS		
W	Brandon Pfaadt, Amarillo, Reno	11
L	Drey Jameson, Reno, Amarillo	13
#ERA	Tommy Henry, Reno	3.74
G	Blake Rogers, Amarillo, Reno	48
GS	Brandon Pfaadt, Amarillo, Reno	29
SV	2 tied	13
IP	Brandon Pfaadt, Amarillo, Reno	167
BB	Liam Norris	61
SO	Brandon Pfaadt, Amarillo, Reno	218
#AVG	Yilber Diaz, Hillsboro, Visalia	.201

2022 PERFORMANCE

General Manager: Mike Hazen. **Farm Director:** Josh Barfield. **Scouting Director:** Ian Rebhan.

Class	Team	League	W	L	PCT	Finish	Manager
Majors	Arizona Diamondbacks	National League	74	88	.457	t- 9th (15)	Torey Lovullo
Triple-A	Reno Aces	Pacific Coast	85	63	.574	1st (10)	Gil Velazquez
Double-A	Amarillo Sod Poodles	Texas	68	69	.496	[illegible] (10)	Shawn Roof
High-A	Hillsboro Hops	Northwest	60	70	.462	4th (6)	Vince Harrison
Low-A	Visalia Rawhide	California	45	87	.341	8th (8)	Jorge Cortes
Rookie	ACL D-backs Black	Arizona Complex	23	32	.418	14th (18)	Rolando Arnedo
Rookie	ACL D-backs Red	Arizona Complex	20	34	.370	16th (18)	Dee Garner
Overall 2022 Minor League Record			362	410	.469	24th (30)	

ORGANIZATION STATISTICS

ARIZONA DIAMONDBACKS

NATIONAL LEAGUE

Batting	B-T	HT	WT	DOB	AVG	vLH	vRH	G	AB	R	H	2B	3B	HR	RBI	BB	HBP	SH	SF	SO	SB	CS	SLG	OBP
Alek Thomas	L-L	5-11	175	4-28-00	.231	.198	.241	113	381	45	88	17	1	8	39	22	3	0	5	74	4	3	.344	.275
Buddy Kennedy	R-R	6-1	190	10-5-98	.217	.256	.175	30	83	10	18	2	2	1	12	8	1	0	2	23	0	0	.325	.287
Carson Kelly	R-R	6-2	212	7-14-94	.211	.197	.221	104	317	40	67	18	0	7	35	29	4	0	4	71	2	0	.334	.282
Christian Walker	R-R	6-0	208	3-28-91	.242	.261	.236	160	583	84	141	25	2	36	94	69	8	0	7	131	2	2	.477	.327
Cooper Hummel	B-R	5-10	198	11-28-94	.176	.149	.196	66	176	20	31	8	3	3	17	23	1	0	1	64	4	1	.307	.274
Corbin Carroll	L-L	5-10	165	8-21-00	.260	.179	.289	32	104	13	27	9	2	4	14	8	3	0	0	31	2	1	.500	.330
Daulton Varsho	L-R	5-10	207	7-2-96	.235	.221	.240	151	531	79	125	23	3	27	74	46	7	2	5	145	16	6	.443	.302
David Peralta	L-L	6-1	210	8-14-87	.248	.114	.267	87	278	29	69	19	2	12	41	27	2	0	3	74	1	2	.460	.316
Drew Ellis	R-R	6-3	205	12-1-95	.154	.250	.111	6	13	2	2	1	0	0	1	1	0	0	0	6	0	0	.231	.214
Emmanuel Rivera	R-R	6-2	225	6-29-96	.227	.227	.227	39	132	22	30	8	0	6	18	12	3	0	1	37	1	2	.424	.304
Geraldo Perdomo	B-R	6-2	203	10-22-99	.195	.237	.177	148	431	58	84	10	2	5	40	50	5	12	2	103	9	2	.262	.285
Grayson Greiner	R-R	6-6	238	10-11-92	.167	--	.167	2	6	0	1	0	0	0	0	2	0	0	0	3	0	0	.167	.375
Jake Hager	R-R	6-1	170	3-4-93	.240	.350	.167	28	50	4	12	2	0	0	3	8	0	1	0	17	0	0	.280	.345
Jake McCarthy	L-L	6-2	215	7-30-97	.283	.281	.284	99	321	53	91	16	3	8	43	23	6	3	1	76	23	3	.427	.342
Jordan Luplow	R-R	6-1	195	9-26-93	.176	.171	.181	83	205	26	36	5	0	11	28	25	3	0	1	60	5	1	.361	.274
Jose Herrera	B-R	5-10	217	2-24-97	.189	.286	.167	47	111	9	21	2	0	0	5	9	0	4	0	34	0	0	.207	.250
Josh Rojas	L-R	6-1	207	6-30-94	.269	.243	.277	125	443	66	119	25	1	9	56	55	2	5	5	98	23	3	.391	.349
Ketel Marte	B-R	6-1	210	10-12-93	.240	.276	.226	137	492	68	118	42	2	12	52	55	6	0	5	101	5	1	.407	.321
Matt Davidson	R-R	6-3	230	3-26-91	.100	.143	.000	5	10	1	1	0	0	1	1	3	0	0	0	3	0	0	.400	.308
Nick Ahmed	R-R	6-2	201	3-15-90	.231	.063	.306	17	52	7	12	2	0	3	7	2	0	0	0	15	0	1	.442	.259
Pavin Smith	L-L	6-2	208	2-6-96	.220	.226	.219	75	245	24	54	9	0	9	33	28	1	0	3	67	1	0	.367	.300
Sergio Alcantara	B-R	5-9	151	7-10-96	.241	.268	.233	71	170	23	41	8	1	6	26	10	1	2	3	45	1	0	.406	.283
2-team total (22 San Diego Padres)					.220	.214	.221	93	205	26	45	8	1	6	29	12	1	2	4	57	1	2	.356	.261
Seth Beer	L-R	6-3	213	9-18-96	.189	.250	.176	38	111	4	21	3	0	1	9	11	3	0	1	31	0	0	.243	.278
Stone Garrett	R-R	6-2	195	11-22-95	.276	.304	.233	27	76	13	21	8	0	4	10	3	1	0	1	27	3	1	.539	.309
Wilmer Difo	B-R	5-11	200	4-2-92	.000	.000	.000	3	6	0	0	0	0	0	0	0	0	0	0	1	0	0	.000	.000
Yonny Hernandez	B-R	5-9	140	5-4-98	.083	.000	.118	12	24	2	2	0	0	0	0	2	0	2	0	4	2	0	.083	.154

Pitching	B-T	HT	WT	DOB	W	L	ERA	G	GS	CG	SV	IP	H	R	ER	HR	BB	SO	AVG	vLH	vRH	K/9	BB/9
Madison Bumgarner	R-L	6-4	257	8-1-89	7	15	4.88	30	30	0	0	159	179	97	86	25	49	112	.281	.263	.286	6.35	2.78
Humberto Castellanos	R-R	5-11	222	4-3-98	3	2	5.68	11	9	0	0	44	50	29	28	7	12	32	.289	.256	.316	6.50	2.44
Zach Davies	R-R	6-0	180	2-7-93	2	5	4.09	27	27	0	0	134	122	66	61	21	52	102	.241	.222	.255	6.83	3.48
Chris Devenski	R-R	6-3	211	11-13-90	2	1	7.59	10	0	0	0	11	14	9	9	2	1	9	.318	.308	.323	7.59	0.84
2-team total (3 Philadelphia Phillies)					2	1	8.59	13	0	0	0	15	21	14	14	3	1	12	.339	.316	.349	7.36	0.61
Luis Frias	R-R	6-3	245	5-23-98	1	1	10.59	15	0	0	0	17	23	20	20	1	17	14	.319	.357	.295	7.41	9.00
Paul Fry	L-L	6-0	205	7-26-92	0	0	9.00	1	0	0	0	1	2	1	1	0	2	2	.400	--	.400	18.00	18.00
Zac Gallen	R-R	6-2	189	8-3-95	12	4	2.54	31	31	0	0	184	121	56	52	15	47	192	.186	.146	.222	9.39	2.30
Tyler Gilbert	L-L	6-3	223	12-22-93	0	3	5.24	8	7	0	0	34	33	21	20	8	10	20	.250	.212	.263	5.24	2.62
Kevin Ginkel	L-R	6-4	235	3-24-94	1	1	3.38	30	0	0	1	29	27	14	11	1	11	30	.243	.200	.263	9.20	3.38
Jake Hager	R-R	6-1	170	3-4-93	0	0	7.71	3	0	0	0	2	3	2	2	0	0	1	.300	.500	.167	3.86	0.00
Tommy Henry	L-L	6-3	205	7-29-97	3	4	5.36	9	9	0	0	47	47	28	28	10	21	36	.263	.371	.236	6.89	4.02
Tyler Holton	L-L	6-2	200	6-13-96	0	0	3.00	10	0	0	0	9	8	3	3	1	2	6	.222	.091	.280	6.00	2.00
Drey Jameson	R-R	6-0	165	8-17-97	3	0	1.48	4	4	0	0	24	20	4	4	2	7	24	.222	.170	.279	8.88	2.59
Carson Kelly	R-R	6-2	212	7-14-94	0	0	7.71	4	0	0	0	5	9	4	4	1	2	0	.409	.222	.538	0.00	3.86
Merrill Kelly	R-R	6-2	202	10-14-88	13	8	3.37	33	33	0	0	200	167	77	75	21	61	177	.226	.229	.224	7.95	2.74
Ian Kennedy	R-R	6-0	210	12-19-84	4	7	5.36	57	0	0	10	50	57	33	30	11	22	44	.278	.253	.292	7.87	3.93
Dallas Keuchel	L-L	6-2	205	1-1-88	0	2	9.64	4	4	0	0	19	27	22	20	4	7	18	.329	.083	.371	8.68	3.38
Joe Mantiply	R-L	6-4	219	3-1-91	2	5	2.85	69	0	0	2	60	59	22	19	6	6	61	.255	.247	.260	9.15	0.90
Corbin Martin	R-R	6-2	225	12-28-95	0	1	4.84	7	2	0	0	22	25	14	12	3	12	21	.291	.294	.288	8.46	4.84
Mark Melancon	R-R	6-1	215	3-28-85	3	10	4.66	62	0	0	18	56	63	37	29	5	21	35	.281	.278	.283	5.63	3.38
Keynan Middleton	R-R	6-3	215	9-12-93	1	2	5.29	18	0	0	0	17	16	13	10	5	3	15	.250	.333	.224	7.94	1.59
Reyes Moronta	R-R	5-10	265	1-6-93	2	2	4.50	17	0	0	2	14	13	9	7	0	8	11	.241	.235	.243	7.07	5.14
2-team total (22 Los Angeles Dodgers)					2	2	4.30	39	0	0	2	38	30	20	18	5	18	38	.214	.174	.234	9.08	4.30

Kyle Nelson	L-L	6-1	175	7-8-96	2	1	2.19	43	1	0	0	37	26	10	9	1	14	30	.194	.194	.194	7.30	3.41
Ryne Nelson	R-R	6-3	184	2-1-98	1	1	1.47	3	3	0	0	18	9	4	3	2	6	16	.145	.156	.133	7.85	2.95
Matt Peacock	R-R	6-1	185	2-27-94	0	0	6.75	2	0	0	0	3	3	2	2	1	2	2	.273	.200	.333	6.75	6.75
Oliver Perez	L-L	6-3	225	8-15-81	1	1	15.75	7	0	0	0	4	8	9	7	1	1	1	.444	.444	.444	2.25	2.25
Sean Poppen	R-R	6-3	210	3-15-94	2	2	4.40	29	0	0	0	29	27	15	14	5	12	22	.265	.333	.236	6.91	3.77
Noe Ramirez	R-R	6-3	205	12-22-89	5	4	5.22	55	0	0	0	50	45	32	29	9	26	51	.245	.300	.218	9.18	4.68
Caleb Smith	R-L	6-0	207	7-28-91	1	3	4.11	44	1	0	0	70	57	35	32	14	39	65	.218	.170	.246	8.36	5.01
Edwin Uceta	R-R	6-0	155	1-9-98	0	0	5.82	10	0	0	0	17	14	12	11	2	7	13	.215	.233	.200	6.88	3.71
Luke Weaver	R-R	6-2	183	8-21-93	1	1	7.71	12	1	0	0	16	24	14	14	1	5	19	.329	.433	.256	10.47	2.76
J.B. Wendelken	R-R	6-1	242	3-24-93	2	1	5.28	29	0	0	0	29	25	18	17	4	14	21	.234	.184	.261	6.52	4.34
Taylor Widener	L-R	6-0	203	10-24-94	0	1	3.63	14	0	0	0	17	22	8	7	2	5	14	.297	.087	.392	7.27	2.60

Fielding

Catcher	PCT	G	PO	A	E	DP	PB
Greiner	.941	2	15	1	1	0	0
Herrera	.983	46	275	18	5	1	3
Hummel	1.000	18	94	3	0	0	4
Kelly	1.000	100	707	35	0	4	3
Varsho	.980	31	140	10	3	2	3

First Base	PCT	G	PO	A	E	DP
Beer	.974	5	38	0	1	4
Luplow	1.000	1	2	0	0	0
Rivera	1.000	4	15	2	0	0
Smith	1.000	10	60	7	0	9
Walker	.996	150	1109	78	5	106

Second Base	PCT	G	PO	A	E	DP
Alcantara	.956	18	17	26	2	5
Difo	1.000	1	3	2	0	0
Hager	1.000	16	19	28	0	7
Hernandez	1.000	2	0	2	0	0
Kennedy	.973	22	38	34	2	10
Marte	.976	94	135	196	8	49
Perdomo	1.000	2	5	6	0	1
Rojas	.972	26	49	56	3	13

Third Base	PCT	G	PO	A	E	DP
Alcantara	.937	35	25	64	6	8
Davidson	1.000	3	2	1	0	0
Ellis	.917	6	7	4	1	0
Hager	1.000	7	1	9	0	0
Hernandez	1.000	10	8	12	0	1
Kennedy	1.000	2	0	2	0	0
Luplow	1.000	1	0	1	0	0
Perdomo	1.000	6	7	13	0	1
Rivera	1.000	29	18	49	0	0
Rojas	.946	89	68	159	13	17

Shortstop	PCT	G	PO	A	E	DP
Ahmed	.983	16	16	41	1	6
Alcantara	.974	20	12	25	1	5
Difo	1.000	2	0	1	0	0
Hager	1.000	4	1	6	0	2
Perdomo	.973	140	169	329	14	83

Outfield	PCT	G	PO	A	E	DP
Carroll	.978	32	43	1	1	0
Garrett	1.000	13	15	0	0	0
Hummel	.970	23	30	2	1	0
Luplow	.982	68	103	7	2	1
McCarthy	.993	91	146	4	1	1
Peralta	.988	75	158	2	2	1
Smith	.976	43	79	2	2	1
Thomas	.991	112	311	4	3	2
Varsho	.989	125	271	8	3	0

RENO ACES — *TRIPLE-A*

PACIFIC COAST LEAGUE

Batting	B-T	HT	WT	DOB	AVG	vLH	vRH	G	AB	R	H	2B	3B	HR	RBI	BB	HBP	SH	SF	SO	SB	CS	SLG	OBP
Blaze Alexander	R-R	6-0	160	6-11-99	.259	.200	.294	7	27	8	7	1	0	2	4	4	3	0	0	8	0	0	.519	.412
Seth Beer	L-R	6-3	213	9-18-96	.242	.229	.247	90	331	56	80	20	1	14	62	44	21	0	6	68	0	1	.435	.361
Braden Bishop	R-R	6-1	178	8-22-93	.232	.277	.209	37	138	19	32	3	1	2	11	15	1	0	0	31	7	1	.312	.312
Dominic Canzone	L-R	6-1	190	8-16-97	.284	.300	.277	88	331	61	94	18	1	16	68	28	5	0	0	74	14	2	.489	.349
Corbin Carroll	L-L	5-10	165	8-21-00	.287	.333	.271	33	129	25	37	11	0	7	22	24	3	0	1	36	11	2	.535	.408
Leandro Cedeno	R-R	6-2	195	8-22-98	.291	.063	.385	14	55	8	16	2	0	2	10	2	1	0	0	14	1	0	.436	.328
Juan Centeno	L-R	5-9	195	11-16-89	.333	.286	.346	10	33	6	11	2	0	1	9	3	1	0	0	4	0	1	.485	.405
C.J. Chatham	R-R	6-4	185	12-22-94	.167	.250	.125	3	12	2	2	0	0	0	1	0	0	0	0	3	0	0	.167	.167
Jancarlos Cintron	R-R	5-8	170	12-1-94	.353	.478	.308	65	252	43	89	21	3	3	29	16	2	1	1	36	7	6	.496	.395
Matt Davidson	R-R	6-3	230	3-26-91	.386	.300	.412	11	44	8	17	1	0	8	12	6	1	0	0	14	0	0	.955	.471
2-team total (75 Las Vegas Aviators)					.310	.317	.306	86	323	67	100	10	1	32	66	44	14	0	1	102	0	0	.644	.414
Wilmer Difo	B-R	5-11	200	4-2-92	.269	.379	.219	72	279	33	75	15	0	7	43	20	0	1	6	41	4	2	.398	.311
Camden Duzenack	R-R	5-9	170	3-8-95	.261	.270	.258	95	318	51	83	20	3	13	55	20	3	5	3	74	10	3	.465	.308
Drew Ellis	R-R	6-3	205	12-1-95	.217	.191	.229	42	143	27	31	12	1	4	28	33	2	0	1	38	2	0	.399	.369
2-team total (70 Tacoma Rainiers)					.226	.190	.239	112	385	61	87	27	2	19	67	74	5	0	4	117	6	3	.455	.355
Stuart Fairchild	R-R	6-0	205	3-17-96	.162	.125	.172	10	37	3	6	2	0	2	3	4	2	0	0	15	0	1	.378	.279
3-team total (5 Sacramento River Cats, 4 Tacoma Rainiers)					.232	.200	.241	19	69	9	16	3	0	4	7	10	6	0	0	26	2	1	.449	.376
Dominic Fletcher	L-L	5-9	185	9-2-97	.301	.230	.329	101	396	70	119	29	8	5	38	42	4	1	6	88	5	6	.452	.368
Stone Garrett	R-R	6-2	195	11-22-95	.275	.214	.300	103	389	73	107	22	4	28	95	33	3	0	6	105	15	2	.568	.332
Juan Graterol	R-R	6-1	225	2-14-89	.255	.244	.260	38	137	17	35	8	0	2	13	5	4	0	1	12	3	0	.358	.299
Grayson Greiner	R-R	6-6	238	10-11-92	.232	.205	.243	45	151	20	35	6	0	6	20	18	1	0	0	67	1	0	.391	.318
Sergio Gutierrez	B-R	6-1	195	1-18-01	.000	--	.000	1	1	0	0	0	0	0	0	0	0	0	0	1	0	0	.000	.000
Jake Hager	R-R	6-1	170	3-4-93	.261	.289	.249	72	261	38	68	19	0	5	45	32	3	2	5	60	8	2	.391	.342
Nick Heath	L-L	6-1	190	11-27-93	.207	.214	.200	7	29	3	6	0	0	2	4	0	0	0	0	10	1	1	.414	.207
Yonny Hernandez	B-R	5-9	140	5-4-98	.244	.286	.225	70	250	49	61	6	6	1	31	35	7	3	0	47	30	5	.328	.353
2-team total (1 Round Rock Express)					.241	.286	.222	71	253	49	61	6	6	1	31	35	7	3	0	47	30	5	.324	.349
Jose Herrera	B-R	5-10	217	2-24-97	.341	.379	.323	26	91	16	31	3	0	2	14	12	1	0	0	10	0	0	.440	.423
Cooper Hummel	B-R	5-10	198	11-28-94	.310	.308	.311	33	129	31	40	8	1	6	19	24	2	0	1	40	3	4	.527	.423
Carson Kelly	R-R	6-2	212	7-14-94	.353	.333	.357	5	17	4	6	2	0	2	3	4	0	0	1	1	0	0	.824	.455
Buddy Kennedy	R-R	6-1	190	10-5-98	.261	.302	.246	93	330	55	86	14	3	7	40	54	3	0	7	76	8	4	.385	.363
Lyle Lin	R-R	6-1	200	6-26-97	--	--	--	1	0	0	0	0	0	0	0	0	1	0	0	0	0	0	--	1.000
Jordan Luplow	R-R	6-1	195	9-26-93	.289	.294	.286	10	45	10	13	3	0	6	14	2	1	0	0	9	0	0	.756	.333
Jake McCarthy	L-L	6-2	215	7-30-97	.369	.340	.385	36	141	33	52	11	3	5	27	19	4	1	0	22	11	4	.596	.457
Dominic Miroglio	R-R	6-0	205	3-10-95	.257	.291	.245	63	214	35	55	14	2	10	37	25	3	0	1	31	1	0	.481	.342
Channy Ortiz	B-R	5-10	165	4-11-99	.083	.000	.100	3	12	2	1	0	0	0	0	0	0	0	0	2	0	0	.083	.083
Yadiel Rivera	R-R	6-3	190	5-2-92	.190	.192	.189	25	79	8	15	1	0	2	8	5	0	0	1	21	2	0	.278	.235
Josh Rojas	L-R	6-1	207	6-30-94	.400	.000	.667	2	5	2	2	1	0	0	2	4	0	0	0	1	1	0	.600	.667
Pavin Smith	L-L	6-2	208	2-6-96	.412	.500	.333	4	17	5	7	1	0	1	6	0	0	0	0	1	0	0	.647	.412
Drew Stankiewicz	B-R	5-10	160	6-18-93	.190	.083	.233	13	42	6	8	2	2	1	12	7	0	1	0	16	2	1	.405	.306

Alek Thomas	L-L	5-11	175	4-28-00	.322	.350	.307	27	115	25	37	11	1	4	19	14	1	0	1	18	5	2	.539	.397
Cole Tucker	B-R	6-3	200	7-3-96	.237	.206	.250	35	114	14	27	4	0	2	13	11	0	0	3	35	4	2	.325	.297

Pitching	B-T	HT	WT	DOB	W	L	ERA	G	GS	CG	SV	IP	H	R	ER	HR	BB	SO	AVG	vLH	vRH	K/9	BB/9
Miguel Aguilar	L-L	5-8	194	9-26-91	3	2	5.44	46	1	0	5	46	51	31	28	9	19	34	.277	.320	.248	6.60	3.69
Jeff Bain	R-R	6-4	200	3-3-96	1	2	3.28	12	7	0	0	25	20	9	9	4	8	28	.211	.231	.186	10.22	2.92
Caleb Baragar	R-L	6-3	215	4-9-94	3	1	5.51	43	3	0	1	47	45	31	29	15	29	50	.250	.250	.250	9.51	5.51
J.B. Bukauskas	R-R	6-0	208	10-11-96	0	1	2.66	21	0	0	1	20	21	6	6	1	4	19	.284	.333	.204	8.41	1.77
Stefan Crichton	R-R	6-3	208	2-29-92	0	0	8.10	4	0	0	0	3	4	4	3	0	1	2	.267	.333	.167	5.40	2.70
Chris Devenski	R-R	6-3	211	11-13-90	0	0	7.36	6	0	0	0	7	7	6	6	3	2	9	.250	.167	.273	11.05	2.45
Camden Duzenack	R-R	5-9	170	3-8-95	0	0	6.75	2	0	0	0	1	2	1	1	0	0	0	.333	.500	.000	0.00	0.00
Luis Frias	R-R	6-3	245	5-23-98	3	2	3.99	27	3	0	0	47	44	26	21	6	26	74	.238	.289	.196	14.07	4.94
Paul Fry	L-L	6-0	205	7-26-92	1	0	4.40	29	0	0	0	29	27	15	14	2	15	28	.243	.235	.250	8.79	4.71
Tyler Gilbert	L-L	6-3	223	12-22-93	4	4	7.57	11	10	0	0	44	55	37	37	11	24	26	.309	.375	.264	5.32	4.91
Kevin Ginkel	L-R	6-4	235	3-24-94	2	1	1.17	30	0	0	9	31	23	6	4	1	12	45	.211	.196	.224	13.21	3.52
Josh Green	R-R	6-3	211	8-31-95	0	1	8.49	8	1	0	0	12	16	11	11	1	12	6	.348	.200	.400	4.63	9.26
Tommy Henry	L-L	6-3	205	7-29-97	4	4	3.74	21	21	0	0	113	103	47	47	11	45	103	.242	.228	.248	8.20	3.58
Tyler Holton	L-L	6-2	200	6-13-96	5	0	4.43	24	2	0	1	45	39	23	22	5	17	43	.238	.206	.257	8.66	3.43
Drey Jameson	R-R	6-0	165	8-17-97	5	12	6.95	22	21	0	0	114	139	91	88	21	42	109	.299	.343	.253	8.61	3.32
Keone Kela	R-R	6-1	220	4-16-93	0	1	5.00	9	0	0	1	9	7	5	5	2	5	11	.206	.294	.118	11.00	5.00
2-team total (7 Oklahoma City Dodgers)					1	2	5.74	16	0	0	1	16	14	11	10	2	15	16	.233	.292	.194	9.19	8.62
Mack Lemieux	L-L	6-3	205	9-6-96	1	0	4.19	19	0	0	0	19	20	10	9	4	12	20	.270	.161	.349	9.31	5.59
Justin Lewis	R-R	6-7	205	8-10-95	1	0	5.25	11	0	0	0	12	11	7	7	1	6	10	.239	.148	.368	7.50	4.50
Jesus Liranzo	R-R	6-2	225	3-7-95	0	2	8.36	15	0	0	1	14	18	13	13	4	10	22	.310	.379	.241	14.14	6.43
Corbin Martin	R-R	6-2	225	12-28-95	6	7	6.08	17	17	0	0	77	86	60	52	15	30	79	.284	.313	.255	9.23	3.51
Justin Martinez	R-R	6-3	180	7-30-01	1	0	3.86	3	0	0	0	5	3	3	2	0	5	8	.167	.182	.143	15.43	9.64
Ryan Meisinger	R-R	6-4	235	5-4-94	1	2	6.14	13	0	0	0	15	19	10	10	5	7	16	.311	.286	.333	9.82	4.30
Humberto Mejia	R-R	6-4	244	3-3-97	1	1	9.60	9	0	0	0	15	25	16	16	4	4	6	.368	.429	.325	3.60	2.40
Keynan Middleton	R-R	6-3	215	9-12-93	2	0	2.12	17	0	0	1	17	8	4	4	1	7	24	.140	.192	.097	12.71	3.71
Kyle Nelson	L-L	6-1	175	7-8-96	0	0	0.00	3	0	0	0	3	2	0	0	0	4	5	.200	.167	.250	16.88	13.50
Ryne Nelson	R-R	6-3	184	2-1-98	10	5	5.43	26	26	0	0	136	142	88	82	25	47	128	.264	.287	.241	8.47	3.11
Deyni Olivero	R-R	6-1	165	1-7-98	2	1	3.81	5	5	0	0	28	30	12	12	5	10	14	.273	.262	.289	4.45	3.18
Matt Peacock	R-R	6-1	185	2-27-94	1	1	9.00	3	0	0	0	4	7	4	4	1	0	2	.389	.375	.400	4.50	0.00
Brandon Pfaadt	R-R	6-4	220	10-15-98	5	1	2.63	10	10	0	0	62	47	18	18	9	14	74	.210	.233	.185	10.80	2.04
Sean Poppen	R-R	6-3	210	3-15-94	0	3	4.62	21	0	0	1	25	26	15	13	1	7	19	.274	.212	.349	6.75	2.49
Yadiel Rivera	R-R	6-3	190	5-2-92	0	0	0.00	1	0	0	0	1	2	0	0	0	0	0	.400	.500	.333	0.00	0.00
Blake Rogers	R-R	6-2	200	2-23-94	1	0	5.14	6	0	0	0	7	7	4	4	0	2	8	.269	.400	.091	10.29	2.57
Caleb Smith	R-L	6-0	207	7-28-91	1	0	0.93	4	0	0	0	10	8	1	1	1	1	8	.242	.250	.238	7.45	0.93
Dan Straily	R-R	6-2	220	12-1-88	3	3	6.35	15	12	0	1	62	63	46	44	14	30	53	.257	.276	.243	7.65	4.33
Mitchell Stumpo	R-R	6-2	205	6-17-96	1	2	3.53	45	0	0	8	43	27	17	17	4	31	51	.178	.139	.219	10.59	6.44
Edwin Uceta	R-R	6-0	155	1-9-98	6	1	4.86	28	5	0	0	50	35	29	27	9	30	70	.198	.156	.241	12.60	5.40
Luke Weaver	R-R	6-2	183	8-21-93	0	0	3.00	2	1	0	0	6	6	2	2	1	2	5	.273	.308	.222	7.50	3.00
Jacob Webb	R-R	6-2	210	8-15-93	0	0	10.13	6	0	0	0	5	8	6	6	1	3	7	.348	.222	.429	11.81	5.06
Ryan Weiss	R-R	6-4	210	12-10-96	0	0	7.45	7	1	0	0	10	14	8	8	5	7	10	.326	.357	.267	9.31	6.52
J.B. Wendelken	R-R	6-1	242	3-24-93	5	1	2.63	20	0	0	4	24	11	8	7	0	9	33	.138	.105	.167	12.38	3.38
Taylor Widener	L-R	6-0	203	10-24-94	2	2	5.40	27	0	0	0	37	40	24	22	5	12	47	.274	.359	.207	11.54	2.95
Blake Workman	R-R	6-3	195	10-8-97	4	0	4.64	27	2	0	0	33	39	21	17	2	11	35	.300	.265	.339	9.55	3.00

Fielding

Catcher	PCT	G	PO	A	E	DP	PB
Centeno	1.000	9	82	5	0	0	0
Duzenack	1.000	2	3	0	0	0	0
Graterol	.990	34	280	8	3	0	1
Greiner	.990	39	362	18	4	3	2
Herrera	.995	22	211	7	1	1	1
Hummel	.958	3	23	0	1	0	0
Kelly	1.000	3	19	2	0	0	0
Lin	1.000	1	6	0	0	0	0
Miroglio	.995	47	379	19	2	3	1
Rivera	1.000	11	51	7	0	5	
Smith	1.000	2	14	2	0	1	

First Base	PCT	G	PO	A	E	DP
Beer	.994	66	457	26	3	56
Canzone	.995	26	174	11	1	18
Cedeno	1.000	5	40	0	0	2
Centeno	.000	1	0	0	0	0
Chatham	1.000	1	9	0	0	1
Davidson	1.000	9	66	2	0	3
Difo	1.000	3	12	1	0	0
Duzenack	1.000	2	8	0	0	1
Ellis	1.000	13	79	7	0	11
Garrett	.833	1	4	1	1	1
Graterol	1.000	1	3	0	0	0
Hager	.978	8	39	5	1	4
McCarthy	1.000	3	9	1	0	0
Miroglio	.987	10	70	4	1	4

Second Base	PCT	G	PO	A	E	DP
Alexander	1.000	1	2	6	0	0
Chatham	1.000	2	4	5	0	1
Cintron	.988	42	52	109	2	31
Difo	1.000	4	13	12	0	7
Duzenack	1.000	14	10	35	0	5
Ellis	1.000	3	4	6	0	1
Hager	1.000	6	10	16	0	1
Hernandez	.990	44	87	105	2	33
Kennedy	.987	23	28	48	1	7
Ortiz	.941	3	9	7	1	2
Rivera	.941	4	5	11	1	2
Stankiewicz	.923	3	5	7	1	5
Tucker	1.000	7	6	7	0	2

Third Base	PCT	G	PO	A	E	DP
Alexander	.000	1	0	0	0	0
Cintron	1.000	14	7	11	0	2
Difo	.946	21	11	24	2	3
Duzenack	.960	17	10	14	1	1
Ellis	.920	23	15	31	4	1
Hager	.930	14	14	26	3	8
Hernandez	.964	11	10	17	1	1
Kennedy	.940	45	24	70	6	7
Rivera	1.000	1	1	3	0	1
Rojas	.000	1	0	0	0	0
Stankiewicz	.958	9	9	14	1	2
Tucker	1.000	1	1	1	0	0

Shortstop	PCT	G	PO	A	E	DP
Alexander	1.000	6	5	11	0	3
Cintron	1.000	4	7	6	0	0
Difo	.965	37	48	91	5	23
Duzenack	.970	19	21	44	2	9
Hager	.971	47	58	111	5	26
Hernandez	1.000	12	14	25	0	4
Rivera	.955	8	5	16	1	3
Tucker	.987	24	28	46	1	10

Outfield	PCT	G	PO	A	E	DP
Bishop	1.000	33	54	1	0	0
Canzone	.959	54	87	6	4	1
Carroll	.988	33	81	4	1	1
Duzenack	.974	49	71	3	2	1
Fairchild	1.000	8	16	1	0	0
Fletcher	.979	99	279	4	6	4
Garrett	.993	73	133	8	1	1
Hager	1.000	4	10	1	0	1
Heath	1.000	7	4	0	0	0
Hummel	.962	19	49	2	2	3
Kennedy	.882	9	15	0	2	0

Luplow	1.000	9	16	1	0	0
McCarthy	.969	32	63	0	2	0
Smith	1.000	1	2	0	0	0
Stankiewicz	1.000	1	2	0	0	0
Thomas	.987	29	78	0	1	0
Tucker	1.000	1	2	0	0	0

AMARILLO SOD POODLES — DOUBLE-A

TEXAS LEAGUE

Batting	B-T	HT	WT	DOB	AVG	vLH	vRH	G	AB	R	H	2B	3B	HR	RBI	BB	HBP	SH	SF	SO	SB	CS	SLG	OBP
Blaze Alexander	R-R	6-0	160	6-11-99	.306	.328	.300	88	317	48	97	17	3	17	54	33	10	2	1	92	10	6	.539	.388
Jorge Barrosa	B-L	5-9	165	2-17-01	.276	.252	.284	110	434	85	120	30	2	12	51	65	4	5	2	80	22	11	.438	.374
Dominic Canzone	L-R	6-1	190	8-16-97	.400	.429	.390	15	55	18	22	7	0	6	20	8	0	0	0	6	1	0	.855	.476
Corbin Carroll	L-L	5-10	165	8-21-00	.313	.250	.333	58	227	62	71	11	8	16	39	41	7	0	2	68	20	3	.643	.430
Leandro Cedeno	R-R	6-2	195	8-22-98	.310	.232	.333	109	426	86	132	18	0	30	93	42	5	0	6	112	0	0	.563	.374
Juan Centeno	L-R	5-9	195	11-16-89	.302	.233	.319	81	311	52	94	22	1	14	58	17	6	2	1	58	1	1	.514	.349
Jancarlos Cintron	R-R	5-8	170	12-1-94	.311	.242	.330	38	148	30	46	13	0	4	30	9	1	4	2	23	7	2	.480	.350
Dairon Cuevas	B-R	6-1	155	4-5-02	.222	.000	.286	5	9	2	2	0	0	0	1	0	0	1	0	4	1	0	.222	.222
Jose Curpa	R-R	5-9	160	3-9-00	.214	.167	.250	8	14	4	3	1	0	0	0	1	0	0	0	3	1	0	.286	.267
Nick Dalesandro	R-R	6-1	175	10-3-96	.275	.294	.269	84	280	44	77	12	1	2	37	24	1	2	5	66	35	3	.346	.329
Deyvison De Los Santos	R-R	6-1	185	6-21-03	.231	.286	.219	10	39	5	9	2	0	1	6	5	1	0	0	9	0	0	.359	.333
Eduardo Diaz	R-R	6-2	175	7-19-97	.263	.263	.263	105	426	69	112	29	3	11	71	29	8	1	2	116	14	7	.423	.320
Tristin English	R-R	6-3	208	5-14-97	.274	.353	.251	62	230	34	63	10	0	6	29	29	9	0	1	47	2	1	.396	.375
Roby Enriquez	L-L	6-2	210	3-21-97	.326	.289	.333	73	264	42	86	15	1	7	47	19	10	1	3	44	6	4	.470	.389
Dominic Fletcher	L-L	5-9	185	9-2-97	.346	.350	.345	32	127	28	44	6	2	7	34	13	1	0	1	25	4	2	.591	.408
Ti_Quan Forbes	R-R	6-4	225	8-26-96	.261	.303	.247	93	352	52	92	13	2	9	50	20	9	1	4	97	7	5	.386	.314
Jeison Guzman	B-R	6-2	205	10-8-98	.292	.600	.211	8	24	3	7	2	0	1	1	1	1	0	0	6	1	0	.500	.346
2-team total (14 Northwest Arkansas Naturals)					.246	.263	.240	22	69	11	17	3	0	2	6	10	1	0	0	24	2	1	.377	.350
Jordan Howard	B-R	5-11	160	2-25-96	--	--	--	1	0	1	0	0	0	0	0	1	0	0	0	0	0	1	--	1.000
Jordan Lawlar	R-R	6-2	190	7-17-02	.212	.077	.236	20	85	18	18	0	0	4	11	10	1	0	1	28	2	1	.353	.299
Lyle Lin	R-R	6-1	200	6-26-97	.182	.333	.125	4	11	4	2	0	0	0	2	2	0	0	1	6	0	0	.182	.286
Gary Mattis	R-R	5-11	175	2-1-98	.273	--	.273	3	11	3	3	0	0	0	0	0	0	0	0	1	1	0	.273	.273
Shane Muntz	R-R	6-4	240	2-23-99	.286	.500	.200	2	7	0	2	0	0	0	0	1	0	0	0	2	0	0	.286	.375
Elvis Peralta	L-R	5-9	160	12-7-96	.186	.100	.212	15	43	9	8	1	1	0	6	4	1	0	1	16	2	0	.256	.265
Caleb Roberts	L-R	6-1	195	2-9-00	.323	.125	.391	9	31	4	10	2	1	0	5	2	0	0	0	6	0	1	.452	.364
Drew Stankiewicz	B-R	5-10	160	6-18-93	.233	.173	.256	87	300	52	70	17	0	13	54	37	0	3	3	91	5	2	.420	.315
Tim Tawa	R-R	6-0	196	4-7-99	.197	.193	.199	60	218	26	43	7	0	5	23	25	2	0	1	57	3	2	.298	.285
A.J. Vukovich	R-R	6-5	210	7-20-01	.295	.182	.333	11	44	6	13	0	0	2	9	1	0	0	0	13	1	0	.432	.311
Andy Yerzy	L-R	6-3	215	7-5-98	.220	.130	.248	86	291	45	64	15	1	12	38	50	3	0	2	85	1	0	.402	.338

Pitching	B-T	HT	WT	DOB	W	L	ERA	G	GS	CG	SV	IP	H	R	ER	HR	BB	SO	AVG	vLH	vRH	K/9	BB/9
Kyle Backhus	L-L	6-4	185	1-31-98	2	2	4.05	11	0	0	3	13	9	8	6	0	8	17	.184	.188	.182	11.48	5.40
Jeff Bain	R-R	6-4	200	3-3-96	8	1	3.80	33	0	0	2	45	42	23	19	10	11	49	.250	.222	.263	9.80	2.20
Cam Booser	L-L	6-3	225	5-4-92	1	1	6.48	19	0	0	0	25	26	18	18	5	22	30	.274	.263	.281	10.80	7.92
Ross Carver	R-R	6-2	191	8-27-99	2	5	9.50	9	9	0	0	36	48	40	38	15	15	31	.331	.361	.301	7.75	3.75
Slade Cecconi	R-R	6-4	219	6-24-99	7	6	4.37	26	25	0	0	130	139	76	63	22	32	127	.266	.298	.243	8.81	2.22
Keegan Curtis	R-R	6-0	175	9-30-95	1	3	8.44	14	0	0	0	16	21	15	15	4	9	14	.304	.154	.395	7.88	5.06
2-team total (16 Tulsa Drillers)					3	4	7.75	30	1	0	1	34	43	30	29	6	17	32	.299	.261	.316	8.55	4.54
Brett de Geus	R-R	6-2	190	11-4-97	2	1	5.96	17	0	0	0	23	24	15	15	3	16	16	.282	.262	.302	6.35	6.35
Roby Enriquez	L-L	6-2	210	3-21-97	0	0	18.00	1	0	0	0	1	2	2	2	1	1	1	.500	1.000	.333	9.00	9.00
Ti_Quan Forbes	R-R	6-4	225	8-26-96	0	0	9.00	1	0	0	0	1	2	1	1	1	0	0	.500	.500	.500	0.00	0.00
Liu Fuenmayor	L-L	5-11	170	2-2-99	1	1	21.21	6	0	0	0	5	6	11	11	3	7	1	.375	.600	.273	1.93	13.50
Junior Garcia	L-L	5-11	220	10-1-95	1	1	7.86	24	0	0	4	26	36	24	23	9	12	28	.321	.303	.329	9.57	4.10
Josh Green	R-R	6-3	211	8-31-95	1	2	6.65	30	1	0	0	47	56	41	35	7	17	38	.295	.350	.255	7.23	3.23
Kenny Hernandez	L-L	6-1	197	6-24-98	4	4	6.26	23	4	0	0	46	64	34	32	9	21	42	.327	.238	.368	8.22	4.11
Jamison Hill	R-R	6-1	180	3-28-99	1	0	6.30	5	4	0	0	20	26	14	14	4	8	12	.321	.321	.321	5.40	3.60
Drey Jameson	R-R	6-0	165	8-17-97	2	1	2.41	4	4	0	0	19	13	5	5	0	4	23	.197	.261	.163	11.09	1.93
Bryce Jarvis	L-R	6-2	195	12-26-97	3	6	8.27	25	25	0	0	107	141	104	98	27	60	110	.325	.337	.315	9.28	5.06
Levi Kelly	R-R	6-4	205	5-14-99	0	1	40.50	2	0	0	0	1	4	6	6	1	4	2	.500	.667	.400	13.50	27.00
Dillon Larsen	R-L	6-5	230	7-9-98	0	1	7.20	2	0	0	0	5	5	4	4	0	4	4	.294	.333	.286	7.20	7.20
Mack Lemieux	L-L	6-3	205	9-6-96	0	3	4.81	23	0	0	1	24	29	15	13	5	15	20	.326	.333	.322	7.40	5.55
Garrett Leonard	R-R	6-3	190	9-25-96	0	0	24.75	5	0	0	0	4	13	14	11	4	7	1	.565	.500	.588	2.25	15.75
Justin Lewis	R-R	6-7	205	8-10-95	2	2	5.15	28	0	0	0	37	32	27	21	16	23	42	.224	.224	.223	10.31	5.65
Kai-Wei Lin	R-R	5-10	175	3-19-96	0	0	4.41	11	0	0	0	16	16	9	8	4	7	18	.262	.250	.268	9.92	3.86
Justin Martinez	R-R	6-3	180	7-30-01	1	0	4.15	2	0	0	0	4	6	2	2	0	2	8	.316	.750	.200	16.62	4.15
Kyle Mora	R-R	6-3	220	7-9-98	0	0	5.40	3	1	0	0	7	5	4	4	3	6	8	.200	.125	.235	10.80	8.10
Deyni Olivero	R-R	6-1	165	1-7-98	2	9	6.19	20	20	0	0	96	114	69	66	16	34	77	.297	.335	.268	7.22	3.19
Danny Oriente	R-R	6-0	190	10-8-97	0	0	0.00	2	0	0	0	1	0	0	0	0	0	0	.000	.000	.000	0.00	0.00
Yorvin Pantoja	L-L	5-11	175	9-22-97	0	1	11.12	9	0	0	1	11	15	14	14	6	9	7	.319	.167	.371	5.56	7.15
Elvis Peralta	L-R	5-9	160	12-7-96	0	0	54.00	1	0	0	0	1	4	4	4	2	0	0	.667	1.000	.600	0.00	0.00
Brandon Pfaadt	R-R	6-4	220	10-15-98	6	6	4.53	19	19	0	0	105	113	55	53	19	19	144	.274	.337	.228	12.30	1.62
Austin Pope	R-R	6-3	210	10-26-98	1	1	8.49	18	0	0	0	30	33	34	28	9	17	31	.280	.360	.221	9.40	5.16
Jake Rice	L-L	6-1	220	7-19-97	1	0	9.36	24	0	0	0	25	35	27	26	9	18	22	.343	.382	.324	7.92	6.48
Blake Rogers	R-R	6-2	200	2-23-94	4	4	3.61	42	0	0	13	47	38	25	19	6	20	59	.225	.257	.202	11.22	3.80
Andrew Saalfrank	L-L	6-3	205	8-18-97	1	0	5.14	13	0	0	0	14	12	10	8	2	9	17	.211	.182	.229	10.93	5.79

Matt Tabor	R-R	6-2	180	7-14-98	0	0	27.00	1	1	0	0	2	5	5	5	0	2	2	.556	.600	.500	10.80	10.80
Brent Teller	R-R	6-2	195	9-21-96	3	0	4.76	19	2	0	2	40	42	23	21	8	23	46	.269	.286	.258	10.44	5.22
Ty Tice	L-R	5-9	185	7-4-96	1	2	6.45	22	0	0	1	22	29	18	16	5	11	26	.309	.316	.304	10.48	4.43
Justin Vernia	R-R	6-2	205	9-22-95	0	1	10.80	5	1	0	0	12	21	14	14	3	1	13	.412	.200	.500	10.03	0.77
Blake Walston	L-L	6-5	175	6-28-01	7	3	5.16	21	21	1	0	106	115	63	61	16	39	110	.280	.292	.275	9.31	3.30
Ryan Weiss	R-R	6-4	210	12-10-96	1	0	4.76	10	0	0	0	17	18	11	9	2	1	15	.265	.280	.256	7.94	0.53
Blake Workman	R-R	6-3	195	10-8-97	2	1	4.32	13	0	0	2	17	15	8	8	6	3	20	.242	.273	.225	10.80	1.62
Andy Yerzy	L-R	6-3	215	7-5-98	0	0	0.00	1	0	0	0	1	1	0	0	0	0	0	.333	.500	.000	0.00	0.00

Fielding

Catcher	PCT	G	PO	A	E	DP	PB
Centeno	.997	62	543	36	2	5	7
Dalesandro	.981	48	388	31	8	1	5
Lin	1.000	4	37	2	0	0	0
Roberts	1.000	5	25	0	0	0	0
Yerzy	.996	31	256	12	1	1	1

First Base	PCT	G	PO	A	E	DP
Canzone	.947	3	17	1	1	2
Cedeno	.996	63	444	30	2	53
De Los Santos	.952	4	16	4	1	2
English	.986	20	134	9	2	23
Muntz	1.000	1	12	0	0	3
Roberts	1.000	2	9	0	0	0
Yerzy	.974	48	317	15	9	36

Second Base	PCT	G	PO	A	E	DP
Alexander	.985	11	33	31	1	10
Cintron	.976	18	32	51	2	11
Cuevas	.923	3	5	7	1	1
Curpa	1.000	1	2	1	0	1
Forbes	1.000	8	10	25	0	7
Guzman	.882	5	5	10	2	2
Howard	1.000	1	0	1	0	1
Peralta	1.000	12	23	25	0	12
Stankiewicz	.984	43	70	113	3	25
Tawa	.968	42	55	95	5	29

Third Base	PCT	G	PO	A	E	DP
Alexander	.923	8	3	9	1	1
Cintron	.923	7	2	10	1	0
Curpa	1.000	4	2	7	0	0
De Los Santos	.778	6	2	5	2	0
English	.963	25	16	36	2	3
Forbes	.953	84	59	122	9	16
Guzman	.000	1	0	0	0	0
Peralta	1.000	2	0	5	0	0
Stankiewicz	1.000	3	1	3	0	2
Vukovich	.833	4	1	4	1	0

Shortstop	PCT	G	PO	A	E	DP
Alexander	.948	70	103	186	16	38
Cintron	.964	15	23	31	2	8
Guzman	1.000	2	1	4	0	1
Lawlar	.953	17	31	50	4	13
Stankiewicz	.960	36	53	91	6	23

Outfield	PCT	G	PO	A	E	DP
Barrosa	.989	108	255	7	3	0
Canzone	1.000	8	16	1	0	0
Carroll	.983	46	108	5	2	1
Cedeno	1.000	2	1	0	0	0
Dalesandro	.957	33	64	2	3	1
Diaz	.971	91	155	11	5	2
English	.833	11	12	3	3	0
Enriquez	.964	59	101	6	4	1
Fletcher	.982	26	53	3	1	0
Mattis	1.000	2	1	0	0	0
Oriente	1.000	1	3	0	0	0
Roberts	.900	4	9	0	1	0
Stankiewicz	.909	6	10	0	1	0
Tawa	1.000	21	31	0	0	0
Vukovich	1.000	7	11	1	0	0

HILLSBORO HOPS

HIGH CLASS A

NORTHWEST LEAGUE

Batting	B-T	HT	WT	DOB	AVG	vLH	vRH	G	AB	R	H	2B	3B	HR	RBI	BB	HBP	SH	SF	SO	SB	CS	SLG	OBP
Axel Andueza	R-R	6-0	163	10-27-98	.150	.143	.152	12	40	9	6	1	0	0	3	6	1	0	0	11	1	0	.175	.277
Jorge Barrosa	B-L	5-9	165	2-17-01	.300	.444	.258	10	40	5	12	3	0	1	6	2	1	0	0	5	4	1	.450	.349
Ryan Bliss	R-R	5-9	165	12-13-99	.214	.180	.224	110	426	68	91	19	3	10	37	43	10	1	4	118	31	12	.343	.298
Spencer Brickhouse	L-R	6-4	235	4-10-98	.188	.091	.203	24	80	8	15	3	0	4	10	4	1	0	0	34	0	0	.375	.235
Neyfy Castillo	R-R	6-3	175	3-2-01	.249	.265	.245	82	309	35	77	13	2	11	29	31	4	0	0	115	15	9	.411	.326
Sheng-Ping Chen	L-R	5-9	165	10-27-00	.364	.333	.367	9	33	10	12	2	0	1	7	5	1	0	0	4	3	0	.515	.462
Cam Coursey	L-R	5-8	155	8-25-98	.250	.222	.256	71	212	31	53	12	1	1	25	42	4	0	3	43	3	4	.330	.379
Dairon Cuevas	B-R	6-1	155	4-5-02	.000	.000	.000	2	7	0	0	0	0	0	0	1	0	0	0	6	0	0	.000	.125
Jose Curpa	R-R	5-9	160	3-9-00	.225	.222	.226	33	80	13	18	2	1	1	11	18	6	0	0	27	5	2	.313	.404
Joshua Day	R-R	6-2	200	3-25-00	.235	.000	.286	4	17	1	4	1	0	0	2	1	0	0	1	5	1	0	.294	.263
Deyvison De Los Santos	R-R	6-1	185	6-21-03	.278	.279	.278	38	158	24	44	9	0	9	33	7	0	0	1	54	1	0	.506	.307
Adrian Del Castillo	L-R	5-11	208	9-27-99	.199	.246	.187	77	286	30	57	17	2	7	30	31	5	0	2	70	5	0	.346	.287
Tristin English	R-R	6-3	208	5-14-97	.261	.333	.242	42	153	23	40	6	1	6	20	9	3	0	1	39	1	1	.431	.313
Roby Enriquez	L-L	6-2	210	3-21-97	.196	.286	.179	15	46	6	9	0	0	1	2	4	3	0	0	10	0	0	.261	.302
Jordan Lawlar	R-R	6-2	190	7-17-02	.288	.370	.262	30	111	31	32	8	2	3	17	16	2	0	1	33	13	1	.477	.385
Lyle Lin	R-R	6-1	200	6-26-97	.183	.172	.186	37	126	10	23	3	0	0	13	9	2	0	1	30	0	0	.206	.246
Gavin Logan	L-R	5-11	212	1-14-00	.235	.250	.233	11	34	2	8	3	0	0	7	8	0	0	1	11	1	0	.324	.372
Ramses Malave	R-R	5-11	175	9-29-00	.191	.118	.211	47	157	23	30	10	0	3	9	16	1	0	1	64	1	1	.312	.269
Gary Mattis	R-R	5-11	175	2-1-98	.235	.300	.220	16	51	6	12	4	0	1	4	2	1	0	0	15	4	0	.373	.278
Elian Miranda	R-R	6-1	200	5-31-99	.130	.063	.151	24	69	7	9	3	0	2	9	2	2	0	1	21	1	0	.261	.176
Shane Muntz	R-R	6-4	240	2-23-99	.097	.200	.077	21	62	5	6	3	0	0	4	7	1	0	2	17	1	0	.145	.194
Danny Oriente	R-R	6-0	190	10-8-97	.232	.167	.250	58	194	20	45	6	0	1	31	23	5	0	4	35	9	4	.278	.323
Channy Ortiz	B-R	5-10	165	4-11-99	.224	.100	.255	66	201	24	45	10	2	2	17	25	5	2	2	52	5	4	.323	.322
Wilderd Patino	R-R	6-1	175	7-18-01	.288	.300	.286	19	73	14	21	5	0	1	11	4	2	1	0	25	13	2	.397	.342
Elvis Peralta	L-R	5-9	160	12-7-96	.200	.000	.286	3	10	0	2	1	0	0	0	0	0	0	0	3	0	1	.300	.200
Leodany Perez	R-R	5-10	160	5-13-00	.182	.000	.200	6	11	1	2	1	0	0	2	2	0	0	0	5	1	0	.273	.308
Jacen Roberson	L-L	6-1	192	5-23-00	.175	.333	.146	18	57	7	10	2	0	2	6	5	1	0	0	32	3	0	.316	.254
Caleb Roberts	L-R	6-1	195	2-9-00	.234	.205	.243	111	389	57	91	24	3	9	55	60	13	0	3	127	17	5	.380	.353
Fox Semones	R-R	6-0	175	12-3-97	.233	.083	.290	32	86	14	20	4	0	3	18	6	0	3	0	39	6	0	.384	.283
Tim Tawa	R-R	6-0	196	4-7-99	.282	.308	.273	58	213	32	60	8	1	8	30	31	2	0	1	36	8	4	.441	.377
A.J. Vukovich	R-R	6-5	210	7-20-01	.274	.236	.286	106	424	55	116	26	2	15	69	18	4	0	2	105	35	4	.450	.308
Jarrod Watkins	L-R	6-1	180	4-25-97	.252	.231	.258	33	115	15	29	7	1	1	13	14	6	0	1	26	5	1	.357	.360

Pitching	B-T	HT	WT	DOB	W	L	ERA	G	GS	CG	SV	IP	H	R	ER	HR	BB	SO	AVG	vLH	vRH	K/9	BB/9
Luke Albright	R-R	6-4	215	12-13-99	6	10	5.49	26	26	0	0	123	125	80	75	17	56	130	.262	.284	.243	9.51	4.10
Jose Alcantara	R-R	6-2	180	8-3-99	2	0	2.97	29	0	0	1	36	29	15	12	3	15	39	.228	.254	.206	9.66	3.72
Bobby Ay	R-R	6-3	190	5-28-97	0	1	7.36	22	0	0	0	22	11	22	18	1	28	25	.145	.154	.135	10.23	11.45
Kyle Backhus	L-L	6-4	185	1-31-98	1	3	3.00	29	0	0	3	39	36	15	13	1	18	61	.250	.212	.272	14.08	4.15
Zach Barnes	R-R	6-0	180	4-10-99	0	0	6.75	1	0	0	0	1	1	1	1	0	2	2	.200	.500	.000	13.50	13.50
Ross Carver	R-R	6-2	191	8-27-99	2	5	3.10	15	15	1	0	81	55	33	28	8	27	97	.186	.196	.177	10.73	2.99

Yilber Diaz	R-R	6-0	190	8-19-00	0	1	4.85	8	8	0	0	30	22	18	16	1	17	29	.204	.140	.246	8.80	5.16
Hugh Fisher	R-L	6-6	210	2-11-99	3	5	8.01	39	0	0	0	39	39	41	35	4	32	52	.253	.140	.320	11.90	7.32
Julio Frias	L-L	6-2	160	6-1-98	1	3	7.54	23	0	0	0	23	12	22	19	1	36	30	.152	.111	.186	11.91	14.29
Liu Fuenmayor	L-L	5-11	170	2-2-99	3	1	2.57	16	0	0	1	21	16	6	6	1	5	24	.216	.235	.200	10.29	2.14
Jackson Goddard	R-R	6-3	220	12-12-96	2	0	4.09	20	1	0	0	22	26	14	10	2	16	26	.283	.242	.305	10.64	6.55
Conor Grammes	R-R	6-1	200	7-13-97	1	1	8.50	12	0	0	0	18	14	20	17	2	13	33	.209	.250	.186	16.50	6.50
Kenny Hernandez	L-L	6-1	197	6-24-98	2	2	2.86	9	8	0	0	50	43	17	16	3	16	39	.242	.263	.231	6.97	2.86
Jamison Hill	R-R	6-1	180	3-28-99	7	7	4.35	21	21	0	0	103	82	56	50	9	46	115	.216	.210	.223	10.02	4.01
Dillon Larsen	R-L	6-5	230	7-9-98	1	1	4.30	22	0	0	1	29	21	14	14	3	24	36	.208	.133	.239	11.05	7.36
Justin Martinez	R-R	6-3	180	7-30-01	1	2	2.67	13	0	0	1	27	21	10	8	1	14	44	.216	.268	.179	14.67	4.67
Junior Mieses	R-R	6-1	168	10-15-99	1	2	6.06	11	0	0	0	16	10	12	11	3	15	23	.175	.214	.138	12.67	8.27
Christian Montes De Oca	R-R	6-4	230	8-30-99	0	3	3.42	24	0	0	9	26	25	11	10	3	9	43	.236	.286	.203	14.70	3.08
Gerald Ogando	R-R	6-2	180	7-28-00	3	1	3.62	19	0	0	0	27	21	11	11	3	9	27	.216	.128	.276	8.89	2.96
Deyni Olivero	R-R	6-1	165	1-7-98	0	1	2.60	3	3	0	0	17	10	5	5	0	4	14	.169	.086	.292	7.27	2.08
Chad Patrick	R-R	6-1	205	8-14-98	3	0	3.77	6	6	0	0	29	26	14	12	1	10	30	.234	.200	.268	9.42	3.14
Austin Pope	R-R	6-3	210	10-26-98	3	1	1.35	11	0	0	3	13	8	2	2	1	2	15	.178	.130	.227	10.13	1.35
Scott Randall	R-R	6-0	172	8-3-98	6	7	3.82	21	21	0	0	108	101	46	46	14	25	104	.248	.292	.209	8.64	2.08
Jake Rice	L-L	6-1	220	7-19-97	3	0	2.57	11	0	0	1	14	8	4	4	0	6	21	.167	.167	.167	13.50	3.86
Andrew Saalfrank	L-L	6-3	205	8-18-97	3	2	2.95	25	0	0	0	40	32	19	13	2	18	53	.211	.170	.232	12.03	4.08
Jose Santamaria	R-R	6-2	190	11-26-98	0	1	6.19	21	0	0	0	32	36	26	22	7	18	23	.275	.333	.215	6.47	5.06
Avery Short	R-L	6-1	205	3-14-01	1	3	4.68	10	6	0	1	25	24	14	13	4	16	29	.250	.333	.206	10.44	5.76
Listher Sosa	R-R	6-4	208	9-6-01	0	0	5.40	2	0	0	0	5	5	3	3	0	1	7	.250	.273	.222	12.60	1.80
Collin Sullivan	R-R	6-1	211	9-19-97	1	2	7.71	14	0	0	0	16	19	15	14	6	13	24	.279	.233	.316	13.22	7.16
Brent Teller	R-R	6-2	195	9-21-96	1	0	3.60	1	1	0	0	5	3	2	2	0	1	4	.167	.143	.182	7.20	1.80
Marcos Tineo	R-R	6-0	165	3-14-97	2	5	5.65	33	10	0	0	72	64	47	45	6	40	92	.237	.244	.232	11.55	5.02
Blake Walston	L-L	6-5	175	6-28-01	1	0	2.55	4	4	0	0	18	13	5	5	0	7	27	.200	.269	.154	13.75	3.57

Fielding

Catcher	PCT	G	PO	A	E	DP	PB
Del Castillo	.998	54	517	38	1	2	15
Lin	1.000	11	92	7	0	0	1
Logan	1.000	5	47	2	0	1	0
Malave	.992	36	345	29	3	2	6
Muntz	1.000	2	7	0	0	0	2
Roberts	.983	28	277	14	5	0	9

First Base	PCT	G	PO	A	E	DP
Andueza	.951	9	73	5	4	5
Brickhouse	1.000	23	186	10	0	16
Castillo	.984	20	120	3	2	8
De Los Santos	1.000	7	54	3	0	6
English	.979	5	43	4	1	6
Lin	.986	22	134	9	2	14
Logan	1.000	1	3	0	0	1
Miranda	.987	12	73	3	1	3
Muntz	.960	9	43	5	2	8
Roberts	.993	22	141	11	1	18
Watkins	1.000	6	33	4	0	4

Second Base	PCT	G	PO	A	E	DP
Bliss	1.000	24	41	64	0	17
Chen	1.000	2	6	1	0	1
Coursey	.978	41	55	81	3	20
Cuevas	1.000	2	3	3	0	1
Curpa	.962	14	17	33	2	10
Ortiz	.986	23	30	40	1	10
Peralta	1.000	1	1	1	0	0
Perez	1.000	1	0	2	0	0
Semones	1.000	2	5	5	0	1
Tawa	.984	19	20	42	1	8
Watkins	1.000	14	20	25	0	8

Third Base	PCT	G	PO	A	E	DP
Chen	1.000	4	7	3	0	1
Coursey	1.000	4	0	4	0	0
Curpa	1.000	4	0	4	0	0
De Los Santos	.944	29	15	36	3	4
English	.960	9	6	18	1	2
Ortiz	1.000	5	4	7	0	2
Peralta	1.000	1	1	1	0	0
Semones	1.000	1	0	1	0	0
Vukovich	.903	76	54	104	17	9
Watkins	1.000	1	0	1	0	0

Shortstop	PCT	G	PO	A	E	DP
Bliss	.962	84	131	197	13	47
Chen	.857	2	2	4	1	1
Curpa	.941	6	5	11	1	1
Day	1.000	4	6	7	0	1
Lawlar	.953	27	29	53	4	16
Ortiz	.935	8	13	16	2	3

Outfield	PCT	G	PO	A	E	DP
Barrosa	.944	9	17	0	1	0
Castillo	1.000	59	85	4	0	1
Coursey	1.000	9	13	0	0	0
Curpa	.923	8	12	0	1	0
English	1.000	24	47	3	0	0
Enriquez	1.000	15	23	0	0	0
Mattis	1.000	10	11	0	0	0
Oriente	.986	45	69	2	1	1
Ortiz	.979	32	45	1	1	0
Patino	.977	19	41	1	1	0
Peralta	1.000	1	5	0	0	0
Perez	1.000	4	4	1	0	0
Roberson	.972	18	34	1	1	0
Roberts	.982	60	104	7	2	1
Semones	.957	24	43	2	2	2
Tawa	.988	41	79	2	1	1
Vukovich	.980	25	46	3	1	0
Watkins	1.000	4	7	0	0	0

VISALIA RAWHIDE

LOW CLASS A

CALIFORNIA LEAGUE

Batting	B-T	HT	WT	DOB	AVG	vLH	vRH	G	AB	R	H	2B	3B	HR	RBI	BB	HBP	SH	SF	SO	SB	CS	SLG	OBP
Juan Batista	R-R	6-1	175	1-9-01	.180	.200	.172	28	89	9	16	3	2	1	5	6	3	1	0	49	7	1	.292	.255
Sheng-Ping Chen	L-R	5-9	165	10-27-00	.221	.238	.216	79	298	39	66	19	1	3	35	25	3	2	0	94	5	4	.322	.288
Gavin Conticello	L-R	6-4	195	6-11-03	.210	.150	.224	30	105	16	22	3	2	1	12	14	5	0	1	38	1	1	.305	.328
Juan Corniel	B-R	5-11	150	10-2-02	.246	.250	.245	76	313	42	77	11	3	2	33	25	0	0	1	66	4	7	.319	.301
Dairon Cuevas	B-R	6-1	155	4-5-02	.167	.250	.125	3	12	1	2	0	0	0	0	0	0	0	0	7	0	0	.167	.167
Jose Curpa	R-R	5-9	160	3-9-00	.286	.500	.000	2	7	0	2	0	0	0	2	0	0	0	0	0	1	0	.286	.286
Joshua Day	R-R	6-2	200	3-25-00	.319	.333	.317	20	72	9	23	3	0	2	13	12	3	0	0	21	3	0	.444	.437
Deyvison De Los Santos	R-R	6-1	185	6-21-03	.329	.352	.320	78	316	43	104	18	2	12	67	22	3	0	8	84	4	1	.513	.370
Adrian Del Castillo	L-R	5-11	208	9-27-99	.333	.250	.357	5	18	2	6	2	0	0	1	3	0	0	1	6	0	0	.444	.409
J.J. D'Orazio	R-R	6-1	170	12-28-01	.221	.266	.206	78	263	29	58	18	0	2	24	39	3	0	5	70	0	2	.312	.323
Deivi Estrada	B-R	5-10	155	1-17-01	.181	.250	.154	23	72	5	13	3	0	0	1	2	0	0	0	30	0	1	.222	.203
Junior Franco	L-L	5-9	165	9-13-02	.254	.233	.261	103	409	54	104	20	0	14	57	33	4	0	2	112	28	8	.406	.315
Kevin Graham	L-R	6-1	195	8-12-99	.245	.083	.268	25	94	20	23	2	1	5	17	11	0	0	1	21	0	1	.447	.321
Sergio Gutierrez	B-R	6-1	195	1-18-01	.169	.186	.164	56	183	28	31	7	2	6	20	32	4	0	0	96	2	2	.328	.306
Alvin Guzman	R-R	6-1	166	10-20-01	.202	.233	.193	70	267	30	54	14	1	3	31	17	3	1	2	103	12	9	.296	.256
Glenallen Hill Jr.	B-R	5-9	170	9-30-00	.149	.103	.165	37	114	15	17	2	1	2	7	17	3	0	1	57	3	2	.237	.274
Brett Johnson	L-R	5-11	195	1-6-00	.223	.368	.187	28	94	17	21	6	0	1	10	23	3	0	2	28	9	1	.319	.385

Jordan Lawlar	R-R	6-2	190	7-17-02	.351	.422	.326	44	174	44	61	9	4	9	32	27	5	0	2	48	24	4	.603	.447
Ramses Malave	R-R	5-11	175	9-29-00	.286	.286	.286	10	35	3	10	1	0	2	8	5	2	0	0	11	2	0	.486	.405
David Martin	L-R	6-1	185	10-28-00	.200	.500	.167	6	20	3	4	2	0	0	2	2	2	0	0	4	0	0	.300	.333
Gary Mattis	R-R	5-11	175	2-1-98	.279	.143	.315	18	68	12	19	5	1	1	11	3	3	0	1	19	2	1	.426	.333
Ivan Melendez	R-R	6-3	225	1-24-00	.207	.067	.236	25	87	11	18	3	1	3	8	10	9	0	0	20	0	0	.368	.349
Shane Muntz	R-R	6-4	240	2-23-99	.300	.522	.224	26	90	14	27	6	0	4	15	14	5	0	2	28	0	0	.500	.414
Angel Ortiz	L-L	6-0	180	10-3-02	.200	--	.200	3	10	3	2	0	0	0	1	2	0	0	0	2	0	0	.200	.333
Channy Ortiz	B-R	5-10	165	4-11-99	.130	.182	.116	19	54	4	7	4	1	0	6	7	4	0	1	21	1	1	.241	.273
Wildord Patino	R-R	6-1	175	7-18-01	.290	.343	.274	75	293	54	85	16	2	8	42	23	16	3	3	84	54	7	.440	.370
Manuel Pena	L-R	6-1	170	12-5-03	.248	.240	.250	36	137	17	34	7	1	0	17	20	0	1	0	41	1	3	.314	.344
Jacen Roberson	L-L	6-1	192	5-23-00	.225	.242	.220	50	151	29	34	9	0	5	24	37	1	0	3	59	3	2	.384	.375
Danyer Sanabria	L-L	6-1	155	3-7-02	.207	.185	.213	35	116	16	24	5	2	2	13	10	1	1	1	40	1	1	.336	.273
Oscar Santos	R-R	5-9	175	9-24-00	.206	.219	.201	69	223	25	46	10	1	9	27	28	3	0	2	104	3	0	.381	.301
Fox Semones	R-R	6-0	175	12-3-97	.000	.000	.000	1	4	0	0	0	0	0	0	0	0	0	0	3	0	0	.000	.000
Daniel Torres	R-R	5-9	150	1-10-02	.097	.125	.087	10	31	1	3	0	0	0	1	3	1	0	0	14	0	0	.097	.200
Jean Walters	B-R	5-11	155	8-13-01	.198	.262	.176	72	248	32	49	5	3	0	19	16	2	6	1	58	5	3	.242	.251

Pitching	B-T	HT	WT	DOB	W	L	ERA	G	GS	CG	SV	IP	H	R	ER	HR	BB	SO	AVG	vLH	vRH	K/9	BB/9
Enmanuel Acosta	R-R	6-2	200	6-6-99	0	1	9.53	12	0	0	2	17	19	19	18	2	13	17	.288	.208	.333	9.00	6.88
Jose Alcantara	R-R	6-2	180	8-3-99	2	1	4.43	13	0	0	0	20	18	12	10	1	21	35	.234	.320	.192	15.49	9.30
Jhosmer Alvarez	R-R	6-1	155	6-29-01	0	3	5.59	5	0	0	0	10	15	6	6	1	6	6	.385	.429	.360	5.59	5.59
Zach Barnes	R-R	6-0	180	4-10-99	1	2	9.35	19	0	0	0	26	30	28	27	2	25	33	.291	.315	.265	11.42	8.65
Juan Batista	R-R	6-1	175	1-9-01	0	0	0.00	1	0	0	0	0	1	2	0	0	1	0	.333	.000	.500	0.00	27.00
Jose Cabrera	R-R	6-3	190	5-30-02	2	4	6.51	7	7	0	0	37	39	33	27	4	11	30	.260	.239	.277	7.23	2.65
Dylan Castaneda	R-R	6-2	190	7-16-01	0	1	19.06	3	0	0	0	6	14	12	12	3	4	8	.452	.429	.471	12.71	6.35
Bryan Castillo	R-R	6-3	185	1-18-99	0	0	15.43	3	0	0	0	5	9	10	8	0	6	6	.409	.375	.429	11.57	11.57
Adrian Del Moral	R-R	6-1	190	2-17-99	0	1	6.07	13	0	0	0	30	22	26	20	3	29	35	.220	.250	.206	10.62	8.80
Yilber Diaz	R-R	6-0	190	8-19-00	4	2	3.56	11	9	0	1	48	34	21	19	4	21	70	.199	.242	.171	13.13	3.94
Joe Elbis	R-R	6-1	150	9-24-02	0	2	9.00	3	3	0	0	10	13	10	10	0	4	14	.289	.444	.250	12.60	3.60
Lorenzo Encarnacion	R-R	5-11	175	11-9-01	0	0	3.86	1	0	0	0	2	2	1	1	1	0	3	.222	.250	.000	11.57	0.00
Deivi Estrada	B-R	5-10	155	1-17-01	0	1	--	1	0	0	0	0	1	1	0	0	1	0	1.000	--	1.000	--	--
Liu Fuenmayor	L-L	5-11	170	2-2-99	0	0	24.30	4	0	0	0	3	12	10	9	1	2	5	.545	.625	.500	13.50	5.40
Spencer Giesting	L-L	6-4	200	7-2-01	0	1	6.08	7	4	0	0	13	11	9	9	2	8	16	.229	.238	.222	10.80	5.40
Miguel Gil	R-R	6-1	160	5-12-01	2	3	3.54	11	1	0	2	28	21	17	11	2	26	39	.204	.079	.277	12.54	8.36
Landon Green	R-R	6-1	200	9-21-99	0	0	3.00	4	0	0	0	9	7	3	3	0	5	10	.206	.211	.200	10.00	5.00
Jamison Hill	R-R	6-1	180	3-28-99	0	1	4.50	1	0	0	0	4	4	3	2	0	2	2	.286	.500	.125	4.50	4.50
Brock Jones	L-L	6-1	180	6-14-01	0	2	8.74	5	4	0	0	11	17	15	11	1	13	12	.333	.385	.316	9.53	10.32
Yu-Min Lin	L-L	5-11	160	7-12-03	2	0	2.97	7	7	0	0	33	31	14	11	2	16	50	.254	.371	.207	13.50	4.32
Jean Marcelino	R-R	6-2	170	7-19-00	1	1	14.66	11	0	0	0	12	12	20	19	0	23	12	.267	.294	.250	9.26	17.74
Eric Mendez	R-R	6-0	175	12-3-99	4	1	3.97	44	0	0	1	66	43	36	29	8	49	64	.184	.244	.146	8.77	6.72
Carlos Meza	L-L	6-1	155	2-10-01	6	4	6.31	38	1	0	2	67	67	54	47	8	43	89	.254	.273	.250	11.96	5.78
Junior Mieses	R-R	6-1	168	10-15-99	1	2	6.75	28	0	0	8	37	36	33	28	5	26	55	.254	.250	.255	13.26	6.27
Christian Montes De Oca	R-R	6-4	230	8-30-99	0	0	2.03	10	0	0	4	13	10	4	3	2	4	28	.200	.357	.139	18.90	2.70
Kyle Mora	R-R	6-3	220	7-9-98	1	1	9.00	5	0	0	0	10	15	11	10	2	2	9	.333	.360	.300	8.10	1.80
Alfred Morillo	R-R	6-3	190	11-14-01	2	2	4.75	23	0	0	0	36	31	26	19	1	20	47	.225	.204	.238	11.75	5.00
Liam Norris	L-L	6-4	215	8-13-01	1	8	7.33	20	18	0	0	66	59	59	54	11	61	84	.235	.222	.239	11.40	8.28
Channy Ortiz	B-R	5-10	165	4-11-99	0	0	6.75	2	0	0	0	1	3	1	1	0	2	0	.429	.333	.500	0.00	13.50
Peniel Otano	R-R	6-4	190	10-7-00	3	7	5.86	23	14	0	0	83	101	73	54	8	42	68	.297	.380	.241	7.37	4.55
Chad Patrick	R-R	6-1	205	8-14-98	0	2	3.46	4	4	0	0	13	12	6	5	2	5	17	.245	.308	.174	11.77	3.46
Yaifer Perdomo	L-L	5-10	160	8-16-01	1	5	6.39	26	14	0	0	75	77	57	53	15	48	91	.265	.351	.234	10.97	5.79
Dylan Ray	R-R	6-3	230	5-9-01	0	3	7.71	6	6	0	0	12	16	14	10	5	3	14	.314	.357	.261	10.80	2.31
Danyer Sanabria	L-L	6-1	155	3-7-02	0	0	13.50	2	0	0	0	1	2	2	1	0	2	1	.400	1.000	.250	13.50	27.00
David Sanchez	R-R	6-1	175	1-6-99	1	2	6.53	25	0	0	3	21	19	23	15	2	27	17	.241	.217	.250	7.40	11.76
Rael Santos	R-R	6-3	165	3-29-01	0	3	8.72	26	0	0	0	32	27	32	31	4	48	40	.227	.222	.228	11.25	13.50
Avery Short	R-L	6-1	205	3-14-01	0	4	4.91	8	8	0	0	33	39	24	18	3	10	42	.279	.226	.294	11.45	2.73
Diomede Sierra	L-L	6-2	170	9-11-01	3	5	5.13	19	19	0	0	74	73	56	42	8	48	81	.252	.153	.277	9.90	5.86
Listher Sosa	R-R	6-4	208	9-6-01	3	5	3.42	36	0	0	2	68	57	38	26	6	30	65	.224	.223	.225	8.56	3.95
Josh Swales	R-R	6-2	195	10-28-01	3	5	7.14	18	13	0	0	63	81	54	50	7	37	48	.313	.296	.323	6.86	5.29
Luis Tejeda	R-R	6-3	170	2-14-01	1	1	6.03	23	0	0	0	34	42	36	23	4	19	24	.300	.314	.292	6.29	4.98
Alex Valdez	R-R	6-2	185	12-24-99	0	1	7.48	20	0	0	1	28	34	30	23	4	17	40	.283	.310	.269	13.01	5.53
Jean Walters	B-R	5-11	155	8-13-01	1	0	3.86	7	0	0	0	7	6	4	3	1	1	3	.240	.400	.133	3.86	1.29

Fielding

Catcher	PCT	G	PO	A	E	DP	PB
Del Castillo	.980	4	48	2	1	0	1
D'Orazio	.984	66	625	67	11	6	10
Gutierrez	.964	28	270	28	11	2	7
Malave	.973	8	64	7	2	0	4
Martin	1.000	5	48	8	0	1	1
Muntz	.980	8	85	11	2	1	4
Santos	.972	17	165	9	5	2	8

First Base	PCT	G	PO	A	E	DP
Batista	.939	8	42	4	3	3
Conticello	.943	7	32	1	2	2
Curpa	1.000	1	4	0	0	0
De Los Santos	.970	14	96	0	3	9
D'Orazio	.964	5	25	2	1	5
Gutierrez	.962	18	120	7	5	13
Melendez	1.000	14	120	10	0	12
Muntz	.990	14	96	8	1	12
Ortiz	.917	2	10	1	1	1
Sanabria	.992	33	221	16	2	26
Santos	.981	18	97	8	2	11
Torres	.984	8	56	4	1	7
Walters	1.000	6	26	1	0	0

Second Base	PCT	G	PO	A	E	DP
Chen	.983	57	109	122	4	43
Corniel	.931	14	28	39	5	6
Cuevas	1.000	1	0	1	0	0
Curpa	1.000	1	1	0	0	0
Day	.952	5	8	12	1	2
Hill Jr.	.750	3	2	1	1	2
Ortiz	1.000	7	13	10	0	6
Pena	.952	26	44	55	5	13
Semones	1.000	1	3	2	0	2
Torres	1.000	3	1	3	0	0
Walters	.968	28	57	64	4	20

Third Base	PCT	G	PO	A	E	DP
Chen	.864	12	4	15	3	1
Conticello	.884	25	15	46	8	4
Day	.500	1	1	1	2	0
De Los Santos	.915	59	26	104	12	8
Melendez	.870	10	6	14	3	0
Ortiz	1.000	2	0	3	0	0
Pena	1.000	3	1	1	0	0
Walters	.969	27	13	50	2	7

Shortstop	PCT	G	PO	A	E	DP
Chen	1.000	5	1	2	0	0
Corniel	.897	61	63	138	23	23
Day	.947	9	15	21	2	8
Lawlar	.859	37	35	87	20	18
Ortiz	.943	10	9	24	2	6
Pena	.889	8	14	10	3	4
Walters	.947	8	9	9	1	4

Outfield	PCT	G	PO	A	E	DP
Batista	1.000	20	19	0	0	0
Chen	1.000	1	1	0	0	0
Cuevas	1.000	3	2	0	0	0
Estrada	1.000	10	17	0	0	0
Franco	.940	100	147	9	10	2
Graham	.977	22	40	3	1	2
Guzman	.983	68	162	9	3	0
Hill Jr.	.897	26	35	0	4	0
Johnson	.980	27	47	3	1	1
Mattis	1.000	14	20	0	0	0
Ortiz	1.000	1	2	0	0	0
Patino	.973	69	142	3	4	1
Roberson	.961	43	71	3	3	0
Sanabria	1.000	3	1	0	0	0
Walters	1.000	7	4	1	0	0

ACL D-BACKS BLACK — ROOKIE

ARIZONA COMPLEX LEAGUE

Batting	B-T	HT	WT	DOB	AVG	vLH	vRH	G	AB	R	H	2B	3B	HR	RBI	BB	HBP	SH	SF	SO	SB	CS	SLG	OBP
Blaze Alexander	R-R	6-0	160	6-11-99	.250	.333	.200	3	8	1	2	0	0	1	1	1	0	0	0	2	0	0	.625	.333
Juan Aparicio	R-R	6-0	165	9-25-02	.282	.313	.274	29	78	13	22	3	2	0	6	9	0	1	0	19	1	0	.372	.356
Juan Batista	R-R	6-1	175	1-9-01	.000	--	.000	1	2	0	0	0	0	0	0	1	0	0	0	0	0	0	.000	.333
2-team total (20 ACL D-backs Red)					.125	.182	.108	21	48	5	6	2	1	0	4	6	1	0	1	23	2	0	.208	.232
Johan Benitez	B-R	6-3	170	8-7-03	.282	.143	.297	21	71	4	20	8	0	1	12	7	1	0	1	20	1	0	.437	.350
2-team total (32 ACL D-backs Red)					.269	.200	.278	53	182	23	49	11	1	1	20	21	4	0	3	62	5	1	.357	.352
Alexander Benua	R-R	6-2	185	10-19-03	.243	.125	.258	23	74	7	18	5	1	0	6	8	1	1	1	19	8	1	.338	.321
Diosfran Cabeza	B-R	5-10	155	5-13-03	.274	.188	.304	39	124	17	34	5	2	0	21	22	1	0	2	22	4	1	.347	.383
2-team total (5 ACL D-backs Red)					.281	.182	.314	44	135	18	38	5	2	0	21	23	1	0	2	26	4	1	.348	.385
Ricardo Caldera	R-R	6-1	175	4-6-02	.177	.118	.200	28	62	8	11	1	1	1	7	15	0	0	0	31	1	0	.274	.338
Dominic Canzone	L-R	6-1	190	8-16-97	.250	.000	.400	3	8	2	2	0	1	0	1	1	0	0	0	3	0	0	.500	.333
Neyfy Castillo	R-R	6-3	175	3-2-01	.333	.250	.500	2	6	0	2	0	0	0	0	0	0	0	0	4	0	0	.333	.333
Christian Cerda	R-R	6-0	190	12-27-02	.206	.000	.233	15	34	5	7	3	0	0	1	8	0	0	1	7	0	0	.294	.349
Alberto Ciprian	R-R	5-11	160	11-5-02	.200	.130	.220	37	105	15	21	5	0	0	8	16	4	0	0	45	1	1	.248	.328
Cam Coursey	L-R	5-8	155	8-25-98	.167	.000	.333	2	6	1	1	1	0	0	2	1	0	0	0	3	0	0	.333	.286
Dairon Cuevas	B-R	6-1	155	4-5-02	.167	.111	.182	18	42	8	7	1	1	0	2	3	1	0	0	23	1	0	.238	.239
Jose Curpa	R-R	5-9	160	3-9-00	.300	.200	.320	12	30	4	9	2	0	0	5	4	0	0	1	6	4	1	.367	.371
Adrian Del Castillo	L-R	5-11	208	9-27-99	.273	.000	.300	4	11	0	3	1	0	0	0	1	0	0	0	4	0	0	.364	.333
Deivi Estrada	B-R	5-10	155	1-17-01	.350	.222	.455	6	20	2	7	1	1	0	3	2	0	0	0	7	1	0	.500	.409
2-team total (7 ACL D-backs Red)					.293	.294	.292	13	41	8	12	3	1	1	6	6	1	0	0	16	2	1	.488	.396
Jose Fernandez	R-R	6-3	165	9-22-03	.204	.185	.210	31	108	17	22	2	3	1	11	9	1	0	2	27	1	0	.306	.267
2-team total (19 ACL D-backs Red)					.217	.156	.238	50	175	24	38	7	3	1	15	14	5	0	2	51	2	0	.309	.291
Juan Garcia	B-R	5-10	165	5-28-03	.250	--	.250	3	4	0	1	0	0	0	0	1	0	0	0	2	0	1	.250	.400
2-team total (12 ACL D-backs Red)					.171	.333	.156	15	35	4	6	2	1	0	1	3	1	0	0	15	1	2	.286	.256
Dominic Gonnella	L-R	5-11	205	9-16-01	.167	.182	.162	17	48	8	8	3	0	0	4	7	1	0	0	19	1	2	.229	.286
Coleton Horner	R-R	6-0	165	7-8-97	.360	.300	.375	17	50	4	18	3	0	0	8	5	1	0	1	13	0	1	.420	.421
2-team total (4 ACL D-backs Red)					.357	.300	.370	21	56	4	20	3	0	0	9	6	1	0	1	15	0	1	.411	.422
David Martin	L-R	6-1	185	10-28-00	.188	.000	.214	6	16	1	3	0	0	0	1	2	2	0	0	4	0	0	.188	.350
2-team total (1 ACL D-backs Red)					.211	.000	.235	7	19	1	4	1	0	0	1	2	2	0	0	5	0	0	.263	.348
Asdrubal Martinez	R-R	5-11	170	1-4-02	.212	.143	.244	26	66	11	14	2	0	0	8	7	0	0	0	25	1	0	.242	.288
Gary Mattis	R-R	5-11	175	2-1-98	.262	.333	.250	17	42	9	11	1	1	1	4	8	1	1	0	13	9	0	.405	.392
Ivan Melendez	R-R	6-3	225	1-24-00	.000	--	.000	1	1	1	0	0	0	0	0	2	1	0	0	0	0	0	.000	.750
2-team total (3 ACL D-backs Red)					.200	.250	.167	4	10	2	2	0	0	0	0	3	1	0	0	5	0	0	.200	.429
Angel Ortiz	L-L	6-0	180	10-3-02	.247	.179	.268	50	166	25	41	9	3	2	28	13	0	0	0	35	4	3	.373	.302
Ronny Polanco	R-R	5-11	180	8-23-03	.241	.250	.239	52	174	24	42	9	2	3	17	12	1	0	0	56	1	3	.368	.294
Jacen Roberson	L-L	6-1	192	5-23-00	.083	.000	.143	6	12	1	1	0	0	0	0	5	1	0	0	7	0	0	.083	.389
2-team total (1 ACL D-backs Red)					.133	.000	.200	7	15	3	2	0	1	0	0	5	2	0	0	8	1	0	.267	.409
Adrian Rodriguez	R-R	6-0	170	10-21-03	.205	.200	.206	14	39	7	8	0	2	0	2	6	0	0	0	14	3	1	.308	.311
Fox Semones	R-R	6-0	175	12-3-97	.333	.000	.375	3	9	0	3	1	0	0	2	0	0	0	0	5	1	0	.444	.333
2-team total (5 ACL D-backs Red)					.250	.000	.286	8	24	1	6	1	0	1	6	1	0	0	0	13	1	0	.417	.280
Luis Suero	R-R	6-2	165	5-25-03	.156	.250	.125	11	32	2	5	1	0	0	1	4	0	0	0	15	3	0	.188	.250
Cole Tucker	B-R	6-3	200	7-3-96	.167	--	.167	4	12	2	2	0	0	0	0	1	0	0	0	3	1	0	.167	.231
Jarrod Watkins	L-R	6-1	180	4-25-97	.239	.267	.232	25	71	8	17	3	1	0	3	9	1	0	0	12	1	0	.310	.333

Pitching	B-T	HT	WT	DOB	W	L	ERA	G	GS	CG	SV	IP	H	R	ER	HR	BB	SO	AVG	vLH	vRH	K/9	BB/9
Enmanuel Acosta	R-R	6-2	200	6-6-99	0	0	9.00	1	0	0	0	1	2	1	1	1	0	3	.400	--	.400	27.00	0.00
2-team total (6 ACL D-backs Red					0	0	3.00	7	0	0	1	6	9	4	2	1	4	9	.333	.167	.381	13.50	6.00
Darlin Almonte	L-L	5-7	150	12-16-02	2	1	6.75	11	0	0	0	12	9	11	9	0	12	13	.209	.182	.219	9.75	9.00
Lisandro Almonte	R-R	6-1	170	6-11-02	0	1	4.18	10	5	0	0	28	29	17	13	3	11	35	.261	.275	.254	11.25	3.54
Axel Andueza	R-R	6-0	163	10-27-98	0	0	59.40	2	0	0	0	2	8	11	11	2	2	3	.615	1.000	.500	16.20	10.80
2-team total (9 ACL D-backs Red)					0	1	16.88	11	0	0	0	11	25	20	20	2	4	10	.463	.471	.459	8.44	3.38
Juan Aparicio	R-R	6-0	165	9-25-02	0	0	0.00	1	0	0	0	0	2	0	0	0	0	1	.667	.500	1.000	27.00	0.00
Zach Barnes	R-R	6-0	180	4-10-99	1	0	0.00	2	0	0	0	3	1	0	0	0	2	5	.100	.250	.000	15.00	6.00
J.B. Bukauskas	R-R	6-0	208	10-11-96	0	0	0.00	1	1	0	0	1	0	0	0	0	0	1	.000	.000	--	9.00	0.00
2-team total (1 ACL D-backs Red)					0	0	0.00	2	1	0	0	2	1	0	0	0	0	3	.143	.000	.333	13.50	0.00

Jose Cabrera	R-R	6-3	190	5-30-02	3	3	3.19	7	7	1	0	37	30	15	13	6	7	33	.219	.179	.257	8.10	1.72
Abraham Calzadilla	R-R	6-1	170	12-12-01	2	0	2.25	9	0	0	0	12	7	9	3	0	11	15	.159	.200	.125	11.25	8.25
2-team total (4 ACL D-backs Red)					2	0	2.20	13	0	0	0	16	11	13	4	2	12	18	.175	.259	.111	9.92	6.61
Dylan Castaneda	R-R	6-2	190	7-16-01	0	4	4.76	4	4	0	0	17	18	11	9	1	7	13	.281	.281	.281	6.88	3.71
2-team total (5 ACL D-backs Red)					0	4	3.65	9	6	0	0	37	37	17	15	2	12	39	.262	.267	.259	9.49	2.92
Gustavo Del Pozo	R-R	6-5	190	12-17-99	1	1	11.05	15	0	0	0	15	25	21	18	3	14	15	.397	.375	.404	9.20	8.59
Luis Diaz	R-R	6-5	230	3-9-01	1	0	4.03	15	0	0	5	22	19	14	10	0	15	33	.241	.219	.255	13.30	6.04
Spencer Giesting	L-L	6-4	200	7-2-01	0	0	13.50	2	0	0	0	2	3	3	3	1	2	3	.333	.333	.333	13.50	9.00
Conor Grammes	R-R	6-1	200	7-13-97	0	0	0.00	1	0	0	0	1	1	0	0	0	0	3	.250	--	.250	27.00	0.00
2-team total (1 ACL D-backs Red)					0	1	16.20	2	0	0	0	2	5	3	3	1	1	4	.500	.667	.429	21.60	5.40
Landon Green	R-R	6-1	200	9-21-99	2	0	2.57	7	0	0	0	14	11	4	4	0	2	22	.208	.158	.235	14.14	1.29
Jean Herrera	R-R	6-0	178	11-14-00	0	0	0.00	2	0	0	1	3	5	0	0	0	0	5	.357	.167	.500	15.00	0.00
2-team total (5 ACL D-backs Red)					0	0	5.14	7	0	0	2	14	21	8	8	1	6	17	.362	.429	.300	10.93	3.86
Edgar Isea	R-R	6-3	185	8-20-02	2	4	6.35	11	8	0	0	34	36	27	24	3	27	47	.265	.304	.224	12.44	7.15
Ian Kennedy	R-R	6-0	210	12-19-84	0	0	27.00	1	1	0	0	1	5	3	3	0	0	2	.625	1.000	.400	18.00	0.00
Dallas Keuchel	L-L	6-2	205	1-1-88	0	1	2.57	1	1	1	0	7	5	3	2	0	1	13	.192	.000	.217	16.71	1.29
2-team total (1 ACL D-backs Red)					0	2	4.50	2	2	1	0	12	12	7	6	0	2	17	.250	.214	.265	12.75	1.50
Jesus Liranzo	R-R	6-2	225	3-7-95	0	0	0.00	1	0	0	0	1	0	0	0	0	1	2	.000		.000	18.00	9.00
Asdrubal Martinez	R-R	5-11	170	1-4-02	0	0	18.00	1	0	0	0	1	1	2	2	0	2	0	1.000	--	1.000	0.00	18.00
Justin Martinez	R-R	6-3	180	7-30-01	0	1	18.00	1	0	0	0	1	2	3	2	1	0	1	.400	.500	.333	9.00	0.00
2-team total (1 ACL D-backs Red)					0	1	9.00	2	0	0	0	2	2	3	2	1	1	2	.286	.250	.333	9.00	4.50
Kyle Mora	R-R	6-3	220	7-9-98	1	1	3.12	9	0	0	0	17	19	9	6	2	3	20	.279	.276	.282	10.38	1.56
2-team total (3 ACL D-backs Red)					1	1	2.22	12	0	0	0	24	23	10	6	2	4	32	.242	.237	.246	11.84	1.48
Osvaldo Morel	R-R	6-3	195	6-17-01	0	1	5.40	5	0	0	0	5	2	3	3	1	7	6	.118	.250	.000	10.80	12.60
Kenny Ogg	R-R	6-1	185	7-4-97	3	1	5.26	15	0	0	4	26	34	21	15	1	7	22	.327	.313	.339	7.71	2.45
Chad Patrick	R-R	6-1	205	8-14-98	2	0	0.00	3	0	0	0	5	3	1	0	0	2	7	.200	.333	.111	13.50	3.86
Yoscar Pimentel	R-R	6-2	160	11-3-01	0	0	4.91	5	2	0	0	7	8	4	4	0	0	10	.276	.167	.353	12.27	0.00
Sarlin Polanco	R-R	6-1	190	2-23-02	0	0	9.31	12	0	0	0	10	10	16	10	1	12	12	.256	.250	.261	11.17	11.17
2-team total (2 ACL D-backs Red)					0	0	10.32	14	0	0	0	11	10	19	13	1	18	14	.233	.235	.231	11.12	14.29
Hansel Rincon	R-R	6-1	160	8-23-02	0	5	7.61	10	6	0	0	37	55	36	31	3	5	27	.348	.400	.307	6.63	1.23
Arturo Roque	R-R	6-1	155	12-2-00	0	1	6.00	2	2	0	0	6	5	4	4	0	6	6	.238	.000	.313	9.00	9.00
2-team total (10 ACL D-backs Red)					3	2	2.78	12	3	0	1	32	27	14	10	2	16	40	.221	.231	.217	11.13	4.45
Avery Short	R-L	6-1	205	3-14-01	0	0	0.00	1	0	0	0	1	0	0	0	0	0	0	.000	.000	.000	0.00	0.00
Caleb Smith	R-L	6-0	207	7-28-91	0	1	3.00	1	1	0	0	3	2	1	1	0	1	3	.200	.250	.167	9.00	3.00
Tyler Stone	L-R	5-10	190	7-1-99	0	0	10.13	2	0	0	0	3	3	3	3	1	3	5	.273	.500	.143	16.88	10.13
2-team total (3 ACL D-backs Red)					0	0	16.88	5	0	0	0	5	10	11	10	1	7	7	.385	.500	.313	11.81	11.81
Luis Tejeda	R-R	6-3	170	2-14-01	0	0	0.00	2	0	0	0	3	3	0	0	0	1	4	.300	.667	.143	13.50	3.38
Brent Teller	R-R	6-2	195	9-21-96	0	2	5.40	3	2	0	0	12	13	8	7	3	2	15	.271	.143	.324	11.57	1.54
Armando Vasquez	L-L	5-11	160	5-4-01	2	3	4.45	9	7	0	0	30	32	18	15	1	16	30	.274	.419	.221	8.90	4.75
Jarrod Watkins	L-R	6-1	180	4-25-97	0	0	0.00	1	0	0	0	0	1	0	0	0	0	1	.333	--	.333	27.00	0.00
Ricardo Yan	R-R	6-4	180	11-14-02	1	1	3.75	9	8	0	0	24	17	13	10	1	12	31	.202	.250	.179	11.63	4.50

Fielding

C: Caldera 28, Cerda 8, Castillo 4, Horner 17, Martin 4. **1B:** Aparicio 7, Cabeza 7, Ciprian 10, Garcia 1, Ortiz 18, Polanco 1, Watkins 11. **2B:** Aparicio 3, Benitez 2, Coursey 1, Cuevas 1, Curpa 3, Polanco 46, Rodriguez 1, Tucker 2. **3B:** Aparicio 16, Benitez 3, Cabeza 18, Ciprian 4, Curpa 2, Garcia 1, Rodriguez 8, Tucker 1, Watkins 4. **SS:** Alexander 3, Benitez 15, Cuevas 2, Curpa 1, Fernandez 31, Rodriguez 3, Tucker 1. **OF:** Aparicio 1, Batista 1,Benua 23, Cabeza 3, Canzone 3, Castillo 2, Ciprian 11, Cuevas 12, Curpa 6, Estrada 6, Gonnella 14, Martinez 25, Mattis 14, Ortiz 28, Roberson 5, Semones 3, Suero 9, Watkins 7.

ACL D-BACKS RED — *ROOKIE*

ARIZONA COMPLEX LEAGUE

Batting	B-T	HT	WT	DOB	AVG	vLH	vRH	G	AB	R	H	2B	3B	HR	RBI	BB	HBP	SH	SF	SO	SB	CS	SLG	OBP
Franyel Baez	B-R	6-3	170	3-1-03	.143	.000	.174	40	112	6	16	0	1	1	9	12	1	0	0	64	2	0	.188	.232
Juan Batista	R-R	6-1	175	1-9-01	.130	.182	.114	20	46	5	6	2	1	0	4	5	1	0	1	23	2	0	.217	.226
2-team total (1 ACL D-backs Black)					.125	.182	.108	21	48	5	6	2	1	0	4	6	1	0	1	23	2	0	.208	.232
Johan Benitez	B-R	6-3	170	8-7-03	.261	.231	.265	32	111	19	29	3	1	0	8	14	3	0	2	42	4	1	.306	.354
2-team total (21 ACL D-backs Black)					.269	.200	.278	53	182	23	49	11	1	1	20	21	4	0	3	62	5	1	.357	.352
Diosfran Cabeza	B-R	5-10	155	5-13-03	.364	.000	.400	5	11	1	4	0	0	0	0	1	0	0	0	4	0	0	.364	.417
2-team total (39 ACL D-backs Black)					.281	.182	.314	44	135	18	38	5	2	0	21	23	1	0	2	26	4	1	.348	.385
Luis Caicuto	R-R	5-10	160	3-5-03	.352	.318	.362	30	91	11	32	4	1	1	8	10	3	2	0	13	2	2	.451	.433
Corbin Carroll	L-L	5-10	165	8-21-00	.500	--	.500	2	6	2	3	0	0	1	1	2	0	0	0	3	0	0	1.000	.625
Kenny Castillo	R-R	6-2	170	5-13-04	.255	.200	.264	42	141	16	36	6	1	2	16	10	1	1	1	39	5	0	.355	.307
Gavin Conticello	L-R	6-4	195	6-11-03	.246	.250	.245	37	126	17	31	7	2	2	19	15	2	0	3	47	3	1	.381	.329
Joshua Day	R-R	6-2	200	3-25-00	.000	.000	.000	2	4	0	0	0	0	0	0	1	0	0	0	0	0	0	.000	.200
Wilmer Difo	B-R	5-11	200	4-2-92	.250	--	.250	2	4	0	1	0	0	0	0	2	0	0	0	1	0	0	.250	.500
Deivi Estrada	B-R	5-10	155	1-17-01	.238	.375	.154	7	21	6	5	2	0	1	3	4	1	0	0	9	1	1	.476	.385
2-team total (6 ACL D-backs Black)					.293	.294	.292	13	41	8	12	3	1	1	6	6	1	0	0	16	2	1	.488	.396
Jose Fernandez	R-R	6-3	165	9-22-03	.239	.111	.286	19	67	7	16	5	0	0	4	5	4	0	0	24	1	0	.313	.329
2-team total (31 ACL D-backs Black)					.217	.156	.238	50	175	24	38	7	3	1	15	14	5	0	2	51	2	0	.309	.291
Juan Garcia	B-R	5-10	165	5-28-03	.161	.333	.143	12	31	4	5	2	1	0	1	2	1	0	0	13	1	1	.290	.235
2-team total (3 ACL D-backs Black)					.171	.333	.156	15	35	4	6	2	1	0	1	3	1	0	0	15	1	2	.286	.256
Jakob Goldfarb	L-R	6-2	210	6-23-96	.258	.429	.236	22	62	8	16	3	1	0	8	8	8	0	0	23	8	3	.339	.410
Kevin Graham	L-R	6-1	195	8-12-99	.000	.000	.000	2	4	0	0	0	0	0	0	0	0	0	0	2	0	0	.000	.000
Glenallen Hill Jr.	B-R	5-9	170	9-30-00	.200	.000	.250	1	5	0	1	0	0	0	0	0	0	0	0	1	0	0	.200	.200

Coleton Horner	R-R	6-0	165	7-8-97	.333	--	.333	4	6	0	2	0	0	0	1	1	0	0	0	2	0	0	.333	.429
2-team total (17 ACL D-backs Black)					.357	.300	.370	21	56	4	20	3	0	0	9	6	1	0	1	15	0	1	.411	.422
Brett Johnson	L-R	5-11	195	1-6-00	.182	.000	.500	4	11	1	2	1	1	0	2	2	0	0	0	4	0	0	.455	.308
Jordan Lawlar	R-R	6-2	190	7-17-02	.368	.000	.500	6	19	5	7	1	1	0	2	4	1	0	0	6	0	0	.526	.500
Gavin Logan	L-R	5-11	212	1-14-00	.286	.000	.375	8	21	3	6	2	0	0	1	4	0	0	0	6	0	0	.381	.400
David Martin	L-R	6-1	185	10-28-00	.333	--	.333	1	3	0	1	1	0	0	0	0	0	0	0	1	0	0	.667	.333
2-team total (6 ACL D-backs Black)					.211	.000	.235	7	19	1	4	1	0	0	1	2	2	0	0	5	0	0	.263	.348
Ivan Melendez	R-R	6-3	225	1-24-00	.222	.250	.200	3	9	1	2	0	0	0	0	1	0	0	0	5	0	0	.222	.300
2-team total (1 ACL D-backs Black)					.200	.250	.167	4	10	2	2	0	0	0	0	3	1	0	0	5	0	0	.200	.429
Jefferson Pena	R-R	5-8	160	1-13-04	.169	.056	.220	19	59	9	10	1	0	1	6	7	0	0	0	28	2	1	.237	.258
Manuel Pena	L-R	6-1	170	12-5-03	.284	.250	.290	32	116	25	33	3	3	4	28	10	0	0	2	30	4	1	.466	.336
Marco Pernalete	R-R	6-4	175	9-12-02	.216	.200	.218	33	97	17	21	6	0	1	14	6	2	0	0	36	1	1	.309	.276
Jacen Roberson	L-L	6-1	192	5-23-00	.333	--	.333	1	3	2	1	0	1	0	0	0	1	0	0	1	1	0	1.000	.500
2-team total (6 ACL D-backs Black)					.133	.000	.200	7	15	3	2	0	1	0	0	5	2	0	0	8	1	0	.267	.409
Anderdson Rojas	L-R	5-10	150	3-8-04	.179	.167	.185	12	39	1	7	2	0	0	3	2	1	0	0	9	3	0	.231	.238
Luis Rubio	R-R	5-10	155	1-10-02	.255	.235	.259	39	102	19	26	4	1	0	12	11	2	1	0	22	3	1	.314	.339
Danyer Sanabria	L-L	6-1	155	3-7-02	.373	.429	.355	25	83	11	31	5	2	1	14	6	0	0	0	16	1	0	.518	.416
Fox Semones	R-R	6-0	175	12-3-97	.200	.000	.231	5	15	1	3	0	0	1	4	1	0	0	0	8	0	0	.400	.250
2-team total (3 ACL D-backs Black)					.250	.000	.286	8	24	1	6	1	0	1	6	1	0	0	0	13	1	0	.417	.280
Daniel Torres	R-R	5-9	150	1-10-02	.311	.294	.314	33	103	17	32	7	0	0	16	10	4	0	1	27	4	3	.379	.390
Jean Walters	B-R	5-11	155	8-13-01	.242	.143	.269	12	33	3	8	1	0	0	1	2	0	1	0	11	3	0	.273	.286

Pitching	**B-T**	**HT**	**WT**	**DOB**	**W**	**L**	**ERA**	**G**	**GS**	**CG**	**SV**	**IP**	**H**	**R**	**ER**	**HR**	**BB**	**SO**	**AVG**	**vLH**	**vRH**	**K/9**	**BB/9**
Enmanuel Acosta	R-R	6-2	200	6-6-99	0	0	1.80	6	0	0	1	5	7	3	1	0	4	6	.318	.167	.375	10.80	7.20
2-team total (1 ACL D-backs Black)					0	0	3.00	7	0	0	1	6	9	4	2	1	4	9	.333	.167	.381	13.50	6.00
Axel Andueza	R-R	6-0	163	10-27-98	0	1	9.00	9	0	0	0	9	17	9	9	0	2	7	.415	.357	.444	7.00	2.00
2-team total (2 ACL D-backs Black)					0	1	16.88	11	0	0	0	11	25	20	20	2	4	10	.463	.471	.459	8.44	3.38
J.B. Bukauskas	R-R	6-0	208	10-11-96	0	0	0.00	1	0	0	0	1	1	0	0	0	0	2	.250	.000	.333	18.00	0.00
2-team total (1 ACL D-backs Black)					0	0	0.00	2	1	0	0	2	1	0	0	0	0	3	.143	.000	.333	13.50	0.00
Abraham Calzadilla	R-R	6-1	170	12-12-01	0	0	2.08	4	0	0	0	4	4	4	1	2	1	3	.211	.429	.083	6.23	2.08
2-team total (9 ACL D-backs Black)					2	0	2.20	13	0	0	0	16	11	13	4	2	12	18	.175	.259	.111	9.92	6.61
Dylan Castaneda	R-R	6-2	190	7-16-01	0	0	2.70	5	2	0	0	20	19	6	6	1	5	26	.247	.250	.245	11.70	2.25
2-team total (4 ACL D-backs Black)					0	4	3.65	9	6	0	0	37	37	17	15	2	12	39	.262	.267	.259	9.49	2.92
Junior Cerda	R-R	5-11	170	6-15-00	3	1	2.93	13	1	0	0	40	33	18	13	5	18	41	.228	.353	.160	9.23	4.05
Billy Corcoran	R-R	6-8	220	8-21-99	1	0	9.00	4	0	0	0	7	13	8	7	1	1	10	.406	.500	.313	12.86	1.29
Fredely De Dios	R-R	6-2	165	11-3-00	0	0	9.82	11	0	0	0	11	15	12	12	1	14	10	.349	.333	.360	8.18	11.45
Chris Devenski	R-R	6-3	211	11-13-90	0	0	0.00	3	3	0	0	3	1	0	0	0	0	3	.100	.000	.143	9.00	0.00
Lorenzo Encarnacion	R-R	5-11	175	11-9-01	2	2	6.04	11	7	0	0	48	54	37	32	5	18	61	.277	.314	.248	11.52	3.40
Jackson Goddard	R-R	6-3	220	12-12-96	0	0	0.00	1	0	0	0	1	0	0	0	0	0	1	.000	.000	.000	9.00	0.00
Conor Grammes	R-R	6-1	200	7-13-97	0	1	40.50	1	0	0	0	1	4	3	3	1	1	1	.667	.667	.667	13.50	13.50
2-team total (1 ACL D-backs Black)					0	1	16.20	2	0	0	0	2	5	3	3	1	1	4	.500	.667	.429	21.60	5.40
Gunnar Groen	R-R	6-6	220	7-1-97	2	3	5.63	12	0	0	0	24	21	17	15	2	13	34	.233	.208	.242	12.75	4.88
Jean Herrera	R-R	6-0	178	11-14-00	0	0	6.55	5	0	0	1	11	16	8	8	1	6	12	.364	.500	.227	9.82	4.91
2-team total (2 ACL D-backs Black)					0	0	5.14	7	0	0	2	14	21	8	8	1	6	17	.362	.429	.300	10.93	3.86
Jesus Jimenez	R-R	6-2	185	10-2-02	2	0	6.57	10	0	0	0	12	17	10	9	0	5	12	.321	.381	.281	8.76	3.65
Brock Jones	L-L	6-1	180	6-14-01	3	3	5.30	9	6	0	0	37	36	22	22	4	20	40	.257	.185	.274	9.64	4.82
Keone Kela	R-R	6-1	220	4-16-93	0	0	0.00	3	2	0	0	3	0	0	0	0	2	4	.000	.000	.000	12.00	6.00
Dallas Keuchel	L-L	6-2	205	1-1-88	0	1	7.20	1	1	0	0	5	7	4	4	0	1	4	.318	.273	.364	7.20	1.80
2-team total (1 ACL D-backs Black)					0	2	4.50	2	2	1	0	12	12	7	6	0	2	17	.250	.214	.265	12.75	1.50
Yu-Min Lin	L-L	5-11	160	7-12-03	0	2	2.35	7	7	0	0	23	9	10	6	0	6	41	.118	.154	.111	16.04	2.35
Justin Martinez	R-R	6-3	180	7-30-01	0	0	0.00	1	0	0	0	1	0	0	0	0	1	1	.000	.000	--	9.00	9.00
2-team total (1 ACL D-backs Black)					0	1	9.00	2	0	0	0	2	2	3	2	1	1	2	.286	.250	.333	9.00	4.50
Keynan Middleton	R-R	6-3	215	9-12-93	0	0	0.00	1	1	0	0	1	1	0	0	0	0	2	.250	1.000	.000	18.00	0.00
Kyle Mora	R-R	6-3	220	7-9-98	0	0	0.00	3	0	0	0	7	4	1	0	0	1	12	.148	.111	.167	15.43	1.29
2-team total (9 ACL D-backs Black)					1	1	2.22	12	0	0	0	24	23	10	6	2	4	32	.242	.237	.246	11.84	1.48
Alfred Morillo	R-R	6-3	190	11-14-01	0	0	0.00	2	0	0	1	2	0	0	0	0	1	3	.000	.000	.000	16.20	5.40
Gerald Ogando	R-R	6-2	180	7-28-00	0	0	0.00	2	0	0	0	3	2	1	0	0	0	0	.167	.000	.222	0.00	0.00
Sarlin Polanco	R-R	6-1	190	2-23-02	0	0	16.20	2	0	0	0	2	0	3	3	0	6	2	.000	.000	.000	10.80	32.40
2-team total (12 ACL D-backs Black)					0	0	10.32	14	0	0	0	11	10	19	13	1	18	14	.233	.235	.231	11.12	14.29
Austin Pope	R-R	6-3	210	10-26-98	0	0	0.00	1	0	0	0	1	0	0	0	0	1	1	.000	--	.000	13.50	13.50
Dylan Ray	R-R	6-3	230	5-9-01	0	0	0.00	2	2	0	0	2	0	0	0	0	1	3	.000	.000	.000	13.50	4.50
Arturo Roque	R-R	6-1	155	12-2-00	3	1	2.05	10	1	0	1	26	22	10	6	2	10	34	.218	.265	.194	11.62	3.42
2-team total (2 ACL D-backs Black)					3	2	2.78	12	3	0	1	32	27	14	10	2	16	40	.221	.231	.217	11.13	4.45
Luis Rubio	R-R	5-10	155	1-10-02	0	1	27.00	2	0	0	0	1	2	4	3	1	0	1	.400	.000	.667	9.00	0.00
Gemil Santa	R-R	5-11	160	11-26-02	1	5	11.19	10	7	0	0	23	30	30	29	1	28	31	.323	.375	.283	11.96	10.80
Eli Saul	L-R	6-5	215	8-16-01	0	1	3.00	3	0	0	0	3	3	1	1	0	4	3	.250	.400	.143	9.00	12.00
Jacob Steinmetz	R-R	6-5	220	7-19-03	0	7	7.88	11	7	0	0	24	28	22	21	1	20	27	.304	.263	.333	10.13	7.50
Tyler Stone	L-R	5-10	190	7-1-99	0	0	23.63	3	0	0	0	3	7	8	7	0	4	2	.467	.500	.444	6.75	13.50
2-team total (2 ACL D-backs Black)					0	0	16.88	5	0	0	0	5	10	11	10	1	7	7	.385	.500	.313	11.81	11.81
Collin Sullivan	R-R	6-1	211	9-19-97	0	1	3.60	4	0	0	0	5	6	2	2	0	2	4	.333	.286	.364	7.20	3.60
Alex Valdez	R-R	6-2	185	12-24-99	3	0	3.95	9	0	0	0	14	15	12	6	1	4	21	.273	.276	.269	13.83	2.63
Wyatt Wendell	R-R	6-5	215	2-11-00	0	4	3.38	7	7	0	0	16	15	8	6	0	5	13	.263	.176	.300	7.31	2.81

Fielding

C: Caicuto 20, Castillo 29, Garcia 1, Goldfarb 2, Horner 1, Logan 5, Martin 1. **1B:** Goldfarb 3, Melendez 3, Sanabria 23, Torres 26. **2B:** Benitez 7, Cabeza 3, Garcia 6, Hill Jr. 1, Pena 19, Rojas 8, Rubio 5, Semones 5, Torres 5. **3B:** Benitez 4, Conticello 33, Day 2, Garcia 2, Pena 2, Rojas 3, Walters 12. **SS:** Benitez

16, Difo 2, Fernandez 19, Garcia 2, Lawlar 6, Pena 10, Rojas 2, Torres 1. **OF:** Andueza 1, Baez 41, Batista 20, Cabeza 1, Carroll 1, Estrada 6, Goldfarb 19, Graham 2, Hill Jr. 1, Johnson 3, Pena 18, Pernalete 26, Roberson 1, Rubio 32, Sanabria 3.

DSL D-BACKS BLACK — ROOKIE

DOMINICAN SUMMER LEAGUE

Batting	B-T	HT	WT	DOB	AVG	vLH	vRH	G	AB	R	H	2B	3B	HR	RBI	BB	HBP	SH	SF	SO	SB	CS	SLG	OBP
Moises Alcala	B-R	5-9	155	2-10-03	.308	.667	.261	10	26	5	8	0	0	1	5	6	0	0	0	7	0	1	.423	.438
2-team total (25 DSL D-backs Red)					.303	.438	.277	35	99	18	30	5	0	4	12	13	2	0	0	24	2	2	.475	.395
Jose Alpuria	B-R	6-2	160	2-12-05	.175	.250	.149	48	137	23	24	3	2	1	13	19	9	0	0	52	6	3	.248	.315
Ronal Antigua	R-R	6-1	180	1-27-03	.177	.217	.154	29	62	10	11	4	0	0	10	18	3	0	2	27	4	0	.242	.376
2-team total (11 DSL D-backs Red)					.181	.207	.167	40	83	14	15	5	0	0	13	22	3	0	4	32	5	0	.241	.357
Juan Aparicio	R-R	6-0	165	9-25-02	.219	.333	.174	11	32	5	7	2	0	0	5	10	1	1	1	9	1	1	.281	.409
Gabriel Araujo	R-R	6-0	175	9-7-04	.300	.250	.318	12	30	6	9	1	1	0	3	5	3	0	1	4	0	2	.400	.436
2-team total (30 DSL D-backs Red)					.257	.300	.241	42	109	13	28	7	2	1	23	10	7	0	1	22	2	4	.385	.354
Alberto Barriga	R-R	5-9	155	11-15-04	.250	.229	.261	42	104	27	26	10	3	0	15	21	2	1	2	18	6	7	.404	.380
Riquelmin Cabral	B-R	5-10	165	5-12-03	.272	.288	.265	53	184	41	50	10	4	4	30	21	5	0	0	24	15	8	.435	.362
Albert Carpio	R-R	5-9	150	8-12-05	.239	.200	.255	28	71	14	17	3	0	0	10	16	4	1	1	13	9	3	.282	.402
2-team total (10 DSL D-backs Red)					.216	.182	.225	38	102	16	22	3	1	0	10	16	4	1	1	21	9	4	.265	.341
Anderson Colmenarez	B-R	5-8	145	1-12-04	.311	.059	.386	27	74	17	23	7	0	0	14	14	4	0	0	9	5	3	.405	.446
2-team total (11 DSL D-backs Red)					.278	.077	.352	38	97	17	27	7	0	0	16	17	4	0	0	15	5	3	.351	.407
Abdias De La Cruz	R-R	6-3	175	11-3-04	.179	.171	.181	47	151	28	27	5	1	2	23	31	1	0	1	54	5	5	.265	.321
Andy Encarnacion	R-R	6-1	160	1-18-05	.500	--	.500	1	4	2	2	1	0	0	2	1	0	0	0	1	1	0	.750	.600
2-team total (51 DSL D-backs Red)					.226	.200	.235	52	159	35	36	10	2	1	20	23	2	0	3	42	3	4	.333	.326
Diego Gonzalez	R-R	5-7	150	7-18-05	.138	.250	.120	17	29	3	4	0	0	0	3	10	0	0	1	10	0	0	.138	.350
2-team total (9 DSL D-backs Red)					.143	.222	.125	26	49	6	7	0	0	0	3	14	0	0	1	16	0	0	.143	.328
Jiter Heredia	R-R	5-11	170	1-29-03	.059	.200	.000	10	17	3	1	0	0	1	2	2	2	0	0	9	0	0	.235	.238
2-team total (14 DSL D-backs Red)					.091	.100	.087	24	33	3	3	0	0	1	3	4	2	0	0	16	1	0	.182	.231
Jakey Josepha	L-R	6-2	135	5-15-04	.368	.500	.344	12	38	5	14	1	0	1	9	8	0	1	1	4	5	1	.474	.468
2-team total (39 DSL D-backs Red)					.311	.400	.288	51	148	20	46	5	1	1	31	25	1	2	3	32	12	1	.378	.407
Jansel Luis	B-R	6-0	170	3-6-05	.462	.500	.444	4	13	2	6	1	0	0	4	0	1	0	1	2	1	0	.538	.467
2-team total (43 DSL D-backs Red)					.345	.378	.336	47	174	35	60	7	1	1	18	12	5	0	2	23	9	3	.414	.399
Modeifi Marte	R-R	6-1	200	7-31-02	.304	.286	.311	55	181	37	55	10	1	7	42	17	8	0	2	23	10	5	.486	.385
Omar Moya	R-R	5-10	165	5-6-05	.269	.250	.273	23	52	5	14	3	0	0	6	3	5	0	1	15	1	0	.327	.361
Jonathan Nava	R-R	5-11	165	9-15-03	.300	.500	.167	4	10	0	3	0	0	0	3	2	0	0	0	3	1	1	.300	.417
Yerald Nin	L-R	6-0	170	8-18-05	.000	--	.000	1	3	1	0	0	0	0	0	2	0	0	0	1	0	0	.000	.400
2-team total (47 DSL D-backs Red)					.230	.176	.244	48	165	31	38	6	1	3	18	22	2	0	1	41	13	4	.333	.326
Jefferson Pena	R-R	5-8	160	1-13-04	.291	.424	.229	29	103	22	30	8	2	0	10	17	4	0	0	26	5	4	.408	.411
Alejandro Rios	R-R	5-11	150	3-30-05	.161	.333	.120	12	31	4	5	2	0	0	4	1	1	0	0	8	0	0	.226	.212
2-team total (14 DSL D-backs Red)					.097	.154	.083	26	62	5	6	2	0	0	7	5	2	0	0	17	0	1	.129	.188
Carlos Sanchez	L-L	5-9	150	1-29-04	.130	.100	.139	20	46	4	6	1	0	0	3	4	0	0	0	11	2	1	.152	.200
2-team total (9 DSL D-backs Red)					.178	.188	.175	29	73	9	13	1	0	0	3	5	0	0	0	18	6	2	.192	.231
Kevin Santos	L-L	6-0	180	1-9-04	.260	.000	.291	40	96	18	25	4	3	2	21	19	1	0	2	35	3	0	.427	.381
Luis Suero	R-R	6-2	165	5-25-03	.235	.250	.231	5	17	5	4	1	0	0	0	2	0	0	0	10	2	0	.294	.316
Cristofer Torin	R-R	5-10	155	5-26-05	.333	.256	.358	50	159	45	53	12	2	0	26	37	4	0	2	20	21	6	.434	.465

Pitching	B-T	HT	WT	DOB	W	L	ERA	G	GS	CG	SV	IP	H	R	ER	HR	BB	SO	AVG	vLH	vRH	K/9	BB/9
Luis Aguilar	R-R	5-11	150	2-18-05	4	1	6.04	13	1	0	1	22	13	16	15	0	18	16	.181	.152	.205	6.45	7.25
2-team total (2 DSL D-backs Red)					4	1	5.47	15	1	0	1	26	16	17	16	0	18	22	.184	.190	.178	7.52	6.15
Jose Aguirre	R-R	6-1	170	10-11-03	0	0	9.00	1	0	0	0	2	1	2	2	1	2	3	.143	.200	.000	13.50	9.00
2-team total (12 DSL D-backs Red)					0	2	2.90	13	7	0	0	40	31	19	13	2	18	38	.218	.190	.241	8.48	4.02
Jonathan Almonte	R-R	6-0	175	8-9-00	0	0	1.50	4	0	0	1	6	5	1	1	0	1	7	.227	.125	.286	10.50	1.50
Eric Basabe	L-L	5-10	150	9-24-02	0	0	81.00	1	0	0	0	0	2	3	3	0	2	1	.667	1.000	.500	27.00	54.00
2-team total (8 DSL D-backs Red)					1	0	12.27	9	0	0	1	7	7	10	10	0	13	12	.250	.375	.200	14.73	15.95
Victor Basora	R-R	6-3	170	2-4-02	6	0	1.93	18	0	0	2	37	31	12	8	1	14	40	.225	.333	.161	9.64	3.38
Victor Brea	L-L	6-4	170	10-8-02	0	0	27.00	1	0	0	0	1	4	4	4	1	2	1	.500	1.000	.429	6.75	13.50
2-team total (9 DSL D-backs Red)					1	1	6.14	10	0	0	0	15	13	12	10	1	16	10	.236	.462	.167	6.14	9.82
Miguel Camacho	R-R	6-5	205	2-4-02	0	0	4.50	6	0	0	0	8	8	6	4	0	5	5	.276	.273	.278	5.63	5.63
2-team total (6 DSL D-backs Red)					0	0	6.46	12	0	0	0	15	16	13	11	0	7	11	.276	.200	.316	6.46	4.11
Jesus Camejo	R-R	6-0	180	2-20-01	1	2	4.96	16	1	0	3	16	13	10	9	2	13	13	.220	.316	.175	7.16	7.16
Rolando Casihis	L-L	6-1	170	9-2-01	2	0	6.75	9	0	0	0	15	12	15	11	0	16	15	.222	.100	.250	9.20	9.82
2-team total (8 DSL D-backs Red)					2	0	4.73	17	1	0	0	32	23	23	17	2	20	38	.198	.160	.209	10.58	5.57
Eric Dominguez	L-L	6-3	180	1-12-03	0	0	6.00	1	1	0	0	3	2	2	2	0	2	2	.182	.200	.167	6.00	6.00
2-team total (10 DSL D-backs Red)					4	2	2.97	11	7	0	0	39	23	15	13	1	25	29	.174	.179	.173	6.64	5.72
Rancel Duarte	R-R	6-2	195	11-30-02	0	1	13.50	1	0	0	0	3	5	4	4	1	0	3	.417	.500	.375	10.13	0.00
2-team total (15 DSL D-backs Red)					1	2	6.75	16	0	0	0	20	23	20	15	1	15	22	.288	.393	.231	9.90	6.75
Jiter Heredia	R-R	5-11	170	1-29-03	1	0	16.20	2	0	0	0	2	3	3	3	0	3	0	.429	.000	.500	0.00	16.20
2-team total (7 DSL D-backs Red)					2	3	7.27	9	0	0	1	9	9	9	7	1	13	4	.273	.111	.333	4.15	13.50
Cesar Jimenez	R-R	6-1	170	7-18-05	3	2	2.91	11	9	0	0	46	45	15	15	3	13	38	.263	.235	.289	7.38	2.53
Onias Jimenez	R-R	6-1	170	5-23-04	0	1	8.53	7	2	0	0	13	12	15	12	1	12	15	.261	.273	.250	10.66	8.53
2-team total (1 DSL D-backs Red)					0	1	7.90	8	2	0	0	14	14	15	12	1	12	15	.280	.308	.250	9.88	7.90
Jediah Kwidama	R-R	6-3	185	7-30-02	0	1	4.76	5	0	0	0	6	5	6	3	1	8	4	.217	.375	.133	6.35	12.71
Alexis Liebano	R-R	6-1	175	3-8-03	2	0	1.04	6	0	0	2	9	3	1	1	0	1	7	.111	.143	.077	7.27	1.04
Jose Linares	R-R	6-0	170	12-12-01	1	0	0.00	2	0	0	0	5	1	0	0	0	1	4	.063	.000	.111	7.20	1.80
2-team total (13 DSL D-backs Red)					4	2	1.23	15	0	0	0	29	13	8	4	0	9	40	.127	.171	.104	12.27	2.76

Moises Lira	R-R	6-1	160	10-18-04	1	1	2.92	11	11	0	0	37	30	14	12	3	19	22	.221	.241	.205	5.35	4.62
2-team total (1 DSL D-backs Red)					1	1	2.93	12	11	0	0	40	34	15	13	3	21	25	.228	.254	.209	5.63	4.73
Teofilo Mendez	R-R	5-11	170	10-8-01	5	1	1.71	21	0	0	4	26	21	9	5	1	10	22	.219	.231	.205	7.52	3.42
Amauri Otero	L-L	6-1	175	2-19-05	1	1	17.23	8	0	0	1	16	31	31	30	2	13	16	.443	.636	.407	9.19	7.47
2-team total (2 DSL D-backs Red)					1	1	13.72	10	0	0	1	20	32	32	31	3	15	19	.381	.583	.347	8.41	6.64
Adonys Perez	L-L	6-3	185	10-10-03	0	0	10.80	3	0	0	0	3	6	4	4	0	2	3	.375	.400	.364	8.10	5.40
Kelly Reyes	R-R	6-1	165	1-6-03	1	0	5.40	13	0	0	0	12	5	7	7	0	21	19	.132	.300	.071	14.66	16.20
Brayan Rodriguez	R-R	6-3	175	3-6-05	0	3	10.38	7	4	0	0	9	10	14	10	0	9	10	.323	.471	.143	10.38	9.35
Jandel Sanchez	L-L	6-4	185	6-20-02	1	0	5.91	8	0	0	1	11	11	7	7	0	10	12	.275	.111	.323	10.13	8.44
2-team total (1 DSL D-backs Red)					1	0	7.59	9	0	0	1	11	11	9	9	0	14	12	.275	.111	.323	10.13	11.81
Vince Sanchez	R-R	6-0	185	8-25-04	2	2	2.49	11	11	0	0	43	35	14	12	1	15	37	.235	.256	.211	7.68	3.12
Gemil Santa	R-R	5-11	160	11-26-02	0	0	2.84	2	2	0	0	6	7	2	2	0	3	5	.269	.250	.278	7.11	4.26
Geral Siri	R-R	5-10	170	5-17-02	0	1	6.75	2	0	0	0	3	1	2	2	0	2	5	.111	.000	.143	16.88	6.75
Brayan Suarez	R-R	6-0	175	4-30-04	0	0	9.00	4	1	0	0	5	7	7	5	0	5	6	.368	.400	.357	10.80	9.00
2-team total (8 DSL D-backs Red)					0	1	4.66	12	5	0	1	19	17	13	10	0	9	27	.258	.292	.238	12.57	4.19
Jesus Suarez	R-R	6-2	170	10-1-02	0	0	0.00	2	0	0	0	2	2	0	0	0	0	1	.333	1.000	.200	5.40	0.00
2-team total (18 DSL D-backs Red)					1	3	3.42	20	0	0	1	26	22	15	10	2	13	15	.237	.250	.228	5.13	4.44
Vitico Valdez	R-R	6-4	175	11-6-03	3	1	2.48	10	5	0	1	36	30	14	10	1	20	26	.227	.284	.155	6.44	4.95
Deyer Zapata	L-L	6-0	150	12-4-03	4	2	2.44	12	10	0	0	44	36	13	12	2	21	51	.229	.225	.231	10.35	4.26

Fielding

C: Alcala 9, Barriga 39, Moya 10, Nava 3, Rios 10. **1B:** Aparicio 4, Cabral 8, Josepha 5, Marte 44. **2B:** Aparicio 2, Barriga 2, Carpio 8, Colmenarez 15, Gonzalez 14, Luis 2, Torin 28. **3B:** Aparicio 2, Cabral 39, Carpio 4, Colmenarez 8, De La Cruz 7, Torin 2. **SS:** Aparicio 1, Carpio 13, De La Cruz 29, Nin 1, Torin 22. **OF:** Alpuria 48, Antigua 29, Araujo 13, Carpio 6, Encarnacion 1, Heredia 5, Josepha 8, Pena 29, Sanchez 20 Santos 36, Suero 6.

DSL D-BACKS RED — *ROOKIE*

DOMINICAN SUMMER LEAGUE

Batting	B-T	HT	WT	DOB	AVG	vLH	vRH	G	AB	R	H	2B	3B	HR	RBI	BB	HBP	SH	SF	SO	SB	CS	SLG	OBP
Moises Alcala	B-R	5-9	155	2-10-03	.301	.385	.283	25	73	13	22	5	0	3	7	7	2	0	0	17	2	1	.493	.378
2-team total (10 DSL D-backs Black)					.303	.438	.277	35	99	18	30	5	0	4	12	13	2	0	0	24	2	2	.475	.395
Ronal Antigua	R-R	6-1	180	1-27-03	.190	.167	.200	11	21	4	4	1	0	0	3	4	0	0	2	5	1	0	.238	.296
2-team total (29 DSL D-backs Black)					.181	.207	.167	40	83	14	15	5	0	0	13	22	3	0	4	32	5	0	.241	.357
Gabriel Araujo	R-R	6-0	175	9-7-04	.241	.318	.211	30	79	7	19	6	1	1	20	5	4	0	0	18	2	2	.380	.318
2-team total (12 DSL D-backs Black)					.257	.300	.241	42	109	13	28	7	2	1	23	10	7	0	1	22	2	4	.385	.354
Alexander Benua	R-R	6-2	185	10-19-03	.290	.294	.289	31	100	33	29	6	0	1	11	12	8	0	1	26	13	4	.380	.405
Albert Carpio	R-R	5-9	150	8-12-05	.161	.000	.172	10	31	2	5	0	1	0	0	0	0	0	0	8	0	1	.226	.161
2-team total (28 DSL D-backs Black)					.216	.182	.225	38	102	16	22	3	1	0	10	16	4	1	1	21	9	4	.265	.341
Anderson Colmenarez	B-R	5-8	145	1-12-04	.174	.111	.214	11	23	0	4	0	0	0	2	3	0	0	0	6	0	0	.174	.269
2-team total (27 DSL D-backs Black)					.278	.077	.352	38	97	17	27	7	0	0	16	17	4	0	0	15	5	3	.351	.407
Jose Colmenarez	R-R	6-1	170	9-4-04	.231	.042	.315	28	78	8	18	5	0	0	15	5	3	0	2	11	2	1	.295	.295
Eskoly De Jesus	L-L	6-2	185	9-7-03	.163	.120	.179	38	92	7	15	4	1	2	12	13	0	0	0	39	1	0	.293	.267
Lewin De La Cruz	B-R	5-10	160	8-7-03	.216	.000	.242	13	37	5	8	1	0	1	7	4	0	0	2	10	1	0	.324	.279
Adrian De Leon	R-R	5-7	180	2-9-04	.158	.000	.200	7	19	3	3	1	0	0	5	4	0	0	0	4	1	1	.211	.304
Andy Encarnacion	R-R	6-1	160	1-18-05	.219	.200	.226	51	155	33	34	9	2	1	18	22	2	0	3	41	2	4	.323	.319
2-team total (1 DSL D-backs Black)					.226	.200	.235	52	159	35	36	10	2	1	20	23	2	0	3	42	3	4	.333	.326
Juan Garcia	B-R	5-10	165	5-28-03	.154	.000	.222	4	13	2	2	0	0	0	0	5	1	0	0	2	2	0	.154	.421
Diego Gonzalez	R-R	5-7	150	7-18-05	.150	.200	.133	9	20	3	3	0	0	0	0	4	0	0	0	6	0	0	.150	.292
2-team total (17 DSL D-backs Black)					.143	.222	.125	26	49	6	7	0	0	0	3	14	0	0	1	16	0	0	.143	.328
Jakey Josepha	L-R	6-2	135	5-15-04	.291	.375	.267	39	110	15	32	4	1	0	22	17	1	1	2	28	7	0	.345	.385
2-team total (12 DSL D-backs Black)					.311	.400	.288	51	148	20	46	5	1	1	31	25	1	2	3	32	12	1	.378	.407
Jansel Luis	B-R	6-0	170	3-6-05	.335	.364	.328	43	161	33	54	6	1	1	14	12	4	0	1	21	8	3	.404	.393
2-team total (4 DSL D-backs Black)					.345	.378	.336	47	174	35	60	7	1	1	18	12	5	0	2	23	9	3	.414	.399
Yerald Nin	L-R	6-0	170	8-18-05	.235	.176	.250	47	162	30	38	6	1	3	18	20	2	0	1	40	13	4	.340	.324
2-team total (1 DSL D-backs Black)					.230	.176	.244	48	165	31	38	6	1	3	18	22	2	0	1	41	13	4	.333	.326
Alejandro Rios	R-R	5-11	150	3-30-05	.032	.000	.043	14	31	1	1	0	0	0	3	4	1	0	0	9	0	1	.032	.167
2-team total (12 DSL D-backs Black)					.097	.154	.083	26	62	5	6	2	0	0	7	5	2	0	0	17	0	1	.129	.188
Anderdson Rojas	L-R	5-10	150	3-8-04	.353	.238	.379	32	116	24	41	7	4	1	23	6	2	0	2	13	6	4	.509	.389
Daniel Salmeron	L-R	6-1	170	9-4-02	.114	.083	.130	12	35	1	4	1	0	0	0	0	0	0	0	8	1	0	.143	.114
Carlos Sanchez	L-L	5-9	150	1-29-04	.259	.333	.238	9	27	5	7	0	0	0	0	1	0	0	0	7	4	1	.259	.286
2-team total (20 DSL D-backs Black)					.178	.188	.175	29	73	9	13	1	0	0	3	5	0	0	0	18	6	2	.192	.231
Ruben Santana	R-R	6-0	190	2-16-05	.316	.448	.279	43	133	35	42	5	4	1	17	25	4	0	1	33	15	1	.436	.436
Robinson Vargas	R-R	5-11	160	6-7-03	.218	.138	.240	50	133	24	29	10	2	1	24	29	9	0	3	43	2	3	.346	.385
Bernardo Zabala	R-R	5-11	190	8-24-03	.139	.000	.179	14	36	4	5	0	0	1	2	2	0	0	0	12	1	0	.222	.184

Pitching	B-T	HT	WT	DOB	W	L	ERA	G	GS	CG	SV	IP	H	R	ER	HR	BB	SO	AVG	vLH	vRH	K/9	BB/9
Isidro Adon	R-R	6-1	225	7-30-01	0	1	13.50	5	0	0	0	2	1	3	3	0	9	2	.167	.500	.000	9.00	40.50
Luis Aguilar	R-R	5-11	150	2-18-05	0	0	2.25	2	0	0	0	4	3	1	1	0	0	6	.200	.333	.000	13.50	0.00
2-team total (13 DSL D-backs Black)					4	1	5.47	15	1	0	1	26	16	17	16	0	18	22	.184	.190	.178	7.52	6.15
Jose Aguirre	R-R	6-1	170	10-11-03	0	2	2.58	12	7	0	0	38	30	17	11	1	16	35	.222	.190	.247	8.22	3.76
2-team total (1 DSL D-backs Black)					0	2	2.90	13	7	0	0	40	31	19	13	2	18	38	.218	.190	.241	8.48	4.02
Jeffrey Amparo	R-R	6-3	175	9-24-04	0	0	13.50	2	2	0	0	1	1	2	2	0	4	1	.250	.000	.333	6.75	27.00
Eric Basabe	L-L	5-10	150	9-24-02	1	0	9.00	8	0	0	1	7	5	7	7	0	11	11	.200	.286	.167	14.14	14.14
2-team total (1 DSL D-backs Black)					1	0	12.27	9	0	0	1	7	7	10	10	0	13	12	.250	.375	.200	14.73	15.95
Victor Brea	L-L	6-4	170	10-8-02	1	1	4.05	9	0	0	0	13	9	8	6	0	14	9	.191	.417	.114	6.08	9.45
2-team total (1 DSL D-backs Black)					1	1	6.14	10	0	0	0	15	13	12	10	1	16	10	.236	.462	.167	6.14	9.82

Miguel Camacho	R-R	6-5	205	2-4-02	0	0	8.59	6	0	0	0	7	8	7	7	0	2	6	.276	.111	.350	7.36	2.45
2-team total (6 DSL D-backs Black)					0	0	6.46	12	0	0	0	15	16	13	11	0	7	11	.276	.200	.316	6.46	4.11
Rolando Casihis	L-L	6-1	170	9-2-01	0	0	3.06	8	1	0	0	18	11	8	6	2	4	23	.177	.200	.170	11.72	2.04
2-team total (9 DSL D-backs Black)					2	0	4.73	17	1	0	0	32	23	23	17	2	20	38	.198	.160	.209	10.58	5.57
Eric Dominguez	L-L	6-3	180	1-12-03	4	2	2.72	10	6	0	0	36	21	13	11	1	23	27	.174	.174	.173	6.69	5.70
2-team total (1 DSL D-backs Black)					4	2	2.97	11	7	0	0	39	23	15	13	1	25	29	.174	.179	.173	6.64	5.72
Rancel Duarte	R-R	6-2	195	11-30-02	1	1	5.71	15	0	0	0	17	18	16	11	0	15	19	.265	.375	.205	9.87	7.79
2-team total (1 DSL D-backs Black)					1	2	6.75	16	0	0	0	20	23	20	15	1	15	22	.288	.393	.231	9.90	6.75
Miguel Gonzalez	R-R	6-4	220	9-6-02	1	1	2.25	8	0	0	0	12	7	4	3	0	9	9	.179	.267	.125	6.75	6.75
Jiter Heredia	R-R	5-11	170	1-29-03	1	3	3.14	7	0	0	1	7	6	6	4	1	10	4	.231	.125	.278	5.14	12.86
2-team total (2 DSL D-backs Black)					2	3	7.27	9	0	0	1	9	9	9	7	1	13	4	.273	.111	.333	4.13	13.50
Axel Hernandez	R-R	6-2	150	5-14-05	0	4	13.50	5	2	0	0	7	13	12	10	1	9	6	.433	.500	.400	8.10	12.15
Jean Herrera	R-R	6-0	178	11-14-00	5	1	0.81	13	0	0	1	33	24	5	3	1	1	37	.200	.205	.198	9.99	0.27
Daniel Jean	L-L	6-1	185	3-24-03	2	0	9.00	16	0	0	1	25	29	31	25	1	22	24	.299	.235	.313	8.64	7.92
Onias Jimenez	R-R	6-1	170	5-23-04	0	0	0.00	1	0	0	0	1	2	0	0	0	0	0	.500	.500	--	0.00	0.00
2-team total (7 DSL D-backs Black)					0	1	7.90	8	2	0	0	14	14	15	12	1	12	15	.280	.308	.250	9.88	7.90
Jose Linares	R-R	6-0	170	12-12-01	3	2	1.48	13	0	0	0	24	12	8	4	0	8	36	.140	.214	.103	13.32	2.96
2-team total (2 DSL D-backs Black)					4	2	1.23	15	0	0	0	29	13	8	4	0	9	40	.127	.171	.104	12.27	2.76
Moises Lira	R-R	6-1	160	10-18-04	0	0	3.00	1	0	0	0	3	4	1	1	0	2	3	.308	.400	.250	9.00	6.00
2-team total (11 DSL D-backs Black)					1	1	2.93	12	11	0	0	40	34	15	13	3	21	25	.228	.254	.209	5.63	4.73
Yan Mago	R-R	6-0	160	11-17-03	0	1	7.90	12	6	0	0	27	21	24	24	3	35	28	.226	.135	.286	9.22	11.52
Carlos Nunez	R-R	6-3	190	1-29-03	0	1	10.57	7	5	0	0	8	3	10	9	0	27	10	.136	.167	.100	11.74	31.70
Amauri Otero	L-L	6-1	175	2-19-05	0	0	1.93	2	0	0	0	5	1	1	1	1	2	3	.071	.000	.077	5.79	3.86
2-team total (8 DSL D-backs Black)					1	1	13.72	10	0	0	1	20	32	32	31	3	15	19	.381	.583	.347	8.41	6.64
Nixon Parra	R-R	6-2	170	1-7-04	0	3	11.25	12	4	0	0	28	38	36	35	7	23	36	.317	.340	.300	11.57	7.39
Hamlet Peralta	R-R	6-7	210	7-26-02	0	0	20.25	3	0	0	0	3	4	6	6	0	5	4	.364	.250	.429	13.50	16.88
Gregori Ramirez	R-R	6-3	170	9-12-04	0	1	4.91	4	4	0	0	7	7	4	4	2	7	2	.280	.286	.278	2.45	8.59
Santiago Ramirez	R-R	6-2	190	8-30-04	0	2	2.73	10	10	0	0	30	26	21	9	0	16	28	.224	.214	.230	8.49	4.85
Jandel Sanchez	L-L	6-4	185	6-20-02	0	0	--	1	0	0	0	0	0	2	2	0	4	0	--	--	--	--	--
2-team total (8 DSL D-backs Black)					1	0	7.59	9	0	0	1	11	11	9	9	0	14	12	.275	.111	.323	10.13	11.81
Maicor Serrano	R-R	6-2	180	2-3-04	3	3	6.52	12	3	0	0	29	32	24	21	3	26	21	.291	.289	.292	6.52	8.07
Brayan Suarez	R-R	6-0	175	4-30-04	0	1	3.14	8	4	0	1	14	10	6	5	0	4	21	.213	.263	.179	13.19	2.51
2-team total (4 DSL D-backs Black)					0	1	4.66	12	5	0	1	19	17	13	10	0	9	27	.258	.292	.238	12.57	4.19
Jesus Suarez	R-R	6-2	170	10-1-02	1	3	3.65	18	0	0	1	25	20	15	10	2	13	14	.230	.229	.231	5.11	4.74
2-team total (2 DSL D-backs Black)					1	3	3.42	20	0	0	1	26	22	15	10	2	13	15	.237	.250	.228	5.13	4.44
Armando Vasquez	L-L	5-11	160	5-4-01	0	0	0.00	2	2	0	0	7	3	0	0	0	3	5	.136	.000	.176	6.75	4.05
Juan Veloz	R-R	6-0	155	10-21-04	0	2	18.00	2	2	0	0	2	4	4	4	1	3	2	.444	.333	.667	9.00	13.50

Fielding

C: Alcala 20, Colmenarez 17, Rios 14, Salmeron 10, Zabala 7. **1B:** Colmenarez 8, Josepha 23, Rojas 1, Vargas 29, Zabala 4. **2B:** Carpio 3, Colmenarez 4, De La Cruz 6, Garcia 1, Gonzalez 8, Luis 24, Nin 13, Rojas 4, Zabala 1. **3B:** Carpio 1, Colmenarez 5, De La Cruz 4, Rojas 8, Santana 38, Vargas 6. **SS:** Carpio 4, Colmenarez 1, Garcia 3, Gonzalez 1, Luis 15, Nin 33, Rojas 3. **OF:** Antigua 9, Araujo 29, Benua 30, Carpio 1, De Jesus 26, Encarnacion 51, Heredia 6, Josepha 12, Rojas 15, Sanchez 10, Vargas 6.

Atlanta Braves

SEASON IN A SENTENCE: Defending a World Series championship was the ultimate goal for the 2022 Braves. While the team fell short of that after an NLDS loss to the Phillies in four games, Atlanta did win the NL East for the fifth consecutive year and won 100 games (101-61) for the first time since 2003.

HIGH POINT: The Braves entered their penultimate series against the division-rival Mets in second place and needed to win the series to preserve a chance at re-claiming the division title. Atlanta proceeded to sweep New York and clinched the division two games later with a 2-1 win over the Marlins—after being 10.5 games out on June 1.

LOW POINT: The entirety of April was the worst stretch of the season for the Braves. The team went 10-12 (.455 W%), split a four-game series with the Reds and Padres and lost three-game sets to the Nationals, Dodgers and Marlins.

NOTABLE ROOKIES: The Braves had two legitimate contenders for NL Rookie of the Year, with OF Michael Harris and RHP Spencer Strider. The duo finished 1-2 in the award voting. Harris provided Gold Glove-caliber defense in center field while narrowly missing a 20-20 season and amassed 4.8 fWAR in just 114 games. Strider used a lethal fastball/slider combination to strike out 38.3% of batters faced—the highest rate in baseball among pitchers with 100-plus innings.

KEY TRANSACTIONS: 1B Matt Olson didn't completely fill the Freddie Freeman void at first base, but he was 20% better than league average as a hitter and a source for big power (34 HR) and RBIs (103) in the middle of the lineup. Atlanta sent catcher Shea Langeliers, outfielder Cristian Pache and righthanders Ryan Cusick and Joey Estes to Oakland for Olson in March, and immediately extended him to an eight-year, $168 million extension. The Braves continued locking down their young player core by extending Harris to an eight-year, $72 million extension, Strider to a six-year, $75 million extension and 3B Austin Riley to a 10 year, $212 million extension—the biggest in franchise history.

ON THE FARM: Atlanta's farm is as bad as it's been in years and one of the worst in baseball, but that's largely a product of graduating top talents (Harris, Strider) and trading others (Langeliers, Pache) for established stars. The reinforcements are finally slowing, but there's still some big league ready pitching depth in the upper minors.

OPENING DAY PAYROLL: $184,630,000 (8th).

PLAYERS OF THE YEAR

MAJOR LEAGUE

Austin Riley
3B
.273/.349/.528
38 HR, 39 2B, 93 RBIs
325 TB led NL

MINOR LEAGUE

Vaughn Grissom
SS
(HiA/AA)
.324/.405/.494
14 HR, 27 SB in 96 G

ORGANIZATION LEADERS

Batting		***Minimum 250 AB**
MAJORS		
*AVG	Michael Harris	.297
*OPS	Austin Riley	.878
HR	Austin Riley	38
RBI	Matt Olson	103
MINORS		
*AVG	Vaughn Grissom, Mississippi, Rome	.324
*OBP	Justyn-Henry Malloy, Rome, Mississippi, Gwinnett	.408
*SLG	Vaughn Grissom, Mississippi, Rome	.494
*OPS	Vaughn Grissom, Mississippi, Rome	.899
R	Cal Conley, Augusta, Rome	94
H	Cody Milligan, Mississippi, Rome	143
TB	Justyn-Henry Malloy, Rome, Mississippi, Gwinnett	217
2B	Justyn-Henry Malloy, Rome, Mississippi, Gwinnett	28
3B	Geraldo Quintero, Augusta, Rome	9
HR	Drew Lugbauer, Mississippi	28
RBI	Drew Lugbauer, Mississippi	82
BB	Justyn-Henry Malloy, Rome, Mississippi, Gwinnett	97
SO	Drew Lugbauer, Mississippi	212
SB	Cal Conley, Augusta, Rome	36

Pitching		**#Minimum 75 IP**
MAJORS		
W	Kyle Wright	21
#ERA	Max Fried	2.48
SO	Charlie Morton	205
SV	Kenley Jansen	41
MINORS		
W	Dylan Dodd, Rome, Mississippi, Gwinnett	12
W	Tanner Gordon, Mississippi, Rome	12
L	Jared Shuster, Mississippi, Gwinnett	10
#ERA	Andrew Hoffmann, Rome	2.36
G	Tyler Ferguson, Mississippi, Gwinnett	52
GS	Alan Rangel, Mississippi, Gwinnett	27
SV	Michael Tonkin, Gwinnett	16
IP	Dylan Dodd, Rome, Mississippi, Gwinnett	142
BB	Royber Salinas, Augusta, Rome	63
SO	Royber Salinas, Augusta, Rome	175
#AVG	Royber Salinas, Augusta, Rome	.187

2022 PERFORMANCE

General Manager: Alex Anthopoulos. **Farm Director:** Ben Sestanovich. **Scouting Director:** Dana Brown.

Class	Team	League	W	L	PCT	Finish	Manager
Majors	Atlanta Braves	National	101	61	.623	2nd (15)	Brian Snitker
Triple-A	Gwinnett Stripers	International	69	79	.466	15th (20)	Matt Tuiasosopo
Double-A	Mississippi Braves	Southern	62	74	.456	6th (8)	Bruce Crabbe
High-A	Rome Braves	South Atlantic	74	54	.578	3rd (12)	Kanekoa Texeira
Low-A	Augusta GreenJackets	Carolina	69	62	.527	4th (12)	Nestor Perez
Rookie	FCL Braves	Florida Complex	20	35	.364	13th (16)	Cody Gabella
Overall 2022 Minor League Record			330	328	.502	15th (30)	

ORGANIZATION STATISTICS

ATLANTA BRAVES

NATIONAL LEAGUE

Batting	B-T	HT	WT	DOB	AVG	vLH	vRH	G	AB	R	H	2B	3B	HR	RBI	BB	HBP	SH	SF	SO	SB	CS	SLG	OBP
Ronald Acuna Jr.	R-R	6-0	205	12-18-97	.266	.234	.275	119	467	71	124	24	0	15	50	53	10	0	3	126	29	11	.413	.351
Ehire Adrianza	B-R	6-1	198	8-21-89	.154	.333	.100	6	13	3	2	1	0	0	0	3	0	0	0	3	0	0	.231	.313
2-team total (31 Washington Nationals)					.175	.184	.169	37	97	8	17	3	0	0	7	11	1	0	1	25	1	0	.206	.264
Ozzie Albies	B-R	5-8	165	1-7-97	.247	.250	.245	64	247	36	61	16	0	8	35	16	2	0	4	47	3	5	.409	.294
Orlando Arcia	R-R	6-0	187	8-4-94	.244	.213	.257	68	209	25	51	9	0	9	30	21	2	0	2	51	0	0	.416	.316
Rylan Bannon	R-R	5-8	180	4-22-96	--	--	--	1	0	0	0	0	0	0	0	0	0	0	0	0	0	0	--	--
Robinson Cano	L-R	6-0	212	10-22-82	.154	--	.154	9	26	1	4	1	0	0	0	1	0	0	0	4	0	0	.192	.185
3-team total (12 New York Mets, 12 San Diego Padres)					.150	.222	.143	33	100	5	15	1	0	1	4	4	0	0	0	25	0	0	.190	.183
William Contreras	R-R	6-0	180	12-24-97	.278	.354	.247	97	334	51	93	14	1	20	45	39	1	0	2	104	2	0	.506	.354
Travis Demeritte	R-R	6-0	180	9-30-94	.213	.308	.175	26	89	9	19	2	0	3	6	6	0	0	1	32	0	0	.337	.260
Alex Dickerson	L-L	6-2	226	5-26-90	.121	--	.121	13	33	3	4	0	0	1	2	3	0	0	0	9	0	0	.212	.194
Adam Duvall	R-R	6-1	215	9-4-88	.213	.233	.206	86	287	39	61	16	1	12	36	21	5	0	2	101	0	2	.401	.276
Travis d'Arnaud	R-R	6-2	210	2-10-89	.268	.341	.246	107	396	61	106	25	1	18	60	19	11	0	0	90	0	0	.472	.319
Mike Ford	L-R	6-0	225	7-4-92	.000	--	.000	5	7	0	0	0	0	0	0	1	0	0	0	2	0	0	.000	.125
2-team total (1 San Francisco Giants)					.091	--	.091	6	11	0	1	0	0	0	2	1	0	0	0	2	0	0	.091	.167
Phil Gosselin	R-R	6-1	188	10-3-88	.261	.300	.231	12	23	4	6	0	0	0	0	1	0	0	0	6	0	0	.261	.292
Vaughn Grissom	R-R	6-3	210	1-5-01	.291	.333	.273	41	141	24	41	6	0	5	18	11	3	0	1	34	5	2	.440	.353
Robbie Grossman	B-L	6-0	209	9-16-89	.217	.244	.204	46	138	16	30	6	0	5	22	18	0	0	1	39	3	1	.370	.306
Michael Harris II	L-L	6-0	195	3-7-01	.297	.238	.323	114	414	75	123	27	3	19	64	21	5	1	0	107	20	2	.514	.339
Guillermo Heredia	R-L	5-10	195	1-31-91	.158	.162	.154	74	76	12	12	3	1	3	8	6	0	0	0	32	0	0	.342	.220
Matt Olson	L-R	6-5	225	3-29-94	.240	.235	.242	162	616	86	148	44	0	34	103	75	4	0	4	170	0	0	.477	.325
Marcell Ozuna	R-R	6-1	225	11-12-90	.226	.200	.236	124	470	56	106	19	0	23	56	31	2	0	4	122	2	1	.413	.274
Manny Pina	R-R	6-0	222	6-5-87	.143	.000	.200	5	14	1	2	0	0	0	2	1	1	0	1	1	0	0	.143	.235
Austin Riley	R-R	6-3	240	4-2-97	.273	.329	.255	159	615	90	168	39	2	38	93	57	17	0	4	168	2	0	.528	.349
Eddie Rosario	L-R	6-1	180	9-28-91	.212	.143	.221	80	250	27	53	12	1	5	24	17	0	0	3	68	3	0	.328	.259
Dansby Swanson	R-R	6-1	190	2-11-94	.277	.297	.270	162	640	99	177	32	1	25	96	49	3	0	4	182	18	7	.447	.329
Chadwick Tromp	R-R	5-8	221	3-21-95	.750	1.000	.000	1	4	0	3	2	0	0	3	0	0	0	0	0	0	0	1.250	.750

Pitching	B-T	HT	WT	DOB	W	L	ERA	G	GS	CG	SV	IP	H	R	ER	HR	BB	SO	AVG	vLH	vRH	K/9	BB/9
Ian Anderson	R-R	6-3	170	5-2-98	10	6	5.00	22	22	0	0	112	115	63	62	12	54	97	.264	.211	.313	7.82	4.35
Orlando Arcia	R-R	6-0	187	8-4-94	0	0	0.00	1	0	0	0	1	0	0	0	0	1	0	.000	.000	.000	0.00	9.00
Silvino Bracho	R-R	5-10	190	7-17-92	0	0	6.23	3	0	0	0	4	3	3	3	2	1	4	.188	.000	.273	8.31	2.08
Jesse Chavez	R-R	6-1	175	8-21-83	3	3	2.72	46	1	0	0	53	49	18	16	5	14	61	.244	.230	.254	10.36	2.38
2-team total (3 Chicago Cubs)					3	3	3.07	49	1	0	0	59	56	22	20	6	16	64	.251	.268	.238	9.82	2.45
Jesus Cruz	R-R	6-1	230	4-15-95	0	0	6.23	7	0	0	0	9	8	6	6	3	4	6	.235	.294	.176	6.23	4.15
Tucker Davidson	L-L	6-2	215	3-25-96	1	2	6.46	4	3	0	0	15	15	11	11	0	13	10	.254	.091	.292	5.87	7.63
Bryce Elder	R-R	6-2	220	5-19-99	2	4	3.17	10	9	1	0	54	44	19	19	4	23	47	.222	.231	.215	7.83	3.83
Mike Ford	L-R	6-0	225	7-4-92	0	0	18.00	1	0	0	0	1	1	2	2	1	1	0	.250	.333	.000	0.00	9.00
Max Fried	L-L	6-4	190	1-18-94	14	7	2.48	30	30	0	0	185	156	55	51	12	32	170	.225	.206	.231	8.26	1.55
Raisel Iglesias	R-R	6-2	190	1-4-90	0	0	0.34	28	0	0	1	26	17	2	1	0	5	30	.185	.175	.192	10.25	1.71
Jay Jackson	R-R	6-1	195	10-27-87	0	0	0.00	2	0	0	0	1	1	0	0	0	0	1	.200	.000	.333	6.75	0.00
Kenley Jansen	B-R	6-5	265	9-30-87	5	2	3.38	65	0	0	41	64	45	25	24	8	22	85	.192	.213	.175	11.95	3.09
Dylan Lee	L-L	6-3	214	8-1-94	5	1	2.13	46	0	0	0	51	40	16	12	5	10	59	.212	.158	.248	10.48	1.78
Tyler Matzek	L-L	6-3	230	10-19-90	4	2	3.50	42	0	0	1	44	26	21	17	3	29	36	.173	.212	.153	7.42	5.98
Collin McHugh	R-R	6-2	191	6-19-87	3	2	2.60	58	0	0	0	69	51	20	20	5	14	75	.203	.182	.220	9.74	1.82
A.J. Minter	L-L	6-0	215	9-2-93	5	4	2.06	75	0	0	5	70	49	21	16	5	15	94	.198	.132	.222	12.09	1.93
Charlie Morton	R-R	6-5	215	11-12-83	9	6	4.34	31	31	0	0	172	149	85	83	28	63	205	.233	.229	.236	10.73	3.30
Kyle Muller	R-L	6-7	250	10-7-97	1	1	8.03	3	3	0	0	12	13	11	11	2	8	12	.260	.000	.295	8.76	5.84
Sean Newcomb	L-L	6-5	255	6-12-93	0	0	7.20	3	0	0	0	5	7	4	4	1	4	4	.318	.182	.455	7.20	7.20
2-team total (17 Chicago Cubs)					2	1	8.78	20	1	0	0	28	33	28	27	8	19	28	.287	.311	.271	9.11	6.18
Jake Odorizzi	R-R	6-2	190	3-27-90	2	3	5.24	10	10	0	0	46	54	29	27	9	18	40	.290	.273	.310	7.77	3.50
Darren O'Day	R-R	6-4	220	10-22-82	2	2	4.15	28	0	0	0	22	19	12	10	3	10	26	.238	.167	.268	10.80	4.15
Will Smith	R-L	6-5	255	7-10-89	0	1	4.38	41	0	0	5	37	35	25	18	7	21	41	.240	.222	.250	9.97	5.11
Jackson Stephens	R-R	6-2	220	5-11-94	3	3	3.69	39	1	0	2	54	49	32	22	3	23	47	.238	.283	.202	7.88	3.86

Spencer Strider	R-R	6-0	195	10-28-98	11	5	2.67	31	20	0	0	132	86	42	39	7	45	202	.180	.202	.156	13.81	3.08
Freddy Tarnok	R-R	6-3	185	11-24-98	0	0	0.00	1	0	0	0	1	1	0	0	0	0	1	.333	.333	--	13.50	0.00
Tyler Thornburg	R-R	5-11	190	9-29-88	0	0	3.86	9	0	0	0	9	12	6	4	0	5	10	.293	.308	.286	9.64	4.82
William Woods	R-R	6-3	190	12-29-98	0	0	0.00	2	0	0	0	2	2	0	0	0	1	2	.286	.500	.200	9.00	4.50
Kyle Wright	R-R	6-4	215	10-2-95	21	5	3.19	30	30	0	0	180	156	67	64	19	53	174	.232	.234	.230	8.68	2.65
Kirby Yates	L-R	5-10	205	3-25-87	0	0	5.14	9	0	0	0	7	6	4	4	2	5	6	.222	.111	.278	7.71	6.43
Huascar Ynoa	R-R	6-2	220	5-28-98	0	2	13.50	2	2	0	0	7	11	10	10	2	6	8	.355	.313	.400	10.80	8.10
Danny Young	L-L	6-3	200	5-27-94	0	0	0.00	1	0	0	0	3	4	0	0	0	0	1	.333	.429	.200	3.38	0.00

Fielding

Catcher	PCT	G	PO	A	E	DP	PB
Contreras	.986	60	559	10	8	1	3
d'Arnaud	.998	99	956	23	2	2	3
Pina	1.000	5	50	2	0	0	1
Tromp	.857	1	6	0	1	0	0

First Base	PCT	G	PO	A	E	DP
Olson	.994	162	1209	101	8	104
Riley	.818	1	7	2	2	0

Second Base	PCT	G	PO	A	E	DP
Adrianza	1.000	4	4	10	0	2
Albies	.987	64	81	151	3	33
Arcia	.979	50	60	127	4	26
Bannon	.000	1	0	0	0	0
Cano	.968	8	11	19	1	5
Gosselin	.964	10	11	16	1	5
Grissom	.973	40	57	87	4	14

Third Base	PCT	G	PO	A	E	DP
Adrianza	1.000	1	1	2	0	0
Arcia	.875	4	2	5	1	0
Riley	.964	159	97	283	14	20

Shortstop	PCT	G	PO	A	E	DP
Adrianza	.000	1	0	0	0	0
Arcia	1.000	1	0	1	0	0
Grissom	1.000	2	3	4	0	2
Swanson	.986	161	193	391	8	77

Outfield	PCT	G	PO	A	E	DP
Acuna Jr.	.975	93	150	4	4	0
Arcia	1.000	6	8	0	0	0
Contreras	--	1	0	0	0	0
Demeritte	1.000	26	52	2	0	0
Dickerson	--	1	0	0	0	0
Duvall	.989	90	174	3	2	2
Gosselin	--	1	0	0	0	0
Grossman	.987	48	75	0	1	0
Harris II	.992	114	252	3	2	0
Heredia	.984	64	60	0	1	0
Ozuna	.988	52	78	1	1	0
Rosario	.952	69	99	1	5	0

GWINNETT STRIPERS — *TRIPLE-A*

INTERNATIONAL LEAGUE

Batting	B-T	HT	WT	DOB	AVG	vLH	vRH	G	AB	R	H	2B	3B	HR	RBI	BB	HBP	SH	SF	SO	SB	CS	SLG	OBP
Ronald Acuna Jr.	R-R	6-0	205	12-18-97	.368	.250	.400	6	19	4	7	1	0	0	1	6	0	0	0	6	3	0	.421	.520
Ehire Adrianza	B-R	6-1	198	8-21-89	.273	.000	.333	3	11	1	3	0	0	0	0	1	0	0	0	3	0	0	.273	.333
2-team total (5 Rochester Red Wings)					.286	.250	.300	8	28	4	8	1	0	1	4	2	1	1	0	7	1	0	.429	.355
Ozzie Albies	B-R	5-8	165	1-7-97	.333	.429	.300	7	27	4	9	0	1	1	6	0	0	0	0	6	0	0	.519	.333
Orlando Arcia	R-R	6-0	187	8-4-94	.231	.500	.111	4	13	4	3	1	0	0	0	3	0	0	0	6	0	0	.308	.375
Rylan Bannon	R-R	5-8	180	4-22-96	.328	.222	.367	21	67	12	22	4	0	2	19	14	2	0	2	13	4	0	.478	.447
2-team total (78 Norfolk Tides)					.249	.234	.254	99	342	57	85	18	1	13	77	59	7	0	3	100	10	1	.421	.367
Ryan Casteel	R-R	5-11	205	6-6-91	.217	.268	.195	69	235	41	51	9	1	17	47	26	3	0	0	69	0	0	.481	.303
Hendrik Clementina	R-R	6-0	250	6-17-97	.154	.263	.109	20	65	5	10	0	0	2	11	5	1	0	0	26	0	0	.246	.225
William Contreras	R-R	6-0	180	12-24-97	.292	.154	.343	13	48	2	14	3	0	0	8	3	0	0	0	10	0	0	.354	.333
Justin Dean	R-R	5-8	185	12-6-96	.204	.067	.256	19	54	3	11	2	0	0	5	3	1	0	1	15	5	1	.241	.254
Travis Demeritte	R-R	6-0	180	9-30-94	.207	.290	.183	38	140	14	29	11	2	2	13	17	0	0	1	54	6	0	.357	.291
Delino DeShields	R-R	5-9	190	8-16-92	.220	.248	.208	109	337	61	74	12	0	1	26	76	5	4	4	116	35	11	.264	.367
Alex Dickerson	L-L	6-2	226	5-26-90	.239	.235	.241	92	322	36	77	20	2	12	43	29	3	0	3	76	1	0	.425	.305
Joe Dunand	R-R	6-2	205	9-20-95	.205	.263	.176	70	229	28	47	12	1	4	15	27	4	0	0	78	4	1	.319	.300
2-team total (20 Jacksonville Jumbo Shrimp)					.214	.253	.196	90	295	43	63	18	1	6	24	37	6	0	1	105	6	1	.342	.313
Mike Ford	L-R	6-0	225	7-4-92	.238	.273	.226	14	42	2	10	6	0	0	3	11	0	0	0	7	0	0	.381	.396
Ryan Goins	L-R	5-10	180	2-13-88	.217	.214	.217	90	300	22	65	12	0	0	25	12	0	2	3	69	0	1	.257	.244
Yariel Gonzalez	B-R	6-1	190	6-1-94	.168	.125	.187	33	107	7	18	4	0	0	8	8	2	0	2	28	2	0	.206	.235
Phil Gosselin	R-R	6-1	188	10-3-88	.297	.315	.289	49	182	25	54	13	2	5	24	16	3	0	3	40	4	0	.473	.358
Greyson Jenista	L-R	6-4	210	12-7-96	.206	.196	.210	96	321	44	66	12	0	14	33	25	3	0	1	125	2	2	.374	.269
Justyn-Henry Malloy	R-R	6-3	212	2-19-00	.280	.333	.250	8	25	5	7	1	0	1	6	7	0	0	1	5	2	0	.440	.424
Jake Marisnick	R-R	6-4	220	3-30-91	.235	.278	.220	17	68	8	16	1	1	1	3	3	3	0	0	18	7	1	.324	.297
2-team total (7 Indianapolis Indians)					.240	.320	.211	24	96	10	23	3	1	1	3	5	4	0	0	31	7	1	.323	.305
Taylor Motter	R-R	6-1	195	9-18-89	.259	.362	.210	42	147	30	38	11	0	12	36	29	0	0	4	39	2	0	.578	.372
2-team total (39 Louisville Bats)					.254	.365	.206	81	279	42	71	15	0	20	54	48	0	0	6	73	2	0	.523	.357
John Nogowski	R-L	6-0	245	1-5-93	.234	.167	.261	40	124	14	29	5	0	2	14	18	3	0	3	29	6	1	.323	.338
2-team total (47 Rochester Red Wings)					.266	.227	.280	87	286	42	76	17	0	4	38	51	6	0	8	53	12	3	.367	.379
Arden Pabst	R-R	6-1	205	3-14-95	.000	.000	.000	1	3	0	0	0	0	0	0	0	0	0	0	2	0	0	.000	.000
Hernan Perez	R-R	6-1	213	3-26-91	.269	.300	.256	86	323	53	87	15	1	9	39	22	3	0	4	74	20	3	.406	.318
Kramer Robertson	R-R	5-10	166	9-20-94	.300	.429	.250	13	50	9	15	3	0	1	6	7	1	0	0	10	4	3	.420	.397
3-team total (81 Memphis Redbirds, 22 Syracuse Mets)					.239	.275	.222	116	410	81	98	16	1	11	47	84	20	0	0	103	30	8	.363	.393
Eddie Rosario	L-R	6-1	180	9-28-91	.273	.231	.300	8	33	4	9	2	0	0	5	4	0	0	0	11	0	0	.333	.351
Braden Shewmake	L-R	6-4	190	11-19-97	.259	.271	.254	76	278	37	72	14	2	7	25	23	2	0	4	57	9	0	.399	.316
Chadwick Tromp	R-R	5-8	221	3-21-95	.253	.324	.223	70	249	34	63	11	0	12	41	16	0	0	1	55	0	1	.442	.297
Preston Tucker	L-L	6-0	210	7-6-90	.267	.303	.255	75	270	37	72	16	0	9	47	30	6	0	5	49	1	0	.426	.347
Pat Valaika	R-R	6-0	200	9-9-92	.242	.298	.217	114	421	51	102	23	0	10	54	38	1	0	6	96	2	1	.368	.303
Drew Waters	B-R	6-2	185	12-30-98	.246	.355	.194	49	191	26	47	7	3	5	16	16	1	0	2	57	5	1	.393	.305
2-team total (31 Omaha Storm Chasers)					.265	.293	.252	80	313	55	83	12	5	12	33	36	2	0	2	98	18	1	.450	.343
Tyler White	R-R	5-11	238	10-29-90	.227	.290	.193	28	88	9	20	2	0	3	12	20	0	0	4	19	1	0	.352	.357
2-team total (75 Nashville Sounds)					.230	.244	.222	103	357	48	82	13	2	16	58	70	4	0	6	88	5	1	.412	.357

Pitching	B-T	HT	WT	DOB	W	L	ERA	G	GS	CG	SV	IP	H	R	ER	HR	BB	SO	AVG	vLH	vRH	K/9	BB/9
R.J. Alaniz	R-R	6-4	220	6-14-91	3	1	3.81	20	0	0	2	26	20	15	11	4	9	41	.208	.222	.196	14.19	3.12
Ian Anderson	R-R	6-3	170	5-2-98	1	2	5.40	4	4	0	0	22	25	14	13	2	10	23	.287	.139	.392	9.55	4.15
Brad Brach	R-R	6-6	215	4-12-86	3	1	4.88	21	0	0	3	24	27	13	13	3	10	26	.290	.286	.294	9.75	3.75

Silvino Bracho	R-R	5-10	190	7-17-92	2	1	2.08	20	4	0	0	26	21	6	6	2	6	34	.214	.256	.182	11.77	2.08
2-team total (18 Worcester Red Sox)					2	4	2.67	38	5	0	0	57	50	18	17	4	10	70	.234	.253	.220	10.99	1.57
Brandon Brennan	R-R	6-4	207	7-26-91	1	1	6.91	24	0	0	0	27	40	23	21	5	17	33	.333	.365	.309	10.87	5.60
Thomas Burrows	L-L	6-2	230	9-14-94	4	3	5.50	32	0	0	0	34	32	25	21	4	12	41	.239	.292	.188	10.75	3.15
Jesus Cruz	R-R	6-1	230	4-15-95	2	1	4.23	28	0	0	1	28	20	13	13	4	16	39	.192	.265	.127	12.69	5.20
Tucker Davidson	L-L	6-2	215	3-25-96	3	7	4.59	15	15	0	0	80	82	43	41	14	24	96	.259	.247	.265	10.76	2.69
Jasseel De La Cruz	R-R	6-1	195	6-26-97	0	2	8.03	7	4	0	0	12	20	14	11	1	7	11	.351	.346	.355	8.03	5.11
Dawson Dimon	R-R	6-1	185	5-17-99	0	0	0.00	1	0	0	0	1	0	0	0	0	0	0	.000	--	.000	0.00	0.00
Dylan Dodd	L-L	6-2	210	6-6-98	1	0	4.05	1	1	0	0	7	5	3	3	1	1	7	.200	.000	.227	9.45	1.35
Bryce Elder	R-R	6-2	220	5-19-99	6	5	4.46	18	17	0	0	105	93	55	52	14	32	97	.234	.269	.200	8.31	2.74
Seth Elledge	R-R	6-3	240	5-20-96	1	5	3.88	43	0	0	3	46	35	23	20	3	16	63	.211	.238	.194	12.24	3.11
Tyler Ferguson	R-R	6-4	225	10-5-93	0	5	6.63	20	0	0	0	19	20	16	14	0	25	20	.286	.333	.261	9.47	11.84
Jay Jackson	R-R	6-1	195	10-27-87	2	0	2.29	19	0	0	1	20	18	5	5	2	4	25	.240	.172	.283	11.44	1.83
Odalvi Javier	R-R	6-0	180	9-4-96	0	0	1.23	5	0	0	0	7	4	1	1	0	6	11	.160	.154	.167	13.50	7.36
Connor Johnstone	R-R	6-1	195	10-4-94	4	2	3.43	32	8	0	1	66	64	29	25	5	23	39	.254	.305	.218	5.35	3.15
Nolan Kingham	R-R	6-4	210	8-18-96	4	3	4.29	27	14	0	0	71	70	37	34	10	12	55	.255	.254	.255	6.94	1.51
Dylan Lee	L-L	6-3	214	8-1-94	1	1	2.30	14	0	0	2	16	14	5	4	2	2	23	.237	.258	.214	13.21	1.15
Tyler Matzek	L-L	6-3	230	10-19-90	0	0	0.00	2	0	0	0	2	0	0	0	0	0	5	.000	.000	.000	22.50	0.00
Kyle Muller	R-L	6-7	250	10-7-97	6	8	3.41	23	23	1	0	135	119	53	51	14	40	159	.240	.197	.266	10.63	2.67
Darren O'Day	R-R	6-4	220	10-22-82	0	0	2.57	7	0	0	0	7	3	2	2	2	4	8	.125	.167	.111	10.29	5.14
Roel Ramirez	R-R	6-0	235	5-26-95	1	1	4.91	21	0	0	1	22	26	12	12	1	9	29	.302	.219	.352	11.86	3.68
Alan Rangel	R-R	6-2	170	8-21-97	0	0	6.00	1	1	0	0	3	4	2	2	0	2	5	.308	.500	.143	15.00	6.00
Jared Shuster	L-L	6-3	210	8-3-98	1	3	4.25	10	9	0	0	49	43	26	23	10	16	39	.239	.271	.227	7.21	2.96
Brandyn Sittinger	R-R	6-1	200	6-6-94	1	3	6.26	23	0	0	0	27	35	19	19	6	13	29	.318	.455	.227	9.55	4.28
Mike Soroka	R-R	6-5	225	8-4-97	0	2	6.43	5	5	0	0	21	20	15	15	3	7	17	.253	.289	.220	7.29	3.00
Jackson Stephens	R-R	6-2	220	5-11-94	1	0	3.00	1	1	0	0	6	4	2	2	0	0	7	.190	.429	.071	10.50	0.00
Freddy Tarnok	R-R	6-3	185	11-24-98	2	1	3.68	10	8	0	0	44	38	18	18	7	17	49	.228	.221	.233	10.02	3.48
Michael Tonkin	R-R	6-7	220	11-19-89	5	2	3.17	47	0	0	16	48	38	20	17	3	15	73	.215	.198	.231	13.59	2.79
Touki Toussaint	R-R	6-3	215	6-20-96	2	2	6.26	13	8	0	0	42	42	30	29	7	25	53	.259	.321	.198	11.45	5.40
Nick Vincent	R-R	5-10	185	7-12-86	1	5	5.12	17	1	0	0	19	29	16	11	5	4	27	.345	.364	.333	12.57	1.86
2-team total (28 Toledo Mud Hens)					6	5	2.39	45	1	0	5	49	44	19	13	5	9	55	.239	.226	.250	10.10	1.65
Darius Vines	R-R	6-1	190	4-30-98	1	0	3.21	7	5	0	0	34	29	12	12	1	14	29	.228	.261	.190	7.75	3.74
Victor Vodnik	R-R	6-0	200	10-9-99	2	0	2.93	24	0	0	2	28	26	10	9	2	16	33	.252	.217	.281	10.73	5.20
Jacob Webb	R-R	6-2	210	8-15-93	2	3	5.34	28	0	0	3	30	24	19	18	4	6	35	.212	.222	.203	10.38	1.78
Allan Winans	R-R	6-2	165	8-10-95	0	1	6.00	4	3	0	0	15	14	10	10	2	6	16	.246	.276	.214	9.60	3.60
William Woods	R-R	6-3	190	12-29-98	1	1	5.19	18	0	0	0	17	13	14	10	3	9	16	.200	.300	.114	8.31	4.67
Kirby Yates	L-R	5-10	205	3-25-87	0	0	1.69	5	0	0	0	5	2	1	1	0	2	4	.111	.000	.167	6.75	3.38
Huascar Ynoa	R-R	6-2	220	5-28-98	5	6	5.68	18	17	0	0	78	73	51	49	14	35	87	.246	.268	.226	10.08	4.06
Danny Young	L-L	6-3	200	5-27-94	0	1	3.24	11	0	0	0	8	5	3	3	0	4	17	.172	.000	.385	18.36	4.32

Fielding

Catcher	PCT	G	PO	A	E	DP	PB
Casteel	.989	57	541	17	6	1	6
Clementina	.977	19	166	7	4	1	1
Contreras	1.000	8	80	1	0	1	2
Dimon	1.000	1	7	0	0	0	0
Tromp	.988	68	630	37	8	3	8

First Base	PCT	G	PO	A	E	DP
Casteel	1.000	2	8	1	0	1
Dunand	.989	11	84	7	1	9
Ford	.960	8	66	6	3	3
Gonzalez	1.000	8	69	3	0	5
Gosselin	.987	8	69	9	1	4
Jenista	.986	19	133	11	2	6
Motter	1.000	7	58	6	0	5
Nogowski	.993	39	268	27	2	29
Perez	.978	11	79	9	2	3
Valaika	1.000	20	147	10	0	14
White	1.000	22	146	16	0	13

Second Base	PCT	G	PO	A	E	DP
Albies	1.000	4	2	10	0	1
Bannon	.857	3	7	5	2	2
DeShields	1.000	1	1	0	0	0
Goins	.992	38	39	87	1	15
Gonzalez	1.000	8	11	10	0	2
Gosselin	.875	2	0	7	1	0
Motter	1.000	11	13	27	0	7
Perez	.964	27	40	67	4	18
Robertson	.968	8	11	19	1	2
Shewmake	.964	9	7	20	1	5
Valaika	.989	48	63	111	2	20

Third Base	PCT	G	PO	A	E	DP
Bannon	.909	16	9	31	4	3
Dunand	.981	55	36	116	3	14
Goins	1.000	1	1	4	0	1
Gonzalez	.943	16	6	27	2	4
Gosselin	.956	29	24	41	3	7
Motter	.929	6	5	8	1	2
Perez	.971	13	6	27	1	3
Robertson	.909	5	2	8	1	0
Valaika	.955	15	9	33	2	2

Shortstop	PCT	G	PO	A	E	DP
Adrianza	1.000	3	2	10	0	2
Arcia	.667	2	0	2	1	0
Goins	.980	53	62	130	4	21
Motter	1.000	1	1	1	0	1
Perez	.862	9	3	22	4	3
Shewmake	.967	65	67	171	8	24
Valaika	.949	23	21	54	4	8

Outfield	PCT	G	PO	A	E	DP
Acuna Jr.	1.000	4	3	0	0	0
Contreras	1.000	2	2	0	0	0
Dean	.972	19	30	5	1	3
Demeritte	1.000	31	66	2	0	0
DeShields	.994	107	179	1	1	0
Dickerson	.969	60	92	1	3	0
Gonzalez	1.000	2	2	0	0	0
Gosselin	1.000	8	4	0	0	0
Jenista	.991	76	101	4	1	0
Malloy	1.000	7	12	0	0	0
Marisnick	1.000	13	28	4	0	1
Motter	.900	11	15	3	2	0
Nogowski	1.000	1	1	0	0	0
Perez	.982	30	51	4	1	1
Rosario	.917	3	11	0	1	0
Tucker	1.000	49	59	3	0	1
Waters	.990	45	99	4	1	1

MISSISSIPPI BRAVES — *DOUBLE-A*

SOUTHERN LEAGUE

Batting	B-T	HT	WT	DOB	AVG	vLH	vRH	G	AB	R	H	2B	3B	HR	RBI	BB	HBP	SH	SF	SO	SB	CS	SLG	OBP
CJ Alexander	L-R	6-5	215	7-17-96	.258	.143	.293	68	271	41	70	11	0	15	43	14	1	0	3	63	13	2	.465	.294
Logan Brown	L-R	6-0	195	9-14-96	.198	.080	.217	54	182	20	36	4	1	1	22	15	1	0	2	47	0	0	.247	.260
Cade Bunnell	L-R	6-0	190	5-14-97	.301	.333	.293	43	146	24	44	11	2	8	32	31	0	0	1	58	0	1	.568	.421
Hendrik Clementina	R-R	6-0	250	6-17-97	.243	.233	.247	69	267	28	65	9	1	11	34	18	3	0	3	98	1	0	.408	.296
Jordan Cowan	L-R	6-0	160	4-13-95	.219	.174	.231	33	114	10	25	5	0	0	7	14	2	0	0	27	2	1	.263	.315

Justin Dean	R-R	5-8	185	12-6-96	.234	.205	.244	78	274	44	64	12	4	3	27	40	6	0	2	97	19	5	.339	.342
Riley Delgado	R-R	5-10	175	2-22-95	.272	.291	.267	109	371	51	101	13	1	2	30	31	8	0	2	57	3	1	.329	.340
Jesse Franklin V	L-L	6-1	215	12-1-98	.236	.455	.182	15	55	6	13	1	1	2	9	6	3	0	2	18	2	0	.400	.333
Yariel Gonzalez	B-R	6-1	190	6-1-94	.257	.229	.263	66	257	28	66	12	0	9	31	24	1	0	2	53	4	0	.409	.320
Vaughn Grissom	R-R	6-3	210	1-5-01	.363	.211	.403	22	91	10	33	3	1	3	12	4	3	0	0	14	7	1	.516	.408
Michael Harris II	L-L	6-0	195	3-7-01	.305	.190	.341	43	174	33	53	16	2	5	33	17	3	0	2	39	11	3	.506	.372
Trey Harris	R-R	5-11	220	1-15-96	.238	.259	.230	59	189	25	45	8	1	2	16	18	11	1	1	38	4	3	.323	.338
Tyler Krieger	B-R	6-2	190	1-16-94	.136	.400	.059	7	22	2	3	1	0	0	0	4	0	2	0	8	1	1	.182	.269
Drew Lugbauer	L-R	6-3	220	8-23-96	.213	.175	.226	128	474	71	101	25	0	28	82	75	6	0	0	212	0	0	.443	.328
Justyn-Henry Malloy	R-R	6-3	212	2-19-00	.268	.333	.250	54	190	35	51	11	0	6	31	43	2	0	3	60	0	0	.421	.403
Jalen Miller	R-R	6-0	190	12-19-96	.235	.213	.245	91	327	49	77	22	2	8	44	48	3	1	0	85	17	5	.388	.339
Cody Milligan	L-R	5-10	170	12-23-98	.271	.266	.273	68	273	37	74	10	1	1	21	32	2	0	6	58	14	0	.326	.345
Andrew Moritz	L-R	5-11	180	12-22-96	.285	.222	.301	84	302	47	86	16	1	2	34	35	2	0	3	69	6	1	.364	.360
Arden Pabst	R-R	6-1	205	3-14-95	.296	.167	.400	8	27	3	8	2	0	2	6	1	0	0	0	9	0	0	.593	.321
Jacob Pearson	L-R	6-1	185	6-1-98	.122	.200	.113	29	90	11	11	8	0	0	7	19	0	0	2	26	4	1	.211	.270
Jefrey Ramos	R-R	6-1	185	2-10-99	.172	.158	.176	27	87	9	15	2	0	1	5	8	4	1	0	20	0	1	.230	.273
Landon Stephens	R-R	6-2	204	3-15-98	.114	.080	.130	23	79	6	9	1	0	3	6	9	2	0	1	38	0	0	.241	.220
Javier Valdes	R-R	5-10	205	11-19-98	.231	.261	.218	23	78	13	18	3	1	2	11	17	3	0	0	21	1	0	.372	.388
Luke Waddell	L-R	5-9	180	7-13-98	.272	.276	.271	41	162	20	44	10	0	2	29	23	1	0	1	22	3	2	.370	.364

Pitching	B-T	HT	WT	DOB	W	L	ERA	G	GS	CG	SV	IP	H	R	ER	HR	BB	SO	AVG	vLH	vRH	K/9	BB/9
Troy Bacon	R-R	6-0	165	9-26-96	5	1	3.89	23	1	0	0	44	48	19	19	8	24	41	.271	.239	.292	8.39	4.91
Logan Brown	L-R	6-0	195	9-14-96	0	0	0.00	1	0	0	0	0	0	0	0	0	0	0	.000	.000	--	0.00	0.00
Jason Creasy	R-R	6-4	197	5-13-92	0	1	5.17	14	0	0	1	16	17	10	9	2	7	12	.283	.160	.371	6.89	4.02
Jasseel De La Cruz	R-R	6-1	195	6-26-97	1	0	6.75	7	0	0	0	8	10	7	6	0	2	5	.323	.313	.333	5.63	2.25
Hayden Deal	L-L	6-4	210	11-4-94	3	2	4.12	31	4	0	0	59	55	30	27	2	26	53	.248	.213	.268	8.08	3.97
Indigo Diaz	R-R	6-5	250	10-14-98	3	4	3.08	49	0	0	4	50	29	20	17	4	31	63	.167	.120	.202	11.42	5.62
Dylan Dodd	L-L	6-2	210	6-6-98	2	4	3.11	9	9	0	0	46	46	18	16	3	13	55	.258	.295	.239	10.68	2.53
Tyler Ferguson	R-R	6-4	225	10-5-93	3	1	3.69	32	0	0	3	32	24	16	13	1	15	44	.200	.173	.221	12.51	4.26
Tanner Gordon	L-R	6-5	215	10-26-97	9	6	5.31	21	21	1	0	98	106	62	58	16	37	97	.275	.263	.284	8.88	3.39
Jake Higginbotham	L-L	6-0	190	1-11-96	2	5	4.73	48	0	0	3	51	59	30	27	5	18	48	.291	.273	.299	8.42	3.16
Coleman Huntley	R-R	6-4	225	3-10-93	2	1	3.39	36	0	0	0	61	53	27	23	6	26	79	.232	.223	.241	11.66	3.84
Odalvi Javier	R-R	6-0	180	9-4-96	2	5	2.75	42	1	0	1	52	36	20	16	2	16	58	.190	.179	.198	9.97	2.75
Nolan Kingham	R-R	6-4	210	8-18-96	1	4	5.54	5	5	0	0	26	38	17	16	4	5	18	.349	.396	.304	6.23	1.73
Justin Maese	R-R	6-3	190	10-24-96	2	6	4.70	50	0	0	11	54	57	34	28	7	23	69	.268	.314	.225	11.57	3.86
Roddery Munoz	R-R	6-2	210	4-14-00	0	0	9.82	3	3	0	0	11	12	14	12	3	5	14	.261	.207	.353	11.45	4.09
A.J. Puckett	R-R	6-4	200	5-27-95	2	5	7.36	33	5	0	0	59	82	51	48	7	25	74	.331	.328	.333	11.35	3.84
Alan Rangel	R-R	6-2	170	8-21-97	5	8	5.26	26	26	0	0	115	122	74	67	15	50	139	.270	.316	.228	10.91	3.92
Trey Riley	L-R	6-3	205	4-21-98	1	1	8.10	7	0	0	0	7	9	6	6	1	9	5	.321	.214	.429	6.75	12.15
Lisandro Santos	L-L	6-1	227	7-24-98	2	1	5.89	17	0	0	0	18	17	14	12	3	11	21	.239	.233	.244	10.31	5.40
Jared Shuster	L-L	6-3	210	8-3-98	6	7	2.78	17	16	1	0	91	65	30	28	8	22	106	.198	.259	.167	10.52	2.18
Freddy Tarnok	R-R	6-3	185	11-24-98	2	2	4.31	15	15	0	0	63	54	32	30	8	27	75	.228	.292	.176	10.77	3.88
Darius Vines	R-R	6-1	190	4-30-98	7	4	3.95	20	20	0	0	107	100	53	47	16	30	127	.244	.220	.263	10.68	2.52
Victor Vodnik	R-R	6-0	200	10-9-99	0	0	0.00	7	0	0	1	7	4	0	0	0	3	14	.160	.273	.071	18.00	3.86
Kyle Wilcox	R-R	6-3	195	6-14-94	0	1	2.77	13	0	0	0	13	7	4	4	1	15	18	.163	.158	.167	12.46	10.38
Allan Winans	R-R	6-2	165	8-10-95	1	4	2.44	8	8	1	0	44	43	19	12	2	9	44	.247	.275	.223	8.93	1.83
William Woods	R-R	6-3	190	12-29-98	0	1	10.80	3	1	0	0	5	7	6	6	2	2	7	.318	.231	.444	12.60	3.60
Kirby Yates	L-R	5-10	205	3-25-87	0	0	0.00	2	1	0	0	2	2	0	0	0	0	4	.250	.400	.000	18.00	0.00
Justin Yeager	L-R	6-4	215	1-20-98	1	0	3.79	38	0	0	6	40	26	21	17	5	23	54	.181	.210	.159	12.05	5.13

Fielding

Catcher	PCT	G	PO	A	E	DP	PB
Brown	.990	51	489	28	5	2	8
Clementina	.989	65	693	33	8	2	1
Cowan	1.000	1	8	1	0	0	0
Pabst	.958	3	22	1	1	1	0
Valdes	.980	17	138	6	3	0	1

First Base	PCT	G	PO	A	E	DP
Alexander	1.000	3	17	3	0	2
Bunnell	1.000	3	24	3	0	3
Lugbauer	.987	124	840	58	12	69
Stephens	1.000	6	47	2	0	5

Second Base	PCT	G	PO	A	E	DP
Brown	1.000	1	3	0	0	0
Bunnell	1.000	6	11	17	0	2
Cowan	1.000	14	20	33	0	4
Delgado	1.000	27	32	48	0	8
Gonzalez	.958	16	33	35	3	10
Grissom	1.000	1	1	4	0	1
Krieger	.941	5	5	11	1	2
Miller	.966	30	58	55	4	11
Milligan	.982	28	41	66	2	19
Waddell	1.000	9	16	22	0	5

Third Base	PCT	G	PO	A	E	DP
Alexander	.929	62	35	110	11	12
Cowan	1.000	14	10	15	0	1
Delgado	.972	59	42	96	4	12
Gonzalez	1.000	4	2	7	0	0

Shortstop	PCT	G	PO	A	E	DP
Bunnell	.954	33	49	76	6	22
Cowan	1.000	4	4	17	0	3
Delgado	1.000	8	6	19	0	3
Gonzalez	.947	42	57	86	8	10
Grissom	.937	21	16	43	4	6
Waddell	.929	29	30	61	7	9

Outfield	PCT	G	PO	A	E	DP
Dean	.980	76	144	4	3	1
Franklin V	1.000	14	20	1	0	0
Harris II	.989	44	90	3	1	1
Harris	.988	45	78	3	1	0
Malloy	1.000	51	77	2	0	0
Miller	1.000	18	22	1	0	0
Milligan	.989	40	84	2	1	1
Moritz	.968	69	117	4	4	2
Pearson	1.000	25	38	1	0	1
Ramos	.914	20	31	1	3	0
Stephens	1.000	13	26	1	0	1

ROME BRAVES — *HIGH CLASS A*

SOUTH ATLANTIC LEAGUE

Batting	B-T	HT	WT	DOB	AVG	vLH	vRH	G	AB	R	H	2B	3B	HR	RBI	BB	HBP	SH	SF	SO	SB	CS	SLG	OBP
Cade Bunnell	L-R	6-0	190	5-14-97	.185	.196	.182	71	222	36	41	6	1	7	24	56	4	0	3	108	3	0	.315	.354

Drew Campbell	L-L	5-11	180	11-10-97	.271	.213	.282	97	369	51	100	10	4	7	50	37	3	1	3	88	15	7	.377	.340
Willie Carter	R-R	6-0	215	4-8-97	.221	.243	.215	52	172	25	38	4	0	7	28	16	6	0	4	66	5	2	.366	.303
Nick Clarno	R-R	6-0	205	6-25-98	.313	--	.313	5	16	2	5	3	0	0	2	3	0	0	0	3	0	0	.500	.421
Cal Conley	B-R	5-10	185	7-17-99	.260	.033	.306	44	177	32	46	10	1	6	25	19	2	0	1	50	13	1	.429	.337
Jordan Cowan	L-R	6-0	160	4-13-95	.077	.250	.000	4	13	1	1	0	0	0	3	2	1	0	0	2	1	0	.077	.250
Victor De Hoyos	R-R	5-9	170	2-23-98	.286	--	.286	2	7	2	2	0	0	0	1	1	0	0	0	2	0	0	.286	.375
Jose Dilone	L-R	6-0	165	10-9-00	.000	--	.000	2	3	1	0	0	0	0	0	2	0	0	0	3	0	0	.000	.400
Dawson Dimon	R-R	6-1	185	5-17-99	1.000	--	1.000	1	1	0	1	0	0	0	0	1	0	0	0	0	0	0	1.000	1.000
Caleb Durbin	R-R	5-8	175	2-22-00	.220	.227	.218	32	109	15	24	7	1	1	15	8	6	0	1	15	3	2	.330	.306
Rusber Estrada	R-R	6-0	215	6-5-95	.100	.000	.111	5	10	0	1	0	0	0	0	2	0	0	0	2	0	0	.100	.250
Vaughn Grissom	R-R	6-3	210	1-5-01	.312	.258	.326	74	298	62	93	17	1	11	55	32	14	0	0	40	20	4	.407	.401
Bryson Horne	L-R	6-3	220	3-6-99	.244	.246	.243	100	373	44	91	19	1	11	52	33	4	0	3	110	4	1	.389	.310
Brian Klein	L-R	5-11	190	6-1-98	.250	.500	.200	8	24	5	6	1	0	1	3	5	1	0	0	9	0	0	.417	.400
Justyn-Henry Malloy	R-R	6-3	212	2-19-00	.304	.417	.271	71	263	51	80	16	0	10	44	47	4	0	6	73	3	0	.479	.409
Brandol Mezquita	R-R	6-0	170	7-14-01	.193	.333	.176	17	57	2	11	0	1	0	5	6	1	0	2	23	0	1	.228	.273
Cody Milligan	L-R	5-10	170	12-23-98	.329	.222	.358	55	210	55	69	17	3	1	15	49	2	0	1	46	7	1	.452	.458
Andrew Moritz	L-R	5-11	180	12-22-96	.250	.500	.214	8	16	5	4	1	0	0	2	9	1	0	1	2	1	1	.313	.519
Kadon Morton	R-R	6-2	195	11-19-00	.188	.000	.231	5	16	1	3	0	0	1	4	1	0	0	0	6	0	0	.375	.235
Keshawn Ogans	R-R	5-9	180	8-26-01	.167	1.000	.130	7	24	3	4	1	0	0	1	3	0	0	1	7	0	0	.200	.250
Brandon Parker	R-R	6-1	205	5-27-99	.153	.000	.170	16	59	8	9	3	0	0	7	4	1	0	1	22	0	0	.203	.215
Jacob Pearson	L-R	6-1	185	6-1-98	.266	.302	.258	67	256	39	68	16	0	4	21	30	7	1	2	57	21	8	.375	.356
Beau Philip	R-R	6-0	200	10-23-98	.221	.162	.235	111	375	53	83	9	0	12	57	62	6	1	5	131	13	3	.341	.337
Geraldo Quintero	B-R	5-8	155	10-10-01	.238	.250	.236	22	80	12	19	4	0	2	12	10	4	0	1	22	8	3	.363	.347
Zade Richardson	R-R	6-1	200	5-10-00	.000	.000	.000	1	2	1	0	0	0	0	0	2	0	0	0	1	0	0	.000	.500
Christian Robinson	L-L	6-2	211	11-23-99	.261	.333	.245	67	234	34	61	14	1	4	33	29	3	0	1	78	7	2	.380	.348
Landon Stephens	R-R	6-2	204	3-15-98	.224	.171	.239	88	321	52	72	15	1	19	70	54	14	0	3	107	2	2	.455	.357
Tyler Tolve	L-R	6-1	200	7-16-00	.261	.191	.275	75	287	42	75	14	5	12	47	30	5	0	3	104	8	1	.470	.338
Javier Valdes	R-R	5-10	205	11-19-98	.263	.289	.257	54	186	32	49	7	0	11	34	21	13	0	1	33	0	0	.478	.376
Braulio Vasquez	R-R	6-0	210	4-13-99	.000	--	.000	3	7	1	0	0	0	0	0	0	0	0	0	5	0	0	.000	.000
Drew Waters	B-R	6-2	185	12-30-98	.364	.000	.444	3	11	5	4	1	0	1	2	1	0	0	0	3	0	0	.727	.417
Ethan Workinger	R-R	6-3	185	10-19-01	.167	--	.167	2	6	1	1	0	0	0	0	1	0	0	0	1	0	0	.167	.286
Adam Zebrowski	R-R	6-3	230	9-28-00	.114	.400	.067	11	35	2	4	0	0	1	3	3	0	0	1	11	0	0	.200	.179

Pitching	B-T	HT	WT	DOB	W	L	ERA	G	GS	CG	SV	IP	H	R	ER	HR	BB	SO	AVG	vLH	vRH	K/9	BB/9
R.J. Alaniz	R-R	6-4	220	6-14-91	0	0	0.00	1	0	0	0	1	0	0	0	0	0	2	.000	.000	--	18.00	0.00
Ronaldo Alesandro	R-R	6-0	170	5-7-98	1	0	4.50	4	0	0	0	6	6	4	3	1	3	7	.273	.182	.364	10.50	4.50
Alec Barger	R-R	6-2	201	3-24-98	3	1	4.38	38	0	0	5	49	51	26	24	5	22	69	.262	.231	.282	12.59	4.01
Marrick Crouse	R-R	6-3	200	5-2-97	0	0	36.00	2	0	0	0	2	3	8	8	1	5	6	.333	1.000	.250	27.00	22.50
Luis De Avila	L-L	5-9	215	5-29-01	6	8	3.49	24	24	1	0	126	115	57	49	11	45	129	.241	.262	.235	9.19	3.21
Isrrael De La Cruz	B-R	5-11	175	6-15-97	1	1	5.33	21	0	0	1	27	31	20	16	2	16	22	.277	.333	.247	7.33	5.33
Dylan Dodd	L-L	6-2	210	6-6-98	9	5	3.44	16	16	0	0	89	85	41	34	6	17	91	.245	.236	.248	9.20	1.72
Benjamin Dum	L-R	6-0	215	9-30-96	3	0	3.86	37	0	0	3	47	48	22	20	6	16	44	.264	.254	.270	8.49	3.09
R.J. Freure	R-R	6-1	210	7-6-97	2	0	4.50	22	0	0	0	26	17	13	13	3	20	30	.185	.294	.121	10.38	6.92
Tanner Gordon	L-R	6-5	215	10-26-97	3	1	1.64	4	4	0	0	22	18	5	4	1	0	36	.220	.303	.163	14.73	0.00
Andrew Hoffmann	R-R	6-5	210	2-2-00	7	2	2.36	15	15	0	0	80	63	23	21	9	21	90	.217	.227	.211	10.13	2.36
Grant Holmes	L-R	6-0	226	3-22-96	0	0	0.00	2	0	0	0	2	1	0	0	0	0	3	.143	.000	.167	13.50	0.00
Landon Leach	R-R	6-4	220	7-12-99	1	1	9.00	5	1	0	0	11	12	15	11	2	11	6	.279	.313	.259	4.91	9.00
Jake McSteen	R-L	6-0	215	3-12-96	5	1	4.90	37	3	0	3	61	67	37	33	10	13	72	.271	.143	.329	10.68	1.93
Ian Mejia	R-R	6-3	205	1-31-00	0	1	4.66	3	3	0	0	10	11	5	5	0	4	9	.282	.278	.286	8.38	3.72
Jose Montilla	R-R	6-1	235	6-4-98	3	1	2.35	12	2	0	0	23	19	8	6	1	5	18	.224	.233	.218	7.04	1.96
Roddery Munoz	R-R	6-2	210	4-14-00	8	4	4.03	19	19	1	0	89	85	48	40	9	37	105	.244	.257	.235	10.58	3.73
Rolddy Munoz	R-R	6-2	183	4-14-00	0	0	6.23	6	0	0	0	9	10	6	6	3	7	14	.278	.333	.250	14.54	7.27
J.J. Niekro	R-R	6-0	185	1-28-98	3	2	4.88	9	9	0	0	48	52	28	26	5	16	37	.281	.246	.298	6.94	3.00
Darren O_Day	R-R	6-4	220	10-22-82	1	0	0.00	1	0	0	0	1	0	0	0	0	0	1	.000	.000	.000	9.00	0.00
Miguel Pena	L-R	6-1	190	11-26-98	0	0	2.70	7	0	0	0	10	8	3	3	1	4	11	.216	.200	.227	9.90	3.60
Trey Riley	L-R	6-3	205	4-21-98	3	3	4.75	33	0	0	4	36	37	24	19	6	25	42	.257	.294	.237	10.50	6.25
Royber Salinas	R-R	6-3	205	4-10-01	5	7	4.11	20	20	0	0	85	63	47	39	6	51	123	.202	.234	.181	12.97	5.38
Lisandro Santos	L-L	6-1	227	7-24-98	2	4	3.40	20	4	0	2	48	37	21	18	4	25	81	.211	.255	.195	15.29	4.72
Davis Schwab	L-L	6-4	230	1-27-97	2	0	4.56	36	0	0	0	49	50	26	25	6	37	60	.265	.220	.281	10.95	6.75
Alex Segal	L-L	6-4	190	3-18-98	3	1	0.79	9	0	0	0	11	15	3	1	1	6	11	.326	.400	.306	8.74	4.76
Austin Smith	R-R	6-4	210	6-22-99	2	3	4.62	45	0	0	13	49	38	25	25	4	18	61	.209	.227	.198	11.28	3.33
Mike Soroka	R-R	6-5	225	8-4-97	0	0	0.00	1	1	0	0	4	1	0	0	0	0	8	.071	.000	.091	18.00	0.00
Dylan Spain	R-R	6-6	205	6-21-98	0	5	5.30	36	7	0	2	56	63	38	33	11	13	60	.276	.232	.308	9.64	2.09
Malcolm Van Buren	R-R	6-4	185	7-5-98	1	3	4.55	28	0	0	0	30	13	20	15	0	45	57	.127	.250	.071	17.29	13.65
Justin Yeager	L-R	6-4	215	1-20-98	0	0	0.75	11	0	0	3	12	3	3	1	1	9	27	.077	.118	.045	20.25	6.75

Fielding

Catcher	PCT	G	PO	A	E	DP	PB
Clarno	.971	3	32	2	1	0	1
Estrada	.970	4	31	1	1	0	0
Tolve	.993	68	653	46	5	3	8
Valdes	.991	50	515	33	5	1	8
Zebrowski	1.000	8	80	8	0	2	0

First Base	PCT	G	PO	A	E	DP
Bunnell	.992	34	239	10	2	16
Horne	.995	81	584	23	3	52
Philip	1.000	1	7	0	0	0
Stephens	1.000	15	104	5	0	13
Vasquez	1.000	1	9	0	0	2

Second Base	PCT	G	PO	A	E	DP
Bunnell	.988	18	30	50	1	10
Conley	.938	2	8	7	1	4
Cowan	1.000	1	1	0	0	0
Durbin	.991	24	48	63	1	19
Grissom	1.000	6	10	14	0	3
Klein	1.000	8	9	16	0	3
Milligan	.966	29	42	70	4	11
Ogans	.909	3	4	6	1	1
Philip	.971	30	35	64	3	12

Quintero	.935	11	9	20	2	4

Third Base	PCT	G	PO	A	E	DP
Bunnell	.929	9	1	12	1	1
Cowan	1.000	2	0	3	0	0
Dilone	1.000	1	2	1	0	0
Durbin	.900	5	2	7	1	0
Grissom	.950	6	4	15	1	0
Malloy	.864	51	28	80	17	4
Philip	.929	50	38	79	9	6
Quintero	.722	6	2	11	5	2

Shortstop	PCT	G	PO	A	E	DP
Bunnell	1.000	9	7	18	0	1
Conley	.948	42	46	99	8	17
Cowan	1.000	1	0	1	0	0
Durbin	1.000	1	1	7	0	3
Grissom	.963	55	79	128	8	30
Ogans	1.000	2	1	7	0	3
Philip	.958	21	25	43	3	11

Outfield	PCT	G	PO	A	E	DP
Bunnell	--	1	0	0	0	0
Campbell	.987	97	147	2	2	1
Carter	.960	33	47	1	2	0
Malloy	1.000	3	2	0	0	0
Mezquita	1.000	17	32	2	0	2
Milligan	.923	26	47	1	4	0
Moritz	1.000	8	12	0	0	0
Morton	.929	5	13	0	1	0
Parker	1.000	15	18	0	0	0
Pearson	.993	65	139	0	1	0
Robinson	.962	63	100	2	4	0
Stephens	.977	61	83	2	2	0
Tolve	1.000	1	1	0	0	0
Waters	1.000	2	2	0	0	0
Workinger	1.000	2	5	0	0	0

AUGUSTA GREENJACKETS — LOW CLASS A

CAROLINA LEAGUE

Batting	B-T	HT	WT	DOB	AVG	vLH	vRH	G	AB	R	H	2B	3B	HR	RBI	BB	HBP	SH	SF	SO	SB	CS	SLG	OBP
Ignacio Alvarez	R-R	6-0	190	4-11-03	.294	.250	.302	15	51	14	15	2	1	0	6	19	1	0	0	9	4	1	.373	.493
Mahki Backstrom	L-L	6-5	220	10-10-01	.205	.140	.218	79	263	48	54	15	5	10	48	56	5	0	0	124	8	5	.414	.355
Drake Baldwin	L-R	6-1	210	3-28-01	.247	.417	.217	21	81	13	20	3	0	0	6	18	2	0	0	22	1	0	.284	.396
Antonio Barranca	R-R	6-3	215	7-25-01	.125	.091	.133	18	56	6	7	2	0	1	7	12	5	0	0	26	0	0	.214	.329
Connor Blair	R-R	6-0	215	5-6-98	.200	.243	.187	50	160	34	32	6	0	7	25	34	5	0	1	60	3	1	.369	.355
Cal Conley	B-R	5-10	185	7-17-99	.246	.317	.228	75	309	62	76	10	6	10	40	25	5	4	6	59	23	7	.414	.307
Victor De Hoyos	R-R	5-9	170	2-23-98	.200	.294	.170	22	70	11	14	3	0	2	10	6	1	0	0	23	1	0	.329	.273
Caleb Durbin	R-R	5-8	175	2-22-00	.249	.259	.247	73	273	57	68	15	1	7	47	42	13	0	5	35	28	3	.388	.369
Rusber Estrada	R-R	6-0	215	6-5-95	.246	.294	.227	19	61	8	15	5	0	4	10	14	1	0	0	18	0	1	.525	.395
E.J. Exposito	R-R	6-0	190	5-4-01	.234	.286	.225	26	94	15	22	3	0	3	11	17	3	0	0	26	2	3	.362	.368
Francisco Floyd	R-R	6-1	167	5-25-02	.252	.034	.311	35	135	23	34	5	0	3	24	20	0	0	1	64	6	2	.356	.346
Justin Janas	L-R	6-3	205	9-18-00	.232	.111	.247	23	82	12	19	4	0	1	14	7	3	0	1	21	0	0	.317	.312
Andrew Keck	R-R	6-3	225	12-12-99	.267	.000	.286	4	15	1	4	0	0	0	2	1	0	0	0	1	1	0	.267	.313
Kevin Kilpatrick Jr.	R-R	6-0	186	11-25-00	.287	.385	.270	21	87	16	25	7	1	1	10	7	2	0	0	21	7	1	.425	.354
Brian Klein	L-R	5-11	190	6-1-98	.223	.148	.240	41	148	18	33	9	1	2	17	17	1	0	2	45	2	1	.338	.304
David McCabe	B-R	6-4	230	3-25-00	.260	.143	.279	26	100	14	26	6	0	1	23	15	0	0	3	27	0	2	.350	.347
Brandol Mezquita	R-R	6-0	170	7-14-01	.281	.257	.288	87	331	57	93	14	4	3	46	41	10	0	6	101	14	5	.375	.371
Kadon Morton	R-R	6-2	195	11-19-00	.227	.216	.230	107	352	57	80	11	4	12	47	56	6	0	2	139	12	5	.384	.341
Keshawn Ogans	R-R	5-9	180	8-26-01	.286	.214	.302	18	77	13	22	2	0	1	9	5	5	0	1	12	9	0	.351	.364
Harry Owen	R-R	6-3	225	3-7-02	.000	--	.000	2	7	0	0	0	0	0	0	1	1	0	0	1	0	0	.000	.222
Stephen Paolini	L-L	6-2	195	11-23-00	.218	.172	.226	111	394	60	86	18	3	7	47	64	5	0	5	128	18	9	.332	.331
Brandon Parker	R-R	6-1	205	5-27-99	.282	.245	.293	65	213	44	60	10	4	10	40	45	10	0	4	59	5	4	.507	.423
Geraldo Quintero	B-R	5-8	155	10-10-01	.262	.241	.269	91	362	61	95	22	9	6	47	48	7	0	2	69	26	8	.423	.358
Cesar Rodriguez	B-R	5-10	160	12-26-00	.000	.000	.000	1	2	1	0	0	0	0	0	2	0	0	0	0	0	0	.000	.500
Eliezel Stevens	L-R	6-0	185	10-8-00	.421	.385	.432	17	57	13	24	3	1	2	18	6	1	0	1	20	0	0	.614	.477
Braulio Vasquez	R-R	6-0	210	4-13-99	.263	.365	.233	65	228	36	60	16	3	2	25	30	4	2	1	49	26	5	.386	.357
Noah Williams	B-R	6-2	180	4-12-04	.353	.000	.375	5	17	2	6	2	0	0	2	2	1	0	0	2	1	2	.471	.450
Ethan Workinger	R-R	6-3	185	10-19-01	.270	.313	.255	17	63	10	17	4	2	2	15	6	0	0	1	20	1	0	.492	.329
Adam Zebrowski	R-R	6-3	230	9-28-00	.238	.205	.244	75	265	51	63	15	2	10	53	54	4	0	3	74	3	0	.423	.371

Pitching	B-T	HT	WT	DOB	W	L	ERA	G	GS	CG	SV	IP	H	R	ER	HR	BB	SO	AVG	vLH	vRH	K/9	BB/9
James Acuna	R-R	6-5	180	9-18-97	4	2	3.17	28	2	0	1	60	37	25	21	4	32	67	.179	.184	.174	10.11	4.83
Ronaldo Alesandro	R-R	6-0	170	5-7-98	0	3	4.25	18	0	0	2	30	17	17	14	1	18	42	.167	.184	.151	12.74	5.46
Kris Anglin	L-L	5-11	175	8-9-01	3	5	5.93	12	7	0	0	30	28	24	20	6	19	36	.231	.216	.238	10.68	5.64
Jorge Bautista	R-R	6-0	155	12-10-00	2	4	8.78	9	8	0	0	40	67	41	39	5	11	30	.383	.390	.378	6.75	2.48
Blake Burkhalter	R-R	6-0	204	9-19-00	1	0	0.00	2	1	0	0	4	1	0	0	0	0	7	.071	.200	.000	14.54	0.00
Cedric De Grandpre	R-R	6-2	210	1-25-02	0	1	12.71	3	2	0	0	6	8	9	8	0	4	8	.308	.357	.250	12.71	6.35
Isrrael De La Cruz	B-R	5-11	175	6-15-97	2	0	3.31	9	0	0	0	16	8	6	6	1	5	21	.140	.095	.167	11.57	2.76
Benjamin Dum	L-R	6-0	215	9-30-96	1	0	0.00	3	0	0	0	6	2	0	0	0	0	6	.105	.200	.071	9.53	0.00
Darling Florentino	R-R	6-0	210	5-25-01	2	1	6.35	22	0	0	1	34	41	28	24	3	20	32	.299	.350	.260	8.47	5.29
Rob Griswold	R-R	6-1	185	7-13-98	5	4	4.12	39	0	0	9	59	49	36	27	7	19	58	.216	.275	.168	8.85	2.90
Landon Harper	R-R	6-1	176	4-8-01	0	1	7.20	4	4	0	0	10	17	8	8	1	2	6	.362	.409	.320	5.40	1.80
Elison Joseph	R-R	6-0	170	1-24-01	3	2	3.32	14	0	0	0	19	15	9	7	0	20	24	.211	.161	.250	11.37	9.47
Landon Leach	R-R	6-4	220	7-12-99	1	3	3.61	11	11	0	0	42	40	23	17	3	17	42	.248	.167	.305	8.93	3.61
Juan Mateo	R-R	5-11	190	9-9-92	4	3	4.53	34	0	0	5	52	44	34	26	3	32	49	.228	.282	.185	8.54	5.57
Ian Mejia	R-R	6-3	205	1-31-00	0	0	3.00	2	2	0	0	6	4	3	2	1	1	4	.190	.100	.273	6.00	1.50
Jose Montilla	R-R	6-1	235	6-4-98	1	0	2.25	6	1	0	0	8	6	2	2	1	3	9	.194	.308	.111	10.13	3.38
Rolddy Munoz	R-R	6-2	183	4-14-00	1	3	5.84	26	2	0	1	49	61	39	32	5	17	65	.295	.320	.273	11.86	3.10
Owen Murphy	R-R	6-1	190	9-27-03	0	1	7.71	3	3	0	0	7	5	6	6	0	6	10	.192	.182	.200	12.86	7.71
J.J. Niekro	R-R	6-0	185	1-28-98	7	1	2.09	15	8	0	0	73	58	19	17	6	17	77	.217	.211	.222	9.45	2.09
Tyler Owens	R-R	5-10	185	1-9-01	5	3	5.20	32	4	0	5	62	67	39	36	6	28	67	.277	.243	.307	9.67	4.04
Miguel Pena	L-R	6-1	190	11-26-98	2	1	3.13	21	0	0	1	32	29	11	11	4	12	41	.246	.313	.200	11.65	3.41
Jordano Perez	R-R	6-0	162	9-2-00	4	2	3.72	10	10	0	0	46	41	20	19	3	11	40	.229	.171	.278	7.83	2.15
JR Ritchie	R-R	6-2	185	6-26-03	0	0	2.70	3	3	0	0	10	7	3	3	1	4	10	.212	.313	.118	9.00	3.60
Estarlin Rodriguez	R-R	6-0	180	10-24-99	2	2	6.40	31	0	0	3	65	67	47	46	13	38	62	.264	.299	.238	8.63	5.29
Rainiery Rodriguez	B-R	6-2	170	8-28-00	4	5	5.86	13	9	0	0	58	67	42	38	8	14	43	.286	.256	.316	6.63	2.16
Royber Salinas	R-R	6-3	205	4-10-01	0	1	1.52	5	5	0	0	24	10	6	4	1	12	52	.127	.118	.133	19.77	4.56
Alex Segal	L-L	6-4	190	3-18-98	0	0	2.16	7	0	0	0	8	6	3	2	0	4	13	.188	.125	.250	14.04	4.32

Adam Shoemaker	L-L	6-6	205	8-24-02	0	0	14.40	3	3	0	0	5	7	8	8	0	5	7	.333	.375	.308	12.60	9.00
William Silva	R-R	6-0	185	8-2-01	0	1	15.43	2	0	0	0	2	5	4	4	0	3	3	.500	.500	.500	11.57	11.57
AJ Smith-Shawver	R-R	6-3	205	11-20-02	3	4	5.11	17	17	0	0	69	54	43	39	4	39	103	.215	.220	.210	13.50	5.11
Samuel Strickland	R-L	6-2	218	3-26-99	5	2	3.41	14	11	0	0	61	63	30	23	3	20	60	.259	.271	.255	8.90	2.97
Ben Thompson	R-R	6-5	220	12-21-97	0	0	0.00	4	0	0	0	4	6	0	0	0	2	5	.353	.250	.444	11.25	4.50
Malcolm Van Buren	R-R	6-4	185	7-5-98	0	0	15.00	3	0	0	0	3	1	5	5	0	8	5	.100	.143	.000	15.00	24.00
Luis Vargas	R-R	5-11	196	5-2-02	4	4	3.75	22	17	0	0	96	86	48	40	10	42	106	.236	.213	.252	9.94	3.94
Peyton Williams	R-R	6-1	180	5-6-98	3	3	4.62	34	1	0	1	49	47	28	25	5	24	57	.250	.253	.247	10.54	4.44

Fielding

Catcher	PCT	G	PO	A	E	DP	PB
Baldwin	.987	16	139	11	2	1	3
Barranca	.977	14	121	7	3	0	3
De Hoyos	.981	19	147	5	3	1	3
Estrada	.989	17	169	13	2	1	1
Owen	.923	1	10	2	1	0	0
Zebrowski	.979	69	672	44	15	4	4

First Base	PCT	G	PO	A	E	DP
Backstrom	.979	68	514	39	12	38
Blair	1.000	1	4	0	0	0
Janas	.992	15	117	8	1	9
Vasquez	.989	49	341	23	4	29
Workinger	1.000	3	16	1	0	1

Second Base	PCT	G	PO	A	E	DP
Conley	.833	4	7	3	2	1
Durbin	.983	32	42	72	2	15
Exposito	.954	13	16	46	3	5
Floyd	1.000	7	11	24	0	6
Klein	.983	20	28	30	1	7
Ogans	.982	12	19	37	1	6
Quintero	.974	30	46	67	3	13
Stevens	.893	15	13	37	6	3

Third Base	PCT	G	PO	A	E	DP
Alvarez	1.000	5	4	5	0	0
Durbin	.949	24	16	40	3	7
Floyd	.889	7	3	13	2	1
Klein	.897	17	8	27	4	1
McCabe	.920	21	12	34	4	2
Quintero	.876	58	41	93	19	7

Shortstop	PCT	G	PO	A	E	DP
Alvarez	.970	10	19	13	1	3
Conley	.951	67	92	158	13	30
Durbin	1.000	16	27	37	0	11
Exposito	.965	14	18	37	2	10
Floyd	.960	19	23	49	3	5
Ogans	.955	6	7	14	1	2

Outfield	PCT	G	PO	A	E	DP
Blair	.918	35	44	1	4	0
Keck	1.000	3	3	0	0	0
Kilpatrick Jr.	1.000	21	33	1	0	0
Mezquita	.963	77	126	4	5	1
Morton	.971	102	179	21	6	5
Paolini	.984	104	185	3	3	1
Parker	.971	37	63	3	2	0
Vasquez	.833	4	3	2	1	0
Williams	1.000	5	5	0	0	0
Workinger	1.000	15	27	2	0	0

FCL BRAVES

ROOKIE

FLORIDA COMPLEX LEAGUE

Batting	B-T	HT	WT	DOB	AVG	vLH	vRH	G	AB	R	H	2B	3B	HR	RBI	BB	HBP	SH	SF	SO	SB	CS	SLG	OBP
Cory Acton	L-R	6-0	175	3-22-99	.219	.167	.231	12	32	7	7	2	0	0	3	8	0	0	0	14	0	2	.281	.375
Ignacio Alvarez	R-R	6-0	190	4-11-03	.279	.091	.344	15	43	11	12	1	1	1	5	7	1	0	0	6	4	0	.419	.392
Drake Baldwin	L-R	6-1	210	3-28-01	.375	.000	.429	3	8	2	3	2	0	0	3	1	0	0	1	3	0	0	.625	.400
Antonio Barranca	R-R	6-3	215	7-25-01	.160	.294	.133	34	100	14	16	5	0	2	16	26	5	0	2	41	6	2	.270	.353
Leonel Callez	R-R	5-11	165	1-25-01	.135	.222	.107	13	37	4	5	1	0	0	0	3	1	0	0	12	0	0	.162	.220
2-team total (5 FCL Blue Jays)					.140	.167	.132	18	50	4	7	1	1	0	0	4	1	0	0	16	0	1	.200	.218
Jair Casanova	R-R	6-0	170	11-14-03	.289	.207	.308	45	149	18	43	5	1	1	16	24	3	0	3	34	0	1	.356	.391
Jeremy Celedonio	R-R	6-0	183	12-26-01	.176	.667	.129	13	34	5	6	0	1	2	8	8	4	0	0	14	5	0	.412	.391
Nick Clarno	R-R	6-0	205	6-25-98	.000	--	.000	1	1	0	0	0	0	0	0	1	0	0	0	1	0	0	.000	.500
Tyler Collins	L-R	5-11	180	3-6-03	.167	--	.167	4	12	4	2	1	0	0	1	4	0	0	0	6	2	0	.250	.375
Jordan Cowan	L-R	6-0	160	4-13-95	.368	.571	.250	6	19	3	7	1	1	0	1	2	1	0	0	3	0	0	.526	.455
Deivy De Castro	B-R	5-9	160	4-26-03	.125	.000	.143	11	24	6	3	0	1	0	0	6	0	0	0	11	0	1	.208	.300
Anderson De Los Santos	B-R	6-0	190	7-28-02	.184	.219	.169	37	103	15	19	3	0	2	11	13	2	0	0	19	4	5	.272	.288
Jose Dilone	L-R	6-0	165	10-9-00	.188	.185	.188	36	112	20	21	3	1	2	14	25	3	0	0	41	11	3	.286	.350
Dawson Dimon	R-R	6-1	185	5-17-99	.200	.000	.222	3	10	0	2	0	0	0	0	2	0	0	0	4	0	0	.200	.333
E.J. Exposito	R-R	6-0	190	5-4-01	.182	.000	.200	4	11	0	2	1	0	0	0	0	0	0	0	3	0	0	.273	.182
Francisco Floyd	R-R	6-1	167	5-25-02	.205	.190	.209	24	88	18	18	2	1	2	8	10	1	0	0	34	9	2	.318	.293
Wilfrank Graciano	R-R	5-10	155	2-18-03	.080	.000	.098	19	50	4	4	0	0	0	2	2	3	0	0	24	2	0	.080	.164
Christian Jackson	R-R	6-2	185	10-23-03	.148	.111	.167	9	27	2	4	1	0	0	3	2	0	0	0	14	1	0	.185	.207
Justin Janas	L-R	6-3	205	9-18-00	.200	.000	.222	4	10	0	2	1	0	0	2	0	2	0	0	2	1	1	.300	.333
Luis Jose	L-L	5-10	165	12-3-02	.156	.111	.174	24	64	2	10	3	0	0	5	9	0	0	0	29	1	1	.203	.260
Andrew Keck	R-R	6-3	225	12-12-99	.200	.500	.125	4	10	0	2	0	0	0	1	1	0	0	0	4	0	0	.200	.273
Kevin Kilpatrick Jr.	R-R	6-0	186	11-25-00	.320	.714	.167	10	25	3	8	2	0	0	0	4	0	0	0	7	3	0	.400	.414
Tyler Krieger	B-R	6-2	190	1-16-94	.167	.000	.200	2	6	0	1	0	0	0	2	0	0	0	0	1	0	0	.167	.167
David McCabe	B-R	6-4	230	3-25-00	.000	.000	.000	2	6	1	0	0	0	0	0	1	0	0	0	0	0	0	.000	.143
Luis Moreno	R-R	5-11	160	12-9-02	.139	.207	.116	39	115	17	16	0	2	0	10	13	9	0	1	33	6	0	.174	.275
Keshawn Ogans	R-R	5-9	180	8-26-01	.143	1.000	.000	3	7	2	1	0	0	0	0	1	0	0	0	4	0	0	.143	.250
Harry Owen	R-R	6-3	225	3-7-02	.222	.286	.182	7	18	2	4	0	0	1	1	4	0	0	0	2	0	0	.389	.364
Arden Pabst	R-R	6-1	205	3-14-95	.176	.333	.143	12	34	5	6	0	0	3	6	6	2	0	1	10	1	0	.441	.326
Cesar Rodriguez	B-R	5-10	160	12-26-00	.250	.143	.298	21	68	5	17	2	0	0	6	3	0	0	0	14	0	0	.279	.282
Eliezel Stevens	L-R	6-0	185	10-8-00	.246	.200	.255	18	57	6	14	5	0	0	10	8	0	0	0	21	2	1	.333	.338
Ambioris Tavarez	R-R	6-0	168	11-12-03	.277	.231	.288	17	65	12	18	4	0	1	8	3	0	0	1	28	3	1	.385	.304
Alexander Then	B-R	5-11	156	12-11-01	.247	.091	.305	28	81	14	20	3	0	0	7	9	2	1	0	25	5	2	.284	.337
Noah Williams	B-R	6-2	180	4-12-04	.233	.286	.217	10	30	1	7	1	0	0	1	4	0	0	0	13	2	0	.267	.324
Ethan Workinger	R-R	6-3	185	10-19-01	.239	.270	.229	42	155	20	37	10	3	4	27	13	3	0	1	31	2	5	.419	.308
Bryson Worrell	B-R	6-2	226	11-7-98	.333	.250	.348	10	27	1	9	2	2	0	8	5	1	0	0	9	0	1	.556	.455

Pitching	B-T	HT	WT	DOB	W	L	ERA	G	GS	CG	SV	IP	H	R	ER	HR	BB	SO	AVG	vLH	vRH	K/9	BB/9
Kris Anglin	L-L	5-11	175	8-9-01	1	1	2.86	5	4	0	0	22	21	10	7	3	7	20	.250	.194	.283	8.18	2.86
2-team total (1 FCL Tigers)					1	1	3.13	6	5	0	0	23	23	11	8	3	8	20	.258	.212	.286	7.83	3.13
Jorge Bautista	R-R	6-0	155	12-10-00	0	4	2.41	8	7	0	0	37	23	12	10	1	8	45	.176	.236	.132	10.85	1.93
Chad Bryant	R-R	6-0	210	8-3-99	0	3	4.50	9	2	0	0	18	14	10	9	0	10	16	.215	.258	.176	8.00	5.00

Brent Burgess	R-R	6-0	200	5-2-97	0	0	5.40	6	1	0	0	5	6	3	3	0	5	8	.300	.300	.300	14.40	9.00
Blake Burkhalter	R-R	6-0	204	9-19-00	0	0	54.00	1	0	0	0	0	3	2	2	0	1	0	.750	.500	1.000	0.00	27.00
Jason Creasy	R-R	6-4	197	5-13-92	1	1	3.57	15	0	0	0	18	13	8	7	2	2	33	.197	.143	.237	16.81	1.02
Wilker Cubillan	R-R	6-4	175	1-14-01	1	4	9.86	17	0	0	3	21	25	24	23	0	23	23	.313	.263	.357	9.86	9.86
Cedric De Grandpre	R-R	6-2	210	1-25-02	0	0	0.00	2	0	0	0	3	1	0	0	0	0	4	.100	.000	.333	12.00	0.00
Jasseel De La Cruz	R-R	6-1	195	6-26-97	0	1	6.00	6	1	0	0	6	6	6	4	2	3	12	.240	.231	.250	18.00	4.50
Anderson De Los Santos	B-R	6-0	190	7-28-02	0	0	--	0	0	0	0	0	0	0	0	0	0	0	--	--	--	--	--
Giomar Diaz	R-R	6-2	190	11-23-02	1	1	3.63	16	0	0	1	22	11	12	9	2	10	21	.143	.214	.102	8.46	4.03
Adel Dilone	R-R	6-3	207	10-7-00	0	1	9.19	11	0	0	2	16	15	18	16	2	12	18	.246	.233	.258	10.34	6.89
Jason Franks	R-R	6-3	200	1-23-99	1	0	8.10	6	0	0	0	7	9	6	6	2	4	12	.333	.357	.308	16.20	5.40
Rolando Gutierrez	L-L	6-2	190	4-6-02	0	2	4.76	6	4	0	0	17	16	10	9	1	8	12	.250	.211	.267	6.35	4.24
Landon Harper	R-R	6-1	176	4-8-01	1	0	0.00	1	0	0	0	1	0	0	0	0	0	0	.000	.000	--	0.00	0.00
Hayden Harris	L-L	6-0	186	3-2-99	1	0	3.86	6	0	0	0	5	3	3	2	1	6	6	.188	.222	.143	11.57	11.57
Miguel Hernandez	R-R	6-0	174	10-1-02	0	3	6.17	10	3	0	1	23	21	16	16	1	17	28	.247	.370	.190	10.80	6.56
Grant Holmes	L-R	6-0	226	3-22-96	0	1	16.20	1	1	0	0	2	2	3	3	0	1	1	.286	.000	.500	5.40	5.40
Jay Jackson	R-R	6-1	195	10-27-87	0	0	4.50	2	1	0	0	2	1	2	1	0	0	1	.167	.500	.000	4.50	0.00
Elison Joseph	R-R	6-0	170	1-24-01	3	0	5.87	14	0	0	5	15	14	10	10	2	8	20	.250	.240	.258	11.74	4.70
Seth Keller	R-R	5-10	180	5-26-04	0	0	18.00	2	1	0	0	2	0	4	4	0	5	1	.000	.000	.000	4.50	22.50
Landon Leach	R-R	6-4	220	7-12-99	0	0	0.00	1	1	0	0	2	0	0	0	0	0	1	.000	.000	.000	4.50	0.00
Ian Mejia	R-R	6-3	205	1-31-00	0	0	0.00	1	1	0	0	1	1	0	0	0	0	0	.333	.500	.000	0.00	0.00
Jose Montilla	R-R	6-1	235	6-4-98	0	0	0.00	2	0	0	0	2	0	0	0	0	0	1	.000	.000	.000	3.86	0.00
Cesari Moreno	R-R	6-4	214	12-21-01	0	3	12.42	14	3	0	0	17	15	24	23	2	28	19	.254	.259	.250	10.26	15.12
Owen Murphy	R-R	6-1	190	9-27-03	0	0	0.00	2	2	0	0	5	2	0	0	0	0	7	.118	.100	.143	12.60	0.00
Efrain Polanco	R-R	5-10	165	2-23-03	0	0	11.15	13	0	0	0	15	16	20	19	2	22	9	.271	.250	.286	5.28	12.91
Hunter Riggins	R-R	6-3	205	8-10-98	0	0	3.00	2	1	0	0	3	2	1	1	0	1	4	.182	.250	.143	12.00	3.00
JR Ritchie	R-R	6-2	185	6-26-03	0	0	0.00	2	2	0	0	4	2	0	0	0	1	4	.125	.182	.000	8.31	2.08
Albert Rivas	R-R	6-0	155	2-18-03	3	2	4.85	13	4	0	0	43	48	27	23	2	10	45	.277	.290	.269	9.49	2.11
Rainiery Rodriguez	B-R	6-2	170	8-28-00	1	0	0.00	3	2	0	0	10	5	0	0	0	0	10	.135	.133	.136	8.71	0.00
Andy Samuelson	L-L	6-4	185	5-20-99	0	0	108.00	1	0	0	0	0	0	4	4	0	5	1	.000	--	.000	27.00	135.00
Andres Sanchez	R-R	6-2	185	8-10-02	3	2	6.52	8	0	0	0	19	22	16	14	0	13	12	.289	.212	.349	5.59	6.05
Alex Segal	L-L	6-4	190	3-18-98	1	0	4.26	5	1	0	0	6	2	3	3	0	1	10	.095	.000	.133	14.21	1.42
Adam Shoemaker	L-L	6-6	205	8-24-02	0	5	5.73	10	8	0	0	33	32	22	21	1	19	30	.260	.333	.242	8.18	5.18
William Silva	R-R	6-0	185	8-2-01	2	0	0.00	3	0	0	0	4	2	0	0	0	2	2	.143	.143	.143	4.50	4.50
Kevin Solano	R-R	6-2	187	4-8-02	0	1	9.82	15	0	0	1	18	26	21	20	3	14	21	.347	.300	.364	10.31	6.87
Samuel Strickland	R-L	6-2	218	3-26-99	0	0	10.80	1	1	0	0	2	2	2	2	1	1	1	.286	.000	.400	5.40	5.40
Alexander Then	B-R	5-11	156	12-11-01	0	0	0.00	1	0	0	0	0	0	0	0	0	0	0	.000	--	.000	0.00	0.00
Ben Thompson	R-R	6-5	220	12-21-97	0	0	0.00	1	0	0	0	1	1	3	0	0	0	2	.200	.000	.250	18.00	0.00
Kyle Wilcox	R-R	6-3	195	6-14-94	0	0	0.00	4	1	0	0	4	1	0	0	0	5	6	.091	.000	.125	14.73	12.27
Allan Winans	R-R	6-2	165	8-10-95	0	0	0.00	2	1	0	0	5	2	0	0	0	2	5	.125	.000	.182	9.00	3.60
William Woods	R-R	6-3	190	12-29-98	0	0	3.00	3	1	0	0	3	3	1	1	0	0	4	.273	.167	.400	12.00	0.00
Kirby Yates	L-R	5-10	205	3-25-87	0	0	0.00	1	1	0	0	1	0	0	0	0	0	2	.000	.000	.000	18.00	0.00

Fielding

C: Baldwin 3, Barranca 29, Callez 5, Clarno 1, Dimon 2, Keck 1, Owen 7, Pabst 5, Rodriguez 7. **1B:** Callez 9, Dilone 19, Janas 4, Pabst 4, Rodriguez 12, Stevens 7, Workinger 4. **2B:** Acton 11, Cowan 1, De Los Santos 4, Exposito 1, Graciano 2, Moreno 17, Ogans 2, Stevens 8, Then 14. **3B:** Alvarez 13, Cowan 1, De Los Santos 6, Dilone 17, Floyd 3, Graciano 8, McCabe 2, Moreno 7, Then 8. **SS:** Cowan 3, Exposito 2, Floyd 24, Graciano 2, Krieger 1, Moreno 11, Ogans 1, Tavarez 14, Then 4. **OF:** Casanova 39, Celedonio 10, Collins 3, De Castro 11, De Los Santos 26, Jackson 7, Jose 21, Keck 3, Kilpatrick Jr. 9, Willliams 8, Workinger 36, Worrell 9.

DSL BRAVES — ROOKIE

DOMINICAN SUMMER LEAGUE

Batting	B-T	HT	WT	DOB	AVG	vLH	vRH	G	AB	R	H	2B	3B	HR	RBI	BB	HBP	SH	SF	SO	SB	CS	SLG	OBP
Diego Benitez	R-R	6-1	180	11-19-04	.196	.080	.221	43	138	25	27	6	0	2	27	29	10	0	5	37	3	2	.283	.363
Elian Cortorreal	B-R	5-10	160	11-8-04	.190	.118	.214	48	137	18	26	5	2	1	19	45	0	0	2	37	8	2	.277	.386
Leiker Figueroa	R-R	5-11	155	1-12-05	.211	.139	.232	49	161	22	34	3	2	0	11	19	6	0	1	38	17	7	.255	.316
Elian Garcia	L-L	5-10	175	10-31-04	.111	.053	.127	35	90	17	10	3	0	0	8	21	8	0	1	37	1	2	.144	.325
Douglas Glod	R-R	5-10	185	1-20-05	.202	.348	.160	32	104	23	21	6	2	2	13	22	2	0	0	36	3	3	.356	.352
Robert Gonzalez	L-R	6-0	175	12-22-04	.264	.351	.246	55	212	41	56	9	4	2	26	25	1	0	2	51	12	5	.373	.342
Yorlis Lendor	B-R	6-6	215	11-29-03	.203	.250	.192	20	64	6	13	1	0	2	14	10	1	0	1	30	2	0	.313	.316
Gabriel Liendo	L-R	5-10	150	1-9-03	.123	.091	.130	23	57	3	7	1	0	0	4	12	5	0	0	18	3	2	.140	.324
Maximo Maria	R-R	6-2	185	10-1-04	.201	.133	.220	51	139	28	28	6	1	4	14	34	6	1	0	58	12	4	.345	.380
Alexander Martinez	R-R	5-11	170	11-16-04	.244	.206	.254	43	164	21	40	9	0	2	26	12	0	0	0	33	2	1	.335	.295
Yorfran Nieves	R-R	6-0	145	2-26-03	.184	.200	.181	36	87	21	16	5	1	0	9	14	8	0	0	26	7	2	.264	.349
Josnaider Orellana	R-R	5-11	175	9-26-04	.197	.000	.221	25	76	14	15	3	0	0	7	14	4	0	0	24	0	1	.237	.351
Alen Pineda	R-R	5-10	180	11-4-04	.105	.111	.103	29	76	6	8	2	0	0	7	22	7	0	1	21	2	0	.132	.349
Luis Sanchez	R-R	5-9	165	1-16-04	.287	.167	.303	34	101	20	29	3	0	1	16	21	7	0	3	10	13	1	.347	.432
Cristian Suarez	R-R	6-2	162	7-7-05	.226	.222	.227	39	124	12	28	5	0	1	14	21	4	0	1	21	4	2	.290	.353

Pitching	B-T	HT	WT	DOB	W	L	ERA	G	GS	CG	SV	IP	H	R	ER	HR	BB	SO	AVG	vLH	vRH	K/9	BB/9
Genderson Almonte	R-R	6-2	170	12-13-03	2	1	2.66	13	4	0	2	24	14	11	7	3	15	21	.169	.240	.138	7.99	5.70
Jose Chavez	R-R	6-0	185	12-23-03	3	1	1.91	15	0	0	8	33	32	16	7	3	17	34	.260	.194	.283	9.27	4.64
Adel Dilone	R-R	6-3	207	10-7-00	0	0	2.84	4	0	0	1	6	6	4	2	1	2	7	.273	.200	.294	9.95	2.84
Didier Fuentes	R-R	6-0	170	6-17-05	1	1	2.25	11	11	0	0	44	35	13	11	2	10	50	.217	.220	.216	10.23	2.05
Anthony Garcia	R-R	6-2	200	3-28-02	2	3	6.25	10	9	0	0	32	32	26	22	0	20	35	.256	.238	.265	9.95	5.68
Rolando Gutierrez	L-L	6-2	190	4-6-02	2	1	1.38	7	6	0	0	26	15	9	4	0	6	26	.158	.150	.160	9.00	2.08

Wellington Guzman	R-R	5-10	170	12-29-04	1	4	2.84	15	0	0	3	32	31	15	10	2	12	21	.261	.233	.276	5.97	3.41
Jhancarlos Lara	R-R	6-3	190	1-15-03	1	1	1.78	10	9	0	0	30	20	9	6	0	26	38	.182	.189	.178	11.27	7.71
Jhonny Martinez	R-R	5-10	172	10-17-04	3	2	4.28	14	1	0	0	27	23	24	13	0	24	32	.215	.237	.203	10.54	7.90
Yorfran Nieves	R-R	6-0	145	2-26-03	0	0	0.00	1	0	0	1	1	0	0	0	0	1	0	.000	--	.000	0.00	13.50
Jose Ojeda	R-R	5-10	170	5-15-05	3	1	3.00	11	1	0	0	24	22	11	8	1	14	15	.250	.172	.288	5.63	5.25
Bernie Orozco	R-R	6-3	205	7-25-04	0	0	27.00	1	0	0	0	0	1	1	1	0	1	1	.500	.000	1.000	27.00	27.00
Hayder Ortiz	R-R	6-0	160	11-14-01	0	1	2.45	5	3	0	1	7	3	3	2	0	12	8	.136	.250	.071	9.82	14.73
Marco Patino	R-R	6-0	175	11-17-04	3	2	2.84	13	0	0	2	25	26	11	8	2	10	22	.257	.176	.299	7.82	3.55
Miguel Perez	R-R	6-0	168	3-2-04	0	0	0.00	3	1	0	0	5	3	0	0	0	0	3	.176	.333	.091	5.06	0.00
Yorvi Pirela	R-R	6-0	160	1-3-05	7	1	3.92	13	1	0	0	39	46	22	17	3	13	28	.305	.300	.306	6.46	3.00
Davis Polo	R-R	6-1	150	10-27-04	2	2	5.03	10	2	0	0	20	18	12	11	1	6	26	.234	.250	.226	11.90	2.75
Francisco Romero	R-R	6-2	170	10-28-03	2	1	3.99	15	1	0	0	29	19	17	13	0	18	26	.192	.200	.188	7.98	5.52
Andres Sanchez	R-R	6-2	185	8-10-02	0	0	0.00	2	2	0	0	6	3	0	0	0	1	3	.150	.167	.143	4.50	1.50
Juan Sanchez	R-R	6-2	180	5-21-03	2	2	3.68	13	0	0	1	29	21	13	12	0	20	28	.210	.194	.217	8.59	6.14
Jhonly Taveras	R-R	6-1	180	12-16-04	2	0	3.05	12	9	0	0	44	28	19	15	4	30	39	.185	.100	.216	7.92	6.09

Fielding

C: Martinez 32, Orellana 12, Pineda 17. **1B:** Liendo 6, Nieves 13, Orellana 4, Pineda 7, Suarez 36. **2B:** Cortorreal 45, Figueroa 7, Liendo 6, Nieves 5, Sanchez 4. **3B:** Cortorreal 2, Figueroa 21, Nieves 17, Sanchez 25. **SS:** Benitez 39, Cortorreal 2, Figueroa 20, Sanchez 3. **OF:** Garcia 35, Glod 29, Gonzalez 56, Lendor 4, Liendo 7, Maria 51, Nieves 1, Pineda 1.

Baltimore Orioles

SEASON IN A SENTENCE: A five-year stretch as baseball's worst team ended in thrilling fashion as the Orioles posted their first winning season since 2016. A resurgent pitching staff, particularly in the bullpen, and the debut of 2019 first-round pick Adley Rutschman pushed Baltimore into postseason contention until the season's final week and spelled the end to the depths of the rebuild.

HIGH POINT: The Orioles had a 10-game winning streak in July to get them over .500 and stayed hot in August. On Sept. 3, they drew more than 30,000 fans on a Saturday night to witness an 8-1 drubbing of Oakland, as the Orioles closed to within 1.5 games of the third and final wild card, and their 71-61 record put them 10 games over .500 for the first time since May 12, 2017.

LOW POINT: Signs of a turnaround stirred when Rutschman debuted on May 21, but inertia proved powerful. Despite improved play and a 14-12 June, the Orioles still were nine games under .500 after closer Jorge Lopez blew back-to-back games in Minnesota in a pair of walk-off losses.

NOTABLE ROOKIES: Rutschman lived up to the hype, with an .806 OPS, 35 doubles, 13 home runs and an 'it' factor of confidence and leadership that made believers out of teammates and opponents alike. Righthander Felix Bautista, a late bloomer at 27, burst onto the bullpen scene with dominant 100 mph heat and went 4-4, 2.19 with 15 saves, becoming the closer in the second half. Righty Kyle Bradish had ups and downs during a 4-7, 4.90 season that included 16.2 scoreless innings in two starts against the 106-win Astros. Minor League Player of the Year Gunnar Henderson hit .259/.348/.440 in a 34-game September and October sneak preview.

KEY TRANSACTIONS: GM Mike Elias, manager Brandon Hyde and the coaching staff did tremendous work in improving waiver wire pickups such as lefty Cionel Perez (1.40 ERA in 58 IP), righty Austin Voth (5-4, 3.04 in 83 IP) and righty reliever Bryan Baker (3.49 ERA in 70 IP). Despite contending, the Orioles traded Lopez (Minnesota) and franchise stalwart Trey Mancini (Houston) prior to the August deadline, netting a solid prospect haul.

ON THE FARM: Baltimore's farm system remains one of the best in baseball with players like Henderson, righthander Grayson Rodriguez and 2022 top pick Jackson Holliday providing a next wave of impact talent.

OPENING DAY PAYROLL: $58,083,184 (29th).

PLAYERS OF THE YEAR

MAJOR LEAGUE

Adley Rutschman
C

.254/.362/.445
One of five rookie Cs in history with 5 WAR

MINOR LEAGUE

Gunnar Henderson
SS

(AA/AAA)
.297/.416/.531
19 HR, 22 SB in 112 G

ORGANIZATION LEADERS

Batting — ***Minimum 250 AB**

MAJORS

*AVG	Trey Mancini	.268
*OPS	Adley Rutschman	.806
HR	Anthony Santander	33
RBI	Anthony Santander	89

MINORS

*AVG	Frederick Bencosme, Aberdeen, Delmarva, FCL Orioles	.311
*OBP	Gunnar Henderson, Bowie, Norfolk	.416
*SLG	Gunnar Henderson, Bowie, Norfolk	.531
*OPS	Gunnar Henderson, Bowie, Norfolk	.946
R	Colton Cowser, Aberdeen, Bowie, Norfolk	114
H	Joey Ortiz, Bowie, Norfolk	153
TB	Jordan Westburg, Bowie, Norfolk	270
2B	Jordan Westburg, Bowie, Norfolk	39
3B	Gunnar Henderson, Bowie, Norfolk	7
HR	Connor Norby, Aberdeen, Bowie, Norfolk	29
RBI	Jordan Westburg, Bowie, Norfolk	106
BB	Colton Cowser, Aberdeen, Bowie, Norfolk	94
SO	Colton Cowser, Aberdeen, Bowie, Norfolk	174
SB	Luis Valdez, Delmarva, Aberdeen	71

PITCHING — **#Minimum 75 IP**

MAJORS

W	Jordan Lyles	12
#ERA	Austin Voth	3.04
SO	Jordan Lyles	144
SV	Jorge Lopez	19

MINORS

W	Peter Van Loon, Aberdeen	11
L	Conor Grady, Delmarva	10
L	Garrett Stallings	10
#ERA	Grayson Rodriguez, Norfolk, Bowie, Aberdeen	2.62
G	Cole Uvila, Norfolk	42
GS	Drew Rom, Bowie, Norfolk	25
SV	Cole Uvila, Norfolk	12
IP	Drew Rom, Bowie, Norfolk	120
BB	Dan Hammer, Delmarva, Aberdeen	73
SO	Drew Rom, Bowie, Norfolk	144
#AVG	Grayson Rodriguez, Norfolk, Bowie, Aberdeen	.176

2022 PERFORMANCE

General Manager: Mike Elias. **Farm Director:** Matt Blood. **Scouting Director:** Brad Ciolek

Class	Team	League	W	L	PCT	Finish	Manager
Majors	Baltimore Orioles	American	83	79	.512	7th (15)	Brandon Hyde
Triple-A	Norfolk Tides	International	74	76	.493	12th (15)	Buck Britton
Double-A	Bowie Baysox	Eastern	68	70	.493	7th (12)	Kyle Moore
High-A	Aberdeen IronBirds	South Atlantic	78	54	.591	2nd (12)	Roberto Mercado
Low-A	Delmarva Shorebirds	Carolina	49	81	.377	12th (12)	Felipe Alou Jr.
Rookie	FCL Orioles	Florida Complex	16	39	.291	15th (16)	C. Frias/ M. Packer
Overall 2022 Minor League Record			334	388	.463	25th (30)	

ORGANIZATION STATISTICS

BALTIMORE ORIOLES

AMERICAN LEAGUE

Batting	B-T	HT	WT	DOB	AVG	vLH	vRH	G	AB	R	H	2B	3B	HR	RBI	BB	HBP	SH	SF	SO	SB	CS	SLG	OBP
Jesus Aguilar	R-R	6-3	277	6-30-90	.224	.100	.310	16	49	2	11	1	0	1	2	1	0	0	0	13	0	0	.306	.240
Jonathan Arauz	B-R	6-0	195	8-3-98	.179	.000	.185	9	28	2	5	0	0	1	4	1	0	0	0	9	0	0	.286	.207
2-team total (6 Boston Red Sox)					.132	.000	.147	15	38	3	5	0	0	1	5	1	0	1	1	12	0	0	.211	.150
Rylan Bannon	R-R	5-8	180	4-22-96	.143	.250	.000	4	14	0	2	0	0	0	0	0	1	0	0	5	0	0	.143	.200
Anthony Bemboom	L-R	6-2	200	1-18-90	.115	.182	.098	22	52	4	6	2	0	1	1	6	0	1	0	17	0	0	.212	.207
Robinson Chirinos	R-R	6-1	220	6-5-84	.179	.213	.151	67	195	10	35	9	0	4	22	19	4	1	1	67	1	0	.287	.265
Yusniel Diaz	R-R	6-1	215	10-7-96	.000	--	.000	1	1	0	0	0	0	0	0	0	0	0	0	1	0	0	.000	.000
Kelvin Gutierrez	R-R	6-2	215	8-28-94	.143	.111	.200	12	28	2	4	1	0	0	3	4	0	0	0	8	1	0	.179	.250
Austin Hays	R-R	6-0	205	7-5-95	.250	.247	.252	145	535	66	134	35	2	16	60	34	10	0	3	114	2	4	.413	.306
Gunnar Henderson	L-R	6-2	210	6-29-01	.259	.130	.290	34	116	12	30	7	1	4	18	16	0	0	0	34	1	1	.440	.348
Richie Martin	R-R	6-0	190	12-22-94	.167	.222	.143	13	30	4	5	0	2	0	3	3	0	0	0	10	3	1	.300	.242
Jorge Mateo	R-R	6-0	182	6-23-95	.221	.203	.228	150	494	63	109	25	7	13	50	27	5	3	2	147	35	9	.379	.267
Ryan McKenna	R-R	5-11	195	2-14-97	.237	.270	.215	105	156	23	37	10	0	2	11	11	2	2	1	55	2	1	.340	.294
Ryan Mountcastle	R-R	6-4	230	2-18-97	.250	.239	.254	145	555	62	139	28	1	22	85	43	4	0	7	154	4	1	.423	.305
Cedric Mullins	L-L	5-8	175	10-1-94	.258	.209	.279	156	608	89	157	32	4	16	64	47	9	1	5	126	34	10	.403	.318
Tyler Nevin	R-R	6-4	225	5-29-97	.197	.231	.174	58	157	17	31	4	0	2	16	20	4	0	3	46	0	0	.261	.299
Rougned Odor	L-R	5-11	200	2-3-94	.207	.190	.211	135	426	49	88	19	3	13	53	32	10	0	4	109	6	1	.357	.275
Chris Owings	R-R	5-10	185	8-12-91	.107	.172	.037	27	56	6	6	2	0	0	0	10	1	1	0	24	1	0	.143	.254
Brett Phillips	L-R	6-0	195	5-30-94	.118	.000	.125	8	17	1	2	2	0	0	1	0	0	0	0	9	0	0	.235	.118
2-team total (75 Tampa Bay Rays)					.144	.000	.174	83	201	22	29	6	0	5	15	16	3	4	1	94	7	0	.249	.217
Adley Rutschman	B-R	6-2	220	2-6-98	.254	.173	.280	113	398	70	101	35	1	13	42	65	4	0	3	86	4	0	.445	.362
Anthony Santander	B-R	6-2	235	10-19-94	.240	.293	.221	152	574	78	138	24	0	33	89	55	13	0	5	122	0	2	.455	.318
DJ Stewart	L-R	6-0	210	11-30-93	.000	--	.000	3	3	0	0	0	0	0	0	0	0	0	0	2	0	0	.000	.000
Kyle Stowers	L-L	6-3	200	1-2-98	.253	.500	.247	34	91	11	23	4	1	3	11	5	2	0	0	29	0	0	.418	.306
Ramon Urias	R-R	6-0	190	6-3-94	.248	.222	.259	118	403	50	100	17	1	16	51	30	5	3	4	98	1	0	.414	.305
Terrin Vavra	L-R	6-1	200	5-12-97	.258	.222	.263	40	89	14	23	2	1	1	12	12	0	0	2	19	0	1	.337	.340

Pitching	B-T	HT	WT	DOB	W	L	ERA	G	GS	CG	SV	IP	H	R	ER	HR	BB	SO	AVG	vLH	vRH	K/9	BB/9
Keegan Akin	L-L	5-11	235	4-1-95	3	3	3.20	45	1	0	2	82	69	35	29	10	20	77	.227	.185	.254	8.49	2.20
Logan Allen	R-L	6-3	200	5-23-97	0	0	10.80	3	0	0	0	2	3	2	2	0	2	1	.375	1.000	.286	5.40	10.80
2-team total (4 Cleveland Guardians)					1	0	5.87	7	0	0	0	8	12	5	5	0	5	7	.353	.545	.261	8.22	5.87
Bryan Baker	R-R	6-6	245	12-2-94	4	3	3.49	66	2	0	1	70	60	29	27	3	26	76	.230	.225	.233	9.82	3.36
Mike Baumann	R-R	6-4	235	9-10-95	1	3	4.72	13	4	0	0	34	43	19	18	3	9	23	.314	.275	.337	6.03	2.36
Felix Bautista	R-R	6-5	190	6-20-95	4	4	2.19	65	0	0	15	66	38	18	16	7	23	88	.167	.149	.176	12.06	3.15
Kyle Bradish	R-R	6-4	220	9-12-96	4	7	4.90	23	23	0	0	118	119	68	64	17	46	111	.265	.235	.280	8.49	3.52
Yennier Cano	R-R	6-4	185	3-9-94	0	1	18.69	3	0	0	0	4	9	9	9	0	5	7	.409	.429	.400	14.54	10.38
2-team total (10 Minnesota Twins)					1	1	11.50	13	0	0	0	18	26	23	23	3	16	21	.333	.407	.294	10.50	8.00
Marcos Diplan	R-R	6-0	200	9-18-96	0	0	1.59	5	0	0	0	6	4	2	1	0	5	8	.182	.100	.250	12.71	7.94
Chris Ellis	L-R	6-5	205	9-22-92	0	0	10.38	2	2	0	0	4	5	5	5	0	6	2	.278	.333	.250	4.15	12.46
Paul Fry	L-L	6-0	205	7-26-92	0	0	6.00	12	0	0	0	12	9	9	8	1	7	12	.209	.250	.194	9.00	5.25
Rico Garcia	R-R	5-9	201	1-10-94	0	0	4.50	6	0	0	0	8	8	4	4	2	3	2	.250	.188	.313	2.25	3.38
Logan Gillaspie	R-R	6-2	220	4-17-97	1	0	3.12	17	0	0	0	17	20	8	6	1	3	10	.294	.208	.341	5.19	1.56
DL Hall	L-L	6-2	195	9-19-98	1	1	5.93	11	1	0	1	14	17	9	9	0	6	19	.298	.429	.256	12.51	3.95
Louis Head	R-R	6-1	180	4-23-90	0	0	1.80	5	0	0	0	5	6	1	1	0	4	3	.286	.000	.353	5.40	7.20
Joey Krehbiel	R-R	6-3	240	12-20-92	5	5	3.90	56	0	0	1	58	53	28	25	9	18	45	.242	.238	.245	7.02	2.81
Dean Kremer	R-R	6-2	200	1-7-96	8	7	3.23	22	21	1	0	125	123	48	45	11	34	87	.262	.271	.258	6.25	2.44
Travis Lakins Sr.	R-R	6-1	220	6-29-94	0	1	9.58	6	0	0	0	10	14	11	11	3	6	8	.326	.333	.321	6.97	5.23
Zac Lowther	L-L	6-2	235	4-30-96	0	0	8.44	1	0	0	0	5	8	6	5	0	2	1	.348	.364	.333	1.69	3.38
Jordan Lyles	R-R	6-5	230	10-19-90	12	11	4.42	32	32	1	0	179	196	94	88	26	52	144	.276	.278	.275	7.24	2.61
Ryan McKenna	R-R	5-11	195	2-14-97	0	0	13.50	2	0	0	0	1	5	2	2	0	1	0	.714	.667	.750	0.00	6.75
John Means	L-L	6-3	235	4-24-93	0	0	3.38	2	2	0	0	8	8	3	3	0	2	7	.258	.143	.292	7.88	2.25
Chris Owings	R-R	5-10	185	8-12-91	0	0	9.00	1	0	0	0	1	2	1	1	0	0	0	.400	.333	.500	0.00	0.00
Cionel Perez	R-L	5-11	162	4-21-96	7	1	1.40	66	0	0	1	58	46	11	9	2	21	55	.220	.224	.218	8.58	3.28
Jake Reed	R-R	6-2	195	9-29-92	1	0	6.35	8	0	0	0	6	7	6	4	0	1	5	.292	.500	.273	7.94	1.59

Denyi Reyes	R-R	6-4	255	11-2-96	0	0	2.35	3	1	0	0	8	8	2	2	0	1	3	.267	.200	.300	3.52	1.17
Cody Sedlock	R-R	6-4	220	6-19-95	0	0	15.00	1	0	0	0	3	6	5	5	0	1	3	.400	.500	.364	9.00	3.00
Beau Sulser	R-R	6-2	195	5-5-94	0	0	3.55	6	0	0	0	13	16	5	5	2	3	9	.320	.435	.222	6.39	2.13
Dillon Tate	R-R	6-2	195	5-1-94	4	4	3.05	67	0	0	5	74	57	29	25	6	16	60	.213	.265	.190	7.33	1.95
Nick Vespi	L-L	6-3	215	10-10-95	5	0	4.10	25	0	0	1	26	29	12	12	5	8	28	.284	.362	.218	9.57	2.73
Austin Voth	R-R	6-2	215	6-26-92	5	4	3.04	22	17	0	0	83	77	30	28	10	25	72	.244	.252	.239	7.81	2.71
Spenser Watkins	R-R	6-2	185	8-27-92	5	6	4.70	23	20	0	0	105	119	59	55	11	30	63	.281	.297	.269	5.38	2.56
Alex Wells	L-L	6-1	195	2-27-97	0	0	4.91	2	0	0	0	4	5	2	2	2	0	6	.313	.250	.333	14.73	0.00
Tyler Wells	R-R	6-8	255	8-26-94	7	7	4.25	23	23	0	0	104	90	49	49	16	28	76	.231	.193	.263	6.60	2.43
Bruce Zimmermann	L-L	6-1	215	2-9-95	2	5	5.99	15	13	0	0	74	97	52	49	21	12	49	.321	.352	.315	5.99	1.47

Fielding

Catcher	PCT	G	PO	A	E	DP	PB
Bemboom	.977	21	121	4	3	0	0
Chirinos	.994	66	459	21	3	2	3
Rutschman	.989	93	670	35	8	3	2

First Base	PCT	G	PO	A	E	DP
Aguilar	1.000	6	42	6	0	4
Mancini	1.000	29	215	13	0	22
Mountcastle	.995	124	963	74	5	111
Nevin	1.000	8	67	3	0	6

Second Base	PCT	G	PO	A	E	DP
Arauz	1.000	1	3	0	0	0
Henderson	1.000	3	6	10	0	3
Martin	.963	10	9	17	1	2
Odor	.969	129	209	296	16	73
Owings	1.000	11	17	22	0	11
Urias	1.000	21	26	50	0	12
Vavra	.978	15	24	21	1	8

Third Base	PCT	G	PO	A	E	DP
Arauz	.889	6	6	10	2	1
Bannon	1.000	3	3	11	0	1
Gutierrez	.960	10	5	19	1	5
Henderson	1.000	24	24	33	0	6
Nevin	.960	44	35	60	4	6
Odor	1.000	2	3	2	0	0
Owings	1.000	2	1	3	0	0
Urias	.969	98	54	197	8	25

Shortstop	PCT	G	PO	A	E	DP
Arauz	1.000	1	0	2	0	0
Henderson	.970	7	8	24	1	5
Martin	.900	2	0	9	1	1
Mateo	.972	149	181	417	17	91
Owings	.931	8	8	19	2	4
Urias	.933	8	4	10	1	1

Outfield	PCT	G	PO	A	E	DP
Diaz	1.000	1	1	0	0	0
Hays	.996	150	276	8	1	0
Mancini	.970	13	30	2	1	0
McKenna	.981	91	101	4	2	0
Mullins	1.000	150	358	9	0	4
Nevin	.800	3	4	0	1	0
Owings	1.000	1	2	0	0	0
Phillips	1.000	6	11	0	0	0
Santander	.987	122	215	5	3	1
Stowers	1.000	25	39	0	0	0
Vavra	1.000	12	13	1	0	0

NORFOLK TIDES — *TRIPLE-A*

INTERNATIONAL LEAGUE

Batting	B-T	HT	WT	DOB	AVG	vLH	vRH	G	AB	R	H	2B	3B	HR	RBI	BB	HBP	SH	SF	SO	SB	CS	SLG	OBP
Jonathan Arauz	B-R	6-0	195	8-3-98	.250	.176	.304	11	40	4	10	3	0	0	6	4	1	0	0	9	1	0	.325	.333
2-team total (24 Worcester Red Sox)					.205	.163	.225	35	132	15	27	8	0	0	9	11	1	0	0	22	2	0	.265	.271
Rylan Bannon	R-R	5-8	180	4-22-96	.229	.237	.226	78	275	45	63	14	1	11	58	45	5	0	1	87	6	1	.407	.347
2-team total (21 Gwinnett Stripers)					.249	.234	.254	99	342	57	85	18	1	13	77	59	7	0	3	100	10	1	.421	.367
Anthony Bemboom	L-R	6-2	200	1-18-90	.228	.167	.247	34	123	18	28	6	0	3	15	10	2	0	2	28	0	0	.350	.292
Cristopher Cespedes	R-R	6-3	200	5-18-98	.125	.000	.143	3	8	0	1	0	0	0	1	1	0	0	0	4	0	0	.125	.222
Colton Cowser	L-R	6-3	195	3-20-00	.219	.189	.235	27	105	23	23	7	0	5	11	13	6	0	0	38	0	0	.429	.339
Greg Cullen	L-R	5-10	190	11-13-96	.317	.304	.322	28	82	19	26	2	1	2	7	14	2	1	0	25	1	0	.439	.429
Brett Cumberland	B-R	5-11	200	6-25-95	.226	.250	.215	41	137	22	31	4	0	4	21	17	6	0	0	44	0	0	.343	.338
Yusniel Diaz	R-R	6-1	215	10-7-96	.251	.237	.260	70	247	40	62	9	0	6	34	36	1	0	2	66	9	4	.360	.346
Patrick Dorrian	L-R	6-2	188	6-26-96	.161	.140	.170	46	149	11	24	7	0	3	15	19	0	0	0	58	2	0	.268	.256
2-team total (48 Nashville Sounds)					.206	.202	.208	94	310	39	64	14	2	14	40	42	1	0	0	111	4	1	.400	.303
Shayne Fontana	L-L	6-2	195	6-21-97	.180	.154	.188	18	61	8	11	2	0	1	6	6	2	0	1	20	0	1	.262	.271
Cam Gallagher	R-R	6-3	230	12-6-92	.059	.000	.083	5	17	1	1	1	0	0	3	3	0	0	0	8	0	0	.118	.200
2-team total (10 Omaha Storm Chasers)					.140	.095	.172	15	50	4	7	2	0	2	8	6	0	0	0	20	0	0	.300	.232
AJ Graffanino	L-R	6-2	170	7-16-97	.154	.167	.143	4	13	0	2	0	0	0	0	0	0	0	0	6	0	0	.154	.154
Cadyn Grenier	R-R	5-11	188	10-31-96	.199	.173	.212	104	316	51	63	18	2	5	34	62	5	6	3	99	12	4	.316	.337
Kelvin Gutierrez	R-R	6-2	215	8-28-94	.242	.261	.232	60	211	34	51	8	2	6	26	24	0	0	3	51	5	2	.384	.315
Adam Hall	R-R	5-11	165	5-22-99	.333	.000	1.000	2	3	1	1	1	0	0	0	1	0	0	0	0	0	0	.667	.500
Dylan Harris	L-L	5-9	190	1-14-97	.115	.086	.128	38	113	19	13	6	0	3	14	20	1	0	2	47	2	2	.248	.250
Gunnar Henderson	L-R	6-2	210	6-29-01	.288	.253	.307	65	250	60	72	13	4	11	41	38	5	0	2	78	10	1	.504	.390
Chris Hudgins	R-R	6-1	190	3-2-96	.100	.000	.125	7	20	0	2	1	0	0	1	2	1	0	0	12	0	0	.150	.217
Jahmai Jones	R-R	6-0	210	8-4-97	.212	.300	.190	27	99	15	21	5	1	2	7	14	5	0	0	23	2	1	.343	.339
Shed Long Jr.	L-R	5-8	184	8-22-95	.211	.154	.240	22	76	9	16	5	0	0	11	11	1	0	0	24	2	2	.276	.318
Richie Martin	R-R	6-0	190	12-22-94	.250	.232	.259	80	292	51	73	20	6	2	25	32	9	0	1	66	29	5	.380	.341
Ryan McKenna	R-R	5-11	195	2-14-97	.273	.250	.280	8	33	5	9	0	0	3	6	4	0	0	1	14	0	2	.545	.342
Robert Neustrom	L-L	6-2	208	11-12-96	.231	.208	.240	101	368	41	85	18	1	15	61	29	7	1	4	69	14	2	.408	.297
Tyler Nevin	R-R	6-4	225	5-29-97	.291	.286	.294	44	165	30	48	8	1	7	36	21	4	0	1	36	4	0	.479	.382
Connor Norby	R-R	5-10	187	6-8-00	.359	.200	.414	9	39	7	14	2	0	4	7	3	0	0	0	5	0	1	.718	.405
Jacob Nottingham	R-R	6-2	220	4-3-95	.229	.255	.217	89	301	41	69	12	1	15	51	37	12	0	4	98	12	3	.425	.333
Joseph Ortiz	R-R	5-11	175	7-14-98	.346	.486	.275	26	104	22	36	7	2	4	14	9	1	0	1	17	6	1	.567	.400
Brett Phillips	L-R	6-0	195	5-30-94	.277	.316	.261	24	65	16	18	1	2	6	17	17	3	0	3	25	1	0	.631	.432
Johnny Rizer	L-L	6-0	192	11-7-96	.194	.143	.216	22	72	13	14	0	0	5	12	8	1	0	0	27	1	1	.403	.284
Cody Roberts	R-R	6-1	195	6-16-96	.375	.400	.368	7	24	3	9	2	0	1	3	4	0	0	0	6	0	0	.583	.464
Ramon Rodriguez	R-R	5-11	194	10-30-98	.588	.500	.667	5	17	4	10	1	0	1	6	0	0	0	0	2	0	0	.824	.588
Adley Rutschman	B-R	6-2	220	2-6-98	.233	.200	.250	12	43	5	10	0	0	3	7	7	3	0	0	6	0	0	.442	.377
DJ Stewart	L-R	6-0	210	11-30-93	.256	.267	.250	29	86	18	22	2	0	6	17	16	3	0	0	28	2	0	.488	.390
Kyle Stowers	L-L	6-3	200	1-2-98	.264	.326	.240	95	349	54	92	29	3	19	78	45	8	1	4	104	3	2	.527	.357
Davis Tavarez	R-R	6-2	235	1-7-99	.333	.400	.000	2	6	1	2	0	0	0	0	0	0	0	0	0	0	0	.333	.333
Beau Taylor	L-R	5-11	205	2-13-90	.183	.120	.217	23	71	11	13	1	0	2	5	19	0	0	1	27	0	0	.282	.352
Terrin Vavra	L-R	6-1	200	5-12-97	.324	.242	.369	45	173	34	56	14	1	2	18	28	6	1	0	36	5	1	.451	.435

BALTIMORE ORIOLES

Jordan Westburg	R-R	6-3	203	2-18-99	.273	.242	.290	91	362	64	99	25	3	18	74	44	6	0	1	90	9	3	.508	.361

Pitching	B-T	HT	WT	DOB	W	L	ERA	G	GS	CG	SV	IP	H	R	ER	HR	BB	SO	AVG	vLH	vRH	K/9	BB/9
Logan Allen	R-L	6-3	200	5-23-97	1	0	8.51	21	0	0	0	24	38	28	23	4	11	21	.358	.313	.397	7.77	4.07
Diogenes Almengo	R-R	6-2	190	6-2-95	3	0	5.85	15	0	0	0	20	18	14	13	3	18	17	.254	.179	.302	7.65	8.10
Mike Baumann	R-R	6-4	235	9-10-95	2	6	4.20	20	9	0	1	60	54	33	28	6	25	81	.231	.200	.252	12.15	3.75
Cameron Bishop	L-L	6-4	215	2-14-96	0	1	1.93	3	0	0	0	9	9	4	2	1	3	5	.265	.250	.269	4.82	2.89
Kyle Bradish	R-R	6-4	220	9-12-96	2	1	1.83	4	4	0	0	20	12	6	4	1	4	23	.169	.233	.071	10.53	1.83
Kyle Brnovich	L-R	6-2	190	10-20-97	0	0	5.63	2	2	0	0	8	5	5	5	1	7	4	.167	.000	.294	4.50	7.88
Yennier Cano	R-R	6-4	185	3-9-94	0	1	4.32	11	0	0	1	17	17	11	8	3	8	20	.254	.229	.281	10.80	4.32
2-team total (20 St. Paul Saints)					1	2	2.90	31	0	0	4	40	33	17	13	5	14	45	.226	.211	.243	10.04	3.12
Anthony Castro	R-R	6-2	185	4-13-95	0	0	2.16	8	0	0	0	8	8	2	2	0	6	8	.258	.333	.227	8.64	6.48
2-team total (28 Columbus Clippers)					1	3	3.55	36	0	0	3	38	33	17	15	2	26	47	.234	.298	.190	11.13	6.16
Ryan Conroy	R-R	6-3	190	12-31-96	2	3	5.84	24	2	0	0	37	45	26	24	5	24	35	.310	.308	.313	8.51	5.84
Greg Cullen	L-R	5-10	190	11-13-96	0	0	6.75	2	0	0	0	1	2	1	1	1	0	0	.333	.500	.250	0.00	0.00
Marcos Diplan	R-R	6-0	200	9-18-96	2	0	2.03	20	0	0	2	27	20	9	6	2	17	28	.204	.245	.163	9.45	5.74
Chris Ellis	L-R	6-5	205	9-22-92	0	0	0.00	1	1	0	0	4	0	0	0	0	1	5	.000	.000	.000	11.25	2.25
Rico Garcia	R-R	5-9	201	1-10-94	3	1	2.34	18	2	0	3	35	25	10	9	6	14	40	.197	.200	.194	10.38	3.63
Logan Gillaspie	R-R	6-2	220	4-17-97	5	3	5.09	22	0	0	1	35	39	20	20	2	9	38	.279	.282	.275	9.68	2.29
Conner Greene	R-R	6-4	195	4-4-95	0	1	10.61	16	0	0	0	19	27	28	22	4	21	18	.346	.273	.400	8.68	10.13
DL Hall	L-L	6-2	195	9-19-98	3	7	4.70	22	18	0	0	77	62	47	40	10	49	125	.212	.188	.223	14.67	5.75
Ryan Hartman	L-L	6-3	234	4-21-94	1	0	4.76	3	1	0	0	11	15	6	6	2	3	8	.326	.250	.385	6.35	2.38
Matt Harvey	R-R	6-4	220	3-27-89	6	1	4.31	10	10	2	0	54	52	27	26	14	24	43	.254	.283	.226	7.12	3.98
Louis Head	R-R	6-1	180	4-23-90	1	1	7.04	14	0	0	0	15	11	12	12	1	17	19	.212	.250	.179	11.15	9.98
Chris Hudgins	R-R	6-1	190	3-2-96	0	0	0.00	1	0	0	0	1	0	0	0	0	0	0	.000	--	.000	0.00	0.00
Blaine Knight	R-R	6-3	165	6-28-96	4	4	7.38	34	7	0	0	72	103	64	59	11	39	70	.338	.366	.316	8.75	4.88
Dean Kremer	R-R	6-2	200	1-7-96	0	0	0.00	2	2	0	0	7	1	0	0	0	2	13	.045	.000	.091	16.71	2.57
Travis Lakins Sr.	R-R	6-1	220	6-29-94	0	1	8.68	5	2	0	0	9	15	9	9	3	8	7	.375	.444	.318	6.75	7.71
David Lebron	R-R	5-11	190	9-7-93	0	1	135.00	1	0	0	0	0	6	6	5	0	0	1	.750	.667	1.000	27.00	0.00
Zac Lowther	L-L	6-2	235	4-30-96	1	5	10.31	17	9	0	0	44	75	53	50	10	23	46	.381	.425	.355	9.48	4.74
Isaac Mattson	R-R	6-2	205	7-14-95	1	0	6.62	19	0	0	0	18	12	13	13	4	20	14	.200	.160	.229	7.13	10.19
Kirk McCarty	L-L	5-8	185	10-12-95	0	1	6.75	1	1	0	0	4	5	3	3	1	0	2	.313	.333	.308	4.50	0.00
2-team total (17 Columbus Clippers)					4	2	3.58	18	9	0	0	65	62	30	26	12	23	55	.253	.224	.269	7.58	3.17
Morgan McSweeney	R-R	6-4	210	9-21-97	4	2	4.18	25	0	0	0	28	23	14	13	5	15	20	.219	.250	.197	6.43	4.82
Tim Naughton	R-R	6-3	195	11-14-95	0	2	5.60	16	0	0	0	18	13	11	11	3	15	25	.200	.154	.231	12.74	7.64
Ofelky Peralta	R-R	6-5	195	4-20-97	1	2	10.34	9	0	0	0	16	27	19	18	1	14	9	.409	.484	.343	5.17	8.04
Denyi Reyes	R-R	6-4	255	11-2-96	0	7	7.17	15	10	0	1	54	74	46	43	13	8	54	.323	.333	.313	9.00	1.33
Grayson Rodriguez	L-R	6-5	220	11-16-99	6	1	2.20	14	14	0	0	70	44	17	17	2	21	97	.178	.164	.190	12.53	2.71
Drew Rom	L-L	6-2	170	12-15-99	1	1	4.54	7	7	1	0	38	38	20	19	1	18	43	.268	.277	.263	10.27	4.30
Phoenix Sanders	R-R	5-10	205	6-5-95	0	0	18.00	2	0	0	0	2	4	4	4	1	1	2	.400	.500	.375	9.00	4.50
2-team total (25 Durham Bulls)					0	0	6.19	27	1	0	1	32	43	23	22	7	3	38	.316	.291	.333	10.69	0.84
Cody Sedlock	R-R	6-4	220	6-19-95	4	1	5.47	14	10	0	0	54	55	39	33	4	28	62	.266	.360	.195	10.27	4.64
2-team total (14 Toledo Mud Hens)					5	3	4.84	28	12	0	0	80	75	50	43	7	44	81	.250	.290	.216	9.11	4.95
Kevin Smith	R-L	6-5	200	5-13-97	0	5	4.66	19	6	0	2	48	45	27	25	9	34	44	.245	.197	.274	8.19	6.33
Beau Sulser	R-R	6-2	195	5-5-94	2	2	4.70	17	3	0	0	44	53	24	23	4	12	46	.303	.321	.286	9.41	2.45
2-team total (3 Indianapolis Indians)					3	4	4.13	20	6	1	0	57	64	30	26	5	14	60	.284	.301	.270	9.53	2.22
Cole Uvila	R-R	6-3	206	1-30-94	2	4	3.48	42	0	0	12	44	37	22	17	0	27	45	.224	.176	.258	9.20	5.52
Chris Vallimont	R-R	6-5	220	3-18-97	6	7	5.38	16	12	0	0	72	73	48	43	11	23	67	.262	.262	.261	8.38	2.88
Nick Vespi	L-L	6-3	215	10-10-95	2	1	0.00	26	0	0	8	29	12	3	0	0	5	36	.126	.051	.179	11.30	1.57
Matt Vogel	R-R	6-0	185	7-27-95	2	1	5.14	27	0	0	0	28	30	20	16	4	14	38	.263	.304	.235	12.21	4.50
Spenser Watkins	R-R	6-2	185	8-27-92	1	0	2.84	4	4	0	0	13	8	6	4	2	3	12	.174	.158	.185	8.53	2.13
Ryan Watson	R-R	6-5	215	11-15-97	0	0	3.65	7	0	0	0	12	8	6	5	1	8	8	.174	.222	.143	5.84	5.84
Alex Wells	L-L	6-1	195	2-27-97	1	0	4.76	4	2	0	0	11	11	6	6	2	3	7	.250	.071	.333	5.56	2.38
Bruce Zimmermann	L-L	6-1	215	2-9-95	5	2	3.77	14	12	0	0	76	83	35	32	6	18	74	.270	.260	.276	8.72	2.12

Fielding

Catcher	PCT	G	PO	A	E	DP	PB
Bemboom	.993	27	254	17	2	2	8
Cumberland	.978	21	176	4	4	1	3
Gallagher	.980	5	47	3	1	0	0
Hudgins	.951	6	53	5	3	0	2
Nottingham	.991	57	538	25	5	3	9
Roberts	.939	6	44	2	3	0	2
Rodriguez	1.000	5	41	1	0	0	0
Rutschman	.977	8	85	1	2	0	0
Taylor	1.000	17	144	5	0	0	2

First Base	PCT	G	PO	A	E	DP
Cumberland	.983	9	54	4	1	6
Dorrian	.993	41	265	36	2	34
Grenier	1.000	18	121	10	0	13
Gutierrez	.982	41	257	14	5	20
Henderson	1.000	3	23	1	0	2
Nevin	1.000	15	95	6	0	7
Nottingham	.995	25	169	12	1	22
Rutschman	.913	2	20	1	2	2
Stewart	.975	5	39	0	1	4

Second Base	PCT	G	PO	A	E	DP
Arauz	1.000	2	2	3	0	2
Bannon	.947	6	7	11	1	2
Cullen	.951	15	15	43	3	9
Graffanino	1.000	3	0	5	0	1
Grenier	.987	25	30	46	1	9
Henderson	.962	6	8	17	1	3
Jones	.987	16	31	45	1	9
Long Jr.	.973	10	10	26	1	7
Martin	.951	19	31	47	4	14
Norby	.957	6	6	16	1	2
Ortiz	1.000	5	13	20	0	8
Vavra	.969	22	35	60	3	16
Westburg	.967	24	28	60	3	9

Third Base	PCT	G	PO	A	E	DP
Arauz	.909	5	3	7	1	2
Bannon	.862	53	25	75	16	7
Cullen	1.000	3	0	3	0	0
Dorrian	1.000	1	0	1	0	0
Grenier	1.000	11	6	11	0	1
Gutierrez	.862	14	11	14	4	1
Henderson	.945	21	18	34	3	9
Nevin	.932	25	24	31	4	8
Westburg	.943	21	7	26	2	3

Shortstop	PCT	G	PO	A	E	DP
Arauz	1.000	2	1	5	0	1
Grenier	.955	27	32	53	4	15
Henderson	.961	32	53	70	5	17
Martin	.977	32	48	79	3	10
Ortiz	1.000	17	24	36	0	8
Westburg	.946	41	56	85	8	23

Outfield	PCT	G	PO	A	E	DP
Cespedes	1.000	2	6	0	0	0
Cowser	.970	29	63	1	2	0

Diaz	.976	62	116	6	3	1
Fontana	1.000	17	46	1	0	0
Grenier	1.000	20	24	2	0	0
Hall	1.000	1	2	0	0	0
Harris	.985	38	64	2	1	0
Jones	1.000	6	11	1	0	0
Long Jr.	1.000	14	21	1	0	0
Martin	1.000	20	34	3	0	0
McKenna	1.000	8	16	1	0	0
Neustrom	.975	86	154	5	4	0
Nevin	1.000	4	1	1	0	0
Norby	1.000	1	4	0	0	0
Phillips	1.000	23	39	1	0	0
Rizer	.952	21	40	0	2	0
Stewart	1.000	15	34	2	0	0
Stowers	.962	95	174	4	7	0
Tavarez	1.000	2	2	0	0	0
Taylor	--	1	0	0	0	0
Vavra	1.000	20	29	0	0	0

BOWIE BAYSOX

DOUBLE-A

EASTERN LEAGUE

Batting	B-T	HT	WT	DOB	AVG	vLH	vRH	G	AB	R	H	2B	3B	HR	RBI	BB	HBP	SH	SF	SO	SB	CS	SLG	OBP
Andres Angulo	R-R	5-10	181	9-5-97	.324	.500	.313	9	34	2	11	3	0	1	5	2	0	0	0	4	0	0	.500	.361
Cristopher Cespedes	R-R	6-3	200	5-18-98	.197	.250	.188	26	76	13	15	4	0	2	7	14	1	0	0	21	0	0	.329	.330
Colton Cowser	L-R	6-3	195	3-20-00	.341	.278	.357	49	176	49	60	10	0	10	33	36	9	0	3	57	2	2	.568	.469
Greg Cullen	L-R	5-10	190	11-13-96	.235	.267	.230	36	102	13	24	5	0	5	15	23	3	1	2	23	0	0	.431	.385
Andrew Daschbach	R-R	6-3	225	10-22-97	.191	.240	.183	103	329	46	63	11	0	15	46	55	14	0	4	165	2	0	.362	.328
Patrick Dorrian	L-R	6-2	188	6-26-96	.000	--	.000	1	4	0	0	0	0	0	0	0	0	0	0	1	0	0	.000	.000
Shayne Fontana	L-L	6-2	195	6-21-97	.278	.269	.280	43	133	30	37	6	0	7	27	27	6	0	2	48	3	2	.481	.417
Chris Givin	R-R	6-2	185	3-21-97	.200	.200	.200	14	45	6	9	3	0	3	8	7	1	0	0	14	1	0	.467	.321
AJ Graffanino	L-R	6-2	170	7-16-97	.226	.167	.232	22	62	6	14	0	0	2	6	6	1	0	0	13	3	0	.323	.304
2-team total (15 Reading Fightin Phils)					.217	.083	.233	37	115	14	25	3	1	2	11	9	1	0	1	26	5	0	.313	.278
Adam Hall	R-R	5-11	165	5-22-99	.253	.241	.255	50	182	26	46	11	0	1	13	18	11	0	1	58	16	1	.330	.354
Maverick Handley	R-R	5-9	190	3-10-98	.236	.273	.228	78	259	43	61	12	1	11	45	36	11	1	1	64	6	2	.417	.352
Dylan Harris	L-L	5-9	190	1-14-97	.315	.400	.293	20	73	11	23	6	0	3	9	9	1	0	0	22	2	1	.521	.398
Hudson Haskin	R-R	6-2	200	12-31-98	.264	.258	.265	109	387	58	102	23	3	15	56	43	24	5	7	101	5	3	.455	.367
Gunnar Henderson	L-R	6-2	210	6-29-01	.312	.147	.358	47	157	41	49	11	3	8	35	41	4	0	6	38	12	2	.573	.452
Darell Hernaiz	R-R	6-1	190	8-3-01	.113	.500	.082	13	53	6	6	1	0	1	8	5	0	0	1	16	1	1	.189	.186
Michael Mantecon	R-R	5-11	192	2-2-02	.091	.250	.000	3	11	3	1	0	0	0	1	1	0	0	0	3	0	0	.091	.167
Coby Mayo	R-R	6-5	215	12-10-01	.250	.318	.236	34	128	21	32	4	0	5	20	12	4	0	1	50	0	0	.398	.331
J.D. Mundy	L-R	6-0	210	5-14-98	.218	.139	.232	67	234	23	51	15	0	8	39	28	2	0	4	85	0	0	.385	.302
Connor Norby	R-R	5-10	187	6-8-00	.298	.333	.290	64	252	58	75	14	2	17	46	34	6	0	4	59	10	2	.571	.389
Joseph Ortiz	R-R	5-11	175	7-14-98	.269	.246	.273	111	435	69	117	28	4	15	71	41	5	1	3	81	2	1	.455	.337
Cesar Prieto	L-R	5-9	175	5-10-99	.255	.246	.257	90	368	44	94	22	0	4	37	15	6	0	0	58	2	5	.348	.296
John Rhodes	R-R	6-0	200	8-15-00	.189	.200	.186	25	90	12	17	3	2	0	9	12	1	0	1	22	0	0	.267	.288
Cody Roberts	R-R	6-1	195	6-16-96	.260	.184	.275	73	242	32	63	16	0	7	39	25	4	0	3	75	0	0	.413	.336
Ramon Rodriguez	R-R	5-11	194	10-30-98	.286	--	.286	2	7	1	2	2	0	0	0	0	0	0	0	0	0	0	.571	.286
Adley Rutschman	B-R	6-2	220	2-6-98	.417	.000	.455	3	12	5	5	2	0	0	2	2	0	0	0	1	0	0	.583	.500
Davis Tavarez	R-R	6-2	235	1-7-99	.179	.000	.208	8	28	3	5	1	0	1	2	1	0	0	0	8	0	0	.321	.207
Ramon Urias	R-R	6-0	190	6-3-94	.000	.000	.000	2	7	0	0	0	0	0	0	1	0	0	0	3	0	0	.000	.125
Zach Watson	R-R	6-0	160	6-25-97	.199	.269	.186	95	331	40	66	12	3	8	32	20	4	4	4	123	5	2	.326	.251
Toby Welk	R-R	6-2	205	5-2-97	.224	.318	.207	39	143	21	32	10	0	4	24	14	1	0	2	46	0	0	.378	.294
Jordan Westburg	R-R	6-3	203	2-18-99	.247	.125	.273	47	182	32	45	14	0	9	32	26	1	0	0	57	3	0	.473	.344
Donta Williams	L-L	5-10	185	6-30-99	.250	.000	.333	3	8	3	2	1	0	1	3	4	0	0	1	2	0	0	.750	.462

Pitching	B-T	HT	WT	DOB	W	L	ERA	G	GS	CG	SV	IP	H	R	ER	HR	BB	SO	AVG	vLH	vRH	K/9	BB/9
Justin Armbruester	R-R	6-4	235	10-21-98	4	1	3.69	14	10	0	2	63	49	29	26	13	16	63	.210	.245	.187	8.95	2.27
Cameron Bishop	L-L	6-4	215	2-14-96	1	2	3.57	6	0	0	1	18	12	7	7	0	12	27	.194	.217	.179	13.75	6.11
Kyle Bradish	R-R	6-4	220	9-12-96	1	0	0.00	2	2	0	0	8	1	0	0	0	0	9	.040	.063	.000	10.13	0.00
Tyler Burch	R-R	6-2	190	9-2-97	0	5	5.40	33	0	0	2	45	45	33	27	10	17	45	.249	.257	.243	9.00	3.40
Ryan Conroy	R-R	6-3	190	12-31-96	2	2	5.94	10	0	0	0	17	19	12	11	2	6	22	.284	.310	.263	11.88	3.24
Noah Denoyer	B-R	6-5	225	2-17-98	1	2	2.61	14	3	0	2	52	30	16	15	8	11	69	.167	.160	.171	12.02	1.92
Jensen Elliott	R-R	6-6	231	4-8-97	6	3	4.56	32	0	0	2	51	72	31	26	7	14	36	.332	.325	.336	6.31	2.45
Rico Garcia	R-R	5-9	201	1-10-94	1	0	1.35	4	0	0	0	7	5	1	1	0	4	11	.200	.125	.235	14.85	5.40
Logan Gillaspie	R-R	6-2	220	4-17-97	1	0	3.38	6	0	0	0	8	7	3	3	0	4	11	.233	.235	.231	12.38	4.50
DL Hall	L-L	6-2	195	9-19-98	0	1	4.91	1	1	0	0	4	3	2	2	0	1	6	.214	.000	.231	14.73	2.45
Brenan Hanifee	R-R	6-5	215	5-29-98	2	1	4.03	10	10	0	0	38	29	18	17	4	12	35	.204	.241	.179	8.29	2.84
Ryan Hartman	L-L	6-3	234	4-21-94	0	0	4.50	1	1	0	0	4	2	2	2	1	0	2	.143	.143	.143	4.50	0.00
Matt Harvey	R-R	6-4	220	3-27-89	2	0	2.70	2	2	0	0	10	9	3	3	2	0	16	.237	.273	.222	14.40	0.00
Nolan Hoffman	R-R	6-4	190	8-9-97	2	2	4.24	18	0	0	0	23	25	15	11	1	7	22	.278	.306	.259	8.49	2.70
Dean Kremer	R-R	6-2	200	1-7-96	0	0	0.00	1	1	0	0	2	1	0	0	0	0	5	.143	.000	.250	22.50	0.00
Travis Lakins Sr.	R-R	6-1	220	6-29-94	0	0	27.00	1	0	0	0	1	1	3	3	1	2	0	.250	--	.250	0.00	18.00
Conner Loeprich	R-R	6-3	215	9-13-97	3	1	4.50	32	3	0	6	72	73	36	36	10	27	77	.257	.256	.258	9.63	3.38
Easton Lucas	L-L	6-4	180	9-23-96	3	1	4.76	32	0	0	1	57	50	32	30	6	25	65	.236	.203	.254	10.32	3.97
Jake Lyons	R-R	6-5	280	8-19-98	0	0	6.00	1	1	0	0	3	4	2	2	1	0	4	.286	.333	.200	12.00	0.00
Chayce McDermott	L-R	6-3	197	8-22-98	1	1	6.08	6	6	0	0	27	17	18	18	7	20	36	.179	.224	.130	12.15	6.75
Clayton McGinness	R-R	6-1	180	1-13-97	1	2	5.46	20	0	0	4	28	28	18	17	3	12	25	.267	.302	.242	8.04	3.86
Griffin McLarty	L-R	6-3	185	8-10-98	3	4	6.04	28	3	0	2	45	43	33	30	8	31	50	.257	.319	.214	10.07	6.25
Morgan McSweeney	R-R	6-4	210	9-21-97	1	2	3.86	13	0	0	1	19	18	9	8	1	11	23	.261	.167	.311	11.09	5.30
Zach Peek	R-R	6-3	190	5-6-98	0	3	3.57	11	11	0	0	45	41	20	18	3	13	40	.243	.202	.288	7.94	2.58
Hector Perez	R-R	6-3	223	6-6-96	0	3	5.27	12	0	0	3	14	13	8	8	3	5	19	.255	.263	.250	12.51	3.29
Shelton Perkins	R-R	5-10	215	1-28-97	1	4	3.28	28	0	0	3	36	22	18	13	2	25	37	.173	.164	.182	9.34	6.31
Cade Povich	L-L	6-3	185	4-12-00	2	2	6.94	6	5	0	0	23	21	18	18	5	11	26	.231	.176	.263	10.03	4.24
Jake Prizina	L-L	6-0	190	1-24-97	3	1	2.93	17	0	0	0	31	29	12	10	3	7	29	.250	.159	.306	8.51	2.05
Wes Robertson	R-R	6-2	190	3-11-96	0	0	4.50	2	0	0	0	2	1	1	1	0	1	2	.167	.000	.250	9.00	4.50

Grayson Rodriguez	L-R	6-5	220	11-16-99	0	1	9.64	2	2	0	0	5	2	5	5	0	5	11	.125	.000	.182	21.21	9.64
Drew Rom	L-L	6-2	170	12-15-99	7	2	4.37	19	18	0	0	82	92	44	40	9	29	101	.280	.228	.307	11.04	3.17
Garrett Stallings	R-R	6-2	200	8-8-97	6	10	6.28	26	22	1	0	119	140	90	83	27	29	124	.286	.345	.236	9.38	2.19
Adam Stauffer	R-R	6-7	240	1-13-99	4	2	3.41	25	2	0	1	63	55	26	24	6	31	74	.234	.269	.205	10.52	4.41
Chris Vallimont	R-R	6-5	220	3-18-97	1	0	0.69	3	3	0	0	13	5	1	1	0	4	18	.119	.148	.067	12.46	2.77
Gregori Vasquez	R-R	6-1	185	9-8-97	0	0	0.00	1	0	0	1	2	1	0	0	0	1	1	.167	.000	.250	4.50	4.50
Antonio Velez	L-L	6-1	195	3-31-97	1	7	6.14	11	10	0	0	48	52	36	33	12	13	51	.277	.333	.250	9.50	2.42
Ryan Watson	R-R	6-5	215	11-15-97	7	5	3.41	20	18	0	1	95	81	39	36	15	21	100	.229	.204	.251	9.47	1.99
Alex Wells	L-L	6-1	195	2-27-97	0	0	0.00	1	1	0	0	3	3	0	0	0	0	2	.300	.200	.400	6.75	0.00
Brandon Young	R-R	6-6	210	8-19-98	1	0	2.03	3	3	0	0	13	13	3	3	2	6	10	.255	.286	.217	6.75	4.05

Fielding

Catcher	PCT	G	PO	A	E	DP	PB
Angulo	.986	8	67	2	1	0	0
Handley	.982	68	628	41	12	3	7
Mantecon	1.000	2	13	1	0	0	1
Roberts	.992	61	558	48	5	5	10
Rodriguez	1.000	2	18	0	0	0	0
Rutschman	1.000	2	25	1	0	0	1

First Base	PCT	G	PO	A	E	DP
Daschbach	.995	80	558	42	3	41
Mayo	1.000	2	14	1	0	0
Mundy	.983	51	336	20	6	27
Welk	.973	11	70	3	2	5

Second Base	PCT	G	PO	A	E	DP
Cullen	.958	11	21	25	2	8
Givin	1.000	3	2	3	0	0
Graffanino	1.000	6	6	12	0	2
Hall	1.000	4	5	11	0	1
Norby	.968	56	74	107	6	16
Ortiz	.986	21	26	47	1	10
Prieto	.987	24	32	44	1	13
Urias	1.000	1	2	2	0	0
Westburg	.984	16	22	41	1	9

Third Base	PCT	G	PO	A	E	DP
Cullen	.875	11	5	9	2	0
Dunlan	1.000	1	0	3	0	0
Givin	1.000	3	4	2	0	1
Graffanino	.800	3	1	3	1	0
Henderson	.966	27	12	45	2	5
Mayo	.821	20	8	24	7	0
Ortiz	1.000	2	1	3	0	0
Prieto	.963	58	40	89	5	6
Urias	.500	1	0	1	1	0
Westburg	.955	16	10	32	2	3

Shortstop	PCT	G	PO	A	E	DP
Givin	1.000	4	0	10	0	1
Graffanino	1.000	4	7	4	0	1
Henderson	.921	18	27	43	6	4
Hernaiz	.979	13	16	31	1	2
Ortiz	.976	85	107	214	8	40
Prieto	1.000	5	4	2	0	0
Westburg	.968	13	8	22	1	3

Outfield	PCT	G	PO	A	E	DP
Cespedes	.971	27	33	0	1	0
Cowser	.979	45	91	3	2	2
Cullon	1.000	6	6	0	0	0
Daschbach	1.000	15	23	0	0	0
Fontana	.968	36	57	3	2	0
Givin	1.000	3	8	0	0	0
Graffanino	1.000	9	13	0	0	0
Hall	.943	23	32	1	2	0
Harris	.932	20	38	3	3	1
Haskin	.986	104	205	4	3	1
Norby	1.000	7	9	0	0	0
Rhodes	.975	24	37	2	1	0
Roberts	1.000	3	8	1	0	0
Tavarez	1.000	8	16	0	0	0
Watson	.995	93	187	3	1	0
Welk	1.000	19	35	2	0	0
Williams	--	2	0	0	0	0

ABERDEEN IRONBIRDS — *HIGH CLASS A*

SOUTH ATLANTIC LEAGUE

Batting	B-T	HT	WT	DOB	AVG	vLH	vRH	G	AB	R	H	2B	3B	HR	RBI	BB	HBP	SH	SF	SO	SB	CS	SLG	OBP
Andres Angulo	R-R	5-10	181	9-5-97	.189	.182	.190	17	53	3	10	2	0	1	6	5	0	0	0	13	1	0	.283	.259
Jonathan Arauz	B-R	6-0	195	8-3-98	.100	--	.100	3	10	1	1	0	0	0	1	1	0	0	1	2	0	0	.100	.167
Dylan Beavers	L-R	6-4	206	8-11-01	.286	.000	.364	4	14	0	4	0	0	0	2	2	0	0	0	5	0	0	.286	.375
Isaac Bellony	B-R	6-2	220	12-15-01	.169	.094	.190	51	148	17	25	4	2	4	18	14	4	0	3	78	0	0	.304	.254
Frederick Bencosme	L-R	6-0	160	12-25-02	.154	.167	.152	12	39	5	6	2	1	0	2	2	0	0	0	9	0	1	.256	.195
TT Bowens	R-R	6-4	235	5-27-98	.248	.318	.232	106	355	51	88	20	5	7	45	66	9	0	3	126	3	1	.392	.376
Collin Burns	L-R	5-11	187	5-20-00	.269	.206	.285	82	309	49	83	20	0	6	34	27	6	0	2	57	13	3	.392	.337
Billy Cook	R-R	6-1	200	1-7-99	.221	.215	.223	112	389	49	86	21	6	15	65	34	10	1	3	139	25	4	.422	.298
Maxwell Costes	R-R	6-1	215	7-30-99	.375	.500	.250	2	8	3	3	0	0	0	2	2	0	0	0	2	0	0	.375	.500
Colton Cowser	L-R	6-3	195	3-20-00	.258	.143	.295	62	229	42	59	19	2	4	22	45	3	0	1	79	16	1	.410	.385
Trendon Craig	R-R	6-1	195	7-11-00	.258	.292	.247	27	97	11	25	3	1	0	10	9	0	0	0	34	7	2	.309	.321
Greg Cullen	L-R	5-10	190	11-13-96	--	--	--	1	0	1	0	0	0	0	0	1	0	0	0	0	0	0	--	1.000
Brett Cumberland	B-R	5-11	200	6-25-95	.125	.000	.167	4	8	0	1	0	0	0	1	2	1	0	0	5	0	1	.125	.364
Isaac De Leon	R-R	6-3	209	11-7-01	.170	.286	.121	15	47	6	8	0	1	0	4	7	2	0	0	22	1	0	.213	.304
Yusniel Diaz	R-R	6-1	215	10-7-96	.286	.250	.300	5	14	1	4	1	0	1	3	3	0	0	1	4	0	0	.571	.389
Jud Fabian	R-L	6-1	195	9-27-00	.167	.167	.167	8	24	1	4	1	0	0	4	5	0	0	1	8	0	2	.208	.300
Shayne Fontana	L-L	6-2	195	6-21-97	.258	.143	.292	9	31	4	8	0	0	2	6	6	1	0	0	12	2	0	.452	.395
Chris Givin	R-R	6-2	185	3-21-97	.217	.222	.216	29	92	13	20	2	0	0	6	11	2	0	2	15	1	1	.239	.308
AJ Graffanino	L-R	6-2	170	7-16-97	.200	.182	.208	13	35	3	7	0	0	0	6	7	1	0	0	2	2	0	.200	.349
Wilkin Grullon	R-R	6-0	220	11-28-99	.174	.300	.139	16	46	5	8	2	0	0	3	5	0	0	0	20	0	0	.217	.255
Darell Hernaiz	R-R	6-1	190	8-3-01	.305	.394	.269	60	226	41	69	13	3	5	29	22	5	0	2	43	22	3	.456	.376
Brayan Hernandez	L-R	6-1	225	11-11-01	.000	.000	.000	1	2	0	0	0	0	0	0	0	0	0	0	2	0	0	.000	.000
Ryan Higgins	R-R	6-1	200	1-25-00	.190	.176	.194	25	84	10	16	4	1	2	7	5	3	0	1	29	0	2	.333	.258
Heston Kjerstad	L-R	6-3	205	2-12-99	.233	.256	.225	43	163	28	38	8	2	3	20	16	4	0	3	47	1	0	.362	.312
Shed Long Jr.	L-R	5-8	184	8-22-95	.188	.500	.000	5	16	1	3	0	1	0	0	4	0	0	0	8	0	0	.313	.350
Michael Mantecon	R-R	5-11	192	2-2-02	.160	.000	.182	8	25	0	4	1	0	0	2	0	0	0	0	8	0	0	.200	.160
Coby Mayo	R-R	6-5	215	12-10-01	.251	.210	.264	68	255	50	64	16	2	14	49	27	3	0	3	62	5	1	.494	.326
Connor Norby	R-R	5-10	187	6-8-00	.237	.212	.242	48	186	27	44	7	2	8	20	18	3	0	2	50	6	3	.425	.311
Connor Pavolony	R-R	6-1	195	10-25-99	.197	.263	.178	60	173	26	34	5	2	5	26	38	6	0	2	64	1	1	.335	.356
Erison Placencia	R-R	6-1	170	12-31-01	.164	.118	.182	20	61	6	10	1	0	1	1	7	0	0	0	30	1	0	.230	.250
Cesar Prieto	L-R	5-9	175	5-10-99	.340	.160	.403	25	97	13	33	6	0	7	20	5	2	0	1	16	3	1	.619	.381
Adam Retzbach	R-R	6-4	220	11-13-00	.083	.250	.000	3	12	2	1	0	1	0	1	0	0	0	0	7	0	0	.250	.083
John Rhodes	R-R	6-0	200	8-15-00	.259	.278	.255	58	201	43	52	15	2	5	35	35	9	0	2	50	16	0	.428	.389
Ramon Rodriguez	R-R	5-11	194	10-30-98	.242	.200	.252	56	182	21	44	2	1	2	21	15	3	1	3	25	7	1	.297	.305
Adley Rutschman	B-R	6-2	220	2-6-98	.429	--	.429	5	14	2	6	3	0	0	1	2	0	0	1	1	0	0	.643	.471
Davis Tavarez	R-R	6-2	235	1-7-99	.286	.214	.305	46	133	16	38	8	1	5	22	8	3	0	0	39	1	0	.474	.340

Jacob Teter	L-L	6-6	225	2-26-99	.285	.154	.317	37	130	16	37	10	0	4	26	15	1	0	3	43	1	0	.454	.356
Luis Valdez	B-R	5-11	165	1-22-00	.233	.286	.217	20	60	8	14	0	1	1	5	5	0	1	1	21	12	1	.317	.288
Terrin Vavra	L-R	6-1	200	5-12-97	.188	--	.188	5	16	5	3	3	0	0	1	4	0	0	1	3	1	0	.375	.333
Max Wagner	R-R	6-0	215	8-19-01	.167	.400	.077	5	18	3	3	0	0	0	1	0	0	0	1	5	1	0	.167	.158
Toby Welk	R-R	6-2	205	5-2-97	.444	.500	.438	5	18	3	8	2	0	1	6	0	0	0	1	2	0	0	.722	.421
Donta Williams	L-L	5-10	185	6-30-99	.222	.158	.238	86	284	48	63	14	4	4	42	51	6	0	3	85	23	5	.342	.349

Pitching	B-T	HT	WT	DOB	W	L	ERA	G	GS	CG	SV	IP	H	R	ER	HR	BB	SO	AVG	vLH	vRH	K/9	BB/9
Justin Armbruester	R-R	6-4	235	10-21-98	2	1	4.02	12	12	0	0	54	42	25	24	8	18	63	.215	.299	.172	10.57	3.02
Carson Carter	R-R	6-4	212	8-6-97	0	2	8.71	9	0	0	0	21	21	20	20	5	13	28	.247	.263	.234	12.19	5.66
Noah Denoyer	B-R	6-5	225	2-17-98	4	0	4.00	6	1	0	0	18	19	9	8	0	6	27	.268	.250	.275	13.50	3.00
Jensen Elliott	R-R	6-6	231	4-8-97	1	0	3.00	4	0	0	0	12	8	4	4	2	1	12	.186	.154	.200	9.00	0.75
Daniel Federman	L-R	6-1	205	9-18-98	0	3	4.20	11	4	0	2	30	32	16	14	4	6	39	.264	.240	.282	11.70	1.80
Ignacio Feliz	R-R	6-1	180	10-23-99	5	2	4.18	26	11	0	1	93	63	47	43	9	55	135	.190	.213	.174	13.11	5.34
Rico Garcia	R-R	5-9	201	1-10-94	0	0	0.00	2	1	0	0	4	1	0	0	0	0	9	.077	.000	.143	20.25	0.00
Connor Gillispie	R-R	5-11	185	11-10-97	8	5	3.79	25	14	0	0	97	72	47	41	18	48	113	.204	.200	.206	10.45	4.44
Thomas Girard	R-R	5-11	195	5-4-99	1	0	6.08	11	0	0	1	13	12	9	9	1	9	14	.235	.158	.281	9.45	6.08
DL Hall	L-L	6-2	195	9-19-98	0	0	0.00	1	1	0	0	4	2	0	0	0	0	6	.154	.000	.200	13.50	0.00
Dan Hammer	R-R	6-2	210	9-10-97	3	1	5.89	13	3	0	0	37	36	25	24	3	36	41	.252	.193	.291	10.06	8.84
Brenan Hanifee	R-R	6-5	215	5-29-98	0	0	3.38	1	1	0	0	3	3	1	1	0	1	2	.273	.333	.250	6.75	3.38
Ryan Hartman	L-L	6-3	234	4-21-94	0	0	0.00	1	1	0	0	3	1	0	0	0	1	4	.100	.500	.000	12.00	3.00
Matt Harvey	R-R	6-4	220	3-27-89	0	0	0.00	1	1	0	0	6	4	0	0	0	0	4	.200	.286	.154	6.00	0.00
Dylan Heid	R-R	6-1	180	5-18-98	0	0	4.76	4	0	0	0	6	4	3	3	0	4	12	.200	.182	.222	19.06	6.35
Nolan Hoffman	R-R	6-4	190	8-9-97	0	0	0.00	1	0	0	0	2	0	0	0	0	2	1	.000	--	.000	4.50	9.00
Daniel Lloyd	R-R	6-3	232	8-8-00	3	4	4.11	17	2	0	0	46	48	30	21	4	13	53	.261	.232	.278	10.37	2.54
Jake Lyons	R-R	6-5	280	8-19-98	4	1	4.43	14	4	0	1	43	35	23	21	6	20	43	.222	.210	.229	9.07	4.22
Chayce McDermott	L-R	6-3	197	8-22-98	0	1	3.60	2	2	0	0	5	3	2	2	1	1	10	.167	.154	.200	18.00	1.80
2-team total (19 Asheville Tourists)					6	2	5.38	21	12	0	0	77	60	50	46	10	44	124	.207	.262	.165	14.49	5.14
Clayton McGinness	R-R	6-1	180	1-13-97	1	0	0.98	11	0	0	6	18	6	3	2	1	4	21	.102	.083	.114	10.31	1.96
Griffin McLarty	L-R	6-3	185	8-10-98	0	0	4.15	3	1	0	0	9	4	4	4	2	5	13	.138	.286	.091	13.50	5.19
Xavier Moore	R-R	6-2	175	1-7-99	2	4	1.36	30	0	0	10	33	18	11	5	1	15	58	.157	.163	.152	15.82	4.09
Alex Pham	R-R	5-11	165	10-10-99	5	2	5.66	11	0	0	0	21	18	14	13	2	11	30	.247	.222	.261	13.06	4.79
Jean Pinto	R-R	5-11	175	1-9-01	4	6	3.83	24	19	0	2	92	79	48	39	11	46	103	.227	.190	.248	10.11	4.52
Cade Povich	L-L	6-3	185	4-12-00	2	0	0.00	2	2	0	0	12	4	0	0	0	2	15	.103	.000	.154	11.25	1.50
Jake Prizina	L-L	6-0	190	1-24-97	1	1	4.82	15	0	0	2	28	28	16	15	1	9	29	.259	.286	.250	9.32	2.89
Rickey Ramirez	R-R	6-0	168	10-20-96	3	0	4.24	27	0	0	2	47	53	27	22	1	30	41	.288	.216	.336	7.91	5.79
Denyi Reyes	R-R	6-4	255	11-2-96	0	0	0.00	1	1	0	0	1	0	0	0	0	0	2	.000	.000	--	18.00	0.00
Nick Richmond	R-R	6-4	195	4-2-98	0	1	3.54	16	0	0	2	20	15	10	8	0	9	20	.217	.231	.209	8.85	3.98
Wes Robertson	R-R	6-2	190	3-11-96	2	2	6.08	21	0	0	2	27	26	22	18	2	16	27	.268	.154	.345	9.11	5.40
Grayson Rodriguez	L-R	6-5	220	11-16-99	0	0	0.00	1	1	0	0	1	1	0	0	0	2	1	.250	--	.250	6.75	13.50
Houston Roth	R-R	6-3	220	3-9-98	10	5	4.49	26	16	0	0	100	93	53	50	10	42	108	.243	.246	.242	9.69	3.77
Nick Roth	R-R	5-10	175	8-28-96	1	2	5.59	24	0	0	4	29	39	22	18	2	4	33	.322	.313	.329	10.24	1.24
Kade Strowd	R-R	6-2	175	9-17-97	2	1	1.20	12	0	0	1	15	10	6	2	2	6	21	.192	.353	.114	12.60	3.60
Davis Tavarez	R-R	6-2	235	1-7-99	0	0	0.00	1	0	0	0	1	0	0	0	0	0	1	.000	--	.000	9.00	0.00
Carlos Tavera	R-R	6-1	195	10-6-98	3	3	4.40	16	16	0	0	57	43	28	28	8	34	81	.205	.203	.206	12.72	5.34
Peter Van Loon	R-R	6-5	210	2-18-99	11	4	3.25	24	14	0	0	89	80	37	32	7	32	97	.242	.259	.230	9.85	3.25
Gregori Vasquez	R-R	6-1	185	9-8-97	0	0	2.35	20	0	0	5	38	34	11	10	4	10	25	.234	.188	.258	5.87	2.35
Antonio Velez	L-L	6-1	195	3-31-97	0	2	4.50	4	3	0	0	14	18	11	7	1	3	15	.290	.353	.267	9.64	1.93
Tyler Wells	R-R	6-8	255	8-26-94	0	1	3.86	1	1	0	0	2	1	1	1	0	0	3	.125	.000	.167	11.57	0.00

Fielding

Catcher	PCT	G	PO	A	E	DP	PB
Angulo	.987	16	140	7	2	1	3
Cumberland	1.000	2	12	1	0	0	0
Grullon	.983	14	114	5	2	0	3
Hernandez	1.000	1	8	0	0	0	0
Mantecon	.969	4	29	2	1	1	1
Pavolony	.981	56	546	26	11	1	4
Retzbach	1.000	3	36	2	0	1	2
Rodriguez	.998	46	477	27	1	3	2
Rutschman	.950	3	19	0	1	0	0

First Base	PCT	G	PO	A	E	DP
Bellony	.880	5	21	1	3	3
Bowens	.990	85	556	42	6	51
Cook	1.000	4	12	1	0	0
Costes	1.000	2	12	0	0	1
De Leon	1.000	8	54	4	0	2
Higgins	1.000	3	23	3	0	4
Rodriguez	1.000	4	22	1	0	1
Teter	.984	27	179	8	3	19

Second Base	PCT	G	PO	A	E	DP
Arauz	1.000	1	4	4	0	1
Bencosme	1.000	2	3	7	0	1
Burns	1.000	5	10	5	0	1
Cook	.915	27	35	51	8	9
De Leon	1.000	1	1	3	0	0
Givin	1.000	9	14	16	0	3
Graffanino	.933	6	14	14	2	6
Hernaiz	.968	17	19	42	2	7
Long Jr.	1.000	2	4	2	0	1
Norby	.992	40	54	73	1	16
Placencia	.929	6	3	10	1	0
Prieto	.970	7	17	15	1	2
Rhodes	1.000	1	1	1	0	1
Valdez	.919	19	28	40	6	6
Vavra	1.000	2	3	1	0	1

Third Base	PCT	G	PO	A	E	DP
Arauz	.000	1	0	0	0	0
Bowens	1.000	2	1	5	0	0
Cook	.750	2	1	2	1	0
Cullen	.000	1	0	0	0	0
De Leon	1.000	6	3	4	0	0
Givin	1.000	15	8	20	0	3
Graffanino	.000	1	0	0	0	0
Hernaiz	1.000	18	14	29	0	3
Higgins	.914	19	8	24	3	0
Long Jr.	.000	1	0	0	0	0
Mayo	.924	61	31	90	10	3
Placencia	1.000	10	11	11	0	2
Prieto	1.000	2	1	1	0	0
Vavra	1.000	1	0	1	0	0
Wagner	1.000	5	2	6	0	1

Shortstop	PCT	G	PO	A	E	DP
Arauz	1.000	1	0	1	0	0
Bencosme	.815	10	9	13	5	2
Burns	.961	74	95	174	11	35
De Leon	1.000	1	0	2	0	0
Givin	1.000	6	4	17	0	2
Graffanino	1.000	5	3	8	0	2
Hernaiz	.977	25	35	50	2	9
Norby	.000	1	0	0	0	0
Placencia	1.000	5	3	12	0	3
Prieto	.970	10	10	22	1	3

Outfield	PCT	G	PO	A	E	DP
Beavers	1.000	4	4	0	0	0
Bellony	.938	37	58	2	4	0
Bowens	1.000	2	2	0	0	0
Burns	1.000	1	1	0	0	0

Cook	.974	72	145	6	4	2
Cowser	.964	56	78	3	3	0
Craig	.971	23	34	0	1	0
Diaz	1.000	4	2	0	0	0
Fabian	1.000	7	9	1	0	0
Fontana	.941	7	16	0	1	0
Graffanino	--	1	0	0	0	0
Higgins	.833	3	5	0	1	0
Kjerstad	.969	31	58	4	2	0
Mantecon	1.000	4	4	0	0	0
Norby	1.000	3	1	0	0	0
Rhodes	.978	55	85	5	2	1
Tavarez	.940	36	46	1	3	0
Vavra	1.000	2	5	0	0	0
Welk	1.000	3	2	0	0	0
Williams	.972	79	137	4	4	0

DELMARVA SHOREBIRDS — *LOW CLASS A*

CAROLINA LEAGUE

Batting	B-T	HT	WT	DOB	AVG	vLH	vRH	G	AB	R	H	2B	3B	HR	RBI	BB	HBP	SH	SF	SO	SB	CS	SLG	OBP
Stiven Acevedo	R-R	6-4	185	8-2-02	.168	.158	.170	38	131	18	22	5	1	1	11	15	1	0	0	52	7	1	.244	.259
Silas Ardoin	R-R	6-0	215	9-19-00	.227	.000	.256	12	44	5	10	1	0	0	8	8	1	0	1	18	0	0	.250	.352
Dylan Beavers	L-R	6-4	206	8-11-01	.359	.571	.333	16	64	13	23	7	2	0	13	12	1	0	0	11	6	1	.531	.468
Isaac Bellony	B-R	6-2	220	12-15-01	.289	.200	.307	50	180	27	52	11	1	6	34	32	0	0	1	69	3	2	.461	.394
Frederick Bencosme	L-R	6-0	160	12-25-02	.336	.310	.340	59	220	29	74	8	2	3	29	27	1	1	1	31	8	5	.432	.410
Cristopher Cespedes	R-R	6-3	200	5-18-98	.333	.500	.313	5	18	6	6	0	0	0	1	4	0	0	0	7	0	1	.333	.455
Maxwell Costes	R-R	6-1	215	7-30-99	.150	.000	.158	8	20	5	3	1	0	0	2	10	2	0	0	10	0	0	.200	.469
Trendon Craig	R-R	6-1	195	7-11-00	.262	.300	.256	59	206	34	54	6	3	2	33	35	6	0	0	72	8	7	.350	.385
Adam Crampton	R-R	6-1	183	5-24-01	.234	.333	.224	18	64	10	15	3	0	0	10	8	2	0	0	17	0	2	.281	.338
Josue Cruz	L-L	6-5	231	12-25-00	.132	.053	.153	28	91	10	12	2	0	1	10	18	1	0	0	53	0	0	.187	.282
Greg Cullen	L-R	5-10	190	11-13-96	.276	.167	.304	9	29	4	8	0	1	0	3	4	0	0	0	4	0	0	.345	.364
Isaac De Leon	R-R	6-3	209	11-7-01	.229	.204	.234	94	323	48	74	21	1	8	52	68	5	0	5	120	5	0	.375	.367
Mishael Deson	R-R	6-4	211	7-7-02	.230	.316	.216	76	270	25	62	5	0	2	26	37	3	0	3	93	10	3	.270	.326
Jud Fabian	R-L	6-1	195	9-27-00	.386	.250	.400	10	44	16	17	7	2	3	9	8	0	0	0	9	0	0	.841	.481
Wilkin Grullon	R-R	6-0	220	11-28-99	.222	.500	.212	18	54	5	12	4	0	3	6	5	1	0	0	15	0	0	.463	.300
Darell Hernaiz	R-R	6-1	190	8-3-01	.283	.300	.280	32	127	25	36	7	2	6	25	8	3	0	0	22	9	0	.512	.341
Brayan Hernandez	L-R	6-1	225	11-11-01	.177	.048	.207	37	113	8	20	4	0	3	8	6	2	0	0	45	0	0	.292	.231
Ryan Higgins	R-R	6-1	200	1-25-00	.203	.200	.203	45	153	25	31	8	2	2	18	21	3	0	0	52	4	2	.320	.311
Douglas Hodo III	R-R	6-0	185	9-25-00	.200	.222	.194	13	40	7	8	1	0	0	1	12	2	0	0	16	4	0	.225	.407
Jackson Holliday	L-R	6-1	175	12-4-03	.238	.100	.281	12	42	8	10	4	0	0	6	15	0	0	0	10	1	1	.333	.439
Heston Kjerstad	L-R	6-3	205	2-12-99	.463	.375	.472	22	80	17	37	9	0	2	17	13	4	0	1	17	0	0	.650	.551
Shed Long Jr.	L-R	5-8	184	8-22-95	--	--	--	1	0	0	0	0	0	0	0	0	1	0	0	0	0	0	--	1.000
Michael Mantecon	R-R	5-11	192	2-2-02	.198	.176	.202	35	116	10	23	3	0	1	6	6	0	0	1	40	1	1	.250	.236
Roberto Martinez	B-R	6-0	145	1-16-03	.234	.222	.236	38	124	11	29	11	0	2	16	10	5	0	1	51	1	2	.371	.314
Erison Placencia	R-R	6-1	170	12-31-01	.135	.167	.130	21	52	3	7	0	0	0	2	5	1	0	1	31	1	1	.135	.220
Elio Prado	R-R	6-0	160	11-29-01	.197	.185	.198	66	234	27	46	6	2	1	25	39	10	0	1	63	3	2	.252	.335
Moises Ramirez	R-R	6-4	235	2-1-02	.147	.059	.160	40	136	8	20	6	0	0	10	11	5	0	1	63	0	1	.191	.235
Adam Retzbach	R-R	6-4	220	11-13-00	.200	.333	.185	10	30	6	6	2	0	0	0	10	3	0	0	14	1	0	.267	.442
Noelberth Romero	R-R	6-0	183	12-5-01	.230	.309	.216	104	383	50	88	16	1	9	48	30	2	0	3	81	17	7	.347	.287
Anthony Servideo	L-R	5-10	175	3-11-99	.129	.000	.138	9	31	1	4	0	0	1	4	1	0	0	0	17	0	0	.226	.156
Davis Tavarez	R-R	6-2	235	1-7-99	.212	.250	.203	27	99	10	21	4	0	2	11	6	0	0	1	31	1	0	.313	.255
Reed Trimble	B-R	6-0	180	6-6-00	.291	.154	.330	31	117	19	34	6	0	2	18	13	0	0	3	28	2	0	.393	.353
Luis Valdez	B-R	5-11	165	1-22-00	.271	.242	.276	95	377	71	102	13	4	2	20	39	6	0	2	95	59	14	.342	.347
Max Wagner	R-R	6-0	215	8-19-01	.250	.000	.261	13	48	9	12	2	2	1	8	9	4	0	1	13	0	0	.438	.403
Creed Willems	L-R	6-0	225	6-4-03	.190	.118	.203	68	221	21	42	9	4	4	23	14	9	0	2	68	0	0	.321	.264
Carter Young	B-R	6-0	180	1-24-01	.246	.571	.207	14	65	11	16	5	1	1	7	5	0	0	1	13	0	0	.400	.296

Pitching	B-T	HT	WT	DOB	W	L	ERA	G	GS	CG	SV	IP	H	R	ER	HR	BB	SO	AVG	vLH	vRH	K/9	BB/9
Darlin Alcantara	R-R	6-3	180	9-20-01	0	2	6.00	8	6	0	2	24	27	25	16	3	22	16	.287	.250	.342	6.00	8.25
Harol Arias	R-R	6-2	180	11-7-02	0	2	8.10	2	2	0	0	7	12	9	6	0	6	4	.364	.333	.389	5.40	8.10
Carter Baumler	R-R	6-2	195	1-31-02	0	0	1.54	4	4	0	0	12	7	3	2	0	7	20	.171	.267	.115	15.43	5.40
Jared Beck	L-L	7-0	225	7-1-00	1	0	3.60	4	0	0	0	10	11	6	4	0	5	10	.282	.250	.304	9.00	4.50
Hugo Beltran	R-R	6-1	190	6-13-00	4	5	2.58	27	0	0	0	38	44	20	11	1	16	34	.286	.287	.284	7.98	3.76
Joel Benitez	R-R	6-2	175	7-21-00	3	2	11.63	13	0	0	0	22	26	31	28	4	19	27	.295	.263	.355	11.22	7.89
Randy Beriguete	R-R	6-4	221	11-2-02	1	1	9.45	9	0	0	0	13	16	15	14	0	12	12	.302	.368	.133	8.10	8.10
Trace Bright	R-R	6-4	199	10-26-00	0	0	2.35	3	0	0	1	8	2	3	2	0	4	5	.091	.154	.000	5.87	4.70
Carson Carter	R-R	6-4	212	8-6-97	0	2	6.41	12	0	0	0	20	24	15	14	3	8	18	.300	.286	.316	8.24	3.66
Moises Chace	R-R	6-1	213	6-9-03	3	5	4.98	19	14	0	1	60	47	39	33	1	42	64	.213	.169	.275	9.65	6.34
Cooper Chandler	R-R	6-2	200	8-12-98	0	0	11.25	3	0	0	0	4	7	5	5	0	1	3	.368	.385	.333	6.75	2.25
Wyatt Cheney	R-R	6-0	185	1-10-01	0	0	--	1	0	0	0	0	1	0	0	0	1	0	1.000	1.000	--	--	--
Deivy Cruz	L-L	5-11	154	2-13-04	1	1	4.02	13	12	0	0	54	45	33	24	3	37	52	.224	.182	.244	8.72	6.20
Shane Davis	R-R	6-3	185	8-26-99	1	6	4.07	13	12	0	0	55	44	34	25	4	29	68	.212	.202	.225	11.06	4.72
Juan De Los Santos	R-R	6-3	250	5-25-02	2	9	4.29	22	21	0	0	80	72	46	38	7	41	84	.237	.256	.213	9.49	4.63
Daniel Federman	L-R	6-1	205	9-18-98	0	6	6.59	10	7	0	0	41	50	30	30	7	12	41	.291	.295	.286	9.00	2.63
Graham Firoved	R-R	6-1	185	9-26-99	0	0	9.00	1	0	0	1	1	2	1	1	0	1	1	.400	.400	--	9.00	9.00
Keagan Gillies	R-R	6-8	255	1-27-98	1	2	6.46	7	4	0	0	15	20	12	11	3	7	17	.303	.342	.250	9.98	4.11
Thomas Girard	R-R	5-11	195	5-4-99	2	0	5.54	20	0	0	0	26	26	19	16	3	22	30	.257	.234	.278	10.38	7.62
Conor Grady	R-R	6-2	215	10-31-98	6	10	5.46	24	15	0	0	96	103	77	58	10	45	100	.270	.251	.293	9.41	4.23
Dan Hammer	R-R	6-2	210	9-10-97	2	3	5.44	12	6	0	0	43	26	27	26	7	37	51	.171	.198	.141	10.67	7.74
Dylan Heid	R-R	6-1	180	5-18-98	2	2	4.55	10	0	0	1	32	26	16	16	3	22	43	.213	.260	.133	12.22	6.25
Ryan Hennen	R-L	6-0	180	9-30-97	0	0	6.00	3	0	0	0	6	7	4	4	0	1	5	.280	.455	.143	7.50	1.50
2-team total (10 Columbia Fireflies)					2	2	3.94	13	0	0	0	32	37	16	14	2	5	42	.282	.342	.258	11.81	1.41
Tyler Joyner	R-R	6-4	225	5-10-96	0	0	1.93	2	2	0	0	5	4	1	1	1	1	4	.250	.125	.375	7.71	1.93
Carson King	R-R	6-2	207	12-5-99	0	2	14.09	5	0	0	0	8	16	15	12	2	8	8	.421	.476	.353	9.39	9.39
Kelvin LaRoche	R-R	5-11	170	7-31-99	2	1	5.87	7	0	0	1	15	20	12	10	0	2	10	.294	.283	.318	5.87	1.17

Yeancarlos Lleras	R-R	6-0	170	7-22-00	0	0	--	2	0	0	0	0	1	6	6	0	7	0	1.000	--	1.000	--	--
Daniel Lloyd	R-R	6-3	232	8-8-00	0	1	4.21	13	0	0	2	26	24	17	12	1	10	27	.240	.196	.286	9.47	3.51
Ryan Long	R-R	6-6	240	10-19-99	7	5	3.10	21	10	0	1	73	60	30	25	6	31	73	.217	.222	.211	9.04	3.84
Hector Lopez	R-R	6-2	275	10-4-01	0	1	15.19	4	0	0	0	5	9	10	9	2	7	3	.391	.400	.385	5.06	11.81
Jake Lyons	R-R	6-5	280	8-19-98	2	0	3.38	2	0	0	0	5	5	2	2	0	4	8	.250	.000	.417	13.50	6.75
Michael Mantecon	R-R	5-11	192	2-2-02	0	0	0.00	1	0	0	0	1	1	0	0	0	1	2	.250	.000	.500	18.00	9.00
Alejandro Mendez	R-R	6-5	254	2-28-01	0	0	8.79	28	0	0	1	42	48	49	41	3	47	45	.286	.289	.282	9.64	10.07
Eduard Monroy	L-L	5-11	198	10-8-01	0	0	8.58	18	0	0	1	28	42	40	27	7	25	29	.326	.383	.293	9.21	7.94
Hayden Nierman	B-R	6-2	170	1-27-00	0	0	0.00	1	0	0	0	1	0	0	0	0	1	1	.000	.000	--	9.00	9.00
Trey Nordmann	R-R	6-5	220	2-13-01	1	0	27.00	3	0	0	0	1	0	3	3	0	6	1	.000	.000	.000	9.00	54.00
Juan Nunez	R-R	5-11	190	12-7-00	0	0	1.23	4	4	0	0	15	7	3	2	0	13	7	.146	.136	.154	4.30	7.98
Miguel Padilla	R-R	6-2	180	4-13-02	1	1	4.63	9	1	0	1	23	17	13	12	2	15	20	.205	.265	.118	7.71	5.79
Hector Perez	R-R	6-3	223	6-6-96	1	0	2.55	9	0	0	0	18	9	5	5	1	14	25	.153	.143	.167	12.74	7.13
Alex Pham	R-R	5-11	165	10-10-99	0	0	1.59	6	0	0	2	11	8	2	2	0	7	15	.190	.115	.313	11.91	5.56
Edgar Portes	R-R	6-2	165	10-2-02	0	6	6.32	18	8	0	0	57	56	47	40	11	37	49	.251	.208	.301	7.74	5.84
Preston Price	L-R	6-1	190	8-18-97	0	0	5.17	19	0	0	5	38	39	31	22	2	21	28	.258	.269	.247	6.57	4.93
Raul Rangel	R-R	6-4	200	10-9-02	0	1	5.79	3	1	0	0	5	3	4	3	0	5	7	.167	.091	.286	13.50	9.64
Denyi Reyes	R-R	6-4	255	11-2-96	1	0	1.80	1	1	0	0	5	3	1	1	0	1	5	.167	.214	.000	9.00	1.80
Nick Richmond	R-R	6-4	195	4-2-98	0	0	3.86	3	0	0	0	5	2	2	2	0	2	6	.125	.200	.000	11.57	3.86
Yaqui Rivera	R-R	6-2	150	7-19-03	3	3	6.17	16	0	0	2	35	38	26	24	2	17	46	.268	.310	.200	11.83	4.37
Reese Sharp	R-R	6-3	220	8-7-00	0	0	3.12	5	0	0	1	9	8	3	3	1	11	16	.250	.250	.250	16.62	11.42
Angel Vargas	R-R	6-1	173	12-1-01	0	2	11.79	16	0	0	0	24	41	37	31	3	21	25	.363	.295	.442	9.51	7.99
Cameron Weston	R-R	6-2	215	8-27-00	2	0	3.18	5	0	0	0	11	6	5	4	1	3	11	.150	.240	.000	8.74	2.38

Fielding

Catcher	PCT	G	PO	A	E	DP	PB
Ardoin	1.000	9	79	4	0	0	1
Grullon	.964	14	103	4	4	1	6
Hernandez	.973	32	266	26	8	0	8
Mantecon	.990	31	282	20	3	1	7
Retzbach	1.000	6	45	6	0	0	1
Willems	.989	47	397	40	5	2	9

First Base	PCT	G	PO	A	E	DP
Bellony	1.000	1	6	0	0	1
Costes	1.000	5	38	0	0	2
Crampton	1.000	1	7	2	0	0
Cruz	.951	27	188	7	10	15
De Leon	1.000	14	92	5	0	7
Grullon	1.000	1	4	0	0	0
Hernandez	1.000	1	1	0	0	0
Higgins	.967	16	82	6	3	5
Mantecon	.000	1	0	0	0	0
Martinez	.969	25	151	3	5	13
Placencia	1.000	6	33	2	0	1
Ramirez	.985	21	131	3	2	7
Retzbach	1.000	4	24	3	0	2
Romero	.941	5	30	2	2	5
Willems	.975	12	69	8	2	7

Second Base	PCT	G	PO	A	E	DP
Bencosme	.976	10	14	26	1	7
Crampton	1.000	8	13	22	0	4
Cullen	.921	7	17	18	3	6
Hernaiz	.867	7	8	18	4	1
Holliday	.938	4	3	12	1	2
Long Jr.	.000	1	0	0	1	0
Mantecon	.000	1	0	0	0	0
Martinez	.909	6	10	10	2	1
Placencia	1.000	3	1	2	0	2
Romero	.946	31	48	75	7	9
Servideo	1.000	2	4	2	0	0
Valdez	.961	60	90	131	9	14
Young	.939	6	10	21	2	3

Third Base	PCT	G	PO	A	E	DP
Bencosme	.833	7	8	7	3	3
Crampton	1.000	5	6	6	0	2
De Leon	.859	48	49	61	18	4
Hernaiz	.833	3	4	1	1	0
Placencia	.857	4	1	5	1	0
Ramirez	.813	15	5	21	6	2
Romero	.883	45	37	54	12	4
Valdez	1.000	1	0	1	0	0
Wagner	1.000	9	7	14	0	0

Shortstop	PCT	G	PO	A	E	DP
Bencosme	.874	39	61	57	17	8
Crampton	.867	4	7	6	2	1
De Leon	.891	32	48	58	13	15
Hernaiz	.940	20	32	31	4	7
Holliday	.969	8	13	18	1	7
Placencia	.846	3	4	7	2	1
Romero	.870	14	17	30	7	4
Servideo	.833	2	0	5	1	2
Valdez	.857	1	1	5	1	1
Young	1.000	8	17	11	0	3

Outfield	PCT	G	PO	A	E	DP
Acevedo	.987	38	75	3	1	1
Beavers	1.000	15	31	2	0	0
Bellony	.977	43	82	3	2	0
Cespedes	1.000	4	7	0	0	0
Craig	1.000	52	88	1	0	0
Deson	.955	66	103	2	5	0
Fabian	1.000	8	24	1	0	1
Hernandez	1.000	1	1	0	0	0
Higgins	.982	25	50	5	1	0
Hodo III	1.000	13	31	1	0	1
Kjerstad	.938	16	29	1	2	0
Mantecon	--	1	0	0	0	0
Martinez	--	2	0	0	0	0
Prado	.970	59	122	6	4	2
Romero	--	1	0	0	0	0
Tavarez	1.000	17	23	2	0	0
Trimble	.960	20	44	4	2	0
Valdez	.963	44	75	2	3	1

FCL ORIOLES — ROOKIE

FLORIDA COMPLEX LEAGUE

Batting	B-T	HT	WT	DOB	AVG	vLH	vRH	G	AB	R	H	2B	3B	HR	RBI	BB	HBP	SH	SF	SO	SB	CS	SLG	OBP
Stiven Acevedo	R-R	6-4	185	8-2-02	.269	.333	.256	16	52	8	14	5	0	2	10	10	1	0	0	13	5	1	.481	.397
Jesus Alvarado	L-L	5-9	176	1-16-03	.255	.250	.256	21	47	9	12	1	0	0	4	10	1	0	0	20	1	2	.277	.397
Andres Angulo	R-R	5-10	181	9-5-97	.267	1.000	.214	5	15	3	4	1	0	0	0	1	1	0	0	4	0	0	.333	.353
Silas Ardoin	R-R	6-0	215	9-19-00	.000	--	.000	4	8	1	0	0	0	0	1	9	0	0	0	2	0	0	.000	.529
Samuel Basallo	L-R	6-3	180	8-13-04	.278	.367	.258	43	158	22	44	5	0	6	32	15	4	0	3	37	1	0	.424	.350
Dylan Beavers	L-R	6-4	206	8-11-01	.111	.000	.167	3	9	1	1	1	0	0	0	2	1	0	0	2	0	0	.222	.333
Frederick Bencosme	L-R	6-0	160	12-25-02	.375	.333	.400	2	8	2	3	0	1	0	0	0	1	0	0	0	0	0	.625	.444
Eruviel Castillo	R-R	6-1	150	12-10-03	.127	.154	.121	29	79	7	10	2	0	0	4	10	3	0	0	23	0	0	.152	.250
Teudis Cortorreal	L-L	6-1	170	12-15-03	.151	.200	.146	23	53	5	8	1	0	0	0	7	1	0	0	15	0	1	.170	.262
Maxwell Costes	R-R	6-1	215	7-30-99	.240	.667	.105	9	25	4	6	0	0	0	0	9	0	0	0	2	1	0	.240	.441
Adam Crampton	R-R	6-1	183	5-24-01	.125	--	.125	3	8	2	1	0	0	0	0	4	1	0	0	2	1	0	.125	.462
Rolphy Cruz	B-R	5-11	164	9-21-02	.213	.111	.239	31	89	10	19	5	0	0	13	7	1	0	2	25	2	4	.270	.273
Brett Cumberland	B-R	5-11	200	6-25-95	.429	--	.429	2	7	0	3	0	0	0	0	0	1	0	0	1	1	0	.429	.500
Anderson De Los Santos	R-R	5-11	185	1-11-04	.242	.148	.268	39	124	20	30	11	0	2	17	23	4	0	2	23	5	3	.379	.373
Yusniel Diaz	R-R	6-1	215	10-7-96	.200	--	.200	2	5	0	1	1	0	0	0	1	0	0	0	1	0	0	.400	.333
Jud Fabian	R-L	6-1	195	9-27-00	.500	1.000	.444	4	10	2	5	1	0	0	3	6	0	0	1	4	1	0	.600	.647
Shayne Fontana	L-L	6-2	195	6-21-97	.167	--	.167	2	6	0	1	0	0	0	0	0	0	0	0	1	0	1	.167	.167

Luis Gonzalez	L-L	6-4	185	11-2-02	.212	.226	.208	43	137	23	29	3	3	2	20	29	6	0	2	66	8	3	.321	.368
Victor Gonzalez	R-R	5-10	155	10-8-02	.120	.500	.087	17	25	9	3	0	0	1	4	10	1	0	0	9	3	0	.240	.389
Wilkin Grullon	R-R	6-0	220	11-28-99	.250	--	.250	2	8	1	2	1	0	0	2	0	1	0	0	2	0	0	.375	.333
Kevin Guerrero	R-R	6-3	165	4-17-04	.145	.100	.156	37	110	12	16	1	0	1	15	29	0	0	1	48	5	2	.182	.321
Adam Hall	R-R	5-11	165	5-22-99	.385	.750	.318	9	26	6	10	2	0	0	5	1	1	0	2	4	1	1	.462	.400
Brayan Hernandez	L-R	6-1	225	11-11-01	.231	.167	.242	15	39	5	9	4	0	2	4	5	1	0	0	13	0	0	.487	.333
Maikol Hernandez	R-R	6-3	175	10-4-03	.155	.161	.154	42	148	20	23	7	0	0	10	19	7	0	1	59	7	2	.203	.280
Julio Herrera	L-R	6-2	180	11-20-00	.283	.167	.300	18	46	8	13	5	0	2	11	5	0	0	0	13	2	1	.522	.353
Douglas Hodo III	R-R	6-0	185	9-25-00	.143	.000	.167	2	7	0	1	0	0	0	0	1	1	0	0	2	0	0	.143	.333
Jackson Holliday	L-R	6-1	175	12-4-03	.409	.333	.438	8	22	6	9	1	0	1	3	10	0	0	1	2	3	0	.591	.576
Junior Lara	L-L	5-11	165	1-27-04	.242	.571	.203	26	66	10	16	3	1	0	1	6	0	1	0	17	6	1	.318	.306
Shed Long Jr.	L-R	5-8	184	8-22-95	.000	.000	.000	3	7	1	0	0	0	0	1	1	0	0	0	3	0	0	.000	.125
Michael Mantecon	R-R	5-11	192	2-2-02	.667	.000	1.000	1	3	1	2	0	0	0	0	1	0	0	0	1	0	0	.667	.750
Roberto Martinez	B-R	6-0	145	1-16-03	.000	.000	.000	4	7	1	0	0	0	0	0	1	0	0	0	2	0	0	.000	.125
Coby Mayo	R-R	6-5	215	12-10-01	.000	--	.000	2	5	1	0	0	0	0	0	1	0	0	0	2	0	0	.000	.167
Erison Placencia	R-R	6-1	170	12-31-01	.000	--	.000	2	4	0	0	0	0	0	2	2	1	0	0	0	0	0	.000	.429
Moises Ramirez	R-R	6-4	235	2-1-02	.242	.333	.233	13	33	4	8	2	0	0	1	1	2	0	0	11	0	0	.303	.306
Adam Retzbach	R-R	6-4	220	11-13-00	.286	.000	.400	3	7	2	2	0	0	0	2	3	1	0	0	0	1	0	.286	.545
Ricardo Rivera	L-R	5-10	176	9-29-02	.000	--	.000	2	3	0	0	0	0	0	0	1	0	0	0	0	0	0	.000	.250
Carlos Rodriguez	R-R	5-11	195	10-14-03	.214	.250	.208	28	56	7	12	2	0	2	16	17	2	0	2	18	1	0	.357	.403
Anthony Servideo	L-R	5-10	175	3-11-99	.119	.000	.135	15	42	5	5	1	0	0	1	15	0	0	0	16	0	0	.143	.351
DJ Stewart	L-R	6-0	210	11-30-93	.429	.000	.462	5	14	2	6	1	0	0	1	3	1	0	0	1	0	0	.500	.556
Dax Stubbs	R-R	5-10	165	5-21-03	.105	.000	.111	10	19	3	2	0	0	1	1	4	0	0	0	12	1	0	.263	.261
Angel Tejada	R-R	5-10	160	1-30-04	.281	.333	.273	30	89	12	25	4	1	3	13	3	5	0	1	18	5	3	.449	.337
Reed Trimble	B-R	6-0	180	6-6-00	.000	.000	.000	2	6	0	0	0	0	0	0	0	0	0	0	2	0	0	.000	.000
Max Wagner	R-R	6-0	215	8-19-01	.500	--	.500	1	4	0	2	1	0	0	2	0	0	0	0	0	1	0	.750	.500
Toby Welk	R-R	6-2	205	5-2-97	.333	.000	.375	4	9	1	3	2	0	0	0	1	0	0	0	2	0	0	.556	.400
Carter Young	B-R	6-0	180	1-24-01	.286	.333	.273	4	14	0	4	0	0	0	1	1	0	0	0	4	0	0	.286	.333

Pitching	B-T	HT	WT	DOB	W	L	ERA	G	GS	CG	SV	IP	H	R	ER	HR	BB	SO	AVG	vLH	vRH	K/9	BB/9
Darlin Alcantara	R-R	6-3	180	9-20-01	1	2	5.63	4	3	0	0	16	16	10	10	1	14	18	.258	.276	.242	10.13	7.88
Cesar Alvarez	R-R	6-1	175	9-11-02	0	0	0.00	1	1	0	0	4	2	0	0	0	0	5	.143	.000	.200	11.25	0.00
Harol Arias	R-R	6-2	180	11-7-02	2	3	4.89	11	8	0	0	46	49	29	25	3	21	31	.269	.221	.305	6.07	4.11
Hugo Beltran	R-R	6-1	190	6-13-00	0	0	1.69	3	0	0	3	5	2	1	1	0	0	6	.118	.286	.000	10.13	0.00
Randy Beriguete	R-R	6-4	221	11-2-02	0	1	5.28	7	0	0	1	15	15	12	9	2	10	11	.242	.250	.237	6.46	5.87
Trace Bright	R-R	6-4	199	10-26-00	0	0	0.00	1	1	0	0	2	0	0	0	0	0	4	.000	.000	.000	18.00	0.00
Wyatt Cheney	R-R	6-0	185	1-10-01	1	0	0.00	1	0	0	0	1	0	0	0	0	0	2	.000	.000	.000	18.00	0.00
Deivy Cruz	L-L	5-11	154	2-13-04	0	2	2.77	3	3	0	0	13	8	6	4	1	8	17	.186	.222	.176	11.77	5.54
Noah Denoyer	B-R	6-5	225	2-17-98	0	0	0.00	1	1	0	0	2	1	0	0	0	0	3	.143	.333	.000	13.50	0.00
Pablo Falconett	R-R	6-2	220	10-28-00	0	0	--	1	0	0	0	0	0	1	1	0	1	0	--	--	--	--	--
Graham Firoved	R-R	6-1	185	9-26-99	0	0	9.00	1	0	0	0	1	0	1	1	0	2	0	.000	.000	.000	0.00	18.00
Elchero Francisca	R-R	6-4	160	8-10-02	1	3	8.10	18	0	0	0	27	32	28	24	3	14	27	.296	.200	.353	9.11	4.73
Orlando Fulgencio	R-R	5-11	168	9-6-00	1	1	7.90	9	0	0	0	14	11	13	12	0	17	15	.229	.250	.222	9.88	11.20
Keagan Gillies	R-R	6-8	255	1-27-98	0	0	0.00	2	1	0	0	5	2	0	0	0	0	5	.118	.111	.125	9.00	0.00
Jarlin Guerrero	R-R	6-0	180	11-25-99	0	2	4.76	4	3	0	0	17	19	11	9	2	3	11	.284	.182	.333	5.82	1.59
Brenan Hanifee	R-R	6-5	215	5-29-98	0	1	3.00	2	2	0	0	3	3	1	1	0	2	3	.273	.333	.200	9.00	6.00
Ryan Hartman	L-L	6-3	234	4-21-94	0	1	4.50	2	1	0	0	4	10	3	2	0	1	2	.500	.750	.333	4.50	2.25
Dylan Heid	R-R	6-1	180	5-18-98	1	0	2.25	2	0	0	0	4	2	1	1	0	5	9	.143	.000	.167	20.25	11.25
Ryan Hennen	R-L	6-0	180	9-30-97	0	0	0.00	1	1	0	0	2	1	0	0	0	0	5	.143	.250	.000	22.50	0.00
Omar Hernandez	L-L	5-8	155	1-24-04	1	0	7.13	17	1	0	0	24	24	20	19	3	33	21	.276	.375	.238	7.88	12.38
Nolan Hoffman	R-R	6-4	190	8-9-97	0	0	0.00	1	0	0	0	2	3	0	0	0	0	2	.333	.000	.429	9.00	0.00
Preston Johnson	R-R	6-4	250	3-11-00	0	0	0.00	1	0	0	0	1	2	0	0	0	0	0	.500	.500	.500	0.00	0.00
Carson King	R-R	6-2	207	12-5-99	0	0	9.00	1	1	0	0	2	3	2	2	0	3	1	.429	.333	.500	4.50	13.50
Adrion Lacle	L-L	6-1	175	11-6-02	0	5	11.35	11	5	0	0	23	37	31	29	4	18	21	.394	.316	.413	8.22	7.04
Travis Lakins Sr.	R-R	6-1	220	6-29-94	0	0	5.40	2	2	0	0	2	1	1	1	0	1	0	.167	.000	.250	0.00	5.40
Anthony Morillo	R-R	6-2	170	2-7-02	0	0	27.00	2	0	0	0	1	2	4	4	1	3	1	.333	.000	.500	6.75	20.25
Hayden Nierman	B-R	6-2	170	1-27-00	0	0	0.00	1	0	0	0	1	0	0	0	0	0	2	.000	.000	.000	18.00	0.00
Trey Nordmann	R-R	6-5	220	2-13-01	0	0	0.00	1	0	0	0	1	0	0	0	0	2	1	.000	.000	.000	9.00	18.00
Juan Nunez	R-R	5-11	190	12-7-00	0	0	3.00	2	1	0	0	6	9	6	2	2	1	9	.321	.308	.333	13.50	1.50
2-team total (8 FCL Twins)					0	2	4.54	10	8	0	0	36	36	25	18	4	11	56	.250	.281	.225	14.13	2.78
Miguel Padilla	R-R	6-2	180	4-13-02	2	1	3.79	5	3	0	0	19	19	9	8	1	5	23	.271	.148	.349	10.89	2.37
Hector Perez	R-R	6-3	223	6-6-96	0	0	0.00	1	1	0	0	2	1	0	0	0	0	4	.143	.000	.333	18.00	0.00
Alex Pham	R-R	5-11	165	10-10-99	0	0	0.00	1	0	0	0	1	0	0	0	0	0	1	.000	.000	--	9.00	0.00
Oscar Pierret	R-R	6-2	190	3-12-01	0	0	34.71	6	0	0	0	5	6	19	18	1	15	6	.300	.333	.286	11.57	28.93
Junior Pina	R-R	6-4	170	12-19-02	1	3	6.56	16	4	0	2	36	29	30	26	3	31	40	.225	.170	.256	10.09	7.82
Yonatan Pineda	R-R	6-1	196	12-7-01	0	2	10.32	18	0	0	2	23	26	28	26	2	31	22	.299	.308	.295	8.74	12.31
Elvis Polanco	L-L	5-10	165	9-16-03	0	3	8.84	16	0	0	0	18	21	22	18	0	25	17	.292	.444	.241	8.35	12.27
Raul Rangel	R-R	6-4	200	10-9-02	1	1	6.48	5	3	0	0	8	6	6	6	1	9	11	.214	.273	.176	11.88	9.72
Yaqui Rivera	R-R	6-2	150	7-19-03	0	0	0.00	3	0	0	0	3	1	1	0	0	3	3	.111	.000	.143	9.00	9.00
Juan Rojas	L-L	6-0	165	1-31-04	1	0	0.00	3	2	0	0	9	4	0	0	0	5	12	.148	.000	.190	12.46	5.19
2-team total (8 FCL Twins)					2	2	2.79	11	7	0	0	39	27	12	12	3	9	50	.197	.105	.232	11.64	2.09
Brayner Sanchez	R-R	6-4	189	6-2-01	1	3	7.83	8	0	0	0	23	27	21	20	3	18	25	.293	.342	.259	9.78	7.04
Issac Solano	R-R	6-6	195	10-23-01	0	4	6.90	15	4	0	1	30	35	25	23	2	28	30	.313	.289	.328	9.00	8.40
Kade Strowd	R-R	6-2	175	9-17-97	0	0	0.00	1	1	0	0	2	0	0	0	0	0	3	.000	.000	.000	13.50	0.00
Angel Tejada	R-R	5-10	160	1-30-04	0	0	0.00	1	0	0	0	1	0	0	0	0	0	3	.000	.000	.000	27.00	0.00

Jordany Vasquez	R-R	6-0	165	1-10-01	1	1	10.50	12	1	0	1	18	23	27	21	0	24	25	.324	.387	.275	12.50	12.00
Antonio Velez	L-L	6-1	195	3-31-97	1	0	0.00	1	0	0	0	2	2	0	0	0	0	2	.286	.000	.500	9.00	0.00
Alex Wells	L-L	6-1	195	2-27-97	0	0	0.00	1	1	0	0	1	0	0	0	0	0	2	.000	--	.000	18.00	0.00

Fielding

C: Angulo 2, Ardoin, 3, Basallo, 32, Cumberland 1, Grullon 1, Hernandez 5, Herrera 8, Mantecon 1, Retzbach 3, Rivera 2, Rodriguez 10. **1B:** Basallo 10, Castillo 14, Costes 6, Grullon 1, Hernandez 6, Herrera 9, Ramirez 5, Rodriguez 10. **2B:** Bencosme 2, Crampton 1, Cruz 19, Gonzalez 6, Hernandez 3, Holliday 1, Long Jr. 1, Martinez 2, Placencia 1, Servideo 3, Stubbs 8, Tejada 17, Young 2. **3B:** Castillo 10, Costes 3, Cruz 3, De Los Santos 34, Hernandez 3, Long Jr. 1, Mayo 1, Ramirez 5, Tejada 4, Wagner 1. **SS:** Crampton 3, Cruz 7, De Los Santos 1, Gonzalez 10, Hernandez 31, Holliday 6, Martinez 1, Placencia 1, Servideo 3, Young 2. **OF:** Acevedo 16, Alvarado 21, Beavers 4, Cortorreal 18, Diaz 1, Fabian 4, Fontana 1, Gonzalez 45, Guerrero 36, Hall 2, Herrera 1, Hodo 2, Lara 25, Stewart 3, Tejada 7, Trimble 1, Welk 2.

DSL ORIOLES — ROOKIE

Batting	B-T	HT	WT	DOB	AVG	vLH	vRH	G	AB	R	H	2B	3B	HR	RBI	BB	HBP	SH	SF	SO	SB	CS	SLG	OBP
Frailyn Abreu	R-R	6-0	180	12-24-01	.173	.250	.150	22	52	10	9	2	0	2	6	12	3	0	0	19	2	1	.327	.358
Leandro Arias	B-R	6-1	155	2-5-05	.217	.100	.234	46	157	25	34	7	2	1	15	27	4	0	1	41	10	3	.306	.344
Kenny Baez	R-R	5-11	185	9-26-02	.194	.167	.196	24	62	9	12	1	0	0	11	13	1	1	0	18	0	1	.210	.342
2-team total (1 DSL BAL Orange)					.188	.167	.190	25	64	9	12	1	0	0	11	13	2	1	0	19	0	1	.203	.342
Cristian Benavides	R-R	6-0	155	5-11-05	.295	.412	.277	38	129	30	38	4	2	2	10	17	2	1	1	39	9	1	.403	.383
Yasmil Bucce	B-R	5-11	168	8-13-04	.230	.294	.217	35	100	13	23	5	0	2	8	15	1	0	1	21	1	0	.340	.333
Edrei Campos	L-R	6-1	165	5-8-05	.250	--	.250	2	8	0	2	0	1	0	2	0	0	0	0	4	1	0	.500	.250
2-team total (43 DSL BAL Orange)					.200	.176	.207	45	150	13	30	7	1	1	15	7	1	1	1	39	5	2	.200	.239
Elis Cuevas	B-R	5-11	150	11-8-04	.315	.300	.317	30	73	18	23	5	1	1	11	20	3	0	0	22	3	1	.452	.479
2-team total (11 DSL BAL Orange)					.265	.214	.274	41	98	19	26	5	1	1	14	22	3	0	0	32	3	3	.367	.415
Luis De La Cruz	L-R	6-2	190	10-15-02	.291	.250	.297	33	86	9	25	5	0	0	12	10	5	0	0	17	3	2	.349	.396
Aron Estrada	B-R	5-8	142	1-13-05	.368	.526	.342	45	136	33	50	12	3	3	31	29	5	0	4	23	4	3	.566	.483
Hector Jimenez	R-R	5-11	155	2-8-04	.235	.091	.257	37	81	19	19	5	0	0	6	13	7	0	0	28	9	3	.296	.386
Juan Martinez	R-R	6-4	175	9-19-04	.116	.077	.123	28	86	9	10	3	0	0	8	13	2	0	1	31	0	2	.151	.245
Ronnie Martinez	R-R	6-0	185	11-11-02	.181	.091	.197	28	72	15	13	2	0	3	7	11	2	0	0	25	1	0	.333	.306
Jose Noguera	R-R	6-2	189	2-24-05	.156	.143	.159	27	77	5	12	2	0	0	12	10	3	0	2	30	1	0	.182	.272
Raylin Ramos	R-R	6-1	180	12-1-04	.288	.308	.285	47	156	25	45	9	2	2	35	15	5	0	5	21	8	5	.410	.359
Adriam Santos	R-R	5-11	165	10-28-04	.083	.167	.067	16	36	2	3	0	0	0	0	2	1	0	0	18	0	1	.083	.154
Braylin Tavera	R-R	6-2	175	2-19-05	.243	.304	.231	47	144	24	35	5	0	2	14	36	5	0	0	47	7	4	.319	.411
Alfredo Velasquez	R-R	5-11	153	9-30-04	.296	.207	.315	48	159	28	47	6	4	1	21	13	7	0	2	12	14	3	.403	.370
Carlos Vicioso	L-R	5-10	160	12-6-02	.143	.100	.160	15	35	3	5	2	1	0	3	5	0	0	0	11	4	1	.257	.250
2-team total (26 DSL BAL Orange)					.241	.214	.250	41	116	18	28	4	3	2	10	16	0	0	1	32	20	5	.379	.331

Pitching	B-T	HT	WT	DOB	W	L	ERA	G	GS	CG	SV	IP	H	R	ER	HR	BB	SO	AVG	vLH	vRH	K/9	BB/9
Anthony Bello	R-R	6-1	209	4-4-99	2	2	3.56	7	7	1	0	30	26	13	12	0	10	29	.226	.186	.250	8.60	2.97
2-team total (1 DSL BAL Orange)					2	2	3.18	8	8	1	0	34	28	13	12	0	13	35	.217	.178	.238	9.26	3.44
Ezequiel Bonilla	R-R	6-1	160	8-12-05	1	1	4.32	11	4	0	1	25	24	16	12	2	16	25	.250	.255	.245	9.00	5.76
Darwin Caballero	R-R	6-3	190	7-15-00	4	0	1.57	9	0	0	1	23	17	4	4	1	8	9	.227	.258	.205	3.52	3.13
Yeiber Cartaya	R-R	6-5	165	1-20-03	0	0	7.90	9	3	0	1	14	9	13	12	1	12	14	.188	.154	.200	9.22	7.90
2-team total (1 DSL BAL Orange)					0	0	7.47	10	3	0	1	16	12	15	13	1	12	15	.214	.143	.238	8.62	6.89
Francisco Crispin	R-R	6-6	190	12-9-02	0	1	3.00	2	0	0	0	3	2	3	1	0	5	5	.182	.333	.000	15.00	15.00
2-team total (8 DSL BAL Orange)					0	5	5.40	10	2	0	0	27	33	21	16	0	21	20	.311	.425	.242	6.75	7.09
Luis De Leon	L-L	6-3	168	4-14-03	3	4	6.00	9	5	0	0	24	15	18	16	0	13	37	.179	.222	.167	13.88	4.88
2-team total (1 DSL BAL Orange)					4	4	5.14	10	5	0	0	28	16	18	16	0	13	45	.165	.208	.151	14.46	4.18
Cesar Espinal	R-R	6-2	165	8-25-05	2	3	5.49	11	0	0	0	20	19	13	12	1	14	16	.271	.324	.212	7.32	6.41
Pedro Figueroa	R-R	6-1	202	6-3-02	0	2	5.40	11	0	0	1	15	9	12	9	0	17	12	.184	.250	.162	7.20	10.20
Joldanny Genao	R-R	6-4	168	8-1-02	2	2	4.15	14	1	0	1	35	29	26	16	4	17	30	.225	.259	.197	7.79	4.41
Duany Gomez	R-R	6-5	186	9-30-00	2	3	3.69	13	3	0	0	32	34	17	13	1	13	28	.272	.211	.324	7.96	3.69
Jarlin Guerrero	R-R	6-0	180	11-25-99	2	1	3.06	4	4	0	0	18	21	13	6	0	3	19	.269	.174	.309	9.68	1.53
Ronal Herrera	R-R	6-2	180	3-10-03	0	2	7.90	13	0	0	1	14	9	16	12	1	21	14	.173	.125	.194	9.22	13.83
Miguel Mesa	R-R	6-2	188	2-5-03	0	1	5.06	4	1	0	1	5	5	4	3	0	5	4	.263	.455	.000	6.75	8.44
Oscar Moreta	R-R	6-2	180	10-12-03	0	1	6.75	1	0	0	0	3	4	2	2	1	1	2	.400	1.000	.250	6.75	3.38
2-team total (12 DSL BAL Orange)					1	4	4.15	13	0	0	1	26	24	16	12	2	15	30	.240	.306	.203	10.38	5.19
Luis Osorio	R-R	6-2	170	1-31-03	1	3	4.13	13	10	0	0	52	47	29	24	0	26	34	.250	.277	.229	5.85	4.47
Juan Pena	R-R	6-3	180	1-13-05	1	0	7.36	11	0	0	1	15	13	16	12	1	18	9	.241	.154	.321	5.52	11.05
Jose Ramirez	L-L	6-3	180	5-23-03	0	4	3.98	12	12	0	0	52	38	31	23	2	42	73	.205	.175	.219	12.63	7.27
Geronimo Rombley	R-R	6-5	200	4-20-04	1	0	2.08	6	0	0	1	9	9	2	2	0	7	9	.281	.364	.238	9.35	7.27
Wilton Rondon	R-R	6-2	185	9-10-02	0	0	18.00	1	0	0	0	1	1	2	2	0	2	0	.333	.000	1.000	0.00	18.00
2-team total (11 DSL BAL Orange)					1	1	4.43	12	0	0	0	20	19	13	10	0	15	16	.244	.231	.250	7.08	6.64
Welington Santana	R-R	6-3	182	5-20-01	0	2	5.09	12	0	0	0	18	18	14	10	1	22	12	.265	.296	.244	6.11	11.21
Jairo Vasquez	R-R	6-1	160	1-16-02	2	2	4.78	10	7	0	0	32	29	20	17	2	18	33	.248	.235	.258	9.28	5.06

Fielding

C: Baez 1, Beato 3, Cuevas 1, Mordan 30, Nolaya 32. **1B:** Aguasvivas 27, Celedonio 2, Cosma 25, Mordan 9, Nolaya 3, Peguero 1, Reyes 3. **2B:** Amparo 8, Celedonio 11, Peguero 48, Reyes 1. **3B:** Aguasvivas 8, Campos 23, Celedonio 21, Cosma 8, Cuevas 5, Peguero 1, Reyes 2. **SS:** Amparo 44, Campos 19, Peguero 1. **OF:** Feliciano 42, Mata 39, Nolaya 1, Pena 27, Ruiz 25, Sandoval 1, Sosa 37, Vicioso 27.

Boston Red Sox

SEASON IN A SENTENCE: Did an era end at Fenway Park? The Mookie Betts-less core of Boston's 2018 World Series champs petered to a last-place AL East finish thanks to (injury- and performance-based) pitching woes and a lineup lacking power at the corners.

HIGH POINT: After a slow start, Boston ripped off a 20-win June, starting the month with a seven-game win streak and capped by a three-game sweep in Cleveland. Boston's record peaked at 42-31, good for third-best in the AL behind the Astros and Yankees.

LOW POINT: The Red Sox collapsed in an 8-19 July, giving up 6.7 runs per game in the month as their pitching fell apart, particularly against fellow AL East contenders. A four-game sweep in Tampa featured several close losses, but the bottom hit with a three-loss stretch in New York and at Fenway against Toronto, losses by scores of 14-1, 13-2 and 28-5. The 23-run loss to Toronto was the worst loss in Sox history, the most runs allowed and didn't even include a position player pitching.

NOTABLE ROOKIES: Touted prospect Jarren Duran got his second, longer shot at an everyday job and didn't hold it, stirring controversy with anti-Covid vaccine comments but more with indifferent, below-par defense and hitting. Righthanders Kutter Crawford (3-6, 5.47) and Bryan Bello (2-8, 4.71) combined for 23 starts and showed they could help in the future but weren't quite ready to help a contender now.

KEY TRANSACTIONS: Despite the poor July on the mound, the Red Sox added hitters at the trade deadline and got a spark from outfielder Tommy Pham, while absorbing Eric Hosmer's contract from the Padres. Boston's biggest offseason free-agent addition was Trevor Story, the former Rockies shortstop who shifted to second base for Boston. His first season (.238/.303/.434, 13 SB, 16 HR) was injury-plagued and uneven. Righty Michael Wacha (11-2, 3.32) was the club's best starter on a one-year deal. Trading Hunter Renfroe to Milwaukee to repatriate Jackie Bradley Jr. to Boston brought a 2018 hero back but didn't work out as the Sox missed Renfroe's thump, while Bradley was released in August.

ON THE FARM: Ceddanne Rafaela emerged as a breakout prospect. His bat is impressive with a line-drive swing that generate some power, but it's his defense at shortstop and in center that should earn him a role in Boston.

OPENING DAY PAYROLL: $211,865,559 (sixth).

PLAYERS OF THE YEAR

MAJOR LEAGUE

Xander Bogaerts
SS

.307/.377/.456
15 HR, 38 2B in 150 G
Third in AL in AVG

MINOR LEAGUE

Ceddanne Rafaela
OF

(HiA/AA)
.299/.342/.539
21 HR, 28 SB in 116 G

ORGANIZATION LEADERS

Batting — *Minimum 250 AB

MAJORS		
*AVG	Xander Bogaerts	.307
*OPS	Rafael Devers	.879
HR	Rafael Devers	27
RBI	Rafael Devers	88
MINORS		
*AVG	Ceddanne Rafaela, Portland, Greenville	.299
*OBP	Niko Kavadas, Salem, Greenville, Portland	.443
*SLG	Niko Kavadas, Salem, Greenville, Portland	.547
*OPS	Niko Kavadas, Salem, Greenville, Portland	.990
R	Eddinson Paulino	96
H	Ceddanne Rafaela, Portland, Greenville	144
TB	Ceddanne Rafaela, Portland, Greenville	259
2B	Eddinson Paulino	35
3B	3 tied	10
HR	Nicholas Northcut, Greenville, Portland	30
RBI	Niko Kavadas, Salem, Greenville, Portland	86
RBI	Ceddanne Rafaela, Portland, Greenville	86
BB	Niko Kavadas, Salem, Greenville, Portland	102
SO	Tyler McDonough	162
SB	David Hamilton, Portland	70

Pitching — #Minimum 75 IP

MAJORS		
W	Michael Wacha	11
#ERA	Michael Wacha	3.32
SO	Nick Pivetta	175
SV	3 tied	8
MINORS		
W	3 tied	10
L	Victor Santos, Portland, Worcester	12
L	Yusniel Padron-Artiles, Greenville, Portland	12
#ERA	Brayan Bello, Worcester, Portland	2.34
G	Andrew Politi, Worcester, Portland	50
GS	Chris Murphy, Portland, Worcester	28
SV	Kaleb Ort, Worcester	16
IP	Chris Murphy, Portland, Worcester	152
BB	Chris Murphy, Portland, Worcester	72
SO	Shane Drohan, Greenville, Portland	157
#AVG	Brayan Bello, Worcester, Portland	.186

2022 PERFORMANCE

General Manager: Brian O'Halloran. **Farm Director:** Brian Abraham. **Scouting Director:** Mike Rikard.

Class	Team	League	W	L	PCT	Finish	Manager
Majors	Boston Red Sox	American	78	84	.481	t-9th (15)	Alex Cora
Triple-A	Worcester Red Sox	International	75	73	.507	9th (20)	Chad Tracy
Double-A	Portland Sea Dogs	Eastern	75	63	.543	5th (12)	Chad Epperson
High-A	Greenville Drive	South Atlantic	52	78	.400	11th (12)	Iggy Suarez
Low-A	Salem Red Sox	Carolina	64	66	.492	7th (12)	Luke Montz
Rookie	FCL Red Sox	Florida Complex	35	20	.636	3rd (16)	J. Gonzalez/ T. Kotchman
Overall 2022 Minor League Record			381	339	.529	6th (30)	

ORGANIZATION STATISTICS

BOSTON RED SOX

AMERICAN LEAGUE

Batting	B-T	HT	WT	DOB	AVG	vLH	vRH	G	AB	R	H	2B	3B	HR	RBI	BB	HBP	SH	SF	SO	SB	CS	SLG	OBP
Abraham Almonte	B-R	5-10	223	6-27-89	.257	.000	.300	15	35	7	9	2	0	1	2	1	1	0	0	12	1	0	.400	.297
Jonathan Arauz	B-R	6-0	195	8-3-98	.000	.000	.000	6	10	1	0	0	0	0	1	0	0	1	1	3	0	0	.000	.000
2-team total (9 Baltimore Orioles)					.132	.000	.147	15	38	3	5	0	0	1	5	1	0	1	1	12	0	0	.211	.150
Christian Arroyo	R-R	6-1	210	5-30-95	.286	.295	.281	87	280	32	80	16	1	6	36	13	3	2	2	49	5	1	.414	.322
Xander Bogaerts	R-R	6-2	218	10-1-92	.307	.382	.286	150	557	84	171	38	0	15	73	57	10	0	7	118	8	2	.456	.377
Jackie Bradley Jr.	L-R	5-10	196	4-19-90	.210	.132	.229	92	271	21	57	19	1	3	29	17	0	2	0	58	2	3	.321	.257
2-team total (40 Toronto Blue Jays)					.203	.164	.214	132	344	30	70	23	1	4	38	24	0	2	0	77	2	3	.311	.255
Triston Casas	L-R	6-4	252	1-15-00	.197	.211	.193	27	76	11	15	1	0	5	12	19	0	0	0	23	1	0	.408	.358
Yu Chang	R-R	6-1	180	8-18-95	.150	.200	.133	11	20	3	3	2	0	0	1	5	1	0	0	7	0	0	.250	.346
3-team total (4 Cleveland Guardians, 36 Tampa Bay Rays)					.222	.176	.253	51	126	14	28	5	0	3	13	12	1	0	2	41	0	0	.333	.291
Franchy Cordero	L-R	6-3	226	9-2-94	.219	.162	.229	84	242	36	53	17	1	8	29	28	1	2	2	92	4	1	.397	.300
Bobby Dalbec	R-R	6-4	227	6-29-95	.215	.240	.204	117	317	40	68	9	2	12	39	29	3	0	4	118	3	0	.369	.283
Jaylin Davis	R-R	5-11	205	7-1-94	.333	.308	.364	12	24	4	8	1	0	0	2	3	0	0	0	11	0	0	.375	.407
Rafael Devers	L-R	6-0	240	10-24-96	.295	.272	.304	141	555	84	164	42	1	27	88	50	6	0	3	114	3	1	.521	.358
Jeter Downs	R-R	5-11	195	7-27-98	.154	.154	.154	14	39	4	6	1	0	1	4	1	0	0	1	21	0	0	.256	.171
Jarren Duran	L-R	6-2	212	9-5-96	.221	.184	.229	58	204	23	45	14	3	3	17	14	4	0	1	63	7	1	.363	.283
Enrique Hernandez	R-R	5-11	190	8-24-91	.222	.224	.221	93	361	48	80	24	0	6	45	34	3	0	4	71	0	2	.338	.291
Eric Hosmer	L-L	6-4	226	10-24-89	.244	.294	.214	14	45	6	11	3	0	0	4	4	1	0	0	9	0	0	.311	.320
J.D. Martinez	R-R	6-3	230	8-21-87	.274	.319	.261	139	533	76	146	43	1	16	62	52	5	0	5	145	0	0	.448	.341
Reese McGuire	L-R	6-0	218	3-2-95	.337	.500	.310	36	98	13	33	5	1	3	12	6	1	1	1	23	1	0	.500	.377
2-team total (53 Chicago White Sox)					.269	.262	.271	89	249	25	67	14	1	3	22	12	3	6	3	56	1	0	.369	.307
Tommy Pham	R-R	6-1	223	3-8-88	.234	.239	.232	53	214	32	50	12	0	6	24	14	6	0	1	67	1	1	.374	.298
Kevin Plawecki	R-R	6-2	208	2-26-91	.217	.119	.252	61	157	15	34	8	0	1	12	14	2	1	1	28	0	0	.287	.287
2-team total (3 Texas Rangers)					.220	.133	.252	64	168	15	37	8	0	1	13	14	2	1	1	32	0	0	.286	.286
Rob Refsnyder	R-R	6-0	205	3-26-91	.307	.359	.270	57	153	25	47	11	0	6	21	15	6	0	3	46	1	1	.497	.384
Yolmer Sanchez	B-R	6-0	210	6-29-92	.108	.111	.107	14	37	1	4	0	0	0	2	5	0	2	0	13	0	2	.108	.214
Travis Shaw	L-R	6-4	230	4-16-90	.000	--	.000	7	19	0	0	0	0	0	0	0	0	0	0	7	0	0	.000	.000
Trevor Story	R-R	6-2	213	11-15-92	.238	.253	.233	94	357	53	85	22	0	16	66	32	3	0	4	122	13	0	.434	.303
Christian Vazquez	R-R	5-9	205	8-21-90	.282	.291	.279	84	294	33	83	20	0	8	42	18	3	0	3	51	1	2	.432	.327
2-team total (35 Houston Astros)					.274	.304	.264	119	398	41	109	23	0	9	52	22	3	0	3	69	1	4	.399	.315
Alex Verdugo	L-L	6-0	192	5-15-96	.280	.266	.285	152	593	75	166	39	1	11	74	42	3	0	6	86	1	3	.405	.328
Connor Wong	R-R	6-1	181	5-19-96	.188	.111	.233	27	48	8	9	3	0	1	7	5	1	1	1	16	0	0	.313	.273

Pitching	B-T	HT	WT	DOB	W	L	ERA	G	GS	CG	SV	IP	H	R	ER	HR	BB	SO	AVG	vLH	vRH	K/9	BB/9
Matt Barnes	R-R	6-4	208	6-17-90	0	4	4.31	44	0	0	8	40	36	22	19	2	21	34	.240	.217	.256	7.71	4.76
Eduard Bazardo	R-R	6-0	165	9-1-95	1	0	2.76	12	0	0	0	16	12	5	5	4	4	11	.203	.167	.229	6.06	2.20
Brayan Bello	R-R	6-1	170	5-17-99	2	8	4.71	13	11	1	0	57	75	34	30	1	27	55	.315	.295	.329	8.63	4.24
Jackie Bradley Jr.	L-R	5-10	196	4-19-90	0	0	9.00	1	0	0	0	1	1	1	1	0	3	1	.250	.000	.333	9.00	27.00
Ryan Brasier	R-R	6-0	227	8-26-87	0	3	5.78	68	0	0	1	62	68	43	40	9	13	64	.280	.306	.269	9.24	1.88
Kutter Crawford	R-R	6-1	209	4-1-96	3	6	5.47	21	12	0	0	77	81	49	47	12	29	77	.269	.275	.265	8.96	3.38
Tyler Danish	R-R	6-0	200	9-12-94	3	1	5.13	32	0	0	0	40	40	24	23	7	12	32	.255	.275	.245	7.14	2.68
Austin Davis	L-L	6-4	235	2-3-93	2	1	5.47	50	3	0	0	54	56	36	33	5	29	61	.260	.198	.299	10.10	4.80
2-team total (2 Minnesota Twins)					2	1	5.79	52	3	0	0	56	57	39	36	5	33	64	.258	.198	.293	10.29	5.30
Jake Diekman	R-L	6-4	195	1-21-87	5	1	4.23	44	0	0	1	38	27	22	18	5	30	51	.203	.188	.212	11.97	7.04
2-team total (26 Chicago White Sox)					5	4	4.99	70	0	0	1	58	52	40	32	9	42	79	.241	.250	.234	12.33	6.55
Nathan Eovaldi	R-R	6-2	217	2-13-90	6	3	3.87	20	20	2	0	109	115	55	47	21	20	103	.264	.232	.284	8.48	1.65
Jeurys Familia	R-R	6-3	240	10-10-89	1	2	6.10	10	0	0	0	10	10	8	7	1	7	8	.263	.182	.296	6.97	6.10
Michael Feliz	R-R	6-4	250	6-28-93	0	0	2.70	1	0	0	0	3	1	2	1	1	2	4	.091	.250	.000	10.80	5.40
Franklin German	R-R	6-2	195	9-22-97	0	0	18.00	5	0	0	0	4	7	8	8	2	4	4	.368	.333	.385	9.00	9.00
Darwinzon Hernandez	L-L	6-2	255	12-17-96	0	1	21.60	7	0	0	0	7	14	17	16	4	8	9	.424	.417	.429	12.15	10.80
Rich Hill	L-L	6-5	221	3-11-80	8	7	4.27	26	26	0	0	124	125	67	59	15	37	109	.258	.277	.255	7.89	2.68
Tanner Houck	R-R	6-5	230	6-29-96	5	4	3.15	32	4	0	8	60	49	22	21	3	22	56	.226	.259	.205	8.40	3.30

Zack Kelly	R-R	6-3	205	3-3-95	1	0	3.95	13	0	0	0	14	14	6	6	2	4	11	.259	.208	.300	7.24	2.63
Reese McGuire	L-R	6-0	218	3-2-95	0	0	0.00	1	0	0	0	1	0	0	0	0	0	0	.000	.000	.000	0.00	0.00
Kaleb Ort	R-R	6-4	240	2-5-92	1	2	6.35	25	0	0	1	28	35	23	20	4	15	27	.302	.200	.366	8.58	4.76
Nick Pivetta	R-R	6-5	214	2-14-93	10	12	4.56	33	33	1	0	180	175	91	91	27	73	175	.253	.252	.254	8.77	3.66
Kevin Plawecki	R-R	6-2	208	2-26-91	0	0	0.00	1	0	0	0	1	1	0	0	0	0	0	.250	.000	.333	0.00	0.00
Hansel Robles	R-R	6-0	220	8-13-90	1	3	5.84	26	0	0	2	25	25	19	16	5	14	21	.260	.188	.297	7.66	5.11
Chris Sale	L-L	6-6	183	3-30-89	0	1	3.18	2	2	0	0	6	5	3	2	0	1	5	.217	.000	.294	7.94	1.59
Yolmer Sanchez	B-R	6-0	210	6-29-92	0	0	9.00	1	0	0	0	1	3	1	1	0	0	0	.500	.500	.500	0.00	0.00
Hirokazu Sawamura	R-R	6-0	212	4-3-88	1	1	3.73	49	0	0	0	51	45	23	21	4	27	40	.238	.188	.267	7.11	4.80
John Schreiber	R-R	6-2	210	3-5-94	4	4	2.22	64	0	0	8	65	45	19	16	3	19	74	.195	.198	.193	10.25	2.63
Connor Seabold	R-R	6-2	190	1-24-96	0	4	11.29	5	5	0	0	18	35	24	23	5	8	19	.402	.414	.397	9.33	3.93
Matt Strahm	R-L	6-2	190	11-12-91	4	4	3.83	50	0	0	4	45	38	24	19	5	17	52	.224	.229	.221	10.48	3.43
Phillips Valdez	R-R	6-2	160	11-16-91	0	1	4.41	13	0	0	0	16	12	11	8	0	7	13	.207	.103	.310	7.16	3.86
Michael Wacha	R-R	6-6	215	7-1-91	11	2	3.32	23	23	1	0	127	111	49	47	18	31	104	.233	.188	.265	7.35	2.19
Garrett Whitlock	R-R	6-5	225	6-11-96	4	2	3.45	31	9	0	6	78	65	32	30	10	15	82	.222	.192	.244	9.42	1.72
Josh Winckowski	R-R	6-4	202	6-28-98	5	7	5.89	15	14	0	0	70	85	47	46	10	27	44	.300	.285	.315	5.63	3.45

Fielding

Catcher	PCT	G	PO	A	E	DP	PB
McGuire	.996	32	223	12	1	2	1
Plawecki	1.000	58	396	14	0	1	1
Vazquez	.991	78	610	33	6	4	3
Wong	.986	20	129	7	2	0	1

First Base	PCT	G	PO	A	E	DP
Arroyo	1.000	9	41	0	0	0
Casas	.995	27	176	8	1	17
Chang	1.000	1	6	0	0	1
Cordero	.977	53	316	31	8	37
Dalbec	.997	89	557	42	2	56
Hosmer	.989	14	81	8	1	8
Shaw	1.000	3	24	1	0	1
Vazquez	1.000	9	45	2	0	4

Second Base	PCT	G	PO	A	E	DP
Arauz	1.000	3	3	4	0	2
Arroyo	.993	40	64	87	1	23
Chang	1.000	4	2	6	0	2
Dalbec	1.000	2	1	2	0	0
Downs	.952	8	7	13	1	1
Hernandez	1.000	11	14	20	0	4
Sanchez	.984	14	26	34	1	11
Story	.984	94	157	215	6	50
Vazquez	1.000	1	1	0	0	0
Wong	.000	2	0	0	0	0

Third Base	PCT	G	PO	A	E	DP
Arroyo	1.000	10	4	11	0	2
Dalbec	.933	24	11	31	3	1
Devers	.964	138	124	255	14	29
Downs	.929	6	4	9	1	2
Wong	.000	1	0	0	0	0

Shortstop	PCT	G	PO	A	E	DP
Arauz	1.000	3	0	1	0	0
Arroyo	.939	14	12	19	2	1
Bogaerts	.983	146	170	401	10	78
Chang	1.000	7	5	12	0	1
Dalbec	1.000	1	0	6	0	1
Downs	1.000	3	1	1	0	0
Hernandez	1.000	10	4	23	0	5

Outfield	PCT	G	PO	A	E	DP
Almonte	1.000	9	14	0	0	0
Arroyo	1.000	17	18	1	0	0
Bradley Jr.	1.000	100	172	3	0	2
Cordero	.962	40	50	0	2	0
Davis	1.000	8	12	0	0	0
Duran	.992	58	132	0	1	0
Hernandez	1.000	80	196	1	0	1
Pham	.966	51	77	8	3	0
Refsnyder	.973	51	71	1	2	0
Verdugo	.981	154	248	8	5	1

WORCESTER RED SOX — *TRIPLE-A*

INTERNATIONAL LEAGUE

Batting	B-T	HT	WT	DOB	AVG	vLH	vRH	G	AB	R	H	2B	3B	HR	RBI	BB	HBP	SH	SF	SO	SB	CS	SLG	OBP
Abraham Almonte	B-R	5-10	223	6-27-89	.291	.214	.317	32	110	30	32	4	1	7	24	36	1	0	0	29	5	2	.536	.469
2-team total (48 Nashville Sounds)					.293	.238	.314	80	294	66	86	15	1	18	66	61	3	0	2	77	6	2	.534	.417
Jonathan Arauz	B-R	6-0	195	8-3-98	.185	.154	.197	24	92	11	17	5	0	0	3	7	0	0	0	13	1	0	.239	.242
2-team total (11 Norfolk Tides)					.205	.163	.225	35	132	15	27	8	0	0	9	11	1	0	0	22	2	0	.265	.271
Christian Arroyo	R-R	6-1	210	5-30-95	.000	.000	.000	2	6	0	0	0	0	0	0	0	0	0	0	3	0	0	.000	.000
Roldani Baldwin	R-R	5-11	211	3-16-96	.167	.143	.176	11	24	3	4	2	0	1	2	2	0	0	0	7	0	0	.375	.231
Cam Cannon	R-R	5-10	205	10-16-97	.257	.455	.167	12	35	2	9	2	0	0	3	1	0	1	0	10	1	0	.314	.278
Triston Casas	L-R	6-4	252	1-15-00	.273	.224	.289	72	264	45	72	20	1	11	38	46	3	0	4	68	0	0	.481	.382
Pedro Castellanos	R-R	6-3	244	12-11-97	.269	.296	.260	60	227	31	61	10	2	5	29	7	6	0	1	47	1	0	.396	.307
Franchy Cordero	L-R	6-3	226	9-2-94	.325	.300	.333	31	117	23	38	10	0	7	36	15	1	0	3	42	4	2	.590	.397
Kole Cottam	R-R	6-3	235	5-30-97	.178	.375	.135	14	45	4	8	5	0	0	2	5	0	0	0	17	0	0	.289	.260
Ricardo Cubillan	B-R	6-0	155	2-1-98	.000	--	.000	1	4	0	0	0	0	0	0	0	0	0	0	0	0	0	.000	.000
Bobby Dalbec	R-R	6-4	227	6-29-95	.250	.182	.270	13	48	8	12	0	0	5	8	3	1	0	1	14	1	0	.563	.302
Jaylin Davis	R-R	5-11	205	7-1-94	.203	.257	.186	88	296	43	60	12	3	7	24	43	5	0	2	107	1	4	.334	.312
Jeter Downs	R-R	5-11	195	7-27-98	.197	.281	.173	81	284	56	56	11	1	16	33	38	12	0	1	99	18	4	.412	.316
Jarren Duran	L-R	6-2	212	9-5-96	.283	.276	.287	68	279	49	79	16	6	10	38	26	2	0	0	73	18	3	.491	.349
Ryan Fitzgerald	L-R	6-0	185	6-17-94	.219	.191	.231	127	452	55	99	26	4	16	72	49	10	1	8	135	6	5	.400	.304
Devlin Granberg	R-R	6-2	224	9-8-95	.260	.235	.270	46	177	20	46	10	1	3	18	14	5	0	0	44	4	1	.379	.332
Deivy Grullon	R-R	5-11	240	2-17-96	.250	.350	.194	20	56	6	14	5	0	3	13	6	0	0	1	23	0	0	.500	.317
Enrique Hernandez	R-R	5-11	190	8-24-91	.000	--	.000	1	4	0	0	0	0	0	0	0	0	0	0	2	0	0	.000	.000
Ronaldo Hernandez	R-R	6-1	230	11-11-97	.261	.260	.261	105	410	50	107	27	0	17	63	21	2	0	4	92	0	3	.451	.297
Johan Mieses	R-R	6-2	185	7-13-95	.271	.288	.263	60	192	32	52	15	0	12	35	32	5	0	1	63	5	0	.536	.387
Jose Peraza	R-R	6-0	210	4-30-94	.214	.000	.222	8	28	2	6	1	0	0	2	0	2	0	0	4	0	0	.250	.267
2-team total (63 Scranton/Wilkes-Barre RailRiders)					.236	.200	.249	71	237	22	56	13	0	5	31	12	7	0	3	31	3	1	.354	.290
Hudson Potts	R-R	6-3	205	10-28-98	.200	.200	--	2	5	1	1	1	0	0	0	1	0	0	0	1	0	0	.400	.333
Roberto Ramos	L-R	6-3	220	12-28-94	.158	.069	.187	39	120	16	19	7	0	5	16	21	1	0	1	54	0	0	.342	.287
Rob Refsnyder	R-R	6-0	205	3-26-91	.306	.268	.321	42	147	31	45	14	0	6	28	28	5	0	2	42	4	0	.524	.429
Yolmer Sanchez	B-R	6-0	210	6-29-92	.247	.261	.242	78	247	43	61	12	1	9	33	50	3	1	2	67	6	1	.413	.377
2-team total (22 Syracuse Mets)					.246	.250	.245	100	325	49	80	16	1	10	40	60	7	1	3	86	6	1	.394	.372
Nick Sogard	B-R	6-1	180	9-9-97	.259	.340	.234	65	201	26	52	13	1	0	21	30	2	1	3	45	9	1	.333	.356
Christin Stewart	L-R	6-0	220	12-10-93	.237	.208	.245	103	338	55	80	15	0	19	55	61	8	0	2	130	9	2	.450	.364
Enmanuel Valdez	L-R	5-9	191	12-28-98	.237	.213	.246	44	173	26	41	9	1	7	30	19	0	0	2	48	3	0	.422	.309
Grant Williams	L-R	5-10	180	10-3-95	.216	.182	.231	53	148	16	32	3	0	0	15	6	1	0	2	31	7	2	.236	.248

Izzy Wilson	L-R	6-3	185	3-6-98	.143	.000	.250	3	7	2	1	1	0	0	2	1	0	0	0	1	0	0	.286	.250
Connor Wong	R-R	6-1	181	5-19-96	.288	.282	.290	81	323	47	93	20	0	15	44	27	4	0	1	80	7	3	.489	.349

Pitching	**B-T**	**HT**	**WT**	**DOB**	**W**	**L**	**ERA**	**G**	**GS**	**CG**	**SV**	**IP**	**H**	**R**	**ER**	**HR**	**BB**	**SO**	**AVG**	**vLH**	**vRH**	**K/9**	**BB/9**
Matt Barnes	R-R	6-4	208	6-17-90	0	0	10.80	2	0	0	0	2	4	2	2	0	2	2	.571	.000	1.000	10.80	10.80
Eduard Bazardo	R-R	6-0	165	9-1-95	2	4	3.45	37	4	0	1	57	65	28	22	5	19	60	.280	.211	.358	9.42	2.98
Brayan Bello	R-R	6-1	170	5-17-99	6	2	2.76	11	10	0	0	59	46	18	18	3	24	81	.214	.267	.178	12.43	3.68
Silvino Bracho	R-R	5-10	190	7-17-92	0	3	3.16	18	1	0	0	31	29	12	11	2	4	36	.250	.250	.250	10.34	1.15
2-team total (20 Gwinnett Stripers)					2	4	2.67	38	5	0	0	57	50	18	17	4	10	70	.234	.253	.220	10.99	1.57
Ryan Brasier	R-R	6-0	227	8-26-87	0	0	0.00	2	0	0	0	2	0	0	0	0	0	3	.000	.000	.000	13.50	0.00
Taylor Cole	R-R	6-1	200	8-20-89	2	0	5.14	19	2	0	0	28	28	16	16	2	19	27	.267	.250	.279	8.68	6.11
Kutter Crawford	R-R	6-1	209	4-1-96	1	0	5.18	6	4	0	0	24	29	16	14	5	6	23	.282	.244	.310	8.51	2.22
Tyler Danish	R-R	6-0	200	9-12-94	0	0	5.68	6	0	0	0	6	8	4	4	0	3	9	.333	.300	.357	12.79	4.26
Nathan Eovaldi	R-R	6-2	217	2-13-90	0	0	7.50	2	2	0	0	6	8	5	5	2	2	8	.320	.250	.385	12.00	3.00
Jeurys Familia	R-R	6-3	240	10-10-89	0	0	0.00	1	0	0	0	1	0	0	0	0	0	3	.000	--	.000	27.00	0.00
Michael Feliz	R-R	6-4	250	6-28-93	0	1	3.28	18	3	0	0	25	20	10	9	1	9	28	.225	.189	.250	10.22	3.28
2-team total (18 St. Paul Saints)					3	2	2.74	36	3	0	2	49	32	18	15	1	19	52	.186	.191	.183	9.49	3.47
Durbin Feltman	R-R	6-0	208	4-18-97	3	5	7.63	40	0	0	1	48	53	44	41	12	24	56	.272	.305	.240	10.43	4.47
Franklin German	R-R	6-2	195	9-22-97	2	1	2.58	32	0	0	7	38	20	11	11	2	16	46	.154	.149	.159	10.80	3.76
Darin Gillies	R-R	6-4	220	11-6-92	0	1	21.00	6	0	0	0	6	14	14	14	2	5	7	.438	.214	.611	10.50	7.50
Jay Groome	L-L	6-6	262	8-23-98	1	1	3.94	3	3	0	0	16	17	7	7	2	7	15	.274	.348	.231	8.44	3.94
Kyle Hart	L-L	6-5	200	11-23-92	5	2	5.63	9	4	1	0	38	41	26	24	7	19	32	.270	.259	.277	7.51	4.46
Geoff Hartlieb	R-R	6-5	240	12-9-93	3	6	5.16	40	3	0	0	61	60	36	35	8	25	64	.254	.252	.257	9.44	3.69
Darwinzon Hernandez	L-L	6-2	255	12-17-96	0	3	5.73	23	7	0	0	33	22	23	21	3	27	51	.188	.167	.200	13.91	7.36
Derek Holland	B-L	6-2	223	10-9-86	0	2	6.35	10	0	0	0	11	8	9	8	1	7	13	.195	.133	.231	10.32	5.56
2-team total (20 Buffalo Bisons)					0	3	5.77	30	6	0	3	39	38	28	25	7	20	38	.262	.175	.318	8.77	4.62
Brian Keller	R-R	6-3	210	6-21-94	6	5	3.27	31	20	0	0	113	80	48	41	8	53	126	.200	.237	.161	10.04	4.22
Zack Kelly	R-R	6-3	205	3-3-95	6	3	2.72	44	0	0	3	50	34	23	15	2	25	72	.191	.216	.167	13.05	4.53
Brett Kennedy	R-R	6-0	200	8-4-94	0	0	0.00	2	0	0	0	1	1	0	0	0	2	1	.200	.000	.500	6.75	13.50
Carlos Martinez	R-R	6-0	200	9-21-91	0	2	20.77	2	2	0	0	4	9	10	10	1	3	4	.409	.400	.417	8.31	6.23
Bryan Mata	R-R	6-3	238	5-3-99	2	0	3.47	5	5	0	0	23	19	9	9	0	15	30	.224	.255	.184	11.57	5.79
Chris Murphy	L-L	6-1	175	6-5-98	3	6	5.50	15	15	0	0	75	77	55	46	8	41	58	.266	.278	.261	6.93	4.90
James Norwood	R-R	6-2	215	12-24-93	0	1	4.87	15	0	0	0	20	19	13	11	0	11	24	.247	.244	.250	10.62	4.87
Kaleb Ort	R-R	6-4	240	2-5-92	2	2	2.88	39	0	0	16	41	28	16	13	1	18	53	.193	.191	.195	11.73	3.98
Thomas Pannone	L-L	6-1	205	4-28-94	5	3	4.57	14	12	0	0	63	71	34	32	7	8	70	.283	.217	.315	10.00	1.14
Andrew Politi	R-R	6-0	193	6-4-96	4	0	2.41	38	2	0	4	56	38	16	15	4	19	63	.194	.177	.210	10.13	3.05
Chris Sale	L-L	6-6	183	3-30-89	0	0	2.45	1	1	0	0	4	3	1	1	0	5	5	.231	.250	.222	12.27	12.27
Victor Santos	R-R	6-1	191	7-12-00	3	4	4.95	9	9	1	0	44	47	24	24	6	14	47	.276	.262	.302	9.69	2.89
Hirokazu Sawamura	R-R	6-0	212	4-3-88	0	0	0.00	1	0	0	0	1	0	0	0	0	1	0	.000	.000	.000	0.00	9.00
John Schreiber	R-R	6-2	210	3-5-94	2	1	1.46	7	0	0	0	12	9	4	2	2	3	15	.200	.167	.238	10.95	2.19
Connor Seabold	R-R	6-2	190	1-24-96	8	2	3.32	19	19	0	0	87	79	35	32	7	19	89	.237	.250	.225	9.24	1.97
Chase Shugart	L-R	5-10	198	10-24-96	3	3	6.82	20	1	0	0	32	39	26	24	5	11	29	.302	.250	.368	8.24	3.13
Caleb Simpson	R-R	6-4	231	9-15-91	1	3	9.11	20	0	0	0	28	32	30	28	4	18	29	.288	.324	.233	9.43	5.86
Matt Strahm	R-L	6-2	190	11-12-91	0	0	0.00	1	0	0	0	1	0	0	0	0	0	1	.000	.000	.000	9.00	0.00
Josh Taylor	L-L	6-5	245	3-2-93	0	2	3.68	8	4	0	0	7	10	5	3	1	2	8	.313	.455	.238	9.82	2.45
Jake Thompson	R-R	6-1	215	9-22-94	1	0	5.40	16	0	0	0	22	19	14	13	0	20	24	.241	.317	.158	9.97	8.31
Phillips Valdez	R-R	6-2	160	11-16-91	1	0	3.06	14	0	0	0	18	11	6	6	0	14	19	.193	.316	.132	9.68	7.13
Michael Wacha	R-R	6-6	215	7-1-91	0	0	0.00	1	1	0	0	5	0	0	0	0	1	8	.000	.000	.000	15.43	1.93
Brandon Walter	L-L	6-2	200	9-8-96	1	1	8.22	2	2	0	0	8	9	7	7	0	4	7	.281	.286	.280	8.22	4.70
Garrett Whitlock	R-R	6-5	225	6-11-96	0	0	9.00	1	0	0	0	2	6	2	2	0	0	3	.500	.286	.800	13.50	0.00
Josh Winckowski	R-R	6-4	202	6-28-98	2	4	3.82	13	12	1	0	61	57	38	26	4	18	62	.244	.279	.200	9.10	2.64

Fielding

Catcher	**PCT**	**G**	**PO**	**A**	**E**	**DP**	**PB**
Baldwin	1.000	6	50	1	0	0	2
Cottam	.979	12	90	3	2	0	1
Grullon	.991	14	111	4	1	1	1
Hernandez	.991	67	651	36	6	6	13
Wong	.984	54	529	30	9	3	9

First Base	**PCT**	**G**	**PO**	**A**	**E**	**DP**
Baldwin	1.000	2	2	1	0	1
Casas	.990	63	465	38	5	42
Castellanos	.989	37	261	12	3	39
Cordero	1.000	3	21	0	0	0
Dalbec	1.000	9	52	5	0	2
Fitzgerald	.988	10	73	6	1	6
Granberg	1.000	3	15	1	0	3
Ramos	.989	28	165	10	2	6

Second Base	**PCT**	**G**	**PO**	**A**	**E**	**DP**
Arauz	.972	16	10	25	1	5
Cubillan	1.000	1	2	4	0	0
Downs	1.000	1	3	3	0	0
Fitzgerald	.990	25	44	57	1	18
Peraza	1.000	3	1	9	0	0
Sanchez	.964	56	73	112	7	25
Sogard	.981	11	21	31	1	10
Valdez	.993	39	44	98	1	21
Williams	.818	4	6	3	2	1
Wong	.500	1	0	1	1	0

Third Base	**PCT**	**G**	**PO**	**A**	**E**	**DP**
Baldwin	1.000	1	2	3	0	0
Cannon	1.000	10	9	19	0	4
Dalbec	.833	4	1	4	1	1
Downs	1.000	3	3	3	0	1
Fitzgerald	.969	37	23	40	2	4
Potts	1.000	2	0	5	0	1
Sanchez	1.000	17	14	30	0	2
Sogard	.977	49	56	73	3	22
Valdez	1.000	3	0	2	0	0
Williams	.947	34	24	65	5	9

Shortstop	**PCT**	**G**	**PO**	**A**	**E**	**DP**
Arauz	1.000	8	5	17	0	0
Arroyo	1.000	1	0	2	0	1
Downs	.966	78	75	177	9	30
Fitzgerald	.964	36	48	87	5	20
Peraza	.957	5	7	15	1	3
Sanchez	1.000	11	14	19	0	3
Sogard	1.000	5	6	5	0	0
Williams	.946	11	8	27	2	8

Outfield	**PCT**	**G**	**PO**	**A**	**E**	**DP**
Almonte	.972	23	33	2	1	1
Castellanos	1.000	17	23	3	0	0
Cordero	1.000	28	42	2	0	1
Davis	.982	87	158	3	3	0
Duran	.987	65	144	6	2	3
Fitzgerald	1.000	27	34	0	0	0
Granberg	1.000	46	68	4	0	1
Mieses	.985	39	62	4	1	1
Refsnyder	.966	34	54	2	2	1
Stewart	.987	94	142	5	2	1
Valdez	1.000	3	4	0	0	0
Wilson	1.000	2	2	1	0	0

PORTLAND SEA DOGS

DOUBLE-A

EASTERN LEAGUE

BOSTON RED SOX

Batting	B-T	HT	WT	DOB	AVG	vLH	vRH	G	AB	R	H	2B	3B	HR	RBI	BB	HBP	SH	SF	SO	SB	CS	SLG	OBP
Wilyer Abreu	L-L	6-0	217	6-24-99	.242	.167	.255	40	128	25	31	5	0	4	19	36	0	0	4	45	8	2	.375	.399
Christian Arroyo	R-R	6-1	210	5-30-95	.500	--	.500	2	4	1	2	0	0	0	2	2	0	0	0	0	1	0	.500	.667
Alex Binelas	L-R	6-3	225	5-26-00	.166	.000	.181	55	211	30	35	10	1	11	35	25	1	1	3	78	0	0	.379	.254
Cam Cannon	R-R	5-10	205	10-16-97	.211	.235	.207	35	109	10	23	5	0	0	4	14	3	0	0	25	3	1	.257	.317
Pedro Castellanos	R-R	6-3	244	12-11-97	.279	.200	.293	61	240	23	67	18	1	8	42	7	3	0	4	56	0	0	.463	.303
Kole Cottam	R-R	6-3	235	5-30-97	.271	.316	.262	64	229	27	62	15	2	2	26	23	5	0	0	65	0	3	.380	.350
Ricardo Cubillan	B-R	6-0	155	2-1-98	.069	.000	.100	16	29	2	2	0	0	0	0	6	0	1	0	11	0	0	.069	.229
Wil Dalton	R-R	6-0	182	8-27-97	.193	.200	.191	69	192	28	37	12	1	6	21	18	7	0	2	80	6	3	.359	.283
Tyler Dearden	L-R	6-2	185	7-6-98	.263	.158	.277	94	316	40	83	16	1	8	47	49	6	0	5	103	0	2	.396	.367
Tyler Esplin	L-R	6-3	230	7-6-99	.214	.333	.182	5	14	2	3	0	0	0	0	3	0	0	0	5	0	0	.214	.353
Devlin Granberg	R-R	6-2	224	9-8-95	.304	.267	.308	40	135	25	41	11	4	1	10	20	9	0	0	22	4	1	.467	.427
David Hamilton	L-R	5-10	175	9-29-97	.251	.262	.249	119	463	81	116	16	9	12	42	56	6	5	1	119	70	8	.402	.338
Enrique Hernandez	R-R	5-11	190	8-24-91	.250	.667	.111	4	12	0	3	2	0	0	2	1	0	0	0	4	0	0	.417	.308
Brandon Howlett	R-R	6-1	205	9-12-99	.167	.000	.188	27	78	5	13	1	1	0	4	11	1	0	0	42	0	0	.205	.278
Niko Kavadas	L-R	6-1	235	10-27-98	.222	.600	.197	24	81	9	18	3	0	2	10	16	3	0	0	40	0	0	.333	.370
Christian Koss	R-R	6-1	182	1-27-98	.260	.149	.278	125	488	69	127	22	5	17	84	25	12	0	6	137	16	5	.430	.309
Matthew Lugo	R-R	6-1	187	5-9-01	.083	.000	.091	3	12	1	1	1	0	0	1	0	0	0	0	4	0	0	.167	.083
Elih Marrero	B-R	5-9	185	6-21-97	.207	.082	.239	79	246	32	51	10	0	2	16	39	2	1	1	74	18	5	.272	.319
Nicholas Northcut	R-R	6-1	206	6-13-99	.208	.222	.205	26	101	12	21	5	0	4	17	4	1	0	0	37	1	0	.376	.245
Hudson Potts	R-R	6-3	205	10-28-98	.234	.231	.235	75	269	36	63	17	0	14	44	24	1	0	2	92	1	0	.454	.297
Ceddanne Rafaela	R-R	5-8	152	9-18-00	.278	.295	.275	71	284	45	79	15	6	12	50	16	6	1	6	62	14	5	.500	.324
Oscar Rangel	L-R	5-11	184	5-27-98	.077	.000	.091	5	13	1	1	0	0	0	1	2	0	0	0	6	0	0	.077	.200
Tyreque Reed	R-R	6-1	250	6-6-97	.198	.200	.197	50	167	18	33	7	0	6	25	18	2	0	0	64	0	0	.347	.283
Rob Refsnyder	R-R	6-0	205	3-26-91	.750	1.000	.667	2	4	4	3	1	0	2	3	3	0	0	0	0	0	0	2.500	.857
Stephen Scott	L-R	5-11	207	5-23-97	.238	.375	.226	59	206	40	49	11	1	7	31	43	3	0	4	50	7	1	.403	.371
Nick Sogard	B-R	6-1	180	9-9-97	.250	.290	.243	60	200	33	50	9	1	4	22	31	4	0	0	43	9	3	.365	.362
Trevor Story	R-R	6-2	213	11-15-92	.600	1.000	.500	2	5	3	3	1	0	1	3	1	0	0	1	1	0	0	1.400	.571
Izzy Wilson	L-R	6-3	185	3-6-98	.215	.133	.224	95	307	50	66	15	3	13	44	40	2	1	1	98	13	4	.410	.309

Pitching	B-T	HT	WT	DOB	W	L	ERA	G	GS	CG	SV	IP	H	R	ER	HR	BB	SO	AVG	vLH	vRH	K/9	BB/9
Matt Barnes	R-R	6-4	208	6-17-90	2	0	3.00	3	0	0	0	3	2	1	1	0	1	4	.182	.000	.286	12.00	3.00
Brayan Bello	R-R	6-1	170	5-17-99	4	2	1.69	7	7	1	0	37	18	8	7	3	12	48	.140	.181	.088	11.57	2.89
Taylor Broadway	R-R	5-11	205	4-8-97	1	0	1.50	5	0	0	1	6	2	1	1	1	0	10	.105	.167	.077	15.00	0.00
Zach Bryant	R-R	6-1	210	6-5-98	1	4	7.64	28	0	0	0	33	31	29	28	9	24	30	.248	.372	.183	8.18	6.55
Brendan Cellucci	L-L	6-4	211	6-30-98	0	0	0.00	2	0	0	0	2	2	0	0	0	0	3	.250	.250	.250	11.57	0.00
Casey Cobb	R-R	5-10	200	6-27-96	1	0	54.00	1	0	0	0	0	2	2	2	0	1	0	.667	--	.667	0.00	27.00
Ricardo Cubillan	B-R	6-0	155	2-1-98	0	0	0.00	1	0	0	0	1	0	0	0	0	1	1	.000	--	.000	9.00	9.00
Tyler Danish	R-R	6-0	200	9-12-94	0	0	1.93	4	0	0	0	5	4	1	1	0	5	6	.235	.000	.286	11.57	9.64
Shane Drohan	L-L	6-3	195	1-7-99	1	1	3.38	5	5	0	0	24	21	13	9	5	11	21	.233	.233	.233	7.88	4.13
Ryan Fernandez	R-R	6-0	170	6-11-98	1	1	4.97	10	0	0	3	13	12	9	7	3	2	16	.240	.211	.258	11.37	1.42
Franklin German	R-R	6-2	195	9-22-97	3	1	3.18	11	0	0	0	11	6	7	4	0	3	18	.158	.118	.190	14.29	2.38
Michael Gettys	R-R	6-1	217	10-22-95	2	0	0.48	18	0	0	7	19	10	3	1	0	8	8	.167	.192	.147	3.86	3.86
Darin Gillies	R-R	6-4	220	11-6-92	0	0	10.80	6	0	0	0	5	9	7	6	0	4	5	.375	.538	.182	9.00	7.20
Rio Gomez	L-L	6-0	190	10-20-94	2	1	6.55	24	2	0	0	33	39	25	24	8	16	41	.302	.216	.337	11.18	4.36
Jay Groome	L-L	6-6	262	8-23-98	3	4	3.52	16	14	0	0	77	58	33	30	11	38	81	.207	.268	.182	9.51	4.46
Kyle Hart	L-L	6-5	200	11-23-92	2	1	4.91	15	6	0	0	44	40	25	24	6	14	42	.242	.224	.250	8.59	2.86
Rich Hill	L-L	6-5	221	3-11-80	0	0	3.00	1	1	0	0	3	4	1	1	1	0	5	.286	.667	.182	15.00	0.00
Brett Kennedy	R-R	6-0	200	8-4-94	3	6	3.94	23	12	0	5	75	74	38	33	8	27	60	.257	.306	.226	7.17	3.23
Chih-Jung Liu	B-R	6-0	185	4-7-99	0	0	4.91	1	1	0	0	4	2	2	2	1	3	2	.167	.167	.167	4.91	7.36
Joan Martinez	R-R	6-3	195	8-29-96	0	2	5.94	30	0	0	2	33	31	22	22	6	21	39	.250	.234	.260	10.53	5.67
Bryan Mata	R-R	6-3	238	5-3-99	5	2	1.85	10	9	0	0	49	35	14	10	4	23	58	.202	.210	.198	10.73	4.25
Oddanier Mosqueda	L-L	5-10	155	5-6-99	5	3	4.30	45	0	0	2	59	46	29	28	9	20	76	.212	.184	.227	11.66	3.07
Chris Murphy	L-L	6-1	175	6-5-98	4	5	2.58	15	13	0	0	77	46	28	22	6	31	91	.170	.155	.176	10.68	3.64
Brendan Nail	R-L	6-0	190	10-18-95	3	2	3.76	40	0	0	2	41	36	20	17	4	20	49	.235	.211	.250	10.84	4.43
Wyatt Olds	R-R	6-0	183	8-5-99	0	0	3.86	1	1	0	0	5	2	2	2	0	5	3	.167	.167	.167	5.79	9.64
Yusniel Padron-Artiles	R-R	6-0	215	11-12-97	0	0	9.58	3	2	0	0	10	16	11	11	2	1	6	.356	.381	.333	5.23	0.87
Andrew Politi	R-R	6-0	193	6-4-96	0	1	2.03	12	0	0	4	13	7	4	3	2	3	20	.152	.130	.174	13.50	2.03
Chris Sale	L-L	6-6	183	3-30-89	0	0	2.25	1	1	0	0	4	4	1	1	0	0	7	.267	.000	.364	15.75	0.00
Victor Santos	R-R	6-1	191	7-12-00	7	8	4.97	19	16	1	0	101	103	62	56	17	20	79	.259	.251	.266	7.02	1.78
Cody Scroggins	R-R	6-0	195	8-17-96	0	0	8.38	9	0	0	1	10	11	9	9	2	6	13	.289	.167	.346	12.10	5.59
Sterling Sharp	R-R	6-3	182	5-30-95	1	1	3.18	7	7	0	0	34	32	15	12	2	12	31	.256	.283	.231	8.21	3.18
Chase Shugart	L-R	5-10	198	10-24-96	2	2	3.77	25	0	0	5	31	29	17	13	3	10	34	.244	.259	.231	9.87	2.90
Caleb Simpson	R-R	6-4	231	9-15-91	1	0	2.92	10	0	0	0	12	9	6	4	0	5	14	.205	.267	.172	10.22	3.65
Dylan Spacke	B-R	6-0	194	3-11-98	2	5	5.65	32	5	0	0	65	66	45	41	8	39	60	.265	.305	.229	8.27	5.37
Josh Taylor	L-L	6-5	245	3-2-93	0	1	9.64	5	3	0	0	5	10	5	5	2	1	4	.455	.400	.471	7.71	1.93
Jake Thompson	R-R	6-1	215	9-22-94	0	1	2.03	17	1	0	3	27	20	6	6	1	11	32	.206	.233	.194	10.80	3.71
Brian Van Belle	R-R	6-3	185	9-3-96	6	4	4.69	16	15	0	0	79	88	45	41	16	12	80	.279	.328	.243	9.15	1.37
Michael Wacha	R-R	6-6	215	7-1-91	0	0	4.15	1	1	0	0	4	4	2	2	0	2	5	.250	.000	.308	10.38	4.15
Jacob Wallace	R-R	6-1	190	8-13-98	8	2	3.81	47	0	0	1	57	35	27	24	7	49	76	.178	.175	.179	12.07	7.78
Brandon Walter	L-L	6-2	200	9-8-96	2	2	2.88	9	9	0	0	50	36	20	16	6	3	68	.191	.164	.203	12.24	0.54
Thad Ward	R-R	6-3	192	1-16-97	0	1	2.43	7	7	0	0	33	28	13	9	3	14	41	.230	.273	.205	11.07	3.78

Jacob Webb	L-R	6-5	246	3-23-99	0	0	6.00	2	0	0	0	3	4	2	2	1	0	4	.308	.286	.333	12.00	0.00
Garrett Whitlock	R-R	6-5	225	6-11-96	0	0	0.00	1	0	0	0	2	1	0	0	0	0	1	.143	.000	.500	4.50	0.00
Ryan Zeferjahn	R-R	6-5	209	2-28-98	3	0	0.84	6	0	0	0	11	3	1	1	1	4	7	.094	.125	.063	5.91	3.38

Fielding

Catcher	PCT	G	PO	A	E	DP	PB
Cottam	1.000	30	262	18	0	3	2
Marrero	.988	74	718	45	9	4	4
Rangel	1.000	1	1	0	0	0	0
Scott	.989	34	326	23	4	0	4

First Base	PCT	G	PO	A	E	DP
Binelas	1.000	10	64	2	0	7
Castellanos	.989	31	262	13	3	25
Cottam	1.000	7	38	4	0	6
Kavadas	.992	16	124	8	1	13
Northcut	1.000	5	48	2	0	10
Potts	.995	53	371	24	2	37
Reed	.993	22	139	7	1	16

Second Base	PCT	G	PO	A	E	DP
Arroyo	1.000	1	0	2	0	0
Cannon	.971	18	27	40	2	13
Cubillan	.938	10	13	17	2	7
Hamilton	.981	63	106	158	5	40
Koss	.975	27	49	66	3	18
Lugo	.900	2	4	5	1	2
Sogard	.983	25	50	68	2	21
Story	1.000	2	3	7	0	2

Third Base	PCT	G	PO	A	E	DP
Binelas	.975	40	14	65	2	5
Cannon	1.000	10	4	19	0	2
Cubillan	.000	2	0	0	1	0
Howlett	.903	15	5	23	3	1
Koss	.945	23	12	40	3	5
Lugo	1.000	1	0	1	0	0
Northcut	.921	18	12	23	3	3
Potts	.952	20	11	29	2	3
Sogard	1.000	20	7	21	0	0

Shortstop	PCT	G	PO	A	E	DP
Cubillan	1.000	3	1	6	0	2
Hamilton	.955	54	68	143	10	35
Koss	.937	69	97	172	18	40
Rafaela	.982	12	17	39	1	12
Sogard	1.000	3	2	11	0	2

Outfield	PCT	G	PO	A	E	DP
Abreu	1.000	45	67	1	0	0
Castellanos	.971	19	31	3	1	0
Dalton	.972	72	99	4	3	1
Dearden	.962	81	95	5	4	1
Esplin	1.000	5	4	0	0	0
Granberg	.985	37	63	1	1	0
Hamilton	1.000	2	4	0	0	0
Hernandez	1.000	4	4	0	0	0
Howlett	1.000	10	11	0	0	0
Koss	1.000	6	11	1	0	0
Rafaela	.986	60	142	3	2	0
Reed	1.000	7	2	1	0	0
Refsnyder	1.000	2	3	0	0	0
Sogard	.971	16	33	1	1	1
Wilson	.975	94	150	6	4	1

GREENVILLE DRIVE — *HIGH CLASS A*

SOUTH ATLANTIC LEAGUE

Batting	B-T	HT	WT	DOB	AVG	vLH	vRH	G	AB	R	H	2B	3B	HR	RBI	BB	HBP	SH	SF	SO	SB	CS	SLG	OBP
Alex Binelas	L-R	6-3	225	5-26-00	.245	.323	.232	58	216	41	53	10	1	14	43	38	1	0	4	69	8	0	.495	.355
Ricardo Cubillan	B-R	6-0	155	2-1-98	.059	.000	.063	6	17	4	1	0	0	0	0	5	0	0	0	4	1	0	.059	.273
Joe Davis	R-R	6-0	230	10-31-96	.239	.196	.249	75	280	38	67	5	0	18	44	17	5	0	1	63	0	0	.450	.294
Nick Decker	L-L	6-0	207	10-2-99	.122	.132	.120	71	222	36	27	8	0	6	18	40	7	0	0	112	11	2	.239	.275
Alex Erro	B-R	5-10	182	12-5-97	.301	.318	.297	40	123	20	37	4	2	2	20	14	1	0	1	29	2	1	.415	.374
Tyler Esplin	L-R	6-3	230	7-6-99	.245	.333	.227	30	106	15	26	7	3	0	6	13	0	1	1	34	0	0	.368	.325
Max Ferguson	L-R	6-1	180	8-23-99	.181	.125	.196	23	72	18	13	2	0	1	10	21	1	0	1	26	6	0	.250	.368
Antoni Flores	R-R	6-1	207	10-14-00	.218	.182	.227	36	110	15	24	2	0	1	9	24	3	0	1	34	0	0	.264	.370
Jose Garcia	R-R	5-11	225	5-3-98	.176	.400	.083	5	17	4	3	2	0	0	2	1	0	0	0	8	0	0	.294	.222
Jaxx Groshans	R-R	6-0	200	7-20-98	.164	.130	.169	53	165	19	27	5	3	5	21	27	1	0	1	57	0	0	.321	.284
Nathan Hickey	L-R	6-0	210	11-23-99	.252	.261	.250	34	115	19	29	6	0	9	23	24	5	0	2	39	0	0	.539	.397
Brandon Howlett	R-R	6-1	205	9-12-99	.194	.200	.193	34	103	16	20	10	0	3	12	26	5	0	1	47	0	0	.379	.378
Gilberto Jimenez	B-R	5-11	212	7-8-00	.268	.215	.279	99	380	49	102	18	2	5	34	18	3	5	1	100	20	9	.366	.306
Blaze Jordan	R-R	6-2	220	12-19-02	.301	.214	.316	25	93	12	28	1	0	4	11	11	2	0	0	27	1	0	.441	.387
Niko Kavadas	L-R	6-1	235	10-27-98	.308	.296	.312	37	120	27	37	4	0	10	28	32	7	0	2	42	0	0	.592	.472
Matthew Lugo	R-R	6-1	187	5-9-01	.288	.284	.288	114	466	76	134	25	10	18	78	35	7	0	3	100	20	7	.500	.344
Marcelo Mayer	L-R	6-3	188	12-12-02	.265	.267	.265	25	98	15	26	4	1	4	13	17	1	0	0	29	1	0	.449	.379
Tyler McDonough	B-R	5-10	180	4-2-99	.230	.310	.211	114	457	60	105	23	4	9	48	48	6	3	1	162	21	5	.357	.311
Nicholas Northcut	R-R	6-1	206	6-13-99	.223	.250	.217	77	296	43	66	13	0	26	58	21	5	0	0	114	0	0	.530	.286
Ceddanne Rafaela	R-R	5-8	152	9-18-00	.330	.241	.345	45	197	37	65	17	4	9	36	10	2	0	0	51	14	2	.594	.368
Corey Rosier	L-R	5-10	180	9-7-99	.163	.200	.157	23	80	8	13	6	0	1	4	11	1	0	0	31	7	1	.275	.272
Stephen Scott	L-R	5-11	207	5-23-97	.188	.292	.163	37	128	17	24	8	1	3	14	23	0	0	3	28	2	1	.336	.305
Phillip Sikes	R-R	6-2	190	4-27-99	.248	.348	.231	44	157	21	39	11	1	6	20	25	1	0	2	44	8	0	.446	.351
Nick Yorke	R-R	6-0	200	4-2-02	.231	.182	.244	80	337	48	78	10	1	11	45	33	2	0	1	94	8	4	.365	.303

Pitching	B-T	HT	WT	DOB	W	L	ERA	G	GS	CG	SV	IP	H	R	ER	HR	BB	SO	AVG	vLH	vRH	K/9	BB/9
Jacinto Arredondo	R-R	5-9	170	12-7-97	3	1	6.30	32	0	0	2	50	66	41	35	6	22	48	.316	.250	.345	8.64	3.96
Maceo Campbell	R-R	6-1	215	6-17-99	0	2	9.82	8	0	0	0	11	8	12	12	2	13	13	.195	.091	.233	10.64	10.64
Brendan Cellucci	L-L	6-4	211	6-30-98	3	4	4.50	43	10	0	0	62	54	35	31	6	44	82	.238	.203	.253	11.90	6.39
Casey Cobb	R-R	5-10	200	6-27-96	3	4	6.00	33	2	0	0	60	74	49	40	10	25	57	.302	.307	.299	8.55	3.75
Joe Davis	R-R	6-0	230	10-31-96	0	0	0.00	1	0	0	0	1	2	0	0	0	1	0	.500	1.000	.333	0.00	13.50
Jordan DiValerio	R-R	6-1	200	10-9-97	4	0	5.32	29	0	0	1	68	82	50	40	12	15	67	.293	.356	.256	8.91	2.00
Shane Drohan	L-L	6-3	195	1-7-99	6	7	4.00	22	20	0	0	106	91	56	47	15	40	136	.226	.287	.201	11.58	3.41
Juan Daniel Encarnacion	R-R	6-2	173	3-30-01	0	0	3.60	2	2	0	0	10	7	4	4	1	3	10	.200	.375	.148	9.00	2.70
Ryan Fernandez	R-R	6-0	170	6-11-98	1	2	4.00	25	0	0	7	27	28	13	12	3	9	40	.262	.361	.211	13.33	3.00
Michael Gettys	R-R	6-1	217	10-22-95	2	1	3.34	22	0	0	0	30	39	15	11	3	7	23	.325	.214	.385	6.98	2.12
Wikelman Gonzalez	R-R	6-0	167	3-25-02	0	0	2.65	4	4	0	0	17	13	5	5	0	6	23	.213	.250	.195	12.18	3.18
Luis Guerrero	R-R	6-0	215	8-5-00	0	2	2.08	7	0	0	1	13	11	5	3	0	3	19	.216	.143	.243	13.15	2.08
Graham Hoffman	R-R	6-3	211	12-26-98	0	0	3.00	3	0	0	0	3	5	1	1	0	1	5	.357	.000	.417	15.00	3.00
Robert Kwiatkowski	R-R	6-1	190	6-8-97	2	4	6.75	30	0	0	1	33	55	30	25	1	18	25	.369	.459	.307	6.75	4.86
Austin Lambright	L-L	6-3	205	8-26-94	2	0	10.89	19	0	0	0	19	24	24	23	3	15	21	.316	.421	.281	9.95	7.11
Chih-Jung Liu	B-R	6-0	185	4-7-99	4	11	6.10	25	21	0	0	100	112	71	68	27	46	106	.284	.333	.253	9.51	4.13
Bryan Lucas	R-R	6-2	160	12-13-97	0	0	0.00	1	0	0	0	1	1	0	0	0	1	0	.500	.000	1.000	0.00	13.50
Bryan Mata	R-R	6-3	238	5-3-99	0	1	4.00	3	3	0	0	9	6	4	4	1	6	15	.182	.000	.300	15.00	6.00
Alexander Montero	R-R	6-3	180	9-21-97	0	0	13.50	3	0	0	0	3	3	4	4	1	0	0	.273	.200	.333	0.00	0.00

Wyatt Olds	R-R	6-0	183	8-5-99	4	9	6.01	26	25	0	0	106	106	80	71	9	59	130	.260	.272	.252	11.00	4.99
Yusniel Padron-Artiles	R-R	6-0	215	11-12-97	3	12	5.95	23	20	0	0	107	121	73	71	26	34	115	.278	.249	.297	9.64	2.85
Aaron Perry	R-R	5-11	175	6-7-99	0	0	0.00	3	0	0	0	3	1	0	0	0	1	3	.100	.000	.143	9.00	3.00
Jorge Rodriguez	L-L	5-11	171	8-25-00	0	0	5.40	1	0	0	0	3	2	2	2	0	2	3	.182	.400	.000	8.10	5.40
Devon Roedahl	R-R	6-2	225	11-29-96	4	7	9.38	27	0	0	1	39	59	47	41	4	18	33	.337	.375	.315	7.55	4.12
Cody Scroggins	R-R	6-0	195	8-17-96	2	0	4.35	35	0	0	6	41	42	21	20	3	27	51	.263	.238	.278	11.10	5.88
Joey Stock	R-R	6-5	210	9-8-97	2	2	4.86	10	0	0	0	17	14	9	9	3	15	19	.246	.167	.303	10.26	8.10
Nate Tellier	R-R	5-9	180	6-5-98	0	0	27.00	1	0	0	0	0	1	1	1	0	2	0	.500	1.000	.000	0.00	54.00
Tyler Uberstine	R-R	6-1	200	6-1-99	1	1	2.43	7	7	0	0	33	25	12	9	2	14	35	.203	.250	.169	9.45	3.78
Brian Van Belle	R-R	6-3	183	9-3-96	3	2	6.14	12	9	0	0	59	83	43	40	17	8	55	.331	.295	.353	8.44	1.23
Thad Ward	R-R	6-3	192	1-16-97	0	1	5.14	2	2	0	0	7	9	6	4	0	4	6	.300	.455	.211	7.71	5.14
Jacob Webb	L-R	6-5	246	3-23-99	1	1	3.72	24	0	0	7	29	23	15	12	3	9	45	.211	.216	.208	13.97	2.79
Ryan Zeferjahn	R-R	6-5	209	2-28-98	2	4	5.79	28	5	0	1	61	58	41	39	6	29	73	.252	.265	.242	10.83	4.30

Fielding

Catcher	PCT	G	PO	A	E	DP	PB
Erro	.973	18	170	13	5	0	2
Garcia	.981	5	47	4	1	0	0
Groshans	.995	48	416	22	2	2	6
Hickey	.985	30	302	17	5	2	4
Scott	.983	33	334	19	6	1	3

First Base	PCT	G	PO	A	E	DP
Binelas	.992	29	221	14	2	14
Davis	1.000	33	195	5	0	27
Jordan	.986	13	72	1	1	6
Kavadas	.976	30	188	13	5	15
Northcut	.989	27	173	12	2	18

Second Base	PCT	G	PO	A	E	DP
Cubillan	1.000	5	6	15	0	5
Ferguson	1.000	6	9	12	0	2
Flores	.959	14	21	26	2	10
Lugo	.955	7	9	12	1	1
McDonough	.964	29	49	59	4	14
Rafaela	1.000	1	2	1	0	0
Yorke	.997	68	130	166	1	36

Third Base	PCT	G	PO	A	E	DP
Binelas	.949	23	15	41	3	5
Cubillan	1.000	1	0	1	0	0
Flores	.889	16	9	23	4	1
Howlett	.923	15	19	17	3	4
Jordan	.882	9	7	8	2	1
Lugo	.880	25	10	34	6	2
Northcut	.935	42	36	65	7	2

Shortstop	PCT	G	PO	A	E	DP
Ferguson	.977	10	18	24	1	7
Flores	1.000	5	10	10	0	3
Lugo	.923	73	83	157	20	28
Mayer	.974	21	28	48	2	10
McDonough	.929	12	19	20	3	4
Northcut	.800	1	1	3	1	0
Rafaela	.976	9	12	29	1	6

Outfield	PCT	G	PO	A	E	DP
Decker	.974	60	105	8	3	1
Erro	1.000	19	19	3	0	1
Esplin	.985	30	59	6	1	1
Ferguson	1.000	7	22	1	0	0
Howlett	.957	15	21	1	1	0
Jimenez	.949	95	176	11	10	2
McDonough	.980	69	137	8	3	1
Rafaela	1.000	32	61	3	0	0
Rosier	.976	22	40	1	1	0
Sikes	.980	43	91	7	2	0

SALEM RED SOX

LOW CLASS A

CAROLINA LEAGUE

Batting	B-T	HT	WT	DOB	AVG	vLH	vRH	G	AB	R	H	2B	3B	HR	RBI	BB	HBP	SH	SF	SO	SB	CS	SLG	OBP
Roman Anthony	L-R	6-3	200	5-13-04	.189	.000	.200	10	37	2	7	2	0	0	5	5	0	0	1	4	0	0	.243	.279
Darel Belen	R-R	6-4	204	5-21-00	.102	.091	.105	32	98	8	10	2	0	3	10	11	3	0	1	51	1	1	.214	.212
Brainer Bonaci	B-R	5-10	164	7-9-02	.262	.279	.257	108	397	86	104	19	6	6	50	89	3	0	5	89	28	6	.385	.397
Allan Castro	B-R	6-1	170	5-24-03	.188	.000	.194	10	32	7	6	1	2	0	4	6	0	0	0	11	0	0	.344	.316
Juan Chacon	R-R	6-2	171	12-4-02	.129	.000	.133	8	31	4	4	1	0	0	1	3	0	0	0	13	1	0	.161	.206
Jonathan Diaz	L-R	5-11	170	7-7-99	.381	1.000	.350	8	21	5	8	3	1	0	4	6	0	0	0	5	1	0	.619	.519
Matt Donlan	R-R	6-3	213	11-9-99	.148	.000	.174	8	27	2	4	1	0	0	1	3	1	0	1	5	0	0	.185	.250
Jose Garcia	R-R	5-11	225	5-3-98	.216	.263	.205	32	102	11	22	5	0	3	14	12	2	0	2	38	0	0	.353	.305
Bryan Gonzalez	R-R	6-2	220	9-18-01	.234	.226	.238	32	111	11	26	5	0	1	9	15	0	0	0	35	5	2	.306	.325
Nathan Hickey	L-R	6-0	210	11-23-99	.271	.290	.266	41	140	31	38	12	0	7	39	39	1	0	2	39	0	1	.507	.429
Blaze Jordan	R-R	6-2	220	12-19-02	.286	.328	.278	95	370	48	106	29	3	8	57	37	5	0	3	67	4	1	.446	.357
Niko Kavadas	L-R	6-1	235	10-27-98	.286	.235	.297	59	192	35	55	18	1	14	48	54	6	0	2	70	1	1	.609	.453
Ahbram Liendo	B-R	5-8	170	2-1-04	.333	.000	.353	6	18	6	6	0	0	0	4	3	0	0	1	1	0	0	.333	.409
Eduardo Lopez	B-R	6-0	187	5-8-02	.234	.288	.220	76	286	39	67	12	2	4	27	36	5	0	5	78	9	5	.332	.325
Marcelo Mayer	L-R	6-3	188	12-12-02	.286	.308	.282	66	252	46	72	26	1	9	40	51	2	0	3	78	16	0	.504	.406
Daniel McElveny	R-R	6-0	190	4-21-03	.167	.211	.151	22	72	13	12	6	0	0	10	21	2	0	3	29	0	1	.250	.357
Chase Meidroth	R-R	5-10	170	7-23-01	.309	.400	.293	19	68	15	21	5	0	4	12	12	3	0	2	9	4	2	.559	.424
Yorberto Mejicano	R-R	5-11	185	11-21-00	.262	.333	.245	68	252	38	66	11	1	5	37	20	4	0	1	52	7	2	.373	.325
Kier Meredith	L-L	5-10	200	9-12-99	.265	.286	.262	65	185	35	49	6	1	1	22	35	13	0	1	35	25	0	.324	.415
Tyler Miller	L-R	6-2	193	12-17-99	.219	.174	.227	114	430	61	94	10	1	13	59	37	6	1	6	130	22	2	.337	.286
Eddinson Paulino	L-R	5-10	155	7-2-02	.266	.200	.278	114	463	96	123	35	10	13	66	64	6	1	5	105	27	5	.469	.359
Luis Ravelo	B-R	6-1	187	11-5-03	.240	.000	.261	7	25	4	6	1	0	1	6	2	1	0	0	8	0	0	.400	.321
Mikey Romero	L-R	6-1	175	1-12-04	.349	1.000	.333	9	43	6	15	4	3	0	11	1	0	0	0	11	1	0	.581	.364
Johnfrank Salazar	R-R	6-1	159	8-5-03	.257	.143	.283	19	74	9	19	3	1	0	8	5	1	3	0	17	0	0	.324	.313
Phillip Sikes	R-R	6-2	190	4-27-99	.258	.400	.225	50	159	36	41	18	4	5	28	28	7	0	1	55	12	1	.516	.390
Karson Simas	R-R	6-6	175	6-2-01	.197	.143	.211	78	279	40	55	10	4	1	24	25	3	0	1	107	15	1	.272	.269
Miguel Ugueto	R-R	6-2	185	9-3-02	.311	.364	.304	22	90	11	28	7	1	0	12	4	0	0	3	17	3	1	.411	.330
Eduardo Vaughan	R-R	6-3	179	1-12-02	.191	.308	.171	27	89	15	17	2	0	0	8	21	1	0	2	33	4	0	.213	.345

Pitching	B-T	HT	WT	DOB	W	L	ERA	G	GS	CG	SV	IP	H	R	ER	HR	BB	SO	AVG	vLH	vRH	K/9	BB/9
Angel Bastardo	R-R	6-1	175	6-18-02	3	4	4.50	22	22	0	0	82	82	49	41	4	45	85	.264	.277	.252	9.33	4.94
Adenys Bautista	R-R	6-3	170	8-6-98	2	2	4.19	30	0	0	1	43	33	28	20	6	25	43	.204	.222	.189	9.00	5.23
Maceo Campbell	R-R	6-1	215	6-17-99	4	3	5.30	24	0	0	1	37	39	25	22	2	26	46	.269	.292	.247	11.09	6.27
Felix Cepeda	R-R	6-3	170	7-15-00	3	4	6.20	28	2	0	2	49	39	37	34	3	49	55	.214	.202	.227	10.03	8.94
Nathanael Cruz	R-R	6-2	175	2-4-03	0	0	7.85	8	3	0	1	18	20	16	16	6	13	15	.278	.250	.292	7.36	6.38
Luis De La Rosa	R-R	6-1	170	7-6-02	2	2	4.72	11	0	0	1	34	31	22	18	2	12	38	.235	.321	.177	9.96	3.15
Osvaldo De La Rosa	R-R	6-4	240	10-28-97	7	1	4.47	32	1	0	2	52	54	26	26	4	24	46	.274	.281	.267	7.91	4.13

Jordan DiValerio	R-R	6-1	200	10-9-97	0	0	36.00	1	0	0	0	1	4	4	4	0	1	1	.571	.500	1.000	9.00	9.00
Hunter Dobbins	R-R	6-2	185	8-30-99	0	5	5.22	17	17	0	0	69	82	44	40	6	22	68	.301	.311	.292	8.87	2.87
Juan Daniel Encarnacion	R-R	6-2	173	3-30-01	10	5	4.09	24	23	0	0	103	95	53	47	3	39	119	.242	.245	.239	10.36	3.40
Jhonny Felix	B-R	6-0	180	9-4-98	0	0	9.72	15	0	0	1	17	14	23	18	0	30	20	.230	.333	.107	10.80	16.20
Wikelman Gonzalez	R-R	6-0	167	3-25-02	4	3	4.54	21	21	1	0	81	63	46	41	2	48	98	.212	.255	.169	10.84	5.31
Luis Guerrero	R-R	6-0	215	8-5-00	4	3	4.18	18	0	0	6	24	15	13	11	1	14	37	.174	.205	.143	14.07	5.32
Graham Hoffman	R-R	6-3	211	12-26-98	2	2	3.48	23	0	0	1	34	28	14	13	1	20	41	.219	.300	.121	10.96	5.35
Gabriel Jackson	R-R	6-2	180	9-7-01	7	8	5.27	25	13	0	0	94	111	65	55	6	39	65	.289	.276	.302	6.22	3.73
Blake Loubier	R-R	6-5	189	10-13-00	1	3	7.43	31	0	0	1	53	71	49	44	7	30	43	.324	.308	.339	7.26	5.06
Bryan Lucas	R-R	6-2	160	12-13-97	1	1	2.27	14	0	0	0	32	22	9	8	1	14	27	.191	.174	.203	7.67	3.98
Bryan Mata	R-R	6-3	238	5-3-99	0	0	0.00	1	1	0	0	2	0	1	0	0	2	2	.000	.000	.000	9.00	9.00
Alexander Montero	R-R	6-3	180	9-21-97	0	2	5.54	8	0	0	0	13	16	9	8	1	6	14	.314	.250	.391	9.69	4.15
Luis Perales	R-R	6-1	160	4-14-03	0	1	3.38	4	4	0	0	11	10	7	4	1	11	16	.250	.455	.000	13.50	9.28
Barbaro Pinero	R-R	6-0	190	6-18-99	0	0	--	3	0	0	0	0	3	11	9	0	6	0	.600	.600	--	--	--
Jose Ramirez	R-R	6-0	142	3-28-01	0	1	7.50	3	0	0	0	6	4	7	5	0	8	7	.174	.167	.182	10.50	12.00
Elmer Rodriguez-Cruz	L-R	6-3	160	8-18-03	0	0	1.50	2	2	0	0	6	3	1	1	0	3	6	.143	.167	.111	9.00	4.50
Reidis Sena	R-R	5-10	160	4-7-01	0	1	5.91	11	10	0	0	21	27	23	14	3	12	21	.307	.317	.298	8.86	5.06
Phillip Sikes	R-R	6-2	190	4-27-99	0	0	0.00	2	0	0	0	2	1	0	0	0	0	2	.167	.250	.000	10.80	0.00
Joey Stock	R-R	6-5	210	9-8-97	3	2	2.08	22	1	0	4	43	28	12	10	4	15	53	.181	.167	.197	11.01	3.12
Miguel Suero	R-R	6-1	185	1-4-97	4	2	6.39	28	0	0	1	44	53	34	31	3	22	38	.303	.345	.261	7.83	4.53
Luis Talavera	R-R	6-3	175	2-6-02	0	0	5.06	4	0	0	0	11	10	12	6	1	6	2	.238	.381	.095	1.69	5.06
Nate Tellier	R-R	5-9	180	6-5-98	0	1	9.92	13	0	0	1	16	18	21	18	2	15	27	.273	.367	.194	14.88	8.27
Christopher Troye	R-R	6-4	225	2-8-99	1	4	4.86	26	0	0	1	33	19	21	18	0	24	50	.164	.200	.131	13.50	6.48
Tyler Uberstine	R-R	6-1	200	6-1-99	4	4	4.63	14	8	0	1	58	56	32	30	5	21	66	.248	.278	.220	10.18	3.24
Michael Valera	R-R	6-2	176	2-12-99	1	0	6.35	2	0	0	0	6	5	4	4	0	4	7	.227	.231	.222	11.12	6.35
Thad Ward	R-R	6-3	192	1-16-97	0	0	0.00	2	2	0	0	6	2	0	0	0	1	10	.100	.500	.056	15.00	1.50
Jacob Webb	L-R	6-5	246	3-23-99	1	2	2.19	18	0	0	3	25	21	10	6	0	19	39	.223	.294	.140	14.23	6.93

Fielding

Catcher	PCT	G	PO	A	E	DP	PB
Diaz	1.000	5	53	6	0	1	0
Donlan	.988	8	79	5	1	1	1
Garcia	.986	31	270	11	4	2	2
Hickey	.989	27	260	14	3	0	6
McElveny	.988	19	155	12	2	0	3
Mejicano	.982	44	405	30	8	1	13

First Base	PCT	G	PO	A	E	DP
Jordan	.982	34	251	20	5	20
Kavadas	.994	42	301	23	2	30
Mejicano	.981	7	50	2	1	5
Miller	.990	47	361	17	4	36
Salazar	.947	3	17	1	1	3

Second Base	PCT	G	PO	A	E	DP
Bonaci	.955	57	73	159	11	33
Liendo	1.000	1	3	0	0	0
Meidroth	1.000	13	21	41	0	8
Paulino	.975	30	47	72	3	16
Ravelo	1.000	2	2	3	0	1
Romero	.864	4	5	14	3	1
Salazar	1.000	4	6	10	0	2
Simas	.918	24	24	65	8	10

Third Base	PCT	G	PO	A	E	DP
Bonaci	.867	10	3	10	2	0
Jordan	.951	50	36	41	4	3
Liendo	.917	5	4	7	1	0
Miller	1.000	26	18	39	0	5
Paulino	.938	34	25	50	5	3
Salazar	.900	12	10	17	3	5

Shortstop	PCT	G	PO	A	E	DP
Bonaci	.966	31	36	77	4	8
Mayer	.956	58	80	138	10	42
Paulino	.947	36	57	85	8	20
Ravelo	.813	3	5	8	3	2
Romero	1.000	3	3	6	0	2

Outfield	PCT	G	PO	A	E	DP
Anthony	.950	8	19	0	1	0
Belen	.893	26	41	9	6	0
Bonaci	--	1	0	0	0	0
Castro	1.000	10	19	0	0	0
Chacon	1.000	8	13	1	0	0
Gonzalez	.957	31	45	0	2	1
Lopez	.985	69	119	11	2	1
Meredith	.987	62	72	3	1	1
Miller	.935	29	42	1	3	0
Paulino	.913	14	19	2	2	1
Sikes	1.000	49	94	3	0	2
Simas	.972	57	139	0	4	0
Ugueto	.963	19	26	0	1	0
Vaughan	1.000	27	38	2	0	0

FCL RED SOX — *ROOKIE*

FLORIDA COMPLEX LEAGUE

Batting	B-T	HT	WT	DOB	AVG	vLH	vRH	G	AB	R	H	2B	3B	HR	RBI	BB	HBP	SH	SF	SO	SB	CS	SLG	OBP
Roman Anthony	L-R	6-3	200	5-13-04	.429	.182	.542	10	35	5	15	2	0	0	7	4	0	0	1	4	1	0	.486	.475
Miguel Bleis	R-R	6-3	170	3-1-04	.301	.250	.312	40	153	28	46	14	4	5	27	10	3	0	1	45	18	3	.542	.353
Brooks Brannon	R-R	6-0	210	5-4-04	.462	.400	.500	5	13	6	6	1	2	0	5	2	0	0	0	5	0	0	.846	.533
Cam Cannon	R-R	5-10	205	10-16-97	.231	.000	.300	4	13	3	3	1	0	0	1	1	0	0	0	1	0	0	.308	.286
Triston Casas	L-R	6-4	252	1-15-00	.429	.000	.500	4	14	3	6	3	0	1	3	3	0	0	0	2	0	0	.857	.529
Allan Castro	B-R	6-1	170	5-24-03	.279	.433	.228	39	122	19	34	4	4	3	17	13	3	0	3	32	8	2	.451	.355
Juan Chacon	R-R	6-2	171	12-4-02	.225	.261	.217	41	138	21	31	10	0	1	25	26	3	0	4	53	21	3	.319	.351
Cutter Coffey	R-R	6-2	190	5-21-04	.125	.167	.100	11	32	7	4	1	0	0	0	7	1	0	0	11	1	0	.156	.300
Tyler Esplin	L-R	6-3	230	7-6-99	.333	.000	.400	3	6	1	2	1	0	0	1	2	0	0	0	1	0	0	.500	.500
Albert Feliz	R-R	6-2	200	4-13-02	.194	.167	.200	19	36	4	7	0	1	1	4	8	0	0	0	13	0	0	.333	.341
Jhostynxon Garcia	R-R	6-0	163	12-11-02	.188	.375	.153	31	101	18	19	5	2	3	17	18	4	0	2	38	4	2	.366	.328
Bryan Gonzalez	R-R	6-2	220	9-18-01	.071	.000	.083	9	28	4	2	0	0	0	2	4	1	0	1	12	1	2	.071	.206
Alexis Hernandez	R-R	6-1	170	10-5-02	.218	.368	.169	26	78	15	17	4	0	1	6	10	3	0	1	17	5	3	.308	.326
Lyonell James	R-R	6-3	165	10-14-02	.340	.389	.329	34	100	19	34	7	1	0	19	17	2	0	1	17	2	1	.430	.442
Ahbram Liendo	B-R	5-8	170	2-1-04	.219	.172	.231	45	146	26	32	11	1	0	19	30	3	0	0	47	12	5	.308	.363
Enderso Lira	R-R	6-1	185	10-11-03	.129	.071	.146	21	62	4	8	1	0	0	6	7	2	0	0	20	0	0	.145	.239
Naysbel Marcano	R-R	6-0	175	5-23-02	.200	.400	.160	18	30	3	6	1	0	1	3	5	1	0	0	14	0	0	.333	.333
Daniel McElveny	R-R	6-0	190	4-21-03	.250	.273	.245	21	64	13	16	10	1	0	6	15	1	0	0	26	5	0	.438	.400
Chase Meidroth	R-R	5-10	170	7-23-01	.375	.333	.400	3	8	4	3	0	0	0	3	2	1	0	0	2	0	0	.375	.545
Juan Montero	R-R	5-11	180	6-10-02	.258	.400	.231	18	31	2	8	5	0	0	10	3	4	0	1	12	0	0	.419	.385
Luis Ravelo	B-R	6-1	187	11-5-03	.187	.200	.184	31	107	19	20	1	2	0	6	17	0	1	0	31	6	3	.234	.298
Mikey Romero	L-R	6-1	175	1-12-04	.250	.222	.259	10	36	5	9	3	0	1	6	7	0	0	0	4	1	0	.417	.372

Ronald Rosario	R-R	6-0	175	1-1-03	.244	.000	.278	20	41	5	10	2	0	0	5	7	3	0	0	11	0	0	.293	.392
Johnfrank Salazar	R-R	6-1	159	8-5-03	.327	.296	.338	32	101	21	33	8	2	0	16	17	3	0	1	9	3	0	.446	.434
Danny Santana	B-R	5-11	195	11-7-90	.286	.250	.294	7	21	3	6	2	0	0	5	4	0	0	0	5	0	0	.381	.400
Miguel Ugueto	R-R	6-2	185	9-3-02	.500	1.000	.333	1	4	0	2	0	0	0	2	0	0	0	0	0	1	0	.500	.500
Freddy Valdez	R-R	6-3	212	12-6-01	.192	.222	.186	22	52	7	10	2	0	1	9	6	2	0	3	14	0	0	.288	.286
Eduardo Vaughan	R-R	6-3	179	1-12-02	.120	.231	.081	21	50	5	6	2	0	0	1	8	0	0	0	22	3	0	.160	.241
B.J. Vela	R-R	5-9	175	10-2-99	.342	.273	.370	21	38	8	13	4	0	0	6	7	4	0	1	8	2	0	.447	.480
Diego Viloria	R-R	5-10	165	2-23-03	.138	.333	.050	12	29	3	4	0	0	0	0	1	2	0	0	4	0	0	.138	.219
Alex Zapete	R-R	6-0	180	9-11-01	.246	.214	.255	26	65	10	16	6	0	0	10	10	1	0	3	17	1	0	.338	.342

Pitching	B-T	HT	WT	DOB	W	L	ERA	G	GS	CG	SV	IP	H	R	ER	HR	BB	SO	AVG	vLH	vRH	K/9	BB/9
Bell, Brock	R-R	6-4	215	3-18-98	0	1	2.77	8	8	0	0	13	10	4	4	0	4	11	.222	.235	.214	7.62	2.77
Blalock, Bradley	R-R	6-2	190	12-25-00	0	2	6.75	4	3	0	0	7	5	6	5	0	4	4	.208	.143	.235	5.40	5.40
Cepeda, Felix	R-R	6-3	170	7-15-00	2	4	6.16	10	8	0	0	38	39	30	26	4	20	29	.265	.236	.283	6.87	4.74
Duke, Mason	R-R	5-10	210	10-21-96	2	1	2.82	13	0	0	0	22	25	8	7	1	5	17	.281	.306	.264	6.85	2.01
Fisher, Devon	R-R	6-0	215	5-1-96	1	0	0.00	3	0	0	0	4	6	0	0	0	0	6	.400	.250	.455	13.50	0.00
Gomez, Anyelo	R-R	6-1	185	3-1-93	0	0	7.36	3	0	0	0	4	3	4	3	1	5	6	.200	.000	.300	14.73	12.27
Groome, Jay	L-L	6-6	220	8-23-98	0	0	0.00	2	2	0	0	2	2	0	0	0	0	3	.250	.000	.333	13.50	0.00
Guedez, Yoelvis	R-R	5-11	175	9-8-00	2	1	1.60	14	0	0	3	34	25	6	6	0	5	36	.202	.189	.211	9.62	1.34
Harrington, Reed	R-R	6-5	200	8-8-98	0	0	4.91	4	0	0	0	4	4	2	2	0	2	4	.267	.250	.273	9.82	4.91
Jimenez, Eddie	R-R	6-2	230	8-9-95	1	0	2.89	14	0	0	0	19	18	6	6	1	7	23	.254	.409	.184	11.09	3.38
Jimenez, Richardson	R-R	5-11	173	9-30-99	1	1	6.75	2	0	0	0	4	4	4	3	0	1	6	.250	.333	.200	13.50	2.25
Larez, Jose	R-R	6-4	195	1-12-97	1	0	3.72	7	0	0	0	10	8	4	4	0	7	8	.211	.167	.231	7.45	6.52
LoBrutto, Dominic	L-L	6-1	185	5-31-96	0	0	0.00	2	1	0	0	3	1	0	0	0	0	4	.111	.333	.000	13.50	0.00
Loubier, Blake	R-R	6-5	190	10-13-00	0	1	5.54	6	6	0	0	13	14	8	8	1	7	15	.286	.261	.308	10.38	4.85
Martinez, Algenis	R-R	6-1	185	9-12-93	0	0	3.00	2	0	0	0	3	2	1	1	0	1	1	.167	.286	.000	3.00	3.00
Montero, Alexander	R-R	6-3	180	9-21-97	0	2	5.75	10	5	0	0	20	25	17	13	1	12	22	.305	.419	.235	9.74	5.31
Perry, Aaron	R-R	5-11	175	6-7-99	0	2	3.00	9	5	0	0	21	11	9	7	0	19	18	.155	.143	.163	7.71	8.14
Reyes, Gregorio	L-L	6-3	170	1-22-99	3	2	3.05	11	8	0	0	41	39	20	14	4	6	36	.244	.182	.267	7.84	1.31
Rodriguez, Jorge	L-L	5-11	170	8-25-00	6	2	1.91	11	6	0	0	47	35	13	10	2	9	58	.202	.167	.216	11.11	1.72
Roedahl, Devon	R-R	6-2	225	11-29-96	0	2	4.09	16	0	0	3	22	20	11	10	2	5	27	.227	.189	.255	11.05	2.05
Schneider, Zach	R-R	6-0	180	1-27-97	1	2	2.28	17	0	0	4	24	20	9	6	1	4	33	.222	.290	.173	12.55	1.52
Spacke, Dylan	B-R	6-0	180	3-11-98	2	1	3.10	12	0	0	0	20	20	10	7	0	3	23	.256	.219	.283	10.18	1.33
Sutherland, Casey	R-R	6-3	205	10-18-96	1	0	0.66	11	0	0	1	27	17	2	2	1	1	26	.174	.118	.234	8.56	0.33
Walter, Brandon	L-L	6-2	200	9-8-96	4	1	2.70	13	0	0	0	33	26	11	10	2	8	39	.208	.241	.198	10.53	2.16

Fielding

C: Brannon 5, Lira 18, Marcano 11, McElveny 13, Montero 14, Rosario 8, Viloria 12. **1B:** Casas 3, Feliz 12, Hernandez 16, James 15, Marcano 6, Montero 4, Rosario 8, Santana 3, Zapete 5. **2B:** Cannon 2, Coffey 3, Liendo 28, Meidroth 2, Ravelo 3, Romero 2, Salazar 10, Vela 10, Zapete 7. **3B:** Cannon 1, Coffey 3, James 20, Liendo 3, Salazar 15, Vela 10, Zapete 13. **SS:** Coffey 3, Liendo 17, Ravelo 29, Romero 6, Salazar 9. **OF:** Anthony 8, Bleis 38, Castro 36, Chacon 41, Esplin 2, Feliz 5, Garcia 21, Gonzalez 5, Hernandez 7, Santana 1, Valdez 14, Vaughan 17.

DSL BOS BLUE — *ROOKIE*

Batting	B-T	HT	WT	DOB	AVG	vLH	vRH	G	AB	R	H	2B	3B	HR	RBI	BB	HBP	SH	SF	SO	SB	CS	SLG	OBP
Marvin Alcantara	R-R	5-10	157	11-2-04	.302	.333	.294	53	189	49	57	15	0	1	29	29	5	0	1	33	14	2	.397	.406
Albertson Asigen	R-R	5-10	175	8-27-01	.313	.303	.314	55	192	41	60	5	4	0	27	33	4	0	4	42	15	2	.380	.416
Rivaldo Avila	R-R	6-0	172	9-11-02	.267	.158	.289	34	116	18	31	6	2	1	36	10	2	0	3	31	2	2	.379	.328
Karim Ayubi	R-R	0-0	0	12-8-03	.248	.200	.254	44	145	29	36	6	3	0	22	26	15	0	2	48	11	4	.331	.410
Josue Castillo	B-R	5-9	162	10-29-03	.129	.333	.107	20	31	9	4	0	0	0	3	12	0	1	1	13	4	0	.129	.364
Fraymi De Leon	B-R	5-10	155	9-28-04	.218	.250	.210	50	179	29	39	1	1	2	21	21	10	3	1	61	20	8	.268	.332
Kelvin Diaz	R-R	6-0	148	3-17-03	.242	.303	.228	46	178	41	43	12	4	6	30	16	10	0	3	55	20	3	.455	.333
Jhaydel Flores	B-R	6-0	176	2-23-05	.246	.250	.245	24	61	5	15	4	0	0	6	3	2	0	1	10	1	1	.311	.299
Andy Lugo	B-R	5-11	160	3-15-04	.318	.295	.324	56	220	52	70	11	2	2	30	11	8	0	3	35	21	2	.414	.368
Jose Mendez	R-R	6-1	153	11-16-02	.285	.333	.274	48	130	20	37	9	1	1	19	26	0	0	1	33	6	3	.392	.401
Helison Mota	B-R	5-11	160	9-24-03	.230	.214	.232	41	113	23	26	5	2	1	19	30	4	0	1	50	5	3	.336	.405
Yevganni Reinita	L-R	5-7	135	10-17-02	.167	.125	.176	26	42	6	7	2	0	0	5	14	1	1	0	11	1	1	.214	.386
Diego Rodriguez	B-R	6-0	150	6-20-03	.262	.286	.259	30	61	20	16	2	3	0	12	15	0	1	1	17	2	1	.393	.403
Miguel Rojas	R-R	5-9	157	1-4-02	.305	.313	.304	26	95	14	29	6	0	0	10	10	1	0	0	16	1	0	.368	.377
Anger Romero	R-R	6-0	185	3-16-05	.467	1.000	.429	7	15	2	7	1	0	0	3	3	0	0	2	2	0	1	.533	.500
Armando Sierra	R-R	6-2	189	1-17-04	.314	.313	.314	51	188	37	59	15	0	5	48	25	3	0	2	22	3	1	.473	.399

Pitching	B-T	HT	WT	DOB	W	L	ERA	G	GS	CG	SV	IP	H	R	ER	HR	BB	SO	AVG	vLH	vRH	K/9	BB/9
Wandy Abreu	R-R	6-4	238	6-8-02	8	0	1.22	18	0	0	1	37	25	7	5	2	11	45	.191	.245	.159	10.95	2.68
Stiwar Adames	L-L	6-2	180	8-8-02	9	1	2.37	16	0	0	1	38	31	12	10	1	15	32	.218	.174	.240	7.58	3.55
Ali Ascanio	R-R	6-1	185	11-18-03	5	1	3.69	17	2	0	0	32	30	21	13	1	25	32	.250	.236	.262	9.09	7.11
Yizreel Burnet	R-R	0-0	0	1-15-04	0	0	2.57	5	3	0	0	7	2	2	2	0	4	10	.095	.000	.143	12.86	5.14
Luis Cohen	R-R	6-0	172	5-26-03	0	1	2.89	13	12	0	0	47	36	16	15	0	14	42	.208	.292	.149	8.10	2.70
Willian Colmenares	R-R	6-0	183	2-3-05	2	2	3.79	13	12	0	0	40	45	18	17	1	18	40	.308	.409	.225	8.93	4.02
Ruben De La Cruz	R-R	5-10	150	1-14-05	2	2	3.04	14	0	0	2	24	14	9	8	0	20	21	.179	.162	.195	7.99	7.61
Inmer Lobo	L-L	6-1	193	2-12-04	2	0	0.82	5	5	0	0	22	15	2	2	1	2	28	.190	.167	.200	11.45	0.82
Carlos Mendoza	R-R	6-1	150	12-26-04	0	0	2.79	9	0	0	0	10	7	4	3	0	7	11	.189	.318	.000	10.24	6.52
Henry Morales	L-R	6-3	185	10-4-01	2	2	5.40	18	0	0	2	32	33	20	19	2	19	23	.277	.269	.288	6.54	5.40
Cristian Nunez	R-R	6-5	210	10-22-02	3	0	1.11	11	9	0	0	32	19	7	4	0	12	32	.174	.175	.174	8.91	3.34
Daniel Nunez	L-L	6-2	175	4-5-03	1	2	6.52	16	4	0	0	29	20	22	21	1	36	31	.200	.286	.167	9.62	11.17
Andres Ortuno	R-R	6-3	167	9-20-01	2	0	1.11	17	1	0	6	24	13	6	3	1	7	27	.159	.220	.098	9.99	2.59
Jean Carlos Reyes	R-R	6-2	203	12-17-03	2	2	5.08	12	11	0	0	39	39	24	22	0	22	34	.267	.344	.207	7.85	5.08

Denison Sanchez	R-R	6-1	164	8-30-05	1	1	8.31	15	1	0	0	17	17	27	16	3	25	14	.243	.206	.278	7.27	12.98
Giancarlos Santana	R-R	6-1	180	11-6-01	2	0	4.07	17	0	0	2	24	24	12	11	1	9	13	.258	.295	.224	4.81	3.33
Cesar Soto	R-R	6-0	170	1-20-02	2	1	5.79	18	0	0	1	28	33	21	18	0	19	25	.295	.277	.308	8.04	6.11
Elvis Soto	R-R	6-0	174	3-2-04	1	1	3.42	15	0	0	3	24	15	10	9	2	9	31	.179	.216	.149	11.79	3.42

Fielding

C: Avila 29, Rojas 26, Romero 7. **1B:** Flores 2, Mendez 41, Sierra 27. **2B:** Alcantara 29, Castillo 7, De Leon 9, Flores 1, Lugo 2, Mendez 4, Reinita 22, Rodriguez 5. **3B:** Alcantara 2, Flores 11, Lugo 6, Mendez 4, Mota 40, Rodriguez 7. **SS:** Alcantara 22, De Leon 41, Flores 4, Mendez 2, Rodriguez 2. **OF:** Asigen 51, Ayubi 36, Diaz 41, Lugo 37, Mendez 1, Rodriguez 15, Sierra 11.

DSL BOS RED — ROOKIE

Batting	B-T	HT	WT	DOB	AVG	vLH	vRH	G	AB	R	H	2B	3B	HR	RBI	BB	HBP	SH	SF	SO	SB	CS	SLG	OBP
Yosander Asencio	B-R	5-11	160	11-14-04	.280	.280	.280	50	150	35	42	7	4	0	17	46	4	1	1	52	15	3	.380	.458
Frank Astacio	R-R	5-11	150	10-14-00	.324	.353	.315	27	71	12	23	4	3	1	16	9	1	0	1	10	4	2	.507	.402
Freili Encarnacion	R-R	6-2	181	1-26-05	.255	.133	.286	41	149	31	38	8	0	3	23	15	5	0	4	51	9	1	.369	.335
Natanael Eusebio	L-L	6-0	160	7-2-05	.188	.231	.171	24	48	6	9	2	0	1	3	10	2	0	0	27	0	1	.292	.350
Renny Flores	R-R	5-9	170	4-1-03	.225	.231	.222	16	40	8	9	2	0	0	7	13	1	0	0	13	0	1	.275	.426
Jhon Garcia	R-R	6-2	168	10-10-02	.245	.571	.196	18	53	7	13	4	0	1	7	5	1	0	1	18	0	0	.377	.317
Johanfran Garcia	R-R	6-0	196	12-8-04	.268	.455	.233	40	138	26	37	7	1	0	23	21	1	0	1	25	0	1	.333	.366
Axel James	L-R	5-11	153	1-25-02	.317	.423	.280	29	101	15	32	8	5	1	21	7	1	0	0	28	10	1	.525	.367
Yohander Linarez	B-R	5-11	160	3-19-05	.267	.189	.289	46	165	22	44	9	2	1	21	11	2	0	2	37	2	2	.364	.317
Jose Liriano	L-R	6-2	216	6-26-03	.228	.148	.246	42	149	26	34	5	2	2	19	21	1	0	3	36	1	0	.329	.322
Enmanuel Martinez	R-R	5-11	194	5-24-04	.261	.250	.265	28	88	9	23	6	0	0	11	5	2	0	0	11	1	0	.330	.316
Franyer Noria	R-R	5-10	135	9-24-04	.299	.200	.325	34	97	21	29	5	2	0	11	15	1	1	0	24	9	0	.392	.398
Cristofher Paniagua	R-R	6-2	170	11-8-04	.240	.182	.250	19	75	10	18	0	0	1	5	6	2	0	0	20	4	1	.280	.313
Ronny Ramirez	R-R	5-11	175	11-11-03	.309	.444	.270	29	81	21	25	2	0	1	14	19	6	0	3	15	1	4	.370	.459
Jancel Santana	B-R	6-0	157	8-17-05	.184	.257	.162	43	152	25	28	7	1	2	16	18	8	1	0	56	12	2	.283	.303
Claudio Simon	R-R	5-10	170	12-9-01	.211	.276	.195	45	147	30	31	4	1	1	15	16	7	0	0	45	31	3	.272	.318
Natanael Yuten	L-L	6-2	143	10-9-04	.307	.317	.304	50	199	30	61	11	2	1	24	17	5	1	1	43	4	6	.397	.374

Pitching	B-T	HT	WT	DOB	W	L	ERA	G	GS	CG	SV	IP	H	R	ER	HR	BB	SO	AVG	vLH	vRH	K/9	BB/9
Frank Astacio	R-R	5-11	150	10-14-00	0	1	0.00	1	0	0	0	1	1	1	0	0	0	2	.250	--	.250	18.00	0.00
Royman Blanco	R-R	6-1	170	4-17-01	4	2	1.07	16	0	0	3	34	31	10	4	1	6	22	.244	.236	.250	5.88	1.60
Darlyn De La Cruz	R-R	6-4	210	11-26-02	1	1	3.04	10	9	0	0	27	17	11	9	0	18	28	.185	.250	.150	9.45	6.08
Junior Delanda	R-R	5-10	156	3-29-03	2	1	7.59	14	0	0	3	21	25	19	18	3	16	16	.294	.351	.250	6.75	6.75
Eduardo Diaz	L-L	6-1	175	6-1-02	0	0	0.00	1	0	0	0	1	1	0	0	0	1	0	.333	--	.333	0.00	13.50
Jogly Garcia	R-R	6-1	175	9-8-03	4	1	4.28	13	1	0	0	34	41	20	16	1	8	25	.304	.254	.347	6.68	2.14
Smil Guzman	R-R	6-0	193	4-4-04	1	2	3.98	12	12	0	0	41	35	22	18	4	22	41	.233	.182	.306	9.07	4.87
Andres Jimenez	R-R	6-2	203	1-4-05	1	1	3.60	11	1	0	1	20	21	13	8	0	20	21	.280	.342	.216	9.45	9.00
Irving Medina	R-R	6-1	175	6-12-03	3	2	5.27	15	0	0	0	27	31	20	16	2	13	29	.279	.268	.286	9.55	4.28
Alvaro Mejias	R-R	0-0	0	9-13-03	1	1	1.23	8	8	0	0	29	16	7	4	0	7	39	.157	.154	.159	11.97	2.15
Simon Pacheco	R-R	5-11	164	6-14-02	6	3	0.77	17	0	0	5	35	17	6	3	0	3	42	.145	.136	.151	10.80	0.77
Eybersson Polanco	R-R	6-0	170	9-3-03	2	1	1.78	12	12	0	0	51	31	10	10	0	17	50	.179	.173	.184	8.88	3.02
Ovis Portes	R-R	6-4	167	12-3-04	3	0	1.21	11	1	0	0	22	17	5	3	0	11	28	.210	.167	.235	11.28	4.43
Dennis Reguillo	R-R	5-11	165	9-9-03	0	3	5.57	11	11	0	0	32	35	26	20	0	16	26	.269	.328	.212	7.24	4.45
Carlos Reyes	R-R	6-3	190	9-17-01	1	2	4.05	16	0	0	0	27	23	18	12	2	19	37	.228	.185	.243	12.49	6.41
Yonfi Rodriguez	R-R	5-10	160	7-30-02	4	0	3.07	16	0	0	1	44	32	19	15	3	26	36	.205	.230	.189	7.36	5.32
Cesar Ruiz	R-R	6-3	170	6-4-03	0	0	7.50	5	4	0	0	12	10	11	10	0	17	14	.244	.188	.280	10.50	12.75
Starlin Santos	L-L	6-3	180	5-13-02	3	2	3.82	14	0	0	2	33	28	16	14	0	15	34	.220	.133	.247	9.27	4.09

Fielding

C: Flores 16, Garcia 21, Martinez 28. **1B:** Astacio 11, Garcia 12, Garcia 8, Liriano 32, Simon 2. **2B:** Asencio 2, Linarez 3, Noria 13, Santana 38, Simon 6. **3B:** Astacio 15, Encarnacion 8, Linarez 10, Noria 18, Simon 15. **SS:** Encarnacion 25, Linarez 33, Santana 4. **OF:** Asencio 45, Eusebio 23, James 17, Paniagua 19, Ramirez 25, Simon 23, Yuten 46.

Chicago Cubs

SEASON IN A SENTENCE: The Cubs tied an MLB record by using 42 different pitchers in the first full year of their rebuild and were never competitive, falling under .500 two weeks into the season and remaining there the rest of the year.

HIGH POINT: Christopher Morel made his MLB debut on May 7 and homered in his first at-bat, turning around a full-count fastball from the Pirates' Chase De Jong and sending it 417 feet onto Waveland Avenue beyond the left-field bleachers at Wrigley Field. Morel received a standing ovation as he rounded the bases and was so excited he missed first base and had to go back to touch it.

LOW POINT: The Cubs lost 10 straight games from June 4-16, their longest losing streak of the season. Within that streak was a particularly brutal four-game stretch that signified just how far the franchise had fallen from its 2015-20 glory years. The Cubs lost games by scores 18-4, 12-5 and 19-5 and twice had to use first baseman Frank Schwindel on the mound just to get through the game.

NOTABLE ROOKIE: Morel remained in the majors after his smashing debut and led all Cubs rookies with 16 home runs, 47 RBIs and 10 stolen bases while playing five different positions, primarily center field. The 23-year-old Dominican struggled with strikeouts and slumped down the stretch, but he solidified his place in the Cubs' plans with his power, speed and defensive versatility.

KEY TRANSACTIONS: The Cubs signed Japanese outfielder Seiya Suzuki to a five-year, $85 million contract in March, the largest contract ever for a Japanese position player. Suzuki finished third on the Cubs with a .262 batting average and .770 OPS despite missing six weeks with a finger injury and was batting second in the order by the end of the season. The Cubs were once again active sellers at the trade deadline, trading veteran relievers Chris Martin, Scott Effross, Mychal Givens and David Robertson for prospects. They curiously held on to catcher Willson Contreras and outfielder Ian Happ, however, their two best trade chips.

ON THE FARM: Cubs domestic affiliates combined to go 315-287 (.523) during the regular season, 10th-best out of 30 organizations. Their talent in the lower levels was particularly apparent as High-A South Bend won the Midwest League championship and Low-A Myrtle Beach finished with the second-best record in the Carolina League.

OPENING DAY PAYROLL: $146,203,500 (15th).

PLAYERS OF THE YEAR

MAJOR LEAGUE

Nico Hoerner SS

.281/.327/.410
10 HR, 20 SB in 135 G
11 SO% second in NL

MINOR LEAGUE

Pete Crow-Armstrong, OF

(LoA/HiA)
.312/.376/.520
16 HR, 32 SB in 101 G

ORGANIZATION LEADERS

Batting		*Minimum 250 AB
MAJORS		
*AVG	Nico Hoerner	.281
*OPS	Willson Contreras	.815
HR	Patrick Wisdom	25
RBI	Ian Happ	72
MINORS		
*AVG	Darius Hill, Tennessee, Iowa	.314
*OBP	B.J. Murray, South Bend, Myrtle Beach	.410
*SLG	Matt Mervis, Iowa, Tennessee, South Bend	.606
*OPS	Matt Mervis, Iowa, Tennessee, South Bend	.984
R	Matt Mervis, Iowa, Tennessee, South Bend	92
H	Darius Hill, Tennessee, Iowa	166
TB	Matt Mervis, Iowa, Tennessee, South Bend	310
2B	Matt Mervis, Iowa, Tennessee, South Bend	40
3B	Pete Crow-Armstrong, South Bend, Myrtle Beach	10
HR	Alexander Canario, Iowa, Tennessee, South Bend	37
RBI	Matt Mervis, Iowa, Tennessee, South Bend	119
BB	Chase Strumpf, Tennessee	73
SO	Chase Strumpf, Tennessee	162
SB	Jake Slaughter, Tennessee, South Bend	36

Pitching		#Minimum 75 IP
MAJORS		
W	Keegan Thompson	10
#ERA	Adrian Sampson	3.11
SO	Justin Steele	126
SV	David Robertson	14
MINORS		
W	Luis Devers, Myrtle Beach, South Bend	13
L	Richard Gallardo, Myrtle Beach, South Bend, Tennessee	10
#ERA	Luis Devers, Myrtle Beach, South Bend	1.91
G	Ben Leeper, Iowa	42
GS	Caleb Kilian, Iowa	26
GS	DJ Herz, South Bend, Tennessee	26
SV	Ben Leeper, Iowa	11
IP	Richard Gallardo, Myrtle Beach, South Bend, Tennessee	122
BB	DJ Herz, South Bend, Tennessee	70
SO	DJ Herz, South Bend, Tennessee	141
SO	Porter Hodge, Myrtle Beach, South Bend	141
#AVG	DJ Herz, South Bend, Tennessee	.170

2022 PERFORMANCE

General Manager: Carter Hawkins. **Farm Director:** Matt Dorey. **Scouting Director:** Dan Kantrovitz.

Class	Team	League	W	L	PCT	Finish	Manager
Majors	Chicago Cubs	National	74	88	.457	t-9th (15)	David Ross
Triple-A	Iowa Cubs	International	68	81	.456	16th (20)	Marty Pevey
Double-A	Tennessee Smokies	Southern	71	66	.518	4th (8)	Michael Ryan
High-A	South Bend Cubs	Midwest	73	58	.557	t-3rd (12)	Lance Rymel
Low-A	Myrtle Beach Pelicans	Carolina	78	53	.595	3rd (12)	Buddy Bailey
Rookie	ACL Cubs	Arizona Complex	25	29	.463	11th (18)	Edgar Perez
Overall 2022 Minor League Record			360	362	.499	17th (30)	

ORGANIZATION STATISTICS

CHICAGO CUBS

NATIONAL LEAGUE

Batting	B-T	HT	WT	DOB	AVG	vLH	vRH	G	AB	R	H	2B	3B	HR	RBI	BB	HBP	SH	SF	SO	SB	CS	SLG	OBP
David Bote	R-R	6-1	205	4-7-93	.259	.182	.289	41	116	15	30	8	0	4	12	6	4	0	1	45	1	0	.431	.315
Willson Contreras	R-R	6-1	225	5-13-92	.243	.219	.251	113	416	65	101	23	2	22	55	45	24	0	2	103	4	2	.466	.349
Narciso Crook	R-R	6-3	220	7-12-95	.250	.200	.333	4	8	1	2	1	0	0	2	0	0	0	1	3	0	0	.375	.222
Jackson Frazier	R-R	5-11	212	9-6-94	.216	.250	.154	19	37	4	8	3	0	0	1	7	1	0	0	11	1	0	.297	.356
Yan Gomes	R-R	6-2	212	7-19-87	.235	.241	.232	86	277	23	65	12	0	8	31	8	3	1	4	47	2	0	.365	.260
Ian Happ	B-R	6-0	205	8-12-94	.271	.305	.261	158	573	72	155	42	2	17	72	58	6	0	4	149	9	4	.440	.342
Michael Hermosillo	R-R	6-0	205	1-17-95	.115	.074	.147	31	61	7	7	2	0	0	4	7	4	1	0	27	1	0	.148	.250
Jason Heyward	L-L	6-5	240	8-9-89	.204	.217	.202	48	137	15	28	5	1	1	10	11	3	0	0	32	1	0	.277	.278
P.J. Higgins	R-R	5-10	195	5-10-93	.229	.219	.234	74	201	23	46	11	1	6	30	22	2	3	1	58	0	0	.383	.310
Nico Hoerner	R-R	6-1	200	5-13-97	.281	.294	.276	135	481	60	135	22	5	10	55	28	6	0	2	57	20	2	.410	.327
Nick Madrigal	R-R	5-8	175	3-5-97	.249	.256	.244	59	209	19	52	7	0	0	7	14	3	2	0	27	3	1	.282	.305
Zach McKinstry	L-R	6-0	180	4-29-95	.206	.214	.206	47	155	17	32	6	3	4	12	13	1	2	0	48	7	0	.361	.272
2-team total (10 Los Angeles Dodgers)					.199	.188	.200	57	166	21	33	6	3	5	14	16	1	2	0	52	7	0	.361	.273
Christopher Morel	R-R	5-11	145	6-24-99	.235	.190	.251	113	379	55	89	19	4	16	47	38	3	3	2	137	10	7	.433	.308
Rafael Ortega	L-R	5-11	180	5-15-91	.241	.211	.242	118	316	35	76	14	1	7	35	44	2	1	7	74	12	7	.358	.331
Esteban Quiroz	L-R	5-6	199	2-17-92	.275	.500	.235	14	40	3	11	0	0	0	3	4	2	1	0	9	1	1	.275	.370
Franmil Reyes	R-R	6-5	265	7-7-95	.234	.313	.217	48	175	19	41	8	2	5	19	16	1	0	1	53	0	1	.389	.301
Alfonso Rivas	L-L	5-11	190	9-13-96	.235	.069	.257	101	251	27	59	5	2	3	25	29	4	1	2	87	6	1	.307	.322
Frank Schwindel	R-R	6-1	220	6-29-92	.229	.211	.236	75	271	23	62	11	0	8	36	19	0	0	2	58	0	0	.358	.277
Andrelton Simmons	R-R	6-2	195	9-4-89	.173	.050	.218	35	75	8	13	1	0	0	7	7	0	3	0	13	4	0	.187	.244
Seiya Suzuki	R-R	5-11	182	8-18-94	.262	.269	.259	111	397	54	104	22	2	14	46	42	4	0	3	110	9	5	.433	.336
Ildemaro Vargas	B-R	6-0	180	7-16-91	.130	.125	.133	10	23	4	3	0	1	1	4	3	0	0	0	2	0	0	.348	.231
2-team total (53 Washington Nationals)					.263	.253	.269	63	209	19	55	13	1	4	23	8	3	1	1	23	3	1	.392	.299
Nelson Velazquez	R-R	6-0	190	12-26-98	.205	.197	.211	77	185	20	38	7	3	6	26	19	2	0	0	65	5	2	.373	.286
Jonathan Villar	B-R	6-0	233	5-2-91	.222	.200	.229	46	153	19	34	6	2	2	15	11	0	0	2	42	6	0	.327	.271
Patrick Wisdom	R-R	6-2	220	8-27-91	.207	.250	.191	134	469	67	97	28	0	25	66	53	9	1	2	183	8	4	.426	.298
Jared Young	L-R	6-2	185	7-9-95	.263	--	.263	6	19	2	5	2	0	0	0	3	0	0	0	7	1	0	.368	.364

Pitching	B-T	HT	WT	DOB	W	L	ERA	G	GS	CG	SV	IP	H	R	ER	HR	BB	SO	AVG	vLH	vRH	K/9	BB/9
Adbert Alzolay	R-R	6-1	208	3-1-95	2	1	3.38	6	0	0	0	13	9	5	5	1	2	19	.184	.176	.188	12.83	1.35
Javier Assad	R-R	6-1	200	7-30-97	2	2	3.11	9	8	0	0	38	35	14	13	4	20	30	.240	.290	.202	7.17	4.78
Steven Brault	L-L	6-0	195	4-29-92	0	0	3.00	9	0	0	0	9	8	4	3	0	5	8	.242	.067	.389	8.00	5.00
Kervin Castro	R-R	6-0	185	2-7-99	0	1	7.59	8	0	0	0	11	11	9	9	3	5	7	.268	.333	.231	5.91	4.22
2-team total (2 San Francisco Giants)					0	1	10.22	10	0	0	0	12	15	14	14	3	7	11	.300	.353	.273	8.03	5.11
Jesse Chavez	R-R	6-1	175	8-21-83	0	0	6.35	3	0	0	0	6	7	4	4	1	2	3	.318	.600	.083	4.76	3.18
2-team total (46 Atlanta Braves)					3	3	3.07	49	1	0	0	59	56	22	20	6	16	64	.251	.268	.238	9.82	2.45
Matt Dermody	R-L	6-5	190	7-4-90	0	0	18.00	1	0	0	0	1	2	2	2	0	2	1	.400	.000	.500	9.00	18.00
Scott Effross	R-R	6-2	202	12-28-93	1	4	2.66	47	1	0	1	44	36	19	13	2	11	50	.220	.132	.261	10.23	2.25
Anderson Espinoza	R-R	6-0	190	3-9-98	0	2	5.40	7	0	0	0	18	14	11	11	4	16	19	.215	.296	.158	9.33	7.85
Jeremiah Estrada	B-R	6-1	185	11-1-98	0	0	3.18	5	0	0	0	6	6	2	2	1	3	8	.286	.333	.267	12.71	4.76
Luke Farrell	L-R	6-6	200	6-7-91	0	0	4.09	4	2	0	0	11	12	5	5	2	3	9	.267	.304	.227	7.36	2.45
2-team total (2 Cincinnati Reds)					0	0	5.40	6	2	0	0	15	18	10	9	3	7	14	.286	.324	.241	8.40	4.20
Mychal Givens	R-R	6-0	230	5-13-90	6	2	2.66	40	0	0	2	41	32	15	12	5	19	51	.216	.222	.213	11.29	4.20
2-team total (19 New York Mets)					7	3	3.38	59	1	0	2	61	56	27	23	8	25	71	.247	.273	.233	10.42	3.67
Robert Gsellman	R-R	6-4	200	7-18-93	0	2	4.70	8	0	0	1	15	17	10	8	2	3	9	.279	.333	.243	5.28	1.76
Kyle Hendricks	R-R	6-3	190	12-7-89	4	6	4.80	16	16	0	0	84	85	45	45	15	24	66	.260	.291	.226	7.04	2.56
Brandon Hughes	B-L	6-2	215	12-1-95	2	3	3.12	57	0	0	8	58	42	22	20	11	21	68	.200	.226	.183	10.61	3.28
Caleb Kilian	R-R	6-4	180	6-2-97	0	2	10.32	3	3	0	0	11	11	15	13	0	12	9	.262	.308	.188	7.15	9.53
Mark Leiter Jr.	R-R	6-0	210	3-13-91	2	7	3.99	35	4	0	3	68	52	32	30	10	25	73	.210	.176	.248	9.71	3.33
Brendon Little	L-L	6-2	195	8-11-96	0	1	40.50	1	0	0	0	1	2	3	3	1	1	0	.500	--	.500	0.00	13.50
Chris Martin	R-R	6-8	225	6-2-86	1	0	4.31	34	0	0	0	31	38	16	15	5	4	40	.297	.302	.292	11.49	1.15
2-team total (26 Los Angeles Dodgers)					4	1	3.05	60	0	0	2	56	50	20	19	6	5	74	.230	.232	.229	11.89	0.80
Conner Menez	L-L	6-2	206	5-29-95	0	0	0.00	1	0	0	0	1	1	0	0	0	0	1	.250	.000	.500	9.00	0.00

Wade Miley	L-L	6-2	220	11-13-86	2	2	3.16	9	8	0	0	37	31	20	13	3	14	28	.218	.147	.241	6.81	3.41
Alec Mills	R-R	6-4	205	11-30-91	0	1	9.68	7	2	0	0	18	28	20	19	7	3	11	.364	.390	.333	5.60	1.53
Sean Newcomb	L-L	6-5	255	6-12-93	2	1	9.13	17	1	0	0	23	26	24	23	7	15	24	.280	.353	.237	9.53	5.96
2-team total (3 Atlanta Braves)					2	1	8.78	20	1	0	0	28	33	28	27	8	19	28	.287	.311	.271	9.11	6.18
Daniel Norris	L-L	6-2	207	4-25-93	0	4	6.90	27	1	0	0	30	23	28	23	7	21	43	.207	.176	.233	12.90	6.30
Nicholas Padilla	R-R	6-2	220	12-24-96	0	0	5.40	1	0	0	0	2	2	1	1	0	2	1	.286	.667	.000	5.40	10.80
Franmil Reyes	R-R	6-5	265	7-7-95	0	0	0.00	1	0	0	0	1	0	0	0	0	0	1	.000	--	.000	9.00	0.00
Ethan Roberts	R-R	5-10	180	7-4-97	0	1	8.22	9	0	0	0	8	10	7	7	3	6	9	.323	.250	.348	10.57	7.04
David Robertson	R-R	5-11	195	4-9-85	3	0	2.23	36	0	0	14	40	23	10	10	4	19	51	.162	.156	.169	11.38	4.24
2-team total (22 Philadelphia Phillies)					4	3	2.40	58	0	0	20	64	39	18	17	6	35	81	.173	.168	.179	11.45	4.95
Manuel Rodriguez	R-R	5-11	210	8-6-96	2	0	3.29	14	0	0	4	14	10	6	5	1	9	8	.208	.222	.205	5.27	5.93
Michael Rucker	R-R	6-1	195	4-27-94	3	1	3.95	41	0	0	0	55	50	25	24	8	20	50	.242	.259	.230	8.23	3.29
Adrian Sampson	R-R	6-2	210	10-7-91	4	5	3.11	21	19	0	0	104	101	40	36	10	27	73	.253	.230	.276	6.30	2.33
Frank Schwindel	R-R	6-1	220	6-29-92	0	0	18.00	3	0	0	0	3	8	6	6	4	1	0	.471	.500	.444	0.00	3.00
Andrelton Simmons	R-R	6-2	195	9-4-89	0	0	45.00	1	0	0	0	1	5	5	5	0	1	0	.833	--	.833	0.00	9.00
Drew Smyly	L-L	6-2	188	6-13-89	7	8	3.47	22	22	0	0	106	101	46	41	16	26	91	.243	.191	.258	7.70	2.20
Locke St. John	L-L	6-3	180	1-31-93	0	0	13.50	1	0	0	0	2	3	3	3	2	0	4	.333	.500	.286	18.00	0.00
Justin Steele	L-L	6-2	205	7-11-95	4	7	3.18	24	24	0	0	119	111	53	42	8	50	126	.244	.232	.248	9.53	3.78
Eric Stout	L-L	6-3	205	3-27-93	0	0	4.91	2	0	0	0	4	3	2	2	1	1	6	.214	.200	.222	14.73	2.45
2-team total (18 Pittsburgh Pirates)					0	0	5.64	20	0	0	1	22	25	15	14	2	16	25	.275	.158	.358	10.07	6.45
Marcus Stroman	R-R	5-7	180	5-1-91	6	7	3.50	25	25	0	0	139	123	61	54	16	36	119	.234	.257	.210	7.72	2.34
Matt Swarmer	R-R	6-5	195	9-25-93	2	3	5.03	11	5	0	0	34	33	26	19	12	20	36	.250	.250	.250	9.53	5.29
Keegan Thompson	R-R	6-1	210	3-13-95	10	5	3.76	29	17	0	1	115	103	54	48	16	43	108	.239	.237	.241	8.45	3.37
Erich Uelmen	R-R	6-3	195	5-19-96	2	1	4.67	25	0	0	1	27	25	15	14	3	12	21	.248	.308	.210	7.00	4.00
Hayden Wesneski	R-R	6-3	210	12-5-97	3	2	2.18	6	4	0	0	33	24	9	8	3	7	33	.198	.159	.221	9.00	1.91
Rowan Wick	L-R	6-3	234	11-9-92	4	7	4.22	64	0	0	9	64	79	37	30	9	29	69	.305	.341	.272	9.70	4.08

Fielding

Catcher	PCT	G	PO	A	E	DP	PB
Contreras	.994	72	605	46	4	7	7
Gomes	.989	69	576	35	7	5	2
Higgins	.991	34	200	10	2	2	3

First Base	PCT	G	PO	A	E	DP
Bote	1.000	6	26	2	0	1
Higgins	1.000	38	235	14	0	20
Rivas	.998	92	608	33	1	57
Schwindel	1.000	48	353	13	0	39
Wisdom	1.000	18	95	7	0	6
Young	1.000	2	17	0	0	2

Second Base	PCT	G	PO	A	E	DP
Bote	1.000	18	20	33	0	11
Madrigal	.996	59	106	144	1	46
McKinstry	1.000	19	30	49	0	8
Morel	.990	33	39	57	1	11
Quiroz	.982	12	25	31	1	9
Simmons	1.000	18	16	20	0	5
Vargas	1.000	3	2	5	0	1
Villar	.958	29	37	54	4	15

Third Base	PCT	G	PO	A	E	DP
Bote	.975	16	10	29	1	5
Higgins	.727	4	2	6	3	0
Hoerner	.000	1	0	0	0	0
McKinstry	.938	21	12	33	3	4
Morel	.918	18	14	31	4	4
Villar	.905	15	2	17	2	1
Wisdom	.948	105	66	187	14	28

Shortstop	PCT	G	PO	A	E	DP
Hoerner	.974	133	127	358	13	58
McKinstry	1.000	9	8	13	0	4
Morel	.953	13	13	28	2	5
Simmons	.980	18	14	36	1	5
Vargas	.966	6	14	14	1	4
Villar	.833	2	4	6	2	2

Outfield	PCT	G	PO	A	E	DP
Crook	1.000	3	4	0	0	0
Frazier	.929	7	12	1	1	0
Happ	.990	149	277	8	3	1
Hermosillo	.944	31	51	0	3	0
Heyward	1.000	47	91	1	0	0
Morel	.975	58	112	4	3	1
Ortega	.993	97	133	4	1	0
Reyes	1.000	1	2	0	0	0
Rivas	1.000	3	2	0	0	0
Suzuki	.981	106	201	3	4	2
Velazquez	.958	69	89	2	4	0
Wisdom	1.000	14	17	0	0	0
Young	--	1	0	0	0	0

IOWA CUBS — *TRIPLE-A*

INTERNATIONAL LEAGUE

Batting	B-T	HT	WT	DOB	AVG	vLH	vRH	G	AB	R	H	2B	3B	HR	RBI	BB	HBP	SH	SF	SO	SB	CS	SLG	OBP
David Bote	R-R	6-1	205	4-7-93	.252	.250	.252	38	143	14	36	8	1	3	22	10	5	0	2	39	5	1	.385	.319
Alexander Canario	R-R	6-1	165	5-7-00	.231	.353	.188	20	65	16	15	2	0	6	14	13	4	1	1	21	3	0	.538	.386
Erick Castillo	R-R	5-11	178	2-25-93	.237	.179	.256	36	114	7	27	2	0	0	12	5	5	2	1	22	0	0	.254	.296
Narciso Crook	R-R	6-3	220	7-12-95	.260	.277	.254	101	362	61	94	21	3	19	67	36	11	0	0	124	13	6	.492	.345
Brennen Davis	R-R	6-4	210	11-2-99	.191	.205	.186	43	141	16	27	6	0	4	13	23	6	0	4	52	0	1	.319	.322
Zach Davis	B-R	5-11	175	6-29-94	.210	.216	.206	48	100	23	21	4	0	0	7	14	4	1	1	26	17	0	.250	.328
Greg Deichmann	L-R	6-2	205	5-31-95	.214	.161	.229	78	257	27	55	10	0	7	33	20	1	2	2	91	8	4	.335	.271
Donnie Dewees	L-L	5-11	205	9-29-93	.286	.000	.308	13	42	8	12	1	1	1	6	3	0	0	0	9	4	0	.429	.333
Christian Donahue	L-R	5-8	180	5-4-95	.176	.500	.133	6	17	3	3	0	0	1	2	1	0	0	0	8	0	0	.353	.222
Jackson Frazier	R-R	5-11	212	9-6-94	.190	.174	.196	66	232	26	44	8	0	6	35	25	6	0	2	92	5	0	.302	.283
Robel Garcia	B-R	6-0	195	3-28-93	.295	.231	.320	41	139	26	41	7	1	12	30	24	0	0	2	51	0	1	.619	.394
Trent Giambrone	R-R	5-8	175	12-20-93	.188	.243	.165	89	256	32	48	10	1	3	20	30	4	0	2	74	11	3	.270	.281
Michael Hermosillo	R-R	6-0	205	1-17-95	.400	.286	.462	6	20	7	8	3	1	1	3	4	1	0	1	7	1	1	.800	.500
John Hicks	R-R	6-2	230	8-31-89	.261	.250	.264	95	357	49	93	25	2	20	56	26	2	0	2	108	10	4	.510	.313
P.J. Higgins	R-R	5-10	195	5-10-93	.417	.316	.453	22	72	9	30	8	0	1	17	12	1	0	1	16	1	0	.569	.500
Darius Hill	L-L	6-1	190	8-17-97	.318	.284	.328	89	343	48	109	23	4	3	35	21	3	2	4	53	4	2	.434	.358
Levi Jordan	R-R	5-8	170	9-24-95	.249	.288	.233	81	273	41	68	15	1	7	25	21	1	2	0	53	9	2	.388	.305
Dixon Machado	R-R	6-1	190	2-22-92	.312	.317	.310	86	340	46	106	20	1	2	31	46	5	0	0	41	10	3	.394	.402
Nick Madrigal	R-R	5-8	175	3-5-97	.308	.429	.281	12	39	8	12	1	0	0	5	3	1	0	0	5	0	0	.333	.372
Nelson Maldonado	R-R	5-10	195	8-13-96	.229	.204	.236	64	231	24	53	15	0	5	34	16	1	2	3	50	3	0	.359	.279
Scott McKeon	R-R	6-0	185	10-30-97	.379	.444	.350	8	29	4	11	3	0	0	2	1	0	0	0	9	0	0	.483	.400
Matt Mervis	L-R	6-4	225	4-16-98	.297	.271	.307	57	209	41	62	15	1	15	39	25	5	0	1	35	0	0	.593	.383
Tyler Payne	R-R	5-11	210	10-25-92	.298	.250	.309	48	151	14	45	10	1	1	15	8	1	2	1	36	0	0	.397	.335
Esteban Quiroz	L-R	5-6	199	2-17-92	.212	.217	.211	40	118	13	25	4	0	3	13	24	4	0	2	35	0	0	.322	.358

Alfonso Rivas	L-L	5-11	190	9-13-96	.298	.125	.357	26	94	15	28	6	1	1	10	10	1	0	1	28	0	0	.415	.368
Frank Schwindel	R-R	6-1	220	6-29-92	.216	.333	.160	10	37	5	8	3	0	1	4	0	0	0	0	8	0	0	.378	.216
Carlos Sepulveda	L-R	5-10	170	8-27-96	.245	.083	.293	24	53	3	13	2	0	0	9	8	1	0	1	9	1	0	.283	.349
Andrelton Simmons	R-R	6-2	195	9-4-89	.133	.000	.154	12	45	3	6	0	0	1	2	4	1	0	0	13	1	2	.200	.220
Seiya Suzuki	R-R	5-11	182	8-18-94	.444	1.000	.167	3	9	2	4	2	0	1	3	2	0	0	0	4	0	0	1.000	.545
Ildemaro Vargas	B-R	6-0	180	7-16-91	.279	.313	.273	25	104	16	29	3	4	1	7	7	0	0	1	12	1	0	.413	.321
2-team total (48 Rochester Red Wings)					.245	.270	.235	73	278	37	68	14	4	3	25	27	0	1	3	37	3	2	.356	.308
Luis Vazquez	R-R	6-1	165	10-10-99	.179	.074	.228	27	84	7	15	4	0	1	7	4	0	2	2	21	2	0	.262	.211
Nelson Velazquez	R-R	6-0	190	12-26-98	.211	.139	.241	34	123	21	26	7	0	6	15	13	1	0	1	50	7	2	.415	.290
Jared Young	L-R	6-2	185	7-9-95	.230	.223	.232	109	400	61	92	21	2	17	59	40	9	2	4	110	3	2	.420	.311

Pitching	B-T	HT	WT	DOB	W	L	ERA	G	GS	CG	SV	IP	H	R	ER	HR	BB	SO	AVG	vLH	vRH	K/9	BB/9
Cory Abbott	R-R	6-1	210	9-20-95	0	1	4.50	2	2	0	0	6	4	3	3	2	2	6	.190	.200	.182	9.00	3.00
2-team total (10 Rochester Red Wings)					0	5	4.98	12	8	0	0	34	34	23	19	6	19	40	.254	.255	.253	10.49	4.98
Adbert Alzolay	R-R	6-1	208	3-1-95	0	1	6.75	4	4	0	0	9	10	7	7	1	6	12	.278	.250	.300	11.57	5.79
Javier Assad	R-R	6-1	200	7-30-97	1	2	2.95	8	7	0	0	37	31	13	12	4	7	37	.223	.230	.218	9.08	1.72
James Bourque	R-R	6-4	215	7-9-93	0	0	3.24	7	1	0	0	8	4	3	3	0	9	16	.143	.167	.125	17.28	9.72
Steven Brault	L-L	6-0	195	4-29-92	2	0	12.00	7	0	0	0	6	11	8	8	1	5	6	.393	.182	.529	9.00	7.50
Kervin Castro	R-R	6-0	185	2-7-99	2	0	1.32	8	0	0	1	14	7	2	2	0	7	18	.163	.200	.143	11.85	4.61
Danis Correa	R-R	5-11	150	8-26-99	2	1	5.40	12	0	0	0	17	17	12	10	3	10	24	.258	.370	.179	12.96	5.40
Matt Dermody	R-L	6-5	190	7-4-90	6	3	3.74	20	13	0	0	79	85	33	33	11	18	70	.269	.237	.287	7.94	2.04
Raynel Espinal	R-R	6-3	215	10-6-91	0	0	16.20	2	0	0	0	3	6	6	6	1	3	4	.400	.750	.273	10.80	8.10
2-team total (6 Louisville Bats)					0	1	6.26	8	3	0	0	23	23	16	16	4	10	26	.267	.333	.220	10.17	3.91
Anderson Espinoza	R-R	6-0	190	3-9-98	1	5	8.31	8	6	0	1	26	32	25	24	7	19	24	.314	.419	.268	8.31	6.58
Jeremiah Estrada	B-R	6-1	185	11-1-98	0	0	0.00	6	0	0	2	6	6	0	0	0	1	12	.250	.333	.200	18.00	1.50
Luke Farrell	L-R	6-6	200	6-7-91	3	4	5.03	17	11	0	0	59	58	33	33	10	28	49	.258	.300	.224	7.47	4.27
2-team total (1 Louisville Bats)					3	4	4.95	18	11	0	0	60	58	33	33	10	28	51	.254	.294	.222	7.65	4.20
Stephen Gonsalves	L-L	6-5	218	7-8-94	1	0	4.26	8	0	0	0	13	9	6	6	2	11	21	.196	.143	.219	14.92	7.82
Robert Gsellman	R-R	6-4	200	7-18-93	1	4	6.21	10	9	0	0	29	29	22	20	3	11	22	.269	.260	.276	6.83	3.41
Jonathan Holder	R-R	6-2	232	6-9-93	1	1	10.00	14	0	0	0	18	29	20	20	2	11	19	.358	.214	.434	9.50	5.50
Bryan Hudson	L-L	6-8	220	5-8-97	1	2	4.11	31	0	0	1	46	40	24	21	4	22	58	.231	.278	.198	11.35	4.30
Brandon Hughes	B-L	6-2	215	12-1-95	1	0	0.00	5	0	0	0	10	4	0	0	0	2	12	.118	.188	.056	10.45	1.74
Kyle Johnson	R-R	6-4	220	9-19-93	1	0	0.00	2	0	0	0	3	1	0	0	0	1	4	.100	.000	.125	12.00	3.00
Caleb Kilian	R-R	6-4	180	6-2-97	5	4	4.22	26	26	0	0	107	108	56	50	7	59	125	.262	.298	.230	10.55	4.98
Ben Leeper	R-R	6-0	195	6-15-97	3	3	4.50	42	0	0	11	46	35	25	23	11	19	57	.208	.194	.217	11.15	3.72
Brandon Leibrandt	L-L	6-4	190	12-13-92	2	2	5.89	10	5	0	1	37	46	24	24	9	11	24	.317	.300	.326	5.89	2.70
Mark Leiter Jr.	R-R	6-0	210	3-13-91	0	3	5.32	6	6	0	0	22	21	13	13	4	6	32	.241	.167	.311	13.09	2.45
Brendon Little	L-L	6-2	195	8-11-96	4	5	4.29	36	0	0	1	50	50	26	24	4	26	49	.262	.236	.277	8.76	4.65
Kevin McCarthy	R-R	6-3	210	2-22-92	0	0	9.00	3	0	0	0	4	3	4	4	0	3	4	.231	.286	.167	9.00	6.75
Dakota Mekkes	R-R	6-7	275	11-6-94	1	3	6.25	26	1	0	1	32	34	27	22	4	23	26	.276	.380	.205	7.39	6.54
Conner Menez	L-L	6-2	206	5-29-95	2	0	2.14	11	1	0	0	21	16	8	5	0	8	25	.203	.088	.289	10.71	3.43
Wade Miley	L-L	6-2	220	11-13-86	0	0	2.81	4	4	0	0	16	13	6	5	1	4	12	.220	.150	.256	6.75	2.25
Alec Mills	R-R	6-4	205	11-30-91	0	2	4.97	4	4	0	0	13	17	7	7	2	3	11	.315	.450	.235	7.82	2.13
Sean Newcomb	L-L	6-5	255	6-12-93	1	1	3.38	12	1	0	1	24	12	10	9	1	18	31	.148	.133	.157	11.63	6.75
Daniel Norris	L-L	6-2	207	4-25-93	0	0	0.00	2	0	0	0	3	3	1	0	0	1	5	.250	.333	.000	15.00	3.00
2-team total (3 Toledo Mud Hens)					0	0	1.54	5	3	0	0	12	8	3	2	0	3	10	.186	.200	.174	7.71	2.31
Nicholas Padilla	R-R	6-2	220	12-24-96	1	0	1.23	10	0	0	1	15	8	2	2	0	8	17	.160	.294	.091	10.43	4.91
2-team total (7 Charlotte Knights)					1	0	1.74	17	0	0	1	21	12	5	4	1	12	23	.169	.273	.122	10.02	5.23
CD Pelham	R-L	6-6	238	2-21-95	0	0	4.66	8	0	0	0	10	6	5	5	0	9	8	.188	.364	.095	7.45	8.38
Eury Ramos	R-R	6-3	152	10-10-97	1	0	10.05	13	0	0	0	14	18	20	16	3	20	8	.300	.167	.389	5.02	12.56
Peyton Remy	L-R	6-2	170	8-20-96	0	0	0.00	1	0	0	0	1	0	0	0	0	2	0	.000	--	.000	0.00	18.00
Samuel Reyes	R-R	5-11	180	3-13-96	0	1	21.60	1	0	0	0	2	4	5	4	1	1	1	.400	.667	.286	5.40	5.40
Ethan Roberts	R-R	5-10	180	7-4-97	0	0	0.00	1	0	0	0	0	0	0	0	0	0	0	.000	--	.000	0.00	0.00
Manuel Rodriguez	R-R	5-11	210	8-6-96	1	0	9.00	5	0	0	1	5	8	5	5	2	1	10	.381	.500	.222	18.00	1.80
Aneuris Rosario	R-R	6-0	165	3-4-95	3	3	6.00	23	0	0	2	30	27	26	20	6	18	28	.241	.240	.242	8.40	5.40
Michael Rucker	R-R	6-1	195	4-27-94	1	0	1.17	10	0	0	0	15	15	3	2	0	8	13	.250	.280	.229	7.63	4.70
Adrian Sampson	R-R	6-2	210	10-7-91	0	3	3.81	8	6	0	0	28	29	15	12	6	7	18	.259	.264	.254	5.72	2.22
Cam Sanders	R-R	6-2	175	12-9-96	1	8	5.45	29	11	0	0	74	56	47	45	9	49	75	.207	.213	.204	9.08	5.93
Wyatt Short	L-L	5-8	180	10-14-94	6	2	3.53	26	8	0	0	74	62	32	29	7	33	67	.223	.259	.208	8.15	4.01
Locke St. John	L-L	6-3	180	1-31-93	0	1	5.14	5	0	0	0	7	7	4	4	1	6	8	.250	.083	.375	10.29	7.71
2-team total (29 Syracuse Mets)					2	6	5.88	34	1	0	1	49	44	37	32	9	29	43	.239	.179	.274	7.90	5.33
Eric Stout	L-L	6-3	205	3-27-93	2	2	3.94	16	1	0	2	30	18	13	13	4	22	48	.168	.128	.191	14.56	6.67
2-team total (11 Indianapolis Indians)					3	2	2.93	27	1	0	5	43	29	14	14	4	29	63	.186	.143	.210	13.19	6.07
Marcus Stroman	R-R	5-7	180	5-1-91	0	0	16.88	1	1	0	0	3	7	5	5	0	1	2	.467	.222	.833	6.75	3.38
Matt Swarmer	R-R	6-5	195	9-25-93	3	3	3.87	21	15	0	0	81	70	39	35	9	33	86	.227	.201	.247	9.52	3.65
Keegan Thompson	R-R	6-1	210	3-13-95	0	0	3.86	1	1	0	0	2	1	1	1	0	1	4	.125	.000	.200	15.43	3.86
Cayne Ueckert	R-R	6-3	195	5-28-96	3	1	7.74	39	1	0	0	50	54	48	43	12	52	63	.276	.301	.257	11.34	9.36
Erich Uelmen	R-R	6-3	195	5-19-96	3	3	2.79	28	0	0	6	42	29	19	13	2	23	52	.197	.191	.203	11.14	4.93
Hayden Wesneski	R-R	6-3	210	12-5-97	0	2	5.66	5	4	0	0	21	17	13	13	1	8	23	.227	.162	.289	10.02	3.48
2-team total (19 Scranton/Wilkes-Barre RailRiders)					6	9	3.92	24	23	0	0	110	92	51	48	10	36	106	.227	.241	.213	8.65	2.94
Blake Whitney	R-R	6-3	185	5-25-96	2	5	6.75	17	0	0	0	24	28	22	18	6	13	19	.283	.342	.246	7.13	4.88
Eric Yardley	R-R	6-0	170	8-18-90	0	0	17.36	5	0	0	0	5	12	10	9	1	3	2	.444	.571	.308	3.86	5.79
2-team total (32 Buffalo Bisons)					3	2	5.79	37	0	0	0	37	43	28	24	4	20	33	.291	.431	.200	7.96	4.82

Fielding

Catcher	PCT	G	PO	A	E	DP	PB
Castillo	.988	35	312	20	4	4	3
Hicks	.988	67	614	38	8	3	10
Higgins	.992	13	123	8	1	1	4
Payne	.997	41	342	13	1	4	3

First Base	PCT	G	PO	A	E	DP
Crook	.984	9	52	8	1	3
Garcia	1.000	3	18	2	0	2
Hicks	1.000	9	59	3	0	8
Higgins	1.000	3	23	2	0	1
Maldonado	.994	22	170	7	1	15
Mervis	.993	53	374	28	3	39
Payne	1.000	2	19	0	0	1
Rivas	.985	9	57	10	1	12
Schwindel	1.000	6	25	5	0	2
Young	.990	42	271	20	3	18

Second Base	PCT	G	PO	A	E	DP
Bote	.982	16	15	40	1	6
Deichmann	1.000	1	2	6	0	0
Donahue	1.000	2	1	6	0	3
Garcia	.955	4	8	13	1	1
Giambrone	.953	65	77	107	9	25
Jordan	.986	29	25	48	1	12
Machado	1.000	9	19	27	0	11
Madrigal	1.000	10	13	20	0	7
McKeon	.875	1	3	4	1	0
Quiroz	.974	20	29	47	2	12
Sepulveda	.960	10	9	15	1	3
Vargas	1.000	5	8	9	0	0
Young	.875	6	5	9	2	4

Third Base	PCT	G	PO	A	E	DP
Bote	.875	14	5	23	4	1
Donahue	1.000	4	5	4	0	1
Garcia	.919	26	15	42	5	3
Giambrone	1.000	12	3	12	0	1
Hicks	1.000	2	0	1	0	1
Higgins	1.000	3	1	3	0	0
Jordan	.935	35	22	50	5	7
Machado	1.000	5	2	5	0	1
McKeon	.875	4	1	6	1	1
Quiroz	.962	9	7	18	1	1
Sepulveda	1.000	7	4	6	0	0
Vargas	.889	2	3	5	1	0
Young	.968	41	33	57	3	7

Shortstop	PCT	G	PO	A	E	DP
Bote	1.000	3	2	9	0	4
Jordan	.962	24	21	54	3	9
Machado	.990	73	104	180	3	30
McKeon	1.000	3	3	10	0	4
Sepulveda	.909	5	3	7	1	0
Simmons	.909	8	7	13	2	3
Vargas	.955	18	19	45	3	16
Vazquez	.990	27	45	58	1	12

Outfield	PCT	G	PO	A	E	DP
Canario	1.000	16	29	1	0	0
Crook	.980	87	147	3	3	1
Davis	.973	39	67	4	2	0
Davis	.984	37	62	0	1	0
Deichmann	.964	80	128	7	5	0
Dewees	1.000	14	20	0	0	0
Frazier	.959	44	66	4	3	1
Garcia	1.000	2	2	0	0	0
Giambrone	1.000	6	9	1	0	0
Hermosillo	1.000	3	8	0	0	0
Hill	.994	82	170	5	1	2
Maldonado	1.000	6	9	0	0	0
Rivas	1.000	11	10	0	0	0
Suzuki	1.000	2	2	0	0	0
Velazquez	.988	35	79	2	1	0
Young	1.000	24	39	3	0	0

TENNESSEE SMOKIES — DOUBLE-A

SOUTHERN LEAGUE

Batting	B-T	HT	WT	DOB	AVG	vLH	vRH	G	AB	R	H	2B	3B	HR	RBI	BB	HBP	SH	SF	SO	SB	CS	SLG	OBP
Miguel Amaya	R-R	6-2	230	3-9-99	.278	.240	.292	28	97	15	27	6	1	4	19	14	3	0	2	28	0	0	.485	.379
D.J. Artis	L-L	5-9	165	3-20-97	.333	.500	.250	2	6	1	2	0	1	0	2	3	0	0	0	1	2	1	.667	.556
Cam Balego	R-R	5-11	205	6-12-95	.160	.190	.138	16	50	9	8	1	0	1	5	12	0	1	1	10	0	1	.240	.317
Bryce Ball	L-R	6-6	240	7-8-98	.265	.210	.285	131	486	77	129	31	2	11	76	69	2	0	4	121	1	4	.405	.357
Bradlee Beesley	R-R	5-10	180	2-21-98	.246	.263	.238	36	122	19	30	11	0	4	21	9	3	0	0	36	10	1	.434	.313
Alexander Canario	R-R	6-1	165	5-7-00	.248	.246	.249	81	310	51	77	18	2	24	61	36	2	0	2	91	17	3	.552	.329
Zach Davis	B-R	5-11	175	6-29-94	.312	.286	.327	22	77	17	24	4	0	0	5	9	2	1	1	24	17	0	.364	.393
Christian Donahue	L-R	5-8	180	5-4-95	.154	.273	.130	22	65	5	10	1	0	0	2	8	0	1	0	22	2	2	.169	.247
Darius Hill	L-L	6-1	190	8-17-97	.308	.229	.336	44	185	34	57	13	1	6	18	13	2	1	0	24	3	2	.486	.360
Levi Jordan	R-R	5-8	170	9-24-95	.353	.481	.293	24	85	22	30	7	1	6	24	12	3	0	1	11	1	2	.671	.446
Nelson Maldonado	R-R	5-10	195	8-13-96	.359	.395	.346	39	142	28	51	16	0	7	31	13	1	0	2	37	3	0	.620	.411
Matt Mervis	L-R	6-4	225	4-16-98	.300	.210	.340	53	203	34	61	16	1	14	51	20	4	0	3	46	2	0	.596	.370
Christopher Morel	R-R	5-11	145	6-24-99	.306	.200	.337	28	108	22	33	5	1	7	20	10	3	1	0	30	3	3	.565	.380
Yonathan Perlaza	B-R	5-11	170	11-10-98	.255	.246	.259	124	470	81	120	36	3	23	73	72	4	0	1	127	15	6	.491	.358
Cole Roederer	L-L	6-0	180	9-24-99	.243	.263	.238	53	181	25	44	7	0	8	30	17	3	1	3	55	3	4	.414	.314
Jake Slaughter	R-R	6-3	200	10-24-96	.293	.287	.295	86	328	60	96	17	1	20	68	37	17	0	4	83	28	8	.534	.389
Chase Strumpf	R-R	6-1	170	3-8-98	.234	.243	.231	116	393	73	92	22	2	21	57	73	19	0	1	162	2	2	.461	.379
Luis Vazquez	R-R	6-1	165	10-10-99	.237	.238	.237	86	325	43	77	14	2	8	36	23	4	3	3	78	7	7	.366	.293
Nelson Velazquez	R-R	6-0	190	12-26-98	.288	.400	.250	22	80	16	23	4	1	9	17	14	0	0	0	33	5	2	.700	.394
Jake Washer	R-R	6-0	220	2-23-96	.188	.211	.178	18	64	6	12	0	0	3	14	1	0	0	0	26	0	0	.328	.200
Andy Weber	L-R	6-1	190	7-24-97	.300	.281	.306	76	280	47	84	12	1	4	25	24	3	0	1	74	6	2	.393	.360
Harrison Wenson	R-R	6-3	235	4-21-95	.163	.143	.168	38	123	13	20	5	0	5	16	13	2	1	0	69	2	0	.325	.254
Bryce Windham	L-R	6-1	190	9-25-96	.202	.238	.189	79	253	40	51	10	0	4	31	44	2	3	2	44	2	1	.289	.322
Delvin Zinn	R-R	5-10	170	5-29-97	.137	.200	.115	49	117	14	16	5	0	0	7	15	4	0	2	34	12	3	.179	.254

Pitching	B-T	HT	WT	DOB	W	L	ERA	G	GS	CG	SV	IP	H	R	ER	HR	BB	SO	AVG	vLH	vRH	K/9	BB/9
Javier Assad	R-R	6-1	200	7-30-97	4	1	2.51	15	14	0	0	72	68	23	20	6	28	74	.254	.213	.288	9.29	3.52
Max Bain	R-R	6-5	240	9-25-97	2	2	7.50	16	5	0	0	36	39	32	30	9	39	32	.285	.393	.197	8.00	9.75
Hunter Bigge	R-R	6-1	205	6-12-98	1	0	6.32	12	0	0	3	16	15	11	11	1	14	23	.259	.250	.267	13.21	8.04
Ben Brown	R-R	6-6	210	9-9-99	3	0	4.06	7	7	0	0	31	33	15	14	3	13	44	.273	.245	.294	12.77	3.77
Burl Carraway	L-L	6-0	173	5-27-99	0	0	9.00	10	0	0	1	10	9	12	10	1	24	7	.265	.455	.174	6.30	21.60
Chris Clarke	R-R	6-7	215	5-13-98	7	5	4.93	20	17	0	1	97	125	58	53	10	20	87	.311	.325	.300	8.10	1.86
Danis Correa	R-R	5-11	150	8-26-99	1	3	2.93	26	0	0	7	40	27	18	13	2	22	40	.191	.197	.187	9.00	4.95
Christian Donahue	L-R	5-8	180	5-4-95	0	0	0.00	1	0	0	0	0	2	0	0	0	0	0	.667	1.000	.500	0.00	0.00
Anderson Espinoza	R-R	6-0	190	3-9-98	1	4	7.11	13	12	0	0	44	40	37	35	10	25	54	.245	.244	.247	10.96	5.08
Jeremiah Estrada	B-R	6-1	185	11-1-98	1	0	1.86	13	0	0	2	19	11	5	4	0	9	27	.167	.226	.114	12.57	4.19
Richard Gallardo	R-R	6-1	180	9-6-01	0	0	6.75	1	1	0	0	4	3	3	3	3	2	6	.200	.333	.111	13.50	4.50
Ben Hecht	R-R	6-2	170	5-31-95	1	2	12.46	12	0	0	0	13	15	20	18	3	16	12	.313	.474	.207	8.31	11.08
DJ Herz	R-L	6-2	175	1-4-01	1	4	8.24	9	9	0	0	32	24	33	29	5	33	42	.209	.250	.193	11.94	9.38
Bailey Horn	L-L	6-2	210	1-15-98	1	3	3.46	28	0	0	4	42	37	16	16	5	27	58	.231	.250	.221	12.53	5.83
Bryan Hudson	L-L	6-8	220	5-8-97	3	1	2.08	8	0	0	3	13	10	4	3	1	5	18	.222	.190	.250	12.46	3.46
Brandon Hughes	B-L	6-2	215	12-1-95	0	0	0.00	5	0	0	1	6	1	0	0	0	1	10	.048	.000	.083	14.21	1.42
Ryan Jensen	R-R	6-0	190	11-23-97	2	4	4.25	17	17	0	0	59	44	29	28	5	39	60	.204	.212	.197	9.10	5.92

Kyle Johnson	R-R	6-4	220	9-19-93	3	3	7.91	32	0	0	3	47	57	46	41	10	37	35	.310	.294	.323	6.75	7.14
Bryan King	R-L	6-1	184	11-5-96	0	2	2.51	9	0	0	0	14	15	6	4	1	8	11	.268	.111	.342	6.91	5.02
Scott Kobos	L-L	6-2	200	8-3-97	2	1	5.06	12	0	0	1	16	12	10	9	3	19	24	.218	.250	.200	13.50	10.69
Graham Lawson	R-R	6-1	225	6-7-96	1	1	7.50	18	0	0	1	24	28	23	20	3	23	27	.277	.326	.236	10.13	8.63
Brandon Leibrandt	L-L	6-4	190	12-13-92	2	2	3.31	11	3	0	0	33	35	13	12	5	5	44	.285	.327	.257	12.12	1.38
Zac Leigh	R-R	6-0	170	11-14-97	0	0	3.86	10	0	0	1	12	7	5	5	1	8	21	.171	.091	.200	16.20	6.17
Eduarniel Nunez	R-R	6-2	170	6-7-99	0	1	6.75	11	0	0	0	15	18	14	11	1	14	11	.295	.269	.314	6.75	8.59
Nicholas Padilla	R-R	6-2	220	12-24-96	1	1	2.82	15	0	0	2	22	16	9	7	0	14	25	.195	.278	.130	10.07	5.64
CD Pelham	R-L	6-6	238	2-21-95	2	1	4.26	21	0	0	2	32	26	15	15	4	16	33	.226	.222	.227	9.38	4.55
Walker Powell	R-R	6-8	210	6-11-96	4	2	1.96	10	4	0	0	41	27	11	9	2	13	38	.181	.221	.148	8.27	2.83
Eury Ramos	R-R	6-3	152	10-10-97	1	1	0.56	12	0	0	0	16	11	2	1	0	7	19	.216	.136	.276	10.69	3.94
Peyton Remy	L-R	6-2	170	8-20-96	8	5	6.77	29	10	0	0	94	94	83	71	18	47	114	.255	.247	.261	10.88	4.48
Samuel Reyes	R-R	5-11	180	3-13-96	5	1	4.47	26	0	0	1	50	46	28	25	9	23	64	.243	.254	.237	11.44	4.11
Cam Sanders	R-R	6-2	175	12-9-96	1	1	3.38	6	6	0	0	24	13	10	9	3	11	36	.151	.225	.087	13.50	4.13
Wyatt Short	L-L	5-8	180	10-14-94	1	0	1.29	3	0	0	0	7	7	1	1	0	5	4	.304	.300	.308	5.14	6.43
Dalton Stambaugh	R-L	6-0	195	2-11-97	7	2	6.19	22	5	0	0	68	80	50	47	11	35	57	.296	.265	.310	7.51	4.61
Riley Thompson	L-R	6-4	210	7-9-96	2	5	4.42	19	19	0	0	57	47	30	28	8	32	64	.230	.207	.250	10.11	5.05
Dauris Valdez	R-R	6-8	254	10-22-95	0	0	0.00	2	0	0	0	3	3	0	0	0	1	4	.300	.167	.500	13.50	3.38
Jake Washer	R-R	6-0	220	2-23-96	0	1	0.00	1	0	0	0	0	1	1	0	0	1	0	.500	--	.500	0.00	27.00
Harrison Wenson	R-R	6-3	235	4-21-95	0	0	0.00	2	0	0	0	1	0	0	0	0	1	0	.000	.000	.000	0.00	6.75
Blake Whitney	R-R	6-3	185	5-25-96	3	2	2.80	18	0	0	1	45	35	17	14	3	14	55	.212	.239	.191	11.00	2.80
Jordan Wicks	L-L	6-3	220	9-1-99	0	3	4.18	8	8	0	0	28	24	14	13	5	11	35	.224	.314	.181	11.25	3.54
Jarod Wright	R-R	6-3	205	12-15-96	0	2	7.50	3	0	0	0	6	3	5	5	1	7	1	.158	.167	.154	1.50	10.50
Delvin Zinn	R-R	5-10	170	5-29-97	0	0	18.00	1	0	0	0	1	2	2	2	0	2	0	.500	.000	.667	0.00	18.00

Fielding

Catcher	PCT	G	PO	A	E	DP	PB
Balego	.964	15	121	11	5	2	2
Washer	.990	9	97	6	1	0	4
Wenson	.985	36	375	28	6	2	7
Windham	.983	78	747	47	14	9	7

First Base	PCT	G	PO	A	E	DP
Balego	1.000	1	3	0	0	0
Ball	.993	81	526	52	4	61
Maldonado	1.000	13	82	5	0	11
Mervis	.997	36	274	25	1	33
Slaughter	1.000	1	2	0	0	0
Strumpf	1.000	3	8	0	0	0
Washer	.909	3	8	2	1	3
Weber	1.000	6	41	3	0	6

Second Base	PCT	G	PO	A	E	DP
Donahue	.909	15	21	29	5	10
Jordan	1.000	7	17	17	0	7
Slaughter	.977	12	19	23	1	7
Strumpf	.980	59	92	150	5	42
Vazquez	1.000	1	2	4	0	2
Weber	.955	28	47	58	5	22
Zinn	.984	19	25	36	1	7

Third Base	PCT	G	PO	A	E	DP
Jordan	1.000	12	11	24	0	4
Morel	.800	4	0	4	1	2
Slaughter	.935	69	29	101	9	7
Strumpf	.943	55	29	86	7	8
Zinn	1.000	1	0	1	0	0

Shortstop	PCT	G	PO	A	E	DP
Morel	.960	6	7	17	1	5
Vazquez	.971	85	129	235	11	60
Weber	.932	36	40	84	9	23
Zinn	.980	14	20	28	1	6

Outfield	PCT	G	PO	A	E	DP
Artis	1.000	2	2	0	0	0
Beesley	.980	36	48	2	1	0
Canario	.982	82	160	7	3	1
Davis	.977	22	43	0	1	0
Donahue	1.000	6	8	1	0	0
Hill	.988	43	81	2	1	0
Maldonado	1.000	9	9	0	0	0
Morel	.946	18	34	1	2	0
Perlaza	.987	119	210	10	3	3
Roederer	1.000	53	81	1	0	0
Slaughter	1.000	6	4	0	0	0
Velazquez	.949	20	36	1	2	0
Zinn	1.000	8	11	0	0	0

SOUTH BEND CUBS

HIGH CLASS A

MIDWEST LEAGUE

Batting	B-T	HT	WT	DOB	AVG	vLH	vRH	G	AB	R	H	2B	3B	HR	RBI	BB	HBP	SH	SF	SO	SB	CS	SLG	OBP
Pablo Aliendo	R-R	6-0	170	5-29-01	.267	.267	.267	89	318	34	85	16	1	7	35	26	7	2	0	77	3	1	.390	.336
Edmond Americaan	L-L	6-1	170	3-26-97	.214	.222	.211	11	28	3	6	2	0	0	0	1	0	0	0	12	2	0	.286	.241
Bradlee Beesley	R-R	5-10	180	2-21-98	.263	.156	.333	21	80	14	21	3	1	2	6	6	1	0	0	20	3	2	.400	.322
Grayson Byrd	L-R	6-3	205	6-16-96	.074	.000	.095	7	27	3	2	1	0	0	1	0	0	0	0	12	0	0	.111	.074
Owen Caissie	L-R	6-4	190	7-8-02	.254	.242	.258	105	378	57	96	21	1	11	58	50	5	0	0	124	11	6	.402	.349
Alexander Canario	R-R	6-1	165	5-7-00	.281	.219	.316	24	89	17	25	6	0	7	22	10	1	0	0	35	3	0	.584	.360
Pete Crow-Armstrong	L-L	6-0	184	3-25-02	.287	.362	.271	63	265	50	76	15	7	9	34	14	6	0	3	69	19	7	.498	.333
Brennen Davis	R-R	6-4	210	11-2-99	.130	.167	.118	5	23	0	3	0	0	0	2	0	0	0	0	8	0	0	.130	.130
Ed Howard	R-R	6-2	185	1-28-02	.244	.250	.241	23	82	8	20	1	1	1	11	9	1	0	1	19	3	0	.317	.323
Caleb Knight	R-R	5-11	220	1-2-96	.231	.303	.205	38	121	17	28	5	0	1	10	12	16	0	0	27	2	2	.298	.376
Kevin Made	R-R	5-10	160	9-10-02	.162	.360	.114	37	130	14	21	6	1	1	14	19	0	1	1	31	3	0	.246	.267
Scott McKeon	R-R	6-0	185	10-30-97	.165	.167	.165	45	133	19	22	3	0	2	7	18	3	1	0	57	6	2	.233	.279
Matt Mervis	L-R	6-4	225	4-16-98	.350	.375	.338	27	100	17	35	9	0	7	29	5	2	0	1	26	0	0	.650	.389
BJ Murray Jr.	B-R	6-0	205	1-5-00	.273	.189	.293	56	187	22	51	8	1	5	28	36	0	0	1	46	8	4	.406	.388
Jordan Nwogu	R-R	6-3	230	3-10-99	.265	.288	.257	88	325	59	86	17	7	15	51	37	12	0	4	90	19	6	.498	.357
Casey Opitz	B-R	5-11	200	7-30-98	.202	.207	.200	36	114	16	23	6	0	3	11	22	0	1	1	42	0	0	.333	.328
Fabian Pertuz	R-R	6-0	156	9-1-00	.237	.162	.261	113	427	54	101	27	3	8	59	22	8	1	3	123	13	3	.370	.285
Yohendrick Pinango	L-L	5-11	170	5-7-02	.250	.242	.253	115	464	65	116	24	2	13	63	30	1	0	0	88	14	1	.394	.297
Cole Roederer	L-L	6-0	180	9-24-99	.197	.292	.135	14	61	8	12	5	1	1	5	4	0	0	1	19	3	0	.361	.242
Yeison Santana	R-R	5-11	170	12-7-00	.248	.340	.218	61	206	28	51	5	1	1	17	32	3	4	0	43	15	11	.296	.357
Jonathan Sierra	L-L	6-3	190	10-17-98	.255	.186	.277	55	184	16	47	8	0	3	21	18	0	0	1	33	0	1	.348	.320
Jake Slaughter	R-R	6-3	200	10-24-96	.247	.179	.289	20	73	15	18	4	0	3	12	10	1	0	0	22	8	0	.425	.345
Luis Verdugo	R-R	6-0	160	10-12-00	.269	.270	.269	107	368	43	99	27	1	5	41	46	3	1	4	70	4	4	.389	.352
Jake Washer	R-R	6-0	220	2-23-96	.300	.370	.274	46	170	33	51	10	0	14	34	15	3	0	1	52	1	0	.606	.365

Pitching	B-T	HT	WT	DOB	W	L	ERA	G	GS	CG	SV	IP	H	R	ER	HR	BB	SO	AVG	vLH	vRH	K/9	BB/9
Jose Albertos	R-R	6-1	185	11-7-98	0	0	0.00	2	0	0	0	2	1	0	0	0	3	5	.143	.000	.200	19.29	11.57
Max Bain	R-R	6-5	240	9-25-97	1	0	2.84	6	2	0	0	19	8	6	6	2	11	21	.127	.118	.138	9.95	5.21
Hunter Bigge	R-R	6-1	205	6-12-98	6	2	4.82	29	0	0	7	37	29	21	20	5	24	47	.212	.208	.215	11.33	5.79
Chris Clarke	R-R	6-7	215	5-13-98	3	1	3.42	6	4	0	0	24	22	10	9	2	5	23	.247	.184	.325	8.75	1.90
Yovanny Cruz	R-R	6-0	180	8-23-99	0	0	3.24	7	0	0	0	8	9	4	3	1	2	7	.273	.188	.353	7.56	2.16
Brad Deppermann	R-R	6-0	195	6-15-96	3	1	4.42	16	0	0	1	18	17	11	9	0	15	20	.246	.242	.250	9.82	7.36
Luis Devers	R-R	6-3	178	4-24-00	4	0	1.05	11	8	0	0	51	29	6	6	1	12	47	.167	.154	.177	8.24	2.10
Manuel Espinoza	R-R	5-11	150	11-17-00	3	5	4.86	17	11	0	0	67	58	45	36	11	31	68	.230	.222	.239	9.18	4.19
Jeremiah Estrada	B-R	6-1	185	11-1-98	2	2	1.17	15	0	0	5	23	14	6	3	1	10	39	.177	.225	.120	15.26	3.91
Kohl Franklin	R-R	6-4	195	9-9-99	3	7	6.88	23	23	0	0	69	72	60	53	8	41	75	.264	.260	.268	9.74	5.32
Richard Gallardo	R-R	6-1	180	9-6-01	0	4	3.73	7	6	0	0	31	35	21	13	6	12	14	.269	.226	.299	4.02	3.45
DJ Herz	R-L	6-2	175	1-4-01	2	2	2.26	17	17	0	0	64	33	18	16	3	37	99	.150	.137	.156	13.99	5.23
Porter Hodge	R-R	6-4	230	2-21-01	3	3	2.01	8	7	0	0	40	26	10	9	3	16	51	.187	.210	.169	11.38	3.57
Bailey Horn	L-L	6-2	210	1-15-98	0	0	0.00	5	0	0	0	10	2	0	0	0	5	16	.065	.077	.056	14.40	4.50
Gabriel Jaramillo	R-R	6-1	176	11-3-98	1	1	4.01	17	0	0	0	25	20	12	11	4	10	20	.220	.237	.208	7.30	3.65
Chris Kachmar	R-R	6-3	180	9-3-96	1	0	2.25	3	1	0	0	4	2	2	1	0	3	5	.143	.200	.111	11.25	6.75
Adam Laskey	R-L	6-3	205	3-9-98	6	0	4.26	19	0	0	0	32	29	17	15	1	21	36	.248	.216	.259	10.23	5.97
Zac Leigh	R-R	6-0	170	11-14-97	2	0	2.35	17	0	0	4	23	16	8	6	2	8	32	.186	.189	.184	12.52	3.13
Luke Little	L-L	6-8	220	8-30-00	0	1	0.69	4	3	0	0	13	6	3	1	0	6	17	.143	.154	.138	11.77	4.15
Riley Martin	L-L	6-1	215	3-19-98	7	5	3.89	27	1	0	1	69	53	33	30	4	39	93	.209	.213	.207	12.07	5.06
Michael McAvene	R-R	6-3	207	8-24-97	2	1	3.73	21	0	0	1	31	23	13	13	2	17	39	.207	.167	.238	11.20	4.88
Wade Miley	L-L	6-2	220	11-13-86	0	0	9.00	2	2	0	0	6	11	7	6	0	1	3	.393	.600	.348	4.50	1.50
Joe Nahas	R-R	6-1	185	11-14-99	4	3	4.19	24	5	0	0	86	77	48	40	9	40	74	.238	.249	.225	7.74	4.19
Eduarniel Nunez	R-R	6-2	170	6-7-99	5	4	3.73	30	0	0	4	41	35	17	17	1	25	46	.230	.224	.237	10.10	5.49
Nicholas Padilla	R-R	6-2	220	12-24-96	1	0	1.80	7	0	0	1	10	4	3	2	0	5	18	.125	.118	.133	16.20	4.50
Daniel Palencia	R-R	5-11	160	2-5-00	1	3	3.94	21	20	0	0	75	56	36	33	7	35	98	.204	.176	.231	11.71	4.18
Walker Powell	R-R	6-8	210	6-11-96	3	0	3.93	13	0	0	2	34	29	16	15	1	5	24	.230	.215	.246	6.29	1.31
Sheldon Reed	L-R	6-2	205	7-30-97	2	2	5.67	24	0	0	4	27	25	18	17	2	14	37	.240	.222	.254	12.33	4.67
Bailey Reid	R-R	6-2	195	7-3-98	1	2	9.00	14	0	0	1	18	18	19	18	4	16	24	.254	.219	.282	12.00	8.00
Jake Reindl	R-R	6-1	190	1-15-97	0	0	2.84	5	0	0	0	6	5	3	2	0	3	8	.217	.250	.200	11.37	4.26
Tyler Schlaffer	R-R	6-1	180	5-24-01	0	0	3.60	1	1	0	0	5	5	2	2	1	1	2	.278	.250	.300	3.60	1.80
Drew Smyly	L-L	6-2	188	6-13-89	0	1	6.75	1	1	0	0	4	4	3	3	2	0	6	.250	.333	.200	13.50	0.00
Dalton Stambaugh	R-L	6-0	195	2-11-97	1	0	2.76	9	3	0	2	29	24	9	9	2	11	26	.226	.250	.216	7.98	3.38
Didier Vargas	R-L	6-0	175	3-13-99	0	1	6.51	11	0	0	0	28	28	22	20	2	12	28	.267	.379	.224	9.11	3.90
Jordan Wicks	L-L	6-3	220	9-1-99	4	3	3.65	16	16	0	0	67	66	32	27	5	17	86	.256	.313	.229	11.61	2.30
Jarod Wright	R-R	6-3	205	12-15-96	2	4	5.35	15	0	0	2	39	39	25	23	5	17	23	.265	.271	.260	5.35	3.96
Alfredo Zarraga	R-R	5-11	158	11-16-00	0	0	0.00	1	0	0	0	1	1	0	0	0	2	1	.200	.500	.000	6.75	13.50

Fielding

Catcher	PCT	G	PO	A	E	DP	PB
Aliendo	.991	88	898	64	9	5	7
Knight	.973	15	131	11	4	4	2
Opitz	.996	26	235	16	1	0	1
Washer	.970	4	29	3	1	0	0

First Base	PCT	G	PO	A	E	DP
Byrd	.974	7	37	1	1	2
Knight	1.000	17	141	6	0	14
Mervis	.977	27	191	21	5	20
Murray Jr.	.993	40	261	28	2	30
Opitz	1.000	8	70	2	0	10
Sierra	.975	15	109	8	3	7
Slaughter	1.000	7	53	3	0	4
Washer	1.000	11	72	7	0	8

Second Base	PCT	G	PO	A	E	DP
McKeon	.958	25	32	60	4	16
Pertuz	.977	45	85	123	5	32
Santana	.959	57	75	137	9	24
Slaughter	1.000	3	6	7	0	2
Verdugo	.750	1	0	3	1	0

Third Base	PCT	G	PO	A	E	DP
McKeon	1.000	8	6	14	0	0
Murray Jr.	.882	9	4	11	2	2
Pertuz	.857	3	0	6	1	0
Slaughter	1.000	10	6	9	0	0
Verdugo	.928	105	63	157	17	16

Shortstop	PCT	G	PO	A	E	DP
Howard	.961	23	29	45	3	15
Made	.960	35	46	98	6	25
McKeon	.917	11	10	12	2	2
Pertuz	.955	64	79	133	10	31
Santana	1.000	1	3	2	0	1

Outfield	PCT	G	PO	A	E	DP
Americaan	1.000	8	13	0	0	0
Beesley	.935	17	29	0	2	0
Caissie	.988	99	162	4	2	1
Canario	.929	18	23	3	2	0
Crow-Armstrong	.985	59	130	3	2	0
Davis	1.000	4	8	0	0	0
Nwogu	.936	67	101	1	7	0
Pinango	.979	91	133	5	3	1
Roederer	1.000	14	37	0	0	0
Sierra	.976	31	39	1	1	0

MYRTLE BEACH PELICANS — *LOW CLASS A*

CAROLINA LEAGUE

Batting	B-T	HT	WT	DOB	AVG	vLH	vRH	G	AB	R	H	2B	3B	HR	RBI	BB	HBP	SH	SF	SO	SB	CS	SLG	OBP
Kevin Alcantara	R-R	6-6	188	7-12-02	.273	.318	.265	112	428	76	117	19	6	15	85	55	6	0	6	123	14	3	.451	.360
Moises Ballesteros	L-R	5-10	195	11-8-03	.248	.071	.274	31	109	17	27	7	0	3	15	18	0	0	2	28	0	1	.394	.349
Parker Chavers	L-R	5-11	185	7-25-98	.244	.333	.237	35	127	16	31	9	2	2	12	5	2	0	2	33	4	2	.394	.279
Pete Crow-Armstrong	L-L	6-0	184	3-25-02	.354	.591	.316	38	158	39	56	5	3	7	27	22	3	0	0	33	13	4	.557	.443
Miguel Fabrizio	L-R	5-11	178	9-26-00	.152	.250	.145	21	66	8	10	3	1	2	13	9	0	0	0	21	0	0	.318	.253
Reivaj Garcia	B-R	5-11	175	8-12-01	.300	.000	.333	3	10	3	3	1	0	0	1	0	0	0	0	1	0	0	.400	.300
Ethan Hearn	L-R	5-10	200	8-31-00	.213	.250	.209	85	286	47	61	14	6	12	41	42	7	1	2	115	13	1	.430	.326
Frank Hernandez	R-R	5-11	185	12-10-01	.089	.071	.097	16	45	4	4	0	0	0	2	7	2	1	0	12	1	0	.089	.241
Josue Huma	B-R	6-1	175	3-17-00	.253	.278	.246	66	253	45	64	9	1	4	33	26	0	0	1	44	7	1	.344	.321
Kevin Made	R-R	5-10	160	9-10-02	.266	.286	.264	57	222	41	59	14	0	9	30	27	5	0	3	49	0	1	.450	.354
Peter Matt	R-R	6-2	220	5-22-98	.230	.200	.237	20	74	8	17	2	0	2	11	7	0	0	2	23	0	0	.338	.289
Haydn McGeary	R-R	6-5	235	10-9-99	.292	.286	.293	12	48	5	14	5	0	1	8	4	0	0	0	12	0	0	.458	.346
Scott McKeon	R-R	6-0	185	10-30-97	.212	.214	.211	15	52	9	11	3	1	0	5	2	2	2	0	18	1	0	.308	.268
Juan Mora	R-R	5-9	176	9-30-99	.269	.196	.285	81	312	56	84	19	2	7	48	27	11	1	3	69	6	3	.410	.346

BJ Murray Jr.	B-R	6-0	205	1-5-00	.305	.333	.300	39	128	31	39	11	0	3	25	26	6	0	1	31	0	0	.461	.441
Ezequiel Pagan	L-R	6-1	163	7-8-00	.292	.309	.289	104	384	59	112	15	5	11	68	40	7	4	3	57	13	4	.443	.366
Reginald Preciado	B-R	6-4	185	5-16-03	.199	.118	.208	46	166	20	33	6	2	2	24	10	5	2	2	69	3	2	.295	.262
Malcom Quintero	B-R	6-0	165	7-29-00	.226	.292	.209	34	115	18	26	5	0	1	17	18	0	1	3	42	1	1	.296	.324
Pedro Ramirez	B-R	5-9	165	4-1-04	.268	.000	.306	10	41	7	11	0	0	0	1	2	3	0	0	6	4	0	.268	.348
Alejandro Rivero	R-R	6-2	200	6-8-97	.230	.238	.226	26	74	11	17	1	1	1	8	8	7	4	2	28	1	1	.311	.352
Cole Roederer	L-L	6-0	180	9-24-99	.467	--	.467	4	15	4	7	2	0	0	2	4	0	0	1	2	2	0	.600	.550
Yeison Santana	R-R	5-11	170	12-7-00	.300	.273	.306	18	60	17	18	4	0	0	7	10	1	0	0	16	3	0	.367	.408
Wally Soto	L-R	5-10	170	1-5-03	--	--	--	1	0	0	0	0	0	0	0	0	0	0	0	0	0	0	--	--
Liam Spence	R-R	6-1	190	4-9-98	.208	.200	.210	41	120	23	25	3	0	3	21	23	1	2	3	34	3	0	.308	.333
Felix Stevens	R-R	6-4	225	7-30-99	.222	.231	.220	73	252	32	56	13	1	11	43	32	2	0	4	96	1	1	.413	.310
James Triantos	R-R	6-1	195	1-29-03	.272	.213	.283	113	456	74	124	19	6	7	50	39	6	0	3	81	20	3	.386	.335
Matt Warkentin	R-L	6-6	250	1-28-97	.234	.444	.169	24	77	13	18	6	0	0	13	14	1	0	2	31	0	0	.312	.351
Jacob Wetzel	L-L	5-11	215	3-26-00	.211	.176	.218	99	336	63	71	14	1	10	51	60	9	1	2	80	14	3	.348	.344

Pitching	B-T	HT	WT	DOB	W	L	ERA	G	GS	CG	SV	IP	H	R	ER	HR	BB	SO	AVG	vLH	vRH	K/9	BB/9
Michael Arias	R-R	6-0	155	11-15-01	0	1	4.50	2	2	0	0	4	4	3	2	0	6	5	.267	.400	.200	11.25	13.50
Yovanny Cabrera	R-R	6-2	180	3-22-01	2	2	4.91	10	0	0	0	18	16	11	10	3	14	16	.229	.240	.222	7.85	6.87
Luis Devers	R-R	6-3	178	4-24-00	9	3	2.58	15	14	0	0	66	57	26	19	3	14	75	.235	.211	.256	10.18	1.90
Richard Gallardo	R-R	6-1	180	9-6-01	6	6	4.05	18	18	0	0	87	84	49	39	8	29	84	.251	.262	.244	8.72	3.01
Angel Gonzalez	R-R	6-2	175	8-26-02	1	2	5.29	25	0	0	3	32	30	23	19	4	28	30	.250	.286	.225	8.35	7.79
Jose Miguel Gonzalez	R-R	6-2	173	12-5-97	6	3	5.45	22	2	0	2	69	68	47	42	10	43	86	.257	.270	.245	11.16	5.58
Saul Gonzalez	R-R	6-7	235	12-28-99	1	1	3.63	7	1	0	0	17	15	8	7	1	12	19	.242	.185	.286	9.87	6.23
Angel Hernandez	L-L	6-2	180	5-6-00	4	3	5.79	21	0	0	2	37	26	26	24	4	31	55	.194	.209	.187	13.26	7.47
Porter Hodge	R-R	6-4	230	2-21-01	4	2	3.00	17	17	0	0	69	54	31	23	1	39	90	.210	.235	.190	11.74	5.09
Nick Hull	R-R	6-0	205	8-21-99	0	1	4.15	3	3	0	0	9	7	4	4	0	3	6	.233	.273	.211	6.23	3.12
Tanner Jesson-Dalton	R-R	6-2	195	8-25-96	0	1	6.00	7	0	0	0	12	8	9	8	0	12	16	.195	.286	.100	12.00	9.00
Bryan King	R-L	6-1	184	11-5-96	0	0	0.00	5	0	0	3	8	5	0	0	0	1	11	.172	.200	.143	12.38	1.13
Grant Kipp	R-R	6-6	220	11-11-99	0	1	6.05	5	5	0	0	19	17	16	13	3	7	17	.224	.179	.250	7.91	3.26
Adam Laskey	R-L	6-3	205	3-9-98	3	0	0.00	19	0	0	4	26	17	1	0	0	7	28	.183	.111	.200	9.69	2.42
Luke Little	L-L	6-8	220	8-30-00	1	4	2.91	20	19	0	0	53	37	25	17	0	32	84	.188	.182	.190	14.35	5.47
Riley Martin	L-L	6-1	215	3-19-98	1	0	0.68	4	0	0	0	13	3	2	1	0	4	27	.068	.000	.097	18.23	2.70
Brody McCullough	R-R	6-4	205	6-30-00	1	0	1.80	4	0	0	0	5	2	1	1	0	2	9	.118	.000	.182	16.20	3.60
Anthony Mendez	R-R	6-1	190	8-4-02	0	1	4.02	9	0	0	1	16	18	8	7	3	11	13	.286	.353	.207	7.47	6.32
Gregori Montano	R-R	5-11	175	8-18-99	2	2	4.12	13	0	0	0	20	11	9	9	0	25	22	.180	.240	.139	10.07	11.44
Koen Moreno	R-R	6-2	170	8-1-01	0	2	13.76	7	5	0	0	17	23	26	26	4	25	23	.324	.267	.366	12.18	13.24
Johzan Oquendo	R-R	6-2	180	1-6-01	3	2	4.94	31	0	0	3	58	59	36	32	2	37	88	.266	.265	.267	13.58	5.71
Mathew Peters	R-R	6-4	215	12-28-00	0	0	0.00	1	0	0	0	1	1	0	0	0	2	1	.250	--	.250	9.00	18.00
Walker Powell	R-R	6-8	210	6-11-96	4	0	2.37	7	1	0	0	19	12	6	5	0	3	25	.174	.129	.211	11.84	1.42
Sheldon Reed	L-R	6-2	205	7-30-97	0	0	0.00	9	0	0	4	12	2	0	0	0	3	23	.059	.071	.050	17.74	2.31
Jake Reindl	R-R	6-1	190	1-15-97	0	0	0.90	7	0	0	2	10	4	1	1	0	6	19	.121	.133	.111	17.10	5.40
Alejandro Rivero	R-R	6-2	200	6-8-97	0	0	0.00	1	0	0	0	1	1	0	0	0	0	0	.333	.333	--	0.00	0.00
Luis Angel Rodriguez	L-L	6-1	190	9-10-99	6	1	4.43	23	5	0	0	69	51	35	34	7	51	106	.202	.167	.218	13.83	6.65
Jose Romero	R-R	5-10	185	4-20-01	0	1	54.00	2	0	0	0	2	5	12	12	1	5	2	.455	.800	.167	9.00	22.50
Oliver Roque	R-R	6-3	180	1-10-02	0	1	10.38	2	1	0	0	4	6	6	5	0	3	3	.300	.250	.333	6.23	6.23
Andricson Salvador	L-L	5-11	180	7-24-00	0	0	5.40	3	0	0	1	3	5	5	2	0	4	5	.313	.500	.250	13.50	10.80
Tyler Santana	R-R	6-1	205	5-13-98	11	1	2.28	24	8	0	1	99	77	27	25	3	31	93	.212	.220	.206	8.48	2.83
Frankie Scalzo Jr.	R-R	6-3	185	11-25-99	3	4	4.63	23	0	0	2	45	38	27	23	2	25	64	.224	.215	.229	12.90	5.04
Tyler Schlaffer	R-R	6-1	180	5-24-01	4	3	3.82	18	18	0	0	75	52	37	32	10	32	84	.193	.218	.172	10.04	3.82
Bryan Serra	L-R	5-10	173	9-7-98	0	0	0.00	1	0	0	0	1	0	0	0	0	1	0	.000	.000	--	0.00	13.50
Sam Thoresen	R-R	6-3	210	9-21-98	0	1	16.20	2	2	0	0	2	3	6	3	0	3	3	.333	.000	.600	16.20	16.20
Didier Vargas	R-L	6-0	175	3-13-99	2	2	3.10	8	8	0	0	41	41	19	14	5	10	37	.265	.231	.276	8.19	2.21
Chase Watkins	L-L	6-4	215	10-4-99	3	2	3.47	25	2	0	1	57	56	26	22	3	25	70	.256	.246	.260	11.05	3.95
Jarod Wright	R-R	6-3	205	12-15-96	0	0	4.50	12	0	0	1	26	26	14	13	3	16	26	.263	.271	.255	9.00	5.54
Alfredo Zarraga	R-R	5-11	158	11-16-00	1	0	2.08	16	0	0	4	17	10	4	4	1	7	28	.164	.111	.206	14.54	3.63

Fielding

Catcher	PCT	G	PO	A	E	DP	PB
Ballesteros	.985	18	171	21	3	3	4
Fabrizio	.964	4	26	1	1	0	1
Hearn	.985	80	859	58	14	4	11
Quintero	.983	31	319	18	6	2	4
Serra	1.000	1	3	0	0	0	0
Soto	1.000	1	3	0	0	0	0

First Base	PCT	G	PO	A	E	DP
Fabrizio	1.000	15	91	8	0	10
McGeary	.987	9	70	4	1	8
Murray Jr.	.980	19	138	10	3	14
Rivero	1.000	3	22	1	0	2
Spence	1.000	20	134	11	0	12
Stevens	.976	50	372	33	10	25
Warkentin	.987	20	138	14	2	18

Second Base	PCT	G	PO	A	E	DP
Huma	.984	17	25	36	1	11
McKeon	1.000	2	0	4	0	1
Mora	.980	72	88	161	5	31
Preciado	.983	16	15	43	1	7
Ramirez	.976	8	15	25	1	5
Santana	.935	15	15	28	3	5
Spence	.941	6	9	7	1	1

Third Base	PCT	G	PO	A	E	DP
Garcia	1.000	2	1	2	0	0
Huma	1.000	7	1	12	0	2
McKeon	.727	6	0	8	3	1
Murray Jr.	.955	11	6	15	1	1
Rivero	1.000	1	0	1	0	0
Spence	1.000	4	2	5	0	1
Triantos	.900	104	39	132	19	9

Shortstop	PCT	G	PO	A	E	DP
Huma	.961	32	48	76	5	11
Made	.976	50	78	123	5	35
McKeon	.880	7	6	16	3	4
Preciado	.909	28	24	66	9	14
Rivero	1.000	9	11	25	0	6
Santana	.000	1	0	0	0	0
Spence	.906	9	9	20	3	4

Outfield	PCT	G	PO	A	E	DP
Alcantara	.964	92	184	5	7	0
Chavers	1.000	34	38	3	0	0
Crow-Armstrong	.944	32	64	3	4	1
Hernandez	.933	15	13	1	1	1
Matt	.962	16	24	1	1	0
Pagan	.964	96	156	5	6	2
Rivero	1.000	12	21	0	0	0
Roederer	1.000	4	9	0	0	0
Spence	1.000	3	1	0	0	0
Stevens	1.000	7	8	1	0	0
Wetzel	.945	94	100	4	6	0

ACL CUBS

ROOKIE

ARIZONA COMPLEX LEAGUE

Batting	B-T	HT	WT	DOB	AVG	vLH	vRH	G	AB	R	H	2B	3B	HR	RBI	BB	HBP	SH	SF	SO	SB	CS	SLG	OBP
Brayan Altuve	R-R	5-11	160	1-22-03	.158	.231	.143	27	76	8	12	2	0	1	6	8	1	0	0	30	5	1	.224	.247
Miguel Amaya	R-R	6-2	230	3-9-99	.216	.250	.212	12	37	4	8	0	0	2	4	7	0	0	0	13	0	0	.378	.341
Moises Ballesteros	L-R	5-10	195	11-8-03	.268	.308	.262	32	97	12	26	5	0	7	18	13	0	0	0	19	0	0	.536	.355
Parker Chavers	L-R	5-11	185	7-25-98	.267	.000	.286	5	15	4	4	0	0	0	2	1	0	0	1	4	2	0	.267	.294
Ke'Shun Collier	L-R	5-8	160	12-21-00	.500	.600	.400	3	10	3	5	1	0	0	1	1	0	0	0	3	1	0	.600	.545
Raino Coran	R-R	6-4	210	5-13-02	.169	.500	.136	24	65	9	11	1	1	1	8	9	0	0	0	33	0	2	.262	.270
Brennen Davis	R-R	6-4	210	11-2-99	.143	.333	.000	5	14	2	2	0	0	1	2	2	1	0	0	5	0	0	.357	.294
Miguel Fabrizio	L-R	5-11	178	9-26-00	.294	.286	.296	14	34	12	10	1	1	1	6	10	1	0	0	19	3	2	.471	.467
Reivaj Garcia	B-R	5-11	175	8-12-01	.267	.667	.222	10	30	5	8	1	0	1	8	4	0	0	1	4	1	0	.400	.343
Andy Garriola	R-R	6-5	235	12-15-99	.083	.333	.000	4	12	1	1	1	0	0	0	1	0	0	0	7	0	0	.167	.154
Dilan Granadillo	B-R	5-9	175	5-18-01	.174	.375	.132	26	46	5	8	1	0	1	6	6	1	0	0	17	1	1	.261	.283
Michael Hermosillo	R-R	6-0	205	1-17-95	.214	.000	.273	4	14	2	3	0	0	0	0	0	0	0	0	6	2	0	.214	.214
Cristian Hernandez	R-R	6-2	175	12-13-03	.261	.333	.248	44	157	21	41	4	1	3	21	13	2	0	3	53	6	3	.357	.320
Frank Hernandez	R-R	5-11	185	12-10-01	.305	.222	.320	24	59	7	18	3	0	0	5	8	2	0	0	15	3	1	.356	.406
Josue Huma	B-R	6-1	175	3-17-00	.000	.000	--	1	1	0	0	0	0	0	0	0	0	0	0	0	0	0	.000	.000
Haydn McGeary	R-R	6-5	235	10-9-99	.222	.200	.231	6	18	1	4	1	0	0	3	3	0	0	0	6	0	0	.278	.333
Ismael Mena	L-L	6-3	185	11-30-02	.264	.294	.258	34	110	20	29	8	0	0	13	10	1	0	0	29	7	6	.336	.331
Fredy Montenegro	R-R	5-10	160	9-12-03	.333	.000	.500	4	3	0	1	0	0	0	1	0	0	0	0	0	0	0	.333	.333
Cristian More	L-L	5-10	170	8-11-01	.300	.267	.306	34	100	19	30	8	2	1	21	10	4	1	3	19	9	2	.450	.376
Rafael Morel	R-R	6-0	170	11-22-01	.278	.412	.257	39	126	20	35	7	2	0	15	13	4	0	2	41	4	2	.365	.359
Carlos Morfa	R-R	6-2	190	12-2-00	.200	.000	.233	17	35	7	7	1	0	1	4	6	1	0	0	14	0	0	.314	.333
Christian Olivo	R-R	5-11	168	10-29-03	.193	.267	.178	36	88	16	17	1	1	0	6	12	5	2	0	20	10	2	.227	.324
Miguel Pabon	R-R	6-0	165	8-30-00	.162	.000	.172	30	68	13	11	2	0	1	8	20	1	0	2	30	0	0	.235	.352
Christopher Paciolla	R-R	6-2	185	3-16-04	.143	.143	.143	7	21	2	3	0	0	1	3	2	2	0	0	7	1	0	.286	.280
Reginald Preciado	B-R	6-4	185	5-16-03	.212	.375	.160	10	33	5	7	2	1	0	4	4	0	0	0	14	0	0	.333	.297
Ronnier Quintero	L-R	5-10	175	11-13-02	.162	.167	.161	19	37	4	6	0	0	0	3	8	0	0	0	11	0	0	.162	.311
Esteban Quiroz	L-R	5-6	199	2-17-92	.750	.500	.833	4	8	6	6	2	0	0	1	3	1	0	0	0	2	0	1.000	.833
Pedro Ramirez	B-R	5-9	165	4-1-04	.329	.217	.350	43	146	26	48	9	5	4	14	17	0	0	0	26	11	4	.541	.399
Alejandro Rivero	R-R	6-2	200	6-8-97	.217	.000	.227	11	23	5	5	0	0	2	8	2	6	0	1	7	0	0	.478	.406
Joanfran Rojas	R-R	5-10	160	9-19-01	.083	.500	.000	8	12	4	1	1	0	0	1	3	0	0	0	4	1	0	.167	.267
Bryan Serra	L-R	5-10	173	9-7-98	.333	--	.333	4	6	1	2	0	1	0	0	2	0	0	0	1	0	0	.667	.500
Wally Soto	L-R	5-10	170	1-5-03	.111	--	.111	8	9	0	1	0	0	0	1	2	0	0	0	5	0	0	.111	.273
Liam Spence	R-R	6-1	190	4-9-98	.158	.250	.151	21	57	8	9	3	1	1	8	8	2	0	0	15	0	0	.298	.284
Anderson Suriel	L-L	6-1	175	4-11-03	.258	.000	.296	14	31	5	8	0	0	0	5	4	1	0	0	5	2	1	.258	.361
Esmarly Tatis	B-R	5-10	165	4-11-00	.318	.000	.333	11	22	5	7	1	1	0	4	4	0	0	1	3	1	2	.455	.407
Matt Warkentin	R-L	6-6	250	1-28-97	.667	1.000	.500	1	3	0	2	0	0	0	0	1	0	0	0	0	0	0	.667	.750

Pitching	B-T	HT	WT	DOB	W	L	ERA	G	GS	CG	SV	IP	H	R	ER	HR	BB	SO	AVG	vLH	vRH	K/9	BB/9
Jose Alcila	R-R	5-11	170	4-5-00	0	2	11.42	9	0	0	1	9	17	12	11	0	6	17	.415	.545	.367	17.65	6.23
Elian Almanzar	L-R	6-4	210	2-1-00	1	1	2.12	17	0	0	0	17	6	5	4	1	19	19	.120	.087	.148	10.06	10.06
Adbert Alzolay	R-R	6-1	208	3-1-95	0	0	3.00	1	1	0	0	3	3	1	1	0	0	4	.231	.250	.200	12.00	0.00
Michael Arias	R-R	6-0	155	11-15-01	0	3	4.85	8	8	0	0	13	5	9	7	2	16	18	.119	.143	.095	12.46	11.08
Rony Baez	R-R	6-0	180	4-21-99	1	0	1.04	9	0	0	0	9	8	4	1	1	2	11	.222	.125	.250	11.42	2.08
Steven Brault	L-L	6-0	195	4-29-92	0	0	0.00	1	0	0	0	1	1	0	0	0	0	2	.250	--	.250	18.00	0.00
Yovanny Cabrera	R-R	6-2	180	3-22-01	1	1	5.68	6	2	0	0	13	11	9	8	1	10	21	.224	.267	.158	14.92	7.11
Yovanny Cruz	R-R	6-0	180	8-23-99	1	0	5.06	3	0	0	0	5	4	3	3	1	0	13	.200	.111	.273	21.94	0.00
Wilson Cunningham	L-L	6-8	185	5-19-03	0	0	0.00	2	0	0	0	2	1	0	0	0	2	3	.200	1.000	.000	16.20	10.80
Brad Deppermann	R-R	6-0	195	6-15-96	0	0	0.00	2	0	0	0	4	1	0	0	0	2	2	.091	.143	.000	4.91	4.91
Wilfri Figuereo	R-R	6-0	172	5-11-01	2	1	4.86	13	0	0	0	17	15	15	9	0	15	29	.246	.206	.296	15.66	8.10
Dominic Hambley	R-R	6-2	230	4-24-03	1	1	7.67	14	2	0	0	27	24	24	23	0	25	31	.242	.293	.207	10.33	8.33
Ben Hecht	R-R	6-2	170	5-31-95	1	0	2.08	4	0	0	0	4	3	4	1	0	4	9	.176	.333	.091	18.69	8.31
Jonathan Holder	R-R	6-2	232	6-9-93	0	0	0.00	2	1	0	0	3	1	0	0	0	1	4	.100	.200	.000	12.00	3.00
Nick Hull	R-R	6-0	205	8-21-99	1	0	0.00	1	0	0	0	1	1	0	0	0	0	1	.250	.000	.333	9.00	0.00
Chris Kachmar	R-R	6-3	180	9-3-96	0	0	1.93	3	2	0	0	5	4	1	1	0	2	4	.235	.200	.286	7.71	3.86
Grant Kipp	R-R	6-6	220	11-11-99	0	0	0.00	1	1	0	0	2	2	0	0	0	0	2	.250	.250	.250	9.00	0.00
Anthony Martinez	R-R	6-3	175	1-10-00	1	3	8.35	15	0	0	1	18	21	19	17	2	19	20	.292	.458	.208	9.82	9.33
Brody McCullough	R-R	6-4	205	6-30-00	1	0	0.00	1	0	0	0	2	2	0	0	0	0	3	.286	.000	.500	13.50	0.00
Anthony Mendez	R-R	6-1	190	8-4-02	1	0	3.18	8	0	0	0	11	8	4	4	1	8	13	.216	.263	.167	10.32	6.35
Gregori Montano	R-R	5-11	175	8-18-99	0	0	2.25	7	0	0	0	8	8	2	2	1	1	13	.250	.100	.318	14.63	1.13
Gleiber Morales	R-R	5-10	165	9-28-02	0	1	7.00	11	1	0	0	18	21	17	14	2	6	22	.304	.414	.225	11.00	3.00
Koen Moreno	R-R	6-2	170	8-1-01	0	0	4.09	5	5	0	0	11	6	6	5	1	15	16	.162	.182	.133	13.09	12.27
Kenyi Perez	R-R	6-2	165	8-9-01	0	4	5.63	11	10	0	0	24	14	16	15	0	29	30	.175	.107	.212	11.25	10.88
Mathew Peters	R-R	6-4	215	12-28-00	0	0	27.00	1	0	0	0	0	1	1	1	0	2	1	.500	.000	1.000	27.00	54.00
Starlyn Pichardo	R-R	6-0	175	1-12-04	2	1	8.64	11	4	0	0	25	20	24	24	4	28	24	.230	.300	.170	8.64	10.08
Erian Rodriguez	R-R	6-3	190	11-23-01	2	2	11.57	11	1	0	0	12	15	17	15	1	10	15	.306	.412	.250	11.57	7.71
Manuel Rodriguez	R-R	5-11	210	8-6-96	0	0	0.00	2	0	0	0	3	3	0	0	0	2	5	.273	.000	.500	15.00	6.00
Cristian Rojas	R-R	6-1	153	7-29-02	0	3	5.40	11	0	0	0	22	19	13	13	2	17	26	.235	.313	.184	10.80	7.06
Jose Romero	R-R	5-10	185	4-20-01	2	1	2.01	9	2	0	0	22	10	5	5	1	12	29	.133	.190	.061	11.69	4.84
Oliver Roque	R-R	6-3	180	1-10-02	1	1	3.26	17	2	0	3	30	17	13	11	0	11	39	.160	.217	.117	11.57	3.26
Andricson Salvador	L-L	5-11	180	7-24-00	2	2	6.10	7	0	0	1	10	8	7	7	2	3	16	.200	.000	.258	13.94	2.61
Tomy Sanchez	R-R	5-8	163	2-9-03	3	0	0.98	13	0	0	0	18	8	6	2	0	13	19	.133	.227	.079	9.33	6.38

Marino Santy	L-L	5-11	170	3-4-02	0	0	3.45	8	4	0	0	16	4	7	6	0	24	13	.091	.167	.079	7.47	13.79
Joel Sierra	R-R	6-1	190	12-31-01	0	0	13.50	1	1	0	0	1	0	1	1	0	2	2	.000	.000	.000	27.00	27.00
Alberto Sojo	R-R	5-11	160	9-23-00	0	1	15.00	7	0	0	0	6	10	10	10	0	3	6	.370	.222	.444	9.00	4.50
Sam Thoresen	R-R	6-3	210	9-21-98	0	1	15.75	4	2	0	0	4	8	8	7	0	11	6	.421	.000	.500	13.50	24.75
Kevin Valdez	R-R	6-4	185	11-13-01	0	0	9.00	4	3	0	0	7	4	9	7	0	5	13	.154	.273	.067	16.71	6.43
Didier Vargas	R-L	6-0	175	3-13-99	1	0	0.53	8	2	0	0	17	4	1	1	0	8	26	.073	.000	.093	13.76	4.24

Fielding

C: Ballesteros 24, Granadillo 26, McGeary 2, Montenegro 1, Pabon 13, Quintero 16, Soto 5. **1B:** Fabrizio 12, Garcia 3, McGeary 3, Pabon 15, Rivero 10, Serra 1, Spence 11, Suriel 9, Warkentin 1. **2B:** Garcia 4, Hernandez 5, Morel 1, Olivo 6, Paciolla 2, Quiroz 3, Ramirez 26, Rojas 3, Serra 1, Spence 3, Tatis 9. **3B:** Garcia 1, Morel 38, Paciolla 3, Ramirez 13, Rojas 2, Tatis 1. **SS:** Garcia 2, Hernandez 37, Olivo 3, Paciolla 2, Preciado 8, Rojas 2, Spence 6. **OF:** Altuve 23, Chavers 5, Collier 3, Coran 21, Davis 2, Garriola 4, Hermosillo 3, Hernandez 24, Mena 32, More 33, Morfa 11, Olvio 28, Suriel 4.

DSL CUBS BLUE — *ROOKIE*

Batting	B-T	HT	WT	DOB	AVG	vLH	vRH	G	AB	R	H	2B	3B	HR	RBI	BB	HBP	SH	SF	SO	SB	CS	SLG	OBP
Josefrailin Alcantara	L-R	5-11	150	11-12-04	.136	.143	.134	40	118	18	16	2	3	2	10	17	7	0	0	47	21	4	.254	.282
Carlos Altuve	R-R	5-11	192	1-6-05	.321	.500	.250	13	28	1	9	2	0	0	3	3	0	0	0	5	0	1	.393	.387
2-team total (17 DSL Cubs Red)					.297	.471	.234	30	64	3	19	2	0	0	9	4	1	0	0	11	0	1	.328	.348
Albert Belliard	L-L	5-8	150	11-18-04	.155	.158	.155	37	103	6	16	5	0	0	6	7	2	1	0	28	5	3	.204	.223
Abel De Leon	R-R	5-11	180	8-20-04	.197	.333	.152	28	61	3	12	3	0	1	4	10	2	0	0	27	2	2	.295	.329
Jairo Diaz	L-R	5-10	180	7-14-04	.196	.211	.192	38	97	13	19	2	1	0	9	11	0	0	2	22	2	0	.237	.273
Jose Escobar	L-R	5-10	165	9-13-04	.288	.200	.308	36	111	19	32	4	4	3	23	8	3	0	0	22	12	2	.477	.352
2-team total (14 DSL Cubs Red)					.295	.176	.328	50	156	28	46	5	7	4	33	12	5	0	2	30	14	3	.494	.360
Moises Febrillet	R-R	6-2	165	11-1-04	.181	.143	.190	41	105	18	19	6	1	0	7	14	2	0	1	40	12	4	.257	.287
Daniel Ferreira	R-R	5-10	170	10-2-03	.176	.050	.198	48	131	14	23	3	2	0	14	25	1	0	1	56	7	4	.229	.310
Dilver Gomez	R-R	5-10	190	1-15-04	.255	.182	.273	26	55	5	14	1	3	0	7	7	2	0	0	21	3	1	.382	.359
Raul Guzman	L-L	5-11	145	10-18-03	.276	.346	.256	40	116	29	32	3	4	0	9	20	2	0	1	34	8	4	.371	.388
Jose Herrera	R-R	5-11	162	4-3-03	.223	.375	.192	34	94	15	21	5	1	6	18	14	5	0	2	28	2	3	.489	.348
Geuri Lubo	R-R	6-2	185	9-24-03	.261	.067	.292	33	111	11	29	8	0	3	24	3	4	0	1	21	8	3	.414	.303
Luis Maza	L-R	5-10	150	10-10-02	.222	.250	.219	18	36	5	8	2	0	0	2	8	1	0	1	11	3	1	.278	.370
2-team total (22 DSL Cubs Red)					.200	.091	.216	40	85	10	17	3	0	0	5	26	2	0	2	30	5	5	.235	.391
Fredy Montenegro	R-R	5-10	160	9-12-03	.188	--	.188	6	16	3	3	0	0	0	1	2	0	0	0	0	0	0	.188	.278
Jefferson Rojas	R-R	5-10	150	4-25-05	.303	.484	.254	45	145	27	44	6	3	1	19	16	6	0	2	18	15	2	.407	.391
Sandy Sanchez	B-R	5-10	150	7-15-05	.245	.211	.253	35	106	17	26	2	2	0	6	14	1	2	0	22	11	4	.302	.339
Esmarly Tatis	B-R	5-10	165	4-11-00	.303	.286	.308	9	33	5	10	3	1	0	4	2	1	0	1	3	2	2	.455	.351
Jerry Torres	L-R	6-1	185	10-4-02	.143	.000	.167	41	105	13	15	2	0	0	12	22	2	0	1	21	4	5	.162	.300
Edward Vargas	R-R	6-2	165	1-22-04	.257	.364	.237	23	70	9	18	2	0	0	3	6	0	0	0	14	6	2	.286	.316

Pitching	B-T	HT	WT	DOB	W	L	ERA	G	GS	CG	SV	IP	H	R	ER	HR	BB	SO	AVG	vLH	vRH	K/9	BB/9
Gabriel Agrazal	R-R	6-1	185	9-10-03	0	1	2.30	12	11	0	0	47	35	14	12	2	14	37	.203	.230	.189	7.09	2.68
David Bracho	R-R	6-0	160	2-24-05	0	4	8.86	9	8	0	0	21	23	23	21	3	16	18	.291	.208	.327	7.59	6.75
Diego Dugarte	R-R	6-1	182	11-8-02	3	2	2.92	12	5	0	0	37	20	24	12	2	24	20	.155	.163	.151	4.86	5.84
Leury Gomez	R-R	6-2	160	9-16-02	3	3	3.42	16	0	0	1	26	23	16	10	2	12	27	.235	.276	.217	9.23	4.10
Charbel Gonzalez	R-R	6-2	180	3-13-04	0	0	9.53	3	0	0	0	6	4	7	6	2	11	4	.235	.333	.182	6.35	17.47
2-team total (6 DSL Cubs Red)					2	0	6.32	9	1	0	1	16	12	15	11	3	26	17	.226	.278	.200	9.77	14.94
Yoendris Gonzalez	R-R	5-11	215	11-27-02	0	1	4.50	3	2	0	0	4	4	3	2	0	2	7	.286	.167	.375	15.75	4.50
Zhiorman Imbriano	L-L	6-0	180	1-30-03	1	0	6.50	9	1	0	1	18	16	13	13	1	14	15	.246	.300	.236	7.50	7.00
Jair Jimenez	R-R	6-1	172	4-9-02	4	1	6.12	14	0	0	4	25	24	24	17	1	25	22	.255	.080	.319	7.92	9.00
Joel Jimenez	R-R	6-0	160	7-23-00	1	4	6.67	10	3	0	0	27	27	24	20	2	24	30	.248	.270	.236	10.00	8.00
Adrian Martinez	R-R	6-2	190	10-24-02	1	4	10.13	14	8	0	0	35	51	49	39	2	32	31	.340	.404	.311	8.05	8.31
Fredy Montenegro	R-R	5-10	160	9-12-03	0	0	0.00	1	0	0	0	0	1	0	0	0	0	0	.500	.000	1.000	0.00	0.00
Abel Moya	R-R	6-1	172	6-6-01	4	0	4.33	15	0	0	1	35	35	20	17	2	16	26	.265	.317	.242	6.62	4.08
Eligio Paredes	R-R	6-1	190	7-10-02	0	3	3.45	9	9	0	0	29	25	16	11	0	11	36	.240	.395	.152	11.30	3.45
Welington Quintero	R-R	6-0	185	12-17-00	1	1	5.12	15	0	0	2	32	33	24	18	3	17	29	.264	.359	.221	8.24	4.83
Jensi Ramirez	R-R	5-11	170	12-31-03	0	1	13.50	5	0	0	0	7	8	15	11	2	9	8	.258	.077	.389	9.82	11.05
Luis R. Reyes	R-R	6-0	185	10-22-02	2	6	4.80	18	0	0	4	30	25	21	16	2	16	38	.229	.194	.247	11.40	4.80
Alfredo Romero	R-R	6-3	175	6-27-03	2	2	3.43	7	3	0	0	21	10	11	8	3	12	21	.137	.100	.151	9.00	5.14
2-team total (1 DSL Cubs Red)					3	2	3.52	8	3	0	0	23	13	12	9	3	13	24	.159	.125	.172	9.39	5.09
Adrian Santana	R-R	6-1	165	9-4-03	1	1	2.92	8	0	0	1	12	14	7	4	0	5	7	.269	.231	.282	5.11	3.65
2-team total (2 DSL Cubs Red)					1	1	4.50	10	0	0	1	14	16	10	7	0	11	9	.276	.214	.295	5.79	7.07
Jerry Torres	L-R	6-1	185	10-4-02	0	0	20.25	2	0	0	0	3	8	6	6	1	2	1	.500	.667	.400	3.38	6.75
Yafrerlyn Vasquez	R-R	6-1	190	3-18-04	0	3	7.24	12	10	0	0	27	22	25	22	1	29	28	.208	.143	.239	9.22	9.55

Fielding

C: Altuve 5, De Leon 27, Diaz 30, Gomez 17, Montenegro 2. **1B:** Altuve 7, Diaz 5, Gomez 1, Herrera 31, Montenegro 4, Sanchez 1, Torres 17. **2B:** Escobar 6, Febrillet 3, Lubo 2, Maza 8, Rojas 26, Sanchez 20, Tatis 4. **3B:** Diaz 1, Escobar 7, Febrillet 31, Lubo 2, Maza 10, Rojas 5, Sanchez 8, Tatis 3. **SS:** Escobar 26, Febrillet 5, Lubo 28, Rojas 4, Sanchez 3, Tatis 2. **OF:** Alcantara 31, Belliard 36, Ferreira 46, Guzman 37, Torres 20, Vargas 16.

DSL CUBS RED — ROOKIE

Batting	B-T	HT	WT	DOB	AVG	vLH	vRH	G	AB	R	H	2B	3B	HR	RBI	BB	HBP	SH	SF	SO	SB	CS	SLG	OBP
Yoanis Aleksandrov	R-R	6-2	220	7-29-04	.021	.125	.000	19	47	2	1	0	0	0	1	1	2	0	0	35	0	0	.021	.080
Carlos Altuve	R-R	5-11	192	1-6-05	.278	.444	.222	17	36	2	10	0	0	0	6	1	1	0	0	6	0	0	.278	.316
2-team total (13 DSL Cubs Blue)					.297	.471	.234	30	64	3	19	2	0	0	9	4	1	0	0	11	0	1	.328	.348
Daniel Benschop	R-R	6-2	185	5-26-05	.221	.259	.209	34	113	10	25	4	1	0	4	7	3	0	1	27	5	5	.274	.282
Andres Bonolis	R-R	6-0	175	5-28-04	.250	--	.250	3	4	1	1	0	0	0	1	0	0	0	0	0	0	0	.250	.250
Elizaul Chalas	B-R	5-10	150	1-8-05	.247	.286	.240	40	89	16	22	6	1	1	11	13	2	0	1	24	9	3	.371	.352
Andrws Cruz	R-R	5-10	150	12-3-02	.229	.176	.244	45	153	27	35	6	1	1	9	19	1	0	1	14	23	5	.301	.316
Darlyn De Leon	L-R	5-8	150	2-11-05	.196	.200	.194	48	143	25	28	2	3	0	9	22	5	0	1	40	15	2	.252	.322
Joan Delgado	R-R	5-11	165	12-7-04	.250	.300	.235	29	88	10	22	7	3	0	13	9	1	0	0	36	7	3	.398	.327
Yidel Diaz	R-R	5-10	203	11-3-04	.205	.269	.186	39	112	13	23	3	2	2	14	13	3	0	1	39	3	2	.321	.302
Jose Escobar	L-R	5-10	165	9-13-04	.311	.143	.387	14	45	9	14	1	3	1	10	4	2	0	2	8	2	1	.533	.377
2-team total (36 DSL Cubs Blue)					.295	.176	.328	50	156	28	46	5	7	4	33	12	5	0	2	30	14	3	.494	.360
Alexis Hernandez	R-R	6-1	155	12-27-04	.244	.267	.237	36	123	19	30	6	0	2	13	16	1	0	1	27	10	4	.341	.333
Oferman Hernandez	L-R	6-0	160	10-15-03	.250	.217	.263	32	80	11	20	4	0	0	12	20	2	1	1	19	7	2	.300	.408
Erbin Jaque	R-R	5-9	170	9-7-02	.213	.114	.245	49	141	26	30	4	2	2	15	10	15	0	0	53	22	4	.312	.331
Luis Maza	L-R	5-10	150	10-10-02	.184	.000	.214	22	49	5	9	1	0	0	3	18	1	0	1	19	2	4	.204	.406
2-team total (18 DSL Cubs Blue)					.200	.091	.216	40	85	10	17	3	0	0	5	26	2	0	2	30	5	5	.235	.391
Josias Ramirez	R-R	6-0	155	7-8-05	.133	.056	.158	32	75	10	10	1	1	2	7	13	3	0	1	38	1	2	.253	.283
Carlos Ramos	R-R	5-10	170	12-14-03	.235	.138	.274	45	102	22	24	5	1	0	11	23	5	0	0	12	5	5	.304	.400
Lizardo Ruiz	R-R	5-11	165	8-20-02	.306	.333	.300	25	62	9	19	4	1	2	14	8	2	0	0	7	2	2	.500	.403
Adan Sanchez	R-R	6-0	205	5-24-05	.328	.387	.310	47	131	21	43	4	2	0	28	24	7	0	2	26	4	3	.389	.451
Julio Valdez	R-R	6-2	212	1-14-05	.160	.150	.164	25	81	11	13	2	0	0	4	6	2	0	0	32	1	1	.185	.236

Pitching	B-T	HT	WT	DOB	W	L	ERA	G	GS	CG	SV	IP	H	R	ER	HR	BB	SO	AVG	vLH	vRH	K/9	BB/9
Melvyn Amador	L-L	5-10	172	1-8-04	0	4	5.50	12	12	0	0	34	31	33	21	1	30	22	.242	.258	.237	5.77	7.86
Juan Bello	R-R	6-1	173	4-6-04	0	2	4.02	9	8	0	0	31	24	16	14	3	7	34	.205	.118	.241	9.77	2.01
Yohan Crispin	R-R	6-2	175	7-15-01	0	0	4.26	14	0	0	5	19	14	12	9	3	9	24	.203	.214	.195	11.37	4.26
Kenneddy Delgado	R-R	6-0	170	9-21-03	2	1	4.66	13	0	0	5	19	15	15	10	0	18	22	.221	.200	.229	10.24	8.38
Charbel Gonzalez	R-R	6-2	180	3-13-04	2	0	4.50	6	1	0	1	10	8	8	5	1	15	13	.222	.250	.208	11.70	13.50
2-team total (3 DSL Cubs Blue)					2	0	6.32	9	1	0	1	16	12	15	11	3	26	17	.226	.278	.200	9.77	14.94
Stanley Guzman	R-R	6-3	170	12-28-99	0	3	4.79	14	0	0	2	21	13	17	11	0	14	35	.173	.214	.149	15.24	6.10
Scarlyn Lebron	R-R	6-3	178	1-2-02	4	2	2.41	17	0	0	0	34	24	16	9	2	10	39	.198	.244	.171	10.43	2.67
Fraimin Marte	R-R	6-3	170	7-21-01	4	3	3.79	17	0	0	2	36	24	16	15	1	23	37	.197	.176	.205	9.34	5.80
Wilme Mora	R-R	6-5	180	6-28-03	1	1	5.59	6	3	0	0	10	9	7	6	0	11	16	.243	.267	.227	14.90	10.24
David Olivo	R-R	6-0	170	9-28-02	1	0	8.38	14	0	0	0	19	27	23	18	1	27	18	.338	.478	.281	8.38	12.57
Carlos Ramos	R-R	5-10	170	12-14-03	0	0	0.00	1	0	0	0	0	0	0	0	0	1	1	.000	.000	--	27.00	27.00
Luis A. Reyes	R-R	6-3	220	10-23-03	3	4	7.07	13	3	0	0	28	38	28	22	3	16	36	.325	.319	.329	11.57	5.14
Samuel Rodriguez	L-L	6-3	178	9-2-01	0	1	11.15	8	3	0	0	15	25	23	19	1	10	16	.338	.385	.328	9.39	5.87
Wilber Rodriguez	R-R	6-4	220	1-9-00	1	1	1.35	8	0	0	0	13	7	2	2	0	5	20	.152	.200	.129	13.50	3.38
Yenrri Rojas	R-R	6-1	186	11-30-03	0	6	4.28	12	12	0	0	48	57	27	23	1	14	28	.305	.345	.287	5.21	2.61
Alfredo Romero	R-R	6-3	175	6-27-03	1	0	4.50	1	0	0	0	2	3	1	1	0	1	3	.333	.250	.400	13.50	4.50
2-team total (7 DSL Cubs Blue)					3	2	3.52	8	3	0	0	23	13	12	9	3	13	24	.159	.125	.172	9.39	5.09
Lizardo Ruiz	R-R	5-11	165	8-20-02	0	0	0.00	1	0	0	0	0	0	0	0	0	0	1	.000	.000	--	27.00	0.00
Adrian Santana	R-R	6-1	165	9-4-03	0	0	16.20	2	0	0	0	2	2	3	3	0	6	2	.333	.000	.400	10.80	32.40
2-team total (8 DSL Cubs Blue)					1	1	4.50	10	0	0	1	14	16	10	7	0	11	9	.276	.214	.295	5.79	7.07
Freilyn Silverio	R-R	6-3	180	1-24-05	0	3	4.70	10	10	0	0	31	22	18	16	3	14	39	.200	.178	.215	11.45	4.11
Runelvis Toribio	R-R	6-1	155	5-2-03	3	3	3.74	13	0	0	0	22	14	10	9	1	28	31	.194	.087	.245	12.88	11.63
Kevin Valdez	R-R	6-4	185	11-13-01	0	3	1.63	8	8	0	0	28	15	14	5	0	17	38	.153	.174	.147	12.36	5.53
Irving Vazquez	R-R	6-3	195	7-13-03	0	1	6.55	16	0	0	0	22	15	22	16	1	28	23	.192	.071	.260	9.41	11.45

Fielding

C: Aleksandrov 7, Altuve 7, Diaz 30, Ramos 24, Sanchez 29. **1B:** Altuve 6, Chalas 1, Cruz 1, Diaz 17, Hernandez 13, Ramos 19, Ruiz 21, Sanchez 6. **2B:** Chalas 27, Cruz 15, De Leon 2, Delgado 10, Escobar 4, Hernandez 3, Maza 7, Ramos 3. **3B:** Chalas 10, Cruz 11, De Leon 3, Delgado 5, Diaz 1, Escobar 7, Maza 12, Ramos 4, Ruiz 3, Sanchez 11. **SS:** Cruz 23, Delgado 9, Escobar 1, Hernandez 31, Ruiz 1. **OF:** Benschop 34, Bonolis 3, De Leon 36, Hernandez 22, Jaque 45, Ramirez 30, Valdez 23.

Chicago White Sox

SEASON IN A SENTENCE: Widely favored to win the AL Central and carrying a club-record payroll estimated at $192 million, the White Sox stumbled out of the gates, struggled to surmount the .500 mark and never sustained positive momentum thanks in part to key injuries, a teamwide power outage and poor performances by several stars. Hall of Fame manager Tony La Russa didn't make it to the finish line as the White Sox came in second.

HIGH POINT: Andrew Vaughn, whose 17 homers led the White Sox, hit a grand slam to power the Sox to an 11-5 win at Detroit, getting Chicago to 76-71 ahead of a day off and subsequent three-game series against Cleveland. The victory brought the Sox to a season-high five games better than .500 and within 3.5 games of first place.

LOW POINT: Two sweeps stand out. The Guardians swept the White Sox in the subsequent series to kick off a season-long eight-game Sox losing streak that essentially ended the AL Central race. A late-August home sweep against the Diamondbacks was the last series La Russa managed; health issues (and the team's September rally under interim manager Miguel Cairo) kept him off the bench the rest of the way.

NOTABLE ROOKIES: Righty Davis Martin provided consistent length as a spot-starter and long man, going at least five innings in 10 of his 14 outings (nine starts). Corner slugger Jake Burger had injuries to both wrists sideline him in early July after a solid start, where he showed intriguing power. Lefty Tanner Banks and righty Jimmy Lambert (older brother of Rockies righthander Peter Lambert) combined for 100 solid bullpen innings.

KEY TRANSACTIONS: Veteran Johnny Cueto, signed in spring training for depth, proved a godsend in the rotation, going 8-10, 3.35 while ranking third on the team in innings. The White Sox lost shortstop Tim Anderson to injury in early August but were able to add veteran Elvis Andrus from Oakland, and Andrus contributed nine homers in just 43 games.

ON THE FARM: The White Sox had arguably the worst farm system in baseball a year ago. Now, it's still bottom tier, but significantly improved. Fast=developing shortstop Colson Montgomery has established himself as one of the better shortstop prospects in the minors as he lept three levels in 2022.

OPENING DAY PAYROLL: $190,370,219 (seventh)

PLAYERS OF THE YEAR

MAJOR LEAGUE

Dylan Cease
RHP
14-8, 2.20 ERA
227 SO, 78 BB, 184 IP
Career-best 1.11 WHIP

MINOR LEAGUE

Colson Montgomery, SS
(LoA/HiA/AA)
.274/.381/.429
11 HR in 96 G

ORGANIZATION LEADERS

Batting — *Minimum 250 AB

MAJORS

*AVG	José Abreu	.304
*OPS	Eloy Jiménez	.858
HR	Andrew Vaughn	17
RBI	Andrew Vaughn	76

MINORS

*AVG	Lenyn Sosa, Birmingham, Charlotte	.315
*OBP	Raudy Read, Birmingham, Charlotte	.396
*SLG	Raudy Read, Birmingham, Charlotte	.557
*OPS	Raudy Read, Birmingham, Charlotte	.953
R	Craig Dedelow, Birmingham, Charlotte	88
H	Lenyn Sosa, Birmingham, Charlotte	152
TB	Mark Payton, Charlotte	254
2B	Luis Mieses, Winston-Salem, Birmingham	39
3B	Loidel Chapelli, Winston-Salem	7
HR	Craig Dedelow, Birmingham, Charlotte	27
RBI	Mark Payton, Charlotte	95
BB	Craig Dedelow, Birmingham, Charlotte	70
SO	Craig Dedelow, Birmingham, Charlotte	214
SB	Duke Ellis, Winston-Salem, Birmingham	57

Pitching — #Minimum 75 IP

MAJORS

W	Dylan Cease	14
#ERA	Dylan Cease	2.20
SO	Dylan Cease	227
SV	Liam Hendriks	37

MINORS

W	Scott Blewett, Birmingham, Charlotte	8
L	3 tied	11
#ERA	Tommy Sommer, Kannapolis, Winston-Salem	2.71
G	Andrew Perez, Charlotte	59
GS	Sean Burke, Birmingham, Winston-Salem, Charlotte	26
GS	Andrew Dalquist, Winston-Salem, Birmingham	26
SV	Adisyn Coffey, Kannapolis	7
IP	John Parke, Charlotte	134
BB	Jason Bilous, Birmingham, Charlotte	79
SO	Sean Burke, Birmingham, Winston-Salem, Charlotte	137
#AVG	Tommy Sommer, Kannapolis, Winston-Salem	.208

2022 PERFORMANCE

General Manager: Rick Hahn. **Farm Director:** Chris Getz. **Scouting Director:** Mike Shirley.

Class	Team	League	W	L	PCT	Finish	Manager
Majors	Chicago White Sox	American	81	81	.500	8th (15)	Tony La Russa
Triple-A	Charlotte Knights	International	58	92	.387	20th (20)	Julio Mosquera
Double-A	Birmingham Barons	Southern	61	77	.442	8th (8)	Justin Jirschele
High-A	Winston-Salem Dash	South Atlantic	58	74	.439	10th (12)	Lorenzo Bundy
Low-A	Kannapolis Cannon Ballers	Carolina	58	74	.439	9th (12)	Guillermo Quiroz
Rookie	ACL White Sox	Arizona Complex	26	28	.481	9th (18)	Pat Leyland
Overall 2022 Minor League Record			293	371	.441	28th (30)	

ORGANIZATION STATISTICS

CHICAGO WHITE SOX

AMERICAN LEAGUE

Batting	B-T	HT	WT	DOB	AVG	vLH	vRH	G	AB	R	H	2B	3B	HR	RBI	BB	HBP	SH	SF	SO	SB	CS	SLG	OBP
Jose Abreu	R-R	6-3	235	1-29-87	.304	.294	.307	157	601	85	183	40	0	15	75	62	12	0	4	110	0	0	.446	.378
Tim Anderson	R-R	6-1	185	6-23-93	.301	.397	.281	79	332	50	100	13	0	6	25	14	5	0	0	55	13	0	.395	.339
Elvis Andrus	R-R	6-0	210	8-26-88	.271	.349	.246	43	181	25	49	8	0	9	28	9	1	0	0	30	11	0	.464	.309
2-team total (106 Oakland Athletics)					.249	.283	.236	149	535	66	133	32	0	17	58	39	3	0	0	92	18	4	.404	.303
Jake Burger	R-R	6-2	230	4-10-96	.250	.326	.224	51	168	20	42	9	1	8	26	10	3	1	1	56	0	0	.458	.302
Adam Engel	R-R	6-2	215	12-9-91	.224	.141	.259	119	245	32	55	13	1	2	17	11	4	0	0	76	12	4	.310	.269
Leury Garcia	B-R	5-8	190	3-18-91	.210	.188	.216	97	300	38	63	8	0	3	20	7	3	2	3	65	2	0	.267	.233
Romy Gonzalez	R-R	6-1	215	9-6-96	.238	.314	.200	32	105	15	25	4	1	2	11	2	1	0	1	39	0	1	.352	.257
Yasmani Grandal	B-R	6-2	225	11-8-88	.202	.257	.186	99	327	15	66	7	0	5	27	45	2	0	2	79	1	0	.269	.301
Josh Harrison	R-R	5-8	190	7-8-87	.256	.250	.258	119	386	50	99	19	2	7	27	21	14	2	2	71	2	1	.370	.317
Adam Haseley	L-L	6-1	190	4-12-96	.238	.000	.263	14	21	4	5	0	0	0	2	3	0	1	0	7	0	0	.238	.333
Eloy Jimenez	R-R	6-4	240	11-27-96	.295	.300	.293	84	292	40	86	12	0	16	54	28	3	0	4	72	0	0	.500	.358
Reese McGuire	L-R	6-0	218	3-2-95	.225	.143	.244	53	151	12	34	9	0	0	10	6	2	5	2	33	0	0	.285	.261
2-team total (36 Boston Red Sox)					.269	.262	.271	89	249	25	67	14	1	3	22	12	3	6	3	56	1	0	.369	.307
Danny Mendick	R-R	5-10	195	9-28-93	.289	.360	.264	31	97	22	28	4	1	3	15	7	1	1	0	23	1	0	.443	.343
Yoan Moncada	B-R	6-2	225	5-27-95	.212	.241	.204	104	397	41	84	18	1	12	51	32	2	1	1	114	2	0	.353	.273
Mark Payton	L-L	5-8	180	12-7-91	.143	.000	.150	8	21	3	3	0	0	0	1	4	0	0	0	4	0	0	.143	.280
Carlos Perez	R-R	5-11	205	9-10-96	.222	.000	.267	7	18	0	4	2	0	0	2	0	0	0	0	2	0	0	.333	.222
AJ Pollock	R-R	6-1	210	12-5-87	.245	.286	.231	138	489	61	120	26	1	14	56	32	2	0	4	98	3	1	.389	.292
Luis Robert	R-R	6-2	220	8-3-97	.284	.354	.266	98	380	54	108	18	0	12	56	17	3	0	1	77	11	3	.426	.319
Gavin Sheets	L-L	6-5	230	4-23-96	.241	.171	.250	124	377	34	91	19	0	15	53	27	3	0	3	86	0	0	.411	.295
Lenyn Sosa	R-R	6-0	180	1-25-00	.114	.000	.148	11	35	3	4	1	0	1	1	1	0	0	0	12	0	0	.229	.139
Andrew Vaughn	R-R	6-0	215	4-3-98	.271	.307	.260	134	510	60	138	28	1	17	76	31	9	0	5	96	0	0	.429	.321
Seby Zavala	R-R	5-11	205	8-28-93	.270	.216	.284	61	178	22	48	14	0	2	21	19	3	3	2	64	0	0	.382	.347

Pitching	B-T	HT	WT	DOB	W	L	ERA	G	GS	CG	SV	IP	H	R	ER	HR	BB	SO	AVG	vLH	vRH	K/9	BB/9
Tanner Banks	R-L	6-1	210	10-24-91	2	0	3.06	35	0	0	0	53	42	25	18	5	18	49	.213	.246	.199	8.32	3.06
Aaron Bummer	L-L	6-3	215	9-21-93	2	1	2.36	32	0	0	2	27	30	11	7	2	10	30	.288	.231	.323	10.13	3.38
Ryan Burr	R-R	6-4	220	5-28-94	1	1	6.00	8	0	0	0	9	8	7	6	3	4	7	.229	.286	.190	7.00	4.00
Dylan Cease	R-R	6-2	195	12-28-95	14	8	2.20	32	32	1	0	184	126	55	45	16	78	227	.190	.219	.163	11.10	3.82
Kyle Crick	L-R	6-4	225	11-30-92	2	0	4.02	14	0	0	0	16	10	7	7	0	11	19	.189	.286	.125	10.91	6.32
Johnny Cueto	R-R	5-11	229	2-15-86	8	10	3.35	25	24	1	0	158	161	66	59	15	33	102	.267	.277	.258	5.80	1.88
Jake Diekman	R-L	6-4	195	1-21-87	0	3	6.52	26	0	0	0	19	25	18	14	4	12	28	.301	.325	.279	13.03	5.59
2-team total (44 Boston Red Sox)					5	4	4.99	70	0	0	1	58	52	40	32	9	42	79	.241	.250	.234	12.33	6.55
Matt Foster	R-R	6-0	215	1-27-95	1	2	4.40	48	0	0	1	45	43	25	22	6	17	42	.247	.279	.226	8.40	3.40
Lucas Giolito	R-R	6-6	245	7-14-94	11	9	4.90	30	30	0	0	162	171	92	88	24	61	177	.272	.217	.312	9.85	3.40
Kendall Graveman	R-R	6-2	200	12-21-90	3	4	3.18	65	0	0	6	65	65	29	23	5	26	66	.257	.260	.254	9.14	3.60
Josh Harrison	R-R	5-8	190	7-8-87	0	0	18.00	3	0	0	0	3	9	6	6	1	2	2	.563	.750	.500	6.00	6.00
Liam Hendriks	R-R	6-0	235	2-10-89	4	4	2.81	58	0	0	37	58	44	22	18	7	16	85	.210	.219	.202	13.27	2.50
Joe Kelly	R-R	6-1	174	6-9-88	1	3	6.08	43	1	0	1	37	36	26	25	2	23	53	.252	.239	.263	12.89	5.59
Dallas Keuchel	L-L	6-2	205	1-1-88	2	5	7.88	8	8	0	0	32	49	33	28	6	20	20	.343	.429	.322	5.63	5.63
2-team total (2 Texas Rangers)					2	7	9.00	10	10	0	0	42	67	47	42	7	24	27	.358	.436	.338	5.79	5.14
Michael Kopech	R-R	6-3	210	4-30-96	5	9	3.54	25	25	0	0	119	85	53	47	15	57	105	.198	.214	.186	7.92	4.30
Jimmy Lambert	R-R	6-2	190	11-18-94	1	2	3.26	42	2	0	0	47	40	18	17	4	24	45	.227	.225	.230	8.62	4.60
Reynaldo Lopez	R-R	6-1	225	1-4-94	6	4	2.76	61	1	0	0	65	51	24	20	1	11	63	.218	.239	.204	8.68	1.52
Lance Lynn	B-R	6-5	270	5-12-87	8	7	3.99	21	21	0	0	122	119	65	54	19	19	124	.247	.249	.245	9.17	1.41
Davis Martin	L-R	6-2	200	1-4-97	3	6	4.83	14	9	0	0	63	63	36	34	8	19	48	.259	.273	.243	6.82	2.70
Jose Ruiz	R-R	6-1	245	10-21-94	1	0	4.60	63	0	0	0	61	53	32	31	9	33	68	.231	.225	.236	10.09	4.90
Anderson Severino	L-L	5-10	190	9-17-94	0	0	6.14	6	0	0	0	7	7	5	5	0	4	9	.250	.250	.250	11.05	4.91
Bennett Sousa	L-L	6-3	220	4-6-95	3	0	8.41	25	0	0	1	20	25	20	19	3	10	12	.301	.378	.239	5.31	4.43
Vince Velasquez	R-R	6-3	212	6-7-92	3	3	4.78	27	9	0	0	75	68	42	40	11	25	69	.235	.222	.245	8.24	2.99

Fielding

Catcher	PCT	G	PO	A	E	DP	PB
Grandal	.993	71	546	17	4	1	8
McGuire	.995	52	401	19	2	2	2
Perez	.981	6	50	2	1	0	1
Zavala	.996	58	474	24	2	5	4

First Base	PCT	G	PO	A	E	DP
Abreu	.989	128	954	51	11	96
Grandal	.969	5	29	2	1	5
Sheets	1.000	13	68	2	0	1
Vaughn	1.000	23	150	10	0	13
Zavala	1.000	2	4	3	0	0

Second Base	PCT	G	PO	A	E	DP
Burger	1.000	3	1	1	0	1
Garcia	.983	47	72	105	3	21
Gonzalez	.989	25	34	55	1	8
Harrison	.971	90	120	186	9	34
Mendick	1.000	6	8	9	0	3
Sosa	1.000	6	9	6	0	3
Vaughn	1.000	2	0	1	0	0

Third Base	PCT	G	PO	A	E	DP
Burger	.934	37	20	65	6	4
Garcia	.938	6	8	7	1	0
Harrison	.926	23	15	35	4	2
Mendick	1.000	2	2	4	0	0
Moncada	.980	101	82	163	5	18

Shortstop	PCT	G	PO	A	E	DP
Anderson	.962	79	99	203	12	38
Andrus	.994	42	58	104	1	17
Garcia	.932	19	18	37	4	10
Gonzalez	1.000	3	7	11	0	2
Harrison	.000	2	0	0	0	0
Mendick	1.000	22	24	47	0	9
Sosa	1.000	5	6	7	0	4

Outfield	PCT	G	PO	A	E	DP
Engel	.982	115	165	1	3	0
Garcia	.952	28	40	0	2	0
Gonzalez	1.000	3	1	0	0	0
Harrison	--	2	0	0	0	0
Haseley	1.000	12	19	0	0	0
Jimenez	1.000	30	49	0	0	0
Mendick	--	1	0	0	0	0
Payton	1.000	10	11	0	0	0
Pollock	.981	158	247	7	5	3
Robert	.991	91	208	1	2	0
Sheets	.977	88	163	6	4	0
Vaughn	.970	89	129	1	4	0

CHARLOTTE KNIGHTS

INTERNATIONAL LEAGUE

TRIPLE-A

Batting	B-T	HT	WT	DOB	AVG	vLH	vRH	G	AB	R	H	2B	3B	HR	RBI	BB	HBP	SH	SF	SO	SB	CS	SLG	OBP
Micker Adolfo	R-R	6-4	225	9-11-96	.231	.228	.233	96	338	47	78	18	0	15	37	25	2	0	1	130	8	4	.417	.287
Tim Anderson	R-R	6-1	185	6-23-93	.333	.375	.206	4	15	0	5	0	0	0	1	0	0	0	0	5	0	0	.333	.333
Luis Alexander Basabe	B-R	6-0	180	8-26-96	.080	.000	.133	9	25	3	2	0	1	0	0	1	0	0	0	15	0	0	.160	.115
Jake Burger	R-R	6-2	230	4-10-96	.253	.250	.255	39	146	22	37	0	2	5	16	18	4	0	0	34	0	1	.384	.351
D.J. Burt	R-R	5-9	160	10-13-95	.207	.250	.200	13	29	4	6	1	0	0	3	4	0	0	0	8	5	0	.241	.303
Nick Ciuffo	L-R	6-0	205	3-7-95	.277	.176	.308	42	141	16	39	4	0	5	20	8	2	0	0	47	0	0	.411	.325
Oscar Colas	L-L	6-1	209	9-17-98	.387	.250	.474	7	31	5	12	2	0	2	4	2	0	0	0	12	1	1	.645	.424
Craig Dedelow	L-R	6-4	210	11-15-94	.174	.240	.148	29	86	19	15	2	1	5	15	16	2	0	1	41	6	2	.395	.314
Xavier Fernandez	R-R	5-11	245	7-15-95	.238	.224	.245	49	168	22	40	12	0	2	17	12	0	0	0	24	2	1	.345	.289
Jameson Fisher	L-R	6-2	210	12-18-93	.149	.111	.158	14	47	5	7	2	0	0	5	6	0	0	0	20	0	1	.191	.245
Leury Garcia	B-R	5-8	190	3-18-91	.250	.000	.333	1	4	0	1	0	0	0	0	0	0	0	0	2	0	0	.250	.250
Logan Glass	R-R	6-4	215	4-9-01	.250	.000	.263	8	20	5	5	1	0	1	4	0	0	0	0	10	0	0	.450	.250
Romy Gonzalez	R-R	6-1	215	9-6-96	.198	.200	.197	33	121	15	24	5	0	4	10	13	1	0	0	45	5	2	.339	.281
Yasmani Grandal	B-R	6-2	225	11-8-88	.379	.350	.444	9	29	6	11	1	0	2	5	9	0	0	0	2	0	0	.621	.526
Adam Haseley	L-L	6-1	190	4-12-96	.239	.258	.228	110	418	59	100	19	4	15	63	32	9	1	3	78	18	3	.411	.305
Eloy Jimenez	R-R	6-4	240	11-27-96	.246	.308	.227	17	57	8	14	0	0	2	6	6	0	0	0	12	0	0	.351	.317
Ryder Jones	L-R	6-2	221	6-7-94	.196	.203	.194	67	214	22	42	5	0	7	27	19	4	0	5	79	0	1	.318	.269
Patrick Kivlehan	R-R	6-2	215	12-22-89	.417	.500	.375	3	12	4	5	1	0	2	3	3	0	0	0	1	0	0	1.000	.533
Danny Mendick	R-R	5-10	195	9-28-93	.303	.200	.321	9	33	9	10	4	0	1	2	3	1	0	0	12	2	2	.515	.378
Yermin Mercedes	R-R	5-11	245	2-14-93	.230	.333	.203	25	87	14	20	5	0	4	13	20	1	0	1	24	5	1	.425	.376
Yoan Moncada	B-R	6-2	225	5-27-95	.318	.000	.467	6	22	5	7	1	0	2	5	2	0	0	1	7	0	1	.636	.360
Tyler Neslony	L-R	6-1	190	2-13-94	.266	.163	.353	27	94	10	25	4	0	2	11	7	0	0	0	24	4	2	.372	.317
Mark Payton	L-L	5-8	180	12-7-91	.293	.323	.276	119	471	85	138	31	5	25	95	54	6	2	6	76	15	6	.539	.369
Carlos Perez	R-R	5-11	205	9-10-96	.254	.273	.242	109	418	53	106	17	1	21	76	34	7	0	6	40	2	2	.450	.316
Raudy Read	R-R	6-0	220	10-29-93	.313	.333	.308	10	32	5	10	1	0	1	4	3	0	0	0	7	0	0	.438	.371
Zach Remillard	R-R	6-2	185	2-21-94	.280	.243	.299	131	418	83	117	19	2	9	52	57	8	3	5	109	19	7	.400	.373
Laz Rivera	R-R	6-1	185	9-20-94	.237	.182	.265	80	232	35	55	9	1	7	32	23	8	1	1	61	9	7	.375	.326
Luis Robert	R-R	6-2	220	8-3-97	.200	--	.200	1	5	0	1	0	0	0	0	0	0	0	0	2	0	0	.200	.200
Blake Rutherford	L-R	6-3	205	5-2-97	.271	.260	.276	116	439	57	119	26	2	13	58	21	5	0	2	91	8	5	.428	.310
Yolbert Sanchez	R-R	5-11	176	3-3-97	.280	.301	.270	113	443	44	124	16	1	3	40	27	3	1	3	71	11	9	.341	.324
Gavin Sheets	L-L	6-5	230	4-23-96	.270	.462	.167	9	37	6	10	4	0	2	7	2	0	0	0	6	0	0	.541	.308
Dwight Smith Jr.	L-R	6-0	210	10-26-92	.236	.261	.219	14	55	6	13	2	0	1	5	5	0	0	0	13	0	0	.327	.300
Lenyn Sosa	R-R	6-0	180	1-25-00	.296	.284	.303	57	226	30	67	12	0	9	31	18	2	0	1	43	3	4	.469	.352
Andrew Vaughn	R-R	6-0	215	4-3-98	.286	.000	.333	2	7	3	2	0	0	2	2	2	0	0	0	1	0	0	1.143	.444
Seby Zavala	R-R	5-11	205	8-28-93	.282	.317	.267	41	142	26	40	12	0	8	16	26	1	0	0	60	0	0	.535	.396

Pitching	B-T	HT	WT	DOB	W	L	ERA	G	GS	CG	SV	IP	H	R	ER	HR	BB	SO	AVG	vLH	vRH	K/9	BB/9
Yoan Aybar	L-L	6-2	210	7-3-97	1	3	8.90	33	0	0	0	31	34	33	31	8	31	36	.274	.310	.242	10.34	8.90
Tanner Banks	R-L	6-1	210	10-24-91	0	1	2.65	9	2	0	0	17	17	5	5	1	5	24	.258	.258	.257	12.71	2.65
Wes Benjamin	R-L	6-2	210	7-26-93	2	0	3.82	7	7	0	0	31	28	18	13	6	12	32	.237	.158	.275	9.39	3.52
Jason Bilous	R-R	6-2	185	8-11-97	1	4	10.23	12	5	0	0	22	27	30	25	4	24	27	.300	.306	.293	11.05	9.82
Scott Blewett	R-R	6-6	245	4-10-96	1	1	12.75	3	3	0	0	12	24	17	17	4	4	10	.414	.560	.303	7.50	3.00
Aaron Bummer	L-L	6-3	215	9-21-93	0	0	9.00	2	0	0	0	2	3	2	2	0	1	2	.333	.286	.500	9.00	4.50
Sean Burke	R-R	6-6	230	12-18-99	0	2	11.57	2	2	0	0	7	12	11	9	1	3	7	.375	.333	.412	9.00	3.86
Ryan Burr	R-R	6-4	220	5-28-94	0	0	0.00	2	0	0	0	2	2	0	0	0	1	2	.286	.000	.333	10.80	5.40
Will Carter	L-R	6-3	195	1-18-93	3	3	4.97	27	1	0	1	29	31	19	16	3	26	29	.282	.333	.254	9.00	8.07
Kyle Crick	L-R	6-4	225	11-30-92	1	0	2.70	6	0	0	0	7	3	3	2	1	4	9	.130	.167	.091	12.15	5.40
Declan Cronin	R-R	6-4	225	9-24-97	1	0	3.52	27	0	0	1	23	26	10	9	2	5	12	.289	.270	.302	4.70	1.96
Johnny Cueto	R-R	5-11	229	2-15-86	0	1	5.17	4	4	0	0	16	15	9	9	3	4	17	.254	.161	.357	9.77	2.30
Craig Dedelow	L-R	6-4	210	11-15-94	0	0	0.00	1	0	0	0	1	1	0	0	0	0	1	.250	.333	.000	9.00	0.00
Rafael Dolis	R-R	6-4	235	1-10-88	1	1	5.02	28	0	0	0	29	24	17	16	2	14	28	.229	.200	.246	8.79	4.40
Johan Dominguez	R-R	6-4	190	1-18-96	0	1	2.35	2	2	0	0	8	6	2	2	1	4	13	.214	.143	.286	15.26	4.70
Brandon Finnegan	L-L	5-11	216	4-14-93	1	2	6.13	31	3	0	0	40	44	30	27	3	27	45	.286	.306	.268	10.21	6.13
Matt Foster	R-R	6-0	215	1-27-95	1	0	0.82	11	0	0	2	11	7	1	1	0	2	14	.179	.200	.158	11.45	1.64
Lincoln Henzman	R-R	6-2	205	7-4-95	2	4	4.91	41	7	0	1	59	74	41	32	5	29	43	.306	.288	.321	6.60	4.45

CHICAGO WHITE SOX

Tyler Johnson	R-R	6-3	210	8-21-95	0	0	14.29	6	0	0	0	6	4	9	9	0	9	6	.190	.200	.182	9.53	14.29
Ryder Jones	L-R	6-2	221	6-7-94	0	0	0.00	1	0	0	0	1	0	0	0	0	0	1	.000	.000	.000	9.00	0.00
Joe Kelly	R-R	6-1	174	6-9-88	0	0	0.00	3	0	0	0	3	0	0	0	0	1	3	.000	.000	.000	9.00	3.00
Patrick Kivlehan	R-R	6-2	215	12-22-89	0	0	0.00	1	0	0	0	1	0	0	0	0	0	0	.000	.000	.000	0.00	0.00
Brody Koerner	R-R	6-2	220	10-17-93	0	5	10.57	9	4	0	0	23	34	29	27	5	17	22	.340	.245	.447	8.61	6.65
Kyle Kubat	L-L	6-1	195	12-4-92	7	4	5.51	37	17	0	0	101	107	72	62	22	52	85	.274	.273	.275	7.55	4.62
Jimmy Lambert	R-R	6-2	190	11-18-94	0	3	9.24	5	5	0	0	13	21	14	13	8	5	12	.368	.320	.406	8.53	3.55
Lance Lynn	B-R	6-5	270	5-12-87	0	1	9.00	3	3	0	0	10	15	10	10	2	2	8	.357	.238	.476	7.20	1.80
Jhan Marinez	R-R	6-1	200	8-12-88	0	1	7.88	14	1	0	0	24	29	23	21	6	12	22	.296	.327	.261	8.25	4.50
Parker Markel	R-R	6-5	240	9-15-90	1	3	10.29	24	0	0	1	21	28	26	24	5	18	27	.311	.317	.306	11.57	7.71
Davis Martin	L-R	6-2	200	1-4-97	3	5	6.11	13	13	0	0	53	60	40	36	11	18	66	.284	.296	.267	11.21	3.06
Kade McClure	R-R	6-7	220	2-12-96	4	4	4.97	44	5	0	1	87	95	56	48	17	28	96	.270	.268	.272	9.93	2.90
Steven Moyers	R-L	6-0	190	9-27-93	1	2	7.31	14	3	0	0	28	38	24	23	8	15	22	.322	.256	.360	6.99	4.76
Zach Muckenhirn	L-L	6-0	205	2-27-95	3	1	3.11	47	0	0	2	55	51	19	19	9	23	56	.242	.244	.240	9.16	3.76
Tobias Myers	R-R	6-0	193	8-5-98	0	6	15.92	7	7	0	0	13	28	24	23	5	15	11	.418	.424	.412	7.62	10.38
2-team total (14 Columbus Clippers)					1	15	7.77	21	21	0	0	73	101	71	63	15	48	51	.322	.329	.315	6.29	5.92
Edgar Navarro	R-R	6-1	180	2-5-98	0	0	12.00	3	0	0	0	3	5	4	4	0	2	3	.357	.286	.429	9.00	6.00
J.B. Olson	L-R	6-2	195	2-15-95	1	4	5.59	47	15	0	2	66	75	42	41	10	28	53	.284	.359	.224	7.23	3.82
Nicholas Padilla	R-R	6-2	220	12-24-96	0	0	3.00	7	0	0	0	6	4	3	2	1	4	6	.190	.200	.188	9.00	6.00
2-team total (10 Iowa Cubs)					1	0	1.74	17	0	0	1	21	12	5	4	1	12	23	.169	.273	.122	10.02	5.23
John Parke	L-L	6-4	220	1-3-95	3	11	6.90	28	25	0	0	134	180	105	103	24	41	100	.326	.313	.334	6.70	2.75
Sammy Peralta	L-L	6-2	205	5-10-98	0	1	4.50	5	0	0	0	6	8	3	3	1	3	8	.320	.364	.286	12.00	4.50
Andrew Perez	L-L	6-2	215	7-25-97	3	4	5.74	59	1	0	2	63	60	40	40	13	27	72	.250	.250	.250	10.34	3.88
Lane Ramsey	R-R	6-9	245	7-16-96	1	1	5.66	19	0	0	4	21	21	15	13	3	17	21	.269	.265	.273	9.15	7.40
Raudy Read	R-R	6-0	220	10-29-93	0	0	36.00	1	0	0	0	1	5	4	4	1	0	0	.625	.750	.500	0.00	0.00
Yacksel Rios	R-R	6-3	215	6-27-93	4	3	4.91	30	1	0	3	33	31	20	18	4	29	38	.248	.239	.253	10.36	7.91
Hunter Schryver	L-L	6-1	205	4-3-95	2	1	3.89	33	0	0	2	37	30	20	16	3	20	33	.221	.148	.268	8.03	4.86
Anderson Severino	L-L	5-10	190	9-17-94	3	4	11.40	37	0	0	0	30	37	40	38	6	42	34	.301	.271	.328	10.20	12.60
Bennett Sousa	L-L	6-3	220	4-6-95	2	1	3.95	28	0	0	6	27	22	14	12	4	12	35	.216	.167	.259	11.52	3.95
Jonathan Stiever	R-R	6-2	210	5-12-97	0	0	0.00	3	2	0	0	3	0	0	0	0	0	1	.000	.000	.000	3.00	0.00
Emilio Vargas	R-R	6-3	220	8-12-96	0	3	6.61	8	5	0	0	33	36	25	24	8	13	29	.283	.270	.297	7.99	3.58
Vince Velasquez	R-R	6-3	212	6-7-92	0	0	4.76	4	0	0	0	6	5	3	3	0	4	7	.227	.364	.091	11.12	6.35
Dan Winkler	R-R	6-3	205	2-2-90	5	0	4.18	29	0	0	2	28	25	14	13	3	15	30	.245	.261	.232	9.64	4.82
Mike Wright Jr.	R-R	6-6	240	1-3-90	0	1	4.64	8	7	0	0	21	18	11	11	4	11	14	.234	.250	.224	5.91	4.64

Fielding

Catcher	PCT	G	PO	A	E	DP	PB
Ciuffo	.991	41	310	19	3	2	3
Fernandez	.992	16	116	4	1	0	5
Grandal	1.000	5	33	5	0	0	1
Perez	.990	83	715	46	8	3	5
Read	1.000	2	1	0	0	0	0
Zavala	1.000	13	116	5	0	0	2

First Base	PCT	G	PO	A	E	DP
Dedelow	.986	20	134	9	2	18
Fernandez	.995	26	192	10	1	28
Fisher	.982	12	103	6	2	15
Grandal	1.000	6	15	0	0	0
Jones	.994	22	149	9	1	14
Kivlehan	.964	3	25	2	1	0
Mercedes	1.000	9	77	4	0	12
Read	1.000	4	29	0	0	2
Remillard	.987	21	145	9	2	14
Rivera	1.000	5	27	1	0	4
Sheets	.983	8	55	4	1	3
Zavala	.991	27	223	7	2	26

Second Base	PCT	G	PO	A	E	DP
Burger	1.000	1	1	1	0	0
Burt	1.000	5	6	10	0	1
Gonzalez	1.000	2	5	8	0	4
Jones	1.000	1	0	2	0	0
Mendick	1.000	1	1	3	0	2
Remillard	.953	16	28	54	4	13
Rivera	.979	36	57	85	3	23
Sanchez	.971	70	98	200	9	43
Sosa	.953	23	40	61	5	16

Third Base	PCT	G	PO	A	E	DP
Burger	.961	35	15	58	3	5
Burt	1.000	3	0	4	0	0
Gonzalez	.500	1	1	0	1	0
Jones	.963	37	18	59	3	9
Mendick	.000	2	0	0	0	0
Moncada	.938	5	1	14	1	0
Remillard	.928	44	41	75	9	11
Rivera	.902	33	17	38	6	5
Sanchez	.857	3	1	5	1	1

Shortstop	PCT	G	PO	A	E	DP
Anderson	1.000	2	0	6	0	2
Gonzalez	.961	25	34	65	4	11
Mendick	.833	5	3	12	3	2
Remillard	.975	52	58	134	5	27
Rivera	1.000	3	6	7	0	4
Sanchez	.983	40	66	105	3	32
Sosa	.971	33	45	89	4	20

Outfield	PCT	G	PO	A	E	DP
Adolfo	.966	89	141	1	5	0
Basabe	1.000	7	16	1	0	0
Burt	1.000	3	6	0	0	0
Colas	.929	6	13	0	1	0
Dedelow	1.000	9	25	1	0	0
Glass	.900	6	9	0	1	0
Haseley	1.000	101	191	4	0	1
Jimenez	1.000	5	3	0	0	0
Mendick	1.000	1	3	0	0	0
Neslony	.975	23	37	2	1	0
Payton	.979	109	224	6	5	1
Remillard	1.000	3	5	0	0	0
Rutherford	.988	92	159	6	2	0
Smith Jr.	.944	9	17	0	1	0
Vaughn	.667	1	2	0	1	0

BIRMINGHAM BARONS — *DOUBLE-A*

SOUTHERN LEAGUE

Batting	B-T	HT	WT	DOB	AVG	vLH	vRH	G	AB	R	H	2B	3B	HR	RBI	BB	HBP	SH	SF	SO	SB	CS	SLG	OBP
D.J. Burt	R-R	5-9	160	10-13-95	.268	.305	.253	78	276	53	74	12	1	3	21	40	3	2	1	53	39	7	.351	.366
Moises Castillo	R-R	6-1	170	7-14-99	.236	.277	.220	63	233	37	55	13	0	2	29	32	1	1	2	46	7	1	.318	.328
Yoelqui Cespedes	R-R	5-9	205	9-24-97	.258	.256	.258	119	458	65	118	29	1	17	59	29	23	0	2	154	33	12	.437	.332
Oscar Colas	L-L	6-1	209	9-17-98	.306	.362	.284	51	206	39	63	9	1	14	33	14	5	0	0	54	1	2	.563	.364
Luis Curbelo	R-R	6-3	185	11-10-97	.175	.207	.165	37	114	14	20	5	0	6	24	8	0	0	0	58	0	0	.377	.230
Ian Dawkins	R-R	5-11	205	7-6-95	.236	.324	.195	65	225	35	53	14	0	5	29	18	3	0	0	53	9	2	.364	.301
Craig Dedelow	L-R	6-4	210	11-15-94	.232	.225	.235	104	383	69	89	16	4	22	68	54	7	0	5	173	10	4	.467	.334
Alex Destino	L-L	6-2	215	10-24-95	.239	.224	.243	66	222	26	53	9	1	5	31	39	2	0	2	84	0	0	.356	.355
Duke Ellis	L-L	6-2	180	1-16-98	318	.143	.400	9	22	8	7	1	0	1	2	3	1	1	0	8	7	1	.500	.423
Xavier Fernandez	R-R	5-11	245	7-15-95	.311	.258	.330	30	119	9	37	3	0	2	15	11	0	0	1	20	0	0	.387	.366
DJ Gladney	R-R	6-3	195	7-14-01	.193	.133	.214	16	57	6	11	2	0	1	5	1	0	0	0	23	1	0	.281	.207

Ivan Gonzalez	R-R	5-9	190	10-28-96	.208	.316	.172	24	77	10	16	6	0	0	9	7	1	0	0	13	0	0	.286	.282
Yasmani Grandal	B-R	6-2	225	11-8-88	.429	.500	.400	3	7	1	3	0	0	1	4	6	0	0	0	2	0	0	.857	.692
Adam Hackenberg	R-R	6-1	225	9-8-99	.167	.222	.152	13	42	3	7	1	0	1	2	3	1	0	0	14	0	0	.262	.239
Wes Kath	L-R	6-3	200	8-3-02	.170	.000	.186	13	47	1	8	1	0	0	3	4	1	0	0	23	0	0	.191	.250
Luis Mieses	L-L	6-3	180	5-31-00	.299	.226	.333	23	97	12	29	5	0	3	16	4	1	0	0	20	1	0	.443	.333
Colson Montgomery	L-R	6-4	205	2-27-02	.146	.091	.162	14	48	5	7	1	0	2	7	2	1	0	1	15	0	0	.292	.192
JJ Muno	L-R	6-0	190	12-21-93	.234	.254	.228	94	278	49	65	10	1	4	33	37	15	0	1	77	29	8	.320	.353
Tyler Neslony	L-R	6-1	190	2-13-94	.326	.186	.378	64	258	49	84	26	3	11	44	31	3	0	0	48	16	5	.578	.404
Tyler Osik	R-R	5-10	203	11-15-96	.200	.200	.200	14	45	5	9	1	0	2	3	6	2	0	0	19	1	1	.356	.321
Bryan Ramos	R-R	6-2	190	3-12-02	.225	.200	.236	21	80	8	18	3	0	3	12	5	1	0	0	15	0	1	.375	.279
Cornelius Randolph	L-R	5-11	205	6-2-97	.118	.000	.160	11	34	2	4	2	0	0	1	4	0	0	0	19	0	1	.176	.211
Raudy Read	R-R	6-0	220	10-29-93	.302	.359	.279	78	275	40	83	21	1	17	67	43	5	0	6	61	0	0	.571	.398
Jose Rodriguez	R-R	5-11	175	5-13-01	.280	.282	.278	104	440	75	123	21	6	11	68	38	3	1	1	66	40	10	.430	.340
Jagger Rusconi	B-R	5-11	165	7-18-96	.232	.267	.215	28	95	11	22	4	0	0	9	13	4	0	2	32	1	3	.274	.342
Yolbert Sanchez	R-R	5-11	176	3-3-97	.353	.400	.341	14	51	7	18	1	0	0	6	13	3	0	0	7	0	0	.373	.507
Evan Skoug	L-R	5-11	200	10-21-95	.233	.179	.252	69	215	39	50	15	0	11	25	37	10	0	1	76	2	1	.456	.369
Lenyn Sosa	R-R	6-0	180	1-25-00	.331	.333	.330	62	257	47	85	10	2	14	48	21	5	0	6	40	0	0	.549	.384
Wilfred Veras	R-R	6-2	180	11-15-02	.267	.333	.256	12	45	5	12	3	0	3	5	3	0	0	0	14	0	0	.533	.313

Pitching	B-T	HT	WT	DOB	W	L	ERA	G	GS	CG	SV	IP	H	R	ER	HR	BB	SO	AVG	vLH	vRH	K/9	BB/9
Angel Acevedo	R-R	6-1	205	9-19-98	0	0	18.00	1	0	0	0	2	4	4	4	1	1	1	.444	.500	.400	4.50	4.50
Skylar Arias	L-L	6-3	204	6-30-97	0	0	54.00	1	0	0	0	0	1	3	2	0	1	1	.500	.000	1.000	27.00	27.00
Yoan Aybar	L-L	6-2	210	7-3-97	0	1	8.10	10	0	0	0	10	11	10	9	2	8	15	.262	.294	.240	13.50	7.20
Jason Bilous	R-R	6-2	185	8-11-97	5	7	5.27	19	16	0	0	84	78	54	49	10	55	104	.241	.226	.258	11.19	5.92
Scott Blewett	R-R	6-6	245	4-10-96	7	6	5.03	24	22	0	0	111	122	69	62	13	44	99	.277	.265	.289	8.03	3.57
Taylor Broadway	R-R	5-11	205	4-8-97	3	2	4.74	37	0	0	1	49	58	28	26	8	14	74	.289	.291	.286	13.50	2.55
Sean Burke	R-R	6-6	230	12-18-99	2	7	4.81	19	19	0	0	73	72	45	39	11	33	99	.259	.264	.254	12.21	4.07
Hansen Butler	R-R	5-11	180	10-30-95	0	1	11.66	10	0	0	0	15	20	19	19	4	19	8	.323	.207	.424	4.91	11.66
Will Carter	L-R	6-3	195	1-18-93	0	0	7.36	2	0	0	0	4	4	3	3	2	1	5	.267	.429	.125	12.27	2.45
Declan Cronin	R-R	6-4	225	9-24-97	1	2	3.86	22	1	0	1	28	25	12	12	2	14	24	.238	.184	.286	7.71	4.50
Andrew Dalquist	R-R	6-1	175	11-13-00	0	2	3.38	4	4	0	0	13	11	7	5	1	11	11	.224	.217	.231	7.43	7.43
Garrett Davila	L-L	6-2	180	1-17-97	6	5	4.97	29	11	0	0	89	93	55	49	7	47	88	.273	.220	.303	8.93	4.77
Theo Denlinger	R-R	6-3	240	7-10-96	1	2	4.70	32	0	0	5	38	34	21	20	6	18	49	.233	.250	.220	11.50	4.23
Johan Dominguez	R-R	6-4	190	1-18-96	0	0	0.00	1	1	0	0	5	3	0	0	0	0	7	.167	.167	.167	12.60	0.00
Fraser Ellard	L-L	6-4	205	11-6-97	1	0	4.28	33	0	0	3	40	40	23	19	0	26	46	.270	.158	.341	10.35	5.85
Caleb Freeman	R-R	6-1	195	2-23-98	0	0	8.79	15	0	0	0	14	13	14	14	1	14	15	.232	.346	.133	9.42	8.79
Brian Glowicki	R-R	5-11	190	10-19-94	2	3	4.18	23	3	0	0	32	23	15	15	4	22	31	.209	.224	.197	8.63	6.12
Haylen Green	L-L	5-11	185	8-12-97	0	1	13.50	1	0	0	0	2	3	3	3	1	1	3	.333	.000	.429	13.50	4.50
Lincoln Henzman	R-R	6-2	205	7-4-95	0	0	3.21	9	0	0	2	14	13	6	5	2	7	18	.255	.208	.296	11.57	4.50
Trey Jeans	L-L	5-10	195	1-31-96	2	1	6.05	16	0	0	0	19	19	16	13	2	18	20	.260	.400	.188	9.31	8.38
Jared Kelley	R-R	6-3	230	10-3-01	0	2	4.50	3	3	0	0	12	13	6	6	2	7	12	.317	.267	.346	9.00	5.25
Kyle Kubat	L-L	6-1	195	12-4-92	0	0	4.15	2	1	0	0	4	2	2	2	0	4	4	.133	.000	.200	8.31	8.31
Davis Martin	L-R	6-2	200	1-4-97	2	1	3.00	5	5	0	0	24	23	9	8	4	7	33	.242	.250	.235	12.38	2.63
Alejandro Mateo	R-R	6-2	210	1-18-94	1	0	0.00	6	0	0	0	8	4	1	0	0	8	9	.143	.143	.143	10.57	9.39
Cristian Mena	R-R	6-2	170	12-21-02	0	1	6.30	3	3	0	0	10	16	8	7	1	1	13	.364	.308	.444	11.70	0.90
Steven Moyers	R-L	6-0	190	9-27-93	5	3	5.61	9	8	0	0	43	63	32	27	7	10	36	.350	.419	.328	7.48	2.08
JJ Muno	L-R	6-0	190	12-21-93	0	1	7.27	10	0	0	0	9	14	9	7	2	2	3	.350	.391	.294	3.12	2.08
Edgar Navarro	R-R	6-1	180	2-5-98	4	2	3.53	35	0	0	3	43	29	25	17	3	36	54	.185	.216	.157	11.22	7.48
J.B. Olson	L-R	6-2	195	2-15-95	0	1	12.27	3	1	0	0	4	4	5	5	1	3	4	.267	.143	.375	9.82	7.36
Karan Patel	R-R	6-0	215	1-2-97	0	0	13.50	1	0	0	0	1	3	2	2	0	3	3	.500	.333	.667	20.25	20.25
Felix Paulino	R-R	6-1	185	3-24-95	4	4	3.29	33	1	0	1	68	54	25	25	8	19	67	.220	.202	.236	8.82	2.50
Sammy Peralta	L-L	6-2	205	5-10-98	4	3	3.70	29	0	0	4	56	47	28	23	5	19	68	.228	.275	.204	10.93	3.05
Kaleb Roper	R-R	6-0	193	11-22-95	2	6	7.78	30	11	0	0	83	116	77	72	16	42	84	.332	.291	.370	9.07	4.54
Garrett Schoenle	L-L	6-5	185	6-21-98	0	1	2.25	4	4	0	0	16	14	4	4	2	4	17	.237	.235	.238	9.56	2.25
Luke Shilling	R-R	6-4	230	11-18-97	1	0	11.74	9	0	0	0	8	8	14	10	2	10	10	.276	.077	.438	11.74	11.74
Yoelvin Silven	R-R	6-1	176	6-26-99	4	2	7.71	36	0	0	0	47	63	42	40	13	18	52	.321	.340	.303	10.03	3.47
Kohl Simas	R-R	6-1	190	12-22-99	0	0	9.95	6	0	0	0	6	10	7	7	3	4	6	.385	.308	.462	8.53	5.68
Chase Solesky	R-R	6-3	201	9-26-97	0	0	1.50	2	0	0	0	6	6	1	1	0	3	8	.250	.091	.385	12.00	4.50
Felipe Tejada	R-R	6-1	190	2-27-98	0	1	9.00	3	0	0	0	3	4	3	3	0	3	3	.400	.333	.429	9.00	9.00
Matthew Thompson	R-R	6-3	195	8-11-00	0	2	5.33	7	7	0	0	25	26	15	15	3	11	31	.265	.174	.346	11.01	3.91
Vince Vannelle	R-R	5-10	202	12-19-97	0	1	11.37	7	0	0	0	6	10	8	8	1	9	7	.385	.308	.462	9.95	12.79
Emilio Vargas	R-R	6-3	220	8-12-96	4	6	5.20	18	14	0	0	80	77	47	46	10	41	87	.252	.225	.274	9.83	4.63
Norge Vera	R-R	6-4	185	6-1-00	0	0	5.63	3	3	0	0	8	5	5	5	0	12	12	.179	.133	.231	13.50	13.50

Fielding

Catcher	PCT	G	PO	A	E	DP	PB
Fernandez	.984	22	173	14	3	2	1
Gonzalez	.981	23	202	9	4	3	2
Hackenberg	.972	13	127	11	4	0	4
Osik	1.000	2	13	1	0	0	0
Read	.988	25	228	15	3	2	6
Skoug	.988	60	613	31	8	4	8

First Base	PCT	G	PO	A	E	DP
Curbelo	.995	26	177	15	1	10
Dedelow	1.000	11	76	8	0	9
Destino	.969	50	356	22	12	38
Fernandez	1.000	5	31	1	0	5
Gladney	1.000	15	86	8	0	13
Mieses	.933	3	13	1	1	0
Osik	1.000	8	43	5	0	1
Read	.989	25	167	17	2	14

Second Base	PCT	G	PO	A	E	DP
Burt	.979	12	18	28	1	6
Castillo	.972	29	39	65	3	12
Muno	.982	24	44	67	2	14
Ramos	.933	8	12	16	2	4
Rodriguez	.973	43	77	105	5	23
Rusconi	.975	7	13	26	1	7
Sanchez	1.000	8	11	20	0	3
Sosa	.980	9	23	25	1	10

Third Base	PCT	G	PO	A	E	DP
Burt	.947	63	43	100	8	11

Curbelo	1.000	2	1	0	0	0
Kath	1.000	13	16	15	0	3
Muno	.924	39	22	75	8	11
Ramos	.905	10	3	16	2	0
Sanchez	1.000	4	1	11	0	1
Sosa	.964	13	6	21	1	3

Shortstop	PCT	G	PO	A	E	DP
Castillo	.945	33	44	60	6	13
Montgomery	.953	14	20	21	2	6
Muno	1.000	2	5	3	0	0
Rodriguez	.950	53	76	113	10	26
Sosa	.986	35	52	85	2	15

Outfield	PCT	G	PO	A	E	DP
Cespedes	.992	110	223	14	2	5
Colas	.987	44	71	7	1	1
Dawkins	1.000	62	112	3	0	0
Dedelow	.987	87	140	12	2	2
Ellis	.933	6	13	1	1	0
Gladney	--	3	0	0	0	0
Mieses	1.000	19	41	2	0	0
Muno	1.000	20	31	2	0	1
Neslony	.975	45	72	7	2	1
Randolph	1.000	11	22	0	0	0
Rusconi	1.000	16	26	0	0	0
Veras	1.000	1	2	0	0	0

WINSTON-SALEM DASH

HIGH CLASS A

SOUTH ATLANTIC LEAGUE

Batting	B-T	HT	WT	DOB	AVG	vLH	vRH	G	AB	R	H	2B	3B	HR	RBI	BB	HBP	SH	SF	SO	SB	CS	SLG	OBP
Andy Atwood	R-R	6-1	195	11-15-96	.212	.000	.230	16	66	5	14	4	0	0	5	4	0	0	0	22	2	1	.273	.257
James Beard	R-R	5-10	170	9-24-00	.178	.667	.143	15	45	8	8	2	0	2	5	8	0	0	0	20	3	2	.356	.302
Brandon Bossard	R-R	6-1	185	6-10-97	.151	.250	.138	26	73	9	11	3	0	2	3	14	2	1	0	31	1	1	.274	.303
D.J. Burt	R-R	5-9	160	10-13-95	.238	.000	.278	6	21	5	5	0	2	0	3	6	0	0	0	7	3	0	.429	.407
Moises Castillo	R-R	6-1	170	7-14-99	.280	.333	.271	47	164	32	46	4	0	1	16	27	3	0	2	37	1	2	.323	.388
Oscar Colas	L-L	6-1	209	9-17-98	.311	.400	.297	59	244	37	76	13	3	7	42	22	1	0	1	54	1	1	.475	.369
Luis Curbelo	R-R	6-3	185	11-10-97	.167	.100	.179	18	66	8	11	1	0	1	1	6	2	0	0	26	0	0	.227	.257
Duke Ellis	L-L	6-2	180	1-16-98	.273	.288	.269	100	374	75	102	17	3	7	27	45	7	2	2	108	50	8	.390	.360
Keegan Fish	B-R	5-11	190	9-19-99	.127	.095	.133	37	126	11	16	5	0	3	13	11	5	0	2	49	1	0	.238	.222
Ivan Gonzalez	R-R	5-9	190	10-28-96	.189	.167	.194	12	37	4	7	2	0	1	3	4	0	0	0	10	0	0	.324	.268
Shawn Goosenberg	R-R	6-1	195	12-5-99	.256	.250	.257	23	78	11	20	4	0	3	11	9	1	0	0	31	4	0	.423	.341
Adam Hackenberg	R-R	6-1	225	9-8-99	.231	.174	.242	78	277	32	64	10	0	7	28	32	10	0	4	70	1	1	.343	.328
Riley Jepson	L-R	6-4	230	4-27-97	.119	.000	.132	13	42	1	5	1	0	0	5	9	0	0	1	13	1	0	.143	.269
Jason Matthews	R-R	6-0	187	4-9-97	.209	.217	.208	91	301	41	63	16	1	2	17	36	9	1	2	110	6	1	.289	.310
Harvin Mendoza	L-L	6-2	185	2-18-99	.182	.130	.189	102	363	30	66	8	2	10	36	39	7	0	1	83	0	0	.298	.273
Luis Mieses	L-L	6-3	180	5-31-00	.281	.176	.301	106	420	54	118	34	0	12	72	24	4	0	3	72	0	0	.448	.324
Colson Montgomery	L-R	6-4	205	2-27-02	.258	.160	.280	37	132	22	34	4	1	5	14	26	3	0	2	26	1	0	.417	.387
Taishi Nakawake	R-R	5-11	185	6-20-98	.200	.000	.222	6	20	2	4	0	0	0	1	1	1	0	1	6	1	1	.200	.261
Ben Norman	L-R	6-2	200	2-15-98	.229	.361	.201	58	205	26	47	10	0	9	28	24	1	0	1	73	6	2	.410	.312
Tyler Osik	R-R	5-10	203	11-15-96	.310	.404	.289	89	313	45	97	14	2	10	53	32	11	0	3	77	3	2	.463	.390
Bryan Ramos	R-R	6-2	190	3-12-02	.275	.203	.291	99	382	64	105	16	1	19	74	40	6	0	4	71	1	0	.471	.350
Colby Smelley	R-R	6-2	195	3-15-00	.203	.000	.218	16	59	2	12	2	0	0	9	6	0	0	0	17	1	0	.237	.277
Terrell Tatum	L-L	6-0	167	7-27-99	.255	.059	.290	32	110	18	28	7	1	3	20	20	1	0	1	38	10	3	.418	.371
Caberea Weaver	R-R	6-3	180	12-1-99	.176	.214	.169	55	182	19	32	5	1	3	16	15	4	1	1	77	14	3	.264	.252
Alsander Womack	R-R	5-9	205	3-16-99	.272	.172	.285	76	268	42	73	7	1	8	41	38	3	0	5	47	4	3	.396	.363

Pitching	B-T	HT	WT	DOB	W	L	ERA	G	GS	CG	SV	IP	H	R	ER	HR	BB	SO	AVG	vLH	vRH	K/9	BB/9
Angel Acevedo	R-R	6-1	205	9-19-98	1	0	0.90	5	0	0	0	10	5	1	1	0	3	4	.147	.250	.115	3.60	2.70
Luis Amaya	L-L	5-11	160	8-26-98	3	0	3.33	34	0	0	3	46	45	21	17	3	26	62	.257	.188	.283	12.13	5.09
Skylar Arias	L-L	6-3	204	6-30-97	2	1	3.91	24	0	0	4	23	14	11	10	1	17	37	.173	.250	.148	14.48	6.65
Brandon Bossard	R-R	6-1	185	6-10-97	0	0	0.00	1	0	0	0	0	1	0	0	0	0	0	.500	.000	1.000	0.00	0.00
Cooper Bradford	R-R	5-11	180	4-13-98	4	1	3.84	37	1	0	0	59	59	31	25	7	28	65	.261	.239	.270	9.97	4.30
Taylor Broadway	R-R	5-11	205	4-8-97	0	0	10.13	3	0	0	1	3	4	3	3	0	2	3	.333	.000	.500	10.13	6.75
Sean Burke	R-R	6-6	230	12-18-99	2	1	2.89	6	5	0	0	28	24	9	9	3	12	31	.242	.324	.200	9.96	3.86
Zach Cable	R-R	6-0	215	10-22-97	1	1	5.65	13	0	0	2	14	12	9	9	2	15	13	.231	.250	.222	8.16	9.42
Isaiah Carranza	R-R	6-5	180	3-2-97	1	2	11.40	17	0	0	1	15	22	25	19	4	9	21	.324	.320	.326	12.60	5.40
Andrew Dalquist	R-R	6-1	175	11-13-00	3	9	6.95	22	22	0	0	91	106	74	70	22	53	69	.304	.299	.306	6.85	5.26
Theo Denlinger	R-R	6-3	240	7-10-96	1	0	3.60	8	0	0	0	10	9	4	4	1	3	17	.225	.231	.222	15.30	2.70
Hunter Dollander	R-R	6-0	232	11-24-96	1	1	7.11	3	3	0	0	13	15	11	10	2	1	15	.283	.294	.278	10.66	0.71
Fraser Ellard	L-L	6-4	205	11-6-97	3	1	3.78	14	0	0	1	17	15	10	7	2	9	12	.238	.179	.286	6.48	4.86
Nick Gallagher	R-R	6-3	200	9-9-95	2	0	3.93	11	0	0	0	18	13	8	8	3	11	17	.200	.100	.244	8.35	5.40
Brooks Gosswein	L-L	6-2	205	10-9-98	0	4	7.41	5	5	0	0	17	24	18	14	2	12	12	.353	.500	.321	6.35	6.35
Haylen Green	L-L	5-11	185	8-12-97	0	2	5.40	5	0	0	0	7	10	5	4	1	1	6	.345	.167	.391	8.10	1.35
Everhett Hazelwood	R-R	6-2	210	5-12-99	3	0	7.64	24	0	0	0	33	43	34	28	6	15	25	.301	.278	.308	6.82	4.09
Trey Jeans	L-L	5-10	195	1-31-96	1	1	2.49	17	1	0	2	22	16	11	6	3	10	34	.198	.087	.241	14.12	4.15
Gil Luna	L-L	5-10	173	7-29-99	1	1	6.00	8	0	0	2	6	7	4	4	2	5	7	.304	.125	.400	10.50	7.50
Ty Madrigal	L-L	6-0	190	3-5-97	1	2	4.99	42	0	0	2	49	49	29	27	7	30	52	.268	.163	.306	9.62	5.55
Alejandro Mateo	R-R	6-2	210	1-18-94	0	0	2.03	12	0	0	0	13	11	3	3	1	5	15	.229	.133	.273	10.13	3.38
Cristian Mena	R-R	6-2	170	12-21-02	1	3	4.65	10	10	0	0	41	39	22	21	4	22	47	.252	.250	.253	10.40	4.87
Jordan Mikel	R-R	6-5	190	3-24-99	0	3	4.28	15	6	0	0	40	33	20	19	6	17	28	.226	.208	.237	6.30	3.83
Luis Moncada	L-L	6-1	150	2-28-98	2	4	6.75	24	9	0	0	60	74	51	45	5	31	48	.305	.429	.267	7.20	4.65
Edgar Navarro	R-R	6-1	180	2-5-98	0	0	1.13	7	0	0	1	8	3	1	1	0	3	12	.115	.111	.118	13.50	3.38
Tyler Osik	R-R	5-10	203	11-15-96	0	0	0.00	1	0	0	0	1	2	0	0	0	0	0	.400	--	.400	0.00	0.00
Karan Patel	R-R	6-0	215	1-2-97	3	5	4.58	37	4	0	1	59	46	34	30	7	43	74	.217	.190	.228	11.29	6.56
Wilber Perez	R-R	6-2	170	11-3-97	2	1	8.15	35	0	0	0	50	49	45	45	9	38	53	.253	.159	.304	9.60	6.89
Chase Plymell	R-R	6-4	205	5-29-98	1	4	7.81	20	0	0	2	28	40	26	24	3	18	29	.331	.321	.333	9.43	5.86
Garrett Schoenle	L-L	6-5	185	6-21-98	1	6	5.67	15	10	0	1	46	43	32	29	8	18	51	.236	.313	.220	9.98	3.52
Jonah Scolaro	L-L	5-10	193	8-3-98	0	1	16.20	2	1	0	0	2	4	3	3	0	1	3	.444	1.000	.375	16.20	5.40
Luke Shilling	R-R	6-4	230	11-18-97	0	1	10.13	3	1	0	0	3	3	3	3	1	3	2	.333	.250	.400	6.75	10.13
Yoelvin Silven	R-R	6-1	176	6-26-99	1	0	0.00	2	0	0	0	5	3	0	0	0	1	4	.176	.200	.167	7.20	1.80

Chase Solesky	R-R	6-3	201	9-26-97	4	8	4.24	24	24	0	0	110	116	55	52	15	31	80	.273	.252	.285	6.53	2.53
Tommy Sommer	L-L	6-4	220	9-25-98	2	2	2.64	9	9	0	0	48	31	14	14	5	14	42	.190	.206	.186	7.93	2.64
Matthew Thompson	R-R	6-3	195	8-11-00	4	5	4.70	18	18	0	0	84	82	52	44	13	29	73	.258	.220	.280	7.79	3.09
Jesus Valles	R-R	6-3	178	12-15-97	3	1	4.67	15	1	0	0	35	37	19	18	7	12	22	.285	.354	.244	5.71	3.12
Vince Vannelle	R-R	5-10	202	12-19-97	4	2	1.82	24	0	0	4	30	24	8	6	2	9	31	.218	.179	.232	9.40	2.73
Norge Vera	R-R	6-4	185	6-1-00	0	1	8.10	2	2	0	0	3	2	3	3	0	4	5	.182	.250	.143	13.50	10.80

Fielding

Catcher	PCT	G	PO	A	E	DP	PB
Fish	.986	27	202	12	3	1	1
Gonzalez	.976	6	40	1	1	1	0
Hackenberg	.990	75	647	76	7	6	9
Osik	.987	18	146	7	2	0	5
Smelley	.989	10	84	5	1	0	1

First Base	PCT	G	PO	A	E	DP
Curbelo	1.000	9	69	2	0	8
Jepson	1.000	4	28	3	0	5
Mendoza	.987	100	729	33	10	81
Mieses	.968	9	58	3	2	4
Osik	1.000	14	101	5	0	9

Second Base	PCT	G	PO	A	E	DP
Atwood	1.000	4	10	5	0	2
Bossard	.970	24	47	51	3	17
Burt	1.000	3	9	9	0	4
Castillo	1.000	1	2	1	0	0
Goosenberg	.963	20	37	41	3	11
Matthews	.991	24	40	70	1	25
Womack	.986	59	102	117	3	32

Third Base	PCT	G	PO	A	E	DP
Atwood	1.000	2	3	5	0	2
Burt	1.000	2	1	2	0	0
Curbelo	.933	8	4	10	1	3
Matthews	.929	32	20	58	6	6
Ramos	.954	86	73	153	11	14
Womack	1.000	4	4	5	0	0

Shortstop	PCT	G	PO	A	E	DP
Atwood	.925	10	7	30	3	5
Castillo	.964	44	71	114	7	30
Matthews	.958	36	33	104	6	19
Montgomery	.938	37	46	90	9	17
Nakawake	.931	6	9	18	2	4

Outfield	PCT	G	PO	A	E	DP
Beard	1.000	15	28	0	0	0
Burt	1.000	1	2	0	0	0
Colas	.982	54	106	4	2	2
Ellis	.961	97	164	7	7	0
Gonzalez	.750	1	2	1	1	0
Jepson	1.000	9	11	0	0	0
Mieses	.985	88	184	9	3	1
Norman	.991	60	107	1	1	0
Tatum	.965	29	51	4	2	3
Weaver	1.000	56	100	6	0	2

KANNAPOLIS CANNON BALLERS — LOW CLASS A

CAROLINA LEAGUE

Batting	B-T	HT	WT	DOB	AVG	vLH	vRH	G	AB	R	H	2B	3B	HR	RBI	BB	HBP	SH	SF	SO	SB	CS	SLG	OBP
Andy Atwood	R-R	6-1	195	11-15-96	.286	.333	.279	35	119	21	34	4	1	5	12	18	4	0	1	21	9	3	.462	.394
Benyamin Bailey	R-R	6-4	215	9-18-01	.215	.273	.208	86	288	30	62	11	1	6	37	46	3	0	7	94	0	1	.323	.323
Brooks Baldwin	B-R	6-2	175	8-15-00	.225	.250	.222	17	71	10	16	2	0	0	4	6	0	0	0	19	1	0	.254	.286
James Beard	R-R	5-10	170	9-24-00	.163	.132	.168	71	240	34	39	5	1	4	15	43	4	1	2	118	25	7	.242	.298
Brandon Bossard	R-R	6-1	185	6-10-97	.185	.429	.100	8	27	2	5	0	0	1	1	5	2	0	0	11	1	0	.296	.353
Jacob Burke	R-R	6-1	208	2-26-01	.269	.600	.247	22	78	13	21	6	1	1	12	6	8	0	0	20	4	2	.410	.380
Troy Claunch	R-R	6-0	210	9-1-98	.254	.250	.255	15	59	8	15	1	0	0	6	6	1	0	0	17	0	0	.271	.333
Tim Elko	R-R	6-4	240	12-27-98	.271	.000	.297	17	70	8	19	4	0	2	7	2	0	0	0	28	0	0	.414	.292
Keegan Fish	B-R	5-11	190	9-19-99	.238	.000	.250	7	21	2	5	0	0	0	2	7	0	0	0	8	1	0	.238	.429
DJ Gladney	R-R	6-3	195	7-14-01	.243	.169	.257	106	407	60	99	17	4	18	65	44	5	0	4	150	10	1	.437	.322
Logan Glass	R-R	6-4	215	4-9-01	.186	.111	.198	62	199	23	37	7	3	8	16	18	12	0	1	96	9	1	.372	.291
Ivan Gonzalez	R-R	5-9	190	10-28-96	.281	.250	.288	19	64	9	18	4	0	3	13	5	1	0	0	12	0	1	.484	.343
Jayson Gonzalez	R-R	6-2	220	4-26-99	.125	.000	.143	13	48	3	6	1	0	0	5	4	0	0	0	32	0	0	.146	.192
Misael Gonzalez	R-R	6-0	175	5-23-01	.176	.256	.160	75	233	29	41	8	3	4	26	33	10	0	1	101	13	4	.288	.303
Wes Kath	L-R	6-3	200	8-3-02	.238	.279	.230	99	383	56	91	20	1	13	42	60	3	0	3	148	2	0	.397	.343
Chase Krogman	L-L	5-11	180	2-27-01	.172	.154	.176	17	64	5	11	0	2	1	8	6	1	0	1	23	1	0	.281	.250
Johnabiell Laureano	R-R	6-0	180	10-11-00	.240	.200	.250	7	25	0	6	3	0	0	2	1	1	2	0	12	0	0	.360	.296
Daniel Millwee	R-R	5-10	205	8-2-95	.000	.000	.000	2	8	0	0	0	0	0	0	0	0	0	0	3	0	0	.000	.000
Colson Montgomery	L-R	6-4	205	2-27-02	.324	.321	.324	45	170	31	55	12	1	4	26	26	6	0	3	42	0	1	.476	.424
Samil Polanco	L-R	6-0	160	2-21-00	.224	.083	.248	73	254	27	57	14	2	4	35	14	4	0	3	44	2	1	.343	.273
Wilber Sanchez	R-R	5-10	160	2-21-02	.162	.244	.150	101	359	46	58	10	2	2	22	55	3	1	2	96	38	8	.217	.277
Colby Smelley	R-R	6-2	195	3-15-00	.274	.280	.272	87	307	48	84	20	1	4	35	45	15	0	2	86	0	1	.384	.390
Jordan Sprinkle	R-R	5-11	180	3-6-01	.237	.300	.229	22	93	11	22	3	0	1	4	6	1	1	0	21	8	1	.301	.290
Terrell Tatum	L-L	6-0	167	7-27-99	.320	.750	.238	10	25	6	8	2	0	0	1	11	0	0	0	11	6	1	.400	.528
Nick Thornquist	R-R	5-8	175	9-23-97	.238	.100	.257	27	84	11	20	3	2	3	14	18	0	0	1	32	0	0	.429	.369
Victor Torres	R-R	6-0	180	7-29-00	.236	.231	.237	50	178	17	42	8	1	7	28	6	4	1	1	47	0	0	.410	.275
Michael Turner	L-R	6-2	205	8-18-98	.000	--	.000	2	5	3	0	0	0	0	0	3	0	0	0	2	0	0	.000	.375
Wilfred Veras	R-R	6-2	180	11-15-02	.266	.302	.260	101	394	58	105	19	2	17	67	27	6	0	6	118	5	0	.454	.319
Caberea Weaver	R-R	6-3	180	12-1-99	.191	.250	.179	13	47	7	9	2	0	3	5	3	1	0	0	19	0	0	.426	.255
Alsander Womack	R-R	5-9	205	3-16-99	.211	.125	.273	7	19	2	4	1	0	0	2	2	0	0	0	3	1	1	.263	.286

Pitching	B-T	HT	WT	DOB	W	L	ERA	G	GS	CG	SV	IP	H	R	ER	HR	BB	SO	AVG	vLH	vRH	K/9	BB/9
Angel Acevedo	R-R	6-1	205	9-19-98	2	2	5.52	27	0	0	1	60	61	40	37	4	26	56	.263	.315	.231	8.35	3.88
Eric Adler	R-R	6-2	190	10-12-00	0	0	5.40	4	0	0	0	3	5	2	2	0	7	5	.357	.167	.500	13.50	18.90
Andy Atwood	R-R	6-1	195	11-15-96	0	0	0.00	1	0	0	0	0	1	0	0	0	1	0	.500	--	.500	0.00	27.00
Brandon Bossard	R-R	6-1	185	6-10-97	0	0	0.00	1	0	0	0	1	1	0	0	0	0	1	.250	.500	.000	9.00	0.00
Jeremiah Burke	R-R	6-2	195	5-16-98	0	1	3.24	3	3	0	0	8	6	4	3	2	1	8	.194	.200	.182	8.64	1.08
Dylan Burns	R-R	6-1	194	12-29-96	1	1	1.35	4	4	0	0	20	11	7	3	0	10	13	.159	.226	.105	5.85	4.50
Zach Cable	R-R	6-0	215	10-22-97	0	2	20.57	8	0	0	1	7	10	16	16	0	10	4	.333	.364	.316	5.14	12.86
Jonathan Cannon	R-R	6-6	213	7-19-00	0	0	1.42	3	3	0	0	6	4	1	1	0	2	3	.200	.273	.111	4.26	2.84
Martin Carrasco	R-R	6-0	165	11-22-99	0	1	3.65	3	3	0	0	12	12	5	5	1	3	16	.245	.250	.235	11.68	2.19
Brian Carrion	R-R	6-2	180	1-1-99	0	1	15.75	3	0	0	0	4	7	9	7	1	5	3	.389	.400	.385	6.75	11.25
Adisyn Coffey	R-R	6-2	185	1-22-99	4	3	5.23	32	0	0	7	31	37	23	18	2	16	36	.296	.373	.227	10.45	4.65
Homer Cruz	R-R	6-0	175	9-21-99	0	0	54.00	2	0	0	0	1	5	6	6	1	3	1	.625	1.000	.571	9.00	27.00
Hunter Dollander	R-R	6-0	232	11-24-96	4	3	3.40	9	5	0	0	42	38	17	16	4	10	43	.242	.310	.186	9.14	2.13

Christian Edwards	R-R	6-3	205	3-4-99	0	1	7.58	17	0	0	0	19	24	20	16	3	18	17	.320	.370	.292	8.05	8.53
Rigo Fernandez	L-L	6-0	190	11-27-97	0	0	5.03	14	0	0	1	20	20	11	11	2	9	22	.270	.211	.291	10.07	4.12
Nick Gallagher	R-R	6-3	200	9-9-95	0	1	0.00	9	0	0	2	9	3	1	0	0	2	16	.094	.125	.063	15.43	1.93
Brooks Gosswein	L-L	6-2	205	10-9-98	3	6	4.94	19	18	0	0	82	83	53	45	8	45	77	.262	.177	.290	8.45	4.94
Haylen Green	L-L	5-11	185	8-12-97	3	1	4.07	33	0	0	1	55	51	29	25	5	16	53	.244	.174	.279	8.62	2.60
Everhett Hazelwood	R-R	6-2	210	5-12-99	1	1	3.10	10	0	0	0	20	15	9	7	0	11	20	.205	.179	.235	8.85	4.87
Liam Jenkins	R-R	6-8	225	4-9-97	2	1	5.14	21	0	0	3	28	19	18	16	0	32	33	.200	.244	.167	10.61	10.29
Jose Jimenez	L-L	6-3	195	8-31-02	0	1	4.50	3	1	0	0	10	10	7	5	0	7	7	.256	.200	.276	6.30	6.30
Jared Kelley	R-R	6-3	230	10-3-01	1	4	3.34	18	18	0	0	65	52	30	24	6	40	59	.218	.179	.243	8.21	5.57
Logan Lyle	L-L	5-11	202	2-1-98	1	0	2.08	2	0	0	0	4	2	1	1	0	3	5	.143	.000	.154	10.38	6.23
Drew McDaniel	R-R	6-2	185	8-26-00	0	0	10.80	3	0	0	0	3	8	5	4	0	4	4	.421	.333	.571	10.80	10.80
Cristian Mena	R-R	6-2	170	12-21-02	1	2	2.68	11	11	0	0	54	45	17	16	2	15	66	.227	.247	.212	11.07	2.52
Tyson Messer	R-R	6-0	215	1-7-97	5	4	5.22	28	0	0	0	29	20	18	17	5	24	29	.204	.163	.236	8.90	7.36
Jordan Mikel	R-R	6-5	190	3-24-99	0	0	3.00	2	0	0	0	6	4	2	2	1	1	10	.200	.200	.200	15.00	1.50
Luis Moncada	L-L	6-1	150	2-28-98	0	0	3.00	2	0	0	0	6	4	2	2	0	2	4	.200	.000	.250	6.00	3.00
Shane Murphy	L-L	6-5	210	1-19-01	0	0	10.38	3	2	0	0	4	7	5	5	0	2	1	.350	.375	.333	2.08	4.15
Noah Owen	L-R	6-4	200	10-1-00	5	10	5.16	23	19	0	0	106	125	69	61	20	32	83	.287	.319	.263	7.03	2.71
Jake Palisch	L-L	6-4	215	8-19-98	0	0	0.00	2	0	0	0	2	1	0	0	0	0	5	.143	.000	.167	22.50	0.00
Bowen Plagge	R-R	6-2	212	4-11-98	3	5	5.97	25	0	0	3	57	50	43	38	4	39	62	.231	.193	.258	9.73	6.12
Chase Plymell	R-R	6-4	205	5-29-98	2	3	4.19	15	0	0	3	34	39	18	16	2	7	43	.285	.255	.305	11.27	1.83
Samil Polanco	L-R	6-0	160	2-21-00	0	0	9.00	2	0	0	0	2	2	2	2	1	0	1	.250	.000	.286	4.50	0.00
Kole Ramage	R-R	6-1	205	9-11-98	0	1	4.70	6	0	0	0	8	8	6	4	0	2	4	.267	.200	.333	4.70	2.35
Lane Ramsey	R-R	6-9	245	7-16-96	0	1	9.00	3	0	0	0	3	4	3	3	1	2	3	.333	.500	.167	9.00	6.00
Johnny Ray	R-R	6-2	220	10-10-98	1	1	4.35	3	1	0	0	10	12	6	5	2	4	17	.300	.353	.261	14.81	3.48
Garrett Schoenle	L-L	6-5	185	6-21-98	3	1	1.57	11	0	0	0	23	10	5	4	0	12	33	.127	.138	.120	12.91	4.70
Jonah Scolaro	L-L	5-10	193	8-3-98	2	1	2.31	6	4	0	0	23	19	9	6	2	10	34	.224	.235	.216	13.11	3.86
Billy Seidl	R-R	6-0	220	11-9-99	1	0	0.00	5	0	0	1	5	2	0	0	0	4	6	.125	.091	.200	10.80	7.20
Kohl Simas	R-R	6-1	190	12-22-99	2	2	3.65	16	15	0	0	62	51	29	25	7	25	76	.226	.202	.246	11.09	3.65
Tommy Sommer	L-L	6-4	220	9-25-98	4	5	2.75	15	14	0	0	75	61	30	23	7	27	87	.218	.242	.206	10.39	3.23
Tristan Stivors	R-R	6-4	220	9-22-98	0	0	6.00	3	0	0	0	3	3	2	2	0	5	4	.300	.250	.333	12.00	15.00
Nick Thornquist	R-R	5-8	175	9-23-97	0	0	0.00	1	0	0	0	1	0	0	0	0	0	0	.000	--	.000	0.00	0.00
Jesus Valles	R-R	6-3	178	12-15-97	3	3	5.32	14	1	0	1	47	60	29	28	4	11	39	.309	.318	.303	7.42	2.09
Vince Vannelle	R-R	5-10	202	12-19-97	0	0	0.00	4	0	0	1	6	4	0	0	0	2	13	.182	.000	.333	18.47	2.84
Manuel Veloz	R-R	6-2	185	1-28-01	2	1	1.04	5	2	0	0	17	9	5	2	1	4	16	.150	.200	.114	8.31	2.08
Norge Vera	R-R	6-4	185	6-1-00	0	2	1.88	8	8	0	0	24	12	5	5	1	15	35	.143	.175	.114	13.13	5.63
Frander Veras	L-R	6-5	185	10-8-98	2	2	6.26	23	0	0	3	27	21	22	19	2	17	27	.206	.333	.127	8.89	5.60

Fielding

Catcher	PCT	G	PO	A	E	DP	PB
Claunch	1.000	8	75	7	0	3	2
Fish	.971	7	65	2	2	0	1
Gonzalez	.995	19	182	14	1	0	0
Millwee	1.000	2	21	3	0	0	0
Smelley	.977	22	201	16	5	1	6
Thornquist	.978	26	211	14	5	2	4
Torres	.990	49	434	41	5	2	5
Turner	1.000	1	8	0	0	0	0

First Base	PCT	G	PO	A	E	DP
Elko	.980	15	139	8	3	13
Gladney	.992	60	477	26	4	41
Gonzalez	.957	3	19	3	1	2
Veras	.984	54	411	17	7	38

Second Base	PCT	G	PO	A	E	DP
Atwood	.988	22	30	54	1	16
Baldwin	1.000	3	6	5	0	2
Bossard	1.000	3	4	2	0	1
Polanco	.957	55	65	113	8	23
Sanchez	.968	47	71	113	6	27
Womack	1.000	7	8	14	0	1

Third Base	PCT	G	PO	A	E	DP
Baldwin	1.000	6	5	10	0	1
Gonzalez	.889	10	4	12	2	0
Kath	.910	95	73	159	23	18
Polanco	1.000	2	3	4	0	1
Veras	.904	19	18	29	5	4

Shortstop	PCT	G	PO	A	E	DP
Atwood	1.000	10	13	24	0	4
Bossard	.958	5	8	15	1	3
Montgomery	.941	41	31	112	9	19
Polanco	1.000	1	1	4	0	0
Sanchez	.965	55	65	154	8	27
Sprinkle	.977	21	23	61	2	12

Outfield	PCT	G	PO	A	E	DP
Bailey	.978	84	127	5	3	0
Baldwin	.941	6	16	0	1	0
Beard	.975	70	148	5	4	1
Burke	.982	22	53	3	1	2
Gladney	.965	43	81	2	3	0
Glass	.983	62	111	2	2	1
Gonzalez	.975	73	116	1	3	0
Krogman	.944	17	29	5	2	0
Laureano	1.000	7	15	0	0	0
Tatum	.952	10	19	1	1	1
Weaver	1.000	15	26	1	0	1

ACL WHITE SOX — ROOKIE

ARIZONA COMPLEX LEAGUE

Batting	B-T	HT	WT	DOB	AVG	vLH	vRH	G	AB	R	H	2B	3B	HR	RBI	BB	HBP	SH	SF	SO	SB	CS	SLG	OBP
Alvaro Aguero	R-R	6-0	160	3-19-03	.212	.182	.219	47	170	24	36	4	2	7	19	10	2	0	0	66	12	3	.382	.264
Matt Archer	R-R	5-10	180	8-13-00	.533	.500	.545	4	15	1	8	0	0	0	5	1	1	0	1	0	1	0	.533	.556
Brooks Baldwin	B-R	6-2	175	8-15-00	.209	.182	.219	10	43	7	9	2	0	0	1	6	0	0	0	10	1	0	.256	.306
Ruben Benavides	R-R	6-1	178	8-9-01	.194	.333	.182	15	36	4	7	3	0	0	1	7	0	0	0	19	0	0	.278	.326
Jhoneiker Betancourt	R-R	6-1	174	5-2-00	.230	.222	.231	22	61	7	14	5	1	1	11	5	5	0	0	15	0	0	.393	.338
Dario Borrero	L-L	6-5	190	11-13-03	.313	.152	.353	46	166	12	52	8	1	0	13	7	2	0	0	29	1	2	.373	.349
Brandon Bossard	R-R	6-1	185	6-10-97	.000	.000	.000	1	4	0	0	0	0	0	0	0	0	0	0	1	0	0	.000	.000
Jacob Burke	R-R	6-1	208	2-26-01	.333	.667	.267	5	18	2	6	1	0	1	2	3	1	0	0	4	0	0	.556	.455
Cameron Butler	R-R	6-0	175	10-3-02	.201	.167	.208	43	144	26	29	5	1	2	11	24	1	0	0	71	11	2	.292	.320
Mario Camilletti	L-R	5-9	195	4-19-99	.250	.000	.333	2	4	1	1	0	0	0	0	2	1	0	0	0	1	0	.250	.571
Troy Claunch	R-R	6-0	210	9-1-98	.400	.200	.600	4	10	3	4	1	0	0	1	6	0	0	0	2	0	0	.500	.625
Tim Elko	R-R	6-4	240	12-27-98	.154	.250	.111	7	26	4	4	0	0	3	9	1	0	0	0	13	0	0	.500	.185
Anthony Espinoza	R-R	5-10	165	9-27-01	.195	.313	.169	27	87	10	17	1	0	2	9	10	0	0	0	29	0	1	.276	.278
Jayson Gonzalez	R-R	6-2	220	4-26-99	.233	.333	.228	20	60	11	14	2	1	0	3	11	1	0	0	28	0	0	.300	.361
Romy Gonzalez	R-R	6-1	215	9-6-96	.471	.600	.417	5	17	5	8	0	0	4	10	1	1	0	0	2	0	0	1.176	.526

CHICAGO WHITE SOX

Manuel Guariman	R-R	6-0	196	2-9-04	.190	.250	.167	20	58	4	11	3	0	0	6	3	2	0	1	14	1	0	.241	.250
Roberth Gutierrez	R-R	6-0	170	11-8-01	.042	.250	.000	10	24	2	1	0	0	0	0	2	0	1	0	12	1	0	.042	.115
Enoy Jimenez	R-R	5-10	160	11-8-00	.500	--	.500	1	2	1	1	0	0	0	0	0	0	0	0	1	0	0	.500	.500
Chase Krogman	L-L	5-11	180	2-27-01	.239	.214	.245	20	67	8	16	3	1	0	7	7	1	0	0	23	0	0	.313	.320
Chris Lanzilli	R-R	6-2	225	6-18-98	.333	.333	.333	7	24	4	8	1	0	2	5	4	0	0	0	4	0	0	.625	.429
Johnabiell Laureano	R-R	6-0	180	10-11-00	.266	.333	.255	19	64	7	17	2	1	1	7	7	1	0	0	25	0	0	.375	.347
Drake Logan	R-R	6-4	205	9-5-00	.150	.000	.200	6	20	2	3	0	1	0	2	5	0	0	0	10	0	0	.250	.320
Javier Mora	R-R	5-11	170	3-23-03	.297	.350	.278	19	74	13	22	5	1	2	12	6	1	0	0	23	1	0	.473	.358
Taishi Nakawake	R-R	5-11	185	6-20-98	.261	.250	.263	6	23	3	6	0	0	0	1	3	0	0	0	3	1	0	.261	.346
Ben Norman	L-R	6-2	200	2-15-98	.421	.500	.385	5	19	4	8	3	0	1	5	1	0	0	0	6	1	0	.737	.450
Luis Pineda	R-R	6-1	209	3-19-02	.266	.360	.246	40	143	19	38	2	0	6	23	8	1	0	1	41	0	0	.406	.307
Victor Quezada	R-R	6-1	185	12-27-03	.151	.083	.168	36	119	13	18	1	0	4	10	17	0	0	1	67	0	1	.261	.255
Jordan Sprinkle	R-R	5-11	180	3-6-01	.385	1.000	.273	5	13	4	5	0	0	0	0	3	2	0	0	3	1	0	.385	.556
Layant Tapia	R-R	6-1	160	1-4-02	.236	.297	.220	48	178	28	42	12	1	5	26	20	1	0	3	69	7	0	.399	.312
Elijah Tatis	R-R	5-11	155	9-27-01	.146	.182	.133	14	41	3	6	1	0	1	4	0	0	0	0	19	0	0	.244	.146
Caberea Weaver	R-R	6-3	180	12-1-99	.174	.000	.250	7	23	5	4	1	0	1	3	1	1	0	0	7	0	0	.348	.240
Bryce Willits	L-R	6-2	200	8-25-99	.182	.000	.200	3	11	2	2	0	1	0	0	2	0	0	0	3	0	0	.364	.308

Pitching	B-T	HT	WT	DOB	W	L	ERA	G	GS	CG	SV	IP	H	R	ER	HR	BB	SO	AVG	vLH	vRH	K/9	BB/9
Axel Acevedo	R-R	6-2	170	9-23-00	0	0	15.75	10	0	0	1	8	14	15	14	2	10	14	.368	.300	.393	15.75	11.25
Mason Adams	R-R	6-0	200	2-23-00	0	0	7.36	3	0	0	0	4	5	3	3	0	1	4	.357	.500	.250	9.82	2.45
Eric Adler	R-R	6-2	190	10-12-00	0	0	6.75	2	0	0	0	1	0	1	1	0	2	3	.000	.000	.000	20.25	13.50
Skylar Arias	L-L	6-3	204	6-30-97	0	0	0.00	1	0	0	0	1	1	1	0	0	0	2	.250	--	.250	18.00	0.00
Erick Bello	R-R	5-11	170	8-18-02	1	4	5.20	18	0	0	3	28	27	19	16	1	19	34	.255	.316	.221	11.06	6.18
Ben Beutel	L-L	6-0	165	9-2-99	0	0	5.40	5	0	0	0	5	7	4	3	1	3	7	.318	.429	.267	12.60	5.40
Jeremiah Burke	R-R	6-2	195	5-16-98	0	1	5.14	3	3	0	0	7	5	4	4	0	2	5	.208	.250	.200	6.43	2.57
Dylan Burns	R-R	6-1	194	12-29-96	3	3	3.97	12	11	0	0	59	59	28	26	6	19	69	.261	.280	.252	10.53	2.90
Jonathan Cannon	R-R	6-6	213	7-19-00	0	0	0.00	1	0	0	1	1	0	0	0	0	1	1	.000	.000	.000	9.00	9.00
Martin Carrasco	R-R	6-0	165	11-22-99	0	2	5.19	6	3	0	0	9	11	6	5	2	3	12	.289	.235	.333	12.46	3.12
Brian Carrion	R-R	6-2	180	1-1-99	0	0	5.14	3	1	0	0	7	9	4	4	0	2	8	.333	.250	.400	10.29	2.57
Oriel Castro	L-L	6-0	175	5-5-01	1	1	4.50	8	1	0	1	12	17	7	6	2	5	10	.340	.333	.343	7.50	3.75
Anderson Comas	L-L	6-3	185	2-10-00	1	0	6.35	11	0	0	0	11	12	9	8	0	11	13	.279	.300	.273	10.32	8.74
Homer Cruz	R-R	6-0	175	9-21-99	2	2	7.45	12	0	0	0	19	24	18	16	3	12	18	.312	.318	.309	8.38	5.59
Hunter Dollander	R-R	6-0	232	11-24-96	2	0	0.82	2	2	0	0	11	5	1	1	1	1	15	.132	.000	.161	12.27	0.82
Christian Edwards	R-R	6-3	205	3-4-99	1	0	4.50	11	2	0	0	24	20	12	12	1	11	30	.227	.192	.242	11.25	4.13
Caleb Freeman	R-R	6-1	195	2-23-98	0	0	0.00	3	0	0	0	3	0	0	0	0	1	3	.000	.000	.000	9.00	3.00
Nick Gallagher	R-R	6-3	200	9-9-95	0	0	5.79	4	1	0	0	5	2	3	3	1	1	4	.125	.000	.154	7.71	1.93
Ethan Hammerberg	L-R	6-5	250	12-18-00	0	0	0.00	6	0	0	0	6	1	0	0	0	1	9	.056	.200	.000	13.50	1.50
Eric Hildebrand	R-R	6-0	180	1-4-00	0	0	40.50	1	0	0	0	1	3	3	3	0	0	0	.600	.667	.500	0.00	0.00
Carlos Hinestroza	R-R	6-1	190	2-4-03	1	0	6.32	16	0	0	0	16	16	12	11	5	8	14	.267	.364	.211	8.04	4.60
Jose Jimenez	L-L	6-3	195	8-31-02	2	3	5.23	10	9	0	0	43	48	27	25	3	13	38	.286	.275	.291	7.95	2.72
Gil Luna	L-L	5-10	173	7-29-99	0	0	27.00	1	0	0	0	0	1	2	1	0	1	0	.500	.000	1.000	0.00	27.00
Alejandro Mateo	R-R	6-2	210	1-18-94	1	1	3.60	4	2	0	0	5	5	3	2	0	0	5	.238	.000	.357	9.00	0.00
Connor McCullough	R-R	6-1	185	10-5-99	0	0	0.00	1	0	0	1	1	0	0	0	0	0	0	.000	--	.000	0.00	0.00
Drew McDaniel	R-R	6-2	185	8-26-00	0	0	4.50	2	0	0	0	2	2	1	1	0	0	3	.286	1.000	.167	13.50	0.00
Matthew McGarry	R-R	6-3	205	4-1-97	0	0	3.00	3	0	0	0	3	3	2	1	0	3	1	.300	.500	.250	3.00	9.00
Mark McLaughlin	R-R	6-3	205	2-14-01	0	0	0.00	1	0	0	0	1	0	0	0	0	0	1	.000	.000	.000	9.00	0.00
Kade Mechals	R-R	5-11	185	10-28-97	0	0	0.00	1	0	0	0	1	0	0	0	0	1	0	.000	.000	--	0.00	9.00
Jordan Mikel	R-R	6-5	190	3-24-99	0	0	0.00	1	0	0	0	1	0	0	0	0	0	0	.000	.000	.000	0.00	0.00
Shane Murphy	L-L	6-5	210	1-19-01	0	0	3.00	2	0	0	0	3	3	1	1	0	2	2	.273	.000	.300	6.00	6.00
Yohemy Nolasco	R-R	6-3	160	7-12-03	0	2	4.93	13	9	0	0	35	37	22	19	5	13	26	.272	.296	.256	6.75	3.38
Jake Palisch	L-L	6-4	215	8-19-98	0	0	0.00	3	0	0	0	3	0	0	0	0	1	7	.000	.000	.000	21.00	3.00
Kole Ramage	R-R	6-1	205	9-11-98	0	0	3.38	3	0	0	0	3	2	1	1	0	1	4	.200	.333	.143	13.50	3.38
Lane Ramsey	R-R	6-9	245	7-16-96	0	0	10.80	2	0	0	0	2	1	3	2	0	2	4	.167	.000	.250	21.60	10.80
Jose Rodulfo	R-R	6-0	165	8-20-00	2	0	2.70	13	0	0	0	20	12	7	6	1	9	22	.176	.077	.200	9.90	4.05
Billy Seidl	R-R	6-0	220	11-9-99	1	0	2.25	3	0	0	0	4	2	1	1	0	2	2	.167	.000	.222	4.50	4.50
Luke Shilling	R-R	6-4	230	11-18-97	0	0	0.00	3	0	0	0	3	1	0	0	0	3	8	.100	.250	.000	24.00	9.00
Tristan Stivors	R-R	6-4	220	9-22-98	0	0	0.00	1	0	0	0	1	0	0	0	0	0	3	.000	.000	.000	27.00	0.00
Jake Suddreth	R-R	6-3	215	4-22-97	1	3	4.63	12	0	0	1	12	14	12	6	2	8	16	.280	.333	.250	12.34	6.17
Emerson Talavera	R-R	5-10	160	10-1-02	4	1	2.77	17	0	0	3	26	18	9	8	3	4	36	.196	.172	.206	12.46	1.38
Manuel Veloz	R-R	6-2	185	1-28-01	3	5	6.30	13	10	0	0	50	60	37	35	6	27	43	.296	.297	.295	7.74	4.86
Frander Veras	L-R	6-5	185	10-8-98	0	0	2.25	4	0	0	0	4	5	1	1	0	1	4	.333	.400	.300	9.00	2.25

Fielding

C: Benavides 9, Betancourt 5, Claunch 3, Guariman 19, Pineda 28. **1B:** Benavides 3, Betancourt 9, Borrero 39, Elko 3, Gonzalez 5. **2B:** Archer 2, Baldwin 4, Camilletti 2, Espinoza 18, Gonzalez 1, Gutierrez 5, Mora 16, Nakawake 4, Tatis 8. **3B:** Espinoza 7, Gonzalez 9, Logan 5, Quezada 31, Tatis 1, Willits 3. **SS:** Bossard 1, Espinoza 2, Gonzalez 2, Nakawake 3, Sprinkle 3, Tapia 45. **OF:** Aguero 47, Baldwin 8, Borrero 6, Burke 5, Butler 41, Gutierrez 4, Jimenez 1, Krogman 19, Lanzilli 7, Laureano 18, Norman 3, Tatis 4, Weaver 5.

DSL WHITE SOX — *ROOKIE*

DOMINICAN SUMMER LEAGUE

Batting	B-T	HT	WT	DOB	AVG	vLH	vRH	G	AB	R	H	2B	3B	HR	RBI	BB	HBP	SH	SF	SO	SB	CS	SLG	OBP
Ricardo Aguilar	R-R	6-0	180	12-13-02	.147	.000	.179	18	34	6	5	2	0	0	4	5	3	1	0	13	0	0	.206	.310
Leandro Alsinois	R-R	5-10	175	9-6-04	.250	.071	.282	32	92	13	23	7	2	2	14	15	2	0	1	22	2	4	.435	.364
Godwin Bennett	R-R	6-2	170	10-4-02	.306	.263	.314	41	121	33	37	9	0	11	36	23	5	0	2	45	5	1	.653	.430

Ryan Burrowes	R-R	6-2	170	8-17-04	.266	.227	.272	47	158	38	42	9	1	3	18	25	10	0	3	34	12	0	.392	.393
Ryan Castillo	L-R	6-1	170	1-28-05	.274	.077	.310	27	84	12	23	3	0	0	11	8	0	1	1	30	2	1	.310	.333
Loidel Chapelli	L-R	5-8	187	12-20-01	.344	.379	.336	46	154	41	53	7	7	8	29	27	2	0	0	22	10	3	.636	.448
Cesar D_Oleo	R-R	6-0	180	1-5-05	.276	.214	.295	25	58	11	16	3	0	0	5	20	1	0	0	18	5	4	.328	.468
Roberth Gutierrez	R-R	6-0	170	11-8-01	.208	.200	.211	10	24	4	5	2	0	0	3	8	0	0	1	9	0	0	.292	.394
Arxy Hernandez	R-R	6-2	170	7-29-03	.277	.226	.289	49	159	31	44	7	1	1	24	18	5	0	1	34	4	2	.352	.366
Erick Hernandez	L-L	6-0	170	1-15-05	.227	.158	.238	38	141	21	32	7	1	0	8	17	6	0	1	37	4	3	.291	.333
Ronny Hernandez	R-R	6-1	200	11-9-04	.268	.273	.267	34	97	20	26	7	0	6	22	18	2	0	3	21	0	0	.526	.383
Carlos Jimenez	L-L	6-4	220	2-3-02	.343	.200	.374	45	140	24	48	10	3	5	37	15	4	0	5	31	3	4	.564	.409
Randel Mondesi	R-R	6-3	190	12-4-02	.238	.280	.229	46	130	21	31	4	1	4	21	17	2	1	1	41	5	4	.377	.333
Juan Oviedo	R-R	5-10	150	1-30-04	.283	.286	.282	15	46	8	13	2	0	0	6	13	0	0	0	11	0	2	.326	.441
Arnold Prado	R-R	6-3	194	11-20-04	.345	.429	.318	29	87	15	30	5	1	1	11	16	2	0	0	23	2	1	.460	.457
Edwin Ramos	R-R	6-2	194	10-16-04	.215	.231	.212	27	79	10	17	1	0	0	11	11	6	1	1	23	0	1	.228	.351
Guillermo Rodriguez	R-R	5-9	156	9-3-04	.237	.267	.230	40	156	22	37	4	2	1	14	9	2	0	0	31	7	4	.308	.287

Pitching	**B-T**	**HT**	**WT**	**DOB**	**W**	**L**	**ERA**	**G**	**GS**	**CG**	**SV**	**IP**	**H**	**R**	**ER**	**HR**	**BB**	**SO**	**AVG**	**vLH**	**vRH**	**K/9**	**BB/9**
Ricardo Aguilar	R-R	6-0	180	12-13-02	0	0	9.00	1	0	0	0	1	2	1	1	0	0	1	.400	1.000	.250	9.00	0.00
Frankeli Arias	L-L	6-0	170	4-5-03	4	1	3.33	13	5	1	0	49	42	27	18	4	12	50	.227	.176	.238	9.25	2.22
Francisco Benitez	R-R	6-2	187	9-15-00	1	0	7.27	5	0	0	0	9	16	15	7	1	8	6	.348	.294	.379	6.23	8.31
Ricardo Brizuela	R-R	6-3	198	6-30-03	4	2	5.02	15	4	0	1	38	39	24	21	3	15	48	.269	.269	.269	11.47	3.58
Oriel Castro	L-L	6-0	175	5-5-01	1	0	1.59	6	0	0	1	11	6	3	2	0	6	14	.162	.222	.143	11.12	4.76
Halan Dishmey	R-R	6-6	210	11-11-04	3	1	7.15	8	0	0	0	11	12	9	9	0	15	8	.273	.333	.231	6.35	11.91
Jorge Ferrer	L-L	6-3	180	9-5-00	2	2	6.16	10	0	0	0	19	23	22	13	2	15	18	.291	.071	.338	8.53	7.11
Ricardo Gomez	R-R	6-3	158	11-9-04	3	3	5.70	17	2	0	2	30	30	25	19	3	18	29	.256	.245	.266	8.70	5.40
Daniel Gonzalez	L-L	6-3	160	11-27-01	3	2	5.24	21	1	0	5	45	46	29	26	7	24	49	.271	.282	.267	9.87	4.84
Jeremy Gonzalez	L-L	6-0	168	4-1-05	0	2	5.90	11	7	0	0	29	38	31	19	1	18	26	.314	.333	.311	8.07	5.59
Juan Jimenez	R-R	6-2	194	9-11-02	0	1	2.70	13	5	0	2	23	17	12	7	1	8	26	.200	.206	.196	10.03	3.09
Jesus Mendez	R-R	5-11	180	7-30-04	0	2	5.00	8	6	0	1	9	10	6	5	0	4	9	.294	.286	.300	9.00	4.00
Jose Mendoza	R-R	6-2	175	3-15-04	4	1	3.72	18	3	0	2	39	37	20	16	4	22	47	.255	.264	.250	10.94	5.12
Edwin Peralta	R-R	6-3	175	5-10-01	4	0	6.48	17	0	0	0	25	32	22	18	3	12	15	.299	.214	.354	5.40	4.32
Ronny Robles	R-R	6-2	180	11-11-01	0	4	5.32	13	8	0	0	44	38	36	26	2	29	38	.226	.293	.163	7.77	5.93
Gabriel Rodriguez	R-R	5-11	172	11-20-02	3	3	3.64	13	10	1	0	54	50	27	22	3	23	58	.251	.255	.248	9.61	3.81
Jose Rodriguez	R-R	6-3	200	7-26-00	0	1	5.40	5	2	0	1	5	6	6	3	0	7	4	.286	.000	.500	7.20	12.60
Marcelo Valladares	R-R	6-4	187	8-28-04	0	0	13.50	2	2	0	0	2	3	3	3	0	0	2	.429	.667	.250	9.00	0.00
Fernando Vargas	R-R	6-2	185	8-3-02	0	1	9.72	8	3	0	0	8	9	14	9	0	10	13	.281	.250	.300	14.04	10.80

Fielding

C: Aguilar 10, Hernandez 32, Oviedo 13, Ramos 12. **1B:** Aguilar 4, Burrowes 1, Gutierrez 3, Jimenez 39, Oviedo 1, Prado 1, Ramos 13. **2B:** Burrowes 10, Castillo 9, Chapelli 33, Gutierrez 1, Rodriguez 10. **3B:** Castillo 14, Gutierrez 1, Hernandez 46. **SS:** Burrowes 32, Hernandez 2, Rodriguez 27. **OF:** Alsinois 31, Bennett 27, Burrowes 1, D'Oleo 24, Gutierrez 6, Hernandez 37, Mondesi 41, Prado 29.

Cincinnati Reds

SEASON IN A SENTENCE: The Reds recorded a winning record in only one month (May, 15-13), and as a result they went on to post their sixth consecutive losing season despite a pitching staff that ranked among the top 10 in the majors in team ERA (4.18).

HIGH POINT: The Reds' offense was the catalyst for the 15-13 record the team compiled during May. They posted nine runs or more in seven games that month, which was a clear bright spot in a season that saw them finish 16 games out of first place in the NL Central. The team also rattled off a season-high six game winning streak in June.

LOW POINT: Any hope Reds fans had coming into the season barely made it past Opening Day. COO Phil Castellini asked "Well, where are you gonna go?" when questioned about the team's rebuild. Cincinnati then went 3-22 to begin the year. The Reds were 14.5 games out of first place by the first week of May.

NOTABLE ROOKIES: Slugging outfielder Aristides Aquino became the first player in major league history to hit 13 homers in his first 100 career plate appearances. He continued to mash, posting a .891 OPS in 56 games for the Reds. Top prospect Nick Senzel saw action in the outfield for Cincinnati, but he ended up on the shelf in September due to a torn right labrum. He finished the year with 12 home runs and a .742 OPS.

KEY TRANSACTIONS: Before the season, Cincinnati dealt outfielder Jesse Winker and third baseman Eugenio Suarez to the Mariners for outfielder Jake Fraley, lefthander Brandon Williamson and righthander Connor Phillips. Cincinnati made further major moves at the trade deadline. Luis Castillo was shipped to Seattle, bringing back four prospects led by shortstops Noelvi Marte and Edwin Arroyo. When Tyler Stephenson fractured his thumb in June, the Reds struggled to find anyone who could catch competently. The team ended up using six other catchers. All six were helpless at the plate.

DOWN ON THE FARM: Shortstop Elly De La Cruz flirted with a 30-30 season as he earned a midseason promotion to Double-A Chattanooga. He ended up settling for 28 home runs to go with 47 stolen bases. Hard-throwing righthander Joe Boyle had a truly fascinating season. He held opponents to a .141 batting average, but his control issues meant he allowed 84 walks compared to just 46 hits in 100.2 innings.

OPENING DAY PAYROLL: $128,815,238 (15th).

PLAYERS OF THE YEAR

MAJOR LEAGUE

Alexis Diaz
RHP

1.84 ERA, 10 SV
83 SO, 33 BB in 63 IP
Led all rookies in ERA

MINOR LEAGUE

Elly De La Cruz
SS

(HiA/AA)
.304/.359/.586
28 HR, 47 SB in 120 G

ORGANIZATION LEADERS

Batting — *Minimum 250 AB

MAJORS

*AVG	Brandon Drury	.274
*OPS	Brandon Drury	.855
HR	Brandon Drury	20
RBI	Kyle Farmer	78

MINORS

*AVG	Elly De La Cruz, Dayton, Chattanooga	.304
*OBP	Matt McLain, Chattanooga	.363
*SLG	Elly De La Cruz, Dayton, Chattanooga	.586
*OPS	Elly De La Cruz, Dayton, Chattanooga	.945
R	Elly De La Cruz, Dayton, Chattanooga	87
H	Elly De La Cruz, Dayton, Chattanooga	143
TB	Elly De La Cruz, Dayton, Chattanooga	276
2B	Elly De La Cruz, Dayton, Chattanooga	31
3B	Elly De La Cruz, Dayton, Chattanooga	9
HR	Elly De La Cruz, Dayton, Chattanooga	28
RBI	Elly De La Cruz, Dayton, Chattanooga	86
BB	Allan Cerda, Dayton, Chattanooga	84
SO	Allan Cerda, Dayton, Chattanooga	168
SB	Michael Siani, Chattanooga, Louisville	52

Pitching — #Minimum 75 IP

MAJORS

W	Alexis Diaz	7
#ERA	Luis Castillo	2.86
SO	Hunter Greene	164
SV	Alexis Diaz	10

MINORS

W	Andrew Abbott, Chattanooga, Dayton	10
L	Randy Wynne, Louisville	11
#ERA	Joe Boyle, Dayton, Chattanooga	2.86
G	Eddy Demurias, Louisville	55
GS	Brandon Williamson, Chattanooga, Louisville	27
GS	Eduardo Salazar, Chattanooga	27
SV	Fernando Cruz, Louisville	23
IP	Randy Wynne, Louisville	133
BB	Joe Boyle, Dayton, Chattanooga	84
SO	Andrew Abbott, Chattanooga, Dayton	159
#AVG	Joe Boyle, Dayton, Chattanooga	.141

2022 PERFORMANCE

General Manager: Nick Krall. **Farm Director:** Shawn Pender. **Scouting Director:** Brad Meador.

Class	Team	League	W	L	PCT	Finish	Manager
Majors	Cincinnati Reds	National	62	100	.383	t-13th (15)	David Bell
Triple-A	Louisville Bats	International	60	90	.400	19th (20)	Pat Kelly
Double-A	Chattanooga Lookouts	Southern	61	75	.449	7th (8)	Jose Moreno
High-A	Dayton Dragons	Midwest	67	61	.523	7th (12)	Bryan LaHair
Low-A	Daytona Tortugas	Florida State	54	74	.422	10th (10)	Gookie Dawkins
Rookie	ACL Reds	Arizona Complex	32	19	.627	2nd (18)	Julio Morillo
Overall 2022 Minor League Record			298	345	.463	26th (30)	

ORGANIZATION STATISTICS

CINCINNATI REDS

NATIONAL LEAGUE

Batting	B-T	HT	WT	DOB	AVG	vLH	vRH	G	AB	R	H	2B	3B	HR	RBI	BB	HBP	SH	SF	SO	SB	CS	SLG	OBP
Albert Almora Jr.	R-R	6-2	190	4-16-94	.223	.224	.223	64	215	26	48	10	1	5	29	17	1	1	1	46	3	2	.349	.282
Aristides Aquino	R-R	6-4	220	4-22-94	.197	.170	.214	80	259	24	51	13	0	10	30	17	0	0	0	101	2	3	.363	.246
Jose Barrero	R-R	6-2	175	4-5-98	.152	.146	.153	48	165	13	25	3	0	2	10	9	0	0	0	76	4	1	.206	.195
Ronnie Dawson	L-R	6-2	217	5-19-95	.000	--	.000	1	3	0	0	0	0	0	0	0	0	0	0	2	0	0	.000	.000
Stuart Fairchild	R-R	6-0	205	3-17-96	.279	.286	.275	38	86	13	24	4	1	5	6	8	5	0	0	29	0	2	.523	.374
2-team total (5 San Francisco Giants)					.255	.250	.259	43	94	14	24	4	1	5	6	8	5	0	0	32	0	2	.479	.346
Kyle Farmer	R-R	6-0	205	8-17-90	.255	.309	.235	145	526	58	134	25	1	14	78	33	16	2	6	99	4	3	.386	.315
Jake Fraley	L-L	6-0	195	5-25-95	.259	.143	.277	68	216	33	56	9	0	12	28	26	3	0	2	54	4	1	.468	.344
TJ Friedl	L-L	5-10	180	8-14-95	.240	.333	.232	72	225	33	54	10	5	8	25	20	7	0	6	40	7	2	.436	.314
Aramis Garcia	R-R	6-1	228	1-12-93	.213	.385	.159	47	108	6	23	2	0	1	4	3	2	2	0	34	0	1	.259	.248
Jonathan India	R-R	6-0	200	12-15-96	.249	.260	.245	103	386	48	96	16	2	10	41	31	14	0	0	94	3	4	.378	.327
Mark Kolozsvary	R-R	5-8	180	9-4-95	.200	.167	.250	10	20	3	4	2	0	1	3	1	0	0	0	9	0	0	.450	.238
Alejo Lopez	B-R	5-10	170	5-5-96	.262	.256	.264	61	145	15	38	5	1	1	10	9	2	0	0	21	3	1	.331	.314
Colin Moran	L-R	6-4	225	10-1-92	.211	.273	.195	42	109	11	23	3	0	5	23	16	0	0	3	30	0	0	.376	.305
Taylor Motter	R-R	6-1	195	9-18-89	.167	.200	.000	2	6	0	1	0	0	0	0	0	0	0	0	3	0	0	.167	.167
Mike Moustakas	L-R	6-0	225	9-11-88	.214	.207	.216	78	252	30	54	12	0	7	25	24	6	0	3	75	2	0	.345	.295
Tyler Naquin	L-R	6-2	195	4-24-91	.246	.186	.264	56	187	29	46	12	2	7	33	13	3	1	0	53	3	2	.444	.305
2-team total (49 New York Mets)					.229	.180	.241	105	310	47	71	19	4	11	46	19	4	1	0	93	4	2	.423	.282
Chris Okey	R-R	5-11	200	12-29-94	.167	.000	.250	7	12	3	2	0	0	0	0	0	1	0	0	5	0	0	.167	.231
Michael Papierski	B-R	6-3	224	2-26-96	.159	.100	.177	34	82	6	13	1	0	1	4	9	0	2	0	22	0	0	.207	.242
2-team total (5 San Francisco Giants)					.143	.095	.157	39	91	7	13	1	0	1	4	10	0	2	0	26	0	0	.187	.228
Matt Reynolds	R-R	6-1	200	12-3-90	.246	.205	.263	92	244	31	60	10	1	3	23	26	1	0	1	78	5	0	.332	.320
2-team total (1 New York Mets)					.246	.205	.263	93	244	31	60	10	1	3	23	26	1	0	1	78	5	0	.332	.320
JT Riddle	L-R	6-1	190	10-12-91	.250	.000	.333	2	4	0	1	0	0	0	0	0	0	0	0	1	0	0	.250	.250
Chuckie Robinson	R-R	5-11	221	12-14-94	.136	.182	.125	25	59	3	8	2	0	2	5	0	0	1	0	17	0	0	.271	.136
Austin Romine	R-R	6-1	216	11-22-88	.147	.000	.192	37	95	8	14	2	0	3	9	2	1	1	0	36	0	0	.263	.173
2-team total (11 St. Louis Cardinals)					.149	.036	.183	48	121	10	18	3	0	3	9	4	1	1	0	43	0	0	.248	.183
Max Schrock	L-R	5-9	185	10-12-94	.154	.500	.125	13	26	1	4	0	0	0	1	1	0	0	0	6	0	0	.154	.185
Nick Senzel	R-R	6-1	205	6-29-95	.231	.241	.226	110	373	45	86	13	0	5	25	30	5	2	1	76	8	5	.306	.296
Michael Siani	L-L	6-1	188	7-16-99	.167	--	.167	9	24	1	4	0	0	0	0	0	0	0	0	7	0	1	.167	.167
Donovan Solano	R-R	5-8	210	12-17-87	.284	.301	.277	80	278	22	79	16	0	4	24	19	5	0	2	61	0	0	.385	.339
Spencer Steer	R-R	5-11	185	12-7-97	.211	.316	.184	28	95	12	20	5	0	2	8	11	2	0	0	26	0	1	.326	.306
Tyler Stephenson	R-R	6-4	225	8-16-96	.319	.346	.307	50	166	24	53	9	0	6	35	12	3	0	2	47	1	0	.482	.372
Joey Votto	L-R	6-2	220	9-10-83	.205	.214	.201	91	322	31	66	18	1	11	41	44	10	0	0	97	0	0	.370	.319

Pitching	B-T	HT	WT	DOB	W	L	ERA	G	GS	CG	SV	IP	H	R	ER	HR	BB	SO	AVG	vLH	vRH	K/9	BB/9
Chase Anderson	R-R	6-1	210	11-30-87	2	4	6.38	9	7	0	0	24	17	18	17	3	15	23	.205	.184	.222	8.63	5.63
Graham Ashcraft	L-R	6-2	240	2-11-98	5	6	4.89	19	19	0	0	105	119	61	57	11	30	71	.281	.232	.323	6.09	2.57
Luis Castillo	R-R	6-2	200	12-12-92	4	4	2.86	14	14	0	0	85	63	30	27	7	28	90	.201	.199	.202	9.53	2.96
Luis Cessa	R-R	6-0	208	4-25-92	4	4	4.57	46	10	0	0	81	76	44	41	14	28	59	.250	.247	.253	6.58	3.12
Fernando Cruz	R-R	6-2	205	3-28-90	0	1	1.23	14	2	0	0	15	9	3	2	1	9	21	.167	.154	.179	12.89	5.52
Ross Detwiler	R-L	6-5	210	3-6-86	0	2	4.44	30	0	0	1	26	31	13	13	5	10	28	.287	.275	.298	9.57	3.42
Alexis Diaz	R-R	6-2	224	9-28-96	7	3	1.84	59	0	0	10	64	28	18	13	5	33	83	.131	.158	.107	11.73	4.66
Phillip Diehl	L-L	6-2	169	7-16-94	0	0	11.12	5	0	0	0	6	8	7	7	3	3	3	.320	.167	.462	4.76	4.76
Kyle Dowdy	R-R	6-1	195	2-3-93	0	0	0.00	2	0	0	0	6	5	0	0	0	3	3	.217	.231	.200	4.26	4.26
Daniel Duarte	R-R	6-0	170	12-4-96	0	0	10.13	3	0	0	0	3	3	3	3	1	3	2	.300	.667	.143	6.75	10.13
Robert Dugger	R-R	6-0	198	7-3-95	0	1	6.75	3	1	0	0	11	11	8	8	3	7	12	.268	.292	.235	10.13	5.91
Justin Dunn	R-R	6-2	185	9-22-95	1	3	6.10	7	7	0	0	31	32	21	21	11	17	21	.276	.322	.228	6.10	4.94
Raynel Espinal	R-R	6-3	215	10-6-91	0	1	7.71	2	0	0	0	5	6	4	4	1	1	5	.316	.167	.571	9.64	1.93
Buck Farmer	L-R	6-4	232	2-20-91	2	2	3.83	44	0	0	2	47	36	21	20	2	25	54	.211	.226	.202	10.34	4.79
Luke Farrell	L-R	6-6	200	6-7-91	0	0	9.00	2	0	0	0	4	6	5	4	1	4	5	.333	.364	.286	11.25	9.00
2-team total (4 Chicago Cubs)					0	0	5.40	6	2	0	0	15	18	10	9	3	7	14	.286	.324	.241	8.40	4.20
Ian Gibaut	R-R	6-3	250	11-19-93	1	2	4.67	33	0	0	1	35	38	18	18	3	18	48	.279	.283	.276	12.46	4.67

Hunter Greene	R-R	6-5	230	8-6-99	5	13	4.44	24	24	1	0	126	104	64	62	24	48	164	.222	.205	.239	11.75	3.44
Vladimir Gutierrez	R-R	6-1	190	9-18-95	1	6	7.61	10	8	0	0	37	46	31	31	8	24	29	.313	.364	.257	7.12	5.89
Ryan Hendrix	R-R	6-3	215	12-16-94	0	0	5.40	9	0	0	0	8	9	5	5	0	6	9	.300	.294	.308	9.72	6.48
Jeff Hoffman	R-R	6-5	235	1-8-93	2	0	3.83	35	1	0	0	45	40	22	19	5	23	45	.235	.242	.231	9.07	4.63
Joel Kuhnel	R-R	6-4	280	2-19-95	2	3	6.36	53	0	0	1	58	67	41	41	8	14	56	.291	.270	.305	8.69	2.17
Derek Law	R-R	6-3	225	9-14-90	2	2	4.08	15	0	0	0	18	19	8	8	2	7	15	.271	.286	.262	7.64	3.57
Nick Lodolo	L-L	6-6	205	2-5-98	4	7	3.66	19	19	0	0	103	90	44	42	13	39	131	.235	.109	.252	11.41	3.40
Alejo Lopez	B-R	5-10	170	5-5-96	0	0	6.75	3	0	0	0	3	2	2	2	2	0	0	.200	.333	.000	0.00	0.00
Mike Minor	R-L	6-4	210	12-26-87	4	12	6.06	19	19	0	0	98	120	72	66	24	40	76	.296	.232	.316	6.98	3.67
Dauri Moreta	R-R	6-2	185	4-15-96	0	2	5.40	35	1	0	1	38	32	24	23	10	13	39	.227	.224	.229	9.16	3.05
Connor Overton	L-R	6-0	190	7-24-93	1	0	2.73	6	4	0	0	33	21	10	10	1	11	14	.188	.167	.207	3.82	3.00
Matt Reynolds	R-R	6-1	200	12-3-90	0	0	6.75	2	0	0	0	1	3	1	1	0	0	0	.500	.500	.500	0.00	0.00
Reiver Sanmartin	L-L	6-2	160	4-15-96	4	4	6.32	45	4	0	0	57	66	43	40	8	29	47	.293	.247	.324	7.42	4.58
Tony Santillan	R-R	6-3	240	4-15-97	0	1	5.49	21	0	0	4	20	23	14	12	1	12	21	.299	.344	.267	9.61	5.49
Max Schrock	L-R	5-9	185	10-12-94	0	0	45.00	1	0	0	0	1	7	5	5	2	0	0	.700	--	.700	0.00	0.00
Lucas Sims	R-R	6-2	225	5-10-94	1	0	9.45	6	0	0	1	7	5	7	7	0	6	5	.217	.125	.267	6.75	8.10
Jared Solomon	R-R	6-2	200	6-10-97	0	0	10.80	9	0	0	0	8	8	10	10	3	5	9	.242	.238	.250	9.72	5.40
Hunter Strickland	R-R	6-3	225	9-24-88	3	3	4.91	66	0	0	7	62	61	37	34	8	33	60	.253	.282	.229	8.66	4.76
Art Warren	R-R	6-3	230	3-23-93	2	3	6.50	39	0	0	3	36	37	29	26	6	22	40	.264	.197	.324	10.00	5.50
Justin Wilson	L-L	6-2	205	8-18-87	0	1	2.45	5	0	0	0	4	3	1	1	0	0	7	.231	.286	.167	17.18	0.00
T.J. Zeuch	R-R	6-7	245	8-1-95	0	3	15.19	3	3	0	0	11	24	18	18	5	7	5	.453	.304	.567	4.22	5.91

Fielding

Catcher	PCT	G	PO	A	E	DP	PB
Garcia	.994	41	303	12	2	1	0
Kolozsvary	1.000	9	53	0	0	0	2
Okey	.968	7	30	0	1	0	1
Papierski	.996	34	250	13	1	1	2
Robinson	.993	25	140	5	1	0	1
Romine	.997	37	291	12	1	2	1
Stephenson	1.000	45	385	16	0	1	2

First Base	PCT	G	PO	A	E	DP
Drury	1.000	9	46	5	0	8
Farmer	.000	2	0	0	0	0
Garcia	1.000	5	7	1	0	0
Moran	1.000	25	118	18	0	10
Moustakas	1.000	24	167	14	0	10
Reynolds	1.000	13	72	9	0	7
Solano	1.000	26	194	19	0	25
Steer	1.000	9	50	5	0	5
Stephenson	1.000	1	1	0	0	0
Votto	.998	76	492	48	1	40

Second Base	PCT	G	PO	A	E	DP
Drury	1.000	20	13	30	0	5
India	.966	86	104	177	10	31
Lopez	.976	33	34	46	2	13
Motter	1.000	1	1	0	0	0
Reynolds	.956	36	47	62	5	13
Schrock	1.000	2	2	2	0	0
Senzel	1.000	1	0	2	0	0
Solano	.952	7	7	13	1	2
Steer	.960	5	9	15	1	6

Third Base	PCT	G	PO	A	E	DP
Drury	.963	62	33	71	4	10
Farmer	.979	36	32	61	2	8
Lopez	1.000	8	4	14	0	1
Moran	1.000	14	6	15	0	1
Motter	.500	2	0	3	3	0
Moustakas	.978	25	16	28	1	2
Reynolds	1.000	14	6	11	0	2
Riddle	1.000	1	2	4	0	0
Senzel	1.000	2	1	1	0	0
Solano	.977	16	14	29	1	3
Steer	.960	14	6	18	1	1

Shortstop	PCT	G	PO	A	E	DP
Barrero	.965	48	58	108	6	26
Drury	1.000	2	2	1	0	0
Farmer	.979	98	106	215	7	50
Reynolds	.988	23	26	53	1	5

Outfield	PCT	G	PO	A	E	DP
Almora Jr.	.986	68	135	5	2	0
Aquino	.968	78	140	12	5	4
Drury	--	1	0	0	0	0
Fairchild	1.000	39	50	0	0	0
Fraley	.976	52	82	1	2	0
Friedl	.992	64	123	4	1	1
Lopez	1.000	6	9	0	0	0
Naquin	1.000	43	74	3	0	0
Pham	.975	83	150	7	4	1
Reynolds	1.000	14	18	0	0	0
Schrock	1.000	5	8	0	0	0
Senzel	.984	101	236	3	4	2
Siani	1.000	9	13	0	0	0

LOUISVILLE BATS — *TRIPLE-A*

INTERNATIONAL LEAGUE

Batting	B-T	HT	WT	DOB	AVG	vLH	vRH	G	AB	R	H	2B	3B	HR	RBI	BB	HBP	SH	SF	SO	SB	CS	SLG	OBP
Albert Almora Jr.	R-R	6-2	190	4-16-94	.296	.258	.320	20	81	9	24	4	0	0	7	2	0	0	0	8	0	0	.346	.313
Trey Amburgey	R-R	6-2	210	10-24-94	.226	.262	.209	39	133	19	30	4	1	7	12	15	0	0	1	46	0	1	.429	.302
Aristides Aquino	R-R	6-4	220	4-22-94	.312	.273	.318	22	77	18	24	6	0	8	19	9	4	0	1	33	2	1	.701	.407
Jose Barrero	R-R	6-2	175	4-5-98	.209	.192	.214	55	220	27	46	8	1	9	24	11	5	0	1	89	5	2	.377	.262
Jake Bauers	L-L	6-1	195	10-6-95	.135	.053	.156	29	96	7	13	4	0	3	12	19	0	0	1	33	4	2	.271	.276
2-team total (32 Scranton/Wilkes-Barre RailRiders)					.183	.140	.195	61	202	21	37	6	1	8	28	39	1	0	2	76	8	3	.342	.316
Lorenzo Cedrola	R-R	5-8	152	1-12-98	.267	.252	.273	124	475	64	127	20	5	4	41	13	12	2	2	84	15	6	.356	.303
Allen Cordoba	R-R	6-2	235	12-6-95	.162	.143	.169	34	99	15	16	2	0	3	13	9	5	0	1	22	9	3	.273	.263
Ashton Creal	R-R	6-1	205	3-23-99	.200	.000	.250	2	5	2	1	0	0	0	0	1	0	0	0	1	1	0	.200	.333
Ronnie Dawson	L-R	6-2	217	5-19-95	.252	.231	.258	116	393	58	99	23	0	11	43	42	11	0	2	112	11	3	.394	.339
Michael De Leon	B-R	6-1	160	1-14-97	.233	.164	.259	64	202	22	47	9	0	3	13	19	1	0	0	49	0	0	.322	.302
Joe Deluca	B-R	6-3	235	8-29-95	.000	.000	.000	1	2	0	0	0	0	0	0	0	0	0	0	2	0	0	.000	.000
Stuart Fairchild	R-R	6-0	205	3-17-96	.273	.250	.278	34	121	23	33	6	1	7	16	10	3	0	2	34	5	1	.512	.338
Jake Fraley	L-L	6-0	195	5-25-95	.268	.333	.241	12	41	8	11	0	0	1	4	7	0	0	0	14	1	0	.341	.375
James Free	B-R	6-2	205	4-14-98	.176	.200	.167	5	17	1	3	1	0	0	0	0	0	0	0	6	0	0	.235	.176
TJ Friedl	L-L	5-10	180	8-14-95	.278	.231	.294	64	205	33	57	9	3	8	38	28	3	4	1	48	10	2	.468	.371
Aramis Garcia	R-R	6-1	228	1-12-93	.190	.500	.158	5	21	2	4	2	0	1	4	1	0	0	0	9	0	0	.429	.227
Isiah Gilliam	B-R	6-3	220	7-23-96	.253	.235	.262	53	158	26	40	10	3	6	35	20	1	0	1	58	4	0	.468	.339
Miguel Hernandez	R-R	6-0	194	4-13-99	.239	.200	.250	22	67	7	16	1	0	1	4	7	0	0	0	18	0	0	.299	.311
TJ Hopkins	R-R	6-0	195	1-16-97	.255	.292	.243	25	94	11	24	5	0	4	14	8	1	0	0	29	2	0	.436	.320
Jonathan India	R-R	6-0	200	12-15-96	.167	.250	.125	4	12	0	2	0	0	0	2	3	0	0	0	4	0	0	.167	.333
Mark Kolozsvary	R-R	5-8	180	9-4-95	.168	.154	.172	42	119	14	20	6	0	3	7	13	8	2	0	44	0	0	.294	.293
Sandy Leon	B-R	5-10	235	3-13-89	.222	.324	.132	26	72	5	16	3	0	1	7	10	1	0	1	12	0	0	.306	.321
2-team total (4 Columbus Clippers)					.226	.316	.152	30	84	7	19	3	0	2	11	14	1	0	1	14	0	0	.333	.340
Steven Leyton	R-R	5-10	165	12-17-98	.208	.000	.238	7	24	2	5	3	1	0	3	0	0	0	0	7	0	0	.417	.208

Alejo Lopez	B-R	5-10	170	5-5-96	.256	.265	.254	46	160	14	41	8	0	3	22	17	2	0	3	21	2	0	.363	.330
Alex McGarry	L-L	6-2	202	5-11-98	.208	.167	.222	8	24	2	5	2	0	0	0	2	0	0	0	6	0	0	.292	.269
Colin Moran	L-R	6-4	225	10-1-92	.249	.182	.263	53	193	21	48	11	0	7	26	18	0	0	2	54	0	0	.415	.310
Taylor Motter	R-R	6-1	195	9-18-89	.250	.368	.202	39	132	12	33	4	0	8	18	19	0	0	2	34	0	0	.462	.340
2-team total (42 Gwinnett Stripers)					.254	.365	.206	81	279	42	71	15	0	20	54	48	0	0	6	73	2	0	.523	.357
Tyler Naquin	L-R	6-2	195	4-24-91	.308	.000	.333	4	13	2	4	1	1	1	2	3	0	0	0	4	0	0	.769	.438
Chris Okey	R-R	5-11	200	12-29-94	.220	.138	.247	41	118	18	26	4	3	2	14	10	0	0	1	39	0	1	.356	.279
Michael Papierski	B-R	6-3	224	2-26-96	.298	.400	.270	17	47	6	14	2	0	3	13	9	1	0	0	12	0	0	.532	.421
Stephen Piscotty	R-R	6-4	211	1-14-91	.250	.400	.190	24	88	8	22	3	0	5	14	7	1	0	0	24	0	0	.455	.313
Juniel Querecuto	B-R	5-9	195	9-19-92	.256	.322	.237	108	398	52	102	27	2	11	34	29	2	0	3	80	10	5	.417	.308
Matt Reynolds	R-R	6-1	200	12-3-90	.300	.333	.286	3	10	0	3	0	0	0	1	1	0	0	0	1	0	0	.300	.364
2-team total (8 Syracuse Mets)					.185	.250	.158	11	27	1	5	0	0	1	4	4	0	0	1	6	0	0	.296	.281
JT Riddle	L-R	6-1	190	10-12-91	.208	.333	.185	27	96	7	20	4	1	3	5	5	1	0	2	22	0	0	.365	.250
2-team total (61 Syracuse Mets)					.241	.291	.225	88	332	39	80	21	2	11	35	10	4	0	4	71	0	0	.416	.269
Leonardo Rivas	B-R	5-10	150	10-10-97	.243	.237	.245	39	140	19	34	7	0	2	12	23	0	1	0	46	8	0	.336	.350
Chuckie Robinson	R-R	5-11	221	12-14-94	.253	.286	.242	27	87	11	22	5	1	2	12	5	1	0	0	19	0	0	.402	.301
Cristian Santana	R-R	6-2	175	2-24-97	.271	.337	.252	121	457	49	124	22	0	11	67	35	5	0	7	112	1	1	.392	.325
Max Schrock	L-R	5-9	185	10-12-94	.304	.267	.315	20	69	14	21	3	0	2	9	3	1	0	0	10	0	0	.435	.342
Nick Senzel	R-R	6-1	205	6-29-95	.000	.000	.000	4	10	1	0	0	0	0	1	1	1	0	0	3	0	0	.000	.167
Michael Siani	L-L	6-1	188	7-16-99	.250	.500	.219	8	36	6	9	0	0	2	6	1	0	0	1	5	3	0	.417	.263
Donovan Solano	R-R	5-8	210	12-17-87	.345	.250	.381	9	29	2	10	4	0	1	3	2	2	0	1	4	0	0	.586	.412
Spencer Steer	R-R	5-11	185	12-7-97	.293	.444	.257	23	92	14	27	7	0	3	13	9	3	0	0	23	1	0	.467	.375
2-team total (48 St. Paul Saints)					.259	.330	.228	71	290	53	75	17	1	15	45	37	7	0	2	66	3	0	.479	.354
Tyler Stephenson	R-R	6-4	225	8-16-96	.267	--	.267	4	15	1	4	1	0	0	1	0	0	0	0	8	0	0	.333	.267
Robbie Tenerowicz	R-R	6-1	185	1-6-95	.170	.125	.194	14	47	7	8	2	1	0	6	5	4	0	0	12	0	0	.255	.304
Joey Votto	L-R	6-2	220	9-10-83	.250	.000	.333	2	4	1	1	0	0	0	1	3	0	0	0	2	0	0	.250	.571
Jonathan Willems	R-R	5-11	190	11-7-98	.200	--	.200	2	5	0	1	1	0	0	0	0	0	0	0	2	0	0	.400	.200
Eric Yang	R-R	5-11	185	3-26-98	.308	.600	.207	13	39	3	12	2	0	0	5	3	0	1	0	14	0	0	.359	.357

Pitching	**B-T**	**HT**	**WT**	**DOB**	**W**	**L**	**ERA**	**G**	**GS**	**CG**	**SV**	**IP**	**H**	**R**	**ER**	**HR**	**BB**	**SO**	**AVG**	**vLH**	**vRH**	**K/9**	**BB/9**
Graham Ashcraft	L-R	6-2	240	2-11-98	3	2	2.29	8	8	0	0	35	42	24	9	0	17	35	.280	.315	.247	8.92	4.33
Michael Byrne	R-R	6-3	205	4-16-97	0	0	3.86	5	0	0	0	5	6	2	2	0	4	5	.300	.200	.400	9.64	7.71
Luis Castillo	R-R	6-2	200	12-12-92	0	0	0.00	2	2	0	0	8	5	0	0	0	5	12	.172	.235	.083	13.50	5.63
Fernando Cruz	R-R	6-2	205	3-28-90	4	4	2.89	51	0	0	23	56	39	22	18	4	19	66	.198	.172	.218	10.61	3.05
Michael De Leon	B-R	6-1	160	1-14-97	0	0	0.00	1	0	0	0	0	0	0	0	0	0	0	.000	--	.000	0.00	0.00
Eddy Demurias	R-R	6-0	184	8-1-97	4	2	3.95	55	0	0	1	55	52	28	24	5	33	59	.254	.288	.232	9.71	5.43
Ross Detwiler	R-L	6-5	210	3-6-86	1	0	3.86	7	0	0	0	7	6	3	3	0	5	7	.261	.286	.222	9.00	6.43
Phillip Diehl	L-L	6-2	169	7-16-94	2	1	4.24	25	0	0	0	23	18	12	11	4	8	30	.209	.216	.204	11.57	3.09
2-team total (13 Syracuse Mets)					2	3	5.90	38	0	0	1	40	39	29	26	8	18	39	.255	.292	.227	8.85	4.08
Kyle Dowdy	R-R	6-1	195	2-3-93	1	3	3.96	48	0	0	1	52	47	29	23	3	31	56	.240	.186	.270	9.63	5.33
Daniel Duarte	R-R	6-0	170	12-4-96	0	1	9.39	10	0	0	0	8	8	8	8	1	6	7	.276	.250	.294	8.22	7.04
Robert Dugger	R-R	6-0	198	7-3-95	2	1	4.65	14	7	0	0	50	49	28	26	5	26	39	.263	.266	.261	6.97	4.65
2-team total (5 Durham Bulls)					2	3	4.48	19	12	0	0	66	62	37	33	7	33	52	.253	.235	.270	7.06	4.48
Justin Dunn	R-R	6-2	185	9-22-95	0	3	6.21	8	8	0	0	29	31	26	20	4	18	27	.267	.352	.194	8.38	5.59
Raynel Espinal	R-R	6-3	215	10-6-91	0	1	4.58	6	3	0	0	20	17	10	10	3	7	22	.239	.281	.205	10.07	3.20
2-team total (2 Iowa Cubs)					0	1	6.26	8	3	0	0	23	23	16	16	4	10	26	.267	.333	.220	10.17	3.91
Buck Farmer	L-R	6-4	232	2-20-91	0	3	3.63	20	0	0	1	22	18	9	9	4	9	34	.217	.211	.222	13.70	3.63
Luke Farrell	L-R	6-6	200	6-7-91	0	0	0.00	1	0	0	0	1	0	0	0	0	0	2	.000	.000	.000	18.00	0.00
2-team total (17 Iowa Cubs)					3	4	4.95	18	11	0	0	60	58	33	33	10	28	51	.254	.294	.222	7.65	4.20
Bernardo Flores Jr.	L-L	6-4	190	8-23-95	0	1	7.13	5	5	0	0	18	24	15	14	3	12	13	.333	.320	.340	6.62	6.11
Pedro Garcia	R-R	5-11	220	3-21-95	1	0	10.80	9	0	0	0	7	12	8	8	1	3	8	.387	.400	.375	10.80	4.05
Zack Godley	R-R	6-3	250	4-21-90	1	0	8.06	14	2	0	0	22	31	23	20	5	19	29	.323	.341	.309	11.69	7.66
Hunter Greene	R-R	6-5	230	8-6-99	0	0	2.57	3	3	0	0	7	6	2	2	0	2	15	.222	.250	.143	19.29	2.57
Ryan Hendrix	R-R	6-3	215	12-16-94	1	1	5.12	42	0	0	0	39	33	23	22	3	31	53	.228	.237	.221	12.34	7.22
Nick Howard	R-R	6-4	215	4-6-93	0	2	10.80	14	0	0	0	13	25	20	16	1	14	14	.391	.371	.414	9.45	9.45
Ricky Karcher	R-R	6-4	230	9-18-97	2	3	3.98	32	0	0	4	32	25	16	14	2	19	46	.219	.213	.224	13.07	5.40
Joel Kuhnel	R-R	6-4	280	2-19-95	0	1	2.61	10	0	0	3	10	9	3	3	1	1	7	.220	.368	.091	6.10	0.87
Derek Law	R-R	6-3	225	9-14-90	0	0	1.13	6	0	0	0	8	4	1	1	0	3	3	.160	.000	.182	3.38	3.38
2-team total (33 Toledo Mud Hens)					1	3	2.87	39	0	0	15	47	41	16	15	2	13	47	.237	.224	.245	9.00	2.49
Ben Lively	R-R	6-4	190	3-5-92	2	5	4.09	18	18	0	0	77	76	36	35	6	28	79	.256	.266	.247	9.23	3.27
Nick Lodolo	L-L	6-6	205	2-5-98	0	0	2.53	3	3	0	0	11	12	3	3	0	2	16	.279	.500	.120	13.50	1.69
Diomar Lopez	R-R	5-11	165	12-15-96	0	1	14.29	6	0	0	0	6	8	11	9	2	5	4	.308	.300	.313	6.35	7.94
Deck McGuire	R-R	6-6	220	6-23-89	4	5	6.32	20	14	0	0	74	74	54	52	12	43	60	.262	.254	.270	7.30	5.23
Mike Minor	R-L	6-4	210	12-26-87	1	2	3.38	4	4	0	0	16	15	7	6	3	1	20	.234	.158	.267	11.25	0.56
Dauri Moreta	R-R	6-2	185	4-15-96	3	4	3.95	28	0	0	1	27	31	16	12	6	12	28	.295	.321	.269	9.22	3.95
Justin Nicolino	L-L	6-3	195	11-22-91	4	6	5.82	20	18	0	0	85	99	55	55	17	28	54	.293	.324	.279	5.72	2.96
Ryan Nutof	L-R	6-2	190	11-2-95	0	0	4.15	4	0	0	0	4	3	2	2	1	5	2	.200	.333	.000	4.15	10.38
Connor Overton	L-R	6-0	190	7-24-93	2	3	2.70	6	4	0	0	27	22	12	8	4	5	31	.218	.220	.217	10.46	1.69
Riley O'Brien	R-R	6-4	180	2-6-95	0	0	6.00	1	0	0	0	3	2	2	2	1	1	4	.182	.500	.111	12.00	3.00
Pedro Payano	R-R	6-2	170	9-27-94	2	4	3.26	50	0	0	0	61	53	25	22	6	40	62	.236	.233	.237	9.20	5.93
Matt Pidich	R-R	6-2	220	12-25-94	5	4	7.26	32	0	0	0	40	47	36	32	6	20	46	.290	.203	.373	10.44	4.54
Julio Pinto	R-R	6-3	223	11-18-95	0	2	10.43	16	0	0	0	15	18	21	17	1	16	15	.316	.267	.370	9.20	9.82
Jacques Pucheu	L-L	6-2	210	1-1-97	0	0	16.20	1	0	0	0	2	5	3	3	1	2	2	.500	.500	.500	10.80	10.80
Reiver Sanmartin	L-L	6-2	160	4-15-96	2	2	7.36	7	2	0	0	18	24	16	15	2	4	26	.316	.370	.286	12.76	1.96
Lucas Sims	R-R	6-2	225	5-10-94	0	0	2.25	4	2	0	0	4	2	1	1	1	1	5	.143	.400	.000	11.25	2.25

Jared Solomon	R-R	6-2	200	6-10-97	3	2	8.93	41	0	0	0	40	48	42	40	12	29	44	.294	.286	.301	9.82	6.47
Carson Spiers	R-R	6-3	205	11-11-97	2	1	7.41	5	1	0	0	17	26	16	14	3	6	15	.342	.419	.242	7.94	3.18
Levi Stoudt	R-R	6-1	195	12-4-97	0	2	3.32	6	6	0	0	19	17	7	7	0	10	15	.243	.333	.162	7.11	4.74
Art Warren	R-R	6-3	230	3-23-93	0	0	0.00	1	0	0	0	1	1	0	0	0	1	1	.250	.500	.000	9.00	9.00
Brandon Williamson	R-L	6-6	210	4-2-98	1	5	4.07	13	13	0	0	55	53	27	25	4	37	49	.251	.345	.218	7.97	6.02
Randy Wynne	R-R	6-1	180	3-9-93	6	11	4.75	26	22	0	0	133	153	75	70	28	34	85	.287	.295	.281	5.77	2.31
T.J. Zeuch	R-R	6-7	245	8-1-95	0	1	3.63	5	5	0	0	22	18	10	9	2	10	26	.220	.294	.167	10.48	4.03
2-team total (5 Memphis Redbirds)					0	5	7.34	10	10	0	0	42	57	36	34	8	21	46	.337	.422	.256	9.94	4.54
Kyle Zimmer	R-R	6-3	225	9-13-91	1	1	6.90	33	0	0	0	30	31	24	23	3	28	29	.265	.259	.270	8.70	8.40

Fielding

Catcher	PCT	G	PO	A	E	DP	PB
Deluca	1.000	1	1	0	0	0	0
Garcia	1.000	3	22	1	0	0	1
Kolozsvary	.989	41	330	19	4	3	5
Leon	.995	26	207	9	1	0	2
Okey	.987	41	290	8	4	0	4
Papierski	1.000	16	142	8	0	3	0
Robinson	.988	27	230	11	3	1	2
Stephenson	.962	3	25	0	1	0	1
Yang	.990	12	96	1	1	1	0

First Base	PCT	G	PO	A	E	DP
Bauers	.974	21	139	10	4	14
Cordoba	.980	21	133	17	3	8
De Leon	.992	35	232	21	2	31
Free	1.000	2	6	0	0	1
Gilliam	1.000	1	1	0	0	0
McGarry	1.000	6	34	4	0	10
Moran	1.000	29	167	21	0	17
Motter	1.000	3	20	1	0	2
Papierski	.000	1	0	0	0	0
Reynolds	1.000	1	2	0	0	0
Santana	.992	34	232	19	2	26
Steer	1.000	2	11	2	0	2
Tenerowicz	1.000	9	54	2	0	2

Second Base	PCT	G	PO	A	E	DP
Cordoba	1.000	2	1	2	0	0
De Leon	.974	11	12	26	1	8
Hernandez	1.000	1	1	1	0	0
India	.933	4	8	6	1	2
Leyton	.964	7	13	14	1	2
Lopez	.981	31	44	57	2	11
Motter	.957	8	11	11	1	3
Querecuto	.973	39	57	89	4	21
Reynolds	1.000	1	3	4	0	2
Riddle	.985	15	24	40	1	8
Rivas	.978	29	62	72	3	26
Schrock	1.000	9	13	27	0	6
Steer	1.000	5	12	13	0	3
Willems	1.000	2	2	4	0	0

Third Base	PCT	G	PO	A	E	DP
Cordoba	.000	2	0	0	0	0
De Leon	.923	6	3	9	1	2
Lopez	.938	7	4	11	1	0
Moran	1.000	11	4	14	0	1
Motter	1.000	5	0	7	0	1
Querecuto	.955	21	13	50	3	3
Riddle	1.000	3	3	6	0	1
Rivas	.933	6	4	10	1	1
Santana	.946	81	54	121	10	17
Schrock	.833	3	3	2	1	1
Solano	1.000	6	2	3	0	0
Steer	.950	8	6	13	1	4

Shortstop	PCT	G	PO	A	E	DP
Barrero	.946	51	67	125	11	28
De Leon	.875	7	4	10	2	0
Hernandez	.885	21	20	34	7	4
Lopez	1.000	1	1	2	0	1
Motter	.956	16	17	48	3	11
Querecuto	.971	46	58	112	5	29
Reynolds	1.000	1	1	2	0	2
Riddle	.800	4	5	7	3	2
Solano	1.000	1	2	0	0	1
Steer	1.000	7	10	12	0	2

Outfield	PCT	G	PO	A	E	DP
Almora Jr.	.980	16	48	0	1	0
Amburgey	1.000	30	53	3	0	0
Aquino	.974	20	36	2	1	0
Bauers	.941	10	16	0	1	0
Cedrola	.992	123	237	10	2	2
Cordoba	1.000	5	6	2	0	0
Creal	1.000	2	5	0	0	0
Dawson	.985	94	187	5	3	2
Fairchild	.987	35	73	1	1	0
Fraley	1.000	8	12	0	0	0
Friedl	1.000	63	118	2	0	1
Gilliam	.958	14	22	1	1	1
Hopkins	1.000	27	62	1	0	0
Lopez	1.000	5	9	0	0	0
Naquin	1.000	3	8	0	0	0
Piscotty	.955	15	20	1	1	1
Querecuto	--	1	0	0	0	0
Rivas	1.000	2	7	0	0	0
Schrock	1.000	5	9	1	0	1
Senzel	1.000	3	5	0	0	0
Siani	1.000	8	16	1	0	0
Steer	1.000	1	4	0	0	0

CHATTANOOGA LOOKOUTS

DOUBLE-A

SOUTHERN LEAGUE

Batting	B-T	HT	WT	DOB	AVG	vLH	vRH	G	AB	R	H	2B	3B	HR	RBI	BB	HBP	SH	SF	SO	SB	CS	SLG	OBP
Allan Cerda	R-R	6-3	170	11-24-99	.198	.053	.253	62	207	36	41	9	0	11	25	42	7	0	1	77	4	1	.401	.350
Quin Cotton	R-R	5-11	200	3-31-98	.213	.194	.219	38	127	16	27	8	0	3	11	12	3	0	1	53	5	4	.346	.294
Elly De La Cruz	B-R	6-5	200	1-11-02	.305	.295	.310	47	190	34	58	17	3	8	34	16	0	0	1	64	19	2	.553	.357
Michael De Leon	B-R	6-1	160	1-14-97	.266	.243	.275	32	128	10	34	11	0	2	19	7	0	0	1	32	0	0	.398	.301
Christian Encarnacion-Strand	R-R	6-0	224	12-1-99	.309	.167	.372	35	136	13	42	6	1	7	29	6	4	0	2	38	0	0	.522	.351
James Free	B-R	6-2	205	4-14-98	.261	.245	.265	63	211	22	55	7	0	8	27	14	3	0	2	53	0	1	.408	.313
Isiah Gilliam	B-R	6-3	220	7-23-96	.288	.242	.305	62	229	42	66	14	1	12	33	29	4	0	1	84	9	1	.515	.376
Miguel Hernandez	R-R	6-0	194	4-13-99	.300	.400	.267	5	20	3	6	1	0	0	2	1	0	0	0	7	0	0	.350	.333
Rece Hinds	R-R	6-4	215	9-5-00	.310	.167	.348	6	29	3	9	2	1	2	4	0	0	0	0	12	0	1	.655	.310
TJ Hopkins	R-R	6-0	195	1-16-97	.260	.316	.241	101	373	57	97	21	2	17	66	40	6	0	6	117	6	5	.464	.336
Jacob Hurtubise	L-R	6-0	180	12-11-97	.250	.273	.244	63	156	27	39	2	2	1	9	23	12	2	1	41	16	3	.308	.385
Ivan Johnson	B-R	6-0	190	10-11-98	.261	.310	.246	50	180	32	47	12	3	4	25	13	4	0	0	66	4	1	.428	.325
Mark Kolozsvary	R-R	5-8	180	9-4-95	.100	.250	.000	4	10	4	1	0	0	0	2	4	1	0	0	4	0	0	.100	.400
Steven Leyton	R-R	5-10	165	12-17-98	.133	.000	.154	3	15	1	2	0	0	0	0	0	0	0	0	4	0	0	.133	.133
Matt Lloyd	L-R	6-1	205	3-17-96	.187	.316	.143	20	75	10	14	5	0	2	14	10	1	0	0	25	1	0	.333	.291
Quincy McAfee	R-R	5-11	185	9-16-97	.217	.197	.224	77	254	36	55	11	1	6	29	34	8	0	5	82	2	4	.339	.322
Alex McGarry	L-L	6-2	202	5-11-98	.256	.323	.231	61	238	34	61	11	3	16	41	16	2	0	0	73	9	1	.529	.309
Matt McLain	R-R	5-11	180	8-6-99	.232	.222	.235	103	371	67	86	21	5	17	58	70	8	0	3	127	27	3	.453	.363
Nick Quintana	R-R	5-10	180	10-13-97	.233	.222	.237	53	189	27	44	11	0	4	20	29	3	1	0	48	0	4	.354	.344
Brian Rey	R-R	5-11	170	2-22-98	.255	.190	.300	15	51	4	13	2	0	1	6	0	2	0	0	8	0	1	.353	.283
Leonardo Rivas	B-R	5-10	150	10-10-97	.216	.327	.172	56	171	23	37	6	1	5	23	16	4	2	4	35	10	5	.351	.292
Chuckie Robinson	R-R	5-11	221	12-14-94	.276	.290	.271	31	116	13	32	5	0	3	13	9	1	0	0	30	4	2	.397	.333
Michael Siani	L-L	6-1	188	7-16-99	.252	.265	.248	121	456	76	115	19	7	12	49	64	7	1	3	90	49	12	.404	.351
Robbie Tenerowicz	R-R	6-1	185	1-6-95	.288	.293	.286	45	146	26	42	10	0	6	22	27	11	0	3	39	1	0	.479	.428
Francisco Urbaez	R-R	5-11	195	10-13-97	.280	.273	.283	46	164	30	46	11	1	3	22	21	1	0	1	31	2	1	.415	.364
Daniel Vellojin	L-R	5-11	160	3-15-00	.191	.083	.229	29	94	12	18	2	1	4	14	16	0	2	0	34	0	1	.362	.309
Jonathan Willems	R-R	5-11	190	11-7-98	.133	.125	.143	6	15	1	2	0	1	0	1	1	3	0	0	7	0	0	.267	.316
Garrett Wolforth	B-R	6-4	220	10-13-97	.237	.300	.214	11	38	5	9	2	0	2	4	4	0	0	0	14	0	0	.447	.310

Eric Yang	R-R	5-11	185	3-26-98	.170	.065	.210	35	112	13	19	6	0	2	15	16	1	1	0	35	2	0	.277	.279

Pitching	B-T	HT	WT	DOB	W	L	ERA	G	GS	CG	SV	IP	H	R	ER	HR	BB	SO	AVG	vLH	vRH	K/9	BB/9
Andrew Abbott	L-L	6-0	180	6-1-99	7	7	4.75	20	20	1	0	91	84	52	48	7	41	119	.248	.227	.261	11.77	4.05
Graham Ashcraft	L-R	6-2	240	2-11-98	0	1	6.00	1	1	0	0	3	4	2	2	0	1	6	.308	.143	.500	18.00	3.00
Sam Benschoter	R-R	6-3	215	3-17-98	0	1	13.50	1	1	0	0	4	3	6	6	1	4	4	.200	.167	.222	9.00	9.00
Joe Boyle	R-R	6-7	240	8-14-99	0	2	4.85	6	5	0	0	26	21	16	14	3	25	31	.228	.213	.244	10.73	8.65
Stevie Branche	R-R	6-4	205	5-18-97	2	3	5.97	28	0	0	1	35	34	27	23	6	35	46	.260	.220	.292	11.94	9.09
Michael Byrne	R-R	6-3	205	4-16-97	2	5	4.61	37	0	0	2	57	58	35	29	7	24	68	.257	.286	.237	10.80	3.81
Manuel Cachutt	R-R	6-0	185	6-7-97	0	0	1.50	4	0	0	0	6	4	1	1	0	3	3	.190	.333	.083	4.50	4.50
Connor Curlis	L-L	6-1	180	11-29-96	3	9	6.34	32	19	0	1	111	123	82	78	25	37	124	.279	.294	.269	10.08	3.01
Andy Fisher	L-L	6-1	185	1-9-96	3	0	4.09	39	0	0	3	44	43	20	20	3	32	55	.267	.211	.318	11.25	6.55
Pedro Garcia	R-R	5-11	220	3-21-95	2	2	2.17	40	0	0	12	50	38	17	12	3	19	58	.211	.234	.194	10.51	3.44
Myles Gayman	R-R	6-4	200	2-19-98	0	0	18.41	6	0	0	0	7	17	17	15	4	6	9	.425	.526	.333	11.05	7.36
Ricky Karcher	R-R	6-4	230	9-18-97	3	2	3.24	20	0	0	6	25	20	12	9	1	21	42	.213	.268	.170	15.12	7.56
JC Keys	R-R	5-10	173	10-9-96	3	3	6.10	26	0	0	0	41	43	33	28	6	33	45	.269	.254	.280	9.80	7.19
Evan Kravetz	L-L	6-8	240	12-19-96	0	0	4.22	11	0	0	2	21	22	11	10	3	14	26	.268	.212	.306	10.97	5.91
Diomar Lopez	R-R	5-11	165	12-15-96	0	1	67.50	1	0	0	0	1	4	5	5	1	1	1	.667	.500	1.000	13.50	13.50
Sam McWilliams	R-R	6-7	230	9-4-95	0	5	8.50	7	5	0	0	18	21	19	17	2	15	18	.304	.282	.333	9.00	7.50
Miguel Medrano	R-R	6-0	165	1-4-98	0	0	5.17	6	0	0	2	16	12	9	9	1	14	21	.207	.250	.167	12.06	8.04
Mike Minor	R-L	6-4	210	12-26-87	0	1	32.40	1	1	0	0	2	5	6	6	2	1	1	.500	.333	.571	5.40	5.40
Ryan Nutof	L-R	6-2	190	11-2-95	6	2	2.96	39	0	0	2	55	51	26	18	2	29	65	.244	.221	.263	10.70	4.77
Ryan Olson	R-R	6-2	195	11-22-94	0	1	8.74	10	1	0	0	11	12	12	11	1	15	7	.279	.263	.292	5.56	11.91
Connor Phillips	R-R	6-2	190	5-4-01	1	5	4.93	12	12	0	0	46	48	26	25	3	34	60	.268	.268	.268	11.82	6.70
Matt Pidich	R-R	6-2	220	12-25-94	0	0	8.18	10	0	0	0	11	13	10	10	2	6	11	.277	.222	.310	9.00	4.91
Julio Pinto	R-R	6-3	223	11-18-95	5	0	3.69	25	0	0	1	32	33	19	13	4	16	43	.264	.304	.232	12.22	4.55
Jacques Pucheu	L-L	6-2	210	1-1-97	0	1	10.38	2	1	0	0	4	6	5	5	0	3	5	.316	.200	.357	10.38	6.23
Christian Roa	R-R	6-4	220	4-2-99	2	0	1.06	3	3	0	0	17	5	2	2	1	7	19	.093	.120	.069	10.06	3.71
Eduardo Salazar	R-R	6-2	177	5-5-98	6	10	5.16	27	27	0	0	126	130	78	72	11	64	111	.270	.271	.270	7.95	4.58
Ricky Salinas	R-R	6-2	220	3-26-96	5	4	5.60	31	2	0	1	71	73	48	44	10	47	59	.261	.305	.221	7.51	5.99
Jared Solomon	R-R	6-2	200	6-10-97	0	0	0.00	5	0	0	3	7	2	0	0	0	1	6	.091	.083	.100	7.71	1.29
Carson Spiers	R-R	6-3	205	11-11-97	2	5	4.99	22	22	0	0	105	114	66	58	24	39	90	.279	.318	.236	7.74	3.35
Spencer Stockton	B-R	6-3	210	4-24-96	3	3	4.04	25	1	0	0	49	42	25	22	6	22	51	.236	.224	.243	9.37	4.04
Levi Stoudt	R-R	6-1	195	12-4-97	1	0	0.00	1	1	0	0	5	2	0	0	0	0	6	.125	.250	.083	10.80	0.00
Vin Timpanelli	R-R	6-2	210	10-2-98	0	0	7.00	11	0	0	0	18	20	16	14	4	21	25	.294	.371	.212	12.50	10.50
Brandon Williamson	R-L	6-6	210	4-2-98	5	2	4.14	14	14	0	0	67	61	31	31	5	40	74	.242	.240	.244	9.89	5.35

Fielding

Catcher	PCT	G	PO	A	E	DP	PB
Free	.988	42	395	30	5	6	8
Kolozsvary	1.000	4	40	3	0	0	0
Robinson	.993	29	276	27	2	2	2
Vellojin	.983	29	283	15	5	2	5
Yang	.978	35	328	23	8	3	3

First Base	PCT	G	PO	A	E	DP
De Leon	.986	11	63	6	1	4
Encarnacion-Strand	.970	12	92	4	3	15
Free	1.000	16	83	3	0	4
Gilliam	1.000	2	20	1	0	4
Lloyd	1.000	15	84	13	0	9
McAfee	.969	5	25	6	1	5
McGarry	.988	46	304	19	4	26
Tenerowicz	1.000	24	141	8	0	16
Urbaez	1.000	4	20	3	0	5
Wolforth	1.000	9	55	0	0	7

Second Base	PCT	G	PO	A	E	DP
Hernandez	1.000	1	2	3	0	1
Johnson	.994	42	66	96	1	26
Leyton	1.000	3	5	10	0	3
McAfee	.987	23	24	51	1	13
McLain	.972	23	23	46	2	15
Quintana	.958	8	10	13	1	7
Rivas	1.000	9	5	19	0	2
Urbaez	.952	29	37	62	5	12
Willems	1.000	5	5	9	0	1

Third Base	PCT	G	PO	A	E	DP
De La Cruz	.885	10	9	14	3	4
De Leon	.944	14	13	21	2	0
Encarnacion-Strand	1.000	15	10	18	0	4
Lloyd	1.000	1	1	1	0	1
McAfee	.909	22	16	24	4	4
Quintana	.947	36	30	60	5	7
Rivas	.963	17	3	23	1	3
Tenerowicz	.953	21	15	26	2	2
Urbaez	.923	5	7	5	1	2

Shortstop	PCT	G	PO	A	E	DP
De La Cruz	.939	30	40	68	7	19
De Leon	1.000	5	3	12	0	3
Hernandez	1.000	3	4	5	0	1
Johnson	.833	2	4	1	1	0
McAfee	.917	3	4	7	1	2
McLain	.957	74	108	135	11	37
Rivas	.953	24	31	50	4	9

Outfield	PCT	G	PO	A	E	DP
Cerda	.959	62	116	2	5	0
Cotton	.982	33	53	1	1	0
Gilliam	1.000	38	73	1	0	0
Hinds	1.000	6	13	0	0	0
Hopkins	.987	90	153	3	2	0
Hurtubise	.981	59	102	2	2	1
Lloyd	--	1	0	0	0	0
McAfee	1.000	20	27	3	0	0
Rey	1.000	7	14	0	0	0
Rivas	1.000	4	5	0	0	0
Siani	.985	111	248	7	4	2
Urbaez	--	1	0	0	0	0

DAYTON DRAGONS — HIGH CLASS A

MIDWEST LEAGUE

Batting	B-T	HT	WT	DOB	AVG	vLH	vRH	G	AB	R	H	2B	3B	HR	RBI	BB	HBP	SH	SF	SO	SB	CS	SLG	OBP
Jay Allen II	R-R	6-2	190	11-22-02	.230	.167	.242	18	74	13	17	1	2	0	8	4	4	1	1	19	12	4	.297	.301
Albert Almora Jr.	R-R	6-2	190	4-16-94	.313	.333	.300	4	16	2	5	0	0	0	2	0	0	0	0	4	1	0	.313	.313
Tyler Callihan	L-R	6-1	205	6-22-00	.232	.192	.245	56	211	27	49	12	4	4	20	17	3	1	1	61	6	2	.384	.297
Allan Cerda	R-R	6-3	170	11-24-99	.219	.203	.225	62	201	38	44	13	1	13	31	42	6	0	0	91	3	3	.488	.369
Quin Cotton	R-R	5-11	200	3-31-98	.145	.190	.127	22	76	7	11	2	0	2	6	10	0	1	0	36	2	0	.250	.244
Ashton Creal	R-R	6-1	205	3-23-99	.211	.229	.204	57	161	22	34	9	1	2	13	19	7	0	4	52	14	6	.317	.314
Elly De La Cruz	B-R	6-5	200	1-11-02	.302	.277	.313	73	281	53	85	14	6	20	52	24	1	0	0	94	28	4	.609	.359
Jake Fraley	L-L	6-0	195	5-25-95	.000	--	.000	1	1	1	0	0	0	0	0	1	1	0	0	0	1	0	.000	.667
Austin Hendrick	L-L	6-0	195	6-15-01	.222	.178	.239	73	261	39	58	17	0	14	48	29	6	0	3	107	14	5	.448	.311
Rece Hinds	R-R	6-4	215	9-5-00	.235	.230	.237	67	247	33	58	9	4	10	26	23	4	0	0	107	13	5	.425	.310
Ruben Ibarra	R-R	6-5	290	4-26-99	.188	.238	.172	25	85	11	16	3	0	4	8	7	2	0	0	21	1	0	.365	.266

Hayden Jones	L-R	6-0	215	4-27-00	.067	.000	.071	4	15	2	1	0	0	1	1	0	0	0	0	7	0	0	.267	.067
Steven Leyton	R-R	5-10	165	12-17-98	.293	.409	.250	23	82	14	24	8	1	3	16	3	3	1	2	18	3	0	.524	.333
Noelvi Marte	R-R	6-1	181	10-16-01	.292	.417	.277	30	106	12	31	4	0	4	13	17	2	0	1	23	10	3	.443	.397
J.V. Martinez	R-R	6-0	219	11-8-98	.249	.288	.231	60	189	21	47	15	1	4	20	15	3	0	1	57	1	0	.402	.313
Quincy McAfee	R-R	5-11	185	9-16-97	.191	.200	.189	19	68	13	13	1	0	2	4	12	3	0	0	17	0	0	.294	.337
Alex McGarry	L-L	6-2	202	5-11-98	.286	.277	.290	41	154	23	44	10	3	11	37	10	2	0	1	57	6	3	.604	.335
Matheu Nelson	R-R	5-11	209	1-14-99	.219	.253	.205	82	283	40	62	13	2	8	24	24	11	1	2	108	1	0	.364	.303
Nick Quintana	R-R	5-10	180	10-13-97	.257	.271	.252	59	183	29	47	12	0	6	32	33	1	0	1	52	5	0	.421	.372
Brian Rey	R-R	5-11	170	2-22-98	.233	.200	.244	15	60	8	14	3	1	1	8	0	3	0	0	8	0	0	.367	.270
Jack Rogers	L-L	6-2	205	4-5-99	.097	.000	.120	21	62	9	6	1	1	0	4	12	1	0	0	29	3	2	.145	.253
Justice Thompson	R-R	6-4	205	7-8-00	.247	.228	.255	90	291	45	72	15	2	7	34	49	5	0	1	117	20	7	.385	.364
Jose Torres	R-R	6-0	171	9-28-99	.234	.242	.232	107	397	53	93	14	2	13	46	28	4	0	7	116	26	4	.378	.287
Michael Trautwein	L-R	6-1	185	9-13-99	.152	.071	.169	29	79	7	12	1	0	0	8	8	1	0	1	33	0	0	.165	.236
Michel Triana	L-R	6-3	230	11-23-99	.213	.211	.213	25	94	19	20	4	2	7	19	7	2	0	1	34	2	0	.521	.279
Daniel Vellojin	L-R	5-11	160	3-15-00	.271	.263	.275	21	70	10	19	2	0	5	10	13	1	0	0	24	0	2	.514	.393
Joey Votto	L-R	6-2	220	9-10-83	.143	.000	.200	2	7	1	1	0	0	0	0	1	0	0	0	3	0	0	.143	.250
Jonathan Willems	R-R	5-11	190	11-7-98	.183	.108	.224	33	104	9	19	6	0	2	6	3	3	0	0	35	2	0	.298	.227
Garrett Wolforth	B-R	6-4	220	10-13-97	.177	.311	.126	69	220	25	39	11	1	9	36	28	7	1	1	107	1	2	.359	.289

Pitching	B-T	HT	WT	DOB	W	L	ERA	G	GS	CG	SV	IP	H	R	ER	HR	BB	SO	AVG	vLH	vRH	K/9	BB/9
Andrew Abbott	L-L	6-0	180	6-1-99	3	0	0.67	5	4	0	0	27	16	2	2	1	7	40	.168	.174	.167	13.33	2.33
Julian Aguiar	L-R	6-3	180	6-5-01	0	1	6.75	2	2	0	0	8	8	7	6	1	5	10	.276	.200	.316	11.25	5.63
Frainger Aranguren	R-R	6-2	190	3-17-97	4	1	2.91	10	0	0	0	22	21	9	7	2	10	12	.263	.195	.333	4.98	4.15
Donovan Benoit	R-R	6-3	203	1-22-99	3	4	4.00	33	0	0	13	45	32	22	20	3	22	61	.198	.209	.189	12.20	4.40
Sam Benschoter	R-R	6-3	215	3-17-98	1	1	4.32	4	4	0	0	17	17	10	8	0	5	23	.262	.333	.172	12.42	2.70
Dennis Boatman	R-R	6-5	225	11-20-99	3	2	3.14	9	0	0	1	14	11	6	5	2	3	18	.208	.190	.219	11.30	1.88
Bryce Bonnin	R-R	6-2	190	10-11-98	1	1	2.52	6	5	0	0	25	11	9	7	5	12	28	.133	.103	.159	10.08	4.32
Joe Boyle	R-R	6-7	240	8-14-99	3	4	2.17	17	17	0	0	75	25	20	18	3	59	122	.107	.110	.104	14.71	7.11
Manuel Cachutt	R-R	6-0	185	6-7-97	2	1	4.73	23	0	0	2	46	33	26	24	5	21	27	.194	.155	.222	5.32	4.14
Luis Castillo	R-R	6-2	200	12-12-92	0	0	3.86	1	1	0	0	2	2	1	1	0	3	4	.286	.250	.333	15.43	11.57
Jean Correa	R-R	6-1	145	2-16-98	0	0	0.00	3	1	0	0	7	1	0	0	0	5	7	.048	.143	.000	9.00	6.43
Justin Dunn	R-R	6-2	185	9-22-95	0	0	4.50	1	1	0	0	2	3	1	1	0	1	1	.375	.250	.500	4.50	4.50
Thomas Farr	R-R	6-0	203	4-29-99	4	6	4.80	22	20	0	0	99	111	57	53	15	37	102	.291	.312	.276	9.24	3.35
Myles Gayman	R-R	6-4	200	2-19-98	3	1	2.94	24	0	0	1	49	48	16	16	5	10	53	.259	.303	.229	9.73	1.84
Jake Gilbert	R-R	6-7	220	12-1-96	5	3	5.77	30	0	0	0	53	54	43	34	4	35	59	.266	.321	.230	10.02	5.94
Jake Gozzo	R-R	6-5	221	1-5-97	1	0	3.95	25	0	0	3	41	28	20	18	8	24	36	.187	.185	.188	7.90	5.27
Steve Hajjar	R-L	6-5	240	8-7-00	0	1	6.43	2	2	0	0	7	4	5	5	0	6	10	.167	.000	.182	12.86	7.71
Nick Hanson	R-R	6-6	205	6-10-98	0	1	9.53	5	0	0	1	6	8	9	6	0	8	5	.333	.313	.375	7.94	12.71
Owen Holt	R-R	6-3	225	4-22-99	0	0	2.45	4	0	0	0	7	5	2	2	0	3	7	.192	.214	.167	8.59	3.68
Evan Kravetz	L-L	6-8	240	12-19-96	4	5	4.19	17	8	0	1	62	58	36	29	8	27	77	.243	.194	.262	11.12	3.90
James Marinan	R-R	6-5	239	10-10-98	3	3	7.88	26	4	0	0	54	67	52	47	11	31	55	.302	.343	.267	9.22	5.20
J.V. Martinez	R-R	6-0	219	11-8-98	0	0	18.00	1	0	0	0	1	3	2	2	0	1	1	.500	.750	.000	9.00	9.00
Miguel Medrano	R-R	6-0	165	1-4-98	2	5	7.79	12	6	0	0	35	35	32	30	7	25	34	.265	.273	.260	8.83	6.49
Chase Petty	R-R	6-1	190	4-4-03	1	2	4.40	7	7	0	0	31	27	15	15	2	7	33	.231	.200	.254	9.68	2.05
Connor Phillips	R-R	6-2	190	5-4-01	4	3	2.95	12	12	0	0	64	39	23	21	5	32	90	.181	.163	.195	12.66	4.50
James Proctor	R-R	6-5	215	7-18-98	4	4	5.10	11	11	0	0	48	50	33	27	3	24	40	.260	.279	.245	7.55	4.53
Jacques Pucheu	L-L	6-2	210	1-1-97	1	1	6.30	3	0	0	0	10	11	8	7	1	5	6	.262	.318	.200	5.40	4.50
Javi Rivera	R-R	6-1	195	11-27-99	1	1	5.12	5	5	0	0	19	15	12	11	4	7	23	.211	.242	.184	10.71	3.26
Christian Roa	R-R	6-4	220	4-2-99	4	3	4.14	17	17	0	0	74	59	37	34	5	48	83	.218	.211	.222	10.09	5.84
Braxton Roxby	R-R	6-3	215	3-12-99	3	0	4.84	19	0	0	3	22	20	13	12	0	10	32	.238	.250	.231	12.90	4.03
Carson Rudd	R-R	6-5	190	9-17-98	1	4	8.88	20	0	0	3	24	26	26	24	9	14	33	.268	.273	.264	12.21	5.18
Jayvien Sandridge	L-L	6-5	220	2-11-99	1	1	5.63	11	0	0	0	16	7	10	10	0	17	24	.130	.056	.167	13.50	9.56
Jake Stevenson	R-R	6-4	225	3-24-97	1	1	10.13	26	0	0	1	27	29	31	30	5	36	29	.290	.313	.269	9.79	12.15
Spencer Stockton	B-R	6-3	210	4-24-96	3	0	1.76	7	1	0	0	15	11	3	3	0	3	17	.193	.222	.167	9.98	1.76
Vin Timpanelli	R-R	6-2	210	10-2-98	1	1	3.94	21	0	0	2	30	22	17	13	3	19	54	.202	.238	.179	16.38	5.76
Art Warren	R-R	6-3	230	3-23-93	0	0	0.00	3	0	0	0	3	1	0	0	0	0	4	.091	.500	.000	12.00	0.00

Fielding

Catcher	PCT	G	PO	A	E	DP	PB
Jones	1.000	2	18	2	0	1	0
Nelson	.993	74	757	44	6	6	4
Trautwein	1.000	23	200	17	0	4	1
Vellojin	.974	14	140	8	4	0	6
Wolforth	.989	19	176	11	2	0	7

First Base	PCT	G	PO	A	E	DP
Ibarra	1.000	20	106	8	0	13
Martinez	.986	34	200	12	3	15
McAfee	1.000	2	12	0	0	1
McGarry	.993	18	131	4	1	14
Rogers	1.000	8	48	5	0	8
Triana	.995	22	172	10	1	14
Votto	1.000	2	10	0	0	0
Wolforth	.995	32	205	12	1	18

Second Base	PCT	G	PO	A	E	DP
Callihan	.978	23	38	53	2	11
Leyton	1.000	9	9	24	0	3
McAfee	.917	3	4	7	1	1
Quintana	.975	19	24	55	2	9
Torres	.954	49	65	120	9	21
Willems	.971	29	35	64	3	13

Third Base	PCT	G	PO	A	E	DP
Callihan	.900	29	18	45	7	5
De La Cruz	.926	14	9	16	2	2
Leyton	.919	11	7	27	3	2
Martinez	.947	25	10	26	2	3
McAfee	1.000	8	3	15	0	2
Quintana	.966	40	23	63	3	6
Triana	.857	3	2	4	1	0
Willems	1.000	2	0	6	0	0

Shortstop	PCT	G	PO	A	E	DP
De La Cruz	.935	54	78	110	13	28
Leyton	1.000	1	0	1	0	0
Marte	.974	23	23	52	2	14
McAfee	.750	1	2	1	1	0
Torres	.975	49	50	109	4	24

Outfield	PCT	G	PO	A	E	DP
Allen II	1.000	16	27	0	0	0
Cerda	.958	54	87	5	4	1
Cotton	.976	22	40	0	1	0
Creal	.947	55	89	1	5	0
Fraley	1.000	1	2	0	0	0
Hendrick	.937	64	112	6	8	1
Hinds	.966	54	75	10	3	3
McAfee	1.000	6	10	1	0	0
McGarry	1.000	6	11	0	0	0

Rey	1.000	13	17	1	0	0	Thompson	.975	85	150	4	4	1	Wolforth	1.000	5	5	1	0	0
Rogers	.882	12	15	0	2	0	Trautwein	1.000	1	2	0	0	0							

DAYTONA TORTUGAS

LOW CLASS A

FLORIDA STATE LEAGUE

Batting	B-T	HT	WT	DOB	AVG	vLH	vRH	G	AB	R	H	2B	3B	HR	RBI	BB	HBP	SH	SF	SO	SB	CS	SLG	OBP
Jay Allen II	R-R	6-2	190	11-22-02	.224	.224	.224	73	241	48	54	13	2	3	21	40	12	4	2	73	31	6	.332	.359
Sebastian Almonte	R-R	6-0	185	10-22-99	.127	.080	.148	26	79	7	10	2	1	0	1	7	1	0	1	36	1	4	.177	.205
Edwin Arroyo	B-B	6-0	175	8-25-03	.227	.280	.208	27	97	16	22	6	3	1	16	9	2	0	1	31	4	2	.381	.303
Johnny Ascanio	B-R	5-10	150	7-4-03	.229	.211	.241	16	48	10	11	0	0	0	2	6	0	0	0	11	0	0	.229	.315
Wilfred Astudillo	B-R	5-11	209	3-14-00	.227	.282	.207	50	150	12	34	8	0	0	19	9	2	0	0	22	1	1	.280	.280
Justin Boyd	R-R	6-0	201	3-30-01	.183	.136	.204	21	71	11	13	4	0	0	4	8	0	0	1	29	5	0	.239	.263
Austin Callahan	L-R	6-3	215	6-6-01	.256	.167	.289	59	203	30	52	15	1	5	22	21	2	0	4	49	5	2	.414	.326
Tyler Callihan	L-R	6-1	205	6-22-00	.282	.278	.284	32	117	18	33	7	0	3	13	10	0	0	1	19	9	1	.419	.336
Fidel Castro	L-R	6-3	175	12-26-98	.211	.071	.256	45	114	13	24	2	1	4	9	11	5	0	0	54	3	2	.351	.308
Luis Chevalier	B-R	5-11	160	1-18-02	.100	.182	.069	19	40	3	4	0	0	0	0	8	0	0	0	19	1	1	.100	.250
Yerlin Confidan	L-L	6-3	170	12-16-02	.246	.438	.184	22	65	10	16	3	1	1	9	11	0	0	0	22	1	1	.369	.355
Ashton Creal	R-R	6-1	205	3-23-99	.214	.200	.218	21	70	8	15	4	1	2	6	6	3	1	1	25	7	1	.386	.300
Joe Deluca	B-R	6-3	235	8-29-95	.143	.250	.000	2	7	2	1	1	0	0	0	1	0	0	0	2	0	0	.286	.250
Blake Dunn	R-R	6-0	210	9-5-98	.290	.379	.250	33	93	22	27	5	1	4	16	24	7	3	0	29	18	1	.495	.468
Trey Faltine	R-R	6-2	198	1-8-01	.237	.333	.213	21	59	12	14	6	0	1	10	14	3	0	2	24	1	0	.390	.397
Ilvin Fernandez	R-R	6-1	160	9-8-01	.175	.125	.196	29	80	7	14	1	0	1	3	7	1	2	0	25	2	0	.225	.250
Rafael Franco	R-R	6-2	155	6-20-01	.114	.100	.120	16	35	4	4	0	0	1	2	4	0	1	0	10	0	0	.200	.205
Austin Hendrick	L-L	6-0	195	6-15-01	.205	.237	.191	36	127	19	26	4	0	7	21	14	3	0	1	58	2	0	.402	.297
Cade Hunter	L-R	6-2	200	11-29-00	.308	.000	.400	8	26	5	8	1	0	2	8	2	0	0	0	7	3	0	.577	.357
Ruben Ibarra	R-R	6-5	290	4-26-99	.286	.257	.295	42	140	21	40	7	0	7	26	17	5	0	2	42	2	1	.486	.378
Hayden Jones	L-R	6-0	215	4-27-00	.243	.310	.222	72	243	31	59	12	0	9	31	19	3	0	1	77	2	2	.403	.305
Danny Lantigua	B-R	6-1	165	3-7-99	.118	.000	.162	17	51	5	6	1	0	1	5	3	0	0	0	23	1	0	.196	.167
Steven Leyton	R-R	5-10	165	12-17-98	.246	.278	.233	51	187	25	46	12	4	8	28	2	3	0	0	39	3	0	.481	.266
Wendell Marrero	L-L	6-2	195	11-28-00	.260	.200	.274	25	77	6	20	6	0	0	11	8	1	0	1	27	2	0	.338	.333
Junior Melo	R-R	6-2	175	5-10-97	.000	.000	.000	1	3	0	0	0	0	0	0	0	0	0	0	2	0	0	.000	.000
Braylin Minier	L-R	6-0	160	6-11-03	.194	.280	.175	45	139	11	27	6	0	3	11	7	0	0	0	50	0	1	.302	.233
Jamal O'Guinn	R-R	6-4	220	1-19-99	.216	.207	.219	70	213	21	46	14	0	3	27	40	5	1	2	71	3	2	.324	.350
Yassel Pino	R-R	6-2	200	10-4-01	.221	.292	.194	53	172	25	38	5	2	5	20	25	1	0	6	50	1	2	.360	.314
Reyny Reyes	R-R	6-2	185	3-20-99	.147	.227	.113	25	75	9	11	1	0	0	2	8	2	0	1	21	3	0	.160	.244
Hector Rodriguez	L-R	5-8	186	3-11-04	.289	.333	.267	13	45	7	13	4	2	0	6	2	0	0	0	10	1	1	.467	.319
2-team total (2 St. Lucie Mets)					.269	.313	.250	15	52	8	14	4	2	0	6	3	0	0	0	10	1	1	.423	.309
Jack Rogers	L-L	6-2	205	4-5-99	.285	.288	.283	72	253	42	72	17	5	10	43	25	4	0	1	104	4	2	.510	.357
Andruw Salcedo	B-R	5-11	175	9-29-02	.154	.333	.059	11	26	4	4	0	0	0	4	5	0	0	0	11	0	0	.154	.290
Debby Santana	R-R	6-2	185	8-24-00	.045	.143	.000	8	22	2	1	0	0	0	0	1	2	0	0	17	0	0	.045	.160
Gus Steiger	R-R	5-11	185	4-20-99	.287	.371	.253	34	122	21	35	7	1	0	12	13	1	1	0	32	12	3	.361	.360
Logan Tanner	R-R	6-0	215	11-10-00	.211	.250	.195	16	57	9	12	3	0	1	7	12	0	0	1	20	1	0	.316	.343
Justice Thompson	R-R	6-4	205	7-8-00	.257	.375	.222	9	35	3	9	1	0	0	0	4	0	0	0	17	3	1	.286	.333
Michael Trautwein	L-R	6-1	185	9-13-99	.240	.667	.182	11	25	2	6	0	0	2	5	2	0	0	0	11	0	0	.480	.296
Michel Triana	L-R	6-3	230	11-23-99	.201	.159	.215	82	288	33	58	9	4	7	33	30	8	1	3	97	10	4	.333	.292
Daniel Vellojin	L-R	5-11	160	3-15-00	.129	.125	.130	20	62	7	8	0	0	1	4	13	0	0	0	21	3	1	.177	.280
Jonathan Willems	R-R	5-11	190	11-7-98	.080	.000	.091	9	25	2	2	0	0	1	1	2	0	0	0	7	1	2	.200	.148

Pitching	B-T	HT	WT	DOB	W	L	ERA	G	GS	CG	SV	IP	H	R	ER	HR	BB	SO	AVG	vLH	vRH	K/9	BB/9
Kevin Abel	R-R	6-1	195	2-19-99	1	3	6.97	11	5	0	0	31	34	29	24	4	29	52	.276	.244	.295	15.10	8.42
Juan Manuel Abril	R-R	6-0	160	3-11-98	1	1	4.57	15	0	0	2	22	20	12	11	2	20	22	.250	.250	.250	9.14	8.31
Jose Acuna	R-R	6-2	175	10-20-02	0	1	3.16	7	5	0	0	31	17	13	11	1	10	35	.160	.091	.192	10.05	2.87
2-team total (2 St. Lucie Mets)					0	1	2.75	9	7	0	0	39	21	14	12	1	15	47	.157	.118	.170	10.75	3.43
Julian Aguiar	L-R	6-3	180	6-5-01	7	7	3.16	23	15	0	0	88	82	45	31	12	22	103	.240	.242	.240	10.49	2.24
Frainger Aranguren	R-R	6-2	190	3-17-97	1	1	1.42	3	0	0	0	6	3	2	1	0	2	1	.150	.077	.286	1.42	2.84
Sam Benschoter	R-R	6-3	215	3-17-98	3	3	4.01	14	9	0	0	52	44	24	23	6	18	80	.223	.229	.221	13.94	3.14
Dennis Boatman	R-R	6-5	225	11-20-99	4	6	3.38	20	0	0	5	29	22	15	11	3	15	42	.212	.125	.250	12.89	4.60
Trey Braithwaite	R-R	6-3	220	9-23-97	1	0	1.50	3	0	0	0	6	5	1	1	0	2	5	.217	.385	.000	7.50	3.00
Ryan Cardona	R-R	6-1	200	5-7-00	4	4	3.36	25	7	0	5	75	55	29	28	6	50	92	.207	.217	.201	11.04	6.00
Tanner Cooper	R-R	6-3	215	9-8-99	4	5	3.55	22	15	0	1	84	80	37	33	12	21	75	.248	.272	.237	8.07	2.26
Jean Correa	R-R	6-1	145	2-16-98	2	0	2.08	3	0	0	0	9	4	2	2	0	5	8	.138	.143	.133	8.31	5.19
Reynardo Cruz	R-R	6-2	165	10-24-01	0	3	5.40	14	6	0	0	40	30	27	24	3	27	38	.219	.188	.236	8.55	6.08
Jose Franco	R-R	6-2	175	11-25-00	1	6	4.44	20	13	0	0	77	76	38	38	13	39	104	.259	.277	.252	12.16	4.56
Arij Fransen	R-R	6-3	190	5-20-01	2	6	6.46	13	6	0	0	39	47	34	28	9	17	28	.299	.267	.313	6.46	3.92
Alberto Gonzalez	R-R	6-1	180	7-26-99	0	2	5.06	5	0	0	0	5	3	4	3	0	5	8	.176	.000	.200	13.50	8.44
Shane Gustafson	R-R	6-5	190	10-10-98	1	1	6.10	4	0	0	1	10	17	8	7	2	4	7	.370	.286	.385	6.10	3.48
Owen Holt	R-R	6-3	225	4-22-99	2	1	2.41	20	0	0	3	37	26	10	10	2	13	42	.193	.222	.178	10.13	3.13
Bryce Hubbart	L-L	6-1	181	6-28-01	1	0	0.00	3	0	0	0	6	1	0	0	0	3	10	.056	.000	.077	15.88	4.76
Alexander Johnson	R-R	6-6	220	7-2-00	1	2	7.08	9	4	0	0	20	18	17	16	1	20	23	.240	.263	.232	10.18	8.85
Brett Lockwood	L-R	6-4	220	4-15-97	4	4	5.82	25	0	0	0	51	66	33	33	1	30	38	.319	.321	.318	6.71	5.29
Zach Maxwell	R-R	6-6	275	1-26-01	0	0	6.75	3	0	0	0	5	4	4	4	0	7	7	.190	.176	.250	11.81	11.81
Yomil Maysonet	R-R	6-1	180	1-9-00	2	1	9.31	6	0	0	0	10	7	11	10	2	13	7	.200	.133	.250	6.52	12.10
Joseph Menefee	L-L	6-2	220	10-6-99	0	0	2.70	3	0	0	0	3	8	1	1	0	1	4	.500	.667	.400	10.80	2.70
Luis Mey	R-R	6-2	160	6-24-01	4	1	5.65	34	0	0	2	43	45	32	27	3	32	58	.274	.294	.265	12.14	6.70

CINCINNATI REDS

Andrew Moore	L-R	6-5	205	8-11-99	0	0	12.54	6	2	0	0	9	12	14	13	1	12	14	.308	.474	.150	13.50	11.57
Hunter Parks	R-R	6-4	187	4-28-01	4	6	4.70	25	14	0	1	82	75	45	43	7	53	94	.241	.265	.230	10.28	5.79
Jose Peralta	R-R	6-1	170	10-2-99	0	1	3.86	2	0	0	0	2	2	2	1	0	3	0	.250	.000	.286	0.00	11.57
Chase Petty	R-R	6-1	190	4-4-03	0	4	3.06	18	13	0	0	68	57	25	23	5	24	63	.233	.197	.249	8.38	3.19
Nicolo Pinazzi	L-L	6-2	195	10-25-99	0	0	9.00	1	0	0	0	3	3	3	3	0	2	6	.250	.600	.000	18.00	6.00
Javi Rivera	R-R	6-1	195	11-27-99	2	3	2.81	19	11	0	0	74	52	26	23	4	18	88	.197	.125	.224	10.75	2.20
Carson Rudd	R-R	6-5	190	9-17-98	2	1	2.77	8	3	0	0	26	12	9	8	1	16	38	.135	.158	.118	13.15	5.54
Jayvien Sandridge	L-L	6-5	220	2-11-99	0	1	1.46	17	0	0	3	25	12	9	4	0	18	43	.135	.000	.158	15.69	6.57

Fielding

Catcher	PCT	G	PO	A	E	DP	PB
Astudillo	.994	37	324	35	2	2	4
Deluca	1.000	1	11	0	0	0	0
Hunter	1.000	5	38	3	0	1	2
Jones	.989	45	430	38	5	6	9
Melo	1.000	1	5	0	0	0	0
Salcedo	1.000	9	68	9	0	0	0
Tanner	.980	14	143	5	3	2	1
Trautwein	1.000	7	57	4	0	0	1
Vellojin	.977	18	159	13	4	1	2

First Base	PCT	G	PO	A	E	DP
Astudillo	1.000	1	8	0	0	0
Callahan	1.000	4	18	1	0	2
Ibarra	.989	36	254	14	3	31
Marrero	1.000	2	13	2	0	4
Pino	.997	45	314	17	1	35
Reyes	1.000	1	7	0	0	0
Rogers	.975	14	75	4	2	1
Triana	.995	29	189	19	1	16

Second Base	PCT	G	PO	A	E	DP
Almonte	.972	20	35	34	2	7
Ascanio	.968	14	22	39	2	13
Callihan	.991	28	49	61	1	18
Chevalier	1.000	8	8	16	0	4
Faltine	.962	9	7	18	1	4
Fernandez	1.000	4	1	7	0	0
Leyton	.988	23	32	47	1	13
Minier	.973	19	32	39	2	6
Reyes	.957	12	22	22	2	10
Willems	1.000	5	7	11	0	2

Third Base	PCT	G	PO	A	E	DP
Almonte	.818	3	3	6	2	2
Callahan	.946	51	29	77	6	9
Callihan	1.000	1	2	1	0	0
Fernandez	.857	4	6	6	2	1
Leyton	.750	1	0	3	1	0
Minier	.958	11	10	13	1	2
Reyes	1.000	9	5	10	0	0
Santana	.818	4	3	6	2	0
Triana	.933	46	28	69	7	9
Willems	1.000	3	1	3	0	0

Shortstop	PCT	G	PO	A	E	DP
Almonte	1.000	3	3	3	0	1
Arroyo	.977	25	26	60	2	12
Faltine	.968	8	15	15	1	6
Fernandez	.957	21	24	43	3	7
Leyton	.957	29	24	65	4	13
Minier	.951	15	15	24	2	7
Reyes	.917	3	3	8	1	0
Steiger	.975	30	38	80	3	17

Outfield	PCT	G	PO	A	E	DP
Allen II	.986	71	133	3	2	1
Boyd	1.000	21	31	2	0	0
Castro	.958	46	60	8	3	2
Chevalier	1.000	8	11	0	0	0
Confidan	.850	16	15	2	3	0
Creal	.939	23	43	3	3	0
Dunn	.977	35	41	1	1	0
Franco	1.000	15	13	1	0	1
Hendrick	1.000	37	49	1	0	0
Lantigua	1.000	10	12	0	0	0
Marrero	.875	21	27	1	4	0
O'Guinn	1.000	55	75	1	0	0
Rodriguez	.958	12	22	1	1	0
Rogers	.923	47	46	2	4	0
Steiger	1.000	1	2	0	0	0
Thompson	1.000	6	12	0	0	0
Trautwein	1.000	3	5	0	0	0

ACL REDS — ROOKIE

ARIZONA COMPLEX LEAGUE

Batting	B-T	HT	WT	DOB	AVG	vLH	vRH	G	AB	R	H	2B	3B	HR	RBI	BB	HBP	SH	SF	SO	SB	CS	SLG	OBP
Victor Acosta	B-R	5-11	170	6-10-04	.214	.200	.217	10	28	5	6	4	0	0	1	5	1	0	0	7	0	0	.357	.353
2-team total (32 ACL Padres)					.237	.161	.259	42	139	22	33	7	2	2	12	21	3	1	1	37	5	7	.360	.348
Deivid Alcantara	R-R	6-2	180	6-14-03	.242	.250	.240	27	62	12	15	3	1	2	11	15	6	0	0	28	7	2	.419	.434
Ariel Almonte	L-L	6-1	170	12-1-03	.286	.240	.296	42	140	28	40	11	0	6	24	21	3	0	0	49	1	0	.493	.390
Sebastian Almonte	R-R	6-0	185	10-22-99	.088	.333	.036	21	34	6	3	0	0	0	3	7	2	0	0	17	2	3	.088	.279
Donovan Antonia	R-R	5-10	182	8-13-03	.261	.278	.257	29	88	24	23	8	0	4	18	14	3	0	1	20	3	2	.489	.377
Edwin Arroyo	B-B	6-0	175	8-25-03	.000	--	.000	2	6	1	0	0	0	0	1	2	0	0	1	2	2	0	.000	.222
Johnny Ascanio	B-R	5-10	150	7-4-03	.344	.125	.377	20	61	12	21	3	2	0	10	8	1	0	1	18	5	2	.459	.423
Leonardo Balcazar	R-R	0-0	0	6-17-04	.322	.526	.290	42	143	25	46	6	2	4	26	18	5	0	2	42	13	1	.476	.411
Justin Boyd	R-R	6-0	201	3-30-01	.667	--	.667	1	3	2	2	1	0	0	0	0	0	0	0	0	1	0	1.000	.667
Luis Chevalier	B-R	5-11	160	1-18-02	.125	.250	.083	6	16	1	2	0	0	0	2	2	0	0	0	5	1	0	.125	.222
Cam Collier	L-R	6-2	210	11-20-04	.370	.500	.348	9	27	7	10	1	0	2	4	7	1	0	0	6	0	2	.630	.514
Yerlin Confidan	L-L	6-3	170	12-16-02	.227	.500	.200	9	22	3	5	2	0	1	2	5	0	0	0	9	0	3	.455	.370
Yan Contreras	R-R	6-2	185	1-30-01	.000	--	.000	2	2	0	0	0	0	0	0	4	1	0	0	2	0	0	.000	.714
Blake Dunn	R-R	6-0	210	9-5-98	.077	.000	.091	4	13	0	1	0	0	0	1	1	0	0	0	3	2	0	.077	.143
Trey Faltine	R-R	6-2	198	1-8-01	.500	--	.500	1	2	1	1	0	0	0	0	1	0	0	0	0	0	0	.500	.667
Ilvin Fernandez	R-R	6-1	160	9-8-01	.273	1.000	.000	4	11	1	3	1	0	0	3	0	0	0	0	2	1	0	.364	.273
Rafael Franco	R-R	6-2	155	6-20-01	.000	.000	.000	4	8	2	0	0	0	0	0	2	0	0	0	4	0	0	.000	.200
Juan Garcia	R-R	5-11	185	5-3-03	.333	.600	.263	10	24	3	8	1	0	1	6	3	2	0	1	6	0	0	.500	.433
Miguel Hernandez	R-R	6-0	194	4-13-99	.275	.273	.276	12	40	11	11	2	0	2	10	5	0	0	0	9	1	0	.475	.356
Rece Hinds	R-R	6-4	215	9-5-00	.063	.000	.071	6	16	2	1	0	0	0	0	2	1	0	0	6	2	2	.063	.211
Cade Hunter	L-R	6-2	200	11-29-00	.400	.000	.462	6	15	5	6	2	1	1	5	5	1	0	0	4	0	0	.867	.571
Wencer Inirio	R-R	6-3	190	10-28-02	.171	.167	.172	26	76	9	13	3	0	1	5	8	3	0	1	33	0	0	.250	.273
Carlos Jorge	L-R	5-10	160	9-22-03	.261	.235	.265	42	119	32	31	7	2	7	21	25	6	1	3	41	27	4	.529	.405
Wendell Marrero	L-L	6-2	195	11-28-00	.250	.308	.234	22	60	15	15	4	1	2	11	16	6	0	0	22	0	0	.450	.451
Junior Melo	R-R	6-2	175	5-10-97	.267	.600	.100	5	15	1	4	0	0	0	3	2	0	0	0	1	0	0	.267	.353
Braylin Minier	L-R	6-0	160	6-11-03	.320	.286	.333	7	25	5	8	2	0	1	7	4	0	0	0	8	0	1	.520	.414
Diego Omana	R-R	5-11	165	1-10-03	.138	.333	.115	10	29	2	4	1	0	0	2	1	0	0	0	4	0	0	.172	.167
Yassel Pino	R-R	6-2	200	10-4-01	.200	--	.200	4	15	3	3	0	1	1	4	2	0	0	1	5	1	0	.533	.278
Brian Rey	R-R	5-11	170	2-22-98	.241	.000	.250	9	29	8	7	1	0	0	4	5	3	0	0	9	5	0	.276	.405
Hector Rodriguez	L-R	5-8	186	3-11-04	.400	.000	.455	7	25	7	10	4	2	0	4	3	0	0	0	0	3	2	.720	.464
Andruw Salcedo	B-R	5-11	175	9-29-02	.213	.364	.188	28	80	8	17	2	0	0	6	12	2	0	1	24	0	0	.238	.326
Jose Serrano	R-R	6-0	180	10-14-03	.244	.286	.236	32	86	14	21	4	0	1	12	13	1	0	0	35	1	0	.326	.350
Sal Stewart	R-R	6-3	215	12-7-03	.292	.667	.238	8	24	5	7	4	0	0	5	4	0	0	0	5	0	0	.458	.393

Junior Tamares	L-R	6-0	165	9-26-01	.214	.500	.167	8	14	2	3	0	0	0	1	2	0	0	0	6	0	0	.214	.313
Logan Tanner	R-R	6-0	215	11-10-00	.000	--	.000	1	3	0	0	0	0	0	0	0	0	0	0	2	0	0	.000	.000
Malvin Valdez	R-R	6-2	178	10-14-03	.219	.200	.223	39	114	23	25	3	2	1	11	16	4	0	0	38	10	1	.307	.336

Pitching	B-T	HT	WT	DOB	W	L	ERA	G	GS	CG	SV	IP	H	R	ER	HR	BB	SO	AVG	vLH	vRH	K/9	BB/9
Kevin Abel	R-R	6-1	195	2-19-99	1	0	1.17	2	1	0	0	8	3	1	1	0	5	14	.115	.333	.087	16.43	5.87
Juan Manuel Abril	R-R	6-0	160	3-11-98	0	0	0.00	1	0	0	0	1	1	0	0	0	1	2	.250	.000	.500	18.00	9.00
Frainger Aranguren	R-R	6-2	190	3-17-97	2	1	5.21	10	0	0	0	19	28	18	11	2	9	21	.329	.276	.357	9.95	4.26
Sam Benschoter	R-R	6-3	215	3-17-98	0	1	6.35	3	3	0	0	6	3	4	4	1	4	11	.150	.250	.000	17.47	6.35
Parker Brahms	R-R	6-3	209	12-2-97	3	0	2.70	7	1	0	1	17	14	11	5	0	5	22	.209	.452	.000	11.88	2.70
Trey Braithwaite	R-R	6-3	220	9-23-97	1	0	0.00	2	0	0	0	2	2	0	0	0	1	2	.250	.500	.167	9.00	4.50
Jean Correa	R-R	6-1	145	2-16-98	0	0	4.15	2	0	0	0	4	5	2	2	0	2	3	.313	.333	.000	6.23	4.15
Vladimir Davila	R-R	5-11	158	9-10-02	1	0	5.40	2	0	0	0	5	7	6	3	0	1	2	.304	.316	.250	3.60	1.80
Arij Fransen	R-R	6-3	190	5-20-01	1	2	7.71	9	7	0	0	26	34	27	22	4	13	18	.315	.385	.275	6.31	4.56
Alberto Gonzalez	R-R	6-1	180	7-26-99	1	0	3.24	8	0	0	1	8	6	5	3	1	2	17	.188	.300	.136	18.36	2.16
Shane Gustafson	R-R	6-5	190	10-10-98	1	1	3.38	7	0	0	0	24	21	11	9	1	4	18	.221	.250	.171	6.75	1.50
Nick Hanson	R-R	6-6	205	6-10-98	0	0	0.00	2	1	0	0	2	0	0	0	0	2	2	.000	--	.000	9.00	9.00
Johnathan Harmon	R-R	6-5	195	9-4-00	0	0	0.00	2	1	0	0	2	1	0	0	0	0	2	.143	.000	.333	9.00	0.00
Rob Hensey	L-L	6-4	220	9-29-99	0	0	0.00	2	0	0	0	2	3	0	0	0	0	3	.375	.000	.500	13.50	0.00
Bryce Hubbart	L-L	6-1	181	6-28-01	0	0	5.40	2	1	0	0	2	2	1	1	0	3	2	.333	1.000	.200	10.80	16.20
Kenya Huggins	R-R	6-3	215	12-12-02	0	1	0.00	1	1	0	0	1	2	2	0	1	0	3	.400	.333	.500	27.00	0.00
Brody Jessee	R-R	6-4	217	12-1-00	0	1	5.40	2	0	0	0	2	0	1	1	0	1	1	.000	.000	--	5.40	5.40
Nick Lodolo	L-L	6-6	205	2-5-98	0	0	4.50	1	1	0	0	2	4	1	1	0	1	2	.444	--	.444	9.00	4.50
Jefferson Lopez	R-R	6-1	185	2-18-01	4	1	1.50	14	0	0	2	24	16	5	4	0	6	29	.195	.214	.185	10.88	2.25
Nestor Lorant	R-R	6-2	175	5-4-02	5	1	4.05	11	2	0	0	33	32	17	15	2	15	47	.256	.308	.219	12.69	4.05
Jared Lyons	R-R	6-1	190	9-27-00	0	0	0.00	2	2	0	0	2	1	0	0	0	0	4	.167	.200	.000	18.00	0.00
Juan Martinez	R-R	6-1	160	12-30-02	1	0	4.91	6	1	0	0	18	29	16	10	2	4	16	.363	.316	.405	7.85	1.96
Zach Maxwell	R-R	6-6	275	1-26-01	0	0	0.00	2	0	0	1	2	1	0	0	0	1	3	.167	.000	.333	13.50	4.50
Yomil Maysonet	R-R	6-1	180	1-9-00	3	0	2.61	13	0	0	4	21	9	6	6	1	10	28	.130	.152	.111	12.19	4.35
Jake McMahill	R-R	6-2	197	3-2-98	0	0	0.00	3	0	0	0	3	0	0	0	0	2	2	.000	.000	.000	6.00	6.00
Sam McWilliams	R-R	6-7	230	9-4-95	0	0	54.00	2	0	0	0	1	0	4	4	0	4	0	.000	.000	.000	0.00	54.00
Joseph Menefee	L-L	6-2	220	10-6-99	0	0	0.00	2	0	0	0	2	1	0	0	0	0	2	.143	.000	.250	9.00	0.00
Jose Montero	R-R	6-2	180	7-14-03	0	0	10.13	1	0	0	0	3	9	4	3	1	0	5	.500	.625	.400	16.88	0.00
Andrew Moore	L-R	6-5	205	8-11-99	0	0	0.00	1	0	0	0	0	0	0	0	0	0	1	.000	--	.000	27.00	0.00
Ryan Olson	R-R	6-2	195	11-22-94	0	0	4.70	7	2	0	0	8	6	7	4	2	4	9	.200	.200	.200	10.57	4.70
Mason Pelio	R-R	6-3	230	7-15-00	0	0	0.00	2	2	0	0	2	1	0	0	0	2	2	.167	.167	--	9.00	9.00
Jose Peralta	R-R	6-1	170	10-2-99	2	1	4.74	15	0	0	1	25	22	19	13	2	13	26	.227	.250	.208	9.49	4.74
Matt Pidich	R-R	6-2	220	12-25-94	0	0	0.00	1	0	0	0	1	1	0	0	0	0	3	.250	.333	.000	27.00	0.00
Nicolo Pinazzi	L-L	6-2	195	10-25-99	3	1	4.54	11	5	0	0	40	28	25	20	2	26	67	.190	.171	.198	15.20	5.90
Jacques Pucheu	L-L	6-2	210	1-1-97	2	1	3.13	5	3	0	0	23	17	9	8	1	6	29	.205	.190	.210	11.35	2.35
Martin Salazar	R-R	6-2	175	5-27-00	0	1	9.82	2	2	0	0	7	10	9	8	1	0	9	.303	.294	.313	11.05	0.00
Adam Serwinowski	L-L	6-5	190	6-7-04	0	0	0.00	1	0	0	0	1	1	0	0	0	1	1	.333	.000	.500	9.00	9.00
Easton Sikorski	R-R	6-0	210	1-12-00	0	0	0.00	2	0	0	0	2	1	0	0	0	0	5	.143	.500	.000	22.50	0.00
Jermaine Vanheyningen	R-R	6-6	220	11-20-98	0	1	5.23	9	5	0	0	10	7	6	6	0	16	13	.200	.238	.143	11.32	13.94
Ben Walmsley	L-L	5-10	202	12-2-04	0	4	6.10	11	7	0	0	21	25	15	14	0	10	24	.291	.150	.333	10.45	4.35
Cory Wilder	R-R	6-3	195	10-12-94	1	1	6.17	9	0	0	0	12	10	8	8	2	9	23	.222	.143	.292	17.74	6.94
T.J. Zeuch	R-R	6-7	245	8-1-95	0	0	0.00	3	3	0	0	4	2	0	0	0	1	8	.154	.111	.250	18.00	2.25

Fielding

C: Garcia 10, Hunter 6, Melo 1, Omana 10, Salcedo 28, Tanner 1. **1B:** Almonte 6, Antonia 1, Ascanio 1, Fernandez 3, Inirio 25, Marrero 10, Melo 2, Pino 4, Serrano 8. **2B:** Acosta 1, Almonte 4, Antonia 1, Ascanio 6, Balcazar 4, Chevalier 2, Fernandez 1, Hernandez 2, Jorge 33, Minier 2, Rey 1, Rodriguez 1, Serrano 1. **3B:** Almonte 5, Ascanio 8, Chevalier 1, Collier 7, Jorge 1, Minier 6, Serrano 24, Stewart 6. **SS:** Acosta 8, Almonte 4, Arroyo 1, Ascanio 1, Balcazar 31, Chevalier 2, Faltine 1, Hernandez 8, Jorge 1. **OF:** Alcantara 25, Almonte 37, Almonte 5, Antonia 20, Boyd 1, Confidan 9, Dunn 4, Franco 3, Hinds 4, Marrero 11, Rey 6, Rodriguez 6, Tamares 5, Valdez 38.

DSL REDS

ROOKIE

DOMINICAN SUMMER LEAGUE

Batting	B-T	HT	WT	DOB	AVG	vLH	vRH	G	AB	R	H	2B	3B	HR	RBI	BB	HBP	SH	SF	SO	SB	CS	SLG	OBP
Ricardo Cabrera	R-R	5-11	178	10-31-04	.253	.240	.256	45	150	30	38	6	5	1	19	13	14	1	2	40	5	4	.380	.363
Ray-Jacson Chirino	R-R	6-1	175	12-24-02	.252	.160	.274	42	131	22	33	9	0	1	23	21	4	0	2	44	1	1	.344	.367
Christopher Consoro	B-R	6-0	156	9-19-03	.048	.000	.059	11	21	1	1	0	1	0	0	4	0	0	0	12	1	0	.143	.200
Jesus Correa	B-R	5-8	167	9-8-04	.333	.375	.321	10	36	7	12	1	2	0	5	4	2	0	0	6	0	4	.472	.429
Iverson Espinoza	R-R	5-10	155	1-6-03	.243	.333	.226	28	74	13	18	2	2	0	9	9	5	0	0	14	5	3	.324	.364
Gabriel Gomes	R-R	5-9	170	3-31-04	.500	--	.500	3	4	1	2	0	0	0	0	3	0	0	0	2	0	0	.500	.714
Henry Guerrero	R-R	6-0	191	10-19-04	.206	.500	.175	21	63	8	13	1	0	0	5	4	6	0	0	14	1	0	.222	.315
Eddy Isturiz	R-R	0-0	0	1-16-04	.271	.400	.245	23	59	12	16	3	1	1	11	1	0	0	0	21	1	1	.407	.283
Luis Leones	L-L	5-10	155	6-12-03	.296	.308	.293	24	71	6	21	3	0	1	6	4	2	1	1	27	0	1	.380	.346
Diego Omana	R-R	5-11	165	1-10-03	.273	.000	.316	14	44	5	12	3	0	0	4	4	1	0	0	6	0	1	.341	.347
Esmith Pineda	R-R	5-10	183	11-13-04	.367	.400	.364	15	49	10	18	2	0	3	13	7	1	0	0	9	2	1	.592	.456
Adrian Reyes	B-R	6-1	215	11-26-04	.197	.138	.212	45	142	14	28	12	1	3	22	28	1	0	0	56	1	2	.359	.333
Luis Reyes	R-R	5-11	193	11-15-03	.275	.571	.212	14	40	6	11	2	0	2	15	12	1	0	0	8	0	0	.475	.453
Brayan Rijo	R-R	0-0	0	11-24-03	.253	.160	.271	45	158	26	40	6	0	0	14	8	4	4	1	52	9	4	.291	.304
Gilberto Rojas	R-R	6-1	165	1-19-05	.222	.400	.171	15	45	4	10	1	0	0	1	7	0	0	0	8	0	0	.244	.327
Carlos Sanchez	L-R	6-0	177	1-12-05	.355	.240	.381	46	138	42	49	4	1	2	26	40	3	0	1	28	14	4	.442	.505
Jesus Torres	R-R	6-0	160	10-2-02	.262	.304	.250	35	103	18	27	8	2	1	17	5	9	0	2	35	9	1	.408	.345

Anthuan Valencia	R-R	5-8	177	10-14-04	.150	.167	.146	39	120	24	18	1	0	0	14	31	3	0	2	32	8	2	.158	.333
Javier Velasquez	B-R	6-1	170	10-1-02	.154	.143	.158	12	26	2	4	0	0	0	1	3	0	0	0	6	0	1	.154	.241

Pitching	**B-T**	**HT**	**WT**	**DOB**	**W**	**L**	**ERA**	**G**	**GS**	**CG**	**SV**	**IP**	**H**	**R**	**ER**	**HR**	**BB**	**SO**	**AVG**	**vLH**	**vRH**	**K/9**	**BB/9**
Eddy Alcantara	L-L	6-5	180	2-11-00	1	1	4.58	11	0	0	1	20	19	12	10	2	13	23	.257	.095	.321	10.53	5.95
Joneiker Arellano	R-R	5-11	155	2-20-05	1	2	4.43	11	9	0	0	45	53	26	22	2	13	42	.288	.265	.314	8.46	2.62
Jonathan Batista	R-R	6-3	195	2-28-02	0	1	3.32	11	4	0	0	22	19	11	8	3	11	20	.229	.146	.310	8.31	4.57
Luis Castro	R-R	6-4	180	3-31-02	1	0	3.00	2	0	0	0	3	1	3	1	0	8	3	.091	.200	.000	9.00	24.00
Jesus Colina	R-R	5-11	170	3-21-05	0	0	3.86	6	0	0	0	7	5	4	3	0	5	9	.200	.125	.235	11.57	6.43
Vladimir Davila	R-R	5-11	158	9-10-02	1	2	3.52	9	6	0	0	31	32	16	12	2	7	37	.264	.234	.284	10.86	2.05
Jean Diaz	R-R	6-0	170	1-24-03	1	1	15.88	5	0	0	1	6	14	10	10	0	3	6	.438	.368	.538	9.53	4.76
Abraham Gaitan	R-R	6-2	180	--	0	1	4.50	2	0	0	0	4	4	4	2	0	2	2	.267	.500	.182	4.50	4.50
Cristian Galindo	L-L	6-2	150	10-14-02	4	0	2.25	11	1	0	0	28	19	11	7	1	9	41	.183	.160	.190	13.18	2.89
Khristian Guevara	L-L	6-3	150	8-24-04	2	2	3.60	8	2	0	0	20	20	10	8	2	3	22	.250	.118	.286	9.90	1.35
Lisnerkin Lantigua	R-R	6-0	181	9-1-04	2	4	3.90	11	6	0	0	32	39	18	14	0	16	30	.312	.309	.314	8.35	4.45
Anyer Laureano	R-R	6-2	188	12-29-02	1	3	6.46	12	0	0	0	15	14	16	11	0	19	16	.233	.158	.268	9.39	11.15
David Lorduy	R-R	6-0	198	10-15-03	1	2	4.04	12	7	0	0	36	43	24	16	2	18	37	.293	.288	.295	9.34	4.54
Juan Martinez	R-R	6-1	160	12-30-02	0	3	5.03	6	5	0	0	20	23	19	11	0	5	26	.267	.325	.217	11.90	2.29
Jose Montero	R-R	6-2	180	7-14-03	2	2	2.92	10	10	0	0	37	34	21	12	2	11	48	.238	.339	.160	11.68	2.68
Nelfri Payano	R-R	5-10	179	11-9-04	4	2	6.62	13	0	0	0	18	18	14	13	1	11	21	.273	.152	.394	10.70	5.60
Ricardo Quintana	R-R	5-11	160	11-1-02	2	0	1.74	6	0	0	1	10	6	4	2	0	9	11	.162	.263	.056	9.58	7.84
Marwin Ramirez	R-R	6-2	175	9-10-00	1	0	4.20	13	0	0	4	15	12	10	7	1	8	11	.218	.200	.229	6.60	4.80
Edmundo Rodriguez	L-L	6-0	160	10-8-03	0	0	5.79	4	0	0	0	5	2	4	3	0	4	7	.118	.000	.182	13.50	7.71
Roberto Ros	R-R	5-10	150	7-6-00	0	0	13.50	1	0	0	0	2	3	4	3	0	3	4	.300	.167	.500	18.00	13.50
Kelvin Valdez	R-R	6-3	200	5-8-03	0	0	7.20	4	0	0	0	5	4	6	4	0	7	9	.200	.143	.231	16.20	12.60
Javier Velasquez	B-R	6-1	170	10-1-02	0	0	9.00	1	0	0	0	2	4	3	2	0	1	2	.364	.000	.571	9.00	4.50
Wilder Zapata	R-R	6-4	170	12-26-01	0	0	19.29	3	0	0	0	2	4	5	5	1	4	4	.333	.000	.571	15.43	15.43

Fielding

C: Gomes 2, Guerrero 15, Isturiz 12, Rojas 14. **1B:** Chirino 42, Isturiz 1, Reyes 11. **2B:** Consoro 3, Correa 10, Espinoza 4, Valencia 36. **3B:** Consoro 3, Espinoza 22, Reyes 12, Sanchez 18. **SS:** Cabrera 44, Consoro 5, Valencia 4. **OF:** Espinoza 1, Leones 25, Pineda 13, Reyes 27, Rijo 45, Sanchez 27, Torres 16, Velasquez 7.

Cleveland Guardians

SEASON IN A SENTENCE: Armed with a new franchise nickname and the youngest roster in the major leagues, Cleveland rallied behind star third baseman Jose Ramirez and veteran manager Terry Francona to a strong finish and the American League Central crown.

HIGH POINT: The Guardians went 40-21 after Aug. 1 and put the division title away in mid-September. They won 4 of 5 against Minnesota in Cleveland, including a 7-6, 15-inning walk-off win to finish a Sept. 17 doubleheader sweep, then swept the White Sox in three games in Chicago. A subsequent sweep of the host Rangers completed a season-long seven-game win streak at exactly the right time of year.

LOW POINT: After sweeping Tampa Bay in two home games in the wild card series, Cleveland won two of the first three games against the Yankees in the Division Series. Gerrit Cole shut down Cleveland in Game 4, however, and Aaron Civale wasn't up to the task in the winner-take-all Game 5. He gave up a first-inning three-run homer to Giancarlo Stanton, and the Guardians couldn't recover in a 5-1 season-ending defeat.

NOTABLE ROOKIES: Outfield offense had been a major shortcoming for several seasons in Cleveland, but rookies helped rectify that in 2022. Steven Kwan posted 5.5 WAR while emerging as one of the game's best contact hitters and leadoff men, with a .298/.373/.400 slash line and 19 stolen bases. Kwan also won a Gold Glove in left field. Oscar Gonzalez, called up in late May, hit safely in 14 of his first 15 games, hit 11 homers and batted .296/.327/.461 with 27 doubles. Lefthander Konnor Pilkington provided rotation depth with 11 starts and posted a 3.88 ERA.

KEY TRANSACTIONS: The Guardians jettisoned veteran Franmil Reyes during the season and didn't add any payroll or significant players as the season went on from outside the organization, relying instead on their deep farm system for reinforcements such as Nolan Jones (86 at-bats), Tyler Freeman (77) and Will Brennan (42), with Brennan making the postseason roster.

ON THE FARM: Even after promoting a wave of rookies to key roles in 2022, the Guardians' farm system remains impressively deep. Righthander Daniel Espino was in the midst of a breakout season when he was shut down with a knee and shoulder injury. Bo Naylor had a breakout season at the plate.

OPENING DAY PAYROLL: $60,388,900 (28th).

PLAYERS OF THE YEAR

MAJOR LEAGUE

Andres Gimenez
2B
.297/.371/.466
17 HR, 20 SB in 146 G
Won first Gold Glove

MINOR LEAGUE

Bo Naylor
C
(AA/AAA)
.263/.392/.496
21 HR, 20 SB in 118 G

ORGANIZATION LEADERS

Batting		***Minimum 250 AB**
MAJORS		
*AVG	Steven Kwan	.298
*OPS	Jose Ramirez	.869
HR	Jose Ramirez	29
RBI	Jose Ramirez	126
MINORS		
*AVG	Will Brennan, Columbus, Akron	.314
*OBP	Will Benson, Columbus	.426
*SLG	Johnathan Rodríguez, Lake County, Akron	.540
*OPS	Will Benson, Columbus	.948
R	George Valera, Akron, Columbus	89
H	Will Brennan, Columbus, Akron	166
TB	Will Brennan, Columbus, Akron	253
2B	Will Brennan, Columbus, Akron	40
3B	Isaiah Greene, Lynchburg	8
HR	Jhonkensy Noel, Akron, Lake County, Columbus	32
RBI	Will Brennan, Columbus, Akron	107
BB	Isaiah Greene, Lynchburg	97
SO	Jhonkensy Noel, Akron, Lake County, Columbus	150
SB	Isaiah Greene, Lynchburg	39

Pitching		**#Minimum 75 IP**
MAJORS		
W	Cal Quantrill	15
#ERA	Shane Bieber	2.88
SO	Shane Bieber	198
SV	Emmanuel Clase	42
MINORS		
W	Randy Labaut, Lake County, Akron	11
L	Franco Aleman, Lynchburg	10
#ERA	Gavin Williams, Akron, Lake County	1.96
G	Kevin Kelly, Columbus, Akron	48
G	Nic Enright, Columbus, Akron	48
GS	Peyton Battenfield, Columbus	28
SV	Cade Smith, Akron, Lake County	13
IP	Peyton Battenfield, Columbus	154
BB	Doug Nikhazy, Lake County, Akron	79
SO	Logan Allen, Akron, Columbus	177
#AVG	Gavin Williams, Akron, Lake County	.173

2022 PERFORMANCE

General Manager: Mike Chernoff. **Farm Director:** Rob Cerfolio. **Scouting Director:** Scott Barnsby.

Class	Team	League	W	L	PCT	Finish	Manager
Majors	Cleveland Guardians	American	92	70	.568	3rd (15)	Terry Francona
Triple-A	Columbus Clippers	International	85	64	.570	4th (20)	Andy Tracy
Double-A	Akron RubberDucks	Eastern	79	59	.572	3rd (12)	Rouglas Odor
High-A	Lake County Captains	Midwest	76	53	.589	1st (12)	Greg DiCenzo
Low-A	Lynchburg Hillcats	Carolina	63	68	.481	8th (12)	Omir Santos
Rookie	ACL Guardians	Arizona Complex	28	24	.538	7th (18)	Jordan Smith
Overall 2022 Minor League Record			379	339	.528	7th (30)	

ORGANIZATION STATISTICS

CLEVELAND GUARDIANS

AMERICAN LEAGUE

Batting	B-T	HT	WT	DOB	AVG	vLH	vRH	G	AB	R	H	2B	3B	HR	RBI	BB	HBP	SH	SF	SO	SB	CS	SLG	OBP
Gabriel Arias	R-R	6-1	217	2-27-00	.191	.174	.208	16	47	9	9	1	1	1	5	8	1	1	0	16	1	0	.319	.321
Will Benson	L-L	6-5	230	6-16-98	.182	.000	.200	28	55	8	10	1	0	0	3	3	2	1	0	19	0	0	.200	.250
Bobby Bradley	L-R	6-1	225	5-29-96	.118	.250	.077	8	17	1	2	0	0	0	0	0	0	0	0	9	0	0	.118	.118
Will Brennan	L-L	6-0	200	2-2-98	.357	.167	.389	11	42	6	15	1	1	1	8	2	1	0	0	4	2	1	.500	.400
Alex Call	R-R	5-11	188	9-27-94	.167	.400	.000	12	12	2	2	0	0	0	0	4	0	0	0	4	0	0	.167	.375
Yu Chang	R-R	6-1	180	8-18-95	.000	.000	.000	4	10	0	0	0	0	0	0	0	0	0	0	7	0	0	.000	.000
3-team total (11 Boston Red Sox, 36 Tampa Bay Rays)					.222	.176	.253	51	126	14	28	5	0	3	13	12	1	0	2	41	0	0	.333	.291
Ernie Clement	R-R	6-0	170	3-22-96	.200	.200	.200	64	145	18	29	3	0	0	6	11	2	2	1	24	0	1	.221	.264
2-team total (6 Oakland Athletics)					.184	.192	.176	70	163	19	30	4	0	0	6	11	2	2	1	26	0	1	.209	.243
Tyler Freeman	R-R	6-0	190	5-21-99	.247	.259	.240	24	77	9	19	3	0	0	3	4	4	0	1	11	1	0	.286	.314
Andres Gimenez	L-R	5-11	161	9-4-98	.297	.336	.286	146	491	66	146	26	3	17	69	34	25	4	3	112	20	3	.466	.371
Oscar Gonzalez	R-R	6-4	240	1-10-98	.296	.266	.308	91	362	39	107	27	0	11	43	15	3	0	2	75	1	2	.461	.327
Austin Hedges	R-R	6-1	223	8-18-92	.163	.147	.168	105	294	26	48	4	0	7	30	25	6	10	3	78	2	0	.248	.241
Nolan Jones	L-R	6-4	195	5-7-98	.244	.000	.259	28	86	10	21	5	0	2	13	8	0	0	0	31	0	0	.372	.309
Steven Kwan	L-L	5-9	170	9-5-97	.298	.285	.303	147	563	89	168	25	7	6	52	62	7	2	4	60	19	5	.400	.373
Bryan Lavastida	R-R	6-0	200	11-27-98	.083	.000	.100	6	12	0	1	0	0	0	0	3	0	0	0	4	0	0	.083	.267
Sandy Leon	B-R	5-10	235	3-13-89	.133	.143	.125	9	15	0	2	0	0	0	0	6	0	0	0	4	0	0	.133	.381
Luke Maile	R-R	6-3	225	2-6-91	.221	.300	.199	76	181	19	40	10	0	3	17	19	3	0	3	54	0	0	.326	.301
Oscar Mercado	R-R	6-2	197	12-16-94	.208	.200	.215	54	120	17	25	6	1	4	16	5	1	0	1	28	2	2	.375	.244
Owen Miller	R-R	6-0	185	11-15-96	.243	.212	.258	130	424	53	103	26	1	6	51	32	7	0	9	93	2	0	.351	.301
Bo Naylor	L-R	6-0	205	2-21-00	.000	.000	.000	5	8	0	0	0	0	0	0	0	0	0	0	5	0	0	.000	.000
Josh Naylor	L-L	5-11	250	6-22-97	.256	.173	.283	122	449	47	115	28	0	20	79	38	6	0	5	80	6	1	.452	.319
Richie Palacios	L-R	5-10	180	5-16-97	.232	.000	.236	54	112	7	26	6	0	0	10	9	1	0	1	20	2	0	.286	.293
Jose Ramirez	B-R	5-9	190	9-17-92	.280	.236	.295	157	601	90	168	44	5	29	126	69	6	0	9	82	20	7	.514	.355
Franmil Reyes	R-R	6-5	265	7-7-95	.213	.167	.228	70	263	24	56	9	0	9	28	14	1	0	2	104	2	0	.350	.254
Amed Rosario	R-R	6-2	190	11-20-95	.283	.295	.279	153	637	86	180	26	9	11	71	25	4	0	4	111	18	4	.403	.312
Myles Straw	R-R	5-10	178	10-17-94	.221	.264	.207	152	535	72	118	22	3	0	32	54	1	2	4	87	21	1	.273	.291

Pitching	B-T	HT	WT	DOB	W	L	ERA	G	GS	CG	SV	IP	H	R	ER	HR	BB	SO	AVG	vLH	vRH	K/9	BB/9
Logan Allen	R-L	6-3	200	5-23-97	1	0	4.50	4	0	0	0	6	9	3	3	0	3	6	.346	.500	.250	9.00	4.50
2-team total (3 Baltimore Orioles)					1	0	5.87	7	0	0	0	8	12	5	5	0	5	7	.353	.545	.261	8.22	5.87
Shane Bieber	R-R	6-3	200	5-31-95	13	8	2.88	31	31	1	0	200	172	70	64	18	36	198	.230	.221	.238	8.91	1.62
Anthony Castro	R-R	6-2	185	4-13-95	0	0	7.43	12	0	0	0	13	19	15	11	5	10	12	.345	.474	.278	8.10	6.75
Aaron Civale	R-R	6-2	215	6-12-95	5	6	4.92	20	20	0	0	97	93	58	53	14	22	98	.249	.240	.257	9.09	2.04
Emmanuel Clase	R-R	6-2	206	3-18-98	3	4	1.36	77	0	0	42	73	43	18	11	3	10	77	.167	.179	.158	9.54	1.24
Ernie Clement	R-R	6-0	170	3-22-96	0	0	18.00	2	0	0	0	2	6	4	4	2	0	0	.600	1.000	.500	0.00	0.00
Xzavion Curry	R-R	6-0	195	7-27-98	0	1	5.79	2	2	0	0	9	13	7	6	1	6	3	.325	.375	.250	2.89	5.79
Enyel De Los Santos	R-R	6-3	235	12-25-95	5	0	3.04	50	0	0	1	53	40	18	18	3	17	61	.208	.209	.208	10.29	2.87
Hunter Gaddis	R-R	6-6	260	4-9-98	0	2	18.41	2	2	0	0	7	15	15	15	7	3	5	.405	.556	.357	6.14	3.68
Ian Gibaut	R-R	6-3	250	11-19-93	0	0	0.00	1	0	0	0	1	1	0	0	0	0	0	.200	.500	.000	0.00	0.00
Anthony Gose	L-L	6-0	200	8-10-90	3	0	4.71	22	0	0	0	21	15	13	11	4	14	28	.197	.200	.196	12.00	6.00
Sam Hentges	L-L	6-6	245	7-18-96	3	2	2.32	57	0	0	1	62	41	17	16	3	19	72	.186	.143	.215	10.45	2.76
James Karinchak	R-R	6-3	215	9-22-95	2	0	2.08	38	0	0	3	39	22	9	9	2	21	62	.161	.129	.194	14.31	4.85
Sandy Leon	B-R	5-10	235	3-13-89	0	0	0.00	1	0	0	0	2	0	0	0	0	0	0	.000	.000	.000	0.00	0.00
Kirk McCarty	L-L	5-8	185	10-12-95	4	3	4.54	13	2	0	0	38	37	23	19	11	13	26	.259	.129	.295	6.21	3.11
Triston McKenzie	R-R	6-5	165	8-2-97	11	11	2.96	31	30	0	0	191	138	65	63	25	44	190	.201	.194	.205	8.94	2.07
Eli Morgan	R-R	5-10	190	5-13-96	5	3	3.38	50	1	0	0	67	46	29	25	10	13	72	.192	.196	.189	9.72	1.76
Cody Morris	R-R	6-4	205	11-4-96	1	2	2.28	7	5	0	0	24	21	8	6	3	12	23	.241	.256	.229	8.75	4.56
Konnor Pilkington	L-L	6-3	240	9-12-97	1	2	3.88	15	11	0	0	58	53	30	25	6	32	50	.238	.256	.234	7.76	4.97
Zach Plesac	R-R	6-3	220	1-21-95	3	12	4.31	25	24	0	0	132	136	74	63	19	38	100	.260	.288	.231	6.84	2.60
Cal Quantrill	L-R	6-3	195	2-10-95	15	5	3.38	32	32	0	0	186	178	78	70	21	47	128	.254	.228	.274	6.18	2.27
Yohan Ramirez	R-R	6-4	212	5-6-95	0	0	4.50	1	0	0	0	2	3	1	1	0	1	1	.333	.000	.429	4.50	4.50
2-team total (7 Seattle Mariners)					1	0	6.97	8	0	0	0	10	10	8	8	3	7	11	.244	.286	.222	9.58	6.10

Nick Sandlin	R-R	5-11	175	1-10-97	5	2	2.25	46	0	0	0	44	27	13	11	2	24	41	.176	.231	.149	8.39	4.91
Bryan Shaw	B-R	6-1	226	11-8-87	6	2	5.40	60	2	0	1	58	58	38	35	9	26	52	.252	.271	.239	8.02	4.01
Trevor Stephan	R-R	6-5	225	11-25-95	6	5	2.69	66	0	0	3	64	57	24	19	3	18	82	.238	.280	.207	11.59	2.54
Tanner Tully	L-L	6-2	205	11-30-94	0	0	6.00	3	0	0	0	6	8	4	4	1	6	2	.333	.286	.353	3.00	9.00
Alex Young	L-L	6-3	220	9-9-93	0	0	0.00	1	0	0	0	0	1	0	0	0	0	1	.500	.000	1.000	27.00	0.00

Fielding

Catcher	PCT	G	PO	A	E	DP	PB
Hedges	.994	105	824	35	5	5	1
Lavastida	1.000	6	36	1	0	0	0
Leon	1.000	8	50	2	0	0	0
Maile	1.000	76	484	23	0	2	1
Naylor	1.000	4	16	2	0	0	0

First Base	PCT	G	PO	A	E	DP
Arias	1.000	1	6	1	0	0
Bradley	.969	7	31	0	1	1
Chang	1.000	2	4	2	0	1
Clement	1.000	5	9	2	0	1
Miller	.989	80	497	48	6	49
Naylor	.991	88	647	51	6	65

Second Base	PCT	G	PO	A	E	DP
Arias	.938	3	4	11	1	0
Chang	1.000	2	1	4	0	0
Clement	.936	15	21	23	3	7
Freeman	.933	4	6	8	1	1
Gimenez	.984	125	226	317	9	70
Miller	.952	25	33	46	4	10
Palacios	1.000	2	2	1	0	1

Third Base	PCT	G	PO	A	E	DP
Arias	.882	9	8	7	2	1
Chang	.000	1	0	0	0	0
Clement	.984	26	19	43	1	6
Freeman	.850	11	6	11	3	3
Miller	1.000	4	0	4	0	2
Ramirez	.970	127	91	234	10	27

Shortstop	PCT	G	PO	A	E	DP
Arias	.750	3	1	5	2	0
Freeman	1.000	7	12	13	0	5
Gimenez	1.000	18	14	46	0	6
Rosario	.977	140	152	358	12	62

Outfield	PCT	G	PO	A	E	DP
Benson	.967	20	29	0	1	0
Brennan	1.000	10	17	0	0	0
Call	1.000	10	7	0	0	0
Clement	1.000	11	13	1	0	0
Gonzalez	.963	84	155	3	6	1
Jones	1.000	22	48	2	0	1
Kwan	.986	150	266	8	4	3
Mercado	.988	52	79	1	1	0
Naylor	1.000	5	10	1	0	0
Palacios	1.000	25	43	2	0	1
Reyes	1.000	14	23	1	0	0
Rosario	.818	6	9	0	2	0
Straw	.995	152	371	12	2	2

COLUMBUS CLIPPERS — TRIPLE-A

INTERNATIONAL LEAGUE

Batting	B-T	HT	WT	DOB	AVG	vLH	vRH	G	AB	R	H	2B	3B	HR	RBI	BB	HBP	SH	SF	SO	SB	CS	SLG	OBP
Anthony Alford	R-R	6-1	215	7-20-94	.167	.000	.200	8	30	6	5	0	0	2	2	3	0	0	0	13	1	0	.367	.242
2-team total (3 Indianapolis Indians)					.184	.200	.179	11	38	9	7	0	0	4	4	6	0	0	0	15	2	0	.500	.295
Gabriel Arias	R-R	6-1	217	2-27-00	.240	.243	.239	77	288	46	69	9	0	13	36	25	6	0	4	78	5	1	.406	.310
Will Benson	L-L	6-5	230	6-16-98	.278	.250	.287	89	316	75	88	20	3	17	45	75	7	2	1	91	16	4	.522	.426
Bobby Bradley	L-R	6-1	225	5-29-96	.174	.195	.167	47	167	24	29	10	0	7	30	19	5	0	7	74	0	1	.359	.268
Will Brennan	L-L	6-0	200	2-2-98	.316	.244	.337	93	393	53	124	28	3	9	68	33	2	0	5	53	15	1	.471	.367
Trenton Brooks	L-L	6-0	195	7-3-95	.273	.226	.286	87	293	46	80	21	1	11	48	41	3	2	1	55	1	0	.464	.367
Seth Caddell	R-R	5-10	190	5-29-99	.500	--	.500	3	2	1	1	1	0	0	0	0	0	0	0	1	0	0	1.000	.500
Alex Call	R-R	5-11	188	9-27-94	.280	.229	.293	71	239	56	67	16	1	11	46	49	11	1	5	50	6	0	.494	.418
2-team total (5 Rochester Red Wings)					.292	.231	.307	76	257	62	75	18	1	13	52	51	12	1	6	55	9	1	.521	.423
Yu Chang	R-R	6-1	180	8-18-95	.167	.500	.125	6	18	1	3	1	0	0	4	5	0	0	1	5	0	0	.222	.333
Ernie Clement	R-R	6-0	170	3-22-96	.238	.400	.200	21	80	13	19	2	1	4	17	6	0	1	0	8	0	0	.438	.291
Gavin Collins	R-R	5-11	205	7-17-95	.235	.212	.244	41	119	15	28	4	0	4	16	12	5	1	2	28	0	1	.370	.326
Jonathan Engelmann	R-R	6-3	205	9-18-96	.250	.500	.214	4	16	2	4	2	0	0	1	1	0	0	0	4	0	0	.375	.294
Zac Fascia	L-R	6-1	225	9-15-98	.000	.000	--	1	1	0	0	0	0	0	0	0	0	0	0	0	0	0	.000	.000
Jose Fermin	R-R	5-11	200	3-29-99	.215	.155	.231	90	270	60	58	11	0	6	31	42	9	6	3	46	9	4	.322	.336
Ike Freeman	R-R	5-10	195	6-17-98	.194	.222	.185	13	36	8	7	1	0	3	6	12	0	1	0	20	0	0	.472	.396
Tyler Freeman	R-R	6-0	190	5-21-99	.279	.241	.288	72	297	51	83	7	0	6	44	25	19	1	1	32	6	2	.364	.371
David Fry	R-R	6-2	215	11-20-95	.256	.260	.255	119	422	64	108	27	2	17	74	39	10	2	6	92	2	0	.450	.329
Oscar Gonzalez	R-R	6-4	240	1-10-98	.282	.225	.299	41	174	21	49	8	2	9	33	6	1	0	1	26	0	0	.506	.308
Daniel Johnson	L-L	5-10	200	7-11-95	.217	.200	.224	17	69	6	15	2	0	3	11	0	0	0	0	24	1	1	.377	.217
3-team total (26 Rochester Red Wings, 14 Syracuse Mets)					.187	.174	.191	57	203	18	38	4	1	5	25	12	1	0	3	71	2	2	.291	.233
Nolan Jones	L-R	6-4	195	5-7-98	.276	.259	.281	55	214	44	59	11	1	9	43	31	1	1	1	64	4	1	.463	.368
Bryan Lavastida	R-R	6-0	200	11-27-98	.224	.217	.226	39	147	24	33	6	2	4	16	16	4	0	1	35	2	1	.374	.315
Sandy Leon	B-R	5-10	235	3-13-89	.250	.250	.250	4	12	2	3	0	0	1	4	4	0	0	0	2	0	0	.500	.438
2-team total (26 Louisville Bats)					.226	.316	.152	30	84	7	19	3	0	2	11	14	1	0	1	14	0	0	.333	.340
Luke Maile	R-R	6-3	225	2-6-91	.563	.400	.636	6	16	6	9	2	0	2	6	4	0	0	0	3	0	0	1.063	.650
Oscar Mercado	R-R	6-2	197	12-16-94	.281	.263	.287	49	167	25	47	7	3	5	31	18	4	0	1	28	9	4	.449	.363
Bo Naylor	L-R	6-0	205	2-21-00	.257	.203	.278	66	245	44	63	14	2	15	47	37	6	0	2	75	9	1	.514	.366
Josh Naylor	L-L	5-11	250	6-22-97	.200	.000	.308	6	20	4	4	2	0	0	5	5	0	0	0	0	0	0	.300	.360
Jhonkensy Noel	R-R	6-3	250	7-15-01	.176	.500	.133	4	17	2	3	1	0	0	0	1	0	0	0	7	0	0	.235	.222
Victor Nova	L-R	5-11	194	1-6-00	.143	.000	.200	2	7	0	1	1	0	0	0	0	0	0	0	3	0	0	.286	.143
Richie Palacios	L-R	5-10	180	5-16-97	.279	.275	.281	45	179	34	50	10	5	4	36	24	2	1	0	43	12	2	.458	.371
Franmil Reyes	R-R	6-5	265	7-7-95	.313	.000	.323	8	32	6	10	2	0	2	7	2	0	0	1	7	0	2	.563	.343
Mike Rivera	R-R	5-9	200	12-12-95	.204	.300	.179	19	49	5	10	0	1	0	8	8	1	0	2	17	0	0	.245	.317
Brayan Rocchio	B-R	5-10	170	1-13-01	.234	.303	.212	33	137	21	32	6	0	5	16	12	1	1	1	21	2	3	.387	.298
Eric Rodriguez	R-R	6-1	195	7-28-98	.000	.000	.000	1	4	0	0	0	0	0	0	0	0	0	0	3	0	0	.000	.000
Chris Roller	R-R	6-0	190	10-8-96	.333	--	.333	3	6	1	2	0	0	0	0	2	1	0	0	1	1	0	.333	.556
Daniel Schneemann	L-R	6-0	185	1-23-97	.000	.000	.000	2	7	0	0	0	0	0	0	1	0	0	0	2	0	0	.000	.125
Jose Tena	L-R	5-11	190	3-20-01	.368	.000	.438	5	19	7	7	2	0	1	2	4	0	0	0	4	0	0	.632	.478
Mitchell Tolman	L-R	5-10	195	6-8-94	.251	.207	.264	112	358	57	90	25	2	11	49	49	7	5	3	85	6	2	.425	.350
George Valera	L-L	6-0	195	11-13-00	.221	.190	.232	42	154	25	34	8	0	9	23	22	2	0	1	45	0	0	.448	.324

Pitching	B-T	HT	WT	DOB	W	L	ERA	G	GS	CG	SV	IP	H	R	ER	HR	BB	SO	AVG	vLH	vRH	K/9	BB/9
Logan Allen	R-L	6-0	190	9-5-98	4	4	6.49	14	14	0	0	60	64	45	43	8	29	73	.269	.220	.282	11.01	4.37
Jaime Arias	R-L	6-0	210	1-21-99	0	0	5.40	2	1	0	0	3	2	2	2	0	2	4	.182	.167	.200	10.80	5.40

Peyton Battenfield	R-R	6-4	224	8-10-97	8	6	3.63	28	28	0	0	154	138	67	62	17	57	109	.240	.242	.239	6.38	3.34
Robert Broom	R-R	6-1	190	9-17-96	2	1	7.71	16	0	0	0	16	16	14	14	2	11	10	.267	.263	.268	5.51	6.06
Seth Caddell	R-R	5-10	190	5-29-99	0	0	27.00	1	0	0	0	1	2	3	3	0	2	0	.400	--	.400	0.00	18.00
Anthony Castro	R-R	6-2	185	4-13-95	1	3	3.94	28	0	0	3	30	25	15	13	2	20	39	.227	.292	.177	11.83	6.07
2-team total (8 Norfolk Tides)					1	3	3.55	36	0	0	3	38	33	17	15	2	26	47	.234	.298	.190	11.13	6.16
Aaron Civale	R-R	6-2	215	6-12-95	0	0	4.73	4	4	0	0	13	14	9	7	2	4	18	.264	.238	.281	12.15	2.70
Kevin Coulter	R-R	6-5	230	8-12-96	0	1	8.10	3	0	0	0	3	4	4	3	1	6	1	.333	.333	.333	2.70	16.20
Xzavion Curry	R-R	6-0	195	7-27-98	4	1	4.58	12	10	0	0	53	50	29	27	9	23	54	.244	.295	.205	9.17	3.91
Brett Daniels	R-R	6-0	208	2-25-96	2	2	7.16	11	0	0	0	16	19	15	13	1	8	15	.284	.310	.263	8.27	4.41
Enyel De Los Santos	R-R	6-3	235	12-25-95	1	0	4.91	4	0	0	2	4	4	2	2	1	2	8	.286	.333	.200	19.64	4.91
Zach Draper	L-L	6-3	200	10-18-94	3	0	3.55	10	2	0	0	13	12	6	5	2	4	8	.261	.192	.350	5.68	2.84
Nic Enright	R-R	6-3	205	1-8-97	4	0	2.68	29	1	0	1	37	30	12	11	5	6	50	.216	.220	.213	12.16	1.46
Hunter Gaddis	R-R	6-6	260	4-9-98	4	3	3.60	9	9	0	0	45	27	20	18	5	15	56	.171	.190	.160	11.20	3.00
Justin Garza	R-R	5-10	170	3-20-94	2	3	4.64	37	0	0	7	43	33	24	22	6	19	50	.220	.130	.260	10.55	4.01
Ian Gibaut	R-R	6-3	250	11-19-93	2	0	3.20	17	0	0	3	20	16	8	7	0	8	19	.229	.158	.313	8.69	3.66
Ian Hamilton	R-R	6-1	200	6-16-95	0	4	6.27	15	0	0	1	19	17	14	13	3	11	24	.236	.217	.245	11.57	5.30
2-team total (23 St. Paul Saints)					2	7	3.61	38	0	0	2	47	33	23	19	6	19	60	.191	.177	.202	11.41	3.61
Tim Herrin	L-L	6-6	230	10-8-96	1	3	4.98	34	2	0	1	47	46	28	26	6	17	64	.250	.271	.237	12.26	3.26
Jake Jewell	R-R	6-2	217	5-16-93	2	2	2.49	36	0	0	4	43	29	14	12	0	15	48	.182	.145	.206	9.97	3.12
2-team total (9 St. Paul Saints)					2	2	3.21	45	0	0	5	56	41	25	20	1	21	65	.197	.167	.218	10.45	3.38
James Karinchak	R-R	6-3	215	9-22-95	1	0	5.73	12	0	0	0	11	10	7	7	0	11	17	.244	.348	.111	13.91	9.00
Kevin Kelly	R-R	6-2	200	11-28-97	2	0	2.73	32	1	0	1	33	28	12	10	1	13	43	.220	.412	.151	11.73	3.55
Ben Krauth	L-L	6-0	190	3-10-94	3	1	4.43	18	0	0	2	22	14	11	11	3	8	23	.182	.143	.214	9.27	3.22
Eli Lingos	L-L	5-11	200	5-21-96	1	0	3.32	17	1	0	0	22	14	8	8	2	8	19	.187	.257	.125	7.89	3.32
Kyle Marman	R-R	6-3	195	3-3-97	0	0	8.10	2	0	0	0	3	2	3	3	2	1	4	.167	.667	.000	10.80	2.70
Kirk McCarty	L-L	5-8	185	10-12-95	4	1	3.38	17	8	0	0	61	57	27	23	11	23	53	.249	.220	.265	7.78	3.38
2-team total (1 Norfolk Tides)					4	2	3.58	18	9	0	0	65	62	30	26	12	23	55	.253	.224	.269	7.58	3.17
Nick Mikolajchak	R-R	6-2	215	11-21-97	5	2	3.04	47	0	0	6	50	38	20	17	3	29	50	.210	.157	.243	8.94	5.19
Andrew Misiaszek	R-L	6-2	215	8-24-97	3	1	3.64	25	3	0	0	30	29	13	12	3	17	42	.266	.225	.290	12.74	5.16
Eric Mock	R-R	6-2	215	7-12-96	0	0	0.00	2	0	0	0	2	0	0	0	0	1	0	.000	.000	.000	0.00	5.40
Cody Morris	R-R	6-4	205	11-4-96	0	0	2.35	6	3	0	1	15	5	4	4	2	6	30	.096	.167	.059	17.61	3.52
Tobias Myers	R-R	6-0	193	8-5-98	1	9	6.00	14	14	0	0	60	73	47	40	10	33	40	.296	.303	.289	6.00	4.95
2-team total (7 Charlotte Knights)					1	15	7.77	21	21	0	0	73	101	71	63	15	48	51	.322	.329	.315	6.29	5.92
Nathan Ocker	R-R	6-0	190	12-3-96	0	0	54.00	1	0	0	0	0	0	2	2	0	3	0	.000	.000	--	0.00	81.00
Luis Oviedo	R-R	6-5	250	5-15-99	1	1	5.79	3	0	0	0	5	3	3	3	2	5	5	.176	.250	.154	9.64	9.64
Konnor Pilkington	L-L	6-3	240	9-12-97	3	5	5.88	13	12	0	0	57	59	40	37	8	26	58	.266	.279	.261	9.21	4.13
Aaron Pinto	L-R	5-10	210	7-3-96	3	2	4.91	28	1	0	1	37	42	24	20	5	20	46	.278	.443	.167	11.29	4.91
Zach Plesac	R-R	6-3	220	1-21-95	1	0	0.00	1	1	0	0	5	2	0	0	0	0	5	.118	.000	.154	9.00	0.00
Thomas Ponticelli	R-R	6-1	205	4-15-97	0	0	1.54	17	1	0	1	23	14	4	4	0	14	19	.182	.143	.214	7.33	5.40
Yohan Ramirez	R-R	6-4	212	5-6-95	1	0	4.35	11	0	0	0	10	3	5	5	0	10	13	.097	.100	.095	11.32	8.71
2-team total (5 Indianapolis Indians)					2	0	2.87	16	0	0	0	16	4	5	5	0	12	17	.083	.154	.057	9.77	6.89
Nick Sandlin	R-R	5-11	175	1-10-97	0	0	8.31	5	0	0	0	4	3	4	4	1	4	3	.214	.500	.100	6.23	8.31
Adam Scott	L-L	6-4	230	10-10-95	4	3	6.33	37	13	0	1	75	79	59	53	13	45	84	.264	.223	.283	10.04	5.38
Tanner Tully	L-L	6-2	205	11-30-94	8	6	4.72	24	20	1	0	122	142	70	64	12	26	98	.288	.265	.298	7.23	1.92
Carlos Vargas	R-R	6-4	210	10-13-99	1	0	0.90	8	0	0	0	10	8	1	1	1	5	16	.222	.294	.158	14.40	4.50
Alex Young	L-L	6-3	220	9-9-93	3	0	3.66	30	0	0	1	32	30	14	13	5	7	47	.242	.269	.222	13.22	1.97

Fielding

Catcher	PCT	G	PO	A	E	DP	PB
Collins	1.000	27	195	11	0	3	6
Fascia	1.000	1	2	0	0	0	0
Fry	.993	12	129	7	1	3	2
Lavastida	.993	35	278	22	2	1	6
Leon	1.000	4	25	3	0	1	0
Maile	1.000	6	46	3	0	0	0
Naylor	.994	56	579	35	4	1	5
Rivera	.983	19	110	6	2	0	1
Rodriguez	1.000	1	11	0	0	1	0

First Base	PCT	G	PO	A	E	DP
Arias	.984	10	59	4	1	6
Benson	1.000	3	16	2	0	4
Bradley	1.000	36	288	12	0	31
Brooks	.994	61	446	17	3	34
Chang	1.000	2	8	0	0	1
Collins	1.000	2	5	0	0	1
Freeman	.958	3	22	1	1	2
Fry	.986	38	257	19	4	26
Naylor	1.000	2	5	0	0	1
Noel	1.000	2	18	0	0	3

Second Base	PCT	G	PO	A	E	DP
Arias	1.000	2	1	5	0	0
Chang	1.000	2	2	7	0	1
Clement	.968	9	11	19	1	3
Fermin	.980	27	41	59	2	12
Freeman	.909	8	10	20	3	4
Freeman	1.000	33	56	83	0	27
Palacios	.933	3	4	10	1	2
Rocchio	1.000	8	7	15	0	4
Tena	1.000	1	1	1	0	0
Tolman	.988	65	108	140	3	36

Third Base	PCT	G	PO	A	E	DP
Arias	.897	14	7	19	3	2
Chang	.750	1	2	1	1	0
Clement	.909	8	5	15	2	0
Fermin	.955	59	39	88	6	18
Freeman	1.000	3	1	2	0	0
Fry	.951	63	38	116	8	13
Nova	.000	1	0	0	0	0
Schneemann	1.000	1	0	3	0	0
Tolman	.840	10	7	14	4	1

Shortstop	PCT	G	PO	A	E	DP
Arias	.965	43	43	94	5	14
Clement	1.000	6	6	22	0	0
Freeman	.976	35	47	77	3	20
Rocchio	.932	26	20	48	5	12
Schneemann	1.000	1	2	4	0	2
Tena	1.000	4	6	11	0	2
Tolman	.946	40	52	106	9	19

Outfield	PCT	G	PO	A	E	DP
Alford	.909	8	19	1	2	0
Arias	.875	7	14	0	2	0
Benson	.975	77	153	6	4	2
Brennan	.977	80	167	2	4	1
Brooks	1.000	6	7	1	0	1
Call	.983	57	115	3	2	1
Engelmann	1.000	4	10	1	0	1
Gonzalez	1.000	36	63	7	0	0
Johnson	.963	13	25	1	1	0
Jones	.901	44	58	6	7	1
Mercado	.962	44	99	1	4	1
Naylor	1.000	4	6	0	0	0
Nova	1.000	1	1	0	0	0
Palacios	.972	42	67	3	2	1
Reyes	1.000	3	2	0	0	0
Roller	1.000	3	3	0	0	0
Valera	1.000	34	63	2	0	0

AKRON RUBBERDUCKS

DOUBLE-A

EASTERN LEAGUE

Batting	B-T	HT	WT	DOB	AVG	vLH	vRH	G	AB	R	H	2B	3B	HR	RBI	BB	HBP	SH	SF	SO	SB	CS	SLG	OBP
Will Brennan	L-L	6-0	200	2-2-98	.311	.304	.313	36	135	16	42	12	1	4	39	17	1	0	4	16	5	2	.504	.382
Seth Caddell	R-R	5-10	190	5-29-99	.100	.200	.086	14	40	3	4	1	0	0	2	5	0	0	0	19	0	0	.125	.200
Yu Chang	R-R	6-1	180	8-18-95	.200	.000	.500	2	5	0	1	0	0	0	0	0	0	0	0	2	0	0	.200	.200
Raynel Delgado	L-R	6-2	200	4-4-00	.229	.175	.241	65	210	26	48	7	2	3	29	30	6	1	1	50	11	5	.324	.340
Jonathan Engelmann	R-R	6-3	205	9-18-96	.178	.185	.176	39	118	18	21	7	0	6	18	11	4	0	0	39	3	0	.390	.271
Julian Escobedo	L-L	6-0	190	6-10-98	.215	.200	.218	118	377	52	81	17	2	7	40	40	12	3	6	86	15	6	.326	.306
Ike Freeman	R-R	5-10	195	6-17-98	.167	.167	.167	11	36	4	6	3	0	0	2	6	0	0	0	15	0	0	.250	.286
Marcos Gonzalez	R-R	5-11	190	10-12-99	.237	.294	.216	38	131	19	31	7	0	3	15	10	3	1	1	39	0	0	.359	.303
Oscar Gonzalez	R-R	6-4	240	1-10-98	.133	.125	.143	5	15	3	2	1	0	0	1	2	0	0	0	4	0	0	.200	.235
Quentin Holmes	R-R	6-2	195	7-7-99	.242	.143	.269	11	33	6	8	0	1	0	1	2	0	0	0	11	3	1	.303	.286
Bryan Lavastida	R-R	6-0	200	11-27-98	.195	.196	.195	45	174	22	34	4	2	5	14	12	3	0	2	45	5	1	.328	.257
Angel Lopez	R-R	5-9	180	3-14-97	.152	.250	.118	14	46	4	7	1	0	0	2	3	0	1	0	19	0	0	.174	.204
Angel Martinez	B-R	6-0	165	1-27-02	.244	.400	.194	24	82	10	20	6	1	3	17	12	4	2	3	18	2	1	.451	.356
Bo Naylor	L-R	6-0	205	2-21-00	.271	.250	.275	52	170	29	46	12	2	6	21	45	3	0	2	46	11	3	.471	.427
Jhonkensy Noel	R-R	6-3	250	7-15-01	.242	.313	.224	67	240	43	58	16	2	13	42	30	6	0	2	63	2	0	.488	.338
Victor Nova	L-R	5-11	194	1-6-00	.125	.111	.128	34	104	12	13	7	0	0	4	17	0	3	0	38	2	0	.192	.248
Micah Pries	L-R	6-4	210	2-27-98	.266	.305	.257	122	448	63	119	29	5	18	73	42	11	0	3	117	20	4	.473	.341
Brayan Rocchio	B-R	5-10	170	1-13-01	.265	.239	.272	99	373	62	99	21	1	13	48	42	9	2	6	81	12	6	.432	.349
Eric Rodriguez	R-R	6-1	195	7-28-98	.190	.357	.151	50	147	13	28	6	0	2	12	10	2	2	1	45	0	0	.272	.250
Johnathan Rodriguez	R-R	6-3	180	11-4-99	.206	.231	.198	28	107	10	22	7	2	5	15	5	0	0	1	43	0	1	.449	.239
Chris Roller	R-R	6-0	190	10-8-96	.212	.304	.192	76	259	31	55	14	2	4	26	30	7	2	3	72	6	3	.328	.308
Daniel Schneemann	L-R	6-0	185	1-23-97	.205	.141	.218	112	380	57	78	11	2	6	38	46	0	3	7	99	20	4	.292	.286
Jose Tena	L-R	5-11	190	3-20-01	.264	.336	.244	127	516	74	136	25	6	13	66	25	3	1	5	138	8	5	.411	.299
George Valera	L-L	6-0	195	11-13-00	.264	.263	.264	90	330	64	87	17	3	15	59	52	3	0	2	100	2	4	.470	.367

Pitching	B-T	HT	WT	DOB	W	L	ERA	G	GS	CG	SV	IP	H	R	ER	HR	BB	SO	AVG	vLH	vRH	K/9	BB/9
Logan Allen	R-L	6-0	190	9-5-98	5	3	3.33	13	13	0	0	73	58	27	27	9	22	104	.216	.222	.215	12.82	2.71
Manuel Alvarez	R-R	6-3	225	9-17-95	2	3	9.79	26	0	0	0	30	32	35	33	4	27	33	.262	.286	.250	9.79	8.01
2-team total (8 Binghamton Rumble Ponies)					3	3	7.65	34	0	0	1	40	42	39	34	4	31	50	.261	.281	.250	11.25	6.98
Jaime Arias	R-L	6-0	210	1-21-99	0	1	6.34	13	11	0	0	44	58	33	31	7	16	33	.312	.357	.292	6.75	3.27
Tanner Bibee	R-R	6-2	205	3-5-99	6	1	1.83	13	13	1	0	74	51	17	15	4	14	81	.194	.175	.208	9.90	1.71
Robert Broom	R-R	6-1	190	9-17-96	5	2	3.47	28	0	0	4	47	39	25	18	2	23	39	.225	.286	.197	7.52	4.44
Tanner Burns	R-R	6-0	210	12-28-98	3	7	3.55	21	21	0	0	89	75	39	35	14	45	92	.227	.202	.241	9.34	4.57
Joey Cantillo	L-L	6-4	225	12-18-99	4	3	1.93	14	13	0	0	61	38	17	13	2	28	87	.178	.113	.200	12.91	4.15
Kevin Coulter	R-R	6-5	230	8-12-96	2	0	6.28	11	0	0	0	14	23	12	10	3	5	11	.371	.273	.425	6.91	3.14
Xzavion Curry	R-R	6-0	195	7-27-98	5	3	3.65	13	11	0	0	69	56	32	28	9	19	80	.218	.264	.176	10.43	2.48
Brett Daniels	R-R	6-0	208	2-25-96	4	1	2.98	28	2	0	3	45	34	19	15	3	27	50	.211	.256	.195	9.93	5.36
Jonathan Engelmann	R-R	6-3	205	9-18-96	0	0	81.00	1	0	0	0	1	3	6	6	1	3	1	.750	.000	1.000	13.50	40.50
Nic Enright	R-R	6-3	205	1-8-97	1	1	3.14	19	0	0	10	29	19	12	10	2	8	37	.186	.174	.196	11.62	2.51
Daniel Espino	R-R	6-2	225	1-5-01	1	0	2.45	4	4	0	0	18	9	5	5	4	4	35	.141	.278	.087	17.18	1.96
Hunter Gaddis	R-R	6-6	260	4-9-98	4	3	4.24	15	14	0	0	76	63	37	36	12	26	102	.223	.243	.210	12.03	3.07
Nick Gallagher	R-R	6-3	200	9-9-95	0	0	12.46	7	0	0	0	9	13	12	12	1	6	7	.342	.182	.407	7.27	6.23
Zach Hart	R-R	6-4	235	5-17-97	1	0	0.00	1	0	0	0	2	1	0	0	0	2	3	.125	.000	.250	11.57	7.71
Tim Herrin	L-L	6-6	230	10-8-96	0	1	2.01	12	0	0	1	22	17	5	5	1	6	37	.210	.138	.250	14.91	2.42
Mason Hickman	R-R	6-6	228	12-23-98	1	1	2.77	10	0	0	4	13	9	5	4	0	9	16	.196	.188	.200	11.08	6.23
Jared Janczak	R-R	6-1	215	6-23-95	2	0	2.00	9	0	0	0	9	4	2	2	0	6	11	.129	.071	.176	11.00	6.00
Jordan Jones	R-R	6-2	195	10-2-97	2	0	4.26	3	0	0	0	6	4	4	3	1	4	6	.182	.000	.235	8.53	5.68
Kevin Kelly	R-R	6-2	200	11-28-97	3	2	1.11	16	0	0	3	24	14	5	3	0	9	32	.157	.147	.164	11.84	3.33
Randy Labaut	L-L	6-1	205	10-1-96	4	1	5.01	18	0	0	0	32	18	19	18	3	24	37	.162	.091	.192	10.30	6.68
Eli Lingos	L-L	5-11	200	5-21-96	1	2	3.02	21	2	0	1	42	33	15	14	4	12	34	.212	.147	.230	7.34	2.59
Kyle Marman	R-R	6-3	195	3-3-97	5	2	4.41	42	0	0	4	51	39	26	25	6	29	66	.209	.277	.172	11.65	5.12
Jake Miednik	R-L	5-11	190	5-1-96	0	1	9.00	2	0	0	0	2	3	3	2	1	2	2	.375	.500	.333	9.00	9.00
Andrew Misiaszek	R-L	6-2	215	8-24-97	2	1	0.56	17	0	0	0	32	20	3	2	1	8	48	.187	.132	.217	13.50	2.25
Doug Nikhazy	L-L	6-0	205	8-11-99	0	2	11.57	3	3	0	0	9	14	12	12	1	11	10	.359	.429	.344	9.64	10.61
Luis Oviedo	R-R	6-5	250	5-15-99	0	4	5.44	21	7	0	1	51	46	33	31	8	38	54	.235	.195	.263	9.47	6.66
2-team total (2 Altoona Curve)					0	4	5.64	23	7	0	1	53	49	35	33	8	39	56	.241	.221	.256	9.57	6.66
Aaron Pinto	L-R	5-10	210	7-3-96	1	0	6.06	11	0	0	0	16	20	14	11	2	12	23	.303	.533	.235	12.67	6.61
Thomas Ponticelli	R-R	6-1	205	4-15-97	2	5	5.25	22	8	0	2	48	50	34	28	8	20	44	.263	.262	.264	8.25	3.75
Jerson Ramirez	R-R	6-1	210	11-24-98	5	2	6.68	31	0	0	4	31	31	23	23	5	26	34	.263	.313	.229	9.87	7.55
Eric Rodriguez	R-R	6-1	195	7-28-98	0	0	54.00	1	0	0	0	0	2	2	2	2	0	0	.667	1.000	.000	0.00	0.00
Alex Royalty	R-R	6-3	190	3-19-97	0	0	54.00	1	0	0	0	0	1	2	2	0	2	1	.500	--	.500	27.00	54.00
Cade Smith	R-R	6-5	225	5-9-99	2	1	2.89	24	0	0	8	37	23	13	12	1	21	55	.181	.125	.215	13.26	5.06
Carlos Vargas	R-R	6-4	210	10-13-99	3	3	4.81	19	0	0	1	24	25	15	13	1	12	21	.269	.343	.224	7.77	4.44
Gavin Williams	L-R	6-6	255	7-26-99	3	3	2.31	16	16	0	0	70	44	21	18	9	26	82	.176	.220	.147	10.54	3.34

Fielding

Catcher	PCT	G	PO	A	E	DP	PB
Caddell	.972	8	61	8	2	2	1
Lavastida	.993	41	392	26	3	2	5
Lopez	.989	9	83	3	1	0	1
Naylor	.996	42	458	19	2	2	2
Rodriguez	.993	48	406	13	3	2	2

First Base	PCT	G	PO	A	E	DP
Delgado	1.000	13	80	3	0	2
Engelmann	1.000	2	7	0	0	0
Freeman	1.000	1	6	0	0	0
Gonzalez	1.000	22	135	7	0	8
Noel	1.000	9	52	4	0	3
Pries	.987	92	579	48	8	71

Second Base	PCT	G	PO	A	E	DP
Delgado	1.000	1	2	2	0	0
Freeman	1.000	6	9	15	0	3
Martinez	.947	19	28	26	3	7

Nova	.000	1	0	0	0	0
Rocchio	.960	44	65	101	7	22
Schneemann	1.000	23	43	50	0	16
Tena	.971	47	56	77	4	16

Third Base	PCT	G	PO	A	E	DP
Chang	1.000	1	0	1	0	0
Delgado	.940	37	26	52	5	4
Freeman	1.000	1	1	0	0	0
Gonzalez	.833	5	2	3	1	1
Nova	.985	29	23	43	1	3

Schneemann	.986	71	47	97	2	10

Shortstop	PCT	G	PO	A	E	DP
Martinez	.938	4	2	13	1	2
Rocchio	.939	51	75	94	11	25
Schneemann	.976	15	18	23	1	3
Tena	.936	71	73	145	15	29

Outfield	PCT	G	PO	A	E	DP
Brennan	.983	34	58	1	1	0
Engelmann	.980	29	47	1	1	0
Escobedo	.983	108	229	5	4	1
Gonzalez	1.000	4	3	0	0	0
Holmes	1.000	10	20	0	0	0
Noel	.979	49	89	3	2	1
Pries	.958	12	21	2	1	1
Rodriguez	1.000	27	53	2	0	1
Roller	.994	66	158	5	1	2
Valera	.988	85	152	7	2	2

LAKE COUNTY CAPTAINS — HIGH CLASS A

MIDWEST LEAGUE

Batting	B-T	HT	WT	DOB	AVG	vLH	vRH	G	AB	R	H	2B	3B	HR	RBI	BB	HBP	SH	SF	SO	SB	CS	SLG	OBP
Michael Amditis	R-R	5-11	190	8-14-97	.184	.188	.183	56	163	18	30	8	0	2	26	29	0	0	3	48	0	0	.270	.303
Aaron Bracho	B-R	5-11	175	4-24-01	.184	.154	.191	80	261	25	48	13	1	8	34	28	5	1	4	91	1	0	.333	.272
Seth Caddell	R-R	5-10	190	5-29-99	.000	--	.000	1	3	0	0	0	0	0	0	0	0	0	0	1	0	0	.000	.000
Christian Cairo	R-R	5-8	170	6-11-01	.198	.154	.209	58	187	30	37	8	1	2	19	41	7	0	0	64	10	2	.283	.362
Raynel Delgado	L-R	6-2	200	4-4-00	.263	.138	.303	39	118	17	31	5	2	2	14	16	4	3	2	25	5	4	.390	.364
Zac Fascia	L-R	6-1	225	9-15-98	.171	.100	.200	30	70	1	12	2	0	0	6	5	0	0	1	24	0	0	.200	.224
Petey Halpin	L-R	6-0	185	5-26-02	.262	.269	.259	105	382	68	100	21	4	6	36	45	5	0	1	92	16	7	.385	.346
Korey Holland	R-R	5-11	170	1-1-00	.217	.190	.224	80	254	30	55	15	3	9	32	11	0	1	0	105	6	3	.406	.249
Quentin Holmes	R-R	6-2	195	7-7-99	.182	.444	.000	8	22	2	4	1	0	0	1	2	0	0	0	10	0	1	.227	.250
Cesar Idrogo	B-R	5-11	170	3-26-01	.292	.250	.300	8	24	3	7	0	0	1	5	2	0	0	0	4	0	0	.417	.346
Connor Kokx	R-R	6-1	200	2-24-00	.234	.245	.232	88	273	50	64	11	2	7	28	43	6	1	1	64	12	7	.366	.350
Angel Martinez	B-R	6-0	165	1-27-02	.288	.276	.294	77	281	46	81	17	3	10	27	40	5	3	2	58	10	6	.477	.384
Joe Naranjo	L-L	5-8	198	5-11-01	.235	.198	.250	119	425	72	100	16	3	18	59	82	5	0	2	131	6	0	.414	.364
Jhonkensy Noel	R-R	6-3	250	7-15-01	.219	.222	.218	62	228	35	50	9	0	19	42	18	4	0	2	80	1	0	.509	.286
Wilfri Peralta	B-R	6-0	155	12-10-00	--	--	--	1	0	1	0	0	0	0	0	0	0	0	0	0	0	0	--	--
Alexfri Planez	R-R	6-2	180	8-17-01	.251	.220	.261	89	346	50	87	21	0	19	63	16	4	0	4	89	7	1	.477	.289
Micael Ramirez	R-R	5-11	170	6-8-99	.210	.250	.200	73	224	23	47	6	0	3	22	31	0	1	0	50	1	1	.277	.306
Gabriel Rodriguez	R-R	6-2	162	2-22-02	.272	.268	.273	94	320	45	87	15	2	9	38	34	3	0	4	72	4	2	.416	.343
Johnathan Rodriguez	R-R	6-3	180	11-4-99	.292	.250	.307	79	295	48	86	16	2	21	59	22	3	0	1	92	2	0	.573	.346
Alan Romero	L-R	5-10	165	10-27-01	.000	--	.000	1	1	0	0	0	0	0	0	0	0	0	0	0	0	0	.000	.000
Milan Tolentino	L-R	6-0	185	11-17-01	.221	.246	.212	66	244	39	54	18	0	3	28	44	2	0	1	92	21	2	.332	.344
Yordys Valdes	B-R	6-0	170	8-16-01	.243	.167	.258	11	37	4	9	1	0	0	2	2	0	0	1	10	0	1	.270	.275

Pitching	B-T	HT	WT	DOB	W	L	ERA	G	GS	CG	SV	IP	H	R	ER	HR	BB	SO	AVG	vLH	vRH	K/9	BB/9
Alaska Abney	R-R	6-1	205	5-5-00	7	2	2.54	42	0	0	3	50	22	17	14	5	28	58	.135	.141	.131	10.51	5.07
Jaime Arias	R-L	6-0	210	1-21-99	1	4	5.56	14	3	0	0	34	33	21	21	4	15	37	.252	.171	.281	9.79	3.97
Trey Benton	R-R	6-4	209	6-18-98	2	1	2.63	26	0	0	8	27	24	14	8	5	20	25	.231	.170	.294	8.23	6.59
Tanner Bibee	R-R	6-2	205	3-5-99	2	1	2.59	12	12	0	0	59	50	22	17	8	13	86	.233	.287	.195	13.12	1.98
Rodney Boone	L-L	6-1	195	4-9-00	5	4	4.80	13	13	1	0	66	62	37	35	16	21	74	.240	.234	.243	10.14	2.88
Serafino Brito	R-R	6-0	200	4-28-97	0	1	3.38	3	0	0	0	5	7	4	2	0	1	5	.292	.571	.176	8.44	1.69
Raymond Burgos	L-L	6-5	170	11-29-98	8	3	2.08	37	0	0	1	65	52	21	15	2	22	67	.220	.222	.219	9.28	3.05
Damon Casetta-Stubbs	R-R	6-4	225	7-22-99	1	0	4.85	8	0	0	0	13	14	7	7	3	6	8	.286	.300	.276	5.54	4.15
Aaron Davenport	R-R	6-0	185	7-25-00	7	6	4.21	23	23	1	0	107	89	52	50	13	52	118	.227	.236	.219	9.93	4.37
Jack DeGroat	R-R	6-2	195	11-29-96	0	0	4.87	18	0	0	1	20	19	16	11	4	16	11	.250	.270	.231	4.87	7.08
Will Dion	L-L	5-10	180	4-17-00	0	1	0.71	2	2	0	0	13	7	1	1	1	3	15	.167	.000	.241	10.66	2.13
Brian Eichhorn	R-R	6-1	225	8-15-97	1	0	2.08	6	0	0	0	9	6	2	2	1	3	11	.188	.250	.150	11.42	3.12
Zach Hart	R-R	6-4	235	5-17-97	6	4	5.08	31	0	0	4	44	37	33	25	6	27	59	.222	.179	.250	11.98	5.48
Mason Hickman	R-R	6-6	228	12-23-98	2	5	4.40	19	10	0	2	59	53	29	29	11	28	87	.235	.292	.192	13.20	4.25
Elvis Jerez	R-R	6-4	185	2-5-00	0	0	3.68	7	0	0	1	7	5	4	3	0	5	7	.208	.154	.273	8.59	6.14
Jordan Jones	R-R	6-2	195	10-2-97	3	2	5.55	28	1	0	4	47	44	30	29	10	25	46	.250	.244	.255	8.81	4.79
Randy Labaut	L-L	6-1	205	10-1-96	7	1	1.89	20	0	0	2	38	22	13	8	5	13	52	.163	.073	.202	12.32	3.08
Jack Leftwich	R-R	6-4	220	9-26-98	4	0	3.12	10	10	0	0	49	33	19	17	4	14	56	.188	.215	.165	10.29	2.57
Tommy Mace	R-R	6-6	230	11-11-98	1	5	4.55	22	21	0	0	85	74	48	43	13	38	75	.233	.216	.246	7.94	4.02
Braunny Munoz	R-R	6-1	170	8-20-00	0	0	6.35	2	0	0	0	6	5	4	4	1	4	4	.250	.250	.250	6.35	6.35
Doug Nikhazy	L-L	6-0	205	8-11-99	4	4	3.19	21	21	0	0	93	59	37	33	8	68	118	.182	.126	.205	11.42	6.58
Nathan Ocker	R-R	6-0	190	12-3-96	2	0	2.70	5	0	0	0	10	5	3	3	2	1	10	.143	.133	.150	9.00	0.90
Davis Sharpe	R-R	6-4	215	1-30-00	5	1	2.35	23	0	0	3	46	34	14	12	6	7	48	.209	.176	.232	9.39	1.37
Cade Smith	R-R	6-5	225	5-9-99	2	1	3.00	20	0	0	5	24	15	10	8	0	14	44	.172	.091	.222	16.50	5.25
Hunter Stanley	R-R	6-0	190	11-25-97	2	1	1.84	4	0	0	0	15	11	3	3	1	5	14	.212	.412	.114	8.59	3.07
Lenny Torres	R-R	6-1	190	10-15-00	1	3	6.00	14	4	0	0	33	34	34	22	7	28	36	.260	.263	.257	9.82	7.64
Matt Turner	L-L	6-4	180	8-4-99	1	2	6.69	28	0	0	0	39	46	34	29	7	28	30	.284	.255	.297	6.92	6.46
Gavin Williams	L-R	6-6	255	7-26-99	2	1	1.40	9	9	0	0	45	25	7	7	0	14	67	.167	.222	.135	13.40	2.80

Fielding

Catcher	PCT	G	PO	A	E	DP	PB
Amditis	.984	53	517	29	9	4	9
Caddell	1.000	1	13	0	0	0	0
Fascia	.979	24	127	10	3	2	4
Ramirez	.985	69	615	43	10	4	8

First Base	PCT	G	PO	A	E	DP
Bracho	1.000	12	66	5	0	6
Naranjo	.991	114	689	54	7	74
Noel	.981	6	45	7	1	5

Second Base	PCT	G	PO	A	E	DP
Bracho	.971	61	88	110	6	31
Cairo	1.000	19	36	45	0	11
Delgado	.982	15	26	29	1	6
Martinez	.988	23	36	47	1	10
Peralta	1.000	1	1	0	0	0
Rodriguez	.889	5	5	11	2	5

	PCT	G	PO	A	E	DP
Tolentino	.963	11	12	14	1	5
Valdes	.960	7	8	16	1	3

Third Base	PCT	G	PO	A	E	DP
Cairo	1.000	7	0	10	0	0
Delgado	.914	18	9	23	3	4
Martinez	1.000	4	4	6	0	0
Noel	.854	24	15	20	6	1
Rodriguez	.942	72	36	95	8	8
Tolentino	.958	12	9	14	1	3

Shortstop	PCT	G	PO	A	E	DP
Cairo	.977	27	32	54	2	16
Delgado	.900	1	4	5	1	0
Martinez	.948	50	67	98	9	24
Rodriguez	1.000	3	0	5	0	0
Tolentino	.974	45	47	104	4	18
Valdes	.875	5	2	5	1	2

Outfield	PCT	G	PO	A	E	DP
Halpin	.978	103	216	9	5	2
Holland	.991	61	108	2	1	2
Holmes	1.000	5	12	0	0	0
Idrogo	1.000	5	6	0	0	0
Kokx	.994	77	152	4	1	1
Noel	.955	18	19	2	1	1
Planez	.986	70	134	8	2	3
Rodriguez	.949	62	105	6	6	2

LYNCHBURG HILLCATS — *LOW CLASS A*

CAROLINA LEAGUE

Batting	B-T	HT	WT	DOB	AVG	vLH	vRH	G	AB	R	H	2B	3B	HR	RBI	BB	HBP	SH	SF	SO	SB	CS	SLG	OBP
Wuilfredo Antunez	L-R	6-0	150	5-16-02	.333	1.000	.200	5	6	0	2	1	0	0	0	4	0	0	0	2	0	0	.500	.600
Will Bartlett	R-R	6-3	215	2-2-01	.212	.156	.219	80	260	46	55	21	1	3	34	56	5	0	3	88	3	0	.335	.358
Juan Benjamin	B-R	5-8	150	4-25-03	.300	.429	.000	3	10	2	3	0	0	0	2	3	0	0	0	2	0	0	.300	.462
Jordan Brown	R-R	6-3	185	9-9-01	.182	.143	.189	32	88	14	16	6	0	2	3	11	2	0	0	34	1	0	.318	.287
Jorge Burgos	L-L	6-0	165	12-26-01	.278	.182	.293	105	396	54	110	18	3	6	66	56	3	0	4	85	6	2	.384	.368
Joe Donovan	R-R	5-11	180	1-20-99	.200	.056	.216	58	185	28	37	10	1	6	33	18	6	0	2	59	2	0	.362	.289
Luis Durango	L-L	5-10	135	4-8-03	.189	.265	.175	71	217	37	41	4	2	0	9	32	10	2	0	38	20	8	.226	.320
Jake Fox	L-R	6-0	185	2-12-03	.247	.208	.253	104	380	74	94	25	4	5	44	74	11	0	5	90	21	3	.374	.381
Dayan Frias	B-R	5-7	140	6-25-02	.239	.286	.231	120	443	64	106	18	2	6	46	65	7	2	2	129	8	5	.330	.344
Angel Genao	B-R	5-9	150	5-19-04	.179	.200	.174	8	28	3	5	1	0	0	3	4	1	0	0	5	0	1	.214	.303
Isaiah Greene	L-L	6-1	180	8-29-01	.226	.215	.229	114	371	65	84	14	8	4	43	97	6	0	2	114	39	4	.340	.393
Cesar Idrogo	B-R	5-11	170	3-26-01	.337	.417	.306	27	86	15	29	8	1	1	16	11	3	0	2	20	0	0	.488	.422
Joe Lampe	L-R	6-1	185	12-5-00	.100	--	.100	3	10	0	1	0	0	0	1	1	0	0	0	6	0	0	.100	.182
Marlin Made	L-L	5-10	165	4-16-01	.162	.077	.180	20	74	7	12	0	1	0	1	5	0	0	0	23	0	0	.189	.215
Richard Paz	L-R	5-7	150	6-12-01	.230	.171	.241	80	265	33	61	12	1	2	45	39	9	0	4	61	0	1	.306	.344
Wilfri Peralta	B-R	6-0	155	12-10-00	.206	.182	.211	52	155	12	32	8	2	0	18	12	0	0	1	56	0	2	.284	.262
Victor Planchart	B-R	5-8	165	5-17-01	.252	.250	.253	64	226	29	57	13	3	2	30	26	3	0	0	61	1	0	.363	.337
Skeiling Rodriguez	L-R	6-0	175	2-26-01	.171	.000	.182	20	70	9	12	3	0	0	5	6	0	0	1	30	0	1	.214	.234
Lexer Saduy	L-L	5-10	148	10-14-02	.222	.000	.286	9	36	7	8	1	0	0	1	5	0	0	0	12	0	0	.250	.317
Junior Sanquintin	B-R	6-0	172	1-8-02	.224	.250	.217	69	259	28	58	10	4	8	40	26	5	0	2	88	1	1	.386	.305
Milan Tolentino	L-R	6-0	185	11-17-01	.333	.381	.327	47	168	33	56	12	0	1	26	32	1	0	4	44	8	1	.423	.434
Carson Tucker	R-R	6-2	180	1-24-02	.137	.111	.139	38	117	12	16	5	1	1	9	18	1	0	0	55	5	0	.222	.257
Yordys Valdes	B-R	6-0	170	8-16-01	.243	.221	.248	101	387	52	94	12	2	3	56	37	3	2	3	89	13	7	.307	.312

Pitching	B-T	HT	WT	DOB	W	L	ERA	G	GS	CG	SV	IP	H	R	ER	HR	BB	SO	AVG	vLH	vRH	K/9	BB/9
Franco Aleman	R-R	6-6	235	6-26-00	3	10	6.31	24	8	0	1	56	69	45	39	6	18	75	.292	.330	.268	12.13	2.91
Reny Artiles	R-R	6-0	160	1-17-02	2	4	10.99	15	3	0	0	29	31	41	35	3	46	23	.270	.263	.276	7.22	14.44
Trey Benton	R-R	6-4	209	6-18-98	1	2	1.13	13	0	0	4	16	5	4	2	0	6	27	.094	.074	.115	15.19	3.38
Rodney Boone	L-L	6-1	195	4-9-00	3	0	1.85	10	10	0	0	49	37	13	10	2	8	63	.214	.250	.197	11.65	1.48
Serafino Brito	R-R	6-0	200	4-28-97	0	0	7.36	3	0	0	0	4	6	4	3	1	2	3	.353	.429	.300	7.36	4.91
Damon Casetta-Stubbs	R-R	6-4	225	7-22-99	1	2	9.25	11	0	0	1	24	39	27	25	4	22	19	.364	.368	.360	7.03	8.14
Trenton Denholm	R-R	5-11	180	11-29-99	5	5	4.79	23	23	0	0	98	110	57	52	8	40	107	.284	.246	.316	9.86	3.69
Will Dion	L-L	5-10	180	4-17-00	8	4	2.26	23	23	0	0	115	88	39	29	8	31	142	.207	.195	.211	11.08	2.42
Brian Eichhorn	R-R	6-1	225	8-15-97	1	1	5.40	5	0	0	0	7	8	5	4	0	4	7	.296	.467	.083	9.45	5.40
Yeury Gervacio	L-L	6-1	168	7-1-99	5	1	6.02	31	0	0	1	55	60	39	37	6	25	81	.270	.235	.291	13.17	4.07
Elvis Jerez	R-R	6-4	185	2-5-00	2	2	2.22	27	0	0	9	28	15	10	7	0	17	40	.149	.163	.138	12.71	5.40
Reid Johnston	L-R	6-3	218	4-7-99	4	6	3.94	24	16	0	0	112	102	61	49	10	24	122	.234	.285	.191	9.80	1.93
Jack Leftwich	R-R	6-4	220	9-26-98	4	2	2.39	14	5	1	0	60	43	20	16	1	10	84	.199	.096	.279	12.53	1.49
Jake Miller	R-R	6-2	210	7-14-00	0	1	4.81	9	9	0	0	34	30	18	18	7	10	43	.242	.190	.295	11.50	2.67
Sergio Morillo	R-R	6-3	190	9-13-99	0	1	5.82	14	0	0	1	22	23	14	14	1	15	39	.264	.220	.304	16.20	6.23
Braunny Munoz	R-R	6-1	170	8-20-00	3	4	3.60	28	2	0	0	65	64	28	26	7	17	59	.264	.277	.254	8.17	2.35
Wilfri Peralta	B-R	6-0	155	12-10-00	0	0	0.00	1	0	0	0	0	0	0	0	0	0	0	.000	.000	--	0.00	0.00
Zach Pettway	R-R	6-2	215	1-29-99	1	1	2.00	14	0	0	1	27	23	8	6	1	8	38	.228	.122	.300	12.67	2.67
Tomas Reyes	L-L	5-11	150	9-23-99	0	1	9.39	4	1	0	0	8	14	11	8	1	3	6	.378	.500	.345	7.04	3.52
Alonzo Richardson	R-R	5-11	165	10-7-02	2	3	6.55	7	6	0	0	33	34	24	24	7	16	25	.268	.286	.256	6.82	4.36
Davis Sharpe	R-R	6-4	215	1-30-00	3	2	1.42	15	0	0	1	25	19	6	4	1	5	39	.207	.282	.151	13.86	1.78
Tyler Thornton	L-R	6-3	200	7-8-00	4	1	3.63	30	0	0	2	35	15	14	14	4	21	58	.128	.123	.133	15.06	5.45
Samuel Vasquez	R-R	6-3	170	9-20-99	1	2	9.55	19	0	0	1	22	31	24	23	3	20	23	.330	.395	.275	9.55	8.31
Wardquelin Vasquez	R-R	6-3	194	7-25-01	1	1	8.44	3	0	0	0	5	6	5	5	1	4	6	.261	.429	.188	10.13	6.75
Hugo Villalobos	R-R	5-10	170	7-27-01	3	1	2.25	17	0	0	2	32	30	8	8	3	16	50	.246	.292	.193	14.06	4.50
Miguel Vinicio	R-R	6-3	170	9-1-99	1	2	3.28	16	0	0	5	25	19	10	9	1	14	24	.213	.268	.167	8.76	5.11
Ryan Webb	L-L	6-1	202	4-19-99	1	1	3.92	11	10	0	0	41	45	23	18	2	25	57	.274	.326	.254	12.41	5.44
Josh Wolf	R-R	6-3	170	9-1-00	1	2	6.35	11	5	0	0	23	21	18	16	1	19	21	.247	.282	.217	8.34	7.54
Juan Zapata	R-R	6-1	198	11-19-98	3	6	3.76	23	10	0	0	81	76	40	34	2	23	66	.244	.207	.277	7.30	2.55

Fielding

Catcher	PCT	G	PO	A	E	DP	PB
Donovan	.989	44	409	36	5	2	5
Paz	.986	60	615	39	9	1	9
Planchart	.971	32	311	29	10	3	2

First Base	PCT	G	PO	A	E	DP
Bartlett	.987	68	491	41	7	36
Made	.955	3	20	1	1	3
Peralta	1.000	12	54	0	0	7
Planchart	1.000	11	67	6	0	6
Sanquintin	.976	45	311	20	8	24

Second Base	PCT	G	PO	A	E	DP
Benjamin	.875	3	1	6	1	1

Fox	.985	61	65	127	3	23
Frias	.980	25	36	63	2	12
Peralta	.818	9	4	14	4	1
Tolentino	.963	9	11	15	1	5
Tucker	.974	13	10	28	1	1
Valdes	.980	26	31	65	2	17

Third Base	PCT	G	PO	A	E	DP
Fox	.800	6	3	5	2	1
Frias	.929	51	35	70	8	6
Genao	1.000	2	0	6	0	1
Peralta	.881	31	20	32	7	4
Sanquintin	.000	1	0	0	0	0

Tolentino	.931	13	14	13	2	2
Tucker	.950	10	5	14	1	1
Valdes	.843	26	13	30	8	1

Shortstop	PCT	G	PO	A	E	DP
Fox	1.000	5	2	9	0	2
Frias	.926	42	52	86	11	18
Genao	.875	6	6	15	3	2
Tolentino	.938	22	30	45	5	12
Tucker	.935	12	14	29	3	6
Valdes	.973	48	67	111	5	19

Outfield	PCT	G	PO	A	E	DP
Antunez	.857	4	5	1	1	0
Brown	.952	29	40	0	2	0
Burgos	.958	101	149	12	7	1
Durango	.993	69	129	7	1	2
Fox	1.000	31	57	3	0	0
Greene	.948	108	161	2	9	1
Idrogo	.952	25	35	5	2	1
Lampe	1.000	3	6	0	0	0
Made	.933	13	14	0	1	0
Rodriguez	.957	17	21	1	1	0
Saduy	1.000	9	17	0	0	0

ACL GUARDIANS — *ROOKIE*

ARIZONA COMPLEX LEAGUE

Batting	B-T	HT	WT	DOB	AVG	vLH	vRH	G	AB	R	H	2B	3B	HR	RBI	BB	HBP	SH	SF	SO	SB	CS	SLG	OBP
Fran Alduey	B-R	5-7	140	1-7-04	.153	.111	.161	33	111	15	17	0	1	2	9	8	1	0	1	28	8	1	.225	.215
Wuilfredo Antunez	L-R	6-0	150	5-16-02	.295	.231	.308	21	78	21	23	3	2	4	13	19	2	0	0	17	11	4	.538	.444
Gabriel Arias	R-R	6-1	217	2-27-00	.231	.667	.100	5	13	2	3	1	0	0	0	3	1	0	0	7	1	0	.308	.412
Jose Baez	B-R	5-9	146	8-30-02	.225	.600	.171	16	40	6	9	2	0	0	2	12	1	0	0	16	2	0	.275	.415
Juan Benjamin	B-R	5-8	150	4-25-03	.300	.222	.315	33	110	25	33	3	5	3	22	25	2	0	2	27	8	5	.500	.432
Christian Cairo	R-R	5-8	170	6-11-01	.200	.000	.214	5	15	1	3	0	0	0	2	4	0	0	0	3	0	0	.200	.368
Erick Caripa	R-R	6-1	160	1-29-03	.208	.250	.200	10	24	4	5	0	0	0	2	5	3	0	0	13	0	0	.208	.406
Maick Collado	B-R	5-11	160	12-24-02	.310	.333	.306	35	126	20	39	9	0	2	15	24	2	0	1	24	2	1	.429	.425
Angel Contreras	B-R	5-7	142	1-14-03	.150	.000	.170	25	60	11	9	1	0	1	8	11	17	0	1	23	1	0	.217	.416
Jose Devers	R-R	5-9	140	5-17-03	.200	.100	.218	20	65	14	13	1	1	1	7	7	3	0	1	15	6	2	.292	.303
Edgar Gamargo	R-R	5-10	172	2-1-02	.000	--	.000	3	2	0	0	0	0	0	0	0	0	0	0	0	0	0	.000	.000
Angel Genao	B-R	5-9	150	5-19-04	.322	.333	.320	38	149	22	48	6	1	2	18	16	3	1	2	40	6	3	.416	.394
Esteban Gonzalez	L-R	5-8	150	3-19-03	.263	.143	.286	38	133	21	35	4	0	1	16	14	6	0	2	32	5	8	.316	.355
Wilmer Hernandez	R-R	5-11	165	9-10-02	.333	.500	.320	10	27	4	9	1	0	0	7	5	0	0	0	3	0	0	.370	.438
Robert Lopez	L-R	5-10	150	1-2-04	.195	.167	.200	25	87	6	17	3	0	0	9	11	2	0	0	26	1	1	.230	.300
Marlin Made	L-L	5-10	165	4-16-01	.205	.182	.210	22	73	14	15	1	0	4	14	10	1	0	1	19	1	0	.384	.306
Manuel Mejias	B-R	5-7	166	6-13-04	.269	.308	.264	31	104	14	28	7	0	1	19	14	2	0	0	15	0	0	.365	.367
Angel Mendoza	L-L	5-10	160	10-9-02	.113	.000	.127	21	62	11	7	2	1	0	3	10	1	0	0	32	1	0	.177	.247
Jose Pastrano	B-R	5-9	145	9-12-02	.242	.200	.250	22	62	13	15	0	1	1	12	15	2	0	0	20	4	2	.323	.405
Simon Rodriguez	L-R	5-9	135	9-23-02	.183	.077	.198	35	109	21	20	3	2	5	16	23	1	0	2	48	9	2	.385	.326
Alan Romero	L-R	5-10	165	10-27-01	.000	--	.000	1	3	0	0	0	0	0	0	0	0	0	0	2	0	0	.000	.000
Sterling Romero	L-L	5-10	145	3-2-02	.258	.167	.271	25	97	10	25	5	0	1	10	2	1	0	1	38	3	2	.340	.277
Lexer Saduy	L-L	5-10	148	10-14-02	.282	.200	.295	33	103	22	29	3	1	1	13	20	3	0	2	27	9	4	.359	.406

Pitching	B-T	HT	WT	DOB	W	L	ERA	G	GS	CG	SV	IP	H	R	ER	HR	BB	SO	AVG	vLH	vRH	K/9	BB/9
Austin Aldeano	R-R	6-1	180	6-6-04	0	0	0.00	1	1	0	0	4	2	0	0	0	0	5	.154	.286	.000	11.25	0.00
Luis Almonte	R-R	5-10	184	7-19-99	1	2	2.25	17	0	0	5	16	14	8	4	2	5	23	.233	.222	.238	12.94	2.81
Albert Breton	R-R	6-3	165	10-7-00	1	3	8.06	14	2	0	1	22	28	24	20	2	12	23	.289	.421	.203	9.27	4.84
Abel Brito	R-R	6-1	175	3-4-01	1	3	6.75	10	7	0	0	37	39	31	28	3	18	41	.264	.226	.291	9.88	4.34
Jack DeGroat	R-R	6-2	195	11-29-96	1	0	0.00	4	0	0	0	6	1	0	0	0	2	8	.053	.000	.071	12.00	3.00
Brian Eichhorn	R-R	6-1	225	8-15-97	0	0	0.00	3	0	0	0	4	2	0	0	0	1	7	.133	.143	.125	15.75	2.25
Daniel Figueroa	R-R	6-0	172	9-25-00	2	0	6.75	15	0	0	1	19	24	18	14	3	9	19	.304	.385	.264	9.16	4.34
Mike Garcia	R-R	6-4	183	8-11-00	0	3	7.13	7	6	0	0	18	24	14	14	1	9	8	.329	.267	.372	4.08	4.58
Yorman Gomez	R-R	5-11	167	11-10-02	3	1	3.76	11	10	0	0	38	35	18	16	2	8	44	.238	.222	.245	10.33	1.88
Ethan Hankins	R-R	6-6	200	5-23-00	0	0	0.00	1	1	0	0	1	0	0	0	0	0	1	.000	--	.000	9.00	0.00
Zach Jacobs	R-R	6-1	170	9-9-01	0	0	3.86	2	0	0	0	2	3	1	1	1	1	2	.300	.400	.200	7.71	3.86
Sergio Morillo	R-R	6-3	190	9-13-99	2	0	1.59	4	1	0	0	6	3	1	1	0	3	6	.158	.167	.154	9.53	4.76
Cody Morris	R-R	6-4	205	11-4-96	0	0	0.00	3	3	0	0	6	4	1	0	0	0	9	.190	.111	.250	13.50	0.00
Darlin Noboa	R-R	6-1	175	2-19-00	1	0	2.78	17	0	0	0	23	19	12	7	3	9	27	.213	.160	.234	10.72	3.57
Steven Perez	L-L	6-0	155	4-21-01	2	2	5.04	16	1	0	0	30	39	23	17	1	16	32	.312	.280	.320	9.49	4.75
Zach Pettway	R-R	6-2	215	1-29-99	0	0	2.08	6	1	0	0	9	9	4	2	1	0	11	.250	.364	.200	11.42	0.00
Bienvenido Polanco	R-R	6-1	170	10-3-01	0	0	1.80	7	0	0	0	10	6	4	2	0	4	10	.171	.250	.130	9.00	3.60
Tomas Reyes	L-L	5-11	150	9-23-99	2	2	5.14	8	0	0	0	14	17	8	8	1	4	14	.304	.412	.256	9.00	2.57
Alonzo Richardson	R-R	5-11	165	10-7-02	5	0	1.93	8	4	0	0	37	35	13	8	2	9	36	.243	.256	.238	8.68	2.17
Adrian Rodriguez	R-R	5-11	155	8-21-00	1	0	7.50	6	0	0	0	6	6	5	5	4	3	7	.250	.400	.211	10.50	4.50
Felipito Santos	R-R	6-2	180	7-20-99	0	0	5.03	16	0	0	1	20	18	12	11	2	14	16	.237	.385	.160	7.32	6.41
Victor Soteldo	R-R	6-1	165	8-27-01	2	1	1.96	17	0	0	4	23	18	8	5	0	4	26	.207	.226	.196	10.17	1.57
Lenny Torres	R-R	6-1	190	10-15-00	0	1	54.00	1	0	0	0	0	1	3	2	0	1	1	.333	.000	.500	27.00	27.00
Adam Tulloch	L-L	6-2	200	7-1-00	0	1	37.80	2	0	0	0	2	8	8	7	1	2	1	.571	1.000	.500	5.40	10.80
Wardquelin Vasquez	R-R	6-3	194	7-25-01	2	1	2.28	9	6	0	0	43	24	16	11	4	16	47	.157	.244	.120	9.76	3.32
Tommy Ventimiglia	R-R	6-4	205	10-1-03	1	4	10.27	16	5	0	0	24	17	34	27	2	39	33	.189	.129	.220	12.55	14.83
Jhon Vergara	R-R	6-3	170	4-4-00	0	0	0.00	4	0	0	0	5	1	1	0	0	4	2	.077	.167	.000	3.86	7.71
Miguel Vinicio	R-R	6-3	170	9-1-99	0	0	0.00	4	0	0	0	5	0	0	0	0	2	6	.000	.000	.000	10.13	3.38
Ryan Webb	L-L	6-1	202	4-19-99	0	0	3.86	4	4	0	0	9	14	6	4	1	5	11	.350	.143	.462	10.61	4.82
Josh Wolf	R-R	6-3	170	9-1-00	1	0	0.00	1	0	0	0	3	1	0	0	0	2	4	.100	.200	.000	12.00	6.00

Fielding

C: Gamargo 3, Hernandez 10, Lopez 22, Mejias 24, Romero 1. **1B:** Collado 20, Contreras 23, Made 12. **2B:** Alduey 21, Baez 2, Benjamin 17, Cairo 2,

Genao 7, Pastrano 7. **3B:** Alduey 6, Arias 1, Baez 8, Benjamin 8, Collado 13, Devers 9, Pastrano 10. **SS:** Alduey 3, Arias 3, Baez 1, Benjamin 2, Cairo 2, Contreras 1, Devers 12, Genao 30, Pastrano 4. **OF:** Antunez 20, Baez 2, Caripa 7, Gonzalez 34, Made 7, Mendoza 18, Rodriguez 30, Romero 18, Saduy 31

DSL CLE BLUE — ROOKIE

DOMINICAN SUMMER LEAGUE

Batting	B-T	HT	WT	DOB	AVG	vLH	vRH	G	AB	R	H	2B	3B	HR	RBI	BB	HBP	SH	SF	SO	SB	CS	SLG	OBP
Luis Aparicio	L-L	5-9	160	1-11-05	.213	.273	.194	12	47	6	10	2	0	1	4	6	0	0	0	4	2	1	.319	.302
2-team total (14 DSL CLE Red)					.209	.286	.194	26	86	11	18	2	0	1	7	12	1	1	2	10	5	4	.267	.307
Nelson Aranguren	R-R	5-11	183	8-26-03	.315	.294	.319	28	89	14	28	9	0	1	10	11	4	0	1	22	0	0	.449	.410
Gueile Borrome	L-R	5-10	155	12-18-04	.198	.182	.202	39	131	14	26	4	2	0	13	20	3	0	1	37	7	3	.260	.316
Jose Cedeno	L-R	5-7	140	3-1-05	.317	.471	.292	40	123	32	39	8	1	1	27	27	7	0	2	17	0	0	.423	.459
Oscar Cedeno	B-R	5-7	138	8-2-03	.284	.400	.254	25	74	15	21	2	2	0	13	8	5	0	3	13	6	1	.365	.378
2-team total (6 DSL CLE Red)					.253	.375	.225	31	87	15	22	2	3	0	15	10	5	0	3	16	7	1	.345	.352
Jhoan Gomez	B-R	5-6	130	10-29-02	.176	.300	.146	17	51	4	9	1	0	0	8	7	1	0	1	9	1	1	.196	.283
Jose Gomez	L-L	5-9	142	2-5-05	.287	.429	.276	28	94	24	27	2	7	2	12	16	6	0	0	36	6	4	.521	.422
Brayan Guedez	L-R	5-8	135	12-7-04	.200	.250	.192	8	30	3	6	1	0	0	3	1	1	0	0	3	4	0	.233	.250
2-team total (27 DSL CLE Red)					.248	.346	.225	35	137	23	34	5	1	0	20	12	5	0	0	31	11	4	.299	.331
Carlos Gutierrez	L-L	5-6	135	6-18-04	.240	.368	.217	43	125	22	30	9	3	0	20	14	3	0	3	24	5	3	.360	.324
Reyden Hidalgo	L-R	0-0	0	5-17-04	.216	.000	.238	30	111	14	24	4	0	0	11	11	3	1	2	10	6	0	.252	.299
Yorfran John	B-R	5-10	163	9-14-04	.273	.667	.224	18	55	6	15	1	0	0	3	6	0	0	1	12	1	1	.291	.339
David Leon	L-R	5-11	156	2-2-04	.257	.111	.279	24	70	13	18	3	2	0	8	16	1	0	0	18	1	0	.357	.402
Miguel Lopez	B-R	5-6	135	8-20-04	.111	.000	.125	4	9	1	1	1	0	0	3	1	0	0	0	3	0	0	.222	.200
2-team total (18 DSL CLE Red)					.273	.231	.283	22	66	7	18	3	3	0	13	10	3	1	0	12	3	2	.409	.392
Alberto Mendez	L-R	5-9	146	11-29-04	.256	.313	.248	39	133	24	34	4	2	2	18	32	2	0	0	44	5	1	.361	.407
Jeffrey Mercedes	B-R	5-8	146	10-2-04	.252	.313	.243	36	119	19	30	9	3	2	25	11	5	0	2	20	1	3	.429	.336
Moises Molero	L-L	5-9	145	2-19-05	.215	.296	.199	47	163	24	35	3	1	1	16	24	4	0	4	45	3	3	.264	.323
Jesus Montilla	B-R	5-8	130	2-29-04	.164	.250	.144	37	110	14	18	3	2	0	14	22	3	0	1	28	5	1	.227	.316
Samuel Parra	L-L	5-10	155	5-7-03	.286	.211	.301	36	112	23	32	11	1	0	11	16	4	0	1	31	1	2	.402	.391
Erickson Sarita	L-L	5-7	140	11-9-02	.266	.167	.280	32	94	16	25	5	0	1	17	13	6	0	0	23	5	1	.351	.389
Nomar Velasquez	L-R	5-9	158	5-21-05	.242	.333	.222	41	132	21	32	1	1	1	12	19	5	1	2	21	19	4	.288	.354

Pitching	B-T	HT	WT	DOB	W	L	ERA	G	GS	CG	SV	IP	H	R	ER	HR	BB	SO	AVG	vLH	vRH	K/9	BB/9
Neiver Acosta	R-R	6-1	184	7-23-03	1	0	4.43	18	0	0	3	22	15	14	11	0	17	31	.190	.167	.200	12.49	6.85
Austin Aldeano	R-R	6-1	180	6-6-04	3	2	2.31	11	11	0	0	47	43	17	12	1	12	33	.253	.178	.309	6.36	2.31
Bryant Capellan	R-R	6-5	217	1-3-02	2	1	12.09	18	0	0	0	22	33	31	30	4	28	15	.359	.333	.369	6.04	11.28
Wagner Castillo	R-R	6-0	180	9-23-03	2	2	5.74	17	0	0	3	27	25	20	17	4	13	26	.236	.173	.296	8.78	4.39
Miguel Cordones	R-R	6-6	180	9-16-99	1	2	3.51	14	2	0	0	33	37	19	13	2	9	34	.276	.204	.325	9.18	2.43
Luis Flores	L-L	6-1	160	10-5-03	3	1	3.20	19	0	0	1	25	26	12	9	0	22	32	.271	.273	.271	11.37	7.82
Frederic Garcia	R-R	6-4	195	12-17-00	2	3	4.14	12	10	0	0	41	28	20	19	1	23	61	.193	.239	.154	13.28	5.01
Luis Garcia	R-R	6-1	175	8-15-02	3	3	4.54	17	2	0	1	34	32	20	17	2	12	41	.241	.185	.278	10.96	3.21
Yonaiker Garcia	R-R	5-11	165	12-15-00	4	1	4.11	16	0	0	2	35	30	17	16	2	10	34	.231	.255	.217	8.74	2.57
2-team total (1 DSL CLE Red)					4	1	4.38	17	0	0	2	37	34	19	18	2	10	36	.243	.260	.233	8.76	2.43
Evelio Hernandez	R-R	5-11	167	9-3-03	0	2	2.16	11	11	0	0	42	30	14	10	3	16	53	.200	.234	.184	11.45	3.46
Melkis Hernandez	L-L	6-0	186	1-18-05	1	6	5.94	12	11	0	0	33	26	29	22	1	38	33	.213	.200	.216	8.91	10.26
Frank Lopez	L-L	5-9	156	7-25-02	0	0	7.11	6	0	0	0	6	5	7	5	0	8	6	.238	.125	.308	8.53	11.37
Diego Navarro	R-R	5-11	176	12-29-02	0	0	13.50	1	1	0	0	1	3	3	2	0	2	1	.429	.500	.000	6.75	13.50
Kenny Pinto	L-L	6-0	160	5-8-03	2	2	6.87	12	12	0	0	37	43	33	28	1	33	28	.299	.182	.320	6.87	8.10
Jose Ramirez	R-R	5-11	155	9-3-04	3	1	3.63	16	0	0	2	22	14	17	9	0	18	19	.177	.097	.229	7.66	7.25
Jose Ruviera	R-R	6-3	168	9-4-01	0	2	5.87	11	0	0	1	15	17	16	10	0	16	10	.288	.381	.237	5.87	9.39
2-team total (3 DSL CLE Red)					0	2	6.10	14	0	0	1	21	19	20	14	1	23	12	.257	.357	.196	5.23	10.02
Juan Sosa	L-L	6-2	200	4-23-03	1	1	11.37	19	0	0	1	19	22	29	24	2	36	17	.306	.111	.333	8.05	17.05
Julio Zapata	R-R	6-1	184	11-22-02	3	0	1.82	19	0	0	2	30	16	7	6	0	15	25	.158	.222	.123	7.58	4.55

Fielding

C: Aranguren 15, Cedeno 35, Leon 16. **1B:** Aranguren 14, Cedeno 17, Gomez 10, Hidalgo 3, Leon 7, Mendez 3, Mercedes 4, Montilla 3, Parra 4, Velasquez 2. **2B:** Borrome 19, Gomez 2, Guedez 1, Hidalgo 12, John 2, Mendez 11, Mercedes 7, Montilla 2, Velasquez 7. **3B:** Borrome 9, Guedez 1, Hidalgo 4, John 3, Mendez 12, Mercedes 11, Montilla 10, Velasquez 13. **SS:** Borrome 6, Guedez 5, Hidalgo 3, John 7, Mendez 12, Mercedes 10, Montilla 14, Velasquez 8. **OF:** Aparicio 15, Cedeno 5, Gomez 6, Gomez 26, Gutierrez 36, Hidalgo 6, Lopez 3, Mercedes 4, Molero 45, Montilla 4, Parra 27, Sarita 27.

DSL CLE RED — ROOKIE

DOMINICAN SUMMER LEAGUE

Batting	B-T	HT	WT	DOB	AVG	vLH	vRH	G	AB	R	H	2B	3B	HR	RBI	BB	HBP	SH	SF	SO	SB	CS	SLG	OBP
Lerwin Andrade	B-R	5-7	137	3-21-04	.225	.235	.222	34	89	17	20	2	0	0	6	18	3	0	1	31	6	6	.247	.369
Luis Aparicio	L-L	5-9	160	1-11-05	.205	.333	.194	14	39	5	8	0	0	0	3	6	1	1	2	6	3	3	.205	.313
2-team total (12 DSL CLE Blue)					.209	.286	.194	26	86	11	18	2	0	1	7	12	1	1	2	10	5	4	.267	.307
Oscar Cedeno	B-R	5-7	138	8-2-03	.077	.000	.083	6	13	0	1	0	1	0	2	2	0	0	0	3	1	0	.231	.200
2-team total (25 DSL CLE Blue)					.253	.375	.225	31	87	15	22	2	3	0	15	10	5	0	3	16	7	1	.345	.352
Jaison Chourio	B-R	6-1	162	5-19-05	.280	.167	.306	40	132	32	37	7	3	1	28	40	1	0	2	22	14	4	.402	.446
Christopher Espinola	L-L	5-7	165	9-19-03	.336	.263	.346	40	146	24	49	8	5	3	22	14	2	0	2	28	10	1	.521	.396
Brayan Guedez	L-R	5-8	135	12-7-04	.262	.364	.235	27	107	20	28	4	1	0	17	11	4	0	0	28	7	4	.318	.352
2-team total (8 DSL CLE Blue)					.248	.346	.225	35	137	23	34	5	1	0	20	12	5	0	0	31	11	4	.299	.331
Pedro Hernandez	R-R	5-7	137	10-17-04	.256	.188	.265	35	129	26	33	3	0	0	10	30	3	0	0	30	4	3	.279	.407
Victor Izturis	L-R	5-9	165	3-22-05	.252	.188	.262	37	119	24	30	7	0	0	25	20	8	0	3	16	0	1	.311	.387

Yanki Jean-Baptiste	B-R	5-11	185	11-18-04	.209	.250	.202	30	110	24	23	5	3	3	18	16	4	0	2	53	5	1	.391	.326
Miguel Lopez	B-R	5-6	135	8-20-04	.298	.250	.311	18	57	6	17	2	3	0	10	9	3	1	0	9	3	2	.439	.420
2-team total (4 DSL CLE Blue)					.273	.231	.283	22	66	7	18	3	3	0	13	10	3	1	0	12	3	2	.409	.392
Alex Paredes	L-R	6-0	165	5-11-05	.178	.000	.216	14	45	3	8	3	1	0	7	4	0	0	0	16	1	0	.289	.245
Ronald Pena	R-R	0-0	0	8-14-04	.268	.417	.233	40	127	25	34	7	4	1	16	21	2	1	1	30	11	4	.409	.377
Richard Polanco	B-R	5-9	150	10-29-03	.213	.111	.229	41	127	15	27	7	1	1	16	31	2	0	0	37	8	3	.307	.375
Emerson Purroy	B-R	5-9	146	2-25-04	.205	.130	.223	38	117	18	24	5	2	1	16	30	1	0	2	29	5	3	.308	.367
Rafael Ramirez	L-R	6-0	159	7-22-05	.247	.300	.240	47	170	27	42	6	4	2	23	25	5	0	0	34	11	4	.365	.360
Kevin Rivas	B-R	5-7	128	4-7-03	.270	.296	.261	36	115	21	31	3	4	1	15	18	3	0	0	51	10	1	.391	.382
Yefri Rivera	B-R	5-8	142	2-12-04	.280	.261	.284	38	118	23	33	5	0	0	19	17	2	0	0	18	8	2	.322	.380
Alan Romero	L-R	5-10	165	10-27-01	.222	.000	.250	6	18	1	4	1	0	0	1	4	0	0	0	7	0	1	.278	.364
Emilio Taveras	R-R	5-10	175	9-18-02	.183	.188	.182	21	60	15	11	2	1	2	12	17	0	0	1	15	2	0	.350	.359

Pitching	B-T	HT	WT	DOB	W	L	ERA	G	GS	CG	SV	IP	H	R	ER	HR	BB	SO	AVG	vLH	vRH	K/9	BB/9
Eudry Alcantara	R-R	5-11	150	12-27-04	1	0	6.35	4	0	0	0	6	4	5	4	1	3	4	.235	.500	.091	6.35	4.76
Pedro Almanzar	R-R	5-10	165	11-5-02	3	3	3.57	13	7	0	0	40	43	27	16	1	8	42	.254	.235	.274	9.37	1.79
Lerwin Andrade	B-R	5-7	137	3-21-04	0	0	0.00	1	0	0	0	0	0	0	0	0	0	0	.000	--	.000	0.00	0.00
Dahan Batista	R-R	6-1	170	3-15-00	0	1	5.56	8	0	0	1	11	15	10	7	2	4	6	.294	.313	.286	4.76	3.18
Franklin Bolivar	R-R	5-10	160	4-5-05	0	2	13.26	16	0	0	0	19	18	32	28	2	29	17	.254	.296	.227	8.05	13.74
Jose Contreras	R-R	6-2	175	5-13-02	1	7	10.85	12	12	0	0	34	46	46	41	0	33	31	.315	.311	.318	8.21	8.74
Robert Cruz	R-R	6-3	170	4-11-00	2	2	6.29	15	2	0	1	34	37	26	24	2	19	27	.276	.283	.272	7.08	4.98
Olmandi Diaz	R-R	5-10	155	7-27-02	2	4	8.42	14	6	0	1	36	59	37	34	6	6	24	.358	.327	.373	5.94	1.49
Logan Franco	R-R	6-3	170	10-11-99	1	2	7.89	15	0	0	0	22	34	27	19	3	17	24	.333	.370	.304	9.97	7.06
Jogly Garcia	R-R	6-1	170	9-8-03	0	3	3.51	9	9	0	0	33	34	25	13	0	24	28	.258	.256	.258	7.56	6.48
Victor Garcia	R-R	6-0	168	2-8-03	0	1	8.64	7	7	0	0	17	33	25	16	1	15	16	.407	.290	.480	8.64	8.10
Yonaiker Garcia	R-R	5-11	165	12-15-00	0	0	9.00	1	0	0	0	2	4	2	2	0	0	2	.400	.333	.429	9.00	0.00
2-team total (16 DSL CLE Blue)					4	1	4.38	17	0	0	2	37	34	19	18	2	10	36	.243	.260	.233	8.76	2.43
Diovel Mariano	R-R	6-1	175	2-23-04	1	0	3.21	19	0	0	1	28	30	15	10	3	8	19	.270	.171	.316	6.11	2.57
Erick Padilla	R-R	5-10	145	11-26-03	0	3	4.23	16	0	0	1	28	24	19	13	0	18	25	.238	.260	.216	8.13	5.86
Felix Polanco	L-L	6-2	190	6-26-00	1	0	5.25	16	1	0	0	24	20	18	14	2	18	31	.217	.211	.219	11.63	6.75
Jose Ruviera	R-R	6-3	168	9-4-01	0	0	6.75	3	0	0	0	5	2	4	4	1	7	2	.133	.286	.000	3.38	11.81
2-team total (11 DSL CLE Blue)					0	2	6.10	14	0	0	1	21	19	20	14	1	23	12	.257	.357	.196	5.23	10.02
Rodarni Salvador	R-R	6-3	158	4-1-05	2	1	2.88	16	0	0	0	25	26	18	8	1	8	22	.263	.273	.255	7.92	2.88
Abrahan Tejada	R-R	5-10	151	12-11-04	0	5	7.68	10	10	0	0	36	42	36	31	4	17	33	.278	.143	.343	8.17	4.21
Javier Tovar	R-R	5-10	184	11-4-01	0	0	1.04	5	5	0	0	17	12	5	2	0	6	18	.188	.219	.156	9.35	3.12
Dielmon Urena	R-R	6-6	166	5-15-01	0	2	12.05	18	0	0	0	22	16	33	29	0	48	21	.213	.190	.222	8.72	19.94
Adauri Vicente	R-R	6-2	188	12-18-00	1	1	5.27	12	0	0	1	14	13	20	8	2	12	15	.236	.130	.313	9.88	7.90
Kendeglys Virguez	R-R	6-2	160	5-6-04	2	5	8.06	17	0	0	0	22	25	26	20	2	19	30	.269	.269	.269	12.09	7.66

Fielding

C: Izturis 36, Paredes 11, Romero 3, Taveras 15. **1B:** Andrade 7, Cedeno 5, Lopez 8, Paredes 6, Polanco 17, Purroy 1, Rivas 11, Rivera 6, Romero 4, Taveras 5. **2B:** Andrade 6, Guedez 6, Hernandez 6, Jean-Baptiste 6, Polanco 5, Purroy 20, Ramirez 5, Rivas 6, Rivera 2. **3B:** Andrade 5, Guedez 10, Hernandez 6, Jean-Baptiste 9, Polanco 6, Purroy 3, Ramirez 10, Rivas 5, Rivera 9. **SS:** Guedez 6, Hernandez 13, Jean-Baptiste 13, Lopez 1, Polanco 1, Purroy 2, Ramirez 25, Rivas 1, Rivera 1. **OF:** Andrade 16, Aparicio 11, Cedeno 1, Chourio 39, Espinola 40, Hernandez 4, Lopez 9, Pena 34, Polanco 3, Purroy 6, Rivas 7, Rivera 19.

Colorado Rockies

SEASON IN A SENTENCE: After three consecutive seasons of finishing 4th in the NL West the Rockies bottomed out in 2022 with their first last place finish since 2015.

HIGH POINT: The Rockies went 16-11 over the first month of the season, which meant they left the month third in the very competitive NL West.

LOW POINT: In the days following the trade deadline the Rockies were heavily criticized as they left a second consecutive trade deadline without acquiring young talent. At the time the Rockies were last in the NL West and 25.5 games out of the division lead. This all culminated on August 3rd as the Rockies lost their fifth consecutive game, a sign of things to come over the final two months of the season. The Rockies would finish with a record of 68-94, 43 games back of the Dodgers in the NL West.

NOTABLE ROOKIES: While the Rockies didn't get much in the way of immediate returns from rookie players this season they did see a talented crop of young players debut in the major leagues. Elehuris Montero hit six home runs and slugged .432 over 53 games. Michael Toglia debuted in late August and showed promise over the final month. Top prospect Ezequiel Tovar made his major league debut on September 23 just two months after his 21st birthday.

KEY TRANSACTIONS: While the Rockies were less active on the trade market during the season, they made a flurry of moves following the end of the offseason lockout. The Rockies signed former Cubs star Kris Bryant and traded Raimel Tapia and Adrian Pinto for slugger Randal Grichuk in the days preceding the ratification of the collective bargaining agreement.

ON THE FARM: Several players took major steps forwarded highlighted by a talented group of infielders, spearheaded by shortstop Ezequiel Tovar. He hit .318/.386/.545 over 66 games with Double-A Hartford as the youngest player to begin his season in the Eastern League. Adael Amador was a standout with a Low-A Fresno team loaded with Top 30 Rockies prospects including Victor Juarez, Benny Montgomery, Warming Bernabel, Yanquiel Fernandez and Hunter Goodman among others. The Rockies made five selections inside the top 100 picks in the draft, adding righthander Gabriel Hughes in the first round as well as a pair of highly productive college outfielders in Florida's Sterlin Thompson and Tennessee's Jordan Beck.

OPENING DAY PAYROLL: $158,887,118 (17th).

PLAYERS OF THE YEAR

MAJOR LEAGUE

Brendan Rodgers
2B
.266/.325/.408
13 HR in 137 G
Won first Gold Glove

MINOR LEAGUE

Adael Amador
SS
(LoA)
.292/.415/.445
15 HR, 26 SB in 115 G

ORGANIZATION LEADERS

Batting — *Minimum 250 AB

MAJORS		
*AVG	Yonathan Daza	.301
*OPS	C.J. Cron	.783
HR	C.J. Cron	29
RBI	C.J. Cron	102
MINORS		
*AVG	Wynton Bernard, Albuquerque	.333
*OBP	Adael Amador, Fresno	.415
*SLG	Sean Bouchard, Albuquerque	.635
*OPS	Sean Bouchard, Albuquerque	1.038
R	Adael Amador, Fresno	100
H	Hunter Goodman, Fresno, Spokane, Hartford	154
TB	Hunter Goodman, Fresno, Spokane, Hartford	299
2B	Julio Carreras, Spokane, Hartford	42
3B	Wynton Bernard, Albuquerque	8
HR	Hunter Goodman, Fresno, Spokane, Hartford	36
RBI	Yanquiel Fernandez, Fresno	109
BB	Adael Amador, Fresno	87
SO	Brenton Doyle, Hartford, Albuquerque	171
SB	Braiden Ward, Spokane, Fresno	57

Pitching — #Minimum 75 IP

MAJORS		
W	German Marquez	9
W	Kyle Freeland	9
#ERA	Kyle Freeland	4.53
SO	German Marquez	150
SV	Daniel Bard	34
MINORS		
W	Case Williams, Fresno, Spokane, Hartford	11
L	3 tied	9
#ERA	Austin Kitchen, Spokane, Hartford	3.32
G	Zach Lee, Albuquerque	64
GS	Karl Kauffmann, Hartford, Albuquerque	28
SV	Gavin Hollowell, Hartford	16
IP	Karl Kauffmann, Hartford, Albuquerque	142
BB	Karl Kauffmann	79
SO	Noah Davis, Hartford, Albuquerque	154
#AVG	Joe Rock, Spokane, Hartford	.223

2022 PERFORMANCE

General Manager: Bill Schmidt. **Farm Director:** Chris Forbes. **Scouting Director:** Danny Montgomery.

Class	Team	League	W	L	PCT	Finish	Manager
Majors	Colorado Rockies	National League	68	94	.420	12th (15)	Bud Black
Triple-A	Albuquerque Isotopes	Pacific Coast	62	86	.419	10th (10)	Warren Schaeffer
Double-A	Hartford Yard Goats	Eastern	77	60	.562	4th (12)	Chris Denorfia
High-A	Spokane Indians	Northwest	64	66	.492	3rd (6)	Scott Little
Low-A	Fresno Grizzlies	California	83	49	.629	1st (8)	Robinson Cancel
Rookie	ACL Rockies	Arizona Complex	34	19	.642	3rd (18)	Fred Ocasio
Overall 2022 Minor League Record			395	325	.549	2nd (30)	

ORGANIZATION STATISTICS

COLORADO ROCKIES

NATIONAL LEAGUE

Batting	B-T	HT	WT	DOB	AVG	vLH	vRH	G	AB	R	H	2B	3B	HR	RBI	BB	HBP	SH	SF	SO	SB	CS	SLG	OBP
Wynton Bernard	R-R	6-2	195	9-24-90	.286	.214	.321	12	42	9	12	1	0	0	3	0	0	0	0	8	3	1	.310	.286
Charlie Blackmon	L-L	6-3	221	7-1-86	.264	.304	.247	135	530	60	140	22	6	16	78	32	8	4	3	109	4	1	.419	.314
Sean Bouchard	R-R	6-3	215	5-16-96	.297	.207	.356	27	74	9	22	6	0	3	11	21	1	0	1	25	0	0	.500	.454
Kris Bryant	R-R	6-5	230	1-4-92	.306	.333	.287	42	160	28	49	12	0	5	14	17	2	0	2	27	0	0	.475	.376
C.J. Cron	R-R	6-4	235	1-5-90	.257	.208	.280	150	575	79	148	28	3	29	102	43	8	0	5	164	0	0	.468	.315
Yonathan Daza	R-R	6-2	207	2-28-94	.301	.341	.279	113	372	56	112	21	2	2	34	26	4	1	5	58	0	3	.384	.349
Elias Diaz	R-R	6-1	223	11-17-90	.228	.278	.197	105	351	29	80	18	2	9	51	25	2	0	3	82	0	1	.368	.281
Randal Grichuk	R-R	6-2	216	8-13-91	.259	.308	.234	141	506	60	131	21	3	19	73	24	6	0	2	127	4	0	.425	.299
Garrett Hampson	R-R	5-11	196	10-10-94	.211	.296	.164	90	199	29	42	7	3	2	15	21	1	3	2	63	12	2	.307	.287
Sam Hilliard	L-L	6-5	236	2-21-94	.184	.107	.199	70	174	26	32	6	1	2	14	23	1	0	2	57	5	1	.264	.280
Jose Iglesias	R-R	5-11	195	1-5-90	.292	.295	.290	118	439	48	128	30	0	3	47	17	8	0	3	56	2	3	.380	.328
Connor Joe	R-R	6-0	205	8-16-92	.238	.259	.226	111	404	56	96	20	4	7	28	55	7	0	1	97	6	2	.359	.338
Ryan McMahon	L-R	6-2	219	12-14-94	.246	.228	.253	153	529	67	130	23	3	20	67	60	5	0	3	158	7	3	.414	.327
Elehuris Montero	R-R	6-3	235	8-17-98	.233	.261	.215	53	176	21	41	15	1	6	20	8	1	0	0	60	0	0	.432	.270
Dom Nunez	L-R	6-1	212	1-17-95	.121	.000	.138	14	33	3	4	1	0	0	2	6	0	0	2	10	0	0	.152	.244
Brendan Rodgers	R-R	6-0	204	8-9-96	.266	.317	.239	137	527	72	140	30	3	13	63	46	3	0	5	101	0	0	.408	.325
Brian Serven	R-R	6-0	207	5-5-95	.203	.227	.196	62	187	19	38	4	1	6	16	13	2	2	1	44	0	0	.332	.261
Michael Toglia	B-L	6-5	226	8-16-98	.216	.200	.224	31	111	10	24	8	2	2	12	9	0	0	0	44	1	1	.378	.275
Ezequiel Tovar	R-R	6-0	162	8-1-01	.212	.364	.136	9	33	2	7	1	0	1	2	2	0	0	0	9	0	0	.333	.257
Alan Trejo	R-R	6-2	205	5-30-96	.271	.167	.298	35	118	15	32	6	0	4	17	5	2	0	0	31	1	2	.424	.312

Pitching	B-T	HT	WT	DOB	W	L	ERA	G	GS	CG	SV	IP	H	R	ER	HR	BB	SO	AVG	vLH	vRH	K/9	BB/9
Daniel Bard	R-R	6-4	215	6-25-85	6	4	1.79	57	0	0	34	60	35	15	12	3	25	69	.162	.174	.147	10.29	3.73
Jake Bird	R-R	6-3	200	12-4-95	2	4	4.91	38	0	0	0	48	45	29	26	7	23	42	.249	.244	.253	7.93	4.34
Ty Blach	R-L	6-1	215	10-20-90	1	0	5.89	24	1	0	1	44	51	29	29	4	11	29	.291	.179	.361	5.89	2.23
Jhoulys Chacin	R-R	6-3	215	1-7-88	4	2	7.61	35	0	0	0	47	55	44	40	7	21	37	.282	.250	.308	7.04	3.99
Alex Colome	R-R	6-1	225	12-31-88	2	7	5.74	53	0	0	4	47	57	36	30	5	22	32	.300	.275	.318	6.13	4.21
Noah Davis	R-R	6-2	195	4-22-97	0	0	18.00	1	0	0	0	1	3	2	2	1	1	2	.500	.667	.333	18.00	9.00
Carlos Estevez	R-R	6-6	277	12-28-92	4	4	3.47	62	0	0	2	57	44	27	22	7	23	54	.211	.216	.204	8.53	3.63
Ryan Feltner	R-R	6-4	190	9-2-96	4	9	5.83	20	19	0	0	97	102	65	63	16	35	84	.266	.250	.283	7.77	3.24
Kyle Freeland	L-L	6-4	204	5-14-93	9	11	4.53	31	31	0	0	175	193	96	88	19	53	131	.281	.315	.271	6.75	2.73
Lucas Gilbreath	L-L	6-1	185	3-5-96	2	0	4.19	47	0	0	0	43	37	22	20	2	26	49	.242	.186	.277	10.26	5.44
Austin Gomber	L-L	6-5	220	11-23-93	5	7	5.56	33	17	0	0	125	137	80	77	20	34	95	.281	.221	.304	6.86	2.45
Ashton Goudeau	R-R	6-6	220	7-23-92	1	0	7.08	12	0	0	1	20	25	18	16	3	10	16	.305	.231	.339	7.08	4.43
Randal Grichuk	R-R	6-2	216	8-13-91	0	0	0.00	1	0	0	0	1	0	0	0	0	0	0	.000	--	.000	0.00	0.00
Gavin Hollowell	R-R	6-7	215	11-4-97	0	2	7.71	6	0	0	0	7	7	7	6	1	4	8	.259	.250	.267	10.29	5.14
Tyler Kinley	R-R	6-4	220	1-31-91	1	1	0.75	25	0	0	0	24	21	5	2	0	6	27	.226	.119	.314	10.13	2.25
Chad Kuhl	R-R	6-3	205	9-10-92	6	11	5.72	27	27	1	0	137	155	91	87	25	58	110	.284	.264	.306	7.23	3.81
Dinelson Lamet	R-R	6-3	228	7-18-92	1	1	4.05	19	0	0	0	20	14	9	9	2	10	29	.189	.171	.212	13.05	4.50
2-team total (13 San Diego Padres)					1	2	6.12	32	0	0	0	32	30	23	22	4	19	45	.242	.241	.242	12.53	5.29
Justin Lawrence	R-R	6-3	213	11-25-94	3	1	5.70	38	0	0	1	43	44	27	27	3	22	48	.265	.316	.218	10.13	4.64
German Marquez	R-R	6-1	230	2-22-95	9	13	4.95	31	31	0	0	182	185	109	100	30	63	150	.263	.279	.245	7.43	3.12
Antonio Senzatela	R-R	6-1	236	1-21-95	3	7	5.07	19	19	0	0	92	133	56	52	9	23	54	.349	.332	.369	5.26	2.24
Brian Serven	R-R	6-0	207	5-5-95	0	0	0.00	1	0	0	0	1	0	0	0	0	1	0	.000	--	.000	0.00	9.00
Jordan Sheffield	R-R	5-10	190	6-1-95	0	0	0.00	2	0	0	0	2	2	0	0	0	2	1	.333	.250	.500	4.50	9.00
Chad Smith	R-R	6-4	200	6-8-95	0	1	7.50	15	0	0	0	18	16	15	15	2	15	23	.239	.320	.190	11.50	7.50
Robert Stephenson	R-R	6-3	205	2-24-93	2	1	6.04	45	0	0	0	45	53	34	30	8	13	37	.291	.294	.289	7.46	2.62
2-team total (13 Pittsburgh Pirates)					2	2	5.43	58	0	0	0	58	63	39	35	10	14	55	.275	.260	.288	8.53	2.17
Jose Urena	R-R	6-2	208	9-12-91	3	8	5.14	17	17	0	0	89	102	57	51	10	38	60	.289	.330	.239	6.04	3.83
2-team total (4 Milwaukee Brewers)					3	8	5.01	21	17	0	0	97	109	62	54	11	43	63	.285	.329	.234	5.85	3.99

Fielding

Catcher	PCT	G	PO	A	E	DP	PB
Diaz	.985	104	672	52	11	3	3
Nunez	.990	14	93	5	1	0	0
Serven	.989	59	415	26	5	2	2

First Base	PCT	G	PO	A	E	DP
Cron	.994	121	1033	59	7	113

Joe	.988	24	150	20	2	14
McMahon	1.000	1	2	0	0	0
Montero	.991	16	100	10	1	10
Serven	1.000	1	3	0	0	0
Toglia	1.000	15	114	11	0	8

Second Base	PCT	G	PO	A	E	DP
Hampson	.976	10	15	26	1	3
McMahon	1.000	10	14	26	0	8
Rodgers	.984	134	218	411	10	99
Trejo	1.000	13	21	37	0	5

Third Base	PCT	G	PO	A	E	DP
Hampson	1.000	7	7	16	0	1
McMahon	.953	145	88	257	17	29
Montero	.943	23	13	37	3	5
Trejo	1.000	2	1	5	0	1

Shortstop	PCT	G	PO	A	E	DP
Hampson	.968	32	33	57	3	15
Iglesias	.981	116	123	298	8	73
Tovar	.971	9	14	20	1	2
Trejo	.949	20	20	55	4	13

Outfield	PCT	G	PO	A	E	DP
Bernard	1.000	12	25	1	0	0
Blackmon	.957	51	83	7	4	3
Bouchard	1.000	26	53	0	0	0
Bryant	.955	30	42	0	2	0
Daza	.977	120	252	3	6	1
Grichuk	.981	158	260	3	5	0
Hampson	1.000	36	56	1	0	0
Hilliard	1.000	76	118	3	0	1
Joe	1.000	66	132	7	0	0
Toglia	1.000	17	20	1	0	0

ALBUQUERQUE ISOTOPES — *TRIPLE-A*

PACIFIC COAST LEAGUE

Batting	B-T	HT	WT	DOB	AVG	vLH	vRH	G	AB	R	H	2B	3B	HR	RBI	BB	HBP	SH	SF	SO	SB	CS	SLG	OBP
Wynton Bernard	R-R	6-2	195	9-24-90	.333	.371	.321	108	429	95	143	31	8	21	92	39	2	0	5	67	30	5	.590	.387
Bret Boswell	L-R	6-0	198	10-4-94	.247	.232	.252	85	287	44	71	15	1	12	34	38	3	0	1	98	6	1	.432	.340
Sean Bouchard	R-R	6-3	215	5-16-96	.300	.278	.309	69	260	61	78	15	6	20	56	44	4	0	4	70	12	2	.635	.404
Kris Bryant	R-R	6-5	230	1-4-92	.150	.222	.091	6	20	2	3	2	0	0	0	2	0	0	0	8	0	0	.250	.227
Yonathan Daza	R-R	6-2	207	2-28-94	.333	.500	.300	3	12	3	4	0	0	0	1	1	0	0	0	4	0	0	.333	.385
Brenton Doyle	R-R	6-3	200	5-14-98	.389	.375	.393	9	36	8	14	1	2	3	9	5	0	0	0	13	0	0	.778	.463
Garrett Hampson	R-R	5-11	196	10-10-94	.400	--	.400	2	10	1	4	1	0	0	5	1	0	0	0	2	1	0	.500	.455
LJ Hatch	R-R	5-11	175	5-18-94	.280	.250	.288	49	161	32	45	6	1	8	21	15	3	1	0	56	2	1	.478	.352
Jimmy Herron	R-L	6-1	195	7-27-96	.266	.222	.280	41	143	30	38	8	2	4	14	17	2	0	1	32	7	1	.434	.350
Tyler Hill	R-R	6-0	195	3-4-96	.273	.000	.375	9	22	3	6	1	1	1	2	1	0	0	0	6	1	0	.545	.304
Sam Hilliard	L-L	6-5	236	2-21-94	.308	.455	.279	37	133	27	41	5	2	13	32	21	2	0	2	39	4	1	.669	.405
Kyle Holder	L-R	6-1	204	5-25-94	.197	.200	.197	45	152	13	30	4	1	2	11	15	2	0	1	43	0	1	.276	.276
Tim Lopes	R-R	5-11	180	6-24-94	.271	.397	.223	70	266	52	72	15	3	9	34	23	4	1	4	69	10	5	.451	.333
Willie MacIver	R-R	6-2	205	10-28-96	.143	.500	.105	6	21	1	3	0	0	0	0	2	0	0	0	8	0	0	.143	.217
Elehuris Montero	R-R	6-3	235	8-17-98	.310	.388	.282	65	255	44	79	10	2	15	54	27	10	0	4	63	4	2	.541	.392
Coco Montes	R-R	6-1	200	10-7-96	.274	.267	.276	111	420	82	115	27	4	20	77	50	7	0	2	131	13	1	.500	.359
Jonathan Morales	R-R	5-11	200	1-29-95	.308	.333	.300	86	308	34	95	11	0	9	46	37	4	0	4	57	0	0	.432	.385
Dom Nunez	L-R	6-1	212	1-17-95	.223	.111	.254	62	247	36	55	13	3	5	29	34	2	0	2	70	1	1	.360	.319
Carlos Perez	R-R	6-0	210	10-27-90	.254	.252	.255	117	456	75	116	28	1	31	87	54	8	0	4	100	0	0	.524	.341
D.J. Peterson	R-R	6-1	210	12-31-91	.249	.278	.238	89	313	51	78	19	0	20	66	37	8	0	2	98	1	0	.502	.342
Scott Schebler	L-R	6-1	228	10-6-90	.243	.192	.259	57	214	32	52	5	5	7	28	17	4	0	3	69	3	0	.411	.307
Brian Serven	R-R	6-0	207	5-5-95	.273	.313	.262	23	77	18	21	3	0	5	11	16	2	0	1	15	0	0	.506	.406
Taylor Snyder	R-R	6-2	165	9-28-94	.194	.229	.181	38	129	17	25	3	1	4	14	8	0	0	1	63	2	0	.326	.239
Michael Toglia	B-L	6-5	226	8-16-98	.333	.450	.283	17	66	11	22	7	0	7	17	9	0	0	0	22	0	1	.758	.413
Ezequiel Tovar	R-R	6-0	162	8-1-01	.333	.333	.333	5	21	3	7	0	0	1	2	2	0	0	0	2	0	0	.476	.391
Alan Trejo	R-R	6-2	205	5-30-96	.296	.356	.279	67	274	46	81	20	1	16	52	10	6	0	3	64	2	2	.551	.331
Ryan Vilade	R-R	6-2	226	2-18-99	.249	.327	.219	99	369	64	92	15	4	5	38	52	4	1	4	69	10	6	.352	.345
Colton Welker	R-R	6-1	235	10-9-97	.324	.444	.286	10	37	9	12	1	0	2	7	6	1	0	1	7	0	0	.514	.422

Pitching	B-T	HT	WT	DOB	W	L	ERA	G	GS	CG	SV	IP	H	R	ER	HR	BB	SO	AVG	vLH	vRH	K/9	BB/9
Logan Allen	R-L	6-3	200	5-23-97	1	3	6.43	6	6	0	0	28	33	20	20	8	9	25	.297	.132	.384	8.04	2.89
Jake Bird	R-R	6-3	200	12-4-95	2	2	2.77	22	0	0	2	26	16	10	8	3	9	34	.170	.125	.194	11.77	3.12
Ty Blach	R-L	6-1	215	10-20-90	1	5	4.50	15	1	0	0	36	44	23	18	3	8	20	.301	.269	.319	5.00	2.00
Ben Bowden	L-L	6-4	249	10-21-94	0	0	8.22	7	0	0	0	8	6	7	7	1	6	11	.222	.300	.176	12.91	7.04
2-team total (22 Sacramento River Cats)					1	1	7.32	29	0	0	0	36	30	29	29	9	21	52	.227	.246	.213	13.12	5.30
Logan Cozart	R-R	6-2	215	1-27-93	1	0	9.82	27	0	0	1	26	37	30	28	9	14	30	.339	.355	.333	10.52	4.91
Noah Davis	R-R	6-2	195	4-22-97	0	0	1.93	1	1	0	0	5	6	1	1	0	2	2	.375	.444	.286	3.86	3.86
Matt Dennis	R-R	6-1	210	1-3-95	5	5	7.00	32	6	0	0	80	104	64	62	15	38	52	.323	.376	.296	5.87	4.29
Frank Duncan	R-R	6-4	215	1-30-92	0	2	17.58	6	6	0	0	14	37	29	28	4	12	14	.463	.512	.410	8.79	7.53
Ryan Feltner	R-R	6-4	190	9-2-96	5	1	3.83	11	11	0	0	52	49	25	22	5	18	60	.246	.244	.248	10.45	3.14
Julian Fernandez	R-R	6-6	233	12-5-95	2	5	6.63	58	0	0	1	57	54	46	42	15	32	65	.243	.235	.248	10.26	5.05
Will Gaddis	R-R	6-1	185	3-12-96	0	0	10.24	6	0	0	0	10	16	12	11	1	4	4	.372	.400	.348	3.72	3.72
Lucas Gilbreath	L-L	6-1	185	3-5-96	1	1	9.64	5	0	0	0	5	8	5	5	0	2	6	.364	.000	.500	11.57	3.86
Brandon Gold	R-R	6-3	203	9-16-94	6	8	7.25	29	22	0	0	108	146	88	87	30	45	73	.322	.332	.315	6.08	3.75
Ashton Goudeau	R-R	6-6	220	7-23-92	0	7	9.51	20	15	0	0	64	101	71	68	15	23	44	.357	.377	.340	6.16	3.22
Nate Griep	R-R	6-2	210	10-11-93	0	1	9.64	29	0	0	0	23	34	25	25	8	20	19	.343	.400	.305	7.33	7.71
JD Hammer	R-R	6-3	202	7-12-94	1	1	5.94	53	0	0	0	47	52	35	31	9	30	47	.283	.290	.279	9.00	5.74
Heath Holder	R-R	6-6	211	8-23-92	2	0	7.91	32	0	0	0	39	38	34	34	8	24	47	.255	.271	.244	10.94	5.59
Karl Kauffmann	R-R	6-2	200	8-15-97	4	5	6.05	13	13	0	0	64	70	48	43	11	45	60	.272	.341	.235	8.44	6.33
Nick Kennedy	R-L	6-1	200	6-20-96	1	2	8.71	42	0	0	0	41	62	43	40	7	27	30	.346	.309	.369	6.53	5.88
Chad Kuhl	R-R	6-3	205	9-10-92	1	0	0.00	1	1	0	0	5	3	0	0	0	4	6	.176	.111	.250	10.80	7.20
Peter Lambert	R-R	6-2	208	4-18-97	0	2	6.23	4	4	0	0	9	11	6	6	0	6	11	.314	.167	.391	11.42	6.23
Justin Lawrence	R-R	6-3	213	11-25-94	1	0	3.07	28	0	0	1	29	17	11	10	2	13	49	.165	.122	.194	15.03	3.99
Zach Lee	R-R	6-3	195	9-13-91	4	6	5.14	64	0	0	12	61	62	41	35	7	27	62	.259	.277	.246	9.10	3.96
Brett Matthews	R-R	6-5	219	4-23-98	0	0	0.00	1	0	0	0	1	0	0	0	0	2	0	.000	--	.000	0.00	27.00
Zach Neal	R-R	6-3	220	11-9-88	6	6	6.87	29	21	0	0	117	146	92	89	28	28	95	.302	.313	.294	7.33	2.16
Corey Oswalt	R-R	6-5	250	9-3-93	0	2	7.63	4	4	0	0	15	23	13	13	7	4	9	.343	.238	.391	5.28	2.35
2-team total (6 Sacramento River Cats)					1	4	7.39	10	5	0	0	28	38	25	23	13	9	26	.317	.171	.376	8.36	2.89
Dillon Overton	L-L	6-2	175	8-17-91	2	7	8.60	12	11	0	0	45	65	49	43	11	16	39	.335	.333	.336	7.80	3.20

Joel Peguero	R-R	5-11	160	5-5-97	1	0	5.19	18	0	0	1	17	24	10	10	2	11	19	.329	.318	.333	9.87	5.71
Riley Pint	R-R	6-5	225	11-6-97	0	1	3.00	3	0	0	0	3	3	1	1	0	2	3	.273	.333	.000	9.00	6.00
PJ Poulin	R-L	6-1	195	7-25-96	3	0	8.10	21	0	0	0	20	31	21	18	4	13	24	.360	.400	.333	10.80	5.85
Garrett Schilling	R-R	6-2	185	10-25-95	0	1	45.00	1	1	0	0	1	5	5	5	1	1	0	.625	1.000	.571	0.00	9.00
Antonio Senzatela	R-R	6-1	236	1-21-95	1	0	5.00	2	2	0	0	9	12	5	5	2	2	0	.343	.333	.357	0.00	2.00
Jordan Sheffield	R-R	5-10	190	6-1-95	0	0	11.12	27	1	0	0	23	32	32	28	12	20	19	.337	.206	.410	7.54	7.94
Chad Smith	R-R	6-4	200	6-8-95	1	2	3.09	32	0	0	12	35	27	13	12	6	11	40	.216	.318	.160	10.29	2.83
Riley Smith	R-R	6-1	207	1-15-95	4	7	8.06	19	17	1	0	93	136	86	83	18	25	80	.345	.381	.315	7.77	2.43
Robert Stephenson	R-R	6-3	205	2-24-93	0	0	0.00	1	0	0	0	1	0	0	0	0	0	0	.000	.000	.000	0.00	0.00
Reagan Todd	L-L	6-3	218	8-30-95	6	3	5.24	49	0	0	0	46	44	32	27	5	28	61	.247	.293	.214	11.85	5.44
Jose Urena	R-R	6-2	208	9-12-91	0	1	7.29	5	5	0	0	21	33	18	17	1	12	14	.375	.471	.315	6.00	5.14

Fielding

Catcher	PCT	G	PO	A	E	DP	PB
MacIver	1.000	6	43	1	0	0	0
Morales	.991	41	318	30	3	4	0
Nunez	.983	52	374	21	7	0	7
Perez	.996	31	253	13	1	1	0
Serven	.978	22	210	9	5	2	2

First Base	PCT	G	PO	A	E	DP
Bouchard	.994	21	157	16	1	14
Montero	.994	20	153	19	1	13
Morales	1.000	9	58	11	0	8
Perez	.995	23	186	11	1	24
Peterson	.990	63	466	28	5	71
Snyder	1.000	1	4	0	0	1
Toglia	1.000	13	117	6	0	11
Welker	1.000	4	25	5	0	2

Second Base	PCT	G	PO	A	E	DP
Boswell	.986	16	24	46	1	16
Hampson	.600	1	2	1	2	1
Hatch	.975	16	38	40	2	16
Holder	1.000	23	35	67	0	12
Lopes	.982	40	56	111	3	21
Montes	.988	38	62	97	2	31
Snyder	.947	12	15	21	2	5
Trejo	.980	10	19	31	1	13

Third Base	PCT	G	PO	A	E	DP
Boswell	.959	30	25	46	3	2
Hatch	1.000	2	2	2	0	1
Lopes	.951	11	13	26	2	4
Montero	.908	37	17	52	7	0
Montes	.963	35	15	89	4	10
Morales	.948	26	15	58	4	13
Snyder	.929	5	3	10	1	1
Trejo	1.000	3	0	4	0	0
Welker	.917	6	3	8	1	0

Shortstop	PCT	G	PO	A	E	DP
Hatch	.971	27	51	82	4	22
Holder	.968	22	31	60	3	18
Lopes	.750	2	2	1	1	0
Montes	.962	37	54	96	6	23
Snyder	.846	5	8	14	4	2
Tovar	.920	5	8	15	2	5
Trejo	.971	53	76	156	7	42

Outfield	PCT	G	PO	A	E	DP
Bernard	.995	105	201	2	1	0
Boswell	1.000	38	72	1	0	0
Bouchard	.987	43	76	2	1	1
Bryant	1.000	5	4	0	0	0
Daza	1.000	2	7	0	0	0
Doyle	1.000	9	20	2	0	0
Hampson	1.000	1	1	0	0	0
Herron	.987	41	74	1	1	0
Hill	1.000	7	12	0	0	0
Hilliard	1.000	31	71	3	0	1
Lopes	.933	13	13	1	1	0
Perez	1.000	8	16	0	0	0
Schebler	1.000	49	70	0	0	0
Snyder	1.000	16	22	0	0	0
Toglia	1.000	3	7	0	0	0
Vilade	.983	97	164	9	3	4

HARTFORD YARD GOATS — *DOUBLE-A*

EASTERN LEAGUE

Batting	B-T	HT	WT	DOB	AVG	vLH	vRH	G	AB	R	H	2B	3B	HR	RBI	BB	HBP	SH	SF	SO	SB	CS	SLG	OBP
Jack Blomgren	R-R	5-10	180	9-27-98	.353	.600	.250	6	17	3	6	2	0	1	5	2	0	1	0	5	0	1	.647	.421
Julio Carreras	R-R	6-2	190	1-12-00	.233	.182	.245	19	60	11	14	5	1	0	13	5	1	2	0	21	2	0	.350	.303
Isaac Collins	B-R	5-9	185	7-22-97	.221	.307	.195	110	375	69	83	24	4	5	32	58	8	6	1	90	30	8	.347	.337
Daniel Cope	R-R	6-0	195	6-15-97	.252	.237	.257	44	151	20	38	7	1	7	26	14	1	0	1	45	1	0	.450	.317
Kyle Datres	R-R	6-0	205	1-5-96	.260	.262	.259	93	308	53	80	15	0	15	49	36	9	0	3	91	23	3	.455	.351
Niko Decolati	R-R	6-1	215	8-12-97	.199	.211	.194	44	141	26	28	6	1	1	17	24	3	0	0	43	9	2	.277	.327
Brenton Doyle	R-R	6-3	200	5-14-98	.246	.255	.244	123	471	74	116	21	3	23	68	23	6	1	6	158	23	3	.450	.287
Max George	R-R	5-10	190	4-7-96	.056	--	.056	8	18	3	1	1	0	0	0	0	2	0	0	7	0	0	.111	.150
Hunter Goodman	R-R	6-1	210	10-8-99	.227	.500	.214	12	44	5	10	0	0	2	4	3	0	0	0	12	1	0	.364	.277
Jameson Hannah	L-L	5-9	185	8-10-97	.273	.217	.289	29	99	16	27	5	1	1	4	12	0	1	0	25	7	0	.374	.351
Jimmy Herron	R-L	6-1	195	7-27-96	.259	.138	.282	54	185	27	48	9	1	9	30	28	6	1	1	37	7	2	.465	.373
Tyler Hill	R-R	6-0	195	3-4-96	.204	.185	.209	44	113	19	23	2	0	3	18	15	0	1	2	32	12	1	.301	.292
Grant Lavigne	L-R	6-4	220	8-27-99	.245	.283	.235	57	208	29	51	7	2	5	24	32	1	0	1	66	0	0	.370	.347
Willie MacIver	R-R	6-2	205	10-28-96	.231	.282	.218	98	346	42	80	18	0	15	50	37	7	2	4	106	10	3	.413	.315
Daniel Montano	L-R	6-1	204	3-31-99	.252	.228	.258	82	305	46	77	16	1	13	39	49	1	1	3	101	5	2	.439	.355
Coco Montes	R-R	6-1	200	10-7-96	.245	.200	.250	15	49	5	12	1	0	0	1	10	1	0	0	13	2	0	.265	.383
Cristopher Navarro	R-R	6-0	170	6-14-99	.207	.000	.240	9	29	4	6	1	0	0	0	1	0	0	0	7	0	0	.241	.233
Aaron Schunk	R-R	6-2	205	7-24-97	.258	.278	.253	122	450	62	116	32	1	14	77	36	5	0	6	115	6	2	.427	.316
Hunter Stovall	R-R	5-8	170	9-5-96	.267	.247	.273	108	393	48	105	27	3	9	55	34	1	5	2	91	10	5	.420	.326
Michael Toglia	B-L	6-5	226	8-16-98	.234	.217	.239	97	363	63	85	13	1	23	66	51	2	0	4	127	7	1	.466	.329
Ezequiel Tovar	R-R	6-0	162	8-1-01	.318	.356	.307	66	264	39	84	15	3	13	47	25	5	0	1	64	17	3	.545	.386
Zac Veen	L-R	6-4	190	12-12-01	.177	.150	.183	34	124	12	22	4	0	1	7	14	1	0	2	42	5	5	.234	.262

Pitching	B-T	HT	WT	DOB	W	L	ERA	G	GS	CG	SV	IP	H	R	ER	HR	BB	SO	AVG	vLH	vRH	K/9	BB/9
Michael Baird	R-R	6-5	210	7-9-95	3	2	4.10	17	12	0	0	68	62	32	31	16	19	73	.238	.273	.209	9.66	2.51
Jared Biddy	R-R	6-2	180	7-25-96	4	1	2.08	29	0	0	0	43	36	12	10	3	16	41	.234	.236	.232	8.52	3.32
Nick Bush	L-L	6-0	195	8-23-96	7	6	3.68	19	19	1	0	100	100	45	41	17	16	98	.256	.271	.250	8.79	1.44
Blair Calvo	R-R	6-3	195	2-27-96	4	2	3.09	29	0	0	0	35	33	12	12	2	11	47	.254	.270	.239	12.09	2.83
Dugan Darnell	L-R	6-2	205	6-26-97	4	1	5.29	38	0	0	0	48	46	30	28	9	33	68	.245	.224	.262	12.84	6.23
Noah Davis	R-R	6-2	195	4-22-97	8	8	5.54	26	26	1	0	133	133	86	82	26	60	152	.260	.298	.230	10.26	4.05
Fineas Del Bonta-Smith	R-R	6-0	190	2-2-97	5	1	3.96	36	0	0	0	50	42	23	22	11	12	55	.226	.231	.222	9.90	2.16
Will Ethridge	R-R	6-5	240	12-20-97	1	1	3.42	7	6	0	0	26	17	10	10	4	16	14	.183	.158	.200	4.78	5.47
Trent Fennell	R-R	6-5	205	11-26-95	2	2	6.35	21	1	0	0	40	30	28	28	8	32	37	.216	.263	.183	8.39	7.26
Will Gaddis	R-R	6-1	185	3-12-96	5	0	4.89	37	0	0	1	50	55	31	27	4	15	35	.284	.275	.291	6.34	2.72
Blake Goldsberry	R-R	6-4	220	5-21-97	0	0	9.00	2	0	0	0	2	2	2	2	1	0	1	.250	.200	.333	4.50	0.00
Noah Gotsis	R-R	6-0	190	6-17-96	5	8	5.45	23	13	1	0	79	80	49	48	9	21	62	.262	.227	.289	7.03	2.38

Tyler Hill	R-R	6-0	195	3-4-96	0	0	18.00	1	0	0	0	1	3	2	2	1	0	0	.500	.000	.600	0.00	0.00
Gavin Hollowell	R-R	6-7	215	11-4-97	4	2	3.14	42	0	0	16	49	30	18	17	3	14	64	.179	.253	.112	11.84	2.59
Boby Johnson	R-R	6-1	185	4-8-97	0	1	12.00	5	0	0	0	6	10	9	8	1	3	6	.357	.375	.333	9.00	4.50
Stephen Jones	R-R	6-4	195	7-30-97	3	1	2.64	47	0	0	8	58	39	18	17	6	24	67	.188	.191	.184	10.40	3.72
Karl Kauffmann	R-R	6-2	200	8-15-97	5	4	4.06	15	15	0	0	78	71	36	35	9	34	84	.245	.268	.224	9.73	3.94
Nick Kennedy	R-L	6-1	200	6-20-96	1	0	0.96	8	0	0	4	9	4	1	1	1	1	9	.129	.200	.063	8.68	0.96
Mitchell Kilkenny	R-R	6-4	206	3-24-97	5	7	5.56	24	24	0	0	102	118	67	63	23	34	76	.288	.280	.295	6.71	3.00
Austin Kitchen	L-L	6-0	200	2-11-97	0	1	3.43	14	0	0	0	21	15	9	8	5	7	16	.192	.086	.279	6.86	3.00
Tony Locey	R-R	6-3	239	7-29-98	2	5	12.11	14	8	0	0	36	60	50	48	8	28	29	.377	.386	.373	7.32	7.07
Riley Pint	R-R	6-5	225	11-6-97	2	1	4.64	38	0	0	0	43	31	23	22	4	29	55	.209	.211	.208	11.60	6.12
PJ Poulin	R-L	6-1	195	7-25-96	5	1	2.21	34	0	0	6	41	28	13	10	4	12	55	.189	.263	.143	12.17	2.66
Joe Rock	L-L	6-6	200	7-29-00	0	0	10.13	2	2	0	0	8	9	9	9	2	5	11	.273	.188	.353	12.38	5.63
Mike Ruff	R-R	6-2	212	3-31-98	1	3	6.75	7	7	0	0	31	38	25	23	6	13	26	.309	.250	.347	7.63	3.82
Garrett Schilling	R-R	6-2	185	10-25-95	1	1	6.59	11	3	0	0	27	29	20	20	5	15	23	.276	.305	.239	7.57	4.94
Case Williams	R-R	6-3	210	2-16-02	0	1	6.00	1	1	0	0	6	6	4	4	1	1	12	.250	.462	.000	18.00	1.50

Fielding

Catcher	PCT	G	PO	A	E	DP	PB
Cope	.994	41	345	13	2	1	0
George	1.000	2	12	2	0	1	0
Goodman	1.000	2	23	1	0	0	1
MacIver	.992	92	856	45	7	6	4

First Base	PCT	G	PO	A	E	DP
Datres	1.000	7	51	4	0	3
Goodman	1.000	4	20	2	0	1
Lavigne	.987	41	284	12	4	24
Toglia	.993	86	647	28	5	70

Second Base	PCT	G	PO	A	E	DP
Blomgren	1.000	5	6	14	0	4
Collins	.989	78	97	183	3	46
George	.000	1	0	0	0	0
Montes	.923	7	7	5	1	2
Navarro	1.000	1	2	1	0	1
Schunk	.966	10	13	15	1	5
Stovall	.980	40	53	94	3	21

Third Base	PCT	G	PO	A	E	DP
Datres	.909	6	1	9	1	0
Montes	1.000	7	3	11	0	1
Navarro	.923	4	3	9	1	0
Schunk	.951	112	89	165	13	18
Stovall	.871	12	6	21	4	1

Shortstop	PCT	G	PO	A	E	DP
Carreras	.957	19	18	26	2	5
Montes	1.000	1	2	2	0	2
Navarro	1.000	4	4	6	0	1
Stovall	.985	52	81	113	3	27
Tovar	.976	64	94	151	6	42

Outfield	PCT	G	PO	A	E	DP
Collins	.981	30	50	1	1	0
Datres	.979	29	46	1	1	0
Decolati	.978	43	86	5	2	0
Doyle	.987	116	293	8	4	0
Hannah	1.000	28	45	3	0	0
Herron	1.000	43	70	0	0	0
Hill	1.000	19	28	0	0	0
Montano	1.000	74	129	1	0	0
Stovall	1.000	3	6	0	0	0
Toglia	1.000	6	7	0	0	0
Veen	.945	33	51	1	3	0

SPOKANE INDIANS — *HIGH CLASS A*

NORTHWEST LEAGUE

Batting	B-T	HT	WT	DOB	AVG	vLH	vRH	G	AB	R	H	2B	3B	HR	RBI	BB	HBP	SH	SF	SO	SB	CS	SLG	OBP
Warming Bernabel	R-R	6-0	180	6-6-02	.305	.355	.284	26	105	18	32	7	0	4	17	2	0	0	1	17	2	2	.486	.315
Cuba Bess	L-R	6-2	215	9-29-97	.100	.000	.125	3	10	2	1	0	0	1	2	0	0	0	0	6	0	0	.400	.100
Trevor Boone	R-R	6-2	210	9-9-97	.231	.341	.156	35	108	14	25	6	0	5	16	4	2	1	1	57	4	0	.426	.270
Julio Carreras	R-R	6-2	190	1-12-00	.289	.267	.296	110	402	59	116	37	2	11	59	31	9	7	1	106	17	5	.473	.352
Jose Cordova	R-R	6-0	180	1-11-00	.167	.000	.250	2	6	0	1	0	0	0	0	0	1	0	0	1	0	0	.167	.286
Eddy Diaz	R-R	6-0	175	2-14-00	.261	.267	.259	97	376	57	98	18	4	5	39	30	12	8	5	87	36	14	.370	.331
Mateo Gil	R-R	6-1	180	7-24-00	.247	.279	.237	48	174	23	43	6	2	6	26	15	0	0	1	48	0	2	.408	.305
Hunter Goodman	R-R	6-1	210	10-8-99	.315	.362	.300	49	197	39	62	16	1	12	34	11	1	0	2	61	1	0	.589	.351
Nic Kent	R-R	6-2	185	4-10-00	.206	.190	.211	53	170	16	35	7	0	1	13	11	2	2	3	48	9	4	.265	.258
Grant Lavigne	L-R	6-4	220	8-27-99	.315	.333	.310	68	241	41	76	16	3	5	38	36	2	1	2	68	2	3	.469	.406
AJ Lewis	R-R	5-10	195	5-31-98	.152	.250	.095	11	33	2	5	2	0	0	1	4	0	0	0	13	0	1	.212	.243
Robby Martin Jr.	L-R	6-3	190	8-17-99	.212	.205	.213	84	278	30	59	20	1	5	36	20	1	1	2	92	3	4	.345	.266
Daniel Montano	L-R	6-1	204	3-31-99	.321	.286	.333	32	109	21	35	11	4	1	22	20	0	2	2	25	1	0	.523	.420
Cristopher Navarro	R-R	6-0	170	6-14-99	.150	.032	.188	43	127	10	19	2	0	0	4	12	0	2	0	37	0	0	.165	.223
Ronaiker Palma	R-R	5-10	180	1-2-00	.300	.379	.272	65	227	28	68	9	1	4	31	12	2	3	3	27	4	3	.401	.336
Bladimir Restituyo	R-R	5-10	151	7-2-01	.280	.324	.265	105	396	55	111	16	5	8	44	11	3	8	5	87	22	10	.407	.301
Drew Romo	B-R	6-1	205	8-29-01	.254	.294	.242	101	374	52	95	19	5	5	58	35	5	0	6	81	18	3	.372	.321
Benjamin Sems	L-R	6-3	200	2-16-98	.163	.222	.149	31	92	17	15	1	1	3	8	7	5	0	0	38	2	1	.293	.260
Colin Simpson	L-R	5-9	228	7-23-96	.300	.375	.285	95	330	53	99	17	4	17	60	36	3	0	4	78	7	1	.530	.370
Yorvis Torrealba	R-R	6-0	195	7-14-97	.156	.143	.167	24	64	8	10	2	0	0	2	7	1	1	0	16	5	3	.188	.250
Zac Veen	L-R	6-4	190	12-12-01	.269	.315	.257	92	342	72	92	19	3	11	60	50	5	0	3	90	50	4	.439	.368
Braiden Ward	L-R	5-10	160	1-18-99	.211	.200	.213	61	185	43	39	5	3	0	7	21	17	2	0	58	31	5	.270	.345

Pitching	B-T	HT	WT	DOB	W	L	ERA	G	GS	CG	SV	IP	H	R	ER	HR	BB	SO	AVG	vLH	vRH	K/9	BB/9
Tyler Ahearn	R-R	6-2	202	8-25-98	1	2	3.86	9	0	0	4	9	8	4	4	1	4	11	.242	.200	.278	10.61	3.86
Anderson Amarista	R-R	6-1	185	9-15-98	2	1	2.16	3	3	0	0	17	10	6	4	2	7	13	.164	.045	.231	7.02	3.78
Jared Biddy	R-R	6-2	180	7-25-96	0	0	1.93	3	0	0	0	5	5	2	1	0	1	4	.313	.400	.273	7.71	1.93
Anderson Bido	R-R	6-3	205	5-7-99	1	4	4.50	38	0	0	4	46	49	25	23	6	12	49	.271	.354	.206	9.59	2.35
Fineas Del Bonta-Smith	R-R	6-0	190	2-2-97	0	0	2.57	5	0	0	1	7	6	2	2	0	2	10	.231	.100	.313	12.86	2.57
Will Ethridge	R-R	6-5	240	12-20-97	5	6	5.65	16	16	1	0	86	86	55	54	18	33	76	.265	.293	.234	7.95	3.45
Blake Goldsberry	R-R	6-4	220	5-21-97	1	0	2.03	23	0	0	3	31	22	8	7	3	9	38	.193	.205	.187	11.03	2.61
Mason Green	L-L	6-1	195	2-5-99	2	4	6.75	9	9	0	0	39	51	33	29	6	19	35	.317	.345	.302	8.15	4.42
Robinson Hernandez	R-R	6-0	186	6-11-99	3	4	5.92	33	0	0	1	52	57	35	34	8	22	51	.277	.237	.310	8.88	3.83
Boby Johnson	R-R	6-1	185	4-8-97	2	2	3.45	34	0	0	2	47	50	25	18	9	17	55	.269	.299	.242	10.53	3.26
Austin Kitchen	L-L	6-0	200	2-11-97	5	1	3.28	22	4	0	2	60	57	28	22	10	16	55	.247	.233	.255	8.20	2.39
Shelby Lackey	R-R	6-3	190	7-8-97	0	3	4.93	41	0	0	4	46	39	28	25	3	30	49	.229	.221	.237	9.66	5.91
Tony Locey	R-R	6-3	239	7-29-98	4	1	3.09	12	12	0	0	67	41	32	23	8	39	64	.174	.175	.174	8.60	5.24
Adam McKillican	R-R	6-5	225	1-9-98	3	0	1.64	32	0	0	0	44	32	12	8	2	18	48	.200	.203	.198	9.82	3.68

Chris McMahon	R-R	6-2	217	2-4-99	1	0	7.00	4	4	0	0	18	30	14	14	4	2	16	.385	.541	.244	8.00	1.00
Juan Mejia	R-R	6-3	200	7-4-00	1	1	6.75	13	0	0	0	16	16	15	12	2	8	17	.291	.167	.387	9.56	4.50
Anderson Pilar	R-R	6-2	210	3-2-98	5	3	4.16	30	3	0	1	63	60	32	29	6	21	59	.250	.252	.248	8.47	3.02
Tanner Propst	L-L	6-0	190	6-7-98	0	2	9.00	21	0	0	0	23	27	23	23	5	15	24	.303	.222	.358	9.39	5.87
Andrew Quezada	L-R	6-1	185	6-28-97	9	4	4.28	21	19	0	0	103	113	55	49	13	35	85	.284	.320	.253	7.43	3.06
Joe Rock	L-L	6-6	200	7-29-00	7	8	4.43	20	20	1	0	108	87	63	53	10	45	109	.219	.213	.222	9.11	3.76
Raymells Rosa	R-R	6-2	180	12-6-98	0	0	2.70	10	0	0	0	10	8	4	3	0	7	11	.211	.250	.182	9.90	6.30
Mike Ruff	R-R	6-2	212	3-31-98	6	6	4.25	16	16	0	0	83	72	40	39	12	28	81	.233	.232	.234	8.82	3.05
Evan Shawver	R-L	6-0	175	9-11-99	1	7	5.01	12	12	0	0	50	48	31	28	8	21	55	.245	.231	.252	9.83	3.75
Luke Taggart	R-R	6-3	228	10-10-97	2	1	2.53	22	0	0	5	32	27	10	9	1	8	44	.227	.293	.164	12.38	2.25
Will Tribucher	L-L	6-3	210	9-23-96	0	0	4.32	7	0	0	0	8	8	4	4	0	3	10	.235	.214	.250	10.80	3.24
Sam Weatherly	L-L	6-4	205	5-28-99	0	0	4.50	1	1	0	0	4	6	2	2	1	1	5	.333	.500	.286	11.25	2.25
Ryley Widell	L-L	6-3	236	6-1-97	1	4	10.42	5	5	0	0	19	31	23	22	6	10	29	.365	.250	.410	13.74	4.74
Case Williams	R-R	6-3	210	2-16-02	2	2	5.57	6	6	0	0	32	39	22	20	6	11	33	.287	.224	.322	9.19	3.06

Fielding

Catcher	PCT	G	PO	A	E	DP	PB
Cordova	1.000	2	15	1	0	0	1
Goodman	1.000	17	153	9	0	1	2
Lewis	1.000	2	14	2	0	0	1
Palma	.990	58	467	36	5	3	7
Romo	.985	57	510	25	8	2	8

First Base	PCT	G	PO	A	E	DP
Boone	.917	3	10	1	1	2
Gil	1.000	3	8	1	0	0
Goodman	.985	26	175	16	3	10
Lavigne	.993	61	428	26	3	46
Simpson	.991	42	297	33	3	30

Second Base	PCT	G	PO	A	E	DP
Diaz	.974	96	146	222	10	51
Gil	1.000	8	7	15	0	2
Kent	.979	29	39	54	2	12
Sems	1.000	3	2	1	0	0

Third Base	PCT	G	PO	A	E	DP
Bernabel	.941	25	23	41	4	2
Carreras	.875	3	1	6	1	2
Gil	.909	19	17	33	5	0
Kent	.951	17	12	27	2	3
Lewis	1.000	4	1	6	0	0
Navarro	.890	40	28	61	11	3
Sems	.849	29	17	45	11	6

Shortstop	PCT	G	PO	A	E	DP
Carreras	.958	106	150	256	18	47
Gil	1.000	16	27	38	0	11
Kent	.941	7	4	12	1	3
Navarro	1.000	3	5	3	0	1

Outfield	PCT	G	PO	A	E	DP
Bess	1.000	3	6	0	0	0
Boone	.977	28	40	2	1	0
Gil	1.000	6	11	0	0	0
Lewis	--	1	0	0	0	0
Martin Jr.	.992	72	122	6	1	1
Montano	.981	30	47	6	1	2
Restituyo	.984	104	235	4	4	1
Simpson	.963	18	25	1	1	0
Torrealba	1.000	25	32	1	0	0
Veen	.987	79	140	8	2	2
Ward	1.000	51	94	3	0	0

FRESNO GRIZZLIES — *LOW CLASS A*

CALIFORNIA LEAGUE

Batting	B-T	HT	WT	DOB	AVG	vLH	vRH	G	AB	R	H	2B	3B	HR	RBI	BB	HBP	SH	SF	SO	SB	CS	SLG	OBP
Adael Amador	B-R	6-0	160	4-11-03	.292	.343	.277	115	449	100	131	24	0	15	57	87	11	3	5	67	26	12	.445	.415
EJ Andrews Jr.	R-R	6-1	210	9-28-00	.231	.264	.217	80	247	41	57	15	2	4	33	28	2	1	3	78	9	1	.356	.311
Jordan Beck	R-R	6-3	225	4-19-01	.282	.286	.280	11	39	11	11	2	0	2	9	13	0	0	0	9	0	0	.487	.462
Warming Bernabel	R-R	6-0	180	6-6-02	.317	.302	.320	65	262	52	83	19	0	10	54	29	5	0	4	39	21	6	.504	.390
Cuba Bess	L-R	6-2	215	9-29-97	.156	.190	.145	27	90	11	14	4	1	0	11	15	3	0	3	32	2	1	.222	.288
Trevor Boone	R-R	6-2	210	9-9-97	.234	.240	.232	38	107	24	25	6	1	8	26	14	2	0	0	47	2	0	.533	.333
Juan Brito	B-R	5-11	162	9-24-01	.286	.283	.287	107	402	91	115	29	6	11	72	78	8	3	6	71	17	9	.470	.407
Yanquiel Fernandez	L-L	6-2	198	1-1-03	.284	.289	.283	112	475	76	135	33	5	21	109	39	4	0	5	114	5	1	.507	.340
Braxton Fulford	R-R	5-11	190	12-9-98	.268	.220	.284	104	366	82	98	17	2	15	53	51	18	1	4	92	13	2	.448	.380
Hunter Goodman	R-R	6-1	210	10-8-99	.291	.339	.279	73	282	53	82	17	1	22	68	26	10	0	3	78	4	2	.592	.368
Juan Guerrero	R-R	6-1	160	9-10-01	.274	.308	.264	113	453	89	124	24	4	14	89	39	6	1	7	85	18	8	.437	.335
Zach Kokoska	L-L	6-1	200	10-20-98	.249	.242	.251	92	309	61	77	14	4	13	40	34	10	3	2	73	17	2	.447	.341
AJ Lewis	R-R	5-10	195	5-31-98	.278	.324	.256	39	115	25	32	8	0	5	33	31	5	0	2	32	0	2	.478	.444
Benny Montgomery	R-R	6-4	200	9-9-02	.313	.382	.292	56	233	48	73	20	3	6	42	21	10	0	0	71	9	1	.502	.394
Bryant Quijada	R-R	5-10	167	7-2-99	.243	.194	.259	50	148	21	36	10	0	2	18	22	5	3	4	30	0	0	.351	.352
Aiverson Rodriguez	R-R	6-0	170	4-1-02	.207	.182	.216	44	135	23	28	8	1	3	12	20	1	5	2	31	3	1	.348	.310
Benjamin Sems	L-R	6-3	200	2-16-98	.245	.231	.248	60	192	38	47	10	2	5	32	30	11	1	2	64	3	1	.396	.374
Sterlin Thompson	L-R	6-4	200	6-26-01	.348	.176	.448	11	46	9	16	4	0	1	4	3	0	0	1	12	2	0	.500	.380
Yorvis Torrealba	R-R	6-0	195	7-14-97	.343	.500	.296	29	105	23	36	10	1	1	18	13	0	0	1	14	6	4	.486	.412
Braiden Ward	L-R	5-10	160	1-18-99	.367	.192	.415	39	120	33	44	6	1	4	19	13	16	0	1	25	26	0	.533	.487

Pitching	B-T	HT	WT	DOB	W	L	ERA	G	GS	CG	SV	IP	H	R	ER	HR	BB	SO	AVG	vLH	vRH	K/9	BB/9
Tyler Ahearn	R-R	6-2	202	8-25-98	4	2	3.63	28	0	0	5	35	28	17	14	2	17	36	.212	.308	.172	9.35	4.41
Luis Amoroso	R-R	6-1	192	12-12-99	3	5	3.84	45	0	0	2	77	68	38	33	5	26	68	.231	.226	.234	7.91	3.03
Zak Baayoun	L-L	6-1	180	5-1-98	0	0	12.00	2	0	0	0	3	5	4	4	1	2	3	.385	.333	.400	9.00	6.00
Gabriel Barbosa	R-R	6-0	183	1-22-02	1	0	5.40	1	0	0	0	5	7	3	3	0	0	3	.318	.500	.214	5.40	0.00
McCade Brown	R-R	6-6	225	8-15-00	4	4	5.22	18	18	0	0	90	90	56	52	10	23	118	.256	.270	.248	11.84	2.31
Jarrod Cande	R-R	6-2	215	8-16-99	4	6	4.93	19	15	0	0	80	86	57	44	9	22	92	.265	.250	.276	10.31	2.46
Brayan Castillo	R-R	6-0	145	9-11-00	4	4	5.62	22	22	0	0	99	103	72	62	12	51	89	.265	.319	.233	8.06	4.62
Angel Chivilli	R-R	6-2	162	7-28-02	2	1	2.88	23	0	0	10	25	26	9	8	1	6	28	.257	.195	.300	10.08	2.16
Joel Condreay	L-R	6-3	210	7-5-96	3	0	1.25	20	0	0	7	22	17	6	3	2	7	24	.230	.185	.255	9.97	2.91
Blake Goldsberry	R-R	6-4	220	5-21-97	0	0	2.45	3	0	0	0	4	3	1	1	1	0	5	.214	.000	.333	12.27	0.00
Noah Gotsis	R-R	6-0	190	6-17-96	2	1	1.64	5	0	0	0	11	11	6	2	0	4	14	.256	.000	.333	11.45	3.27
Mason Green	L-L	6-1	195	2-5-99	5	3	3.07	13	13	0	0	73	64	29	25	2	32	71	.239	.294	.226	8.71	3.93
Jaden Hill	R-R	6-4	234	12-22-99	0	0	2.45	3	3	0	0	7	7	2	2	0	2	14	.259	.364	.188	17.18	2.45
Gabriel Hughes	R-R	6-4	220	8-22-01	0	0	0.00	1	1	0	0	3	1	0	0	0	1	1	.100	.250	.000	3.00	3.00
Victor Juarez	R-R	6-0	173	6-19-03	6	5	4.98	21	21	0	0	103	102	62	57	15	33	100	.263	.280	.253	8.74	2.88
Cullen Kafka	R-R	6-4	210	4-16-99	6	4	5.11	19	13	0	0	81	106	51	46	3	32	80	.315	.336	.302	8.89	3.56

Bryce McGowan	R-R	6-1	205	3-20-00	2	0	7.44	30	0	0	0	33	38	31	27	3	33	39	.290	.381	.247	10.74	9.09
Juan Mejia	R-R	6-3	200	7-4-00	2	2	3.71	31	0	0	6	34	29	15	14	2	19	43	.236	.214	.247	11.38	5.03
Ever Moya	L-L	6-5	220	5-25-99	1	2	5.72	39	0	0	1	46	49	38	29	5	35	33	.277	.222	.295	6.50	6.90
Tanner Propst	L-L	6-0	190	6-7-98	1	0	5.59	11	0	0	0	10	7	6	6	0	12	6	.206	.167	.214	5.59	11.17
Felix Ramires	L-L	6-4	175	9-26-99	3	2	6.11	33	0	0	1	35	45	29	24	2	30	42	.315	.333	.306	10.70	7.64
Tyler Ras	B-R	6-4	205	11-9-99	5	2	4.91	39	0	0	0	51	54	36	28	8	26	49	.267	.235	.284	8.59	4.56
Francis Rivera	R-R	6-4	160	9-14-00	2	0	2.84	16	0	0	0	19	20	7	6	0	5	13	.270	.406	.167	6.16	2.37
Gabriel Rodriguez	L-L	6-1	193	4-9-99	2	0	9.42	16	0	0	0	14	14	18	15	1	25	20	.259	.235	.270	12.56	15.70
Raymollc Roca	R-R	6-2	180	12-6-98	0	0	54.00	1	0	0	0	0	1	2	2	1	2	0	.500	--	.500	0.00	54.00
Sergio Sanchez	R-R	6-0	180	1-13-01	8	3	4.42	46	0	0	2	71	59	41	35	3	47	77	.223	.269	.193	9.71	5.93
Evan Shawver	R-L	6-0	175	9-11-99	2	0	1.13	3	3	0	0	16	12	2	2	0	5	15	.207	.375	.143	8.44	2.81
Jordy Vargas	R-R	6-3	153	11-6-03	2	0	3.65	6	6	0	0	25	20	15	10	5	13	24	.225	.206	.236	8.76	4.74
Ryley Widell	L-L	6-3	236	6-1-97	0	1	6.75	1	1	0	0	4	6	3	3	1	0	5	.333	.375	.300	11.25	0.00
Case Williams	R-R	6-3	210	2-16-02	9	2	4.22	16	16	0	0	90	91	47	42	13	34	90	.262	.303	.240	9.03	3.41

Fielding

Catcher	PCT	G	PO	A	E	DP	PB
Fulford	.997	88	778	77	3	9	12
Goodman	.987	24	212	15	3	0	6
Lewis	.778	3	7	0	2	0	0
Quijada	.986	26	202	17	3	2	5

First Base	PCT	G	PO	A	E	DP
Bess	.992	15	113	15	1	11
Boone	.986	24	129	10	2	17
Goodman	.977	48	323	24	8	33
Lewis	1.000	29	205	17	0	21
Quijada	1.000	22	145	19	0	7
Sems	.975	6	38	1	1	2

Second Base	PCT	G	PO	A	E	DP
Amador	.941	7	15	17	2	4
Brito	.972	102	190	257	13	67
Lewis	.889	2	1	7	1	1
Rodriguez	.935	15	27	31	4	10
Sems	1.000	11	16	16	0	2

Third Base	PCT	G	PO	A	E	DP
Bernabel	.912	64	48	117	16	17
Bess	.917	13	9	24	3	1
Lewis	.571	2	2	2	3	0
Rodriguez	.800	19	9	35	11	3
Sems	.937	28	22	37	4	2
Thompson	.875	11	4	17	3	1

Shortstop	PCT	G	PO	A	E	DP
Amador	.945	108	120	255	22	47
Brito	1.000	4	5	13	0	3
Rodriguez	.813	10	13	13	6	3
Sems	.929	16	20	45	5	10

Outfield	PCT	G	PO	A	E	DP
Andrews Jr.	.954	63	121	3	6	0
Beck	1.000	9	24	0	0	0
Boone	1.000	11	17	0	0	0
Fernandez	.947	90	173	7	10	2
Guerrero	.965	89	157	7	6	2
Kokoska	.991	61	112	3	1	2
Lewis	--	1	0	0	0	0
Montgomery	.989	44	90	3	1	0
Torrealba	1.000	12	15	1	0	0
Ward	.980	35	48	2	1	1

ACL ROCKIES — ROOKIE

ARIZONA COMPLEX LEAGUE

Batting	B-T	HT	WT	DOB	AVG	vLH	vRH	G	AB	R	H	2B	3B	HR	RBI	BB	HBP	SH	SF	SO	SB	CS	SLG	OBP
Jordan Beck	R-R	6-3	225	4-19-01	.306	.273	.316	15	49	9	15	5	0	1	10	8	0	0	0	11	0	0	.469	.404
Austin Bernard	B-R	5-10	195	3-14-96	.194	.167	.200	11	31	1	6	0	0	1	5	5	0	0	0	10	0	0	.290	.306
Cuba Bess	L-R	6-2	215	9-29-97	.333	.143	.371	27	84	17	28	2	2	6	18	17	3	0	1	25	3	0	.619	.457
Jesus Bugarin	R-R	5-10	180	12-2-01	.337	.222	.357	51	184	34	62	9	5	4	24	15	2	0	1	50	7	6	.505	.391
Jose Cordova	R-R	6-0	180	1-11-00	.163	.000	.171	15	43	2	7	0	0	0	4	2	2	0	0	10	0	0	.163	.234
Fadriel Cruz	L-R	5-10	170	11-12-00	.176	.500	.133	20	51	7	9	4	1	0	3	12	1	0	0	20	4	1	.294	.344
Brad Cumbest	R-R	6-6	235	7-13-00	.059	.000	.063	6	17	3	1	0	0	0	0	3	0	0	0	8	0	0	.059	.200
Eddy Diaz	R-R	6-0	175	2-14-00	.267	.000	.286	4	15	2	4	0	0	1	3	0	1	0	0	2	1	0	.467	.313
Francisco Garcia	R-R	6-0	190	11-10-02	.188	.176	.189	39	128	17	24	4	1	1	9	13	3	0	0	43	0	3	.258	.278
Gabriel Gil	R-R	5-10	173	3-9-01	.160	.000	.200	11	25	1	4	1	0	1	3	0	1	0	0	12	0	0	.320	.192
Mateo Gil	R-R	6-1	180	7-24-00	.241	.143	.273	10	29	8	7	3	1	1	1	5	1	0	0	11	1	0	.517	.371
Kody Huff	R-R	5-10	198	12-11-00	.160	.000	.167	9	25	4	4	2	0	0	5	3	2	0	0	9	1	0	.240	.300
Parker Kelly	R-R	6-3	220	3-18-99	.250	.500	.200	9	24	4	6	3	1	0	2	3	1	0	0	10	0	0	.458	.357
Tim Lopes	R-R	5-11	180	6-24-94	.444	--	.444	3	9	5	4	1	0	2	5	1	0	0	0	0	1	0	1.222	.500
Luis Mendez	L-R	5-11	157	10-30-02	.254	.229	.259	52	197	26	50	9	3	6	28	18	4	0	2	57	8	4	.421	.326
Skyler Messinger	R-R	6-3	220	11-1-98	.375	.800	.263	10	24	4	9	0	0	0	3	1	1	1	0	3	0	1	.375	.423
Benny Montgomery	R-R	6-4	200	9-9-02	.273	.600	.176	6	22	3	6	1	1	0	2	0	0	0	0	6	0	0	.409	.273
Jesus Ordonez	R-R	5-8	180	12-26-99	.259	.125	.280	38	116	16	30	11	0	4	21	14	4	0	2	15	1	4	.457	.353
Francisco Ortiz	R-R	6-0	160	9-15-99	.231	.429	.207	24	65	8	15	2	0	1	5	11	1	0	1	28	0	1	.308	.346
Luis Paredes	L-L	5-10	170	3-21-04	.180	.333	.165	31	100	11	18	5	0	0	10	10	1	0	2	50	2	4	.230	.257
Jean Perez	R-R	5-10	178	7-20-02	.230	.222	.232	35	87	16	20	4	0	1	6	5	4	1	1	27	4	0	.310	.299
Gerard Ramos	R-R	6-3	175	1-19-01	.000	.000	.000	1	4	0	0	0	0	0	0	0	0	0	0	2	0	0	.000	.000
Ryan Ritter	R-R	6-2	200	11-10-00	.320	.000	.364	8	25	9	8	4	1	1	4	2	2	0	0	3	2	0	.680	.414
Aiverson Rodriguez	R-R	6-0	170	4-1-02	.338	.385	.328	22	80	10	27	3	1	1	7	5	1	0	0	20	2	1	.438	.384
Taylor Snyder	R-R	6-2	165	9-28-94	.300	.333	.296	9	30	6	9	4	0	3	5	1	0	0	0	11	0	0	.733	.323
Cole Stilwell	R-R	6-1	215	2-18-00	.000	.000	--	2	1	0	0	0	0	0	0	2	1	0	0	0	0	0	.000	.750
Sterlin Thompson	L-R	6-4	200	6-26-01	.273	.100	.311	15	55	9	15	3	0	1	6	2	3	0	1	16	1	0	.382	.328
Ryan Vilade	R-R	6-2	226	2-18-99	.300	.000	.429	3	10	3	3	1	0	1	3	1	0	0	0	3	1	1	.700	.364
Anthony Walters	R-R	6-1	185	12-17-97	.176	.000	.182	17	34	8	6	0	0	2	3	8	2	0	0	18	0	0	.353	.364
Cole Zabowski	L-L	6-5	240	11-5-97	.255	.000	.308	18	47	7	12	4	0	1	7	11	2	0	2	11	0	0	.404	.403

Pitching	B-T	HT	WT	DOB	W	L	ERA	G	GS	CG	SV	IP	H	R	ER	HR	BB	SO	AVG	vLH	vRH	K/9	BB/9
Blake Adams	R-R	6-2	215	9-11-00	1	0	1.69	5	0	0	1	5	4	1	1	0	3	4	.222	.200	.231	6.75	5.06
Zach Agnos	R-R	6-0	210	8-15-00	0	0	9.00	1	0	0	0	1	2	1	1	1	0	1	.500	.500	.500	9.00	0.00
Anderson Amarista	R-R	6-1	185	9-15-98	1	0	3.72	7	2	0	0	19	15	10	8	1	1	28	.197	.250	.167	13.03	0.47
Gabriel Barbosa	R-R	6-0	183	1-22-02	5	0	3.46	11	6	0	1	39	42	17	15	3	4	38	.276	.298	.263	8.77	0.92
Austin Becker	R-R	6-5	215	9-2-99	0	0	0.00	2	0	0	0	2	0	0	0	0	0	3	.000	.000	.000	13.50	0.00
Blair Calvo	R-R	6-3	195	2-27-96	1	0	0.00	2	0	0	0	2	3	0	0	0	0	2	.333	.250	.400	9.00	0.00

Angel Chivilli	R-R	6-2	162	7-28-02	1	1	1.15	9	0	0	0	16	10	3	2	0	4	23	.182	.182	.182	13.21	2.30
Caleb Franzen	L-L	6-3	200	6-10-01	0	0	0.00	1	0	0	0	1	0	0	0	0	0	0	.000	--	.000	0.00	0.00
Blake Goldsberry	R-R	6-4	220	5-21-97	0	0	2.25	4	0	0	0	4	5	1	1	0	0	5	.333	.286	.375	11.25	0.00
Nate Hadley	R-R	5-11	182	12-7-95	2	0	1.29	18	0	0	2	21	20	5	3	0	6	24	.238	.143	.286	10.29	2.57
Brady Hill	L-R	6-0	180	11-10-00	0	0	18.00	1	0	0	0	1	2	2	2	1	2	3	.400	.333	.500	27.00	18.00
Jaden Hill	R-R	6-4	234	12-22-99	0	0	3.48	7	7	0	0	10	11	4	4	0	4	11	.282	.368	.200	9.58	3.48
Tyler Hoffman	R-R	6-0	182	9-1-99	0	0	2.08	3	0	0	0	4	1	1	1	0	0	7	.071	.000	.143	14.54	0.00
Braxton Hyde	R-R	6-3	195	6-6-01	0	0	0.00	1	0	0	0	1	0	0	0	0	0	1	.000	.000	.000	9.00	0.00
Brett Matthews	R-R	6-5	219	4-23-98	1	1	3.00	16	1	0	2	24	19	9	8	1	4	29	.221	.115	.267	10.88	1.50
Chris McMahon	R-R	6-2	217	2-4-99	0	0	2.53	4	2	0	0	11	17	4	3	1	3	9	.386	.412	.370	7.59	2.53
Bryan Mena	R-R	6-2	185	6-14-04	2	2	4.54	9	5	0	0	36	39	20	18	1	11	32	.265	.298	.244	8.07	2.78
Helcris Olivarez	L-L	6-2	192	8-8-00	0	0	0.00	1	1	0	0	2	0	0	0	0	0	1	.000	.000	.000	4.50	0.00
Alberto Pacheco	L-L	6-1	176	11-29-02	5	4	3.13	11	8	0	0	46	39	22	16	1	15	57	.222	.283	.190	11.15	2.93
Davis Palermo	R-R	6-2	180	12-16-99	0	0	6.75	2	0	0	0	1	1	1	1	1	2	2	.200	.000	.250	13.50	13.50
Carson Palmquist	L-L	6-3	185	10-17-00	0	0	0.00	1	0	0	0	1	0	0	0	0	2	1	.000	--	.000	9.00	18.00
Bryan Perez	R-R	6-2	167	9-8-03	1	3	9.00	4	3	0	0	12	21	15	12	1	2	9	.375	.455	.324	6.75	1.50
Michael Petersen	R-R	6-7	195	5-16-94	0	0	0.00	1	1	0	0	1	0	0	0	0	0	2	.000	.000	.000	18.00	0.00
Michael Prosecky	L-L	6-3	200	2-28-01	0	0	0.00	1	0	0	0	1	0	0	0	0	0	1	.000	.000	.000	9.00	0.00
Javier Ramos	R-R	6-6	210	10-15-99	1	0	0.00	1	0	0	0	1	0	0	0	0	1	1	.000	--	.000	9.00	9.00
Francis Rivera	R-R	6-4	160	9-14-00	2	2	4.15	15	0	0	7	17	24	10	8	1	6	23	.320	.226	.386	11.94	3.12
Gabriel Rodriguez	L-L	6-1	193	4-9-99	1	0	3.60	7	0	0	1	5	4	2	2	0	6	6	.211	.000	.267	10.80	10.80
Raymells Rosa	R-R	6-2	180	12-6-98	1	0	2.38	12	0	0	0	11	7	3	3	0	4	15	.167	.250	.115	11.91	3.18
Garrett Schilling	R-R	6-2	185	10-25-95	0	0	2.57	3	2	0	0	7	5	2	2	1	2	12	.208	.167	.250	15.43	2.57
Carson Skipper	L-L	6-2	211	8-12-99	0	0	0.00	2	0	0	0	2	1	0	0	0	0	2	.143	1.000	.000	9.00	0.00
Tyler Statler	R-R	6-6	230	7-1-01	1	1	6.20	11	1	0	0	20	25	19	14	0	10	21	.309	.333	.294	9.30	4.43
Cole Stringer	L-L	6-0	175	8-10-96	1	1	3.60	7	2	0	0	10	10	6	4	0	6	14	.256	.375	.226	12.60	5.40
Luke Summers	R-R	6-0	215	7-11-98	1	1	3.31	16	0	0	1	16	11	7	6	1	1	22	.186	.167	.200	12.12	0.55
Carlos Torres	R-R	6-4	240	5-3-01	0	0	2.08	4	0	0	1	4	2	1	1	0	2	2	.133	.143	.125	4.15	4.15
Will Tribucher	L-L	6-3	210	9-23-96	2	1	3.12	7	1	0	0	9	6	3	3	1	1	15	.188	.444	.087	15.58	1.04
Jordy Vargas	R-R	6-3	153	11-6-03	2	1	2.36	7	5	0	0	27	13	8	7	0	4	40	.141	.111	.161	13.50	1.35
Sam Weatherly	L-L	6-4	205	5-28-99	0	1	3.52	4	2	0	0	8	8	3	3	1	1	18	.250	.167	.269	21.13	1.17
Ryley Widell	L-L	6-3	236	6-1-97	2	0	2.51	8	4	0	0	29	26	8	8	2	3	37	.243	.316	.227	11.62	0.94

Fielding

C: Bernard 8, Cordova 6, Gil 9, Huff 9, Ordonez 26, Ortiz 3, Stilwell 2. **1B:** Bess 12, Cordova 3, Kelly 9, Ortiz 18, Ramos 1, Zabowski 14. **2B:** Diaz 3, Gil 3, Lopes 1, Mendez 5, Perez 21, Rodriguez 18, Snyder 6, Walters 8. **3B:** Garcia 34, Gil 5, Lopes 1, Messinger 10, Perez 6, Rodriguez 1, Snyder 1, Walters 3. **SS:** Diaz 1, Mendez 46, Perez 1, Ritter 6, Rodriguez 1. **OF:** Beck 14, Bess 15, Bugarin 51, Cordova 1, Cruz 20, Cumbest 2, Lopes 1, Montgomery 5, Paredes 31, Perez 10, Snyder 1, Thompson 15, Vilade 2, Walters 2.

DSL COLORADO — *ROOKIE*

DOMINICAN SUMMER LEAGUE

Batting	B-T	HT	WT	DOB	AVG	vLH	vRH	G	AB	R	H	2B	3B	HR	RBI	BB	HBP	SH	SF	SO	SB	CS	SLG	OBP
Elisandro Alcantara	R-R	6-0	175	10-29-02	.000	--	.000	1	3	1	0	0	0	0	0	1	1	0	0	1	1	0	.000	.400
2-team total (56 DSL Rockies)					.276	.306	.269	57	192	41	53	10	4	7	37	29	9	1	1	73	9	3	.479	.394
Cruzmel Arias	R-R	5-11	176	2-20-04	.286	.350	.274	44	133	22	38	5	0	1	13	14	7	1	0	27	6	8	.346	.383
Oscar Aude	R-R	6-0	176	5-14-03	.194	.214	.190	55	186	24	36	4	1	6	26	22	3	1	3	42	5	6	.323	.285
Erick Bautista	R-R	6-2	197	2-18-05	.257	.176	.267	51	148	34	38	7	4	9	36	26	6	2	0	65	7	3	.541	.389
2-team total (4 DSL Rockies)					.244	.158	.255	55	160	37	39	7	4	10	39	28	7	2	0	70	7	4	.525	.379
Bryant Betancourt	L-R	5-11	170	10-12-03	.355	.278	.367	44	138	34	49	11	0	11	36	27	4	2	4	21	0	3	.674	.462
Jairold Carlito	L-R	6-0	150	4-21-02	.068	.000	.077	26	44	10	3	0	1	1	5	17	2	0	1	22	3	1	.182	.344
Gabriel Gil	R-R	5-10	173	3-9-01	.318	.500	.278	8	22	2	7	3	0	0	4	5	0	0	0	6	2	0	.455	.444
Jorluis Guerra	R-R	5-11	165	1-11-04	.286	.300	.283	42	119	18	34	6	0	1	12	14	4	4	0	27	3	1	.361	.380
Roynier Hernandez	L-R	5-11	180	12-6-04	.245	.286	.240	56	200	38	49	9	0	0	14	37	0	1	2	35	8	4	.290	.360
2-team total (1 DSL Rockies)					.249	.286	.244	57	201	39	50	9	0	0	14	38	0	1	2	35	8	4	.294	.365
Dyan Jorge	R-R	6-3	170	3-18-03	.319	.333	.317	49	191	35	61	11	1	4	20	23	4	0	0	31	13	10	.450	.404
2-team total (4 DSL Rockies)					.320	.333	.318	53	206	37	66	13	1	4	25	24	4	0	0	35	13	10	.451	.402
Robert Mendoza	B-R	6-0	175	10-9-01	.231	.200	.234	33	104	19	24	4	0	3	13	13	6	0	1	31	2	1	.356	.347
Pedro Mota	R-R	6-1	160	9-24-01	.125	.000	.167	3	8	0	1	0	0	0	0	0	3	0	0	3	0	1	.125	.364
2-team total (28 DSL Rockies)					.195	.118	.214	31	87	19	17	4	0	0	8	24	6	2	1	28	2	1	.241	.398
Luis Paredes	L-L	5-10	170	3-21-04	.139	.125	.143	11	36	3	5	0	0	2	6	5	0	0	0	15	0	1	.306	.244
Oswal Rada	R-R	6-1	200	2-17-03	.241	.267	.236	30	87	5	21	2	0	1	8	7	2	2	0	22	0	2	.299	.313
Felix Tena	R-R	6-0	196	9-27-03	.286	.320	.280	54	182	28	52	9	2	7	24	10	9	0	3	45	11	9	.473	.348
2-team total (4 DSL Rockies)					.288	.333	.280	58	191	35	55	10	2	7	25	11	14	0	3	46	11	10	.471	.365
Gabriel Terrero	L-R	6-3	169	12-21-03	.190	.000	.211	13	42	4	8	2	0	2	8	3	1	0	0	19	1	0	.381	.261
2-team total (30 DSL Rockies)					.177	.000	.202	43	130	25	23	4	0	4	20	23	8	1	0	47	10	1	.300	.335
Ronny Ugarte	L-R	6-3	205	12-10-04	.273	.278	.273	49	161	29	44	18	0	7	31	21	6	0	2	38	3	1	.516	.374

Pitching	B-T	HT	WT	DOB	W	L	ERA	G	GS	CG	SV	IP	H	R	ER	HR	BB	SO	AVG	vLH	vRH	K/9	BB/9
Gerson Balbino	R-R	6-0	167	4-15-05	0	3	3.86	12	11	0	0	40	43	26	17	4	13	33	.274	.362	.222	7.49	2.95
Jose Barcenas	R-R	6-0	180	9-7-02	0	1	13.50	1	0	0	0	2	3	4	3	2	1	2	.375	.250	.500	9.00	4.50
2-team total (10 DSL Rockies)					3	2	13.22	11	0	0	0	16	28	29	24	4	8	17	.364	.370	.360	9.37	4.41
Jerald Cabrera	R-R	6-1	185	8-26-01	0	0	0.00	1	0	0	0	2	2	0	0	0	1	2	.286	.500	.000	10.80	5.40
2-team total (14 DSL Rockies)					1	0	6.89	15	0	0	0	16	24	13	12	1	11	10	.358	.407	.325	5.74	6.32
Luichi Casilla	L-L	6-2	180	12-26-04	0	0	1.19	7	7	0	0	23	20	6	3	0	11	28	.235	.417	.205	11.12	4.37
Wuardo Fernandez	R-R	6-1	168	12-14-00	1	2	3.86	23	0	0	14	23	23	15	10	1	10	23	.264	.265	.264	8.87	3.86

2-team total (2 DSL Rockies)					2	2	3.55	25	0	0	15	25	23	16	10	1	13	27	.242	.243	.241	9.59	4.62
Claudio Galva	R-R	6-3	176	10-13-03	0	0	2.45	10	10	0	0	37	26	12	10	2	15	40	.197	.185	.205	9.82	3.68
2-team total (2 DSL Rockies)					0	0	2.43	12	11	0	0	41	29	13	11	2	17	43	.200	.210	.193	9.52	3.76
Aneudis George	R-R	6-1	172	9-27-03	3	1	3.42	20	0	0	0	26	27	14	10	2	6	27	.260	.244	.270	9.23	2.05
Keider Herrera	R-R	5-11	168	1-7-05	4	4	7.26	14	0	0	0	31	43	27	25	3	11	29	.328	.345	.316	8.42	3.19
Angel Jimenez	R-R	6-2	190	7-4-03	5	1	3.32	11	6	0	0	41	29	17	15	3	7	47	.199	.235	.167	10.40	1.55
Johandry Milano	L-L	6-1	160	2-9-03	3	1	1.35	14	0	0	0	33	19	6	5	0	7	36	.164	.261	.140	9.72	1.89
2-team total (1 DSL Rockies)					3	1	1.27	15	0	0	0	35	20	6	5	0	8	37	.163	.261	.140	9.42	2.04
Alan Perdomo	R-R	6-4	150	8-24-01	4	2	4.43	17	0	0	2	22	24	13	11	3	5	18	.286	.172	.315	7.25	2.01
2-team total (1 DSL Rockies)					4	2	5.25	18	0	0	2	24	27	16	14	3	5	18	.293	.212	.339	6.75	1.88
Doilin Perez	R-R	6-4	200	5-10-05	0	1	4.12	9	7	0	0	20	19	12	9	3	10	19	.253	.344	.186	8.69	4.58
2-team total (1 DSL Rockies)					0	1	3.92	10	7	0	1	21	19	12	9	3	10	21	.244	.324	.182	9.15	4.35
Enmanuel Pio	R-R	5-11	145	4-11-00	3	0	4.39	19	0	0	0	27	26	13	13	5	7	24	.263	.279	.250	8.10	2.36
Enger Sanchez	R-R	6-5	170	5-23-03	3	2	2.50	11	7	0	0	36	31	18	10	2	9	29	.226	.237	.218	7.25	2.25
Kenebell Sevelen	R-R	6-3	190	8-17-04	0	0	9.00	7	0	0	0	9	15	13	9	1	5	11	.349	.381	.318	11.00	5.00
2-team total (3 DSL Rockies)					0	0	9.00	10	0	0	0	11	18	15	11	1	8	13	.353	.417	.296	10.64	6.55
Luis Tejeda	R-R	6-2	170	12-13-01	1	3	5.65	13	5	0	1	37	41	26	23	6	15	31	.295	.320	.260	8.35	3.60
Ervin Torres	L-L	6-0	185	11-3-04	4	0	2.79	12	5	0	0	39	37	13	12	1	4	28	.247	.303	.231	6.52	0.93
Cesar Vargas	R-R	6-4	176	12-1-04	3	0	8.05	12	1	0	0	19	25	20	17	1	10	13	.313	.371	.267	6.16	4.74
Bill Villanueva	L-R	6-2	147	1-20-05	0	5	12.56	15	1	0	0	14	22	23	20	5	15	10	.355	.400	.324	6.28	9.42

Fielding

C: Arias 4, Betancourt 18, Gil 7, Mendoza 15, Rada 25. **1B:** Arias 4, Betancourt 9, Mendoza 6, Rada 5, Terrero 4, Ugarte 40. **2B:** Arias 11, Guerra 5, Hernandez 45. **3B:** Arias 17, Guerra 36, Mota 3, Terrero 7. **SS:** Hernandez 11, Jorge 49. **OF:** Alcantara 1, Arias 14, Aude 51, Bautista 54, Carlito 20, Guerra 1, Paredes 7, Tena 53.

DSL ROCKIES — ROOKIE

DOMINICAN SUMMER LEAGUE

Batting	B-T	HT	WT	DOB	AVG	vLH	vRH	G	AB	R	H	2B	3B	HR	RBI	BB	HBP	SH	SF	SO	SB	CS	SLG	OBP
Elisandro Alcantara	R-R	6-0	175	10-29-02	.280	.306	.275	56	189	40	53	10	4	7	37	28	8	1	1	72	8	3	.487	.394
2-team total (1 DSL Colorado)					.276	.306	.269	57	192	41	53	10	4	7	37	29	9	1	1	73	9	3	.479	.394
Erick Bautista	R-R	6-2	197	2-18-05	.083	.000	.100	4	12	3	1	0	0	1	3	2	1	0	0	5	0	1	.333	.267
2-team total (51 DSL Colorado)					.244	.158	.255	55	160	37	39	7	4	10	39	28	7	2	0	70	7	4	.525	.379
Derek Bernard	L-R	6-0	190	8-9-05	.308	.222	.326	56	214	49	66	12	2	4	25	21	3	2	1	66	11	4	.439	.377
Juan Castillo	R-R	6-1	170	1-16-03	.307	.286	.310	35	101	11	31	5	0	0	12	9	6	4	1	21	3	3	.356	.393
Jose Colina	B-R	5-8	155	2-25-04	.556	.667	.500	4	9	1	5	0	0	0	2	1	2	0	1	1	0	0	.556	.615
Angel Feliz	L-R	6-1	157	3-2-04	.212	.182	.220	18	52	10	11	2	0	2	10	10	1	2	0	19	3	0	.365	.349
Esneider Gomez	R-R	5-11	185	9-18-02	.267	.226	.275	54	180	35	48	12	0	0	28	18	13	0	6	30	8	2	.333	.364
Roynier Hernandez	L-R	5-11	180	12-6-04	1.000	--	1.000	1	1	1	1	0	0	0	0	1	0	0	0	0	0	0	1.000	1.000
2-team total (56 DSL Colorado)					.249	.286	.244	57	201	39	50	9	0	0	14	38	0	1	2	35	8	4	.294	.365
Sandry Hernandez	R-R	5-11	155	2-28-03	.293	.194	.315	58	198	42	58	16	3	1	34	19	7	2	4	39	14	7	.419	.368
Kelvin HIdalgo	R-R	6-2	166	3-1-05	.269	.237	.276	59	223	48	60	12	3	5	33	26	6	0	2	50	15	7	.417	.358
Michael James	L-R	5-11	170	12-4-01	.288	.333	.282	40	118	28	34	7	1	3	27	29	4	1	3	33	10	5	.441	.435
Dyan Jorge	R-R	6-3	170	3-18-03	.333	--	.333	4	15	2	5	2	0	0	5	1	0	0	0	4	0	0	.467	.375
2-team total (49 DSL Colorado)					.320	.333	.318	53	206	37	66	13	1	4	25	24	4	0	0	35	13	10	.451	.402
Franklin Lopez	R-R	5-9	170	11-19-04	.291	.111	.312	30	86	21	25	6	0	0	21	19	5	2	2	23	2	0	.360	.438
Pedro Mota	R-R	6-1	160	9-24-01	.203	.133	.219	28	79	19	16	4	0	0	8	24	3	2	1	25	2	0	.253	.402
2-team total (3 DSL Colorado)					.195	.118	.214	31	87	19	17	4	0	0	8	24	6	2	1	28	2	1	.241	.398
Ronny Novas	L-R	5-10	165	11-20-00	.220	.200	.225	20	50	5	11	0	0	0	8	7	1	1	1	8	5	2	.220	.322
Moises Paiva	R-R	5-7	150	3-11-03	.250	.000	.333	3	8	0	2	1	0	0	1	0	0	1	0	1	0	0	.375	.250
Andy Perez	L-R	6-3	165	6-3-04	.302	.333	.296	58	222	33	67	11	2	2	32	11	3	4	9	35	11	8	.396	.331
Felix Tena	R-R	6-0	196	9-27-03	.333	.500	.286	4	9	7	3	1	0	0	1	1	5	0	0	1	0	1	.444	.600
2-team total (54 DSL Colorado)					.288	.333	.280	58	191	35	55	10	2	7	25	11	14	0	3	46	11	10	.471	.365
Gabriel Terrero	L-R	6-3	169	12-21-03	.170	.000	.197	30	88	21	15	2	0	2	12	20	7	1	0	28	9	1	.261	.365
2-team total (13 DSL Colorado)					.177	.000	.202	43	130	25	23	4	0	4	20	23	8	1	0	47	10	1	.300	.335

Pitching	B-T	HT	WT	DOB	W	L	ERA	G	GS	CG	SV	IP	H	R	ER	HR	BB	SO	AVG	vLH	vRH	K/9	BB/9
Jose Barcenas	R-R	6-0	180	9-7-02	3	1	13.19	10	0	0	0	14	25	25	21	2	7	15	.362	.391	.348	9.42	4.40
2-team total (1 DSL Colorado)					3	2	13.22	11	0	0	0	16	28	29	24	4	8	17	.364	.370	.360	9.37	4.41
Cristian Brioso	R-R	6-0	188	6-14-01	0	0	0.00	2	0	0	0	2	1	0	0	0	2	1	.143	.000	.250	4.50	9.00
Jerald Cabrera	R-R	6-1	185	8-26-01	1	0	7.71	14	0	0	0	14	22	13	12	1	10	8	.367	.391	.351	5.14	6.43
2-team total (1 DSL Colorado)					1	0	6.89	15	0	0	0	16	24	13	12	1	11	10	.358	.407	.325	5.74	6.32
Rony Cruz	R-R	6-1	196	3-3-04	2	2	3.06	11	10	0	0	35	39	16	12	1	10	33	.277	.295	.263	8.41	2.55
Jesus De La Rosa	L-L	6-2	170	5-28-02	1	0	6.00	5	0	0	1	6	4	5	4	1	8	9	.190	.000	.250	13.50	12.00
Janer Feliciano	R-R	6-3	220	8-8-01	2	0	7.02	18	0	0	0	17	16	15	13	2	17	25	.250	.259	.243	13.50	9.18
Wuardo Fernandez	R-R	6-1	168	12-14-00	1	0	0.00	2	0	0	1	2	0	1	0	0	3	4	.000	.000	.000	18.00	13.50
2-team total (23 DSL Colorado)					2	2	3.55	25	0	0	15	25	23	16	10	1	13	27	.242	.243	.241	9.59	4.62
Claudio Galva	R-R	6-3	176	10-13-03	0	0	2.25	2	1	0	0	4	3	1	1	0	2	3	.231	.375	.000	6.75	4.50
2-team total (10 DSL Colorado)					0	0	2.43	12	11	0	0	41	29	13	11	2	17	43	.200	.210	.193	9.52	3.76
Kevin Garcia	L-L	6-0	170	11-25-99	5	0	2.09	17	0	0	1	43	35	17	10	6	19	56	.217	.256	.205	11.72	3.98
Redinson Gomez	R-R	6-2	170	7-26-04	3	5	3.94	10	10	0	0	46	45	29	20	3	9	43	.254	.310	.227	8.47	1.77
Marcos Herrera	R-R	6-2	182	10-11-04	3	2	4.24	11	8	0	0	34	26	19	16	5	15	29	.210	.224	.200	7.68	3.97
Welinton Herrera	L-L	6-0	166	4-3-04	5	1	2.93	20	1	0	2	43	33	19	14	0	14	54	.213	.167	.227	11.30	2.93
Bladimir Lopez	R-R	6-2	205	7-31-03	0	0	8.10	11	0	0	0	10	11	15	9	1	12	6	.282	.294	.273	5.40	10.80
Ismael Luciano	R-R	6-0	170	3-4-03	2	3	4.31	11	10	1	0	48	45	35	23	3	25	49	.250	.292	.226	9.19	4.69

Johandry Milano	L-L	6-1	160	2-9-03	0	0	0.00	1	0	0	0	2	1	0	0	0	1	1	.143	--	.143	4.50	4.50
2-team total (14 DSL Colorado)					3	1	1.27	15	0	0	0	35	20	6	5	0	8	37	.163	.261	.140	9.42	2.04
Wilny Moron	R-R	6-0	175	12-28-00	3	1	5.11	25	0	0	11	25	32	14	14	2	11	24	.314	.300	.319	8.76	4.01
Manuel Olivares	R-R	5-11	145	12-4-01	5	1	3.36	11	11	0	0	56	59	23	21	4	9	63	.280	.283	.277	10.07	1.44
Alan Perdomo	R-R	6-4	150	8-24-01	0	0	16.20	1	0	0	0	2	3	3	3	1	0	0	.375	.500	.250	0.00	0.00
2-team total (17 DSL Colorado)					4	2	5.25	18	0	0	2	24	27	16	14	3	5	18	.293	.212	.339	6.75	1.88
Doilin Perez	R-R	6-4	200	5-10-05	0	0	0.00	1	0	0	1	1	0	0	0	0	0	2	.000	.000	.000	18.00	0.00
2-team total (9 DSL Colorado)					0	1	3.92	10	7	0	1	21	19	12	9	3	10	21	.244	.324	.182	9.15	4.35
Willians Romero	R-R	6-1	190	2-7-05	0	0	25.07	6	0	0	0	5	6	13	13	0	11	3	.333	.125	.500	5.79	21.21
Isaac Rudecindo	R-R	6-2	210	1-27-01	2	0	1.63	27	0	0	4	28	19	6	5	1	14	36	.192	.194	.190	11.71	4.55
Kenebell Sevelen	R-R	6-3	190	8-17-04	0	0	9.00	3	0	0	0	2	3	2	2	0	3	2	.375	.667	.200	9.00	13.50
2-team total (7 DSL Colorado)					0	0	9.00	10	0	0	0	11	18	15	11	1	8	13	.353	.417	.296	10.64	6.55
Yoan Valdez	R-R	6-1	187	8-19-05	2	1	3.79	12	9	0	0	38	33	22	16	3	10	23	.228	.222	.231	5.45	2.37
Juan Vargas	R-R	6-3	180	10-10-00	1	2	11.74	7	0	0	0	8	12	14	10	3	8	7	.333	.375	.321	8.22	9.39

Fielding

C: Castillo 31, Gomez 12, Lopez 21. **1B:** Castillo 1, Gomez 37, Mota 8, Terrero 15. **2B:** Bernard 50, Colina 2, Hernandez 1, Jorge 1, Mota 6, Perez 1. **3B:** Gomez 1, Hidalgo 26, Mota 7, Perez 26. **SS:** Hidalgo 29, Jorge 2, Perez 29. **OF:** Alcantara 58, Bautista 4, Feliz 16, Gomez 2, Hernandez 57, James 32, Novas 15, Paiva 1, Tena 4, Terrero 4.

Detroit Tigers

SEASON IN A SENTENCE: A chic preseason dark horse pick after an active offseason and strong 2021 finish, the Tigers never got hot, finishing last in the major leagues in runs and only one game out of the AL Central basement.

HIGH POINT: The Tigers knew 39-year-old, future Hall of Famer Miguel Cabrera would reach the 3,000-hit milestone early in the season, and he did it with a single to right field on April 23 against the Rockies. Detroit won the game 13-0 to improve to 6-7, getting within a game of .500—which the club would never do again. Cabrera also was named to the All-Star Game by commissioner Rob Manfred.

LOW POINT: Detroit's offense provided many with 22 shutouts along the way. Two came during the season-long eight-game losing streak in the first half of August. On Aug. 7, six Rays combined to three-hit the Tigers in a 7-0 loss, with Tampa scoring seven runs in the ninth. Five days later, Chicago's Michael Kopech no-hit Detroit for six innings, and while the Tigers managed three hits against the bullpen, they still lost 2-0.

NOTABLE ROOKIES: Detroit saw its top two hitting prospects, 2020 No. 1 overall pick Spencer Torkleson and 2019 first-rounder Riley Greene, reach the big leagues. Greene, who played a smooth center field, showed off above-average tools while posting a league-average season (.253/.321/.362). Torkelson struggled significantly enough to be sent back to Triple-A for a month and batted just .203/.285/.319 with eight home runs. On the mound, righty Beau Brieske, a 27th-round pick in 2019, held his own in 15 starts, while 2017 first-rounder Alex Faedo (1-5, 5.53 in 12 starts) did not.

KEY TRANSACTIONS: Detroit loaded up in the offseason, but outfielder Austin Meadows (vertigo) was never right, shortstop Javier Baez (and his $144 million contract) produced a lot of outs with a .278 OBP, and lefthander Eduardo Rodriguez, the top import on the mound, left the team in May for undisclosed personal reasons, returning to pitch well in August. The season of setbacks led to the dismissal of general manager Al Avila. Former Giants GM Scott Harris named in late September as the club's new president of baseball operation.

ON THE FARM: Righthanders Jackson Jobe, Wilmer Flores and Ty Madden were among the Tigers' best performers as the system remains dominated by pitching.

OPENING DAY PAYROLL: $129,543,200 (20th).

PLAYERS OF THE YEAR

MAJOR LEAGUE

Tarik Skubal
LHP

7-8, 3.52 ERA
117 SO, 32 BB, 118 IP
Career-best 2.96 FIP

MINOR LEAGUE

Wilmer Flores
RHP

(HiA/AA)
2.79 ERA, 1.01 WHIP
130 SO, 23 BB, 103 IP

ORGANIZATION LEADERS

Batting		***Minimum 250 AB**
MAJORS		
*AVG	Harold Castro	.271
*OPS	Eric Haase	.748
HR	Javier Baez	17
RBI	Javier Baez	67
MINORS		
*AVG	Kerry Carpenter, Erie, Toledo	.313
*OBP	Carlos Mendoza, West Michigan, Lakeland	.425
*SLG	Kerry Carpenter, Erie, Toledo	.645
*OPS	Kerry Carpenter, Erie, Toledo	1.025
R	Josh Lester, Toledo	84
H	Josh Lester, Toledo	137
TB	Josh Lester, Toledo	267
2B	Josh Lester, Toledo	39
3B	Wenceel Perez, West Michigan, Erie	10
HR	Quincy Nieporte, Erie	31
RBI	Josh Lester, Toledo	99
BB	Zack Short, Toledo	88
SO	Gage Workman, Erie	206
SB	Gage Workman, Erie	30

Pitching		**#Minimum 75 IP**
MAJORS		
W	Tarik Skubal	7
W	Alex Lange	7
#ERA	Tarik Skubal	3.52
SO	Tarik Skubal	117
SV	Gregory Soto	30
MINORS		
W	Carlos Guzman, West Michigan, Erie	9
L	Nivaldo Rodriguez, Toledo	8
#ERA	Chance Kirby, Erie	2.62
G	Miguel Diaz, Toledo	58
GS	Austin Bergner, Erie, Toledo	26
GS	Ty Madden, West Michigan, Erie	26
SV	Derek Law, Toledo	15
IP	Chance Kirby, Erie	127
BB	Austin Bergner, Erie, Toledo	47
SO	Reese Olson, Erie	168
#AVG	Chance Kirby, Erie	.197

2022 PERFORMANCE

General Manager: Al Avila. **Farm Director:** Dan Lunetta. **Scouting Director:** Scott Pleis.

Class	Team	League	W	L	PCT	Finish	Manager
Majors	Detroit Tigers	American	66	96	.407	13th (15)	A.J. Hinch
Triple-A	Toledo Mud Hens	International	87	63	.580	3rd (20)	Lloyd McClendon
Double-A	Erie SeaWolves	Eastern	80	58	.580	2nd (12)	Gabe Alvarez
High-A	West Michigan Whitecaps	Midwest	72	59	.550	5th (12)	Brayan Pena
Low-A	Lakeland Flying Tigers	Florida State	66	64	.508	6th (10)	Andrew Graham
Rookie	FCL Tigers	Florida Complex	18	37	.327	14th (16)	Mike Alvarez
Overall 2022 Minor League Record			376	344	.522	t-9th (30)	

ORGANIZATION STATISTICS

DETROIT TIGERS

AMERICAN LEAGUE

Batting	B-T	HT	WT	DOB	AVG	vLH	vRH	G	AB	R	H	2B	3B	HR	RBI	BB	HBP	SH	SF	SO	SB	CS	SLG	OBP
Akil Baddoo	L-L	6-1	214	8-16-98	.204	.231	.198	73	201	30	41	3	2	2	9	24	0	0	0	64	9	6	.269	.289
Javier Baez	R-R	6-0	190	12-1-92	.238	.301	.217	144	555	64	132	27	4	17	67	26	6	0	3	147	9	2	.393	.278
Tucker Barnhart	B-R	5-11	192	1-7-91	.221	.238	.216	94	281	16	62	10	0	1	16	25	1	1	0	74	0	0	.267	.287
Miguel Cabrera	R-R	6-4	267	4-18-83	.254	.289	.243	112	397	25	101	10	0	5	43	28	3	0	5	101	1	0	.317	.305
Daz Cameron	R-R	6-2	185	1-15-97	.219	.300	.182	21	64	6	14	3	1	1	8	5	1	0	0	20	2	0	.344	.286
Jeimer Candelario	B-R	6-1	216	11-24-93	.217	.235	.210	124	429	49	93	19	2	13	50	28	6	0	4	109	0	1	.361	.272
Kerry Carpenter	L-R	6-2	220	9-2-97	.252	.217	.263	31	103	16	26	4	1	6	10	6	3	0	1	32	0	0	.485	.310
Harold Castro	L-R	5-10	195	11-30-93	.271	.303	.266	120	420	37	114	21	2	7	47	17	1	3	2	79	0	1	.381	.300
Willi Castro	B-R	6-1	206	4-24-97	.241	.250	.237	112	365	47	88	18	2	8	31	15	8	1	3	82	9	4	.367	.284
Kody Clemens	L-R	6-1	200	5-15-96	.145	.273	.116	57	117	13	17	4	0	5	17	8	0	0	2	33	1	0	.308	.197
Brendon Davis	R-R	6-4	185	7-28-97	.200	.400	.000	3	10	2	2	0	0	0	0	1	0	0	0	3	1	0	.200	.273
Dustin Garneau	R-R	6-2	205	8-13-87	.300	.333	.000	8	10	1	3	1	0	0	1	1	0	0	0	4	0	0	.400	.364
Riley Greene	L-L	6-3	200	9-28-00	.253	.303	.232	93	376	46	95	18	4	5	42	36	3	0	3	120	1	4	.362	.321
Robbie Grossman	B-L	6-0	209	9-16-89	.205	.364	.143	83	273	24	56	13	1	2	23	38	6	0	3	90	3	1	.282	.313
Eric Haase	R-R	5-10	210	12-18-92	.254	.281	.239	110	323	41	82	17	1	14	44	24	1	0	3	97	0	0	.443	.305
Derek Hill	R-R	6-2	190	12-30-95	.229	.370	.161	31	83	8	19	2	0	1	3	5	0	3	1	28	3	0	.289	.270
Ryan Kreidler	R-R	6-4	208	11-12-97	.178	.240	.146	26	73	8	13	1	0	1	6	6	1	2	2	22	0	1	.233	.244
Josh Lester	L-R	6-3	180	7-17-94	.000	.000	.000	2	5	0	0	0	0	0	0	0	0	0	0	3	0	0	.000	.000
Austin Meadows	L-L	6-3	225	5-3-95	.250	.229	.258	36	128	9	32	6	2	0	11	16	3	0	0	17	0	1	.328	.347
Victor Reyes	B-R	6-5	194	10-5-94	.254	.238	.260	92	315	27	80	19	3	3	34	13	4	0	4	77	2	2	.362	.289
Jonathan Schoop	R-R	6-1	247	10-16-91	.202	.186	.207	131	481	48	97	23	1	11	38	19	6	0	4	107	5	0	.322	.239
Zack Short	R-R	5-10	180	5-29-95	.000	.000	.000	6	9	2	0	0	0	0	2	2	0	0	2	5	1	0	.000	.154
Spencer Torkelson	R-R	6-1	220	8-26-99	.203	.216	.198	110	360	38	73	16	1	8	28	37	5	0	2	99	0	1	.319	.285

Pitching	B-T	HT	WT	DOB	W	L	ERA	G	GS	CG	SV	IP	H	R	ER	HR	BB	SO	AVG	vLH	vRH	K/9	BB/9
Tyler Alexander	R-L	6-2	203	7-14-94	4	11	4.81	27	17	0	0	101	108	58	54	18	25	61	.275	.260	.280	5.44	2.23
Jacob Barnes	R-R	6-2	231	4-14-90	3	1	6.10	22	0	0	0	21	21	14	14	3	9	10	.269	.143	.340	4.35	3.92
2-team total (1 New York Yankees)					3	1	5.64	23	0	0	0	22	23	14	14	3	9	12	.271	.167	.327	4.84	3.63
Tucker Barnhart	B-R	5-11	192	1-7-91	0	0	9.00	1	0	0	0	1	3	1	1	0	0	0	.600	.500	.667	0.00	0.00
Beau Brieske	R-R	6-3	200	4-5-98	3	6	4.19	15	15	0	0	82	73	39	38	14	25	54	.236	.206	.260	5.95	2.76
Drew Carlton	R-R	6-1	215	9-8-95	0	0	2.08	5	0	0	0	9	4	4	2	1	0	7	.129	.143	.118	7.27	0.00
Luis Castillo	R-R	6-3	212	3-10-95	0	0	0.00	3	0	0	0	4	2	0	0	0	0	4	.143	.167	.125	9.82	0.00
Harold Castro	L-R	5-10	195	11-30-93	0	0	4.50	4	0	0	0	4	6	2	2	0	1	1	.400	.000	.500	2.25	2.25
Andrew Chafin	R-L	6-2	235	6-17-90	2	3	2.83	64	0	0	3	57	48	26	18	5	19	67	.222	.233	.214	10.52	2.98
Jose Cisnero	R-R	6-3	258	4-11-89	1	0	1.08	28	0	0	0	25	15	4	3	0	19	23	.176	.161	.185	8.28	6.84
Kody Clemens	L-R	6-1	200	5-15-96	0	0	3.86	7	0	0	0	7	12	3	3	0	1	1	.375	.308	.421	1.29	1.29
Angel De Jesus	R-R	6-4	200	2-13-97	0	0	2.13	8	0	0	0	13	9	3	3	2	4	7	.188	.214	.176	4.97	2.84
Miguel Diaz	R-R	6-0	224	11-28-94	0	0	2.45	3	0	0	0	4	1	1	1	0	2	3	.083	.000	.167	7.36	4.91
Alex Faedo	R-R	6-5	225	11-12-95	1	5	5.53	12	12	0	0	54	63	34	33	7	25	44	.293	.283	.304	7.38	4.19
Jason Foley	R-R	6-4	215	11-1-95	1	0	3.88	60	0	0	0	60	72	27	26	2	11	43	.298	.349	.269	6.41	1.64
Michael Fulmer	R-R	6-3	224	3-15-93	3	4	3.20	41	0	0	2	39	29	17	14	1	20	39	.203	.298	.140	8.92	4.58
2-team total (26 Minnesota Twins)					5	6	3.39	67	0	0	3	64	59	27	24	4	28	61	.247	.337	.188	8.62	3.96
Bryan Garcia	R-R	6-1	205	4-19-95	2	0	3.54	4	4	0	0	20	14	8	8	3	10	17	.200	.147	.250	7.52	4.43
Rony Garcia	R-R	6-3	200	12-19-97	3	3	4.41	16	8	0	0	51	40	27	25	9	13	48	.213	.183	.242	8.47	2.29
Garrett Hill	R-R	6-0	185	1-16-96	3	3	4.03	17	8	0	0	60	53	29	27	8	29	40	.231	.178	.266	5.97	4.33
Drew Hutchison	L-R	6-3	215	8-22-90	3	9	4.53	28	18	0	0	105	114	58	53	15	42	68	.273	.301	.251	5.81	3.59
Joe Jimenez	R-R	6-3	277	1-17-95	3	2	3.49	62	0	0	2	57	49	24	22	4	13	77	.226	.253	.206	12.23	2.06
Alex Lange	R-R	6-3	202	10-2-95	7	4	3.41	71	0	0	0	63	47	30	24	5	31	82	.203	.189	.213	11.65	4.41
Derek Law	R-R	6-3	225	9-14-90	0	1	4.50	2	0	0	0	2	4	5	1	1	1	2	.444	.500	.429	9.00	4.50
Matt Manning	R-R	6-6	195	1-28-98	2	3	3.43	12	12	0	0	63	55	27	24	6	19	48	.231	.226	.236	6.86	2.71
Casey Mize	R-R	6-3	212	5-1-97	0	1	5.40	2	2	0	0	10	13	6	6	1	2	4	.302	.133	.393	3.60	1.80
Daniel Norris	L-L	6-2	207	4-25-93	2	0	3.45	14	2	0	0	29	22	11	11	4	8	23	.214	.176	.232	7.22	2.51
Wily Peralta	R-R	6-1	255	5-8-89	2	0	2.58	28	1	0	0	38	34	12	11	2	24	32	.241	.235	.244	7.51	5.63

Michael Pineda	R-R	6-7	280	1-18-89	2	7	5.79	11	11	0	0	47	58	31	30	13	8	26	.304	.306	.301	5.01	1.54
Eduardo Rodriguez	L-L	6-2	231	4-7-93	5	5	4.05	17	17	0	0	91	87	49	41	12	34	72	.247	.299	.235	7.12	3.36
Elvin Rodriguez	R-R	6-3	160	3-31-98	0	4	10.62	7	5	0	0	30	42	35	35	12	15	25	.331	.327	.333	7.58	4.55
Tarik Skubal	R-L	6-3	240	11-20-96	7	8	3.52	21	21	0	0	118	104	53	46	9	32	117	.237	.250	.234	8.95	2.45
Gregory Soto	L-L	6-1	234	2-11-95	2	11	3.28	64	0	0	30	60	49	32	22	2	34	60	.225	.245	.218	8.95	5.07
Will Vest	R-R	6-0	180	6-6-95	3	3	4.00	59	2	0	1	63	62	30	28	6	22	63	.262	.255	.266	9.00	3.14
Joey Wentz	L-L	6-5	220	10-6-97	2	2	3.03	7	7	0	0	33	23	13	11	2	13	27	.195	.167	.205	7.44	3.58

Fielding

Catcher	PCT	G	PO	A	E	DP	PB
Barnhart	.996	92	653	29	3	3	3
Garneau	1.000	7	23	1	0	0	0
Haase	.987	84	527	23	7	2	6

First Base	PCT	G	PO	A	E	DP
Castro	.990	50	354	27	4	47
Clemens	1.000	13	53	5	0	4
Schoop	1.000	2	9	1	0	0
Torkelson	.998	109	805	51	2	76

Second Base	PCT	G	PO	A	E	DP
Castro	.952	14	26	33	3	8
Castro	1.000	16	16	21	0	3
Clemens	1.000	9	13	21	0	6
Kreidler	1.000	2	3	7	0	0
Schoop	.994	129	207	313	3	86

Short	1.000	2	7	3	0	3

Third Base	PCT	G	PO	A	E	DP
Barnhart	.000	1	0	0	0	0
Candelario	.961	117	75	197	11	17
Castro	.935	25	23	35	4	4
Castro	.909	6	4	6	1	3
Clemens	.962	17	5	20	1	6
Davis	1.000	1	0	2	0	0
Kreidler	.971	13	9	25	1	4
Lester	1.000	1	0	1	0	0

Shortstop	PCT	G	PO	A	E	DP
Baez	.954	133	187	354	26	76
Castro	.957	19	15	29	2	5
Castro	.943	16	10	23	2	5
Kreidler	1.000	13	9	34	0	6

Short	1.000	4	1	9	0	1

Outfield	PCT	G	PO	A	E	DP
Baddoo	.988	66	166	0	2	0
Cameron	1.000	21	45	1	0	1
Carpenter	1.000	20	34	1	0	1
Castro	1.000	4	3	0	0	0
Castro	.988	83	157	6	2	2
Clemens	1.000	9	14	1	0	0
Davis	1.000	2	1	0	0	0
Greene	.992	93	241	0	2	0
Grossman	.988	80	167	1	2	0
Haase	1.000	11	15	1	0	0
Hill	1.000	30	79	2	0	1
Kreidler	--	1	0	0	0	0
Meadows	1.000	33	79	1	0	0
Reyes	.988	90	161	2	2	0

TOLEDO MUD HENS — TRIPLE-A

INTERNATIONAL LEAGUE

Batting	B-T	HT	WT	DOB	AVG	vLH	vRH	G	AB	R	H	2B	3B	HR	RBI	BB	HBP	SH	SF	SO	SB	CS	SLG	OBP
Akil Baddoo	L-L	6-1	214	8-16-98	.300	.300	.300	30	110	14	33	9	2	3	15	19	1	0	1	26	7	4	.500	.405
Daz Cameron	R-R	6-2	185	1-15-97	.240	.241	.240	98	383	56	92	24	2	10	50	37	5	0	5	123	19	4	.392	.312
Jeimer Candelario	B-R	6-1	216	11-24-93	.375	.500	.357	4	16	3	6	2	0	1	3	2	0	0	1	3	0	0	.688	.421
Kerry Carpenter	L-R	6-2	220	9-2-97	.331	.333	.330	35	118	17	39	11	1	8	27	17	2	0	1	17	2	7	.644	.420
Willi Castro	B-R	6-1	206	4-24-97	.265	.222	.280	8	34	2	9	2	0	0	1	2	0	0	0	10	3	1	.324	.306
Kody Clemens	L-R	6-1	200	5-15-96	.274	.209	.299	60	241	41	66	12	6	13	43	20	0	1	2	71	5	2	.535	.327
Brendon Davis	R-R	6-4	185	7-28-97	.232	.282	.212	103	367	54	85	19	2	14	47	55	7	0	1	104	6	4	.409	.342
Michael De La Cruz	B-R	5-10	190	5-15-93	.000	--	.000	1	3	0	0	0	0	0	0	0	0	0	0	1	0	0	.000	.000
Dustin Garneau	R-R	6-2	205	8-13-87	.195	.316	.131	52	164	21	32	9	0	7	21	17	8	0	2	52	1	0	.378	.298
Riley Greene	L-L	6-3	200	9-28-00	.274	.273	.275	15	62	10	17	4	0	1	6	6	0	0	0	14	3	0	.387	.338
Robbie Grossman	B-L	6-0	209	9-16-89	.143	.000	.167	2	7	1	1	0	0	1	1	1	0	0	0	2	0	0	.571	.250
Derek Hill	R-R	6-2	190	12-30-95	.223	.138	.250	31	121	19	27	5	2	2	10	9	0	1	1	32	2	1	.347	.275
Corey Joyce	R-R	6-1	190	8-19-98	.625	.600	.636	7	16	8	10	2	0	2	8	5	1	0	0	3	1	0	1.125	.727
Jose King	L-R	5-10	182	1-16-99	.000	--	.000	1	3	0	0	0	0	0	0	0	0	0	0	2	0	0	.000	.000
Ryan Kreidler	R-R	6-4	208	11-12-97	.213	.193	.221	56	202	29	43	12	2	8	22	36	9	0	3	72	15	1	.411	.352
Ryan Lavarnway	R-R	6-3	239	8-7-87	.281	.250	.291	44	146	20	41	11	0	5	26	23	3	0	2	34	0	0	.459	.385
2-team total (40 Jacksonville Jumbo Shrimp)					.245	.260	.239	84	278	34	68	15	0	11	44	40	7	0	2	69	0	0	.417	.352
Josh Lester	L-R	6-3	180	7-17-94	.246	.272	.235	145	557	84	137	39	2	29	99	51	5	0	7	137	7	3	.479	.311
Andre Lipcius	R-R	6-1	190	5-22-98	.302	.250	.324	46	159	18	48	13	1	3	24	25	0	0	4	33	1	3	.453	.388
Jack Lopez	R-R	5-10	160	12-16-92	.167	.183	.162	95	293	32	49	13	2	6	34	12	2	3	1	118	11	2	.287	.205
Austin Meadows	L-L	6-3	225	5-3-95	.147	.118	.176	10	34	4	5	0	0	1	4	4	0	0	1	7	0	0	.235	.231
Dane Myers	R-R	6-2	205	3-8-96	.256	.300	.242	14	43	5	11	3	0	0	5	1	2	0	0	15	1	1	.326	.304
Brady Policelli	R-R	5-10	195	6-24-95	.196	.182	.200	29	51	14	10	1	1	2	4	7	1	0	0	16	0	1	.373	.305
Chris Rabago	R-R	5-11	204	4-22-93	.178	.154	.182	31	90	10	16	1	0	2	7	8	3	2	0	32	1	0	.256	.267
Victor Reyes	B-R	6-5	194	10-5-94	.333	.000	.450	8	27	9	9	1	0	3	5	4	0	0	1	2	1	1	.704	.406
Jacob Robson	L-R	5-10	182	11-20-94	.192	.179	.195	53	151	21	29	9	2	3	17	28	0	0	0	67	13	4	.338	.318
Dylan Rosa	R-R	6-2	200	6-27-96	.143	.100	.156	26	42	8	6	0	0	2	6	4	0	1	2	23	2	0	.286	.208
Ali Sanchez	R-R	6-1	200	1-20-97	.268	.200	.290	44	142	23	38	9	0	2	21	22	2	0	2	48	1	0	.373	.369
2-team total (30 Memphis Redbirds)					.262	.247	.269	74	252	38	66	14	0	6	33	35	2	0	2	77	2	0	.389	.354
Jonathan Schoop	R-R	6-1	247	10-16-91	.222	1.000	.125	3	9	0	2	1	0	0	0	2	0	0	0	0	0	0	.333	.364
Zack Short	R-R	5-10	180	5-29-95	.229	.289	.207	128	459	79	105	31	1	11	60	88	5	1	6	149	11	5	.373	.355
Trayce Thompson	R-R	6-3	225	3-15-91	.299	.391	.270	25	97	17	29	7	1	8	19	7	1	0	0	30	1	1	.639	.352
Spencer Torkelson	R-R	6-1	220	8-26-99	.229	.286	.202	35	131	18	30	6	0	5	18	23	1	0	0	41	1	1	.389	.348
John Valente	R-R	5-11	190	6-23-95	.293	.389	.267	82	249	37	73	14	2	2	26	23	2	2	2	25	14	2	.390	.355
Jamie Westbrook	R-R	5-9	193	6-18-95	.248	.254	.246	120	419	55	104	21	0	11	48	53	14	0	4	80	1	2	.377	.349
2-team total (3 Nashville Sounds)					.254	.258	.253	123	429	58	109	22	0	11	48	54	14	0	4	80	1	2	.382	.353

Pitching	B-T	HT	WT	DOB	W	L	ERA	G	GS	CG	SV	IP	H	R	ER	HR	BB	SO	AVG	vLH	vRH	K/9	BB/9
Tyler Alexander	R-L	6-2	203	7-14-94	1	1	8.00	5	1	0	0	9	12	8	8	1	1	8	.308	.313	.304	8.00	1.00
Chase Anderson	R-R	6-1	210	11-30-87	4	3	4.63	17	15	0	0	70	70	41	36	14	27	62	.255	.265	.245	7.97	3.47
2-team total (10 Durham Bulls)					7	3	4.50	27	16	0	1	80	77	47	40	16	29	72	.246	.245	.247	8.10	3.26
Jacob Barnes	R-R	6-2	231	4-14-90	0	0	3.00	5	0	0	0	6	7	2	2	0	2	12	.280	.222	.313	18.00	3.00
2-team total (10 Scranton/Wilkes-Barre RailRiders)					1	1	2.57	15	0	0	0	14	11	5	4	0	6	20	.208	.174	.233	12.86	3.86
Austin Bergner	R-R	6-5	210	5-1-97	1	3	6.91	8	7	0	0	29	26	22	22	5	16	28	.239	.219	.267	8.79	5.02

Nolan Blackwood	R-R	6-5	185	3-16-95	2	1	3.81	44	0	0	0	50	50	23	21	9	19	38	.260	.343	.216	6.89	3.44
Beau Brieske	R-R	6-3	200	4-5-98	0	2	4.15	4	4	0	0	17	17	8	8	3	5	19	.266	.281	.250	9.87	2.60
Drew Carlton	R-R	6-1	215	9-8-95	4	3	4.78	46	2	0	2	58	58	33	31	9	11	67	.254	.287	.228	10.34	1.70
Luis Castillo	R-R	6-3	212	3-10-95	4	1	1.74	40	0	0	0	41	39	10	8	2	11	39	.253	.250	.255	8.49	2.40
Andrew Chafin	R-L	6-2	235	6-17-90	1	0	0.00	1	0	0	0	1	0	0	0	0	0	2	.000	--	.000	18.00	0.00
Jose Cisnero	R-R	6-3	258	4-11-89	1	0	3.18	6	0	0	0	6	3	2	2	0	1	6	.150	.400	.067	9.53	1.59
Angel De Jesus	R-R	6-4	200	2-13-97	5	1	4.15	44	0	0	1	48	34	26	22	4	20	44	.195	.153	.225	8.31	3.78
Miguel Del Pozo	L-L	6-1	205	10-14-92	5	2	3.88	55	0	0	7	53	44	25	23	4	16	66	.229	.195	.257	11.14	2.70
Bubba Derby	L-R	5-11	185	2-24-94	0	0	6.23	3	1	0	0	4	8	3	3	0	2	2	.400	.444	.364	4.15	4.15
Miguel Diaz	R-R	6-0	224	11-28-94	4	5	4.29	58	0	0	7	65	59	39	31	5	30	69	.240	.228	.252	9.55	4.15
Alex Faedo	R-R	6-5	225	11-12-95	1	0	0.00	1	1	0	0	5	4	0	0	0	0	8	.222	.125	.300	14.40	0.00
Jason Foley	R-R	6-4	215	11-1-95	1	0	3.60	4	0	0	0	5	5	2	2	1	1	6	.250	.273	.222	10.80	1.80
Bryan Garcia	R-R	6-1	205	4-19-95	5	3	3.80	39	11	0	1	85	77	36	36	11	34	69	.242	.252	.234	7.28	3.59
Rony Garcia	R-R	6-3	200	12-19-97	0	0	6.75	2	0	0	0	4	2	3	3	0	1	2	.143	.100	.250	4.50	2.25
Dario Gardea	R-R	6-2	210	1-29-99	0	0	0.00	1	0	0	0	1	1	0	0	0	0	2	.250	.250	--	18.00	0.00
Chi Chi Gonzalez	R-R	6-3	210	1-15-92	0	1	5.48	5	4	0	0	21	24	13	13	4	8	18	.293	.286	.300	7.59	3.38
3-team total (5 S./Wilkes-Barre RailRiders, 8 St. Paul Saints)					2	3	4.03	18	14	0	0	80	82	38	36	8	27	71	.265	.280	.247	7.95	3.02
Garrett Hill	R-R	6-0	185	1-16-96	2	2	4.06	8	8	0	0	38	31	20	17	4	15	46	.220	.194	.241	10.99	3.58
Tim Holdgrafer	R-R	6-1	180	7-31-96	0	0	33.75	1	0	0	0	1	3	5	5	0	2	0	.429	.600	.000	0.00	13.50
Zac Houston	R-R	6-5	260	11-30-94	1	1	7.50	17	0	0	0	18	20	16	15	3	17	24	.278	.324	.237	12.00	8.50
Sam Howard	R-L	6-4	195	3-5-93	2	1	3.18	40	0	0	0	34	25	15	12	6	20	41	.203	.169	.241	10.85	5.29
2-team total (2 Indianapolis Indians)					2	2	3.19	42	1	0	0	37	27	16	13	6	21	42	.205	.171	.242	10.31	5.15
Drew Hutchison	L-R	6-3	215	8-22-90	1	1	3.95	6	3	0	0	14	11	6	6	2	3	19	.220	.179	.273	12.51	1.98
Nick Kuzia	R-R	6-4	190	2-7-96	2	0	3.68	6	0	0	0	7	7	5	3	0	2	5	.226	.250	.200	6.14	2.45
A.J. Ladwig	R-R	6-5	220	12-24-92	0	1	9.82	1	0	0	0	4	5	4	4	1	1	4	.313	.333	.300	9.82	2.45
Derek Law	R-R	6-3	225	9-14-90	1	3	3.23	33	0	0	15	39	37	15	14	2	10	44	.250	.234	.262	10.15	2.31
2-team total (6 Louisville Bats)					1	3	2.87	39	0	0	15	47	41	16	15	2	13	47	.237	.224	.245	9.00	2.49
Jesus Liranzo	R-R	6-2	225	3-7-95	0	0	17.18	4	0	0	0	4	5	7	7	1	3	5	.313	.375	.250	12.27	7.36
Andrew Magno	R-L	5-11	190	4-30-98	0	0	0.00	1	0	0	0	0	0	0	0	0	0	0	.000	--	.000	0.00	0.00
Matt Manning	R-R	6-6	195	1-28-98	1	1	2.66	6	6	0	0	20	19	6	6	0	10	23	.257	.234	.296	10.18	4.43
Michael Mariot	R-R	6-0	190	10-20-88	3	1	5.40	7	4	0	0	27	28	16	16	6	11	20	.277	.325	.246	6.75	3.71
2-team total (11 Lehigh Valley IronPigs)					7	2	4.90	18	15	0	0	79	77	44	43	15	32	56	.257	.264	.250	6.38	3.65
Casey Mize	R-R	6-3	212	5-1-97	0	0	40.50	1	1	0	0	1	4	3	3	1	0	0	.667	.667	.667	0.00	0.00
Joe Navilhon	R-R	6-0	200	7-13-93	0	1	5.23	6	3	0	0	10	10	6	6	2	8	13	.250	.263	.238	11.32	6.97
Daniel Norris	L-L	6-2	207	4-25-93	0	0	2.08	3	3	0	0	9	5	2	2	0	2	5	.161	.091	.200	5.19	2.08
2-team total (2 Iowa Cubs)					0	0	1.54	5	3	0	0	12	8	3	2	0	3	10	.186	.200	.174	7.71	2.31
Carlos Pena	L-L	5-11	160	9-7-98	0	0	5.40	2	0	0	0	3	4	2	2	0	4	2	.286	.500	.125	5.40	10.80
Wily Peralta	R-R	6-1	255	5-8-89	0	0	3.38	5	0	0	1	5	7	2	2	0	3	8	.304	.313	.286	13.50	5.06
Michael Pineda	R-R	6-7	280	1-18-89	1	2	4.68	7	6	0	0	25	30	13	13	2	5	21	.297	.327	.269	7.56	1.80
Ricardo Pinto	R-R	6-0	195	1-20-94	3	1	3.58	20	0	0	0	33	34	13	13	4	13	39	.276	.317	.238	10.74	3.58
Brady Policelli	R-R	5-10	195	6-24-95	0	0	0.00	1	0	0	0	0	0	0	0	0	1	0	.000	--	.000	0.00	27.00
Daniel Ponce de Leon	R-R	6-3	200	1-16-92	3	0	1.69	3	3	0	0	16	9	3	3	0	5	15	.158	.176	.130	8.44	2.81
2-team total (7 Rochester Red Wings)					4	3	4.23	10	10	0	0	45	38	22	21	3	17	51	.225	.179	.264	10.28	3.43
Alex Powers	R-R	6-4	205	2-26-92	1	0	11.57	5	0	0	0	7	8	9	9	0	6	9	.276	.154	.375	11.57	7.71
Chris Rabago	R-R	5-11	204	4-22-93	0	0	18.00	1	0	0	0	1	3	2	2	0	1	1	.600	1.000	.333	9.00	9.00
Eduardo Rodriguez	L-L	6-2	231	4-7-93	1	0	0.60	3	3	0	0	15	8	1	1	0	2	26	.154	.136	.167	15.60	1.20
Elvin Rodriguez	R-R	6-3	160	3-31-98	6	4	4.98	23	21	0	0	99	115	58	55	17	36	91	.292	.265	.315	8.24	3.26
Nivaldo Rodriguez	R-R	6-1	214	4-16-97	3	8	6.92	19	15	0	0	65	95	56	50	16	31	49	.339	.373	.312	6.78	4.29
Ramon Rosso	R-R	6-4	240	6-9-96	0	0	0.00	1	0	0	0	1	0	0	0	0	2	1	.000	.000	.000	9.00	18.00
Ricardo Sanchez	L-L	5-10	220	4-11-97	1	1	5.55	5	5	0	0	24	31	16	15	3	7	20	.307	.262	.339	7.40	2.59
2-team total (21 Lehigh Valley IronPigs)					7	5	4.95	26	26	0	0	116	133	71	64	13	41	103	.287	.274	.295	7.97	3.17
Cody Sedlock	R-R	6-4	220	6-19-95	1	2	3.51	14	2	0	0	26	20	11	10	3	16	19	.215	.163	.273	6.66	5.61
2-team total (14 Norfolk Tides)					5	3	4.84	28	12	0	0	80	75	50	43	7	44	81	.250	.290	.216	9.11	4.95
Logan Shore	R-R	6-2	215	12-28-94	2	4	5.68	25	6	0	0	52	63	39	33	12	24	39	.293	.280	.304	6.71	4.13
Markus Solbach	R-R	6-5	205	8-26-91	1	1	0.82	2	2	0	0	11	6	3	1	0	1	9	.154	.143	.182	7.36	0.82
Shea Spitzbarth	R-R	6-1	215	10-4-94	5	0	3.27	36	2	0	0	44	30	16	16	4	28	34	.194	.200	.187	6.95	5.73
Will Vest	R-R	6-0	180	6-6-95	0	0	0.00	1	0	0	0	1	1	0	0	0	0	1	.250	.000	.333	9.00	0.00
Nick Vincent	R-R	5-10	185	7-12-86	5	0	0.61	28	0	0	5	30	15	3	2	0	5	28	.150	.137	.163	8.49	1.52
2-team total (17 Gwinnett Stripers)					6	5	2.39	45	1	0	5	49	44	19	13	5	9	55	.239	.226	.250	10.10	1.65
Joey Wentz	L-L	6-5	220	10-6-97	2	2	3.17	12	11	0	0	48	37	17	17	6	20	53	.211	.308	.155	9.87	3.72

Fielding

Catcher	PCT	G	PO	A	E	DP	PB
Garneau	.998	51	444	26	1	2	10
Lavarnway	1.000	22	201	8	0	1	2
Policelli	1.000	27	133	11	0	0	5
Rabago	.987	29	206	18	3	1	1
Sanchez	.997	38	307	22	1	2	2

First Base	PCT	G	PO	A	E	DP
Clemens	.987	11	75	3	1	3
De La Cruz	1.000	1	5	0	0	0
Lavarnway	1.000	1	3	1	0	1
Lester	.996	104	780	74	3	74
Rabago	1.000	1	4	0	0	0
Sanchez	.962	4	24	1	1	1
Torkelson	.996	31	224	18	1	25

Second Base	PCT	G	PO	A	E	DP
Castro	1.000	2	0	3	0	1
Clemens	.960	25	34	63	4	11
Joyce	1.000	1	0	1	0	0
King	1.000	1	1	2	0	0
Kreidler	.984	12	29	32	1	9
Lester	1.000	5	8	16	0	3
Lipcius	.976	20	32	48	2	10
Lopez	.955	14	15	27	2	7
Policelli	.000	1	0	0	0	0
Schoop	1.000	2	5	2	0	1
Short	.966	15	25	31	2	7
John Valente	.981	22	18	33	1	5
Jamie Westbrook	.982	42	51	109	3	22

Third Base	PCT	G	PO	A	E	DP
Candelario	.917	3	5	6	1	0
Castro	.000	1	0	0	0	0
Clemens	1.000	13	8	22	0	8
Davis	.972	44	39	64	3	5
Joyce	.500	1	0	1	1	0
Kreidler	.935	11	9	20	2	4

	PCT	G	PO	A	E	DP
Lester	1.000	7	6	12	0	1
Lipcius	.903	25	21	35	6	4
Lopez	1.000	7	5	8	0	1
Myers	.923	6	6	6	1	1
Valente	.952	42	31	49	4	2

Shortstop	PCT	G	PO	A	E	DP
Castro	1.000	2	2	6	0	0
Davis	1.000	10	17	22	0	7
Joyce	1.000	2	1	1	0	1
Kreidler	.976	26	37	87	3	14
Lopez	.933	10	23	19	3	5
Short	.978	109	136	261	9	57

Outfield	PCT	G	PO	A	E	DP
Baddoo	1.000	29	63	2	0	1
Cameron	.987	98	233	2	3	0
Carpenter	1.000	31	52	1	0	0
Castro	1.000	3	7	0	0	0
Clemens	1.000	13	25	0	0	0
Davis	.958	47	88	3	4	2
Greene	1.000	15	31	1	0	0
Grossman	--	1	0	0	0	0
Hill	1.000	28	62	3	0	0
Lester	.974	25	34	3	1	0
Lopez	.991	65	108	7	1	1
Meadows	1.000	7	5	2	0	0
Myers	1.000	7	11	0	0	0
Reyes	1.000	5	8	0	0	0
Robson	1.000	49	75	3	0	1
Rosa	.875	16	14	0	2	0
Short	.938	9	14	1	1	0
Thompson	.978	21	41	3	1	1
Valente	1.000	7	10	1	0	1
Westbrook	.875	7	7	0	1	0

ERIE SEAWOLVES — *DOUBLE-A*

EASTERN LEAGUE

Batting	B-T	HT	WT	DOB	AVG	vLH	vRH	G	AB	R	H	2B	3B	HR	RBI	BB	HBP	SH	SF	SO	SB	CS	SLG	OBP
Ulrich Bojarski	R-R	6-3	212	9-15-98	.000	.000	.000	1	3	0	0	0	0	0	0	1	0	0	0	3	0	0	.000	.250
Daniel Cabrera	L-L	6-3	200	9-5-98	.206	.169	.214	96	355	37	73	14	3	5	33	40	2	0	3	80	6	0	.304	.288
Kerry Carpenter	L-R	6-2	220	9-2-97	.304	.333	.296	63	240	43	73	16	0	22	48	16	5	0	1	72	1	3	.646	.359
Luis Carpio	R-R	5-11	190	7-11-97	.218	.200	.223	78	243	26	53	14	0	2	20	27	2	0	2	67	8	1	.300	.299
Josh Crouch	R-R	6-0	200	12-7-98	.167	.000	.200	6	24	1	4	0	0	1	4	0	0	0	0	6	0	0	.292	.167
Trei Cruz	B-R	6-2	204	7-5-98	.200	.400	.150	8	25	3	5	0	0	0	0	5	0	0	0	7	1	0	.200	.333
Michael De La Cruz	B-R	5-10	190	5-15-93	.200	.000	.273	20	60	13	12	2	0	2	6	14	2	0	0	10	0	1	.333	.368
Eric De La Rosa	R-R	6-3	186	6-3-97	.225	.175	.238	60	191	30	43	10	2	3	18	14	10	0	2	79	9	3	.346	.309
Dillon Dingler	R-R	6-3	210	9-17-98	.238	.250	.235	107	387	56	92	22	3	14	58	45	12	0	3	143	1	0	.419	.333
Luis Garcia	B-R	5-11	170	10-1-00	.000	.000	.000	4	7	3	0	0	0	0	0	5	0	0	0	3	0	0	.000	.417
2-team total (6 Reading Fightin Phils)					.069	.000	.074	10	29	3	2	0	0	0	1	8	0	1	0	14	0	1	.069	.270
Jake Holton	R-R	6-0	210	3-2-98	.217	.200	.222	7	23	3	5	0	0	0	0	1	2	0	0	8	0	0	.217	.308
Cooper Johnson	R-R	6-1	209	4-25-98	.000	.000	.000	5	16	0	0	0	0	0	0	3	0	0	0	10	0	0	.000	.158
Corey Joyce	R-R	6-1	190	8-19-98	.250	.375	.200	18	56	4	14	2	1	0	4	4	5	0	0	17	1	0	.321	.354
Jose King	L-R	5-10	182	1-16-99	.000	.000	.000	6	12	1	0	0	0	0	0	1	0	0	0	8	0	0	.000	.077
Andre Lipcius	R-R	6-1	190	5-22-98	.264	.283	.259	88	303	52	80	20	1	9	39	61	5	0	3	56	12	1	.426	.392
Parker Meadows	L-R	6-5	205	11-2-99	.275	.211	.294	113	425	64	117	21	6	16	51	52	4	0	8	90	17	2	.466	.354
Dane Myers	R-R	6-2	205	3-8-96	.268	.375	.245	107	407	59	109	18	2	25	72	23	7	2	3	118	20	4	.506	.316
Andrew Navigato	R-R	5-11	188	5-28-98	.252	.262	.250	97	361	63	91	16	0	18	45	25	13	0	6	71	14	2	.446	.319
Quincy Nieporte	R-R	6-1	225	7-29-94	.270	.291	.265	123	459	72	124	25	2	31	91	40	7	0	10	85	2	0	.536	.331
Bryant Packard	L-R	6-3	200	10-6-97	.233	.571	.189	16	60	9	14	3	0	1	7	4	1	0	1	8	0	0	.333	.288
Wenceel Perez	B-R	5-11	203	10-30-99	.307	.348	.299	39	150	28	46	10	5	5	28	15	3	0	3	23	5	4	.540	.374
Chris Rabago	R-R	5-11	204	4-22-93	.209	.250	.203	20	67	5	14	5	1	0	5	7	2	0	0	26	1	0	.313	.303
Dylan Rosa	R-R	6-2	200	6-27-96	.205	.219	.200	35	122	17	25	3	0	7	17	17	1	0	1	65	2	1	.402	.305
Jon Rosoff	L-R	5-9	175	11-14-94	.238	.273	.231	25	63	7	15	2	0	0	2	8	0	0	0	12	0	0	.270	.324
Danny Serretti	B-R	6-1	195	5-7-00	.263	.200	.286	6	19	6	5	0	0	0	2	4	1	0	0	4	2	0	.263	.417
Eduardo Valencia	R-R	6-1	180	1-25-00	.333	--	.333	1	3	0	1	0	0	0	1	1	0	0	0	2	0	0	.333	.500
Gage Workman	B-R	6-3	202	10-24-99	.225	.190	.235	128	475	61	107	30	9	14	68	34	1	1	4	206	30	9	.415	.276

Pitching	B-T	HT	WT	DOB	W	L	ERA	G	GS	CG	SV	IP	H	R	ER	HR	BB	SO	AVG	vLH	vRH	K/9	BB/9
Elvis Alvarado	R-R	6-4	183	2-23-99	5	1	3.97	20	1	0	2	23	16	11	10	2	7	23	.200	.212	.191	9.13	2.78
Austin Bergner	R-R	6-5	210	5-1-97	4	2	2.38	19	19	0	0	91	65	27	24	12	31	93	.195	.172	.213	9.23	3.08
Luis Castillo	R-R	6-3	212	3-10-95	1	0	0.00	3	0	0	0	3	2	0	0	0	0	3	.167	.000	.286	8.10	0.00
Yaya Chentouf	R-R	5-9	205	6-18-97	5	2	2.97	49	0	0	7	58	51	26	19	7	15	65	.231	.316	.183	10.14	2.34
Bubba Derby	L-R	5-11	185	2-24-94	2	0	4.76	17	0	0	4	23	21	12	12	3	5	25	.241	.273	.209	9.93	1.99
Chavez Fernander	R-R	6-3	205	7-7-97	1	1	5.23	15	0	0	0	21	21	13	12	1	8	19	.266	.258	.271	8.27	3.48
Wilmer Flores	R-R	6-4	225	2-20-01	6	4	3.01	19	19	0	0	84	67	36	28	8	21	95	.213	.205	.220	10.22	2.26
Dario Gardea	R-R	6-2	210	1-29-99	0	1	5.54	22	0	0	0	26	32	16	16	4	9	19	.302	.250	.333	6.58	3.12
Sawyer Gipson-Long	R-R	6-4	225	12-12-97	2	2	4.54	7	7	0	0	36	37	20	18	7	9	35	.270	.322	.231	8.83	2.27
Carlos Guzman	R-R	6-1	210	5-16-98	0	0	0.00	2	0	0	0	1	0	0	0	0	0	1	.000	.000	.000	6.75	0.00
Garrett Hill	R-R	6-0	185	1-16-96	2	0	2.25	7	7	0	0	32	19	9	8	3	10	52	.167	.113	.231	14.63	2.81
J.T. Hintzen	R-R	6-0	185	6-1-96	1	1	9.45	6	0	0	0	7	4	7	7	1	7	8	.167	.308	.000	10.80	9.45
Tim Holdgrafer	R-R	6-1	180	7-31-96	0	1	5.06	3	0	0	0	5	7	6	3	1	1	4	.304	.375	.267	6.75	1.69
Zac Houston	R-R	6-5	260	11-30-94	1	6	4.41	31	0	0	4	35	25	21	17	6	23	64	.195	.250	.158	16.62	5.97
Brant Hurter	L-L	6-6	250	9-6-98	0	2	7.90	4	2	0	0	14	21	14	12	1	4	17	.350	.222	.373	11.20	2.63
Chance Kirby	R-R	5-11	165	7-19-95	8	3	2.62	29	21	1	0	127	90	40	37	14	29	116	.197	.209	.189	8.22	2.06
Nick Kuzia	R-R	6-4	190	2-7-96	4	4	5.18	35	1	0	0	49	45	32	28	6	28	49	.241	.250	.234	9.06	5.18
A.J. Ladwig	R-R	6-5	220	12-24-92	0	1	3.27	4	2	0	0	11	10	5	4	1	4	10	.244	.444	.087	8.18	3.27
Billy Lescher	R-R	6-4	215	9-17-95	1	1	4.79	32	0	0	1	36	33	19	19	3	9	33	.248	.263	.237	8.33	2.27
Ty Madden	R-R	6-3	215	2-21-00	2	2	2.78	7	7	0	0	36	28	13	11	6	12	49	.217	.250	.198	12.36	3.03
Andrew Magno	R-L	5-11	190	4-30-98	0	0	5.79	4	0	0	0	5	4	4	3	1	2	4	.235	.000	.308	7.71	3.86
Gerson Moreno	R-R	6-0	218	9-10-95	4	2	3.32	48	1	0	8	57	33	22	21	5	33	96	.171	.208	.147	15.16	5.21
Joe Navilhon	R-R	6-0	200	7-13-93	6	0	5.36	33	0	0	0	44	47	26	26	10	10	50	.278	.320	.245	10.31	2.06
Reese Olson	R-R	6-1	160	7-31-99	8	6	4.14	26	25	0	0	120	109	65	55	15	38	168	.237	.212	.259	12.64	2.86

Carlos Pena	L-L	5-11	160	9-7-98	0	0	81.00	1	0	0	0	0	3	4	3	1	1	1	.600	1.000	.500	27.00	27.00
J.T. Perez	L-L	6-4	215	10-26-95	0	1	7.36	6	0	0	0	7	5	6	6	2	4	4	.185	.071	.308	4.91	4.91
Alex Powers	R-R	6-4	205	2-26-92	0	0	14.73	6	0	0	0	7	13	12	12	4	2	11	.382	.471	.294	13.50	2.45
Jon Rosoff	L-R	5-9	175	11-14-94	0	1	11.57	3	0	0	0	2	3	4	3	0	2	1	.300	.400	.200	3.86	7.71
Markus Solbach	R-R	6-5	205	8-26-91	3	4	4.57	15	15	0	0	63	63	34	32	11	19	62	.252	.252	.252	8.86	2.71
Shea Spitzbarth	R-R	6-1	215	10-4-94	1	0	0.93	8	0	0	0	10	4	1	1	0	4	12	.125	.167	.100	11.17	3.72
Jared Tobey	R-L	6-4	225	3-11-96	0	1	6.23	6	0	0	0	9	8	6	6	1	2	6	.267	.188	.357	6.23	2.08
Brendan White	R-R	5-11	185	11-18-98	6	5	2.67	48	0	0	9	67	44	25	20	3	17	73	.182	.196	.169	9.76	2.27
Adam Wolf	L-L	6-6	215	12-26-96	5	4	2.72	35	11	0	4	89	79	30	27	6	37	92	.234	.221	.239	9.27	3.73
Kyle Zurak	R-R	6-1	208	11-28-94	2	0	6.32	13	0	0	0	16	22	11	11	3	10	13	.349	.387	.313	7.47	5.74
2-team total (13 Somerset Patriots)					4	1	4.50	26	0	0	0	34	35	19	17	3	18	35	.267	.322	.222	9.26	4.76

Fielding

Catcher	PCT	G	PO	A	E	DP	PB
Crouch	1.000	2	28	0	0	0	0
De La Cruz	.986	14	138	7	2	1	1
Dingler	.989	82	834	47	10	4	9
Johnson	1.000	5	44	4	0	0	1
Rabago	1.000	18	159	18	0	0	0
Rosoff	.990	18	186	4	2	0	1
Valencia	1.000	1	10	1	0	0	0

First Base	PCT	G	PO	A	E	DP
Holton	1.000	6	40	1	0	3
Lipcius	1.000	1	6	1	0	2
Myers	.995	51	349	20	2	27
Navigato	1.000	1	6	2	0	1
Nieporte	.995	82	558	40	3	38

Second Base	PCT	G	PO	A	E	DP
Carpio	.982	45	65	96	3	16
Cruz	1.000	1	1	2	0	0
Garcia	1.000	2	1	4	0	1
King	1.000	2	1	3	0	0
Lipcius	.967	14	23	35	2	6
Navigato	.978	48	77	145	5	30
Perez	.940	30	46	63	7	5
Rosoff	1.000	1	0	1	0	0

Third Base	PCT	G	PO	A	E	DP
Carpio	1.000	5	2	5	0	1
Cruz	.778	6	3	11	4	3
Joyce	.947	10	9	9	1	2
King	.000	1	0	0	0	0
Lipcius	.932	61	63	73	10	7
Myers	.950	8	10	9	1	0
Workman	.956	49	28	80	5	9

Shortstop	PCT	G	PO	A	E	DP
Carpio	.963	26	28	51	3	7
Garcia	.833	2	0	5	1	1
Joyce	1.000	3	2	7	0	1
King	1.000	1	0	1	0	0
Navigato	.985	21	22	43	1	5
Serretti	.947	6	4	14	1	2
Workman	.943	80	85	197	17	29

Outfield	PCT	G	PO	A	E	DP
Bojarski	--	1	0	0	0	0
Cabrera	.986	95	137	4	2	1
Carpenter	.964	55	78	2	3	0
De La Rosa	.981	59	103	3	2	2
Meadows	.988	112	251	4	3	2
Myers	.963	47	71	6	3	0
Navigato	1.000	18	21	0	0	0
Packard	.950	11	17	2	1	0
Rosa	.983	31	58	1	1	0
Rosoff	--	2	0	0	0	0

WEST MICHIGAN WHITECAPS — HIGH CLASS A

MIDWEST LEAGUE

Batting	B-T	HT	WT	DOB	AVG	vLH	vRH	G	AB	R	H	2B	3B	HR	RBI	BB	HBP	SH	SF	SO	SB	CS	SLG	OBP
Eliezer Alfonzo	B-R	5-10	155	9-23-99	.354	.333	.361	12	48	11	17	1	0	2	10	6	1	1	2	6	0	0	.500	.421
Akil Baddoo	L-L	6-1	214	8-16-98	.000	.000	.000	3	10	0	0	0	0	0	0	1	0	0	0	5	0	0	.000	.091
Chase Barbary	R-R	6-2	180	4-7-97	.227	.167	.250	10	22	2	5	2	0	0	0	1	1	0	0	7	0	0	.318	.292
Lazaro Benitez	R-R	5-9	190	10-15-99	.143	.125	.154	11	21	2	3	1	0	0	1	3	0	0	1	7	0	1	.190	.240
Justice Bigbie	R-R	6-2	200	1-24-99	.387	.556	.318	9	31	6	12	4	0	1	7	2	1	0	0	6	0	1	.613	.441
Ulrich Bojarski	R-R	6-3	212	9-15-98	.170	.200	.153	33	94	14	16	3	0	7	17	8	3	0	1	45	1	0	.426	.255
Daniel Cabrera	L-L	6-3	200	9-5-98	.346	.174	.395	24	104	17	36	6	1	3	13	8	0	0	2	16	1	0	.510	.386
Esney Chacon	R-R	6-1	160	3-17-00	.214	.176	.225	43	145	15	31	3	2	0	7	10	1	2	1	37	1	2	.262	.268
Josh Crouch	R-R	6-0	200	12-7-98	.290	.256	.300	90	335	43	97	22	0	10	61	38	5	0	4	56	1	0	.445	.366
Trei Cruz	B-R	6-2	204	7-5-98	.233	.195	.244	109	386	63	90	19	4	8	52	76	0	0	5	111	15	4	.365	.355
Dustin Garneau	R-R	6-2	205	8-13-87	.083	--	.083	4	12	1	1	0	0	0	2	4	1	0	0	2	0	0	.083	.353
Jake Holton	R-R	6-0	210	3-2-98	.262	.212	.277	109	381	67	100	19	3	13	69	71	15	0	2	86	5	5	.430	.397
Carlos Irigoyen	R-R	6-2	165	3-21-01	.203	.222	.195	24	59	5	12	3	0	0	4	3	0	0	1	28	0	0	.254	.238
Cooper Johnson	R-R	6-1	209	4-25-98	.192	.357	.156	23	78	7	15	3	0	1	4	10	3	0	0	26	0	0	.269	.308
Corey Joyce	R-R	6-1	190	8-19-98	.240	.111	.276	63	208	45	50	9	2	9	32	47	10	0	3	52	6	5	.433	.399
Jace Jung	L-R	6-0	205	10-4-00	.231	.161	.260	30	108	16	25	6	1	1	13	25	0	0	1	28	1	0	.333	.373
Colt Keith	L-R	6-3	211	8-14-01	.301	.263	.310	48	193	38	58	14	3	9	31	22	0	0	1	42	4	0	.544	.370
Jose King	L-R	5-10	182	1-16-99	.244	.345	.226	59	193	19	47	10	2	4	27	8	3	2	4	54	2	3	.378	.279
Ryan Kreidler	R-R	6-4	208	11-12-97	.231	.500	.111	4	13	3	3	2	0	0	4	4	0	0	0	3	2	0	.385	.412
Ben Malgeri	R-R	6-1	215	1-12-00	.236	.146	.261	116	373	63	88	16	4	4	45	57	24	2	6	116	12	8	.332	.367
Parker Meadows	L-R	6-5	205	11-2-99	.230	.083	.265	14	61	16	14	4	1	4	7	4	1	1	0	18	0	0	.525	.288
Carlos Mendoza	L-R	5-7	165	12-14-99	.247	.235	.250	53	162	25	40	4	2	0	16	37	7	4	3	30	4	5	.296	.402
Chris Meyers	L-R	6-3	210	4-27-99	.256	.143	.292	23	86	14	22	3	1	2	8	8	1	0	0	28	0	1	.384	.326
Jimmy Mojica	R-R	6-0	175	5-4-00	.190	.333	.167	8	21	2	4	0	0	0	1	2	0	0	0	4	0	0	.190	.261
Austin Murr	L-L	6-2	218	1-26-99	.224	.254	.218	113	402	50	90	23	0	2	43	57	3	2	3	55	10	2	.296	.323
Andrew Navigato	R-R	5-11	188	5-28-98	.288	.250	.300	15	52	8	15	5	2	0	11	6	2	0	2	14	1	2	.462	.371
Izaac Pacheco	L-R	6-4	225	11-18-02	.183	.167	.190	18	60	9	11	2	0	3	13	9	0	0	4	17	0	1	.367	.274
Bryant Packard	L-R	6-3	200	10-6-97	.266	.162	.284	65	241	43	64	12	2	6	44	11	7	1	3	47	24	3	.407	.313
Wenceel Perez	B-R	5-11	203	10-30-99	.286	.319	.277	55	206	35	59	13	5	9	38	27	0	0	3	38	13	1	.529	.364
Jon Rosoff	L-R	5-9	175	11-14-94	.267	.000	.364	4	15	1	4	2	0	0	2	0	0	0	0	1	0	0	.400	.267
Mike Rothenberg	B-R	6-3	215	10-5-98	.184	.286	.167	14	49	2	9	2	0	1	4	3	0	0	0	18	0	0	.286	.231
Jonathan Schoop	R-R	6-1	247	10-16-91	.429	.000	.600	2	7	2	3	1	0	0	0	2	0	0	0	0	0	0	.571	.556
Austin Schultz	R-R	5-9	200	2-21-00	.048	.000	.071	7	21	3	1	0	0	0	1	5	0	0	0	12	1	0	.048	.231
Danny Serretti	B-R	6-1	195	5-7-00	.289	.300	.286	10	38	9	11	4	0	0	4	6	2	0	0	11	1	1	.395	.413
Eduardo Valencia	R-R	6-1	180	1-25-00	.200	.250	.167	10	30	7	6	0	0	2	4	4	1	0	0	8	0	0	.400	.314

Pitching	B-T	HT	WT	DOB	W	L	ERA	G	GS	CG	SV	IP	H	R	ER	HR	BB	SO	AVG	vLH	vRH	K/9	BB/9
Elvis Alvarado	R-R	6-4	183	2-23-99	3	1	1.86	23	0	0	7	29	25	8	6	1	7	32	.229	.192	.263	9.93	2.17
Jack Anderson	R-R	6-3	197	11-23-99	0	1	3.00	18	0	0	4	21	24	10	7	1	6	22	.282	.323	.259	9.43	2.57

Gio Arriera	R-R	6-2	236	6-7-98	8	1	4.79	35	0	0	0	41	33	22	22	5	31	38	.226	.246	.213	8.27	6.75
Michael Bienlien	R-R	6-3	246	3-19-98	1	2	6.63	15	0	0	0	19	26	16	14	4	15	24	.317	.375	.280	11.37	7.11
Cameron Brown	L-R	6-2	165	5-12-98	0	0	3.38	2	0	0	0	3	3	1	1	0	3	4	.273	.000	.300	13.50	10.13
Garrett Burhenn	R-R	6-3	215	9-12-99	0	1	7.43	4	3	0	0	13	21	12	11	2	7	9	.356	.400	.324	6.08	4.73
Chavez Fernander	R-R	6-3	205	7-7-97	2	3	4.03	26	0	0	1	29	23	15	13	0	13	28	.217	.114	.268	8.69	4.03
Wilmer Flores	R-R	6-4	225	2-20-01	1	0	1.83	6	5	0	0	20	14	5	4	2	2	35	.192	.222	.174	16.02	0.92
Dario Gardea	R-R	6-2	210	1-29-99	1	1	1.76	24	0	0	2	31	20	7	6	3	5	40	.179	.257	.143	11.74	1.47
Carlos Guzman	R-R	6-1	210	5-16-98	9	6	4.16	25	23	1	0	106	90	56	49	11	34	89	.233	.233	.233	7.56	2.89
Aaron Haase	R-R	5-8	193	5-24-00	0	0	18.00	1	0	0	0	1	1	2	2	0	2	1	.250	--	.250	9.00	18.00
Tim Holdgrafer	R-R	6-1	180	7-31-96	0	1	3.27	10	0	0	0	11	10	6	4	1	3	12	.238	.286	.214	9.82	2.45
Blake Holub	R-R	6-6	230	10-23-98	0	0	5.68	6	0	0	0	6	7	4	4	0	4	7	.304	.333	.286	9.95	5.68
Brant Hurter	L-L	6-6	250	9-6-98	4	1	3.20	11	10	0	0	51	44	19	18	2	11	62	.234	.217	.239	11.01	1.95
Carlos Irigoyen	R-R	6-2	165	3-21-01	0	0	13.50	1	0	0	0	1	1	1	1	1	1	0	.333	.000	.500	0.00	13.50
Jackson Jobe	R-R	6-2	190	7-30-02	2	0	1.15	3	3	0	0	16	10	5	2	2	5	10	.175	.320	.063	5.74	2.87
Ty Madden	R-R	6-3	215	2-21-00	6	4	3.10	19	19	0	0	87	69	33	30	10	26	84	.212	.177	.242	8.69	2.69
Andrew Magno	R-L	5-11	190	4-30-98	2	2	2.37	47	0	0	12	49	33	15	13	1	31	62	.190	.200	.183	11.31	5.66
Jordan Marks	L-R	6-2	220	4-29-99	0	4	5.98	11	8	0	1	41	41	30	27	10	6	38	.252	.276	.238	8.41	1.33
Trevin Michael	R-R	6-2	200	9-15-97	1	0	7.71	8	0	0	0	9	9	8	8	3	4	11	.265	.273	.261	10.61	3.86
Keider Montero	R-R	6-1	145	7-6-00	7	7	4.51	25	25	0	0	104	100	60	52	12	37	101	.253	.220	.278	8.77	3.21
Williander Moreno	R-R	6-0	160	3-13-99	0	0	4.91	5	0	0	0	7	10	4	4	2	2	5	.323	.267	.375	6.14	2.45
Hendry Nunez	R-R	6-4	180	7-22-99	1	1	5.01	26	0	0	0	32	22	21	18	4	22	29	.198	.257	.171	8.07	6.12
Jack O_Loughlin	L-L	6-5	223	3-14-00	2	1	4.01	27	6	0	0	52	43	29	23	4	27	50	.229	.186	.248	8.71	4.70
Carlos Pena	L-L	5-11	160	9-7-98	1	1	4.32	4	1	0	0	8	9	4	4	0	6	18	.257	.250	.261	19.44	6.48
RJ Petit	R-R	6-8	300	9-23-99	2	1	4.10	40	0	0	1	42	37	25	19	5	14	46	.226	.173	.250	9.94	3.02
Angel Reyes	R-R	6-2	205	10-17-97	0	1	5.82	19	0	0	1	22	20	15	14	3	9	14	.241	.219	.255	5.82	3.74
Gabriel Sequeira	L-L	6-0	200	8-18-97	5	3	3.12	46	0	0	2	49	44	22	17	4	26	55	.242	.205	.273	10.10	4.78
Andrew Shaps	L-L	6-1	185	12-5-95	0	0	5.40	16	0	0	0	17	13	11	10	0	19	15	.224	.143	.270	8.10	10.26
2-team total (3 Great Lakes Loons)					0	1	6.05	19	0	0	0	19	16	16	13	0	25	22	.229	.160	.267	10.24	11.64
Dylan Smith	R-R	6-2	180	5-28-00	8	6	4.00	20	19	0	0	83	78	42	37	6	21	86	.244	.237	.249	9.29	2.27
Ted Stuka	R-R	6-7	225	5-13-97	1	3	7.03	23	0	0	0	24	24	19	19	1	26	26	.267	.366	.184	9.62	9.62
Bryce Tassin	R-R	6-2	209	1-11-97	2	3	4.85	38	1	0	1	56	59	33	30	3	17	47	.267	.279	.259	7.60	2.75
Jared Tobey	R-L	6-4	225	3-11-96	1	2	4.38	30	0	0	2	25	23	14	12	6	20	30	.250	.261	.239	10.95	7.30
Matt Walker	L-L	6-3	217	6-15-98	2	2	4.40	11	6	0	0	31	33	15	15	3	13	33	.287	.242	.305	9.68	3.82
Joey Wentz	L-L	6-5	220	10-6-97	0	0	1.80	2	2	0	0	5	2	1	1	0	2	4	.125	.000	.154	7.20	3.60

Fielding

Catcher	PCT	G	PO	A	E	DP	PB
Alfonzo	.980	9	95	5	2	0	0
Barbary	.968	6	58	2	2	0	4
Crouch	.991	71	596	48	6	5	5
Garneau	1.000	2	19	0	0	0	1
Johnson	.995	22	165	18	1	2	3
Rosoff	1.000	4	41	1	0	1	1
Rothenberg	1.000	13	121	9	0	0	2
Valencia	1.000	6	65	0	0	1	1

First Base	PCT	G	PO	A	E	DP
Bigbie	1.000	6	39	5	0	3
Holton	.993	69	500	38	4	43
Meyers	1.000	21	179	11	0	14
Murr	.988	40	321	11	4	26
Valencia	1.000	1	2	0	0	1

Second Base	PCT	G	PO	A	E	DP
Cruz	.962	6	9	16	1	6
Irigoyen	1.000	6	4	9	0	1
Joyce	1.000	8	7	16	0	3
Jung	.992	27	41	76	1	13
Keith	.982	13	19	37	1	8
King	.971	20	28	40	2	13
Mendoza	1.000	23	40	45	0	15
Navigato	.857	2	4	2	1	0
Perez	.961	30	47	76	5	13
Schoop	1.000	1	1	3	0	0

Third Base	PCT	G	PO	A	E	DP
Cruz	.955	28	24	39	3	6
Irigoyen	1.000	7	4	5	0	0
Joyce	1.000	8	5	4	0	1
Keith	.929	27	19	33	4	3
King	.955	35	23	61	4	7
Mendoza	.943	11	8	25	2	2
Navigato	1.000	2	3	5	0	0
Pacheco	.921	15	12	23	3	3
Perez	.750	7	3	12	5	1

Shortstop	PCT	G	PO	A	E	DP
Cruz	.957	70	63	158	10	21
Irigoyen	.857	3	1	5	1	1
Joyce	.948	38	50	96	8	31
King	1.000	2	3	5	0	0
Kreidler	1.000	3	5	7	0	0
Navigato	.958	8	8	15	1	2
Pacheco	1.000	2	3	5	0	0
Serretti	.972	10	12	23	1	3

Outfield	PCT	G	PO	A	E	DP
Baddoo	1.000	2	3	0	0	0
Benitez	.875	11	14	0	2	0
Bojarski	1.000	29	30	2	0	0
Cabrera	.977	22	41	1	1	1
Chacon	.970	44	63	2	2	1
Holton	1.000	17	26	2	0	1
Irigoyen	1.000	2	6	0	0	0
King	1.000	3	4	0	0	0
Malgeri	.992	116	234	1	2	0
Meadows	1.000	13	23	0	0	0
Mendoza	1.000	18	27	3	0	0
Mojica	1.000	7	10	0	0	0
Murr	.971	76	129	3	4	0
Navigato	--	1	0	0	0	0
Packard	1.000	61	99	2	0	1
Schultz	1.000	7	7	0	0	0

LAKELAND FLYING TIGERS — *LOW CLASS A*

FLORIDA STATE LEAGUE

Batting	B-T	HT	WT	DOB	AVG	vLH	vRH	G	AB	R	H	2B	3B	HR	RBI	BB	HBP	SH	SF	SO	SB	CS	SLG	OBP
Eliezer Alfonzo	B-R	5-10	155	9-23-99	.185	.333	.143	7	27	3	5	1	0	0	0	1	0	0	0	6	0	0	.222	.214
Lazaro Benitez	R-R	5-9	190	10-15-99	.221	.333	.193	42	136	17	30	11	1	2	16	11	5	0	3	35	4	1	.360	.297
Justice Bigbie	R-R	6-2	200	1-24-99	.258	.268	.255	91	330	37	85	17	5	2	41	28	13	0	1	89	4	2	.358	.339
Roberto Campos	R-R	6-2	200	6-14-03	.258	.225	.266	112	403	52	104	26	5	5	50	40	2	0	3	97	7	3	.385	.326
Esney Chacon	R-R	6-1	160	3-17-00	.337	.333	.338	30	92	17	31	4	1	1	12	10	0	0	0	23	6	2	.435	.402
Josh Crouch	R-R	6-0	200	12-7-98	.333	.250	.357	11	36	7	12	3	0	0	5	5	1	0	1	10	0	0	.417	.419
Daneurys De La Cruz	R-R	5-10	160	4-27-01	.204	.229	.199	61	201	21	41	9	1	2	13	32	5	0	0	92	2	0	.289	.328
Jose De La Cruz	R-R	6-1	216	1-3-02	.202	.268	.187	92	307	31	62	10	1	10	42	29	8	0	1	132	3	3	.339	.287
Eric De La Rosa	R-R	6-3	186	6-3-97	.067	.250	.000	4	15	2	1	0	0	0	0	1	0	0	0	4	1	0	.067	.125
Manuel Garcia	R-R	5-11	170	1-28-00	.167	.200	.161	12	36	3	6	0	0	0	6	4	0	0	0	10	0	0	.167	.250
Luke Gold	R-R	6-0	220	10-10-00	.200	.125	.213	19	55	5	11	2	0	0	11	9	2	0	3	17	0	0	.236	.319

Alvaro Gonzalez	B-R	6-0	165	9-16-00	.187	.037	.229	43	123	17	23	7	0	3	17	15	5	0	1	43	0	1	.317	.299
Peyton Graham	R-R	6-3	185	1-26-01	.270	.353	.253	27	100	19	27	5	1	1	13	10	2	0	1	29	7	1	.370	.345
Riley Greene	L-L	6-3	200	9-28-00	.333	--	.333	2	6	0	2	0	0	0	2	1	0	0	0	0	1	1	.333	.429
Derek Hill	R-R	6-2	190	12-30-95	.000	.000	.000	3	9	2	0	0	0	0	0	2	1	0	0	3	1	0	.000	.250
Andrew Jenkins	R-R	6-0	217	11-3-00	.227	.222	.229	14	44	9	10	3	0	0	3	5	2	0	0	12	2	0	.295	.333
Dom Johnson	R-R	5-9	185	3-7-01	.273	.300	.261	10	33	8	9	1	0	2	6	2	1	0	1	10	4	0	.485	.324
Iverson Leonardo	L-L	6-0	173	8-21-01	.186	.000	.216	16	43	5	8	1	1	0	8	5	2	0	2	9	2	0	.256	.288
Kingston Liniak	R-R	6-2	200	11-11-99	.163	.286	.136	28	80	11	13	4	0	0	9	17	0	0	0	21	1	3	.213	.309
Carlos Mendoza	L-R	5-7	165	12-14-99	.288	.259	.294	46	146	34	42	8	1	2	18	41	2	0	0	28	8	3	.397	.450
Chris Meyers	L-R	6-3	210	4-27-99	.290	.091	.333	17	62	11	18	3	2	3	16	9	0	0	0	8	3	0	.548	.380
Izaac Pacheco	L-R	6-4	225	11-18-02	.267	.214	.281	88	330	54	88	21	2	8	39	38	1	0	2	80	12	4	.415	.342
Carlos Pelegrin	R-R	6-2	180	6-21-00	.286	.500	.200	3	7	0	2	0	0	0	0	2	0	0	0	3	1	0	.286	.444
Adinso Reyes	R-R	6-1	195	10-22-01	.187	.200	.185	22	75	11	14	1	0	4	4	8	0	0	0	35	0	0	.360	.265
Mike Rothenberg	B-R	6-3	215	10-5-98	.217	.196	.224	57	180	21	39	8	0	5	23	29	2	0	0	67	0	1	.344	.332
Alonzo Rubalcaba	R-R	6-0	210	2-22-00	.227	.200	.235	7	22	2	5	1	0	0	2	2	1	0	0	9	0	0	.273	.320
Cristian Santana	R-R	6-0	165	11-25-03	.215	.195	.219	80	265	52	57	13	0	9	30	54	18	0	3	88	10	5	.366	.379
Austin Schultz	R-R	5-9	200	2-21-00	.222	.250	.215	55	153	21	34	6	1	2	20	20	8	1	2	58	10	1	.314	.339
Manuel Sequera	R-R	6-1	170	9-28-02	.232	.256	.226	116	457	59	106	28	1	19	64	20	11	0	3	110	4	5	.422	.279
Danny Serretti	B-R	6-1	195	5-7-00	.375	.571	.320	11	32	11	12	4	0	2	7	14	0	0	0	6	4	1	.688	.565
Seth Stephenson	R-R	5-9	165	1-10-01	.233	1.000	.179	10	30	5	7	0	0	0	1	1	2	0	0	8	9	0	.233	.303
Eduardo Valencia	R-R	6-1	180	1-25-00	.243	.381	.220	45	144	17	35	7	0	4	20	17	1	1	1	30	1	0	.375	.325
Frank Veliz	R-R	5-11	160	9-10-99	.208	.333	.158	17	53	6	11	3	1	1	3	5	1	1	0	21	0	0	.358	.288

Pitching	B-T	HT	WT	DOB	W	L	ERA	G	GS	CG	SV	IP	H	R	ER	HR	BB	SO	AVG	vLH	vRH	K/9	BB/9
Elvis Alvarado	R-R	6-4	183	2-23-99	0	1	2.25	6	0	0	1	8	7	2	2	0	4	8	.226	.100	.286	9.00	4.50
Jack Anderson	R-R	6-3	197	11-23-99	3	3	3.72	21	0	0	2	39	33	18	16	3	8	50	.229	.224	.232	11.64	1.86
Kris Anglin	L-L	5-11	175	8-9-01	0	1	10.38	2	2	0	0	4	5	5	5	1	4	5	.278	.500	.167	10.38	8.31
Michael Bienlien	R-R	6-3	246	3-19-98	2	1	2.86	20	0	0	2	35	30	13	11	3	15	35	.226	.226	.225	9.09	3.89
Cameron Brown	L-R	6-2	165	5-12-98	3	2	0.55	20	0	0	3	33	25	9	2	0	15	31	.203	.263	.176	8.54	4.13
Garrett Burhenn	R-R	6-3	215	9-12-99	4	5	3.43	18	17	1	0	79	74	37	30	12	19	103	.243	.264	.230	11.78	2.17
Ulices Campos	R-R	5-10	170	12-14-01	1	0	3.18	3	1	0	0	11	7	5	4	3	7	10	.175	.176	.174	7.94	5.56
Andrew Chafin	R-L	6-2	235	6-17-90	0	0	0.00	1	1	0	0	1	1	0	0	0	0	0	.333	.500	.000	0.00	0.00
Jose Cisnero	R-R	6-3	258	4-11-89	0	1	40.50	1	0	0	0	1	3	4	3	0	2	0	.750	1.000	.667	0.00	27.00
Nick Davila	R-R	6-3	202	11-21-98	3	5	3.65	13	11	0	0	57	65	35	23	7	13	53	.278	.293	.270	8.42	2.06
Jack Dellinger	R-R	6-4	210	2-12-98	0	0	27.00	1	0	0	0	1	2	4	3	0	1	0	.400	.500	.000	0.00	9.00
Bubba Derby	L-R	5-11	185	2-24-94	1	0	0.00	2	0	0	0	3	2	0	0	0	0	3	.182	.400	.000	9.00	0.00
Jose Diaz	R-R	6-5	200	5-12-00	2	0	0.00	4	0	0	1	6	3	0	0	0	3	11	.136	.000	.176	15.63	4.26
Alex Faedo	R-R	6-5	225	11-12-95	1	1	2.53	3	1	0	0	11	6	3	3	0	3	12	.162	.154	.167	10.13	2.53
Wilmer Fenelon	R-R	6-3	170	10-18-00	0	0	9.00	5	0	0	0	4	9	7	4	1	5	6	.409	.333	.438	13.50	11.25
Aaron Haase	R-R	5-8	193	5-24-00	2	1	2.65	26	0	0	5	34	27	14	10	6	14	51	.214	.267	.185	13.50	3.71
Wilkel Hernandez	R-R	6-3	195	4-13-99	3	5	4.50	14	13	0	0	44	48	27	22	4	16	51	.279	.306	.264	10.43	3.27
J.T. Hintzen	R-R	6-0	185	6-1-96	1	1	5.19	3	1	0	0	9	10	5	5	0	6	8	.286	.158	.438	8.31	6.23
Tim Holdgrafer	R-R	6-1	180	7-31-96	0	0	0.00	3	0	0	1	5	0	0	0	0	1	5	.000	.000	.000	9.00	1.80
Blake Holub	R-R	6-6	230	10-23-98	2	1	6.31	26	4	0	6	46	44	34	32	5	27	61	.249	.261	.241	12.02	5.32
Brant Hurter	L-L	6-6	250	9-6-98	3	3	2.98	10	6	0	0	42	34	16	14	4	6	57	.213	.200	.214	12.12	1.28
Edgardo Ibarra	L-L	6-0	160	6-2-03	0	0	12.27	2	0	0	0	4	6	5	5	1	1	5	.375	.400	.364	12.27	2.45
Francisco Jimenez	R-R	6-2	194	3-23-99	0	2	10.80	4	0	0	0	5	5	7	6	1	4	8	.263	.111	.400	14.40	7.20
Marco Jimenez	R-R	5-11	239	12-6-99	1	1	7.23	9	6	0	0	24	28	20	19	2	18	31	.280	.262	.293	11.79	6.85
Jackson Jobe	R-R	6-2	190	7-30-02	2	5	4.52	18	18	0	0	62	59	41	31	12	25	71	.251	.260	.244	10.36	3.65
Billy Lescher	R-R	6-4	215	9-17-95	1	0	4.32	9	1	0	0	8	8	4	4	0	3	12	.258	.273	.250	12.96	3.24
Matt Manning	R-R	6-6	195	1-28-98	0	0	0.00	1	1	0	0	2	1	0	0	0	1	0	.167	.000	.200	0.00	4.50
Carlos Marcano	R-R	6-2	150	7-8-03	3	3	4.68	29	0	0	2	42	47	31	22	2	18	41	.275	.455	.190	8.72	3.83
Jordan Marks	L-R	6-2	220	4-29-99	0	1	6.35	7	4	0	0	17	21	12	12	2	8	16	.300	.400	.225	8.47	4.24
Tyler Mattison	R-R	6-4	235	9-5-99	7	0	5.23	24	0	0	1	33	25	21	19	2	17	46	.210	.268	.179	12.67	4.68
Troy Melton	R-R	6-4	210	12-3-00	0	0	0.00	2	2	0	0	5	3	0	0	0	0	5	.188	.200	.167	9.00	0.00
Trevin Michael	R-R	6-2	200	9-15-97	0	0	0.00	1	0	0	0	2	1	0	0	0	0	4	.167	.500	.000	18.00	0.00
Jake Miller	L-L	6-2	185	6-27-01	0	3	8.59	5	5	0	0	15	23	14	14	5	3	21	.348	.278	.375	12.89	1.84
Joe Miller	L-L	5-10	195	3-13-00	0	0	6.10	4	4	0	0	10	13	9	7	1	6	12	.289	.286	.289	10.45	5.23
Williander Moreno	R-R	6-0	160	3-13-99	4	4	2.98	25	6	0	4	63	66	25	21	4	14	65	.261	.258	.263	9.24	1.99
Hendry Nunez	R-R	6-4	180	7-22-99	0	0	1.86	7	0	0	0	10	6	2	2	0	8	10	.188	.273	.143	9.31	7.45
Carlos Pena	L-L	5-11	160	9-7-98	4	4	3.87	19	15	0	0	86	68	41	37	7	32	99	.216	.145	.241	10.36	3.35
Wily Peralta	R-R	6-1	255	5-8-89	0	0	0.00	1	1	0	0	2	1	0	0	0	0	2	.167	.000	.333	9.00	0.00
RJ Petit	R-R	6-8	300	9-23-99	1	0	2.19	9	0	0	4	12	9	3	3	1	4	16	.205	.286	.167	11.68	2.92
Erick Pinales	R-R	6-2	185	1-27-99	4	2	3.14	34	0	0	3	43	29	18	15	1	44	62	.193	.163	.208	12.98	9.21
Patrick Pridgen	R-R	6-4	220	3-26-99	0	0	24.30	4	0	0	1	3	9	9	9	1	3	8	.474	.500	.462	21.60	8.10
Angel Reyes	R-R	6-2	205	10-17-97	3	1	2.45	11	3	0	0	26	16	9	7	1	13	22	.178	.259	.143	7.71	4.56
Paul Richan	R-R	6-2	200	3-26-97	0	1	1.50	3	3	0	0	6	3	1	1	0	2	6	.150	.125	.167	9.00	3.00
Eduardo Rodriguez	L-L	6-2	231	4-7-93	0	0	3.00	1	1	0	0	3	3	1	1	0	1	5	.231	.333	.200	15.00	3.00
Erick Rodriguez	R-R	5-10	185	3-21-02	1	4	4.80	32	0	0	4	45	46	29	24	8	15	47	.257	.250	.261	9.40	3.00
Andy Santana	R-R	6-3	190	10-27-99	0	0	6.43	10	0	0	0	14	19	13	10	3	10	11	.328	.273	.361	7.07	6.43
Dylan Smith	R-R	6-2	180	5-28-00	0	0	0.00	2	2	0	0	5	3	0	0	0	0	3	.167	.167	.167	5.40	0.00
Ted Stuka	R-R	6-7	225	5-13-97	0	0	24.30	3	0	0	0	3	4	10	9	0	8	4	.308	.750	.111	10.80	21.60
Cristhian Tortosa	L-L	6-4	170	10-30-98	3	2	5.76	22	0	0	1	30	25	25	19	4	21	46	.221	.192	.230	13.96	6.37
Matt Walker	L-L	6-3	217	6-15-98	1	0	3.52	14	1	0	0	23	20	12	9	1	12	20	.238	.308	.225	7.83	4.70

Fielding

Catcher	PCT	G	PO	A	E	DP	PB
Alfonzo	.979	5	42	4	1	0	0
Crouch	1.000	9	83	16	0	1	2
De La Cruz	.975	32	290	16	8	1	8
Garcia	.948	11	86	6	5	0	2
Rothenberg	.993	41	413	35	3	4	4
Rubalcaba	1.000	7	73	3	0	0	2
Valencia	.972	27	261	20	8	1	1

First Base	PCT	G	PO	A	E	DP
Bigbie	.993	58	390	25	3	34
De La Cruz	.980	14	91	5	2	8
Gonzalez	1.000	1	3	0	0	0
Jenkins	.981	14	99	3	2	11
Meyers	.984	15	124	3	2	7
Rothenberg	.986	12	67	6	1	2
Valencia	1.000	16	106	3	0	10

Second Base	PCT	G	PO	A	E	DP
Gold	1.000	8	7	16	0	4
Gonzalez	.952	39	72	68	7	15
Graham	1.000	5	6	16	0	2
Mendoza	.923	13	25	23	4	6
Santana	.961	29	55	69	5	19
Sequera	.940	21	33	45	5	5
Serretti	.957	4	12	10	1	3
Veliz	.957	14	29	16	2	6

Third Base	PCT	G	PO	A	E	DP
Gold	.867	7	2	11	2	0
Gonzalez	.000	1	0	0	1	0
Graham	.600	2	1	2	2	0
Mendoza	.972	18	6	29	1	1
Pacheco	.947	63	43	135	10	11
Reyes	.897	21	8	44	6	7
Santana	.839	11	9	17	5	2
Sequera	.727	6	3	5	3	0
Serretti	1.000	1	1	1	0	1
Veliz	.800	3	0	4	1	0

Shortstop	PCT	G	PO	A	E	DP
Graham	.922	14	19	40	5	9
Pacheco	.879	18	15	43	8	3
Reyes	1.000	1	1	2	0	0
Santana	.923	34	31	65	8	8
Sequera	.916	60	62	123	17	22
Serretti	.909	5	1	9	1	1

Outfield	PCT	G	PO	A	E	DP
Benitez	.912	40	51	1	5	0
Bigbie	.864	14	19	0	3	0
Campos	.987	103	150	6	2	2
Chacon	.962	31	48	3	2	1
De La Cruz	.953	76	116	6	6	1
De La Rosa	1.000	2	3	1	0	0
Greene	1.000	1	1	0	0	0
Hill	1.000	2	4	0	0	0
Johnson	1.000	10	16	0	0	0
Leonardo	.875	18	21	0	3	0
Liniak	1.000	29	54	1	0	0
Mendoza	.933	15	27	1	2	0
Pelegrin	1.000	3	6	0	0	0
Schultz	.964	56	76	5	3	0
Stephenson	1.000	10	18	1	0	0

FCL TIGERS

ROOKIE

FLORIDA COMPLEX LEAGUE

Batting	B-T	HT	WT	DOB	AVG	vLH	vRH	G	AB	R	H	2B	3B	HR	RBI	BB	HBP	SH	SF	SO	SB	CS	SLG	OBP
Yoneiry Acevedo	B-R	5-10	150	12-4-00	.194	.167	.200	27	62	14	12	1	0	0	3	10	1	0	0	23	5	0	.210	.315
Eliezer Alfonzo	B-R	5-10	155	9-23-99	.500	--	.500	2	6	3	3	0	0	0	0	2	0	0	0	0	0	0	.500	.625
Abel Bastidas	B-R	6-2	165	11-24-03	.260	.167	.277	44	154	18	40	10	2	3	26	24	1	0	1	33	4	6	.409	.361
Lazaro Benitez	R-R	5-9	190	10-15-99	.333	.000	.412	6	21	2	7	3	1	0	7	0	1	0	0	4	0	1	.571	.364
Jesus Bolivar	R-R	6-0	165	3-23-02	.169	.118	.182	29	83	8	14	4	0	0	5	5	3	0	1	30	2	2	.217	.239
Colin Burgess	R-R	5-8	195	11-10-00	.333	.667	.167	3	9	0	3	1	0	0	3	2	0	0	0	2	0	0	.444	.455
Cesar Calderon	R-R	6-2	170	11-1-01	.183	.222	.176	22	60	11	11	3	0	3	7	8	1	0	0	21	3	0	.383	.290
Clayton Campbell	R-R	6-0	209	9-11-03	.149	.125	.153	37	101	10	15	5	0	1	9	21	5	0	2	33	0	2	.228	.318
Daneurys De La Cruz	R-R	5-10	160	4-27-01	.211	.200	.214	7	19	1	4	2	0	0	5	0	1	0	1	7	0	0	.316	.238
Jose De La Cruz	R-R	6-1	216	1-3-02	.238	.333	.222	6	21	5	5	2	0	1	3	1	1	0	0	11	1	0	.476	.304
Michael De La Cruz	B-R	5-10	190	5-15-93	.333	.000	.389	6	21	5	7	2	1	1	6	3	0	0	0	4	1	0	.667	.417
Raudy De Los Santos	R-R	5-11	155	3-18-03	.198	.286	.180	33	121	16	24	4	2	0	4	9	1	0	0	25	7	1	.264	.260
Adonis Figuereo	L-L	6-2	206	5-5-01	.120	.000	.136	22	50	5	6	2	0	3	9	10	2	0	0	23	0	2	.340	.290
Manuel Garcia	R-R	5-11	170	1-28-00	.254	.250	.255	23	59	10	15	5	0	1	5	10	8	0	0	10	2	3	.390	.429
Luke Gold	R-R	6-0	220	10-10-00	.200	.333	.143	3	10	0	2	0	0	0	0	1	1	0	0	2	0	0	.200	.333
Alvaro Gonzalez	B-R	6-0	165	9-16-00	.174	.333	.150	8	23	4	4	3	0	0	1	5	1	0	0	10	0	0	.304	.345
Carlos Irigoyen	R-R	6-2	165	3-21-01	.139	.000	.161	11	36	3	5	1	1	0	4	0	2	0	0	17	2	0	.222	.184
Andrew Jenkins	R-R	6-0	217	11-3-00	.250	.000	.320	9	32	3	8	2	1	0	3	5	3	0	0	6	0	0	.375	.400
Dom Johnson	R-R	5-9	185	3-7-01	.045	.200	.000	5	22	1	1	0	0	0	0	1	1	0	0	8	0	0	.045	.125
Tyler Johnson	L-L	6-1	220	10-25-99	.200	.500	.125	4	10	0	2	0	0	0	0	4	1	0	0	8	0	0	.200	.467
Iverson Leonardo	L-L	6-0	173	8-21-01	.248	.267	.245	31	109	15	27	6	0	5	17	11	1	0	1	28	4	2	.440	.320
Kingston Liniak	R-R	6-2	200	11-11-99	.296	.600	.227	9	27	6	8	2	0	2	2	4	0	0	0	5	0	0	.593	.387
J.D. McLaughlin	R-R	6-3	195	12-28-00	.273	.167	.289	14	44	6	12	2	0	1	9	3	1	0	1	12	4	1	.386	.327
Chris Meyers	L-R	6-3	210	4-27-99	.286	1.000	.231	4	14	2	4	0	0	1	1	0	1	0	0	2	0	0	.500	.333
Jimmy Mojica	R-R	6-0	175	5-4-00	.280	.400	.250	21	50	9	14	1	0	1	3	7	2	0	0	18	2	0	.360	.390
Carlos Pelegrin	R-R	6-2	180	6-21-00	.236	.200	.240	36	110	17	26	4	1	2	9	15	1	0	0	35	3	1	.345	.333
Jose Reina	R-R	6-2	160	2-28-01	.252	.400	.226	42	135	21	34	11	0	1	19	15	3	1	1	41	8	2	.356	.338
Adinso Reyes	R-R	6-1	195	10-22-01	.333	.217	.362	32	117	19	39	6	0	5	21	12	1	0	2	32	1	3	.513	.394
Cristian Santana	R-R	6-0	165	11-25-03	.200	--	.200	2	5	3	1	0	0	1	2	4	0	0	0	3	0	1	.800	.556
Sergio Tapia	R-R	5-10	160	8-24-02	.288	.308	.283	23	66	12	19	5	1	1	12	10	0	0	2	10	2	1	.439	.372
Moises Valero	R-R	6-2	185	3-1-02	.286	.095	.330	37	112	18	32	5	1	2	11	12	2	0	0	35	4	3	.402	.365
Frank Veliz	R-R	5-11	160	9-10-99	.189	.000	.226	15	37	4	7	0	0	1	4	5	1	0	0	11	0	0	.270	.302

Pitching	B-T	HT	WT	DOB	W	L	ERA	G	GS	CG	SV	IP	H	R	ER	HR	BB	SO	AVG	vLH	vRH	K/9	BB/9
Max Alba	R-R	6-5	215	7-15-99	0	0	10.80	2	0	0	0	2	2	2	2	0	2	3	.286	.500	.000	16.20	10.80
Kris Anglin	L-L	5-11	175	8-9-01	0	0	9.00	1	1	0	0	1	2	1	1	0	1	0	.400	.500	.333	0.00	9.00
2-team total (5 FCL Braves)					1	1	3.13	6	5	0	0	23	23	11	8	3	8	20	.258	.212	.286	7.83	3.13
Joel Baez	R-R	6-4	185	8-19-02	0	2	13.22	15	1	0	0	16	22	27	24	2	17	11	.306	.345	.279	6.06	9.37
Adolfo Bauza	R-R	6-2	160	9-27-00	1	1	7.07	7	1	0	0	14	10	12	11	0	14	6	.204	.133	.235	3.86	9.00
Luis Bellorin	R-R	5-11	170	7-26-00	0	1	6.48	16	0	0	1	17	18	13	12	0	19	11	.290	.308	.278	5.94	10.26
Ulices Campos	R-R	5-10	170	12-14-01	0	1	2.84	11	9	0	0	38	27	14	12	3	14	40	.197	.255	.163	9.47	3.32
Rayner Castillo	R-R	6-3	180	6-30-04	1	5	8.02	11	10	0	0	43	56	38	38	8	18	34	.320	.338	.305	7.17	3.80
Jesus Cruz	R-R	6-4	185	10-8-00	1	2	8.39	11	1	0	0	25	17	24	23	3	22	27	.193	.162	.216	9.85	8.03
Jack Dellinger	R-R	6-4	210	2-12-98	2	1	1.76	13	0	0	1	15	8	6	3	0	13	12	.148	.227	.094	7.04	7.63
Bubba Derby	L-R	5-11	185	2-24-94	1	0	3.86	2	0	0	0	2	2	1	1	0	1	1	.222	.333	.167	3.86	3.86
Daniele Di Monte	R-R	6-2	187	2-16-02	2	3	8.85	10	3	0	0	20	16	24	20	0	25	10	.222	.226	.220	4.43	11.07
Jose Diaz	R-R	6-5	200	5-12-00	2	1	3.00	17	0	0	1	24	13	10	8	3	15	34	.160	.310	.077	12.75	5.63

Wilmer Fenelon	R-R	6-3	170	10-18-00	0	0	15.00	5	0	0	0	3	2	6	5	1	4	5	.154	.200	.125	15.00	12.00
Wilmer A. Fenelon	R-R	6-3	175	6-12-03	4	3	6.89	14	0	0	1	16	20	18	12	0	19	19	.308	.370	.263	10.91	10.91
Quinn Gudaitis	R-R	6-7	225	4-10-99	0	0	9.00	2	0	0	0	2	2	2	2	0	2	1	.250	.000	.333	4.50	9.00
Martin Herrera	L-R	6-0	175	9-22-00	1	1	5.52	15	0	0	0	15	16	10	9	1	9	13	.291	.211	.333	7.98	5.52
Connor Holden	R-R	6-5	240	6-25-98	0	0	9.00	2	0	0	0	2	2	2	2	1	2	1	.286	.200	.500	4.50	9.00
Edgardo Ibarra	L-L	6-0	160	6-2-03	1	2	2.65	11	4	0	1	37	26	14	11	3	20	36	.205	.234	.188	8.68	4.82
Francisco Jimenez	R-R	6-2	194	3-23-99	0	0	5.56	16	0	0	1	23	21	15	14	5	8	27	.241	.147	.302	10.72	3.18
Marco Jimenez	R-R	5-11	239	12-6-99	0	1	4.63	4	4	0	0	12	11	7	6	2	7	15	.256	.350	.174	11.57	5.40
Jordan Marks	L-R	6-2	220	4-29-99	0	0	4.50	1	1	0	0	2	1	1	1	1	0	2	.143	.000	.250	9.00	0.00
Jack Masloff	L-L	6-2	185	6-9-00	0	0	0.00	2	0	0	0	2	0	0	0	0	0	3	.000	--	.000	13.50	0.00
Tyler Mattison	R-R	6-4	235	9-5-99	0	1	1.29	3	1	0	1	7	4	1	1	0	2	8	.167	.182	.154	10.29	2.57
Trevin Michael	R-R	6-2	200	9-15-97	0	0	0.00	1	0	0	0	1	1	1	0	0	0	2	.333	--	.333	18.00	0.00
Joe Miller	L-L	5-10	195	3-13-00	0	0	0.00	1	0	0	0	2	0	0	0	0	0	0	.000	.000	.000	0.00	0.00
Albert Oliva	R-R	6-2	194	10-18-02	0	0	6.75	2	0	0	0	3	3	2	2	0	3	4	.273	.143	.500	13.50	10.13
Martin Olivas	R-R	6-1	170	7-25-01	0	1	6.75	6	0	0	0	5	10	5	4	0	4	3	.417	.556	.333	5.06	6.75
Cole Patten	R-R	6-4	194	8-5-99	0	0	33.75	1	1	0	0	1	5	5	5	1	1	3	.556	.500	.571	20.25	6.75
Jose Peraza	R-R	5-11	160	10-29-01	0	0	15.19	5	0	0	0	5	6	10	9	0	10	3	.261	.375	.200	5.06	16.88
Cleiverth Perez	L-L	6-0	211	2-5-00	2	1	6.27	14	2	0	1	19	20	16	13	1	6	16	.260	.323	.217	7.71	2.89
Franklin Perez	R-R	6-3	197	12-6-97	0	4	9.59	10	10	0	0	25	26	29	27	4	29	18	.289	.293	.286	6.39	10.30
Patrick Pridgen	R-R	6-4	220	3-26-99	0	0	0.00	2	0	0	0	2	1	0	0	0	1	2	.143	.000	.200	9.00	4.50
Gabriel Reyes	L-L	6-1	170	7-1-03	0	5	5.29	10	6	0	0	32	37	20	19	2	9	29	.282	.275	.288	8.07	2.51
Andy Santana	R-R	6-3	190	10-27-99	0	0	2.89	16	0	0	2	19	19	8	6	1	10	14	.260	.214	.289	6.75	4.82
Cristhian Tortosa	L-L	6-4	170	10-30-98	0	0	3.52	7	0	0	1	8	3	4	3	1	4	15	.111	.222	.056	17.61	4.70
Chris Williams Jr.	L-L	6-2	205	3-3-00	0	1	16.20	2	0	0	0	2	4	4	3	0	2	2	.444	.250	.600	10.80	10.80

Fielding

C: Alfonzo 2, Burgess 3, Campbell 9, De La Cruz 7, De La Cruz 1, Garcia 20, Tapia 16, Valero 11. **1B:** Calderon 12, Campbell 15, Garcia 3, Jenkins 7, Johnson 2, Meyers 3, Olivas 1, Valero 21. **2B:** Acevedo 20, Bastidas 11, De Los Santos 14, Gold 1, Gonzalez 8, Santana 1, Veliz 10. **3B:** Bastidas 6, Calderon 6, Campbell 13, De Los Santos 5, Gold 2, Irigoyen 8, Olivas 1, Reyes 15, Veliz 6. **SS:** Acevedo 4, Bastidas 25, Calderon 1, De Los Santos 16, Irigoyen 3, Reyes 11, Santana 1. **OF:** Benitez 4, Bolivar 28, De La Cruz 5, De Los Santos 1, Figuereo 16, Johnson 4, Leonardo 24, Liniak 6, McLaughlin 13, Mojica 19, Pelegrin 33, Reina 40.

DSL TIGERS 1 — *ROOKIE*

DOMINICAN SUMMER LEAGUE

Batting	B-T	HT	WT	DOB	AVG	vLH	vRH	G	AB	R	H	2B	3B	HR	RBI	BB	HBP	SH	SF	SO	SB	CS	SLG	OBP
Sebastian Bautista	R-R	6-3	190	5-17-03	.266	.111	.291	24	64	11	17	6	0	0	7	13	3	0	2	26	1	2	.359	.402
Yoan Bravo	R-R	6-1	165	10-14-01	.204	.333	.182	45	103	17	21	3	0	1	10	18	3	0	0	26	4	2	.262	.339
Josue Briceno	L-R	6-4	200	9-23-04	.280	.273	.281	30	100	12	28	4	0	3	10	11	1	0	1	22	1	2	.410	.354
2-team total (14 DSL Tigers 2)					.234	.200	.238	44	145	15	34	8	0	4	16	13	1	0	2	37	1	2	.372	.298
Jose Cardozo	R-R	5-10	150	9-18-03	.146	.333	.094	21	41	6	6	1	0	1	5	5	5	0	0	17	3	0	.244	.314
2-team total (3 DSL Tigers 2)					.163	.300	.128	24	49	7	8	1	0	1	5	5	7	0	0	19	3	0	.245	.328
Jensy De Leon	R-R	6-0	175	5-14-04	.178	.100	.194	43	118	12	21	8	0	1	11	8	10	0	0	30	5	2	.271	.287
Yimmy Diaz	B-R	5-10	155	2-19-04	.272	.348	.259	49	162	30	44	6	1	3	20	27	4	0	1	30	7	6	.377	.387
Antonio Dominguez	R-R	5-9	150	4-25-01	.283	.357	.269	26	92	16	26	9	1	2	18	4	4	0	1	18	2	0	.467	.337
Geury Estevez	B-R	6-0	180	2-20-02	.333	.500	.250	2	6	2	2	0	0	0	0	0	0	0	0	0	0	0	.333	.333
2-team total (33 DSL Tigers 2)					.258	.357	.241	35	97	21	25	1	1	0	18	12	3	0	0	18	3	0	.289	.357
Nomar Fana	B-R	5-11	175	9-28-02	.257	.273	.252	50	140	25	36	11	1	3	16	25	1	0	1	49	8	5	.414	.371
Samuel Gil	R-R	5-9	165	11-1-04	.333	.000	.400	3	12	1	4	1	1	0	3	0	0	0	0	3	0	1	.583	.333
2-team total (47 DSL Tigers 2)					.260	.176	.280	50	177	33	46	11	3	2	29	25	3	0	0	36	7	1	.390	.361
Ricardo Hurtado	R-R	5-10	180	5-23-03	.000	--	.000	2	4	0	0	0	0	0	0	0	1	0	0	0	0	0	.000	.200
2-team total (33 DSL Tigers 2)					.198	.143	.203	35	81	10	16	7	0	0	8	21	12	0	0	12	2	1	.284	.430
Andri Leon	L-L	6-0	150	2-28-03	.235	.500	.200	5	17	1	4	0	1	0	3	0	1	0	1	3	1	0	.353	.263
2-team total (50 DSL Tigers 2)					.283	.346	.272	55	173	31	49	11	2	2	30	12	9	0	4	46	6	6	.405	.354
Abelaldo Lopez	R-R	6-1	160	9-5-02	.173	.167	.174	37	110	18	19	2	0	4	12	15	4	0	1	60	5	2	.300	.292
Delvis Matos	R-R	5-11	165	11-9-04	.120	.111	.122	37	100	9	12	4	0	0	6	5	4	0	0	44	1	2	.160	.193
Franyerber Montilla	B-R	6-0	160	4-15-05	.210	.222	.207	54	176	29	37	8	4	3	21	38	1	0	1	62	11	6	.352	.352
Jose Ochoa	R-R	5-9	162	7-25-03	.238	.227	.240	46	126	21	30	6	3	0	10	13	6	0	0	38	6	5	.333	.338
Javier Osorio	R-R	6-0	165	3-29-05	.175	.148	.181	46	154	17	27	5	0	1	12	16	7	0	1	68	15	3	.227	.281
Reylin Perez	B-R	5-11	160	10-5-04	.333	1.000	.000	3	3	2	1	1	0	0	2	2	0	0	0	1	0	0	.667	.600
2-team total (47 DSL Tigers 2)					.306	.250	.315	50	147	42	45	15	3	7	32	38	3	0	0	54	7	3	.592	.457
Junior Quezada	R-R	6-0	165	2-3-05	.125	.000	.167	5	16	2	2	0	0	0	1	1	0	0	0	7	1	1	.125	.176
2-team total (36 DSL Tigers 2)					.264	.211	.275	41	121	16	32	1	2	0	18	16	3	0	1	27	6	3	.306	.362
Fraudy Rodriguez	R-R	5-9	163	9-8-01	.105	.000	.111	10	19	2	2	2	0	0	1	1	2	0	0	11	0	0	.211	.227
2-team total (2 DSL Tigers 2)					.125	.000	.130	12	24	6	3	2	0	1	4	5	2	0	0	12	0	0	.333	.323
Justin Rodriguez	R-R	5-10	155	3-11-04	.421	.250	.467	5	19	3	8	4	0	0	3	0	0	0	0	9	0	0	.632	.421
2-team total (43 DSL Tigers 2)					.262	.296	.255	48	168	31	44	15	3	2	22	16	5	0	1	66	5	1	.423	.342
Samuel Rojas	R-R	5-10	190	11-6-02	.248	.333	.225	34	101	11	25	10	0	1	11	10	6	0	2	24	0	1	.376	.345
2-team total (3 DSL Tigers 2)					.255	.333	.233	37	110	11	28	10	0	1	12	10	6	0	2	28	0	1	.373	.344
Heison Sanchez	L-R	6-0	170	9-6-04	.200	.000	.231	6	15	3	3	2	0	0	1	9	0	0	0	4	1	2	.333	.500
2-team total (40 DSL Tigers 2)					.234	.100	.256	46	145	26	34	9	2	2	15	26	8	0	0	46	4	3	.366	.380
Manuel Santana	R-R	6-0	175	10-30-04	.161	.083	.182	20	56	4	9	2	0	1	6	7	2	0	0	32	0	0	.250	.277

Pitching	B-T	HT	WT	DOB	W	L	ERA	G	GS	CG	SV	IP	H	R	ER	HR	BB	SO	AVG	vLH	vRH	K/9	BB/9
Jorge Boyer	L-L	6-4	182	4-15-03	0	0	--	1	0	0	0	0	0	3	1	0	2	0	--	--	--	--	--
2-team total (18 DSL Tigers 2)					1	3	7.11	19	0	0	1	19	14	25	15	1	24	29	.203	.222	.200	13.74	11.37

DETROIT TIGERS

Jaison Brete	R-R	6-1	160	4-27-01	1	2	3.62	19	2	0	1	37	37	25	15	2	16	43	.253	.245	.258	10.37	3.86
Ignacio Briceno	L-L	5-11	155	6-4-01	0	0	0.00	1	0	0	0	2	4	0	0	0	0	0	.571	1.000	.500	0.00	0.00
2-team total (16 DSL Tigers 2)					6	1	1.59	17	0	0	3	28	21	9	5	0	6	30	.210	.214	.209	9.53	1.91
Luis Camilo	L-L	5-9	178	7-22-02	1	2	5.52	12	0	0	1	15	10	11	9	1	19	16	.189	.500	.116	9.82	11.66
Ronny Chalas	R-R	5-10	162	8-19-02	2	2	2.20	22	0	0	7	33	24	10	8	1	13	35	.209	.275	.173	9.64	3.58
Eddy Felix	R-R	6-2	180	8-23-03	1	0	1.93	8	1	0	1	14	8	3	3	1	4	19	.167	.083	.194	12.21	2.57
Antonio Florido	R-R	6-1	175	2-15-05	3	3	9.00	13	6	0	0	21	32	24	21	3	18	14	.352	.258	.400	6.00	7.71
Pedro Garcia	R-R	6-1	190	2-27-02	0	0	0.00	1	0	0	0	3	2	0	0	0	1	0	.222	--	.222	0.00	3.00
2-team total (12 DSL Tigers 2)					4	2	3.16	13	10	0	0	51	36	18	18	3	11	46	.195	.106	.190	0.06	1.93
Xiomer Guacache	R-R	6-3	195	2-11-04	0	2	8.76	4	3	0	0	12	19	14	12	2	9	6	.345	.412	.316	4.38	6.57
2-team total (7 DSL Tigers 2)					1	4	8.88	11	3	0	0	25	37	28	25	4	15	22	.349	.333	.356	7.82	5.33
Eiker Huizi	R-R	6-0	155	9-24-00	1	3	6.75	18	1	0	0	28	32	23	21	3	20	28	.311	.389	.269	9.00	6.43
Luis Lopez	R-R	5-11	170	12-1-00	0	0	0.00	1	0	0	0	1	0	0	0	0	0	0	.000	.000	.000	0.00	0.00
2-team total (4 DSL Tigers 2)					0	0	7.04	5	0	0	0	8	8	7	6	1	5	4	.276	.250	.294	4.70	5.87
Jaime Marin	R-R	5-11	165	12-25-00	4	1	3.98	18	0	0	0	32	32	18	14	0	9	46	.262	.209	.291	13.07	2.56
2-team total (2 DSL Tigers 2)					5	1	3.74	20	0	0	1	34	34	18	14	0	10	46	.264	.208	.296	12.30	2.67
Anderson Melendez	R-R	6-1	170	10-12-02	0	0	1.80	2	2	0	0	5	3	1	1	1	4	8	.167	.143	.102	14.40	7.20
Donal Montas	R-R	6-3	190	5-5-02	1	0	5.40	2	0	0	0	5	6	3	3	0	2	4	.286	.200	.364	7.20	3.60
2-team total (10 DSL Tigers 2)					1	1	2.97	12	9	0	0	39	28	17	13	5	12	42	.188	.145	.218	9.61	2.75
Henry Montilla	R-R	6-1	170	4-12-02	0	2	1.35	5	1	0	0	13	7	7	2	0	4	13	.163	.167	.160	8.78	2.70
2-team total (8 DSL Tigers 2)					1	3	2.18	13	3	0	0	33	25	14	8	0	13	34	.212	.240	.191	9.27	3.55
Edwin Moreno	R-R	6-1	170	2-8-03	1	0	3.00	1	0	0	0	3	3	1	1	0	1	4	.231	.500	.111	12.00	3.00
2-team total (13 DSL Tigers 2)					3	3	5.54	14	8	0	1	37	40	27	23	3	16	47	.268	.302	.250	11.33	3.86
Frank Moreno	R-R	6-2	185	10-16-02	1	5	4.86	12	12	0	0	37	43	31	20	1	20	25	.283	.346	.250	6.08	4.86
Franklin Paulino	R-R	6-3	160	7-24-03	0	0	0.00	1	0	0	0	1	1	1	0	0	0	1	.200	.000	.333	9.00	0.00
Jorger Petri	L-L	5-10	155	11-3-04	0	1	6.75	16	2	0	0	25	35	24	19	4	16	24	.321	.333	.319	8.53	5.68
Juan Polanco	R-R	6-1	205	12-30-00	0	1	0.00	5	0	0	0	6	2	1	0	0	4	7	.105	.200	.071	10.50	6.00
2-team total (10 DSL Tigers 2)					2	2	0.45	15	0	0	2	20	13	2	1	0	8	20	.188	.304	.130	9.00	3.60
Wanmer Ramirez	R-R	6-1	190	1-6-04	0	5	5.04	12	12	0	0	45	49	32	25	3	18	28	.277	.318	.252	5.64	3.63
Andres Ramos	R-R	5-11	180	3-26-05	1	2	7.88	7	0	0	0	8	10	11	7	0	9	3	.294	.500	.250	3.38	10.13
Jose Rivas	R-R	5-11	160	12-20-01	1	1	0.00	12	0	0	1	19	16	2	0	0	2	16	.239	.292	.209	7.45	0.93
Jesus A. Rodriguez	L-L	5-11	145	10-15-03	1	5	5.36	12	12	0	0	40	36	26	24	2	20	51	.234	.200	.240	11.38	4.46
Moises Rodriguez	R-R	6-2	170	3-3-02	0	1	4.22	13	0	0	2	21	15	12	10	1	15	12	.211	.240	.196	5.06	6.33
Keni Salgado	R-R	6-2	165	11-18-03	2	0	5.87	13	0	0	0	15	12	10	10	1	8	15	.218	.063	.282	8.80	4.70
Gabriel Torres	R-R	6-1	160	8-13-03	1	0	3.75	6	6	0	0	24	25	11	10	0	6	30	.258	.143	.304	11.25	2.25
Elvin Valerio	R-R	6-5	225	8-29-02	0	0	12.00	3	0	0	0	3	4	5	4	0	5	5	.333	.250	.375	15.00	15.00
2-team total (8 DSL Tigers 2)					0	0	5.95	11	5	0	0	20	20	14	13	1	10	20	.263	.281	.250	9.15	4.58

Fielding

C: Briceno 15, Hurtado 1, Rodriguez 8, Rojas 26, Santana 18. **1B:** Bravo 29, Briceno 6, De Leon 4, Dominguez 20, Estevez 2, Hurtado 1, Rodriguez 2, Rojas 7. **2B:** Cardozo 6, De Leon 10, Diaz 16, Montilla 26, Osorio 8, Perez 1, Sanchez 2. **3B:** Bravo 9, Cardozo 10, De Leon 19, Diaz 20, Montilla 2, Rodriguez 3, Sanchez 3. **SS:** Bravo 1, De Leon 2, Diaz 10, Gil 1, Montilla 18, Osorio 34, Perez 1. **OF:** Bautista 21, Bravo 7, Fana 51, Leon 5, Lopez 37, Matos 36, Ochoa 43, Quezada 5.

DSL TIGERS 2 — *ROOKIE*

DOMINICAN SUMMER LEAGUE

Batting	B-T	HT	WT	DOB	AVG	vLH	vRH	G	AB	R	H	2B	3B	HR	RBI	BB	HBP	SH	SF	SO	SB	CS	SLG	OBP
Josue Briceno	L-R	6-4	200	9-23-04	.133	.000	.146	14	45	3	6	4	0	1	6	2	0	0	1	15	0	0	.289	.167
2-team total (30 DSL Tigers 1)					.234	.200	.238	44	145	15	34	8	0	4	16	13	1	0	2	37	1	2	.372	.298
Jose Cardozo	R-R	5-10	150	9-18-03	.250	.000	.286	3	8	1	2	0	0	0	0	0	2	0	0	2	0	0	.250	.400
2-team total (21 DSL Tigers 1)					.163	.300	.128	24	49	7	8	1	0	1	5	5	7	0	0	19	3	0	.245	.328
Angel Cruz	R-R	5-11	165	9-27-01	.290	.545	.241	21	69	9	20	7	0	0	8	3	3	0	0	17	0	2	.391	.347
Geury Estevez	B-R	6-0	180	2-20-02	.253	.333	.241	33	91	19	23	1	1	0	18	12	3	0	0	18	3	0	.286	.358
2-team total (2 DSL Tigers 1)					.258	.357	.241	35	97	21	25	1	1	0	18	12	3	0	0	18	3	0	.289	.357
Samuel Gil	R-R	5-9	165	11-1-04	.255	.188	.271	47	165	32	42	10	2	2	26	25	3	0	0	33	7	0	.376	.363
2-team total (3 DSL Tigers 1)					.260	.176	.280	50	177	33	46	11	3	2	29	25	3	0	0	36	7	1	.390	.361
Ricardo Hurtado	R-R	5-10	180	5-23-03	.208	.143	.214	33	77	10	16	7	0	0	8	21	11	0	0	12	2	1	.299	.440
2-team total (2 DSL Tigers 1)					.198	.143	.203	35	81	10	16	7	0	0	8	21	12	0	0	12	2	1	.284	.430
Andri Leon	L-L	6-0	150	2-28-03	.288	.333	.280	50	156	30	45	11	1	2	27	12	8	0	3	43	5	6	.410	.363
2-team total (5 DSL Tigers 1)					.283	.346	.272	55	173	31	49	11	2	2	30	12	9	0	4	46	6	6	.405	.354
Jesus Machado	R-R	5-10	152	3-24-03	.286	.300	.283	46	119	25	34	4	1	0	14	18	7	1	0	32	12	5	.336	.410
Dany Martinez	R-R	5-11	170	6-30-03	.226	.400	.192	12	31	5	7	2	0	0	4	5	1	0	0	13	0	0	.290	.351
Randy Perea	R-R	5-11	150	1-21-04	.293	.083	.333	40	75	22	22	1	1	0	10	13	1	0	1	27	6	2	.333	.400
Reylin Perez	B-R	5-11	160	10-5-04	.306	.211	.320	47	144	40	44	14	3	7	30	36	3	0	0	53	7	3	.590	.454
2-team total (3 DSL Tigers 1)					.306	.250	.315	50	147	42	45	15	3	7	32	38	3	0	0	54	7	3	.592	.457
Junior Quezada	R-R	6-0	165	2-3-05	.286	.267	.289	36	105	14	30	1	2	0	17	15	3	0	1	20	5	2	.333	.387
2-team total (5 DSL Tigers 1)					.264	.211	.275	41	121	16	32	1	2	0	18	16	3	0	1	27	6	3	.306	.362
Elian Riera	L-L	5-10	150	2-23-04	.140	.250	.119	23	50	9	7	1	0	0	7	6	1	0	1	18	3	3	.160	.241
Fraudy Rodriguez	R-R	5-9	163	9-8-01	.200	--	.200	2	5	4	1	0	0	1	3	4	0	0	0	1	0	0	.800	.556
2-team total (10 DSL Tigers 1)					.125	.000	.130	12	24	6	3	2	0	1	4	5	2	0	0	12	0	0	.333	.323
Justin Rodriguez	R-R	5-10	155	3-11-04	.242	.304	.230	43	149	28	36	11	3	2	19	16	5	0	1	57	5	1	.396	.333
2-team total (5 DSL Tigers 1)					.262	.296	.255	48	168	31	44	15	3	2	22	16	5	0	1	66	5	1	.423	.342
Samuel Rojas	R-R	5-10	190	11-6-02	.333	.333	.333	3	9	0	3	0	0	0	1	0	0	0	0	4	0	0	.333	.333

2-team total (34 DSL Tigers 1)					.255	.333	.233	37	110	11	28	10	0	1	12	10	6	0	2	28	0	1	.373	.344
Newremberg Rondon	R-R	5-11	170	7-10-03	.270	.125	.295	35	111	13	30	6	0	1	18	13	4	0	0	22	1	0	.351	.367
Heison Sanchez	L-R	6-0	170	9-6-04	.238	.111	.259	40	130	23	31	7	2	2	14	17	8	0	0	42	3	1	.369	.361
2-team total (6 DSL Tigers 1)					.234	.100	.256	46	145	26	34	9	2	2	15	26	8	0	0	46	4	3	.366	.380
Yoel Viloria	B-R	5-10	160	4-25-03	.262	.333	.250	25	65	18	17	1	1	1	9	14	3	0	2	16	2	1	.354	.405

Pitching	**B-T**	**HT**	**WT**	**DOB**	**W**	**L**	**ERA**	**G**	**GS**	**CG**	**SV**	**IP**	**H**	**R**	**ER**	**HR**	**BB**	**SO**	**AVG**	**vLH**	**vRH**	**K/9**	**BB/9**
Yeremi Bastardo	L-L	5-9	160	1-13-02	0	1	4.97	11	0	0	0	13	14	11	7	0	9	13	.292	.200	.316	9.24	6.39
Jorge Boyer	L-L	6-4	182	4-15-03	1	3	6.63	18	0	0	1	19	14	22	14	1	22	29	.203	.222	.200	13.74	10.42
2-team total (1 DSL Tigers 1)					1	3	7.11	19	0	0	1	19	14	25	15	1	24	29	.203	.222	.200	13.74	11.37
Ignacio Briceno	L-L	5-11	155	6-4-01	6	1	1.69	16	0	0	3	27	17	9	5	0	6	30	.183	.154	.188	10.13	2.03
2-team total (1 DSL Tigers 1)					6	1	1.59	17	0	0	3	28	21	9	5	0	6	30	.210	.214	.209	9.53	1.91
Gregoris Chalas	R-R	5-10	143	8-12-00	0	0	5.47	11	4	0	0	26	26	19	16	0	14	24	.255	.324	.221	8.20	4.78
Juan Cordero	R-R	6-0	165	7-24-02	4	1	2.70	10	0	0	0	20	22	10	6	0	4	17	.282	.250	.296	7.65	1.80
Jose Florian	R-R	5-11	155	2-3-04	2	2	4.74	11	0	0	1	19	20	11	10	0	10	17	.274	.174	.320	8.05	4.74
Pedro Garcia	R-R	6-1	190	2-27-02	4	2	3.35	12	10	0	0	48	34	18	18	5	10	46	.193	.186	.197	8.57	1.86
2-team total (1 DSL Tigers 1)					4	2	3.16	13	10	0	0	51	36	18	18	5	11	46	.195	.186	.198	8.06	1.93
Xiomer Guacache	R-R	6-3	195	2-11-04	1	2	9.00	7	0	0	0	13	18	14	13	2	6	16	.353	.250	.400	11.08	4.15
2-team total (4 DSL Tigers 1)					1	4	8.88	11	3	0	0	25	37	28	25	4	15	22	.349	.333	.356	7.82	5.33
Abraham Landaeta	R-R	6-2	175	11-29-00	2	2	4.15	9	6	0	0	22	21	15	10	0	7	23	.244	.282	.213	9.55	2.91
Bryant Landaeta	R-R	6-2	175	11-27-03	1	1	2.70	10	3	0	2	27	25	8	8	0	7	17	.266	.188	.306	5.74	2.36
Luis Lopez	R-R	5-11	170	12-1-00	0	0	8.10	4	0	0	0	7	8	7	6	1	5	4	.308	.300	.313	5.40	6.75
2-team total (1 DSL Tigers 1)					0	0	7.04	5	0	0	0	8	8	7	6	1	5	4	.276	.250	.294	4.70	5.87
Jaime Marin	R-R	5-11	165	12-25-00	1	0	0.00	2	0	0	1	2	2	0	0	0	1	0	.286	.200	.500	0.00	4.50
2-team total (18 DSL Tigers 1)					5	1	3.74	20	0	0	1	34	34	18	14	0	10	46	.264	.208	.296	12.30	2.67
Donal Montas	R-R	6-3	190	5-5-02	0	1	2.62	10	9	0	0	34	22	14	10	5	10	38	.172	.135	.197	9.96	2.62
2-team total (2 DSL Tigers 1)					1	1	2.97	12	9	0	0	39	28	17	13	5	12	42	.188	.145	.218	9.61	2.75
Henry Montilla	R-R	6-1	170	4-12-02	1	1	2.75	8	2	0	0	20	18	7	6	0	9	21	.240	.281	.209	9.61	4.12
2-team total (5 DSL Tigers 1)					1	3	2.18	13	3	0	0	33	25	14	8	0	13	34	.212	.240	.191	9.27	3.55
Edwin Moreno	R-R	6-1	170	2-8-03	2	3	5.77	13	8	0	1	34	37	26	22	3	15	43	.272	.286	.264	11.27	3.93
2-team total (1 DSL Tigers 1)					3	3	5.54	14	8	0	1	37	40	27	23	3	16	47	.268	.302	.250	11.33	3.86
Eliseo Mota	R-R	6-2	185	11-7-02	1	2	7.16	8	3	0	0	16	28	18	13	3	9	14	.373	.321	.404	7.71	4.96
Juan Polanco	R-R	6-1	205	12-30-00	2	1	0.64	10	0	0	2	14	11	1	1	0	4	13	.220	.333	.156	8.36	2.57
2-team total (5 DSL Tigers 1)					2	2	0.45	15	0	0	2	20	13	2	1	0	8	20	.188	.304	.130	9.00	3.60
Juan Ruiz	R-R	5-11	216	11-3-03	0	0	0.90	3	2	0	0	10	5	1	1	0	3	13	.143	.273	.083	11.70	2.70
Rolando Sirit	R-R	6-3	165	11-12-01	1	2	2.89	5	4	0	0	9	8	5	3	0	4	16	.222	.286	.182	15.43	3.86
Elvin Valerio	R-R	6-5	225	8-29-02	0	0	4.86	8	5	0	0	17	16	9	9	1	5	15	.250	.286	.222	8.10	2.70
2-team total (3 DSL Tigers 1)					0	0	5.95	11	5	0	0	20	20	14	13	1	10	20	.263	.281	.250	9.15	4.58
Darwyn Zambrano	R-R	6-2	175	7-27-00	2	0	2.63	15	0	0	1	24	13	7	7	4	8	26	.165	.174	.161	9.75	3.00

Fielding

C: Briceno 1, Hurtado 25, Martinez 7, Rodriguez 2, Rojas 2, Rondon 26. **1B:** Briceno 3, Estevez 27, Hurtado 8, Leon 1, Rojas 1, Rondon 8, Viloria 17. **2B:** Cruz 9, Estevez 3, Gil 16, Perez 11, Rodriguez 6, Sanchez 14. **3B:** Cardozo 2, Cruz 8, Estevez 2, Rodriguez 30, Sanchez 15. **SS:** Gil 26, Perez 29, Sanchez 2. **OF:** Leon 50, Machado 44, Perea 34, Quezada 36, Riera 17, Viloria 8

Houston Astros

SEASON IN A SENTENCE: Houston started strong, stayed hot and entered the postseason as the American League favorite. While other 100-win teams bowed out quickly in the playoffs, the Astros didn't lose an AL playoff game and beat the Phillies in six gams to win the second World Series championship in franchise history.

HIGH POINT: After sweeping the Mariners and Yankees to win their fourth pennant in six seasons, the Astros lost two of the first three against Philadelphia. That's when righthander Cristian Javier changed the trajectory of the Series, throwing six no-hit innings one night after the Phillies had put up seven runs. Relievers Bryan Abreu, Rafael Montero and Ryan Pressly pitched an inning apiece to complete the first World Series no-hitter since Don Larsen's 1956 perfect game.

LOW POINT: Only when they were down 2-1 to the Phillies did the Astros ever seem truly down. Houston did play the postseason under a cloud of uncertainty, as owner Jim Crane didn't reward manager Dusty Baker or general manager James Click with contract extensions during the season. The two sides parted ways in November, when Click declined to take Crane's one-year contract offer.

NOTABLE ROOKIES: Jeremy Peña was tasked with replacing Carlos Correa at shortstop, and he thrived defensively and hit 22 homers during a .253/.289/.426 season. Then came the postseason, when Peña came up with big hit after big hit in Correa-like fashion to earn MVP honors in both the AL Championship Series and the World Series. He became the first rookie position player to win the World Series honor. Several other rookies made the postseason rosters, including DH David Hensley, catcher Korey Lee and righthander Hunter Brown, but still remain prospects.

KEY TRANSACTIONS: Houston let Correa walk and generally worked the margins of the roster while continuing to develop its young core. An injury to Michael Brantley and uncertainly in center field led the Astros to trade Jose Siri to Tampa, making Chas McCormick the primary center fielder. Veteran additions such as DH/first baseman Trey Mancini and lefty reliever Will Smith had their moments, but Smith didn't even pitch in the postseason for the dominant Astros.

ON THE FARM: Brown was one of the best pitchers in Triple-A and looks MLB-ready.

OPENING DAY PAYROLL: $174,356,000 (10th).

PLAYERS OF THE YEAR

MAJOR LEAGUE

Yordan Alvarez
OF
.306/.406/.613
37 HR, 78 BB, 97 RBIs
1.019 OPS second in AL

MINOR LEAGUE

Hunter Brown
RHP
(AAA)
2.55 ERA, 1.09 WHIP
134 SO, 45 BB, 106 IP

ORGANIZATION LEADERS

Batting		*Minimum 250 AB
MAJORS		
*AVG	Yordan Alvarez	.306
*OPS	Yordan Alvarez	1.019
HR	Yordan Alvarez	37
RBI	Kyle Tucker	107
MINORS		
*AVG	Enmanuel Valdez, Corpus Christi, Sugar Land	.327
*OBP	David Hensley, Sugar Land	.420
*SLG	Enmanuel Valdez, Corpus Christi, Sugar Land	.606
*OPS	Enmanuel Valdez, Corpus Christi, Sugar Land	1.016
R	Corey Julks, Sugar Land	100
H	Justin Dirden, Corpus Christi, Sugar Land	144
TB	Justin Dirden, Corpus Christi, Sugar Land	266
2B	Justin Dirden, Corpus Christi, Sugar Land	40
3B	Rabel Colon, DSL Astros Orange	8
HR	Corey Julks, Sugar Land	31
RBI	Justin Dirden, Corpus Christi, Sugar Land	101
BB	David Hensley, Sugar Land	80
SO	Tyler Whitaker, Fayetteville	180
SB	Pedro León, Sugar Land	38

Pitching		#Minimum 75 IP
MAJORS		
W	Justin Verlander	18
#ERA	Justin Verlander	1.75
SO	Cristian Javier	194
SO	Framber Valdez	194
SV	Ryan Pressly	33
MINORS		
W	3 tied	9
L	Alex Santos, Fayetteville	11
#ERA	Hunter Brown, Sugar Land	2.55
G	Nick Hernandez, Sugar Land, Corpus Christi	51
GS	Misael Tamarez, Corpus Christi, Sugar Land	23
SV	Enoli Paredes, Sugar Land	12
IP	Chad Donato, Sugar Land	125
BB	Misael Tamarez, Corpus Christi, Sugar Land	70
SO	Spencer Arrighetti, Asheville, Corpus Christi	152
#AVG	Edinson Batista, Fayetteville, Asheville	.178

2022 PERFORMANCE

General Manager: James Click. **Farm Director:** Pete Putila. **Scouting Director:** Kris Gross

Class	Team	League	W	L	PCT	Finish	Manager
Majors	Houston Astros	American	106	56	.654	1st (15)	Dusty Baker
Triple-A	Sugar Land Space Cowboys	Pacific Coast	73	75	.493	5th (10)	Mickey Storey
Double-A	Corpus Christi Hooks	Texas	63	74	.460	9th (10)	Gregorio Petit
High-A	Asheville Tourists	South Atlantic	62	69	.473	8th (12)	Nate Shaver
Low-A	Fayetteville Woodpeckers	Carolina	55	75	.423	10th (12)	Dickie Joe Thon
Rookie	FCL Astros Orange	Florida Complex	26	28	.481	9th (16)	Carlos Lugo
Rookie	FCL Astros Blue	Florida Complex	15	38	.283	16th (16)	Ricky Rivera
Overall 2022 Minor League Record			353	419	.457	27th (30)	

ORGANIZATION STATISTICS

HOUSTON ASTROS

AMERICAN LEAGUE

Batting	B-T	HT	WT	DOB	AVG	vLH	vRH	G	AB	R	H	2B	3B	HR	RBI	BB	HBP	SH	SF	SO	SB	CS	SLG	OBP
Jose Altuve	R-R	5-6	166	5-6-90	.300	.340	.285	141	527	103	158	39	0	28	57	66	10	0	1	87	18	1	.533	.387
Yordan Alvarez	L-R	6-5	225	6-27-97	.306	.321	.299	135	470	95	144	29	2	37	97	78	6	0	7	106	1	1	.613	.406
Michael Brantley	L-L	6-2	209	5-15-87	.288	.295	.285	64	243	28	70	14	1	5	26	31	1	1	1	30	1	1	.416	.370
Alex Bregman	R-R	6-0	192	3-30-94	.259	.225	.277	155	548	93	142	38	0	23	93	87	11	0	10	77	1	2	.454	.366
Jason Castro	L-R	6-3	215	6-18-87	.115	.000	.130	34	78	6	9	2	0	1	3	8	1	0	1	40	1	0	.179	.205
Aledmys Diaz	R-R	6-1	195	8-1-90	.243	.267	.233	92	305	35	74	13	0	12	38	18	2	0	2	53	1	1	.403	.287
Yainer Diaz	R-R	6-0	195	9-21-98	.125	.000	.167	6	8	0	1	1	0	0	1	1	0	0	0	2	0	0	.250	.222
Mauricio Dubon	R-R	6-0	173	7-19-94	.208	.224	.200	83	197	21	41	8	0	3	16	12	1	3	3	26	2	3	.294	.254
Niko Goodrum	B-R	6-3	215	2-28-92	.116	.000	.139	15	43	2	5	2	0	0	1	2	0	0	0	23	1	0	.163	.156
Yuli Gurriel	R-R	6-0	215	6-9-84	.242	.265	.232	146	545	53	132	40	0	8	53	30	6	0	3	73	8	0	.360	.288
David Hensley	R-R	6-6	190	3-28-96	.345	.333	.353	16	29	7	10	2	1	1	5	5	0	0	0	6	0	0	.586	.441
Taylor Jones	R-R	6-7	230	12-6-93	.000	--	.000	1	1	0	0	0	0	0	0	0	0	0	0	0	0	0	.000	.000
Korey Lee	R-R	6-2	210	7-25-98	.160	.182	.143	12	25	1	4	2	0	0	4	1	0	0	0	9	0	0	.240	.192
Martin Maldonado	R-R	6-0	230	8-16-86	.186	.212	.176	113	344	40	64	12	0	15	45	22	7	4	2	116	0	0	.352	.248
Trey Mancini	R-R	6-3	230	3-18-92	.176	.192	.168	51	165	17	29	7	0	8	22	18	1	0	2	49	0	0	.364	.258
J.J. Matijevic	L-R	6-0	206	11-14-95	.209	.111	.224	32	67	7	14	2	0	2	5	2	2	0	0	25	1	0	.328	.254
Chas McCormick	R-L	6-0	208	4-19-95	.245	.340	.207	119	359	47	88	12	2	14	44	46	1	0	1	106	4	3	.407	.332
Jake Meyers	R-L	6-0	200	6-18-96	.227	.250	.214	52	150	13	34	6	2	1	15	7	2	0	1	54	2	1	.313	.269
Jeremy Pena	R-R	6-0	202	9-22-97	.253	.286	.241	136	521	72	132	20	2	22	63	22	6	1	5	135	11	2	.426	.289
Joe Perez	R-R	6-2	198	8-12-99	.000	--	.000	1	1	0	0	0	0	0	0	0	0	0	0	1	0	0	.000	.000
Jose Siri	R-R	6-2	175	7-22-95	.178	.057	.220	48	135	18	24	4	2	3	10	9	2	0	1	48	6	1	.304	.238
2-team total (56 Tampa Bay Rays)					.213	.156	.232	104	301	53	64	13	2	7	24	20	3	0	1	108	14	2	.339	.268
Kyle Tucker	L-R	6-4	199	1-17-97	.257	.228	.275	150	544	71	140	28	1	30	107	59	1	0	2	95	25	4	.478	.330
Christian Vazquez	R-R	5-9	205	8-21-90	.250	.348	.222	35	104	8	26	3	0	1	10	4	0	0	0	18	0	2	.308	.278
2-team total (84 Boston Red Sox)					.274	.304	.264	119	398	41	109	23	0	9	52	22	3	0	3	69	1	4	.399	.315

Pitching	B-T	HT	WT	DOB	W	L	ERA	G	GS	CG	SV	IP	H	R	ER	HR	BB	SO	AVG	vLH	vRH	K/9	BB/9
Bryan Abreu	R-R	6-1	225	4-22-97	4	0	1.94	55	0	0	2	60	45	16	13	2	26	88	.207	.189	.225	13.13	3.88
Pedro Baez	R-R	6-0	232	3-11-88	0	0	11.57	3	0	0	0	2	5	6	3	0	3	2	.417	.667	.167	7.71	11.57
Brandon Bielak	L-R	6-2	208	4-2-96	0	0	3.65	5	0	0	0	12	11	5	5	2	4	12	.234	.150	.296	8.76	2.92
Ronel Blanco	R-R	6-0	180	8-31-93	0	0	7.11	7	0	0	0	6	8	5	5	1	4	7	.296	.333	.267	9.95	5.68
Hunter Brown	R-R	6-2	212	8-29-98	2	0	0.89	7	2	0	0	20	15	2	2	0	7	22	.205	.136	.310	9.74	3.10
Luis Garcia	R-R	6-1	244	12-13-96	15	8	3.72	28	28	0	0	157	131	70	65	23	47	157	.222	.234	.213	8.98	2.69
Cristian Javier	R-R	6-1	213	3-26-97	11	9	2.54	30	25	0	0	149	89	44	42	17	52	194	.170	.189	.147	11.74	3.15
Seth Martinez	R-R	6-2	200	8-29-94	1	1	2.09	29	0	0	0	39	26	10	9	3	14	38	.187	.280	.135	8.84	3.26
Phil Maton	R-R	6-2	206	3-25-93	0	2	3.84	67	0	0	0	66	58	34	28	10	24	73	.237	.242	.232	10.01	3.29
Lance McCullers Jr.	L-R	6-1	202	10-2-93	4	2	2.27	8	8	0	0	48	37	12	12	4	22	50	.215	.165	.258	9.44	4.15
Rafael Montero	R-R	6-0	190	10-17-90	5	2	2.37	71	0	0	14	68	47	22	18	3	23	73	.193	.158	.225	9.61	3.03
Parker Mushinski	L-L	6-0	218	11-22-95	0	0	3.68	7	0	0	0	7	5	3	3	0	3	8	.192	.250	.143	9.82	3.68
Hector Neris	R-R	6-2	227	6-14-89	6	4	3.72	70	0	0	3	65	49	29	27	3	17	79	.205	.205	.205	10.88	2.34
Jake Odorizzi	R-R	6-2	190	3-27-90	4	3	3.75	12	12	0	0	60	52	29	25	5	17	46	.231	.218	.243	6.90	2.55
Enoli Paredes	R-R	5-11	171	9-28-95	0	0	3.00	3	0	0	0	3	3	1	1	0	3	2	.273	.333	.200	6.00	9.00
Ryan Pressly	R-R	6-2	206	12-15-88	3	3	2.98	50	0	0	33	48	30	17	16	4	13	65	.181	.178	.184	12.10	2.42
Will Smith	R-L	6-5	255	7-10-89	0	2	3.27	24	0	0	0	22	23	10	8	2	4	24	.271	.239	.308	9.82	1.64
Ryne Stanek	R-R	6-4	226	7-26-91	2	1	1.15	59	0	0	1	55	36	8	7	2	31	62	.188	.175	.198	10.21	5.10
Blake Taylor	L-L	6-3	220	8-17-95	1	1	3.94	19	0	0	0	16	15	7	7	1	10	9	.234	.219	.250	5.06	5.63
Jose Urquidy	R-R	6-0	217	5-1-95	13	8	3.94	29	28	0	0	164	154	74	72	29	38	134	.244	.226	.260	7.34	2.08
Framber Valdez	R-L	5-11	239	11-19-93	17	6	2.82	31	31	3	0	201	166	71	63	11	67	194	.223	.192	.229	8.67	3.00
Justin Verlander	R-R	6-5	235	2-20-83	18	4	1.75	28	28	0	0	175	116	43	34	12	29	185	.186	.163	.208	9.51	1.49

Fielding

Catcher	PCT	G	PO	A	E	DP	PB
Castro	.986	30	200	10	3	2	1
Diaz	1.000	2	2	1	0	0	0
Lee	.986	12	73	0	1	0	2
Maldonado	.998	113	1025	49	2	3	9
Vazquez	.992	30	253	7	2	1	0

First Base	PCT	G	PO	A	E	DP
Diaz	1.000	6	45	2	0	4
Goodrum	1.000	4	24	1	0	0
Gurriel	.996	142	1057	45	4	106
Mancini	1.000	10	66	1	0	3
Matijevic	1.000	10	36	1	0	2

Second Base	PCT	G	PO	A	E	DP
Altuve	.979	135	159	269	9	67
Diaz	1.000	22	19	38	0	3
Dubon	.962	16	8	17	1	5
Goodrum	.970	10	15	17	1	6
Hensley	1.000	5	2	3	0	0

Third Base	PCT	G	PO	A	E	DP
Bregman	.983	154	144	263	7	39
Diaz	1.000	10	1	8	0	1
Hensley	1.000	3	0	2	0	1
Perez	1.000	1	0	1	0	0

Shortstop	PCT	G	PO	A	E	DP
Diaz	.966	18	14	43	2	8
Dubon	.968	17	19	42	2	6
Hensley	1.000	2	1	2	0	1
Pena	.963	134	146	347	19	64

Outfield	PCT	G	PO	A	E	DP
Alvarez	.977	56	79	7	2	1
Brantley	1.000	29	59	1	0	0
Diaz	.974	29	36	1	1	0
Dubon	.976	57	81	2	2	1
Hensley	1.000	1	1	0	0	0
Mancini	1.000	18	23	0	0	0
Matijevic	--	1	0	0	0	0
McCormick	.995	141	187	3	1	0
Meyers	.983	51	119	0	2	0
Siri	.991	46	114	0	1	0
Tucker	.990	147	287	8	3	1

SUGAR LAND SPACE COWBOYS — TRIPLE-A

PACIFIC COAST LEAGUE

Batting	B-T	HT	WT	DOB	AVG	vLH	vRH	G	AB	R	H	2B	3B	HR	RBI	BB	HBP	SH	SF	SO	SB	CS	SLG	OBP
Jose Altuve	R-R	5-6	166	5-6-90	.429	.500	.400	2	7	1	3	1	0	0	0	1	0	0	0	2	0	0	.571	.500
Jose Alvarez	R-R	6-1	180	6-4-00	--	--	--	1	0	1	0	0	0	0	0	0	0	0	0	0	0	0	--	--
Franklin Barreto	R-R	5-10	208	2-27-96	.162	.208	.149	73	241	27	39	7	1	6	21	30	2	0	1	102	11	4	.274	.259
Lewis Brinson	R-R	6-5	212	5-8-94	.299	.416	.264	85	331	61	99	21	2	22	63	26	4	2	1	102	5	3	.574	.356
2-team total (2 Sacramento River Cats)					.298	.407	.264	87	339	62	101	21	2	22	63	27	4	2	1	106	5	3	.566	.356
Marty Costes	R-R	5-9	200	12-18-95	.258	.228	.269	61	213	36	55	13	0	5	22	24	10	0	1	46	10	4	.390	.359
Alex De Goti	R-R	6-0	192	8-19-94	.253	.226	.262	135	494	77	125	28	3	9	69	73	5	1	4	104	8	2	.377	.352
Aledmys Diaz	R-R	6-1	195	8-1-90	.167	.000	.182	3	12	1	2	0	0	1	1	1	0	0	0	1	0	0	.417	.231
Edwin Diaz	R-R	6-2	223	8-25-95	.227	.161	.253	30	110	12	25	5	1	3	17	8	0	1	1	46	0	0	.373	.277
Yainer Diaz	R-R	6-0	195	9-21-98	.294	.220	.318	48	201	38	59	9	1	16	48	13	3	0	2	39	1	0	.587	.342
Justin Dirden	L-R	6-3	209	7-16-97	.242	.281	.229	32	128	18	31	8	0	4	28	10	2	1	1	40	5	1	.398	.305
Rolando Espinosa	R-R	6-0	177	1-5-01	.056	.000	.059	5	18	3	1	0	0	0	0	2	0	0	0	8	0	0	.056	.150
Niko Goodrum	B-R	6-3	215	2-28-92	.311	.400	.267	13	45	12	14	3	0	2	5	17	0	0	0	14	2	0	.511	.500
David Hensley	R-R	6-6	190	3-28-96	.298	.345	.285	104	379	80	113	30	4	10	57	80	2	0	3	103	20	7	.478	.420
Taylor Jones	R-R	6-7	230	12-6-93	.263	.260	.263	74	274	52	72	17	0	12	43	35	12	0	1	78	0	0	.456	.370
2-team total (7 Sacramento River Cats)					.262	.263	.261	81	298	57	78	21	0	12	48	40	12	0	1	86	0	0	.453	.370
Corey Julks	R-R	6-1	185	2-27-96	.270	.227	.284	130	523	100	141	21	4	31	89	56	10	0	1	128	22	5	.503	.351
AJ Lee	R-R	6-0	200	5-26-97	.000	--	.000	2	4	0	0	0	0	0	0	0	0	0	0	2	0	0	.000	.000
Korey Lee	R-R	6-2	210	7-25-98	.238	.240	.237	104	404	74	96	20	2	25	76	36	5	0	1	127	12	1	.483	.307
Pedro Leon	R-R	5-10	170	5-28-98	.228	.135	.256	115	413	71	94	27	3	17	63	71	19	0	1	145	38	18	.431	.365
Scott Manea	R-R	5-11	237	12-21-95	.196	.211	.192	89	285	38	56	9	2	4	34	43	7	0	2	92	0	1	.284	.315
J.J. Matijevic	L-R	6-0	206	11-14-95	.285	.261	.294	64	246	46	70	16	2	16	54	33	2	0	1	68	10	2	.561	.372
Alex McKenna	R-R	6-2	204	9-6-97	.217	.186	.227	53	184	18	40	9	0	2	23	24	3	0	1	66	6	3	.299	.316
Jake Meyers	R-L	6-0	200	6-18-96	.306	.300	.307	38	144	26	44	6	1	7	18	25	0	0	1	30	2	0	.507	.406
Michael Papierski	B-R	6-3	224	2-26-96	.211	.087	.254	26	90	12	19	3	0	1	15	14	2	0	2	9	0	0	.278	.324
2-team total (14 Sacramento River Cats)					.210	.139	.234	40	143	17	30	5	0	3	28	17	2	0	3	27	0	0	.308	.297
Joe Perez	R-R	6-2	198	8-12-99	.483	.333	.550	8	29	6	14	1	0	1	6	6	0	0	0	6	0	0	.621	.571
Cesar Salazar	L-R	5-9	185	3-15-96	.203	.308	.174	17	59	2	12	1	0	0	6	5	1	0	1	13	0	0	.220	.273
Jose Siri	R-R	6-2	175	7-22-95	.296	.188	.327	16	71	17	21	3	2	9	22	6	0	0	1	20	2	0	.775	.346
Dillon Thomas	L-L	6-1	215	12-10-92	.267	.000	.444	5	15	3	4	1	0	1	1	1	1	0	0	4	0	0	.533	.353
2-team total (108 Salt Lake Bees)					.271	.264	.273	113	414	75	112	23	2	18	78	56	18	0	4	127	6	4	.466	.378
Ronaldo Urdaneta	R-R	5-10	155	11-18-98	.300	.200	.400	4	10	2	3	0	0	0	2	2	0	0	0	3	2	0	.300	.417
Enmanuel Valdez	L-R	5-9	191	12-28-98	.296	.250	.311	38	159	26	47	10	1	10	32	11	2	0	1	29	1	1	.560	.347

Pitching	B-T	HT	WT	DOB	W	L	ERA	G	GS	CG	SV	IP	H	R	ER	HR	BB	SO	AVG	vLH	vRH	K/9	BB/9
Jonathan Bermudez	L-L	6-2	237	10-16-95	2	4	8.96	19	14	0	0	67	85	68	67	16	37	65	.310	.250	.335	8.69	4.95
2-team total (5 Sacramento River Cats)					2	7	9.00	24	19	0	0	81	100	82	81	23	44	81	.304	.217	.345	9.00	4.89
Brandon Bielak	L-R	6-2	208	4-2-96	3	6	3.15	23	14	0	0	89	82	39	31	5	43	86	.243	.255	.233	8.73	4.36
Ronel Blanco	R-R	6-0	180	8-31-93	4	7	3.63	44	0	0	5	45	35	23	18	8	19	58	.212	.222	.206	11.69	3.83
Hunter Brown	R-R	6-2	212	8-29-98	9	4	2.55	23	14	0	1	106	70	35	30	5	45	134	.186	.207	.167	11.38	3.82
Brett Conine	R-R	6-3	218	10-16-96	6	3	6.86	29	14	0	0	106	142	88	81	19	55	87	.316	.340	.298	7.36	4.66
Devin Conn	R-R	5-11	169	4-3-97	0	0	3.86	11	0	0	0	14	13	6	6	2	10	6	.271	.250	.286	3.86	6.43
Alex De Goti	R-R	6-0	192	8-19-94	0	0	0.00	1	0	0	0	1	2	0	0	0	0	0	.500	1.000	.333	0.00	0.00
Chad Donato	R-R	6-0	195	6-3-95	4	8	5.34	29	18	0	2	125	122	83	74	20	60	101	.252	.219	.273	7.29	4.33
Shawn Dubin	R-R	6-1	171	9-6-95	3	5	4.78	23	12	0	0	58	52	33	31	3	32	80	.243	.225	.254	12.34	4.94
Jimmy Endersby	R-R	6-1	194	1-16-98	2	3	7.66	12	8	0	0	45	55	38	38	12	26	33	.304	.318	.292	6.65	5.24
J.P. France	R-R	6-0	216	4-4-95	3	4	3.90	34	15	0	3	111	99	51	48	15	51	136	.233	.243	.226	11.06	4.15
Layne Henderson	R-R	6-4	200	6-8-96	0	0	1.93	6	0	0	0	9	6	2	2	1	2	12	.182	.200	.167	11.57	1.93
Nick Hernandez	R-R	6-1	212	12-30-94	5	5	3.92	48	0	0	0	60	38	32	26	8	30	77	.179	.235	.142	11.61	4.53
Tyler Ivey	R-R	6-4	195	5-12-96	0	1	10.38	5	2	0	0	13	18	16	15	3	8	17	.316	.333	.296	11.77	5.54
Josh James	R-R	6-3	234	3-8-93	1	0	7.01	28	0	0	4	26	32	21	20	4	17	29	.296	.313	.283	10.17	5.96
Seth Martinez	R-R	6-2	200	8-29-94	2	1	3.60	14	0	0	0	15	10	7	6	2	6	15	.185	.100	.235	9.00	3.60
Lance McCullers Jr.	L-R	6-1	202	10-2-93	0	0	7.15	3	3	0	0	11	13	10	9	2	7	14	.283	.211	.333	11.12	5.56
Colin McKee	R-R	6-3	225	6-21-94	0	0	3.77	12	0	0	0	14	10	12	6	0	14	13	.192	.333	.118	8.16	8.79
Adam Morgan	L-L	6-1	200	2-27-90	1	1	3.12	9	0	0	0	9	8	5	3	1	1	10	.242	.154	.300	10.38	1.04
Parker Mushinski	L-L	6-0	218	11-22-95	2	2	2.66	38	0	0	0	41	28	17	12	3	19	41	.193	.200	.189	9.07	4.20
Jake Odorizzi	R-R	6-2	190	3-27-90	0	0	6.00	1	1	0	0	3	2	2	2	0	2	4	.182	.000	.333	12.00	6.00

Jon Olczak	R-R	6-0	180	11-14-93	4	4	4.66	47	2	0	0	66	71	39	34	14	21	77	.272	.252	.288	10.55	2.88
Enoli Paredes	R-R	5-11	171	9-28-95	5	4	2.63	50	0	0	12	55	34	24	16	4	31	81	.176	.235	.134	13.34	5.10
Ryan Pressly	R-R	6-2	206	12-15-88	0	0	0.00	1	0	0	0	1	0	0	0	0	0	0	.000	.000	.000	0.00	0.00
Joe Record	R-R	6-3	232	1-12-95	4	1	5.45	29	0	0	0	38	44	26	23	3	19	38	.289	.339	.258	9.00	4.50
Zac Rosscup	R-L	6-2	220	6-9-88	2	1	3.10	26	0	0	0	29	23	11	10	0	17	35	.217	.229	.211	10.86	5.28
Matt Ruppenthal	R-R	6-4	225	10-21-95	0	1	23.63	2	0	0	0	3	7	8	7	1	2	3	.500	.250	.600	10.13	6.75
Peter Solomon	R-R	6-4	211	8-16-96	8	6	5.20	23	18	0	0	97	97	72	56	17	44	88	.257	.259	.255	8.16	4.08
Misael Tamarez	R-R	6-1	206	1-16-00	1	1	2.50	4	4	0	0	18	6	5	5	2	15	20	.105	.083	.111	10.00	7.50
Blake Taylor	L-L	6-3	220	8-17-95	2	0	5.06	11	1	0	0	11	6	6	6	1	7	7	.176	.143	.185	5.91	5.91
Jojanse Torres	R-R	6-2	188	8-4-95	0	1	15.19	6	0	0	0	5	10	9	9	2	14	7	.417	.500	.375	11.81	23.63
Forrest Whitley	R-R	6-7	238	9-15-97	0	2	7.09	10	8	0	0	33	32	26	26	2	25	36	.250	.224	.271	9.82	6.82

Fielding

Catcher	PCT	G	PO	A	E	DP	PB
Diaz	.996	27	239	5	1	0	3
Lee	.994	66	678	36	4	4	13
Manea	.994	34	301	8	2	2	1
Papierski	1.000	11	119	4	0	0	1
Salazar	.990	11	94	3	1	2	0

First Base	PCT	G	PO	A	E	DP
De Goti	1.000	1	6	0	0	1
Diaz	1.000	1	1	0	0	0
Diaz	.986	10	64	6	1	7
Goodrum	1.000	3	25	2	0	4
Hensley	.993	18	125	14	1	8
Jones	.996	36	225	28	1	27
Lee	1.000	1	5	1	0	1
Manea	.987	34	208	15	3	23
Matijevic	.994	41	283	24	2	26
Papierski	.986	9	64	7	1	4
Salazar	1.000	1	6	0	0	0
Valdez	.968	6	24	6	1	2

Second Base	PCT	G	PO	A	E	DP
Altuve	1.000	2	0	5	0	0
Barreto	.977	35	55	75	3	18
De Goti	.991	29	37	68	1	20
Diaz	.983	13	27	32	1	8
Espinosa	.667	4	3	3	3	1
Goodrum	.800	4	4	4	2	1
Hensley	.977	23	38	47	2	13
Julks	.813	4	6	7	3	1
Lee	1.000	2	0	3	0	0
Leon	.947	20	24	47	4	6
Urdaneta	1.000	3	3	2	0	0
Valdez	.981	18	14	38	1	5

Third Base	PCT	G	PO	A	E	DP
Barreto	.964	13	8	19	1	5
De Goti	.955	34	25	60	4	8
Diaz	1.000	3	3	7	0	2
Espinosa	1.000	1	0	1	0	0
Hensley	.981	24	17	36	1	3
Jones	.889	23	13	35	6	4
Julks	.912	49	24	69	9	9
Perez	.875	5	3	11	2	2
Valdez	1.000	3	0	3	0	1

Shortstop	PCT	G	PO	A	E	DP
Barreto	.968	26	31	60	3	13
De Goti	.984	73	83	165	4	33
Diaz	1.000	1	1	2	0	0
Diaz	.982	15	17	39	1	10
Goodrum	.909	3	4	6	1	1
Hensley	.949	33	35	58	5	10
Leon	.727	3	5	3	3	1

Outfield	PCT	G	PO	A	E	DP
Brinson	.974	73	150	1	4	0
Costes	.957	55	86	3	4	0
Diaz	1.000	1	2	0	0	0
Diaz	1.000	2	2	0	0	0
Dirden	.972	30	68	1	2	0
Espinosa	--	1	0	0	0	0
Goodrum	1.000	2	1	0	0	0
Hensley	.889	6	8	0	1	0
Jones	1.000	10	18	1	0	0
Julks	.983	67	115	1	2	0
Lee	1.000	2	2	0	0	0
Leon	.980	86	187	5	4	1
Matijevic	.971	19	34	0	1	0
McKenna	.990	53	96	1	1	0
Meyers	1.000	30	83	1	0	0
Perez	1.000	2	6	0	0	0
Salazar	1.000	1	4	0	0	0
Siri	1.000	14	50	0	0	0
Thomas	1.000	5	6	0	0	0
Valdez	.933	9	14	0	1	0

CORPUS CHRISTI HOOKS — DOUBLE-A

TEXAS LEAGUE

Batting	B-T	HT	WT	DOB	AVG	vLH	vRH	G	AB	R	H	2B	3B	HR	RBI	BB	HBP	SH	SF	SO	SB	CS	SLG	OBP
Wilyer Abreu	L-L	6-0	217	6-24-99	.249	.250	.249	89	329	81	82	24	0	15	54	78	4	0	0	108	23	1	.459	.399
Ross Adolph	L-R	6-1	190	12-17-96	.246	.294	.235	59	183	32	45	6	3	5	29	49	13	0	1	76	8	5	.393	.435
Jose Alvarez	R-R	6-1	180	6-4-00	.253	.267	.246	29	95	13	24	4	0	1	9	11	1	0	0	33	2	1	.326	.336
Bryan Arias	R-R	6-0	205	6-6-97	.220	.288	.200	92	291	31	64	17	0	6	45	43	8	0	3	98	11	1	.340	.333
Matthew Barefoot	R-L	6-0	205	9-20-97	.000	--	.000	1	4	0	0	0	0	0	0	0	0	0	0	1	0	0	.000	.000
Luke Berryhill	R-R	6-1	227	5-28-98	.256	.270	.251	96	352	67	90	18	0	12	60	63	11	0	6	122	5	2	.409	.380
Jordan Brewer	R-L	6-1	204	8-1-97	.193	.148	.207	31	109	14	21	6	0	1	8	10	3	0	1	39	6	0	.275	.276
Edwin Diaz	R-R	6-2	223	8-25-95	.168	.081	.196	44	149	20	25	2	1	9	24	17	1	0	2	60	2	0	.376	.254
Yainer Diaz	R-R	6-0	195	9-21-98	.316	.278	.326	57	244	37	77	13	3	9	48	21	0	0	2	40	1	0	.504	.367
Justin Dirden	L-R	6-3	209	7-16-97	.324	.242	.354	92	349	64	113	32	5	20	73	41	13	1	3	94	7	2	.616	.411
Rolando Espinosa	R-R	6-0	177	1-5-01	.000	--	.000	3	4	0	0	0	0	0	0	0	0	0	0	2	0	0	.000	.000
Luis Guerrero	R-R	5-11	195	11-9-98	.080	.143	.070	20	50	8	4	0	0	1	3	12	0	0	1	31	3	0	.140	.254
Quincy Hamilton	L-L	5-10	190	6-12-98	.206	.179	.214	34	126	15	26	5	0	4	19	19	2	0	0	34	7	2	.341	.320
Grae Kessinger	R-R	6-2	204	8-25-97	.211	.229	.205	121	421	72	89	13	2	16	58	69	5	2	3	113	23	10	.366	.327
AJ Lee	R-R	6-0	200	5-26-97	.333	--	.333	1	3	0	1	0	0	0	0	0	0	0	0	0	0	0	.333	.333
Alex McKenna	R-R	6-2	204	9-6-97	.246	.269	.237	53	183	29	45	9	4	4	28	29	4	0	2	62	10	3	.404	.358
Joe Perez	R-R	6-2	198	8-12-99	.265	.159	.299	64	257	30	68	16	0	6	28	26	1	0	0	70	3	0	.397	.335
Cesar Salazar	L-R	5-9	185	3-15-96	.277	.278	.276	85	307	56	85	17	0	16	54	24	14	0	6	58	8	3	.489	.350
Scott Schreiber	R-R	6-3	230	10-13-95	.143	.091	.161	12	42	6	6	2	1	2	5	3	2	0	0	11	0	0	.381	.234
C.J. Stubbs	R-R	6-3	207	11-12-96	.211	.188	.218	41	133	22	28	2	2	11	25	17	6	0	2	60	8	1	.504	.323
Ronaldo Urdaneta	R-R	5-10	155	11-18-98	.100	.091	.111	6	20	4	2	1	0	0	2	3	0	0	0	10	2	0	.150	.217
Enmanuel Valdez	L-R	5-9	191	12-28-98	.357	.319	.372	44	168	40	60	16	0	11	45	34	1	0	2	47	4	2	.649	.463
Will Wagner	L-R	6-0	210	7-29-98	.251	.183	.278	72	251	40	63	12	2	6	28	35	9	2	1	57	5	1	.386	.361
Shay Whitcomb	R-R	6-3	202	9-28-98	.219	.272	.202	118	461	67	101	22	2	19	60	36	6	0	3	165	20	2	.399	.283

Pitching	B-T	HT	WT	DOB	W	L	ERA	G	GS	CG	SV	IP	H	R	ER	HR	BB	SO	AVG	vLH	vRH	K/9	BB/9
Jose Alvarez	R-R	6-1	180	6-4-00	0	1	27.00	1	0	0	0	2	6	6	6	1	2	1	.600	.250	.833	4.50	9.00
Bryan Arias	R-R	6-0	205	6-6-97	0	0	0.00	2	0	0	0	2	3	0	0	0	0	1	.375	.500	.250	5.40	0.00
Spencer Arrighetti	R-R	6-2	186	1-2-00	1	1	3.43	5	4	0	0	21	13	8	8	3	9	28	.181	.172	.186	12.00	3.86
Jose Betances	R-R	6-0	170	10-17-99	0	1	9.00	1	0	0	0	2	1	4	2	0	4	1	.143	.000	.200	4.50	18.00
Jose Bravo	R-R	6-3	213	6-10-97	9	4	4.49	24	16	0	1	108	115	61	54	16	34	99	.267	.262	.272	8.22	2.82
Tyler Brown	R-R	6-4	242	10-2-98	1	8	6.78	17	10	0	2	65	77	51	49	16	28	71	.289	.314	.273	9.83	3.88

Chandler Casey	R-R	6-2	195	5-30-96	3	1	5.82	21	0	0	1	34	37	23	22	5	20	22	.282	.347	.244	5.82	5.29
Adrian Chaidez	R-R	6-1	180	6-10-99	4	3	6.37	22	12	0	0	78	75	59	55	17	54	81	.255	.194	.288	9.39	6.26
Franny Cobos	R-R	5-9	182	2-1-01	0	0	8.31	6	0	0	0	13	19	12	12	3	7	16	.358	.389	.343	11.08	4.85
Devin Conn	R-R	5-11	169	4-3-97	7	3	2.92	35	0	0	7	52	36	21	17	5	21	46	.193	.167	.207	7.91	3.61
Cody Deason	R-R	6-4	214	12-26-96	5	5	6.14	21	14	0	0	78	91	66	53	5	46	72	.297	.333	.271	8.34	5.33
Jimmy Endersby	R-R	6-1	194	1-16-98	2	5	3.88	16	12	0	0	72	65	38	31	8	39	66	.240	.282	.211	8.25	4.88
Freylin Garcia	R-R	6-3	170	12-6-97	0	1	5.01	18	0	0	1	23	25	15	13	3	16	30	.281	.162	.365	11.57	6.17
Ruben Garcia	R-R	6-4	220	8-2-96	0	0	17.36	5	0	0	0	5	8	9	9	1	9	6	.364	.200	.412	11.57	17.36
Cesar Gomez	L-R	6-3	195	7-9-98	0	2	5.82	5	3	0	1	22	26	19	14	3	6	19	.286	.233	.333	7.89	2.49
Layne Henderson	R-R	6-4	200	6-8-96	5	4	3.89	28	0	0	0	44	32	22	19	4	22	56	.204	.209	.200	11.45	4.50
Nick Hernandez	R-R	6-1	212	12-30-94	0	0	0.00	3	0	0	0	4	0	0	0	0	1	8	.000	.000	.000	16.62	2.08
Michael Horrell	R-R	6-3	195	12-18-96	1	1	5.46	22	0	0	1	28	41	20	17	2	23	27	.345	.375	.324	8.68	7.39
Angel Macuare	R-R	6-2	250	3-3-00	1	4	8.76	6	5	0	0	25	31	24	24	3	14	23	.307	.295	.316	8.39	5.11
Lance McCullers Jr.	L-R	6-1	202	10-2-93	0	0	4.50	1	1	0	0	2	3	1	1	0	0	3	.333	.500	.200	13.50	0.00
Jaime Melendez	L-R	5-8	190	9-26-01	2	8	5.01	23	16	0	0	74	59	44	41	7	51	106	.219	.221	.218	12.95	6.23
Jayden Murray	R-R	6-1	190	4-11-97	0	2	4.28	6	6	0	0	27	24	14	13	3	11	26	.235	.342	.172	8.56	3.62
Jake Odorizzi	R-R	6-2	190	3-27-90	1	0	0.00	1	1	0	0	5	3	0	0	0	0	6	.176	.111	.250	10.80	0.00
Joe Record	R-R	6-3	232	1-12-95	1	0	3.22	16	1	0	4	22	16	8	8	0	14	26	.208	.233	.191	10.48	5.64
Julio Robaina	L-L	5-11	170	3-23-01	2	6	6.81	23	17	0	0	81	93	71	61	11	61	84	.291	.128	.343	9.37	6.81
Matt Ruppenthal	R-R	6-4	225	10-21-95	6	2	4.13	43	0	0	1	61	42	30	28	3	41	84	.197	.110	.243	12.39	6.05
Jonathan Sprinkle	R-R	6-6	237	7-8-98	4	2	5.88	39	0	0	2	49	44	34	32	4	34	70	.237	.259	.218	12.86	6.24
Misael Tamarez	R-R	6-1	206	1-16-00	3	6	4.62	24	19	0	1	103	76	55	53	18	55	122	.204	.238	.178	10.63	4.79
Jojanse Torres	R-R	6-2	188	8-4-95	0	2	8.54	33	0	0	2	39	52	46	37	11	32	41	.323	.333	.315	9.46	7.38
Derek West	R-R	6-5	257	12-2-96	5	2	4.82	32	0	0	4	47	44	27	25	3	29	52	.246	.236	.252	10.03	5.59

Fielding

Catcher	PCT	G	PO	A	E	DP	PB
Alvarez	.985	9	60	5	1	0	1
Berryhill	.972	41	396	15	12	2	2
Diaz	.983	23	216	18	4	3	2
Salazar	.989	52	494	37	6	2	1
Stubbs	.982	16	151	9	3	2	5

First Base	PCT	G	PO	A	E	DP
Alvarez	.960	3	22	2	1	5
Arias	.995	27	174	15	1	28
Berryhill	.986	32	192	20	3	27
Brewer	.987	10	75	2	1	9
Diaz	1.000	2	19	0	0	1
Diaz	1.000	26	184	21	0	12
Perez	1.000	4	29	0	0	7
Salazar	.990	16	99	4	1	11
Schreiber	1.000	1	3	0	0	1
Stubbs	1.000	14	84	3	0	14
Wagner	.978	9	44	0	1	2

Second Base	PCT	G	PO	A	E	DP
Arias	.909	7	9	11	2	6
Diaz	1.000	10	17	19	0	5
Espinosa	1.000	1	0	3	0	0
Kessinger	.977	7	15	27	1	9
Salazar	.929	3	4	9	1	6
Urdaneta	1.000	2	3	3	0	2
Valdez	.943	19	27	39	4	10
Wagner	.981	41	58	94	3	27
Whitcomb	.987	55	88	140	3	31

Third Base	PCT	G	PO	A	E	DP
Alvarez	.000	1	0	0	1	0
Arias	.878	25	10	33	6	1
Diaz	1.000	9	3	14	0	0
Espinosa	1.000	2	1	1	0	0
Kessinger	1.000	15	10	32	0	8
Lee	.667	1	1	1	1	0
Perez	.927	40	28	48	6	2
Urdaneta	.800	2	1	3	1	0
Valdez	1.000	14	12	17	0	3
Wagner	.938	21	13	32	3	5
Whitcomb	.946	15	8	27	2	3

Shortstop	PCT	G	PO	A	E	DP
Diaz	.909	18	26	34	6	9
Kessinger	.950	88	123	178	16	56
Wagner	.000	1	0	0	0	0
Whitcomb	.984	33	46	78	2	27

Outfield	PCT	G	PO	A	E	DP
Abreu	.970	83	156	6	5	1
Adolph	.989	53	90	1	1	0
Alvarez	.909	15	28	2	3	1
Arias	.974	21	37	1	1	1
Berryhill	1.000	4	5	0	0	0
Brewer	1.000	18	30	0	0	0
Diaz	1.000	6	12	0	0	0
Dirden	.993	84	138	1	1	0
Guerrero	1.000	16	28	2	0	0
Hamilton	.962	35	71	5	3	2
McKenna	.979	51	93	2	2	0
Perez	.920	17	22	1	2	0
Salazar	1.000	6	8	0	0	0
Schreiber	1.000	8	10	0	0	0
Stubbs	.923	7	12	0	1	0
Valdez	1.000	6	8	0	0	0

ASHEVILLE TOURISTS

HIGH CLASS A

SOUTH ATLANTIC LEAGUE

Batting	B-T	HT	WT	DOB	AVG	vLH	vRH	G	AB	R	H	2B	3B	HR	RBI	BB	HBP	SH	SF	SO	SB	CS	SLG	OBP
Jose Alvarez	R-R	6-1	180	6-4-00	.254	.263	.250	18	67	10	17	3	1	1	15	3	0	0	0	15	1	0	.373	.286
Colin Barber	L-L	6-0	200	12-4-00	.298	.234	.316	63	218	35	65	10	1	7	33	30	11	0	1	57	7	4	.450	.408
Tim Borden II	R-R	6-2	200	9-1-99	.298	.200	.319	15	57	10	17	1	0	6	17	4	4	0	0	29	1	0	.632	.385
Jordan Brewer	R-L	6-1	204	8-1-97	.247	.267	.242	24	81	20	20	3	1	5	16	15	6	0	1	25	5	2	.494	.398
Deury Carrasco	L-R	6-0	182	9-20-99	.202	.129	.218	52	173	28	35	10	2	4	19	32	2	0	1	69	7	1	.353	.332
Kenedy Corona	R-R	5-11	184	3-21-00	.290	.442	.257	62	245	56	71	15	3	10	37	28	5	0	1	63	20	6	.498	.373
J.C. Correa	R-R	6-0	200	9-15-98	.309	.250	.322	105	404	59	125	29	1	8	64	37	3	0	9	36	1	2	.446	.364
Marty Costes	R-R	5-9	200	12-18-95	.313	.000	.455	4	16	3	5	2	0	1	5	2	0	0	0	2	0	0	.625	.389
Zach Daniels	R-R	6-1	220	1-23-99	.282	.282	.282	95	358	76	101	15	1	23	64	48	4	0	2	127	22	5	.522	.371
Cristian Gonzalez	R-R	6-4	210	10-22-01	.227	.160	.243	104	409	54	93	18	1	10	48	29	4	0	3	127	1	2	.350	.283
Luis Guerrero	R-R	5-11	195	11-9-98	.223	.268	.214	65	242	46	54	6	4	7	29	27	1	0	0	100	14	3	.368	.304
Quincy Hamilton	L-L	5-10	190	6-12-98	.321	.378	.307	49	187	44	60	15	1	7	30	37	6	0	3	39	12	2	.524	.442
AJ Lee	R-R	6-0	200	5-26-97	.235	.250	.232	47	153	26	36	2	2	5	19	15	4	0	1	62	3	0	.373	.318
Joey Loperfido	L-R	6-4	195	5-11-99	.354	.571	.317	26	96	19	34	8	1	3	24	13	2	0	2	25	2	2	.552	.434
Miguel Palma	R-R	5-10	170	1-4-02	.327	.263	.341	27	104	15	34	4	1	7	29	7	2	0	0	22	0	0	.587	.381
Nerio Rodriguez	R-R	6-2	230	9-21-99	.291	.350	.281	39	134	25	39	8	0	8	24	18	3	0	1	40	0	0	.530	.385

Michael Sandle	R-R	5-11	185	9-21-98	.268	.261	.270	114	470	79	126	23	5	10	57	40	13	0	1	112	23	3	.402	.342
Luis Santana	R-R	5-9	196	7-20-99	.297	.275	.303	97	343	58	102	23	2	11	62	38	13	0	2	69	11	4	.472	.386
Juan Santander	R-R	6-2	180	12-9-02	.286	--	.286	2	7	1	2	0	0	0	1	0	0	0	0	2	0	0	.286	.286
Chad Stevens	R-R	6-4	215	2-3-99	.248	.242	.250	85	322	55	80	16	1	12	60	30	4	0	3	101	12	5	.416	.318
C.J. Stubbs	R-R	6-3	207	11-12-96	.217	.286	.194	42	138	29	30	5	0	10	27	24	4	0	1	68	6	1	.471	.347
Will Wagner	L-R	6-0	210	7-29-98	.276	.200	.290	45	163	22	45	7	1	4	25	32	1	0	3	41	3	1	.405	.392
Justin Williams	R-R	6-3	215	6-26-00	.216	.154	.227	26	88	6	19	6	0	2	11	5	1	0	0	41	1	2	.352	.266

Pitching	B-T	HT	WT	DOB	W	L	ERA	G	GS	CG	SV	IP	H	R	ER	HR	BB	SO	AVG	vLH	vRH	K/9	BB/9
Spencer Arrighetti	R-R	6-2	186	1-2-00	6	5	5.04	22	13	0	2	86	88	55	48	6	46	124	.259	.260	.258	13.03	4.83
Edinson Batista	R-R	6-2	185	5-19-02	1	0	3.14	3	2	0	0	14	9	6	5	2	9	14	.180	.143	.207	8.79	5.65
Jose Betances	R-R	6-0	170	10-17-99	3	3	6.49	29	0	0	3	35	25	26	25	2	34	44	.191	.203	.181	11.42	8.83
Walker Brockhouse	R-R	6-4	197	2-22-99	0	0	10.50	5	0	0	0	6	7	7	7	1	3	4	.304	.273	.333	6.00	4.50
Aaron Brown	R-R	6-4	220	3-19-99	4	9	5.28	25	14	0	2	109	129	73	64	21	34	95	.291	.313	.274	7.84	2.81
Adrian Chaidez	R-R	6-1	180	6-10-99	0	0	2.53	6	2	0	0	21	13	10	6	0	6	30	.169	.233	.128	12.66	2.53
Jacob Coats	R-R	6-6	235	6-4-98	0	1	7.34	25	0	0	1	34	37	30	28	5	28	43	.274	.238	.306	11.27	7.34
Franny Cobos	R-R	5-9	182	2-1-01	1	2	7.39	13	1	0	0	28	29	25	23	5	19	28	.274	.184	.351	9.00	6.11
Danny Cody	R-R	6-3	195	3-6-97	3	4	8.59	31	0	0	6	37	45	41	35	5	33	28	.304	.286	.318	6.87	8.10
Tommy DeJuneas	R-R	6-1	210	10-24-95	0	0	3.38	2	0	0	0	3	0	1	1	0	5	1	.000	.000	.000	3.38	16.88
Jacob DeLabio	R-R	6-5	205	9-19-97	0	0	0.00	5	0	0	2	5	5	0	0	0	4	4	.263	.333	.200	6.75	6.75
Kasey Ford	L-R	6-6	275	1-10-98	2	1	3.24	5	0	0	1	8	7	4	3	0	7	10	.241	.200	.263	10.80	7.56
Ray Gaither	R-R	6-4	224	3-4-98	0	2	3.92	13	8	0	2	41	38	23	18	5	21	52	.236	.205	.261	11.32	4.57
Cesar Gomez	L-R	6-3	195	7-9-98	7	4	4.56	21	11	0	2	77	79	43	39	11	22	76	.263	.277	.252	8.88	2.57
Colton Gordon	L-L	6-4	225	12-20-98	2	0	2.66	4	3	0	1	20	13	6	6	2	3	29	.178	.000	.236	12.84	1.33
Kyle Gruller	R-R	6-3	234	5-21-98	1	1	8.36	15	0	0	1	14	11	13	13	2	14	19	.212	.200	.222	12.21	9.00
Ryan Gusto	R-R	6-4	213	3-11-99	4	5	6.55	18	9	0	1	66	73	48	48	13	28	72	.275	.240	.309	9.82	3.82
Ernesto Jaquez	R-R	6-2	190	6-11-99	3	5	7.29	17	11	0	0	58	62	56	47	12	39	47	.266	.243	.286	7.29	6.05
Alfredi Jimenez	R-R	6-1	176	10-19-99	1	3	8.55	5	3	0	0	20	32	21	19	6	3	19	.352	.300	.377	8.55	1.35
Rhett Kouba	R-R	6-0	180	9-3-99	5	3	4.53	14	7	0	0	56	55	38	28	8	22	65	.250	.208	.282	10.51	3.56
AJ Lee	R-R	6-0	200	5-26-97	0	0	23.14	2	0	0	0	2	7	6	6	2	1	0	.583	.500	.625	0.00	3.86
Juan Pablo Lopez	L-L	6-4	222	2-17-99	1	1	10.61	12	5	0	0	28	48	38	33	1	20	29	.372	.333	.395	9.32	6.43
Chayce McDermott	L-R	6-3	197	8-22-98	6	1	5.50	19	10	0	0	72	57	48	44	9	43	114	.210	.274	.164	14.25	5.38
2-team total (2 Aberdeen IronBirds)					6	2	5.38	21	12	0	0	77	60	50	46	10	44	124	.207	.262	.165	14.49	5.14
Cole McDonald	L-R	6-1	218	3-11-97	2	6	6.86	28	5	0	1	60	61	49	46	7	50	100	.258	.317	.215	14.92	7.46
Christian Mejias	R-R	6-0	160	5-19-99	1	4	8.01	10	4	0	0	30	36	30	27	6	17	34	.295	.316	.277	10.09	5.04
Hunter Peck	L-L	6-2	195	5-5-97	0	2	9.13	14	0	0	1	24	35	28	24	8	19	22	.347	.484	.286	8.37	7.23
Luis Santana	R-R	5-9	196	7-20-99	0	0	0.00	3	0	0	0	3	1	0	0	0	1	1	.111	.000	.500	3.00	3.00
Diosmerky Taveras	R-R	6-5	256	9-23-99	5	3	4.76	23	12	0	0	76	65	43	40	3	49	92	.227	.186	.261	10.94	5.83
Heitor Tokar	R-R	6-6	276	10-25-00	3	4	8.02	20	11	0	0	76	102	79	68	13	32	64	.313	.273	.342	7.55	3.77
Palmer Wenzel	R-R	6-1	195	2-11-97	1	0	9.00	14	0	0	2	16	23	18	16	0	16	12	.319	.313	.325	6.75	9.00
Derek West	R-R	6-5	257	12-2-96	0	0	2.25	7	0	0	2	8	6	2	2	1	5	16	.207	.231	.188	18.00	5.63

Fielding

Catcher	PCT	G	PO	A	E	DP	PB
Alvarez	.992	12	123	8	1	1	2
Correa	.986	65	622	29	9	3	22
Palma	.980	15	143	2	3	0	3
Rodriguez	1.000	20	181	8	0	0	0
Santander	1.000	1	11	0	0	0	2
Stubbs	.978	21	202	20	5	2	6

First Base	PCT	G	PO	A	E	DP
Alvarez	1.000	4	16	1	0	1
Correa	1.000	1	7	0	0	1
Lee	.984	29	179	10	3	16
Loperfido	.972	5	32	3	1	5
Palma	1.000	11	64	4	0	6
Rodriguez	.982	16	100	12	2	8
Santana	.995	28	188	7	1	18
Stubbs	1.000	16	122	6	0	13
Wagner	1.000	11	92	11	0	6
Williams	.982	15	103	6	2	6

Second Base	PCT	G	PO	A	E	DP
Borden II	1.000	1	2	1	0	0
Carrasco	.973	10	10	26	1	9
Correa	.961	20	37	37	3	9
Guerrero	.952	41	65	93	8	17
Lee	1.000	5	7	11	0	3
Loperfido	1.000	3	11	6	0	3
Santana	.972	29	35	71	3	13
Stevens	.968	17	27	34	2	4
Wagner	.979	12	16	31	1	8

Third Base	PCT	G	PO	A	E	DP
Borden II	.864	9	6	13	3	2
Carrasco	.811	20	8	22	7	4
Correa	.903	15	6	22	3	2
Gonzalez	1.000	11	4	15	0	1
Lee	.870	8	7	13	3	2
Santana	.938	19	7	38	3	8
Stevens	.827	29	16	51	14	5
Wagner	.976	16	17	24	1	1
Williams	.913	10	5	16	2	1

Shortstop	PCT	G	PO	A	E	DP
Borden II	.900	4	3	6	1	1
Carrasco	.920	18	22	47	6	10
Gonzalez	.943	76	84	165	15	31
Stevens	.961	34	32	66	4	13

Outfield	PCT	G	PO	A	E	DP
Barber	.988	54	78	1	1	1
Brewer	.978	21	45	0	1	0
Carrasco	--	1	0	0	0	0
Corona	.959	56	113	4	5	1
Costes	1.000	4	8	1	0	1
Daniels	.973	79	137	5	4	1
Guerrero	.978	22	45	0	1	0
Hamilton	.989	44	89	5	1	1
Loperfido	1.000	13	23	1	0	0
Sandle	.985	106	185	6	3	3
Santana	.870	12	18	2	3	0
Stubbs	1.000	2	1	0	0	0

FAYETTEVILLE WOODPECKERS — *LOW CLASS A*

CAROLINA LEAGUE

Batting	B-T	HT	WT	DOB	AVG	vLH	vRH	G	AB	R	H	2B	3B	HR	RBI	BB	HBP	SH	SF	SO	SB	CS	SLG	OBP
Jose Alvarez	R-R	6-1	180	6-4-00	.333	.200	.342	23	78	13	26	4	1	1	12	13	0	0	0	19	5	1	.449	.429
Logan Cerny	R-R	6-1	185	9-28-99	.253	.268	.250	86	316	59	80	16	4	15	54	47	7	0	2	110	35	7	.472	.360
Ryan Clifford	L-L	6-3	200	7-20-03	.268	.167	.286	12	41	5	11	2	0	1	5	10	0	0	0	15	0	0	.390	.412
Zach Cole Jr.	L-R	6-2	190	8-4-00	.211	.250	.205	28	95	10	20	5	0	2	11	16	6	0	0	31	15	3	.326	.359
Kenedy Corona	R-R	5-11	184	3-21-00	.261	.429	.226	45	165	32	43	9	1	9	30	21	1	0	1	43	8	2	.491	.346
Zach Dezenzo	R-R	6-4	220	5-11-00	.255	.333	.238	27	102	13	26	3	0	4	15	12	2	0	1	37	4	0	.402	.342

Rolando Espinosa	R-R	6-0	177	1-5-01	.143	.000	.150	8	21	1	3	1	0	0	0	3	1	0	0	10	4	1	.190	.280
John Garcia	R-R	6-0	190	9-25-00	.174	.500	.143	8	23	1	4	3	0	0	3	0	3	0	0	11	0	0	.304	.269
Drew Gilbert	L-L	5-9	185	9-27-00	.238	.500	.176	6	21	4	5	0	0	1	2	1	0	0	0	0	3	1	.381	.273
Freddy Guilamo	R-R	5-11	160	12-10-00	.120	.103	.123	55	183	14	22	5	0	5	14	14	1	0	1	84	1	1	.230	.186
Jaxon Hallmark	R-R	5-10	175	10-2-98	.201	.256	.188	61	199	24	40	4	2	2	15	31	5	0	2	92	20	5	.271	.321
Quincy Hamilton	L-L	5-10	190	6-12-98	.291	.292	.291	36	134	22	39	8	0	6	19	20	5	0	1	27	8	0	.485	.400
Jackson Loftin	R-R	6-2	195	5-14-00	.179	.083	.197	23	78	9	14	3	1	2	9	9	4	0	0	26	6	1	.321	.297
Joey Loperfido	L-R	6-4	195	5-11-99	.304	.339	.296	82	296	51	90	17	3	9	45	40	9	0	3	76	30	9	.473	.399
Roilan Machandy	R-R	6-0	170	5-18-01	.000	.000	.000	1	4	0	0	0	0	0	0	0	0	0	0	2	0	0	.000	.000
Victor Mascai	L-R	6-2	209	2-10-01	.216	.314	.195	65	204	29	44	12	0	9	32	36	0	0	2	80	2	0	.407	.331
Garrett McGowan	L-L	6-4	215	4-14-99	.115	.067	.125	26	87	7	10	3	0	0	8	7	6	0	1	30	0	0	.149	.228
Jacob Melton	L-L	6-3	208	9-7-00	.324	.357	.316	19	71	11	23	6	0	4	13	11	2	0	1	20	4	2	.577	.424
Leosdany Molina	R-R	6-0	182	1-9-00	.214	.216	.214	116	457	54	98	16	2	6	37	32	9	0	3	113	22	5	.298	.277
Cody Orr	R-R	6-2	212	4-2-99	.192	.250	.181	78	261	34	50	7	1	2	14	37	10	0	2	90	25	5	.249	.313
Miguel Palma	R-R	5-10	170	1-4-02	.224	.212	.227	58	205	28	46	11	0	6	29	26	5	0	2	40	0	0	.366	.324
Collin Price	R-R	6-6	205	11-15-99	.290	.250	.296	19	62	7	18	5	0	2	10	7	1	0	0	17	0	0	.468	.371
Yeuris Ramirez	R-R	6-0	170	11-28-98	.199	.161	.205	70	216	25	43	6	1	6	25	25	11	0	2	97	12	4	.319	.311
Rainier Rivas	L-L	6-3	220	6-29-01	.152	.138	.156	40	138	10	21	3	0	4	13	7	1	0	0	52	1	0	.261	.199
Tommy Sacco Jr.	B-R	5-10	185	5-21-99	.198	.105	.221	25	96	14	19	4	1	2	6	11	0	0	0	26	7	1	.323	.280
Tyler Whitaker	R-R	6-4	190	8-2-02	.187	.164	.191	122	460	48	86	19	3	11	54	41	10	0	4	180	16	4	.313	.266
Justin Williams	R-R	6-3	215	6-26-00	.244	.412	.224	43	160	20	39	8	0	3	20	17	2	0	2	55	0	1	.350	.320
Ryan Wrobleski	R-R	6-1	196	2-2-00	.167	.000	.208	18	60	3	10	4	0	0	2	6	3	0	1	22	0	0	.233	.271

Pitching	B-T	HT	WT	DOB	W	L	ERA	G	GS	CG	SV	IP	H	R	ER	HR	BB	SO	AVG	vLH	vRH	K/9	BB/9
Shea Barry	R-R	6-2	195	12-22-97	0	6	8.68	20	8	0	0	57	67	65	55	6	53	51	.295	.317	.283	8.05	8.37
Edinson Batista	R-R	6-2	185	5-19-02	8	3	2.60	21	8	0	0	93	59	30	27	3	43	113	.177	.225	.147	10.90	4.15
Valente Bellozo	R-R	5-10	170	1-4-00	3	2	1.73	10	5	0	0	42	28	10	8	1	17	43	.193	.114	.267	9.29	3.67
Jose Betances	R-R	6-0	170	10-17-99	1	0	2.38	6	0	0	3	11	4	3	3	0	10	22	.108	.000	.160	17.47	7.94
A.J. Blubaugh	R-R	6-2	180	7-4-00	2	1	4.85	3	1	0	0	13	11	7	7	0	3	20	.224	.167	.258	13.85	2.08
Walker Brockhouse	R-R	6-4	197	2-22-99	0	1	2.57	3	0	0	0	7	6	3	2	0	3	4	.240	.333	.100	5.14	3.86
Carlos Calderon	R-R	6-0	175	10-4-01	4	6	4.13	26	14	0	0	105	86	57	48	9	60	113	.222	.218	.224	9.72	5.16
Jacob Coats	R-R	6-6	235	6-4-98	2	1	1.84	7	0	0	0	15	10	7	3	1	11	21	.185	.200	.179	12.89	6.75
Franny Cobos	R-R	5-9	182	2-1-01	1	1	1.98	4	2	0	0	14	5	3	3	0	5	18	.109	.000	.167	11.85	3.29
Jacob DeLabio	R-R	6-5	205	9-19-97	1	3	2.45	16	0	0	2	22	20	9	6	1	11	26	.241	.233	.245	10.64	4.50
Nolan DeVos	R-R	6-0	185	8-11-00	2	0	1.50	4	1	0	0	12	7	2	2	0	6	21	.167	.200	.136	15.75	4.50
Ian Foggo	R-R	6-1	200	6-1-98	0	0	3.60	4	0	0	1	5	3	3	2	0	11	14	.167	.286	.091	25.20	19.80
Kasey Ford	L-R	6-6	275	1-10-98	2	2	5.73	22	0	0	2	33	30	22	21	4	19	44	.236	.295	.205	12.00	5.18
Freylin Garcia	R-R	6-3	170	12-6-97	3	0	5.20	18	0	0	2	28	28	18	16	0	14	34	.252	.282	.236	11.06	4.55
Ronny Garcia	R-R	6-3	170	12-2-99	0	0	0.49	10	0	0	1	18	8	1	1	0	9	12	.129	.125	.132	5.89	4.42
Brett Gillis	R-R	6-2	215	9-29-99	0	0	0.00	2	0	0	0	3	0	0	0	0	3	4	.000	.000	.000	13.50	10.13
Colton Gordon	L-L	6-4	225	12-20-98	0	0	2.21	5	3	0	0	20	13	5	5	1	3	27	.183	.304	.125	11.95	1.33
Tyler Guilfoil	R-R	6-4	215	1-19-00	0	0	0.00	4	1	0	2	12	4	0	0	0	5	21	.108	.059	.150	16.20	3.86
Ryan Gusto	R-R	6-4	213	3-11-99	2	0	2.63	5	4	0	0	24	15	9	7	1	8	24	.169	.184	.157	9.00	3.00
Josh James	R-R	6-3	234	3-8-93	0	0	0.00	2	2	0	0	2	0	0	0	0	0	6	.000	.000	.000	27.00	0.00
Ernesto Jaquez	R-R	6-2	190	6-11-99	0	2	2.45	4	2	0	1	18	9	6	5	1	8	29	.145	.154	.139	14.24	3.93
Rhett Kouba	R-R	6-0	180	9-3-99	1	0	2.40	4	3	0	0	15	11	4	4	1	5	20	.200	.296	.107	12.00	3.00
Zack Matthews	B-R	6-0	205	1-31-99	2	4	9.12	14	4	0	0	26	23	29	26	5	26	39	.237	.167	.306	13.68	9.12
Christian Mejias	R-R	6-0	160	5-19-99	4	1	2.45	10	5	0	0	44	29	12	12	3	16	51	.187	.196	.182	10.43	3.27
Deylen Miley	R-R	6-2	210	1-25-98	3	8	4.64	24	15	0	0	83	70	49	43	5	59	111	.226	.227	.225	11.99	6.37
Peyton Plumlee	R-R	6-3	201	2-10-97	0	0	0.00	1	0	0	0	2	1	1	0	0	0	2	.143	.000	.167	10.80	0.00
Yeuris Ramirez	R-R	6-0	170	11-28-98	0	0	13.50	2	0	0	0	1	3	2	2	0	1	0	.429	.000	.600	0.00	6.75
Fabricio Reina	R-R	6-3	175	2-26-00	3	3	6.75	26	0	0	0	28	26	30	21	2	23	33	.234	.171	.271	10.61	7.39
Bryant Salgado	R-R	6-1	205	3-2-00	6	7	4.75	23	13	0	0	89	92	58	47	8	42	86	.262	.282	.252	8.70	4.25
Alimber Santa	R-R	5-10	163	5-3-03	0	0	--	1	0	0	0	0	1	1	1	0	2	0	1.000	1.000	--	--	--
Alex Santos II	R-R	6-4	194	2-10-02	0	11	5.99	23	14	0	1	83	74	61	55	15	37	104	.229	.198	.248	11.32	4.03
Jayson Schroeder	R-R	6-2	196	11-14-99	0	5	8.23	29	0	0	3	27	27	32	25	1	61	23	.267	.349	.207	7.57	20.09
Andre Scrubb	R-R	6-4	270	1-13-95	0	1	4.05	5	0	0	0	7	4	3	3	0	4	8	.160	.267	.000	10.80	5.40
Nic Swanson	R-R	6-2	180	7-8-99	3	4	4.99	24	12	0	0	83	78	48	46	13	50	93	.248	.190	.287	10.08	5.42
Austin Temple	R-R	6-4	180	8-24-99	0	0	10.80	4	0	0	1	3	4	4	4	2	0	4	.286	.200	.333	10.80	0.00
Miguel Ullola	R-R	6-1	184	6-19-02	2	2	3.25	22	11	0	2	72	39	30	26	3	55	120	.157	.151	.160	15.00	6.88
Palmer Wenzel	R-R	6-1	195	2-11-97	0	1	6.94	8	0	0	1	12	10	10	9	1	9	8	.238	.357	.179	6.17	6.94
Forrest Whitley	R-R	6-7	238	9-15-97	0	0	0.00	2	2	0	0	5	1	0	0	0	0	7	.059	.000	.100	12.60	0.00

Fielding

Catcher	PCT	G	PO	A	E	DP	PB
Alvarez	.973	10	99	11	3	1	2
Garcia	.987	6	71	5	1	0	1
Guilamo	.983	50	531	38	10	2	17
Palma	.985	42	433	28	7	3	5
Price	.980	10	89	9	2	1	1
Wrobleski	.988	13	156	11	2	1	2

First Base	PCT	G	PO	A	E	DP
Alvarez	1.000	5	32	3	0	2
Clifford	1.000	2	14	1	0	1
Dezenzo	1.000	5	31	1	0	3
Garcia	1.000	2	2	1	0	0
Guilamo	.923	5	36	0	3	2
Loperfido	.990	27	178	15	2	14
Mascai	.969	45	295	14	10	23
McGowan	.982	18	108	4	2	11
Orr	.750	1	2	1	1	0
Palma	1.000	14	95	3	0	4
Ramirez	1.000	1	1	0	0	0
Rivas	1.000	2	8	0	0	0
Williams	.989	15	86	8	1	3

Second Base	PCT	G	PO	A	E	DP
Dezenzo	.857	3	3	3	1	0
Espinosa	1.000	3	0	3	0	1
Hallmark	.940	24	45	49	6	13
Loftin	1.000	7	15	14	0	6
Loperfido	.966	26	31	55	3	5
Molina	.950	18	23	34	3	5
Orr	.972	13	16	19	1	2
Ramirez	.947	36	38	70	6	12
Sacco Jr.	1.000	13	18	15	0	2

Third Base	PCT	G	PO	A	E	DP

Dezenzo	.974	15	14	23	1	5
Hallmark	.895	12	7	10	2	1
Loftin	1.000	6	6	5	0	0
Molina	1.000	1	2	0	0	0
Orr	.889	30	18	46	8	2
Ramirez	.940	20	16	31	3	2
Sacco Jr.	.778	4	4	3	2	1
Whitaker	.970	27	26	38	2	3
Williams	.929	22	16	36	4	2

Shortstop	PCT	G	PO	A	E	DP
Loftin	1.000	8	7	26	0	3
Molina	.951	95	126	207	17	32
Orr	1.000	1	0	1	0	0
Sacco Jr.	1.000	6	6	10	0	1
Whitaker	.902	22	15	40	6	5

Outfield	PCT	G	PO	A	E	DP
Alvarez	.714	6	5	0	2	0
Cerny	.977	70	121	6	3	1
Clifford	.900	9	8	1	1	0
Cole Jr.	1.000	26	44	6	0	1
Corona	.984	33	55	6	1	1
Espinosa	1.000	5	10	0	0	0
Gilbert	1.000	5	8	1	0	0
Hallmark	1.000	26	41	3	0	2
Hamilton	.977	28	41	1	1	0
Loperfido	.964	30	50	4	2	1
Machandy	1.000	1	2	0	0	0
Mascai	1.000	7	5	0	0	0
McGowan	1.000	6	1	1	0	0
Melton	1.000	16	29	1	0	1
Orr	1.000	31	52	4	0	1
Price	1.000	3	2	0	0	0
Rivas	.957	30	45	0	2	0
Whitaker	.990	70	97	4	1	1
Wrobleski	1.000	4	4	0	0	0

FCL ASTROS BLUE

ROOKIE

FLORIDA COMPLEX LEAGUE

Batting	B-T	HT	WT	DOB	AVG	vLH	vRH	G	AB	R	H	2B	3B	HR	RBI	BB	HBP	SH	SF	SO	SB	CS	SLG	OBP
Ross Adolph	L-R	6-1	190	12-17-96	.250	--	.250	1	4	0	1	0	0	0	0	0	1	0	0	3	0	0	.250	.400
2-team total (6 FCL Astros Orange)					.286	1.000	.250	7	21	3	6	0	1	0	2	6	2	0	0	7	3	2	.381	.483
Colin Barber	L-L	6-0	200	12-4-00	.000	.000	.000	1	3	0	0	0	0	0	0	0	0	0	0	0	0	0	.000	.000
2-team total (2 FCL Astros Orange)					.200	.000	.286	3	10	0	2	0	0	0	0	0	0	0	0	1	0	0	.200	.200
Luke Berryhill	R-R	6-1	227	5-28-98	.000	.000	.000	1	3	0	0	0	0	0	0	0	0	0	0	0	0	0	.000	.000
2-team total (2 FCL Astros Orange)					.250	.000	.286	3	8	2	2	1	0	0	0	2	0	0	0	0	0	0	.375	.400
Tim Borden II	R-R	6-2	200	9-1-99	.259	.500	.240	11	27	9	7	1	0	0	4	7	2	0	1	8	3	0	.296	.432
Fernando Caldera	R-R	5-11	170	10-10-02	.143	--	.143	4	7	1	1	1	0	0	0	1	0	0	0	3	0	0	.286	.250
2-team total (36 FCL Astros Orange)					.277	.278	.276	40	94	20	26	5	1	4	20	13	3	0	3	40	3	1	.479	.372
Everette Cooper	R-R	6-0	165	9-16-02	.308	.500	.273	4	13	3	4	0	0	0	0	0	0	0	0	6	0	0	.308	.308
2-team total (25 FCL Astros Orange)					.127	.056	.151	29	71	7	9	0	0	0	3	4	6	0	0	33	1	1	.127	.235
Marty Costes	R-R	5-9	200	12-18-95	.250	--	.250	2	4	0	1	0	0	0	0	0	1	0	0	1	0	0	.250	.400
2-team total (2 FCL Astros Orange)					.444	1.000	.375	4	9	0	4	0	0	0	0	0	1	0	0	1	1	1	.444	.500
Narbe Cruz	R-R	6-3	181	10-1-00	.227	.286	.222	30	97	8	22	5	0	1	9	7	1	0	0	16	1	3	.309	.286
2-team total (19 FCL Astros Orange)					.263	.333	.254	49	156	16	41	13	0	2	21	10	2	0	0	28	5	3	.385	.315
Richel Del Rosario	R-R	6-0	191	2-27-04	.245	.200	.250	38	98	18	24	5	1	0	8	14	9	0	1	27	6	4	.316	.385
Omar Diaz	L-L	6-1	180	9-23-01	.210	.500	.178	46	119	13	25	4	2	1	7	20	1	0	0	40	2	1	.303	.329
Yamal Encarnacion	B-R	5-8	150	9-8-03	.273	.133	.286	52	176	21	48	7	2	1	13	22	3	0	0	32	9	9	.352	.363
John Garcia	R-R	6-0	190	9-25-00	.000	.000	.000	8	22	1	0	0	0	0	0	3	2	0	0	7	0	1	.000	.185
Adonis Giron	R-R	5-10	190	2-22-01	.198	.571	.165	28	86	5	17	4	0	0	9	5	3	0	1	22	2	1	.244	.263
Niko Goodrum	B-R	6-3	215	2-28-92	.364	.000	.400	4	11	5	4	2	0	0	3	3	0	0	0	5	1	0	.545	.500
2-team total (3 FCL Astros Orange)					.235	.000	.250	7	17	7	4	2	0	0	4	7	0	0	0	9	1	0	.353	.458
Dexter Jordan	R-R	6-0	193	10-30-99	.200	.111	.217	22	55	9	11	3	0	2	7	11	2	0	0	22	9	2	.364	.353
Jackson Loftin	R-R	6-2	195	5-14-00	.250	.000	.267	4	16	1	4	0	0	0	2	1	1	0	0	5	1	0	.250	.333
Dauri Lorenzo	B-R	5-9	186	10-29-02	.250	.333	.245	34	100	14	25	4	0	1	12	17	0	0	3	21	0	4	.320	.350
2-team total (5 FCL Astros Orange)					.272	.333	.269	39	114	20	31	5	1	1	15	21	0	0	3	22	0	4	.360	.377
Roilan Machandy	R-R	6-0	170	5-18-01	.000	--	.000	1	3	0	0	0	0	0	0	0	0	0	0	1	0	0	.000	.000
2-team total (48 FCL Astros Orange)					.242	.207	.250	49	149	36	36	8	2	1	13	16	10	0	0	58	23	9	.342	.354
Yohander Martinez	R-R	5-10	175	1-8-02	.235	.000	.258	46	136	18	32	0	1	2	19	30	9	0	2	22	5	5	.294	.401
Jacob Melton	L-L	6-3	208	9-7-00	.000	--	.000	4	17	0	0	0	0	0	0	0	0	0	0	6	1	0	.000	.000
Christopher Morales	R-R	6-1	170	9-30-02	.143	.250	.129	13	35	3	5	2	0	0	0	4	3	0	0	20	0	0	.200	.286
2-team total (14 FCL Astros Orange)					.159	.200	.153	27	69	8	11	2	1	0	1	8	5	0	0	38	0	2	.217	.293
Freudis Nova	R-R	6-1	178	1-12-00	.500	--	.500	1	4	1	2	1	0	0	0	0	0	0	0	0	0	0	.750	.500
2-team total (2 FCL Astros Orange)					.500	--	.500	3	6	2	3	1	0	1	1	1	1	0	0	1	0	0	1.167	.625
Josue Payano	R-R	5-10	150	6-22-03	.222	.000	.250	23	63	8	14	1	0	1	4	3	4	0	0	29	4	5	.286	.300
2-team total (11 FCL Astros Orange)					.237	.182	.244	34	93	11	22	2	0	1	4	6	5	0	0	41	5	8	.290	.317
Frank Perez	R-R	6-2	180	12-24-01	.000	--	.000	1	1	1	0	0	0	0	0	2	1	0	0	1	1	0	.000	.750
2-team total (44 FCL Astros Orange)					.189	.174	.192	45	122	23	23	5	2	4	17	16	14	0	0	58	4	2	.361	.349
Joe Perez	R-R	6-2	198	8-12-99	.333	--	.333	4	12	1	4	2	0	0	1	2	0	0	0	2	1	0	.500	.429
2-team total (7 FCL Astros Orange)					.316	.333	.313	11	38	3	12	3	0	0	3	2	0	0	0	9	1	0	.395	.350
Luis Perez	R-R	5-10	193	10-24-02	.210	.385	.192	49	143	19	30	7	2	3	18	32	0	0	1	54	17	2	.350	.352
2-team total (1 FCL Astros Orange)					.205	.333	.191	50	146	19	30	7	2	3	18	32	0	0	1	55	17	2	.342	.346
Juan Santander	R-R	6-2	180	12-9-02	.168	.000	.180	38	107	9	18	4	0	1	9	14	2	0	0	28	1	1	.234	.276
Scott Schreiber	R-R	6-3	230	10-13-95	.417	--	.417	4	12	3	5	0	0	0	0	2	1	0	0	1	1	0	.417	.533
2-team total (7 FCL Astros Orange)					.419	--	.419	11	31	8	13	1	0	1	5	7	1	0	0	9	2	1	.548	.538
Ricardo Toro	R-R	6-1	170	2-24-01	.246	.417	.230	47	134	22	33	5	0	5	21	14	10	0	2	23	3	1	.396	.356

Pitching	B-T	HT	WT	DOB	W	L	ERA	G	GS	CG	SV	IP	H	R	ER	HR	BB	SO	AVG	vLH	vRH	K/9	BB/9
Valente Bellozo	R-R	5-10	170	1-4-00	0	1	18.00	1	1	0	0	1	4	2	2	0	0	2	.571	.667	.500	18.00	0.00
2-team total (4 FCL Astros Orange)					0	2	7.71	5	5	0	0	7	11	6	6	0	1	11	.367	.333	.381	14.14	1.29
Reimy Beltre	R-R	6-3	170	12-12-00	3	1	2.43	10	4	0	1	37	21	11	10	0	26	44	.167	.174	.163	10.70	6.32
2-team total (3 FCL Astros Orange)					3	1	2.86	13	5	0	1	44	26	16	14	0	33	53	.172	.170	.173	10.84	6.75
A.J. Blubaugh	R-R	6-2	180	7-4-00	0	0	3.18	3	2	0	0	6	3	2	2	0	3	4	.167	.250	.100	6.35	4.76
Gerardo Bojorquez	R-R	6-3	195	10-23-97	0	1	27.00	1	1	0	0	1	2	2	2	0	0	0	.500	1.000	.333	0.00	0.00
Walker Brockhouse	R-R	6-4	197	2-22-99	3	3	3.83	12	3	0	0	40	37	26	17	2	25	49	.243	.224	.252	11.03	5.63
Tyler Brown	R-R	6-4	242	10-2-98	0	0	0.00	1	0	0	0	3	2	0	0	0	1	2	.200	.000	.333	6.00	3.00
2-team total (1 FCL Astros Orange)					0	0	1.93	2	1	0	0	5	7	2	1	0	1	3	.368	.375	.364	5.79	1.93
Yefri Carrillo	R-R	6-2	170	1-13-01	0	4	8.59	11	6	0	0	29	33	33	28	4	18	36	.280	.302	.267	11.05	5.52

Yeremi Ceballos	L-L	6-2	165	12-21-98	0	1	27.00	1	0	0	0	1	3	3	3	0	0	1	.600	1.000	.500	9.00	0.00
2-team total (1 FCL Astros Orange)					0	1	13.50	2	0	0	0	2	3	3	3	0	2	4	.375	.500	.333	18.00	9.00
Willy Collado	R-R	6-2	168	3-30-98	0	0	0.00	1	1	0	0	0	0	0	0	0	2	0	.000	--	.000	0.00	54.00
Jacob DeLabio	R-R	6-5	205	9-19-97	0	0	0.00	1	1	0	0	1	0	0	0	0	0	1	.000	.000	.000	9.00	0.00
2-team total (1 FCL Astros Orange)					0	0	0.00	2	1	0	0	3	0	0	0	0	0	5	.000	.000	.000	15.00	0.00
Nolan DeVos	R-R	6-0	185	8-11-00	0	0	3.86	2	1	0	0	2	2	1	1	0	3	1	.250	.000	.333	3.86	11.57
Kevin Dickey	B-L	6-4	195	3-31-98	0	0	0.00	2	1	0	0	3	1	1	0	0	3	4	.100	.000	.167	12.00	9.00
2-team total (1 FCL Astros Orange)					0	0	0.00	3	1	0	0	4	2	1	0	0	3	5	.154	.000	.222	11.25	6.75
Johan Figuereo	R-R	6-0	172	6-27-00	0	0	0.00	1	0	0	1	1	0	0	0	0	0	0	.000	--	.000	0.00	0.00
2-team total (12 FCL Astros Orange)					2	3	7.99	13	2	0	1	33	40	34	29	7	18	22	.299	.391	.250	6.06	4.96
Ray Gaither	R-R	6-4	224	3-4-98	1	0	6.75	2	2	0	0	4	3	3	3	1	1	5	.214	.167	.250	11.25	2.25
2-team total (1 FCL Astros Orange)					1	0	4.50	3	3	0	0	6	5	3	3	1	1	8	.227	.182	.273	12.00	1.50
Ronny Garcia	R-R	6-3	170	12-2-99	1	4	3.29	10	6	0	0	38	39	18	14	2	12	52	.262	.233	.274	12.21	2.82
Brett Gillis	R-R	6-2	215	9-29-99	0	0	3.38	2	1	0	0	3	2	2	1	0	1	6	.200	.250	.167	20.25	3.38
Colton Gordon	L-L	6-4	225	12-20-98	0	1	0.00	4	4	0	0	7	3	1	0	0	1	11	.120	.143	.111	14.14	1.29
2-team total (2 FCL Astros Orange)					0	1	2.08	6	5	0	0	13	9	4	3	1	2	22	.188	.200	.184	15.23	1.38
Tyler Gullfoll	R-R	6-4	215	1-19-00	1	0	2.45	2	0	0	0	4	1	1	1	1	2	6	.083	.250	.000	14.73	4.91
2-team total (1 FCL Astros Orange)					2	0	1.59	3	0	0	0	6	1	1	1	1	2	10	.056	.143	.000	15.88	3.18
Carlos Hiraldo	R-R	6-2	170	6-28-98	0	2	12.46	8	0	0	0	13	15	19	18	4	18	14	.273	.118	.342	9.69	12.46
2-team total (1 FCL Astros Orange)					0	2	11.25	9	0	0	0	16	17	21	20	4	21	17	.258	.143	.311	9.56	11.81
Michael Horrell	R-R	6-3	195	12-18-96	0	1	27.00	1	1	0	0	1	2	2	2	0	1	1	.667	1.000	.500	13.50	13.50
2-team total (1 FCL Astros Orange)					0	1	10.80	2	1	0	0	2	2	2	2	0	1	1	.333	.500	.250	5.40	5.40
Marshall Hunt	R-R	6-3	200	7-8-99	0	2	4.70	3	0	0	0	8	5	7	4	2	3	9	.192	.143	.211	10.57	3.52
2-team total (8 FCL Astros Orange)					1	2	3.90	11	2	0	0	30	19	17	13	7	14	36	.183	.154	.200	10.80	4.20
Alfredi Jimenez	R-R	6-1	176	10-19-99	0	2	10.80	2	2	0	0	2	2	3	2	0	2	2	.286	.333	.250	10.80	10.80
Roger Jorge	R-R	6-1	180	4-3-01	0	1	11.48	7	1	0	0	13	13	17	17	5	17	11	.260	.400	.167	7.43	11.48
2-team total (3 FCL Astros Orange)					0	2	7.77	10	1	0	0	22	18	22	19	6	21	23	.225	.333	.160	9.41	8.59
Eurys Martich	R-R	6-3	206	8-20-02	0	2	4.58	9	0	0	1	18	16	14	9	3	28	17	.250	.250	.250	8.66	14.26
Yohander Martinez	R-R	5-10	175	1-8-02	0	0	0.00	1	0	0	1	1	0	0	0	0	0	1	.000	.000	.000	9.00	0.00
Colin McKee	R-R	6-3	225	6-21-94	0	0	0.00	1	0	0	0	1	0	0	0	0	0	0	.000	.000	.000	0.00	0.00
2-team total (3 FCL Astros Orange)					0	0	1.59	4	1	0	0	6	3	1	1	0	2	8	.158	.167	.154	12.71	3.18
Alex Palmer	B-R	5-10	160	5-15-98	0	0	0.00	3	1	0	0	6	1	0	0	0	1	14	.053	.200	.000	21.00	1.50
Bryan Perez	R-R	5-11	160	4-14-00	3	1	2.92	17	0	0	1	25	19	13	8	1	17	29	.211	.222	.208	10.58	6.20
Peyton Plumlee	R-R	6-3	201	2-10-97	0	0	0.00	1	1	0	0	1	1	0	0	0	0	1	.250	.000	.500	9.00	0.00
Johangel Ramirez	R-R	6-2	193	9-10-01	1	4	5.72	11	1	0	0	28	30	24	18	0	14	22	.268	.300	.250	6.99	4.45
Juan Soto	R-R	6-2	209	4-30-03	0	1	5.01	13	3	0	2	41	35	34	23	4	34	48	.222	.311	.165	10.45	7.40
Danny Subero	R-R	6-4	194	11-2-01	0	1	4.97	6	0	0	1	13	11	10	7	2	8	12	.229	.316	.172	8.53	5.68
Blake Taylor	L-L	6-3	220	8-17-95	0	0	0.00	1	1	0	0	1	0	0	0	0	0	2	.000	.000	.000	18.00	0.00
Austin Temple	R-R	6-4	180	8-24-99	1	0	0.00	2	0	0	0	3	2	0	0	0	0	5	.182	.333	.125	15.00	0.00
2-team total (1 FCL Astros Orange)					1	0	0.00	3	1	0	0	7	2	0	0	0	0	10	.091	.143	.067	12.86	0.00
Ricardo Toro	R-R	6-1	170	2-24-01	0	0	27.00	1	0	0	0	1	2	3	3	1	1	0	.400	1.000	.250	0.00	9.00
Luis Vega	R-R	6-3	165	11-16-01	1	5	5.80	12	7	0	0	45	45	39	29	10	23	43	.256	.232	.267	8.60	4.60
Forrest Whitley	R-R	6-7	238	9-15-97	0	0	13.50	1	1	0	0	2	3	3	3	0	2	2	.333	.000	.429	9.00	9.00

Fielding

C: Berryhill 1, Caldera 2, Garcia 6, Santander 25, Toro 25. **1B:** Berryhill 1, Caldera 2, Cruz 7, Del Rosario 1, Diaz 14, Garcia 1, Giron 2, Jordan 1, Martinez 3, Payano 6, Santander 5, Schreiber 2, Toro 20. **2B:** Borden 2, Cruz 16, Del Rosario 1, Encarnacion 13, Jordan 2, Lorenzo 16, Martinez 5, Payano 4. **3B:** Borden 2, Cruz 6, Del Rosario 8, Encarnacion 8, Loftin 1, Martinez 28, Payano 4, Perez 3, Toro 1. **SS:** Borden 4, Cruz 1, Del Rosario 1, Encarnacion 18, Goodrum 3, Loftin 3, Lorenzo 18, Martinez 10. **OF:** Barber 1, Cooper 2, Costes 1, Del Rosario 22, Diaz 34, Encarnacion 19, Giron 20, Jordan 4, Machandy 1, Martinez 1, Melton 4, Morales 8, Payano 8, Perez 1, Perez 46, Santander 3, Schreiber 1.

FCL ASTROS ORANGE — *ROOKIE*

FLORIDA COMPLEX LEAGUE

Batting	B-T	HT	WT	DOB	AVG	vLH	vRH	G	AB	R	H	2B	3B	HR	RBI	BB	HBP	SH	SF	SO	SB	CS	SLG	OBP
Ross Adolph	L-R	6-1	190	12-17-96	.294	1.000	.250	6	17	3	5	0	1	0	2	6	1	0	0	4	3	2	.412	.500
2-team total (1 FCL Astros Blue)					.286	1.000	.250	7	21	3	6	0	1	0	2	6	2	0	0	7	3	2	.381	.483
Ricardo Balogh	B-R	6-3	175	7-9-02	.277	.419	.247	52	177	14	49	5	3	0	34	11	0	0	3	50	3	1	.339	.314
Colin Barber	L-L	6-0	200	12-4-00	.286	.000	.400	2	7	0	2	0	0	0	0	0	0	0	0	1	0	0	.286	.286
2-team total (1 FCL Astros Blue)					.200	.000	.286	3	10	0	2	0	0	0	0	0	0	0	0	1	0	0	.200	.200
Luke Berryhill	R-R	6-1	227	5-28-98	.400	--	.400	2	5	2	2	1	0	0	0	2	0	0	0	0	0	0	.600	.571
2-team total (1 FCL Astros Blue)					.250	.000	.286	3	8	2	2	1	0	0	0	2	0	0	0	0	0	0	.375	.400
Fernando Caldera	R-R	5-11	170	10-10-02	.287	.278	.290	36	87	19	25	4	1	4	20	12	3	0	3	37	3	1	.494	.381
2-team total (4 FCL Astros Blue)					.277	.278	.276	40	94	20	26	5	1	4	20	13	3	0	3	40	3	1	.479	.372
Ryan Clifford	L-L	6-3	200	7-20-03	.222	.250	.219	13	36	8	8	3	0	1	5	12	2	0	0	16	2	0	.389	.440
Zach Cole Jr.	L-R	6-2	190	8-4-00	.150	.000	.176	5	20	3	3	1	0	0	1	0	0	0	0	6	2	0	.200	.150
Everette Cooper	R-R	6-0	165	9-16-02	.086	.000	.119	25	58	4	5	0	0	0	3	4	6	0	0	27	1	1	.086	.221
2-team total (4 FCL Astros Blue)					.127	.056	.151	29	71	7	9	0	0	0	3	4	6	0	0	33	1	1	.127	.235
Marty Costes	R-R	5-9	200	12-18-95	.600	1.000	.500	2	5	0	3	0	0	0	0	0	0	0	0	0	1	1	.600	.600
2-team total (2 FCL Astros Blue)					.444	1.000	.375	4	9	0	4	0	0	0	0	0	1	0	0	1	1	1	.444	.500
Narbe Cruz	R-R	6-3	181	10-1-00	.322	.364	.313	19	59	8	19	8	0	1	12	3	1	0	0	12	4	0	.508	.365
2-team total (30 FCL Astros Blue)					.263	.333	.254	49	156	16	41	13	0	2	21	10	2	0	0	28	5	3	.385	.315
Luis Encarnacion	R-R	5-8	170	9-25-02	.264	.227	.271	40	140	32	37	9	0	5	29	14	3	0	1	19	1	1	.436	.342
Rolando Espinosa	R-R	6-0	177	1-5-01	.243	.286	.235	45	140	31	34	3	1	6	32	29	3	0	3	50	32	5	.407	.377
Drew Gilbert	L-L	5-9	185	9-27-00	.455	.667	.375	4	11	5	5	1	0	1	4	3	1	0	0	2	3	0	.818	.600
Richi Gonzalez	R-R	6-2	182	12-29-02	.250	.292	.241	50	136	24	34	7	0	2	18	17	3	0	1	47	15	6	.346	.344

Niko Goodrum	B-R	6-3	215	2-28-92	.000	--	.000	3	6	2	0	0	0	0	1	4	0	0	0	4	0	0	.000	.400
2-team total (4 FCL Astros Blue)					.235	.000	.250	7	17	7	4	2	0	0	4	7	0	0	0	9	1	0	.353	.458
Freddy Guilamo	R-R	5-11	160	12-10-00	.211	.250	.200	9	19	3	4	0	0	1	2	3	1	0	0	8	1	1	.368	.348
Carlos Hurtado	R-R	6-0	170	5-18-01	.237	.333	.208	31	93	11	22	5	0	0	6	3	1	0	0	11	3	0	.290	.268
Dauri Lorenzo	B-R	5-9	186	10-29-02	.429	--	.429	5	14	6	6	1	1	0	3	4	0	0	0	1	0	0	.643	.556
2-team total (34 FCL Astros Blue)					.272	.333	.269	39	114	20	31	5	1	1	15	21	0	0	3	22	0	4	.360	.377
Roilan Machandy	R-R	6-0	170	5-18-01	.247	.207	.256	48	146	36	36	8	2	1	13	16	10	0	0	57	23	9	.349	.360
2-team total (1 FCL Astros Blue)					.242	.207	.250	49	149	36	36	8	2	1	13	16	10	0	0	58	23	9	.342	.354
Christopher Morales	R-R	6-1	170	9-30-02	.176	.167	.179	14	34	5	6	0	1	0	1	4	2	0	0	18	0	2	.235	.300
2-team total (13 FCL Astros Blue)					.159	.200	.153	27	69	8	11	2	1	0	1	8	5	0	0	38	0	2	.217	.293
Hector Nieves	L-R	6-3	185	7-8-03	.212	.174	.224	32	99	11	21	1	0	1	9	11	3	0	3	29	4	2	.253	.302
Freudis Nova	R-R	6-1	178	1-12-00	.500	--	.500	2	2	1	1	0	0	1	1	1	1	0	0	1	0	0	2.000	.750
2-team total (1 FCL Astros Blue)					.500	--	.500	3	6	2	3	1	0	1	1	1	1	0	0	1	0	0	1.167	.625
Josue Payano	R-R	5-10	150	6-22-03	.267	.500	.231	11	30	3	8	1	0	0	0	3	1	0	0	12	1	3	.300	.353
2-team total (23 FCL Astros Blue)					.237	.182	.244	34	93	11	22	2	0	1	4	6	5	0	0	41	5	8	.290	.317
Frank Perez	R-R	6-2	180	12-24-01	.190	.174	.194	44	121	22	23	5	2	4	17	14	13	0	0	57	3	2	.364	.338
2-team total (1 FCL Astros Blue)					.189	.174	.192	45	122	23	23	5	2	4	17	16	14	0	0	58	4	2	.361	.349
Joe Perez	R-R	6-2	198	8-12-99	.308	.333	.300	7	26	2	8	1	0	0	2	0	0	0	0	7	0	0	.346	.308
2-team total (4 FCL Astros Blue)					.316	.333	.313	11	38	3	12	3	0	0	3	2	0	0	0	9	1	0	.395	.350
Luis Perez	R-R	5-10	193	10-24-02	.000	.000	.000	1	3	0	0	0	0	0	0	0	0	0	0	1	0	0	.000	.000
2-team total (49 FCL Astros Blue)					.205	.333	.191	50	146	19	30	7	2	3	18	32	0	0	1	55	17	2	.342	.346
Tommy Sacco Jr.	B-R	5-10	185	5-21-99	.000	.000	.000	1	3	1	0	0	0	0	0	0	1	0	0	2	1	0	.000	.250
Scott Schreiber	R-R	6-3	230	10-13-95	.421	--	.421	7	19	5	8	1	0	1	5	5	0	0	0	8	1	1	.632	.542
2-team total (4 FCL Astros Blue)					.419	--	.419	11	31	8	13	1	0	1	5	7	1	0	0	9	2	1	.548	.538
Ronaldo Urdaneta	R-R	5-10	155	11-18-98	.150	.158	.148	29	80	15	12	1	1	0	4	21	5	0	0	24	10	0	.188	.358

Pitching	B-T	HT	WT	DOB	W	L	ERA	G	GS	CG	SV	IP	H	R	ER	HR	BB	SO	AVG	vLH	vRH	K/9	BB/9
Jose Andujar	R-R	5-10	158	2-10-02	0	2	6.75	13	3	0	2	28	20	25	21	3	35	37	.202	.278	.159	11.89	11.25
Valente Bellozo	R-R	5-10	170	1-4-00	0	1	6.00	4	4	0	0	6	7	4	4	0	1	9	.304	.167	.353	13.50	1.50
2-team total (1 FCL Astros Blue)					0	2	7.71	5	5	0	0	7	11	6	6	0	1	11	.367	.333	.381	14.14	1.29
Reimy Beltre	R-R	6-3	170	12-12-00	0	0	5.14	3	1	0	0	7	5	5	4	0	7	9	.200	.143	.222	11.57	9.00
2-team total (10 FCL Astros Blue)					3	1	2.86	13	5	0	1	44	26	16	14	0	33	53	.172	.170	.173	10.84	6.75
Tyler Brown	R-R	6-4	242	10-2-98	0	0	5.40	1	1	0	0	2	5	2	1	0	0	1	.556	.750	.400	5.40	0.00
2-team total (1 FCL Astros Blue)					0	0	1.93	2	1	0	0	5	7	2	1	0	1	3	.368	.375	.364	5.79	1.93
Riley Cabral	R-R	5-11	211	1-25-97	0	0	0.00	1	1	0	0	1	0	0	0	0	1	0	.000	.000	.000	0.00	9.00
Yeremi Ceballos	L-L	6-2	165	12-21-98	0	0	0.00	1	0	0	0	1	0	0	0	0	2	3	.000	.000	.000	27.00	18.00
2-team total (1 FCL Astros Blue)					0	1	13.50	2	0	0	0	2	3	3	3	0	2	4	.375	.500	.333	18.00	9.00
Jacob DeLabio	R-R	6-5	205	9-19-97	0	0	0.00	1	0	0	0	2	0	0	0	0	0	4	.000	.000	.000	18.00	0.00
2-team total (1 FCL Astros Blue)					0	0	0.00	2	1	0	0	3	0	0	0	0	0	5	.000	.000	.000	15.00	0.00
Kevin Dickey	B-L	6-4	195	3-31-98	0	0	0.00	1	0	0	0	1	1	0	0	0	0	1	.333	--	.333	9.00	0.00
2-team total (2 FCL Astros Blue)					0	0	0.00	3	1	0	0	4	2	1	0	0	3	5	.154	.000	.222	11.25	6.75
Shawn Dubin	R-R	6-1	171	9-6-95	0	0	0.00	2	2	0	0	2	2	0	0	0	0	2	.250	.500	.000	9.00	0.00
Carlos Espinosa	R-R	6-2	188	8-8-01	1	2	2.60	11	4	0	2	28	20	8	8	1	10	28	.200	.258	.174	9.11	3.25
Johan Figuereo	R-R	6-0	172	6-27-00	2	3	8.24	12	2	0	0	32	40	34	29	7	18	22	.305	.391	.259	6.25	5.12
2-team total (1 FCL Astros Blue)					2	3	7.99	13	2	0	1	33	40	34	29	7	18	22	.299	.391	.250	6.06	4.96
Ian Foggo	R-R	6-1	200	6-1-98	2	3	1.98	19	0	0	6	27	17	11	6	0	25	37	.175	.286	.130	12.18	8.23
Ray Gaither	R-R	6-4	224	3-4-98	0	0	0.00	1	1	0	0	2	2	0	0	0	0	3	.250	.200	.333	13.50	0.00
2-team total (2 FCL Astros Blue)					1	0	4.50	3	3	0	0	6	5	3	3	1	1	8	.227	.182	.273	12.00	1.50
Elvis Garcia	R-R	6-0	165	9-24-02	1	3	6.61	5	2	0	0	16	16	16	12	1	10	11	.232	.222	.238	6.06	5.51
Colton Gordon	L-L	6-4	225	12-20-98	0	0	4.50	2	1	0	0	6	6	3	3	1	1	11	.261	.333	.250	16.50	1.50
2-team total (4 FCL Astros Blue)					0	1	2.08	6	5	0	0	13	9	4	3	1	2	22	.188	.200	.184	15.23	1.38
Freddy Guilamo	R-R	5-11	160	12-10-00	0	0	0.00	1	0	0	0	1	0	0	0	0	0	0	.000	--	.000	0.00	0.00
Tyler Guilfoil	R-R	6-4	215	1-19-00	1	0	0.00	1	0	0	0	2	0	0	0	0	0	4	.000	.000	.000	18.00	0.00
2-team total (2 FCL Astros Blue)					2	0	1.59	3	0	0	0	6	1	1	1	1	2	10	.056	.143	.000	15.88	3.18
Carlos Hiraldo	R-R	6-2	170	6-28-98	0	0	6.00	1	0	0	0	3	2	2	2	0	3	3	.182	.250	.143	9.00	9.00
2-team total (8 FCL Astros Blue)					0	2	11.25	9	0	0	0	16	17	21	20	4	21	17	.258	.143	.311	9.56	11.81
Kevin Holcomb	R-R	6-5	210	1-5-99	4	2	5.28	9	3	0	0	29	30	19	17	2	13	24	.275	.225	.304	7.45	4.03
Michael Horrell	R-R	6-3	195	12-18-96	0	0	0.00	1	0	0	0	1	0	0	0	0	0	0	.000	.000	.000	0.00	0.00
2-team total (1 FCL Astros Blue)					0	1	10.80	2	1	0	0	2	2	2	2	0	1	1	.333	.500	.250	5.40	5.40
Marshall Hunt	R-R	6-3	200	7-8-99	1	0	3.63	8	2	0	0	22	14	10	9	5	11	27	.179	.156	.196	10.88	4.43
2-team total (3 FCL Astros Blue)					1	2	3.90	11	2	0	0	30	19	17	13	7	14	36	.183	.154	.200	10.80	4.20
Roger Jorge	R-R	6-1	180	4-3-01	0	1	2.08	3	0	0	0	9	5	5	2	1	4	12	.167	.200	.150	12.46	4.15
2-team total (7 FCL Astros Blue)					0	2	7.77	10	1	0	0	22	18	22	19	6	21	23	.225	.333	.160	9.41	8.59
Zack Matthews	B-R	6-0	205	1-31-99	0	0	0.00	1	1	0	0	1	0	0	0	0	0	2	.000	--	.000	18.00	0.00
Colin McKee	R-R	6-3	225	6-21-94	0	0	1.93	3	1	0	0	5	3	1	1	0	2	8	.188	.250	.167	15.43	3.86
2-team total (1 FCL Astros Blue)					0	0	1.59	4	1	0	0	6	3	1	1	0	2	8	.158	.167	.154	12.71	3.18
Cristofer Mezquita	L-L	6-0	175	6-6-00	3	1	2.60	12	5	1	0	52	46	17	15	1	24	49	.240	.240	.239	8.48	4.15
Mark Moclair	R-R	6-2	205	3-13-97	3	4	3.21	10	4	0	0	34	22	21	12	0	15	45	.179	.146	.195	12.03	4.01
Jeremy Molero	R-R	6-2	170	11-8-99	2	2	3.13	12	4	0	0	32	16	16	11	0	18	46	.145	.128	.155	13.07	5.12
Jose Nodal	L-L	6-3	195	7-16-02	5	3	3.18	14	5	0	1	51	43	24	18	5	21	53	.230	.192	.257	9.35	3.71
Daniel Pacheco	R-R	5-10	214	12-4-01	0	0	30.00	4	2	0	0	3	4	10	10	2	8	2	.308	.000	.444	6.00	24.00
Frank Perez	R-R	6-2	180	12-24-01	0	1	18.00	1	0	0	0	1	2	3	2	0	2	2	.333	.000	.400	18.00	18.00
Zac Rosscup	R-L	6-2	220	6-9-88	0	0	27.00	1	1	0	0	1	3	3	3	0	0	1	.429	.333	.500	9.00	0.00
Alimber Santa	R-R	5-10	163	5-3-03	0	0	9.00	2	1	0	0	2	3	2	2	0	0	4	.333	.500	.200	18.00	0.00
Austin Temple	R-R	6-4	180	8-24-99	0	0	0.00	1	1	0	0	4	0	0	0	0	0	5	.000	.000	.000	11.25	0.00

2-team total (2 FCL Astros Blue)					1	0	0.00	3	1	0	0	7	2	0	0	0	0	10	.091	.143	.067	12.86	0.00
Ronaldo Urdaneta	R-R	5-10	155	11-18-98	0	0	0.00	1	0	0	0	1	0	0	0	0	1	1	.000	.000	.000	9.00	9.00
Logan VanWey	R-R	6-2	205	2-14-99	1	0	0.00	4	2	0	0	8	1	0	0	0	3	16	.040	.000	.077	18.00	3.38

Fielding

C: Berryhill 1, Caldera 28, Encarnacion 12, Guilamo 5, Hurtado 22. **1B:** Balogh 35, Berryhill 1, Caldera 1, Clifford 1, Encarnacion 11, Espinosa 3, Goodrum 1, Guilamo 1, Hurtado 9, Schreiber 5. **2B:** Balogh 2, Cruz 11, Encarnacion 13, Espinosa 10, Goodrum 1, Lorenzo 3, Nieves 4, Payano 8, Perez 1, Urdaneta 15. **3B:** Balogh 20, Cruz 6, Encarnacion 10, Espinosa 4, Gonzalez 2, Lorenzo 1, Machandy 10, Nieves 1, Payano 2, Perez 6, Sacco Jr. 1, Urdaneta 6. **SS:** Balogh 2, Cruz 2, Espinosa 28, Goodrum 1, Machandy 1, Nieves 26, Nova 2, Payano 1, Urdaneta 4. **OF:** Adolph 5, Balogh 1, Barber 2, Caldera 1, Clifford 9, Cole Jr. 5, Cooper 19, Costes 2, Encarnacion 4, Espinosa 10, Gilbert 2, Gonzalez 48, Guilamo 2, Machandy 42, Morales 9, Perez 34, Perez 1, Urdaneta 1.

DSL HOU BLUE — ROOKIE

DOMINICAN SUMMER LEAGUE

Batting	B-T	HT	WT	DOB	AVG	vLH	vRH	G	AB	R	H	2B	3B	HR	RBI	BB	HBP	SH	SF	SO	SB	CS	SLG	OBP
Jose Arias	R-R	5-10	170	11-3-04	.115	.067	.127	33	78	7	9	0	2	1	5	5	5	0	0	45	10	3	.205	.216
2-team total (24 DSL HOU Orange)					.164	.103	.180	57	140	18	23	6	2	1	12	10	7	0	0	76	14	5	.257	.255
Daniel Castro	B-R	5-10	190	10-21-03	.206	.280	.190	51	141	19	29	4	2	4	11	18	9	0	0	39	5	5	.318	.333
Carlos Cauro	R-R	6-2	184	6-14-05	.191	.500	.161	25	68	6	13	2	0	0	5	11	2	0	1	21	0	1	.221	.317
Andy Colon	R-R	6-1	176	1-5-04	.127	.296	.087	55	142	10	18	4	1	1	8	16	5	0	0	85	11	3	.190	.239
Luis Colon	B-R	5-8	160	12-2-03	.135	.500	.065	19	37	6	5	1	1	0	1	5	2	0	0	18	2	6	.216	.273
Axell De Paula	R-R	5-10	178	10-18-04	.224	.276	.211	55	143	17	32	7	0	4	14	12	9	0	0	66	12	7	.357	.323
Victor Diaz	R-R	5-10	175	11-25-01	.000	--	.000	1	2	1	0	0	0	0	0	1	0	0	0	1	0	0	.000	.333
2-team total (34 DSL HOU Orange)					.271	.471	.221	35	85	16	23	4	0	3	13	13	0	0	0	19	6	1	.424	.367
Jesus Fernandez	R-R	6-0	150	8-26-03	.139	.143	.138	58	151	22	21	5	1	1	13	31	3	0	3	45	13	5	.205	.293
Sandro Gaston	R-R	6-3	210	12-16-02	.319	.500	.293	47	141	31	45	14	1	12	37	22	4	0	2	41	3	4	.688	.420
Kenni Gomez	L-R	5-11	185	5-14-05	.294	.143	.318	37	102	20	30	5	2	4	24	18	1	0	1	28	10	5	.500	.402
Alberto Hernandez	R-R	6-0	169	2-4-04	.235	.290	.222	56	166	23	39	6	2	3	22	20	5	0	2	27	9	7	.349	.332
Marco Marcelino	R-R	5-9	190	10-30-04	.184	.000	.220	18	49	11	9	0	0	0	4	11	0	0	3	17	6	0	.184	.317
Karniel Pratt	R-R	5-10	170	1-3-05	.210	.200	.212	54	143	24	30	6	0	1	8	33	3	0	0	60	12	5	.273	.369
Rafael Ramirez	R-R	6-1	185	11-9-04	.153	.286	.121	52	144	13	22	3	1	3	17	15	4	0	1	40	7	3	.250	.250
Jose Robledo	B-R	5-7	188	9-14-03	.200	.111	.224	41	125	15	25	2	1	1	10	4	2	0	1	39	8	2	.256	.235
Brayan Sanchez	R-R	6-0	195	12-19-04	.222	.000	.267	9	18	1	4	0	0	0	0	2	0	0	0	7	1	1	.222	.300
2-team total (29 DSL HOU Orange)					.183	.000	.228	38	71	11	13	3	0	1	7	21	6	0	1	29	2	2	.268	.404
Andrews Sosa	R-R	5-10	160	1-7-05	.233	.300	.212	19	43	11	10	1	0	0	3	9	3	0	0	11	4	2	.256	.400

Pitching	B-T	HT	WT	DOB	W	L	ERA	G	GS	CG	SV	IP	H	R	ER	HR	BB	SO	AVG	vLH	vRH	K/9	BB/9
Dawill Almonte	R-R	5-9	168	10-19-01	2	0	2.77	12	5	0	1	39	31	14	12	2	10	38	.215	.217	.213	8.77	2.31
2-team total (1 DSL HOU Orange)					2	0	2.68	13	5	0	2	40	31	14	12	2	10	41	.209	.214	.203	9.15	2.23
Henry Bibieca	R-R	6-1	176	12-15-02	0	4	14.09	8	0	0	0	8	11	20	12	2	8	7	.297	.353	.250	8.22	9.39
Jonaiker Castellar	R-R	5-10	141	5-23-02	0	0	2.89	7	0	0	1	9	10	5	3	1	2	8	.286	.211	.375	7.71	1.93
Anthony Cruz	R-R	5-11	179	8-19-02	1	2	4.79	9	2	0	0	21	16	13	11	2	13	24	.195	.233	.154	10.45	5.66
Marcos Eusebio	R-R	6-1	180	9-5-00	0	2	6.75	8	4	0	0	24	24	23	18	5	26	28	.261	.256	.265	10.50	9.75
Daniel Familia	R-R	6-0	203	9-5-02	0	0	0.00	4	0	0	0	3	3	1	0	0	3	1	.250	.250	.250	2.70	8.10
Jesus Fernandez	R-R	6-0	150	8-26-03	0	1	10.13	4	0	0	0	3	7	5	3	0	0	1	.538	.636	.000	3.38	0.00
Franklin Gil	R-R	5-11	155	1-6-03	4	0	1.88	12	0	0	3	14	14	4	3	1	4	18	.264	.167	.345	11.30	2.51
Edwin Gonzalez	R-R	6-2	153	7-19-04	0	0	5.40	5	2	0	0	12	13	11	7	0	5	12	.271	.389	.200	9.26	3.86
Pedro Marquez	R-R	5-11	172	12-7-01	2	0	7.53	7	2	0	0	14	13	15	12	1	14	12	.245	.226	.273	7.53	8.79
Sandy Mejia	R-R	6-0	160	1-3-04	2	3	4.20	12	7	0	0	41	30	19	19	2	29	44	.205	.200	.209	9.74	6.42
Abel Mendez	R-R	6-4	205	4-4-03	0	4	9.75	14	4	0	1	24	26	27	26	0	36	26	.286	.150	.392	9.75	13.50
Oswald Mori	R-R	6-4	185	6-20-02	1	2	4.40	9	1	0	1	14	9	8	7	0	10	16	.180	.154	.208	10.05	6.28
Alain Pena	R-R	5-11	155	4-10-03	2	5	3.29	12	7	0	0	38	32	18	14	0	20	39	.222	.174	.267	9.16	4.70
Engel Daniel Peralta	R-R	6-4	190	6-3-04	1	1	2.05	10	1	0	0	22	11	6	5	0	10	24	.149	.111	.170	9.82	4.09
Chanderson Perez	R-R	6-0	195	9-22-01	3	2	6.26	16	0	0	0	23	28	23	16	1	10	20	.289	.400	.192	7.83	3.91
Darwin Rosario	R-R	6-3	180	6-15-00	0	0	0.00	1	1	0	0	1	0	0	0	0	1	1	.000	.000	.000	9.00	9.00
Leomar Rosario	R-R	6-6	217	6-11-03	0	2	6.43	11	5	0	0	28	21	22	20	1	27	29	.210	.178	.236	9.32	8.68
Wilmy Sanchez	R-R	5-9	193	12-17-03	3	0	2.12	12	4	0	3	34	27	10	8	2	15	49	.213	.200	.222	12.97	3.97
Yeriel Santos	R-R	6-0	165	11-20-03	0	3	2.27	12	7	0	0	40	25	16	10	1	24	41	.179	.203	.160	9.30	5.45
Jose Serrano	R-R	6-2	212	2-14-04	0	1	4.91	7	0	0	1	11	13	7	6	1	4	7	.295	.281	.333	5.73	3.27
Euris Vasquez	R-R	6-0	163	10-24-03	0	2	6.14	5	0	0	0	7	8	8	5	1	7	7	.296	.250	.333	8.59	8.59
2-team total (4 DSL HOU Orange)					0	3	9.53	9	0	0	0	11	15	15	12	3	10	10	.326	.348	.304	7.94	7.94
Luis Victorino	R-R	6-0	167	8-18-02	2	3	2.88	12	6	0	1	34	27	16	11	2	14	38	.227	.167	.268	9.96	3.67
Elvin Villega	R-R	6-2	173	7-13-02	0	0	0.00	2	2	0	0	2	2	0	0	0	0	2	.250	.400	.000	9.00	0.00

Fielding

C: Castro 28, Cauro 11, Diaz 1, Gaston 26, Sanchez 4, Sosa 11. **1B:** Castro 18, Cauro 9, Colon 14, Colon 1, Fernandez 14, Gaston 23, Gomez 1, Sanchez 3. **2B:** Colon 9, Fernandez 15, Hernandez 8, Pratt 5, Ramirez 7, Robledo 24. **3B:** Fernandez 26, Hernandez 13, Ramirez 25, Robledo 9. **SS:** Colon 5, Fernandez 5, Hernandez 34, Ramirez 15, Robledo 8. **OF:** Arias 32, Castro 2, Colon 44, Colon 1, De Paula 45, Familia 2, Gomez 26, Marcelino 17, Pratt 51.

DSL HOU ORANGE — ROOKIE

DOMINICAN SUMMER LEAGUE

Batting	B-T	HT	WT	DOB	AVG	vLH	vRH	G	AB	R	H	2B	3B	HR	RBI	BB	HBP	SH	SF	SO	SB	CS	SLG	OBP
Carlos Arcila	R-R	5-11	155	1-2-04	.229	.194	.240	47	131	25	30	4	1	2	22	24	10	0	2	36	12	6	.321	.383
Jose Arias	R-R	5-10	170	11-3-04	.226	.143	.250	24	62	11	14	6	0	0	7	5	2	0	0	31	4	2	.323	.304
2-team total (33 DSL HOU Blue)					.164	.103	.180	57	140	18	23	6	2	1	12	10	7	0	0	76	14	5	.257	.255
Luis Baez	R-R	6-1	205	1-11-04	.305	.283	.312	58	203	40	62	19	2	9	43	14	2	0	3	56	10	7	.552	.351

Samuel Capellan	R-R	5-11	155	1-5-05	.265	.286	.262	29	68	11	18	3	0	1	7	11	1	0	1	23	9	2	.353	.370
Rabel Colon	L-R	6-0	175	8-29-03	.280	.192	.296	53	168	32	47	6	8	1	18	23	4	0	1	53	20	4	.429	.378
Darwin De Leon	R-R	5-9	156	10-31-03	.274	.211	.289	31	95	19	26	2	0	5	18	13	1	0	2	17	9	3	.453	.360
Victor Diaz	R-R	5-10	175	11-25-01	.277	.471	.227	34	83	15	23	4	0	3	13	12	0	0	0	18	6	1	.434	.368
2-team total (1 DSL HOU Blue)					.271	.471	.221	35	85	16	23	4	0	3	13	13	0	0	0	19	6	1	.424	.367
Wilton Lara	R-R	5-11	175	1-21-04	.227	.200	.234	50	132	23	30	7	0	3	14	11	5	0	0	36	14	7	.348	.311
Waner Luciano	R-R	6-1	170	1-13-05	.229	.389	.187	56	170	32	39	11	2	6	32	34	9	0	1	42	9	2	.424	.383
Brayan Nolasco	R-R	5-9	178	9-24-03	.121	.130	.118	50	116	16	14	0	0	2	11	11	6	0	0	43	9	4	.172	.233
Alejandro Nunez	L-R	5-10	179	9-8-04	.293	.308	.289	56	181	41	53	4	4	2	23	20	10	1	0	26	20	5	.392	.393
Roiner Quintana	R-R	5-11	157	6-20-05	.202	.269	.181	40	109	17	22	3	1	3	15	15	0	0	1	23	10	3	.330	.296
Anderson Sanchez	R-R	6-1	170	11-6-03	.200	.211	.197	42	90	18	18	2	1	1	14	25	1	0	0	38	7	5	.278	.379
Brayan Sanchez	R-R	6-0	195	12-19-04	.170	.000	.214	29	53	10	9	3	0	1	7	19	6	0	1	22	1	1	.283	.430
2-team total (9 DSL HOU Blue)					.183	.000	.228	38	71	11	13	3	0	1	7	21	6	0	1	29	2	2	.268	.404
Kedaur Trujillo	R-R	5-11	188	3-2-04	.379	.250	.413	22	58	11	22	7	1	2	11	8	0	0	2	8	5	2	.638	.441
Jancel Villarroel	R-R	5-8	176	1-17-05	.381	.500	.333	10	21	10	8	1	1	1	3	9	0	1	0	5	2	2	.667	.567

Pitching	**B-T**	**HT**	**WT**	**DOB**	**W**	**L**	**ERA**	**G**	**GS**	**CG**	**SV**	**IP**	**H**	**R**	**ER**	**HR**	**BB**	**SO**	**AVG**	**vLH**	**vRH**	**K/9**	**BB/9**
Dawill Almonte	R-R	5-9	168	10-19-01	0	0	0.00	1	0	0	1	1	0	0	0	0	0	3	.000	.000	.000	20.25	0.00
2-team total (12 DSL HOU Blue)					2	0	2.68	13	5	0	2	40	31	14	12	2	10	41	.209	.214	.203	9.15	2.23
Carlos Arcila	R-R	5-11	155	1-2-04	0	0	1.50	4	0	0	0	6	5	2	1	0	2	2	.263	.308	.167	3.00	3.00
Jose Arias	R-R	5-10	170	11-3-04	0	1	5.40	2	0	0	0	2	2	1	1	0	0	1	.333	.333	.333	5.40	0.00
Amilcar Chirinos	R-R	6-3	200	11-7-01	2	0	1.44	12	7	0	0	31	23	5	5	1	12	46	.209	.250	.172	13.21	3.45
Rabel Colon	L-R	6-0	175	8-29-03	0	0	9.00	1	0	0	0	1	0	1	1	0	4	1	.000	.000	.000	9.00	36.00
Enrique Coronel	R-R	6-0	175	8-25-00	0	0	5.30	7	3	0	0	19	19	11	11	1	11	27	.264	.237	.294	13.02	5.30
Hector Cuevas	R-R	6-6	223	8-24-01	1	2	10.95	12	4	0	0	25	27	32	30	1	31	33	.278	.295	.264	12.04	11.31
Freilyn De Pena	R-R	5-10	173	3-13-03	2	0	4.32	7	0	0	2	8	9	5	4	1	8	12	.265	.313	.222	12.96	8.64
Jose Fleury	R-R	6-0	185	3-8-02	2	0	1.42	10	4	0	0	38	27	8	6	1	4	60	.193	.250	.150	14.21	0.95
Jose Guedez	R-R	6-0	169	9-27-01	2	0	0.69	7	2	0	1	26	15	2	2	0	8	36	.165	.183	.129	12.46	2.77
David Landeta	R-R	6-2	244	3-28-03	1	2	6.64	10	1	0	1	20	25	16	15	3	6	26	.298	.269	.344	11.51	2.66
Mauricio Maican	R-R	5-10	150	12-28-03	3	2	6.35	13	3	0	1	23	15	17	16	1	29	40	.185	.225	.146	15.88	11.51
Angelo Martinez	R-R	6-1	155	6-17-00	1	0	9.49	8	0	0	0	12	8	13	13	1	15	20	.182	.000	.348	14.59	10.95
Carlos Mateo	R-R	6-1	164	12-16-03	2	1	2.63	10	4	0	1	27	23	11	8	1	13	33	.232	.238	.228	10.87	4.28
Abel Mercedes	R-R	6-1	185	6-29-02	2	4	5.35	12	7	0	0	37	33	28	22	0	24	57	.241	.241	.241	13.86	5.84
Carlos Montes	R-R	6-2	180	4-16-04	0	1	45.00	3	2	0	0	2	5	10	10	0	9	1	.500	.500	--	4.50	40.50
Juan Nunez	R-R	6-0	155	10-13-03	2	2	6.48	13	0	0	2	17	15	14	12	1	16	15	.254	.233	.276	8.10	8.64
Michael Perez	R-R	6-4	243	2-21-04	4	0	3.47	13	1	0	2	23	15	10	9	1	16	33	.183	.158	.205	12.73	6.17
Raimy Rodriguez	R-R	6-1	185	7-16-05	3	2	3.94	13	4	0	1	30	26	21	13	0	14	32	.226	.271	.179	9.71	4.25
Cesar Rojas	R-R	6-3	162	5-12-02	0	1	13.89	11	3	0	0	12	10	24	18	1	33	13	.233	.118	.308	10.03	25.46
Anderson Sanchez	R-R	6-1	170	11-6-03	0	0	18.00	1	0	0	0	2	6	4	4	0	1	3	.545	.500	.571	13.50	4.50
Liz Sanchez	L-L	5-9	190	4-11-01	3	0	4.41	13	3	0	0	33	22	22	16	0	27	39	.190	.148	.202	10.74	7.44
Yanquiel Sanchez	L-L	6-3	200	1-28-01	1	1	2.73	10	7	0	0	26	26	9	8	1	11	37	.263	.053	.313	12.65	3.76
Wander Severino	R-R	6-0	163	10-24-03	5	3	4.21	15	4	0	2	36	33	19	17	2	20	34	.248	.246	.250	8.42	4.95
Euris Vasquez	R-R	6-0	163	10-24-03	0	1	15.75	4	0	0	0	4	7	7	7	2	3	3	.368	.455	.250	6.75	6.75
2-team total (5 DSL HOU Blue)					0	3	9.53	9	0	0	0	11	15	15	12	3	10	10	.326	.348	.304	7.94	7.94

Fielding

C: Arcila 24, Diaz 20, Sanchez 21, Trujillo 13, Villarroel 7. **1B:** Arcila 25, Arias 1, Diaz 9, Lara 6, Luciano 5, Nolasco 7, Sanchez 19, Sanchez 12, Trujillo 6. **2B:** Arcila 4, Arias 1, Capellan 13, De Leon 23, Lara 11, Luciano 4, Nunez 14, Quintana 3. **3B:** Arcila 2, De Leon 3, Lara 12, Luciano 48, Nunez 2, Trujillo 1. **SS:** Capellan 3, De Leon 7, Lara 18, Luciano 2, Nunez 39. **OF:** Arias 21, Baez 50, Capellan 1, Colon 43, Nolasco 38, Nunez 1, Quintana 37, Rojas 1, Sanchez 22, Sanchez 1

Kansas City Royals

SEASON IN A SENTENCE: After entering the season with hopes of making a significant stride forward, the Royals had a losing record in every month, fell to 20 games below .500 by early June and saw the end of the Dayton Moore era while enduring their seventh consecutive losing season.

HIGH POINT: Pitching development remains an organizational weakness, making Brady Singer's improvement one of the season's brightest lights. He won six straight decisions during one stretch in August and September, including an outing with six scoreless, one-hit innings in Kauffman Stadium Aug. 14 against the 111-win Dodgers. Singer went 10-5, 3.23 overall and ranked sixth among American League pitchers with 4.5 WAR.

LOW POINT: Kansas City finished last in the AL in most of the important pitching categories, from ERA (4.70) to walks per nine (3.7) to fewest strikeouts per nine (7.6). But the offense had its own woes, including three straight shutouts July 26-28, two to the Angels and one at Yankees Stadium, after the club had won 12 of its first 22 games in the month. The Royals were shut out 16 times.

NOTABLE ROOKIES: Rookies dominated the lineup, especially in the second half, when it featured as many as seven at a time. Bobby Witt Jr., the club's top prospect entering the season, had his issues but flashed premium tools during a .254/.294/.428 season that included 20 home runs and 30 stolen bases. Catcher/outfielder M.J. Melendez was the lone Royal to draw more than 40 walks (he had 66) in a .217/.313/.393 campaign with 18 home runs, while slugger Vinnie Pasquantino walked more than he struck out and slugged 10 homers in 72 games while batting .295/.383/.450.

KEY TRANSACTIONS: As the season neared its end, new club CEO John Sherman fired Moore, who had taken over baseball operations in 2006, and elevated general manager J.J. Piccolo to the top spot. Piccolo soon thereafter fired manager Mike Matheny and pitching coach Cal Eldred.

ON THE FARM: The Royals have promoted a wave of prospects to the majors, but the promotions have left the farm system quite then. Kansas City has invested plenty of draft capital in pitching prospects, but many of them struggled in 2022. First-round outfielder Gavin Cross had a solid debut and outfielder Tyler Gentry impressed across two levels.

OPENING DAY PAYROLL: $94,932,900 (23rd).

PLAYERS OF THE YEAR

MAJOR LEAGUE

Brady Singer
RHP
10-5, 3.23 ERA
150 SO, 35 BB, 153 IP
Career-best 1.14 WHIP

MINOR LEAGUE

Tyler Gentry
OF
(HiA/AA)
.326/.422/.542
21 HR, 86 RBIs in 108 G

ORGANIZATION LEADERS

Batting — ***Minimum 250 AB**

MAJORS		
*AVG	Andrew Benintendi	.320
*OPS	Andrew Benintendi	.785
HR	Salvador Perez	23
RBI	Bobby Witt	80
MINORS		
*AVG	Tyler Gentry, Northwest Arkansas, Quad Cities	.326
*OBP	Logan Porter, Northwest Arkansas, Omaha	.442
*SLG	Vinnie Pasquantino, Omaha	.561
*OPS	Tyler Gentry, Northwest Arkansas, Quad Cities	.965
R	Maikel Garcia, Northwest Arkansas, Omaha	104
R	Nick Loftin, Northwest Arkansas, Omaha	104
H	Maikel Garcia, Northwest Arkansas, Omaha	139
TB	Brewer Hicklen, Omaha	241
2B	Maikel Garcia, Northwest Arkansas, Omaha	34
3B	Tyler Tolbert, Quad Cities	10
HR	Brewer Hicklen, Omaha	28
RBI	Tyler Gentry, Northwest Arkansas, Quad Cities	86
BB	Logan Porter, Northwest Arkansas, Omaha	87
SO	Brewer Hicklen, Omaha	202
SB	Tyler Tolbert, Quad Cities	60

Pitching — **#Minimum 75 IP**

MAJORS		
W	Brady Singer	10
#ERA	Brady Singer	3.23
SO	Brady Singer	150
SV	Scott Barlow	24
MINORS		
W	Emilio Marquez, Quad Cities, Northwest Arkansas, Omaha	11
L	Alec Marsh, Northwest Arkansas, Omaha	16
#ERA	Emilio Marquez, Quad Cities, Northwest Arkansas, Omaha	3.77
G	Andres Nunez, Omaha	54
GS	Alec Marsh, Northwest Arkansas, Omaha	27
SV	Kasey Kalich, Quad Cities, Northwest Arkansas, Omaha	10
IP	Austin Cox, Omaha	147
BB	Anthony Veneziano, Northwest Arkansas	66
SO	Alec Marsh, Northwest Arkansas, Omaha	156
#AVG	Drew Parrish, Northwest Arkansas, Omaha	.211

2022 PERFORMANCE

General Manager: J.J. Picollo. **Farm Director:** Lonnie Goldberg. **Scouting Director:** Danny Ontiveros.

Class	Team	League	W	L	PCT	Finish	Manager
Majors	Kansas City Royals	American	65	97	.401	14th (15)	Mike Matheny
Triple-A	Omaha Storm Chasers	International	71	78	.477	14th (20)	Scott Thorman
Double-A	Northwest Arkansas Naturals	Texas	58	79	.423	10th (10)	Chris Widger
High-A	Quad Cities River Bandits	Midwest	54	78	.409	11th (12)	Brooks Conrad
Low-A	Columbia Fireflies	Carolina	52	79	.397	11th (12)	Tony Pena Jr.
Rookie	ACL Royals	Arizona Complex	25	30	.455	13th (18)	Omar Ramirez
Overall 2022 Minor League Record			308	415	.426	t-29th (30)	

ORGANIZATION STATISTICS

KANSAS CITY ROYALS

AMERICAN LEAGUE

Batting	B-T	HT	WT	DOB	AVG	vLH	vRH	G	AB	R	H	2B	3B	HR	RBI	BB	HBP	SH	SF	SO	SB	CS	SLG	OBP
Dairon Blanco	R-R	6-0	170	4-26-93	.286	.667	.000	5	7	1	2	0	0	0	2	0	0	0	0	4	1	0	.286	.286
Hunter Dozier	R-R	6-4	220	8-22-91	.236	.252	.230	129	462	51	109	26	4	12	41	34	3	0	1	125	4	3	.387	.292
Nate Eaton	R-R	5-11	185	12-22-96	.264	.300	.250	44	106	16	28	4	3	1	12	10	2	1	3	30	11	1	.387	.331
Freddy Fermin	R-R	5-10	200	5-16-95	.000	--	.000	3	7	1	0	0	0	0	0	0	0	0	0	3	0	1	.000	.000
Cam Gallagher	R-R	6-3	230	12-6-92	.214	.167	.250	18	42	1	9	5	0	0	5	3	0	2	0	13	0	0	.333	.267
Maikel Garcia	R-R	6-0	145	3-3-00	.318	.500	.214	9	22	1	7	1	0	0	2	1	0	0	0	5	0	0	.364	.348
Brewer Hicklen	R-R	6-2	208	2-9-96	.000	.000	.000	6	4	1	0	0	0	0	0	0	0	0	0	4	0	0	.000	.000
Kyle Isbel	L-R	5-11	190	3-3-97	.211	.204	.213	106	256	32	54	10	4	5	28	16	3	1	2	75	9	6	.340	.264
Nicky Lopez	L-R	5-11	180	3-13-95	.227	.207	.234	142	436	51	99	12	4	0	20	29	4	10	1	63	13	3	.273	.281
Michael Massey	L-R	6-0	190	3-22-98	.243	.200	.254	52	173	16	42	9	1	4	17	9	8	2	2	46	3	0	.376	.307
MJ Melendez	L-R	6-1	190	11-29-98	.217	.295	.193	129	460	57	100	21	3	18	62	66	1	0	7	131	2	3	.393	.313
Adalberto Mondesi	B-R	6-1	200	7-27-95	.140	.000	.171	15	50	3	7	0	0	0	3	4	0	0	0	20	5	0	.140	.204
Edward Olivares	R-R	6-2	190	3-6-96	.286	.283	.287	53	161	24	46	8	0	4	15	10	2	0	1	36	2	3	.410	.333
Ryan O'Hearn	L-L	6-3	220	7-26-93	.239	.200	.244	67	134	14	32	6	1	1	16	8	2	0	1	35	0	0	.321	.290
Vinnie Pasquantino	L-L	6-4	245	10-10-97	.295	.352	.279	72	258	25	76	10	0	10	26	35	3	0	2	34	1	0	.450	.383
Salvador Perez	R-R	6-3	255	5-10-90	.254	.278	.246	114	445	48	113	23	1	23	76	18	7	0	3	109	0	0	.465	.292
Nick Pratto	L-L	6-1	215	10-6-98	.184	.222	.172	49	158	18	29	9	1	7	20	19	1	1	3	66	0	0	.386	.271
Emmanuel Rivera	R-R	6-2	225	6-29-96	.237	.288	.212	63	198	24	47	8	3	6	22	11	2	0	0	46	0	0	.399	.284
Sebastian Rivero	R-R	6-1	210	11-16-98	.154	.375	.056	17	26	2	4	0	0	0	1	2	0	1	0	10	0	0	.154	.214
Brent Rooker	R-R	6-4	225	11-1-94	.160	.214	.091	14	25	1	4	1	0	0	2	3	1	0	0	7	0	0	.200	.276
Carlos Santana	B-R	5-11	215	4-8-86	.216	.298	.186	52	176	17	38	10	0	4	21	36	0	0	0	28	0	0	.341	.349
2-team total (79 Seattle Mariners)					.202	.265	.178	131	431	52	87	18	0	19	60	71	2	0	2	88	0	0	.376	.316
Michael A. Taylor	R-R	6-4	215	3-26-91	.254	.238	.260	124	414	49	105	10	3	9	43	35	2	2	3	109	4	2	.357	.313
Drew Waters	B-R	6-2	185	12-30-98	.240	.222	.246	32	96	14	23	6	1	5	18	12	0	0	0	40	0	0	.479	.324
Bobby Witt Jr.	R-R	6-1	200	6-14-00	.254	.234	.260	150	591	82	150	31	6	20	80	30	6	0	5	135	30	7	.428	.294

Pitching	B-T	HT	WT	DOB	W	L	ERA	G	GS	CG	SV	IP	H	R	ER	HR	BB	SO	AVG	vLH	vRH	K/9	BB/9
Albert Abreu	R-R	6-2	190	9-26-95	0	0	4.15	4	0	0	0	4	6	2	2	1	4	3	.353	.167	.455	6.23	8.31
3-team total (22 New York Yankees, 7 Texas Rangers)					2	2	3.26	33	0	0	0	39	35	15	14	5	22	38	.243	.191	.268	8.84	5.12
Scott Barlow	R-R	6-3	210	12-18-92	7	4	2.18	69	0	0	24	74	52	23	18	9	22	77	.198	.211	.187	9.32	2.66
Ronald Bolanos	R-R	6-2	230	8-23-96	0	0	4.42	8	0	0	0	18	20	9	9	2	12	12	.286	.296	.279	5.89	5.89
Jake Brentz	L-L	6-1	205	9-14-94	0	3	23.63	8	0	0	0	5	11	15	14	1	10	9	.423	.300	.500	15.19	16.88
Kris Bubic	L-L	6-3	225	8-19-97	3	13	5.58	28	27	0	0	129	156	87	80	18	63	110	.306	.372	.287	7.67	4.40
Max Castillo	R-R	6-2	280	5-4-99	0	2	9.16	5	4	0	0	19	23	19	19	4	10	17	.307	.277	.357	8.20	4.82
2-team total (9 Toronto Blue Jays)					0	2	5.95	14	6	0	0	39	38	28	26	8	15	37	.252	.259	.242	8.47	3.43
Taylor Clarke	R-R	6-4	217	5-13-93	3	1	4.04	47	0	0	3	49	50	25	22	6	8	48	.260	.250	.267	8.82	1.47
Dylan Coleman	R-R	6-5	230	9-16-96	5	2	2.78	68	0	0	0	68	47	26	21	5	37	71	.194	.230	.169	9.40	4.90
Jose Cuas	R-R	6-3	195	6-28-94	4	2	3.58	47	0	0	1	38	39	18	15	2	24	34	.264	.350	.231	8.12	5.73
Hunter Dozier	R-R	6-4	220	8-22-91	0	0	18.00	1	0	0	0	1	2	2	2	1	1	0	.400	--	.400	0.00	9.00
Amir Garrett	R-L	6-5	239	5-3-92	3	1	4.96	60	0	0	0	45	28	26	25	0	32	49	.177	.106	.228	9.73	6.35
Zack Greinke	R-R	6-2	200	10-21-83	4	9	3.68	26	26	0	0	137	157	65	56	14	27	73	.286	.286	.286	4.80	1.77
Foster Griffin	R-L	6-3	225	7-27-95	0	0	12.46	5	0	0	0	4	6	7	6	0	4	2	.375	.200	.455	4.15	8.31
2-team total (1 Toronto Blue Jays)					0	0	8.53	6	0	0	0	6	7	7	6	0	5	4	.304	.125	.400	5.68	7.11
Jonathan Heasley	R-R	6-3	225	1-27-97	4	10	5.28	21	21	0	0	104	108	67	61	19	47	70	.267	.269	.265	6.06	4.07
Carlos Hernandez	R-R	6-4	245	3-11-97	0	5	7.39	27	7	0	0	56	72	48	46	7	31	35	.314	.214	.389	5.63	4.98
Brad Keller	R-R	6-5	255	7-27-95	6	14	5.09	35	22	0	1	140	153	86	79	17	57	102	.277	.255	.295	6.57	3.67
Jackson Kowar	R-R	6-5	200	10-4-96	0	0	9.77	7	0	0	0	16	27	17	17	4	11	17	.380	.500	.327	9.77	6.32
Nicky Lopez	L-R	5-11	180	3-13-95	0	0	18.00	1	0	0	0	1	3	2	2	2	0	0	.500	.667	.333	0.00	0.00
Daniel Lynch	L-L	6-6	200	11-17-96	4	13	5.13	27	27	0	0	132	155	79	75	21	52	122	.290	.308	.287	8.34	3.55
Daniel Mengden	R-R	6-1	215	2-19-93	0	1	5.14	5	1	0	1	7	10	5	4	1	1	8	.333	.286	.348	10.29	1.29
Wyatt Mills	R-R	6-4	214	1-25-95	0	1	4.79	19	0	0	0	21	21	11	11	1	10	20	.266	.345	.220	8.71	4.35
2-team total (8 Seattle Mariners)					0	1	4.60	27	0	0	0	29	26	15	15	1	13	26	.243	.316	.203	7.98	3.99
Anthony Misiewicz	R-L	6-1	196	11-1-94	1	1	4.11	15	0	0	0	15	13	8	7	3	4	19	.224	.217	.229	11.15	2.35

2-team total (17 Seattle Mariners)					1	2	4.34	32	0	0	0	29	27	15	14	4	10	27	.248	.255	.241	8.38	3.10
Joel Payamps	R-R	6-2	225	4-7-94	2	3	3.16	29	0	0	0	43	46	19	15	5	16	33	.274	.214	.304	6.96	3.38
2-team total (12 Oakland Athletics)					3	6	3.23	41	0	0	0	56	60	24	20	7	16	41	.273	.188	.311	6.63	2.59
Matt Peacock	R-R	6-1	185	2-27-94	0	0	4.91	7	0	0	0	7	9	4	4	0	2	4	.290	.308	.278	4.91	2.45
Brady Singer	R-R	6-5	215	8-4-96	10	5	3.23	27	24	0	0	153	140	58	55	18	35	150	.246	.233	.259	8.80	2.05
Collin Snider	R-R	6-4	195	10-10-95	4	2	6.55	42	0	0	0	34	40	25	25	3	15	22	.301	.302	.300	5.77	3.93
Gabe Speier	L-L	5-11	200	4-12-95	0	1	2.33	17	1	0	0	19	16	5	5	2	5	14	.225	.200	.239	6.52	2.33
Josh Staumont	R-R	6-3	200	12-21-93	3	3	6.45	42	0	0	3	38	37	28	27	3	29	43	.261	.277	.247	10.27	6.93
Michael A. Taylor	R-R	6-4	215	3-26-91	0	0	9.00	1	0	0	0	2	5	2	2	1	2	2	.455	.500	.429	9.00	9.00
Arodys Vizcaino	R-R	6-0	245	11-13-90	0	0	6.35	7	0	0	0	6	4	4	4	1	7	3	.182	.182	.182	4.76	11.12
Luke Weaver	R-R	6-2	183	8-21-93	0	0	5.59	14	0	0	0	19	28	15	12	0	8	19	.341	.300	.381	8.84	3.72
Angel Zerpa	L-L	6-0	220	9-27-99	2	1	1.64	3	2	0	0	11	9	3	2	2	3	3	.220	.400	.194	2.45	2.45

Fielding

Catcher	PCT	G	PO	A	E	DP	PB
Fermin	1.000	3	16	1	0	0	0
Gallagher	.991	18	108	6	1	0	1
Melendez	.990	78	467	27	5	3	6
Perez	.995	77	548	30	3	3	1
Rivero	1.000	17	70	2	0	0	0

First Base	PCT	G	PO	A	E	DP
Dozier	.997	42	290	22	1	33
O'Hearn	1.000	13	62	5	0	9
Pasquantino	.993	37	273	16	2	37
Pratto	1.000	43	297	26	0	32
Rivera	1.000	1	2	1	0	0
Santana	.994	42	330	26	2	31

Second Base	PCT	G	PO	A	E	DP
Lopez	.989	68	122	152	3	41
Massey	.982	48	95	123	4	37
Merrifield	.983	61	94	134	4	39

Third Base	PCT	G	PO	A	E	DP
Dozier	.920	27	8	38	4	4
Eaton	.966	15	9	19	1	6
Lopez	1.000	30	17	36	0	2
Massey	1.000	1	0	1	0	0
Rivera	.976	57	39	123	4	14
Witt Jr.	.976	55	32	90	3	7

Shortstop	PCT	G	PO	A	E	DP
Garcia	.917	8	11	11	2	1
Lopez	.982	52	62	153	4	42
Mondesi	1.000	15	18	45	0	10
Witt Jr.	.959	98	113	259	16	51

Outfield	PCT	G	PO	A	E	DP
Benintendi	1.000	91	162	2	0	0
Blanco	1.000	3	6	0	0	0
Dozier	1.000	44	59	0	0	0
Eaton	.980	31	47	3	1	0
Hicklen	1.000	5	2	0	0	0
Isbel	.979	108	184	2	4	1
Melendez	.972	38	67	2	2	0
Merrifield	1.000	39	84	1	0	0
Olivares	.987	40	76	1	1	0
O'Hearn	1.000	13	14	0	0	0
Pratto	1.000	8	11	0	0	0
Rooker	1.000	7	7	1	0	1
Taylor	.990	123	289	8	3	0
Waters	1.000	33	63	2	0	0

OMAHA STORM CHASERS — *TRIPLE-A*

INTERNATIONAL LEAGUE

Batting	B-T	HT	WT	DOB	AVG	vLH	vRH	G	AB	R	H	2B	3B	HR	RBI	BB	HBP	SH	SF	SO	SB	CS	SLG	OBP
Dairon Blanco	R-R	6-0	170	4-26-93	.301	.338	.291	107	366	63	110	20	3	14	61	35	6	2	5	98	45	7	.486	.367
Jose Briceno	R-R	6-1	225	9-19-92	.252	.243	.255	41	131	18	33	8	0	4	21	6	3	0	1	31	0	0	.405	.298
Gabriel Cancel	R-R	6-0	205	12-8-96	.221	.241	.216	78	267	36	59	15	0	5	32	28	5	0	2	97	6	2	.333	.305
Angelo Castellano	R-R	6-0	165	1-13-95	.218	.200	.225	59	174	25	38	8	0	3	19	21	5	2	1	37	6	2	.316	.318
Ivan Castillo	B-R	5-9	179	5-30-95	.242	.196	.259	113	392	58	95	23	0	6	37	45	3	3	4	53	9	4	.347	.322
Clay Dungan	L-R	6-1	190	6-2-96	.208	.171	.222	127	452	64	94	22	4	9	52	47	10	2	4	100	17	2	.334	.294
Nate Eaton	R-R	5-11	185	12-22-96	.295	.296	.295	54	200	33	59	10	3	9	32	21	6	0	2	48	11	4	.510	.376
Freddy Fermin	R-R	5-10	200	5-16-95	.270	.328	.253	87	296	44	80	17	0	15	56	46	1	0	5	62	1	0	.480	.365
Cam Gallagher	R-R	6-3	230	12-6-92	.182	.125	.235	10	33	3	6	1	0	2	5	3	0	0	0	12	0	0	.394	.250
2-team total (5 Norfolk Tides)					.140	.095	.172	15	50	4	7	2	0	2	8	6	0	0	0	20	0	0	.300	.232
Maikel Garcia	R-R	6-0	145	3-3-00	.274	.242	.282	40	164	41	45	10	0	7	28	17	1	1	3	42	12	5	.463	.341
Saul Garza	R-R	6-3	227	4-9-98	.000	.000	.000	2	8	1	0	0	0	0	0	0	0	0	0	6	0	0	.000	.000
Jimmy Govern	R-R	5-11	190	12-11-96	.218	.180	.229	64	216	29	47	13	2	6	22	12	3	0	1	52	3	1	.380	.267
William Hancock	L-R	6-2	200	10-31-96	.143	.133	.146	27	56	8	8	1	0	0	4	8	2	1	0	25	0	0	.161	.273
Brewer Hicklen	R-R	6-2	208	2-9-96	.248	.271	.239	130	480	85	119	30	4	28	85	58	17	1	3	202	35	2	.502	.348
Kyle Isbel	L-R	5-11	190	3-3-97	.250	.000	.385	5	20	4	5	2	0	1	4	2	1	0	0	3	0	1	.500	.348
Rubendy Jaquez	B-R	5-11	174	2-13-99	.143	.000	.167	2	7	1	1	0	1	0	1	1	0	0	0	2	0	0	.429	.250
JaCoby Jones	R-R	6-2	211	5-10-92	.214	.294	.185	38	126	12	27	6	0	4	13	9	1	0	1	55	2	0	.357	.270
Nick Loftin	R-R	6-1	180	9-25-98	.216	.038	.252	38	153	26	33	7	0	5	19	10	4	0	1	41	5	2	.359	.280
Michael Massey	L-R	6-0	190	3-22-98	.325	.321	.327	33	126	21	41	13	0	7	29	13	2	0	2	35	4	0	.595	.392
MJ Melendez	L-R	6-1	190	11-29-98	.167	.111	.183	21	78	7	13	4	0	2	6	13	0	0	0	22	3	0	.295	.286
Edward Olivares	R-R	6-2	190	3-6-96	.269	.364	.232	21	78	13	21	7	0	1	11	8	0	0	0	14	2	1	.397	.337
Vinnie Pasquantino	L-L	6-4	245	10-10-97	.277	.261	.284	73	264	52	73	17	2	18	70	40	3	0	6	39	3	1	.561	.371
Salvador Perez	R-R	6-3	255	5-10-90	.500	--	.500	3	8	1	4	1	0	0	0	1	0	0	0	3	0	0	.625	.556
Logan Porter	R-R	6-0	200	7-12-95	.301	.238	.315	35	113	19	34	8	0	3	17	28	4	0	1	30	0	0	.451	.452
Nick Pratto	L-L	6-1	215	10-6-98	.228	.247	.221	82	303	57	69	10	3	17	47	59	10	0	2	114	8	2	.449	.369
Roman Quinn	B-R	5-10	175	5-14-93	.250	.000	.300	7	24	5	6	0	0	2	4	6	1	0	1	10	1	0	.500	.406
3-team total (1 Durham Bulls, 6 Lehigh Valley IronPigs)					.295	.200	.345	14	44	15	13	3	0	4	10	15	1	0	1	15	1	1	.636	.475
John Rave	L-L	6-0	185	12-30-97	.195	.231	.179	11	41	6	8	2	0	2	6	2	0	0	0	13	1	0	.390	.233
Jakson Reetz	R-R	6-0	205	1-3-96	.257	.364	.237	21	70	11	18	3	0	5	15	7	3	0	2	22	0	0	.514	.341
2-team total (19 Nashville Sounds)					.235	.242	.233	40	136	16	32	6	1	8	24	9	5	0	3	36	1	0	.471	.301
Emmanuel Rivera	R-R	6-2	225	6-29-96	.307	.269	.327	20	75	12	23	5	1	3	5	10	0	0	0	16	1	0	.520	.388
Brent Rooker	R-R	6-4	225	11-1-94	.338	.522	.263	20	80	16	27	8	0	9	32	9	3	0	0	25	0	1	.775	.424
Michael A. Taylor	R-R	6-4	215	3-26-91	.250	.000	.286	2	8	1	2	0	0	0	2	1	0	0	0	2	0	0	.250	.333
Drew Waters	B-R	6-2	185	12-30-98	.295	.189	.341	31	122	29	36	5	2	7	17	20	1	0	0	41	13	0	.541	.399
2-team total (49 Gwinnett Stripers)					.265	.293	.252	80	313	55	83	12	5	12	33	36	2	0	2	98	18	1	.450	.343

Pitching	B-T	HT	WT	DOB	W	L	ERA	G	GS	CG	SV	IP	H	R	ER	HR	BB	SO	AVG	vLH	vRH	K/9	BB/9
Ronald Bolanos	R-R	6-2	230	8-23-96	0	4	6.26	28	4	0	0	42	59	32	29	6	18	34	.343	.338	.348	7.34	3.89
Colten Brewer	R-R	6-4	222	10-29-92	1	1	4.76	36	0	0	1	40	36	21	21	7	18	42	.243	.210	.267	9.53	4.08

Kris Bubic	L-L	6-3	225	8-19-97	0	2	6.59	3	3	0	0	14	14	10	10	2	4	17	.264	.381	.188	11.20	2.63
Angelo Castellano	R-R	6-0	165	1-13-95	0	0	0.00	1	0	0	0	1	1	0	0	0	0	1	.250	.000	.333	9.00	0.00
Max Castillo	R-R	6-2	280	5-4-99	1	1	8.44	7	6	0	0	21	35	24	20	3	9	22	.354	.341	.364	9.28	3.80
2-team total (5 Buffalo Bisons)					3	1	4.07	12	9	0	0	49	45	26	22	5	19	51	.239	.207	.264	9.43	3.51
Taylor Clarke	R-R	6-4	217	5-13-93	0	0	0.00	1	0	0	0	1	1	0	0	0	0	1	.250	.000	.333	9.00	0.00
Dylan Coleman	R-R	6-5	230	9-16-96	0	0	0.00	1	0	0	0	1	0	0	0	0	1	1	.000	.000	.000	9.00	9.00
Austin Cox	L-L	6-4	235	3-28-97	7	7	4.21	29	24	1	1	147	161	80	69	20	50	105	.273	.257	.281	6.41	3.05
Jose Cuas	R-R	6-3	195	6-28-94	0	3	1.61	22	0	0	3	22	17	7	4	1	7	21	.205	.237	.178	8.46	2.82
Yefri Del Rosario	R-R	6-2	180	9-23-99	1	0	2.70	9	0	0	0	10	10	4	3	1	3	6	.250	.350	.150	5.40	2.70
Josh Dye	L-L	6-5	180	9-14-96	5	3	4.48	48	6	0	0	62	71	32	31	14	16	58	.287	.221	.336	8.37	2.31
Sam Freeman	R-L	5-11	180	6-24-87	3	2	1.50	34	0	0	1	36	23	9	6	2	21	32	.177	.219	.136	8.00	5.25
Amir Garrett	R-L	6-5	239	5-3-92	0	0	0.00	2	0	0	0	2	0	0	0	0	0	1	.000	.000	.000	4.50	0.00
Jimmy Govern	R-R	5-11	190	12-11-96	0	0	0.00	1	0	0	0	1	1	1	0	0	0	0	.333	1.000	.000	0.00	0.00
Zack Greinke	R-R	6-2	200	10-21-83	2	0	2.25	2	2	0	0	12	7	3	3	1	1	8	.171	.357	.074	6.00	0.75
Foster Griffin	R-L	6-3	225	7-27-95	4	0	1.93	20	0	0	0	28	19	8	6	2	6	32	.188	.231	.161	10.29	1.93
2-team total (18 Buffalo Bisons)					6	0	2.10	38	0	0	1	51	40	14	12	3	15	57	.208	.222	.198	9.99	2.63
Zach Haake	R-R	6-7	220	10-8-96	1	1	6.75	5	1	0	0	7	10	9	5	0	8	10	.333	.308	.353	13.50	10.80
Patrick Halligan	R-R	6-6	230	10-4-99	0	0	0.00	1	0	0	0	2	1	0	0	0	0	3	.143	.333	.000	11.57	0.00
Jonathan Heasley	R-R	6-3	225	1-27-97	1	2	4.35	9	9	0	0	39	35	22	19	7	10	45	.236	.219	.250	10.30	2.29
Carlos Hernandez	R-R	6-4	245	3-11-97	2	4	3.78	12	11	0	0	50	39	24	21	7	19	44	.207	.167	.240	7.92	3.42
Kasey Kalich	R-R	6-3	220	4-25-98	0	0	9.00	1	0	0	0	1	1	1	1	0	2	2	.250	.000	.333	18.00	18.00
Jackson Kowar	R-R	6-5	200	10-4-96	4	10	6.16	20	20	0	0	83	95	67	57	14	43	88	.287	.270	.301	9.50	4.64
Richard Lovelady	L-L	6-0	185	7-7-95	0	0	0.00	3	0	0	0	3	1	0	0	0	1	7	.100	.333	.000	21.00	3.00
Daniel Lynch	L-L	6-6	200	11-17-96	0	0	3.86	2	2	0	0	7	7	3	3	0	3	8	.259	.182	.313	10.29	3.86
Emilio Marquez	L-L	5-8	170	4-28-98	0	0	27.00	1	0	0	0	1	6	6	3	0	1	1	.600	.667	.500	9.00	9.00
Alec Marsh	R-R	6-2	220	5-14-98	1	1	1.80	2	2	0	0	10	5	2	2	1	5	9	.135	.182	.115	8.10	4.50
Marcelo Martinez	L-L	6-2	190	8-10-96	5	6	6.70	27	15	0	0	95	104	78	71	21	46	98	.270	.333	.227	9.25	4.34
Daniel Mengden	R-R	6-1	215	2-19-93	7	7	5.20	25	20	0	0	109	106	65	63	24	56	93	.257	.244	.269	7.68	4.62
Wyatt Mills	R-R	6-4	214	1-25-95	2	1	2.57	13	0	0	1	14	7	5	4	2	10	23	.149	.278	.069	14.79	6.43
Anthony Misiewicz	R-L	6-1	196	11-1-94	2	1	4.05	8	0	0	0	7	3	3	3	2	1	7	.136	.111	.154	9.45	1.35
Charlie Neuweiler	R-R	6-1	205	2-8-99	0	0	27.00	1	0	0	0	1	2	2	2	0	3	0	.500	.500	--	0.00	40.50
Andres Nunez	R-R	6-4	240	9-20-95	5	4	3.61	54	0	0	7	62	64	30	25	5	17	69	.266	.207	.302	9.96	2.45
Drew Parrish	L-L	5-11	200	12-8-97	3	8	5.62	17	15	0	0	74	69	54	46	15	44	51	.247	.277	.235	6.23	5.38
Joel Payamps	R-R	6-2	225	4-7-94	0	0	6.23	3	0	0	0	4	5	3	3	0	1	6	.263	.286	.250	12.46	2.08
Brad Peacock	R-R	6-1	207	2-2-88	2	1	1.64	35	0	0	7	38	33	9	7	2	16	45	.229	.305	.176	10.57	3.76
2-team total (20 St. Paul Saints)					5	4	2.26	55	0	0	15	60	47	19	15	5	26	67	.216	.244	.195	10.11	3.92
Matt Peacock	R-R	6-1	185	2-27-94	0	1	4.50	8	0	0	0	10	13	7	5	2	3	8	.295	.375	.250	7.20	2.70
2-team total (14 Buffalo Bisons)					1	3	4.21	22	0	0	0	26	30	16	12	5	7	23	.280	.239	.311	8.06	2.45
Brady Singer	R-R	6-5	215	8-4-96	1	0	3.29	3	3	0	0	14	8	5	5	3	4	11	.163	.250	.135	7.24	2.63
Eric Skoglund	L-L	6-7	215	10-26-92	0	0	5.63	6	0	0	0	8	6	5	5	1	5	4	.222	.091	.313	4.50	5.63
Collin Snider	R-R	6-4	195	10-10-95	2	1	5.40	20	0	0	0	22	18	15	13	1	16	13	.231	.263	.220	5.40	6.65
Andres Sotillet	R-R	6-1	215	3-2-97	3	0	1.70	28	0	0	0	37	20	8	7	3	16	31	.165	.184	.157	7.54	3.89
Gabe Speier	L-L	5-11	200	4-12-95	1	3	14.51	30	0	0	0	27	51	44	43	11	12	34	.402	.362	.425	11.48	4.05
Josh Staumont	R-R	6-3	200	12-21-93	0	0	0.00	2	0	0	0	2	1	0	0	0	1	4	.143	.000	.250	18.00	4.50
Domingo Tapia	R-R	6-3	263	8-4-91	0	0	3.60	5	0	0	0	5	3	2	2	0	3	2	.188	.143	.222	3.60	5.40
Jace Vines	R-R	6-3	215	9-4-94	0	0	7.24	14	0	0	0	14	13	12	11	2	10	20	.236	.217	.250	13.17	6.59
Arodys Vizcaino	R-R	6-0	245	11-13-90	0	0	1.76	16	0	0	7	15	12	3	3	1	6	19	.211	.179	.241	11.15	3.52
Nathan Webb	R-R	6-2	215	8-20-97	0	0	23.14	3	0	0	0	2	5	6	6	1	4	2	.455	.333	.500	7.71	15.43
Ryan Weiss	R-R	6-4	210	12-10-96	2	2	7.82	30	0	0	0	36	49	33	31	6	16	34	.325	.351	.309	8.58	4.04
Zach Willeman	R-R	6-2	219	3-27-96	3	2	6.27	34	0	0	0	37	36	33	26	6	29	38	.250	.233	.262	9.16	6.99
Stephen Woods Jr.	R-R	6-2	195	6-10-95	0	0	0.00	3	0	0	0	3	1	0	0	0	1	6	.111	.500	.000	18.00	3.00
Angel Zerpa	L-L	6-0	220	9-27-99	0	0	1.17	6	6	0	0	8	2	1	1	0	4	0	.083	.000	.167	0.00	4.70

Fielding

Catcher	PCT	G	PO	A	E	DP	PB
Briceno	.991	37	295	21	3	0	4
Fermin	.992	69	576	36	5	4	4
Gallagher	.985	10	58	8	1	1	1
Hancock	.991	18	101	5	1	2	3
Melendez	.985	15	125	5	2	1	0
Perez	1.000	1	6	0	0	0	0
Reetz	.989	11	91	2	1	0	1

First Base	PCT	G	PO	A	E	DP
Briceno	.941	3	16	0	1	4
Cancel	.986	12	67	6	1	9
Castellano	.968	14	117	4	4	12
Pasquantino	.997	34	272	25	1	25
Porter	1.000	33	260	14	0	24
Pratto	.982	58	455	23	9	42

Second Base	PCT	G	PO	A	E	DP
Cancel	.969	39	65	93	5	21
Castellano	1.000	2	1	7	0	2
Castillo	.981	23	42	59	2	13
Dungan	.981	62	99	155	5	35
Massey	.992	28	48	71	1	20

Third Base	PCT	G	PO	A	E	DP
Cancel	.846	5	1	10	2	1
Castellano	.943	15	6	44	3	6
Dungan	.945	40	29	75	6	8
Eaton	.929	4	2	11	1	0
Govern	.921	44	27	66	8	7
Jaquez	1.000	2	2	5	0	0
Loftin	.872	24	8	33	6	3
Massey	.833	2	1	9	2	2
Porter	.000	1	0	0	1	0
Rivera	.956	19	14	29	2	0

Shortstop	PCT	G	PO	A	E	DP
Castellano	.973	20	30	42	2	14
Castillo	.974	89	99	238	9	48
Dungan	.909	6	7	13	2	3
Garcia	.952	39	41	97	7	20

Outfield	PCT	G	PO	A	E	DP
Blanco	.978	94	177	3	4	0
Cancel	.933	12	14	0	1	0
Castellano	1.000	7	13	0	0	0
Dungan	.938	18	14	1	1	0
Eaton	.976	49	75	5	2	1
Govern	1.000	6	11	1	0	0
Hicklen	.981	134	242	15	5	2
Isbel	.900	3	9	0	1	0
Jones	1.000	38	78	0	0	0
Loftin	.897	13	26	0	3	0
Melendez	1.000	2	7	1	0	0
Olivares	1.000	21	30	1	0	0
Pratto	.971	21	32	1	1	0
Quinn	1.000	7	13	0	0	0
Rave	1.000	11	12	0	0	0
Reetz	--	1	0	0	0	0
Rooker	.962	14	24	1	1	0
Taylor	1.000	1	2	0	0	0
Waters	.983	25	59	0	1	0

NORTHWEST ARKANSAS NATURALS

DOUBLE-A

TEXAS LEAGUE

Batting	B-T	HT	WT	DOB	AVG	vLH	vRH	G	AB	R	H	2B	3B	HR	RBI	BB	HBP	SH	SF	SO	SB	CS	SLG	OBP
CJ Alexander	L-R	6-5	215	7-17-96	.272	.239	.283	46	184	31	50	7	2	10	44	12	1	0	4	48	6	2	.495	.313
Parker Bates	L-R	6-1	205	11-16-97	.111	.500	.000	3	9	1	1	0	0	0	0	2	0	1	0	4	2	0	.111	.273
Brhet Bewley	R-R	5-11	182	1-30-97	.225	.227	.225	37	111	12	25	5	0	3	11	17	0	1	2	32	0	0	.351	.323
Tucker Bradley	L-L	6-0	206	5-6-98	.293	.272	.298	110	396	73	116	22	3	12	53	55	3	5	1	84	19	6	.455	.382
Angelo Castellano	R-R	6-0	165	1-13-95	.160	.148	.164	30	94	9	15	3	1	0	3	14	0	1	1	24	1	3	.213	.266
Tyler Cropley	R-R	5-11	185	12-10-95	.163	.214	.141	31	92	7	15	5	0	2	7	8	5	0	2	22	0	0	.283	.262
Nate Eaton	R-R	5-11	185	12-22-96	.271	.300	.264	37	140	23	38	4	1	4	19	11	3	2	3	29	12	1	.400	.331
Maikel Garcia	R-R	6-0	145	3-3-00	.291	.333	.282	78	323	63	94	24	1	4	33	41	0	3	2	60	27	3	.409	.369
Tyler Gentry	R-R	6-2	210	2-1-99	.321	.394	.296	73	274	57	88	16	0	16	63	40	10	0	7	66	8	4	.555	.417
Robbie Glendinning	R-R	6-2	196	10-6-95	.252	.274	.246	118	428	77	108	21	1	19	76	75	10	1	4	168	11	3	.439	.373
Ryan Grotjohn	L-R	6-2	175	4-25-95	.162	.100	.172	34	68	10	11	2	0	2	9	13	1	0	2	34	3	0	.279	.298
Jeison Guzman	B-R	6-2	205	10-8-98	.222	.143	.258	14	45	8	10	1	0	1	5	9	0	0	0	18	1	1	.311	.352
2-team total (8 Amarillo Sod Poodles)					.246	.263	.240	22	69	11	17	3	0	2	6	10	1	0	0	24	2	1	.377	.350
Diego Hernandez	L-L	6-0	150	11-21-00	.298	.353	.278	32	124	23	37	4	0	2	11	12	1	1	3	28	13	4	.379	.357
Nick Loftin	R-R	6-1	180	9-25-98	.270	.315	.259	90	363	78	98	17	1	12	47	45	5	6	5	57	24	4	.421	.354
Michael Massey	L-R	6-0	190	3-22-98	.305	.395	.282	54	220	36	67	15	0	9	48	21	1	0	6	54	9	2	.495	.359
Seuly Matias	R-R	6-3	225	9-4-98	.225	.189	.238	99	347	49	78	15	3	16	62	48	10	0	7	139	6	1	.424	.330
Morgan McCullough	L-R	5-9	180	12-19-97	.242	.208	.253	30	99	15	24	7	0	2	9	13	4	0	1	30	1	2	.374	.350
Jake Means	R-R	6-2	215	4-14-96	.208	.200	.210	107	375	55	78	22	0	11	48	49	5	0	1	119	10	1	.355	.307
Logan Porter	R-R	6-0	200	7-12-95	.301	.308	.300	77	259	46	78	18	0	10	45	59	6	0	3	73	0	2	.486	.437
John Rave	L-L	6-0	185	12-30-97	.262	.281	.257	111	389	66	102	13	2	14	73	63	2	2	5	115	22	6	.414	.364
Sebastian Rivero	R-R	6-1	210	11-16-98	.218	.189	.227	42	156	22	34	15	0	5	27	15	3	1	3	38	1	0	.410	.294
Gavin Stupienski	L-R	6-1	220	3-12-94	.228	.143	.240	20	57	5	13	3	0	1	12	3	1	0	0	22	2	0	.333	.279
Luca Tresh	R-R	6-0	193	1-11-00	.253	.476	.186	24	91	16	23	4	0	5	14	13	2	0	0	25	1	0	.462	.358

Pitching	B-T	HT	WT	DOB	W	L	ERA	G	GS	CG	SV	IP	H	R	ER	HR	BB	SO	AVG	vLH	vRH	K/9	BB/9
Adrian Alcantara	R-R	6-1	178	8-29-99	1	0	10.13	2	2	0	0	8	10	9	9	2	4	7	.323	.250	.348	7.88	4.50
Brhet Bewley	R-R	5-11	182	1-30-97	0	0	0.00	1	0	0	0	1	1	0	0	0	1	0	.250	1.000	.000	0.00	6.75
Dante Biasi	L-L	6-0	205	12-4-97	6	5	4.09	22	15	0	0	84	72	41	38	7	54	86	.236	.255	.227	9.25	5.81
Jonathan Bowlan	R-R	6-6	240	12-1-96	1	3	6.92	9	9	0	0	39	51	33	30	7	17	30	.317	.333	.302	6.92	3.92
Jake Brentz	L-L	6-1	205	9-14-94	0	0	27.00	2	0	0	0	1	1	3	3	0	1	1	.250	.000	.333	9.00	9.00
Holden Capps	R-L	6-2	180	3-24-95	0	3	7.46	16	0	0	0	25	33	22	21	2	22	24	.320	.368	.292	8.53	7.82
Christian Chamberlain	L-L	5-10	173	7-20-99	3	0	7.71	20	0	0	0	28	35	25	24	4	27	33	.297	.364	.271	10.61	8.68
Christian Cosby	R-R	6-5	215	12-21-96	1	0	14.81	6	0	0	0	10	18	17	17	5	7	9	.375	.350	.393	7.84	6.10
Tyler Cropley	R-R	5-11	185	12-10-95	0	0	0.00	3	0	0	0	3	0	0	0	0	0	0	.000	.000	.000	0.00	0.00
Yefri Del Rosario	R-R	6-2	180	9-23-99	6	3	4.76	38	0	0	6	62	68	35	33	8	26	47	.275	.314	.246	6.79	3.75
Jonah Dipoto	R-R	6-1	225	9-3-96	3	0	3.68	42	0	0	3	64	51	32	26	6	52	84	.213	.215	.211	11.87	7.35
C.J. Eldred	R-R	6-2	220	5-6-95	0	0	4.38	7	0	0	0	12	16	7	6	0	3	7	.320	.389	.281	5.11	2.19
Zach Haake	R-R	6-7	220	10-8-96	1	1	5.45	14	1	0	0	33	39	21	20	3	17	30	.289	.250	.313	8.18	4.64
Andrew Hoffmann	R-R	6-5	210	2-2-00	2	4	6.64	9	9	0	0	39	50	32	29	5	20	30	.313	.368	.262	6.86	4.58
Kasey Kalich	R-R	6-3	220	4-25-98	2	2	7.71	10	0	0	1	12	7	11	10	0	17	13	.175	.231	.148	10.03	13.11
Will Klein	R-R	6-5	230	11-28-99	1	1	10.51	30	3	0	0	44	55	56	51	6	51	55	.313	.380	.258	11.34	10.51
Asa Lacy	L-L	6-4	215	6-2-99	1	2	11.25	11	3	0	0	20	9	27	25	2	28	25	.132	.130	.133	11.25	12.60
Richard Lovelady	L-L	6-0	185	7-7-95	0	0	0.00	1	0	0	0	1	0	0	0	0	0	2	.000	.000	.000	18.00	0.00
Emilio Marquez	L-L	5-8	170	4-28-98	1	1	5.21	9	0	0	2	19	22	13	11	1	9	14	.278	.200	.305	6.63	4.26
Alec Marsh	R-R	6-2	220	5-14-98	1	15	7.32	25	25	0	0	114	137	101	93	27	54	147	.290	.362	.227	11.57	4.25
Marcelo Martinez	L-L	6-2	190	8-10-96	1	0	2.57	3	3	0	0	14	6	4	4	2	7	17	.125	.154	.114	10.93	4.50
Noah Murdock	R-R	6-8	205	8-20-98	0	6	9.00	7	7	0	0	30	43	30	30	9	20	25	.344	.403	.286	7.50	6.00
Charlie Neuweiler	R-R	6-1	205	2-8-99	0	0	15.00	2	0	0	0	3	5	5	5	0	3	3	.417	.250	.500	9.00	9.00
Drew Parrish	L-L	5-11	200	12-8-97	4	3	2.13	10	10	0	0	55	31	16	13	5	14	48	.160	.210	.136	7.85	2.29
Matt Peacock	R-R	6-1	185	2-27-94	0	1	9.00	1	0	0	0	1	3	2	1	0	1	0	.500	1.000	.000	0.00	9.00
Walter Pennington	L-L	6-2	205	4-14-98	6	3	5.66	33	1	0	2	62	75	47	39	4	29	52	.310	.263	.331	7.55	4.21
Zack Phillips	L-L	6-0	170	7-11-98	2	2	6.26	20	3	0	0	46	49	35	32	7	22	37	.280	.189	.320	7.24	4.30
T.J. Sikkema	L-L	6-0	221	7-25-98	0	5	7.44	8	8	0	0	33	42	34	27	6	15	29	.313	.036	.387	7.99	4.13
Eric Skoglund	L-L	6-7	215	10-26-92	2	0	4.50	4	0	0	0	6	8	3	3	3	1	6	.320	.250	.353	9.00	1.50
Patrick Smith	L-L	6-2	215	10-14-96	0	1	72.00	3	0	0	0	1	4	10	8	0	7	0	.571	.400	1.000	0.00	63.00
Andres Sotillet	R-R	6-1	215	3-2-97	3	0	1.13	19	0	0	4	32	22	4	4	0	8	30	.193	.178	.203	8.44	2.25
Gabe Speier	L-L	5-11	200	4-12-95	0	0	0.00	1	0	0	0	1	1	0	0	0	0	2	.250	.000	1.000	18.00	0.00
Anthony Veneziano	L-L	6-5	205	9-1-97	6	9	5.72	26	25	1	0	123	133	90	78	24	66	129	.273	.273	.272	9.46	4.84
Nathan Webb	R-R	6-2	215	8-20-97	0	2	9.57	20	0	0	1	26	43	36	28	4	20	30	.364	.500	.278	10.25	6.84
Zach Willeman	R-R	6-2	219	3-27-96	0	2	5.16	16	0	0	1	23	21	14	13	4	9	25	.256	.263	.250	9.93	3.57
Stephen Woods Jr.	R-R	6-2	195	6-10-95	2	0	4.50	38	0	0	1	58	66	42	29	5	49	69	.281	.277	.284	10.71	7.60
Angel Zerpa	L-L	6-0	220	9-27-99	2	5	4.36	13	13	0	0	64	70	34	31	7	21	69	.276	.333	.249	9.70	2.95

Fielding

Catcher	PCT	G	PO	A	E	DP	PB
Cropley	.996	28	234	12	1	2	4
Porter	.997	36	353	19	1	4	2
Rivero	.985	41	358	27	6	3	9
Stupienski	.982	12	107	4	2	1	1
Tresh	.980	23	187	13	4	3	5

First Base	PCT	G	PO	A	E	DP
Alexander	1.000	32	236	16	0	26
Bradley	1.000	2	4	1	0	1
Glendinning	.988	67	469	37	6	58
Means	.992	20	112	11	1	15
Porter	.993	20	127	8	1	6
Stupienski	1.000	6	20	1	0	1

KANSAS CITY ROYALS

Second Base	PCT	G	PO	A	E	DP
Bewley	.918	22	29	49	7	12
Castellano	.962	7	11	14	1	4
Glendinning	.939	24	40	53	6	14
Grotjohn	.947	6	10	8	1	4
Loftin	.951	19	42	36	4	7
Massey	1.000	46	76	110	0	30
McCullough	1.000	15	23	33	0	10
Means	1.000	6	9	9	0	3

Third Base	PCT	G	PO	A	E	DP
Alexander	.913	10	5	16	2	2
Bewley	.900	6	4	5	1	0
Eaton	.969	23	17	45	2	7
Glendinning	.920	12	7	16	2	1
Grotjohn	1.000	4	1	1	0	0
Loftin	1.000	4	2	4	0	1
McCullough	.895	5	3	14	2	3
Means	.926	74	50	138	15	14
Porter	1.000	6	4	13	0	0

Shortstop	PCT	G	PO	A	E	DP
Castellano	.958	22	23	45	3	8
Eaton	1.000	2	1	7	0	1
Garcia	.975	78	88	185	7	42
Grotjohn	.926	7	11	14	2	4
Guzman	.860	13	13	24	6	9
Loftin	.947	6	3	15	1	1
McCullough	.975	10	18	21	1	4
Means	.926	7	10	15	2	3

Outfield	PCT	G	PO	A	E	DP
Bates	1.000	3	14	0	0	0
Bewley	--	1	0	0	0	0
Bradley	.977	90	160	7	4	0
Castellano	1.000	1	2	0	0	0
Eaton	.963	11	22	4	1	1
Gentry	.984	54	115	9	2	3
Grotjohn	1.000	10	10	0	0	0
Hernandez	.957	29	67	0	3	0
Loftin	.971	56	129	4	4	1
Matias	.966	69	135	6	5	1
Rave	.978	100	174	6	4	1

QUAD CITIES RIVER BANDITS — HIGH CLASS A

MIDWEST LEAGUE

Batting	B-T	HT	WT	DOB	AVG	vLH	vRH	G	AB	R	H	2B	3B	HR	RBI	BB	HBP	SH	SF	SO	SB	CS	SLG	OBP
Jack Alexander	R-R	6-0	212	5-30-00	.219	.143	.228	17	64	9	14	3	0	2	8	4	0	0	0	21	0	0	.359	.265
Parker Bates	L-R	6-1	205	11-16-97	.227	.267	.218	73	238	36	54	9	4	9	34	27	7	0	1	71	9	4	.412	.322
Darryl Collins	L-R	6-2	185	9-16-01	.269	.200	.277	26	93	15	25	1	2	1	13	17	1	0	4	26	3	0	.355	.374
Burle Dixon	L-L	6-5	185	10-15-98	.177	.217	.166	68	215	18	38	12	0	2	18	23	2	2	2	107	11	2	.260	.260
Kale Emshoff	R-R	6-2	228	5-2-98	.224	.231	.222	100	361	40	81	19	0	12	46	39	11	0	4	148	2	2	.377	.316
Felix Familia	R-R	6-2	205	10-13-98	.225	.333	.194	11	40	4	9	2	0	2	3	0	0	0	0	7	0	0	.425	.225
Saul Garza	R-R	6-3	227	4-9-98	.192	.118	.207	30	104	11	20	5	0	0	11	13	3	0	0	35	0	0	.240	.300
Tyler Gentry	R-R	6-2	210	2-1-99	.336	.361	.326	35	128	22	43	6	1	5	23	20	3	0	1	39	2	2	.516	.434
Herard Gonzalez	B-R	5-11	167	5-16-01	.238	.240	.238	113	407	61	97	9	7	9	61	65	2	5	4	114	14	8	.361	.343
Kyle Hayes	R-R	6-2	190	10-8-97	.000	.000	.000	4	13	0	0	0	0	0	0	1	2	0	0	5	0	0	.000	.188
Diego Hernandez	L-L	6-0	150	11-21-00	.279	.293	.275	83	330	55	92	17	4	7	29	27	6	7	1	72	27	8	.418	.343
Rubendy Jaquez	B-R	5-11	174	2-13-99	.221	.250	.214	26	86	10	19	1	2	1	10	3	0	2	0	15	2	3	.314	.247
Morgan McCullough	L-R	5-9	180	12-19-97	.241	.209	.250	64	191	26	46	9	3	5	23	34	7	2	3	54	7	4	.398	.370
Juan Carlos Negret	R-R	6-1	190	6-19-99	.222	.292	.196	91	329	43	73	16	1	18	68	35	4	0	9	94	1	0	.441	.297
Dillan Shrum	R-L	6-0	200	3-4-98	.238	.159	.260	97	311	44	74	22	1	16	54	52	17	0	3	129	1	0	.469	.373
Tyler Tolbert	R-R	6-0	160	1-27-98	.224	.273	.210	116	447	79	100	20	10	4	36	55	5	5	5	125	60	0	.340	.313
River Town	L-R	5-11	181	7-8-99	.250	.385	.230	26	100	15	25	2	1	2	14	9	2	0	3	17	4	0	.350	.316
Luca Tresh	R-R	6-0	193	1-11-00	.273	.324	.257	80	300	48	82	15	1	14	54	41	2	0	4	85	3	3	.470	.360
Enrique Valdez	L-R	6-0	185	5-15-01	.149	.111	.158	14	47	2	7	2	0	1	4	5	1	0	1	19	3	0	.255	.241
Cam Williams	B-R	6-2	195	2-7-98	.156	.163	.154	58	186	29	29	6	1	12	26	29	4	0	0	105	4	1	.392	.283
Peyton Wilson	B-R	5-9	180	11-1-99	.268	.221	.281	88	340	60	91	16	3	14	44	41	8	0	1	97	23	2	.456	.359

Pitching	B-T	HT	WT	DOB	W	L	ERA	G	GS	CG	SV	IP	H	R	ER	HR	BB	SO	AVG	vLH	vRH	K/9	BB/9
Adrian Alcantara	R-R	6-1	178	8-29-99	7	5	4.57	22	16	1	0	108	105	62	55	19	36	123	.254	.266	.246	10.22	2.99
Jack Aldrich	L-L	5-11	204	6-12-99	0	2	4.85	5	0	0	0	13	14	7	7	1	4	6	.292	.211	.345	4.15	2.77
Parker Bates	L-R	6-1	205	11-16-97	0	0	0.00	1	0	0	0	1	0	0	0	0	0	0	.000	.000	--	0.00	0.00
Harrison Beethe	R-R	6-5	220	4-3-98	0	3	15.00	24	0	0	0	21	28	36	35	2	33	24	.326	.357	.310	10.29	14.14
Jonathan Bowlan	R-R	6-6	240	12-1-96	0	0	0.00	1	1	0	0	4	6	0	0	0	1	6	.333	.444	.222	13.50	2.25
Noah Cameron	L-L	6-3	220	7-17-99	2	1	3.48	9	9	0	0	31	27	15	12	2	7	53	.229	.267	.216	15.39	2.03
Delvin Capellan	R-R	6-1	167	12-6-98	1	0	3.78	11	0	0	0	17	12	8	7	1	13	23	.197	.158	.214	12.42	7.02
Eric Cerantola	R-R	6-5	225	5-2-00	0	1	5.00	3	3	0	0	9	11	6	5	1	8	7	.297	.273	.333	7.00	8.00
Christian Chamberlain	L-L	5-10	173	7-20-99	0	1	4.29	13	4	0	0	21	12	10	10	5	20	39	.164	.150	.170	16.71	8.57
Chandler Champlain	R-R	6-5	220	7-23-99	1	3	9.84	8	7	0	0	32	58	35	35	3	11	22	.414	.356	.442	6.19	3.09
Christian Cosby	R-R	6-5	215	12-21-96	0	2	16.88	4	0	0	1	5	11	10	10	1	5	4	.458	.556	.400	6.75	8.44
Mitch Ellis	B-R	6-3	200	8-22-95	0	0	9.00	3	0	0	0	5	7	5	5	1	5	8	.333	.333	.333	14.40	9.00
William Fleming	R-R	6-6	220	3-6-99	3	4	5.10	11	11	0	0	55	63	31	31	9	18	39	.285	.316	.268	6.42	2.96
Tyson Guerrero	L-L	6-1	188	2-16-99	0	3	6.17	6	6	0	0	23	24	19	16	5	10	22	.258	.217	.271	8.49	3.86
Zach Haake	R-R	6-7	220	10-8-96	0	1	2.38	4	4	0	0	11	10	6	3	1	3	11	.222	.167	.259	8.74	2.38
Patrick Halligan	R-R	6-6	230	10-4-99	1	5	5.34	23	4	0	0	56	66	37	33	12	12	39	.292	.300	.287	6.31	1.94
Parker Harm	L-L	6-2	208	2-2-97	0	2	6.23	15	0	0	0	22	14	19	15	0	21	28	.187	.136	.208	11.63	8.72
Kasey Kalich	R-R	6-3	220	4-25-98	3	3	2.65	25	0	0	9	34	23	12	10	0	19	35	.192	.213	.178	9.26	5.03
Rylan Kaufman	L-L	6-4	225	6-23-99	1	7	5.15	19	19	0	0	94	91	59	54	12	47	100	.252	.253	.252	9.54	4.48
Rito Lugo	L-L	5-10	185	11-3-95	1	3	3.72	9	3	0	0	29	32	12	12	3	8	30	.296	.273	.302	9.31	2.48
Emilio Marquez	L-L	5-8	170	4-28-98	10	2	2.88	24	0	0	3	56	39	18	18	9	15	74	.191	.172	.200	11.82	2.40
Chazz Martinez	L-L	6-3	210	1-6-00	0	0	10.80	4	0	0	1	3	4	4	4	0	2	4	.286	.000	.308	10.80	5.40
Morgan McCullough	L-R	5-9	180	12-19-97	0	0	0.00	1	0	0	0	0	0	0	0	0	0	0	.000	.000	--	0.00	0.00
Caden Monke	L-L	6-3	170	9-2-99	0	5	6.04	30	1	0	4	67	71	49	45	11	35	75	.275	.213	.301	10.07	4.70
Yohanse Morel	R-R	6-0	170	8-23-00	2	2	4.08	10	0	0	0	18	20	10	8	0	10	21	.290	.278	.303	10.70	5.09
Noah Murdock	R-R	6-8	205	8-20-98	0	1	5.36	10	10	0	0	40	41	28	24	3	24	39	.261	.322	.224	8.70	5.36
Charlie Neuweiler	R-R	6-1	205	2-8-99	6	7	4.94	25	17	0	0	95	100	57	52	5	41	82	.276	.263	.288	7.80	3.90
Anderson Paulino	R-R	6-2	200	9-12-98	4	7	4.59	36	6	0	2	65	67	38	33	3	20	54	.262	.311	.227	7.52	2.78
Walter Pennington	L-L	6-2	205	4-14-98	0	0	0.00	3	0	0	1	6	2	0	0	0	1	9	.111	.143	.091	14.29	1.59
Zack Phillips	L-L	6-0	170	7-11-98	2	1	6.30	7	0	0	0	10	15	9	7	2	4	8	.366	.600	.333	7.20	3.60
Ruben Ramirez	R-R	6-0	190	11-14-98	0	2	4.39	15	0	0	1	27	22	13	13	2	12	23	.229	.276	.209	7.76	4.05
Anthony Simonelli	R-R	6-2	200	12-23-98	4	0	5.21	26	2	0	0	67	81	43	39	13	24	69	.297	.248	.326	9.22	3.21
Eric Skoglund	L-L	6-7	215	10-26-92	0	0	6.23	2	2	0	0	4	5	3	3	1	3	5	.278	.429	.182	10.38	6.23

Patrick Smith	L-L	6-2	215	10-14-96	0	1	2.20	14	0	0	0	16	8	4	4	0	11	21	.148	.167	.139	11.57	6.06
Chase Wallace	R-R	6-2	195	11-13-98	3	1	7.34	22	0	0	0	34	43	30	28	7	23	23	.305	.386	.250	6.03	6.03
Beck Way	R-R	6-4	200	8-6-99	3	3	3.79	7	7	0	0	36	24	17	15	1	17	47	.189	.217	.173	11.86	4.29

Fielding

Catcher	PCT	G	PO	A	E	DP	PB
Alexander	.987	15	139	10	2	1	2
Emshoff	.995	58	525	34	3	3	6
Familia	1.000	3	23	3	0	0	0
Garza	.944	6	48	3	3	1	0
Hayes	1.000	4	40	2	0	0	0
Tresh	.998	49	410	24	1	4	2

First Base	PCT	G	PO	A	E	DP
Bates	.000	1	0	0	0	0
Familia	.985	8	62	3	1	4
Garza	.990	12	92	5	1	7
Shrum	.992	94	726	55	6	67
Williams	.989	23	165	10	2	13

Second Base	PCT	G	PO	A	E	DP
Gonzalez	.959	62	99	137	10	30
Jaquez	1.000	2	3	6	0	1
McCullough	.985	18	22	42	1	8
Wilson	.969	51	73	112	6	23

Third Base	PCT	G	PO	A	E	DP
Gonzalez	.939	38	21	56	5	3
Jaquez	.974	21	15	23	1	4
McCullough	.972	32	17	52	2	4
Valdez	.955	8	3	18	1	2
Williams	.903	37	15	69	9	5

Shortstop	PCT	G	PO	A	E	DP
Jaquez	.800	1	1	3	1	0
McCullough	.983	14	16	42	1	7
Tolbert	.967	113	157	316	16	60
Valdez	.947	5	7	11	1	3

Outfield	PCT	G	PO	A	E	DP
Bates	.993	71	136	6	1	2
Collins	1.000	25	37	1	0	0
Dixon	1.000	63	81	2	0	0
Gentry	1.000	27	44	1	0	0
Hernandez	.975	80	150	8	4	2
Carlos Negret	1.000	73	126	4	0	0
Town	1.000	26	34	4	0	2
Wilson	.973	35	65	7	2	2

COLUMBIA FIREFLIES — *LOW CLASS A*

CAROLINA LEAGUE

Batting	B-T	HT	WT	DOB	AVG	vLH	vRH	G	AB	R	H	2B	3B	HR	RBI	BB	HBP	SH	SF	SO	SB	CS	SLG	OBP
Yeudi Advincola	R-R	6-1	170	10-9-01	.182	.200	.179	15	44	6	8	1	2	0	2	3	2	3	0	18	4	3	.295	.265
Gary Camarillo	R-R	6-1	157	7-5-01	.128	.100	.135	25	94	8	12	2	0	3	10	3	2	0	1	51	2	1	.245	.170
Wilmin Candelario	B-R	5-11	195	9-11-01	.184	.100	.197	23	76	9	14	3	1	0	6	12	1	0	0	35	10	2	.250	.303
Darryl Collins	L-R	6-2	185	9-16-01	.235	.400	.211	49	162	19	38	12	3	0	16	35	1	2	5	30	5	3	.346	.365
Tyler Cropley	R-R	5-11	185	12-10-95	.273	1.000	.200	3	11	1	3	0	0	0	0	0	0	0	0	1	1	0	.273	.273
Gavin Cross	L-L	6-3	210	2-13-01	.293	.143	.318	26	99	20	29	5	2	7	22	22	1	0	1	31	4	2	.596	.423
Jaswel De Los Santos	L-R	6-1	185	1-28-02	.143	.273	.123	28	84	13	12	2	0	2	6	14	2	2	0	39	7	0	.238	.280
Dayton Dooney	B-R	6-0	190	8-21-99	.148	.133	.150	42	149	17	22	3	1	5	16	21	1	0	1	59	1	2	.282	.256
Felix Familia	R-R	6-2	205	10-13-98	.164	.222	.154	20	61	7	10	2	0	0	2	8	0	1	0	16	1	2	.197	.261
Omar Florentino	B-R	5-9	170	10-26-01	.192	.150	.200	48	130	20	25	3	1	0	7	23	5	2	1	38	13	3	.231	.333
Francis Grullon	B-R	5-10	187	10-13-00	.160	.111	.171	14	50	7	8	1	0	0	4	6	0	0	0	16	0	0	.180	.250
Kyle Hayes	R-R	6-2	190	10-8-97	.137	.250	.123	25	73	5	10	2	0	2	8	9	4	0	0	30	1	0	.247	.267
Omar Hernandez	R-R	5-11	170	12-10-01	.231	.241	.229	85	320	40	74	15	1	1	31	26	2	5	1	78	18	3	.294	.292
David Hollie	R-R	6-2	205	10-25-99	.241	.000	.286	32	108	19	26	6	2	3	13	9	4	0	1	50	8	1	.417	.320
Rubendy Jaquez	B-R	5-11	174	2-13-99	.268	.313	.259	27	97	8	26	3	2	1	12	7	1	0	0	16	7	2	.371	.324
Carter Jensen	L-R	6-1	210	7-3-03	.226	.236	.225	113	393	66	89	24	2	11	50	83	4	0	5	103	8	6	.382	.363
Edgar Martinez	L-R	5-10	180	2-14-01	.250	.125	.263	24	88	13	22	1	3	1	5	8	1	1	0	38	5	0	.364	.320
Erick Pena	L-R	6-3	205	2-20-03	.149	.149	.150	82	281	25	42	10	1	9	36	41	1	1	2	121	6	5	.288	.258
Guillermo Quintana	R-R	6-1	180	3-16-01	.240	.304	.230	114	417	53	100	21	0	8	54	57	3	0	6	76	19	5	.348	.331
Jean Ramirez	L-L	5-10	190	10-25-00	.276	.229	.285	57	214	44	59	6	1	6	21	28	2	11	0	39	37	11	.397	.365
Joshua Rivera	R-R	5-11	185	1-30-99	.206	.095	.233	32	107	11	22	3	1	0	7	12	2	1	0	38	2	3	.252	.298
Lizandro Rodriguez	B-R	5-11	180	11-16-02	.290	.300	.288	18	62	13	18	4	1	1	5	8	2	0	0	11	1	1	.435	.389
River Town	L-R	5-11	181	7-8-99	.248	.243	.249	81	282	47	70	18	3	12	45	52	14	4	4	64	18	3	.461	.386
Levi Usher	L-R	6-0	210	6-25-00	.074	.000	.080	8	27	3	2	1	0	0	3	3	0	0	1	8	1	0	.111	.161
Enrique Valdez	L-R	6-0	185	5-15-01	.256	.200	.263	82	285	39	73	19	1	6	37	23	3	1	4	85	19	6	.393	.314
Javier Vaz	L-R	5-9	151	9-22-00	.260	.444	.220	27	100	14	26	6	1	1	12	20	1	0	0	14	4	3	.370	.388
Daniel Vazquez	R-R	6-0	150	12-15-03	.195	.186	.196	77	293	25	57	10	0	0	31	28	0	2	4	86	10	5	.229	.262
Cayden Wallace	R-R	6-1	205	8-7-01	.294	.267	.298	27	109	15	32	7	3	2	16	12	1	0	0	22	8	1	.468	.369

Pitching	B-T	HT	WT	DOB	W	L	ERA	G	GS	CG	SV	IP	H	R	ER	HR	BB	SO	AVG	vLH	vRH	K/9	BB/9
Jack Aldrich	L-L	5-11	204	6-12-99	4	0	3.95	23	0	0	3	43	44	21	19	4	14	42	.257	.143	.313	8.72	2.91
Wander Arias	R-R	6-4	230	11-3-99	3	5	5.20	22	5	0	4	81	88	60	47	12	33	74	.281	.277	.285	8.19	3.65
Luinder Avila	R-R	6-3	195	8-21-01	6	10	4.54	26	26	1	0	115	102	66	58	10	49	97	.234	.209	.251	7.59	3.83
Mason Barnett	R-R	6-0	218	11-7-00	1	0	0.00	3	0	0	0	7	0	0	0	0	1	11	.000	.000	.000	14.14	1.29
Luis Barroso	R-R	6-3	165	9-7-98	4	8	5.23	36	0	0	9	52	51	39	30	6	14	59	.248	.264	.235	10.28	2.44
Jonatan Bernal	R-R	6-1	194	6-29-02	2	2	4.70	9	4	0	0	38	44	24	20	4	8	27	.291	.360	.257	6.34	1.88
Daury Cabrera	R-R	6-4	230	10-23-00	1	0	3.72	5	0	0	0	10	9	6	4	3	3	10	.231	.154	.385	9.31	2.79
Noah Cameron	L-L	6-3	220	7-17-99	0	1	3.72	7	7	0	0	29	22	14	12	3	9	39	.208	.286	.188	12.10	2.79
Delvin Capellan	R-R	6-1	167	12-6-98	2	3	5.82	18	0	0	1	39	54	35	25	5	14	35	.327	.284	.363	8.15	3.26
Eric Cerantola	R-R	6-5	225	5-2-00	1	2	5.48	7	7	0	0	21	24	14	13	4	6	29	.293	.366	.220	12.23	2.53
Shane Connolly	L-L	6-2	175	2-13-99	1	2	6.05	23	0	0	1	39	42	31	26	5	23	33	.276	.367	.233	7.68	5.35
Heribert Garcia	R-R	6-0	220	10-2-99	7	3	6.09	19	0	0	1	65	81	46	44	13	17	55	.302	.315	.294	7.62	2.35
Patrick Halligan	R-R	6-6	230	10-4-99	0	2	7.15	3	0	0	0	11	14	9	9	2	2	9	.286	.211	.333	7.15	1.59
Ryan Hennen	R-L	6-0	180	9-30-97	2	2	3.46	10	0	0	0	26	30	12	10	2	4	37	.283	.296	.278	12.81	1.38
2-team total (3 Delmarva Shorebirds)					2	2	3.94	13	0	0	0	32	37	16	14	2	5	42	.282	.342	.258	11.81	1.41
Isaiah Henry	R-R	6-3	212	3-22-99	0	0	7.71	4	0	0	0	5	6	7	4	0	6	5	.333	.300	.375	9.64	11.57
Ben Hernandez	R-R	6-2	205	7-1-01	1	7	5.38	23	23	0	0	77	83	56	46	7	40	71	.280	.325	.250	8.30	4.68
Eduardo Herrera	B-R	5-9	179	1-5-00	0	0	0.00	1	0	0	0	2	0	0	0	0	2	3	.000	.000	.000	13.50	9.00
Tim Holdgrafer	R-R	6-1	180	7-31-96	1	1	5.82	8	0	0	0	17	21	12	11	0	6	17	.300	.227	.333	9.00	3.18
Rubendy Jaquez	B-R	5-11	174	2-13-99	0	0	0.00	1	0	0	0	0	0	0	0	0	0	0	.000	.000	--	0.00	0.00
Brandon Johnson	R-R	6-0	195	6-12-99	0	0	9.00	4	0	0	1	5	7	6	5	1	3	3	.350	.333	.357	5.40	5.40

Rylan Kaufman	L-L	6-4	225	6-23-99	1	2	5.49	6	3	0	0	20	24	17	12	1	13	26	.304	.333	.297	11.90	5.95
Ben Kudrna	R-R	6-3	175	1-30-03	2	5	3.48	17	17	0	0	72	66	32	28	4	32	61	.239	.218	.255	7.59	3.98
Cooper McKeehan	L-L	6-1	195	3-28-01	0	0	2.25	5	0	0	0	8	5	2	2	0	5	10	.161	.222	.136	11.25	5.63
John McMillon	L-R	6-3	230	1-27-98	1	2	6.10	26	0	0	0	31	17	23	21	2	38	45	.167	.211	.141	13.06	11.03
Frank Mozzicato	L-L	6-3	175	6-19-03	2	6	4.30	19	19	0	0	69	55	43	33	6	51	89	.219	.217	.220	11.61	6.65
Shane Panzini	R-R	6-3	220	10-30-01	0	4	5.00	17	17	0	0	63	66	40	35	9	38	66	.277	.303	.259	9.43	5.43
Oscar Rayo	L-L	6-1	180	1-13-02	1	1	3.91	8	0	0	1	23	25	11	10	4	6	20	.275	.226	.300	7.83	2.35
Joshua Rivera	R-R	5-11	185	1-30-99	0	0	0.00	1	0	0	0	1	0	0	0	0	0	1	.000	.000	.000	6.75	0.00
Ben Sears	R-R	6-5	208	6-15-00	0	0	3.29	7	0	0	0	14	11	5	5	1	2	11	.224	.188	.242	7.24	1.32
Matt Stil	R-R	6-3	190	7-5-00	2	1	4.55	16	1	0	0	28	21	19	14	2	37	31	.210	.114	.262	10.08	12.04
Samuel Valerio	R-R	6-4	230	10-8-01	0	3	10.21	12	2	0	0	27	31	35	31	3	31	33	.272	.268	.276	10.87	10.21
Chase Wallace	R-R	6-2	195	11-13-98	0	0	3.00	4	0	0	0	6	6	4	2	0	5	4	.250	.375	.188	6.00	7.50
Ben Wereski	L-L	6-2	210	10-26-97	4	6	4.42	26	0	0	2	57	55	36	28	9	16	62	.250	.343	.209	9.79	2.53
Marlin Willis	L-L	6-4	190	6-5-98	3	1	4.93	27	0	0	0	42	37	28	23	3	39	63	.234	.239	.232	13.50	8.36

Fielding

Catcher	PCT	G	PO	A	E	DP	PB
Cropley	.941	2	14	2	1	0	0
Familia	.980	5	46	3	1	0	2
Hayes	1.000	23	166	12	0	1	1
Hernandez	.985	59	542	61	9	6	5
Jensen	.978	46	395	43	10	6	9

First Base	PCT	G	PO	A	E	DP
Dooney	1.000	4	28	2	0	2
Familia	.968	14	83	9	3	6
Hayes	1.000	1	6	0	0	0
Jaquez	1.000	4	26	2	0	2
Quintana	.984	110	825	53	14	80

Second Base	PCT	G	PO	A	E	DP
Advincola	1.000	3	5	5	0	2
Dooney	.947	31	41	66	6	18
Florentino	.951	38	59	78	7	18
Grullon	.953	12	14	27	2	3
Jaquez	.920	6	12	11	2	3
Martinez	.933	15	36	34	5	13
Rivera	1.000	7	13	22	0	6
Rodriguez	.989	17	33	57	1	13
Vaz	1.000	7	12	22	0	1

Third Base	PCT	G	PO	A	E	DP
Advincola	.800	5	3	5	2	1
Florentino	.778	4	1	6	2	1
Jaquez	.852	12	7	16	4	0
Martinez	.000	1	0	0	0	0
Rivera	.875	6	0	7	1	0
Rodriguez	.833	1	0	5	1	0
Valdez	.896	80	66	124	22	11
Wallace	.950	25	18	39	3	4

Shortstop	PCT	G	PO	A	E	DP
Advincola	1.000	6	13	15	0	3
Candelario	.875	23	27	57	12	12
Florentino	.846	4	5	6	2	2
Martinez	.667	2	1	1	1	1
Rivera	.984	19	27	36	1	8
Valdez	.750	1	1	2	1	0
Vazquez	.929	77	105	196	23	45

Outfield	PCT	G	PO	A	E	DP
Camarillo	.962	25	48	2	2	0
Collins	.987	47	73	1	1	0
Cross	.964	22	51	2	2	0
De Los Santos	.932	27	53	2	4	0
Hollie	.971	30	64	4	2	3
Martinez	.917	7	10	1	1	0
Pena	.974	81	184	2	5	1
Ramirez	.975	58	113	5	3	2
Town	.916	75	112	8	11	0
Usher	1.000	7	10	0	0	0
Vaz	.971	20	31	3	1	1

ACL ROYALS — *ROOKIE*

ARIZONA COMPLEX LEAGUE

Batting	B-T	HT	WT	DOB	AVG	vLH	vRH	G	AB	R	H	2B	3B	HR	RBI	BB	HBP	SH	SF	SO	SB	CS	SLG	OBP
Yeudi Advincola	R-R	6-1	170	10-9-01	.390	.333	.407	23	77	12	30	4	1	0	14	5	0	0	0	14	9	1	.468	.427
Jack Alexander	R-R	6-0	212	5-30-00	.250	.333	.200	3	8	1	2	0	0	1	3	1	1	0	0	4	0	0	.625	.400
Giullianno Allende	L-L	6-2	165	9-4-03	.143	.000	.167	2	7	0	1	0	0	0	0	0	0	0	0	1	1	0	.143	.143
Parker Bates	L-R	6-1	205	11-16-97	.211	.000	.250	6	19	1	4	1	0	1	1	4	0	0	0	3	1	0	.421	.348
Junior Calderon	R-R	6-0	205	12-9-01	.273	.125	.301	32	99	12	27	11	1	3	22	12	1	0	5	22	2	2	.495	.342
Wilmin Candelario	B-R	5-11	195	9-11-01	.273	.231	.286	31	110	19	30	6	3	4	15	6	1	0	0	47	10	3	.491	.316
Ryan Cepero	R-R	6-1	180	2-11-03	.130	.167	.125	20	54	5	7	2	0	1	4	3	0	0	0	25	0	0	.222	.175
Austin Charles	R-R	6-6	215	11-13-03	.273	.000	.375	3	11	1	3	0	0	0	0	0	0	0	0	4	0	0	.273	.273
Darnel Collins	L-L	6-1	200	7-12-04	.213	.143	.225	26	94	14	20	4	1	0	10	8	0	0	0	24	0	0	.277	.275
Darryl Collins	L-R	6-2	185	9-16-01	.227	.429	.133	6	22	2	5	1	0	0	1	4	0	0	0	5	1	0	.273	.346
Tyler Cropley	R-R	5-11	185	12-10-95	.200	.500	.000	2	5	0	1	1	0	0	0	1	0	0	0	0	0	0	.400	.333
Gavin Cross	L-L	6-3	210	2-13-01	.500	.667	.429	3	10	4	5	2	0	1	3	2	0	0	0	2	0	0	1.000	.583
Jaswel De Los Santos	L-R	6-1	185	1-28-02	.280	.250	.286	21	82	9	23	3	2	2	8	8	1	0	1	24	8	1	.439	.348
German Duarte	R-R	6-0	198	10-30-02	.000	.000	.000	3	8	0	0	0	0	0	0	0	0	0	0	3	0	0	.000	.000
Hayden Dunhurst	L-R	5-11	220	9-19-00	.429	.250	.667	3	7	2	3	2	0	0	1	3	0	0	0	2	0	0	.714	.600
Omar Florentino	B-R	5-9	170	10-26-01	.231	.000	.250	5	13	3	3	0	0	1	1	2	0	0	0	1	1	0	.462	.333
Saul Garza	R-R	6-3	227	4-9-98	.167	.250	.143	5	18	2	3	0	0	0	1	1	0	0	0	6	0	0	.167	.211
Francis Grullon	B-R	5-10	187	10-13-00	.500	--	.500	2	4	1	2	1	0	0	2	0	0	0	0	1	0	0	.750	.500
Diego Guzman	R-R	6-1	200	9-12-03	.198	.333	.161	34	111	10	22	3	3	1	12	12	1	0	0	43	3	3	.306	.282
Jeison Guzman	B-R	6-2	205	10-8-98	.200	--	.200	3	10	1	2	0	0	0	0	1	0	0	0	4	0	0	.200	.273
David Hollie	R-R	6-2	205	10-25-99	.286	.000	.348	9	28	8	8	2	0	1	6	7	0	0	0	10	1	0	.464	.429
Roger Leyton	R-R	6-1	200	2-3-03	.274	.278	.274	36	124	23	34	13	2	3	19	14	4	0	2	29	6	3	.484	.361
Diego Maican	R-R	6 3	235	10 24 00	.000	.000	.000	2	6	1	0	0	0	0	0	0	1	0	0	2	0	0	.000	.143
Junior Marin	R-R	6-2	240	3-15-04	.315	.353	.307	30	92	15	29	7	1	0	6	9	1	0	1	31	3	1	.413	.379
Edgar Martinez	L-R	5-10	180	2-14-01	.198	.125	.213	26	91	9	18	5	2	1	9	8	2	1	1	37	5	0	.330	.275
Brennon McNair	R-R	6-1	185	9-15-02	.231	.174	.241	42	156	28	36	5	4	6	19	17	5	0	2	50	7	3	.429	.322
Omar Nuel	R-R	6-1	210	5-12-03	.228	.200	.234	30	92	17	21	4	0	6	16	7	1	0	0	38	8	0	.467	.290
Enmanuel Pire	R-R	5-10	180	5-18-01	.270	.200	.296	14	37	4	10	2	0	0	2	3	1	0	1	12	1	0	.324	.333
Lizandro Rodriguez	B-R	5-11	180	11-16-02	.317	.294	.323	25	82	17	26	4	1	5	12	9	3	0	1	16	5	3	.573	.400
Milo Rushford	L-L	6-1	185	2-12-04	.200	.000	.250	3	10	0	2	1	0	0	1	1	0	0	0	2	1	0	.300	.273
Dionmy Salon	R-R	6-2	215	11-18-01	.348	.600	.304	20	66	7	23	3	0	2	7	8	4	0	0	19	0	0	.485	.449
Rothaikeg Seijas	R-R	5-11	170	7-22-02	.214	.000	.265	22	42	7	9	4	0	0	3	6	3	0	0	18	2	0	.310	.353
Gabriel Silva	R-R	5-10	218	12-10-03	.185	.231	.176	23	81	11	15	5	0	3	11	5	3	0	1	32	0	0	.358	.256
Levi Usher	L-R	6-0	210	6-25-00	.167	--	.167	8	24	2	4	0	1	0	0	4	0	0	0	9	1	0	.250	.286

Javier Vaz	L-R	5-9	151	9-22-00	.250	.500	.167	2	8	2	2	1	0	0	0	1	1	0	0	3	1	0	.375	.400
Cayden Wallace	R-R	6-1	205	8-7-01	.286	.333	.250	3	7	3	2	1	0	0	1	3	0	0	0	1	0	0	.429	.500
Cam Williams	B-R	6-2	195	2-7-98	.208	.000	.227	8	24	5	5	1	1	1	3	8	1	0	0	8	1	1	.458	.424

Pitching	B-T	HT	WT	DOB	W	L	ERA	G	GS	CG	SV	IP	H	R	ER	HR	BB	SO	AVG	vLH	vRH	K/9	BB/9
Mack Anglin	R-R	6-4	220	7-5-00	0	0	0.00	1	0	0	0	1	0	0	0	0	0	1	.000	.000	.000	9.00	0.00
Brandon Barker	R-R	6-3	210	8-20-92	0	0	9.00	1	1	0	0	1	3	1	1	0	0	3	.500	.000	.750	27.00	0.00
Mason Barnett	R-R	6-0	218	11-7-00	0	0	0.00	1	1	0	0	1	0	0	0	0	0	1	.000	--	.000	9.00	0.00
Jonathan Bowlan	R-R	6-6	240	12-1-96	0	1	5.12	7	7	0	0	19	29	11	11	1	4	26	.354	.344	.360	12.10	1.86
Daury Cabrera	R-R	6-4	230	10-23-00	2	6	5.98	13	4	0	0	44	55	33	29	3	17	47	.294	.333	.264	9.69	3.50
Noah Cameron	L-L	6-3	220	7-17-99	0	1	3.18	3	3	0	0	6	9	2	2	1	0	7	.346	.400	.333	11.12	0.00
Jose Catano	L-L	6-3	193	6-10-01	2	3	3.76	12	3	0	0	38	33	17	16	3	13	50	.224	.310	.203	11.74	3.05
Luis Cepeda	L-L	6-1	175	10-12-00	3	1	2.49	8	4	0	0	22	19	7	6	3	6	24	.224	.000	.260	9.97	2.49
Julio Cruz	R-R	6-0	195	7-26-00	0	0	0.00	2	0	0	0	1	0	0	0	0	0	0	.000	.000	.000	0.00	0.00
Andres Diaz	R-R	6-1	215	7-6-01	3	2	4.55	11	0	0	2	28	23	17	14	4	3	39	.213	.256	.185	12.69	0.98
C.J. Eldred	R-R	6-2	220	5-6-95	0	1	4.50	5	4	0	0	10	9	5	5	0	5	9	.243	.400	.185	8.10	4.50
Ruben Garcia	R-R	6-4	220	8-2-96	0	0	0.00	1	0	0	0	1	1	0	0	0	0	1	.333	.000	1.000	9.00	0.00
Adrian Gonzalez	R-R	6-2	170	9-30-00	0	0	6.75	5	0	0	0	4	6	3	3	0	5	3	.375	.250	.417	6.75	11.25
Zach Haake	R-R	6-7	220	10-8-96	0	0	3.60	2	1	0	0	5	5	2	2	1	0	8	.238	.000	.313	14.40	0.00
Parker Harm	L-L	6-2	208	2-2-97	0	0	13.50	2	0	0	0	2	1	3	3	1	2	4	.111	.000	.125	18.00	9.00
Isaiah Henry	R-R	6-3	212	3-22-99	0	0	108.00	1	0	0	0	0	3	4	4	1	2	0	.750	.000	1.000	0.00	54.00
Miguel Hernandez	R-R	6-0	174	10-26-01	0	0	7.71	5	0	0	0	5	7	5	4	1	2	4	.318	.375	.286	7.71	3.86
Eduardo Herrera	B-R	5-9	179	1-5-00	0	0	0.00	1	0	0	1	1	1	0	0	0	0	3	.250	.000	.333	27.00	0.00
Brandon Johnson	R-R	6-0	195	6-12-99	0	0	0.00	1	0	0	0	1	0	0	0	0	0	2	.000	.000	.000	18.00	0.00
Asa Lacy	L-L	6-4	215	6-2-99	1	0	9.00	4	2	0	0	8	4	10	8	1	14	10	.143	.231	.067	11.25	15.75
Rito Lugo	L-L	5-10	185	11-3-95	0	0	1.42	6	5	0	0	13	8	2	2	0	1	18	.178	.357	.097	12.79	0.71
Chazz Martinez	L-L	6-3	210	1-6-00	0	0	6.00	2	0	0	0	3	2	2	2	0	1	1	.182	.000	.286	3.00	3.00
Juan Martinez	R-R	5-11	195	4-6-01	0	0	8.64	8	0	0	0	8	8	10	8	1	8	17	.222	.167	.250	18.36	8.64
Cooper McKeehan	L-L	6-1	195	3-28-01	0	0	0.00	1	0	0	0	1	1	0	0	0	1	1	.250	1.000	.000	9.00	9.00
Pablo Mujica	L-L	6-0	180	6-26-01	5	2	3.13	11	1	0	0	32	21	13	11	2	16	44	.184	.069	.224	12.51	4.55
Elvis Novas	R-R	6-0	205	9-2-02	0	2	4.50	10	1	0	0	30	28	18	15	3	8	30	.239	.231	.244	9.00	2.40
Marcus Olivarez	R-R	6-3	200	9-12-98	0	0	0.00	3	0	0	0	4	1	0	0	0	1	6	.077	.167	.000	13.50	2.25
Luilly Ovalle	R-R	6-3	170	10-13-00	0	0	6.75	5	2	0	0	7	9	6	5	2	2	9	.290	.333	.250	12.15	2.70
Dario Peralta	R-R	6-1	210	10-12-00	0	1	10.05	12	0	0	2	14	22	23	16	3	7	16	.338	.419	.265	10.05	4.40
Luis Polanco	R-R	6-3	225	8-10-00	0	0	4.38	11	0	0	1	12	11	6	6	0	5	19	.239	.400	.161	13.86	3.65
Ruben Ramirez	R-R	6-0	190	11-14-98	0	0	0.00	1	0	0	0	1	0	0	0	0	0	1	.000	.000	--	9.00	0.00
Ryan Ramsey	R-L	6-0	195	1-18-01	0	0	0.00	1	0	0	0	2	1	0	0	0	1	3	.143	.000	.200	13.50	4.50
Oscar Rayo	L-L	6-1	180	1-13-02	1	0	0.00	1	0	0	0	4	2	0	0	0	0	8	.133	.000	.167	18.00	0.00
Nicholas Regalado	R-R	6-2	215	5-15-02	0	0	4.50	4	0	0	0	4	6	5	2	0	0	7	.300	.667	.143	15.75	0.00
David Sandlin	R-R	6-4	215	2-21-01	0	0	0.00	1	1	0	0	2	1	0	0	0	0	3	.143	.250	.000	13.50	0.00
Osiris Santana	R-R	5-11	158	10-11-01	1	2	3.32	18	0	0	5	22	20	12	8	2	4	26	.222	.200	.240	10.80	1.66
Wesley Scott	R-R	6-1	185	3-2-01	0	0	11.57	3	0	0	0	2	1	3	3	0	4	4	.143	.000	.250	15.43	15.43
Ben Sears	R-R	6-5	208	6-15-00	1	0	0.00	1	0	0	0	2	2	0	0	0	0	2	.250	.000	.500	9.00	0.00
Anthony Simonelli	R-R	6-2	200	12-23-98	0	0	1.50	3	3	0	0	6	5	1	1	0	0	3	.250	.250	.250	4.50	0.00
Eric Skoglund	L-L	6-7	215	10-26-92	0	2	11.57	3	3	0	0	5	9	7	6	2	0	9	.375	.125	.500	17.36	0.00
Adrian Solano	R-R	6-1	180	10-17-99	2	0	2.16	5	1	0	0	8	8	4	2	1	1	6	.235	.417	.136	6.48	1.08
Samuel Valerio	R-R	6-4	230	10-8-01	0	2	13.50	7	0	0	1	7	10	12	11	2	7	13	.333	.538	.176	15.95	8.59
Mauricio Veliz	R-R	6-2	220	7-17-02	2	3	2.36	13	5	0	1	46	32	19	12	4	12	37	.193	.246	.155	7.29	2.36
Luis Villar	L-L	5-10	195	11-8-00	0	0	9.64	7	0	0	1	5	6	5	5	3	0	3	.316	.400	.286	5.79	0.00
Daniel Vitriago	L-L	5-10	200	12-5-00	0	0	1.69	7	2	0	0	11	9	2	2	0	0	15	.225	.167	.235	12.66	0.00
Nathan Webb	R-R	6-2	215	8-20-97	2	1	5.79	4	1	0	0	5	3	3	3	0	3	7	.188	.000	.429	13.50	5.79

Fielding

C: Alexander 2, Cropley 2, Duarte 2, Dunhurst 3, Garza 1, Pire 14, Salon 18, Silva 17. **1B:** Calderon 24, Collins 25, Garza 2, Maican 2, Williams 3. **2B:** Cepero 3, Florentino 5, Grullon 2, Guzman 22, Martinez 3, Rodriguez 24, Vaz 1. **3B:** Calderon 4, Guzman 14, Martinez 11, McNair 26, Wallace 3, Williams 4. **SS:** Advincola 20, Cepero 17, Charles 3, Guzman 3, Martinez 2, McNair 13, Rodriguez 1. **OF:** Allende 2, Bates 5, Candelario 29, Collins 3, Cross 3, De Los Santos 21, Hollie 7, Leyton 32, Marin 21, Martinez 7, Nuel 22, Rushford 3, Seijas 19, Usher 9, Vaz 1

DSL KC GLASS — ROOKIE

DOMINICAN SUMMER LEAGUE

Batting	B-T	HT	WT	DOB	AVG	vLH	vRH	G	AB	R	H	2B	3B	HR	RBI	BB	HBP	SH	SF	SO	SB	CS	SLG	OBP
Marino Castillo	L-R	5-11	150	10-13-02	.253	.200	.265	31	83	13	21	1	0	0	7	8	5	0	0	20	5	4	.265	.354
2-team total (12 DSL KC Stewart)					.274	.235	.280	43	117	22	32	3	0	0	11	14	8	0	0	26	12	6	.299	.388
Steven Cespedes	L-R	5-9	170	10-23-03	.250	.400	.211	7	24	3	6	1	0	0	0	3	0	0	0	7	0	1	.292	.333
2-team total (19 DSL KC Stewart)					.286	.308	.281	26	70	10	20	5	0	0	5	14	0	0	1	13	0	1	.357	.400
Jose Chacon	R-R	6-0	165	11-29-02	.189	.000	.217	41	106	11	20	4	0	1	7	20	10	0	0	23	1	3	.255	.368
Luis Echenique	L-L	5-11	175	11-25-02	.500	--	.500	1	2	0	1	0	0	0	1	0	0	0	0	0	0	0	.500	.500
2-team total (22 DSL KC Stewart)					.255	.250	.256	23	47	12	12	1	1	0	8	12	1	0	0	1	3	2	.319	.417
Jeffry Filion	R-R	5-11	185	10-23-02	.000	.000	.000	4	8	1	0	0	0	0	0	1	0	0	0	6	0	0	.000	.111
2-team total (15 DSL KC Stewart)					.050	.000	.067	19	40	4	2	1	1	0	3	8	0	0	1	16	2	0	.125	.204
Eduardo Garcia	L-R	6-1	183	9-10-01	.000	.000	.000	4	9	0	0	0	0	0	0	3	0	0	0	7	0	0	.000	.250
2-team total (49 DSL KC Stewart)					.216	.148	.229	53	171	24	37	9	1	2	24	23	4	0	7	55	3	0	.316	.312
Manuel German	R-R	6-1	220	4-29-05	.209	.167	.217	41	110	15	23	8	0	3	17	16	3	0	3	32	1	0	.364	.318
2-team total (5 DSL KC Stewart)					.190	.143	.200	46	126	16	24	9	0	3	18	17	5	0	3	37	1	0	.333	.305

Ricson Gonzalez	R-R	6-0	170	6-16-05	.241	.222	.243	27	79	8	19	4	0	0	8	7	3	0	0	13	1	0	.291	.326
2-team total (3 DSL KC Stewart)					.222	.167	.231	30	90	8	20	4	0	0	8	7	4	0	0	16	1	0	.267	.307
Aldrin Lucas	R-R	5-10	165	2-7-03	.207	.188	.211	36	92	12	19	1	1	3	14	18	4	1	1	28	2	0	.337	.357
2-team total (1 DSL KC Stewart)					.213	.188	.218	37	94	12	20	1	1	3	14	19	4	1	1	28	2	0	.340	.364
Jose Medina	B-R	5-10	185	4-16-05	.120	.000	.143	11	25	3	3	1	0	0	1	5	0	0	0	11	0	0	.160	.267
2-team total (26 DSL KC Stewart)					.293	.188	.313	37	99	20	29	3	1	0	11	22	3	0	0	25	0	1	.343	.435
Raimel Medina	R-R	5-11	165	11-15-04	.252	.100	.276	51	143	16	36	6	0	1	13	19	5	0	1	30	15	2	.315	.357
Charles Nova	R-R	5-10	155	1-15-05	.223	.333	.198	38	112	14	25	3	0	0	11	16	2	0	3	22	4	3	.250	.323
Josi Novas	R-R	6-4	180	2-12-05	.205	.000	.223	36	112	15	23	10	1	4	23	12	1	0	2	47	5	2	.420	.283
2-team total (8 DSL KC Stewart)					.221	.000	.242	44	136	25	30	13	3	4	28	18	1	0	2	57	7	2	.449	.312
Juan Olmos	R-R	6-2	175	11-22-04	.163	.111	.175	17	49	7	8	0	1	1	6	5	2	0	0	20	0	0	.265	.268
Alexander Orasma	B-R	6-0	165	11-19-04	.217	.238	.212	40	106	8	23	4	0	0	7	10	0	2	1	26	7	1	.255	.282
Angel Parra	L-L	6-0	156	1-26-04	.122	.286	.088	12	41	5	5	1	0	1	2	5	0	0	0	15	2	0	.220	.217
2-team total (22 DSL KC Stewart)					.243	.158	.260	34	115	12	28	6	0	2	11	12	3	0	0	25	8	2	.348	.331
Jhonny Perdomo	R-R	5-10	168	6-9-02	.306	.130	.339	49	147	31	45	8	0	1	18	19	8	0	1	30	17	4	.381	.411
Henry Ramos	L-L	6-1	175	9-20-04	.193	.107	.211	51	161	20	31	6	0	0	15	30	3	0	2	42	18	1	.230	.327
Ivan Sosa	R-R	--	--	9-9-04	.069	.000	.083	11	29	2	2	1	0	0	1	4	0	0	1	13	1	0	.103	.176
2-team total (41 DSL KC Stewart)					.183	.167	.188	52	180	22	33	9	1	2	17	16	3	1	3	52	4	3	.278	.257
Luis Tejeda	R-R	6-0	169	2-18-04	.000	.000	.000	3	6	0	0	0	0	0	0	0	0	0	0	0	0	0	.000	.000
2-team total (5 DSL KC Stewart)					.200	.000	.273	8	15	4	3	0	0	0	3	3	0	0	1	2	1	1	.200	.316
Erick Torres	R-R	5-10	160	12-20-04	.266	.346	.252	51	173	36	46	7	2	3	16	21	6	2	0	35	14	5	.382	.365
Yeison Vargas	R-R	0-0	0	9-10-03	.243	.200	.250	28	70	14	17	0	2	1	5	11	2	0	1	23	1	3	.343	.357
2-team total (11 DSL KC Stewart)					.231	.250	.227	39	104	21	24	3	2	2	10	17	2	1	1	36	1	4	.356	.347

Pitching	B-T	HT	WT	DOB	W	L	ERA	G	GS	CG	SV	IP	H	R	ER	HR	BB	SO	AVG	vLH	vRH	K/9	BB/9
Felix Arronde	R-R	6-3	185	4-25-03	1	8	6.94	12	12	0	0	35	40	31	27	4	13	50	.276	.282	.270	12.86	3.34
Dioni Baez	R-R	6-2	185	1-24-03	0	0	4.26	3	0	0	0	6	7	3	3	0	3	7	.318	.500	.167	9.95	4.26
2-team total (10 DSL KC Stewart)					2	4	8.31	13	3	0	0	26	36	29	24	0	18	19	.336	.339	.333	6.58	6.23
Andy Basora	R-R	6-3	155	4-13-05	0	2	11.57	2	0	0	0	2	4	5	3	0	2	3	.364	.667	.250	11.57	7.71
2-team total (11 DSL KC Stewart)					1	3	3.33	13	0	0	0	27	30	20	10	0	13	24	.273	.340	.222	8.00	4.33
Wilson Betemit Jr.	R-R	6-1	170	7-27-03	2	2	1.35	11	4	0	0	33	17	7	5	1	10	34	.153	.140	.162	9.18	2.70
2-team total (1 DSL KC Stewart)					2	2	1.30	12	4	0	0	35	17	7	5	1	10	35	.149	.136	.157	9.09	2.60
Emilio Castillo	L-L	5-10	150	10-18-02	0	0	0.00	2	0	0	0	2	1	0	0	0	3	1	.167	--	.167	4.50	13.50
2-team total (12 DSL KC Stewart)					1	1	2.67	14	6	0	0	30	27	10	9	0	17	36	.233	.250	.229	10.68	5.04
Jeremy Castro	R-R	6-4	190	11-16-02	0	1	2.13	7	0	0	0	13	3	6	3	0	12	12	.073	.105	.045	8.53	8.53
2-team total (1 DSL KC Stewart)					0	1	3.14	8	0	0	0	14	4	8	5	0	15	15	.087	.091	.083	9.42	9.42
Frandy Cuevas	L-L	5-11	180	1-19-02	2	1	5.29	10	0	0	2	17	15	13	10	1	14	17	.250	.333	.205	9.00	7.41
2-team total (1 DSL KC Stewart)					2	1	4.74	11	0	0	2	19	16	13	10	1	14	21	.239	.292	.209	9.95	6.63
Weskendry Espinoza	R-R	6-1	185	3-18-02	1	1	8.25	5	1	0	0	12	18	12	11	2	5	8	.360	.400	.333	6.00	3.75
2-team total (7 DSL KC Stewart)					1	1	7.28	12	7	0	1	30	41	26	24	2	14	25	.333	.348	.316	7.58	4.25
Leonel Ferrand	L-L	6-4	190	7-12-03	0	1	3.55	5	5	0	0	13	16	6	5	1	5	8	.327	.273	.370	5.68	3.55
2-team total (7 DSL KC Stewart)					0	3	5.23	12	8	0	0	31	39	23	18	2	14	27	.307	.294	.312	7.84	4.06
Jhonny Gomez	R-R	5-11	180	8-27-02	3	0	3.00	12	0	0	2	21	21	10	7	1	4	18	.250	.268	.233	7.71	1.71
Jose Gutierrez	R-R	6-1	155	5-24-03	0	2	4.50	3	2	0	0	10	14	7	5	1	2	11	.318	.303	.364	9.90	1.80
2-team total (4 DSL KC Stewart)					0	3	3.06	7	5	0	0	18	15	8	6	1	2	14	.217	.262	.148	7.13	1.02
Henson Leal	R-R	6-1	176	9-19-03	1	1	3.00	5	0	0	1	12	8	5	4	0	4	10	.182	.300	.083	7.50	3.00
2-team total (7 DSL KC Stewart)					1	2	3.91	12	0	0	1	23	23	13	10	1	10	18	.253	.378	.167	7.04	3.91
Jemir Leal	R-R	6-2	155	4-7-03	2	2	5.82	12	0	0	1	22	29	14	14	1	9	17	.326	.189	.423	7.06	3.74
Ricardito Lorenzo	L-L	6-3	200	8-3-03	0	0	0.00	2	0	0	1	3	3	0	0	0	0	1	.250	.333	.222	3.00	0.00
2-team total (10 DSL KC Stewart)					1	1	6.35	12	5	0	1	28	36	29	20	0	19	21	.298	.393	.269	6.67	6.04
Yunior Marte	R-R	6-5	210	9-8-03	0	3	5.49	11	8	0	1	20	26	14	12	1	3	10	.302	.342	.271	4.58	1.37
Luis Martinez	L-L	6-1	180	9-17-03	0	0	10.13	2	0	0	0	3	7	7	3	0	2	3	.467	.333	.556	10.13	6.75
2-team total (9 DSL KC Stewart)					0	1	5.89	11	0	0	0	18	16	18	12	0	23	26	.235	.308	.218	12.76	11.29
Ismael Michel	R-R	6-3	175	2-14-02	1	0	4.80	8	0	0	1	15	9	8	8	1	8	21	.173	.316	.091	12.60	4.80
2-team total (3 DSL KC Stewart)					2	0	4.64	11	0	0	1	21	18	12	11	1	10	27	.225	.360	.164	11.39	4.22
Fraynel Nova	R-R	6-0	190	5-22-02	0	1	2.75	8	5	0	0	20	17	9	6	1	5	19	.230	.172	.267	8.69	2.29
Victor Pena	L-L	5-11	165	12-21-02	8	0	0.99	13	1	0	2	27	13	5	3	1	6	42	.138	.130	.141	13.83	1.98
Alvaro Pineda	R-R	6-2	170	6-30-04	0	0	0.00	2	0	0	0	2	1	0	0	0	0	1	.125	.333	.000	4.50	0.00
2-team total (9 DSL KC Stewart)					1	5	6.39	11	6	0	1	25	33	19	18	2	5	14	.311	.353	.292	4.97	1.78
Yimi Presinal	R-R	5-11	175	9-18-04	2	1	2.05	10	5	0	0	31	31	10	7	0	10	16	.270	.296	.246	4.70	2.93
Oscar Rayo	L-L	6-1	180	1-13-02	0	0	0.53	5	5	0	0	17	13	2	1	0	3	22	.217	.188	.227	11.65	1.59
Emmanuel Reyes	R-R	6-0	180	5-16-04	2	1	0.96	11	10	0	0	47	28	12	5	1	4	47	.165	.206	.137	9.06	0.77
2-team total (1 DSL KC Stewart)					2	1	0.91	12	11	0	0	49	29	12	5	1	4	52	.162	.200	.138	9.49	0.73
David Rodriguez	L-L	5-11	152	9-27-03	2	0	3.86	9	0	0	0	19	19	20	8	2	7	16	.271	.375	.241	7.71	3.38
2-team total (4 DSL KC Stewart)					2	0	3.00	13	0	0	2	24	21	20	8	2	7	19	.241	.333	.217	7.13	2.63
Edinson Salgado	L-L	6-0	150	1-6-05	0	0	4.50	1	0	0	0	2	4	1	1	0	1	0	.444	.600	.250	0.00	4.50
2-team total (9 DSL KC Stewart)					1	3	11.12	10	0	0	0	17	24	25	21	2	18	18	.320	.455	.264	9.53	9.53
Junior Sanchez	R-R	6-2	180	2-2-05	1	0	2.45	4	0	0	0	7	6	2	2	0	5	5	.250	.267	.222	6.14	6.14
2-team total (7 DSL KC Stewart)					1	2	4.21	11	5	0	1	26	26	17	12	0	16	16	.271	.306	.206	5.61	5.61
Yenfri Sosa	L-L	6-0	170	12-29-03	0	0	3.98	11	0	0	1	20	23	12	9	1	9	23	.280	.316	.270	10.18	3.98
2-team total (1 DSL KC Stewart)					0	0	3.91	12	0	0	1	23	24	13	10	1	12	27	.267	.300	.257	10.57	4.70
Luis Valdez	R-R	6-0	170	10-25-04	2	1	2.77	12	1	0	1	26	15	10	8	1	10	22	.161	.133	.175	7.62	3.46
Richy Valdez	R-R	6-1	180	7-29-05	1	0	0.00	1	0	0	0	2	0	0	0	0	0	0	.000	.000	--	0.00	0.00
2-team total (12 DSL KC Stewart)					1	4	8.24	13	11	0	0	32	43	39	29	1	25	25	.328	.375	.293	7.11	7.11
Jheremy Vicente	R-R	6-1	170	10-1-03	0	0	0.00	1	0	0	1	2	0	0	0	0	0	1	.000	.000	.000	4.50	0.00

2-team total (11 DSL KC Stewart)	0	4	4.19	12	7	0	1	34	24	21	16	0	25	26	.198	.246	.150	6.82	6.55

Fielding

C: Cespedes 7, Filion 4, Gonzalez 25, Lucas 13, Medina 9, Olmos 11. **1B:** Garcia 1, German 40, Lucas 24. **2B:** Nova 21, Novas 1, Orasma 9, Perdomo 19, Vargas 14. **3B:** Chacon 38, Orasma 12, Perdomo 16, Vargas 1. **SS:** Nova 9, Novas 29, Orasma 18, Sosa 11. **OF:** Castillo 29, Echenique 1, Medina 50, Parra 13, Ramos 50, Tejeda 2, Torres 48

DSL KC STEWART — ROOKIE

DOMINICAN SUMMER LEAGUE

Batting	B-T	HT	WT	DOB	AVG	vLH	vRH	G	AB	R	H	2B	3B	HR	RBI	BB	HBP	SH	SF	SO	SB	CS	SLG	OBP
Meiver Borges	R-R	5-10	165	10-12-02	.261	.800	.111	9	23	2	6	0	0	1	3	5	0	0	0	3	0	1	.391	.393
Osman Bravo	R-R	5-11	170	6-16-04	.263	.333	.250	8	19	2	5	2	0	0	4	3	2	0	1	5	0	0	.368	.400
Marino Castillo	L-R	5-11	150	10-13-02	.324	.500	.313	12	34	9	11	2	0	0	4	6	3	0	0	6	7	2	.382	.465
2-team total (31 DSL KC Glass)					.274	.235	.280	43	117	22	32	3	0	0	11	14	8	0	0	26	12	6	.299	.388
Jorge Celado	R-R	6-0	163	1-14-03	.268	.250	.271	22	71	5	19	4	0	0	9	6	1	0	0	20	1	1	.324	.333
Steven Cespedes	L-R	5-9	170	10-23-03	.304	.250	.316	19	46	7	14	4	0	0	5	11	0	0	1	6	0	0	.391	.431
2-team total (7 DSL KC Glass)					.286	.308	.281	26	70	10	20	5	0	0	5	14	0	0	1	13	0	1	.357	.400
Ethan De Cuba	B-R	6-0	145	4-14-03	.203	.184	.209	55	172	31	35	5	1	0	13	37	4	1	0	38	34	4	.244	.357
Luis Echenique	L-L	5-11	175	11-25-02	.244	.250	.243	22	45	12	11	1	1	0	7	12	1	0	0	1	3	2	.311	.414
2-team total (1 DSL KC Glass)					.255	.250	.256	23	47	12	12	1	1	0	8	12	1	0	0	1	3	2	.319	.417
Yosmi Fernandez	B-R	5-11	165	4-15-04	.196	.103	.218	54	148	18	29	7	1	0	11	27	3	1	0	57	10	8	.257	.331
Jeffry Filion	R-R	5-11	185	10-23-02	.063	.000	.077	15	32	3	2	1	1	0	3	7	0	0	1	10	2	0	.156	.225
2-team total (4 DSL KC Glass)					.050	.000	.067	19	40	4	2	1	1	0	3	8	0	0	1	16	2	0	.125	.204
Eduardo Garcia	L-R	6-1	183	9-10-01	.228	.167	.239	49	162	24	37	9	1	2	24	20	4	0	7	48	3	0	.333	.316
2-team total (4 DSL KC Glass)					.216	.148	.229	53	171	24	37	9	1	2	24	23	4	0	7	55	3	0	.316	.312
Manuel German	R-R	6-1	220	4-29-05	.063	.000	.077	5	16	1	1	1	0	0	1	1	2	0	0	5	0	0	.125	.211
2-team total (41 DSL KC Glass)					.190	.143	.200	46	126	16	24	9	0	3	18	17	5	0	3	37	1	0	.333	.305
Ricson Gonzalez	R-R	6-0	170	6-16-05	.091	.000	.125	3	11	0	1	0	0	0	0	0	1	0	0	3	0	0	.091	.167
2-team total (27 DSL KC Glass)					.222	.167	.231	30	90	8	20	4	0	0	8	7	4	0	0	16	1	0	.267	.307
Aldrin Lucas	R-R	5-10	165	2-7-03	.500	--	.500	1	2	0	1	0	0	0	0	1	0	0	0	0	0	0	.500	.667
2-team total (36 DSL KC Glass)					.213	.188	.218	37	94	12	20	1	1	3	14	19	4	1	1	28	2	0	.340	.364
Jose Medina	B-R	5-10	185	4-16-05	.351	.250	.371	26	74	17	26	2	1	0	10	17	3	0	0	14	0	1	.405	.489
2-team total (11 DSL KC Glass)					.293	.188	.313	37	99	20	29	3	1	0	11	22	3	0	0	25	0	1	.343	.435
Jairo Mendez	L-L	6-0	155	10-6-02	.279	.080	.318	49	154	25	43	10	2	2	24	21	1	2	2	51	11	3	.409	.365
Josi Novas	R-R	6-4	180	2-12-05	.292	.000	.333	8	24	10	7	3	2	0	5	6	0	0	0	10	2	0	.583	.433
2-team total (36 DSL KC Glass)					.221	.000	.242	44	136	25	30	13	3	4	28	18	1	0	2	57	7	2	.449	.312
Angel Parra	L-L	6-0	156	1-26-04	.311	.083	.355	22	74	7	23	5	0	1	9	7	3	0	0	10	6	2	.419	.393
2-team total (12 DSL KC Glass)					.243	.158	.260	34	115	12	28	6	0	2	11	12	3	0	0	25	8	2	.348	.331
Angel Pierre	R-R	6-0	170	9-19-03	.300	.333	.294	33	100	23	30	11	4	2	19	21	2	0	2	31	9	5	.550	.424
Angel Santana	R-R	5-10	160	4-27-03	.254	.318	.241	46	134	15	34	6	1	0	17	17	5	0	2	28	6	5	.313	.354
Ivan Sosa	R-R	--	--	9-9-04	.205	.194	.208	41	151	20	31	8	1	2	16	12	3	1	2	39	3	3	.311	.274
2-team total (11 DSL KC Glass)					.183	.167	.188	52	180	22	33	9	1	2	17	16	3	1	3	52	4	3	.278	.257
Luis Tejeda	R-R	6-0	169	2-18-04	.333	.000	.375	5	9	4	3	0	0	0	3	3	0	0	1	2	1	1	.333	.462
2-team total (3 DSL KC Glass)					.200	.000	.273	8	15	4	3	0	0	0	3	3	0	0	1	2	1	1	.200	.316
Francisco Ulloa	R-R	5-11	170	10-18-03	.151	.231	.138	40	93	15	14	0	0	1	8	26	5	1	1	33	7	2	.183	.360
Keine Urdaneta	R-R	5-11	150	1-24-05	.147	.143	.147	40	116	17	17	2	0	0	7	15	3	2	2	31	12	4	.164	.257
Yeison Vargas	R-R	0-0	0	9-10-03	.206	.333	.179	11	34	7	7	3	0	1	5	6	0	1	0	13	0	1	.382	.325
2-team total (28 DSL KC Glass)					.231	.250	.227	39	104	21	24	3	2	2	10	17	2	1	1	36	1	4	.356	.347

Pitching	B-T	HT	WT	DOB	W	L	ERA	G	GS	CG	SV	IP	H	R	ER	HR	BB	SO	AVG	vLH	vRH	K/9	BB/9
Dioni Baez	R-R	6-2	185	1-24-03	2	4	9.61	10	3	0	0	20	29	26	21	0	15	12	.341	.306	.389	5.49	6.86
2-team total (3 DSL KC Glass)					2	4	8.31	13	3	0	0	26	36	29	24	0	18	19	.336	.339	.333	6.58	6.23
Andy Basora	R-R	6-3	155	4-13-05	1	1	2.55	11	0	0	0	25	26	15	7	0	11	21	.263	.318	.218	7.66	4.01
2-team total (2 DSL KC Glass)					1	3	3.33	13	0	0	0	27	30	20	10	0	13	24	.273	.340	.222	8.00	4.33
Wilson Betemit Jr.	R-R	6-1	170	7-27-03	0	0	0.00	1	0	0	0	1	0	0	0	0	0	1	.000	.000	.000	6.75	0.00
2-team total (11 DSL KC Glass)					2	2	1.30	12	4	0	0	35	17	7	5	1	10	35	.149	.136	.157	9.09	2.60
Emilio Castillo	L-L	5-10	150	10-18-02	1	1	2.86	12	6	0	0	28	26	10	9	0	14	35	.236	.250	.233	11.12	4.45
2-team total (2 DSL KC Glass)					1	1	2.67	14	6	0	0	30	27	10	9	0	17	36	.233	.250	.229	10.68	5.04
Jeremy Castro	R-R	6-4	190	11-16-02	0	0	10.80	1	0	0	0	2	1	2	2	0	3	3	.200	.000	.500	16.20	16.20
2-team total (7 DSL KC Glass)					0	1	3.14	8	0	0	0	14	4	8	5	0	15	15	.087	.091	.083	9.42	9.42
Frandy Cuevas	L-L	5-11	180	1-19-02	0	0	0.00	1	0	0	0	2	1	0	0	0	0	4	.143	.000	.250	18.00	0.00
2-team total (10 DSL KC Glass)					2	1	4.74	11	0	0	2	19	16	13	10	1	14	21	.239	.292	.209	9.95	6.63
Luis Echenique	L-L	5-11	175	11-25-02	0	1	6.75	7	0	0	0	8	12	7	6	0	3	7	.364	.000	.400	7.88	3.38
Weskendry Espinoza	R-R	6-1	185	3-18-02	0	0	6.62	7	6	0	1	18	23	14	13	0	9	17	.315	.326	.296	8.66	4.58
2-team total (5 DSL KC Glass)					1	1	7.28	12	7	0	1	30	41	26	24	2	14	25	.333	.348	.316	7.58	4.25
Leonel Ferrand	L-L	6-4	190	7-12-03	0	2	6.38	7	3	0	0	18	23	17	13	1	9	19	.295	.333	.288	9.33	4.42
2-team total (5 DSL KC Glass)					0	3	5.23	12	8	0	0	31	39	23	18	2	14	27	.307	.294	.312	7.84	4.06
Jesus Franco	L-L	6-1	170	3-4-05	0	3	15.55	11	0	0	0	11	23	30	19	1	23	7	.411	.600	.370	5.73	18.82
Jose Gutierrez	R-R	6-1	155	5-24-03	0	1	1.17	4	3	0	0	8	1	1	1	0	0	3	.040	.111	.000	3.52	0.00
2-team total (3 DSL KC Glass)					0	3	3.06	7	5	0	0	18	15	8	6	1	2	14	.217	.262	.148	7.13	1.02
Henson Leal	R-R	6-1	176	9-19-03	0	1	4.91	7	0	0	0	11	15	8	6	1	6	8	.319	.471	.233	6.55	4.91
2-team total (5 DSL KC Glass)					1	2	3.91	12	0	0	1	23	23	13	10	1	10	18	.253	.378	.167	7.04	3.91
Ricardito Lorenzo	L-L	6-3	200	8-3-03	1	1	7.11	10	5	0	0	25	33	29	20	0	19	20	.303	.400	.274	7.11	6.75
2-team total (2 DSL KC Glass)					1	1	6.35	12	5	0	1	28	36	29	20	0	19	21	.298	.393	.269	6.67	6.04
Luis Martinez	L-L	6-1	180	9-17-03	0	1	5.17	9	0	0	0	16	9	11	9	0	21	23	.170	.286	.152	13.21	12.06

2-team total (2 DSL KC Glass)					0	1	5.89	11	0	0	0	18	16	18	12	0	23	26	.235	.308	.218	12.76	11.29
Juan Mejia	R-R	6-3	180	11-24-03	0	0	16.20	2	0	0	0	2	5	3	3	0	1	1	.556	1.000	.500	5.40	5.40
Eslahiber Mendez	R-R	5-11	160	12-9-03	0	2	12.15	6	0	0	0	7	5	11	9	0	18	10	.217	.250	.182	13.50	24.30
Ismael Michel	R-R	6-3	175	2-14-02	1	0	4.26	3	0	0	0	6	9	4	3	0	2	6	.321	.500	.273	8.53	2.84
2-team total (8 DSL KC Glass)					2	0	4.64	11	0	0	1	21	18	12	11	1	10	27	.225	.360	.164	11.39	4.22
Juan Ozuna	L-L	5-10	165	10-26-04	2	0	3.91	12	0	0	0	25	24	14	11	1	12	24	.247	.357	.229	8.53	4.26
Yeri Perez	R-R	6-3	180	10-16-04	1	0	4.32	11	0	0	0	25	18	13	12	1	22	14	.202	.224	.175	5.04	7.92
Alvaro Pineda	R-R	6-2	170	6-30-04	1	5	6.94	9	6	0	1	23	32	19	18	2	5	13	.327	.355	.313	5.01	1.93
2-team total (2 DSL KC Glass)					1	5	6.39	11	6	0	1	25	33	19	18	2	5	14	.311	.353	.292	4.97	1.78
Wermer Pineda	R-R	6-4	171	10-27-02	1	1	6.00	13	0	0	2	18	25	16	12	0	11	12	.333	.289	.378	6.00	5.50
Sebastian Ramirez	L-L	6-2	180	10-1-03	2	1	4.70	9	3	0	0	23	13	12	12	3	15	23	.160	.143	.167	9.00	5.87
Emmanuel Reyes	R-R	6-0	180	5-16-04	0	0	0.00	1	1	0	0	3	1	0	0	0	0	5	.111	.000	.143	16.88	0.00
2-team total (11 DSL KC Glass)					2	1	0.91	12	11	0	0	49	29	12	5	1	4	52	.162	.200	.138	9.49	0.73
David Rodriguez	L-L	5-11	152	9-27-03	0	0	0.00	4	0	0	2	5	2	0	0	0	0	3	.118	.000	.133	5.06	0.00
2-team total (9 DSL KC Glass)					2	0	3.00	13	0	0	2	24	21	20	8	2	7	19	.241	.333	.217	7.13	2.63
Edwin Rodriguez	R-R	6-2	170	8-24-03	2	2	8.77	13	1	0	0	26	30	30	25	2	20	26	.288	.220	.333	9.12	7.01
Edinson Salgado	L-L	6-0	150	1-6-05	1	3	12.00	9	0	0	0	15	20	24	20	2	17	18	.303	.412	.265	10.80	10.20
2-team total (1 DSL KC Glass)					1	3	11.12	10	0	0	0	17	24	25	21	2	18	18	.320	.455	.264	9.53	9.53
Junior Sanchez	R-R	6-2	180	2-2-05	0	2	4.91	7	5	0	1	18	20	15	10	0	11	11	.278	.319	.200	5.40	5.40
2-team total (4 DSL KC Glass)					1	2	4.21	11	5	0	1	26	26	17	12	0	16	16	.271	.306	.206	5.61	5.61
Jeremmy Santos	R-R	6-6	180	3-10-05	1	3	7.80	12	0	0	0	15	13	18	13	0	14	13	.228	.281	.160	7.80	8.40
Yenfri Sosa	L-L	6-0	170	12-29-03	0	0	3.38	1	0	0	0	3	1	1	1	0	3	4	.125	.000	.143	13.50	10.13
2-team total (11 DSL KC Glass)					0	0	3.91	12	0	0	1	23	24	13	10	1	12	27	.267	.300	.257	10.57	4.70
Richy Valdez	R-R	6-1	180	7-29-05	0	4	8.80	12	11	0	0	30	43	39	29	1	25	25	.344	.420	.293	7.58	7.58
2-team total (1 DSL KC Glass)					1	4	8.24	13	11	0	0	32	43	39	29	1	25	25	.328	.375	.293	7.11	7.11
Jheremy Vicente	R-R	6-1	170	10-1-03	0	4	4.45	11	7	0	0	32	24	21	16	0	25	25	.209	.259	.158	6.96	6.96
2-team total (1 DSL KC Glass)					0	4	4.19	12	7	0	1	34	24	21	16	0	25	26	.198	.246	.150	6.82	6.55

Fielding

C: Borges 8, Bravo 7, Cespedes 14, Filion 15, Gonzalez 3, Lucas 1, Medina 24, Santana 1. **1B:** Celado 13, Garcia 15, German 4, Santana 31. **2B:** Fernandez 42, Pierre 1, Ulloa 1, Urdaneta 16, Vargas 5. **3B:** Garcia 19, Pierre 26, Santana 1, Urdaneta 17. **SS:** Fernandez 11, Ferrand 1, Novas 8, Pierre 6, Sosa 36, Urdaneta 3. **OF:** Castillo 12, De Cuba 55, Echenique 16, Mendez 46, Parra 23, Santana 10, Tejeda 5, Ulloa 34, Urdaneta 1

Los Angeles Angels

SEASON IN A SENTENCE: As Talking Heads famously sang, same as it ever was in Anaheim, as the Angels continued to squander two generational talents. Mike Trout finished second in the American League in homers while Shohei Ohtani improved upon his 2021 MVP season, but the Angels had their seventh consecutive losing season nonetheless.

HIGH POINT: A 27-17 start generated enthusiasm that maybe this season would be different, a stretch that included lefty Reid Detmers throwing the season's lone complete-game no-hitter May 10 against Tampa. Closer Raisel Iglesias had 11 saves in those 27 victories, the last of them a 5-3 win against the Rangers that included an eight-inning start by Noah Syndergaard. Any Ohtani outing was a high point as he went 15-9, 2.33, qualified for the ERA title with 166 innings, struck out 219 . . . and also hit 34 homers in a .273/.356/.519 season.

LOW POINT: A 14-game losing streak immediately signaled that indeed, this would not be a different season. Manager Joe Maddon was fired June 7 after the 12th loss and vented publicly about his firing and the state of the game in general. Trout struggled with a back injury that prompted him to miss a month, and third baseman Anthony Rendon missed all but six games after May with right wrist surgery. Despite Trout and Ohtani, the Angels ranked 13th in the AL in runs and dead last with 1,539 strikeouts.

NOTABLE ROOKIES: The Angels really didn't have any aside from Detmers, their 2020 first-round pick. He threw the no-hitter and made 25 starts in a 7-6, 3.77 season as part of the club's six-man rotation.

KEY TRANSACTIONS: Phil Nevin replaced Madden, first on an interim basis, then with a full-time contract to return in 2023. GM Perry Minasian was active at the trade deadline, dealing Iglesias to his previous employer (the Braves) while sending Syndergaard and outfielder Brandon Marsh to the Phillies in separate deals for catcher Logan O'Hoppe and outfielder Mickey Moniak, the 2016 draft's No. 1 overall pick and a SoCal native.

ON THE FARM: For the first time in years, the Angels are rich in catching prospects thanks to the midseason acquisition of O'Hoppe and the emergence of teenager Edgar Quero. Shortstop Zach Neto reached Double-A in his draft year.

OPENING DAY PAYROLL: $181,888,095 (ninth).

PLAYERS OF THE YEAR

MAJOR LEAGUE

Shohei Ohtani
DH/RHP
.273/.356/.519
34 HR, 30 2B, 95 RBIs
2.33 ERA, 219 SO, 166 IP

MINOR LEAGUE

Edgar Quero
C
(Low-A)
.312/.435/.530
17 HR, 35 2B in 111 G

ORGANIZATION LEADERS

Batting — ***Minimum 250 AB**

MAJORS

*AVG	Mike Trout	.283
*OPS	Mike Trout	.999
HR	Mike Trout	40
RBI	Shohei Ohtani	95

MINORS

*AVG	BJ Boyd, Inland Empire, Salt Lake	.337
*OBP	Edgar Quero, Inland Empire	.435
*SLG	Edgar Quero, Inland Empire	.530
*OPS	Edgar Quero, Inland Empire	.965
R	Edgar Quero, Inland Empire	86
H	Kean Wong, Salt Lake	130
TB	Edgar Quero, Inland Empire	219
2B	Edgar Quero, Inland Empire	35
3B	David Calabrese, Inland Empire	7
HR	Jake Gatewood, Salt Lake	22
RBI	Dillon Thomas, Salt Lake	77
BB	Jeremy Arocho, Inland Empire	79
SO	Bryce Teodosio, Rocket City	166
SB	Kean Wong, Salt Lake	41

Pitching — **#Minimum 75 IP**

MAJORS

W	Shohei Ohtani	15
#ERA	Shohei Ohtani	2.33
SO	Shohei Ohtani	219
SV	Raisel Iglesias	16

MINORS

W	Connor Van Scoyoc, Inland Empire	11
L	Adam Seminaris, Tri-City, Rocket City, Salt Lake	11
L	Jose Salvador, Tri-City, Inland Empire	11
#ERA	Chase Silseth, Rocket City	2.28
G	Kolton Ingram, Rocket City	50
GS	Jose Salvador, Tri-City, Inland Empire	24
SV	Eric Torres, Rocket City	22
IP	Cesar Valdez, Salt Lake	146
BB	Kelvin Caceres, Inland Empire	54
SO	Jose Salvador, Tri-City, Inland Empire	152
#AVG	Kelvin Caceres, Inland Empire	.170

2022 PERFORMANCE

General Manager: Perry Minasian. **Farm Director:** Joey Prebynski. **Scouting Director:** Tim McIlvaine.

Class	Team	League	W	L	PCT	Finish	Manager
Majors	Los Angeles Angels	American	73	89	.451	11th (15)	J. Maddon/P. Nevin
Triple-A	Salt Lake Bees	Pacific Coast	70	80	.467	8th (10)	Lou Marson
Double-A	Rocket City Trash Pandas	Southern	81	57	.587	1st (8)	Andy Schatzley
High-A	Tri-City Dust Devils	Northwest	58	71	.450	t-5th (6)	Jack Howell
Low-A	Inland Empire 66ers	California	70	62	.530	4th (8)	Dave Stapleton
Rookie	ACL Angels	Arizona Complex	33	21	.611	5th (18)	Ever Magallanes
Overall 2022 Minor League Record			347	316	.523	8th (30)	

ORGANIZATION STATISTICS

LOS ANGELES ANGELS

AMERICAN LEAGUE

Batting	B-T	HT	WT	DOB	AVG	vLH	vRH	G	AB	R	H	2B	3B	HR	RBI	BB	HBP	SH	SF	SO	SB	CS	SLG	OBP
Jo Adell	R-R	6-3	215	4-8-99	.224	.204	.236	88	268	22	60	12	2	8	27	11	4	0	1	107	4	2	.373	.264
Ryan Aguilar	L-L	6-2	168	9-11-94	.136	.000	.150	7	22	2	3	1	0	0	2	2	1	0	1	14	0	0	.182	.231
Matt Duffy	R-R	6-2	190	1-15-91	.250	.239	.257	77	228	14	57	8	0	2	16	17	2	0	0	50	0	0	.311	.308
Steven Duggar	L-R	6-1	187	11-4-93	.053	.000	.063	9	19	3	1	0	1	0	0	3	0	0	0	13	0	0	.158	.182
2-team total (8 Texas Rangers)					.111	.000	.133	17	36	5	4	0	1	0	0	5	0	0	0	25	1	1	.167	.220
David Fletcher	R-R	5-9	185	5-31-94	.255	.250	.257	61	216	20	55	9	1	2	17	7	3	2	0	16	1	0	.333	.288
Mike Ford	L-R	6-0	225	7-4-92	.231	.280	.212	28	91	8	21	4	0	3	5	8	0	0	0	26	0	0	.374	.293
2-team total (16 Seattle Mariners)					.217	.259	.204	44	120	9	26	5	0	3	8	16	1	0	0	38	0	0	.333	.314
Phil Gosselin	R-R	6-1	188	10-3-88	.098	.103	.091	22	51	2	5	0	1	0	2	1	1	0	0	18	0	0	.137	.132
Monte Harrison	R-R	6-3	225	8-10-95	.182	.000	.286	9	11	5	2	0	0	1	3	2	1	0	0	8	1	0	.455	.357
Juan Lagares	R-R	6-2	219	3-17-89	.183	.136	.211	20	60	4	11	2	1	0	0	2	0	0	0	15	0	0	.250	.210
David MacKinnon	R-R	6-2	200	12-15-94	.189	.133	.227	16	37	0	7	0	0	0	6	5	0	0	1	12	0	0	.189	.279
2-team total (6 Oakland Athletics)					.140	.077	.208	22	50	2	7	0	0	0	6	6	0	0	1	17	0	0	.140	.228
Brandon Marsh	L-R	6-4	215	12-18-97	.226	.192	.237	93	292	34	66	9	2	8	37	22	3	3	3	117	8	2	.353	.284
Jack Mayfield	R-R	5-11	190	9-30-90	.186	.179	.190	23	70	8	13	1	1	1	6	3	1	0	0	17	1	0	.271	.230
Mickey Moniak	L-R	6-2	195	5-13-98	.200	.143	.208	19	60	9	12	2	1	3	6	1	1	0	0	25	1	0	.417	.226
Shohei Ohtani	L-R	6-4	210	7-5-94	.273	.263	.278	157	586	90	160	30	6	34	95	72	5	0	3	161	11	9	.519	.356
Logan O'Hoppe	R-R	6-2	185	2-9-00	.286	.400	.222	5	14	1	4	0	0	0	2	2	0	0	0	3	0	0	.286	.375
Anthony Rendon	R-R	6-1	200	6-6-90	.229	.239	.225	47	166	15	38	10	0	5	24	23	2	0	2	35	2	0	.380	.326
Luis Rengifo	B-R	5-10	195	2-26-97	.264	.315	.238	127	489	45	129	22	4	17	52	17	4	1	0	79	6	2	.429	.294
Jose Rojas	L-R	6-0	200	2-24-93	.125	.000	.137	22	56	1	7	2	0	0	1	0	1	0	0	19	0	0	.161	.140
Austin Romine	R-R	6-1	216	11-22-88	.250	.500	.167	3	8	0	2	0	0	0	0	0	0	1	0	3	0	0	.250	.250
Magneuris Sierra	L-L	5-11	178	4-7-96	.165	.121	.190	45	91	7	15	1	3	0	5	4	0	1	0	25	6	1	.242	.200
Livan Soto	L-R	6-0	160	6-22-00	.400	.261	.500	18	55	9	22	5	1	1	9	2	0	1	1	13	1	1	.582	.414
Max Stassi	R-R	5-10	200	3-15-91	.180	.162	.190	102	333	32	60	12	1	9	30	38	2	1	1	112	0	0	.303	.267
Michael Stefanic	R-R	5-10	180	2-24-96	.197	.094	.310	25	61	5	12	2	0	0	0	5	2	1	0	12	0	0	.230	.279
Kurt Suzuki	R-R	5-11	210	10-4-83	.180	.088	.210	51	139	10	25	4	0	4	15	15	2	1	2	29	0	0	.295	.266
Matt Thaiss	L-R	6-0	215	5-6-95	.217	.000	.259	29	69	9	15	1	0	2	8	11	0	0	1	24	1	0	.319	.321
Dillon Thomas	L-L	6-1	215	12-10-92	.091	.000	.111	8	11	1	1	0	0	0	0	2	1	0	0	6	0	0	.091	.286
Mike Trout	R-R	6-2	235	8-7-91	.283	.310	.273	119	438	85	124	28	2	40	80	54	6	0	1	139	1	0	.630	.369
Andrew Velazquez	B-R	5-9	170	7-14-94	.196	.224	.183	125	322	37	63	8	0	9	28	15	3	6	3	119	17	1	.304	.236
Jonathan Villar	B-R	6-0	233	5-2-91	.163	.154	.167	13	49	6	8	0	0	1	3	4	0	1	0	17	1	0	.224	.226
Tyler Wade	L-R	6-1	188	11-23-94	.218	.227	.216	67	147	22	32	5	0	1	8	10	1	5	0	33	8	5	.272	.272
Chad Wallach	R-R	6-2	246	11-4-91	.143	.100	.160	12	35	3	5	1	0	1	4	4	0	1	0	9	0	0	.257	.231
Jared Walsh	L-L	6-0	210	7-30-93	.215	.200	.220	118	423	41	91	18	2	15	44	27	4	0	0	138	2	1	.374	.269
Taylor Ward	R-R	6-1	200	12-14-93	.281	.268	.286	135	495	73	139	22	2	23	65	60	4	0	5	120	5	3	.473	.360
Aaron Whitefield	R-R	6-4	210	9-2-96	.000	.000	.000	5	11	0	0	0	0	0	0	0	0	0	0	5	0	0	.000	.000

Pitching	B-T	HT	WT	DOB	W	L	ERA	G	GS	CG	SV	IP	H	R	ER	HR	BB	SO	AVG	vLH	vRH	K/9	BB/9
Kyle Barraclough	R-R	6-3	229	5-23-90	0	1	3.00	8	0	0	0	9	7	3	3	0	4	9	.219	.333	.150	9.00	4.00
Jaime Barria	R-R	6-1	210	7-18-96	3	3	2.61	35	1	0	0	79	63	29	23	11	19	54	.217	.225	.212	6.13	2.16
Archie Bradley	R-R	6-4	215	8-10-92	0	1	4.82	21	0	0	2	19	17	13	10	1	7	15	.239	.143	.302	7.23	3.38
Jesse Chavez	R-R	6-1	175	8-21-83	1	0	7.59	11	0	0	0	11	15	12	9	2	4	10	.326	.286	.360	8.44	3.38
Tucker Davidson	L-L	6-2	215	3-25-96	1	5	6.87	8	8	0	0	37	39	28	28	7	22	23	.271	.324	.255	5.65	5.40
Reid Detmers	L-L	6-2	210	7-8-99	7	6	3.77	25	25	1	0	129	110	56	54	13	46	122	.231	.209	.237	8.51	3.21
Jhonathan Diaz	L-L	6-0	170	9-13-96	1	1	2.93	4	3	0	0	15	13	5	5	1	10	11	.236	.100	.267	6.46	5.87
Phil Gosselin	R-R	6-1	188	10-3-88	0	0	0.00	1	0	0	0	1	0	0	0	0	0	0	.000	.000	.000	0.00	0.00
Jimmy Herget	R-R	6-3	170	9-9-93	2	1	2.48	49	1	0	9	69	48	20	19	4	15	63	.196	.229	.174	8.22	1.96
Raisel Iglesias	R-R	6-2	190	1-4-90	2	6	4.04	39	0	0	16	36	29	18	16	5	9	48	.216	.217	.216	12.11	2.27
Janson Junk	R-R	6-1	177	1-15-96	1	1	6.48	3	2	0	0	8	10	6	6	1	3	11	.294	.250	.333	11.88	3.24
Michael Lorenzen	R-R	6-3	217	1-4-92	8	6	4.24	18	18	0	0	98	81	48	46	11	44	85	.224	.233	.217	7.83	4.05
Aaron Loup	L-L	5-11	210	12-19-87	0	5	3.84	65	0	0	1	59	54	38	25	4	22	52	.235	.238	.233	7.98	3.38
Jose Marte	R-R	6-3	180	6-14-96	0	0	7.36	11	0	0	0	11	8	9	9	2	18	15	.200	.214	.192	12.27	14.73
Mike Mayers	R-R	6-2	220	12-6-91	1	1	5.68	24	3	0	0	51	52	35	32	15	18	45	.259	.242	.273	7.99	3.20

Jack Mayfield	R-R	5-11	190	9-30-90	0	0	0.00	1	0	0	0	1	1	0	0	0	0	0	.250	.250	--	0.00	0.00
Brian Moran	L-L	6-4	225	9-30-88	0	0	54.00	1	0	0	0	0	3	2	2	1	1	0	.750	.667	1.000	0.00	27.00
Shohei Ohtani	L-R	6-4	210	7-5-94	15	9	2.33	28	28	0	0	166	124	45	43	14	44	219	.203	.221	.188	11.87	2.39
Oliver Ortega	R-R	6-0	165	10-2-96	1	3	3.71	27	0	0	1	34	32	18	14	5	18	33	.250	.188	.288	8.74	4.76
Elvis Peguero	R-R	6-5	208	3-20-97	0	0	6.75	13	0	0	0	17	23	16	13	4	5	12	.319	.269	.348	6.23	2.60
Jose Quijada	L-L	5-11	215	11-9-95	0	5	3.98	42	0	0	3	41	25	19	18	5	21	52	.172	.115	.204	11.51	4.65
Gerardo Reyes	R-R	5-11	195	5-13-93	0	0	4.50	2	0	0	0	2	3	1	1	1	3	0	.333	.000	.375	0.00	13.50
Kenny Rosenberg	L-L	6-1	195	7-9-95	0	0	4.22	3	1	0	0	11	9	5	5	1	6	8	.225	.250	.214	6.75	5.06
Patrick Sandoval	L-L	6-3	190	10-18-96	6	9	2.91	27	27	1	0	149	139	56	48	8	60	151	.246	.151	.271	9.14	3.63
Chase Silseth	R-R	6-0	217	5-18-00	1	3	6.59	7	7	0	0	29	33	21	21	7	12	24	.287	.353	.234	7.53	3.77
Jose Suarez	L-L	5-10	225	1-3-98	8	8	3.96	22	20	0	0	109	103	49	48	14	33	103	.243	.202	.256	8.50	2.72
Noah Syndergaard	L-R	6-6	242	8-29-92	5	8	3.83	15	15	0	0	80	75	36	34	9	22	64	.244	.258	.233	7.20	2.48
Ryan Tepera	R-R	6-1	195	11-3-87	5	4	3.61	59	0	0	6	57	42	27	23	7	20	47	.202	.193	.208	7.38	3.14
Touki Toussaint	R-R	6-3	215	6-20-96	1	1	4.62	8	2	0	0	25	15	13	13	2	19	26	.176	.233	.145	9.24	6.75
Cesar Valdez	R-R	6-2	225	3-17-85	0	0	9.00	1	0	0	0	1	2	2	1	0	0	0	.400	.000	.667	0.00	0.00
Nash Walters	R-R	6-5	210	5-18-97	0	0	0.00	1	0	0	0	0	1	0	0	0	1	0	.500	1.000	.000	0.00	27.00
Andrew Wantz	R-R	6-4	235	10-13-95	2	1	3.22	42	1	0	0	50	37	19	18	8	21	52	.206	.246	.180	9.30	3.75
Austin Warren	R-R	6-0	170	2-5-96	2	0	5.63	14	0	0	0	16	19	10	10	3	5	9	.306	.278	.318	5.06	2.81
Zack Weiss	R-R	6-3	210	6-16-92	0	1	3.38	12	0	0	0	13	7	6	5	2	7	18	.152	.238	.080	12.15	4.73
Rob Zastryzny	R-L	6-3	205	3-26-92	0	0	6.00	5	0	0	0	3	2	3	2	0	1	2	.182	.200	.167	6.00	3.00

Fielding

Catcher	PCT	G	PO	A	E	DP	PB
O'Hoppe	1.000	5	43	1	0	0	0
Romine	1.000	3	19	2	0	0	0
Stassi	.992	97	826	26	7	7	8
Suzuki	.997	44	341	10	1	1	2
Thaiss	1.000	14	96	3	0	0	0
Wallach	1.000	12	80	3	0	0	0

First Base	PCT	G	PO	A	E	DP
Aguilar	1.000	1	3	0	0	1
Duffy	.991	21	105	3	1	7
Ford	1.000	27	178	9	0	21
Gosselin	1.000	3	16	1	0	3
MacKinnon	1.000	7	28	1	0	4
Suzuki	1.000	1	2	0	0	1
Thaiss	1.000	11	57	3	0	4
Walsh	.994	118	842	46	5	83

Second Base	PCT	G	PO	A	E	DP
Duffy	.953	17	14	27	2	10
Fletcher	.993	44	59	88	1	18
Mayfield	.970	11	21	11	1	5
Rengifo	.978	99	139	210	8	66
Stefanic	1.000	22	32	31	0	5
Wade	.978	31	43	47	2	9

Third Base	PCT	G	PO	A	E	DP
Duffy	.969	42	31	62	3	9
Gosselin	1.000	17	5	20	0	1
MacKinnon	1.000	5	2	6	0	0
Mayfield	1.000	8	1	14	0	0
Rendon	.948	47	31	78	6	7
Rengifo	.941	39	26	54	5	7
Rojas	1.000	12	6	15	0	3
Soto	1.000	1	0	1	0	0
Thaiss	1.000	3	2	3	0	1
Villar	.917	13	6	27	3	5
Wade	.935	12	5	24	2	3
Ward	.000	2	0	0	0	0

Shortstop	PCT	G	PO	A	E	DP
Fletcher	1.000	36	20	75	0	13
Rengifo	.941	19	11	21	2	3
Soto	.963	18	17	35	2	7
Velazquez	.979	124	106	271	8	44
Wade	.978	19	12	32	1	8

Outfield	PCT	G	PO	A	E	DP
Adell	.966	84	139	5	5	1
Aguilar	1.000	8	12	0	0	0
Duggar	1.000	10	12	0	0	0
Harrison	.889	9	7	1	1	0
Lagares	.958	22	22	1	1	0
Marsh	.983	98	173	1	3	1
Mayfield	1.000	6	8	1	0	1
Moniak	1.000	20	26	1	0	1
Rengifo	1.000	6	2	0	0	0
Rojas	.909	7	10	0	1	0
Sierra	1.000	47	70	2	0	0
Thomas	1.000	10	9	0	0	0
Trout	.996	111	250	2	1	0
Wade	1.000	14	11	0	0	0
Walsh	1.000	2	1	0	0	0
Ward	.983	134	277	6	5	1
Whitefield	1.000	6	5	0	0	0

SALT LAKE BEES — *TRIPLE-A*

PACIFIC COAST LEAGUE

Batting	B-T	HT	WT	DOB	AVG	vLH	vRH	G	AB	R	H	2B	3B	HR	RBI	BB	HBP	SH	SF	SO	SB	CS	SLG	OBP
Jo Adell	R-R	6-3	215	4-8-99	.239	.200	.252	40	155	35	37	15	0	13	33	20	3	0	2	56	3	2	.587	.333
BJ Boyd	L-R	5-11	230	7-16-93	.111	.000	.143	2	9	1	1	1	0	0	1	0	0	0	0	4	0	0	.222	.111
Michael Cruz	L-R	5-11	210	1-13-96	1.000	--	1.000	1	1	0	1	1	0	0	1	0	0	0	0	0	0	0	2.000	1.000
Brendon Davis	R-R	6-4	185	7-28-97	.243	.282	.227	36	136	24	33	10	1	6	25	18	2	0	3	31	2	2	.463	.333
Pedro Diaz	R-R	6-3	210	1-9-99	.000	--	.000	1	1	0	0	0	0	0	0	0	0	0	0	1	0	0	.000	.000
Matt Duffy	R-R	6-2	190	1-15-91	.171	.167	.174	10	35	4	6	0	0	1	2	2	1	0	0	8	0	0	.257	.237
Steven Duggar	L-R	6-1	187	11-4-93	.147	.100	.167	10	34	3	5	1	0	2	2	3	0	0	0	14	1	0	.353	.216
3-team total (11 R. R. Express, 14 Sacramento River Cats)					.182	.184	.183	35	121	16	22	4	0	4	12	17	1	0	1	45	6	0	.314	.286
Colby Fitch	L-R	5-11	215	7-27-95	.218	.154	.238	20	55	8	12	3	1	2	8	2	8	0	1	27	0	0	.418	.333
David Fletcher	R-R	5-9	185	5-31-94	.204	.154	.222	13	49	3	10	1	0	0	1	2	0	0	0	7	1	0	.224	.235
Mike Ford	L-R	6-0	225	7-4-92	.217	.000	.227	6	23	2	5	1	0	0	0	1	0	0	0	5	0	0	.261	.250
3-team total (3 Sacramento River Cats, 11 Tacoma Rainiers)					.254	.214	.263	20	71	12	18	2	0	2	5	12	1	0	0	10	0	0	.366	.369
Jake Gatewood	R-R	6-5	190	9-25-95	.211	.210	.211	108	394	56	83	18	3	22	66	23	5	2	4	140	2	3	.439	.261
Jose Gomez	R-R	5-11	175	12-10-96	.225	.231	.224	30	102	14	23	7	2	2	13	7	1	2	0	27	2	0	.392	.282
Monte Harrison	R-R	6-3	225	8-10-95	.236	.225	.240	82	288	52	68	13	2	9	40	39	1	0	3	113	28	4	.389	.326
Torii Hunter Jr.	R-R	6-2	180	6-7-95	.266	.280	.261	29	94	14	25	3	2	1	7	7	1	1	0	32	8	2	.372	.324
Kyle Kasser	L-R	5-10	191	10-12-95	.299	.381	.268	28	77	12	23	6	1	1	10	12	1	0	1	16	1	0	.442	.396
Juan Lagares	R-R	6-2	219	3-17-89	.308	.714	.158	7	26	3	8	2	1	0	6	3	0	0	0	4	0	1	.462	.379
David MacKinnon	R-R	6-2	200	12-15-94	.324	.329	.323	63	225	47	73	19	4	14	45	42	2	0	4	51	2	2	.631	.429
2-team total (16 Las Vegas Aviators)					.318	.333	.312	79	289	53	92	24	4	15	54	49	3	0	5	63	2	2	.585	.416
Braxton Martinez	R-R	6-3	220	3-3-94	.211	.375	.091	6	19	1	4	2	0	0	2	5	0	0	0	3	0	0	.316	.375
Orlando Martinez	L-L	6-0	185	2-17-98	.250	.231	.257	67	244	27	61	12	4	5	34	19	1	0	3	59	3	3	.393	.303
Jack Mayfield	R-R	5-11	190	9-30-90	.247	.246	.247	54	223	31	55	14	3	6	31	12	3	1	2	47	6	3	.417	.292
Mickey Moniak	L-R	6-2	195	5-13-98	.333	.500	.286	2	9	2	3	1	0	2	4	0	0	0	0	0	0	0	1.111	.333
Anthony Mulrine	R-R	6-1	205	3-30-98	.159	.182	.154	20	63	3	10	2	0	0	4	3	3	1	0	24	1	0	.190	.232
Jake Palomaki	B-R	5-10	175	7-17-95	.304	.321	.298	90	316	53	96	13	1	2	30	39	5	2	2	56	10	3	.370	.387

Carlos Reina	B-R	6-0	175	12-11-98	.000	.000	.000	2	7	0	0	0	0	0	0	1	0	0	0	4	0	0	.000	.125
Luis Rengifo	B-R	5-10	195	2-26-97	.313	.400	.275	24	99	19	31	5	2	4	15	12	0	0	1	24	2	2	.525	.384
William Rivera	R-R	6-3	184	4-21-00	.000	.000	.000	1	3	1	0	0	0	0	0	1	0	0	0	1	1	0	.000	.250
Jose Rojas	L-R	6-0	200	2-24-93	.275	.234	.294	62	247	46	68	13	3	18	50	29	1	0	3	58	5	2	.571	.350
2-team total (7 Sacramento River Cats)					.274	.256	.283	69	274	51	75	15	3	20	52	31	1	0	3	64	5	2	.569	.346
Austin Romine	R-R	6-1	216	11-22-88	.273	.400	.167	10	33	7	9	1	0	1	4	5	0	1	0	8	0	0	.394	.368
Magneuris Sierra	L-L	5-11	178	4-7-96	.297	.279	.303	76	279	49	83	10	4	7	45	24	4	1	3	51	22	5	.437	.358
Michael Stefanic	R-R	5-10	180	2-24-96	.314	.325	.309	77	287	50	90	14	3	4	37	48	8	0	3	22	4	2	.425	.422
Matt Thaiss	L-R	6-0	215	5-6-95	.268	.198	.296	77	284	46	76	16	3	10	48	43	2	0	3	61	7	0	.451	.364
Dillon Thomas	L-L	6-1	215	12-10-92	.271	.280	.268	108	399	72	108	22	2	17	77	55	17	0	4	123	6	4	.464	.379
2-team total (5 Sugar Land Space Cowboys)					.271	.264	.273	113	414	75	112	23	2	18	78	56	18	0	4	127	6	4	.466	.378
Andrew Velazquez	B-R	5-9	170	7-14-94	.313	.571	.111	5	16	7	5	3	0	1	6	4	0	0	0	5	2	0	.688	.450
Tyler Wade	L-R	6-1	188	11-23-94	.250	--	.250	2	4	1	1	1	0	0	0	0	0	0	0	2	0	0	.500	.250
Chad Wallach	R-R	6-2	246	11-4-91	.219	.317	.174	89	319	40	70	16	1	9	43	36	5	0	5	95	3	0	.361	.304
Kean Wong	L-R	5-9	189	4-17-95	.262	.345	.228	128	497	70	130	18	4	3	53	61	2	1	4	125	41	6	.332	.342

Pitching	B-T	HT	WT	DOB	W	L	ERA	G	GS	CG	SV	IP	H	R	ER	HR	BB	SO	AVG	vLH	vRH	K/9	BB/9
Jonathan Aro	R-R	6-0	235	10-10-90	4	7	6.03	40	7	0	3	63	74	47	42	4	21	51	.290	.264	.313	7.32	3.02
Kyle Barraclough	R-R	6-3	229	5-23-90	4	3	3.00	41	0	0	2	45	31	16	15	3	28	61	.193	.219	.170	12.20	5.60
Archie Bradley	R-R	6-4	215	8-10-92	1	0	3.18	4	0	0	0	6	6	2	2	1	0	3	.261	.200	.308	4.76	0.00
Ty Buttrey	L-R	6-6	240	3-31-93	0	0	5.94	34	0	0	2	36	38	27	24	2	23	30	.270	.286	.254	7.43	5.70
Davis Daniel	R-R	6-1	190	6-11-97	6	7	4.49	21	21	0	0	102	92	59	51	14	32	83	.236	.250	.222	7.30	2.81
Grant Dayton	L-L	6-2	210	11-25-87	1	0	5.56	34	0	0	0	34	36	23	21	4	17	33	.273	.269	.275	8.74	4.50
Reid Detmers	L-L	6-2	210	7-8-99	0	0	1.50	1	1	0	0	6	3	1	1	1	1	14	.143	.000	.188	21.00	1.50
Jhonathan Diaz	L-L	6-0	170	9-13-96	3	1	4.98	10	10	0	0	47	44	28	26	4	20	46	.246	.089	.299	8.81	3.83
Colby Fitch	L-R	5-11	215	7-27-95	0	0	9.00	1	0	0	0	1	2	1	1	0	1	1	.400	.667	.000	9.00	9.00
Janson Junk	R-R	6-1	177	1-15-96	1	7	4.64	16	15	0	0	74	77	41	38	9	18	69	.266	.296	.239	8.43	2.20
Jake Kalish	B-L	6-2	210	7-9-91	10	2	2.87	23	11	0	0	85	77	29	27	6	19	72	.244	.181	.276	7.65	2.02
Kyle Kasser	L-R	5-10	191	10-12-95	0	0	0.00	1	0	0	0	0	0	0	0	0	0	0	.000	.000	--	0.00	0.00
Dylan King	R-R	6-3	247	12-5-96	0	1	6.75	1	1	0	0	4	4	3	3	0	5	1	.286	.250	.300	2.25	11.25
Luis Ledo	R-R	6-4	240	5-28-95	2	0	0.96	8	0	0	0	9	5	1	1	1	8	6	.167	.067	.267	5.79	7.71
Jake Lee	R-R	6-4	215	6-30-95	0	2	5.85	9	7	0	0	20	23	14	13	1	6	17	.288	.326	.243	7.65	2.70
Michael Lorenzen	R-R	6-3	217	1-4-92	0	2	10.80	2	2	0	0	7	10	8	8	2	2	8	.333	.333	.333	10.80	2.70
Jose Marte	R-R	6-3	180	6-14-96	0	2	5.45	34	0	0	3	35	27	23	21	4	23	46	.211	.233	.191	11.94	5.97
Mike Mayers	R-R	6-2	220	12-6-91	0	3	6.27	8	8	0	0	33	30	27	23	7	17	34	.236	.250	.220	9.27	4.64
Kodi Medeiros	L-L	6-1	195	5-25-96	0	0	10.80	10	0	0	0	12	17	14	14	5	5	9	.327	.200	.406	6.94	3.86
Cristopher Molina	R-R	6-3	170	6-10-97	0	1	6.43	4	3	0	0	14	14	11	10	3	8	14	.264	.343	.111	9.00	5.14
Brian Moran	L-L	6-4	225	9-30-88	5	2	4.07	45	1	0	0	49	49	25	22	7	14	52	.257	.288	.240	9.62	2.59
Oliver Ortega	R-R	6-0	165	10-2-96	2	1	5.96	23	0	0	2	26	34	18	17	3	8	27	.321	.291	.353	9.47	2.81
Elvis Peguero	R-R	6-5	208	3-20-97	4	1	2.84	38	0	0	5	44	34	18	14	2	13	50	.210	.225	.198	10.15	2.64
Robinson Pina	R-R	6-4	224	11-26-98	0	2	29.45	3	2	0	0	4	9	12	12	4	7	5	.474	.444	.500	12.27	17.18
Gerardo Reyes	R-R	5-11	195	5-13-93	3	4	3.74	46	0	0	6	46	35	23	19	5	33	58	.211	.246	.186	11.43	6.50
Keith Rogalla	R-R	6-3	205	9-15-95	0	1	5.24	20	0	0	0	22	27	14	13	1	21	20	.290	.432	.163	8.06	8.46
Kenny Rosenberg	L-L	6-1	195	7-9-95	2	5	3.16	14	13	1	0	63	50	27	22	9	27	62	.216	.172	.231	8.90	3.88
Adam Seminaris	R-L	6-0	191	10-19-98	2	5	5.24	9	9	0	0	34	43	20	20	5	16	27	.309	.196	.366	7.08	4.19
Ryan Smith	L-L	5-11	185	8-13-97	2	6	6.75	32	10	0	1	79	90	67	59	17	35	81	.285	.264	.296	9.27	4.00
Jose Suarez	L-L	5-10	225	1-3-98	1	1	8.64	4	3	0	0	17	18	16	16	3	8	17	.269	.333	.239	9.18	4.32
Wander Suero	R-R	6-4	216	9-15-91	2	3	6.08	20	0	0	2	24	35	19	16	2	9	15	.350	.415	.305	5.70	3.42
Touki Toussaint	R-R	6-3	215	6-20-96	0	1	3.95	9	3	0	0	14	13	7	6	3	11	9	.265	.278	.258	5.93	7.24
Cesar Valdez	R-R	6-2	225	3-17-85	10	5	3.94	23	23	3	0	146	138	69	64	14	22	123	.249	.255	.242	7.56	1.35
Nash Walters	R-R	6-5	210	5-18-97	0	1	6.75	7	0	0	1	5	5	5	4	2	4	4	.238	.333	.167	6.75	6.75
Andrew Wantz	R-R	6-4	235	10-13-95	1	1	2.87	10	0	0	0	16	11	5	5	3	3	17	.208	.263	.176	9.77	1.72
Austin Warren	R-R	6-0	170	2-5-96	2	0	2.12	29	0	0	1	34	23	9	8	2	17	30	.185	.127	.232	7.94	4.50
Zack Weiss	R-R	6-3	210	6-16-92	2	3	4.50	43	0	0	3	50	44	29	25	6	21	65	.226	.289	.179	11.70	3.78
Rob Zastryzny	R-L	6-3	205	3-26-92	0	0	2.25	8	0	0	0	8	8	2	2	0	1	9	.258	.333	.211	10.13	1.13

Fielding

Catcher	PCT	G	PO	A	E	DP	PB
Cruz	.000	1	0	0	0	0	0
Fitch	.992	16	125	6	1	2	0
Mulrine	.984	20	175	8	3	1	0
Reina	1.000	2	19	0	0	0	1
Romine	1.000	9	60	4	0	0	0
Thaiss	.982	45	372	18	7	1	4
Wallach	.988	60	528	25	7	2	4

First Base	PCT	G	PO	A	E	DP
Davis	.000	1	0	0	0	0
Duffy	1.000	2	10	1	0	1
Fitch	1.000	1	4	0	0	0
Ford	1.000	5	36	0	0	6
Gatewood	.988	38	309	26	4	32
Kasser	1.000	4	29	4	0	2
MacKinnon	1.000	57	418	33	0	43
Martinez	.964	4	22	5	1	2
Rojas	.996	28	222	12	1	19
Thaiss	.981	6	51	1	1	5
Thomas	1.000	1	1	0	0	0
Wallach	.976	7	38	3	1	4
Wong	1.000	3	15	2	0	1

Second Base	PCT	G	PO	A	E	DP
Davis	1.000	1	1	2	0	0
Duffy	1.000	1	0	1	0	0
Fletcher	1.000	3	3	4	0	0
Gomez	.941	4	7	9	1	3
Kasser	.952	19	12	28	2	7
Mayfield	.840	8	5	16	4	0
Palomaki	.971	20	27	40	2	14
Rengifo	1.000	5	5	13	0	3
Rojas	1.000	1	2	2	0	1
Stefanic	.989	68	104	159	3	37
Velazquez	1.000	1	1	0	0	0
Wong	.986	31	57	83	2	16

Third Base	PCT	G	PO	A	E	DP
Davis	.886	10	10	21	4	4
Duffy	.889	4	4	4	1	0
Gatewood	.938	25	26	34	4	3

Gomez	.985	25	16	50	1	5
Mayfield	1.000	12	12	23	0	4
Rengifo	1.000	3	2	3	0	1
Rojas	.867	11	9	17	4	3
Stefanic	1.000	6	6	19	0	1
Thaiss	1.000	1	1	1	0	0
Wong	.958	60	37	124	7	16

Shortstop	PCT	G	PO	A	E	DP
Davis	.844	9	9	18	5	2
Fletcher	.941	7	6	10	1	3
Gatewood	.961	14	14	35	2	6
Gomez	1.000	2	3	7	0	1
Mayfield	.976	31	23	59	2	9
Palomaki	.976	74	95	192	7	40
Rengifo	.970	16	15	49	2	9
Velazquez	1.000	3	3	3	0	1
Wade	1.000	1	2	3	0	0

Outfield	PCT	G	PO	A	E	DP
Adell	.970	38	64	1	2	1
Boyd	1.000	2	2	1	0	0
Davis	.968	15	30	0	1	0
Diaz	--	1	0	0	0	0
Duggar	1.000	9	20	1	0	1
Gatewood	.955	36	63	0	3	0
Harrison	.967	76	173	4	6	2
Hunter Jr.	.977	24	42	0	1	0
Kasser	--	1	0	0	0	0
Lagares	1.000	6	10	0	0	0
Martinez	.978	63	128	5	3	2
Moniak	1.000	2	7	0	0	0
Rivera	1.000	1	1	0	0	0
Rojas	.963	17	26	0	1	0
Sierra	.994	72	161	7	1	3
Thomas	.970	87	160	3	5	3
Velazquez	1.000	1	1	0	0	0
Wong	1.000	8	15	0	0	0

ROCKET CITY TRASH PANDAS — DOUBLE-A

SOUTHERN LEAGUE

Batting	B-T	HT	WT	DOB	AVG	vLH	vRH	G	AB	R	H	2B	3B	HR	RBI	BB	HBP	SH	SF	SO	SB	CS	SLG	OBP
Jordyn Adams	R-R	6-2	181	10-18-99	.249	.316	.224	62	209	33	52	7	2	4	20	21	4	0	2	70	15	0	.359	.326
Ryan Aguilar	L-L	6-2	168	9-11-94	.271	.275	.270	93	291	56	79	13	3	15	50	66	6	0	1	103	11	3	.491	.415
Trey Cabbage	L-R	6-3	204	5-3-97	.327	.189	.395	30	113	21	37	6	1	10	32	20	2	0	1	47	10	2	.664	.434
Gustavo Campero	B-R	5-6	182	9-20-97	.250	.500	.125	6	12	1	3	0	0	0	0	1	1	0	0	1	1	0	.250	.357
Sonny DiChiara	R-R	6-1	263	7-29-99	.195	.094	.233	36	118	7	23	2	0	1	10	25	6	0	0	55	1	1	.237	.362
Jose Gomez	R-R	5-11	175	12-10-96	.260	.250	.263	80	281	35	73	18	0	5	27	22	8	0	1	71	6	7	.377	.330
Zach Humphreys	R-R	5-10	195	10-9-97	.248	.333	.223	69	230	43	57	7	1	7	28	51	1	0	3	57	8	3	.378	.382
Torii Hunter Jr.	R-R	6-2	180	6-7-95	.249	.283	.236	54	169	25	42	7	3	7	21	12	4	1	2	57	16	2	.450	.310
Jeremiah Jackson	R-R	6-0	165	3-26-00	.215	.231	.210	87	307	44	66	16	0	14	44	38	4	0	2	77	7	4	.404	.308
Kevin Maitan	B-R	6-2	190	2-12-00	.261	.218	.275	114	399	54	104	20	1	11	45	41	7	0	3	140	3	3	.398	.338
Braxton Martinez	R-R	6-3	220	3-3-94	.202	.206	.201	74	267	37	54	13	0	9	36	40	3	0	2	93	0	1	.352	.311
Orlando Martinez	L-L	6-0	185	2-17-98	.305	.229	.330	39	141	25	43	7	1	4	33	18	0	0	4	33	6	4	.454	.374
Anthony Mulrine	R-R	6-1	205	3-30-98	.160	.147	.164	45	144	19	23	5	0	1	12	19	6	0	0	43	0	0	.215	.284
Zach Neto	R-R	6-0	185	1-31-01	.320	.360	.309	30	122	22	39	9	0	4	23	8	5	0	1	29	4	2	.492	.382
Logan O'Hoppe	R-R	6-2	185	2-9-00	.306	.387	.269	29	98	24	30	3	0	11	33	29	3	0	1	22	1	2	.673	.473
Preston Palmeiro	L-R	5-11	180	1-22-95	.263	.274	.259	113	407	53	107	31	0	8	60	47	5	0	4	82	1	2	.398	.343
Kyren Paris	R-R	6-0	180	11-11-01	.359	.222	.400	14	39	11	14	2	0	3	8	10	2	0	0	14	5	0	.641	.510
Livan Soto	L-R	6-0	160	6-22-00	.281	.270	.284	119	456	69	128	17	1	6	57	71	5	5	6	102	18	8	.362	.379
Bryce Teodosio	R-L	6-3	220	6-18-99	.192	.173	.200	112	369	48	71	10	0	14	41	43	11	1	1	166	28	5	.333	.295
Aaron Whitefield	R-R	6-4	210	9-2-96	.262	.211	.278	79	301	56	79	18	3	9	38	36	3	0	4	93	29	10	.432	.343

Pitching	B-T	HT	WT	DOB	W	L	ERA	G	GS	CG	SV	IP	H	R	ER	HR	BB	SO	AVG	vLH	vRH	K/9	BB/9
Glenn Albanese Jr.	R-R	6-7	223	10-22-98	0	0	4.66	5	0	0	0	10	8	5	5	3	6	9	.222	.105	.353	8.38	5.59
Ivan Armstrong	R-R	6-5	247	7-27-00	0	1	10.13	6	0	0	0	8	12	9	9	2	6	8	.375	.286	.444	9.00	6.75
Sam Bachman	R-R	6-1	235	9-30-99	1	1	3.92	12	12	0	0	44	41	24	19	4	25	30	.248	.221	.273	6.18	5.15
Ky Bush	L-L	6-6	240	11-12-99	7	4	3.67	21	21	0	0	103	93	45	42	14	29	101	.237	.276	.219	8.83	2.53
Cooper Criswell	R-R	6-6	200	7-24-96	0	1	7.20	1	1	0	0	5	6	4	4	1	2	5	.300	.200	.400	9.00	3.60
Coleman Crow	R-R	6-0	175	12-30-00	9	3	4.85	24	23	0	0	128	133	72	69	20	35	128	.263	.257	.268	9.00	2.46
Jack Dashwood	L-L	6-6	240	11-17-97	1	1	4.92	31	1	0	0	60	53	35	33	9	21	84	.230	.232	.230	12.53	3.13
Mason Erla	R-R	6-4	200	8-19-97	5	6	4.28	16	16	0	0	82	88	42	39	9	19	64	.274	.283	.265	7.02	2.09
Jimmy Herget	R-R	6-3	170	9-9-93	1	0	4.50	3	0	0	0	4	2	2	2	1	2	4	.154	.222	.000	9.00	4.50
Aaron Hernandez	R-R	6-1	170	12-2-96	3	4	5.48	35	3	0	3	48	47	31	29	8	20	50	.253	.190	.304	9.44	3.78
Connor Higgins	R-L	6-5	240	7-21-96	0	0	24.30	4	0	0	0	3	5	9	9	2	12	4	.357	.500	.250	10.80	32.40
Kolton Ingram	L-L	5-9	170	10-21-96	6	2	2.67	50	0	0	10	61	39	21	18	6	17	73	.186	.141	.205	10.83	2.52
Nick Jones	L-L	6-6	209	1-22-99	3	0	4.11	31	0	0	1	35	27	17	16	2	26	44	.211	.180	.231	11.31	6.69
Ben Joyce	R-R	6-5	225	9-17-00	1	0	2.08	13	0	0	1	13	11	4	3	0	4	20	.220	.273	.179	13.85	2.77
Brett Kerry	R-R	6-0	213	4-12-99	5	7	4.46	25	20	0	1	103	112	53	51	19	30	118	.279	.315	.245	10.31	2.62
Brent Killam	L-L	5-11	180	3-26-98	2	3	8.39	9	7	0	0	34	48	36	32	11	13	37	.329	.256	.359	9.70	3.41
Luis Ledo	R-R	6-4	240	5-28-95	5	3	4.00	29	0	0	4	36	26	18	16	6	17	41	.202	.167	.232	10.25	4.25
Zach Linginfelter	L-R	6-5	220	4-10-97	2	1	6.54	24	0	0	0	32	28	23	23	1	20	38	.241	.318	.194	10.80	5.68
Landon Marceaux	R-R	6-0	199	10-8-99	0	1	7.94	2	2	0	0	6	6	5	5	1	2	4	.273	.200	.333	6.35	3.18
Braxton Martinez	R-R	6-3	220	3-3-94	0	0	13.50	2	0	0	0	1	4	2	2	0	1	0	.500	.200	1.000	0.00	6.75
Sean McLaughlin	L-R	5-11	195	5-16-94	5	4	4.94	38	1	0	0	58	53	34	32	8	19	63	.242	.228	.254	9.72	2.93
Cristopher Molina	R-R	6-3	170	6-10-97	3	1	6.75	18	1	0	2	43	55	32	32	12	16	45	.322	.375	.283	9.49	3.38
Luke Murphy	R-R	6-5	190	11-5-99	7	2	2.62	37	0	0	1	45	25	13	13	0	26	52	.164	.148	.176	10.48	5.24
Braden Olthoff	R-R	6-4	241	3-12-99	3	6	4.91	14	8	0	1	62	66	36	34	7	23	30	.273	.308	.240	4.33	3.32
Adam Seminaris	R-L	6-0	191	10-19-98	3	4	4.70	8	7	0	0	31	37	17	16	0	14	27	.301	.314	.295	7.92	4.11
Chase Silseth	R-R	6-0	217	5-18-00	7	0	2.28	15	15	0	0	83	52	23	21	11	27	110	.182	.172	.191	11.93	2.93
Eric Torres	L-L	6-0	195	9-22-99	2	2	1.59	42	0	0	22	51	25	13	9	3	23	81	.143	.121	.154	14.29	4.06

Fielding

Catcher	PCT	G	PO	A	E	DP	PB
Campero	1.000	1	9	0	0	0	0
Humphreys	.986	65	585	48	9	2	8
Mulrine	.996	45	424	22	2	1	5
O'Hoppe	.985	27	250	11	4	2	1

First Base	PCT	G	PO	A	E	DP
Aguilar	.962	11	45	5	2	7
Cabbage	1.000	12	74	6	0	8
DiChiara	1.000	20	146	6	0	20
Humphreys	.000	1	0	0	0	0
Maitan	1.000	25	159	11	0	26
Martinez	.994	42	296	13	2	27
Palmeiro	.994	43	282	27	2	28

Second Base	PCT	G	PO	A	E	DP
Gomez	.982	43	61	107	3	27
Jackson	.979	33	55	88	3	17
Palmeiro	.976	14	17	24	1	7
Paris	.980	13	19	30	1	6

Soto	.990	42	72	117	2	37

Third Base	PCT	G	PO	A	E	DP
Gomez	.943	25	16	34	3	9
Jackson	.966	10	5	23	1	4
Maitan	.950	89	38	113	8	7
Palmeiro	.903	16	7	21	3	1
Soto	.875	7	2	12	2	2

Shortstop	PCT	G	PO	A	E	DP
Gomez	.976	11	11	30	1	5
Jackson	.910	31	49	72	12	27
Neto	.914	28	35	71	10	22
Soto	.970	68	79	182	8	36

Outfield	PCT	G	PO	A	E	DP
Adams	.971	62	98	3	3	0
Aguilar	.978	74	133	2	3	0
Cabbage	1.000	10	20	0	0	0
Gomez	1.000	3	5	0	0	0
Hunter Jr.	1.000	47	59	1	0	0
Jackson	.917	9	10	1	1	0
Martinez	.983	35	55	4	1	0
Palmeiro	--	1	0	0	0	0
Teodosio	.989	110	261	5	3	0
Whitefield	.984	75	122	5	2	1

TRI-CITY DUST DEVILS — *HIGH CLASS A*

NORTHWEST LEAGUE

Batting	B-T	HT	WT	DOB	AVG	vLH	vRH	G	AB	R	H	2B	3B	HR	RBI	BB	HBP	SH	SF	SO	SB	CS	SLG	OBP
Jordyn Adams	R-R	6-2	181	10-18-99	.228	.265	.218	58	219	31	50	11	3	0	22	21	5	2	2	54	18	3	.306	.308
Casey Dana	R-R	6-4	215	5-31-99	.209	.133	.225	21	86	14	18	3	2	1	9	2	2	1	0	18	0	2	.326	.244
Francisco Del Valle	L-L	6-1	211	8-18-98	.216	.250	.210	26	97	7	21	3	0	1	10	4	0	0	0	21	1	0	.278	.248
Osmy Gregorio	R-R	6-2	186	5-27-98	.255	.272	.250	113	444	58	113	18	6	2	44	32	3	3	4	125	22	8	.336	.306
Jose Guzman	B-R	5-11	182	9-15-00	.202	.136	.221	62	198	26	40	9	1	1	14	36	3	0	1	69	14	3	.273	.332
Kyle Kasser	L-R	5-10	191	10-12-95	.272	.255	.276	66	243	24	66	6	0	1	17	35	0	2	2	31	15	3	.309	.361
D'Shawn Knowles	B-R	6-0	165	1-16-01	.234	.243	.231	84	321	44	75	10	2	1	26	32	3	7	2	101	13	4	.287	.307
Kyle Lovelace	R-R	5-10	163	8-3-98	.107	.050	.120	33	103	4	11	0	0	0	9	8	1	1	2	47	2	1	.107	.175
Gabe Matthews	L-R	6-2	231	11-24-97	.227	.160	.244	113	388	56	88	26	0	14	64	65	16	0	6	139	3	1	.402	.356
Christian Molfetta	R-R	5-10	195	10-17-96	.200	.211	.197	60	190	21	38	8	1	1	19	22	4	3	1	65	1	2	.268	.295
Mitch Nay	R-R	6-3	200	9-20-93	.160	.167	.158	31	119	11	19	2	0	2	8	11	2	0	0	47	0	0	.227	.242
Zach Neto	R-R	6-0	185	1-31-01	.200	.000	.294	7	25	2	5	0	1	1	4	4	2	0	0	4	1	0	.400	.355
Kyren Paris	R-R	6-0	180	11-11-01	.229	.154	.247	89	328	58	75	18	5	8	32	49	9	5	0	117	28	4	.387	.345
Mike Peabody	L-R	6-4	206	10-1-98	.205	.203	.205	92	308	42	63	13	1	8	48	34	15	2	4	106	12	6	.331	.310
Dylan Phillips	L-L	6-0	220	6-16-99	.333	.000	.375	10	18	6	6	3	0	0	3	5	1	0	0	6	1	0	.500	.500
Straton Podaras	R-R	6-1	200	12-9-97	.194	.216	.188	59	170	31	33	10	0	8	19	38	8	0	1	58	6	1	.394	.364
Jose Reyes	L-R	6-2	180	9-22-00	.130	.000	.158	6	23	2	3	1	0	1	4	0	0	0	0	6	0	0	.304	.130
Steven Rivas	L-L	6-1	218	6-28-99	.244	.259	.241	82	299	31	73	20	1	8	50	12	2	2	1	107	4	1	.398	.277
Evan Russell	R-R	5-11	195	7-26-98	.273	.500	.222	7	22	4	6	2	0	0	1	4	0	0	0	7	1	0	.364	.385
Christian Sepulveda	R-R	6-5	205	1-5-98	.252	.269	.247	35	123	18	31	13	1	1	17	5	5	0	2	31	2	2	.398	.304
Joe Stewart	R-R	6-4	207	5-6-98	.232	.280	.220	33	125	11	29	6	1	1	17	10	3	0	1	43	7	1	.320	.302
Brendan Tinsman	R-R	6-2	225	12-6-99	.304	.500	.263	7	23	3	7	0	0	0	0	1	1	0	0	3	1	0	.304	.360
Mike Wilson	L-R	6-0	200	3-29-98	.184	.125	.195	15	49	8	9	2	1	3	6	6	1	0	0	25	1	0	.449	.286
Edwin Yon	R-R	6-8	237	7-24-98	.231	.212	.238	52	182	20	42	7	3	6	23	11	3	0	0	86	2	0	.401	.286
Kenyon Yovan	R-R	6-2	221	12-28-97	.194	.194	.194	28	93	7	18	5	2	1	10	6	0	0	1	38	0	0	.323	.240

Pitching	B-T	HT	WT	DOB	W	L	ERA	G	GS	CG	SV	IP	H	R	ER	HR	BB	SO	AVG	vLH	vRH	K/9	BB/9
Glenn Albanese Jr.	R-R	6-7	223	10-22-98	1	1	3.41	27	0	0	5	37	34	14	14	2	11	44	.241	.250	.233	10.70	2.68
Mason Albright	L-L	6-0	190	11-26-02	0	0	9.00	3	0	0	0	4	5	5	4	0	5	4	.294	.571	.100	9.00	11.25
Ivan Armstrong	R-R	6-5	247	7-27-00	1	3	1.93	13	0	0	6	14	12	5	3	1	3	19	.235	.222	.250	12.21	1.93
Nathan Burns	R-R	6-1	200	6-1-99	1	2	5.33	30	0	0	3	27	24	17	16	2	15	32	.233	.261	.211	10.67	5.00
Ryan Costeiu	R-R	6-0	200	11-28-00	3	5	3.42	16	10	0	1	68	60	29	26	7	19	81	.239	.235	.243	10.67	2.50
Dakota Donovan	R-R	6-6	255	7-25-97	4	2	3.40	34	0	0	6	45	36	19	17	2	19	54	.221	.183	.250	10.80	3.80
Brandon Dufault	R-R	6-5	204	10-19-98	1	2	4.93	34	0	0	3	46	43	35	25	5	28	65	.249	.247	.250	12.81	5.52
Emilker Guzman	R-R	5-10	184	2-10-99	3	5	1.98	40	0	0	3	50	39	21	11	2	19	63	.205	.260	.171	11.34	3.42
Houston Harding	L-L	6-1	230	5-22-98	2	0	4.58	23	0	0	0	37	36	22	19	5	17	43	.252	.306	.223	10.37	4.10
Connor Higgins	R-L	6-5	240	7-21-96	0	1	8.78	12	0	0	0	13	20	17	13	2	10	13	.351	.250	.405	8.78	6.75
Nick Jones	L-L	6-6	209	1-22-99	1	1	5.63	8	0	0	1	8	6	6	5	0	5	13	.194	.000	.316	14.63	5.63
Brent Killam	L-L	5-11	180	3-26-98	2	4	4.89	10	10	0	0	46	54	27	25	10	16	50	.295	.417	.252	9.78	3.13
Dylan King	R-R	6-3	247	12-5-96	2	2	2.32	20	4	0	0	50	33	14	13	4	17	69	.185	.136	.227	12.34	3.04
Zac Kristofak	R-R	5-9	189	12-8-97	1	3	3.82	34	9	0	0	64	63	29	27	6	20	60	.263	.264	.262	8.48	2.83
Landon Marceaux	R-R	6-0	199	10-8-99	4	5	2.65	16	16	1	0	85	64	30	25	5	14	69	.204	.190	.219	7.31	1.48
Victor Mederos	R-R	6-2	227	6-8-01	0	1	5.63	6	6	0	0	16	15	13	10	1	9	15	.242	.235	.250	8.44	5.06
Kyle Molnar	R-R	6-3	220	11-14-96	4	0	2.61	22	0	0	1	38	30	16	11	0	18	35	.216	.224	.211	8.29	4.26
Nick Mondak	L-L	6-4	203	6-2-98	3	7	5.16	21	21	0	0	98	108	58	56	17	18	92	.278	.264	.286	8.48	1.66
Braden Olthoff	R-R	6-4	241	3-12-99	2	3	3.13	9	9	0	0	46	40	19	16	3	10	43	.234	.253	.211	8.41	1.96
Dylan Phillips	L-L	6-0	220	6-16-99	1	1	5.14	4	0	0	0	7	8	4	4	0	0	6	.296	.222	.333	7.71	0.00
Robinson Pina	R-R	6-4	224	11 26 98	6	6	3.31	18	13	0	1	82	71	34	30	7	24	117	.231	.169	.275	12.89	2.64
Jose Salvador	L-L	6-2	170	9-21-99	4	7	4.58	14	14	0	0	71	76	39	36	10	30	84	.276	.302	.265	10.70	3.82
Hayden Seig	R-R	6-5	227	9-10-98	3	2	6.34	26	0	0	0	33	53	29	23	4	13	26	.371	.379	.365	7.16	3.58
Adam Seminaris	R-L	6-0	191	10-19-98	2	2	0.98	7	5	0	0	37	27	8	4	2	8	43	.205	.176	.222	10.55	1.96
Jake Smith	R-R	6-4	200	10-4-99	2	5	3.72	27	7	0	0	68	59	36	28	6	30	78	.227	.229	.225	10.37	3.99
John Swanda	R-R	6-2	185	3-18-99	5	1	5.76	6	5	0	0	30	33	19	19	3	4	22	.284	.237	.333	6.67	1.21
Greg Veliz	L-R	6-2	200	4-10-97	0	0	9.00	4	0	0	0	6	9	6	6	1	3	3	.346	.300	.375	4.50	4.50

Fielding

Catcher	PCT	G	PO	A	E	DP	PB
Lovelace	.986	32	266	20	4	1	3
Molfetta	.986	33	320	21	5	2	1
Podaras	.984	58	564	44	10	6	11
Russell	.972	6	64	6	2	0	1
Tinsman	1.000	5	45	3	0	0	2

First Base	PCT	G	PO	A	E	DP
Matthews	.991	105	755	56	7	68
Nay	.980	8	44	5	1	2
Sepulveda	1.000	8	43	4	0	6
Yovan	1.000	14	54	11	0	6

Second Base	PCT	G	PO	A	E	DP
Gregorio	.982	43	58	104	3	18

Guzman	.950	31	50	64	6	16
Kasser	.973	24	44	66	3	12
Paris	.958	26	37	55	4	16
Sepulveda	1.000	6	18	8	0	2

Third Base	PCT	G	PO	A	E	DP
Gregorio	.905	8	3	16	2	0
Guzman	.889	23	10	38	6	1
Kasser	.952	40	32	86	6	9
Molfetta	.921	23	4	31	3	2
Nay	.939	13	11	20	2	1
Sepulveda	.959	20	12	35	2	1

Yovan	1.000	6	2	12	0	2

Shortstop	PCT	G	PO	A	E	DP
Gregorio	.980	46	77	117	4	30
Guzman	1.000	5	6	5	0	1
Knowles	.939	11	13	18	2	3
Neto	.952	6	8	12	1	1
Paris	.931	60	77	111	14	25
Sepulveda	.500	1	0	1	1	0

Outfield	PCT	G	PO	A	E	DP
Adams	.989	49	85	3	1	2
Dana	.903	18	25	3	3	0
Del Valle	1.000	21	33	3	0	0
Gregorio	.952	13	17	3	1	1
Knowles	1.000	69	138	5	0	2
Molfetta	--	1	0	0	0	0
Peabody	.988	82	159	3	2	1
Reyes	1.000	3	3	1	0	0
Rivas	.977	64	118	8	3	0
Stewart	.983	31	55	3	1	1
Wilson	1.000	10	15	0	0	0
Yon	.961	35	46	3	2	0

INLAND EMPIRE 66ERS

LOW CLASS A

CALIFORNIA LEAGUE

Batting	B-T	HT	WT	DOB	AVG	vLH	vRH	G	AB	R	H	2B	3B	HR	RBI	BB	HBP	SH	SF	SO	SB	CS	SLG	OBP
Jeremy Arocho	B-R	5-10	165	10-6-98	.231	.197	.244	85	251	53	58	14	1	0	32	79	4	1	1	58	32	5	.295	.421
Werner Blakely	L-R	6-3	185	2-21-02	.295	.302	.292	55	183	36	54	13	2	5	40	45	6	0	1	70	24	2	.470	.447
Jose Bonilla	R-R	6-0	185	4-2-02	.151	.217	.129	32	93	4	14	2	1	0	5	4	3	0	1	41	0	0	.194	.208
BJ Boyd	L-R	5-11	230	7-16-93	.345	.324	.353	68	255	48	88	20	2	6	50	31	6	0	3	35	9	4	.510	.424
David Calabrese	L-R	5-11	160	9-26-02	.250	.237	.255	112	424	68	106	23	7	7	64	50	3	0	11	116	26	2	.387	.326
Trent Deveaux	R-R	6-0	160	5-4-00	.185	.143	.200	19	54	5	10	2	0	0	5	5	1	0	0	16	1	0	.222	.267
Myles Emmerson	R-R	5-11	185	5-15-98	.238	.216	.247	74	256	31	61	11	0	2	32	29	2	0	1	59	6	1	.305	.319
Tucker Flint	L-L	6-2	215	4-5-01	.287	.400	.259	30	101	24	29	8	0	3	20	23	6	0	1	40	6	1	.455	.443
Luke Franzoni	R-R	6-2	220	12-20-99	.167	.167	.167	13	42	7	7	3	0	0	3	9	0	0	0	21	0	0	.238	.314
Starlin Gill	R-R	5-10	150	3-16-00	.173	.209	.156	51	133	27	23	2	0	1	13	19	5	3	2	34	8	4	.211	.296
Denzer Guzman	R-R	6-1	180	2-8-04	.176	.250	.154	5	17	2	3	0	0	0	2	6	0	0	0	10	1	0	.176	.391
D'Shawn Knowles	B-R	6-0	165	1-16-01	.328	.414	.306	38	137	25	45	9	2	1	23	24	2	1	1	38	9	2	.445	.433
Tate Kolwyck	R-R	5-11	195	12-27-99	.196	.071	.250	14	46	9	9	4	0	1	7	9	1	1	0	16	1	0	.348	.339
Carson Matthews	R-R	5-10	180	1-27-00	.181	.192	.175	29	83	14	15	3	0	2	6	12	4	0	0	31	2	2	.289	.313
Vojtech Mensik	R-R	6-0	182	5-24-98	.214	.214	.214	54	159	32	34	4	2	0	19	27	8	2	0	48	15	3	.264	.356
Darwin Moreno	R-R	6-2	175	1-26-02	.154	.167	.143	15	39	5	6	1	0	1	5	4	2	1	0	22	0	0	.256	.267
Adrian Placencia	B-R	5-11	155	6-2-03	.254	.278	.245	104	382	83	97	23	2	13	64	76	8	0	2	142	21	8	.427	.387
Edgar Quero	B-R	5-11	170	4-6-03	.312	.275	.326	111	413	86	129	35	2	17	75	73	21	0	6	91	12	5	.530	.435
Alexander Ramirez	R-R	6-2	180	8-29-02	.229	.256	.219	118	475	67	109	24	5	8	59	31	11	0	3	160	21	8	.352	.290
Jadiel Sanchez	B-R	6-2	185	5-10-01	.309	.455	.273	15	55	7	17	3	1	0	6	4	3	0	1	11	0	1	.400	.381
Quentin Selma	L-R	6-3	205	6-8-98	.203	.156	.216	40	143	20	29	7	2	3	15	14	2	1	2	45	0	1	.343	.280
Max Stassi	R-R	5-10	200	3-15-91	.375	.000	.500	2	8	2	3	1	0	1	2	0	0	0	0	2	0	0	.875	.375
Arol Vera	B-R	6-2	170	9-12-02	.207	.172	.221	120	487	71	101	16	4	4	59	53	6	1	4	149	19	7	.281	.291
Kevin Watson Jr.	L-R	6-1	190	5-25-99	.237	.212	.246	68	194	39	46	4	5	7	43	33	6	0	3	64	10	2	.418	.360

Pitching	B-T	HT	WT	DOB	W	L	ERA	G	GS	CG	SV	IP	H	R	ER	HR	BB	SO	AVG	vLH	vRH	K/9	BB/9
Mason Albright	L-L	6-0	190	11-26-02	0	4	9.00	12	12	0	0	48	72	54	48	12	23	53	.348	.318	.356	9.94	4.31
Stiward Aquino	R-R	6-6	170	6-20-99	2	2	7.39	20	0	0	1	28	26	26	23	5	29	32	.241	.300	.206	10.29	9.32
Archie Bradley	R-R	6-4	215	8-10-92	1	0	0.00	1	0	0	0	1	0	0	0	0	0	1	.000	.000	.000	9.00	0.00
Kelvin Caceres	R-R	6-1	180	1-26-00	3	2	3.84	36	5	0	4	77	46	46	33	5	54	117	.170	.173	.168	13.62	6.28
Chase Chaney	R-R	6-1	180	12-16-99	5	5	2.77	30	11	0	3	91	92	35	28	3	17	81	.256	.261	.252	8.01	1.68
Caden Dana	L-R	6-4	215	12-17-03	0	0	27.00	1	1	0	0	2	6	5	5	0	1	2	.545	.625	.333	10.80	5.40
Michael Darrell-Hicks	R-R	6-5	220	11-13-97	2	1	10.61	7	0	0	0	9	9	12	11	1	8	10	.237	.250	.222	9.64	7.71
Leonard Garcia	L-L	6-2	165	8-11-03	1	1	6.83	12	1	0	2	28	36	22	21	1	25	37	.319	.353	.313	12.04	8.13
Max Gieg	R-R	6-5	230	6-8-01	1	0	5.06	13	0	0	1	16	15	9	9	2	7	20	.250	.267	.233	11.25	3.94
Starlin Gill	R-R	5-10	150	3-16-00	0	0	9.00	3	0	0	0	4	3	4	4	0	2	2	.200	.200	.200	4.50	4.50
Julio Goff	R-R	5-10	200	1-11-00	7	9	5.51	25	17	0	2	111	121	83	68	12	44	115	.275	.259	.286	9.32	3.57
Fernando Guanare	R-R	6-1	140	6-21-03	3	5	6.60	25	14	0	1	74	87	64	54	9	33	71	.296	.297	.295	8.67	4.03
Gabriel Hernandez	R-R	6-1	160	1-22-02	2	3	4.95	34	1	0	1	64	60	39	35	9	35	41	.250	.264	.242	5.80	4.95
Alejandro Hidalgo	R-R	6-1	160	5-22-03	0	3	4.62	10	10	0	0	39	34	21	20	3	19	58	.225	.212	.232	13.38	4.38
Jack Kochanowicz	L-R	6-6	220	12-22-00	4	4	4.99	17	9	0	0	58	57	36	32	6	18	53	.253	.286	.236	8.27	2.81
Michael Lorenzen	R-R	6-3	217	1-4-92	0	0	3.00	1	1	0	0	6	4	2	2	1	2	5	.200	.143	.231	7.50	3.00
Jean Carlos Lucas	R-R	6-3	185	12-2-00	0	0	12.38	7	0	0	0	8	15	16	11	1	7	9	.385	.385	.385	10.13	7.88
Jorge Marcheco	R-R	6-1	185	8-6-02	0	1	4.76	3	3	0	0	11	8	6	6	1	3	14	.186	.130	.250	11.12	2.38
Alex Martinez	R-R	5-10	170	9-15-02	2	2	7.36	17	0	0	0	22	26	23	18	1	17	32	.306	.258	.333	13.09	6.95
Carson Matthews	R-R	5-10	180	1-27-00	0	0	0.00	1	0	0	0	0	0	0	0	0	0	1	.000	.000	--	27.00	0.00
Matthew McMillan	L-R	6-5	220	11-24-99	2	1	5.71	18	0	0	0	35	33	26	22	2	30	33	.254	.306	.234	8.57	7.79
Kyle Molnar	R-R	6-3	220	11-14-96	1	0	1.42	6	0	0	0	13	11	2	2	0	3	12	.224	.300	.205	8.53	2.13
Daniel Nunan	L-L	6-6	215	5-25-00	0	0	3.51	20	0	0	0	33	25	14	13	4	10	29	.203	.094	.242	7.83	2.70
Roman Phansalkar	R-R	6-1	195	6-2-98	2	0	5.29	12	0	0	0	17	14	11	10	2	12	14	.219	.222	.216	7.41	6.35
Jose Quijada	L-L	5-11	215	11-9-95	0	0	0.00	3	0	0	0	3	1	0	0	0	1	5	.100	.000	.250	15.00	3.00
Dayan Reinoso	R-R	6-1	210	8-27-98	1	3	3.56	25	0	0	7	30	24	14	12	1	20	32	.226	.279	.190	9.49	5.93
Jose Salvador	L-L	6-2	170	9-21-99	2	4	2.66	10	10	0	0	47	42	20	14	2	15	68	.228	.204	.238	12.93	2.85
Hayden Seig	R-R	6-5	227	9-10-98	4	1	0.82	9	0	0	3	11	11	3	1	0	2	12	.262	.556	.182	9.82	1.64
Blake Seigler	R-R	6-3	205	2-16-98	4	0	4.15	22	0	0	2	30	26	17	14	3	25	41	.228	.150	.270	12.16	7.42
Jose Soriano	R-R	6-3	220	10-20-98	0	0	5.40	3	3	0	0	5	6	3	3	0	2	6	.286	.364	.200	10.80	3.60
Jared Southard	R-R	6-2	220	10-4-00	0	0	12.38	8	0	0	0	8	19	11	11	2	8	4	.487	.647	.364	4.50	9.00
John Swanda	R-R	6-2	185	3-18-99	2	0	4.50	2	0	0	0	8	7	5	4	1	1	7	.233	.167	.250	7.88	1.13
Connor Van Scoyoc	R-R	6-6	210	11-26-99	11	5	4.28	23	22	0	0	120	103	63	57	10	39	140	.226	.201	.239	10.50	2.93

Pitching	B-T	HT	WT	DOB	W	L	ERA	G	GS	CG	SV	IP	H	R	ER	HR	BB	SO	AVG	vLH	vRH	K/9	BB/9
Greg Veliz	L-R	6-2	200	4-10-97	2	1	4.50	9	0	0	0	10	9	5	5	1	7	13	.231	.182	.250	11.70	6.30
Joey Walsh	L-L	6-1	224	10-5-97	5	4	5.34	29	12	0	1	84	80	55	50	19	40	93	.251	.226	.260	9.92	4.27
Kenyon Yovan	R-R	6-2	221	12-28-97	1	1	2.35	12	0	0	4	15	7	5	4	0	5	28	.137	.167	.121	16.43	2.93

Fielding

Catcher	PCT	G	PO	A	E	DP	PB
Emmerson	.993	55	517	50	4	6	9
Quero	.985	80	719	62	12	0	4
Stassi	1.000	1	13	1	0	0	0
Watson Jr.	.952	5	20	0	1	0	1

First Base	PCT	G	PO	A	E	DP
Arocho	.953	6	41	0	2	3
Bonilla	.976	19	116	6	3	12
Emmerson	.959	12	66	4	3	6
Flint	.971	24	152	18	5	16
Franzoni	.963	7	48	4	2	5
Gill	1.000	22	122	8	0	13
Matthews	1.000	2	11	0	0	1
Selma	.993	40	264	16	2	32
Watson Jr.	.980	14	92	6	2	9

Second Base	PCT	G	PO	A	E	DP
Arocho	.943	12	13	20	2	5
Gill	.976	21	38	42	2	12
Kolwyck	1.000	6	8	12	0	1
Matthews	1.000	2	0	1	0	0
Mensik	.974	11	13	24	1	5
Placencia	.971	67	104	162	8	46
Vera	.977	23	43	42	2	12

Third Base	PCT	G	PO	A	E	DP
Arocho	.947	39	23	66	5	6
Blakely	.842	34	23	41	12	2
Bonilla	.821	10	5	18	5	3
Gill	1.000	4	1	4	0	0
Kolwyck	1.000	7	3	11	0	0
Matthews	.857	11	2	16	3	1
Mensik	.881	39	19	55	10	5
Vera	1.000	1	2	2	0	0

Shortstop	PCT	G	PO	A	E	DP
Gill	.000	1	0	0	0	0
Guzman	.882	5	6	9	2	2
Knowles	.783	4	1	17	5	1
Mensik	1.000	5	3	11	0	2
Placencia	.918	32	28	62	8	13
Vera	.963	93	127	233	14	56

Outfield	PCT	G	PO	A	E	DP
Arocho	.962	30	49	1	2	1
Boyd	1.000	47	81	0	0	0
Calabrese	.973	113	249	2	7	1
Deveaux	.958	18	22	1	1	0
Flint	.889	5	8	0	1	0
Franzoni	--	1	0	0	0	0
Knowles	.976	34	78	2	2	0
Matthews	.800	9	7	1	2	1
Moreno	1.000	14	12	2	0	0
Ramirez	.980	118	235	6	5	3
Sanchez	.957	11	22	0	1	0
Watson Jr.	.970	21	32	0	1	0

ACL ANGELS — *ROOKIE*

ARIZONA COMPLEX LEAGUE

Batting	B-T	HT	WT	DOB	AVG	vLH	vRH	G	AB	R	H	2B	3B	HR	RBI	BB	HBP	SH	SF	SO	SB	CS	SLG	OBP
Matt Coutney	L-R	6-1	230	7-8-99	.231	.200	.238	9	26	5	6	1	0	1	1	6	0	0	0	11	0	0	.385	.375
Casey Dana	R-R	6-4	215	5-31-99	.429	--	.429	2	7	1	3	1	0	0	1	0	0	0	0	0	0	0	.571	.429
Pedro Diaz	R-R	6-3	210	1-9-99	.233	.000	.241	11	30	4	7	1	0	0	1	1	2	0	0	17	0	0	.267	.303
Isaias Falcon	R-R	5-10	165	10-26-00	.194	.000	.212	18	36	6	7	1	0	0	4	2	0	0	0	19	1	2	.222	.237
Cristian Garcia	B-R	6-1	168	7-26-04	.236	.250	.235	49	165	26	39	6	2	2	29	17	3	1	3	43	1	1	.333	.314
Ben Gobbel	R-R	6-1	190	11-2-99	.184	.667	.152	13	49	8	9	1	0	0	4	4	2	0	1	11	1	1	.204	.268
Denzer Guzman	R-R	6-1	180	2-8-04	.286	.261	.290	52	192	38	55	11	3	3	33	15	2	0	2	44	3	1	.422	.341
Edwin Hidalgo	R-R	0-0	0	8-12-03	.158	.167	.154	6	19	2	3	1	0	0	0	1	0	0	0	3	0	0	.211	.200
Mason Holt	R-R	5-11	190	10-20-98	.296	.250	.304	16	54	9	16	3	1	0	9	4	3	0	0	20	6	0	.389	.377
Jorge Jimenez	R-R	5-9	150	6-9-02	.255	.286	.250	15	47	6	12	1	1	1	5	4	1	0	0	10	2	1	.383	.327
Kleiver Lopez	R-R	0-0	0	7-14-04	.093	.125	.086	15	43	4	4	1	0	0	1	2	2	0	0	15	1	0	.116	.170
Johan Macias	B-R	5-9	150	1-6-03	.322	.385	.315	42	121	19	39	7	2	2	20	10	1	4	3	25	2	3	.463	.370
Orlando Martinez	L-L	6-0	185	2-17-98	.455	--	.455	4	11	4	5	3	0	0	2	1	0	0	0	4	0	0	.727	.500
Darwin Moreno	R-R	6-2	175	1-26-02	.000	.000	.000	2	4	0	0	0	0	0	0	1	0	0	0	3	0	0	.000	.200
Kristin Munroe	R-R	6-1	175	8-6-04	.213	.167	.220	14	47	5	10	1	0	0	4	5	2	0	0	25	2	0	.234	.315
Mitch Nay	R-R	6-3	200	9-20-93	.462	1.000	.364	5	13	3	6	1	0	2	4	2	0	0	0	1	0	0	1.000	.533
Jesus Ortega	R-R	6-0	170	1-18-01	.189	.111	.198	29	90	15	17	5	0	0	7	9	2	3	1	33	0	1	.244	.275
Kyren Paris	R-R	6-0	180	11-11-01	.143	--	.143	2	7	1	1	0	0	1	2	2	0	0	0	3	0	0	.571	.333
Dylan Phillips	L-L	6-0	220	6-16-99	.241	.000	.259	11	29	4	7	2	1	0	4	4	0	0	2	9	0	0	.379	.314
Carlos Reina	B-R	6-0	175	12-11-98	.222	.000	.250	10	27	3	6	1	0	0	5	4	0	1	3	7	1	0	.259	.294
Jose Reyes	L-R	6-2	180	9-22-00	.303	.150	.333	38	122	19	37	5	1	4	16	5	0	0	0	29	2	1	.459	.331
Steven Rivas	L-L	6-1	218	6-28-99	.333	--	.333	3	12	3	4	0	0	1	3	1	0	0	0	4	0	0	.583	.385
William Rivera	R-R	6-3	184	4-21-00	.333	.000	.400	4	6	1	2	0	0	0	0	1	1	0	0	2	0	2	.333	.500
Gabriel Rodriguez	R-R	6-1	154	9-29-02	.176	.200	.172	11	34	4	6	1	0	1	5	4	0	0	1	8	0	0	.294	.256
Jorge Ruiz	L-L	5-10	164	6-30-04	.335	.308	.339	53	203	36	68	12	2	0	23	12	4	2	1	20	8	2	.414	.382
Evan Russell	R-R	5-11	195	7-26-98	.143	.250	.100	5	14	1	2	1	0	0	1	4	0	0	0	5	0	0	.214	.333
Anthony Scull	L-L	6-0	165	1-26-04	.306	.000	.314	13	36	8	11	0	2	0	6	5	0	0	0	11	1	1	.417	.390
Quentin Selma	L-R	6-3	205	6-8-98	.071	.000	.083	4	14	1	1	0	0	0	1	1	0	0	0	7	0	0	.071	.133
Christian Sepulveda	R-R	6-5	205	1-5-98	.283	.200	.295	35	120	25	34	8	3	6	23	11	6	0	0	35	7	0	.550	.372
Michael Stefanic	R-R	5-10	180	2-24-96	.231	.500	.111	4	13	2	3	0	0	0	1	1	0	0	0	1	0	0	.231	.286
Brendan Tinsman	R-R	6-2	225	12-6-99	.250	.000	.333	6	20	2	5	1	0	0	5	1	1	0	0	6	0	0	.300	.318
Yeremi Villahermosa	B-R	5-9	150	10-16-02	.253	.000	.278	28	79	12	20	2	0	0	12	7	1	0	4	25	2	1	.278	.308
Mike Wilson	L-R	6-0	200	3-29-98	.500	.500	.500	5	14	9	7	2	2	2	6	3	1	0	0	4	0	0	1.357	.611

Pitching	B-T	HT	WT	DOB	W	L	ERA	G	GS	CG	SV	IP	H	R	ER	HR	BB	SO	AVG	vLH	vRH	K/9	BB/9
Mason Albright	L-L	6-0	190	11-26-02	1	0	3.00	2	0	0	0	3	3	1	1	0	0	2	.250	.200	.286	6.00	0.00
Jose Aleman	R-R	6-1	165	2-1-03	1	1	5.23	7	0	0	0	10	11	10	6	0	10	6	.282	.267	.292	5.23	8.71
Stiward Aquino	R-R	6-6	170	6-20-99	0	1	10.80	2	0	0	0	3	3	4	4	0	5	5	.231	.000	.333	13.50	13.50
Ivan Armstrong	R-R	6-5	247	7-27-00	2	0	0.00	9	0	0	2	11	2	0	0	0	2	12	.057	.000	.087	9.82	1.64
Milleran Cedano	L-L	6-0	165	3-23-03	0	0	0.00	1	1	0	0	5	1	0	0	0	1	6	.067	.200	.000	11.57	1.93
Sandi Charle	R-R	6-5	180	9-5-02	1	0	3.31	14	0	0	0	33	27	14	12	2	12	45	.216	.286	.171	12.40	3.31
Daniel Cordero	R-R	6-2	170	4-23-03	0	0	8.22	5	0	0	0	8	11	9	7	1	8	9	.333	.200	.391	10.57	9.39
Cooper Criswell	R-R	6-6	200	7-24-96	0	0	2.08	5	5	0	0	13	11	3	3	0	2	19	.224	.280	.167	13.15	1.38
Caden Dana	L-R	6-4	215	12-17-03	0	0	1.35	3	3	0	0	7	6	1	1	0	0	6	.240	.200	.267	8.10	0.00
Manuel De La Rosa	R-R	6-2	210	4-17-02	0	0	4.50	7	0	0	0	12	11	6	6	0	9	10	.234	.188	.258	7.50	6.75
Pedro Diaz	R-R	6-3	210	1-9-99	0	0	0.00	1	0	0	0	1	1	0	0	0	2	0	.333	.000	.500	0.00	27.00
Dakota Donovan	R-R	6-6	255	7-25-97	0	0	0.00	2	0	0	0	3	5	0	0	0	0	4	.417	.200	.571	12.00	0.00
Emmanuel Duran	R-R	6-1	182	10-9-00	1	1	2.66	14	0	0	1	20	23	9	6	1	11	23	.291	.188	.362	10.18	4.87

Leonard Garcia	L-L	6-2	165	8-11-03	2	2	7.20	9	5	0	0	30	38	27	24	4	9	34	.302	.189	.348	10.20	2.70
Yendy Gomez	R-R	6-2	170	12-19-03	1	2	10.69	7	2	0	0	16	22	23	19	2	13	13	.328	.409	.289	7.31	7.31
Jenrry Gonzalez	L-L	5-10	185	6-7-01	3	0	0.89	15	0	0	4	20	9	4	2	1	5	32	.130	.100	.143	14.16	2.21
Keythel Key	R-R	6-3	180	10-10-03	0	0	16.20	1	0	0	0	2	0	3	3	0	2	3	.000	.000	.000	16.20	10.80
Brent Killam	L-L	5-11	180	3-26-98	0	1	3.38	2	2	0	0	5	6	2	2	0	1	7	.273	.250	.286	11.81	1.69
Jake Lee	R-R	6-4	215	6-30-95	1	0	0.00	3	1	0	0	4	1	0	0	0	1	7	.077	.333	.000	15.75	2.25
Jean Carlos Lucas	R-R	6-3	185	12-2-00	2	1	1.13	4	0	0	0	8	4	6	1	2	1	13	.138	.167	.130	14.63	1.13
Jorge Marcheco	R-R	6-1	185	8-6-02	5	2	3.20	11	8	0	0	51	42	21	18	3	12	76	.223	.171	.259	13.50	2.13
Alex Martinez	R-R	5-10	170	9-15-02	1	0	0.00	3	0	0	0	4	1	0	0	0	1	8	.077	.000	.167	18.00	2.25
Quinton Martinez	L-L	6-4	190	1-23-99	0	0	3.60	3	0	0	0	5	6	2	2	0	1	4	.273	.200	.333	7.20	1.80
C.J. Mayhue	R-L	5-11	181	1-22-01	1	0	0.00	2	0	0	0	2	2	0	0	0	3	1	.333	.000	.400	5.40	16.20
Victor Morin	R-R	6-6	190	10-30-02	1	1	9.22	7	5	0	0	14	17	15	14	0	9	17	.304	.455	.206	11.20	5.93
Luis Nunez	R-R	6-2	175	9-19-01	3	0	0.99	15	0	0	1	27	17	4	3	0	8	35	.175	.161	.182	11.52	2.63
Adrian Pena	R-R	6-4	180	11-11-02	2	1	4.29	10	2	0	0	21	14	11	10	0	17	32	.187	.226	.159	13.71	7.29
Andrew Peters	R-R	6-2	191	11-25-98	0	0	0.00	2	2	0	0	3	0	0	0	0	0	0	.000	.000	.000	0.00	0.00
Dylan Phillips	L-L	6-0	220	6-16-99	0	1	13.50	2	0	0	0	1	4	2	2	0	1	2	.500	.333	.600	13.50	6.75
Kenny Rosenberg	L-L	6-1	195	7-9-95	0	2	7.50	3	2	0	0	6	8	5	5	1	1	6	.320	.375	.294	9.00	1.50
Dawry Segura	R-R	6-2	140	8-5-03	0	0	9.35	7	0	0	0	9	18	9	9	1	2	7	.429	.286	.500	7.27	2.08
Jose Soriano	R-R	6-3	220	10-20-98	0	0	0.00	4	4	0	0	8	4	0	0	0	2	11	.148	.167	.133	12.38	2.25
John Swanda	R-R	6-2	185	3-18-99	1	0	0.00	3	2	0	0	6	2	0	0	0	0	7	.100	.100	.100	10.50	0.00
Gabriel Tapia	R-R	6-1	160	5-20-02	0	1	6.32	7	0	0	0	16	14	13	11	0	11	18	.233	.250	.225	10.34	6.32
Walbert Urena	R-R	6-0	170	1-25-04	3	4	3.86	12	10	0	0	37	25	24	16	2	32	45	.187	.135	.220	10.85	7.71
Luis Viloria	L-L	5-10	150	9-24-03	1	0	3.14	10	0	0	1	14	12	5	5	1	3	17	.226	.313	.189	10.67	1.88
Kenyon Yovan	R-R	6-2	221	12-28-97	0	0	0.00	5	0	0	0	5	4	0	0	0	1	11	.222	.333	.111	19.80	1.80

Fielding

C: Hidalgo 4, Reina 10, Rodriguez 8, Russell 4, Tinsman 4, Villahermosa 28. **1B:** Coutney 9, Diaz 2, Garcia 21, Selma 2, Sepulveda 23. **2B:** Gobbel 1, Jimenez 8, Lopez 13, Macias 31, Paris 2, Stefanic 3. **3B:** Garcia 24, Gobbel 12, Macias 3, Munroe 4, Nay 3, Sepulveda 11. **SS:** Guzman 48, Lopez 2, Macias 5. **OF:** Dana 2, Diaz 1, Falcon 17, Holt 17, Martinez 3, Moreno 2, Munroe 9, Ortega 30, Reyes 30, Rivas 2, Rivera 1, Ruiz 54, Scull 11, Wilson 5.

DSL ANGELS — *ROOKIE*

DOMINICAN SUMMER LEAGUE

Batting	B-T	HT	WT	DOB	AVG	vLH	vRH	G	AB	R	H	2B	3B	HR	RBI	BB	HBP	SH	SF	SO	SB	CS	SLG	OBP
Eiver Betancourt	L-R	5-11	185	10-2-03	.000	--	.000	2	2	0	0	0	0	0	0	0	0	0	0	0	0	0	.000	.000
Kevyn Castillo	L-L	5-10	170	6-12-05	.225	.250	.214	12	40	7	9	3	0	0	5	6	1	1	0	17	4	2	.300	.340
Jorge Chirinos	R-R	6-0	170	5-11-03	.162	.000	.200	21	37	8	6	2	0	0	2	2	3	0	1	17	0	1	.216	.256
Dewis De Jesus	R-R	5-10	140	3-10-05	.222	.000	.273	13	27	5	6	2	0	0	3	5	0	0	0	5	0	1	.296	.344
Randy De Jesus	R-R	6-4	210	2-13-05	.272	.360	.258	52	184	33	50	13	1	7	43	20	6	0	0	45	5	3	.467	.362
Athanael Duarte	R-R	5-10	165	11-11-04	.210	.250	.202	41	124	20	26	6	1	3	23	22	2	0	1	27	12	2	.347	.336
Wilifer Estrella	B-R	5-11	160	12-5-04	.230	.294	.214	45	87	20	20	1	1	0	6	10	1	3	0	29	5	5	.264	.316
Jerson Florentino	R-R	5-7	155	10-23-04	.209	.214	.208	51	148	30	31	6	2	0	15	19	5	0	2	25	7	0	.277	.316
Dario Laverde	L-R	5-10	160	2-26-05	.298	.208	.315	45	151	35	45	4	6	0	28	21	7	0	2	19	9	4	.404	.403
Jonathan Linares	B-R	6-0	200	4-2-05	.289	.240	.308	31	90	16	26	5	1	0	18	16	4	1	1	16	3	2	.367	.414
Junior Manon	L-R	5-10	165	2-6-03	.303	.286	.308	26	66	17	20	4	0	3	11	21	3	0	1	25	4	1	.500	.484
Juan Mota	L-R	6-2	160	10-23-03	.205	.333	.175	24	78	8	16	1	0	0	9	6	0	0	1	17	2	2	.218	.259
Capri Ortiz	R-R	6-0	150	4-1-05	.241	.184	.255	53	191	28	46	7	5	2	26	14	4	3	1	52	16	8	.361	.305
Nelson Rada	L-L	5-10	160	8-24-05	.311	.103	.356	50	164	50	51	12	3	1	26	26	14	2	0	26	27	6	.439	.446
Ramon Ramirez	L-L	6-2	195	1-30-05	.272	.161	.299	55	158	35	43	14	3	4	38	37	2	0	1	48	2	5	.475	.414
Eliezer Rivero	R-R	6-0	180	3-29-05	.284	.333	.279	23	67	13	19	3	0	0	5	5	3	1	0	12	2	2	.328	.360
Anthony Scull	L-L	6-0	165	1-26-04	.000	.000	--	1	1	0	0	0	0	0	0	0	0	0	0	1	0	0	.000	.000
Luis Torres	R-R	6-3	210	1-12-04	.345	.395	.333	59	203	47	70	20	1	8	41	17	6	0	3	35	8	5	.571	.406

Pitching	B-T	HT	WT	DOB	W	L	ERA	G	GS	CG	SV	IP	H	R	ER	HR	BB	SO	AVG	vLH	vRH	K/9	BB/9
Adrian Acosta	R-R	6-1	170	5-20-05	2	1	6.25	13	7	0	1	32	29	27	22	4	23	37	.236	.250	.227	10.52	6.54
Sadiel Baro	L-L	6-2	177	11-10-04	4	3	4.08	12	9	0	1	53	54	37	24	3	18	60	.254	.261	.251	10.19	3.06
Yhonkervix Castillo	L-L	6-1	158	9-28-02	2	0	1.57	11	0	0	1	23	18	4	4	1	5	26	.225	.231	.224	10.17	1.96
Manuel Cazorla	L-L	6-2	170	1-3-05	4	1	3.47	12	12	0	0	49	48	33	19	1	21	45	.244	.260	.238	8.21	3.83
Jorge Chirinos	R-R	6-0	170	5-11-03	0	0	0.00	1	0	0	0	1	3	0	0	0	0	2	.500	.000	.600	13.50	0.00
Nixon Encarnacion	R-R	6-2	178	12-30-04	3	1	3.28	9	9	0	0	36	30	19	13	1	21	43	.238	.204	.260	10.85	5.30
Miguel Gomez	R-R	6-3	175	1-5-05	1	1	6.60	11	0	0	0	15	14	16	11	2	15	9	.233	.167	.278	5.40	9.00
Bryan Hernandez	R-R	6-1	145	5-25-04	0	1	12.21	12	3	0	0	14	12	22	19	1	25	19	.218	.091	.303	12.21	16.07
Joel Hurtado	R-R	6-2	180	2-6-01	1	1	3.50	5	4	0	0	18	12	8	7	3	9	21	.190	.259	.139	10.50	4.50
David Lopez	L-L	6-4	160	10-8-04	1	0	2.89	12	0	0	0	19	10	8	6	0	17	17	.169	.077	.196	8.20	8.20
Haminton Mendez	R-R	6-1	177	6-5-04	1	1	6.52	15	0	0	2	19	20	17	14	3	8	19	.270	.333	.227	8.84	3.72
Diego Perez	L-R	6-3	170	7-7-03	0	2	7.07	12	0	0	2	14	14	17	11	0	9	8	.264	.333	.219	5.14	5.79
Santiago Quintero	L-L	6-3	180	4-16-05	2	4	3.89	12	7	0	2	44	39	33	19	2	27	48	.245	.313	.238	9.82	5.52
Yokelvin Reyes	L-L	6-1	195	3-29-04	0	2	10.80	8	0	0	0	12	21	16	14	0	6	12	.375	.500	.341	9.26	4.63
Alejandro Rodriguez	L-L	6-0	170	11-15-04	2	1	5.23	14	0	0	1	21	18	14	12	1	26	27	.247	.313	.228	11.76	11.32
Andre Sanchez	R-R	5-10	140	2-5-03	5	2	5.11	13	2	0	1	44	33	27	25	2	23	47	.208	.311	.167	9.61	4.70
Edinson Valdespina	R-R	6-6	190	5-31-04	2	2	5.03	11	7	0	0	39	36	29	22	2	21	36	.240	.357	.170	8.24	4.81
Marco Vega	R-R	6-2	165	10-25-04	5	2	2.88	14	0	0	4	25	22	12	8	1	5	27	.247	.235	.255	9.72	1.80

Fielding

C: Chirinos 3, Laverde 27, Linares 17, Rivero 17. **1B:** Betancourt 1, Chirinos 5, Manon 4, Mota 5, Torres 54. **2B:** De Jesus 5, Duarte 5, Florentino 44, Manon 12. **3B:** Duarte 35, Florentino 2, Manon 5, Mota 20. **SS:** De Jesus 6, Florentino 6, Ortiz 52. **OF:** Castillo 12, Chirinos 8, De Jesus 53, Estrella 43, Rada 49, Ramirez 45, Scull 1, Torres 8

Los Angeles Dodgers

SEASON IN A SENTENCE: The Dodgers overcame injuries to Walker Buehler and Clayton Kershaw and poor seasons from Cody Bellinger and Max Muncy to win a franchise-record 111 games, but their season ended in disappointment after they were upset by the rival Padres in the National League Division Series.

HIGH POINT: Kershaw added another accolade to his illustrious career on April 30 when he passed Hall of Famer Don Sutton to become the Dodgers' all-time strikeout leader at 2,697.

LOW POINT: The Dodgers led the Padres 3-0 in the seventh inning of Game 4 of the NL Division Series and appeared poised to tie the series, but their bullpen collapsed as the Padres scored five runs in the seventh inning to take the lead. The shell-shocked Dodgers failed to respond and were eliminated with a 5-3 loss, their earliest playoff exit since 2019. Manager Dave Roberts' decision to pull starter Tyler Anderson after five scoreless innings and failure to get a reliever up in time to replace a struggling Yency Almonte added further scrutiny to his ability to manage a staff in the postseason.

NOTABLE ROOKIE: The Dodgers overwhelmingly rode their veteran stars to a franchise-record 111 wins and didn't give much playing time to rookies. Righthander Ryan Pepiot was their most significant rookie contributor, going 3-0, 3.47 in nine appearances (seven starts) while showing swing-and-miss stuff but also shoddy control.

KEY TRANSACTIONS: The Dodgers signed all-star first baseman Freddie Freeman to a six-year, $162 million contract before the season. Freeman subsequently led the National League in hits, runs, doubles and on-base percentage and finished one percentage point shy of the NL batting title in his first season in Los Angeles. The Dodgers also made an astute pickup with the signing of Anderson, who went 15-5, 2.57 and made his first all-star team. The Dodgers traded outfielder A.J. Pollock to the White Sox for closer Craig Kimbrel before the season, but Kimbrel pitched so poorly he lost the closer's job and was left off the Dodgers' playoff roster.

ON THE FARM: Six Dodgers affiliates posted winning records during the season, the most of any organization. That included all four full-season affiliates, with High-A Great Lakes and Triple-A Oklahoma City both finishing one game back of the best records in their respective leagues.

OPENING DAY PAYROLL: 284,730,745 (1st).

PLAYERS OF THE YEAR

MAJOR LEAGUE

Mookie Betts
OF
.269/.340/.533
35 HR, 40 2B, 117 R
Won sixth Gold Glove

MINOR LEAGUE

Miguel Vargas
3B
(Triple-A)
.304/.404/.511
17 HR, 32 2B in 113 G

ORGANIZATION LEADERS

Batting		*Minimum 250 AB
MAJORS		
*AVG	Freddie Freeman	.325
*OPS	Freddie Freeman	.918
HR	Mookie Betts	35
RBI	Freddie Freeman	100
RBI	Trea Turner	100
MINORS		
*AVG	Miguel Vargas, Oklahoma City	.304
*OBP	Austin Gauthier, Rancho Cucamonga, Great Lakes	.441
*SLG	James Outman, Tulsa, Oklahoma City	.586
*OPS	James Outman, Tulsa, Oklahoma City	.978
R	Michael Busch, Oklahoma City, Tulsa	118
H	Michael Busch, Oklahoma City, Tulsa	151
TB	Michael Busch, Oklahoma City, Tulsa	285
2B	Michael Busch, Oklahoma City, Tulsa	38
3B	Drew Avans, Oklahoma City	12
HR	Jason Martin, Oklahoma City	32
HR	Michael Busch, Oklahoma City, Tulsa	32
RBI	Michael Busch, Oklahoma City, Tulsa	108
BB	Austin Gauthier, Rancho Cucamonga, Great Lakes	103
SO	Leonel Valera, Tulsa, Great Lakes	176
SB	Drew Avans, Oklahoma City	40

Pitching		#Minimum 75 IP
MAJORS		
W	Julio Urias	17
#ERA	Tony Gonsolin	2.14
SO	Julio Urias	166
SV	Craig Kimbrel	22
MINORS		
W	Alec Gamboa, Tulsa	11
L	Landon Knack, Tulsa	10
#ERA	Gavin Stone, Great Lakes, Tulsa, Oklahoma City	1.48
G	Nick Robertson, Tulsa, Oklahoma City	53
GS	Nick Nastrini, Great Lakes, Tulsa	27
SV	Carson Fulmer, Oklahoma City	12
IP	Gavin Stone, Great Lakes, Tulsa, Oklahoma City	122
BB	Andre Jackson, Oklahoma City	61
SO	Nick Nastrini, Great Lakes, Tulsa	169
#AVG	Nick Nastrini, Great Lakes, Tulsa	.180

2022 PERFORMANCE

General Manager: Brandon Gomes. **Farm Director:** Will Rhymes. **Scouting Director:** Billy Gasparino.

Class	Team	League	W	L	PCT	Finish	Manager
Majors	Los Angeles Dodgers	National	111	51	.685	1st (15)	Dave Roberts
Triple-A	Oklahoma City Dodgers	Pacific Coast	84	66	.560	3rd (10)	Travis Barbary
Double-A	Tulsa Drillers	Texas	69	67	.507	4th (10)	Scott Hennessey
High-A	Great Lakes Loons	Midwest	76	55	.580	2nd (12)	Austin Chubb
Low-A	Rancho Cucamonga Quakes	California	68	64	.515	5th (8)	John Shoemaker
Rookie	ACL Dodgers	Arizona Complex	25	29	.463	t-11th (18)	Jair Fernandez
Overall 2022 Minor League Record			393	328	.545	4th (30)	

ORGANIZATION STATISTICS

LOS ANGELES DODGERS

NATIONAL LEAGUE

Batting	B-T	HT	WT	DOB	AVG	vLH	vRH	G	AB	R	H	2B	3B	HR	RBI	BB	HBP	SH	SF	SO	SB	CS	SLG	OBP
Hanser Alberto	R-R	5-11	215	10-17-92	.244	.279	.173	73	156	13	38	9	2	2	15	3	0	0	0	25	0	1	.365	.258
Eddy Alvarez	L-R	5-9	185	1-30-90	.160	.000	.174	14	25	1	4	0	0	0	3	0	0	1	1	9	1	0	.160	.154
Austin Barnes	R-R	5-10	187	12-28-89	.212	.182	.230	62	179	31	38	6	0	8	26	27	3	2	1	37	2	1	.380	.324
Cody Bellinger	L-L	6-4	203	7-13-95	.210	.213	.209	144	504	70	106	27	3	19	68	38	2	0	6	150	14	3	.389	.265
Mookie Betts	R-R	5-9	180	10-7-92	.269	.308	.255	142	572	117	154	40	3	35	82	55	8	0	4	104	12	2	.533	.340
Freddie Freeman	L-R	6-5	220	9-12-89	.325	.294	.338	159	612	117	199	47	2	21	100	84	5	0	7	102	13	3	.511	.407
Joey Gallo	L-R	6-5	250	11-19-93	.162	.143	.165	44	117	16	19	4	1	7	23	16	3	0	1	57	1	0	.393	.277
Jake Lamb	L-R	6-3	215	10-9-90	.239	.000	.254	25	67	10	16	5	1	2	4	8	2	0	0	24	0	1	.433	.338
Gavin Lux	L-R	6-2	190	11-23-97	.276	.263	.280	129	421	66	116	20	7	6	42	47	0	0	3	95	7	2	.399	.346
Zach McKinstry	L-R	6-0	180	4-29-95	.091	.000	.111	10	11	4	1	0	0	1	2	3	0	0	0	4	0	0	.364	.286
2-team total (47 Chicago Cubs)					.199	.188	.200	57	166	21	33	6	3	5	14	16	1	2	0	52	7	0	.361	.273
Max Muncy	L-R	6-0	215	8-25-90	.196	.178	.202	136	464	69	91	22	1	21	69	90	5	0	6	141	2	0	.384	.329
James Outman	L-R	6-3	215	5-14-97	.462	.000	.500	4	13	6	6	2	0	1	3	2	1	0	0	7	0	0	.846	.563
Kevin Pillar	R-R	6-0	200	1-4-89	.083	.333	.000	4	12	1	1	1	0	0	0	1	0	0	0	4	0	0	.167	.154
Edwin Rios	L-R	6-3	220	4-21-94	.244	.231	.247	27	86	12	21	1	0	7	17	5	1	0	0	36	0	1	.500	.293
Will Smith	R-R	5-10	195	3-28-95	.260	.300	.247	137	508	68	132	26	3	24	87	56	10	0	4	96	1	0	.465	.343
Chris Taylor	R-R	6-1	196	8-29-90	.221	.193	.233	118	402	45	89	25	3	10	43	44	5	0	3	160	10	1	.373	.304
Trayce Thompson	R-R	6-3	225	3-15-91	.268	.188	.320	74	205	35	55	14	1	13	39	30	2	0	2	86	4	0	.537	.364
2-team total (6 San Diego Padres)					.256	.174	.308	80	219	36	56	14	1	13	41	32	2	0	2	93	4	1	.507	.353
Justin Turner	R-R	5-11	202	11-23-84	.278	.275	.279	128	468	61	130	36	0	13	81	50	6	0	8	89	3	0	.438	.350
Trea Turner	R-R	6-2	185	6-30-93	.298	.298	.298	160	652	101	194	39	4	21	100	45	3	0	6	131	27	3	.466	.343
Miguel Vargas	R-R	6-3	205	11-17-99	.170	.174	.167	18	47	4	8	1	0	1	8	2	0	0	1	13	1	0	.255	.200
Tony Wolters	L-R	5-10	195	6-9-92	.000	--	.000	2	4	0	0	0	0	0	0	0	0	0	0	3	0	0	.000	.000

Pitching	B-T	HT	WT	DOB	W	L	ERA	G	GS	CG	SV	IP	H	R	ER	HR	BB	SO	AVG	vLH	vRH	K/9	BB/9
Hanser Alberto	R-R	5-11	215	10-17-92	0	0	4.09	10	0	0	0	11	10	5	5	2	3	1	.238	.211	.261	0.82	2.45
Yency Almonte	R-R	6-5	223	6-4-94	0	0	1.02	33	0	0	1	35	18	4	4	2	10	33	.150	.071	.192	8.41	2.55
Tyler Anderson	L-L	6-2	220	12-30-89	15	5	2.57	30	28	0	0	179	145	57	51	14	34	138	.221	.234	.218	6.95	1.71
Phil Bickford	R-R	6-4	200	7-10-95	2	1	4.72	60	0	0	0	61	53	33	32	12	14	67	.233	.247	.227	9.89	2.07
Justin Bruihl	L-L	6-2	215	6-26-97	1	1	3.80	24	0	0	1	24	22	11	10	4	6	13	.253	.234	.275	4.94	2.28
Walker Buehler	R-R	6-2	185	7-28-94	6	3	4.02	12	12	1	0	65	67	30	29	8	17	58	.263	.271	.252	8.03	2.35
Garrett Cleavinger	R-L	6-1	220	4-23-94	0	1	10.38	4	0	0	0	4	6	7	5	1	3	7	.333	.500	.250	14.54	6.23
Robbie Erlin	R-L	5-11	200	10-8-90	0	0	9.00	2	0	0	0	2	2	2	2	1	1	1	.250	.400	.000	4.50	4.50
Caleb Ferguson	R-L	6-3	226	7-2-96	1	0	1.82	37	1	0	0	35	23	9	7	1	17	37	.187	.243	.163	9.61	4.41
Tony Gonsolin	R-R	6-3	205	5-14-94	16	1	2.14	24	24	0	0	130	79	32	31	11	35	119	.172	.163	.184	8.22	2.42
Brusdar Graterol	R-R	6-1	265	8-26-98	2	4	3.26	46	1	0	4	50	39	20	18	3	10	43	.215	.292	.165	7.79	1.81
Shane Greene	R-R	6-4	200	11-17-88	1	0	0.00	1	0	0	0	2	2	0	0	0	0	1	.250	.250	.250	4.50	0.00
Michael Grove	R-R	6-3	200	12-18-96	1	0	4.60	7	6	0	0	29	32	21	15	6	10	24	.260	.275	.241	7.36	3.07
Andrew Heaney	L-L	6-2	200	6-5-91	4	4	3.10	16	14	0	0	73	60	34	25	14	19	110	.214	.230	.210	13.62	2.35
Heath Hembree	R-R	6-4	220	1-13-89	1	1	7.94	6	0	0	0	6	9	6	5	1	3	5	.360	.462	.250	7.94	4.76
2-team total (20 Pittsburgh Pirates)					3	1	7.36	26	0	0	0	22	26	19	18	6	17	17	.299	.452	.214	6.95	6.95
Daniel Hudson	R-R	6-3	215	3-9-87	2	3	2.22	25	0	0	5	24	17	7	6	1	5	30	.193	.174	.214	11.10	1.85
Andre Jackson	R-R	6-3	210	5-1-96	0	0	1.86	4	0	0	1	10	9	3	2	0	4	9	.243	.167	.280	8.38	3.72
Tommy Kahnle	R-R	6-1	230	8-7-89	0	0	2.84	13	0	0	1	13	5	4	4	2	3	14	.128	.154	.077	9.95	2.13
Clayton Kershaw	L-L	6-4	225	3-19-88	12	3	2.28	22	22	0	0	126	96	36	32	10	23	137	.206	.254	.198	9.76	1.64
Craig Kimbrel	R-R	6-0	215	5-28-88	6	7	3.75	63	0	0	22	60	51	31	25	4	28	72	.227	.261	.193	10.80	4.20
Chris Martin	R-R	6-8	225	6-2-86	3	1	1.46	26	0	0	2	25	12	4	4	1	1	34	.135	.111	.151	12.41	0.36
2-team total (34 Chicago Cubs)					4	1	3.05	60	0	0	2	56	50	20	19	6	5	74	.230	.232	.229	11.89	0.80
Dustin May	R-R	6-6	180	9-6-97	2	3	4.50	6	6	0	0	30	21	17	15	3	14	29	.194	.148	.241	8.70	4.20
Reyes Moronta	R-R	5-10	265	1-6-93	0	0	4.18	22	0	0	0	24	17	11	11	5	10	27	.198	.138	.228	10.27	3.80
2-team total (17 Arizona Diamondbacks)					2	2	4.30	39	0	0	2	38	30	20	18	5	18	38	.214	.174	.234	9.08	4.30
Ryan Pepiot	R-R	6-3	215	8-21-97	3	0	3.47	9	7	0	0	36	26	15	14	6	27	42	.200	.239	.159	10.40	6.69

Evan Phillips	R-R	6-2	215	9-11-94	7	3	1.14	64	0	0	2	63	33	11	8	2	15	77	.155	.170	.142	11.00	2.14
David Price	L-L	6-5	215	8-26-85	2	0	2.45	40	0	0	2	40	38	11	11	6	9	37	.242	.271	.224	8.26	2.01
Jake Reed	R-R	6-2	195	9-29-92	0	0	1.93	5	0	0	1	5	6	1	1	0	1	2	.316	.429	.250	3.86	1.93
2-team total (5 New York Mets)					1	0	7.36	10	0	0	1	11	10	9	9	2	7	8	.238	.417	.167	6.55	5.73
Blake Treinen	R-R	6-5	225	6-30-88	1	1	1.80	5	0	0	0	5	1	1	1	1	1	6	.063	.000	.111	10.80	1.80
Julio Urias	L-L	6-0	225	8-12-96	17	7	2.16	31	31	0	0	175	127	51	42	23	41	166	.199	.178	.204	8.54	2.11
Alex Vesia	L-L	6-1	209	4-11-96	5	0	2.15	63	0	0	1	54	37	14	13	2	24	79	.187	.130	.217	13.09	3.98
Mitch White	R-R	6-3	210	12-28-94	1	2	3.70	15	10	0	0	56	51	25	23	6	19	47	.237	.225	.248	7.55	3.05

Fielding

Catcher	PCT	G	PO	A	E	DP	PB
Barnes	.993	55	521	12	4	3	2
Smith	.997	109	968	32	3	6	4
Wolters	1.000	1	5	1	0	0	0

First Base	PCT	G	PO	A	E	DP
Alberto	1.000	3	7	1	0	1
Freeman	.996	159	1155	91	5	100
Gallo	1.000	1	1	0	0	0
Lamb	1.000	2	4	0	0	2
Muncy	1.000	3	4	1	0	1
Rios	1.000	4	5	1	0	1
Vargas	1.000	8	35	3	0	2

Second Base	PCT	G	PO	A	E	DP
Alberto	.966	37	32	54	3	14
Barnes	.000	1	0	0	0	0
Betts	1.000	7	9	15	0	7
Lux	.973	102	148	180	9	45
McKinstry	1.000	2	1	1	0	0
Muncy	.981	31	35	69	2	13
Taylor	1.000	22	27	53	0	8
Wolters	.000	1	0	0	0	0

Third Base	PCT	G	PO	A	E	DP
Alberto	1.000	20	17	23	0	3
Alvarez	1.000	5	2	5	0	2
McKinstry	.000	1	0	0	0	0
Muncy	.955	84	51	161	10	25
Rios	1.000	4	2	4	0	0
Taylor	1.000	3	0	1	0	0
Turner	.961	66	33	138	7	16
Vargas	.000	1	0	0	0	0

Shortstop	PCT	G	PO	A	E	DP
Alberto	1.000	5	4	4	0	2
Alvarez	.000	1	0	0	0	0
Lux	1.000	9	3	11	0	3
McKinstry	1.000	1	1	2	0	1
Taylor	.000	1	0	0	0	0
Turner	.969	160	174	334	16	54

Outfield	PCT	G	PO	A	E	DP
Alberto	--	1	0	0	0	0
Alvarez	.917	6	11	0	1	0
Bellinger	.991	144	322	2	3	0
Betts	.994	136	298	8	2	4
Gallo	.983	42	55	2	1	0
Lamb	1.000	9	3	0	0	0
Lux	1.000	28	29	0	0	0
McKinstry	1.000	4	6	0	0	0
Outman	1.000	4	3	0	0	0
Pillar	1.000	5	7	0	0	0
Taylor	.988	100	165	3	2	2
Thompson	1.000	76	119	1	0	1
Vargas	.900	7	9	0	1	0

OKLAHOMA CITY DODGERS — *TRIPLE-A*

PACIFIC COAST LEAGUE

Batting	B-T	HT	WT	DOB	AVG	vLH	vRH	G	AB	R	H	2B	3B	HR	RBI	BB	HBP	SH	SF	SO	SB	CS	SLG	OBP
Eddy Alvarez	L-R	5-9	185	1-30-90	.322	.237	.345	47	177	40	57	9	4	8	29	28	9	1	0	55	3	3	.554	.439
Jacob Amaya	R-R	6-0	180	9-3-98	.259	.293	.247	84	294	46	76	10	1	8	45	49	4	0	4	83	3	1	.381	.368
Drew Avans	L-L	5-10	195	6-13-96	.282	.294	.279	119	432	94	122	17	12	7	48	61	7	3	1	129	40	7	.426	.379
Andy Burns	R-R	6-2	205	8-7-90	.223	.289	.192	90	283	44	63	14	0	7	37	46	1	0	2	86	5	3	.346	.331
Michael Busch	L-R	6-1	210	11-9-97	.266	.240	.276	111	444	87	118	32	0	21	79	50	5	0	5	131	3	2	.480	.343
Omar Estevez	R-R	5-10	185	2-25-98	.216	.306	.177	52	162	24	35	10	0	3	24	12	2	0	2	40	1	1	.333	.275
Hunter Feduccia	L-R	6-2	215	6-5-97	.240	.182	.256	40	150	25	36	14	0	7	25	17	1	0	0	45	0	0	.473	.321
Ty Kelly	B-R	6-0	180	7-20-88	.180	.091	.205	22	50	6	9	2	1	0	4	6	0	0	1	16	0	0	.260	.263
Jake Lamb	L-R	6-3	215	10-9-90	.290	.400	.270	61	231	44	67	12	0	15	50	39	3	0	3	74	1	1	.537	.395
Devin Mann	R-R	6-3	180	2-11-97	.258	.323	.238	44	132	25	34	5	3	5	26	21	3	0	0	36	0	0	.455	.372
Hamlet Marte	R-R	5-10	180	2-3-94	.083	.000	.091	7	12	0	1	0	0	0	1	2	0	0	0	8	0	1	.083	.214
Jason Martin	L-R	5-9	185	9-5-95	.285	.284	.285	129	470	100	134	25	5	32	107	68	1	1	4	135	8	5	.564	.374
Zach McKinstry	L-R	6-0	180	4-29-95	.335	.311	.342	48	191	36	64	9	4	4	25	27	2	0	3	33	0	3	.487	.417
Max Muncy	L-R	6-0	215	8-25-90	.143	.000	.154	4	14	1	2	0	0	1	2	3	0	0	0	6	0	0	.357	.294
Ryan Noda	L-L	6-3	217	3-30-96	.259	.246	.263	135	464	86	120	23	1	25	90	92	15	0	3	162	20	4	.474	.395
James Outman	L-R	6-3	215	5-14-97	.292	.208	.336	57	212	42	62	14	6	15	61	32	4	0	3	63	6	1	.627	.390
Kevin Pillar	R-R	6-0	200	1-4-89	.315	.419	.288	42	149	42	47	7	3	10	40	20	3	0	4	22	2	1	.604	.398
Edwin Rios	L-R	6-3	220	4-21-94	.259	.288	.248	48	189	32	49	17	0	9	39	20	5	0	4	66	0	1	.492	.339
Stefen Romero	R-R	6-2	220	10-17-88	.265	.237	.281	30	102	18	27	8	0	3	22	11	4	0	2	24	1	0	.431	.353
Chris Taylor	R-R	6-1	196	8-29-90	.429	.600	.000	2	7	2	3	0	0	2	3	0	1	0	0	0	0	0	1.286	.500
Tomas Telis	B-R	5-8	220	6-18-91	.287	.300	.281	80	275	34	79	9	0	2	36	30	5	1	2	31	0	0	.342	.365
Miguel Vargas	R-R	6-3	205	11-17-99	.304	.351	.291	113	438	100	133	32	4	17	82	71	6	0	5	76	16	5	.511	.404
Tony Wolters	L-R	5-10	195	6-9-92	.230	.222	.232	61	204	21	47	9	1	0	29	26	2	0	2	58	0	0	.284	.321

Pitching	B-T	HT	WT	DOB	W	L	ERA	G	GS	CG	SV	IP	H	R	ER	HR	BB	SO	AVG	vLH	vRH	K/9	BB/9
Jose Adames	R-R	6-2	165	1-17-93	2	1	6.14	18	0	0	1	22	22	17	15	1	23	37	.259	.286	.246	15.14	9.41
Yency Almonte	R-R	6-5	223	6-4-94	0	1	4.00	14	0	0	3	18	14	8	8	3	1	28	.209	.438	.137	14.00	0.50
Yadier Alvarez	R-R	6-3	175	3-7-96	3	1	6.20	23	0	0	0	25	28	23	17	1	23	22	.289	.216	.333	8.03	8.39
Pedro Baez	R-R	6-0	232	3-11-88	0	1	14.29	7	0	0	0	6	13	9	9	1	2	3	.433	.429	.435	4.76	3.18
Dellin Betances	R-R	6-8	265	3-23-88	0	3	11.08	15	1	0	0	13	10	17	16	2	14	12	.204	.211	.200	8.31	9.69
Phil Bickford	R-R	6-4	200	7-10-95	0	0	9.00	6	0	0	0	5	4	5	5	2	3	6	.222	.125	.300	10.80	5.40
Justin Bruihl	L-L	6-2	215	6-26-97	3	1	3.56	25	1	0	0	30	32	15	12	2	20	24	.264	.309	.227	7.12	5.93
Beau Burrows	R-R	6-2	210	9-18-96	8	6	7.18	31	16	0	1	100	123	85	80	18	60	95	.303	.265	.327	8.52	5.38
Dakota Chalmers	R-R	6-3	175	10-8-96	1	0	8.31	13	0	0	0	13	15	13	12	1	19	15	.273	.320	.233	10.38	13.15
Garrett Cleavinger	R-L	6-1	220	4-23-94	0	2	2.79	22	1	0	1	29	20	9	9	4	17	47	.192	.182	.197	14.59	5.28
Keegan Curtis	R-R	6-0	175	9-30-95	2	1	4.05	3	1	0	0	7	9	3	3	0	0	10	.310	.222	.350	13.50	0.00
Danny Duffy	L-L	6-3	205	12-21-88	0	0	7.36	4	0	0	0	4	4	3	3	0	2	6	.267	.400	.200	14.73	4.91
Jon Duplantier	L-R	6-4	229	7-11-94	5	3	4.80	34	14	0	0	94	85	56	50	18	57	109	.235	.298	.195	10.47	5.48
Robbie Erlin	R-L	5-11	200	10-8-90	5	4	7.01	21	14	0	0	77	95	63	60	14	35	69	.296	.237	.314	8.06	4.09
Caleb Ferguson	R-L	6-3	226	7-2-96	0	1	7.36	10	2	0	0	7	10	8	6	1	4	13	.313	.375	.292	15.95	4.91
Carson Fulmer	R-R	6-0	210	12-13-93	6	6	2.86	49	1	0	12	57	36	28	18	4	35	62	.177	.257	.135	9.85	5.56

Sam Gaviglio	R-R	6-1	215	5-22-90	6	4	6.35	17	9	0	1	67	83	56	47	12	26	67	.303	.394	.242	9.05	3.51
Tony Gonsolin	R-R	6-3	205	5-14-94	0	0	0.00	1	1	0	0	2	1	0	0	0	0	2	.167	.333	.000	9.00	0.00
Victor Gonzalez	L-L	6-0	180	11-16-95	1	0	3.09	12	0	0	0	12	10	4	4	1	5	10	.222	.200	.233	7.71	3.86
Brusdar Graterol	R-R	6-1	265	8-26-98	1	0	0.00	4	0	0	0	4	1	0	0	0	1	4	.091	--	.091	9.82	2.45
Shane Greene	R-R	6-4	200	11-17-88	0	1	5.87	7	0	0	0	8	13	5	5	0	4	9	.351	.333	.360	10.57	4.70
Michael Grove	R-R	6-3	200	12-18-96	1	4	4.07	14	12	0	0	60	56	32	27	10	21	68	.247	.286	.224	10.26	3.17
Justin Hagenman	R-R	6-3	205	10-7-96	4	2	6.08	41	2	0	1	53	60	36	36	8	21	55	.286	.273	.293	9.28	3.54
Andrew Heaney	L-L	6-2	200	6-5-91	0	1	1.23	2	2	0	0	7	4	1	1	0	0	10	.160	.200	.133	12.27	0.00
Heath Hembree	R-R	6-4	220	1-13-89	1	0	4.82	10	0	0	1	9	7	5	5	2	2	14	.200	.154	.227	13.50	1.93
Andre Jackson	R-R	6-3	210	5-1-96	2	7	5.00	21	19	0	1	76	68	48	42	10	61	76	.234	.211	.247	9.04	7.26
Tommy Kahnle	R-R	6-1	230	8-7-89	1	0	3.72	10	0	0	0	10	8	4	4	2	3	10	.216	.214	.217	9.31	2.79
Marshall Kasowski	L-R	6-3	215	3-10-95	1	0	3.70	47	1	0	0	56	37	23	23	3	39	68	.192	.254	.162	10.93	6.27
Keone Kela	R-R	6-1	220	4-16-93	1	1	6.75	7	0	0	0	7	7	6	5	0	10	5	.269	.286	.263	6.75	13.50
2-team total (9 Reno Aces)					1	2	5.74	16	0	0	1	16	14	11	10	2	15	16	.233	.292	.194	9.19	8.62
Ty Kelly	B-R	6-0	180	7-20-88	0	0	18.00	1	0	0	0	1	3	2	2	0	1	0	.600	1.000	.333	0.00	9.00
Jose Martinez	R-R	6-0	194	4-23-99	0	1	12.00	1	1	0	0	3	3	4	4	0	3	5	.250	.222	.333	15.00	9.00
Dustin May	R-R	6-6	180	9-6-97	1	0	1.89	5	5	0	0	19	14	4	4	2	6	33	.192	.273	.157	15.63	2.84
Bobby Miller	L-R	6-5	220	4-5-99	1	1	3.38	4	4	1	0	21	17	10	8	4	6	28	.218	.100	.292	11.81	2.53
Reyes Moronta	R-R	5-10	265	1-6-93	1	0	2.70	11	0	0	2	10	8	3	3	1	9	17	.216	.000	.276	15.30	8.10
Darien Nunez	L-L	6-2	205	3-19-93	1	0	7.71	3	0	0	0	5	5	4	4	1	2	6	.278	.333	.250	11.57	3.86
Aaron Ochsenbein	R-R	6-3	225	2-29-96	1	3	6.97	17	1	0	0	21	23	18	16	3	15	17	.277	.280	.276	7.40	6.53
Ryan Pepiot	R-R	6-3	215	8-21-97	9	1	2.56	19	17	0	0	91	62	27	26	10	36	114	.193	.194	.193	11.23	3.55
Yefry Ramirez	R-R	6-2	215	11-28-93	2	1	3.76	8	7	1	0	41	35	20	17	5	11	30	.232	.170	.265	6.64	2.43
Jake Reed	R-R	6-2	195	9-29-92	2	0	0.87	10	0	0	0	10	8	1	1	0	3	11	.211	.200	.214	9.58	2.61
Nick Robertson	R-R	6-6	265	7-16-98	0	0	2.31	9	0	0	2	12	10	4	3	0	3	15	.222	.167	.242	11.57	2.31
Hansel Robles	R-R	6-0	220	8-13-90	1	0	8.00	20	1	0	0	18	16	16	16	2	14	18	.232	.217	.239	9.00	7.00
Logan Salow	L-L	6-1	185	9-27-94	0	0	6.00	3	1	0	0	3	1	3	2	1	4	4	.091	.000	.167	12.00	12.00
Gavin Stone	R-R	6-1	175	10-15-98	2	1	1.16	6	6	0	0	23	14	5	3	1	8	33	.169	.179	.164	12.73	3.09
Blake Treinen	R-R	6-5	225	6-30-88	0	0	4.50	7	0	0	0	6	8	5	3	0	1	9	.296	.444	.222	13.50	1.50
Bobby Wahl	R-R	6-3	216	3-21-92	0	0	15.43	6	0	0	0	5	5	8	8	2	6	6	.278	.500	.100	11.57	11.57
Mark Washington	R-R	6-7	205	3-22-96	1	2	5.61	27	1	0	0	34	42	21	21	5	15	30	.321	.250	.367	8.02	4.01
Mitch White	R-R	6-3	210	12-28-94	2	0	0.00	2	2	0	0	12	3	0	0	0	2	10	.081	.071	.111	7.71	1.54
Mike Wright Jr.	R-R	6-6	240	1-3-90	2	3	4.46	10	6	0	0	34	35	20	17	3	20	26	.267	.286	.256	6.82	5.24
Daniel Zamora	L-L	6-3	195	4-15-93	4	2	3.86	51	1	0	3	63	58	36	27	5	27	71	.242	.188	.271	10.14	3.86

Fielding

Catcher	PCT	G	PO	A	E	DP	PB
Feduccia	1.000	32	323	13	0	2	1
Marte	.917	3	11	0	1	0	0
Telis	.992	63	557	30	5	0	5
Wolters	.985	60	566	32	9	4	4

First Base	PCT	G	PO	A	E	DP
Burns	1.000	8	47	2	0	2
Lamb	1.000	34	236	16	0	24
Mann	1.000	5	27	5	0	5
Noda	.994	104	760	37	5	75
Telis	1.000	1	2	0	0	0
Vargas	1.000	3	13	0	0	1

Second Base	PCT	G	PO	A	E	DP
Alvarez	.982	13	31	24	1	3
Amaya	1.000	4	6	4	0	1
Burns	.963	12	25	27	2	5
Busch	.963	93	138	200	13	62
Estevez	.857	2	3	3	1	2
Kelly	1.000	11	7	16	0	4
Mann	.963	8	9	17	1	3
McKinstry	1.000	5	7	9	0	3
Muncy	1.000	2	2	5	0	1
Taylor	1.000	1	1	1	0	0
Vargas	1.000	7	10	15	0	5
Wolters	1.000	1	2	0	0	0

Third Base	PCT	G	PO	A	E	DP
Alvarez	1.000	4	3	7	0	2
Burns	.925	20	9	28	3	2
Kelly	1.000	3	0	3	0	0
Lamb	.833	3	1	4	1	0
Mann	.968	18	9	21	1	4
McKinstry	1.000	2	3	0	0	0
Muncy	1.000	2	0	3	0	0
Rios	.881	33	24	65	12	11
Taylor	.000	1	0	0	0	0
Vargas	.919	74	46	124	15	8

Shortstop	PCT	G	PO	A	E	DP
Alvarez	.975	22	30	47	2	14
Amaya	.960	80	76	190	11	37
Burns	.952	12	11	29	2	9
Estevez	1.000	4	3	5	0	1
Mann	1.000	1	0	2	0	0
McKinstry	.934	33	37	77	8	8

Outfield	PCT	G	PO	A	E	DP
Alvarez	1.000	7	12	1	0	0
Avans	.976	118	242	6	6	0
Burns	.943	28	30	3	2	0
Busch	.944	11	17	0	1	0
Estevez	1.000	23	30	1	0	0
Kelly	1.000	1	1	0	0	0
Lamb	1.000	3	3	0	0	0
Mann	1.000	14	12	1	0	0
Martin	.973	119	211	4	6	2
McKinstry	1.000	7	14	1	0	1
Noda	.957	21	22	0	1	0
Outman	.991	53	111	2	1	0
Pillar	.985	34	66	1	1	0
Romero	.973	19	35	1	1	0
Taylor	--	1	0	0	0	0
Vargas	.963	23	26	0	1	0

TULSA DRILLERS — *DOUBLE-A*

TEXAS LEAGUE

Batting	B-T	HT	WT	DOB	AVG	vLH	vRH	G	AB	R	H	2B	3B	HR	RBI	BB	HBP	SH	SF	SO	SB	CS	SLG	OBP
Ismael Alcantara	R-R	6-1	165	9-25-98	.235	.182	.261	10	34	4	8	0	1	3	5	7	2	0	0	11	2	1	.559	.395
Jacob Amaya	R-R	6-0	180	9-3-98	.264	.362	.230	49	182	39	48	10	3	9	26	32	0	0	2	29	3	1	.500	.370
Abiatal Avelino	R-R	6-0	210	2-14-95	.230	.242	.224	60	209	30	48	10	0	7	26	14	4	1	2	38	9	1	.378	.288
Kenneth Betancourt	R-R	5-8	160	2-5-00	.253	.217	.267	25	83	9	21	3	0	0	7	3	0	1	0	19	1	1	.289	.279
Chris Betts	L-R	6-2	215	3-10-97	.146	.080	.172	27	89	14	13	4	0	5	14	13	0	0	0	48	0	0	.360	.255
Michael Busch	L-R	6-1	210	11-9-97	.306	.333	.295	31	108	31	33	6	0	11	29	24	4	0	1	36	1	0	.667	.445
Wladimir Chalo	R-R	5-8	197	4-21-00	.000	.000	.000	1	4	0	0	0	0	0	0	0	0	0	0	3	0	0	.000	.000
Jonny DeLuca	R-R	6-0	200	7-10-98	.298	.364	.268	25	104	22	31	5	3	7	20	8	3	2	2	17	5	0	.606	.359
Hunter Feduccia	L-R	6-2	215	6-5-97	.236	.227	.240	43	144	21	34	6	1	8	26	24	0	0	2	38	0	0	.458	.341
Kody Hoese	R-R	6-4	200	7-13-97	.232	.228	.233	77	289	32	67	10	2	5	34	20	1	0	3	76	1	1	.332	.281
Ryan January	L-R	6-3	210	5-27-97	.143	.313	.098	27	77	12	11	1	0	3	10	19	3	0	0	30	0	0	.273	.333
Ty Kelly	B-R	6-0	180	7-20-88	.063	.000	.091	5	16	0	1	0	0	0	0	1	0	0	0	3	0	0	.063	.118

Jeren Kendall	L-R	5-11	190	2-4-96	.162	.105	.173	84	234	34	38	9	2	6	19	34	4	0	1	99	26	4	.295	.278
Brandon Lewis	R-R	6-2	222	10-23-98	.209	.202	.212	110	397	60	83	19	0	24	71	28	7	0	4	147	0	1	.438	.271
Devin Mann	R-R	6-3	180	2-11-97	.267	.273	.266	74	243	45	65	16	0	11	35	43	5	0	3	50	1	2	.469	.384
James Outman	L-R	6-3	215	5-14-97	.295	.269	.304	68	261	59	77	17	1	16	45	38	6	0	2	89	7	3	.552	.394
Andy Pages	R-R	6-1	212	12-8-00	.236	.316	.211	132	487	69	115	29	3	26	80	62	15	0	7	140	6	3	.468	.336
Buddy Reed	B-R	6-4	218	4-27-95	.274	.323	.245	28	84	20	23	6	0	2	6	8	0	1	0	30	9	1	.417	.337
Kekai Rios	R-R	5-11	205	6-6-97	.250	.500	.167	3	8	0	2	0	0	0	0	2	0	0	0	1	0	0	.250	.400
Carson Taylor	B-R	6-2	205	6-2-99	.253	.254	.252	76	269	31	68	11	0	4	23	29	4	0	1	67	0	0	.338	.333
Leonel Valera	R-R	6-2	210	7-9-99	.290	.349	.269	88	321	61	93	12	5	13	62	33	4	0	2	119	22	1	.480	.361
Ryan Ward	L-R	5-11	200	2-23-98	.255	.257	.254	116	459	62	117	18	2	28	78	39	5	0	2	116	5	1	.486	.319
Justin Yurchak	L-R	6-1	204	9-17-96	.282	.213	.300	110	393	52	111	22	0	8	48	53	5	0	0	61	2	1	.399	.375

Pitching	B-T	HT	WT	DOB	W	L	ERA	G	GS	CG	SV	IP	H	R	ER	HR	BB	SO	AVG	vLH	vRH	K/9	BB/9
Jose Adames	R-R	6-2	165	1-17-93	1	3	3.60	22	0	0	0	25	17	14	10	1	17	35	.198	.214	.190	12.60	6.12
Abiatal Avelino	R-R	6-0	210	2-14-95	0	0	0.00	5	0	0	1	5	2	0	0	0	2	0	.133	.143	.125	0.00	3.60
Clayton Beeter	R-R	6-2	220	10-9-98	0	3	5.75	18	16	0	0	52	48	37	33	10	35	88	.235	.256	.221	15.33	6.10
Jake Cantleberry	L-L	6-1	180	8-8-97	1	0	6.08	10	0	0	0	13	13	9	9	1	12	5	.277	.200	.364	3.38	8.10
Keegan Curtis	R-R	6-0	175	9-30-95	2	1	7.13	16	1	0	1	18	22	15	14	2	8	18	.293	.400	.255	9.17	4.08
2-team total (14 Amarillo Sod Poodles)					3	4	7.75	30	1	0	1	34	43	30	29	6	17	32	.299	.261	.316	8.55	4.54
Tanner Dodson	B-R	6-1	160	5-9-97	4	0	8.39	29	0	0	1	34	45	33	32	2	36	29	.326	.296	.345	7.60	9.44
Austin Drury	L-L	5-11	190	8-13-97	4	1	4.34	28	0	0	1	37	43	26	18	2	35	30	.287	.321	.266	7.23	8.44
Nick Frasso	R-R	6-5	200	10-18-98	0	0	5.40	4	4	0	0	12	12	7	7	1	7	10	.261	.261	.261	7.71	5.40
Alec Gamboa	B-L	6-1	205	1-17-97	11	4	5.91	30	6	0	1	88	87	60	58	11	47	72	.257	.285	.239	7.34	4.79
Cameron Gibbens	L-R	6-8	194	7-4-95	0	0	25.58	9	0	0	0	6	1	18	18	0	25	9	.053	.250	.000	12.79	35.53
Michael Grove	R-R	6-3	200	12-18-96	0	1	2.76	5	5	0	0	16	11	8	5	1	5	22	.180	.263	.143	12.12	2.76
Justin Hagenman	R-R	6-3	205	10-7-96	1	1	2.79	5	0	0	0	10	7	3	3	1	1	10	.189	.357	.087	9.31	0.93
Andrew Heaney	L-L	6-2	200	6-5-91	0	0	0.00	1	1	0	0	5	2	0	0	0	1	9	.118	.167	.091	16.20	1.80
Jose Hernandez	L-L	6-3	205	12-31-97	3	2	3.96	36	2	0	0	39	30	18	17	7	18	47	.219	.232	.206	10.94	4.19
Kyle Hurt	R-R	6-3	240	5-30-98	1	5	9.29	12	8	0	0	31	35	35	32	3	37	45	.280	.234	.328	13.06	10.74
Melvin Jimenez	B-R	6-0	170	7-23-99	1	0	10.57	8	0	0	0	8	9	9	9	2	7	9	.281	.333	.261	10.57	8.22
Landon Knack	L-R	6-2	220	7-15-97	2	10	5.01	17	17	0	0	65	64	40	36	8	27	80	.257	.247	.263	11.13	3.76
Jordan Leasure	R-R	6-3	215	8-15-98	2	2	3.65	44	0	0	5	49	38	24	20	8	19	63	.208	.156	.235	11.49	3.47
Lael Lockhart	B-L	6-3	225	12-31-97	1	1	4.93	8	5	0	0	35	30	20	19	2	20	29	.226	.204	.238	7.53	5.19
Kevin Malisheski	R-R	6-3	220	9-7-97	0	1	9.00	9	0	0	0	12	17	12	12	4	12	15	.347	.348	.346	11.25	9.00
Jose Martinez	R-R	6-0	194	4-23-99	3	2	4.81	27	5	0	0	58	57	32	31	5	29	40	.256	.315	.214	6.21	4.50
Bobby Miller	L-R	6-5	220	4-5-99	6	6	4.45	20	19	0	0	91	78	49	45	8	31	117	.223	.209	.234	11.57	3.07
Nick Nastrini	R-R	6-3	215	2-18-00	1	1	4.15	6	6	0	0	30	14	14	14	5	16	42	.140	.179	.091	12.46	4.75
Aaron Ochsenbein	R-R	6-3	225	2-29-96	2	0	2.57	13	0	0	2	14	7	5	4	2	1	12	.149	.364	.083	7.71	0.64
Cole Percival	R-R	6-5	220	2-26-99	0	0	12.00	12	0	0	0	15	19	20	20	3	19	8	.317	.435	.243	4.80	11.40
Zack Plunkett	R-R	6-2	225	2-16-96	1	1	14.81	6	0	0	0	10	19	18	17	5	3	5	.388	.412	.375	4.35	2.61
2-team total (17 Midland RockHounds)					3	2	7.07	23	0	0	0	36	44	35	28	10	10	25	.297	.304	.293	6.31	2.52
Adolfo Ramirez	R-R	6-0	165	6-1-99	0	0	3.21	4	0	0	0	14	10	5	5	3	7	19	.192	.250	.143	12.21	4.50
Nick Robertson	R-R	6-6	265	7-16-98	1	3	4.88	44	2	0	7	55	52	33	30	7	27	72	.244	.210	.265	11.71	4.39
John Rooney	R-L	6-5	215	1-28-97	4	7	6.15	24	17	0	0	98	105	85	67	19	48	99	.278	.273	.280	9.09	4.41
Emmet Sheehan	R-R	6-5	220	11-15-99	0	0	4.15	2	2	0	0	4	2	3	2	1	3	5	.133	.000	.200	10.38	6.23
Gavin Stone	R-R	6-1	175	10-15-98	6	4	1.60	14	13	0	0	73	59	16	13	1	30	107	.219	.248	.191	13.13	3.68
Gus Varland	L-R	6-1	205	11-6-96	4	4	6.11	41	7	0	2	71	79	54	48	11	37	85	.289	.245	.316	10.83	4.71
Mark Washington	R-R	6-7	205	3-22-96	3	0	1.16	15	0	0	4	23	9	3	3	0	10	22	.120	.069	.152	8.49	3.86
Guillermo Zuniga	R-R	6-5	230	10-10-98	4	4	4.77	48	0	0	11	55	47	32	29	12	30	66	.227	.282	.189	10.87	4.94

Fielding

Catcher	PCT	G	PO	A	E	DP	PB
Avelino	1.000	1	1	0	0	0	0
Betts	.996	25	243	9	1	1	1
Chalo	.889	1	8	0	1	0	0
Feduccia	1.000	35	312	13	0	1	4
January	.979	21	180	7	4	0	4
Rios	1.000	3	21	1	0	0	1
Taylor	.990	58	562	12	6	3	6

First Base	PCT	G	PO	A	E	DP
Lewis	.990	61	448	33	5	30
Mann	1.000	1	8	2	0	1
Ward	1.000	3	20	1	0	2
Yurchak	.987	75	498	39	7	43

Second Base	PCT	G	PO	A	E	DP
Avelino	.968	25	43	48	3	13
Betancourt	.986	22	28	45	1	9
Busch	.968	26	31	59	3	11
Hoese	1.000	8	6	16	0	1
Lewis	.000	1	0	0	0	0
Mann	.973	58	78	137	6	24
Valera	1.000	2	2	5	0	0

Third Base	PCT	G	PO	A	E	DP
Avelino	.975	28	24	53	2	4
Hoese	.972	69	40	98	4	9
Lewis	.929	34	24	55	6	8
Mann	.824	5	3	11	3	0
Pages	.000	1	0	0	0	0
Valera	.867	6	2	11	2	1

Shortstop	PCT	G	PO	A	E	DP
Amaya	.969	49	48	109	5	18
Avelino	1.000	2	4	4	0	1
Betancourt	.750	2	3	3	2	1
Hoese	1.000	1	2	2	0	1
Mann	.889	4	6	10	2	2
Valera	.920	78	79	151	20	28

Outfield	PCT	G	PO	A	E	DP
Alcantara	1.000	10	25	2	0	0
Avelino	1.000	3	3	0	0	0
Busch	1.000	2	4	0	0	0
DeLuca	.914	24	29	3	3	0
Kelly	1.000	4	11	0	0	0
Kendall	.980	78	146	3	3	0
Mann	1.000	2	4	0	0	0
Outman	.977	65	121	4	3	2
Pages	.962	119	187	14	8	5
Reed	1.000	24	39	0	0	0
Ward	.970	88	155	5	5	0
Yurchak	.917	8	11	0	1	0

GREAT LAKES LOONS

HIGH CLASS A

MIDWEST LEAGUE

Batting	B-T	HT	WT	DOB	AVG	vLH	vRH	G	AB	R	H	2B	3B	HR	RBI	BB	HBP	SH	SF	SO	SB	CS	SLG	OBP
Ismael Alcantara	R-R	6-1	165	9-25-98	.187	.203	.183	97	321	41	60	10	3	5	36	21	10	6	3	96	11	6	.283	.256
Diego Cartaya	R-R	6-3	219	9-7-01	.251	.157	.278	62	231	43	58	13	0	13	41	40	9	0	2	75	1	0	.476	.379
Zac Ching	R-R	5-9	180	5-29-97	.190	.154	.200	19	58	6	11	4	0	0	11	8	1	0	2	24	2	0	.259	.290
Alex De Jesus	R-R	6-2	170	3-22-02	.282	.250	.293	50	195	27	55	11	2	4	26	28	2	0	1	65	0	1	.421	.376
Aldrich De Jongh	L-R	5-9	185	9-1-98	.216	.212	.216	63	204	35	44	5	1	9	25	32	2	0	1	61	3	0	.382	.326
Jonny DeLuca	R-R	6-0	200	7-10-98	.245	.284	.233	73	277	51	68	17	2	18	51	37	5	0	2	56	12	2	.516	.343
Luis Yanel Diaz	R-R	5-11	170	9-9-99	.196	.190	.198	34	107	17	21	4	2	6	20	10	1	1	0	32	4	3	.439	.271
Yunior Garcia	R-R	6-0	198	7-29-01	.152	.000	.200	10	33	2	5	0	0	0	1	0	0	0	1	12	0	0	.152	.147
Austin Gauthier	R-R	6-0	188	5-7-99	.177	.294	.133	21	62	9	11	3	0	1	5	15	2	0	2	18	2	2	.274	.346
Max Hewitt	L-R	6-0	182	9-14-97	.125	.100	.133	21	40	6	5	3	0	0	3	7	1	0	0	17	0	0	.200	.271
Ryan January	L-R	6-3	210	5-27-97	.206	.229	.198	41	126	22	26	7	0	5	21	31	7	0	0	57	0	0	.381	.390
Damon Keith	R-R	6-3	195	5-28-00	.204	.143	.220	31	103	16	21	4	1	5	14	21	0	0	0	33	0	1	.408	.339
Sauryn Lao	R-R	6-2	182	8-14-99	.169	.188	.163	18	59	7	10	2	0	1	4	7	0	0	0	17	0	0	.254	.258
Eddys Leonard	R-R	5-11	195	11-10-00	.264	.261	.265	127	496	80	131	32	4	15	61	45	21	0	4	119	4	4	.435	.348
Hector Martinez	R-R	6-0	135	8-22-00	.250	.000	.500	1	4	1	1	0	0	0	0	0	0	0	0	0	0	0	.250	.250
Edwin Mateo	B-L	5-9	160	11-18-98	.214	.262	.191	60	192	18	41	10	0	2	14	16	2	1	1	47	3	2	.297	.280
Jose Ramos	R-R	6-1	200	1-1-01	.240	.172	.262	95	362	63	87	19	3	19	74	39	5	0	1	133	2	0	.467	.322
Harold Restituyo	R-R	6-2	185	9-1-00	.215	.333	.170	19	65	11	14	1	0	0	5	8	0	0	0	24	1	0	.231	.301
Kekai Rios	R-R	5-11	205	6-6-97	.218	.271	.202	68	216	26	47	8	1	4	24	27	4	0	0	65	0	0	.319	.316
Leonel Valera	R-R	6-2	210	7-9-99	.211	.100	.239	42	147	20	31	3	2	5	21	15	3	0	2	57	11	0	.361	.293
Imanol Vargas	L-R	6-3	215	6-29-98	.268	.190	.290	116	381	65	102	20	1	18	63	80	8	0	1	145	5	0	.467	.404
Jorbit Vivas	L-R	5-10	171	3-9-01	.269	.222	.285	128	479	73	129	19	7	10	66	63	21	0	6	58	2	1	.401	.374
Joe Vranesh	R-R	6-2	200	1-23-98	.147	.167	.140	21	68	8	10	1	0	3	8	3	2	0	1	33	2	0	.294	.203
Juan Zabala	R-R	5-10	190	7-3-99	.444	1.000	.000	3	9	1	4	1	0	0	2	2	0	0	0	1	0	0	.556	.545

Pitching	B-T	HT	WT	DOB	W	L	ERA	G	GS	CG	SV	IP	H	R	ER	HR	BB	SO	AVG	vLH	vRH	K/9	BB/9
Aldry Acosta	R-R	6-4	235	9-7-99	1	2	0.74	20	1	0	0	24	18	6	2	0	11	16	.202	.176	.218	5.92	4.07
Carlos Alejo	R-R	6-1	230	8-23-99	1	0	16.20	10	0	0	0	7	8	14	12	2	11	7	.286	.300	.278	9.45	14.85
Jeff Belge	L-L	6-5	225	12-4-97	3	3	3.66	29	1	0	5	32	22	13	13	2	17	50	.191	.211	.182	14.06	4.78
Jake Cantleberry	L-L	6-1	180	8-8-97	3	1	4.32	24	0	0	3	33	23	18	16	5	24	39	.192	.179	.198	10.53	6.48
Ben Casparius	R-R	6-0	208	2-11-99	1	4	6.45	18	9	0	0	60	71	48	43	11	32	67	.291	.260	.313	10.05	4.80
Hyun-il Choi	R-R	6-2	215	5-27-00	0	1	6.00	1	1	0	0	3	4	3	2	0	0	4	.308	.273	.500	12.00	0.00
Carlos De Los Santos	R-R	6-2	170	11-18-00	0	0	0.00	1	0	0	0	1	0	0	0	0	0	2	.000	.000	.000	27.00	0.00
Reinaldo De Paula	R-R	5-11	177	10-20-98	0	1	6.75	4	0	0	0	5	4	5	4	0	5	5	.222	.273	.143	8.44	8.44
Cole Duensing	L-R	6-4	195	6-16-98	3	5	3.68	34	1	0	0	44	44	22	18	5	15	48	.256	.271	.245	9.82	3.07
Carlos Duran	R-R	6-7	230	7-30-01	1	3	4.25	14	13	0	0	49	43	25	23	6	24	68	.235	.253	.221	12.58	4.44
Braydon Fisher	R-R	6-4	180	7-26-00	4	4	4.75	36	0	0	1	47	33	29	25	3	37	64	.192	.174	.204	12.17	7.04
Nick Frasso	R-R	6-5	200	10-18-98	0	0	1.59	2	2	0	0	6	5	1	1	0	0	9	.238	.200	.250	14.29	0.00
Ben Harris	L-L	6-1	195	2-22-00	3	0	1.93	22	3	0	4	28	9	6	6	1	15	48	.100	.161	.068	15.43	4.82
Jose Hernandez	L-L	6-3	205	12-31-97	1	2	2.14	15	0	0	8	21	17	11	5	1	7	22	.207	.250	.185	9.43	3.00
Max Hewitt	L-R	6-0	182	9-14-97	0	0	0.00	1	0	0	0	1	1	0	0	0	1	1	.333	.333	--	9.00	9.00
Michael Hobbs	R-R	6-3	215	7-10-99	7	1	3.08	19	0	0	1	26	18	9	9	2	12	24	.191	.159	.220	8.20	4.10
Kyle Hurt	R-R	6-3	240	5-30-98	4	2	2.21	13	11	1	0	41	21	11	10	1	22	64	.151	.129	.169	14.16	4.87
Antonio Knowles	R-R	6-1	190	1-15-00	3	4	4.74	36	0	0	0	44	34	27	23	2	36	63	.200	.172	.217	12.98	7.42
Ronan Kopp	L-L	6-7	250	7-29-02	0	1	1.93	3	2	0	0	5	3	4	1	0	6	6	.167	.143	.182	11.57	11.57
Jordan Leasure	R-R	6-3	215	8-15-98	0	0	1.93	5	0	0	2	9	4	2	2	0	5	21	.125	.167	.071	20.25	4.82
Lael Lockhart	B-L	6-3	225	12-31-97	2	3	3.16	19	11	0	0	77	77	32	27	5	21	85	.258	.253	.261	9.94	2.45
Kevin Malisheski	R-R	6-3	220	9-7-97	1	0	4.09	15	1	0	0	22	9	10	10	1	19	28	.122	.167	.063	11.45	7.77
Nick Nastrini	R-R	6-3	215	2-18-00	5	3	3.86	21	21	0	0	86	61	38	37	12	39	127	.192	.183	.200	13.24	4.07
Cole Percival	R-R	6-5	220	2-26-99	3	2	3.77	26	6	0	1	57	55	31	24	5	27	60	.242	.224	.258	9.42	4.24
Robbie Peto	R-R	6-4	225	7-10-98	6	1	4.11	22	4	0	1	66	47	30	30	6	50	54	.202	.188	.212	7.40	6.85
Adolfo Ramirez	R-R	6-0	165	6-1-99	1	0	1.46	4	2	0	0	12	4	2	2	0	3	16	.105	.111	.100	11.68	2.19
River Ryan	R-R	6-2	195	8-17-98	1	1	1.93	5	3	0	0	14	9	7	3	2	8	22	.176	.042	.296	14.14	5.14
Adam Scoggins	L-L	6-3	220	1-21-98	1	1	6.11	21	0	0	0	18	18	15	12	1	21	19	.265	.286	.255	9.68	10.70
Andrew Shaps	L-L	6-1	185	12-5-95	0	1	10.13	3	0	0	0	3	3	5	3	0	6	7	.250	.250	.250	23.63	20.25
2-team total (16 West Michigan Whitecaps)					0	1	6.05	19	0	0	0	19	16	16	13	0	25	22	.229	.160	.267	10.24	11.64
Emmet Sheehan	R-R	6-5	220	11-15-99	7	2	2.83	18	12	0	0	64	41	25	20	2	28	101	.180	.171	.188	14.28	3.96
Julian Smith	R-L	6-4	210	6-3-97	3	0	5.29	39	0	0	3	51	53	36	30	11	30	54	.265	.277	.259	9.53	5.29
Gavin Stone	R-R	6-1	175	10-15-98	1	1	1.44	6	6	0	0	25	19	5	4	1	6	28	.204	.167	.256	10.08	2.16
Christian Suarez	L-L	5-11	160	11-25-00	0	0	0.00	1	0	0	0	1	0	0	0	0	0	1	.000	.000	.000	9.00	0.00
Ryan Sublette	R-R	6-2	190	10-1-98	7	1	2.98	41	1	0	8	54	41	21	18	4	33	87	.203	.157	.239	14.41	5.47
Joan Valdez	R-R	6-4	175	3-10-99	0	0	2.45	4	0	0	0	4	1	1	1	0	9	5	.083	.000	.167	12.27	22.09
Kendall Williams	R-R	6-6	205	8-24-00	3	5	4.15	23	20	0	0	93	89	52	43	12	48	76	.252	.271	.233	7.33	4.63

Fielding

Catcher	PCT	G	PO	A	E	DP	PB
Cartaya	.989	41	428	24	5	1	3
Hewitt	1.000	2	17	2	0	0	0
January	.988	29	304	12	4	0	1
Rios	.997	62	623	26	2	1	8
Zabala	1.000	2	15	1	0	0	0

First Base	PCT	G	PO	A	E	DP
Alcantara	.958	3	21	2	1	4
Ching	.947	12	45	9	3	3
Yanel Diaz	.895	3	16	1	2	1
Garcia	1.000	5	32	2	0	3
Hewitt	.973	7	33	3	1	3
Lao	1.000	3	7	1	0	0
Vargas	.983	104	651	57	12	66
Vranesh	1.000	1	1	1	0	1

Second Base	PCT	G	PO	A	E	DP
Alcantara	.000	1	0	0	0	0

Ching	1.000	2	1	3	0	0
Yanel Diaz	1.000	2	2	0	0	0
Gauthier	.983	14	29	30	1	8
Hewitt	1.000	9	7	15	0	3
Lao	.933	10	20	22	3	11
Leonard	.929	8	5	21	2	3
Valera	1.000	1	0	1	0	0
Vivas	.987	91	117	185	4	35

Third Base	PCT	G	PO	A	E	DP
Ching	1.000	3	0	5	0	0
De Jesus	.848	39	18	49	12	1
Yanel Diaz	.898	20	22	31	6	3
Gauthier	.727	3	5	3	3	2
Lao	.833	5	4	6	2	1
Leonard	.944	7	6	11	1	0
Martinez	1.000	1	1	2	0	1
Valera	.913	21	19	23	4	1
Vivas	.841	33	22	36	11	4

Shortstop	PCT	G	PO	A	E	DP
De Jesus	1.000	3	2	3	0	2
Yanel Diaz	1.000	4	4	8	0	1
Gauthier	1.000	3	0	4	0	0
Leonard	.951	104	125	186	16	41
Valera	.900	19	23	31	6	9

Outfield	PCT	G	PO	A	E	DP
Alcantara	.990	88	192	7	2	4
De Jongh	.972	46	68	1	2	1
DeLuca	.982	67	107	4	2	0
Yanel Diaz	.917	6	10	1	1	0
Garcia	1.000	1	3	0	0	0
Keith	.940	32	42	5	3	0
Leonard	.857	4	11	1	2	1
Mateo	.988	55	81	0	1	0
Ramos	.988	84	150	8	2	1
Restituyo	.964	16	27	0	1	0
Vranesh	.909	7	10	0	1	0

RANCHO CUCAMONGA QUAKES — *LOW CLASS A*

CALIFORNIA LEAGUE

Batting	B-T	HT	WT	DOB	AVG	vLH	vRH	G	AB	R	H	2B	3B	HR	RBI	BB	HBP	SH	SF	SO	SB	CS	SLG	OBP
Chris Alleyne	B-R	5-10	190	11-13-98	.234	.265	.223	29	128	23	30	7	2	3	17	13	1	0	1	38	9	1	.391	.308
Juan Alonso	R-R	6-0	180	11-3-03	.235	.364	.174	10	34	7	8	3	0	1	6	4	2	0	0	15	1	1	.412	.350
Javier Armas	L-R	5-10	155	8-27-03	.235	.000	.286	6	17	4	4	2	0	0	3	6	0	0	0	10	0	0	.353	.435
Kenneth Betancourt	R-R	5-8	160	2-5-00	.278	.259	.283	81	277	58	77	19	1	4	44	32	2	1	3	47	7	1	.397	.354
Nick Biddison	R-R	5-10	190	7-30-00	.276	.333	.260	31	123	20	34	6	2	4	20	16	3	0	1	32	6	1	.455	.371
Julio Carrion	R-R	6-2	185	12-29-98	.246	.222	.254	73	244	50	60	9	1	10	47	41	9	0	2	99	5	1	.414	.372
Diego Cartaya	R-R	6-3	219	9-7-01	.260	.250	.263	33	131	31	34	9	1	9	31	23	9	0	0	44	0	0	.550	.405
Alex De Jesus	R-R	6-2	170	3-22-02	.259	.289	.248	37	143	34	37	9	1	7	22	32	1	0	0	50	2	0	.483	.398
Luis Yanel Diaz	R-R	5-11	170	9-9-99	.277	.226	.291	74	282	55	78	14	1	11	59	33	4	0	5	85	27	5	.450	.355
Rayne Doncon	R-R	6-2	176	9-22-03	.250	.250	.250	11	40	6	10	0	0	3	8	3	0	0	0	5	0	0	.475	.302
Yeiner Fernandez	R-R	5-9	170	9-19-02	.292	.303	.288	89	363	76	106	16	2	10	68	46	10	0	4	55	3	2	.430	.383
Alex Freeland	B-R	6-2	200	8-24-01	.313	.333	.308	8	32	7	10	1	0	3	6	2	2	0	0	11	2	0	.625	.389
Kyle Froemke	R-R	6-4	200	12-15-98	.247	.350	.215	25	85	17	21	5	0	3	6	11	3	0	0	35	1	1	.412	.354
Yunior Garcia	R-R	6-0	198	7-29-01	.305	.306	.305	87	334	58	102	28	1	13	74	33	9	0	0	75	2	0	.512	.383
Austin Gauthier	R-R	6-0	188	5-7-99	.287	.237	.304	84	300	81	86	18	4	6	49	88	9	0	0	81	10	1	.433	.461
Marco Hernandez	R-R	6-2	170	6-22-98	.228	.067	.286	20	57	10	13	3	0	2	11	14	3	0	0	14	0	1	.386	.405
Gaige Howard	L-R	6-2	220	5-22-98	.238	.278	.231	36	126	29	30	5	1	1	29	30	3	0	0	22	4	1	.317	.396
Damon Keith	R-R	6-3	195	5-28-00	.299	.387	.274	88	334	75	100	23	4	12	65	69	11	0	2	95	5	3	.500	.433
Griffin Lockwood-Powell	R-R	6-2	195	2-23-98	.276	.192	.304	33	105	19	29	4	0	7	26	23	5	0	2	31	0	0	.514	.422
Hector Martinez	R-R	6-0	135	8-22-00	.200	.182	.205	32	95	14	19	5	0	1	14	9	0	0	1	25	0	2	.284	.267
Sean McLain	R-R	5-11	170	3-22-01	.175	.053	.227	17	63	7	11	1	0	1	4	8	3	0	0	19	4	1	.238	.297
Kyle Nevin	R-R	6-4	200	8-22-01	.174	.294	.135	18	69	12	12	6	1	0	10	4	2	0	2	15	2	0	.290	.234
Jorge Puerta	R-R	5-11	178	12-5-01	.000	.000	.000	1	4	0	0	0	0	0	0	0	0	0	0	2	0	0	.000	.000
Nelson Quiroz	B-R	5-8	194	11-5-01	.341	.125	.389	12	44	9	15	2	0	4	9	6	0	0	0	5	0	0	.659	.420
Jose Ramos	R-R	6-1	200	1-1-01	.277	.192	.302	28	112	20	31	3	3	6	23	18	5	0	3	36	2	0	.518	.391
Luis Rodriguez	R-R	6-2	175	9-16-02	.241	.288	.226	110	431	61	104	20	1	11	67	65	5	0	5	159	3	1	.369	.344
Dalton Rushing	L-R	6-1	220	2-21-01	.424	.538	.384	28	99	27	42	11	0	8	30	21	6	0	2	21	1	0	.778	.539
Jake Vogel	R-R	5-11	165	10-12-01	.236	.308	.212	109	432	72	102	22	9	1	49	52	9	0	6	111	19	7	.336	.327
Taylor Young	R-R	5-9	170	8-6-98	.292	.296	.291	29	106	24	31	4	1	2	13	27	4	0	0	25	11	0	.406	.453

Pitching	B-T	HT	WT	DOB	W	L	ERA	G	GS	CG	SV	IP	H	R	ER	HR	BB	SO	AVG	vLH	vRH	K/9	BB/9
Axel Acevedo	R-R	6-2	170	9-23-00	0	0	7.71	2	0	0	0	2	1	2	2	0	2	5	.125	.000	.200	19.29	7.71
Horacio Andujar	R-R	6-2	161	1-14-99	0	1	--	1	0	0	0	0	4	7	7	1	3	0	1.000	1.000	1.000	--	--
Heisell Baro	R-R	6-1	185	2-20-02	3	0	5.40	15	0	0	0	23	26	14	14	1	14	23	.299	.304	.290	8.87	5.40
Kelvin Bautista	L-L	5-11	155	7-7-99	1	4	6.17	42	0	0	1	54	49	43	37	2	49	55	.238	.220	.245	9.17	8.17
Octavio Becerra	L-L	6-3	209	2-3-01	1	0	0.79	6	0	0	0	11	7	1	1	0	7	11	.184	.111	.207	8.74	5.56
Kenneth Betancourt	R-R	5-8	160	2-5-00	0	0	0.00	3	0	0	1	2	0	0	0	0	1	0	.000	.000	.000	0.00	5.40
Maddux Bruns	L-L	6-2	205	6-20-02	0	3	5.68	21	21	0	0	44	36	30	28	1	45	67	.226	.200	.233	13.60	9.14
Chris Campos	R-R	5-10	170	8-13-00	0	0	6.75	4	4	0	0	5	5	4	4	1	1	5	.250	.182	.333	8.44	1.69
Ben Casparius	R-R	6-0	208	2-11-99	1	2	2.73	9	7	0	0	30	15	16	9	3	14	43	.146	.133	.155	13.04	4.25
Yamil Castillo	R-R	6-1	200	8-18-99	4	1	5.23	21	0	0	1	33	25	19	19	7	21	37	.210	.189	.227	10.19	5.79
Carlos De Los Santos	R-R	6-2	170	11-18-00	5	0	4.53	36	2	0	1	44	37	24	22	0	32	58	.224	.262	.185	11.95	6.60
Reinaldo De Paula	R-R	5-11	177	10-20-98	2	0	2.89	21	0	0	3	28	20	13	9	2	9	29	.196	.216	.176	9.32	2.89
Danny Duffy	L L	6 3	205	12-21-88	0	0	0.00	1	1	0	0	1	0	0	0	0	0	2	.000	.000	.000	18.00	0.00
Jonathan Edwards	R-R	6-6	185	1-26-00	1	1	11.42	10	0	0	1	9	10	17	11	2	19	16	.278	.300	.250	16.62	19.73
Gabe Emmett	R-R	6-5	175	5-22-01	1	2	8.81	19	2	0	0	32	35	35	31	1	25	30	.278	.328	.220	8.53	7.11
Frankelyn Feliz	R-R	6-1	170	12-24-01	1	0	9.00	1	0	0	0	2	1	2	2	0	2	2	.125	.333	.000	9.00	9.00
Braydon Fisher	R-R	6-4	180	7-26-00	0	0	3.38	3	0	0	0	5	2	2	2	0	3	8	.105	.000	.200	13.50	5.06
Osvanni Gutierrez	R-R	6-1	170	5-24-01	1	0	13.09	10	0	0	1	11	16	17	16	4	9	13	.340	.259	.450	10.64	7.36
Roque Gutierrez	R-R	5-9	177	9-7-02	0	0	9.45	9	0	0	0	13	20	16	14	3	5	14	.323	.364	.300	9.45	3.38
Ben Harris	L-L	6-1	195	2-22-00	1	1	5.53	22	0	0	3	28	23	18	17	1	22	59	.223	.440	.154	19.19	7.16
Andrew Heaney	L-L	6-2	200	6-5-91	0	0	13.50	1	1	0	0	3	6	4	4	2	0	2	.462	.500	.444	6.75	0.00
Edgardo Henriquez	R-R	6-4	200	6-24-02	2	3	4.54	14	13	0	0	36	39	21	18	2	18	44	.275	.279	.270	11.10	4.54
Peter Heubeck	R-R	6-3	170	7-22-02	0	1	7.39	15	13	0	0	32	22	26	26	7	25	42	.196	.250	.125	11.94	7.11
Joel Ibarra	R-R	6-0	176	7-10-02	3	2	5.95	10	4	0	0	20	16	15	13	3	15	22	.222	.220	.226	10.07	6.86
Madison Jeffrey	L-R	6-0	190	3-14-00	2	3	6.00	41	0	0	4	42	29	35	28	3	44	55	.193	.182	.205	11.79	9.43
Tommy Kahnle	R-R	6-1	230	8-7-89	0	0	2.45	5	3	0	0	4	5	1	1	0	0	4	.313	.250	.375	9.82	0.00

Clayton Kershaw	L-L	6-4	225	3-19-88	0	0	2.25	1	1	0	0	4	3	1	1	1	1	7	.200	.000	.300	15.75	2.25
Ronan Kopp	L-L	6-7	250	7-29-02	5	2	2.81	24	9	0	1	58	36	21	18	3	37	102	.170	.158	.174	15.92	5.77
Jimmy Lewis	R-R	6-6	200	11-2-00	0	1	7.94	7	0	0	0	11	7	10	10	1	13	11	.179	.182	.176	8.74	10.32
Huei-Sheng Lin	R-R	6-2	198	10-9-98	1	2	6.71	17	5	0	0	52	59	44	39	12	32	57	.278	.282	.274	9.80	5.50
Jacob Meador	R-R	6-0	183	10-26-00	0	1	4.05	5	2	0	0	7	4	3	3	2	1	10	.174	.235	.000	13.50	1.35
Orlando Ortiz-Mayr	R-R	6-3	195	12-6-97	2	4	6.79	20	3	0	0	61	64	52	46	8	32	81	.266	.294	.229	11.95	4.72
Robbie Peto	R-R	6-4	225	7-10-98	0	0	2.87	5	0	0	0	16	11	7	5	0	9	18	.216	.143	.267	10.34	5.17
Darlin Pinales	R-R	6-4	240	8-28-02	1	0	1.59	3	1	0	0	11	8	2	2	0	2	9	.211	.318	.063	7.15	1.59
Adolfo Ramirez	R-R	6-0	165	6-1-99	5	0	3.51	16	1	0	0	41	33	19	16	3	14	56	.216	.304	.122	12.29	3.07
Livan Reinoso	R-R	6-1	185	8-27-98	0	1	5.79	4	0	0	1	5	2	4	3	0	3	5	.154	.200	.000	9.64	5.79
Benony Robles	L-L	6-4	185	10-1-00	6	3	5.86	25	6	0	0	78	84	68	51	10	42	79	.273	.281	.269	9.08	4.83
Jerming Rosario	R-R	6-1	175	5-8-02	5	6	6.64	26	14	0	0	85	89	73	63	9	60	112	.266	.287	.240	11.81	6.33
River Ryan	R-R	6-2	195	8-17-98	1	3	2.67	10	10	0	0	34	29	15	10	2	13	48	.228	.194	.262	12.83	3.48
Martin Santana	R-R	6-4	165	1-30-01	4	5	5.70	37	0	0	0	47	41	37	30	3	36	55	.225	.174	.278	10.46	6.85
Christian Suarez	L-L	5-11	160	11-25-00	4	6	4.30	36	0	0	0	59	58	40	28	4	34	77	.256	.247	.260	11.81	5.22
Joan Valdez	R-R	6-4	175	3-10-99	3	1	3.92	32	1	0	4	41	39	24	18	4	30	57	.250	.292	.220	12.41	6.53
Luis Valdez	L-L	6-2	158	7-18-03	0	1	7.20	2	2	0	0	5	6	6	4	0	2	8	.273	.500	.083	14.40	3.60
Kendall Williams	R-R	6-6	205	8-24-00	0	1	5.29	4	4	0	0	17	14	11	10	5	5	20	.219	.150	.250	10.59	2.65
Justin Wrobleski	L-L	6-1	194	7-14-00	1	2	5.40	3	2	0	0	7	8	4	4	1	5	5	.364	.333	.400	6.75	6.75
Jhan Zambrano	R-R	6-3	165	12-21-01	1	1	11.40	9	0	0	0	15	24	21	19	4	7	18	.343	.412	.278	10.80	4.20

Fielding

Catcher	PCT	G	PO	A	E	DP	PB
Cartaya	.997	23	261	36	1	1	7
Fernandez	.974	62	644	65	19	8	15
Hernandez	.985	18	193	9	3	0	3
Lockwood-Powell	.967	10	85	4	3	0	1
Quiroz	.981	11	94	10	2	0	3
Rushing	.995	17	180	15	1	2	7

First Base	PCT	G	PO	A	E	DP
Betancourt	1.000	10	79	4	0	5
Biddison	.000	1	0	0	0	0
Carrion	.985	50	307	27	5	20
Yanel Diaz	1.000	6	22	2	0	3
Froemke	1.000	5	27	5	0	2
Garcia	.978	38	256	13	6	10
Howard	1.000	1	1	0	0	1
Lockwood-Powell	.977	20	119	9	3	10
Nevin	.988	11	80	5	1	10
Puerta	1.000	1	7	1	0	0
Rushing	1.000	5	32	1	0	2

Second Base	PCT	G	PO	A	E	DP
Armas	.952	5	9	11	1	2
Betancourt	.989	52	59	113	2	15
Carrion	1.000	2	0	2	0	1
Yanel Diaz	1.000	2	0	3	0	0
Fernandez	.938	17	32	43	5	10
Freeland	1.000	2	3	6	0	1
Froemke	.909	3	3	7	1	1
Garcia	.000	2	0	0	0	0
Gauthier	.947	19	21	33	3	3
Martinez	.909	14	13	27	4	4
Young	.979	26	42	53	2	12

Third Base	PCT	G	PO	A	E	DP
Betancourt	.857	6	4	8	2	1
Biddison	.913	19	9	33	4	2
Carrion	.900	20	16	29	5	3
De Jesus	.864	11	7	12	3	3
Yanel Diaz	.893	51	41	93	16	8
Freeland	.000	1	0	0	0	0
Froemke	.846	19	12	21	6	2
Martinez	.909	15	7	23	3	2

Shortstop	PCT	G	PO	A	E	DP
Armas	1.000	1	2	1	0	0
Betancourt	.897	10	17	18	4	0
De Jesus	.938	11	11	19	2	1
Yanel Diaz	.842	11	8	24	6	3
Doncon	.966	10	13	15	1	5
Freeland	.929	6	15	11	2	4
Gauthier	.932	69	81	139	16	24
Martinez	1.000	3	2	2	0	1
McLain	.885	16	23	31	7	8
Young	1.000	3	2	8	0	1

Outfield	PCT	G	PO	A	E	DP
Alleyne	.942	28	46	3	3	2
Alonso	1.000	10	11	1	0	0
Betancourt	--	1	0	0	0	0
Biddison	.919	15	28	6	3	3
Carrion	--	1	0	0	0	0
Yanel Diaz	.909	9	9	1	1	0
Garcia	.810	19	14	3	4	1
Howard	.981	34	52	1	1	0
Keith	.953	77	116	6	6	0
Nevin	1.000	6	5	0	0	0
Ramos	.956	30	41	2	2	1
Rodriguez	.944	84	108	11	7	4
Vogel	.973	110	174	6	5	0

ACL DODGERS — *ROOKIE*

ARIZONA COMPLEX LEAGUE

Batting	B-T	HT	WT	DOB	AVG	vLH	vRH	G	AB	R	H	2B	3B	HR	RBI	BB	HBP	SH	SF	SO	SB	CS	SLG	OBP
Chris Alleyne	B-R	5-10	190	11-13-98	.250	--	.250	2	4	0	1	0	0	0	0	0	0	0	0	2	0	0	.250	.250
Juan Alonso	R-R	6-0	180	11-3-03	.288	.409	.262	41	125	33	36	7	1	2	22	40	7	0	2	47	12	2	.408	.477
Javier Armas	L-R	5-10	155	8-27-03	.221	.083	.250	28	68	7	15	1	1	1	8	5	0	2	0	23	6	1	.309	.274
Nick Biddison	R-R	5-10	190	7-30-00	.000	.000	.000	2	4	0	0	0	0	0	0	0	0	0	0	1	0	0	.000	.000
Roger Caraballo	R-R	6-1	185	8-14-01	.194	.227	.185	32	103	15	20	6	0	3	9	7	3	0	0	35	2	0	.340	.265
Wladimir Chalo	R-R	5-8	197	4-21-00	.333	1.000	.273	5	12	1	4	0	0	0	2	2	1	0	0	4	0	0	.333	.467
Cameron Decker	B-R	6-1	205	9-22-03	.083	.200	.000	4	12	2	1	0	0	0	0	0	1	0	0	6	0	0	.083	.154
Wilman Diaz	R-R	6-2	182	11-15-03	.168	.282	.139	50	197	26	33	5	0	2	15	12	1	0	1	80	3	2	.223	.218
Rayne Doncon	R-R	6-2	176	9-22-03	.256	.297	.247	51	199	28	51	16	1	9	38	15	0	0	1	38	6	2	.482	.307
Miguel Droz	R-R	6-0	170	10-2-01	.224	.188	.235	19	67	5	15	4	0	0	8	2	2	0	1	26	0	0	.284	.264
Julio Enrique	R-R	6-1	184	2-21-00	.172	.118	.186	29	87	17	15	3	2	2	7	4	6	0	0	31	12	0	.322	.258
Andy Espinosa	R-R	5-11	195	1-25-03	.209	.261	.195	35	110	22	23	9	1	5	20	13	4	0	0	45	1	1	.445	.315
Kyle Froemke	R-R	6-4	200	12-15-98	.111	.500	.063	9	18	1	2	0	0	0	3	0	0	0	2	8	0	0	.111	.100
Jesus Galiz	R-R	6-0	183	12-19-03	.235	.154	.250	27	85	15	20	8	0	4	13	11	3	0	0	25	0	0	.471	.343
Kody Hoese	R-R	6-4	200	7-13-97	.300	--	.300	3	10	1	3	1	0	1	2	0	0	0	0	4	0	0	.700	.300
Jose Izarra	R-R	6-0	175	3-7-02	.391	.800	.278	7	23	4	9	1	0	0	1	1	1	0	0	7	1	0	.435	.440
Sauryn Lao	R-R	6-2	182	8-14-99	.250	.000	.286	2	8	0	2	0	0	0	0	2	0	0	0	2	0	0	.250	.400
Thayron Liranzo	B-R	6-3	195	7-5-03	.236	.040	.276	41	148	23	35	11	1	8	30	21	2	0	0	42	0	0	.486	.339
Griffin Lockwood-Powell	R-R	6-2	195	2-23-98	.400	.500	.375	5	10	4	4	1	0	1	2	8	0	0	0	4	0	0	.800	.667
Sean McLain	R-R	5-11	170	3-22-01	.000	.000	.000	2	4	0	0	0	0	0	0	0	1	0	0	1	0	0	.000	.200
Luis Morales	R-R	5-9	162	12-6-00	.268	.500	.222	34	97	17	26	4	2	2	13	8	2	0	1	29	3	0	.412	.333
Kyle Nevin	R-R	6-4	200	8-22-01	.000	.000	.000	2	4	0	0	0	0	0	0	0	0	0	0	1	0	0	.000	.000
Chris Newell	L-L	6-3	200	4-23-01	.220	.300	.194	11	41	5	9	3	0	1	2	1	1	0	0	11	3	3	.366	.256
Jorge Puerta	R-R	5-11	178	12-5-01	.247	.143	.271	24	73	10	18	4	0	2	9	14	3	0	1	18	1	0	.384	.385

Buddy Reed	B-R	6-4	218	4-27-95	.267	.200	.300	4	15	3	4	1	0	0	2	1	0	0	0	3	2	0	.333	.313
Simon Reid	L-R	6-1	200	4-19-01	.300	.000	.333	3	10	1	3	1	0	0	1	0	0	0	0	1	0	0	.400	.300
Harold Restituyo	R-R	6-2	185	9-1-00	.360	.333	.366	14	50	5	18	2	0	1	7	6	1	0	1	12	1	1	.460	.431
Frank Rodriguez	R-R	5-11	197	9-28-01	.236	.357	.207	25	72	9	17	4	0	2	10	9	2	1	1	25	0	0	.375	.333
Dalton Rushing	L-R	6-1	220	2-21-01	.000	.000	.000	2	5	0	0	0	0	0	0	1	0	0	0	1	0	0	.000	.167
Victor Sosa	L-L	6-1	165	1-7-03	.213	.500	.171	15	47	4	10	2	0	1	6	4	0	0	0	15	1	0	.319	.275
Logan Wagner	B-R	6-1	200	3-9-04	.220	.222	.220	15	50	8	11	1	0	0	6	7	1	0	0	12	2	1	.240	.328
Taylor Young	R-R	5-9	170	8-6-98	.000	--	.000	2	2	1	0	0	0	0	0	2	0	0	0	1	1	0	.000	.500

Pitching	B-T	HT	WT	DOB	W	L	ERA	G	GS	CG	SV	IP	H	R	ER	HR	BB	SO	AVG	vLH	vRH	K/9	BB/9
Horacio Andujar	R-R	6-2	161	1-14-99	1	1	2.01	13	0	0	0	22	17	7	5	2	6	23	.213	.316	.180	9.27	2.42
Pedro Baez	R-R	6-0	232	3-11-88	0	0	3.38	5	4	0	0	5	3	2	2	0	2	4	.158	.100	.222	6.75	3.38
Heisell Baro	R-R	6-1	185	2-20-02	1	0	4.76	7	0	0	0	11	12	6	6	2	1	19	.273	.300	.265	15.09	0.79
Dellin Betances	R-R	6-8	265	3-23-88	0	0	7.36	4	4	0	0	4	6	3	3	0	0	7	.400	.571	.250	17.18	0.00
Jeisson Cabrera	R-R	6-2	170	9-5-98	0	0	1.93	5	4	0	0	5	3	1	1	0	3	10	.188	.333	.154	19.29	5.79
Chris Campos	R-R	5-10	170	8-13-00	1	0	0.00	2	1	0	0	2	0	0	0	0	0	4	.000	.000	.000	18.00	0.00
Yamil Castillo	R-R	6-1	200	8-18-99	0	0	0.00	2	0	0	0	2	1	0	0	0	0	4	.167	.000	.200	18.00	0.00
Fran Castro	R-R	6-0	175	7-9-00	1	1	4.41	13	0	0	0	16	14	9	8	1	6	21	.230	.368	.167	11.57	3.31
Hyun-il Choi	R-R	6-2	215	5-27-00	0	0	0.00	1	0	0	0	1	0	0	0	0	0	0	.000	--	.000	0.00	0.00
Daniel Cruz	R-R	6-3	185	10-5-97	0	0	0.00	2	0	0	0	2	1	0	0	0	0	2	.143	.333	.000	9.00	0.00
Reinaldo De Paula	R-R	5-11	177	10-20-98	1	0	0.00	3	0	0	0	3	2	0	0	0	1	5	.167	.143	.200	13.50	2.70
Tanner Dodson	B-R	6-1	160	5-9-97	0	0	5.40	1	0	0	0	2	0	1	1	0	2	2	.000	--	.000	10.00	10.80
Jack Dreyer	R-L	6-2	205	2-27-99	0	0	1.50	12	0	0	0	12	8	2	2	2	3	13	.182	.111	.200	9.75	2.25
Danny Duffy	L-L	6-3	205	12-21-88	0	0	4.50	2	2	0	0	2	2	1	1	0	2	3	.250	1.000	.143	13.50	9.00
Carlos Duran	R-R	6-7	230	7-30-01	0	0	0.00	1	1	0	0	1	0	0	0	0	0	1	.000	.000	.000	9.00	0.00
Jonathan Edwards	R-R	6-6	185	1-26-00	1	0	2.70	3	0	0	0	3	2	1	1	0	3	3	.167	.000	.200	8.10	8.10
Gabe Emmett	R-R	6-5	175	5-22-01	0	0	2.08	2	0	0	0	4	5	1	1	0	0	5	.278	.250	.286	10.38	0.00
Frankelyn Feliz	R-R	6-1	170	12-24-01	1	0	5.68	12	0	0	0	13	17	14	8	1	13	13	.315	.412	.270	9.24	9.24
Cameron Gibbens	L-R	6-8	194	7-4-95	0	0	27.00	1	0	0	0	0	1	1	1	0	3	1	.500	1.000	.000	27.00	81.00
Jorge Gonzalez	R-R	6-5	203	8-30-02	0	6	9.00	14	2	0	0	25	29	29	25	4	13	29	.299	.207	.338	10.44	4.68
Victor Gonzalez	L-L	6-0	180	11-16-95	0	0	0.00	1	0	0	0	1	1	0	0	0	0	2	.250	--	.250	18.00	0.00
Osvanni Gutierrez	R-R	6-1	170	5-24-01	1	0	1.80	6	0	0	0	10	4	2	2	1	2	10	.121	.125	.120	9.00	1.80
Roque Gutierrez	R-R	5-9	177	9-7-02	2	0	2.49	15	0	0	6	22	16	7	6	2	6	29	.208	.345	.125	12.05	2.49
Andrew Heaney	L-L	6-2	200	6-5-91	0	0	3.60	1	1	0	0	5	5	2	2	2	0	8	.263	.000	.333	14.40	0.00
Heath Hembree	R-R	6-4	220	1-13-89	0	1	4.50	2	0	0	0	2	2	1	1	1	0	4	.286	.333	.250	18.00	0.00
Joel Ibarra	R-R	6-0	176	7-10-02	2	1	2.12	9	0	0	1	17	17	6	4	0	4	28	.262	.250	.268	14.82	2.12
Breyln Jones	R-R	6-2	180	10-15-00	0	0	8.22	7	0	0	0	8	8	7	7	1	16	7	.267	.308	.235	8.22	18.78
Jimmy Lewis	R-R	6-6	200	11-2-00	1	2	8.56	7	4	0	0	14	16	15	13	2	11	13	.281	.375	.212	8.56	7.24
Carlos Martinez	R-R	6-3	190	11-9-01	1	0	3.22	14	1	0	2	22	14	9	8	2	10	36	.177	.214	.157	14.51	4.03
Maximo Martinez	R-R	6-2	185	6-21-04	0	1	13.50	2	2	0	0	5	5	7	7	0	1	6	.263	.222	.300	11.57	1.93
Francisco Mateo	R-R	5-8	185	2-10-00	0	0	10.80	2	0	0	0	2	3	2	2	0	1	2	.375	1.000	.167	10.80	5.40
Alberluis Matos	L-L	6-0	175	9-30-01	1	1	3.60	9	0	0	0	10	7	4	4	0	10	15	.189	.364	.115	13.50	9.00
Dustin May	R-R	6-6	180	9-6-97	0	0	0.00	1	1	0	0	2	0	0	0	0	0	3	.000	.000	.000	13.50	0.00
Garrett McDaniels	L-L	6-2	180	12-15-99	0	1	18.00	1	0	0	0	1	1	2	2	0	2	1	.250	.000	.333	9.00	18.00
Jacob Meador	R-R	6-0	183	10-26-00	0	0	4.50	2	1	0	0	2	4	3	1	0	1	4	.364	.500	.333	18.00	4.50
Darlin Pinales	R-R	6-4	240	8-28-02	1	2	3.03	10	4	0	0	30	21	13	10	0	16	33	.196	.171	.208	10.01	4.85
Kelvin Ramirez	R-R	6-4	187	6-10-01	1	2	6.75	14	0	0	1	20	26	15	15	1	7	24	.317	.343	.298	10.80	3.15
Livan Reinoso	R-R	6-1	185	8-27-98	1	0	0.00	3	0	0	0	3	0	0	0	0	2	2	.000	.000	.000	6.00	6.00
Christian Romero	R-R	6-3	195	12-11-02	1	1	4.91	10	1	0	0	22	22	12	12	3	2	28	.256	.375	.210	11.45	0.82
Waylin Santana	R-R	6-1	155	3-13-03	0	4	10.13	9	5	0	0	21	28	24	24	2	8	21	.315	.286	.328	8.86	3.38
David Tiburcio	R-R	6-2	195	12-29-01	2	2	3.80	8	3	0	0	21	24	11	9	4	5	23	.264	.156	.322	9.70	2.11
Rafael Tua	R-R	5-10	145	10-26-01	0	1	7.45	9	0	0	0	10	14	10	8	4	4	17	.326	.235	.385	15.83	3.72
Luis Valdez	L-L	6-2	158	7-18-03	3	0	2.86	8	5	0	0	28	22	9	9	2	1	37	.212	.167	.230	11.75	0.32
Callum Wallace	R-R	6-3	190	4-6-04	0	0	3.27	11	0	0	0	11	7	5	4	1	4	13	.194	.182	.200	10.64	3.27
Justin Wrobleski	L-L	6-1	194	7-14-00	0	1	1.80	10	8	0	0	15	12	3	3	0	0	21	.211	.286	.186	12.60	0.00
Reynaldo Yean	R-R	6-4	190	1-4-04	0	0	0.00	3	0	0	0	3	2	0	0	0	3	5	.182	.000	.250	15.00	9.00
Jhan Zambrano	R-R	6-3	165	12-21-01	1	1	3.86	10	0	0	0	16	14	10	7	4	8	16	.246	.250	.243	8.82	4.41

Fielding

C: Chalo 4, Galiz 16, Liranzo 20, Puerta 2, Reid 3, Rodriguez 17, Rushing 1. **1B:** Caraballo 1, Decker 3, Froemke 6, Liranzo 7, Lockwood-Powell 5, Nevin 1, Puerta 16, Rodriguez 8, Sosa 14. **2B:** Armas 10, Diaz 14, Doncon 21, Espinosa 7, Izarra 2, Wagner 5. **3B:** Armas 5, Decker 1, Droz 17, Espinosa 22, Froemke 1, Hoese 3, Izarra 2, Lao 2, Wagner 9. **SS:** Diaz 34, Doncon 15, Droz 3, Izarra 4, McLain 2, Young 2. **OF:** Alleyne 2, Alonso 39, Armas 11, Biddison 2, Caraballo 32, Enrique 28, Morales 34, Nevin 1, Newell 11, Puerta 5, Reed 3, Restituyo 13

DSL LAD BAUTISTA — *ROOKIE*

DOMINICAN SUMMER LEAGUE

Batting	B-T	HT	WT	DOB	AVG	vLH	vRH	G	AB	R	H	2B	3B	HR	RBI	BB	HBP	SH	SF	SO	SB	CS	SLG	OBP
Agustin Acosta	L-R	6-2	173	9-7-04	.239	.286	.231	46	138	31	33	4	2	4	19	33	5	0	0	43	12	5	.384	.403
Alexander Albertus	R-R	6-1	176	10-27-04	.304	.350	.293	40	112	25	34	3	2	0	16	32	4	0	2	21	6	0	.366	.467
Daniel Arrias	L-L	5-10	170	11-30-03	.100	.200	.080	17	30	6	3	0	0	0	2	7	3	0	0	4	1	2	.100	.325
Carlos Avila	R-R	0-0	0	12-4-03	.308	.294	.311	35	120	22	37	5	1	2	23	15	6	0	0	18	4	3	.417	.411
Luis Barett	R-R	5-11	165	11-25-03	.237	.333	.207	13	38	7	9	4	0	0	5	2	1	0	0	5	2	0	.342	.293
2-team total (30 DSL LAD Mega)					.215	.267	.208	43	121	32	26	5	0	1	9	25	6	0	0	23	6	2	.281	.375
Elio Campos	R-R	5-9	157	1-2-04	.390	.200	.417	16	41	13	16	3	0	0	6	8	0	0	0	1	4	0	.463	.490
Luis Castaneda	R-R	5-11	163	2-24-04	.193	.091	.217	22	57	9	11	2	0	0	6	9	3	1	0	16	0	1	.228	.333

2-team total (1 DSL LAD Mega)					.193	.091	.217	23	57	9	11	2	0	0	6	10	3	1	0	16	0	1	.228	.343
Josue De Paula	L-L	6-3	185	5-24-05	.349	.355	.348	53	186	42	65	13	2	5	30	32	3	0	2	31	16	6	.522	.448
Angel Diaz	R-R	5-11	180	2-4-04	.310	.375	.298	37	100	13	31	13	1	1	17	10	6	0	1	22	1	3	.490	.402
Derlin Figueroa	L-R	6-0	163	9-7-03	.233	.167	.243	15	43	4	10	3	1	2	10	4	1	1	1	9	4	2	.488	.306
2-team total (28 DSL LAD Mega)					.296	.217	.311	43	142	31	42	5	1	9	38	21	3	1	2	35	8	4	.535	.393
Jose Hernandez	R-R	6-1	145	4-30-03	.188	.167	.200	5	16	3	3	1	1	0	2	2	1	0	0	1	1	0	.375	.316
2-team total (15 DSL LAD Mega)					.226	.063	.283	20	62	10	14	5	1	1	10	9	1	0	3	16	1	0	.387	.320
Roger Lasso	B-R	6-0	180	2-27-04	.201	.160	.210	47	149	27	30	6	0	5	24	24	4	0	3	41	2	4	.342	.322
Umar Male	R-R	5-10	175	5-14-01	.200	.273	.176	18	45	8	9	0	0	2	5	8	1	0	0	21	1	0	.333	.333
Mairoshendrick Martinus	R-R	6-3	161	2-3-05	.264	.333	.255	52	182	43	48	6	5	7	38	19	4	0	6	47	10	5	.467	.336
Yorfran Medina	R-R	6-4	195	1-25-05	.181	.100	.194	26	72	11	13	3	0	2	13	6	5	0	0	26	1	2	.306	.289
Oswaldo Osorio	L-R	6-1	171	4-12-05	.239	.167	.254	44	138	42	33	4	5	6	24	39	8	0	2	44	11	7	.471	.428
Jeral Perez	R-R	6-0	179	11-6-04	.278	.241	.286	47	176	38	49	11	2	8	28	24	3	0	2	34	5	2	.500	.371
Victor Rodrigues	R-R	6-3	203	9-23-04	.237	.350	.221	44	156	24	37	8	1	2	29	15	6	0	2	29	4	1	.340	.324

Pitching	B-T	HT	WT	DOB	W	L	ERA	G	GS	CG	SV	IP	H	R	ER	HR	BB	SO	AVG	vLH	vRH	K/9	BB/9
Dailoui Abad	R-R	6-0	168	5-2-02	2	1	6.14	17	0	0	2	22	27	18	15	3	12	19	.300	.419	.237	7.77	4.91
2-team total (1 DSL LAD Mega)					2	1	5.92	18	0	0	2	24	28	19	16	3	13	20	.289	.371	.242	7.40	4.81
Edgar Aviles	R-R	6-2	150	1-20-05	1	0	0.00	2	0	0	0	3	2	0	0	0	3	0	.182	.000	.333	0.00	8.10
2-team total (15 DSL LAD Mega)					4	0	5.18	17	0	0	0	24	17	17	14	3	17	21	.195	.156	.238	7.77	6.29
Aldrin Batista	R-R	6-2	185	5-4-03	1	1	1.55	13	11	0	0	41	26	18	7	1	23	38	.179	.180	.179	8.41	5.09
Peter Bonilla	L-L	6-3	195	12-16-04	6	0	1.95	18	0	0	0	32	23	11	7	3	11	37	.209	.000	.221	10.30	3.06
Felix Cabrera	L-L	6-3	170	4-8-02	2	1	6.75	16	0	0	0	23	33	20	17	0	14	21	.333	.000	.375	8.34	5.56
Steven Castillo	R-R	6-2	195	9-15-04	2	1	6.14	10	0	0	0	15	19	10	10	1	5	14	.311	.316	.310	8.59	3.07
Nicolas Cruz	R-R	5-11	160	4-23-04	1	0	3.00	1	0	0	0	3	2	1	1	1	0	3	.182	.500	.000	9.00	0.00
2-team total (14 DSL LAD Mega)					5	0	3.63	15	0	0	1	22	27	14	9	3	4	20	.290	.310	.281	8.06	1.61
Yuliangel De La Cruz	R-R	6-3	158	1-24-05	2	1	7.78	12	3	0	0	20	26	22	17	2	11	14	.310	.320	.305	6.41	5.03
2-team total (3 DSL LAD Mega)					2	1	7.13	15	4	0	0	24	30	25	19	2	17	15	.303	.333	.290	5.63	6.38
Joldelanio De Los Santos	R-R	6-0	175	9-21-03	1	2	7.94	16	3	0	0	23	24	25	20	0	19	13	.258	.200	.279	5.16	7.54
Dilan Figueredo	R-R	6-0	174	3-28-03	0	1	5.40	4	0	0	0	3	5	2	2	0	5	7	.357	.000	.625	18.90	13.50
2-team total (8 DSL LAD Mega)					0	2	5.19	12	6	0	0	17	16	12	10	2	20	18	.250	.150	.295	9.35	10.38
Juan Hernandez	R-R	6-2	187	11-19-02	0	0	16.20	2	0	0	0	2	1	3	3	0	4	2	.167	.333	.000	10.80	21.60
Wilkerson Hernandez	R-R	6-3	185	9-30-03	1	0	7.45	9	0	0	0	10	10	9	8	2	6	4	.286	.214	.333	3.72	5.59
2-team total (1 DSL LAD Mega)					1	0	8.44	10	0	0	0	11	12	11	10	3	6	5	.300	.313	.292	4.22	5.06
Jhonny Jimenez	R-R	6-5	180	11-9-03	3	1	11.70	14	3	0	0	20	21	28	26	3	21	19	.266	.348	.232	8.55	9.45
Luis Joseph	R-R	6-4	176	4-22-03	0	0	2.70	4	2	0	0	7	7	2	2	1	0	6	.280	.333	.231	8.10	0.00
2-team total (4 DSL LAD Mega)					0	2	4.96	8	6	0	0	16	16	12	9	4	3	16	.254	.286	.229	8.82	1.65
Sean Linan	R-R	6-0	185	11-7-04	4	1	2.08	15	0	0	1	26	14	6	6	0	11	27	.161	.182	.148	9.35	3.81
Jesus Luna	R-R	6-6	165	11-6-00	3	1	2.10	18	0	0	4	26	18	14	6	0	9	29	.191	.086	.254	10.17	3.16
Ricardo Montero	R-R	6-6	237	2-17-04	0	4	6.38	14	13	0	0	37	36	33	26	1	26	27	.271	.283	.264	6.63	6.38
Accimias Morales	R-R	6-5	190	9-13-04	1	2	3.19	12	12	0	0	37	38	19	13	0	3	24	.262	.267	.260	5.89	0.74
Kinn Omosako	R-R	6-4	210	6-24-04	0	0	0.61	13	1	0	0	15	13	1	1	0	8	10	.250	.083	.300	6.14	4.91
Pedro Santillan	R-R	6-4	200	7-7-01	0	2	7.23	17	0	0	0	19	26	20	15	0	14	8	.321	.464	.245	3.86	6.75
Ben Serunkuma	R-R	5-10	170	9-19-01	2	1	2.11	12	0	0	0	21	18	8	5	1	3	19	.222	.150	.246	8.02	1.27
Enrike Sevilya	R-R	6-3	195	7-27-05	0	2	4.11	12	0	0	0	15	8	7	7	0	17	6	.157	.214	.135	3.52	9.98
Yoryi Simarra	R-R	6-1	174	11-18-04	1	2	5.23	12	8	0	0	33	31	19	19	2	18	33	.272	.341	.233	9.09	4.96
Missael Soto	R-R	0-0	0	9-21-03	1	1	6.39	8	0	0	0	13	13	13	9	2	4	13	.255	.154	.289	9.24	2.84
Luis Valdez	L-L	6-2	158	7-18-03	0	0	0.00	3	3	0	0	10	4	0	0	0	0	6	.118	.250	.100	5.40	0.00

Fielding

C: Avila 16, Diaz 22, Rodrigues 24. **1B:** Avila 16, Castaneda 5, Diaz 15, Figueroa 1, Hernandez 4, Medina 11, Rodrigues 18. **2B:** Albertus 14, Campos 2, Castaneda 13, Figueroa 5, Martinus 7, Osorio 9, Perez 17. **3B:** Albertus 12, Campos 1, Castaneda 4, Figueroa 4, Hernandez 1, Male 1, Martinus 15, Osorio 14, Perez 9. **SS:** Albertus 7, Martinus 23, Osorio 16, Perez 15. **OF:** Acosta 42, Arrias 16, Barett 15, Campos 9, De Paula 41, Figueroa 2, Lasso 46, Male 10, Medina 18

DSL LAD MEGA — *ROOKIE*

DOMINICAN SUMMER LEAGUE

Batting	B-T	HT	WT	DOB	AVG	vLH	vRH	G	AB	R	H	2B	3B	HR	RBI	BB	HBP	SH	SF	SO	SB	CS	SLG	OBP
Luis Barett	R-R	5-11	165	11-25-03	.205	.167	.208	30	83	25	17	1	0	1	4	23	5	0	0	18	4	2	.253	.405
2-team total (13 DSL LAD Bautista)					.215	.267	.208	43	121	32	26	5	0	1	9	25	6	0	0	23	6	2	.281	.375
Luis Castaneda	R-R	5-11	163	2-24-04	--	--	--	1	0	0	0	0	0	0	0	1	0	0	0	0	0	0	--	1.000
2-team total (22 DSL LAD Bautista)					.193	.091	.217	23	57	9	11	2	0	0	6	10	3	1	0	16	0	1	.228	.343
Natanael Castillo	R-R	6-0	150	11-6-04	.176	.000	.203	25	74	11	13	2	0	0	8	11	3	0	1	18	0	2	.203	.303
Miguel Dominguez	R-R	6-0	195	2-20-04	.235	.143	.254	27	81	21	19	5	0	3	12	22	4	0	0	26	1	0	.407	.421
Derlin Figueroa	L-R	6-0	163	9-7-03	.323	.235	.341	28	99	27	32	2	0	7	28	17	2	0	1	26	4	2	.556	.429
2-team total (15 DSL LAD Bautista)					.296	.217	.311	43	142	31	42	5	1	9	38	21	3	1	2	35	8	4	.535	.393
Darol Garcia	R-R	5-11	178	9-12-02	.359	.300	.373	31	103	25	37	2	1	1	11	22	0	1	0	21	7	4	.427	.472
Luis Guerra	R-R	6-1	180	10-4-03	.268	.200	.283	49	168	41	45	10	0	3	28	24	2	0	1	28	1	2	.381	.364
Eduardo Guerrero	B-R	6-2	165	5-9-05	.297	.423	.274	44	172	40	51	4	0	1	35	23	3	0	4	32	6	4	.337	.381
Jose Hernandez	R-R	6-1	145	4-30-03	.239	.000	.306	15	46	7	11	4	0	1	8	7	0	0	3	15	0	0	.391	.321
2-team total (5 DSL LAD Bautista)					.226	.063	.283	20	62	10	14	5	1	1	10	9	1	0	3	16	1	0	.387	.320
Jose Meza	R-R	6-1	160	4-22-03	.267	.241	.272	51	187	42	50	8	2	6	37	22	5	0	4	41	9	3	.428	.353
Samuel Munoz	L-R	6-3	190	9-22-04	.347	.200	.366	47	173	39	60	12	5	1	42	26	4	0	7	34	4	5	.491	.429
Raynerd Ortega	R-R	6-1	154	7-8-05	.233	.077	.250	36	133	19	31	4	0	1	13	23	2	0	0	40	3	2	.286	.354
Javier Pena	R-R	6-0	185	9-10-04	.158	.000	.176	11	38	3	6	0	0	0	2	2	0	0	1	12	1	0	.158	.195

Jorge Puerta	R-R	5-11	178	12-5-01	.431	.556	.405	15	51	13	22	8	0	4	21	10	3	0	0	2	0	0	.824	.547
Carlos Rojas	R-R	6-0	165	7-25-02	.300	.286	.303	46	160	33	48	17	1	1	36	30	5	0	6	16	2	0	.438	.413
Edwin Sanchez	R-R	6-3	180	8-2-04	.234	.150	.250	44	128	30	30	7	0	5	29	30	6	0	3	35	3	3	.406	.395
German Tapia	R-R	6-2	170	9-19-03	.219	.000	.259	11	32	8	7	1	1	0	5	7	1	0	1	10	1	2	.313	.366
2-team total (26 DSL Tampa Bay)					.295	.211	.314	37	105	30	31	4	1	2	16	30	4	0	2	27	4	6	.410	.461
Jefferson Valladares	R-R	6-0	190	5-30-02	.333	.250	.344	45	147	36	49	8	2	3	30	16	19	0	1	30	5	6	.476	.459

Pitching	**B-T**	**HT**	**WT**	**DOB**	**W**	**L**	**ERA**	**G**	**GS**	**CG**	**SV**	**IP**	**H**	**R**	**ER**	**HR**	**BB**	**SO**	**AVG**	**vLH**	**vRH**	**K/9**	**BB/9**
Dailoui Abad	R-R	6-0	168	5-2-02	0	0	3.86	1	0	0	0	2	1	1	1	0	1	1	.143	.000	.333	3.86	3.86
2-team total (17 DSL LAD Bautista)					2	1	5.92	18	0	0	2	24	28	19	16	3	13	20	.289	.371	.242	7.40	4.81
Guillermo Arvizu	L-L	6-4	242	8-28-02	1	2	5.46	15	6	0	0	31	37	21	19	3	13	40	.306	.294	.308	11.49	3.73
Edgar Aviles	R-R	6-2	150	1-20-05	3	0	6.00	15	0	0	0	21	15	17	14	3	14	21	.197	.175	.222	9.00	6.00
2-team total (2 DSL LAD Bautista)					4	0	5.18	17	0	0	0	24	17	17	14	3	17	21	.195	.156	.238	7.77	6.29
Alvaro Benua	R-R	6-4	198	1-11-03	4	0	4.75	12	3	0	0	30	20	19	16	0	27	42	.189	.313	.135	12.46	8.01
Moises Brito	L-L	6-5	215	7-9-02	1	0	1.59	4	1	0	0	11	6	3	2	1	0	13	.150	.333	.118	10.32	0.00
2-team total (12 DSL Blue Jays)					3	4	1.79	16	3	0	1	40	27	11	8	2	1	45	.185	.258	.165	10.04	0.22
Ilmerson Colon	L-L	6-2	167	3-10-05	0	0	7.00	8	0	0	1	9	10	7	7	2	7	13	.323	.000	.400	13.00	7.00
Nicolas Cruz	R-R	5-11	160	4-23-04	4	0	3.72	14	0	0	1	19	25	13	8	2	4	17	.305	.280	.316	7.91	1.86
2-team total (1 DSL LAD Bautista)					5	0	3.63	15	0	0	1	22	27	14	9	3	4	20	.290	.310	.281	8.06	1.61
Yuliangel De La Cruz	R-R	6-3	158	1-24-05	0	0	4.15	3	1	0	0	4	4	3	2	0	6	1	.267	.400	.200	2.08	12.46
2-team total (12 DSL LAD Bautista)					2	1	7.13	15	4	0	0	24	30	25	19	2	17	15	.303	.333	.290	5.63	6.38
Anderson Estevez	R-R	6-2	185	12-12-04	1	2	8.27	14	0	0	1	21	26	24	19	2	26	21	.317	.406	.260	9.15	11.32
Dilan Figueredo	R-R	6-0	174	3-28-03	0	1	5.14	8	6	0	0	14	11	10	8	2	15	11	.220	.214	.222	7.07	9.64
2-team total (4 DSL LAD Bautista)					0	2	5.19	12	6	0	0	17	16	12	10	2	20	18	.250	.150	.295	9.35	10.38
Domingo Geronimo	R-R	5-11	150	10-7-04	1	2	2.35	16	0	0	1	23	20	9	6	1	8	25	.233	.206	.250	9.78	3.13
Joseilyn Gonzalez	R-R	5-11	160	4-8-02	2	2	6.66	17	1	0	0	26	29	24	19	3	8	25	.282	.452	.208	8.77	2.81
Jholbran Herder	R-R	6-2	170	11-2-04	1	1	2.56	12	12	0	0	39	31	15	11	1	12	33	.215	.286	.170	7.68	2.79
Wilkerson Hernandez	R-R	6-3	185	9-30-03	0	0	18.00	1	0	0	0	1	2	2	2	1	0	1	.400	1.000	.000	9.00	0.00
2-team total (9 DSL LAD Bautista)					1	0	8.44	10	0	0	0	11	12	11	10	3	6	5	.300	.313	.292	4.22	5.06
Wuillians Herrera	R-R	6-4	183	3-12-04	1	0	13.21	16	0	0	1	16	19	29	23	0	25	16	.292	.167	.366	9.19	14.36
Luis Joseph	R-R	6-4	176	4-22-03	0	2	6.52	4	4	0	0	10	9	10	7	3	3	10	.237	.250	.227	9.31	2.79
2-team total (4 DSL LAD Bautista)					0	2	4.96	8	6	0	0	16	16	12	9	4	3	16	.254	.286	.229	8.82	1.65
Edgar Leon	R-R	6-3	170	12-29-04	1	3	2.97	13	10	0	0	30	24	17	10	1	22	21	.222	.214	.227	6.23	6.53
Carlos Martinez	R-R	6-3	190	11-9-01	0	0	0.00	2	0	0	0	3	2	2	0	0	1	5	.182	.333	.125	16.88	3.38
Arod McKenzie	L-L	6-3	165	5-25-05	2	1	7.79	12	2	0	0	17	19	16	15	1	16	9	.284	.667	.266	4.67	8.31
Lesther Medrano	R-R	6-2	185	3-5-03	4	2	4.82	16	0	0	2	28	35	24	15	5	5	26	.324	.385	.290	8.36	1.61
Roiger Mujica	R-R	6-2	180	7-24-05	0	0	6.52	15	8	0	0	19	18	19	14	2	17	19	.243	.321	.196	8.84	7.91
Jose Rodriguez	B-R	6-6	200	7-18-01	5	0	0.47	17	0	0	2	19	7	1	1	1	5	30	.113	.091	.125	14.21	2.37
Luciano Romero	R-R	6-2	190	1-8-05	1	2	6.16	15	5	0	0	19	26	22	13	0	26	20	.329	.308	.340	9.47	12.32
Angel Tello	R-R	6-4	165	1-26-04	0	0	3.54	17	0	0	0	20	21	8	8	1	12	16	.288	.227	.314	7.08	5.31
Jefferson Valladares	R-R	6-0	190	5-30-02	1	0	0.00	1	0	0	0	1	0	1	0	0	1	1	.000	.000	.000	6.75	6.75
Michael Vilchez	R-R	6-3	180	6-3-04	1	1	3.57	17	0	0	1	23	20	13	9	0	14	20	.238	.192	.259	7.94	5.56
Reynaldo Yean	R-R	6-4	190	1-4-04	3	1	3.38	17	0	0	2	21	9	10	8	1	11	36	.122	.154	.104	15.19	4.64

Fielding

C: Dominguez 20, Pena 1, Puerta 1, Rojas 29, Valladares 10. **1B:** Figueroa 6, Hernandez 4, Puerta 12, Rojas 14, Valladares 23. **2B:** Castaneda 1, Castillo 9, Figueroa 6, Garcia 9, Guerra 14, Guerrero 14, Hernandez 1, Ortega 11, Pena 1. **3B:** Castillo 3, Figueroa 8, Garcia 7, Guerra 28, Guerrero 1, Hernandez 6, Ortega 6, Valladares 5. **SS:** Castillo 10, Garcia 7, Guerrero 26, Hernandez 2, Ortega 18. **OF:** Barett 30, Figueroa 6, Garcia 5, Guerra 9, Meza 49, Munoz 28, Puerta 2, Sanchez 43, Tapia 11, Valladares 6.

Miami Marlins

SEASON IN A SENTENCE: The Marlins floundered among the other Beasts of the East, finishing with a 69-93 record that placed them in fourth place, ahead of only the Nationals.

HIGH POINT: Sandy Alcantara's tour de force season placed him firmly among the best starters in the sport and earned him a spot among the National League's Cy Young Award finalists. Alcantara pitched a league-high 228.1 innings, including six complete games. He finished with a 14-9, 2.28 record and 207 strikeouts.

LOW POINT: Any time Alcantara was not on the mound was a low point. The team scored just 586 runs, the third-fewest in the sport and fewest in the National League. The Marlins also made changes to their braintrust during and after the season. The team fired VP of player development Gary Denbo in July, then did the same with farm director Geoff DeGroot and professional scouting director Hadi Raad after the season. Toward the end of September, manager Don Mattingly informed the club he would retire instead of returning for 2023.

NOTABLE ROOKIE: Righthander Edward Cabrera has long had potential but has seen his progress stunted by injuries. When he got the chance this year, he shined. Cabrera finished 6-4, 3.01 with 75 strikeouts in 71 innings. The Marlins also got production from unheralded rookie infielder Charles LeBlanc. LeBlanc, 26, hit four home runs and produced an OPS of .723. The Marlins also gave extended auditions to some of their top prospects, including outfielders JJ Bleday, Peyton Burdick and Jordan Groshans, who were largely underwhelming. Catcher Nick Fortes cracked nine home runs in 72 games.

KEY TRANSACTIONS: Miami made one deal at the trade deadline, spinning relievers Anthony Bass and Zach Pop to the Blue Jays for Groshans.

ON THE FARM: The Marlins' farm system was thinned by injuries and graduations, but one man stood tall above the rest: Eury Perez. The towering teenaged righthander dominated much older competition nearly all season long, save for a stretch before he went on the injured list. Perez finished with 110 strikeouts and just 25 walks in 77 innings, firmly establishing himself as one of the best pitching prospects in the game. Righty Max Meyer also made his big league debut but required Tommy John surgery in August. Miami selected Louisiana State slugger Jacob Berry with their first-round selection in the draft.

OPENING DAY PAYROLL: $79,775,000 (26th)

PLAYERS OF THE YEAR

MAJOR LEAGUE

Sandy Alcantara
RHP

14-9, 2.28 ERA
207 SO, 50 BB, 229 IP
Led NL in IP, also 6 CG

MINOR LEAGUE

Eury Perez
RHP

(AA/LoA)
3.97 ERA, 1.14 WHIP
110 SO, 25 BB, 77 IP

ORGANIZATION LEADERS

Batting — *Minimum 250 AB

MAJORS		
* AVG	Garrett Cooper	.261
* OPS	Garrett Cooper	.752
HR	Jesus Aguilar	15
RBI	Garrett Cooper	50
MINORS		
* AVG	Willians Astudillo, Jacksonville	.307
* OBP	Kyle Castillo, Beloit, Jupiter	.406
* SLG	Willians Astudillo, Jacksonville	.541
* OPS	Willians Astudillo, Jacksonville	.912
R	Nasim Nuñez, Beloit, Pensacola	75
H	Brian Miller, Jacksonville	119
TB	Jerar Encarnacion, Jacksonville, Pensacola	194
2B	Luis Aviles, Jacksonville, Pensacola	26
	Victor Mesa Jr., Beloit	26
3B	Brian Miller, Jacksonville	9
HR	Griffin Conine, Pensacola	24
RBI	Griffin Conine, Pensacola	74
BB	Zach Zubia, Jupiter, Beloit	96
SO	Griffin Conine, Pensacola	183
SB	Nasim Nuñez, Beloit, Pensacola	70

Pitching — #Minimum 75 IP

MAJORS		
W	Sandy Alcantara	14
# ERA	Sandy Alcantara	2.28
SO	Sandy Alcantara	207
SV	Tanner Scott	20
MINORS		
W	M.D. Johnson, Beloit	9
	Matthew Kent, Jacksonville	9
	Bryan Hoeing, Jacksonville, Pensacola	9
L	Matthew Kent, Jacksonville	11
# ERA	George Soriano, Jacksonville, Pensacola	2.72
G	Eli Villalobos, Pensacola, Jacksonville	52
GS	Jeff Lindgren, Pensacola, Jacksonville	27
SV	Eli Villalobos, Pensacola, Jacksonville	14
IP	Matthew Kent, Jacksonville	144.1
BB	Sandro Bargallo, Jupiter	70
SO	Dax Fulton, Beloit, Pensacola	150
# AVG	Eli Villalobos, Pensacola, Jacksonville	.191

2022 PERFORMANCE

General Manager: Kim Ng. **Farm Director:** Gary Denbo. **Scouting Director:** DJ Svihlik

Class	Team	League	W	L	PCT	Finish	Manager
Majors	Miami Marlins	National	69	93	.426	11th (15)	Don Mattingly
Triple-A	Jacksonville Jumbo Shrimp	International	80	69	.537	6th (20)	Daren Brown
Double-A	Pensacola Blue Wahoos	Southern	68	63	.519	3rd (8)	Kevin Randel
High-A	Beloit Sky Carp	Midwest	62	67	.481	8th (12)	Jorge Hernandez
Low-A	Jupiter Hammerheads	Florida State	63	66	.488	7th (10)	Angel Espada
Rookie	FCL Marlins	Florida Complex	31	24	.564	6th (16)	Luis Dorante
Overall 2022 Minor League Record			355	354	.501	16th (30)	

ORGANIZATION STATISTICS

MIAMI MARLINS

MIAMI MARLINS

NATIONAL LEAGUE

Batting	B-T	HT	WT	DOB	AVG	vLH	vRH	G	AB	R	H	2B	3B	HR	RBI	BB	HBP	SH	SF	SO	SB	CS	SLG	OBP
Jesus Aguilar	R-R	6-3	277	6-30-90	.236	.217	.241	113	415	37	98	18	0	15	49	27	4	0	5	106	1	0	.388	.286
Brian Anderson	R-R	6-3	208	5-19-93	.222	.247	.215	98	338	43	75	16	1	8	28	37	7	0	1	101	1	0	.346	.311
Willians Astudillo	R-R	5-9	225	10-14-91	.241	.214	.250	21	54	5	13	0	0	1	4	1	0	0	0	3	1	0	.296	.255
Jon Berti	R-R	5-10	190	1-22-90	.240	.232	.243	102	358	47	86	17	3	4	28	42	3	0	1	89	41	5	.338	.324
JJ Bleday	L-L	6-3	205	11-10-97	.167	.163	.168	65	204	21	34	10	2	5	16	30	2	0	2	67	4	1	.309	.277
Peyton Burdick	R-R	6-0	205	2-26-97	.207	.242	.186	32	92	8	19	4	0	4	11	8	2	0	0	35	1	0	.380	.284
Jazz Chisholm Jr.	L-R	5-11	184	2-1-98	.254	.143	.275	60	213	39	54	10	4	14	45	21	3	0	3	66	12	5	.535	.325
Garrett Cooper	R-R	6-5	235	12-25-90	.261	.228	.270	119	414	37	108	33	2	9	50	40	10	0	5	119	0	0	.415	.337
Bryan De La Cruz	R-R	6-2	175	12-16-96	.252	.184	.277	115	329	38	83	20	0	13	43	19	2	0	4	90	4	0	.432	.294
Lewin Diaz	L-L	6-4	217	11-19-96	.169	.071	.178	58	160	12	27	4	0	5	11	11	1	0	2	54	1	0	.288	.224
Joe Dunand	R-R	6-2	205	9-20-95	.300	.500	.167	3	10	2	3	1	0	1	1	0	1	0	0	3	0	0	.700	.364
Jerar Encarnacion	R-R	6-4	250	10-22-97	.182	.160	.192	23	77	7	14	3	0	3	14	3	0	0	1	32	2	0	.338	.210
Nick Fortes	R-R	5-11	198	11-11-96	.230	.213	.237	72	217	41	50	6	1	9	24	18	5	0	0	45	5	3	.392	.304
Avisail Garcia	R-R	6-4	250	6-12-91	.224	.219	.225	98	357	31	80	9	0	8	35	17	4	0	2	109	4	0	.317	.266
Erik Gonzalez	R-R	6-3	205	8-31-91	.189	.091	.231	16	37	4	7	1	0	0	3	4	0	0	0	12	1	0	.216	.268
Jordan Groshans	R-R	6-3	200	11-10-99	.262	.300	.255	17	61	9	16	0	0	1	2	4	0	0	0	13	0	0	.311	.308
Billy Hamilton	R-R	6-0	160	9-9-90	.077	.000	.111	20	13	9	1	0	0	0	0	1	0	1	0	8	7	0	.077	.143
Payton Henry	R-R	6-2	215	6-24-97	.143	.100	.167	15	28	2	4	0	0	0	4	5	2	0	0	8	0	0	.143	.314
Charles Leblanc	R-R	6-3	195	6-3-96	.263	.239	.273	48	156	18	41	10	0	4	11	12	1	0	0	53	4	2	.404	.320
Miguel Rojas	R-R	6-0	188	2-24-89	.236	.215	.243	140	471	34	111	19	2	6	36	26	6	1	3	61	9	3	.323	.283
Jesus Sanchez	L-R	6-3	222	10-7-97	.214	.145	.229	98	313	38	67	14	3	13	36	26	3	0	1	92	1	0	.403	.280
Jorge Soler	R-R	6-4	235	2-25-92	.207	.203	.209	72	270	32	56	13	0	13	34	31	3	0	1	90	0	2	.400	.295
Jacob Stallings	R-R	6-5	225	12-22-89	.223	.210	.225	114	346	25	77	12	0	4	34	29	6	1	2	83	0	1	.292	.292
Joey Wendle	L-R	6-1	195	4-26-90	.259	.230	.266	101	347	27	90	24	1	3	32	15	5	1	3	50	12	3	.360	.297
Luke Williams	R-R	6-1	186	8-9-96	.235	.243	.231	71	115	20	27	4	1	1	3	9	0	0	0	40	11	4	.313	.290
2-team total (8 San Francisco Giants)					.236	.244	.232	79	127	21	30	5	1	1	6	9	0	0	0	44	11	4	.315	.287

Pitching	B-T	HT	WT	DOB	W	L	ERA	G	GS	CG	SV	IP	H	R	ER	HR	BB	SO	AVG	vLH	vRH	K/9	BB/9
Sandy Alcantara	R-R	6-5	200	9-7-95	14	9	2.28	32	32	6	0	229	174	67	58	16	50	207	.212	.196	.231	8.15	1.97
Shawn Armstrong	R-R	6-2	225	9-11-90	0	0	10.80	7	0	0	0	7	10	10	8	1	3	5	.333	.364	.316	6.75	4.05
Willians Astudillo	R-R	5-9	225	10-14-91	0	0	0.00	2	0	0	0	2	0	0	0	0	2	0	.000	.000	.000	0.00	9.00
Anthony Bass	R-R	6-2	205	11-1-87	2	3	1.41	45	0	0	0	45	32	10	7	1	10	45	.198	.262	.155	9.07	2.01
Anthony Bender	R-R	6-4	205	2-3-95	1	3	3.26	22	0	0	6	19	17	7	7	3	8	17	.250	.357	.175	7.91	3.72
Richard Bleier	L-L	6-3	215	4-16-87	2	2	3.55	55	1	0	1	51	63	22	20	3	10	32	.301	.256	.336	5.68	1.78
Huascar Brazoban	R-R	6-3	155	10-15-89	1	1	3.09	27	0	0	0	32	26	13	11	3	21	40	.222	.256	.205	11.25	5.91
Jeff Brigham	R-R	6-0	195	2-16-92	0	1	3.38	16	0	0	1	24	22	10	9	3	10	28	.244	.229	.255	10.50	3.75
Edward Cabrera	R-R	6-5	217	4-13-98	6	4	3.01	14	14	0	0	72	44	24	24	10	33	75	.177	.168	.185	9.42	4.14
Daniel Castano	L-L	6-3	231	9-17-94	1	3	4.04	10	7	0	0	36	42	20	16	5	9	20	.292	.267	.303	5.05	2.27
Jake Fishman	L-L	6-3	195	2-8-95	0	0	4.09	7	0	0	0	11	13	5	5	0	0	6	.289	.313	.276	4.91	0.00
Dylan Floro	L-R	6-2	203	12-27-90	1	3	3.02	56	0	0	10	54	48	23	18	4	15	48	.235	.293	.202	8.05	2.52
Braxton Garrett	R-L	6-2	202	8-5-97	3	7	3.58	17	17	0	0	88	86	38	35	9	24	90	.254	.173	.280	9.20	2.45
Louis Head	R-R	6-1	180	4-23-90	0	0	7.23	23	0	0	1	24	26	19	19	4	11	23	.271	.314	.246	8.75	4.18
Elieser Hernandez	R-R	6-0	214	5-3-95	3	6	6.35	20	10	0	0	62	67	48	44	19	22	60	.269	.273	.264	8.66	3.18
Bryan Hoeing	R-R	6-6	210	10-19-96	1	1	12.08	8	1	0	0	13	19	17	17	5	5	6	.352	.333	.361	4.26	3.55
Jordan Holloway	R-R	6-6	230	6-13-96	0	0	3.38	1	0	0	0	3	3	1	1	0	1	2	.300	.000	.375	6.75	3.38
A.J. Ladwig	R-R	6-5	220	12-24-92	0	0	10.80	1	0	0	0	3	6	4	4	2	0	0	.400	.333	.444	0.00	0.00
Pablo Lopez	L-R	6-4	225	3-7-96	10	10	3.75	32	32	0	0	180	157	78	75	21	53	174	.234	.249	.218	8.70	2.65
Jesus Luzardo	L-L	6-0	218	9-30-97	4	7	3.32	18	18	0	0	100	69	40	37	10	35	120	.191	.203	.189	10.76	3.14
Max Meyer	L-R	6-0	196	3-12-99	0	1	7.50	2	2	0	0	6	7	5	5	2	2	6	.292	.182	.385	9.00	3.00
Tommy Nance	R-R	6-6	235	3-19-91	2	3	4.33	35	2	0	0	44	45	22	21	5	21	57	.265	.184	.330	11.75	4.33
Andrew Nardi	L-L	6-3	215	8-18-98	1	1	9.82	13	0	0	0	15	25	17	16	5	14	24	.362	.435	.326	14.73	8.59
Nick Neidert	R-R	6-1	202	11-20-96	0	1	3.60	1	1	0	0	5	5	2	2	1	0	3	.250	.308	.143	5.40	0.00
Steven Okert	L-L	6-2	202	7-9-91	5	5	2.98	60	0	0	0	51	34	19	17	7	26	63	.186	.239	.152	11.05	4.56
Zach Pop	R-R	6-4	220	9-20-96	2	0	3.60	18	0	0	0	20	23	9	8	1	2	14	.288	.300	.280	6.30	0.90

Cody Poteet	R-R	6-1	190	7-30-94	0	1	3.86	12	2	0	0	28	23	12	12	4	11	21	.223	.245	.200	6.75	3.54
Trevor Rogers	L-L	6-5	217	11-13-97	4	11	5.47	23	23	0	0	107	116	69	65	15	45	106	.274	.194	.298	8.92	3.79
Tanner Scott	R-L	6-0	235	7-22-94	4	5	4.31	67	0	0	20	63	55	34	30	5	46	90	.236	.231	.238	12.93	6.61
Cole Sulser	R-R	6-1	190	3-12-90	1	4	5.29	39	0	0	2	34	39	23	20	6	16	38	.295	.207	.365	10.06	4.24
Jimmy Yacabonis	R-R	6-3	225	3-21-92	1	1	6.75	9	0	0	0	9	12	8	7	3	5	15	.300	.154	.370	14.46	4.82
Aneurys Zabala	R-R	6-3	259	12-21-96	0	0	0.00	2	0	0	0	3	3	0	0	0	1	2	.333	.333	.333	6.75	3.38

Fielding

Catcher	PCT	G	PO	A	E	DP	PB
Fortes	1.000	59	464	19	0	3	1
Henry	1.000	15	78	8	0	0	1
Stallings	.998	110	918	24	2	2	0

First Base	PCT	G	PO	A	E	DP
Aguilar	.992	57	432	38	4	42
Astudillo	1.000	3	3	0	0	0
Cooper	.995	59	411	28	2	43
Diaz	1.000	56	378	32	0	40
Fortes	1.000	1	2	0	0	0
Gonzalez	1.000	1	2	0	0	1
Leblanc	1.000	8	30	0	0	4
Rojas	1.000	10	27	3	0	4
Williams	1.000	1	1	0	0	0

Second Base	PCT	G	PO	A	E	DP
Anderson	1.000	1	1	0	0	0
Astudillo	.842	8	6	10	3	4
Berti	.994	47	67	99	1	28
Chisholm Jr.	.982	60	93	123	4	21
Dunand	1.000	2	2	6	0	0
Gonzalez	1.000	2	6	3	0	1
Hamilton	.000	2	0	0	0	0
Leblanc	1.000	26	34	50	0	11
Wendle	.990	33	39	62	1	17
Williams	1.000	14	13	31	0	5

Third Base	PCT	G	PO	A	E	DP
Aguilar	1.000	4	1	3	0	0
Anderson	.937	48	20	99	8	7
Astudillo	1.000	10	2	8	0	1
Berti	.975	37	14	63	2	5
Dunand	1.000	1	1	3	0	0
Gonzalez	1.000	7	3	9	0	1
Groshans	.981	17	15	37	1	3
Hamilton	.000	1	0	0	0	0
Leblanc	.964	13	7	20	1	2
Wendle	.955	43	19	65	4	10
Williams	1.000	23	8	18	0	1

Shortstop	PCT	G	PO	A	E	DP
Berti	1.000	10	5	14	0	1
Gonzalez	1.000	8	2	15	0	2
Rojas	.987	136	184	340	7	74
Wendle	.975	34	46	72	3	22

Outfield	PCT	G	PO	A	E	DP
Anderson	.977	44	81	4	2	2
Berti	1.000	19	27	0	0	0
Bleday	.991	64	113	1	1	0
Burdick	1.000	31	46	0	0	0
De La Cruz	.972	122	168	5	5	1
Encarnacion	.946	20	33	2	2	0
Garcia	.985	86	129	3	2	1
Hamilton	1.000	11	6	0	0	0
Sanchez	.994	91	168	5	1	0
Soler	1.000	57	89	4	0	0
Williams	1.000	25	34	1	0	0

JACKSONVILLE JUMBO SHRIMP — *TRIPLE-A*

INTERNATIONAL LEAGUE

Batting	B-T	HT	WT	DOB	AVG	vLH	vRH	G	AB	R	H	2B	3B	HR	RBI	BB	HBP	SH	SF	SO	SB	CS	SLG	OBP
Brian Anderson	R-R	6-3	208	5-19-93	.231	.167	.286	7	26	4	6	2	0	2	2	2	0	0	0	10	0	0	.538	.286
Willians Astudillo	R-R	5-9	225	10-14-91	.307	.351	.292	75	283	36	87	18	0	16	53	17	13	0	2	16	4	1	.541	.371
Luis Aviles Jr.	R-R	6-2	210	3-16-95	.246	.128	.285	56	191	18	47	12	3	7	21	10	1	0	0	52	7	1	.450	.287
Jon Berti	R-R	5-10	190	1-22-90	.071	.000	.100	4	14	2	1	0	0	0	0	3	0	0	0	7	1	0	.071	.235
JJ Bleday	L-L	6-3	205	11-10-97	.228	.221	.232	85	302	54	69	13	0	20	52	60	5	0	0	99	1	1	.470	.365
Bryson Brigman	R-R	5-11	180	6-19-95	.251	.278	.240	105	382	54	96	15	3	8	38	22	5	1	3	91	9	3	.369	.299
Peyton Burdick	R-R	6-0	205	2-26-97	.214	.270	.186	99	364	74	78	16	5	15	58	53	9	0	3	120	13	3	.409	.326
Santiago Chavez	R-R	5-11	205	8-5-95	.208	.241	.198	35	120	14	25	7	0	1	10	6	2	0	2	33	0	0	.292	.254
Bryan De La Cruz	R-R	6-2	175	12-16-96	.320	.533	.229	13	50	10	16	3	0	4	10	4	0	0	0	13	1	0	.620	.370
Isan Diaz	L-R	5-11	201	5-27-96	.000	.000	.000	2	7	0	0	0	0	0	0	1	0	0	0	6	0	0	.000	.125
Lewin Diaz	L-L	6-4	217	11-19-96	.252	.264	.247	82	325	55	82	19	1	19	64	32	5	0	6	75	0	0	.492	.323
Ray-Patrick Didder	R-R	5-9	199	10-1-94	.240	.357	.197	32	104	12	25	2	0	2	14	7	3	0	0	36	4	1	.317	.307
Joe Dunand	R-R	6-2	205	9-20-95	.242	.200	.255	20	66	15	16	6	0	2	9	10	2	0	1	27	2	0	.424	.354
2-team total (70 Gwinnett Stripers)					.214	.253	.196	90	295	43	63	18	1	6	24	37	6	0	1	105	6	1	.342	.313
Jerar Encarnacion	R-R	6-4	250	10-22-97	.265	.325	.241	68	264	43	70	12	0	14	40	29	0	0	4	87	0	1	.470	.333
Nick Fortes	R-R	5-11	198	11-11-96	.257	.242	.264	28	105	13	27	4	0	3	13	11	3	0	1	17	1	0	.381	.342
Avisail Garcia	R-R	6-4	250	6-12-91	.250	.167	.313	8	28	3	7	2	0	0	2	5	0	0	1	11	2	0	.321	.353
Erik Gonzalez	R-R	6-3	205	8-31-91	.284	.342	.256	99	370	42	105	19	1	4	38	28	2	0	2	86	9	2	.373	.336
Norel Gonzalez	L-R	6-1	240	6-26-94	.255	.194	.277	39	137	15	35	9	1	6	24	10	4	0	1	38	0	1	.467	.322
Jordan Groshans	R-R	6-3	200	11-10-99	.301	.333	.289	31	113	14	34	7	0	2	10	19	0	0	1	19	1	0	.416	.398
2-team total (67 Buffalo Bisons)					.266	.278	.262	98	353	44	94	15	0	3	34	54	2	0	3	65	3	0	.334	.364
Devin Hairston	R-R	5-8	175	4-7-96	.205	.250	.188	14	44	6	9	3	0	1	4	6	0	0	1	19	0	2	.341	.294
Billy Hamilton	R-R	6-0	160	9-9-90	.333	.333	--	1	3	0	1	1	0	0	1	0	0	0	0	2	0	0	.667	.333
2-team total (2 St. Paul Saints)					.200	.143	.333	3	10	2	2	2	0	0	1	1	0	0	0	6	1	0	.400	.273
Payton Henry	R-R	6-2	215	6-24-97	.239	.353	.204	21	71	13	17	3	0	1	9	7	3	0	2	28	0	0	.324	.325
Bubba Hollins	R-R	6-0	200	12-6-95	.364	.000	.571	4	11	3	4	2	0	0	1	3	0	0	0	0	0	0	.545	.500
Alex Jackson	R-R	6-2	215	12-25-95	.000	.000	.000	1	4	0	0	0	0	0	0	0	0	0	0	1	0	0	.000	.000
2-team total (31 Nashville Sounds)					.217	.222	.214	32	106	9	23	8	1	2	18	12	3	0	2	29	1	0	.368	.309
Troy Johnston	L-L	6-0	205	6-22-97	.155	.208	.137	29	97	9	15	5	0	4	8	18	1	0	0	24	1	0	.330	.293
Ryan Lavarnway	R-R	6-3	239	8-7-87	.205	.268	.176	40	132	14	27	4	0	6	18	17	4	0	0	35	0	0	.371	.314
2-team total (44 Toledo Mud Hens)					.245	.260	.239	84	278	34	68	15	0	11	44	40	7	0	2	69	0	0	.417	.352
Charles Leblanc	R-R	6-3	195	6-3-96	.302	.297	.304	87	318	47	96	20	1	14	45	35	6	0	1	98	6	0	.503	.381
Ynmanol Marinez	R-R	6-0	190	4-12-01	.333	.000	.400	2	6	2	2	1	0	0	0	1	0	0	0	2	0	0	.500	.429
David Martinez	R-R	5-10	195	10-16-96	.000	.000	.000	1	3	0	0	0	0	0	0	1	0	0	0	2	0	0	.000	.250
Jan Mercado	R-R	6-0	200	8-28-99	1.000	--	1.000	1	2	0	2	0	0	0	0	0	0	0	0	0	0	0	1.000	1.000
Victor Victor Mesa	R-R	5-11	188	7-20-96	.200	.318	.164	32	95	7	19	1	0	1	8	5	1	0	2	13	9	2	.242	.243
Brian Miller	L-R	6-1	196	8-20-95	.292	.287	.293	108	408	67	119	19	9	7	45	37	1	2	4	77	26	6	.434	.349
J.D. Orr	L-L	5-11	185	9-11-96	.545	--	.545	3	11	3	6	1	0	0	1	0	0	0	0	1	1	0	.636	.545
J.D. Osborne	R-R	6-1	215	7-13-95	.250	1.000	.000	2	4	0	1	0	0	0	0	1	0	0	0	1	0	0	.250	.400
Lorenzo Quintana	R-R	5-10	205	3-1-89	.246	.304	.217	60	240	41	59	12	1	14	54	17	5	0	3	55	0	0	.479	.306
Dalvy Rosario	R-R	6-0	185	7-22-00	.381	.375	.385	7	21	6	8	1	1	0	2	3	0	0	1	6	2	0	.524	.440
Jesus Sanchez	L-R	6-3	222	10-7-97	.308	.261	.327	42	159	30	49	7	0	6	27	21	3	0	0	39	4	1	.465	.399

Demetrius Sims	R-R	6-3	220	7-14-95	.211	.163	.239	35	114	14	24	2	1	2	6	8	2	1	1	56	5	0	.298	.272
Joey Wendle	L-R	6-1	195	4-26-90	.333	.400	.300	4	15	1	5	1	0	1	3	0	1	0	1	4	0	0	.600	.353
Luke Williams	R-R	6-1	186	8-9-96	.167	.143	.200	4	12	3	2	0	0	1	1	5	0	0	0	5	5	0	.417	.412

Pitching	B-T	HT	WT	DOB	W	L	ERA	G	GS	CG	SV	IP	H	R	ER	HR	BB	SO	AVG	vLH	vRH	K/9	BB/9
Richard Bleier	L-L	6-3	215	4-16-87	0	0	0.00	1	1	0	0	1	2	0	0	0	0	2	.333	.333	--	13.50	0.00
Huascar Brazoban	R-R	6-3	155	10-15-89	2	0	3.18	27	0	0	0	45	32	16	16	6	16	59	.198	.208	.188	11.71	3.18
Jeff Brigham	R-R	6-0	195	2-16-92	3	3	3.98	30	1	0	1	43	35	21	19	8	21	69	.222	.206	.233	14.44	4.40
Parker Bugg	R-R	6-6	210	10-26-94	2	0	3.18	26	3	0	0	40	30	14	14	4	20	43	.211	.221	.203	9.76	4.54
Edward Cabrera	R-R	6-5	217	4-13-98	2	2	3.77	6	6	0	0	29	21	13	12	2	12	39	.202	.255	.151	12.24	3.77
Paul Campbell	L-R	6-0	210	7-26-95	0	2	11.25	2	1	0	0	8	9	10	10	2	5	9	.281	.261	.333	10.13	5.63
Daniel Castano	L-L	6-3	231	9-17-94	3	0	4.24	7	6	0	0	34	33	19	16	10	11	38	.250	.241	.257	10.06	2.91
Grant Dayton	L-L	6-2	210	11-25-87	0	1	2.35	12	0	0	1	15	10	6	4	1	5	24	.179	.167	.192	14.09	2.93
Tommy Eveld	R-R	6-5	214	12-30-93	1	2	3.38	23	1	0	0	35	28	17	13	6	10	31	.217	.242	.194	8.05	2.60
Jake Fishman	L-L	6-3	195	2-8-95	4	1	2.25	33	0	0	1	56	39	21	14	4	20	54	.194	.173	.220	8.68	3.21
Dylan Floro	L-R	6-2	203	12-27-90	0	0	2.70	3	1	0	0	3	2	1	1	0	1	4	.167	.000	.250	10.80	2.70
Robert Garcia	R-L	6-4	225	6-14-96	1	5	4.06	44	0	0	7	58	49	31	26	5	30	60	.233	.190	.287	9.36	4.68
Braxton Garrett	R-L	6-2	202	8-5-97	2	3	3.15	7	7	0	0	34	28	13	12	3	9	29	.219	.212	.224	7.60	2.36
Elieser Hernandez	R-R	6-0	214	5-3-95	4	4	4.11	12	11	0	0	57	51	31	26	8	17	68	.236	.264	.209	10.74	2.68
Colton Hock	R-R	6-5	230	3-15-96	1	1	3.47	14	1	0	0	23	22	9	9	2	7	23	.244	.163	.319	8.87	2.70
Bryan Hoeing	R-R	6-6	210	10-19-96	7	5	5.07	18	17	0	0	94	100	56	53	14	35	49	.280	.291	.267	4.69	3.35
Jordan Holloway	R-R	6-6	230	6-13-96	0	1	6.62	8	2	0	0	18	12	13	13	4	16	24	.197	.226	.167	12.23	8.15
Matthew Kent	L-L	6-0	180	9-13-92	9	11	4.99	28	25	0	0	144	167	91	80	17	38	80	.290	.300	.284	4.99	2.37
Jeff Lindgren	R-R	6-1	200	9-17-96	3	3	5.29	15	15	0	0	68	72	45	40	11	28	49	.274	.333	.221	6.49	3.71
Jesus Luzardo	L-L	6-0	218	9-30-97	0	0	2.08	2	2	0	0	9	3	2	2	0	4	9	.100	.143	.063	9.35	4.15
Anthony Maldonado	R-R	6-4	220	2-6-98	1	0	1.74	15	0	0	3	21	13	4	4	1	5	28	.178	.346	.085	12.19	2.18
Max Meyer	L-R	6-0	196	3-12-99	3	4	3.72	12	12	0	0	58	39	25	24	5	19	65	.188	.139	.247	10.09	2.95
Cody Mincey	R-R	5-11	180	4-23-92	1	3	6.38	4	4	0	0	18	18	14	13	4	9	10	.257	.316	.188	4.91	4.42
Bryan Mitchell	L-R	6-2	215	4-19-91	1	1	9.78	9	3	0	0	19	35	23	21	4	13	16	.385	.279	.479	7.45	6.05
Tommy Nance	R-R	6-6	235	3-19-91	0	0	3.18	4	1	0	1	6	2	3	2	1	2	6	.111	.143	.091	9.53	3.18
Andrew Nardi	L-L	6-3	215	8-18-98	3	0	2.84	24	0	0	7	32	14	10	10	3	14	45	.131	.100	.158	12.79	3.98
Nick Neidert	R-R	6-1	202	11-20-96	4	0	1.96	14	8	0	1	46	39	15	10	6	9	48	.227	.216	.238	9.39	1.76
Zach Pop	R-R	6-4	220	9-20-96	0	1	2.22	19	0	0	0	24	28	8	6	0	8	20	.298	.333	.265	7.40	2.96
2-team total (4 Buffalo Bisons)					0	1	2.57	23	0	0	0	28	31	11	8	0	12	25	.284	.302	.268	8.04	3.86
Cody Poteet	R-R	6-1	190	7-30-94	0	0	0.00	2	2	0	0	5	3	0	0	0	0	6	.167	.200	.125	11.57	0.00
Josh Rogers	L-L	6-3	211	7-10-94	4	4	4.75	9	9	0	0	47	47	26	25	6	21	32	.258	.339	.220	6.08	3.99
2-team total (3 Rochester Red Wings)					4	7	6.03	12	12	0	0	60	65	42	40	13	24	39	.274	.329	.248	5.88	3.62
Trevor Rogers	L-L	6-5	217	11-13-97	1	1	5.63	2	2	0	0	8	7	5	5	1	2	14	.226	.444	.136	15.75	2.25
Jackson Rose	R-R	6-2	185	4-25-96	0	0	9.82	2	0	0	0	4	9	4	4	2	2	4	.450	.500	.400	9.82	4.91
Josh Simpson	L-L	6-2	190	8-19-97	2	0	4.38	10	0	0	0	12	10	6	6	0	5	23	.233	.160	.333	16.78	3.65
George Soriano	R-R	6-2	210	3-24-99	4	2	2.49	32	0	0	8	47	31	15	13	2	23	49	.194	.176	.209	9.38	4.40
Will Stewart	L-L	6-2	190	7-14-97	6	5	5.69	25	7	0	0	68	83	51	43	4	38	61	.305	.295	.315	8.07	5.03
Cole Sulser	R-R	6-1	190	3-12-90	0	1	5.68	6	0	0	0	6	8	4	4	2	2	10	.296	.250	.364	14.21	2.84
Eli Villalobos	R-R	6-4	195	6-26-97	2	0	1.04	12	0	0	6	17	11	3	2	1	8	26	.183	.227	.158	13.50	4.15
Jimmy Yacabonis	R-R	6-3	225	3-21-92	4	3	3.42	18	0	0	2	24	19	10	9	1	11	35	.218	.273	.163	13.31	4.18
2-team total (8 Durham Bulls)					6	4	3.31	26	0	0	2	33	24	13	12	1	14	43	.205	.255	.167	11.85	3.86
Aneurys Zabala	R-R	6-3	259	12-21-96	0	0	9.51	17	1	0	0	24	23	25	25	3	28	30	.261	.333	.204	11.41	10.65

Fielding

Catcher	PCT	G	PO	A	E	DP	PB
Astudillo	1.000	5	36	0	0	0	0
Chavez	.984	34	287	16	5	2	3
Fortes	.996	24	230	15	1	1	2
Henry	1.000	20	154	6	0	0	0
Jackson	1.000	1	10	0	0	0	0
Lavarnway	.994	36	292	20	2	2	3
Mercado	1.000	1	4	0	0	0	0
Quintana	.987	34	292	13	4	1	2

First Base	PCT	G	PO	A	E	DP
Astudillo	1.000	1	5	0	0	1
Diaz	.990	82	643	60	7	78
Dunand	1.000	3	26	2	0	5
Encarnacion	.982	13	104	4	2	14
Gonzalez	.991	14	98	11	1	12
Johnston	.991	29	215	7	2	24
Leblanc	.986	8	70	2	1	1

Second Base	PCT	G	PO	A	E	DP
Astudillo	.929	6	10	16	2	5
Aviles Jr.	1.000	12	20	34	0	9
Berti	1.000	1	0	4	0	0
Brigman	.976	87	121	204	8	53
Diaz	1.000	2	3	2	0	0
Didder	1.000	6	10	17	0	3
Gonzalez	.962	8	4	21	1	5
Groshans	.971	9	13	20	1	5
Hairston	1.000	2	1	5	0	2
Leblanc	.988	17	27	55	1	11
Wendle	.875	1	4	3	1	1
Williams	1.000	2	1	8	0	1

Third Base	PCT	G	PO	A	E	DP
Anderson	1.000	2	1	0	0	0
Astudillo	.945	30	25	44	4	7
Aviles Jr.	.926	26	17	33	4	1
Berti	.667	1	1	1	1	0
Didder	1.000	3	1	10	0	2
Dunand	.977	14	14	28	1	5
Gonzalez	1.000	19	6	40	0	2
Groshans	.963	12	8	18	1	2
Hollins	.900	4	4	5	1	2
Leblanc	.963	38	18	59	3	10
Marinez	1.000	2	0	2	0	0
Sims	1.000	5	1	5	0	0
Wendle	.000	1	0	0	0	0
Williams	.889	2	3	5	1	1

Shortstop	PCT	G	PO	A	E	DP
Aviles Jr.	1.000	5	7	10	0	3
Berti	1.000	1	2	3	0	1
Brigman	.966	14	17	40	2	16
Didder	.976	21	22	59	2	11
Gonzalez	.962	59	76	149	9	46
Groshans	.974	10	13	25	1	7
Hairston	.951	12	6	33	2	4
Sims	.983	30	39	80	2	15
Wendle	1.000	1	2	1	0	1

Outfield	PCT	G	PO	A	E	DP
Anderson	1.000	3	1	1	0	0
Aviles Jr.	.923	9	11	1	1	0
Berti	1.000	1	2	0	0	0
Bleday	.976	85	157	5	4	1
Burdick	.989	87	171	9	2	4
De La Cruz	.963	12	23	3	1	2
Didder	1.000	1	1	0	0	0
Encarnacion	.936	52	99	3	7	0
Garcia	1.000	5	10	1	0	0
Gonzalez	.960	14	24	0	1	0
Hamilton	1.000	1	2	0	0	0
Leblanc	.980	25	48	1	1	0
Mesa	1.000	32	59	2	0	0
Miller	.982	92	159	7	3	3
Orr	.750	3	3	0	1	0
Rosario	.941	6	15	1	1	0
Sanchez	1.000	38	70	2	0	0

PENSACOLA BLUE WAHOOS — DOUBLE-A

SOUTHERN LEAGUE

Batting	B-T	HT	WT	DOB	AVG	vLH	vRH	G	AB	R	H	2B	3B	HR	RBI	BB	HBP	SH	SF	SO	SB	CS	SLG	OBP
Luis Aviles Jr.	R-R	6-2	210	3-16-95	.267	.270	.267	46	172	26	46	14	0	7	25	9	2	0	4	48	7	2	.471	.305
Will Banfield	R-R	6-1	207	11-18-99	.267	.147	.317	31	116	14	31	5	1	3	16	5	2	0	3	25	0	0	.405	.302
Davis Bradshaw	L-R	6-3	175	4-25-98	.286	.235	.299	27	84	16	24	6	0	0	7	13	2	1	0	20	5	0	.357	.394
Hayden Cantrelle	B-R	5-11	175	11-25-98	.185	.167	.194	28	92	14	17	5	0	3	10	14	3	1	0	40	6	4	.337	.312
Santiago Chavez	R-R	5-11	205	8-5-95	.138	.214	.114	17	58	5	8	1	0	2	8	5	2	0	0	20	0	0	.259	.231
Marcus Chiu	R-R	6-2	208	1-13-97	.193	.238	.179	25	88	12	17	4	0	3	11	5	4	0	0	30	2	0	.341	.268
Griffin Conine	L-R	6-1	210	7-11-97	.215	.198	.221	118	414	55	89	15	2	24	74	74	4	0	4	183	1	1	.435	.337
Jose Devers	L-R	6-0	174	12-7-99	.210	.190	.215	58	233	33	49	10	4	2	28	14	4	0	2	46	3	0	.313	.265
Ray-Patrick Didder	R-R	5-9	199	10-1-94	.241	.308	.222	77	286	42	69	8	1	10	28	27	17	0	3	83	22	4	.381	.339
Jerar Encarnacion	R-R	6-4	250	10-22-97	.358	.379	.352	31	120	26	43	3	0	8	18	13	2	0	1	35	4	2	.583	.426
Cobie Fletcher-Vance	R-R	5-8	195	8-24-97	.243	.302	.224	106	395	40	96	20	0	4	43	28	7	0	6	67	2	3	.324	.300
Norel Gonzalez	L-R	6-1	240	6-26-94	.257	.200	.269	55	202	25	52	10	0	9	44	23	3	0	1	47	2	2	.441	.341
Devin Hairston	R-R	5-8	175	4-7-96	.225	.176	.238	26	80	7	18	5	0	0	11	6	1	0	0	28	1	0	.288	.287
Bubba Hollins	R-R	6-0	200	12-6-95	.231	.273	.217	66	221	26	51	8	0	2	21	18	8	0	1	57	3	0	.294	.310
Troy Johnston	L-L	6-0	205	6-22-97	.292	.239	.311	85	329	42	96	20	1	10	49	32	7	1	7	71	3	0	.450	.360
Thomas Jones	R-R	6-3	220	12-9-97	.176	.200	.168	62	193	33	34	11	1	8	23	27	8	1	2	90	5	3	.368	.300
Paul McIntosh	R-R	6-1	220	11-20-97	.258	.179	.283	90	318	66	82	25	1	13	51	55	8	0	2	75	10	5	.465	.379
Jan Mercado	R-R	6-0	200	8-28-99	.176	.333	.120	10	34	5	6	0	1	0	2	3	3	1	0	12	1	0	.235	.300
Victor Victor Mesa	R-R	5-11	188	7-20-96	.228	.204	.236	54	206	26	47	6	1	2	22	16	6	4	6	40	26	2	.296	.295
Nasim Nunez	B-R	5-9	158	8-18-00	.261	.257	.262	38	142	22	37	6	0	0	14	24	2	1	2	36	21	5	.303	.371
J.D. Orr	L-L	5-11	185	9-11-96	.237	.160	.256	81	253	42	60	11	1	1	15	46	6	4	2	59	39	7	.300	.365
J.D. Osborne	R-R	6-1	215	7-13-95	.243	.265	.237	42	148	17	36	8	1	5	20	11	4	0	0	49	0	0	.412	.313
Demetrius Sims	R-R	6-3	220	7-14-95	.318	.304	.323	29	85	13	27	9	0	1	14	12	4	0	1	27	5	2	.459	.422
Jorge Soler	R-R	6-4	235	2-25-92	.429	.333	.500	2	7	3	3	0	0	2	3	1	0	0	0	1	0	0	1.286	.500

Pitching	B-T	HT	WT	DOB	W	L	ERA	G	GS	CG	SV	IP	H	R	ER	HR	BB	SO	AVG	vLH	vRH	K/9	BB/9
Anthony Bender	R-R	6-4	205	2-3-95	0	0	4.50	3	0	0	0	2	3	1	1	0	1	2	.333	.500	.286	9.00	4.50
Dylan Bice	L-R	6-4	220	8-17-97	1	1	5.23	24	0	0	3	31	27	18	18	5	18	33	.233	.215	.255	9.58	5.23
Parker Bugg	R-R	6-6	210	10-26-94	1	1	4.00	4	0	0	0	9	8	5	4	0	12	11	.235	.176	.294	11.00	12.00
Edward Cabrera	R-R	6-5	217	4-13-98	0	0	0.00	2	2	0	0	6	0	0	0	0	1	8	.000	.000	.000	12.00	1.50
Tyler Eckberg	R-R	6-4	220	9-4-97	1	0	0.00	2	0	0	0	4	1	0	0	0	1	3	.083	.200	.000	7.36	2.45
Justin Evans	R-R	6-0	185	9-9-96	1	0	1.59	7	0	0	0	11	5	3	2	0	10	12	.132	.130	.133	9.53	7.94
Dax Fulton	L-L	6-7	225	10-16-01	1	1	2.57	4	3	0	0	21	9	9	6	2	7	30	.125	.105	.132	12.86	3.00
Robert Garcia	R-L	6-4	225	6-14-96	0	0	0.00	2	0	0	0	5	1	0	0	0	0	4	.067	.333	.000	7.71	0.00
Colton Hock	R-R	6-5	230	3-15-96	5	3	3.72	32	0	0	10	36	33	18	15	4	8	30	.231	.221	.242	7.43	1.98
Bryan Hoeing	R-R	6-6	210	10-19-96	2	1	0.35	4	4	0	0	26	20	4	1	0	4	26	.211	.204	.217	9.12	1.40
Chandler Jozwiak	L-L	6-0	185	2-15-99	1	0	3.60	7	0	0	0	10	6	4	4	0	7	19	.171	.100	.200	17.10	6.30
Zach King	L-L	6-6	228	4-30-98	2	6	8.22	11	11	0	0	46	60	43	42	7	30	46	.317	.259	.344	9.00	5.87
A.J. Ladwig	R-R	6-5	220	12-24-92	8	5	4.13	16	15	0	0	89	112	49	41	11	7	63	.304	.300	.310	6.35	0.71
Zack Leban	R-R	6-2	235	5-30-96	1	3	6.40	21	0	0	0	32	28	24	23	6	16	42	.231	.300	.164	11.69	4.45
Jeff Lindgren	R-R	6-1	200	9-17-96	4	1	3.15	12	12	1	0	69	56	26	24	7	25	67	.225	.228	.221	8.78	3.28
Anthony Maldonado	R-R	6-4	220	2-6-98	3	3	3.67	27	0	0	1	42	33	19	17	8	15	58	.216	.213	.219	12.53	3.24
Robinson Martinez	R-R	6-0	190	3-20-98	2	1	3.15	14	0	0	1	20	18	10	7	3	8	25	.234	.257	.214	11.25	3.60
Zach McCambley	L-R	6-2	220	5-4-99	6	8	5.65	19	19	0	0	94	83	67	59	12	52	101	.237	.266	.205	9.67	4.98
Andrew McInvale	R-R	6-2	195	11-3-96	2	3	7.13	22	2	0	1	35	37	30	28	4	24	36	.270	.284	.254	9.17	6.11
Josan Mendez	R-R	6-2	180	7-10-00	0	0	1.50	3	0	0	0	6	5	1	1	0	1	5	.250	.333	.214	7.50	1.50
Jorge Mercedes	R-R	6-3	185	7-1-00	0	1	3.86	2	0	0	0	2	0	1	1	0	3	4	.000	--	.000	15.43	11.57
Cody Mincey	R-R	5-11	180	4-23-92	5	7	5.10	19	17	0	0	95	110	57	54	17	30	76	.291	.336	.230	7.17	2.83
Bryan Mitchell	L-R	6-2	215	4-19-91	1	0	4.95	4	4	0	0	20	21	16	11	2	6	17	.273	.257	.286	7.65	2.70
Tyler Mitzel	R-R	6-4	210	5-10-96	1	1	14.90	10	0	0	0	10	20	19	16	3	5	8	.444	.407	.500	7.45	4.66
Patrick Monteverde	R-L	6-2	190	9-24-97	1	0	4.99	6	6	0	0	31	37	18	17	5	6	32	.301	.195	.354	9.39	1.76
Tommy Nance	R-R	6-6	235	3-19-91	0	0	0.00	1	0	0	0	2	1	0	0	0	0	2	.167	.500	.000	9.00	0.00
Andrew Nardi	L-L	6-3	215	8-18-98	2	2	1.40	13	0	0	2	19	15	4	3	1	4	31	.214	.156	.263	14.43	1.86
Luis Palacios	L-L	6-2	160	7-1-00	1	0	2.70	2	2	0	0	10	4	3	3	2	4	9	.121	.200	.107	8.10	3.60
Eury Perez	R-R	6-8	220	4-15-03	3	3	4.08	17	17	0	0	75	62	36	34	9	25	106	.223	.205	.244	12.72	3.00
Brady Puckett	R-R	6-8	220	7-31-95	0	0	10.80	11	0	0	0	10	15	13	12	1	10	12	.341	.292	.400	10.80	9.00
Sean Reynolds	L-R	6-8	240	4-19-98	2	0	5.11	24	0	0	4	25	22	16	14	3	10	27	.234	.279	.196	9.85	3.65
Josh Roberson	R-R	6-3	175	5-12-96	0	1	0.00	3	0	0	0	3	4	4	0	0	2	2	.364	.400	.333	6.75	6.75
2-team total (28 Montgomery Biscuits)					2	7	6.68	31	2	0	2	34	39	34	25	4	25	39	.289	.339	.247	10.43	6.68
Trevor Rogers	L-L	6-5	217	11-13-97	0	0	6.75	2	2	0	0	8	10	7	6	2	0	11	.294	.154	.381	12.38	0.00
Josh Simpson	L-L	6-2	190	8-19-97	5	2	3.88	40	0	0	2	56	31	24	24	5	29	89	.164	.143	.179	14.39	4.69
George Soriano	R-R	6-2	210	3-24-99	0	2	3.10	8	6	0	0	29	25	15	10	2	17	36	.227	.302	.128	11.17	5.28
Will Stewart	L-L	6-2	190	7-14-97	1	1	4.23	6	5	0	0	28	24	14	13	3	9	22	.231	.132	.288	7.16	2.93
Eli Villalobos	R-R	6-4	195	6-26-97	3	2	3.38	40	0	0	8	61	41	26	23	9	21	75	.193	.135	.257	11.01	3.08
Jimmy Yacabonis	R-R	6-3	225	3-21-92	0	0	0.00	1	0	0	0	1	1	0	0	0	1	0	.333	1.000	.000	0.00	9.00
Jefry Yan	L-L	6-3	185	8-17-96	2	4	4.89	38	4	0	2	57	49	36	31	3	47	88	.231	.205	.250	13.89	7.42
Aneurys Zabala	R-R	6-3	259	12-21-96	0	0	12.00	3	0	0	0	3	6	4	4	0	3	4	.429	.333	.500	12.00	9.00

Fielding

Catcher	PCT	G	PO	A	E	DP	PB
Banfield	.993	27	270	15	2	3	2
Chavez	.989	17	165	15	2	1	3
McIntosh	.979	69	665	32	15	9	5
Mercado	.991	10	95	10	1	0	1
Osborne	.989	10	86	6	1	0	3

First Base	PCT	G	PO	A	E	DP
Chiu	.994	24	169	7	1	9
Encarnacion	.966	4	26	2	1	2
Gonzalez	.983	15	106	9	2	9
Hollins	.926	9	59	4	5	6
Johnston	.994	64	472	46	3	48
McIntosh	1.000	1	16	0	0	2
Osborne	.989	15	86	5	1	12

Second Base	PCT	G	PO	A	E	DP
Aviles Jr.	1.000	1	1	0	0	0
Cantrelle	.971	24	15	52	2	4
Devers	.982	47	62	99	3	30
Didder	1.000	15	19	34	0	9
Fletcher-Vance	.974	26	46	67	3	14
Nunez	.917	4	5	6	1	0
Sims	.967	18	22	37	2	8

Third Base	PCT	G	PO	A	E	DP
Aviles Jr.	.909	11	8	12	2	0
Cantrelle	.000	1	0	0	1	0
Didder	1.000	2	2	2	0	1
Fletcher-Vance	.963	72	49	105	6	13
Hollins	.947	43	27	63	5	2
Sims	.923	6	3	9	1	0

Shortstop	PCT	G	PO	A	E	DP
Aviles Jr.	.945	31	54	83	8	25
Devers	.667	2	0	2	1	0
Didder	.959	35	39	54	4	18
Hairston	1.000	26	33	67	0	19
Nunez	.947	34	35	72	6	9
Sims	1.000	4	5	9	0	2

Outfield	PCT	G	PO	A	E	DP
Bradshaw	.959	26	46	1	2	0
Conine	.990	106	176	13	2	2
Didder	.970	20	31	1	1	0
Encarnacion	.964	27	47	6	2	1
Gonzalez	.972	19	34	1	1	0
Johnston	1.000	11	20	1	0	0
Jones	.992	60	123	1	1	1
Mesa	.982	54	106	5	2	0
Orr	.966	77	133	9	5	1
Sims	--	1	0	0	0	0
Soler	1.000	1	2	0	0	0

BELOIT SKY CARP — *HIGH-A*

MIDWEST LEAGUE

Batting	B-T	HT	WT	DOB	AVG	vLH	vRH	G	AB	R	H	2B	3B	HR	RBI	BB	HBP	SH	SF	SO	SB	CS	SLG	OBP
Brady Allen	R-L	6-1	218	9-3-99	.206	.400	.172	9	34	3	7	0	1	0	4	4	0	0	0	9	0	0	.265	.289
Tanner Allen	L-R	5-11	190	6-5-98	.209	.280	.188	59	215	23	45	9	3	3	21	14	4	0	2	38	2	0	.321	.268
Will Banfield	R-R	6-1	207	11-18-99	.204	.238	.194	71	269	29	55	13	1	8	36	11	3	0	6	68	1	1	.349	.239
Davis Bradshaw	L-R	6-3	175	4-25-98	.310	.366	.299	70	245	23	76	8	3	1	24	16	7	4	2	36	8	6	.380	.367
Kyler Castillo	R-R	5-11	185	10-29-97	.280	.271	.283	66	214	28	60	7	1	1	27	30	4	0	3	50	2	1	.336	.375
Marcus Chiu	R-R	6-2	208	1-13-97	.232	.242	.228	79	259	35	60	12	0	9	34	23	13	0	1	84	1	0	.382	.324
Jose Estrada	R-R	5-10	175	5-5-00	.250	.667	.000	2	8	1	2	1	0	1	4	0	0	0	0	4	0	0	.750	.250
Bennett Hostetler	R-R	6-0	195	9-23-97	.232	.160	.256	101	371	49	86	18	1	9	53	31	16	0	3	90	3	0	.358	.316
Osiris Johnson	R-R	6-1	198	10-18-00	.200	.083	.233	16	55	6	11	1	0	0	1	4	1	0	0	16	2	0	.218	.267
Ynmanol Marinez	R-R	6-0	190	4-12-01	.259	.209	.272	114	425	60	110	14	3	10	56	27	6	0	2	115	3	1	.376	.311
Jan Mercado	R-R	6-0	200	8-28-99	.170	.000	.235	14	47	4	8	2	0	1	6	4	2	0	0	26	0	0	.277	.264
Victor Mesa Jr.	L-L	6-0	195	9-8-01	.243	.308	.221	121	460	53	112	26	3	5	50	53	4	2	6	100	10	4	.346	.323
Tevin Mitchell	R-R	6-1	170	5-2-97	.051	.059	.049	28	78	2	4	0	1	1	7	6	0	1	0	44	1	0	.115	.119
Cody Morissette	L-R	6-0	175	1-16-00	.232	.300	.211	84	336	48	78	17	0	13	51	33	7	0	3	90	4	1	.399	.311
Nasim Nunez	B-R	5-9	158	8-18-00	.247	.229	.253	85	300	53	74	11	3	2	27	71	1	4	2	103	49	11	.323	.390
J.D. Orr	L-L	5-11	185	9-11-96	.286	.357	.250	16	42	6	12	3	1	0	0	7	1	0	0	8	10	2	.405	.400
Federico Polanco	L-R	5-10	155	3-20-01	.160	.172	.156	38	119	15	19	4	1	1	8	14	3	0	0	44	1	0	.235	.265
Nic Ready	R-R	6-3	239	2-13-97	.000	--	.000	1	3	0	0	0	0	0	0	0	0	0	0	2	0	0	.000	.000
Dalvy Rosario	R-R	6-0	185	7-22-00	.251	.245	.252	113	427	56	107	18	5	9	53	24	7	2	7	117	28	7	.379	.297
Jose Salas	B-R	6-2	191	4-26-03	.230	.190	.242	48	191	29	44	7	1	4	17	20	5	1	0	41	18	0	.340	.319
Angeudis Santos	B-R	6-1	168	9-19-01	.313	.333	.308	6	16	4	5	0	0	1	3	4	0	0	0	5	1	0	.500	.450
Harrison Spohn	R-R	6-3	185	12-3-98	.385	.750	.222	5	13	2	5	0	0	1	3	6	0	0	0	4	0	1	.615	.579
Zach Zubia	R-R	6-4	230	11-4-97	.230	.333	.207	33	100	18	23	3	0	5	16	30	1	0	4	33	0	0	.410	.400

Pitching	B-T	HT	WT	DOB	W	L	ERA	G	GS	CG	SV	IP	H	R	ER	HR	BB	SO	AVG	vLH	vRH	K/9	BB/9
Luarbert Arias	R-R	6-2	176	12-12-00	1	1	6.75	3	0	0	0	5	5	4	4	2	1	6	.227	.111	.308	10.13	1.69
Gabe Bierman	R-R	6-2	200	9-3-99	1	1	2.25	2	2	0	0	12	4	5	3	0	2	11	.103	.111	.095	8.25	1.50
Raul Brito	R-R	6-1	180	5-23-97	4	3	3.10	33	0	0	1	52	42	25	18	1	18	55	.219	.267	.179	9.46	3.10
Tyler Eckberg	R-R	6-4	220	9-4-97	1	3	4.00	11	0	0	1	18	23	12	8	1	2	23	.307	.333	.289	11.50	1.00
Justin Evans	R-R	6-0	185	9-9-96	5	1	2.77	27	0	0	2	39	37	16	12	2	18	55	.253	.193	.292	12.69	4.15
Evan Fitterer	R-R	6-3	192	6-26-00	4	7	4.28	22	22	0	0	107	102	56	51	8	46	80	.250	.231	.264	6.71	3.86
Dax Fulton	L-L	6-7	225	10-16-01	5	6	4.07	20	20	0	0	97	104	51	44	6	35	120	.276	.313	.263	11.10	3.24
Matt Givin	R-R	6-3	180	6-17-99	3	3	5.05	28	1	0	0	52	56	30	29	3	7	51	.277	.298	.263	8.88	1.22
M.D. Johnson	R-R	6-5	190	7-7-97	9	9	3.46	20	20	0	0	112	89	46	43	12	28	125	.218	.237	.200	10.04	2.25
Chandler Jozwiak	L-L	6-0	185	2-15-99	5	0	1.85	23	0	0	6	34	22	11	7	0	10	31	.185	.135	.207	8.21	2.65
Zach King	L-L	6-6	228	4-30-98	4	3	2.77	12	12	0	0	65	51	23	20	5	27	87	.219	.258	.205	12.05	3.74
Robinson Martinez	R-R	6-0	190	3-20-98	0	2	5.19	28	0	0	4	35	25	22	20	6	20	51	.197	.151	.230	13.24	5.19
Andrew McInvale	R-R	6-2	195	11-3-96	0	2	8.10	6	0	0	0	7	6	6	6	3	2	9	.240	.286	.222	12.15	2.70
Josan Mendez	R-R	6-2	180	7-10-00	2	1	2.89	30	0	0	0	47	48	24	15	2	11	32	.258	.293	.231	6.17	2.12
Jorge Mercedes	R-R	6-3	185	7-1-00	0	0	1.93	4	0	0	0	5	1	1	1	1	2	8	.067	.000	.125	15.43	3.86
Tyler Mitzel	R-R	6-4	210	5-10-96	2	1	2.77	26	0	0	2	49	36	17	15	5	7	67	.198	.149	.231	12.39	1.29
Chris Mokma	R-R	6-4	210	2-11-01	3	6	7.71	20	8	0	0	61	82	60	52	14	24	50	.314	.283	.335	7.42	3.56
Patrick Monteverde	R-L	6-2	190	9-24-97	3	4	2.51	15	15	0	0	79	62	24	22	8	26	90	.215	.276	.188	10.25	2.96
Patrick Murphy	L-L	6-1	205	3-7-97	0	1	11.25	3	0	0	0	4	7	7	5	0	2	4	.333	.250	.353	9.00	4.50
Luis Palacios	L-L	6-2	160	7-1-00	3	2	4.85	7	7	0	0	39	45	21	21	7	7	33	.294	.212	.317	7.62	1.62
Hunter Perdue	R-R	6-3	210	3-4-99	1	2	6.20	5	4	0	0	20	17	14	14	3	12	16	.233	.200	.256	7.08	5.31
Brady Puckett	R-R	6-8	220	7-31-95	2	2	3.09	21	0	0	2	32	21	14	11	1	17	40	.193	.171	.206	11.25	4.78
Sean Reynolds	L-R	6-8	240	4-19-98	0	1	3.25	26	0	0	6	28	17	10	10	2	14	39	.170	.136	.196	12.69	4.55
Jackson Rose	R-R	6-2	185	4-25-96	2	2	1.80	23	8	0	1	55	39	20	11	4	8	58	.195	.214	.176	9.49	1.31
Edgar Sanchez	R-R	6-1	190	8-2-00	0	1	4.07	6	6	0	0	24	22	12	11	0	14	20	.250	.393	.183	7.40	5.18
Jake Schrand	R-R	6-0	180	8-8-99	1	1	3.86	5	0	0	1	7	8	3	3	2	3	4	.286	.273	.294	5.14	3.86
Joey Steele	R-R	6-2	195	11-15-95	0	0	1.93	8	0	0	0	9	4	2	2	1	2	9	.125	.133	.118	8.68	1.93
Jake Walters	R-R	6-0	190	3-11-96	1	2	4.50	6	4	0	1	24	27	13	12	2	12	24	.281	.216	.322	9.00	4.50
Caleb Wurster	L-L	5-11	182	9-21-98	0	0	6.35	5	0	0	0	6	6	4	4	0	5	9	.273	.000	.353	14.29	7.94

Fielding

Catcher	PCT	G	PO	A	E	DP	PB
Banfield	.994	48	491	34	3	3	3
Estrada	1.000	2	12	1	0	0	0
Hostetler	.983	68	597	53	11	5	14
Mercado	1.000	12	115	7	0	0	3

First Base	PCT	G	PO	A	E	DP
Chiu	.994	77	574	45	4	52
Marinez	.981	17	151	5	3	11
Polanco	.957	7	42	3	2	7
Ready	1.000	1	7	0	0	0
Zubia	.982	28	203	15	4	20

Second Base	PCT	G	PO	A	E	DP
Morissette	.964	68	82	160	9	35
Polanco	.957	24	39	51	4	14
Rosario	.883	19	24	44	9	8
Salas	.943	14	23	27	3	9
Santos	.857	3	2	4	1	0
Spohn	1.000	4	9	6	0	3

Third Base	PCT	G	PO	A	E	DP
Marinez	.932	75	37	128	12	7
Morissette	1.000	13	10	22	0	1
Rosario	.961	30	22	52	3	2
Salas	1.000	11	8	18	0	3
Santos	1.000	3	2	2	0	0

Shortstop	PCT	G	PO	A	E	DP
Marinez	1.000	3	4	3	0	0
Nunez	.947	84	116	190	17	42
Rosario	.937	27	44	60	7	15
Salas	.984	16	14	48	1	11
Spohn	1.000	1	1	1	0	0

Outfield	PCT	G	PO	A	E	DP
Allen	1.000	7	17	0	0	0
Allen	1.000	50	65	2	0	0
Bradshaw	.946	67	99	6	6	0
Castillo	.956	66	104	4	5	0
Johnson	.938	16	30	0	2	0
Mesa Jr.	.992	112	254	7	2	1
Mitchell	.970	26	31	1	1	0
Orr	.929	15	24	2	2	0
Rosario	.969	34	61	2	2	0

JUPITER HAMMERHEADS — *LOW-A*

FLORIDA STATE LEAGUE

Batting	B-T	HT	WT	DOB	AVG	vLH	vRH	G	AB	R	H	2B	3B	HR	RBI	BB	HBP	SH	SF	SO	SB	CS	SLG	OBP
Brady Allen	R-L	6-1	218	9-3-99	.251	.247	.252	108	386	55	97	16	2	8	52	55	5	0	4	118	6	1	.365	.349
Tanner Allen	L-R	5-11	190	6-5-98	.179	.053	.220	25	78	9	14	2	2	0	7	9	2	0	0	13	0	0	.256	.281
Brian Anderson	R-R	6-3	208	5-19-93	.000	--	.000	1	2	1	0	0	0	0	1	2	0	0	0	1	0	0	.000	.500
Cameron Barstad	L-R	6-1	195	11-29-00	.233	.154	.253	55	189	21	44	17	0	3	22	25	5	0	2	87	0	0	.370	.335
Jacob Berry	B-R	6-0	212	5-5-01	.264	.345	.240	33	125	19	33	7	0	3	24	13	7	0	3	23	1	1	.392	.358
Jon Berti	R-R	5-10	190	1-22-90	.167	.000	.250	2	6	0	1	1	0	0	0	0	0	0	0	1	0	0	.333	.167
Jorge Caballero	R-R	6-1	170	1-10-00	.290	.325	.283	74	238	29	69	6	3	3	23	27	4	1	1	70	1	1	.378	.370
Yiddi Cappe	R-R	6-3	175	9-17-02	.278	.206	.298	37	158	18	44	5	1	3	15	6	0	0	3	22	7	1	.380	.299
Kyler Castillo	R-R	5-11	185	10-29-97	.343	.571	.317	24	70	12	24	3	1	1	9	16	5	0	0	13	1	1	.457	.495
Javeon Cody	R-R	6-3	205	7-29-99	.234	.240	.233	47	145	18	34	5	2	1	11	11	1	1	1	54	6	1	.317	.291
Garrett Cooper	R-R	6-5	235	12-25-90	.375	--	.375	3	8	2	3	0	0	0	1	3	0	0	0	1	0	0	.375	.545
Jose Devers	L-R	6-0	174	12-7-99	.167	.000	.200	2	6	1	1	0	0	0	0	0	0	0	0	3	0	0	.167	.167
Isan Diaz	L-R	5-11	201	5-27-96	.000	.000	.000	2	5	0	0	0	0	0	0	1	0	1	0	2	0	0	.000	.167
Jose Estrada	R-R	5-10	175	5-5-00	.132	.182	.123	21	68	4	9	0	0	0	6	4	2	0	1	17	0	0	.132	.200
Payton Henry	R-R	6-2	215	6-24-97	.111	--	.111	3	9	0	1	0	0	0	1	2	1	0	0	3	0	0	.111	.333
Osiris Johnson	R-R	6-1	198	10-18-00	.247	.200	.256	66	247	35	61	10	0	5	28	19	3	1	5	48	8	1	.348	.303
Ian Lewis	B-R	5-10	177	2-4-03	.265	.130	.309	51	185	21	49	7	3	2	21	22	3	0	3	45	16	1	.368	.347
Hudson Livesey	B-R	6-0	170	8-9-99	.200	.000	.286	5	10	2	2	1	0	0	1	1	0	0	0	4	0	0	.300	.273
Chase Luttrell	L-L	6-1	200	6-1-00	.157	.200	.143	26	83	7	13	2	0	1	12	6	0	0	1	28	0	0	.217	.211
Joe Mack	L-R	6-1	210	12-27-02	.231	.091	.263	35	121	18	28	4	1	3	12	29	1	0	1	40	0	0	.355	.382
David Martinez	R-R	5-10	195	10-16-96	.125	--	.125	3	8	0	1	0	0	0	0	3	1	0	0	5	0	0	.125	.417
Jan Mercado	R-R	6-0	200	8-28-99	.206	.200	.208	20	63	7	13	4	0	1	6	5	0	0	0	33	0	0	.317	.265
Torin Montgomery	R-R	6-3	230	5-2-01	.250	.321	.225	31	108	17	27	7	0	3	16	10	4	0	0	32	0	0	.398	.336
Federico Polanco	L-R	5-10	155	3-20-01	.265	.000	.310	10	34	5	9	3	0	1	4	3	0	0	0	13	1	1	.441	.324
Sam Praytor	R-R	5-10	205	4-4-99	.318	--	.318	7	22	2	7	0	0	0	2	3	2	0	0	3	0	0	.318	.444
Cristhian Rodriguez	L-R	6-1	160	12-23-01	.201	.208	.199	71	239	13	48	8	2	1	17	25	0	0	1	97	1	2	.264	.275
Jose Salas	B-R	6-2	191	4-26-03	.267	.310	.257	61	221	40	59	13	3	5	24	23	9	1	3	54	15	1	.421	.355
Javier Sanoja	R-R	5-9	150	9-3-02	.239	.340	.214	73	268	37	64	6	4	3	25	13	1	0	4	41	9	6	.325	.273
Carlos Santiago	B-R	5-11	145	7-24-01	.237	.289	.224	52	194	17	46	6	1	4	28	7	2	0	3	61	2	1	.340	.267
Angeudis Santos	B-R	6-1	168	9-19-01	.200	.216	.196	59	185	23	37	8	2	1	21	22	2	1	0	55	8	2	.281	.292
Jake Thompson	L-R	6-0	207	3-3-98	.292	.385	.266	34	120	23	35	13	0	3	16	20	1	0	0	32	0	1	.475	.397
Kahlil Watson	L-R	5-9	178	4-16-03	.231	.271	.223	83	324	50	75	16	5	9	44	27	4	0	3	127	16	3	.395	.296
Joey Wendle	L-R	6-1	195	4-26-90	.429	1.000	.333	2	7	1	3	1	0	0	3	1	0	0	0	1	0	0	.571	.500
Zach Zubia	R-R	6-4	230	11-4-97	.232	.250	.228	81	237	36	55	14	0	7	33	66	3	0	1	82	0	0	.380	.404

Pitching	B-T	HT	WT	DOB	W	L	ERA	G	GS	CG	SV	IP	H	R	ER	HR	BB	SO	AVG	vLH	vRH	K/9	BB/9
Luarbert Arias	R-R	6-2	176	12-12-00	3	0	3.08	26	1	0	0	53	38	21	18	3	21	66	.199	.200	.198	11.28	3.59
Sandro Bargallo	L-L	6-1	180	12-29-01	2	3	3.51	22	20	0	0	82	60	44	32	3	70	96	.208	.263	.188	10.54	7.68
Anthony Bender	R-R	6-4	205	2-3-95	0	0	0.00	2	2	0	0	2	0	0	0	0	1	4	.000	.000	.000	15.43	3.86
Gabe Bierman	R-R	6-2	200	9-3-99	6	6	4.76	20	17	0	0	96	88	55	51	10	47	105	.238	.216	.249	9.81	4.39
Richard Bleier	L-L	6-3	215	4-16-87	0	0	0.00	1	0	0	0	1	0	0	0	0	2	0	.000	--	.000	0.00	18.00
Edward Cabrera	R-R	6-5	217	4-13-98	0	0	0.00	1	1	0	0	4	1	0	0	0	3	7	.083	.000	.091	15.75	6.75
A.J. Candelario	R-R	6-0	165	12-17-97	0	2	6.23	7	0	0	2	9	10	7	6	1	5	15	.294	.000	.417	15.58	5.19
Kyle Crigger	R-R	6-2	180	6-4-99	2	1	3.14	10	0	0	1	14	12	7	5	1	5	10	.231	.250	.219	6.28	3.14
Juan Diaz	L-L	6-0	175	6-19-98	0	2	2.89	3	3	0	0	9	7	3	3	0	4	5	.219	.125	.250	4.82	3.86
Tyler Eckberg	R-R	6-4	220	9-4-97	3	1	2.11	21	0	0	6	38	44	11	9	1	7	45	.288	.243	.302	10.57	1.64
Breidy Encarnacion	R-R	6-3	185	11-9-00	1	0	9.00	2	0	0	0	3	3	3	3	0	4	6	.273	.500	.143	18.00	12.00
Tommy Eveld	R-R	6-5	214	12-30-93	0	0	0.00	3	0	0	1	5	1	0	0	0	0	6	.067	.000	.077	11.57	0.00
Justin Fall	L-L	6-6	240	6-11-99	8	7	3.71	18	14	0	1	87	87	41	36	1	21	78	.252	.288	.242	8.04	2.16
Dylan Floro	L-R	6-2	203	12-27-90	0	1	10.80	2	2	0	0	2	2	3	2	0	1	0	.250	.500	.000	0.00	5.40
Braxton Garrett	R-L	6-2	202	8-5-97	0	0	6.75	1	1	0	0	3	3	2	2	2	2	5	.250	.000	.375	16.88	6.75
Cade Gibson	L-L	6-2	195	2-18-98	1	0	0.00	4	0	0	0	8	4	0	0	0	4	10	.148	.200	.136	11.74	4.70
Elieser Hernandez	R-R	6-0	214	5-3-95	0	0	0.00	1	1	0	0	1	1	0	0	0	0	2	.250	.000	.500	18.00	0.00
Jordan Holloway	R-R	6-6	230	6-13-96	0	0	6.75	2	2	0	0	4	4	3	3	1	4	5	.286	.500	.125	11.25	9.00

Yeuris Jimenez	R-R	6-3	218	3-23-01	1	4	4.04	36	0	0	1	56	39	29	25	6	27	69	.193	.224	.178	11.16	4.37
Marcus Johnson	R-R	6-6	200	12-11-00	1	2	5.11	3	2	0	0	12	7	7	7	2	7	24	.159	.000	.212	17.51	5.11
Holt Jones	R-R	6-8	235	5-8-99	1	4	5.04	8	7	0	0	30	29	21	17	5	24	35	.252	.290	.238	10.38	7.12
Chandler Jozwiak	L-L	6-0	185	2-15-99	1	0	2.70	10	0	0	0	13	8	4	4	1	3	17	.170	.091	.194	11.48	2.03
Cole Kirschsieper	R-L	5-11	170	12-27-00	0	1	9.00	2	0	0	0	4	7	5	4	1	2	6	.350	.333	.353	13.50	4.50
Maycold Leon	L-L	6-1	160	4-29-02	0	1	3.72	6	0	0	0	10	8	6	4	1	6	11	.216	.273	.192	10.24	5.59
Jesus Luzardo	L-L	6-0	218	9-30-97	0	0	3.00	1	1	0	0	3	2	1	1	1	0	3	.200	.000	.286	9.00	0.00
Manuel Medina	L-L	5-10	140	3-25-02	0	0	0.87	4	0	0	0	10	5	1	1	0	3	15	.152	.222	.125	13.06	2.61
Max Meyer	L-R	6-0	196	3-12-99	0	0	3.00	1	1	0	0	3	1	1	1	0	0	4	.091	.000	.143	12.00	0.00
Karson Milbrandt	R-R	6-2	190	4-21-04	0	0	9.00	1	1	0	0	2	2	2	2	0	1	1	.250	.000	.286	4.50	4.50
Jacob Miller	R-R	6-2	180	8-10-03	0	1	0.00	1	1	0	0	2	1	1	0	0	0	3	.125	.000	.143	13.50	0.00
Bryan Mitchell	L-R	6-2	215	4-19-91	0	0	0.00	1	0	0	0	1	0	0	0	0	1	1	.000	--	.000	13.50	13.50
Chris Mokma	R-R	6-4	210	2-11-01	4	1	3.58	6	5	0	0	33	20	15	13	4	13	33	.174	.171	.176	9.09	3.58
Euri Montero	R-R	6-4	170	3-28-02	1	0	6.39	7	0	0	0	13	17	9	9	1	5	7	.333	.333	.333	4.97	3.55
Patrick Murphy	L-L	6-1	205	3-7-97	1	1	3.00	18	0	0	5	24	19	9	8	1	11	25	.221	.286	.200	9.38	4.13
Tommy Nance	R-R	6-6	235	3-19-91	0	0	2.25	3	2	0	0	4	1	1	1	1	1	4	.077	.000	.100	9.00	2.25
Luis Palacios	L-L	6-2	160	7-1-00	4	5	4.03	14	12	1	0	83	86	39	37	11	5	82	.265	.270	.263	8.93	0.54
Eury Perez	R-R	6-8	220	4-15-03	0	0	0.00	1	1	0	0	2	1	0	0	0	0	4	.143	.000	.167	18.00	0.00
Jared Pettitte	L-L	6-3	218	5-28-98	0	1	14.14	8	0	0	0	7	6	14	11	1	15	11	.240	.400	.200	14.14	19.29
Natanael Polanco	R-R	6-1	170	4-24-03	0	0	3.00	4	0	0	0	9	8	3	3	1	2	4	.235	.294	.176	4.00	2.00
Jared Poland	R-R	6-0	215	1-12-00	0	0	1.80	3	3	0	0	10	6	3	2	1	2	9	.182	.125	.200	8.10	1.80
Cody Poteet	R-R	6-1	190	7-30-94	0	0	0.00	1	1	0	0	2	0	0	0	0	1	4	.000	.000	.000	18.00	4.50
Yoilan Quinonez	R-R	6-4	200	8-11-99	1	2	5.45	24	0	0	3	35	38	23	21	3	10	40	.268	.160	.326	10.38	2.60
Jean Reyes	R-R	5-11	165	8-16-02	1	0	2.95	9	0	0	0	18	10	7	6	0	15	16	.167	.208	.139	7.85	7.36
Juan Reynoso	R-R	6-0	165	4-4-04	0	4	7.18	9	6	0	0	26	24	26	21	6	19	27	.235	.250	.227	9.23	6.49
Josh Roberson	R-R	6-3	175	5-12-96	1	1	11.25	4	1	0	1	4	6	6	5	0	6	8	.333	.250	.357	18.00	13.50
Edgar Sanchez	R-R	6-1	190	8-2-00	5	3	4.24	15	13	0	0	70	58	41	33	4	26	74	.220	.272	.197	9.51	3.34
Jake Schrand	R-R	6-0	180	8-8-99	5	1	3.56	27	0	0	2	43	41	17	17	5	15	43	.253	.264	.248	9.00	3.14
Cason Sherrod	R-R	6-4	215	6-25-96	0	0	9.00	2	0	0	0	2	2	2	2	0	0	0	.286	1.000	.000	0.00	0.00
Dale Stanavich	L-L	5-11	175	6-23-99	0	3	14.54	8	0	0	0	9	11	15	14	1	8	6	.333	.200	.391	6.23	8.31
Joey Steele	R-R	6-2	195	11-15-95	2	0	1.59	8	0	0	1	11	4	2	2	1	1	17	.108	.091	.115	13.50	0.79
Cole Sulser	R-R	6-1	190	3-12-90	0	0	0.00	2	1	0	0	2	0	0	0	0	0	6	.000	.000	.000	23.14	0.00
Edison Suriel	L-L	5-10	185	10-24-98	1	5	5.79	24	0	0	1	42	47	34	27	4	25	51	.280	.222	.295	10.93	5.36
Evan Taylor	L-L	6-4	250	12-26-99	0	1	2.92	9	0	0	0	12	8	5	4	1	7	19	.186	.214	.172	13.86	5.11
Dameivi Tineo	L-L	6-3	170	8-1-03	0	2	9.53	3	2	0	0	6	4	6	6	0	14	5	.211	.500	.133	7.94	22.24
Jake Walters	R-R	6-0	190	3-11-96	2	0	2.08	5	5	0	0	22	18	7	5	1	4	20	.237	.000	.333	8.31	1.66
Josh White	R-R	6-1	205	11-24-00	0	0	5.14	6	0	0	0	7	7	5	4	0	5	10	.241	.273	.222	12.86	6.43
Caleb Wurster	L-L	5-11	182	9-21-98	4	0	2.60	29	0	0	9	35	27	14	10	1	17	45	.209	.171	.227	11.68	4.41

Fielding

Catcher	PCT	G	PO	A	E	DP	PB
Barstad	.986	50	436	41	7	3	8
Estrada	.985	20	174	23	3	1	1
Henry	1.000	2	18	3	0	0	0
Mack	.979	30	302	17	7	1	8
Martinez	.962	3	22	3	1	0	1
Mercado	.975	20	177	18	5	1	2
Praytor	1.000	6	61	5	0	1	1

First Base	PCT	G	PO	A	E	DP
Cooper	1.000	2	10	2	0	1
Montgomery	.982	30	215	7	4	22
Polanco	1.000	4	28	2	0	8
Rodriguez	.990	15	94	3	1	4
Santiago	1.000	6	31	0	0	3
Thompson	1.000	2	14	1	0	0
Zubia	.990	78	568	35	6	53

Second Base	PCT	G	PO	A	E	DP
Berti	1.000	1	1	2	0	0
Devers	1.000	2	2	4	0	1
Diaz	1.000	1	1	4	0	0
Johnson	.800	2	2	2	1	0
Lewis	.956	29	57	52	5	10
Polanco	1.000	2	5	5	0	1
Salas	.930	12	17	23	3	5
Sanoja	.976	47	87	118	5	36
Santiago	.944	5	11	6	1	1
Santos	.975	22	33	46	2	13
Watson	.960	23	29	43	3	8

Third Base	PCT	G	PO	A	E	DP
Anderson	1.000	1	0	1	0	0
Berry	.929	24	9	43	4	2
Berti	1.000	1	1	3	0	0
Cappe	.786	9	2	9	3	0
Diaz	.500	1	0	1	1	0
Lewis	.946	14	7	28	2	2
Polanco	1.000	1	4	1	0	0
Rodriguez	.906	36	20	57	8	6
Salas	.951	16	5	34	2	1
Sanoja	.963	14	6	20	1	3
Santiago	.956	18	10	33	2	0
Santos	.750	8	5	7	4	0
Wendle	1.000	1	1	1	0	0

Shortstop	PCT	G	PO	A	E	DP
Cappe	.965	21	14	41	2	11
Lewis	.750	2	1	2	1	1
Rodriguez	.931	14	18	36	4	8
Salas	.967	25	32	56	3	17
Santiago	.967	27	23	66	3	17
Santos	1.000	1	0	1	0	0
Watson	.909	46	51	89	14	21
Wendle	1.000	1	1	2	0	0

Outfield	PCT	G	PO	A	E	DP
Allen	.988	102	167	1	2	0
Allen	1.000	24	32	2	0	0
Caballero	.991	75	102	5	1	0
Castillo	1.000	23	32	2	0	1
Cody	.969	43	63	0	2	0
Johnson	.991	58	108	7	1	1
Luttrell	1.000	26	45	0	0	0
Sanoja	1.000	10	28	1	0	0
Santos	.968	17	29	1	1	1
Thompson	1.000	30	32	1	0	1

FCL MARLINS — *ROOKIE*

FLORIDA COMPLEX LEAGUE

Batting	B-T	HT	WT	DOB	AVG	vLH	vRH	G	AB	R	H	2B	3B	HR	RBI	BB	HBP	SH	SF	SO	SB	CS	SLG	OBP
Steven Adderley	R-R	6-0	160	12-5-02	.034	--	.034	18	29	2	1	0	0	0	1	3	0	0	0	11	3	1	.034	.125
Andre Arthur	R-R	6-4	185	6-9-03	.192	.000	.227	15	26	5	5	0	1	0	2	4	4	0	0	13	1	0	.269	.382
Jacob Berry	B-R	6-0	212	5-5-01	.125	.000	.133	4	16	1	2	0	0	0	2	1	1	0	0	6	0	0	.125	.222
Spencer Bramwell	R-R	5-10	220	1-10-99	.059	.000	.063	5	17	2	1	0	0	0	1	2	0	0	0	8	0	0	.059	.158
Diowill Burgos	L-R	6-1	207	1-29-01	.221	.250	.216	29	86	9	19	6	1	2	15	12	0	0	0	28	0	0	.384	.316
Yiddi Cappe	R-R	6-3	175	9-17-02	.305	.500	.279	30	118	23	36	7	0	6	25	9	3	0	2	19	6	4	.517	.364
Arquimedes Cumana	R-R	6-3	175	4-28-00	.238	.000	.294	22	42	5	10	1	0	0	6	6	3	0	0	14	1	0	.262	.373

Jose Estrada	R-R	5-10	175	5-5-00	.200	.333	.179	14	45	6	9	4	0	1	5	4	0	0	0	5	0	0	.356	.265
Jose Garcia	B-R	6-1	190	10-4-01	.143	.000	.167	7	7	2	1	1	0	0	0	3	0	0	0	5	0	0	.286	.400
Payton Henry	R-R	6-2	215	6-24-97	.417	1.000	.364	5	12	4	5	1	0	2	3	1	1	0	0	3	0	0	1.000	.500
Jesus Hernandez	R-R	5-11	150	2-20-04	.245	.167	.255	18	53	9	13	0	2	0	3	7	0	0	0	15	5	0	.321	.333
Ronald Hernandez	B-R	6-1	155	10-23-03	.236	.091	.263	41	140	14	33	4	1	2	22	14	6	0	1	32	2	1	.321	.329
Renny Hidalgo	R-R	5-9	165	9-5-02	.232	.143	.246	43	151	24	35	9	0	1	15	17	3	0	0	37	6	3	.311	.322
Osiris Johnson	R-R	6-1	198	10-18-00	.222	.000	.250	3	9	0	2	0	0	0	0	2	0	0	0	2	0	1	.222	.364
Carmine Lane	R-R	6-1	200	3-28-01	.000	.000	.000	3	6	0	0	0	0	0	0	2	0	0	0	3	0	0	.000	.250
Chase Luttrell	L-L	6-1	200	6-1-00	.500	1.000	.333	1	4	0	2	0	0	0	2	0	0	0	0	1	0	0	.500	.500
Joe Mack	L-R	6-1	210	12-27-02	.296	.000	.320	9	27	2	8	0	0	2	3	4	0	0	0	7	0	0	.519	.387
Jordan McCants	L-R	6-1	165	5-21-02	.245	.286	.238	50	196	32	48	9	5	0	11	24	1	1	2	57	8	2	.342	.327
Jhonny Melenciano	L-R	6-0	155	12-13-01	.287	.375	.278	39	87	9	25	5	1	1	16	15	0	3	1	23	9	4	.402	.388
Victor Victor Mesa	R-R	5-11	188	7-20-96	.250	--	.250	3	8	1	2	0	0	0	1	3	0	0	0	3	3	0	.250	.455
Torin Montgomery	R-R	6-3	230	5-2-01	.375	1.000	.333	4	16	4	6	1	0	1	3	1	0	0	0	4	0	0	.625	.412
Cody Morissette	L-R	6-0	175	1-16-00	.333	--	.333	2	6	1	2	1	0	0	1	0	0	0	0	1	0	0	.500	.333
Yolinson Pena	R-R	5-11	175	9-16-00	.000	--	.000	5	3	0	0	0	0	0	0	0	0	0	0	3	0	0	.000	.000
Federico Polanco	L-R	5-10	155	3-20-01	.429	.000	.462	4	14	2	6	1	1	0	4	1	0	0	0	7	0	0	.643	.467
Lorenzo Quintana	R-R	5-10	205	3-1-89	.125	--	.125	4	8	0	1	0	0	0	0	2	0	0	0	0	0	0	.125	.300
Tyler Rando	R-R	5-10	202	3-12-98	.125	--	.125	4	8	1	1	1	0	0	0	0	0	0	0	2	0	0	.250	.125
Brett Roberts	R-R	6-0	182	3-12-01	.256	.000	.282	13	43	7	11	1	0	3	9	5	0	0	0	8	1	0	.488	.333
Cristhian Rodriguez	L-R	6-1	160	12-23-01	.152	.071	.169	22	79	12	12	3	0	0	6	6	1	0	0	26	1	0	.190	.221
Miguel Rodriguez	R-R	6-0	160	11-8-02	.125	.000	.143	3	8	1	1	0	0	0	0	0	0	0	0	2	0	0	.125	.125
Richard Roman	R-R	6-1	210	12-22-01	.184	.250	.176	12	38	3	7	2	0	0	5	5	1	0	0	9	0	0	.237	.295
Junior Sanchez	L-R	5-11	177	12-18-02	.161	.200	.158	24	62	6	10	0	1	0	4	10	1	0	0	6	2	0	.194	.288
Javier Sanoja	R-R	5-9	150	9-3-02	.318	.143	.344	28	107	27	34	10	1	3	19	13	0	1	3	6	9	3	.514	.382
Carlos Santiago	B-R	5-11	145	7-24-01	.343	.700	.281	16	67	14	23	10	1	1	10	5	0	0	1	17	1	0	.567	.384
Angeudis Santos	B-R	6-1	168	9-19-01	.211	.000	.229	13	38	6	8	0	1	2	5	6	0	0	0	13	2	1	.421	.318
Harrison Spohn	R-R	6-3	185	12-3-98	.143	.500	.115	9	28	3	4	2	0	1	2	4	0	0	0	7	0	0	.321	.250
Kahlil Watson	L-R	5-9	178	4-16-03	.273	.000	.300	5	11	4	3	2	0	1	3	5	1	0	1	5	0	0	.727	.500
Noah Williamson	R-R	6-4	220	8-23-00	.217	.143	.225	41	143	27	31	13	3	2	20	16	10	0	2	71	6	4	.392	.333
Joshua Zamora	R-R	5-11	190	5-18-99	.188	.000	.214	7	16	1	3	0	0	0	5	4	2	0	0	3	0	1	.188	.409

Pitching	B-T	HT	WT	DOB	W	L	ERA	G	GS	CG	SV	IP	H	R	ER	HR	BB	SO	AVG	vLH	vRH	K/9	BB/9
Stiven Almanzar	R-R	5-10	155	12-24-01	1	2	3.14	8	0	0	1	14	15	7	5	0	6	12	.294	.357	.270	7.53	3.77
Luis Baldiris	L-L	5-11	150	5-7-04	0	0	9.00	1	0	0	0	2	1	2	2	0	2	2	.143	--	.143	9.00	9.00
Anthony Bender	R-R	6-4	205	2-3-95	0	0	0.00	1	1	0	0	1	0	0	0	0	0	3	.000	.000	.000	27.00	0.00
Yoelvis Burguillos	R-R	6-2	150	9-7-02	0	1	10.13	3	0	0	0	3	8	9	3	0	2	2	.471	.333	.545	6.75	6.75
Ike Buxton	R-R	6-3	208	7-18-00	0	0	9.64	3	0	0	0	5	3	5	5	0	8	5	.200	.200	.200	9.64	15.43
Kyle Crigger	R-R	6-2	180	6-4-99	0	0	0.00	1	0	0	0	1	2	0	0	0	0	2	.400	.250	1.000	18.00	0.00
Wander De La Rosa	B-R	6-0	160	10-22-01	2	1	3.63	10	1	0	0	17	16	12	7	1	6	13	.250	.238	.256	6.75	3.12
Juan Diaz	L-L	6-0	175	6-19-98	1	1	5.68	6	3	0	0	19	23	14	12	4	6	24	.295	.308	.292	11.37	2.84
Mario Doble	R-R	6-4	178	11-1-00	1	1	4.58	10	0	0	0	20	16	15	10	2	9	16	.219	.154	.255	7.32	4.12
Franyer Duarte	R-R	6-0	160	2-2-04	3	1	3.94	11	0	0	0	30	20	15	13	1	17	14	.190	.088	.239	4.25	5.16
Breidy Encarnacion	R-R	6-3	185	11-9-00	0	0	1.93	12	4	0	2	28	15	6	6	1	8	34	.153	.216	.115	10.93	2.57
Justin Fall	L-L	6-6	240	6-11-99	0	0	8.10	1	1	0	0	3	5	4	3	0	0	4	.333	.000	.385	10.80	0.00
Cade Gibson	L-L	6-2	195	2-18-98	0	0	1.29	4	1	0	0	7	4	1	1	0	2	10	.167	.000	.286	12.86	2.57
Jack Gowen	R-R	6-1	220	10-29-99	1	0	2.45	3	0	0	0	4	0	2	1	0	6	6	.000	.000	.000	14.73	14.73
Louis Head	R-R	6-1	180	4-23-90	0	0	0.00	1	1	0	0	1	0	0	0	0	0	2	.000	.000	.000	18.00	0.00
Elieser Hernandez	R-R	6-0	214	5-3-95	0	0	0.00	1	1	0	0	1	0	0	0	0	0	1	.000	.000	.000	9.00	0.00
Jordan Holloway	R-R	6-6	230	6-13-96	0	0	0.00	1	1	0	0	2	1	0	0	0	0	5	.167	.000	.250	22.50	0.00
Marcus Johnson	R-R	6-6	200	12-11-00	0	1	8.31	2	2	0	0	4	5	4	4	0	4	5	.294	.000	.417	10.38	8.31
Holt Jones	R-R	6-8	235	5-8-99	0	1	2.25	2	1	0	0	4	7	2	1	0	1	4	.438	.500	.417	9.00	2.25
Cole Kirschsieper	R-L	5-11	170	12-27-00	1	0	0.00	2	1	0	0	3	3	0	0	0	0	4	.231	.333	.200	12.00	0.00
Zack Leban	R-R	6-2	235	5-30-96	1	0	0.00	2	0	0	0	4	1	0	0	0	1	5	.083	.250	.000	12.27	2.45
Maycold Leon	L-L	6-1	160	4-29-02	4	0	0.92	9	0	0	0	20	12	2	2	1	3	17	.171	.188	.167	7.78	1.37
Collin Lowe	R-R	6-4	210	9-11-98	1	0	1.59	4	2	0	0	11	10	2	2	0	2	9	.227	.286	.200	7.15	1.59
Manuel Medina	L-L	5-10	140	3-25-02	3	1	3.00	11	1	0	1	30	22	10	10	2	2	41	.200	.360	.153	12.30	0.60
Jorge Mercedes	R-R	6-3	185	7-1-00	2	2	2.63	15	5	0	1	24	12	8	7	0	17	43	.152	.125	.164	16.13	6.38
Jacob Miller	R-R	6-2	180	8-10-03	0	1	7.36	3	3	0	0	4	4	5	3	1	2	3	.250	.250	.250	7.36	4.91
Euri Montero	R-R	6-4	170	3-28-02	0	0	2.93	8	0	0	2	15	13	5	5	0	1	9	.232	.235	.231	5.28	0.59
Jhonaiker Osorio	L-R	6-0	160	9-2-00	1	0	2.92	9	0	0	2	12	10	4	4	0	2	13	.222	.188	.241	9.49	1.46
Jared Pettitte	L-L	6-3	218	5-28-98	1	0	0.00	3	0	0	0	4	0	0	0	0	1	4	.000	.000	.000	9.00	2.25
Natanael Polanco	R-R	6-1	170	4-24-03	1	1	4.00	11	0	0	1	18	18	9	8	2	3	17	.254	.333	.220	8.50	1.50
Jared Poland	R-R	6-0	215	1-12-00	0	0	0.00	2	1	0	0	3	3	0	0	0	3	2	.273	.500	.143	6.75	10.13
Matt Pushard	R-R	6-4	245	10-27-97	1	1	14.73	5	0	0	0	4	4	6	6	1	8	6	.250	.167	.300	14.73	19.64
Jean Reyes	R-R	5-11	165	8-16-02	0	1	2.61	7	0	0	1	10	8	7	3	2	3	14	.200	.100	.233	12.19	2.61
Juan Reynoso	R-R	6-0	165	4-4-04	0	0	1.93	3	3	0	0	9	3	2	2	1	7	5	.107	.125	.100	4.82	6.75
Jose Rojas	R-R	6-0	160	4-19-03	0	0	27.00	1	0	0	0	1	4	3	3	1	0	1	.571	--	.571	9.00	0.00
Yoelvis Sanchez	L-L	6-2	163	4-27-02	0	0	13.50	1	0	0	0	1	1	1	1	0	2	1	.333	.000	.500	13.50	27.00
Jhoniel Serrano	R-R	0-0	0	10-17-03	1	4	9.17	12	8	0	0	34	36	40	35	5	22	29	.263	.333	.203	7.60	5.77
Cason Sherrod	R-R	6-4	215	6-25-96	1	0	0.00	6	3	0	0	9	6	2	0	0	0	11	.176	.143	.200	11.00	0.00
Cristian Sierra	R-R	6-5	212	4-1-98	0	1	8.64	8	0	0	0	8	4	11	8	0	12	16	.138	.000	.167	17.28	12.96
Dale Stanavich	L-L	5-11	175	6-23-99	1	0	0.00	2	0	0	0	2	0	0	0	0	0	4	.000	.000	.000	18.00	0.00
Joey Steele	R-R	6-2	195	11-15-95	1	0	0.00	3	1	0	0	5	1	0	0	0	0	5	.063	.000	.077	9.00	0.00
Tristan Stevens	R-R	6-2	200	12-8-97	0	0	0.00	3	0	0	1	4	3	0	0	0	0	3	.214	.250	.200	6.75	0.00

Dameivi Tineo	L-L	6-3	170	8-1-03	2	0	0.86	6	5	0	0	21	8	2	2	0	5	24	.116	.000	.182	10.29	2.14
Williams Valencia	R-R	6-0	167	7-21-00	0	1	2.93	11	0	0	4	15	11	6	5	0	5	12	.204	.235	.189	7.04	2.93
Henry Valencio	R-R	6-1	170	5-11-99	0	1	5.93	10	0	0	0	14	10	9	9	0	12	11	.204	.167	.216	7.24	7.90
Jake Walters	R-R	6-0	190	3-11-96	0	1	2.45	4	3	0	0	7	7	3	2	0	1	8	.233	.286	.217	9.82	1.23
Josh White	R-R	6-1	205	11-24-00	0	0	9.00	3	0	0	0	4	7	4	4	1	3	6	.389	.333	.417	13.50	6.75
Alex Williams	L-R	6-3	220	10-22-99	0	0	0.00	2	2	0	0	5	0	0	0	0	0	5	.000	.000	.000	9.00	0.00

Fielding

C: Bramwell 3, Cumana 13, Estrada 10, Garcia 4, Henry 2, Hernandez 30, Mack 5, Quintana 2, Rando 3. **1B:** Burgos 13, Cumana 8, Estrada 4, Garcia 2, Montgomery 3, Pena 3, Polanco 2, Roberts 7, Rodriguez 11, Santiago 9, Zamora 3. **2B:** McCants 32, Morissette 1, Sanchez 19, Sanoja 4, Zamora 4. **3B:** Berry 3, Cappe 12, Garcia 1, Hernandez 12, Morissette 1, Pena 2, Polanco 1, Roberts 1, Rodriguez 5, Sanoja 12, Santiago 4, Santos 1, Spohn 4, Zamora 1. **SS:** Burgos 1, Cappe 15, Hernandez 6, McCants 12, Rodriguez 6, Rodriguez 1, Sanoja 7, Santiago 3, Santos 1, Spohn 5, Watson 5. **OF:** Adderley 11, Arthur 14, Burgos 12, Hidalgo 44, Johnson 3, Luttrell 1, Melenciano 38, Mesa 3, Roman 11, Sanoja 5, Santos 10, Williamson 41.

DSL MARLINS — *ROOKIE*

DOMINICAN SUMMER LEAGUE

Batting	B-T	HT	WT	DOB	AVG	vLH	vRH	G	AB	R	H	2B	3B	HR	RBI	BB	HBP	SH	SF	SO	SB	CS	SLG	OBP
Lisandro Bonifacio	B-R	6-0	155	8-12-05	.137	.241	.108	41	131	19	18	3	0	1	8	26	4	1	1	51	6	3	.183	.296
Byron Chourio	B-R	6-2	171	5-20-05	.344	.429	.319	51	183	47	63	9	0	1	23	25	5	0	4	27	19	7	.410	.429
Oscar Colina	R-R	6-0	150	1-28-04	.221	.310	.196	44	136	29	30	2	0	0	11	27	4	0	1	29	25	5	.235	.363
Kengri De Los Santos	R-R	6-1	179	9-11-04	.279	.400	.242	15	43	4	12	3	1	0	4	2	1	0	0	10	0	2	.395	.326
2-team total (4 DSL Miami)					.232	.385	.186	19	56	5	13	3	1	0	5	3	1	0	0	18	0	2	.321	.283
Kendry Feliz	R-R	5-11	160	11-17-04	.254	.364	.232	44	134	25	34	5	1	3	22	32	5	1	1	38	8	2	.373	.413
Jose Gerardo	R-R	6-1	179	6-12-05	.284	.455	.245	50	176	44	50	12	1	11	31	33	8	0	1	66	18	1	.551	.417
Julio Henriquez	R-R	6-0	190	11-4-04	.266	.296	.257	41	128	21	34	6	2	1	22	17	9	0	4	30	3	3	.367	.380
2-team total (9 DSL Miami)					.255	.265	.252	50	153	23	39	7	3	1	24	23	12	0	4	36	4	3	.359	.385
Jesus Hernandez	R-R	5-11	150	2-20-04	.250	.176	.270	23	80	10	20	3	0	1	13	12	0	0	3	5	6	2	.325	.337
Jose Monserrate	R-R	6-0	176	9-20-04	.292	.207	.308	55	185	33	54	12	2	2	35	23	8	0	4	35	14	5	.411	.386
Gregory Mota	R-R	6-3	172	12-20-04	.250	.231	.253	26	88	13	22	2	0	2	13	10	2	0	0	40	3	2	.341	.340
Nestor Rios	R-R	5-9	175	1-4-05	.202	.000	.227	31	109	17	22	5	0	1	12	6	7	0	1	32	0	1	.275	.285
Jose Rivera	B-R	6-0	145	11-17-04	.142	.156	.137	41	127	15	18	3	0	1	20	17	3	0	3	40	1	1	.189	.253
Juan Rodriguez	R-R	6-0	160	6-18-04	.208	.125	.232	25	72	11	15	1	0	1	10	6	2	0	2	15	1	1	.264	.280
Carlos Sanchez	B-R	5-9	175	9-20-04	.245	.333	.223	42	151	22	37	5	1	4	26	18	1	0	4	32	6	1	.371	.322

Pitching	B-T	HT	WT	DOB	W	L	ERA	G	GS	CG	SV	IP	H	R	ER	HR	BB	SO	AVG	vLH	vRH	K/9	BB/9
Andelzon Abad	L-L	6-0	155	6-19-04	1	6	6.91	11	7	0	0	27	29	30	21	2	26	32	.266	.238	.273	10.54	8.56
Jhon Cabral	R-R	6-1	172	8-9-05	0	3	8.74	10	10	0	0	23	16	27	22	0	36	17	.211	.179	.229	6.75	14.29
Willian Campos	R-R	6-3	175	9-24-04	0	0	0.00	4	0	0	0	9	8	1	0	0	1	6	.229	.200	.250	6.23	1.04
2-team total (8 DSL Miami)					1	1	5.49	12	0	0	0	20	24	13	12	0	9	17	.293	.194	.353	7.78	4.12
Luis Cesar	L-L	6-3	183	2-24-04	0	1	1.80	2	2	0	0	5	1	3	1	0	4	3	.067	.000	.125	5.40	7.20
Juan De La Cruz	R-R	6-3	180	3-4-05	3	2	4.17	11	10	0	0	41	38	24	19	3	18	28	.248	.313	.219	6.15	3.95
Rodolfo De La Cruz	R-R	6-2	193	2-19-04	1	2	4.58	11	6	0	0	37	34	20	19	1	22	32	.245	.217	.258	7.71	5.30
Eliazar Dishmey	R-R	6-1	175	10-25-04	0	2	2.74	10	3	0	1	23	19	9	7	1	11	37	.211	.267	.183	14.48	4.30
Eiver Espinoza	R-R	6-6	168	1-11-04	2	0	1.35	10	1	0	0	20	16	10	3	0	15	19	.203	.219	.191	8.55	6.75
Angel Hernandez	R-R	6-2	194	1-24-04	2	1	4.58	10	0	0	0	18	16	9	9	0	9	14	.242	.385	.150	7.13	4.58
Gerardo Hernandez	R-R	0-0	0	10-16-03	0	0	18.00	1	0	0	0	2	4	4	4	0	1	2	.400	.000	.444	9.00	4.50
2-team total (10 DSL Miami)					1	2	7.23	11	0	0	0	19	22	21	15	2	14	14	.289	.304	.283	6.75	6.75
Leandro Hernandez	R-R	6-1	170	1-27-02	2	0	1.13	5	0	0	2	8	3	2	1	0	0	11	.115	.000	.176	12.38	0.00
Elvin Jimenez	R-R	6-2	210	3-19-05	2	0	0.00	6	0	0	0	7	4	0	0	0	9	7	.160	.000	.235	8.59	11.05
Julio Mendez	L-L	5-11	180	1-7-05	0	3	1.93	8	8	0	0	23	15	11	5	1	12	34	.181	.267	.162	13.11	4.63
2-team total (1 DSL Miami)					0	3	2.13	9	9	0	0	25	17	12	6	1	13	36	.189	.294	.164	12.79	4.62
Franklyn Moreta	R-R	6-0	160	1-11-04	3	0	2.93	9	0	0	1	15	17	6	5	0	5	14	.283	.333	.256	8.22	2.93
2-team total (2 DSL Miami)					3	1	2.95	11	0	0	2	18	22	10	6	0	6	15	.297	.333	.277	7.36	2.95
Lester Nin	R-R	6-0	195	11-15-03	3	0	1.51	8	7	0	0	36	17	8	6	2	6	40	.140	.214	.118	10.09	1.51
Michael Perez	R-R	6-3	160	9-5-02	3	0	3.09	6	0	0	0	12	9	4	4	1	3	9	.205	.250	.179	6.94	2.31
Albert Polanco	R-R	6-2	174	6-30-05	2	0	1.57	7	0	0	0	23	14	9	4	0	6	31	.169	.115	.193	12.13	2.35
Luifer Romero	L-L	6-2	160	12-9-04	1	1	5.57	8	1	0	0	21	28	19	13	1	6	25	.318	.500	.278	10.71	2.57
Braulio Salas	R-R	6-2	175	11-5-04	0	0	10.13	3	0	0	0	5	13	7	6	1	2	4	.481	1.000	.300	6.75	3.38
Elian Serrata	R-R	6-0	160	1-27-02	0	0	47.25	5	0	0	0	3	7	14	14	3	5	2	.467	.714	.250	6.75	16.88
2-team total (8 DSL Miami)					1	1	9.17	13	0	0	0	18	18	20	18	3	6	22	.261	.414	.150	11.21	3.06
Alfonso Suriel	L-L	6-2	155	7-3-03	2	0	5.46	10	2	0	1	28	31	20	17	2	7	33	.274	.056	.316	10.61	2.25
Fraylin Suriel	R-R	6-1	170	5-21-04	1	2	6.23	11	0	0	2	17	14	15	12	2	15	5	.222	.286	.190	2.60	7.79
Roosevelt Trinidad	R-R	6-5	200	5-15-03	2	1	5.14	10	0	0	1	21	20	17	12	3	8	21	.233	.172	.263	9.00	3.43
Nicolas Uriepero	R-R	6-2	209	3-3-05	0	0	3.86	1	0	0	0	2	1	1	1	0	2	3	.143	.000	.167	11.57	7.71
Mado Villegas	R-R	5-11	165	7-6-03	1	2	3.42	11	0	0	0	24	19	13	9	2	4	20	.218	.206	.226	7.61	1.52

Fielding

C: Rios 24, Rodriguez 10, Sanchez 25. **1B:** Henriquez 34, Rodriguez 13, Sanchez 11. **2B:** Bonifacio 7, De Los Santos 12, Feliz 22, Hernandez 7, Rivera 14. **3B:** Bonifacio 8, De Los Santos 1, Feliz 18, Hernandez 9, Mota 23. **SS:** Bonifacio 27, Hernandez 4, Rivera 27. **OF:** Chourio 42, Colina 43, Feliz 1, Gerardo 32, Henriquez 7, Monserrate 50.

DSL MIAMI — ROOKIE

DOMINICAN SUMMER LEAGUE

Batting	B-T	HT	WT	DOB	AVG	vLH	vRH	G	AB	R	H	2B	3B	HR	RBI	BB	HBP	SH	SF	SO	SB	CS	SLG	OBP
Greyber Altamirano	L-R	6-2	145	10-15-04	.231	.267	.224	29	91	9	21	2	0	0	10	7	1	0	2	13	4	0	.253	.287
Reiner Chourio	L-R	5-10	155	12-12-03	.261	.250	.265	32	88	15	23	5	1	1	10	14	1	0	1	33	2	2	.375	.365
Kengri De Los Santos	R-R	6-1	179	9-11-04	.077	.333	.000	4	13	1	1	0	0	0	1	1	0	0	0	8	0	0	.077	.143
2-team total (15 DSL Marlins)					.232	.385	.186	19	56	5	13	3	1	0	5	3	1	0	0	18	0	2	.321	.283
Edward Duran	R-R	5-10	170	5-29-04	.224	.265	.212	41	147	20	33	10	1	0	12	19	3	0	0	26	3	1	.306	.325
Danny Gonzalez	R-R	6-0	160	11-26-04	.154	.000	.200	14	39	8	6	2	1	1	7	12	2	0	1	14	5	1	.333	.370
Julio Henriquez	R-R	6-0	190	11-4-04	.200	.143	.222	9	25	2	5	1	1	0	2	6	3	0	0	6	1	0	.320	.412
2-team total (41 DSL Marlins)					.255	.265	.252	50	153	23	39	7	3	1	24	23	12	0	4	36	4	3	.359	.385
Deivis Mosquera	R-R	6-2	178	11-5-04	.239	.200	.247	38	113	18	27	4	2	2	11	17	5	0	0	29	5	2	.363	.363
Cherif Neymour	B-R	5-11	150	3-4-05	.196	.152	.208	40	153	30	30	12	2	0	10	13	5	0	1	63	22	1	.301	.279
Kevin Novoa	R-R	5-11	175	8-27-04	.200	.000	.219	10	35	3	7	1	0	1	3	0	1	0	0	9	0	0	.314	.222
Victor Ortega	R-R	6-1	200	1-19-04	.320	.429	.278	10	25	2	8	1	0	0	2	8	1	0	0	4	0	2	.360	.500
Antony Peguero	R-R	6-0	175	6-14-05	.286	.233	.301	50	196	24	56	10	1	5	33	13	8	0	0	35	7	6	.423	.355
Robert Perez	R-R	6-2	165	4-27-04	.171	.107	.191	36	117	17	20	6	0	4	17	16	3	0	1	48	6	2	.325	.285
Germain Ruiz	R-R	6-3	155	12-25-02	.250	.350	.229	39	116	20	29	6	1	3	9	13	7	0	0	41	10	4	.397	.360
Mauricio Serrano	B-R	--	--	5-17-05	.169	.167	.170	28	65	8	11	3	0	0	6	18	0	0	1	21	5	1	.215	.345
Toby Simmons	B-L	5-11	175	12-2-04	.272	.268	.273	51	180	35	49	10	5	4	26	28	3	0	2	66	22	5	.450	.376
Yoffry Solano	B-R	5-10	155	11-4-04	.320	.350	.313	30	103	17	33	4	2	0	11	10	3	0	1	19	4	2	.398	.393
Marco Vargas	L-R	6-0	170	5-14-05	.319	.439	.284	53	182	30	58	13	3	2	38	35	0	0	4	32	14	6	.456	.421
Derek Vegas	R-R	6-2	175	12-22-01	.289	.364	.274	40	128	18	37	7	0	1	12	15	5	0	1	24	1	1	.367	.383

Pitching	B-T	HT	WT	DOB	W	L	ERA	G	GS	CG	SV	IP	H	R	ER	HR	BB	SO	AVG	vLH	vRH	K/9	BB/9
Josue Arias	L-L	6-2	165	5-5-05	0	7	13.30	12	8	0	0	23	23	38	34	2	37	25	.258	.167	.282	9.78	14.48
Luis Baldiris	L-L	5-11	150	5-7-04	0	0	4.71	12	0	0	0	21	15	15	11	4	16	32	.185	.000	.205	13.71	6.86
Rafael Brito	R-R	6-7	175	3-27-03	0	4	18.60	13	0	0	0	15	26	38	31	2	32	8	.394	.400	.391	4.80	19.20
Willian Campos	R-R	6-3	175	9-24-04	1	1	9.82	8	0	0	0	11	16	12	12	0	8	11	.340	.188	.419	9.00	6.55
2-team total (4 DSL Marlins)					1	1	5.49	12	0	0	0	20	24	13	12	0	9	17	.293	.194	.353	7.78	4.12
Rafael Castaneda	R-R	6-4	165	5-18-04	0	0	5.40	3	0	0	0	5	3	3	3	1	3	2	.167	.250	.143	3.60	5.40
Walin Castillo	R-R	6-3	175	1-2-05	1	3	2.70	10	9	0	0	33	28	16	10	3	9	36	.224	.240	.213	9.72	2.43
Jose Fernandez	R-R	6-1	155	10-16-03	0	1	5.53	10	4	0	0	28	30	21	17	1	15	34	.275	.286	.269	11.06	4.88
Johandry Fuente	R-R	6-0	185	12-29-02	1	0	9.00	12	0	0	0	18	19	23	18	2	23	19	.260	.353	.232	9.50	11.50
Julio Garcia	R-R	6-0	170	12-28-04	0	0	1.42	4	0	0	0	6	4	1	1	0	2	9	.190	.143	.214	12.79	2.84
Gerardo Hernandez	R-R	0-0	0	10-16-03	1	2	5.94	10	0	0	0	17	18	17	11	2	13	12	.273	.318	.250	6.48	7.02
2-team total (1 DSL Marlins)					1	2	7.23	11	0	0	0	19	22	21	15	2	14	14	.289	.304	.283	6.75	6.75
Luis Lopez	R-R	6-3	185	10-8-01	1	1	4.41	12	0	0	5	16	18	9	8	1	4	9	.281	.227	.310	4.96	2.20
Liomar Martinez	R-R	6-2	165	6-25-05	1	2	4.13	9	2	0	0	24	28	14	11	2	8	14	.286	.367	.250	5.25	3.00
Julio Mendez	L-L	5-11	180	1-7-05	0	0	4.50	1	1	0	0	2	2	1	1	0	1	2	.286	.500	.200	9.00	4.50
2-team total (8 DSL Marlins)					0	3	2.13	9	9	0	0	25	17	12	6	1	13	36	.189	.294	.164	12.79	4.62
Franklyn Moreta	R-R	6-0	160	1-11-04	0	1	3.00	2	0	0	1	3	5	4	1	0	1	1	.357	.333	.375	3.00	3.00
2-team total (9 DSL Marlins)					3	1	2.95	11	0	0	2	18	22	10	6	0	6	15	.297	.333	.277	7.36	2.95
Juan Ortega	R-R	6-2	170	6-3-05	1	5	11.86	12	1	0	0	22	30	35	29	2	25	12	.330	.160	.394	4.91	10.23
Johan Palacios	R-R	6-9	--	12-26-04	0	3	6.15	11	11	0	0	34	33	27	23	2	21	30	.262	.310	.238	8.02	5.61
Luis Ramirez	R-R	6-3	175	2-19-02	4	1	3.14	9	0	0	0	14	13	7	5	1	9	14	.236	.273	.212	8.79	5.65
Erinson Reyes	R-R	6-1	187	11-18-01	0	1	9.42	14	0	0	0	14	20	17	15	1	15	10	.328	.350	.317	6.28	9.42
Darwin Rodriguez	R-R	6-1	180	11-10-04	0	3	10.50	11	10	0	0	24	29	29	28	2	26	23	.296	.188	.348	8.63	9.75
Jose Rojas	R-R	6-0	160	4-19-03	3	1	5.57	14	0	0	0	21	21	13	13	0	11	19	.273	.267	.277	8.14	4.71
Cristian Rueda	R-R	6-1	180	1-5-05	0	1	13.02	15	0	0	0	19	35	28	27	4	11	16	.389	.412	.375	7.71	5.30
Elian Serrata	R-R	6-0	160	1-27-02	1	1	2.40	8	0	0	0	15	11	6	4	0	1	20	.204	.318	.125	12.00	0.60
2-team total (5 DSL Marlins)					1	1	9.17	13	0	0	0	18	18	20	18	3	6	22	.261	.414	.150	11.21	3.06
Santiago Suarez	R-R	6-2	175	1-11-05	1	1	2.31	11	11	0	0	39	36	15	10	1	6	38	.250	.283	.231	8.77	1.38
Riskiel Tineo	R-R	6-3	190	2-27-03	3	0	2.81	13	1	0	3	32	26	11	10	1	2	29	.217	.233	.208	8.16	0.56
Jonas Uzcategui	L-L	6-0	155	10-30-04	1	0	6.23	7	1	0	0	13	12	9	9	1	13	18	.245	.308	.222	12.46	9.00

Fielding

C: Duran 30, Novoa 7, Ortega 6, Vegas 17. **1B:** Duran 11, Henriquez 2, Novoa 3, Ortega 4, Ruiz 21, Vegas 22. **2B:** Altamirano 7, Chourio 3, De Los Santos 4, Neymour 16, Serrano 15, Solano 6, Vargas 14. **3B:** Altamirano 3, Chourio 24, Serrano 10, Solano 7, Vargas 22. **SS:** Altamirano 15, Neymour 22, Solano 14, Vargas 12. **OF:** Chourio 2, Gonzalez 12, Henriquez 8, Mosquera 34, Peguero 38, Perez 31, Ruiz 19, Simmons 44.

Milwaukee Brewers

SEASON IN A SENTENCE: The Brewers got off to a 32-19 start by the end of May but finished 86-76 and one game back in the wild card race, missing the playoffs for the first time since 2017.

HIGH POINT: Heading into the trade deadline, the Brewers were well positioned to win the National League Central. They won seven games in an eight-game stretch ending on July 30 with a 9-4 victory over the Red Sox, boosting their lead in the division to four games ahead of the Cardinals.

LOW POINT: From August on, the Brewers went 29-31. With the Cardinals going 22-7 in August, the Brewers by the end of the month dropped to six games back in the NL Central as the Phillies and Padres jumped ahead of them in the wild card race.

NOTABLE ROOKIES: The Brewers received little help from rookies, especially among hitters. The most promising of their 2022 rookies was Aaron Ashby, who entered the year as the organization's top prospect and finished with a 4.44 ERA and 126 strikeouts in 107.1 innings. Two rookies who took unconventional paths—29-year-old righthander Jason Alexander and 27-year-old Peter Strzelecki—found roles in Milwaukee, with Strzelecki the more effective of the two with a 2.83 ERA in 35 innings of relief.

KEY TRANSACTIONS: Lefthander Josh Hader made his fourth all-star team in 2022 before Milwaukee sent him to the Padres at the trade deadline in exchange for righthander Dinelson Lamet, lefthander Taylor Rogers, outfielder Esteury Ruiz and lefthander Robert Gasser. They replaced Hader in their bullpen at the same time by trading for Matt Bush, sending one of their top pitching prospects in lefthander Antoine Kelly to the Rangers along with utilityman Mark Mathias.

ON THE FARM: Center fielder Jackson Chourio had the most spectacular rise for any prospect in baseball in 2022. After playing in the Dominican Summer League in 2021, Chourio rocketed through the farm system, reaching Double-A as an 18-year-old and showcasing his power/speed combination to become one of baseball's premier prospects. Their 2021 first-round pick, Sal Frelick, reached Triple-A as he hit .331/.403/.480 across three levels. With shortstop Brice Turang and outfielders Joey Wiemer and Esteury Ruiz in Triple-A and center fielder Garrett Mitchell getting a taste of the majors in 2022, the Brewers have several young position players in line to help in 2023.

OPENING DAY PAYROLL: $132,189,909 (19th).

PLAYERS OF THE YEAR

MAJOR LEAGUE

Corbin Burnes
RHP
12-8, 2.94 ERA
243 SO, 51 BB, 202 IP
Led NL in SO

MINOR LEAGUE

Jackson Chourio
OF
(LoA/HiA/AA)
.288/.342/.538
20 HR, 30 2B in 99 G

ORGANIZATION LEADERS

Batting		*Minimum 250 AB
MAJORS		
* AVG	Hunter Renfroe	.255
* OPS	Hunter Renfroe	.807
HR	Rowdy Tellez	35
RBI	Willy Adames	98
MINORS		
* AVG	Sal Frelick, Biloxi, Nashville, Wisconsin	.331
* OBP	Sal Frelick, Biloxi, Nashville, Wisconsin	.403
* SLG	Jakson Reetz, Biloxi, Nashville	.589
* OPS	Jakson Reetz, Biloxi, Nashville	.953
* R	Sal Frelick, Biloxi, Nashville, Wisconsin	90
H	Sal Frelick, Biloxi, Nashville, Wisconsin	131
TB	Sal Frelick, Biloxi, Nashville, Wisconsin	236
2B	Joey Wiemer, Biloxi, Nashville	34
3B	Tristan Peters, Wisconsin	8
HR	Jakson Reetz, Biloxi, Nashville	25
RBI	Jon Singleton, Nashville	87
BB	Jon Singleton, Nashville	117
SO	Joe Gray Jr., Wisconsin	177
SB	Brice Turang, Nashville	34

Pitching		#Minimum 75 IP
MAJORS		
W	Brandon Woodruff	13
# ERA	Corbin Burnes	2.94
SO	Corbin Burnes	243
SV	Josh Hader	29
MINORS		
W	Caleb Boushley, Nashville	12
L	Nick Bennett, Biloxi, Nashville	12
# ERA	Brandon Knarr, Biloxi, Wisconsin	2.83
G	Hobie Harris, Nashville	53
GS	Justin Jarvis, Wisconsin, Biloxi	28
SV	Cam Robinson, Wisconsin, Biloxi, Nashville	25
IP	Brandon Knarr, Biloxi, Wisconsin	146.1
BB	Justin Jarvis, Wisconsin, Biloxi	66
SO	Brandon Knarr, Biloxi, Wisconsin	152
# AVG	Antoine Kelly, Wisconsin	.189

2022 PERFORMANCE

General Manager: Matt Arnold. **Farm Director:** Tom Flanagan. **Scouting Director:** Tod Johnson.

Class	Team	League	W	L	PCT	Finish	Manager
Majors	Milwaukee Brewers	National	86	76	.531	7th (15)	Craig Counsell
Triple-A	Nashville Sounds	International	91	58	.611	1st (20)	Rick Sweet
Double-A	Biloxi Shuckers	Southern	67	68	.496	5th (8)	Mike Guerrero
High-A	Wisconsin Timber Rattlers	Midwest	69	60	.535	6th (12)	Joe Ayrault
Low-A	Carolina Mudcats	Carolina	69	62	.527	t-4th (12)	Victor Estevez
Rookie	ACL Brewers Gold	Arizona Complex	32	21	.604	6th (18)	David Tufo
Rookie	ACL Brewers Blue	Arizona Complex	19	34	.358	17th (18)	Rafael Neda
Overall 2022 Minor League Record			396	372	.516	13th (30)	

ORGANIZATION STATISTICS

MILWAUKEE BREWERS

NATIONAL LEAGUE

Batting	B-T	HT	WT	DOB	AVG	vLH	vRH	G	AB	R	H	2B	3B	HR	RBI	BB	HBP	SH	SF	SO	SB	CS	SLG	OBP
Willy Adames	R-R	6-0	210	9-2-95	.238	.224	.243	139	563	83	134	31	0	31	98	49	1	0	4	166	8	3	.458	.298
Mike Brosseau	R-R	5-10	205	3-15-94	.255	.274	.217	70	141	15	36	5	0	6	23	14	5	0	0	48	2	0	.418	.344
Lorenzo Cain	R-R	6-2	214	4-13-86	.179	.068	.228	43	145	17	26	5	0	1	9	8	2	0	1	36	2	2	.234	.231
Victor Caratini	B-R	6-1	215	8-17-93	.199	.168	.218	96	272	26	54	12	0	9	34	31	9	1	1	67	0	0	.342	.300
Jonathan Davis	R-R	5-8	190	5-12-92	.224	.250	.217	37	76	9	17	1	0	0	4	14	0	1	0	26	7	1	.237	.344
Mario Feliciano	R-R	6-1	200	11-20-98	.250	--	.250	2	4	0	1	0	0	0	0	1	0	0	0	1	0	0	.250	.400
Keston Hiura	R-R	6-0	202	8-2-96	.226	.188	.254	80	234	34	53	8	1	14	32	23	8	0	1	111	5	2	.449	.316
Alex Jackson	R-R	6-2	215	12-25-95	.250	.375	.000	5	12	0	3	0	0	0	0	0	0	0	0	7	0	0	.250	.250
Mark Mathias	R-R	6-0	200	8-2-94	.125	.167	.000	6	16	2	2	0	0	1	4	0	0	0	1	4	1	0	.313	.118
Andrew McCutchen	R-R	5-11	195	10-10-86	.237	.221	.243	134	515	66	122	25	0	17	69	57	4	0	4	124	8	6	.384	.316
Garrett Mitchell	L-R	6-3	215	9-4-98	.311	.500	.298	28	61	9	19	3	0	2	9	6	0	1	0	28	8	0	.459	.373
Omar Narvaez	L-R	5-11	220	2-10-92	.206	.212	.205	84	262	21	54	12	1	4	23	29	3	1	1	57	0	0	.305	.292
Jace Peterson	L-R	6-0	215	5-9-90	.236	.281	.230	113	288	44	68	14	2	8	34	33	2	2	3	85	12	1	.382	.316
Hunter Renfroe	R-R	6-1	230	1-28-92	.255	.258	.254	125	474	62	121	23	1	29	72	39	4	2	3	121	1	1	.492	.315
Pablo Reyes	R-R	5-8	175	9-5-93	.267	.167	.333	6	15	1	4	0	0	0	0	1	0	0	0	2	0	0	.267	.313
Esteury Ruiz	R-R	6-0	169	2-15-99	.000	.000	.000	3	8	2	0	0	0	0	0	1	0	0	0	2	0	0	.000	.111
2-team total (14 San Diego Padres)					.171	.190	.143	17	35	3	6	1	1	0	2	1	0	0	0	7	1	2	.257	.194
Pedro Severino	R-R	6-1	235	7-20-93	.222	.214	.250	8	18	0	4	2	0	0	1	3	0	0	0	7	0	0	.333	.333
Tyrone Taylor	R-R	6-0	194	1-22-94	.233	.225	.237	120	373	49	87	21	3	17	51	22	7	0	3	102	3	2	.442	.286
Rowdy Tellez	L-L	6-4	255	3-16-95	.219	.209	.222	153	529	67	116	23	0	35	89	62	5	0	3	121	2	1	.461	.306
Luis Urias	R-R	5-9	186	6-3-97	.239	.269	.226	119	406	54	97	17	1	16	47	50	11	0	5	99	1	2	.404	.335
Kolten Wong	L-R	5-7	185	10-10-90	.251	.138	.277	134	430	65	108	24	4	15	47	46	14	2	5	88	17	6	.430	.339
Christian Yelich	L-R	6-3	195	12-5-91	.252	.258	.249	154	575	99	145	25	4	14	57	88	5	1	2	162	19	3	.383	.355

Pitching	B-T	HT	WT	DOB	W	L	ERA	G	GS	CG	SV	IP	H	R	ER	HR	BB	SO	AVG	vLH	vRH	K/9	BB/9
Jason Alexander	R-R	6-3	200	3-1-93	2	3	5.40	18	11	0	0	72	88	47	43	12	28	46	.312	.331	.297	5.78	3.52
Aaron Ashby	R-L	6-2	181	5-24-98	2	10	4.44	27	19	0	1	107	106	62	53	15	47	126	.254	.250	.254	10.57	3.94
Luke Barker	R-R	6-3	230	3-11-92	0	0	11.25	3	0	0	0	4	7	5	5	2	0	3	.368	.364	.375	6.75	0.00
Brad Boxberger	R-R	5-10	211	5-27-88	4	3	2.95	70	0	0	1	64	52	23	21	6	27	68	.223	.248	.203	9.56	3.80
Mike Brosseau	R-R	5-10	205	3-15-94	0	0	0.00	3	0	0	0	3	2	0	0	0	1	0	.167	.000	.286	0.00	3.00
Corbin Burnes	R-R	6-3	225	10-22-94	12	8	2.94	33	33	0	0	202	144	73	66	23	51	243	.197	.203	.190	10.83	2.27
Matt Bush	R-R	5-9	180	2-8-86	0	2	4.30	25	1	0	2	23	16	15	11	6	8	29	.193	.207	.185	11.35	3.13
Victor Caratini	B-R	6-1	215	8-17-93	0	0	27.00	1	0	0	0	1	2	3	3	0	1	0	.400	.500	.333	0.00	9.00
Jake Cousins	R-R	6-4	185	7-14-94	2	1	2.70	12	0	0	0	13	10	4	4	1	8	21	.204	.238	.179	14.18	5.40
Chi Chi Gonzalez	R-R	6-3	210	1-15-92	0	1	6.35	4	2	0	0	11	12	8	8	3	4	8	.273	.235	.296	6.35	3.18
Trevor Gott	R-R	5-10	182	8-26-92	3	4	4.14	45	0	0	0	46	35	25	21	8	12	44	.205	.212	.200	8.67	2.36
Jandel Gustave	R-R	6-3	220	10-12-92	2	0	3.86	27	0	0	0	28	25	13	12	4	11	27	.236	.207	.247	8.68	3.54
Josh Hader	L-L	6-3	180	4-7-94	1	4	4.24	37	0	0	29	34	26	16	16	7	12	59	.203	.250	.192	15.62	3.18
2-team total (19 San Diego Padres)					2	5	5.22	56	0	0	36	50	43	30	29	8	21	81	.225	.209	.230	14.58	3.78
Adrian Houser	R-R	6-3	222	2-2-93	6	10	4.73	22	21	0	0	103	103	66	54	8	47	69	.258	.307	.217	6.05	4.12
Trevor Kelley	R-R	6-2	210	10-20-92	1	0	6.08	18	0	0	0	24	25	17	16	7	9	23	.260	.257	.262	8.75	3.42
Eric Lauer	R-L	6-3	228	6-3-95	11	7	3.69	29	29	0	0	159	135	71	65	27	59	157	.228	.216	.230	8.91	3.35
Jake McGee	L-L	6-4	229	8-6-86	0	0	6.35	6	0	0	0	6	7	4	4	2	1	4	.292	.333	.267	6.35	1.59
3-team total (24 S.F. Giants, 12 Washington Nationals)					1	3	6.81	42	0	0	3	37	41	29	28	6	12	25	.275	.306	.260	6.08	2.92
J.C. Mejia	R-R	6-5	240	8-26-96	0	0	23.14	2	0	0	0	2	5	6	6	0	5	1	.455	.400	.500	3.86	19.29
Hoby Milner	L-L	6-3	175	1-13-91	3	3	3.76	67	0	0	0	65	61	29	27	5	15	64	.250	.253	.248	8.91	2.09
Freddy Peralta	R-R	5-11	199	6-4-96	4	4	3.58	18	17	0	0	78	54	31	31	6	27	86	.190	.145	.222	9.92	3.12
Luis Perdomo	R-R	6-2	201	5-9-93	3	0	3.80	14	0	0	0	24	24	10	10	4	3	12	.261	.353	.207	4.56	1.14
Jace Peterson	L-R	6-0	215	5-9-90	0	0	0.00	1	0	0	0	1	0	0	0	0	0	0	.000	.000	.000	0.00	0.00
Pablo Reyes	R-R	5-8	175	9-5-93	0	0	0.00	1	0	0	0	1	0	0	0	0	0	0	.000	.000	.000	0.00	0.00
Taylor Rogers	L-L	6-3	190	12-17-90	3	3	5.48	24	0	0	3	23	20	16	14	6	10	36	.238	.048	.302	14.09	3.91
2-team total (42 San Diego Padres)					4	8	4.76	66	0	0	31	64	57	38	34	7	19	84	.238	.167	.263	11.75	2.66

Connor Sadzeck	R-R	6-7	235	10-1-91	0	0	9.00	2	0	0	0	3	4	3	3	2	1	2	.333	.000	.500	6.00	3.00
Miguel Sanchez	R-R	6-3	205	12-31-93	1	1	4.05	12	0	0	0	13	12	7	6	3	8	9	.245	.300	.207	6.08	5.40
Ethan Small	L-L	6-4	215	2-14-97	0	0	7.11	2	2	0	0	6	8	5	5	1	8	7	.320	.333	.318	9.95	11.37
Peter Strzelecki	R-R	6-2	195	10-24-94	2	1	2.83	30	0	0	1	35	28	13	11	2	15	40	.220	.222	.220	10.29	3.86
Brent Suter	L-L	6-4	213	8-29-89	5	3	3.78	54	0	0	0	67	58	32	28	9	22	53	.236	.200	.250	7.16	2.97
Justin Topa	R-R	6-4	200	3-7-91	0	0	4.91	7	0	0	0	7	9	6	4	0	4	4	.290	.250	.304	4.91	4.91
Jose Urena	R-R	6-2	208	9-12-91	0	0	3.52	4	0	0	0	8	7	5	3	1	5	3	.241	.308	.188	3.52	5.87
2-team total (17 Colorado Rockies)					3	8	5.01	21	17	0	0	97	109	62	54	11	43	63	.285	.329	.234	5.85	3.99
Devin Williams	R-R	6-2	200	9-21-94	6	4	1.93	65	0	0	15	61	31	17	13	2	30	96	.151	.207	.110	14.24	4.45
Brandon Woodruff	L-R	6-4	243	2-10-93	13	4	3.05	27	27	0	0	153	122	56	52	18	42	190	.215	.190	.237	11.15	2.47

Fielding

Catcher	PCT	G	PO	A	E	DP	PB
Caratini	.995	90	737	38	4	3	5
Feliciano	1.000	2	12	2	0	1	0
Jackson	1.000	4	34	0	0	0	0
Narvaez	.993	83	704	32	5	3	5
Severino	1.000	4	38	3	0	1	2

First Base	PCT	G	PO	A	E	DP
Brosseau	1.000	3	13	0	0	1
Caratini	1.000	2	6	2	0	1
Hiura	.986	33	202	12	3	22
Peterson	1.000	5	19	0	0	1
Renfroe	.000	1	0	0	0	0
Severino	1.000	2	2	0	0	0
Tellez	.998	139	946	81	2	86

Second Base	PCT	G	PO	A	E	DP
Hiura	.921	14	17	18	3	4
Mathias	1.000	6	10	10	0	1
Peterson	1.000	3	1	3	0	1
Urias	.992	46	52	73	1	16
Wong	.963	131	182	255	17	60

Third Base	PCT	G	PO	A	E	DP
Brosseau	.934	55	22	63	6	8
Peterson	.980	86	53	144	4	13
Reyes	1.000	2	1	6	0	2
Urias	.940	73	33	125	10	8

Shortstop	PCT	G	PO	A	E	DP
Adames	.973	136	178	334	14	68
Brosseau	.917	4	4	7	1	2
Reyes	.750	3	0	3	1	0
Urias	.966	24	33	53	3	11
Wong	1.000	1	3	0	0	0

Outfield	PCT	G	PO	A	E	DP
Cain	.976	42	80	1	2	1
Davis	.982	34	56	0	1	0
Hiura	.900	5	9	0	1	0
McCutchen	1.000	53	88	1	0	0
Mitchell	.976	28	40	1	1	0
Peterson	1.000	15	24	1	0	0
Renfroe	.982	118	210	11	4	2
Ruiz	1.000	3	2	0	0	0
Taylor	1.000	127	234	5	0	3
Yelich	.995	115	189	2	1	1

MILWAUKEE BREWERS

NASHVILLE SOUNDS

TRIPLE-A

INTERNATIONAL LEAGUE

Batting	B-T	HT	WT	DOB	AVG	vLH	vRH	G	AB	R	H	2B	3B	HR	RBI	BB	HBP	SH	SF	SO	SB	CS	SLG	OBP
Willy Adames	R-R	6-0	210	9-2-95	.333	1.000	.200	2	6	1	2	0	0	1	1	2	0	0	0	1	0	0	.833	.500
Abraham Almonte	B-R	5-10	223	6-27-89	.293	.250	.313	48	184	36	54	11	0	11	42	25	2	0	2	48	1	0	.533	.380
2-team total (32 Worcester Red Sox)					.293	.238	.314	80	294	66	86	15	1	18	66	61	3	0	2	77	6	2	.534	.417
Mike Brosseau	R-R	5-10	205	3-15-94	.333	.500	.286	2	9	1	3	1	0	0	0	0	0	0	0	2	0	0	.444	.333
Yeison Coca	B-R	5-11	182	5-22-99	--	--	--	1	0	1	0	0	0	0	0	0	0	0	0	0	0	0	--	--
David Dahl	L-R	6-2	197	4-1-94	.294	.329	.278	67	252	44	74	15	1	9	41	26	0	0	2	62	3	0	.468	.357
2-team total (18 Rochester Red Wings)					.279	.271	.283	85	319	54	89	20	1	10	51	34	1	0	5	84	4	0	.442	.345
Jonathan Davis	R-R	5-8	190	5-12-92	.293	.238	.310	48	184	27	54	11	1	4	22	28	5	1	3	44	14	1	.429	.395
Cam Devanney	R-R	6-1	195	4-13-97	.306	.357	.286	13	49	10	15	4	0	3	11	5	0	0	2	14	0	0	.571	.357
Brent Diaz	R-R	6-1	205	3-22-96	.250	.500	.000	3	12	3	3	0	0	0	1	0	0	0	0	5	0	1	.250	.250
Patrick Dorrian	L-R	6-2	188	6-26-96	.248	.261	.243	48	161	28	40	7	2	11	25	23	1	0	0	53	2	1	.522	.346
2-team total (46 Norfolk Tides)					.206	.202	.208	94	310	39	64	14	2	14	40	42	1	0	0	111	4	1	.400	.303
Mario Feliciano	R-R	6-1	200	11-20-98	.274	.318	.254	77	285	31	78	14	0	6	38	18	5	0	2	52	2	2	.386	.326
Sal Frelick	L-R	5-10	180	4-19-00	.365	.394	.350	46	189	38	69	11	2	4	25	19	5	1	1	16	9	3	.508	.435
Keston Hiura	R-R	6-0	202	8-2-96	.319	.227	.400	13	47	8	15	1	0	6	18	9	3	0	0	15	0	3	.723	.458
Alex Jackson	R-R	6-2	215	12-25-95	.225	.242	.217	31	102	9	23	8	1	2	18	12	3	0	2	28	1	0	.382	.319
2-team total (1 Jacksonville Jumbo Shrimp)					.217	.222	.214	32	106	9	23	8	1	2	18	12	3	0	2	29	1	0	.368	.309
Nick Kahle	R-R	5-10	210	2-28-98	.375	.500	.333	4	8	1	3	1	0	0	1	0	0	0	0	2	0	0	.500	.375
Matt Lipka	R-R	6-1	215	4-15-92	.258	.269	.254	32	93	15	24	3	2	2	5	11	0	1	0	27	12	1	.398	.337
2-team total (45 Rochester Red Wings)					.228	.196	.241	77	197	39	45	6	4	2	11	25	2	2	0	62	26	1	.330	.321
Mark Mathias	R-R	6-0	200	8-2-94	.318	.346	.305	50	170	20	54	8	1	8	30	27	4	0	1	48	8	3	.518	.421
Garrett Mitchell	L-R	6-3	215	9-4-98	.342	.222	.413	20	73	15	25	6	0	1	9	10	2	0	0	18	9	0	.466	.435
Andruw Monasterio	R-R	6-0	193	5-30-97	.237	.302	.217	68	219	34	52	15	1	1	17	27	1	0	2	64	6	3	.329	.321
Omar Narvaez	L-R	5-11	220	2-10-92	.375	.167	1.000	2	8	1	3	1	0	0	2	0	0	0	0	1	0	0	.500	.375
Brian Navarreto	R-R	6-0	237	12-29-94	.269	.258	.273	43	130	21	35	1	0	4	18	10	1	0	1	20	1	0	.369	.324
Dustin Peterson	R-R	6-2	210	9-10-94	.143	.000	.167	3	7	1	1	1	0	0	0	4	0	0	0	1	0	0	.286	.455
2-team total (102 Lehigh Valley IronPigs)					.243	.274	.231	105	400	50	97	23	2	9	47	44	3	0	1	102	6	2	.378	.321
Corey Ray	L-L	6-0	196	9-22-94	.199	.188	.202	37	136	14	27	9	1	5	23	6	0	0	1	48	7	0	.390	.231
Jakson Reetz	R-R	6-0	205	1-3-96	.212	.182	.227	19	66	5	14	3	1	3	9	2	2	0	1	14	1	0	.424	.254
2-team total (21 Omaha Storm Chasers)					.235	.242	.233	40	136	16	32	6	1	8	24	9	5	0	3	36	1	0	.471	.301
Pablo Reyes	R-R	5-8	175	9-5-93	.273	.273	.273	99	385	63	105	27	2	11	59	39	6	1	1	67	15	7	.439	.348
Esteury Ruiz	R-R	6-0	169	2-15-99	.329	.451	.263	37	146	30	48	10	0	3	19	14	4	3	0	29	25	5	.459	.402
Pedro Severino	R-R	6-1	235	7-20-93	.308	.282	.321	31	117	20	36	10	0	4	17	6	2	0	1	27	2	0	.496	.349
Jon Singleton	L-L	6-2	230	9-18-91	.219	.168	.247	134	456	84	100	22	2	24	87	117	1	0	7	161	3	1	.434	.375
Tyrone Taylor	R-R	6-0	194	1-22-94	.375	.500	.250	2	8	1	3	0	0	0	0	0	0	0	0	1	1	0	.375	.375
Brice Turang	L-R	6-0	173	11-21-99	.286	.293	.282	131	532	89	152	24	2	13	78	65	0	0	6	118	34	2	.412	.360
Jamie Westbrook	R-R	5-9	193	6-18-95	.500	.500	.500	3	10	3	5	1	0	0	0	1	0	0	0	0	0	0	.600	.545
2-team total (120 Toledo Mud Hens)					.254	.258	.253	123	429	58	109	22	0	11	48	54	14	0	4	80	1	2	.382	.353
Tyler White	R-R	5-11	238	10-29-90	.230	.228	.232	75	269	39	62	11	2	13	46	50	4	0	2	69	4	1	.431	.357
2-team total (28 Gwinnett Stripers)					.230	.244	.222	103	357	48	82	13	2	16	58	70	4	0	6	88	5	1	.412	.357
Garrett Whitley	R-R	6-1	195	3-13-97	.196	.192	.198	48	148	29	29	8	0	3	13	36	2	0	0	66	9	2	.311	.360
Joey Wiemer	R-R	6-5	215	2-11-99	.287	.259	.304	43	150	24	43	15	1	6	30	21	0	0	3	34	6	2	.520	.368

Weston Wilson	R-R	6-3	215	9-11-94	.228	.240	.224	118	416	63	95	21	0	11	54	39	3	0	4	131	17	4	.358	.297

Pitching	B-T	HT	WT	DOB	W	L	ERA	G	GS	CG	SV	IP	H	R	ER	HR	BB	SO	AVG	vLH	vRH	K/9	BB/9
Jason Alexander	R-R	6-3	200	3-1-93	8	2	2.84	13	10	0	0	63	58	22	20	5	17	47	.244	.242	.245	6.68	2.42
Robbie Baker	R-R	6-1	211	1-31-95	0	1	12.00	2	1	0	0	3	6	4	4	2	2	2	.429	.200	1.000	6.00	6.00
Luke Barker	R-R	6-3	230	3-11-92	5	0	3.60	23	0	0	3	25	20	11	10	2	10	28	.213	.214	.212	10.08	3.60
Nick Bennett	L-L	6-4	210	9-1-97	0	1	81.00	1	0	0	0	1	2	6	6	0	4	1	.500	.333	1.000	13.50	54.00
Alec Bettinger	R-R	6-2	210	7-13-95	2	4	6.49	13	6	0	0	35	41	31	25	9	21	21	.299	.350	.260	5.45	5.45
Caleb Boushley	R-R	6-3	190	10-1-93	12	2	3.25	25	25	0	0	127	106	47	46	12	43	91	.226	.219	.231	6.43	3.04
Rex Brothers	L-L	6-0	205	12-18-87	0	0	17.36	7	0	0	0	3	8	9	9	2	8	6	.421	.400	.500	11.57	15.43
Zack Brown	R-R	6-1	199	12-15-94	2	0	3.93	49	0	0	3	50	41	26	22	4	19	51	.223	.218	.227	9.12	3.40
Victor Castaneda	R-R	6-1	185	8-27-98	2	0	5.14	3	3	0	0	14	14	8	8	1	5	8	.246	.323	.154	5.14	3.21
Luis Contreras	R-R	6-1	175	4-29-96	0	0	8.00	9	0	0	0	9	8	8	8	2	9	14	.229	.294	.167	14.00	9.00
Jake Cousins	R-R	6-4	185	7-14-94	1	0	2.78	21	0	0	1	23	15	8	7	2	11	31	.181	.222	.161	12.31	4.37
Lucas Erceg	L-R	6-3	196	5-1-95	2	1	3.43	33	2	0	1	39	34	15	15	3	23	42	.234	.295	.190	9.61	5.26
Dylan File	R-R	6-1	205	6-4-96	8	6	4.57	26	19	0	0	114	107	60	58	13	34	95	.244	.259	.226	7.48	2.68
Pablo Garabitos	L-L	6-1	170	7-30-00	0	0	6.00	1	0	0	0	3	2	2	2	1	3	1	.222	.250	.200	3.00	9.00
Robert Gasser	L-L	6-1	185	5-31-99	2	2	4.44	5	5	0	0	26	26	14	13	1	16	31	.255	.273	.250	10.59	5.47
Trevor Gott	R-R	5-10	182	8-26-92	0	0	0.00	3	0	0	0	4	2	0	0	0	1	5	.154	.333	.100	12.27	2.45
Jandel Gustave	R-R	6-3	220	10-12-92	0	0	2.25	4	0	0	0	4	4	1	1	0	0	3	.267	.429	.125	6.75	0.00
Matt Hardy	L-R	6-0	170	7-15-95	3	1	4.15	32	0	0	0	35	37	18	16	3	15	32	.287	.306	.275	8.31	3.89
Hobie Harris	R-R	6-3	200	6-23-93	4	3	2.04	53	0	0	8	53	29	19	12	5	28	56	.164	.135	.193	9.51	4.75
Kent Hasler	R-R	5-10	205	10-15-95	0	0	9.00	1	0	0	0	1	2	1	1	0	0	1	.400	.250	1.000	9.00	0.00
Tyler Herb	R-R	6-3	200	4-28-92	7	7	5.06	20	14	1	1	91	120	56	51	11	25	89	.317	.342	.293	8.83	2.48
Adrian Houser	R-R	6-3	222	2-2-93	0	1	3.24	3	3	0	0	8	6	6	3	1	7	10	.200	.250	.167	10.80	7.56
Thomas Jankins	R-R	6-3	220	7-2-95	0	1	7.04	13	1	0	0	15	23	13	12	2	6	16	.359	.276	.429	9.39	3.52
Nick Kahle	R-R	5-10	210	2-28-98	0	0	9.00	1	0	0	0	1	1	1	1	1	0	0	.250	.250	--	0.00	0.00
Trevor Kelley	R-R	6-2	210	10-20-92	3	3	2.36	34	0	0	9	34	29	11	9	2	10	42	.225	.123	.306	11.01	2.62
Josh Lindblom	R-R	6-4	240	6-15-87	9	7	4.05	26	24	0	0	133	120	62	60	23	47	133	.238	.248	.229	8.98	3.17
Matt Lipka	R-R	6-1	215	4-15-92	0	0	9.00	1	0	0	0	1	1	1	1	1	0	0	.250	.000	.500	0.00	0.00
J.C. Mejia	R-R	6-5	240	8-26-96	0	3	2.76	24	0	0	1	29	15	11	9	3	13	33	.150	.205	.107	10.13	3.99
Andy Otero	L-L	5-9	165	6-3-92	0	1	3.41	16	0	0	1	34	31	13	13	2	13	16	.246	.226	.260	4.19	3.41
Freddy Peralta	R-R	5-11	199	6-4-96	0	0	1.69	2	2	0	0	5	4	2	1	1	1	8	.200	.182	.222	13.50	1.69
Angel Perdomo	L-L	6-8	265	5-7-94	0	0	0.00	3	0	0	0	2	0	0	0	0	6	5	.000	.000	.000	19.29	23.14
2-team total (21 Durham Bulls)					4	2	1.97	24	2	0	0	32	16	12	7	2	18	53	.150	.083	.203	14.91	5.06
Luis Perdomo	R-R	6-2	201	5-9-93	2	0	2.67	24	3	0	4	30	21	9	9	2	4	33	.193	.179	.208	9.79	1.19
Cam Robinson	R-R	6-1	194	9-6-99	0	0	6.92	11	0	0	0	13	16	10	10	1	8	16	.314	.300	.323	11.08	5.54
Trevor Rosenthal	R-R	6-2	230	5-29-90	0	0	18.00	3	0	0	0	2	4	4	4	2	3	2	.444	.333	.667	9.00	13.50
Connor Sadzeck	R-R	6-7	235	10-1-91	1	1	0.96	24	0	0	3	28	17	5	3	2	12	35	.172	.231	.106	11.25	3.86
2-team total (17 Rochester Red Wings)					1	4	2.20	41	0	0	3	49	34	14	12	8	20	56	.193	.273	.131	10.29	3.67
Miguel Sanchez	R-R	6-3	205	12-31-93	4	2	3.79	17	0	0	1	19	16	8	8	2	6	18	.235	.200	.263	8.53	2.84
Ethan Small	L-L	6-4	215	2-14-97	7	6	4.46	27	21	0	0	103	82	57	51	8	58	114	.217	.237	.206	9.96	5.07
Peter Strzelecki	R-R	6-2	195	10-24-94	4	0	2.84	27	0	0	3	32	18	10	10	4	10	50	.168	.208	.136	14.21	2.84
Justin Topa	R-R	6-4	200	3-7-91	2	0	4.34	17	0	0	0	19	23	9	9	0	8	17	.307	.419	.227	8.20	3.86
Zach Vennaro	R-R	6-6	220	6-3-96	1	0	10.80	3	0	0	0	5	6	6	6	1	4	3	.333	.545	.000	5.40	7.20
Marcus Walden	R-R	5-10	198	9-13-88	0	3	4.53	16	9	0	0	60	59	31	30	5	19	52	.252	.233	.272	7.84	2.87
Nash Walters	R-R	6-5	210	5-18-97	0	0	0.00	2	0	0	0	1	1	0	0	0	0	0	.200	.000	.250	0.00	0.00
Tyler White	R-R	5-11	238	10-29-90	0	0	45.00	1	0	0	0	1	7	5	5	1	0	0	.778	1.000	.667	0.00	0.00
Brandon Woodruff	L-R	6-4	243	2-10-93	0	0	3.38	1	1	0	0	3	2	1	1	0	1	7	.200	.333	.000	23.63	3.38

Fielding

Catcher	PCT	G	PO	A	E	DP	PB
Diaz	1.000	3	23	0	0	1	0
Feliciano	.989	65	509	17	6	1	14
Jackson	.991	23	216	14	2	0	1
Kahle	.929	2	11	2	1	0	0
Narvaez	1.000	1	8	1	0	0	0
Navarreto	.997	39	290	17	1	4	1
Reetz	.990	9	93	2	1	1	0
Severino	.986	18	135	5	2	0	3

First Base	PCT	G	PO	A	E	DP
Hiura	1.000	1	7	0	0	0
Peterson	1.000	1	8	1	0	1
Severino	.962	3	22	3	1	5
Singleton	.994	111	841	89	6	79
White	.995	27	181	13	1	25
Wilson	.980	8	46	4	1	1

Second Base	PCT	G	PO	A	E	DP
Devanney	1.000	1	2	1	0	0
Dorrian	.961	13	18	31	2	4
Hiura	.923	7	13	11	2	5
Mathias	.992	32	50	80	1	16
Monasterio	.982	24	43	66	2	23
Reyes	.986	50	87	130	3	30
Turang	1.000	7	6	27	0	5
Westbrook	.889	3	5	11	2	1
Wilson	1.000	16	27	44	0	10

Third Base	PCT	G	PO	A	E	DP
Brosseau	1.000	2	3	3	0	0
Devanney	1.000	5	4	6	0	1
Dorrian	.961	33	17	57	3	5
Mathias	.929	17	17	22	3	4
Monasterio	.974	15	7	30	1	2
Reyes	1.000	17	15	32	0	4
Turang	1.000	8	0	15	0	2
White	.917	7	2	9	1	0
Wilson	.963	53	31	73	4	6

Shortstop	PCT	G	PO	A	E	DP
Adames	1.000	2	5	2	0	1
Devanney	1.000	8	6	18	0	5
Monasterio	.945	26	26	60	5	11
Reyes	.954	14	23	39	3	9
Turang	.974	104	139	271	11	52
Wilson	1.000	1	1	3	0	1

Outfield	PCT	G	PO	A	E	DP
Almonte	.983	37	57	2	1	0
Dahl	1.000	63	116	3	0	3
Davis	.991	45	108	2	1	0
Frelick	1.000	40	57	2	0	1
Hiura	1.000	5	9	0	0	0
Lipka	.952	27	59	1	3	0
Mitchell	1.000	17	20	1	0	0
Peterson	1.000	2	3	0	0	0
Ray	.989	37	81	6	1	2
Reetz	1.000	8	13	0	0	0
Reyes	.975	18	38	1	1	0
Ruiz	1.000	32	65	0	0	0
Taylor	--	1	0	0	0	0
Turang	1.000	14	19	0	0	0
Whitley	1.000	45	88	2	0	1
Wiemer	.986	36	70	3	1	1
Wilson	.973	43	67	4	2	0

BILOXI SHUCKERS

DOUBLE-A

SOUTHERN LEAGUE

Batting	B-T	HT	WT	DOB	AVG	vLH	vRH	G	AB	R	H	2B	3B	HR	RBI	BB	HBP	SH	SF	SO	SB	CS	SLG	OBP
Noah Campbell	B-R	6-1	200	6-6-99	.262	.088	.298	60	195	30	51	15	1	2	22	31	1	1	1	58	6	3	.379	.364
Jackson Chourio	R-R	6-1	165	3-11-04	.087	.091	.083	6	23	0	2	1	0	0	4	2	0	0	1	11	2	1	.130	.154
Wes Clarke	R-R	6-2	228	10-13-99	.254	.286	.244	16	59	9	15	2	0	5	9	7	0	0	1	21	0	0	.542	.328
Yeison Coca	B-R	5-11	182	5-22-99	.211	.190	.219	72	232	28	49	12	1	1	16	30	1	2	3	76	10	3	.284	.301
Cam Devanney	R-R	6-1	195	4-13-97	.259	.300	.245	115	402	59	104	28	1	20	57	43	9	0	5	96	6	2	.483	.340
Brent Diaz	R-R	6-1	205	3-22-96	.261	.229	.273	55	180	20	47	8	0	7	28	15	7	0	0	48	4	1	.422	.342
Thomas Dillard	B-R	6-0	230	8-28-97	.233	.235	.232	121	425	67	99	29	1	12	67	81	8	0	2	157	14	2	.391	.364
Terence Doston	L-R	5-10	160	9-22-00	.276	.192	.300	47	116	17	32	2	0	2	13	11	2	1	0	35	5	2	.345	.349
Sal Frelick	L-R	5-10	180	4-19-00	.317	.273	.331	52	224	40	71	12	3	5	25	20	4	0	2	33	9	2	.464	.380
Gabe Holt	L-R	5-11	175	1-7-98	.205	.215	.202	81	288	31	59	11	0	0	17	20	1	1	2	25	10	3	.243	.257
Nick Kahle	R-R	5-10	210	2-28-98	.236	.167	.259	22	72	11	17	4	0	4	15	7	1	1	1	23	0	0	.458	.309
Jason Lopez	R-R	5-10	160	3-16-98	.202	.273	.167	33	99	10	20	5	0	2	13	12	0	0	1	28	0	0	.313	.286
Tristen Lutz	R-R	6-2	210	8-22-98	.259	.295	.247	71	255	30	66	11	0	12	58	34	4	0	2	88	1	1	.443	.353
Ashton McGee	L-R	6-1	215	11-19-98	.135	.111	.140	20	52	6	7	2	0	1	4	15	0	0	1	32	0	0	.231	.324
Garrett Mitchell	L-R	6-3	215	9-4-98	.277	.295	.270	44	166	29	46	9	2	4	25	16	4	0	1	52	7	1	.428	.353
Andruw Monasterio	R-R	6-0	193	5-30-97	.316	.308	.319	42	158	35	50	7	0	8	27	25	4	0	1	26	9	2	.513	.420
Ethan Murray	R-R	6-0	201	5-13-00	.257	.222	.269	10	35	8	9	3	0	1	2	7	0	0	0	9	2	0	.429	.381
Corey Ray	L-L	6-0	196	9-22-94	.237	.200	.252	38	152	21	36	8	0	8	21	14	1	0	3	51	3	3	.447	.300
Jakson Reetz	R-R	6-0	205	1-3-96	.281	.315	.271	64	231	48	65	16	0	22	58	26	16	0	0	72	1	1	.636	.392
Pedro Severino	R-R	6-1	235	7-20-93	.435	1.000	.350	6	23	4	10	0	0	1	4	4	0	0	0	4	1	0	.565	.519
Luis Urias	R-R	5-9	186	6-3-97	.148	.125	.158	7	27	4	4	1	0	0	2	3	1	0	0	7	0	0	.185	.258
Felix Valerio	R-R	5-7	165	12-26-00	.228	.258	.219	113	417	60	95	14	2	12	51	48	7	0	8	80	30	9	.357	.313
Zavier Warren	B-R	6-1	215	1-8-99	.250	.179	.281	28	92	9	23	3	0	2	11	12	1	0	1	27	3	0	.348	.340
Garrett Whitley	R-R	6-1	195	3-13-97	.245	.318	.212	40	143	21	35	8	1	7	22	22	1	0	0	49	10	3	.462	.349
Joey Wiemer	R-R	6-5	215	2-11-99	.243	.256	.238	84	334	57	81	19	1	15	47	34	5	0	1	113	25	1	.440	.321
Freddy Zamora	R-R	6-1	190	11-1-98	.209	.200	.211	24	91	10	19	4	0	1	5	5	3	0	1	22	4	0	.286	.270

Pitching	B-T	HT	WT	DOB	W	L	ERA	G	GS	CG	SV	IP	H	R	ER	HR	BB	SO	AVG	vLH	vRH	K/9	BB/9
Clayton Andrews	L-L	5-6	160	1-4-97	0	2	9.72	7	0	0	0	8	7	9	9	0	7	16	.226	.182	.250	17.28	7.56
Robbie Baker	R-R	6-1	211	1-31-95	1	0	3.52	6	0	0	1	8	7	3	3	1	1	8	.250	.100	.333	9.39	1.17
Nick Bennett	L-L	6-4	210	9-1-97	7	11	4.79	25	24	0	0	124	122	72	66	20	44	125	.254	.172	.303	9.07	3.19
Justin Bullock	R-R	6-2	195	5-12-99	0	2	6.35	9	9	0	0	28	40	21	20	7	16	16	.345	.333	.358	5.08	5.08
Victor Castaneda	R-R	6-1	185	8-27-98	4	6	3.97	23	22	1	0	107	97	53	47	16	47	110	.240	.265	.215	9.28	3.97
Harold Chirino	R-R	6-2	173	1-12-98	3	3	3.29	44	0	0	3	52	44	24	19	4	25	50	.228	.265	.187	8.65	4.33
Luis Contreras	R-R	6-1	175	4-29-96	3	2	3.00	26	0	0	1	42	30	14	14	2	21	59	.199	.139	.253	12.64	4.50
Lucas Erceg	L-R	6-3	196	5-1-95	1	3	6.55	16	2	0	1	22	30	23	16	3	14	27	.313	.404	.224	11.05	5.73
Taylor Floyd	R-R	6-1	185	12-8-97	0	1	7.83	21	0	0	0	23	29	24	20	2	21	25	.309	.296	.325	9.78	8.22
Robert Gasser	L-L	6-1	185	5-31-99	1	1	2.21	4	4	0	0	20	14	7	5	2	8	26	.194	.190	.196	11.51	3.54
Matt Hardy	L-R	6-0	170	7-15-95	1	0	2.25	6	0	0	0	8	9	2	2	1	1	9	.273	.250	.294	10.13	1.13
Kent Hasler	R-R	5-10	205	10-15-95	1	3	4.91	29	0	0	0	37	33	28	20	7	17	44	.243	.246	.239	10.80	4.17
Tyler Herb	R-R	6-3	200	4-28-92	3	1	1.31	7	6	0	0	34	29	7	5	2	9	35	.230	.200	.262	9.17	2.36
Arnaldo Hernandez	R-R	6-0	175	2-9-96	5	2	7.03	39	0	0	1	49	63	40	38	8	30	66	.312	.300	.324	12.21	5.55
J.T. Hintzen	R-R	6-0	185	6-1-96	4	3	5.31	27	0	0	0	39	36	29	23	6	20	32	.237	.207	.271	7.38	4.62
Robbie Hitt	R-R	6-2	205	6-21-96	4	3	4.80	42	0	0	1	51	50	32	27	3	26	54	.253	.267	.241	9.59	4.62
Justin Jarvis	R-R	6-2	183	2-20-00	2	1	2.70	4	4	0	0	20	15	6	6	1	15	16	.217	.189	.250	7.20	6.75
Brandon Knarr	R-L	5-10	217	6-2-98	4	6	3.64	16	16	0	0	89	88	45	36	10	34	87	.253	.275	.241	8.80	3.44
Carlos Luna	R-R	6-1	208	9-25-96	5	6	5.35	28	14	0	1	109	122	68	65	17	38	111	.279	.296	.260	9.14	3.13
James Meeker	R-R	6-4	222	3-22-95	0	0	0.00	2	0	0	0	2	0	0	0	0	0	0	.000	.000	.000	0.00	0.00
J.C. Mejia	R-R	6-5	240	8-26-96	0	0	0.00	2	0	0	0	2	0	0	0	0	0	3	.000	.000	.000	16.20	0.00
Ryan Middendorf	L-R	6-6	220	12-22-97	0	2	5.59	6	0	0	1	10	11	6	6	1	9	12	.289	.235	.333	11.17	8.38
Andy Otero	L-L	5-9	165	6-3-92	1	1	3.44	7	6	0	0	34	39	16	13	4	11	34	.289	.273	.297	9.00	2.91
Cam Robinson	R-R	6-1	194	9-6-99	0	0	1.23	13	0	0	6	15	8	2	2	0	5	16	.167	.185	.143	9.82	3.07
TJ Shook	R-R	6-4	217	5-29-98	4	2	5.71	18	17	0	0	80	88	53	51	18	46	75	.274	.286	.261	8.40	5.15
Abner Uribe	R-R	6-2	200	6-20-00	0	0	0.00	2	0	0	0	3	2	0	0	0	4	4	.182	.200	.167	12.00	12.00
Zach Vennaro	R-R	6-6	220	6-3-96	5	2	4.93	46	0	0	11	49	48	29	27	3	31	53	.262	.315	.209	9.67	5.66
Nash Walters	R-R	6-5	210	5-18-97	6	3	4.60	42	0	0	1	47	44	26	24	3	15	66	.244	.292	.190	12.64	2.87
Noah Zavolas	R-R	6-1	190	5-11-96	2	2	6.57	14	11	0	2	62	71	48	45	13	24	56	.293	.297	.289	8.17	3.50

Fielding

Catcher	PCT	G	PO	A	E	DP	PB
Clarke	1.000	3	24	4	0	2	0
Diaz	.987	47	417	26	6	1	7
Kahle	.984	19	172	9	3	0	2
Lopez	.982	30	242	31	5	3	7
Reetz	.984	40	356	23	6	2	4
Severino	1.000	3	27	0	0	0	2

First Base	PCT	G	PO	A	E	DP
Campbell	1.000	8	43	7	0	1
Clarke	1.000	10	72	3	0	8
Devanney	.971	4	33	0	1	3
Dillard	.981	95	679	49	14	57
McGee	1.000	9	68	3	0	9
Severino	1.000	1	5	0	0	1
Warren	.989	12	84	5	1	10

Second Base	PCT	G	PO	A	E	DP
Coca	1.000	10	24	22	0	5
Holt	.982	44	53	108	3	26
Valerio	.977	82	118	219	8	38
Zamora	1.000	2	3	5	0	2

Third Base	PCT	G	PO	A	E	DP
Campbell	.667	2	1	1	1	0
Coca	.975	52	42	75	3	4
Devanney	.949	45	25	68	5	5
Holt	.818	12	2	16	4	0
McGee	.810	10	6	11	4	1
Urias	.875	3	2	5	1	1
Valerio	1.000	3	1	5	0	0
Warren	.943	17	8	25	2	1

Shortstop	PCT	G	PO	A	E	DP
Coca	1.000	4	6	7	0	4
Devanney	.962	60	82	118	8	30
Monasterio	.941	38	63	81	9	14

Murray	.971	10	16	18	1	4
Urias	1.000	2	1	4	0	1
Zamora	.903	23	40	62	11	17

Outfield	PCT	G	PO	A	E	DP
Campbell	.936	43	44	0	3	0
Chourio	.909	5	10	0	1	0
Coca	1.000	5	6	1	0	0
Devanney	1.000	4	4	0	0	0
Dillard	1.000	6	4	1	0	0
Doston	1.000	44	74	1	0	0
Frelick	.983	51	112	3	2	1
Holt	.857	4	6	0	1	0
Kahle	--	1	0	0	0	0
Lutz	.963	55	73	4	3	1
Mitchell	.978	41	86	3	2	1
Ray	.968	35	59	1	2	0
Reetz	1.000	11	14	1	0	1
Valerio	1.000	9	14	0	0	0
Whitley	1.000	39	74	2	0	0
Wiemer	.974	82	177	11	5	2

WISCONSIN TIMBER RATTLERS — HIGH A

MIDWEST LEAGUE

Batting	B-T	HT	WT	DOB	AVG	vLH	vRH	G	AB	R	H	2B	3B	HR	RBI	BB	HBP	SH	SF	SO	SB	CS	SLG	OBP
Jose Acosta	B-R	5-10	170	3-20-00	.216	.268	.198	67	218	29	47	6	2	8	24	24	1	3	2	73	10	6	.372	.294
Jadher Areinamo	R-R	5-10	160	11-28-03	.077	.000	.091	7	26	0	2	1	0	0	1	0	0	0	0	8	0	0	.115	.077
Micah Bello	R-R	5-11	165	7-21-00	.206	.238	.190	20	63	9	13	4	0	2	12	5	1	0	0	27	1	0	.365	.275
Tyler Black	L-R	6-2	190	7-26-00	.281	.303	.273	64	231	45	65	13	4	4	35	45	5	0	2	44	13	6	.424	.406
Mike Brosseau	R-R	5-10	205	3-15-94	.357	.143	.571	5	14	3	5	1	0	0	1	5	0	0	1	3	0	0	.429	.500
Jackson Chourio	R-R	6-1	165	3-11-04	.252	.250	.252	31	127	24	32	6	0	8	24	11	2	0	2	31	4	1	.488	.317
Arbert Cipion	R-R	6-2	186	5-9-00	.213	.214	.212	59	188	20	40	9	2	2	20	10	1	0	0	56	13	2	.314	.256
Wes Clarke	R-R	6-2	228	10-13-99	.223	.175	.244	83	273	27	61	19	0	9	52	57	4	0	4	83	0	1	.392	.361
Yeison Coca	B-R	5-11	182	5-22-99	.056	.000	.083	15	36	8	2	1	0	0	1	6	0	0	0	14	1	0	.083	.190
Jonathan Davis	R-R	5-8	190	5-12-92	.000	--	.000	1	3	0	0	0	0	0	0	0	0	0	0	0	0	0	.000	.000
Terence Doston	L-R	5-10	160	9-22-00	.182	.222	.154	7	22	3	4	0	0	0	0	1	0	0	0	6	0	0	.182	.217
Sal Frelick	L-R	5-10	180	4-19-00	.291	.211	.317	21	79	12	23	5	1	2	9	13	0	0	0	14	6	3	.456	.391
Eduardo Garcia	R-R	6-2	160	7-10-02	.248	.200	.259	26	105	11	26	3	0	5	17	0	3	0	0	40	1	0	.419	.269
Joe Gray Jr.	R-R	6-1	214	3-12-00	.193	.164	.203	123	462	58	89	21	4	15	54	51	7	0	7	177	17	2	.353	.279
Alex Hall	B-R	5-11	204	6-8-99	.181	.094	.226	30	94	11	17	6	0	1	14	12	1	0	1	42	0	1	.277	.278
Tayden Hall	L-R	6-4	215	1-12-03	.233	.333	.208	9	30	6	7	2	1	0	2	4	1	0	1	8	0	0	.367	.333
Ernesto Martinez	L-L	6-6	250	6-20-99	.237	.273	.229	21	59	10	14	3	0	2	9	16	1	0	1	21	8	1	.390	.403
Ashton McGee	L-R	6-1	215	11-19-98	.237	.244	.234	56	186	20	44	8	1	4	24	23	2	0	0	70	2	0	.355	.327
Reidy Mercado	B-R	5-11	153	1-6-01	.239	.313	.218	22	71	9	17	0	0	0	4	1	0	1	0	21	4	0	.239	.250
Ben Metzinger	R-R	6-0	195	6-26-99	.222	.214	.224	25	90	15	20	2	0	3	8	10	2	0	0	30	1	0	.344	.314
Darrien Miller	L-R	6-0	186	3-10-01	.224	.148	.251	89	304	58	68	12	1	12	40	49	24	2	2	84	6	1	.388	.372
Ethan Murray	R-R	6-0	201	5-13-00	.213	.264	.193	94	315	36	67	19	1	5	33	34	6	1	4	97	14	4	.327	.298
Tristan Peters	L-R	6-0	180	2-29-00	.306	.311	.304	90	330	61	101	22	8	7	51	45	2	0	6	61	13	6	.485	.386
Jace Peterson	L-R	6-0	215	5-9-90	.222	1.000	.125	3	9	1	2	2	0	0	0	1	1	0	0	3	0	0	.444	.364
Antonio Pinero	R-R	6-2	195	3-15-99	.185	.157	.195	60	200	19	37	5	0	3	17	10	2	1	1	59	5	1	.255	.230
Jeferson Quero	R-R	5-10	165	10-8-02	.313	.200	.329	20	83	10	26	4	1	4	14	2	0	0	0	15	0	0	.530	.329
Zack Raabe	R-R	5-10	180	8-18-99	.269	.500	.227	10	26	7	7	2	1	0	2	7	0	0	1	5	0	1	.423	.412
Carlos Rodriguez	L-L	6-0	186	12-7-00	.268	.182	.306	42	142	23	38	10	1	3	21	18	3	0	3	35	10	3	.415	.355
Zavier Warren	B-R	6-1	215	1-8-99	.220	.168	.239	100	373	48	82	26	2	10	46	37	6	0	3	81	6	1	.381	.298
Kolten Wong	L-R	5-7	185	10-10-90	.167	.200	.000	2	6	2	1	0	0	1	1	1	0	0	0	1	0	0	.667	.286

Pitching	B-T	HT	WT	DOB	W	L	ERA	G	GS	CG	SV	IP	H	R	ER	HR	BB	SO	AVG	vLH	vRH	K/9	BB/9
Robbie Baker	R-R	6-1	211	1-31-95	1	3	3.61	34	0	0	4	52	55	24	21	4	11	56	.272	.303	.243	9.63	1.89
Justin Bullock	R-R	6-2	195	5-12-99	1	2	5.32	5	5	0	0	22	24	13	13	3	3	15	.273	.333	.209	6.14	1.23
Alexander Cornielle	R-R	6-2	180	8-22-01	1	0	2.08	3	3	0	0	17	16	4	4	2	6	21	.250	.158	.289	10.90	3.12
Stiven Cruz	R-R	6-2	165	11-14-01	1	1	0.47	4	4	0	0	19	6	1	1	1	6	20	.097	.095	.098	9.47	2.84
Taylor Floyd	R-R	6-1	185	12-8-97	5	3	3.93	20	0	0	0	34	22	16	15	2	23	42	.188	.205	.178	11.01	6.03
Tyler Gillies	R-R	6-2	190	6-6-95	0	1	6.58	23	0	0	0	26	27	20	19	4	16	29	.265	.321	.204	10.04	5.54
Trevor Gott	R-R	5-10	182	8-26-92	0	1	13.50	2	0	0	0	2	4	3	3	0	0	3	.444	.200	.750	13.50	0.00
Miguel Guerrero	R-R	6-5	216	7-15-00	2	3	7.22	19	0	0	0	34	44	32	27	6	21	31	.310	.357	.264	8.29	5.61
Kent Hasler	R-R	5-10	205	10-15-95	3	0	2.04	14	0	0	0	18	11	5	4	0	9	26	.172	.080	.231	13.25	4.58
Justin Jarvis	R-R	6-2	183	2-20-00	9	8	4.02	24	24	0	0	121	105	64	54	19	51	134	.231	.203	.258	9.97	3.79
Brannon Jordan	R-R	6-2	190	7-20-98	0	1	7.20	4	0	0	0	5	10	5	4	0	2	3	.400	.600	.350	5.40	3.60
Antoine Kelly	L-L	6-5	205	12-5-99	2	4	3.86	19	19	0	0	91	60	43	39	6	52	119	.189	.189	.188	11.77	5.14
Justin King	L-L	6-1	215	12-19-97	1	1	12.27	5	0	0	0	4	6	5	5	0	3	4	.353	.500	.308	9.82	7.36
Brandon Knarr	R-L	5-10	217	6-2-98	7	2	1.57	10	10	0	0	57	43	10	10	4	13	65	.203	.236	.191	10.20	2.04
Max Lazar	R-R	6-1	200	6-3-99	1	0	4.22	11	6	0	1	32	32	18	15	5	11	19	.252	.183	.313	5.34	3.09
Joey Matulovich	R-R	6-3	208	7-6-97	5	1	5.83	37	0	0	1	59	62	39	38	6	24	64	.271	.333	.220	9.82	3.68
Ashton McGee	L-R	6-1	215	11-19-98	0	0	9.00	2	0	0	0	2	4	2	2	1	0	1	.400	.000	.500	4.50	0.00
James Meeker	R-R	6-4	222	3-22-95	4	4	2.45	42	2	0	17	62	51	21	17	1	17	57	.217	.171	.254	8.23	2.45
Ryan Middendorf	L-R	6-6	220	12-22-97	2	0	2.31	5	0	0	0	12	9	3	3	1	1	17	.205	.304	.095	13.11	0.77
Ryne Moore	R-R	6-4	210	11-27-98	2	4	6.82	7	6	0	0	30	34	27	23	4	9	26	.288	.233	.320	7.71	2.67
Karlos Morales	L-L	6-3	170	8-10-99	1	1	1.74	6	0	0	1	10	9	2	2	0	7	9	.231	.111	.267	7.84	6.10
Zach Mort	R-R	6-0	214	5-22-97	7	4	4.99	24	6	0	1	79	81	45	44	10	23	73	.260	.246	.269	8.28	2.61
Jeison Pena	R-R	6-1	165	9-14-02	0	0	6.75	3	0	0	0	3	4	3	2	0	8	2	.333	.250	.375	6.75	27.00
Israel Puello	R-R	6-3	200	10-10-00	1	4	5.55	12	12	0	0	58	54	40	36	11	34	50	.245	.218	.263	7.71	5.25
Cam Robinson	R-R	6-1	194	9-6-99	3	1	1.45	28	0	0	19	37	21	7	6	0	17	52	.163	.148	.176	12.54	4.10
Carlos Rodriguez	R-R	6-0	180	11-27-01	3	1	1.98	7	7	0	0	36	21	9	8	0	13	45	.168	.189	.159	11.15	3.22
Brady Schanuel	R-R	6-1	196	2-21-97	0	2	2.96	29	5	0	0	55	30	21	18	3	50	57	.161	.192	.139	9.38	8.23
TJ Shook	R-R	6-4	217	5-29-98	2	1	2.41	7	4	0	0	34	23	10	9	4	11	43	.190	.171	.216	11.50	2.94
Cristian Sierra	R-R	6-5	212	4-1-98	1	0	7.56	6	0	0	0	8	10	11	7	2	10	8	.286	.273	.308	8.64	10.80
Russell Smith	L-L	6-7	255	9-10-98	2	5	4.87	15	15	0	0	68	63	44	37	8	27	62	.236	.303	.209	8.17	3.56
Christian Tripp	R-R	6-7	220	3-13-97	1	2	5.47	19	0	0	0	26	19	20	16	2	24	19	.194	.136	.241	6.49	8.20

Brandon Woodruff	L-R	6-4	243	2-10-93	1	0	1.80	1	1	0	0	5	2	1	1	1	1	7	.118	.100	.143	12.60	1.80

Fielding

Catcher	PCT	G	PO	A	E	DP	PB
Clarke	.976	28	233	14	6	1	2
Hall	.996	26	259	14	1	1	1
Miller	.995	68	615	36	3	9	2
Quero	1.000	13	111	8	0	0	1

First Base	PCT	G	PO	A	E	DP
Acosta	1.000	7	15	0	0	2
Clarke	.990	40	286	12	3	20
Hall	1.000	3	15	0	0	3
Hall	.972	6	34	1	1	0
Martinez	.985	20	125	3	2	8
McGee	.995	50	350	15	2	18
Warren	.989	12	88	1	1	4

Second Base	PCT	G	PO	A	E	DP
Acosta	.982	52	74	86	3	16
Areinamo	.950	6	13	6	1	1
Black	.965	30	50	59	4	12
Coca	.976	11	13	27	1	0
Murray	.990	29	33	71	1	15
Pinero	.857	2	2	4	1	2
Raabe	1.000	4	7	5	0	1
Wong	1.000	1	0	2	0	0

Third Base	PCT	G	PO	A	E	DP
Black	.938	6	6	9	1	0
Brosseau	1.000	3	0	4	0	1
Metzinger	.936	23	15	29	3	3
Murray	.947	11	7	11	1	2
Peterson	.667	2	0	2	1	0
Pinero	1.000	9	4	10	0	2
Warren	.932	83	57	121	13	6

Shortstop	PCT	G	PO	A	E	DP
Areinamo	1.000	1	1	1	0	1
Coca	1.000	2	0	5	0	0
Garcia	.952	25	24	56	4	9
Murray	.945	56	72	136	12	19
Pinero	.964	50	49	110	6	14

Outfield	PCT	G	PO	A	E	DP
Acosta	.933	9	13	1	1	0
Bello	1.000	13	22	3	0	0
Black	.964	15	26	1	1	0
Chourio	1.000	24	70	1	0	0
Cipion	.981	59	100	3	2	2
Davis	1.000	1	4	0	0	0
Doston	1.000	7	24	1	0	1
Frelick	1.000	17	34	3	0	0
Gray Jr.	.968	111	233	8	8	3
Hall	1.000	2	3	0	0	0
McGee	--	1	0	0	0	0
Mercado	1.000	21	33	0	0	0
Peters	1.000	75	120	2	0	0
Peterson	--	1	0	0	0	0
Raabe	1.000	5	8	1	0	1
Rodriguez	.988	41	78	2	1	2

CAROLINA MUDCATS — LOW-A

CAROLINA LEAGUE

Batting	B-T	HT	WT	DOB	AVG	vLH	vRH	G	AB	R	H	2B	3B	HR	RBI	BB	HBP	SH	SF	SO	SB	CS	SLG	OBP
Willy Adames	R-R	6-0	210	9-2-95	.500	--	.500	1	2	1	1	0	0	1	2	1	0	0	0	1	0	0	2.000	.667
Jadher Areinamo	R-R	5-10	160	11-28-03	.299	.320	.292	28	97	16	29	2	0	0	11	9	3	0	1	14	2	1	.320	.373
Jace Avina	R-R	6-2	180	6-6-03	.245	.333	.222	28	102	17	25	4	2	5	25	12	3	0	2	42	2	3	.471	.336
Micah Bello	R-R	5-11	165	7-21-00	.356	.263	.400	18	59	13	21	6	0	2	13	7	2	0	1	14	2	0	.559	.435
Eric Brown Jr.	R-R	5-10	190	12-19-00	.262	.250	.266	23	84	16	22	4	1	3	7	11	4	0	1	17	15	2	.440	.370
Jean Carmona	B-R	6-1	183	10-31-99	.167	.214	.156	26	78	9	13	2	1	1	4	15	3	1	1	33	5	2	.256	.320
Luis Castillo	L-L	5-11	175	10-11-03	.250	.158	.272	28	100	15	25	2	0	3	12	11	2	0	0	25	4	2	.360	.336
Jesus Chirinos	R-R	6-0	165	7-27-01	.237	.185	.250	117	405	60	96	13	0	12	55	69	0	0	6	152	3	1	.358	.344
Jackson Chourio	R-R	6-1	165	3-11-04	.324	.293	.330	62	250	51	81	23	5	12	47	19	1	0	1	76	10	2	.600	.373
Arbert Cipion	R-R	6-2	186	5-9-00	.292	.125	.330	34	130	26	38	6	3	4	22	17	4	0	0	31	9	4	.477	.391
Eduarqui Fernandez	R-R	6-2	176	11-20-01	.252	.250	.253	34	123	16	31	5	2	3	13	12	3	0	1	52	6	3	.398	.331
Alberis Ferrer	R-R	6-1	150	12-17-00	.184	.056	.203	43	136	23	25	2	2	5	27	15	2	0	2	66	7	0	.338	.271
Eduardo Garcia	R-R	6-2	160	7-10-02	.262	.246	.266	85	347	43	91	13	3	10	48	19	5	0	1	122	14	2	.403	.309
Jesus Garcia	R-R	5-7	163	10-2-02	.097	--	.097	11	31	4	3	0	0	0	0	3	2	0	0	9	1	0	.097	.222
Alex Hall	B-R	5-11	204	6-8-99	.104	.091	.108	15	48	4	5	1	0	1	3	6	0	0	0	25	1	0	.188	.204
Branlyn Jaraba	R-R	6-2	196	3-20-02	.228	.083	.267	17	57	7	13	3	0	3	11	2	2	0	0	20	1	1	.439	.279
Oswal Leones	L-R	6-0	165	10-6-00	.194	.178	.199	57	196	21	38	9	1	2	25	21	3	0	2	59	8	2	.281	.279
Hendry Mendez	L-L	6-2	175	11-7-03	.244	.229	.248	105	377	47	92	11	1	5	39	62	5	0	2	70	7	8	.318	.357
Robert Moore	B-R	5-9	170	3-31-02	.264	.250	.267	27	110	14	29	8	0	3	14	13	2	0	0	28	6	2	.418	.352
Hedbert Perez	L-L	5-10	160	4-4-03	.216	.213	.217	105	407	53	88	23	2	15	57	30	2	0	2	132	9	6	.393	.272
Jeferson Quero	R-R	5-10	165	10-8-02	.278	.309	.271	75	284	44	79	18	1	6	43	28	3	0	4	61	10	2	.412	.345
Zack Raabe	R-R	5-10	180	8-18-99	.228	.216	.230	76	250	39	57	14	0	0	26	51	4	0	3	53	7	0	.284	.364
Jose Sibrian	R-R	5-11	175	10-24-98	.244	.189	.262	68	217	33	53	13	0	2	26	21	7	0	0	36	0	0	.332	.331
Luis Silva	R-R	6-0	178	7-6-01	.170	.121	.183	55	153	14	26	7	0	0	12	12	1	0	1	53	4	2	.216	.234
Jheremy Vargas	R-R	5-10	160	5-10-03	.179	.186	.177	87	257	47	46	8	0	3	29	49	7	0	1	80	9	4	.245	.325

Pitching	B-T	HT	WT	DOB	W	L	ERA	G	GS	CG	SV	IP	H	R	ER	HR	BB	SO	AVG	vLH	vRH	K/9	BB/9
Jakob Brustoski	L-L	6-2	240	3-20-99	1	0	12.86	21	0	0	0	21	19	30	30	2	36	48	.235	.192	.255	20.57	15.43
Alexander Cornielle	R-R	6-2	180	8-22-01	9	7	3.19	22	19	0	0	102	81	47	36	10	53	124	.218	.232	.208	10.98	4.69
Stiven Cruz	R-R	6-2	165	11-14-01	3	5	4.60	15	15	0	0	72	77	38	37	13	18	89	.274	.270	.277	11.07	2.24
Leoni De La Cruz	L-L	6-0	175	5-22-98	1	1	3.38	11	0	0	3	21	14	9	8	2	11	21	.187	.211	.179	8.86	4.64
Jeferson Figueroa	R-R	6-0	180	8-22-00	1	7	6.81	21	12	0	1	77	74	66	58	10	42	94	.246	.233	.254	11.03	4.93
Pablo Garabitos	L-L	6-1	170	7-30-00	6	1	1.61	24	0	0	0	56	38	13	10	1	16	61	.189	.269	.161	9.80	2.57
Jesus Garcia	R-R	5-7	163	10-2-02	0	0	4.50	1	0	0	0	2	4	1	1	0	0	0	.364	.500	.200	0.00	0.00
Arielbi Gonzalez	R-R	5-10	180	11-16-02	0	1	8.00	3	1	0	0	9	11	8	8	3	4	4	.314	.308	.318	4.00	4.00
Miguel Guerrero	R-R	6-5	216	7-15-00	3	1	1.50	14	0	0	0	24	19	4	4	1	12	31	.221	.269	.200	11.63	4.50
Logan Henderson	R-R	5-11	194	3-2-02	0	1	4.63	5	5	0	0	12	14	6	6	0	6	18	.286	.273	.296	13.89	4.63
Yujanyer Herrera	R-R	6-3	175	8-17-03	0	1	9.82	4	2	0	0	15	23	18	16	1	13	9	.377	.273	.436	5.52	7.98
Edwin Jimenez	R-R	6-3	175	12-12-01	4	7	4.75	25	17	0	0	114	119	68	60	17	41	104	.272	.305	.247	8.23	3.25
Brannon Jordan	R-R	6-2	190	7-20-98	3	1	4.06	24	5	0	5	58	47	30	26	3	37	71	.223	.236	.213	11.08	5.77
Max Lazar	R-R	6-1	200	6-3-99	0	1	2.57	3	2	0	0	7	6	3	2	1	1	6	.240	.182	.286	7.71	1.29
Ryan Middendorf	L-R	6-6	220	12-22-97	0	0	0.00	4	0	0	1	8	5	0	0	0	2	13	.179	.200	.167	14.63	2.25
Jacob Misiorowski	R-R	6-7	190	4-3-02	0	0	5.40	2	2	0	0	2	1	1	1	0	7	3	.167	.500	.000	16.20	37.80
Junior Montero	R-R	6-3	175	9-20-98	6	1	4.78	26	0	0	2	32	16	17	17	2	29	39	.150	.206	.123	10.97	8.16
Ryne Moore	R-R	6-4	210	11-27-98	0	1	2.31	6	6	0	0	35	26	13	9	1	11	38	.202	.224	.177	9.77	2.83
Karlos Morales	L-L	6-3	170	8-10-99	2	3	2.52	26	0	0	5	36	29	17	10	2	15	46	.215	.128	.261	11.61	3.79
Fernando Olguin	R-R	5-9	155	3-4-01	4	3	5.30	20	10	0	0	70	72	49	41	10	29	70	.271	.323	.241	9.04	3.75

Jeison Pena	R-R	6-1	165	9-14-02	3	0	2.33	14	0	0	1	27	17	11	7	0	20	35	.185	.120	.209	11.67	6.67
Israel Puello	R-R	6-3	200	10-10-00	3	7	5.51	13	6	0	1	49	48	34	30	7	17	61	.257	.277	.237	11.20	3.12
Brandon Ramey	R-R	6-3	170	8-31-00	0	1	7.71	8	0	0	0	9	8	9	8	1	13	7	.229	.263	.188	6.75	12.54
Carlos Rodriguez	R-R	6-0	180	11-27-01	3	4	3.53	19	13	0	1	71	53	31	28	7	27	84	.213	.198	.222	10.60	3.41
Yerlin Rodriguez	R-R	6-2	172	3-22-02	0	0	18.00	3	0	0	1	4	6	8	8	0	8	4	.375	.500	.300	9.00	18.00
Miguel Segura	R-R	6-1	160	2-15-02	2	2	4.38	22	10	0	0	74	59	39	36	7	61	64	.220	.228	.214	7.78	7.42
Trevor Tietz	R-R	6-3	205	7-14-00	0	1	5.33	24	0	0	4	25	21	15	15	1	15	33	.221	.238	.208	11.72	5.33
Christian Tripp	R-R	6-7	220	3-13-97	3	0	3.28	16	0	0	2	25	18	9	9	1	12	32	.200	.273	.130	11.68	4.38
Alexander Vallecillo	R-R	6-2	150	7-1-02	1	3	9.00	6	4	0	0	20	28	21	20	3	13	17	.337	.290	.365	7.65	5.85
Michele Vassalotti	R-R	6-2	180	8-2-00	9	2	2.64	33	0	0	7	48	29	22	14	1	24	56	.170	.169	.170	10.57	4.53
Cameron Wagoner	R-R	6-5	187	6-21-01	2	0	0.77	3	1	0	0	12	12	1	1	1	1	16	.273	.273	.273	12.34	0.77
Tyler Woessner	R-R	6-4	230	10-26-99	0	0	5.40	1	1	0	0	2	2	1	1	0	2	2	.286	.500	.200	10.80	10.80
Jolon Zhao	R-R	5-10	180	8-29-01	0	0	36.00	2	0	0	0	1	2	4	4	0	5	2	.400	.500	.000	18.00	45.00

Fielding

Catcher	PCT	G	PO	A	E	DP	PB
Garcia	.963	6	73	4	3	0	0
Hall	.987	15	140	15	2	2	1
Quero	.986	53	516	50	8	2	4
Sibrian	.992	63	592	63	5	4	8
Silva	1.000	1	1	0	0	0	0

First Base	PCT	G	PO	A	E	DP
Chirinos	.982	113	687	41	13	53
Garcia	1.000	1	6	0	0	0
Jaraba	1.000	4	29	0	0	3
Silva	.991	19	104	1	1	8

Second Base	PCT	G	PO	A	E	DP
Areinamo	.892	9	16	17	4	8
Brown Jr.	1.000	3	6	7	0	2
Carmona	.909	4	6	4	1	1
Ferrer	1.000	4	7	9	0	2
Moore	.952	15	20	39	3	8
Raabe	.966	69	90	110	7	24
Silva	1.000	2	3	2	0	1
Vargas	.990	29	41	57	1	10

Third Base	PCT	G	PO	A	E	DP
Areinamo	.955	15	11	31	2	2
Carmona	.833	15	12	18	6	2
Ferrer	.802	27	21	44	16	4
Jaraba	.852	11	8	15	4	3
Silva	.989	34	32	60	1	7
Vargas	.890	39	30	51	10	4

Shortstop	PCT	G	PO	A	E	DP
Areinamo	1.000	4	5	10	0	2
Brown Jr.	.950	17	37	39	4	9
Carmona	1.000	3	2	2	0	0
Ferrer	.875	4	4	3	1	2
Garcia	.956	80	112	146	12	22
Moore	.973	12	17	19	1	8
Vargas	.896	16	25	18	5	3

Outfield	PCT	G	PO	A	E	DP
Avina	1.000	27	61	0	0	0
Bello	.900	13	17	1	2	1
Carmona	--	1	0	0	0	0
Castillo	1.000	20	19	3	0	1
Chourio	.988	57	159	5	2	1
Cipion	.954	32	57	5	3	3
Fernandez	1.000	34	72	1	0	0
Leones	.983	41	56	1	1	0
Mendez	1.000	87	132	4	0	1
Perez	.987	88	146	9	2	3
Silva	1.000	1	1	0	0	0

ACL BREWERS BLUE — *ROOKIE*

ARIZONA COMPLEX LEAGUE

Batting	B-T	HT	WT	DOB	AVG	vLH	vRH	G	AB	R	H	2B	3B	HR	RBI	BB	HBP	SH	SF	SO	SB	CS	SLG	OBP
Jace Avina	R-R	6-2	180	6-6-03	.294	.357	.286	36	119	27	35	8	1	10	29	15	15	0	0	51	2	0	.630	.436
Jhonnys Cabrera	R-R	5-11	150	6-5-02	.235	.000	.250	25	51	11	12	2	0	4	10	14	3	0	0	23	0	0	.510	.426
Larry Ernesto	B-R	6-2	175	9-12-00	.000	--	.000	1	1	0	0	0	0	0	0	0	0	0	0	1	0	0	.000	.000
Eduarqui Fernandez	R-R	6-2	176	11-20-01	.257	.231	.260	31	113	21	29	10	1	5	17	11	0	0	0	51	4	0	.496	.323
Jesus Garcia	R-R	5-7	163	10-2-02	.273	--	.273	5	11	2	3	0	0	0	1	1	2	0	0	2	0	1	.273	.429
Nader Garcia	L-R	5-9	160	5-14-02	.125	--	.125	3	8	1	1	1	0	0	2	0	0	0	0	2	0	0	.250	.125
2-team total (6 ACL Brewers Gold)					.250	.000	.267	9	16	4	4	2	0	0	2	2	0	0	0	3	0	0	.375	.333
Daniel Guilarte	R-R	6-0	160	10-29-03	.306	.308	.306	36	124	17	38	8	0	0	20	19	1	0	0	31	8	3	.371	.403
Jonatan Guzman	R-R	6-0	155	11-25-03	.236	.125	.252	41	127	13	30	4	0	1	18	6	5	0	0	32	6	2	.291	.297
Tayden Hall	L-R	6-4	215	1-12-03	.424	.800	.357	10	33	7	14	4	0	0	5	6	0	0	0	6	0	0	.545	.513
2-team total (1 ACL Brewers Gold)					.368	.800	.303	11	38	7	14	4	0	0	5	6	0	0	0	8	0	0	.474	.455
Alex Jackson	R-R	6-2	215	12-25-95	1.000	--	1.000	1	1	1	1	1	0	0	0	1	0	0	0	0	0	0	2.000	1.000
Oswal Leones	L-R	6-0	165	10-6-00	.250	.250	.250	9	24	3	6	1	0	0	1	8	0	0	0	6	2	2	.292	.438
Darlin Lora	R-R	5-10	175	7-23-03	.242	.000	.267	11	33	6	8	0	1	0	2	4	0	0	0	7	0	0	.303	.324
Quinton Low	L-R	6-6	215	9-5-02	.254	.000	.279	43	114	20	29	7	1	2	16	16	5	0	0	35	0	0	.386	.370
Ernesto Martinez	L-L	6-6	250	6-20-99	.263	.000	.333	7	19	4	5	0	0	3	8	6	0	0	0	7	0	0	.737	.440
Luis Medina	L-L	6-2	168	2-24-03	.239	.167	.253	35	109	15	26	2	0	3	15	6	1	0	2	33	3	2	.339	.280
Reidy Mercado	B-R	5-11	153	1-6-01	.247	.143	.257	24	81	12	20	4	0	0	9	14	1	0	0	22	8	2	.296	.365
Ben Metzinger	R-R	6-0	195	6-26-99	.250	.000	.286	3	8	0	2	0	1	0	0	2	0	0	0	3	0	0	.500	.400
2-team total (1 ACL Brewers Gold)					.333	.000	.364	4	12	2	4	0	1	0	2	3	0	0	0	4	0	0	.500	.467
Garrett Mitchell	L-R	6-3	215	9-4-98	.083	.000	.100	4	12	5	1	1	0	0	0	4	1	0	0	4	1	0	.167	.353
Robert Moore	B-R	5-9	170	3-31-02	.091	--	.091	3	11	1	1	1	0	0	1	1	1	0	0	1	0	0	.182	.231
2-team total (1 ACL Brewers Gold)					.133	--	.133	4	15	3	2	1	0	0	2	2	1	0	0	2	1	0	.200	.278
Jason Ollarve	L-R	5-10	160	5-20-04	.375	.000	.400	5	16	2	6	0	0	0	4	4	0	0	0	3	2	0	.375	.500
2-team total (18 ACL Brewers Gold)					.247	.000	.269	23	73	7	18	1	0	1	12	7	2	0	2	15	3	1	.301	.321
Beyker Pastran	R-R	5-10	162	4-1-03	.186	.063	.204	45	129	21	24	2	2	0	14	16	3	0	2	38	1	0	.233	.287
Alexander Perez	R-R	5-9	140	3-12-03	.239	.176	.246	44	155	25	37	12	1	4	23	13	4	0	1	30	12	4	.406	.312
Ney Serrano	R-R	6-0	150	5-8-04	.212	.167	.215	40	113	25	24	5	0	3	14	21	4	0	1	51	5	2	.336	.353
Felipe Valderrama	R-R	6-0	170	7-24-04	.207	.273	.191	21	58	12	12	2	0	2	8	6	4	0	0	24	1	1	.345	.324
Jheremy Vargas	R-R	5-10	160	5-10-03	.250	.667	.207	11	32	5	8	2	0	1	1	6	0	0	0	12	2	3	.406	.368
Matthew Wood	L-R	5-10	190	3-2-01	.200	--	.200	2	5	0	1	0	0	0	1	0	0	0	0	0	0	0	.200	.200
Jamal Zalm	R-R	5-10	155	9-21-02	.202	.250	.198	34	94	20	19	4	2	1	10	18	1	0	0	36	5	0	.319	.336

Pitching	B-T	HT	WT	DOB	W	L	ERA	G	GS	CG	SV	IP	H	R	ER	HR	BB	SO	AVG	vLH	vRH	K/9	BB/9
Logan Adams	R-R	6-6	231	12-7-99	0	0	0.00	1	1	0	0	1	1	0	0	0	0	1	.250	.000	.500	9.00	0.00
Jared Albir	R-R	6-2	161	8-27-02	0	5	6.81	9	7	0	0	36	47	33	27	3	18	39	.324	.373	.298	9.84	4.54
Jonathan Beymer	R-R	6-2	180	8-26-98	1	1	2.25	3	0	0	0	4	4	2	1	0	1	5	.267	.333	.250	11.25	2.25

Ryan Brady	R-R	6-1	185	3-23-99	0	0	2.25	3	1	0	0	4	2	1	1	0	1	8	.154	.333	.000	18.00	2.25
Jhonnys Cabrera	R-R	5-11	150	6-5-02	0	0	0.00	1	0	0	0	2	2	1	0	0	1	0	.286	.333	.250	0.00	5.40
Junior Castillo	L-L	5-10	160	1-28-03	1	2	11.42	16	1	0	0	17	25	28	22	2	27	19	.325	.421	.293	9.87	14.02
Jose Chavez	R-R	6-2	150	1-9-03	0	1	6.00	20	0	0	0	24	26	20	16	0	18	24	.257	.326	.207	9.00	6.75
Jake Cousins	R-R	6-4	185	7-14-94	0	0	0.00	1	0	0	0	1	0	0	0	0	0	2	.000	--	.000	18.00	0.00
Samuel Dario	R-R	6-3	175	12-23-02	3	2	5.40	22	0	0	1	32	37	22	19	3	20	35	.298	.321	.279	9.95	5.68
Leoni De La Cruz	L-L	6-0	175	5-22-98	0	1	2.33	14	0	0	1	19	16	6	5	1	8	26	.229	.000	.262	12.10	3.72
Brian Fitzpatrick	B-L	6-7	230	6-1-00	0	0	2.45	2	1	0	0	4	1	1	1	0	1	7	.083	.333	.000	17.18	2.45
Andy Garcia	R-R	6-0	160	1-16-02	0	5	7.22	10	6	0	0	29	29	30	23	2	26	31	.269	.326	.226	9.73	8.16
Rafael Garcia	R-R	6-1	158	4-28-01	0	0	54.00	3	3	0	0	1	6	8	8	1	4	1	.600	.500	.667	6.75	27.00
Arielbi Gonzalez	R-R	5-10	180	11-16-02	1	1	3.22	11	6	0	0	45	38	18	16	4	14	47	.221	.244	.213	9.47	2.82
Logan Henderson	R-R	5-11	194	3-2-02	0	0	0.00	2	2	0	0	2	1	0	0	0	0	5	.125	.000	.250	22.50	0.00
Yujanyer Herrera	R-R	6-3	175	8-17-03	2	3	5.36	11	8	0	0	44	48	31	26	2	10	46	.277	.323	.225	9.48	2.06
Justin King	L-L	6-1	215	12-19-97	0	0	0.00	1	0	0	0	1	1	0	0	0	1	3	.250	.000	.333	27.00	9.00
2-team total (4 ACL Brewers Gold)					1	1	0.00	5	0	0	0	5	4	1	0	0	2	7	.267	.000	.364	13.50	3.86
Max Lazar	R-R	6-1	200	6-3-99	0	0	0.00	1	1	0	0	1	1	0	0	0	0	1	.250	.000	.333	9.00	0.00
Quinton Low	L-R	6-6	215	9-5-02	0	0	0.82	10	0	0	2	11	3	1	1	1	5	16	.081	.095	.063	13.09	4.09
Raul Mendoza	R-R	5-11	168	12-9-00	0	0	4.50	7	0	0	0	10	12	6	5	2	8	11	.308	.267	.333	9.90	7.20
2-team total (12 ACL Brewers Gold)					2	1	5.33	19	0	0	3	25	30	18	15	4	18	22	.309	.341	.286	7.82	6.39
Nick Merkel	R-R	6-7	255	7-3-98	0	2	3.52	3	3	0	0	8	8	6	3	0	2	4	.286	.278	.300	4.70	2.35
Angel Perdomo	L-L	6-8	265	5-7-94	0	0	0.00	2	0	0	0	2	1	0	0	0	0	3	.143	.000	.200	13.50	0.00
Michael Perdomo	R-R	6-0	170	11-22-01	1	0	5.40	6	0	0	0	8	9	6	5	0	4	6	.273	.182	.318	6.48	4.32
2-team total (12 ACL Brewers Gold)					2	0	6.75	18	0	0	0	21	23	20	16	3	16	12	.274	.214	.333	5.06	6.75
Anthony Perez	R-R	6-3	190	10-28-01	2	1	6.23	13	1	0	0	26	26	20	18	3	16	36	.260	.220	.317	12.46	5.54
Jesus Rivero	R-R	6-1	175	5-14-03	4	5	6.90	16	5	0	0	30	19	27	23	1	27	46	.179	.146	.207	13.80	8.10
Edrian Robinson	R-R	6-5	170	3-1-02	0	0	3.86	2	0	0	0	2	3	1	1	0	2	2	.300	.333	.286	7.71	7.71
Phili Silverio	R-R	6-2	190	7-27-01	0	1	33.75	1	0	0	0	1	3	5	5	0	3	0	.429	.000	.600	0.00	20.25
2-team total (16 ACL Brewers Gold)					1	3	7.48	17	0	0	1	22	23	19	18	2	18	26	.274	.310	.255	10.80	7.48
Trevor Tietz	R-R	6-3	205	7-14-00	0	1	2.70	2	0	0	0	3	4	3	1	1	1	8	.267	.500	.111	21.60	2.70
2-team total (17 ACL Brewers Gold)					6	1	4.10	19	0	0	3	26	32	16	12	5	9	39	.291	.308	.276	13.33	3.08
Alexander Vallecillo	R-R	6-2	150	7-1-02	4	3	3.82	8	7	0	0	38	40	18	16	4	11	45	.276	.281	.272	10.75	2.63

Fielding

C: Cabrera 18, Garcia 3, Garcia 2, Hall 5, Jackson 1, Lora 8, Ollarve 4, Valderrama 19, Wood 2. **1B:** Cabrera 3, Hall 3, Low 30, Martinez 5, Pastran 14, Perez 1, Vargas 2. **2B:** Cabrera 1, Guilarte 2, Guzman 20, Pastran 2, Perez 21, Serrano 9, Zalm 4. **3B:** Guilarte 2, Guzman 7, Metzinger 3, Pastran 15, Perez 11, Serrano 15, Vargas 4, Zalm 1. **SS:** Guilarte 31, Moore 3, Perez 5, Serrano 15, Vargas 3. **OF:** Avina 31, Ernesto 1, Fernandez 27, Hall 1, Leones 9, Medina 34, Mercado 21, Mitchell 3, Pastran 10, Perez 1, Vargas 3, Zalm 30.

ACL BREWERS GOLD — *ROOKIE*

ARIZONA COMPLEX LEAGUE

Batting	B-T	HT	WT	DOB	AVG	vLH	vRH	G	AB	R	H	2B	3B	HR	RBI	BB	HBP	SH	SF	SO	SB	CS	SLG	OBP
Luke Adams	R-R	6-4	210	4-24-04	.375	.400	.370	11	32	9	12	3	0	1	7	7	2	0	0	8	9	1	.563	.512
Jadher Areinamo	R-R	5-10	160	11-28-03	.323	.471	.300	34	127	31	41	10	3	1	21	19	2	0	1	19	4	4	.472	.416
Gregory Barrios	R-R	6-0	180	4-8-04	.291	.364	.281	48	175	33	51	5	2	0	26	17	4	0	4	30	13	0	.343	.360
Miguel Briceno	R-R	5-9	155	7-6-03	.328	.364	.319	25	58	5	19	4	1	0	10	7	0	0	3	17	1	0	.431	.382
Eric Brown Jr.	R-R	5-10	190	12-19-00	.308	.000	.333	4	13	7	4	3	0	0	1	4	0	0	0	4	4	0	.538	.471
Jose Caballero	R-R	5-10	140	3-26-03	.292	.200	.306	37	113	23	33	3	0	0	10	19	3	0	1	22	9	1	.319	.404
Luis Castillo	L-L	5-11	175	10-11-03	.297	.231	.305	33	118	21	35	9	2	3	27	17	1	0	1	28	1	0	.483	.387
Eduarh Colina	R-R	5-11	160	6-6-03	.191	.444	.170	37	115	19	22	6	0	1	9	11	6	0	0	53	1	0	.270	.295
Blayberg Diaz	R-R	5-11	190	1-31-03	.185	.071	.202	35	108	13	20	1	0	3	21	17	4	0	5	22	5	0	.278	.306
Alberis Ferrer	R-R	6-1	150	12-17-00	.231	.000	.273	4	13	3	3	1	0	0	2	2	0	0	0	6	0	0	.308	.333
Nader Garcia	L-R	5-9	160	5-14-02	.375	.000	.429	6	8	3	3	1	0	0	0	2	0	0	0	1	0	0	.500	.500
2-team total (3 ACL Brewers Blue)					.250	.000	.267	9	16	4	4	2	0	0	2	2	0	0	0	3	0	0	.375	.333
Tayden Hall	L-R	6-4	215	1-12-03	.000	--	.000	1	5	0	0	0	0	0	0	0	0	0	0	2	0	0	.000	.000
2-team total (10 ACL Brewers Blue)					.368	.800	.303	11	38	7	14	4	0	0	5	6	0	0	0	8	0	0	.474	.455
Branlyn Jaraba	R-R	6-2	196	3-20-02	.244	.154	.262	24	78	11	19	3	0	0	4	6	5	0	1	33	0	0	.282	.333
Diego Larez	R-R	6-1	165	12-9-02	.190	.182	.192	36	84	26	16	4	0	2	9	21	7	0	0	32	7	1	.310	.393
Rafael Martinez	B-R	5-11	170	9-20-01	.232	.250	.229	19	56	9	13	2	1	0	6	9	1	0	1	27	2	0	.304	.343
Ben Metzinger	R-R	6-0	195	6-26-99	.500	--	.500	1	4	2	2	0	0	0	2	1	0	0	0	1	0	0	.500	.600
2-team total (3 ACL Brewers Blue)					.333	.000	.364	4	12	2	4	0	1	0	2	3	0	0	0	4	0	0	.500	.467
Robert Moore	B-R	5-9	170	3-31-02	.250	--	.250	1	4	2	1	0	0	0	1	1	0	0	0	1	1	0	.250	.400
2-team total (3 ACL Brewers Blue)					.133	--	.133	4	15	3	2	1	0	0	2	2	1	0	0	2	1	0	.200	.278
Kaylan Nicasia	B-R	6-2	176	4-10-02	.232	.353	.215	43	138	25	32	7	3	5	30	23	1	0	2	41	2	4	.435	.341
Satchell Norman	R-R	5-10	200	7-22-02	.344	1.000	.323	10	32	6	11	2	0	0	3	5	1	0	0	8	4	1	.406	.447
Jason Ollarve	L-R	5-10	160	5-20-04	.211	.000	.231	18	57	5	12	1	0	1	8	3	2	0	2	12	1	1	.281	.266
2-team total (5 ACL Brewers Blue)					.247	.000	.269	23	73	7	18	1	0	1	12	7	2	0	2	15	3	1	.301	.321
Dylan O'Rae	L-R	5-9	160	2-14-04	.308	.000	.348	8	26	6	8	0	0	0	3	6	0	0	1	7	4	1	.308	.424
Jesus Parra	R-R	6-2	184	8-30-02	.217	.250	.212	41	138	14	30	13	0	3	26	8	5	0	4	47	3	0	.377	.277
Carlos Roa	R-R	5-11	165	9-4-01	.211	.167	.216	20	57	11	12	2	1	2	7	9	0	0	0	19	6	0	.386	.318
Reece Walling	L-R	6-6	202	9-22-03	.143	.250	.129	13	35	8	5	0	0	0	4	13	0	0	0	19	1	0	.143	.375

Pitching	B-T	HT	WT	DOB	W	L	ERA	G	GS	CG	SV	IP	H	R	ER	HR	BB	SO	AVG	vLH	vRH	K/9	BB/9
Clayton Andrews	L-L	5-6	160	1-4-97	0	0	0.00	2	0	0	0	2	0	0	0	0	0	3	.000	--	.000	13.50	0.00
Patricio Aquino	R-R	6-0	175	5-1-03	2	1	4.72	8	7	0	0	34	30	22	18	3	16	49	.233	.194	.274	12.84	4.19
Kevin Briceno	R-R	6-1	160	10-15-02	2	1	3.00	6	3	0	0	21	18	8	7	3	9	17	.228	.350	.186	7.29	3.86

Jakob Brustoski	L-L	6-2	240	3-20-99	0	0	9.35	7	0	0	0	9	8	9	9	0	10	17	.235	.000	.348	17.65	10.38
Gerson Calzadilla	R-R	5-11	155	4-5-03	4	2	3.94	11	8	0	0	48	46	23	21	5	19	38	.251	.276	.218	7.13	3.56
Yorman Galindez	R-R	6-1	160	2-3-03	3	2	6.45	13	4	0	0	38	40	28	27	3	26	50	.276	.300	.253	11.95	6.21
Delson Guzman	R-R	5-11	160	9-10-02	1	0	2.57	4	1	0	1	7	3	3	2	0	5	9	.120	.250	.000	11.57	6.43
Justin King	L-L	6-1	215	12-19-97	1	1	0.00	4	0	0	0	4	3	1	0	0	1	4	.273	.000	.375	9.82	2.45
2-team total (1 ACL Brewers Blue)					1	1	0.00	5	0	0	0	5	4	1	0	0	2	7	.267	.000	.364	13.50	3.86
Fraudy Maldonado	L-L	6-0	155	3-21-03	0	1	7.32	15	0	0	2	20	21	20	16	1	12	24	.280	.400	.250	10.98	5.49
Domingo Mejia	R-R	6-3	175	8-31-01	0	2	7.88	4	4	0	0	16	17	15	14	2	9	14	.262	.400	.220	7.88	5.06
Raul Mendoza	R-R	5-11	168	12-9-00	2	1	5.87	12	0	0	3	15	18	12	10	2	10	11	.310	.385	.250	6.46	5.87
2-team total (7 ACL Brewers Blue)					2	1	5.33	19	0	0	3	25	30	18	15	4	18	22	.309	.341	.286	7.82	6.39
Ryan Middendorf	L-R	6-6	220	12-22-97	1	1	1.38	7	0	0	0	13	10	2	2	0	1	19	.204	.174	.231	13.15	0.69
Fray Morelo	R-R	6-2	178	5-23-02	1	0	9.28	13	0	0	1	21	26	24	22	5	20	21	.310	.172	.382	8.86	8.44
Henrison Mota	R-R	6-3	193	7-4-03	1	1	3.62	10	9	0	0	32	18	27	13	0	39	44	.161	.154	.164	12.25	10.86
Jeison Pena	R-R	6-1	165	9-14-02	0	1	4.32	7	2	0	1	17	13	10	8	1	4	27	.210	.250	.196	14.58	2.16
Michael Perdomo	R-R	6-0	170	11-22-01	1	0	7.62	12	0	0	0	13	14	14	11	3	12	6	.275	.226	.350	4.15	8.31
2-team total (6 ACL Brewers Blue)					2	0	6.75	18	0	0	0	21	23	20	16	3	16	12	.274	.214	.333	5.06	6.75
Carlos Roa	R-R	5-11	165	9-4-01	0	0	18.00	1	0	0	0	1	3	2	2	0	0	1	.600	.500	.667	9.00	0.00
Yerlin Rodriguez	R-R	6-2	172	3-22-02	4	3	5.47	10	4	0	0	26	24	25	16	0	17	31	.235	.243	.231	10.59	5.81
Phili Silverio	R-R	6-2	190	7-27-01	1	2	5.75	16	0	0	1	20	20	14	13	2	15	26	.260	.333	.220	11.51	6.64
2-team total (1 ACL Brewers Blue)					1	3	7.48	17	0	0	1	22	23	19	18	2	18	26	.274	.310	.255	10.80	7.48
Shane Smith	R-R	6-4	235	4-4-00	0	0	6.00	3	3	0	0	3	6	2	2	0	3	4	.429	.556	.200	12.00	9.00
Scott Sunitsch	L-L	6-1	205	6-16-96	0	0	0.00	1	1	0	0	1	1	0	0	0	0	1	.333	--	.333	9.00	0.00
Trevor Tietz	R-R	6-3	205	7-14-00	6	0	4.30	17	0	0	3	23	28	13	11	4	8	31	.295	.283	.306	12.13	3.13
2-team total (2 ACL Brewers Blue)					6	1	4.10	19	0	0	3	26	32	16	12	5	9	39	.291	.308	.276	13.33	3.08
Justin Topa	R-R	6-4	200	3-7-91	1	0	0.00	1	0	0	0	1	0	0	0	0	0	1	.000	.000	.000	9.00	0.00
Caden Vire	L-L	6-6	170	9-9-03	0	2	9.82	7	2	0	0	11	10	15	12	1	15	11	.233	.167	.258	9.00	12.27
Cameron Wagoner	R-R	6-5	187	6-21-01	1	0	3.38	4	2	0	0	8	4	3	3	0	1	8	.143	.063	.250	9.00	1.13
Tyler Wehrle	R-R	6-3	220	5-18-00	0	0	6.00	2	1	0	0	3	3	2	2	1	1	2	.250	.167	.333	6.00	3.00
Tyler Woessner	R-R	6-4	230	10-26-99	0	0	0.00	3	2	0	0	6	2	0	0	0	1	11	.105	.100	.111	16.50	1.50

Fielding

C: Diaz 28, Garcia 2, Norman 7, Ollarve 18. **1B:** Adams 1, Diaz 3, Hall 1, Jaraba 16, Nicasia 2, Parra 35. **2B:** Areinamo 10, Barrios 18, Briceno 11, Caballero 14, Nicasia 1, O'Rae 5, Roa 1. **3B:** Adams 7, Areinamo 7, Briceno 13, Caballero 6, Ferrer 2, Jaraba 7, Metzinger 1, Nicasia 5, Parra 4, Roa 9. **SS:** Areinamo 12, Barrios 24, Brown Jr. 4, Caballero 13, O'Rae 3. **OF:** Adams 3, Castillo 29, Colina 38, Larez 34, Martinez 18, Nicasia 30, Walling 13.

DSL BREWERS 1 — ROOKIE

DOMINICAN SUMMER LEAGUE

Batting	B-T	HT	WT	DOB	AVG	vLH	vRH	G	AB	R	H	2B	3B	HR	RBI	BB	HBP	SH	SF	SO	SB	CS	SLG	OBP
Miguel Briceno	R-R	5-9	155	7-6-03	.294	.250	.308	5	17	4	5	2	0	0	1	3	0	0	0	2	0	1	.412	.400
Duncan Garcia	R-R	6-1	170	10-31-03	.246	.314	.229	55	179	26	44	13	2	4	20	23	5	0	2	60	19	9	.408	.344
Deylin Gomez	R-R	5-11	185	6-1-05	.131	.050	.156	33	84	7	11	0	0	1	3	5	4	0	1	43	1	1	.167	.213
Gery Holguin	R-R	6-0	160	8-3-05	.191	.143	.201	53	162	23	31	1	0	2	16	36	4	0	1	53	6	4	.235	.350
Roman La Torre	L-R	5-10	160	5-4-05	.209	.000	.215	24	67	7	14	5	0	0	7	7	2	0	0	11	0	0	.284	.303
Luis Lara	B-R	5-9	155	11-17-04	.260	.244	.265	58	200	39	52	11	4	2	21	21	5	0	3	28	7	7	.385	.341
Darlin Lora	R-R	5-10	175	7-23-03	.200	.250	.182	5	15	1	3	0	0	0	1	0	1	0	0	3	3	0	.200	.250
Edgardo Ordonez	L-R	5-11	155	9-24-03	.290	.261	.299	35	100	19	29	6	0	2	16	18	1	0	1	27	1	0	.410	.400
Jose Pena	B-R	6-0	155	2-21-05	.139	.105	.146	39	101	7	14	3	0	0	8	15	4	0	1	62	2	1	.168	.273
Angel Pereira	R-R	5-10	176	3-30-05	.236	.250	.232	41	123	22	29	4	1	0	16	15	13	0	1	34	5	8	.285	.375
Erick Reyes	R-R	5-10	145	4-17-04	.500	--	.500	1	2	0	1	0	0	0	0	0	0	0	0	0	1	0	.500	.500
2-team total (32 DSL Brewers 2)					.176	.059	.216	33	68	21	12	2	1	2	8	24	1	0	1	25	14	1	.324	.394
Arnys Rodriguez	B-R	5-11	173	8-12-03	.220	.217	.221	40	109	19	24	5	0	1	16	23	2	0	2	41	4	2	.294	.360
Richard Rojas	R-R	5-10	155	1-19-04	.218	.375	.179	44	119	10	26	7	0	0	20	11	5	0	3	44	6	0	.277	.304
Juan Rosa	R-R	6-2	200	5-22-03	.100	--	.100	5	10	0	1	0	0	0	0	0	0	0	0	5	0	0	.100	.100
Jhonny Severino	R-R	6-3	185	11-8-04	.268	.405	.232	48	179	26	48	11	1	3	25	14	4	0	1	55	10	1	.391	.333
Ludwin Tejada	L-R	5-10	175	5-12-05	.269	.222	.279	19	52	5	14	1	0	0	5	10	0	0	0	7	1	0	.288	.387
2-team total (3 DSL Brewers 2)					.283	.222	.294	22	60	7	17	1	1	0	6	10	0	0	0	9	2	0	.333	.386
Fabricio Valera	L-R	6-2	174	9-21-04	.132	.111	.138	14	38	2	5	0	0	0	2	17	2	0	0	13	1	0	.132	.421
Luis Watter	R-R	5-8	150	1-10-03	.259	.212	.275	45	135	19	35	5	1	0	10	19	1	0	0	37	9	0	.311	.355

Pitching	B-T	HT	WT	DOB	W	L	ERA	G	GS	CG	SV	IP	H	R	ER	HR	BB	SO	AVG	vLH	vRH	K/9	BB/9
Gregory Baez	R-R	6-3	180	12-29-01	1	2	5.61	16	0	0	3	26	28	16	16	2	15	36	.272	.300	.245	12.62	5.26
Kevin Briceno	R-R	6-1	160	10-15-02	2	2	1.29	6	6	0	0	28	16	5	4	2	5	31	.168	.133	.185	9.96	1.61
Jesael Cabrera	R-R	6-0	155	10-22-03	2	3	4.09	8	0	0	1	22	20	15	10	1	11	21	.247	.190	.267	8.59	4.50
Royer Cabrera	R-R	5-11	170	10-30-04	1	1	9.64	7	3	0	0	14	21	17	15	1	12	9	.356	.346	.364	5.79	7.71
Justin Caceres	R-R	6-1	168	11-13-04	1	2	6.97	16	0	0	1	31	36	29	24	2	19	25	.283	.409	.217	7.26	5.52
Cristofher Carrasco	R-R	5-10	175	12-24-02	1	1	5.40	4	1	0	0	10	10	6	6	1	6	17	.256	.231	.269	15.30	5.40
Braudin Ciprian	R-R	6-2	220	3-20-01	0	1	4.91	3	0	0	0	4	2	8	2	0	4	2	.125	.143	.111	4.91	9.82
2-team total (8 DSL Brewers 2)					0	1	5.56	11	0	0	0	11	12	15	7	0	9	9	.245	.214	.257	7.15	7.15
Jhofez Mejias	L-L	5-10	150	10-28-03	2	2	4.08	13	3	0	1	29	32	20	13	2	13	34	.278	.333	.270	10.67	4.08
Raul Mendoza	R-R	5-11	168	12-9-00	0	0	0.00	1	0	0	0	1	1	0	0	0	0	1	.250	.333	.000	9.00	0.00
Osbriel Mogollon	L-L	5-10	160	4-1-04	2	3	2.74	12	10	0	0	46	22	15	14	1	24	57	.149	.079	.173	11.15	4.70
Michael Perdomo	R-R	6-0	170	11-22-01	1	0	0.00	1	0	0	0	2	0	1	0	0	0	2	.000	.000	.000	10.80	0.00
Anthony Perez	R-R	6-3	190	10-28-01	0	2	9.00	2	2	0	0	7	9	8	7	0	3	3	.333	.417	.267	3.86	3.86
Bryan Rivera	R-R	6-1	170	6-17-05	1	0	5.63	7	5	0	0	24	26	17	15	3	11	26	.280	.258	.290	9.75	4.13
Leonardo Rivera	R-R	6-3	170	10-12-03	2	3	6.48	15	0	0	1	25	23	21	18	3	17	20	.250	.192	.273	7.20	6.12

Aneuris Rodriguez	R-R	6-3	185	6-14-04	1	1	3.89	10	7	0	0	35	27	21	15	1	18	33	.213	.259	.178	8.57	4.67
Manuel Rodriguez	R-R	6-2	175	8-8-05	1	5	4.54	12	5	0	3	36	36	25	18	3	9	24	.259	.216	.284	6.06	2.27
Dikember Sanchez	R-R	5-11	160	2-20-04	3	1	4.97	13	0	0	1	25	22	16	14	0	19	21	.229	.158	.276	7.46	6.75
Ranwell Smith	R-R	5-11	140	8-23-05	0	4	6.20	9	6	0	0	25	25	22	17	2	21	19	.269	.212	.300	6.93	7.66
Wande Torres	L-L	6-3	190	1-31-05	1	4	3.79	11	11	0	0	40	28	21	17	1	33	45	.200	.233	.191	10.04	7.36
Hamlet Vasquez	R-R	6-3	175	9-9-02	0	0	3.32	8	0	0	0	19	19	15	7	0	13	16	.257	.286	.231	7.58	6.16
2-team total (7 DSL Brewers 2)					1	0	3.96	15	0	0	0	25	30	19	11	0	16	21	.303	.311	.296	7.56	5.76

Fielding

C: La Torre 20, Lora 4, Ordonez 25, Rosa 2, Tejada 16. **1B:** Lora 1, Ordonez 5, Pena 7, Reyes 1, Rodriguez 36, Rojas 10, Tejada 3. **2B:** Briceno 2, Holguin 12, Pena 20, Pereira 15, Rojas 7, Severino 1, Watter 5. **3B:** Briceno 2, Holguin 16, Pena 1, Pereira 10, Rodriguez 1, Rojas 15, Severino 9, Watter 6. **SS:** Holguin 19, Pena 2, Pereira 4, Rojas 6, Severino 29. **OF:** Garcia 52, Gomez 30, Lara 53, Pena 2, Pereira 2, Rodriguez 2, Rojas 4, Valera 7, Watter 36.

DSL BREWERS 2 — ROOKIE

DOMINICAN SUMMER LEAGUE

Batting	B-T	HT	WT	DOB	AVG	vLH	vRH	G	AB	R	H	2B	3B	HR	RBI	BB	HBP	SH	SF	SO	SB	CS	SLG	OBP
Juan Baez	R-R	5-11	175	6-27-05	.268	.256	.271	54	198	33	53	9	0	3	22	17	2	0	4	31	17	6	.359	.326
Johan Barrios	R-R	6-3	180	1-8-05	.292	.000	.330	34	120	22	35	3	2	0	13	11	0	0	0	31	3	4	.350	.351
Reminton Batista	B-R	5-10	175	1-28-05	.252	.235	.256	46	159	31	40	4	3	1	13	23	2	0	3	53	18	5	.333	.348
Mendy Ferreira	R-R	6-0	165	1-27-03	.212	.353	.176	35	85	15	18	4	0	1	14	7	0	0	3	28	11	3	.294	.263
Jose Gonzalez	R-R	5-10	165	10-2-02	.188	.150	.194	42	128	14	24	5	0	1	13	17	2	0	4	40	4	2	.250	.285
Irving Igualas	L-R	6-0	175	7-27-03	.231	.147	.254	48	160	13	37	4	1	1	18	16	0	0	2	63	8	5	.288	.298
Estefano Lozano	R-R	6-0	182	2-7-04	.100	--	.100	5	10	1	1	0	0	0	0	2	1	0	0	6	0	0	.100	.308
Eric Martinez	R-R	6-0	175	4-6-04	.272	.250	.277	37	114	19	31	9	1	3	18	10	6	1	2	31	1	2	.447	.356
Demetrio Nadal	R-R	5-7	125	7-3-04	.239	.250	.237	48	142	30	34	2	3	1	11	22	10	0	2	29	17	3	.317	.375
Francisco Nina	R-R	6-5	175	9-6-04	.212	.375	.170	36	118	17	25	4	0	1	10	12	3	0	0	38	5	2	.271	.301
Brayan Oropeza	R-R	6-1	175	11-18-03	.220	.143	.246	28	82	14	18	5	0	3	13	16	4	0	1	23	1	0	.390	.369
Yeison Perez	L-L	5-10	165	1-13-04	.331	.276	.346	42	136	29	45	15	4	7	40	16	4	0	3	38	3	1	.654	.409
Edgardo Reyes	R-R	6-2	168	12-16-04	.145	.059	.169	28	76	3	11	1	0	0	5	10	5	0	0	28	1	0	.158	.286
Erick Reyes	R-R	5-10	145	4-17-04	.167	.059	.204	32	66	21	11	2	1	2	8	24	1	0	1	25	13	1	.318	.391
2-team total (1 DSL Brewers 1)					.176	.059	.216	33	68	21	12	2	1	2	8	24	1	0	1	25	14	1	.324	.394
Donis Rodriguez	B-R	5-8	150	8-30-05	.176	.125	.188	33	85	14	15	1	0	0	8	22	3	0	2	23	9	3	.188	.357
Edwin Tamoy	R-R	6-0	170	10-20-04	.244	.091	.300	14	41	7	10	1	0	1	3	2	1	0	0	10	0	0	.341	.295
Ludwin Tejada	L-R	5-10	175	5-12-05	.375	--	.375	3	8	2	3	0	1	0	1	0	0	0	0	2	1	0	.625	.375
2-team total (19 DSL Brewers 1)					.283	.222	.294	22	60	7	17	1	1	0	6	10	0	0	0	9	2	0	.333	.386
Jamal Zalm	R-R	5-10	155	9-21-02	.316	1.000	.235	4	19	3	6	1	0	0	2	1	0	0	0	2	0	0	.368	.350

Pitching	B-T	HT	WT	DOB	W	L	ERA	G	GS	CG	SV	IP	H	R	ER	HR	BB	SO	AVG	vLH	vRH	K/9	BB/9
Braudin Ciprian	R-R	6-2	220	3-20-01	0	0	5.87	8	0	0	0	8	10	7	5	0	5	7	.303	.286	.308	8.22	5.87
2-team total (3 DSL Brewers 1)					0	1	5.56	11	0	0	0	11	12	15	7	0	9	9	.245	.214	.257	7.15	7.15
Daniel Corniel	R-R	6-0	177	7-7-04	1	4	4.97	10	9	0	0	42	40	31	23	3	14	47	.244	.235	.250	10.15	3.02
Nelson Cuevas	R-R	6-2	145	4-25-01	1	4	2.78	18	0	0	4	23	20	13	7	1	11	21	.233	.200	.246	8.34	4.37
Felipe De Los Santos	R-R	6-0	180	11-29-02	2	1	3.47	6	4	0	0	23	17	9	9	2	14	27	.207	.182	.224	10.41	5.40
Franddy De Los Santos	R-R	6-2	175	3-3-04	0	1	13.91	11	0	0	0	11	10	19	17	1	23	16	.244	.364	.200	13.09	18.82
David Dominguez	L-L	6-2	185	11-10-03	4	0	3.76	13	0	0	0	26	19	12	11	3	14	30	.200	.267	.188	10.25	4.78
Stanley Encarnacion	R-R	6-1	185	11-22-01	1	4	5.40	14	1	0	0	28	27	18	17	1	9	27	.257	.359	.197	8.58	2.86
Anthony Flores	L-L	5-11	165	10-21-04	2	5	5.97	11	7	0	0	35	36	30	23	0	22	30	.275	.176	.309	7.79	5.71
Dencer Geraldo	R-R	6-1	160	3-5-03	1	0	6.16	12	6	0	0	31	31	26	21	0	21	25	.279	.208	.345	7.34	6.16
Jose Meneses	L-L	6-1	150	3-9-05	2	2	3.68	14	0	0	0	22	15	11	9	1	21	19	.197	.063	.233	7.77	8.59
Daurys Mora	R-R	5-10	180	1-20-04	1	3	5.50	10	9	0	0	34	37	23	21	3	11	31	.276	.317	.258	8.13	2.88
Roman Perez	R-R	6-4	180	10-26-00	0	1	6.45	16	0	0	3	22	22	18	16	3	15	27	.250	.241	.254	10.88	6.04
Anfernny Reyes	L-L	6-3	170	2-23-04	2	0	1.54	11	11	0	0	47	45	18	8	0	24	48	.251	.162	.275	9.26	4.63
Reybert Reyes	R-R	6-3	183	1-20-03	0	2	9.49	11	0	0	0	12	15	15	13	0	11	11	.294	.381	.233	8.03	8.03
Waldin Rodriguez	R-R	6-3	176	1-5-02	3	1	5.79	17	0	0	3	19	16	12	12	1	14	19	.246	.250	.244	9.16	6.75
Darling Solano	R-R	6-1	165	12-25-03	1	3	6.42	11	7	0	1	34	22	30	24	1	30	49	.179	.244	.141	13.10	8.02
Hamlet Vasquez	R-R	6-3	175	9-9-02	1	0	6.00	7	0	0	0	6	11	4	4	0	3	5	.440	.400	.467	7.50	4.50
2-team total (8 DSL Brewers 1)					1	0	3.96	15	0	0	0	25	30	19	11	0	16	21	.303	.311	.296	7.56	5.76
Jeral Vizcaino	R-R	6-1	155	1-7-02	5	1	1.46	12	5	0	0	37	25	8	6	2	13	38	.191	.196	.187	9.24	3.16

Fielding

C: Lozano 2, Martinez 27, Oropeza 22, Tamoy 13, Tejada 2. **1B:** Martinez 5, Oropeza 5, Perez 30, Reyes 13, Reyes 9, Tejada 1, Zalm 1. **2B:** Baez 5, Nadal 22, Reyes 6, Reyes 5, Rodriguez 25, Zalm 1. **3B:** Baez 10, Barrios 23, Nadal 7, Reyes 6, Reyes 13, Rodriguez 2, Zalm 1. **SS:** Baez 37, Barrios 8, Nadal 16. **OF:** Batista 42, Ferreira 26, Gonzalez 36, Igualas 42, Nina 31, Perez 10, Rodriguez 1

Minnesota Twins

SEASON IN A SENTENCE: Minnesota led the American League Central from mid-April through much of the season and stood tied with Cleveland as late as Sept. 4. The Twins' injuries, especially to the lineup, and the Guardians' fast finish led to a September collapse as Minnesota finished 14 games out, in third place, with a record just five games better than 2021.

HIGH POINT: The Twins held first place for 92 days but peaked in May, when center fielder Byron Buxton was on fire. His walk-off home run off Chicago's Liam Hendriks on April 24 was one of his more electrifying moments, as was a walk-off against the Orioles July 1 that blunted the blow of a previous series loss to Cleveland.

LOW POINT: A 6-13 mark against the Guardians was punctuated in that September swoon, when Minnesota was swept at home and lost four of five at Cleveland to finish off the race. The latter series included an excruciating 7-6 15-inning loss on Sept. 17, the longest extra-inning game in MLB in 2022. It capped a doubleheader sweep and snuffed the Twins' last hope.

NOTABLE ROOKIES: Joe Ryan was the club's steadiest starting pitcher, overcoming a bout with Covid to lead the club in wins (13), innings (147) and strikeouts (151, a franchise rookie record). Jhoan Duran saved Minnesota's bullpen, ranking second among all relievers in Win Probability Added (4.6) while going 2-4, 1.86 with eight saves and breaking all the Twins records for hardest pitches thrown. Corner infielder Jose Miranda rallied from a slow start to lead the team in RBIs (66) during a .268/.325/.426 campaign with 15 homers.

KEY TRANSACTIONS: Minnesota raised hopes by signing shortstop Carlos Correa when the lockout ended to a three-year, $105.3 million contract with opt-outs after every season When he injured his finger, top prospect Royce Lewis was promoted to the majors for the first time but re-injured the same anterior cruciate ligament that cost him the 2021 season. Injuries to players from Lewis to August deadline acquisition Tyler Mahle to spring trade pickup Chris Paddack crippled the Twins, who lost more than 2,300 days to the injured list, second-most in baseball.

ON THE FARM: Injuries hurt at the minor league level too, but before he was shut down with a knee injury, outfielder Emmanuel Rodriguez was one of the best young hitters in Class A.

OPENING DAY PAYROLL: $136,908,190 (16th).

PLAYERS OF THE YEAR

MAJOR LEAGUE

Carlos Correa
SS

.291/.366/.467
22 HR, 24 2B in 136 G
5.2 oWAR 10th in AL

MINOR LEAGUE

Louie Varland
RHP

(AA/AAA)
3.06 ERA, 1.26 WHIP
146 SO, 42 BB, 126 IP

MIKE JANES/FOUR SEAM IMAGES

ORGANIZATION LEADERS

Batting — *Minimum 250 AB

MAJORS		
* AVG	Luis Arraez	.316
* OPS	Carlos Correa	.834
HR	Byron Buxton	28
RBI	Jose Miranda	66
MINORS		
* AVG	Christian Encarnacion-Strand, Cedar Rapids, Wichita	.302
* OBP	Edouard Julien, Wichita	.441
* SLG	Christian Encarnacion-Strand, Cedar Rapids, Wichita	.612
* OPS	Christian Encarnacion-Strand, Cedar Rapids, Wichita	.987
R	Michael Helman, St. Paul, Wichita	101
H	Anthony Prato, Wichita, Cedar Rapids	136
TB	Matt Wallner, Wichita, St. Paul	248
2B	Matt Wallner, Wichita, St. Paul	32
3B	Anthony Prato, Wichita, Cedar Rapids	8
HR	Chris Williams, Wichita, St. Paul	28
RBI	Matt Wallner, Wichita, St. Paul	95
BB	Edouard Julien, Wichita	98
SO	Matt Wallner, Wichita, St. Paul	170
SB	Mikey Perez, Fort Myers, Cedar Rapids, St. Paul	48

Pitching — #Minimum 75 IP

MAJORS		
W	Joe Ryan	13
# ERA	Sonny Gray	3.08
SO	Joe Ryan	151
SV	Emilio Pagan	9
MINORS		
W	Kody Funderburk, Wichita	10
	Brent Headrick, Cedar Rapids, Wichita	10
L	Travis Adams, Fort Myers, Cedar Rapids	8
	Cade Povich, Cedar Rapids	8
# ERA	Cody Laweryson, Wichita, Cedar Rapids	1.62
G	Evan Sisk, St. Paul, Wichita	50
GS	Brent Headrick, Cedar Rapids, Wichita	23
	Louie Varland, Wichita, St. Paul	23
SV	Austin Schulfer, St. Paul, Wichita	8
	Brad Peacock, St. Paul	8
IP	Louie Varland, Wichita, St. Paul	126.1
BB	Daniel Gossett, Wichita, St. Paul	50
SO	Louie Varland, Wichita, St. Paul	146
# AVG	Cody Laweryson, Wichita, Cedar Rapids	.198

2022 PERFORMANCE

General Manager: Thad Levine. **Farm Director:** Alex Hassan. **Scouting Director:** Sean Johnson.

Class	Team	League	W	L	PCT	Finish	Manager
Majors	Minnesota Twins	American	78	84	.481	t-9th (15)	Rocco Baldelli
Triple-A	St. Paul Saints	International	74	75	.497	t-10th (15)	Toby Gardenhire
Double-A	Wichita Wind Surge	Texas	78	59	.569	1st (10)	Ramon Borrego
High-A	Cedar Rapids Kernels	Midwest	73	58	.557	3rd (12)	Brian Dinkelman
Low-A	Fort Myers Mighty Mussels	Florida State	69	59	.539	2nd (10)	Brian Meyer
Rookie	FCL Twins	Florida Complex	25	30	.455	12th (16)	Seth Feldman
Overall 2022 Minor League Record			351	309	.532	5th (30)	

ORGANIZATION STATISTICS

MINNESOTA TWINS

AMERICAN LEAGUE

Batting	B-T	HT	WT	DOB	AVG	vLH	vRH	G	AB	R	H	2B	3B	HR	RBI	BB	HBP	SH	SF	SO	SB	CS	SLG	OBP
Luis Arraez	L-R	5-10	175	4-8-97	.316	.266	.330	144	547	88	173	31	1	8	49	50	3	0	3	43	4	4	.420	.375
Tim Beckham	R-R	6-0	215	1-27-90	.080	.077	.083	12	25	1	2	0	0	0	1	0	0	0	0	9	0	0	.080	.080
Byron Buxton	R-R	6-2	190	12-18-93	.224	.252	.211	92	340	61	76	13	3	28	51	34	7	0	1	116	6	0	.526	.306
Jake Cave	L-L	6-0	200	12-4-92	.213	.273	.199	54	164	17	35	7	3	5	20	11	0	0	2	49	2	0	.384	.260
Gilberto Celestino	R-L	6-0	170	2-13-99	.238	.213	.251	122	311	30	74	12	1	2	24	32	2	2	0	77	4	1	.302	.313
Mark Contreras	L-R	6-0	195	1-24-95	.121	.071	.136	28	58	9	7	1	0	3	6	1	1	0	1	21	1	0	.293	.148
Carlos Correa	R-R	6-4	220	9-22-94	.291	.299	.289	136	522	70	152	24	1	22	64	61	3	0	4	121	0	1	.467	.366
Kyle Garlick	R-R	6-1	210	1-26-92	.233	.243	.224	66	150	23	35	3	0	9	18	8	3	0	1	48	0	0	.433	.284
Jose Godoy	L-R	5-11	200	10-13-94	.000	.000	.000	2	3	2	0	0	0	0	0	2	0	0	0	2	0	0	.000	.000
2-team total (8 Pittsburgh Pirates)					.050	.000	.056	10	20	3	1	0	0	0	1	2	0	0	0	9	0	0	.050	.136
Nick Gordon	L-R	6-0	160	10-24-95	.272	.267	.329	138	405	45	110	28	4	9	50	19	10	3	6	105	6	4	.427	.316
Caleb Hamilton	R-R	6-0	185	2-5-95	.056	.143	.000	22	18	5	1	0	0	1	1	4	0	1	0	14	0	0	.222	.227
Billy Hamilton	R-R	6-0	160	9-9-90	.000	.000	.000	17	7	4	0	0	0	0	0	1	0	0	0	4	3	1	.125	.000
2-team total (20 Miami Marlins)					.050	.000	.083	37	20	13	1	0	0	0	0	2	0	1	0	12	10	1	.050	.136
Ryan Jeffers	R-R	6-4	235	6-3-97	.208	.307	.167	67	212	25	44	10	1	7	27	23	0	1	0	62	0	0	.363	.285
Max Kepler	L-L	6-4	225	2-10-93	.227	.243	.221	115	388	54	88	18	1	9	43	49	5	0	4	66	3	2	.348	.318
Alex Kirilloff	L-L	6-2	195	11-9-97	.250	.167	.267	45	144	14	36	7	0	3	21	5	4	0	2	36	0	0	.361	.290
Trevor Larnach	L-R	6-4	223	2-26-97	.231	.277	.212	51	160	22	37	13	0	5	18	18	0	0	2	57	0	0	.406	.306
Sandy Leon	B-R	5-10	235	3-13-89	.179	.250	.116	25	56	6	10	3	0	0	4	7	0	2	0	23	0	0	.232	.270
2-team total (9 Cleveland Guardians)					.169	.250	.116	34	71	6	12	3	0	0	4	13	0	2	0	27	0	0	.211	.298
Royce Lewis	R-R	6-2	200	6-5-99	.300	.375	.281	12	40	5	12	4	0	2	5	1	0	0	0	5	0	0	.550	.317
Jose Miranda	R-R	6-2	210	6-29-98	.268	.275	.265	125	444	45	119	25	0	15	66	28	10	0	1	91	1	1	.426	.325
Jermaine Palacios	R-R	6-0	145	7-19-96	.143	.133	.150	30	70	8	10	0	0	2	6	4	0	1	2	27	0	0	.229	.184
Jorge Polanco	B-R	5-11	208	7-5-93	.235	.226	.240	104	375	54	88	16	0	16	56	64	2	0	4	95	3	3	.405	.346
Gary Sanchez	R-R	6-2	230	12-2-92	.205	.165	.219	128	419	42	86	24	0	16	61	40	7	0	5	136	2	0	.377	.282
Miguel Sanó	R-R	6-4	272	5-11-93	.083	.087	.081	20	60	1	5	0	0	1	3	9	1	0	1	25	1	0	.133	.211
Gio Urshela	R-R	6-0	215	10-11-91	.285	.291	.283	144	501	61	143	27	3	13	64	41	2	0	7	96	1	0	.429	.338
Matt Wallner	L-R	6-5	220	12-12-97	.228	.118	.275	18	57	4	13	3	0	2	10	6	2	0	0	25	1	0	.386	.323

Pitching	B-T	HT	WT	DOB	W	L	ERA	G	GS	CG	SV	IP	H	R	ER	HR	BB	SO	AVG	vLH	vRH	K/9	BB/9
Jorge Alcala	R-R	6-3	205	7-28-95	0	0	0.00	2	0	0	0	2.1	2	0	0	0	2	2	.250	1.000	.000	7.71	7.71
Chris Archer	R-R	6-2	195	9-26-88	2	8	4.56	25	25	0	0	102.2	87	56	52	12	48	84	.228	.190	.254	7.36	4.21
Dylan Bundy	B-R	6-1	225	11-15-92	8	8	4.89	29	29	0	0	140	151	79	76	24	28	94	.271	.254	.284	6.04	1.80
Yennier Cano	R-R	6-4	185	3-9-94	1	0	9.22	10	0	0	0	13.2	17	14	14	3	11	14	.304	.400	.250	9.22	7.24
2-team total (3 Baltimore Orioles)					1	1	11.50	13	0	0	0	18	26	23	23	3	16	21	.333	.407	.294	8.00	10.50
Jharel Cotton	R-R	5-11	200	1-19-92	2	2	2.83	25	0	0	0	35	23	13	11	7	16	31	.185	.214	.162	7.97	4.11
2-teams (5 San Francisco Giants)					4	2	3.56	30	0	0	0	43	34	20	17	7	20	39	.218	.239	.202	8.16	4.19
Danny Coulombe	L-L	5-10	190	10-26-89	0	0	1.46	10	0	0	0	12.1	7	3	2	0	9	9	.163	.167	.160	6.57	6.57
Austin Davis	L-R	6-4	235	2-3-93	0	0	16.20	2	0	0	0	1.2	1	3	3	0	4	3	.167	.000	.160	16.20	21.60
2-teams (50 games Boston Red Sox)					2	1	5.79	52	3	0	0	56	57	39	36	5	33	64	.258	.198	.293	10.29	5.30
Tyler Duffey	R-R	6-3	220	12-27-90	2	4	4.91	40	0	0	2	44	45	24	24	8	15	39	.268	.271	.265	7.98	3.07
Jhoan Duran	R-R	6-5	230	1-8-98	2	4	1.86	57	0	0	8	67.2	50	15	14	6	16	89	.207	.204	.209	11.84	2.13
Michael Fulmer	R-R	6-3	224	3-15-93	2	2	3.70	26	0	0	1	24.1	30	10	10	3	8	22	.313	.395	.259	8.14	2.96
2-teams (41 Detroit Tigers)					2	2	3.70	67	0	0	3	63.2	59	27	24	4	28	61	.247	.337	.188	8.62	3.96
Chi Chi González	R-R	6-3	210	1-15-92	0	0	7.71	2	2	0	0	7	12	6	6	2	0	4	.387	.333	.421	5.14	0.00
3-teams (4 Milwaukee Brewers, 1 New York Yankees)					0	1	5.87	7	5	0	0	23	28	15	15	5	7	15	.304	.275	.327	5.87	2.74
Nick Gordon	L-R	6-0	160	10-24-95	0	0	22.09	4	0	0	0	3.2	10	9	9	2	4	0	.476	.250	.529	0.00	9.82
Sonny Gray	R-R	5-10	195	11-7-89	8	5	3.08	24	24	0	0	119.2	99	44	41	11	36	117	.224	.250	.244	8.80	2.71
Ian Hamilton	R-R	6-1	200	6-16-95	0	0	6.75	1	0	0	0	2.2	3	2	2	1	1	0	.300	.000	.333	0.00	3.38
Ronny Henriquez	R-R	5-10	155	6-20-00	0	1	2.31	3	0	0	0	11.2	8	4	3	1	3	9	.178	.130	.227	6.94	2.31
Griffin Jax	R-R	6-2	195	11-22-94	7	4	3.36	65	0	0	1	72.1	56	29	27	7	20	78	.212	.189	.224	9.71	2.49
Jorge López	R-R	6-3	200	2-10-93	0	1	4.37	23	0	0	4	22.2	23	11	11	1	14	18	.271	.250	.286	7.15	5.56
2-teams (44 Baltimore Orioles)					4	7	2.54	67	0	0	23	71	53	26	20	4	31	72	.206	.218	.199	9.13	3.93
Tyler Mahle	R-R	6-3	210	9-29-94	1	1	4.41	4	4	0	0	16.1	13	8	8	4	4	12	.220	.063	.279	6.61	2.20

2-teams (19 Cincinnati Reds)					6	8	4.40	23	23	0	0	120.2	104	61	59	16	43	126	.230	.192	.268	9.40	3.21
Trevor Megill	L-R	6-3	200	2-10-93	4	3	4.80	39	0	0	0	45	50	29	24	4	17	49	.282	.250	.307	9.80	3.40
Juan Minaya	R-R	6-4	210	9-18-90	1	0	5.59	6	0	0	0	9.2	8	6	6	0	5	11	.216	.125	.286	10.24	4.66
Jovani Moran	L-L	6-1	167	4-24-97	0	1	2.21	31	0	0	1	40.2	25	11	10	0	18	54	.172	.229	.144	11.95	3.98
Bailey Ober	R-R	6-9	260	7-12-95	2	3	3.21	11	11	0	0	56	48	22	20	4	11	51	.227	.258	.205	8.20	1.77
Chris Paddack	R-R	6-5	217	1-8-96	1	2	4.03	5	5	0	0	22.1	25	10	10	0	2	20	.284	.324	.259	8.06	0.81
Emilio Pagán	L-R	6-2	208	5-7-91	4	6	4.43	59	0	0	9	63	60	36	31	12	26	84	.245	.213	.270	12.00	3.71
Jermaile Palacios	R-R	6-0	145	7-19-96	0	0	0.00	2	0	0	0	0.2	1	0	0	0	0	1	.333	.000	.500	13.50	0.00
Dereck Rodríguez	R-R	6-0	208	6-5-92	0	1	3.52	2	0	0	0	7.2	7	5	3	3	4	4	.250	.444	.158	4.70	4.70
Jhon Romero	R-R	5-10	195	1-17-95	0	0	3.60	4	0	0	0	5	9	2	2	0	1	6	.391	.625	.267	10.80	1.80
Joe Ryan	R-R	6-2	205	6-5-96	13	8	3.55	27	27	0	0	147	115	60	58	20	47	151	.211	.202	.219	9.24	2.88
Aaron Sanchez	R-R	6-4	212	7-1-92	0	1	4.71	8	3	0	0	28.2	31	16	15	2	7	25	.274	.262	.282	7.85	2.20
2-teams (7 Washington Nationals)					3	4	6.60	15	10	0	0	60	78	46	44	8	15	41	.324	.265	.364	6.15	2.25
Cole Sands	R-R	6-3	215	7-17-97	0	3	5.87	11	3	0	1	30.2	35	21	20	4	13	28	.276	.218	.319	8.22	3.82
Devin Smeltzer	R-L	6-3	195	9-7-95	5	2	3.71	15	12	0	0	70.1	67	30	29	13	19	40	.253	.308	.239	5.12	2.43
Joe Smith	R-R	6-2	211	3-22-84	1	1	4.61	34	0	0	0	27.1	33	18	14	7	9	17	.297	.303	.295	5.60	2.96
Cody Stashak	R-R	6-2	180	6-4-94	3	0	3.86	11	0	0	0	16.1	16	7	7	1	0	15	.250	.320	.205	8.27	0.00
Caleb Thielbar	R-L	6-0	205	1-31-87	4	3	3.49	67	0	0	1	59.1	51	26	23	5	18	80	.226	.225	.226	12.13	2.73
Tyler Thornburg	R-R	5-11	190	9-29-88	0	1	2.79	5	0	0	0	9.2	4	4	3	1	6	4	.121	.143	.213	3.72	5.59
2-teams (9 Atlanta Braves)					0	1	3.32	14	0	0	0	19	16	10	7	1	11	14	.216	.222	.213	6.63	5.21
Louie Varland	L-R	6-1	205	12-9-97	1	2	3.81	5	5	0	0	26	26	11	11	4	6	21	.263	.262	.263	7.27	2.08
Josh Winder	R-R	6-5	210	10-11-96	4	6	4.70	15	11	0	0	67	69	37	35	11	18	47	.264	.238	.282	6.31	2.42
Simeon Woods Richardson	R-R	6-3	210	9-27-00	0	1	3.60	1	1	0	0	5	3	3	2	1	2	3	.167	.125	.200	5.40	3.60

Fielding

Catcher	PCT	G	PO	A	E	DP	PB
Godoy	1.000	2	7	1	0	0	0
Hamilton	1.000	11	31	0	0	0	0
Jeffers	.994	59	475	14	3	2	5
Leon	.989	25	183	3	2	0	3
Sanchez	.994	91	678	37	4	4	4

First Base	PCT	G	PO	A	E	DP
Arraez	1.000	65	437	21	0	42
Beckham	1.000	2	8	1	0	2
Hamilton	1.000	6	17	1	0	2
Kirilloff	1.000	18	103	5	0	11
Miranda	.994	77	505	28	3	45
Palacios	1.000	1	5	0	0	1
Sanchez	1.000	1	0	1	0	0
Sano	.986	19	131	5	2	9

Second Base	PCT	G	PO	A	E	DP
Arraez	.992	41	44	75	1	17
Gordon	.966	36	46	67	4	16
Hamilton	1.000	1	2	0	0	0
Palacios	.864	12	7	12	3	2
Polanco	.979	97	167	215	8	55

Third Base	PCT	G	PO	A	E	DP
Arraez	.941	7	5	11	1	1
Gordon	1.000	1	0	2	0	0
Miranda	.952	34	18	41	3	6
Palacios	.000	1	0	0	0	0
Urshela	.983	136	100	237	6	25

Shortstop	PCT	G	PO	A	E	DP
Correa	.983	132	157	307	8	51
Gordon	.933	17	9	19	2	7
Lewis	.952	11	12	28	2	4
Palacios	.930	14	7	33	3	4
Polanco	1.000	6	1	8	0	0
Urshela	1.000	2	0	1	0	0

Outfield	PCT	G	PO	A	E	DP
Beckham	1.000	4	3	0	0	0
Buxton	1.000	57	133	3	0	2
Cave	.989	59	85	6	1	1
Celestino	.984	126	238	4	4	0
Contreras	.980	25	45	3	1	0
Garlick	.985	50	66	1	1	0
Gordon	.982	100	161	3	3	1
Hamilton	1.000	6	3	0	0	0
Kepler	.991	113	225	5	2	1
Kirilloff	.978	29	43	1	1	0
Larnach	1.000	44	83	4	0	0
Lewis	1.000	1	3	0	0	0
Wallner	.935	16	29	0	2	0

ST. PAUL SAINTS — *TRIPLE-A*

INTERNATIONAL LEAGUE

Batting	B-T	HT	WT	DOB	AVG	vLH	vRH	G	AB	R	H	2B	3B	HR	RBI	BB	HBP	SH	SF	SO	SB	CS	SLG	OBP
John Andreoli	R-R	6-1	218	6-9-90	.197	.149	.210	74	233	45	46	8	1	13	32	49	1	1	1	101	13	2	.408	.338
2-team total (36 Lehigh Valley IronPigs)					.184	.169	.188	110	337	60	62	11	2	15	43	78	1	3	2	150	19	3	.362	.337
David Banuelos	R-R	6-0	205	10-1-96	.204	.214	.200	55	181	25	37	7	0	8	26	15	2	1	0	61	0	1	.376	.273
Andrew Bechtold	R-R	6-1	185	4-18-96	.220	.259	.209	36	118	17	26	3	0	5	18	18	0	0	0	43	0	0	.373	.324
Tim Beckham	R-R	6-0	215	1-27-90	.413	.326	.458	34	126	18	52	6	0	5	31	14	3	0	0	31	2	1	.579	.483
Stevie Berman	R-R	6-2	225	11-28-94	.000	--	.000	1	3	0	0	0	0	0	0	1	0	0	0	0	0	0	.000	.250
2-team total (67 Buffalo Bisons)					.212	.203	.217	68	212	27	45	14	0	8	28	37	7	1	4	64	1	0	.392	.342
Braden Bishop	R-R	6-1	178	8-22-93	.229	.277	.197	41	118	17	27	5	1	4	16	9	2	0	1	35	5	1	.390	.292
Jake Cave	L-L	6-0	200	12-4-92	.273	.317	.252	85	322	63	88	20	7	14	57	43	7	0	1	93	10	0	.509	.370
Gilberto Celestino	R-L	6-0	170	2-13-99	.000	.000	.000	2	7	0	0	0	0	0	0	2	0	0	0	3	1	0	.000	.222
Mark Contreras	L-R	6-0	195	1-24-95	.237	.238	.236	102	376	64	89	21	1	15	59	37	8	0	2	125	23	2	.418	.317
Derek Fisher	L-R	6-3	215	8-21-93	.158	.083	.183	27	95	13	15	5	0	3	11	12	1	0	0	37	0	0	.305	.259
Kyle Garlick	R-R	6-1	210	1-26-92	.250	.429	.154	11	40	5	10	1	1	3	7	6	0	0	0	16	0	0	.550	.348
Jose Godoy	L-R	5-11	200	10-13-94	.197	.178	.207	43	137	13	27	5	0	3	14	13	1	0	0	41	0	0	.299	.272
2-team total (10 Indianapolis Indians)					.227	.200	.240	53	176	20	40	6	0	6	26	14	2	0	1	48	0	0	.364	.290
Billy Hamilton	R-R	6-0	160	9-9-90	.143	.000	.333	2	7	2	1	1	0	0	0	1	0	0	0	4	1	0	.286	.250
2-team total (1 Jacksonville Jumbo Shrimp)					.200	.143	.333	3	10	2	2	2	0	0	1	1	0	0	0	6	1	0	.400	.273
Caleb Hamilton	R-R	6-0	185	2-5-95	.233	.321	.172	62	206	34	48	10	0	11	43	43	1	0	1	67	1	0	.442	.367
Michael Helman	R-R	6-1	195	5-23-96	.250	.261	.245	96	368	67	92	17	1	14	40	40	3	0	4	80	30	5	.416	.325
Wander Javier	R-R	6-1	165	12-29-98	.100	.000	.111	7	20	1	2	0	0	1	3	3	1	0	1	13	0	0	.250	.240
Ryan Jeffers	R-R	6-4	235	6-3-97	.229	.500	.148	9	35	5	8	1	0	3	7	4	0	0	0	4	1	0	.514	.308
Alex Kirilloff	L-L	6-2	195	11-9-97	.359	.476	.303	35	131	33	47	7	0	10	32	22	4	0	0	26	1	0	.641	.465
Nash Knight	B-R	6-0	205	9-20-92	.226	.207	.233	36	115	17	26	7	0	2	11	17	2	0	0	46	0	0	.339	.336
Trevor Larnach	L-R	6-4	223	2-26-97	.222	.375	.179	10	36	1	8	0	0	0	2	4	0	0	1	11	0	0	.222	.293
Royce Lewis	R-R	6-2	200	6-5-99	.313	.259	.327	34	131	30	41	12	1	5	14	18	3	0	1	32	12	2	.534	.405
Kevin Merrell	L-R	6-1	180	12-14-95	.256	.286	.240	12	39	7	10	0	0	3	7	3	0	0	0	6	0	1	.487	.310
Jose Miranda	R-R	6-2	210	6-29-98	.256	.333	.243	21	86	10	22	10	0	2	12	5	1	0	3	14	0	0	.442	.295
Roy Morales	R-R	6-2	195	6-25-95	.301	.290	.309	47	163	26	49	7	0	4	34	26	4	0	1	24	3	1	.417	.407

Frank Nigro	R-R	6-4	200	8-1-97	.200	--	.200	5	10	1	2	0	0	0	0	0	0	1	0	7	0	0	.200	.200
Jermaine Palacios	R-R	6-0	145	7-19-96	.283	.315	.268	102	392	70	111	28	0	14	60	34	1	0	1	102	12	9	.462	.341
Mikey Perez	R-R	6-0	185	8-24-99	1.000	--	1.000	1	1	1	1	0	0	1	3	0	0	0	0	0	0	0	4.000	1.000
Jorge Polanco	B-R	5-11	208	7-5-93	.500	.500	--	1	2	0	1	0	0	0	1	1	0	0	0	0	0	0	.500	.667
Daniel Robertson	R-R	5-11	210	3-22-94	.183	.500	.104	17	60	8	11	2	0	1	10	7	1	0	0	13	0	0	.267	.279
2-team total (41 Lehigh Valley IronPigs)					.209	.326	.177	58	201	31	42	13	0	6	26	23	4	0	1	53	0	1	.363	.301
Jake Rucker	R-R	6-1	195	9-14-99	.115	.333	.087	9	26	3	3	0	0	1	3	2	1	0	1	10	1	0	.231	.200
Miguel Sano	R-R	6-4	272	5-11-93	.348	.000	.364	8	23	5	8	2	0	3	7	3	0	0	0	10	0	0	.826	.423
Dalton Shuffield	R-R	5-9	170	3-31-99	.271	.273	.270	14	48	5	13	3	2	2	9	3	0	0	0	14	1	0	.542	.314
Chance Sisco	L-R	6-3	210	2-24-95	.194	.167	.200	10	31	4	6	2	0	1	3	5	0	0	1	10	0	0	.355	.297
Elliot Soto	R-R	5-9	160	8-21-89	.223	.250	.211	92	301	48	67	20	2	4	32	40	3	0	0	77	9	1	.342	.320
Spencer Steer	R-R	5-11	185	12-7-97	.242	.300	.211	48	198	39	48	10	1	12	32	28	4	0	2	43	2	0	.485	.345
2-team total (23 Louisville Bats)					.259	.330	.228	71	290	53	75	17	1	15	45	37	7	0	2	66	3	0	.479	.354
Cole Sturgeon	L-L	6-0	180	9-17-91	.247	.208	.264	48	174	20	43	7	4	1	25	15	2	1	2	29	7	3	.351	.311
Curtis Terry	R-R	6-2	258	10-6-96	.250	.198	.275	80	296	41	74	19	2	10	32	40	5	0	1	56	0	0	.429	.348
Matt Wallner	L-R	6-5	220	12-12-97	.247	.271	.237	50	190	29	47	17	3	6	31	35	4	0	0	63	1	0	.463	.376
Chris Williams	R-R	6-1	225	11-23-96	.192	.154	.205	42	151	21	29	5	0	10	31	21	1	0	3	54	0	0	.424	.290
Ernie Yake	L-R	5-10	175	11-20-97	.267	.300	.200	6	15	3	4	0	0	0	3	1	0	0	1	1	0	0	.267	.294

Pitching	B-T	HT	WT	DOB	W	L	ERA	G	GS	CG	SV	IP	H	R	ER	HR	BB	SO	AVG	vLH	vRH	K/9	BB/9
Melvi Acosta	R-R	6-1	215	6-2-95	0	0	0.00	1	0	0	0	2	1	0	0	0	2	1	.167	.000	.333	4.50	9.00
Jordan Balazovic	R-R	6-5	215	9-17-98	0	7	7.39	22	21	0	0	71	102	66	58	20	35	76	.336	.401	.281	9.68	4.46
David Banuelos	R-R	6-0	205	10-1-96	0	0	0.00	1	0	0	0	0	0	0	0	0	0	0	.000	--	.000	0.00	0.00
Tyler Bashlor	R-R	6-0	195	4-16-93	2	1	3.86	7	0	0	0	7	5	4	3	1	9	7	.200	.143	.222	9.00	11.57
Tyler Beck	R-R	6-1	190	11-16-95	0	0	16.88	2	0	0	1	3	4	5	5	2	4	4	.333	.375	.250	13.50	13.50
Yennier Cano	R-R	6-4	185	3-9-94	1	1	1.90	20	0	0	3	24	16	6	5	2	6	25	.203	.195	.211	9.51	2.28
2-team total (11 Norfolk Tides)					1	2	2.90	31	0	0	4	40	33	17	13	5	14	45	.226	.211	.243	10.04	3.12
Jharel Cotton	R-R	5-11	200	1-19-92	4	1	2.88	22	0	0	1	25	17	8	8	4	10	39	.187	.180	.195	14.04	3.60
Danny Coulombe	L-L	5-10	190	10-26-89	0	0	9.00	1	0	0	0	1	2	1	1	1	0	1	.400	.500	.000	9.00	0.00
Randy Dobnak	R-R	6-1	230	1-17-95	1	2	5.40	8	3	0	0	20	18	12	12	3	16	19	.240	.222	.250	8.55	7.20
Jake Faria	R-R	6-4	230	7-30-93	1	2	7.48	12	9	0	0	43	52	40	36	9	27	39	.297	.237	.366	8.10	5.61
Michael Feliz	R-R	6-4	250	6-28-93	3	1	2.19	18	0	0	2	25	12	8	6	0	10	24	.145	.194	.115	8.76	3.65
2-team total (18 Worcester Red Sox)					3	2	2.74	36	3	0	2	49	32	18	15	1	19	52	.186	.191	.183	9.49	3.47
Chi Chi Gonzalez	R-R	6-3	210	1-15-92	2	2	3.44	8	5	0	0	37	32	16	14	3	14	35	.237	.254	.221	8.59	3.44
3-team total (5 S./W.-B. RailRiders, 5 Toledo Mud Hens)					2	3	4.03	18	14	0	0	80	82	38	36	8	27	71	.265	.280	.247	7.95	3.02
Jordan Gore	B-R	6-0	180	8-3-94	0	1	7.47	15	0	0	1	16	23	14	13	2	13	10	.354	.375	.333	5.74	7.47
Daniel Gossett	R-R	6-0	185	11-13-92	2	2	8.63	13	5	0	0	32	47	34	31	6	21	23	.348	.364	.328	6.40	5.85
Ian Hamilton	R-R	6-1	200	6-16-95	2	3	1.88	23	0	0	1	29	16	9	6	3	8	36	.158	.161	.156	11.30	2.51
2-team total (15 Columbus Clippers)					2	7	3.61	38	0	0	2	47	33	23	19	6	19	60	.191	.177	.202	11.41	3.61
Ben Heller	R-R	6-3	210	8-5-91	0	0	21.60	3	0	0	0	2	4	5	4	2	3	3	.400	.000	.500	16.20	16.20
Ronny Henriquez	R-R	5-10	155	6-20-00	3	4	5.66	24	14	0	1	95	99	60	60	19	33	106	.266	.233	.292	10.01	3.12
Griffin Jax	R-R	6-2	195	11-22-94	1	0	0.00	1	0	0	0	2	0	0	0	0	1	2	.000	.000	.000	9.00	4.50
Jake Jewell	R-R	6-2	217	5-16-93	0	0	5.68	9	0	0	1	13	12	11	8	1	6	17	.245	.227	.259	12.08	4.26
2-team total (36 Columbus Clippers)					2	2	3.21	45	0	0	5	56	41	25	20	1	21	65	.197	.167	.218	10.45	3.38
Ariel Jurado	R-R	6-2	240	1-30-96	2	2	3.54	14	7	0	1	53	40	23	21	7	12	44	.211	.239	.184	7.43	2.03
Nash Knight	B-R	6-0	205	9-20-92	0	0	9.00	1	0	0	0	1	2	1	1	0	0	0	.400	.333	.500	0.00	0.00
Ryan Mason	R-R	6-6	215	10-4-94	0	0	3.18	5	0	0	0	6	3	3	2	1	6	9	.150	.125	.167	14.29	9.53
Trevor Megill	L-R	6-8	250	12-5-93	0	2	3.00	10	0	0	2	12	11	6	4	2	4	16	.282	.278	.286	12.00	3.00
Juan Minaya	R-R	6-4	210	9-18-90	1	5	6.98	29	1	0	4	40	41	33	31	6	20	36	.265	.267	.263	8.10	4.50
2-team total (6 Rochester Red Wings)					1	7	6.29	35	1	0	4	49	46	37	34	8	26	42	.250	.244	.255	7.77	4.81
Roy Morales	R-R	6-2	195	6-25-95	0	0	0.00	1	0	0	0	0	0	0	0	0	1	0	.000	.000	--	0.00	27.00
Jovani Moran	L-L	6-1	167	4-24-97	1	2	6.00	20	0	0	0	24	25	16	16	2	14	43	.260	.214	.296	16.13	5.25
Matt Mullenbach	R-R	6-4	195	10-6-96	0	0	9.00	2	0	0	0	3	5	3	3	0	1	3	.385	.250	.444	9.00	3.00
Bailey Ober	R-R	6-9	260	7-12-95	0	1	4.66	2	2	0	0	10	5	6	5	2	2	13	.147	.333	.080	12.10	1.86
Brad Peacock	R-R	6-1	207	2-2-88	3	3	3.38	20	0	0	8	21	14	10	8	3	10	22	.189	.129	.233	9.28	4.22
2-team total (35 Omaha Storm Chasers)					5	4	2.26	55	0	0	15	60	47	19	15	5	26	67	.216	.244	.195	10.11	3.92
Jake Petricka	R-R	6-4	218	6-5-88	0	1	4.18	21	0	0	2	24	24	12	11	1	8	22	.253	.289	.220	8.37	3.04
Wladimir Pinto	R-R	5-11	170	2-12-98	3	4	2.08	25	0	0	1	35	26	17	8	3	27	43	.198	.254	.147	11.16	7.01
JC Ramirez	R-R	6-4	220	8-16-88	3	0	5.66	16	2	0	0	35	34	22	22	6	21	28	.262	.291	.240	7.20	5.40
Dereck Rodriguez	R-R	6-0	208	6-5-92	8	4	4.75	23	16	0	0	95	93	54	50	13	32	92	.254	.228	.277	8.75	3.04
Joe Ryan	R-R	6-2	205	6-5-96	0	0	0.00	1	1	0	0	3	1	0	0	0	0	4	.091	.167	.000	12.00	0.00
Aaron Sanchez	R-R	6-4	212	7-1-92	3	2	3.80	10	10	0	0	47	43	24	20	7	15	33	.246	.250	.242	6.27	2.85
2-team total (3 Rochester Red Wings)					4	2	3.75	13	13	0	0	62	60	30	26	9	20	43	.260	.234	.283	6.21	2.89
Mario Sanchez	R-R	6-1	166	10-31-94	6	4	4.24	28	13	0	1	91	78	45	43	12	26	70	.231	.252	.216	6.90	2.56
Cole Sands	R-R	6-3	215	7-17-97	3	6	5.55	19	13	0	0	62	78	42	38	9	24	72	.310	.299	.320	10.51	3.50
Austin Schulfer	R-R	6-2	175	12-22-95	4	3	5.23	29	1	0	1	33	30	20	19	4	13	31	.256	.256	.257	8.54	3.58
Evan Sisk	L-L	6-2	209	4-23-97	2	1	2.08	31	0	0	0	35	19	11	8	0	18	43	.164	.088	.237	11.16	4.67
Devin Smeltzer	R-L	6-3	195	9-7-95	3	4	7.56	15	9	0	0	50	64	44	42	10	16	47	.309	.259	.329	8.46	2.88
Brock Stewart	L-R	6-3	220	10-3-91	0	1	6.14	7	0	0	0	7	9	6	5	2	1	11	.290	.333	.273	13.50	1.23
Drew Strotman	R-R	6-3	195	9-3-96	3	2	6.44	39	0	0	0	50	53	40	36	6	33	58	.266	.296	.246	10.37	5.90
Caleb Thielbar	R-L	6-0	205	1-31-87	0	0	0.00	1	0	0	0	1	0	0	0	0	0	1	.000	.000	.000	9.00	0.00
Tyler Thornburg	R-R	5-11	190	9-29-88	1	0	5.65	13	0	0	0	14	17	12	9	1	6	15	.288	.267	.295	9.42	3.77
Lewis Thorpe	R-L	6-1	218	11-23-95	0	0	43.20	1	1	0	0	2	6	8	8	2	2	2	.545	.800	.333	10.80	10.80
Louie Varland	L-R	6-1	205	12-9-97	1	1	1.69	4	4	0	0	21	15	5	4	1	3	27	.192	.069	.265	11.39	1.27
Tyler Viza	R-R	6-3	170	10-21-94	3	0	7.08	15	0	0	0	20	25	17	16	3	7	21	.294	.304	.282	9.30	3.10

Josh Winder	R-R	6-5	210	10-11-96	0	0	3.38	5	5	0	0	16	11	7	6	3	6	11	.186	.158	.200	6.19	3.38
Hunter Wood	R-R	6-1	175	8-12-93	0	0	2.08	8	0	0	0	9	2	2	2	1	10	10	.071	.000	.133	10.38	10.38
Simeon Woods Richardson	R-R	6-3	210	9-27-00	2	0	2.21	7	7	0	0	37	21	10	9	2	10	38	.165	.186	.155	9.33	2.45

Fielding

Catcher	PCT	G	PO	A	E	DP	PB
Banuelos	.988	51	471	27	6	4	6
Bechtold	1.000	8	58	4	0	0	2
Berman	1.000	1	10	0	0	0	0
Godoy	.991	38	329	15	3	2	5
Hamilton	.986	31	267	15	4	2	5
Jeffers	.952	4	37	3	2	0	1
Morales	1.000	9	64	6	0	0	1
Nigro	1.000	4	27	1	0	0	0
Sisco	1.000	7	54	5	0	2	0
Williams	.926	6	50	0	4	0	0

First Base	PCT	G	PO	A	E	DP
Bechtold	1.000	6	44	0	0	3
Beckham	1.000	5	22	2	0	2
Hamilton	1.000	4	4	1	0	0
Helman	.947	5	16	2	1	0
Kirilloff	.983	14	107	6	2	9
Knight	1.000	6	35	4	0	6
Miranda	1.000	5	47	2	0	4
Morales	.995	25	175	7	1	19
Palacios	1.000	1	2	1	0	0
Sano	.985	6	65	1	1	4
Terry	.989	60	414	40	5	42
Williams	1.000	26	196	12	0	16

Second Base	PCT	G	PO	A	E	DP
Banuelos	1.000	1	1	2	0	1
Bechtold	.969	9	17	14	1	4
Beckham	.911	10	18	23	4	5
Helman	.994	36	55	101	1	21
Knight	.966	9	13	15	1	4
Merrell	1.000	10	5	18	0	1
Palacios	1.000	2	3	6	0	1
Polanco	1.000	1	1	2	0	0
Robertson	.970	11	11	21	1	5
Rucker	1.000	4	4	5	0	2
Shuffield	.933	10	11	17	2	3
Soto	1.000	33	50	75	0	20
Steer	.952	15	15	45	3	6
Yake	1.000	4	7	12	0	2

Third Base	PCT	G	PO	A	E	DP
Bechtold	.966	12	8	20	1	0
Beckham	.857	9	4	14	3	1
Hamilton	.955	11	9	12	1	1
Helman	1.000	15	9	22	0	3
Javier	1.000	1	1	4	0	1
Knight	.960	18	7	41	2	1
Lewis	1.000	2	0	4	0	0
Merrell	.000	1	0	0	0	0
Miranda	.933	14	13	29	3	6
Palacios	.909	33	28	62	9	6
Robertson	1.000	2	2	4	0	2
Rucker	.833	4	1	4	1	0
Soto	.966	12	11	17	1	1
Steer	.932	26	10	45	4	5

Shortstop	PCT	G	PO	A	E	DP
Bechtold	1.000	1	1	3	0	0
Beckham	1.000	2	5	6	0	0
Helman	.962	13	18	33	2	5
Javier	.960	6	9	15	1	5
Lewis	.957	26	33	56	4	10
Palacios	.942	56	60	120	11	20
Robertson	1.000	1	1	3	0	1
Shuffield	1.000	4	7	7	0	3
Soto	.975	43	54	102	4	21
Steer	1.000	4	5	14	0	3

Outfield	PCT	G	PO	A	E	DP
Andreoli	.979	69	143	0	3	0
Bishop	.984	37	57	4	1	2
Cave	.987	81	149	6	2	0
Celestino	1.000	2	1	1	0	0
Contreras	.982	91	159	8	3	3
Fisher	1.000	24	36	2	0	1
Garlick	1.000	7	5	0	0	0
Hamilton	1.000	1	1	0	0	0
Helman	.986	28	64	4	1	3
Kirilloff	.971	15	32	1	1	0
Knight	1.000	3	2	0	0	0
Larnach	1.000	7	10	0	0	0
Lewis	1.000	3	7	1	0	0
Merrell	.500	1	1	1	2	0
Morales	--	1	0	0	0	0
Palacios	1.000	9	14	2	0	0
Soto	1.000	6	7	1	0	0
Sturgeon	.960	38	68	4	3	2
Wallner	.976	40	78	4	2	1
Williams	.833	6	5	0	1	0

WICHITA WIND SURGE — *DOUBLE-A*

TEXAS LEAGUE

Batting	B-T	HT	WT	DOB	AVG	vLH	vRH	G	AB	R	H	2B	3B	HR	RBI	BB	HBP	SH	SF	SO	SB	CS	SLG	OBP
Andrew Bechtold	R-R	6-1	185	4-18-96	.238	.293	.218	87	320	43	76	13	0	14	41	45	0	0	1	93	2	1	.409	.331
Leobaldo Cabrera	R-R	6-1	170	1-21-98	.223	.262	.210	83	256	35	57	11	1	7	27	28	4	0	0	89	6	3	.355	.309
Jair Camargo	R-R	5-10	230	7-1-99	.239	.245	.236	46	176	24	42	5	0	12	33	16	2	0	2	66	4	2	.472	.306
Christian Encarnacion-Strand	R-R	6-0	224	12-1-99	.333	.188	.395	13	54	11	18	2	1	5	17	4	2	0	0	14	1	1	.685	.400
Seth Gray	L-R	6-3	205	5-30-98	.091	.143	.067	7	22	2	2	0	0	1	1	4	0	0	0	10	0	0	.227	.231
Michael Helman	R-R	6-1	195	5-23-96	.278	.262	.284	39	144	34	40	6	2	6	20	21	0	0	1	32	10	0	.472	.367
Will Holland	R-R	5-10	181	4-18-98	.235	.242	.231	31	98	21	23	1	2	3	14	17	2	0	0	39	11	2	.378	.359
Alex Isola	R-R	6-1	215	7-22-98	.286	.343	.259	58	210	33	60	9	0	10	40	32	1	0	4	45	0	1	.471	.377
Edouard Julien	L-R	6-2	195	4-30-99	.300	.210	.332	113	400	77	120	19	3	17	67	98	6	0	4	125	19	7	.490	.441
DaShawn Keirsey Jr.	L-L	6-2	195	5-13-97	.271	.282	.267	121	425	61	115	26	3	7	48	32	7	0	4	108	42	7	.395	.329
Nash Knight	B-R	6-0	205	9-20-92	.275	.154	.316	13	51	8	14	3	1	1	2	5	0	0	0	20	0	0	.431	.339
2-team total (2 Frisco RoughRiders)					.254	.125	.302	15	59	8	15	3	1	1	2	5	0	0	0	23	0	0	.390	.313
Trevor Larnach	L-R	6-4	223	2-26-97	.125	.000	.167	2	8	1	1	0	0	1	3	1	0	0	0	3	0	0	.500	.222
Brooks Lee	B-R	6-2	205	2-14-01	.375	1.000	.167	2	8	1	3	0	0	0	0	0	0	0	0	2	0	0	.375	.375
Austin Martin	R-R	6-0	185	3-23-99	.241	.237	.243	90	336	59	81	13	3	2	32	47	21	0	2	54	34	5	.315	.367
Kevin Merrell	L-R	6-1	180	12-14-95	.265	.276	.260	32	102	16	27	3	0	4	12	11	1	2	2	17	2	2	.412	.336
Roy Morales	R-R	6-2	195	6-25-95	.333	.000	.412	5	21	5	7	1	0	0	3	3	0	0	0	2	1	0	.381	.417
Dennis Ortega	R-R	6-3	230	6-11-97	.238	.306	.210	43	168	17	40	8	1	2	24	15	2	0	0	51	4	0	.333	.308
Daniel Ozoria	B-R	5-9	165	8-24-00	.226	.182	.235	22	62	7	14	1	0	0	6	3	0	3	0	20	3	2	.242	.262
Anthony Prato	R-R	5-10	186	5-11-98	.294	.333	.281	87	296	51	87	22	3	3	31	45	11	1	3	71	10	2	.419	.403
Aaron Sabato	R-R	6-2	230	6-4-99	.179	.217	.164	23	84	13	15	4	0	5	18	10	3	0	2	31	2	0	.405	.283
Kyle Schmidt	R-R	6-0	205	7-13-97	.180	.154	.189	27	100	8	18	0	0	1	10	6	3	0	0	34	0	0	.210	.248
Yunior Severino	B-R	6-1	189	10-3-99	.273	.205	.298	37	143	19	39	8	0	8	25	14	1	0	2	48	0	1	.497	.338
Spencer Steer	R-R	5-11	185	12-7-97	.307	.327	.295	35	137	27	42	13	1	8	30	14	4	0	1	23	1	3	.591	.385
Cole Sturgeon	L-L	6-0	180	9-17-91	.249	.164	.278	67	261	37	65	9	0	8	46	26	3	0	2	45	4	2	.375	.322
Dillon Tatum	R-R	6-0	220	5-24-00	.222	.500	.143	2	9	2	2	1	0	0	2	0	0	0	0	3	0	0	.333	.222
Kennie Taylor	R-R	5-11	170	10-20-96	.037	.125	.000	9	27	3	1	0	0	0	0	5	0	0	0	14	0	0	.037	.188
Matt Wallner	L-R	6-5	220	12-12-97	.299	.276	.307	78	268	61	80	15	1	21	64	62	7	0	5	107	8	5	.597	.436
Chris Williams	R-R	6-1	225	11-23-96	.277	.379	.249	75	271	41	75	16	1	18	58	42	1	0	3	90	2	2	.542	.372
Ernie Yake	L-R	5-10	175	11-20-97	.244	.211	.254	28	86	12	21	7	0	0	8	7	1	0	0	9	4	2	.326	.309

Pitching	B-T	HT	WT	DOB	W	L	ERA	G	GS	CG	SV	IP	H	R	ER	HR	BB	SO	AVG	vLH	vRH	K/9	BB/9
Melvi Acosta	R-R	6-1	215	6-2-95	2	1	5.73	12	0	0	0	22	25	15	14	2	10	15	.298	.190	.405	6.14	4.09
Argenis Angulo	R-R	6-3	225	2-26-94	2	2	7.63	14	0	0	1	15	21	14	13	3	15	24	.323	.393	.270	14.09	8.80
Denny Bentley	L-L	6-2	195	5-28-98	6	3	3.79	33	0	0	1	38	32	19	16	2	26	47	.229	.190	.256	11.13	6.16

Michael Boyle	R-L	6-3	200	4-12-94	0	0	16.20	5	0	0	0	5	10	9	9	3	3	2	.400	.455	.357	3.60	5.40
Jordan Brink	L-R	6-0	200	3-18-93	1	0	2.70	4	0	0	0	3	4	1	1	0	3	3	.308	.600	.125	8.10	8.10
Andrew Cabezas	R-R	5-10	175	12-5-96	2	0	3.13	24	0	0	0	32	22	13	11	2	12	27	.200	.245	.164	7.67	3.41
Matt Canterino	R-R	6-2	222	12-14-97	0	1	1.83	11	10	0	0	34	17	8	7	1	22	50	.142	.208	.090	13.11	5.77
Danny Coulombe	L-L	5-10	190	10-26-89	0	0	0.00	1	1	0	0	1	0	0	0	0	1	0	.000	.000	.000	0.00	9.00
Steven Cruz	R-R	6-7	225	6-15-99	1	4	5.14	46	0	0	4	56	54	35	32	4	35	72	.252	.213	.280	11.57	5.63
Blayne Enlow	R-R	6-3	170	3-21-99	1	3	4.40	24	10	0	3	57	60	33	28	4	30	64	.270	.242	.291	10.05	4.71
Zach Featherstone	L-L	6-2	215	12-18-95	1	0	21.32	7	0	0	0	6	16	16	15	2	9	6	.485	.333	.571	8.53	12.79
Kody Funderburk	L-L	6-4	230	11-27-96	10	5	2.94	32	17	0	0	107	98	39	35	8	44	103	.244	.227	.255	8.66	3.70
Osiris German	R-R	6-1	170	11-2-98	3	3	3.33	37	1	0	2	46	46	19	17	5	17	49	.258	.176	.309	9.59	3.33
Sawyer Gipson-Long	R-R	6-4	225	12-12-97	3	4	7.17	8	7	0	0	38	46	30	30	5	6	35	.293	.314	.276	8.36	1.43
Jordan Gore	B-R	6-0	180	8-3-94	2	1	4.50	27	0	0	2	30	26	17	15	2	25	31	.226	.173	.270	9.30	7.50
Daniel Gossett	R-R	6-0	185	11-13-92	3	1	2.26	14	11	1	0	68	44	22	17	4	29	71	.181	.190	.173	9.44	3.86
Ben Gross	R-R	6-1	210	10-5-96	3	1	4.03	10	3	0	0	22	22	17	10	2	15	23	.262	.229	.286	9.27	6.04
Brent Headrick	L-L	6-6	235	12-17-97	2	3	4.81	10	8	0	0	43	47	24	23	11	12	59	.273	.306	.260	12.35	2.51
Ryan Horstman	L-L	6-2	220	7-20-92	0	0	6.75	3	0	0	0	3	3	2	2	0	5	1	.300	.000	.429	3.38	16.88
Steven Klimek	L-R	6-3	205	4-4-94	1	1	7.82	23	0	0	1	25	34	24	22	3	18	18	.324	.244	.375	6.39	6.39
Cody Laweryson	L-R	6-4	205	5-10-98	5	0	1.06	19	8	0	0	60	41	7	7	2	15	69	.197	.211	.186	10.41	2.26
Brandon Lawson	L-R	6-3	205	12-13-94	0	2	18.47	4	3	0	0	6	19	15	13	2	8	3	.487	.571	.440	4.26	11.37
Casey Legumina	R-R	6-2	195	6-19-97	2	5	4.93	30	13	0	3	73	78	43	40	11	32	76	.265	.302	.232	9.37	3.95
Hunter McMahon	R-R	6-3	185	4-9-98	0	2	24.55	4	0	0	0	4	9	11	10	2	4	4	.450	.556	.364	9.82	9.82
Tyler Palm	R-R	6-9	226	12-10-94	0	0	0.00	1	0	0	0	1	0	0	0	0	0	2	.000	.000	.000	18.00	0.00
Francis Peguero	R-R	6-1	185	8-11-97	3	0	5.30	17	0	0	1	19	20	11	11	0	3	13	.282	.217	.313	6.27	1.45
Alex Phillips	R-R	6-4	220	12-16-94	2	0	2.42	18	0	0	2	22	17	8	6	3	11	35	.205	.235	.184	14.10	4.43
Aaron Rozek	L-L	6-2	225	8-20-95	2	0	5.82	6	4	0	0	17	23	11	11	3	7	14	.319	.227	.360	7.41	3.71
Bryan Sammons	L-L	6-4	235	4-27-95	3	6	5.76	37	1	0	2	50	47	39	32	14	18	59	.239	.192	.269	10.62	3.24
Alex Scherff	B-R	6-3	205	2-5-98	0	2	5.27	25	0	0	2	27	26	24	16	5	15	28	.250	.298	.211	9.22	4.94
Austin Schulfer	R-R	6-2	175	12-22-95	0	0	0.39	15	0	0	7	23	11	2	1	0	4	30	.134	.097	.157	11.74	1.57
Evan Sisk	L-L	6-2	209	4-23-97	3	0	0.95	19	0	0	1	28	16	3	3	2	11	33	.160	.080	.240	10.48	3.49
Chris Vallimont	R-R	6-5	220	3-18-97	0	2	9.95	7	6	0	0	19	28	24	21	2	23	20	.329	.250	.415	9.47	10.89
Louie Varland	L-R	6-1	205	12-9-97	7	4	3.34	20	19	0	0	105	102	46	39	14	39	119	.251	.276	.229	10.20	3.34
Tyler Viza	R-R	6-3	170	10-21-94	5	0	0.49	9	0	0	0	18	11	1	1	0	6	29	.172	.148	.189	14.24	2.95
Simeon Woods Richardson	R-R	6-3	210	9-27-00	3	3	3.06	16	15	0	0	71	56	25	24	4	26	77	.217	.190	.241	9.81	3.31

Fielding

Catcher	PCT	G	PO	A	E	DP	PB
Bechtold	.985	39	370	20	6	3	7
Camargo	.985	35	360	29	6	1	3
Isola	.982	18	164	4	3	0	1
Morales	1.000	3	30	1	0	0	0
Ortega	.980	11	93	6	2	0	2
Schmidt	.993	18	136	9	1	1	4
Tatum	1.000	2	28	0	0	0	0
Williams	.982	18	149	12	3	2	1

First Base	PCT	G	PO	A	E	DP
Bechtold	1.000	10	56	4	0	3
Gray	.971	5	33	1	1	6
Helman	1.000	6	33	6	0	6
Isola	.983	17	108	5	2	10
Merrell	1.000	4	33	0	0	2
Morales	.909	1	10	0	1	3
Ortega	.982	18	103	7	2	6
Prato	1.000	6	38	2	0	0
Sabato	1.000	19	139	7	0	5
Schmidt	1.000	1	10	0	0	1
Williams	.992	57	347	22	3	23

Second Base	PCT	G	PO	A	E	DP
Bechtold	1.000	1	3	2	0	1
Helman	1.000	5	6	13	0	4
Julien	.971	94	129	174	9	28
Knight	1.000	3	3	5	0	0
Martin	.970	7	13	19	1	3
Merrell	1.000	8	7	16	0	2
Ozoria	1.000	1	1	0	0	1
Prato	1.000	6	11	21	0	5
Severino	1.000	2	0	5	0	0
Steer	1.000	6	10	15	0	4
Yake	1.000	7	6	15	0	1

Third Base	PCT	G	PO	A	E	DP
Bechtold	.968	35	32	60	3	9
Encarnacion-Strand	.913	8	6	15	2	2
Gray	1.000	1	0	1	0	0
Helman	.900	14	10	17	3	0
Knight	1.000	2	2	2	0	0
Merrell	.875	9	5	9	2	2
Ozoria	.889	4	3	5	1	0
Prato	.897	19	9	26	4	2
Severino	.948	34	19	54	4	4
Steer	.951	17	12	27	2	5
Yake	1.000	2	2	2	0	0

Shortstop	PCT	G	PO	A	E	DP
Knight	1.000	7	10	18	0	6
Lee	1.000	2	1	5	0	2
Martin	.922	70	94	118	18	19
Merrell	1.000	9	4	12	0	1
Ozoria	.870	15	17	23	6	2
Prato	1.000	12	19	22	0	3
Steer	.895	9	5	12	2	0
Yake	1.000	18	19	47	0	8

Outfield	PCT	G	PO	A	E	DP
Cabrera	1.000	73	119	6	0	0
Helman	1.000	17	63	0	0	0
Holland	1.000	32	59	1	0	0
Keirsey Jr.	.996	116	273	7	1	1
Larnach	1.000	1	3	0	0	0
Martin	1.000	9	28	0	0	0
Prato	.976	45	76	6	2	1
Sturgeon	.990	57	90	7	1	1
Taylor	1.000	8	13	0	0	0
Wallner	.962	67	117	9	5	2

CEDAR RAPIDS KERNELS — HIGH-A

MIDWEST LEAGUE

Batting	B-T	HT	WT	DOB	AVG	vLH	vRH	G	AB	R	H	2B	3B	HR	RBI	BB	HBP	SH	SF	SO	SB	CS	SLG	OBP
Jair Camargo	R-R	5-10	230	7-1-99	.296	.263	.312	28	115	16	34	5	0	6	16	3	0	0	0	37	0	0	.496	.314
Christian Encarnacion-Strand	R-R	6-0	224	12-1-99	.296	.229	.322	74	294	52	87	23	3	20	68	30	5	0	1	85	7	1	.599	.370
Kyler Fedko	R-R	6-2	195	9-21-99	.231	.243	.228	84	320	54	74	16	3	8	38	39	5	0	2	69	9	2	.375	.322
Willie Joe Garry Jr.	L-L	6-2	187	5-29-00	.210	.122	.236	60	181	32	38	10	6	2	14	31	4	4	0	68	15	4	.365	.338
Seth Gray	L-R	6-3	205	5-30-98	.245	.185	.262	113	417	61	102	14	1	16	67	46	16	0	1	155	13	5	.398	.342
Will Holland	R-R	5-10	181	4-18-98	.225	.250	.216	85	276	45	62	12	4	6	35	39	7	1	4	98	21	4	.362	.331
Wander Javier	R-R	6-1	165	12-29-98	.209	.253	.198	109	392	48	82	14	5	12	59	30	6	0	4	129	5	3	.362	.273
Brooks Lee	B-R	6-2	205	2-14-01	.289	.316	.282	25	97	14	28	4	0	4	12	16	1	0	0	18	0	2	.454	.395
Charles Mack	L-R	6-0	190	11-12-99	.166	.167	.166	57	193	20	32	9	1	5	23	18	2	0	0	73	0	1	.301	.244
Jeferson Morales	R-R	5-8	170	5-13-99	.207	.154	.227	69	241	33	50	11	2	7	31	23	13	0	5	71	5	1	.357	.305
Dylan Neuse	R-R	5-10	180	12-22-98	.177	.175	.178	61	186	25	33	4	0	3	17	25	3	0	0	57	11	1	.247	.285

Frank Nigro	R-R	6-4	200	8-1-97	.286	.000	.333	4	7	0	2	0	0	0	1	2	0	0	0	2	0	0	.286	.444
Daniel Ozoria	B-R	5-9	165	8-24-00	.000	--	.000	1	3	0	0	0	0	0	0	0	0	0	0	2	0	0	.000	.000
Mikey Perez	R-R	6-0	185	8-24-99	.221	.292	.197	28	95	18	21	3	0	2	7	16	4	0	0	26	16	2	.316	.357
Anthony Prato	R-R	5-10	186	5-11-98	.271	.182	.299	45	181	46	49	8	5	7	33	22	2	0	4	59	12	4	.486	.349
Jake Rucker	R-R	6-1	195	9-14-99	.262	.234	.270	55	206	29	54	16	2	6	35	22	6	1	4	52	5	5	.447	.345
Aaron Sabato	R-R	6-2	230	6-4-99	.226	.250	.217	80	288	50	65	13	0	17	57	49	8	0	3	111	2	1	.448	.351
Kyle Schmidt	R-R	6-0	205	7-13-97	.000	--	.000	1	3	0	0	0	0	0	0	1	0	0	0	1	0	0	.000	.250
Yunior Severino	B-R	6-1	189	10-3-99	.283	.250	.294	46	159	30	45	9	2	11	40	25	6	0	1	43	0	0	.572	.398
Dalton Shuffield	R-R	5-9	170	3-31-99	.292	1.000	.227	8	24	3	7	0	0	1	2	4	0	0	0	10	2	0	.417	.393
Alerick Soularie	R-R	6-0	175	7-5-99	.227	.130	.257	91	330	68	75	15	3	10	39	18	7	0	4	106	18	5	.382	.334
Kennie Taylor	R-R	5-11	170	10-20-96	.216	.167	.233	28	97	15	21	2	1	1	5	8	1	0	0	32	1	3	.289	.283
Pat Winkel	L-R	6-1	200	1-27-00	.254	.140	.286	54	197	21	50	9	0	6	30	23	0	0	1	62	1	0	.391	.330

Pitching	B-T	HT	WT	DOB	W	L	ERA	G	GS	CG	SV	IP	H	R	ER	HR	BB	SO	AVG	vLH	vRH	K/9	BB/9
Melvi Acosta	R-R	6-1	215	6-2-95	1	0	1.47	13	0	0	1	18	13	5	3	0	9	12	.213	.179	.242	5.89	4.42
Travis Adams	R-R	6-1	197	1-19-00	2	3	4.88	7	7	0	0	31	34	20	17	4	11	39	.272	.327	.229	11.20	3.16
Pierce Banks	R-R	6-0	205	3-31-98	0	0	13.50	1	1	0	0	2	5	4	3	2	3	2	.417	.444	.333	9.00	13.50
Malik Barrington	R-R	6-2	236	10-8-97	1	1	10.80	2	0	0	0	3	5	4	4	1	0	2	.385	.500	.286	5.40	0.00
Denny Bentley	L-L	6-2	195	5-28-98	1	1	3.06	13	0	0	2	18	14	6	6	0	4	26	.219	.207	.229	13.25	2.04
Andrew Cabezas	R-R	5-10	175	12-5-96	1	2	3.63	12	0	0	0	17	14	11	7	3	3	26	.209	.206	.212	13.50	1.56
David Festa	R-R	6-6	185	3-8-00	7	3	2.71	16	13	0	0	80	67	29	24	5	28	75	.233	.240	.225	8.47	3.16
Osiris German	R-R	6-1	170	11-2-98	0	0	1.17	6	0	0	5	8	6	1	1	0	0	10	.214	.214	.214	11.74	0.00
Sawyer Gipson-Long	R-R	6-4	225	12-12-97	5	2	1.99	10	10	0	0	50	33	11	11	4	13	52	.185	.170	.205	9.42	2.36
Regi Grace	L-R	6-2	215	12-10-99	0	0	13.50	3	0	0	0	3	6	5	4	0	3	3	.462	.429	.500	10.13	10.13
Bradley Hanner	R-R	6-4	210	2-10-99	7	4	4.60	39	1	0	2	59	46	35	30	4	27	65	.216	.229	.204	9.97	4.14
Brent Headrick	L-L	6-6	235	12-17-97	8	2	2.34	15	15	0	0	65	45	17	17	7	13	77	.188	.200	.183	10.61	1.79
Cody Laweryson	L-R	6-4	205	5-10-98	1	0	2.57	16	2	0	1	35	25	12	10	0	12	42	.200	.254	.138	10.80	3.09
Casey Legumina	R-R	6-2	195	6-19-97	0	1	4.05	3	3	0	0	13	10	6	6	0	4	16	.204	.212	.188	10.80	2.70
Hunter McMahon	R-R	6-3	185	4-9-98	3	0	1.19	19	1	0	2	38	21	8	5	1	4	36	.162	.117	.200	8.60	0.96
Bobby Milacki	R-R	6-2	210	11-6-96	6	1	2.83	38	0	0	3	64	54	21	20	4	22	68	.227	.217	.237	9.61	3.11
Derek Molina	L-R	6-3	206	7-27-97	2	2	3.57	37	0	0	5	53	46	24	21	6	22	54	.235	.276	.208	9.17	3.74
Sean Mooney	R-R	6-1	200	1-11-98	2	3	3.30	18	12	0	0	60	45	29	22	7	30	82	.205	.250	.159	12.30	4.50
Matt Mullenbach	R-R	6-4	195	10-6-96	1	1	1.29	20	0	0	0	28	22	8	4	0	8	26	.206	.196	.214	8.36	2.57
Frank Nigro	R-R	6-4	200	8-1-97	0	0	0.00	1	0	0	0	1	0	0	0	0	2	2	.000	.000	--	18.00	18.00
Jaylen Nowlin	L-L	6-1	180	1-29-01	1	1	4.40	3	3	0	0	14	13	7	7	2	7	22	.241	.063	.316	13.81	4.40
Jon Olsen	R-R	6-2	190	5-13-97	1	1	4.76	16	3	0	0	23	22	13	12	0	8	30	.242	.282	.212	11.91	3.18
Tyler Palm	R-R	6-9	226	12-10-94	0	0	4.50	35	2	0	0	52	58	32	26	2	26	39	.290	.279	.302	6.75	4.50
Samuel Perez	L-L	5-11	205	11-29-99	0	0	2.35	6	1	0	0	8	7	2	2	1	3	6	.250	.125	.300	7.04	3.52
Cade Povich	L-L	6-3	185	4-12-00	6	8	4.46	16	16	0	0	79	71	47	39	9	26	107	.234	.286	.215	12.24	2.97
Luis Rijo	R-R	6-1	200	9-6-98	0	4	10.80	6	6	0	0	15	24	20	18	2	9	11	.353	.400	.326	6.60	5.40
Miguel Rodriguez	R-R	6-2	180	2-25-99	2	1	3.36	39	1	0	4	56	48	25	21	13	24	67	.225	.230	.221	10.70	3.83
Orlando Rodriguez	R-R	6-2	195	12-16-95	4	1	2.97	26	6	0	0	61	46	23	20	6	26	75	.207	.270	.165	11.13	3.86
Aaron Rozek	L-L	6-2	225	8-20-95	7	6	4.83	18	16	0	0	73	76	45	39	14	25	68	.265	.280	.258	8.42	3.10
Ryan Shreve	R-R	6-6	215	6-23-98	1	3	3.08	28	2	0	1	38	29	21	13	2	15	39	.207	.226	.192	9.24	3.55
John Stankiewicz	R-R	6-4	230	9-8-98	2	4	5.86	11	10	0	0	43	50	28	28	5	16	37	.289	.280	.300	7.74	3.35
Matthew Swain	R-R	6-7	225	8-20-97	1	3	6.15	23	0	0	0	34	34	25	23	5	21	34	.254	.267	.243	9.09	5.61

Fielding

Catcher	PCT	G	PO	A	E	DP	PB
Camargo	.991	21	202	15	2	1	4
Mack	.980	44	422	21	9	2	3
Morales	.981	19	195	9	4	0	5
Nigro	1.000	3	25	4	0	0	0
Schmidt	1.000	1	8	0	0	0	0
Winkel	.984	46	410	19	7	0	5

First Base	PCT	G	PO	A	E	DP
Encarnacion-Strand	1.000	2	2	0	0	0
Gray	1.000	38	272	19	0	22
Mack	.957	9	37	8	2	7
Perez	1.000	2	17	4	0	1
Rucker	.994	22	166	8	1	8
Sabato	.990	63	443	41	5	24

Second Base	PCT	G	PO	A	E	DP
Gray	1.000	1	1	1	0	0
Javier	1.000	2	4	9	0	0
Perez	.976	17	26	55	2	8
Prato	.966	28	38	77	4	7
Rucker	1.000	7	10	15	0	2
Severino	.960	31	36	59	4	9
Shuffield	1.000	8	11	10	0	2
Soularie	.971	42	50	82	4	12

Third Base	PCT	G	PO	A	E	DP
Encarnacion-Strand	.863	55	51	81	21	7
Gray	.938	49	37	84	8	9
Javier	.833	7	1	9	2	0
Ozoria	1.000	1	0	3	0	1
Prato	1.000	3	1	3	0	0
Rucker	.952	19	12	28	2	1
Severino	1.000	1	0	1	0	0

Shortstop	PCT	G	PO	A	E	DP
Holland	.982	15	19	35	1	7
Javier	.956	96	123	201	15	35
Lee	.939	20	26	36	4	4
Perez	1.000	2	3	2	0	0

Outfield	PCT	G	PO	A	E	DP
Fedko	.964	80	130	5	5	0
Garry Jr.	.971	60	93	7	3	1
Gray	1.000	6	4	0	0	0
Holland	.983	70	172	6	3	1
Morales	.987	44	74	2	1	1
Neuse	.990	51	93	7	1	3
Perez	1.000	2	1	0	0	0
Prato	.939	17	31	0	2	0
Rucker	1.000	3	2	0	0	0
Severino	--	2	0	0	0	0
Soularie	.959	47	69	1	3	1
Taylor	.976	28	40	1	1	0

FORT MYERS MIGHTY MUSSELS — *LOW-A*

FLORIDA STATE LEAGUE

Batting	B-T	HT	WT	DOB	AVG	vLH	vRH	G	AB	R	H	2B	3B	HR	RBI	BB	HBP	SH	SF	SO	SB	CS	SLG	OBP
Carlos Aguiar	L-L	6-2	175	8-28-01	.243	.308	.228	44	140	21	34	9	2	10	24	9	0	0	0	66	3	6	.550	.289
Luis Baez	R-R	5-11	170	11-23-00	.215	.189	.221	66	177	29	38	2	2	1	22	28	2	0	0	63	20	3	.266	.329
Nate Baez	R-R	6-1	191	5-17-01	.288	.286	.289	16	52	7	15	4	0	3	11	4	1	0	1	15	0	1	.538	.345
Tim Beckham	R-R	6-0	215	1-27-90	.286	.333	.250	2	7	3	2	0	0	1	3	2	0	0	0	2	0	0	.714	.444
Noah Cardenas	R-R	6-1	195	9-10-99	.261	.314	.246	99	310	42	81	18	1	9	43	73	15	0	3	70	11	5	.413	.421

Keoni Cavaco	R-R	6-2	195	6-2-01	.231	.297	.215	99	368	34	85	18	5	11	59	22	2	0	4	138	7	4	.397	.275
Rubel Cespedes	L-R	6-2	210	8-29-00	.290	.325	.284	74	255	33	74	15	0	4	28	17	4	0	3	57	1	1	.396	.341
Kyler Fedko	R-R	6-2	195	9-21-99	.318	.261	.338	26	88	19	28	5	1	2	16	17	1	0	3	22	4	1	.466	.422
Jesus Feliz	R-R	6-0	185	6-7-00	.167	.286	.118	7	24	3	4	2	0	0	1	2	0	0	0	6	0	0	.250	.231
Zach Huffins	R-R	6-1	185	6-16-99	.143	.000	.167	9	21	2	3	1	0	1	3	5	1	0	0	11	1	1	.333	.333
Noah Miller	B-R	6-1	190	11-12-02	.211	.236	.204	108	383	62	81	12	4	2	24	76	6	0	4	110	23	7	.279	.348
Dylan Neuse	R-R	5-10	180	12-22-98	.211	.161	.237	31	90	15	19	3	0	2	6	15	1	0	0	25	2	4	.311	.330
Frank Nigro	R-R	6-4	200	8-1-97	.125	.143	.000	4	8	1	1	0	0	0	0	6	0	0	0	6	1	1	.125	.500
Ricardo Olivar	R-R	5-10	176	8-10-01	.222	.000	.250	3	9	0	2	0	0	0	1	1	0	0	0	3	0	0	.222	.300
Jorel Ortega	R-R	6-0	194	1-22-01	1.000	1.000	--	1	1	0	1	0	0	0	2	0	0	0	0	0	0	0	1.000	1.000
Daniel Ozoria	B-R	5-9	165	8-24-00	.264	.313	.247	47	129	22	34	5	0	1	12	13	1	0	1	47	17	3	.326	.333
Mikey Perez	R-R	6-0	185	8-24-99	.225	.222	.225	81	258	43	58	20	1	8	37	27	14	0	2	66	32	5	.403	.329
Nelson Roberto	R-R	6-2	220	10-27-00	.145	.154	.143	26	83	10	12	2	1	3	9	5	2	0	0	43	0	0	.301	.211
Alex Rodriguez	R-R	5-11	205	9-10-98	.250	.000	.333	1	4	0	1	0	0	0	1	0	0	0	0	1	0	0	.250	.250
Emmanuel Rodriguez	L-L	5-10	210	2-28-03	.272	.313	.260	47	136	35	37	5	3	9	25	57	4	0	2	52	11	5	.551	.492
Kala_i Rosario	R-R	6-1	205	7-2-02	.239	.200	.249	109	373	53	89	21	3	12	46	34	11	0	1	136	7	2	.408	.320
Ben Ross	R-R	6-1	180	6-6-01	.257	.188	.276	22	74	17	19	5	0	3	13	13	1	0	1	19	6	0	.446	.371
Jake Rucker	R-R	6-1	195	9-14-99	.225	.200	.232	60	218	37	49	9	4	2	17	33	6	0	3	53	13	7	.330	.338
Alec Sayre	R-R	6-1	195	10-5-00	.267	.200	.280	12	30	6	8	2	0	0	4	14	0	0	1	8	1	1	.333	.489
Kyle Schmidt	R-R	6-0	205	7-13-97	.244	.333	.217	28	90	8	22	4	0	4	20	7	0	0	1	24	0	0	.422	.296
Tanner Schobel	R-R	5-10	170	6-4-01	.242	.292	.227	28	99	11	24	3	0	1	10	18	2	0	1	23	6	1	.303	.367
LaRon Smith	R-R	6-2	200	9-16-00	.197	.278	.163	25	61	6	12	7	0	1	8	9	4	0	2	30	0	1	.361	.329
Dillon Tatum	R-R	6-0	220	5-24-00	.175	.093	.196	72	211	30	37	8	0	6	19	41	7	0	3	90	0	2	.299	.324
Misael Urbina	R-R	6-0	190	4-26-02	.246	.184	.268	50	191	28	47	16	1	5	22	23	0	0	3	51	9	4	.419	.323
Ernie Yake	L-R	5-10	175	11-20-97	.257	.250	.259	13	35	2	9	0	0	0	4	3	1	0	2	6	4	2	.257	.317

Pitching	B-T	HT	WT	DOB	W	L	ERA	G	GS	CG	SV	IP	H	R	ER	HR	BB	SO	AVG	vLH	vRH	K/9	BB/9
Travis Adams	R-R	6-1	197	1-19-00	4	5	3.50	15	15	0	0	69	57	28	27	4	15	69	.224	.302	.185	8.96	1.95
Jorge Alcala	R-R	6-3	205	7-28-95	0	1	0.00	1	0	0	0	1	2	1	0	0	0	1	.333	.667	.000	9.00	0.00
Develson Aria	L-L	6-0	155	3-20-01	0	0	0.00	2	0	0	0	3	0	0	0	0	2	4	.000	.000	.000	12.00	6.00
Jordan Balazovic	R-R	6-5	215	9-17-98	0	0	18.00	1	0	0	0	2	4	4	4	1	2	1	.400	.500	.375	4.50	9.00
Malik Barrington	R-R	6-2	236	10-8-97	3	5	3.17	31	3	0	5	54	38	25	19	3	25	71	.196	.250	.169	11.83	4.17
Michael Boyle	R-L	6-3	200	4-12-94	1	0	0.00	2	1	0	0	2	1	0	0	0	2	4	.111	.000	.167	15.43	7.71
Logan Campbell	R-R	6-2	205	7-22-99	0	1	10.80	4	0	0	0	3	5	4	4	1	7	6	.333	.200	.400	16.20	18.90
Jordan Carr	B-L	6-2	210	7-17-97	6	2	3.84	14	10	0	0	61	62	29	26	4	11	42	.266	.160	.295	6.20	1.62
Tomas Cleto	R-R	6-2	206	10-9-00	0	0	3.68	5	4	0	0	15	12	8	6	1	6	13	.226	.267	.211	7.98	3.68
Randy Dobnak	R-R	6-1	230	1-17-95	0	0	0.00	1	1	0	0	2	1	0	0	0	0	0	.143	.000	.167	0.00	0.00
Blayne Enlow	R-R	6-3	170	3-21-99	0	0	16.20	1	1	0	0	2	5	7	3	1	1	1	.417	.250	.500	5.40	5.40
Anthony Escobar	R-R	5-11	230	8-25-00	0	1	8.74	19	0	0	1	23	32	28	22	2	18	23	.344	.419	.306	9.13	7.15
David Festa	R-R	6-6	185	3-8-00	2	1	1.50	5	5	0	0	24	12	5	4	1	6	33	.148	.174	.138	12.38	2.25
Regi Grace	L-R	6-2	215	12-10-99	4	3	4.45	33	3	0	2	57	60	36	28	4	27	74	.264	.177	.311	11.75	4.29
Sonny Gray	R-R	5-10	195	11-7-89	0	0	0.00	1	1	0	0	3	1	0	0	0	0	5	.091	.500	.000	15.00	0.00
Steve Hajjar	R-L	6-5	240	8-7-00	2	2	2.47	12	12	0	0	44	25	14	12	3	22	71	.168	.185	.164	14.63	4.53
Jackson Hicks	R-R	6-3	225	2-15-98	5	3	2.98	36	0	0	0	51	45	32	17	3	22	58	.226	.186	.248	10.17	3.86
Kyle Jones	L-R	6-1	200	2-7-00	1	0	0.00	1	0	0	0	3	2	0	0	0	0	5	.182	.000	.250	15.00	0.00
Ariel Jurado	R-R	6-2	240	1-30-96	0	0	0.00	1	1	0	0	4	1	0	0	0	2	4	.077	.000	.200	9.00	4.50
A.J. Labas	R-R	6-3	223	12-8-98	1	1	7.20	5	1	0	0	10	14	8	8	0	3	14	.333	.231	.379	12.60	2.70
Johnathan Lavallee	R-R	6-4	240	8-11-99	2	1	4.81	13	2	0	2	24	20	14	13	0	16	23	.222	.281	.190	8.51	5.92
Zebby Matthews	R-R	6-5	210	5-22-00	0	0	0.00	1	0	0	0	2	0	0	0	0	0	4	.000	.000	.000	18.00	0.00
Hunter McMahon	R-R	6-3	185	4-9-98	1	0	2.23	20	0	0	5	32	20	8	8	5	8	36	.182	.222	.162	10.02	2.23
Juan Mendez	R-R	6-4	240	10-18-98	3	4	5.05	32	0	0	3	46	35	28	26	4	31	58	.211	.174	.225	11.27	6.02
Matt Mullenbach	R-R	6-4	195	10-6-96	3	0	2.12	10	0	0	1	17	17	7	4	1	3	20	.266	.389	.217	10.59	1.59
Jaylen Nowlin	L-L	6-1	180	1-29-01	4	3	3.65	19	11	0	0	57	47	25	23	2	29	89	.221	.250	.213	14.14	4.61
Bailey Ober	R-R	6-9	260	7-12-95	0	0	1.29	2	2	0	0	7	4	1	1	1	1	6	.167	.286	.118	7.71	1.29
Pierson Ohl	R-R	6-1	180	9-10-99	6	7	3.53	20	18	0	0	92	95	41	36	5	13	101	.268	.246	.278	9.92	1.28
Mike Paredes	R-R	5-11	185	7-27-00	7	4	3.27	24	13	0	1	85	81	34	31	11	16	63	.253	.274	.243	6.64	1.69
Samuel Perez	L-L	5-11	205	11-29-99	2	4	3.20	24	0	0	1	45	35	21	16	5	15	40	.213	.243	.205	8.00	3.00
Zaquiel Puentes	R-R	6-1	160	12-30-00	0	2	8.36	9	0	0	0	14	13	13	13	3	9	17	.245	.231	.250	10.93	5.79
Marco Raya	R-R	6-1	170	8-7-02	3	2	3.05	19	17	0	0	65	47	25	22	8	23	76	.199	.244	.171	10.52	3.18
Niklas Rimmel	R-R	6-3	200	7-5-99	4	1	1.98	29	1	0	4	41	28	14	9	2	19	52	.188	.178	.192	11.41	4.17
John Stankiewicz	R-R	6-4	230	9-8-98	3	0	0.83	4	4	0	0	22	11	3	2	0	5	31	.147	.188	.136	12.88	2.08
Cody Stashak	R-R	6-2	180	6-4-94	0	0	0.00	1	0	0	0	1	0	0	0	0	0	2	.000	.000	.000	18.00	0.00
Brock Stewart	L-R	6-3	220	10-3-91	0	0	9.64	3	1	0	0	5	3	5	5	2	3	3	.188	.333	.154	5.79	5.79
Matthew Swain	R-R	6-7	225	8-20-97	2	1	0.00	14	0	0	7	21	4	1	0	0	5	31	.062	.167	.021	13.29	2.14
John Wilson	L-L	6-0	195	7-17-97	0	4	3.83	30	0	0	2	49	53	29	21	2	22	34	.277	.240	.291	6.20	4.01
Josh Winder	R-R	6-5	210	10-11-96	0	1	18.00	1	1	0	0	2	3	4	4	1	2	3	.333	1.000	.250	13.50	9.00

Fielding

Catcher	PCT	G	PO	A	E	DP	PB
Baez	1.000	9	68	1	0	0	0
Cardenas	.987	57	512	37	7	3	0
Nigro	1.000	3	19	2	0	0	0
Olivar	1.000	2	10	0	0	0	0
Rodriguez	1.000	1	10	0	0	0	0
Schmidt	.984	14	118	4	2	0	1
Smith	.950	7	55	2	3	1	3
Tatum	.995	45	405	30	2	2	7

First Base	PCT	G	PO	A	E	DP
Baez	1.000	3	16	2	0	2
Cardenas	.995	25	168	17	1	16
Cespedes	1.000	22	145	6	0	16
Feliz	1.000	6	37	1	0	2
Perez	.976	7	40	1	1	4
Ross	1.000	1	2	0	0	0
Rucker	.992	21	111	11	1	10
Schmidt	1.000	14	101	5	0	12
Smith	.990	15	96	7	1	8
Tatum	.986	22	137	6	2	11

Second Base	PCT	G	PO	A	E	DP
Cespedes	.991	35	48	65	1	11
Ozoria	.949	18	45	30	4	11
Perez	.970	50	69	94	5	27
Ross	1.000	4	9	6	0	3
Rucker	1.000	2	4	1	0	1
Schobel	1.000	19	26	51	0	10
Yake	1.000	6	9	12	0	1

Third Base	PCT	G	PO	A	E	DP
Cavaco	.892	80	59	114	21	12
Cespedes	.833	8	4	6	2	0
Feliz	.833	1	1	4	1	1
Ozoria	.875	4	2	5	1	0
Perez	.643	5	4	5	5	0
Ross	.800	2	2	2	1	0
Rucker	.941	24	15	33	3	3
Schobel	.800	6	2	6	2	0
Yake	1.000	2	0	4	0	0

Shortstop	PCT	G	PO	A	E	DP
Beckham	1.000	1	2	4	0	2
Miller	.980	98	104	234	7	41
Ozoria	.967	8	10	19	1	4
Perez	.750	8	5	16	7	3
Ross	1.000	8	9	13	0	4
Schobel	.857	3	2	4	1	1
Yake	1.000	4	2	10	0	0

Outfield	PCT	G	PO	A	E	DP
Aguiar	1.000	38	54	3	0	1
Baez	.992	64	124	5	1	1
Cespedes	1.000	3	3	1	0	0
Fedko	.931	22	27	0	2	0
Huffins	1.000	8	18	0	0	0
Neuse	1.000	32	54	4	0	1
Olivar	1.000	1	2	0	0	0
Ozoria	1.000	10	14	1	0	0
Perez	--	1	0	0	0	0
Roberto	1.000	20	28	0	0	0
Rodriguez	.970	41	63	1	2	1
Rosario	.941	96	135	9	9	2
Ross	1.000	6	11	0	0	0
Rucker	1.000	9	15	0	0	0
Sayre	.941	12	16	0	1	0
Urbina	.978	42	89	1	2	0

FCL TWINS — *ROOKIE*

FLORIDA COMPLEX LEAGUE

Batting	B-T	HT	WT	DOB	AVG	vLH	vRH	G	AB	R	H	2B	3B	HR	RBI	BB	HBP	SH	SF	SO	SB	CS	SLG	OBP
Carlos Aguiar	L-L	6-2	175	8-28-01	.167	.000	.200	2	6	1	1	1	0	0	0	1	0	0	0	1	1	0	.333	.286
Nate Baez	R-R	6-1	191	5-17-01	.222	.200	.250	3	9	0	2	1	0	0	1	1	0	0	0	3	0	0	.333	.300
Jair Camargo	R-R	5-10	230	7-1-99	.273	.333	.250	3	11	1	3	1	1	0	1	1	0	0	0	4	0	0	.545	.333
Wilfri Castro	R-R	5-11	165	3-21-01	.222	.100	.250	19	54	9	12	1	0	2	7	8	0	0	0	14	0	0	.352	.323
Andres Centeno	R-R	6-1	183	10-23-03	.228	.176	.236	42	123	22	28	6	2	1	21	24	2	0	2	52	4	2	.333	.358
Deiner Contreras	R-R	6-0	198	4-14-04	.056	.000	.063	8	18	3	1	0	0	0	0	1	0	0	0	9	0	0	.056	.105
Andrew Cossetti	R-R	6-0	215	1-31-00	.000	.000	.000	1	2	1	0	0	0	0	0	1	1	0	0	0	0	0	.000	.500
Rafael Cruz	R-R	6-1	166	11-13-03	.203	.125	.216	18	59	8	12	3	1	2	11	6	3	0	0	17	0	1	.390	.309
Danny De Andrade	R-R	5-11	173	4-10-04	.242	.414	.208	48	178	27	43	9	1	4	23	19	6	0	1	34	4	2	.371	.333
Jefferson De La Cruz	L-L	6-1	176	11-26-03	.207	.083	.227	30	87	11	18	0	1	1	7	9	4	0	0	31	5	0	.264	.310
Gregory Duran	L-R	6-2	201	10-8-02	.188	.278	.172	41	117	17	22	6	1	3	12	24	2	0	0	49	2	3	.333	.336
Jesus Feliz	R-R	6-0	185	6-7-00	.000	--	.000	2	4	0	0	0	0	0	0	1	1	0	0	2	0	0	.000	.333
Willie Joe Garry Jr.	L-L	6-2	187	5-29-00	.150	.000	.167	5	20	1	3	0	0	0	2	2	0	0	0	8	2	0	.150	.227
Alex Isola	R-R	6-1	215	7-22-98	.167	--	.167	3	6	2	1	0	0	1	3	3	0	0	0	2	0	0	.667	.444
Brooks Lee	B-R	6-2	205	2-14-01	.353	--	.353	4	17	2	6	2	0	0	3	0	0	0	0	0	0	0	.471	.353
Reynaldo Madrigal	R-R	6-1	174	9-23-03	.000	.000	.000	5	11	1	0	0	0	0	0	4	2	0	0	6	1	1	.000	.353
Austin Martin	R-R	6-0	185	3-23-99	.250	.000	.333	2	8	1	2	1	0	0	3	2	0	0	0	1	1	1	.375	.400
Fredy Michel	B-R	5-10	154	7-10-04	.163	.125	.171	40	129	21	21	3	0	2	7	26	3	0	0	59	15	6	.233	.316
Jeferson Morales	R-R	5-8	170	5-13-99	.222	--	.222	3	9	1	2	0	0	1	4	1	0	0	0	2	0	0	.556	.300
Frank Nigro	R-R	6-4	200	8-1-97	.111	.333	.000	5	9	1	1	0	0	0	0	3	0	0	0	5	1	0	.111	.333
Ricardo Olivar	R-R	5-10	176	8-10-01	.349	.600	.316	40	129	16	45	12	3	5	23	18	5	0	2	33	5	5	.605	.442
Dennis Ortega	R-R	6-3	230	6-11-97	.500	--	.500	3	10	2	5	1	0	0	2	1	0	0	0	1	0	0	.600	.545
Jorel Ortega	R-R	6-0	194	1-22-01	.000	--	.000	2	4	0	0	0	0	0	0	2	0	0	0	3	0	0	.000	.333
Jankel Ortiz	B-R	6-0	170	6-14-04	.250	.500	.200	4	12	2	3	1	0	0	1	4	0	0	0	4	0	0	.333	.438
Alexander Pena	R-R	6-2	175	4-12-02	.317	.222	.344	25	82	12	26	7	1	3	15	5	3	0	1	29	0	1	.537	.374
Ismael Perez	L-L	5-11	175	12-16-03	.206	.133	.217	39	107	16	22	6	2	0	16	18	0	0	1	32	3	1	.299	.317
Breilin Ramirez	R-R	6-1	170	9-6-02	.172	.091	.182	35	99	9	17	4	0	2	10	17	2	1	0	40	0	0	.273	.305
Giovanny Rivero	B-R	5-10	173	10-19-03	.071	.333	.000	17	28	2	2	0	0	0	0	4	0	0	0	12	0	0	.071	.188
Daniel Robertson	R-R	5-11	210	3-22-94	.318	.333	.316	7	22	7	7	3	0	2	9	5	0	0	0	3	0	1	.727	.444
2-team total (2 FCL Phillies)					.296	.250	.304	9	27	8	8	3	0	2	9	6	1	0	0	5	0	1	.630	.441
Alex Rodriguez	R-R	5-11	205	9-10-98	.095	--	.095	10	21	4	2	0	0	1	2	4	1	0	0	10	0	0	.238	.269
Ben Ross	R-R	6-1	180	6-6-01	.111	--	.111	2	9	1	1	1	0	0	0	1	0	0	0	3	0	0	.222	.200
Miguel Sano	R-R	6-4	272	5-11-93	.313	.333	.300	5	16	3	5	1	0	2	4	3	0	0	0	2	1	0	.750	.421
Alec Sayre	R-R	6-1	195	10-5-00	.182	.000	.222	3	11	2	2	0	1	0	3	2	0	0	0	5	0	0	.364	.308
Tanner Schobel	R-R	5-10	170	6-4-01	.200	--	.200	4	15	3	3	1	0	0	1	1	0	0	0	3	1	0	.267	.250
Dalton Shuffield	R-R	5-9	170	3-31-99	.500	--	.500	3	10	4	5	0	0	1	2	3	0	0	0	0	0	0	.800	.615
LaRon Smith	R-R	6-2	200	9-16-00	.000	--	.000	1	3	0	0	0	0	0	0	1	0	0	0	1	0	0	.000	.250
Malfrin Sosa	R-R	6-1	198	9-13-02	.197	.077	.226	20	66	14	13	4	0	1	5	8	1	0	0	26	0	0	.303	.293
Yonardy Soto	R-L	5-11	180	1-31-03	.204	.176	.208	39	113	18	23	8	0	3	15	18	0	0	0	46	2	2	.354	.313
Misael Urbina	R-R	6-0	190	4-26-02	.250	.222	.258	10	40	3	10	4	0	0	5	2	3	0	1	9	1	1	.350	.326
Amilcar Vasquez	B-R	5-8	170	12-26-01	.194	.125	.217	15	31	4	6	1	0	0	2	4	4	0	0	4	0	0	.226	.359
Ernie Yake	L-R	5-10	175	11-20-97	.071	.333	.000	4	14	2	1	0	0	0	1	1	0	0	0	6	1	0	.071	.133

Pitching	B-T	HT	WT	DOB	W	L	ERA	G	GS	CG	SV	IP	H	R	ER	HR	BB	SO	AVG	vLH	vRH	K/9	BB/9
Develson Aria	L-L	6-0	155	3-20-01	1	3	5.34	11	7	0	0	29	30	24	17	3	13	39	.261	.176	.296	12.24	4.08
Pierce Banks	R-R	6-0	205	3-31-98	1	2	2.63	8	0	0	0	14	11	5	4	2	3	14	.212	.316	.152	9.22	1.98
Tyler Bashlor	R-R	6-0	195	4-16-93	0	0	0.00	1	0	0	0	1	0	0	0	0	0	0	.000	.000	.000	0.00	0.00
Tyler Beck	R-R	6-1	190	11-16-95	0	0	0.00	1	0	0	0	1	0	0	0	0	0	1	.000	.000	--	9.00	0.00
Cole Bellair	R-R	6-1	230	4-8-97	1	1	1.61	14	0	0	0	22	17	9	4	1	6	20	.218	.243	.195	8.06	2.42
Miguelangel Boadas	R-R	6-1	181	12-7-02	3	2	5.53	12	0	0	2	28	34	21	17	2	9	25	.296	.288	.302	8.13	2.93
Michael Boyle	R-L	6-3	200	4-12-94	1	0	0.00	3	0	0	0	4	4	0	0	0	1	4	.267	.000	.308	9.00	2.25
Matt Canterino	R-R	6-2	222	12-14-97	0	0	3.38	2	2	0	0	3	3	1	1	1	1	4	.300	.000	.429	13.50	3.38
Tomas Cleto	R-R	6-2	206	10-9-00	1	2	4,55	9	2	0	2	30	27	15	15	1	3	31	.227	.317	.179	9.40	0.91
C.J. Culpepper	R-R	6-3	193	11-2-01	0	0	0.00	1	0	0	0	1	0	0	0	0	1	1	.000	.000	.000	9.00	9.00

Randy Dobnak	R-R	6-1	230	1-17-95	0	0	0.00	2	2	0	0	3	4	0	0	0	0	4	.308	.200	.375	12.00	0.00
Jacob Edwards	L-L	5-9	190	7-31-00	0	0	0.00	2	0	0	0	2	1	0	0	0	3	1	.143	.000	.167	4.50	13.50
Rafael Feliz	R-R	6-0	160	11-20-00	0	0	0.00	1	0	0	0	1	0	0	0	0	1	2	.000	.000	.000	18.00	9.00
Tanner Gaff	L-R	6-4	220	5-13-98	1	0	4.15	5	0	0	0	4	6	2	2	0	1	6	.353	.222	.500	12.46	2.08
Giovahniey German	R-R	6-2	165	10-8-00	0	2	14.73	3	0	0	0	4	5	8	6	2	7	2	.357	.667	.273	4.91	17.18
Regi Grace	L-R	6-2	215	12-10-99	0	0	0.00	1	0	0	0	1	1	0	0	0	0	1	.333	--	.333	9.00	0.00
Steve Hajjar	R-L	6-5	240	8-7-00	0	0	21.60	1	1	0	0	2	3	5	4	0	4	2	.375	.500	.250	10.80	21.60
Ben Heller	R-R	6-3	210	8-5-91	0	1	6.43	4	2	0	0	7	5	6	5	0	7	6	.192	.167	.200	7.71	9.00
Ryan Horstman	L-L	6-2	220	7-20-92	1	0	1.29	5	4	0	0	7	3	2	1	0	0	8	.130	.167	.118	10.29	0.00
Kyle Jones	L-R	6-1	200	2-7-00	0	0	0.00	1	0	0	0	1	0	0	0	0	0	0	.000	--	.000	0.00	0.00
John Klein	R-R	6-5	225	4-22-02	0	0	0.00	2	0	0	0	2	1	0	0	0	1	2	.125	.500	.000	9.00	4.50
A.J. Labas	R-R	6-3	223	12-8-98	0	0	0.00	3	1	0	0	4	1	0	0	0	0	4	.077	.000	.111	9.00	0.00
Yon Landaeta	R-R	6-1	170	3-16-00	1	2	5.03	10	0	0	0	20	13	12	11	0	22	28	.188	.222	.167	12.81	10.07
Johnathan Lavallee	R-R	6-4	240	8-11-99	1	0	2.89	3	1	0	0	9	8	3	3	0	2	6	.216	.278	.158	5.79	1.93
Cleiber Maldonado	L-L	6-1	200	11-20-03	2	1	3.54	9	2	0	0	20	18	13	8	2	11	18	.225	.100	.243	7.97	4.87
Zebby Matthews	R-R	6-5	210	5-22-00	0	0	0.00	1	0	0	0	1	1	0	0	0	0	2	.250	.500	.000	18.00	0.00
Brayan Medina	R-R	6-1	180	10-6-02	1	0	6.46	10	7	0	0	24	19	21	17	1	20	24	.216	.237	.200	9.13	7.61
Ricky Mineo	R-R	6-5	225	8-22-00	0	0	0.00	1	0	0	0	1	0	0	0	0	0	1	.000	--	.000	9.00	0.00
Danny Moreno	R-R	6-1	180	10-10-99	0	2	5.76	15	0	0	2	25	32	25	16	0	9	21	.305	.389	.261	7.56	3.24
Andrew Morris	R-R	6-0	195	9-1-01	0	0	0.00	1	0	0	0	1	0	0	0	0	0	1	.000	.000	--	9.00	0.00
Jack Noble	R-R	6-2	200	4-2-00	1	0	0.00	2	0	0	0	2	3	0	0	0	1	3	.333	.333	.333	13.50	4.50
Juan Nunez	R-R	5-11	190	12-7-00	0	2	4.85	8	7	0	0	30	27	19	16	2	10	47	.233	.275	.200	14.26	3.03
2-team total (2 FCL Orioles)					0	2	4.54	10	8	0	0	36	36	25	18	4	11	56	.250	.281	.225	14.13	2.78
Jose Olivares	R-R	6-1	199	1-18-03	2	2	4.01	10	4	0	1	34	28	17	15	4	17	40	.217	.224	.213	10.69	4.54
Jon Olsen	R-R	6-2	190	5-13-97	0	0	1.04	6	0	0	0	9	6	1	1	0	2	8	.200	.143	.217	8.31	2.08
Francis Peguero	R-R	6-1	185	8-11-97	0	1	12.46	4	0	0	0	4	8	6	6	0	0	5	.400	.556	.273	10.38	0.00
Elpidio Perez	L-L	6-3	248	11-11-98	3	0	3.86	11	0	0	0	12	11	7	5	0	8	20	.234	.200	.250	15.43	6.17
Alex Phillips	R-R	6-4	220	12-16-94	2	0	0.00	2	0	0	0	2	0	0	0	0	0	2	.000	.000	.000	9.00	0.00
Leyner Ponce	R-R	6-1	190	12-22-00	0	0	5.40	5	0	0	0	3	2	3	2	0	5	3	.154	.222	.000	8.10	13.50
Zaquiel Puentes	R-R	6-1	160	12-30-00	1	0	0.00	2	0	0	0	2	0	0	0	0	2	1	.000	.000	.000	4.50	9.00
Wilker Reyes	L-L	6-0	170	2-25-02	0	2	6.43	11	1	0	0	21	32	21	15	2	8	31	.344	.294	.355	13.29	3.43
Luis Rijo	R-R	6-1	200	9-6-98	0	0	1.20	6	5	0	0	15	12	2	2	0	3	18	.214	.143	.238	10.80	1.80
Isaiah Rivera	L-R	6-2	215	5-26-98	0	1	3.52	15	0	0	4	15	12	7	6	0	5	25	.207	.208	.206	14.67	2.93
Juan Rojas	L-L	6-0	165	1-31-04	1	2	3.60	8	5	0	0	30	23	12	12	3	4	38	.209	.125	.244	11.40	1.20
2-team total (3 FCL Orioles)					2	2	2.79	11	7	0	0	39	27	12	12	3	9	50	.197	.105	.232	11.64	2.09
Brock Stewart	L-R	6-3	220	10-3-91	0	1	9.00	1	1	0	0	2	3	2	2	0	0	2	.333	.000	.600	9.00	0.00
Jesus Toledo	L-L	5-11	180	8-25-99	0	0	0.00	1	1	0	0	1	0	0	0	0	1	0	.000	--	.000	0.00	9.00
Zach Veen	L-L	6-0	180	4-18-01	0	1	3.00	3	0	0	0	3	2	1	1	1	0	4	.182	.333	.125	12.00	0.00
Ricardo Velez	R-R	6-1	180	8-21-98	0	0	3.68	8	0	0	0	7	7	3	3	0	4	12	.241	.000	.438	14.73	4.91
Hunter Wood	R-R	6-1	175	8-12-93	0	0	0.00	1	0	0	0	1	1	0	0	0	0	3	.250	.333	.000	27.00	0.00

Fielding

C: Baez 3, Camargo 2, Castro 10, Contreras 6, Cossetti 1, Isola 3, Morales 2, Nigro 5, Olivar 10, Ortega 2, Rivero 16, Rodriguez 8, Smith 1, Vasquez 13. **1B:** Cruz 3, Duran 22, Ortega 1, Pena 14, Ramirez 21, Sano 4, Soto 2. **2B:** Duran 1, Feliz 1, Michel 28, Olivar 4, Ortega 1, Ortiz 1, Pena 3, Rivero 1, Robertson 1, Schobel 2, Shuffield 2, Soto 18, Yake 1. **3B:** Cruz 12, De Andrade 13, Duran 1, Ortega 1, Pena 7, Ramirez 9, Robertson 3, Ross 1, Soto 17, Yake 1. **SS:** De Andrade 37, Lee 3, Martin 2, Michel 12, Ortiz 3, Robertson 1, Schobel 1, Shuffield 1, Yake 1. **OF:** Aguiar 2, Centeno 41, De La Cruz 29, Duran 16, Garry Jr. 4, Madrigal 5, Olivar 23, Perez 34, Sayre 3, Sosa 16, Urbina 8.

DSL TWINS — *ROOKIE*

DOMINICAN SUMMER LEAGUE

Batting	B-T	HT	WT	DOB	AVG	vLH	vRH	G	AB	R	H	2B	3B	HR	RBI	BB	HBP	SH	SF	SO	SB	CS	SLG	OBP
Bryan Acuna	R-R	6-0	176	8-11-05	.310	.381	.298	43	145	33	45	12	0	0	16	20	5	0	1	36	9	4	.393	.409
Rafael Cruz	R-R	6-1	166	11-13-03	.349	.222	.375	34	106	27	37	5	3	7	27	17	3	0	2	29	5	4	.651	.445
Junior Del Valle	R-R	5-11	173	3-23-04	.290	.286	.291	38	93	20	27	5	1	1	12	12	4	0	2	16	3	3	.398	.387
Denyerbe Gervis	B-R	5-8	139	9-5-03	.272	.158	.295	42	114	21	31	5	3	1	12	17	1	0	1	30	8	7	.395	.368
Harold Grant	R-R	5-11	160	10-29-04	.298	.190	.320	45	121	22	36	6	3	3	23	14	1	0	2	36	10	8	.471	.370
Yilber Herrera	B-R	5-11	145	1-15-05	.181	.200	.176	43	116	15	21	6	3	1	11	30	1	0	2	40	10	6	.310	.349
Junior Marino	R-R	5-11	165	8-19-04	.295	.353	.279	34	78	16	23	5	0	0	9	8	3	2	3	13	5	2	.359	.370
Yasser Mercedes	R-R	6-2	175	11-16-04	.355	.286	.370	41	155	34	55	13	3	4	20	18	1	0	2	35	30	5	.555	.420
Anderson Nova	L-L	6-0	165	2-14-05	.355	.300	.365	40	124	20	44	8	2	1	19	21	3	0	1	26	1	3	.476	.456
Daniel Pena	R-R	5-11	205	3-9-05	.304	.160	.336	46	135	30	41	7	0	1	22	13	10	0	1	22	4	3	.378	.403
Isaac Pena	B-R	5-10	160	12-27-03	.341	.300	.349	46	129	24	44	4	4	0	20	21	2	1	3	14	4	10	.434	.432
Ricardo Pena	R-R	6-0	180	5-30-05	.227	.357	.192	29	66	12	15	2	0	3	13	7	1	0	1	23	2	1	.394	.307
Jesus Peraza	R-R	6-0	170	11-8-04	.246	.000	.271	28	65	4	16	2	0	0	12	6	4	0	1	24	3	3	.277	.342
Jose Rodriguez	R-R	6-2	196	6-10-05	.289	.343	.277	55	190	39	55	15	3	13	49	21	3	0	5	52	5	0	.605	.361
Luis Rodriguez	B-R	5-10	169	9-15-03	.232	.273	.225	34	82	13	19	5	2	0	10	12	1	0	1	25	3	5	.341	.333
Javier Roman	R-R	6-0	155	3-26-03	.109	.143	.104	29	55	2	6	0	0	0	6	6	4	1	1	21	1	1	.109	.242
Juan Zapata	B-R	5-9	140	12-5-04	.173	.000	.231	33	52	11	9	1	1	0	2	7	2	0	0	17	3	2	.231	.295

Pitching	B-T	HT	WT	DOB	W	L	ERA	G	GS	CG	SV	IP	H	R	ER	HR	BB	SO	AVG	vLH	vRH	K/9	BB/9
Jose Betancourt	R-R	6-3	182	12-16-04	0	0	6.00	5	2	0	1	3	2	5	2	0	7	5	.154	.100	.333	15.00	21.00
Julio Bonilla	R-R	6-3	180	11-15-00	3	0	3.91	9	2	0	0	25	24	17	11	5	7	24	.250	.271	.229	8.53	2.49
Jose Brito	R-R	6-1	168	9-19-99	1	3	3.68	12	0	0	1	15	17	12	6	0	12	16	.274	.321	.235	9.82	7.36
Roger Duran	R-R	6-1	185	8-25-04	4	0	2.22	10	5	0	0	28	26	9	7	0	14	23	.243	.306	.211	7.31	4.45
Cristian Jimenez	R-R	6-2	180	5-16-04	1	2	3.38	10	7	0	1	37	36	22	14	1	7	49	.242	.167	.284	11.81	1.69

Cesar Lares	L-L	6-0	155	7-3-03	2	3	2.93	11	11	0	0	46	31	16	15	0	20	71	.188	.306	.155	13.89	3.91
Bianger Liendo	R-R	6-1	175	3-7-04	1	1	4.91	11	0	0	0	15	14	11	8	1	9	19	.255	.429	.147	11.66	5.52
Jeferson Lopez	R-R	6-1	174	11-22-04	0	1	4.50	15	3	0	2	24	28	13	12	2	3	29	.280	.256	.295	10.88	1.13
Leonardo Lugo	R-R	5-11	170	9-11-04	3	3	10.94	15	1	0	1	26	31	36	32	5	24	34	.290	.234	.333	11.62	8.20
Eider Machuca	R-R	6-2	190	8-11-04	0	2	16.20	13	1	0	0	13	20	27	24	1	25	23	.333	.286	.359	15.53	16.88
Junior Marino	R-R	5-11	165	8-19-04	0	1	5.40	2	0	0	0	5	5	5	3	0	2	0	.278	.111	.444	0.00	3.60
Juan Mercedes	R-R	5-10	181	1-7-02	1	0	5.51	12	1	0	1	16	15	18	10	5	16	26	.231	.250	.222	14.33	8.82
Anthony Narvaez	R-R	6-1	175	7-30-03	2	0	3.62	11	4	0	1	27	26	15	11	0	10	39	.245	.227	.258	12.84	3.29
José Ojo	R-R	6-0	170	5-17-01	1	0	4.40	11	1	0	1	14	7	16	7	1	15	13	.140	.200	.114	8.16	9.42
Miguel Olivares	R-R	6-1	180	9-19-03	1	2	1.44	12	8	0	0	50	27	13	8	0	20	54	.157	.131	.162	9.72	3.60
Oscar Paredes	R-R	6-0	176	10-2-03	2	4	6.99	13	6	0	1	28	41	30	22	3	20	25	.347	.413	.306	7.94	6.35
Orlando Rubio	R-R	6-0	170	1-3-04	5	2	3.94	14	1	0	1	32	22	21	14	1	21	36	.193	.143	.241	10.13	5.91
Eduardo Soriano	R-R	6-1	190	10-4-02	1	2	2.13	11	1	0	1	25	22	10	6	3	7	19	.229	.278	.200	6.75	2.49
Ledwin Taveras	R-R	6-2	175	3-1-05	4	2	3.70	10	6	0	0	41	31	21	17	3	10	33	.203	.175	.222	7.19	2.18

Fielding

C: Pena 10, Pena 28, Peraza 28, Roman 22. **1B:** Cruz 10, Pena 30, Pena 9, Pena 2, Rodriguez 17, Roman 2. **2B:** Gervis 18, Grant 9, Herrera 25, Marino 8, Pena 4, Rodriguez 2, Zapata 19. **3B:** Cruz 25, Gervis 11, Pena 25, Rodriguez 9, Zapata 4. **SS:** Acuna 42, Herrera 17, Pena 6, Zapata 7. **OF:** Del Valle 35, Gervis 15, Grant 22, Marino 13, Mercedes 40, Nova 33, Pena 1, Rodriguez 51, Rodriguez 3, Zapata 1.

MINNESOTA TWINS

New York Mets

SEASON IN A SENTENCE: The Mets won the second-most games in franchise history, made the postseason for the first time since 2016 and bolstered a farm system that now ranks top 10 in the game—but an air of disappointment hovers over the season based on the way it ended.

HIGH POINT: In a season filled with improbable come-from-behind victories, the Mets' 101st and final win in might have been the most meaningful. Only the 108-win 1986 Mets won more often.

LOW POINT: While losing to the Padres in in the NL Wild Card Series was disappointing, that fate could have been avoided had the Mets won one of three games in Atlanta during the final weekend of the regular season. Instead, the Mets got swept—despite having Max Scherzer, Jacob deGrom and Chris Bassitt on the mound—and lost the NL East division tiebreaker to the Braves, who also won 101 games but took the season series 10-9.

NOTABLE ROOKIE: The Mets' farm system has produced few new contributors since delivering Jeff McNeil in 2018 and Pete Alonso in 2019. That trend could change in 2023, because three of the system's top four prospects debuted late in 2022 but did not graduate. No. 1 prospect Francisco Alvarez made the biggest impact. The 20-year-old Venezuelan catcher was the youngest player in MLB in 2022—he homered and doubled in 12 at-bats—and also the youngest to bat 100 times at Triple-A. Third basemen Brett Baty and Mark Vientos also debuted.

KEY TRANSACTIONS: New general manager Billy Eppler wisely targeted free agents without qualifying offers attached and signed them to short-term deals. In a flurry of pre-lockout activity, the Mets signed Max Scherzer, Starling Marte, Eduardo Escobar and Mark Canha. That quartet produced nearly 13 WAR in 2022. The Mets held onto all their key prospects at the trade deadline as they targeted modest power upgrades like Tyler Naquin, Darin Ruf and Daniel Vogelbach.

ON THE FARM: Mets minor league affiliates went 348-369 (.485), 10th worst in baseball—but there are signs of hope. The 2022 draft helped. First-round catcher Kevin Parada and second-round righthander Blade Tidwell helped Low-A St. Lucie win the Florida State League title. High-A Brooklyn posted a similar record but lost in the South Atlantic League playoffs. Double-A Binghamton and Triple-A Syracuse finished deep in the second division.

OPENING DAY PAYROLL: $265,998,338 (2nd).

PLAYERS OF THE YEAR

MAJOR LEAGUE

Francisco Lindor
SS

.270/.339/.449
26 HR, 16 SB in 161 G
Career-high 107 RBIs

MINOR LEAGUE

Brett Baty
3B

(AA/AAA)
.315/.410/.533
19 HR, 22 2B in 95 G

ORGANIZATION LEADERS

Batting		*Minimum 250 AB
MAJORS		
* AVG	Jeff McNeil	.326
* OPS	Pete Alonso	.869
HR	Pete Alonso	40
RBI	Pete Alonso	131
MINORS		
* AVG	Brett Baty, Binghamton, Syracuse	.315
* OBP	Brett Baty, Binghamton, Syracuse	.410
* SLG	Brett Baty, Binghamton, Syracuse	.533
* OPS	Brett Baty, Binghamton, Syracuse	.943
R	Brett Baty, Binghamton, Syracuse	76
H	Alex Ramirez, St. Lucie, Brooklyn	140
TB	Ronny Mauricio, Binghamton	240
2B	Alex Ramirez, St. Lucie, Brooklyn	30
3B	Alex Ramirez, St. Lucie, Brooklyn	7
HR	Francisco Alvarez, Binghamton, Syracuse	27
RBI	Ronny Mauricio, Binghamton	98
BB	Francisco Alvarez, Binghamton, Syracuse	70
	Wyatt Young, Binghamton, Syracuse, Brooklyn	70
SO	Carlos Dominguez, St. Lucie	173
SB	Omar De Los Santos, St. Lucie	70

Pitching		#Minimum 75 IP
MAJORS		
W	Chris Bassitt	15
	Carlos Carrasco	15
# ERA	Max Scherzer	2.29
SO	Max Scherzer	173
SV	Edwin Diaz	32
MINORS		
W	Dominic Hamel, St. Lucie, Brooklyn	10
L	Junior Santos, Brooklyn	13
# ERA	Nick Zwack, Brooklyn, St. Lucie	2.36
G	Michel Otañez, Syracuse, Binghamton	45
GS	Jose Butto, Binghamton, Syracuse	25
SV	Grant Hartwig, Bing., Brook., St. Lucie, Syracuse	13
IP	Jose Butto, Binghamton, Syracuse	129
BB	Dominic Hamel, St. Lucie, Brooklyn	54
SO	Dominic Hamel, St. Lucie, Brooklyn	145
# AVG	Dominic Hamel, St. Lucie, Brooklyn	.196

2022 PERFORMANCE

General Manager: Billy Eppler. **Farm Director:** Kevin Howard. **Scouting Director:** Marc Tramuta.

Class	Team	League	W	L	PCT	Finish	Manager
Majors	New York Mets	National	101	61	.623	4th (15)	Buck Showalter
Triple-A	Syracuse Mets	International	64	85	.430	18th (20)	Kevin Boles
Double-A	Binghamton Rumble Ponies	Eastern	53	83	.390	11th (12)	Reid Brignac
High-A	Brooklyn Cyclones	South Atlantic	70	62	.530	5th (12)	Luis Rivera
Low-A	St. Lucie Mets	Florida State	73	56	.566	1st (10)	Robbie Robinson
Rookie	FCL Mets	Florida Complex	33	22	.600	t-4th (16)	Endy Chavez
Overall 2022 Minor League Record			348	369	.485	21st (30)	

ORGANIZATION STATISTICS

NEW YORK METS

NATIONAL LEAGUE

Batting	B-T	HT	WT	DOB	AVG	vLH	vRH	G	AB	R	H	2B	3B	HR	RBI	BB	HBP	SH	SF	SO	SB	CS	SLG	OBP
Pete Alonso	R-R	6-3	245	12-7-94	.271	.247	.279	160	597	95	162	27	0	40	131	67	12	0	9	128	5	1	.518	.352
Francisco Alvarez	R-R	5-10	233	11-19-01	.167	.000	.250	5	12	3	2	1	0	1	1	2	0	0	0	4	0	0	.500	.286
Brett Baty	L-R	6-3	210	11-13-99	.184	.111	.207	11	38	4	7	0	0	2	5	2	1	0	0	8	0	0	.342	.244
Travis Blankenhorn	L-R	6-2	235	8-3-96	.000	--	.000	1	3	0	0	0	0	0	0	0	0	0	0	1	0	0	.000	.000
Mark Canha	R-R	6-2	209	2-15-89	.266	.241	.280	140	462	71	123	24	0	13	61	48	28	0	4	97	3	1	.403	.367
Robinson Cano	L-R	6-0	212	10-22-82	.195	.222	.188	12	41	3	8	0	0	1	3	2	0	0	0	11	0	0	.268	.233
3-team total (9 Atlanta Braves, 12 San Diego Padres)					.150	.222	.143	33	100	5	15	1	0	1	4	4	0	0	0	25	0	0	.190	.183
J.D. Davis	R-R	6-3	218	4-27-93	.238	.223	.253	66	181	26	43	8	1	4	21	20	4	0	2	66	1	1	.359	.324
2-team total (49 San Francisco Giants)					.248	.245	.252	115	318	46	79	16	1	12	35	39	6	0	2	122	1	1	.418	.340
Eduardo Escobar	B-R	5-10	193	1-5-89	.240	.259	.231	136	495	58	119	26	4	20	69	40	1	0	6	129	0	2	.430	.295
Terrance Gore	R-R	5-7	160	6-8-91	.143	.000	.167	10	7	1	1	0	0	0	0	0	0	1	0	3	3	0	.143	.143
Luis Guillorme	L-R	5-10	190	9-27-94	.273	.214	.296	102	297	33	81	12	1	2	17	34	2	2	0	46	1	0	.340	.351
Ender Inciarte	L-L	5-11	190	10-29-90	.125	.000	.200	11	8	1	1	0	0	0	0	0	0	0	0	0	0	0	.125	.125
Travis Jankowski	L-R	6-2	190	6-15-91	.167	.188	.158	43	54	11	9	0	0	0	2	8	1	0	0	9	3	0	.167	.286
Khalil Lee	L-L	5-10	170	6-26-98	.500	--	.500	2	2	1	1	0	0	1	3	0	0	0	0	0	0	0	2.000	.500
Francisco Lindor	B-R	5-11	190	11-14-93	.270	.271	.269	161	630	98	170	25	5	26	107	59	10	0	7	133	16	6	.449	.339
Deven Marrero	R-R	6-0	190	8-25-90	.000	.000	.000	5	6	0	0	0	0	0	0	0	0	0	0	3	1	0	.000	.000
Starling Marte	R-R	6-1	195	10-9-88	.292	.302	.287	118	466	76	136	24	5	16	63	26	13	0	0	97	18	9	.468	.347
Patrick Mazeika	L-R	6-3	210	10-14-93	.191	.300	.172	24	68	4	13	4	0	1	6	2	0	2	0	9	0	0	.294	.214
James McCann	R-R	6-3	220	6-13-90	.195	.092	.257	61	174	19	34	6	0	3	18	11	4	0	2	46	3	0	.282	.257
Jeff McNeil	L-R	6-1	195	4-8-92	.326	.312	.332	148	533	73	174	39	1	9	62	40	11	0	5	61	4	0	.454	.382
Tyler Naquin	L-R	6-2	195	4-24-91	.203	.167	.210	49	123	18	25	7	2	4	13	6	1	0	0	40	1	0	.390	.246
2-team total (56 Cincinnati Reds)					.229	.180	.241	105	310	47	71	19	4	11	46	19	4	1	0	93	4	2	.423	.282
Tomas Nido	R-R	6-0	211	4-12-94	.239	.259	.227	98	284	31	68	15	0	3	28	14	1	12	2	76	0	0	.324	.276
Brandon Nimmo	L-R	6-3	206	3-27-93	.274	.264	.280	151	580	102	159	30	7	16	64	71	16	3	3	116	3	2	.433	.367
Michael Perez	L-R	5-10	195	8-7-92	.143	.000	.154	6	14	2	2	0	0	0	3	2	0	0	0	6	0	0	.143	.250
2-team total (39 Pittsburgh Pirates)					.149	.115	.158	45	121	10	18	0	0	6	14	10	0	1	0	32	1	0	.298	.214
Nick Plummer	L-L	5-10	200	7-31-96	.138	.000	.200	14	29	4	4	1	0	2	6	1	1	0	0	12	0	0	.379	.194
Matt Reynolds	R-R	6-1	200	12-3-90	--	--	--	1	0	0	0	0	0	0	0	0	0	0	0	0	0	0	--	--
2-team total (92 Cincinnati Reds)					.246	.205	.263	93	244	31	60	10	1	3	23	26	1	0	1	78	5	0	.332	.320
Darin Ruf	R-R	6-2	232	7-28-86	.152	.149	.158	29	66	6	10	3	0	0	7	5	1	0	2	20	0	0	.197	.216
2-team total (90 San Francisco Giants)					.204	.222	.188	119	334	52	68	12	0	11	45	45	6	0	3	105	2	0	.338	.307
Yolmer Sanchez	B-R	6-0	210	6-29-92	--	--	--	3	0	0	0	0	0	0	0	0	0	0	0	0	0	0	--	--
Dominic Smith	L-L	6-0	239	6-15-95	.194	.176	.197	58	134	11	26	10	1	0	17	12	4	0	2	37	0	0	.284	.276
Mark Vientos	R-R	6-4	185	12-11-99	.167	.222	.111	16	36	3	6	1	0	1	3	5	0	0	0	12	0	0	.278	.268
Daniel Vogelbach	L-R	6-0	270	12-17-92	.255	.125	.262	55	149	18	38	9	0	6	25	33	1	0	0	47	0	0	.436	.393

Pitching	B-T	HT	WT	DOB	W	L	ERA	G	GS	CG	SV	IP	H	R	ER	HR	BB	SO	AVG	vLH	vRH	K/9	BB/9
R.J. Alvarez	R-R	6-1	230	6-8-91	0	1	11.57	1	0	0	0	2	4	3	3	2	3	2	.400	.400	.400	7.71	11.57
Chris Bassitt	R-R	6-5	217	2-22-89	15	9	3.42	30	30	0	0	182	159	71	69	19	49	167	.234	.247	.224	8.27	2.43
Jose Butto	R-R	6-1	202	3-19-98	0	0	15.75	1	1	0	0	4	9	7	7	2	2	5	.429	.500	.385	11.25	4.50
Carlos Carrasco	R-R	6-4	224	3-21-87	15	7	3.97	29	29	0	0	152	161	71	67	17	41	152	.272	.249	.289	9.00	2.43
Alex Claudio	L-L	6-3	188	1-31-92	0	0	0.00	3	0	0	0	3	1	0	0	0	2	2	.091	.000	.167	5.40	5.40
Sam Clay	L-L	6-3	238	6-21-93	0	0	0.00	1	0	0	0	1	1	1	0	0	1	2	.200	.000	.333	18.00	9.00
2-team total (6 Washington Nationals)					0	0	8.44	7	0	0	0	5	4	6	5	1	4	5	.200	.125	.250	8.44	6.75
Jacob deGrom	L-R	6-4	180	6-19-88	5	4	3.08	11	11	0	0	64	40	22	22	9	8	102	.175	.165	.184	14.27	1.12
Edwin Diaz	R-R	6-3	165	3-22-94	3	1	1.31	61	0	0	32	62	34	9	9	3	18	118	.160	.101	.202	17.13	2.61
Nate Fisher	L-L	6-1	205	5-28-96	0	0	0.00	1	0	0	0	3	1	0	0	0	2	1	.111	.250	.000	3.00	6.00
Mychal Givens	R-R	6-0	230	5-13-90	1	1	4.79	19	1	0	0	21	24	12	11	3	6	20	.304	.391	.268	8.71	2.61
2-team total (40 Chicago Cubs)					7	3	3.38	59	1	0	2	61	56	27	23	8	25	71	.247	.273	.233	10.42	3.67
Colin Holderman	R-R	6-7	240	10-8-95	4	0	2.04	15	0	0	0	18	11	6	4	0	7	18	.186	.217	.167	9.17	3.57
2-team total (9 Pittsburgh Pirates)					5	0	3.81	24	0	0	0	28	20	14	12	0	14	24	.206	.195	.214	7.62	4.45
Tommy Hunter	R-R	6-3	250	7-3-86	0	1	2.42	18	0	0	0	22	21	8	6	4	6	22	.241	.269	.230	8.87	2.42
Yoan Lopez	R-R	6-3	208	1-2-93	1	0	5.73	8	0	0	0	11	14	8	7	2	5	10	.311	.333	.300	8.18	4.09

Seth Lugo	R-R	6-4	225	11-17-89	3	2	3.60	62	0	0	3	65	58	26	26	9	18	69	.233	.167	.279	9.55	2.49
Trevor May	R-R	6-5	240	9-23-89	2	0	5.04	26	0	0	1	25	27	14	14	4	9	30	.265	.283	.250	10.80	3.24
Adonis Medina	R-R	6-1	187	12-18-96	1	0	6.08	14	0	0	1	24	30	18	16	2	6	17	.306	.286	.317	6.46	2.28
Tylor Megill	R-R	6-7	230	7-28-95	4	2	5.13	15	9	0	0	47	46	27	27	7	13	51	.253	.293	.205	9.70	2.47
Bryce Montes de Oca	R-R	6-7	265	4-23-96	0	0	10.80	3	0	0	0	3	7	4	4	0	2	6	.412	.222	.625	16.20	5.40
Stephen Nogosek	R-R	6-2	205	1-11-95	1	1	2.45	12	0	0	0	22	20	10	6	4	7	21	.230	.214	.244	8.59	2.86
Adam Ottavino	B-R	6-5	246	11-22-85	6	3	2.06	66	0	0	3	66	48	15	15	6	16	79	.204	.301	.160	10.83	2.19
David Peterson	L-L	6-6	240	9-3-95	7	5	3.83	28	19	0	0	106	93	50	45	11	48	126	.236	.176	.252	10.73	4.09
Jake Reed	R-R	6-2	195	9-29-92	1	0	11.37	5	0	0	0	6	4	8	8	2	6	6	.174	.400	.111	8.53	8.53
2-team total (5 Los Angeles Dodgers)					1	0	7.36	10	0	0	1	11	10	9	9	2	7	8	.238	.417	.167	6.55	5.73
Sean Reid-Foley	R-R	6-3	230	8-30-95	0	0	5.40	7	0	0	0	10	7	6	6	1	7	8	.194	.217	.154	7.20	6.30
Joely Rodriguez	L-L	6-1	200	11-14-91	2	4	4.47	55	0	0	0	50	42	28	25	3	26	57	.226	.233	.220	10.19	4.65
Darin Ruf	R-R	6-2	232	7-28-86	0	0	0.00	1	0	0	0	2	1	0	0	0	0	0	.143	.500	.000	0.00	0.00
Max Scherzer	R-R	6-3	208	7-27-84	11	5	2.29	23	23	0	0	145	108	39	37	13	24	173	.207	.196	.215	10.71	1.49
Chasen Shreve	L-L	6-4	180	7-12-90	1	1	6.49	25	0	0	0	26	27	19	19	6	10	29	.262	.296	.224	9.91	3.42
Drew Smith	R-R	6-2	190	9-24-93	3	3	3.33	44	0	0	0	46	38	17	17	9	15	53	.222	.268	.200	10.37	2.93
Thomas Szapucki	R-L	6-2	210	6-12-96	0	1	60.75	1	1	0	0	1	7	9	9	4	3	2	.700	1.000	.571	13.50	20.25
2-team total (10 San Francisco Giants)					0	1	7.20	11	1	0	0	15	19	12	12	6	7	18	.317	.375	.278	10.80	4.20
Taijuan Walker	R-R	6-4	235	8-13-92	12	5	3.49	29	29	0	0	157	143	63	61	15	45	132	.240	.242	.239	7.55	2.57
Trevor Williams	R-R	6-3	235	4-25-92	3	5	3.21	30	9	0	1	90	87	34	32	12	23	84	.253	.319	.209	8.43	2.31
Rob Zastryzny	R-L	6-3	205	3-26-92	0	0	9.00	1	0	0	0	1	1	1	1	0	0	1	.250	.500	.000	9.00	0.00

Fielding

Catcher	PCT	G	PO	A	E	DP	PB
Alvarez	1.000	2	12	0	0	0	0
Mazeika	.994	22	158	4	1	1	1
McCann	.993	60	524	16	4	4	1
Nido	.994	96	859	27	5	3	3
Perez	1.000	6	30	4	0	1	0

First Base	PCT	G	PO	A	E	DP
Alonso	.992	134	913	92	8	102
Canha	1.000	1	1	0	0	0
Davis	.964	4	26	1	1	1
Mazeika	1.000	2	2	0	0	0
McCann	1.000	3	9	2	0	2
Ruf	1.000	9	43	1	0	1
Smith	1.000	37	145	15	0	15

Second Base	PCT	G	PO	A	E	DP
Cano	1.000	7	7	11	0	3
Escobar	1.000	2	2	0	0	0
Guillorme	.996	67	95	151	1	40
McNeil	.992	106	160	223	3	55

Third Base	PCT	G	PO	A	E	DP
Baty	.933	11	7	21	2	1
Canha	1.000	1	0	1	0	0
Davis	.923	12	4	8	1	2
Escobar	.958	130	91	184	12	19
Guillorme	.979	22	12	34	1	5
Marrero	1.000	1	1	1	0	1
McNeil	1.000	1	1	0	0	0
Sanchez	1.000	2	0	1	0	0
Vientos	1.000	2	0	2	0	1

Shortstop	PCT	G	PO	A	E	DP
Guillorme	.955	15	3	18	1	3
Lindor	.985	159	198	385	9	82
Marrero	1.000	3	1	1	0	0
Sanchez	.500	1	0	1	1	0

Outfield	PCT	G	PO	A	E	DP
Canha	1.000	140	194	3	0	1
Gore	1.000	6	5	0	0	0
Inciarte	1.000	10	9	0	0	0
Jankowski	1.000	41	38	0	0	0
Lee	--	2	0	0	0	0
Marte	.995	118	209	9	1	1
McNeil	.989	47	85	3	1	1
Naquin	.964	42	53	0	2	0
Nimmo	1.000	151	304	4	0	1
Plummer	1.000	9	7	1	0	0
Reynolds	--	1	0	0	0	0
Ruf	1.000	7	6	0	0	0

SYRACUSE METS — *TRIPLE-A*

INTERNATIONAL LEAGUE

Batting	B-T	HT	WT	DOB	AVG	vLH	vRH	G	AB	R	H	2B	3B	HR	RBI	BB	HBP	SH	SF	SO	SB	CS	SLG	OBP
Francisco Alvarez	R-R	5-10	233	11-19-01	.234	.333	.178	45	158	31	37	6	0	9	31	34	5	0	2	52	0	0	.443	.382
Brett Baty	L-R	6-3	210	11-13-99	.364	.375	.357	6	22	3	8	0	0	0	1	3	1	0	0	6	0	1	.364	.462
Travis Blankenhorn	L-R	6-2	235	8-3-96	.267	.238	.285	91	329	44	88	20	0	15	55	32	6	1	1	88	10	1	.465	.342
Cody Bohanek	R-R	6-1	195	7-2-95	.176	.157	.184	56	176	27	31	7	1	2	15	18	8	0	1	70	9	2	.261	.281
Quinn Brodey	L-L	6-1	195	12-1-95	.200	.222	.189	35	110	16	22	5	3	4	15	6	0	0	0	37	7	1	.409	.241
Jose Colina	B-R	6-2	250	3-26-98	.100	.200	.067	7	20	2	2	0	0	0	3	3	2	0	0	10	0	0	.100	.280
Carlos Cortes	L-B	5-7	197	6-30-97	.168	.212	.149	34	107	11	18	4	0	1	8	7	2	0	1	24	0	0	.234	.231
Nick Dini	R-R	5-8	190	7-27-93	.232	.328	.185	50	177	31	41	5	0	11	37	21	3	0	0	36	1	0	.446	.323
Johneshwy Fargas	R-R	6-1	180	12-15-94	.227	.311	.184	38	132	22	30	5	0	5	21	6	5	2	1	39	10	2	.379	.285
Branden Fryman	R-R	6-2	176	3-16-98	.158	.200	.143	7	19	0	3	1	0	0	1	0	0	0	0	10	0	1	.211	.158
Nic Gaddis	R-R	5-11	171	10-12-96	1.000	1.000	1.000	1	2	2	2	2	0	0	0	3	0	0	0	0	0	0	2.000	1.000
Terrance Gore	R-R	5-7	160	6-8-91	.241	.235	.244	26	58	15	14	0	0	0	4	6	0	2	0	19	9	2	.241	.313
Luis Guillorme	L-R	5-10	190	9-27-94	.417	1.000	.364	4	12	1	5	0	0	0	1	1	0	0	0	1	0	0	.417	.462
Ender Inciarte	L-L	5-11	190	10-29-90	.188	.250	.167	4	16	2	3	1	0	0	0	1	0	0	0	3	2	0	.250	.235
2-team total (34 Scranton/Wilkes-Barre RailRiders)					.244	.222	.253	38	119	14	29	3	1	4	11	14	0	0	0	20	6	2	.387	.323
Travis Jankowski	L-R	6-2	190	6-15-91	.237	.194	.250	36	131	27	31	3	1	1	6	31	1	1	0	36	15	1	.298	.387
Daniel Johnson	L-L	5-10	200	7-11-95	.136	.000	.162	14	44	4	6	1	0	1	6	1	1	0	2	23	0	0	.227	.167
3-team total (17 Columbus Clippers, 26 Rochester Red Wings)					.187	.174	.191	57	203	18	38	4	1	5	25	12	1	0	3	71	2	2	.291	.233
Gosuke Katoh	L-R	6-1	200	10-8-94	.223	.230	.219	80	287	42	64	15	2	9	32	32	4	1	0	72	7	1	.383	.310
2-team total (1 Buffalo Bisons)					.219	.228	.215	81	292	42	64	15	2	9	34	32	4	1	0	73	7	1	.377	.305
Khalil Lee	L-L	5-10	170	6-26-98	.211	.178	.226	100	355	48	75	25	0	10	37	47	14	0	1	139	14	3	.366	.326
Tzu-Wei Lin	L-R	5-9	180	2-15-94	.152	.189	.127	28	92	8	14	3	0	2	8	13	0	1	0	28	4	1	.250	.257
Juan Loyo	R-R	5-11	180	3-16-99	.167	.500	.000	4	12	0	2	0	0	0	0	1	0	0	0	7	0	0	.167	.231
Jake Mangum	B-L	6-1	179	3-8-96	.333	.375	.321	33	138	22	46	11	1	2	21	7	1	0	2	23	7	1	.471	.365
Deven Marrero	R-R	6-0	190	8-25-90	.229	.308	.185	44	144	23	33	1	2	3	19	20	0	2	0	34	5	1	.326	.323
Patrick Mazeika	L-R	6-3	210	10-14-93	.261	.244	.271	33	111	10	29	2	0	2	12	15	7	0	0	18	0	0	.333	.383
Nick Meyer	R-R	6-1	200	2-18-97	.247	.220	.256	51	158	25	39	9	0	3	23	25	3	2	1	40	11	3	.361	.358
Daniel Palka	L-L	6-2	230	10-28-91	.263	.252	.268	109	395	68	104	18	0	26	79	48	1	0	1	105	0	2	.506	.344
Michael Perez	L-R	5-10	195	8-7-92	.183	.176	.186	17	60	3	11	2	0	2	10	3	1	0	1	18	0	0	.317	.231

2-team total (8 Indianapolis Indians)					.208	.200	.211	25	77	6	16	3	0	2	12	13	1	0	1	23	0	0	.325	.326
Nick Plummer	L-L	5-10	200	7-31-96	.238	.241	.236	65	235	29	56	12	0	7	41	25	8	0	2	80	8	4	.379	.330
Matt Reynolds	R-R	6-1	200	12-3-90	.118	.200	.083	8	17	1	2	0	0	1	3	3	0	0	1	5	0	0	.294	.238
2-team total (3 Louisville Bats)					.185	.250	.158	11	27	1	5	0	0	1	4	4	0	0	1	6	0	0	.296	.281
JT Riddle	L-R	6-1	190	10-12-91	.254	.281	.244	61	236	32	60	17	1	8	30	5	3	0	2	49	0	0	.436	.276
2-team total (27 Louisville Bats)					.241	.291	.225	88	332	39	80	21	2	11	35	10	4	0	4	71	0	0	.416	.269
Carlos Rincon	R-R	6-3	190	10-14-97	.218	.226	.216	39	147	22	32	10	0	5	13	9	1	0	0	50	0	2	.388	.268
Luke Ritter	R-R	5-11	187	2-15-97	.160	.176	.150	26	94	9	15	4	0	2	8	13	1	0	0	32	2	2	.266	.269
Kramer Robertson	R-R	5-10	166	9-20-91	.240	.179	.277	22	75	16	18	0	1	1	7	17	4	0	0	14	4	2	.307	.406
3-team total (13 Gwinnett Stripers, 81 Memphis Redbirds)					.239	.275	.222	116	410	81	98	16	1	11	47	84	20	0	0	103	30	8	.363	.393
Manny Rodriguez	R-R	5-10	166	7-4-96	.216	.250	.212	11	37	2	8	0	0	2	4	1	0	0	0	12	1	0	.378	.237
Matt Rudick	L-L	5-9	170	7-2-98	.133	.000	.167	5	15	3	2	1	0	0	0	2	1	0	0	3	0	0	.200	.278
Yolmer Sanchez	B-R	6-0	210	6-29-92	.244	.222	.255	22	78	6	19	4	0	1	7	10	4	0	1	19	0	0	.333	.355
2-team total (78 Worcester Red Sox)					.246	.250	.245	100	325	49	80	16	1	10	40	60	7	1	3	86	6	1	.394	.372
Warren Saunders	R-R	6-3	205	12-15-98	.176	.200	.167	5	17	0	3	0	0	0	2	0	0	0	0	9	0	0	.176	.176
Hayden Senger	R-R	6-1	210	4-3-97	.261	.250	.263	6	23	1	6	1	0	0	0	0	0	0	0	7	0	0	.304	.261
Dominic Smith	L-L	6-0	239	6-15-95	.281	.196	.315	54	218	42	62	11	0	10	38	25	4	0	1	39	4	1	.472	.367
Mark Vientos	R-R	6-4	185	12-11-99	.280	.330	.259	101	378	66	106	16	1	24	72	44	3	0	2	122	0	2	.519	.350
Wyatt Young	L-R	5-7	160	12-5-99	.352	.292	.383	19	71	14	25	3	0	1	7	11	1	1	0	13	2	0	.437	.446

Pitching	B-T	HT	WT	DOB	W	L	ERA	G	GS	CG	SV	IP	H	R	ER	HR	BB	SO	AVG	vLH	vRH	K/9	BB/9
Tim Adleman	R-R	6-5	225	11-13-87	2	1	6.04	17	9	0	0	45	46	33	30	10	16	39	.261	.250	.269	7.86	3.22
Manuel Alvarez	R-R	6-3	225	9-17-95	0	0	13.50	1	0	0	0	1	2	1	1	0	2	0	.500	1.000	.333	0.00	27.00
R.J. Alvarez	R-R	6-1	230	6-8-91	4	3	3.55	40	0	0	4	46	34	23	18	3	29	44	.209	.235	.189	8.67	5.72
Jose Butto	R-R	6-1	202	3-19-98	1	1	2.45	8	7	0	0	37	26	10	10	3	9	30	.198	.193	.203	7.36	2.21
Trevor Cahill	R-R	6-4	223	3-1-88	0	1	6.52	8	6	0	0	19	25	18	14	4	19	17	.321	.344	.304	7.91	8.84
Alex Claudio	L-L	6-3	188	1-31-92	3	2	3.91	34	0	0	2	48	46	27	21	7	15	42	.249	.205	.280	7.82	2.79
Sam Clay	L-L	6-3	238	6-21-93	4	1	3.97	19	0	0	0	23	22	11	10	1	10	25	.265	.160	.310	9.93	3.97
2-team total (21 Rochester Red Wings)					5	3	3.56	40	0	0	0	43	44	18	17	3	17	45	.265	.200	.302	9.42	3.56
Trey Cobb	R-R	6-1	190	6-24-94	6	5	5.33	31	1	0	3	51	48	36	30	6	24	40	.251	.213	.279	7.11	4.26
Jacob deGrom	L-R	6-4	180	6-19-88	0	1	4.50	2	2	0	0	8	4	5	4	2	4	10	.148	.100	.176	11.25	4.50
Yennsy Diaz	R-R	6-1	210	11-15-96	0	2	6.75	20	0	0	0	28	27	22	21	3	19	22	.257	.163	.323	7.07	6.11
Phillip Diehl	L-L	6-2	169	7-16-94	0	2	8.27	13	0	0	1	16	21	17	15	4	10	9	.313	.393	.256	4.96	5.51
2-team total (25 Louisville Bats)					2	3	5.90	38	0	0	1	40	39	29	26	8	18	39	.255	.292	.227	8.85	4.08
Justin Dillon	R-R	6-3	225	9-5-93	0	0	5.49	15	1	0	1	20	22	14	12	1	11	21	.289	.314	.268	9.61	5.03
Nate Fisher	L-L	6-1	205	5-28-96	1	2	4.34	18	11	0	0	56	60	29	27	6	23	40	.276	.306	.265	6.43	3.70
Mychal Givens	R-R	6-0	230	5-13-90	0	0	0.00	1	1	0	0	1	0	0	0	0	0	2	.000	.000	.000	18.00	0.00
Harol Gonzalez	R-R	6-0	160	3-2-95	0	5	8.13	8	7	0	0	28	34	25	25	5	13	15	.298	.267	.333	4.88	4.23
Cole Gordon	L-R	6-5	226	10-2-95	0	0	9.00	1	1	0	0	2	2	2	2	1	2	1	.250	.333	.200	4.50	9.00
Connor Grey	R-R	6-0	180	5-6-94	5	6	6.38	26	24	0	0	104	131	77	74	12	43	88	.308	.303	.313	7.59	3.71
David Griffin	R-R	6-0	205	7-16-96	0	2	12.86	2	2	0	0	7	14	10	10	3	2	6	.438	.429	.444	7.71	2.57
Grant Hartwig	R-R	6-5	235	12-18-97	2	0	0.00	2	0	0	0	3	0	0	0	0	2	4	.000	.000	.000	12.00	6.00
Josh Hejka	R-R	6-1	175	3-20-97	0	1	8.53	2	2	0	0	6	7	6	6	2	2	7	.292	.385	.182	9.95	2.84
Colin Holderman	R-R	6-7	240	10-8-95	1	0	2.51	11	0	0	3	14	9	5	4	2	3	17	.176	.182	.172	10.67	1.88
2-team total (3 Indianapolis Indians)					1	0	2.60	14	0	0	3	17	11	6	5	2	5	21	.177	.231	.139	10.90	2.60
Tommy Hunter	R-R	6-3	250	7-3-86	1	0	4.61	8	0	0	0	14	16	9	7	2	1	14	.267	.160	.343	9.22	0.66
Alec Kisena	L-R	6-5	268	10-12-95	0	0	8.44	1	1	0	0	5	7	6	5	2	2	4	.304	.200	.500	6.75	3.38
Yoan Lopez	R-R	6-3	208	1-2-93	2	2	5.14	29	0	0	2	35	41	22	20	4	15	38	.285	.415	.209	9.77	3.86
Joey Lucchesi	L-L	6-5	225	6-6-93	0	0	1.80	2	2	0	0	5	4	1	1	0	1	3	.211	.250	.200	5.40	1.80
Trevor May	R-R	6-5	240	9-23-89	0	0	6.00	3	0	0	0	3	3	2	2	0	1	3	.273	.250	.286	9.00	3.00
Adonis Medina	R-R	6-1	187	12-18-96	1	0	4.65	18	2	0	1	31	36	19	16	4	17	33	.283	.281	.286	9.58	4.94
Tylor Megill	R-R	6-7	230	7-28-95	0	0	14.73	4	1	0	0	4	5	6	6	0	3	3	.313	.222	.429	7.36	7.36
Andrew Mitchell	L-L	6-1	200	10-23-94	0	0	5.17	10	0	0	0	16	18	10	9	3	12	14	.295	.321	.273	8.04	6.89
Bryce Montes de Oca	R-R	6-7	265	4-23-96	2	2	3.44	30	0	0	8	34	24	14	13	0	24	56	.195	.182	.206	14.82	6.35
Mike Montgomery	L-L	6-5	220	7-1-89	2	10	6.72	22	17	0	0	70	76	60	52	9	33	54	.273	.283	.267	6.98	4.26
Stephen Nogosek	R-R	6-2	205	1-11-95	2	0	2.30	31	0	0	4	43	31	13	11	2	15	53	.200	.177	.215	11.09	3.14
Eric Orze	R-R	6-4	195	8-21-97	4	3	5.13	32	0	0	1	47	42	32	27	11	14	64	.232	.129	.297	12.17	2.66
Michel Otanez	R-R	6-4	218	7-3-97	4	1	6.37	31	0	0	2	30	28	25	21	4	35	38	.239	.234	.243	11.53	10.62
Felix Pena	R-R	6-2	220	2-25-90	1	5	4.06	8	6	0	0	31	32	17	14	3	9	26	.274	.352	.206	7.55	2.61
David Peterson	L-L	6-6	240	9-3-95	2	3	4.85	6	6	0	0	26	33	16	14	1	10	34	.303	.278	.315	11.77	3.46
Jake Reed	R-R	6-2	195	9-29-92	0	0	5.73	8	0	0	0	11	11	8	7	1	5	11	.244	.353	.179	9.00	4.09
Jose Rodriguez	R-R	6-2	175	8-29-95	2	3	4.95	29	11	0	0	76	79	45	42	14	36	68	.270	.270	.270	8.02	4.24
Antonio Santos	R-R	6-3	223	10-6-96	1	0	8.49	8	0	0	0	12	19	11	11	3	5	8	.358	.353	.361	6.17	3.86
Max Scherzer	R-R	6-3	208	7-27-84	0	0	2.45	1	1	0	0	4	3	1	1	1	1	7	.214	.167	.250	17.18	2.45
Drew Smith	R-R	6-2	190	9-24-93	0	0	0.00	3	0	0	0	3	2	0	0	0	1	4	.182	.200	.167	12.00	3.00
Locke St. John	L-L	6-3	180	1-31-93	2	5	6.00	29	1	0	1	42	37	33	28	8	23	35	.237	.200	.257	7.50	4.93
2-team total (5 Iowa Cubs)					2	6	5.88	34	1	0	1	49	44	37	32	9	29	43	.239	.179	.274	7.90	5.33
Thomas Szapucki	R-L	6-2	210	6-12-96	2	6	3.38	18	16	0	0	64	54	25	24	5	29	87	.230	.238	.226	12.23	4.08
Jesus Vargas	R-R	6-2	175	8-18-98	0	1	12.15	2	2	0	0	7	12	9	9	2	3	5	.400	.400	.400	6.75	4.05
Anthony Vizcaya	R-R	6-0	220	10-24-93	2	1	6.08	10	0	0	0	13	15	9	9	4	7	12	.300	.294	.303	8.10	4.73
Josh Walker	L-L	6-6	225	12-1-94	2	2	6.91	9	0	0	0	14	18	12	11	2	7	23	.316	.300	.324	14.44	4.40
Jordan Yamamoto	R-R	6-0	185	5-11-96	2	1	8.27	7	3	0	0	16	25	15	15	3	7	15	.357	.441	.278	8.27	3.86
Joe Zanghi	R-R	6-3	240	12-1-94	0	0	4.19	15	0	0	1	19	14	11	9	3	16	16	.200	.188	.211	7.45	7.45
Rob Zastryzny	R-L	6-3	205	3-26-92	1	5	3.61	26	6	0	1	47	48	26	19	6	19	59	.261	.185	.292	11.22	3.61

Fielding

Catcher	PCT	G	PO	A	E	DP	PB
Alvarez	.990	33	276	22	3	1	7
Colina	1.000	3	25	1	0	0	0
Dini	.977	40	368	16	9	1	3
Gaddis	1.000	1	9	0	0	0	1
Loyo	1.000	4	21	1	0	1	0
Mazeika	.991	13	110	3	1	1	0
Meyer	.991	39	309	21	3	5	5
Perez	.993	15	129	16	1	1	1
Senger	1.000	6	38	3	0	0	1

First Base	PCT	G	PO	A	E	DP
Blankenhorn	1.000	1	11	0	0	2
Colina	1.000	4	21	3	0	0
Katoh	.985	10	61	6	1	8
Mazeika	.986	9	70	2	1	7
Meyer	.974	5	34	4	1	6
Palka	.993	45	264	27	2	35
Rincon	.979	11	89	5	2	8
Ritter	1.000	6	37	2	0	3
Smith	.991	39	300	41	3	21
Vientos	.987	27	215	18	3	33

Second Base	PCT	G	PO	A	E	DP
Blankenhorn	.964	31	51	55	4	18
Bohanek	1.000	19	29	46	0	13
Fryman	1.000	3	8	4	0	1
Katoh	.982	66	114	159	5	49
Lin	1.000	5	7	10	0	6
Marrero	.972	8	17	18	1	6
Reynolds	1.000	2	2	2	0	1
Riddle	1.000	5	7	10	0	3
Ritter	.688	3	3	8	5	0
Robertson	.923	3	2	10	1	1
Rodriguez	.966	5	12	16	1	5
Sanchez	1.000	4	4	11	0	0
Saunders	.952	5	8	12	1	4

Third Base	PCT	G	PO	A	E	DP
Baty	.889	4	1	7	1	1
Bohanek	.960	25	19	53	3	6
Fryman	.667	2	0	2	1	0
Guillorme	.000	2	0	0	0	0
Katoh	1.000	1	0	1	0	0
Lin	1.000	5	4	4	0	0
Marrero	.925	14	12	25	3	5
Riddle	.947	9	4	14	1	0
Ritter	.941	18	22	26	3	1
Robertson	.900	6	3	6	1	0
Sanchez	.969	10	10	21	1	2
Vientos	.922	59	36	82	10	10

Shortstop	PCT	G	PO	A	E	DP
Bohanek	.885	15	18	36	7	10
Fryman	1.000	1	0	3	0	0
Guillorme	1.000	1	0	2	0	0
Lin	.928	17	14	50	5	11
Marrero	.980	23	30	66	2	14
Reynolds	1.000	5	9	14	0	6
Riddle	.984	46	55	127	3	22
Robertson	.984	12	17	44	1	13
Rodriguez	.917	6	7	15	2	2
Sanchez	.939	8	10	21	2	2
Young	.914	19	22	42	6	10

Outfield	PCT	G	PO	A	E	DP
Baty	1.000	2	3	1	0	0
Blankenhorn	1.000	50	89	1	0	0
Brodey	.967	33	55	4	2	1
Cortes	.929	28	49	3	4	2
Fargas	.968	36	59	2	2	0
Gore	.972	20	34	1	1	0
Inciarte	1.000	3	6	0	0	0
Jankowski	1.000	34	68	1	0	0
Johnson	.960	13	24	0	1	0
Katoh	1.000	5	8	2	0	0
Lee	.957	98	172	6	8	0
Lin	.833	2	5	0	1	0
Mangum	.987	32	73	2	1	1
Palka	1.000	27	36	0	0	0
Plummer	.967	61	89	0	3	0
Rincon	1.000	19	33	0	0	0
Rudick	1.000	5	13	0	0	0

NEW YORK METS

BINGHAMTON RUMBLE PONIES — DOUBLE-A

EASTERN LEAGUE

Batting	B-T	HT	WT	DOB	AVG	vLH	vRH	G	AB	R	H	2B	3B	HR	RBI	BB	HBP	SH	SF	SO	SB	CS	SLG	OBP
Francisco Alvarez	R-R	5-10	233	11-19-01	.277	.296	.271	67	253	43	70	16	0	18	47	36	3	0	4	71	0	0	.553	.368
Zach Ashford	L-R	5-10	175	2-9-97	.250	.210	.260	94	320	38	80	19	1	5	42	30	4	0	3	79	10	1	.363	.319
Brett Baty	L-R	6-3	210	11-13-99	.312	.243	.330	89	340	73	106	22	0	19	59	46	8	0	0	98	2	3	.544	.406
Cody Bohanek	R-R	6-1	195	7-2-95	.190	.273	.173	22	63	12	12	5	0	0	3	17	3	0	0	23	0	2	.270	.386
Quinn Brodey	L-L	6-1	195	12-1-95	.182	.154	.189	19	66	6	12	6	0	1	9	2	2	0	0	28	3	1	.318	.229
Jose Colina	B-R	6-2	250	3-26-98	.000	.000	.000	4	9	1	0	0	0	0	1	3	0	0	1	6	0	0	.000	.231
Carlos Cortes	L-B	5-7	197	6-30-97	.241	.274	.233	89	332	44	80	18	3	11	47	35	3	0	4	100	0	1	.413	.316
Jefrey De Los Santos	L-R	6-0	154	5-30-03	.500	--	.500	1	2	1	1	0	0	0	0	1	0	0	0	1	0	0	.500	.667
Antoine Duplantis	L-L	5-11	180	9-5-96	.132	.125	.134	26	91	5	12	1	1	1	7	5	1	1	1	28	0	1	.198	.184
Johneshwy Fargas	R-R	6-1	180	12-15-94	.197	.290	.167	38	127	24	25	4	0	3	11	17	8	1	2	35	18	0	.299	.325
Branden Fryman	R-R	6-2	176	3-16-98	.120	.000	.188	8	25	1	3	0	0	0	0	0	0	0	0	7	0	0	.120	.120
Nic Gaddis	R-R	5-11	171	10-12-96	.181	.250	.171	29	94	10	17	1	0	2	10	11	5	0	1	30	1	0	.255	.297
Rowdey Jordan	B-R	5-10	190	1-27-99	.208	.278	.193	29	106	11	22	4	1	2	6	12	2	1	1	33	2	2	.321	.298
Gregory Leal	R-R	6-0	171	2-14-03	.000	--	.000	1	3	0	0	0	0	0	0	0	0	0	0	2	0	0	.000	.000
Juan Loyo	R-R	5-11	180	3-16-99	--	--	--	1	0	0	0	0	0	0	0	0	1	0	0	0	0	0	--	1.000
Jake Mangum	B-L	6-1	179	3-8-96	.273	.318	.253	36	143	20	39	4	4	2	13	12	2	1	0	34	7	2	.399	.338
Ronny Mauricio	B-R	6-3	166	4-4-01	.259	.226	.267	123	509	71	132	26	2	26	89	24	4	0	4	125	20	11	.472	.296
James McCann	R-R	6-3	220	6-13-90	.263	.333	.250	9	38	5	10	2	0	1	3	3	0	0	0	17	0	0	.395	.317
Brandon McIlwain	R-R	6-1	205	5-31-98	.219	.258	.211	50	192	27	42	8	0	4	17	20	5	0	1	64	3	2	.323	.307
Nick Meyer	R-R	6-1	200	2-18-97	.209	.077	.231	28	91	16	19	1	1	3	14	20	0	1	1	20	3	1	.341	.348
Matt O'Neill	R-R	6-0	205	8-20-97	.316	.000	.375	8	19	5	6	2	0	1	5	1	0	0	0	7	0	0	.579	.350
Luke Ritter	R-R	5-11	187	2-15-97	.215	.190	.220	100	363	52	78	17	3	13	54	46	13	0	3	133	7	2	.386	.322
Manny Rodriguez	R-R	5-10	166	7-4-96	.167	.217	.153	31	108	12	18	8	1	3	7	4	1	0	1	48	1	0	.343	.202
Hayden Senger	R-R	6-1	210	4-3-97	.238	.250	.235	77	265	31	63	14	2	5	31	21	9	0	2	99	3	0	.362	.313
Jeremy Vasquez	L-L	6-1	205	7-17-96	.238	.171	.254	104	365	28	87	20	0	3	47	44	3	0	3	71	0	0	.318	.323
Matt Winaker	L-L	6-1	195	11-29-95	.163	.167	.163	68	202	31	33	6	2	3	22	34	11	2	3	57	2	1	.257	.312
Wyatt Young	L-R	5-7	160	12-5-99	.257	.233	.262	98	374	60	96	20	4	6	34	56	1	1	2	89	5	2	.380	.353

Pitching	B-T	HT	WT	DOB	W	L	ERA	G	GS	CG	SV	IP	H	R	ER	HR	BB	SO	AVG	vLH	vRH	K/9	BB/9
Manuel Alvarez	R-R	6-3	225	9-17-95	1	0	0.93	8	0	0	1	10	10	4	1	0	4	17	.256	.267	.250	15.83	3.72
2-team total (26 Akron RubberDucks)					3	3	7.65	34	0	0	1	40	42	39	34	4	31	50	.261	.281	.250	11.25	6.98
Cody Bohanek	R-R	6-1	195	7-2-95	0	0	0.00	1	0	0	0	1	0	0	0	0	0	0	.000	.000	.000	0.00	0.00
Garrison Bryant	L-R	6-3	202	12-3-98	3	3	6.96	9	8	0	0	43	45	33	33	10	17	21	.273	.301	.250	4.43	3.59
Jose Butto	R-R	6-1	202	3-19-98	6	5	4.00	20	18	0	0	92	86	44	41	14	35	108	.244	.246	.243	10.53	3.41
Yeizo Campos	R-R	5-11	175	4-29-96	4	2	6.23	29	0	0	0	48	44	34	33	7	25	47	.243	.280	.212	8.87	4.72
Jose Chacin	R-R	6-4	192	3-25-97	4	9	5.67	23	20	0	0	102	110	67	64	15	33	94	.272	.279	.267	8.32	2.92
Trey Cobb	R-R	6-1	190	6-24-94	2	1	0.47	9	0	0	0	19	12	3	1	0	4	26	.176	.206	.147	12.10	1.86
Justin Courtney	R-R	6-5	225	7-24-96	0	0	3.68	6	0	0	0	7	9	3	3	0	3	10	.290	.300	.286	12.27	3.68
Tony Dibrell	R-R	6-3	190	11-8-95	2	2	4.55	8	6	0	0	30	25	18	15	3	21	39	.225	.173	.271	11.83	6.37

Andrew Edwards	L-L	6-2	216	5-12-97	2	0	5.00	14	0	0	0	18	19	10	10	3	11	24	.271	.179	.333	12.00	5.50
Nate Fisher	L-L	6-1	205	5-28-96	0	1	3.77	12	2	0	0	29	19	14	12	3	11	40	.181	.188	.178	12.56	3.45
Kevin Gadea	R-R	6-5	240	12-6-94	0	2	11.74	11	0	0	0	15	28	29	20	3	17	15	.378	.448	.333	8.80	9.98
Jordan Geber	R-R	6-3	205	7-31-99	0	1	13.50	1	0	0	0	2	4	3	3	3	1	3	.444	.250	.600	13.50	4.50
Harol Gonzalez	R-R	6-0	160	3-2-95	0	0	2.25	1	1	0	0	4	3	1	1	0	1	4	.214	.400	.111	9.00	2.25
David Griffin	R-R	6-0	205	7-16-96	1	7	5.46	19	14	0	1	64	70	41	39	8	29	51	.281	.277	.285	7.13	4.06
Brooks Hall	R-R	6-5	235	6-26-90	0	0	7.04	4	3	0	1	15	18	13	12	4	9	12	.310	.250	.367	7.04	5.28
Grant Hartwig	R-R	6-5	235	12-18-97	0	2	1.14	16	0	0	3	24	14	8	3	0	11	34	.167	.147	.180	12.93	4.18
Josh Hejka	R-R	6-1	175	3-20-97	4	2	4.99	25	0	0	1	40	49	28	22	4	18	38	.302	.364	.260	8.62	4.08
Tommy Hunter	R-R	6-3	250	7-3-86	0	0	0.00	1	0	0	0	1	1	0	0	0	0	2	.250	.000	.500	18.00	0.00
Alec Kisena	L-R	6-5	268	10-12-95	2	7	5.76	15	11	0	0	59	57	40	38	12	20	48	.252	.261	.246	7.28	3.03
Michael Krauza	R-R	6-1	200	8-7-97	2	0	2.70	6	0	0	0	7	8	3	2	0	4	6	.296	.250	.333	8.10	5.40
Justin Lasko	R-R	6-4	208	3-16-97	3	3	7.16	13	4	0	0	44	63	36	35	7	19	28	.339	.387	.315	5.73	3.89
Joey Lucchesi	L-L	6-5	225	6-6-93	0	1	6.75	2	0	0	0	3	5	4	2	0	1	4	.417	.667	.167	13.50	3.38
Trevor May	R-R	6-5	240	9-23-89	0	0	0.00	1	0	0	0	1	1	0	0	0	0	1	.250	.500	.000	9.00	0.00
Tylor Megill	R-R	6-7	230	7-28-95	0	0	3.18	3	2	0	0	6	3	2	2	1	0	11	.158	.000	.300	17.47	0.00
Brian Metoyer	R-R	6-3	173	11-13-98	1	0	9.02	6	0	0	0	7	6	8	8	3	8	11	.231	.091	.333	13.50	9.82
Andrew Mitchell	L-L	6-1	200	10-23-94	1	1	7.71	13	0	0	3	14	13	12	12	2	10	16	.250	.273	.244	10.29	6.43
Bryce Montes de Oca	R-R	6-7	265	4-23-96	1	1	3.12	14	1	0	3	17	11	8	6	0	14	24	.180	.200	.167	12.46	7.27
Dedniel Nunez	R-R	6-2	180	6-5-96	1	0	3.49	23	0	0	2	28	36	11	11	4	13	43	.298	.273	.318	13.66	4.13
Carlos Ocampo	R-R	6-2	181	9-3-98	0	0	9.00	1	0	0	0	3	4	3	3	1	0	2	.308	.167	.429	6.00	0.00
Cam Opp	L-L	5-10	185	11-4-95	0	0	8.10	4	0	0	0	7	11	6	6	0	7	3	.379	.667	.250	4.05	9.45
Michel Otanez	R-R	6-4	218	7-3-97	0	1	1.80	14	0	0	6	15	12	4	3	0	6	20	.222	.136	.281	12.00	3.60
Hunter Parsons	R-R	6-2	215	6-24-97	1	2	5.31	24	1	0	0	39	36	25	23	5	26	42	.243	.264	.232	9.69	6.00
Mitch Ragan	R-R	6-0	216	4-1-97	1	3	5.71	25	6	0	0	52	52	36	33	10	33	52	.261	.261	.261	9.00	5.71
Marcel Renteria	R-R	5-11	185	9-27-94	0	2	15.12	3	3	0	0	8	15	14	14	2	8	13	.375	.571	.333	14.04	8.64
Oscar Rojas	R-R	5-11	200	5-5-99	0	1	27.00	2	1	0	0	1	4	4	3	0	1	0	.500	1.000	.200	0.00	9.00
Antonio Santos	R-R	6-3	223	10-6-96	3	3	4.70	21	0	0	0	31	31	17	16	4	14	35	.265	.222	.292	10.27	4.11
Max Scherzer	R-R	6-3	208	7-27-84	0	0	4.50	2	2	0	0	8	7	5	4	1	2	14	.219	.200	.222	15.75	2.25
Drew Smith	R-R	6-2	190	9-24-93	0	0	0.00	1	0	0	0	1	1	0	0	0	0	2	.250	.250	--	18.00	0.00
Willy Taveras	R-R	5-11	163	1-20-98	1	2	5.40	24	0	0	0	45	58	34	27	12	9	36	.310	.259	.349	7.20	1.80
Alex Valverde	R-R	6-2	185	9-26-96	2	8	5.79	23	17	0	0	87	95	57	56	18	37	98	.283	.266	.294	10.14	3.83
Jesus Vargas	R-R	6-2	175	8-18-98	2	8	6.47	17	12	0	1	65	77	56	47	13	15	53	.286	.282	.290	7.30	2.07
Kyle Wilson	R-R	6-1	185	9-27-96	0	0	0.00	1	1	0	0	2	2	0	0	0	0	3	.250	.333	.200	11.57	0.00
Jordan Yamamoto	R-R	6-0	185	5-11-96	1	1	4.55	14	3	0	2	32	33	20	16	7	10	34	.260	.311	.232	9.66	2.84
Joe Zanghi	R-R	6-3	240	12-1-94	2	2	2.70	21	0	0	1	30	19	10	9	3	14	46	.178	.050	.254	13.80	4.20

Fielding

Catcher	PCT	G	PO	A	E	DP	PB
Francisco Alvarez	.987	46	450	22	6	1	3
Jose Colina	1.000	3	31	0	0	0	2
Nic Gaddis	1.000	9	71	10	0	1	1
Gregory Leal	.917	1	9	2	1	1	0
Juan Loyo	.000	1	0	0	0	0	0
James McCann	.983	7	53	5	1	1	1
Nick Meyer	.953	23	191	14	10	2	1
Matt O'Neill	1.000	7	30	3	0	1	1
Hayden Senger	.987	50	419	20	6	5	7

First Base	PCT	G	PO	A	E	DP
Cody Bohanek	1.000	2	15	0	0	0
Luke Ritter	.994	24	159	10	1	14
Jeremy Vasquez	.976	82	515	24	13	58
Matt Winaker	.995	31	194	15	1	9

Second Base	PCT	G	PO	A	E	DP
Jefrey De Los Santos	1.000	1	1	0	0	0
Branden Fryman	.957	5	8	14	1	3
Luke Ritter	.965	27	33	50	3	6
Manny Rodriguez	1.000	16	23	40	0	12
Wyatt Young	.984	89	129	182	5	42

Third Base	PCT	G	PO	A	E	DP
Brett Baty	.920	68	56	104	14	8
Cody Bohanek	1.000	3	4	5	0	0
Nic Gaddis	.951	21	20	38	3	6
Luke Ritter	.880	40	28	45	10	6
Manny Rodriguez	.818	6	1	8	2	1
Wyatt Young	.000	1	0	0	0	0

Shortstop	PCT	G	PO	A	E	DP
Cody Bohanek	.933	8	10	18	2	3
Branden Fryman	.857	3	2	4	1	1
Ronny Mauricio	.936	112	151	212	25	52
Manny Rodriguez	.966	7	12	16	1	5
Wyatt Young	.941	8	1	15	1	1

Outfield	PCT	G	PO	A	E	DP
Zach Ashford	.989	92	182	4	2	1
Brett Baty	1.000	9	19	1	0	0
Cody Bohanek	1.000	8	17	1	0	1
Quinn Brodey	1.000	19	48	2	0	1
Carlos Cortes	.983	78	157	12	3	1
Antoine Duplantis	1.000	26	45	0	0	0
Johneshwy Fargas	.978	36	86	2	2	1
Rowdey Jordan	1.000	27	51	3	0	0
Jake Mangum	1.000	34	73	1	0	0
Brandon McIlwain	.985	49	127	1	2	0
Matt Winaker	1.000	33	62	1	0	0

BROOKLYN CYCLONES

HIGH-A

SOUTH ATLANTIC LEAGUE

Batting	B-T	HT	WT	DOB	AVG	vLH	vRH	G	AB	R	H	2B	3B	HR	RBI	BB	HBP	SH	SF	SO	SB	CS	SLG	OBP
Jose Colina	B-R	6-2	250	3-26-98	.000	.000	.000	1	2	1	0	0	0	0	0	1	0	0	0	1	0	0	.000	.333
Stanley Consuegra	R-R	6-2	167	9-24-00	.239	.316	.213	56	226	33	54	13	2	5	27	18	5	0	0	62	4	2	.381	.309
Eduardo Escobar	B-R	5-10	193	1-5-89	.286	.000	.500	2	7	1	2	0	0	0	1	0	0	0	0	1	0	0	.286	.286
Branden Fryman	R-R	6-2	176	3-16-98	.186	.167	.188	22	70	6	13	0	1	2	7	7	0	0	1	19	6	1	.300	.256
Nic Gaddis	R-R	5-11	171	10-12-96	.204	.220	.200	67	225	38	46	14	1	6	36	40	6	0	3	54	2	2	.356	.336
Justin Guerrera	R-R	5-9	185	1-11-00	.104	.125	.094	16	48	5	5	0	0	2	5	5	2	0	0	20	1	1	.229	.218
Gregory Guerrero	R-R	6-0	186	1-20-99	.273	.250	.278	10	22	2	6	1	0	1	6	5	1	0	0	10	0	0	.455	.429
Rowdey Jordan	B-R	5-10	190	1-27-99	.262	.250	.266	67	244	33	64	17	3	2	27	40	1	0	0	59	12	4	.381	.368
Juan Loyo	R-R	5-11	180	3-16-99	.308	.600	.125	6	13	4	4	0	0	0	1	2	2	0	0	5	0	0	.308	.471
William Lugo	R-R	6-3	215	1-2-02	.267	.200	.308	28	105	18	28	7	0	4	18	13	1	0	2	27	0	0	.448	.347
Brandon McIlwain	R-R	6-1	205	5-31-98	.298	.333	.289	48	161	17	48	7	6	3	16	14	10	0	0	45	12	5	.472	.389
Jose Mena	R-R	6-0	208	12-22-96	.239	.253	.234	83	306	31	73	12	0	8	35	11	4	0	0	67	0	0	.356	.274
Tanner Murphy	R-R	6-4	199	5-1-98	.232	.357	.210	32	95	10	22	4	2	2	8	6	4	0	1	34	1	0	.379	.302
Shervyen Newton	B-R	6-4	209	4-24-99	.199	.160	.211	96	327	47	65	13	3	8	46	39	8	0	3	134	1	1	.330	.297
Matt O'Neill	R-R	6-0	205	8-20-97	.175	.180	.173	69	206	29	36	6	4	2	25	44	3	0	1	81	0	1	.272	.327

Jaylen Palmer	R-R	6-4	208	7-31-00	.184	.159	.191	102	315	45	58	13	2	9	35	50	12	0	0	147	22	3	.324	.318
Jose Peroza	R-R	6-1	221	6-15-00	.271	.320	.254	115	398	42	108	23	2	8	52	48	7	1	5	110	4	1	.399	.356
Alex Ramirez	R-R	6-3	170	1-13-03	.278	.262	.284	54	227	22	63	17	1	5	34	16	2	0	1	54	4	7	.427	.329
Wilmer Reyes	R-R	6-0	161	12-22-97	.205	.240	.196	34	127	15	26	4	0	1	13	6	1	1	1	36	5	3	.260	.244
Carlos Rincon	R-R	6-3	190	10-14-97	.286	.400	.000	3	7	1	2	1	0	0	2	4	0	0	0	1	0	0	.429	.545
Matt Rudick	L-L	5-9	170	7-2-98	.243	.293	.225	83	300	50	73	18	4	3	28	45	16	0	5	58	17	5	.360	.366
Warren Saunders	R-R	6-3	205	12-15-98	.189	.154	.200	33	106	10	20	6	1	1	4	8	2	0	0	32	0	1	.292	.259
JT Schwartz	L-R	6-4	215	12-17-99	.273	.259	.276	109	400	57	109	25	4	6	49	46	7	0	2	89	3	3	.400	.356
Joe Suozzi	R-R	6-3	215	2-28-98	.221	.210	.225	75	231	34	51	7	4	8	32	24	12	0	1	86	8	4	.390	.325
Fernando Villalobos	L-R	6-0	195	6-24-02	.222	--	.222	3	9	3	2	0	0	0	0	2	0	0	0	6	0	0	.222	.364
Wyatt Young	L-R	5-7	160	12-5-99	.214	.250	.200	5	14	1	3	0	0	0	1	3	1	0	0	2	0	1	.214	.389

Pitching	B-T	HT	WT	DOB	W	L	ERA	G	GS	CG	SV	IP	H	R	ER	HR	BB	SO	AVG	vLH	vRH	K/9	BB/9
Daison Acosta	R-R	6-2	160	8-24-98	5	6	4.84	31	10	0	10	71	53	40	38	0	44	69	.210	.245	.187	8.79	5.60
Keyshawn Askew	L-L	6-4	190	1-5-00	1	0	3.66	5	4	0	0	20	15	8	8	0	9	28	.217	.192	.233	12.81	4.12
Garrison Bryant	L-R	6-3	202	12-3-98	5	1	3.18	15	9	0	0	65	57	23	23	5	19	58	.239	.196	.267	8.03	2.63
Jose Chacin	R-R	6-4	192	3-25-97	0	1	1.53	4	4	0	0	18	14	5	3	1	3	22	.206	.200	.211	11.21	1.53
Nolan Clenney	L-R	6-2	200	6-16-96	3	4	4.92	33	2	0	1	68	60	37	37	7	22	87	.232	.222	.238	11.57	2.93
Jeffrey Colon	R-R	6-1	170	11-9-99	1	0	1.07	6	3	0	2	25	13	3	3	2	7	27	.153	.233	.109	9.59	2.49
Justin Courtney	R-R	6-5	225	7-24-96	5	3	4.21	33	0	0	6	47	49	23	22	5	23	45	.269	.273	.267	8.62	4.40
Andrew Edwards	L-L	6-2	216	5-12-97	0	1	10.80	3	0	0	0	3	5	4	4	1	1	6	.333	.286	.375	16.20	2.70
Benito Garcia	R-R	6-0	165	3-10-00	0	0	7.71	2	0	0	0	5	5	4	4	0	0	4	.263	.333	.200	7.71	0.00
David Griffin	R-R	6-0	205	7-16-96	2	0	1.57	7	2	0	0	23	11	5	4	1	4	27	.138	.063	.188	10.57	1.57
Dylan Hall	R-R	6-5	210	9-7-97	0	2	4.84	16	0	0	4	22	20	14	12	2	8	28	.235	.333	.163	11.28	3.22
Dominic Hamel	R-R	6-2	206	3-2-99	5	1	2.59	11	11	0	0	56	35	17	16	0	25	74	.180	.152	.206	11.96	4.04
Brendan Hardy	R-R	6-4	170	12-15-99	1	0	3.48	17	0	0	0	21	12	8	8	0	17	29	.167	.241	.116	12.63	7.40
Grant Hartwig	R-R	6-5	235	12-18-97	1	0	0.59	11	0	0	7	15	9	1	1	1	6	24	.173	.050	.250	14.09	3.52
Josh Hejka	R-R	6-1	175	3-20-97	1	0	0.00	6	0	0	1	8	5	0	0	0	2	10	.179	.182	.176	11.74	2.35
Tommy Hunter	R-R	6-3	250	7-3-86	0	0	0.00	2	1	0	0	3	1	0	0	0	1	2	.100	.167	.000	6.00	3.00
Nate Jones	R-R	6-1	200	1-6-97	1	0	3.86	6	0	0	1	12	11	5	5	2	5	7	.244	.308	.219	5.40	3.86
Daniel Juarez	L-L	5-11	155	9-28-00	1	0	0.00	5	0	0	0	4	4	1	0	0	3	3	.250	.125	.375	6.23	6.23
Michael Krauza	R-R	6-1	200	8-7-97	0	0	0.00	1	0	0	0	1	0	0	0	0	0	0	.000	--	.000	0.00	0.00
Nathan Lavender	L-L	6-2	210	1-20-00	2	2	2.48	16	0	0	2	29	21	9	8	1	15	37	.202	.195	.206	11.48	4.66
Trey McLoughlin	R-R	6-2	210	6-11-99	1	0	5.11	4	0	0	1	12	11	7	7	3	5	14	.224	.176	.250	10.22	3.65
Luis Moreno	R-R	6-2	170	5-29-99	4	7	2.92	16	14	0	0	77	61	32	25	7	23	70	.216	.215	.216	8.18	2.69
Colby Morris	R-R	6-3	190	5-17-97	1	1	6.43	9	0	0	0	14	14	10	10	2	12	14	.275	.143	.324	9.00	7.71
Carlos Ocampo	R-R	6-2	181	9-3-98	0	2	3.86	3	3	0	0	7	6	6	3	0	8	6	.240	.286	.222	7.71	10.29
Cam Opp	L-L	5-10	185	11-4-95	1	3	5.23	16	0	0	1	31	32	20	18	5	19	26	.274	.293	.263	7.55	5.52
Hunter Parsons	R-R	6-2	215	6-24-97	3	0	1.83	12	0	0	2	20	14	4	4	1	4	25	.197	.250	.176	11.44	1.83
Oscar Rojas	R-R	5-11	200	5-5-99	5	4	4.22	17	10	0	0	53	61	29	25	4	16	50	.288	.293	.285	8.44	2.70
Evy Ruibal	R-R	6-4	232	9-29-95	0	1	6.94	12	0	0	0	12	13	10	9	1	8	12	.289	.385	.250	9.26	6.17
Franklin Sanchez	R-R	6-6	183	9-12-00	1	1	3.18	4	0	0	0	6	6	3	2	0	4	5	.286	.125	.385	7.94	6.35
Junior Santos	R-R	6-7	244	8-16-01	8	13	4.47	26	23	0	0	117	126	67	58	4	44	105	.272	.295	.254	8.10	3.39
Reyson Santos	R-R	6-0	218	1-22-99	0	0	7.79	16	0	0	1	17	17	15	15	3	19	12	.266	.333	.239	6.23	9.87
Christian Scott	R-R	6-4	215	6-15-99	0	0	3.80	6	5	0	0	21	21	9	9	0	10	25	.247	.176	.294	10.55	4.22
Carson Seymour	R-R	6-6	260	12-16-98	1	5	3.68	11	9	0	0	51	45	25	21	8	12	65	.228	.198	.252	11.40	2.10
Sammy Tavarez	R-R	6-7	225	10-20-98	3	1	2.88	32	0	0	5	41	19	18	13	1	33	56	.138	.122	.146	12.39	7.30
Jesus Vargas	R-R	6-2	175	8-18-98	2	1	2.03	7	1	0	0	27	21	7	6	1	6	31	.216	.222	.213	10.46	2.03
Mike Vasil	L-R	6-5	225	3-19-00	1	1	5.13	8	8	0	0	33	24	21	19	3	15	44	.197	.135	.243	11.88	4.05
Jordan Yamamoto	R-R	6-0	185	5-11-96	0	0	7.50	3	0	0	0	6	6	5	5	3	3	8	.273	.400	.235	12.00	4.50
Nick Zwack	L-L	6-3	230	8-1-98	5	1	1.84	14	13	0	1	64	44	15	13	2	16	72	.193	.242	.175	10.18	2.26

Fielding

Catcher	PCT	G	PO	A	E	DP	PB
Colina	1.000	1	7	1	0	1	1
Gaddis	.987	22	217	12	3	1	3
Loyo	.923	5	35	1	3	0	0
Mena	.992	54	483	38	4	0	15
O'Neill	.992	52	478	31	4	0	3
Villalobos	1.000	2	17	0	0	0	1

First Base	PCT	G	PO	A	E	DP
Guerrero	1.000	3	21	1	0	3
Saunders	1.000	3	20	4	0	3
Schwartz	.989	104	769	55	9	70
Suozzi	.989	23	162	11	2	19

Second Base	PCT	G	PO	A	E	DP
Fryman	1.000	15	30	38	0	11
Gaddis	.962	13	22	29	2	4
Guerrera	.938	16	22	38	4	7
Guerrero	.947	6	9	9	1	2
Jordan	.978	10	21	23	1	7
Newton	1.000	2	5	8	0	3
Peroza	.986	54	80	137	3	25
Reyes	.971	8	12	21	1	4
Saunders	1.000	12	16	26	0	9
Young	1.000	3	2	5	0	1

Third Base	PCT	G	PO	A	E	DP
Fryman	1.000	4	8	7	0	0
Gaddis	.875	21	11	45	8	8
Lugo	.946	25	20	33	3	2
Palmer	.933	19	6	22	2	1
Peroza	.963	52	23	82	4	5
Saunders	.848	13	7	21	5	1

Shortstop	PCT	G	PO	A	E	DP
Escobar	1.000	1	2	3	0	2
Fryman	.889	3	5	11	2	1
Lugo	1.000	2	5	10	0	2
Newton	.962	95	118	232	14	47
Peroza	1.000	8	10	22	0	5
Reyes	.939	24	35	72	7	15
Young	1.000	2	2	3	0	0

Outfield	PCT	G	PO	A	E	DP
Consuegra	.969	52	86	9	3	0
Guerrero	1.000	2	2	0	0	0
Jordan	1.000	50	73	1	0	0
McIlwain	.943	43	65	1	4	0
Murphy	1.000	24	40	1	0	0
Palmer	1.000	76	107	1	0	0
Ramirez	.955	51	82	3	4	1
Reyes	1.000	2	2	0	0	0
Rudick	1.000	72	117	2	0	1
Suozzi	.948	34	51	4	3	1

ST. LUCIE METS — *LOW-A*

FLORIDA STATE LEAGUE

Batting	B-T	HT	WT	DOB	AVG	vLH	vRH	G	AB	R	H	2B	3B	HR	RBI	BB	HBP	SH	SF	SO	SB	CS	SLG	OBP
Ronis Aybar	L-R	6-0	180	1-13-00	.250	.500	.200	5	12	3	3	0	0	0	2	0	1	0	0	5	1	0	.250	.308
Raul Beracierta	R-R	6-1	215	5-24-99	.300	.313	.295	93	317	55	95	12	1	13	39	22	4	0	1	83	1	1	.467	.352
Cesar Berbesi	L-R	6-0	160	4-13-00	.111	.250	.071	6	18	4	2	1	0	1	2	7	0	0	0	5	2	0	.333	.360
Oscar Campos	R-R	5-10	170	12-8-96	.625	1.000	.500	3	8	1	5	0	0	0	0	0	0	0	0	1	0	0	.625	.625
Stanley Consuegra	R-R	6-2	167	9-24-00	.251	.215	.263	66	255	38	64	14	4	8	32	26	3	0	3	77	8	8	.431	.324
Omar De Los Santos	R-R	6-1	172	8-8-99	.271	.240	.281	111	431	75	117	23	5	16	62	35	10	0	2	151	70	15	.459	.339
Carlos Dominguez	R-R	6-1	190	10-11-99	.233	.198	.246	111	390	54	91	15	0	20	65	37	16	0	1	173	22	10	.426	.324
Chase Estep	L-R	6-0	200	4-12-00	.214	.296	.175	24	84	14	18	4	0	4	13	13	1	0	1	23	0	1	.405	.323
Branden Fryman	R-R	6-2	176	3-16-98	.000	.000	.000	4	11	1	0	0	0	0	0	1	1	0	0	5	1	0	.000	.154
Justin Guerrera	R-R	5-9	185	1-11-00	.200	.100	.234	82	275	36	55	9	1	11	40	41	7	0	1	120	5	4	.360	.318
Gregory Guerrero	R-R	6-0	186	1-20-99	.204	.429	.167	15	49	0	10	4	0	0	2	2	0	0	0	20	0	0	.286	.235
Daniel Johnson	L-L	5-10	200	7-11-95	.421	.000	.444	5	19	1	8	3	0	0	1	2	0	0	0	6	0	0	.579	.476
Kevin Kendall	L-R	5-10	175	6-25-99	.111	.000	.143	3	9	0	1	0	0	0	0	0	0	0	0	5	0	0	.111	.111
Andriel Lantigua	R-R	6-1	190	11-29-03	.000	--	.000	1	3	0	0	0	0	0	0	0	0	0	0	2	0	0	.000	.000
Gregory Leal	R-R	6-0	171	2-14-03	.182	.200	.176	7	22	2	4	1	0	0	0	1	0	0	0	12	0	0	.227	.217
Khalil Lee	L-L	5-10	170	6-26-98	.241	.500	.200	8	29	5	7	3	1	0	2	3	3	0	0	11	1	3	.414	.371
Tzu-Wei Lin	L-R	5-9	180	2-15-94	.238	.125	.308	7	21	4	5	1	0	1	2	6	0	0	0	7	1	0	.429	.407
Juan Loyo	R-R	5-11	180	3-16-99	.200	.000	.231	10	30	6	6	0	0	0	2	3	1	0	0	11	0	0	.200	.294
William Lugo	R-R	6-3	215	1-2-02	.261	.200	.280	84	314	47	82	18	2	10	45	37	5	0	1	90	0	0	.427	.347
Brad Malm	R-R	6-1	185	8-19-99	.170	.125	.194	16	47	4	8	3	0	0	6	4	1	0	1	19	0	0	.234	.245
Blaine McIntosh	L-L	6-4	180	6-9-01	.300	.273	.316	9	30	1	9	1	0	0	3	5	2	1	0	15	1	2	.333	.432
Tanner Murphy	R-R	6-4	199	5-1-98	.240	.148	.274	32	100	18	24	4	1	3	15	17	4	0	3	30	6	1	.390	.363
Shervyen Newton	B-R	6-4	209	4-24-99	.298	.250	.306	24	84	12	25	9	0	4	16	10	1	1	1	29	0	0	.548	.375
Drake Osborn	R-R	5-10	190	7-22-98	.221	.214	.222	28	86	11	19	4	0	3	16	9	2	0	3	15	1	0	.372	.300
Kevin Parada	R-R	6-1	197	8-3-01	.276	.125	.333	10	29	5	8	1	0	1	5	10	1	0	1	12	0	1	.414	.463
Karell Paz	B-R	6-3	215	8-11-99	1.000	--	1.000	1	1	0	1	0	1	0	3	0	0	0	0	0	0	0	3.000	1.000
Vincent Perozo	L-R	6-0	170	3-6-03	.129	.231	.056	9	31	4	4	1	1	1	6	1	2	0	1	8	0	0	.323	.200
Alex Ramirez	R-R	6-3	170	1-13-03	.284	.277	.286	67	271	40	77	13	6	6	37	28	5	0	2	68	17	9	.443	.359
JT Riddle	L-R	6-1	190	10-12-91	.083	.000	.111	3	12	1	1	1	0	0	2	0	0	0	0	5	0	0	.167	.083
Jose Rivera	R-R	5-9	190	9-7-99	.226	.250	.214	30	84	11	19	1	0	1	5	29	2	0	0	37	1	3	.274	.435
Hector Rodriguez	L-R	5-8	186	3-11-04	.143	.000	.167	2	7	1	1	0	0	0	0	1	0	0	0	0	0	0	.143	.250
2-team total (13 Daytona Tortugas)					.269	.313	.250	15	52	8	14	4	2	0	6	3	0	0	0	10	1	1	.423	.309
Matt Rudick	L-L	5-9	170	7-2-98	--	--	--	1	0	0	0	0	0	0	0	0	0	0	0	0	0	0	--	--
Eduardo Salazar	R-R	6-3	167	12-15-00	.228	.389	.189	29	92	6	21	2	1	2	5	5	3	0	0	29	0	1	.337	.290
Warren Saunders	R-R	6-3	205	12-15-98	.237	.222	.239	22	76	12	18	6	0	1	6	7	2	0	0	19	0	0	.355	.318
Brady Smith	R-R	6-1	210	11-18-98	.136	.000	.172	29	81	8	11	3	0	1	5	10	2	0	0	38	0	0	.210	.247
D_Andre Smith	R-R	5-9	180	5-10-01	.256	.250	.258	13	43	10	11	3	1	2	6	3	2	0	1	13	1	1	.512	.327
Albert Suarez	L-R	5-11	150	11-30-99	.094	.083	.096	25	64	6	6	1	0	0	2	8	1	0	2	15	0	1	.109	.200
Rhylan Thomas	L-L	6-0	170	4-15-00	.077	.000	.083	6	13	1	1	0	0	0	0	3	0	1	0	3	0	0	.077	.250
Junior Tilien	R-R	6-1	168	9-9-02	.248	.264	.242	84	323	44	80	13	1	12	44	30	0	0	0	81	3	0	.406	.312
Fernando Villalobos	L-R	6-0	195	6-24-02	.146	.120	.155	34	96	14	14	1	0	4	12	29	0	0	0	36	0	0	.281	.344
Kevin Villavicencio	R-R	5-10	172	11-24-03	.239	.077	.267	26	88	11	21	7	0	1	4	1	0	0	0	26	1	2	.352	.247
Jack-Thomas Wold	L-L	5-10	220	9-16-99	.203	.175	.213	61	227	29	46	12	1	6	29	19	2	0	0	50	2	1	.344	.270

Pitching	B-T	HT	WT	DOB	W	L	ERA	G	GS	CG	SV	IP	H	R	ER	HR	BB	SO	AVG	vLH	vRH	K/9	BB/9
Jose Acuna	R-R	6-2	175	10-20-02	0	0	1.13	2	2	0	0	8	4	1	1	0	5	12	.143	1.000	.111	13.50	5.63
2-team total (7 Daytona Tortugas)					0	1	2.75	9	7	0	0	39	21	14	12	1	15	47	.157	.118	.170	10.75	3.43
Miguel Alfonseca	R-R	6-0	190	2-13-00	2	1	5.20	23	0	0	0	36	38	23	21	3	24	47	.270	.250	.280	11.64	5.94
Keyshawn Askew	L-L	6-4	190	1-5-00	4	0	1.93	13	4	0	1	47	28	16	10	3	19	64	.176	.160	.183	12.34	3.66
Javier Atencio	L-L	6-0	160	11-26-01	2	0	2.27	10	8	0	1	40	30	13	10	1	23	48	.208	.179	.219	10.89	5.22
Jace Beck	R-R	6-9	200	6-14-00	0	1	2.37	17	0	0	1	19	11	5	5	2	17	22	.167	.167	.167	10.42	8.05
Robert Colina	R-R	5-11	175	4-24-01	0	5	7.99	10	6	0	0	33	42	29	29	4	17	41	.311	.322	.303	11.30	4.68
Jeffrey Colon	R-R	6-1	170	11-9-99	3	0	3.23	13	4	0	2	47	41	20	17	2	11	57	.227	.215	.239	10.84	2.09
Joshua Cornielly	R-R	6-2	175	1-15-01	5	3	5.21	31	0	0	3	47	48	28	27	8	25	53	.264	.324	.228	10.22	4.82
Levi David	R-R	6-5	220	6-14-99	1	2	10.03	14	0	0	1	12	2	13	13	0	24	15	.059	.000	.080	11.57	18.51
Felipe De La Cruz	L-L	6-0	160	5-26-01	0	0	0.00	2	0	0	1	4	2	0	0	0	0	9	.154	.250	.111	20.25	0.00
Jacob deGrom	L-R	6-4	180	6-19-88	0	0	0.00	2	2	0	0	5	3	0	0	0	0	11	.176	.250	.111	21.21	0.00
Joel Diaz	R-R	6-2	208	2-26-04	3	2	5.86	16	10	0	0	55	62	37	36	7	25	51	.284	.321	.263	8.30	4.07
Tony Dibrell	R-R	6-3	190	11-8-95	0	0	0.00	3	3	0	0	6	2	0	0	0	2	9	.105	.182	.000	14.29	3.18
Justin Dillon	R-R	6-3	225	9-5-93	1	1	9.00	2	0	0	0	3	2	3	3	0	1	0	.182	.000	.200	0.00	3.00
Benito Garcia	R-R	6-0	165	3-10-00	2	3	6.10	10	0	0	1	21	20	17	14	2	4	28	.256	.250	.259	12.19	1.74
Jordan Geber	R-R	6-3	205	7-31-99	1	0	5.00	6	4	0	0	27	31	18	15	3	11	25	.290	.283	.295	8.33	3.67
Paul Gervase	R-R	6-10	230	5-23-00	1	1	6.10	7	0	0	0	10	11	7	7	1	7	14	.262	.294	.240	12.19	6.10
Dan Goggin	R-R	6-2	206	6-9-97	0	0	5.40	6	0	0	1	8	5	5	5	0	10	5	.192	.250	.143	5.40	10.80
Raimon Gomez	R-R	6-2	175	9-6-01	4	5	3.78	24	2	0	3	48	43	23	20	1	20	54	.243	.275	.222	10.20	3.78
Harol Gonzalez	R-R	6-0	160	3-2-95	0	0	3.52	3	2	0	0	8	6	3	3	1	2	5	.231	.250	.214	5.87	2.35
Saul Gonzalez	R-R	6-7	235	12-28-99	2	1	2.81	14	1	0	1	26	24	9	8	0	7	29	.253	.293	.222	10.17	2.45
Dylan Hall	R-R	6-5	210	9-7-97	1	1	1.52	18	0	0	2	24	21	5	4	0	10	21	.241	.219	.255	7.99	3.80
Dominic Hamel	R-R	6-2	206	3-2-99	5	2	3.84	14	13	0	0	63	48	29	27	5	29	71	.209	.207	.210	10.09	4.12
Brendan Hardy	R-R	6-4	170	12-15-99	0	0	1.08	6	0	0	1	8	3	1	1	0	4	17	.107	.125	.083	18.36	4.32
Grant Hartwig	R-R	6-5	235	12-18-97	3	0	4.30	10	0	0	3	15	15	8	7	0	5	21	.259	.273	.250	12.89	3.07

Nate Jones	R-R	6-1	200	1-6-97	1	1	4.84	16	0	0	3	22	24	14	12	1	8	18	.282	.286	.280	7.25	3.22
Daniel Juarez	L-L	5-11	155	9-28-00	3	1	1.85	26	0	0	4	39	21	10	8	2	21	56	.163	.135	.174	12.92	4.85
Michael Krauza	R-R	6-1	200	8-7-97	1	2	6.75	9	0	0	0	9	10	7	7	4	5	15	.278	.313	.250	14.46	4.82
Kolby Kubichek	R-R	6-0	180	11-28-99	1	0	2.93	6	0	0	0	15	12	5	5	1	8	17	.207	.250	.184	9.98	4.70
Nathan Lavender	L-L	6-2	210	1-20-00	4	1	0.48	10	0	0	1	19	11	1	1	0	11	30	.177	.385	.122	14.46	5.30
Joey Lucchesi	L-L	6-5	225	6-6-93	1	0	0.00	4	2	0	0	5	3	1	0	0	1	5	.176	.250	.154	9.00	1.80
Nick MacDonald	R-R	6-1	175	6-11-98	0	1	10.80	2	0	0	0	2	4	4	2	0	3	1	.400	.000	.571	5.40	16.20
Trey McLoughlin	R-R	6-2	210	6-11-99	4	2	3.26	22	1	0	4	39	32	15	14	6	8	46	.221	.161	.265	10.71	1.86
Mike Montgomery	L-L	6-5	220	7-1-89	0	1	4.91	2	2	0	0	4	4	4	2	0	2	5	.250	.000	.308	12.27	4.91
Luis Moreno	R-R	6-2	170	5-29-99	4	0	2.68	9	3	0	1	40	36	15	12	1	20	37	.245	.283	.218	8.26	4.46
Dedniel Nunez	R-R	6-2	180	6-5-96	0	0	0.00	3	0	0	0	5	1	0	0	0	0	6	.059	.000	.083	11.57	0.00
Carlos Ocampo	R-R	6-2	181	9-3-98	0	1	18.90	3	1	0	0	3	6	7	7	1	3	4	.400	.571	.250	10.80	8.10
Douglas Orellana	R-R	6-1	196	5-1-02	0	0	6.00	3	0	0	0	6	6	5	4	0	7	8	.286	.167	.333	12.00	10.50
Eric Orze	R-R	6-4	195	8-21-97	0	0	0.00	2	0	0	0	3	2	0	0	0	0	5	.182	.333	.000	15.00	0.00
Layonel Ovalles	R-R	6-3	216	6-16-03	0	1	6.23	5	3	0	1	17	15	12	12	3	12	22	.227	.231	.225	11.42	6.23
Jawilme Ramirez	R-R	6-2	170	11-28-01	1	0	0.00	2	0	0	0	3	2	0	0	0	4	3	.182	.167	.200	8.10	10.80
Jake Reed	R-R	6-2	195	9-29-92	0	0	0.00	2	1	0	0	2	1	0	0	0	0	4	.167	.500	.000	18.00	0.00
Joe Joe Rodriguez	R-R	6-1	200	10-12-99	0	0	6.75	1	0	0	0	1	1	1	1	0	3	0	.200	--	.200	0.00	20.25
Franklin Sanchez	R-R	6-6	183	9-12-00	1	1	3.90	13	7	0	0	30	22	13	13	1	17	37	.204	.205	.203	11.10	5.10
Reyson Santos	R-R	6-0	218	1-22-99	0	0	4.91	12	0	0	1	15	13	8	8	1	6	14	.228	.037	.400	8.59	3.68
Christian Scott	R-R	6-4	215	6-15-99	3	3	4.82	12	4	1	0	37	40	21	20	2	12	52	.272	.214	.325	12.54	2.89
Carson Seymour	R-R	6-6	260	12-16-98	4	0	1.19	7	4	0	0	30	23	6	4	0	9	27	.209	.250	.182	8.01	2.67
Tyler Stuart	R-R	6-9	250	10-8-99	0	0	13.50	2	1	0	0	3	4	4	4	0	3	6	.364	.500	.333	20.25	10.13
Joander Suarez	R-R	6-3	223	2-27-00	0	2	7.20	4	2	0	0	10	17	10	8	0	6	13	.370	.240	.524	11.70	5.40
Dylan Tebrake	R-R	6-3	225	7-13-99	0	0	0.00	2	0	0	0	3	3	0	0	0	0	6	.273	.222	.500	20.25	0.00
Blade Tidwell	R-R	6-4	207	6-8-01	0	1	2.16	4	4	0	0	8	4	2	2	0	6	9	.143	.083	.188	9.72	6.48
Mike Vasil	L-R	6-5	225	3-19-00	3	1	2.19	9	8	0	0	37	26	12	9	1	11	39	.193	.129	.247	9.49	2.68
Jordany Ventura	R-R	6-0	162	7-6-00	0	0	5.40	3	3	0	0	7	7	4	4	0	2	10	.259	.273	.250	13.50	2.70
Jaison Vilera	R-R	6-0	188	6-19-97	0	2	10.80	3	2	0	0	7	10	9	8	0	9	9	.313	.278	.357	12.15	12.15
Josh Walker	L-L	6-6	225	12-1-94	1	0	1.35	3	1	0	0	7	3	1	1	0	3	12	.136	.143	.133	16.20	4.05
Kyle Wilson	R-R	6-1	185	9-27-96	0	0	5.40	2	1	0	0	3	1	2	2	1	2	6	.091	.143	.000	16.20	5.40
Calvin Ziegler	R-R	6-0	205	10-3-02	0	6	4.44	16	16	0	0	47	26	26	23	3	35	70	.166	.191	.146	13.50	6.75
Nick Zwack	L-L	6-3	230	8-1-98	1	1	4.97	4	2	0	0	13	14	8	7	1	2	24	.280	.214	.306	17.05	1.42

Fielding

Catcher	PCT	G	PO	A	E	DP	PB
Beracierta	1.000	8	57	3	0	0	3
Campos	1.000	3	24	2	0	0	0
Lantigua	1.000	1	4	0	0	0	0
Leal	.964	6	48	5	2	0	0
Loyo	.982	10	105	2	2	0	0
Osborn	.988	28	304	19	4	2	3
Parada	1.000	6	60	3	0	1	1
Perozo	1.000	6	69	4	0	0	1
Rivera	1.000	15	130	10	0	0	4
Smith	.996	27	250	13	1	1	6
Villalobos	.991	29	296	25	3	4	6

First Base	PCT	G	PO	A	E	DP
Beracierta	.994	47	321	11	2	34
Guerrero	.981	7	51	0	1	4
Lugo	.971	9	63	5	2	5
Malm	1.000	3	12	3	0	0
Perozo	1.000	2	10	3	0	1
Salazar	.983	10	53	4	1	7
Saunders	1.000	2	18	0	0	1
Smith	1.000	1	2	0	0	0
Wold	.995	56	348	28	2	38

Second Base	PCT	G	PO	A	E	DP
Berbesi	1.000	3	6	6	0	2
Guerrera	.935	39	51	78	9	23
Guerrero	1.000	7	6	5	0	2
Malm	.900	4	4	5	1	1
Newton	.833	1	1	4	1	1
Rivera	1.000	9	10	10	0	3
Rodriguez	1.000	1	2	4	0	1
Saunders	1.000	12	14	24	0	3
Smith	.955	12	18	24	2	3
Suarez	.958	13	21	25	2	7
Tilien	.970	27	38	60	3	20
Villavicencio	1.000	7	8	21	0	8

Third Base	PCT	G	PO	A	E	DP
Estep	.950	24	10	28	2	2
Guerrera	.900	35	20	43	7	5
Guerrero	1.000	2	1	2	0	0
Lugo	.935	54	35	65	7	11
Malm	1.000	1	2	3	0	0
Rivera	1.000	1	0	1	0	0
Salazar	.800	3	2	2	1	1
Saunders	.500	2	0	1	1	0
Suarez	.938	8	6	9	1	1
Tilien	.000	1	0	0	0	0
Villavicencio	.909	4	4	6	1	0

Shortstop	PCT	G	PO	A	E	DP
Fryman	1.000	3	4	4	0	1
Kendall	1.000	2	1	4	0	1
Lin	.923	6	10	14	2	5
Lugo	.969	23	29	64	3	15
Malm	.929	9	9	17	2	3
Newton	.940	21	26	53	5	10
Riddle	.857	2	2	4	1	0
Suarez	1.000	4	3	3	0	1
Tilien	.933	51	54	100	11	21
Villavicencio	.983	15	14	45	1	5

Outfield	PCT	G	PO	A	E	DP
Aybar	1.000	4	5	0	0	0
Beracierta	.923	18	24	0	2	0
Consuegra	.972	61	94	9	3	2
De Los Santos	.976	96	148	17	4	1
Dominguez	.977	99	159	11	4	3
Johnson	.875	4	7	0	1	0
Kendall	.667	1	2	0	1	0
Lee	1.000	5	7	0	0	0
McIntosh	1.000	7	10	0	0	0
Murphy	.985	30	65	2	1	0
Ramirez	.970	60	96	1	3	0
Rodriguez	1.000	2	2	0	0	0
Rudick	--	1	0	0	0	0
Salazar	1.000	9	13	0	0	0
Suarez	--	1	0	0	0	0
Thomas	1.000	6	13	1	0	0
Wold	--	1	0	0	0	0

FCL METS — *ROOKIE*

FLORIDA COMPLEX LEAGUE

Batting	B-T	HT	WT	DOB	AVG	vLH	vRH	G	AB	R	H	2B	3B	HR	RBI	BB	HBP	SH	SF	SO	SB	CS	SLG	OBP
Ronis Aybar	L-R	6-0	180	1-13-00	.180	.095	.203	31	100	11	18	3	3	2	18	14	3	0	1	45	6	4	.330	.297
Dyron Campos	R-R	5-10	155	12-26-00	.135	.200	.125	11	37	5	5	0	0	2	6	3	1	0	0	11	1	0	.297	.220
Luis Castillo	L-R	6-1	180	11-13-01	.136	.000	.167	23	59	12	8	2	0	3	9	24	1	0	0	24	0	0	.322	.393
Francis De Leon	R-R	0-0	0	10-4-03	.109	.000	.125	18	46	9	5	0	0	0	3	4	3	0	1	23	3	1	.109	.222
Jefrey De Los Santos	L-R	6-0	154	5-30-03	.205	.192	.208	43	132	20	27	4	2	3	14	15	1	0	2	41	5	4	.333	.287
Chase Estep	L-R	6-0	200	4-12-00	.333	.500	.000	1	3	1	1	0	0	0	0	1	0	0	0	1	0	0	.333	.500
Tommy Gomez	R-R	5-10	188	4-21-04	.190	.167	.194	14	42	6	8	3	0	1	7	5	1	0	1	14	2	0	.333	.286
Terrance Gore	R-R	5-7	160	6-8-91	.250	.000	.273	4	12	3	3	2	0	0	1	3	0	0	0	3	1	0	.417	.400

Gregory Guerrero	R-R	6-0	186	1-20-99	.167	.000	.182	8	24	6	4	1	0	0	1	7	0	0	0	8	0	0	.208	.355
Adrian Hernandez	R-R	5-9	210	2-8-01	.100	--	.100	3	10	1	1	0	0	0	3	4	0	0	0	4	0	0	.100	.357
Jose Hernandez	R-R	5-11	190	5-13-02	.081	.125	.069	13	37	1	3	1	0	0	0	5	3	0	0	18	1	0	.108	.244
Andriel Lantigua	R-R	6-1	190	11-29-03	.125	.000	.152	22	56	7	7	2	0	0	3	7	4	0	0	25	0	0	.161	.269
Wilfredo Lara	R-R	5-10	180	4-28-04	.235	.200	.241	42	136	19	32	7	3	1	13	17	4	0	0	34	8	3	.353	.338
Gregory Leal	R-R	6-0	171	2-14-03	.083	.000	.091	5	12	2	1	1	0	0	3	1	0	0	1	7	0	0	.167	.143
Tzu-Wei Lin	L-R	5-9	180	2-15-94	.000	.000	.000	1	3	0	0	0	0	0	0	2	0	0	0	2	0	0	.000	.400
Franklin Linares	R-R	6-0	165	11-5-00	.333	.500	.167	4	12	3	4	1	0	0	0	0	2	0	0	2	4	1	.417	.429
Brad Malm	R-R	6-1	185	8-19-99	.286	--	.286	2	7	0	2	2	0	0	0	0	0	0	0	2	0	0	.571	.286
Jake Mangum	B-L	6-1	179	3-8-96	.429	.500	.400	3	7	1	3	0	1	0	1	3	2	0	0	0	0	0	.714	.667
Yeral Martinez	L-R	6-3	220	10-30-02	.230	.063	.268	27	87	15	20	2	0	5	13	7	2	0	3	37	0	0	.425	.293
Blaine McIntosh	L-L	6-4	180	6-9-01	.231	.143	.253	33	104	16	24	5	1	3	14	21	5	0	0	26	7	5	.385	.385
Nick Morabito	R-R	5-11	185	5-7-03	.091	.000	.105	6	22	1	2	1	0	0	2	2	0	0	0	14	1	0	.136	.167
Scott Ota	L-L	5-11	195	8-16-97	.143	1.000	.077	4	14	4	2	1	0	0	1	3	0	0	0	2	2	0	.214	.294
Kevin Parada	R-R	6-1	197	8-3-01	.273	.600	.000	3	11	1	3	2	0	0	3	2	1	0	0	1	0	0	.455	.429
Karell Paz	B-R	6-3	215	8-11-99	.286	.000	.314	18	56	14	16	4	2	3	8	5	2	0	1	11	2	1	.589	.359
Vincent Perozo	L-R	6-0	170	3-6-03	.283	.222	.301	36	120	22	34	7	2	4	22	11	10	0	1	32	1	0	.475	.387
Jacob Reimer	R-R	6-2	205	2-22-04	.261	.400	.222	7	23	5	6	0	1	1	7	6	0	0	0	3	0	0	.478	.414
Wilmer Reyes	R-R	6-0	161	12-22-97	.242	.333	.222	10	33	6	8	3	0	2	6	4	0	1	0	9	0	0	.515	.324
Hector Rodriguez	L-R	5-8	186	3-11-04	.349	.529	.315	27	106	19	37	4	4	3	16	6	0	0	1	10	12	3	.547	.381
Adrian Rubio	B-R	6-2	175	12-10-02	.227	.100	.333	9	22	3	5	2	0	0	1	4	2	0	0	11	1	1	.318	.393
Matt Rudick	L-L	5-9	170	7-2-98	.000	.000	.000	1	3	0	0	0	0	0	0	1	0	0	0	2	0	0	.000	.250
Eduardo Salazar	R-R	6-3	167	12-15-00	.270	.125	.310	11	37	4	10	0	1	1	4	3	0	0	0	6	1	0	.405	.325
Eric Santana	B-R	6-0	180	11-2-02	.151	.143	.154	31	86	11	13	1	0	2	13	16	0	0	0	41	3	0	.233	.284
D_Andre Smith	R-R	5-9	180	5-10-01	.000	--	.000	2	7	0	0	0	0	0	0	1	0	0	0	2	0	0	.000	.125
Rhylan Thomas	L-L	6-0	170	4-15-00	.257	.222	.269	10	35	5	9	1	0	0	2	5	1	0	0	2	2	1	.286	.366
Kevin Villavicencio	R-R	5-10	172	11-24-03	.250	.346	.228	41	140	19	35	7	0	1	12	21	5	0	0	30	7	4	.321	.367
Jett Williams	R-R	5-8	175	11-3-03	.250	.222	.261	10	32	7	8	1	1	1	6	4	3	0	2	6	6	0	.438	.366
Matt Winaker	L-L	6-1	195	11-29-95	.200	.200	--	2	5	1	1	0	0	1	1	2	1	0	0	1	0	0	.800	.500

Pitching	B-T	HT	WT	DOB	W	L	ERA	G	GS	CG	SV	IP	H	R	ER	HR	BB	SO	AVG	vLH	vRH	K/9	BB/9
Jose Acuna	R-R	6-2	175	10-20-02	3	0	3.16	6	3	0	0	26	18	10	9	2	7	36	.196	.056	.230	12.62	2.45
Miguel Alfonseca	R-R	6-0	190	2-13-00	2	0	2.25	3	1	0	0	8	7	3	2	0	1	4	.250	.250	.250	4.50	1.13
Eli Ankeney	L-L	6-0	200	1-10-01	0	0	0.00	3	0	0	0	3	0	0	0	0	0	6	.000	.000	.000	16.20	0.00
Javier Atencio	L-L	6-0	160	11-26-01	0	0	0.00	3	3	0	0	4	4	0	0	0	2	8	.250	.600	.091	18.00	4.50
Luke Bartnicki	L-L	6-3	220	1-7-00	0	0	0.00	1	0	0	0	1	0	0	0	0	1	2	.000	.000	.000	18.00	9.00
Jace Beck	R-R	6-9	200	6-14-00	1	0	0.00	1	0	0	0	1	1	0	0	0	0	1	.200	.000	.250	6.75	0.00
Connor Brandon	R-R	6-3	220	3-26-01	0	0	0.00	2	1	0	0	2	1	0	0	0	1	1	.167	.000	.500	4.50	4.50
Richard Brito	R-R	6-4	190	11-5-98	0	1	2.45	4	3	0	0	4	4	3	1	0	1	5	.235	.000	.333	12.27	2.45
Trevor Cahill	R-R	6-4	223	3-1-88	0	0	6.75	1	1	0	0	1	1	1	1	0	1	4	.200	--	.200	27.00	6.75
Jean Calderon	R-R	6-0	220	11-15-00	1	0	5.74	7	2	0	1	16	13	10	10	1	5	21	.213	.150	.244	12.06	2.87
Robert Colina	R-R	5-11	175	4-24-01	1	0	1.59	4	2	0	0	17	11	3	3	0	3	22	.186	.200	.176	11.65	1.59
Candido Cuevas	R-R	6-1	202	4-24-04	0	1	14.40	3	0	0	0	5	10	8	8	0	5	4	.455	.455	.455	7.20	9.00
Levi David	R-R	6-5	220	6-14-99	0	1	12.00	4	0	0	0	3	3	6	4	1	5	7	.231	.333	.143	21.00	15.00
Felipe De La Cruz	L-L	6-0	160	5-26-01	1	2	4.83	10	6	0	0	32	32	21	17	3	16	44	.262	.250	.266	12.51	4.55
Tony Dibrell	R-R	6-3	190	11-8-95	0	0	0.00	1	1	0	0	1	0	0	0	0	0	1	.000	.000	.000	9.00	0.00
Justin Dillon	R-R	6-3	225	9-5-93	0	0	0.00	1	1	0	0	1	1	0	0	0	1	1	.250	.000	.333	9.00	9.00
Benito Garcia	R-R	6-0	165	3-10-00	1	1	3.18	9	0	0	4	11	11	8	4	1	4	9	.224	.385	.167	7.15	3.18
Saul Garcia	R-R	6-2	180	6-11-03	2	2	4.94	14	2	0	1	31	30	22	17	1	23	46	.254	.257	.253	13.35	6.68
Paul Gervase	R-R	6-10	230	5-23-00	0	0	0.00	1	0	0	0	1	0	0	0	0	0	2	.000	.000	.000	18.00	0.00
Jose Gomez	R-R	6-4	177	1-24-04	2	0	4.30	7	0	0	0	15	11	7	7	1	14	14	.220	.250	.211	8.59	8.59
Harol Gonzalez	R-R	6-0	160	3-2-95	0	0	0.00	1	1	0	0	1	0	0	0	0	0	1	.000	.000	.000	9.00	0.00
Brian Gursky	R-L	6-1	205	2-4-98	1	0	0.00	2	0	0	0	3	1	2	0	0	2	3	.111	.000	.167	10.13	6.75
Kolby Kubichek	R-R	6-0	180	11-28-99	2	0	1.15	9	0	0	3	16	12	4	2	0	6	17	.203	.143	.237	9.77	3.45
Joey Lancellotti	R-R	5-11	205	1-15-98	0	0	4.76	6	0	0	1	6	5	3	3	1	3	8	.250	.200	.300	12.71	4.76
Douglas Orellana	R-R	6-1	196	5-1-02	3	4	3.96	11	6	0	0	36	22	19	16	2	21	55	.172	.231	.146	13.62	5.20
Layonel Ovalles	R-R	6-3	216	6-16-03	1	2	2.76	11	1	0	1	29	26	15	9	0	5	44	.230	.200	.239	13.50	1.53
Jonaiker Palacios	R-R	6-0	170	5-7-03	2	2	3.77	9	0	0	0	14	15	9	6	1	5	16	.263	.211	.289	10.05	3.14
Jawilme Ramirez	R-R	6-2	170	11-28-01	1	0	0.84	11	6	0	1	43	27	7	4	1	6	40	.179	.054	.219	8.37	1.26
Brawny Reyes	R-R	6-3	165	3-7-03	0	1	5.56	7	2	0	0	11	11	8	7	0	7	8	.275	.200	.320	6.35	5.56
Kevin Ribon	R-R	6-0	157	9-20-02	1	1	5.14	13	0	0	1	14	11	8	8	1	7	8	.216	.190	.233	5.14	4.50
Joe Joe Rodriguez	R-R	6-1	200	10-12-99	2	0	1.42	3	0	0	0	6	5	1	1	0	2	6	.238	.333	.200	8.53	2.84
Luis Rodriguez	R-R	6-4	175	2-27-03	3	2	1.41	16	0	0	0	32	20	14	5	2	14	37	.174	.233	.139	10.41	3.94
Manny Rodriguez	R-R	5-10	166	7-4-96	0	1	20.25	4	1	0	0	3	4	7	6	0	5	1	.308	.167	.429	3.38	16.88
Chris Santiago	R-R	6-2	215	6-18-01	0	0	0.00	3	0	0	0	3	0	0	0	0	3	2	.000	.000	.000	6.00	9.00
Claudio Scotti	R-R	6-4	210	7-8-98	1	0	7.59	5	2	0	0	11	8	10	9	0	12	13	.211	.545	.074	10.97	10.13
Tyler Stuart	R-R	6-9	250	10-8-99	0	0	0.00	1	1	0	0	1	0	0	0	0	0	1	.000	.000	.000	9.00	0.00
Joander Suarez	R-R	6-3	223	2-27-00	1	1	3.97	6	3	0	0	11	13	6	5	2	3	12	.283	.313	.267	9.53	2.38
Dylan Tebrake	R-R	6-3	225	7-13-99	0	0	0.00	2	1	0	0	2	2	0	0	0	0	2	.222	.000	.333	9.00	0.00
Blade Tidwell	R-R	6-4	207	6-8-01	0	0	0.00	1	1	0	0	1	0	0	0	0	1	2	.000	.000	.000	18.00	9.00
Mike Vasil	L-R	6-5	225	3-19-00	0	0	0.00	1	1	0	0	1	1	0	0	0	0	2	.250	1.000	.000	18.00	0.00
Christopher Vasquez	R-R	6-0	160	3-17-01	1	0	1.42	13	0	0	2	19	12	4	3	0	6	21	.174	.136	.191	9.95	2.84
Jordany Ventura	R-R	6-0	162	7-6-00	0	0	0.00	1	1	0	0	2	0	0	0	0	0	3	.000	.000	.000	13.50	0.00
Zebulon Vermillion	L-R	6-5	240	10-26-98	0	0	0.00	1	0	0	0	1	0	0	0	0	0	0	.000	.000	.000	0.00	0.00
Josh Walker	L-L	6-6	225	12-1-94	0	0	0.00	1	1	0	0	1	0	0	0	0	1	3	.000	.000	.000	27.00	9.00

Kyle Wilson	R-R	6-1	185	9-27-96	0	0	0.00	1	1	0	0	1	0	0	0	0	1	1	.000	--	.000	9.00	9.00

Fielding

C: Gomez 7, Hernandez 5, Lantigua 21, Leal 3, Parada 2, Perozo 25. **1B:** Campos 3, Castillo 9, Gomez 1, Guerrero 2, Hernandez 3, Lara 2, Martinez 20, Paz 7, Perozo 6, Salazar 10. **2B:** Castillo 1, De Los Santos 24, Guerrero 4, Lara 6, Linares 1, Reyes 2, Rodriguez 2, Rubio 7, Smith 2, Villavicencio 13. **3B:** Castillo 13, Estep 1, Guerrero 3, Lara 33, Malm 1, Paz 1, Reimer 5, Rubio 2, Salazar 1, Villavicencio 2. **SS:** De Los Santos 18, Lara 1, Lin 1, Linares 1, Malm 1, Reyes 4, Villavicencio 25, Williams 8. **OF:** Aybar 30, Campos 10, De Leon 16, Gore 3, Linares 1, Mangum 3, Martinez 4, McIntosh 30, Morabito 5, Paz 9, Reyes 3, Rodriguez 24, Rudick 1, Santana 28, Thomas 9, Winaker 1

DSL METS 1 — ROOKIE

DOMINICAN SUMMER LEAGUE

Batting	B-T	HT	WT	DOB	AVG	vLH	vRH	G	AB	R	H	2B	3B	HR	RBI	BB	HBP	SH	SF	SO	SB	CS	SLG	OBP
Jostyn Almonte	R-R	5-11	193	5-10-03	.209	.200	.212	19	43	7	9	0	0	0	1	9	4	0	0	13	2	1	.209	.393
2-team total (19 DSL Mets 2)					.263	.250	.266	38	95	21	25	2	0	2	13	24	5	0	0	34	7	4	.347	.435
Jose Aular	R-R	5-11	175	1-2-04	.258	.125	.272	30	89	13	23	1	1	0	8	5	4	0	0	15	1	2	.292	.327
Jesus Baez	R-R	5-10	180	2-26-05	.255	.313	.244	30	98	23	25	6	0	2	12	17	2	0	1	24	3	3	.378	.373
2-team total (24 DSL Mets 2)					.242	.216	.248	54	186	36	45	9	0	7	34	26	3	0	2	46	8	6	.403	.341
Jaycey Benita	R-R	6-1	157	12-30-02	.130	.333	.100	13	23	5	3	0	1	0	1	5	1	0	0	13	2	1	.217	.310
2-team total (15 DSL Mets 2)					.246	.455	.196	28	57	12	14	3	1	2	8	12	1	0	0	22	3	3	.439	.386
Samuel Camacaro	B-R	6-0	179	11-23-03	.139	.143	.138	19	36	4	5	0	1	0	4	8	0	2	3	9	2	1	.194	.277
2-team total (26 DSL Mets 2)					.200	.125	.221	45	110	19	22	1	1	1	10	22	2	2	4	26	6	2	.255	.333
Dyron Campos	R-R	5-10	155	12-26-00	.309	.333	.306	16	55	14	17	5	1	1	13	5	0	0	1	16	3	0	.491	.361
2-team total (25 DSL Mets 2)					.300	.296	.301	41	140	29	42	10	3	5	28	13	1	0	3	37	5	1	.521	.357
Lewis Castillo	R-R	6-0	163	6-23-03	.265	.200	.276	14	34	4	9	2	0	0	3	4	3	1	1	4	3	1	.324	.381
2-team total (15 DSL Mets 2)					.295	.412	.268	29	88	13	26	2	0	0	11	15	3	1	1	10	9	4	.318	.411
Sebastian Castro	L-R	6-3	185	8-27-04	.174	.059	.192	44	121	25	21	6	4	0	10	42	2	0	0	58	7	3	.289	.394
Yohairo Cuevas	L-L	6-3	172	9-16-03	.277	.259	.281	51	166	29	46	12	1	2	31	27	0	0	2	43	7	3	.398	.374
Manuel Guance	R-R	5-10	150	11-6-03	.225	.000	.250	16	40	10	9	1	0	0	5	14	1	0	1	19	6	2	.250	.429
2-team total (20 DSL Mets 2)					.270	.167	.293	36	100	18	27	4	0	2	13	22	2	0	1	41	13	2	.370	.408
Angel Guerrero	L-R	6-1	185	11-17-03	.241	.400	.205	20	54	6	13	5	1	0	10	3	2	0	2	18	1	1	.370	.295
Robert Hendrick	R-R	6-2	190	4-22-03	.111	.000	.125	4	9	1	1	0	0	0	0	3	2	0	0	6	0	0	.111	.429
2-team total (22 DSL Mets 2)					.133	.133	.133	26	60	11	8	3	0	1	8	14	7	0	0	27	0	2	.233	.358
Yonatan Henriquez	B-R	6-0	185	10-12-04	.247	.294	.237	31	93	16	23	3	0	2	14	18	5	0	2	27	5	6	.344	.390
Mike Ibarguen	R-R	0-0	0	3-25-04	.109	.143	.104	30	55	9	6	1	1	1	4	8	1	0	1	28	2	3	.218	.231
2-team total (8 DSL Mets 2)					.132	.182	.123	38	76	14	10	1	1	3	8	15	3	0	1	35	3	3	.289	.295
Simon Juan	R-R	6-2	195	7-13-05	.219	.211	.221	53	201	32	44	9	3	2	23	20	7	0	1	54	16	1	.323	.310
Jose Marcano	R-R	6-0	160	5-6-04	.245	.143	.262	21	49	7	12	2	0	0	6	5	1	0	1	15	6	2	.286	.321
2-team total (1 DSL Mets 2)					.264	.125	.289	22	53	9	14	2	0	1	9	5	1	0	1	16	7	2	.358	.333
Frederick Marte	B-R	6-1	160	2-20-04	.152	.143	.154	14	33	7	5	2	0	0	5	6	1	0	1	9	1	1	.212	.293
2-team total (25 DSL Mets 2)					.185	.278	.167	39	108	20	20	5	0	0	8	20	3	0	1	23	8	3	.231	.326
Yohenny Mata	R-R	6-2	175	6-3-04	.239	.000	.271	40	109	13	26	6	0	0	13	9	4	0	1	12	2	2	.294	.317
Germain Noriega	L-L	5-9	140	12-12-03	.278	.333	.267	20	54	9	15	0	2	0	3	5	2	0	0	10	3	0	.352	.361
2-team total (24 DSL Mets 2)					.277	.320	.267	44	141	27	39	3	2	0	11	15	4	0	1	26	11	2	.326	.360
Carlos Oviedo	R-R	6-2	210	8-20-04	.222	--	.222	3	9	0	2	1	0	0	2	2	0	0	0	2	0	0	.333	.364
2-team total (36 DSL Mets 2)					.268	.238	.274	39	127	20	34	13	0	2	21	17	2	0	2	32	0	1	.417	.358
Orangel Rodriguez	R-R	6-2	180	4-1-05	.286	--	.286	6	21	1	6	0	0	1	5	1	0	0	0	5	0	0	.429	.318
2-team total (7 DSL Mets 2)					.286	.000	.303	13	35	3	10	0	0	2	10	3	0	0	1	7	0	0	.457	.333
Dangelo Sarmiento	R-R	6-2	160	1-4-05	.296	.273	.299	32	108	21	32	5	1	1	16	13	2	0	3	21	9	3	.389	.373
2-team total (2 DSL Mets 2)					.295	.273	.297	34	112	21	33	6	1	1	16	13	3	0	3	22	9	4	.393	.374
Daniel Silva	B-R	6-2	200	1-12-05	.250	.000	.333	7	12	1	3	0	0	0	0	3	0	0	0	5	0	0	.250	.400
Christopher Suero	R-R	6-0	205	1-27-04	.204	.211	.203	38	98	23	20	7	0	1	12	25	4	0	0	29	4	2	.306	.386
Enrique Valdez	R-R	6-0	180	9-1-01	.195	.250	.189	15	41	5	8	3	0	2	8	10	2	0	0	14	2	0	.415	.377
2-team total (21 DSL Mets 2)					.129	.167	.123	36	93	15	12	4	0	3	14	26	4	0	1	40	4	1	.269	.339
Jeisel Vargas	R-R	5-7	155	12-2-04	.056	.000	.067	9	18	0	1	0	0	0	1	0	1	0	0	9	0	1	.056	.105
Ruben Yustiz	R-R	6-2	175	1-2-04	.077	.200	.048	12	26	0	2	0	0	0	1	4	0	1	1	10	0	0	.077	.194
2-team total (1 DSL Mets 2)					.103	.200	.083	13	29	2	3	0	0	0	1	5	0	1	1	10	0	0	.103	.229

Pitching	B-T	HT	WT	DOB	W	L	ERA	G	GS	CG	SV	IP	H	R	ER	HR	BB	SO	AVG	vLH	vRH	K/9	BB/9
Eris Albino	R-R	6-6	223	1-24-04	0	0	13.50	4	0	0	0	4	4	7	6	0	6	5	.250	.286	.222	11.25	13.50
2-team total (10 DSL Mets 2)					2	1	6.41	14	6	0	0	27	9	21	19	0	34	25	.103	.097	.107	8.44	11.48
Wellington Aracena	R-R	6-3	180	12-27-04	0	1	8.04	7	3	0	0	16	17	19	14	1	15	14	.270	.217	.300	8.04	8.62
2-team total (5 DSL Mets 2)					1	2	6.84	12	5	0	0	25	26	30	19	1	23	28	.260	.194	.297	10.08	8.28
Juan Arnaud	R-R	6-2	164	6-22-03	2	1	3.28	12	1	0	0	25	24	15	9	1	22	25	.255	.268	.245	9.12	8.03
2-team total (6 DSL Mets 2)					3	2	5.87	18	1	0	1	31	33	26	20	3	30	34	.273	.286	.264	9.98	8.80
Jorge Avendano	L-L	6-1	175	9-23-03	0	2	1.50	10	2	0	0	24	14	8	4	0	14	27	.165	.250	.145	10.13	5.25
2-team total (7 DSL Mets 2)					0	2	3.27	17	2	0	0	33	27	19	12	0	21	38	.216	.227	.214	10.36	5.73
Jaycey Benita	R-R	6-1	157	12-30-02	0	0	0.00	1	0	0	0	1	0	0	0	0	0	1	.000	--	.000	13.50	0.00
2-team total (1 DSL Mets 2)					0	0	0.00	2	0	0	0	1	0	0	0	0	0	1	.000	--	.000	9.00	0.00
Richard Cardoza	L-L	6-0	150	6-1-04	0	2	18.90	3	1	0	0	3	5	7	7	0	6	3	.385	.000	.500	8.10	16.20
2-team total (12 DSL Mets 2)					0	3	6.75	15	1	0	0	19	14	18	14	0	20	23	.206	.154	.218	11.09	9.64
Welvis Colon	R-R	6-0	194	8-12-01	2	0	1.59	6	0	0	0	6	5	1	1	0	7	7	.263	.500	.154	11.12	11.12
Estarlin Escalante	R-R	6-4	235	8-22-03	0	0	40.50	1	0	0	0	1	1	3	3	0	4	1	.333	.000	.500	13.50	54.00
2-team total (17 DSL Mets 2)					2	1	5.40	18	4	0	0	38	39	26	23	4	23	45	.264	.255	.267	10.57	5.40
Wilson Esterlin	R-R	6-3	160	8-17-04	5	1	2.70	12	5	0	0	37	22	12	11	2	22	48	.171	.070	.221	11.78	5.40
Andinson Ferrer	R-R	6-3	180	5-5-04	2	1	1.80	18	1	0	0	30	15	6	6	1	19	46	.150	.186	.123	13.80	5.70

Rodolfo Garrido	R-R	6-1	176	9-23-04	3	3	4.20	14	12	0	0	41	30	24	19	1	28	46	.204	.208	.200	10.18	6.20
Cristofer Gomez	R-R	6-4	222	5-13-03	3	0	0.40	15	0	0	6	23	8	1	1	0	9	37	.110	.130	.100	14.69	3.57
Franklin Gomez	L-L	6-0	145	7-6-05	0	4	4.97	10	8	0	0	25	26	18	14	2	19	29	.271	.240	.282	10.30	6.75
2-team total (3 DSL Mets 2)					2	4	3.67	13	9	0	0	34	33	19	14	2	21	42	.260	.188	.284	11.01	5.50
Jose Gomez	R-R	6-4	177	1-24-04	0	0	3.00	2	2	0	0	3	1	1	1	0	1	4	.125	.000	.200	12.00	3.00
Wilson Lopez	R-R	6-1	216	7-15-02	3	1	4.85	16	5	0	1	30	19	17	16	1	22	41	.186	.237	.156	12.44	6.67
Gregori Louis	L-L	6-3	161	10-28-02	1	0	3.46	11	0	0	0	13	11	5	5	2	6	23	.229	.385	.171	15.92	4.15
2-team total (2 DSL Mets 2)					1	0	3.52	13	0	0	1	15	14	6	6	2	7	25	.246	.429	.186	14.67	4.11
Yohenny Mata	R-R	6-2	175	6-3-04	0	0	0.00	1	0	0	0	1	2	0	0	0	0	1	.500	.500	.500	9.00	0.00
Franciso Mercado	R-R	6-2	150	12-7-03	0	0	3.86	3	0	0	0	5	7	2	2	1	3	6	.350	.333	.353	11.57	5.79
2-team total (10 DSL Mets 2)					0	1	4.71	13	0	0	0	21	26	13	11	1	11	27	.302	.391	.270	11.57	4.71
Ernesto Mercedes	R-R	6-2	180	10-14-03	0	2	3.72	14	9	0	0	36	27	21	15	1	29	41	.197	.207	.190	10.16	7.18
Juan Oramas	R-R	6-3	170	7-14-05	0	2	3.00	4	4	0	0	15	12	6	5	2	4	15	.226	.250	.216	9.00	2.40
2-team total (8 DSL Mets 2)					0	5	3.89	12	12	0	0	39	35	19	17	2	11	41	.233	.275	.212	9.38	2.52
Jonaiker Palacios	R-R	6-0	170	5-7-03	1	0	0.79	6	0	0	2	11	9	2	1	0	6	10	.257	.182	.292	7.94	4.76
Jeremy Peguero	L-L	6-2	175	5-3-02	1	0	2.40	9	1	0	0	15	6	5	4	0	10	16	.122	.100	.128	9.60	6.00
2-team total (13 DSL Mets 2)					5	3	3.13	22	1	0	1	37	25	18	13	0	22	46	.187	.179	.189	11.09	5.30
Cesar Rivera	L-L	6-3	190	4-16-05	0	3	11.17	9	0	0	0	10	11	15	12	0	18	7	.314	.200	.360	6.52	16.76
Arlison Rodriguez	L-L	6-5	220	3-5-03	4	3	4.78	18	0	0	3	26	29	19	14	1	9	30	.266	.286	.263	10.25	3.08
Jorge Rodriguez	R-R	6-3	180	12-18-01	2	0	6.08	6	2	0	0	13	18	11	9	0	5	8	.316	.333	.300	5.40	3.38
2-team total (8 DSL Mets 2)					2	2	6.44	14	9	0	0	36	43	34	26	1	16	38	.279	.321	.257	9.41	3.96
Marcos Rodriguez	L-L	6-3	176	10-28-02	1	0	6.97	8	0	0	0	10	10	13	8	1	13	12	.244	.286	.235	10.45	11.32
2-team total (9 DSL Mets 2)					2	0	7.25	17	0	0	0	22	23	25	18	2	29	29	.274	.286	.271	11.69	11.69
Wander Rosario	R-R	6-7	185	7-6-04	1	1	18.69	5	0	0	0	4	7	13	9	1	11	6	.350	.333	.353	12.46	22.85
2-team total (7 DSL Mets 2)					2	2	16.03	12	0	0	0	11	14	25	19	1	24	10	.326	.250	.355	8.44	20.25
Roberto Sanchez	L-L	6-1	162	3-7-03	0	0	7.71	2	0	0	0	2	3	2	2	0	2	3	.333	.000	.375	11.57	7.71
2-team total (12 DSL Mets 2)					0	0	2.00	14	0	0	1	18	11	5	4	0	15	21	.180	.000	.216	10.50	7.50
Frelianderson Seijas	R-R	6-1	160	2-10-05	0	0	7.24	11	0	0	1	14	18	11	11	1	6	17	.321	.421	.270	11.20	3.95
2-team total (4 DSL Mets 2)					1	0	6.11	15	0	0	1	18	19	12	12	1	8	22	.268	.364	.224	11.21	4.08
Jose Sequera	R-R	6-2	160	11-24-04	0	0	36.00	1	0	0	0	1	0	4	4	0	4	1	.000	.000	.000	9.00	36.00
2-team total (4 DSL Mets 2)					0	1	21.00	5	0	0	0	3	5	9	7	0	9	4	.385	.375	.400	12.00	27.00
Omar Victorino	R-R	6-2	170	6-9-05	0	1	2.70	3	3	0	0	10	8	6	3	0	4	9	.216	.125	.241	8.10	3.60
2-team total (10 DSL Mets 2)					1	3	5.11	13	11	0	0	37	30	25	21	2	32	37	.222	.227	.220	9.00	7.78
Johan Villegas	L-L	6-2	160	3-7-05	0	0	5.40	6	0	0	0	7	6	4	4	0	9	6	.231	.500	.182	8.10	12.15
2-team total (9 DSL Mets 2)					0	0	3.24	15	0	0	1	17	12	8	6	0	24	16	.211	.300	.191	8.64	12.96

Fielding

C: Aular 20, Marcano 5, Oviedo 1, Rodriguez 4, Silva 1, Suero 31, Yustiz 8. **1B:** Aular 9, Castillo 5, Cuevas 34, Hendrick 4, Marcano 12, Mata 2, Oviedo 2, Suero 2, Valdez 3, Yustiz 2. **2B:** Baez 5, Camacaro 8, Castillo 7, Guance 7, Henriquez 13, Marte 5, Mata 9, Sarmiento 6, Valdez 8. **3B:** Baez 1, Camacaro 3, Castillo 5, Castro 5, Guance 3, Henriquez 16, Marcano 5, Marte 4, Mata 25, Sarmiento 1, Valdez 3. **SS:** Baez 24, Camacaro 8, Henriquez 3, Marte 6, Mata 2, Sarmiento 26. **OF:** Almonte 9, Benita 6, Campos 14, Castro 40, Cuevas 22, Gomez 1, Guerrero 19, Ibarguen 25, Juan 47, Marcano 1, Mata 1, Noriega 13

DSL METS 2 — ROOKIE

DOMINICAN SUMMER LEAGUE

Batting	B-T	HT	WT	DOB	AVG	vLH	vRH	G	AB	R	H	2B	3B	HR	RBI	BB	HBP	SH	SF	SO	SB	CS	SLG	OBP
Jostyn Almonte	R-R	5-11	193	5-10-03	.308	.333	.304	19	52	14	16	2	0	2	12	15	1	0	0	21	5	3	.462	.471
2-team total (19 DSL Mets 1)					.263	.250	.266	38	95	21	25	2	0	2	13	24	5	0	0	34	7	4	.347	.435
Jesus Baez	R-R	5-10	180	2-26-05	.227	.143	.254	24	88	13	20	3	0	5	22	9	1	0	1	22	5	3	.432	.303
2-team total (30 DSL Mets 1)					.242	.216	.248	54	186	36	45	9	0	7	34	26	3	0	2	46	8	6	.403	.341
Jaycey Benita	R-R	6-1	157	12-30-02	.324	.500	.269	15	34	7	11	3	0	2	7	7	0	0	0	9	1	2	.588	.439
2-team total (13 DSL Mets 1)					.246	.455	.196	28	57	12	14	3	1	2	8	12	1	0	0	22	3	3	.439	.386
Samuel Camacaro	B-R	6-0	179	11-23-03	.230	.118	.263	26	74	15	17	1	0	1	6	14	2	0	1	17	4	1	.284	.363
2-team total (19 DSL Mets 1)					.200	.125	.221	45	110	19	22	1	1	1	10	22	2	2	4	26	6	2	.255	.333
Dyron Campos	R-R	5-10	155	12-26-00	.294	.286	.297	25	85	15	25	5	2	4	15	8	1	0	2	21	2	1	.541	.354
2-team total (16 DSL Mets 1)					.300	.296	.301	41	140	29	42	10	3	5	28	13	1	0	3	37	5	1	.521	.357
Lewis Castillo	R-R	6-0	163	6-23-03	.315	.500	.262	15	54	9	17	0	0	0	8	11	0	0	0	6	6	3	.315	.431
2-team total (14 DSL Mets 1)					.295	.412	.268	29	88	13	26	2	0	0	11	15	3	1	1	10	9	4	.318	.411
Luis Castillo	L-R	6-1	180	11-13-01	.195	.222	.188	17	41	15	8	2	2	1	4	15	3	1	0	14	3	0	.415	.441
Willy Fanas	B-R	6-2	190	1-23-04	.257	.292	.247	32	101	16	26	2	1	0	10	11	1	0	2	24	10	3	.297	.330
Joel Flores	R-R	6-1	175	4-28-03	.156	.250	.138	35	96	17	15	5	1	2	8	13	5	0	1	39	3	3	.292	.287
Manuel Guance	R-R	5-10	150	11-6-03	.300	.214	.326	20	60	8	18	3	0	2	8	8	1	0	0	22	7	0	.450	.391
2-team total (16 DSL Mets 1)					.270	.167	.293	36	100	18	27	4	0	2	13	22	2	0	1	41	13	2	.370	.408
Robert Hendrick	R-R	6-2	190	4-22-03	.137	.143	.135	22	51	10	7	3	0	1	8	11	5	0	0	21	0	2	.255	.343
2-team total (4 DSL Mets 1)					.133	.133	.133	26	60	11	8	3	0	1	8	14	7	0	0	27	0	2	.233	.358
Mike Ibarguen	R-R	0-0	0	3-25-04	.190	.250	.176	8	21	5	4	0	0	2	4	7	2	0	0	7	1	0	.476	.433
2-team total (30 DSL Mets 1)					.132	.182	.123	38	76	14	10	1	1	3	8	15	3	0	1	35	3	3	.289	.295
Jose Marcano	R-R	6-0	160	5-6-04	.500	.000	.667	1	4	2	2	0	0	1	3	0	0	0	0	1	1	0	1.250	.500
2-team total (21 DSL Mets 1)					.264	.125	.289	22	53	9	14	2	0	1	9	5	1	0	1	16	7	2	.358	.333
Gustavo Marquez	R-R	0-0	0	10-4-03	.174	.150	.180	37	109	15	19	5	1	0	10	11	10	0	2	36	6	0	.239	.303
Frederick Marte	B-R	6-1	160	2-20-04	.200	.364	.172	25	75	13	15	3	0	0	3	14	2	0	0	14	7	2	.240	.341
2-team total (14 DSL Mets 1)					.185	.278	.167	39	108	20	20	5	0	0	8	20	3	0	1	23	8	3	.231	.326
Gerald Mejia	B-R	6-0	156	6-14-03	.214	.100	.278	11	28	8	6	1	1	1	5	9	1	0	0	14	6	0	.429	.421
Jose Melendez	R-R	0-0	0	10-3-03	.215	.429	.163	38	107	9	23	5	0	1	15	5	5	0	2	19	3	1	.290	.277
Germain Noriega	L-L	5-9	140	12-12-03	.276	.313	.268	24	87	18	24	3	0	0	8	10	2	0	1	16	8	2	.310	.360

2-team total (20 DSL Mets 1)					.277	.320	.267	44	141	27	39	3	2	0	11	15	4	0	1	26	11	2	.326	.360
Carlos Oviedo	R-R	6-2	210	8-20-04	.271	.238	.278	36	118	20	32	12	0	2	19	15	2	0	2	30	0	1	.424	.358
2-team total (3 DSL Mets 1)					.268	.238	.274	39	127	20	34	13	0	2	21	17	2	0	2	32	0	1	.417	.358
Karell Paz	B-R	6-3	215	8-11-99	.341	.300	.355	15	41	5	14	0	2	1	11	3	4	0	2	7	3	4	.512	.420
Yoandy Perez	L-R	6-0	155	8-17-04	.223	.346	.189	41	121	20	27	7	3	0	14	20	1	0	1	51	8	0	.331	.336
Orangel Rodriguez	R-R	6-2	180	4-1-05	.286	.000	.333	7	14	2	4	0	0	1	5	2	0	0	1	2	0	0	.500	.353
2-team total (6 DSL Mets 1)					.286	.000	.303	13	35	3	10	0	0	2	10	3	0	0	1	7	0	0	.457	.333
Jeffry Rosa	R-R	6-1	190	9-11-04	.216	.083	.235	33	97	11	21	6	0	3	8	7	7	0	0	47	3	1	.371	.315
Dangelo Sarmiento	R-R	6-2	160	1-4-05	.250	--	.250	2	4	0	1	1	0	0	0	0	1	0	0	1	0	1	.500	.400
2-team total (32 DSL Mets 1)					.295	.273	.297	34	112	21	33	6	1	1	16	13	3	0	3	22	9	4	.393	.374
Francisco Toledo	R-R	5-10	160	4-23-05	.293	.154	.357	15	41	9	12	1	1	1	6	4	1	0	0	7	4	1	.439	.370
Enrique Valdez	R-R	6-0	180	9-1-01	.077	.125	.068	21	52	10	4	1	0	1	6	16	2	0	1	26	2	1	.154	.310
2-team total (15 DSL Mets 1)					.129	.167	.123	36	93	15	12	4	0	3	14	26	4	0	1	40	4	1	.269	.339
Ruben Yustiz	R-R	6-2	175	1-2-04	.333	--	.333	1	3	2	1	0	0	0	0	1	0	0	0	0	0	0	.333	.500
2-team total (12 DSL Mets 1)					.103	.200	.083	13	29	2	3	0	0	0	1	5	0	1	1	10	0	0	.103	.229

Pitching	B-T	HT	WT	DOB	W	L	ERA	G	GS	CG	SV	IP	H	R	ER	HR	BB	SO	AVG	vLH	vRH	K/9	BB/9
Eris Albino	R-R	6-6	223	1-24-04	2	1	5.16	10	6	0	0	23	5	14	13	0	28	20	.070	.042	.085	7.94	11.12
2-team total (4 DSL Mets 1)					2	1	6.41	14	6	0	0	27	9	21	19	0	34	25	.103	.097	.107	8.44	11.48
Wellington Aracena	R-R	6-3	180	12-27-04	1	1	4.82	5	2	0	0	9	9	11	5	0	8	14	.243	.154	.292	13.50	7.71
2-team total (7 DSL Mets 1)					1	2	6.84	12	5	0	0	25	26	30	19	1	23	28	.260	.194	.297	10.08	8.28
Juan Arnaud	R-R	6-2	164	6-22-03	1	1	16.50	6	0	0	1	6	9	11	11	2	8	9	.333	.375	.316	13.50	12.00
2-team total (12 DSL Mets 1)					3	2	5.87	18	1	0	1	31	33	26	20	3	30	34	.273	.286	.264	9.98	8.80
Jorge Avendano	L-L	6-1	175	9-23-03	0	0	8.00	7	0	0	0	9	13	11	8	0	7	11	.325	.167	.353	11.00	7.00
2-team total (10 DSL Mets 1)					0	2	3.27	17	2	0	0	33	27	19	12	0	21	38	.216	.227	.214	10.36	5.73
Jaycey Benita	R-R	6-1	157	12-30-02	0	0	0.00	1	0	0	0	0	0	0	0	0	0	0	--	--	--	0.00	0.00
2-team total (1 DSL Mets 1)					0	0	0.00	2	0	0	0	1	0	0	0	0	0	1	.000	--	.000	9.00	0.00
Carlos Brito	R-R	6-5	192	2-24-02	0	0	23.63	4	0	0	0	3	2	8	7	0	11	4	.200	.500	.000	13.50	37.13
Richard Cardoza	L-L	6-0	150	6-1-04	0	1	4.11	12	0	0	0	15	9	11	7	0	14	20	.164	.200	.156	11.74	8.22
2-team total (3 DSL Mets 1)					0	3	6.75	15	1	0	0	19	14	18	14	0	20	23	.206	.154	.218	11.09	9.64
Yoerison Cepeda	R-R	6-4	195	10-14-01	2	3	5.34	21	0	0	2	29	25	21	17	1	19	32	.231	.233	.231	10.05	5.97
Jose Chirinos	R-R	6-3	170	10-16-04	0	4	4.91	12	8	0	0	33	31	26	18	6	18	29	.246	.174	.288	7.91	4.91
Candido Cuevas	R-R	6-1	202	4-24-04	1	2	3.56	11	7	0	0	30	26	19	12	1	16	38	.224	.262	.203	11.27	4.75
Yoelin Disla	R-R	6-5	195	9-24-03	3	2	5.19	19	0	0	0	26	14	18	15	1	30	34	.161	.143	.169	11.77	10.38
Estarlin Escalante	R-R	6-4	235	8-22-03	2	1	4.78	17	4	0	0	38	38	23	20	4	19	44	.262	.261	.263	10.51	4.54
2-team total (1 DSL Mets 1)					2	1	5.40	18	4	0	0	38	39	26	23	4	23	45	.264	.255	.267	10.57	5.40
Franklin Gomez	L-L	6-0	145	7-6-05	2	0	0.00	3	1	0	0	9	7	1	0	0	2	13	.226	.000	.292	13.00	2.00
2-team total (10 DSL Mets 1)					2	4	3.67	13	9	0	0	34	33	19	14	2	21	42	.260	.188	.284	11.01	5.50
Gregori Louis	L-L	6-3	161	10-28-02	0	0	3.86	2	0	0	1	2	3	1	1	0	1	2	.333	1.000	.250	7.71	3.86
2-team total (11 DSL Mets 1)					1	0	3.52	13	0	0	1	15	14	6	6	2	7	25	.246	.429	.186	14.67	4.11
Franciso Mercado	R-R	6-2	150	12-7-03	0	1	4.96	10	0	0	0	16	19	11	9	0	8	21	.288	.400	.239	11.57	4.41
2-team total (3 DSL Mets 1)					0	1	4.71	13	0	0	0	21	26	13	11	1	11	27	.302	.391	.270	11.57	4.71
Juan Oramas	R-R	6-3	170	7-14-05	0	3	4.44	8	8	0	0	24	23	13	12	0	7	26	.237	.286	.210	9.62	2.59
2-team total (4 DSL Mets 1)					0	5	3.89	12	12	0	0	39	35	19	17	2	11	41	.233	.275	.212	9.38	2.52
Jeremy Peguero	L-L	6-2	175	5-3-02	4	3	3.63	13	0	0	1	22	19	13	9	0	12	30	.224	.222	.224	12.09	4.84
2-team total (9 DSL Mets 1)					5	3	3.13	22	1	0	1	37	25	18	13	0	22	46	.187	.179	.189	11.09	5.30
Brawny Reyes	R-R	6-3	165	3-7-03	0	0	6.43	3	3	0	0	7	7	5	5	1	5	10	.250	.200	.278	12.86	6.43
Jorge Rodriguez	R-R	6-3	180	12-18-01	0	2	6.65	8	7	0	0	23	25	23	17	1	11	30	.258	.308	.239	11.74	4.30
2-team total (6 DSL Mets 1)					2	2	6.44	14	9	0	0	36	43	34	26	1	16	38	.279	.321	.257	9.41	3.96
Marcos Rodriguez	L-L	6-3	176	10-28-02	1	0	7.50	9	0	0	0	12	13	12	10	1	16	17	.302	.286	.306	12.75	12.00
2-team total (8 DSL Mets 1)					2	0	7.25	17	0	0	0	22	23	25	18	2	29	29	.274	.286	.271	11.69	11.69
Wander Rosario	R-R	6-7	185	7-6-04	1	1	14.21	7	0	0	0	6	7	12	10	0	13	4	.304	.222	.357	5.68	18.47
2-team total (5 DSL Mets 1)					2	2	16.03	12	0	0	0	11	14	25	19	1	24	10	.326	.250	.355	8.44	20.25
Roberto Sanchez	L-L	6-1	162	3-7-03	0	0	1.15	12	0	0	1	16	8	3	2	0	13	18	.154	.000	.186	10.34	7.47
2-team total (2 DSL Mets 1)					0	0	2.00	14	0	0	1	18	11	5	4	0	15	21	.180	.000	.216	10.50	7.50
Frelianderson Seijas	R-R	6-1	160	2-10-05	1	0	2.25	4	0	0	0	4	1	1	1	0	2	5	.067	.000	.083	11.25	4.50
2-team total (11 DSL Mets 1)					1	0	6.11	15	0	0	1	18	19	12	12	1	8	22	.268	.364	.224	11.21	4.08
Jose Sequera	R-R	6-2	160	11-24-04	0	1	13.50	4	0	0	0	2	5	5	3	0	5	3	.455	.429	.500	13.50	22.50
2-team total (1 DSL Mets 1)					0	1	21.00	5	0	0	0	3	5	9	7	0	9	4	.385	.375	.400	12.00	27.00
Brian Sierra	R-R	6-3	188	1-5-04	1	2	4.82	8	0	0	1	9	8	5	5	0	9	6	.267	.357	.188	5.79	8.68
Krisspy Valdez	R-R	6-9	215	11-23-03	1	2	5.54	17	3	0	1	26	21	19	16	1	26	29	.231	.222	.236	10.04	9.00
Omar Victorino	R-R	6-2	170	6-9-05	1	2	6.00	10	8	0	0	27	22	19	18	2	28	28	.224	.250	.210	9.33	9.33
2-team total (3 DSL Mets 1)					1	3	5.11	13	11	0	0	37	30	25	21	2	32	37	.222	.227	.220	9.00	7.78
Johan Villegas	L-L	6-2	160	3-7-05	0	0	1.80	9	0	0	1	10	6	4	2	0	15	10	.194	.167	.200	9.00	13.50
2-team total (6 DSL Mets 1)					0	0	3.24	15	0	0	1	17	12	8	6	0	24	16	.211	.300	.191	8.64	12.96

Fielding

C: Flores 5, Melendez 29, Oviedo 19, Rodriguez 5, Toledo 14. **1B:** Castillo 3, Flores 11, Hendrick 12, Marcano 1, Melendez 5, Oviedo 17, Paz 7, Perez 4, Valdez 7. **2B:** Camacaro 1, Castillo 8, Castillo 2, Guance 18, Marte 7, Perez 17, Valdez 9. **3B:** Baez 3, Camacaro 14, Castillo 7, Castillo 11, Guance 2, Marte 13, Melendez 5, Perez 1, Valdez 5. **SS:** Baez 19, Camacaro 12, Castillo 1, Marte 5, Perez 22, Sarmiento 1. **OF:** Almonte 15, Benita 10, Campos 24, Cepeda 1, Escalante 1, Fanas 25, Flores 21, Ibarguen 8, Marquez 29, Mejia 9, Noriega 21, Paz 6, Rosa 26, Sanchez 1

New York Yankees

SEASON IN A SENTENCE: The Yankees rode Aaron Judge's record-breaking season to a division title and a spot in the American League Championship Series before being swept by the eventual world champion Astros.

HIGH POINT: From open to close, Judge's season was one of the greatest in franchise history. The unquestioned peak, however, came on Oct. 4, when Judge slammed his 62nd home run of the season. The home run broke the American League and franchise records, set by Roger Maris in 1961. It was his last home run of the regular season, capping a year when he produced 10.6 wins above replacement, as measured by Baseball Reference.

LOW POINT: The Yankees were no-hit by the Astros on June 25. Houston's Cristian Javier, Bryan Abreu and Ryan Pressly silenced New York's bats that day, then again four months later when Javier led Houston in a shutout of the Yankees in the third game of the American League Championship Series.

NOTABLE ROOKIES: The Yankees got help late in the season from infielders Oswaldo Cabrera and Oswald Peraza. The former bounced around the diamond, including some of his first professional experience in the outfield. The latter ranks as one of the team's top prospects and had the look of a solid defender at shortstop.

KEY TRANSACTIONS: Before the season, New York shipped catcher Gary Sanchez and infielder Gio Urshela to Minnesota in exchange for third baseman Josh Donaldson, shortstop Isiah Kiner-Falefa and catcher Ben Rortvedt. At midseason, the team further bolstered its pitching staff by acquiring righthanders Frankie Montas (Athletics), Lou Trivino (Athletics) and Scott Effross (Cubs). The Yankees also added outfield help by sending lefty Jordan Montgomery to St. Louis for Harrison Bader, who showed well in the postseason.

ON THE FARM: The Yankees' farm is headed by a strong group, including shortstops Anthony Volpe and Oswald Peraza, as well as outfielders Jasson Dominguez and Everson Pereira. The system was thinned by the glut of trades the team made to acquire help during its playoff run. The system also got a boost from the addition of first-rounder Spencer Jones—a powerful athletic outfielder from Vanderbilt—as well as the rise of teenage righthander Luis Serna, who showed uncommon pitchability and a dastardly changeup in the Rookie-level Florida Complex League.

OPENING DAY PAYROLL: $236,838,214 (3rd).

PLAYERS OF THE YEAR

MAJOR LEAGUE

Aaron Judge
OF

.311/.425/.686
AL record 62 HR
MLB Player of the Year

MINOR LEAGUE

Anthony Volpe
SS

(AA/AAA)
.249/.342/.460
21 HR, 50 SB in 132 G

ORGANIZATION LEADERS

Batting — ***Minimum 250 AB**

MAJORS

* AVG	Aaron Judge	.311
* OPS	Aaron Judge	1.111
HR	Aaron Judge	62
RBI	Aaron Judge	131

MINORS

* AVG	Andres Chaparro, FCL, Tampa, Somerset	.296
* OBP	Anthony Seigler, Tampa, Hudson Valley	.405
* SLG	Andres Chaparro, FCL, Tampa, Somerset	.592
* OPS	Andres Chaparro, FCL, Tampa, Somerset	.962
R	Jasson Dominguez, Tampa, Hudson Valley, Somerset	92
H	Anthony Volpe, Somerset, Scranton/Wilkes-Barre	127
TB	Anthony Volpe, Somerset, Scranton/Wilkes-Barre	235
2B	Anthony Volpe, Somerset, Scranton/Wilkes-Barre	35
3B	Everson Pereira, Hudson Valley, Somerset	9
HR	Tyler Hardman, Hudson Valley, Somerset	22
RBI	Tyler Hardman, Hudson Valley, Somerset	81
BB	Anthony Seigler, Tampa, Hudson Valley	91
SO	Anthony Garcia, Tampa	156
SB	Anthony Volpe, Somerset, Scranton/Wilkes-Barre	50

Pitching — **#Minimum 75 IP**

MAJORS

W	Jameson Taillon	14
# ERA	Nestor Cortes	2.44
SO	Gerrit Cole	257
SV	Clay Holmes	20

MINORS

W	Sean Boyle, Somerset, Scranton/Wilkes-Barre	13
L	Will Warren, Hudson Valley, Somerset	9
	Blas Castano, Hudson Valley, Somerset	9
# ERA	Ken Waldichuk, Somerset, Scranton/Wilkes-Barre	2.71
G	Zach Greene, Scranton	48
GS	Sean Boyle, Somerset, Scranton/Wilkes-Barre	27
SV	Carson Coleman, Hudson Valley, Somerset	19
IP	Sean Boyle, Somerset, Scranton/Wilkes-Barre	155.1
BB	Matt Krook, Scranton/Wilkes-Barre	73
SO	Sean Boyle, Somerset, Scranton/Wilkes-Barre	160
# AVG	Juan Carela, Tampa, Hudson Valley	.191

2022 PERFORMANCE

General Manager: Brian Cashman. **Farm Director:** Kevin Reese. **Scouting Director:** Damon Oppenheimer.

Class	Team	League	W	L	PCT	Finish	Manager
Majors	New York Yankees	American	99	63	.611	2nd (15)	Aaron Boone
Triple-A	Scranton/Wilkes-Barre RailRiders	International	83	67	.553	5th (20)	Doug Davis
Double-A	Somerset Patriots	Eastern	83	53	.610	1st (12)	Dan Fiorito
High-A	Hudson Valley Renegades	South Atlantic	71	59	.546	4th (12)	Tyson Blaser
Low-A	Tampa Tarpons	Florida State	61	67	.477	8th (10)	Rachel Balkovec
Rookie	FCL Yankees	Florida Complex	38	17	.691	2nd (16)	Sergio Santos
Overall 2022 Minor League Record			393	324	.548	3rd (30)	

ORGANIZATION STATISTICS

NEW YORK YANKEES

AMERICAN LEAGUE

Batting	B-T	HT	WT	DOB	AVG	vLH	vRH	G	AB	R	H	2B	3B	HR	RBI	BB	HBP	SH	SF	SO	SB	CS	SLG	OBP
Miguel Andujar	R-R	6-0	211	3-2-95	.229	.211	.241	27	96	9	22	2	0	1	8	3	0	0	1	22	4	0	.281	.250
Harrison Bader	R-R	6-0	210	6-3-94	.217	.400	.195	14	46	3	10	3	0	0	9	2	0	0	1	15	2	1	.283	.245
Andrew Benintendi	L-L	5-9	180	7-6-94	.254	.250	.256	33	114	14	29	9	1	2	12	13	1	1	2	25	4	1	.404	.331
Rob Brantly	L-R	6-0	191	7-14-89	.333	--	.333	1	3	0	1	1	0	0	0	0	0	0	0	0	0	0	.667	.333
Oswaldo Cabrera	B-R	6-0	200	3-1-99	.247	.286	.238	44	154	21	38	8	1	6	19	15	0	1	1	44	3	2	.429	.312
Matt Carpenter	L-R	6-4	210	11-26-85	.305	.333	.295	47	128	28	39	9	0	15	37	19	5	1	1	35	0	0	.727	.412
Josh Donaldson	R-R	6-1	210	12-8-85	.222	.217	.223	132	478	59	106	28	0	15	62	54	8	0	6	148	2	2	.374	.308
Estevan Florial	L-R	6-1	195	11-25-97	.097	.250	.074	17	31	4	3	0	0	0	1	3	1	0	0	13	2	0	.097	.200
Joey Gallo	L-R	6-5	250	11-19-93	.159	.102	.178	82	233	32	37	4	1	12	24	40	0	0	0	106	2	0	.339	.282
Marwin Gonzalez	B-R	6-1	205	3-14-89	.185	.207	.175	86	184	20	34	7	0	6	18	14	4	3	2	54	3	0	.321	.255
Ronald Guzman	L-L	6-5	235	10-20-94	.000	.000	.000	3	6	0	0	0	0	0	0	0	0	0	0	5	0	0	.000	.000
Aaron Hicks	B-R	6-1	205	10-2-89	.216	.234	.209	130	384	54	83	9	2	8	40	62	4	1	2	109	10	3	.313	.330
Kyle Higashioka	R-R	6-1	202	4-20-90	.227	.254	.216	83	229	27	52	7	0	10	31	12	1	2	4	52	0	1	.389	.264
Aaron Judge	R-R	6-7	282	4-26-92	.311	.274	.322	157	570	133	177	28	0	62	131	111	6	0	5	175	16	3	.686	.425
Isiah Kiner-Falefa	R-R	5-11	190	3-23-95	.261	.264	.260	142	483	66	126	20	0	4	48	35	5	3	5	72	22	4	.327	.314
DJ LeMahieu	R-R	6-4	220	7-13-88	.261	.285	.253	125	467	74	122	18	0	12	46	67	4	1	2	71	4	3	.377	.357
Tim Locastro	R-R	6-1	200	7-14-92	.186	.200	.179	38	43	13	8	1	0	2	4	2	1	0	0	7	8	2	.349	.239
Oswald Peraza	R-R	6-0	200	6-15-00	.306	.222	.325	18	49	8	15	3	0	1	2	6	2	0	0	9	2	0	.429	.404
Anthony Rizzo	L-L	6-3	240	8-8-89	.224	.233	.220	130	465	77	104	21	1	32	75	58	23	0	2	101	6	5	.480	.338
Giancarlo Stanton	R-R	6-6	245	11-8-89	.211	.184	.220	110	398	53	84	7	0	31	78	50	0	0	3	137	0	0	.462	.297
Gleyber Torres	R-R	6-1	205	12-13-96	.257	.255	.257	140	526	73	135	28	1	24	76	39	3	1	3	129	10	5	.451	.310
Jose Trevino	R-R	5-10	215	11-28-92	.248	.304	.233	115	335	39	83	12	1	11	43	15	2	0	1	62	2	1	.388	.283

Pitching	B-T	HT	WT	DOB	W	L	ERA	G	GS	CG	SV	IP	H	R	ER	HR	BB	SO	AVG	vLH	vRH	K/9	BB/9
Albert Abreu	R-R	6-2	190	9-26-95	2	2	3.16	22	0	0	0	26	25	10	9	2	6	26	.255	.258	.254	9.12	2.10
3-team total (4 Kansas City Royals, 7 Texas Rangers)					2	2	3.26	33	0	0	0	39	35	15	14	5	22	38	.243	.191	.268	8.84	5.12
Anthony Banda	L-L	6-2	220	8-10-93	0	0	40.50	2	0	0	0	1	2	3	3	0	5	1	.500	.000	.667	13.50	67.50
2-team total (7 Toronto Blue Jays)					0	1	7.71	9	1	0	0	7	9	6	6	1	8	8	.321	.231	.400	10.29	10.29
Manny Banuelos	R-L	5-10	215	3-13-91	0	0	2.16	4	0	0	1	8	7	2	2	0	3	8	.219	.143	.240	8.64	3.24
Luke Bard	R-R	6-3	200	11-13-90	0	0	0.00	1	0	0	0	1	0	0	0	0	0	0	.000	.000	.000	0.00	0.00
2-team total (8 Tampa Bay Rays)					1	1	1.80	9	0	0	0	15	7	3	3	0	7	8	.143	.176	.125	4.80	4.20
Jacob Barnes	R-R	6-2	231	4-14-90	0	0	0.00	1	0	0	0	2	2	0	0	0	0	2	.286	.500	.200	10.80	0.00
2-team total (22 Detroit Tigers)					3	1	5.64	23	0	0	0	22	23	14	14	3	9	12	.271	.167	.327	4.84	3.63
Zack Britton	L-L	6-1	200	12-22-87	0	0	13.50	3	0	0	0	1	1	1	1	0	6	1	.333	.000	1.000	13.50	81.00
Miguel Castro	R-R	6-7	201	12-24-94	5	0	4.03	34	0	0	0	29	27	16	13	2	15	31	.243	.243	.243	9.62	4.66
Aroldis Chapman	L-L	6-4	218	2-28-88	4	4	4.46	43	0	0	9	36	24	18	18	4	28	43	.188	.162	.198	10.65	6.94
Gerrit Cole	R-R	6-4	220	9-8-90	13	8	3.50	33	33	0	0	201	154	81	78	33	50	257	.209	.182	.229	11.53	2.24
Nestor Cortes	R-L	5-11	210	12-10-94	12	4	2.44	28	28	1	0	158	108	44	43	16	38	163	.189	.110	.202	9.27	2.16
Scott Effross	R-R	6-2	202	12-28-93	0	0	2.13	13	0	0	3	13	9	4	3	1	4	12	.196	.111	.250	8.53	2.84
Domingo German	R-R	6-2	181	8-4-92	2	5	3.61	15	14	0	0	72	65	31	29	11	19	58	.236	.230	.243	7.22	2.36
Luis Gil	R-R	6-2	185	6-3-98	0	0	9.00	1	1	0	0	4	5	4	4	0	2	5	.294	.167	.364	11.25	4.50
Chi Chi Gonzalez	R-R	6-3	210	1-15-92	0	0	1.93	1	1	0	0	5	4	1	1	0	3	3	.235	.273	.167	5.79	5.79
2-team total (2 Minnesota Twins)					0	0	5.40	3	3	0	0	12	16	7	7	2	3	7	.333	.304	.360	5.40	2.31
Marwin Gonzalez	B-R	6-1	205	3-14-89	0	0	0.00	1	0	0	0	0	0	0	0	0	0	0	.000	--	.000	0.00	0.00
Chad Green	L-R	6-3	215	5-24-91	1	1	3.00	14	0	0	1	15	13	6	5	1	5	16	.241	.316	.200	9.60	3.00
Shane Greene	R-R	6-4	200	11-17-88	0	0	18.00	1	0	0	0	1	1	2	2	1	1	1	.250	--	.250	9.00	9.00
Clay Holmes	R-R	6-5	245	3-27-93	7	4	2.54	62	0	0	20	64	45	21	18	2	20	65	.196	.250	.159	9.19	2.83
Michael King	R-R	6-3	210	5-25-95	6	3	2.29	34	0	0	1	51	35	15	13	3	16	66	.192	.179	.200	11.65	2.82
Jonathan Loaisiga	R-R	5-11	165	11-2-94	2	3	4.13	50	0	0	2	48	43	25	22	3	19	37	.234	.243	.228	6.94	3.56
Lucas Luetge	L-L	6-4	205	3-24-87	4	4	2.67	50	0	0	2	57	63	19	17	4	17	60	.276	.269	.280	9.42	2.67
Ron Marinaccio	R-R	6-2	205	7-1-95	1	0	2.05	40	0	0	0	44	22	12	10	2	24	56	.149	.146	.152	11.45	4.91
David McKay	R-R	6-3	205	3-31-95	0	0	0.00	2	0	0	0	2	1	0	0	0	2	1	.143	.000	.333	4.50	9.00

3-team total (1 Oakland Athletics, 1 Tampa Bay Rays)					0	0	6.75	4	0	0	0	7	8	5	5	1	4	3	.296	.250	.333	4.05	5.40
Frankie Montas	R-R	6-2	255	3-21-93	1	3	6.35	8	8	0	0	40	46	28	28	6	15	33	.288	.297	.281	7.49	3.40
Jordan Montgomery	L-L	6-6	228	12-27-92	3	3	3.69	21	21	0	0	115	103	48	47	15	23	97	.236	.200	.244	7.61	1.81
Wandy Peralta	L-L	6-0	227	7-27-91	3	4	2.72	56	0	0	4	56	42	19	17	2	17	47	.208	.155	.237	7.51	2.72
Clarke Schmidt	R-R	6-1	200	2-20-96	5	5	3.12	29	3	0	2	58	46	23	20	5	23	56	.222	.268	.192	8.74	3.59
JP Sears	R-L	5-11	180	2-19-96	3	0	2.05	7	2	0	0	22	14	5	5	1	5	15	.184	.214	.177	6.14	2.05
2-team total (10 Oakland Athletics)					6	3	3.86	17	11	0	0	70	67	31	30	8	23	51	.256	.265	.254	6.56	2.96
Luis Severino	R-R	6-2	218	2-20-94	7	3	3.18	19	19	0	0	102	72	37	36	14	30	112	.196	.196	.195	9.88	2.65
Jameson Taillon	R-R	6-5	230	11-18-91	14	5	3.91	32	32	0	0	177	168	78	77	26	32	151	.246	.235	.253	7.66	1.62
Lou Trivino	R-R	6-5	235	10-1-91	1	2	1.66	25	0	0	1	22	18	6	4	1	10	22	.222	.273	.203	9.14	4.15
Ryan Weber	R-R	6-1	175	8-12-90	0	0	0.84	5	0	0	1	11	6	1	1	1	1	3	.167	.083	.208	2.53	0.84
Greg Weissert	R-R	6-2	215	2-4-95	3	0	5.56	12	0	0	0	11	6	7	7	1	5	11	.146	.000	.222	8.74	3.97

Fielding

Catcher	PCT	G	PO	A	E	DP	PB
Brantly	1.000	1	9	0	0	0	0
Higashioka	.993	82	669	21	5	2	6
Trevino	.993	112	828	32	6	1	2

First Base	PCT	G	PO	A	E	DP
Andujar	.000	1	0	0	0	0
Cabrera	1.000	3	9	1	0	0
Carpenter	1.000	5	24	1	0	1
Gonzalez	.976	14	71	9	2	7
Guzman	1.000	3	16	1	0	1
LeMahieu	.996	35	230	13	1	16
Rizzo	.995	120	919	72	5	71

Second Base	PCT	G	PO	A	E	DP
Cabrera	.929	3	5	8	1	3
Gonzalez	1.000	3	0	1	0	0
LeMahieu	.986	41	53	91	2	21
Peraza	1.000	4	5	5	0	2
Torres	.985	124	192	270	7	50

Third Base	PCT	G	PO	A	E	DP
Cabrera	1.000	3	7	6	0	0
Carpenter	1.000	2	1	3	0	1
Donaldson	.961	104	78	220	12	17
Gonzalez	1.000	12	4	23	0	0
Kiner-Falefa	.909	6	2	8	1	0
LeMahieu	.992	47	23	106	1	7

Shortstop	PCT	G	PO	A	E	DP
Cabrera	1.000	4	2	11	0	0
Gonzalez	1.000	20	14	33	0	4
Kiner-Falefa	.970	138	149	331	15	51
Peraza	1.000	12	11	22	0	4
Torres	.889	6	4	4	1	0

Outfield	PCT	G	PO	A	E	DP
Andujar	1.000	19	39	0	0	0
Bader	1.000	14	31	0	0	0
Benintendi	1.000	33	52	2	0	0
Cabrera	1.000	36	53	7	0	0
Carpenter	1.000	15	25	0	0	0
Florial	1.000	16	24	2	0	0
Gallo	.991	84	108	2	1	0
Gonzalez	1.000	36	41	1	0	1
Hicks	.996	136	221	4	1	1
Judge	1.000	151	275	6	0	1
Locastro	1.000	27	22	1	0	0
Stanton	.983	38	56	2	1	0

SCRANTON/WILKES-BARRE RAILRIDERS — TRIPLE-A

INTERNATIONAL LEAGUE

Batting	B-T	HT	WT	DOB	AVG	vLH	vRH	G	AB	R	H	2B	3B	HR	RBI	BB	HBP	SH	SF	SO	SB	CS	SLG	OBP
Evan Alexander	L-L	6-2	175	2-26-98	.121	.125	.118	29	33	12	4	1	0	0	0	7	0	0	0	13	5	1	.152	.275
Armando Alvarez	R-R	6-1	195	7-14-94	.278	.290	.272	91	299	48	83	20	0	18	55	20	0	0	4	71	4	2	.525	.319
Miguel Andujar	R-R	6-0	211	3-2-95	.285	.360	.257	71	277	42	79	17	0	13	51	17	2	0	1	35	5	0	.487	.330
Jake Bauers	L-L	6-1	195	10-6-95	.226	.208	.232	32	106	14	24	2	1	5	16	20	1	0	1	43	4	1	.406	.352
2-team total (29 Louisville Bats)					.183	.140	.195	61	202	21	37	6	1	8	28	39	1	0	2	76	8	3	.342	.316
Chad Bell	L-R	6-3	210	3-4-97	.197	.200	.196	22	66	7	13	3	0	1	4	10	1	0	0	28	0	0	.288	.312
Michael Beltre	B-R	6-3	220	7-3-95	.283	.118	.361	22	53	10	15	5	0	2	9	11	1	0	0	16	6	0	.491	.415
Greg Bird	L-R	6-3	220	11-9-92	.218	.196	.226	59	206	16	45	8	1	6	22	31	2	0	1	61	2	0	.354	.325
Rob Brantly	L-R	6-0	191	7-14-89	.269	.194	.288	59	182	18	49	10	1	1	22	11	7	0	1	32	1	0	.352	.333
Josh Breaux	R-R	6-1	220	10-7-97	.239	.289	.219	41	159	20	38	4	2	6	21	12	1	0	0	49	1	0	.403	.297
Oswaldo Cabrera	B-R	6-0	200	3-1-99	.262	.246	.270	47	183	29	48	12	3	8	29	19	3	2	1	55	10	3	.492	.340
Derek Dietrich	L-R	6-2	205	7-18-89	.250	.211	.265	44	136	16	34	13	1	3	21	7	8	0	3	41	0	0	.426	.318
Oliver Dunn	L-R	5-10	185	9-2-97	.071	.167	.000	7	14	2	1	0	0	1	2	4	1	0	0	8	0	0	.286	.316
Phillip Evans	R-R	5-10	210	9-10-92	.244	.245	.243	103	361	45	88	17	0	9	33	31	5	0	3	57	2	2	.366	.310
Estevan Florial	L-R	6-1	195	11-25-97	.283	.222	.305	101	403	66	114	31	2	15	46	54	1	2	1	140	39	10	.481	.368
David Freitas	R-R	6-2	250	3-18-89	.239	.132	.293	36	113	9	27	6	0	2	9	12	0	0	1	23	0	0	.345	.310
Ronald Guzman	L-L	6-5	235	10-20-94	.255	.300	.237	105	322	51	82	24	0	16	53	41	5	0	4	100	2	0	.478	.344
Ender Inciarte	L-L	5-11	190	10-29-90	.252	.219	.268	34	103	12	26	2	1	4	11	13	0	0	0	17	4	2	.408	.336
2-team total (4 Syracuse Mets)					.244	.222	.253	38	119	14	29	3	1	4	11	14	0	0	0	20	6	2	.387	.323
Ryan LaMarre	R-L	6-1	215	11-21-88	.297	.273	.306	53	155	33	46	10	0	5	21	21	9	0	1	42	7	2	.458	.409
Tim Locastro	R-R	6-1	200	7-14-92	.240	.244	.238	47	167	27	40	13	2	3	18	12	11	0	0	38	7	1	.395	.332
Max McDowell	R-R	6-1	208	1-12-94	.193	.230	.175	66	187	17	36	10	0	2	16	23	4	0	1	50	3	1	.278	.293
Chris Owings	R-R	5-10	185	8-12-91	.235	.256	.229	59	187	27	44	7	1	8	30	18	1	0	2	52	5	2	.412	.303
Jose Peraza	R-R	6-0	210	4-30-94	.239	.203	.253	63	209	20	50	12	0	5	29	12	5	0	3	27	3	1	.368	.293
2-team total (8 Worcester Red Sox)					.236	.200	.249	71	237	22	56	13	0	5	31	12	7	0	3	31	3	1	.354	.290
Oswald Peraza	R-R	6-0	200	6-15-00	.259	.252	.262	99	386	57	100	16	0	19	50	34	7	1	1	100	33	5	.448	.329
Cristian Perez	R-R	5-10	170	10-26-98	.125	.000	.200	3	8	2	1	0	0	0	0	1	0	0	0	4	1	0	.125	.222
Blake Perkins	B-R	5-11	181	9-10-96	.244	.200	.254	30	86	16	21	4	1	3	14	17	5	2	4	26	4	0	.419	.384
Matt Pita	R-R	5-10	175	4-21-97	.198	.000	.250	40	86	11	17	4	0	5	15	8	1	0	1	27	3	1	.419	.271
Ben Rortvedt	L-R	5-10	205	9-25-97	.221	.204	.230	42	154	21	34	9	0	6	20	18	2	1	2	57	0	0	.396	.307
Anthony Volpe	R-R	5-11	180	4-28-01	.236	.238	.235	22	89	15	21	4	1	3	5	8	2	0	0	30	6	1	.404	.313
Tyler Wade	L-R	6-1	188	11-23-94	.227	.167	.253	42	141	26	32	6	1	4	16	27	1	0	1	35	15	1	.369	.353

Pitching	B-T	HT	WT	DOB	W	L	ERA	G	GS	CG	SV	IP	H	R	ER	HR	BB	SO	AVG	vLH	vRH	K/9	BB/9
Albert Abreu	R-R	6-2	190	9-26-95	0	0	2.70	4	0	0	0	3	5	1	1	0	2	5	.333	.000	.500	13.50	5.40
Evan Alexander	L-L	6-2	175	2-26-98	0	0	0.00	1	0	0	0	1	0	0	0	0	0	0	.000	--	.000	0.00	0.00
Anthony Banda	L-L	6-2	220	8-10-93	0	3	6.14	6	1	0	0	7	7	6	5	0	6	8	.259	.300	.235	9.82	7.36
Manny Banuelos	R-L	5-10	215	3-13-91	0	2	2.35	7	5	0	0	31	22	10	8	0	12	30	.202	.114	.262	8.80	3.52

Luke Bard	R-R	6-3	200	11-13-90	1	1	3.09	9	0	0	2	12	12	8	4	2	5	11	.261	.273	.250	8.49	3.86
2-team total (19 Durham Bulls)					1	1	4.29	28	1	0	2	36	30	21	17	9	10	38	.224	.155	.276	9.59	2.52
Jacob Barnes	R-R	6-2	231	4-14-90	1	1	2.25	10	0	0	0	8	4	3	2	0	4	8	.143	.143	.143	9.00	4.50
2-team total (5 Toledo Mud Hens)					1	1	2.57	15	0	0	0	14	11	5	4	0	6	20	.208	.174	.233	12.86	3.86
Sean Boyle	R-R	6-1	205	10-29-96	5	1	3.61	9	8	0	0	47	47	19	19	10	14	43	.261	.344	.178	8.18	2.66
Braden Bristo	R-R	6-0	180	11-1-94	3	3	4.56	41	1	0	1	53	52	34	27	6	31	64	.250	.188	.308	10.80	5.23
Jhony Brito	R-R	6-2	160	2-17-98	6	2	3.31	18	15	0	0	71	59	26	26	5	24	53	.229	.194	.264	6.75	3.06
Zack Britton	L-L	6-1	200	12-22-87	0	0	0.00	4	0	0	0	3	2	0	0	0	2	2	.182	.250	.143	5.40	5.40
Miguel Castro	R-R	6-7	201	12-24-94	0	0	0.00	3	0	0	0	3	1	0	0	0	2	5	.111	.250	.000	15.00	6.00
Aroldis Chapman	L-L	6-4	218	2-28-88	0	0	0.00	1	0	0	0	1	0	0	0	0	0	2	.000	.000	.000	18.00	0.00
Jimmy Cordero	R-R	6-4	240	10-19-91	1	1	2.09	32	0	0	6	39	25	12	9	2	13	50	.181	.172	.189	11.64	3.03
Tyler Duffey	R-R	6-3	220	12-27-90	1	1	10.50	7	0	0	1	6	11	7	7	1	1	8	.379	.429	.333	12.00	1.50
Scott Effross	R-R	6-2	202	12-28-93	0	1	18.00	1	0	0	0	1	3	2	2	1	0	0	.500	.333	.667	0.00	0.00
Carlos Espinal	R-R	5-11	175	10-21-96	0	2	4.37	13	0	0	1	23	20	12	11	1	16	19	.238	.286	.190	7.54	6.35
Deivi Garcia	R-R	5-9	163	5-19-99	2	4	7.96	14	7	0	0	37	40	37	33	7	24	39	.276	.338	.211	9.40	5.79
Domingo German	R-R	6-2	181	8-4-92	1	0	0.00	2	2	0	0	10	4	0	0	0	1	5	.125	.067	.176	4.50	0.90
Luis Gil	R-R	6-2	185	6-3-98	0	3	7.89	6	6	0	0	22	21	20	19	6	15	31	.244	.245	.243	12.88	6.23
Michael Gomez	R-R	6-3	210	8-15-96	3	5	4.84	44	0	0	0	61	65	40	33	4	33	54	.274	.297	.257	7.92	4.84
Chi Chi Gonzalez	R-R	6-3	210	1-15-92	0	0	3.63	5	5	0	0	22	26	9	9	1	5	18	.280	.309	.237	7.25	2.01
3-team total (8 St. Paul Saints, 5 Toledo Mud Hens)					2	3	4.03	18	14	0	0	80	82	38	36	8	27	71	.265	.280	.247	7.95	3.02
Shane Greene	R-R	6-4	200	11-17-88	2	1	5.40	20	0	0	3	27	26	16	16	3	15	30	.252	.308	.219	10.13	5.06
Zach Greene	R-R	6-1	215	8-29-96	9	0	3.42	48	4	0	0	68	51	33	26	11	32	96	.201	.205	.197	12.64	4.21
Ronald Guzman	L-L	6-5	235	10-20-94	0	0	0.00	1	0	0	0	0	0	0	0	0	2	1	.000	--	.000	27.00	54.00
Matt Krook	L-L	6-4	225	10-21-94	10	7	4.09	29	22	0	0	139	120	71	63	19	73	155	.233	.172	.261	10.06	4.74
Trevor Lane	L-L	5-11	185	4-26-94	0	2	2.08	20	0	0	0	22	21	12	5	2	13	25	.256	.196	.333	10.38	5.40
Jonathan Loaisiga	R-R	5-11	165	11-2-94	0	0	9.00	1	0	0	0	1	3	1	1	0	0	2	.500	.500	.500	18.00	0.00
Josh Maciejewski	R-L	6-3	175	8-14-95	0	1	13.50	1	1	0	0	3	2	4	4	1	2	2	.200	.000	.286	6.75	6.75
Ron Marinaccio	R-R	6-2	205	7-1-95	1	0	2.79	8	0	0	0	10	10	3	3	3	4	21	.250	.333	.158	19.55	3.72
Reggie McClain	R-R	6-2	180	11-16-92	0	1	7.56	17	0	0	0	17	17	15	14	0	18	16	.262	.265	.258	8.64	9.72
David McKay	R-R	6-3	205	3-31-95	3	0	2.91	17	0	0	1	22	15	7	7	3	11	26	.195	.225	.162	10.80	4.57
2-team total (4 Durham Bulls)					3	0	3.86	21	0	0	1	26	21	11	11	4	12	29	.221	.245	.196	10.17	4.21
Shelby Miller	R-R	6-3	225	10-10-90	2	2	1.71	16	0	0	4	21	13	6	4	1	6	25	.171	.205	.135	10.71	2.57
Matt Minnick	R-L	6-2	210	3-11-96	0	0	6.75	1	0	0	0	1	2	1	1	1	0	1	.400	--	.400	6.75	0.00
Jose Mujica	R-R	6-2	249	6-29-96	3	1	4.39	35	1	0	3	53	43	28	26	14	16	47	.216	.213	.219	7.93	2.70
Vinny Nittoli	R-R	6-1	210	11-11-90	4	1	3.44	22	4	0	0	37	26	15	14	5	13	44	.202	.176	.218	10.80	3.19
3-team total (10 Buffalo Bisons, 5 Lehigh Valley IronPigs)					4	1	3.81	37	4	0	2	52	40	23	22	7	14	64	.213	.181	.238	11.08	2.42
Matt Pita	R-R	5-10	175	4-21-97	0	0	0.00	1	0	0	0	0	0	0	0	0	0	0	.000	--	.000	0.00	0.00
Emmanuel Ramirez	R-R	6-2	190	7-15-94	1	0	11.05	8	0	0	0	7	12	9	9	2	5	10	.375	.385	.368	12.27	6.14
Stephen Ridings	R-R	6-8	220	8-14-95	0	0	0.00	1	0	0	0	1	1	0	0	0	0	2	.250	.000	.500	18.00	0.00
Richard Rodriguez	R-R	6-4	220	3-4-90	3	1	3.86	17	0	0	0	23	15	10	10	3	7	24	.181	.209	.150	9.26	2.70
Danny Salazar	R-R	6-0	195	1-11-90	0	0	3.86	2	1	0	0	2	2	1	1	1	2	4	.222	.000	.333	15.43	7.71
Clarke Schmidt	R-R	6-1	200	2-20-96	2	1	3.27	8	8	0	0	33	26	13	12	1	9	46	.205	.230	.182	12.55	2.45
JP Sears	R-L	5-11	180	2-19-96	1	1	1.67	11	9	0	0	43	24	12	8	3	7	55	.155	.141	.167	11.51	1.47
Shawn Semple	R-R	6-1	220	10-9-95	1	1	11.45	4	1	0	0	11	22	14	14	5	6	6	.400	.333	.425	4.91	4.91
Luis Severino	R-R	6-2	218	2-20-94	0	0	4.15	1	1	0	0	4	4	2	2	0	1	6	.235	.286	.200	12.46	2.08
Chasen Shreve	L-L	6-4	180	7-12-90	1	0	1.93	5	0	0	0	5	1	1	1	0	1	5	.067	.143	.000	9.64	1.93
Mitch Spence	R-R	6-1	185	5-6-98	3	2	3.86	10	10	0	0	51	52	24	22	5	16	48	.260	.290	.226	8.42	2.81
Ken Waldichuk	L-L	6-4	220	1-8-98	2	3	3.59	11	11	0	0	48	38	20	19	5	23	70	.218	.157	.244	13.22	4.34
Ryan Weber	R-R	6-1	175	8-12-90	3	4	3.86	15	8	0	0	40	43	23	17	6	5	27	.272	.238	.295	6.13	1.13
Greg Weissert	R-R	6-2	215	2-4-95	2	1	1.69	42	0	0	18	48	24	9	9	3	19	70	.149	.160	.138	13.13	3.56
Hayden Wesneski	R-R	6-3	210	12-5-97	6	7	3.51	19	19	0	0	90	75	38	35	9	28	83	.227	.259	.195	8.33	2.81
2-team total (5 Iowa Cubs)					6	9	3.92	24	23	0	0	110	92	51	48	10	36	106	.227	.241	.213	8.65	2.94

Fielding

Catcher	PCT	G	PO	A	E	DP	PB
Brantly	.997	30	286	9	1	2	1
Breaux	.990	25	190	11	2	0	0
Freitas	.986	23	205	2	3	0	4
McDowell	.989	58	500	20	6	2	3
Rortvedt	.989	27	251	8	3	0	2

First Base	PCT	G	PO	A	E	DP
Alvarez	.951	6	38	1	2	2
Bauers	1.000	15	124	7	0	9
Bell	.978	13	82	7	2	3
Bird	.984	34	230	15	4	20
Brantly	1.000	4	13	0	0	0
Evans	1.000	9	35	4	0	7
Guzman	.992	87	585	42	5	50

Second Base	PCT	G	PO	A	E	DP
Alvarez	1.000	4	1	7	0	0
Bell	.900	7	5	13	2	1
Cabrera	.990	21	28	69	1	15
Dietrich	1.000	26	30	45	0	10
Dunn	1.000	3	4	3	0	0
Evans	1.000	9	16	23	0	6
Owings	.976	36	52	71	3	12
Peraza	.955	35	42	65	5	16
Peraza	.941	10	13	19	2	2
Perez	1.000	2	2	2	0	0
Wade	.941	9	9	23	2	7

Third Base	PCT	G	PO	A	E	DP
Alexander	.000	1	0	0	0	0
Alvarez	.937	73	50	127	12	14
Andujar	.935	19	11	32	3	1
Bell	1.000	3	0	3	0	0
Cabrera	.913	6	5	16	2	2
Dietrich	1.000	13	3	17	0	0
Evans	.947	39	28	80	6	4
Owings	1.000	1	0	1	0	0
Peraza	.889	4	3	5	1	1
Wade	1.000	1	0	1	0	0

Shortstop	PCT	G	PO	A	E	DP
Cabrera	1.000	15	15	40	0	7
Owings	.947	5	4	14	1	1
Peraza	1.000	12	10	31	0	4
Peraza	.971	89	108	193	9	47
Perez	1.000	1	1	0	0	0
Volpe	.969	21	21	42	2	5
Wade	.962	10	5	20	1	0

Outfield	PCT	G	PO	A	E	DP
Alexander	.967	19	29	0	1	0
Alvarez	1.000	1	1	0	0	0
Andujar	.986	46	72	0	1	0
Bauers	1.000	16	25	1	0	1
Beltre	.969	22	30	1	1	0
Cabrera	.889	3	8	0	1	0
Dunn	1.000	3	2	0	0	0
Evans	.961	46	66	7	3	0
Florial	.990	102	201	2	2	2
Inciarte	.981	31	49	2	1	0
LaMarre	.960	51	69	3	3	0
Locastro	.973	43	72	0	2	0

Owings	1.000	19	31	1	0	0	Perkins	1.000	29	58	0	0	0	Wade	1.000	24	31	3	0	0
Peraza	.909	10	10	0	1	0	Pita	1.000	32	47	2	0	0							

SOMERSET PATRIOTS — DOUBLE-A

EASTERN LEAGUE

Batting	B-T	HT	WT	DOB	AVG	vLH	vRH	G	AB	R	H	2B	3B	HR	RBI	BB	HBP	SH	SF	SO	SB	CS	SLG	OBP
Harrison Bader	R-R	6-0	210	6-3-94	.286	.400	.250	6	21	4	6	2	0	1	4	2	0	0	0	3	1	0	.524	.348
Jesus Bastidas	R-R	5-10	145	9-14-98	.240	.181	.256	111	396	56	95	18	1	18	55	38	12	0	3	115	11	7	.427	.323
Chad Bell	L-R	6-3	210	3-4-97	.249	.217	.256	71	249	37	62	8	0	14	40	29	1	0	1	98	0	3	.450	.329
Michael Beltre	B-R	6-3	220	7-3-95	.227	.163	.248	54	172	33	39	7	1	7	30	25	2	0	4	63	23	3	.401	.325
Josh Breaux	R-R	6-1	220	10-7-97	.204	.209	.202	53	211	24	43	10	0	13	29	19	1	0	0	64	1	0	.436	.273
Max Burt	R-R	6-2	185	8-28-96	.205	.172	.214	85	268	40	55	12	0	11	32	18	7	0	4	86	19	2	.373	.269
Andres Chaparro	R-R	6-1	200	5-4-99	.289	.351	.277	64	239	36	69	16	0	19	52	25	6	0	1	54	3	0	.594	.369
Derek Dietrich	L-R	6-2	205	7-18-89	.290	.286	.292	18	62	17	18	5	0	7	18	9	5	0	0	23	0	0	.710	.421
Jasson Dominquez	B-R	5-10	190	2-7-03	.105	.286	.000	5	19	5	2	0	1	1	1	3	0	0	0	5	1	0	.368	.227
Elijah Dunham	L-L	6-0	213	5-29-98	.248	.195	.262	110	415	67	103	26	3	17	63	59	7	0	4	103	37	7	.448	.348
Oliver Dunn	L-R	5-10	185	9-2-97	.333	.333	.333	29	66	12	22	8	1	2	16	10	1	0	0	26	3	1	.576	.429
Rodolfo Duran	R-R	5-9	181	2-19-98	.222	.250	.216	53	203	20	45	12	0	9	33	11	2	0	2	53	0	0	.414	.266
Mickey Gasper	B-R	5-10	205	10-11-95	.266	.295	.259	70	214	34	57	14	1	8	27	44	9	0	3	53	3	2	.453	.407
Tyler Hardman	R-R	6-3	204	1-27-99	.067	.000	.083	4	15	0	1	0	0	0	2	0	0	0	1	6	0	0	.067	.063
Brandon Lockridge	R-R	6-1	185	3-14-97	.230	.267	.222	108	418	67	96	18	1	14	49	36	7	0	3	125	18	4	.378	.300
James Nelson	R-R	6-2	180	10-18-97	.000	--	.000	2	5	2	0	0	0	0	0	2	1	0	0	2	0	0	.000	.375
Everson Pereira	R-R	6-0	191	4-10-01	.283	.364	.275	29	113	21	32	4	3	5	13	9	1	0	0	37	2	2	.504	.341
Cristian Perez	R-R	5-10	170	10-26-98	.211	.000	.235	5	19	0	4	1	0	0	1	0	0	0	0	6	0	0	.263	.211
Blake Perkins	B-R	5-11	181	9-10-96	.247	.310	.227	71	243	43	60	14	2	12	36	37	1	0	2	66	17	2	.469	.346
Matt Pita	R-R	5-10	175	4-21-97	.000	--	.000	2	7	0	0	0	0	0	0	1	0	0	0	3	0	0	.000	.125
Jeisson Rosario	L-L	6-1	191	10-22-99	.243	.254	.241	104	362	46	88	19	4	11	39	64	5	0	2	82	12	7	.409	.363
Giancarlo Stanton	R-R	6-6	245	11-8-89	.000	--	.000	2	7	0	0	0	0	0	0	0	0	0	0	3	0	0	.000	.000
Trey Sweeney	L-R	6-4	200	4-24-00	.233	.273	.219	11	43	6	10	1	0	2	5	7	0	0	0	10	2	1	.395	.340
Saul Torres	R-R	6-2	190	2-19-99	.000	.000	.000	2	6	0	0	0	0	0	1	0	1	0	0	3	0	0	.000	.143
Anthony Volpe	R-R	5-11	180	4-28-01	.251	.213	.259	110	422	71	106	31	4	18	60	57	10	0	8	88	44	6	.472	.348
Eric Wagaman	R-R	6-4	210	8-14-97	.340	.364	.333	17	53	13	18	3	0	4	6	4	1	0	0	8	1	0	.623	.397
Austin Wells	L-R	6-2	220	7-12-99	.261	.184	.277	55	211	34	55	8	1	12	43	29	5	0	2	58	7	0	.479	.360

Pitching	B-T	HT	WT	DOB	W	L	ERA	G	GS	CG	SV	IP	H	R	ER	HR	BB	SO	AVG	vLH	vRH	K/9	BB/9
Albert Abreu	R-R	6-2	190	9-26-95	1	0	0.00	1	0	0	0	1	1	0	0	0	0	2	.250	.000	.500	18.00	0.00
Clayton Beeter	R-R	6-2	220	10-9-98	0	0	2.13	7	7	0	0	25	16	6	6	1	11	41	.176	.261	.089	14.57	3.91
Sean Boyle	R-R	6-1	205	10-29-96	8	4	3.75	19	19	0	0	108	91	52	45	15	20	117	.226	.250	.209	9.75	1.67
Jhony Brito	R-R	6-2	160	2-17-98	5	2	2.36	8	8	0	0	42	36	14	11	4	11	38	.232	.132	.284	8.14	2.36
Zack Britton	L-L	6-1	200	12-22-87	0	0	0.00	1	0	0	0	1	0	0	0	0	0	2	.000	--	.000	18.00	0.00
Blas Castano	R-R	5-10	162	9-8-98	0	1	27.00	1	1	0	0	2	7	9	5	4	1	2	.538	.571	.500	10.80	5.40
Miguel Castro	R-R	6-7	201	12-24-94	0	0	10.80	3	0	0	0	2	5	2	2	0	1	2	.500	.714	.000	10.80	5.40
Aroldis Chapman	L-L	6-4	218	2-28-88	0	0	0.00	4	0	0	0	4	2	0	0	0	2	7	.154	.167	.143	15.75	4.50
Carson Coleman	R-R	6-2	190	4-7-98	2	3	2.86	35	0	0	15	44	30	16	14	2	10	69	.191	.162	.213	14.11	2.05
Nelvin Correa	R-R	6-1	170	1-25-97	0	0	0.00	5	0	0	0	6	1	0	0	0	2	5	.059	.000	.143	7.94	3.18
Kaleb Cowart	B-R	6-3	225	6-2-92	2	0	4.20	15	0	0	0	15	9	7	7	1	16	14	.167	.174	.161	8.40	9.60
Derek Craft	R-R	6-8	220	7-11-96	1	4	4.40	27	0	0	5	29	24	18	14	4	17	35	.226	.214	.234	10.99	5.34
Nick Ernst	R-R	6-3	195	8-27-96	6	0	4.37	39	0	0	2	60	49	31	29	8	35	71	.222	.242	.206	10.71	5.28
Carlos Espinal	R-R	5-11	175	10-21-96	2	0	3.11	24	0	0	1	38	26	14	13	6	16	43	.195	.232	.169	10.27	3.82
Deivi Garcia	R-R	5-9	163	5-19-99	2	1	5.40	6	6	0	0	27	20	19	16	6	8	37	.196	.222	.182	12.49	2.70
Domingo German	R-R	6-2	181	8-4-92	0	0	1.23	2	2	0	0	7	4	1	1	0	0	6	.160	.182	.143	7.36	0.00
Michael Gomez	R-R	6-3	210	8-15-96	0	0	0.00	2	0	0	0	4	1	0	0	0	4	5	.083	.000	.100	11.25	9.00
Yoendrys Gomez	R-R	6-3	175	10-15-99	1	0	3.86	4	4	0	0	16	14	7	7	1	6	19	.230	.324	.111	10.47	3.31
Steven Jennings	R-R	6-2	175	11-13-98	3	3	4.19	46	0	0	5	67	62	36	31	7	14	67	.249	.231	.262	9.05	1.89
Barrett Loseke	R-R	6-0	170	11-12-96	7	3	3.50	37	2	0	1	64	60	31	25	8	25	73	.248	.260	.239	10.21	3.50
Josh Maciejewski	R-L	6-3	175	8-14-95	4	1	2.88	14	1	0	1	34	29	15	11	2	12	48	.223	.200	.233	12.58	3.15
Ron Marinaccio	R-R	6-2	205	7-1-95	0	0	0.00	1	0	0	0	1	0	0	0	0	0	3	.000	.000	.000	27.00	0.00
Aaron McGarity	R-R	6-3	185	1-31-95	3	0	2.30	11	0	0	0	16	9	4	4	1	5	24	.167	.083	.233	13.79	2.87
Luis Medina	R-R	6-1	175	5-3-99	4	3	3.38	17	17	0	0	72	46	32	27	4	40	81	.179	.183	.175	10.13	5.00
Matt Minnick	R-L	6-2	210	3-11-96	5	3	1.81	35	0	0	3	60	25	14	12	5	19	62	.124	.130	.121	9.35	2.87
Jose Mujica	R-R	6-2	249	6-29-96	0	1	2.25	6	0	0	2	8	3	3	2	2	2	11	.111	.133	.083	12.38	2.25
Tanner Myatt	R-R	6-7	220	5-21-98	4	2	4.30	22	0	0	0	29	17	19	14	3	21	30	.170	.267	.091	9.20	6.44
Emmanuel Ramirez	R-R	6-2	190	7-15-94	4	1	1.93	26	0	0	2	37	21	9	8	4	11	45	.168	.175	.162	10.85	2.65
Stephen Ridings	R-R	6-8	220	8-14-95	0	0	0.00	1	0	0	0	1	1	0	0	0	0	2	.250	.000	.500	18.00	0.00
Charlie Ruegger	R-R	6-6	218	7-14-97	0	0	15.00	3	0	0	0	3	6	5	5	1	2	5	.400	.600	.300	15.00	6.00
Matt Sauer	R-R	6-4	195	1-21-99	0	2	7.84	4	4	0	0	21	22	18	18	5	7	34	.268	.194	.314	14.81	3.05
Shawn Semple	R-R	6-1	220	10-9-95	1	0	4.63	6	0	0	0	12	10	6	6	1	1	5	.227	.130	.333	3.86	0.77
Luis Severino	R-R	6-2	218	2-20-94	0	0	4.50	1	1	0	0	4	4	2	2	1	0	4	.250	.167	.300	9.00	0.00

Mitch Spence	R-R	6-1	185	5-6-98	3	5	5.24	17	15	0	0	79	86	49	46	12	26	79	.274	.252	.291	9.00	2.96
Randy Vasquez	R-R	6-0	165	11-3-98	2	7	3.90	25	25	0	0	115	106	56	50	11	41	120	.239	.246	.233	9.36	3.20
Ken Waldichuk	L-L	6-4	220	1-8-98	4	0	1.26	6	6	0	0	29	16	6	4	2	10	46	.158	.087	.179	14.44	3.14
Will Warren	R-R	6-2	175	6-16-99	7	6	4.02	18	18	0	0	94	89	54	42	8	33	83	.251	.280	.227	7.95	3.16
Kyle Zurak	R-R	6-1	208	11-28-94	2	1	2.95	13	0	0	0	18	13	8	6	0	8	22	.191	.250	.150	10.80	3.93
2-team total (13 Erie SeaWolves)					4	1	4.50	26	0	0	0	34	35	19	17	3	18	35	.267	.322	.222	9.26	4.76

Fielding

Catcher	PCT	G	PO	A	E	DP	PB
Breaux	.993	38	376	21	3	0	1
Duran	.983	46	429	32	8	3	8
Gasper	.993	13	130	6	1	1	0
Torres	.958	2	22	1	1	0	3
Wells	.986	38	400	27	6	4	3

First Base	PCT	G	PO	A	E	DP
Bell	.993	36	257	30	2	21
Burt	.968	12	84	7	3	9
Chaparro	.967	14	84	4	3	8
Dietrich	1.000	8	60	7	0	2
Gasper	.991	57	407	34	4	31
Hardman	1.000	1	6	1	0	0
Wagaman	.987	10	71	3	1	9

Second Base	PCT	G	PO	A	E	DP
Bastidas	.973	92	131	228	10	54
Bell	.944	4	7	10	1	1
Burt	.968	23	22	39	2	4
Dietrich	.947	6	9	9	1	2
Dunn	1.000	12	14	21	0	2
Perez	.917	3	5	6	1	0
Pita	1.000	1	1	0	0	0

Third Base	PCT	G	PO	A	E	DP
Bastidas	.833	2	3	2	1	0
Bell	.908	29	20	39	6	2
Burt	.929	46	21	83	8	4
Chaparro	.925	48	20	66	7	7
Dietrich	.818	4	3	6	2	1
Dunn	.857	5	3	9	2	0
Hardman	1.000	3	2	2	0	0
Nelson	1.000	2	1	0	0	0
Perez	.667	2	0	2	1	1

Shortstop	PCT	G	PO	A	E	DP
Bastidas	.903	19	22	34	6	4
Burt	1.000	3	3	2	0	1
Sweeney	.974	10	8	30	1	5
Volpe	.971	106	133	240	11	51

Outfield	PCT	G	PO	A	E	DP
Bader	1.000	4	12	0	0	0
Beltre	.970	40	65	0	2	0
Burt	1.000	1	2	0	0	0
Dominguez	1.000	2	9	0	0	0
Dunham	.993	96	141	6	1	1
Dunn	.952	13	20	0	1	0
Lockridge	.990	97	190	2	2	1
Pereira	.978	24	43	1	1	0
Perkins	.992	60	120	6	1	2
Pita	1.000	1	1	0	0	0
Rosario	.957	89	148	9	7	1

HUDSON VALLEY RENEGADES — *HIGH CLASS A*

SOUTH ATLANTIC LEAGUE

Batting	B-T	HT	WT	DOB	AVG	vLH	vRH	G	AB	R	H	2B	3B	HR	RBI	BB	HBP	SH	SF	SO	SB	CS	SLG	OBP
Kyle Battle	R-R	6-1	190	12-4-97	.321	.333	.316	8	28	4	9	4	0	0	5	3	0	0	0	9	4	2	.464	.387
Cooper Bowman	R-R	6-0	205	1-25-00	.217	.122	.236	80	299	54	65	15	1	8	35	55	5	0	5	97	35	6	.355	.343
Benjamin Cowles	R-R	6-1	180	2-15-00	.221	.267	.210	23	77	11	17	2	1	0	8	12	2	0	1	31	0	1	.273	.337
Pat DeMarco	R-R	5-9	192	3-10-98	.231	.255	.225	66	229	18	53	11	0	1	16	12	1	0	3	67	5	3	.293	.269
Jasson Dominguez	B-R	5-10	190	2-7-03	.306	.282	.314	40	157	33	48	6	4	6	22	23	2	0	2	34	17	1	.510	.397
Tyler Hardman	R-R	6-3	204	1-27-99	.262	.247	.266	107	397	53	104	16	2	22	79	40	3	0	7	136	14	4	.479	.329
Spencer Henson	R-R	6-2	235	11-3-97	.211	.167	.222	71	242	37	51	10	1	10	37	32	5	0	3	86	2	1	.384	.312
Carlos Narvaez	R-R	6-0	190	11-26-98	.194	.146	.205	79	248	37	48	12	1	11	35	45	5	0	2	87	4	2	.383	.327
James Nelson	R-R	6-2	180	10-18-97	.221	.333	.203	49	149	19	33	6	0	2	23	31	3	0	1	56	16	7	.302	.364
Aaron Palensky	R-R	5-11	190	9-22-98	.251	.233	.256	77	219	46	55	13	3	10	34	34	7	0	0	79	9	3	.475	.369
Everson Pereira	R-R	6-0	191	4-10-01	.274	.231	.284	73	288	55	79	13	6	9	43	34	2	0	1	87	19	5	.455	.354
Cristian Perez	R-R	5-10	170	10-26-98	.171	.000	.217	26	76	7	13	2	0	0	5	2	0	0	1	22	2	0	.197	.190
Grant Richardson	L-L	6-2	210	7-13-99	.208	.188	.214	35	130	19	27	3	1	10	28	10	5	0	1	54	2	0	.477	.288
Ben Rortvedt	L-R	5-10	205	9-25-97	.083	.000	.111	4	12	3	1	0	0	0	0	3	0	0	0	6	0	0	.083	.267
T.J. Rumfield	L-R	6-5	225	5-17-00	.284	.267	.289	52	197	27	56	13	0	4	34	29	3	0	2	45	4	2	.411	.381
Aldenis Sanchez	R-R	6-1	165	9-26-98	.257	.254	.258	96	315	40	81	9	2	1	32	42	4	0	2	105	32	9	.308	.350
Anthony Seigler	B-B	6-0	200	6-20-99	.235	.218	.240	72	238	49	56	15	0	4	32	66	4	0	8	64	11	7	.349	.399
Trey Sweeney	L-R	6-4	200	4-24-00	.241	.259	.236	100	390	70	94	18	4	14	51	59	7	0	1	108	29	2	.415	.350
Eduardo Torrealba	R-R	5-8	140	3-26-99	.216	.286	.197	72	232	26	50	8	3	2	30	19	4	0	0	41	14	3	.302	.286
Saul Torres	R-R	6-2	190	2-19-99	.150	.500	.111	7	20	2	3	0	1	0	1	2	0	0	0	12	0	0	.250	.227
Eric Wagaman	R-R	6-4	210	8-14-97	.233	.308	.213	52	180	18	42	7	0	9	26	25	2	0	1	34	2	0	.422	.332
Austin Wells	L-R	6-2	220	7-12-99	.323	.261	.342	28	99	21	32	7	0	6	16	19	0	0	1	27	9	0	.576	.429

Pitching	B-T	HT	WT	DOB	W	L	ERA	G	GS	CG	SV	IP	H	R	ER	HR	BB	SO	AVG	vLH	vRH	K/9	BB/9
Blane Abeyta	R-R	6-3	185	9-4-98	5	8	4.47	23	20	0	0	105	105	58	52	6	52	88	.261	.295	.236	7.57	4.47
Nelson L. Alvarez	R-R	6-4	220	6-11-98	5	2	2.85	35	0	0	4	54	35	21	17	3	32	65	.184	.225	.155	10.90	5.37
Edgar Barclay	L-L	5-10	200	5-25-98	7	4	1.74	28	4	0	1	67	41	16	13	0	20	86	.177	.154	.190	11.50	2.67
Bryan Blanton	R-R	6-0	190	12-19-95	0	1	7.90	10	0	0	1	14	14	15	12	1	18	13	.264	.231	.296	8.56	11.85
Juan Carela	R-R	6-3	186	12-15-01	1	4	7.71	7	7	0	0	28	25	24	24	4	17	21	.238	.304	.186	6.75	5.46
Blas Castano	R-R	5-10	162	9-8-98	5	8	3.49	21	20	1	0	106	99	48	41	8	33	101	.247	.316	.187	8.60	2.81
Carson Coleman	R-R	6-2	190	4-7-98	0	0	0.47	9	0	0	4	19	7	1	1	1	9	26	.115	.077	.143	12.10	4.19
Nelvin Correa	R-R	6-1	170	1-25-97	2	2	1.49	28	0	0	4	42	31	13	7	1	19	38	.205	.186	.217	8.08	4.04
Harold Cortijo	R-R	6-2	180	9-29-98	0	0	9.64	4	0	0	1	5	4	5	5	0	3	7	.235	.250	.222	13.50	5.79
Bailey Dees	R-R	6-8	250	2-5-99	0	0	3.18	3	0	0	0	6	3	4	2	0	2	8	.143	.200	.091	12.71	3.18
Wellington Diaz	R-R	6-4	190	4-25-97	2	2	3.97	20	0	0	0	23	18	14	10	3	18	21	.222	.270	.182	8.34	7.15
Richard Fitts	R-R	6-3	215	12-17-99	4	0	0.55	5	5	0	0	33	17	3	2	1	3	38	.152	.116	.174	10.36	0.82
Michael Giacone	L-L	6-0	175	10-23-96	3	0	1.86	6	0	0	0	10	3	2	2	1	2	15	.097	.083	.105	13.97	1.86
Carlos Gomez	R-R	6-1	175	6-14-98	2	3	3.40	29	0	0	4	48	35	21	18	2	29	48	.198	.213	.186	9.06	5.48
Yoendrys Gomez	R-R	6-3	175	10-15-99	0	0	1.93	10	10	0	0	28	20	7	6	0	12	27	.204	.224	.184	8.68	3.86
Trevor Holloway	R-R	6-2	200	6-22-97	0	0	2.00	4	0	0	0	9	5	2	2	0	5	6	.161	.125	.200	6.00	5.00
Rodney Hutchison	R-R	6-5	225	8-9-96	1	1	3.38	12	0	0	1	16	12	6	6	1	8	18	.218	.208	.226	10.13	4.50
Alex Mauricio	R-R	6-0	180	9-24-96	4	0	4.78	26	0	0	6	38	35	22	20	3	21	46	.246	.250	.244	10.99	5.02
Kevin Milam	R-R	6-0	200	2-13-98	0	0	8.18	8	0	0	0	11	14	10	10	1	7	12	.304	.222	.357	9.82	5.73
Ryan Miller	R-R	6-0	180	3-28-96	2	3	5.75	25	0	0	2	36	29	27	23	7	18	50	.230	.175	.275	12.50	4.50

Jhonatan Munoz	R-R	5-10	200	8-10-99	5	1	4.58	27	1	0	0	55	53	30	28	8	25	51	.261	.304	.234	8.35	4.09
Tanner Myatt	R-R	6-7	220	5-21-98	1	0	1.65	17	0	0	4	27	12	8	5	2	18	40	.133	.152	.123	13.17	5.93
Jack Neely	R-R	6-8	225	6-5-00	1	0	0.00	4	0	0	0	5	0	0	0	0	1	8	.000	.000	.000	15.43	1.93
Josue Panacual	R-R	5-10	158	1-13-02	3	5	4.99	13	10	0	1	61	68	37	34	5	34	41	.282	.292	.273	6.02	4.99
Charlie Ruegger	R-R	6-6	218	7-14-97	2	2	4.74	20	0	0	1	25	28	14	13	3	15	21	.289	.320	.255	7.66	5.47
Enrique Santana	R-R	5-11	190	9-23-97	0	0	0.00	3	0	0	0	4	3	0	0	0	2	4	.214	.111	.400	9.00	4.50
Matt Sauer	R-R	6-4	195	1-21-99	5	3	3.77	18	18	1	0	88	75	45	37	8	35	100	.229	.275	.196	10.19	3.57
Shawn Semple	R-R	6-1	220	10-9-95	3	0	2.40	4	1	0	0	15	14	5	4	1	5	16	.233	.250	.222	9.60	3.00
T.J. Sikkema	L-L	6-0	221	7-25-98	1	1	2.48	11	10	0	0	36	21	12	10	3	9	54	.165	.146	.174	13.38	2.23
Leif Strom	R-R	6-6	240	5-17-97	0	1	6.23	6	1	0	0	9	6	6	6	0	11	13	.207	.286	.133	13.50	11.42
Will Warren	R-R	6-2	175	6-16-99	2	3	3.60	8	8	0	0	35	30	16	14	2	9	42	.234	.180	.284	10.80	2.31
Beck Way	R-R	6-4	200	8-6-99	5	5	3.73	15	15	0	0	72	55	32	30	9	26	80	.212	.222	.204	9.95	3.24

Fielding

Catcher	PCT	G	PO	A	E	DP	PB
Narvaez	.986	64	573	40	9	4	5
Rortvedt	1.000	2	12	0	0	0	0
Seigler	.995	47	391	28	2	3	9
Torres	1.000	4	34	0	0	0	1
Wells	1.000	21	210	15	0	5	1

First Base	PCT	G	PO	A	E	DP
Hardman	1.000	11	51	4	0	1
Henson	.989	48	331	28	4	33
Rumfield	.990	41	298	14	3	30
Wagaman	.993	37	279	21	2	33

Second Base	PCT	G	PO	A	E	DP
Bowman	.996	58	120	156	1	41
Cowles	.984	15	32	28	1	8
Perez	1.000	3	3	3	0	0
Torrealba	1.000	56	104	162	0	36

Third Base	PCT	G	PO	A	E	DP
Hardman	.942	98	64	130	12	16
Nelson	.875	22	10	25	5	3
Perez	.950	8	7	12	1	0
Torrealba	.889	10	6	10	2	0

Shortstop	PCT	G	PO	A	E	DP
Bowman	.983	17	20	37	1	10
Cowles	.875	8	3	18	3	4
Perez	.935	14	20	38	4	6
Sweeney	.948	87	110	219	18	49
Torrealba	.909	6	12	18	3	1

Outfield	PCT	G	PO	A	E	DP
Battle	1.000	8	12	2	0	0
DeMarco	.990	68	90	6	1	2
Dominguez	.988	35	80	5	1	3
Nelson	.972	25	35	0	1	0
Palensky	.990	72	93	4	1	0
Pereira	.973	66	106	3	3	1
Richardson	1.000	35	73	2	0	0
Sanchez	.970	92	152	7	5	1

TAMPA TARPONS — *LOW CLASS A*

FLORIDA STATE LEAGUE

Batting	B-T	HT	WT	DOB	AVG	vLH	vRH	G	AB	R	H	2B	3B	HR	RBI	BB	HBP	SH	SF	SO	SB	CS	SLG	OBP
Tayler Aguilar	L-L	6-0	205	8-15-00	.169	.048	.220	20	71	11	12	5	0	3	8	10	1	0	0	25	3	0	.366	.280
Brett Barrera	R-R	6-1	217	5-7-01	.274	.231	.293	23	84	8	23	6	0	1	10	2	0	0	1	17	1	0	.381	.287
Kyle Battle	R-R	6-1	190	12-4-97	.173	.211	.158	43	133	14	23	8	0	2	11	14	5	0	1	40	16	2	.278	.275
Beau Brewer	R-R	6-3	215	10-28-01	.167	.000	.222	3	12	1	2	0	0	0	0	0	0	0	0	1	0	0	.167	.167
Marcos Cabrera	R-R	6-3	189	10-10-01	.196	.233	.183	97	337	43	66	9	2	14	40	46	5	0	2	148	19	8	.359	.300
Oswaldo Cabrera	B-R	6-0	200	3-1-99	.364	.200	.500	4	11	1	4	1	0	1	2	3	0	0	0	1	3	1	.727	.500
Connor Cannon	R-R	6-5	240	5-16-98	.154	.143	.157	39	117	12	18	3	0	3	9	11	12	0	2	62	0	0	.256	.289
Andres Chaparro	R-R	6-1	200	5-4-99	.412	.625	.222	5	17	4	7	1	0	1	2	0	0	0	0	2	1	0	.647	.412
Roberto Chirinos	R-R	5-11	172	9-8-00	.198	.239	.183	54	172	17	34	8	2	0	17	13	2	0	0	60	7	2	.267	.262
Benjamin Cowles	R-R	6-1	180	2-15-00	.289	.356	.265	70	225	36	65	16	3	7	33	31	6	0	1	72	14	5	.480	.388
Juan Crisp	R-R	6-1	170	5-23-00	.500	--	.500	1	4	2	2	1	0	0	3	0	0	0	0	2	0	0	.750	.500
Jasson Dominguez	B-R	5-10	190	2-7-03	.265	.221	.280	75	275	54	73	17	2	9	36	46	2	0	1	89	19	6	.440	.373
Christopher Familia	L-L	5-11	170	6-10-00	.207	.162	.228	36	116	15	24	3	0	5	21	11	4	0	1	27	4	0	.362	.295
Anthony Garcia	B-R	6-5	204	9-5-00	.195	.067	.238	95	298	56	58	8	1	14	42	83	2	0	1	156	21	5	.369	.372
Antonio Gomez	R-R	6-2	210	11-13-01	.252	.295	.235	89	325	36	82	10	2	8	48	35	6	0	4	100	1	3	.369	.332
Ryder Green	R-R	6-0	200	5-5-00	.238	.143	.286	6	21	4	5	0	0	1	2	2	0	0	0	7	1	1	.381	.304
Alex Guerrero	L-R	6-0	185	3-10-00	.091	.000	.167	3	11	0	1	0	0	0	0	0	0	0	0	5	0	0	.091	.091
Spencer Jones	L-L	6-7	225	5-14-01	.325	.360	.310	22	83	18	27	5	0	3	8	10	2	0	0	18	10	0	.494	.411
Alan Mejia	R-R	6-0	165	7-20-01	.173	.211	.161	25	81	7	14	2	0	1	9	7	0	0	1	33	2	0	.235	.236
Ben Rice	L-R	6-2	205	2-22-99	.267	.200	.295	68	206	32	55	9	0	9	36	28	6	0	2	41	4	1	.442	.368
Grant Richardson	L-L	6-2	210	7-13-99	.253	.256	.252	55	178	28	45	10	1	6	32	20	7	0	1	68	14	2	.421	.350
Ben Rortvedt	L-R	5-10	205	9-25-97	.500	--	.500	2	4	1	2	0	0	1	1	1	0	0	0	1	0	0	1.250	.600
T.J. Rumfield	L-R	6-5	225	5-17-00	.100	.000	.167	4	10	0	1	0	0	0	1	0	0	0	0	2	0	0	.100	.100
Raimfer Salinas	R-R	6-0	175	12-31-00	.225	.200	.234	64	191	24	43	7	0	5	25	22	7	0	1	73	3	2	.340	.326
Luis Santos	R-R	5-8	160	1-4-00	.206	.205	.207	57	165	19	34	6	1	2	16	21	2	0	0	35	7	3	.291	.303
Madison Santos	L-R	5-10	165	9-6-99	.191	.154	.206	75	235	32	45	7	3	5	31	61	1	0	0	110	17	9	.311	.360
Anthony Seigler	B-B	6-0	200	6-20-99	.237	.278	.224	25	76	12	18	6	0	3	13	25	0	0	0	18	5	0	.434	.426
Jared Serna	R-R	5-8	168	6-1-02	.179	.278	.095	12	39	6	7	2	0	0	2	3	1	0	1	15	1	1	.231	.250
Alexander Vargas	B-R	5-11	148	10-29-01	.203	.182	.211	100	389	59	79	14	2	8	33	35	3	0	4	123	27	13	.311	.271
Austin Wells	L-R	6-2	220	7-12-99	.231	.250	.222	9	26	5	6	2	0	2	6	8	0	0	0	5	0	0	.538	.412

Pitching	B-T	HT	WT	DOB	W	L	ERA	G	GS	CG	SV	IP	H	R	ER	HR	BB	SO	AVG	vLH	vRH	K/9	BB/9
Ryan Anderson	L-L	6-6	205	9-9-98	3	7	4.26	35	0	0	0	61	51	33	29	8	25	64	.219	.222	.218	9.39	3.67
Kris Bow	R-R	6-4	225	11-27-00	0	0	4.91	3	0	0	0	4	3	2	2	0	1	4	.214	.400	.111	9.82	2.45
Will Brian	L-L	5-11	220	4-25-99	0	0	0.00	1	0	0	0	1	0	0	0	0	0	4	.000	.000	.000	27.00	0.00
Zack Britton	L-L	6-1	200	12-22-87	0	0	3.86	3	1	0	0	2	2	1	1	0	0	3	.250	.000	.333	11.57	0.00
Alex Bustamante	R-R	6-3	195	6-22-00	1	0	2.08	3	0	0	0	4	2	1	1	0	4	5	.133	.167	.111	10.38	8.31
Yorlin Calderon	R-R	6-3	155	8-17-01	2	0	2.84	4	3	1	0	19	14	6	6	2	7	21	.203	.250	.178	9.95	3.32
Juan Carela	R-R	6-3	186	12-15-01	7	2	2.96	16	14	0	0	79	49	36	26	5	35	110	.175	.210	.161	12.53	3.99
Yon Castro	R-R	6-0	203	5-23-99	2	6	3.59	22	20	0	1	88	77	41	35	11	31	103	.239	.204	.254	10.57	3.18
Chandler Champlain	R-R	6-5	220	7-23-99	2	5	4.30	16	15	0	0	73	72	38	35	11	19	94	.251	.241	.257	11.54	2.33
Harold Cortijo	R-R	6-2	180	9-29-98	5	1	4.14	35	0	0	3	54	48	27	25	3	27	59	.241	.266	.230	9.77	4.47
Bailey Dees	R-R	6-8	250	2-5-99	4	3	3.31	31	0	0	0	52	35	23	19	4	24	62	.186	.121	.215	10.80	4.18

Richard Fitts	R-R	6-3	215	12-17-99	3	8	5.01	17	17	0	0	79	73	47	44	13	17	93	.239	.247	.236	10.59	1.94
Domingo German	R-R	6-2	181	8-4-92	0	0	0.00	1	1	0	0	3	1	0	0	0	0	0	.100	.250	.000	0.00	0.00
Carlos Gomez	R-R	6-1	175	6-14-98	1	0	1.42	9	0	0	2	19	12	3	3	1	7	30	.171	.250	.140	14.21	3.32
Shane Gray	R-R	6-3	215	4-18-00	0	0	0.00	1	0	0	0	1	1	0	0	0	1	1	.250	.000	.500	9.00	9.00
Sean Hermann	R-R	6-0	160	6-13-03	0	0	2.66	4	4	0	0	20	19	8	6	5	7	16	.253	.216	.289	7.08	3.10
Trevor Holloway	R-R	6-2	200	6-22-97	5	2	2.49	29	1	0	4	43	40	16	12	4	19	46	.242	.208	.259	9.55	3.95
Zach Kohn	R-R	6-4	190	9-30-97	3	0	6.75	4	0	0	0	4	2	4	3	0	4	5	.143	.200	.111	11.25	9.00
Jonathan Loaisiga	R-R	5-11	165	11-2-94	0	0	0.00	1	1	0	0	1	0	0	0	0	0	1	.000	.000	.000	9.00	0.00
Shaine McNeely	L-R	6-4	210	5-10-98	0	2	9.00	6	0	0	0	6	9	8	6	2	4	11	.333	.300	.353	16.50	6.00
Leam Mendez	L-R	6-2	196	1-21-00	1	1	4.97	7	0	0	0	13	13	7	7	3	5	16	.265	.238	.286	11.37	3.55
Zach Messinger	R-R	6-6	225	10-4-99	1	8	4.30	31	16	0	2	84	68	43	40	5	45	112	.221	.247	.210	12.05	4.84
Kevin Milam	R-R	6-0	200	2-13-98	5	3	4.09	21	0	0	0	33	36	20	15	4	7	46	.277	.367	.250	12.55	1.91
Kenlly Montas	R-R	6-0	187	5-31-96	0	0	9.64	3	0	0	0	5	6	6	5	0	4	7	.300	.250	.313	13.50	7.71
Jack Neely	R-R	6-8	225	6-5-00	3	1	3.94	34	0	0	7	46	38	24	20	3	25	79	.221	.364	.172	15.57	4.93
Nick Paciorek	R-R	6-2	195	6-1-98	0	1	25.07	7	0	0	0	5	13	15	13	1	4	4	.500	.273	.667	7.71	7.71
Josue Panacual	R-R	5-10	158	1-13-02	1	2	3.38	7	7	0	0	29	23	15	11	0	14	37	.205	.240	.195	11.35	4.30
Eric Reyzelman	R-R	6-2	188	6-27-01	0	0	6.00	3	0	0	0	3	2	2	2	0	3	7	.200	.000	.333	21.00	9.00
Osiel Rodriguez	R-R	6-2	210	11-22-01	0	1	16.88	2	0	0	0	3	6	5	5	1	1	4	.429	.500	.333	13.50	3.38
Enrique Santana	R-R	5-11	190	9-23-97	0	1	2.10	23	0	0	0	26	22	13	6	0	26	31	.229	.233	.227	10.87	9.12
Luis Severino	R-R	6-2	218	2-20-94	1	0	0.00	1	0	0	0	2	1	0	0	0	0	3	.167	.000	.200	13.50	0.00
Kevin Stevens	R-R	6-2	225	1-26-98	0	1	2.08	4	0	0	0	4	6	2	1	0	4	2	.333	.250	.400	4.15	8.31
Joel Valdez	L-L	6-4	171	4-28-00	1	0	2.10	6	6	0	0	26	13	8	6	1	15	37	.148	.042	.188	12.97	5.26
Gerrit van Zijll	L-L	6-4	210	8-2-96	2	2	3.10	15	0	0	3	20	15	8	7	3	10	25	.214	.111	.250	11.07	4.43
Danny Watson	R-R	6-7	235	10-6-00	5	5	4.01	38	0	0	1	58	45	30	26	3	36	66	.216	.362	.160	10.18	5.55
Tyrone Yulie	R-R	6-4	180	8-4-01	3	5	4.97	22	22	0	0	87	73	55	48	6	55	87	.225	.238	.217	9.00	5.69

Fielding

Catcher	PCT	G	PO	A	E	DP	PB
Crisp	1.000	1	12	0	0	0	0
Gomez	.983	70	670	67	13	5	9
Rice	.989	37	331	26	4	1	9
Rortvedt	1.000	1	8	1	0	0	0
Seigler	.995	18	192	21	1	2	1
Wells	1.000	6	51	7	0	1	0

First Base	PCT	G	PO	A	E	DP
Cannon	.978	25	169	7	4	16
Chirinos	1.000	1	7	0	0	1
Garcia	.973	88	541	35	16	39
Guerrero	1.000	2	10	2	0	2
Rice	.989	15	86	4	1	7
Rumfield	1.000	3	12	0	0	1

Second Base	PCT	G	PO	A	E	DP
Barrera	.983	20	19	40	1	4
Cabrera	1.000	1	0	1	0	0
Chirinos	.982	26	46	62	2	9
Cowles	.975	35	49	67	3	14
Santos	.979	39	63	77	3	17
Serna	.976	12	13	27	1	7

Third Base	PCT	G	PO	A	E	DP
Barrera	.500	2	0	2	2	1
Brewer	.800	2	1	3	1	1
Cabrera	.929	91	55	140	15	18
Chaparro	.833	3	2	3	1	1
Chirinos	1.000	12	9	17	0	0
Cowles	.912	14	11	20	3	4
Santos	.909	10	5	5	1	0

Shortstop	PCT	G	PO	A	E	DP
Cabrera	1.000	1	2	1	0	0
Chirinos	.902	15	23	23	5	8
Cowles	1.000	21	28	35	0	2
Santos	.941	5	8	8	1	4
Vargas	.928	88	76	182	20	26

Outfield	PCT	G	PO	A	E	DP
Aguilar	1.000	17	35	0	0	0
Battle	1.000	41	68	0	0	0
Cabrera	--	1	0	0	0	0
Dominguez	.954	65	120	4	6	0
Familia	.941	32	48	0	3	0
Green	1.000	6	8	1	0	0
Jones	.972	18	34	1	1	1
Mejia	.963	26	26	0	1	0
Richardson	.987	53	70	4	1	2
Salinas	.969	60	94	1	3	1
Santos	1.000	1	0	1	0	0
Santos	.975	71	117	1	3	0

FCL YANKEES — *ROOKIE*

FLORIDA COMPLEX LEAGUE

Batting	B-T	HT	WT	DOB	AVG	vLH	vRH	G	AB	R	H	2B	3B	HR	RBI	BB	HBP	SH	SF	SO	SB	CS	SLG	OBP
Tayler Aguilar	L-L	6-0	205	8-15-00	.143	.000	.200	3	7	2	1	0	0	0	0	2	0	0	0	1	1	0	.143	.333
Daury Arias	L-L	5-10	172	8-7-01	.228	.143	.250	48	171	39	39	10	0	5	28	34	9	0	3	39	5	4	.374	.378
Brett Barrera	R-R	6-1	217	5-7-01	.111	.000	.143	3	9	1	1	0	0	0	0	0	0	0	0	1	0	0	.111	.111
Mauro Bonifacio	R-R	6-6	252	8-31-01	.000	.000	.000	11	20	2	0	0	0	0	0	6	1	0	0	15	0	0	.000	.259
Beau Brewer	R-R	6-3	215	10-28-01	.207	.125	.238	9	29	2	6	2	0	0	5	2	0	0	0	2	0	0	.276	.258
Oswaldo Cabrera	B-R	6-0	200	3-1-99	.333	.000	.500	1	3	1	1	0	0	0	1	0	0	0	1	1	0	0	.333	.250
Connor Cannon	R-R	6-5	240	5-16-98	.300	.000	.333	4	10	2	3	0	0	2	2	2	0	0	0	3	0	0	.900	.417
Andres Chaparro	R-R	6-1	200	5-4-99	.250	--	.250	2	4	0	1	0	0	0	1	0	0	0	0	2	0	0	.250	.250
Roberto Chirinos	R-R	5-11	172	9-8-00	.167	.000	.333	2	6	1	1	0	0	0	1	1	0	0	0	2	0	0	.167	.286
Pedro Diaz	R-R	6-2	202	11-6-97	.357	.000	.385	9	28	9	10	2	1	0	6	5	0	0	1	13	2	0	.500	.441
Brenny Escanio	B-R	5-9	145	12-16-02	.216	.174	.226	39	116	20	25	8	2	2	20	26	2	0	1	28	9	2	.371	.366
Kelvin Espino	L-R	6-1	193	12-8-01	.316	.375	.300	17	38	7	12	0	0	4	4	7	0	0	0	9	0	1	.632	.422
Christopher Familia	L-L	5-11	170	6-10-00	.297	.333	.290	21	74	25	22	5	0	6	20	18	4	0	0	12	0	1	.608	.458
Osmany Fleitas	R-R	5-9	133	1-7-02	.286	.500	.250	9	14	3	4	1	0	0	1	2	0	0	0	5	1	0	.357	.375
Rafael Flores	R-R	6-4	220	11-7-00	.429	.000	.500	4	14	4	6	1	0	2	6	0	0	0	0	3	0	0	.929	.429
Alex Garcia	B-R	5-10	155	12-8-01	.273	.222	.308	8	22	4	6	1	0	0	4	3	0	0	0	6	2	1	.318	.360
Alex Guerrero	L-R	6-0	185	3-10-00	.273	.200	.294	8	22	5	6	1	0	2	4	5	0	0	0	9	0	0	.591	.407
Anthony Hall	L-L	6-2	200	2-9-01	.000	--	.000	1	1	0	0	0	0	0	0	0	0	0	0	0	0	0	.000	.000
Spencer Jones	L-L	6-7	225	5-14-01	.500	.750	.333	3	10	3	5	1	0	1	4	1	0	0	0	2	2	0	.900	.545
D_Vaughn Knowles	R-R	5-10	161	1-16-01	.154	.000	.182	9	13	2	2	0	0	0	1	2	0	0	1	9	1	1	.154	.250
Jackson Lyon	R-R	5-10	175	5-18-00	.167	.000	.200	5	18	2	3	2	0	0	2	0	1	0	0	3	0	0	.278	.211
Omar Martinez	L-R	5-11	192	7-5-01	.282	.500	.254	20	71	15	20	2	1	3	17	13	2	0	1	14	1	1	.465	.402
Nelson Medina	R-R	6-2	175	9-14-00	.311	.111	.361	19	45	11	14	2	3	2	8	7	2	0	0	17	2	1	.622	.426
Alan Mejia	R-R	6-0	165	7-20-01	.213	.313	.196	34	108	12	23	5	1	2	14	16	1	0	3	42	1	1	.333	.313
Felix Negueis	R-R	6-0	200	12-29-00	.287	.200	.309	32	101	22	29	13	2	4	29	17	1	0	2	36	7	1	.574	.388

Pablo Olivares	R-R	6-0	160	1-27-98	.133	.000	.167	7	15	1	2	0	0	0	0	3	1	0	0	1	1	2	.133	.316
Jake Palmer	L-L	5-10	185	11-19-98	.300	.333	.286	5	10	0	3	0	0	0	1	5	4	0	0	0	1	0	.300	.632
Dayro Perez	R-R	6-2	180	1-31-02	.250	.161	.276	38	136	35	34	8	0	3	15	28	3	0	0	54	16	4	.375	.389
Agustin Ramirez	R-R	6-0	210	9-10-01	.304	.269	.310	44	168	34	51	14	1	6	51	23	2	0	4	31	13	2	.506	.386
Jesus Rodriguez	R-R	5-10	182	4-23-02	.348	.280	.364	37	132	29	46	10	4	4	24	15	5	0	0	14	8	3	.576	.434
Angel Rojas	R-R	6-0	160	11-26-00	.143	.000	.167	9	14	6	2	1	0	0	1	2	1	0	0	6	5	1	.214	.294
Ronny Rojas	B-R	6-1	180	8-23-01	.168	.130	.181	32	95	16	16	5	0	4	13	21	2	0	1	38	3	1	.347	.328
Hemmanuel Rosario	R-R	6-2	200	8-21-00	.500	.000	.571	5	8	5	4	1	0	0	1	3	2	0	0	2	1	0	.625	.692
Stanley Rosario	L-R	6-2	195	12-1-00	.231	.000	.250	6	13	0	3	1	0	0	1	0	0	0	0	7	0	1	.308	.231
T.J. Rumfield	L-R	6-5	225	5-17-00	.000	.000	.000	1	2	0	0	0	0	0	0	0	0	0	0	0	0	0	.000	.000
Edward Sanchez	R-R	5-11	165	3-28-01	.077	.000	.091	8	13	2	1	0	0	1	2	3	1	0	0	5	1	1	.308	.294
Jared Serna	R-R	5-8	168	6-1-02	.302	.500	.266	37	129	40	39	9	1	6	28	25	6	0	0	24	16	4	.527	.438
Sincere Smith	R-R	5-11	170	3-13-00	.261	.000	.286	10	23	3	6	1	0	0	2	2	1	0	0	10	3	0	.304	.346
Dionys Vallejo	R-R	6-2	159	5-25-00	.286	.500	.250	10	14	2	4	1	0	0	1	2	1	0	0	4	2	0	.357	.412
Carlos Verdecia	B-R	5-11	170	3-16-02	.200	--	.200	2	5	0	1	0	0	0	0	0	0	0	0	4	0	0	.200	.200

Pitching	D-T	HT	WT	DOB	W	L	ERA	G	GS	CG	SV	IP	H	R	ER	HR	BB	SO	AVG	vLH	vRH	K/9	BB/9
Luis Arejula	R-R	6-1	170	2-20-02	0	0	3.24	8	2	0	0	17	17	6	6	2	4	16	.266	.217	.293	8.64	2.16
Cole Ayers	R-R	6-3	185	8-17-99	1	0	5.68	13	0	0	1	19	20	15	12	2	11	17	.267	.148	.333	8.05	5.21
Kris Bow	R-R	6-4	225	11-27-00	0	0	0.00	1	0	0	0	1	0	0	0	0	2	0	.000	--	.000	0.00	18.00
Will Brian	L-L	5-11	220	4-25-99	0	0	27.00	1	0	0	0	1	2	2	2	0	1	1	.500	--	.500	13.50	13.50
Alex Bustamante	R-R	6-3	195	6-22-00	0	0	13.50	1	0	0	0	1	0	1	1	0	1	2	.000	--	.000	27.00	13.50
Yorlin Calderon	R-R	6-3	155	8-17-01	4	1	4.38	10	3	0	0	39	41	21	19	6	9	54	.268	.236	.286	12.46	2.08
Kaleb Cowart	B-R	6-3	225	6-2-92	0	0	0.00	1	0	0	0	1	0	0	0	0	0	3	.000	.000	.000	20.25	0.00
Yoljeldriz Diaz	R-R	5-11	165	7-14-01	1	0	21.60	1	0	0	0	2	1	4	4	0	5	2	.167	--	.167	10.80	27.00
Steven Fulgencio	R-R	6-2	175	10-5-00	0	1	16.88	4	0	0	0	3	7	7	5	0	3	3	.467	.750	.364	10.13	10.13
Ocean Gabonia	R-R	6-1	175	7-31-01	1	0	3.86	9	0	0	1	12	14	8	5	0	1	14	.298	.313	.290	10.80	0.77
Yoendrys Gomez	R-R	6-3	175	10-15-99	0	0	0.00	1	1	0	0	3	3	0	0	0	0	3	.300	.333	.286	10.13	0.00
Nolberto Henriquez	R-R	6-4	170	10-16-99	3	4	4.64	19	0	0	2	21	20	14	11	2	14	18	.250	.161	.306	7.59	5.91
Sean Hermann	R-R	6-0	160	6-13-03	2	0	2.43	6	6	0	0	33	28	12	9	3	6	41	.222	.255	.197	11.07	1.62
Matt Keating	R-R	6-1	215	12-8-00	0	0	0.00	1	0	0	0	1	0	0	0	0	1	2	.000	.000	.000	18.00	9.00
Zach Kohn	R-R	6-4	190	9-30-97	0	0	1.04	7	0	0	0	9	5	1	1	1	1	9	.185	.333	.111	9.35	1.04
Justin Lange	R-R	6-4	220	9-11-01	3	1	6.44	12	12	0	0	36	29	29	26	2	30	51	.215	.229	.207	12.63	7.43
Aaron McGarity	R-R	6-3	185	1-31-95	0	0	0.00	3	0	0	0	3	1	0	0	0	0	4	.091	.000	.143	10.80	0.00
Shaine McNeely	L-R	6-4	210	5-10-98	2	0	2.89	7	0	0	0	9	10	3	3	0	0	14	.263	.231	.280	13.50	0.00
Leam Mendez	L-R	6-2	196	1-21-00	1	2	3.78	14	0	0	4	17	17	8	7	1	5	21	.274	.316	.256	11.34	2.70
Nick Paciorek	R-R	6-2	195	6-1-98	2	0	0.00	2	0	0	0	3	1	0	0	0	1	6	.125	.000	.143	20.25	3.38
Sebastian Perrone	R-R	5-11	180	4-8-00	3	2	5.70	18	0	0	2	24	29	21	15	1	24	27	.290	.278	.297	10.27	9.13
Leonardo Pestana	R-R	6-4	198	7-30-98	0	0	--	1	1	0	0	0	0	2	2	0	1	0	--	--	--	--	--
Manny Ramirez	R-R	5-11	215	11-21-99	1	0	8.31	6	0	0	0	4	7	4	4	0	8	8	.412	.250	.462	16.62	16.62
Eric Reyzelman	R-R	6-2	188	6-27-01	0	0	9.00	1	0	0	0	1	1	1	1	0	1	1	.250	.333	.000	9.00	9.00
Osiel Rodriguez	R-R	6-2	210	11-22-01	6	0	3.34	11	0	0	1	32	28	14	12	2	7	38	.231	.220	.239	10.58	1.95
Richard Rodriguez	R-R	6-4	220	3-4-90	0	0	5.40	1	1	0	0	2	2	1	1	1	0	2	.286	.333	.250	10.80	0.00
Carlos Rosario	R-R	6-2	170	6-26-00	0	0	4.91	4	0	0	0	4	3	2	2	0	4	3	.231	.000	.429	7.36	9.82
Hemmanuel Rosario	R-R	6-2	200	8-21-00	0	1	54.00	1	0	0	0	0	1	3	2	1	1	0	.500	.500	--	0.00	27.00
Brock Selvidge	R-L	6-3	205	8-28-02	3	1	2.95	11	9	0	0	43	37	17	14	2	17	53	.233	.250	.223	11.18	3.59
Montana Semmel	R-R	6-4	225	1-1-02	2	2	2.08	16	0	0	3	22	10	6	5	1	5	23	.135	.107	.152	9.55	2.08
Luis Serna	R-R	5-11	162	7-20-04	0	0	1.96	11	10	0	0	41	33	16	9	0	17	56	.221	.143	.269	12.19	3.70
Kevin Stevens	R-R	6-2	225	1-26-98	0	1	81.00	1	0	0	0	0	2	3	3	0	0	1	.667	.500	1.000	27.00	0.00
Joel Valdez	L-L	6-4	171	4-28-00	1	1	4.82	7	7	0	0	28	21	20	15	1	17	43	.206	.111	.215	13.82	5.46
Alfred Vega	R-R	6-1	169	1-19-01	0	0	1.15	7	2	0	0	16	8	3	2	0	4	22	.143	.043	.212	12.64	2.30
Luis Velasquez	R-R	5-10	155	7-1-01	2	0	1.76	8	1	0	0	15	8	3	3	0	9	22	.157	.160	.154	12.91	5.28

Fielding

C: Flores 2, Martinez 15, Ramirez 31, Rodriguez 6, Rosario 1. **1B:** Cannon 2, Diaz 5, Guerrero 7, Martinez 5, Rodriguez 29, Rojas 8, Rumfield 1, Vallejo 4. **2B:** Barrera 3, Chirinos 1, Escanio 14, Fleitas 3, Garcia 7, Rojas 1, Sanchez 1, Serna 28, Smith 4, Vallejo 1, Verdecia 2. **3B:** Brewer 9, Chaparro 1, Chirinos 1, Escanio 2, Fleitas 1, Rojas 6, Rojas 24, Sanchez 5, Serna 7, Smith 6, Vallejo 2. **SS:** Escanio 23, Fleitas 5, Garcia 1, Perez 32, Rojas 1, Sanchez 2, Vallejo 1. **OF:** Aguilar 3, Arias 44, Bonifacio 9, Espino 12, Familia 16, Hall 1, Jones 3, Knowles 9, Lyon 5, Medina 19, Mejia 33, Negueis 23, Olivares 5, Palmer 5, Rosario 6, Vallejo 1.

DSL NYY BOMBERS — *ROOKIE*

DOMINICAN SUMMER LEAGUE

Batting	B-T	HT	WT	DOB	AVG	vLH	vRH	G	AB	R	H	2B	3B	HR	RBI	BB	HBP	SH	SF	SO	SB	CS	SLG	OBP
Gabriel Bersing	R-R	6-1	195	10-17-02	.286	.200	.300	10	35	7	10	0	3	3	10	2	1	0	1	16	1	1	.714	.333
2-team total (35 DSL NYY Yankees)					.211	.242	.202	45	152	25	32	2	4	7	24	12	2	0	1	64	4	3	.414	.275
Enger Castellano	R-R	6-0	190	12-2-02	.202	.308	.174	58	188	36	38	16	2	3	30	40	11	0	4	62	10	6	.356	.366
Johan Contreras	R-R	6-1	218	3-10-05	.327	.500	.268	22	55	6	18	3	0	2	12	6	0	0	0	19	0	0	.491	.393
John Cruz	L-L	6-3	171	8-29-05	.225	.206	.230	54	169	38	38	8	3	5	24	48	6	0	1	62	10	5	.396	.411
Edinson Duran	R-R	5-7	180	7-22-02	.341	.389	.328	29	85	17	29	7	2	5	30	11	5	0	2	19	2	1	.647	.437
Andry Javier	B-R	5-10	160	2-13-04	.111	.077	.122	26	54	4	6	1	1	0	4	10	0	0	1	12	3	2	.167	.246
Joshua Leito	R-R	5-10	170	3-20-05	.069	.000	.083	16	29	7	2	1	0	0	4	12	1	0	0	18	2	1	.103	.357
Joel Mendez	R-R	6-1	180	1-28-03	.205	.250	.193	59	205	44	42	12	5	5	36	35	5	0	4	90	4	4	.385	.329
Fidel Montero	R-R	6-0	178	12-19-03	.154	.189	.146	56	195	41	30	7	0	7	19	48	5	0	0	93	40	9	.297	.335
Hans Montero	R-R	5-11	160	12-25-03	.180	.158	.185	31	111	14	20	2	2	1	6	24	5	0	2	39	16	5	.261	.345

Luis Ogando	R-R	5-10	175	10-11-03	.300	.286	.304	34	100	17	30	6	1	2	17	15	5	0	0	19	15	3	.440	.417
Juan Rosa	R-R	6-0	189	11-18-02	.104	.000	.135	40	115	16	12	2	0	3	12	27	1	0	0	74	7	2	.200	.280
Juan Sanchez	L-R	5-11	190	3-21-03	.236	.222	.239	22	55	5	13	4	0	2	10	8	1	0	0	7	4	0	.418	.344
Oscar Silverio	L-R	5-9	170	10-25-01	.254	.231	.259	26	67	13	17	5	0	0	8	19	0	0	1	19	3	1	.328	.414
Luis Suarez	R-R	5-9	143	10-5-04	.188	.238	.172	34	85	20	16	4	1	0	10	23	5	0	3	29	16	3	.259	.379
Enmanuel Tejeda	R-R	5-11	158	12-25-04	.289	.182	.321	46	142	35	41	6	7	3	22	41	5	0	0	25	11	6	.493	.463
Engelth Urena	R-R	6-0	196	8-17-04	.226	.200	.231	11	31	8	7	2	0	3	12	5	1	0	0	6	0	1	.581	.351
Carlos Verdecia	B-R	5-11	170	3-16-02	.227	.000	.238	8	22	4	5	3	0	1	3	6	0	0	0	8	2	2	.500	.393

Pitching	B-T	HT	WT	DOB	W	L	ERA	G	GS	CG	SV	IP	H	R	ER	HR	BB	SO	AVG	vLH	vRH	K/9	BB/9
Gerardo Abrego	R-R	6-3	190	4-16-01	2	1	2.77	14	3	0	0	39	24	22	12	3	29	58	.169	.100	.196	13.38	6.69
Chalniel Arias	R-R	6-3	165	9-11-03	1	1	3.69	15	2	0	3	32	24	21	13	0	16	44	.211	.214	.208	12.51	4.55
Angel Benitez	R-R	6-7	204	9-10-03	0	0	1.06	5	5	0	0	17	9	3	2	0	7	24	.150	.111	.167	12.71	3.71
Ruben Castillo	R-R	6-1	160	6-18-01	2	4	2.54	16	0	0	3	28	21	13	8	1	8	35	.200	.250	.178	11.12	2.54
Keninson Diaz	R-R	6-2	180	3-30-04	2	2	8.68	12	0	0	0	19	18	25	18	1	16	23	.243	.280	.224	11.09	7.71
Edinson Duran	R-R	5-7	180	7-22-02	0	0	0.00	1	0	0	0	1	1	0	0	0	0	1	.200	.000	.333	6.75	0.00
Domingo Feliz	R-R	6-1	185	--	1	0	16.20	1	0	0	0	2	2	3	3	0	4	1	.333	.500	.250	5.40	21.60
2-team total (6 DSL NYY Yankees)					1	1	12.60	7	0	0	0	10	9	14	14	1	12	13	.237	.417	.154	11.70	10.80
Omar Gonzalez	R-R	6-4	175	7-25-05	1	0	0.44	6	5	0	0	20	6	1	1	0	9	36	.091	.000	.143	15.93	3.98
Daniel Guerrero	R-R	6-4	204	1-26-04	1	4	6.18	12	9	0	0	39	43	32	27	3	25	43	.269	.278	.264	9.84	5.72
Diego Hernandez	R-R	6-0	154	8-12-04	4	2	2.10	12	5	0	0	34	24	16	8	2	14	48	.188	.214	.174	12.58	3.67
Carlos Herrera	R-R	5-10	165	9-1-02	0	0	40.50	1	0	0	0	1	1	3	3	0	2	0	.500	1.000	.000	0.00	27.00
Franyer Herrera	L-L	6-0	165	5-3-05	0	0	4.50	1	0	0	0	2	2	3	1	0	0	1	.222	1.000	.125	4.50	0.00
2-team total (7 DSL NYY Yankees)					2	1	2.40	8	0	0	0	15	11	10	4	0	5	19	.196	.250	.175	11.40	3.00
Andry Javier	B-R	5-10	160	2-13-04	0	0	0.00	1	0	0	0	1	2	1	0	0	1	2	.286	.500	.200	13.50	6.75
Jordy Luciano	R-R	5-10	160	7-22-01	0	0	3.38	3	0	0	0	5	6	6	2	0	4	8	.250	.333	.200	13.50	6.75
2-team total (12 DSL NYY Yankees)					2	4	4.50	15	0	0	0	24	17	19	12	2	20	41	.191	.172	.200	15.38	7.50
Rafaelin Nivar	L-L	5-10	160	10-21-01	2	1	3.68	12	0	0	0	15	11	11	6	2	14	24	.190	.222	.175	14.73	8.59
Alexis Paulino	R-R	6-0	175	5-5-03	1	2	9.20	13	0	0	0	29	36	38	30	3	26	38	.310	.366	.280	11.66	7.98
Edwar Polimir	L-L	5-11	145	11-5-00	2	3	4.42	12	8	0	0	39	33	20	19	1	23	59	.237	.100	.261	13.73	5.35
Miguel Pozo	L-L	5-11	155	9-9-01	1	7	4.53	12	11	0	0	48	39	31	24	4	19	70	.214	.214	.214	13.22	3.59
Pedro Rodriguez	L-L	5-10	145	8-11-02	3	2	3.92	13	0	0	1	21	17	16	9	1	12	25	.215	.133	.234	10.89	5.23
Ronald Roman	L-L	6-3	185	10-10-01	0	0	10.50	8	0	0	0	6	7	9	7	1	12	10	.292	.000	.318	15.00	18.00
2-team total (2 DSL NYY Yankees)					0	0	12.54	10	0	0	0	9	10	16	13	2	19	11	.270	.000	.313	10.61	18.32
Hansel Rosario	R-R	6-4	174	8-5-02	1	2	5.40	11	4	0	0	25	17	19	15	1	31	30	.198	.250	.172	10.80	11.16
Daniel Salas	R-R	6-3	189	2-16-03	0	0	7.36	4	0	0	0	4	2	4	3	1	11	5	.154	.400	.000	12.27	27.00
Geralmi Santana	R-R	6-3	173	12-7-00	3	2	5.54	13	8	0	1	50	53	41	31	4	14	60	.268	.246	.278	10.73	2.50
Oscar Silverio	L-R	5-9	170	10-25-01	0	0	0.00	1	0	0	0	1	0	0	0	0	0	0	.000	--	.000	0.00	0.00

Fielding

C: Bersing 8, Contreras 13, Duran 5, Sanchez 19, Silverio 19, Urena 8. **1B:** Bersing 1, Castellano 31, Contreras 1, Duran 24, Herrera 1, Silverio 6. **2B:** Cruz 1, Javier 15, Leito 6, Ogando 10, Suarez 21, Tejeda 10, Verdecia 5. **3B:** Castellano 23, Javier 6, Leito 8, Ogando 20, Suarez 3, Tejeda 4, Verdecia 2. **SS:** Javier 1, Montero 25, Ogando 2, Suarez 6, Tejeda 27. **OF:** Cruz 49, Javier 2, Leito 1, Mendez 49, Montero 46, Rosa 42.

DSL NYY YANKEES — *ROOKIE*

DOMINICAN SUMMER LEAGUE

Batting	B-T	HT	WT	DOB	AVG	vLH	vRH	G	AB	R	H	2B	3B	HR	RBI	BB	HBP	SH	SF	SO	SB	CS	SLG	OBP
Ramiro Altagracia	R-R	5-11	180	1-18-04	.175	.244	.151	47	160	21	28	8	0	1	21	32	3	0	3	62	16	2	.244	.318
Roderick Arias	B-R	6-2	178	9-9-04	.194	.071	.238	31	108	25	21	6	2	3	11	28	4	0	0	46	10	2	.370	.379
David Beckles	R-R	6-3	215	4-23-04	.276	.275	.276	52	174	35	48	6	0	5	28	31	2	0	2	58	10	2	.397	.388
Gabriel Bersing	R-R	6-1	195	10-17-02	.188	.250	.169	35	117	18	22	2	1	4	14	10	1	0	0	48	3	2	.325	.258
2-team total (10 DSL NYY Bombers)					.211	.242	.202	45	152	25	32	2	4	7	24	12	2	0	1	64	4	3	.414	.275
Keiner Delgado	B-R	5-8	145	1-5-04	.310	.424	.281	52	168	50	52	16	4	3	28	58	10	0	2	28	34	8	.506	.504
Johan Ferreira	R-R	5-11	190	10-5-02	.207	.333	.172	27	82	13	17	6	0	0	15	11	2	0	0	29	10	0	.280	.316
Santiago Gomez	R-R	5-11	160	4-5-04	.230	.241	.226	43	122	22	28	5	2	3	14	28	5	0	0	39	22	5	.377	.394
Diomedes Hernandez	R-R	5-11	165	2-6-05	.229	.190	.245	24	70	13	16	5	1	0	12	10	2	0	0	15	4	0	.329	.341
Carlos Herrera	R-R	5-10	165	9-1-02	.121	.000	.160	14	33	5	4	1	0	0	4	8	1	0	0	13	1	2	.152	.310
2-team total (2 DSL NYY Bombers)					.114	.000	.148	16	35	5	4	1	0	0	4	8	1	0	0	15	1	2	.143	.295
Jhon Imbert	R-R	6-1	172	9-1-03	.115	.048	.140	32	78	20	9	1	0	2	9	34	2	0	0	41	8	2	.205	.395
Andres Lacruz	B-R	5-10	158	1-25-05	.190	.308	.138	20	42	10	8	1	1	0	7	8	2	0	1	12	1	3	.262	.340
Juan Matheus	B-R	5-10	155	4-29-04	.252	.467	.186	45	127	30	32	10	3	4	33	41	3	0	1	37	15	7	.472	.442
Willy Montero	R-R	6-4	202	8-4-04	.262	.222	.274	53	191	35	50	9	1	4	25	36	7	0	1	61	16	4	.382	.396
Manuel Palencia	R-R	6-0	175	9-5-02	.323	.281	.337	39	130	24	42	7	1	0	26	19	1	0	1	10	4	2	.392	.411
Louis Pierre	L-L	6-2	160	9-12-04	.169	.063	.204	19	65	11	11	1	1	1	8	15	3	0	0	28	2	0	.262	.349
Abrahan Ramirez	L-R	5-9	150	10-8-04	.333	.400	.311	25	60	15	20	4	3	0	16	11	2	0	2	15	4	4	.500	.440
Ricardo Rodriguez	R-R	6-1	155	11-16-04	.139	.125	.143	15	36	6	5	0	0	0	5	7	1	0	1	12	2	1	.139	.289

Pitching	B-T	HT	WT	DOB	W	L	ERA	G	GS	CG	SV	IP	H	R	ER	HR	BB	SO	AVG	vLH	vRH	K/9	BB/9
Brian Arias	R-R	6-0	177	11-18-03	0	2	4.00	7	5	0	0	18	16	9	8	1	11	19	.246	.286	.227	9.50	5.50
Wilfrido Bido	R-R	5-10	170	6-4-04	2	1	1.96	11	5	0	0	37	24	10	8	3	9	33	.179	.229	.151	8.10	2.21
Franklin Corniel	R-R	6-2	165	10-8-01	0	0	4.50	2	0	0	0	2	1	1	1	0	2	2	.167	.500	.000	9.00	9.00
Ernesto Disla	R-R	6-2	170	3-8-04	0	2	14.46	9	0	0	0	9	17	21	15	4	9	9	.395	.214	.483	8.68	8.68
Domingo Feliz	R-R	6-1	185	--	0	1	11.88	6	0	0	0	8	7	11	11	1	8	12	.219	.400	.136	12.96	8.64
2-team total (1 DSL NYY Bombers)					1	1	12.60	7	0	0	0	10	9	14	14	1	12	13	.237	.417	.154	11.70	10.80
Donys Garcia	R-R	6-2	175	2-18-01	8	0	3.61	13	0	0	1	42	33	20	17	1	13	57	.208	.268	.159	12.12	2.76

Alejandro Gomez	R-R	6-4	180	8-3-02	6	1	2.28	13	0	0	1	47	33	19	12	1	23	63	.196	.157	.214	11.98	4.37
Franyer Herrera	L-L	6-0	165	5-3-05	2	1	2.08	7	0	0	0	13	9	7	3	0	5	18	.191	.200	.188	12.46	3.46
2-team total (1 DSL NYY Bombers)					2	1	2.40	8	0	0	0	15	11	10	4	0	5	19	.196	.250	.175	11.40	3.00
Carlos Lagrange	R-R	6-7	195	5-25-03	0	1	3.00	11	10	0	0	33	10	13	11	1	19	43	.094	.063	.108	11.73	5.18
Henry Lalane	L-L	6-7	211	5-18-04	3	3	2.98	11	11	0	0	48	35	24	16	0	14	52	.202	.114	.233	9.68	2.61
Jordy Luciano	R-R	5-10	160	7-22-01	2	4	4.82	12	0	0	0	19	11	13	10	2	16	33	.169	.100	.200	15.91	7.71
2-team total (3 DSL NYY Bombers)					2	4	4.50	15	0	0	0	24	17	19	12	2	20	41	.191	.172	.200	15.38	7.50
Edinzo Marquez	R-R	6-2	208	12-16-04	0	0	4.15	5	2	0	0	13	8	6	6	1	8	16	.186	.273	.138	11.08	5.54
Sabier Marte	R-R	6-5	167	2-10-04	1	1	4.15	10	4	0	1	30	35	22	14	3	3	38	.271	.340	.232	11.27	0.89
Christopher Medina	R-R	6-1	185	3-21-04	1	1	7.88	9	0	0	0	8	8	8	7	0	15	12	.250	.273	.238	13.50	16.88
Jordarlin Mendoza	R-R	6-0	175	11-14-03	1	1	2.95	13	12	0	0	55	44	23	18	3	19	77	.223	.250	.208	12.60	3.11
Jan Pena	R-R	6-4	180	6-15-00	1	3	2.70	16	0	0	5	27	25	15	8	1	9	23	.253	.279	.232	7.76	3.04
Michael Peres	L-L	6-0	180	9-18-03	3	3	7.76	12	1	0	0	27	24	30	23	3	16	33	.238	.263	.232	11.14	5.40
Ronald Roman	L-L	6-3	185	10-10-01	0	0	16.20	2	0	0	0	3	3	7	6	1	7	1	.231	.000	.300	2.70	18.90
2-team total (8 DSL NYY Bombers)					0	0	12.54	10	0	0	0	9	10	16	13	2	19	11	.270	.000	.313	10.61	18.32
Luis Urbano	L-L	6-2	163	10-1-02	0	0	5.68	11	0	0	0	13	16	13	8	1	17	8	.286	.433	.244	5.68	12.08
Christian Zazueta	R-R	6-3	163	10-7-04	0	3	7.59	8	8	0	0	21	24	20	18	4	6	25	.276	.297	.260	10.55	2.53

Fielding

C: Bersing 11, Hernandez 12, Herrera 5, Palencia 31, Rodriguez 10. **1B:** Bersing 23, Ferreira 22, Herrera 8, Imbert 12. **2B:** Delgado 18, Gomez 12, Imbert 1, Matheus 13, Ramirez 19. **3B:** Ferreira 4, Gomez 19, Imbert 6, Matheus 30. **SS:** Arias 26, Delgado 26, Gomez 7, Matheus 1. **OF:** Altagracia 41, Beckles 53, Ferreira 1, Imbert 16, Lacruz 20, Montero 44, Pierre 17, Ramirez 1, Rodriguez 1.

Oakland Athletics

SEASON IN A SENTENCE: After four consecutive winning seasons, the Athletics shed payroll and talent before and after the lockout. While ownership focused on the franchise's future home, the club turned in its first 100-loss season since 1979.

HIGH POINT: Oakland's re-tooled roster got off to a competitive start, including winning three out of four in its first home series of the season, against Baltimore. Young veteran Paul Blackburn won the finale of that series with rookie relievers Domingo Acevedo, Zack Jackson and Dany Jimenez finishing the last win that left the A's at 8-6.

LOW POINT: The team's .627 OPS was the lowest since the club moved to the Bay Area in 1968 (predating the DH). The A's scored just 20 runs during a 10-game losing streak to open June, capped by a walk-off 3-2 loss at Cleveland, to drop to 20-40 and cement their last-place status.

NOTABLE ROOKIES: Oakland used a franchise-record 64 players, 34 of them classified as rookies. The most important were shortstop Nick Allen (Oakland's 2017 third-round pick), who struggled offensively but shined with the glove (96th percentile Outs Above Average); outfielder Cristian Pache, who struggled significantly after being acquired from Atlanta, and fellow former Brave Shea Langeliers, a catcher who could replace Sean Murphy if the A's trade their 2022 all-star. Acevedo, Jackson and lefty A.J. Puk, all rookies, led the club in appearances while Jimenez took over as the closer in the second half.

KEY TRANSACTIONS: The A's allowed manager Bob Melvin to take the Padres' managerial post. When the lockout ended, Oakland traded first baseman Matt Olson (Braves), righthander Chris Bassitt (Mets) and third baseman Matt Chapman (Toronto). Olson went to his hometown Atlanta for Langeliers, Pache, righthander Ryan Cusick and lefthander Joey Estes. The primary return for Chapman was infielder Kevin Smith and righthander Gunnar Hoglund. Bassitt netted pitchers Adam Oller and another two-time high pick, 2020 second-rounder J.T. Ginn. During the season, Oakland traded righthanders Frankie Montas and Lou Trivino to the Yankees, netting intriguing lefthanders J.P. Sears and Ken Waldichuk in a four-player package.

ON THE FARM: The addition of prospects in trades were needed because the system remains thin in homegrown talent.

OPENING DAY PAYROLL: $48,056,154 (30th).

PLAYERS OF THE YEAR

MAJOR LEAGUE

Sean Murphy
C

.250/.332/.426
18 HR, 37 2B in 148 G
116 G caught led AL

MINOR LEAGUE

Shea Langeliers
C

(Triple-A)
.283/.366/.510
19 HR, 56 RBIs in 92 G

ORGANIZATION LEADERS

Batting — *Minimum 250 AB

MAJORS		
* AVG	Sean Murphy	.250
* OPS	Sean Murphy	.759
HR	Seth Brown	25
RBI	Seth Brown	73
MINORS		
* AVG	Jordan Diaz, Midland, Las Vegas	.326
* OBP	Matt Davidson, Las Vegas	.405
* SLG	Matt Davidson, Las Vegas	.595
* OPS	Matt Davidson, Las Vegas	1.000
R	Junior Perez, Stockton	74
H	Jordan Diaz, Midland, Las Vegas	160
TB	Jordan Diaz, Midland, Las Vegas	253
	Tyler Soderstrom, Lansing, Midland, Las Vegas	
2B	Jordan Diaz, Midland, Las Vegas	34
3B	Luis Barrera, Las Vegas	7
HR	Tyler Soderstrom, Lansing, Midland, Las Vegas	29
RBI	Tyler Soderstrom, Lansing, Midland, Las Vegas	105
BB	Junior Perez, Stockton	70
SO	Max Muncy, Stockton, Lansing	169
SB	Junior Perez, Stockton	32

Pitching — #Minimum 75 IP

MAJORS		
W	Cole Irvin	9
# ERA	Frankie Montas	3.18
SO	Cole Irvin	128
SV	Dany Jimenez	11
MINORS		
W	Jack Cushing, Midland, Las Vegas	12
L	3 tied	11
# ERA	Jack Owen, Stockton, Lansing	3.38
G	Garrett Acton, Midland, Las Vegas	51
GS	Collin Wiles, Las Vegas	26
SV	Hunter Breault, Stockton, Las Vegas	10
	Trayson Kubo, Lansing, Midland	
IP	Collin Wiles, Las Vegas	143.1
BB	Stevie Emanuels, Stockton, Lansing	62
SO	Kyle Virbitsky, Stockton, Lansing	140
# AVG	Kyle Virbitsky, Stockton, Lansing	.2697

2022 PERFORMANCE

General Manager: David Forst. **Farm Director:** Ed Sprague. **Scouting Director:** Eric Kubota.

Class	Team	League	W	L	PCT	Finish	Manager
Majors	Oakland Athletics	American	60	102	.370	15th (15)	Mark Kotsay
Triple-A	Las Vegas Aviators	Pacific Coast	71	79	.473	7th (10)	Fran Riordan
Double-A	Midland RockHounds	Texas	66	71	.482	8th (10)	Bobby Crosby
High-A	Lansing Lugnuts	Midwest	54	77	.412	10th (12)	Phillip Pohl
Low-A	Stockton Ports	California	45	87	.341	t-7th (8)	Franklin Font
Rookie	ACL Athletics	Arizona Complex	20	34	.370	t-15th (18)	Adam Rosales
Overall 2022 Minor League Record			282	380	.426	t-29th (30)	

ORGANIZATION STATISTICS

OAKLAND ATHLETICS

AMERICAN LEAGUE

Batting	B-T	HT	WT	DOB	AVG	vLH	vRH	G	AB	R	H	2B	3B	HR	RBI	BB	HBP	SH	SF	SO	SB	CS	SLG	OBP
Austin Allen	L-R	6-2	219	1-16-94	.071	.200	.000	5	14	1	1	0	0	0	0	1	1	0	0	9	0	0	.071	.188
Nick Allen	R-R	5-8	166	10-8-98	.207	.276	.179	100	299	31	62	13	0	4	19	19	1	6	1	64	3	2	.291	.256
Elvis Andrus	R-R	6-0	210	8-26-88	.237	.255	.230	106	354	41	84	24	0	8	30	30	2	0	0	62	7	4	.373	.301
2-team total (43 Chicago White Sox)					.249	.283	.236	149	535	66	133	32	0	17	58	39	3	0	0	92	18	4	.404	.303
Luis Barrera	L-L	6-0	195	11-15-95	.234	.143	.243	32	77	3	18	5	0	1	7	6	1	0	1	17	3	0	.338	.294
Christian Bethancourt	R-R	6-3	205	9-2-91	.249	.266	.233	56	169	23	42	11	0	4	19	10	2	1	0	41	4	1	.385	.298
2-team total (45 Tampa Bay Rays)					.252	.252	.251	101	318	39	80	17	0	11	34	12	2	1	0	80	5	1	.409	.283
Skye Bolt	B-R	6-2	180	1-15-94	.198	.188	.203	42	106	10	21	2	0	4	13	7	2	0	1	30	5	0	.330	.259
Jonah Bride	R-R	5-10	200	12-27-95	.204	.185	.213	58	162	17	33	4	0	1	6	19	4	1	1	32	1	0	.247	.301
Seth Brown	L-L	6-1	223	7-13-92	.230	.174	.243	150	500	55	115	26	3	25	73	51	3	0	1	146	11	2	.444	.305
Conner Capel	L-L	6-1	185	5-19-97	.371	.500	.364	13	35	6	13	0	1	2	9	4	0	0	1	8	1	1	.600	.425
Ernie Clement	R-R	6-0	170	3-22-96	.056	.125	.000	6	18	1	1	1	0	0	0	0	0	0	0	2	0	0	.111	.056
2-team total (64 Cleveland Guardians)					.184	.192	.176	70	163	19	30	4	0	0	6	11	2	2	1	26	0	1	.209	.243
Matt Davidson	R-R	6-3	230	3-26-91	.167	.125	.188	8	24	2	4	0	0	1	2	0	0	0	0	10	0	1	.292	.167
Jordan Diaz	R-R	5-10	175	8-13-00	.265	.250	.273	15	49	3	13	3	0	0	1	2	0	0	0	7	0	0	.327	.294
Dermis Garcia	R-R	6-3	200	1-7-98	.207	.167	.225	39	116	13	24	6	0	5	20	8	1	0	0	55	0	0	.388	.264
Drew Jackson	R-R	6-2	200	7-28-93	.000	.000	--	3	3	0	0	0	0	0	0	0	0	0	0	1	0	0	.000	.000
Tony Kemp	L-R	5-6	160	10-31-91	.235	.219	.238	147	497	61	117	24	2	7	46	45	8	5	3	69	11	1	.334	.307
Shea Langeliers	R-R	6-0	205	11-18-97	.218	.276	.204	40	142	14	31	10	1	6	22	9	0	0	2	53	0	0	.430	.261
Ramon Laureano	R-R	5-11	203	7-15-94	.211	.210	.211	94	346	49	73	18	0	13	34	25	12	0	0	104	11	6	.376	.287
Christian Lopes	R-R	6-0	211	10-1-92	.000	.000	.000	4	9	0	0	0	0	0	0	1	0	0	0	5	0	0	.000	.100
Jed Lowrie	B-R	6-0	180	4-17-84	.180	.184	.178	50	167	14	30	5	0	3	16	15	0	0	2	39	1	0	.263	.245
Vimael Machin	L-R	5-11	185	9-25-93	.220	.154	.224	73	223	26	49	12	0	1	13	25	2	0	3	47	1	1	.287	.300
David MacKinnon	R-R	6-2	200	12-15-94	.000	.000	.000	6	13	2	0	0	0	0	0	1	0	0	0	5	0	0	.000	.071
2-team total (16 Los Angeles Angels)					.140	.077	.208	22	50	2	7	0	0	0	6	6	0	0	1	17	0	0	.140	.228
Mickey McDonald	L-R	6-2	175	6-2-95	.000	.000	.000	4	4	0	0	0	0	0	0	2	0	0	0	3	0	0	.000	.333
Billy McKinney	L-L	6-1	205	8-23-94	.096	.111	.093	23	52	3	5	1	0	1	4	4	0	0	1	16	0	0	.173	.158
Nate Mondou	L-R	5-10	205	3-24-95	.000	--	.000	1	2	0	0	0	0	0	0	1	0	0	0	1	0	0	.000	.333
Sean Murphy	R-R	6-3	228	10-4-94	.250	.242	.252	148	537	67	134	37	2	18	66	56	13	0	5	124	1	0	.426	.332
Sheldon Neuse	R-R	6-0	232	12-10-94	.214	.181	.235	89	271	25	58	4	2	4	26	20	2	0	0	80	6	1	.288	.273
Cristian Pache	R-R	6-2	215	11-19-98	.166	.220	.138	91	241	18	40	5	2	3	18	15	1	3	0	70	2	2	.241	.218
Chad Pinder	R-R	6-2	210	3-29-92	.235	.260	.218	111	361	38	85	18	0	12	42	14	0	1	2	118	2	0	.385	.263
Stephen Piscotty	R-R	6-4	211	1-14-91	.190	.190	.190	42	126	12	24	4	0	5	14	9	2	0	2	48	2	0	.341	.252
Kevin Smith	R-R	6-0	190	7-4-96	.180	.260	.135	47	139	9	25	9	1	2	13	7	0	3	2	42	4	0	.302	.216
Cal Stevenson	L-L	5-10	175	9-12-96	.167	.200	.164	23	60	5	10	3	0	0	1	8	0	2	1	23	1	1	.217	.261
Cody Thomas	L-R	6-4	211	10-8-94	.267	1.000	.185	10	30	1	8	0	0	0	0	2	0	0	0	12	0	0	.267	.313
Stephen Vogt	L-R	6-0	216	11-1-84	.161	.000	.170	70	168	18	27	4	1	7	23	17	2	0	4	46	1	0	.321	.241

Pitching	B-T	HT	WT	DOB	W	L	ERA	G	GS	CG	SV	IP	H	R	ER	HR	BB	SO	AVG	vLH	vRH	K/9	BB/9
Domingo Acevedo	R-R	6-7	240	3-6-94	4	4	3.33	70	0	0	4	68	50	26	25	9	17	58	.206	.215	.201	7.71	2.26
Christian Bethancourt	R-R	6-3	205	9-2-91	0	0	0.00	1	0	0	0	1	0	0	0	0	1	0	.000	.000	.000	0.00	9.00
2-team total (3 Tampa Bay Rays)					0	0	2.25	4	0	0	0	4	6	1	1	1	1	1	.333	.143	.455	2.25	2.25
Paul Blackburn	R-R	6-1	196	12-4-93	7	6	4.28	21	21	0	0	111	110	53	53	15	30	89	.255	.260	.250	7.19	2.43
Ryan Castellani	R-R	6-4	218	4-1-96	0	0	0.00	3	0	0	0	3	2	1	0	0	0	1	.182	--	.182	3.38	0.00
Tyler Cyr	R-R	6-1	205	5-5-93	1	0	2.08	11	0	0	0	13	9	3	3	1	5	16	.196	.083	.235	11.08	3.46
Justin Grimm	R-R	6-3	210	8-16-88	0	0	4.11	15	0	0	0	15	18	8	7	1	7	11	.295	.296	.294	6.46	4.11
Cole Irvin	L-L	6-4	217	1-31-94	9	13	3.98	30	30	0	0	181	174	87	80	25	36	128	.251	.229	.257	6.36	1.79
Zach Jackson	R-R	6-4	230	12-25-94	2	3	3.00	54	0	0	3	48	28	18	16	1	33	67	.171	.143	.188	12.56	6.19
Daulton Jefferies	L-R	6-0	182	8-2-95	1	7	5.72	8	8	0	0	39	46	26	25	4	8	28	.286	.243	.322	6.41	1.83
Dany Jimenez	R-R	6-1	182	12-23-93	3	4	3.41	34	0	0	11	34	23	16	13	2	18	34	.183	.178	.185	8.91	4.72
James Kaprielian	R-R	6-3	225	3-2-94	5	9	4.23	26	26	0	0	134	121	68	63	16	59	98	.239	.237	.241	6.58	3.96
Jared Koenig	R-L	6-5	235	1-24-94	1	3	5.72	10	5	0	0	39	40	25	25	4	15	22	.260	.303	.248	5.03	3.43
Adam Kolarek	L-L	6-3	215	1-14-89	0	1	4.58	15	0	0	0	18	20	9	9	1	8	9	.294	.276	.308	4.58	4.08

Jacob Lemoine	R-R	6-5	220	11-28-93	0	0	7.71	9	0	0	0	16	18	15	14	4	7	13	.273	.414	.162	7.16	3.86
Zach Logue	L-L	6-0	165	4-23-96	3	8	6.79	14	10	0	0	57	68	44	43	13	20	42	.293	.235	.309	6.63	3.16
Parker Markel	R-R	6-5	240	9-15-90	0	0	0.00	3	0	0	0	3	1	0	0	0	5	3	.125	.000	.167	9.00	15.00
Adrian Martinez	R-R	6-2	215	12-10-96	4	6	6.24	12	12	0	0	58	69	42	40	13	19	53	.295	.297	.293	8.27	2.97
David McKay	R-R	6-3	205	3-31-95	0	0	3.38	1	0	0	0	3	4	1	1	0	0	2	.364	.429	.250	6.75	0.00
3-team total (2 New York Yankees, 1 Tampa Bay Rays)					0	0	6.75	4	0	0	0	7	8	5	5	1	4	3	.296	.250	.333	4.05	5.40
Sam Moll	L-L	5-9	190	1-3-92	2	1	2.91	53	0	0	0	43	33	16	14	5	22	46	.205	.169	.238	9.55	4.57
Sheldon Neuse	R-R	6-0	232	12-10-94	0	0	0.00	3	0	0	0	4	1	0	0	0	0	0	.083	.167	.000	0.00	0.00
Adam Oller	R-R	6-4	225	10-17-94	2	8	6.30	19	14	0	0	74	82	55	52	17	39	46	.280	.262	.292	5.57	4.72
Joel Payamps	R-R	6-2	225	4-7-94	1	3	3.46	12	0	0	0	13	14	5	5	2	0	8	.269	.077	.333	5.54	0.00
2-team total (29 Kansas City Royals)					3	6	3.23	41	0	0	0	56	60	24	20	7	16	41	.273	.188	.311	6.63	2.59
Chad Pinder	R-R	6-2	210	3-29-92	0	0	27.00	1	0	0	0	1	2	3	3	0	2	0	.500	.500	.500	0.00	18.00
Austin Pruitt	R-R	5-10	185	8-31-89	0	1	4.23	39	1	0	1	55	48	29	26	11	9	38	.226	.203	.241	6.18	1.46
A.J. Puk	L-L	6-7	248	4-25-95	4	3	3.12	62	0	0	4	66	53	27	23	7	23	76	.217	.153	.252	10.31	3.12
Norge Ruiz	R-R	5-10	180	3-15-94	0	1	7.11	14	0	0	0	19	30	16	15	4	7	18	.361	.441	.306	8.53	3.32
JP Sears	R-L	5-11	180	2-19-96	3	3	4.69	10	9	0	0	48	53	26	25	7	18	36	.285	.286	.285	6.75	3.38
2-team total (7 New York Yankees)					6	3	3.86	17	11	0	0	70	67	31	30	8	23	51	.256	.265	.254	6.56	2.96
Sam Selman	R-L	6-2	198	11-14-90	0	0	4.91	16	0	0	0	18	16	10	10	4	5	18	.232	.241	.225	8.84	2.45
Kirby Snead	L-L	6-1	218	10-7-94	1	1	5.84	46	0	0	1	45	56	31	29	5	22	35	.308	.314	.304	7.05	4.43
Domingo Tapia	R-R	6-3	263	8-4-91	0	0	8.47	11	0	0	0	17	25	16	16	1	14	12	.338	.324	.350	6.35	7.41
Ken Waldichuk	L-L	6-4	220	1-8-98	2	2	4.93	7	7	0	0	35	32	19	19	5	10	33	.244	.138	.275	8.57	2.60
Collin Wiles	R-R	6-4	222	5-30-94	0	0	4.66	4	0	0	0	10	11	6	5	1	2	9	.289	.333	.269	8.38	1.86

Fielding

Catcher	PCT	G	PO	A	E	DP	PB
Allen	1.000	4	24	3	0	1	0
Bethancourt	1.000	14	79	6	0	0	1
Langeliers	.993	17	126	10	1	2	0
Murphy	.991	116	878	40	8	4	2
Vogt	.992	19	115	8	1	2	0

First Base	PCT	G	PO	A	E	DP
Bethancourt	.995	31	180	14	1	20
Bride	1.000	5	21	1	0	0
Brown	.993	84	538	44	4	51
Davidson	1.000	1	6	0	0	1
Diaz	1.000	1	6	0	0	1
Garcia	1.000	35	230	14	0	29
Lowrie	1.000	3	28	1	0	1
MacKinnon	1.000	5	29	5	0	2
McKinney	1.000	7	37	4	0	2
Neuse	.980	13	94	4	2	7
Pinder	1.000	3	26	0	0	2
Vogt	1.000	17	88	4	0	8

Second Base	PCT	G	PO	A	E	DP
Allen	.975	43	69	87	4	19
Bride	.990	32	38	64	1	15
Diaz	.956	12	20	23	2	9
Kemp	.990	89	126	171	3	35
Lopes	1.000	2	0	4	0	2
Lowrie	1.000	2	3	8	0	2
Machin	.000	1	0	0	0	0
Mondou	.000	1	0	0	0	0
Neuse	.931	23	31	36	5	10
Pinder	.000	1	0	0	0	0

Third Base	PCT	G	PO	A	E	DP
Bride	.930	21	9	31	3	1
Clement	1.000	4	3	7	0	1
Davidson	.846	6	3	8	2	1
Jackson	.000	1	0	0	0	0
Machin	.964	68	42	119	6	16
Neuse	.935	44	25	75	7	12
Pinder	1.000	9	2	4	0	0
Smith	.991	39	32	74	1	9

Shortstop	PCT	G	PO	A	E	DP
Allen	.978	60	68	197	6	40
Andrus	.977	101	114	262	9	48
Clement	1.000	1	1	2	0	0
Machin	.000	1	0	0	1	0
Neuse	1.000	2	2	6	0	0
Smith	.962	10	11	14	1	3

Outfield	PCT	G	PO	A	E	DP
Barrera	.941	33	47	1	3	0
Bolt	1.000	43	88	0	0	0
Brown	.985	87	127	2	2	2
Capel	1.000	13	37	0	0	0
Clement	--	1	0	0	0	0
Garcia	.667	1	2	0	1	0
Jackson	1.000	3	2	0	0	0
Kemp	.991	65	112	4	1	2
Laureano	.990	105	190	5	2	0
Lopes	1.000	2	1	0	0	0
McDonald	1.000	2	2	0	0	0
McKinney	1.000	14	19	1	0	1
Pache	.995	90	197	1	1	0
Pinder	.994	94	150	3	1	1
Piscotty	1.000	33	65	0	0	0
Stevenson	1.000	25	45	0	0	0
Thomas	1.000	10	18	0	0	0

LAS VEGAS AVIATORS — TRIPLE-A

PACIFIC COAST LEAGUE

Batting	B-T	HT	WT	DOB	AVG	vLH	vRH	G	AB	R	H	2B	3B	HR	RBI	BB	HBP	SH	SF	SO	SB	CS	SLG	OBP
Austin Allen	L-R	6-2	219	1-16-94	.271	.138	.310	35	129	17	35	11	0	5	26	12	4	1	1	37	0	0	.473	.349
Nick Allen	R-R	5-8	166	10-8-98	.266	.346	.231	46	173	31	46	10	0	2	16	27	2	4	0	34	10	2	.358	.371
Luis Barrera	L-L	6-0	195	11-15-95	.263	.275	.257	85	312	55	82	16	7	8	45	29	3	1	3	68	9	3	.436	.329
Marty Bechina	R-R	6-0	200	10-31-96	.100	.083	.111	11	30	3	3	0	0	1	2	6	1	0	0	12	0	1	.200	.270
Christian Bethancourt	R-R	6-3	205	9-2-91	.263	.500	.154	5	19	3	5	2	0	2	2	2	0	0	0	4	0	0	.684	.333
Skye Bolt	B-R	6-2	180	1-15-94	.326	.290	.344	24	95	15	31	7	0	4	23	7	2	0	0	23	1	1	.526	.385
Jonah Bride	R-R	5-10	200	12-27-95	.393	.438	.378	18	61	14	24	6	0	2	10	13	4	0	0	12	0	0	.590	.526
Conner Capel	L-L	6-1	185	5-19-97	.321	.286	.357	7	28	4	9	2	0	0	4	3	1	0	0	8	2	1	.393	.406
Matt Davidson	R-R	6-3	230	3-26-91	.297	.319	.287	75	279	59	83	9	1	24	54	38	13	0	1	88	0	0	.595	.405
2-team total (11 Reno Aces)					.310	.317	.306	86	323	67	100	10	1	32	66	44	14	0	1	102	0	0	.644	.414
Jordan Diaz	R-R	5-10	175	8-13-00	.348	.412	.321	26	112	19	39	8	1	4	25	6	1	0	1	15	0	0	.545	.383
Vince Fernandez	L-R	6-3	210	7-25-95	.248	.181	.268	102	311	61	77	18	5	15	49	36	11	0	2	120	4	0	.482	.344
Dermis Garcia	R-R	6-3	200	1-7-98	.264	.269	.261	68	239	51	63	15	1	13	44	32	2	0	5	83	4	1	.498	.349
Zack Gelof	R-R	6-3	205	10-19-99	.257	.400	.200	9	35	7	9	1	0	5	5	3	0	0	0	11	1	0	.714	.316
Drew Jackson	R-R	6-2	200	7-28-93	.243	.291	.215	50	148	19	36	5	0	1	14	23	2	0	0	56	8	1	.297	.353
2-team total (10 Sacramento River Cats)					.236	.288	.200	60	178	26	42	6	0	4	19	24	2	0	0	71	8	1	.337	.333
Dalton Kelly	L-L	6-3	200	8-4-94	.219	.287	.193	98	310	49	68	12	2	15	48	44	6	0	0	118	7	3	.416	.328
Shea Langeliers	R-R	6-0	205	11-18-97	.283	.257	.296	92	353	62	100	19	2	19	56	43	4	0	2	88	5	1	.510	.366
Ramon Laureano	R-R	5-11	203	7-15-94	.135	.000	.217	10	37	10	5	2	0	0	2	5	2	0	0	11	2	0	.189	.273
Christian Lopes	R-R	6-0	211	10-1-92	.257	.273	.248	53	187	24	48	14	1	2	22	23	4	0	2	56	4	1	.374	.347
Hansen Lopez	R-R	5-9	170	7-3-00	.000	--	.000	1	1	0	0	0	0	0	0	0	0	0	0	1	0	0	.000	.000
Jed Lowrie	B-R	6-0	180	4-17-84	.316	.333	.313	5	19	5	6	0	0	2	3	2	0	0	0	4	0	0	.632	.381
Vimael Machin	L-R	5-11	185	9-25-93	.324	.299	.335	64	256	41	83	16	3	4	49	33	1	0	2	30	0	0	.457	.401

David MacKinnon	R-R	6-2	200	12-15-94	.297	.357	.280	16	64	6	19	5	0	1	9	7	1	0	1	12	0	0	.422	.370
2-team total (63 Salt Lake Bees)					.318	.333	.312	79	289	53	92	24	4	15	54	49	3	0	5	63	2	2	.585	.416
Kyle McCann	L-R	6-2	217	12-2-97	.167	.250	.125	7	24	4	4	2	0	1	1	3	1	0	0	9	0	0	.375	.286
Mickey McDonald	L-R	6-2	175	6-2-95	.267	.153	.311	67	210	37	56	9	1	2	17	32	4	5	1	55	7	4	.348	.372
Billy McKinney	L-L	6-1	205	8-23-94	.295	.235	.317	69	251	48	74	13	5	12	49	36	6	0	0	83	2	0	.530	.396
Nate Mondou	L-R	5-10	205	3-24-95	.283	.330	.267	108	385	59	109	30	3	7	64	46	13	0	5	83	1	1	.431	.374
Jose Mujica	R-R	6-0	164	3-28-01	.250	.333	.000	1	4	1	1	0	0	0	0	0	0	0	0	3	0	0	.250	.250
Sheldon Neuse	R-R	6-0	232	12-10-94	.398	.393	.400	25	108	14	43	6	1	5	20	3	0	0	2	22	2	0	.611	.407
Cristian Pache	R-R	6-2	215	11-19-98	.248	.326	.216	41	157	15	39	8	1	4	20	11	1	0	2	39	1	1	.389	.298
Elvis Peralta	L-R	5-9	160	12-7-96	.000	.000	.000	3	3	1	0	0	0	0	0	0	0	0	0	2	0	0	.000	.000
Stephen Piscotty	R-R	6-4	211	1-14-91	.381	.500	.368	5	21	2	8	1	0	0	1	1	1	0	0	3	0	0	.429	.435
Buddy Reed	B-R	6-4	218	4-27-95	.196	.167	.212	20	51	5	10	0	0	0	3	4	0	1	0	16	1	0	.196	.255
Max Schuemann	R-R	6-1	186	6-11-97	.143	.091	.167	11	35	5	5	2	0	1	2	6	0	0	0	16	1	1	.286	.268
JJ Schwarz	R-R	6-1	205	3-28-96	.207	.188	.231	12	29	3	6	0	0	1	5	4	0	0	1	11	0	0	.310	.294
William Simoneit	R-R	6-4	235	10-14-96	.293	.250	.310	18	41	11	12	4	0	0	7	8	0	0	1	13	0	0	.390	.400
Kevin Smith	R-R	6-0	190	7-4-96	.268	.320	.247	86	332	44	89	16	2	13	49	29	4	1	4	112	6	1	.446	.331
Tyler Soderstrom	L-R	6-2	200	11-24-01	.297	.000	.393	9	37	2	11	1	0	1	6	1	0	0	0	13	0	0	.405	.316
Cal Stevenson	L-L	5-10	175	9-12-96	.322	.222	.348	24	87	23	28	2	2	4	19	14	1	0	2	12	7	1	.529	.413
Beau Taylor	L-R	5-11	205	2-13-90	.250	.276	.239	27	100	20	25	6	0	4	13	16	4	0	0	28	0	0	.430	.375
Eric Thames	L-R	5-11	235	11-10-86	.274	.231	.293	22	84	9	23	6	0	3	16	7	1	0	0	35	0	0	.452	.337
Cody Thomas	L-R	6-4	211	10-8-94	.200	.167	.207	10	35	3	7	3	0	1	8	2	1	0	1	13	0	0	.371	.256
Stephen Vogt	L-R	6-0	216	11-1-84	.278	.000	.385	5	18	3	5	1	0	1	2	1	0	0	0	6	0	0	.500	.316

Pitching	B-T	HT	WT	DOB	W	L	ERA	G	GS	CG	SV	IP	H	R	ER	HR	BB	SO	AVG	vLH	vRH	K/9	BB/9
Garrett Acton	L-R	6-2	215	6-15-98	2	6	5.53	32	2	0	3	42	46	32	26	12	15	50	.279	.375	.218	10.63	3.19
Hunter Breault	R-R	6-2	228	6-12-99	0	0	9.82	6	0	0	0	7	14	8	8	3	2	4	.389	.313	.450	4.91	2.45
Aaron Brown	L-L	6-2	223	6-20-92	7	4	4.77	46	1	0	3	66	57	42	35	13	39	71	.231	.218	.238	9.68	5.32
Ryan Castellani	R-R	6-4	218	4-1-96	2	1	11.97	26	0	0	3	29	40	45	39	6	40	25	.320	.321	.319	7.67	12.27
Bryce Conley	R-R	6-3	200	8-22-94	0	1	7.36	6	0	0	0	7	9	6	6	3	5	9	.310	.400	.263	11.05	6.14
Jeff Criswell	R-R	6-4	225	3-10-99	0	1	4.22	2	2	0	0	11	10	5	5	0	3	4	.263	.143	.333	3.38	2.53
Jack Cushing	R-R	6-3	195	12-3-96	1	3	14.14	6	6	0	0	21	43	34	33	11	7	20	.402	.346	.455	8.57	3.00
Tyler Cyr	R-R	6-1	205	5-5-93	0	0	5.40	4	0	0	0	5	7	3	3	1	5	8	.333	.250	.353	14.40	9.00
Ty Damron	L-L	6-2	200	7-28-94	2	1	5.11	8	5	0	0	25	29	14	14	5	11	21	.290	.333	.271	7.66	4.01
Parker Dunshee	R-R	6-0	215	2-12-95	5	11	9.22	31	20	0	0	111	140	117	114	38	56	92	.304	.337	.280	7.44	4.53
Hogan Harris	R-L	6-3	230	12-26-96	1	3	6.35	8	8	0	0	28	31	21	20	6	17	39	.277	.357	.250	12.39	5.40
Grant Holmes	L-R	6-0	226	3-22-96	1	2	8.27	28	3	0	0	37	57	34	34	10	14	26	.356	.354	.358	6.32	3.41
Brent Honeywell Jr.	R-R	6-2	195	3-31-95	0	3	7.79	11	0	0	0	17	28	15	15	7	7	21	.373	.280	.420	10.90	3.63
Brian Howard	R-R	6-9	213	4-25-95	3	1	6.72	42	3	0	0	70	83	55	52	14	32	65	.297	.328	.273	8.40	4.13
Dany Jimenez	R-R	6-1	182	12-23-93	0	0	0.00	2	0	0	0	2	0	0	0	0	0	4	.000	--	.000	18.00	0.00
James Kaprielian	R-R	6-3	225	3-2-94	0	1	9.35	2	2	0	0	9	12	9	9	1	5	7	.353	.357	.350	7.27	5.19
Gabe Klobosits	L-R	6-8	254	5-16-95	0	1	7.59	11	0	0	1	11	12	10	9	3	6	12	.279	.182	.381	10.13	5.06
Jared Koenig	R-L	6-5	235	1-24-94	6	6	4.71	20	18	0	0	107	112	57	56	13	30	104	.269	.258	.272	8.75	2.52
Adam Kolarek	L-L	6-3	215	1-14-89	2	3	6.10	37	0	0	2	41	42	29	28	4	16	39	.269	.215	.308	8.49	3.48
Jacob Lemoine	R-R	6-5	220	11-28-93	2	1	4.95	26	2	0	1	36	42	21	20	5	22	26	.294	.400	.217	6.44	5.45
Zach Logue	L-L	6-0	165	4-23-96	3	6	8.12	17	17	0	0	79	119	74	71	25	38	59	.352	.370	.346	6.75	4.35
Parker Markel	R-R	6-5	240	9-15-90	3	0	1.89	17	0	0	1	19	13	5	4	2	10	28	.191	.158	.204	13.26	4.74
Adrian Martinez	R-R	6-2	215	12-10-96	5	7	5.72	18	18	1	0	90	94	64	57	24	33	100	.270	.271	.269	10.04	3.31
David McKay	R-R	6-3	205	3-31-95	0	0	7.11	5	0	0	0	6	9	5	5	2	2	5	.360	.313	.444	7.11	2.84
Mason Miller	R-R	6-5	200	8-24-98	0	1	5.40	2	2	0	0	5	5	3	3	2	1	7	.294	.375	.222	12.60	1.80
Nate Mondou	L-R	5-10	205	3-24-95	0	0	13.50	1	0	0	0	1	1	2	2	1	1	0	.200	.000	.333	0.00	6.75
Adam Oller	R-R	6-4	225	10-17-94	3	0	3.69	7	7	0	0	32	29	17	13	0	17	32	.242	.250	.229	9.09	4.83
Colin Peluse	R-R	6-3	230	6-11-98	0	1	37.80	1	1	0	0	2	7	7	7	2	1	1	.538	.500	.556	5.40	5.40
Chester Pimentel	R-R	6-5	210	11-12-95	1	1	3.48	9	0	0	1	10	6	5	4	1	7	8	.171	.231	.136	6.97	6.10
Austin Pruitt	R-R	5-10	185	8-31-89	1	0	3.27	12	0	0	1	22	20	10	8	0	2	20	.238	.200	.265	8.18	0.82
Miguel Romero	R-R	6-0	202	4-23-94	2	1	7.76	38	2	0	0	53	72	48	46	9	30	32	.329	.402	.276	5.40	5.06
Norge Ruiz	R-R	5-10	180	3-15-94	5	1	3.73	31	0	0	2	41	36	18	17	5	16	39	.229	.190	.255	8.56	3.51
JP Sears	R-L	5-11	180	2-19-96	0	0	1.93	1	1	0	0	5	4	1	1	0	0	5	.235	.167	.273	9.64	0.00
Sam Selman	R-L	6-2	198	11-14-90	2	0	2.83	28	0	0	6	35	20	11	11	2	18	36	.164	.150	.171	9.26	4.63
Kirby Snead	L-L	6-1	218	10-7-94	2	0	4.61	11	0	0	1	14	13	7	7	1	3	20	.245	.167	.286	13.17	1.98
Domingo Tapia	R-R	6-3	263	8-4-91	0	0	1.76	27	0	0	4	31	25	12	6	1	12	29	.219	.271	.182	8.51	3.52
Beau Taylor	L-R	5-11	205	2-13-90	0	0	0.00	1	0	0	0	1	1	0	0	0	0	0	.333	--	.333	0.00	0.00
Ken Waldichuk	L-L	6-4	220	1-8-98	0	1	3.38	4	4	0	0	19	20	9	7	3	3	21	.267	.286	.259	10.13	1.45
Jake Walkinshaw	R-R	6-3	200	7-7-96	1	0	3.44	6	0	0	1	18	21	9	7	3	4	11	.280	.316	.243	5.40	1.96
Collin Wiles	R-R	6-4	222	5-30-94	9	11	5.40	26	26	1	0	143	175	100	86	27	27	106	.298	.278	.317	6.66	1.70

Fielding

Catcher	PCT	G	PO	A	E	DP	PB
Allen	.989	21	166	6	2	2	1
Bethancourt	.969	3	29	2	1	0	2
Bride	1.000	1	10	0	0	0	2
Langeliers	.988	79	630	41	8	6	4
McCann	1.000	3	22	2	0	0	0
Schwarz	.974	5	36	1	1	0	0
Simoneit	1.000	14	84	3	0	1	1
Soderstrom	.955	5	40	2	2	0	0
Taylor	.995	24	201	10	1	2	2
Vogt	1.000	3	18	1	0	0	0

First Base	PCT	G	PO	A	E	DP
Allen	1.000	1	5	1	0	0
Bethancourt	1.000	1	6	0	0	1
Bride	1.000	3	27	2	0	5
Davidson	1.000	23	195	9	0	19
Diaz	1.000	3	26	0	0	3
Garcia	.983	47	321	21	6	40
Kelly	.997	40	262	30	1	27
Lowrie	1.000	2	10	0	0	2
Machin	1.000	1	7	0	0	0
MacKinnon	1.000	4	29	3	0	6
McCann	.964	4	27	0	1	3
McKinney	1.000	16	124	6	0	8
Mujica	1.000	1	9	0	0	1
Neuse	1.000	1	4	0	0	0

Schwarz	1.000	1	5	2	0	0
Soderstrom	1.000	3	30	1	0	1
Thames	1.000	11	75	7	0	7
Vogt	1.000	1	2	1	0	0

Second Base	PCT	G	PO	A	E	DP
Allen	1.000	7	17	15	0	9
Bride	1.000	5	7	7	0	3
Davidson	1.000	1	1	1	0	1
Diaz	1.000	3	6	3	0	0
Gelof	.944	9	12	22	2	3
Jackson	.971	9	11	22	1	5
Lopes	.985	17	32	35	1	7
Lowrie	.000	1	0	0	0	0
Machin	.978	11	20	25	1	6
McDonald	1.000	1	0	2	0	0
Mondou	.978	80	123	186	7	48
Neuse	1.000	4	8	7	0	3
Peralta	1.000	2	1	0	0	0
Schuemann	.975	10	12	27	1	10

Third Base	PCT	G	PO	A	E	DP
Bechina	1.000	6	11	15	0	4
Bride	1.000	7	2	15	0	1
Davidson	.959	31	19	74	4	4
Diaz	.667	3	1	5	3	0
Jackson	1.000	1	1	3	0	0
Lopes	1.000	7	5	17	0	3
Machin	.901	36	21	70	10	14
MacKinnon	.955	10	3	18	1	2
McDonald	.969	24	19	43	2	1
Mondou	.968	13	6	24	1	2
Neuse	.972	13	9	26	1	5
Simoneit	1.000	1	0	1	0	1
Smith	1.000	7	6	7	0	1

Shortstop	PCT	G	PO	A	E	DP
Allen	.987	39	44	112	2	16
Jackson	.902	13	13	33	5	9
Lopes	1.000	1	4	8	0	4
Machin	.971	16	21	46	2	6
Mondou	1.000	2	6	4	0	1
Neuse	1.000	3	6	11	0	0
Smith	.969	78	99	218	10	50

Outfield	PCT	G	PO	A	E	DP
Barrera	.961	84	163	8	7	0
Bechina	1.000	5	6	0	0	0
Bolt	.974	21	37	1	1	0
Capel	1.000	8	8	2	0	0
Fernandez	.946	87	157	2	9	1
Garcia	.500	1	1	0	1	0
Jackson	.983	27	54	3	1	0
Kelly	1.000	55	72	0	0	0
Laureano	.944	8	16	1	1	0
Lopes	1.000	26	41	1	0	0
McDonald	.988	40	83	2	1	0
McKinney	.989	43	92	1	1	0
Mondou	1.000	9	11	2	0	0
Pache	.987	41	75	2	1	0
Piscotty	1.000	3	6	0	0	0
Reed	.882	20	26	4	4	1
Schuemann	1.000	1	5	0	0	0
Stevenson	1.000	25	49	3	0	0
Thomas	1.000	5	6	0	0	0

MIDLAND ROCKHOUNDS — DOUBLE-A

TEXAS LEAGUE

Batting	B-T	HT	WT	DOB	AVG	vLH	vRH	G	AB	R	H	2B	3B	HR	RBI	BB	HBP	SH	SF	SO	SB	CS	SLG	OBP
Marty Bechina	R-R	6-0	200	10-31-96	.227	.286	.207	78	273	35	62	13	1	7	30	31	9	0	0	102	7	5	.359	.326
Austin Beck	R-R	6-1	200	11-21-98	.230	.111	.268	21	74	5	17	1	0	1	5	2	0	0	0	27	2	0	.284	.250
Jonah Bride	R-R	5-10	200	12-27-95	.315	.438	.281	19	73	18	23	9	0	4	22	11	1	0	2	11	0	0	.603	.402
Marcos Brito	B-R	6-0	165	3-6-00	.000	--	.000	5	6	1	0	0	0	0	0	0	0	0	0	1	0	0	.000	.000
Chase Calabuig	L-L	5-11	185	12-10-95	.313	.300	.318	110	380	54	119	25	2	6	48	47	5	0	2	56	3	1	.437	.394
Logan Davidson	B-R	6-3	185	12-26-97	.252	.260	.250	111	424	72	107	21	1	14	56	53	3	0	4	134	4	1	.406	.337
Jordan Diaz	R-R	5-10	175	8-13-00	.319	.300	.325	94	379	48	121	26	0	15	58	22	4	0	2	61	0	0	.507	.361
Jeremy Eierman	R-R	6-0	205	9-10-96	.203	.200	.205	72	290	37	59	13	0	14	44	18	1	0	3	104	3	3	.393	.250
Devin Foyle	L-L	6-3	190	11-18-96	.243	.206	.252	54	189	26	46	9	0	2	24	29	4	0	1	38	0	0	.323	.354
Zack Gelof	R-R	6-3	205	10-19-99	.271	.316	.258	87	354	54	96	16	2	13	61	47	0	0	1	110	9	2	.438	.356
Jalen Greer	R-R	6-3	185	7-19-01	.000	--	.000	1	2	0	0	0	0	0	0	0	0	0	0	1	0	0	.000	.000
Michael Guldberg	R-R	6-0	171	6-22-99	.277	.400	.250	52	166	27	46	7	1	0	18	18	3	1	3	35	4	3	.331	.353
Brett Harris	R-R	6-3	208	6-24-98	.286	.276	.289	84	315	51	90	15	2	10	45	31	7	5	2	62	11	5	.441	.361
Hansen Lopez	R-R	5-9	170	7-3-00	.333	.500	.000	1	3	0	1	0	0	0	1	1	0	0	0	0	0	0	.333	.500
Kyle McCann	L-R	6-2	217	12-2-97	.238	.224	.242	98	370	61	88	18	0	20	65	53	6	0	1	144	2	0	.449	.342
Mickey McDonald	L-R	6-2	175	6-2-95	.323	.357	.313	16	62	10	20	4	0	1	6	6	3	2	0	15	4	0	.435	.408
Max Schuemann	R-R	6-1	186	6-11-97	.290	.338	.273	79	290	62	84	13	3	8	39	50	17	6	4	84	23	5	.438	.418
JJ Schwarz	R-R	6-1	205	3-28-96	.304	.300	.305	68	247	31	75	17	0	8	38	37	2	0	4	68	2	1	.470	.393
Shane Selman	R-L	5-11	198	8-30-96	.211	.242	.201	82	270	41	57	13	1	11	41	25	8	0	3	96	2	0	.389	.294
William Simoneit	R-R	6-4	235	10-14-96	.258	.190	.275	64	209	42	54	14	0	5	28	38	7	0	2	59	2	2	.397	.387
Tyler Soderstrom	L-R	6-2	200	11-24-01	.278	.242	.290	36	133	17	37	1	2	8	28	10	1	0	3	33	0	1	.496	.327
Jake Suddleson	R-R	6-3	205	12-30-97	.243	.375	.207	11	37	4	9	1	0	1	5	5	1	0	1	13	0	0	.351	.341
Sahid Valenzuela	B-R	5-9	165	9-16-97	.211	.278	.194	25	90	14	19	4	0	4	11	5	0	0	0	17	0	1	.389	.253

Pitching	B-T	HT	WT	DOB	W	L	ERA	G	GS	CG	SV	IP	H	R	ER	HR	BB	SO	AVG	vLH	vRH	K/9	BB/9
Garrett Acton	L-R	6-2	215	6-15-98	1	3	4.23	19	0	0	6	28	29	16	13	3	14	42	.269	.268	.269	13.66	4.55
Austin Briggs	R-L	6-1	205	10-11-95	3	2	4.26	28	0	0	6	32	33	29	15	4	21	32	.266	.225	.286	9.09	5.97
Wandisson Charles	R-R	6-4	263	9-7-96	2	0	11.43	30	0	0	0	37	57	51	47	6	38	34	.350	.419	.307	8.27	9.24
Chase Cohen	L-R	6-1	183	4-26-97	5	4	3.41	44	1	0	7	58	48	25	22	5	31	67	.227	.263	.207	10.40	4.81
Calvin Coker	R-R	6-3	174	3-6-96	0	0	0.00	1	0	0	0	2	1	0	0	0	0	1	.143	.333	.000	4.50	0.00
Bryce Conley	R-R	6-3	200	8-22-94	2	4	4.50	35	0	0	4	48	59	30	24	3	24	46	.307	.308	.307	8.63	4.50
Jeff Criswell	R-R	6-4	225	3-10-99	2	6	4.21	12	9	0	0	58	61	28	27	6	24	57	.274	.256	.285	8.90	3.75
Jack Cushing	R-R	6-3	195	12-3-96	11	3	3.67	19	19	1	0	110	112	53	45	8	32	95	.257	.272	.245	7.75	2.61
Ryan Cusick	R-R	6-6	235	11-12-99	1	6	7.02	12	9	0	0	41	53	36	32	4	30	43	.319	.310	.324	9.44	6.59
Ty Damron	L-L	6-2	200	7-28-94	6	4	4.11	19	18	0	0	92	102	50	42	13	32	71	.284	.287	.283	6.95	3.13
Michael Danielak	R-R	6-4	215	3-16-94	4	3	3.98	41	1	0	3	75	77	38	33	8	27	63	.266	.250	.279	7.59	3.25
J.T. Ginn	R-R	6-2	200	5-20-99	1	4	6.11	10	10	0	0	35	38	28	24	3	14	41	.264	.339	.207	10.44	3.57
Wander Guante	R-R	6-1	180	6-15-00	0	1	40.50	1	1	0	0	1	7	6	6	2	1	0	.636	.600	.667	0.00	6.75
Charles Hall	R-R	5-10	170	9-6-94	2	2	2.43	23	0	0	3	33	21	14	9	5	26	42	.178	.286	.101	11.34	7.02
Hogan Harris	R-L	6-3	230	12-26-96	1	0	1.67	8	7	0	0	32	15	6	6	0	19	48	.136	.167	.122	13.36	5.29
Nick Highberger	R-R	5-11	200	11-4-93	2	1	6.43	39	0	0	0	56	62	46	40	4	45	50	.279	.264	.290	8.04	7.23
Trayson Kubo	R-R	6-0	180	9-26-97	0	0	1.93	3	0	0	0	5	4	1	1	0	1	7	.250	.273	.200	13.50	1.93
David Leal	L-L	6-5	250	4-22-97	4	6	4.84	20	19	0	0	115	138	66	62	12	14	77	.297	.278	.303	6.01	1.09
Aiden McIntyre	R-R	6-5	220	8-27-95	0	0	18.00	1	0	0	0	1	2	2	2	0	2	0	.400	1.000	.250	0.00	18.00
Luis Medina	R-R	6-1	175	5-3-99	1	4	11.76	7	7	0	0	21	35	28	27	3	22	26	.389	.370	.409	11.32	9.58
Matt Milburn	R-R	6-3	210	7-29-93	3	8	6.07	29	12	0	0	99	130	76	67	14	31	70	.321	.362	.286	6.34	2.81
Colin Peluse	R-R	6-3	230	6-11-98	10	6	5.38	23	21	0	1	119	133	78	71	17	28	92	.278	.286	.272	6.98	2.12

Chester Pimentel	R-R	6-5	210	11-12-95	2	0	4.82	23	0	0	2	28	30	15	15	2	27	40	.265	.239	.284	12.86	8.68
Zack Plunkett	R-R	6-2	225	2-16-96	2	1	3.91	17	0	0	0	25	25	17	11	5	7	20	.253	.256	.250	7.11	2.49
2-team total (6 Tulsa Drillers)					3	2	7.07	23	0	0	0	36	44	35	28	10	10	25	.297	.304	.293	6.31	2.52
Dalton Sawyer	L-L	6-5	210	11-22-93	0	0	3.09	8	0	0	0	12	8	6	4	2	8	12	.211	.214	.208	9.26	6.17
Shane Selman	R-L	5-11	198	8-30-96	0	0	27.00	3	0	0	0	3	8	9	9	1	6	1	.500	.800	.364	3.00	18.00
William Simoneit	R-R	6-4	235	10-14-96	0	1	27.00	1	0	0	0	1	2	4	3	1	2	0	.667	--	.667	0.00	18.00
Trey Supak	R-R	6-5	268	5-31-96	0	0	1.59	3	3	0	0	6	3	1	1	0	5	8	.158	.375	.000	12.71	7.94
Jack Weisenburger	R-R	6-3	220	10-8-97	1	0	4.82	8	0	0	3	9	6	5	5	2	3	11	.176	.250	.136	10.61	2.89
Brock Whittlesey	R-R	6-3	210	2-27-97	0	2	12.46	8	0	0	0	13	24	19	18	3	5	7	.400	.379	.419	4.85	3.46

Fielding

Catcher	PCT	G	PO	A	E	DP	PB
Bride	.987	10	74	1	1	0	2
Lopez	1.000	1	8	1	0	0	0
McCann	.995	48	391	25	2	2	7
Schwarz	1.000	28	220	15	0	3	1
Simoneit	.983	37	321	26	6	3	0
Soderstrom	.991	16	107	4	1	1	1

First Base	PCT	G	PO	A	E	DP
Calabuig	1.000	15	70	4	0	2
Diaz	.983	41	278	15	5	29
McCann	.990	38	270	17	3	29
Schwarz	1.000	11	75	3	0	8
Simoneit	.995	23	190	15	1	26
Soderstrom	.991	17	106	8	1	14

Second Base	PCT	G	PO	A	E	DP
Bechina	1.000	13	24	30	0	9
Bride	.750	1	2	1	1	1
Brito	1.000	2	2	5	0	0
Davidson	.000	1	0	0	0	0
Eierman	.989	18	33	56	1	12
Gelof	.979	53	109	122	5	37
Greer	1.000	1	1	3	0	1
Harris	.966	17	43	41	3	9
Schuemann	.964	24	48	59	4	12
Valenzuela	.978	13	16	29	1	7

Third Base	PCT	G	PO	A	E	DP
Bride	1.000	2	0	5	0	2
Davidson	.887	21	8	39	6	4
Diaz	.818	7	2	7	2	1
Eierman	.942	16	10	39	3	3
Gelof	.922	26	13	34	4	1
Harris	.975	66	42	114	4	15
McCann	.000	1	0	0	1	0
McDonald	1.000	1	0	1	0	0
Schuemann	1.000	1	1	3	0	0

Shortstop	PCT	G	PO	A	E	DP
Bechina	.964	5	9	18	1	3
Davidson	.959	86	134	216	15	57
Eierman	.949	37	55	111	9	17
Schuemann	.919	11	9	25	3	6

Outfield	PCT	G	PO	A	E	DP
Bechina	.977	59	124	2	3	1
Beck	1.000	19	42	1	0	0
Brito	--	1	0	0	0	0
Calabuig	.980	94	189	3	4	1
Diaz	.500	2	1	0	1	0
Foyle	1.000	45	87	4	0	2
Gelof	1.000	1	4	0	0	0
Guldberg	1.000	50	130	3	0	0
McDonald	.963	14	25	1	1	0
Schuemann	.975	42	77	2	2	0
Selman	.994	79	163	10	1	3
Suddleson	1.000	6	9	0	0	0
Valenzuela	1.000	12	14	1	0	0

LANSING LUGNUTS — *HIGH CLASS A*

MIDWEST LEAGUE

Batting	B-T	HT	WT	DOB	AVG	vLH	vRH	G	AB	R	H	2B	3B	HR	RBI	BB	HBP	SH	SF	SO	SB	CS	SLG	OBP
Euribiel Angeles	R-R	5-11	175	5-11-02	.278	.301	.269	97	363	29	101	19	1	2	32	17	4	2	2	58	8	6	.353	.316
Lazaro Armenteros	R-R	6-0	182	5-22-99	.261	.271	.256	56	165	29	43	6	0	10	26	29	2	1	1	86	13	4	.479	.376
Marty Bechina	R-R	6-0	200	10-31-96	.267	.250	.273	13	45	9	12	2	2	0	5	8	3	0	0	15	0	0	.400	.411
Austin Beck	R-R	6-1	200	11-21-98	.247	.424	.195	43	146	23	36	3	0	8	25	15	1	0	5	36	1	0	.432	.311
Cooper Bowman	R-R	6-0	205	1-25-00	.209	.238	.202	33	115	12	24	2	0	3	12	9	4	0	1	38	12	0	.304	.287
Marcos Brito	B-R	6-0	165	3-6-00	.176	.250	.111	6	17	3	3	0	0	0	1	2	1	0	0	9	2	0	.176	.300
Brayan Buelvas	R-R	5-11	155	6-8-02	.195	.213	.190	69	236	28	46	14	1	7	26	17	6	0	1	57	7	4	.352	.265
Jonny Butler	L-R	6-1	200	2-12-99	.244	.083	.284	37	119	16	29	8	1	2	21	15	0	0	2	33	4	0	.378	.324
Lawrence Butler	L-R	6-3	210	7-10-00	.270	.205	.295	81	293	52	79	19	3	11	41	40	0	0	0	105	13	5	.468	.357
Alexander Campos	R-R	6-0	178	2-20-00	.304	.389	.275	23	69	14	21	2	0	2	9	14	0	0	0	18	1	0	.420	.422
Denzel Clarke	R-R	6-5	220	5-1-00	.209	.122	.233	51	187	30	39	9	2	8	21	28	2	0	1	79	16	1	.406	.317
Matt Cross	R-R	6-1	205	7-28-98	.180	.191	.174	43	133	17	24	4	1	6	19	13	1	0	4	53	0	0	.361	.252
Brett Harris	R-R	6-3	208	6-24-98	.304	.385	.276	29	102	22	31	7	0	7	18	19	1	0	1	21	0	0	.578	.415
Hansen Lopez	R-R	5-9	170	7-3-00	.146	.000	.167	14	41	2	6	0	0	0	5	4	0	0	0	17	0	0	.146	.222
Gabriel Maciel	B-R	5-10	185	1-10-99	.275	.227	.301	62	211	31	58	11	3	1	16	23	4	4	0	34	7	2	.370	.357
Patrick McColl	L-R	6-6	215	6-22-97	.194	.179	.198	73	211	25	41	7	2	2	15	28	2	1	1	74	1	0	.275	.293
Jared McDonald	R-R	6-2	180	12-5-96	.232	.224	.235	84	298	34	69	15	0	9	41	28	6	1	5	106	1	2	.372	.306
Shane McGuire	L-R	6-0	195	4-12-99	.236	.176	.247	33	110	16	26	5	1	1	13	26	4	0	2	18	2	0	.327	.394
Max Muncy	R-R	6-1	180	8-25-02	.226	.250	.221	42	168	19	38	12	2	3	19	18	2	0	2	60	13	1	.375	.305
Kevin Richards	R-R	6-2	160	1-8-00	.176	.050	.229	22	68	6	12	3	1	1	8	3	2	0	2	21	1	1	.294	.227
Tyler Soderstrom	L-R	6-2	200	11-24-01	.260	.210	.283	89	335	47	87	19	3	20	71	29	4	0	3	99	0	0	.513	.323
Drew Swift	R-R	6-0	165	2-15-99	.253	.197	.280	59	221	38	56	8	1	1	16	30	4	0	1	61	21	2	.312	.352
Sahid Valenzuela	B-R	5-9	165	9-16-97	.197	.258	.182	49	152	16	30	6	0	0	11	11	2	2	0	39	1	2	.237	.261
Jack Winkler	R-R	6-2	185	11-4-98	.267	.304	.248	60	206	31	55	9	1	4	25	22	6	0	0	37	4	2	.379	.355
Joshwan Wright	R-R	5-8	170	11-9-00	.274	.286	.270	81	274	30	75	13	4	1	22	17	2	1	2	46	5	3	.361	.319

Pitching	B-T	HT	WT	DOB	W	L	ERA	G	GS	CG	SV	IP	H	R	ER	HR	BB	SO	AVG	vLH	vRH	K/9	BB/9
Edward Baram	R-R	6-3	205	6-2-97	1	1	7.58	15	0	0	0	19	19	21	16	3	20	10	.260	.211	.314	4.74	9.47
Blake Beers	R-R	6-4	215	7-15-98	0	4	4.08	10	10	0	0	53	50	26	24	4	24	49	.243	.233	.252	8.32	4.08
Osvaldo Berrios	R-R	6-2	200	11-29-99	5	8	6.17	27	11	0	3	93	103	69	64	16	33	79	.270	.279	.259	7.62	3.18
Calvin Coker	R-R	6-3	174	3-6-96	1	0	3.00	12	0	0	3	18	21	7	6	2	7	17	.280	.231	.306	8.50	3.50
Jeff Criswell	R-R	6-4	225	3-10-99	2	3	3.78	10	10	1	0	50	37	24	21	7	18	58	.206	.247	.168	10.44	3.24
T.J. Czyz	R-R	6-2	175	9-12-00	1	0	3.38	4	0	0	0	5	4	2	2	0	4	7	.211	.000	.308	11.81	6.75
Micah Dallas	R-R	6-2	215	4-14-00	0	0	1.35	4	0	0	0	7	2	1	1	1	0	8	.095	.000	.154	10.80	0.00
Joe DeMers	R-R	6-1	240	11-9-96	3	3	5.68	28	0	0	0	52	66	36	33	4	12	33	.320	.351	.295	5.68	2.06
Stevie Emanuels	R-R	6-5	210	1-30-99	3	8	6.62	17	12	0	0	69	90	57	51	11	45	73	.310	.333	.287	9.48	5.84
Joey Estes	R-R	6-2	190	10-8-01	3	7	4.55	20	20	0	0	91	86	47	46	17	30	92	.250	.247	.253	9.10	2.97
Christian Fernandez	R-R	6-2	170	8-11-99	0	3	6.91	8	6	0	0	29	31	22	22	4	17	26	.274	.220	.317	8.16	5.34
James Gonzalez	L-L	6-2	257	9-15-00	0	0	11.88	5	1	0	0	8	13	11	11	1	6	5	.351	.294	.400	5.40	6.48

Diego Granado	R-R	6-1	200	1-13-97	1	2	6.08	27	1	0	0	40	50	33	27	2	26	40	.299	.313	.287	9.00	5.85
Charles Hall	R-R	5-10	170	9-6-94	0	0	12.00	3	0	0	0	3	3	4	4	0	0	4	.231	.200	.250	12.00	0.00
Hogan Harris	R-L	6-3	230	12-26-96	0	1	1.38	7	7	0	0	13	5	4	2	0	7	18	.114	.154	.097	12.46	4.85
Grant Holman	R-R	6-6	250	5-31-00	1	4	4.66	9	7	0	0	37	38	20	19	2	5	35	.262	.271	.253	8.59	1.23
Angello Infante	R-R	6-1	180	4-16-99	4	2	4.29	39	0	0	6	50	55	30	24	3	24	42	.279	.237	.317	7.51	4.29
Jorge Juan	R-R	6-8	200	3-6-99	0	0	4.86	6	4	0	0	17	10	9	9	3	8	20	.169	.150	.179	10.80	4.32
Trayson Kubo	R-R	6-0	180	9-26-97	4	4	4.44	36	0	0	10	47	38	25	23	4	33	54	.218	.260	.188	10.41	6.36
Mac Lardner	R-L	6-4	195	12-29-97	2	4	4.55	19	8	0	0	57	62	35	29	8	21	58	.270	.284	.263	9.10	3.30
David Leal	L-L	6-5	250	4-22-97	2	1	2.08	5	2	0	0	22	12	6	5	2	3	27	.158	.160	.157	11.22	1.25
Daniel Martinez	L-R	5-11	190	7-28-98	1	4	9.00	30	1	0	0	39	49	41	39	12	27	35	.310	.309	.312	8.08	6.23
Patrick McColl	L-R	6-6	215	6-22-97	0	0	14.21	6	0	0	0	6	13	11	10	3	1	0	.419	.267	.563	0.00	1.42
Mason Miller	R-R	6-5	200	8-24-98	0	1	3.86	3	3	0	0	7	3	3	3	1	2	13	.125	.000	.188	16.71	2.57
Kumar Nambiar	L-L	5-11	188	4-17-98	6	5	5.55	43	0	0	0	60	49	41	37	5	32	62	.228	.263	.209	9.30	4.80
Jack Owen	L-L	6-2	204	5-26-98	6	1	3.35	11	9	1	0	51	43	21	19	3	14	44	.224	.261	.203	7.76	2.47
Shohei Tomioka	R-R	6-0	190	2-29-96	0	4	7.32	21	2	0	2	36	49	32	29	6	19	29	.333	.262	.384	7.32	4.79
Kyle Virbitsky	R-R	6-7	235	10-8-98	2	3	4.31	7	7	0	0	40	35	20	19	9	10	41	.236	.246	.230	9.30	2.27
Jake Walkinshaw	R-R	6-3	200	7-7-96	3	1	3.83	9	8	0	0	40	37	18	17	5	11	43	.242	.271	.223	9.68	2.48
Jacob Watters	R-R	6-4	230	3-3-01	0	0	0.00	2	2	0	0	3	1	1	0	0	3	2	.091	.333	.000	6.00	9.00
Brock Whittlesey	R-R	6-3	210	2-27-97	3	2	2.90	33	0	0	3	50	54	24	16	5	19	30	.276	.368	.217	5.44	3.44
Joshwan Wright	R-R	5-8	170	11-9-00	0	1	27.00	1	0	0	0	1	4	4	3	0	1	0	.667	.667	.667	0.00	9.00

Fielding

Catcher	PCT	G	PO	A	E	DP	PB
Cross	.981	31	232	23	5	3	5
Lopez	.975	11	67	12	2	0	1
McDonald	.992	48	361	26	3	3	5
McGuire	.989	17	162	16	2	2	0
Soderstrom	.996	31	230	17	1	1	5

First Base	PCT	G	PO	A	E	DP
Butler	.987	11	68	6	1	8
Cross	.979	13	80	14	2	8
McColl	.987	50	362	22	5	29
McDonald	1.000	10	69	4	0	2
McGuire	.974	10	72	4	2	4
Soderstrom	.993	39	273	10	2	30
Winkler	.944	2	17	0	1	2

Second Base	PCT	G	PO	A	E	DP
Angeles	.980	34	55	95	3	19
Bowman	.976	24	27	54	2	6
Brito	1.000	2	2	4	0	2
Campos	1.000	3	3	12	0	1
Harris	1.000	4	5	7	0	2
Swift	1.000	24	51	50	0	15
Valenzuela	.970	28	38	58	3	15
Wright	.986	21	24	46	1	10

Third Base	PCT	G	PO	A	E	DP
Angeles	.923	5	5	7	1	1
Bechina	.889	4	2	6	1	1
Bowman	.500	1	0	1	1	0
Campos	.875	19	12	23	5	3
Harris	.911	23	24	27	5	6
Valenzuela	.842	15	12	20	6	2
Winkler	.955	39	32	53	4	5
Wright	.898	32	31	48	9	7

Shortstop	PCT	G	PO	A	E	DP
Angeles	.969	49	53	101	5	16
Bowman	1.000	6	10	14	0	3
Muncy	.947	35	48	76	7	10
Swift	.966	31	43	70	4	17
Winkler	.904	12	18	29	5	7

Outfield	PCT	G	PO	A	E	DP
Armenteros	.988	45	83	0	1	0
Bechina	1.000	8	15	0	0	0
Beck	1.000	34	64	6	0	2
Brito	.889	5	8	0	1	0
Buelvas	.977	65	127	2	3	1
Butler	1.000	30	55	1	0	1
Butler	.974	58	100	11	3	3
Clarke	.993	48	143	0	1	0
Maciel	.983	60	117	0	2	0
McColl	1.000	13	19	1	0	0
Richards	1.000	24	24	1	0	0
Valenzuela	1.000	3	5	0	0	0
Winkler	1.000	3	3	0	0	0
Wright	.977	28	42	1	1	1

STOCKTON PORTS — *LOW CLASS A*

CALIFORNIA LEAGUE

Batting	B-T	HT	WT	DOB	AVG	vLH	vRH	G	AB	R	H	2B	3B	HR	RBI	BB	HBP	SH	SF	SO	SB	CS	SLG	OBP
Wilson Alvarez	R-R	5-10	155	5-19-98	.235	.222	.238	18	51	4	12	3	0	0	6	6	0	4	1	16	1	0	.294	.310
Danny Bautista	R-R	6-2	185	9-20-00	.264	.354	.232	99	367	48	97	24	2	5	37	34	13	7	2	72	10	8	.381	.346
Marcos Betancourt	R-R	6-0	165	1-17-01	.133	.333	.083	5	15	0	2	1	0	0	2	0	0	0	0	8	0	0	.200	.133
Jonah Bride	R-R	5-10	200	12-27-95	.250	.000	.273	3	12	2	3	0	0	0	0	2	0	0	0	2	0	0	.250	.357
Marcos Brito	B-R	6-0	165	3-6-00	.208	.188	.213	27	96	16	20	1	1	2	8	20	2	2	0	47	2	0	.302	.356
Nick Brueser	R-L	6-3	212	9-29-98	.160	.188	.151	56	187	17	30	6	0	6	19	30	6	1	1	88	1	1	.289	.295
Alexander Campos	R-R	6-0	178	2-20-00	.250	.154	.282	32	104	15	26	3	1	1	14	19	4	0	3	28	3	1	.327	.377
Denzel Clarke	R-R	6-5	220	5-1-00	.295	.297	.294	42	156	37	46	14	2	7	26	28	7	0	2	56	14	2	.545	.420
Jalen Greer	R-R	6-3	185	7-19-01	.160	.273	.130	50	156	9	25	4	0	1	6	16	1	1	0	80	7	0	.205	.243
Ramon Laureano	R-R	5-11	203	7-15-94	.250	.500	.200	3	12	0	3	0	0	0	0	0	0	0	0	3	0	0	.250	.250
Luis Marinez	R-R	6-1	155	10-11-01	.250	.000	1.000	1	4	1	1	0	0	0	1	1	0	0	0	2	0	0	.250	.400
Ramon Martinez	R-R	6-0	170	11-17-01	.163	.133	.176	16	49	4	8	1	0	0	1	5	0	0	1	26	1	1	.184	.236
Cameron Masterman	R-R	6-2	225	5-5-99	.231	.304	.206	24	91	14	21	6	0	2	13	8	1	0	1	36	0	1	.363	.297
Shane McGuire	L-R	6-0	195	4-12-99	.290	.316	.283	50	176	20	51	7	2	1	21	32	6	0	2	42	4	2	.369	.412
Brennan Milone	R-R	6-1	198	5-6-01	.310	.286	.316	27	100	13	31	4	0	1	8	14	1	0	0	21	1	0	.380	.400
Jose Mujica	R-R	6-0	164	3-28-01	.091	.000	.167	3	11	0	1	0	0	0	0	1	0	0	0	5	0	0	.091	.167
Max Muncy	R-R	6-1	180	8-25-02	.230	.211	.236	81	304	50	70	16	1	16	51	51	7	1	2	109	6	5	.447	.352
Jhoan Paulino	R-R	6-1	176	6-11-01	.222	.250	.214	91	320	36	71	18	0	8	38	21	3	1	6	105	1	2	.353	.271
Junior Perez	R-R	6-1	165	7-4-01	.249	.209	.260	116	398	74	99	21	2	15	62	70	5	2	7	148	32	7	.425	.363
Pedro Pineda	R-R	6-1	170	9-6-03	.188	.167	.192	42	144	22	27	3	3	4	13	17	8	1	1	77	5	1	.333	.306
Robert Puason	R-R	6-3	165	9-11-02	.185	.109	.208	55	200	25	37	8	0	2	18	13	3	0	2	77	5	4	.255	.243
Mariano Ricciardi	L-R	5-7	170	6-29-98	.241	.263	.233	52	158	23	38	5	0	1	11	26	0	1	1	40	2	5	.291	.346
Kevin Richards	R-R	6-2	160	1-8-00	.256	.250	.258	56	219	33	56	9	2	10	34	19	3	0	2	55	3	2	.452	.321
CJ Rodriguez	R-R	5-10	200	7-7-00	.266	.340	.246	73	241	32	64	11	0	3	34	44	4	0	6	56	0	1	.349	.380
Dereck Salom	R-R	5-10	135	2-22-01	.226	.235	.224	23	84	8	19	3	0	0	8	9	2	1	1	13	1	2	.262	.313
T.J. Schofield-Sam	L-R	6-1	185	6-20-01	.259	.300	.249	109	409	51	106	23	3	6	55	22	18	0	5	79	8	5	.374	.322
Tommy Stevenson	R-R	6-4	225	9-13-00	.239	.238	.239	23	92	9	22	6	0	2	11	7	0	0	0	38	0	0	.370	.293
Daniel Susac	R-R	6-4	218	5-14-01	.286	.227	.303	25	98	14	28	7	0	1	13	7	2	0	0	25	0	0	.388	.346

Caeden Trenkle	L-L	5-10	179	6-29-01	.304	.360	.289	27	115	20	35	3	3	1	15	11	1	1	2	31	5	3	.409	.364
Cooper Uhl	R-R	5-10	185	10-19-97	.167	.050	.190	47	120	12	20	3	0	2	12	20	9	3	0	45	0	1	.242	.329

Pitching	B-T	HT	WT	DOB	W	L	ERA	G	GS	CG	SV	IP	H	R	ER	HR	BB	SO	AVG	vLH	vRH	K/9	BB/9
Mark Adamiak	R-R	6-4	230	12-15-00	0	0	13.50	1	0	0	0	2	5	3	3	0	1	3	.500	.600	.400	13.50	4.50
Wilson Alvarez	R-R	5-10	155	5-19-98	0	0	3.60	4	0	0	0	5	2	2	2	0	2	5	.125	.000	.154	9.00	3.60
Luke Anderson	R-R	6-2	205	8-5-98	8	7	5.81	27	13	0	0	96	118	75	62	17	58	111	.295	.260	.317	10.41	5.44
Edward Baram	R-R	6-3	205	6-2-97	0	1	6.11	14	0	0	1	18	16	15	12	2	11	19	.232	.161	.289	9.68	5.60
Tyler Baum	R-R	6-2	193	1-14-98	1	1	18.75	25	0	0	0	24	34	55	50	2	46	29	.327	.250	.368	10.88	17.25
Danny Bautista	R-R	6-2	185	9-20-00	0	0	9.00	1	0	0	0	1	2	1	1	0	0	0	.500	1.000	.333	0.00	0.00
Blake Beers	R-R	6-4	215	7-15-98	2	2	4.08	7	6	0	0	40	38	19	18	7	7	51	.250	.292	.231	11.57	1.59
Hunter Breault	R-R	6-2	228	6-12-99	2	6	3.72	44	0	0	10	58	69	43	24	9	17	64	.288	.356	.248	9.93	2.64
Serafino Brito	R-R	6-0	200	4-28-97	1	3	2.84	21	0	0	2	25	19	13	8	3	9	39	.194	.216	.180	13.86	3.20
Luis Carrasco	R-R	6-1	180	12-19-01	0	0	13.50	2	0	0	0	1	5	3	2	0	0	2	.417	.750	.250	13.50	0.00
Alexis Cedano	R-R	6-0	180	11-12-97	0	1	12.39	17	0	0	1	20	36	33	28	6	12	21	.364	.481	.319	9.30	5.31
Aaron Cohn	R-R	6-0	195	10-30-98	3	4	4.95	41	0	0	2	56	71	38	31	10	17	43	.300	.333	.282	6.87	2.72
Calvin Coker	R-R	6-3	174	3-6-96	1	0	1.76	11	0	0	2	15	18	7	3	1	2	16	.265	.219	.306	9.39	1.17
Clark Cota	R-R	6-2	230	10-6-96	2	2	5.96	37	0	0	2	48	53	34	32	10	28	44	.277	.257	.289	8.19	5.21
Jose Dicochea	R-R	6-3	180	3-21-01	0	2	15.88	3	3	0	0	6	10	10	10	0	9	7	.370	.545	.250	11.12	14.29
Stevie Emanuels	R-R	6-5	210	1-30-99	0	3	5.79	6	3	0	1	28	30	20	18	5	17	32	.275	.341	.235	10.29	5.46
Dheygler Gimenez	R-R	6-2	170	12-3-01	1	6	5.51	12	8	0	0	47	55	47	29	11	30	57	.284	.313	.261	10.84	5.70
James Gonzalez	L-L	6-2	257	9-15-00	1	7	5.48	17	14	0	1	71	71	50	43	11	30	71	.260	.304	.249	9.04	3.82
Carlos Guarate	R-R	6-2	178	3-30-01	2	2	13.20	7	3	0	0	15	30	22	22	5	4	10	.405	.474	.382	6.00	2.40
Gunnar Hoglund	L-R	6-4	220	12-17-99	0	0	0.00	1	1	0	0	3	3	1	0	0	1	1	.250	.333	.222	3.00	3.00
Brent Honeywell Jr.	R-R	6-2	195	3-31-95	0	0	3.00	2	2	0	0	3	4	1	1	0	1	3	.333	.250	.375	9.00	3.00
Cole Irvin	L-L	6-4	217	1-31-94	1	0	1.80	1	1	0	0	5	5	1	1	1	0	6	.250	--	.250	10.80	0.00
Garrett Irvin	L-L	6-0	185	2-18-99	0	0	2.25	6	0	0	0	8	7	2	2	0	3	13	.233	.125	.273	14.63	3.38
Grant Judkins	L-R	6-3	200	8-6-97	3	4	5.43	15	13	0	0	66	72	44	40	12	35	66	.271	.272	.270	8.95	4.75
James Kaprielian	R-R	6-3	225	3-2-94	1	0	3.60	1	1	0	0	5	3	2	2	2	0	6	.167	.000	.214	10.80	0.00
Nolan Long	R-R	6-10	255	1-19-94	0	1	8.10	8	0	0	0	7	4	6	6	0	8	7	.160	.091	.214	9.45	10.80
Mitch Myers	R-R	6-2	200	1-8-99	4	10	5.50	23	22	0	0	124	143	83	76	26	38	98	.285	.286	.285	7.09	2.75
Jack Owen	L-L	6-2	204	5-26-98	3	4	3.41	23	1	0	3	37	35	20	14	5	9	48	.245	.188	.261	11.68	2.19
Jack Perkins	R-R	6-1	220	12-26-99	0	0	2.00	5	1	0	0	9	5	3	2	0	2	11	.161	.182	.150	11.00	2.00
Jake Pfennigs	R-R	6-7	215	9-9-99	0	0	11.12	5	0	0	0	6	13	9	7	0	3	6	.448	.333	.529	9.53	4.76
Blaze Pontes	R-R	6-0	185	1-6-00	0	0	12.00	4	0	0	0	6	9	8	8	1	2	3	.321	.125	.400	4.50	3.00
Mariano Ricciardi	L-R	5-7	170	6-29-98	0	0	11.57	2	0	0	0	2	3	3	3	0	2	2	.300	.333	.286	7.71	7.71
Yehizon Sanchez	R-R	6-2	170	11-16-00	2	8	5.75	22	16	0	0	92	107	71	59	22	38	77	.290	.319	.273	7.51	3.70
Skylar Szynski	L-R	6-2	195	7-14-97	2	1	10.47	26	0	0	0	33	44	42	38	9	36	22	.319	.348	.304	6.06	9.92
Lou Trivino	R-R	6-5	235	10-1-91	0	1	45.00	1	1	0	0	1	5	5	5	1	0	2	.625	.750	.500	18.00	0.00
Cooper Uhl	R-R	5-10	185	10-19-97	0	0	14.54	4	0	0	0	4	6	7	7	0	6	5	.353	.250	.385	10.38	12.46
Robin Vazquez	R-R	6-2	187	4-15-98	0	3	8.76	37	0	0	1	50	78	55	49	8	33	45	.350	.391	.331	8.05	5.90
Kyle Virbitsky	R-R	6-7	235	10-8-98	5	4	4.78	16	15	0	0	87	101	53	46	9	20	99	.285	.279	.289	10.28	2.08
Tyler Watson	R-L	6-6	240	5-22-97	0	0	0.00	1	0	0	0	1	1	2	0	0	1	0	.200	--	.200	0.00	9.00
Chen Zhong-Ao Zhuang	R-R	6-1	190	8-25-00	0	4	4.71	8	8	0	0	42	46	35	22	9	9	43	.267	.288	.255	9.21	1.93

Fielding

Catcher	PCT	G	PO	A	E	DP	PB
Betancourt	1.000	3	29	0	0	0	0
Marinez	1.000	1	9	1	0	1	0
McGuire	.984	29	222	17	4	1	5
Mujica	1.000	3	27	6	0	1	0
Rodriguez	.991	55	480	49	5	6	14
Susac	.960	11	87	9	4	0	3
Uhl	.982	42	348	24	7	2	5

First Base	PCT	G	PO	A	E	DP
Brueser	.987	39	283	29	4	19
McGuire	.986	17	125	20	2	8
Paulino	.992	18	120	12	1	9
Richards	1.000	1	1	0	0	1
Schofield-Sam	.974	39	286	16	8	22
Stevenson	.994	22	156	11	1	15
Uhl	1.000	1	0	1	0	0

Second Base	PCT	G	PO	A	E	DP
Alvarez	.905	16	21	36	6	6
Brito	.955	9	10	11	1	5
Campos	.947	12	12	24	2	7
Greer	.963	12	22	30	2	3
Milone	.944	27	55	63	7	17
Muncy	1.000	2	0	4	0	0
Paulino	.000	1	0	0	0	0
Puason	.951	44	60	94	8	17
Ricciardi	.961	25	32	41	3	8

Third Base	PCT	G	PO	A	E	DP
Bride	1.000	2	1	2	0	0
Campos	.889	9	5	11	2	3
Greer	.800	13	4	16	5	1
Paulino	.891	61	36	86	15	4
Schofield-Sam	.901	55	43	94	15	6

Shortstop	PCT	G	PO	A	E	DP
Brito	.957	7	11	11	1	4
Campos	.828	11	5	19	5	4
Greer	.935	9	14	15	2	1
Muncy	.920	77	100	187	25	32
Puason	.800	11	13	15	7	3
Salom	.928	23	21	56	6	12
Schofield-Sam	.875	3	3	4	1	1

Outfield	PCT	G	PO	A	E	DP
Bautista	.971	98	163	5	5	1
Brito	.923	10	11	1	1	0
Brueser	.944	15	17	0	1	0
Clarke	.989	40	91	2	1	0
Greer	.964	15	27	0	1	0
Laureano	1.000	1	1	0	0	0
Martinez	.938	16	29	1	2	0
Masterman	1.000	16	29	1	0	0
Perez	.964	114	233	10	9	2
Pineda	.967	40	56	2	2	1
Richards	.952	35	58	1	3	0
Schofield-Sam	1.000	4	5	0	0	0
Trenkle	1.000	27	56	2	0	0
Vazquez	--	2	0	0	0	0

ACL ATHLETICS — *ROOKIE*

ARIZONA COMPLEX LEAGUE

Batting	B-T	HT	WT	DOB	AVG	vLH	vRH	G	AB	R	H	2B	3B	HR	RBI	BB	HBP	SH	SF	SO	SB	CS	SLG	OBP
Wilson Alvarez	R-R	5-10	155	5-19-98	.208	.250	.200	9	24	4	5	0	0	0	7	5	1	0	2	8	1	0	.208	.344
Carlos Amaya	R-R	5-10	165	12-28-01	.250	.389	.223	38	112	15	28	9	1	3	17	12	1	0	2	31	2	1	.429	.323
Angel Arevalo	R-R	5-11	160	10-2-03	.229	.222	.230	29	70	11	16	4	0	0	10	14	0	2	1	25	1	2	.286	.353
Austin Beck	R-R	6-1	200	11-21-98	.417	.000	.455	4	12	1	5	1	0	0	0	1	1	0	0	4	0	0	.500	.500

Nelson Beltran	R-R	5-10	160	12-28-01	.269	.360	.245	38	119	33	32	7	2	3	16	16	9	0	0	43	7	2	.437	.396
Marcos Betancourt	R-R	6-0	165	1-17-01	.176	.200	.167	7	17	2	3	2	0	0	3	1	1	0	0	4	0	0	.294	.263
Henry Bolte	R-R	6-3	195	8-4-03	.212	.000	.233	11	33	5	7	0	0	0	2	5	1	0	0	19	0	1	.212	.333
Jose Bonilla	R-R	6-3	180	2-20-01	.000	.000	.000	1	2	0	0	0	0	0	0	0	0	0	0	2	0	0	.000	.000
Marcos Brito	B-R	6-0	165	3-6-00	.267	.250	.273	5	15	2	4	1	0	0	3	5	0	0	0	7	0	1	.333	.450
Brayan Buelvas	R-R	5-11	155	6-8-02	.261	.333	.235	7	23	4	6	1	1	1	4	4	2	0	1	6	4	0	.522	.400
Lawrence Butler	L-R	6-3	210	7-10-00	.111	--	.111	3	9	0	1	0	0	0	0	0	0	0	0	4	0	0	.111	.111
Alexander Campos	R-R	6-0	178	2-20-00	.545	.400	.667	5	11	3	6	1	0	0	2	3	0	0	0	3	1	1	.636	.643
Bjay Cooke	R-R	6-2	187	3-14-03	.256	.429	.219	12	39	7	10	2	4	0	5	6	3	0	0	16	2	0	.513	.396
Cristopher Cruz	R-R	6-0	180	3-28-02	.167	.133	.172	37	102	13	17	3	0	4	16	15	0	0	1	46	1	1	.314	.271
Jasmed Diaz	L-L	6-0	175	4-16-03	.156	.000	.206	20	45	7	7	2	0	0	1	10	1	0	0	32	0	2	.200	.321
Clark Elliott	L-R	6-0	183	9-29-00	.000	--	.000	1	1	1	0	0	0	0	0	1	0	0	0	0	0	0	.000	.500
Jose Escorche	R-R	5-10	145	4-29-02	.278	.333	.267	5	18	4	5	0	0	0	0	1	0	0	0	2	5	0	.278	.316
Devin Foyle	L-L	6-3	190	11-18-96	.000	.000	.000	1	3	0	0	0	0	0	0	1	0	0	0	2	0	0	.000	.250
Carlos Franco	R-R	5-10	150	2-17-03	.236	.067	.270	29	89	11	21	4	1	1	14	10	3	0	0	16	2	0	.337	.333
Luis Freitez	R-R	6-0	180	5-17-03	.218	.154	.231	32	78	9	17	3	0	0	6	8	0	0	0	28	1	0	.256	.291
Jalen Greer	R-R	6-3	185	7-19-01	.182	.000	.250	7	22	5	4	0	0	0	0	2	1	0	0	11	0	0	.182	.280
Yeniel Laboy	L-R	6-3	196	5-11-04	.156	.000	.172	12	32	4	5	0	0	0	2	4	0	0	0	10	2	0	.156	.250
Hansen Lopez	R-R	5-9	170	7-3-00	.412	.500	.385	6	17	6	7	2	0	1	4	3	0	0	0	8	0	0	.706	.500
Davonn Mackey	R-R	6-2	170	10-10-00	.083	.000	.091	9	12	2	1	1	0	0	0	3	0	0	0	7	0	0	.167	.267
Lester Madden	R-R	6-2	190	1-19-99	.130	.333	.100	8	23	3	3	1	0	0	0	2	0	0	0	6	0	0	.174	.200
Luis Marinez	R-R	6-1	155	10-11-01	.136	.143	.135	23	59	11	8	0	1	3	8	16	4	0	1	22	1	1	.322	.350
Ramon Martinez	R-R	6-0	170	11-17-01	.154	.111	.167	14	39	2	6	2	0	0	2	3	2	0	2	21	0	1	.205	.239
Cameron Masterman	R-R	6-2	225	5-5-99	.000	--	.000	2	4	0	0	0	0	0	1	0	0	0	1	4	0	0	.000	.000
Brennan Milone	R-R	6-1	198	5-6-01	.500	1.000	.333	2	4	2	2	1	0	0	1	1	0	0	1	1	0	0	.750	.500
Darlyn Montero	B-R	6-2	170	5-11-02	.241	.130	.262	47	145	25	35	6	2	2	23	15	3	0	1	38	8	2	.352	.323
Jose Mujica	R-R	6-0	164	3-28-01	.283	.053	.333	33	106	16	30	5	1	4	22	9	2	0	1	22	0	0	.462	.347
Pedro Pineda	R-R	6-1	170	9-6-03	.000	--	.000	1	3	0	0	0	0	0	0	0	0	0	0	3	0	0	.000	.000
Robert Puason	R-R	6-3	165	9-11-02	.260	.280	.255	38	127	22	33	6	2	1	9	11	1	0	2	44	6	1	.362	.319
Jorge Romero	R-R	6-2	185	5-30-00	.000	.000	.000	5	10	0	0	0	0	0	0	2	0	0	0	8	0	0	.000	.167
Jamaliel Rosado Jr.	R-R	6-3	195	8-15-03	.182	.000	.200	5	11	1	2	0	0	1	2	1	0	0	0	8	0	0	.455	.250
Dereck Salom	R-R	5-10	135	2-22-01	.221	.235	.218	30	95	10	21	1	2	0	7	10	1	3	1	17	1	2	.274	.299
Saul Sanchez	B-R	5-11	160	1-5-01	.000	--	.000	1	2	1	0	0	0	0	0	0	0	0	0	0	0	0	.000	.000
Tommy Stevenson	R-R	6-4	225	9-13-00	.000	.000	.000	2	5	1	0	0	0	0	0	0	1	0	0	4	0	0	.000	.167
Daniel Susac	R-R	6-4	218	5-14-01	.500	.000	.600	2	6	1	3	1	0	0	2	0	0	0	0	0	0	0	.667	.500
Cody Thomas	L-R	6-4	211	10-8-94	.188	.000	.200	6	16	0	3	1	0	0	2	3	0	0	1	4	0	0	.250	.300
Caeden Trenkle	L-L	5-10	179	6-29-01	.333	--	.333	2	6	1	2	0	0	0	1	0	0	0	0	3	0	0	.333	.333

Pitching	**B-T**	**HT**	**WT**	**DOB**	**W**	**L**	**ERA**	**G**	**GS**	**CG**	**SV**	**IP**	**H**	**R**	**ER**	**HR**	**BB**	**SO**	**AVG**	**vLH**	**vRH**	**K/9**	**BB/9**
Mark Adamiak	R-R	6-4	230	12-15-00	0	1	19.29	3	1	0	0	2	2	5	5	0	3	1	.222	.286	.000	3.86	11.57
Wilson Alvarez	R-R	5-10	155	5-19-98	0	0	0.00	1	0	0	0	1	3	0	0	0	0	1	.429	.750	.000	6.75	0.00
Tyler Baum	R-R	6-2	195	1-14-98	0	0	3.00	2	0	0	1	3	0	1	1	0	1	3	.000	.000	.000	9.00	3.00
Marcos Betancourt	R-R	6-0	165	1-17-01	0	0	9.00	1	0	0	0	1	3	1	1	0	0	0	.600	.500	1.000	0.00	0.00
Reid Birlingmair	L-R	5-10	210	11-13-96	0	1	10.80	2	1	0	0	3	7	4	4	1	0	6	.438	.500	.400	16.20	0.00
Marshall Cantillo	R-R	6-1	183	3-28-01	0	0	21.00	3	0	0	0	3	7	7	7	0	2	2	.500	.167	.750	6.00	6.00
Luis Carrasco	R-R	6-1	180	12-19-01	3	1	1.82	7	2	0	0	25	24	5	5	2	8	18	.264	.309	.194	6.57	2.92
Alexis Cedano	R-R	6-0	180	11-12-97	0	0	4.91	4	0	0	0	4	4	2	2	0	1	2	.308	.300	.333	4.91	2.45
Odue Civada	R-R	6-1	165	4-5-02	0	0	7.16	11	0	0	2	16	23	13	13	2	9	13	.343	.410	.250	7.16	4.96
Ryan Cusick	R-R	6-6	235	11-12-99	0	0	9.00	1	1	0	0	2	3	2	2	0	0	3	.333	.250	1.000	13.50	0.00
T.J. Czyz	R-R	6-2	175	9-12-00	0	0	0.00	2	0	0	0	2	1	0	0	0	2	5	.125	.250	.000	19.29	7.71
Micah Dallas	R-R	6-2	215	4-14-00	0	0	9.00	2	1	0	0	2	3	2	2	0	0	2	.333	.286	.500	9.00	0.00
Dairon De Jesus	R-R	6-3	180	3-27-04	3	1	4.15	10	1	0	1	13	13	9	6	0	7	17	.265	.297	.167	11.77	4.85
Willy De Paula	R-R	6-2	180	4-1-02	0	3	11.37	13	0	0	1	13	17	21	16	0	16	13	.321	.273	.355	9.24	11.37
Jose Dicochea	R-R	6-3	180	3-21-01	1	0	0.00	2	1	0	0	4	2	0	0	0	3	3	.167	.222	.000	7.36	7.36
Luis Florentino	R-R	6-2	190	3-13-00	0	5	5.40	17	0	0	0	22	19	19	13	4	11	30	.226	.324	.149	12.46	4.57
Jake Garland	R-R	6-5	236	9-26-00	0	1	12.00	3	1	0	0	3	4	6	4	0	1	4	.250	.182	.400	12.00	3.00
Roberto Garza	R-R	6-2	175	6-22-02	0	1	3.00	10	0	0	1	15	6	6	5	0	11	20	.122	.107	.143	12.00	6.60
Dheygler Gimenez	R-R	6-2	170	12-3-01	1	1	5.00	3	1	0	0	9	7	5	5	0	1	5	.219	.250	.200	5.00	1.00
J.T. Ginn	R-R	6-2	200	5-20-99	0	0	0.00	2	2	0	0	7	4	1	0	0	0	5	.167	.111	.333	6.43	0.00
Adriel Gonzalez	R-R	6-2	145	4-28-02	1	2	4.31	10	6	0	0	31	34	24	15	2	11	31	.262	.254	.270	8.90	3.16
Jose Gonzalez	R-R	6-0	160	1-5-02	2	4	9.87	14	0	0	0	17	26	21	19	3	6	20	.347	.353	.341	10.38	3.12
Wander Guante	R-R	6-1	180	6-15-00	3	2	4.91	11	3	0	1	44	47	26	24	2	15	44	.278	.303	.258	9.00	3.07
Charles Hall	R-R	5-10	170	9-6-94	0	0	0.00	2	0	0	0	4	2	0	0	0	0	8	.143	.000	.182	18.00	0.00
Moises Hernandez	R-R	0-0	0	2-20-04	0	0	9.22	16	1	0	2	14	12	18	14	0	28	19	.235	.190	.267	12.51	18.44
Gunnar Hoglund	L-R	6-4	220	12-17-99	0	1	0.00	2	2	0	0	5	4	1	0	0	0	7	.200	.273	.111	12.60	0.00
Grant Holman	R-R	6-6	250	5-31-00	0	1	5.40	2	2	0	0	5	5	3	3	1	2	5	.263	.273	.250	9.00	3.60
Garrett Irvin	L-L	6-0	185	2-18-99	0	0	0.00	3	1	0	0	4	2	0	0	0	1	5	.143	.000	.333	11.25	2.25
Jorge Juan	R-R	6-8	200	3-6-99	1	0	0.00	2	0	0	0	4	1	0	0	0	1	8	.077	.111	.000	18.00	2.25
Rafael Kelly	R-R	6-2	190	6-9-97	0	1	27.00	2	2	0	0	2	10	8	7	1	1	4	.556	.500	.600	15.43	3.86
Nolan Long	R-R	6-10	255	1-19-94	0	0	2.08	5	1	0	0	4	3	2	1	0	1	5	.176	.200	.143	10.38	2.08
Ramon Martinez	R-R	6-0	170	11-17-01	0	1	--	1	0	0	0	0	2	4	3	1	1	0	1.000	1.000	1.000	--	--
Aiden McIntyre	R-R	6-5	220	8-27-95	1	0	6.75	5	3	0	0	7	10	6	5	1	3	10	.333	.182	.421	13.50	4.05
Mason Miller	R-R	6-5	200	8-24-98	0	0	0.00	1	1	0	0	2	0	0	0	0	0	5	.000	.000	.000	22.50	0.00
Jack Perkins	R-R	6-1	220	12-26-99	0	1	9.00	1	1	0	0	1	2	1	1	0	0	3	.400	1.000	.000	27.00	0.00
Jake Pfennigs	R-R	6-7	215	9-9-99	0	1	0.00	2	2	0	0	3	1	3	0	0	2	4	.111	.000	.167	13.50	6.75

Blaze Pontes	R-R	6-0	185	1-6-00	0	0	0.00	2	0	0	0	2	0	0	0	0	0	2	.000	.000	.000	9.00	0.00
Zach Rafuse	R-R	6-0	185	12-3-96	0	0	0.00	3	0	0	0	5	2	0	0	0	0	4	.111	.111	.111	7.20	0.00
Brayan Restituyo	L-L	5-11	160	1-17-02	0	1	4.97	10	4	0	0	25	31	20	14	2	14	31	.301	.244	.339	11.01	4.97
Eduardo Rivera	L-L	6-7	237	6-13-03	0	0	3.29	8	3	0	0	14	15	7	5	0	11	22	.263	.353	.225	14.49	7.24
Roger Rodriguez	R-R	6-1	145	9-11-01	1	4	4.91	12	7	0	0	40	45	28	22	5	14	44	.276	.342	.218	9.82	3.12
Trey Supak	R-R	6-5	268	5-31-96	0	0	0.00	1	0	0	0	2	0	0	0	0	1	0	.000	.000	.000	0.00	4.50
Jake Walkinshaw	R-R	6-3	200	7-7-96	0	0	1.93	2	2	0	0	5	5	1	1	0	1	4	.313	.500	.200	7.71	1.93
Jacob Watters	R-R	6-4	230	3-3-01	0	0	0.00	1	0	0	0	1	0	0	0	0	1	1	.000	.000	.000	9.00	9.00
Brandon Withers	R-R	6-0	200	7-4-94	3	0	4.41	10	1	0	1	16	9	9	8	0	10	16	.158	.240	.094	8.82	5.51

Fielding

C: Amaya 18, Betancourt 6, Franco 13, Lopez 3, Marinez 9, Mujica 11, Susac 2. **1B:** Amaya 11, Cruz 5, Franco 8, Lopez 2, Marinez 9, Montero 8, Mujica 15, Stevenson 2. **2B:** Alvarez 9, Arevalo 23, Beltran 1, Brito 1, Campos 1, Cruz 1, Laboy 1, Milone 2, Puason 8, Salom 15. **3B:** Amaya 1, Arevalo 1, Beltran 3, Campos 1, Cruz 9, Laboy 12, Montero 23, Salom 12, Sanchez 1. **SS:** Arevalo 5, Campos 3, Cooke 7, Escorche 5, Greer 3, Montero 1, Puason 29, Rosado Jr. 2, Salom 6. **OF:** Amaya 2, Beck 3, Beltran 35, Bolte 13, Bonilla 1, Brito 4, Buelvas 5, Butler 2, Cooke 2, Cruz 22, Diaz 12, Elliott 1, Freitez 32, Greer 4, Mackey 9, Madden 9, Martinez 15, Masterman 1, Montero 19, Pineda 1, Romero 5, Salom 1, Thomas 4, Trenkle 2

DSL ATHLETICS — *ROOKIE*

DOMINICAN SUMMER LEAGUE

Batting	B-T	HT	WT	DOB	AVG	vLH	vRH	G	AB	R	H	2B	3B	HR	RBI	BB	HBP	SH	SF	SO	SB	CS	SLG	OBP
Bryan Andrade	R-R	6-1	145	2-3-05	.198	.364	.178	34	101	12	20	2	0	0	12	13	4	1	4	19	1	0	.218	.303
Dayker Baldallo	L-R	5-10	135	11-29-03	.160	.000	.190	32	75	15	12	2	0	0	7	20	1	0	1	22	3	0	.187	.340
Erubiel Fuentes	R-R	5-8	170	1-15-03	.233	.238	.232	34	120	24	28	1	0	0	11	17	5	1	0	13	4	2	.242	.352
Moises Gallardo	R-R	6-0	160	4-23-03	.211	.370	.183	58	180	34	38	13	2	6	35	42	9	0	2	69	3	2	.406	.382
Ray Garrett	R-R	5-10	155	3-23-04	.225	.357	.200	28	89	24	20	4	1	0	9	18	5	0	0	21	2	2	.292	.384
Cesar Gonzalez	R-R	6-2	165	1-13-05	.280	.000	.318	22	50	8	14	1	0	0	8	14	6	0	1	8	1	1	.300	.479
Matheus Lelis	R-R	5-9	160	6-12-02	.165	.231	.156	42	103	17	17	3	0	0	13	15	6	0	0	22	1	0	.194	.306
Anderson Machado	R-R	6-1	170	10-10-03	.257	.348	.240	45	144	16	37	5	1	0	24	15	10	0	1	26	1	1	.306	.365
Beyker Martinez	B-R	6-1	165	3-21-04	.184	.143	.190	25	49	8	9	1	0	0	4	13	1	0	2	19	7	0	.204	.354
German Ortiz	B-R	0-0	0	8-2-04	.249	.360	.230	54	177	36	44	6	3	0	26	40	3	0	4	45	6	0	.316	.388
Carlos Pacheco	R-R	5-10	150	11-1-04	.183	.208	.179	52	164	38	30	3	2	0	19	39	7	0	2	43	19	6	.226	.358
Javier Pariguan	R-R	5-10	160	2-5-04	.179	.286	.143	9	28	5	5	1	0	1	5	2	0	0	1	10	0	0	.321	.226
Elvis Rijo	R-R	5-11	165	11-27-03	.252	.238	.255	43	115	17	29	8	0	0	14	18	8	1	1	19	1	3	.322	.387
Angel Rivera	R-R	5-9	175	2-2-03	.347	.389	.338	33	95	26	33	7	1	3	28	21	7	0	2	17	2	0	.537	.488
Joseph Rodriguez	R-R	6-1	165	1-4-03	.270	.154	.287	34	100	22	27	6	0	0	13	25	1	1	0	30	6	0	.330	.421
Jonatan Yan	R-R	6-0	150	11-1-04	.189	.100	.200	34	95	10	18	3	1	1	12	13	1	0	1	12	5	1	.274	.291

Pitching	B-T	HT	WT	DOB	W	L	ERA	G	GS	CG	SV	IP	H	R	ER	HR	BB	SO	AVG	vLH	vRH	K/9	BB/9
Felix Castro	R-R	6-3	180	2-16-04	0	1	4.33	15	2	0	3	27	18	19	13	1	22	30	.184	.341	.070	10.00	7.33
Derek Corro	L-L	5-11	145	11-19-04	1	6	5.63	10	7	0	0	38	50	33	24	3	21	29	.316	.542	.276	6.81	4.93
Eliazar De Los Santos	R-R	6-4	220	8-15-02	0	1	10.03	9	0	0	0	12	15	17	13	2	11	12	.300	.429	.207	9.26	8.49
Richard Fernandez	R-R	6-1	190	9-22-02	1	2	7.41	7	6	0	0	17	19	20	14	2	6	18	.264	.267	.262	9.53	3.18
Manuel Figuereo	R-R	6-5	190	10-15-03	0	1	8.50	11	0	0	0	18	16	22	17	2	18	11	.242	.211	.255	5.50	9.00
Camilo Hernandez	R-R	6-1	190	9-30-03	3	2	7.04	17	0	0	0	31	39	30	24	3	14	24	.295	.190	.378	7.04	4.11
Jefferson Jean	R-R	6-3	170	1-29-05	0	0	4.91	6	6	0	0	7	5	4	4	0	4	9	.185	.200	.176	11.05	4.91
Elvi Lina	R-R	6-2	200	10-17-04	0	0	2.45	3	0	0	0	4	2	2	1	0	4	4	.200	.400	.000	9.82	9.82
Alejandro Manzano	R-R	6-2	165	2-28-02	1	2	6.57	10	7	0	0	37	46	32	27	4	12	38	.295	.373	.257	9.24	2.92
Manuel Perez	R-R	6-2	180	8-29-05	3	1	3.58	11	7	0	0	38	39	21	15	1	15	29	.260	.288	.238	6.93	3.58
Javier Reina	R-R	6-2	165	9-1-03	0	0	10.80	6	0	0	0	7	6	9	8	2	13	6	.240	.429	.167	8.10	17.55
Sulivan Ribeiro	L-L	6-4	218	12-16-03	1	1	3.52	11	10	0	0	31	20	14	12	0	22	24	.194	.269	.169	7.04	6.46
Franyelson Rodriguez	R-R	6-1	160	5-20-02	3	1	2.57	18	1	0	3	35	36	13	10	1	3	25	.252	.180	.290	6.43	0.77
Gimy Rojas	R-R	6-1	145	10-31-03	0	0	5.40	10	0	0	0	17	15	11	10	1	10	13	.254	.269	.242	7.02	5.40
Reynaldo Saa	R-R	6-1	175	12-25-04	5	2	1.37	16	2	0	0	26	11	12	4	1	9	25	.131	.121	.137	8.54	3.08
Carlos Sarmiento	L-L	5-11	145	8-19-03	5	5	3.29	12	9	0	0	52	48	27	19	4	19	48	.244	.256	.241	8.31	3.29
Ramon Vasquez	R-R	5-11	160	12-11-00	0	4	8.02	15	1	0	3	21	24	22	19	4	19	18	.282	.211	.340	7.59	8.02
Gerard Veloz	L-L	6-1	157	11-7-04	3	3	4.15	15	0	0	0	22	12	16	10	0	22	27	.162	.250	.145	11.22	9.14
Wilmi Vizcaino	R-R	6-2	170	5-9-05	0	0	8.56	12	0	0	0	14	13	18	13	0	21	5	.250	.235	.257	3.29	13.83

Fielding

C: Gonzalez 13, Lelis 40, Pariguan 7, Rivera 22. **1B:** Andrade 1, Gonzalez 1, Lelis 5, Machado 34, Ortiz 16, Rivera 7. **2B:** Baldallo 6, Fuentes 18, Garrett 24, Machado 2, Ortiz 4, Rijo 12. **3B:** Andrade 19, Baldallo 2, Fuentes 12, Machado 2, Ortiz 28. **SS:** Andrade 13, Baldallo 24, Fuentes 2, Ortiz 1, Rijo 26. **OF:** Gallardo 45, Garrett 1, Machado 7, Martinez 21, Ortiz 1, Pacheco 48, Rijo 3, Rodriguez 29, Yan 32.

Philadelphia Phillies

SEASON IN A SENTENCE: After a slow start to the season, the Phillies won 87 games to advance to the postseason for the first time since 2011, and eventually made it to the World Series before losing to the Astros in six games.

HIGH POINT: The Phillies bashed five home runs in Game 3 of the World Series to take a 2-1 series lead in the team's first home game in the Fall Classic since 2009.

LOW POINT: The Phillies lost seven of eight games to end the month of May and sat at just 21-29 on the season. Days later the team made the switch from Girardi to Thomson, who won 65 games the rest of the season to take Philadelphia back to the postseason.

NOTABLE ROOKIES: Shortstop Bryson Stott, the team's top hitting prospect heading into the 2022 season, took hold of a starting job at the beginning of June and had a solid showing while displaying above-average defense and adding some timely hits in the postseason. Outfielder Matt Vierling struggled against righthanders but hit .295 against lefthanded pitchers and provided solid defense in the outfield. First baseman Darick Hall hit two home runs in just his second major league game and finished the season with nine in just 42 games, while lefthander Bailey Falter provided a steady presence at the back of the rotation.

KEY TRANSACTIONS: The Phillies signed outfielder Nick Castellanos to a five-year, $100 million deal in the offseason, then made a number of moves at the trade deadline to augment the big league club. The team traded No. 3 prospect Logan O'Hoppe to the Angels for Marsh to upgrade their outfield defense and acquired David Robertson and Noah Syndergaard in subsequent deals.

ON THE FARM: Righthander Andrew Painter announced himself as one of the top pitching prospects in the sport en route to claiming Baseball America's inaugural Minor League Pitcher of the Year Award. Painter rose from Low-A Clearwater to Double-A Reading, where he was joined by a pair of Top 100 Prospects in righthanders Mick Abel and Griff McGarry. Outfielder Johan Rojas provided excellent defense in center field, but struggled offensively before an encouraging stint in the Arizona Fall League. Second baseman Hao Yu Lee made the biggest leap of any player in the system, posting a .799 OPS as a 19-year-old in Low-A and being recognized as the best hitting prospect in the Florida State League by league managers.

OPENING DAY PAYROLL: $224,448,846 (4th).

PLAYERS OF THE YEAR

MAJOR LEAGUE
Aaron Nola
RHP
11-13, 3.25 ERA
235 SO, 29 BB, 205 IP
8.1 SO/BB led MLB

MINOR LEAGUE
Andrew Painter
RHP
(LoA/HiA/AA)
1.56 ERA, 0.89 WHIP
155 SO, 25 BB, 104 IP

ORGANIZATION LEADERS

Batting		*Minimum 250 AB
MAJORS		
* AVG	Bryce Harper	.286
* OPS	Bryce Harper	.877
HR	Kyle Schwarber	46
RBI	Kyle Schwarber	94
MINORS		
* AVG	Yairo Munoz, Lehigh Valley	.311
* OBP	Logan O'Hoppe, Reading	.392
* SLG	Darick Hall, Lehigh Valley	.528
* OPS	Logan O'Hoppe, Reading	.889
R	Johan Rojas, Jersey Shore, Reading	82
H	Johan Rojas, Jersey Shore, Reading	122
TB	Darick Hall, Lehigh Valley	208
2B	Dalton Guthrie, Lehigh Valley	27
3B	Santiago Torres, FCL	8
HR	Darick Hall, Lehigh Valley	28
RBI	Darick Hall, Lehigh Valley	88
BB	Josh Ockimey, Reading, Lehigh Valley	84
SO	Jhailyn Ortiz, Reading	165
SB	Johan Rojas, Jersey Shore, Reading	62

Pitching		#Minimum 75 IP
MAJORS		
W	Zack Wheeler	12
# ERA	Zack Wheeler	2.82
SO	Aaron Nola	235
SV	Corey Knebel	12
MINORS		
W	Mick Abel, Jersey Shore, Reading	8
L	Mick Abel, Jersey Shore, Reading	11
# ERA	Andrew Painter, Clearwater, Jersey Shore, Reading	1.56
G	Brian Marconi, Reading, Lehigh Valley	4.40
GS	Noah Skirrow, Reading, Lehigh Valley	4.36
SV	Brian Marconi, Reading, Lehigh Valley	18
IP	Noah Skirrow, Reading, Lehigh Valley	119.2
BB	Colton Eastman, Reading, Lehigh Valley	66
SO	Andrew Painter, Clearwater, Jersey Shore, Reading	155
# AVG	Ethan Lindow, Reading, Lehigh Valley	.238

2022 PERFORMANCE

General Manager: Sam Fuld. **Farm Director:** Preston Mattingly. **Scouting Director:** Brian Barber.

Class	Team	League	W	L	PCT	Finish	Manager
Majors	Philadelphia Phillies	National	87	75	.537	6th (15)	J. Girardi/ R. Thomson
Triple-A	Lehigh Valley IronPigs	International	76	72	.514	t-7th (20)	Anthony Contreras
Double-A	Reading Fightin Phils	Eastern	61	77	.442	9th (12)	Shawn Williams
High A	Jersey Shore BlueClaws	South Atlantic	51	81	.386	12th (12)	Keith Werman
Low-A	Clearwater Threshers	Florida State	57	71	.445	9th (10)	Marty Malloy
Rookie	FCL Phillies	Florida Complex	26	29	.473	10th (16)	Chris Adamson
Overall 2022 Minor League Record			347	372	0.483	22nd (30)	

ORGANIZATION STATISTICS

PHILADELPHIA PHILLIES

NATIONAL LEAGUE

Batting	B-T	HT	WT	DOB	AVG	vLH	vRH	G	AB	R	H	2B	3B	HR	RBI	BB	HBP	SH	SF	SO	SB	CS	SLG	OBP
Alec Bohm	R-R	6-5	218	8-3-96	.280	.352	.253	152	586	79	164	24	3	13	72	31	4	0	10	110	2	3	.398	.315
Johan Camargo	B-R	6-0	195	12-13-93	.237	.182	.279	52	152	8	36	3	0	3	15	13	0	1	0	37	0	0	.316	.297
Nick Castellanos	R-R	6-4	203	3-4-92	.263	.295	.254	136	524	56	138	27	0	13	62	29	3	0	2	130	7	1	.389	.305
Didi Gregorius	L-R	6-3	205	2-18-90	.210	.164	.226	63	214	17	45	9	4	1	19	13	3	0	2	36	1	0	.304	.263
Dalton Guthrie	R-R	5-11	160	12-23-95	.333	.333	.333	14	21	3	7	0	0	1	5	6	1	0	0	7	1	0	.476	.500
Darick Hall	L-R	6-4	232	7-25-95	.250	.083	.266	42	136	19	34	8	1	9	16	5	1	0	0	44	0	0	.522	.282
Bryce Harper	L-R	6-3	210	10-16-92	.286	.256	.300	99	370	63	106	28	1	18	65	46	3	0	7	87	11	4	.514	.364
Odubel Herrera	L-R	5-11	205	12-29-91	.238	.300	.221	62	185	23	44	9	1	5	21	11	0	0	1	42	6	0	.378	.279
Rhys Hoskins	R-R	6-4	245	3-17-93	.246	.286	.233	156	589	81	145	33	2	30	79	72	6	0	4	169	2	1	.462	.332
Scott Kingery	R-R	5-10	180	4-29-94	--	--	--	1	0	0	0	0	0	0	0	0	0	0	0	0	0	0	--	--
Brandon Marsh	L-R	6-4	215	12-18-97	.288	.174	.312	41	132	15	38	9	2	3	15	6	0	0	0	41	2	2	.455	.319
Nick Maton	L-R	6-2	178	2-18-97	.250	.250	.250	35	72	13	18	2	1	5	17	10	1	0	2	29	0	0	.514	.341
Oscar Mercado	R-R	6-2	197	12-16-94	.000	--	.000	1	1	0	0	0	0	0	0	0	0	0	0	1	0	0	.000	.000
Mickey Moniak	L-R	6-2	195	5-13-98	.130	.000	.150	18	46	4	6	1	0	0	2	3	0	1	0	19	0	0	.152	.184
Yairo Munoz	R-R	5-11	200	1-23-95	.211	.250	.160	29	57	7	12	2	0	3	7	3	0	0	0	10	1	0	.404	.250
Simon Muzziotti	L-L	6-1	175	12-27-98	.143	--	.143	9	7	0	1	0	0	0	0	0	1	1	0	2	0	0	.143	.250
Roman Quinn	B-R	5-10	175	5-14-93	.162	.182	.133	23	37	8	6	1	0	0	3	3	0	0	0	15	4	1	.189	.225
J.T. Realmuto	R-R	6-1	212	3-18-91	.276	.262	.281	139	504	75	139	26	5	22	84	41	12	0	5	119	21	1	.478	.342
Donny Sands	R-R	6-2	190	5-16-96	.000	.000	.000	3	3	0	0	0	0	0	0	1	0	0	0	1	0	0	.000	.250
Kyle Schwarber	L-R	6-0	229	3-5-93	.218	.193	.232	155	577	100	126	21	3	46	94	86	4	0	2	200	10	1	.504	.323
Jean Segura	R-R	5-10	220	3-17-90	.277	.301	.267	98	354	45	98	9	0	10	33	25	7	0	1	58	13	6	.387	.336
Edmundo Sosa	R-R	6-0	210	3-6-96	.315	.419	.174	25	54	9	17	7	1	2	13	1	2	1	1	12	3	0	.593	.345
2-team total (53 St. Louis Cardinals)					.227	.232	.223	78	176	26	40	11	4	2	21	5	7	1	1	50	6	1	.369	.275
Bryson Stott	L-R	6-3	200	10-6-97	.234	.263	.226	127	427	58	100	19	2	10	49	36	1	1	1	89	12	4	.358	.295
Garrett Stubbs	L-R	5-10	170	5-26-93	.264	.333	.244	50	106	19	28	4	1	5	16	14	0	1	0	30	2	0	.462	.350
Matt Vierling	R-R	6-3	205	9-16-96	.246	.295	.217	117	325	41	80	12	2	6	32	23	3	0	6	70	7	4	.351	.297
Bradley Zimmer	L-R	6-4	185	11-27-92	.250	.333	.231	9	16	4	4	1	0	0	0	0	0	0	0	4	0	0	.313	.250

Pitching	B-T	HT	WT	DOB	W	L	ERA	G	GS	CG	SV	IP	H	R	ER	HR	BB	SO	AVG	vLH	vRH	K/9	BB/9
Jose Alvarado	L-L	6-2	245	5-21-95	4	2	3.18	59	0	0	2	51	38	21	18	2	24	81	.203	.237	.188	14.29	4.24
Mark Appel	R-R	6-5	220	7-15-91	0	0	1.74	6	0	0	0	10	9	2	2	0	3	5	.243	.154	.292	4.35	2.61
Andrew Bellatti	R-R	6-1	190	8-5-91	4	4	3.31	59	1	0	2	54	47	25	20	5	25	78	.234	.278	.209	12.92	4.14
Connor Brogdon	R-R	6-6	205	1-29-95	2	2	3.27	47	0	0	2	44	44	16	16	6	11	50	.253	.241	.263	10.23	2.25
Sam Coonrod	R-R	6-1	225	9-22-92	0	0	7.82	12	0	0	0	13	12	12	11	1	7	12	.267	.217	.318	8.53	4.97
Tyler Cyr	R-R	6-1	205	5-5-93	0	0	27.00	1	0	0	0	0	2	1	1	1	0	0	.667	.500	1.000	0.00	0.00
Chris Devenski	R-R	6-3	211	11-13-90	0	0	11.25	3	0	0	0	4	7	5	5	1	0	3	.389	.333	.417	6.75	0.00
2-team total (10 Arizona Diamondbacks)					2	1	8.59	13	0	0	0	15	21	14	14	3	1	12	.339	.316	.349	7.36	0.61
Seranthony Dominguez	R-R	6-1	225	11-25-94	6	5	3.00	54	0	0	9	51	36	18	17	4	22	61	.197	.209	.190	10.76	3.88
Nick Duron	R-R	6-4	190	1-30-96	0	0	0.00	1	0	0	0	1	2	0	0	0	0	1	.500	.000	.667	9.00	0.00
Zach Eflin	R-R	6-6	220	4-8-94	3	5	4.04	20	13	0	1	76	70	38	34	8	15	65	.241	.277	.209	7.73	1.78
Bailey Falter	R-L	6-4	175	4-24-97	6	4	3.86	20	16	0	0	84	85	39	36	16	17	74	.263	.229	.273	7.93	1.82
Jeurys Familia	R-R	6-3	240	10-10-89	1	1	6.09	38	0	0	0	34	48	26	23	6	15	33	.338	.333	.341	8.74	3.97
Kyle Gibson	R-R	6-6	215	10-23-87	10	8	5.05	31	31	0	0	168	176	98	94	24	48	144	.268	.260	.274	7.73	2.58
Darick Hall	L-R	6-4	232	7-25-95	0	0	0.00	1	0	0	0	0	1	0	0	0	0	0	.500	1.000	.000	0.00	0.00
Brad Hand	L-L	6-3	224	3-20-90	3	2	2.80	55	0	0	5	45	37	18	14	2	23	38	.223	.217	.226	7.60	4.60
Damon Jones	L-L	6-5	233	9-30-94	0	0	9.64	4	0	0	0	5	4	5	5	0	5	5	.222	.200	.231	9.64	9.64
Michael Kelly	R-R	6-4	185	9-6-92	0	0	2.25	4	0	0	0	4	3	1	1	1	1	4	.214	.333	.125	9.00	2.25
Corey Knebel	R-R	6-3	224	11-26-91	3	5	3.43	46	0	0	12	45	33	22	17	4	28	41	.202	.163	.241	8.26	5.64
Nick Maton	L-R	6-2	178	2-18-97	0	0	20.25	2	0	0	0	1	4	3	3	0	0	0	.500	.750	.250	0.00	0.00
Francisco Morales	R-R	6-4	185	10-27-99	0	0	7.20	3	0	0	1	5	2	5	4	1	6	3	.143	.200	.111	5.40	10.80
Nick Nelson	R-R	6-1	205	12-5-95	3	2	4.85	47	2	0	1	69	66	38	37	1	36	69	.257	.256	.258	9.04	4.72
Vinny Nittoli	R-R	6-1	210	11-11-90	0	0	0.00	2	0	0	0	2	0	0	0	0	1	1	.000	.000	.000	4.50	4.50
Aaron Nola	R-R	6-2	200	6-4-93	11	13	3.25	32	32	2	0	205	168	75	74	19	29	235	.219	.200	.237	10.32	1.27

James Norwood	R-R	6-2	215	12-24-93	1	0	8.31	20	0	0	0	17	24	17	16	2	9	22	.316	.378	.256	11.42	4.67
Michael Plassmeyer	L-L	6-2	197	11-5-96	0	1	3.68	2	0	0	0	7	9	3	3	1	1	7	.321	.500	.308	8.59	1.23
David Robertson	R-R	5-11	195	4-9-85	1	3	2.70	22	0	0	6	23	16	8	7	2	16	30	.193	.194	.191	11.57	6.17
2-team total (36 Chicago Cubs)					4	3	2.40	58	0	0	20	64	39	18	17	6	35	81	.173	.168	.179	11.45	4.95
JoJo Romero	L-L	5-11	200	9-9-96	0	0	13.50	2	0	0	0	2	4	3	3	1	1	1	.444	.000	.500	4.50	4.50
2-team total (15 St. Louis Cardinals)					0	0	4.96	17	0	0	0	16	13	9	9	3	10	17	.232	.118	.282	9.37	5.51
Bubby Rossman	B-R	6-5	220	6-29-92	0	0	18.00	1	0	0	0	1	1	2	2	1	1	1	.250	--	.250	9.00	9.00
Cristopher Sanchez	L-L	6-1	165	12-12-96	2	2	5.63	15	3	0	1	40	38	25	25	5	17	35	.244	.277	.229	7.88	3.83
Garrett Stubbs	L-R	5-10	170	5-26-93	0	0	17.18	4	0	0	0	4	7	7	7	3	1	1	.412	.333	.455	2.45	2.45
Ranger Suarez	L-L	6-1	217	8-26-95	10	7	3.65	29	29	0	0	155	149	74	63	15	58	129	.249	.197	.263	7.47	3.36
Noah Syndergaard	L-R	6-6	242	8-29-92	5	2	4.12	10	9	1	0	55	63	26	25	5	9	31	.290	.292	.289	5.10	1.48
Zack Wheeler	L-R	6-4	195	5-30-90	12	7	2.82	26	26	0	0	153	125	52	48	13	34	163	.221	.201	.240	9.59	2.00

Fielding

Catcher	PCT	G	PO	A	E	DP	PB
Realmuto	.993	133	1151	49	8	11	2
Sands	1.000	1	1	0	0	0	0
Stubbs	.990	41	285	10	3	1	3

First Base	PCT	G	PO	A	E	DP
Bohm	1.000	10	54	1	0	1
Camargo	1.000	5	17	1	0	6
Hall	1.000	7	40	2	0	5
Hoskins	.990	151	1098	103	12	103
Realmuto	.857	3	6	0	1	0
Vierling	1.000	2	1	0	0	0

Second Base	PCT	G	PO	A	E	DP
Camargo	1.000	9	13	11	0	4
Guthrie	1.000	1	1	1	0	1
Kingery	.000	1	0	0	0	0
Maton	1.000	10	11	20	0	5
Munoz	1.000	14	12	22	0	7
Segura	.990	97	168	216	4	57
Stott	1.000	47	63	106	0	26
Vierling	1.000	4	2	8	0	1

Third Base	PCT	G	PO	A	E	DP
Bohm	.962	135	92	241	13	22
Camargo	.974	13	10	27	1	4
Guthrie	1.000	1	0	3	0	1
Maton	1.000	2	1	4	0	0
Munoz	1.000	8	5	8	0	0
Sosa	1.000	11	9	24	0	1
Stott	.857	2	1	5	1	0
Vierling	.923	5	3	9	1	1

Shortstop	PCT	G	PO	A	E	DP
Camargo	1.000	26	33	48	0	9
Gregorius	.991	61	70	140	2	29
Maton	1.000	2	0	5	0	1
Segura	1.000	1	0	1	0	0
Sosa	.968	8	15	15	1	3
Stott	.975	83	95	183	7	35

Outfield	PCT	G	PO	A	E	DP
Castellanos	1.000	124	222	8	0	3
Guthrie	1.000	12	14	0	0	0
Harper	1.000	8	14	0	0	0
Herrera	.993	66	131	4	1	0
Marsh	1.000	40	80	0	0	0
Maton	1.000	20	25	2	0	0
Mercado	--	1	0	0	0	0
Moniak	1.000	18	36	0	0	0
Munoz	.667	3	2	0	1	0
Muzziotti	.909	8	9	1	1	0
Quinn	.966	23	26	2	1	0
Schwarber	.995	139	182	3	1	0
Sosa	1.000	2	1	0	0	0
Stubbs	--	1	0	0	0	0
Vierling	1.000	128	182	2	0	1
Zimmer	.933	9	14	0	1	0

LEHIGH VALLEY IRONPIGS — *TRIPLE-A*

INTERNATIONAL LEAGUE

Batting	B-T	HT	WT	DOB	AVG	vLH	vRH	G	AB	R	H	2B	3B	HR	RBI	BB	HBP	SH	SF	SO	SB	CS	SLG	OBP
John Andreoli	R-R	6-1	218	6-9-90	.154	.200	.135	36	104	15	16	3	1	2	11	29	0	2	1	49	6	1	.260	.336
2-team total (74 St. Paul Saints)					.184	.169	.188	110	337	60	62	11	2	15	43	78	1	3	2	150	19	3	.362	.337
Jorge Bonifacio	R-R	6-1	220	6-4-93	.240	.224	.246	112	383	44	92	17	1	15	57	47	10	0	4	125	8	2	.407	.336
Edgar Cabral	R-R	5-11	210	9-12-95	.149	.200	.130	24	74	6	11	1	0	2	7	10	0	0	0	25	2	0	.243	.250
Johan Camargo	B-R	6-0	195	12-13-93	.213	.205	.216	41	141	19	30	6	0	2	23	21	1	0	4	25	0	0	.298	.311
Ali Castillo	R-R	5-9	180	6-19-89	.275	.288	.269	61	182	25	50	10	0	0	17	21	0	0	1	23	7	1	.330	.348
Jack Conley	R-R	6-1	190	1-16-97	.125	.167	.100	5	16	1	2	0	0	0	2	2	0	1	0	8	1	0	.125	.222
Karl Ellison	R-R	6-1	195	5-23-95	.056	.143	.000	8	18	1	1	0	0	0	0	4	0	0	0	6	0	0	.056	.227
Freddy Francisco	R-R	5-11	180	2-7-01	.000	--	.000	2	2	0	0	0	0	0	0	0	0	0	0	2	0	0	.000	.000
Vito Friscia	R-R	6-3	225	12-19-96	.063	.000	.067	6	16	1	1	0	0	0	0	2	0	0	0	7	0	0	.063	.167
Sal Gozzo	B-R	6-0	196	3-29-98	.000	.000	--	2	3	0	0	0	0	0	0	1	0	0	0	1	0	0	.000	.250
Didi Gregorius	L-R	6-3	205	2-18-90	.200	.333	.111	5	15	3	3	0	0	1	2	1	1	0	1	1	0	0	.400	.278
Dalton Guthrie	R-R	5-11	160	12-23-95	.302	.267	.318	92	338	64	102	27	1	10	52	24	9	2	1	73	21	6	.476	.363
Darick Hall	L-R	6-4	232	7-25-95	.254	.184	.286	101	394	59	100	24	0	28	88	42	4	0	3	100	6	1	.528	.330
Bryce Harper	L-R	6-3	210	10-16-92	.625	1.000	.571	2	8	3	5	2	0	2	6	2	0	0	0	1	0	1	1.625	.700
Odubel Herrera	L-R	5-11	205	12-29-91	.154	.000	.222	3	13	1	2	1	0	0	1	0	0	0	0	1	0	0	.231	.154
Herbert Iser	L-R	6-3	210	12-14-97	.286	--	.286	3	7	0	2	0	0	0	0	1	0	0	0	2	0	0	.286	.375
Scott Kingery	R-R	5-10	180	4-29-94	.230	.244	.224	95	305	51	70	14	4	7	34	54	2	4	1	108	18	2	.370	.348
Drew Maggi	R-R	6-0	192	5-16-89	.209	.200	.213	66	196	27	41	8	0	0	14	35	6	3	1	54	14	5	.250	.345
2-team total (28 Indianapolis Indians)					.212	.207	.215	94	292	43	62	16	1	0	22	40	9	3	2	84	22	5	.274	.324
Rafael Marchan	B-R	5-9	170	2-25-99	.233	.268	.217	66	232	26	54	17	0	4	29	20	9	0	2	24	1	0	.358	.316
Hunter Markwardt	L-L	6-1	185	8-22-97	--	--	--	1	0	1	0	0	0	0	0	0	0	0	0	0	0	0	--	--
Brandon Marsh	L-R	6-4	215	12-18-97	.429	.000	.600	2	7	3	3	0	0	0	3	1	0	0	0	1	2	0	.429	.500
Nick Maton	L-R	6-2	178	2-18-97	.261	.224	.278	57	211	33	55	20	1	5	35	34	3	0	2	55	3	1	.436	.368
Mickey Moniak	L-R	6-2	195	5-13-98	.277	.150	.317	20	83	14	23	5	0	5	8	8	0	0	0	22	5	3	.518	.341
Yairo Munoz	R-R	5-11	200	1-23-95	.310	.338	.301	72	277	41	86	15	1	6	37	9	3	2	1	48	13	3	.437	.338
Simon Muzziotti	L-L	6-1	175	12-27-98	.313	.200	.364	5	16	2	5	0	0	0	0	2	0	0	0	3	1	0	.313	.389
Josh Ockimey	L-R	6-1	238	10-18-95	.202	.175	.215	53	178	30	36	8	1	8	27	28	2	0	2	58	1	0	.393	.314
Dustin Peterson	R-R	6-2	210	9-10-94	.244	.276	.233	102	393	49	96	22	2	9	47	40	3	0	1	101	6	2	.379	.318
2-team total (3 Nashville Sounds)					.243	.274	.231	105	400	50	97	23	2	9	47	44	3	0	1	102	6	2	.378	.321
Roman Quinn	B-R	5-10	175	5-14-93	.294	.222	.375	6	17	8	5	3	0	1	2	8	0	0	0	4	0	1	.647	.520
3-team total (1 Durham Bulls, 7 Omaha Storm Chasers)					.295	.200	.345	14	44	15	13	3	0	4	10	15	1	0	1	15	1	1	.636	.475
Daniel Robertson	R-R	5-11	210	3-22-94	.220	.258	.209	41	141	23	31	11	0	5	16	16	3	0	1	40	0	1	.404	.311
2-team total (17 St. Paul Saints)					.209	.326	.177	58	201	31	42	13	0	6	26	23	4	0	1	53	0	1	.363	.301
Donny Sands	R-R	6-2	190	5-16-96	.308	.375	.277	57	201	41	62	9	0	5	34	38	0	0	3	44	1	0	.428	.413
Jean Segura	R-R	5-10	220	3-17-90	.200	.000	.222	8	30	3	6	0	0	0	3	6	0	0	0	6	2	0	.200	.333

Chris Sharpe	R-R	6-1	195	6-6-96	.219	.192	.233	51	155	23	34	11	0	3	23	20	4	0	2	55	8	3	.348	.320
Madison Stokes	R-R	6-2	200	4-25-96	.219	.333	.192	11	32	1	7	1	1	0	3	5	0	0	0	14	6	0	.313	.324
Bryson Stott	L-R	6-3	200	10-6-97	.333	.111	.407	9	36	11	12	2	1	2	7	3	0	0	1	10	2	0	.611	.375
Will Toffey	L-R	6-2	205	12-31-94	.242	.221	.250	97	326	48	79	23	4	9	37	48	7	5	2	121	9	2	.420	.350
Ronald Torreyes	R-R	5-8	155	9-2-92	.171	.214	.143	10	35	5	6	1	0	0	3	3	0	0	0	2	0	0	.200	.237
Matt Vierling	R-R	6-3	205	9-16-96	.271	.286	.266	21	85	15	23	6	2	2	9	10	0	0	0	15	8	2	.459	.347
Justin Williams	L-R	6-1	235	8-20-95	.194	.267	.170	19	62	8	12	3	0	0	9	10	2	0	0	20	0	0	.242	.324
Austin Wynns	R-R	6-0	190	12-10-90	.365	.500	.316	33	104	21	38	5	0	3	20	28	1	0	0	18	1	0	.500	.504

Pitching	B-T	HT	WT	DOB	W	L	ERA	G	GS	CG	SV	IP	H	R	ER	HR	BB	SO	AVG	vLH	vRH	K/9	BB/9
Mike Adams	R-R	5-11	175	9-7-94	0	0	13.50	2	0	0	0	2	3	3	3	1	2	1	.375	.250	.500	4.50	9.00
Jose Alvarado	L-L	6-2	245	5-21-95	1	0	0.00	4	0	0	1	4	1	0	0	0	1	5	.083	.167	.000	11.25	2.25
Mark Appel	R-R	6-5	220	7-15-91	6	0	3.15	31	0	0	5	40	33	17	14	4	17	36	.223	.209	.235	8.10	3.83
Aaron Barrett	R-R	6-3	230	1-2-88	1	1	12.83	15	1	0	0	13	23	20	19	5	8	15	.371	.441	.286	10.13	5.40
Andrew Bellatti	R-R	6-1	190	8-5-91	0	0	0.00	2	0	0	0	1	2	0	0	0	0	3	.400	.333	.500	20.25	0.00
Trevor Bettencourt	R-R	6-0	195	7-21-94	0	0	4.32	8	1	0	0	8	13	5	4	2	3	7	.371	.250	.474	7.56	3.24
Connor Brogdon	R-R	6-6	205	1-29-95	0	1	2.89	10	1	0	2	9	8	3	3	0	6	17	.229	.300	.133	16.39	5.79
Ali Castillo	R-R	5-9	180	6-19-89	0	0	13.50	2	0	0	1	1	2	2	2	1	0	1	.333	.000	.500	6.75	0.00
Sam Coonrod	R-R	6-1	225	9-22-92	1	0	8.00	9	0	0	0	9	12	9	8	1	6	5	.316	.370	.182	5.00	6.00
Hans Crouse	L-R	6-4	180	9-15-98	0	3	13.14	5	5	0	0	12	21	18	18	2	6	13	.375	.414	.333	9.49	4.38
Tyler Cyr	R-R	6-1	205	5-5-93	2	3	2.50	35	0	0	6	36	26	13	10	0	18	37	.202	.169	.241	9.25	4.50
Chris Devenski	R-R	6-3	211	11-13-90	0	0	1.04	9	0	0	0	9	4	1	1	1	3	11	.133	.071	.188	11.42	3.12
Kyle Dohy	L-L	6-2	202	9-17-96	0	0	7.41	19	0	0	0	17	22	17	14	2	15	25	.297	.406	.214	13.24	7.94
Seranthony Dominguez	R-R	6-1	225	11-25-94	0	0	0.00	1	0	0	0	1	0	0	0	0	2	1	.000	.000	.000	9.00	18.00
Nick Duron	R-R	6-4	190	1-30-96	4	7	2.77	52	0	0	7	49	45	21	15	3	29	63	.253	.203	.293	11.65	5.36
James Dykstra	L-R	6-3	207	11-22-90	0	0	5.06	6	1	0	0	5	6	3	3	0	4	4	.273	.231	.333	6.75	6.75
Colton Eastman	R-R	6-3	185	8-22-96	1	7	5.83	16	15	1	0	54	41	36	35	4	44	53	.211	.196	.230	8.83	7.33
Zach Eflin	R-R	6-6	220	4-8-94	0	0	4.50	1	1	0	0	2	1	1	1	1	0	3	.143	.333	.000	13.50	0.00
Kent Emanuel	L-L	6-4	225	6-4-92	2	2	2.37	10	10	0	0	49	47	16	13	4	6	44	.250	.234	.261	8.03	1.09
Bailey Falter	R-L	6-4	175	4-24-97	4	1	1.91	9	9	0	0	47	25	10	10	4	6	49	.157	.214	.112	9.38	1.15
Jace Fry	L-L	6-1	209	7-9-93	1	2	6.75	18	0	0	0	16	17	12	12	2	7	20	.283	.308	.265	11.25	3.94
2-team total (15 Rochester Red Wings)					4	2	5.34	33	0	0	0	30	31	18	18	3	15	40	.270	.298	.250	11.87	4.45
Joe Gatto	R-R	6-3	220	6-14-95	3	0	6.62	28	2	0	0	34	36	27	25	6	33	45	.273	.234	.309	11.91	8.74
Ofreidy Gomez	R-R	6-3	230	7-6-95	0	1	8.49	24	3	0	0	23	28	22	22	3	26	27	.295	.366	.241	10.41	10.03
Jonathan Hennigan	L-L	6-4	193	8-27-94	5	3	3.53	45	2	0	0	59	42	23	23	4	38	55	.205	.207	.203	8.44	5.83
Jakob Hernandez	L-L	6-4	260	5-19-96	3	1	4.22	46	0	0	6	49	38	23	23	10	19	69	.216	.191	.241	12.67	3.49
Damon Jones	L-L	6-5	233	9-30-94	0	1	2.25	4	0	0	0	4	2	1	1	0	2	6	.154	.167	.143	13.50	4.50
Michael Kelly	R-R	6-4	185	9-6-92	2	2	5.29	47	1	0	1	51	56	34	30	8	24	66	.279	.232	.324	11.65	4.24
Drew Maggi	R-R	6-0	192	5-16-89	0	0	0.00	1	0	0	0	1	1	0	0	0	0	0	.333	.000	.500	0.00	0.00
Dillon Maples	R-R	6-2	230	5-9-92	1	0	6.28	19	0	0	0	14	9	12	10	0	22	18	.180	.120	.240	11.30	13.81
Brian Marconi	R-L	6-3	175	5-9-97	0	1	3.95	10	1	0	0	14	15	7	6	2	13	11	.288	.286	.290	7.24	8.56
Michael Mariot	R-R	6-0	190	10-20-88	4	1	4.64	11	11	0	0	52	49	28	27	9	21	36	.246	.241	.253	6.19	3.61
2-team total (7 Toledo Mud Hens)					7	2	4.90	18	15	0	0	79	77	44	43	15	32	56	.257	.264	.250	6.38	3.65
James Marvel	R-R	6-4	215	9-17-93	6	7	6.05	35	9	0	0	94	114	67	63	8	31	62	.306	.347	.248	5.96	2.98
Griff McGarry	R-R	6-2	190	6-8-99	0	2	9.00	7	0	0	0	8	7	8	8	2	9	9	.250	.250	.250	10.13	10.13
Erik Miller	L-L	6-5	240	2-13-98	0	1	7.50	10	0	0	0	12	14	10	10	4	14	18	.280	.273	.286	13.50	10.50
Francisco Morales	R-R	6-4	185	10-27-99	3	3	9.58	22	0	0	2	21	24	23	22	1	28	16	.289	.250	.333	6.97	12.19
Yairo Munoz	R-R	5-11	200	1-23-95	0	0	18.00	1	0	0	0	1	1	2	2	0	2	1	.250	.000	.333	9.00	18.00
Jake Newberry	R-R	6-2	200	11-20-94	1	1	3.46	19	4	0	0	26	22	11	10	1	14	15	.227	.216	.239	5.19	4.85
Vinny Nittoli	R-R	6-1	210	11-11-90	0	0	7.94	5	0	0	0	6	8	5	5	2	0	5	.333	.273	.385	7.94	0.00
3-team total (10 Buffalo Bisons, 22 S./W.-B. RailRiders)					4	1	3.81	37	4	0	2	52	40	23	22	7	14	64	.213	.181	.238	11.08	2.42
Braeden Ogle	L-L	6-2	215	7-30-97	2	2	5.30	36	0	0	1	36	40	21	21	1	21	24	.284	.264	.295	6.06	5.30
Corey Oswalt	R-R	6-5	250	9-3-93	2	2	5.56	11	6	0	0	23	28	14	14	1	10	14	.315	.300	.333	5.56	3.97
Jack Perkins	R-R	6-4	200	8-6-97	0	2	14.85	4	3	0	0	7	11	11	11	1	7	8	.379	.600	.143	10.80	9.45
Michael Plassmeyer	L-L	6-2	197	11-5-96	6	3	2.41	16	16	0	0	82	63	26	22	12	23	82	.211	.194	.219	9.00	2.52
JoJo Romero	L-L	5-11	200	9-9-96	0	0	0.00	5	0	0	0	4	3	0	0	0	0	3	.200	.333	.111	6.75	0.00
2-team total (3 Memphis Redbirds)					0	0	0.00	8	0	0	0	7	4	0	0	0	0	8	.160	.222	.125	10.29	0.00
Bubby Rossman	B-R	6-5	220	6-29-92	3	3	6.04	15	5	0	0	25	29	18	17	2	17	27	.284	.280	.288	9.59	6.04
Cristopher Sanchez	L-L	6-1	165	12-12-96	2	2	3.14	15	14	0	0	57	48	24	20	1	20	58	.226	.224	.228	9.10	3.14
Ricardo Sanchez	L-L	5-10	220	4-11-97	6	4	4.79	21	21	0	0	92	102	55	49	10	34	83	.281	.278	.283	8.12	3.33
2-team total (5 Toledo Mud Hens)					7	5	4.95	26	26	0	0	116	133	71	64	13	41	103	.287	.274	.295	7.97	3.17
Tayler Scott	R-R	6-3	185	6-1-92	0	0	15.00	4	0	0	0	3	7	5	5	0	4	4	.438	.500	.333	12.00	12.00
Matt Seelinger	R-R	6-3	190	4-19-95	0	0	0.00	2	1	0	0	2	1	0	0	0	2	4	.167	.250	.000	21.60	10.80
Ryan Sherriff	L-L	6-1	190	5-25-90	1	0	3.18	11	0	0	0	11	12	4	4	1	6	12	.293	.250	.320	9.53	4.76
Jeff Singer	L-L	6-0	200	9-13-93	2	2	7.04	25	1	0	0	31	34	24	24	8	20	29	.281	.278	.284	8.51	5.87
Noah Skirrow	R-R	6-3	215	7-21-98	0	1	3.00	4	4	0	0	21	14	7	7	3	9	18	.192	.167	.226	7.71	3.86
Andrew Vasquez	L-L	6-6	235	9-14-93	0	0	2.25	4	0	0	0	4	3	2	1	0	1	3	.188	.125	.250	6.75	2.25
2-team total (10 Buffalo Bisons)					2	0	2.40	14	0	0	1	15	6	5	4	0	3	18	.115	.087	.138	10.80	1.80
Zach Warren	L-L	6-5	205	6-9-96	1	0	7.94	26	0	0	0	23	23	20	20	1	26	20	.261	.200	.313	7.94	10.32

Fielding

Catcher	PCT	G	PO	A	E	DP	PB
Cabral	.967	18	138	8	5	0	2
Castillo	.000	1	0	0	0	0	0
Conley	1.000	5	43	4	0	0	0
Ellison	1.000	8	49	4	0	1	1
Friscia	1.000	6	39	2	0	1	1
Marchan	.989	56	498	36	6	3	4
Sands	.987	35	283	16	4	1	5
Wynns	1.000	28	213	17	0	2	4

First Base	PCT	G	PO	A	E	DP
Camargo	.979	6	45	1	1	3

Castillo	1.000	1	1	0	0	0
Hall	.999	99	737	60	1	78
Ockimey	.994	40	310	18	2	35
Sands	1.000	1	6	0	0	0
Toffey	1.000	7	27	1	0	2
Vierling	1.000	1	4	0	0	0

Second Base	PCT	G	PO	A	E	DP
Castillo	.994	45	73	101	1	19
Gozzo	1.000	1	4	3	0	3
Guthrie	1.000	2	4	6	0	2
Kingery	.980	48	69	129	4	35
Maggi	.973	20	25	48	2	11
Maton	1.000	9	11	19	0	6
Munoz	.954	17	28	34	3	7
Segura	.947	5	5	13	1	2
Stott	1.000	1	0	5	0	1
Toffey	.000	1	0	0	0	0
Torreyes	1.000	7	10	14	0	3

Third Base	PCT	G	PO	A	E	DP
Camargo	1.000	10	7	13	0	2
Castillo	1.000	11	1	10	0	0
Guthrie	.000	1	0	0	0	0
Maggi	.906	14	8	21	3	2
Maton	1.000	1	2	1	0	0
Munoz	.957	25	20	46	3	6
Robertson	1.000	13	9	19	0	1
Stokes	1.000	1	1	1	0	0
Stott	1.000	1	0	1	0	0
Toffey	.975	82	56	143	5	22
Torreyes	1.000	1	0	1	0	0

Shortstop	PCT	G	PO	A	E	DP
Camargo	1.000	4	5	2	0	0
Castillo	1.000	1	0	1	0	0
Gregorius	1.000	3	2	4	0	2
Guthrie	.889	2	4	4	1	3
Kingery	.972	39	38	102	4	22
Maggi	.954	15	18	44	3	9
Maton	.966	46	73	100	6	28
Munoz	.933	11	12	30	3	2
Robertson	.969	27	28	66	3	10
Stott	1.000	6	14	20	0	8
Toffey	1.000	1	1	6	0	2
Torreyes	.867	2	2	11	2	2

Outfield	PCT	G	PO	A	E	DP
Andreoli	.965	34	53	2	2	0
Bonifacio	.989	101	171	8	2	4
Castillo	1.000	5	4	0	0	0
Guthrie	.989	85	175	11	2	4
Hall	--	1	0	0	0	0
Herrera	1.000	1	4	0	0	0
Maggi	1.000	10	15	0	0	0
Marsh	1.000	1	2	0	0	0
Moniak	1.000	19	40	0	0	0
Munoz	1.000	11	19	1	0	0
Muzziotti	1.000	4	6	1	0	0
Peterson	.971	95	169	1	5	0
Quinn	1.000	5	16	2	0	0
Rossman	--	1	0	0	0	0
Sharpe	.952	47	78	1	4	0
Stokes	1.000	11	23	1	0	0
Toffey	.938	10	15	0	1	0
Vierling	1.000	20	38	1	0	0
Williams	1.000	15	27	0	0	0

PHILADELPHIA PHILLIES

READING FIGHTIN PHILS — *DOUBLE-A*

EASTERN LEAGUE

Batting	B-T	HT	WT	DOB	AVG	vLH	vRH	G	AB	R	H	2B	3B	HR	RBI	BB	HBP	SH	SF	SO	SB	CS	SLG	OBP
Johan Camargo	B-R	6-0	195	12-13-93	.467	.667	.417	4	15	3	7	1	0	0	3	2	0	0	0	1	0	0	.533	.529
Ali Castillo	R-R	5-9	180	6-19-89	.253	.310	.241	42	170	18	43	4	0	0	12	8	1	0	5	23	3	2	.276	.283
Jack Conley	R-R	6-1	190	1-16-97	.239	.289	.228	74	234	21	56	10	3	6	30	31	5	1	0	63	2	2	.385	.341
Aldrem Corredor	L-L	6-0	202	10-27-95	.244	.322	.231	110	393	56	96	11	0	14	70	53	4	1	4	98	0	0	.379	.337
Carlos De La Cruz	R-R	6-8	210	10-6-99	.278	.320	.270	38	151	21	42	12	1	7	23	8	1	0	2	45	1	0	.510	.315
Colby Fitch	L-R	5-11	215	7-27-95	.000	--	.000	2	5	0	0	0	0	0	1	2	0	0	1	3	0	0	.000	.250
Freddy Francisco	R-R	5-11	180	2-7-01	.333	--	.333	1	3	0	1	1	0	0	1	1	0	0	0	1	0	0	.667	.500
Vito Friscia	R-R	6-3	225	12-19-96	.245	.155	.268	83	282	37	69	16	1	10	39	56	4	0	3	87	0	0	.415	.374
Luis Garcia	B-R	5-11	170	10-1-00	.091	--	.091	6	22	0	2	0	0	0	1	3	0	1	0	11	0	1	.091	.200
2-team total (4 Erie SeaWolves)					.069	.000	.074	10	29	3	2	0	0	0	1	8	0	1	0	14	0	1	.069	.270
Sal Gozzo	B-R	6-0	196	3-29-98	.172	.167	.174	46	145	16	25	8	0	1	12	10	3	4	0	56	1	0	.248	.241
AJ Graffanino	L-R	6-2	170	7-16-97	.208	.000	.234	15	53	8	11	3	1	0	5	3	0	0	1	13	2	0	.302	.246
2-team total (22 Bowie Baysox)					.217	.083	.233	37	115	14	25	3	1	2	11	9	1	0	1	26	5	0	.313	.278
Jonathan Guzman	R-R	6-0	156	8-17-99	.168	.167	.169	119	404	32	68	10	4	3	26	24	3	8	1	110	9	5	.235	.220
Herbert Iser	L-R	6-3	210	12-14-97	.278	.500	.213	23	79	9	22	5	0	2	9	9	1	0	0	19	0	0	.418	.360
Albert Jerez	R-R	6-2	165	5-18-01	.222	.500	.000	3	9	1	2	0	0	0	0	0	1	0	0	2	0	0	.222	.300
Matt Kroon	R-R	6-1	195	12-5-96	.000	.000	.000	2	5	0	0	0	0	0	0	1	0	0	0	3	0	1	.000	.167
Hunter Markwardt	L-L	6-1	185	8-22-97	.151	.105	.164	34	86	9	13	2	1	0	4	5	1	3	0	31	1	2	.198	.207
Freylin Minyety	R-R	5-10	185	10-22-99	.161	.100	.173	20	62	6	10	1	0	0	9	10	2	2	0	12	0	0	.177	.297
Mickey Moniak	L-R	6-2	195	5-13-98	.391	.500	.381	5	23	5	9	1	1	1	6	1	0	0	1	6	0	0	.652	.400
Simon Muzziotti	L-L	6-1	175	12-27-98	.259	.267	.258	38	143	23	37	5	4	5	20	19	0	0	3	31	7	3	.455	.339
Josh Ockimey	L-R	6-1	238	10-18-95	.253	.259	.252	65	217	33	55	13	1	9	28	56	0	0	0	76	2	1	.447	.407
Jhailyn Ortiz	R-R	6-3	215	11-18-98	.237	.236	.237	119	448	67	106	25	2	17	61	43	12	0	2	165	9	2	.415	.319
Logan O'Hoppe	R-R	6-2	185	2-9-00	.275	.333	.260	75	262	48	72	11	1	15	45	41	11	0	2	52	6	2	.496	.392
Wendell Rijo	R-R	5-11	170	9-4-95	.266	.164	.291	94	342	57	91	23	1	12	53	41	7	1	4	85	24	7	.444	.353
Johan Rojas	R-R	6-1	165	8-14-00	.260	.267	.259	60	235	42	61	8	5	4	16	21	5	3	0	44	29	4	.387	.333
Chris Sharpe	R-R	6-1	195	6-6-96	.182	.143	.190	29	77	11	14	4	2	1	8	18	3	0	4	26	1	0	.325	.343
Madison Stokes	R-R	6-2	200	4-25-96	.159	.188	.150	41	132	16	21	7	0	4	10	14	3	2	0	62	0	1	.303	.255
McCarthy Tatum	R-R	6-6	210	5-15-96	.206	.389	.167	28	102	15	21	7	1	5	13	9	1	0	0	30	3	0	.441	.277
Kevin Vicuna	R-R	6-0	140	1-14-98	.272	.175	.294	88	312	37	85	15	5	2	37	17	9	0	3	66	9	7	.372	.326
Ethan Wilson	L-L	6-1	210	11-7-99	.214	.222	.213	18	70	7	15	2	0	1	3	5	2	1	0	21	1	2	.286	.286

Pitching	B-T	HT	WT	DOB	W	L	ERA	G	GS	CG	SV	IP	H	R	ER	HR	BB	SO	AVG	vLH	vRH	K/9	BB/9
Mick Abel	R-R	6-5	190	8-18-01	1	3	3.52	5	5	0	0	23	19	9	9	5	12	27	.224	.225	.222	10.57	4.70
Mike Adams	R-R	5-11	175	9-7-94	7	1	5.28	37	4	0	1	61	68	44	36	10	29	58	.280	.254	.306	8.51	4.26
Aidan Anderson	R-R	6-1	195	6-21-97	0	2	11.57	6	2	0	0	9	15	14	12	3	6	3	.375	.389	.364	2.89	5.79
Andrew Baker	R-R	6-3	190	3-24-00	1	0	0.84	6	0	0	0	11	3	1	1	0	5	11	.094	.111	.087	9.28	4.22
Albertus Barber	R-R	6-2	190	2-18-96	0	0	20.25	3	0	0	0	4	9	9	9	2	3	6	.450	.500	.429	13.50	6.75
Trevor Bettencourt	R-R	6-0	195	7-21-94	1	2	3.32	12	1	0	0	19	18	8	7	4	5	20	.247	.226	.262	9.47	2.37
Tyler Carr	R-R	5-10	175	5-1-96	0	0	6.97	8	0	0	0	10	13	8	8	1	6	4	.310	.360	.235	3.48	5.23
Colton Eastman	R-R	6-3	185	8-22-96	1	3	3.26	9	9	0	0	47	41	20	17	8	22	33	.236	.277	.211	6.32	4.21
Kent Emanuel	L-L	6-4	225	6-4-92	0	1	13.50	1	1	0	0	3	8	4	4	0	1	2	.533	.000	.571	6.75	3.38
Ethan Evanko	L-L	6-4	185	6-7-95	1	2	7.24	5	2	0	0	14	20	12	11	4	3	14	.333	.429	.304	9.22	1.98
Julian Garcia	L-R	6-3	206	5-13-95	0	1	8.86	13	0	0	0	21	22	22	21	6	16	23	.278	.227	.343	9.70	6.75
Ofreidy Gomez	R-R	6-3	230	7-6-95	1	2	1.35	14	0	0	2	20	15	8	3	0	7	28	.205	.133	.256	12.60	3.15
Josh Hendrickson	L-L	6-4	215	9-18-97	0	3	8.84	5	5	0	0	18	23	20	18	3	9	20	.299	.407	.240	9.82	4.42
Nick Lackney	L-L	6-4	210	6-5-97	0	0	18.90	3	0	0	0	3	4	7	7	1	7	3	.267	.222	.333	8.10	18.90
Taylor Lehman	L-L	6-8	240	12-30-95	1	1	3.74	15	4	0	0	22	17	9	9	1	7	25	.210	.179	.226	10.38	2.91

Adam Leverett	L-R	6-4	190	9-19-98	5	8	5.54	29	11	0	0	75	83	49	46	14	28	84	.286	.274	.299	10.13	3.38
Ethan Lindow	R-L	6-3	180	10-15-98	5	3	4.20	19	19	0	0	96	95	47	45	12	23	67	.254	.229	.266	6.26	2.15
Brian Marconi	R-L	6-3	175	5-9-97	4	6	4.53	43	0	0	18	44	42	24	22	4	34	57	.251	.206	.283	11.75	7.01
James McArthur	R-R	6-7	230	12-11-96	2	6	5.05	13	13	0	0	57	66	39	32	10	26	65	.289	.298	.282	10.26	4.11
Griff McGarry	R-R	6-2	190	6-8-99	1	3	2.20	8	7	0	0	33	13	10	8	1	20	39	.123	.125	.121	10.74	5.51
Tyler McKay	R-R	6-6	180	8-18-97	2	4	6.47	25	0	0	0	40	46	32	29	6	15	28	.297	.317	.283	6.25	3.35
Erik Miller	L-L	6-5	240	2-13-98	1	0	2.23	22	7	0	0	36	25	9	9	0	17	44	.198	.213	.190	10.90	4.21
McKinley Moore	R-R	6-6	225	8-24-98	4	5	4.35	39	1	0	0	50	50	33	24	3	26	71	.260	.231	.287	12.87	4.71
Francisco Morales	R-R	6-4	185	10-27-99	2	0	1.48	23	0	0	1	30	9	5	5	0	17	54	.092	.087	.096	16.02	5.04
Matt Osterberg	L-L	6-2	200	4-21-99	0	0	0.00	1	0	0	0	1	1	0	0	0	0	0	.200	.000	.333	0.00	0.00
Andrew Painter	R-R	6-7	215	4-10-03	2	1	2.54	5	5	0	0	28	25	8	8	3	2	37	.238	.115	.358	11.75	0.64
Jack Perkins	R-R	6-4	200	8-6-97	3	3	6.87	24	6	0	0	55	66	44	42	10	26	50	.303	.315	.291	8.18	4.25
Carlo Reyes	R-R	6-0	212	7-4-98	0	2	6.17	8	2	0	0	12	16	9	8	1	6	8	.320	.333	.310	6.17	4.63
JoJo Romero	L-L	5-11	200	9-9-96	0	0	3.00	2	0	0	2	3	5	1	1	0	0	4	.385	.000	.500	12.00	0.00
Austin Ross	R-R	6-1	185	8-16-94	0	1	7.36	10	0	0	0	15	22	13	12	3	8	16	.349	.333	.364	9.82	4.91
Bubby Rossman	B-R	6-5	220	6-29-92	2	2	3.02	29	9	0	1	45	29	18	15	3	25	56	.185	.138	.234	11.28	5.04
Andrew Schultz	R-R	6-4	195	7-31-97	0	0	2.45	14	0	0	0	15	13	6	4	0	14	14	.232	.192	.267	8.59	8.59
Brett Schulze	R-R	6-2	180	11-24-97	0	0	2.84	4	0	0	0	6	5	2	2	1	3	8	.208	.429	.118	11.37	4.26
Matt Seelinger	R-R	6-3	190	4-19-95	3	2	3.47	45	1	0	2	62	51	30	24	6	35	75	.220	.272	.169	10.83	5.05
Ryan Sherriff	L-L	6-1	190	5-25-90	0	0	0.00	1	0	0	0	1	0	0	0	0	0	2	.000	.000	.000	18.00	0.00
Noah Skirrow	R-R	6-3	215	7-21-98	5	8	4.65	21	21	0	0	99	107	58	51	10	32	115	.273	.303	.241	10.49	2.92
Billy Sullivan	R-R	6-2	195	4-16-99	5	1	4.59	44	2	0	2	51	50	29	26	5	36	77	.251	.256	.248	13.59	6.35
Zach Warren	L-L	6-5	205	6-9-96	0	0	0.00	5	0	0	0	6	4	0	0	0	0	9	.200	.273	.111	14.29	0.00
Braden Zarbnisky	L-R	6-2	191	12-26-96	1	1	4.60	30	1	0	2	43	39	23	22	14	14	53	.239	.225	.250	11.09	2.93

Fielding

Catcher	PCT	G	PO	A	E	DP	PB
Conley	.995	37	348	24	2	2	6
Francisco	1.000	1	7	2	0	0	0
Friscia	.967	24	196	6	7	1	3
Iser	.995	23	189	10	1	2	4
O'Hoppe	.993	58	571	35	4	4	3

First Base	PCT	G	PO	A	E	DP
Corredor	.987	59	376	14	5	48
De La Cruz	.926	4	24	1	2	0
Friscia	1.000	4	26	0	0	2
Ockimey	.993	63	386	26	3	44
Stokes	.980	8	46	3	1	6
Vicuna	1.000	6	40	2	0	2

Second Base	PCT	G	PO	A	E	DP
Castillo	1.000	4	6	12	0	1
Garcia	1.000	2	2	5	0	0
Gozzo	.989	27	33	56	1	7
Graffanino	1.000	1	0	1	0	0
Minyety	1.000	20	23	43	0	11
Rijo	.979	31	67	70	3	27
Stokes	1.000	4	7	9	0	3
Vicuna	.954	53	82	124	10	33

Third Base	PCT	G	PO	A	E	DP
Camargo	.857	3	2	4	1	0
Castillo	.984	31	20	42	1	5
Gozzo	.913	11	11	10	2	1
Graffanino	1.000	9	1	10	0	1
Jerez	.875	3	3	4	1	0
Rijo	.961	50	32	67	4	7
Stokes	.917	5	4	7	1	2
Tatum	.964	27	14	39	2	8
Vicuna	.750	2	1	2	1	0

Shortstop	PCT	G	PO	A	E	DP
Garcia	.947	4	4	14	1	1
Gozzo	1.000	6	10	18	0	5
Graffanino	1.000	2	6	5	0	2
Guzman	.978	118	144	251	9	62
Stokes	.953	11	18	23	2	5

Outfield	PCT	G	PO	A	E	DP
Castillo	1.000	7	15	2	0	1
Conley	.943	39	40	10	3	2
Corredor	1.000	31	44	3	0	1
De La Cruz	.987	30	74	0	1	0
Friscia	1.000	10	15	3	0	1
Kroon	.833	2	5	0	1	0
Markwardt	.979	32	43	4	1	1
Moniak	1.000	5	8	0	0	0
Muzziotti	.989	37	81	5	1	0
Ortiz	.950	104	186	6	10	0
Rojas	.988	58	158	5	2	0
Sharpe	1.000	31	61	0	0	0
Stokes	1.000	17	30	1	0	0
Vicuna	.974	21	36	2	1	0
Wilson	1.000	15	26	1	0	0

JERSEY SHORE BLUECLAWS — *HIGH CLASS A*

SOUTH ATLANTIC LEAGUE

Batting	B-T	HT	WT	DOB	AVG	vLH	vRH	G	AB	R	H	2B	3B	HR	RBI	BB	HBP	SH	SF	SO	SB	CS	SLG	OBP
Jared Carr	L-R	6-1	180	5-24-99	.216	.239	.211	114	371	46	80	13	1	2	19	46	12	2	1	119	16	9	.272	.321
Arturo De Freitas	R-R	6-0	170	5-28-01	.082	.000	.100	21	61	3	5	1	0	0	4	3	1	0	2	25	0	0	.098	.134
Carlos De La Cruz	R-R	6-8	210	10-6-99	.266	.228	.280	64	214	29	57	10	1	10	24	19	7	0	1	75	5	2	.463	.344
Karl Ellison	R-R	6-1	195	5-23-95	.134	.045	.156	39	112	8	15	4	1	1	8	15	0	1	0	42	1	1	.214	.236
Freddy Francisco	R-R	5-11	180	2-7-01	.087	.111	.071	7	23	2	2	1	0	1	1	1	0	0	0	9	0	0	.261	.125
Luis Garcia	B-R	5-11	170	10-1-00	.168	.176	.165	45	155	24	26	4	1	3	10	30	5	2	1	47	4	4	.265	.319
Sal Gozzo	B-R	6-0	196	3-29-98	.220	.400	.194	12	41	4	9	3	0	0	3	3	1	0	0	15	4	0	.293	.289
Herbert Iser	L-R	6-3	210	12-14-97	.274	.261	.278	32	95	6	26	4	0	2	14	13	1	0	1	23	0	1	.379	.364
Hao Yu Lee	R-R	5-10	190	2-3-03	.257	.000	.265	9	35	5	9	3	1	1	2	5	0	0	0	9	3	0	.486	.350
Marcus Lee Sang	L-L	6-0	200	1-2-01	.254	.200	.268	18	71	11	18	2	1	3	7	5	3	0	0	21	1	2	.437	.329
Rafael Marchan	B-R	5-9	170	2-25-99	.231	.000	.375	4	13	1	3	2	0	0	0	2	0	0	0	2	0	0	.385	.333
Casey Martin	R-R	5-11	175	4-7-99	.181	.169	.184	110	398	42	72	21	2	5	33	22	7	1	3	101	17	2	.281	.235
Nick Matera	R-R	6-2	215	8-29-96	.159	.160	.159	47	151	15	24	9	1	3	20	22	2	0	2	61	0	0	.291	.271
Adony Mejia	R-R	5-11	170	6-9-01	.167	.250	.000	2	6	1	1	0	0	1	1	0	0	0	0	3	0	0	.667	.167
Freylin Minyety	R-R	5-10	185	10-22-99	.188	.190	.187	57	181	15	34	2	1	0	11	21	2	2	1	50	2	5	.210	.278
Andrick Nava	B-R	5-11	175	10-6-01	.243	.133	.273	22	70	8	17	4	1	0	8	10	0	0	2	13	1	0	.329	.329
Leandro Pineda	L-L	6-1	165	6-4-02	.150	.000	.164	16	60	9	9	3	1	0	5	7	2	0	1	19	0	0	.233	.257
Anthony Quirion	R-R	6-2	205	10-29-97	.134	.154	.130	23	67	1	9	2	0	0	3	4	3	0	0	27	0	1	.164	.216
Baron Radcliff	L-R	6-4	228	2-9-99	.237	.206	.244	104	346	44	82	15	2	17	49	60	1	0	1	163	6	2	.439	.350
Johan Rojas	R-R	6-1	165	8-14-00	.230	.208	.236	70	265	40	61	12	2	3	22	21	1	3	2	55	33	1	.325	.287
Kendall Simmons	R-R	6-2	180	4-11-00	.281	.333	.279	17	64	15	18	2	0	3	11	8	0	0	0	15	2	0	.453	.361
D.J. Stewart	R-R	6-2	205	2-2-99	.234	.296	.219	80	273	36	64	14	2	7	34	22	4	0	1	69	17	1	.377	.300
Madison Stokes	R-R	6-2	200	4-25-96	.222	--	.222	3	9	3	2	0	0	0	1	1	2	0	0	1	0	0	.222	.417
McCarthy Tatum	R-R	6-6	210	5-15-96	.264	.133	.284	32	110	17	29	6	1	3	18	6	2	0	0	33	4	2	.418	.314

Nicolas Torres	R-R	5-10	155	9-23-99	.208	.129	.224	58	183	13	38	5	3	1	15	12	2	0	0	49	4	5	.284	.264
Uziel Viloria	B-R	5-9	155	10-6-01	.195	.259	.178	44	128	18	25	4	0	3	10	14	1	0	0	50	1	2	.297	.280
Justin Williams	L-R	6-1	235	8-20-95	.067	--	.067	4	15	2	1	0	0	0	0	3	0	0	0	7	3	0	.067	.222
Ethan Wilson	L-L	6-1	210	11-7-99	.238	.245	.236	112	424	39	101	20	2	7	45	28	4	0	2	93	25	7	.344	.290
Rixon Wingrove	L-R	6-5	260	5-23-00	.251	.250	.251	67	219	28	55	7	2	12	43	26	7	0	0	87	2	1	.466	.349

Pitching	**B-T**	**HT**	**WT**	**DOB**	**W**	**L**	**ERA**	**G**	**GS**	**CG**	**SV**	**IP**	**H**	**R**	**ER**	**HR**	**BB**	**SO**	**AVG**	**vLH**	**vRH**	**K/9**	**BB/9**
Mick Abel	R-R	6-5	190	8-18-01	7	8	4.01	18	18	0	0	85	75	42	38	6	38	103	.230	.223	.234	10.86	4.01
Aidan Anderson	R-R	6-1	195	6-21-97	1	4	3.72	23	0	0	8	29	29	13	12	2	7	26	.254	.194	.282	8.07	2.17
Erubiel Armenta	L-L	6-3	189	3-11-00	3	2	3.60	40	0	0	1	40	22	20	16	2	32	54	.161	.103	.184	12.15	7.20
Andrew Baker	R-R	6-3	190	3-24-00	3	1	4.74	40	0	0	0	44	41	28	23	5	24	61	.237	.262	.223	12.57	4.95
Albertus Barber	R-R	6-2	190	2-18-96	1	0	0.98	16	0	0	0	18	9	3	2	1	7	22	.143	.211	.114	10.80	3.44
Cam Bedrosian	R-R	6-1	225	10-2-91	0	1	19.29	2	0	0	0	2	4	5	5	1	2	4	.400	.200	.600	15.43	7.71
Ben Brown	R-R	6-6	210	9-9-99	3	5	3.08	16	15	0	0	73	53	30	25	7	23	105	.197	.245	.164	12.95	2.84
Joel Cesar	R-R	5-11	191	1-26-96	0	0	13.50	3	0	0	0	3	1	4	4	0	6	3	.111	.333	.000	10.13	20.25
Jordan Fowler	L-L	6-3	180	3-9-99	0	0	0.00	1	0	0	0	2	1	0	0	0	1	2	.125	.000	.167	9.00	4.50
Carlos A Francisco	R-R	6-4	220	7-2-99	1	3	5.13	41	0	0	0	47	35	35	27	2	28	55	.201	.207	.198	10.46	5.32
Tristan Garnett	L-L	6-6	240	3-29-98	0	0	2.08	3	0	0	0	4	6	1	1	0	0	6	.316	.167	.385	12.46	0.00
Kyle Glogoski	R-R	6-2	183	1-6-99	2	6	2.77	16	12	0	0	65	56	29	20	5	20	75	.228	.260	.205	10.38	2.77
Josh Hendrickson	L-L	6-4	215	9-18-97	0	1	5.14	2	2	0	0	7	5	4	4	1	7	7	.208	.200	.211	9.00	9.00
Cristian Hernandez	R-R	6-3	180	9-23-00	5	3	4.70	29	9	0	1	75	79	44	39	7	19	67	.269	.307	.244	8.08	2.29
Jonathan Hughes	R-R	6-2	196	1-8-97	0	5	3.59	35	0	0	8	43	40	22	17	1	16	36	.244	.207	.264	7.59	3.38
Herbert Iser	L-R	6-3	210	12-14-97	0	0	0.00	1	0	0	0	1	0	0	0	0	0	0	.000	.000	.000	0.00	0.00
Sam Jacobsak	R-R	6-5	200	6-11-98	1	0	7.71	4	0	0	0	5	6	6	4	1	2	6	.300	.182	.444	11.57	3.86
Keylan Killgore	L-L	6-3	185	9-30-96	0	0	7.71	3	0	0	0	2	4	2	2	1	1	3	.400	.000	.571	11.57	3.86
Taylor Lehman	L-L	6-8	240	12-30-95	0	0	0.00	3	0	0	0	2	1	0	0	0	1	1	.167	.000	.200	4.50	4.50
Ethan Lindow	R-L	6-3	180	10-15-98	2	0	1.33	8	0	0	0	20	12	4	3	0	7	31	.162	.125	.180	13.72	3.10
Rafael Marcano	L-L	6-1	170	4-20-00	1	5	5.82	10	10	0	0	43	45	31	28	5	22	47	.268	.268	.268	9.76	4.57
Jordi Martinez	L-L	6-2	185	7-18-00	0	1	4.05	2	2	0	0	7	9	7	3	0	1	7	.310	.375	.286	9.45	1.35
Griff McGarry	R-R	6-2	190	6-8-99	3	3	3.86	12	12	0	0	47	33	20	20	6	24	82	.199	.209	.192	15.81	4.63
Christian McGowan	R-R	6-3	205	3-7-00	0	1	4.91	2	2	0	0	7	8	4	4	1	2	7	.320	.125	.412	8.59	2.45
Tyler McKay	R-R	6-6	180	8-18-97	0	0	2.66	15	0	0	0	20	19	7	6	0	8	19	.253	.343	.175	8.41	3.54
Jhordany Mezquita	L-L	6-1	185	1-30-98	0	0	2.51	6	1	0	0	14	11	4	4	2	4	16	.216	.214	.216	10.05	2.51
Scott Moss	L-L	6-6	225	10-6-94	0	1	12.00	1	1	0	0	3	2	4	4	0	3	1	.182	.200	.167	3.00	9.00
Andrew Painter	R-R	6-7	215	4-10-03	3	0	0.98	8	8	1	0	37	25	7	4	2	7	49	.185	.212	.169	12.03	1.72
Dominic Pipkin	R-R	6-4	160	11-5-99	4	7	5.01	30	13	0	0	74	71	52	41	6	51	64	.262	.288	.244	7.82	6.23
Carlo Reyes	R-R	6-0	212	7-4-98	0	2	2.84	20	4	0	0	44	37	15	14	4	13	54	.224	.281	.194	10.96	2.64
Jason Ruffcorn	R-R	6-2	215	7-27-98	0	4	5.80	38	0	0	7	45	37	38	29	4	37	40	.219	.220	.218	8.00	7.40
Matt Russell	R-R	6-2	190	3-28-99	5	9	4.74	18	16	0	0	82	99	54	43	5	35	69	.300	.316	.289	7.60	3.86
Rodolfo Sanchez	R-R	5-10	165	1-12-00	1	1	5.84	11	0	0	0	12	12	8	8	0	9	16	.255	.263	.250	11.68	6.57
Andrew Schultz	R-R	6-4	195	7-31-97	0	3	4.80	31	0	0	1	30	23	19	16	3	20	48	.204	.333	.150	14.40	6.00
Brett Schulze	R-R	6-2	180	11-24-97	0	0	4.05	13	0	0	1	13	11	6	6	1	6	17	.229	.100	.321	11.48	4.05
Victor Vargas	R-R	6-1	175	9-3-00	2	1	2.91	7	7	1	0	34	28	11	11	3	8	26	.226	.277	.195	6.88	2.12
Rixon Wingrove	L-R	6-5	260	5-23-00	0	0	9.00	1	0	0	0	1	3	1	1	0	0	0	.600	1.000	.500	0.00	0.00
J.P. Woodward	L-L	6-6	215	11-13-98	3	4	6.87	32	0	0	0	38	48	35	29	2	16	41	.296	.292	.298	9.71	3.79

Fielding

Catcher	**PCT**	**G**	**PO**	**A**	**E**	**DP**	**PB**
De Freitas	.990	20	183	12	2	1	2
Ellison	.993	39	403	18	3	2	8
Francisco	.970	3	29	3	1	1	3
Iser	.995	24	197	14	1	2	1
Marchan	1.000	3	26	1	0	0	0
Martin	1.000	1	2	0	0	0	0
Matera	.989	21	168	4	2	1	4
Nava	.970	14	124	4	4	1	3
Quirion	.981	20	145	11	3	0	4

First Base	**PCT**	**G**	**PO**	**A**	**E**	**DP**
De La Cruz	.987	22	147	5	2	15
Iser	.857	2	11	1	2	1
Matera	1.000	11	72	4	0	7
Nava	1.000	1	4	0	0	0
Quirion	1.000	2	7	0	0	2
Stewart	.994	25	155	12	1	12
Tatum	1.000	9	53	8	0	7
Torres	1.000	8	52	2	0	6
Viloria	.900	2	8	1	1	2
Wingrove	.995	60	409	17	2	44

Second Base	**PCT**	**G**	**PO**	**A**	**E**	**DP**
Garcia	.925	21	36	50	7	10
Lee	1.000	6	9	10	0	4
Martin	.976	17	27	53	2	10
Minyety	.983	18	20	37	1	7
Quirion	1.000	1	1	1	0	1
Radcliff	.000	1	0	0	0	0
Simmons	.923	8	11	13	2	8
Tatum	.935	7	13	16	2	7
Torres	.967	31	44	73	4	17
Viloria	.965	30	47	62	4	16

Third Base	**PCT**	**G**	**PO**	**A**	**E**	**DP**
Minyety	.916	40	21	66	8	5
Simmons	.923	7	3	9	1	0
Stewart	.907	51	31	66	10	10
Stokes	1.000	1	0	1	0	0
Tatum	.960	15	3	21	1	4
Torres	.810	11	4	13	4	0
Viloria	.714	8	3	7	4	0
Wingrove	.750	1	0	3	1	1

Shortstop	**PCT**	**G**	**PO**	**A**	**E**	**DP**
Garcia	1.000	24	29	55	0	15
Gozzo	.958	12	14	32	2	6
Lee	.923	3	5	7	1	3
Martin	.956	89	93	213	14	37
Minyety	1.000	1	1	0	0	0
Radcliff	1.000	1	2	1	0	2
Stokes	.667	1	2	0	1	0
Tatum	1.000	2	3	1	0	1
Viloria	.778	3	1	6	2	1

Outfield	**PCT**	**G**	**PO**	**A**	**E**	**DP**
Carr	.974	98	181	7	5	2
De La Cruz	.980	31	48	1	1	0
Sang	.967	16	29	0	1	0
Martin	1.000	1	2	0	0	0
Pineda	.966	16	27	1	1	0
Radcliff	.975	76	112	3	3	1
Rojas	.987	63	143	5	2	0
Stokes	1.000	1	5	0	0	0
Torres	1.000	3	5	0	0	0
Williams	1.000	4	7	1	0	0
Wilson	.981	97	144	7	3	0

CLEARWATER THRESHERS — *LOW CLASS A*

FLORIDA STATE LEAGUE

Batting	**B-T**	**HT**	**WT**	**DOB**	**AVG**	**vLH**	**vRH**	**G**	**AB**	**R**	**H**	**2B**	**3B**	**HR**	**RBI**	**BB**	**HBP**	**SH**	**SF**	**SO**	**SB**	**CS**	**SLG**	**OBP**
Matt Alifano	R-R	6-2	195	12-31-00	.196	.222	.189	15	46	3	9	1	0	0	4	4	4	0	0	18	0	0	.217	.315

Alexeis Azuaje	R-R	5-10	155	4-24-02	.285	.120	.321	38	137	23	39	8	1	1	8	6	9	1	0	43	15	4	.380	.355
Jamari Baylor	R-R	5-11	190	8-25-00	.178	.185	.176	89	241	41	43	11	2	6	28	52	13	0	0	100	22	9	.315	.353
Emaarion Boyd	R-R	6-1	177	8-22-03	.429	1.000	.333	2	7	1	3	0	0	0	0	0	1	0	0	0	1	0	.429	.500
Erick Brito	R-R	5-10	134	5-25-02	.228	.227	.229	97	289	28	66	10	4	1	21	27	3	8	0	56	15	6	.301	.301
Chris Burke	L-R	5-11	180	8-16-01	.073	.083	.069	16	41	4	3	1	0	0	0	6	1	1	0	17	1	0	.098	.208
Chad Castillo	L-R	6-4	225	4-19-00	.233	.111	.247	24	86	8	20	8	0	3	8	10	1	0	0	27	0	0	.430	.320
Aldrem Corredor	L-L	6-0	202	10-27-95	.400	.000	.429	5	15	4	6	1	0	0	2	4	0	0	0	5	0	0	.467	.526
Justin Crawford	L-R	6-3	175	1-13-04	.143	.333	.111	5	21	2	3	0	0	0	0	2	0	0	0	9	2	1	.143	.217
Arturo De Freitas	R-R	6-0	170	5-28-01	.228	.306	.197	62	219	26	50	9	1	5	18	17	1	0	1	65	0	1	.347	.286
Cade Fergus	R-R	6-3	195	8-22-00	.168	.059	.192	29	95	14	16	1	1	4	12	14	6	0	0	51	6	1	.326	.313
Wilfredo Flores	L-R	5-10	170	5-14-00	.258	.171	.284	88	302	29	78	10	2	3	30	11	2	0	3	53	8	4	.334	.286
Luis Garcia	B-R	5-11	170	10-1-00	.250	1.000	.000	3	8	1	2	0	0	0	0	2	0	0	0	4	1	0	.250	.400
Yhoswar Garcia	R-R	6-0	150	9-13-01	.206	.304	.184	35	126	26	26	4	3	1	16	14	4	1	1	35	29	6	.310	.303
Odubel Herrera	L-R	5-11	205	12-29-91	.368	1.000	.333	5	19	3	7	2	0	0	2	0	1	0	0	5	0	0	.474	.400
Herbert Iser	L-R	6-3	210	12-14-97	.143	.500	.000	2	7	0	1	0	0	0	1	1	0	0	0	0	0	0	.143	.250
Albert Jerez	R-R	6-2	165	5-18-01	.135	.125	.139	17	52	4	7	1	0	0	3	3	1	1	1	19	2	1	.154	.193
Otto Kemp	R-R	6-0	185	9-9-99	.128	.222	.100	12	39	6	5	0	0	0	1	7	2	0	0	13	0	0	.128	.292
Dakota Kotowski	R-R	6-5	245	3-26-00	.129	.182	.100	9	31	3	4	0	0	2	2	3	0	0	0	13	0	0	.323	.206
Hao Yu Lee	R-R	5-10	190	2-3-03	.283	.222	.299	68	258	37	73	11	1	7	50	36	7	0	1	57	10	7	.415	.384
Marcus Lee Sang	L-L	6-0	200	1-2-01	.259	.246	.263	84	293	45	76	12	1	8	37	33	4	0	3	100	18	7	.389	.339
Ryan Leitch	R-R	6-1	195	8-26-01	.212	.000	.241	9	33	3	7	0	0	2	6	0	0	0	0	16	0	0	.394	.212
Nick Matera	R-R	6-2	215	8-29-96	.167	--	.167	2	6	0	1	0	0	0	0	1	0	0	0	4	0	0	.167	.286
Nick Maton	L-R	6-2	178	2-18-97	.294	.000	.385	4	17	2	5	1	0	0	4	0	0	0	0	0	0	0	.353	.294
Adony Mejia	R-R	5-11	170	6-9-01	.111	.250	.071	6	18	2	2	0	0	0	0	2	1	0	0	8	0	1	.111	.238
Freylin Minyety	R-R	5-10	185	10-22-99	.190	.143	.200	12	42	4	8	0	0	0	2	3	1	0	0	9	1	2	.190	.261
Mickey Moniak	L-R	6-2	195	5-13-98	.400	.667	.286	3	10	1	4	1	1	0	2	0	2	0	1	3	0	0	.700	.462
Simon Muzziotti	L-L	6-1	175	12-27-98	.000	.000	.000	2	8	0	0	0	0	0	0	1	0	0	0	4	0	0	.000	.111
Andrick Nava	B-R	5-11	175	10-6-01	.237	.400	.191	32	114	12	27	3	0	4	19	10	0	0	0	25	0	0	.368	.298
Leandro Pineda	L-L	6-1	165	6-4-02	.219	.193	.226	73	256	34	56	16	6	3	29	32	5	0	6	78	5	3	.363	.311
Anthony Quirion	R-R	6-2	205	10-29-97	.214	.107	.247	34	117	13	25	4	0	6	16	14	10	0	0	44	3	1	.402	.348
Felix Reyes	R-R	6-4	195	3-26-01	.163	.143	.167	14	49	6	8	1	1	1	5	5	0	0	0	18	1	1	.286	.241
Caleb Ricketts	L-R	6-4	225	5-10-00	.259	.273	.257	22	81	13	21	0	0	3	10	11	2	0	0	30	0	0	.370	.362
Wendell Rijo	R-R	5-11	170	9-4-95	.154	--	.154	4	13	0	2	1	0	0	0	1	0	0	0	1	1	0	.231	.214
Jadiel Sanchez	B-R	6-2	185	5-10-01	.236	.143	.259	38	140	13	33	5	2	6	19	10	1	0	3	27	2	2	.429	.286
Donny Sands	R-R	6-2	190	5-16-96	.300	1.000	.222	3	10	1	3	1	0	1	2	1	0	0	0	2	0	0	.700	.364
Troy Schreffler	R-R	6-1	190	10-27-00	.207	.308	.190	27	92	11	19	5	1	1	9	11	3	0	0	32	4	0	.315	.311
Kendall Simmons	R-R	6-2	180	4-11-00	.204	.209	.202	74	270	31	55	12	2	9	36	24	9	3	1	83	9	3	.363	.289
Madison Stokes	R-R	6-2	200	4-25-96	.000	--	.000	1	2	0	0	0	0	0	0	0	1	0	0	0	0	0	.000	.333
McCarthy Tatum	R-R	6-6	210	5-15-96	.375	.750	.250	4	16	6	6	3	0	0	1	1	0	0	0	2	1	0	.563	.412
Nicolas Torres	R-R	5-10	155	9-23-99	.147	.192	.133	37	116	7	17	3	0	0	5	6	2	1	0	32	5	1	.172	.202
Randy Vasquez	L-R	6-0	170	12-16-02	.250	.000	.286	4	8	0	2	0	0	0	0	1	0	0	0	4	1	0	.250	.333
Jordan Viars	L-L	6-4	215	7-18-03	.208	.000	.278	8	24	2	5	0	0	0	3	2	1	0	1	9	0	0	.208	.286
Justin Williams	L-R	6-1	235	8-20-95	.500	--	.500	1	4	2	2	2	0	0	0	0	0	0	0	1	0	1	1.000	.500
Rixon Wingrove	L-R	6-5	260	5-23-00	.111	.000	.136	8	27	1	3	1	0	0	0	3	1	0	0	13	0	0	.148	.226
Micah Yonamine	R-R	6-4	210	10-10-00	.240	.215	.249	78	262	21	63	7	2	4	28	30	4	2	3	87	2	1	.328	.324

Pitching	B-T	HT	WT	DOB	W	L	ERA	G	GS	CG	SV	IP	H	R	ER	HR	BB	SO	AVG	vLH	vRH	K/9	BB/9
Aidan Anderson	R-R	6-1	195	6-21-97	1	0	5.40	2	0	0	0	3	4	2	2	2	0	3	.286	.167	.375	8.10	0.00
Konnor Ash	R-R	5-11	191	3-17-99	1	2	5.36	31	0	0	4	40	36	27	24	3	26	54	.235	.230	.242	12.05	5.80
Cam Bedrosian	R-R	6-1	225	10-2-91	0	0	0.00	2	0	0	0	2	1	0	0	0	2	4	.143	--	.143	18.00	9.00
Carlos Betancourt	R-R	6-1	160	3-27-01	4	1	2.78	26	1	0	2	45	40	16	14	2	16	51	.238	.200	.259	10.13	3.18
Trevor Bettencourt	R-R	6-0	195	7-21-94	0	0	0.00	2	0	0	0	2	1	0	0	0	1	4	.143	.000	.200	18.00	4.50
Malik Binns	R-R	6-7	240	1-15-99	6	0	5.01	17	0	0	0	23	8	13	13	0	25	32	.113	.167	.094	12.34	9.64
Josh Bortka	R-R	6-5	225	7-12-99	0	0	3.00	3	0	0	0	3	4	1	1	0	2	6	.308	.333	.300	18.00	6.00
Jean Cabrera	R-R	6-0	145	10-20-01	2	4	5.24	12	12	0	0	46	54	28	27	8	28	51	.295	.375	.260	9.91	5.44
Eiberson Castellano	R-R	6-3	160	5-9-01	1	3	3.51	17	8	0	0	51	37	24	20	4	18	61	.207	.279	.169	10.69	3.16
Starlyn Castillo	R-R	6-0	210	2-24-02	0	7	11.67	10	8	0	0	27	38	37	35	7	14	29	.333	.380	.297	9.67	4.67
Sam Coonrod	R-R	6-1	225	9-22-92	0	0	0.00	2	1	0	0	2	1	0	0	0	0	4	.143	.000	.200	18.00	0.00
Gabriel Cotto	L-L	6-5	175	5-15-00	3	3	4.57	17	17	0	0	67	58	39	34	7	37	70	.231	.273	.222	9.40	4.97
Jack Dallas	R-R	5-11	200	12-18-98	0	0	0.00	6	0	0	1	8	2	0	0	0	5	10	.087	.125	.067	11.74	5.87
Kent Emanuel	L-L	6-4	225	6-4-92	0	0	0.00	2	2	0	0	6	4	0	0	0	1	6	.190	.167	.200	9.00	1.50
Jordan Fowler	L-L	6-3	180	3-9-99	2	2	2.65	19	6	0	0	54	50	22	16	8	11	51	.244	.370	.208	8.45	1.82
Alex Garbrick	R-R	6-1	210	6-4-98	3	3	5.36	32	0	0	3	44	43	31	26	3	31	56	.265	.292	.254	11.54	6.39
Tristan Garnett	L-L	6-6	240	3-29-98	3	1	1.86	19	0	0	2	29	20	7	6	2	5	43	.196	.167	.205	13.34	1.55
Kyle Glogoski	R-R	6-2	183	1-6-99	1	0	3.00	2	0	0	0	3	1	1	1	1	4	5	.111	.000	.250	15.00	12.00
Daniel Harper	R-R	6-4	225	6-1-99	0	0	1.08	7	0	0	1	8	9	3	1	0	3	7	.281	.250	.300	7.56	3.24
Buddy Hayward	R-R	6-6	225	10-15-98	0	0	3.24	6	0	0	0	8	8	4	3	3	4	13	.235	.273	.217	14.04	4.32
Josh Hendrickson	L-L	6-4	215	9-18-97	0	0	0.00	1	1	0	0	4	1	0	0	0	0	7	.077	.000	.111	15.75	0.00
Sam Jacobsak	R-R	6-5	200	6-11-98	0	1	3.18	12	0	0	0	23	15	10	8	4	6	30	.185	.214	.170	11.91	2.38
Estibenzon Jimenez	R-R	6-1	172	1-25-02	0	0	3.00	2	2	0	0	9	5	3	3	2	2	12	.152	.000	.192	12.00	2.00
Orion Kerkering	R-R	6-2	204	4-4-01	1	0	4.50	5	0	0	0	6	7	3	3	0	0	6	.292	.375	.250	9.00	0.00
Keylan Killgore	L-L	6-3	185	9-30-96	1	0	5.68	5	0	0	1	6	8	4	4	0	1	7	.308	.167	.429	9.95	1.42
Taylor Lehman	L-L	6-8	240	12-30-95	0	0	0.00	1	0	0	0	2	0	0	0	0	0	2	.000	.000	.000	9.00	0.00
Victor Lopez	R-R	6-4	192	9-2-99	7	1	6.03	22	0	0	0	31	35	24	21	5	12	31	.289	.289	.289	8.90	3.45
Fernando Lozano	R-R	6-2	186	1-11-00	2	0	5.51	9	0	0	0	16	20	10	10	1	7	13	.323	.200	.381	7.16	3.86

Rafael Marcano	L-L	6-1	170	4-20-00	1	4	3.80	7	3	0	0	21	25	14	9	0	9	26	.284	.500	.243	10.97	3.80
Jordi Martinez	L-L	6-2	185	7-18-00	3	6	4.25	17	15	0	0	72	79	41	34	6	23	64	.280	.292	.276	8.00	2.88
Gunner Mayer	R-R	6-6	190	7-27-00	1	6	5.18	14	12	0	0	49	39	28	28	10	26	67	.215	.214	.216	12.39	4.81
Tommy McCollum	R-R	6-5	260	6-8-99	1	0	1.45	23	0	0	5	31	11	6	5	3	16	52	.111	.067	.130	15.10	4.65
Alex McFarlane	R-R	6-4	215	6-9-01	0	3	9.00	3	3	0	0	8	12	8	8	1	3	12	.364	.333	.375	13.50	3.38
Alex McKenney	R-R	6-3	245	5-11-99	0	0	8.31	14	0	0	0	17	20	16	16	1	19	13	.303	.348	.279	6.75	9.87
Oswald Medina	R-R	6-0	145	12-2-01	0	4	4.24	9	8	0	0	34	42	23	16	3	6	22	.302	.326	.290	5.82	1.59
Scott Moss	L-L	6-6	225	10-6-94	0	0	0.00	2	2	0	0	6	3	0	0	0	8	5	.167	.000	.231	7.94	12.71
Matt Osterberg	L-L	6-2	200	4-21-99	2	6	3.25	22	12	0	0	64	75	35	23	4	15	52	.293	.140	.324	7.35	2.12
Micah Ottenbreit	R-R	6-4	190	5-7-03	0	1	7.94	2	2	0	0	6	6	5	5	1	5	4	.273	.000	.429	6.35	7.94
Andrew Painter	R-R	6-7	215	4-10-03	1	1	1.40	9	9	0	0	39	17	10	6	0	16	69	.130	.163	.110	16.06	3.72
Nicoly Pina	R-R	6-3	203	10-8-99	0	1	21.60	2	0	0	0	2	2	4	4	0	4	3	.286	.000	.333	16.20	21.60
Alex Rao	R-R	6-4	230	10-25-99	0	0	0.00	2	0	0	0	2	0	0	0	0	0	1	.000	.000	.000	4.50	0.00
JoJo Romero	L-L	5-11	200	9-9-96	2	0	2.25	4	2	0	0	4	4	1	1	0	2	5	.250	.000	.267	11.25	4.50
Rodolfo Sanchez	R-R	5-10	165	1-12-00	4	2	3.12	30	0	0	4	40	32	18	14	3	20	51	.206	.204	.208	11.38	4.46
Brett Schulze	R-R	6-2	180	11-24-97	0	0	0.00	2	0	0	0	3	1	0	0	0	1	4	.100	.000	.125	12.00	3.00
Ryan Sherriff	L-L	6-1	190	5-25-90	0	0	0.00	2	0	0	0	2	1	0	0	0	1	4	.143	--	.143	18.00	4.50
Manuel Urias	R-R	6-6	200	3-8-01	0	0	0.00	3	0	0	0	5	3	1	0	0	1	7	.176	.000	.250	13.50	1.93
Victor Vargas	R-R	6-1	175	9-3-00	0	0	3.48	2	2	0	0	10	10	4	4	1	1	5	.286	.217	.417	4.35	0.87
Andrew Walling	L-L	6-2	220	10-29-99	0	0	6.14	4	0	0	0	7	7	5	5	0	6	9	.259	.125	.316	11.05	7.36
Chase Webster	R-R	6-4	250	9-12-99	0	1	7.71	2	0	0	0	2	1	2	2	0	2	5	.125	.000	.200	19.29	7.71
Jared Wetherbee	L-L	5-10	203	8-14-98	1	1	4.50	19	0	0	1	24	17	14	12	2	26	36	.205	.211	.203	13.50	9.75
Cam Wynne	R-R	6-6	220	1-11-99	0	3	1.25	16	0	0	1	22	20	10	3	2	10	25	.247	.321	.208	10.38	4.15
Gabriel Yanez	L-L	6-3	168	7-22-99	3	4	3.22	33	0	0	2	50	44	25	18	3	13	58	.232	.262	.223	10.37	2.32

Fielding

Catcher	PCT	G	PO	A	E	DP	PB
De Freitas	.994	60	546	78	4	5	6
Leitch	.988	8	73	9	1	0	1
Matera	.955	2	21	0	1	0	0
Mejia	1.000	6	55	7	0	0	1
Nava	1.000	14	119	9	0	1	5
Quirion	1.000	21	235	11	0	3	7
Ricketts	.994	17	155	10	1	2	2
Sands	1.000	2	16	2	0	1	1
Yonamine	.971	4	32	1	1	0	0

First Base	PCT	G	PO	A	E	DP
Baylor	.982	19	109	2	2	8
Castillo	1.000	19	125	9	0	11
Corredor	1.000	4	27	1	0	3
Iser	.947	2	16	2	1	1
Jerez	1.000	2	4	2	0	0
Quirion	.987	9	71	3	1	6
Reyes	1.000	3	12	1	0	2
Torres	1.000	1	7	1	0	1
Wingrove	1.000	5	20	4	0	2
Yonamine	.986	72	482	19	7	44

Second Base	PCT	G	PO	A	E	DP
Azuaje	.951	32	58	59	6	17
Baylor	.934	38	60	68	9	18
Brito	.909	3	3	7	1	1
Garcia	1.000	2	4	4	0	0
Kemp	1.000	2	5	3	0	0
Lee	.968	15	24	37	2	8
Maton	1.000	2	1	5	0	1
Minyety	1.000	4	9	6	0	3
Rijo	1.000	1	0	5	0	1
Simmons	.963	33	66	65	5	18
Torres	.950	4	9	10	1	2

Third Base	PCT	G	PO	A	E	DP
Alifano	.968	15	10	20	1	2
Azuaje	1.000	1	1	1	0	0
Baylor	.800	1	1	3	1	0
Jerez	.909	16	9	21	3	1
Kemp	1.000	9	6	13	0	0
Lee	.917	20	16	39	5	3
Minyety	.947	7	2	16	1	0
Rijo	1.000	1	2	3	0	0
Simmons	.897	33	19	59	9	8
Tatum	1.000	3	3	2	0	0
Torres	.918	25	15	41	5	2
Vasquez	.667	4	1	3	2	0

Shortstop	PCT	G	PO	A	E	DP
Baylor	.821	10	7	16	5	2
Brito	.969	94	123	219	11	41
Garcia	.800	1	1	3	1	1
Lee	.987	23	23	53	1	9
Maton	1.000	1	1	2	0	1
Rijo	1.000	1	0	2	0	1
Simmons	1.000	1	2	2	0	1
Stokes	1.000	1	1	2	0	0

Outfield	PCT	G	PO	A	E	DP
Boyd	1.000	2	2	0	0	0
Burke	1.000	15	27	1	0	0
Castillo	1.000	1	1	0	0	0
Crawford	1.000	5	10	0	0	0
Fergus	.984	29	58	4	1	2
Flores	.985	85	126	2	2	1
Garcia	.987	34	69	5	1	2
Herrera	.857	3	5	1	1	0
Kotowski	1.000	4	7	0	0	0
Sang	.958	80	109	4	5	0
Minyety	1.000	1	1	0	0	0
Moniak	1.000	3	6	1	0	0
Muzziotti	1.000	2	5	0	0	0
Pineda	.976	71	107	14	3	0
Reyes	1.000	4	5	0	0	0
Sanchez	.944	29	46	5	3	0
Schreffler	1.000	28	39	2	0	0
Torres	1.000	7	9	1	0	0
Viars	--	1	0	0	0	0
Williams	1.000	1	2	1	0	0

FCL PHILLIES — ROOKIE

FLORIDA COMPLEX LEAGUE

Batting	B-T	HT	WT	DOB	AVG	vLH	vRH	G	AB	R	H	2B	3B	HR	RBI	BB	HBP	SH	SF	SO	SB	CS	SLG	OBP
Alexeis Azuaje	R-R	5-10	155	4-24-02	.176	.000	.214	5	17	1	3	1	0	0	1	0	0	0	0	5	1	1	.235	.176
Emaarion Boyd	R-R	6-1	177	8-22-03	.345	.455	.278	9	29	6	10	1	0	0	2	5	2	0	0	5	7	2	.379	.472
Justin Crawford	L-R	6-3	175	1-13-04	.297	.357	.261	11	37	6	11	0	1	0	5	5	1	0	0	6	8	3	.351	.395
Jordan Dissin	R-R	6-3	185	5-29-02	.353	.500	.308	10	17	3	6	0	0	0	0	5	2	0	0	6	0	0	.353	.542
Ezra Farmer	L-L	6-0	165	6-10-03	.111	.333	.067	8	18	3	2	1	0	0	3	2	1	0	0	11	1	1	.167	.238
Yemal Flores	R-R	5-11	206	11-22-03	.160	.235	.145	34	100	9	16	2	1	3	13	12	2	0	2	46	3	1	.290	.259
Freddy Francisco	R-R	5-11	180	2-7-01	.500	--	.500	1	2	1	1	0	1	0	0	0	0	0	0	1	0	0	1.500	.500
Luis Garcia	B-R	5-11	170	10-1-00	1.000	--	1.000	1	1	1	1	1	0	0	0	1	0	0	0	0	0	0	2.000	1.000
Yhoswar Garcia	R-R	6-0	150	9-13-01	.333	.500	.250	2	6	0	2	0	0	0	1	1	0	0	0	1	3	1	.333	.429
Diego Gonzalez	R-R	5-11	160	6-7-03	.276	.238	.284	39	123	14	34	8	0	0	9	16	1	0	0	27	4	4	.341	.364
Oscar Gonzalez	R-R	6-0	184	11-21-00	.263	.333	.250	28	76	15	20	3	0	2	12	10	0	0	0	13	0	0	.382	.349
Lou Helmig	L-R	6-5	198	5-1-03	.195	.133	.208	33	87	6	17	3	1	0	13	14	3	0	1	32	4	2	.253	.324
Albert Jerez	R-R	6-2	165	5-18-01	.333	--	.333	1	3	1	1	0	0	1	1	0	1	0	0	1	0	0	1.333	.500
Otto Kemp	R-R	6-0	185	9-9-99	.500	.667	.429	4	10	4	5	0	0	0	2	4	0	0	0	3	2	0	.500	.643
Dakota Kotowski	R-R	6-5	245	3-26-00	.484	.545	.450	11	31	8	15	4	1	0	7	3	1	0	0	10	1	0	.677	.543
Hao Yu Lee	R-R	5-10	190	2-3-03	.500	.500	.500	2	6	4	3	1	0	1	1	2	0	0	0	1	1	0	1.167	.625
Nick Matera	R-R	6-2	215	8-29-96	.167	.400	.000	4	12	1	2	0	0	0	1	1	0	0	0	3	0	0	.167	.231

Adony Mejia	R-R	5-11	170	6-9-01	.212	.200	.214	30	52	10	11	1	0	3	9	9	4	0	0	22	3	1	.404	.369
Cole Moore	L-R	6-2	211	6-14-99	.206	.200	.208	12	34	4	7	3	0	1	7	7	0	0	0	8	0	0	.382	.341
Simon Muzziotti	L-L	6-1	175	12-27-98	.000	--	.000	1	2	0	0	0	0	0	0	0	0	0	0	0	0	0	.000	.000
Ty Penner	L-R	6-4	215	5-1-00	.129	.125	.130	10	31	5	4	1	0	1	3	3	0	0	0	7	0	0	.258	.206
Rickardo Perez	L-R	5-10	172	12-4-03	.349	.412	.333	30	83	5	29	1	0	1	14	7	0	0	3	13	0	1	.398	.387
Jackie Pertuz	L-R	6-0	188	11-1-02	.250	.273	.244	30	56	7	14	6	0	0	6	4	3	0	0	19	0	0	.357	.333
Nikau Pouaka-Grego	L-R	5-10	175	9-13-04	.301	.267	.315	35	103	20	31	6	1	3	16	16	6	0	0	16	2	2	.466	.424
Anthony Quirion	R-R	6-2	205	10-29-97	.227	.333	.211	6	22	1	5	0	0	0	1	1	1	0	0	6	0	0	.227	.292
Felix Reyes	R-R	6-1	195	2-26-01	.241	.261	.237	42	137	26	33	6	1	4	26	4	1	0	1	31	2	2	.387	.266
Wendell Rijo	R-R	5-11	170	9-4-95	.500	--	.500	1	2	1	1	0	0	0	0	2	0	0	0	0	1	0	.500	.750
Bryan Rincon	B-R	5-11	185	2-8-04	.176	.091	.217	12	34	7	6	2	0	2	9	6	1	1	0	7	4	0	.412	.317
Daniel Robertson	R-R	5-11	210	3-22-94	.200	.000	.250	2	5	1	1	0	0	0	0	1	1	0	0	2	0	0	.200	.429
2-team total (7 FCL Twins)					.296	.250	.304	9	27	8	8	3	0	2	9	6	1	0	0	5	0	1	.630	.441
Albert Rodriguez	R-R	6-2	170	12-11-02	.208	.067	.242	32	77	15	16	3	0	1	13	9	3	0	0	33	6	1	.286	.315
Ricardo Rosario	R-R	6-1	160	2-8-03	.240	.118	.265	35	100	14	24	5	1	1	7	13	2	0	1	22	4	3	.340	.336
Jadiel Sanchez	B-R	6-2	185	5-10-01	.500	--	.500	1	2	0	1	1	0	0	0	0	0	0	0	0	0	0	1.000	.500
Jehisbert Sevilla	R-R	5-11	149	3-21-03	.193	.200	.191	43	114	12	22	2	2	0	11	18	2	0	0	21	5	3	.246	.313
Gustavo Sosa	R-R	6-2	203	7-17-01	.133	.250	.091	9	15	2	2	1	0	0	2	4	1	0	2	3	0	0	.200	.318
Madison Stokes	R-R	6-2	200	4-25-96	.300	.200	.400	4	10	2	3	2	0	0	1	1	0	0	0	1	1	0	.500	.364
McCarthy Tatum	R-R	6-6	210	5-15-96	.167	.000	.200	2	6	1	1	1	0	0	1	1	0	0	0	1	0	0	.333	.286
Randy Vasquez	L-R	6-0	170	12-16-02	.204	.227	.198	38	113	21	23	10	3	0	16	18	2	0	0	36	6	1	.345	.323
Jordan Viars	L-L	6-4	215	7-18-03	.240	.172	.256	44	154	28	37	6	1	2	20	17	5	0	3	40	5	0	.331	.330
Justin Williams	L-R	6-1	235	8-20-95	.444	1.000	.375	3	9	2	4	0	0	1	2	0	0	0	0	1	1	0	.778	.444

Pitching	**B-T**	**HT**	**WT**	**DOB**	**W**	**L**	**ERA**	**G**	**GS**	**CG**	**SV**	**IP**	**H**	**R**	**ER**	**HR**	**BB**	**SO**	**AVG**	**vLH**	**vRH**	**K/9**	**BB/9**
Jose Acuna	L-L	6-1	210	9-25-02	0	0	15.95	7	0	0	1	7	7	13	13	0	19	8	.269	.250	.273	9.82	23.32
Samuel Aldegheri	L-L	6-1	180	9-19-01	0	0	1.46	8	4	0	0	12	9	2	2	0	7	17	.191	.333	.171	12.41	5.11
Albertus Barber	R-R	6-2	190	2-18-96	0	1	9.64	5	0	0	0	5	5	6	5	1	3	8	.238	.182	.300	15.43	5.79
Cam Bedrosian	R-R	6-1	225	10-2-91	0	0	9.00	2	1	0	0	2	3	2	2	0	1	3	.333	.000	.429	13.50	4.50
Trevor Bettencourt	R-R	6-0	195	7-21-94	0	0	0.00	1	1	0	0	2	1	0	0	0	0	1	.143	.000	.167	4.50	0.00
Malik Binns	R-R	6-7	240	1-15-99	0	2	6.94	10	0	0	0	12	16	14	9	0	15	13	.372	.231	.433	10.03	11.57
Josh Bortka	R-R	6-5	225	7-12-99	1	0	0.00	2	0	0	0	2	2	0	0	0	1	1	.250	.000	.333	4.50	4.50
Starlyn Castillo	R-R	6-0	210	2-24-02	0	1	5.68	4	3	0	0	13	19	8	8	0	1	15	.333	.222	.385	10.66	0.71
Ty Collins	L-R	6-3	165	8-29-01	2	0	3.86	9	0	0	0	9	10	5	4	0	7	12	.278	.133	.381	11.57	6.75
Jaydenn Estanista	R-R	6-3	180	10-3-01	3	0	2.01	12	5	0	0	31	14	9	7	3	16	35	.139	.182	.118	10.05	4.60
Braeden Fausnaught	L-L	6-3	235	7-29-99	0	0	0.00	2	0	0	0	2	0	0	0	0	0	3	.000	--	.000	13.50	0.00
Eric Garcia	R-R	6-5	230	5-12-00	0	0	7.36	4	0	0	0	4	3	4	3	0	5	6	.188	.333	.154	14.73	12.27
Tristan Garnett	L-L	6-6	240	3-29-98	0	0	0.00	1	0	0	0	2	1	0	0	0	1	0	.200	.000	.250	0.00	5.40
Maikel Garrido	L-L	6-4	175	1-24-00	0	0	5.79	4	0	0	0	5	4	3	3	0	4	5	.222	.400	.154	9.64	7.71
Buddy Hayward	R-R	6-6	225	10-15-98	0	1	10.13	3	0	0	0	3	3	3	3	0	3	3	.273	.333	.250	10.13	10.13
Josh Hendrickson	L-L	6-4	215	9-18-97	0	0	0.00	2	2	0	0	5	0	0	0	0	2	4	.000	.000	.000	7.20	3.60
Sam Jacobsak	R-R	6-5	200	6-11-98	1	1	4.32	6	0	0	0	8	5	4	4	0	1	7	.172	.300	.105	7.56	1.08
DJ Jefferson	R-R	6-5	185	1-9-01	1	0	4.76	7	0	0	0	6	6	3	3	0	3	7	.273	.500	.188	11.12	4.76
Estibenzon Jimenez	R-R	6-1	172	1-25-02	2	2	2.29	12	3	0	1	35	29	12	9	0	10	37	.225	.362	.146	9.42	2.55
Orion Kerkering	R-R	6-2	204	4-4-01	0	0	0.00	1	0	0	0	1	0	0	0	0	1	1	.000	.000	.000	9.00	9.00
Keylan Killgore	L-L	6-3	185	9-30-96	0	0	4.50	2	0	0	0	2	3	1	1	0	1	2	.375	.500	.333	9.00	4.50
Taylor Lehman	L-L	6-8	240	12-30-95	0	0	0.00	2	2	0	0	2	0	0	0	0	0	3	.000	.000	.000	13.50	0.00
Fernando Lozano	R-R	6-2	186	1-11-00	0	0	2.56	11	2	0	2	32	27	9	9	1	5	25	.233	.275	.211	7.11	1.42
Gunner Mayer	R-R	6-6	190	7-27-00	0	0	0.00	3	0	0	0	5	1	0	0	0	4	6	.059	.143	.000	10.13	6.75
Jake McKenna	R-L	6-6	215	4-24-02	0	0	27.00	1	1	0	0	0	0	1	1	0	3	0	.000	--	.000	0.00	81.00
Alex McKenney	R-R	6-3	245	5-11-99	2	0	6.75	2	0	0	0	3	2	2	2	1	2	1	.222	.000	.250	3.38	6.75
Oswald Medina	R-R	6-0	145	12-2-01	1	4	5.66	10	6	0	0	35	46	25	22	6	5	21	.315	.298	.323	5.40	1.29
Daniel Mejia	R-R	6-5	164	4-19-02	1	1	7.31	10	1	0	1	16	19	15	13	3	14	12	.328	.333	.324	6.75	7.88
Scott Moss	L-L	6-6	225	10-6-94	0	1	18.00	3	2	0	0	3	4	6	6	0	4	2	.308	.200	.375	6.00	12.00
Jose Pena Jr.	R-R	6-3	200	7-8-03	1	3	6.59	9	7	0	0	27	23	21	20	2	19	28	.228	.294	.194	9.22	6.26
Jonathan Petit	R-R	6-2	174	4-19-01	3	3	4.50	11	6	0	1	32	28	20	16	3	10	33	.222	.234	.215	9.28	2.81
Nicoly Pina	R-R	6-3	203	10-8-99	1	1	4.11	14	0	0	1	15	9	9	7	0	17	23	.173	.250	.139	13.50	9.98
Alex Rao	R-R	6-4	230	10-25-99	0	0	0.00	1	0	0	0	1	0	1	0	0	1	0	.000	.000	.000	0.00	9.00
JoJo Romero	L-L	5-11	200	9-9-96	0	0	0.00	1	1	0	0	1	0	0	0	0	0	3	.000	.000	.000	27.00	0.00
Mason Ronan	L-L	6-3	222	3-3-00	1	0	2.08	4	0	0	0	4	2	1	1	0	6	6	.143	.000	.167	12.46	12.46
Sergio Sanchez	L-L	6-1	160	12-16-00	0	0	3.24	6	0	0	1	8	9	3	3	0	4	13	.265	.444	.200	14.04	4.32
Brett Schulze	R-R	6-2	180	11-24-97	0	0	3.00	3	0	0	0	3	1	1	1	0	1	5	.091	.000	.167	15.00	3.00
Christopher Soriano	L-L	6-1	160	9-17-01	1	4	4.63	16	0	0	1	23	16	14	12	1	16	20	.195	.263	.175	7.71	6.17
Manuel Urias	R-R	6-6	200	3-8-01	1	1	4.23	11	7	0	0	38	37	18	18	2	9	38	.257	.204	.284	8.92	2.11
Wilson Valdez	R-R	6-2	168	10-25-99	2	0	2.31	11	0	0	3	12	6	3	3	2	6	10	.154	.077	.192	7.71	4.63
Victor Vargas	R-R	6-1	175	9-3-00	1	1	4.82	4	1	0	0	9	8	6	5	1	0	8	.222	.273	.200	7.71	0.00
Giussepe Velasquez	R-R	6-1	170	4-30-03	1	2	9.82	9	0	0	0	11	17	14	12	2	6	10	.395	.313	.444	8.18	4.91
Andrew Walling	L-L	6-2	220	10-29-99	0	0	6.75	3	0	0	1	4	2	3	3	0	3	3	.143	.000	.182	6.75	6.75
Jared Wetherbee	L-L	5-10	203	8-14-98	0	0	0.00	1	0	0	0	1	1	0	0	0	1	2	.250	1.000	.000	18.00	9.00
Cam Wynne	R-R	6-6	220	1-11-99	0	0	13.50	2	0	0	0	2	4	3	3	0	0	1	.400	.250	.500	4.50	0.00

Fielding

C: Dissin 8, Francisco 1, Gonzalez 14, Matera 3, Mejia 26, Perez 13, Pertuz 25, Quirion 4, Sosa 8. **1B:** Gonzalez 4, Helmig 20, Kotowski 2, Mejia 1, Moore 12, Penner 1, Pertuz 1, Reyes 22, Vasquez 4. **2B:** Azuaje 4, Gonzalez 16, Kemp 4, Pouaka-Grego 17, Robertson 1, Sevilla 13, Vasquez 9. **3B:** Gonzalez 8, Jerez 1, Moore 1, Penner 9, Pouaka-Grego 15, Reyes 2, Robertson 1, Tatum 2, Vasquez 27. **SS:** Garcia 1, Gonzalez 14, Lee 2, Pouaka-Grego 2, Rincon 12, Sevilla 30, Stokes 2. **OF:** Boyd 9, Crawford 10, Farmer 7, Flores 30, Garcia 2, Helmig 12, Kotowski 7, Muzziotti 1, Reyes 14, Rodriguez 29, Rosario 38,

Sanchez 1, Stokes 1, Viars 38, Williams 2.

DSL PHILLIES RED — ROOKIE

DOMINICAN SUMMER LEAGUE

Batting	B-T	HT	WT	DOB	AVG	vLH	vRH	G	AB	R	H	2B	3B	HR	RBI	BB	HBP	SH	SF	SO	SB	CS	SLG	OBP
Kliubert Avila	R-R	5-10	170	5-19-03	.214	.333	.197	23	70	10	15	3	1	1	4	11	2	0	0	27	3	2	.329	.337
Deivi Cabrera	R-R	0-0	0	1-26-04	.182	.000	.200	24	55	8	10	1	0	0	7	8	2	2	0	13	4	2	.200	.308
Jose Colmenarez	R-R	5-9	160	11-24-02	.250	.300	.239	29	56	19	14	6	1	2	9	13	7	0	1	17	6	4	.500	.442
Aroon Escobar	R-R	5-11	180	1-1-05	.238	.250	.236	48	143	28	34	4	1	3	21	24	14	1	4	26	11	6	.343	.389
Jhorjan Guevara	R-R	6-2	170	5-19-02	.215	.231	.212	27	79	12	17	4	0	0	7	8	4	0	0	15	4	0	.266	.319
Dariam Gutierrez	R-R	6-1	175	1-26-02	.100	.000	.111	4	10	2	1	1	0	0	1	2	1	0	0	3	3	0	.200	.308
2-team total (40 DSL Phillies White)					.262	.280	.257	44	130	24	34	7	2	2	27	17	4	0	2	30	16	3	.392	.359
Fernando Hernandez	R-R	5-11	165	3-30-03	.179	.133	.185	48	145	21	26	7	2	2	21	20	3	0	2	36	6	3	.297	.288
Jose Leanez	R-R	6-0	145	1-13-03	.237	.200	.243	43	118	19	28	6	2	0	15	10	10	1	0	26	23	4	.322	.348
Jorge Mendez	R-R	5-10	160	8-1-03	.400	.556	.383	34	90	14	36	8	0	1	19	6	11	0	1	9	9	3	.522	.491
Arquedion Muller	R-R	5-10	170	6-19-04	.193	.222	.188	26	57	17	11	2	1	2	12	9	2	0	1	23	6	1	.368	.319
Luis Pelegrin	R-R	5-11	160	2-27-03	.255	.143	.273	22	51	12	13	0	0	2	6	6	7	0	0	14	10	0	.373	.406
Jerffson Pena	L-R	6-2	185	12-16-03	.237	.000	.266	52	156	24	37	7	3	3	14	25	5	0	0	61	20	6	.378	.360
Yoangel Ramos	R-R	6-2	165	1-21-04	.188	.000	.214	26	64	11	12	1	1	2	5	9	2	0	1	25	2	2	.328	.303
Solardo Rodriguez	R-R	5-11	170	11-24-03	.246	.143	.259	23	61	8	15	2	0	0	8	4	0	0	3	11	3	1	.279	.279
Neify Rosario	R-R	6-0	185	9-25-04	.204	.083	.220	35	103	14	21	8	0	1	12	15	6	0	2	33	5	2	.311	.333
Yemil Rosario	R-R	6-2	150	4-12-04	.223	.269	.213	44	148	25	33	5	2	0	14	19	2	0	1	50	18	3	.284	.318
Marco Soto	B-R	5-11	145	3-8-04	.299	.211	.310	49	177	28	53	11	1	0	16	18	4	1	3	25	9	4	.373	.371
Santiago Torres	R-R	6-1	160	9-20-02	.206	.071	.235	45	160	16	33	2	8	0	27	18	5	0	2	32	10	4	.319	.303

Pitching	B-T	HT	WT	DOB	W	L	ERA	G	GS	CG	SV	IP	H	R	ER	HR	BB	SO	AVG	vLH	vRH	K/9	BB/9
Edwar Chirinos	L-L	5-10	160	4-20-05	2	0	2.49	13	1	0	3	25	20	11	7	0	13	33	.222	.158	.239	11.72	4.62
Josbel Garcia	R-R	6-0	165	3-30-04	2	0	4.70	11	0	0	1	23	22	13	12	2	9	15	.247	.297	.212	5.87	3.52
Jeffrey German	R-R	6-3	175	10-26-04	4	1	2.17	11	10	0	0	46	31	13	11	1	21	46	.195	.180	.204	9.07	4.14
Luis Gomez	R-R	6-1	174	5-14-01	3	4	3.86	14	5	0	1	47	58	22	20	4	9	43	.310	.300	.318	8.29	1.74
Luis Gonzalez	R-R	6-0	170	7-15-05	4	5	3.71	11	11	0	0	51	53	25	21	2	5	30	.268	.310	.234	5.29	0.88
Jonh Henriquez	R-R	6-0	187	10-30-99	0	2	3.00	5	0	0	2	6	6	4	2	0	4	7	.261	.091	.417	10.50	6.00
Jean Hernandez	R-R	6-1	185	10-22-02	1	0	6.66	11	4	0	0	26	34	20	19	2	16	15	.347	.349	.345	5.26	5.61
Neyker Ibarra	L-L	5-11	165	3-30-02	0	0	2.25	3	0	0	0	4	5	2	1	0	3	2	.357	.000	.385	4.50	6.75
Jared Loyo	L-L	6-4	175	1-14-03	2	0	3.78	10	0	0	0	17	17	10	7	0	15	18	.258	.308	.245	9.72	8.10
Carlos Millan	R-R	6-2	160	7-19-03	1	0	6.89	10	0	0	0	16	19	13	12	0	9	19	.297	.316	.289	10.91	5.17
Fernando Ortega	R-R	6-4	160	10-10-01	5	3	3.20	11	7	1	2	45	41	22	16	1	13	27	.248	.246	.250	5.40	2.60
Adilson Peralta	R-R	6-4	175	6-17-03	0	2	7.06	7	6	0	0	22	25	17	17	0	11	18	.284	.258	.298	7.48	4.57
Jesus Querales	R-R	6-0	175	2-18-03	2	0	1.64	15	0	0	7	22	14	4	4	1	10	28	.182	.188	.178	11.45	4.09
Ronny Ramirez	L-L	5-10	160	11-3-02	0	0	2.84	12	0	0	0	19	10	7	6	0	14	22	.159	.286	.143	10.42	6.63
Pedro Reyes	R-R	6-3	175	11-26-02	3	0	1.37	7	6	0	0	26	26	6	4	0	6	21	.257	.237	.270	7.18	2.05
Enrique Segura	R-R	6-3	175	12-19-04	5	1	2.32	13	8	0	0	43	36	16	11	1	22	39	.234	.322	.179	8.23	4.64
John Sosa	L-L	6-3	200	2-14-03	0	1	9.45	7	0	0	0	7	1	11	7	0	14	9	.053	.000	.071	12.15	18.90
Edgar Zuniga	R-R	6-2	185	9-15-02	2	4	2.64	14	1	0	2	31	31	15	9	0	4	26	.265	.245	.281	7.63	1.17

Fielding

C: Avila 3, Colmenarez 22, Mendez 32, Rodriguez 18. **1B:** Cabrera 7, Guevara 1, Hernandez 8, Leanez 4, Muller 15, Pelegrin 6, Ramos 14, Rodriguez 1, Rosario 11, Soto 5. **2B:** Cabrera 11, Escobar 20, Hernandez 2, Muller 1, Pelegrin 7, Ramos 2, Rosario 14, Soto 15. **3B:** Cabrera 3, Escobar 14, Hernandez 17, Muller 1, Pelegrin 3, Ramos 8, Rosario 4, Soto 12. **SS:** Cabrera 2, Escobar 12, Hernandez 21, Rosario 10, Soto 18. **OF:** Guevara 25, Gutierrez 3, Leanez 38, Pena 50, Rosario 33, Torres 44.

DSL PHILLIES WHITE — ROOKIE

DOMINICAN SUMMER LEAGUE

Batting	B-T	HT	WT	DOB	AVG	vLH	vRH	G	AB	R	H	2B	3B	HR	RBI	BB	HBP	SH	SF	SO	SB	CS	SLG	OBP
Dervin Andrade	R-R	6-0	200	11-1-03	.203	.111	.230	31	79	9	16	9	0	0	10	9	3	0	1	17	2	0	.316	.304
Erick Barria	R-R	5-11	155	1-31-03	.260	.300	.250	29	50	10	13	1	0	0	7	8	2	0	2	12	4	1	.280	.371
Nolan Beltran	L-R	6-0	160	1-24-05	.226	.130	.244	51	146	24	33	7	0	0	17	31	4	3	2	18	5	3	.274	.372
William Bergolla	L-R	5-11	165	10-20-04	.380	.167	.400	24	71	18	27	3	0	0	14	11	1	0	0	3	2	3	.423	.470
Leny Carela	R-R	6-0	170	10-9-04	.260	.211	.273	38	96	12	25	3	0	0	10	19	0	1	2	18	10	4	.292	.376
Derek Escobar	B-R	5-11	170	1-28-02	.210	.250	.202	45	100	26	21	1	0	1	5	29	4	3	0	29	17	5	.250	.406
Jorge Garcia	L-R	5-11	145	2-6-04	.308	.324	.303	54	156	30	48	12	1	1	28	13	6	0	2	41	8	2	.417	.379
Dariam Gutierrez	R-R	6-1	175	1-26-02	.275	.292	.271	40	120	22	33	6	2	2	26	15	3	0	2	27	13	3	.408	.364
2-team total (4 DSL Phillies Red)					.262	.280	.257	44	130	24	34	7	2	2	27	17	4	0	2	30	16	3	.392	.359
Raylin Heredia	R-R	6-0	174	11-10-03	.273	.231	.286	51	172	27	47	16	5	2	33	13	3	0	2	49	7	1	.459	.332
Andres Hernandez	R-R	6-2	180	3-10-05	.147	.083	.161	27	68	9	10	2	1	0	9	14	2	0	1	23	0	1	.206	.306
Manolfi Jimenez	L-L	6-0	190	11-14-04	.246	.323	.228	49	167	26	41	9	1	2	24	12	2	0	4	28	3	1	.347	.297
Jarol Martinez	R-R	6-2	150	7-19-03	.294	.182	.333	35	85	22	25	3	0	0	10	14	4	0	0	26	3	2	.329	.417
Angel Mata	R-R	6-1	175	1-4-05	.253	.333	.233	33	75	9	19	3	0	1	12	8	1	0	1	8	1	0	.333	.329
Romel Mendez	L-L	6-0	160	1-10-05	.233	.077	.277	21	60	18	14	3	0	0	1	7	3	1	0	10	3	1	.283	.343
Leonardo Rondon	B-R	5-8	160	3-10-04	.340	.455	.309	41	103	16	35	7	2	1	15	10	7	4	1	18	5	3	.476	.430
Ricardo Rosario	R-R	6-1	160	2-8-03	.346	.167	.400	8	26	3	9	3	1	0	3	2	0	1	1	7	3	1	.538	.379
Brahian Silva	R-R	5-11	170	12-30-02	.255	.125	.279	29	51	11	13	3	0	1	9	17	4	1	1	14	3	1	.373	.466
Andres Tabares	L-L	6-1	165	8-25-05	.255	.182	.275	24	51	6	13	0	0	0	6	7	1	1	0	11	3	5	.255	.356
Juan Villavicencio	L-R	5-10	155	11-24-04	.266	.227	.273	46	143	29	38	8	2	2	16	20	1	1	1	35	13	1	.392	.358

Pitching	B-T	HT	WT	DOB	W	L	ERA	G	GS	CG	SV	IP	H	R	ER	HR	BB	SO	AVG	vLH	vRH	K/9	BB/9
Luis Alcala	L-R	6-2	180	9-21-96	1	0	4.91	9	0	0	1	18	17	12	10	2	3	10	.243	.286	.232	4.91	1.47
Saul Alcala	R-R	6-1	158	11-7-00	2	0	1.50	6	0	0	1	12	9	3	2	1	1	9	.205	.286	.167	6.75	0.75
Juan Amarante	L-L	5-10	177	4-14-04	3	0	2.79	15	0	0	2	29	21	10	9	1	10	40	.196	.150	.207	12.41	3.10
Kleyderve Andrade	L-L	5-11	180	12-19-02	0	0	6.14	5	0	0	0	7	8	7	5	0	5	6	.296	.000	.320	7.36	6.14
Joalbert Angulo	L-L	6-5	165	10-30-01	2	0	3.48	4	0	0	0	10	9	5	4	0	5	12	.243	.125	.276	10.45	4.35
Hermes Astudillo	R-R	5-11	160	3-2-02	5	1	3.50	14	0	0	4	18	19	12	7	0	9	20	.284	.267	.288	10.00	4.50
Fliecer Bata	R-R	6-3	190	3-20-04	1	2	3.95	10	10	0	0	41	44	25	18	6	6	35	.265	.304	.245	7.68	1.32
Wilmer Blanco	R-R	6-3	170	2-21-04	0	3	5.70	11	6	0	0	24	25	10	15	1	18	26	.272	.323	.246	9.51	6.85
Javier Fuenmayor	R-R	6-2	170	1-20-03	2	2	3.82	12	4	0	2	38	40	23	16	1	10	27	.268	.224	.290	6.45	2.39
Alexis Garibaldi	L-L	6-4	195	3-19-04	1	0	3.86	9	1	0	0	14	6	6	6	0	15	12	.130	.286	.103	7.71	9.64
Maxwel Hernandez	R-R	6-2	190	5-14-03	3	2	0.72	11	11	0	0	50	24	9	4	1	16	51	.140	.102	.156	9.24	2.90
Diego Linares	R-R	6-2	180	9-29-02	5	1	3.38	13	0	0	1	27	18	13	10	1	6	26	.189	.172	.197	8.78	2.03
Juan Melendez	R-R	6-3	170	7-19-04	0	0	16.55	9	1	0	0	10	16	21	19	1	15	7	.372	.429	.345	6.10	13.06
Douglas Mijares	R-R	6-3	165	4-27-00	6	2	5.14	14	1	0	1	28	33	19	16	2	4	23	.295	.250	.319	7.39	1.29
Danyony Pulido	R-R	6-1	165	10-19-02	2	2	1.82	11	11	0	0	49	32	13	10	2	28	34	.203	.241	.183	6.20	5.11
Miguelangel Rodriguez	R-R	6-4	195	6-2-03	0	0	8.64	6	0	0	0	8	12	11	0	0	9	8	.316	.357	.292	8.64	9.72
Maikel Rosales	R-R	6-2	175	10-14-03	2	0	3.86	11	0	0	0	16	13	8	7	0	9	12	.217	.235	.209	6.61	4.96
Saul Teran	R-R	6-1	165	3-20-02	0	3	4.50	15	4	0	5	32	33	17	16	3	11	36	.264	.359	.221	10.13	3.09
Ezequiel Ventura	R-R	6-1	151	6-20-02	5	1	2.40	11	10	1	0	49	38	15	13	2	18	38	.221	.211	.226	7.03	3.33

Fielding

C: Andrade 22, Mata 31, Rondon 15, Silva 16. **1B:** Andrade 1, Barria 2, Escobar 41, Gutierrez 1, Martinez 13, Rondon 15, Rosario 1. **2B:** Barria 4, Beltran 26, Bergolla 8, Carela 17, Escobar 1, Rondon 2, Villavicencio 16. **3B:** Barria 15, Beltran 3, Bergolla 1, Carela 16, Hernandez 26, Martinez 12, Rondon 1, Villavicencio 5. **SS:** Barria 6, Beltran 23, Bergolla 14, Carela 2, Hernandez 1, Villavicencio 23. **OF:** Garcia 47, Gutierrez 37, Heredia 46, Jimenez 37, Martinez 1, Mendez 12, Rosario 7, Tabares 22.

Pittsburgh Pirates

SEASON IN A SENTENCE: Pirates fans got to see some shiny new toys in one of baseball's best ballparks, but they also had to watch another 100-loss team, as the Bucs lost 100 games in consecutive seasons for the first time since the early 1950s.

HIGH POINT: A three-game sweep of the 111-win Dodgers, in Los Angeles, May 30-June 1 qualifies but also seems fluky. Rookie shortstop O'Neil Cruz has more staying power and was the most entertaining Pirates player in years and must-watch TV. High points included the hardest-hit ball in the Statcast era (dating to 2015), a 122.4 mph single on Aug. 24 against the Braves, and the hardest infield throw in MLB history, clocked at 97.8 mph in a July 14 game in Miami.

LOW POINT: The Pirates' only winning month was October (3-2). And right after that Dodgers sweep and subsequent series win against Arizona, Pittsburgh embarked on a season-long nine-game losing streak, confirmation that the sweep in L.A. was a mirage. The offense generated 20 runs in those nine games en route to ranking last in the National League in OPS (.655) and 14th in runs (591).

NOTABLE ROOKIES: Cruz had plenty of downs with his ups, from his .294 OBP to 126 strikeouts in just 331 at-bats, but his high upside and premium tools shined through. Other Bucs rookies provided power and hit for similarly low averages, such as outfielder Jack Suwinski, whose 19 homers ranked second on the club, and Diego Castillo, who hit 11 bombs while starting in five different defensive spots. Righthander Roansy Contreras looked like a future rotation stalwart, going 5-5, 3.79 in 20 starts and showing a four-pitch power repertoire.

KEY TRANSACTIONS: The Pirates' front office flipped a pair of veteran impending free-agents for prospects at the deadline in DH Dan Vogelbach (Mets) and lefthander Jose Quintana (Cardinals), who had been the club's best starter in the first half. The most trivial (and amusing) transaction goes to infielder Rodolfo Castro, suspended by MLB for a game when his mobile phone fell out of his pants pocket, during a game, when he slid into third base in an August game in Arizona.

ON THE FARM: Catcher Endy Rodriguez began the season as a multi-positional player at High-A Greensboro in deference to 2021 No. 1 pick Henry Davis. By the end of the year, he was the team's breakout prospect who reached Triple-A.

OPENING DAY PAYROLL: $61,661,800 (27th).

PLAYERS OF THE YEAR

MAJOR LEAGUE
Bryan Reynolds
OF
.262/.345/.461
27 HR in 145 G
Career high for HR

MINOR LEAGUE
Endy Rodriguez
C
(HiA/AA/AAA)
.323/.407/.590
25 HR, 39 2B in 125 G

ORGANIZATION LEADERS

Batting — *Minimum 250 AB

MAJORS		
* AVG	Bryan Reynolds	.262
* OPS	Bryan Reynolds	.807
HR	Bryan Reynolds	27
RBI	Bryan Reynolds	62
MINORS		
* AVG	Endy Rodriguez, Greensboro, Altoona, Indianapolis	.323
* OBP	Endy Rodriguez, Greensboro, Altoona, Indianapolis	.407
* SLG	Matt Gorski, Bradenton, Greens., Altoona, Ind.	.598
* OPS	Endy Rodriguez, Greensboro, Altoona, Indianapolis	.996
R	Endy Rodriguez, Greensboro, Altoona, Indianapolis	92
H	Endy Rodriguez, Greensboro, Altoona, Indianapolis	148
TB	Endy Rodriguez, Greensboro, Altoona, Indianapolis	270
2B	Endy Rodriguez, Greensboro, Altoona, Indianapolis	39
3B	Travis Swaggerty, Indianapolis	8
HR	Aaron Shackelford, Altoona, Indianapolis	26
RBI	Endy Rodriguez, Greensboro, Altoona, Indianapolis	95
BB	Andres Alvarez, Altoona	64
SO	Mason Martin, Indianapolis	194
SB	Tsung-Che Cheng, Bradenton	33

Pitching — #Minimum 75 IP

MAJORS		
W	Wil Crowe	6
	Chase De Jong	
# ERA	Jose Quintana	3.50
SO	J.T. Brubaker	147
SV	David Bednar	19
MINORS		
W	Domingo Gonzalez, Greensboro, Altoona	9
L	Adrian Florencio, Greensboro	10
# ERA	Cody Bolton, Indianapolis	3.09
G	Hunter Stratton, Indianapolis	47
GS	Jared Jones, Greensboro	26
SV	Tyler Samaniego, Greensboro, Altoona	14
IP	Luis Ortiz, Altoona, Indianapolis	124.1
BB	Osvaldo Bido, Indianapolis	64
SO	Jared Jones, Greensboro	142
# AVG	Nick Garcia, Greensboro	.2184

2022 PERFORMANCE

General Manager: Ben Cherington. **Farm Director:** John Baker. **Scouting Director:** Joe Delli Carri.

Class	Team	League	W	L	PCT	Finish	Manager
Majors	Pittsburgh Pirates	National	62	100	.383	t-13th (15)	Derek Shelton
Triple-A	Indianapolis Indians	International	74	75	.497	t-10th (15)	Miguel Perez
Double-A	Altoona Curve	Eastern	71	66	.518	6th (12)	Kieran Mattison
High-A	Greensboro Grasshoppers	South Atlantic	50	70	.417	9th (12)	Callix Crabbe
Low-A	Bradenton Marauders	Florida State	67	62	.519	4th (10)	Jonathan Johnston
Rookie	FCL Pirates	Florida Complex	30	25	.545	7th (16)	Jose Mosquera
Overall 2022 Minor League Record			370	346	.517	12th (30)	

ORGANIZATION STATISTICS

PITTSBURGH PIRATES

NATIONAL LEAGUE

Batting	B-T	HT	WT	DOB	AVG	vLH	vRH	G	AB	R	H	2B	3B	HR	RBI	BB	HBP	SH	SF	SO	SB	CS	SLG	OBP
Anthony Alford	R-R	6-1	215	7-20-94	.250	.000	1.000	2	4	0	1	0	0	0	0	0	0	0	0	2	0	0	.250	.250
Greg Allen	B-R	6-0	185	3-15-93	.186	.182	.190	46	118	17	22	4	0	2	8	10	2	3	1	42	8	2	.271	.260
Miguel Andujar	R-R	6-0	211	3-2-95	.250	.444	.185	9	36	4	9	3	1	0	9	2	0	0	2	5	0	1	.389	.275
Ji Hwan Bae	L-R	6-1	185	7-26-99	.333	.000	.423	10	33	5	11	3	0	0	6	2	2	0	0	6	3	0	.424	.405
Diego Castillo	R-R	5-11	185	10-28-97	.206	.239	.167	96	262	28	54	13	0	11	29	14	3	0	4	75	1	1	.382	.251
Rodolfo Castro	B-R	6-0	205	5-21-99	.233	.263	.220	71	253	25	59	8	4	11	27	22	2	0	1	74	5	3	.427	.299
Yu Chang	R-R	6-1	180	8-18-95	.167	.200	.083	18	42	5	7	1	0	1	2	4	3	0	0	18	0	1	.262	.286
Michael Chavis	R-R	5-10	190	8-11-95	.229	.240	.222	129	401	39	92	16	3	14	49	19	2	0	4	126	1	1	.389	.265
Zack Collins	L-R	6-3	220	2-6-95	.040	.000	.043	10	25	2	1	0	0	0	1	3	0	0	1	10	0	0	.040	.138
Oneil Cruz	L-R	6-7	220	10-4-98	.233	.158	.265	87	331	45	77	13	4	17	54	28	1	0	1	126	10	4	.450	.294
Jason Delay	R-R	5-11	200	3-7-95	.213	.242	.191	57	155	17	33	6	0	1	11	9	2	1	0	50	0	2	.271	.265
Ben Gamel	L-L	5-11	180	5-17-92	.232	.175	.252	115	371	42	86	20	2	9	46	48	3	0	1	98	5	1	.369	.324
Jose Godoy	L-R	5-11	200	10-13-94	.059	.000	.067	8	17	1	1	0	0	0	1	0	0	0	0	7	0	0	.059	.059
Ke'Bryan Hayes	R-R	5-10	205	1-28-97	.244	.270	.232	136	505	55	123	24	3	7	41	48	5	0	2	122	20	5	.345	.314
Tyler Heineman	B-R	5-10	190	6-19-91	.211	.255	.184	52	142	14	30	6	0	0	8	8	5	3	0	13	1	0	.254	.277
Andrew Knapp	B-R	6-1	189	11-9-91	.129	.333	.107	11	31	2	4	1	0	0	2	3	1	0	0	9	0	0	.161	.229
2-team total (3 San Francisco Giants)					.143	.250	.129	14	35	4	5	1	0	0	4	5	1	0	1	9	0	0	.171	.262
Bligh Madris	L-R	6-0	208	2-29-96	.177	.190	.174	39	113	10	20	7	0	1	7	10	0	0	0	31	2	1	.265	.244
Tucupita Marcano	L-R	6-0	180	9-16-99	.206	.239	.193	49	160	18	33	6	2	2	13	10	1	5	1	44	2	1	.306	.256
Jake Marisnick	R-R	6-4	220	3-30-91	.234	.150	.324	31	77	9	18	6	0	2	6	4	0	1	0	24	2	1	.390	.272
Cal Mitchell	L-L	6-0	205	3-8-99	.226	.245	.220	69	212	21	48	11	0	5	17	18	0	1	1	52	3	1	.349	.286
Kevin Newman	R-R	6-0	195	8-4-93	.274	.361	.230	78	288	31	79	18	2	2	24	16	2	2	1	48	8	2	.372	.316
Kevin Padlo	R-R	6-2	210	7-15-96	.000	.000	.000	3	11	0	0	0	0	0	0	0	0	0	0	1	0	0	.000	.000
2-team total (4 San Francisco Giants)					.087	.000	.143	7	23	0	2	0	0	0	0	0	0	0	0	5	0	0	.087	.087
Hoy Park	L-R	6-1	200	4-7-96	.216	.125	.233	23	51	7	11	2	0	2	6	4	1	2	2	15	1	0	.373	.276
Liover Peguero	R-R	6-2	200	12-31-00	.333	.500	.000	1	3	0	1	0	0	0	0	1	0	0	0	2	0	0	.333	.500
Michael Perez	L-R	5-10	195	8-7-92	.150	.120	.159	39	107	8	16	0	0	6	11	8	0	1	0	26	1	0	.318	.209
2-team total (6 New York Mets)					.149	.115	.158	45	121	10	18	0	0	6	14	10	0	1	0	32	1	0	.298	.214
Roberto Perez	R-R	5-11	220	12-23-88	.233	.238	.231	21	60	8	14	2	0	2	8	9	0	0	0	25	0	0	.367	.333
Bryan Reynolds	B-R	6-3	205	1-27-95	.262	.273	.258	145	542	74	142	19	4	27	62	56	14	0	2	141	7	3	.461	.345
Canaan Smith-Njigba	L-R	6-0	230	4-30-99	.200	--	.200	3	5	1	1	1	0	0	0	1	1	0	0	0	0	0	.400	.429
Jack Suwinski	L-L	6-2	215	7-29-98	.202	.122	.237	106	326	45	66	11	0	19	38	41	4	0	1	114	4	2	.411	.298
Travis Swaggerty	L-L	5-10	200	8-19-97	.111	.167	.000	5	9	0	1	0	0	0	0	0	0	0	0	4	0	0	.111	.111
Yoshi Tsutsugo	L-R	6-1	225	11-26-91	.171	.175	.168	50	170	11	29	4	0	2	19	19	0	0	4	50	0	0	.229	.249
Cole Tucker	B-R	6-3	200	7-3-96	.175	.071	.204	18	63	3	11	1	1	0	2	0	0	0	0	25	1	0	.222	.175
Josh VanMeter	L-R	5-11	194	3-10-95	.187	.069	.211	67	171	15	32	5	2	3	14	19	0	0	2	45	4	0	.292	.266

Pitching	B-T	HT	WT	DOB	W	L	ERA	G	GS	CG	SV	IP	H	R	ER	HR	BB	SO	AVG	vLH	vRH	K/9	BB/9
Cam Alldred	L-L	6-3	205	7-25-96	0	0	0.00	1	0	0	0	1	1	0	0	0	0	1	.250	.333	.000	9.00	0.00
Anthony Banda	L-L	6-2	220	8-10-93	1	0	6.41	23	0	0	0	20	34	14	14	3	5	22	.374	.405	.352	10.07	2.29
Manny Banuelos	R-L	5-10	215	3-13-91	2	1	4.96	31	0	0	0	33	25	21	18	2	18	34	.214	.216	.212	9.37	4.96
David Bednar	L-R	6-1	250	10-10-94	3	4	2.61	45	0	0	19	52	42	19	15	4	16	69	.218	.188	.239	12.02	2.79
Tyler Beede	R-R	6-2	216	5-23-93	2	5	5.23	25	5	0	0	52	57	32	30	6	23	35	.274	.253	.294	6.10	4.01
2-team total (6 San Francisco Giants)					2	5	5.14	31	5	0	0	61	71	37	35	7	29	39	.284	.267	.300	5.72	4.26
Austin Brice	R-R	6-4	238	6-19-92	0	0	4.05	4	0	0	0	7	4	3	3	0	3	5	.167	.182	.154	6.75	4.05
JT Brubaker	R-R	6-3	185	11-17-93	3	12	4.69	28	28	0	0	144	157	85	75	17	54	147	.271	.269	.272	9.19	3.38
Diego Castillo	R-R	5-11	185	10-28-97	0	0	36.00	2	0	0	0	2	6	8	8	1	3	1	.545	.500	.600	4.50	13.50
Roansy Contreras	R-R	6-0	175	11-7-99	5	5	3.79	21	18	0	0	95	82	45	40	13	39	86	.225	.204	.239	8.15	3.69
Wil Crowe	R-R	6-2	245	9-9-94	6	10	4.38	60	1	0	4	76	68	40	37	8	38	68	.235	.198	.260	8.05	4.50
Chase De Jong	L-R	6-4	230	12-29-93	6	3	2.64	42	0	0	1	72	52	24	21	10	30	59	.204	.209	.200	7.41	3.77
Yerry De Los Santos	R-R	6-2	215	12-12-97	0	3	4.91	26	0	0	3	26	22	18	14	3	11	26	.224	.214	.232	9.12	3.86
Jerad Eickhoff	R-R	6-4	246	7-2-90	0	1	20.77	1	1	0	0	4	10	10	10	2	1	4	.455	.636	.273	8.31	2.08
Junior Fernandez	R-R	6-3	215	3-2-97	0	0	0.00	3	0	0	0	3	1	0	0	0	4	2	.100	.250	.000	5.40	10.80

2-team total (13 St. Louis Cardinals)					0	0	2.41	16	0	0	0	19	18	6	5	3	12	14	.257	.235	.264	6.75	5.79
Aaron Fletcher	L-L	6-0	220	2-25-96	0	1	6.94	9	0	0	0	12	10	9	9	2	4	6	.233	.250	.222	4.63	3.09
Heath Hembree	R-R	6-4	220	1-13-89	2	0	7.16	20	0	0	0	16	17	13	13	5	14	12	.274	.444	.205	6.61	7.71
2-team total (6 Los Angeles Dodgers)					3	1	7.36	26	0	0	0	22	26	19	18	6	17	17	.299	.452	.214	6.95	6.95
Colin Holderman	R-R	6-7	240	10-8-95	1	0	6.75	9	0	0	0	11	9	8	8	0	7	6	.237	.167	.300	5.06	5.91
2-team total (15 New York Mets)					5	0	3.81	24	0	0	0	28	20	14	12	0	14	24	.206	.195	.214	7.62	4.45
Sam Howard	R-L	6-4	195	3-5-93	0	0	9.00	3	0	0	0	2	2	2	2	1	4	1	.286	.500	.000	4.50	18.00
Mitch Keller	R-R	6-2	220	4-4-96	5	12	3.91	31	29	0	0	159	162	77	69	14	60	138	.266	.276	.257	7.81	3.40
Max Kranick	R-R	6-3	220	7-21-97	0	0	0.00	2	0	0	0	5	3	0	0	0	3	4	.188	.000	.375	7.20	5.40
Nick Mears	R-R	6-2	200	10-7-96	0	0	0.00	2	0	0	0	2	1	0	0	0	1	2	.143	.333	.000	9.00	4.50
Luis Ortiz	R-R	6-2	240	1-27-99	0	2	4.50	4	4	0	0	16	8	9	8	1	10	17	.136	.167	.122	9.56	5.63
Johan Oviedo	R-R	6-5	245	3-2-98	2	2	3.23	7	7	0	0	31	23	12	11	1	16	28	.198	.280	.136	8.22	4.70
2-team total (14 St. Louis Cardinals)					4	3	3.21	21	8	0	0	56	49	21	20	5	23	54	.227	.195	.248	8.68	3.70
Dillon Peters	L-L	5-11	195	8-31-92	5	2	4.58	22	4	0	0	39	35	20	20	5	17	26	.241	.160	.284	5.95	3.89
Yohan Ramirez	R-R	6-4	212	5-6-95	3	1	3.67	22	0	0	1	27	22	11	11	1	13	21	.224	.289	.183	7.00	4.33
Robert Stephenson	R-R	6-3	205	2-24-93	0	1	3.38	13	0	0	0	13	10	5	5	2	1	18	.213	.105	.286	12.15	0.68
2-team total (45 Colorado Rockies)					2	2	5.43	58	0	0	0	58	63	39	35	10	14	55	.275	.260	.288	8.53	2.17
Eric Stout	L-L	6-3	205	3-27-93	0	0	5.79	18	0	0	1	19	22	13	12	1	15	19	.286	.152	.386	9.16	7.23
2-team total (2 Chicago Cubs)					0	0	5.64	20	0	0	1	22	25	15	14	2	16	25	.275	.158	.358	10.07	6.45
Beau Sulser	R-R	6-2	195	5-5-94	0	0	3.72	4	0	0	0	10	8	9	4	1	6	10	.211	.235	.190	9.31	5.59
Zach Thompson	R-R	6-7	250	10-23-93	3	10	5.18	29	22	0	0	122	138	76	70	19	46	90	.280	.256	.301	6.66	3.40
Duane Underwood Jr.	R-R	6-2	225	7-20-94	1	6	4.40	51	1	0	1	57	58	35	28	1	25	57	.254	.298	.224	8.95	3.92
Josh VanMeter	L-R	5-11	194	3-10-95	0	0	39.00	3	0	0	0	3	15	13	13	5	2	0	.600	.600	.600	0.00	6.00
Cam Vieaux	L-L	6-3	200	12-5-93	0	0	10.38	8	0	0	0	9	15	11	10	2	5	15	.366	.222	.478	15.58	5.19
Bryse Wilson	R-R	6-1	250	12-20-97	3	9	5.52	25	20	0	0	116	132	80	71	20	32	79	.287	.299	.276	6.15	2.49
Miguel Yajure	R-R	6-1	215	5-1-98	1	1	8.88	12	1	0	1	24	31	26	24	3	16	16	.307	.386	.246	5.92	5.92

Fielding

Catcher	PCT	G	PO	A	E	DP	PB
Collins	1.000	2	10	1	0	0	0
Delay	.978	57	393	15	9	2	0
Godoy	1.000	8	43	2	0	0	0
Heineman	.989	50	340	25	4	2	4
Knapp	.971	11	64	3	2	0	1
Perez	.996	38	264	12	1	1	1
Perez	.994	20	163	4	1	0	1
VanMeter	1.000	1	1	0	0	0	0

First Base	PCT	G	PO	A	E	DP
Castillo	.943	7	30	3	2	3
Chang	1.000	5	40	2	0	3
Chavis	.996	107	679	39	3	66
Collins	1.000	8	36	3	0	5
Gamel	.978	5	43	1	1	5
Madris	1.000	9	60	3	0	4
Padlo	1.000	1	9	0	0	2
Tsutsugo	.993	35	260	15	2	29
VanMeter	.974	21	139	11	4	21
Vogelbach	.857	5	5	1	1	1

Second Base	PCT	G	PO	A	E	DP
Bae	1.000	4	8	11	0	2
Castillo	1.000	28	39	51	0	12
Castro	.966	32	57	84	5	19
Chang	.972	11	14	21	1	5
Chavis	1.000	14	12	12	0	3
Marcano	.989	23	36	52	1	7
Newman	.994	42	73	104	1	32
Park	.974	11	16	21	1	5
Tucker	1.000	6	5	11	0	2
VanMeter	.969	39	44	82	4	22

Third Base	PCT	G	PO	A	E	DP
Castillo	.750	4	0	3	1	0
Castro	.950	24	11	46	3	7
Chavis	.842	9	5	11	3	1
Hayes	.972	133	109	307	12	36
Padlo	1.000	2	2	3	0	2
Park	.889	6	3	5	1	0
VanMeter	1.000	2	1	3	0	0

Shortstop	PCT	G	PO	A	E	DP
Castillo	.950	32	30	65	5	10
Castro	.934	19	18	53	5	9
Cruz	.953	79	135	211	17	54
Hayes	1.000	3	3	1	0	0
Marcano	1.000	1	1	0	0	0
Newman	.955	33	35	71	5	18
Park	1.000	3	3	7	0	2
Peguero	1.000	1	2	3	0	0
Tucker	.750	3	3	3	2	0

Outfield	PCT	G	PO	A	E	DP
Alford	1.000	3	1	0	0	0
Allen	1.000	47	70	0	0	0
Andujar	1.000	4	7	0	0	0
Bae	.818	6	9	0	2	0
Castillo	.972	22	35	0	1	0
Cruz	--	1	0	0	0	0
Gamel	.993	97	140	2	1	0
Madris	1.000	26	41	0	0	0
Marcano	.977	31	40	3	1	1
Marisnick	1.000	30	58	1	0	0
Mitchell	.978	54	86	1	2	1
Park	.800	2	4	0	1	0
Reynolds	.993	128	282	2	2	1
Smith-Njigba	1.000	2	4	0	0	0
Suwinski	.988	113	162	7	2	1
Swaggerty	.500	4	1	0	1	0
Tucker	1.000	12	17	0	0	0
VanMeter	--	1	0	0	0	0

INDIANAPOLIS INDIANS — *TRIPLE-A*

INTERNATIONAL LEAGUE

Batting	B-T	HT	WT	DOB	AVG	vLH	vRH	G	AB	R	H	2B	3B	HR	RBI	BB	HBP	SH	SF	SO	SB	CS	SLG	OBP
Anthony Alford	R-R	6-1	215	7-20-94	.250	.400	.000	3	8	3	2	0	0	2	2	3	0	0	0	2	1	0	1.000	.455
2-team total (8 Columbus Clippers)					.184	.200	.179	11	38	9	7	0	0	4	4	6	0	0	0	15	2	0	.500	.295
Greg Allen	B-R	6-0	185	3-15-93	.429	.500	.333	4	14	4	6	2	0	1	3	0	2	0	0	3	0	0	.786	.500
Ji Hwan Bae	L-R	6-1	185	7-26-99	.289	.325	.274	108	419	81	121	23	6	8	53	48	2	1	3	80	30	8	.430	.362
Carter Bins	R-R	6-0	215	10-7-98	.208	.180	.217	71	245	35	51	13	3	10	32	25	7	0	2	100	2	0	.408	.297
Josh Bissonette	R-R	6-0	185	11-1-96	.213	.188	.222	44	122	18	26	8	0	0	15	20	1	2	0	33	1	0	.279	.329
Diego Castillo	R-R	5-11	185	10-28-97	.246	.286	.232	35	134	21	33	6	0	3	12	14	3	0	0	33	2	1	.358	.331
Rodolfo Castro	B-R	6-0	205	5-21-99	.246	.286	.227	75	272	37	67	13	2	12	40	32	6	0	4	86	6	3	.441	.334
Brendt Citta	R-R	6-2	180	7-12-96	.257	.262	.255	41	144	19	37	10	0	5	27	14	3	0	2	45	0	0	.431	.331
Zack Collins	L-R	6-3	220	2-6-95	.250	--	.250	2	8	2	2	1	0	0	1	1	0	0	1	2	0	1	.375	.300
2-team total (36 Buffalo Bisons)					.198	.195	.200	38	126	17	25	8	1	5	29	33	1	0	5	42	3	1	.397	.358
Oneil Cruz	L-R	6-7	220	10-4-98	.232	.220	.237	55	211	40	49	7	3	9	35	30	4	0	2	56	11	6	.422	.336
Taylor Davis	R-R	5-10	200	11-28-89	.273	.250	.280	40	121	9	33	4	0	0	15	16	1	3	3	21	0	0	.306	.355
Jason Delay	R-R	5-11	200	3-7-95	.220	.167	.250	28	82	10	18	5	1	0	8	8	0	2	1	15	1	0	.305	.286
Ben Gamel	L-L	5-11	180	5-17-92	.226	.125	.261	8	31	8	7	1	0	1	3	2	2	0	0	6	0	0	.355	.314
Jose Godoy	L-R	5-11	200	10-13-94	.333	.300	.345	10	39	7	13	1	0	3	12	1	1	0	1	7	0	0	.590	.357
2-team total (43 St. Paul Saints)					.227	.200	.240	53	176	20	40	6	0	6	26	14	2	0	1	48	0	0	.364	.290

Matt Gorski	R-R	6-4	198	12-22-97	.500	--	.500	1	2	0	1	0	0	0	0	0	0	0	0	1	1	0	.500	.500
Mike Jarvis	R-R	5-10	180	5-12-98	.120	.000	.150	8	25	5	3	1	0	0	1	3	0	0	0	9	0	0	.160	.214
Connor Kaiser	R-R	6-4	195	11-20-96	.222	.250	.200	3	9	2	2	0	0	0	1	2	1	0	0	2	0	0	.222	.417
Bligh Madris	L-R	6-0	208	2-29-96	.294	.267	.306	71	255	34	75	19	4	7	34	29	1	1	2	63	4	2	.482	.366
2-team total (10 Durham Bulls)					.297	.253	.316	81	296	45	88	22	4	11	49	33	1	1	3	74	4	2	.510	.366
Drew Maggi	R-R	6-0	192	5-16-89	.219	.222	.217	28	96	16	21	8	1	0	8	5	3	0	1	30	8	0	.323	.276
2-team total (66 Lehigh Valley IronPigs)					.212	.207	.215	94	292	43	62	16	1	0	22	40	9	3	2	84	22	5	.274	.324
Tucupita Marcano	L-R	6-0	180	9-16-99	.287	.214	.315	25	101	16	29	5	0	3	9	13	0	0	1	16	1	5	.426	.365
Jake Marisnick	R-R	6-4	220	3-30-91	.250	.429	.190	7	28	2	7	2	0	0	0	2	1	0	0	13	0	0	.321	.323
2-team total (17 Gwinnett Stripers)					.240	.320	.211	24	96	10	23	3	1	1	3	5	4	0	0	31	7	1	.323	.305
Mason Martin	L-R	6-0	220	6-2-99	.210	.213	.209	134	481	62	101	29	5	19	74	52	2	0	6	194	12	3	.410	.287
Cal Mitchell	L-L	6-0	205	3-8-99	.339	.333	.341	63	236	33	80	18	2	9	49	17	5	0	3	38	8	1	.547	.391
Kevin Newman	R-R	6-0	195	8-4-93	.396	.400	.394	13	48	6	19	3	0	0	6	3	1	0	1	6	0	0	.458	.434
Malcom Nunez	R-R	5-11	205	3-9-01	.231	.000	.250	5	13	1	3	0	0	1	1	4	0	0	0	5	0	0	.462	.412
Jared Oliva	R-R	6-2	200	11-27-95	.266	.316	.251	99	319	54	85	22	3	8	37	24	4	0	2	77	21	4	.429	.324
Hunter Owen	R-R	5-11	200	9-22-93	.246	.250	.243	18	57	11	14	2	1	1	6	8	3	0	0	20	0	0	.368	.368
Kevin Padlo	R-R	6-2	210	7-15-96	.279	.391	.238	22	86	15	24	7	0	1	15	9	0	0	1	31	3	0	.395	.344
Hoy Park	L-R	6-1	200	4-7-96	.225	.256	.214	89	316	48	71	11	0	10	37	52	0	1	2	99	14	0	.354	.332
Michael Perez	L-R	5-10	195	8-7-92	.294	.333	.286	8	17	3	5	1	0	0	2	10	0	0	0	5	0	0	.353	.556
2-team total (17 Syracuse Mets)					.208	.200	.211	25	77	6	16	3	0	2	12	13	1	0	1	23	0	0	.325	.326
Jamie Ritchie	R-R	6-2	203	4-9-93	.242	.160	.270	35	99	12	24	4	0	0	11	21	0	0	0	20	0	0	.283	.375
Endy Rodriguez	B-R	6-0	170	5-26-00	.455	.333	.474	6	22	2	10	2	1	1	8	0	0	0	1	3	0	0	.773	.435
Blake Sabol	L-R	6-4	225	1-7-98	.296	.333	.286	25	81	13	24	3	1	5	15	17	2	0	1	22	1	0	.543	.426
Aaron Shackelford	L-R	5-10	215	10-16-96	.063	.000	.077	4	16	0	1	0	0	0	0	0	0	0	0	7	0	0	.063	.063
Canaan Smith-Njigba	L-R	6-0	230	4-30-99	.277	.200	.310	52	184	31	51	15	3	1	19	33	0	1	0	52	8	3	.408	.387
Jack Suwinski	L-L	6-2	215	7-29-98	.214	.156	.235	31	117	19	25	5	0	6	18	11	1	0	1	49	1	0	.410	.285
Travis Swaggerty	L-L	5-10	200	8-19-97	.254	.241	.259	107	398	55	101	15	8	9	55	57	1	1	1	117	20	5	.399	.348
Yoshi Tsutsugo	L-R	6-1	225	11-26-91	.440	.375	.471	9	25	4	11	2	0	2	12	9	0	0	2	3	0	0	.760	.556
2-team total (29 Buffalo Bisons)					.301	.267	.321	38	123	19	37	6	0	7	30	28	0	0	3	41	0	1	.520	.422
Cole Tucker	B-R	6-3	200	7-3-96	.135	--	.135	10	37	5	5	1	0	0	4	5	0	0	0	12	1	0	.162	.238
Josh VanMeter	L-R	5-11	194	3-10-95	.161	.000	.217	9	31	6	5	2	0	1	3	7	0	0	0	10	0	1	.323	.316

Pitching	B-T	HT	WT	DOB	W	L	ERA	G	GS	CG	SV	IP	H	R	ER	HR	BB	SO	AVG	vLH	vRH	K/9	BB/9
Cam Alldred	L-L	6-3	205	7-25-96	3	3	4.07	42	2	0	1	66	66	33	30	5	25	62	.260	.231	.276	8.41	3.39
Jeremy Beasley	R-R	6-2	235	11-20-95	0	0	--	1	0	0	0	0	2	3	3	0	1	0	1.000	1.000	1.000	--	--
2-team total (19 Buffalo Bisons)					2	1	2.61	20	3	0	1	38	22	12	11	5	12	43	.165	.197	.139	10.18	2.84
David Bednar	L-R	6-1	250	10-10-94	0	1	3.00	3	1	0	0	3	2	1	1	0	1	4	.182	.000	.250	12.00	3.00
Tyler Beede	R-R	6-2	216	5-23-93	0	0	0.00	1	1	0	0	2	2	0	0	0	0	1	.333	.000	.400	4.50	0.00
Osvaldo Bido	R-R	6-3	175	10-18-95	3	8	4.53	32	25	0	0	111	103	70	56	18	64	122	.242	.224	.254	9.86	5.17
Cody Bolton	R-R	6-3	230	6-19-98	4	2	3.09	30	14	0	0	76	57	32	26	4	40	82	.207	.212	.205	9.75	4.76
Austin Brice	R-R	6-4	238	6-19-92	3	4	5.56	37	2	0	6	44	42	32	27	7	18	53	.244	.277	.224	10.92	3.71
Mike Burrows	R-R	6-2	195	11-8-99	1	4	5.31	12	10	0	0	42	45	27	25	5	12	42	.271	.275	.268	8.93	2.55
Brad Case	R-R	6-6	242	9-13-96	1	1	9.35	6	0	0	0	9	18	9	9	0	3	7	.409	.389	.423	7.27	3.12
Roansy Contreras	R-R	6-0	175	11-7-99	1	1	3.15	9	9	0	0	34	29	13	12	4	13	46	.227	.229	.225	12.06	3.41
Chase De Jong	L-R	6-4	230	12-29-93	1	0	2.08	3	2	0	0	13	7	3	3	0	5	19	.156	.091	.217	13.15	3.46
Yerry De Los Santos	R-R	6-2	215	12-12-97	2	0	1.72	12	0	0	3	16	8	3	3	1	2	20	.148	.050	.206	11.49	1.15
Matt Eckelman	R-R	6-3	281	10-6-93	0	3	7.67	24	2	0	0	32	46	33	27	8	16	27	.331	.328	.333	7.67	4.55
Jerad Eickhoff	R-R	6-4	246	7-2-90	6	7	4.96	28	20	0	0	114	102	68	63	17	30	107	.236	.242	.231	8.42	2.36
Junior Fernandez	R-R	6-3	215	3-2-97	1	0	2.25	6	0	0	0	8	2	2	2	0	6	8	.080	.250	.048	9.00	6.75
2-team total (35 Memphis Redbirds)					2	3	4.87	41	0	0	5	44	49	26	24	4	23	51	.280	.394	.202	10.35	4.67
Aaron Fletcher	L-L	6-0	220	2-25-96	1	1	1.45	14	0	0	1	19	20	6	3	0	6	9	.267	.300	.244	4.34	2.89
Eric Hanhold	R-R	6-5	210	11-1-93	4	4	3.40	44	0	0	10	53	47	28	20	3	24	49	.234	.192	.260	8.32	4.08
Heath Hembree	R-R	6-4	220	1-13-89	1	0	9.00	2	0	0	0	2	2	2	2	0	3	3	.286	.500	.000	13.50	13.50
Colin Holderman	R-R	6-7	240	10-8-95	0	0	3.00	3	0	0	0	3	2	1	1	0	2	4	.182	.500	.000	12.00	6.00
2-team total (11 Syracuse Mets)					1	0	2.60	14	0	0	3	17	11	6	5	2	5	21	.177	.231	.139	10.90	2.60
Sam Howard	R-L	6-4	195	3-5-93	0	1	3.38	2	1	0	0	3	2	1	1	0	1	1	.222	.200	.250	3.38	3.38
2-team total (40 Toledo Mud Hens)					2	2	3.19	42	1	0	0	37	27	16	13	6	21	42	.205	.171	.242	10.31	5.15
Joe Jacques	L-L	6-4	210	3-11-95	4	1	3.62	29	0	0	2	37	35	15	15	4	12	27	.259	.093	.337	6.51	2.89
Nathan Kirby	L-L	6-2	200	11-23-93	0	1	2.74	15	4	0	0	23	22	11	7	1	22	18	.253	.231	.271	7.04	8.61
Max Kranick	R-R	6-3	220	7-21-97	0	1	2.70	3	2	0	0	7	5	3	2	2	2	4	.185	.077	.286	5.40	2.70
Travis MacGregor	R-R	6-4	215	10-15-97	2	3	7.25	23	0	0	0	36	37	37	29	4	27	43	.255	.314	.223	10.75	6.75
Zach Matson	L-L	6-3	225	10-24-95	1	1	5.44	31	10	0	0	41	42	26	25	6	21	29	.259	.210	.290	6.31	4.57
Trey McGough	L-L	6-3	195	3-29-98	1	0	3.06	8	5	0	0	18	15	6	6	4	4	13	.227	.316	.191	6.62	2.04
Nick Mears	R-R	6-2	200	10-7-96	1	1	4.74	23	0	0	0	25	19	14	13	2	17	27	.213	.211	.216	9.85	6.20
Cristofer Melendez	R-R	6-3	226	9-16-97	2	4	4.83	26	0	0	1	32	21	20	17	4	28	43	.189	.214	.174	12.22	7.96
Shea Murray	R-R	6-6	215	11-5-93	0	0	12.71	6	0	0	0	6	15	18	8	2	7	5	.417	.500	.364	7.94	11.12
Luis Ortiz	R-R	6-2	240	1-27-99	0	0	3.60	2	2	0	0	10	4	8	4	1	4	12	.108	.444	.000	10.80	3.60
Johan Oviedo	R-R	6-5	245	3-2-98	0	0	0.79	5	4	0	0	11	8	1	1	0	3	13	.195	.182	.211	10.32	2.38
2-team total (10 Memphis Redbirds)					4	2	4.70	15	14	0	0	61	51	34	32	14	26	64	.225	.212	.239	9.39	3.82
John O'Reilly	R-R	6-5	225	10-4-95	5	3	5.84	41	0	0	1	62	70	47	40	7	24	29	.283	.286	.282	4.23	3.50
Dillon Peters	L-L	5-11	195	8-31-92	0	0	1.17	5	0	0	0	8	5	1	1	0	3	7	.185	.000	.238	8.22	3.52
Quinn Priester	R-R	6-3	210	9-15-00	1	1	3.86	2	2	0	0	9	5	4	4	1	7	10	.156	.200	.118	9.64	6.75
Yohan Ramirez	R-R	6-4	212	5-6-95	1	0	0.00	5	0	0	0	5	1	0	0	0	2	4	.059	.333	.000	6.75	3.38
2-team total (11 Columbus Clippers)					2	0	2.87	16	0	0	0	16	4	5	5	0	12	17	.083	.154	.057	9.77	6.89
Colin Selby	R-R	6-2	220	10-24-97	0	1	3.00	3	0	0	0	3	2	1	1	1	0	2	.182	.000	.286	6.00	0.00

Peter Solomon	R-R	6-4	211	8-16-96	0	1	8.53	4	3	0	0	13	14	13	12	5	10	10	.269	.273	.268	7.11	7.11
Eric Stout	L-L	6-3	205	3-27-93	1	0	0.68	11	0	0	3	13	11	1	1	0	7	15	.224	.176	.250	10.13	4.73
2-team total (16 Iowa Cubs)					3	2	2.93	27	1	0	5	43	29	14	14	4	29	63	.186	.143	.210	13.19	6.07
Hunter Stratton	R-R	6-4	225	11-17-96	2	6	5.71	47	1	0	3	63	54	42	40	8	39	82	.228	.279	.199	11.71	5.57
Beau Sulser	R-R	6-2	195	5-5-94	1	2	2.13	3	3	1	0	13	11	6	3	1	2	14	.220	.211	.226	9.95	1.42
2-team total (17 Norfolk Tides)					3	4	4.13	20	6	1	0	57	64	30	26	5	14	60	.284	.301	.270	9.53	2.22
Noe Toribio	R-R	6-2	194	8-25-99	5	3	6.75	22	2	0	0	44	44	38	33	4	30	31	.270	.352	.229	6.34	6.14
Duane Underwood Jr.	R-R	6-2	225	7-20-94	1	0	0.00	1	0	0	0	2	2	0	0	0	1	2	.250	.000	.500	9.00	4.50
Cam Vieaux	L-L	6-3	200	12-5-93	5	1	3.06	35	1	0	2	50	37	19	17	7	15	47	.207	.175	.224	8.46	2.70
Blake Weiman	R-L	6-3	210	11-5-95	0	1	7.27	12	1	0	0	17	23	15	14	4	3	16	.333	.400	.282	8.31	1.56
Bryse Wilson	R-R	6-1	250	12-20-97	5	0	2.97	6	6	0	0	36	32	12	12	6	6	34	.230	.309	.155	8.42	1.49
Miguel Yajure	R-R	6-1	215	5-1-98	4	4	6.09	16	14	0	0	55	59	38	37	7	23	53	.272	.301	.250	8.73	3.79

Fielding

Catcher	PCT	G	PO	A	E	DP	PB
Bins	.994	58	497	20	3	6	5
Davis	.980	23	188	4	4	1	4
Delay	.986	27	211	8	3	1	1
Godoy	1.000	10	96	8	0	1	1
Perez	1.000	7	51	3	0	0	1
Ritchie	.994	21	159	7	1	0	2
Rodriguez	1.000	3	27	1	0	0	0
Sabol	.982	8	50	4	1	1	1

First Base	PCT	G	PO	A	E	DP
Castillo	1.000	3	30	0	0	1
Citta	.990	14	97	6	1	11
Collins	.933	2	13	1	1	2
Davis	.981	6	50	1	1	5
Madris	.938	12	84	7	6	8
Martin	.990	106	823	53	9	78
Owen	1.000	1	10	1	0	1
Padlo	1.000	2	15	2	0	1
Tsutsugo	1.000	7	40	1	0	7
VanMeter	.917	1	9	2	1	1

Second Base	PCT	G	PO	A	E	DP
Bae	.979	57	102	131	5	32
Bissonette	.980	11	12	37	1	6
Castillo	1.000	5	9	10	0	4
Castro	.963	15	26	52	3	7
Jarvis	.950	4	8	11	1	3
Maggi	.958	10	20	26	2	5
Marcano	.957	12	21	23	2	7
Newman	1.000	6	10	13	0	4
Padlo	1.000	1	2	2	0	1
Park	.990	23	32	67	1	15
Rodriguez	1.000	1	1	1	0	1
Shackelford	1.000	3	4	5	0	1
Tucker	1.000	5	2	9	0	1
VanMeter	1.000	5	11	10	0	4

Third Base	PCT	G	PO	A	E	DP
Bae	.000	1	0	0	0	0
Bissonette	.948	32	24	49	4	5
Castillo	.905	7	5	14	2	0
Castro	.951	32	23	55	4	8
Davis	1.000	9	4	6	0	0
Jarvis	1.000	4	0	5	0	0
Maggi	1.000	5	1	6	0	1
Marcano	1.000	1	1	1	0	0
Nunez	1.000	5	1	7	0	2
Owen	.917	11	8	14	2	3
Padlo	.965	18	12	43	2	7
Park	.914	36	20	65	8	5
Tucker	.500	1	0	1	1	0

Shortstop	PCT	G	PO	A	E	DP
Bae	.976	24	20	60	2	6
Castillo	.960	15	15	33	2	8
Castro	.973	29	31	79	3	14
Cruz	.918	44	39	117	14	19
Kaiser	1.000	3	1	4	0	0
Maggi	.943	13	20	30	3	7
Marcano	.976	10	13	27	1	6
Newman	1.000	6	7	10	0	6
Park	.970	15	13	51	2	13
Tucker	1.000	3	2	6	0	1

Outfield	PCT	G	PO	A	E	DP
Alford	1.000	2	5	0	0	0
Allen	1.000	3	3	0	0	0
Bae	.968	28	61	0	2	0
Bissonette	--	1	0	0	0	0
Castillo	1.000	5	10	0	0	0
Citta	.955	12	21	0	1	0
Cruz	.909	10	20	0	2	0
Gamel	.917	7	10	1	1	1
Gorski	--	1	0	0	0	0
Madris	.979	41	89	3	2	1
Marcano	1.000	2	6	1	0	0
Marisnick	1.000	6	9	0	0	0
Mitchell	1.000	56	76	1	0	0
Oliva	.989	96	175	2	2	1
Park	.917	11	9	2	1	0
Ritchie	.857	8	6	0	1	0
Sabol	.867	12	13	0	2	0
Smith-Njigba	.976	47	83	0	2	0
Suwinski	.979	29	45	2	1	0
Swaggerty	.985	96	190	7	3	0

ALTOONA CURVE — *DOUBLE-A*

EASTERN LEAGUE

Batting	B-T	HT	WT	DOB	AVG	vLH	vRH	G	AB	R	H	2B	3B	HR	RBI	BB	HBP	SH	SF	SO	SB	CS	SLG	OBP
Andres Alvarez	R-R	5-10	175	3-29-97	.220	.183	.227	110	368	53	81	13	2	20	50	64	5	1	5	123	21	1	.429	.339
Daniel Amaral	R-R	6-0	190	3-7-97	.000	.000	--	2	3	0	0	0	0	0	0	0	0	1	0	2	0	0	.000	.000
Carter Bins	R-R	6-0	215	10-7-98	.130	.100	.139	14	46	5	6	4	0	1	4	4	1	0	0	21	2	0	.283	.216
Josh Bissonette	R-R	6-0	185	11-1-96	.167	.333	.111	15	48	4	8	1	0	0	3	5	0	0	0	7	0	1	.188	.245
Brendt Citta	R-R	6-2	180	7-12-96	.225	.237	.223	59	204	28	46	8	2	4	23	25	5	0	1	65	1	2	.343	.323
Henry Davis	R-R	6-2	210	9-21-99	.207	.381	.168	31	116	19	24	8	0	4	18	12	8	0	0	30	3	1	.379	.324
Jason Delay	R-R	5-11	200	3-7-95	.143	.000	.167	2	7	0	1	1	0	0	0	0	0	0	0	3	0	0	.286	.143
Claudio Finol	R-R	5-11	171	4-13-00	.043	.000	.056	9	23	1	1	0	0	0	1	3	0	0	0	6	0	0	.043	.154
Matt Fraizer	L-R	6-3	220	1-12-98	.219	.179	.227	116	439	56	96	18	7	6	44	35	5	1	0	114	18	1	.333	.284
Nick Gonzales	R-R	5-10	195	5-27-99	.263	.321	.248	71	259	47	68	20	1	7	33	43	10	0	4	90	5	3	.429	.383
Matt Gorski	R-R	6-4	198	12-22-97	.277	.172	.304	38	141	27	39	8	2	6	28	15	2	0	0	47	10	2	.489	.354
Grant Koch	R-R	5-10	195	2-5-97	.000	.000	.000	4	11	1	0	0	0	0	0	1	0	0	0	4	0	0	.000	.083
Fabricio Macias	R-R	6-0	188	3-11-98	.255	.324	.235	41	149	20	38	11	0	4	25	5	1	0	2	42	5	4	.409	.280
Tucupita Marcano	L-R	6-0	180	9-16-99	.303	.000	.353	31	99	22	30	7	2	2	13	20	0	1	2	25	4	2	.475	.413
Will Matthiessen	R-R	6-7	230	1-9-98	.171	.143	.176	11	41	4	7	1	0	2	4	1	0	0	0	14	0	0	.341	.190
Malcom Nunez	R-R	5-11	205	3-9-01	.286	.222	.299	29	105	20	30	5	0	5	21	17	1	0	3	27	1	0	.476	.381
Liover Peguero	R-R	6-2	200	12-31-00	.259	.236	.264	121	483	65	125	22	5	10	58	29	4	3	2	111	28	6	.387	.305
Endy Rodriguez	B-R	6-0	170	5-26-00	.356	.391	.347	31	118	27	42	14	0	8	32	18	1	0	1	21	1	0	.678	.442
Blake Sabol	L-R	6-4	225	1-7-98	.281	.239	.291	98	366	61	103	23	5	14	60	38	2	0	6	107	9	2	.486	.347
Lolo Sanchez	R-R	5-11	186	4-23-99	.231	.237	.230	66	212	26	49	6	0	5	24	34	3	3	2	40	7	2	.330	.343
Connor Scott	L-L	6-3	200	10-8-99	.247	.211	.256	109	380	46	94	25	4	7	49	33	2	1	4	92	10	6	.389	.308
Aaron Shackelford	L-R	5-10	215	10-16-96	.239	.294	.224	110	397	66	95	23	1	26	79	40	4	1	1	128	11	2	.499	.314
Dylan Shockley	R-R	5-11	195	4-10-97	.147	.077	.164	24	68	4	10	3	0	0	2	7	6	1	0	34	1	0	.191	.284
Jack Suwinski	L-L	6-2	215	7-29-98	.353	.714	.295	13	51	13	18	8	0	3	13	5	1	0	0	14	1	0	.686	.421
Jared Triolo	R-R	6-3	212	2-8-98	.282	.237	.292	112	425	66	120	21	5	9	39	63	3	0	4	87	24	5	.419	.376

Pitching	B-T	HT	WT	DOB	W	L	ERA	G	GS	CG	SV	IP	H	R	ER	HR	BB	SO	AVG	vLH	vRH	K/9	BB/9
Bear Bellomy	R-R	6-3	220	11-29-96	1	2	7.04	31	0	0	1	55	72	47	43	13	11	44	.312	.312	.311	7.20	1.80
Mike Burrows	R-R	6-2	195	11-8-99	4	2	2.94	12	12	0	0	52	38	17	17	3	19	69	.199	.144	.248	11.94	3.29
Brad Case	R-R	6-6	242	9-13-96	1	3	3.92	30	0	0	1	62	59	35	27	7	22	58	.250	.256	.247	8.42	3.19
Omar Cruz	L-L	6-0	200	1-26-99	3	3	5.03	23	5	0	0	63	61	36	35	9	28	69	.251	.229	.263	9.91	4.02
Nick Dombkowski	R-L	6-2	195	8-9-98	3	1	3.92	22	1	0	1	41	38	26	18	5	11	45	.239	.182	.269	9.80	2.40
Matt Eckelman	R-R	6-3	281	10-6-93	1	0	2.25	4	3	0	0	12	10	3	3	0	5	5	.233	.235	.231	3.75	3.75
J.C. Flowers	R-R	6-3	195	5-19-98	7	6	2.88	33	2	0	3	69	57	26	22	6	24	62	.227	.234	.220	8.13	3.15
Oliver Garcia	R-R	6-3	213	1-8-98	0	0	0.00	3	0	0	0	4	3	1	0	0	2	6	.176	.250	.154	13.50	4.50
Domingo Gonzalez	R-R	6-0	185	9-27-99	0	0	3.00	1	0	0	0	3	2	1	1	0	3	4	.182	.333	.125	12.00	9.00
Joe Jacques	L-L	6-4	210	3-11-95	1	0	0.00	2	1	0	0	3	1	0	0	0	2	4	.111	.000	.167	12.00	6.00
Cameron Junker	R-R	6-5	220	9-3-97	0	0	0.00	4	0	0	0	4	1	0	0	0	1	7	.071	.000	.167	14.54	2.08
Will Kobos	R-R	6-2	180	8-3-97	2	0	3.77	12	1	0	1	14	10	8	6	0	15	18	.200	.217	.185	11.30	9.42
Travis MacGregor	R-R	6-4	215	10-15-97	4	1	3.60	15	3	0	0	45	34	19	18	6	22	60	.210	.246	.188	12.00	4.40
Zach Matson	L-L	6-3	225	10-24-95	2	1	1.84	11	1	0	0	15	7	5	3	1	5	17	.137	.200	.097	10.43	3.07
Enmanuel Mejia	R-R	5-11	185	12-22-98	2	5	5.80	40	1	0	2	50	50	40	32	6	31	51	.262	.337	.200	9.24	5.62
Cristofer Melendez	R-R	6-3	226	9-16-97	1	0	5.23	8	1	0	0	10	7	6	6	1	9	14	.200	.375	.053	12.19	7.84
Carmen Mlodzinski	R-R	6-2	225	2-19-99	6	8	4.78	27	22	0	0	105	109	63	56	10	40	111	.267	.276	.256	9.48	3.42
Kyle Nicolas	R-R	6-4	223	2-22-99	2	4	3.97	24	22	0	0	91	71	43	40	9	47	101	.216	.222	.211	10.03	4.67
Luis Ortiz	R-R	6-2	240	1-27-99	5	9	4.64	24	23	0	0	114	100	63	59	19	34	126	.238	.253	.225	9.92	2.68
Luis Oviedo	R-R	6-5	250	5-15-99	0	0	13.50	2	0	0	0	1	3	2	2	0	1	2	.429	.750	.000	13.50	6.75
2-team total (21 Akron RubberDucks)					0	4	5.64	23	7	0	1	53	49	35	33	8	39	56	.241	.221	.256	9.57	6.66
Jeffrey Passantino	R-R	5-10	225	9-24-95	2	2	3.92	19	3	0	0	41	45	19	18	6	11	33	.273	.230	.321	7.19	2.40
Dillon Peters	L-L	5-11	195	8-31-92	1	0	3.60	4	1	0	0	5	3	2	2	0	0	6	.176	.600	.000	10.80	0.00
Quinn Priester	R-R	6-3	210	9-15-00	4	4	2.87	15	15	0	0	75	68	30	24	4	22	75	.241	.215	.261	8.96	2.63
Austin Roberts	R-R	6-0	205	7-27-98	3	1	4.28	37	3	0	2	48	52	28	23	9	19	56	.268	.231	.301	10.43	3.54
Tyler Samaniego	R-L	6-4	205	1-30-99	3	3	3.52	24	0	0	10	31	15	13	12	2	9	23	.147	.200	.119	6.75	2.64
Colin Selby	R-R	6-2	220	10-24-97	2	2	2.20	26	1	0	8	33	27	13	8	1	14	41	.225	.246	.203	11.30	3.86
Aaron Shortridge	R-R	6-3	196	5-29-97	3	4	4.88	14	14	0	0	55	61	38	30	6	31	37	.285	.308	.262	6.02	5.04
Tahnaj Thomas	R-R	6-4	210	6-16-99	5	4	3.02	37	1	0	3	51	44	18	17	4	20	52	.235	.241	.231	9.24	3.55
Noe Toribio	R-R	6-2	194	8-25-99	3	1	1.85	15	1	0	0	39	29	11	8	2	13	46	.201	.191	.211	10.62	3.00
Duane Underwood Jr.	R-R	6-2	225	7-20-94	0	0	0.00	3	0	0	0	4	3	0	0	0	1	5	.200	.375	.000	11.25	2.25

Fielding

Catcher	PCT	G	PO	A	E	DP	PB
Bins	.991	13	105	4	1	0	3
Davis	.983	20	167	4	3	0	7
Delay	1.000	1	8	0	0	0	0
Koch	1.000	4	33	0	0	0	0
Rodriguez	.990	21	188	18	2	0	4
Sabol	.991	58	542	28	5	1	10
Shockley	.995	23	202	18	1	0	0

First Base	PCT	G	PO	A	E	DP
Citta	.994	44	317	22	2	30
Gorski	.977	6	42	1	1	8
Matthiessen	.978	11	81	8	2	7
Nunez	1.000	22	176	8	0	14
Shackelford	.993	57	386	35	3	28

Second Base	PCT	G	PO	A	E	DP
Alvarez	.991	30	47	58	1	12
Bissonette	1.000	5	8	12	0	2
Finol	1.000	4	0	10	0	0
Gonzales	.972	55	74	133	6	26
Marcano	.923	5	5	7	1	1
Peguero	.899	19	28	43	8	12
Rodriguez	.857	2	3	3	1	2
Shackelford	.968	24	26	64	3	15

Third Base	PCT	G	PO	A	E	DP
Alvarez	.944	44	31	71	6	7
Bissonette	1.000	4	3	6	0	0
Finol	1.000	1	0	1	0	1
Marcano	1.000	3	2	1	0	0
Nunez	1.000	2	0	7	0	2
Triolo	.970	87	65	165	7	15

Shortstop	PCT	G	PO	A	E	DP
Alvarez	1.000	12	10	27	0	3
Bissonette	1.000	1	3	0	0	0
Finol	.500	1	1	0	1	0
Gonzales	.917	14	21	23	4	7
Peguero	.935	94	132	201	23	40
Triolo	.929	19	26	39	5	9

Outfield	PCT	G	PO	A	E	DP
Alvarez	1.000	14	20	0	0	0
Amaral	1.000	1	1	0	0	0
Bissonette	1.000	5	8	0	0	0
Davis	1.000	2	2	0	0	0
Fraizer	1.000	114	250	9	0	4
Gorski	1.000	31	58	3	0	0
Macias	.988	39	80	1	1	0
Marcano	1.000	23	38	1	0	0
Sabol	1.000	10	13	1	0	0
Sanchez	.980	56	92	6	2	2
Scott	.980	103	187	8	4	0
Shackelford	1.000	7	11	0	0	0
Suwinski	1.000	11	14	1	0	0
Triolo	1.000	7	15	2	0	0

GREENSBORO GRASSHOPPERS — *HIGH CLASS A*

SOUTH ATLANTIC LEAGUE

Batting	B-T	HT	WT	DOB	AVG	vLH	vRH	G	AB	R	H	2B	3B	HR	RBI	BB	HBP	SH	SF	SO	SB	CS	SLG	OBP
Francisco Acuna	R-R	5-6	150	1-12-00	.271	.349	.250	63	199	34	54	18	0	6	24	20	8	1	0	52	7	3	.452	.361
Angel Basabe	L-L	6-0	153	12-12-00	.130	.125	.133	7	23	4	3	1	0	1	2	0	0	0	0	8	2	0	.304	.130
Jase Bowen	R-R	6-0	190	9-2-00	.176	.300	.146	27	102	11	18	4	1	3	8	5	0	0	2	35	5	0	.324	.211
Luke Brown	L-R	5-10	195	3-12-99	.165	.250	.152	38	91	10	15	5	1	1	9	5	1	1	2	29	3	0	.275	.212
Henry Davis	R-R	6-2	210	9-21-99	.341	.133	.388	22	82	18	28	3	1	5	22	8	9	0	1	18	5	1	.585	.450
Maikol Escotto	R-R	6-0	180	6-4-02	.164	.214	.153	41	146	17	24	4	2	6	19	9	3	2	0	58	5	3	.342	.228
Yoyner Fajardo	L-R	6-0	179	4-6-99	.260	.171	.274	83	304	38	79	6	3	6	28	36	2	0	1	64	17	13	.359	.341
Claudio Finol	R-R	5-11	171	4-13-00	.196	.400	.146	18	51	5	10	2	1	0	0	2	1	0	0	9	1	0	.275	.241
Jackson Glenn	R-R	5-9	205	10-24-97	.216	.200	.222	86	287	34	62	16	2	4	31	29	5	0	2	86	11	1	.328	.297
Jacob Gonzalez	R-R	6-3	190	6-26-98	.281	.280	.282	88	334	41	94	13	1	9	45	27	9	0	3	49	2	1	.407	.349
Matt Gorski	R-R	6-4	198	12-22-97	.294	.484	.232	37	126	34	37	3	2	17	37	17	1	0	2	39	9	1	.754	.377
Abrahan Gutierrez	R-R	6-0	214	10-31-99	.257	.241	.262	108	377	51	97	22	0	12	56	52	8	0	4	112	4	2	.411	.356
Hudson Head	L-L	6-1	180	4-8-01	.234	.181	.250	106	359	60	84	17	4	10	40	47	13	0	1	141	13	8	.387	.343
Jack Herman	R-R	5-9	190	9-30-99	.230	.257	.218	35	122	13	28	2	0	3	12	12	1	1	0	38	1	1	.320	.304
Luis Hernandez	R-R	5-9	150	9-6-00	--	--	--	1	0	0	0	0	0	0	0	0	1	0	0	0	0	0	--	1.000
Mike Jarvis	R-R	5-10	180	5-12-98	.196	.286	.173	29	102	18	20	3	0	8	21	9	4	0	1	28	12	1	.461	.284
Dariel Lopez	R-R	6-1	183	2-7-02	.286	.179	.316	102	391	58	112	15	1	19	58	21	5	1	2	107	6	4	.476	.329

Fabricio Macias	R-R	6-0	188	3-11-98	.267	.263	.268	24	90	12	24	3	0	5	19	6	0	0	1	19	1	0	.467	.309
Ernny Ordonez	R-R	6-1	210	1-17-99	.212	.234	.205	81	274	32	58	12	1	14	49	13	1	2	0	106	4	3	.416	.250
Hunter Owen	R-R	5-11	200	9-22-93	.250	--	.250	3	8	0	2	1	0	0	2	0	1	0	0	5	0	0	.375	.333
Endy Rodriguez	B-R	6-0	170	5-26-00	.302	.290	.305	88	318	63	96	23	3	16	55	42	7	0	3	77	3	3	.544	.392
Sammy Siani	L-L	5-10	195	12-14-00	.201	.226	.195	82	284	45	57	9	0	7	28	46	3	1	0	121	25	5	.306	.318
Eli Wilson	R-R	6-2	190	7-6-98	.233	.239	.231	59	193	31	45	5	2	6	24	18	6	1	2	56	1	2	.373	.315

Pitching	B-T	HT	WT	DOB	W	L	ERA	G	GS	CG	SV	IP	H	R	ER	HR	BB	SO	AVG	vLH	vRH	K/9	BB/9
Carlos Campos	R-R	6-1	169	5-10-01	0	1	4.50	1	0	0	0	2	2	1	1	0	2	1	.286	.000	.667	4.50	9.00
Jack Carey	R-R	6-0	205	9-20-99	4	6	5.75	33	4	0	1	61	71	49	39	9	27	62	.286	.363	.233	9.15	3.98
Cristian Charle	R-R	6-1	208	6-2-00	2	1	3.10	12	0	0	1	20	16	7	7	2	8	17	.216	.138	.267	7.52	3.54
Ricky DeVito	B-R	6-3	195	8-21-98	3	6	5.40	35	6	0	0	70	63	48	42	6	44	90	.239	.179	.286	11.57	5.66
Nick Dombkowski	R-L	6-2	195	8-9-98	1	0	1.76	10	1	0	0	15	10	4	3	1	6	22	.182	.190	.176	12.91	3.52
Matt Eckelman	R-R	6-3	281	10-6-93	1	0	4.50	9	1	0	0	18	13	10	9	2	14	11	.210	.240	.189	5.50	7.00
Claudio Finol	R-R	5-11	171	4-13-00	0	0	9.00	1	0	0	0	1	1	1	1	1	0	0	.250	.000	.500	0.00	0.00
Adrian Florencio	R-R	6-6	205	10-11-98	1	10	8.07	21	15	0	0	58	82	60	52	17	35	62	.328	.322	.333	9.62	5.43
Santiago Florez	R-R	6-5	222	5-9-00	2	4	6.50	32	5	0	0	64	71	49	46	9	29	61	.280	.224	.320	8.62	4.10
Grant Ford	R-R	6-1	175	3-11-98	1	0	3.60	5	0	0	0	10	6	4	4	0	9	5	.194	.231	.167	4.50	8.10
Nick Garcia	L-R	6-4	215	4-20-99	4	4	3.66	25	23	1	0	113	90	48	46	15	46	109	.219	.200	.234	8.68	3.66
Domingo Gonzalez	R-R	6-0	185	9-27-99	9	3	4.96	28	11	0	0	102	99	59	56	13	42	99	.252	.228	.266	8.76	3.72
Logan Hofmann	L-R	5-10	190	11-18-99	1	1	6.81	26	0	0	0	36	39	33	27	6	36	25	.283	.230	.325	6.31	9.08
Jared Jones	L-R	6-1	180	8-6-01	5	7	4.62	26	26	0	0	123	115	68	63	19	51	142	.246	.259	.237	10.42	3.74
Cameron Junker	R-R	6-5	220	9-3-97	6	3	3.64	42	1	0	12	47	37	23	19	6	24	62	.216	.153	.263	11.87	4.60
Will Kobos	R-R	6-2	180	8-3-97	0	0	9.00	1	0	0	0	2	2	2	2	2	0	1	.250	.000	.500	4.50	0.00
Garrett Leonard	R-R	6-3	190	9-25-96	0	2	9.60	18	1	0	0	30	40	37	32	7	22	27	.323	.250	.375	8.10	6.60
Valentin Linarez	R-R	6-5	226	2-14-00	0	0	2.35	2	2	0	0	8	2	2	2	0	6	7	.087	.100	.077	8.22	7.04
Oliver Mateo	R-R	6-2	170	11-7-97	0	1	5.68	23	0	0	5	19	12	15	12	1	25	30	.182	.208	.167	14.21	11.84
Justin Meis	R-R	6-2	160	11-23-99	4	4	4.44	16	16	0	0	73	57	36	36	10	33	74	.212	.250	.181	9.12	4.07
Dante Mendoza	R-R	6-5	186	12-16-98	0	1	14.54	5	0	0	0	4	9	8	7	4	2	9	.391	.500	.333	18.69	4.15
Michell Miliano	R-R	6-3	185	12-22-99	1	2	7.36	22	0	0	1	26	21	24	21	3	28	37	.214	.317	.140	12.97	9.82
Mitchell Miller	L-L	6-6	185	6-13-97	2	0	2.70	6	0	0	0	10	8	3	3	1	5	11	.235	.167	.273	9.90	4.50
Wandi Montout	R-R	6-5	190	3-21-97	4	4	6.69	29	0	0	0	35	34	29	26	4	29	30	.256	.229	.271	7.71	7.46
Jeffrey Passantino	R-R	5-10	225	9-24-95	0	0	11.25	2	0	0	0	4	7	5	5	1	0	5	.368	.600	.286	11.25	0.00
Quinn Priester	R-R	6-3	210	9-15-00	0	0	16.88	1	1	0	0	3	6	5	5	1	1	3	.429	.000	.500	10.13	3.38
Denny Roman	L-L	5-9	180	9-30-98	1	0	8.86	16	0	0	0	21	25	22	21	3	16	22	.284	.241	.305	9.28	6.75
Tyler Samaniego	R-L	6-4	205	1-30-99	1	1	0.53	14	0	0	4	17	3	3	1	0	11	24	.054	.095	.029	12.71	5.82
Sean Sullivan	R-R	6-1	175	10-2-00	2	5	4.68	20	15	0	1	75	75	46	39	16	27	84	.257	.234	.274	10.08	3.24
Sergio Umana	R-R	6-0	175	5-21-00	0	0	0.00	1	0	0	0	1	0	0	0	0	2	1	.000	.000	.000	9.00	18.00
Eddy Yean	R-R	6-1	180	6-25-01	3	4	6.75	42	0	0	3	53	62	45	40	6	29	60	.292	.287	.296	10.13	4.89

Fielding

Catcher	PCT	G	PO	A	E	DP	PB
Davis	.993	13	131	8	1	0	0
Gutierrez	.989	45	424	20	5	2	3
Rodriguez	.994	51	444	47	3	4	5
Wilson	.991	23	208	20	2	2	2

First Base	PCT	G	PO	A	E	DP
Bowen	1.000	2	10	3	0	1
Glenn	1.000	1	1	0	0	1
Gonzalez	.992	71	505	22	4	49
Gorski	.973	6	34	2	1	5
Gutierrez	.988	21	157	8	2	14
Ordonez	.978	38	210	8	5	21
Owen	1.000	1	6	1	0	2
Rodriguez	.957	3	20	2	1	3

Second Base	PCT	G	PO	A	E	DP
Acuna	1.000	2	3	5	0	2
Escotto	.974	9	16	21	1	2
Fajardo	.977	33	54	73	3	25
Finol	.960	7	8	16	1	2
Glenn	.979	43	74	109	4	26
Jarvis	1.000	9	8	18	0	1
Lopez	.973	18	28	45	2	9
Rodriguez	.969	15	21	42	2	8

Third Base	PCT	G	PO	A	E	DP
Acuna	.000	2	0	0	0	0
Glenn	.949	38	24	50	4	5
Jarvis	1.000	4	3	8	0	0
Lopez	.877	55	23	84	15	9
Ordonez	.895	19	9	25	4	1
Owen	.833	2	2	3	1	1
Wilson	.907	22	8	41	5	1

Shortstop	PCT	G	PO	A	E	DP
Acuna	.972	60	75	134	6	33
Escotto	.945	32	50	71	7	20
Finol	.976	10	11	30	1	4
Glenn	1.000	1	3	2	0	2
Jarvis	.870	10	17	23	6	4
Lopez	.922	25	33	62	8	12

Outfield	PCT	G	PO	A	E	DP
Basabe	1.000	8	8	0	0	0
Bowen	1.000	25	54	1	0	1
Brown	.980	32	48	1	1	1
Fajardo	.970	41	61	3	2	1
Gorski	.981	26	48	3	1	1
Head	.977	98	203	7	5	3
Herman	.949	35	53	3	3	0
Jarvis	.929	7	13	0	1	0
Macias	.821	19	20	3	5	0
Ordonez	.941	29	47	1	3	0
Rodriguez	1.000	13	11	2	0	0
Siani	.993	83	132	11	1	3

BRADENTON MARAUDERS — LOW CLASS A

FLORIDA STATE LEAGUE

Batting	B-T	HT	WT	DOB	AVG	vLH	vRH	G	AB	R	H	2B	3B	HR	RBI	BB	HBP	SH	SF	SO	SB	CS	SLG	OBP
Anthony Alford	R-R	6-1	215	7-20-94	.429	--	.429	2	7	3	3	1	0	1	1	0	0	0	0	0	0	0	1.000	.429
Greg Allen	B-R	6-0	185	3-15-93	.333	.500	.286	3	9	1	3	0	0	0	0	1	1	0	0	3	0	0	.333	.455
Darwin Baez	R-R	6-0	186	11-6-00	.200	.000	.250	3	10	2	2	0	0	0	2	2	0	0	0	4	0	0	.200	.333
Angel Basabe	L-L	6-0	153	12-12-00	.257	.200	.271	25	74	6	19	1	4	0	4	10	1	0	0	13	3	2	.378	.353
Jase Bowen	R-R	6-0	190	9-2-00	.278	.313	.268	98	367	60	102	17	2	14	66	38	8	0	4	110	20	2	.450	.355
Jack Brannigan	R-R	6-0	190	3-11-01	.211	.133	.225	26	95	14	20	3	0	3	14	15	2	0	0	28	6	3	.337	.330
Luke Brown	L-R	5-10	195	3-12-99	.234	.261	.225	33	94	20	22	2	0	1	16	18	4	0	1	28	5	1	.287	.376
Sergio Campana	R-R	6-1	160	3-29-02	.210	.221	.207	100	328	50	69	14	1	7	29	53	8	0	2	150	29	12	.323	.332
Bubba Chandler	B-R	6-2	200	9-14-02	.184	.250	.167	32	76	8	14	3	1	1	8	11	0	0	1	35	3	0	.289	.284
Tsung-Che Cheng	L-R	5-7	154	7-26-01	.270	.192	.290	104	385	79	104	25	7	6	52	63	5	1	4	95	33	6	.418	.376
Nick Cimillo	R-R	6-2	215	2-23-00	.188	.000	.333	8	16	6	3	0	0	0	0	3	3	0	0	5	0	0	.188	.409

Jauri Custodio	R-R	5-10	162	9-21-01	.231	.000	.250	4	13	1	3	0	0	0	0	1	0	0	0	4	0	0	.231	.286
Henry Davis	R-R	6-2	210	9-21-99	.364	.500	.333	5	11	2	4	1	0	1	2	1	2	0	1	2	1	0	.727	.467
Brenden Dixon	R-R	6-1	205	11-20-00	.208	.098	.237	89	289	46	60	12	2	8	36	53	4	0	1	104	6	1	.346	.337
Jasiah Dixon	R-R	5-11	180	8-31-01	.232	.250	.228	45	125	18	29	1	3	0	14	14	3	0	1	43	9	4	.288	.322
Maikol Escotto	R-R	6-0	180	6-4-02	.253	.118	.286	25	87	11	22	6	0	2	13	9	2	0	1	22	3	6	.391	.333
Jakob Goldfarb	L-R	6-2	210	6-23-96	.228	.167	.235	19	57	8	13	0	0	1	8	13	6	0	0	21	0	0	.281	.421
Nick Gonzales	R-R	5-10	195	5-27-99	.000	--	.000	1	3	0	0	0	0	0	1	1	0	0	0	2	0	0	.000	.250
Jacob Gonzalez	R-R	6-3	190	6-26-98	.393	.538	.368	24	89	14	35	11	0	4	16	9	7	0	2	14	0	0	.652	.477
Tres Gonzalez	L-L	5-11	185	10-4-00	.325	.286	.329	24	80	12	26	4	1	0	12	9	3	0	0	12	7	1	.400	.413
Matt Gorski	R-R	6-4	198	12-22-97	.176	.500	.077	5	17	1	3	0	0	1	1	1	0	0	0	6	1	0	.353	.222
Wyatt Hendrie	R-R	5-11	200	2-8-99	.248	.245	.249	81	242	32	60	9	3	4	26	28	9	0	1	83	6	1	.360	.346
Luis Hernandez	R-R	5-9	150	9-6-00	.250	.000	.273	4	12	0	3	0	0	0	0	0	2	0	0	7	0	0	.250	.357
Mike Jarvis	R-R	5-10	180	5-12-98	.231	.218	.236	58	182	21	42	9	3	3	18	14	4	0	0	42	12	4	.363	.300
Juan Jerez	R-R	6-0	160	11-28-01	.212	.246	.203	75	259	38	55	9	3	7	41	25	5	0	3	95	20	2	.351	.291
Termarr Johnson	L-R	5-7	175	6-11-04	.275	.111	.323	14	40	7	11	4	0	1	6	10	0	0	3	13	4	1	.450	.396
Grant Koch	R-R	5-10	195	2-5-97	.229	.150	.254	28	83	6	19	2	0	1	8	14	3	0	1	27	0	0	.289	.356
Fabricio Macias	R-R	6-0	188	3-11-98	.125	.250	.083	5	16	0	2	1	0	0	4	2	0	0	0	3	1	0	.188	.222
Tucupita Marcano	L-R	6-0	180	9-16-99	.000	--	.000	1	3	1	0	0	0	0	0	1	0	0	0	1	0	0	.000	.250
Norkis Marcos	R-R	6-1	170	5-26-01	.182	.270	.156	56	165	20	30	3	2	5	22	20	2	0	1	68	12	4	.315	.277
Alexander Mojica	R-R	6-1	250	8-2-02	.167	.214	.154	40	132	11	22	5	0	4	14	22	2	0	1	50	0	0	.295	.293
Deivis Nadal	B-R	5-11	150	2-8-02	.218	.167	.234	56	193	29	42	12	2	1	16	21	5	2	0	62	11	6	.316	.311
Rodolfo Nolasco	R-R	6-1	175	9-23-01	.239	.224	.244	77	280	40	67	15	2	11	48	37	2	0	2	109	7	4	.425	.330
Geovanny Planchart	R-R	6-0	176	9-17-01	.175	.200	.167	20	57	4	10	0	0	0	1	12	0	0	0	25	0	0	.175	.319
Randy Romero	R-R	5-11	155	8-10-99	.205	.194	.210	42	112	9	23	3	0	1	10	6	1	1	3	32	7	2	.259	.246
Lolo Sanchez	R-R	5-11	186	4-23-99	.400	.000	.500	1	5	1	2	0	0	0	1	0	0	0	0	2	0	0	.400	.400
Tanner Tredaway	R-R	6-1	175	8-24-99	.160	.000	.178	19	50	7	8	1	0	1	10	14	3	0	0	10	2	0	.240	.373
Deion Walker	R-R	6-5	180	8-20-01	.000	--	.000	4	10	1	0	0	0	0	0	4	0	0	0	5	0	1	.000	.286

Pitching	**B-T**	**HT**	**WT**	**DOB**	**W**	**L**	**ERA**	**G**	**GS**	**CG**	**SV**	**IP**	**H**	**R**	**ER**	**HR**	**BB**	**SO**	**AVG**	**vLH**	**vRH**	**K/9**	**BB/9**
Carlos Campos	R-R	6-1	169	5-10-01	0	2	4.34	11	1	0	2	19	23	12	9	4	5	17	.303	.167	.365	8.20	2.41
Bubba Chandler	B-R	6-2	200	9-14-02	1	1	4.15	8	6	0	0	26	20	12	12	3	18	33	.215	.220	.212	11.42	6.23
Cristian Charle	R-R	6-1	208	6-2-00	3	0	2.16	20	0	0	0	33	26	10	8	1	9	40	.210	.178	.228	10.80	2.43
Po-Yu Chen	L-R	6-2	187	10-2-01	4	8	4.58	22	22	0	0	98	88	54	50	8	36	103	.237	.244	.233	9.43	3.29
Xavier Concepcion	R-R	6-2	175	1-22-98	1	0	6.52	7	0	0	1	10	14	7	7	1	6	5	.359	.250	.387	4.66	5.59
Joelvis Del Rosario	R-R	5-11	170	4-16-01	7	4	3.68	20	19	0	0	93	95	47	38	12	25	76	.267	.299	.248	7.35	2.42
Kelvin Disla	R-R	6-0	170	7-5-01	1	0	0.00	2	0	0	0	2	0	0	0	0	4	0	.000	.000	.000	0.00	21.60
Nick Dombkowski	R-L	6-2	195	8-9-98	1	0	1.69	4	0	0	0	11	7	2	2	1	2	19	.184	.333	.138	16.03	1.69
Wilber Dotel	R-R	6-3	178	9-25-02	0	0	10.38	2	0	0	0	4	2	5	5	0	9	3	.154	.200	.125	6.23	18.69
Grant Ford	R-R	6-1	175	3-11-98	0	0	13.50	1	0	0	0	1	1	2	2	0	2	1	.200	.000	.333	6.75	13.50
Darvin Garcia	R-R	6-3	170	4-25-99	3	3	5.76	30	0	0	0	45	43	32	29	6	28	45	.244	.209	.266	8.93	5.56
Ryan Harbin	R-R	6-4	195	8-6-01	1	0	0.00	1	0	0	0	2	1	0	0	0	0	1	.167	.333	.000	4.50	0.00
Jack Hartman	R-R	6-3	205	7-13-98	0	1	6.27	22	0	0	1	19	22	21	13	2	16	19	.289	.185	.347	9.16	7.71
Luigi Hernandez	R-R	6-0	185	9-21-03	0	0	3.86	3	0	0	1	5	5	3	2	1	3	3	.294	.333	.286	5.79	5.79
Sam Howard	R-L	6-4	195	3-5-93	0	0	0.00	1	1	0	0	1	0	0	0	0	1	2	.000	.000	.000	18.00	9.00
Drew Irvine	B-R	6-3	180	12-17-99	0	0	3.18	6	0	0	0	11	7	5	4	1	7	11	.179	.214	.160	8.74	5.56
Joe Jacques	L-L	6-4	210	3-11-95	0	0	0.00	2	0	0	1	3	1	0	0	0	0	4	.111	.000	.125	12.00	0.00
Carlos Jimenez	R-R	6-2	140	7-14-02	1	7	4.13	19	15	0	0	70	60	40	32	7	45	88	.234	.292	.200	11.37	5.81
Will Kobos	R-R	6-2	180	8-3-97	1	0	4.91	3	0	0	0	4	3	2	2	1	3	3	.231	.250	.222	7.36	7.36
Max Kranick	R-R	6-3	220	7-21-97	0	0	4.50	1	1	0	0	2	1	1	1	1	0	3	.143	.500	.000	13.50	0.00
Valentin Linarez	R-R	6-5	226	2-14-00	3	8	4.13	20	17	0	0	81	65	41	37	7	39	88	.220	.274	.186	9.82	4.35
Carlos Lomeli	R-R	6-2	195	3-19-99	6	4	5.40	33	0	0	6	50	56	36	30	7	17	47	.276	.348	.239	8.46	3.06
Brennan Malone	R-R	6-4	205	9-8-00	1	0	13.50	2	0	0	0	2	4	3	3	2	1	3	.400	.500	.250	13.50	4.50
Nick Mears	R-R	6-2	200	10-7-96	1	0	5.06	6	1	0	0	5	4	3	3	0	2	7	.200	.143	.231	11.81	3.38
Justin Meis	R-R	6-2	160	11-23-99	3	4	3.51	10	7	0	0	41	40	26	16	4	14	42	.250	.283	.234	9.22	3.07
Dante Mendoza	R-R	6-5	186	12-16-98	5	2	1.23	21	0	0	3	29	13	8	4	1	15	37	.134	.176	.111	11.35	4.60
Mitchell Miller	L-L	6-6	185	6-13-97	2	1	3.18	17	0	0	1	23	16	9	8	1	11	24	.205	.071	.234	9.53	4.37
Johan Montero	R-R	6-3	187	8-26-99	4	1	3.40	32	0	0	5	48	40	21	18	0	18	50	.220	.279	.190	9.44	3.40
Cy Nielson	R-L	6-3	210	2-25-01	0	0	9.39	6	0	0	0	8	7	9	8	1	8	7	.259	.250	.261	8.22	9.39
Luis Oviedo	R-R	6-5	250	5-15-99	0	0	0.00	2	2	0	0	2	0	0	0	0	3	1	.000	.000	.000	3.86	11.57
Jeffrey Passantino	R-R	5-10	225	9-24-95	1	0	3.00	1	0	0	0	3	3	1	1	1	0	4	.250	.250	.250	12.00	0.00
Luis Peralta	L-L	5-11	170	1-6-01	0	7	6.41	19	18	0	0	60	57	43	43	9	44	97	.249	.193	.267	14.47	6.56
Quinn Priester	R-R	6-3	210	9-15-00	0	0	0.00	1	1	0	0	3	0	0	0	0	0	1	.000	.000	.000	3.00	0.00
Wilkin Ramos	R-R	6-5	165	10-31-00	4	1	3.88	37	1	0	3	51	50	29	22	3	32	58	.253	.333	.217	10.24	5.65
Yoelvis Reyes	L-L	6-2	192	12-10-99	1	1	3.75	6	1	0	1	12	10	5	5	1	7	13	.227	.000	.286	9.75	5.25
Sebastian Rodriguez	R-R	6-0	168	10-17-00	0	1	7.71	3	0	0	0	5	6	4	4	0	6	6	.353	.200	.417	11.57	11.57
Denny Roman	L-L	5-9	180	9-30-98	0	0	1.30	14	0	0	0	28	21	6	4	1	8	28	.212	.238	.205	9.11	2.60
Aaron Shortridge	R-R	6-3	196	5-29-97	0	0	1.00	3	3	0	0	9	7	1	1	0	2	6	.212	.267	.167	6.00	2.00
Anthony Solometo	L-L	6-5	220	12-2-02	5	1	2.64	13	8	0	0	48	31	16	14	0	19	51	.188	.119	.211	9.63	3.59
Jake Sweeney	R-L	6-7	240	6-14-00	1	0	3.38	19	1	0	0	37	29	17	14	3	23	41	.215	.214	.215	9.88	5.54
Yunior Thibo	R-R	6-4	185	6-24-98	4	5	4.42	36	0	0	7	53	46	34	26	2	36	55	.232	.314	.188	9.34	6.11
Sergio Umana	R-R	6-0	175	5-21-00	2	0	2.77	19	2	0	0	39	37	19	12	4	6	33	.242	.258	.231	7.62	1.38
Duane Underwood Jr.	R-R	6-2	225	7-20-94	0	0	5.40	2	2	0	0	2	1	1	1	0	2	0	.167	.333	.000	0.00	10.80
Mike Walsh	R-R	6-2	195	1-17-01	0	0	11.57	3	0	0	0	2	3	3	3	0	4	1	.333	.400	.250	3.86	15.43

Fielding

Catcher	PCT	G	PO	A	E	DP	PB
Baez	1.000	2	14	2	0	0	1
Cimillo	1.000	8	44	4	0	0	0
Davis	1.000	4	26	5	0	0	0
Goldfarb	1.000	10	78	4	0	0	2
Hendrie	.990	71	537	59	6	5	13
Hernandez	.966	4	26	2	1	1	0
Koch	.996	27	247	8	1	1	3
Planchart	.990	19	195	12	2	1	8

First Base	PCT	G	PO	A	E	DP
Bowen	1.000	14	89	3	0	9
Dixon	.990	41	280	25	3	37
Gonzalez	.986	19	134	2	2	13
Jerez	.992	32	233	12	2	20
Marcos	1.000	17	111	7	0	9
Mojica	1.000	11	72	1	0	6
Planchart	1.000	1	9	0	0	1

Second Base	PCT	G	PO	A	E	DP
Bowen	.942	16	18	31	3	7
Cheng	1.000	13	23	31	0	9
Dixon	.940	14	18	29	3	7
Escotto	1.000	10	7	20	0	4
Gonzales	1.000	1	1	1	0	1
Jarvis	.945	34	62	58	7	17
Jerez	.938	4	6	9	1	4
Johnson	.977	12	25	17	1	7
Marcano	1.000	1	1	1	0	0
Marcos	.906	13	19	39	6	9
Nadal	.918	22	34	56	8	17

Third Base	PCT	G	PO	A	E	DP
Bowen	.667	1	2	0	1	0
Brannigan	.948	25	11	44	3	1
Dixon	.930	26	11	42	4	2
Jarvis	1.000	6	7	7	0	1
Jerez	.833	21	12	33	9	5
Marcos	.923	22	22	26	4	0
Mojica	.969	22	13	18	1	1
Nadal	.955	13	3	18	1	0

Shortstop	PCT	G	PO	A	E	DP
Cheng	.972	84	109	236	10	47
Escotto	.933	14	17	39	4	13
Jarvis	.822	11	12	25	8	4
Johnson	1.000	1	3	0	0	0
Marcos	1.000	2	0	3	0	0
Nadal	.897	20	19	33	6	7

Outfield	PCT	G	PO	A	E	DP
Alford	1.000	1	2	0	0	0
Allen	1.000	3	1	0	0	0
Basabe	1.000	19	19	0	0	0
Bowen	.982	63	105	5	2	0
Brown	1.000	32	59	7	0	1
Campana	.974	96	175	9	5	3
Custodio	1.000	4	8	0	0	0
Dixon	.925	42	57	5	5	1
Goldfarb	1.000	2	1	0	0	0
Gonzalez	1.000	24	40	1	0	0
Gorski	1.000	4	1	0	0	0
Hendrie	.667	1	2	0	1	0
Jarvis	1.000	7	8	0	0	0
Macias	1.000	4	5	0	0	0
Nadal	1.000	3	2	0	0	0
Nolasco	.964	67	131	4	5	2
Romero	.982	40	52	3	1	0
Tredaway	.960	18	23	1	1	0
Walker	1.000	4	7	0	0	0

FCL PIRATES — *ROOKIE*

FLORIDA COMPLEX LEAGUE

Batting	B-T	HT	WT	DOB	AVG	vLH	vRH	G	AB	R	H	2B	3B	HR	RBI	BB	HBP	SH	SF	SO	SB	CS	SLG	OBP
Omar Alfonzo	L-R	6-1	180	8-3-03	.144	.179	.132	33	104	9	15	3	0	1	9	17	2	0	0	28	0	0	.202	.276
Franrielis Bastardo	R-R	6-2	196	7-19-02	.174	.167	.176	12	23	3	4	1	0	1	4	2	1	0	1	13	0	0	.348	.259
Braylon Bishop	L-L	6-2	193	4-23-03	.220	.318	.195	36	109	18	24	3	1	1	12	22	2	0	1	36	10	2	.294	.358
Jack Brannigan	R-R	6-0	190	3-11-01	.200	.000	.250	2	5	0	1	0	0	0	0	1	1	0	0	2	0	0	.200	.429
Jesus Castillo	R-B	5-9	144	7-12-03	.352	.457	.312	42	128	23	45	4	0	0	21	17	3	2	0	18	9	6	.383	.439
Bubba Chandler	B-R	6-2	200	9-14-02	.231	.000	.261	14	26	8	6	0	1	3	9	9	1	0	0	6	1	0	.654	.444
Nick Cimillo	R-R	6-2	215	2-23-00	.250	.333	.167	4	12	1	3	0	0	0	2	0	0	0	0	1	0	0	.250	.250
Jauri Custodio	R-R	5-10	162	9-21-01	.345	.375	.340	21	58	7	20	4	3	2	10	6	6	0	0	8	1	2	.621	.457
Henry Davis	R-R	6-2	210	9-21-99	.000	--	.000	1	3	0	0	0	0	0	0	0	1	0	0	1	0	0	.000	.250
Jasiah Dixon	R-R	5-11	180	8-31-01	.286	.000	.333	3	7	1	2	0	0	0	0	0	1	0	0	2	0	0	.286	.375
Rafael Escalante	R-R	5-11	160	9-13-01	.226	.235	.224	36	93	14	21	8	2	0	14	24	4	0	0	23	0	1	.355	.405
Maikol Escotto	R-R	6-0	180	6-4-02	.300	.500	.167	3	10	3	3	0	0	0	0	2	1	0	0	4	3	0	.300	.462
Nick Gonzales	R-R	5-10	195	5-27-99	.429	.500	.333	2	7	1	3	1	1	0	3	0	0	0	0	1	1	0	.857	.429
Tres Gonzalez	L-L	5-11	185	10-4-00	.000	.000	--	1	2	1	0	0	0	0	0	0	1	0	0	0	0	0	.000	.333
A.J. Graham	R-R	6-3	180	10-2-02	.053	.000	.071	7	19	1	1	1	0	0	1	0	0	0	0	9	0	0	.105	.053
Luis Hernandez	R-R	5-9	150	9-6-00	.189	.200	.188	14	37	7	7	0	0	0	2	5	0	0	0	14	0	0	.189	.286
Juan Jerez	R-R	6-0	160	11-28-01	.222	.000	.250	3	9	3	2	1	0	0	0	3	0	0	0	1	0	1	.333	.417
Termarr Johnson	L-R	5-7	175	6-11-04	.130	.000	.150	9	23	0	3	2	0	0	0	6	0	0	0	8	2	0	.217	.310
Solomon Maguire	L-R	5-11	168	3-4-03	.217	.259	.205	37	115	19	25	3	2	0	11	14	2	1	1	25	3	1	.278	.311
Alexander Mojica	R-R	6-1	250	8-2-02	.156	.250	.125	11	32	4	5	1	0	2	6	6	1	0	0	17	0	0	.375	.308
Geovanny Planchart	R-R	6-0	176	9-17-01	.200	.091	.220	25	70	13	14	3	1	0	6	15	2	0	2	15	1	0	.271	.348
Shalin Polanco	L-L	5-11	168	2-6-04	.250	.364	.227	37	132	24	33	7	0	3	17	12	3	0	1	40	7	4	.371	.324
Javier Rivas	R-R	6-3	165	9-1-02	.265	.194	.286	46	155	24	41	9	0	5	29	10	8	0	2	43	4	1	.419	.337
Emilson Rosado	R-R	6-3	229	2-11-01	.167	--	.167	3	6	1	1	0	0	1	1	0	0	0	0	3	0	0	.667	.167
Lolo Sanchez	R-R	5-11	186	4-23-99	.077	.000	.111	4	13	2	1	0	0	0	1	1	1	0	0	3	0	1	.077	.200
Ronny Sanchez	R-R	5-11	191	7-22-02	.153	.115	.167	36	98	10	15	3	1	2	16	4	4	0	2	36	1	1	.265	.213
Luis Tejeda	R-R	5-11	170	8-26-02	.308	.333	.300	13	26	10	8	1	0	0	2	13	0	1	0	8	1	0	.346	.538
Enmanuel Terrero	L-L	5-11	160	9-14-02	.330	.350	.326	35	106	22	35	3	3	1	10	23	0	0	1	17	9	7	.443	.446
Jeral Toledo	B-R	6-0	135	1-22-03	.173	.294	.148	35	98	21	17	5	2	0	11	20	4	0	1	31	5	4	.265	.333
Tanner Tredaway	R-R	6-1	175	8-24-99	.200	--	.200	2	5	1	1	1	0	0	0	0	0	0	0	1	0	0	.400	.200
Esmerlyn Valdez	R-R	6-2	181	1-27-04	.232	.333	.205	33	99	25	23	7	0	3	20	18	5	0	2	29	0	1	.394	.371
Deion Walker	R-R	6-5	180	8-20-01	.231	.000	.261	14	26	5	6	1	0	0	4	9	4	0	2	10	1	1	.269	.463
Lonnie White Jr.	R-R	6-3	212	12-31-02	.286	--	.286	2	7	1	2	1	0	1	3	0	0	0	0	3	0	0	.857	.286

Pitching	B-T	HT	WT	DOB	W	L	ERA	G	GS	CG	SV	IP	H	R	ER	HR	BB	SO	AVG	vLH	vRH	K/9	BB/9
Elijah Birdsong	R-R	6-2	200	10-11-99	0	0	6.75	4	0	0	0	4	2	3	3	1	3	3	.154	.000	.286	6.75	6.75
Carlos Campos	R-R	6-1	169	5-10-01	1	1	2.70	3	0	0	0	3	2	2	1	0	3	1	.182	.333	.000	2.70	8.10
Bubba Chandler	B-R	6-2	200	9-14-02	0	0	0.00	6	5	0	0	15	3	0	0	0	10	27	.061	.077	.043	15.85	5.87
Hung-Leng Chang	R-R	6-3	159	10-7-01	3	1	4.76	8	3	0	1	23	22	14	12	0	8	27	.247	.213	.286	10.72	3.18
Cristopher Cruz	R-R	6-2	170	1-6-03	0	3	7.36	11	10	0	0	29	30	26	24	3	22	23	.261	.188	.313	7.06	6.75
Yoldin De La Paz	L-L	6-0	165	5-10-02	0	0	4.50	1	0	0	0	2	1	1	1	0	1	4	.143	--	.143	18.00	4.50
Enmanuel De Los Santos	R-R	6-4	163	10-14-00	1	2	2.82	10	5	0	0	22	15	14	7	1	18	31	.183	.222	.164	12.49	7.25
Jaycob Deese	R-R	6-1	195	5-30-00	0	0	0.00	3	0	0	0	4	3	1	0	0	1	5	.214	.333	.125	11.25	2.25
Derek Diamond	R-R	6-2	200	1-4-01	0	0	0.00	3	0	0	0	4	3	0	0	0	1	4	.214	.333	.125	9.00	2.25
Miguel Diaz	R-R	6-0	160	8-19-01	1	0	5.65	12	0	0	1	14	12	9	9	4	6	16	.218	.214	.222	10.05	3.77

Kelvin Disla	R-R	6-0	170	7-5-01	1	1	3.29	11	0	0	1	14	10	6	5	0	5	12	.213	.200	.219	7.90	3.29
Wilber Dotel	R-R	6-3	178	9-25-02	2	2	2.62	12	9	0	0	34	24	13	10	1	16	35	.198	.220	.183	9.17	4.19
Alessandro Ercolani	R-R	6-2	185	4-20-04	1	0	1.19	10	8	0	1	30	19	4	4	0	20	39	.184	.103	.234	11.57	5.93
Grant Ford	R-R	6-1	175	3-11-98	0	0	3.00	2	2	0	0	3	3	2	1	0	1	5	.273	.250	.286	15.00	3.00
Jose Garces	R-R	6-2	149	6-9-04	1	2	8.00	10	0	0	0	18	18	25	16	2	21	19	.261	.345	.200	9.50	10.50
Roelmy Garcia	R-R	6-2	172	4-12-03	2	2	11.57	18	0	0	0	16	16	22	21	0	31	25	.258	.227	.275	13.78	17.08
Ryan Harbin	R-R	6-4	195	8-6-01	1	0	5.02	8	0	0	0	14	14	8	8	1	10	14	.269	.310	.217	8.79	6.28
Luigi Hernandez	R-R	6-0	185	9-21-03	3	0	3.98	10	2	0	0	20	17	10	9	1	14	33	.218	.205	.231	14.61	6.20
Drew Irvine	B-R	6-3	180	12-17-99	2	1	1.16	7	0	0	1	12	8	2	2	0	2	10	.195	.333	.138	7.30	1.46
Owen Kellington	L-R	6-3	193	2-5-03	0	1	11.70	6	2	0	0	10	14	13	13	0	9	15	.311	.188	.379	13.50	8.10
Antwone Kelly	R-R	5-10	183	9-1-03	0	1	2.31	10	2	0	0	23	20	10	6	2	10	29	.222	.211	.231	11.19	3.86
Will Kobos	R-R	6-2	180	8-3-97	0	1	9.00	1	1	0	0	1	2	1	1	0	0	3	.400	1.000	.000	27.00	0.00
Nic Laio	R-R	6-5	205	7-28-97	0	0	1.93	3	0	0	0	5	4	1	1	0	3	3	.286	.333	.250	5.79	5.79
Andy Maldonado	R-R	6-4	196	7-21-02	2	0	10.50	4	0	0	0	6	6	8	7	2	6	10	.250	.375	.188	15.00	9.00
Brennan Malone	R-R	6-4	205	9-8-00	0	0	3.00	1	1	0	0	3	4	3	1	0	1	4	.333	.667	.222	12.00	3.00
Adrian Mendez	L-L	6-1	160	3-7-02	0	1	18.90	5	0	0	0	3	4	8	7	0	9	4	.308	.500	.273	10.80	24.30
Michell Miliano	R-R	6-3	185	12-22-99	0	1	1.69	3	0	0	0	5	4	3	1	0	2	6	.190	.100	.273	10.13	3.38
Mitchell Miller	L-L	6-6	185	6-13-97	1	0	0.00	2	0	0	0	2	0	0	0	0	0	4	.000	.000	.000	21.60	0.00
Cy Nielson	R-L	6-3	210	2-25-01	0	0	0.00	1	1	0	0	1	2	0	0	0	0	1	.500	.333	1.000	9.00	0.00
Jorge Ramos	R-R	6-0	150	6-5-02	1	0	1.23	10	0	0	1	15	10	2	2	0	3	18	.189	.300	.121	11.05	1.84
Yoelvis Reyes	L-L	6-2	192	12-10-99	1	2	5.40	7	0	0	0	10	11	10	6	2	8	10	.282	.250	.290	9.00	7.20
Daniel Rivero	R-R	6-0	191	1-22-01	3	1	2.63	14	0	0	2	14	10	5	4	0	9	14	.208	.045	.346	9.22	5.93
Sebastian Rodriguez	R-R	6-0	168	10-17-00	0	0	1.86	7	0	0	0	10	3	2	2	0	6	13	.097	.167	.053	12.10	5.59
Eliecer Romero	R-R	6-0	185	9-8-01	0	0	2.70	12	0	0	2	13	14	4	4	0	4	10	.286	.280	.292	6.75	2.70
Owen Sharts	R-R	6-2	190	11-23-99	1	1	9.00	12	3	0	0	11	6	12	11	0	27	12	.162	.091	.192	9.82	22.09
Joaquin Tejada	R-R	5-11	160	7-16-03	2	0	4.00	12	1	0	0	27	16	12	12	0	17	28	.172	.200	.155	9.33	5.67
Ryan Velazquez	R-R	6-4	225	5-28-99	0	1	13.50	2	0	0	0	1	6	2	2	0	2	0	.750	.750	.750	0.00	13.50
Raydel Velette	R-R	6-6	196	6-20-01	0	0	2.57	8	0	0	1	7	7	2	2	1	3	1	.259	.273	.250	1.29	3.86
Mike Walsh	R-R	6-2	195	1-17-01	0	0	9.00	1	0	0	0	1	1	1	1	0	1	1	.333	.500	.000	9.00	9.00

Fielding

C: Alfonzo 24, Cimillo 4, Davis 1, Escalante 5, Hernandez 14, Planchart 15. **1B:** Alfonzo 7, Bastardo 4, Escalante 6, Jerez 1, Mojica 3, Planchart 7, Rosado 1, Sanchez 34, Valdez 5. **2B:** Castillo 24, Escalante 7, Escotto 1, Gonzales 1, Graham 2, Johnson 3, Rivas 5, Tejeda 4, Toledo 17. **3B:** Brannigan 2, Castillo 7, Escalante 20, Jerez 2, Mojica 6, Rivas 17, Rosado 1, Tejeda 8, Toledo 3. **SS:** Castillo 13, Escotto 2, Graham 4, Johnson 4, Rivas 25, Tejeda 1, Toledo 13. **OF:** Bastardo 6, Bishop 34, Custodio 13, Dixon 3, Gonzalez 1, Maguire 30, Polanco 32, Sanchez 5, Sanchez 1, Terrero 30, Tredaway 2, Valdez 22, Walker 10, White Jr. 2

DSL PIT BLACK — *ROOKIE*

DOMINICAN SUMMER LEAGUE

Batting	B-T	HT	WT	DOB	AVG	vLH	vRH	G	AB	R	H	2B	3B	HR	RBI	BB	HBP	SH	SF	SO	SB	CS	SLG	OBP
Rodolfo De La Cruz	L-L	6-0	160	11-24-03	.170	.100	.183	48	135	23	23	5	2	4	16	27	4	0	0	62	6	4	.326	.325
Robert De Paula	R-R	5-11	193	3-23-03	.190	.095	.210	43	121	15	23	8	1	4	20	8	14	0	3	58	3	0	.372	.308
Kelvin Diaz	R-R	6-0	143	10-3-02	.218	.429	.179	46	133	31	29	13	2	1	20	32	5	0	0	40	17	5	.368	.388
Eybert Escalona	R-R	6-0	180	10-27-02	.357	.750	.292	15	28	6	10	2	0	2	10	8	3	0	0	7	0	0	.643	.538
2-team total (8 DSL PIT Gold)					.333	.700	.237	23	48	11	16	3	0	2	10	12	3	0	0	13	0	1	.521	.492
Ewry Espinal	L-R	6-0	185	12-18-02	.231	.207	.238	53	134	35	31	7	2	4	18	60	5	0	1	61	14	2	.403	.480
Pedro Figuereo	B-R	5-10	150	3-28-03	.111	.000	.130	15	27	1	3	0	0	0	2	3	4	0	0	15	3	1	.111	.294
2-team total (21 DSL PIT Gold)					.136	.167	.130	36	66	10	9	1	0	0	5	15	5	0	0	35	5	2	.152	.337
Rubel Lebron	R-R	5-10	154	9-13-03	.071	.333	.000	5	14	3	1	0	0	0	0	2	1	0	0	4	1	0	.071	.235
Daje Morales	R-R	5-10	155	3-3-05	.219	.214	.220	53	155	25	34	7	4	1	19	31	4	0	0	41	12	7	.335	.363
Christopher Orelin	R-R	5-11	157	1-31-05	.192	.111	.203	23	73	6	14	2	0	0	5	8	1	0	1	19	3	5	.219	.277
Eduardo Oviedo	R-R	6-1	169	9-2-04	.177	.194	.173	52	158	21	28	5	0	4	20	14	8	0	1	55	14	6	.285	.276
Isaac Paulino	R-R	5-11	160	3-10-05	.209	.214	.208	52	148	24	31	6	1	1	16	23	7	0	4	52	7	5	.284	.335
Delfin Ramirez	R-R	6-0	160	9-26-02	.159	.214	.147	35	82	6	13	2	0	1	8	10	1	0	0	37	2	1	.220	.258
Richard Ramirez	R-R	6-0	160	7-3-05	.174	.087	.194	41	121	18	21	6	0	1	7	17	0	0	2	41	2	1	.248	.271
Angel Rodriguez	R-R	6-2	175	10-25-04	.207	.059	.243	30	87	10	18	4	0	1	5	10	4	0	1	26	5	2	.287	.314
Miguel Sosa	R-R	5-11	181	12-4-03	.305	.294	.308	31	82	13	25	8	0	3	17	25	1	0	1	12	3	3	.512	.468
Fabian Urbina	L-R	5-8	175	10-25-01	.100	.333	.000	6	10	1	1	0	0	0	0	3	0	0	0	1	1	0	.100	.308
July Vittini	R-R	6-2	190	5-29-03	.214	.000	.231	6	14	2	3	1	0	0	2	1	0	0	0	6	0	0	.286	.267
Wesley Zapata	B-R	5-10	152	3-2-04	.306	.250	.317	30	98	19	30	12	1	0	16	8	1	0	1	17	5	2	.449	.361
2-team total (24 DSL PIT Gold)					.287	.256	.297	54	171	32	49	17	2	1	28	22	1	1	1	34	6	4	.427	.369

Pitching	B-T	HT	WT	DOB	W	L	ERA	G	GS	CG	SV	IP	H	R	ER	HR	BB	SO	AVG	vLH	vRH	K/9	BB/9
Hader Blanco	L-L	5-11	150	2-14-05	1	3	3.60	15	3	0	1	30	17	19	12	0	29	27	.170	.167	.171	8.10	8.70
Luis Brito	L-L	6-1	164	11-25-01	1	1	7.23	12	0	0	0	24	29	20	19	1	21	19	.312	.222	.321	7.23	7.99
Victor Cabreja	L-L	6-3	180	1-10-02	2	0	6.32	7	2	0	0	16	18	11	11	1	7	21	.310	.143	.364	12.06	4.02
2-team total (7 DSL PIT Gold)					5	0	4.67	14	6	0	0	35	33	18	18	1	15	36	.260	.200	.271	9.35	3.89
Diego Chiquillo	L-L	5-11	185	12-9-02	2	4	3.48	15	7	0	1	31	23	20	12	3	25	47	.205	.179	.214	13.65	7.26
Jarlen De La Paz	L-L	6-4	180	6-4-05	1	2	4.34	13	6	0	0	19	8	12	9	0	17	16	.119	.067	.135	7.71	8.20
Pedro Figuereo	B-R	5-10	150	3-28-03	0	0	0.00	1	0	0	0	1	1	0	0	0	0	0	.250	.000	1.000	0.00	0.00
Juan Fuentes	R-R	6-3	165	9-30-01	0	0	9.95	8	0	0	1	6	8	12	7	0	9	6	.296	.375	.263	8.53	12.79
2-team total (4 DSL PIT Gold)					1	0	13.97	12	0	0	1	10	15	20	15	0	14	8	.349	.385	.333	7.45	13.03
Luis C Gonzalez	L-L	6-0	160	11-19-01	1	0	5.23	6	0	0	0	10	10	6	6	1	8	14	.244	.143	.265	12.19	6.97
2-team total (6 DSL PIT Gold)					2	0	2.74	12	0	0	0	23	14	8	7	1	17	26	.173	.111	.181	10.17	6.65
Lewys Guzman	R-R	6-1	180	2-9-02	0	0	21.81	9	0	0	0	9	14	22	21	0	16	12	.359	.300	.379	12.46	16.62

Yoerys Hernandez	L-L	6-2	185	9-1-03	5	2	4.06	13	0	0	0	31	28	16	14	1	8	26	.239	.217	.245	7.55	2.32
2-team total (1 DSL PIT Gold)					5	2	3.82	14	0	0	0	33	29	16	14	1	8	27	.234	.240	.232	7.36	2.18
Luis Joseph	R-R	6-1	180	6-15-02	1	2	3.27	12	5	0	0	22	20	14	8	0	16	28	.238	.355	.170	11.45	6.55
Wilbur Martinez	R-R	6-2	162	8-3-01	3	1	2.70	12	0	0	3	20	16	10	6	1	12	16	.208	.241	.188	7.20	5.40
2-team total (4 DSL PIT Gold)					4	1	2.05	16	0	0	4	26	20	13	6	1	13	23	.198	.220	.183	7.86	4.44
Greiber Mendez	R-R	6-0	150	4-3-04	5	0	3.78	16	0	0	0	33	36	19	14	3	14	35	.273	.200	.310	9.45	3.78
Dermis Ordonez	R-R	6-1	170	9-5-04	1	0	1.23	5	0	0	0	7	3	2	1	0	9	6	.136	.000	.188	7.36	11.05
2-team total (8 DSL PIT Gold)					1	2	5.25	13	4	0	0	24	11	18	14	0	29	15	.145	.034	.213	5.63	10.88
Adolfo Oviedo	R-R	6-1	165	11-17-04	0	1	4.59	11	9	0	0	33	38	18	17	2	13	30	.277	.297	.270	8.10	3.51
2-team total (1 DSL PIT Gold)					0	1	4.33	12	10	0	0	35	39	18	17	2	14	31	.273	.308	.260	7.90	3.57
Brandison Polanco	R-R	6-2	170	8-1-02	0	4	5.63	12	3	0	0	32	34	24	20	5	8	24	.268	.257	.272	6.75	2.25
Delfin Ramirez	R-R	6-0	160	9-26-02	0	0	0.00	3	0	0	0	3	3	2	0	1	1	3	.231	.200	.250	9.00	3.00
Patricio Ress	R-R	6-2	165	6-26-03	0	1	12.27	1	1	0	0	4	9	6	5	2	0	4	.450	.333	.500	9.82	0.00
2-team total (15 DSL PIT Gold)					3	2	5.73	16	3	0	2	33	41	26	21	6	20	33	.304	.286	.310	9.00	5.45
Jonathan Salazar	R-R	6-3	180	12-22-03	0	6	6.10	11	11	0	0	31	23	26	21	0	16	34	.198	.189	.203	9.87	4.65
Reyson Santos	R-R	6-3	180	9-7-01	0	1	11.93	13	0	0	0	14	20	22	19	2	16	14	.317	.263	.341	8.79	10.05
Alexis Torres	R-R	6-0	153	3-16-03	1	1	4.97	11	3	0	0	25	30	18	14	3	10	21	.288	.314	.275	7.46	3.55
Isaias Uribe	L-L	6-3	172	8-13-02	1	4	4.94	10	9	0	0	31	30	20	17	0	9	33	.259	.280	.253	9.58	2.61
2-team total (3 DSL PIT Gold)					1	4	4.15	13	12	0	0	39	35	21	18	0	14	42	.245	.310	.228	9.69	3.23
Dioris Valdez	R-R	6-1	180	11-16-02	1	0	8.31	6	0	0	0	9	10	13	8	1	6	9	.294	.455	.217	9.35	6.23
2-team total (4 DSL PIT Gold)					1	1	8.56	10	0	0	0	14	16	19	13	2	10	13	.291	.429	.244	8.56	6.59
Eduardo Zapata	R-R	6-2	160	8-27-03	0	0	10.80	2	0	0	0	2	1	2	2	0	5	0	.200	.333	.000	0.00	27.00

Fielding

C: Escalona 4, Ramirez 41, Sosa 13, Urbina 6, Vittini 6. **1B:** De Paula 2, Diaz 5, Escalona 6, Espinal 38, Ramirez 15, Vittini 1. **2B:** Diaz 9, Figuereo 6, Morales 29, Orelin 4, Paulino 7, Ramirez 9, Zapata 1, Zapata 3. **3B:** Diaz 2, Figuereo 6, Morales 8, Orelin 3, Paulino 32, Ramirez 4, Zapata 10. **SS:** Diaz 24, Morales 15, Orelin 15, Paulino 1, Zapata 11. **OF:** De La Cruz 46, De Paula 39, Diaz 1, Espinal 13, Oviedo 52, Ramirez 1, Rodriguez 26, Sosa 19.

DSL PIT GOLD — ROOKIE

DOMINICAN SUMMER LEAGUE

Batting	B-T	HT	WT	DOB	AVG	vLH	vRH	G	AB	R	H	2B	3B	HR	RBI	BB	HBP	SH	SF	SO	SB	CS	SLG	OBP
Roinny Aguiar	B-R	5-6	160	4-1-05	.204	.087	.238	40	103	25	21	6	0	1	12	38	2	3	1	31	18	5	.291	.424
Gustavo Armas	R-R	6-2	175	12-12-03	.157	.179	.150	44	108	21	17	5	1	0	18	29	6	0	0	46	7	1	.222	.364
Tony Blanco Jr.	R-R	6-6	243	5-14-05	.211	.143	.250	8	19	1	4	0	0	1	4	0	0	0	0	10	0	0	.368	.211
Yordany De Los Santos	R-R	6-1	170	2-17-05	.258	.265	.255	59	190	35	49	15	1	1	38	32	6	0	6	45	14	3	.363	.372
Isaias Dipre	R-R	5-11	159	6-7-03	.276	.271	.278	56	174	36	48	17	1	3	32	22	4	0	6	52	14	4	.437	.359
Eybert Escalona	R-R	6-0	180	10-27-02	.300	.667	.143	8	20	5	6	1	0	0	0	4	0	0	0	6	0	1	.350	.417
2-team total (15 DSL PIT Black)					.333	.700	.237	23	48	11	16	3	0	2	10	12	3	0	0	13	0	1	.521	.492
Samuel Escudero	R-R	0-0	0	2-27-04	.284	.250	.300	37	74	16	21	5	0	0	9	16	2	1	1	14	4	1	.351	.419
Pedro Figuereo	B-R	5-10	150	3-28-03	.154	.250	.129	21	39	9	6	1	0	0	3	12	1	0	0	20	2	1	.179	.365
2-team total (15 DSL PIT Black)					.136	.167	.130	36	66	10	9	1	0	0	5	15	5	0	0	35	5	2	.152	.337
Juan Machado	L-R	5-11	145	6-4-03	.311	.280	.327	31	74	26	23	0	1	0	10	20	5	1	2	20	16	4	.338	.475
Lennyn Nunez	B-R	5-10	150	8-8-03	.200	.250	.188	12	20	5	4	1	0	0	2	3	2	0	0	2	5	1	.250	.360
Jhonson Pena	R-R	6-0	155	8-3-02	.248	.219	.261	46	101	26	25	2	4	1	18	27	4	5	3	30	7	2	.376	.415
Axiel Plaz	R-R	5-11	165	8-12-05	.382	.500	.357	32	68	16	26	11	1	3	21	13	4	0	1	16	2	0	.706	.500
Eddy Rodriguez	R-R	6-0	181	11-5-03	.238	.259	.232	48	126	29	30	4	1	6	24	26	13	0	3	35	5	2	.429	.411
Carlos Tirado	L-R	6-1	187	3-13-05	.265	.179	.288	46	132	25	35	8	1	2	24	31	7	0	2	29	3	0	.386	.424
Dioris Valdez	R-R	6-1	180	11-16-02	.000	.000	.000	7	8	0	0	0	0	0	0	1	0	0	0	7	0	0	.000	.111
2-team total (10 DSL PIT Black)					.067	.000	.091	17	15	3	1	1	0	0	0	6	0	0	0	11	1	0	.133	.333
Ruben Vizcaya	R-R	5-10	155	9-30-03	.203	.171	.214	52	153	29	31	4	4	0	22	32	7	3	3	42	13	4	.281	.359
Wesley Zapata	B-R	5-10	152	3-2-04	.260	.259	.261	24	73	13	19	5	1	1	12	14	0	1	0	17	1	2	.397	.379
2-team total (30 DSL PIT Black)					.287	.256	.297	54	171	32	49	17	2	1	28	22	1	1	1	34	6	4	.427	.369
John Zorrilla	R-R	6-1	173	5-23-04	.118	.154	.105	41	102	17	12	3	0	4	15	33	2	0	0	65	5	0	.265	.343

Pitching	B-T	HT	WT	DOB	W	L	ERA	G	GS	CG	SV	IP	H	R	ER	HR	BB	SO	AVG	vLH	vRH	K/9	BB/9
Gilberto Alcala	R-R	6-3	175	10-3-02	0	0	2.88	8	8	0	0	25	18	11	8	0	9	26	.194	.179	.200	9.36	3.24
Victor Cabreja	L-L	6-3	180	1-10-02	3	0	3.32	7	4	0	0	19	15	7	7	0	8	15	.217	.333	.206	7.11	3.79
2-team total (7 DSL PIT Black)					5	0	4.67	14	6	0	0	35	33	18	18	1	15	36	.260	.200	.271	9.35	3.89
Jesus Clode	R-R	6-2	180	8-28-01	6	1	2.41	10	0	0	1	19	11	8	5	0	5	23	.162	.227	.130	11.09	2.41
Darlin Diaz	R-R	6-0	177	11-30-03	4	1	2.84	14	0	0	1	19	15	9	6	1	8	13	.217	.211	.220	6.16	3.79
Luis Faringthon	R-R	5-11	187	5-27-03	2	1	0.41	12	0	0	3	22	13	5	1	0	8	23	.169	.208	.151	9.41	3.27
Juan Fuentes	R-R	6-3	165	9-30-01	1	0	21.60	4	0	0	0	3	7	8	8	0	5	2	.438	.400	.455	5.40	13.50
2-team total (8 DSL PIT Black)					1	0	13.97	12	0	0	1	10	15	20	15	0	14	8	.349	.385	.333	7.45	13.03
Luis C Gonzalez	L-L	6-0	160	11-19-01	1	0	0.71	6	0	0	0	13	4	2	1	0	9	12	.100	.000	.105	8.53	6.39
2-team total (6 DSL PIT Black)					2	0	2.74	12	0	0	0	23	14	8	7	1	17	26	.173	.111	.181	10.17	6.65
Kevison Hernandez	R-R	6-5	188	7-20-02	0	0	2.84	5	4	0	0	13	6	5	4	0	3	20	.136	.176	.111	14.21	2.13
Yoerys Hernandez	L-L	6-2	185	9-1-03	0	0	0.00	1	0	0	0	2	1	0	0	0	0	1	.143	.500	.000	4.50	0.00
2-team total (13 DSL PIT Black)					5	2	3.82	14	0	0	0	33	29	16	14	1	8	27	.234	.240	.232	7.36	2.18
Wilbur Martinez	R-R	6-2	162	8-3-01	1	0	0.00	4	0	0	1	6	4	3	0	0	1	7	.167	.167	.167	9.95	1.42
2-team total (12 DSL PIT Black)					4	1	2.05	16	0	0	4	26	20	13	6	1	13	23	.198	.220	.183	7.86	4.44
Rafael Mendez	R-R	6-3	170	8-14-02	7	0	5.34	14	0	0	0	29	31	20	17	2	17	28	.277	.286	.275	8.79	5.34
Dermis Ordonez	R-R	6-1	170	9-5-04	0	2	7.02	8	4	0	0	17	8	16	13	0	20	9	.148	.043	.226	4.86	10.80
2-team total (5 DSL PIT Black)					1	2	5.25	13	4	0	0	24	11	18	14	0	29	15	.145	.034	.213	5.63	10.88
Yojeiry Osoria	L-L	6-1	188	1-24-03	0	1	2.84	6	4	0	0	13	6	9	4	0	12	22	.146	.100	.161	15.63	8.53
Adolfo Oviedo	R-R	6-1	165	11-17-04	0	0	0.00	1	1	0	0	2	1	0	0	0	1	1	.167	.500	.000	4.50	4.50

2-team total (11 DSL PIT Black)					0	1	4.33	12	10	0	0	35	39	18	17	2	14	31	.273	.308	.260	7.90	3.57
Keneth Quintanilla	R-R	6-0	154	1-21-03	1	2	3.13	10	8	1	0	32	23	14	11	0	13	37	.205	.186	.217	10.52	3.69
Patricio Ress	R-R	6-2	165	6-26-03	3	1	4.91	15	2	0	2	29	32	20	16	4	20	29	.278	.276	.279	8.90	6.14
2-team total (1 DSL PIT Black)					3	2	5.73	16	3	0	2	33	41	26	21	6	20	33	.304	.286	.310	9.00	5.45
Luis Rodriguez	R-R	6-0	185	8-23-04	0	0	0.00	2	0	0	0	2	3	2	0	0	2	2	.250	.333	.222	7.71	7.71
Eliecer Romero	R-R	6-0	185	9-8-01	2	1	0.90	6	0	0	1	10	7	2	1	0	5	10	.212	.100	.261	9.00	4.50
Pitterson Rosa	R-R	6-2	178	11-30-04	0	1	3.22	8	8	0	0	22	13	9	8	0	11	24	.181	.211	.170	9.67	4.43
Alberto Saba	R-R	6-2	160	1-18-05	3	0	3.60	16	1	0	1	30	26	16	12	2	16	25	.226	.368	.156	7.50	4.80
Fares Sanchez	R-R	6-1	170	6-9-04	4	2	1.44	12	1	0	0	31	19	5	5	0	8	16	.174	.104	.169	4.60	2.30
Andres Silvera	R-R	6-0	188	7-20-04	2	1	1.54	11	11	0	0	41	27	8	7	0	6	45	.182	.229	.168	9.88	1.32
Isaias Uribe	L-L	6-3	172	8-13-02	0	0	1.13	3	3	0	0	8	5	1	1	0	5	9	.185	.500	.130	10.13	5.63
2-team total (10 DSL PIT Black)					1	4	4.15	13	12	0	0	39	35	21	18	0	14	42	.245	.310	.228	9.69	3.23
Dioris Valdez	R-R	6-1	180	11-16-02	0	1	9.00	4	0	0	0	5	6	6	5	1	4	4	.286	.333	.278	7.20	7.20
2-team total (6 DSL PIT Black)					1	1	8.56	10	0	0	0	14	16	19	13	2	10	13	.291	.429	.244	8.56	6.59
Wilkin Valdez	R-R	6-5	210	7-14-01	4	0	1.62	15	0	0	3	33	20	9	6	0	25	28	.180	.190	.174	7.56	6.75

Fielding

C: Escalona 8, Escudero 35, Nunez 11, Plaz 26. **1B:** Armas 5, Escudero 1, Figuereo 2, Tirado 46, Valdez 1, Zapata 9. **2B:** Aguiar 33, Figuereo 18, Pena 13, Zapata 4, Zorrilla 1. **3B:** Aguiar 2, De Los Santos 6, Figuereo 1, Pena 21, Zapata 11, Zorrilla 30. **SS:** De Los Santos 54, Pena 1, Zapata 2, Zorrilla 6. **OF:** Armas 26, Blanco Jr. 1, Dipre 36, Machado 29, Pena 12, Rodriguez 40, Vizcaya 51.

St. Louis Cardinals

SEASON IN A SENTENCE: The Cardinals won the Central Division, said goodbye to a pair of legends and underperformed in the playoffs as they were swept in the Wild Card series at the hands of the eventual NL champion Phillies.

HIGH POINT: The month of August was good to the Cardinals as they won 17 of 20 games to begin the month, and overtook the NL Central on Aug. 6th, a lead they would never relinquish. Future Hall of Famer and former MVP Albert Pujols would thrill the fans over this period hitting .324/.386/.743 and slugging 17 home runs over his final 47 regular season games. The home run surge would push Pujols over 700 career home runs, as he completed the feat at Dodger Stadium on September 23rd.

LOW POINT: The Cardinals went 11-13 during the month of July. They experienced their only losing streak of three or more games as they lost four games between July 3-6.

NOTABLE ROOKIES: Infielder Brendan Donovan hit .281 with a .394 on-base percentage and was awarded a Gold Glove for his play in the field at season's end. Highly touted 2018 first round pick Nolan Gorman made his debut, hitting .226/.300/.420 with 13 home runs across 89 games. Juan Yepez hit 12 holes runs and slugged .447 across 76 games. On the pitching side righthander Andre Pallante contributed as both a starter and reliever throughout the year.

KEY TRANSACTIONS: While the Cardinals made few splashes in free agency last winter they did add a group of veteran contributors in lefthander Steven Matz, as well as outfielder Corey Dickenson. Their biggest acquisition of the off-season proved to be the signing of Cardinals Legend Albert Pujols for his swan song in the week leading up to 2022 regular seasons. The Cardinals made a pair of impactful trades at the deadline, shipping homegrown centerfielder Harrison Bader to the Yankees in exchange for lefthanded starter Jordan Montgomery. They acquired a second lefthanded starter in Jose Quintana.

ON THE FARM: The Cardinals had seven players ranked among the Top 100 by season's end. with Jordan Walker, Masyn Winn at 56, Tink Hence at 57, Alec Burleson at 65, Gordon Graceffo at 66, Matthew Liberatore at 71 and Ivan Herrera at 84. While none of these players debuted in 2022, it's conceivable all but Tink Hence could see time with the major league team in 2023.

OPENING DAY PAYROLL: $158,200,00 (12th)

PLAYERS OF THE YEAR

MAJOR LEAGUE

Paul Goldschmidt
1B

.317/.404/.578
35 HR, 115 RBIs, 151 G
.981 OPS led NL

MINOR LEAGUE

Jordan Walker
3B

(Double-A)
.306/.388/.510
19 HR, 31 2B in 119 G

ORGANIZATION LEADERS

Batting		***Minimum 250 AB**
MAJORS		
* AVG	Paul Goldschmidt	.317
* OPS	Paul Goldschmidt	.981
HR	Paul Goldschmidt	35
RBI	Paul Goldschmidt	115
MINORS		
* AVG	Alec Burleson, Memphis	.331
* OBP	Scott Hurst, Memphis	.399
* SLG	Moises Gomez, Springfield, Memphis	.624
* OPS	Moises Gomez, Springfield, Memphis	.996
R	Jordan Walker, Springfield	100
H	Alec Burleson, Memphis	143
TB	Moises Gomez, Springfield, Memphis	276
2B	Masyn Winn, Peoria, Springfield	36
3B	Masyn Winn, Peoria, Springfield	8
HR	Moises Gomez, Springfield, Memphis	39
RBI	Moises Gomez, Springfield, Memphis	94
BB	Mike Antico, Peoria, Springfield	71
SO	Moises Gomez, Springfield, Memphis	174
SB	Mike Antico, Peoria, Springfield	67

Pitching		**#Minimum 75 IP**
MAJORS		
W	Miles Mikolas	12
# ERA	Andre Pallante	3.17
SO	Miles Mikolas	153
SV	Ryan Helsley	19
MINORS		
W	Thomas Parsons, Memphis	12
L	3 tied	12
# ERA	Inohan Paniagua, Palm Beach, Peoria	2.81
G	Zach McAllister, Memphis	56
GS	Michael McGreevy, Peoria, Springfield	28
SV	Freddy Pacheco, Springfield, Memphis	12
IP	Kyle Leahy, Springfield, Memphis	144.2
BB	Kyle Leahy, Springfield, Memphis	72
SO	Austin Love, Peoria	151
# AVG	Gordon Graceffo, Peoria, Springfield	.202
	Thomas Parsons, Memphis	.2023

ST. LOUIS CARDINALS

2022 PERFORMANCE

General Manager: Mike Girsch. **Farm Director:** Gary LaRocque. **Scouting Director:** Randy Flores.

Class	Team	League	W	L	PCT	Finish	Manager
Majors	St. Louis Cardinals	National	93	69	.574	3rd (15)	Oliver Marmol
Triple-A	Memphis Redbirds	International	73	77	.487	13th (20)	Ben Johnson
Double-A	Springfield Cardinals	Texas	68	70	.493	7th (10)	Jose Leger
High-A	Peoria Chiefs	Midwest	56	76	.424	9th (12)	Patrick Anderson
Low-A	Palm Beach Cardinals	Florida State	67	61	.523	3rd (10)	Gary Kendall
Rookie	FCL Cardinals	Florida Complex	25	29	.463	11th (16)	Roberto Espinoza
Overall 2022 Minor League Record			322	339	.487	19th (30)	

ORGANIZATION STATISTICS

ST. LOUIS CARDINALS

NATIONAL LEAGUE

Batting	B-T	HT	WT	DOB	AVG	vLH	vRH	G	AB	R	H	2B	3B	HR	RBI	BB	HBP	SH	SF	SO	SB	CS	SLG	OBP
Nolan Arenado	R-R	6-2	215	4-16-91	.293	.250	.303	148	557	73	163	42	1	30	103	52	7	0	4	72	5	3	.533	.358
Harrison Bader	R-R	6-0	210	6-3-94	.256	.191	.271	72	246	35	63	7	3	5	21	13	4	0	1	47	15	2	.370	.303
Alec Burleson	L-L	6-2	212	11-25-98	.188	.333	.178	16	48	4	9	1	0	1	3	5	0	0	0	9	1	0	.271	.264
Conner Capel	L-L	6-1	185	5-19-97	.176	--	.176	9	17	1	3	0	0	1	2	1	0	0	1	2	0	0	.353	.211
Dylan Carlson	B-L	6-2	205	10-23-98	.236	.305	.207	128	432	56	102	30	4	8	42	45	7	0	4	94	5	2	.380	.316
Paul DeJong	R-R	6-0	205	8-2-93	.157	.151	.159	77	210	19	33	9	0	6	25	21	4	0	2	79	3	2	.286	.245
Ben DeLuzio	R-R	6-3	200	8-9-94	.150	.000	.188	22	20	3	3	1	0	0	0	3	1	1	0	5	0	1	.200	.292
Corey Dickerson	L-R	6-1	200	5-22-89	.267	.077	.286	97	281	28	75	17	1	6	36	12	2	0	2	48	0	0	.399	.300
Brendan Donovan	L-R	6-1	195	1-16-97	.281	.279	.282	126	391	64	110	21	1	5	45	60	14	1	2	70	2	3	.379	.394
Tommy Edman	B-R	5-10	180	5-9-95	.265	.276	.261	153	577	95	153	31	4	13	57	46	5	1	1	111	32	3	.400	.324
Paul Goldschmidt	R-R	6-3	220	9-10-87	.317	.411	.294	151	561	106	178	41	0	35	115	79	5	0	4	141	7	0	.578	.404
Nolan Gorman	L-R	6-1	210	5-10-00	.226	.211	.227	89	283	44	64	13	0	14	35	28	2	0	0	103	1	0	.420	.300
Ivan Herrera	R-R	5-11	220	6-1-00	.111	.000	.143	11	18	0	2	0	0	0	1	2	0	1	1	8	0	0	.111	.190
Andrew Knizner	R-R	6-1	225	2-3-95	.215	.138	.238	97	260	28	56	10	0	4	25	26	6	1	0	62	0	1	.300	.301
Yadier Molina	R-R	5-11	225	7-13-82	.214	.254	.201	80	262	19	56	8	0	5	24	5	2	0	1	40	2	0	.302	.233
Lars Nootbaar	L-R	6-3	210	9-8-97	.228	.273	.217	108	290	53	66	16	3	14	40	51	1	0	5	71	4	1	.448	.340
Tyler O'Neill	R-R	5-11	200	6-22-95	.228	.256	.219	96	334	56	76	11	1	14	58	38	4	0	7	103	14	4	.392	.308
Albert Pujols	R-R	6-3	235	1-16-80	.270	.351	.223	109	307	42	83	14	0	24	68	28	10	0	6	55	1	2	.550	.345
Kramer Robertson	R-R	5-10	166	9-20-94	.000	--	.000	2	1	0	0	0	0	0	1	0	0	0	0	0	0	0	.000	.000
Austin Romine	R-R	6-1	216	11-22-88	.154	.167	.150	11	26	2	4	1	0	0	0	2	0	0	0	7	0	0	.192	.214
2-team total (37 Cincinnati Reds)					.149	.036	.183	48	121	10	18	3	0	3	9	4	1	1	0	43	0	0	.248	.183
Edmundo Sosa	R-R	6-0	210	3-6-96	.189	.118	.239	53	122	17	23	4	3	0	8	4	5	0	0	38	3	1	.270	.244
2-team total (25 Philadelphia Phillies)					.227	.232	.223	78	176	26	40	11	4	2	21	5	7	1	1	50	6	1	.369	.275
Cory Spangenberg	L-R	6-0	195	3-16-91	--	--	--	1	0	0	0	0	0	0	0	0	0	0	0	0	0	0	--	--
Juan Yepez	R-R	6-1	200	2-19-98	.253	.255	.253	76	253	27	64	13	0	12	30	16	1	0	4	61	0	0	.447	.296

Pitching	B-T	HT	WT	DOB	W	L	ERA	G	GS	CG	SV	IP	H	R	ER	HR	BB	SO	AVG	vLH	vRH	K/9	BB/9
Aaron Brooks	R-R	6-4	230	4-27-90	0	0	7.71	5	0	0	0	9	11	8	8	3	2	7	.275	.250	.300	6.75	1.93
Genesis Cabrera	L-L	6-2	180	10-10-96	4	2	4.63	39	0	0	1	45	39	24	23	8	20	32	.231	.214	.239	6.45	4.03
Corey Dickerson	L-R	6-1	200	5-22-89	0	0	0.00	1	0	0	0	1	2	0	0	0	1	0	.400	.667	.000	0.00	9.00
Junior Fernandez	R-R	6-3	215	3-2-97	0	0	2.93	13	0	0	0	15	17	6	5	3	8	12	.283	.231	.298	7.04	4.70
2-team total (3 Pittsburgh Pirates)					0	0	2.41	16	0	0	0	19	18	6	5	3	12	14	.257	.235	.264	6.75	5.79
Jack Flaherty	R-R	6-4	225	10-15-95	2	1	4.25	9	8	0	0	36	36	18	17	4	22	33	.259	.268	.246	8.25	5.50
Giovanny Gallegos	R-R	6-2	215	8-14-91	3	6	3.05	57	0	0	14	59	42	23	20	6	18	73	.197	.226	.175	11.14	2.75
Ryan Helsley	R-R	6-2	230	7-18-94	9	1	1.25	54	0	0	19	65	28	11	9	6	20	94	.128	.141	.118	13.08	2.78
Jordan Hicks	R-R	6-2	220	9-6-96	3	6	4.84	35	8	0	0	61	46	33	33	5	35	63	.210	.232	.197	9.24	5.14
Dakota Hudson	R-R	6-5	215	9-15-94	8	7	4.45	27	26	0	0	140	141	71	69	9	61	78	.273	.263	.281	5.03	3.93
Andrew Knizner	R-R	6-1	225	2-3-95	0	0	0.00	1	0	0	0	1	1	0	0	0	0	0	.333	.000	.500	0.00	0.00
Matthew Liberatore	L-L	6-4	200	11-6-99	2	2	5.97	9	7	0	0	35	42	23	23	5	18	28	.304	.235	.327	7.27	4.67
Steven Matz	R-L	6-2	201	5-29-91	5	3	5.25	15	10	0	0	48	50	28	28	8	10	54	.256	.279	.250	10.13	1.88
T.J. McFarland	L-L	6-3	200	6-8-89	0	0	6.61	28	0	0	0	33	42	26	24	5	11	16	.323	.354	.305	4.41	3.03
Miles Mikolas	R-R	6-4	230	8-23-88	12	13	3.29	33	32	1	0	202	170	81	74	25	39	153	.226	.207	.244	6.81	1.73
Yadier Molina	R-R	5-11	225	7-13-82	0	0	18.00	2	0	0	0	2	6	4	4	2	0	1	.500	.571	.400	4.50	0.00
Jordan Montgomery	L-L	6-6	228	12-27-92	6	3	3.11	11	11	1	0	64	56	24	22	6	13	61	.232	.194	.238	8.62	1.84
James Naile	R-R	6-4	185	2-8-93	0	0	5.00	7	0	0	0	9	8	5	5	2	2	5	.229	.308	.182	5.00	2.00
Packy Naughton	R-L	6-2	195	4-16-96	0	2	4.78	26	3	0	1	32	39	17	17	3	7	31	.295	.163	.373	8.72	1.97
Johan Oviedo	R-R	6-5	245	3-2-98	2	1	3.20	14	1	0	0	25	26	9	9	4	7	26	.260	.081	.365	9.24	2.49
2-team total (7 Pittsburgh Pirates)					4	3	3.21	21	8	0	0	56	49	21	20	5	23	54	.227	.195	.248	8.68	3.70
Andre Pallante	R-R	6-0	203	9-18-98	6	5	3.17	47	10	0	0	108	113	39	38	9	40	73	.274	.246	.295	6.08	3.33
Albert Pujols	R-R	6-3	235	1-16-80	0	0	36.00	1	0	0	0	1	3	4	4	2	1	0	.500	.500	.500	0.00	9.00
Jose Quintana	R-L	6-1	220	1-24-89	3	2	2.01	12	12	0	0	63	54	18	14	1	16	48	.238	.250	.236	6.89	2.30
JoJo Romero	L-L	5-11	200	9-9-96	0	0	3.77	15	0	0	0	14	9	6	6	2	9	16	.191	.125	.226	10.05	5.65
2-team total (2 Philadelphia Phillies)					0	0	4.96	17	0	0	0	16	13	9	9	3	10	17	.232	.118	.282	9.37	5.51

Angel Rondon	R-R	6-1	205	12-1-97	1	0	0.00	1	0	0	0	5	1	0	0	0	3	4	.059	.000	.143	7.20	5.40
Chris Stratton	R-R	6-2	205	8-22-90	5	0	2.78	20	0	0	0	23	22	8	7	0	12	23	.262	.231	.276	9.13	4.76
Zack Thompson	L-L	6-2	215	10-28-97	1	1	2.08	22	1	0	1	35	20	9	8	3	14	27	.164	.146	.176	7.01	3.63
Drew VerHagen	R-R	6-6	230	10-22-90	3	1	6.65	19	0	0	0	22	27	18	16	5	14	18	.300	.353	.268	7.48	5.82
Adam Wainwright	R-R	6-7	230	8-30-81	11	12	3.71	32	32	1	0	192	192	80	79	16	54	143	.261	.256	.265	6.71	2.54
Jake Walsh	R-R	6-1	192	7-20-95	0	1	13.50	3	0	0	0	3	3	4	4	0	2	5	.250	.200	.286	16.88	6.75
Kodi Whitley	R-R	6-3	220	2-21-95	2	0	5.68	14	0	0	0	13	11	8	8	2	9	12	.234	.231	.238	8.53	6.39
Nick Wittgren	R-R	6-2	216	5-29-91	1	0	5.90	29	0	0	1	29	35	19	19	1	10	17	.299	.311	.292	5.28	3.10
Jake Woodford	R-R	6-4	215	10-28-96	4	0	2.23	27	1	0	0	48	43	13	12	1	11	24	.249	.292	.232	4.47	2.05

Fielding

Catcher	PCT	G	PO	A	E	DP	PB
Herrera	1.000	11	49	8	0	0	1
Knizner	.990	90	577	21	6	6	3
Molina	.994	77	512	25	3	6	1
Romine	1.000	10	62	3	0	0	0

First Base	PCT	G	PO	A	E	DP
Burleson	1.000	6	29	2	0	5
Donovan	.971	16	60	6	2	9
Goldschmidt	.999	128	1071	91	1	118
Knizner	1.000	5	13	0	0	1
Molina	.000	1	0	0	0	0
Pujols	1.000	22	157	14	0	19
Yepez	1.000	15	69	7	0	12

Second Base	PCT	G	PO	A	E	DP
DeJong	.875	1	2	5	1	2
Donovan	1.000	38	58	75	0	25
Edman	.991	89	124	210	3	51
Gorman	.975	68	127	181	8	61
Sosa	.000	1	0	0	0	0

Third Base	PCT	G	PO	A	E	DP
Arenado	.968	131	84	283	12	42
Donovan	.960	31	15	80	4	10
Edman	.938	8	5	10	1	2
Sosa	1.000	11	5	13	0	1
Spangenberg	.000	1	0	0	0	0
Yepez	1.000	6	2	6	0	0

Shortstop	PCT	G	PO	A	E	DP
DeJong	.978	75	79	191	6	46
Donovan	.967	7	14	15	1	4
Edman	.994	80	93	215	2	49
Robertson	.000	1	0	0	1	0
Sosa	.972	34	33	70	3	15

Outfield	PCT	G	PO	A	E	DP
Bader	1.000	71	174	3	0	0
Burleson	1.000	11	16	0	0	0
Capel	1.000	7	11	0	0	0
Carlson	.991	135	222	8	2	1
DeLuzio	1.000	18	19	0	0	0
Dickerson	.989	70	88	0	1	0
Donovan	1.000	39	61	4	0	1
Edman	1.000	3	2	0	0	0
Gorman	--	1	0	0	0	0
Nootbaar	.989	102	169	8	2	4
O'Neill	.993	104	147	3	1	0
Yepez	.959	40	45	2	2	1

ST. LOUIS CARDINALS

MEMPHIS REDBIRDS — *TRIPLE-A*

INTERNATIONAL LEAGUE

Batting	B-T	HT	WT	DOB	AVG	vLH	vRH	G	AB	R	H	2B	3B	HR	RBI	BB	HBP	SH	SF	SO	SB	CS	SLG	OBP
Austin Allen	L-R	6-2	219	1-16-94	.318	.167	.333	20	66	7	21	4	0	2	14	9	0	0	1	19	0	0	.470	.395
Harrison Bader	R-R	6-0	210	6-3-94	.000	--	.000	1	3	1	0	0	0	0	0	1	0	0	0	0	0	0	.000	.250
Luken Baker	R-R	6-4	280	3-10-97	.228	.214	.234	124	464	52	106	14	0	21	66	37	5	0	7	129	0	0	.394	.288
Roberto Baldoquin	R-R	5-11	199	5-14-94	.273	.227	.291	23	77	10	21	2	0	0	4	10	3	0	0	12	1	1	.299	.378
Alec Burleson	L-L	6-2	212	11-25-98	.331	.325	.333	109	432	68	143	25	1	20	87	29	3	0	6	67	4	0	.532	.372
Conner Capel	L-L	6-1	185	5-19-97	.258	.202	.281	87	325	52	84	18	3	10	38	50	2	0	0	62	19	8	.425	.361
Dylan Carlson	B-L	6-2	205	10-23-98	.778	1.000	.750	3	9	5	7	3	0	1	4	2	0	0	0	1	0	0	1.444	.818
Clint Coulter	R-R	6-3	225	7-30-93	.297	.255	.315	54	182	26	54	14	1	9	33	15	9	0	1	33	0	1	.533	.377
Paul DeJong	R-R	6-0	205	8-2-93	.249	.208	.261	51	201	36	50	10	0	17	54	20	2	0	7	52	1	1	.552	.313
Ben DeLuzio	R-R	6-3	200	8-9-94	.277	.299	.268	94	364	60	101	16	6	9	49	36	7	0	1	91	30	6	.429	.353
Corey Dickerson	L-R	6-1	200	5-22-89	.308	.250	.333	5	13	2	4	1	0	1	2	1	0	0	0	2	0	0	.615	.357
Brendan Donovan	L-R	6-1	195	1-16-97	.298	.421	.237	16	57	12	17	3	0	1	6	8	0	0	0	8	0	0	.404	.385
Moises Gomez	R-R	5-11	200	8-27-98	.266	.264	.267	60	218	36	58	8	2	16	40	25	0	0	1	84	3	0	.541	.340
Nolan Gorman	L-R	6-1	210	5-10-00	.275	.169	.330	43	171	35	47	5	0	16	26	14	1	0	2	69	3	0	.585	.330
Ivan Herrera	R-R	5-11	220	6-1-00	.268	.254	.274	65	235	41	63	10	1	6	34	38	3	0	2	52	5	1	.396	.374
Scott Hurst	L-R	5-10	175	3-25-96	.286	.221	.305	90	311	55	89	12	2	10	38	54	5	0	1	68	18	8	.434	.399
Matt Koperniak	L-R	6-0	200	2-8-98	.667	--	.667	2	3	1	2	0	0	0	0	1	1	0	0	0	1	0	.667	.800
Irving Lopez	L-R	5-9	175	6-30-95	.263	.125	.278	26	80	13	21	5	0	1	7	8	4	0	0	15	1	0	.363	.359
Evan Mendoza	R-R	6-2	205	6-28-96	.247	.258	.244	109	360	56	89	16	0	4	29	56	1	1	3	56	17	4	.325	.348
Yadier Molina	R-R	5-11	225	7-13-82	.200	.500	.000	2	5	1	1	0	0	0	0	1	1	0	0	0	1	0	.200	.429
Lars Nootbaar	L-R	6-3	210	9-8-97	.222	.118	.261	17	63	13	14	4	0	4	14	10	1	0	3	19	2	0	.476	.325
Tyler O_Neill	R-R	5-11	200	6-22-95	.400	.429	.385	5	20	3	8	2	0	1	2	0	2	0	0	6	0	0	.650	.455
Pedro Pages	R-R	6-1	234	9-17-98	.222	.150	.248	44	153	16	34	8	0	4	16	14	0	0	3	46	0	0	.353	.282
Delvin Perez	R-R	6-3	175	11-24-98	.224	.289	.198	45	134	19	30	4	1	3	13	14	1	0	0	38	8	0	.336	.302
Chase Pinder	R-R	5-11	185	3-16-96	.138	.333	.050	11	29	2	4	2	0	1	4	5	0	0	1	4	1	0	.310	.257
Kramer Robertson	R-R	5-10	166	9-20-94	.228	.281	.204	81	285	56	65	13	0	9	34	60	15	0	0	79	22	3	.368	.389
3-team total (13 Gwinnett Stripers, 22 Syracuse Mets)					.239	.275	.222	116	410	81	98	16	1	11	47	84	20	0	0	103	30	8	.363	.393
Austin Romine	R-R	6-1	216	11-22-88	.318	.200	.417	6	22	1	7	1	0	0	4	0	0	0	0	4	0	0	.364	.318
Ali Sanchez	R-R	6-1	200	1-20-97	.255	.286	.235	30	110	15	28	5	0	4	12	13	0	0	0	29	1	0	.409	.333
2-team total (44 Toledo Mud Hens)					.262	.247	.269	74	252	38	66	14	0	6	33	35	2	0	2	77	2	0	.389	.354
Cory Spangenberg	L-R	6-0	195	3-16-91	.236	.274	.223	106	382	53	90	17	5	10	42	27	3	0	2	135	14	3	.385	.290
Justin Toerner	L-L	5-11	185	8-11-96	.185	.313	.143	23	65	11	12	2	0	1	8	9	2	2	3	24	1	2	.262	.291
Juan Yepez	R-R	6-1	200	2-19-98	.277	.286	.273	50	188	34	52	9	0	16	53	17	2	0	1	46	0	0	.580	.341

Pitching	B-T	HT	WT	DOB	W	L	ERA	G	GS	CG	SV	IP	H	R	ER	HR	BB	SO	AVG	vLH	vRH	K/9	BB/9
Grant Black	R-R	6-5	225	7-21-94	2	2	4.17	23	5	0	1	45	40	25	21	7	18	24	.237	.227	.243	4.76	3.57
Jacob Bosiokovic	R-R	6-5	240	12-21-93	1	1	5.27	15	0	0	3	14	13	9	8	3	4	13	.241	.240	.241	8.56	2.63
Aaron Brooks	R-R	6-4	230	4-27-90	5	4	5.56	15	13	0	0	70	81	45	43	9	20	54	.296	.306	.285	6.98	2.58
Genesis Cabrera	L-L	6-2	180	10-10-96	1	1	7.62	10	0	0	2	13	14	11	11	1	4	15	.264	.188	.297	10.38	2.77
Junior Fernandez	R-R	6-3	215	3-2-97	1	3	5.45	35	0	0	5	36	47	24	22	4	17	43	.313	.403	.241	10.65	4.21
2-team total (6 Indianapolis Indians)					2	3	4.87	41	0	0	5	44	49	26	24	4	23	51	.280	.394	.202	10.35	4.67
Jack Flaherty	R-R	6-4	225	10-15-95	1	2	4.35	3	3	0	0	10	9	6	5	2	3	11	.231	.222	.250	9.58	2.61
Jordan Hicks	R-R	6-2	220	9-6-96	0	0	12.60	4	1	0	0	5	7	7	7	1	4	5	.333	.500	.231	9.00	7.20

Dakota Hudson	R-R	6-5	215	9-15-94	1	1	1.71	3	3	0	0	21	20	7	4	0	8	19	.260	.267	.255	8.14	3.43
Kyle Leahy	B-R	6-5	200	6-4-97	0	0	7.36	1	0	0	0	4	4	3	3	1	1	2	.286	.000	.308	4.91	2.45
Matthew Liberatore	L-L	6-4	200	11-6-99	7	9	5.17	22	22	0	0	115	118	68	66	16	41	116	.269	.241	.282	9.08	3.21
Ryan Loutos	R-R	6-5	215	1-29-99	0	3	6.33	22	2	0	2	27	44	20	19	4	12	29	.373	.422	.342	9.67	4.00
Steven Matz	R-L	6-2	201	5-29-91	0	0	1.84	6	4	0	0	15	9	3	3	1	3	19	.176	.263	.125	11.66	1.84
Zach McAllister	R-R	6-6	240	12-8-87	5	2	3.99	56	0	0	2	68	62	35	30	7	27	90	.242	.247	.239	11.97	3.59
T.J. McFarland	L-L	6-3	200	6-8-89	0	2	4.00	17	0	0	0	18	17	9	8	2	4	15	.254	.182	.324	7.50	2.00
James Nalle	R-R	6-4	185	2-8-93	4	3	3.31	44	3	0	0	73	80	31	27	5	21	64	.276	.282	.271	7.85	2.58
Packy Naughton	R-L	6-2	195	4-16-96	2	1	2.08	11	0	0	0	22	21	6	5	2	5	25	.256	.226	.275	10.38	2.08
Ljay Newsome	R-R	5-11	210	11-8-96	0	0	4.76	4	0	0	0	6	5	4	3	0	1	5	.250	.750	.125	7.94	1.59
Johan Oviedo	R-R	6-5	245	3-2-98	4	2	5.58	10	10	0	0	50	43	33	31	14	23	51	.231	.219	.244	9.18	4.14
2-team total (5 Indianapolis Indians)					4	2	4.70	15	14	0	0	61	51	34	32	14	26	64	.225	.212	.239	9.39	3.82
Freddy Pacheco	R-R	5-11	203	4-17-98	2	2	2.41	26	0	0	4	34	17	12	9	2	12	43	.145	.167	.127	11.50	3.21
Blake Parker	R-R	6-3	225	6-19-85	1	2	6.59	26	0	0	0	27	27	20	20	7	14	36	.255	.333	.190	11.85	4.61
Thomas Parsons	R-R	6-4	220	9-1-95	12	4	4.31	38	17	0	0	136	102	68	65	29	57	110	.204	.212	.198	7.30	3.78
Julian Quezada	R-R	6-9	255	8-25-94	1	1	2.92	17	0	0	0	23	30	8	8	1	11	28	.300	.333	.297	10.22	4.01
Dalton Roach	R-R	6-2	210	4-8-96	0	0	0.00	1	0	0	0	1	2	0	0	0	2	1	.500	.500	.500	9.00	18.00
JoJo Romero	L-L	5-11	200	9-9-96	0	0	0.00	3	0	0	0	3	1	0	0	0	0	5	.100	.000	.143	15.00	0.00
2-team total (5 Lehigh Valley IronPigs)					0	0	0.00	8	0	0	0	7	4	0	0	0	0	8	.160	.222	.125	10.29	0.00
Angel Rondon	R-R	6-1	205	12-1-97	3	1	4.04	18	5	0	0	49	39	25	22	7	33	52	.218	.250	.189	9.55	6.06
Kyle Ryan	L-L	6-5	215	9-25-91	6	1	4.88	39	0	0	1	48	54	28	26	8	29	35	.283	.301	.265	6.56	5.44
Connor Thomas	L-L	5-11	173	5-29-98	6	12	5.47	28	25	1	0	135	172	92	82	16	40	110	.307	.271	.328	7.33	2.67
Zack Thompson	L-L	6-2	215	10-28-97	2	3	4.73	19	10	0	0	53	44	32	28	6	21	67	.219	.179	.239	11.31	3.54
Drew VerHagen	R-R	6-6	230	10-22-90	0	0	5.40	1	1	0	0	2	1	1	1	0	1	2	.167	.000	.250	10.80	5.40
Brandon Waddell	L-L	6-3	180	6-3-94	2	1	3.30	23	0	0	3	30	29	11	11	1	11	33	.257	.317	.189	9.90	3.30
Jake Walsh	R-R	6-1	192	7-20-95	1	0	1.17	13	0	0	6	15	11	3	2	1	7	22	.196	.133	.269	12.91	4.11
Kodi Whitley	R-R	6-3	220	2-21-95	1	0	3.86	30	0	0	3	33	33	16	14	8	16	32	.254	.298	.229	8.82	4.41
Garrett Williams	L-L	6-1	200	9-15-94	0	7	6.85	18	11	0	0	47	54	41	36	5	35	56	.297	.297	.297	10.65	6.65
Jake Woodford	R-R	6-4	215	10-28-96	2	3	3.14	11	10	0	0	43	39	17	15	2	19	39	.244	.247	.240	8.16	3.98
T.J. Zeuch	R-R	6-7	245	8-1-95	0	4	11.64	5	5	0	0	19	39	26	25	6	11	20	.448	.510	.368	9.31	5.12
2-team total (5 Louisville Bats)					0	5	7.34	10	10	0	0	42	57	36	34	8	21	46	.337	.422	.256	9.94	4.54

Fielding

Catcher	PCT	G	PO	A	E	DP	PB
Allen	.992	16	122	7	1	2	2
Coulter	1.000	11	87	4	0	1	1
Herrera	.993	57	502	33	4	2	7
Molina	1.000	1	4	0	0	0	0
Pages	.997	37	302	18	1	2	7
Romine	1.000	5	42	1	0	0	0
Sanchez	.996	27	254	13	1	1	1

First Base	PCT	G	PO	A	E	DP
Baker	.994	118	894	41	6	93
Baldoquin	1.000	5	42	2	0	5
Donovan	.944	5	34	0	2	3
Mendoza	1.000	1	8	1	0	0
Spangenberg	1.000	4	16	1	0	3
Yepez	1.000	20	147	8	0	14

Second Base	PCT	G	PO	A	E	DP
Baldoquin	.981	11	21	32	1	9
Donovan	1.000	3	6	6	0	1
Gorman	.987	34	52	105	2	30
Lopez	.969	5	16	15	1	6
Mendoza	.987	47	96	128	3	34
Perez	.951	9	16	23	2	7
Robertson	.985	18	26	39	1	6
Spangenberg	.957	28	41	69	5	12

Third Base	PCT	G	PO	A	E	DP
Baldoquin	1.000	7	2	9	0	1
Coulter	.846	6	3	8	2	3
Donovan	1.000	7	3	11	0	2
Lopez	.974	18	10	28	1	5
Mendoza	1.000	7	2	8	0	1
Perez	.952	31	18	41	3	8
Robertson	1.000	16	17	27	0	3
Spangenberg	.954	61	42	104	7	9
Yepez	.923	4	4	8	1	0

Shortstop	PCT	G	PO	A	E	DP
DeJong	.964	44	45	118	6	23
Mendoza	.983	54	67	158	4	28
Robertson	.971	46	68	130	6	30
Spangenberg	1.000	7	7	18	0	3

Outfield	PCT	G	PO	A	E	DP
Burleson	.985	76	130	4	2	2
Capel	.974	82	145	6	4	2
Carlson	1.000	2	1	0	0	0
Coulter	.981	28	47	4	1	0
DeLuzio	.995	87	184	3	1	0
Dickerson	1.000	3	6	0	0	0
Donovan	1.000	1	0	1	0	0
Gomez	.980	48	90	6	2	2
Hurst	.987	89	149	7	2	1
Koperniak	1.000	1	2	0	0	0
Mendoza	1.000	1	5	0	0	0
Nootbaar	.957	11	21	1	1	0
O'Neill	1.000	3	4	1	0	0
Perez	1.000	1	1	0	0	0
Pinder	.947	10	17	1	1	0
Spangenberg	1.000	3	6	0	0	0
Toerner	1.000	24	51	2	0	0
Yepez	1.000	8	10	1	0	0

SPRINGFIELD CARDINALS — *DOUBLE-A*

TEXAS LEAGUE

Batting	B-T	HT	WT	DOB	AVG	vLH	vRH	G	AB	R	H	2B	3B	HR	RBI	BB	HBP	SH	SF	SO	SB	CS	SLG	OBP
Mike Antico	L-R	5-10	200	2-16-98	.233	.137	.259	60	240	44	56	12	0	8	31	30	4	0	1	67	30	4	.383	.327
Aaron Antonini	L-R	6-0	200	7-27-98	.188	.208	.175	21	64	8	12	2	0	1	7	7	3	0	0	12	0	0	.266	.297
Roberto Baldoquin	R-R	5-11	199	5-14-94	.203	.265	.179	39	118	16	24	5	0	0	6	15	5	0	0	26	0	1	.246	.319
Jacob Buchberger	R-R	6-2	215	10-1-97	.538	1.000	.250	5	13	3	7	1	0	1	4	5	0	0	0	3	2	2	.846	.667
Dylan Carlson	B-L	6-2	205	10-23-98	.000	--	.000	3	7	0	0	0	0	0	0	1	0	0	0	1	0	0	.000	.125
Jonah Davis	L-R	5-10	181	7-2-97	.146	.217	.119	67	164	34	24	5	2	8	22	26	10	1	0	92	2	0	.348	.300
Nick Dunn	L-R	5-10	185	1-29-97	.271	.256	.275	112	399	69	108	21	3	7	44	63	8	0	2	42	5	2	.391	.379
Moises Gomez	R-R	5-11	200	8-27-98	.321	.309	.325	60	224	53	72	17	0	23	54	27	4	0	2	90	7	3	.705	.401
Matt Koperniak	L-R	6-0	200	2-8-98	.288	.224	.304	106	385	67	111	13	2	14	59	40	5	3	4	82	11	4	.442	.359
Irving Lopez	L-R	5-9	175	6-30-95	.253	.300	.236	49	150	20	38	8	0	2	17	22	3	0	2	27	4	1	.347	.356
Todd Lott	R-R	6-4	235	8-22-97	.191	.211	.181	32	110	15	21	3	0	3	16	7	6	0	0	38	1	1	.300	.276
Malcom Nunez	R-R	5-11	205	3-9-01	.255	.315	.236	85	298	51	76	11	0	17	66	48	2	0	2	71	4	2	.463	.360
Pedro Pages	R-R	6-1	234	9-17-98	.232	.294	.212	42	138	22	32	7	0	6	28	24	1	0	4	56	1	0	.413	.341
Delvin Perez	R-R	6-3	175	11-24-98	.222	.231	.220	50	162	26	36	6	0	2	20	23	2	0	1	48	13	0	.296	.324
Chase Pinder	R-R	5-11	185	3-16-96	.278	.318	.267	62	209	39	58	14	0	10	52	53	2	0	4	56	5	5	.488	.422
Nick Raposo	R-R	5-10	200	6-3-98	.270	.224	.292	59	204	36	55	18	0	7	34	23	1	0	1	55	1	1	.461	.345

Chandler Redmond	L-R	6-1	231	1-9-97	.235	.219	.240	94	327	52	77	11	3	21	79	39	1	0	3	111	0	1	.480	.316
Errol Robinson	R-R	5-11	170	10-1-94	.269	.286	.262	39	119	21	32	4	0	1	12	25	1	0	0	42	12	3	.328	.400
Julio E. Rodriguez	R-R	6-0	245	6-11-97	.252	.197	.279	68	218	33	55	7	0	11	50	47	2	0	2	64	2	0	.436	.387
Edmundo Sosa	R-R	6-0	210	3-6-96	.375	--	.375	2	8	1	3	0	0	0	0	0	1	0	0	0	0	0	.375	.444
Justin Toerner	L-L	5-11	185	8-11-96	.236	.296	.215	66	212	41	50	11	0	6	34	47	10	0	1	75	9	0	.373	.396
Jordan Walker	R-R	6-5	220	5-22-02	.306	.283	.313	119	461	100	141	31	3	19	68	58	9	0	8	116	22	5	.510	.388
Brady Whalen	L-R	6-4	180	1-15-98	.306	.333	.300	29	98	20	30	11	3	0	15	7	1	1	1	20	5	0	.480	.355
Masyn Winn	R-R	5-11	180	3-21-02	.258	.276	.253	86	345	69	89	25	1	11	48	50	1	2	5	86	28	5	.432	.349

Pitching	B-T	HT	WT	DOB	W	L	ERA	G	GS	CG	SV	IP	H	R	ER	HR	BB	SO	AVG	vLH	vRH	K/9	BB/9
John Beller	L-L	5-11	175	3-6-99	3	1	6.75	15	0	0	0	16	11	14	12	2	14	17	.193	.167	.212	9.56	7.88
Grant Black	R-R	6-5	225	7-21-94	3	3	3.69	22	0	0	1	32	31	24	13	4	17	33	.242	.255	.234	9.38	4.83
Michael Brettell	R-R	6-3	195	7-13-97	5	3	5.58	45	0	0	1	71	80	50	44	5	34	58	.294	.304	.288	7.35	4.31
Gianluca Dalatri	R-R	6-6	250	4-4-98	0	0	8.03	7	0	0	0	12	17	11	11	4	11	11	.347	.333	.357	8.03	8.03
Edgar Escobar	R-R	6-1	220	1-20-97	7	12	6.73	28	20	0	0	124	145	96	93	23	50	98	.295	.295	.294	7.09	3.62
Jack Flaherty	R-R	6-4	225	10-15-95	0	0	2.16	4	4	0	0	17	13	4	4	0	4	23	.213	.300	.129	12.42	2.16
Gordon Graceffo	R-R	6-4	210	3-17-00	7	4	3.94	18	18	1	0	94	76	44	41	16	24	83	.217	.230	.207	7.98	2.31
Logan Gragg	R-R	6-5	200	8-8-98	1	1	6.07	17	4	0	4	43	50	31	29	13	17	42	.286	.306	.272	8.79	3.56
Andre Granillo	R-R	6-4	245	5-12-00	0	1	22.50	3	0	0	1	2	7	5	5	0	2	5	.538	.667	.429	22.50	9.00
Sean Kealey	L-L	6-7	225	10-15-97	1	2	5.89	14	0	0	0	18	25	16	12	3	15	28	.329	.433	.261	13.75	7.36
Kyle Leahy	B-R	6-5	200	6-4-97	10	7	5.23	27	26	0	0	141	155	90	82	22	71	144	.280	.249	.304	9.19	4.53
Irving Lopez	L-R	5-9	175	6-30-95	0	0	0.00	1	0	0	0	0	0	0	0	0	0	0	.000	.000	--	0.00	0.00
Ryan Loutos	R-R	6-5	215	1-29-99	1	1	1.61	15	0	0	3	22	14	5	4	0	10	26	.175	.231	.148	10.48	4.03
Connor Lunn	R-R	6-3	215	7-8-98	4	7	6.61	21	17	0	0	82	104	65	60	15	24	78	.313	.321	.307	8.60	2.64
Kevin Marnon	R-L	6-7	245	3-16-94	0	0	19.50	7	0	0	0	6	13	13	13	1	11	4	.433	.417	.444	6.00	16.50
Steven Matz	R-L	6-2	201	5-29-91	0	0	7.71	2	2	0	0	2	3	2	2	0	4	3	.273	--	.273	11.57	15.43
Michael McGreevy	L-R	6-4	215	7-8-00	6	4	4.64	20	20	0	0	99	109	55	51	14	26	76	.284	.298	.274	6.91	2.36
Freddy Pacheco	R-R	5-11	203	4-17-98	1	5	3.81	24	0	0	8	28	20	18	12	4	16	41	.208	.216	.203	13.02	5.08
Tyler Pike	L-L	6-0	180	1-26-94	5	4	5.05	36	1	0	3	62	58	35	35	8	34	79	.248	.217	.268	11.41	4.91
Johan Quezada	R-R	6-9	255	8-25-94	1	0	7.20	23	0	0	1	30	33	31	24	2	26	39	.275	.400	.200	11.70	7.80
Dalton Roach	R-R	6-2	210	4-8-96	6	8	4.29	40	11	0	7	99	92	51	47	20	23	95	.246	.263	.234	8.67	2.10
Griffin Roberts	R-R	6-3	210	6-13-96	0	0	10.70	16	0	0	0	18	14	22	21	2	21	23	.222	.286	.171	11.72	10.70
Domingo Robles	L-L	6-2	170	4-29-98	5	5	6.14	30	10	0	1	110	127	77	75	12	42	70	.289	.252	.306	5.73	3.44
Leonardo Taveras	R-R	6-5	190	9-7-98	0	0	6.75	7	0	0	0	9	4	7	7	1	11	10	.133	.154	.118	9.64	10.61
Cory Thompson	R-R	5-11	180	9-23-94	0	0	5.40	10	0	0	0	12	14	7	7	3	4	13	.292	.250	.313	10.03	3.09
Drew VerHagen	R-R	6-6	230	10-22-90	0	0	0.00	1	1	0	0	2	0	0	0	0	0	3	.000	.000	.000	13.50	0.00
Garrett Williams	L-L	6-1	200	9-15-94	1	2	3.94	10	4	0	0	30	17	15	13	6	11	45	.163	.111	.191	13.65	3.34
Michael YaSenka	R-R	6-1	195	5-26-98	1	0	6.75	19	0	0	0	32	30	25	24	6	25	36	.242	.212	.264	10.13	7.03

Fielding

Catcher	PCT	G	PO	A	E	DP	PB
Antonini	.994	18	143	11	1	4	2
Pages	.991	32	291	24	3	3	3
Raposo	1.000	46	341	17	0	2	2
Rodriguez	.991	52	415	22	4	3	5

First Base	PCT	G	PO	A	E	DP
Baldoquin	1.000	3	5	1	0	1
Lott	1.000	2	9	1	0	0
Nunez	.994	68	470	23	3	47
Pages	1.000	1	2	0	0	1
Redmond	.991	49	312	28	3	31
Rodriguez	1.000	3	15	1	0	0
Whalen	1.000	28	191	6	0	24

Second Base	PCT	G	PO	A	E	DP
Baldoquin	1.000	7	10	15	0	2
Dunn	.981	103	175	232	8	72
Lopez	.981	24	41	60	2	13
Perez	1.000	4	5	13	0	1
Redmond	.833	1	1	4	1	0
Robinson	.947	4	7	11	1	3

Third Base	PCT	G	PO	A	E	DP
Baldoquin	.970	15	8	24	1	1
Buchberger	1.000	3	1	7	0	0
Lopez	.946	18	6	29	2	2
Nunez	.929	9	5	8	1	0
Perez	.909	6	0	10	1	0
Robinson	.971	26	18	49	2	6
Walker	.905	70	60	111	18	8
Whalen	.000	1	0	0	0	0

Shortstop	PCT	G	PO	A	E	DP
Baldoquin	.964	14	14	39	2	11
Dunn	.333	1	0	1	2	0
Lopez	1.000	4	9	1	0	0
Perez	.923	34	33	75	9	15
Robinson	.882	9	7	23	4	4
Sosa	1.000	2	4	7	0	3
Winn	.983	84	120	219	6	46

Outfield	PCT	G	PO	A	E	DP
Antico	1.000	52	115	2	0	1
Carlson	1.000	2	2	0	0	0
Davis	.991	60	105	4	1	0
Gomez	.961	54	120	3	5	1
Koperniak	.994	90	163	7	1	1
Lopez	--	2	0	0	0	0
Lott	1.000	28	43	0	0	0
Perez	1.000	11	6	1	0	0
Pinder	.983	51	115	0	2	0
Toerner	.987	65	146	7	2	0
Walker	.984	31	50	10	1	2

PEORIA CHIEFS — *HIGH CLASS A*

MIDWEST LEAGUE

Batting	B-T	HT	WT	DOB	AVG	vLH	vRH	G	AB	R	H	2B	3B	HR	RBI	BB	HBP	SH	SF	SO	SB	CS	SLG	OBP
Mike Antico	L-R	5-10	200	2-16-98	.255	.244	.261	71	274	41	70	19	2	6	32	41	4	0	2	76	37	3	.405	.358
Aaron Antonini	L-R	6-0	200	7-27-98	.222	.206	.227	43	153	21	34	3	0	6	24	17	5	1	5	34	3	1	.359	.311
Jacob Buchberger	R-R	6-2	215	10-1-97	.257	.272	.251	94	350	43	90	9	4	9	51	41	2	0	1	82	16	1	.383	.338
Matt Chamberlain	L-R	6-0	200	10-31-98	.217	.278	.190	37	120	12	26	4	0	2	9	23	4	1	0	48	3	4	.300	.361
Mack Chambers	B-R	6-0	180	8-10-99	.242	.156	.270	79	260	49	63	13	1	6	29	34	2	2	2	60	10	3	.369	.332
Thomas Francisco	L-R	6-0	211	6-26-99	.197	.195	.198	45	157	13	31	8	1	1	27	12	6	0	6	25	0	0	.280	.271
Francisco Hernandez	R-R	5-11	190	10-8-99	.219	.207	.225	96	310	46	68	16	2	5	31	46	5	0	3	100	18	4	.332	.327
Tommy Jew	R-R	6-1	185	10-26-97	.193	.170	.203	106	331	39	64	13	1	7	26	39	3	3	2	120	31	4	.302	.283
L.J. Jones	R-R	6-0	225	6-27-99	.261	.261	.262	102	394	48	103	33	1	13	64	31	10	1	4	90	2	1	.449	.328
Todd Lott	R-R	6-4	235	8-22-97	.260	.288	.252	80	334	52	87	18	2	11	40	19	12	0	2	106	7	2	.425	.322
Aaron McKeithan	R-R	6-1	220	12-13-99	.253	.304	.231	25	75	6	19	3	0	1	7	7	1	0	0	16	0	1	.333	.325
Noah Mendlinger	L-R	5-9	180	8-9-00	.246	.220	.253	72	224	38	55	9	1	2	18	41	11	5	3	42	8	3	.321	.384
Ramon Mendoza	R-R	5-11	174	8-31-00	.229	.184	.246	55	175	22	40	7	2	1	17	22	2	8	1	59	3	1	.309	.320

ST. LOUIS CARDINALS

Tyler Reichenborn	R-R	5-11	180	7-23-98	.250	.243	.253	78	268	39	67	8	1	8	35	37	5	8	2	69	20	6	.377	.349
Zade Richardson	R-R	6-1	200	5-10-00	.139	.200	.095	12	36	2	5	0	0	0	1	3	2	0	0	15	1	0	.139	.244
Luis Rodriguez	R-R	6-0	175	2-26-00	.245	.100	.306	31	102	9	25	1	0	2	13	4	1	0	0	28	0	0	.314	.280
Patrick Romeri	R-R	6-3	195	6-29-01	.193	.143	.203	23	83	9	16	4	0	0	11	8	1	0	1	32	2	0	.241	.269
Carlos Soto	L-R	6-1	225	4-27-99	.181	.179	.182	48	149	17	27	11	0	3	13	26	1	1	2	52	0	1	.315	.303
Wade Stauss	L-R	6-2	225	4-4-99	.203	.222	.196	25	64	11	13	2	0	2	5	11	7	2	0	28	1	1	.328	.378
Osvaldo Tovalin	L-R	6-2	225	10-31-99	.211	.213	.211	64	246	25	52	8	1	7	37	19	6	1	2	46	2	4	.337	.282
Brady Whalen	L-R	6-4	180	1-16-98	.281	.257	.296	23	89	15	25	4	0	3	7	9	0	0	0	12	1	0	.427	.347
Masyn Winn	R-R	5-11	180	3-21-02	.349	.372	.337	33	129	22	45	11	7	1	15	13	1	1	3	29	15	0	.566	.404

Pitching	B-T	HT	WT	DOB	W	L	ERA	G	GS	CG	SV	IP	H	R	ER	HR	BB	SO	AVG	vLH	vRH	K/9	BB/9
John Beller	L-L	5-11	175	3-6-99	2	1	3.04	13	2	0	3	27	15	10	9	2	12	36	.158	.129	.172	12.15	4.05
Gianluca Dalatri	R-R	6-6	250	4-4-98	1	2	2.30	18	0	0	5	27	15	9	7	1	9	37	.161	.244	.096	12.18	2.96
Chris Gerard	R-L	5-10	175	11-23-99	1	2	4.32	8	0	0	0	17	14	10	8	5	8	25	.219	.273	.190	13.50	4.32
Gordon Graceffo	R-R	6-4	210	3-17-00	3	2	0.99	8	8	0	0	46	27	6	5	1	4	56	.170	.138	.188	11.04	0.79
Logan Gragg	R-R	6-5	200	8-8-98	4	4	3.92	13	11	0	0	60	61	29	26	7	10	49	.261	.267	.257	7.39	1.51
Andre Granillo	R-R	6-4	245	5-12-00	1	4	3.63	26	0	0	5	35	27	22	14	3	19	51	.214	.275	.173	13.24	4.93
Nathanael Heredia	L-L	6-3	190	9-10-00	4	4	4.12	41	1	0	0	74	62	39	34	5	54	86	.225	.261	.208	10.41	6.54
Ryan Loutos	R-R	6-5	215	1-29-99	2	2	3.14	9	0	0	4	14	11	7	5	1	3	17	.224	.353	.156	10.67	1.88
Austin Love	R-R	6-3	232	1-26-99	7	12	5.73	26	25	0	0	126	139	80	80	15	52	151	.277	.342	.222	10.81	3.72
Edgar Manzo	R-R	5-11	181	10-24-00	1	2	8.59	12	5	0	1	29	42	30	28	4	17	28	.331	.283	.373	8.59	5.22
Michael McGreevy	L-R	6-4	215	7-8-00	3	1	2.58	8	8	1	0	45	41	14	13	1	4	41	.238	.230	.245	8.14	0.79
Zane Mills	R-R	6-4	220	7-4-00	4	6	4.03	19	19	0	0	103	112	57	46	10	28	69	.277	.307	.249	6.05	2.45
Inohan Paniagua	R-R	6-1	148	2-6-00	2	2	4.42	8	8	0	0	39	34	21	19	8	16	38	.236	.255	.225	8.84	3.72
Wilfredo Pereira	R-R	6-0	197	4-26-99	6	8	5.02	27	18	0	0	118	100	70	66	17	31	129	.227	.260	.200	9.81	2.36
Levi Prater	B-L	6-0	184	6-20-99	0	2	6.21	30	0	0	1	42	34	31	29	7	44	44	.221	.236	.212	9.43	9.43
Jack Ralston	R-R	6-6	231	8-13-97	1	0	3.38	11	0	0	0	13	3	6	5	1	10	25	.073	.167	.000	16.88	6.75
Dionys Rodriguez	L-R	6-0	188	9-3-00	3	11	4.59	27	25	0	0	122	110	67	62	14	53	119	.235	.261	.211	8.80	3.92
Chris Roycroft	R-R	6-8	230	6-21-97	2	2	4.50	19	0	0	1	32	42	20	16	2	16	40	.307	.403	.227	11.25	4.50
Colin Schmid	L-L	6-1	195	8-13-97	0	0	9.17	15	0	0	0	18	23	23	18	6	15	16	.295	.292	.296	8.15	7.64
Enmanuel Solano	R-R	6-1	160	9-23-98	1	3	9.11	20	0	0	0	28	44	36	28	2	22	16	.349	.392	.320	5.20	7.16
Leonardo Taveras	R-R	6-5	190	9-7-98	3	2	5.49	28	0	0	4	41	36	29	25	4	28	67	.229	.260	.202	14.71	6.15
Nick Trogrlic-Iverson	R-R	6-1	175	10-3-97	4	4	3.33	31	0	0	4	70	62	29	26	4	17	67	.230	.250	.216	8.57	2.18
Drew VerHagen	R-R	6-6	230	10-22-90	0	0	0.00	3	2	0	0	4	3	1	0	0	2	3	.200	.250	.143	6.75	4.50
Michael YaSenka	R-R	6-1	195	5-26-98	1	0	5.19	12	0	0	0	26	24	15	15	6	5	26	.238	.205	.263	9.00	1.73

Fielding

Catcher	PCT	G	PO	A	E	DP	PB
Antonini	.989	30	255	22	3	0	0
McKeithan	.995	23	178	11	1	1	1
Richardson	1.000	8	63	0	0	0	0
Rodriguez	.976	23	196	8	5	2	6
Soto	1.000	35	336	15	0	1	6
Stauss	.991	25	206	9	2	0	4

First Base	PCT	G	PO	A	E	DP
Buchberger	.990	14	94	1	1	6
Francisco	1.000	38	254	27	0	22
Jones	.994	26	175	5	1	9
Rodriguez	1.000	7	41	7	0	6
Soto	1.000	5	27	0	0	2
Tovalin	.988	30	232	11	3	21
Whalen	1.000	19	121	4	0	17

Second Base	PCT	G	PO	A	E	DP
Buchberger	.976	24	33	50	2	14
Chambers	.983	18	25	34	1	7
Hernandez	.970	78	126	192	10	35
Mendlinger	.972	9	13	22	1	8
Mendoza	.944	4	3	14	1	2
Tovalin	1.000	1	1	3	0	0

Third Base	PCT	G	PO	A	E	DP
Buchberger	.948	43	21	71	5	6
Chambers	.950	8	8	11	1	0
Mendlinger	.929	62	44	100	11	7
Mendoza	.857	2	1	5	1	1
Tovalin	.939	23	17	29	3	4

Shortstop	PCT	G	PO	A	E	DP
Chambers	.901	50	55	91	16	19
Hernandez	.848	10	14	14	5	3
Mendoza	.982	48	61	103	3	23
Winn	.910	28	25	56	8	12

Outfield	PCT	G	PO	A	E	DP
Antico	.987	70	149	3	2	0
Buchberger	1.000	6	6	0	0	0
Chamberlain	.973	37	68	5	2	1
Jew	.991	103	211	8	2	0
Jones	1.000	13	17	0	0	0
Lott	.979	73	139	4	3	1
Reichenborn	.993	78	142	3	1	2
Romeri	1.000	22	46	0	0	0
Tovalin	1.000	6	7	0	0	0

PALM BEACH CARDINALS — LOW CLASS A

FLORIDA STATE LEAGUE

Batting	B-T	HT	WT	DOB	AVG	vLH	vRH	G	AB	R	H	2B	3B	HR	RBI	BB	HBP	SH	SF	SO	SB	CS	SLG	OBP
Joshua Baez	R-R	6-4	220	6-28-03	.286	.308	.280	20	63	11	18	5	1	3	16	11	4	0	1	30	4	3	.540	.418
Leonardo Bernal	B-R	6-0	200	2-13-04	.256	.286	.250	45	156	22	40	8	1	7	29	12	2	0	1	32	1	1	.455	.316
Jake Burns	L-R	6-0	199	2-17-03	.191	.250	.186	17	47	7	9	4	0	0	2	10	1	1	0	23	0	1	.277	.345
Elijah Cabell	R-R	6-2	225	6-30-99	.162	.121	.172	56	167	24	27	5	0	8	27	40	7	0	2	98	1	0	.335	.343
Matt Chamberlain	L-R	6-0	200	10-31-98	.224	.143	.242	47	152	29	34	9	3	2	25	23	3	1	3	54	6	1	.362	.331
Nathan Church	L-L	5-11	180	7-12-00	.189	.292	.155	27	95	12	18	1	1	0	4	9	5	1	1	14	3	1	.221	.291
Jimmy Crooks III	L-R	6-1	210	7-19-01	.266	.357	.246	23	79	12	21	3	2	3	7	12	5	0	0	22	0	0	.468	.396
Adanson Cruz	R-R	6-2	175	10-6-00	.160	.097	.174	56	175	20	28	7	1	3	15	15	2	1	2	81	2	1	.263	.232
Michael Curialle	R-R	6-2	199	6-16-01	.231	.250	.222	21	65	9	15	4	0	0	5	6	5	0	0	16	2	0	.292	.342
Lizandro Espinoza	R-R	5-7	158	11-20-02	.159	.000	.193	19	69	10	11	1	1	1	3	3	0	1	0	29	1	0	.246	.194
Tre Fletcher	R-R	6-2	200	4-30-01	.000	.000	.000	5	16	0	0	0	0	0	0	0	0	0	0	16	0	0	.000	.000
Thomas Francisco	L-R	6-0	211	6-26-99	.266	.148	.289	45	169	19	45	9	0	5	31	24	1	0	3	27	0	0	.408	.355
Roblin Heredia	L-R	6-0	200	7-22-02	.094	.000	.125	10	32	2	3	0	0	0	0	4	0	0	0	15	1	0	.094	.194
Brandon Hernandez	L-R	6-0	190	8-21-01	.130	.182	.119	41	123	12	16	3	0	0	4	16	1	1	0	58	2	0	.154	.236
Ryan Holgate	L-L	6-2	193	6-8-00	.219	.167	.236	21	73	6	16	3	1	0	5	1	0	0	0	26	2	0	.288	.230
Alex Iadisernia	L-L	5-11	180	10-11-00	.275	.143	.309	21	69	7	19	2	1	0	7	6	2	0	0	21	2	1	.333	.351
Albert Inoa	R-R	5-11	170	12-4-01	.000	--	.000	1	1	0	0	0	0	0	0	0	0	0	0	1	0	0	.000	.000
Carlos Linarez	R-R	6-0	170	10-24-01	.000	.000	.000	2	7	0	0	0	0	0	0	0	0	0	0	2	0	0	.000	.000

Aaron McKeithan	R-R	6-1	220	12-13-99	.284	.289	.282	59	194	23	55	10	1	4	23	27	9	0	2	44	1	0	.407	.392
Ramon Mendoza	R-R	5-11	174	8-31-00	.139	.000	.169	22	72	12	10	2	1	1	5	15	3	1	0	17	2	1	.236	.311
Brody Moore	R-R	5-11	183	7-20-00	.252	.250	.253	32	111	12	28	4	0	0	13	14	0	0	4	28	3	0	.288	.326
Darlin Moquete	R-R	5-11	175	9-19-99	.223	.163	.240	65	220	31	49	7	0	8	28	18	3	0	4	56	5	5	.364	.286
Sander Mora	R-R	5-9	155	2-23-01	.171	.139	.178	72	210	30	36	6	1	3	16	35	1	1	2	71	8	1	.252	.290
Jesus Orecchia	R-R	6-1	175	4-22-01	.283	.500	.237	14	46	6	13	1	0	0	2	8	1	0	0	19	0	0	.304	.400
Hansel Otamendi	R-R	5-9	180	2-15-02	.159	.250	.140	20	69	5	11	3	0	0	6	10	1	0	2	20	1	0	.203	.268
Tyler Reichenborn	R-R	5-11	180	7-23-98	.267	.333	.252	41	150	14	40	3	1	0	15	21	6	1	2	29	1	4	.300	.374
Jeremy Rivas	R-R	6-0	172	3-4-03	.245	.239	.246	117	425	47	104	16	1	2	37	37	4	1	4	104	8	6	.301	.309
Luis Rodriguez	R-R	6-0	175	2-26-00	.225	.077	.259	20	71	4	16	3	0	1	5	2	0	0	0	24	0	0	.310	.247
Patrick Romeri	R-R	6-3	195	6-29-01	.325	.333	.323	24	77	16	25	6	1	5	15	8	0	0	0	20	3	2	.623	.388
Chris Rotondo	R-R	6-0	200	6-15-99	.312	.381	.286	24	77	17	24	4	0	1	7	7	2	0	1	28	3	0	.403	.379
Victor Scott II	L-L	5-11	190	2-12-01	.222	.111	.244	31	108	20	24	4	4	2	12	24	1	5	4	26	13	3	.389	.358
Franklin Soto	R-R	5-11	168	9-23-99	.233	.400	.150	10	30	5	7	0	0	0	4	4	0	0	0	10	1	0	.233	.324
Wade Stauss	L-R	6-2	225	4-4-99	.195	.143	.205	29	87	4	17	2	0	1	5	10	9	2	0	45	0	0	.253	.340
Jhon Torres	R-R	6-4	199	3-29-00	.208	.259	.188	27	96	8	20	5	0	3	15	6	0	0	0	30	0	0	.354	.255
Osvaldo Tovalin	L-R	6-2	225	10-31-99	.313	.313	.314	56	217	28	68	9	2	4	32	17	6	0	1	38	0	1	.429	.378
Brady Whalen	L-R	6-4	180	1-15-98	.288	.297	.286	49	170	24	49	10	1	6	23	23	6	0	1	36	2	0	.465	.390
R.J. Yeager	R-R	6-3	200	10-2-98	.289	.182	.320	28	97	17	28	4	1	3	18	9	3	0	2	19	2	0	.443	.360
Jose Zapata	R-R	5-11	195	2-14-01	.400	--	.400	4	5	0	2	0	0	0	1	0	0	0	0	2	0	0	.400	.400

Pitching	B-T	HT	WT	DOB	W	L	ERA	G	GS	CG	SV	IP	H	R	ER	HR	BB	SO	AVG	vLH	vRH	K/9	BB/9
Trent Baker	R-R	6-3	240	12-28-98	9	7	3.14	25	25	0	0	123	114	53	43	8	48	138	.241	.200	.264	10.07	3.50
Ian Bedell	R-R	6-2	198	9-5-99	0	0	6.75	3	0	0	0	3	6	5	2	0	1	4	.429	.571	.286	13.50	3.38
D.J. Carpenter	R-R	6-8	242	2-8-00	0	0	0.00	2	0	0	1	2	0	0	0	0	0	3	.000	.000	.000	13.50	0.00
Nelfri Contreras	B-L	6-0	177	12-25-98	5	3	5.28	26	0	0	0	31	36	25	18	0	24	40	.279	.231	.300	11.74	7.04
Alex Cornwell	L-L	6-2	200	5-9-99	5	3	5.14	24	10	0	3	70	83	45	40	5	20	78	.295	.329	.284	10.03	2.57
Angel Cuenca	R-R	6-1	160	7-10-01	0	0	3.38	3	0	0	0	5	6	4	2	0	4	3	.316	.333	.308	5.06	6.75
Gianluca Dalatri	R-R	6-6	250	4-4-98	1	0	0.00	8	0	0	1	9	3	0	0	0	3	19	.100	.000	.115	19.00	3.00
Jose Davila	R-R	6-3	177	11-9-02	1	2	3.86	8	7	0	0	35	31	20	15	2	20	20	.240	.263	.222	5.14	5.14
Yonael Dominguez	R-R	6-2	175	10-24-01	0	2	6.30	6	5	0	0	20	21	16	14	1	10	17	.273	.192	.314	7.65	4.50
Roy Garcia	R-R	6-0	190	8-28-00	4	6	5.66	29	1	0	8	56	46	36	35	6	32	71	.223	.235	.216	11.48	5.17
Chris Gerard	R-L	5-10	175	11-23-99	4	3	3.52	20	6	0	0	46	42	21	18	4	26	56	.237	.205	.248	10.96	5.09
Andre Granillo	R-R	6-4	245	5-12-00	3	1	2.87	10	0	0	2	16	10	6	5	2	9	26	.185	.250	.158	14.94	5.17
Carlos Guarate	R-R	6-2	178	3-30-01	5	4	4.18	19	12	0	0	75	79	39	35	11	24	59	.269	.254	.278	7.05	2.87
Diorys Guerrero	L-L	6-1	170	2-1-01	0	0	30.86	3	0	0	0	2	4	8	8	0	6	3	.400	.200	.600	11.57	23.14
Hayes Heinecke	L-L	6-0	210	6-28-99	3	3	3.80	24	1	0	4	43	35	20	18	2	23	55	.229	.222	.231	11.60	4.85
Tink Hence	R-R	6-1	175	8-6-02	0	1	1.38	16	16	0	0	52	31	9	8	1	15	81	.174	.120	.214	13.93	2.58
Matt Hickey	L-R	6-1	165	5-11-98	1	0	1.64	10	0	0	0	11	8	3	2	0	5	10	.205	.200	.208	8.18	4.09
Chris Holba	R-R	6-3	190	8-31-96	0	1	7.20	5	0	0	0	5	9	5	4	0	4	6	.409	.600	.250	10.80	7.20
Tanner Jacobson	R-R	6-1	190	1-24-00	0	0	6.23	4	0	0	0	4	1	3	3	0	7	6	.067	.167	.000	12.46	14.54
Ludwin Jimenez	R-R	6-2	165	8-9-01	1	0	6.00	12	0	0	0	15	7	11	10	1	17	20	.140	.071	.167	12.00	10.20
Edgar Manzo	R-R	5-11	181	10-24-00	2	0	4.26	14	0	0	2	25	29	12	12	4	11	19	.299	.300	.299	6.75	3.91
Andrew Marrero	R-R	5-10	196	5-8-00	0	4	1.27	32	0	0	11	35	17	13	5	1	21	55	.144	.057	.181	14.01	5.35
Zane Mills	R-R	6-4	220	7-4-00	1	2	3.48	7	7	0	0	41	44	17	16	3	7	35	.272	.324	.256	7.62	1.52
Jose Moreno	R-R	6-0	197	8-20-00	1	2	2.65	22	4	0	1	54	48	21	16	0	38	59	.241	.253	.234	9.77	6.29
Ljay Newsome	R-R	5-11	210	11-8-96	0	0	5.40	3	0	0	0	3	6	2	2	0	1	3	.400	.375	.429	8.10	2.70
Edwin Nunez	R-R	6-3	185	11-5-01	1	1	12.15	5	0	0	0	7	8	9	9	1	11	7	.308	.333	.304	9.45	14.85
Inohan Paniagua	R-R	6-1	148	2-6-00	6	4	2.18	17	17	0	0	99	72	33	24	4	23	107	.202	.200	.203	9.73	2.09
Bryan Pope	R-R	6-2	195	1-27-99	3	4	3.96	26	7	0	4	61	76	34	27	6	15	51	.303	.291	.309	7.48	2.20
Jack Ralston	R-R	6-6	231	8-13-97	1	1	5.40	9	0	0	0	12	8	7	7	1	13	11	.186	.200	.179	8.49	10.03
Hancel Rincon	R-R	6-2	160	4-28-02	3	4	4.29	9	8	0	0	42	43	26	20	5	10	33	.264	.302	.245	7.07	2.14
Griffin Roberts	R-R	6-3	210	6-13-96	1	0	7.71	5	0	0	0	5	4	4	4	1	4	10	.235	.143	.300	19.29	7.71
Gustavo J. Rodriguez	R-R	6-3	160	1-8-01	3	2	2.65	27	1	0	3	58	40	20	17	4	26	66	.195	.228	.175	10.30	4.06
Alfredo Ruiz	L-L	6-0	200	3-12-00	3	1	3.53	19	1	0	0	36	31	14	14	5	10	47	.235	.190	.256	11.86	2.52
Omar Sanchez	R-L	5-10	185	4-23-02	0	0	13.50	1	0	0	0	1	2	2	2	0	3	3	.333	.000	.400	20.25	20.25

Fielding

Catcher	PCT	G	PO	A	E	DP	PB
Bernal	.984	37	328	30	6	2	3
Burns	.992	13	116	7	1	2	3
Crooks III	.978	17	163	14	4	5	5
Heredia	.981	10	90	11	2	1	5
Linarez	1.000	1	10	1	0	0	1
McKeithan	.993	28	252	14	2	1	2
Rodriguez	.984	7	57	6	1	0	1
Stauss	.990	21	193	11	2	0	3
Zapata	1.000	1	3	0	0	0	0

First Base	PCT	G	PO	A	E	DP
Francisco	.994	45	303	21	2	33
Holgate	1.000	5	41	4	0	5
Mendoza	1.000	6	41	3	0	6
Orecchia	1.000	8	49	4	0	6
Rodriguez	1.000	9	71	5	0	9
Tovalin	1.000	6	45	3	0	7
Whalen	1.000	47	340	16	0	33
Yeager	.973	6	35	1	1	3

Second Base	PCT	G	PO	A	E	DP
Espinoza	.970	17	29	35	2	9
Hernandez	.982	37	67	94	3	28
Inoa	1.000	1	1	0	0	0
Mendoza	1.000	10	11	16	0	2
Moore	.989	26	34	58	1	12
Moquete	.956	21	40	46	4	10
Mora	.962	18	20	30	2	8
Soto	.880	8	11	11	3	2

Third Base	PCT	G	PO	A	E	DP
Curialle	.909	19	15	25	4	6
Hernandez	1.000	2	1	5	0	0
Linarez	1.000	1	2	3	0	0
Mendoza	1.000	1	0	1	0	0
Moore	1.000	1	0	1	0	0
Mora	.953	48	30	71	5	7
Orecchla	.933	5	5	9	1	1
Tovalin	.949	42	24	70	5	5
Yeager	.917	20	14	30	4	4

Shortstop	PCT	G	PO	A	E	DP
Espinoza	.889	2	3	5	1	1
Mendoza	.857	1	0	6	1	0
Moore	.857	6	8	10	3	2
Mora	.952	5	8	12	1	5
Rivas	.972	117	151	296	13	63
Soto	.857	1	3	3	1	2

Outfield	PCT	G	PO	A	E	DP
Baez	1.000	16	25	3	0	1
Cabell	.985	38	63	4	1	0

Chamberlain	.987	49	75	2	1	0	Mendoza	.875	6	7	0	1	0	Rotondo	.968	18	29	1	1	1
Church	.982	25	52	3	1	2	Moquete	.982	37	52	2	1	0	Scott II	1.000	31	70	1	0	0
Cruz	.976	56	118	3	3	1	Otamendi	.958	20	20	3	1	0	Torres	.955	19	21	0	1	0
Fletcher	1.000	5	3	1	0	0	Reichenborn	.966	41	52	4	2	0	Tovalin	1.000	4	4	1	0	0
Iadisernia	1.000	19	29	1	0	0	Romeri	1.000	24	34	1	0	0	Whalen	1.000	1	2	0	0	0

FCL CARDINALS — ROOKIE

FLORIDA COMPLEX LEAGUE

Batting	B-T	HT	WT	DOB	AVG	vLH	vRH	G	AB	R	H	2B	3B	HR	RBI	BB	HBP	SH	SF	SO	SB	CS	SLG	OBP
Joshua Baez	R-R	6-4	220	6-28-03	.237	.400	.179	12	38	4	9	3	0	1	5	5	0	0	0	14	6	1	.395	.326
Javier Bolivar	R-R	6-2	170	12-19-02	.176	.273	.159	37	74	12	13	2	0	3	9	17	1	0	0	37	4	0	.324	.337
Jake Burns	L-R	6-0	199	2-17-03	.000	.000	.000	5	14	1	0	0	0	0	1	5	0	0	0	6	1	1	.000	.263
Romtres Cabrera	R-R	6-0	182	9-13-03	.100	.182	.082	29	60	8	6	1	0	0	2	10	1	0	0	28	5	2	.117	.239
Won-Bin Cho	L-L	6-3	200	8-20-03	.211	.467	.148	26	76	10	16	3	1	1	3	20	4	0	0	27	6	4	.316	.400
Jose Cordoba	R-R	5-11	165	1-3-03	.236	.130	.265	38	106	18	25	5	0	5	21	15	2	0	2	33	5	4	.425	.336
Adanson Cruz	R-R	6-2	175	10-6-00	.273	.000	.375	5	11	1	3	2	0	0	2	0	0	0	0	2	0	0	.455	.273
Samil De La Rosa	R-R	5-8	175	9-24-03	.241	.143	.265	46	141	25	34	9	1	6	21	13	10	0	1	33	3	4	.447	.345
Fernando Diaz	L-R	6-4	185	1-12-02	.200	.188	.203	26	80	7	16	2	1	2	11	5	1	0	0	34	2	0	.325	.256
Lizandro Espinoza	R-R	5-7	158	11-20-02	.240	.087	.284	29	104	17	25	5	4	1	15	12	2	0	3	29	4	1	.394	.322
Tre Fletcher	R-R	6-2	200	4-30-01	.085	.067	.094	21	47	6	4	0	0	0	1	6	0	0	0	28	3	0	.085	.189
Adari Grant	R-R	5-11	163	1-2-04	.206	.211	.205	37	97	14	20	2	1	0	7	18	3	0	0	39	6	6	.247	.347
Raul Guzman	R-R	6-0	180	9-14-02	.167	.000	.200	24	54	4	9	3	0	0	1	3	4	0	0	28	1	1	.222	.262
Roblin Heredia	L-R	6-0	200	7-22-02	.128	.067	.156	21	47	4	6	2	1	0	6	6	2	0	0	25	0	0	.213	.255
Brandon Hernandez	L-R	6-0	190	8-21-01	.286	.278	.289	22	56	9	16	2	0	0	2	13	1	0	0	13	3	0	.321	.429
Ryan Holgate	L-L	6-2	193	6-8-00	.174	.400	.111	12	23	3	4	1	0	0	1	11	2	1	0	9	1	0	.217	.472
Albert Inoa	R-R	5-11	170	12-4-01	.094	.125	.083	14	32	5	3	0	0	1	1	5	0	0	0	12	0	0	.188	.216
Carlos Linarez	R-R	6-0	170	10-24-01	.221	.286	.207	35	113	11	25	5	0	1	10	6	1	0	0	29	5	2	.292	.267
Jesus Orecchia	R-R	6-1	175	4-22-01	.000	--	.000	4	4	0	0	0	0	0	0	1	0	0	0	1	0	0	.000	.200
Hansel Otamendi	R-R	5-9	180	2-15-02	.108	.000	.114	14	37	4	4	0	0	0	2	7	0	0	0	12	0	0	.108	.250
Luis Pino	R-R	5-11	175	2-7-04	.216	.190	.224	31	97	17	21	5	0	3	17	12	3	0	0	35	4	2	.361	.321
Jeremy Ramos	R-R	6-3	173	4-4-03	.167	.385	.123	29	78	7	13	2	1	0	3	1	1	0	0	31	4	0	.218	.188
Francis Reynoso	R-R	6-5	206	12-26-02	.183	.278	.151	25	71	11	13	4	2	1	11	8	2	0	1	34	0	1	.338	.280
Edgardo Rodriguez	R-R	6-0	207	11-29-00	.200	.143	.231	18	40	3	8	2	0	0	4	3	0	0	0	9	0	0	.250	.256
Patrick Romeri	R-R	6-3	195	6-29-01	.238	.000	.250	7	21	2	5	1	1	0	4	2	0	0	1	7	1	0	.381	.292
Felix Taveras	L-R	6-1	186	3-8-03	.196	.000	.250	21	56	4	11	3	2	0	6	7	1	0	0	28	2	0	.321	.297
Jhon Torres	R-R	6-4	199	3-29-00	.385	1.000	.333	5	13	1	5	0	0	0	2	3	0	0	0	2	0	0	.385	.500
Diego Velasquez	R-R	5-10	175	3-25-02	.000	.000	.000	9	15	2	0	0	0	0	0	1	1	0	0	6	0	0	.000	.118
Jose Zapata	R-R	5-11	195	2-14-01	.188	.000	.200	16	32	3	6	0	0	1	2	0	1	0	0	13	0	0	.281	.212

Pitching	B-T	HT	WT	DOB	W	L	ERA	G	GS	CG	SV	IP	H	R	ER	HR	BB	SO	AVG	vLH	vRH	K/9	BB/9
Benjamin Arias	R-R	6-5	195	11-5-01	1	4	3.64	12	11	0	0	42	50	26	17	3	21	40	.299	.314	.289	8.57	4.50
Chandler Arnold	R-R	6-2	189	11-19-99	0	0	0.00	1	0	0	0	1	1	0	0	0	1	1	.250	.000	.500	9.00	9.00
Ian Bedell	R-R	6-2	198	9-5-99	0	0	0.00	3	2	0	0	3	3	0	0	0	2	6	.250	.200	.286	18.00	6.00
Augusto Calderon	R-R	6-0	190	10-6-00	3	2	7.71	17	0	0	1	23	28	21	20	1	10	30	.292	.382	.242	11.57	3.86
D.J. Carpenter	R-R	6-8	242	2-8-00	0	0	4.50	2	0	0	0	2	3	1	1	0	2	3	.333	.000	.429	13.50	9.00
Alejandro Cervantes	R-R	6-2	189	5-15-01	0	1	4.38	9	1	0	0	12	9	6	6	1	10	20	.205	.227	.182	14.59	7.30
Randel Clemente	R-R	6-3	173	11-17-01	1	0	9.00	18	0	0	2	21	26	24	21	0	13	24	.299	.351	.260	10.29	5.57
Angel Cuenca	R-R	6-1	160	7-10-01	0	1	4.80	15	2	0	1	15	13	8	8	1	7	18	.228	.313	.195	10.80	4.20
Jose Davila	R-R	6-3	177	11-9-02	0	1	2.45	7	6	0	0	29	22	11	8	1	8	34	.202	.268	.162	10.43	2.45
Yonael Dominguez	R-R	6-2	175	10-24-01	3	0	1.84	7	4	0	0	29	17	7	6	2	5	23	.162	.179	.152	7.06	1.53
Ettore Giulianelli	R-R	6-3	190	3-30-03	1	1	2.70	8	0	0	1	10	3	6	3	0	11	9	.097	.125	.087	8.10	9.90
Diorys Guerrero	L-L	6-1	170	2-1-01	2	1	1.52	10	5	0	1	30	19	11	5	1	15	36	.171	.161	.175	10.92	4.55
Hunter Hayes	R-R	6-1	185	8-5-00	0	0	9.00	2	1	0	0	2	3	2	2	0	1	2	.375	.500	.250	9.00	4.50
Chris Holba	R-R	6-3	190	8-31-96	0	0	0.00	3	1	0	0	3	2	0	0	0	0	4	.200	.000	.250	12.00	0.00
Tanner Jacobson	R-R	6-1	190	1-24-00	1	0	0.00	2	0	0	0	2	1	0	0	0	1	2	.143	.000	.250	9.00	4.50
Ludwin Jimenez	R-R	6-2	165	8-9-01	1	2	6.60	13	0	0	0	15	16	12	11	2	5	24	.276	.269	.281	14.40	3.00
Americo Lugo	R-R	6-1	192	8-27-00	1	0	4.42	16	0	0	3	18	24	16	9	1	11	24	.308	.345	.286	11.78	5.40
Ljay Newsome	R-R	5-11	210	11-8-96	1	1	2.70	4	2	0	0	3	5	3	1	0	0	4	.333	.000	.357	10.80	0.00
Edwin Nunez	R-R	6-3	185	11-5-01	0	1	4.05	22	0	0	2	27	20	16	12	1	15	23	.204	.263	.167	7.76	5.06
Wilmer Ortega	R-R	6-1	169	4-4-01	0	2	3.18	14	7	0	1	34	31	13	12	3	9	38	.246	.316	.188	10.06	2.38
Johan Quezada	R-R	6-9	255	8-25-94	0	0	0.00	4	1	0	0	5	1	0	0	0	1	6	.063	.143	.000	10.80	1.80
Jack Ralston	R-R	6-6	231	8-13-97	0	0	0.00	2	1	0	0	2	0	0	0	0	1	2	.000	--	.000	9.00	4.50
Brayan Ramirez	R-R	6-4	200	9-29-01	0	1	5.28	12	0	0	0	15	17	11	9	1	18	19	.279	.111	.349	11.15	10.57
Yordy Richard	R-R	6-1	195	8-27-02	1	1	12.00	13	0	0	0	12	21	20	16	4	12	15	.396	.474	.353	11.25	9.00
Hancel Rincon	R-R	6-2	160	4-28-02	0	4	4.43	6	4	0	0	22	25	13	11	1	5	24	.287	.208	.317	9.67	2.01
Griffin Roberts	R-R	6-3	210	6-13-96	0	0	0.00	2	0	0	0	2	2	0	0	0	1	4	.250	.000	.500	18.00	4.50
Enrique Saldana	R-R	5-11	155	6-26-99	3	3	3.00	13	2	0	0	18	22	11	6	0	4	13	.310	.389	.283	6.50	2.00
Omar Sanchez	R-L	5-10	185	4-23-02	1	1	1.50	15	0	0	0	18	14	5	3	0	14	18	.215	.125	.245	9.00	7.00
Victor Villanueva	R-R	6-1	170	3-26-01	5	1	2.86	15	0	0	1	22	15	8	7	3	10	31	.185	.067	.255	12.68	4.09
Alec Willis	R-R	6-5	220	3-30-03	0	1	1.59	6	4	0	0	11	6	3	2	1	2	16	.140	.133	.143	12.71	1.59

Fielding

C: Burns 3, Heredia 20, Linarez 29, Orecchia 2, Rodriguez 7, Velasquez 8, Zapata 10. **1B:** Bollivar 15, Cordoba 1, Diaz 19, Guzman 1, Linarez 5, Orecchia 1, Reynoso 24, Rodriguez 2, Zapata 4. **2B:** De La Rosa 25, Espinoza 4, Grant 27, Guzman 1, Hernandez 2, Inoa 4. **3B:** Bolivar 16, De La Rosa 20, Diaz 1, Espinoza 2, Guzman 23, Hernandez 2, Inoa 7, Zapata 1. **SS:** Bolivar 10, Espinoza 23, Grant 11, Hernandez 17, Inoa 2. **OF:** Baez 9, Cabrera 26, Cho 23, Cordoba 37, Cruz 5, Fletcher 18, Orecchia 1, Otamendi 14, Pino 22, Ramos 25, Romeri 8, Taveras 13, Torres 2.

DSL CARDINALSROOKIE

DOMINICAN SUMMER LEAGUE

Batting	B-T	HT	WT	DOB	AVG	vLH	vRH	G	AB	R	H	2B	3B	HR	RBI	BB	HBP	SH	SF	SO	SB	CS	SLG	OBP
Arfeni Batista	R-R	6-0	161	9-4-04	.240	.259	.235	39	129	21	31	5	1	1	10	21	2	0	1	45	4	2	.318	.353
Carlos Carmona	R-R	6-2	190	7-1-04	.255	.231	.259	32	94	21	24	3	1	2	15	14	7	0	4	18	4	2	.372	.378
Anyelo Encarnacion	R-R	6-0	164	1-2-04	.323	.333	.321	36	99	39	32	5	4	1	20	33	3	1	2	29	15	3	.485	.496
Justin Guerrero	R-R	6-1	195	5-20-03	.274	.438	.235	23	84	12	23	6	1	1	9	12	2	0	1	17	0	1	.405	.374
Yancel Guerrero	R-R	6-1	169	4-16-04	.267	.185	.292	41	116	41	31	3	2	2	22	30	8	0	0	48	12	2	.379	.448
Maikel Hernandez	B-R	6-0	163	2-20-03	.233	.211	.239	31	90	14	21	6	0	0	8	20	1	0	2	20	0	0	.300	.372
Maycol Justo	B-R	5-10	141	2-2-03	.255	.286	.247	26	106	17	27	5	3	3	20	7	2	0	0	39	2	2	.443	.313
Alejandro Loaiza	R-R	5-11	163	12-23-03	.158	.273	.138	27	76	9	12	2	0	1	7	15	1	0	1	34	1	0	.224	.301
Jonathan Mejia	B-R	6-0	185	4-12-05	.267	.241	.272	45	165	33	44	14	3	5	34	33	10	0	0	48	3	2	.479	.418
Yordalin Pena	R-R	6-3	177	9-17-04	.257	.344	.237	46	167	25	43	8	4	3	25	10	5	0	2	39	8	0	.407	.315
Marcelo Perez	R-R	6-2	181	1-7-04	.197	.235	.186	27	76	12	15	2	1	0	11	20	4	0	0	28	0	2	.250	.390
Yaisel Ramos	R-R	6-4	185	2-20-03	.252	.267	.247	40	119	20	30	4	2	1	10	28	5	0	3	42	8	2	.345	.406
Elias Reynoso	R-R	5-10	158	11-25-03	.182	.158	.188	30	88	14	16	6	1	1	17	25	0	0	0	40	4	1	.307	.363
Luis Rodriguez	R-R	6-1	210	10-7-04	.301	.316	.297	26	93	16	28	4	0	4	19	6	1	0	1	25	0	1	.473	.347
Keshawn Rombley	L-R	6-0	171	8-11-03	.187	.222	.182	26	75	12	14	1	2	1	5	8	1	0	1	28	0	0	.293	.271
Jose Suarez	R-R	6-2	200	8-9-04	.248	.219	.257	39	141	30	35	9	4	6	28	16	2	0	3	46	3	1	.496	.327
Miguel Vargas	L-L	6-0	176	3-14-04	.211	.154	.224	37	133	21	28	2	1	7	27	16	1	0	2	42	6	2	.398	.296

Pitching	B-T	HT	WT	DOB	W	L	ERA	G	GS	CG	SV	IP	H	R	ER	HR	BB	SO	AVG	vLH	vRH	K/9	BB/9
Alexander Beltre	R-L	6-1	169	11-5-02	2	1	2.01	10	8	1	0	40	34	13	9	0	13	46	.224	.226	.223	10.26	2.90
Junior Chirinos	R-R	6-3	190	11-18-04	2	0	4.30	8	0	0	0	15	14	9	7	3	3	14	.259	.200	.294	8.59	1.84
Esteban Contreras	R-R	6-1	187	4-16-03	1	0	5.28	13	0	0	1	15	13	10	9	2	20	24	.236	.276	.192	14.09	11.74
Diego Dominguez	R-R	6-0	178	7-2-04	4	1	5.49	11	0	0	0	20	21	13	12	3	14	16	.292	.345	.256	7.32	6.41
Samuel Fabian	R-R	6-4	177	5-21-03	1	0	6.53	14	0	0	0	21	16	20	15	0	17	16	.211	.226	.200	6.97	7.40
Jovi Galvez	R-R	6-2	223	7-5-04	0	5	16.71	19	1	0	0	14	19	38	26	0	39	11	.333	.310	.357	7.07	25.07
Henry Gomez	R-R	6-1	163	10-17-01	6	1	3.58	15	1	0	1	28	31	16	11	3	8	23	.277	.283	.273	7.48	2.60
Yordy Herrera	L-L	6-2	150	12-2-04	0	1	4.32	13	1	0	1	17	13	11	8	0	21	27	.210	.333	.180	14.58	11.34
Bruno Lopez	R-R	6-4	220	4-18-02	4	1	2.59	19	0	0	2	24	24	15	7	1	15	30	.247	.238	.255	11.10	5.55
Oliver Lopez	R-R	6-2	165	4-1-02	0	2	3.07	14	0	0	0	15	11	10	5	1	23	13	.220	.118	.273	7.98	14.11
Miguel Martinez	R-R	6-0	143	1-26-03	0	2	6.67	17	0	0	3	27	30	21	20	2	16	45	.275	.270	.278	15.00	5.33
Ronny Oliver	R-R	6-2	155	1-1-04	3	1	6.27	11	7	0	0	33	35	24	23	4	18	30	.282	.370	.231	8.18	4.91
Darlin Saladin	R-R	5-11	150	12-28-02	1	4	3.59	12	12	0	0	48	50	27	19	0	26	51	.275	.289	.264	9.63	4.91
Gerado Salas	R-R	6-0	189	2-14-03	3	1	3.61	11	10	0	0	47	38	22	19	4	8	48	.221	.187	.247	9.13	1.52
Leonel Sequera	R-R	6-0	190	8-6-05	0	4	3.47	11	11	0	0	36	35	19	14	1	11	42	.243	.208	.260	10.40	2.72
Juan Severino	R-R	6-0	165	6-6-04	0	0	9.92	14	0	0	0	16	20	19	18	1	18	13	.299	.310	.289	7.16	9.92
Omar Yanez	R-R	6-2	190	12-7-02	3	2	3.34	19	0	0	3	30	32	12	11	3	18	40	.291	.289	.292	12.13	5.46
Nelfy Ynfante	R-R	6-3	168	2-1-05	3	0	1.96	11	8	0	0	41	33	15	9	1	19	39	.219	.286	.179	8.49	4.14

Fielding

C: Guerrero 20, Hernandez 10, Loaiza 20, Rodriguez 17. **1B:** Guerrero 33, Hernandez 21, Loaiza 7, Vargas 1. **2B:** Batista 2, Encarnacion 30, Justo 4, Perez 1, Reynoso 26. **3B:** Batista 25, Encarnacion 1, Guerrero 8, Justo 1, Perez 27. **SS:** Batista 12, Guerrero 1, Justo 16, Mejia 32. **OF:** Carmona 26, Pena 41, Ramos 42, Rombley 18, Suarez 31, Vargas 29.

San Diego Padres

SEASON IN A SENTENCE: While superstar Fernando Tatis Jr. missed the season, first with injury and then a midseason PED suspension, the Padres rallied around new manager Bob Melvin and third baseman Manny Machado to earn a wild-card spot and vanquish the Dodgers in the division series before losing to the Phillies in the National League Championship Series.

HIGH POINT: The postseason berth was the first for the Padres in a full season since 2006. Then San Diego upset the 101-win Mets in the Wild Card Series and took down the 111-win Dodgers in four games, as the Padres bullpen allowed only one run in 16 innings. Josh Hader, acquired at the deadline from the Brewers, clinched the series with saves in each of San Diego's victories.

LOW POINT: Hader inexplicably was still in the bullpen when Bryce Harper hit the game-winning homer in the clinching Game Five of the NLCS. The Padres had steeled themselves for the postseason by adding Hader plus star outfielder Juan Soto among others at the trade deadline, but Tatis soured the mood on Aug. 12 when MLB announced his 80-game suspension for testing positive for clostebol, a banned substance. Tatis had a second wrist surgery and left shoulder surgery after his suspension as he seeks to return in 2023, the third year of his 14-year, $340 million contract.

NOTABLE ROOKIES: Top prospects shortstop C.J. Abrams and lefthander MacKenzie Gore played important roles in the first half before being trasded. Righthanders Steven Wilson and Robert Suarez emerged as key bullpen pieces.

KEY TRANSACTIONS: No team was more aggressive at the deadline than San Diego, which acquired first baseman/DH Josh Bell in the same deal that netted Soto, giving up top prospects Abrams, Gore, outfielder James Woods and right-handed flamethrower Jarlin Susana. Preller successfully pawned off Eric Hosmer and his contract to Boston but the Padres are paying most of Hosmer's remaining contract. The Nats also added versatile Brandon Drury from the Reds and Hader from the Brewers, weathering his August struggles before helping him find his form down the stretch.

ON THE FARM: The Padres ability to regenerate their farm system continues to impress. Shortstop Jackson Merrill stepped up to became the next high-impact Padres prospect after many of his colleagues were traded away.

OPENING DAY PAYROLL: $211,968,286 (fifth).

PLAYERS OF THE YEAR

MAJOR LEAGUE

Manny Machado
3B
.298/.366/.531
32 HR, 37 2B, 102 RBIs
Made 6th all-star team

MINOR LEAGUE

Eguy Rosario
SS
(Triple-A)
.288/.368/.508
22 HR, 21 SB in 124 G

ORGANIZATION LEADERS

Batting		***Minimum 250 AB**
MAJORS		
* AVG	Manny Machado	.298
* OPS	Manny Machado	.898
HR	Manny Machado	32
RBI	Manny Machado	102
MINORS		
* AVG	Esteury Ruiz, El Paso	.333
* OBP	Esteury Ruiz, El Paso	.467
* SLG	Esteury Ruiz, El Paso	.560
* OPS	Esteury Ruiz, El Paso	1.028
R	Eguy Rosario, El Paso	98
H	Connor Hollis, El Paso	160
TB	Eguy Rosario, El Paso	249
2B	Eguy Rosario, El Paso	34
3B	3 tied	8
HR	Brandon Dixon, ACL, San Antonio, El Paso	23
	Marcus Castanon, Lake Elsinore	
RBI	Marcus Castanon, Lake Elsinore	85
BB	Justin Farmer, Lake Elsinore, Fort Wayne	106
SO	Joshua Mears, ACL, Fort Wayne, San Antonio	161
SB	Esteury Ruiz, El Paso	60

Pitching		**#Minimum 75 IP**
MAJORS		
W	Yu Darvish	16
# ERA	Joe Musgrove	2.93
SO	Yu Darvish	197
SV	Taylor Rogers	28
MINORS		
W	4 tied	8
L	4 tied	10
# ERA	Edwuin Bencomo, Fort Wayne, San Antonio	2.96
G	Angel Felipe, San Antonio, El Paso	51
GS	Matt Waldron	25
SV	Angel Felipe, San Antonio, El Paso	14
IP	Jackson Wolf, Fort Wayne, San Antonio	129.2
BB	Noel Vela, Fort Wayne, San Antonio	67
SO	Jackson Wolf, Fort Wayne, San Antonio	142
# AVG	Jackson Wolf, Fort Wayne, San Antonio	.215

2022 PERFORMANCE

General Manager: A.J. Preller. **Farm Director:** Ryley Westman. **Scouting Director:** Chris Kemp.

Class	Team	League	W	L	PCT	Finish	Manager
Majors	San Diego Padres	National	89	73	.549	5th (15)	Bob Melvin
Triple-A	El Paso Chihuahuas	Pacific Coast	85	65	.567	2nd (10)	Jared Sandberg
Double-A	San Antonio Missions	Texas	68	68	.500	5th (10)	Phillip Wellman
High-A	Fort Wayne TinCaps	Midwest	50	80	.385	12th (12)	Brian Esposito
Low-A	Lake Elsinore Storm	California	77	55	.583	2nd (8)	Eric Junge
Rookie	ACL Padres	Arizona Complex	29	25	.537	8th (18)	Lukas Ray
Overall 2022 Minor League Record			345	316	.522	t-9th (30)	

ORGANIZATION STATISTICS

SAN DIEGO PADRES

NATIONAL LEAGUE

Batting	B-T	HT	WT	DOB	AVG	vLH	vRH	G	AB	R	H	2B	3B	HR	RBI	BB	HBP	SH	SF	SO	SB	CS	SLG	OBP
CJ Abrams	L-R	6-2	185	10-3-00	.232	.103	.271	46	125	16	29	5	0	2	11	4	6	2	2	27	1	2	.320	.285
2-team total (44 Washington Nationals)					.246	.157	.287	90	284	33	70	12	2	2	21	5	9	2	2	50	7	4	.324	.280
Sergio Alcantara	B-R	5-9	151	7-10-96	.114	.067	.150	22	35	3	4	0	0	0	3	2	0	0	1	12	0	2	.114	.158
2-team total (71 Arizona Diamondbacks)					.220	.214	.221	93	205	26	45	8	1	6	29	12	1	2	4	57	1	2	.356	.261
Jorge Alfaro	R-R	6-3	230	6-11-93	.246	.269	.238	82	256	25	63	14	0	7	40	11	4	0	3	98	1	0	.383	.285
Jose Azocar	R-R	5-11	181	5-11-96	.257	.243	.274	98	202	24	52	9	3	0	10	12	0	1	1	44	5	6	.332	.298
Matthew Batten	R-R	5-11	180	6-22-95	.105	.200	.000	15	19	0	2	1	0	0	1	2	1	0	0	6	0	0	.158	.227
Matt Beaty	L-R	6-0	215	4-28-93	.093	.333	.075	20	43	6	4	1	1	0	1	2	2	0	0	8	0	0	.163	.170
Josh Bell	B-R	6-4	261	8-14-92	.192	.250	.173	53	177	26	34	5	0	3	14	32	0	0	0	41	0	0	.271	.316
2-team total (103 Washington Nationals)					.266	.276	.261	156	552	78	147	29	3	17	71	81	5	0	6	102	0	1	.422	.362
Luis Campusano	R-R	5-11	232	9-29-98	.250	.278	.233	16	48	4	12	1	0	1	5	1	0	0	1	11	0	0	.333	.260
Robinson Cano	L-R	6-0	212	10-22-82	.091	--	.091	12	33	1	3	0	0	0	1	1	0	0	0	10	0	0	.091	.118
3-team total (9 Atlanta Braves, 12 New York Mets)					.150	.222	.143	33	100	5	15	1	0	1	4	4	0	0	0	25	0	0	.190	.183
Jake Cronenworth	L-R	6-0	187	1-21-94	.239	.232	.241	158	587	88	140	30	4	17	88	70	16	0	8	131	3	0	.390	.332
Brandon Dixon	R-R	6-2	215	1-29-92	.214	.000	.333	5	14	1	3	1	0	0	1	0	0	0	0	5	0	0	.286	.214
Brandon Drury	R-R	6-2	230	8-21-92	.238	.280	.220	46	168	25	40	9	0	8	28	9	4	0	2	42	0	1	.435	.290
Trent Grisham	L-L	5-11	224	11-1-96	.184	.203	.177	152	451	58	83	16	2	17	53	57	7	7	2	150	7	1	.341	.284
Eric Hosmer	L-L	6-4	226	10-24-89	.272	.330	.249	90	335	32	91	16	0	8	40	33	0	0	1	55	0	0	.391	.336
Ha-Seong Kim	R-R	5-9	168	10-17-95	.251	.270	.243	150	517	58	130	29	3	11	59	51	7	3	4	100	12	2	.383	.325
Luis Liberato	L-L	6-1	175	12-18-95	.000	--	.000	7	5	0	0	0	0	0	0	0	0	0	0	3	0	0	.000	.000
Manny Machado	R-R	6-3	218	7-6-92	.298	.259	.313	150	578	100	172	37	1	32	102	63	1	0	2	133	9	1	.531	.366
Nomar Mazara	L-L	6-4	224	4-26-95	.264	.333	.252	55	159	16	42	8	0	2	18	10	2	0	0	40	0	0	.352	.316
Wil Myers	R-R	6-3	207	12-10-90	.261	.264	.259	77	261	29	68	15	0	7	41	21	1	0	3	86	2	1	.398	.315
Austin Nola	R-R	6-0	197	12-28-89	.251	.285	.230	110	347	40	87	15	0	4	40	34	6	1	9	60	2	1	.329	.321
Jurickson Profar	B-R	6-0	184	2-20-93	.243	.259	.237	152	575	82	140	36	2	15	58	73	4	3	3	103	5	1	.391	.331
Brent Rooker	R-R	6-4	225	11-1-94	.000	.000	.000	2	7	0	0	0	0	0	0	0	0	0	0	4	0	0	.000	.000
Eguy Rosario	R-R	5-9	150	8-25-99	.200	.000	.250	7	5	0	1	0	0	0	0	1	0	0	0	2	0	0	.200	.333
Esteury Ruiz	R-R	6-0	169	2-15-99	.222	.235	.200	14	27	1	6	1	1	0	2	0	0	0	0	5	1	2	.333	.222
2-team total (3 Milwaukee Brewers)					.171	.190	.143	17	35	3	6	1	1	0	2	1	0	0	0	7	1	2	.257	.194
Juan Soto	L-L	6-2	224	10-25-98	.236	.185	.265	52	182	31	43	8	1	6	16	44	1	0	0	34	0	0	.390	.388
2-team total (101 Washington Nationals)					.242	.210	.261	153	524	93	127	25	2	27	62	135	4	0	0	96	6	2	.452	.401
Trayce Thompson	R-R	6-3	225	3-15-91	.071	.000	.125	6	14	1	1	0	0	0	2	2	0	0	0	7	0	1	.071	.188
2-team total (74 Los Angeles Dodgers)					.256	.174	.308	80	219	36	56	14	1	13	41	32	2	0	2	93	4	1	.507	.353
Luke Voit	R-R	6-3	255	2-13-91	.225	.172	.246	82	298	38	67	18	0	13	48	39	3	0	4	110	1	1	.416	.317
2-team total (53 Washington Nationals)					.226	.174	.247	135	500	55	113	22	0	22	69	55	7	0	6	179	1	1	.402	.308

Pitching	B-T	HT	WT	DOB	W	L	ERA	G	GS	CG	SV	IP	H	R	ER	HR	BB	SO	AVG	vLH	vRH	K/9	BB/9
Austin Adams	R-R	6-3	220	5-5-91	1	0	0.00	2	0	0	0	2	0	0	0	0	3	2	.000	.000	.000	7.71	11.57
Pedro Avila	R-R	5-11	210	1-14-97	0	0	4.50	2	0	0	0	4	3	3	2	1	1	5	.188	.143	.222	11.25	2.25
Michel Baez	R-R	6-8	220	1-21-96	0	0	0.00	2	0	0	0	2	1	0	0	0	0	2	.143	.000	.200	9.00	0.00
Matthew Batten	R-R	5-11	180	6-22-95	0	0	4.50	2	0	0	0	2	2	1	1	1	0	1	.250	.200	.333	4.50	0.00
Jose Castillo	L-L	6-6	252	1-10-96	0	0	9.00	1	0	0	0	1	1	1	1	0	1	1	.333	.000	.500	9.00	9.00
Mike Clevinger	R-R	6-4	215	12-21-90	7	7	4.33	23	22	0	0	114	102	56	55	20	35	91	.233	.211	.257	7.16	2.76
Nabil Crismatt	R-R	6-1	220	12-25-94	5	2	2.94	50	1	0	0	67	57	29	22	5	22	65	.226	.208	.238	8.69	2.94
Yu Darvish	R-R	6-5	220	8-16-86	16	8	3.10	30	30	0	0	195	148	67	67	22	37	197	.207	.185	.233	9.11	1.71
Luis Garcia	R-R	6-2	240	1-30-87	4	6	3.39	64	0	0	3	61	57	28	23	3	17	68	.243	.247	.239	10.03	2.51
MacKenzie Gore	L-L	6-2	197	2-24-99	4	4	4.50	16	13	0	0	70	66	35	35	7	37	72	.248	.193	.263	9.26	4.76
Javy Guerra	L-R	6-0	185	9-25-95	0	0	18.00	1	0	0	0	2	3	4	4	1	3	1	.333	.286	.500	4.50	13.50
Josh Hader	L-L	6-3	180	4-7-94	1	1	7.31	19	0	0	7	16	17	14	13	1	9	22	.270	.158	.318	12.38	5.06
2-team total (37 Milwaukee Brewers)					2	5	5.22	56	0	0	36	50	43	30	29	8	21	81	.225	.209	.230	14.58	3.78
Tim Hill	R-L	6-4	200	2-10-90	3	0	3.56	55	0	0	0	48	45	20	19	1	14	25	.251	.208	.280	4.69	2.63
Pierce Johnson	R-R	6-2	202	5-10-91	1	2	5.02	15	0	0	0	14	14	8	8	1	8	21	.250	.217	.273	13.19	5.02
Ray Kerr	L-L	6-3	185	9-10-94	0	0	9.00	7	0	0	0	5	3	5	5	1	4	3	.188	.000	.273	5.40	7.20

Reiss Knehr	L-R	6-2	205	11-3-96	0	0	3.95	5	1	0	0	14	11	6	6	1	4	10	.216	.222	.214	6.59	2.63
Dinelson Lamet	R-R	6-3	228	7-18-92	0	1	9.49	13	0	0	0	12	16	14	13	2	9	16	.320	.412	.273	11.68	6.57
2-team total (19 Colorado Rockies)					1	2	6.12	32	0	0	0	32	30	23	22	4	19	45	.242	.241	.242	12.53	5.29
Sean Manaea	R-L	6-5	245	2-1-92	8	9	4.96	30	28	0	0	158	155	95	87	29	50	156	.254	.187	.273	8.89	2.85
Nick Martinez	L-R	6-1	200	8-5-90	4	4	3.47	47	10	0	8	106	96	44	41	15	41	95	.239	.225	.251	8.04	3.47
Adrian Morejon	L-L	5-11	224	2-27-99	5	1	4.24	26	0	0	0	34	31	18	16	4	9	28	.238	.227	.244	7.41	2.38
Joe Musgrove	R-R	6-5	230	12-4-92	10	7	2.93	30	30	0	0	181	154	67	59	22	42	184	.227	.203	.254	9.15	2.09
Wil Myers	R-R	6-3	207	12-10-90	0	0	7.36	1	0	0	0	1	4	3	3	3	0	0	.286	.333	.273	0.00	0.00
Taylor Rogers	L-L	6-3	190	12-17-90	1	5	4.35	42	0	0	28	41	37	22	20	1	9	48	.239	.231	.241	10.45	1.96
2-team total (24 Milwaukee Brewers)					4	8	4.76	66	0	0	31	64	57	38	34	7	19	84	.238	.167	.263	11.75	2.66
Tayler Scott	R-R	6-3	185	6-1-92	0	1	6.75	8	0	0	0	12	19	10	9	1	6	13	.358	.500	.297	9.75	4.50
Blake Snell	L-L	6-4	225	12-4-92	8	10	3.38	24	24	0	0	128	103	51	48	11	51	171	.216	.233	.213	12.02	3.59
Craig Stammen	R-R	6-2	228	3-9-84	1	2	4.43	33	1	0	0	41	45	22	20	9	10	35	.280	.290	.273	7.75	2.21
Robert Suarez	R-R	6-2	210	3-1-91	5	1	2.27	45	0	0	1	48	29	13	12	4	21	61	.176	.181	.172	11.52	3.97
Kyle Tyler	R-R	6-0	185	12-27-96	1	0	0.00	2	0	0	0	4	2	0	0	0	1	2	.154	.200	.125	4.50	2.25
Ryan Weathers	R-L	6-1	230	12-17-99	0	0	9.82	1	1	0	0	4	6	4	4	0	4	3	.353	--	.353	7.36	9.82
Steven Wilson	R-R	6-3	221	8-24-94	4	2	3.06	50	1	0	1	53	36	20	18	7	20	53	.191	.221	.175	9.00	3.40

Fielding

Catcher	PCT	G	PO	A	E	DP	PB
Alfaro	.997	65	544	27	2	4	7
Campusano	.988	10	81	2	1	0	1
Nola	.993	101	833	27	6	3	5

First Base	PCT	G	PO	A	E	DP
Beaty	1.000	3	5	0	0	0
Bell	1.000	21	117	10	0	9
Cronenworth	1.000	20	60	6	0	6
Drury	1.000	21	139	11	0	8
Hosmer	.993	88	609	69	5	59
Myers	1.000	25	154	8	0	17
Voit	.969	11	84	9	3	8

Second Base	PCT	G	PO	A	E	DP
Abrams	.946	13	13	22	2	3
Alcantara	1.000	7	5	4	0	1
Batten	1.000	5	3	2	0	1
Cano	1.000	5	8	13	0	1
Cronenworth	.992	147	205	308	4	77
Drury	1.000	7	15	17	0	4
Nola	1.000	2	1	1	0	1

Third Base	PCT	G	PO	A	E	DP
Alcantara	1.000	6	3	14	0	1
Batten	1.000	7	4	7	0	0
Dixon	1.000	2	0	3	0	0
Drury	.923	5	6	6	1	1
Kim	1.000	24	16	32	0	4
Machado	.966	134	93	217	11	27
Myers	.000	1	0	0	0	0
Nola	.000	1	0	0	0	0
Rosario	.000	4	0	0	0	0

Shortstop	PCT	G	PO	A	E	DP
Abrams	.980	32	34	64	2	8
Alcantara	1.000	8	4	18	0	1
Cronenworth	.966	9	11	17	1	5
Kim	.982	131	120	327	8	59
Rosario	1.000	2	1	2	0	0

Outfield	PCT	G	PO	A	E	DP
Abrams	1.000	3	4	0	0	0
Azocar	.975	105	155	2	4	0
Batten	1.000	1	1	0	0	0
Beaty	1.000	12	9	0	0	0
Dixon	1.000	1	1	0	0	0
Grisham	.994	148	341	3	2	1
Liberato	--	3	0	0	0	0
Mazara	.989	51	93	1	1	0
Myers	.989	52	89	1	1	1
Profar	.984	146	229	10	4	2
Rooker	1.000	2	6	0	0	0
Ruiz	1.000	16	18	0	0	0
Soto	.991	52	112	1	1	0
Thompson	1.000	7	12	0	0	0

EL PASO CHIHUAHUAS — *TRIPLE-A*

PACIFIC COAST LEAGUE

Batting	B-T	HT	WT	DOB	AVG	vLH	vRH	G	AB	R	H	2B	3B	HR	RBI	BB	HBP	SH	SF	SO	SB	CS	SLG	OBP
CJ Abrams	L-R	6-2	185	10-3-00	.314	.267	.327	30	140	35	44	4	1	7	28	8	3	0	0	25	10	3	.507	.364
Shogo Akiyama	L-R	6-0	190	4-16-88	.343	.400	.320	16	70	14	24	2	1	3	21	4	0	0	0	14	2	0	.529	.378
Kelvin Alarcon	B-R	6-1	155	3-6-99	.429	--	.429	2	7	1	3	0	0	0	0	2	0	0	0	1	0	0	.429	.556
Jorge Alfaro	R-R	6-3	230	6-11-93	.267	.333	.250	4	15	5	4	1	0	2	4	1	0	0	0	5	0	0	.733	.313
Jose Azocar	R-R	5-11	181	5-11-96	.306	.344	.288	23	98	11	30	6	0	5	16	7	0	0	0	24	3	1	.520	.352
Matthew Batten	R-R	5-11	180	6-22-95	.289	.287	.290	85	325	63	94	17	1	12	46	47	3	1	2	73	18	2	.458	.382
Matt Beaty	L-R	6-0	215	4-28-93	.270	.222	.278	35	126	19	34	2	1	2	13	14	5	0	0	27	0	0	.349	.366
Luis Campusano	R-R	5-11	232	9-29-98	.298	.293	.299	81	319	62	95	15	1	14	60	33	2	0	4	62	0	0	.483	.363
Robinson Cano	L-R	6-0	212	10-22-82	.333	.211	.364	21	96	20	32	5	0	3	20	7	0	0	1	22	0	0	.479	.375
Michael Cantu	R-R	6-3	225	8-28-95	.196	.192	.197	44	92	10	18	3	0	1	8	11	0	0	0	37	0	0	.261	.282
Jarryd Dale	R-R	6-1	195	9-11-00	.222	.333	.208	10	27	5	6	2	0	0	4	5	0	0	1	7	0	0	.296	.333
Brandon Dixon	R-R	6-2	215	1-29-92	.371	.389	.367	25	97	24	36	9	0	13	32	14	1	0	2	27	3	1	.866	.447
Juan Fernandez	R-R	5-11	205	3-7-99	.440	.429	.444	7	25	2	11	0	0	1	7	2	0	0	0	4	0	0	.560	.481
Cam Gallagher	R-R	6-3	230	12-6-92	.255	.333	.233	16	55	9	14	4	0	1	10	6	0	0	2	11	0	0	.382	.317
C.J. Hinojosa	R-R	5-10	185	7-15-94	.291	.336	.275	122	461	69	134	33	2	17	83	45	7	1	5	86	8	2	.482	.359
Connor Hollis	R-R	5-10	170	11-18-94	.310	.273	.323	24	84	13	26	9	1	0	4	10	1	0	0	14	2	0	.440	.389
Reinaldo Ilarraza	B-R	5-10	150	1-12-99	.279	.100	.314	26	61	10	17	3	0	1	6	8	0	2	1	16	4	0	.377	.357
Adam Kerner	R-R	5-10	180	7-31-98	.000	.000	.000	2	3	1	0	0	0	0	0	0	0	0	0	1	0	0	.000	.000
Taylor Kohlwey	L-L	6-3	200	7-20-94	.297	.264	.308	128	501	87	149	32	4	11	82	68	11	1	6	91	9	3	.443	.389
Domingo Leyba	B-R	5-11	205	9-11-95	.125	.000	.174	10	32	3	4	2	0	1	4	6	0	0	1	6	0	0	.281	.256
Luis Liberato	L-L	6-1	175	12-18-95	.261	.250	.265	99	329	68	86	28	2	20	59	48	2	6	5	99	6	1	.541	.354
Kyle Martin	L-L	6-2	240	11-13-92	.257	.216	.267	79	257	47	66	19	0	17	46	36	3	0	2	85	0	0	.529	.352
Nomar Mazara	L-L	6-4	224	4-26-95	.367	.233	.408	35	128	32	47	14	0	7	27	21	1	0	2	29	0	0	.641	.454
Kelvin Melean	R-R	6-0	195	9-5-98	.255	.231	.265	16	47	11	12	3	0	0	3	5	0	0	1	10	0	0	.319	.321
Thomas Milone	L-L	5-11	190	1-26-95	.229	.161	.245	61	170	24	39	9	3	3	19	28	1	1	0	67	4	3	.371	.342
Wil Myers	R-R	6-3	207	12-10-90	.229	.077	.318	9	35	3	8	1	0	2	3	3	0	0	0	9	0	0	.429	.289
Tirso Ornelas	L-R	6-3	200	3-11-00	.214	.000	.273	3	14	2	3	1	0	0	2	1	0	0	0	2	0	0	.286	.267
Kervin Pichardo	R-R	6-0	180	10-15-01	.213	.206	.217	29	80	14	17	4	1	4	15	10	1	2	0	29	0	0	.438	.308
Alison Quintero	R-R	5-11	175	4-24-00	.000	--	.000	1	1	0	0	0	0	0	0	0	0	0	0	1	0	0	.000	.000
Webster Rivas	R-R	6-1	219	8-8-90	.283	.250	.300	15	46	5	13	2	0	0	8	8	0	0	1	12	0	0	.326	.382
Aderlin Rodriguez	R-R	6-3	210	11-18-91	.272	.325	.256	45	173	28	47	10	0	12	46	14	7	0	5	45	0	0	.538	.342
Brent Rooker	R-R	6-4	225	11-1-94	.272	.236	.283	61	228	55	62	19	0	19	55	37	6	0	2	78	5	1	.605	.385

Eguy Rosario	R-R	5-9	150	8-25-99	.288	.308	.282	124	490	98	141	34	4	22	81	59	7	1	7	109	21	8	.508	.368
Esteury Ruiz	R-R	6-0	169	2-15-99	.315	.421	.293	28	111	30	35	6	0	4	9	20	9	2	0	25	23	4	.477	.457
Jack Stronach	L-R	6-3	195	8-2-97	.375	.000	.429	3	8	4	3	1	0	0	2	1	1	0	0	2	0	0	.500	.500
Brett Sullivan	L-R	6-1	195	2-22-94	.285	.228	.303	113	421	73	120	28	6	9	81	38	3	0	13	58	3	0	.444	.339
Trayce Thompson	R-R	6-3	225	3-15-91	.316	.308	.318	16	57	16	18	4	0	9	17	7	0	0	1	18	1	0	.860	.385
Chase Valentine	R-R	5-11	160	4-22-02	.000	--	.000	2	5	0	0	0	0	0	0	0	0	0	0	4	0	0	.000	.000
Luke Voit	R-R	6-3	255	2-13-91	.000	.000	.000	5	18	1	0	0	0	0	0	2	0	0	0	12	0	0	.000	.100

Pitching	B-T	HT	WT	DOB	W	L	ERA	G	GS	CG	SV	IP	H	R	ER	HR	BB	SO	AVG	vLH	vRH	K/9	BB/9
Pedro Avila	R-R	5-11	210	1-14-97	7	2	4.58	30	24	0	0	112	98	64	57	16	49	124	.232	.248	.223	9.96	3.94
Michel Baez	R-R	6-8	220	1-21-96	1	2	8.44	24	0	0	0	21	27	21	20	3	18	24	.310	.118	.357	10.13	7.59
Carlos Belen	R-R	6-1	250	2-28-96	0	1	2.81	14	0	0	1	16	13	8	5	1	2	8	.213	.267	.196	4.50	1.13
Travis Bergen	L-L	6-1	223	10-8-93	4	0	4.07	25	0	0	1	24	24	13	11	2	25	27	.253	.211	.281	9.99	9.25
Jordan Brink	L-R	6-0	200	3-18-93	2	0	7.66	23	0	0	0	25	31	22	21	4	13	29	.301	.333	.279	10.58	4.74
Michael Cantu	R-R	6-3	225	8-28-95	0	0	27.00	1	0	0	0	1	4	3	3	0	1	0	.571	.667	.500	0.00	9.00
Jose Castillo	L-L	6-6	252	1-10-96	3	2	2.91	43	0	0	3	43	43	16	14	3	20	58	.267	.288	.255	12.05	4.15
Mike Clevinger	R-R	6-4	215	12-21-90	0	0	2.70	2	2	0	0	7	7	2	2	1	2	10	.269	.063	.600	13.50	2.70
Tom Cosgrove	L-L	6-2	190	6-14-96	2	1	4.80	28	0	0	0	30	22	17	16	6	15	43	.200	.156	.231	12.90	4.50
Nabil Crismatt	R-R	6-1	220	12-25-94	1	0	2.45	3	0	0	0	4	2	1	1	1	0	5	.154	.143	.167	12.27	0.00
Thomas Eshelman	R-R	6-2	225	6-20-94	1	2	8.01	13	10	0	0	39	64	38	35	10	2	27	.356	.364	.351	6.18	0.46
Angel Felipe	R-R	6-5	190	8-30-97	2	1	4.43	19	0	0	3	22	13	11	11	0	11	35	.167	.156	.174	14.10	4.43
Heath Fillmyer	R-R	6-1	195	5-16-94	2	1	7.56	5	0	0	0	8	12	8	7	2	7	8	.333	.286	.400	8.64	7.56
Mason Fox	R-R	6-2	170	1-7-97	0	0	5.40	5	0	0	0	5	7	3	3	1	2	10	.318	.167	.375	18.00	3.60
Grant Gavin	R-R	6-2	185	7-10-95	5	0	4.85	33	1	0	4	39	37	26	21	5	27	48	.243	.221	.262	11.08	6.23
MacKenzie Gore	L-L	6-2	197	2-24-99	0	0	0.00	1	1	0	0	5	2	0	0	0	0	7	.125	.000	.200	12.60	0.00
Jay Groome	L-L	6-6	262	8-23-98	3	2	3.16	10	10	0	0	51	52	20	18	4	19	44	.267	.295	.258	7.71	3.33
Tyler Higgins	R-R	6-3	215	4-22-91	1	4	4.97	24	0	0	0	25	26	16	14	6	9	24	.260	.371	.200	8.53	3.20
Alek Jacob	L-R	6-3	190	6-16-98	1	1	6.59	16	0	0	2	14	18	10	10	4	5	18	.305	.385	.283	11.85	3.29
Pierce Johnson	R-R	6-2	202	5-10-91	0	0	1.80	5	0	0	1	5	2	1	1	0	0	6	.118	.286	.000	10.80	0.00
Ray Kerr	L-L	6-3	185	9-10-94	5	0	5.08	46	0	0	3	44	45	29	25	4	36	67	.269	.214	.297	13.60	7.31
Brandon Kintzler	R-R	5-10	200	8-1-84	1	1	22.85	7	0	0	0	4	13	11	11	3	6	3	.520	.556	.500	6.23	12.46
Reiss Knehr	L-R	6-2	205	11-3-96	4	4	6.88	32	15	0	1	88	89	68	67	18	55	92	.259	.318	.214	9.44	5.65
Ian Krol	L-L	6-1	210	5-9-91	1	1	7.46	24	1	0	2	25	31	21	21	6	17	33	.304	.333	.283	11.72	6.04
Dinelson Lamet	R-R	6-3	228	7-18-92	0	1	0.77	11	0	0	0	12	8	2	1	0	5	18	.182	.235	.148	13.89	3.86
Aaron Leasher	L-L	6-3	208	4-28-96	8	6	4.23	35	11	0	0	87	87	47	41	10	38	91	.261	.268	.257	9.38	3.92
Ryan Lillie	R-R	6-0	210	5-1-96	2	1	10.03	6	1	0	0	12	23	15	13	4	8	11	.434	.400	.455	8.49	6.17
Moises Lugo	R-R	6-1	185	1-20-99	2	0	6.10	11	0	0	0	10	11	8	7	2	5	12	.262	.250	.267	10.45	4.35
Evan Miller	L-R	6-2	197	5-23-95	3	5	8.45	46	3	0	3	54	62	55	51	9	28	50	.279	.317	.257	8.28	4.64
Felix Minjarez	R-R	6-3	205	9-13-96	0	0	13.50	2	0	0	0	2	2	4	3	2	1	1	.222	.000	.400	4.50	4.50
Adrian Morejon	L-L	5-11	224	2-27-99	0	0	0.00	2	0	0	0	3	1	0	0	0	0	5	.100	--	.100	15.00	0.00
Aaron Northcraft	R-R	6-3	229	5-28-90	0	0	3.16	30	0	0	0	31	17	11	11	1	21	20	.162	.176	.155	5.74	6.03
Ramon Perez	L-L	6-1	225	7-2-99	0	1	15.00	2	1	0	0	3	8	7	5	0	4	0	.444	1.000	.375	0.00	12.00
Yusmeiro Petit	R-R	6-1	252	11-22-84	1	1	7.71	11	0	0	1	12	18	10	10	3	4	12	.353	.375	.343	9.26	3.09
Drew Pomeranz	R-L	6-5	246	11-22-88	0	0	16.20	2	0	0	0	2	1	3	3	1	3	2	.167	.000	.200	10.80	16.20
Jose Quezada	R-R	5-9	165	9-7-95	2	1	11.49	15	0	0	0	16	19	20	20	4	15	16	.297	.280	.308	9.19	8.62
Webster Rivas	R-R	6-1	219	8-8-90	0	0	0.00	1	0	0	0	1	1	0	0	0	0	0	.333	--	.333	0.00	0.00
Jesse Scholtens	R-R	6-4	230	4-6-94	4	4	4.10	37	15	0	1	83	82	40	38	13	31	92	.254	.228	.273	9.94	3.35
Tayler Scott	R-R	6-3	185	6-1-92	2	1	3.76	33	0	0	3	41	41	22	17	5	11	52	.261	.213	.292	11.51	2.43
Blake Snell	L-L	6-4	225	12-4-92	1	0	1.80	1	1	0	0	5	3	1	1	0	0	7	.167	.000	.188	12.60	0.00
Craig Stammen	R-R	6-2	228	3-9-84	0	0	2.25	2	0	0	0	4	7	1	1	0	0	6	.389	.333	.400	13.50	0.00
Robert Suarez	R-R	6-2	210	3-1-91	0	0	9.00	3	0	0	0	3	4	4	3	2	1	3	.308	.500	.273	9.00	3.00
Wen-Hua Sung	R-R	6-1	235	9-2-96	0	0	1.50	4	0	0	0	6	4	2	1	1	5	6	.182	.200	.143	9.00	7.50
Kyle Tyler	R-R	6-0	185	12-27-96	2	1	4.98	15	2	0	0	22	11	12	12	2	19	27	.151	.118	.179	11.22	7.89
2-team total (4 Sacramento River Cats)					2	1	5.68	19	2	0	0	25	17	16	16	4	22	33	.189	.175	.200	11.72	7.82
Matt Waldron	R-R	6-2	185	9-26-96	3	9	8.44	16	16	0	0	69	92	68	65	12	29	58	.317	.312	.321	7.53	3.76
Ryan Weathers	R-L	6-1	230	12-17-99	7	7	6.73	31	22	0	0	123	163	101	92	31	57	88	.328	.341	.323	6.44	4.17
Luke Westphal	L-L	6-3	230	6-14-89	2	2	4.19	29	14	0	0	69	60	40	32	9	38	82	.231	.224	.235	10.75	4.98
Steven Wilson	R-R	6-3	221	8-24-94	0	0	4.50	2	0	0	0	2	1	1	1	1	0	4	.143	.000	.167	18.00	0.00

Fielding

Catcher	PCT	G	PO	A	E	DP	PB
Alfaro	1.000	1	5	1	0	0	0
Campusano	.987	61	565	23	8	2	4
Cantu	1.000	18	95	0	0	1	0
Fernandez	1.000	1	10	1	0	0	0
Gallagher	1.000	13	127	9	0	1	0
Kerner	1.000	1	3	0	0	0	0
Rivas	1.000	7	57	6	0	0	0
Sullivan	.983	64	566	28	10	6	10

First Base	PCT	G	PO	A	E	DP
Alarcon	1.000	1	9	1	0	1
Batten	1.000	2	7	1	0	2
Cantu	.983	14	57	2	1	8
Fernandez	1.000	1	6	0	0	0
Hollis	1.000	2	8	0	0	1
Kohlwey	.993	45	271	26	2	30
Martin	.994	68	445	27	3	45
Melean	1.000	1	6	0	0	0
Myers	1.000	5	24	2	0	2
Rodriguez	.985	32	235	21	4	26
Voit	1.000	1	5	0	0	0

Second Base	PCT	G	PO	A	E	DP
Abrams	.909	2	3	7	1	2
Batten	.906	10	17	12	3	1
Cano	.926	9	11	14	2	5
Dale	.000	2	0	0	0	0
Hinojosa	.987	40	69	79	2	23
Hollis	.983	16	22	35	1	9
Ilarraza	1.000	6	10	9	0	3
Leyba	1.000	9	9	19	0	4
Melean	1.000	8	9	14	0	4
Pichardo	.727	4	5	3	3	1
Rosario	.951	54	89	123	11	32

Third Base	PCT	G	PO	A	E	DP
Alarcon	1.000	1	1	2	0	0
Batten	.946	34	34	53	5	8
Dale	1.000	2	0	2	0	0
Dixon	.824	8	3	11	3	0
Hinojosa	.974	30	18	58	2	9
Hollis	.929	4	4	9	1	1
Ilarraza	1.000	3	1	9	0	1
Leyba	1.000	1	0	2	0	0
Melean	1.000	6	3	8	0	0
Pichardo	.938	25	8	37	3	7
Rodriguez	1.000	1	0	4	0	1

Rosario	.989	35	24	64	1	8
Sullivan	.967	15	7	22	1	2

Shortstop	PCT	G	PO	A	E	DP
Abrams	.935	26	27	74	7	18
Batten	1.000	36	44	95	0	21
Dale	1.000	3	0	3	0	0
Hinojosa	.958	54	59	173	8	24
Rosario	.946	37	41	98	8	15
Valentine	1.000	1	2	0	0	0

Outfield	PCT	G	PO	A	E	DP
Abrams	1.000	2	7	0	0	0
Akiyama	.969	16	31	0	1	0
Azocar	.969	23	60	2	2	0
Batten	1.000	9	15	0	0	0
Beaty	1.000	24	27	1	0	0
Dale	1.000	5	5	2	0	0
Dixon	1.000	13	31	1	0	0
Hollis	1.000	3	1	0	0	0
Ilarraza	.850	14	17	0	3	0
Kohlwey	.984	93	177	7	3	2
Liberato	.989	97	178	7	2	2
Martin	--	4	0	0	0	0
Mazara	1.000	24	45	0	0	0
Milone	.991	58	104	2	1	1
Myers	1.000	1	2	0	0	0
Ornelas	1.000	1	3	0	0	0
Rooker	.978	51	86	1	2	0
Ruiz	1.000	29	68	0	0	0
Stronach	1.000	1	4	0	0	0
Sullivan	1.000	13	8	2	0	0
Thompson	1.000	16	31	1	0	0

SAN ANTONIO MISSIONS — DOUBLE-A

TEXAS LEAGUE

Batting	D-T	HT	WT	DOB	AVG	vLH	vRH	G	AB	R	H	2B	3B	HR	RBI	BB	HBP	SH	SF	SO	SB	CS	SLG	OBP
Matthew Acosta	L-L	5-11	205	4-1-98	.158	.000	.222	12	38	1	6	2	0	0	4	3	0	0	0	15	2	1	.211	.220
Kelvin Alarcon	B-R	6-1	155	3-6-99	.409	.500	.400	5	22	3	9	3	0	0	2	2	0	0	0	5	1	0	.545	.458
Michael Cantu	R-R	6-3	225	8-28-95	.167	.250	.000	2	6	1	1	0	0	0	0	1	0	0	0	5	0	0	.167	.286
Brandon Dixon	R-R	6-2	215	1-29-92	.367	.389	.363	25	98	23	36	7	2	10	42	12	1	0	3	25	6	0	.786	.430
Rafael Fermin	R-R	6-0	170	12-25-01	.200	--	.200	2	5	1	1	0	0	0	0	0	1	0	0	0	0	0	.200	.333
Juan Fernandez	R-R	5-11	205	3-7-99	.271	.263	.273	103	380	35	103	14	2	0	55	34	10	2	2	72	11	2	.318	.345
Ike Freeman	R-R	5-10	195	6-17-98	.214	.500	.167	4	14	0	3	2	0	0	1	1	1	0	0	4	0	0	.357	.313
Chris Givin	R-R	6-2	185	3-21-97	.239	.217	.244	29	109	14	26	6	0	0	9	13	0	0	0	22	1	0	.294	.320
Wyatt Hoffman	R-R	5-9	170	3-16-99	.200	.000	.333	2	5	0	1	0	0	0	0	1	0	0	0	2	0	0	.200	.333
Connor Hollis	R-R	5-10	170	11-18-94	.333	.358	.325	103	403	82	134	22	3	9	59	62	10	2	2	93	19	12	.469	.432
Korry Howell	R-R	6-3	180	9-1-98	.253	.222	.264	48	146	37	37	8	4	6	20	25	9	2	2	52	12	1	.486	.390
Reinaldo Ilarraza	B-R	5-10	150	1-12-99	.200	.000	.250	3	10	2	2	0	0	1	3	1	0	1	0	5	1	0	.500	.273
Connor Kaiser	R-R	6-4	195	11-20-96	.202	.156	.212	54	178	32	36	7	0	7	28	24	1	3	1	60	9	1	.360	.299
Domingo Leyba	B-R	5-11	205	9-11-95	.266	.244	.273	98	372	57	99	21	1	10	60	59	4	0	9	61	12	1	.409	.365
Tyler Malone	L-R	5-11	190	11-4-97	.333	.000	.400	6	12	3	4	1	0	0	1	5	0	0	0	2	1	0	.417	.529
Joshua Mears	R-R	6-3	230	2-21-01	.169	.273	.153	24	83	9	14	2	0	5	15	10	1	0	0	45	1	0	.373	.266
Kelvin Melean	R-R	6-0	195	9-5-98	.245	.211	.257	41	139	19	34	8	2	2	22	14	1	2	1	36	2	2	.374	.316
Thomas Milone	L-L	5-11	190	1-26-95	.268	.218	.283	61	235	36	63	10	3	6	37	26	5	3	1	68	11	4	.413	.352
Jorge Ona	R-R	6-0	235	12-31-96	.220	.217	.221	69	250	35	55	9	0	8	25	22	7	0	0	103	0	0	.352	.301
Tirso Ornelas	L-R	6-3	200	3-11-00	.288	.344	.274	112	441	62	127	28	2	7	51	43	4	2	2	85	7	2	.408	.355
Willmert Paula	L-R	6-1	165	9-30-01	.000	--	.000	2	4	1	0	0	0	0	0	1	0	0	0	3	0	0	.000	.200
Robbie Podorsky	R-R	5-8	170	1-27-95	.400	.385	.407	10	40	12	16	5	2	0	6	3	1	1	0	9	2	0	.625	.455
Alison Quintero	R-R	5-11	175	4-24-00	.200	.250	.167	5	10	2	2	0	0	0	1	1	0	0	0	4	0	0	.200	.273
Ripken Reyes	B-R	5-10	185	4-1-97	.241	.260	.234	67	191	37	46	7	1	0	16	28	15	10	3	29	7	3	.288	.376
Webster Rivas	R-R	6-1	219	8-8-90	.248	.222	.257	57	202	31	50	14	1	1	27	40	2	0	2	49	1	2	.342	.374
Yorman Rodriguez	R-R	5-10	160	7-23-97	.279	.298	.274	122	491	69	137	25	0	15	83	38	2	0	9	83	5	2	.422	.328
Edwin Rojas	R-R	6-2	170	11-12-01	.333	.364	.300	8	21	3	7	1	1	1	3	1	1	0	0	9	0	1	.619	.391
Agustin Ruiz	L-R	6-2	215	9-23-99	.237	.000	.277	23	76	13	18	3	1	2	9	12	2	0	1	23	2	0	.382	.352
Esteury Ruiz	R-R	6-0	169	2-15-99	.344	.395	.331	49	180	54	62	17	2	9	37	32	14	3	2	40	37	5	.611	.474
Chandler Seagle	R-R	6-0	190	5-23-96	.209	.182	.217	73	239	28	50	12	0	3	22	24	3	8	1	73	2	1	.297	.288
Ethan Skender	R-R	5-11	185	12-22-96	.257	.278	.250	24	74	7	19	3	1	0	7	5	3	1	0	17	5	0	.324	.329
Jack Stronach	L-R	6-3	195	8-2-97	.095	.000	.125	7	21	0	2	0	0	0	2	5	0	2	0	6	0	0	.095	.269
Fernando Tatis Jr.	R-R	6-3	217	1-2-99	.222	--	.222	4	9	2	2	1	1	0	0	4	1	0	0	2	0	0	.556	.500
Wyatt Ulrich	L-R	6-1	170	7-27-96	.209	.125	.229	11	43	7	9	0	0	0	2	4	0	0	0	9	3	0	.209	.277
Mitch Walding	L-R	6-3	190	9-10-92	.045	.000	.056	7	22	0	1	1	0	0	3	7	0	0	0	8	1	0	.091	.276
Juan Zabala	R-R	5-10	190	7-3-99	.375	.333	.381	7	24	5	9	1	0	0	0	4	0	0	0	5	4	2	.417	.464

Pitching	B-T	HT	WT	DOB	W	L	ERA	G	GS	CG	SV	IP	H	R	ER	HR	BB	SO	AVG	vLH	vRH	K/9	BB/9
Lake Bachar	R-R	6-2	219	6-3-95	5	3	6.15	27	7	0	6	45	48	35	31	10	18	44	.271	.241	.298	8.74	3.57
Michel Baez	R-R	6-8	220	1-21-96	4	1	2.41	13	0	0	1	19	10	5	5	3	4	24	.154	.308	.051	11.57	1.93
Carlos Belen	R-R	6-1	250	2-28-96	3	4	4.32	27	0	0	0	42	42	25	20	4	16	33	.259	.319	.215	7.13	3.46
Edwuin Bencomo	R-R	6-2	205	4-14-99	1	0	4.35	11	0	0	0	21	16	10	10	4	9	17	.219	.233	.209	7.40	3.92
Jason Blanchard	R-L	6-0	185	6-25-97	0	0	4.80	6	4	0	0	15	14	9	8	1	8	19	.259	.063	.342	11.40	4.80
Tom Cosgrove	L-L	6-2	190	6-14-96	6	1	2.45	20	0	0	0	26	12	7	7	3	13	39	.140	.116	.163	13.68	4.56
Thomas Eshelman	R-R	6-2	225	6-20-94	3	5	4.58	14	14	2	0	75	94	45	38	8	11	41	.306	.304	.308	4.94	1.33
Angel Felipe	R-R	6-5	190	8-30-97	3	5	3.18	32	0	0	11	40	36	19	14	1	25	49	.240	.288	.202	11.12	5.67
Mason Fox	R-R	6-2	170	1-7-97	4	3	6.04	31	0	0	0	48	49	34	32	6	29	43	.265	.273	.261	8.12	5.48
Grant Gavin	R-R	6-2	185	7-10-95	2	1	4.76	13	0	0	0	17	20	10	9	1	9	15	.303	.440	.220	7.94	4.76
Jordan Guerrero	R-R	6-5	296	8-1-96	0	0	2.25	4	0	0	0	4	2	1	1	0	3	4	.143	.111	.200	9.00	6.75
Henry Henry	R-R	6-4	215	12-17-98	4	1	5.20	34	10	0	0	80	86	48	46	5	55	83	.276	.250	.294	9.38	6.21
Osvaldo Hernandez	L-L	6-0	181	5-15-98	4	3	4.37	36	4	0	0	56	49	31	27	7	24	45	.233	.228	.237	7.28	3.88
Alek Jacob	L-R	6-3	190	6-16-98	1	0	1.83	23	1	0	2	34	27	8	7	1	10	43	.214	.241	.194	11.27	2.62
Brandon Komar	R-R	6-0	200	5-8-99	5	4	6.05	16	14	0	0	74	90	54	50	10	30	54	.304	.326	.287	6.54	3.63
Kevin Kopps	R-R	6-0	200	3-2-97	1	2	4.14	42	3	0	4	54	44	30	25	4	34	60	.219	.174	.252	9.94	5.63
Ben Krauth	L-L	6-0	190	3-10-94	1	4	7.18	9	9	0	0	36	49	32	29	8	21	32	.314	.205	.350	7.93	5.20
Dinelson Lamet	R-R	6-3	228	7-18-92	0	0	3.86	6	0	0	0	7	10	3	3	2	1	9	.323	.333	.316	11.57	1.29
Reggie Lawson	R-R	6-4	205	8-2-97	4	6	5.63	17	17	0	0	62	56	41	39	11	50	55	.240	.219	.255	7.94	7.22
Ryan Lillie	R-R	6-0	210	5-1-96	1	4	4.78	15	6	0	0	38	37	27	20	5	23	29	.266	.254	.275	6.93	5.50
Moises Lugo	R-R	6-1	185	1-20-99	6	0	2.74	28	1	0	2	62	41	22	19	4	34	85	.186	.267	.130	12.27	4.91

Luis Madrazo	R-R	6-4	185	1-16-98	0	0	27.00	1	0	0	0	0	2	1	1	0	0	0	.667	--	.667	0.00	0.00
Dwayne Matos	R-R	6-1	155	11-7-00	1	1	12.00	5	4	0	0	15	22	20	20	3	13	8	.344	.367	.324	4.80	7.80
Seth Mayberry	R-R	6-3	195	6-22-00	0	1	8.44	4	0	0	0	5	10	6	5	2	2	8	.385	.300	.438	13.50	3.38
Felix Minjarez	R-R	6-3	205	9-13-96	1	0	6.09	19	0	0	0	34	39	26	23	6	13	37	.289	.345	.250	9.79	3.44
Gabe Morales	L-L	6-3	175	4-14-99	0	0	5.32	8	5	0	0	22	19	14	13	1	21	23	.232	.226	.235	9.41	8.59
Adrian Morejon	L-L	5-11	224	2-27-99	0	0	0.00	5	0	0	0	7	1	0	0	0	2	8	.050	.000	.063	10.29	2.57
Gabe Mosser	R-R	6-4	185	6-8-96	0	1	4.94	5	5	0	0	24	27	14	13	4	8	12	.293	.237	.333	4.56	3.04
Ramon Perez	L-L	6-1	225	7-2-99	0	1	4.35	6	0	0	0	10	4	7	5	0	10	12	.118	.222	.080	10.45	8.71
Jose Quezada	R-R	5-9	165	9-7-95	1	1	0.64	11	0	0	2	14	10	2	1	1	2	17	.200	.150	.233	10.93	1.29
Fernando Sanchez	L-L	6-0	198	9-13-00	0	0	5.06	3	0	0	0	5	7	3	3	0	6	6	.333	.400	.273	10.13	10.13
Fred Schlichtholz	R-L	6-3	215	9-18-95	0	4	2.04	27	0	0	2	35	36	8	8	3	9	41	.265	.304	.238	10.44	2.29
Ethan Skender	R-R	5-11	185	12-22-96	0	0	0.00	1	0	0	0	1	1	0	0	0	0	0	.250	--	.250	0.00	0.00
Nick Thwaits	R-R	6-2	195	6-27-99	0	0	0.00	1	0	0	0	1	2	1	0	0	0	0	.333	.500	.250	0.00	0.00
Noel Vela	L-L	6-1	185	12-21-98	1	3	6.35	9	4	0	0	23	25	17	16	1	20	24	.284	.281	.286	9.53	7.94
Matt Waldron	R-R	6-2	185	9-26-96	2	1	2.84	9	9	0	0	44	42	16	14	2	10	38	.258	.221	.291	7.71	2.03
Nolan Watson	R-R	6-2	195	1-25-97	4	6	5.84	29	17	0	0	91	100	65	59	8	46	94	.275	.313	.246	9.30	4.55
Jackson Wolf	L-L	6-7	205	4-22-99	0	2	8.44	2	2	0	0	11	12	12	10	1	6	8	.286	.429	.257	6.75	5.06

Fielding

Catcher	PCT	G	PO	A	E	DP	PB
Cantu	.909	1	9	1	1	0	0
Fernandez	1.000	14	90	7	0	0	2
Malone	.973	5	36	0	1	0	0
Quintero	1.000	2	4	0	0	0	0
Rivas	.975	28	260	13	7	2	5
Rodriguez	.986	24	197	13	3	0	2
Seagle	.992	70	567	49	5	3	6
Zabala	1.000	1	12	1	0	1	1

First Base	PCT	G	PO	A	E	DP
Cantu	.917	1	11	0	1	2
Dixon	.979	17	131	8	3	10
Fernandez	.970	32	243	15	8	24
Freeman	1.000	1	9	1	0	2
Ornelas	1.000	1	4	0	0	1
Rivas	.988	9	69	10	1	8
Rodriguez	.990	74	577	38	6	58
Walding	1.000	3	19	2	0	3
Zabala	1.000	1	4	0	0	0

Second Base	PCT	G	PO	A	E	DP
Alarcon	.895	5	7	10	2	4
Fernandez	.850	6	8	9	3	3
Freeman	1.000	2	2	5	0	0
Givin	1.000	13	23	30	0	6
Hoffman	.857	1	4	2	1	1
Hollis	1.000	13	21	35	0	6
Howell	.976	10	14	26	1	6
Leyba	.988	54	90	157	3	37
Melean	.915	12	16	27	4	5
Reyes	.976	21	27	54	2	16
Skender	.973	11	13	23	1	1

Third Base	PCT	G	PO	A	E	DP
Dixon	.786	5	4	7	3	1
Fernandez	.957	30	24	42	3	3
Givin	1.000	1	2	1	0	1
Hollis	.939	67	48	106	10	13
Melean	.911	17	9	32	4	2
Reyes	1.000	3	1	7	0	0
Rivas	1.000	5	1	12	0	2
Rodriguez	.900	7	4	14	2	1
Skender	.857	3	1	5	1	0
Walding	.500	2	0	1	1	0

Shortstop	PCT	G	PO	A	E	DP
Givin	.968	15	19	42	2	7
Hollis	.989	23	37	57	1	17
Howell	.778	3	2	5	2	1
Kaiser	.982	54	80	135	4	36
Leyba	.948	40	50	113	9	21
Melean	1.000	4	3	10	0	1
Tatis Jr.	.778	3	3	4	2	0

Outfield	PCT	G	PO	A	E	DP
Acosta	.900	11	16	2	2	1
Dixon	--	1	0	0	0	0
Fermin	1.000	2	5	0	0	0
Howell	.986	36	69	0	1	0
Ilarraza	.000	3	0	0	1	0
Malone	1.000	1	3	1	0	1
Mears	1.000	24	58	1	0	0
Milone	.992	59	118	2	1	0
Ona	.911	39	46	5	5	0
Ornelas	.990	105	191	3	2	0
Paula	1.000	2	3	0	0	0
Podorsky	1.000	8	22	1	0	1
Reyes	.988	43	72	10	1	3
Rojas	1.000	6	11	1	0	0
Ruiz	1.000	20	23	3	0	0
Ruiz	1.000	42	99	4	0	0
Skender	1.000	7	16	0	0	0
Stronach	1.000	5	8	0	0	0
Ulrich	1.000	11	21	0	0	0

FORT WAYNE TINCAPS — *HIGH CLASS A*

MIDWEST LEAGUE

Batting	B-T	HT	WT	DOB	AVG	vLH	vRH	G	AB	R	H	2B	3B	HR	RBI	BB	HBP	SH	SF	SO	SB	CS	SLG	OBP
Matthew Acosta	L-L	5-11	205	4-1-98	.257	.167	.290	51	179	21	46	9	2	2	20	23	1	0	2	48	7	1	.363	.341
Charlis Aquino	R-R	6-2	165	11-18-01	.214	.308	.133	9	28	3	6	0	0	0	3	0	0	0	0	11	1	1	.214	.214
Olivier Basabe	R-R	5-11	195	7-15-97	.243	.250	.240	77	239	27	58	5	2	5	28	28	4	1	1	61	7	3	.343	.331
Cole Cummings	L-R	6-2	205	6-20-98	.202	.148	.224	58	213	23	43	8	1	6	18	27	6	0	2	61	3	1	.333	.306
Jarryd Dale	R-R	6-1	195	9-11-00	.198	.215	.192	124	435	47	86	17	3	4	35	74	4	2	4	130	27	7	.278	.317
Josttin Diaz	B-R	6-0	170	5-18-02	.280	.455	.143	9	25	5	7	0	0	3	7	2	0	1	0	11	0	0	.640	.333
Lucas Dunn	R-R	6-0	205	4-30-99	.215	.186	.224	81	298	40	64	13	3	4	30	49	6	0	2	97	8	1	.319	.335
Albert Fabian	L-L	6-0	215	12-21-01	.142	.107	.154	29	106	6	15	4	0	4	12	5	3	0	0	43	0	0	.292	.202
Justin Farmer	R-R	6-1	190	12-19-98	.233	.300	.200	17	60	7	14	2	0	1	6	11	2	0	2	24	2	0	.317	.360
Max Ferguson	L-R	6-1	180	8-23-99	.162	.167	.160	27	105	14	17	4	3	3	11	14	2	3	1	31	4	1	.343	.270
Robert Hassell III	L-L	6-2	195	8-15-01	.299	.257	.313	75	304	49	91	19	1	10	55	38	2	0	2	66	20	3	.467	.379
Wyatt Hoffman	R-R	5-9	170	3-16-99	.143	.250	.100	11	28	1	4	0	0	0	0	1	0	0	0	8	1	0	.143	.172
Reinaldo Ilarraza	B-R	5-10	150	1-12-99	.068	.000	.089	28	73	8	5	0	0	0	4	11	3	1	0	31	3	0	.068	.218
Adam Kerner	R-R	5-10	180	7-31-98	.238	.304	.211	26	80	8	19	7	0	2	13	8	0	1	0	21	1	0	.400	.307
Justin Lopez	B-R	6-2	195	5-9-00	.185	.200	.179	32	119	12	22	6	1	1	14	7	1	0	1	29	0	0	.277	.234
Carlos Luis	L-R	6-2	160	9-4-99	.253	.250	.254	24	83	10	21	4	2	0	7	9	0	0	0	19	0	0	.349	.326
Tyler Malone	L-R	5-11	190	11-4-97	.000	.000	.000	3	9	0	0	0	0	0	0	2	0	0	0	6	0	0	.000	.182
Joshua Mears	R-R	6-3	230	2-21-01	.223	.156	.245	52	184	29	41	11	0	14	34	16	6	0	1	90	1	1	.511	.304
Kelvin Melean	R-R	6-0	195	9-5-98	.217	.292	.186	25	83	8	18	0	0	1	4	16	3	0	0	16	0	1	.253	.363
Ripken Reyes	B-R	5-10	185	4-1-97	.223	.231	.220	46	139	21	31	8	3	2	14	19	11	0	0	25	2	1	.367	.361
Corey Rosier	L-R	5-10	180	9-7-99	.263	.220	.281	85	308	69	81	7	8	6	37	54	6	3	2	68	33	4	.396	.381
Agustin Ruiz	L-R	6-2	215	9-23-99	.224	.200	.232	63	210	33	47	12	1	8	30	24	10	0	3	54	1	0	.405	.328
Angel Solarte	R-R	5-11	200	3-29-01	.192	.161	.202	39	125	14	24	4	0	0	12	23	1	0	0	39	2	1	.224	.322
Jack Stronach	L-R	6-3	195	8-2-97	.203	.200	.203	50	158	24	32	11	0	2	14	23	6	1	1	46	0	1	.310	.324
Wyatt Ulrich	L-R	6-1	170	7-27-96	.111	.000	.125	7	18	0	2	0	0	0	0	1	1	0	0	6	0	0	.111	.200
Brandon Valenzuela	B-R	6-0	225	10-2-00	.209	.216	.206	99	345	39	72	14	2	10	47	63	3	0	2	95	0	1	.348	.334

Anthony Vilar	L-R	5-10	190	4-1-99	.226	.152	.254	54	168	17	38	10	0	2	15	30	1	0	3	50	1	1	.321	.342

Pitching	B-T	HT	WT	DOB	W	L	ERA	G	GS	CG	SV	IP	H	R	ER	HR	BB	SO	AVG	vLH	vRH	K/9	BB/9
Edwuin Bencomo	R-R	6-2	205	4-14-99	4	2	2.44	25	0	0	1	55	48	17	15	2	14	50	.236	.217	.250	8.13	2.28
Ryan Bergert	R-R	6-1	210	3-8-00	4	10	5.84	24	24	0	0	103	124	69	67	18	42	129	.290	.302	.281	11.24	3.66
Luke Boyd	R-R	6-2	180	11-21-97	0	4	6.33	30	0	0	4	27	34	25	19	4	18	25	.304	.220	.352	8.33	6.00
Wilton Castillo	R-R	6-7	190	2-12-00	0	0	0.00	2	0	0	1	1	0	0	0	0	0	1	.000	.000	.000	6.75	0.00
Keegan Collett	R-R	6-3	215	7-27-98	1	1	5.40	8	0	0	1	13	11	0	8	0	12	19	.269	.263	.273	12.83	8.10
Efrain Contreras	R-R	5-10	225	1-2-00	0	5	5.74	17	17	0	0	53	64	35	34	7	25	64	.300	.265	.330	10.80	4.22
Danny Denz	L-L	5-9	205	5-20-98	0	2	10.66	10	3	0	0	25	34	32	30	7	22	28	.324	.344	.315	9.95	7.82
Jose Espada	R-R	6-0	170	2-22-97	1	3	4.05	11	7	0	0	40	30	22	18	7	18	58	.201	.246	.170	13.05	4.05
Mason Fox	R-R	6-2	170	1-7-97	0	0	0.00	2	0	0	1	2	0	0	0	0	0	5	.000	.000	.000	22.50	0.00
Robert Gasser	L-L	6-1	185	5-31-99	4	9	4.18	18	18	0	0	90	86	46	42	8	28	115	.252	.216	.262	11.46	2.79
Garrett Hawkins	R-R	6-5	230	2-10-00	0	3	8.80	4	4	0	0	15	22	19	15	6	10	12	.328	.303	.353	7.04	5.87
Alek Jacob	L-R	6-3	190	6-16-98	3	0	0.00	4	0	0	0	9	4	0	0	0	0	16	.129	.200	.095	16.00	0.00
Sam Keating	R-R	6-3	190	8-31-98	2	2	6.00	27	0	0	0	39	34	29	26	3	33	27	.231	.254	.213	6.23	7.62
Adam Kerner	R-R	5-10	180	7-31-98	0	0	0.00	1	0	0	0	0	0	0	0	0	0	0	.000	.000	--	0.00	0.00
Brandon Komar	R-R	6-0	200	5-8-99	1	2	3.71	15	2	0	0	44	30	18	18	4	14	41	.197	.197	.198	8.45	2.89
Walki Lezan	R-R	6-0	165	4-24-02	0	0	10.80	1	0	0	0	2	2	2	2	0	1	1	.333	.333	.333	5.40	5.40
Luis Madrazo	R-R	6-4	185	1-16-98	0	1	5.02	14	0	0	0	29	21	19	16	3	25	24	.208	.298	.130	7.53	7.85
Dwayne Matos	R-R	6-1	155	11-7-00	1	5	6.02	16	7	0	1	55	71	41	37	12	24	43	.309	.322	.300	6.99	3.90
Seth Mayberry	R-R	6-3	195	6-22-00	3	1	4.57	30	0	0	2	41	38	27	21	2	23	61	.238	.233	.240	13.28	5.01
Miguel Mendez	R-R	6-2	165	7-1-02	0	0	6.75	1	0	0	0	1	1	1	1	0	2	1	.200	.000	1.000	6.75	13.50
Felix Minjarez	R-R	6-3	205	9-13-96	4	0	2.91	13	0	0	0	22	14	7	7	2	15	31	.187	.091	.262	12.88	6.23
Gabe Morales	L-L	6-3	175	4-14-99	2	1	3.26	17	0	0	2	39	26	19	14	4	33	59	.190	.196	.186	13.73	7.68
Alan Mundo	R-R	6-2	170	5-27-00	0	0	2.70	5	0	0	0	7	9	2	2	2	1	13	.310	.500	.211	17.55	1.35
Ryan Och	R-L	6-0	205	7-18-98	1	1	3.95	9	0	0	1	14	4	7	6	0	15	26	.093	.143	.069	17.12	9.88
Ramon Perez	L-L	6-1	225	7-2-99	1	3	4.88	28	0	0	3	31	25	18	17	1	17	50	.227	.167	.274	14.36	4.88
Bodi Rascon	L-L	6-5	205	2-3-01	1	2	9.37	4	3	0	0	16	23	17	17	7	7	13	.338	.300	.354	7.16	3.86
Jason Reynolds	R-R	6-3	200	9-25-98	0	0	9.82	6	0	0	0	7	13	11	8	1	10	6	.371	.357	.381	7.36	12.27
Ethan Routzahn	R-R	6-4	225	3-19-98	0	2	4.81	21	0	0	1	24	31	14	13	4	10	20	.307	.286	.318	7.40	3.70
Fred Schlichtholz	R-L	6-3	215	9-18-95	1	0	1.50	4	0	0	0	6	6	1	1	0	0	8	.261	.333	.214	12.00	0.00
Adam Smith	R-R	6-2	180	5-9-00	0	1	1.80	2	2	0	0	5	3	1	1	0	2	5	.176	.286	.100	9.00	3.60
Blake Snell	L-L	6-4	225	12-4-92	0	0	0.00	1	1	0	0	4	2	0	0	0	0	4	.133	.000	.154	9.00	0.00
Wen-Hua Sung	R-R	6-1	235	9-2-96	0	0	2.35	7	0	0	1	8	7	3	2	1	3	9	.233	.250	.222	10.57	3.52
Nick Thwaits	R-R	6-2	195	6-27-99	3	5	3.19	32	0	0	2	62	55	23	22	7	19	53	.235	.301	.191	7.69	2.76
Alexuan Vega	L-L	6-2	160	6-22-99	0	0	0.00	2	0	0	0	4	2	0	0	0	3	3	.167	.250	.125	6.75	6.75
Noel Vela	L-L	6-1	185	12-21-98	6	7	3.83	20	20	0	0	87	74	45	37	6	47	101	.228	.200	.238	10.45	4.86
Jackson Wolf	L-L	6-7	205	4-22-99	7	8	4.01	23	22	0	0	119	91	56	53	16	44	134	.209	.170	.223	10.13	3.33

Fielding

Catcher	PCT	G	PO	A	E	DP	PB
Kerner	.973	19	175	6	5	1	0
Valenzuela	.994	65	613	64	4	4	9
Vilar	1.000	49	455	19	0	4	6

First Base	PCT	G	PO	A	E	DP
Acosta	1.000	10	68	1	0	12
Basabe	.979	15	88	6	2	11
Cummings	.997	49	367	17	1	41
Dunn	.986	10	71	1	1	7
Luis	.980	7	44	4	1	4
Stronach	.984	42	296	14	5	26

Second Base	PCT	G	PO	A	E	DP
Basabe	.923	13	17	31	4	3
Dale	.973	17	23	48	2	12
Dunn	.969	17	24	38	2	9
Ferguson	1.000	8	12	24	0	8
Hoffman	.977	10	17	26	1	8
Ilarraza	.960	13	20	28	2	7
Melean	1.000	14	21	28	0	8
Reyes	.976	41	62	98	4	28
Vilar	1.000	1	0	3	0	0

Third Base	PCT	G	PO	A	E	DP
Basabe	.737	22	7	21	10	1
Diaz	1.000	7	3	6	0	0
Dunn	.944	55	33	84	7	6
Ilarraza	1.000	1	4	0	0	0
Lopez	.950	24	8	30	2	1
Luis	.862	11	5	20	4	5
Melean	1.000	10	4	14	0	4
Reyes	1.000	3	1	1	0	0

Shortstop	PCT	G	PO	A	E	DP
Aquino	1.000	1	1	1	0	0
Dale	.950	106	115	246	19	53
Ferguson	.955	15	23	40	3	11
Ilarraza	1.000	1	0	2	0	0
Lopez	.750	2	2	4	2	1
Melean	1.000	4	7	7	0	3
Reyes	.917	2	4	7	1	2

Outfield	PCT	G	PO	A	E	DP
Acosta	1.000	38	60	5	0	0
Aquino	1.000	8	20	0	0	0
Basabe	1.000	24	41	2	0	0
Fabian	.923	20	23	1	2	0
Farmer	.969	17	31	0	1	0
Ferguson	1.000	2	6	0	0	0
Hassell III	.993	65	136	2	1	0
Ilarraza	1.000	10	9	2	0	1
Malone	1.000	2	4	0	0	0
Mears	1.000	44	84	3	0	1
Rosier	.986	84	135	5	2	0
Ruiz	1.000	51	82	4	0	2
Solarte	1.000	25	42	2	0	1
Ulrich	.800	7	7	1	2	1

LAKE ELSINORE STORM — LOW CLASS A

CALIFORNIA LEAGUE

Batting	B-T	HT	WT	DOB	AVG	vLH	vRH	G	AB	R	H	2B	3B	HR	RBI	BB	HBP	SH	SF	SO	SB	CS	SLG	OBP
Matthew Acosta	L-L	5-11	205	4-1-98	.194	.200	.192	30	103	21	20	3	0	5	13	16	2	3	2	30	7	1	.369	.309
Kelvin Alarcon	B-R	6-1	155	3-6-99	.286	.500	.000	3	7	1	2	0	0	0	0	1	0	0	0	3	0	0	.286	.375
Jared Alvarez-Lopez	R-R	6-2	200	1-18-01	.220	.153	.243	64	232	30	51	13	2	0	30	22	6	1	1	79	2	1	.293	.303
Charlis Aquino	R-R	6-2	165	11-18-01	.220	.353	.185	57	164	30	36	4	1	3	18	11	6	1	0	49	21	4	.311	.293
Colton Bender	R-R	5-9	195	1-13-99	.200	.000	.235	14	40	11	8	1	0	0	5	13	3	0	0	14	1	0	.225	.429
Marcos Castanon	R-R	6-0	195	3-23-99	.261	.291	.251	117	421	82	110	25	0	23	85	80	16	0	2	122	0	3	.485	.397
Nerwilian Cedeno	B-R	5-11	175	3-16-02	.256	.255	.256	71	270	60	69	13	4	6	54	42	4	0	2	79	18	8	.400	.362
Cole Cummings	L-R	6-2	205	6-20-98	.262	.150	.305	43	145	34	38	5	2	6	32	34	7	0	4	53	6	0	.448	.416
Griffin Doersching	R-R	6-4	251	8-12-98	.227	.095	.269	25	88	21	20	1	0	8	19	14	3	0	1	37	0	0	.511	.349
Victor Duarte	R-R	5-11	170	2-23-01	.225	.250	.213	28	89	16	20	5	0	2	13	10	5	0	0	28	0	0	.348	.337

Lucas Dunn	R-R	6-0	205	4-30-99	.293	.396	.237	42	150	28	44	13	5	3	36	30	5	1	2	49	11	4	.507	.422
Albert Fabian	L-L	6-0	215	12-21-01	.278	.298	.272	62	241	48	67	14	2	12	55	29	4	0	2	68	3	5	.502	.362
Justin Farmer	R-R	6-1	190	12-19-98	.224	.294	.199	109	384	88	86	19	2	11	45	95	4	1	3	126	38	6	.370	.381
Max Ferguson	L-R	6-1	180	8-23-99	.247	.247	.247	64	239	63	59	9	5	3	39	61	3	2	2	70	51	4	.364	.403
Michael Green	L-L	6-0	190	6-10-98	.211	.200	.222	7	19	4	4	0	0	1	4	0	2	0	0	9	1	0	.368	.286
Cristian Heredia	R-R	6-3	175	4-12-01	.000	.000	.000	4	9	0	0	0	0	0	0	1	0	0	0	4	0	0	.000	.100
Alejandro Hernandez	R-R	5-11	175	10-19-99	.222	--	.222	7	9	3	2	0	0	0	1	2	0	0	0	1	0	0	.222	.364
Wyatt Hoffman	R-R	5-9	170	3-16-99	.188	.200	.185	40	117	15	22	7	1	1	10	17	4	0	1	44	9	4	.291	.309
Pierce Jones	R-R	6-1	185	6-15-01	.143	.200	.115	28	77	13	11	4	0	1	8	9	5	1	1	20	10	1	.234	.272
Carlos Luis	L-R	6-2	160	9-4-99	.319	.210	.347	83	310	57	99	25	1	6	70	36	3	0	5	64	3	0	.465	.390
Tyler Malone	L-R	5-11	190	11-4-97	.244	.100	.286	20	45	8	11	3	0	1	6	16	1	0	0	12	0	1	.378	.452
Jakob Marsee	L-L	6-0	180	6-28-01	.254	.263	.250	18	67	18	17	6	1	2	8	16	3	0	0	15	12	1	.463	.419
Nathan Martorella	L-L	6-1	224	2-18-01	.288	.333	.273	17	59	10	17	4	0	2	11	12	0	0	1	15	0	0	.458	.403
Jackson Merrill	L-R	6-3	195	4-19-03	.325	.379	.302	45	197	33	64	10	3	5	34	19	1	2	0	42	8	5	.482	.387
Kai Murphy	L-L	5-8	173	8-26-00	.200	.000	.240	13	30	5	6	2	0	0	5	3	0	0	0	4	3	0	.267	.273
Wil Myers	R-R	6-3	207	12-10-90	.333	.333	.333	5	18	5	6	1	0	2	4	2	0	0	0	3	0	0	.722	.400
Graham Pauley	L-R	6-1	200	9-24-00	.328	.308	.333	17	58	14	19	4	0	2	13	12	2	0	0	10	6	3	.500	.458
Kervin Pichardo	R-R	6-0	180	10-15-01	.182	.195	.178	51	148	23	27	9	0	3	14	16	7	0	1	53	5	3	.304	.291
Jurickson Profar	B-R	6-0	184	2-20-93	.000	.000	.000	1	4	1	0	0	0	0	0	1	0	0	0	2	0	0	.000	.200
Alison Quintero	R-R	5-11	175	4-24-00	.250	--	.250	2	4	0	1	0	1	0	0	0	0	0	0	2	0	0	.750	.250
Tyler Robertson	R-R	6-4	200	3-10-00	.143	.000	.167	2	7	1	1	0	0	1	4	0	0	0	0	3	0	0	.571	.143
Ruben Salinas	R-L	6-0	154	1-13-03	.079	.100	.071	11	38	7	3	0	1	0	2	4	0	0	0	24	2	0	.132	.167
Angel Solarte	R-R	5-11	200	3-29-01	.210	.235	.205	27	105	10	22	3	1	0	8	5	4	1	1	24	3	2	.257	.270
Gilberto Vizcarra	R-R	5-10	180	3-1-99	.000	.000	.000	4	14	0	0	0	0	0	1	2	1	0	1	2	0	1	.000	.167
James Wood	L-R	6-7	240	9-17-02	.337	.346	.333	50	193	55	65	19	1	10	45	37	5	0	1	42	15	5	.601	.453
Juan Zabala	R-R	5-10	190	7-3-99	.294	.289	.295	60	211	32	62	8	2	3	26	28	6	1	1	41	19	3	.393	.390
Samuel Zavala	L-L	6-1	175	7-15-04	.254	.414	.204	33	122	24	31	6	2	7	26	19	0	0	0	37	5	3	.508	.355

Pitching	B-T	HT	WT	DOB	W	L	ERA	G	GS	CG	SV	IP	H	R	ER	HR	BB	SO	AVG	vLH	vRH	K/9	BB/9
Kelvin Alarcon	B-R	6-1	155	3-6-99	0	0	9.00	1	0	0	0	1	3	1	1	0	1	1	.500	.000	.600	9.00	9.00
Charlis Aquino	R-R	6-2	165	11-18-01	0	0	10.80	2	0	0	0	2	3	2	2	0	1	1	.429	.333	.500	5.40	5.40
Michel Baez	R-R	6-8	220	1-21-96	0	0	1.17	4	2	0	0	8	3	1	1	0	1	9	.120	.000	.158	10.57	1.17
Matt Boswell	R-R	6-1	210	12-19-98	2	1	3.78	7	3	0	0	17	12	9	7	0	7	17	.197	.280	.139	9.18	3.78
Jose Castillo	L-L	6-6	252	1-10-96	0	0	0.00	5	0	0	0	5	4	1	0	0	1	7	.190	.000	.211	11.81	1.69
Wilton Castillo	R-R	6-7	190	2-12-00	0	2	15.26	3	3	0	0	8	15	13	13	1	6	7	.417	.533	.333	8.22	7.04
Manuel Castro	R-R	5-8	180	5-11-02	1	4	9.66	14	5	0	2	32	42	35	34	6	22	44	.318	.250	.363	12.51	6.25
Mike Clevinger	R-R	6-4	215	12-21-90	0	0	0.00	1	1	0	0	2	1	0	0	0	0	5	.143	.000	.250	22.50	0.00
Keegan Collett	R-R	6-3	215	7-27-98	5	0	3.00	31	0	0	4	45	30	19	15	3	31	82	.184	.206	.170	16.40	6.20
Danny Denz	L-L	5-9	205	5-20-98	0	1	9.82	14	1	0	1	22	25	24	24	5	21	27	.281	.500	.240	11.05	8.59
Mason Feole	L-L	6-1	194	8-28-98	0	1	108.00	1	0	0	0	0	3	4	4	0	3	0	1.000	--	1.000	0.00	81.00
Ruben Galindo	R-R	6-1	175	1-24-01	5	3	5.67	31	5	0	0	67	68	49	42	3	36	77	.264	.312	.228	10.40	4.86
Luis Garcia	R-R	6-2	240	1-30-87	0	0	0.00	2	0	0	0	2	2	0	0	0	0	3	.250	.200	.333	13.50	0.00
Will Geerdes	R-R	6-2	220	3-21-00	1	1	4.40	5	2	0	0	14	14	9	7	0	9	17	.241	.100	.393	10.67	5.65
Jesus Gonzalez	L-L	5-10	160	6-12-01	7	6	5.22	21	19	0	0	91	99	59	53	11	33	69	.282	.288	.281	6.80	3.25
Jordan Guerrero	R-R	6-5	296	8-1-96	0	0	10.80	4	0	0	0	3	6	4	4	1	1	3	.375	.364	.400	8.10	2.70
Garrett Hawkins	R-R	6-5	230	2-10-00	5	5	3.94	17	17	0	0	78	73	40	34	9	20	108	.245	.215	.268	12.52	2.32
Brenden Heiss	R-R	6-0	200	9-15-97	0	0	16.20	5	0	0	0	5	5	9	9	1	14	6	.278	.000	.556	10.80	25.20
Wyatt Hoffman	R-R	5-9	170	3-16-99	0	0	18.00	1	0	0	0	1	3	2	2	1	0	0	.500	.600	.000	0.00	0.00
Aaron Holiday	R-R	6-3	205	5-28-00	5	4	4.42	35	0	0	3	57	52	35	28	7	24	74	.240	.244	.237	11.68	3.79
Jairo Iriarte	R-R	6-2	160	12-15-01	4	7	5.12	21	18	0	0	91	83	56	52	13	42	109	.236	.238	.236	10.74	4.14
Jared Kollar	R-R	6-0	195	7-24-98	0	1	5.27	7	3	0	0	14	16	8	8	2	3	13	.296	.286	.300	8.56	1.98
Austin Krob	L-L	6-3	205	9-20-99	0	0	13.50	2	2	0	0	3	6	5	5	1	2	4	.353	.333	.357	10.80	5.40
Yerry Landinez	B-R	6-1	170	1-20-01	3	2	5.91	30	0	0	3	43	51	38	28	11	19	45	.293	.333	.260	9.49	4.01
Victor Lizarraga	R-R	6-3	180	11-30-03	8	3	3.43	20	19	0	0	94	87	48	36	5	34	95	.244	.216	.268	9.06	3.24
Carter Loewen	R-R	6-4	240	9-28-98	0	0	20.25	2	0	0	0	1	4	3	3	0	2	1	.500	.429	1.000	6.75	13.50
Justin Lopez	B-R	6-2	195	5-9-00	0	0	0.00	4	0	0	2	3	0	0	0	0	2	3	.000	.000	.000	8.10	5.40
Ben Miller	L-L	6-4	225	9-29-99	3	4	3.58	38	0	0	7	55	65	33	22	2	24	45	.294	.294	.294	7.32	3.90
Adrian Morejon	L-L	5-11	224	2-27-99	0	1	10.80	2	2	0	0	3	7	5	4	1	0	7	.412	.250	.462	18.90	0.00
Alan Mundo	R-R	6-2	170	5-27-00	5	1	2.23	27	0	0	3	48	35	13	12	0	20	68	.197	.197	.197	12.66	3.72
Dylan Nedved	R-R	6-2	195	4-23-99	0	1	12.00	7	0	0	0	9	15	14	12	2	10	3	.385	.500	.355	3.00	10.00
Ryan Och	R-L	6-0	205	7-18-98	0	0	3.55	8	0	0	3	13	4	5	5	0	8	22	.100	.222	.065	15.63	5.68
Kervin Pichardo	R-R	6-0	180	10-15-01	0	0	18.00	2	0	0	0	2	5	4	4	1	2	1	.455	.500	.429	4.50	9.00
Drew Pomeranz	R-L	6-5	246	11-22-88	0	0	4.50	2	1	0	0	2	3	1	1	0	0	2	.375	.000	.429	9.00	0.00
Hazahel Quijada	L-L	6-2	185	9-18-97	6	1	4.18	32	0	0	3	52	52	25	24	2	35	57	.264	.278	.261	9.93	6.10
Bodi Rascon	L-L	6-5	205	2-3-01	4	2	4.20	16	14	0	0	64	69	38	30	5	23	57	.270	.200	.291	7.97	3.22
Kobe Robinson	R-R	6-2	160	3-3-01	1	0	3.57	7	3	0	0	23	18	9	9	2	12	31	.220	.200	.234	12.31	4.76
Fernando Sanchez	L-L	6-0	198	9-13-00	0	0	4.05	3	2	0	0	7	5	3	3	0	6	9	.208	.333	.167	12.15	8.10
Blake Snell	L-L	6-4	225	12-4-92	0	0	6.75	1	1	0	0	4	4	4	3	1	2	8	.250	--	.250	18.00	4.50
Duncan Snider	R-R	6-7	235	10-10-97	6	1	4.31	11	6	0	0	48	45	25	23	3	12	57	.250	.284	.217	10.69	2.25
Matt Sparling	R-L	5-11	200	2-24-98	2	1	9.35	14	0	0	0	17	25	21	18	0	18	17	.338	.227	.385	8.83	9.35
Craig Stammen	R-R	6-2	228	3-9-84	0	0	0.00	2	1	0	0	3	0	0	0	0	2	3	.000	.000	.000	10.13	6.75
Matthew Swilley	R-R	6-2	175	12-19-90	1	0	4.50	15	0	0	0	14	15	10	7	1	11	19	.268	.227	.294	12.21	7.07
Levi Thomas	R-R	5-11	185	6-29-98	2	0	4.60	10	2	0	1	31	33	18	16	3	21	40	.282	.225	.312	11.49	6.03
Alexuan Vega	L-L	6-2	160	6-22-99	1	2	8.20	27	0	0	2	53	70	57	48	6	32	34	.314	.277	.324	5.81	5.47
Juan Zabala	R-R	5-10	190	7-3-99	0	0	0.00	1	0	0	0	1	0	0	0	0	1	0	.000	.000	.000	0.00	13.50

SAN DIEGO PADRES

Fielding

Catcher	PCT	G	PO	A	E	DP	PB
Alvarez-Lopez	.993	55	513	42	4	2	18
Aquino	.000	1	0	0	0	0	0
Bender	.963	11	95	8	4	1	1
Duarte	.992	23	240	20	2	2	4
Dunn	1.000	2	9	2	0	0	0
Hernandez	.955	4	19	2	1	0	0
Malone	.958	3	22	1	1	0	2
Quintero	1.000	2	7	0	0	0	1
Vizcarra	.979	4	39	7	1	1	1
Zabala	.987	40	356	26	5	3	1

First Base	PCT	G	PO	A	E	DP
Acosta	1.000	2	13	0	0	1
Alarcon	1.000	2	8	1	0	1
Alvarez-Lopez	1.000	2	5	1	0	2
Castanon	1.000	2	9	0	0	2
Cedeno	.985	11	65	2	1	11
Cummings	.996	26	214	13	1	21
Doersching	.994	19	146	10	1	11
Duarte	.000	1	0	0	0	0
Dunn	.965	7	55	0	2	5
Fabian	1.000	7	28	1	0	3
Luis	.983	52	385	24	7	31
Malone	.917	2	9	2	1	0
Martorella	1.000	7	53	2	0	6
Pichardo	1.000	1	2	0	0	0
Zabala	.971	5	33	0	1	2

Second Base	PCT	G	PO	A	E	DP
Aquino	.947	7	6	12	1	4
Castanon	.962	19	30	46	3	13
Cedeno	.972	59	106	137	7	33
Dunn	.867	3	5	8	2	3
Ferguson	.984	18	24	39	1	8
Hoffman	.987	16	30	45	1	13
Pauley	.967	12	21	38	2	3
Pichardo	.900	9	17	19	4	4

Third Base	PCT	G	PO	A	E	DP
Aquino	.000	2	0	0	0	0
Castanon	.954	85	48	139	9	12
Dunn	.914	21	8	24	3	4
Hoffman	1.000	2	2	1	0	0
Luis	.833	14	6	14	4	1
Pauley	1.000	2	0	4	0	0
Pichardo	.917	21	10	34	4	4
Zabala	1.000	1	1	0	0	0

Shortstop	PCT	G	PO	A	E	DP
Aquino	.934	22	20	51	5	5
Ferguson	.981	40	52	103	3	21
Hoffman	.962	19	22	54	3	10
Luis	1.000	1	2	0	0	0
Merrill	.948	42	61	103	9	27
Pauley	1.000	1	1	1	0	1
Pichardo	.872	17	13	28	6	3

Outfield	PCT	G	PO	A	E	DP
Acosta	.957	26	44	1	2	0
Aquino	.966	20	26	2	1	1
Bender	--	1	0	0	0	0
Dunn	1.000	5	2	0	0	0
Fabian	.910	53	58	3	6	0
Farmer	.983	106	164	8	3	3
Ferguson	1.000	7	14	0	0	0
Green	1.000	7	5	1	0	0
Heredia	1.000	3	2	0	0	0
Hoffman	1.000	3	6	1	0	0
Jones	.958	25	22	1	1	0
Luis	1.000	3	3	1	0	0
Malone	.917	15	21	1	2	0
Marsee	.974	17	36	2	1	0
Martorella	1.000	5	4	0	0	0
Murphy	1.000	13	14	0	0	0
Myers	1.000	1	3	0	0	0
Pauley	1.000	5	3	0	0	0
Pichardo	.867	6	11	2	2	0
Robertson	--	2	0	0	0	0
Salinas	.900	10	9	0	1	0
Solarte	.926	21	24	1	2	0
Wood	.959	45	92	2	4	1
Zavala	.953	32	59	2	3	0

ACL PADRES — *ROOKIE*

ARIZONA COMPLEX LEAGUE

Batting	B-T	HT	WT	DOB	AVG	vLH	vRH	G	AB	R	H	2B	3B	HR	RBI	BB	HBP	SH	SF	SO	SB	CS	SLG	OBP
Victor Acosta	B-R	5-11	170	6-10-04	.243	.154	.271	32	111	17	27	3	2	2	11	16	2	1	1	30	5	7	.360	.346
2-team total (10 ACL Reds)					.237	.161	.259	42	139	22	33	7	2	2	12	21	3	1	1	37	5	7	.360	.348
Kelvin Alarcon	B-R	6-1	155	3-6-99	.272	.250	.281	30	81	11	22	2	0	0	12	11	0	0	3	17	3	0	.296	.347
Matt Beaty	L-R	6-0	215	4-28-93	.000	.000	.000	3	8	0	0	0	0	0	0	1	0	0	0	1	0	0	.000	.111
Eddy Beltre	R-R	5-11	165	4-16-04	.259	.259	.259	28	85	19	22	4	0	0	8	14	5	0	0	26	7	8	.306	.394
Colton Bender	R-R	5-9	195	1-13-99	.225	.050	.294	28	71	14	16	3	0	2	8	18	2	0	0	15	0	0	.352	.396
Jacob Campbell	R-R	6-0	200	5-21-00	.333	.000	.500	6	6	2	2	0	0	0	0	2	4	0	0	2	0	0	.333	.667
Spence Coffman	R-R	6-1	170	1-7-04	.000	.000	.000	5	11	0	0	0	0	0	0	1	0	1	0	4	0	1	.000	.083
Josttin Diaz	B-R	6-0	170	5-18-02	.246	.167	.271	44	126	18	31	5	5	2	18	13	0	0	0	52	4	2	.413	.317
Brandon Dixon	R-R	6-2	215	1-29-92	.667	--	.667	1	3	2	2	0	0	0	0	0	0	0	0	0	0	0	.667	.667
Griffin Doersching	R-R	6-4	251	8-12-98	.400	.000	.444	5	10	4	4	1	0	1	1	2	1	0	0	2	0	0	.800	.538
Albert Fabian	L-L	6-0	215	12-21-01	.444	.400	.500	3	9	2	4	1	0	0	2	1	1	0	0	2	1	0	.556	.545
Michael Green	L-L	6-0	190	6-10-98	.286	.000	.333	5	14	4	4	1	0	0	2	1	1	0	0	7	0	0	.357	.375
Alejandro Hernandez	R-R	5-11	175	10-19-99	.250	.000	.333	4	4	1	1	0	0	0	1	3	0	0	1	0	0	0	.250	.500
Kaden Hollow	L-R	6-1	210	3-17-01	.111	.000	.167	5	9	0	1	0	0	0	2	1	0	0	0	4	0	0	.111	.200
Jonny Homza	R-R	6-0	185	6-13-99	.160	.500	.095	9	25	4	4	2	0	0	2	4	1	0	0	9	1	0	.240	.300
Reinaldo Ilarraza	B-R	5-10	150	1-12-99	.211	.200	.214	7	19	2	4	1	0	1	2	2	1	0	0	9	2	0	.421	.318
Braedon Karpathios	L-L	6-1	186	6-19-03	.211	.000	.267	7	19	2	4	0	0	1	4	2	0	0	0	5	0	0	.368	.286
Lamar King Jr.	R-R	6-3	215	12-7-03	.111	--	.111	4	9	1	1	0	0	0	1	1	1	0	0	2	0	0	.111	.273
Tyler Malone	L-R	5-11	190	11-4-97	.333	--	.333	2	3	0	1	1	0	0	0	0	0	0	0	0	0	0	.667	.333
Jakob Marsee	L-L	6-0	180	6-28-01	.212	.000	.259	13	33	13	7	1	1	0	3	14	0	0	0	10	3	0	.303	.447
Nathan Martorella	L-L	6-1	224	2-18-01	.387	.500	.370	11	31	4	12	4	0	1	10	4	0	0	0	6	0	0	.613	.457
Joshua Mears	R-R	6-3	230	2-21-01	.268	.273	.267	17	56	10	15	6	1	3	10	8	1	0	1	26	2	0	.571	.364
Jackson Merrill	L-R	6-3	195	4-19-03	.433	.556	.381	10	30	5	13	3	1	1	6	1	0	0	0	2	3	0	.700	.452
Juan Murillo	R-R	6-2	180	8-19-02	.308	.185	.351	37	104	22	32	6	0	4	18	5	4	0	0	26	10	0	.481	.363
Kai Murphy	L-L	5-8	173	8-26-00	.357	.667	.273	9	14	5	5	1	0	0	2	3	0	0	0	5	0	0	.429	.471
Devin Ortiz	R-R	6-2	215	2-7-99	.167	.000	.200	5	12	0	2	0	0	0	1	1	0	0	0	1	0	0	.167	.231
Willmert Paula	L-R	6-1	165	9-30-01	.000	.000	.000	1	2	0	0	0	0	0	0	0	0	0	0	0	0	0	.000	.000
Graham Pauley	L-R	6-1	200	9-24-00	.213	.000	.270	15	47	9	10	3	1	2	12	9	0	0	1	7	0	0	.447	.333
Jake Perez	R-R	6-0	165	7-5-00	.208	.300	.186	23	53	10	11	1	1	0	8	8	1	0	1	26	2	1	.264	.317
Matias Polanco	L-R	5-11	175	9-18-00	.500	.500	--	1	2	0	1	0	0	0	0	0	0	0	0	0	0	0	.500	.500
Alison Quintero	R-R	5-11	175	4-24-00	.000	--	.000	2	1	1	0	0	0	0	0	1	0	0	0	1	0	0	.000	.500
Tyler Robertson	R-R	6-4	200	3-10-00	.208	.000	.227	11	24	4	5	0	1	1	5	4	0	0	0	4	0	0	.417	.321
Carlos Rodriguez	B-R	5-10	155	5-12-03	.192	.273	.171	21	52	4	10	2	0	1	8	7	0	0	0	13	1	0	.288	.288
Edwin Rojas	R-R	6-2	170	11-12-01	.216	.143	.233	17	37	7	8	3	0	0	6	6	2	0	0	12	1	1	.297	.356
Ruben Salinas	R-L	6-0	154	1-13-03	.318	.438	.280	37	132	24	42	8	2	4	31	12	1	0	1	43	5	3	.500	.377
Romeo Sanabria	L-R	6-2	200	5-2-02	.083	--	.083	7	12	1	1	1	0	0	0	3	0	0	0	6	0	0	.167	.267
Ethan Skender	R-R	5-11	185	12-22-96	.000	.000	.000	5	12	1	0	0	0	0	0	2	1	0	0	2	0	0	.000	.200
Bryan Torres	R-R	5-9	165	12-11-99	.200	.000	.250	5	10	0	2	0	0	0	1	1	0	0	0	7	0	0	.200	.273
Chase Valentine	R-R	5-11	160	4-22-02	.120	.250	.095	12	25	4	3	1	1	0	0	2	0	0	0	17	0	0	.240	.185

Rosman Verdugo	R-R	6-0	180	2-2-05	.251	.250	.252	52	167	26	42	7	4	7	35	22	2	0	4	69	3	4	.467	.338
Gilberto Vizcarra	R-R	5-10	180	3-1-99	.269	.286	.263	19	52	8	14	4	0	0	10	3	3	0	1	7	1	0	.346	.339
Nick Vogt	R-R	6-1	185	8-4-00	.125	.200	.091	5	16	1	2	0	0	0	0	2	0	0	0	3	1	0	.125	.222
James Wood	L-R	6-7	240	9-17-02	.125	.250	.083	5	16	1	2	0	0	0	0	3	0	0	0	7	1	0	.125	.263
Samuel Zavala	L-L	6-1	175	7-15-04	.345	.400	.333	10	29	6	10	3	1	1	6	4	0	1	1	11	0	0	.621	.412

Pitching	B-T	HT	WT	DOB	W	L	ERA	G	GS	CG	SV	IP	H	R	ER	HR	BB	SO	AVG	vLH	vRH	K/9	BB/9
Luis Acosta	R-R	6-1	175	2-5-01	2	1	4.60	8	0	0	0	16	16	11	8	2	11	19	.267	.273	.263	10.91	6.32
Henry Baez	R-R	6-3	175	10-12-02	1	4	3.82	9	7	0	0	31	28	24	13	0	13	41	.235	.306	.205	12.03	3.82
Wilton Castillo	R-R	6-7	190	2-12-00	0	0	0.00	4	1	0	0	4	3	0	0	0	0	9	.200	.111	.333	20.25	0.00
Manuel Castro	R-R	5-8	180	5-11-02	1	1	0.00	2	0	0	0	9	2	3	0	1	4	11	.069	.143	.045	11.42	4.15
Javier Chacon	L-L	5-11	190	12-24-02	1	1	3.07	11	6	0	0	41	35	21	14	7	19	60	.216	.222	.214	13.17	4.17
Mason Feole	L-L	6-1	194	8-28-98	0	0	0.00	3	0	0	0	3	2	0	0	0	2	7	.182	.000	.250	21.00	6.00
Jeferson Garcia	R-R	6-0	165	2-4-00	0	1	9.64	5	1	0	0	5	6	5	5	1	5	4	.333	.333	.333	7.71	9.64
Jordan Guerrero	R-R	6-5	296	8-1-96	0	0	0.00	2	2	0	0	2	2	0	0	0	0	2	.250	.400	.000	9.00	0.00
Luis Gutierrez	L-L	6-0	175	7-31-03	0	0	2.04	6	2	0	0	18	10	5	4	3	15	10	.189	.167	.195	5.09	7.64
Brenden Heiss	R-R	6-0	200	9-15-97	2	2	6.75	13	0	0	2	16	14	14	12	0	11	18	.233	.389	.167	10.13	6.19
Cristian Heredia	R-R	6-3	175	4-12-01	0	0	0.00	1	0	0	0	1	1	0	0	0	1	1	.250	.500	.000	9.00	9.00
Pierce Johnson	R-R	6-2	202	5-10-91	0	0	0.00	1	1	0	0	1	0	0	0	0	0	1	.000	.000	.000	9.00	0.00
Ian Koenig	L-R	6-2	225	4-10-01	0	0	0.00	1	0	0	0	1	0	0	0	0	0	1	.000	.000	.000	9.00	0.00
Austin Krob	L-L	6-3	205	9-20-99	0	0	0.00	1	0	0	0	1	0	0	0	0	0	0	.000	--	.000	0.00	0.00
Walki Lezan	R-R	6-0	165	4-24-02	3	1	7.90	15	0	0	1	27	33	27	24	4	17	37	.292	.429	.231	12.18	5.60
Carter Loewen	R-R	6-4	240	9-28-98	1	0	0.00	2	0	0	0	2	1	1	0	0	0	2	.143	.333	.000	9.00	0.00
Justin Lopez	B-R	6-2	195	5-9-00	4	0	1.29	5	0	0	1	7	7	2	1	0	3	9	.250	.300	.222	11.57	3.86
Adrian Luna	R-R	6-0	160	7-27-01	3	1	7.03	11	1	0	0	32	31	25	25	5	22	29	.258	.342	.220	8.16	6.19
Miguel Mendez	R-R	6-2	165	7-1-02	0	1	7.97	18	0	0	2	20	19	18	18	1	14	34	.238	.214	.250	15.05	6.20
David Morgan	R-R	6-0	185	10-26-99	0	0	3.00	3	0	0	0	3	3	2	1	0	1	4	.273	.500	.143	12.00	3.00
Juan Murillo	R-R	6-2	180	8-19-02	0	0	0.00	2	0	0	0	2	0	0	0	0	0	4	.000	.000	.000	18.00	0.00
Braden Nett	R-R	6-3	185	6-18-02	0	0	3.00	3	0	0	0	3	2	2	1	0	2	5	.167	.500	.000	15.00	6.00
Ryan Och	R-L	6-0	205	7-18-98	0	1	4.50	2	2	0	0	2	3	1	1	0	1	2	.429	.333	.500	9.00	4.50
Reinier Parra	R-R	6-0	155	5-31-01	3	1	6.23	16	0	0	1	22	23	15	15	2	14	28	.267	.400	.239	11.63	5.82
Joshua Paulina	R-R	6-6	220	2-9-02	0	1	25.58	9	0	0	1	6	14	20	18	1	14	7	.438	.700	.318	9.95	19.89
Jake Perez	R-R	6-0	165	7-5-00	1	0	0.00	1	0	0	0	2	1	0	0	0	1	0	.200	.200	--	0.00	4.50
Drew Pomeranz	R-L	6-5	246	11-22-88	0	0	0.00	1	1	0	0	1	0	0	0	0	0	2	.000	.000	.000	18.00	0.00
Jose Quezada	R-R	5-9	165	9-7-95	0	0	0.00	1	1	0	0	1	0	0	0	0	0	1	.000	--	.000	9.00	0.00
Jose Luis Reyes	R-R	6-3	190	8-20-02	1	0	2.08	5	0	0	0	4	6	3	1	0	4	4	.333	.600	.231	8.31	8.31
Miguel Rondon	R-R	5-11	150	1-26-01	2	4	5.40	11	7	0	0	42	38	27	25	5	16	40	.245	.212	.262	8.64	3.46
Ethan Routzahn	R-R	6-4	225	3-19-98	0	0	9.00	1	1	0	0	1	2	1	1	0	0	1	.400	1.000	.000	9.00	0.00
Elvis Saba	R-R	5-11	180	5-11-00	0	1	15.75	4	2	0	0	4	11	7	7	2	2	3	.478	.500	.462	6.75	4.50
Fernando Sanchez	L-L	6-0	198	9-13-00	1	2	4.87	9	8	0	0	20	16	12	11	2	8	31	.213	.333	.197	13.72	3.54
Matt Sparling	R-L	5-11	200	2-24-98	0	0	0.00	1	0	0	0	1	0	0	0	0	2	2	.000	.000	.000	18.00	18.00
Robert Suarez	R-R	6-2	210	3-1-91	0	0	0.00	1	1	0	0	1	0	0	0	0	0	3	.000	--	.000	27.00	0.00
Jarlin Susana	R-R	6-6	235	3-23-04	0	0	2.45	8	7	0	0	29	15	8	8	1	11	44	.155	.167	.148	13.50	3.38
Evan Sweeting	R-R	6-1	185	10-4-01	2	0	2.20	11	0	0	0	16	11	5	4	2	10	19	.200	.190	.206	10.47	5.51
Levi Thomas	R-R	5-11	185	6-29-98	0	0	0.00	2	2	0	0	5	2	2	0	0	3	5	.125	.000	.182	9.64	5.79
Chase Walter	R-R	6-7	260	7-26-98	0	0	18.00	2	1	0	0	1	0	2	2	0	3	1	.000	.000	.000	9.00	27.00
Riley Yeatman	R-R	6-5	180	2-12-04	1	2	10.13	7	0	0	1	16	19	18	18	7	7	18	.306	.308	.306	10.13	3.94

Fielding

C: Bender 22, Campbell 5, Hernandez 4, Hollow 5, King Jr. 3, Polanco 1, Rodriguez 14, Sanabria 6, Vizcarra 14. **1B:** Alarcon 15, Diaz 26, Dixon 1, Doersching 4, Martorella 10, Ortiz 2, Perez 2, Quintero 1, Rodriguez 6. **2B:** Acosta 9, Alarcon 2, Coffman 3, Diaz 2, Ilarraza 6, Pauley 9, Perez 4, Skender 4, Torres 1, Verdugo 27. **3B:** Alarcon 13, Diaz 15, Ilarraza 1, Ortiz 3, Pauley 7, Perez 13, Robertson 2, Torres 3, Verdugo 14. **SS:** Acosta 27, Coffman 1, Merrill 10, Valentine 11, Verdugo 17. **OF:** Beaty 1, Beltre 25, Diaz 5, Fabian 3, Green 5, Heredia 1, Karpathios 6, Malone 1, Marsee 14, Mears 14, Murillo 29, Murphy 6, Paula 1, Perez 4, Robertson 7, Rojas 16, Salinas 31, Vogt 5, Wood 5, Zavala 8.

DSL PADRES — *ROOKIE*

DOMINICAN SUMMER LEAGUE

Batting	B-T	HT	WT	DOB	AVG	vLH	vRH	G	AB	R	H	2B	3B	HR	RBI	BB	HBP	SH	SF	SO	SB	CS	SLG	OBP
Alain Camou	L-R	5-11	150	11-1-03	.333	.333	.333	55	201	45	67	15	2	1	30	33	2	1	3	22	10	6	.443	.427
Oliver Carrillo	R-R	5-11	210	1-19-02	.328	.286	.337	38	125	28	41	8	2	9	32	26	3	0	1	35	4	0	.640	.452
Jesus Castro	R-R	5-10	158	7-7-04	.233	.000	.286	19	43	8	10	2	0	0	3	10	0	0	1	13	4	1	.279	.370
Oliver Cedeno	B-R	5-10	160	9-10-04	.000	--	.000	2	3	0	0	0	0	0	0	0	0	0	0	0	0	0	.000	.000
Nestor Chevalier	R-R	6-0	165	9-25-04	.184	.143	.194	19	38	5	7	2	0	0	5	5	0	0	0	14	4	1	.237	.279
Kashon Conliffe	R-R	5-11	150	7-5-05	.215	.250	.208	43	121	29	26	4	2	6	26	19	1	1	3	52	14	1	.430	.319
Jose Cordero	R-R	6-1	165	5-24-03	.272	.222	.289	38	103	19	28	3	3	2	10	16	2	0	2	42	12	2	.417	.374
Eizon Delgado	R-R	5-11	170	3-24-04	.000	.000	.000	4	6	1	0	0	0	0	0	2	0	0	0	2	1	0	.000	.250
Estiven Giron	R-R	5-11	170	5-25-05	.250	.417	.208	21	60	8	15	4	1	1	10	7	2	0	2	13	0	0	.400	.338
Oswaldo Linares	R-R	5-11	150	4-28-03	.274	.333	.261	50	146	31	40	7	0	5	31	27	7	0	3	28	3	0	.425	.404
Maikol Munoz	R-R	6-1	155	10-21-03	.288	.355	.275	53	184	32	53	10	1	5	32	21	6	0	2	52	2	2	.435	.376
Adrian Perez	R-R	5-9	165	10-3-02	.237	.263	.231	38	97	17	23	9	0	3	24	19	0	0	1	24	2	2	.423	.359
Yendry Rojas	L-R	6-0	185	1-27-05	.279	.172	.304	46	154	29	43	4	4	0	18	26	0	2	5	23	14	6	.357	.373
Jose Sanabria	R-R	5-10	150	10-30-02	.309	.394	.293	57	207	43	64	12	2	2	25	32	3	2	4	47	7	3	.415	.402
Hugo Sanchez	L-R	6-0	180	11-6-02	.284	.235	.293	41	116	31	33	3	2	2	14	32	2	0	1	31	11	1	.397	.444
Estuar Suero	B-R	6-5	180	8-29-05	.250	.241	.252	47	152	33	38	7	3	3	21	21	2	0	1	52	14	4	.395	.347
Ramses Velazquez	L-L	6-0	180	10-14-04	.000	.000	.000	2	4	1	0	0	0	0	0	1	0	0	0	3	1	0	.000	.200

Heber Villalobos	R-R	5-11	180	9-24-03	.150	.333	.118	10	20	6	3	1	0	0	2	5	1	0	0	4	0	0	.200	.346

Pitching	**B-T**	**HT**	**WT**	**DOB**	**W**	**L**	**ERA**	**G**	**GS**	**CG**	**SV**	**IP**	**H**	**R**	**ER**	**HR**	**BB**	**SO**	**AVG**	**vLH**	**vRH**	**K/9**	**BB/9**
Josmar Acevedo	R-R	6-1	170	12-22-03	1	2	4.88	11	9	0	0	31	32	22	17	3	20	29	.254	.304	.214	8.33	5.74
Luis Acosta	R-R	6-1	175	2-5-01	1	1	4.30	6	0	0	0	15	13	11	7	0	9	12	.245	.333	.200	7.36	5.52
Juan Arias	R-R	6-3	190	6-21-02	0	0	5.01	15	0	0	0	23	26	14	13	0	12	23	.292	.270	.308	8.87	4.63
Joel Asencio	R-R	6-7	180	3-26-03	3	1	7.50	12	0	0	0	18	22	31	15	1	14	18	.286	.333	.244	9.00	7.00
Jhosep Chirinos	R-R	6-4	175	4-17-04	1	0	1.37	12	11	0	0	39	24	10	6	0	19	52	.169	.140	.170	11.90	4.35
Angel Garza	R-R	6-1	200	12-7-04	0	2	6.39	15	3	0	0	31	32	22	22	2	18	32	.274	.213	.314	9.29	5.23
Luis German	R-R	6-2	160	10-14-01	0	1	10.50	7	0	0	0	6	6	7	7	0	8	8	.286	.250	.308	12.00	12.00
Geral Gonzales	R-R	6-0	170	9-20-02	1	0	12.71	6	0	0	0	6	8	8	8	1	8	7	.333	.250	.375	11.12	12.71
Luis Gutierrez	L-L	6-0	175	7-31-03	2	0	2.03	6	0	0	0	13	13	6	3	0	6	12	.250	.182	.268	8.10	4.05
Aldo Leija	R-R	6-2	160	6-30-04	0	3	1.87	12	12	0	0	43	33	14	9	3	8	54	.212	.197	.222	11.22	1.66
Yariel Moreno	R-R	6-5	190	6-28-04	7	0	2.13	12	2	0	0	42	31	11	10	0	17	36	.207	.267	.167	7.65	3.61
Rafael Nava	R-R	5-11	155	6-5-05	0	0	0.00	2	0	0	0	3	0	0	0	0	1	2	.000	.000	.000	6.75	3.38
Francis Pena	R-R	6-1	170	1-25-01	2	2	7.43	14	0	0	2	23	33	22	19	2	15	19	.340	.341	.310	7.43	5.07
Enmanuel Pinales	R-R	6-2	185	4-16-01	2	4	7.75	11	4	0	0	36	54	36	31	6	17	32	.355	.389	.325	8.00	4.25
Jonney Rosario	R-R	5-10	185	7-28-04	3	2	4.01	12	11	0	0	52	51	26	23	4	15	53	.258	.240	.275	9.23	2.61
Xavier Ruiz	R-R	6-1	180	11-19-02	1	2	3.86	9	0	0	1	12	19	18	5	1	6	4	.373	.412	.353	3.09	4.63
Braian Salazar	L-L	6-2	165	6-12-05	0	1	4.30	7	7	0	0	15	12	8	7	2	5	12	.231	.267	.216	7.36	3.07
Jeison Sanchez	R-R	6-0	170	5-12-04	0	0	4.50	10	0	0	0	8	8	5	4	1	5	10	.258	.077	.389	11.25	5.63
Santiago Sojo	R-R	6-4	185	12-24-00	4	1	1.02	16	0	0	7	18	12	5	2	1	7	23	.185	.071	.270	11.72	3.57
Jefren Tejeda	L-L	6-1	170	7-24-03	2	1	4.76	14	0	0	1	23	23	17	12	2	17	26	.271	.318	.254	10.32	6.75
Javier Zenizo	R-R	5-8	160	1-13-03	0	0	6.00	6	0	0	1	6	8	4	4	2	4	6	.308	.364	.267	9.00	6.00

Fielding

C: Castro 10, Giron 2, Linares 46, Villalobos 7. **1B:** Carrillo 10, Castro 7, Giron 11, Munoz 4, Perez 14, Sanabria 2, Sanchez 23, Villalobos 2. **2B:** Camou 53, Chevalier 5, Sanabria 2, Sanchez 5, Villalobos 1. **3B:** Munoz 35, Perez 19, Sanabria 2, Sanchez 11. **SS:** Camou 2, Cedeno 2, Rojas 35, Sanabria 26. **OF:** Carrillo 24, Chevalier 13, Conliffe 35, Cordero 39, Delgado 1, Sanabria 31, Sanchez 8, Suero 44, Velazquez 2

San Francisco Giants

SEASON IN A SENTENCE: After a 2021 season when they won a sport-best 107 games, the Giants fell back to earth in 2022, finished with a .500 winning percentage and missed the playoffs.

HIGH POINT: From June 10-12, the Giants won three straight against the eventual-division champion Dodgers. San Francisco won by an aggregate score of 12-4, including a 2-0 shutout in the finale when Carlos Rodon bested Julio Urias in a battle of premier lefthanded starters.

LOW POINT: From July 21-27, the Giants dropped seven straight games, including four to the Dodgers and three more to the D-backs. While Los Angeles dominated the regular season, Arizona did not. The D-backs won 74 games all season, but 10 of those wins came against San Francisco.

NOTABLE ROOKIES: Catcher Joey Bart continued to struggle at the plate, finishing with a .660 OPS and 11 home runs in 261 at-bats. The highest wins above replacement total, as measured by Baseball Reference, came from third baseman David Villar, an 11th-round pick from 2018 who hit his way to the big leagues. He clubbed nine home runs in 156 at-bats and finished with a .787 OPS, good for an OPS+ of 120.

KEY TRANSACTIONS: The Giants signed Rodon to a two-year deal worth a potential $44 million. The deal came with an opt-out clause, however, which Rodon exercised after the 2022 season.

ON THE FARM: The Giants' season on the farm was filled with unexpected outcomes in both directions. Their high draft picks from 2021—righthander Will Bednar and lefty Matt Mikulski—struggled with injuries and ineffectiveness. Neither made it out of Low-A. On the other side of the coin, outfielders Vaun Brown and Grant McCray had breakout seasons. The former bashed his way from Low-A to Double-A and won the minor league batting title with a .346 average. The latter showed an exciting tool set at both Class A levels and eventually helped High-A Eugene win the Northwest League crown. Third baseman Casey Schmitt also asserted himself as a force at the plate and in the field. The San Diego State alumnus produced an .854 OPS and reached Triple-A by season's end. He played standout defense at third base as well and filled in capably while Marco Luciano was on the injured list. He won Best Defensive Third Baseman in Baseball America's annual Best Tools survey.

OPENING DAY PAYROLL: $157,870,187 (13th)

PLAYERS OF THE YEAR

MAJOR LEAGUE	MINOR LEAGUE
Carlos Rodon	**Kyle Harrison**
LHP	**LHP**
14-8, 2.88 ERA	(HiA/AA)
237 SO, 52 BB, 178 IP	2.71 ERA, 1.13 WHIP
12.0 SO/9 led NL	186 SO, 49 BB, 113 IP

ORGANIZATION LEADERS

Batting		*Minimum 250 AB
MAJORS		
* AVG	Joc Pederson	.274
* OPS	Joc Pederson	.874
HR	Joc Pederson	23
RBI	Wilmer Flores	71
MINORS		
* AVG	Vaun Brown, San Jose, Eugene, Richmond	.346
* OBP	Vaun Brown, San Jose, Eugene, Richmond	.437
* SLG	Vaun Brown, San Jose, Eugene, Richmond	.623
* OPS	Vaun Brown, San Jose, Eugene, Richmond	1.023
R	Grant McCray, San Jose, Eugene	104
H	Grant McCray, San Jose, Eugene	141
TB	Grant McCray, San Jose, Eugene	251
2B	Aeverson Arteaga, San Jose	35
3B	Grant McCray, San Jose, Eugene	9
HR	David Villar, Sacramento	27
RBI	Aeverson Arteaga, San Jose	84
BB	Grant McCray, San Jose, Eugene	67
SO	Tyler Fitzgerald, Richmond	171
SB	Vaun Brown, San Jose, Eugene, Richmond	44

Pitching		#Minimum 75 IP
MAJORS		
W	Logan Webb	15
# ERA	Carlos Rodon	2.88
SO	Carlos Rodon	237
SV	Camilo Doval	27
MINORS		
W	Abel Adames, Eugene	11
L	Kai-Wei Teng, Richmond	12
# ERA	Trevor McDonald, San Jose, Eugene	2.31
G	Joey Marciano, Sacramento	56
GS	Kai-Wei Teng, Richmond	28
SV	Nick Avila, Eugene, Richmond	16
IP	Matt Frisbee, Richmond	139.2
BB	Kai-Wei Teng, Richmond	85
SO	Kyle Harrison, Eugene, Richmond	186
# AVG	Kyle Harrison, Eugene, Richmond	.193

2022 PERFORMANCE

General Manager: Scott Harris. **Farm Director:** Kyle Haines. **Scouting Director:** Michael Holmes.

Class	Team	League	W	L	PCT	Finish	Manager
Majors	San Francisco Giants	National	81	81	.500	8th (15)	Gabe Kapler
Triple-A	Sacramento River Cats	Pacific Coast	65	83	.439	9th (10)	Dave Brundage
Double-A	Richmond Flying Squirrels	Eastern	66	71	.482	8th (12)	Dennis Pelfrey
High-A	Eugene Emeralds	Northwest	81	48	.628	1st (6)	Carlos Valderrama
Low-A	San Jose Giants	California	74	58	.561	3rd (8)	Lipso Nava
Rookie	ACL Giants Black	Arizona Complex	37	17	.685	1st (18)	Jose Montilla
Rookie	ACL Giants Orange	Arizona Complex	18	37	.327	18th (18)	Greg Tagert
Overall 2022 Minor League Record			389	384	.503	14th (30)	

ORGANIZATION STATISTICS

SAN FRANCISCO GIANTS

NATIONAL LEAGUE

Batting	B-T	HT	WT	DOB	AVG	vLH	vRH	G	AB	R	H	2B	3B	HR	RBI	BB	HBP	SH	SF	SO	SB	CS	SLG	OBP
Joey Bart	R-R	6-2	238	12-15-96	.215	.182	.231	97	261	34	56	6	0	11	25	26	4	0	0	112	2	1	.364	.296
Brandon Belt	L-L	6-3	231	4-20-88	.213	.182	.223	78	254	25	54	9	1	8	23	37	6	0	1	81	1	0	.350	.326
Lewis Brinson	R-R	6-5	212	5-8-94	.167	.207	.000	16	36	5	6	2	0	3	4	2	0	1	0	14	1	0	.472	.211
Willie Calhoun	L-R	5-8	200	11-4-94	.125	--	.125	4	8	0	1	0	0	0	1	1	0	0	0	2	0	0	.125	.222
Curt Casali	R-R	6-2	220	11-9-88	.231	.345	.190	41	108	13	25	3	0	4	14	15	1	0	2	36	0	0	.370	.325
Brandon Crawford	L-R	6-1	223	1-21-87	.231	.241	.227	118	407	50	94	15	2	9	52	39	8	0	4	98	1	1	.344	.308
J.D. Davis	R-R	6-3	218	4-27-93	.263	.277	.250	49	137	20	36	8	0	8	14	19	2	0	0	56	0	0	.496	.361
2-team total (66 New York Mets)					.248	.245	.252	115	318	46	79	16	1	12	35	39	6	0	2	122	1	1	.418	.340
Austin Dean	R-R	6-0	215	10-14-93	.375	.333	.500	3	8	1	3	0	0	0	0	1	0	0	0	0	0	0	.375	.444
Mauricio Dubon	R-R	6-0	173	7-19-94	.239	.421	.111	21	46	10	11	1	0	2	8	1	0	0	2	4	0	0	.391	.245
Steven Duggar	L-R	6-1	187	11-4-93	.194	.000	.206	12	36	2	7	3	0	0	4	2	0	0	1	16	4	0	.278	.231
Thairo Estrada	R-R	5-10	185	2-22-96	.260	.283	.250	140	488	71	127	22	2	14	62	33	14	1	5	89	21	6	.400	.322
Stuart Fairchild	R-R	6-0	205	3-17-96	.000	.000	.000	5	8	1	0	0	0	0	0	0	0	0	0	3	0	0	.000	.000
2-team total (38 Cincinnati Reds)					.255	.250	.259	43	94	14	24	4	1	5	6	8	5	0	0	32	0	2	.479	.346
Wilmer Flores	R-R	6-2	213	8-6-91	.229	.223	.231	151	525	72	120	28	1	19	71	59	11	0	7	103	0	0	.394	.316
Mike Ford	L-R	6-0	225	7-4-92	.250	--	.250	1	4	0	1	0	0	0	2	0	0	0	0	0	0	0	.250	.250
2-team total (5 Atlanta Braves)					.091	--	.091	6	11	0	1	0	0	0	2	1	0	0	0	2	0	0	.091	.167
Luis Gonzalez	L-L	6-1	185	9-10-95	.254	.214	.272	98	311	31	79	17	2	4	36	30	4	0	5	75	10	2	.360	.323
Bryce Johnson	B-R	6-1	195	10-27-95	.111	.071	.250	11	18	1	2	0	0	0	2	1	0	0	0	7	0	0	.111	.158
Andrew Knapp	B-R	6-1	189	11-9-91	.250	.000	.333	3	4	2	1	0	0	0	2	2	0	0	1	0	0	0	.250	.429
2-team total (11 Pittsburgh Pirates)					.143	.250	.129	14	35	4	5	1	0	0	4	5	1	0	1	9	0	0	.171	.262
Jason Krizan	L-R	6-0	185	6-28-89	.125	--	.125	3	8	0	1	0	0	0	0	2	0	0	0	3	0	0	.125	.300
Tommy La Stella	L-R	5-11	180	1-31-89	.239	.190	.245	60	180	17	43	14	0	2	14	11	1	0	3	30	0	0	.350	.282
Evan Longoria	R-R	6-1	213	10-7-85	.244	.282	.215	89	266	31	65	13	0	14	42	27	2	0	3	83	0	0	.451	.315
Dixon Machado	R-R	6-1	190	2-22-92	.200	.222	.167	5	15	1	3	0	0	0	0	1	1	0	0	5	0	0	.200	.294
Yermin Mercedes	R-R	5-11	245	2-14-93	.233	.278	.105	31	73	9	17	5	0	1	8	9	1	0	0	17	0	0	.342	.325
Kevin Padlo	R-R	6-2	210	7-15-96	.167	.000	.250	4	12	0	2	0	0	0	0	0	0	0	0	4	0	0	.167	.167
2-team total (3 Pittsburgh Pirates)					.087	.000	.143	7	23	0	2	0	0	0	0	0	0	0	0	5	0	0	.087	.087
Michael Papierski	B-R	6-3	224	2-26-96	.000	.000	.000	5	9	1	0	0	0	0	0	1	0	0	0	4	0	0	.000	.100
2-team total (34 Cincinnati Reds)					.143	.095	.157	39	91	7	13	1	0	1	4	10	0	2	0	26	0	0	.187	.228
Joc Pederson	L-L	6-1	220	4-21-92	.274	.245	.278	134	380	57	104	19	3	23	70	42	7	0	4	100	3	2	.521	.353
Ford Proctor	L-R	6-1	195	12-4-96	.111	.000	.118	7	18	3	2	0	0	1	6	2	0	0	2	3	0	0	.278	.182
Heliot Ramos	R-R	6-1	188	9-7-99	.100	.125	.000	9	20	4	2	0	0	0	0	2	0	0	0	6	0	0	.100	.182
Darin Ruf	R-R	6-2	232	7-28-86	.216	.252	.191	90	268	46	58	9	0	11	38	40	5	0	1	85	2	0	.373	.328
2-team total (29 New York Mets)					.204	.222	.188	119	334	52	68	12	0	11	45	45	6	0	3	105	2	0	.338	.307
Austin Slater	R-R	6-1	204	12-13-92	.264	.277	.246	125	277	49	73	15	2	7	34	40	6	0	2	89	12	1	.408	.366
Ka'ai Tom	L-R	5-9	185	5-29-94	.000	.000	--	1	1	0	0	0	0	0	0	0	0	0	0	0	0	0	.000	.000
David Villar	R-R	6-1	215	1-27-97	.231	.292	.187	52	156	21	36	6	1	9	24	18	6	0	1	58	0	1	.455	.331
Jason Vosler	L-R	6-1	220	9-6-93	.265	.222	.270	36	98	14	26	6	1	4	12	10	2	0	1	29	1	1	.469	.342
LaMonte Wade Jr.	L-L	6-1	205	1-1-94	.207	.100	.225	77	217	29	45	7	1	8	26	26	5	2	1	51	1	0	.359	.305
Donovan Walton	L-R	5-10	190	5-25-94	.158	.133	.164	24	76	8	12	8	0	1	8	1	1	0	0	16	0	0	.303	.179
Luke Williams	R-R	6-1	186	8-9-96	.250	.250	.250	8	12	1	3	1	0	0	3	0	0	0	0	4	0	0	.333	.250
2-team total (71 Miami Marlins)					.236	.244	.232	79	127	21	30	5	1	1	6	9	0	0	0	44	11	4	.315	.287
Austin Wynns	R-R	6-0	190	12-10-90	.259	.234	.276	66	162	14	42	7	0	3	21	10	3	1	1	38	0	0	.358	.313
Mike Yastrzemski	L-L	5-10	178	8-23-90	.214	.179	.227	148	485	73	104	31	2	17	57	61	5	1	6	141	5	1	.392	.305

Pitching	B-T	HT	WT	DOB	W	L	ERA	G	GS	CG	SV	IP	H	R	ER	HR	BB	SO	AVG	vLH	vRH	K/9	BB/9
Scott Alexander	L-L	6-2	195	7-10-89	0	0	1.04	17	4	0	2	17	12	2	2	1	1	10	.194	.107	.265	5.19	0.52
Jose Alvarez	L-L	5-11	195	5-6-89	2	1	5.28	21	0	0	1	15	17	10	9	3	9	15	.270	.240	.289	8.80	5.28
Tyler Beede	R-R	6-2	216	5-23-93	0	0	4.66	6	0	0	0	10	14	5	5	1	6	4	.333	.333	.333	3.72	5.59
2-team total (25 Pittsburgh Pirates)					2	5	5.14	31	5	0	0	61	71	37	35	7	29	39	.284	.267	.300	5.72	4.26
John Brebbia	L-R	6-1	200	5-30-90	6	2	3.18	76	11	0	0	68	71	27	24	5	18	54	.268	.278	.262	7.15	2.38

Kervin Castro	R-R	6-0	185	2-7-99	0	0	27.00	2	0	0	0	2	4	5	5	0	2	4	.444	.500	.429	21.60	10.80
2-team total (8 Chicago Cubs)					0	1	10.22	10	0	0	0	12	15	14	14	3	7	11	.300	.353	.273	8.03	5.11
Alex Cobb	R-R	6-3	205	10-7-87	7	8	3.73	28	28	0	0	150	152	72	62	9	43	151	.262	.269	.256	9.08	2.59
Jharel Cotton	R-R	5-11	200	1-19-92	2	0	6.75	5	0	0	0	8	11	7	6	0	4	8	.344	.364	.333	9.00	4.50
Anthony DeSclafani	R-R	6-2	195	4-18-90	0	2	6.63	5	5	0	0	19	34	21	14	4	4	17	.400	.382	.412	8.05	1.89
Camilo Doval	R-R	6-2	185	7-4-97	6	6	2.53	68	0	0	27	68	54	27	19	4	30	80	.218	.261	.182	10.64	3.99
Jarlin Garcia	L-L	6-3	215	1-18-93	1	4	3.74	58	0	0	1	65	60	34	27	10	18	56	.242	.192	.275	7.75	2.49
Luis Gonzalez	L-L	6-1	185	9-10-95	0	0	5.68	5	0	0	0	6	9	4	4	0	1	0	.310	.286	.318	0.00	1.42
Sean Hjelle	R-R	6-11	228	5-7-97	1	2	5.76	8	0	0	0	25	33	19	16	3	8	28	.311	.205	.373	10.08	2.88
Jakob Junis	R-R	6-3	220	9-16-92	5	7	4.42	23	17	0	0	112	120	57	55	13	25	98	.269	.307	.235	7.88	2.01
Dominic Leone	R-R	5-10	215	10-26-91	4	5	4.01	55	0	0	3	49	55	24	22	6	24	52	.281	.333	.248	9.49	4.38
Zack Littell	R-R	6-4	220	10-5-95	3	3	5.08	39	0	0	1	44	48	25	25	8	13	39	.276	.220	.298	7.92	2.64
Mauricio Llovera	R-R	5-11	224	4-17-96	0	0	4.41	17	1	0	0	16	14	8	8	2	8	20	.219	.207	.229	11.02	4.41
Sam Long	L-L	6-1	185	7-8-95	1	3	3.61	28	6	0	1	42	39	23	17	8	14	33	.238	.423	.152	7.02	2.98
Yunior Marte	R-R	6-2	180	2-2-95	1	1	5.44	39	0	0	0	48	47	32	29	5	22	44	.255	.257	.254	8.25	4.13
Jake McGee	L-L	6-4	229	8-6-86	1	2	7.17	24	0	0	3	21	27	18	17	2	6	11	.303	.276	.317	4.64	2.53
3-team total (6 Mil. Brewers, 12 Wash. Nationals)					1	3	6.81	42	0	0	3	37	41	29	28	6	12	25	.275	.306	.260	6.08	2.92
Shelby Miller	R-R	6-3	225	10-10-90	0	1	6.43	4	0	0	0	7	6	5	5	0	3	14	.222	.267	.167	18.00	3.86
Luis Ortiz	R-R	6-3	230	9-22-95	0	0	1.04	6	0	0	0	9	5	1	1	0	3	6	.167	.111	.190	6.23	3.12
Carlos Rodon	L-L	6-3	245	12-10-92	14	8	2.88	31	31	1	0	178	131	59	57	12	52	237	.202	.179	.207	11.98	2.63
Tyler Rogers	R-R	6-3	181	12-17-90	3	4	3.57	68	0	0	0	76	73	34	30	3	23	49	.253	.317	.208	5.83	2.74
Gregory Santos	R-R	6-2	190	8-28-99	0	0	4.91	2	0	0	0	4	3	2	2	0	3	2	.214	.167	.250	4.91	7.36
Thomas Szapucki	R-L	6-2	210	6-12-96	0	0	1.98	10	0	0	0	14	12	3	3	2	4	16	.240	.286	.207	10.54	2.63
2-team total (1 New York Mets)					0	1	7.20	11	1	0	0	15	19	12	12	6	7	18	.317	.375	.278	10.80	4.20
Andrew Vasquez	L-L	6-6	235	9-14-93	0	0	0.00	1	0	0	0	2	0	0	0	0	1	4	.000	.000	.000	18.00	4.50
Cole Waites	R-R	6-3	180	6-10-98	0	0	3.18	7	0	0	0	6	6	2	2	1	4	4	.286	.333	.267	6.35	6.35
Donovan Walton	L-R	5-10	190	5-25-94	0	0	27.00	1	0	0	0	1	3	3	3	1	1	0	.500	.500	.500	0.00	9.00
Logan Webb	R-R	6-1	220	11-18-96	15	9	2.90	32	32	0	0	192	174	76	62	11	49	163	.240	.263	.216	7.63	2.29
Alex Wood	R-L	6-4	215	1-12-91	8	12	5.10	26	26	0	0	131	132	78	74	17	30	131	.262	.193	.283	9.02	2.07
Austin Wynns	R-R	6-0	190	12-10-90	0	0	13.50	2	0	0	0	2	3	3	3	1	1	0	.333	.250	.400	0.00	4.50
Alex Young	L-L	6-3	220	9-9-93	1	1	2.39	24	1	0	0	26	28	11	7	0	11	20	.277	.348	.218	6.84	3.76

Fielding

Catcher	PCT	G	PO	A	E	DP	PB
Bart	.989	93	656	34	8	4	4
Casali	.993	39	265	21	2	1	1
Knapp	1.000	3	16	1	0	0	0
Mercedes	.000	1	0	0	0	0	0
Papierski	1.000	4	18	2	0	0	0
Proctor	1.000	1	1	0	0	0	0
Wynns	.987	57	423	19	6	0	2

First Base	PCT	G	PO	A	E	DP
Belt	.988	63	458	54	6	35
Casali	1.000	2	3	1	0	0
Davis	1.000	14	76	6	0	6
Flores	.990	45	279	20	3	24
Ford	1.000	1	11	0	0	1
La Stella	1.000	3	21	1	0	2
Mercedes	1.000	4	12	0	0	0
Padlo	1.000	1	6	0	0	1
Papierski	1.000	1	5	0	0	0
Ruf	.992	36	239	14	2	20
Villar	.986	11	62	6	1	8
Vosler	1.000	2	9	2	0	2
Wade Jr.	.982	22	151	13	3	19

Second Base	PCT	G	PO	A	E	DP
Dubon	1.000	1	1	1	0	0
Estrada	.986	102	159	205	5	59
Flores	1.000	61	80	118	0	27
La Stella	.900	3	3	6	1	0
Proctor	1.000	6	3	11	0	1
Villar	.944	6	5	12	1	2
Vosler	1.000	1	0	1	0	0
Walton	1.000	14	13	32	0	4

Third Base	PCT	G	PO	A	E	DP
Davis	.971	18	6	28	1	1
Dubon	1.000	3	0	3	0	0
Estrada	1.000	3	1	4	0	0
Flores	.941	34	14	50	4	5
La Stella	1.000	6	1	3	0	0
Longoria	.966	68	40	129	6	11
Padlo	1.000	3	3	7	0	1
Villar	.932	27	10	58	5	3
Vosler	.984	29	10	52	1	5
Williams	1.000	8	0	6	0	1

Shortstop	PCT	G	PO	A	E	DP
Crawford	.966	116	163	287	16	67
Dubon	1.000	4	6	9	0	2
Estrada	.961	37	40	83	5	19
Machado	1.000	5	2	15	0	1
Vosler	1.000	1	0	3	0	0
Walton	.962	12	13	38	2	4

Outfield	PCT	G	PO	A	E	DP
Brinson	1.000	16	17	1	0	0
Davis	--	2	0	0	0	0
Dean	1.000	4	4	0	0	0
Dubon	1.000	14	17	1	0	0
Duggar	1.000	13	19	0	0	0
Estrada	1.000	19	18	0	0	0
Fairchild	1.000	5	8	0	0	0
Gonzalez	.977	127	167	6	4	0
Johnson	1.000	12	11	1	0	0
Krizan	1.000	3	4	0	0	0
Mercedes	.875	8	7	0	1	0
Pederson	.986	120	137	2	2	0
Ramos	1.000	9	12	0	0	0
Ruf	1.000	31	21	0	0	0
Slater	.981	136	157	1	3	0
Tom	--	1	0	0	0	0
Vosler	1.000	4	1	0	0	0
Wade Jr.	1.000	53	49	2	0	1
Williams	1.000	1	2	0	0	0
Yastrzemski	.989	197	271	9	3	3

SACRAMENTO RIVER CATS — *TRIPLE-A*

PACIFIC COAST LEAGUE

Batting	B-T	HT	WT	DOB	AVG	vLH	vRH	G	AB	R	H	2B	3B	HR	RBI	BB	HBP	SH	SF	SO	SB	CS	SLG	OBP
Joey Bart	R-R	6-2	238	12-15-96	.286	.375	.250	7	28	5	8	0	0	1	4	2	1	0	0	6	0	0	.393	.355
Alex Blandino	R-R	6-0	190	11-6-92	.183	.286	.148	24	82	13	15	5	0	1	9	13	2	0	0	38	1	0	.280	.309
2-team total (47 Tacoma Rainiers)					.195	.316	.153	71	220	37	43	13	1	4	31	56	6	0	3	89	8	2	.318	.368
Lewis Brinson	R-R	6-5	212	5-8-94	.250	.250	.250	2	8	1	2	0	0	0	0	1	0	0	0	4	0	0	.250	.333
2-team total (85 Sugar Land Space Cowboys)					.298	.407	.264	87	339	62	101	21	2	22	63	27	4	2	1	106	5	3	.566	.356
Willie Calhoun	L-R	5-8	200	11-4-94	.291	.245	.313	42	148	24	43	9	0	5	23	19	2	0	1	22	0	0	.453	.376
2-team total (21 Round Rock Express)					.264	.197	.291	63	231	42	61	10	0	10	43	25	2	0	3	35	0	0	.437	.337
Curt Casali	R-R	6-2	220	11-9-88	.000	--	.000	3	7	0	0	0	0	0	0	0	0	0	0	7	0	0	.000	.000
2-team total (5 Tacoma Rainiers)					.200	.000	.211	8	20	3	4	1	0	0	1	3	1	0	0	10	0	0	.250	.333
Brandon Crawford	L-R	6-1	223	1-21-87	.000	.000	.000	2	4	0	0	0	0	0	0	1	0	0	0	1	0	0	.000	.200
Jaylin Davis	R-R	5-11	205	7-1-94	.295	.357	.267	10	44	10	13	3	0	2	7	3	0	0	0	14	3	1	.500	.340
Austin Dean	R-R	6-0	215	10-14-93	.268	.299	.247	115	392	68	105	17	5	17	55	38	8	0	0	94	10	2	.467	.345

Isan Diaz	L-R	5-11	201	5-27-96	.275	.250	.284	83	284	60	78	12	2	23	61	43	4	0	1	82	7	2	.574	.377
Steven Duggar	L-R	6-1	187	11-4-93	.204	.238	.179	14	49	8	10	1	0	1	5	3	1	0	0	18	2	0	.286	.264
3-team total (11 R. R. Express, 10 Salt Lake Bees)					.182	.184	.183	35	121	16	22	4	0	4	12	17	1	0	1	45	6	0	.314	.286
Robert Emery	R-R	6-0	210	10-22-96	.000	--	.000	2	6	0	0	0	0	0	0	0	0	0	0	4	0	0	.000	.000
Stuart Fairchild	R-R	6-0	205	3-17-96	.188	.286	.111	5	16	2	3	1	0	1	1	4	1	0	0	8	2	0	.438	.381
3-team total (10 Reno Aces, 4 Tacoma Rainiers)					.232	.200	.241	19	69	9	16	3	0	4	7	10	6	0	0	26	2	1	.449	.376
Mike Ford	L-R	6-0	225	7-4-92	.000	--	.000	3	7	0	0	0	0	0	0	6	0	0	0	1	0	0	.000	.462
3-team total (6 Salt Lake Bees, 11 Tacoma Rainiers)					.254	.214	.263	20	71	13	18	2	0	2	5	12	1	0	0	10	0	0	.366	.369
Arquimedes Gamboa	B-R	6-0	190	9-23-97	.239	.179	.269	82	255	28	61	12	2	4	29	37	1	2	1	69	7	1	.349	.337
Ricardo Genoves	R-R	6-2	190	5-14-99	.233	.347	.163	38	129	12	30	6	0	3	21	16	1	0	1	39	0	0	.349	.320
Cesar Gonzalez	R-R	5-11	206	5-8-01	.000	.000	.000	1	2	0	0	0	0	0	0	0	0	0	0	1	0	0	.000	.000
Luis Gonzalez	L-L	6-1	185	9-10-95	.289	.308	.286	20	76	15	22	1	0	6	13	15	0	0	1	22	4	2	.539	.402
Drew Jackson	R-R	6-2	200	7-28-93	.200	.278	.083	10	30	7	6	1	0	3	5	1	0	0	0	15	0	0	.533	.226
2-team total (50 Las Vegas Aviators)					.236	.288	.200	60	178	26	42	6	0	4	19	24	2	0	0	71	8	1	.337	.333
Bryce Johnson	B-R	6-1	195	10-27-95	.290	.343	.263	94	307	41	89	11	4	5	36	33	7	2	3	90	31	5	.401	.369
Taylor Jones	R-R	6-7	230	12-6-93	.250	.286	.235	7	24	5	6	4	0	0	5	5	0	0	0	8	0	0	.417	.379
2-team total (74 Sugar Land Space Cowboys)					.262	.263	.261	81	298	57	78	21	0	12	48	40	12	0	1	86	0	0	.453	.370
Andrew Knapp	B-R	6-1	189	11-9-91	.276	.238	.294	34	127	20	35	7	0	8	26	13	2	0	0	35	1	1	.520	.352
2-team total (22 Tacoma Rainiers)					.245	.217	.257	56	208	28	51	14	0	12	37	17	4	0	1	57	1	1	.486	.313
Jason Krizan	L-R	6-0	185	6-28-89	.266	.265	.266	97	357	58	95	30	2	15	55	35	0	0	3	61	1	1	.487	.329
Tommy La Stella	L-R	5-11	180	1-31-89	.316	.250	.333	12	38	8	12	2	0	2	7	9	1	0	0	7	0	0	.526	.458
Evan Longoria	R-R	6-1	213	10-7-85	.333	.333	.333	7	24	3	8	2	0	0	0	1	0	0	0	8	0	0	.417	.360
Dixon Machado	R-R	6-1	190	2-22-92	.231	.180	.268	35	121	14	28	6	0	4	15	7	2	0	1	23	0	0	.380	.282
Shane Matheny	L-R	6-1	205	6-5-96	.170	.100	.222	15	47	5	8	1	0	2	4	3	0	0	0	23	0	0	.319	.220
Wyatt Mathisen	R-R	6-0	217	12-30-93	.170	.114	.195	38	112	19	19	5	0	5	18	16	2	0	4	45	0	0	.348	.276
Patrick Mazeika	L-R	6-3	210	10-14-93	.235	.100	.323	13	51	9	12	2	0	2	6	3	1	0	0	5	0	0	.392	.291
Yermin Mercedes	R-R	5-11	245	2-14-93	.268	.255	.275	37	142	17	38	5	0	8	19	13	1	0	2	34	2	0	.472	.329
Kevin Padlo	R-R	6-2	210	7-15-96	.275	.306	.250	22	80	16	22	3	1	7	16	5	2	0	0	18	3	0	.600	.333
2-team total (38 Tacoma Rainiers)					.245	.257	.240	60	220	34	54	9	2	11	36	23	4	0	1	59	10	2	.455	.327
Michael Papierski	B-R	6-3	224	2-26-96	.208	.231	.200	14	53	5	11	2	0	2	13	3	0	0	1	18	0	0	.358	.246
2-team total (26 Sugar Land Space Cowboys)					.210	.139	.234	40	143	17	30	5	0	3	28	17	2	0	3	27	0	0	.308	.297
Jhonny Pereda	R-R	6-1	202	4-18-96	.272	.312	.248	65	206	23	56	10	0	4	25	35	0	1	4	41	0	1	.379	.371
Ford Proctor	L-R	6-1	195	12-4-96	.267	.211	.295	34	116	19	31	3	0	6	14	24	0	1	1	38	0	0	.448	.390
Heliot Ramos	R-R	6-1	188	9-7-99	.227	.211	.235	108	427	61	97	17	1	11	45	41	7	0	0	112	6	6	.349	.305
Jose Rojas	L-R	6-0	200	2-24-93	.259	.385	.143	7	27	5	7	2	0	2	2	2	0	0	0	6	0	0	.556	.310
2-team total (62 Salt Lake Bees)					.274	.256	.283	69	274	51	75	15	3	20	52	31	1	0	3	64	5	2	.569	.346
Casey Schmitt	R-R	6-2	215	3-1-99	.333	.800	.100	4	15	1	5	1	0	1	3	0	0	0	1	5	0	0	.600	.313
Ka'ai Tom	L-R	5-9	185	5-29-94	.239	.143	.268	78	268	40	64	17	0	10	47	35	6	1	1	80	6	3	.414	.339
David Villar	R-R	6-1	215	1-27-97	.275	.267	.280	84	298	67	82	19	1	27	82	55	11	0	2	93	1	1	.617	.404
Jason Vosler	L-R	6-1	220	9-6-93	.242	.180	.273	94	360	52	87	13	1	18	47	34	2	2	0	100	4	0	.433	.311
LaMonte Wade Jr.	L-L	6-1	205	1-1-94	.250	.211	.280	14	44	11	11	4	0	2	11	10	2	0	2	6	0	0	.477	.397
Steele Walker	L-L	5-11	209	7-30-96	.247	.167	.277	25	89	10	22	5	1	2	14	4	1	0	0	16	2	0	.393	.287
2-team total (50 Round Rock Express)					.268	.208	.291	75	280	42	75	14	1	9	40	24	4	0	1	51	8	3	.421	.333
Donovan Walton	L-R	5-10	190	5-25-94	.225	.217	.229	20	71	10	16	6	0	1	7	12	1	4	0	13	3	0	.352	.345
2-team total (12 Tacoma Rainiers)					.254	.250	.256	32	122	20	31	10	2	2	12	18	1	4	0	19	5	1	.418	.355
Luke Williams	R-R	6-1	186	8-9-96	.378	.313	.429	10	37	8	14	4	0	0	7	3	0	0	1	13	4	2	.486	.415
Will Wilson	R-R	6-0	184	7-21-98	.182	.333	.056	10	33	2	6	2	0	0	2	2	1	0	0	14	0	1	.242	.250
Max Wright	L-R	6-3	215	1-8-98	1.000	--	1.000	1	1	0	1	0	0	0	0	0	0	0	0	0	0	0	1.000	1.000

Pitching	B-T	HT	WT	DOB	W	L	ERA	G	GS	CG	SV	IP	H	R	ER	HR	BB	SO	AVG	vLH	vRH	K/9	BB/9
Scott Alexander	L-L	6-2	195	7-10-89	1	0	0.00	7	0	0	0	8	2	0	0	0	4	8	.087	.125	.067	9.39	4.70
Jose Alvarez	L-L	5-11	195	5-6-89	1	0	4.50	3	0	0	0	4	6	2	2	0	0	3	.375	.600	.273	6.75	0.00
Tristan Beck	R-R	6-4	165	6-24-96	5	8	5.64	20	19	0	0	97	105	66	61	10	29	97	.271	.278	.266	8.97	2.68
Jonathan Bermudez	L-L	6-2	237	10-16-95	0	3	9.22	5	5	0	0	14	15	14	14	7	7	16	.273	.115	.414	10.54	4.61
2-team total (19 Sugar Land Space Cowboys)					2	7	9.00	24	19	0	0	81	100	82	81	23	44	81	.304	.217	.345	9.00	4.89
Spencer Bivens	R-R	6-5	205	6-28-94	1	1	6.75	6	0	0	1	13	15	11	10	2	4	12	.300	.333	.276	8.10	2.70
Ben Bowden	L-L	6-4	249	10-21-94	1	1	7.07	22	0	0	0	28	24	22	22	8	15	41	.229	.234	.224	13.18	4.82
2-team total (7 Albuquerque Isotopes)					1	1	7.32	29	0	0	0	36	30	29	29	9	21	52	.227	.246	.213	13.12	5.30
Bryan Brickhouse	R-R	6-0	195	6-6-92	2	0	9.53	6	2	0	0	11	14	12	12	1	13	9	.292	.320	.261	7.15	10.32
Matt Carasiti	R-R	6-2	205	7-23-91	3	2	8.31	23	0	0	1	22	30	20	20	4	14	28	.323	.333	.316	11.63	5.82
Cody Carroll	R-R	6-5	230	10-15-92	2	1	7.62	31	2	0	0	39	53	33	33	11	28	49	.325	.296	.348	11.31	6.46
Kervin Castro	R-R	6-0	185	2-7-99	0	4	5.57	29	0	0	0	32	31	21	20	4	24	32	.254	.305	.206	8.91	6.68
R.J. Dabovich	R-R	6-3	208	1-11-99	2	0	4.38	23	1	0	1	25	16	15	12	1	20	31	.193	.195	.190	11.31	7.30
Enmanuel De Jesus	L-L	6-3	190	12-10-96	4	5	4.51	35	19	0	0	102	108	59	51	11	51	118	.271	.278	.268	10.45	4.51
Anthony DeSclafani	R-R	6-2	195	4-18-90	0	1	4.76	2	2	0	0	6	8	4	3	0	3	5	.348	.308	.400	7.94	4.76
Raynel Espinal	R-R	6-3	215	10-6-91	5	5	5.29	19	18	0	0	83	87	51	49	16	38	102	.268	.308	.232	11.02	4.10
Aaron Fletcher	L-L	6-0	220	2-25-96	0	1	15.15	15	0	0	0	14	22	26	23	4	14	12	.333	.207	.432	7.90	9.22
Ken Giles	R-R	6-3	197	9-20-90	0	0	3.38	3	0	0	0	3	2	1	1	1	2	2	.200	.333	.000	6.75	6.75
2-team total (8 Tacoma Rainiers)					0	1	8.38	11	0	0	0	10	12	10	9	4	9	8	.293	.348	.222	7.45	8.38
Norwith Gudino	R-R	6-2	200	11-22-95	3	5	8.87	26	6	0	1	48	46	47	47	13	31	60	.250	.276	.227	11.33	5.85
Matt Hall	L-L	6-0	200	7-23-93	1	1	10.80	2	1	0	0	3	6	4	4	0	7	4	.462	.250	.556	10.80	18.90
Trevor Hildenberger	R-R	6-2	205	12-15-90	0	0	2.08	4	1	0	0	4	4	2	1	1	2	2	.235	.100	.429	4.15	4.15
Sean Hjelle	R-R	6-11	228	5-7-97	6	8	4.92	22	22	0	0	97	112	62	53	11	38	80	.287	.343	.242	7.42	3.53
Wei-Chieh Huang	R-R	6-2	175	9-26-93	3	2	4.40	23	13	0	0	72	67	43	35	9	31	89	.241	.218	.260	11.18	3.89
Jakob Junis	R-R	6-3	220	9-16-92	0	1	8.74	3	3	0	0	11	19	11	11	5	4	9	.388	.250	.415	7.15	3.18

Jason Krizan	L-R	6-0	185	6-28-89	0	0	20.25	4	0	0	0	3	9	6	6	1	0	0	.529	.444	.625	0.00	0.00
Zack Littell	R-R	6-4	220	10-5-95	0	1	6.75	13	1	0	0	13	14	10	10	3	4	13	.269	.333	.200	8.78	2.70
Mauricio Llovera	R-R	5-11	224	4-17-96	2	0	0.00	15	0	0	1	20	13	1	0	0	4	28	.178	.167	.184	12.60	1.80
Sam Long	L-L	6-1	185	7-8-95	1	0	4.32	8	3	0	0	17	11	8	8	2	16	16	.180	.083	.243	8.64	8.64
Joey Marciano	L-L	6-5	250	1-11-95	4	2	4.12	56	1	0	9	59	58	31	27	6	33	62	.258	.219	.287	9.46	5.03
Yunior Marte	R-R	6-2	180	2-2-95	1	1	3.16	25	0	0	3	26	9	11	9	4	9	35	.106	.086	.120	12.27	3.16
Jake McGee	L-L	6-4	229	8-6-86	0	0	3.38	3	0	0	0	3	1	1	1	0	1	7	.111	.000	.125	23.63	3.38
Shelby Miller	R-R	6-3	225	10-10-90	0	2	3.62	27	1	0	8	32	25	17	13	3	15	44	.212	.265	.174	12.25	4.18
Tobias Myers	R-R	6-0	193	8-5-98	0	0	9.00	2	1	0	0	3	1	3	3	0	3	3	.100	.167	.000	9.00	9.00
Luis Ortiz	R-R	6-3	230	9-22-95	4	3	4.54	35	4	0	2	67	68	38	34	8	13	72	.260	.241	.274	9.62	1.74
Corey Oswalt	R-R	6-5	250	9-3-93	1	2	7.11	6	1	0	0	13	15	12	10	6	5	17	.283	.071	.359	12.08	3.55
2-team total (4 Albuquerque Isotopes)					1	4	7.39	10	5	0	0	28	38	25	23	13	9	26	.317	.171	.376	8.36	2.89
Joe Palumbo	L-L	6-0	195	10-26-94	0	0	33.75	3	0	0	0	1	6	5	5	0	2	1	.667	.750	.600	6.75	13.50
Michael Plassmeyer	L-L	6-2	197	11-5-96	0	6	7.38	11	10	0	0	46	50	39	38	15	24	47	.279	.178	.313	9.13	4.66
Randy Rodriguez	R-R	6-0	166	9-5-99	0	1	10.50	5	0	0	0	6	3	7	7	0	11	7	.143	.375	.000	10.50	16.50
Angel Rondon	R-R	6-1	205	12-1-97	0	1	10.13	3	0	0	0	3	4	3	3	1	4	4	.364	.250	.429	13.50	13.50
Patrick Ruotolo	R-R	5-10	250	1-16-95	2	4	7.11	27	0	0	2	32	32	26	25	6	17	42	.258	.321	.206	11.94	4.83
Gregory Santos	R-R	6-2	190	8-28-99	1	2	4.91	33	0	0	1	33	29	22	18	4	20	34	.236	.233	.238	9.27	5.45
Michael Stryffeler	R-R	6-2	210	5-22-96	0	2	7.88	18	0	0	0	16	8	14	14	2	17	25	.145	.143	.147	14.06	9.56
Thomas Szapucki	R-L	6-2	210	6-12-96	0	0	1.08	7	0	0	0	8	7	3	1	0	3	15	.226	.125	.261	16.20	3.24
Peter Tago	R-R	6-3	205	7-5-92	1	0	10.00	8	0	0	0	9	12	11	10	1	9	8	.300	.538	.185	8.00	9.00
Daniel Tillo	L-L	6-5	215	6-13-96	0	0	9.82	3	0	0	0	4	7	5	4	0	1	2	.389	571	.273	4.91	2.45
Trenton Toplikar	R-R	6-4	215	5-21-96	0	0	0.00	1	0	0	0	1	0	0	0	0	0	0	.000	--	.000	0.00	0.00
Kyle Tyler	R-R	6-0	185	12-27-96	0	0	9.82	4	0	0	0	4	6	4	4	2	3	6	.353	.500	.273	14.73	7.36
2-team total (15 El Paso Chihuahuas)					2	1	5.68	19	2	0	0	25	17	16	16	4	22	33	.189	.175	.200	11.72	7.82
Andrew Vasquez	L-L	6-6	235	9-14-93	5	0	2.20	14	0	0	1	16	13	4	4	1	5	23	.220	.154	.273	12.67	2.76
Cole Waites	R-R	6-3	180	6-10-98	1	0	0.00	7	0	0	1	8	3	0	0	0	3	11	.120	.154	.083	12.38	3.38
Jeremy Walker	R-R	6-5	235	6-12-95	0	4	6.88	28	0	0	1	35	43	29	27	4	15	38	.307	.322	.296	9.68	3.82
Ryan Walker	R-R	6-2	200	11-26-95	0	1	6.14	7	0	0	0	7	10	5	5	0	3	9	.303	.400	.222	11.05	3.68
Ty Weber	R-R	6-4	220	3-19-98	1	0	4.26	3	0	0	0	6	6	5	3	2	1	3	.240	.188	.333	4.26	1.42
Ronnie Williams	R-R	6-0	170	1-6-96	1	2	7.64	10	9	0	0	33	38	31	28	3	22	31	.295	.275	.317	8.45	6.00
Taylor Williams	B-R	5-11	185	7-21-91	0	0	6.81	27	3	0	0	40	50	31	30	4	17	45	.301	.328	.286	10.21	3.86
2-team total (23 Tacoma Rainiers)					2	1	4.69	50	3	0	1	63	70	35	33	5	24	68	.281	.293	.274	9.66	3.41
Alex Young	L-L	6-3	220	9-9-93	0	0	0.00	3	0	0	0	3	1	0	0	0	2	3	.100	.143	.000	9.00	6.00

Fielding

Catcher	PCT	G	PO	A	E	DP	PB
Bart	1.000	7	59	5	0	1	1
Casali	1.000	2	9	0	0	0	1
Emery	1.000	2	15	1	0	0	1
Genoves	.997	32	328	21	1	0	7
Knapp	.988	25	233	10	3	1	3
Mazeika	.989	8	88	2	1	0	1
Mercedes	1.000	2	10	0	0	0	0
Papierski	.991	11	104	8	1	0	2
Pereda	.993	61	590	17	4	2	17
Proctor	.977	4	40	2	1	0	1

First Base	PCT	G	PO	A	E	DP
Dean	1.000	6	31	4	0	2
Ford	.955	3	20	1	1	1
Genoves	1.000	1	1	0	0	0
Gonzalez	1.000	1	5	0	0	0
Jones	1.000	5	34	4	0	3
Knapp	.976	6	39	2	1	3
Krizan	.989	49	339	15	4	43
Mathisen	.988	13	72	8	1	7
Mazeika	1.000	4	23	0	0	3
Mercedes	.980	21	134	14	3	17
Padlo	1.000	7	44	3	0	5
Papierski	1.000	2	13	0	0	0
Pereda	1.000	1	2	0	0	0
Proctor	1.000	1	4	0	0	0
Rojas	1.000	2	14	0	0	1
Villar	.982	16	95	16	2	12
Vosler	1.000	28	160	8	0	8
Wade Jr.	1.000	4	13	0	0	1

Second Base	PCT	G	PO	A	E	DP
Blandino	.975	17	37	42	2	17
Calhoun	1.000	2	0	2	0	0
Diaz	.983	57	67	105	3	23
Jackson	1.000	1	2	0	0	0
Krizan	.966	28	27	57	3	14
La Stella	.923	8	5	7	1	0
Padlo	1.000	5	7	6	0	3
Proctor	1.000	8	9	19	0	5
Villar	.978	15	14	30	1	7
Vosler	1.000	18	25	46	0	7
Walton	1.000	7	11	13	0	4
Williams	1.000	3	3	3	0	0
Wilson	1.000	3	2	5	0	1

Third Base	PCT	G	PO	A	E	DP
Blandino	1.000	2	0	2	0	0
Diaz	.889	10	7	9	2	1
Jackson	.750	1	1	2	1	1
La Stella	1.000	2	0	1	0	0
Longoria	.889	4	4	4	1	0
Matheny	1.000	1	0	1	0	0
Mathisen	.974	21	9	28	1	8
Padlo	1.000	8	4	13	0	3
Proctor	.972	16	9	26	1	2
Rojas	1.000	3	1	7	0	0
Schmitt	.900	4	4	5	1	1
Villar	.953	51	36	105	7	12
Vosler	.959	34	17	53	3	3
Walton	1.000	1	1	2	0	0
Williams	.500	2	0	1	1	0
Wilson	1.000	2	1	3	0	1

Shortstop	PCT	G	PO	A	E	DP
Blandino	.875	5	2	12	2	3
Crawford	.875	2	3	4	1	2
Diaz	.976	14	17	24	1	4
Gamboa	.955	80	98	177	13	37
Jackson	1.000	1	0	4	0	1
Machado	.962	35	42	86	5	14
Matheny	1.000	2	0	3	0	1
Proctor	1.000	4	7	12	0	3
Walton	.947	7	5	13	1	2
Williams	1.000	2	2	3	0	2
Wilson	1.000	5	2	6	0	0

Outfield	PCT	G	PO	A	E	DP
Brinson	1.000	1	5	0	0	0
Calhoun	1.000	19	17	1	0	0
Davis	1.000	6	7	0	0	0
Dean	.966	94	163	5	6	2
Duggar	1.000	9	14	1	0	0
Fairchild	1.000	5	3	0	0	0
Gamboa	1.000	1	3	0	0	0
Gonzalez	.964	15	27	0	1	0
Jackson	1.000	7	10	0	0	0
Johnson	.989	91	179	1	2	1
Jones	1.000	1	3	0	0	0
Krizan	1.000	1	1	0	0	0
Matheny	1.000	12	17	0	0	0
Mercedes	.667	2	2	0	1	0
Padlo	1.000	6	9	0	0	0
Ramos	.983	103	171	5	3	1
Rojas	1.000	2	4	0	0	0
Tom	.978	68	122	10	3	2
Vosler	1.000	19	30	0	0	0
Wade Jr.	1.000	8	9	0	0	0
Walker	.979	23	47	0	1	0
Walton	1.000	4	1	0	0	0
Williams	.833	4	5	0	1	0

RICHMOND FLYING SQUIRRELS

DOUBLE-A

EASTERN LEAGUE

Batting	B-T	HT	WT	DOB	AVG	vLH	vRH	G	AB	R	H	2B	3B	HR	RBI	BB	HBP	SH	SF	SO	SB	CS	SLG	OBP
Carter Aldrete	R-R	6-2	205	10-12-97	.231	.270	.217	42	143	18	33	8	0	6	24	10	0	1	2	43	1	2	.413	.277
Brett Auerbach	R-R	5-9	185	8-27-98	.220	.284	.205	99	372	54	82	15	0	17	53	48	2	1	2	136	12	6	.398	.311
Vaun Brown	R-R	6-1	215	6-23-98	.000	.000	--	1	2	0	0	0	0	0	0	0	0	0	0	0	0	0	.000	.000
Robert Emery	R-R	6-0	210	10-22-96	.243	.080	.295	35	103	15	25	5	2	4	13	13	8	0	1	28	0	3	.447	.368
Tyler Fitzgerald	R-R	6-3	205	9-15-97	.229	.240	.225	125	455	74	104	20	3	21	58	37	19	3	5	171	20	1	.424	.310
Ricardo Genoves	R-R	6-2	190	5-14-99	.203	.286	.188	53	182	16	37	8	1	7	17	17	4	0	0	58	0	0	.374	.286
Michael Gigliotti	L-L	6-1	180	2-14-96	.215	.250	.209	75	251	49	54	5	3	7	29	51	10	5	2	77	24	6	.343	.366
Jacob Heyward	R-R	6-1	215	8-1-95	.201	.150	.213	102	318	50	64	8	1	11	37	44	4	0	4	123	1	1	.336	.303
Franklin Labour	R-R	6-1	190	5-11-98	.177	.186	.175	75	209	30	37	11	1	7	30	24	3	1	1	99	4	0	.340	.270
Riley Mahan	L-R	6-3	220	12-31-95	.266	.231	.275	23	64	13	17	4	1	3	11	9	3	1	1	32	2	0	.500	.377
Brandon Martorano	R-R	6-2	198	1-6-98	.217	.194	.223	93	323	51	70	16	4	10	46	39	6	0	4	120	11	2	.384	.309
Shane Matheny	L-R	6-1	205	6-5-96	.254	.213	.264	93	315	58	80	13	1	12	47	58	5	3	1	115	4	0	.416	.377
Tristan Peters	L-R	6-0	180	2-29-00	.212	.107	.240	34	132	16	28	7	1	1	17	15	2	0	0	31	5	2	.303	.302
Diego Rincones	R-R	6-0	175	6-14-99	.257	.250	.259	91	334	34	86	12	0	10	47	16	9	0	4	48	0	0	.383	.306
Sean Roby	R-R	6-2	215	7-8-98	.219	.239	.213	89	320	45	70	7	1	25	55	27	4	0	2	140	1	0	.481	.286
Casey Schmitt	R-R	6-2	215	3-1-99	.342	.480	.305	29	120	13	41	10	1	3	16	6	1	0	0	29	2	0	.517	.378
Armani Smith	R-R	6-4	215	7-19-98	.228	.295	.208	75	263	24	60	12	1	2	21	35	2	0	2	89	3	3	.304	.321
Frankie Tostado	L-L	6-2	205	3-31-98	.284	.351	.268	77	292	36	83	16	1	11	41	19	2	0	2	72	3	2	.459	.330
Simon Whiteman	R-R	5-10	165	1-28-97	.165	.069	.214	28	85	10	14	4	0	0	6	8	3	0	0	31	5	1	.212	.260
Will Wilson	R-R	6-0	184	7-21-98	.225	.195	.233	52	191	35	43	6	0	12	27	28	0	0	0	65	2	2	.445	.324

Pitching	B-T	HT	WT	DOB	W	L	ERA	G	GS	CG	SV	IP	H	R	ER	HR	BB	SO	AVG	vLH	vRH	K/9	BB/9
Melvin Adon	L-R	6-3	246	6-9-94	1	0	4.15	10	0	0	0	13	12	9	6	1	6	11	.235	.214	.261	7.62	4.15
Tanner Andrews	R-R	6-3	220	11-15-95	0	0	0.00	4	0	0	0	5	3	0	0	0	3	5	.188	.500	.083	8.44	5.06
Nick Avila	R-R	6-4	195	7-25-97	2	1	1.33	20	0	0	3	27	21	4	4	3	6	27	.223	.200	.245	9.00	2.00
Solomon Bates	R-R	6-2	210	3-16-97	4	1	4.02	23	0	0	0	40	28	18	18	10	21	47	.194	.183	.202	10.49	4.69
Tristan Beck	R-R	6-4	165	6-24-96	0	1	2.57	3	3	0	0	14	10	5	4	1	7	19	.196	.200	.192	12.21	4.50
Bryan Brickhouse	R-R	6-0	195	6-6-92	5	5	4.37	14	14	0	0	68	63	37	33	8	25	72	.244	.266	.223	9.53	3.31
R.J. Dabovich	R-R	6-3	208	1-11-99	4	1	2.70	22	0	0	5	27	18	10	8	1	6	38	.182	.233	.143	12.83	2.03
Jake Dahlberg	L-L	6-0	205	12-1-93	5	7	4.31	21	20	0	0	100	108	54	48	17	30	95	.276	.288	.270	8.52	2.69
Gray Fenter	R-R	6-0	200	1-25-96	0	4	5.13	22	7	0	0	40	28	25	23	4	38	50	.192	.176	.205	11.16	8.48
Matt Frisbee	R-R	6-5	215	11-18-96	6	10	5.16	27	26	1	0	140	149	85	80	23	38	132	.269	.277	.262	8.51	2.45
Evan Gates	R-R	6-0	210	1-13-98	0	0	3.00	7	0	0	0	9	6	3	3	0	5	14	.200	.250	.167	14.00	5.00
John Gavin	R-L	6-6	250	10-10-95	0	0	9.00	6	0	0	0	7	9	8	7	2	4	11	.300	.143	.348	14.14	5.14
Jorge Guzman	R-R	6-1	246	1-28-96	0	0	22.50	2	0	0	0	2	4	5	5	2	2	4	.400	.333	.429	18.00	9.00
Kyle Harrison	R-L	6-2	200	8-12-01	4	2	3.11	18	18	0	0	84	60	30	29	11	39	127	.201	.236	.190	13.61	4.18
Clay Helvey	R-R	6-3	195	2-14-97	1	2	2.20	23	0	0	2	29	18	12	7	1	17	34	.171	.167	.175	10.67	5.34
Wil Jensen	R-R	6-4	180	9-2-97	2	2	4.91	8	5	0	0	29	25	17	16	5	13	22	.229	.231	.228	6.75	3.99
Ryan Murphy	R-R	6-1	190	10-8-99	1	1	9.35	2	2	0	0	9	9	9	9	2	10	7	.265	.364	.217	7.27	10.38
Ofelky Peralta	R-R	6-5	195	4-20-97	0	2	7.16	10	1	0	0	16	19	13	13	1	11	13	.292	.394	.188	7.16	6.06
Travis Perry	R-R	6-4	190	3-8-97	0	0	6.60	13	0	0	0	15	19	11	11	2	8	8	.311	.321	.303	4.80	4.80
Taylor Rashi	R-R	6-4	220	1-15-96	1	3	2.83	30	0	0	1	35	21	13	11	1	13	52	.171	.121	.215	13.37	3.34
Blake Rivera	R-R	6-4	225	1-9-98	4	3	2.70	28	1	0	2	47	30	19	14	2	23	48	.182	.213	.156	9.26	4.44
Randy Rodriguez	R-R	6-0	166	9-5-99	0	1	6.30	6	0	0	0	10	7	10	7	2	8	19	.184	.111	.250	17.10	7.20
Landen Roupp	R-R	6-2	205	9-10-98	2	1	3.76	5	5	0	0	26	19	12	11	3	11	31	.194	.167	.220	10.59	3.76
Frank Rubio	R-R	5-11	185	4-23-95	0	1	4.34	16	0	0	0	19	24	12	9	0	11	16	.316	.333	.300	7.71	5.30
Patrick Ruotolo	R-R	5-10	250	1-16-95	0	0	0.00	2	0	0	1	3	0	0	0	0	0	7	.000	.000	.000	21.00	0.00
John Russell	R-R	6-3	195	10-17-95	0	0	4.50	29	0	0	1	36	43	21	18	4	16	44	.305	.290	.316	11.00	4.00
Tyler Schimpf	R-R	6-4	210	8-7-95	1	0	9.00	14	0	0	0	14	18	18	14	3	23	13	.295	.344	.241	8.36	14.79
Kai-Wei Teng	R-R	6-4	260	12-1-98	6	12	5.22	28	28	0	0	136	122	87	79	14	85	169	.240	.249	.231	11.16	5.61
Daniel Tillo	L-L	6-5	215	6-13-96	0	1	6.00	6	0	0	0	9	11	9	6	1	5	6	.314	.500	.240	6.00	5.00
Trenton Toplikar	R-R	6-4	215	5-21-96	2	1	6.37	21	1	0	0	30	31	21	21	5	16	29	.267	.265	.269	8.80	4.85
Cole Waites	R-R	6-3	180	6-10-98	2	2	1.71	18	0	0	4	21	12	7	4	0	15	38	.162	.069	.222	16.29	6.43
Ryan Walker	R-R	6-2	200	11-26-95	7	2	3.35	43	0	0	2	46	37	22	17	1	24	56	.215	.247	.187	11.04	4.73
Ty Weber	R-R	6-4	220	3-19-98	0	0	6.75	2	0	0	0	4	4	3	3	0	2	3	.250	.200	.273	6.75	4.50
Keaton Winn	R-R	6-4	238	2-20-98	2	3	4.15	6	6	0	0	30	35	14	14	4	6	24	.294	.383	.203	7.12	1.78
Chris Wright	L-L	6-1	205	10-14-98	4	2	3.86	41	0	0	6	56	44	27	24	5	35	76	.218	.184	.238	12.21	5.63

Fielding

Catcher	PCT	G	PO	A	E	DP	PB
Auerbach	1.000	22	192	15	0	1	4
Emery	.982	11	103	5	2	2	1
Genoves	.995	37	393	19	2	1	6
Martorano	.992	74	665	44	6	2	13

First Base	PCT	G	PO	A	E	DP
Aldrete	.984	11	57	5	1	8
Emery	.953	5	40	1	2	6
Genoves	1.000	8	44	3	0	7
Mahan	.983	17	104	10	2	6
Rincones	1.000	1	7	0	0	0
Roby	.986	21	118	18	2	12
Smith	1.000	15	95	4	0	7
Tostado	.996	67	444	35	2	45

Second Base	PCT	G	PO	A	E	DP
Aldrete	.952	11	16	24	2	7
Auerbach	.984	53	76	107	3	20
Fitzgerald	.972	30	41	62	3	16
Mahan	1.000	2	2	2	0	0
Matheny	.972	21	31	39	2	8
Roby	1.000	1	2	0	0	0
Whiteman	1.000	9	13	17	0	6
Wilson	1.000	16	32	31	0	10

Third Base	PCT	G	PO	A	E	DP
Aldrete	1.000	6	2	6	0	0
Auerbach	1.000	13	9	13	0	1
Emery	.000	1	0	0	0	0
Fitzgerald	.944	8	8	9	1	0
Genoves	.000	1	0	0	0	0
Matheny	.909	21	16	44	6	4
Roby	.904	57	30	93	13	9
Schmitt	.965	29	18	37	2	5
Whiteman	.800	5	3	5	2	0

Wilson	1.000	2	3	3 0	0

Shortstop	PCT	G	PO	A	E	DP
Aldrete	.846	3	6	5	2	0
Fitzgerald	.968	87	114	189	10	44
Matheny	.915	17	29	46	7	13
Whiteman	1.000	1	1	2	0	0
Wilson	.944	32	36	66	6	10

Outfield	PCT	G	PO	A	E	DP
Aldrete	1.000	7	6	1	0	0
Auerbach	1.000	15	22	0	0	0
Brown	1.000	1	1	0	0	0
Gigliotti	.988	74	167	2	2	1
Heyward	.977	96	167	3	4	0
Labour	.978	70	128	5	3	2
Matheny	.935	32	56	2	4	0
Peters	.986	33	68	2	1	1
Rincones	.962	36	49	1	2	0
Smith	.988	55	81	2	1	1
Tostado	1.000	5	10	0	0	0
Whiteman	.963	12	25	1	1	0

EUGENE EMERALDS — *HIGH CLASS A*

NORTHWEST LEAGUE

Batting	B-T	HT	WT	DOB	AVG	vLH	vRH	G	AB	R	H	2B	3B	HR	RBI	BB	HBP	SH	SF	SO	SB	CS	SLG	OBP
Carter Aldrete	R-R	6-2	205	10-12-97	.289	.304	.285	74	242	47	70	17	0	15	52	31	2	0	4	60	2	2	.545	.369
Patrick Bailey	B-R	6-1	210	5-29-99	.225	.131	.252	83	267	49	60	14	1	12	51	49	2	0	7	72	1	1	.419	.342
Hunter Bishop	L-R	6-5	210	6-25-98	.235	.211	.242	85	315	51	74	11	2	13	44	31	9	2	1	117	20	2	.406	.320
Rodolfo Bone	R-R	5-10	195	3-22-00	.158	.100	.179	33	114	8	18	4	0	2	12	4	1	0	0	48	0	0	.246	.193
Vaun Brown	R-R	6-1	215	6-23-98	.350	.367	.346	43	157	50	55	10	2	9	34	22	11	0	4	52	21	3	.611	.454
Hayden Cantrelle	B-R	5-11	175	11-25-98	.214	.000	.261	9	28	8	6	4	0	1	4	12	0	0	1	8	3	0	.464	.439
Damon Dues	L-R	6-0	180	6-21-98	.455	1.000	.400	5	11	6	5	0	0	0	2	6	0	1	0	3	3	0	.455	.647
Jared Dupere	L-R	5-11	200	1-23-99	.143	.100	.154	12	49	5	7	3	0	1	9	4	0	0	0	19	1	0	.265	.208
Robert Emery	R-R	6-0	210	10-22-96	.243	.250	.240	33	107	16	26	7	0	1	11	19	4	0	1	36	0	0	.336	.374
Ronaldo Flores	R-R	6-0	175	5-17-02	.182	.000	.222	5	11	1	2	1	0	0	0	0	0	0	0	4	0	0	.273	.182
Najee Gaskins	R-R	6-0	180	9-7-97	.266	.278	.263	30	94	14	25	5	1	0	12	9	6	1	2	38	3	1	.340	.360
Jimmy Glowenke	R-R	5-10	200	6-5-99	.212	.255	.200	75	250	39	53	14	0	12	44	23	9	0	0	88	0	0	.412	.301
Marco Luciano	R-R	6-2	178	9-10-01	.263	.254	.267	57	205	27	54	10	0	10	30	22	2	0	1	51	0	0	.459	.339
Riley Mahan	L-R	6-3	220	12-31-95	.276	.125	.333	8	29	9	8	3	1	2	10	3	0	0	2	14	0	0	.655	.324
Luis Matos	R-R	5-11	160	1-28-02	.211	.237	.202	91	369	55	78	14	1	11	43	27	7	0	4	65	11	3	.344	.275
Grant McCray	L-R	6-2	190	12-7-00	.269	.182	.293	14	52	12	14	2	0	2	10	9	1	0	0	22	8	0	.423	.387
Jairo Pomares	L-R	6-1	185	8-4-00	.254	.262	.252	95	338	49	86	20	0	14	59	36	3	0	2	127	0	0	.438	.330
Ghordy Santos	B-R	6-1	177	9-2-99	.259	.267	.257	64	251	38	65	14	1	6	18	18	3	0	2	83	8	4	.394	.314
Casey Schmitt	R-R	6-2	215	3-1-99	.273	.244	.283	93	333	58	91	14	1	17	59	42	6	0	2	86	1	2	.474	.363
Armani Smith	R-R	6-4	215	7-19-98	.233	.333	.192	24	73	13	17	1	1	4	15	16	1	0	0	24	1	1	.438	.378
Andy Thomas	L-R	6-2	210	6-17-98	.174	.130	.190	24	86	8	15	1	0	1	8	15	1	0	0	25	0	0	.221	.304
2-team total (64 Everett AquaSox)					.238	.197	.251	88	302	41	72	13	0	10	40	58	7	0	0	91	1	0	.381	.373
Luis Toribio	L-R	6-1	185	9-28-00	.209	.195	.213	111	378	57	79	18	1	21	59	52	4	0	3	154	0	0	.429	.309
Simon Whiteman	R-R	5-10	165	1-28-97	.180	.256	.160	61	183	27	33	3	1	1	14	36	3	2	0	64	16	1	.224	.324
Carter Williams	L-R	6-3	210	1-14-98	.277	.290	.274	38	137	18	38	8	0	4	23	7	0	0	2	34	3	1	.423	.308
Max Wright	L-R	6-3	215	1-8-98	.198	.250	.186	26	86	13	17	3	0	4	11	11	3	0	0	27	0	0	.372	.310

Pitching	B-T	HT	WT	DOB	W	L	ERA	G	GS	CG	SV	IP	H	R	ER	HR	BB	SO	AVG	vLH	vRH	K/9	BB/9
Abel Adames	R-R	6-5	190	12-8-95	11	4	4.50	34	1	0	1	62	61	37	31	12	23	65	.253	.210	.284	9.44	3.34
Tanner Andrews	R-R	6-3	220	11-15-95	0	0	2.25	4	0	0	0	4	1	1	1	1	1	8	.077	.167	.000	18.00	2.25
Nick Avila	R-R	6-4	195	7-25-97	2	1	0.95	27	0	0	13	28	19	6	3	1	8	31	.190	.211	.163	9.85	2.54
Prelander Berroa	R-R	5-11	170	4-18-00	0	0	0.68	4	4	0	0	13	5	1	1	0	6	16	.122	.045	.211	10.80	4.05
2-team total (13 Everett AquaSox)					2	2	2.06	17	17	0	0	66	34	16	15	2	38	97	.153	.121	.183	13.29	5.21
Mason Black	R-R	6-3	230	12-10-99	5	3	3.94	16	16	0	0	78	70	37	34	11	28	92	.240	.236	.242	10.66	3.24
Seth Corry	L-L	6-2	195	11-3-98	0	0	3.86	2	2	0	0	2	3	1	1	0	3	1	.300	.400	.200	3.86	11.57
Brooks Crawford	R-R	6-4	215	8-19-96	8	3	3.18	43	0	0	2	57	49	23	20	7	20	64	.239	.211	.256	10.16	3.18
Hunter Dula	L-R	6-1	205	3-8-99	0	0	4.15	4	0	0	0	4	1	2	2	0	7	2	.083	.143	.000	4.15	14.54
Ronaldo Flores	R-R	6-0	175	5-17-02	0	0	0.00	1	0	0	0	1	1	0	0	0	0	0	.200	.000	.500	0.00	0.00
Evan Gates	R-R	6-0	210	1-13-98	0	1	2.78	19	0	0	1	23	18	7	7	3	8	28	.217	.182	.240	11.12	3.18
John Gavin	R-L	6-6	250	10-10-95	1	0	1.80	4	0	0	0	5	3	1	1	0	1	8	.176	.000	.200	14.40	1.80
Jorge Guzman	R-R	6-1	246	1-28-96	0	0	0.00	5	0	0	1	4	2	0	0	0	3	7	.118	.167	.091	14.54	6.23
Kyle Harrison	R-L	6-2	200	8-12-01	0	1	1.55	7	7	0	0	29	19	8	5	2	10	59	.179	.244	.138	18.31	3.10
Clay Helvey	R-R	6-3	195	2-14-97	1	1	3.12	21	0	0	2	26	11	12	9	1	12	40	.121	.082	.167	13.85	4.15
Wil Jensen	R-R	6-4	180	9-2-97	6	3	2.84	15	12	0	0	63	51	25	20	8	16	77	.213	.171	.254	10.94	2.27
Trevor McDonald	R-R	6-2	200	2-26-01	0	0	1.64	2	0	0	0	11	11	5	2	2	2	18	.256	.111	.360	14.73	1.64
Nick Morreale	R-R	6-5	220	7-27-97	8	4	3.33	40	0	0	2	54	45	33	20	5	20	64	.216	.232	.204	10.67	3.33
Ryan Murphy	R-R	6-1	190	10-8-99	1	0	2.90	7	7	0	0	31	20	11	10	1	12	47	.180	.203	.154	13.65	3.48
Tyler Myrick	R-R	6-0	205	6-25-98	0	0	1.00	8	0	0	1	9	6	2	1	0	4	10	.188	.214	.167	10.00	4.00
Mat Olsen	R-R	5-11	185	7-8-00	6	1	4.61	28	0	0	0	41	41	26	21	1	22	59	.258	.323	.213	12.95	4.83
Ofelky Peralta	R-R	6-5	195	4-20-97	1	0	0.00	3	0	0	0	6	1	2	0	0	3	11	.045	.000	.059	15.63	4.26
Randy Rodriguez	R-R	6-0	166	9-5-99	2	3	3.38	16	13	0	0	51	35	21	19	5	24	71	.193	.286	.100	12.61	4.26
Landen Roupp	R-R	6-2	205	9-10-98	3	0	1.67	7	7	0	0	32	19	6	6	1	9	52	.165	.171	.162	14.47	2.51
Juan Sanchez	L-L	6-2	165	11-12-00	3	0	3.76	40	0	0	7	53	42	24	22	3	29	75	.216	.238	.206	12.82	4.96
Carson Seymour	R-R	6-6	260	12-16-98	2	3	3.99	6	6	0	0	29	25	18	13	1	10	43	.229	.158	.268	13.19	3.07
Brett Standlee	R-R	6-4	223	9-14-98	3	2	4.75	40	1	0	1	53	53	33	28	5	23	61	.254	.274	.237	10.36	3.91
Nick Swiney	R-L	6-3	185	2-12-99	4	6	3.84	21	20	0	0	89	63	48	38	7	45	105	.193	.243	.170	10.62	4.55
Daniel Tillo	L-L	6-5	215	6-13-96	0	0	2.08	4	0	0	0	4	3	3	1	0	3	5	.200	.333	.167	10.38	6.23
Cole Waites	R-R	6-3	180	6-10-98	1	1	3.55	13	0	0	1	13	10	5	5	1	4	27	.208	.276	.105	19.18	2.84
Ty Weber	R-R	6-4	220	3-19-98	3	3	3.45	29	2	0	2	63	62	28	24	7	14	55	.252	.196	.295	7.90	2.01
Keaton Winn	R-R	6-4	238	2-20-98	3	2	3.16	8	8	0	0	37	38	15	13	2	10	46	.264	.234	.278	11.19	2.43
Jake Wong	R-R	6-2	218	9-3-96	6	5	4.52	25	17	0	1	98	95	58	49	7	44	108	.252	.247	.256	9.95	4.05
Nick Zwack	L-L	6-3	230	8-1-98	1	1	3.99	6	6	0	0	29	23	14	13	3	16	36	.211	.143	.235	11.05	4.91

Fielding

Catcher	PCT	G	PO	A	E	DP	PB
Bailey	.989	72	762	62	9	2	12
Bone	.988	32	310	19	4	2	8
Emery	.933	4	25	3	2	0	1
Flores	1.000	2	12	1	0	0	0
Thomas	.994	15	165	12	1	0	0
Wright	1.000	10	87	7	0	0	1

First Base	PCT	G	PO	A	E	DP
Aldrete	.972	33	190	22	6	14
Bailey	1.000	1	1	0	0	0
Emery	.981	26	187	16	4	20
Mahan	.963	3	23	3	1	2
Toribio	.972	61	389	26	12	28
Wright	.963	10	78	1	3	6

Second Base	PCT	G	PO	A	E	DP
Aldrete	1.000	1	1	2	0	0
Cantrelle	1.000	8	12	13	0	3
Glowenke	1.000	47	61	99	0	21
Mahan	1.000	3	6	5	0	1
Santos	.958	21	22	46	3	7
Whiteman	.979	51	79	105	4	22

Third Base	PCT	G	PO	A	E	DP
Aldrete	.924	35	20	53	6	2
Dues	1.000	2	1	5	0	1
Glowenke	1.000	9	7	14	0	1
Mahan	1.000	1	2	3	0	0
Santos	.000	1	0	0	0	0
Schmitt	.931	50	37	58	7	4
Toribio	.961	34	15	59	3	7
Whiteman	1.000	1	0	2	0	0

Shortstop	PCT	G	PO	A	E	DP
Aldrete	1.000	3	4	4	0	1
Cantrelle	.833	1	2	3	1	0
Glowenke	.977	13	15	27	1	8
Luciano	.928	51	50	91	11	14
Santos	.804	18	21	24	11	5
Schmitt	.963	40	41	88	5	18
Whiteman	.920	6	8	15	2	3

Outfield	PCT	G	PO	A	E	DP
Aldrete	.500	2	1	0	1	0
Bishop	1.000	68	122	2	0	0
Brown	1.000	36	51	6	0	0
Dues	1.000	3	3	0	0	0
Dupere	.952	11	18	2	1	0
Gaskins	1.000	25	34	1	0	1
Matos	.989	83	168	5	2	1
McCray	.952	13	19	1	1	0
Pomares	.957	80	105	5	5	1
Santos	.968	26	28	2	1	0
Smith	.935	19	29	0	2	0
Whiteman	1.000	2	3	0	0	0
Williams	.955	32	40	2	2	1

SAN JOSE GIANTS

LOW CLASS A

CALIFORNIA LEAGUE

Batting	B-T	HT	WT	DOB	AVG	vLH	vRH	G	AB	R	H	2B	3B	HR	RBI	BB	HBP	SH	SF	SO	SB	CS	SLG	OBP
Aeverson Arteaga	R-R	6-1	170	3-16-03	.270	.293	.265	122	503	87	136	35	2	14	84	49	10	0	3	155	11	6	.431	.345
Victor Bericoto	R-R	6-1	155	12-3-01	.265	.337	.246	107	423	63	112	19	0	12	68	57	3	0	4	108	3	4	.395	.353
Vaun Brown	R-R	6-1	215	6-23-98	.346	.389	.333	59	228	50	79	14	5	14	41	25	8	0	1	67	23	3	.636	.427
Hayden Cantrelle	B-R	5-11	175	11-25-98	.279	.467	.250	35	111	26	31	3	5	2	12	34	2	0	2	37	10	1	.450	.450
Damon Dues	L-R	6-0	180	6-21-98	.368	.000	.378	13	38	17	14	3	1	0	2	19	0	0	0	4	8	2	.500	.579
Jared Dupere	L-R	5-11	200	1-23-99	.289	.348	.276	32	128	26	37	4	1	10	29	14	1	0	0	40	2	0	.570	.364
Ronaldo Flores	R-R	6-0	175	5-17-02	.275	.200	.288	21	69	11	19	1	0	5	10	3	1	0	1	16	1	0	.507	.311
Garrett Frechette	L-L	6-3	210	12-31-00	.255	.188	.269	97	376	44	96	16	3	4	39	19	6	2	5	98	2	2	.346	.298
Najee Gaskins	R-R	6-0	180	9-7-97	.274	.367	.241	40	117	19	32	7	0	1	15	18	7	5	2	38	4	2	.359	.396
P.J. Hilson	R-R	5-11	175	8-25-00	.375	.429	.364	11	40	5	15	1	0	2	11	1	2	0	2	6	2	0	.550	.400
Andrew Kachel	L-R	6-0	170	12-24-00	.286	.000	.333	3	7	2	2	1	0	0	4	2	0	0	0	4	0	0	.429	.444
Abdiel Layer	B-R	6-2	170	8-9-98	.231	.280	.217	30	108	18	25	8	1	5	16	13	1	2	2	43	3	2	.463	.315
Riley Mahan	L-R	6-3	220	12-31-95	.256	.167	.272	39	160	21	41	7	1	7	26	17	3	0	1	54	4	2	.444	.337
Grant McCray	L-R	6-2	190	12-7-00	.291	.264	.298	106	436	92	127	21	9	21	69	58	9	0	4	148	35	10	.525	.383
Wade Meckler	L-R	5-10	178	4-21-00	.439	.167	.552	11	41	9	18	7	0	1	8	9	0	0	0	8	1	0	.683	.540
Zach Morgan	R-R	6-0	180	3-30-00	.250	.500	.167	2	8	2	2	1	1	0	1	1	1	0	0	3	0	0	.625	.400
Yorlis Rodriguez	R-R	6-0	190	7-20-99	.258	.266	.256	105	431	56	111	20	2	16	60	18	4	2	4	91	4	0	.425	.291
Dilan Rosario	R-R	6-0	185	6-16-01	.216	.286	.197	45	162	22	35	2	1	2	19	28	3	1	1	59	4	3	.278	.340
Rayner Santana	R-R	6-2	250	8-15-02	.180	.175	.182	50	172	20	31	3	0	4	16	18	1	1	2	81	3	1	.267	.259
Anyesber Sivira	R-R	5-9	155	1-9-00	.289	.182	.310	39	135	26	39	5	1	4	21	14	7	1	2	37	2	2	.430	.380
Alexander Suarez	R-R	6-2	200	12-20-01	.231	.159	.242	91	308	53	71	14	3	12	47	18	13	1	6	101	13	1	.412	.296
Adrian Sugastey	R-R	6-1	210	10-23-02	.240	.250	.238	75	300	41	72	11	1	5	32	30	10	0	0	53	1	0	.333	.329
Diego Velasquez	B-R	6-1	150	10-1-03	.159	.200	.147	10	44	6	7	1	0	0	0	3	0	0	0	9	0	0	.182	.213
Carter Williams	L-R	6-3	210	1-14-98	.386	.267	.414	42	158	37	61	13	1	7	38	27	6	0	5	26	5	2	.614	.480
Max Wright	L-R	6-3	215	1-8-98	.197	.188	.200	29	76	12	15	6	0	1	6	22	6	0	0	27	0	1	.316	.413
Logan Wyatt	L-R	6-4	230	11-15-97	.191	.000	.231	11	47	5	9	3	0	0	6	5	0	0	1	10	0	0	.255	.264

Pitching	B-T	HT	WT	DOB	W	L	ERA	G	GS	CG	SV	IP	H	R	ER	HR	BB	SO	AVG	vLH	vRH	K/9	BB/9
Melvin Adon	L-R	6-3	246	6-9-94	0	1	1.93	5	0	0	0	5	4	4	1	0	4	7	.222	.222	.222	13.50	7.71
Scott Alexander	L-L	6-2	195	7-10-89	1	0	3.00	3	0	0	0	3	3	1	1	0	0	1	.250	.500	.200	3.00	0.00
Tanner Andrews	R-R	6-3	220	11-15-95	0	0	0.00	2	0	0	0	3	0	0	0	0	2	4	.000	.000	.000	13.50	6.75
Will Bednar	R-R	6-2	230	6-13-00	1	3	4.19	12	12	0	0	43	25	22	20	7	22	51	.167	.159	.172	10.67	4.60
Hayden Birdsong	R-R	6-4	215	8-30-01	1	0	4.50	3	0	0	0	6	8	3	3	0	3	11	.320	.364	.286	16.50	4.50
Spencer Bivens	R-R	6-5	205	6-28-94	2	1	2.70	21	0	0	2	30	20	10	9	3	18	36	.182	.077	.239	10.80	5.40
Mason Black	R-R	6-3	230	12-10-99	1	1	1.57	8	8	0	0	34	25	6	6	1	8	44	.198	.140	.246	11.53	2.10
Jose Cruz	R-R	6-1	178	5-18-00	2	1	2.06	38	0	0	6	52	21	13	12	3	23	86	.119	.098	.130	14.79	3.96
Sam Delaplane	R-R	5-11	175	3-27-95	0	0	14.73	4	0	0	0	4	3	6	6	0	7	11	.188	.286	.111	27.00	17.18
Hunter Dula	L-R	6-1	205	3-8-99	2	4	4.10	35	0	0	7	42	39	25	19	3	19	54	.239	.306	.198	11.66	4.10
Ronaldo Flores	R-R	6-0	175	5-17-02	0	0	0.00	2	0	0	0	2	2	0	0	0	0	0	.250	.400	.000	0.00	0.00
Evan Gates	R-R	6-0	210	1-13-98	5	1	0.76	16	0	0	1	24	5	4	2	2	6	28	.065	.077	.059	10.65	2.28
John Gavin	R-L	6-6	250	10-10-95	1	0	2.53	8	0	0	0	11	9	3	3	0	6	17	.231	.000	.273	14.34	5.06
Jorge Guzman	R-R	6-1	246	1-28-96	0	0	3.00	5	0	0	1	6	7	2	2	0	5	6	.304	.429	.250	9.00	7.50
Trevor Hildenberger	R-R	6-2	205	12-15-90	0	0	18.00	1	0	0	0	1	2	2	2	0	0	1	.400	.333	.500	9.00	0.00
Joe Kemlage	B-L	6-1	220	1-19-99	2	2	4.56	12	4	0	1	47	41	27	24	5	29	48	.232	.237	.230	9.13	5.51
William Kempner	R-R	6-0	222	6-18-01	0	0	6.35	3	2	0	0	6	6	4	4	1	4	6	.273	.222	.308	9.53	6.35
Zack Littell	R-R	6-4	220	10-5-95	0	0	0.00	2	0	0	0	2	2	0	0	0	1	2	.250	1.000	.000	9.00	4.50
Seth Lonsway	L-L	6-2	210	10-7-98	9	3	4.06	26	9	0	1	95	81	57	43	8	51	120	.229	.200	.236	11.33	4.81
Ben Madison	R-R	6-3	205	9-15-97	1	3	3.33	20	0	0	1	27	17	11	10	0	15	47	.179	.237	.140	15.67	5.00
Mikell Manzano	R-R	6-0	140	11-30-02	0	2	23.63	2	1	0	0	3	6	8	7	1	3	4	.429	.400	.444	13.50	10.13
Trevor McDonald	R-R	6-2	200	2-26-01	6	3	2.39	27	10	0	2	90	74	34	24	2	40	102	.223	.260	.199	10.16	3.99

Manuel Mercedes	R-R	6-4	190	9-21-02	4	6	5.13	25	9	0	2	81	67	62	46	7	63	67	.227	.277	.188	7.48	7.03
Matt Mikulski	L-L	6-4	205	5-8-99	4	5	6.95	22	18	0	0	79	94	66	61	12	31	96	.296	.351	.284	10.94	3.53
Spencer Miles	L-R	6-3	180	7-26-00	1	0	6.23	2	0	0	0	4	5	3	3	1	2	5	.294	.200	.333	10.38	4.15
Ryan Murphy	R-R	6-1	190	10-8-99	0	0	10.80	1	0	0	0	2	3	2	2	1	1	3	.375	.250	.500	16.20	5.40
Tyler Myrick	R-R	6-0	205	6-25-98	2	3	3.38	30	0	0	5	32	35	17	12	1	12	31	.276	.347	.231	8.72	3.38
Mat Olsen	R-R	5-11	185	7-8-00	2	0	0.53	8	0	0	2	17	9	2	1	0	3	24	.150	.125	.159	12.71	1.59
Ofelky Peralta	R-R	6-5	195	4-20-97	1	0	3.86	5	0	0	0	7	5	6	3	0	1	7	.200	.333	.077	9.00	1.29
Yoniel Ramirez	R-R	6-0	180	5-27-01	1	0	5.79	9	0	0	0	14	12	9	9	1	10	16	.226	.048	.344	10.29	6.43
Julio Rodriguez	R-R	6-3	180	2-10-00	4	2	4.34	38	0	0	0	48	49	31	23	1	34	63	.263	.194	.307	11.90	6.42
Landen Roupp	R-R	6-2	205	9-10-98	5	2	2.59	14	2	0	0	49	33	14	14	2	17	69	.188	.191	.185	12.76	3.14
JJ Santa Cruz	L-L	6-7	220	1-15-96	1	0	3.72	9	0	0	0	10	11	7	4	0	3	9	.268	.000	.306	8.38	2.79
Rayner Santana	R-R	6-2	250	8-15-02	0	0	0.00	1	0	0	0	1	2	0	0	0	1	1	.400	.333	.500	9.00	9.00
Eric Silva	R-R	6-1	185	10-3-02	3	7	5.88	22	22	0	0	86	77	57	56	11	39	99	.244	.241	.246	10.40	4.10
Liam Simon	R-R	6-4	220	10-16-00	0	0	2.08	2	2	0	0	4	3	1	1	0	4	5	.200	.000	.375	10.38	8.31
Nick Sinacola	L-R	6-2	205	10-29-99	6	6	3.86	25	18	0	0	103	104	53	44	11	39	116	.263	.298	.244	10.17	3.42
Willian Suarez	R-R	6-3	175	3-21-98	1	1	4.76	12	0	0	1	17	13	9	9	1	12	35	.200	.200	.200	18.53	6.35
Ian Villers	R-R	6-6	245	9-1-00	0	0	3.00	3	0	0	0	3	1	2	1	0	4	2	.091	.000	.167	6.00	12.00
Esmerlin Vinicio	L-L	6-2	141	1-31-03	4	0	6.46	24	2	0	1	39	45	30	28	4	26	43	.298	.321	.293	9.92	6.00
Jeremy Walker	R-R	6-5	235	6-12-95	0	0	9.00	1	0	0	0	2	4	2	2	0	0	4	.400	.000	.571	18.00	0.00
Carson Whisenhunt	L-L	6-3	209	10-20-00	0	0	0.00	2	2	0	0	5	5	0	0	0	1	7	.263	.500	.200	13.50	1.93
Keaton Winn	R-R	6-4	238	2-20-98	1	1	4.87	13	11	0	0	41	38	24	22	3	16	55	.247	.172	.300	12.17	3.54

Fielding

Catcher	PCT	G	PO	A	E	DP	PB
Flores	.987	16	146	10	2	1	7
Morgan	1.000	2	27	0	0	0	0
Santana	.984	37	351	20	6	1	15
Sugastey	.987	62	698	61	10	6	8
Wright	.990	20	189	10	2	0	8

First Base	PCT	G	PO	A	E	DP
Bericoto	.977	31	201	12	5	23
Frechette	.990	91	677	33	7	62
Layer	1.000	2	6	1	0	2
Mahan	.970	4	32	0	1	5
Santana	1.000	3	28	2	0	3
Wyatt	.971	8	63	3	2	5

Second Base	PCT	G	PO	A	E	DP
Cantrelle	.992	26	49	70	1	17
Dues	1.000	5	6	11	0	2
Layer	.979	13	21	25	1	8
Mahan	.980	13	24	25	1	11
Rodriguez	.882	4	7	8	2	0
Rosario	.943	38	59	74	8	17
Sivira	.980	32	59	86	3	19
Velasquez	1.000	8	15	28	0	9

Third Base	PCT	G	PO	A	E	DP
Layer	.947	14	9	27	2	2
Mahan	.841	16	8	29	7	2
Rodriguez	.930	98	58	181	18	17
Sivira	1.000	6	3	12	0	0

Shortstop	PCT	G	PO	A	E	DP
Arteaga	.947	118	147	302	25	69
Cantrelle	.917	3	6	5	1	1
Dues	1.000	1	2	0	0	0
Layer	.900	2	5	4	1	1
Rosario	.949	10	17	20	2	5
Velasquez	.667	2	2	2	2	0

Outfield	PCT	G	PO	A	E	DP
Bericoto	.862	57	47	3	8	0
Brown	.987	49	76	1	1	0
Dues	.750	5	2	1	1	0
Dupere	1.000	26	35	1	0	0
Frechette	1.000	2	1	0	0	0
Gaskins	.925	36	36	1	3	0
Hilson	.944	10	17	0	1	0
McCray	.961	93	164	9	7	2
Meckler	1.000	13	14	0	0	0
Suarez	.924	82	130	4	11	1
Williams	.978	38	44	0	1	0

ACL GIANTS BLACK — *ROOKIE*

ARIZONA COMPLEX LEAGUE

Batting	B-T	HT	WT	DOB	AVG	vLH	vRH	G	AB	R	H	2B	3B	HR	RBI	BB	HBP	SH	SF	SO	SB	CS	SLG	OBP
Hunter Bishop	L-R	6-5	210	6-25-98	.000	.000	--	1	2	0	0	0	0	0	0	0	0	0	0	0	0	0	.000	.000
Hayden Cantrelle	B-R	5-11	175	11-25-98	.308	.000	.333	5	13	6	4	3	0	0	3	5	0	0	2	5	0	1	.538	.450
Reggie Crawford	L-L	6-4	235	12-4-00	.158	.167	.154	6	19	2	3	0	0	0	0	2	0	0	0	9	0	0	.158	.238
Jared Dupere	L-R	5-11	200	1-23-99	.254	.000	.262	17	63	13	16	5	1	4	13	7	0	0	0	17	4	0	.556	.329
Javier Francisco	R-R	6-1	162	11-11-02	.151	.063	.171	36	86	12	13	3	1	1	3	11	2	1	0	37	0	0	.244	.263
Harrison Freed	R-R	5-11	205	5-13-98	.270	.286	.268	24	63	10	17	5	0	2	11	6	3	0	2	27	0	0	.444	.351
Thomas Gavello	L-R	5-10	180	6-6-01	.200	.222	.188	9	25	6	5	0	0	1	5	4	3	0	1	12	0	0	.320	.364
Cesar Gonzalez	R-R	5-11	206	5-8-01	.212	.250	.200	14	33	5	7	2	0	0	4	2	0	0	1	11	0	0	.273	.250
P.J. Hilson	R-R	5-11	175	8-25-00	.295	.200	.314	52	183	44	54	12	5	9	27	16	10	0	1	63	13	1	.563	.381
Marco Luciano	R-R	6-2	178	9-10-01	.318	1.000	.211	8	22	6	7	2	0	1	6	4	1	0	0	7	0	0	.545	.444
Wyatt Mathisen	R-R	6-0	217	12-30-93	.375	.667	.200	3	8	5	3	0	0	2	5	4	0	0	0	1	0	0	1.125	.583
Luis Matos	R-R	5-11	160	1-28-02	.429	--	.429	2	7	3	3	1	0	1	4	1	0	0	0	1	0	0	1.000	.500
Wade Meckler	L-R	5-10	178	4-21-00	.289	.222	.310	12	38	12	11	4	0	0	6	11	1	0	0	8	1	0	.395	.460
Tanner O'Tremba	R-R	6-0	212	12-6-99	.229	.500	.148	11	35	9	8	1	0	1	7	2	4	0	0	17	1	0	.343	.341
Jean Pena	R-R	6-1	175	12-22-00	.159	.136	.163	42	126	22	20	4	1	3	18	25	1	0	2	55	0	0	.278	.299
Onil Perez	R-R	6-1	187	9-10-02	.275	.321	.264	47	149	18	41	10	3	0	20	16	2	0	4	30	3	2	.383	.345
Mauricio Pierre	R-R	6-3	180	11-23-03	.232	.300	.220	45	138	15	32	6	0	1	10	10	2	1	0	52	5	3	.297	.293
Elian Rayo	R-R	6-0	202	3-4-03	.238	.276	.229	52	160	24	38	7	2	6	28	26	5	0	1	67	1	0	.419	.359
Samuel Reyes	R-R	6-0	170	1-27-03	.222	.400	.194	15	36	7	8	2	0	0	5	4	3	0	0	15	0	0	.278	.349
Anthony Rodriguez	B-R	6-2	165	9-20-02	.251	.267	.248	52	175	26	44	6	0	6	30	22	2	0	2	69	2	2	.389	.338
Dilan Rosario	R-R	6-0	185	6-16-01	.221	.278	.209	37	104	16	23	8	0	2	13	15	1	0	0	41	1	2	.356	.325
Anyesber Sivira	R-R	5-9	155	1-9-00	.353	--	.353	12	34	8	12	0	1	2	7	4	0	0	0	8	0	0	.588	.421

Pitching	B-T	HT	WT	DOB	W	L	ERA	G	GS	CG	SV	IP	H	R	ER	HR	BB	SO	AVG	vLH	vRH	K/9	BB/9
Cristian Acosta	R-R	6-0	170	9-19-99	1	1	3.24	6	0	0	0	17	15	11	6	0	6	20	.227	.333	.121	10.80	3.24
2-team total (3 ACL Giants Orange)					1	1	4.05	9	0	0	0	20	20	15	9	0	9	23	.253	.371	.159	10.35	4.05
Scott Alexander	L-L	6-2	195	7-10-89	1	0	0.00	3	1	0	0	3	3	0	0	0	0	4	.273	.500	.143	12.00	0.00
John Bertrand	L-L	6-3	205	2-8-98	0	0	0.00	5	1	0	1	8	4	0	0	0	0	8	.143	.000	.235	9.00	0.00
Wilkelma Castillo	R-R	6-0	170	1-6-00	2	2	2.86	20	0	0	4	28	19	11	9	2	8	31	.184	.314	.118	9.85	2.54
John Gavin	R-L	6-6	250	10-10-95	2	0	0.00	6	0	0	2	9	2	0	0	0	3	13	.071	.000	.100	13.00	3.00

Jorge Guzman	R-R	6-1	246	1-28-96	1	0	0.00	4	0	0	0	5	2	0	0	0	1	7	.118	.000	.200	12.60	1.80
Davis Hare	R-R	6-3	219	6-15-99	0	0	0.00	2	0	0	0	2	0	0	0	0	2	3	.000	.000	.000	13.50	9.00
Trevor Hildenberger	R-R	6-2	205	12-15-90	0	0	0.00	1	1	0	0	1	0	0	0	0	0	2	.000	.000	.000	18.00	0.00
Rolfi Jimenez	R-R	6-0	150	10-8-02	6	2	5.44	14	6	0	1	48	59	34	29	6	20	44	.312	.290	.325	8.25	3.75
Jakob Junis	R-R	6-3	220	9-16-92	0	0	2.25	2	2	0	0	4	5	1	1	1	0	4	.278	.400	.125	9.00	0.00
Joe Kemlage	B-L	6-1	220	1-19-99	3	0	0.00	4	3	0	0	16	9	0	0	0	2	25	.161	.063	.200	14.06	1.13
William Kempner	R-R	6-0	222	6-18-01	1	0	2.70	2	0	0	0	3	4	1	1	0	2	5	.333	.500	.250	13.50	5.40
Haydn King	L-L	6-2	205	11-14-98	1	2	1.38	12	0	0	0	13	8	5	2	0	7	17	.170	.083	.200	11.77	4.85
Ben Madison	R-R	6-3	205	9-15-97	1	0	0.00	5	0	0	0	7	3	0	0	0	2	7	.125	.250	.063	9.00	2.57
Nomar Medina	L-L	6-0	190	11-23-02	6	0	2.22	14	12	1	1	65	58	20	16	1	16	70	.243	.273	.234	9.69	2.22
Spencer Miles	L-R	6-3	180	7-26-00	1	0	0.00	3	0	0	0	3	1	1	0	0	1	7	.100	.000	.200	21.00	3.00
Roberto Monegro	R-R	5-10	145	11-15-01	2	2	4.33	9	7	0	0	35	40	18	17	3	9	48	.284	.286	.282	12.23	2.29
Miguel Mora	R-R	6-2	187	11-4-01	4	4	3.29	13	12	0	0	55	43	25	20	0	26	78	.213	.215	.211	12.84	4.28
Ryan Murphy	R-R	6-1	190	10-8-99	0	0	9.00	1	0	0	0	1	2	1	1	1	0	0	.400	.250	1.000	0.00	0.00
Kanoa Pagan	R-R	6-2	190	9-29-98	2	1	1.40	11	0	0	2	19	18	4	3	0	4	31	.250	.286	.227	14.43	1.86
Carson Ragsdale	R-R	6-8	225	5-25-98	1	0	0.00	5	4	0	0	6	3	0	0	0	3	9	.150	.250	.083	14.29	4.76
Austin Reich	R-R	6-3	210	4-15-97	0	1	18.00	1	0	0	0	1	3	2	2	0	1	1	.750	1.000	.667	9.00	9.00
Gregory Santos	R-R	6-2	190	8-28-99	0	0	0.00	2	2	0	0	2	2	0	0	0	0	3	.250	.400	.000	13.50	0.00
Liam Simon	R-R	6-4	220	10-16-00	0	0	2.57	4	0	0	3	7	3	2	2	0	2	7	.120	.071	.182	9.00	2.57
Willian Suarez	R-R	6-3	175	3-21-98	2	0	3.60	14	0	0	1	30	23	14	12	4	12	56	.205	.225	.194	16.80	3.60
Esmerlin Vinicio	L-L	6-2	141	1-31-03	0	1	1.93	4	3	0	0	14	13	4	3	0	6	16	.250	.176	.286	10.29	3.86
Tyler Vogel	R-R	6-0	175	11-16-00	0	1	11.57	4	0	0	0	2	4	4	3	0	5	2	.400	.333	.429	7.71	19.29

Fielding

C: Gavello 2, Gonzalez 8, Perez 44. **1B:** Francisco 10, O'Tremba 3, Pena 41, Rosario 3. **2B:** Cantrelle 5, Francisco 1, Gavello 4, Pena 1, Rodriguez 4, Rosario 32, Sivira 8. **3B:** Francisco 2, Gavello 2, Mathisen 2, Rayo 49. **SS:** Luciano 6, Rodriguez 47, Rosario 4. **OF:** Bishop 1, Dupere 16, Francisco 12, Freed 21, Gonzalez 2, Hilson 50, Matos 2, Meckler 12, O'Tremba 6, Pierre 41, Reyes 8, Sivira 2.

ACL GIANTS ORANGE — *ROOKIE*

ARIZONA COMPLEX LEAGUE

Batting	B-T	HT	WT	DOB	AVG	vLH	vRH	G	AB	R	H	2B	3B	HR	RBI	BB	HBP	SH	SF	SO	SB	CS	SLG	OBP
Kwan Adkins	L-L	6-2	195	10-2-96	.270	.292	.265	37	126	19	34	7	2	5	16	8	4	1	1	38	7	1	.476	.331
Rajean Anza	R-R	5-11	160	5-18-03	.208	.091	.230	28	72	6	15	4	0	1	9	7	0	0	0	23	4	0	.306	.278
Justin Bench	R-R	6-0	185	8-28-99	.500	.000	1.000	1	2	0	1	0	0	0	0	0	0	0	0	0	0	0	.500	.500
Gustavo Cardozo	R-R	6-1	160	10-9-03	.230	.200	.237	26	74	5	17	2	0	0	8	3	1	1	3	23	3	0	.257	.259
Nomar Diaz	R-R	6-1	180	4-15-04	.000	.000	.000	7	12	1	0	0	0	0	0	0	1	0	0	5	0	0	.000	.077
Damon Dues	L-R	6-0	180	6-21-98	.378	.375	.379	12	37	8	14	1	2	0	1	4	0	0	0	12	2	0	.514	.439
Tyler Forner	R-L	5-11	195	10-18-01	.194	.276	.170	44	129	17	25	5	1	1	10	9	2	0	0	61	1	1	.271	.257
Jimmy Glowenke	R-R	5-10	200	6-5-99	.261	.400	.222	8	23	2	6	1	0	0	0	2	1	0	0	5	0	0	.304	.346
Matt Higgins	L-R	6-1	215	7-2-99	.344	.167	.385	10	32	4	11	2	2	0	9	6	1	0	1	9	0	0	.531	.450
Carter Howell	R-R	6-0	200	2-7-99	.310	.375	.286	9	29	8	9	2	0	0	3	4	1	0	0	6	1	0	.379	.412
Andrew Kachel	L-R	6-0	170	12-24-00	.310	.143	.364	10	29	4	9	0	0	0	2	5	0	0	1	2	1	0	.310	.400
Derwin Laya	R-R	6-3	187	9-15-03	.185	.179	.187	51	135	13	25	1	0	3	15	19	1	0	2	49	0	0	.259	.287
Jediael Maduro	L-L	6-1	188	12-26-03	.167	.150	.172	31	78	7	13	5	0	0	6	10	2	1	0	26	0	2	.231	.278
Donovan McIntyre	L-L	6-2	165	12-10-02	.155	.217	.140	45	116	20	18	4	1	2	8	12	8	1	0	63	1	3	.259	.279
Zach Morgan	R-R	6-0	180	3-30-00	.148	.400	.091	9	27	3	4	2	0	0	4	3	0	0	0	8	0	0	.222	.233
Irvin Murr III	R-R	6-4	220	3-12-03	.182	.172	.185	48	137	13	25	3	0	2	5	12	2	0	1	63	0	1	.248	.257
Jairo Pomares	L-R	6-1	185	8-4-00	.533	.333	.583	4	15	5	8	3	0	3	7	1	0	0	0	2	0	0	1.333	.563
Cesar Quintas	R-R	6-1	175	3-25-03	.204	.222	.200	34	93	3	19	2	0	0	7	6	5	2	2	32	0	3	.226	.283
Adrian Sugastey	R-R	6-1	210	10-23-02	.231	.167	.250	9	26	4	6	1	1	0	2	4	0	0	1	5	0	0	.346	.323
Yeiver Torrealba	R-R	5-11	145	10-26-01	.136	.333	.063	11	22	3	3	0	0	0	0	2	1	0	0	9	2	0	.136	.240
Freddy Tremaria	R-R	5-11	165	4-28-03	.151	.154	.150	22	53	6	8	1	0	3	3	2	1	0	0	26	0	0	.340	.196
Diego Velasquez	B-R	6-1	150	10-1-03	.277	.256	.283	52	159	18	44	5	2	1	20	21	4	3	3	31	7	1	.352	.369
Donovan Walton	L-R	5-10	190	5-25-94	.143	.500	.000	3	7	0	1	0	0	0	0	1	1	0	0	1	1	0	.143	.333
Will Wilson	R-R	6-0	184	7-21-98	.500	.833	.409	9	28	6	14	4	0	1	9	4	2	0	0	8	0	0	.750	.588
Logan Wyatt	L-R	6-4	230	11-15-97	.234	.182	.250	18	47	6	11	0	0	0	5	5	0	0	0	11	0	0	.234	.308

Pitching	B-T	HT	WT	DOB	W	L	ERA	G	GS	CG	SV	IP	H	R	ER	HR	BB	SO	AVG	vLH	vRH	K/9	BB/9
Cristian Acosta	R-R	6-0	170	9-19-99	0	0	8.10	3	0	0	0	3	5	4	3	0	3	3	.385	1.000	.273	8.10	8.10
2-team total (6 ACL Giants Black)					1	1	4.05	9	0	0	0	20	20	15	9	0	9	23	.253	.371	.159	10.35	4.05
Melvin Adon	L-R	6-3	246	6-9-94	0	1	3.86	6	3	0	0	7	6	3	3	1	3	10	.250	.167	.333	12.86	3.86
Tanner Andrews	R-R	6-3	220	11-15-95	2	0	1.17	6	0	0	0	8	4	4	1	1	1	13	.148	.167	.133	15.26	1.17
Solomon Bates	R-R	6-2	210	3-16-97	0	0	0.00	2	1	0	0	3	0	0	0	0	0	5	.000	.000	.000	15.00	0.00
Hayden Birdsong	R-R	6-4	215	8-30-01	0	0	1.59	4	0	0	0	6	2	1	1	0	0	12	.118	.125	.111	19.06	0.00
Jason Bonilla	R-R	6-0	165	8-30-98	1	3	3.32	15	0	0	0	22	20	9	8	1	16	31	.238	.200	.265	12.88	6.65
Jack Choate	L-L	6-6	249	4-18-01	1	1	2.25	4	0	0	0	4	2	3	1	0	5	8	.143	.000	.182	18.00	11.25
Lisander De La Cruz	R-R	6-2	185	8-16-01	0	6	4.89	15	6	0	0	35	41	27	19	1	14	44	.285	.309	.270	11.31	3.60
Jorge Garcia	R-R	6-0	185	5-10-02	1	0	2.79	7	0	0	0	10	7	3	3	1	3	14	.189	.235	.150	13.03	2.79
Ken Giles	R-R	6-3	197	9-20-90	0	0	18.00	1	1	0	0	1	2	2	2	0	1	2	.400	.500	.333	18.00	9.00
Wei-Chieh Huang	R-R	6-2	175	9-26-93	0	0	0.00	4	3	0	0	7	2	0	0	0	1	12	.087	.167	.000	14.73	1.23
Gerelmi Maldonado	R-R	6-2	170	12-21-03	0	2	2.27	14	8	0	1	40	32	13	10	3	19	59	.219	.288	.172	13.39	4.31
Mikell Manzano	R-R	6-0	140	11-30-02	3	3	3.93	14	11	0	0	55	56	25	24	4	17	81	.257	.291	.235	13.25	2.78
Rafael Martinez	R-R	6-0	160	4-18-00	0	1	6.00	11	1	0	0	18	26	15	12	0	6	26	.317	.289	.341	13.00	3.00
Luis Moreno	R-R	6-2	174	8-3-98	3	3	4.37	16	0	0	2	23	22	21	11	2	10	24	.244	.324	.189	9.53	3.97
Irvin Murr III	R-R	6-4	220	3-12-03	1	0	0.00	1	0	0	0	2	2	2	0	0	0	0	.333	.667	.000	0.00	0.00

Brayan Palencia	R-R	5-11	142	1-14-03	3	5	4.33	14	6	0	0	44	57	29	21	6	10	42	.320	.247	.376	8.66	2.06
Joe Palumbo	L-L	6-0	195	10-26-94	0	0	2.45	2	0	0	0	4	1	1	1	0	1	5	.091	.143	.000	12.27	2.45
Freddery Paulino	R-R	6-2	181	9-12-00	0	9	8.49	12	8	0	0	41	68	45	39	6	17	26	.368	.419	.341	5.66	3.70
Ofelky Peralta	R-R	6-5	195	4-20-97	0	1	2.16	6	0	0	3	8	7	4	2	1	4	13	.219	.182	.238	14.04	4.32
Yoniel Ramirez	R-R	6-0	180	5-27-01	0	2	2.70	14	0	0	2	17	13	7	5	0	7	26	.210	.261	.179	14.04	3.78
JJ Santa Cruz	L-L	6-7	220	1-15-96	2	0	2.08	5	0	0	0	9	8	3	2	0	3	15	.242	.200	.261	15.58	3.12
Daniel Tillo	L-L	6-5	215	6-13-96	1	0	0.00	6	5	0	0	8	3	0	0	0	4	10	.125	.000	.167	11.74	4.70
Ty Weber	R-R	6-4	220	3-19-98	0	0	3.86	2	1	0	1	7	5	3	3	1	0	6	.192	.182	.200	7.71	0.00
Carson Whisenhunt	L-L	6-3	209	10-20-00	0	0	0.00	2	1	0	0	3	1	0	0	0	0	7	.100	.500	.000	21.00	0.00
Ronnie Williams	R-R	6-0	170	1-6-96	0	0	1.69	5	0	0	0	11	9	2	2	0	2	15	.237	.222	.250	12.66	1.69
Hayden Wynja	L-L	6-9	220	10-14-98	0	0	8.10	3	0	0	0	3	6	3	3	1	0	3	.375	.000	.462	8.10	0.00

Fielding

C: Anza 26, Diaz 7, Morgan 8, Sugastey 7, Tremaria 19. **1B:** Adkins 1, Kachel 3, Maduro 16, Murr 27, Pomares 1, Torrealba 1, Wyatt 15. **2B:** Cardozo 20, Dues 8, Glowenke 6, Kachel 4, Murr 10, Quintas 2, Torrealba 4, Velasquez 7, Walton 1. **3B:** Bench 1, Kachel 6, Laya 48, Murr 4. **SS:** Cardozo 6, Dues 1, Torrealba 3, Velasquez 42, Wilson 7. **OF:** Adkins 34, Bonilla 1, Forner 43, Higgins 9, Howell 9, Maduro 5, McIntyre 41, Quintas 32.

DSL GIANTS BLACK — ROOKIE

DOMINICAN SUMMER LEAGUE

Batting	B-T	HT	WT	DOB	AVG	vLH	vRH	G	AB	R	H	2B	3B	HR	RBI	BB	HBP	SH	SF	SO	SB	CS	SLG	OBP
Randy Arrieta	R-R	5-11	150	11-1-03	.146	.286	.118	33	82	7	12	1	3	0	3	7	1	0	0	34	3	2	.232	.222
Saul Bautista	B-R	6-0	145	4-20-04	.280	.250	.288	33	93	19	26	6	2	0	8	18	0	1	2	32	17	6	.307	.389
Javier Castillo	R-R	6-1	170	11-14-03	.244	.348	.221	39	127	14	31	3	4	2	20	11	1	0	0	20	1	2	.378	.309
Victor Coronil	R-R	6-0	175	9-7-02	.169	.273	.150	27	71	4	12	2	0	2	10	10	2	0	1	34	1	0	.282	.286
Moises De La Rosa	R-R	6-2	190	11-29-04	.265	.182	.289	19	49	12	13	3	2	0	5	9	6	0	0	12	2	2	.408	.438
Alessandro Duran	B-R	5-10	170	7-2-05	.156	.194	.146	45	154	13	24	4	0	0	12	16	2	0	3	42	2	0	.182	.240
Javier Francisco	R-R	6-1	162	11-11-02	.417	.600	.368	9	24	5	10	2	1	1	5	4	0	0	2	0	0	1	.708	.467
Luis Frias	R-R	5-11	155	8-7-04	.258	.321	.240	38	128	33	33	3	0	1	9	16	4	0	1	37	19	7	.305	.356
Audie Jimenez	R-R	6-0	151	12-16-04	.146	.115	.154	44	130	13	19	3	0	0	9	5	3	0	2	35	2	3	.169	.193
2-team total (2 DSL Giants Orange)					.146	.143	.147	46	137	15	20	3	0	0	10	6	4	0	2	37	2	3	.168	.201
Wueslly Lespe	L-R	6-0	165	4-23-03	.198	.200	.197	36	81	20	16	3	2	2	8	19	5	0	2	38	3	1	.358	.374
Eduardo Montero	L-R	5-10	150	10-26-03	.286	.000	.333	2	7	0	2	0	0	0	2	0	0	0	0	2	0	0	.286	.286
2-team total (23 DSL Giants Orange)					.243	.273	.237	25	70	4	17	1	0	0	8	11	0	2	1	17	0	1	.257	.341
Ramon Peralta	R-R	5-11	165	10-2-03	.241	.125	.272	37	116	18	28	4	2	2	23	27	2	0	2	34	8	1	.362	.388
Samuel Rodriguez	B-R	5-11	161	10-22-03	.188	.000	.231	4	16	1	3	1	0	0	1	1	0	0	0	5	0	0	.250	.235
2-team total (1 DSL Giants Orange)					.188	.000	.231	5	16	1	3	1	0	0	1	2	0	0	0	5	0	1	.250	.278
Brandy Rosario	R-R	6-0	145	3-24-04	.140	.167	.137	28	57	3	8	4	0	0	5	6	3	0	1	25	0	1	.211	.254
Eliam Sandoval	L-L	6-2	175	2-4-04	.314	.176	.348	26	86	16	27	4	0	5	16	10	1	0	0	23	5	2	.535	.392
Jean Carlos Sio	L-R	6-0	167	4-3-04	.200	.270	.177	49	150	22	30	7	1	1	10	25	3	0	1	23	16	4	.280	.324
Fabio Villadiego	R-R	5-11	140	3-13-04	.212	.269	.192	38	99	25	21	4	0	3	8	19	7	0	1	25	6	2	.343	.373
Diego Villegas	L-L	6-0	170	3-23-04	.240	.250	.238	10	25	4	6	2	0	0	3	8	1	0	0	7	0	1	.320	.441
Guillermo Williamson	L-L	6-1	200	3-16-04	.234	.265	.227	58	188	27	44	15	0	7	38	30	3	0	3	64	2	1	.426	.344

Pitching	B-T	HT	WT	DOB	W	L	ERA	G	GS	CG	SV	IP	H	R	ER	HR	BB	SO	AVG	vLH	vRH	K/9	BB/9
Anderson Azor	R-R	6-0	162	10-9-03	4	3	5.28	18	3	0	1	31	29	19	18	1	18	27	.261	.227	.284	7.92	5.28
Luis Bermudez	R-R	6-0	165	6-10-04	1	1	1.45	11	10	0	0	43	25	11	7	1	13	39	.169	.213	.138	8.10	2.70
Brayan Cabello	R-R	6-0	155	12-6-03	0	0	0.00	3	0	0	0	5	3	0	0	0	3	3	.176	.200	.167	5.79	5.79
2-team total (14 DSL Giants Orange)					1	1	3.65	17	0	0	3	25	29	16	10	1	16	23	.299	.207	.338	8.39	5.84
Jilber Canas	R-R	6-2	170	2-22-02	1	2	8.10	17	1	0	0	23	24	27	21	0	18	25	.276	.308	.250	9.64	6.94
Jan Caraballo	R-R	6-6	181	10-20-03	1	0	0.87	8	0	0	0	10	11	3	1	0	6	4	.306	.400	.238	3.48	5.23
2-team total (7 DSL Giants Orange)					1	3	4.43	15	0	0	0	20	23	13	10	1	14	12	.307	.429	.234	5.31	6.20
Leandro Castillo	R-R	6-1	160	7-1-02	1	0	6.27	12	0	0	0	19	19	16	13	0	15	18	.271	.233	.300	8.68	7.23
Pavel Duarte	L-L	6-1	164	10-29-03	0	3	10.38	7	1	0	0	9	10	11	10	3	9	9	.278	.400	.258	9.35	9.35
2-team total (8 DSL Giants Orange)					2	4	4.91	15	1	0	0	26	29	17	14	3	19	32	.287	.222	.301	11.22	6.66
Ricardo Estrada	L-L	6-0	170	6-25-02	2	5	5.40	10	10	0	0	42	43	30	25	1	17	38	.274	.206	.293	8.21	3.67
Fernando Estrella	R-R	6-2	145	5-30-03	0	8	12.15	10	9	0	0	27	37	39	36	4	17	24	.339	.282	.371	8.10	5.74
Mauricio Estrella	R-R	6-2	180	4-15-04	2	3	3.29	13	13	0	0	63	57	32	23	3	15	64	.236	.226	.243	9.14	2.14
Marlon Franco	R-R	6-2	165	9-18-02	3	2	6.43	20	1	0	0	28	29	23	20	5	15	28	.259	.271	.250	9.00	4.82
Carlos Gazo	R-R	5-11	170	11-29-03	1	0	2.45	5	0	0	0	7	5	2	2	1	4	5	.185	.182	.188	6.14	4.91
Carlos Gomez	R-R	5-11	165	12-22-04	0	3	9.00	10	0	0	0	13	11	16	13	1	12	15	.220	.333	.171	10.38	8.31
Jose Gonzalez	R-R	6-1	180	6-15-02	0	2	7.27	11	0	0	0	17	22	20	14	2	13	18	.293	.467	.178	9.35	6.75
Johnny Grullon	L-L	6-0	170	7-4-02	1	2	3.12	7	7	0	0	26	17	11	9	0	21	18	.189	.080	.231	6.23	7.27
Juan Morillo	R-R	5-10	145	11-1-02	0	0	13.83	15	0	0	0	14	15	24	21	1	26	9	.268	.211	.297	5.93	17.12
Yonathan Ochoa	R-R	6-3	175	10-18-02	0	0	6.00	3	0	0	0	3	2	2	2	1	1	2	.182	.333	.125	6.00	3.00
2-team total (8 DSL Giants Orange)					1	2	9.00	11	0	0	0	9	16	12	9	1	6	10	.364	.471	.296	10.00	6.00
Alfonso Perez	R-R	6-2	175	8-14-05	0	1	7.56	14	0	0	0	17	22	21	14	0	9	11	.310	.333	.289	5.94	4.86
Melvin Pineda	R-R	5-11	170	5-4-04	0	1	9.00	1	1	0	0	3	3	3	3	0	2	6	.231	.000	.500	18.00	6.00
2-team total (10 DSL Giants Orange)					1	5	3.79	11	11	0	0	38	30	20	16	1	21	56	.213	.283	.170	13.26	4.97
Miguel Ramos	R-R	6-1	204	9-5-04	0	1	2.08	6	4	0	1	17	10	7	4	1	13	22	.167	.200	.150	11.42	6.75
Luis Yepez	R-R	5-11	165	5-7-02	4	1	1.38	20	0	0	6	26	19	6	4	1	9	26	.211	.300	.167	9.00	3.12
Deifran Yriarte	R-R	6-0	180	12-14-04	1	0	9.64	4	0	0	0	5	8	7	5	0	4	5	.400	.375	.417	9.64	7.71

Fielding

C: Castillo 25, Coronil 8, Duran 29, Montero 2. **1B:** Coronil 8, Francisco 3, Lespe 5, Williamson 46. **2B:** Jimenez 20, Lespe 21, Rodriguez 1, Rosario 25, Sio 1. **3B:** Francisco 4, Jimenez 2, Lespe 11, Rosario 3, Sio 46. **SS:** Francisco 3, Jimenez 23, Peralta 35, Rodriguez 3. **OF:** Arrieta 31, Bautista 29, De La Rosa 16, Frias 37, Jimenez 2, Sandoval 24, Villadiego 39, Villegas 10, Williamson 8.

DSL GIANTS ORANGE

ROOKIE

DOMINICAN SUMMER LEAGUE

Batting	B-T	HT	WT	DOB	AVG	vLH	vRH	G	AB	R	H	2B	3B	HR	RBI	BB	HBP	SH	SF	SO	SB	CS	SLG	OBP
Jose Alifonso	R-R	5-8	165	9-16-03	.133	.000	.149	40	98	15	13	3	2	0	5	25	3	2	0	43	10	3	.204	.325
Erick Arosemena	R-R	6-0	170	4-2-05	.178	.357	.151	37	107	10	19	3	1	3	15	11	4	0	1	43	4	1	.308	.276
Jose Astudillo	R-R	5-10	150	2-27-04	.281	.000	.300	10	32	13	9	2	1	0	2	4	1	2	1	4	6	1	.406	.368
Jhosward Camacho	B-R	5-10	146	7-9-04	.280	.211	.292	36	125	23	35	6	1	1	16	18	0	0	1	22	4	2	.368	.368
Estanlin Cassiani	L-L	5-11	155	12-30-02	.375	.423	.367	50	176	40	66	3	2	0	10	14	1	3	1	21	15	7	.415	.422
Brayan Ferrer	B-R	6-0	170	12-26-03	.263	.250	.265	22	57	6	15	2	0	0	9	12	2	0	1	12	5	0	.298	.403
Diego Gonzalez	B-R	5-11	155	9-22-03	.154	.154	.154	23	65	6	10	1	2	0	8	12	3	0	1	16	2	0	.231	.309
Audie Jimenez	R-R	6-0	151	12-16-04	.143	.500	.000	2	7	2	1	0	0	0	1	1	1	0	0	2	0	0	.143	.333
2-team total (44 DSL Giants Black)					.146	.143	.147	46	137	15	20	3	0	0	10	6	4	0	2	37	2	3	.168	.201
Oswaldo Ladera	R-R	6-2	170	2-14-03	.227	.154	.242	49	154	29	35	14	0	3	26	18	13	0	0	63	11	3	.377	.357
Yeison Lemos	R-R	6-0	165	9-6-02	.157	.167	.155	28	89	8	14	2	0	2	11	4	2	0	1	27	2	1	.247	.208
Jediael Maduro	L-L	6-1	188	12-26-03	.359	.300	.379	12	39	11	14	2	0	2	8	8	0	0	0	7	0	0	.564	.468
Eduardo Montero	L-R	5-10	150	10-26-03	.238	.300	.226	23	63	4	15	1	0	0	6	11	0	2	1	15	0	1	.254	.347
2-team total (2 DSL Giants Black)					.243	.273	.237	25	70	4	17	1	0	0	8	11	0	2	1	17	0	1	.257	.341
Lazaro Morales	R-R	5-11	160	4-16-04	.299	.217	.315	40	134	19	40	11	2	1	20	10	10	0	2	30	9	8	.433	.385
Juan Perez	R-R	6-1	182	9-22-04	.222	.143	.240	47	153	25	34	2	0	3	12	14	6	0	0	50	1	2	.294	.312
Jose Ramos	R-R	5-11	143	10-25-02	.272	.333	.258	49	147	30	40	11	1	3	23	29	3	1	1	28	22	1	.422	.400
Ryan Reckley	B-R	5-10	160	9-6-04	.194	.000	.233	11	36	7	7	1	0	0	2	9	1	0	0	10	3	1	.222	.370
Dennys Riera	R-R	5-9	165	2-17-05	.154	.118	.161	35	104	12	16	5	1	2	14	9	3	0	2	32	1	0	.279	.237
Samuel Rodriguez	B-R	5-11	161	10-22-03	--	--	--	1	0	0	0	0	0	0	0	1	0	0	0	0	0	1	--	1.000
2-team total (4 DSL Giants Black)					.188	.000	.231	5	16	1	3	1	0	0	1	2	0	0	0	5	0	1	.250	.278
Juanel Urena	R-R	5-10	165	3-2-04	.155	.000	.175	29	71	6	11	1	0	1	6	16	1	2	1	26	3	7	.211	.315

Pitching	B-T	HT	WT	DOB	W	L	ERA	G	GS	CG	SV	IP	H	R	ER	HR	BB	SO	AVG	vLH	vRH	K/9	BB/9
Brayan Cabello	R-R	6-0	155	12-6-03	1	1	4.50	14	0	0	3	20	26	16	10	1	13	20	.325	.208	.375	9.00	5.85
2-team total (3 DSL Giants Black)					1	1	3.65	17	0	0	3	25	29	16	10	1	16	23	.299	.207	.338	8.39	5.84
Jan Caraballo	R-R	6-6	181	10-20-03	0	3	8.10	7	0	0	0	10	12	10	9	1	8	8	.308	.462	.231	7.20	7.20
2-team total (8 DSL Giants Black)					1	3	4.43	15	0	0	0	20	23	13	10	1	14	12	.307	.429	.234	5.31	6.20
Samir Chires	R-R	6-0	160	9-17-03	3	1	2.45	15	7	0	0	44	39	17	12	1	17	38	.242	.261	.228	7.77	3.48
Pavel Duarte	L-L	6-1	164	10-29-03	2	1	2.12	8	0	0	0	17	19	6	4	0	10	23	.292	.154	.327	12.18	5.29
2-team total (7 DSL Giants Black)					2	4	4.91	15	1	0	0	26	29	17	14	3	19	32	.287	.222	.301	11.22	6.66
Daniel Espinoza	L-L	6-0	168	11-25-03	0	0	14.54	4	0	0	0	4	4	7	7	0	7	4	.235	.000	.286	8.31	14.54
Ankeily Feliz	R-R	6-1	185	6-27-03	3	2	9.37	15	0	0	1	16	22	19	17	5	16	15	.324	.250	.346	8.27	8.82
Junior Flores	R-R	6-1	170	2-13-02	1	1	0.00	10	0	0	2	10	5	2	0	0	4	14	.147	.167	.136	13.03	3.72
Moises Gonzalez	R-R	6-2	175	10-25-02	0	0	8.10	3	0	0	0	3	4	4	3	0	1	5	.286	.200	.333	13.50	2.70
Melvin Javier	R-R	6-5	190	4-25-03	1	1	9.88	12	0	0	0	14	11	16	15	0	13	14	.216	.192	.240	9.22	8.56
Carlos Lopez	L-L	6-0	165	8-31-02	1	1	4.66	15	0	0	2	19	23	18	10	1	17	26	.284	.211	.306	12.10	7.91
Jorge Martinez	R-R	6-0	161	11-6-01	2	3	3.42	12	12	0	0	50	37	26	19	3	22	67	.202	.238	.183	12.06	3.96
Victor Moreno	L-L	6-1	165	1-19-04	0	0	8.74	12	1	0	0	11	9	14	11	0	21	7	.220	.091	.267	5.56	16.68
Ismael Mota	R-R	6-2	165	8-4-01	3	0	3.14	11	11	0	0	43	32	24	15	1	25	55	.213	.271	.176	11.51	5.23
Yonathan Ochoa	R-R	6-3	175	10-18-02	1	2	10.50	8	0	0	0	6	14	10	7	0	5	8	.424	.500	.368	12.00	7.50
2-team total (3 DSL Giants Black)					1	2	9.00	11	0	0	0	9	16	12	9	1	6	10	.364	.471	.296	10.00	6.00
Cesar Perdomo	L-L	6-0	170	2-9-02	1	0	0.60	4	3	0	0	15	9	1	1	0	3	18	.188	.000	.200	10.80	1.80
Argenis Perez	L-L	5-10	140	4-30-03	1	3	4.40	13	2	0	0	29	27	23	14	1	16	29	.250	.357	.234	9.10	5.02
Melvin Pineda	R-R	5-11	170	5-4-04	1	4	3.34	10	10	0	0	35	27	17	13	1	19	50	.211	.326	.146	12.86	4.89
2-team total (1 DSL Giants Black)					1	5	3.79	11	11	0	0	38	30	20	16	1	21	56	.213	.283	.170	13.26	4.97
Carlos Rangel	R-R	6-3	175	3-4-04	1	0	9.82	8	0	0	0	7	5	8	8	0	11	9	.192	.143	.211	11.05	13.50
Jose Rojas	R-R	6-1	145	1-2-04	0	6	6.02	12	12	0	0	46	55	33	31	3	21	37	.309	.324	.298	7.19	4.08
Daniel Rondon	R-R	6-0	190	3-16-03	0	1	48.60	3	0	0	0	2	8	9	9	0	3	1	.615	.500	.714	5.40	16.20
Ken Salas	R-R	6-2	180	7-30-01	1	0	6.57	13	0	0	4	12	18	12	9	0	9	19	.321	.368	.297	13.86	6.57
Erasmo Tortolero	R-R	6-1	188	8-5-02	3	2	6.97	15	0	0	2	21	23	18	16	0	15	11	.291	.306	.279	4.79	6.53

Fielding

C: Ferrer 6, Gonzalez 11, Montero 9, Perez 33. **1B:** Astudillo 2, Camacho 9, Ferrer 15, Gonzalez 12, Maduro 9, Montero 6, Morales 8. **2B:** Alifonso 34, Astudillo 2, Camacho 9, Morales 1, Ramos 7, Riera 12, Rodriguez 1. **3B:** Astudillo 2, Camacho 18, Jimenez 1, Lemos 19, Ramos 16, Riera 8. **SS:** Camacho 1, Jimenez 1, Lemos 8, Ramos 31, Reckley 10, Riera 13. **OF:** Arosemena 31, Cassiani 49, Ladera 41, Maduro 4, Morales 32, Ramos 1, Urena 23

Seattle Mariners

SEASON IN A SENTENCE: Rookie center fielder Julio Rodriguez electrified the league, and the Mariners' pitching staff emerged as one of the best in baseball, helping Seattle win 90 games and a wild card spot to reach the playoffs for the first time since 2001.

HIGH POINT: With the Mariners magic number down to one, catcher Cal Raleigh sent Seattle to the postseason with a two-out, walk-off home run in the bottom of the ninth inning against Oakland on Sept. 30 for 2-1 victory. Raleigh's homer off the right-field foul pole at T-Mobile Park touched off a frenzied celebration in the city of Seattle and cemented his place forever in Mariners lore.

LOW POINT: Days of tension between the Mariners and Angels boiled over on June 26. After Mariners reliever Erik Swanson threw a fastball near Mike Trout's head the previous night, Angels righthander Andrew Wantz threw behind Rodriguez in the first inning and hit Mariners outfielder Jesse Winker in the second inning, touching off an elongated brawl that stopped and started twice. Winker, Rodriguez, shortstop J.P. Crawford and manager Scott Servais were all ejected, with Winker flipping both middle fingers at the Angel Stadium crowd as he departed.

NOTABLE ROOKIE: Rodriguez won the Mariners center field job out of spring training and became baseball's latest young sensation, batting .284 with 28 home runs, 75 RBIs and 25 stolen bases while playing highlight-reel defense. Rodriguez made his first all-star team and became the fastest rookie ever to reach 25 homers and 25 stolen bases, beating a record previously held by Trout.

KEY TRANSACTIONS: Sensing they were ready to compete, the Mariners acquired Winker and slugging third baseman Eugenio Suarez from the Reds in a blockbuster six-player trade just before the start of spring training. They struck another headline deal with the Reds again at the trade deadline, acquiring ace Luis Castillo for a four-prospect package headlined by marquee shortstops Noelvi Marte and Edwin Arroyo. Winker did little in Seattle, but Suarez and Castillo proved to be key.

ON THE FARM: The Mariners' farm system was hurt by the graduations of Rodriguez and righthander George Kirby and various prospect-for-veteran trades, leading to an underwhelming showing on the field. Mariners domestic affiliates went 288-310 (.488), 19th out of 30 teams. Just two of their six affiliates overall made the playoffs.

OPENING DAY PAYROLL: $104,635,506 (22nd).

PLAYERS OF THE YEAR

MAJOR LEAGUE

Julio Rodriguez
OF

.284/.345/.509
28 HR, 25 SB in 132 G
Led rookies in HR

MINOR LEAGUE

Taylor Dollard
RHP

(Double-A)
16-2, 2.25 ERA
131 SO, 31 BB, 144 IP

ORGANIZATION LEADERS

Batting — *Minimum 250 AB

MAJORS

* AVG	Julio Rodriguez	.284
* OPS	Julio Rodriguez	.853
HR	Eugenio Suarez	31
RBI	Eugenio Suarez	87

MINORS

* AVG	Gabriel Gonzalez, ACL, Modesto	.321
* OBP	Harry Ford, Modesto	.425
* SLG	Jarred Kelenic, Tacoma	.557
* OPS	Jarred Kelenic, Tacoma	.922
R	Robert Perez, Modesto, Everett	100
H	Cade Marlowe, Arkansas, Tacoma	143
TB	Cade Marlowe, Arkansas, Tacoma	243
	Robert Perez, Modesto, Everett	243
2B	Jake Scheiner, Arkansas	34
3B	Jonatan Clase, Modesto	11
HR	Robert Perez, Modesto, Everett	27
RBI	Robert Perez, Modesto, Everett	114
BB	Harry Ford, Modesto	88
SO	Dariel Gomez, Everett	163
SB	Jonatan Clase, Modesto	55

Pitching — #Minimum 75 IP

MAJORS

W	Logan Gilbert	13
# ERA	Logan Gilbert	3.20
SO	Robbie Ray	212
SV	Paul Sewald	20

MINORS

W	Taylor Dollard, Arkansas	16
L	Stephen Kolek, Arkansas	13
# ERA	Taylor Dollard, Arkansas	2.25
G	Nick Ramirez, Tacoma	53
	Patrick Weigel, Tacoma	53
GS	Darren McCaughan, Tacoma	28
SV	Nick Ramirez, Tacoma	16
IP	Darren McCaughan, Tacoma	154.1
BB	Stephen Kolek, Arkansas	66
SO	Bryce Miller, Modesto, Everett, Arkansas	163
# AVG	Bryce Miller, Modesto, Everett, Arkansas	.191

2022 PERFORMANCE

General Manager: Jerry Dipoto. **Farm Director:** Andy McKay. **Scouting Director:** Scott Hunter.

Class	Team	League	W	L	PCT	Finish	Manager
Majors	Seattle Mariners	American	90	72	.556	5th (15)	Scott Servais
Triple-A	Tacoma Rainiers	Pacific Coast	72	78	.480	6th (10)	Tim Federowicz
Double-A	Arkansas Travelers	Texas	73	65	.529	3rd (10)	Collin Cowgill
High-A	Everett AquaSox	Northwest	59	72	.450	t-5th (6)	Eric Farris
Low-A	Modesto Nuts	California	66	66	.500	6th (8)	Austin Knight
Rookie	ACL Mariners	Arizona Complex	26	29	.473	10th (18)	Luis Caballero
Overall 2022 Minor League Record			328	337	.493	18th (30)	

ORGANIZATION STATISTICS

SEATTLE MARINERS

AMERICAN LEAGUE

Batting	B-T	HT	WT	DOB	AVG	vLH	vRH	G	AB	R	H	2B	3B	HR	RBI	BB	HBP	SH	SF	SO	SB	CS	SLG	OBP
Curt Casali	R-R	6-2	220	11-9-88	.125	.077	.214	16	40	7	5	1	0	1	3	9	1	0	0	14	0	0	.225	.300
J.P. Crawford	L-R	6-2	202	1-11-95	.243	.221	.253	145	518	57	126	24	3	6	42	68	10	2	5	80	3	2	.336	.339
Drew Ellis	R-R	6-3	205	12-1-95	.333	.500	.000	1	3	0	1	0	0	0	0	0	0	0	0	1	0	0	.333	.333
Stuart Fairchild	R-R	6-0	205	3-17-96	.000	.000	.000	3	3	0	0	0	0	0	0	0	0	0	0	2	0	0	.000	.000
Mike Ford	L-R	6-0	225	7-4-92	.172	.000	.185	16	29	1	5	1	0	0	3	8	1	0	0	12	0	0	.207	.368
2-team total (28 Los Angeles Angels)					.217	.259	.204	44	120	9	26	5	0	3	8	16	1	0	0	38	0	0	.333	.314
Ty France	R-R	5-11	215	7-13-94	.274	.273	.275	140	551	65	151	27	1	20	83	35	21	0	5	94	0	0	.436	.338
Adam Frazier	L-R	5-10	181	12-14-91	.238	.210	.248	156	541	61	129	22	4	3	42	46	5	4	6	73	11	6	.311	.301
Sam Haggerty	B-R	5-11	175	5-26-94	.256	.364	.191	83	176	29	45	9	1	5	23	18	4	1	2	53	13	1	.403	.335
Mitch Haniger	R-R	6-2	214	12-23-90	.246	.246	.245	57	224	31	55	8	0	11	34	20	1	0	2	65	0	0	.429	.308
Travis Jankowski	L-R	6-2	190	6-15-91	.000	--	.000	1	1	0	0	0	0	0	0	0	0	0	0	1	0	0	.000	.000
Jarred Kelenic	L-L	6-1	206	7-16-99	.141	.130	.147	54	163	20	23	5	1	7	17	16	1	0	1	61	5	2	.313	.221
Andrew Knapp	B-R	6-1	189	11-9-91	.000	--	.000	2	4	0	0	0	0	0	0	0	0	0	0	3	0	0	.000	.000
Jake Lamb	L-R	6-3	215	10-9-90	.167	--	.167	16	30	3	5	1	0	1	2	3	1	0	0	14	0	0	.300	.265
Jack Larsen	L-L	6-1	195	1-13-95	.000	--	.000	1	1	0	0	0	0	0	0	0	0	0	0	1	0	0	.000	.000
Kyle Lewis	R-R	6-4	222	7-13-95	.143	.200	.122	18	56	6	8	0	0	3	5	5	1	0	0	19	0	0	.304	.226
Dylan Moore	R-R	6-0	205	8-2-92	.224	.247	.204	104	205	41	46	11	2	6	24	34	13	1	1	75	21	8	.385	.368
Tom Murphy	R-R	6-1	206	4-3-91	.303	.333	.292	14	33	9	10	2	0	1	1	8	0	0	0	13	0	0	.455	.439
Brian O'Keefe	R-R	6-1	210	7-15-93	.333	.333	--	2	3	0	1	0	0	0	0	1	0	0	0	2	0	0	.333	.500
Kevin Padlo	R-R	6-2	210	7-15-96	.200	.111	1.000	6	10	0	2	1	0	0	3	1	0	0	0	5	0	0	.300	.273
Cal Raleigh	B-R	6-3	235	11-26-96	.211	.212	.211	119	370	46	78	20	1	27	63	38	2	0	5	122	1	0	.489	.284
Julio Rodriguez	R-R	6-3	228	12-29-00	.284	.275	.286	132	511	84	145	25	3	28	75	40	8	0	1	145	25	7	.509	.345
Carlos Santana	B-R	5-11	215	4-8-86	.192	.243	.173	79	255	35	49	8	0	15	39	35	2	0	2	60	0	0	.400	.293
2-team total (52 Kansas City Royals)					.202	.265	.178	131	431	52	87	18	0	19	60	71	2	0	2	88	0	0	.376	.316
Steven Souza Jr.	R-R	6-4	225	4-24-89	.158	.000	.214	6	19	0	3	0	0	0	1	0	0	0	0	8	0	0	.158	.158
Eugenio Suarez	R-R	5-11	213	7-18-91	.236	.269	.225	150	543	76	128	24	2	31	87	73	8	0	5	196	0	0	.459	.332
Abraham Toro	B-R	6-0	225	12-20-96	.185	.200	.178	109	324	36	60	13	1	10	35	22	2	0	4	65	2	0	.324	.239
Luis Torrens	R-R	6-0	217	5-2-96	.225	.203	.244	57	151	13	34	2	0	3	15	12	1	0	2	50	0	0	.298	.283
Taylor Trammell	L-L	6-2	220	9-13-97	.196	.100	.220	43	102	15	20	9	0	4	10	13	0	1	1	33	2	1	.402	.284
Justin Upton	R-R	6-1	215	8-25-87	.125	.125	.125	17	48	2	6	1	0	1	3	6	3	0	0	23	0	0	.208	.263
Donovan Walton	L-R	5-10	190	5-25-94	--	--	--	1	0	1	0	0	0	0	0	0	0	0	0	0	0	0	--	--
Marcus Wilson	R-R	6-2	198	8-15-96	.200	.500	.000	3	5	1	1	0	0	0	0	1	0	0	0	4	0	0	.200	.333
Jesse Winker	L-L	6-3	215	8-17-93	.219	.244	.211	136	456	51	100	15	0	14	53	84	4	0	3	103	0	0	.344	.344

Pitching	B-T	HT	WT	DOB	W	L	ERA	G	GS	CG	SV	IP	H	R	ER	HR	BB	SO	AVG	vLH	vRH	K/9	BB/9
Brennan Bernardino	L-L	6-4	180	1-15-92	0	1	3.86	2	0	0	0	2	3	3	1	0	2	0	.300	.667	.143	0.00	7.71
Ryan Borucki	L-L	6-4	210	3-31-94	2	0	4.26	21	0	0	0	19	17	9	9	4	6	13	.239	.206	.270	6.16	2.84
2-team total (11 Toronto Blue Jays)					2	0	5.68	32	0	0	0	25	24	16	16	6	11	21	.247	.184	.313	7.46	3.91
Matthew Boyd	L-L	6-3	223	2-2-91	2	0	1.35	10	0	0	0	13	5	2	2	0	8	13	.116	.125	.105	8.78	5.40
Matt Brash	R-R	6-1	173	5-12-98	4	4	4.44	39	5	0	0	51	46	25	25	3	33	62	.247	.234	.257	11.01	5.86
Diego Castillo	R-R	6-3	268	1-18-94	7	3	3.64	59	0	0	7	54	40	27	22	5	22	53	.203	.243	.181	8.78	3.64
Luis Castillo	R-R	6-2	200	12-12-92	4	2	3.17	11	11	0	0	65	55	26	23	6	17	77	.226	.215	.238	10.61	2.34
Roenis Elias	L-L	6-1	205	8-1-88	0	0	3.52	7	0	0	0	8	7	3	3	1	3	6	.233	.250	.227	7.04	3.52
Matthew Festa	R-R	6-1	195	3-11-93	2	0	4.17	53	0	0	2	54	43	26	25	10	18	64	.218	.211	.223	10.67	3.00
Chris Flexen	R-R	6-3	219	7-1-94	8	9	3.73	33	22	0	2	138	132	61	57	17	51	95	.250	.221	.275	6.21	3.33
Logan Gilbert	R-R	6-6	215	5-5-97	13	6	3.20	32	32	0	0	186	170	71	66	19	49	174	.242	.201	.276	8.43	2.38
Ken Giles	R-R	6-3	197	9-20-90	0	0	0.00	5	0	0	0	4	1	0	0	0	4	6	.071	.000	.167	12.46	8.31
Marco Gonzales	L-L	6-1	205	2-16-92	10	15	4.13	32	32	0	0	183	194	97	84	30	50	103	.271	.280	.268	5.07	2.46
George Kirby	R-R	6-4	215	2-4-98	8	5	3.39	25	25	0	0	130	135	54	49	13	22	133	.264	.210	.324	9.21	1.52
Matt Koch	L-R	6-3	215	11-2-90	0	0	8.31	4	0	0	0	4	5	4	4	2	1	3	.278	.300	.250	6.23	2.08
Wyatt Mills	R-R	6-4	214	1-25-95	0	0	4.15	8	0	0	0	9	5	4	4	0	3	6	.179	.222	.158	6.23	3.12
2-team total (19 Kansas City Royals)					0	1	4.60	27	0	0	0	29	26	15	15	1	13	26	.243	.316	.203	7.98	3.99
Tommy Milone	L-L	6-0	215	2-16-87	1	1	5.40	7	0	0	0	17	14	10	10	4	6	5	.233	.333	.200	2.70	3.24

Anthony Misiewicz	R-L	6-1	196	11-1-94	0	1	4.61	17	0	0	0	14	14	7	7	1	6	8	.275	.286	.261	5.27	3.95
2-team total (15 Kansas City Royals)					1	2	4.34	32	0	0	0	29	27	15	14	4	10	27	.248	.255	.241	8.38	3.10
Andres Munoz	R-R	6-2	222	1-16-99	2	5	2.49	64	0	0	4	65	43	20	18	5	15	96	.189	.157	.223	13.29	2.08
Penn Murfee	R-R	6-2	195	5-2-94	4	0	2.99	64	1	0	0	69	48	23	23	7	18	76	.192	.233	.169	9.87	2.34
Riley O'Brien	R-R	6-4	180	2-6-95	0	0	0.00	1	0	0	0	1	1	0	0	0	1	1	.250	.000	1.000	9.00	9.00
Yohan Ramirez	R-R	6-4	212	5-6-95	1	0	7.56	7	0	0	0	8	7	7	7	3	6	10	.219	.333	.150	10.80	6.48
2-team total (1 Cleveland Guardians)					1	0	6.97	8	0	0	0	10	10	8	8	3	7	11	.244	.286	.222	9.58	6.10
Robbie Ray	L-L	6-2	225	10-1-91	12	12	3.71	32	32	0	0	189	163	80	78	32	62	212	.231	.212	.236	10.10	2.95
Sergio Romo	R-R	5-11	185	3-4-83	0	0	8.16	17	0	0	0	14	18	13	13	6	4	11	.305	.240	.353	6.91	2.51
2-team total (6 Toronto Blue Jays)					0	1	7.50	23	0	0	0	18	19	16	15	7	6	14	.268	.214	.302	7.00	3.00
Paul Sewald	R-R	6-3	219	5-26-90	5	4	2.67	65	0	0	20	64	32	21	19	10	17	72	.146	.167	.130	10.13	2.39
Justus Sheffield	L-L	5-10	224	5-13-96	1	0	3.86	6	1	0	0	12	9	5	5	1	6	7	.209	.143	.241	5.40	4.63
Drew Steckenrider	R-R	6-4	235	1-10-91	0	2	5.65	16	0	0	2	14	21	9	9	2	5	10	.333	.394	.267	6.28	3.14
Erik Swanson	R-R	6-3	222	9-4-93	3	2	1.68	57	1	0	3	54	39	11	10	3	10	70	.202	.200	.205	11.74	1.68
Luis Torrens	R-R	6-0	217	5-2-96	1	0	4.50	2	0	0	0	2	3	2	1	1	0	0	.333	.250	.400	0.00	0.00
Danny Young	L-L	6-3	200	5-27-94	0	0	7.36	2	0	0	0	4	7	3	3	1	2	5	.389	.167	.500	12.27	4.91

Fielding

Catcher	PCT	G	PO	A	E	DP	PB
Casali	.993	15	134	3	1	0	0
Knapp	1.000	2	11	0	0	0	0
Murphy	1.000	12	96	2	0	0	1
O'Keefe	1.000	1	1	0	0	0	0
Raleigh	.994	115	911	28	6	3	3
Torrens	.997	42	271	16	1	1	0

First Base	PCT	G	PO	A	E	DP
Casali	1.000	1	2	0	0	0
Ford	1.000	1	2	0	0	0
France	.997	127	816	72	3	73
Lamb	1.000	2	7	2	0	0
Moore	1.000	8	30	0	0	5
Padlo	1.000	5	15	1	0	2
Santana	1.000	34	243	24	0	23
Toro	1.000	1	5	1	0	1

Second Base	PCT	G	PO	A	E	DP
France	1.000	1	0	1	0	0
Frazier	.986	124	191	238	6	61
Haggerty	1.000	4	3	4	0	1
Moore	1.000	12	11	18	0	5
Toro	.988	55	59	112	2	23
Torrens	1.000	2	0	1	0	0

Third Base	PCT	G	PO	A	E	DP
Ellis	1.000	1	2	2	0	1
France	1.000	6	4	8	0	1
Lamb	.875	4	2	5	1	1
Moore	.000	2	0	0	0	0
Suarez	.971	130	112	226	10	23
Toro	.940	31	23	40	4	3
Walton	.000	1	0	0	0	0

Shortstop	PCT	G	PO	A	E	DP
Crawford	.972	144	162	326	14	70
Frazier	.909	4	4	6	1	0
Moore	.984	26	23	38	1	6

Outfield	PCT	G	PO	A	E	DP
Fairchild	--	2	0	0	0	0
Frazier	1.000	39	54	2	0	0
Haggerty	.992	76	120	2	1	0
Haniger	.981	47	100	2	2	1
Jankowski	--	1	0	0	0	0
Kelenic	.991	51	101	4	1	0
Lamb	1.000	11	12	0	0	0
Larsen	--	1	0	0	0	0
Lewis	1.000	4	13	0	0	0
Moore	1.000	64	94	3	0	0
Rodriguez	.984	130	357	3	6	0
Santana	--	1	0	0	0	0
Souza Jr.	1.000	5	11	1	0	0
Toro	--	1	0	0	0	0
Trammell	1.000	44	71	2	0	0
Upton	1.000	6	8	0	0	0
Wilson	1.000	3	2	0	0	0
Winker	.978	118	176	5	4	0

TACOMA RAINIERS — *TRIPLE-A*

PACIFIC COAST LEAGUE

Batting	B-T	HT	WT	DOB	AVG	vLH	vRH	G	AB	R	H	2B	3B	HR	RBI	BB	HBP	SH	SF	SO	SB	CS	SLG	OBP
Trey Amburgey	R-R	6-2	210	10-24-94	.172	.091	.189	20	64	11	11	1	0	2	7	4	1	0	0	20	1	0	.281	.232
Jake Anchia	R-R	6-1	210	3-5-97	.333	.000	.500	2	6	1	2	2	0	0	0	0	0	0	0	3	0	0	.667	.333
Alex Blandino	R-R	6-0	190	11-6-92	.203	.333	.157	47	138	24	28	8	1	3	22	43	4	0	3	51	7	2	.341	.399
2-team total (24 Sacramento River Cats)					.195	.316	.153	71	220	37	43	13	1	4	31	56	6	0	3	89	8	2	.318	.368
Curt Casali	R-R	6-2	220	11-9-88	.308	.000	.333	5	13	3	4	1	0	0	1	3	1	0	0	3	0	0	.385	.471
2-team total (3 Sacramento River Cats)					.200	.000	.211	8	20	3	4	1	0	0	1	3	1	0	0	10	0	0	.250	.333
Drew Ellis	R-R	6-3	205	12-1-95	.231	.189	.243	70	242	34	56	15	1	15	39	41	3	0	3	79	4	3	.488	.346
2-team total (42 Reno Aces)					.226	.190	.239	112	385	61	87	27	2	19	67	74	5	0	4	117	6	3	.455	.355
Stuart Fairchild	R-R	6-0	205	3-17-96	.438	--	.438	4	16	4	7	0	0	1	3	2	3	0	0	3	0	0	.625	.571
3-team total (10 Reno Aces, 5 Sacramento River Cats)					.232	.200	.241	19	69	9	16	3	0	4	7	10	6	0	0	26	2	1	.449	.376
Mike Ford	L-R	6-0	225	7-4-92	.317	.231	.357	11	41	10	13	1	0	2	5	5	1	0	0	4	0	0	.488	.404
3-team total (3 Sacramento River Cats, 6 Salt Lake Bees)					.254	.214	.263	20	71	12	18	2	0	2	5	12	1	0	0	10	0	0	.366	.369
Zach Green	R-R	6-2	224	3-7-94	.227	.306	.201	91	339	44	77	23	1	18	52	28	5	0	6	113	1	0	.460	.291
Arturo Guerrero	R-R	6-3	165	9-21-00	.400	--	.400	1	5	1	2	0	0	1	2	0	0	0	0	1	0	0	1.000	.400
Sam Haggerty	B-R	5-11	175	5-26-94	.283	.243	.296	39	152	28	43	11	2	6	25	18	4	3	2	34	15	1	.500	.369
Billy Hamilton	R-R	6-0	160	9-9-90	.186	.120	.213	22	86	11	16	2	0	0	5	9	0	0	0	25	4	0	.209	.263
Mitch Haniger	R-R	6-2	214	12-23-90	.238	.200	.250	8	21	5	5	0	0	2	6	10	2	0	0	3	0	0	.524	.515
Scott Heineman	R-R	6-1	220	12-4-92	.190	.138	.211	29	100	16	19	6	0	2	15	11	1	0	0	40	5	3	.310	.277
Derek Hill	R-R	6-2	190	12-30-95	.236	.265	.222	34	106	19	25	5	2	5	19	13	1	1	2	36	6	1	.462	.320
Cesar Izturis Jr.	B-R	5-11	145	11-11-99	.220	.400	.161	15	41	6	9	1	0	0	5	5	0	0	0	11	3	2	.244	.304
Jarred Kelenic	L-L	6-1	206	7-16-99	.295	.296	.295	86	352	58	104	32	3	18	65	35	5	0	2	82	9	4	.557	.365
Andrew Knapp	B-R	6-1	189	11-9-91	.198	.167	.206	22	81	8	16	7	0	4	11	4	2	0	1	22	0	0	.432	.250
2-team total (34 Sacramento River Cats)					.245	.217	.257	56	208	28	51	14	0	12	37	17	4	0	1	57	1	1	.486	.313
Kyle Lewis	R-R	6-4	222	7-13-95	.245	.293	.226	42	147	29	36	4	0	12	34	26	1	0	0	45	0	0	.517	.362
Cade Marlowe	L-R	6-1	210	6-24-97	.250	.235	.257	13	52	8	13	3	1	3	16	7	1	0	0	23	6	0	.519	.350
Mason McCoy	R-R	5-11	185	3-31-95	.256	.294	.244	124	442	72	113	23	5	21	63	50	3	3	5	130	22	3	.473	.332
Erick Mejia	B-R	5-11	195	11-9-94	.261	.261	.261	120	464	72	121	29	3	15	58	49	1	3	4	103	19	7	.433	.330
Dylan Moore	R-R	6-0	205	8-2-92	.250	.000	.333	1	4	1	1	0	0	0	0	0	0	0	0	1	1	0	.250	.250
Josh Morgan	R-R	5-11	185	11-16-95	.220	.000	.283	20	59	6	13	3	0	2	5	12	0	0	2	15	0	0	.373	.342
Joseph Odom	R-R	6-2	215	1-9-92	.231	.224	.233	62	208	30	48	15	0	10	25	28	2	0	0	95	2	0	.447	.328
Brian O'Keefe	R-R	6-1	210	7-15-93	.253	.293	.237	83	316	42	80	19	2	13	40	32	4	0	0	80	1	1	.449	.330
Kevin Padlo	R-R	6-2	210	7-15-96	.229	.211	.235	38	140	18	32	6	1	4	20	18	2	0	1	41	7	2	.371	.323

2-team total (22 Sacramento River Cats)					.245	.257	.240	60	220	34	54	9	2	11	36	23	4	0	1	59	10	2	.455	.327
James Parker	R-R	6-1	200	3-26-00	.000	.000	.000	1	4	0	0	0	0	0	0	0	0	0	0	1	0	0	.000	.000
Miguel Perez	R-R	6-2	170	8-21-00	.172	.000	.227	13	29	4	5	0	0	2	5	5	0	0	0	19	0	0	.379	.294
Cal Raleigh	B-R	6-3	235	11-26-96	.286	.231	.333	7	28	4	8	2	0	1	4	2	0	0	0	7	0	0	.464	.333
Ben Ramirez	L-R	6-3	200	12-2-98	.318	.250	.333	6	22	2	7	0	0	1	2	0	0	0	0	8	0	0	.455	.318
David Sheaffer	R-R	6-2	170	5-9-95	.250	.000	.333	1	4	0	1	0	0	0	0	0	0	0	0	2	0	0	.250	.250
Steven Souza Jr.	R-R	6-4	225	4-24-89	.267	.214	.279	22	75	17	20	5	0	5	17	19	1	0	1	25	3	1	.533	.417
Trent Tingelstad	L-R	5-10	215	6-14-98	.286	--	.286	4	14	0	4	0	1	0	2	3	0	0	0	3	0	0	.429	.412
Abraham Toro	B-R	6-0	225	12-20-96	.241	.313	.214	16	58	6	14	3	1	2	12	10	0	0	0	12	3	0	.431	.353
Luis Torrens	R-R	6-0	217	5-2-96	.279	.357	.255	16	61	7	17	5	0	3	15	5	0	0	2	18	0	0	.508	.324
Taylor Trammell	L-L	6-2	220	9-13-97	.333	.304	.344	22	87	18	29	6	0	5	12	11	0	0	0	17	8	1	.575	.408
Justin Upton	R-R	6-1	215	8-25-87	.200	.200	.200	12	45	8	9	2	0	2	6	6	0	0	1	18	0	0	.378	.288
Jonathan Villar	B-R	6-0	233	5-2-91	.283	.227	.307	37	145	20	41	9	2	6	24	10	0	0	0	34	10	3	.497	.329
Forrest Wall	L-R	6-1	195	11-20-95	.255	.165	.283	120	412	67	105	17	3	6	41	42	8	2	3	125	52	12	.354	.333
Donovan Walton	L-R	5-10	190	5-25-94	.294	.294	.294	12	51	10	15	4	2	1	5	6	0	0	0	6	2	1	.510	.368
2-team total (20 Sacramento River Cats)					.254	.250	.256	32	122	20	31	10	2	2	12	18	1	4	0	19	5	1	.418	.355
Evan White	R-L	6-3	219	4-26-96	.204	.438	.156	28	93	14	19	5	0	7	16	13	1	0	0	23	0	0	.484	.308
Marcus Wilson	R-R	6-2	198	8-15-96	.218	.234	.213	91	293	50	64	18	3	16	47	53	5	0	4	126	14	2	.464	.344

Pitching	B-T	HT	WT	DOB	W	L	ERA	G	GS	CG	SV	IP	H	R	ER	HR	BB	SO	AVG	vLH	vRH	K/9	BB/9
Fernando Abad	L-L	6-2	235	12-17-85	1	1	3.56	40	0	0	0	43	43	21	17	5	12	32	.265	.219	.296	6.70	2.51
Anthony Banda	L-L	6-2	220	8-10-93	0	0	2.25	4	0	0	0	4	1	1	1	1	0	3	.077	.000	.111	6.75	0.00
Jacob Barnes	R-R	6-2	231	4-14-90	0	0	0.00	4	0	0	0	4	4	0	0	0	1	5	.250	.333	.200	11.25	2.25
Jarod Bayless	R-R	6-4	225	12-29-96	0	0	0.00	1	0	0	0	2	0	0	0	0	0	0	.000	.000	.000	0.00	0.00
Brennan Bernardino	L-L	6-4	180	1-15-92	2	0	2.20	23	0	0	2	33	18	10	8	1	10	35	.161	.075	.237	9.64	2.76
Kyle Bird	L-L	6-3	220	4-12-93	6	1	6.66	44	0	0	0	49	60	40	36	7	35	50	.306	.244	.347	9.25	6.47
Matthew Boyd	L-L	6-3	223	2-2-91	1	1	2.25	6	0	0	0	8	4	2	2	1	0	14	.143	.111	.158	15.75	0.00
Matt Brash	R-R	6-1	173	5-12-98	0	1	3.46	22	0	0	3	26	19	14	10	4	14	41	.207	.222	.196	14.19	4.85
John Creel	L-R	6-5	222	7-1-97	0	0	0.00	1	0	0	0	0	0	0	0	0	0	1	.000	--	.000	27.00	0.00
Riley Davis	R-R	6-3	200	11-10-98	0	0	--	1	0	0	0	0	4	5	4	1	1	0	1.000	1.000	--	--	--
Tyler Driver	R-R	6-2	185	2-4-01	0	0	9.00	1	0	0	0	2	3	2	2	0	1	2	.375	1.000	.167	9.00	4.50
Roenis Elias	L-L	6-1	205	8-1-88	3	3	5.12	37	9	0	0	65	70	39	37	8	19	55	.275	.261	.282	7.62	2.63
Drew Ellis	R-R	6-3	205	12-1-95	0	0	0.00	1	0	0	0	1	0	0	0	0	1	0	.000	--	.000	0.00	9.00
Matthew Festa	R-R	6-1	195	3-11-93	1	0	0.00	6	0	0	0	7	2	2	0	0	2	11	.091	.100	.083	14.85	2.70
Mike Ford	L-R	6-0	225	7-4-92	0	0	6.75	2	0	0	0	1	1	1	1	0	1	0	.200	.500	.000	0.00	6.75
Ken Giles	R-R	6-3	197	9-20-90	0	1	10.29	8	0	0	0	7	10	9	8	3	7	6	.323	.353	.286	7.71	9.00
2-team total (3 Sacramento River Cats)					0	1	8.38	11	0	0	0	10	12	10	9	4	9	8	.293	.348	.222	7.45	8.38
Kyle Hill	R-R	5-11	200	5-12-97	0	0	0.00	1	0	0	0	1	0	0	0	0	1	0	.000	.000	.000	0.00	9.00
Chris Jefferson	L-R	6-2	200	1-24-97	0	0	5.19	5	0	0	0	9	12	7	5	0	6	13	.353	.389	.313	13.50	6.23
George Kirby	R-R	6-4	215	2-4-98	0	1	18.00	1	1	0	0	2	5	4	4	0	1	2	.455	.400	1.000	9.00	4.50
Matt Koch	L-R	6-3	215	11-2-90	4	1	3.05	38	0	0	4	38	27	14	13	6	13	50	.196	.235	.157	11.74	3.05
Nick Margevicius	L-L	6-5	225	6-18-96	0	4	7.53	33	7	0	0	49	78	47	41	8	19	51	.355	.303	.382	9.37	3.49
Chris Mazza	R-R	6-4	190	10-17-89	4	3	7.49	15	7	0	0	34	44	29	28	9	13	28	.314	.365	.273	7.49	3.48
Darren McCaughan	R-R	6-1	200	3-18-96	8	9	4.55	28	28	0	0	154	140	82	78	22	42	141	.238	.213	.263	8.22	2.45
Ian McKinney	L-L	5-11	185	11-18-94	0	2	10.07	10	4	0	0	22	27	27	25	5	17	8	.307	.300	.309	3.22	6.85
Juan Mercedes	R-R	6-2	190	4-3-00	0	2	6.30	3	1	0	0	10	14	7	7	0	4	6	.326	.222	.353	5.40	3.60
Wyatt Mills	R-R	6-4	214	1-25-95	1	0	1.83	16	0	0	0	20	12	4	4	1	7	17	.174	.273	.128	7.78	3.20
Tommy Milone	L-L	6-0	215	2-16-87	3	1	2.68	11	10	0	0	40	30	12	12	3	11	38	.208	.368	.151	8.48	2.45
Anthony Misiewicz	R-L	6-1	196	11-1-94	0	0	3.65	13	0	0	0	12	10	5	5	2	6	13	.208	.167	.233	9.49	4.38
Colby Morris	R-R	6-3	190	5-17-97	0	0	27.00	2	0	0	0	3	6	9	9	1	4	2	.429	.600	.333	6.00	12.00
Penn Murfee	R-R	6-2	195	5-2-94	2	0	0.00	5	0	0	2	8	1	0	0	0	2	10	.043	.000	.091	11.25	2.25
Kelvin Nunez	R-R	6-1	170	12-10-99	0	0	6.75	1	0	0	0	3	4	2	2	0	2	0	.308	.333	.300	0.00	6.75
Riley O'Brien	R-R	6-4	180	2-6-95	1	3	7.12	32	1	0	0	37	43	36	29	4	29	43	.287	.279	.292	10.55	7.12
Brayan Perez	L-L	6-0	170	9-5-00	0	0	0.00	1	0	0	0	2	1	0	0	0	1	2	.143	--	.143	9.00	4.50
Daniel Ponce de Leon	R-R	6-3	200	1-16-92	5	8	7.95	16	16	0	0	71	77	64	63	16	42	80	.271	.229	.307	10.09	5.30
Nick Ramirez	L-L	6-4	232	8-1-89	3	4	2.93	53	0	0	16	55	49	21	18	4	15	53	.241	.286	.214	8.62	2.44
Yohan Ramirez	R-R	6-4	212	5-6-95	0	1	9.00	4	0	0	0	6	8	7	6	2	1	7	.308	.273	.333	10.50	1.50
Sergio Romo	R-R	5-11	185	3-4-83	0	0	9.00	1	0	0	0	1	1	1	1	1	0	1	.250	.500	.000	9.00	0.00
Justus Sheffield	L-L	5-10	224	5-13-96	6	8	6.99	24	24	0	0	103	138	85	80	19	47	86	.322	.273	.350	7.51	4.11
Gabriel Sosa	R-R	6-2	182	4-17-01	0	0	0.00	1	0	0	0	1	0	0	0	0	1	0	.000	--	.000	0.00	9.00
Drew Steckenrider	R-R	6-4	235	1-10-91	4	0	4.62	23	0	0	3	25	29	14	13	6	17	21	.274	.200	.370	7.46	6.04
Erik Swanson	R-R	6-3	222	9-4-93	0	0	0.00	1	0	0	0	1	2	0	0	0	0	1	.400	.333	.500	9.00	0.00
Blake Townsend	L-L	6-4	220	4-5-01	0	1	6.75	2	0	0	0	3	4	2	2	0	2	6	.333	.250	.375	20.25	6.75
Phillips Valdez	R-R	6-2	160	11-16-91	1	1	4.22	18	1	0	0	21	26	14	10	3	9	16	.313	.278	.340	6.75	3.80
Fred Villarreal	R-R	5-11	187	4-7-98	0	0	21.60	2	0	0	0	2	4	4	4	0	3	1	.444	.400	.500	5.40	16.20
Konner Wade	L-R	6-3	195	12-3-91	5	7	5.45	24	23	0	0	116	144	72	70	20	27	78	.306	.273	.341	6.07	2.10
Austin Warner	L-L	5-11	185	6-27-94	5	3	5.21	33	12	0	0	86	96	51	50	14	32	72	.288	.288	.288	7.51	3.34
Patrick Weigel	R-R	6-6	240	7-8-94	3	5	4.21	53	1	0	1	62	50	32	29	6	38	63	.222	.271	.186	9.15	5.52
Taylor Williams	B-R	5-11	185	7-21-91	2	1	1.14	23	0	0	1	24	20	4	3	1	7	23	.241	.226	.250	8.75	2.66
2-team total (27 Sacramento River Cats)					2	1	4.69	50	3	0	1	63	70	35	33	5	24	68	.281	.293	.274	9.66	3.41
Marcus Wilson	R-R	6-2	198	8-15-96	0	0	22.50	2	0	0	0	2	3	5	5	0	2	1	.333	.429	.000	4.50	9.00
Asher Wojciechowski	R-R	6-4	235	12-21-88	0	4	8.77	9	5	0	0	26	33	28	25	7	8	23	.308	.267	.339	8.06	2.81
Danny Young	L-L	6-3	200	5-27-94	1	1	3.86	29	0	0	2	28	20	13	12	0	9	40	.196	.211	.188	12.86	2.89

Fielding

Catcher	PCT	G	PO	A	E	DP	PB
Anchia	1.000	2	9	0	0	0	0
Casali	.950	3	18	1	1	0	0
Knapp	.984	19	175	6	3	0	2
Morgan	.988	20	157	6	2	2	1
Odom	.987	35	282	12	4	2	1
O'Keefe	.989	62	525	24	6	2	3
Raleigh	.971	5	32	1	1	0	0
Sheaffer	.909	1	7	3	1	0	0
Torrens	.988	10	76	7	1	0	0

First Base	PCT	G	PO	A	E	DP
Ellis	.993	14	131	15	1	16
Ford	1.000	5	34	4	0	6
Green	.992	69	456	23	4	43
Heineman	.973	5	34	2	1	3
Knapp	1.000	2	15	4	0	4
Mejia	1.000	2	13	1	0	1
Odom	.987	24	148	8	2	13
Padlo	1.000	16	118	6	0	8
Souza Jr.	1.000	2	13	1	0	2
Torrens	1.000	2	12	2	0	2
White	.994	21	166	13	1	23

Second Base	PCT	G	PO	A	E	DP
Blandino	1.000	32	58	94	0	24
Ellis	.976	20	25	56	2	11
Haggerty	.964	29	64	68	5	20
Izturis Jr.	1.000	10	13	25	0	5
Mazza	.000	1	0	0	0	0
McCoy	1.000	7	17	19	0	8
Mejia	.969	8	11	20	1	2
Padlo	1.000	2	4	5	0	1
Parker	1.000	1	0	2	0	0
Ramirez	1.000	1	1	2	0	1
Toro	1.000	9	18	18	0	4
Torrens	1.000	4	3	9	0	1
Villar	.986	27	53	84	2	20
Walton	1.000	2	1	9	0	1

Third Base	PCT	G	PO	A	E	DP
Blandino	1.000	9	7	7	0	1
Ellis	.975	31	21	57	2	8
Green	.977	16	12	31	1	3
McCoy	1.000	1	0	1	0	0
Mejia	.951	63	43	112	8	6
Padlo	.955	19	14	28	2	2
Ramirez	1.000	5	3	13	0	1
Toro	1.000	5	4	12	0	3
Villar	1.000	5	0	10	0	3
Walton	1.000	1	1	2	0	0

Shortstop	PCT	G	PO	A	E	DP
Blandino	1.000	3	5	6	0	3
Ellis	1.000	1	1	1	0	0
Haggerty	.933	7	12	16	2	1
Izturis Jr.	1.000	3	2	5	0	1
McCoy	.986	110	127	304	6	62
Mejia	.973	18	28	44	2	15
Moore	1.000	1	1	3	0	0
Walton	.973	7	15	21	1	6

Outfield	PCT	G	PO	A	E	DP
Amburgey	1.000	16	26	0	0	0
Bird	1.000	2	2	0	0	0
Fairchild	1.000	4	10	0	0	0
Guerrero	1.000	2	3	0	0	0
Haggerty	1.000	2	6	0	0	0
Hamilton	.952	21	39	1	2	0
Haniger	1.000	4	4	1	0	0
Heineman	1.000	23	46	1	0	0
Hill	.985	31	61	3	1	1
Kelenic	.987	75	147	9	2	0
Knapp	1.000	1	1	0	0	0
Lewis	.900	8	9	0	1	0
Marlowe	1.000	13	34	1	0	0
McCoy	1.000	3	5	1	0	0
Mejia	1.000	29	54	2	0	0
Perez	1.000	10	12	0	0	0
Souza Jr.	1.000	13	26	1	0	0
Tingelstad	.857	3	6	0	1	0
Trammell	1.000	18	30	1	0	0
Upton	1.000	6	10	0	0	0
Wall	.996	115	246	2	1	0
Walton	1.000	1	3	0	0	0
Wilson	.994	86	154	8	1	1

ARKANSAS TRAVELERS — DOUBLE-A

TEXAS LEAGUE

Batting	B-T	HT	WT	DOB	AVG	vLH	vRH	G	AB	R	H	2B	3B	HR	RBI	BB	HBP	SH	SF	SO	SB	CS	SLG	OBP
Jake Anchia	R-R	6-1	210	3-5-97	.220	.275	.198	77	287	27	63	9	0	4	40	18	2	0	3	82	1	0	.293	.268
Jose Caballero	R-R	5-10	185	8-30-96	.227	.179	.246	31	97	20	22	4	0	2	12	35	2	0	0	22	15	2	.330	.440
Zach DeLoach	L-R	6-1	205	8-18-98	.258	.229	.270	114	418	79	108	15	3	14	73	71	5	0	5	119	4	1	.409	.369
Patrick Frick	R-R	6-2	200	2-14-97	.228	.226	.229	89	294	44	67	10	1	1	25	35	4	0	6	76	2	1	.279	.313
Connor Hoover	L-R	5-10	185	7-18-96	.176	.153	.183	77	239	25	42	9	1	5	25	32	3	0	3	74	5	3	.285	.278
Cesar Izturis Jr.	B-R	5-11	145	11-11-99	.143	.167	.125	8	28	3	4	0	0	0	2	2	0	0	1	6	0	0	.143	.194
Tanner Kirwer	R-R	6-0	180	3-15-96	.240	.294	.214	96	312	41	75	8	1	5	29	38	7	2	3	97	23	2	.321	.333
Jack Larsen	L-L	6-1	195	1-13-95	.269	.272	.268	116	450	88	121	24	4	10	57	72	3	0	3	107	8	2	.407	.371
Cade Marlowe	L-R	6-1	210	6-24-97	.291	.244	.311	120	447	75	130	18	4	20	86	55	12	0	4	133	36	10	.483	.380
Kaden Polcovich	B-R	5-10	185	2-21-99	.242	.193	.263	118	451	70	109	21	4	12	60	59	13	0	1	118	18	2	.386	.345
Joe Rizzo	L-R	5-10	194	3-31-98	.277	.264	.282	118	488	84	135	30	0	21	69	48	2	0	2	103	2	1	.467	.343
Matt Scheffler	R-R	6-2	190	2-6-98	.250	.288	.236	71	244	44	61	7	3	1	33	45	6	0	3	59	10	2	.316	.376
Jake Scheiner	R-R	6-1	200	8-13-95	.252	.257	.249	127	477	74	120	34	0	21	105	73	9	0	9	119	3	1	.455	.356
David Sheaffer	R-R	6-2	170	5-9-95	.200	.000	.500	2	5	0	1	0	0	0	0	0	0	0	0	1	0	0	.200	.200
Trent Tingelstad	L-R	5-10	215	6-14-98	.300	.400	.200	4	10	1	3	1	0	0	2	4	0	0	0	3	0	0	.400	.500
Riley Unroe	B-R	5-11	180	8-3-95	.264	.250	.269	102	368	63	97	18	4	8	53	59	3	1	3	85	25	5	.399	.367

Pitching	B-T	HT	WT	DOB	W	L	ERA	G	GS	CG	SV	IP	H	R	ER	HR	BB	SO	AVG	vLH	vRH	K/9	BB/9
Peyton Alford	L-L	6-0	190	8-15-97	1	2	5.54	13	2	0	0	26	25	18	16	1	22	26	.263	.323	.234	9.00	7.62
Dayeison Arias	R-R	6-1	160	1-7-97	0	1	3.03	33	1	0	1	33	21	11	11	3	17	42	.183	.173	.190	11.57	4.68
Prelander Berroa	R-R	5-11	170	4-18-00	2	1	4.37	9	9	0	0	35	20	17	17	3	25	53	.167	.176	.159	13.63	6.43
Scott Boches	R-R	6-5	205	10-17-94	0	0	5.74	13	0	0	0	16	16	11	10	4	7	13	.254	.310	.206	7.47	4.02
Isaiah Campbell	R-R	6-4	230	8-15-97	0	4	3.46	14	0	0	1	13	13	6	5	2	2	24	.250	.211	.273	16.62	1.38
Taylor Dollard	R-R	6-3	195	2-17-99	16	2	2.25	27	27	0	0	144	106	42	36	9	31	131	.203	.181	.217	8.19	1.94
David Ellingson	R-R	6-2	200	1-23-95	0	2	9.00	26	0	0	1	28	35	29	28	4	17	26	.315	.310	.319	8.36	5.46
Jake Haberer	R-R	6-2	225	2-9-95	1	2	5.40	45	0	0	0	43	40	30	26	6	29	60	.242	.182	.283	12.46	6.02
Emerson Hancock	R-R	6-4	213	5-31-99	7	4	3.75	21	21	0	0	98	80	48	41	16	38	92	.219	.221	.217	8.42	3.48
Connor Hoover	L-R	5-10	185	7-18-96	0	0	0.00	1	0	0	0	0	0	0	0	0	0	0	.000	.000	--	0.00	0.00
Rodney Hutchison	R-R	6-5	225	8-9-96	0	0	9.00	1	0	0	0	3	6	3	3	0	1	2	.429	.444	.400	6.00	3.00
Connor Jones	R-R	6-3	220	10-10-94	4	8	7.02	17	17	1	0	74	78	59	58	8	49	64	.272	.238	.291	7.75	5.93
Rob Kaminsky	R-L	6-0	195	9-2-94	3	1	4.91	39	0	0	1	37	35	24	20	5	19	39	.248	.320	.209	9.57	4.66
George Kirby	R-R	6-4	215	2-4-98	2	0	1.82	5	5	0	0	25	17	6	5	3	5	32	.195	.188	.200	11.68	1.82
Collin Kober	R-R	6-1	185	9-8-94	4	2	3.38	44	1	0	5	48	32	19	18	6	23	64	.189	.264	.134	12.00	4.31
Stephen Kolek	R-R	6-3	210	4-18-97	6	13	4.51	27	27	0	0	144	140	79	72	10	66	138	.257	.273	.246	8.65	4.13
Travis Kuhn	R-R	5-10	195	5-20-98	3	3	4.10	50	0	0	3	59	43	31	27	3	35	71	.203	.227	.185	10.77	5.31
Bryce Miller	R-R	6-2	180	8-23-98	4	1	3.20	10	10	0	0	51	34	19	18	3	19	61	.191	.215	.172	10.84	3.38
Ben Onyshko	R-L	6-2	205	10-18-96	3	2	4.36	43	0	0	0	54	48	32	26	9	27	44	.239	.136	.308	7.38	4.53
Braden Shipley	R-R	6-1	190	2-22-92	3	1	3.79	47	0	0	0	55	35	29	23	5	36	58	.186	.123	.234	9.55	5.93
Jackson Sigman	R-R	6-2	200	6-13-95	0	0	--	1	0	0	0	0	0	3	3	0	2	0	--	--	--	--	--
Levi Stoudt	R-R	6-1	195	12-4-97	6	6	5.28	18	18	0	0	87	92	52	51	13	22	82	.269	.206	.308	8.48	2.28

Michael Stryffeler	R-R	6-2	210	5-22-96	1	3	2.27	35	0	0	14	36	25	12	9	3	19	57	.195	.163	.215	14.38	4.79
Devin Sweet	B-R	5-11	183	9-6-96	4	6	5.28	43	0	0	1	58	53	37	34	9	23	68	.243	.179	.279	10.55	3.57
Juan Then	R-R	6-1	200	2-7-00	0	1	5.40	10	0	0	0	10	11	6	6	2	3	14	.282	.438	.174	12.60	2.70
Blake Weiman	R-L	6-3	210	11-5-95	3	0	2.67	22	0	0	0	27	17	8	8	2	3	26	.175	.188	.163	8.67	1.00
Robert Winslow	R-R	6-5	215	8-19-97	0	0	0.00	1	0	0	0	1	0	0	0	0	0	1	.000	.000	.000	9.00	0.00

Fielding

Catcher	PCT	G	PO	A	E	DP	PB
Anchila	.991	75	734	38	7	6	12
Scheffler	.989	61	565	37	7	4	11
Sheaffer	1.000	2	12	1	0	0	0

First Base	PCT	G	PO	A	E	DP
Hoover	1.000	18	121	7	0	5
Larsen	.983	10	57	1	1	7
Rizzo	1.000	10	61	8	0	9
Scheffler	1.000	4	19	1	0	1
Scheiner	.993	98	705	58	5	65

Second Base	PCT	G	PO	A	E	DP
Caballero	1.000	1	0	1	0	0
Frick	.984	47	79	103	3	20
Hoover	1.000	9	12	18	0	5
Izturis Jr.	1.000	1	2	2	0	1
Polcovich	.980	78	128	207	7	39
Unroe	1.000	6	12	11	0	3

Third Base	PCT	G	PO	A	E	DP
Frick	.600	7	1	8	6	0
Hoover	.956	19	16	27	2	3
Polcovich	.909	14	9	21	3	2
Rizzo	.970	82	50	142	6	14
Scheiner	.789	9	6	9	4	1
Unroe	1.000	13	8	18	0	3

Shortstop	PCT	G	PO	A	E	DP
Caballero	.939	27	27	65	6	8
Frick	.943	34	32	67	6	12
Hoover	1.000	9	11	22	0	9
Izturis Jr	.957	7	13	9	1	1
Polcovich	.750	2	2	4	2	1
Unroe	.975	62	64	133	5	30

Outfield	PCT	G	PO	A	E	DP
DeLoach	.973	96	174	7	5	2
Hoover	1.000	24	37	0	0	0
Kirwer	.994	95	164	8	1	1
Larsen	.983	72	116	2	2	0
Marlowe	.975	114	267	5	7	1
Rizzo	1.000	1	5	1	0	1
Scheiner	1.000	2	10	0	0	0
Shipley	--	1	0	0	0	0
Tingelstad	1.000	2	3	0	0	0
Unroe	.964	21	26	1	1	0

EVERETT AQUASOX — *HIGH CLASS A*

NORTHWEST LEAGUE

Batting	B-T	HT	WT	DOB	AVG	vLH	vRH	G	AB	R	H	2B	3B	HR	RBI	BB	HBP	SH	SF	SO	SB	CS	SLG	OBP
Cole Barr	R-R	5-11	195	5-23-98	.168	.209	.158	79	208	36	35	8	1	4	24	44	14	0	4	85	15	6	.274	.344
Colin Davis	R-R	6-1	190	2-8-99	.241	.167	.261	9	29	4	7	2	0	1	4	2	0	0	0	8	3	0	.414	.290
Ty Duvall	L-R	5-11	200	7-11-97	.235	.313	.217	29	85	14	20	7	0	3	10	18	0	0	1	34	0	0	.424	.365
Dariel Gomez	L-R	6-4	190	7-15-96	.222	.202	.229	113	409	57	91	20	2	26	65	55	5	0	1	163	0	1	.472	.321
Mitch Haniger	R-R	6-2	214	12-23-90	.333	--	.333	3	9	1	3	0	0	1	2	0	1	0	0	2	0	0	.667	.400
Cesar Izturis Jr.	B-R	5-11	145	11-11-99	.083	.000	.143	4	12	0	1	0	0	0	2	0	0	0	1	4	1	0	.083	.077
Tyler Keenan	L-R	6-4	250	2-27-99	.250	.111	.284	25	92	8	23	4	0	3	14	12	2	0	0	29	0	0	.391	.349
2-team total (15 Vancouver Canadians)					.268	.226	.279	40	142	15	38	11	0	4	18	17	2	0	1	42	0	0	.430	.352
Victor Labrada	L-L	5-9	165	1-16-00	.232	.250	.227	111	401	66	93	15	6	10	31	49	8	2	0	134	27	8	.374	.328
Justin Lavey	R-R	6-1	205	9-23-97	.230	.270	.215	95	331	54	76	18	3	6	33	36	0	0	1	117	24	1	.356	.304
Kyle Lewis	R-R	6-4	222	7-13-95	.444	.667	.333	4	9	4	4	0	0	3	7	1	0	0	1	2	0	0	1.444	.455
Noelvi Marte	R-R	6-1	181	10-16-01	.275	.247	.283	85	342	62	94	19	0	15	55	42	7	0	3	84	13	6	.462	.363
Myles Miller	L-R	6-0	180	5-22-96	.137	.107	.146	45	131	11	18	3	2	0	7	10	0	0	0	58	2	1	.191	.199
Josh Morgan	R-R	5-11	185	11-16-95	.083	.250	.000	3	12	2	1	0	0	1	3	1	0	0	1	2	0	0	.333	.143
Spencer Packard	L-R	6-1	205	10-12-97	.282	.278	.284	69	255	43	72	15	1	12	37	41	9	0	2	47	5	1	.490	.397
James Parker	R-R	6-1	200	3-26-00	.219	.211	.222	107	374	50	82	18	2	13	49	44	3	0	2	139	6	0	.382	.305
Robert Perez Jr.	R-R	6-1	170	6-26-00	.342	.355	.337	35	120	22	41	6	1	7	27	23	9	0	1	34	1	1	.583	.477
Ben Ramirez	L-R	6-3	200	12-2-98	.177	.080	.205	30	113	11	20	5	1	2	8	8	0	0	2	31	0	0	.292	.228
Alberto Rodriguez	L-L	5-11	227	10-6-00	.261	.279	.255	119	472	59	123	28	3	10	46	50	4	0	1	138	6	4	.396	.336
Mike Salvatore	R-R	6-0	186	12-27-96	.168	.300	.132	54	184	17	31	4	1	7	27	24	1	0	2	52	1	0	.315	.265
Axel Sanchez	R-R	6-0	170	12-10-02	.235	.250	.231	8	34	0	8	1	0	0	1	0	0	0	0	9	0	0	.265	.235
David Sheaffer	R-R	6-2	170	5-9-95	.197	.267	.176	16	66	5	13	6	0	1	10	4	0	0	1	22	0	0	.333	.239
Andy Thomas	L-R	6-2	210	6-17-98	.264	.229	.274	64	216	33	57	12	0	9	32	43	6	0	0	66	1	0	.444	.400
2-team total (24 Eugene Emeralds)					.238	.197	.251	88	302	41	72	13	0	10	40	58	7	0	0	91	1	0	.381	.373
Trent Tingelstad	L-R	5-10	215	6-14-98	.209	.227	.203	87	263	28	55	11	1	3	30	46	1	0	1	76	0	0	.293	.328
Abraham Toro	B-R	6-0	225	12-20-96	.500	1.000	.333	2	4	0	2	0	0	0	2	1	0	0	0	0	0	0	.500	.600
Luis Torrens	R-R	6-0	217	5-2-96	.250	.000	.500	1	4	1	1	0	0	1	2	0	0	0	0	0	0	0	1.000	.250
Charlie Welch	R-R	6-0	205	2-8-00	.211	.304	.175	51	166	26	35	9	1	9	32	41	1	0	2	67	0	2	.440	.367

Pitching	B-T	HT	WT	DOB	W	L	ERA	G	GS	CG	SV	IP	H	R	ER	HR	BB	SO	AVG	vLH	vRH	K/9	BB/9
Peyton Alford	L-L	6-0	190	8-15-97	3	1	5.87	24	0	0	0	31	27	22	20	2	20	51	.231	.306	.198	14.97	5.87
Jarod Bayless	R-R	6-4	225	12-29-96	3	3	8.00	28	0	0	0	36	38	35	32	12	18	48	.270	.383	.185	12.00	4.50
Jorge Benitez	L-L	6-2	155	6-2-99	0	1	2.13	11	0	0	3	13	8	4	3	0	6	22	.186	.091	.219	15.63	4.26
Prelander Berroa	R-R	5-11	170	4-18-00	2	2	2.41	13	13	0	0	52	29	15	14	2	32	81	.160	.141	.177	13.93	5.50
2-team total (4 Eugene Emeralds)					2	2	2.06	17	17	0	0	66	34	16	15	2	38	97	.153	.121	.183	13.29	5.21
Isaiah Campbell	R-R	6-4	230	8-15-97	1	0	0.82	19	4	0	10	33	18	4	3	2	10	35	.159	.200	.121	9.55	2.73
Diego Castillo	R-R	6-3	268	1-18-94	0	0	67.50	1	0	0	0	1	3	5	5	0	1	1	.600	.000	.750	13.50	13.50
Luis Curvelo	R-R	6-1	170	10-21-00	3	2	4.82	37	1	0	0	52	45	29	28	9	28	57	.234	.236	.233	9.80	4.82
Julio Dilone	L-R	6-1	196	3-23-00	0	0	3.00	1	0	0	0	3	2	1	1	0	1	3	.200	.200	.200	9.00	3.00
Tyler Driver	R-R	6-2	185	2-4-01	0	0	0.00	2	0	0	0	1	0	0	0	0	3	2	.000	.000	.000	13.50	20.25
Tim Elliott	R-R	6-1	200	10-11-97	1	4	10.45	23	5	0	2	31	53	42	36	9	10	40	.361	.367	.356	11.61	2.90
Michael Flynn	R-R	6-4	185	8-7-96	3	1	7.50	21	4	0	0	36	50	34	30	3	13	33	.329	.299	.353	8.25	3.25
Ken Giles	R-R	6-3	197	9-20-90	0	0	8.44	6	2	0	0	5	7	9	5	1	3	9	.292	.429	.235	15.19	5.06
Kyle Hill	R-R	5-11	200	5-12-97	0	2	2.51	27	0	0	5	32	24	13	9	2	18	41	.203	.194	.214	11.41	5.01
Leon Hunter Jr.	R-R	6-3	253	3-17-97	7	4	4.63	35	0	0	4	47	41	26	24	8	25	52	.240	.221	.259	10.03	4.82
Jordan Jackson	R-R	6-6	204	10-14-98	2	4	4.64	9	9	0	0	43	44	25	22	4	18	35	.263	.254	.269	7.38	3.80
Evan Johnson	R-R	5-11	190	1-17-97	3	0	4.70	27	0	0	2	38	29	22	20	4	26	52	.209	.250	.177	12.21	6.10
Jimmy Joyce	R-R	6-2	210	1-13-99	7	11	5.75	23	23	0	0	113	106	80	72	14	47	133	.247	.247	.246	10.62	3.75

Jimmy Kingsbury	R-R	6-1	187	2-13-99	1	0	5.40	1	1	0	0	5	6	4	3	0	0	2	.273	.273	.273	3.60	0.00
Adam Macko	L-L	6-0	170	12-30-00	0	2	3.99	8	8	0	0	38	33	18	17	4	20	60	.234	.292	.204	14.09	4.70
Bernie Martinez	R-R	6-0	195	12-24-96	0	1	5.00	7	0	0	0	9	9	5	5	1	0	14	.257	.278	.235	14.00	0.00
Brendan McGuigan	R-R	6-2	210	10-9-95	0	3	5.73	19	1	0	0	22	20	18	14	2	16	25	.247	.189	.295	10.23	6.55
Juan Mercedes	R-R	6-2	190	4-3-00	7	8	4.51	22	21	1	0	108	99	59	54	15	30	124	.243	.247	.239	10.37	2.51
Jake Miednik	R-L	5-11	190	5-1-96	0	0	9.00	1	0	0	0	2	1	2	2	0	1	1	.143	.000	.200	4.50	4.50
Bryce Miller	R-R	6-2	180	8-23-98	3	3	3.24	16	15	0	0	78	54	29	28	7	25	99	.194	.222	.163	11.47	2.90
Mike Mokma	R-R	6-7	235	5-6-98	2	1	2.27	26	0	0	1	36	28	12	9	2	12	31	.212	.185	.231	7.82	3.03
Kelvin Nunez	R-R	6-1	170	12-10-99	0	2	10.22	9	0	0	0	12	22	14	14	3	6	16	.407	.417	.400	11.68	4.38
Bryan Pall	R-R	6-1	215	10-28-95	0	1	6.91	11	0	0	0	14	17	14	11	2	10	12	.298	.269	.323	7.53	6.28
Brayan Perez	L-L	6-0	170	9-5-00	2	1	7.47	5	3	0	0	16	19	16	13	2	15	13	.284	.304	.273	7.47	8.62
Logan Rinehart	R-R	6-3	185	9-21-97	3	2	3.98	12	12	0	0	54	46	26	24	5	23	69	.232	.247	.224	11.43	3.81
Max Roberts	L-L	6-6	190	7-23-97	0	5	5.40	34	0	0	1	42	44	30	25	5	24	62	.267	.283	.257	13.39	5.18
Jackson Sigman	R-R	6-2	200	6-13-95	0	1	13.50	2	0	0	0	2	3	3	3	0	3	6	.333	.250	.400	27.00	13.50
Erik Swanson	R-R	6-3	222	9-4-93	0	0	0.00	1	0	0	0	1	0	0	0	0	0	2	.000	.000	.000	18.00	0.00
Andy Thomas	L-R	6-2	210	6-17-98	0	0	0.00	1	0	0	0	1	0	0	0	0	0	0	.000	.000	--	0.00	0.00
Trent Tingelstad	L-R	5-10	215	6-14-98	0	0	0.00	1	0	0	0	1	0	0	0	0	0	0	.000	.000	.000	0.00	0.00
Blake Townsend	L-L	6-4	220	4-5-01	1	0	3.18	4	0	0	0	6	5	4	2	0	3	6	.208	.222	.200	9.53	4.76
Fred Villarreal	R-R	5-11	187	4-7-98	2	1	4.55	33	2	0	0	63	64	37	32	2	26	52	.261	.240	.276	7.39	3.69
Matt Willrodt	R-R	6-4	220	10-19-97	2	3	5.20	26	0	0	3	28	27	21	16	2	14	30	.260	.256	.262	9.76	4.55
Robert Winslow	R-R	6-5	215	8-19-97	0	0	12.60	8	0	0	0	10	14	14	14	1	9	12	.333	.368	.304	10.80	8.10
Bryan Woo	R-R	6-2	205	1-30-00	1	3	4.78	7	7	0	0	32	32	23	17	2	16	46	.254	.364	.195	12.94	4.50

Fielding

Catcher	PCT	G	PO	A	E	DP	PB
Duvall	.981	25	243	13	5	3	9
Morgan	1.000	2	24	0	0	0	1
Sheaffer	.979	11	130	11	3	2	2
Thomas	.995	57	604	52	3	5	7
Torrens	.929	1	12	1	1	1	2
Welch	.997	39	373	20	1	1	13

First Base	PCT	G	PO	A	E	DP
Gomez	.990	93	688	40	7	61
Keenan	.980	7	46	2	1	2
Packard	1.000	4	21	3	0	1
Parker	1.000	12	77	4	0	9
Perez Jr.	.985	15	124	7	2	11
Ramirez	1.000	2	8	1	0	0
Sheaffer	1.000	3	22	2	0	5
Thomas	1.000	1	1	0	0	0

Second Base	PCT	G	PO	A	E	DP
Barr	1.000	4	6	8	0	1
Izturis Jr.	1.000	4	2	5	0	0
Lavey	.943	68	98	133	14	27
Parker	1.000	22	29	67	0	12
Ramirez	1.000	4	7	14	0	2
Salvatore	1.000	30	35	58	0	14
Sanchez	.935	7	11	18	2	2
Toro	1.000	2	1	0	0	0

Third Base	PCT	G	PO	A	E	DP
Barr	.910	55	32	89	12	7
Keenan	1.000	14	7	16	0	0
Lavey	.932	23	12	29	3	2
Packard	.000	1	0	0	0	0
Parker	.936	28	18	55	5	3
Ramirez	.983	19	11	47	1	3
Sanchez	1.000	1	0	3	0	0

Shortstop	PCT	G	PO	A	E	DP
Marte	.918	81	103	164	24	40
Parker	.986	45	46	96	2	26
Ramirez	.857	2	2	4	1	2
Salvatore	.912	7	14	17	3	2

Outfield	PCT	G	PO	A	E	DP
Barr	1.000	9	7	0	0	0
Davis	1.000	8	20	2	0	1
Haniger	1.000	1	1	0	0	0
Labrada	.969	107	177	8	6	1
Miller	1.000	36	47	2	0	1
Packard	.987	56	73	1	1	0
Perez Jr.	1.000	7	6	1	0	0
Ramirez	.833	4	5	0	1	0
Rodriguez	.953	104	159	5	8	2
Sheaffer	1.000	2	2	0	0	0
Tingelstad	.960	79	93	3	4	1

MODESTO NUTS

LOW CLASS A

CALIFORNIA LEAGUE

Batting	B-T	HT	WT	DOB	AVG	vLH	vRH	G	AB	R	H	2B	3B	HR	RBI	BB	HBP	SH	SF	SO	SB	CS	SLG	OBP
Amador Arias	R-R	5-11	143	8-25-00	.183	.203	.176	71	241	39	44	10	1	6	25	30	6	0	2	93	3	4	.307	.287
Edwin Arroyo	B-B	6-0	175	8-25-03	.316	.276	.329	87	364	76	115	19	7	13	67	35	8	0	3	90	21	4	.514	.385
Freuddy Batista	R-R	6-0	182	12-12-99	.266	.230	.275	81	305	56	81	21	2	9	54	31	15	0	1	94	8	1	.436	.361
Randy Bednar	R-L	5-11	200	11-30-98	.217	.206	.220	86	300	42	65	15	2	3	43	29	9	0	6	113	8	2	.310	.299
Walking Cabrera	R-R	6-3	184	8-26-00	.250	.295	.238	95	372	56	93	27	2	5	62	40	3	0	7	102	5	3	.374	.322
Jonatan Clase	B-R	5-8	150	5-23-02	.267	.243	.276	107	423	91	113	22	11	13	49	65	8	0	2	133	55	10	.463	.373
Colin Davis	R-R	6-1	190	2-8-99	.226	.259	.215	60	217	30	49	13	1	4	33	23	3	0	2	58	5	3	.350	.306
Ty Duvall	L-R	5-11	200	7-11-97	.274	.308	.265	22	62	13	17	5	0	1	5	18	3	0	1	18	0	0	.403	.452
Harry Ford	R-R	5-10	200	2-21-03	.274	.337	.254	104	390	89	107	23	4	11	65	88	17	0	4	115	23	5	.438	.425
Gabriel Gonzalez	R-R	5-10	165	1-4-04	.286	.276	.289	32	126	31	36	5	1	2	17	13	11	0	0	21	4	1	.389	.400
Junior Gonzalez	R-R	5-11	186	5-10-00	.150	.143	.154	6	20	2	3	0	1	0	0	0	1	0	0	10	0	0	.250	.190
Cesar Izturis Jr.	B-R	5-11	145	11-11-99	.256	.313	.217	11	39	4	10	2	1	0	7	5	1	0	0	8	1	1	.359	.356
Victor Labrada	L-L	5-9	165	1-16-00	.400	.333	.409	12	50	13	20	5	0	2	13	9	1	0	1	8	3	1	.620	.492
Tyler Locklear	R-R	6-3	210	11-24-00	.282	.176	.325	29	117	19	33	5	0	7	29	7	7	0	2	29	0	0	.504	.353
Gabe Moncada	L-L	6-2	175	12-17-01	.154	.083	.167	21	78	13	12	2	0	2	10	11	2	0	0	28	0	0	.256	.275
Milkar Perez	B-R	5-11	200	10-16-01	.145	.171	.138	54	179	17	26	4	0	0	17	47	1	0	1	59	1	0	.168	.325
Robert Perez Jr.	R-R	6-1	170	6-26-00	.270	.263	.271	92	345	78	93	18	1	20	87	48	12	0	10	108	5	0	.501	.369
Ben Ramirez	L-R	6-3	200	12-2-98	.273	.180	.296	75	304	51	83	17	1	9	58	28	5	0	1	73	2	0	.424	.343
Brett Rodriguez	R-R	6-0	200	5-6-98	.223	.246	.215	80	251	47	56	10	1	4	22	36	13	1	1	105	16	4	.319	.349
Axel Sanchez	R-R	6-0	170	12-10-02	.305	.333	.298	33	131	27	40	13	2	8	37	15	6	0	0	42	4	1	.618	.401
David Sheaffer	R-R	6-2	170	5-9-95	.217	.385	.179	19	69	6	15	4	0	1	8	8	2	0	1	17	0	0	.319	.313
Hogan Windish	R-R	6-1	222	5-10-99	.336	.357	.333	30	119	31	40	11	1	2	31	17	6	0	2	32	4	0	.496	.438
Cole Young	L-R	6-0	180	7-29-03	.385	.286	.406	10	39	11	15	0	0	2	9	4	0	0	2	4	1	2	.538	.422

Pitching	B-T	HT	WT	DOB	W	L	ERA	G	GS	CG	SV	IP	H	R	ER	HR	BB	SO	AVG	vLH	vRH	K/9	BB/9
Ty Adcock	R-R	6-0	213	2-7-97	0	1	9.00	6	1	0	0	6	8	6	6	0	2	6	.320	.250	.353	9.00	3.00
Raul Alcantara	L-L	6-0	167	1-22-01	1	3	4.09	35	0	0	1	51	47	32	23	3	29	51	.239	.152	.265	9.06	5.15
Jose Aquino	L-L	6-3	175	6-27-02	0	0	9.00	1	0	0	0	1	2	1	1	0	1	0	.400	.000	.500	0.00	9.00

Amador Arias	R-R	5-11	143	8-25-00	0	0	0.00	1	0	0	0	0	0	0	0	0	0	1	.000	--	.000	27.00	0.00
Jorge Benitez	L-L	6-2	155	6-2-99	5	2	3.25	25	0	0	11	36	28	17	13	2	12	40	.211	.125	.247	10.00	3.00
Juan Burgos	R-R	6-0	155	12-22-99	0	0	3.96	19	1	0	0	25	18	14	11	1	23	31	.200	.212	.193	11.16	8.28
Sam Carlson	R-R	6-4	195	12-3-98	3	3	4.61	16	11	0	0	57	57	31	29	4	24	60	.266	.264	.269	9.53	3.81
John Creel	L-R	6-5	222	7-1-97	0	0	4.76	3	0	0	0	6	3	3	3	0	3	5	.143	.000	.167	7.94	4.76
Riley Davis	R-R	6-3	200	11-10-98	1	0	3.29	17	0	0	0	27	21	11	10	2	6	23	.208	.278	.169	7.57	1.98
Josias De Los Santos	R-R	6-2	174	7-29-99	1	0	6.75	7	0	0	0	9	11	7	7	0	10	12	.297	.200	.313	11.57	9.64
Tyler Driver	R-R	6-2	185	2-4-01	6	1	3.48	32	0	0	1	54	48	22	21	5	25	48	.236	.296	.197	7.95	4.14
William Fleming	R-R	6-6	220	3-6-99	6	6	4.92	14	14	0	0	68	64	40	37	9	24	59	.249	.315	.201	7.85	3.19
Natanael Garabitos	R-R	6-0	185	8-4-00	2	1	5.11	35	0	0	0	44	33	28	25	3	35	59	.205	.161	.232	12.07	7.16
Jose Geraldo	R-R	5-10	185	12-3-99	1	0	7.23	13	0	0	1	19	21	17	15	1	9	15	.269	.375	.222	7.23	4.34
Joseph Hernandez	R-R	5-11	150	6-15-00	9	5	3.39	24	22	0	0	117	79	47	44	10	54	143	.193	.257	.156	11.03	4.17
Adam Hill	R-R	6-6	225	3-24-97	0	0	27.00	1	0	0	0	1	2	3	3	1	4	1	.400	--	.400	9.00	36.00
Rodney Hutchison	R-R	6-5	225	8-9-96	1	0	2.05	8	0	0	0	22	12	9	5	1	7	15	.148	.143	.151	6.14	2.86
Jordan Jackson	R-R	6-6	204	10-14-98	6	7	3.77	17	14	0	0	76	78	42	32	5	25	81	.259	.287	.240	9.55	2.95
Chris Jefferson	L-R	6-2	200	1-24-97	1	1	3.92	23	0	0	0	39	34	19	17	2	14	49	.233	.259	.217	11.31	3.23
Jimmy Joyce	R-R	6-2	210	1-13-99	0	1	3.24	2	2	0	0	8	6	4	3	0	7	7	.200	.077	.294	7.56	7.56
Jimmy Kingsbury	R-R	6-1	187	2-13-99	1	2	4.28	15	10	0	0	48	47	27	23	1	23	54	.250	.287	.218	10.06	4.28
Holden Laws	L-L	6-2	166	12-8-99	0	1	6.86	14	0	0	0	20	21	19	15	5	10	25	.263	.176	.286	11.44	4.58
Brendan McGuigan	R-R	6-2	210	10-9-95	0	0	2.25	5	0	0	0	4	4	3	1	1	4	6	.250	.167	.300	13.50	9.00
Juan Mercedes	R-R	6-2	190	4-3-00	0	1	2.25	1	0	0	0	4	3	3	1	0	2	7	.200	.667	.083	15.75	4.50
Jake Miednik	R-L	5-11	190	5-1-96	1	3	9.19	10	8	0	0	32	44	40	33	4	20	23	.324	.389	.300	6.40	5.57
Bryce Miller	R-R	6-2	180	8-23-98	0	0	1.69	1	1	0	0	5	5	1	1	0	2	3	.238	.250	.231	5.06	3.38
Andrew Moore	L-R	6-5	205	8-11-99	2	1	1.95	25	0	0	1	32	25	10	7	0	17	58	.217	.206	.222	16.14	4.73
Michael Morales	R-R	6-2	205	8-13-02	5	7	5.91	26	26	0	0	120	143	96	79	14	50	125	.292	.296	.290	9.35	3.74
Kelvin Nunez	R-R	6-1	170	12-10-99	1	4	3.42	26	1	0	3	53	49	22	20	6	11	61	.245	.268	.229	10.42	1.88
Brayan Perez	L-L	6-0	170	9-5-00	6	3	2.90	19	3	0	1	50	56	23	16	5	9	40	.280	.283	.279	7.25	1.63
Adrian Quintana	R-R	6-0	175	11-20-02	1	4	10.42	5	5	0	0	19	35	23	22	2	8	16	.412	.429	.404	7.58	3.79
Stefan Raeth	L-R	6-1	180	8-31-00	0	2	5.63	7	0	0	3	8	7	6	5	1	5	7	.233	.273	.211	7.88	5.63
Max Roberts	L-L	6-6	190	7-23-97	0	0	4.50	4	0	0	0	6	6	3	3	0	3	6	.273	.143	.333	9.00	4.50
Gabriel Sosa	R-R	6-2	182	4-17-01	0	1	4.15	4	0	0	0	4	4	2	2	0	3	5	.250	.000	.333	10.38	6.23
Yeury Tatiz	R-R	6-3	175	11-22-00	5	4	8.38	18	7	0	1	58	73	60	54	7	23	46	.297	.371	.241	7.14	3.57
Blake Townsend	L-L	6-4	220	4-5-01	1	1	4.74	13	0	0	0	19	10	11	10	2	12	20	.154	.143	.159	9.47	5.68
Bryan Woo	R-R	6-2	205	1-30-00	0	1	3.98	6	6	0	0	20	18	9	9	2	6	29	.240	.306	.179	12.84	2.66

Fielding

Catcher	PCT	G	PO	A	E	DP	PB
Batista	.988	44	375	29	5	2	9
Duvall	.989	18	156	17	2	0	5
Ford	.986	54	534	41	8	3	14
Gonzalez	.988	6	77	7	1	0	1
Sheaffer	.990	12	96	7	1	3	0

First Base	PCT	G	PO	A	E	DP
Arias	1.000	2	12	0	0	0
Batista	.950	3	15	4	1	3
Locklear	1.000	5	45	3	0	6
Moncada	.994	21	161	10	1	22
Perez Jr.	.986	83	606	39	9	51
Ramirez	1.000	9	60	2	0	8
Sheaffer	1.000	3	19	3	0	0
Windish	.988	10	77	7	1	10

Second Base	PCT	G	PO	A	E	DP
Arias	.951	46	97	98	10	20
Izturis Jr.	.949	9	13	24	2	6
Ramirez	.964	19	24	29	2	10
Rodriguez	.971	39	51	85	4	18
Sanchez	.944	4	7	10	1	3
Windish	.975	17	33	46	2	13
Young	.923	2	5	7	1	1

Third Base	PCT	G	PO	A	E	DP
Arias	.818	7	4	5	2	1
Izturis Jr.	1.000	1	2	4	0	0
Locklear	.918	22	9	36	4	5
Perez	.864	52	22	80	16	8
Perez Jr.	.833	2	1	4	1	0
Ramirez	.958	44	35	101	6	3
Rodriguez	.667	3	0	4	2	0
Sanchez	.667	1	0	2	1	0
Windish	.786	3	2	9	3	0

Shortstop	PCT	G	PO	A	E	DP
Arias	.917	12	21	23	4	5
Arroyo	.955	84	118	199	15	35
Izturis Jr.	.500	1	0	1	1	0
Sanchez	.936	28	51	81	9	25
Young	.941	8	9	23	2	6

Outfield	PCT	G	PO	A	E	DP
Batista	1.000	1	2	0	0	0
Bednar	.978	76	126	5	3	0
Cabrera	.971	91	158	12	5	1
Clase	.971	100	198	6	6	2
Davis	.972	56	104	2	3	0
Gonzalez	.914	31	50	3	5	0
Labrada	.885	11	23	0	3	0
Ramirez	1.000	2	3	0	0	0
Rodriguez	.981	33	50	2	1	0

ACL MARINERS — *ROOKIE*

ARIZONA COMPLEX LEAGUE

Batting	B-T	HT	WT	DOB	AVG	vLH	vRH	G	AB	R	H	2B	3B	HR	RBI	BB	HBP	SH	SF	SO	SB	CS	SLG	OBP
Starlin Aguilar	L-R	5-11	170	1-26-04	.291	.162	.326	46	175	13	51	6	1	0	20	8	0	0	2	42	0	1	.337	.319
Freuddy Batista	R-R	6-0	182	12-12-99	.083	.000	.111	4	12	2	1	1	0	0	0	0	1	0	0	4	0	0	.167	.154
Asdrubal Bueno	R-R	5-11	170	11-25-01	.158	.154	.159	31	76	8	12	5	1	1	6	9	5	0	0	36	1	0	.289	.289
Jose Caballero	R-R	5-10	185	8-30-96	.600	1.000	.500	2	5	2	3	0	0	0	1	1	1	0	0	1	0	0	.600	.714
Jose Caguana	R-R	5-10	175	4-5-02	.227	.000	.263	16	22	2	5	0	0	2	7	1	0	0	1	12	1	0	.500	.250
Connor Charping	R-R	6-0	210	4-12-99	.182	.333	.125	8	11	0	2	0	0	0	1	2	2	0	0	3	1	0	.182	.400
Ty Duvall	L-R	5-11	200	7-11-97	.154	.000	.182	5	13	3	2	1	0	0	3	5	0	0	0	5	0	0	.231	.389
George Feliz	R-R	5-11	160	9-21-02	.193	.125	.212	43	150	18	29	5	3	2	16	17	2	0	1	54	12	3	.307	.282
Carlos Fernandez	R-R	6-0	160	9-18-01	.135	.364	.038	21	37	6	5	1	0	0	1	3	4	0	0	13	2	1	.162	.273
Gabriel Gonzalez	R-R	5-10	165	1-4-04	.357	.429	.337	35	126	20	45	9	0	5	17	8	6	0	0	21	5	3	.548	.421
Junior Gonzalez	R-R	5-11	186	5-10-00	.123	.077	.135	29	65	7	8	0	2	0	5	10	1	0	1	26	2	0	.185	.247
Arturo Guerrero	R-R	6-3	165	9-21-00	.198	.208	.195	38	111	16	22	6	1	2	11	15	7	0	1	42	7	4	.324	.328
Josh Hood	R-R	6-2	202	7-21-00	.150	.167	.143	8	20	2	3	0	0	0	2	4	0	0	1	7	2	0	.150	.280
Cesar Izturis Jr.	B-R	5-11	145	11-11-99	.313	.556	.256	15	48	8	15	1	0	0	7	3	2	1	2	4	4	0	.333	.364
Bill Knight	R-R	6-1	195	8-24-99	.344	.286	.360	12	32	9	11	1	0	1	6	8	4	0	1	10	5	1	.469	.511
Tatem Levins	L-R	6-0	206	5-29-99	.467	.667	.417	7	15	2	7	0	0	0	2	7	0	0	0	1	0	0	.467	.636

Tyler Locklear	R-R	6-3	210	11-24-00	.333	--	.333	2	6	0	2	1	0	0	2	1	2	0	0	1	0	0	.500	.556
Andrew Miller	R-R	6-4	230	9-2-97	.293	.214	.318	27	58	10	17	2	1	1	5	10	0	0	0	18	3	1	.414	.397
Gabe Moncada	L-L	6-2	175	12-17-01	.310	.240	.330	36	116	12	36	8	2	3	12	17	1	0	1	24	4	2	.491	.400
Josh Morgan	R-R	5-11	185	11-16-95	.375	.500	.333	3	8	2	3	0	0	1	1	1	0	0	0	3	0	0	.750	.444
Gunn Omosako	R-R	6-4	190	5-12-01	.289	.077	.375	21	45	9	13	3	0	0	7	1	3	0	0	22	3	1	.356	.347
Spencer Packard	L-R	6-1	205	10-12-97	.417	1.000	.300	4	12	1	5	1	0	0	4	1	0	0	0	2	0	0	.500	.462
Miguel Perez	R-R	6-2	170	8-21-00	.176	.130	.191	37	91	15	16	4	0	3	12	16	0	0	1	42	2	1	.319	.296
Blake Rambusch	R-R	5-9	175	8-31-99	.313	.500	.286	11	32	6	10	1	0	0	2	5	2	1	1	8	6	1	.344	.425
Edryn Rodriguez	R-R	5-9	150	4-23-03	.241	.125	.270	47	158	26	38	11	0	5	14	13	2	1	2	48	5	4	.405	.303
Luke Roskam	L-R	6-2	218	2-19-98	.154	.333	.100	7	13	3	2	2	0	0	2	5	0	0	0	8	0	0	.308	.389
Mike Salvatore	R-R	6-0	186	12-27-96	.200	--	.200	4	15	0	3	0	0	0	1	2	0	0	1	4	0	0	.200	.278
Axel Sanchez	R-R	6-0	170	12-10-02	.267	.200	.282	27	86	15	23	5	2	2	9	11	1	0	1	20	9	2	.442	.354
Curtis Washington Jr.	R-R	6-2	180	5-22-00	.178	.200	.171	17	45	8	8	1	1	0	2	6	0	0	0	12	7	3	.244	.275
Charlie Welch	R-R	6-0	205	2-8-00	.182	.000	.250	4	11	3	2	0	0	0	1	3	0	0	0	5	0	0	.182	.357
Hogan Windish	R-R	6-1	222	5-10-99	.300	.000	.375	3	10	0	3	2	0	0	4	1	1	0	1	3	0	1	.500	.385
Cole Young	L-R	6-0	180	7-29-03	.333	.250	.353	7	21	6	7	1	1	0	5	4	0	0	1	4	3	0	.476	.423
Nick Zona	R-R	6-2	200	7-9-99	.100	.250	.000	5	10	1	1	0	0	0	0	3	0	0	0	4	0	0	.100	.308

Pitching	B-T	HT	WT	DOB	W	L	ERA	G	GS	CG	SV	IP	H	R	ER	HR	BB	SO	AVG	vLH	vRH	K/9	BB/9
Ty Adcock	R-R	6-0	213	2-7-97	0	0	4.50	2	1	0	0	2	1	1	1	0	2	5	.143	.333	.000	22.50	9.00
Jose Aquino	L-L	6-3	175	6-27-02	0	0	1.80	1	0	0	0	5	4	1	1	0	2	6	.211	.333	.188	10.80	3.60
Drake Batcho	L-L	6-4	215	4-17-00	1	1	23.14	3	0	0	0	2	2	7	6	0	5	3	.200	.500	.125	11.57	19.29
Scott Boches	R-R	6-5	205	10-17-94	0	0	0.00	2	2	0	0	2	1	0	0	0	0	5	.143	.000	.200	22.50	0.00
Juan Burgos	R-R	6-0	155	12-22-99	2	0	0.98	7	2	0	1	18	10	2	2	1	3	15	.156	.185	.135	7.36	1.47
Danny Chang	L-L	6-3	176	2-11-00	0	2	3.79	10	4	0	0	19	10	9	8	0	11	26	.164	.200	.152	12.32	5.21
John Creel	L-R	6-5	222	7-1-97	2	1	3.82	19	0	0	1	33	24	16	14	2	18	40	.207	.158	.231	10.91	4.91
Riley Davis	R-R	6-3	200	11-10-98	1	0	4.50	2	0	0	0	2	2	1	1	1	1	3	.333	.200	1.000	13.50	4.50
Josias De Los Santos	R-R	6-2	174	7-29-99	2	3	4.40	19	0	0	3	31	27	17	15	0	16	40	.229	.211	.238	11.74	4.70
Julio Dilone	L-R	6-1	196	3-23-00	1	2	5.87	10	1	0	0	15	9	11	10	0	14	32	.164	.200	.133	18.78	8.22
Jose Geraldo	R-R	5-10	185	12-3-99	0	3	5.25	10	0	0	1	12	12	9	7	1	4	24	.235	.286	.200	18.00	3.00
Joey Gerber	R-R	6-4	212	5-3-97	0	0	0.00	1	0	0	0	1	2	1	0	0	0	0	.400	.500	.333	0.00	0.00
Adam Hill	R-R	6-6	225	3-24-97	0	0	2.70	3	3	0	0	3	3	3	1	0	4	6	.214	.000	.300	16.20	10.80
Rodney Hutchison	R-R	6-5	225	8-9-96	0	0	2.25	4	0	0	0	8	8	2	2	0	1	13	.258	.214	.294	14.63	1.13
Holden Laws	L-L	6-2	166	12-8-99	0	1	0.63	10	0	0	2	14	9	2	1	0	10	17	.170	.200	.163	10.67	6.28
Abdiel Medina	R-R	5-11	155	1-20-02	2	4	5.80	11	7	0	0	50	61	36	32	7	19	44	.300	.356	.259	7.97	3.44
Jake Miednik	R-L	5-11	190	5-1-96	2	0	3.38	7	0	0	1	13	4	6	5	0	4	18	.093	.222	.059	12.15	2.70
David Morillo	R-R	6-2	168	9-26-01	3	2	2.98	16	8	0	0	42	32	19	14	1	20	44	.219	.130	.272	9.35	4.25
Colby Morris	R-R	6-3	190	5-17-97	3	2	2.23	11	9	0	0	40	34	20	10	6	11	40	.215	.235	.206	8.93	2.45
Juan Querecuto	R-R	6-2	175	9-21-00	2	1	2.65	17	3	0	0	34	22	19	10	0	24	42	.188	.171	.197	11.12	6.35
Adrian Quintana	R-R	6-0	175	11-20-02	1	1	7.11	7	5	0	0	19	24	17	15	5	8	21	.316	.286	.341	9.95	3.79
Logan Rinehart	R-R	6-3	185	9-21-97	1	0	0.00	2	1	0	0	4	4	0	0	0	1	5	.267	.167	.333	11.25	2.25
Gabriel Sosa	R-R	6-2	182	4-17-01	1	1	4.08	13	0	0	1	18	16	11	8	2	5	22	.235	.120	.302	11.21	2.55
Juan Then	R-R	6-1	200	2-7-00	0	0	0.00	2	2	0	0	2	2	1	0	0	2	2	.250	.000	.333	9.00	9.00
Anthony Tomczak	R-R	6-2	200	10-17-00	0	1	9.00	1	0	0	0	1	2	1	1	0	0	1	.400	.500	.333	9.00	0.00
Blake Townsend	L-L	6-4	220	4-5-01	0	0	4.50	1	0	0	0	2	3	1	1	1	1	5	.333	.000	.375	22.50	4.50
Bryan Warzek	L-L	6-0	205	1-17-97	1	4	3.38	14	3	0	1	27	21	20	10	3	14	38	.210	.056	.244	12.83	4.73
Robert Winslow	R-R	6-5	215	8-19-97	1	0	1.23	5	1	0	0	7	2	1	1	0	4	11	.095	.100	.091	13.50	4.91
Bryan Woo	R-R	6-2	205	1-30-00	0	0	0.00	3	3	0	0	5	3	0	0	0	0	9	.176	.333	.091	17.36	0.00

Fielding

C: Batista 2, Caguana 15, Charping 7, Duvall 5, Gonzalez 28, Levins 2, Miller 16, Morgan 2, Roskam 5, Welch 3. **1B:** Bueno 14, Fernandez 5, Levins 3, Miller 12, Moncada 30, Roskam 2, Sanchez 1, Zona 2. **2B:** Bueno 10, Fernandez 8, Hood 1, Izturis Jr. 9, Perez 1, Rambusch 8, Rodriguez 23, Sanchez 1, Windish 2, Young 1, Zona 2. **3B:** Aguilar 38, Bueno 7, Fernandez 6, Hood 4, Izturis Jr. 2, Locklear 1, Rambusch 1, Sanchez 4. **SS:** Caballero 1, Fernandez 3, Hood 2, Izturis Jr. 7, Rambusch 1, Rodriguez 21, Sanchez 20, Young 6, Zona 1. **OF:** Feliz 39, Gonzalez 30, Guerrero 31, Knight 11, Moncada 9, Omosako 15, Packard 2, Perez 29, Rodriguez 1, Washington Jr. 14

DSL MARINERS — *ROOKIE*

DOMINICAN SUMMER LEAGUE

Batting	B-T	HT	WT	DOB	AVG	vLH	vRH	G	AB	R	H	2B	3B	HR	RBI	BB	HBP	SH	SF	SO	SB	CS	SLG	OBP
Michael Arroyo	R-R	5-10	160	11-3-04	.314	.207	.339	49	153	46	48	10	2	4	22	27	16	0	3	33	4	4	.484	.457
Luis Bolivar	R-R	6-1	160	2-9-04	.163	.040	.191	45	135	17	22	3	1	0	7	19	4	1	1	65	5	3	.200	.283
Ricardo Cova	R-R	5-9	145	5-24-04	.307	.357	.295	40	140	16	43	7	2	3	28	9	5	0	0	44	7	1	.450	.370
Juan Cruz	R-R	5-11	140	4-30-04	.234	.182	.242	36	77	20	18	1	1	4	15	10	2	1	0	28	12	3	.429	.337
Joaan De Jesus	R-R	5-10	165	6-15-05	.102	.154	.087	31	59	11	6	1	1	0	6	11	2	0	0	20	1	1	.153	.264
Adrian Garcia	R-R	5-10	180	5-3-05	.213	.067	.250	26	75	9	16	0	0	1	11	12	2	0	1	24	0	2	.253	.333
Carlos Gonzalez	R-R	5-11	175	11-20-03	.179	.053	.207	41	106	14	19	4	0	2	6	26	6	0	1	38	0	0	.274	.367
Martin Gonzalez	R-R	5-10	165	9-28-04	.233	.152	.252	53	172	28	40	7	0	3	24	32	9	0	2	86	2	4	.326	.377
German Guilarte	R-R	5-10	167	3-6-03	.150	.000	.170	27	60	7	9	1	0	0	5	7	7	1	0	21	0	1	.167	.311
Carlos Jimenez	L-L	5-10	170	2-14-03	.255	.188	.269	32	94	26	24	5	3	6	17	28	2	0	2	34	13	5	.564	.429
Bryant Mendez	R-R	5-11	165	9-15-03	.230	.259	.222	48	135	25	31	5	0	5	22	21	4	0	2	41	7	4	.378	.346
Lazaro Montes	L-R	6-3	210	10-22-04	.284	.152	.315	55	176	34	50	13	5	10	41	35	9	0	3	74	3	1	.585	.422
Andy Sosa	R-R	6-2	175	2-13-03	.234	.118	.256	41	107	8	25	4	0	4	20	8	1	0	1	34	3	3	.383	.291
Luis Suisbel	B-R	6-1	190	5-23-03	.216	.242	.208	44	134	21	29	7	1	4	17	17	12	0	0	44	3	2	.373	.356
Dervy Ventura	B-R	5-10	165	1-20-04	.245	.100	.279	45	106	25	26	4	4	0	15	23	2	1	2	24	2	1	.358	.383

Pitching	B-T	HT	WT	DOB	W	L	ERA	G	GS	CG	SV	IP	H	R	ER	HR	BB	SO	AVG	vLH	vRH	K/9	BB/9
Sebastian Barrios	R-R	6-1	165	6-20-04	4	2	3.91	14	0	0	0	23	19	16	10	1	22	18	.226	.268	.186	7.04	8.61
Yensy Bello	R-R	5-10	180	12-2-02	0	0	7.71	12	0	0	0	12	7	10	10	1	15	17	.171	.154	.179	13.11	11.57
Lisander Brito	R-R	6-3	175	7-9-02	2	1	5.52	11	6	0	0	29	28	18	18	3	15	26	.262	.244	.274	7.98	4.60
Kristian Cardozo	R-R	6-2	175	11-10-02	1	3	5.00	10	10	0	0	36	39	25	20	0	18	38	.267	.304	.250	9.50	4.50
Joaan De Jesus	R-R	5-10	165	6-15-05	0	0	0.00	1	0	0	0	0	0	0	0	0	0	0	.000	--	.000	0.00	0.00
Anderson Guevara	R-R	5-10	170	11-4-04	2	2	7.54	20	0	0	4	23	22	22	19	2	23	18	.268	.265	.271	7.15	9.13
Federik Jimenez	R-R	6-0	175	7-27-04	0	0	9.35	7	0	0	0	9	6	11	9	0	13	5	.200	.200	.200	5.19	13.50
Yoryi Jimenez	R-R	6-1	175	10-28-03	2	0	8.24	17	0	0	2	20	27	27	18	2	26	17	.329	.290	.353	7.78	11.90
Aneury Lora	R-R	6-2	155	3-30-04	0	4	4.05	8	7	0	0	20	21	18	9	1	8	22	.273	.226	.304	9.90	3.60
Emmanuel Marcano	R-R	6-0	170	12-4-02	4	1	3.82	16	1	0	2	31	26	13	13	3	12	26	.228	.222	.231	7.63	3.52
Luis Martinez	R-R	5-11	160	8-8-05	1	2	4.43	15	0	0	0	20	23	11	10	0	14	14	.299	.233	.340	6.20	6.20
Jean Munoz	R-R	6-1	155	9-17-02	2	4	4.81	12	11	0	0	49	44	30	26	1	18	58	.239	.167	.292	10.73	3.33
Anyelo Ovando	R-R	6-5	222	12-25-00	4	3	3.24	23	0	0	2	33	22	16	12	1	24	47	.191	.174	.203	12.69	6.48
Juan Pinto	L-L	6-2	165	8-26-04	1	2	4.75	10	10	0	0	30	24	25	16	0	29	33	.224	.059	.256	9.79	8.60
Erick Rodriguez	R-R	6-1	195	11-7-03	0	0	15.63	7	0	0	0	6	9	11	11	2	11	5	.346	.286	.368	7.11	15.63
Wuilliams Rodriguez	R-R	6-4	195	2-20-04	2	2	4.73	8	5	0	0	27	24	14	14	1	10	17	.255	.244	.264	5.74	3.38
Steven Sanchez	R-R	6-0	160	8-19-03	4	1	2.32	17	4	0	3	43	30	13	11	1	12	39	.203	.222	.191	8.23	2.53
Roiber Talavera	R-R	6-0	160	3-31-04	0	0	1.29	6	5	0	0	21	10	5	3	1	7	24	.141	.179	.116	10.29	3.00
Eduardo Tovar	R-R	5-11	165	10-10-03	3	0	2.50	13	0	0	2	18	13	7	5	1	6	23	.203	.185	.216	11.50	3.00
Fran Visamon	R-R	6-4	190	3-3-02	0	0	8.25	11	0	0	0	12	12	11	11	0	6	9	.279	.278	.280	6.75	4.50

Fielding

C: Garcia 26, Gonzalez 17, Guilarte 24. **1B:** Cova 4, Gonzalez 15, Guilarte 1, Mendez 20, Sosa 5, Suisbel 26. **2B:** Arroyo 7, De Jesus 12, Gonzalez 16, Mendez 6, Ventura 30. **3B:** Arroyo 11, Cova 14, De Jesus 10, Gonzalez 5, Mendez 10, Suisbel 15, Ventura 6. **SS:** Arroyo 27, De Jesus 7, Gonzalez 29. **OF:** Bolivar 44, Cova 20, Cruz 33, Gonzalez 1, Guilarte 1, Jimenez 31, Mendez 15, Montes 40, Sosa 18, Ventura 9.

Tampa Bay Rays

SEASON IN A SENTENCE: In an even more competitive AL East, the Rays were once again a playoff team, but the offense never reached the levels of recent years as Tampa Bay took an early playoff exit.

HIGH POINT: Drew Rassmussen struck out 10 Yankees while Wander Franco and Randy Arozarena each doubled twice in a Sept. 9 4-2 Rays' victory. That win cut the Yankees' lead to just 3.5 games and brought the Rays to 20 games above .500. At the time, a late run to claim another Al East crown seemed possible. Tampa Bay went 8-18 the rest of the way and ended up 13 games behind the Yankees.

LOW POINT: With their postseason on the line, the Rays couldn't score a run in 15 innings in a do-or-die Game 2 against the Guardians. The team's offensive issues were placed in clear focus in the game that eliminated them. Tampa Bay had the winning run reach third base in the 10th inning, but couldn't score.

NOTABLE ROOKIES: Infielder/outfielder Vidal Brujan and outfielder Josh Lowe struggled to find firm footholds on the roster.

KEY TRANSACTIONS: The offseason trade of outfielder Austin Meadows to Detroit brought back third baseman Isaac Paredes in return. Paredes' 20 home runs were tied for the team lead. The Rays extended righthander Tyler Glasnow's contract, then watched him return from Tommy John surgery in time to pitch in the playoffs. Righthnader Shane Baz, expected to be one of the team's top pitchers, joined Tyler Glasnow on the injured list with an elbow injury that required Tommy John surgery. Wander Franco also missed nearly half of the season with a hamate bone injury in his hand. Center fielder Jose Siri was acquired from the Astros in a three-team deal at the trade deadline.

ON THE FARM: Tampa Bay's conveyer belt of prospects rolls along. This year it was first baseman Kyle Manzardo who emerged as a bat to watch. Manzardo forced a midseason promotion to Double-A Montgomery after he dominated the South Atlantic League. The Rays once again finished with the best record in the minors, and Low-A Charleston was the Baseball America Minor League Team of the Year. The Carolina League champs' .667 winning percentage was best of all 120 MiLB full-season teams.

OPENING DAY PAYROLL: $68,976,867 (26th).

PLAYERS OF THE YEAR

MAJOR LEAGUE

Shane McClanahan
LHP
12-8, 2.54 ERA
194 SO, 38 BB, 166 IP
0.93 WHIP No. 2 in AL

MINOR LEAGUE

Kyle Manzardo
1B
(HiA/AA)
.327/.426/.617
22 HR, 26 2B in 93 G

ORGANIZATION LEADERS

Batting		*Minimum 250 AB
MAJORS		
* AVG	Harold Ramirez	.300
* OPS	Yandy Diaz	.824
HR	Randy Arozarena	20
	Isaac Paredes	
RBI	Randy Arozarena	89
MINORS		
* AVG	Kyle Manzardo, Bowling Green, Montgomery	.327
* OBP	Kyle Manzardo, Bowling Green, Montgomery	.426
* SLG	Kyle Manzardo, Bowling Green, Montgomery	.617
* OPS	Kyle Manzardo, Bowling Green, Montgomery	1.043
R	Miles Mastrobuoni, Durham	92
H	Miles Mastrobuoni, Durham	152
TB	Miles Mastrobuoni, Durham	238
2B	Osleivis Basabe, Bowling Green, Montgomery	39
3B	Mason Auer, Charleston Bowling Green	12
HR	Tristan Gray, Durham	33
RBI	Tristan Gray, Durham	89
	Heriberto Hernandez, Bowling Green	
BB	Kameron Misner, Montgomery	86
SO	Carson Williams, Charleston	168
SB	Mason Auer, Charleston Bowling Green	48

Pitching		#Minimum 75 IP
MAJORS		
W	Shane McClanahan	12
# ERA	Jeffrey Springs	2.46
SO	Shane McClanahan	194
SV	Jason Adam	8
	Pete Fairbanks	
MINORS		
W	Anthony Molina, Charleston, Bowling Green	14
L	Easton McGee, Durham	9
# ERA	Mason Montgomery, Bowling Green, Montgomery	2.10
G	Dalton Moats, Durham	51
	Chris Muller, Durham	
GS	Taj Bradley, Montgomery, Durham	28
SV	Dusten Knight, Durham	12
IP	Taj Bradley, Montgomery, Durham	133.1
BB	Sandy Gaston, Charleston	56
SO	Mason Montgomery, Bowling Green, Montgomery	171
# AVG	Mason Montgomery, Bowling Green, Montgomery	.196

2022 PERFORMANCE

General Manager: Peter Bendix. **Farm Director:** Jeff McLerran. **Scouting Director:** Rob Metzler.

Class	Team	League	W	L	PCT	Finish	Manager
Majors	Tampa Bay Rays	American	86	76	.531	6th (15)	Kevin Cash
Triple-A	Durham Bulls	International	86	64	.573	2nd (20)	Brady Williams
Double-A	Montgomery Biscuits	Southern	70	61	.534	2nd (0)	Morgan Ensberg
High-A	Bowling Green Hot Rods	South Atlantic	78	52	.600	1st (12)	Jeff Smith
Low-A	Charleston RiverDogs	Carolina	88	44	.667	1st (12)	Blake Butera
Rookie	FCL Rays	Florida Complex	39	16	.709	1st (16)	Rafael Valenzuela
Overall 2022 Minor League Record			411	302	.576	1st (30)	

ORGANIZATION STATISTICS

TAMPA BAY RAYS

AMERICAN LEAGUE

Batting	B-T	HT	WT	DOB	AVG	vLH	vRH	G	AB	R	H	2B	3B	HR	RBI	BB	HBP	SH	SF	SO	SB	CS	SLG	OBP
Jonathan Aranda	L-R	6-0	210	5-23-98	.192	.143	.197	32	78	10	15	4	0	2	6	8	1	0	0	23	0	0	.321	.276
Randy Arozarena	R-R	5-11	185	2-28-95	.263	.317	.249	153	586	72	154	41	3	20	89	46	11	0	2	156	32	12	.445	.327
Christian Bethancourt	R-R	6-3	205	9-2-91	.255	.225	.266	45	149	16	38	6	0	7	15	2	0	0	0	39	1	0	.436	.265
2-team total (56 Oakland Athletics)					.252	.252	.251	101	318	39	80	17	0	11	34	12	2	1	0	80	5	1	.409	.283
Vidal Brujan	B-R	5-10	180	2-9-98	.163	.220	.134	52	147	13	24	5	0	3	16	12	1	0	2	37	5	5	.259	.228
Yu Chang	R-R	6-1	180	8-18-95	.260	.190	.315	36	96	11	25	3	0	3	12	7	0	0	2	27	0	0	.385	.305
3-team total (11 Boston Red Sox, 4 Cleveland Guardians)					.222	.176	.253	51	126	14	28	5	0	3	13	12	1	0	2	41	0	0	.333	.291
Ji-Man Choi	L-R	6-1	260	5-19-91	.233	.294	.223	113	356	36	83	22	0	11	52	58	2	0	3	123	0	0	.388	.341
Yandy Diaz	R-R	6-2	215	8-8-91	.296	.310	.291	137	473	71	140	33	0	9	57	78	6	0	1	60	3	3	.423	.401
Wander Franco	B-R	5-10	189	3-1-01	.277	.304	.269	83	314	46	87	20	3	6	33	26	0	0	4	33	8	0	.417	.328
Kevin Kiermaier	L-R	6-1	210	4-22-90	.228	.256	.221	63	206	28	47	8	0	7	22	14	1	0	0	61	6	1	.369	.281
Brandon Lowe	L-R	5-10	185	7-6-94	.221	.261	.212	65	235	31	52	10	2	8	25	27	3	0	1	61	1	0	.383	.308
Josh Lowe	L-R	6-4	205	2-2-98	.221	.095	.259	52	181	24	40	12	2	2	13	15	1	1	0	66	3	0	.343	.284
Manuel Margot	R-R	5-11	180	9-28-94	.274	.346	.252	89	336	36	92	18	2	4	47	24	2	0	1	68	7	3	.375	.325
Miles Mastrobuoni	L-R	5-11	185	10-31-95	.188	--	.188	8	16	1	3	0	0	0	0	1	0	0	0	6	1	0	.188	.235
Francisco Mejia	B-R	5-8	188	10-27-95	.242	.337	.202	93	289	32	70	22	0	6	31	7	2	0	1	65	0	0	.381	.264
Isaac Paredes	R-R	5-11	213	2-18-99	.205	.231	.196	111	331	48	68	16	0	20	45	44	4	0	2	67	0	1	.435	.304
David Peralta	L-L	6-1	210	8-14-87	.255	.200	.267	47	161	10	41	11	1	0	18	14	2	0	3	40	0	1	.335	.317
Brett Phillips	L-R	6-0	195	5-30-94	.147	.000	.179	75	184	21	27	4	0	5	14	16	3	4	1	85	7	0	.250	.225
2-team total (8 Baltimore Orioles)					.144	.000	.174	83	201	22	29	6	0	5	15	16	3	4	1	94	7	0	.249	.217
Rene Pinto	R-R	5-10	195	11-2-96	.213	.214	.212	25	80	5	17	3	0	2	10	2	1	0	0	35	0	0	.325	.241
Roman Quinn	B-R	5-10	175	5-14-93	.262	.000	.379	21	42	7	11	2	2	0	4	4	1	0	0	21	0	2	.405	.340
Luke Raley	L-R	6-4	235	9-19-94	.197	.273	.180	22	61	7	12	2	0	1	4	7	3	0	1	24	0	0	.279	.306
Harold Ramirez	R-R	5-10	232	9-6-94	.300	.360	.277	120	403	46	121	24	0	6	58	19	9	0	4	72	3	5	.404	.343
Jose Siri	R-R	6-2	175	7-22-95	.241	.238	.242	56	166	35	40	9	0	4	14	11	1	0	0	60	8	1	.367	.292
2-team total (48 Houston Astros)					.213	.156	.232	104	301	53	64	13	2	7	24	20	3	0	1	108	14	2	.339	.268
Taylor Walls	B-R	5-10	185	7-10-96	.172	.164	.175	142	407	53	70	18	2	8	33	52	2	2	2	120	10	3	.285	.268
Mike Zunino	R-R	6-2	235	3-25-91	.148	.135	.154	36	115	7	17	3	0	5	16	6	1	0	1	46	0	0	.304	.195

Pitching	B-T	HT	WT	DOB	W	L	ERA	G	GS	CG	SV	IP	H	R	ER	HR	BB	SO	AVG	vLH	vRH	K/9	BB/9
Jason Adam	R-R	6-3	229	8-4-91	2	3	1.56	67	0	0	8	63	31	12	11	5	17	75	.147	.136	.154	10.66	2.42
Shawn Armstrong	R-R	6-2	225	9-11-90	2	3	3.60	43	3	0	2	55	56	22	22	6	14	61	.264	.282	.255	9.98	2.29
Luke Bard	R-R	6-3	200	11-13-90	1	1	1.93	8	0	0	0	14	7	3	3	0	7	8	.152	.188	.133	5.14	4.50
2-team total (1 New York Yankees)					1	1	1.80	9	0	0	0	15	7	3	3	0	7	8	.143	.176	.125	4.80	4.20
Shane Baz	R-R	6-2	190	6-17-99	1	2	5.00	6	6	0	0	27	27	15	15	5	9	30	.252	.175	.299	10.00	3.00
Jalen Beeks	L-L	5-11	215	7-10-93	2	3	2.80	42	7	0	2	61	49	22	19	7	22	70	.219	.219	.219	10.33	3.25
Christian Bethancourt	R-R	6-3	205	9-2-91	0	0	3.00	3	0	0	0	3	6	1	1	1	0	1	.400	.167	.556	3.00	0.00
2-team total (1 Oakland Athletics)					0	0	2.25	4	0	0	0	4	6	1	1	1	1	1	.333	.143	.455	2.25	2.25
Yu Chang	R-R	6-1	180	8-18-95	0	0	13.50	2	0	0	0	2	6	3	3	1	0	0	.600	.429	1.000	0.00	0.00
JT Chargois	B-R	6-3	200	12-3-90	2	0	2.42	21	3	0	0	22	16	7	6	3	5	17	.203	.214	.200	6.85	2.01
Yonny Chirinos	R-R	6-2	225	12-26-93	1	0	0.00	2	1	0	0	7	7	0	0	0	1	6	.250	.143	.286	7.71	1.29
Garrett Cleavinger	R-L	6-1	220	4-23-94	1	0	2.41	13	0	0	0	19	8	5	5	1	4	25	.125	.105	.133	12.05	1.93
Cooper Criswell	R-R	6-6	200	7-24-96	0	0	2.70	1	1	0	0	3	2	1	1	0	1	4	.167	.000	.200	10.80	2.70
Robert Dugger	R-R	6-0	198	7-3-95	0	0	5.06	1	0	0	0	5	8	3	3	0	0	7	.333	.273	.385	11.81	0.00
Pete Fairbanks	R-R	6-6	225	12-16-93	0	0	1.13	24	0	0	8	24	13	3	3	1	3	38	.159	.189	.133	14.25	1.13
Calvin Faucher	R-R	6-1	190	9-22-95	2	3	5.48	22	0	0	1	21	26	16	13	4	10	21	.289	.419	.220	8.86	4.22
J.P. Feyereisen	R-R	6-2	215	2-7-93	4	0	0.00	22	2	0	1	24	7	1	0	0	5	25	.086	.111	.074	9.25	1.85
Josh Fleming	L-L	6-2	220	5-18-96	2	5	6.43	10	3	0	0	35	54	36	25	5	12	29	.348	.278	.386	7.46	3.09
Ralph Garza Jr.	R-R	6-2	220	4-6-94	2	2	3.34	19	0	0	0	35	38	14	13	4	16	17	.284	.362	.224	4.37	4.11
Tyler Glasnow	L-R	6-8	225	8-23-93	0	0	1.35	2	2	0	0	7	4	1	1	1	2	10	.167	.214	.100	13.50	2.70
Javy Guerra	L-R	6-0	185	9-25-95	2	1	3.38	17	0	0	0	16	13	7	6	2	8	9	.217	.167	.238	5.06	4.50
Kevin Herget	L-R	5-10	185	4-3-91	0	1	7.71	3	0	0	0	7	9	6	6	0	0	4	.321	.231	.400	5.14	0.00
Andrew Kittredge	R-R	6-1	230	3-17-90	3	1	3.15	17	0	0	5	20	15	7	7	4	2	14	.205	.143	.244	6.30	0.90

Corey Kluber	R-R	6-4	215	4-10-86	10	10	4.34	31	31	0	0	164	178	82	79	20	21	139	.274	.279	.270	7.63	1.15
Dusten Knight	R-R	6-0	200	9-7-90	0	1	5.73	6	0	0	0	11	11	8	7	4	4	9	.250	.091	.303	7.36	3.27
Chris Mazza	R-R	6-4	190	10-17-89	1	0	11.81	2	0	0	0	5	9	10	7	3	6	5	.333	.250	.368	8.44	10.13
Shane McClanahan	L-L	6-1	200	4-28-97	12	8	2.54	28	28	0	0	166	116	52	47	19	38	194	.194	.204	.192	10.50	2.06
Easton McGee	R-R	6-6	205	12-26-97	0	0	0.00	1	0	0	0	3	4	1	0	0	0	1	.286	.000	.364	3.00	0.00
David McKay	R-R	6-3	205	3-31-95	0	0	18.00	1	0	0	0	2	3	4	4	1	2	0	.333	.000	.375	0.00	9.00
3-team total (2 New York Yankees, 1 Oakland Athletics)					0	0	6.75	4	0	0	0	7	8	5	5	1	4	3	.296	.250	.333	4.05	5.40
Cristofer Ogando	R-R	6-3	195	10-23-93	0	0	4.15	3	0	0	0	4	4	2	2	0	1	2	.286	.500	.250	4.15	2.08
Luis Patino	R-R	6-1	192	10-26-99	1	2	8.10	6	6	0	0	20	26	18	18	6	13	11	.313	.250	.372	4.95	5.85
Brett Phillips	L-R	6-0	195	5-30-94	0	0	18.00	3	0	0	0	4	9	8	8	3	2	0	.450	.600	.300	0.00	4.50
Colin Poche	L-L	6-3	225	1-17-94	4	2	3.99	65	0	0	7	59	46	30	26	11	22	64	.211	.189	.218	9.82	3.38
Brooks Raley	L-L	6-3	200	6-29-88	1	2	2.68	60	0	0	6	54	37	19	16	3	15	61	.189	.155	.208	10.23	2.52
Drew Rasmussen	R-R	6-1	211	7-27-95	11	7	2.84	28	28	0	0	146	121	51	46	13	31	125	.222	.207	.232	7.71	1.91
Tommy Romero	R-R	6-2	225	7-8-97	1	0	7.71	3	1	0	0	5	3	4	4	2	5	5	.188	.429	.000	9.64	9.64
Phoenix Sanders	R-R	5-10	205	6-5-95	0	0	3.07	8	0	0	0	15	12	5	5	0	3	12	.226	.222	.229	7.36	1.84
Jeffrey Springs	L-L	6-3	218	9-20-92	9	5	2.46	33	25	0	0	135	114	42	37	14	31	144	.222	.248	.215	9.58	2.06
Ryan Thompson	R-R	6-5	210	6-26-92	3	3	3.80	47	0	0	3	43	39	24	18	4	11	39	.234	.196	.250	8.23	2.32
Matt Wisler	R-R	6-3	215	9-12-92	3	3	2.25	39	5	0	1	44	30	18	11	6	14	35	.189	.186	.191	7.16	2.86
Jimmy Yacabonis	R-R	6-3	225	3-21-92	0	0	11.57	5	1	0	0	5	8	7	6	1	5	6	.381	.182	.600	11.57	9.64
Ryan Yarbrough	R-L	6-5	205	12-31-91	3	8	4.50	20	9	0	0	80	88	44	40	12	22	61	.276	.159	.308	6.86	2.48

Fielding

Catcher	PCT	G	PO	A	E	DP	PB
Bethancourt	.990	35	283	17	3	0	1
Mejia	.997	83	619	27	2	2	5
Pinto	.986	25	215	3	3	0	1
Zunino	.997	35	283	9	1	0	2

First Base	PCT	G	PO	A	E	DP
Aranda	1.000	11	41	1	0	3
Bethancourt	1.000	6	28	0	0	2
Chang	.000	1	0	0	0	0
Choi	.996	98	706	30	3	62
Diaz	.992	17	121	8	1	11
Mejia	1.000	2	5	0	0	0
Paredes	.994	29	144	12	1	14
Raley	1.000	3	11	0	0	3
Ramirez	.982	32	214	6	4	11

Second Base	PCT	G	PO	A	E	DP
Aranda	.917	13	21	23	4	4
Brujan	.965	31	46	64	4	18
Chang	.987	26	34	42	1	6
Lowe	.969	53	74	112	6	23
Mastrobuoni	1.000	6	7	7	0	2
Paredes	.992	43	50	78	1	19
Walls	.983	34	47	70	2	18

Third Base	PCT	G	PO	A	E	DP
Aranda	1.000	6	5	4	0	1
Bethancourt	1.000	1	1	0	0	0
Brujan	1.000	1	1	1	0	0
Chang	1.000	6	0	6	0	1
Diaz	.978	102	63	163	5	18
Paredes	.977	50	33	93	3	13
Walls	.966	25	17	40	2	5

Shortstop	PCT	G	PO	A	E	DP
Brujan	1.000	5	7	16	0	2
Chang	1.000	9	10	18	0	2
Franco	.980	72	68	172	5	26
Paredes	1.000	1	0	2	0	1
Walls	.972	92	104	240	10	29

Outfield	PCT	G	PO	A	E	DP
Aranda	--	1	0	0	0	0
Arozarena	.976	129	198	4	5	0
Brujan	.952	21	20	0	1	0
Kiermaier	.993	60	139	2	1	0
Lowe	--	1	0	0	0	0
Lowe	1.000	52	82	2	0	0
Margot	.986	79	134	3	2	0
Mastrobuoni	1.000	3	7	0	0	0
Peralta	1.000	38	57	0	0	0
Phillips	.986	79	141	3	2	1
Quinn	1.000	24	27	0	0	0
Raley	.963	15	24	2	1	0
Ramirez	1.000	29	33	0	0	0
Siri	.992	54	128	1	1	0

DURHAM BULLS

TRIPLE-A

INTERNATIONAL LEAGUE

Batting	B-T	HT	WT	DOB	AVG	vLH	vRH	G	AB	R	H	2B	3B	HR	RBI	BB	HBP	SH	SF	SO	SB	CS	SLG	OBP
Jonathan Aranda	L-R	6-0	210	5-23-98	.318	.291	.331	104	403	71	128	26	1	18	85	45	10	0	7	100	4	0	.521	.394
Ryan Boldt	L-R	6-2	210	11-22-94	.236	.263	.224	67	250	39	59	13	1	7	31	18	5	0	1	78	8	2	.380	.299
Vidal Brujan	B-R	5-10	180	2-9-98	.292	.260	.304	63	257	56	75	14	3	6	21	27	5	0	1	48	26	13	.440	.369
Ruben Cardenas	R-R	6-2	185	10-10-97	.208	.196	.214	82	284	40	59	14	2	16	41	32	1	0	1	93	5	4	.440	.289
Xavier Edwards	B-R	5-10	175	8-9-99	.246	.309	.218	93	349	48	86	19	1	5	33	43	0	7	1	75	7	4	.350	.328
Wander Franco	B-R	5-10	189	3-1-01	.429	.250	.471	7	21	3	9	2	0	0	2	4	0	0	0	3	0	1	.524	.520
Tristan Gray	L-R	6-3	215	3-22-96	.225	.235	.220	124	458	72	103	21	0	33	89	30	8	0	4	159	4	2	.487	.282
Jim Haley	R-R	6-1	195	2-23-95	.231	.242	.224	112	373	61	86	14	5	18	47	35	7	1	3	125	16	2	.440	.306
Garrett Hiott	L-R	5-11	175	7-7-97	.000	.000	.000	1	3	0	0	0	0	0	0	1	0	0	0	2	0	0	.000	.250
Joe Hudson	R-R	6-0	210	5-21-91	.226	.200	.237	49	137	24	31	3	0	11	27	25	1	0	2	49	1	0	.489	.345
Niko Hulsizer	R-R	6-2	225	2-1-97	.179	.167	.188	9	28	5	5	1	0	1	1	5	0	0	0	14	2	1	.321	.303
Diego Infante	R-R	6-2	178	10-22-99	.188	.200	.182	5	16	1	3	0	0	0	0	0	0	0	0	6	2	0	.188	.188
Johan Lopez	R-R	5-10	167	7-28-00	.000	.000	.000	3	4	0	0	0	0	0	0	0	1	0	0	2	0	0	.000	.200
Brandon Lowe	L-R	5-10	185	7-6-94	.313	.000	.385	5	16	3	5	2	0	0	1	0	1	0	0	2	0	0	.438	.353
Josh Lowe	L-R	6-4	205	2-2-98	.315	.324	.311	80	302	51	95	27	2	14	67	44	2	0	3	115	25	2	.556	.402
Bligh Madris	L-R	6-0	208	2-29-96	.317	.167	.379	10	41	11	13	3	0	4	15	4	0	0	1	11	0	0	.683	.370
2-team total (71 Indianapolis Indians)					.297	.253	.316	81	296	45	88	22	4	11	49	33	1	1	3	74	4	2	.510	.366
Manuel Margot	R-R	5-11	180	9-28-94	.263	.000	.385	5	19	6	5	0	0	0	2	4	0	0	0	2	0	0	.263	.391
Miles Mastrobuoni	L-R	5-11	185	10-31-95	.300	.252	.321	129	507	92	152	32	3	16	64	63	1	0	2	95	23	3	.469	.377
Curtis Mead	R-R	6-2	171	10-26-00	.278	.346	.239	20	72	8	20	6	0	3	14	11	1	0	1	17	1	0	.486	.376
Julio Meza	R-R	6-0	165	5-4-99	.500	--	.500	1	4	1	2	0	0	0	2	0	0	0	0	1	0	0	.500	.500
Alexander Ovalles	L-L	6-0	184	10-6-00	.167	.000	.200	3	6	0	1	0	0	0	2	1	0	0	0	2	0	0	.167	.286
Isaac Paredes	R-R	5-11	213	2-18-99	.263	.269	.261	25	95	15	25	7	1	4	18	13	2	0	3	19	0	1	.484	.354
Rene Pinto	R-R	5-10	195	11-2-96	.266	.351	.234	73	282	39	75	26	2	14	54	22	1	0	1	82	1	0	.521	.320
Ford Proctor	L-R	6-1	195	12-4-96	.213	.143	.249	79	268	27	57	7	0	6	28	44	3	1	1	95	3	2	.306	.329
Jordan Qsar	L-R	6-3	195	12-2-95	.205	.143	.233	24	88	12	18	4	1	4	6	3	1	0	0	37	2	2	.409	.239
Roman Quinn	B-R	5-10	175	5-14-93	.667	.500	1.000	1	3	2	2	0	0	1	4	1	0	0	0	1	0	0	1.667	.750
3-team total (6 L. V. IronPigs, 7 Omaha Storm Chasers)					.295	.200	.345	14	44	15	13	3	0	4	10	15	1	0	1	15	1	1	.636	.475
Luke Raley	L-R	6-4	235	9-19-94	.300	.290	.303	63	227	39	68	8	1	14	50	27	12	1	1	73	7	2	.529	.401

Harold Ramirez	R-R	5-10	232	9-6-94	.500	.000	.667	1	4	0	2	1	0	0	0	1	0	0	0	1	0	0	.750	.600
David Rodriguez	R-R	6-1	215	2-25-96	.250	.256	.247	37	116	21	29	7	0	5	12	10	1	0	0	38	0	0	.440	.315
Nate Soria	R-R	5-10	175	11-24-95	.000	--	.000	1	1	0	0	0	0	0	0	0	0	0	0	1	0	0	.000	.000
Cal Stevenson	L-L	5-10	175	9-12-96	.265	.145	.322	57	170	29	45	7	1	2	17	31	0	1	1	42	9	2	.353	.376
Alika Williams	R-R	6-2	180	3-12-99	.176	.500	.133	6	17	1	3	1	0	0	2	4	0	0	0	7	0	1	.235	.333
Brett Wisely	L-R	5-10	180	5-8-99	.238	.250	.235	5	21	3	5	2	0	0	2	1	0	0	1	6	1	0	.333	.261
Grant Witherspoon	L-L	6-3	200	9-27-96	.241	.254	.236	66	224	33	54	14	1	10	28	31	3	0	1	65	5	2	.446	.340

Pitching	B-T	HT	WT	DOB	W	L	ERA	G	GS	CG	SV	IP	H	R	ER	HR	BB	SO	AVG	vLH	vRH	K/9	BB/9
Chase Anderson	R-R	6-1	210	11-30-87	3	0	3.60	10	1	0	1	10	7	6	4	2	2	10	.184	.067	.261	9.00	1.80
2-team total (17 Toledo Mud Hens)					7	3	4.50	27	16	0	1	80	77	47	40	16	29	72	.246	.245	.247	8.10	3.26
Nick Anderson	R-R	6-4	205	7-5-90	1	0	5.63	17	0	0	1	16	20	11	10	5	3	12	.308	.318	.302	6.75	1.69
Shawn Armstrong	R-R	6-2	225	9-11-90	0	0	2.57	7	0	0	2	7	5	2	2	0	2	10	.200	.222	.188	12.86	2.57
Luke Bard	R-R	6-3	200	11-13-90	0	0	4.88	19	1	0	0	24	18	13	13	7	5	27	.205	.083	.288	10.13	1.88
2-team total (9 Scranton/Wilkes-Barre RailRiders)					1	1	4.29	28	1	0	2	36	30	21	17	9	10	38	.224	.155	.276	9.59	2.52
Shane Baz	R-R	6-2	190	6-17-99	0	0	1.38	4	4	0	0	13	8	2	2	1	4	20	.167	.167	.167	13.85	2.77
Seth Blair	R-R	6-2	185	3-3-89	0	3	7.61	21	2	0	1	24	29	21	20	9	13	17	.302	.344	.281	6.46	5.70
Ben Bowden	L-L	6-4	249	10-21-94	4	0	2.45	21	0	0	0	22	19	8	6	2	14	24	.232	.256	.209	9.82	5.73
Taj Bradley	R-R	6-2	190	3-20-01	4	3	3.66	12	12	0	0	59	55	28	24	10	15	53	.240	.275	.217	8.08	2.29
Trevor Brigden	L-R	6-3	210	9-20-95	1	0	2.19	7	0	0	0	12	8	3	3	2	1	17	.186	.286	.138	12.41	0.73
JT Chargois	B-R	6-3	200	12-3-90	1	2	20.65	10	0	0	0	6	10	13	13	1	7	4	.385	.400	.375	6.35	11.12
Yonny Chirinos	R-R	6-2	225	12-26-93	0	0	2.81	5	5	0	0	16	11	5	5	2	6	13	.196	.231	.167	7.31	3.38
Garrett Cleavinger	R-L	6-1	220	4-23-94	0	0	1.00	9	0	0	2	9	2	2	1	0	3	17	.069	.056	.091	17.00	3.00
Cooper Criswell	R-R	6-6	200	7-24-96	2	1	4.17	11	3	0	0	37	31	19	17	3	6	33	.226	.255	.209	8.10	1.47
Adrian De Horta	R-R	6-3	185	3-13-95	0	2	8.79	11	2	0	0	14	16	14	14	3	13	15	.271	.300	.256	9.42	8.16
Robert Dugger	R-R	6-0	198	7-3-95	0	2	3.94	5	5	0	0	16	13	9	7	2	7	13	.220	.120	.294	7.31	3.94
2-team total (14 Louisville Bats)					2	3	4.48	19	12	0	0	66	62	37	33	7	33	52	.253	.235	.270	7.06	4.48
Zack Erwin	L-L	6-5	195	1-24-94	4	5	5.79	32	2	0	0	37	43	26	24	4	16	29	.291	.190	.356	6.99	3.86
Pete Fairbanks	R-R	6-6	225	12-16-93	0	1	3.86	6	0	0	0	5	5	5	2	1	3	7	.227	.111	.308	13.50	5.79
Calvin Faucher	R-R	6-1	190	9-22-95	3	3	3.56	34	4	0	1	43	44	19	17	7	21	52	.260	.275	.250	10.88	4.40
Josh Fleming	L-L	6-2	220	5-18-96	9	2	3.06	15	10	0	0	65	73	23	22	4	14	46	.300	.262	.313	6.40	1.95
Carlos Garcia	R-R	6-3	185	11-28-98	0	0	0.00	1	0	0	0	1	0	0	0	0	0	1	.000	--	.000	6.75	0.00
Ralph Garza Jr.	R-R	6-2	220	4-6-94	3	2	5.64	21	3	0	1	30	31	21	19	6	4	22	.267	.327	.224	6.53	1.19
Chris Gau	L-R	6-2	205	2-3-97	0	1	5.06	8	0	0	0	11	14	6	6	2	9	8	.326	.333	.321	6.75	7.59
Tyler Glasnow	L-R	6-8	225	8-23-93	0	0	1.29	4	4	0	0	7	1	1	1	0	4	14	.045	.143	.000	18.00	5.14
Javy Guerra	L-R	6-0	185	9-25-95	2	0	1.74	43	0	0	9	41	20	10	8	1	16	52	.142	.135	.146	11.32	3.48
Kevin Herget	L-R	5-10	185	4-3-91	8	1	2.95	21	17	0	0	98	105	35	32	13	16	99	.273	.273	.274	9.12	1.47
David Hess	R-R	6-1	215	7-10-93	0	1	27.00	4	0	0	0	4	13	13	13	2	2	4	.520	.667	.474	8.31	4.15
Miller Hogan	R-R	6-2	200	7-18-96	0	1	8.15	6	5	0	0	18	25	16	16	5	10	14	.338	.400	.295	7.13	5.09
Joe Hudson	R-R	6-0	210	5-21-91	0	1	6.00	4	0	0	0	3	5	6	2	3	0	0	.385	.286	.500	0.00	0.00
Andrew Kittredge	R-R	6-1	230	3-17-90	0	0	0.00	1	0	0	0	1	1	0	0	0	0	1	.250	.000	.333	9.00	0.00
Dusten Knight	R-R	6-0	200	9-7-90	4	4	3.42	48	1	0	12	55	40	23	21	7	32	66	.194	.129	.248	10.73	5.20
Jack Labosky	R-R	6-3	235	7-19-96	1	0	6.00	1	0	0	0	3	3	2	2	1	0	2	.273	.333	.250	6.00	0.00
Jose Lopez	L-L	6-1	200	2-15-99	0	0	0.00	2	0	0	0	2	2	0	0	0	2	2	.250	.250	.250	9.00	9.00
Chris Mazza	R-R	6-4	190	10-17-89	1	0	4.85	8	0	0	0	13	16	9	7	0	6	18	.302	.313	.297	12.46	4.15
Easton McGee	R-R	6-6	205	12-26-97	6	9	5.43	27	22	0	0	108	122	71	65	24	20	82	.279	.320	.252	6.85	1.67
Brendan McKay	L-L	6-2	220	12-18-95	0	0	2.25	2	1	0	0	4	2	2	1	0	1	5	.143	.333	.000	11.25	2.25
David McKay	R-R	6-3	205	3-31-95	0	0	9.00	4	0	0	0	4	6	4	4	1	1	3	.333	.333	.333	6.75	2.25
2-team total (17 Scranton/Wilkes-Barre RailRiders)					3	0	3.86	21	0	0	1	26	21	11	11	4	12	29	.221	.245	.196	10.17	4.21
Evan McKendry	R-R	6-3	200	2-6-98	0	0	3.95	3	1	0	0	14	15	7	6	3	4	14	.278	.400	.231	9.22	2.63
Dalton Moats	L-L	6-3	210	5-24-95	1	0	3.60	51	1	0	0	55	48	24	22	10	12	60	.235	.247	.225	9.82	1.96
Chris Muller	R-R	6-5	210	4-22-96	5	3	4.91	51	1	0	2	59	59	37	32	6	34	75	.261	.275	.252	11.51	5.22
Jayden Murray	R-R	6-1	190	4-11-97	0	1	10.38	1	1	0	0	4	8	5	5	1	0	8	.381	.333	.417	16.62	0.00
Cristofer Ogando	R-R	6-3	195	10-23-93	2	1	4.56	41	0	0	3	53	41	31	27	8	26	53	.216	.200	.225	8.94	4.39
Luis Patino	R-R	6-1	192	10-26-99	3	2	4.50	9	9	0	0	34	32	19	17	6	13	34	.246	.180	.288	9.00	3.44
Joel Peguero	R-R	5-11	160	5-5-97	2	1	4.58	32	4	0	0	39	37	23	20	5	24	33	.252	.265	.245	7.55	5.49
Angel Perdomo	L-L	6-8	265	5-7-94	4	2	2.12	21	2	0	0	30	16	12	7	2	12	48	.160	.091	.214	14.56	3.64
2-team total (3 Nashville Sounds)					4	2	1.97	24	2	0	0	32	16	12	7	2	18	53	.150	.083	.203	14.91	5.06
Colin Poche	L-L	6-3	225	1-17-94	0	0	0.00	6	0	0	1	6	1	0	0	0	2	11	.053	.100	.000	16.50	3.00
Tommy Romero	R-R	6-2	225	7-8-97	6	5	3.51	23	13	0	1	67	57	29	26	12	25	58	.230	.257	.211	7.83	3.38
2-team total (6 Rochester Red Wings)					9	6	3.24	29	15	0	1	86	70	34	31	16	34	72	.221	.245	.202	7.53	3.56
Phoenix Sanders	R-R	5-10	205	6-5-95	0	0	5.40	25	1	0	1	30	39	19	18	6	2	36	.310	.283	.329	10.80	0.60
2-team total (2 Norfolk Tides)					0	0	6.19	27	1	0	1	32	43	23	22	7	3	38	.316	.291	.333	10.69	0.84
Justin Sterner	R-R	6-1	215	8-29-96	1	0	12.86	6	0	0	0	7	12	10	10	1	7	9	.387	.200	.476	11.57	9.00
Alan Strong	R-R	6-3	200	10-22-96	1	0	4.50	2	0	0	0	4	5	2	2	0	1	3	.313	.600	.182	6.75	2.25
Ryan Thompson	R-R	6-5	210	6-26-92	0	0	0.00	1	0	0	0	1	1	0	0	0	1	1	.333	.500	.000	9.00	9.00
Jeremy Walker	R-R	6-5	235	6-12-95	0	0	5.91	17	2	0	0	21	29	16	14	1	4	14	.333	.333	.333	5.91	1.69
Joe Wieland	R-R	6-2	205	1-21-90	0	1	3.00	5	3	0	0	12	11	7	4	2	4	8	.250	.316	.200	6.00	3.00
Nathan Wiles	R-R	6-4	228	7-2-98	0	1	12.27	1	1	0	0	4	7	5	5	0	1	4	.389	.286	.455	9.82	2.45
Matt Wisler	R-R	6-3	215	9-12-92	0	0	9.82	4	0	0	0	4	5	4	4	1	2	1	.333	.333	.333	2.45	4.91
Jimmy Yacabonis	R-R	6-3	225	3-21-92	2	1	3.00	8	0	0	0	9	5	3	3	0	3	8	.167	.143	.174	8.00	3.00
2-team total (18 Jacksonville Jumbo Shrimp)					6	4	3.31	26	0	0	2	33	24	13	12	1	14	43	.205	.255	.167	11.85	3.86
Ryan Yarbrough	R-L	6-5	205	12-31-91	2	2	4.55	7	7	0	0	28	32	18	14	3	12	26	.286	.226	.309	8.46	3.90
Tyler Zombro	R-R	5-10	215	9-2-94	0	0	13.50	2	0	0	0	2	6	3	3	1	1	0	.500	.333	.667	0.00	4.50

Fielding

Catcher	PCT	G	PO	A	E	DP	PB
Hudson	.994	37	312	14	2	3	2
Meza	.909	1	9	1	1	0	0
Pinto	.978	54	462	29	11	2	6
Proctor	.975	52	450	17	12	2	10
Rodriguez	.982	13	110	2	2	0	1

First Base	PCT	G	PO	A	E	DP
Aranda	.996	33	232	15	1	28
Gray	1.000	19	137	9	0	10
Haley	.991	72	542	21	5	55
Ovalles	1.000	2	9	2	0	3
Paredes	1.000	2	18	1	0	2
Raley	1.000	27	189	9	0	27
Ramirez	1.000	1	7	1	0	0
Rodriguez	.929	2	12	1	1	1

Second Base	PCT	G	PO	A	E	DP
Aranda	.962	25	42	59	4	18
Brujan	1.000	1	1	2	0	0
Edwards	.978	49	92	133	5	46
Haley	.964	6	16	11	1	3
Lowe	1.000	2	3	4	0	1
Mastrobuoni	.980	57	81	116	4	30
Mead	.960	4	14	10	1	4
Paredes	1.000	6	4	17	0	3
Proctor	1.000	4	4	4	0	1
Williams	1.000	1	1	1	0	0
Wisely	1.000	2	5	4	0	2

Third Base	PCT	G	PO	A	E	DP
Aranda	.957	30	16	50	3	8
Brujan	.900	6	4	5	1	0
Edwards	.981	20	15	37	1	5
Gray	.977	32	28	58	2	8
Haley	.891	24	14	43	7	2
Mastrobuoni	1.000	2	4	2	0	0
Mead	.935	11	10	19	2	3
Paredes	.960	16	12	36	2	4
Proctor	.900	10	4	14	2	3
Wisely	1.000	2	2	2	0	2

Shortstop	PCT	G	PO	A	E	DP
Brujan	.968	40	50	100	5	15
Edwards	.977	20	16	53	2	10
Franco	1.000	4	0	8	0	0
Gray	.953	66	63	160	11	36
Haley	1.000	1	1	3	0	1
Lopez	.900	2	2	7	1	1
Mastrobuoni	.978	13	17	27	1	8
Proctor	.875	4	3	4	1	1
Williams	.923	5	2	10	1	3
Wisely	1.000	1	1	4	0	1

Outfield	PCT	G	PO	A	E	DP
Aranda	1.000	7	15	0	0	0
Boldt	.990	54	100	3	1	0
Brujan	.975	16	38	1	1	0
Cardenas	.968	77	142	9	5	4
Haley	1.000	3	3	0	0	0
Hiott	1.000	1	1	0	0	0
Hulsizer	.857	9	12	0	2	0
Infante	1.000	5	14	1	0	0
Lowe	.985	59	128	2	2	0
Madris	.947	11	17	1	1	0
Margot	1.000	3	3	0	0	0
Mastrobuoni	.992	57	125	3	1	0
Ovalles	1.000	1	1	0	0	0
Qsar	1.000	24	44	1	0	0
Quinn	1.000	1	1	0	0	0
Raley	.973	27	34	2	1	1
Stevenson	1.000	54	130	4	0	2
Witherspoon	.966	60	85	1	3	0

MONTGOMERY BISCUITS — DOUBLE-A

SOUTHERN LEAGUE

Batting	B-T	HT	WT	DOB	AVG	vLH	vRH	G	AB	R	H	2B	3B	HR	RBI	BB	HBP	SH	SF	SO	SB	CS	SLG	OBP
Hill Alexander	R-R	6-2	200	6-13-96	.200	.103	.242	26	95	11	19	5	1	2	12	6	1	0	1	33	2	1	.337	.252
Logan Allen	R-R	5-10	180	8-13-98	.100	--	.100	3	10	2	1	0	0	1	1	1	2	0	0	3	1	0	.400	.308
Roberto Alvarez	R-R	5-11	151	7-28-99	.248	.276	.238	66	222	25	55	9	3	0	22	16	5	1	4	42	1	3	.315	.308
Osleivis Basabe	R-R	6-1	188	9-13-00	.333	.362	.324	57	228	39	76	23	3	0	25	24	3	1	3	25	14	0	.461	.399
Evan Edwards	L-L	6-0	200	6-21-97	.220	.196	.228	66	214	30	47	6	1	12	37	38	6	0	3	90	6	2	.425	.349
Tyler Frank	L-R	6-0	185	1-15-97	.198	.306	.171	53	182	24	36	5	0	2	17	11	4	0	3	60	6	2	.258	.255
Garrett Hiott	L-R	5-11	175	7-7-97	.206	.250	.192	30	102	9	21	6	0	2	8	6	4	3	0	34	4	2	.324	.277
Niko Hulsizer	R-R	6-2	225	2-1-97	.279	.240	.294	71	262	46	73	19	0	18	56	34	3	0	1	102	14	3	.557	.367
Blake Hunt	R-R	6-3	215	11-10-98	.245	.263	.239	81	273	31	67	15	1	5	39	21	7	0	1	70	2	0	.363	.315
Diego Infante	R-R	6-2	178	10-22-99	.273	.229	.295	42	143	25	39	9	0	2	27	19	0	0	1	47	4	3	.378	.356
Greg Jones	B-R	6-2	175	3-7-98	.238	.259	.231	79	319	54	76	19	3	8	40	27	11	0	1	128	37	5	.392	.318
Johan Lopez	R-R	5-10	167	7-28-00	.157	.238	.122	23	70	7	11	3	0	1	3	4	1	1	1	23	2	1	.243	.211
Kyle Manzardo	L-R	6-1	205	7-18-00	.323	.296	.333	30	99	18	32	10	0	5	26	14	3	0	6	19	1	1	.576	.402
Jacson McGowan	R-R	6-3	212	6-18-97	.250	.100	.289	17	48	5	12	4	0	2	6	7	1	0	0	29	2	0	.458	.357
Curtis Mead	R-R	6-2	171	10-26-00	.305	.407	.269	56	210	35	64	21	0	10	36	25	8	0	3	45	6	2	.548	.394
Kameron Misner	L-L	6-4	218	1-8-98	.251	.188	.270	117	415	80	104	25	1	16	62	86	6	0	3	155	32	7	.431	.384
Erik Ostberg	L-R	5-10	225	10-12-95	.216	.182	.225	51	162	19	35	6	2	6	20	24	0	0	1	56	3	1	.389	.316
Alexander Ovalles	L-L	6-0	184	10-6-00	.139	.000	.156	10	36	4	5	1	0	0	1	5	0	0	0	11	1	0	.167	.244
Alejandro Pie	R-R	6-4	175	1-31-02	.143	.000	.158	6	21	2	3	0	0	0	2	2	0	0	0	8	2	0	.143	.217
Jordan Qsar	L-R	6-3	195	12-2-95	.234	.189	.251	78	273	48	64	12	6	13	41	41	5	0	0	120	9	2	.465	.345
Abiezel Ramirez	B-R	5-11	160	1-26-00	.000	--	.000	1	2	0	0	0	0	0	0	0	0	0	0	1	0	0	.000	.000
Austin Shenton	L-R	6-0	205	1-22-98	.236	.196	.248	52	195	28	46	9	1	8	29	28	3	0	2	70	0	0	.415	.338
Ronny Simon	B-R	5-9	150	4-17-00	.271	.300	.260	39	144	25	39	8	2	7	25	11	0	0	4	25	12	2	.500	.314
Alika Williams	R-R	6-2	180	3-12-99	.238	.250	.235	6	21	1	5	1	0	0	2	3	0	0	0	8	1	0	.286	.333
Brett Wisely	L-R	5-10	180	5-8-99	.274	.254	.282	112	430	84	118	23	6	15	56	62	5	1	2	104	31	11	.460	.371
Grant Witherspoon	L-L	6-3	200	9-27-96	.294	.216	.322	49	194	29	57	11	3	7	33	14	2	0	1	47	10	4	.490	.346

Pitching	B-T	HT	WT	DOB	W	L	ERA	G	GS	CG	SV	IP	H	R	ER	HR	BB	SO	AVG	vLH	vRH	K/9	BB/9
Michael Berglund	L-R	6-2	175	7-18-97	0	0	9.00	1	0	0	0	1	1	1	1	1	0	0	.250	.000	.333	0.00	0.00
Taj Bradley	R-R	6-2	190	3-20-01	3	1	1.70	16	16	0	0	74	50	17	14	4	18	88	.189	.227	.150	10.65	2.18
Trevor Brigden	L-R	6-3	210	9-20-95	4	5	3.28	30	0	0	3	47	39	20	17	6	8	63	.224	.203	.242	12.15	1.54
Michael Costanzo	L-L	6-1	190	11-14-95	1	2	7.54	11	0	0	0	23	22	22	19	7	10	15	.239	.171	.281	5.96	3.97
Franklin Dacosta	L-L	5-11	162	2-27-00	0	0	3.00	1	0	0	0	3	3	1	1	1	2	3	.250	.000	.273	9.00	6.00
John Doxakis	R-L	6-4	215	8-20-98	2	7	5.68	20	18	0	0	82	74	56	52	11	45	72	.242	.257	.234	7.87	4.92
Carlos Garcia	R-R	6-3	185	11-28-98	7	1	4.35	39	0	0	3	62	50	32	30	9	29	73	.216	.250	.188	10.60	4.21
Chris Gau	L-R	6-2	205	2-3-97	5	2	2.93	30	1	0	1	46	31	23	15	5	8	53	.185	.227	.127	10.37	1.57
Andrew Gross	R-R	6-4	195	9-19-96	2	3	4.29	36	2	0	3	57	54	37	27	10	25	42	.248	.278	.227	6.67	3.97
Miller Hogan	R-R	6-2	200	7-18-96	0	0	9.00	1	0	0	0	3	5	3	3	1	0	1	.357	.250	1.000	3.00	0.00
Sean Hunley	R-R	6-4	220	7-5-99	7	2	3.55	27	10	0	0	91	95	37	36	4	18	68	.271	.275	.267	6.70	1.77
Joe LaSorsa	L-L	6-5	215	4-29-98	3	0	3.15	19	1	0	1	34	26	12	12	3	3	34	.211	.150	.241	8.91	0.79
Cameron Leonard	R-R	6-4	205	7-26-99	0	0	0.00	1	0	0	0	1	0	0	0	0	0	3	.000	.000	.000	20.25	0.00
Jose Lopez	L-L	6-1	200	2-15-99	8	3	2.60	39	0	0	9	55	32	19	16	1	35	91	.166	.164	.167	14.80	5.69
Evan McKendry	R-R	6-3	200	2-6-98	0	5	4.00	20	18	0	0	81	72	47	36	14	9	83	.229	.208	.248	9.22	1.00
Michael Mercado	R-R	6-4	160	4-15-99	4	8	4.91	24	20	0	0	103	102	57	56	17	36	115	.254	.248	.262	10.08	3.16

Mason Montgomery	L-L	6-2	195	6-17-00	3	1	2.48	11	11	0	0	54	40	15	15	5	16	53	.199	.103	.238	8.78	2.65
Jayden Murray	R-R	6-1	190	4-11-97	8	2	2.83	16	15	0	0	76	65	34	24	9	23	65	.226	.274	.176	7.66	2.71
Erik Ostberg	L-R	5-10	225	10-12-95	0	0	0.00	1	0	0	0	1	1	0	0	0	1	1	.333	--	.333	9.00	9.00
Cody Reed	L-L	6-5	230	4-15-93	1	0	7.71	7	0	0	1	9	7	8	8	2	6	10	.206	.214	.200	9.64	5.79
Evan Reifert	R-R	6-4	190	5-14-99	0	0	21.60	5	0	0	0	3	4	8	8	0	7	5	.333	.429	.200	13.50	18.90
Josh Roberson	R-R	6-3	175	5-12-96	2	6	7.26	28	2	0	2	31	35	30	25	4	23	37	.282	.333	.239	10.74	6.68
2-team total (3 Pensacola Blue Wahoos)					2	7	6.68	31	2	0	2	34	39	34	25	4	25	39	.289	.339	.247	10.43	6.68
Nomar Rojas	R-R	6-4	168	3-30-01	0	0	0.00	1	0	0	0	1	1	0	0	0	0	2	.250	.000	.333	18.00	0.00
Caleb Sampen	R-R	6-2	185	7-23-96	1	3	4.47	14	7	0	0	44	53	22	22	7	9	27	.296	.364	.231	5.48	1.83
Ian Seymour	L-L	6-0	210	12-13-98	0	2	8.10	5	5	0	0	17	22	15	15	2	12	23	.319	.250	.356	12.42	6.48
Justin Sterner	R-R	6-1	215	8-29-96	5	2	2.41	32	0	0	4	41	31	15	11	6	17	56	.209	.234	.190	12.29	3.73
Graeme Stinson	L-L	6-5	250	8-6-97	2	0	2.45	5	0	0	0	7	6	4	2	0	7	9	.222	.200	.235	11.05	8.59
Alan Strong	R-R	6-3	200	10-22-96	2	0	4.19	24	1	0	0	34	35	18	16	3	13	36	.261	.268	.256	9.44	3.41
Zack Trageton	R-R	6-1	225	9-2-98	0	4	7.07	13	4	0	0	28	33	23	22	5	20	19	.295	.271	.321	6.11	6.43
Nathan Witt	R-R	6-4	210	4-19-96	0	2	7.53	25	0	0	0	29	32	27	24	4	27	31	.286	.339	.232	9.73	8.48

Fielding

Catcher	PCT	G	PO	A	E	DP	PB
Alvarez	.996	61	524	24	2	5	8
Berglund	1.000	1	9	0	0	0	0
Hunt	.987	72	646	37	9	3	12
Ostberg	1.000	2	16	2	0	0	0

First Base	PCT	G	PO	A	E	DP
Edwards	.984	49	360	19	6	35
Frank	.987	9	71	6	1	10
Manzardo	1.000	23	177	11	0	7
McGowan	.983	16	107	11	2	8
Mead	.941	3	15	1	1	0
Ostberg	1.000	1	1	0	0	0
Ovalles	1.000	4	33	0	0	3
Shenton	.973	19	94	16	3	12
Wisely	.982	17	99	10	2	8

Second Base	PCT	G	PO	A	E	DP
Basabe	1.000	12	18	29	0	5
Frank	.946	19	24	29	3	6
Lopez	1.000	5	4	12	0	2
Mead	.981	16	21	32	1	3
Pie	.857	1	1	5	1	1
Ramirez	1.000	1	1	2	0	0
Simon	.903	27	27	57	9	12
Wisely	.969	54	74	146	7	37

Third Base	PCT	G	PO	A	E	DP
Basabe	.963	33	21	58	3	6
Frank	.933	10	9	19	2	3
Lopez	.900	8	0	18	2	3
Mead	.949	35	29	45	4	5
Pie	1.000	5	1	5	0	0
Shenton	.965	26	17	38	2	1
Simon	.929	7	7	6	1	0
Wisely	1.000	13	9	17	0	2

Shortstop	PCT	G	PO	A	E	DP
Basabe	.980	13	15	35	1	5
Frank	.951	14	25	33	3	9
Jones	.953	77	117	206	16	30
Lopez	.929	6	12	14	2	5
Williams	.913	6	4	17	2	0
Wisely	.985	18	26	40	1	9

Outfield	PCT	G	PO	A	E	DP
Alexander	.930	22	38	2	3	0
Allen	1.000	3	8	0	0	0
Edwards	1.000	10	18	0	0	0
Hiott	1.000	28	63	2	0	0
Hulsizer	.934	61	81	4	6	0
Infante	.981	36	49	2	1	0
Misner	.992	112	237	10	2	3
Ovalles	1.000	6	12	1	0	0
Qsar	.994	72	154	1	1	1
Wisely	1.000	3	3	0	0	0
Witherspoon	.979	47	89	3	2	2

BOWLING GREEN HOT RODS — *HIGH CLASS A*

SOUTH ATLANTIC LEAGUE

Batting	B-T	HT	WT	DOB	AVG	vLH	vRH	G	AB	R	H	2B	3B	HR	RBI	BB	HBP	SH	SF	SO	SB	CS	SLG	OBP
Mason Auer	R-R	6-1	210	3-1-01	.288	.279	.290	55	226	38	65	8	3	11	31	24	6	0	3	62	24	4	.496	.367
Dru Baker	R-R	5-11	205	3-22-00	.224	.263	.212	22	85	18	19	7	0	3	9	13	0	0	0	27	4	1	.412	.327
Osleivis Basabe	R-R	6-1	188	9-13-00	.315	.310	.316	55	216	41	68	16	2	4	22	16	3	1	0	34	7	5	.463	.370
Michael Berglund	L-R	6-2	175	7-18-97	.224	.214	.225	47	134	25	30	7	0	4	12	25	3	1	0	54	0	0	.366	.358
Beau Brundage	L-R	6-3	170	4-29-97	.215	.333	.193	39	130	16	28	6	3	4	18	8	2	0	2	44	5	1	.400	.268
Logan Driscoll	L-R	6-1	195	11-3-97	.229	.171	.241	60	205	29	47	8	1	7	39	30	6	1	3	53	3	1	.380	.340
Matt Dyer	R-R	6-4	185	7-14-98	.233	.119	.258	62	232	30	54	6	2	4	25	24	9	0	0	86	10	2	.328	.328
Tyler Frank	L-R	6-0	185	1-15-97	.289	.308	.281	14	45	7	13	2	1	0	9	7	2	0	1	10	1	1	.378	.400
Heriberto Hernandez	R-R	6-1	195	12-16-99	.255	.297	.246	119	419	70	107	28	1	24	89	67	8	0	0	155	6	2	.499	.368
Garrett Hiott	L-R	5-11	175	7-7-97	.274	.333	.258	36	113	15	31	7	0	3	8	11	3	0	1	35	9	2	.416	.352
Diego Infante	R-R	6-2	178	10-22-99	.283	.302	.279	67	265	44	75	14	2	11	48	25	0	0	4	82	4	3	.475	.340
Luis Leon	B-R	6-0	175	9-10-98	.176	.214	.165	40	131	20	23	3	1	4	10	22	2	0	0	33	3	1	.305	.303
Johan Lopez	R-R	5-10	167	7-28-00	.236	.194	.245	55	191	32	45	10	0	5	22	27	6	1	2	57	7	2	.366	.345
Kyle Manzardo	L-R	6-1	205	7-18-00	.329	.244	.348	63	225	53	74	16	1	17	55	45	1	0	4	46	0	0	.636	.436
Pedro Martinez	B-R	5-11	165	1-28-01	.233	.250	.231	17	60	9	14	3	0	0	1	8	2	0	0	18	5	1	.283	.343
Tanner Murray	R-R	6-2	190	9-3-99	.276	.283	.275	66	250	33	69	12	2	6	38	13	5	0	2	50	6	4	.412	.322
Alexander Ovalles	L-L	6-0	184	10-6-00	.273	.250	.278	89	315	63	86	18	3	14	62	43	6	1	3	76	9	5	.483	.368
Dillon Paulson	L-L	6-3	200	6-10-97	.163	.000	.171	15	43	8	7	1	0	4	13	10	1	0	3	9	0	0	.465	.316
Alejandro Pie	R-R	6-4	175	1-31-02	.133	.000	.154	4	15	3	2	1	0	0	0	0	0	0	0	6	1	0	.200	.133
Abiezel Ramirez	B-R	5-11	160	1-26-00	.182	.229	.169	51	165	21	30	5	3	3	14	23	2	0	0	54	1	2	.303	.289
Ronny Simon	B-R	5-9	150	4-17-00	.255	.183	.274	70	290	57	74	11	3	15	51	17	2	1	4	74	22	6	.469	.297
Nate Soria	R-R	5-10	175	11-24-95	.255	.143	.289	53	184	18	47	7	0	3	21	11	2	0	1	64	0	0	.342	.303
Gionti Turner	R-R	6-2	178	8-17-00	.223	.438	.184	34	103	18	23	3	1	1	6	9	3	3	1	16	4	2	.301	.302
Alika Williams	R-R	6-2	180	3-12-99	.254	.191	.264	84	323	59	82	10	2	10	58	47	6	0	4	68	6	3	.390	.355

Pitching	B-T	HT	WT	DOB	W	L	ERA	G	GS	CG	SV	IP	H	R	ER	HR	BB	SO	AVG	vLH	vRH	K/9	BB/9
Ben Brecht	L-L	6-7	215	1-7-98	2	2	3.16	11	11	0	0	43	48	20	15	7	6	49	.281	.261	.288	10.34	1.27
Beau Brundage	L-R	6-3	170	4-29-97	0	0	0.00	1	0	0	0	1	1	0	0	0	0	0	.250	--	.250	0.00	0.00
Neraldo Catalina	R-R	6-6	202	6-21-00	0	0	24.00	4	0	0	0	3	5	11	8	0	7	4	.333	.333	.333	12.00	21.00
Franklin Dacosta	L-L	5-11	162	2-27-00	3	3	3.69	24	5	0	1	61	51	26	25	7	18	61	.230	.171	.257	9.00	2.66
John Doxakis	R-L	6-4	215	8-20-98	2	1	2.94	7	7	0	0	34	20	13	11	4	8	41	.168	.063	.207	10.96	2.14
Conor Dryer	L-R	6-3	205	8-18-98	5	2	3.80	29	3	0	3	64	69	33	27	9	16	71	.272	.163	.327	9.98	2.25
Haden Erbe	R-R	6-3	225	8-13-98	0	0	0.00	3	0	0	0	4	0	0	0	0	2	5	.000	.000	.000	11.25	4.50
Andrew Gross	R-R	6-4	195	9-19-96	0	0	0.00	1	0	0	0	2	1	0	0	0	0	2	.200	.000	.250	10.80	0.00
Sean Hunley	R-R	6-4	220	7-5-99	0	0	0.00	1	0	0	0	2	2	0	0	0	0	2	.286	.000	.333	9.00	0.00

Seth Johnson	R-R	6-1	200	9-19-98	1	1	3.00	7	7	0	0	27	23	9	9	4	11	41	.232	.303	.197	13.67	3.67
Joe LaSorsa	L-L	6-5	215	4-29-98	4	3	1.62	21	0	0	7	39	24	11	7	3	7	53	.174	.140	.193	12.23	1.62
Cameron Leonard	R-R	6-4	205	7-26-99	2	5	5.84	27	0	0	4	45	59	33	29	4	12	53	.317	.342	.301	10.68	2.42
Jose Lopez	L-L	6-1	200	2-15-99	0	0	0.00	1	0	0	1	2	1	0	0	0	1	2	.167	--	.167	9.00	4.50
Audry Lugo	R-R	5-11	160	10-29-98	6	1	7.32	25	0	0	1	39	48	34	32	5	28	34	.312	.236	.354	7.78	6.41
Antonio Menendez	R-R	6-4	215	3-11-99	0	0	3.24	6	0	0	3	8	6	3	3	0	3	11	.207	.444	.100	11.88	3.24
Anthony Molina	R-R	6-1	170	1-12-02	13	2	2.94	26	7	0	0	89	85	37	29	10	18	75	.245	.224	.262	7.61	1.83
Mason Montgomery	L-L	6-2	195	6-17-00	3	2	1.81	16	16	0	0	70	49	20	14	6	27	118	.194	.175	.200	15.24	3.49
Addison Moss	R-R	6-1	190	9-10-97	1	0	1.08	5	0	0	0	8	7	6	1	1	4	7	.241	.333	.200	7.56	4.32
Sean Mullen	R-R	6-1	205	9-18-99	4	2	4.44	30	1	0	5	47	43	29	23	7	18	36	.242	.209	.261	6.94	3.47
Victor Munoz	R-R	6-3	160	12-25-00	3	2	4.64	14	6	0	1	43	53	26	22	4	9	29	.308	.318	.302	6.12	1.90
Matthew Peguero	R-R	6-2	200	1-12-00	3	3	4.83	17	2	0	0	32	38	19	17	6	19	24	.306	.429	.227	6.82	5.40
Ben Peoples	L-R	6-1	175	5-1-01	0	2	2.70	2	2	0	0	10	4	3	3	0	4	12	.121	.125	.120	10.80	3.60
Evan Reifert	R-R	6-4	190	5-14-99	6	2	3.67	20	0	0	2	27	19	13	11	2	11	43	.196	.262	.145	14.33	3.67
Nomar Rojas	R-R	6-4	168	3-30-01	1	1	6.13	29	0	0	3	47	57	36	32	4	30	39	.303	.296	.308	7.47	5.74
Jack Snyder	R-R	6-2	205	8-4-98	0	0	8.31	2	0	0	0	4	9	5	4	0	2	3	.429	.556	.333	6.23	4.15
Graeme Stinson	L-L	6-5	250	8-6-97	3	2	4.50	35	0	0	2	56	45	29	28	4	23	75	.217	.147	.252	12.05	3.70
Zack Trageton	R-R	6-1	225	9-2-98	1	1	2.05	5	5	0	0	22	14	8	5	0	13	26	.179	.222	.143	10.64	5.32
Austin Vernon	R-R	6-8	265	2-8-99	0	3	4.50	9	6	0	1	20	12	11	10	1	18	23	.176	.147	.206	10.35	8.10
Kyle Whitten	R-R	6-3	190	9-22-98	4	2	3.76	23	0	0	5	38	35	16	16	5	11	38	.238	.275	.219	8.92	2.58
Patrick Wicklander	R-L	6-1	205	12-31-99	4	5	5.48	18	11	0	1	71	77	46	43	13	25	75	.275	.256	.283	9.55	3.18
Nathan Wiles	R-R	6-4	228	7-2-98	2	2	4.38	23	22	0	0	88	83	44	43	14	11	72	.246	.232	.255	7.34	1.12
Logan Workman	R-R	6-4	215	12-6-98	5	3	3.49	20	19	0	0	90	83	39	35	13	26	81	.249	.278	.221	8.07	2.59

Fielding

Catcher	PCT	G	PO	A	E	DP	PB
Berglund	.987	36	279	20	4	2	4
Driscoll	.992	40	370	25	3	0	6
Dyer	.995	19	189	18	1	2	6
Leon	1.000	21	165	9	0	1	3
Soria	.995	22	204	5	1	1	4

First Base	PCT	G	PO	A	E	DP
Driscoll	1.000	4	26	3	0	1
Dyer	1.000	1	6	1	0	1
Frank	.968	3	29	1	1	3
Hernandez	.978	6	43	2	1	2
Leon	.947	3	16	2	1	2
Manzardo	.993	52	399	16	3	33
Ovalles	.997	43	268	24	1	30
Paulson	1.000	9	69	5	0	5
Soria	.974	15	109	2	3	11

Second Base	PCT	G	PO	A	E	DP
Basabe	.980	14	24	26	1	7
Frank	1.000	6	7	17	0	4
Lopez	1.000	16	18	48	0	6
Martinez	.968	8	12	18	1	1
Murray	.960	21	47	50	4	12
Ramirez	.985	20	26	40	1	16
Simon	.975	38	66	88	4	21
Turner	.977	10	16	26	1	11

Third Base	PCT	G	PO	A	E	DP
Basabe	.963	20	15	37	2	3
Dyer	.625	3	1	4	3	0
Frank	.800	3	1	3	1	0
Leon	.889	4	4	4	1	1
Lopez	.933	24	15	41	4	3
Martinez	1.000	1	1	1	0	1
Murray	.926	25	13	37	4	2
Pie	.875	3	0	7	1	1
Ramirez	.923	24	15	21	3	3
Simon	.935	20	12	46	4	3
Turner	.727	6	3	5	3	0

Shortstop	PCT	G	PO	A	E	DP
Basabe	.950	16	17	40	3	7
Lopez	.984	15	24	38	1	8
Martinez	.931	7	9	18	2	5
Murray	.925	9	12	25	3	6
Ramirez	.833	3	2	8	2	1
Simon	.917	6	10	12	2	4
Turner	1.000	1	0	1	0	0
Williams	.960	77	84	177	11	31

Outfield	PCT	G	PO	A	E	DP
Auer	.978	53	130	4	3	2
Baker	1.000	20	43	1	0	0
Brundage	.985	36	63	1	1	0
Driscoll	.909	6	7	3	1	0
Dyer	1.000	30	64	3	0	0
Hernandez	.962	104	172	6	7	0
Hiott	.986	36	65	4	1	0
Infante	.979	59	89	5	2	0
Ovalles	.988	43	80	1	1	0
Soria	--	1	0	0	0	0
Turner	1.000	14	19	3	0	0

CHARLESTON RIVERDOGS — *LOW CLASS A*

CAROLINA LEAGUE

Batting	B-T	HT	WT	DOB	AVG	vLH	vRH	G	AB	R	H	2B	3B	HR	RBI	BB	HBP	SH	SF	SO	SB	CS	SLG	OBP
Logan Allen	R-R	5-10	180	8-13-98	.215	.136	.235	34	107	20	23	7	1	2	11	14	8	0	2	23	6	0	.355	.344
Mason Auer	R-R	6-1	210	3-1-01	.293	.300	.292	60	232	46	68	13	9	4	31	31	3	0	4	48	24	3	.478	.378
Dru Baker	R-R	5-11	205	3-22-00	.361	.357	.361	25	97	20	35	2	2	3	23	16	2	0	0	21	17	3	.515	.461
Edwin Barragan	R-R	5-7	158	7-2-03	.276	.500	.240	9	29	3	8	1	0	1	4	2	3	0	0	5	1	1	.414	.382
Michael Berglund	L-R	6-2	175	7-18-97	.254	.125	.273	20	63	11	16	3	1	0	4	17	1	1	0	18	3	0	.333	.420
Junior Caminero	R-R	5-11	157	7-5-03	.299	.429	.267	26	107	19	32	2	1	6	20	8	2	0	0	22	5	0	.505	.359
Daiwer Castellanos	L-R	5-11	155	8-16-00	.276	.200	.297	32	116	14	32	5	1	0	15	4	0	1	0	14	7	1	.336	.300
Freddvil Chevez	R-R	6-4	200	3-13-00	.157	.294	.132	28	108	12	17	2	1	1	8	7	1	0	1	29	0	0	.222	.214
Dawson Dimon	R-R	6-1	185	5-17-99	.140	.000	.188	13	43	4	6	1	1	0	6	7	0	0	1	17	0	0	.209	.255
Angel Galarraga	L-R	6-1	178	8-1-02	.192	.125	.222	8	26	3	5	2	0	0	1	3	1	1	0	8	0	0	.269	.300
Christian Johnson	R-R	5-11	180	6-4-01	.226	.000	.250	11	31	5	7	1	0	2	3	3	1	1	0	10	1	2	.452	.314
Brock Jones	L-L	6-0	197	3-28-01	.286	.364	.263	13	49	15	14	4	1	4	12	12	0	0	1	21	9	3	.653	.419
Dominic Keegan	R-R	6-0	210	8-1-00	.261	.250	.267	6	23	4	6	0	0	2	6	2	1	0	0	6	0	0	.522	.346
Luis Leon	B-R	6-0	175	9-10-98	.276	.300	.272	39	134	19	37	6	1	4	23	17	1	0	3	29	0	0	.425	.355
Oneill Manzueta	R-R	6-0	190	2-7-01	.242	.179	.255	111	385	57	93	16	5	9	51	63	3	0	0	144	6	2	.379	.353
Jelfry Marte	B-R	5-10	130	3-27-01	.224	.176	.234	65	201	28	45	6	1	2	15	26	6	4	0	78	10	2	.294	.330
Julio Meza	R-R	6-0	165	5-4-99	.273	.182	.291	20	66	12	18	4	1	1	8	5	3	0	0	18	1	0	.409	.351
Nathan Perry	L-R	6-2	207	7-7-99	.230	.161	.246	45	161	17	37	6	0	5	18	16	2	0	2	30	1	0	.360	.304
Alejandro Pie	R-R	6-4	175	1-31-02	.200	.190	.204	24	75	13	15	3	1	2	11	8	4	0	1	35	4	0	.347	.307
Kenny Piper	R-R	5-10	190	7-12-98	.206	.320	.181	44	141	23	29	5	1	5	21	31	3	1	1	40	6	1	.362	.358
Abiezel Ramirez	B-R	5-11	160	1-26-00	.230	.000	.262	21	74	11	17	3	1	3	17	12	0	0	0	22	7	1	.419	.337
Blake Robertson	L-R	6-5	200	5-19-01	.196	.286	.184	16	56	10	11	4	0	1	5	13	2	0	0	22	3	0	.321	.366
Shane Sasaki	R-R	6-0	165	7-1-00	.324	.304	.328	89	346	71	112	27	3	9	57	49	4	0	3	92	47	4	.497	.410
Nick Schnell	L-R	6-3	180	3-27-00	.257	.321	.241	38	140	25	36	9	0	3	19	20	0	2	2	57	1	3	.386	.346

Bobby Seymour	L-R	6-4	250	10-7-98	.281	.286	.279	95	349	63	98	21	3	12	73	51	5	0	5	98	15	1	.461	.376
Ryan Spikes	R-R	5-9	185	3-13-03	.228	.208	.232	74	290	50	66	11	3	10	33	26	8	0	2	105	17	5	.390	.307
Gionti Turner	R-R	6-2	178	8-17-00	.174	.000	.211	28	86	10	15	1	0	0	7	8	3	0	1	33	4	1	.186	.265
Willy Vasquez	R-R	6-0	191	9-6-01	.256	.305	.245	113	449	78	115	21	9	10	73	36	3	0	4	126	25	3	.410	.313
Carson Williams	R-R	6-2	180	6-25-03	.252	.224	.258	113	452	81	114	22	10	19	70	57	10	1	3	168	28	10	.471	.347

Pitching	B-T	HT	WT	DOB	W	L	ERA	G	GS	CG	SV	IP	H	R	ER	HR	BB	SO	AVG	vLH	vRH	K/9	BB/9
Alex Ayala Jr.	R-L	6-1	195	11-26-01	3	1	4.14	10	2	0	1	37	27	18	17	4	13	44	.200	.220	.191	10.70	3.16
Nick Ditsko	R-R	6-4	225	6-16-02	0	0	4.00	4	4	0	0	9	8	4	4	0	7	5	.242	.364	.182	5.00	7.00
Neraldo Catalina	R-R	6-6	202	6-21-00	1	0	4.33	31	5	0	1	44	23	28	21	0	48	57	.152	.159	.145	11.75	9.89
Yonny Chirinos	R-R	6-2	225	12-26-93	0	1	11.37	3	2	0	0	6	9	9	8	1	2	6	.321	.368	.222	8.53	2.84
Aneudy Cortorreal	R-R	6-3	200	12-13-99	4	2	3.86	39	0	0	1	56	36	31	24	2	53	73	.182	.189	.174	11.73	8.52
Jonny Cuevas	R-R	6-3	200	11-20-00	3	1	4.50	19	1	0	1	56	53	33	28	5	40	43	.247	.189	.303	6.91	6.43
Yoniel Curet	R-R	6-2	190	11-3-02	0	0	4.50	2	2	0	0	6	6	5	3	0	7	10	.261	.214	.333	15.00	10.50
Dawson Dimon	R-R	6-1	185	5-17-99	0	0	0.00	2	0	0	0	2	1	0	0	0	0	1	.167	.000	.333	5.40	0.00
Christian Fernandez	R-R	6-2	170	8-11-99	5	2	2.79	16	8	0	0	58	42	22	18	6	25	87	.201	.179	.223	13.50	3.88
Kamron Fields	R-R	6-2	200	9-24-98	3	0	2.92	34	1	0	2	49	36	25	16	7	41	41	.202	.239	.167	7.48	7.48
Over Galue	R-R	6-2	188	7-31-01	12	2	3.93	28	6	0	1	94	82	46	41	4	51	101	.231	.265	.193	9.67	4.88
Roel Garcia III	R-R	6-4	245	11-21-98	2	1	2.31	7	0	0	2	12	11	6	3	1	2	21	.234	.125	.364	16.20	1.54
Sandy Gaston	R-R	6-3	200	12-16-01	2	4	4.61	31	4	0	3	55	33	30	28	3	56	77	.172	.230	.109	12.68	9.22
JJ Goss	R-R	6-3	185	12-25-00	4	5	4.00	25	25	0	0	101	97	48	45	7	21	101	.257	.273	.239	8.97	1.87
Sean Harney	L-R	6-0	190	7-10-98	1	1	9.00	6	0	0	0	8	10	9	8	0	5	11	.286	.294	.278	12.38	5.63
Antonio Jimenez	L-L	5-11	145	5-6-01	11	5	3.74	26	19	0	0	108	96	50	45	8	51	123	.239	.196	.254	10.22	4.24
Brendan McKay	L-L	6-2	220	12-18-95	0	0	3.12	3	2	0	0	9	7	5	3	2	4	6	.212	.214	.211	6.23	4.15
Antonio Menendez	R-R	6-4	215	3-11-99	2	0	0.83	11	0	0	1	22	17	4	2	1	6	29	.213	.243	.186	12.05	2.49
Anthony Molina	R-R	6-1	170	1-12-02	1	0	5.14	3	0	0	0	7	5	4	4	0	1	10	.200	.125	.333	12.86	1.29
Victor Munoz	R-R	6-3	160	12-25-00	4	2	4.22	10	0	0	0	32	34	21	15	2	10	22	.266	.281	.250	6.19	2.81
Matthew Peguero	R-R	6-2	200	1-12-00	1	0	2.57	3	0	0	0	7	7	4	2	0	5	11	.250	.214	.286	14.14	6.43
Ben Peoples	L-R	6-1	175	5-1-01	5	5	3.11	22	21	0	0	84	69	34	29	9	38	109	.224	.190	.264	11.68	4.07
Juan Rivera	R-R	6-3	220	6-4-98	0	0	8.38	12	0	0	0	10	5	13	9	1	25	9	.156	.150	.167	8.38	23.28
Jack Snyder	R-R	6-2	205	8-4-98	7	2	3.74	34	0	0	9	53	55	26	22	5	17	61	.263	.250	.276	10.36	2.89
Brayden Theriot	R-R	6-2	195	12-19-96	2	1	5.51	12	0	0	1	16	18	11	10	0	7	18	.277	.382	.161	9.92	3.86
Austin Vernon	R-R	6-8	265	2-8-99	9	1	1.69	15	1	0	1	59	32	12	11	6	23	91	.156	.165	.148	13.96	3.53
Kyle Whitten	R-R	6-3	190	9-22-98	1	0	1.86	15	0	0	6	19	13	4	4	1	3	14	.194	.265	.121	6.52	1.40
Daiveyon Whittle	R-R	6-1	236	11-11-99	1	5	4.44	21	15	0	0	73	73	47	36	6	28	60	.259	.239	.278	7.40	3.45
Patrick Wicklander	R-L	6-1	205	12-31-99	3	2	2.96	7	4	0	0	27	22	10	9	3	4	45	.210	.238	.190	14.82	1.32
Cole Wilcox	R-R	6-5	232	7-14-99	0	1	2.45	4	4	0	0	11	8	5	3	1	2	15	.190	.182	.200	12.27	1.64
Junior William	R-R	6-4	187	3-6-00	0	0	3.60	3	0	0	0	5	4	3	2	0	0	3	.211	.000	.400	5.40	0.00
Logan Workman	R-R	6-4	215	12-6-98	1	0	0.77	6	6	0	0	23	15	3	2	0	3	34	.183	.208	.147	13.11	1.16

Fielding

Catcher	PCT	G	PO	A	E	DP	PB
Berglund	.990	19	181	19	2	1	9
Dimon	.972	7	65	5	2	1	4
Galarraga	1.000	6	47	3	0	0	1
Keegan	.985	6	59	5	1	0	1
Leon	.991	31	326	12	3	0	3
Meza	.981	15	146	5	3	2	8
Perry	.994	16	144	12	1	0	2
Piper	.980	35	365	32	8	4	0

First Base	PCT	G	PO	A	E	DP
Chevez	.989	22	169	12	2	20
Marte	.972	4	35	0	1	1
Meza	1.000	1	4	0	0	1
Perry	.975	19	144	10	4	10
Robertson	1.000	13	77	5	0	7
Seymour	.990	75	569	45	6	46

Second Base	PCT	G	PO	A	E	DP
Barragan	.950	6	7	12	1	1
Caminero	.857	2	2	4	1	1
Marte	.939	31	37	56	6	8
Ramirez	.938	20	20	55	5	15
Spikes	.974	60	65	157	6	33
Turner	.960	8	11	13	1	4
Vasquez	.923	10	14	22	3	6

Third Base	PCT	G	PO	A	E	DP
Barragan	.857	3	2	4	1	0
Caminero	.912	17	7	24	3	0
Marte	.951	20	20	19	2	3
Pie	.839	13	10	16	5	2
Spikes	.846	4	5	6	2	0
Turner	.947	8	8	10	1	2
Vasquez	.942	72	51	111	10	14

Shortstop	PCT	G	PO	A	E	DP
Spikes	.969	8	7	24	1	3
Vasquez	.924	17	21	40	5	8
Williams	.968	108	136	252	13	59

Outfield	PCT	G	PO	A	E	DP
Allen	.981	32	51	0	1	0
Auer	.970	54	93	5	3	0
Baker	.974	24	32	5	1	1
Castellanos	.982	33	51	3	1	2
Johnson	1.000	11	16	1	0	1
Jones	1.000	13	30	1	0	0
Manzueta	.957	103	148	8	7	2
Marte	1.000	9	13	0	0	0
Pie	.700	6	7	0	3	0
Sasaki	.972	77	134	3	4	0
Schnell	.983	33	57	2	1	1
Turner	.882	12	15	0	2	0

FCL RAYS — ROOKIE

FLORIDA COMPLEX LEAGUE

Batting	B-T	HT	WT	DOB	AVG	vLH	vRH	G	AB	R	H	2B	3B	HR	RBI	BB	HBP	SH	SF	SO	SB	CS	SLG	OBP
Cesar Aponte	R-R	6-3	160	7-16-02	.000	--	.000	2	2	0	0	0	0	0	0	0	0	0	0	0	0	0	.000	.000
Cristopher Barete	L-L	5-9	155	12-10-01	.357	.000	.500	3	14	5	5	2	0	0	5	0	0	0	0	4	1	0	.500	.357
Edwin Barragan	R-R	5-7	158	7-2-03	.281	.167	.293	24	64	8	18	0	0	0	12	10	1	0	2	11	3	5	.281	.377
Jalen Battles	R-R	6-2	210	12-20-99	.200	.000	.250	5	20	3	4	0	0	0	1	0	0	0	0	2	1	0	.200	.200
Junior Caminero	R-R	5-11	157	7-5-03	.326	.476	.297	36	132	18	43	5	1	5	31	15	4	0	3	21	7	1	.492	.403
Ruben Cardenas	R-R	6-2	185	10-10-97	.615	.000	.667	4	13	7	8	0	0	3	5	4	1	0	0	0	2	0	1.308	.722
Daiwer Castellanos	L-R	5-11	155	8-16-00	.292	.333	.267	8	24	4	7	0	0	0	2	2	0	0	0	2	0	0	.292	.346
Estanli Castillo	R-R	6-3	195	10-7-01	.310	.167	.333	24	87	17	27	9	1	0	18	15	0	0	1	31	4	1	.437	.408
Christian Cerda	R-R	6-0	190	12-27-02	.315	.364	.302	20	54	15	17	5	0	2	12	15	0	0	0	12	5	0	.519	.464
Ryan Cermak	R-R	6-1	205	6-2-01	.273	.333	.263	7	22	5	6	0	1	2	5	1	1	0	0	9	3	0	.636	.333
Carlos Colmenarez	L-R	5-10	170	11-15-03	.254	.190	.267	35	126	36	32	7	3	1	19	17	9	0	1	41	13	2	.381	.379
Willmer De La Cruz	B-R	5-8	168	4-6-03	.283	.091	.305	37	106	22	30	3	1	1	12	19	1	1	0	28	9	4	.358	.397

Daury Del Rosario	B-R	6-0	175	2-14-02	.221	.222	.221	32	86	22	19	3	1	1	9	24	3	0	0	35	5	4	.314	.407
Jhon Diaz	L-L	5-11	160	10-1-02	.225	.318	.209	41	151	24	34	7	4	2	19	12	1	0	1	52	9	4	.364	.285
Matt Dyer	R-R	6-4	185	7-14-98	.333	.000	.400	4	12	2	4	0	0	1	4	1	0	0	0	3	0	1	.583	.385
Evan Edwards	L-L	6-0	200	6-21-97	.421	--	.421	6	19	7	8	0	1	2	11	7	0	0	1	5	1	0	.842	.556
Mario Fernandez	R-R	5-11	172	9-28-00	.133	.000	.143	6	15	3	2	0	0	0	0	1	1	0	0	3	0	0	.133	.235
Wander Franco	B-R	5-10	189	3-1-01	.429	.000	.600	2	7	1	3	1	1	0	1	0	0	0	0	2	0	1	.857	.429
Angel Galarraga	L-R	6-1	178	8-1-02	.156	.250	.146	15	45	4	7	1	0	0	5	4	0	0	0	13	0	1	.178	.224
Garrett Hiott	L-R	5-11	175	7-7-97	.333	--	.333	1	3	2	1	0	0	0	0	1	1	0	0	2	0	0	.333	.600
Xavier Isaac	L-L	6-4	240	12-17-03	.211	.000	.235	5	19	4	4	3	0	0	5	2	0	0	0	3	0	0	.368	.286
Kamren James	R-R	6-2	205	5-25-00	.200	.000	.250	7	20	3	4	0	0	0	3	2	1	0	2	6	2	0	.200	.280
Christian Johnson	R-R	5-11	180	6-4-01	.178	.400	.150	18	45	4	8	3	0	0	5	2	2	1	2	16	0	2	.244	.235
Brock Jones	L-L	6-0	197	3-28-01	.211	.000	.235	6	19	4	4	0	0	0	2	5	0	0	0	6	2	2	.211	.375
Dominic Keegan	R-R	6-0	210	8-1-00	.412	1.000	.375	6	17	2	7	4	0	0	5	3	0	0	0	4	1	0	.647	.500
Kevin Kiermaier	L-R	6-1	210	4-22-90	.000	--	.000	1	2	1	0	0	0	0	0	1	0	0	0	0	0	0	.000	.333
Manuel Margot	R-R	5-11	180	9-28-94	.143	.000	.167	2	7	1	1	0	0	0	0	0	0	0	0	1	0	0	.143	.143
Pedro Martinez	B-R	5-11	165	1-28-01	.125	--	.125	6	16	1	2	1	0	0	1	2	0	0	0	3	2	0	.188	.222
Francisco Mejia	B-R	5-8	188	10-27-95	.000	--	.000	1	3	1	0	0	0	0	0	0	1	0	0	1	0	0	.000	.250
Patrick Merino	R-R	6-2	220	8-13-98	.261	.300	.256	33	92	26	24	4	1	6	24	26	1	0	1	39	9	1	.522	.425
Julio Meza	R-R	6-0	165	5-4-99	.286	.500	.200	3	7	1	2	1	0	0	2	0	1	0	0	3	1	0	.429	.375
Dillon Paulson	L-L	6-3	200	6-10-97	.333	.500	.318	9	24	4	8	2	0	0	4	8	0	0	0	4	0	0	.417	.500
Odalys Peguero	B-R	5-9	172	1-25-03	.260	.400	.241	39	131	30	34	3	3	1	23	28	0	0	2	39	10	2	.351	.385
Alejandro Pie	R-R	6-4	175	1-31-02	.175	.333	.146	16	57	10	10	2	0	0	8	6	3	0	0	24	5	1	.211	.288
Kenny Piper	R-R	5-10	190	7-12-98	.286	--	.286	2	7	1	2	0	0	0	0	0	0	0	0	3	0	0	.286	.286
Jhonny Piron	R-R	6-1	165	2-6-04	.206	.235	.202	41	131	26	27	2	0	3	18	23	2	0	1	42	3	3	.290	.331
Roylems Rangel	R-R	5-8	163	10-17-02	.000	--	.000	1	1	0	0	0	0	0	0	0	0	0	0	0	0	0	.000	.000
Blake Robertson	L-R	6-5	200	5-19-01	.231	--	.231	4	13	1	3	1	0	0	2	0	0	0	0	6	0	1	.308	.231
Felix Salguera	R-R	6-0	171	3-1-02	.212	.222	.211	21	66	10	14	0	1	1	12	4	5	0	0	15	4	1	.288	.307
Joshuan Sandoval	R-R	6-2	215	12-18-97	.000	--	.000	2	3	0	0	0	0	0	0	1	0	0	0	0	0	0	.000	.250
Chandler Simpson	L-R	6-2	170	11-18-00	.370	.500	.333	8	27	5	10	3	0	0	3	6	0	0	1	4	8	0	.481	.471
Gionti Turner	R-R	6-2	178	8-17-00	.263	.333	.250	6	19	4	5	1	0	1	4	2	3	0	0	3	1	1	.474	.417

Pitching	B-T	HT	WT	DOB	W	L	ERA	G	GS	CG	SV	IP	H	R	ER	HR	BB	SO	AVG	vLH	vRH	K/9	BB/9
Alexander Alberto	R-R	6-8	190	11-2-01	1	1	6.44	13	10	0	0	36	36	29	26	1	22	40	.261	.263	.259	9.91	5.45
Emilio Alfonzo	R-R	6-6	170	8-2-00	2	0	3.68	11	2	0	0	15	8	6	6	1	12	13	.163	.100	.207	7.98	7.36
Nick Anderson	R-R	6-4	205	7-5-90	0	0	0.00	2	0	0	0	1	2	1	0	0	1	2	.286	.250	.333	13.50	6.75
Conor Angel	R-R	6-5	190	9-30-99	0	0	54.00	2	0	0	0	1	1	4	4	0	5	0	.333	.000	1.000	0.00	67.50
Alex Ayala Jr.	R-L	6-1	195	11-26-01	1	0	2.70	6	4	0	0	20	15	6	6	0	11	24	.214	.333	.182	10.80	4.95
Hunter Barnhart	R-R	6-2	205	2-14-02	0	0	0.00	1	1	0	0	1	0	0	0	0	0	1	.000	.000	.000	9.00	0.00
Orlando Barrios	R-R	6-6	180	8-27-01	3	0	2.59	12	1	0	2	31	23	10	9	1	12	28	.200	.300	.123	8.04	3.45
Nick Bitsko	R-R	6-4	225	6-16-02	1	2	7.41	10	8	0	0	17	14	16	14	0	20	15	.212	.267	.196	7.94	10.59
Ben Brecht	L-L	6-7	215	1-7-98	0	0	0.00	1	0	0	0	2	0	0	0	0	0	4	.000	.000	.000	18.00	0.00
Nigel Calmes	R-R	6-1	175	9-21-99	0	0	10.13	3	0	0	0	3	6	3	3	0	2	3	.429	.333	.600	10.13	6.75
Linse Carvajal	R-R	6-2	170	12-5-98	0	1	--	1	0	0	0	0	0	3	3	0	3	0	--	--	--	--	--
JT Chargois	B-R	6-3	200	12-3-90	0	0	4.50	2	0	0	0	2	2	1	1	0	0	1	.250	.000	.286	4.50	0.00
Yonny Chirinos	R-R	6-2	225	12-26-93	1	0	0.00	3	0	0	0	4	4	0	0	0	0	3	.267	.250	.286	6.75	0.00
Jake Christianson	R-R	6-3	190	10-22-99	0	0	0.00	2	0	0	1	2	0	0	0	0	1	5	.000	.000	.000	19.29	3.86
Elvis Contreras	L-L	5-11	145	2-13-00	3	2	4.68	13	0	0	1	33	31	18	17	3	11	31	.261	.280	.255	8.54	3.03
Samuel Cruz	R-R	6-3	160	1-9-02	1	0	3.09	9	0	0	0	12	8	4	4	1	12	16	.200	.125	.250	12.34	9.26
Yoniel Curet	R-R	6-2	190	11-3-02	2	1	1.75	13	8	0	0	36	19	10	7	3	21	48	.156	.160	.153	12.00	5.25
Nate Dahle	R-R	6-6	235	10-9-97	0	0	6.75	3	0	0	1	3	3	2	2	0	1	3	.300	.429	.000	10.13	3.38
Duncan Davitt	R-R	6-3	235	9-23-99	0	1	12.46	3	0	0	0	4	7	6	6	1	2	6	.389	.167	.500	12.46	4.15
Manuel De La Rosa	L-L	6-0	155	4-20-03	2	0	4.05	13	1	0	0	33	20	17	15	0	16	37	.174	.200	.167	9.99	4.32
Haden Erbe	R-R	6-3	225	8-13-98	0	0	0.00	1	0	0	0	1	0	0	0	0	0	0	.000	.000	.000	0.00	0.00
Pete Fairbanks	R-R	6-6	225	12-16-93	0	0	9.00	1	0	0	0	1	2	1	1	0	0	2	.400	1.000	.250	18.00	0.00
Roel Garcia III	R-R	6-4	245	11-21-98	0	0	0.00	1	0	0	0	1	0	0	0	0	1	2	.000	--	.000	18.00	9.00
Cristian Guzman	R-R	5-11	153	5-8-02	0	1	5.14	12	0	0	0	14	14	9	8	0	19	11	.269	.150	.344	7.07	12.21
Cade Halemanu	R-R	6-4	215	8-9-00	1	0	0.00	2	0	0	0	3	1	0	0	0	0	5	.100	.200	.000	15.00	0.00
Sean Harney	L-R	6-0	190	7-10-98	0	0	0.00	1	0	0	0	1	0	0	0	0	0	2	.000	.000	.000	18.00	0.00
David Hess	R-R	6-1	215	7-10-93	2	0	3.00	4	0	0	0	6	5	2	2	1	1	7	.227	.250	.200	10.50	1.50
Trevor Martin	R-R	6-5	238	12-15-00	0	0	0.00	1	1	0	0	1	1	0	0	0	1	2	.250	.333	.000	18.00	9.00
Israel Mateo	R-R	5-11	135	11-22-01	0	1	2.84	10	0	0	1	13	8	5	4	1	8	16	.178	.200	.167	11.37	5.68
Brendan McKay	L-L	6-2	220	12-18-95	0	0	3.38	2	2	0	0	3	4	1	1	0	1	3	.364	.400	.333	10.13	3.38
Samuel Mejia	R-R	6-1	160	6-17-02	0	1	2.25	14	0	0	5	20	14	7	5	1	6	22	.189	.242	.146	9.90	2.70
Antonio Menendez	R-R	6-4	215	3-11-99	0	1	2.57	3	2	0	0	7	4	2	2	0	1	8	.167	.143	.176	10.29	1.29
Luis Patino	R-R	6-1	192	10-26-99	0	0	3.00	2	2	0	0	3	3	1	1	0	0	6	.231	.167	.286	18.00	0.00
Matthew Peguero	R-R	6-2	200	1-12-00	0	1	3.86	3	0	0	0	5	5	4	2	0	2	6	.250	.375	.167	11.57	3.86
Cody Reed	L-L	6-5	230	4-15-93	4	0	2.35	6	1	0	0	8	5	4	2	0	1	7	.172	.000	.208	8.22	1.17
Evan Reifert	R-R	6-4	190	5-14-99	1	0	0.00	6	0	0	0	7	2	0	0	0	2	14	.091	.000	.167	18.00	2.57
Juan Rivera	R-R	6-3	220	6-4-98	0	0	2.08	3	0	0	0	4	2	1	1	0	5	4	.154	.000	.222	8.31	10.38
Juan Rodriguez	R-R	6-1	180	8-22-01	5	0	2.87	14	0	0	1	16	6	6	5	0	7	18	.111	.050	.147	10.34	4.02
Michael Sansone	R-L	5-9	195	11-10-99	0	0	0.00	3	0	0	0	4	2	0	0	0	1	4	.167	--	.167	9.82	2.45
Kikito Severino	L-L	5-11	145	8-26-01	2	2	1.41	13	6	0	0	38	32	11	6	1	16	28	.235	.313	.212	6.57	3.76
Aaron Slegers	R-R	6-10	260	9-4-92	0	0	0.00	2	1	0	0	3	0	0	0	0	1	6	.000	.000	.000	20.25	3.38
Andri Tavarez	L-L	6-1	165	5-23-03	4	0	0.75	16	0	0	4	24	12	4	2	0	12	29	.152	.158	.150	10.88	4.50
Joe Wieland	R-R	6-2	205	1-21-90	1	0	0.00	3	0	0	0	7	3	0	0	0	0	7	.130	.000	.176	9.45	0.00

Cole Wilcox	R-R	6-5	232	7-14-99	0	1	7.20	3	3	0	0	5	7	4	4	0	2	9	.318	.500	.214	16.20	3.60
Junior William	R-R	6-4	187	3-6-00	1	0	1.23	6	0	0	1	7	3	2	1	1	1	10	.111	.000	.150	12.27	1.23
Mikey York	R-R	6-2	190	2-24-96	1	0	0.00	3	2	0	0	4	3	0	0	0	1	6	.188	.000	.300	12.46	2.08

Fielding

C: Cerda 19, Fernandez 6, Galarraga 14, Keegan 6, Meza 2, Piper 2, Rangel 1, Salguera 19, Sandoval 1. **1B:** Aponte 1, Del Rosario 32, Edwards 4, Isaac 4, Merino 13, Paulson 5, Robertson 3. **2B:** Barragan 8, Colmenarez 5, De La Cruz 19, James 2, Peguero 23. **3B:** Aponte 1, Barragan 13, Caminero 16, De La Cruz 7, James 5, Peguero 2, Pie 11, Turner 4. **SS:** Battles 4, Caminero 12, Colmenarez 23, De La Cruz 6, Franco 1, Martinez 1, Peguero 12. **OF:** Duarte 3, Cardenas 3, Castellanos 8, Castillo 22, Cermak 7, Diaz 44, Dyer 3, Hiott 1, Johnson 18, Jones 6, Kiermaier 1, Margot 1, Merino 13, Piron 42, Simpson 8, Turner 2.

DSL RAYS — ROOKIE

DOMINICAN SUMMER LEAGUE

Batting	B-T	HT	WT	DOB	AVG	vLH	vRH	G	AB	R	H	2B	3B	HR	RBI	BB	HBP	SH	SF	SO	SB	CS	SLG	OBP
Elis Barreat	R-R	5-9	158	5-22-03	.333	.000	1.000	1	3	0	1	0	0	0	1	1	0	0	0	0	3	0	.333	.500
2-team total (35 DSL Tampa Bay)					.294	.167	.329	36	109	19	32	6	2	2	18	15	9	0	1	16	6	1	.440	.418
Jose Contreras	R-R	6-1	200	5-5-05	.229	.276	.220	53	179	25	41	7	2	2	20	25	4	0	3	64	3	3	.324	.332
Enderson Delgado	B-R	5-11	184	9-21-04	.218	.455	.189	34	101	14	22	3	0	0	9	11	6	0	1	21	2	2	.248	.328
Arison Jimenez	R-R	5-10	153	11-5-02	.263	.353	.244	29	99	22	26	4	0	4	15	13	4	0	0	24	7	1	.424	.371
Larry Martinez	R-R	5-11	170	8-6-05	.232	.286	.224	18	56	8	13	1	0	0	7	7	0	0	0	7	1	1	.250	.317
2-team total (5 DSL Tampa Bay)					.243	.273	.238	23	74	11	18	3	0	0	9	9	2	0	0	11	1	1	.284	.341
Raudelis Martinez	L-R	6-0	180	5-30-02	.293	.333	.286	26	75	15	22	4	2	3	10	16	5	0	1	11	6	2	.520	.443
Enzo Paulino	L-R	5-11	179	5-25-04	.259	.235	.264	54	193	28	50	12	1	2	32	21	3	0	2	40	7	2	.363	.338
Juanfel Peguero	B-R	5-11	142	12-31-04	.258	.250	.259	9	31	5	8	0	0	0	5	7	1	0	0	4	7	4	.258	.410
Jose Pena	R-R	6-0	185	12-24-02	.063	.000	.067	7	16	2	1	0	0	0	3	4	2	0	1	10	0	1	.063	.304
2-team total (18 DSL Tampa Bay)					.165	.167	.164	25	79	11	13	1	0	1	6	10	5	0	1	30	3	5	.215	.295
Jhonny Perez	R-R	5-11	195	3-11-05	.250	.000	.333	2	4	0	1	0	0	0	0	1	1	0	0	3	0	0	.250	.500
2-team total (34 DSL Tampa Bay)					.264	.273	.262	36	106	21	28	5	0	2	10	22	2	0	1	30	6	3	.368	.397
Jose Perez	R-R	5-9	170	3-12-04	.205	.167	.211	31	83	9	17	0	1	0	6	18	2	1	2	11	5	4	.229	.352
2-team total (1 DSL Tampa Bay)					.209	.231	.205	32	86	12	18	0	1	0	6	19	2	1	2	12	5	4	.233	.358
Elias Petiyan	B-R	5-11	160	12-3-01	.339	.333	.340	36	115	26	39	9	3	1	14	17	2	1	1	30	8	3	.496	.430
Narciso Polanco	L-R	5-11	161	10-28-04	.251	.265	.248	52	175	34	44	8	4	2	36	36	4	0	3	52	11	5	.377	.385
Roylems Rangel	R-R	5-8	163	10-17-02	.273	.143	.292	17	55	11	15	4	1	2	5	8	1	1	1	10	0	1	.491	.369
2-team total (13 DSL Tampa Bay)					.253	.111	.286	30	95	16	24	6	1	2	8	15	1	1	3	24	3	1	.400	.351
Jose Sanabria	R-R	6-1	180	2-10-05	.237	.500	.206	10	38	6	9	2	0	0	6	5	0	0	0	8	1	0	.289	.326
Miguel Tamares	B-R	5-10	150	9-6-04	.202	.121	.222	52	168	52	34	6	3	3	12	51	5	1	0	50	30	9	.327	.402
Roosbert Tapia	R-R	6-2	177	6-23-05	.210	.269	.200	58	186	26	39	11	0	2	22	13	3	1	0	47	9	2	.301	.272
Victor Valera	B-R	5-9	146	10-15-02	.264	.316	.256	44	140	26	37	6	0	2	16	15	2	1	3	22	17	5	.350	.338
Neifi Vasquez	R-R	6-4	173	9-22-03	.182	.143	.186	20	66	4	12	2	1	0	4	1	1	0	0	16	2	0	.242	.206
2-team total (23 DSL Tampa Bay)					.175	.115	.188	43	154	17	27	4	1	0	8	8	4	0	0	43	5	0	.214	.235

Pitching	B-T	HT	WT	DOB	W	L	ERA	G	GS	CG	SV	IP	H	R	ER	HR	BB	SO	AVG	vLH	vRH	K/9	BB/9
Emilio Afanador	R-R	6-1	202	2-10-03	1	2	9.30	12	5	0	0	20	20	22	21	3	24	25	.256	.259	.255	11.07	10.62
Landany Alfonseca	R-R	6-1	160	3-9-05	3	1	3.98	17	0	0	1	20	15	13	9	0	19	20	.190	.154	.208	8.85	8.41
Adrian Almonte	L-L	6-4	199	3-4-03	3	0	5.18	17	0	0	1	24	21	15	14	0	19	24	.241	.167	.253	8.88	7.03
Baltazar Arredondo	L-L	6-1	175	1-22-04	0	2	2.96	10	5	0	0	24	17	9	8	1	12	23	.193	.250	.181	8.51	4.44
Cristian Bastardo	R-R	6-2	190	7-4-03	0	0	4.50	5	2	0	0	6	7	3	3	1	4	5	.292	.167	.333	7.50	6.00
Fernando Costume	R-R	6-2	165	5-14-03	2	3	6.20	19	0	0	2	25	28	25	17	0	21	30	.267	.286	.260	10.95	7.66
Christopher Dishmey	R-R	6-2	200	11-12-00	0	0	3.13	7	4	0	0	23	16	9	8	3	14	20	.195	.318	.150	7.83	5.48
Justino Dominguez	R-R	5-11	178	9-26-01	2	0	2.84	8	0	0	0	13	8	5	4	0	6	17	.178	.154	.188	12.08	4.26
2-team total (3 DSL Tampa Bay)					3	0	3.63	11	0	0	0	17	12	9	7	0	15	24	.188	.091	.238	12.46	7.79
Sandy Eusebio	L-L	6-3	192	10-5-01	3	2	7.66	16	0	0	0	22	26	23	19	1	26	24	.292	.350	.275	9.67	10.48
Renaldito Florian	R-R	5-11	161	3-26-02	1	1	3.64	12	5	0	0	30	32	15	12	1	18	32	.267	.333	.241	9.71	5.46
Yonathan Gomez	R-R	6-2	154	8-17-01	1	2	4.50	16	3	0	4	24	23	19	12	0	7	24	.250	.346	.212	9.00	2.63
Luis Hernandez	R-R	6-4	195	4-1-01	1	3	3.60	12	10	0	0	45	42	20	18	4	22	48	.250	.184	.277	9.60	4.40
Danny Hilario	R-R	6-0	185	9-17-04	1	0	10.05	11	0	0	0	14	14	16	16	5	13	14	.250	.429	.190	8.79	8.16
Sebastian Javier	R-R	6-1	185	12-26-03	0	4	5.75	14	10	0	0	36	34	31	23	2	29	27	.243	.297	.223	6.75	7.25
Humberto Jimenez	R-R	6-2	174	9-29-01	1	3	5.22	15	1	0	1	29	29	20	17	2	13	22	.254	.278	.244	6.75	3.99
Anthony Manriquez	R-R	6-2	160	9-18-04	0	3	8.71	15	0	0	0	21	25	22	20	1	13	16	.294	.320	.283	6.97	5.66
Alexander Marte	R-R	6-2	200	1-7-01	0	0	3.86	2	0	0	0	2	0	1	1	0	2	3	.000	.000	.000	11.57	7.71
2-team total (1 DSL Tampa Bay)					0	0	5.40	3	0	0	0	3	2	2	2	0	5	3	.200	.333	.143	8.10	13.50
Chariel Radney	L-L	6-0	189	3-27-05	2	3	4.55	12	8	0	0	32	25	24	16	1	33	38	.225	.286	.216	10.80	9.38
Michael Saturria	R-R	6-4	190	9-1-02	2	3	2.70	20	0	0	4	23	17	14	7	1	19	37	.193	.194	.193	14.27	7.33
Jeromy Sosa	L-L	6-7	175	2-19-03	1	1	6.56	14	3	0	0	23	10	20	17	2	38	33	.132	.133	.131	12.73	14.66
Wander Ventura	R-R	6-2	170	2-26-03	1	1	3.92	12	3	0	0	21	15	10	9	0	13	20	.203	.208	.200	8.71	5.66

Fielding

C: Delgado 19, Martinez 4, Martinez 16, Perez 2, Perez 13, Rangel 12. **1B:** Barreat 1, Delgado 9, Martinez 8, Martinez 6, Paulino 4, Perez 3, Petiyan 15, Polanco 1, Rangel 6, Tapia 10, Valera 6. **2B:** Peguero 3, Perez 7, Polanco 15, Tamares 12, Valera 26. **3B:** Perez 3, Polanco 12, Tamares 6, Tapia 44, Valera 1. **SS:** Peguero 5, Polanco 17, Tamares 34, Valera 7. **OF:** Contreras 51, Jimenez 25, Martinez 1, Paulino 46, Pena 3, Petiyan 19, Polanco 13, Sanabria 9, Vasquez 19.

DSL TAMPA BAY

ROOKIE

DOMINICAN SUMMER LEAGUE

Batting	B-T	HT	WT	DOB	AVG	vLH	vRH	G	AB	R	H	2B	3B	HR	RBI	BB	HBP	SH	SF	SO	SB	CS	SLG	OBP
Luis Ariza	R-R	5-11	155	5-8-04	.239	.324	.216	46	159	29	38	6	1	1	25	23	7	0	2	40	6	2	.308	.356
Nicandro Aybar	B-R	6-1	170	9-8-04	.261	.438	.216	45	157	21	41	6	3	1	14	33	1	0	1	30	9	4	.357	.391
Elis Barreat	R-R	5-9	158	5-22-03	.292	.182	.321	35	106	19	31	6	2	2	17	14	9	0	1	16	3	1	.443	.415
2-team total (1 DSL Rays)					.294	.167	.329	36	109	19	32	6	2	2	18	15	9	0	1	16	6	1	.440	.418
Alexis Feliz	L-R	5-10	155	9-26-02	.198	.080	.239	33	96	14	19	2	1	0	11	16	0	0	2	24	8	2	.240	.307
Ricardo Gonzalez	B-R	6-0	186	7-6-04	.256	.140	.296	44	168	25	43	5	4	3	22	18	2	0	2	32	11	5	.387	.332
Larry Martinez	R-R	5-11	170	8-6-05	.278	.250	.286	5	18	3	5	2	0	0	2	2	2	0	0	4	0	0	.389	.409
2-team total (18 DSL Rays)					.243	.273	.238	23	74	11	18	3	0	0	9	9	2	0	0	11	1	1	.284	.341
Angel Mateo	R-R	6-2	190	2-13-05	.269	.225	.282	52	171	32	46	7	0	7	25	27	10	0	2	36	10	3	.433	.395
Santiago Millan	R-R	6-2	174	5-27-03	.221	.200	.227	35	113	16	25	3	2	6	26	16	2	0	1	42	4	2	.442	.326
Jordany Oliver	R-R	6-0	160	1-11-05	.207	.160	.221	36	111	14	23	3	2	1	14	11	3	0	1	41	11	2	.297	.294
Jose Pena	R-R	6-0	185	12-24-02	.190	.182	.192	18	63	9	12	1	0	1	3	6	3	0	0	20	3	4	.254	.292
2-team total (7 DSL Rays)					.165	.167	.164	25	79	11	13	1	0	1	6	10	5	0	1	30	3	5	.215	.295
Jhonny Perez	R-R	5-11	195	3-11-05	.265	.286	.259	34	102	21	27	5	0	2	10	21	1	0	1	27	6	3	.373	.392
2-team total (2 DSL Rays)					.264	.273	.262	36	106	21	28	5	0	2	10	22	2	0	1	30	6	3	.368	.397
Jose Perez	R-R	5-9	170	3-12-04	.333	1.000	.000	1	3	3	1	0	0	0	0	1	0	0	0	1	0	0	.333	.500
2-team total (31 DSL Rays)					.209	.231	.205	32	86	12	18	0	1	0	6	19	2	1	2	12	5	4	.233	.358
Roylems Rangel	R-R	5-8	163	10-17-02	.225	.091	.276	13	40	5	9	2	0	0	3	7	0	0	2	14	3	0	.275	.327
2-team total (17 DSL Rays)					.253	.111	.286	30	95	16	24	6	1	2	8	15	1	1	3	24	3	1	.400	.351
Nathanael Rodriguez	R-R	6-0	155	12-6-03	.228	.268	.217	51	184	30	42	6	0	5	25	25	1	0	1	35	4	2	.342	.322
Rodrigo Romero	R-R	5-10	150	2-28-05	.128	.000	.154	16	47	7	6	1	0	0	3	12	3	0	0	27	2	1	.149	.339
German Tapia	R-R	6-2	170	9-19-03	.329	.286	.339	26	73	22	24	3	0	2	11	23	3	0	1	17	3	4	.452	.500
2-team total (11 DSL LAD Mega)					.295	.211	.314	37	105	30	31	4	1	2	16	30	4	0	2	27	4	6	.410	.461
Neifi Vasquez	R-R	6-4	173	9-22-03	.170	.105	.188	23	88	13	15	2	0	0	4	7	3	0	0	27	3	0	.193	.255
2-team total (20 DSL Rays)					.175	.115	.188	43	154	17	27	4	1	0	8	8	4	0	0	43	5	0	.214	.235

Pitching	B-T	HT	WT	DOB	W	L	ERA	G	GS	CG	SV	IP	H	R	ER	HR	BB	SO	AVG	vLH	vRH	K/9	BB/9
Jordy Andujar	R-R	6-3	186	2-25-03	1	1	8.84	13	0	0	1	18	26	20	18	6	20	22	.351	.290	.395	10.80	9.82
Ronald Contreras	R-R	6-2	184	6-18-05	1	2	10.13	8	3	0	0	13	15	15	15	0	19	10	.306	.294	.313	6.75	12.83
Justino Dominguez	R-R	5-11	178	9-26-01	1	0	5.79	3	0	0	0	5	4	4	3	0	9	7	.211	.000	.400	13.50	17.36
2-team total (8 DSL Rays)					3	0	3.63	11	0	0	0	17	12	9	7	0	15	24	.188	.091	.238	12.46	7.79
Victor Fransua	R-R	6-1	180	8-13-00	0	1	3.62	16	0	0	7	27	23	12	11	0	19	32	.235	.184	.267	10.54	6.26
Alvaro Gamez	L-L	6-3	175	2-19-05	2	4	5.01	12	8	0	0	32	33	27	18	0	21	19	.264	.192	.283	5.29	5.85
Yeison Garcia	L-L	6-3	183	10-12-04	1	1	12.64	12	4	0	0	16	11	25	22	2	38	16	.204	.462	.122	9.19	21.83
Cristhofer Gonzalez	R-R	6-3	166	12-18-04	3	1	2.55	11	5	0	1	35	32	15	10	1	11	43	.242	.275	.228	10.95	2.80
Angel Guaiquirian	R-R	6-3	174	3-21-03	0	0	1.80	4	0	0	1	5	6	2	1	0	4	1	.300	.375	.250	1.80	7.20
Maikel Hernandez	R-R	6-1	184	6-8-05	2	0	2.70	11	7	0	0	33	26	13	10	1	10	28	.217	.208	.222	7.56	2.70
Ismael Laureano	R-R	6-0	162	7-2-05	1	5	7.11	13	7	0	0	32	30	30	25	5	25	18	.259	.225	.276	5.12	7.11
Egory Manuela	L-L	6-1	180	9-9-03	0	0	10.80	2	2	0	0	2	1	4	2	0	4	4	.143	.500	.000	21.60	21.60
Alexander Marte	R-R	6-2	200	1-7-01	0	0	9.00	1	0	0	0	1	2	1	1	0	3	0	.667	1.000	.500	0.00	27.00
2-team total (2 DSL Rays)					0	0	5.40	3	0	0	0	3	2	2	2	0	5	3	.200	.333	.143	8.10	13.50
Keiner Navas	L-L	6-1	156	2-29-04	1	1	4.74	12	0	0	0	19	23	14	10	2	11	21	.291	.250	.302	9.95	5.21
Moises Palma	R-R	6-4	195	9-1-04	1	0	5.59	11	0	0	0	19	20	12	12	6	9	16	.282	.143	.340	7.45	4.19
Pedro Paulino	R-R	6-1	190	8-6-01	1	2	4.26	8	0	0	0	13	11	10	6	1	10	14	.234	.222	.241	9.95	7.11
Jorman Primera	R-R	6-2	170	12-18-01	3	2	3.66	10	1	0	1	20	12	11	8	3	7	17	.176	.083	.227	7.78	3.20
Geudis Ramos	L-L	6-1	175	2-16-05	1	0	10.95	10	0	0	0	12	11	15	15	2	13	13	.239	.286	.231	9.49	9.49
Andy Rodriguez	R-R	6-1	182	7-28-02	2	0	1.15	5	2	0	0	16	15	3	2	0	6	10	.268	.400	.194	5.74	3.45
Gerlin Rosario	R-R	6-3	211	2-15-02	1	2	2.38	12	7	0	0	53	48	14	14	2	4	35	.240	.195	.271	5.94	0.68
Ramon Sanchez	R-R	6-3	160	11-14-01	1	3	13.50	12	5	0	0	17	21	29	26	5	19	19	.304	.217	.348	9.87	9.87
Roybell Santodomingo	R-R	6-2	170	5-6-01	0	0	0.00	3	1	0	0	5	3	4	0	0	4	4	.188	.167	.200	7.20	7.20
Jesus Ullola	L-L	6-4	185	8-24-05	0	0	27.00	2	2	0	0	2	2	5	5	0	5	0	.400	--	.400	0.00	27.00
Raimund Uzcategui	R-R	6-0	165	11-21-00	1	1	1.78	16	0	0	5	25	24	9	5	0	11	26	.250	.270	.237	9.24	3.91
Edwin Zamudio	L-R	6-2	195	9-17-02	1	5	7.24	12	2	0	0	27	38	28	22	2	12	24	.319	.306	.329	7.90	3.95

Fielding

C: Ariza 29, Martinez 4, Perez 18, Rangel 6. **1B:** Ariza 10, Barreat 18, Feliz 16, Perez 8, Rangel 4. **2B:** Aybar 17, Barreat 12, Feliz 5, Gonzalez 12, Perez 1, Romero 11. **3B:** Aybar 6, Barreat 1, Feliz 8, Gonzalez 10, Rodriguez 29, Romero 2. **SS:** Aybar 17, Gonzalez 22, Rodriguez 15, Romero 3. **OF:** Mateo 50, Millan 29, Oliver 35, Pena 16, Tapia 22, Vasquez 23.

Texas Rangers

SEASON IN A SENTENCE: After spending over $300 million on infielders Corey Seager and Marcus Semien and righthander Jon Gray, the Rangers still spun their wheels and lost 94 games.

HIGH POINT: On Aug. 24, the Rangers produced their peak offensive performance, scoring 16 runs against the Rockies. Silver Slugger Nathaniel Lowe led the way with a three-hit evening that included his 20th home run of the season.

LOW POINT: From Aug. 27-Sept. 5, the Rangers lost a season-worst nine straight games. Six of those losses came against the Red Sox and Tigers, who also finished the season with losing records.

NOTABLE ROOKIES: No one rookie stood out, but the Rangers got contributions from a pair of trade pieces in infielder Ezequiel Duran and righthander Glenn Otto—who came over from the Yankees in the Joey Gallo deal of 2021—as well as speedster Bubba Thompson and lefthander Cole Ragans. The latter's ascension to the big leagues was a testament to perseverance and patience. Ragans, whom Texas selected in the first round of the 2016 draft, battled through multiple arm injuries that kept him out all of 2018 and 2019 before the lost pandemic season of 2020.Third baseman Josh Jung also made his big league debut, which was especially impressive considering he missed most of the season after having shoulder surgery just before the minor league season commenced.

KEY TRANSACTIONS: The Rangers were long rumored to be potential big spenders heading into the winter, and they lived up to those whispers by opening up the checkbook for Seager, Semien and Gray before the lockout put the kibosh on transactions for the rest of the winter.

ON THE FARM: The star of Texas' farm was clearly outfielder Evan Carter. The 2020 first-rounder who shocked the industry has proved the Rangers wise at every turn. The precocious outfielder has shown an enticing blend of skills and polish and arrived at Double-A Frisco in time to help lead the RoughRiders to the Texas League championship. Jack Leiter, the team's first-rounder from 2021, was aggressively assigned to Double-A to begin his pro career and struggled with command and control all season long. Texas again shocked the industry in the draft when they selected Kumar Rocker—Leiter's former co-ace when the pair pitched at Vanderbilt—with the third overall pick before adding high school righthander Brock Porter for big money in the fourth round.

OPENING DAY PAYROLL: $151,477,166 (14th)

PLAYERS OF THE YEAR

MAJOR LEAGUE

Martin Perez
LHP

12-8, 2.89 ERA
169 SO, 69 BB, 196 IP
First-time all-star

MINOR LEAGUE

Evan Carter
OF

(HiA/AA)
.295/.397/.489
12 HR, 28 SB in 106 G

ORGANIZATION LEADERS

Batting		*Minimum 250 AB
MAJORS		
* AVG	Nathaniel Lowe	.302
* OPS	Nathaniel Lowe	.851
HR	Corey Seager	33
RBI	Adolis Garcia	101
MINORS		
* AVG	Yohel Pozo, Round Rock	.320
* OBP	Aaron Zavala, Hickory, Frisco	.420
* SLG	Ezequiel Duran, Frisco, Round Rock	.555
* OPS	Ezequiel Duran, Frisco, Round Rock	.899
R	Aaron Zavala, Hickory, Frisco	89
H	Jonathan Ornelas, Frisco	157
TB	Blaine Crim, Frisco, Round Rock	250
2B	Ezequiel Duran, Frisco, Round Rock	33
3B	Evan Carter, Hickory, Frisco	10
HR	Blaine Crim, Frisco, Round Rock	24
RBI	Blaine Crim, Frisco, Round Rock	96
BB	Trevor Hauver, Hickory, Frisco	93
SO	Marcus Smith, Down East	163
SB	Bubba Thompson, Round Rock	49

Pitching		#Minimum 75 IP
MAJORS		
W	Martin Perez	12
# ERA	Brock Burke	1.97
SO	Martin Perez	169
SV	Joe Barlow	13
MINORS		
W	Triston Polley, Hickory, Frisco	11
L	Tekoah Roby, Hickory	11
# ERA	Mitchell Bratt, Down East	2.45
G	Chase Lee, Frisco, Round Rock	51
GS	Cole Winn, Round Rock	28
SV	Jesus Tinoco, Round Rock	13
IP	Cole Winn, Round Rock	121.2
BB	Cole Winn, Round Rock	87
SO	Mason Englert, Hickory, Frisco	136
# AVG	Mason Englert, Hickory, Frisco	.199

2022 PERFORMANCE

General Manager: Chris Young. **Farm Director:** Josh Bonifay. **Scouting Director:** Kip Fagg.

Class	Team	League	W	L	PCT	Finish	Manager
Majors	Texas Rangers	American	68	94	.420	12th (15)	C. Woodward/T. Beasley
Triple-A	Round Rock Express	Pacific Coast	79	71	.527	4th (10)	Matt Hagen
Double-A	Frisco RoughRiders	Texas	74	63	.540	2nd (10)	Jared Goedert
High-A	Hickory Crawdads	South Atlantic	66	65	.504	6th (12)	Carlos Cardoza
Low-A	Down East Wood Ducks	Carolina	65	66	.496	6th (12)	Steve Mintz
Rookie	ACL Rangers	Arizona Complex	32	22	.593	4th (18)	Carlos Maldonado
Overall 2022 Minor League Record			377	345	.522	t-9th (30)	

ORGANIZATION STATISTICS

TEXAS RANGERS

AMERICAN LEAGUE

Batting	B-T	HT	WT	DOB	AVG	vLH	vRH	G	AB	R	H	2B	3B	HR	RBI	BB	HBP	SH	SF	SO	SB	CS	SLG	OBP
Kole Calhoun	L-L	5-10	205	10-14-87	.196	.208	.193	125	388	36	76	14	1	12	49	27	6	0	3	136	3	2	.330	.257
Willie Calhoun	L-R	5-8	200	11-4-94	.136	.400	.103	18	44	7	6	3	0	1	2	8	1	0	0	6	0	0	.273	.283
Charlie Culberson	R-R	6-1	200	4-10-89	.252	.275	.200	70	115	19	29	6	0	2	12	5	0	4	0	31	2	3	.357	.283
Steven Duggar	L-R	6-1	187	11-4-93	.176	.000	.214	8	17	2	3	0	0	0	0	2	0	0	0	12	1	1	.176	.263
2-team total (9 Los Angeles Angels)					.111	.000	.133	17	36	5	4	0	1	0	0	5	0	0	0	25	1	1	.167	.220
Ezequiel Duran	R-R	5-11	185	5-22-99	.236	.224	.239	58	208	25	49	10	1	5	25	12	0	0	0	54	4	1	.365	.277
Adolis Garcia	R-R	6-1	205	3-2-93	.250	.235	.256	156	605	88	151	34	5	27	101	40	6	0	6	183	25	6	.456	.300
Mitch Garver	R-R	6-1	220	1-15-91	.207	.269	.184	54	188	23	39	7	0	10	24	23	2	0	2	53	1	1	.404	.298
Jonah Heim	B-R	6-4	220	6-27-95	.227	.267	.210	127	406	51	92	20	1	16	48	41	1	0	2	87	2	0	.399	.298
Elier Hernandez	R-R	6-3	197	11-21-94	.182	.176	.188	14	33	4	6	2	0	0	3	1	0	0	1	15	0	0	.242	.200
Sam Huff	R-R	6-5	240	1-14-98	.240	.229	.247	44	121	9	29	4	0	4	10	11	0	0	0	42	1	0	.372	.303
Andy Ibanez	R-R	5-11	205	4-3-93	.218	.214	.221	40	119	13	26	4	0	1	9	9	0	0	0	21	3	0	.277	.273
Josh Jung	R-R	6-2	214	2-12-98	.204	.270	.164	26	98	9	20	4	1	5	14	4	0	0	0	39	2	0	.418	.235
Nathaniel Lowe	L-R	6-4	220	7-7-95	.302	.330	.288	157	593	74	179	26	3	27	76	48	4	0	0	147	2	2	.492	.358
Mark Mathias	R-R	6-0	200	8-2-94	.277	.250	.320	24	65	11	18	3	0	5	16	9	0	0	0	26	2	0	.554	.365
Brad Miller	L-R	6-2	195	10-18-89	.212	.158	.217	81	222	20	47	3	0	7	32	18	0	0	1	70	4	2	.320	.270
Kevin Plawecki	R-R	6-2	208	2-26-91	.273	.333	.250	3	11	0	3	0	0	0	1	0	0	0	0	4	0	0	.273	.273
2-team total (61 Boston Red Sox)					.220	.133	.252	64	168	15	37	8	0	1	13	14	2	1	1	32	0	0	.286	.286
Zach Reks	L-R	6-2	190	11-12-93	.265	.000	.281	16	34	3	9	1	0	0	3	0	0	0	0	10	0	1	.294	.265
Corey Seager	L-R	6-4	215	4-27-94	.245	.225	.254	151	593	91	145	24	1	33	83	58	7	0	5	103	3	0	.455	.317
Marcus Semien	R-R	6-0	195	9-17-90	.248	.250	.247	161	657	101	163	31	5	26	83	53	4	0	10	120	25	8	.429	.304
Josh H. Smith	L-R	5-10	172	8-7-97	.197	.118	.212	73	213	23	42	5	0	2	16	28	7	2	3	50	4	3	.249	.307
Nick Solak	R-R	5-11	185	1-11-95	.207	.250	.158	35	82	14	17	1	0	3	4	7	5	1	0	19	3	2	.329	.309
Leody Taveras	B-R	6-2	195	9-8-98	.261	.264	.260	99	314	39	82	14	2	5	34	21	2	1	3	88	11	5	.366	.309
Bubba Thompson	R-R	6-2	197	6-9-98	.265	.189	.299	55	170	18	45	5	0	1	9	7	2	2	0	56	18	3	.312	.302
Meibrys Viloria	L-R	5-11	225	2-15-97	.159	.200	.155	26	63	10	10	1	0	2	5	11	0	0	1	29	0	0	.270	.280
Steele Walker	L-L	5-11	209	7-30-96	.071	.000	.077	5	14	1	1	0	0	1	1	2	0	0	0	4	0	0	.286	.188
Eli White	R-R	6-3	195	6-26-94	.200	.204	.196	47	105	16	21	2	0	3	10	11	0	0	1	41	12	1	.305	.274

Pitching	B-T	HT	WT	DOB	W	L	ERA	G	GS	CG	SV	IP	H	R	ER	HR	BB	SO	AVG	vLH	vRH	K/9	BB/9
Albert Abreu	R-R	6-2	190	9-26-95	0	0	3.12	7	0	0	0	9	4	3	3	2	12	9	.138	.000	.211	9.35	12.46
3-team total (4 Kansas City Royals, 22 New York Yankees)					2	2	3.26	33	0	0	0	39	35	15	14	5	22	38	.243	.191	.268	8.84	5.12
A.J. Alexy	R-R	6-4	195	4-21-98	1	1	11.57	4	0	0	0	7	10	9	9	1	9	6	.345	.500	.286	7.71	11.57
Kolby Allard	L-L	6-1	195	8-13-97	1	2	7.29	10	0	0	1	21	21	17	17	9	6	19	.263	.278	.258	8.14	2.57
Kohei Arihara	R-R	6-2	210	8-11-92	1	3	9.45	5	4	0	0	20	36	22	21	4	11	14	.387	.348	.426	6.30	4.95
Joe Barlow	R-R	6-2	210	9-28-95	3	1	3.86	35	0	0	13	35	27	18	15	5	13	28	.213	.182	.236	7.20	3.34
Brock Burke	L-L	6-4	210	8-4-96	7	5	1.97	52	0	0	0	82	63	25	18	9	24	90	.211	.192	.218	9.84	2.62
Matt Bush	R-R	5-9	180	2-8-86	2	1	2.95	40	5	0	1	37	27	16	12	5	10	45	.199	.196	.200	11.05	2.45
Charlie Culberson	R R	6 1	200	4 10 89	0	0	0.00	2	0	0	0	2	1	0	0	0	1	0	.143	.000	.200	0.00	4.50
Dane Dunning	R-R	6-4	225	12-20-94	4	8	4.46	29	29	0	0	153	158	80	76	20	62	137	.268	.271	.265	8.04	3.64
Jon Gray	R-R	6-4	225	11-5-91	7	7	3.96	24	24	0	0	127	105	61	56	17	39	134	.222	.248	.201	9.47	2.76
Taylor Hearn	L-L	6-6	230	8-30-94	6	8	5.13	31	13	0	1	100	107	60	57	11	43	97	.268	.270	.267	8.73	3.87
Jonathan Hernandez	R-R	6-3	190	7-6-96	2	3	2.97	29	0	0	4	30	26	14	10	2	17	27	.232	.255	.215	8.01	5.04
Greg Holland	R-R	5-10	210	11-20-85	0	1	7.71	5	0	0	0	5	6	5	4	3	1	5	.333	.333	.333	9.64	1.93
Spencer Howard	R-R	6-3	210	7-28-96	2	4	7.41	10	8	0	0	38	50	33	31	12	15	32	.309	.261	.344	7.65	3.58
Dallas Keuchel	L-L	6-2	205	1-1-88	0	2	12.60	2	2	0	0	10	18	14	14	1	4	7	.409	.455	.394	6.30	3.60
2-team total (8 Chicago White Sox)					2	7	9.00	10	10	0	0	42	67	47	42	7	24	27	.358	.436	.338	5.79	5.14
John King	L-L	6-2	215	9-14-94	1	4	4.03	39	0	0	0	51	61	27	23	5	14	30	.298	.254	.315	5.26	2.45
Jose Leclerc	R-R	6-0	195	12-19-93	0	3	2.83	39	0	0	7	48	33	17	15	5	21	54	.192	.173	.209	10.20	3.97
Brett Martin	L-L	6-4	200	4-28-95	1	7	4.14	55	1	0	3	50	50	27	23	4	18	40	.260	.194	.292	7.20	3.24
Tyson Miller	R-R	6-4	225	7-29-95	1	2	10.97	4	2	0	0	11	16	14	13	1	8	8	.348	.238	.440	6.75	6.75
Matt Moore	L-L	6-3	210	6-18-89	5	2	1.95	63	0	0	5	74	49	20	16	3	38	83	.187	.243	.165	10.09	4.62
Glenn Otto	R-R	6-3	240	3-11-96	7	10	4.64	27	27	0	0	136	119	74	70	21	62	107	.236	.201	.267	7.10	4.11

Spencer Patton	R-R	6-1	200	2-20-88	0	0	3.86	7	0	0	0	7	4	3	3	1	3	5	.174	.143	.188	6.43	3.86
Martin Perez	L-L	6-0	200	4-4-91	12	8	2.89	32	32	1	0	196	178	70	63	11	69	169	.241	.219	.246	7.75	3.16
Cole Ragans	L-L	6-4	190	12-12-97	0	3	4.95	9	9	0	0	40	43	24	22	6	16	27	.272	.222	.282	6.08	3.60
Garrett Richards	R-R	6-2	210	5-27-88	1	1	5.27	32	2	0	1	43	44	28	25	3	13	36	.262	.243	.277	7.59	2.74
Yerry Rodriguez	R-R	6-2	198	10-15-97	0	0	0.00	1	0	0	0	1	1	0	0	0	0	1	.250	1.000	.000	9.00	0.00
Dennis Santana	R-R	6-2	190	4-12-96	3	8	5.22	63	1	0	1	59	50	39	34	2	28	54	.228	.208	.239	8.28	4.30
Josh Sborz	R-R	6-3	215	12-17-93	1	0	6.45	19	1	0	0	22	25	16	16	4	11	32	.284	.294	.278	12.90	4.43
Nick Snyder	R-R	6-4	190	10-10-95	0	0	18.00	2	0	0	0	1	1	2	2	0	3	0	.250	.500	.000	0.00	27.00
Jesus Tinoco	R-R	6-4	258	4-30-95	0	0	2.18	17	2	0	0	21	12	5	5	2	10	18	.167	.130	.184	7.84	4.35

Fielding

Catcher	PCT	G	PO	A	E	DP	PB
Garver	.992	14	119	4	1	0	2
Heim	.997	111	839	37	3	3	3
Huff	.986	29	208	11	3	0	5
Plawecki	.952	3	20	0	1	0	0
Viloria	.970	20	151	10	5	0	1

First Base	PCT	G	PO	A	E	DP
Culberson	1.000	1	1	0	0	0
Hernandez	1.000	1	7	1	0	0
Huff	1.000	6	38	0	0	2
Ibanez	.949	6	34	3	2	2
Lowe	.993	153	1252	70	9	125
Mathias	1.000	3	20	0	0	3

Second Base	PCT	G	PO	A	E	DP
Culberson	.971	11	10	23	1	5
Duran	.957	9	9	13	1	0
Ibanez	1.000	2	2	4	0	0
Semien	.989	148	252	398	7	89
Smith	1.000	2	2	1	0	0
Solak	.000	1	0	0	0	0

Third Base	PCT	G	PO	A	E	DP
Culberson	.907	25	12	37	5	4
Duran	.933	51	31	95	9	6
Ibanez	.961	25	11	62	3	3
Jung	.974	25	19	55	2	6
Mathias	1.000	2	1	3	0	0
Miller	.946	27	5	30	2	5
Smith	.989	36	22	72	1	8

Shortstop	PCT	G	PO	A	E	DP
Culberson	.000	1	0	0	0	0
Seager	.972	144	176	407	17	91
Semien	.971	17	24	43	2	7
Smith	1.000	6	9	13	0	3

Outfield	PCT	G	PO	A	E	DP
Calhoun	1.000	105	160	3	0	1
Calhoun	1.000	5	5	0	0	0
Culberson	.941	12	14	2	1	1
Duggar	1.000	9	10	0	0	0
Garcia	.982	150	269	10	5	1
Hernandez	1.000	8	17	1	0	0
Mathias	1.000	4	3	0	0	0
Miller	1.000	31	35	1	0	0
Reks	1.000	16	12	1	0	0
Smith	1.000	24	30	2	0	1
Solak	1.000	22	29	2	0	0
Taveras	.991	93	211	3	2	1
Thompson	.990	54	96	0	1	0
Walker	1.000	5	10	0	0	0
White	1.000	44	74	3	0	1

ROUND ROCK EXPRESS — *TRIPLE-A*

PACIFIC COAST LEAGUE

Batting	B-T	HT	WT	DOB	AVG	vLH	vRH	G	AB	R	H	2B	3B	HR	RBI	BB	HBP	SH	SF	SO	SB	CS	SLG	OBP
Sherten Apostel	R-R	6-4	235	3-11-99	.224	.150	.255	19	67	12	15	5	0	3	15	10	0	0	0	31	0	0	.433	.325
Diosbel Arias	R-R	6-2	190	7-21-96	.272	.277	.270	77	250	34	68	16	0	5	35	29	3	0	2	68	0	0	.396	.352
Kole Calhoun	L-L	5-10	205	10-14-87	.300	.400	.200	3	10	2	3	1	0	0	0	3	0	0	0	4	0	0	.400	.462
Willie Calhoun	L-R	5-8	200	11-4-94	.217	.059	.258	21	83	18	18	1	0	5	20	6	0	0	2	13	0	0	.410	.264
2-team total (42 Sacramento River Cats)					.264	.197	.291	63	231	42	61	10	0	10	43	25	2	0	3	35	0	0	.437	.337
Matt Carpenter	L-R	6-4	210	11-26-85	.275	.190	.305	21	80	15	22	5	2	6	19	14	0	0	1	20	1	1	.613	.379
Frainyer Chavez	B-R	5-10	170	5-24-99	.227	.333	.188	7	22	1	5	1	1	0	2	0	0	0	0	5	0	1	.364	.227
Blaine Crim	R-R	5-11	200	6-17-97	.278	.294	.270	13	54	5	15	1	0	0	5	2	0	0	1	13	0	0	.296	.298
Ryan Dorow	R-R	6-0	195	8-21-95	.237	.269	.227	112	371	59	88	19	3	6	44	44	4	2	3	97	2	3	.353	.322
Steven Duggar	L-R	6-1	187	11-4-93	.184	.143	.200	11	38	5	7	2	0	1	5	11	0	0	1	13	3	0	.316	.360
3-team total (14 Sacramento River Cats, 10 Salt Lake Bees)					.182	.184	.183	35	121	16	22	4	0	4	12	17	1	0	1	45	6	0	.314	.286
Ezequiel Duran	R-R	5-11	185	5-22-99	.283	.275	.286	33	145	18	41	9	0	9	26	7	1	0	2	43	7	5	.531	.316
Sandro Fabian	R-R	6-1	180	3-6-98	.212	.080	.257	32	99	21	21	6	0	4	13	7	3	0	0	18	0	0	.394	.284
Mitch Garver	R-R	6-1	220	1-15-91	.333	--	.333	1	3	2	1	0	0	0	0	1	0	0	0	2	0	0	.333	.500
Elier Hernandez	R-R	6-3	197	11-21-94	.298	.310	.293	89	319	56	95	21	6	13	57	24	6	0	2	64	10	2	.524	.356
Yonny Hernandez	B-R	5-9	140	5-4-98	.000	--	.000	1	3	0	0	0	0	0	0	0	0	0	0	0	0	0	.000	.000
2-team total (70 Reno Aces)					.241	.286	.222	71	253	49	61	6	6	1	31	35	7	3	0	47	30	5	.324	.349
Sam Huff	R-R	6-5	240	1-14-98	.260	.291	.251	63	246	46	64	4	0	21	50	25	3	0	0	85	0	0	.533	.336
Andy Ibanez	R-R	5-11	205	4-3-93	.255	.258	.255	73	282	38	72	18	1	6	31	28	4	0	1	48	5	2	.390	.330
Josh Jung	R-R	6-2	214	2-12-98	.273	.304	.263	23	99	15	27	7	0	6	24	4	3	0	0	30	1	0	.525	.321
Nash Knight	B-R	6-0	205	9-20-92	.253	.318	.233	29	95	14	24	6	1	2	20	22	3	0	0	32	0	2	.400	.408
Jack Kruger	R-R	6-1	195	10-26-94	.175	.333	.146	20	57	5	10	0	0	0	3	4	1	0	0	17	0	0	.175	.242
J.P. Martinez	L-L	5-9	174	3-21-96	.199	.200	.198	41	141	20	28	7	2	6	19	24	1	1	0	53	14	0	.404	.319
Mark Mathias	R-R	6-0	200	8-2-94	.345	.500	.304	8	29	7	10	2	0	1	4	4	1	0	1	9	5	0	.517	.429
Brad Miller	L-R	6-2	195	10-18-89	.000	--	.000	2	8	1	0	0	0	0	0	1	0	0	0	5	0	0	.000	.111
Konner Piotto	L-R	5-10	195	1-1-98	--	--	--	1	0	0	0	0	0	0	0	0	0	0	0	0	0	0	--	--
Yohel Pozo	R-R	6-0	201	6-14-97	.320	.240	.354	65	253	37	81	21	0	6	38	11	2	0	1	32	0	1	.474	.352
Wilson Ramos	R-R	6-1	241	8-10-87	.222	--	.222	3	9	1	2	0	0	0	0	1	0	0	0	2	0	0	.222	.300
Zach Reks	L-R	6-2	190	11-12-93	.331	.146	.425	34	121	24	40	10	1	6	21	15	4	0	0	36	1	1	.579	.421
Josh Sale	L-R	6-0	215	7-5-91	.229	.179	.244	72	236	33	54	10	1	11	33	37	4	0	0	81	3	2	.419	.343
Josh H. Smith	L-R	5-10	172	8-7-97	.290	.291	.289	55	221	45	64	13	4	6	45	33	6	0	1	54	9	4	.466	.395
Nick Solak	R-R	5-11	185	1-11-95	.278	.258	.286	57	223	38	62	15	1	10	45	30	4	0	2	51	6	0	.489	.371
Nick Tanielu	R-R	5-11	214	9-4-92	.236	.219	.241	89	280	42	66	18	2	6	40	33	3	1	1	62	2	1	.379	.322
Leody Taveras	B-R	6-2	195	9-8-98	.294	.354	.266	49	204	34	60	12	3	7	29	14	0	0	3	48	7	4	.485	.335
Bubba Thompson	R-R	6-2	197	6-9-98	.303	.359	.287	80	346	77	105	12	4	13	48	22	6	0	1	95	49	3	.474	.355
Meibrys Viloria	L-R	5-11	225	2-15-97	.280	.205	.305	54	175	38	49	13	0	5	28	40	3	0	0	49	2	0	.440	.422
Steele Walker	L-L	5-11	209	7-30-96	.277	.226	.297	50	191	32	53	9	0	7	26	20	3	0	1	35	6	3	.435	.353
2-team total (25 Sacramento River Cats)					.268	.208	.291	75	280	42	75	14	1	9	40	24	4	0	1	51	8	3	.421	.333
Davis Wendzel	R-R	6-1	206	5-23-97	.207	.282	.179	85	314	43	65	9	0	17	51	37	0	0	4	94	2	1	.398	.287
Matt Whatley	R-R	5-9	200	1-7-96	.230	.200	.241	29	74	14	17	2	0	2	7	10	0	6	2	22	0	1	.338	.314
Eli White	R-R	6-3	195	6-26-94	.000	.000	.000	3	7	0	0	0	0	0	0	0	0	0	0	3	0	0	.000	.000

Pitching	B-T	HT	WT	DOB	W	L	ERA	G	GS	CG	SV	IP	H	R	ER	HR	BB	SO	AVG	vLH	vRH	K/9	BB/9
Albert Abreu	R-R	6-2	190	9-26-95	0	0	0.00	3	0	0	0	3	1	1	0	0	0	2	.091	.143	.000	6.00	0.00
A.J. Alexy	R-R	6-4	195	4-21-98	6	6	5.91	31	16	0	0	96	108	67	63	25	56	103	.286	.329	.255	9.66	5.25
Kolby Allard	L-L	6-1	195	8-13-97	3	3	4.65	20	20	0	0	89	81	50	46	21	38	113	.237	.170	.264	11.43	3.84
Grant Anderson	R-R	6-0	180	6-21-97	0	0	6.39	8	0	0	0	13	16	10	9	2	5	16	.308	.333	.294	11.37	3.55
Justin Anderson	L-R	6-3	230	9-28-92	0	0	6.00	3	0	0	0	3	2	2	2	1	3	4	.200	.333	.143	12.00	9.00
Kohei Arihara	R-R	6-2	210	8-11-92	3	6	4.86	19	15	0	0	74	80	44	40	10	19	64	.273	.306	.249	7.78	2.31
Jason Bahr	R-R	6-5	195	2-15-95	2	1	5.90	20	0	0	0	40	47	31	26	8	24	46	.299	.333	.277	10.44	5.45
Joe Barlow	R-R	6-2	210	9-28-95	0	0	6.75	2	0	0	0	1	2	1	1	0	1	2	.400	.667	.000	13.50	6.75
Hever Bueno	R-R	6-2	179	11-23-94	3	1	7.82	30	0	0	1	38	41	39	33	7	30	54	.273	.302	.253	12.79	7.11
Kyle Cody	R-R	6-7	225	8-9-94	0	0	3.66	12	2	0	1	20	20	8	8	1	5	21	.274	.250	.289	9.61	2.29
Tyler Duffey	R-R	6-3	220	12-27-90	1	0	0.00	4	0	0	0	5	5	1	0	0	4	5	.250	.125	.333	9.00	7.20
Demarcus Evans	R-R	6-5	265	10-22-96	2	3	3.82	32	0	0	4	33	22	15	14	4	22	44	.182	.227	.156	12.00	6.00
Taylor Hearn	L-L	6-6	230	8-30-94	1	0	6.00	3	2	0	0	12	8	8	8	3	6	20	.190	.000	.267	15.00	4.50
Jonathan Hernandez	R-R	6-3	190	7-6-96	0	2	4.05	15	0	0	0	13	13	7	6	1	13	16	.250	.125	.357	10.80	8.78
Spencer Howard	R-R	6-3	210	7-28-96	3	6	4.73	14	12	0	0	59	53	35	31	6	25	73	.236	.213	.256	11.14	3.81
Lucas Jacobsen	L-L	6-5	190	7-1-95	0	0	1.80	5	1	0	0	5	3	1	1	1	3	10	.158	.143	.167	18.00	5.40
James Jones	L-L	6-3	205	9-24-88	0	0	5.93	16	0	0	1	14	9	12	9	0	13	19	.180	.130	.222	12.51	8.56
Zak Kent	R-R	6-3	208	2-24-98	1	1	1.67	5	5	0	0	27	17	7	5	2	13	23	.181	.189	.175	7.67	4.33
Dallas Keuchel	L-L	6-2	205	1-1-88	1	0	2.31	4	4	0	0	23	13	6	6	1	11	22	.163	.174	.158	8.49	4.24
John King	L-L	6-2	215	9-14-94	2	1	7.27	14	0	0	0	17	20	16	14	5	7	18	.282	.214	.326	9.35	3.63
Jake Latz	R-L	6-2	185	4-8-96	5	5	5.77	19	10	0	0	53	59	36	34	12	31	59	.284	.254	.295	10.02	5.26
Jose Leclerc	R-R	6-0	195	12-19-93	0	1	5.40	7	0	0	0	7	5	4	4	0	5	8	.208	.154	.273	10.80	6.75
Chase Lee	R-R	6-0	170	8-13-98	1	1	5.46	30	0	0	2	31	40	22	19	2	11	41	.308	.241	.355	11.78	3.16
Tyson Miller	R-R	6-4	225	7-29-95	4	7	4.52	29	16	0	1	90	91	51	45	14	40	114	.259	.255	.263	11.44	4.01
Matt Moore	L-L	6-3	210	6-18-89	1	0	0.00	2	0	0	0	5	2	0	0	0	1	7	.133	.333	.083	12.60	1.80
Seth Nordlin	R-R	6-4	213	9-4-97	0	0	6.75	2	1	0	0	4	6	3	3	0	2	3	.375	.500	.250	6.75	4.50
Glenn Otto	R-R	6-3	240	3-11-96	0	1	2.79	3	3	0	0	10	8	4	3	1	3	12	.216	.294	.150	11.17	2.79
Fernery Ozuna	R-R	5-8	170	11-9-95	1	0	9.31	13	0	0	0	19	25	20	20	2	13	23	.333	.345	.326	10.71	6.05
Spencer Patton	R-R	6-1	200	2-20-88	4	2	6.44	24	0	0	1	29	33	24	21	8	17	40	.284	.308	.266	12.27	5.22
Cole Ragans	L-L	6-4	190	12-12-97	3	2	3.32	8	8	0	0	43	34	18	16	4	12	48	.211	.245	.194	9.97	2.49
Garrett Richards	R-R	6-2	210	5-27-88	1	0	9.00	1	0	0	0	1	3	2	1	0	0	1	.500	1.000	.250	9.00	0.00
Daniel Robert	L-R	6-4	210	8-30-94	4	4	6.28	37	0	0	2	39	33	29	27	3	27	48	.228	.238	.220	11.17	6.28
Yerry Rodriguez	R-R	6-2	198	10-15-97	4	1	4.27	49	5	0	4	59	60	31	28	9	32	73	.261	.309	.226	11.14	4.88
Ryder Ryan	R-R	6-2	205	5-11-95	5	4	3.64	47	0	0	1	59	53	30	24	7	29	67	.238	.326	.179	10.16	4.40
Dennis Santana	R-R	6-2	190	4-12-96	0	0	0.00	2	0	0	0	4	2	0	0	0	1	4	.154	.286	.000	9.82	2.45
Josh Sborz	R-R	6-3	215	12-17-93	3	0	1.61	19	1	0	1	22	11	6	4	2	11	30	.147	.214	.061	12.09	4.43
Nick Snyder	R-R	6-4	190	10-10-95	2	2	4.97	41	1	0	2	38	36	23	21	5	18	51	.252	.262	.244	12.08	4.26
Drew Strotman	R-R	6-3	195	9-3-96	1	0	3.86	3	0	0	0	2	3	1	1	0	3	5	.273	.000	.333	19.29	11.57
Nick Tanielu	R-R	5-11	214	9-4-92	0	0	13.50	3	0	0	0	3	7	8	5	0	3	0	.438	.556	.286	0.00	8.10
Tyler Thomas	R-L	6-1	175	12-22-95	1	0	3.00	1	0	0	0	3	2	1	1	1	1	2	.182	.200	.167	6.00	3.00
Tyree Thompson	R-R	6-4	165	6-12-97	0	0	13.50	1	0	0	0	1	2	3	1	1	2	2	.400	.000	.500	27.00	27.00
Jesus Tinoco	R-R	6-4	258	4-30-95	1	2	3.27	35	0	0	13	44	33	16	16	3	17	51	.205	.227	.189	10.43	3.48
Nick Tropeano	R-R	6-4	205	8-27-90	1	1	3.05	12	0	0	0	21	13	8	7	1	17	21	.186	.346	.091	9.15	7.40
Stephen Villines	R-R	6-1	185	7-15-95	0	0	12.38	6	0	0	0	8	12	13	11	4	6	1	.343	.313	.368	1.13	6.75
Dan Winkler	R-R	6-3	205	2-2-90	0	0	3.50	16	0	0	3	18	12	9	7	2	13	26	.185	.318	.116	13.00	6.50
Cole Winn	R-R	6-2	190	11-25-99	9	8	6.51	28	28	0	0	122	125	94	88	13	87	123	.265	.249	.279	9.10	6.44

Fielding

Catcher	PCT	G	PO	A	E	DP	PB
Huff	.990	44	458	25	5	3	7
Kruger	1.000	19	179	3	0	0	2
Piotto	1.000	1	1	0	0	0	0
Pozo	.981	30	294	10	6	0	4
Ramos	1.000	3	25	2	0	0	0
Viloria	.976	39	339	29	9	1	3
Whatley	.984	28	241	13	4	1	5

First Base	PCT	G	PO	A	E	DP
Apostel	.986	16	132	8	2	10
Arias	1.000	5	18	0	0	0
Carpenter	.993	19	131	3	1	16
Crim	.962	7	42	9	2	6
Hernandez	.987	24	147	6	2	16
Ibanez	.996	31	222	11	1	25
Knight	1.000	2	11	1	0	4
Pozo	.983	11	51	6	1	9
Reks	.960	8	48	0	2	6
Sale	.958	13	66	2	3	8
Tanielu	.995	28	179	10	1	18
Viloria	1.000	1	1	1	0	0

Second Base	PCT	G	PO	A	E	DP
Arias	.981	55	74	133	4	37
Chavez	1.000	3	2	4	0	0
Dorow	.979	35	58	79	3	21
Duran	1.000	2	4	6	0	1
Hernandez	1.000	1	2	1	0	0
Ibanez	1.000	3	4	3	0	1
Knight	.978	23	22	66	2	14
Mathias	1.000	6	6	11	0	2
Tanielu	.984	29	49	71	2	21
Wendzel	1.000	1	2	0	0	0

Third Base	PCT	G	PO	A	E	DP
Arias	.963	12	9	17	1	2
Carpenter	.000	1	0	0	1	0
Dorow	.889	6	7	9	2	1
Duran	.833	6	2	13	3	2
Ibanez	.980	27	17	31	1	3
Jung	.974	18	9	28	1	2
Knight	.750	2	2	1	1	0
Miller	.000	1	0	0	0	0
Smith	.929	20	8	31	3	4
Tanielu	.944	27	17	50	4	9
Wendzel	.924	35	20	53	6	5

Shortstop	PCT	G	PO	A	E	DP
Chavez	1.000	4	7	6	0	2
Dorow	.961	72	72	150	9	33
Duran	.970	9	13	19	1	6
Knight	.667	2	0	2	1	1
Smith	.968	17	17	43	2	11
Wendzel	.954	51	67	120	9	27

Outfield	PCT	G	PO	A	E	DP
Calhoun	1.000	2	3	0	0	0
Calhoun	.955	12	21	0	1	0
Duggar	1.000	12	15	0	0	0
Duran	.970	17	31	1	1	0
Fabian	.979	31	44	3	1	1
Hernandez	.992	62	122	3	1	0
Martinez	1.000	40	88	2	0	2
Mathias	1.000	2	1	0	0	0
Reks	1.000	21	37	2	0	1
Sale	.912	39	50	2	5	0
Smith	1.000	19	26	0	0	0
Solak	.986	44	71	0	1	0
Taveras	.978	48	89	0	2	0
Thompson	.988	80	159	1	2	0
Walker	.972	41	70	0	2	0
White	1.000	3	4	0	0	0

FRISCO ROUGHRIDERS — DOUBLE-A

TEXAS LEAGUE

Batting	B-T	HT	WT	DOB	AVG	vLH	vRH	G	AB	R	H	2B	3B	HR	RBI	BB	HBP	SH	SF	SO	SB	CS	SLG	OBP
Luisangel Acuna	R-R	5-10	181	3-12-02	.224	.306	.184	37	152	21	34	6	2	3	18	17	0	0	0	36	12	3	.349	.302
Miguel Aparicio	L-L	6-0	195	3-17-99	.200	.188	.204	23	70	7	14	1	1	1	5	10	3	1	0	25	3	4	.286	.325
Diosbel Arias	R-R	6-2	190	7-21-96	.180	.250	.158	15	50	8	9	1	0	2	5	5	3	0	0	6	1	1	.320	.293
Jax Biggers	L-R	5-11	175	4-7-97	.281	.191	.306	61	217	26	61	15	2	1	24	19	2	1	2	39	5	3	.382	.342
Evan Carter	L-R	6-4	190	8-29-02	.429	.222	.583	6	21	8	9	3	0	1	7	5	1	0	1	0	2	1	.714	.536
Frainyer Chavez	B-R	5-10	170	5-24-99	.291	.323	.250	14	55	7	16	3	0	0	8	5	0	0	1	12	2	0	.345	.344
Blaine Crim	R-R	5-11	200	6-17-97	.295	.406	.262	119	461	81	136	26	0	24	91	49	8	0	13	82	4	0	.508	.363
Ezequiel Duran	R-R	5-11	185	5-22-99	.317	.270	.329	45	183	34	58	24	1	7	31	14	1	0	2	36	7	2	.574	.365
Sandro Fabian	R-R	6-1	180	3-6-98	.258	.228	.267	69	244	39	63	16	1	12	43	19	6	0	2	50	2	0	.480	.325
Justin Foscue	R-R	6-0	205	3-2-99	.288	.340	.270	101	400	60	115	31	1	15	81	45	9	0	6	66	3	4	.483	.367
David Garcia	B-R	5-11	201	2-6-00	.228	.192	.238	66	237	26	54	11	1	5	36	18	5	1	1	66	0	1	.346	.295
Mitch Garver	R-R	6-1	220	1-15-91	.333	.667	.000	2	6	2	2	1	0	0	1	2	0	0	0	1	0	0	.500	.500
Trey Hair	L-R	5-10	185	4-21-95	.244	.231	.247	64	234	37	57	14	0	17	51	18	3	1	2	63	2	3	.521	.304
Dustin Harris	L-R	6-2	185	7-8-99	.257	.369	.229	85	331	58	85	16	2	17	66	42	5	0	4	74	19	5	.471	.346
Trevor Hauver	L-R	6-0	205	11-20-98	.230	.158	.262	21	61	17	14	4	0	4	12	24	0	0	3	22	0	0	.492	.432
Scott Kapers	R-R	5-11	198	11-27-96	.180	.167	.189	20	61	12	11	2	0	3	10	6	7	1	0	21	1	1	.361	.324
Nash Knight	B-R	6-0	205	9-20-92	.125	.000	.200	2	8	0	1	0	0	0	0	0	0	0	0	3	0	0	.125	.125
2-team total (13 Wichita Wind Surge)					.254	.125	.302	15	59	8	15	3	1	1	2	5	0	0	0	23	0	0	.390	.313
J.P. Martinez	L-L	5-9	174	3-21-96	.268	.186	.292	66	254	53	68	7	6	9	26	43	4	0	0	76	25	9	.449	.382
Brad Miller	L-R	6-2	195	10-18-89	.182	--	.182	3	11	3	2	1	0	1	3	2	0	0	0	3	0	0	.545	.308
Jonathan Ornelas	R-R	6-0	196	5-26-00	.299	.358	.281	123	525	84	157	20	2	14	64	45	6	2	2	121	14	6	.425	.360
Konner Piotto	L-R	5-10	195	1-1-98	.500	.333	1.000	1	4	2	2	0	0	0	0	0	0	0	0	1	0	0	.500	.500
Jordan Procyshen	L-R	5-10	185	3-11-93	.222	.233	.218	35	108	18	24	5	0	4	13	16	3	1	1	35	3	2	.380	.336
Thomas Saggese	R-R	5-11	175	4-10-02	.381	.375	.385	5	21	5	8	3	2	1	9	1	0	0	0	3	1	0	.857	.409
Josh Sale	L-R	6-0	215	7-5-91	.000	.000	.000	1	3	0	0	0	0	0	0	1	0	0	0	3	0	0	.000	.250
Josh Stowers	R-R	6-0	200	2-25-97	.222	.179	.235	105	356	58	79	20	2	10	49	49	10	2	2	118	22	5	.374	.331
Kellen Strahm	R-R	6-1	215	4-25-97	.277	.326	.260	104	354	72	98	16	0	10	42	65	6	2	6	95	11	1	.407	.392
Matt Whatley	R-R	5-9	200	1-7-96	.226	.120	.256	32	115	17	26	5	0	2	9	6	1	0	1	25	2	0	.322	.268
Aaron Zavala	L-R	6-0	193	6-24-00	.277	.256	.288	30	112	28	31	8	0	5	21	21	5	0	1	29	4	1	.482	.410

Pitching	B-T	HT	WT	DOB	W	L	ERA	G	GS	CG	SV	IP	H	R	ER	HR	BB	SO	AVG	vLH	vRH	K/9	BB/9
Grant Anderson	R-R	6-0	180	6-21-97	5	0	2.80	39	0	0	6	55	49	19	17	6	16	75	.231	.277	.202	12.35	2.63
Joe Barlow	R-R	6-2	210	9-28-95	1	0	0.00	3	0	0	0	5	1	0	0	0	2	5	.059	.000	.125	8.44	3.38
Cody Bradford	L-L	6-4	197	2-22-98	10	7	5.01	26	26	0	0	119	114	70	66	18	33	124	.248	.314	.220	9.40	2.50
Tim Brennan	R-R	6-4	212	12-18-96	6	3	2.76	19	13	0	0	75	62	27	23	9	13	55	.225	.179	.258	6.60	1.56
Sean Chandler	R-R	6-5	203	1-24-97	0	1	14.29	6	0	0	0	6	5	9	9	1	10	7	.238	.182	.300	11.12	15.88
Frainyer Chavez	B-R	5-10	170	5-24-99	0	0	0.00	1	0	0	0	0	0	0	0	0	0	0	.000	.000	--	0.00	0.00
Marc Church	R-R	6-3	189	3-30-01	1	3	7.20	14	0	0	1	15	18	14	12	4	7	21	.295	.345	.250	12.60	4.20
Joe Corbett	R-R	6-5	230	10-12-96	3	1	4.50	25	0	0	0	30	30	16	15	10	12	30	.265	.273	.261	9.00	3.60
Mason Englert	B-R	6-4	206	11-1-99	1	1	4.11	3	3	0	0	15	14	7	7	1	5	20	.237	.217	.250	11.74	2.93
Kevin Gowdy	R-R	6-4	205	11-16-97	2	3	9.90	32	3	0	0	40	52	44	44	11	31	33	.317	.328	.311	7.43	6.98
Trey Hair	L-R	5-10	185	4-21-95	0	0	18.00	1	0	0	0	1	4	2	2	1	1	0	.571	.333	.750	0.00	9.00
Jonathan Hernandez	R-R	6-3	190	7-6-96	0	0	0.00	1	0	0	0	2	0	0	0	0	1	2	.000	.000	.000	10.80	5.40
Lucas Jacobsen	L-L	6-5	190	7-1-95	0	1	2.45	14	0	0	3	15	9	4	4	2	7	20	.170	.200	.158	12.27	4.30
James Jones	L-L	6-3	205	9-24-88	1	0	0.00	2	0	0	0	2	0	0	0	0	2	5	.000	.000	.000	19.29	7.71
Antoine Kelly	L-L	6-5	205	12-5-99	0	0	7.23	7	5	0	0	19	12	16	15	0	19	24	.194	.000	.240	11.57	9.16
Zak Kent	R-R	6-3	208	2-24-98	2	3	4.68	19	19	0	0	83	83	45	43	11	30	87	.263	.260	.265	9.47	3.27
Jose Leclerc	R-R	6-0	195	12-19-93	1	0	3.86	2	0	0	0	2	4	1	1	0	0	3	.364	.333	.375	11.57	0.00
Chase Lee	R-R	6-0	170	8-13-98	1	1	2.25	21	0	0	5	24	16	7	6	0	8	30	.186	.273	.132	11.25	3.00
Jack Leiter	R-R	6-1	205	4-21-00	3	10	5.54	23	22	0	0	93	88	69	57	11	56	109	.246	.267	.230	10.59	5.44
John Matthews	R-R	6-1	190	1-21-98	0	0	5.40	3	0	0	0	3	2	2	2	0	4	4	.182	.250	.143	10.80	10.80
Seth Nordlin	R-R	6-4	213	9-4-97	2	2	3.44	30	5	0	1	73	68	29	28	7	23	63	.249	.266	.238	7.73	2.82
Fernery Ozuna	R-R	5-8	170	11-9-95	5	0	2.93	35	0	0	9	43	36	17	14	4	9	50	.220	.186	.245	10.47	1.88
Triston Polley	L-L	6-0	190	12-20-96	5	2	4.63	26	0	0	2	35	20	19	18	4	31	34	.171	.182	.164	8.74	7.97
Jordan Procyshen	L-R	5-10	185	3-11-93	0	0	0.00	1	0	0	1	0	0	0	0	0	0	0	.000	--	.000	0.00	0.00
Cole Ragans	L-L	6-4	190	12-12-97	5	3	2.81	10	10	0	0	51	41	18	16	6	19	65	.219	.241	.211	11.40	3.33
Justin Slaten	R-R	6-4	222	9-15-97	1	6	6.93	25	5	0	0	51	49	41	39	6	48	64	.255	.357	.197	11.37	8.53
Josh Smith	L-L	6-5	205	2-5-97	4	1	4.15	26	0	0	0	30	34	18	14	3	14	22	.293	.325	.276	6.53	4.15
Nick Starr	R-R	6-3	225	12-3-96	1	1	2.05	28	0	0	5	31	20	9	7	1	10	25	.183	.275	.130	7.34	2.93
Tyler Thomas	R-L	6-1	175	12-22-95	1	1	6.37	26	0	0	0	41	37	31	29	8	26	51	.240	.217	.255	11.20	5.71
Tai Tiedemann	R-R	6-6	195	5-31-96	5	3	6.20	43	3	0	2	61	73	49	42	12	31	29	.298	.280	.310	4.28	4.57
Ricky Vanasco	R-R	6-3	180	10-13-98	0	0	6.75	2	2	0	0	8	11	8	6	2	5	7	.324	.235	.412	7.88	5.63
Bradford Webb	R-R	6-3	200	4-20-98	0	0	20.25	1	0	0	0	1	1	3	3	0	4	2	.200	.500	.000	13.50	27.00
Avery Weems	R-L	6-2	205	6-6-97	2	6	5.14	26	17	0	0	91	96	62	52	14	32	107	.262	.267	.261	10.58	3.16
Owen White	R-R	6-3	199	8-9-99	3	0	2.49	4	4	0	0	22	19	6	6	1	4	23	.241	.235	.244	9.55	1.66
Matt Wivinis	R-R	6-0	170	7-24-93	0	1	10.13	6	0	0	0	8	13	9	9	4	1	5	.394	.500	.360	5.63	1.13
Grant Wolfram	L-L	6-6	235	12-12-96	3	3	4.42	39	0	0	2	57	49	32	28	3	43	71	.232	.160	.272	11.21	6.79

Fielding

Catcher	PCT	G	PO	A	E	DP	PB
Garcia	.993	61	512	30	4	1	3
Kapers	.990	20	189	6	2	0	0
Piotto	1.000	1	7	0	0	0	0
Procyshen	.983	28	280	8	5	1	5
Whatley	.987	32	285	20	4	0	3

First Base	PCT	G	PO	A	E	DP
Arias	1.000	3	24	1	0	2
Biggers	1.000	1	10	0	0	2
Chavez	1.000	5	37	3	0	3
Crim	.995	102	712	46	4	82
Hair	.966	11	82	2	3	4
Harris	1.000	6	44	6	0	3
Hauver	1.000	3	13	1	0	5
Procyshen	.960	6	45	3	2	4
Saggese	1.000	1	4	0	0	0

Second Base	PCT	G	PO	A	E	DP
Acuna	.966	13	23	33	2	10
Biggers	.963	16	36	43	3	9
Chavez	1.000	3	4	7	0	1
Duran	.982	15	22	34	1	4
Foscue	.978	76	126	183	7	40
Hair	1.000	7	13	16	0	7
Ornelas	.958	4	6	17	1	4
Saggese	1.000	3	9	4	0	3

Third Base	PCT	G	PO	A	E	DP
Arias	1.000	11	11	11	0	2
Biggers	.944	32	21	47	4	5
Chavez	.944	6	5	12	1	2
Crim	1.000	1	1	0	0	0
Duran	.917	4	3	8	1	1
Foscue	.946	12	11	24	2	4
Hair	.956	39	25	61	4	5
Knight	1.000	2	1	2	0	0
Miller	.750	1	1	2	1	1
Ornelas	.956	29	29	57	4	7
Saggese	.667	1	0	2	1	0

Shortstop	PCT	G	PO	A	E	DP
Acuna	.959	24	31	62	4	15
Biggers	.941	3	5	11	1	3
Duran	.956	24	31	55	4	10
Ornelas	.973	86	121	236	10	46

Outfield	PCT	G	PO	A	E	DP
Aparicio	1.000	16	23	1	0	1
Biggers	1.000	7	15	1	0	0
Carter	1.000	5	15	0	0	0
Fabian	.988	47	79	3	1	0
Harris	.941	58	94	1	6	0
Hauver	1.000	13	15	3	0	0
Martinez	1.000	64	126	3	0	0
Ornelas	1.000	4	10	0	0	0
Stowers	.976	99	197	3	5	1
Strahm	.994	82	166	5	1	1
Zavala	.980	24	48	1	1	1

HICKORY CRAWDADS — *HIGH CLASS A*

SOUTH ATLANTIC LEAGUE

Batting	B-T	HT	WT	DOB	AVG	vLH	vRH	G	AB	R	H	2B	3B	HR	RBI	BB	HBP	SH	SF	SO	SB	CS	SLG	OBP
Luisangel Acuna	R-R	5-10	181	3-12-02	.317	.341	.311	54	205	45	65	10	0	8	29	34	1	0	0	60	28	6	.483	.417
Miguel Aparicio	L-L	6-0	195	3-17-99	.143	.214	.095	9	35	5	5	1	0	2	4	1	1	0	0	10	0	0	.343	.189
Angel Aponte	R-R	6-0	170	2-3-00	.259	.273	.254	77	232	44	60	11	1	6	38	24	6	1	4	59	17	5	.392	.338
Zion Bannister	B-R	6-3	189	9-9-01	.222	1.000	.000	6	9	3	2	0	0	0	0	3	0	0	0	2	1	0	.222	.417
Evan Carter	L-R	6-4	190	8-29-02	.287	.203	.310	100	376	78	108	18	10	11	66	59	6	1	5	75	26	12	.476	.388
Frainyer Chavez	B-R	5-10	170	5-24-99	.281	.333	.264	73	231	35	65	9	2	2	32	30	4	0	3	50	13	3	.364	.369
Griffin Cheney	R-R	5-11	185	5-21-99	.160	.000	.190	11	25	7	4	1	0	0	0	5	0	0	0	7	1	1	.200	.300
Jayce Easley	B-R	5-8	151	8-2-99	.230	.257	.223	56	174	38	40	6	1	4	23	38	3	2	3	42	21	4	.345	.372
Randy Florentino	L-R	5-11	182	7-5-00	.242	.148	.262	51	153	24	37	3	1	4	25	21	1	2	3	44	2	0	.353	.331
Cody Freeman	R-R	5-10	180	1-5-01	.234	.202	.243	102	385	51	90	10	1	13	71	40	6	0	5	70	8	5	.366	.312
Jake Guenther	L-L	6-4	230	5-16-97	.181	.200	.178	36	105	21	19	4	0	4	14	11	4	0	2	34	1	1	.333	.279
Josh Hatcher	L-L	6-2	200	9-3-98	.171	.400	.139	13	41	5	7	2	0	0	3	4	0	0	0	11	2	0	.220	.244
Trevor Hauver	L-R	6-0	205	11-20-98	.217	.109	.244	82	276	49	60	13	1	13	58	69	6	0	8	90	2	1	.413	.376
Liam Hicks	L-R	5-11	185	6-2-99	.188	.000	.250	7	16	2	3	0	0	0	4	3	2	0	1	5	0	0	.188	.364
Cristian Inoa	R-R	5-10	165	7-4-99	.278	.227	.291	98	360	55	100	23	1	9	57	35	8	0	6	77	2	5	.422	.350
Scott Kapers	R-R	5-11	198	11-27-96	.261	.273	.258	37	119	18	31	2	1	8	23	7	4	0	1	45	0	1	.496	.321
Daniel Mateo	R-R	6-1	165	7-3-01	.250	.167	.269	9	32	4	8	0	1	1	4	3	1	0	0	13	1	1	.406	.333
Alejandro Osuna	L-L	6-0	185	10-10-02	.282	.214	.297	21	78	14	22	2	0	1	10	6	0	0	4	17	2	3	.346	.318
Yenci Pena	R-R	6-2	193	7-13-00	.136	.000	.150	7	22	1	3	1	0	0	3	0	0	0	0	10	0	0	.182	.136
Konner Piotto	L-R	5-10	195	1-1-98	.308	.000	.400	9	26	5	8	4	0	0	7	3	1	0	1	3	0	0	.462	.387
Obie Ricumstrict	R-R	6-2	175	7-20-98	.188	.200	.182	6	16	0	3	0	0	0	0	2	0	0	0	5	0	1	.188	.278
Keyber Rodriguez	R-R	5-10	178	10-24-00	.247	.241	.249	103	368	55	91	13	1	4	41	34	5	2	3	90	8	4	.321	.317
Thomas Saggese	R-R	5-11	175	4-10-02	.308	.266	.319	98	380	56	117	22	2	14	61	29	4	1	5	94	11	3	.487	.359
Chris Seise	R-R	6-2	196	1-6-99	.246	.228	.251	93	346	55	85	14	2	10	46	37	1	0	2	125	12	3	.384	.319
Aaron Zavala	L-R	6-0	193	6-24-00	.278	.138	.316	81	299	61	83	10	3	11	41	68	8	0	0	79	10	5	.441	.424

Pitching	B-T	HT	WT	DOB	W	L	ERA	G	GS	CG	SV	IP	H	R	ER	HR	BB	SO	AVG	vLH	vRH	K/9	BB/9
Dane Acker	R-R	6-2	189	4-1-99	0	3	10.66	4	4	0	0	13	16	16	15	3	10	17	.308	.320	.296	12.08	7.11
Robby Ahlstrom	L-L	6-3	195	6-19-99	1	6	6.14	13	11	0	0	51	57	42	35	11	21	59	.277	.338	.248	10.34	3.68
Ben Anderson	R-R	6-4	200	5-2-98	5	3	3.51	9	9	0	0	41	36	17	16	3	18	29	.237	.236	.237	6.37	3.95
Michael Brewer	R-R	6-5	215	8-8-00	2	2	3.96	23	0	0	4	25	31	13	11	2	10	31	.304	.304	.304	11.16	3.60
Frainyer Chavez	B-R	5-10	170	5-24-99	0	0	0.00	1	0	0	0	1	0	0	0	0	0	0	.000	.000	.000	0.00	0.00
Marc Church	R-R	6-3	189	3-30-01	2	2	2.91	23	0	0	4	34	28	12	11	7	7	57	.220	.269	.187	15.09	1.85
Gavin Collyer	R-R	6-1	165	5-12-01	0	1	2.45	1	1	0	0	4	2	5	1	1	4	5	.182	.000	.286	12.27	9.82
Joe Corbett	R-R	6-5	230	10-12-96	1	1	2.86	16	0	0	1	22	18	11	7	4	5	32	.214	.219	.212	13.09	2.05
Destin Dotson	L-L	6-7	231	11-17-99	1	2	5.19	28	0	0	2	35	29	20	20	4	32	42	.228	.235	.224	10.90	8.31
Mason Englert	B-R	6-4	206	11-1-99	7	5	3.57	21	21	1	0	103	73	44	41	15	26	116	.193	.168	.212	10.10	2.26
Eris Filpo	R-R	6-3	170	5-3-98	0	0	20.77	3	0	0	0	4	11	10	10	1	4	3	.478	.467	.500	6.23	8.31
2-team total (1 Wilmington Blue Rocks)					0	0	22.50	4	0	0	0	6	17	15	15	3	4	5	.500	.474	.533	7.50	6.00
Ryan Garcia	R-R	6-0	180	1-24-98	1	0	0.00	2	1	0	0	10	4	0	0	0	4	15	.114	.091	.125	13.50	3.60
Kelvin Gonzalez	R-R	6-0	170	12-24-97	0	0	3.00	6	0	0	0	9	8	5	3	3	3	11	.222	.188	.250	11.00	3.00
Larson Kindreich	L-L	6-4	210	6-21-99	1	1	5.40	9	7	0	0	27	18	18	16	4	25	36	.194	.167	.200	12.15	8.44
Nick Krauth	R-R	6-3	170	9-6-99	5	7	4.96	23	17	0	0	89	89	52	49	10	29	70	.263	.267	.260	7.08	2.93
Jesus Linarez	R-R	6-4	216	1-10-97	3	1	4.91	34	1	0	2	59	66	37	32	7	19	44	.289	.299	.282	6.75	2.91
Eudrys Manon	R-R	6-1	160	1-16-98	1	0	7.18	25	0	0	4	26	26	22	21	4	21	35	.252	.310	.213	11.96	7.18
John Matthews	R-R	6-1	190	1-21-98	5	1	4.32	30	1	0	2	75	61	40	36	6	36	68	.221	.198	.239	8.16	4.32
Theo McDowell	L-R	6-4	175	12-2-98	1	1	2.49	17	0	0	2	22	13	7	6	1	9	25	.176	.206	.150	10.38	3.74
Juan Mejia	L-L	5-11	160	1-9-99	0	0	5.12	13	1	0	0	19	18	11	11	3	6	16	.240	.174	.269	7.45	2.79
Damian Mendoza	L-R	6-1	175	1-25-01	0	0	0.00	1	0	0	0	0	0	0	0	0	1	0	.000	.000	--	0.00	27.00
Yohanse Morel	R-R	6-0	170	8-23-00	0	1	6.75	23	0	0	0	28	36	24	21	4	15	30	.305	.259	.344	9.64	4.82
Spencer Mraz	R-R	6-10	245	5-5-98	2	2	5.40	40	0	0	3	55	46	37	33	8	39	68	.229	.244	.216	11.13	6.38
Triston Polley	L-L	6-0	190	12-20-96	6	2	5.67	16	0	0	1	27	30	21	17	4	8	33	.273	.243	.288	11.00	2.67

Tekoah Roby	R-R	6-1	185	9-18-01	3	11	4.64	22	21	0	0	105	95	58	54	19	35	126	.239	.192	.277	10.83	3.01
Josh Smith	L-L	6-5	205	2-5-97	1	1	1.17	6	0	0	0	8	6	1	1	0	4	5	.207	.417	.059	5.87	4.70
Josh Stephan	R-R	6-3	185	11-1-01	2	1	1.54	3	3	0	0	12	7	5	2	1	7	13	.179	.150	.211	10.03	5.40
Leury Tejada	R-R	6-1	160	12-24-99	6	4	4.75	24	0	0	0	47	52	30	25	8	15	48	.269	.250	.286	9.13	2.85
Tyree Thompson	R-R	6-4	165	6-12-97	1	0	6.88	13	0	0	1	17	21	15	13	2	10	16	.296	.152	.421	8.47	5.29
Ricky Vanasco	R-R	6-3	180	10-13-98	3	5	4.48	21	21	0	0	84	78	45	42	12	47	111	.245	.220	.264	11.85	5.02
Bradford Webb	R-R	6-3	200	4-20-98	0	0	4.50	10	2	0	1	18	20	12	9	1	5	24	.270	.194	.326	12.00	2.50
Owen White	R-R	6-3	199	8-9-99	6	2	3.99	11	10	0	0	59	51	27	26	7	19	81	.230	.222	.236	12.43	2.91

Fielding

Catcher	PCT	G	PO	A	E	DP	PB
Florentino	.994	45	448	30	3	3	3
Freeman	.979	46	427	33	10	3	6
Hicks	.968	2	29	1	1	0	0
Kapers	.997	33	298	15	1	1	4
Piotto	.973	8	69	4	2	0	1

First Base	PCT	G	PO	A	E	DP
Chavez	.993	23	138	9	1	13
Florentino	1.000	2	6	3	0	1
Freeman	1.000	1	5	0	0	0
Guenther	.991	34	212	5	2	18
Hatcher	1.000	1	1	0	0	0
Hicks	.923	2	12	0	1	0
Inoa	.991	79	549	22	5	49
Kapers	1.000	3	8	1	0	0

Second Base	PCT	G	PO	A	E	DP
Acuna	.931	9	9	18	2	3
Chavez	.973	39	54	92	4	18
Cheney	.950	6	7	12	1	3
Easley	1.000	5	6	10	0	1
Freeman	1.000	1	1	0	0	0
Inoa	1.000	5	10	7	0	4
Rodriguez	1.000	26	37	63	0	11
Saggese	.978	48	70	109	4	21

Third Base	PCT	G	PO	A	E	DP
Chavez	1.000	2	1	1	0	0
Freeman	.945	42	26	60	5	8
Inoa	.913	11	7	14	2	2
Pena	1.000	4	4	12	0	1
Rodriguez	.929	43	31	74	8	5
Saggese	.946	31	16	54	4	4

Shortstop	PCT	G	PO	A	E	DP
Acuna	.917	37	52	81	12	18
Chavez	.981	10	17	35	1	7
Cheney	.818	3	3	6	2	0
Rodriguez	.983	32	45	74	2	14
Saggese	.947	15	23	48	4	9
Seise	.878	36	47	61	15	16

Outfield	PCT	G	PO	A	E	DP
Aparicio	1.000	8	15	1	0	0
Aponte	.956	73	83	4	4	1
Bannister	1.000	4	2	1	0	0
Carter	.988	83	167	3	2	1
Easley	.964	47	99	7	4	0
Guenther	1.000	3	1	0	0	0
Hatcher	1.000	13	20	0	0	0
Hauver	.983	73	116	2	2	1
Mateo	.944	9	17	0	1	0
Osuna	1.000	19	49	1	0	0
Ricumstrict	1.000	6	8	0	0	0
Rodriguez	1.000	1	1	1	0	0
Zavala	.966	73	109	6	4	1

DOWN EAST WOOD DUCKS — LOW CLASS A

CAROLINA LEAGUE

Batting	B-T	HT	WT	DOB	AVG	vLH	vRH	G	AB	R	H	2B	3B	HR	RBI	BB	HBP	SH	SF	SO	SB	CS	SLG	OBP
Jose Acosta	B-R	5-10	170	3-20-00	.230	.308	.208	23	61	7	14	4	2	2	11	7	1	4	0	21	4	1	.459	.319
Maximo Acosta	R-R	6-1	187	10-29-02	.262	.164	.282	107	404	62	106	26	1	4	35	40	9	2	1	87	44	17	.361	.341
Zion Bannister	B-R	6-3	189	9-9-01	.184	.300	.154	21	49	6	9	1	0	0	4	8	0	0	1	18	2	0	.204	.293
Derwin Barreto	B-R	5-9	160	9-1-00	.203	.200	.204	22	64	12	13	3	0	2	7	16	1	0	2	17	3	1	.344	.361
JoJo Blackmon	L-L	6-0	183	3-31-03	.160	.333	.122	16	50	11	8	0	3	1	9	6	0	1	0	22	2	1	.340	.250
Cameron Cauley	R-R	5-10	170	2-6-03	.209	.208	.209	76	287	36	60	11	3	2	21	38	3	1	2	91	38	5	.289	.306
Danyer Cueva	L-R	6-1	160	5-27-04	.111	.000	.118	5	18	0	2	0	0	0	0	0	0	0	0	5	0	0	.111	.111
Gleider Figuereo	L-R	6-0	165	6-27-04	.208	.250	.200	6	24	0	5	0	0	0	1	2	0	0	0	8	0	0	.208	.269
Yosy Galan	R-R	6-4	200	4-25-01	.206	.206	.206	98	345	56	71	15	1	20	59	39	8	0	2	139	17	6	.429	.299
Liam Hicks	L-R	5-11	185	6-2-99	.273	.231	.280	30	88	11	24	6	0	2	17	26	2	0	4	11	5	1	.409	.433
Daniel Mateo	R-R	6-1	165	7-3-01	.274	.333	.259	98	376	59	103	9	5	11	51	21	5	0	5	99	42	12	.412	.317
Tucker Mitchell	R-R	6-1	210	2-10-01	.185	.160	.191	43	135	16	25	4	1	4	17	20	8	0	0	52	8	2	.319	.325
Ian Moller	R-R	6-0	190	10-26-02	.201	.143	.212	60	184	29	37	6	0	5	22	47	2	0	2	63	18	2	.315	.366
Yeison Morrobel	L-L	6-2	170	12-8-03	.231	.000	.240	8	26	3	6	1	0	0	3	3	0	0	0	6	2	1	.269	.310
Efrenyer Narvaez	R-R	5-11	155	7-25-02	.205	.220	.201	56	210	16	43	6	1	3	22	13	5	0	2	66	5	3	.286	.265
Abimelec Ortiz	L-L	6-0	230	2-22-02	.226	.295	.214	93	292	37	66	8	2	11	39	32	4	0	3	93	6	7	.380	.308
Alejandro Osuna	L-L	6-0	185	10-10-02	.308	.216	.329	76	273	54	84	13	1	8	44	36	5	3	3	51	32	15	.451	.394
Junior Paniagua	R-R	5-10	160	10-8-01	.200	.269	.184	88	280	34	56	14	4	2	20	17	3	2	1	71	7	0	.300	.252
Yenci Pena	R-R	6-2	193	7-13-00	.213	.171	.225	57	164	22	35	4	1	3	14	31	3	0	1	52	8	4	.305	.347
Konner Piotto	L-R	5-10	195	1-1-98	.286	.250	.333	2	7	0	2	0	0	0	0	0	0	0	0	5	0	0	.286	.286
Jose Rodriguez	L-R	6-0	185	10-5-01	.197	.137	.209	87	309	25	61	13	1	4	29	29	7	0	1	87	7	7	.285	.280
Brady Smith	R-R	6-1	210	11-18-98	.200	.143	.214	11	35	4	7	2	0	1	7	6	0	0	0	18	0	0	.343	.317
Marcus Smith	L-L	5-11	185	9-11-00	.179	.145	.186	94	302	42	54	8	1	5	31	66	8	4	5	163	47	8	.262	.336
Xavier Valentin	L-R	5-9	180	8-22-00	.184	.000	.200	17	49	4	9	0	0	1	5	5	1	0	1	27	3	1	.245	.268
Miguel Villarroel	R-R	6-0	165	12-23-01	.323	.263	.333	38	130	22	42	6	0	1	23	17	1	1	0	22	8	3	.392	.405

Pitching	B-T	HT	WT	DOB	W	L	ERA	G	GS	CG	SV	IP	H	R	ER	HR	BB	SO	AVG	vLH	vRH	K/9	BB/9
Jose Acosta	B-R	5-10	170	3-20-00	0	0	0.00	1	0	0	0	0	0	0	0	0	0	0	.000	.000	--	0.00	0.00
Robby Ahlstrom	L-L	6-3	195	6-19-99	1	4	3.55	9	6	0	0	38	43	19	15	2	10	47	.287	.405	.241	11.13	2.37
Mitch Bratt	L-L	6-1	190	7-3-03	5	5	2.45	19	18	0	0	81	66	28	22	4	28	99	.218	.250	.201	11.05	3.12
Michael Brewer	R-R	6-5	215	8-8-00	3	2	0.55	9	0	0	1	16	9	4	1	0	4	19	.150	.077	.206	10.47	2.20
Gavin Collyer	R-R	6-1	165	5-12-01	6	4	4.63	23	21	0	0	101	86	57	52	8	40	110	.230	.269	.198	9.80	3.56
Jose Corniell	R-R	6-3	165	6-22-03	3	5	5.45	22	4	0	3	66	58	40	40	9	34	71	.237	.308	.181	9.68	4.64
Aidan Curry	R-R	6-5	185	7-5-02	0	0	0.00	1	1	0	0	3	1	0	0	0	5	6	.100	.167	.000	16.20	13.50
Destin Dotson	L-L	6-7	231	11-17-99	1	1	4.61	8	0	0	1	14	10	7	7	3	6	25	.192	.158	.212	16.46	3.95
Ryan Garcia	R-R	6-0	180	1-24-98	1	2	2.31	12	12	0	0	47	29	14	12	3	17	59	.177	.123	.220	11.38	3.28
Josh Gessner	R-R	6-1	205	6-25-00	2	4	6.33	13	5	0	1	43	43	35	30	5	26	47	.261	.271	.250	9.91	5.48
Liam Hicks	L-R	5-11	185	6-2-99	0	0	9.00	1	0	0	0	1	2	1	1	1	2	1	.400	.400	--	9.00	18.00
Anthony Hoopii-Tuionetoa	R-R	6-2	190	8-11-00	4	3	3.09	36	0	0	8	44	38	27	15	2	20	67	.229	.224	.232	13.81	4.12
Larson Kindreich	L-L	6-4	210	6-21-99	3	2	2.37	9	5	0	0	38	25	12	10	0	20	55	.187	.182	.189	13.03	4.74
Jackson Leath	R-R	6-1	192	6-20-99	2	4	8.42	28	0	0	1	31	31	36	29	6	23	29	.254	.400	.169	8.42	6.68
Nick Lockhart	R-R	6-6	204	2-12-01	3	3	4.22	30	0	0	2	49	38	26	23	5	17	60	.213	.186	.231	11.02	3.12

Dylan MacLean	R-L	6-4	190	7-12-02	2	0	3.96	21	0	0	0	25	26	18	11	4	8	16	.263	.278	.254	5.76	2.88
D.J. McCarty	R-R	6-2	145	9-9-02	0	1	10.80	1	1	0	0	2	3	3	2	0	2	2	.375	.500	.333	10.80	10.80
Theo McDowell	L-R	6-4	175	12-2-98	4	1	2.77	21	0	0	1	26	13	9	8	1	15	34	.148	.176	.130	11.77	5.19
Juan Mejia	L-L	5-11	160	1-9-99	0	1	10.34	10	0	0	0	16	20	18	18	4	10	19	.303	.182	.364	10.91	5.74
Damian Mendoza	L-R	6-1	175	1-25-01	4	1	2.48	33	0	0	3	62	55	28	17	3	30	59	.241	.245	.238	8.61	4.38
Alberto Mota	R-R	5-11	170	2-17-03	0	0	2.45	7	0	0	1	11	8	3	3	0	9	15	.205	.222	.190	12.27	7.36
Teodoro Ortega	R-R	6-0	145	3-12-00	1	1	5.79	10	0	0	0	14	13	12	9	1	8	19	.255	.217	.286	12.21	5.14
Ivan Oviedo	R-R	6-2	175	10-14-02	0	0	0.00	1	0	0	0	4	2	0	0	0	3	5	.154	.000	.182	10.38	6.23
Adrian Rodriguez	R-R	6-5	192	5-18-01	2	0	3.09	7	0	0	0	12	9	4	4	1	6	16	.214	.211	.217	12.34	4.63
Winston Santos	R-R	6-0	160	4-15-02	7	6	3.49	22	21	0	0	108	89	49	42	8	30	108	.222	.233	.213	8.97	2.49
Florencio Serrano	R-R	6-1	205	2-23-00	0	0	3.86	10	0	0	1	26	23	11	11	2	9	18	.256	.306	.195	6.31	3.16
Josh Smith	L-L	6-5	205	2-5-97	0	0	2.45	3	0	0	1	4	4	2	1	0	0	4	.250	.333	.231	9.82	0.00
Josh Stephan	R-R	6-3	185	11-1-01	4	4	3.34	18	16	0	1	92	77	42	34	10	24	102	.223	.246	.208	10.01	2.36
Leury Tejada	R-R	6-1	160	12-24-99	1	1	5.40	13	0	0	2	25	27	18	15	2	12	29	.270	.214	.310	10.44	4.32
Emiliano Teodo	R-R	6-1	165	2-14-01	3	6	3.09	22	17	0	0	84	51	36	29	7	44	115	.171	.184	.161	12.27	4.70
Xavier Valentin	L-R	5-9	180	8-22-00	0	0	0.00	1	0	0	0	1	0	0	0	0	0	0	.000	.000	--	0.00	0.00
Bradford Webb	R-R	6-3	200	4-20-98	3	3	3.86	11	4	0	1	40	35	20	17	1	19	47	.235	.276	.209	10.66	4.31
Kai Wynyard	R-R	6-0	176	6-22-02	0	2	4.24	12	0	0	2	23	20	12	11	3	10	27	.227	.297	.176	10.41	3.86

Fielding

Catcher	PCT	G	PO	A	E	DP	PB
Hicks	.990	9	94	3	1	0	0
Mitchell	.993	13	133	8	1	1	1
Moller	.984	55	510	39	9	4	9
Narvaez	.982	52	548	48	11	4	16
Smith	.960	4	47	1	2	0	0

First Base	PCT	G	PO	A	E	DP
Hicks	.973	15	100	9	3	12
Mitchell	.992	15	113	5	1	9
Ortiz	.993	74	532	26	4	44
Osuna	.000	1	0	0	0	0
Pena	1.000	4	18	1	0	2
Rodriguez	.993	20	128	5	1	8
Smith	1.000	2	9	0	0	0
Valentin	.875	1	7	0	1	1
Villarroel	.980	6	47	3	1	0

Second Base	PCT	G	PO	A	E	DP
Acosta	.983	16	19	38	1	13
Acosta	.982	29	39	73	2	12
Barreto	.943	10	10	23	2	4
Cauley	.989	28	25	65	1	12
Cueva	1.000	4	4	13	0	1
Paniagua	.965	38	42	69	4	16
Valentin	.935	11	22	21	3	5

Third Base	PCT	G	PO	A	E	DP
Acosta	.818	3	1	8	2	0
Barreto	.692	6	2	7	4	2
Cueva	1.000	1	1	1	0	0
Figuereo	1.000	2	1	4	0	0
Paniagua	.944	50	38	96	8	9
Pena	.882	44	12	63	10	4
Villarroel	.957	33	20	47	3	8

Shortstop	PCT	G	PO	A	E	DP
Acosta	1.000	1	0	3	0	0
Acosta	.942	76	89	172	16	31
Barreto	.933	6	12	16	2	4
Cauley	.951	48	67	108	9	24
Paniagua	1.000	2	3	2	0	0

Outfield	PCT	G	PO	A	E	DP
Bannister	1.000	17	26	2	0	1
Blackmon	.950	14	19	0	1	0
Galan	.965	83	108	3	4	0
Mateo	.966	92	186	10	7	3
Morrobel	1.000	7	11	1	0	0
Ortiz	1.000	11	17	2	0	1
Osuna	.981	61	103	1	2	1
Rodriguez	.958	41	63	6	3	1
Smith	.977	77	166	4	4	0

ACL RANGERS — *ROOKIE*

ARIZONA COMPLEX LEAGUE

Batting	B-T	HT	WT	DOB	AVG	vLH	vRH	G	AB	R	H	2B	3B	HR	RBI	BB	HBP	SH	SF	SO	SB	CS	SLG	OBP
Frandy Almonte	B-R	5-8	150	10-16-03	.217	.125	.250	26	60	18	13	2	0	0	9	18	3	0	2	21	11	0	.250	.410
Miguel Aparicio	L-L	6-0	195	3-17-99	.263	.667	.188	10	38	8	10	2	0	2	10	4	0	0	0	15	2	0	.474	.333
Zion Bannister	B-R	6-3	189	9-9-01	.281	.400	.259	10	32	4	9	3	0	0	4	9	2	0	0	10	0	4	.375	.465
Derwin Barreto	B-R	5-9	160	9-1-00	.091	.000	.100	3	11	2	1	0	0	0	0	2	0	0	0	5	0	0	.091	.231
Beycker Barroso	R-R	5-10	160	1-24-03	.333	.000	.378	15	42	6	14	3	0	1	6	5	2	0	0	5	4	2	.476	.429
JoJo Blackmon	L-L	6-0	183	3-31-03	.265	.242	.273	38	132	29	35	4	4	8	15	22	3	2	0	60	16	1	.538	.382
Hunter Bryan	R-R	6-0	195	4-22-01	.225	.000	.257	16	40	7	9	3	0	0	3	9	1	1	0	24	0	0	.300	.380
Antonio Cabello	R-R	5-10	160	11-1-00	.091	.000	.133	7	22	2	2	0	0	0	1	5	1	0	0	12	0	0	.091	.286
Griffin Cheney	R-R	5-11	185	5-21-99	.226	.375	.174	9	31	3	7	3	1	2	5	3	1	0	0	10	1	0	.581	.314
Danyer Cueva	L-R	6-1	160	5-27-04	.330	.293	.341	44	176	39	58	10	1	5	31	10	3	0	0	40	3	2	.483	.376
Alisson Del Orbe	B-R	6-3	185	9-6-01	.188	.000	.214	5	16	1	3	0	0	0	0	0	0	0	0	10	0	0	.188	.188
Jayce Easley	B-R	5-8	151	8-2-99	.250	.500	.167	3	8	2	2	1	0	0	1	1	3	0	0	2	1	0	.375	.500
Jeferson Espinal	L-L	6-0	180	6-7-02	.255	.000	.304	25	94	13	24	6	2	0	10	10	2	0	0	50	5	4	.362	.340
Jose A. Felix	R-R	5-11	190	7-23-02	.244	.000	.324	15	45	5	11	2	0	1	7	7	0	0	0	22	1	1	.356	.346
Gleider Figuereo	L-R	6-0	165	6-27-04	.280	.148	.316	35	125	29	35	5	5	9	31	15	3	0	3	33	7	1	.616	.363
David Garcia	B-R	5-11	201	2-6-00	.250	.000	.333	4	12	5	3	2	0	0	3	4	1	0	0	3	0	0	.417	.471
Robert Gonzalez	R-R	6-0	175	6-19-01	.220	.111	.240	24	59	9	13	2	0	2	10	9	3	0	2	19	4	1	.356	.342
Anthony Gutierrez	R-R	6-3	180	11-25-04	.259	.333	.228	22	81	13	21	5	2	1	8	3	2	0	1	16	6	3	.407	.299
Josh Hatcher	L-L	6-2	200	9-3-98	.282	.333	.267	9	39	3	11	4	0	0	4	2	0	0	0	13	1	2	.385	.317
Liam Hicks	L-R	5-11	185	6-2-99	.478	.727	.400	13	46	10	22	3	1	1	11	7	3	0	1	6	0	0	.652	.561
Josh Jung	R-R	6-2	214	2-12-98	.240	.167	.263	8	25	4	6	0	0	3	5	3	1	0	0	5	0	0	.600	.345
Andres Mesa	R-R	5-11	170	10-16-02	.243	.250	.241	37	148	21	36	11	1	1	26	8	3	0	1	51	11	3	.351	.294
Tucker Mitchell	R-R	6-1	210	2-10-01	.208	.143	.235	7	24	3	5	1	0	1	4	1	1	0	0	9	0	0	.375	.269
Jesus Moreno	R-R	5-11	170	4-16-01	.271	.087	.329	28	96	19	26	4	1	3	19	7	3	0	2	31	2	1	.427	.333
Yeison Morrobel	L-L	6-2	170	12-8-03	.329	.297	.339	41	152	31	50	13	1	3	21	17	3	0	1	34	5	5	.487	.405
Keithron Moss	B-R	5-11	188	8-20-01	.163	.143	.167	19	49	9	8	1	0	0	2	11	2	0	1	24	10	1	.184	.333
Efrenyer Narvaez	R-R	5-11	155	7-25-02	.286	.375	.250	8	28	6	8	0	1	0	4	4	1	0	0	8	0	0	.357	.394
Ismael Padua	R-R	6-1	180	9-11-02	.226	.182	.239	25	93	12	21	3	1	3	14	7	2	0	0	35	3	0	.376	.294
Chandler Pollard	R-R	6-2	173	5-3-04	.000	.000	.000	2	5	0	0	0	0	0	0	1	2	0	0	2	0	1	.000	.375
Tommy Specht	L-R	6-3	200	6-24-04	.200	.000	.333	3	10	2	2	1	0	0	0	2	0	0	0	6	0	0	.300	.333
Xavier Valentin	L-R	5-9	180	8-22-00	.143	.250	.000	2	7	1	1	0	0	0	0	0	1	0	0	3	2	0	.143	.250
Miguel Villarroel	R-R	6-0	165	12-23-01	.351	.400	.340	15	57	18	20	6	0	1	11	7	2	0	1	5	1	1	.509	.433
Davis Wendzel	R-R	6-1	206	5-23-97	.105	.000	.143	6	19	1	2	2	0	0	1	2	0	0	0	7	0	0	.211	.190

Pitching	B-T	HT	WT	DOB	W	L	ERA	G	GS	CG	SV	IP	H	R	ER	HR	BB	SO	AVG	vLH	vRH	K/9	BB/9
Dane Acker	R-R	6-2	189	4-1-99	0	0	2.08	5	5	0	0	13	7	7	3	1	5	14	.156	.083	.182	9.69	3.46
Ismael Agreda	R-R	6-0	150	10-8-03	2	2	6.91	10	3	0	1	27	31	25	21	5	16	35	.277	.333	.243	11.52	5.27
Michael Alfonso	R-R	6-3	205	1-8-03	0	0	9.22	8	1	0	1	14	21	16	14	4	8	18	.344	.467	.304	11.85	5.27
Biembenido Brito	R-R	6-3	180	2-13-03	0	1	13.50	2	1	0	0	5	5	8	7	1	5	9	.263	.500	.154	17.36	9.64
Seth Clark	R-L	6-3	220	11-18-99	0	0	0.00	1	0	0	0	1	0	0	0	0	0	2	.000	.000	.000	18.00	0.00
Kyle Cody	R-R	6-7	225	8-9-94	1	0	0.84	8	0	0	0	11	9	1	1	0	3	18	.237	.250	.231	15.19	2.53
Aidan Curry	R-R	6-5	185	7-5-02	1	1	4.63	11	9	0	0	35	37	20	18	4	17	50	.270	.366	.229	12.86	4.37
Dane Dunning	R-R	6-4	225	12-20-94	0	0	3.60	1	1	0	0	5	3	2	2	1	1	9	.158	.182	.125	16.20	1.80
Evan Elliott	R-R	6-3	210	1-10-01	0	1	4.82	9	0	0	0	9	8	5	5	1	5	13	.222	.231	.217	12.54	4.82
Josh Gessner	R-R	6-1	205	6-25-00	0	0	0.00	1	1	0	0	5	4	1	0	0	1	9	.222	.250	.214	17.36	1.93
Jose Gonzalez	R-R	6-3	200	8-5-01	0	1	10.24	4	3	0	1	10	13	12	11	2	3	12	.325	.375	.292	11.17	2.79
Kelvin Gonzalez	R-R	6-0	170	12-24-97	1	0	2.84	5	0	0	0	6	8	2	2	0	1	9	.308	.375	.278	12.79	1.42
Nyan Hernandez	L-R	6-2	198	7-11-01	0	2	5.68	9	4	0	0	19	22	14	12	1	13	23	.286	.370	.240	10.89	6.16
James Jones	L-L	6-3	205	9-24-88	3	0	0.00	4	1	0	0	5	3	0	0	0	0	12	.167	.000	.188	21.60	0.00
Bryan Magdaleno	L-L	6-1	202	2-22-01	1	1	4.12	15	0	0	0	20	20	13	9	0	14	18	.260	.182	.273	8.24	6.41
D.J. McCarty	R-R	6-2	145	9-9-02	3	3	5.24	11	10	0	0	46	52	33	27	1	24	51	.283	.329	.254	9.91	4.66
Juan Mejia	L-L	5-11	160	1-9-99	0	0	1.80	3	0	0	0	5	6	1	1	0	1	2	.316	.000	.333	3.60	1.80
Brayan Mendoza	L-L	6-0	155	1-19-04	0	2	7.23	8	3	0	1	19	24	15	15	4	8	18	.312	.417	.292	8.68	3.86
Joseph Montalvo	B-R	6-2	185	5-4-02	4	0	2.31	10	1	0	0	23	22	6	6	1	3	36	.239	.192	.258	13.89	1.16
Jesus Moreno	R-R	5-11	170	4-16-01	0	0	0.00	1	0	0	0	0	0	0	0	0	0	0	.000	.000	--	0.00	0.00
Alberto Mota	R-R	5-11	170	2-17-03	2	0	1.33	16	0	0	4	20	17	6	3	0	9	28	.221	.200	.231	12.39	3.98
Ivan Oviedo	R-R	6-2	175	10-14-02	3	1	3.02	11	5	0	1	45	40	21	15	3	12	50	.230	.235	.228	10.07	2.42
Luis Paulino	L-L	5-10	135	5-2-98	0	3	4.18	14	0	0	0	24	30	15	11	0	9	35	.300	.200	.325	13.31	3.42
Adrian Rodriguez	R-R	6-5	192	5-18-01	3	0	3.18	12	0	0	3	17	9	7	6	0	7	27	.158	.190	.139	14.29	3.71
Josue Rodriguez	L-L	5-11	175	7-30-02	2	1	10.61	8	0	0	0	9	12	13	11	0	10	12	.324	.556	.250	11.57	9.64
Eury Rosado	R-R	6-0	160	11-23-00	1	2	5.50	19	0	0	4	34	44	23	21	6	16	48	.306	.326	.297	12.58	4.19
Florencio Serrano	R-R	6-1	205	2-23-00	0	0	1.50	3	3	0	0	6	5	1	1	0	3	5	.227	.100	.333	7.50	4.50
Justin Slaten	R-R	6-4	222	9-15-97	0	0	0.00	1	0	0	0	1	0	0	0	0	0	2	.000	.000	.000	18.00	0.00
Jose Viola	R-R	6-0	175	4-25-01	0	0	7.71	2	0	0	0	2	1	2	2	0	3	4	.125	.000	.500	15.43	11.57
Bradford Webb	R-R	6-3	200	4-20-98	0	1	7.71	1	1	0	0	2	4	2	2	0	1	2	.400	1.000	.333	7.71	3.86
Matt Wivinis	R-R	6-0	170	7-24-93	1	0	3.78	13	2	0	0	17	19	9	7	3	6	16	.279	.316	.265	8.64	3.24
Kai Wynyard	R-R	6-0	176	6-22-02	4	0	4.86	7	0	0	0	17	12	9	9	1	4	24	.197	.190	.200	12.96	2.16

Fielding

C: Barroso 13, Cabello 6, Felix 3, Garcia 4, Hicks 6, Mitchell 2, Moreno 21, Narvaez 7. **1B:** Barreto 1, Bryan 7, Felix 11, Hatcher 6, Hicks 6, Jung 1, Mesa 4, Mitchell 3, Moreno 6, Moss 4, Valentin 2, Villarroel 8. **2B:** Almonte 6, Bryan 2, Cheney 4, Cueva 7, Del Orbe 1, Mesa 27, Moss 9, Pollard 2, Villarroel 1. **3B:** Almonte 6, Bryan 6, Cheney 4, Del Orbe 4, Figuereo 30, Jung 3, Mesa 2, Moss 3, Villarroel 2. **SS:** Almonte 5, Barreto 2, Cheney 1, Cueva 40, Mesa 5, Moss 1, Villarroel 1, Wendzel 5. **OF:** Almonte 8, Aparicio 9, Bannister 9, Blackmon 38, Easley 3, Espinal 5, Gonzalez 23, Gutierrez 22, Hatcher 2, Mesa 1, Morrobel 38, Padua 15, Specht 3.

DSL TEX BLUE — *ROOKIE*

DOMINICAN SUMMER LEAGUE

Batting	B-T	HT	WT	DOB	AVG	vLH	vRH	G	AB	R	H	2B	3B	HR	RBI	BB	HBP	SH	SF	SO	SB	CS	SLG	OBP
Erick Alvarez	R-R	5-10	150	2-1-05	.000	--	.000	1	1	0	0	0	0	0	0	0	0	0	0	0	0	0	.000	.000
2-team total (51 DSL TEX Red)					.294	.364	.279	52	187	31	55	8	4	4	22	15	6	0	0	26	15	6	.444	.365
Edgar Basabe	R-R	6-0	155	4-27-04	.306	.250	.324	44	134	36	41	5	3	3	14	29	4	0	2	29	18	4	.455	.438
Andy Beato	R-R	0-0	0	11-27-03	.100	.250	.000	7	10	2	1	1	0	0	0	2	1	0	0	6	0	0	.200	.308
Daniel Bruzual	R-R	6-0	170	2-1-05	.202	.167	.211	33	114	6	23	7	2	0	14	2	4	0	2	22	0	1	.298	.238
Roni Cabrera	R-R	6-1	175	7-31-05	.214	.231	.209	37	112	20	24	3	1	2	18	13	3	0	2	32	6	1	.313	.308
Jose De Jesus	B-L	6-1	170	1-8-05	.281	.186	.308	54	199	45	56	5	3	3	27	27	1	0	1	47	14	9	.382	.368
Alfredo Espinoza	R-R	6-0	160	9-23-04	.146	.100	.158	14	48	2	7	2	0	0	2	7	0	1	0	14	0	0	.188	.255
Kleimer Lemos	B-R	6-1	175	6-3-05	.258	.226	.267	42	132	11	34	6	1	1	17	8	1	1	4	28	6	3	.341	.297
Jesus Lopez	L-R	6-1	180	5-24-05	1.000	--	1.000	1	1	0	1	0	0	0	1	0	0	0	0	0	0	0	1.000	1.000
2-team total (37 DSL TEX Red)					.236	.222	.239	38	110	13	26	8	0	3	17	22	4	0	2	17	4	3	.391	.377
Luis Marquez	R-R	5-10	150	8-31-05	.238	.323	.211	42	126	25	30	4	2	3	16	11	6	1	1	26	6	3	.373	.326
Wady Mendez	L-L	6-0	155	10-14-04	.302	.278	.308	49	169	31	51	9	7	4	31	18	4	0	1	48	15	5	.509	.380
Miguel Ojeda Jr.	R-R	6-0	200	6-16-00	.279	.400	.242	20	43	4	12	3	0	0	3	6	0	0	1	6	0	0	.349	.360
2-team total (11 DSL TEX Red)					.300	.294	.302	31	70	8	21	6	0	0	11	11	1	0	2	10	0	1	.386	.393
Keiderson Pavon	R-R	5-7	140	12-11-03	.259	.250	.262	55	158	29	41	5	0	0	18	20	2	2	1	15	13	6	.291	.348
Frank Pena	R-R	6-3	175	11-14-03	.345	.286	.364	12	29	4	10	2	0	0	3	1	1	0	0	7	3	0	.414	.387
Julio Pinto	R-R	5-10	165	6-5-04	.214	.222	.211	50	159	25	34	9	0	0	16	15	6	2	1	21	4	3	.270	.304
Josue Romero	R-R	5-9	190	9-19-02	.267	.250	.273	8	15	3	4	1	0	0	4	5	2	0	1	2	0	0	.333	.478
2-team total (14 DSL TEX Red)					.196	.111	.216	22	46	6	9	1	1	0	6	9	4	0	1	8	0	0	.261	.367
Marcos Torres	L-L	6-3	163	9-30-04	.282	.278	.283	53	181	34	51	9	3	6	33	26	9	0	2	43	13	6	.464	.394
Echedry Vargas	R-R	5-11	170	2-27-05	.301	.409	.270	54	196	40	59	19	5	4	27	13	10	0	4	27	13	5	.510	.368
Oliver Yan	R-R	5-11	155	3-7-05	.065	.125	.043	19	31	4	2	0	1	0	2	0	0	0	0	16	1	1	.129	.065

Pitching	B-T	HT	WT	DOB	W	L	ERA	G	GS	CG	SV	IP	H	R	ER	HR	BB	SO	AVG	vLH	vRH	K/9	BB/9
Ismael Agreda	R-R	6-0	150	10-8-03	1	0	1.80	1	1	0	0	5	0	1	1	0	1	4	.000	.000	.000	7.20	1.80
Jordy Arias	R-R	5-11	185	8-4-05	0	1	2.57	4	3	0	0	14	6	5	4	1	15	16	.136	.375	.083	10.29	9.64
2-team total (5 DSL TEX Red)					2	1	1.41	9	8	1	0	38	15	8	6	1	27	46	.121	.224	.053	10.80	6.34
Wilian Bormie	R-R	6-3	175	2-23-03	0	0	2.57	4	4	0	0	7	3	2	2	1	4	10	.143	.091	.200	12.86	5.14
Biembenido Brito	R-R	6-3	180	2-13-03	1	1	3.63	9	9	0	0	35	23	16	14	2	21	55	.185	.245	.147	14.28	5.45
Enyer Burgos	R-R	6-0	175	6-15-02	0	2	22.09	5	1	0	0	4	8	9	9	0	9	8	.400	.625	.250	19.64	22.09

2-team total (7 DSL TEX Red)					0	6	11.65	12	5	0	0	17	22	25	22	0	24	25	.310	.261	.333	13.24	12.71
Leandro Calderon	R-R	6-1	200	6-17-02	1	1	1.69	9	7	0	0	32	14	7	6	1	16	59	.127	.140	.119	16.59	4.50
2-team total (1 DSL TEX Red)					1	1	1.83	10	7	0	0	34	15	8	7	1	18	63	.127	.128	.127	16.51	4.72
Remy Cesar	R-R	5-11	182	7-11-03	2	3	7.56	11	0	0	0	17	12	15	14	1	16	21	.211	.158	.237	11.34	8.64
2-team total (7 DSL TEX Red)					2	5	8.42	18	0	0	0	26	19	28	24	1	32	25	.213	.194	.224	8.77	11.22
Wilfredo Cordero	R-R	6-2	190	9-30-02	1	1	10.80	8	1	0	1	10	8	14	12	0	17	16	.235	.250	.227	14.40	15.30
2-team total (13 DSL TEX Red)					2	4	9.72	21	1	0	1	25	19	34	27	0	39	34	.211	.212	.211	12.24	14.04
Hayrol Done	R-R	6-2	175	6-30-03	1	0	3.00	3	0	0	0	6	1	2	2	0	5	2	.063	.000	.083	3.00	7.50
2-team total (17 DSL TEX Red)					3	1	4.45	20	0	0	1	32	20	24	16	1	29	23	.180	.205	.167	6.40	8.07
Sebastian Duenas	L-L	6-0	155	5-29-02	1	0	5.23	6	1	0	0	10	6	6	6	1	9	13	.171	.000	.214	11.32	7.84
2-team total (4 DSL TEX Red)					1	0	11.30	10	1	0	0	14	16	22	18	4	13	17	.271	.235	.286	10.67	8.16
Dianye Florentino	R-R	6-4	200	1-7-00	2	0	1.45	21	0	0	10	31	19	10	5	1	14	38	.181	.163	.194	11.03	4.06
2-team total (1 DSL TEX Red)					2	0	1.41	22	0	0	10	32	19	10	5	1	14	39	.176	.159	.188	10.97	3.94
Nyan Hernandez	L-R	6-2	198	7-11-01	1	0	1.80	1	1	0	0	5	0	1	1	0	2	2	.000	.000	.000	3.60	3.60
2-team total (3 DSL TEX Red)					3	0	1.23	4	4	0	0	22	4	3	3	1	9	17	.060	.048	.065	6.95	3.68
Miguel Jorge	R-R	6-2	180	2-16-03	0	0	6.00	3	2	0	0	3	2	2	2	0	4	1	.182	.000	.250	3.00	12.00
Elis Leal	R-R	6-1	170	1-3-02	0	1	15.88	4	0	0	0	6	10	13	10	3	7	1	.345	.364	.333	1.59	11.12
Aneudis Mejia	R-R	5-11	165	12-13-03	2	0	1.17	4	0	0	0	8	7	3	1	0	5	9	.241	.375	.190	10.57	5.87
Peniel Mena	R-R	6-1	160	11-28-00	1	0	6.00	4	0	0	1	6	8	4	4	1	2	6	.333	.308	.364	9.00	3.00
Jesus Mosquera	R-R	6-3	185	7-8-02	1	0	29.25	6	2	0	0	4	5	15	13	0	14	5	.294	.429	.200	11.25	31.50
2-team total (3 DSL TEX Red)					1	1	45.69	9	2	0	0	4	9	25	22	0	24	5	.409	.375	.429	10.38	49.85
Wilkerman Munoz	R-R	6-3	185	11-27-02	2	2	3.21	9	6	0	0	34	27	15	12	1	15	29	.220	.200	.229	7.75	4.01
2-team total (3 DSL TEX Red)					2	2	2.79	12	9	0	0	48	40	18	15	2	18	44	.227	.213	.235	8.19	3.35
German Nunez	R-R	6-3	155	5-24-02	5	0	4.55	17	0	0	2	28	25	15	14	0	7	37	.229	.167	.269	12.04	2.28
Wilker Palma	R-R	6-1	170	5-8-02	0	1	4.50	9	0	0	0	14	9	9	7	1	10	19	.176	.286	.100	12.21	6.43
2-team total (9 DSL TEX Red)					0	4	6.34	18	3	0	1	33	30	27	23	5	22	41	.244	.306	.203	11.30	6.06
Deretd Parra	R-R	6-3	160	6-18-00	4	1	1.78	12	4	0	0	35	20	8	7	0	11	37	.161	.140	.176	9.42	2.80
2-team total (3 DSL TEX Red)					4	3	1.87	15	6	0	0	43	28	11	9	0	13	45	.182	.177	.185	9.35	2.70
Juan Peralta	L-L	5-11	180	8-29-05	0	0	6.75	2	0	0	0	1	4	1	1	0	1	1	.500	1.000	.200	6.75	6.75
Eward Rodriguez	R-R	--	--	9-19-03	2	1	2.42	11	2	0	0	26	27	9	7	0	8	23	.267	.154	.307	7.96	2.77
2-team total (6 DSL TEX Red)					3	3	3.95	17	5	0	0	41	43	23	18	0	13	41	.272	.217	.295	9.00	2.85
Geury Rodriguez	L-L	6-0	155	10-20-04	0	0	0.00	1	0	0	0	1	1	0	0	0	0	1	.250	--	.250	9.00	0.00
2-team total (14 DSL TEX Red)					1	0	8.84	15	1	0	0	19	25	19	19	1	14	29	.325	.154	.359	13.50	6.52
Victor Simeon	R-R	6-2	160	12-4-00	3	1	3.83	10	9	0	0	42	32	19	18	1	25	45	.213	.313	.167	9.57	5.31
Danery Tejada	R-R	6-0	180	10-21-02	1	0	1.64	11	1	0	3	22	16	5	4	0	4	22	.208	.182	.227	9.00	1.64
2-team total (1 DSL TEX Red)					1	0	1.57	12	1	0	3	23	17	5	4	0	5	22	.213	.194	.227	8.61	1.96
Gabriel Torres	L-L	5-11	165	3-14-01	0	0	1.69	2	1	0	0	5	4	1	1	0	4	7	.200	.000	.235	11.81	6.75
2-team total (10 DSL TEX Red)					2	5	4.18	12	9	0	0	47	51	36	22	3	12	57	.259	.205	.272	10.84	2.28
Rayner Urbaez	R-R	6-0	175	2-13-03	2	2	1.89	16	1	0	1	38	23	10	8	1	10	54	.169	.159	.174	12.79	2.37
Jesus Valdez	R-R	6-2	175	5-3-01	3	1	0.55	5	0	0	0	16	7	5	1	1	4	19	.125	.111	.132	10.47	2.20
2-team total (12 DSL TEX Red)					4	3	0.91	17	1	0	1	40	26	18	4	1	9	41	.174	.151	.188	9.30	2.04
Adonis Villavicencio	R-R	6-2	200	12-22-00	1	0	2.45	7	0	0	0	11	10	3	3	0	4	13	.244	.333	.174	10.64	3.27
2-team total (11 DSL TEX Red)					1	1	5.04	18	0	0	1	25	19	15	14	1	20	36	.218	.313	.164	12.96	7.20
Jose Viola	R-R	6-0	175	4-25-01	2	0	1.74	5	3	0	0	21	13	5	4	2	8	26	.181	.115	.217	11.32	3.48
2-team total (10 DSL TEX Red)					3	1	2.32	15	3	0	2	31	22	10	8	2	11	36	.198	.158	.219	10.45	3.19
Oliver Yan	R-R	5-11	155	3-7-05	0	0	0.00	1	0	0	0	1	1	0	0	0	0	0	.333	.000	.500	0.00	0.00

Fielding

C: Beato 6, Bruzual 31, Espinoza 10, Ojeda Jr. 13, Romero 8. **1B:** Beato 1, Espinoza 3, Lemos 33, Marquez 17, Ojeda Jr. 6, Torres 12. **2B:** Lemos 5, Marquez 15, Pavon 25, Pinto 12, Vargas 11. **3B:** Lemos 2, Marquez 6, Pavon 17, Pinto 25, Vargas 11. **SS:** Lemos 2, Marquez 9, Pavon 13, Pinto 14, Vargas 26. **OF:** Alvarez 1, Basabe 36, Cabrera 20, De Jesus 49, Mendez 40, Pena 7, Torres 33, Yan 15.

DSL TEX RED — ROOKIE

DOMINICAN SUMMER LEAGUE

Batting	B-T	HT	WT	DOB	AVG	vLH	vRH	G	AB	R	H	2B	3B	HR	RBI	BB	HBP	SH	SF	SO	SB	CS	SLG	OBP
Erick Alvarez	R-R	5-10	150	2-1-05	.296	.364	.281	51	186	31	55	8	4	4	22	15	6	0	0	26	15	6	.446	.367
2-team total (1 DSL TEX Blue)					.294	.364	.279	52	187	31	55	8	4	4	22	15	6	0	0	26	15	6	.444	.365
Yeremi Cabrera	L-L	5-11	155	7-2-05	.179	.133	.191	47	140	22	25	3	3	2	12	26	5	1	0	29	11	3	.286	.327
Juan Diaz	R-R	6-2	180	1-9-04	.253	.226	.259	46	166	23	42	7	3	2	16	10	4	0	2	19	12	5	.367	.308
Freddy Espinal	L-L	6-0	155	5-21-05	.161	.000	.200	15	31	4	5	0	1	0	0	4	1	0	0	9	0	2	.226	.278
Jaiker Garcia	R-R	6-4	175	12-23-04	.174	.182	.171	39	92	14	16	3	1	0	1	14	2	0	0	40	8	4	.228	.296
Cristian Gonzalez	R-R	6-0	160	2-14-05	.259	.244	.263	51	197	23	51	13	0	4	22	13	6	0	2	34	3	4	.386	.321
Anthony Gutierrez	R-R	6-3	180	11-25-04	.352	.444	.329	23	91	22	32	8	0	3	16	8	2	0	2	18	5	3	.538	.408
Francisco Laya	R-R	6-0	160	10-9-03	.206	.138	.231	39	107	19	22	4	0	1	11	26	4	0	1	26	8	5	.271	.377
Jesus Lopez	L-R	6-1	180	5-24-05	.229	.222	.231	37	109	13	25	8	0	3	16	22	4	0	2	17	4	3	.385	.372
2-team total (1 DSL TEX Blue)					.236	.222	.239	38	110	13	26	8	0	3	17	22	4	0	2	17	4	3	.391	.377
Elian Lozano	R-R	5-11	175	1-2-03	.167	.750	.077	12	30	4	5	0	0	0	2	10	2	0	0	12	2	0	.167	.405
Rafael Marcano	R-R	5-11	165	2-26-02	.180	.083	.204	21	61	6	11	2	1	1	6	7	3	0	0	16	1	1	.295	.296
Gedionne Marlin	R-R	0-0	0	2-5-04	.240	.205	.250	52	167	23	40	13	3	1	23	19	4	0	1	44	5	4	.371	.330
Esteban Mejia	R-R	5-11	165	11-3-04	.267	.333	.248	34	131	20	35	8	3	0	18	10	3	0	1	16	15	1	.374	.331
Miguel Ojeda Jr.	R-R	6-0	200	6-16-00	.333	.143	.400	11	27	4	9	3	0	0	8	5	1	0	1	4	0	1	.444	.441
2-team total (20 DSL TEX Blue)					.300	.294	.302	31	70	8	21	6	0	0	11	11	1	0	2	10	0	1	.386	.393
Hector Osorio	L-L	6-0	150	4-6-05	.276	.000	.308	9	29	2	8	1	0	0	3	8	2	0	0	6	1	1	.310	.462
Joselin Payano	R-R	6-1	160	12-28-04	.176	.200	.170	28	68	6	12	2	0	1	5	11	1	0	1	16	0	2	.250	.296

Hector Pinero	B-R	5-11	155	1-12-03	.158	.167	.156	14	38	7	6	0	0	0	2	5	1	0	0	19	1	0	.158	.273
Josue Romero	R-R	5-9	190	9-19-02	.161	.000	.192	14	31	3	5	0	1	0	2	4	2	0	0	6	0	0	.226	.297
2-team total (8 DSL TEX Blue)					.196	.111	.216	22	46	6	9	1	1	0	6	9	4	0	1	8	0	0	.261	.367
Jeremy Santana	R-R	6-3	180	1-24-04	.214	.208	.216	35	112	9	24	4	0	0	9	18	2	0	0	41	16	5	.250	.333
Yeferson Tineo	B-R	6-0	160	10-10-03	.210	.294	.193	33	100	15	21	2	0	0	11	17	2	0	1	27	7	2	.230	.333

Pitching	B-T	HT	WT	DOB	W	L	ERA	G	GS	CG	SV	IP	H	R	ER	HR	BB	SO	AVG	vLH	vRH	K/9	BB/9
Gerson Angulo	R-R	6-1	180	7-26-02	2	1	5.40	11	2	0	2	13	11	9	8	1	10	26	.224	.125	.273	17.55	6.75
Jordy Arias	R-R	5-11	185	8-4-03	2	0	0.74	5	5	1	0	24	9	3	2	0	12	30	.113	.195	.026	11.10	4.44
2-team total (4 DSL TEX Blue)					2	1	1.41	9	8	1	0	38	15	8	6	1	27	46	.121	.224	.053	10.80	6.34
Yeimison Arias	R-R	6-1	165	1-9-05	1	0	2.76	6	3	0	0	16	12	7	5	0	7	13	.197	.227	.179	7.16	3.86
Julio Ayola	R-R	6-3	173	4-8-02	0	0	7.88	4	0	0	0	8	6	8	7	2	4	5	.207	.364	.111	5.63	4.50
Yefris Baptiste	L-L	6-2	175	11-23-02	1	1	12.96	8	0	0	1	8	7	12	12	1	10	12	.219	.200	.222	12.96	10.80
Enyer Burgos	R-R	6-0	175	6-15-02	0	4	8.78	7	4	0	0	13	14	16	13	0	15	17	.275	.067	.361	11.48	10.13
2-team total (5 DSL TEX Blue)					0	6	11.65	12	5	0	0	17	22	25	22	0	24	25	.310	.261	.333	13.24	12.71
Leandro Calderon	R-R	6-1	200	6-17-02	0	0	3.86	1	0	0	0	2	1	1	1	0	2	4	.125	.000	.250	15.43	7.71
2-team total (9 DSL TEX Blue)					1	1	1.83	10	7	0	0	34	15	8	7	1	18	63	.127	.128	.127	16.51	4.72
Remy Cesar	R-R	5-11	182	7-11-03	0	2	10.00	7	0	0	0	9	7	13	10	0	16	4	.219	.250	.200	4.00	16.00
2-team total (11 DSL TEX Blue)					2	5	8.42	18	0	0	0	26	19	28	24	1	32	25	.213	.194	.224	8.77	11.22
Bawin Colon	R-R	6-3	215	4-14-02	0	0	7.36	3	0	0	0	4	3	3	3	0	5	4	.231	.250	.222	9.82	12.27
Wilfredo Cordero	R-R	6-2	190	9-30-02	1	3	9.00	13	0	0	0	15	11	20	15	0	22	18	.196	.190	.200	10.80	13.20
2-team total (8 DSL TEX Blue)					2	4	9.72	21	1	0	1	25	19	34	27	0	39	34	.211	.212	.211	12.24	14.04
David Davalillo	R-R	6-1	175	9-21-02	0	0	13.50	2	0	0	0	2	3	3	3	1	1	0	.333	.500	.200	0.00	4.50
Hayrol Done	R-R	6-2	175	6-30-03	2	1	4.78	17	0	0	1	26	19	22	14	1	24	21	.200	.229	.183	7.18	8.20
2-team total (3 DSL TEX Blue)					3	1	4.45	20	0	0	1	32	20	24	16	1	29	23	.180	.205	.167	6.40	8.07
Sebastian Duenas	L-L	6-0	155	5-29-02	0	0	27.00	4	0	0	0	4	10	16	12	3	4	4	.417	.400	.429	9.00	9.00
2-team total (6 DSL TEX Blue)					1	0	11.30	10	1	0	0	14	16	22	18	4	13	17	.271	.235	.286	10.67	8.16
Jose Estrada	R-R	6-1	155	3-31-01	0	1	5.06	17	0	0	0	32	21	20	18	2	25	37	.186	.238	.155	10.41	7.03
Dianye Florentino	R-R	6-4	200	1-7-00	0	0	0.00	1	0	0	0	1	0	0	0	0	0	1	.000	.000	.000	9.00	0.00
2-team total (21 DSL TEX Blue)					2	0	1.41	22	0	0	10	32	19	10	5	1	14	39	.176	.159	.188	10.97	3.94
Jaiker Garcia	R-R	6-4	175	12-23-04	0	0	0.00	1	0	0	0	1	1	0	0	0	0	1	.250	.000	.333	6.75	0.00
Orlando Gil	R-R	6-3	165	9-10-01	1	3	2.18	13	7	0	0	45	36	17	11	2	22	53	.216	.213	.217	10.52	4.37
Nyan Hernandez	L-R	6-2	198	7-11-01	2	0	1.06	3	3	0	0	17	4	2	2	1	7	15	.077	.056	.088	7.94	3.71
2-team total (1 DSL TEX Blue)					3	0	1.23	4	4	0	0	22	4	3	3	1	9	17	.060	.048	.065	6.95	3.68
Emmanuel Martinez	L-L	6-1	170	8-28-03	0	1	6.49	8	8	0	0	26	32	21	19	0	18	44	.299	.440	.256	15.04	6.15
Brayan Mendoza	L-L	6-0	155	1-19-04	1	2	1.23	5	5	0	0	22	7	3	3	0	12	26	.101	.125	.098	10.64	4.91
Jesus Mosquera	R-R	6-3	185	7-8-02	0	1	243.00	3	0	0	0	0	4	10	9	0	10	0	.800	.000	1.000	0.00	270.00
2-team total (6 DSL TEX Blue)					1	1	45.69	9	2	0	0	4	9	25	22	0	24	5	.409	.375	.429	10.38	49.85
Wilkerman Munoz	R-R	6-3	185	11-27-02	0	0	1.84	3	3	0	0	15	13	3	3	1	3	15	.245	.238	.250	9.20	1.84
2-team total (9 DSL TEX Blue)					2	2	2.79	12	9	0	0	48	40	18	15	2	18	44	.227	.213	.235	8.19	3.35
Miguel Ojeda Jr.	R-R	6-0	200	6-16-00	0	0	23.63	1	0	0	0	3	9	7	7	2	1	1	.529	.571	.500	3.38	3.38
Wilker Palma	R-R	6-1	170	5-8-02	0	3	7.71	9	3	0	1	19	21	18	16	4	12	22	.292	.321	.273	10.61	5.79
2-team total (9 DSL TEX Blue)					0	4	6.34	18	3	0	1	33	30	27	23	5	22	41	.244	.306	.203	11.30	6.06
Deretd Parra	R-R	6-3	160	6-18-00	0	2	2.25	3	2	0	0	8	8	3	2	0	2	8	.267	.333	.222	9.00	2.25
2-team total (12 DSL TEX Blue)					4	3	1.87	15	6	0	0	43	28	11	9	0	13	45	.182	.177	.185	9.35	2.70
Hector Pinero	B-R	5-11	155	1-12-03	0	0	0.00	1	0	0	0	0	1	0	0	0	1	0	.500	.500	--	0.00	27.00
Eward Rodriguez	R-R	--	--	9-19-03	1	2	6.60	6	3	0	0	15	16	14	11	0	5	18	.281	.300	.270	10.80	3.00
2-team total (11 DSL TEX Blue)					3	3	3.95	17	5	0	0	41	43	23	18	0	13	41	.272	.217	.295	9.00	2.85
Geury Rodriguez	L-L	6-0	155	10-20-04	1	0	9.33	14	1	0	0	18	24	19	19	1	14	28	.329	.154	.367	13.75	6.87
2-team total (1 DSL TEX Blue)					1	0	8.84	15	1	0	0	19	25	19	19	1	14	29	.325	.154	.359	13.50	6.52
Danery Tejada	R-R	6-0	180	10-21-02	0	0	0.00	1	0	0	0	1	1	0	0	0	1	0	.333	.333	--	0.00	9.00
2-team total (11 DSL TEX Blue)					1	0	1.57	12	1	0	3	23	17	5	4	0	5	22	.213	.194	.227	8.61	1.96
Gabriel Torres	L-L	5-11	165	3-14-01	2	5	4.50	10	8	0	0	42	47	35	21	3	8	50	.266	.222	.277	10.71	1.71
2-team total (2 DSL TEX Blue)					2	5	4.18	12	9	0	0	47	51	36	22	3	12	57	.259	.205	.272	10.84	2.28
Jose Felipe Torres	R-R	5-10	150	10-17-04	2	3	2.01	18	2	0	2	45	39	18	10	2	7	41	.232	.276	.209	8.26	1.41
Jesus Valdez	R-R	6-2	175	5-3-01	1	2	1.16	12	1	0	1	23	19	13	3	0	5	22	.204	.171	.224	8.49	1.93
2-team total (5 DSL TEX Blue)					4	3	0.91	17	1	0	1	40	26	18	4	1	9	41	.174	.151	.188	9.30	2.04
Adonis Villavicencio	R-R	6-2	200	12-22-00	0	1	7.07	11	0	0	1	14	9	12	11	1	16	23	.196	.286	.156	14.79	10.29
2-team total (7 DSL TEX Blue)					1	1	5.04	18	0	0	1	25	19	15	14	1	20	36	.218	.313	.164	12.96	7.20
Jose Viola	R-R	6-0	175	4-25-01	1	1	3.48	10	0	0	2	10	9	5	4	0	3	10	.231	.250	.222	8.71	2.61
2-team total (5 DSL TEX Blue)					3	1	2.32	15	3	0	2	31	22	10	8	2	11	36	.198	.158	.219	10.45	3.19

Fielding

C: Lopez 24, Marcano 17, Ojeda Jr. 10, Payano 7, Romero 14. **1B:** Diaz 18, Garcia 14, Lozano 8, Payano 15, Pinero 1, Santana 15, Tineo 1. **2B:** Garcia 6, Gonzalez 13, Marlin 2, Mejia 18, Payano 1, Pinero 10, Tineo 19. **3B:** Garcia 10, Gonzalez 5, Marlin 49, Mejia 2, Tineo 1. **SS:** Garcia 5, Gonzalez 32, Mejia 15, Pinero 1, Tineo 12. **OF:** Alvarez 31, Cabrera 46, Diaz 31, Espinal 5, Gutierrez 19, Laya 39, Osorio 6, Payano 1, Santana 16.

Toronto Blue Jays

SEASON IN A SENTENCE: The Blue Jays finished second in a highly competitive AL East with a record of 92-70, but their season ended at the hands of Mariners as the Jays were swept during the three game wild card series.

HIGH POINT: The Blue Jays ripped off an eight-game winning streak from May 23rd until June 2nd as they swept the Angels and White Sox in the process.

LOW POINT: Following their eight-game winning streak the Blue Jays free-falled for the next month going 15-22 between June 3rd and July 10th. On July 11th the Blue Jays were 16.5 games out of first place in the AL East.

NOTABLE ROOKIES: The Blue Jays relied on a veteran core in 2022 more than in previous seasons. While the Blue Jays top prospect catcher Gabriel Moreno made his debut last summer, he featured in just 25 games, a majority of which came during the final month of the season. The Blue Jays saw players like Vinny Capra and Otto López make their major league debuts, but in short term fill-in roles.

KEY TRANSACTIONS: The Blue Jays signed veteran righthander Kevin Gausman to a five-year contract worth $110 million before the lockout. In the days following the ratification of the new Collective Bargaining Agreement, the Blue Jays got back to work. They shipped their 2021 first-round pick Gunnar Hoglund and two other prospects to the Athletics in exchange for third baseman Matt Chapman. The Blue Jays were one of the more active teams at the trade deadline completing four separate trades leading up to the deadline. The biggest of that quartet being the acquisition of former All-Star second baseman Whit Merrifield from the Royals.

ON THE FARM: Top prospect Gabriel Moreno maintained his status as one of the top catching prospects in the game. Third-round pick Ricky Tiedemann blossomed into one of the best lefthanded pitching prospects in baseball cementing his place among the Top 100 Prospects in the game. While sixth rounder Hayden Junger broke camp with Double-A New Hampshire and is in line to make his major league debut in 2023. After injury plagued seasons in the organization Cuban righthander Yosver Zulueta proved to be a legitimate prospect, starting his season in Low-A Dunedin and climbing to Triple-A Buffalo by year's end.

OPENING DAY PAYROLL: $170,074,000 (11th).

PLAYERS OF THE YEAR

MAJOR LEAGUE

Alek Manoah
RHP
16-7, 2.24 ERA
180 SO, 51 BB, 197 IP
Third in AL ERA race

MINOR LEAGUE

Ricky Tiedemann
LHP
(LoA/HiA/AA)
.2.17 ERA, 0.86 WHIP
117 SO, 29 BB, 79 IP

ORGANIZATION LEADERS

Batting		*Minimum 250 AB
MAJORS		
* AVG	Lourdes Gurriel	.291
* OPS	Vladimir Guerrero Jr.	.818
HR	Vladimir Guerrero Jr.	32
RBI	Vladimir Guerrero Jr.	97
MINORS		
* AVG	Addison Barger, Vancouver., N. Hampshire, Buffalo	.308
* OBP	Tanner Morris, New Hampshire, Buffalo	.399
* SLG	Addison Barger, Vancouver., N. Hampshire, Buffalo	.555
* OPS	Addison Barger, Vancouver., N. Hampshire, Buffalo	.933
R	Addison Barger, Vancouver., N. Hampshire, Buffalo	80
H	Addison Barger, Vancouver., N. Hampshire, Buffalo	144
TB	Addison Barger, Vancouver., N. Hampshire, Buffalo	259
2B	Rafael Lantigua, New Hampshire, Buffalo	35
3B	Steward Berroa, Vancouver, New Hampshire	7
HR	Orelvis Martinez, New Hampshire	30
RBI	Addison Barger, Vancouver., N. Hampshire, Buffalo	91
BB	Spencer Horwitz, New Hampshire, Buffalo	73
SO	Sebastian Espino, New Hampshire	166
SB	Steward Berroa, Vancouver, New Hampshire	47

Pitching		#Minimum 75 IP
MAJORS		
W	Alek Manoah	16
# ERA	Alek Manoah	2.24
SO	Kevin Gausman	205
SV	Jordan Romano	36
MINORS		
W	Andrew Bash, New Hampshire, Buffalo	10
L	Bowden Francis, Buffalo	10
# ERA	Ricky Tiedemann, Dunedin, Vancouver, N. Hampshire	2.24
G	Kyle Johnston, Buffalo	49
GS	Adam Kloffenstein, Vancouver, New Hampshire	24
SV	Matt Gage, Buffalo	12
IP	Thomas Hatch, Buffalo	131
BB	Adam Kloffenstein, Vancouver, New Hampshire	55
SO	Dahian Santos, Dunedin, Vancouver	142
# AVG	Casey Lawrence, Buffalo	.205

2022 PERFORMANCE

General Manager: Ross Atkins. **Farm Director:** Charlie Wilson. **Scouting Director:** Shane Farrell.

Class	Team	League	W	L	PCT	Finish	Manager
Majors	Toronto Blue Jays	American	92	70	.568	4th (15)	C. Montoyo/J. Schneider
Triple-A	Buffalo Bisons	International	76	72	.514	t-7th (20)	C. Candaele/J. Ware
Double-A	New Hampshire Fisher Cats	Eastern	59	79	.428	10th (12)	Cesar Martin
High-A	Vancouver Canadians	Northwest	67	62	.519	2nd (6)	Brent Lavallee
Low-A	Dunedin Blue Jays	Florida State	66	63	.512	5th (10)	Donnie Murphy
Rookie	FCL Blue Jays	Florida Complex	28	27	.509	8th (16)	Jose Mayorga
Overall 2022 Minor League Record			314	341	.479	23rd (30)	

ORGANIZATION STATISTICS

TORONTO BLUE JAYS

AMERICAN LEAGUE

Batting	B-T	HT	WT	DOB	AVG	vLH	vRH	G	AB	R	H	2B	3B	HR	RBI	BB	HBP	SH	SF	SO	SB	CS	SLG	OBP
Bo Bichette	R-R	6-0	190	3-5-98	.290	.262	.295	159	652	91	189	43	1	24	93	41	2	0	2	155	13	8	.469	.333
Cavan Biggio	L-R	6-2	200	4-11-95	.202	.150	.212	97	257	43	52	18	1	6	24	38	6	1	1	85	2	0	.350	.318
Jackie Bradley Jr.	L-R	5-10	196	4-19-90	.178	.250	.151	40	73	9	13	4	0	1	9	7	0	0	0	19	0	0	.274	.250
2-team total (92 Boston Red Sox)					.203	.164	.214	132	344	30	70	23	1	4	38	24	0	2	0	77	2	3	.311	.255
Vinny Capra	R-R	5-8	175	7-7-96	.200	.200	--	8	5	2	1	0	0	0	0	2	0	0	0	1	0	0	.200	.429
Matt Chapman	R-R	6-0	215	4-28-93	.229	.245	.225	155	538	83	123	27	1	27	76	68	10	0	5	170	2	2	.433	.324
Zack Collins	L-R	6-3	220	2-6-95	.194	.182	.197	26	72	7	14	4	0	4	10	6	1	0	0	31	0	0	.417	.266
Santiago Espinal	R-R	5-10	187	11-13-94	.267	.301	.256	135	449	51	120	25	0	7	51	36	2	1	3	68	6	6	.370	.322
Vladimir Guerrero	R-R	6-2	240	3-16-99	.274	.245	.280	160	638	90	175	35	0	32	97	58	6	0	4	116	8	3	.480	.339
Lourdes Gurriel Jr.	R-R	6-4	215	10-10-93	.291	.278	.295	121	453	52	132	32	1	5	52	31	6	0	2	83	3	4	.400	.343
Tyler Heineman	B-R	5-10	190	6-19-91	.267	.000	.500	10	15	2	4	2	0	0	1	0	0	1	0	4	0	0	.400	.267
Teoscar Hernandez	R-R	6-2	215	10-15-92	.267	.286	.262	131	499	71	133	35	1	25	77	34	2	0	0	152	6	3	.491	.316
Danny Jansen	R-R	6-2	215	4-15-95	.260	.226	.272	72	215	34	56	10	0	15	44	25	3	0	5	44	1	0	.516	.339
Gosuke Katoh	L-R	6-1	200	10-8-94	.143	.000	.167	8	7	2	1	1	0	0	0	3	0	1	0	1	0	0	.286	.400
Alejandro Kirk	R-R	5-8	245	11-6-98	.285	.276	.288	139	470	59	134	19	0	14	63	63	4	0	4	58	0	0	.415	.372
Otto Lopez	R-R	5-10	185	10-1-98	.667	1.000	.500	8	9	0	6	0	0	0	3	1	0	0	0	1	0	1	.667	.700
Whit Merrifield	R-R	6-1	195	1-24-89	.281	.233	.297	44	121	19	34	5	0	5	16	8	0	0	1	24	1	2	.446	.323
Gabriel Moreno	R-R	5-11	195	2-14-00	.319	.333	.313	25	69	10	22	1	0	1	7	4	0	0	0	8	0	0	.377	.356
George Springer	R-R	6-3	220	9-19-89	.267	.252	.271	133	513	89	137	22	4	25	76	54	7	0	5	100	14	2	.472	.342
Raimel Tapia	L-L	6-3	175	2-4-94	.265	.262	.266	128	411	47	109	20	3	7	52	16	0	3	1	81	8	2	.380	.292
Bradley Zimmer	L-R	6-4	185	11-27-92	.101	.077	.111	100	89	14	9	4	0	2	5	5	6	1	0	41	3	2	.213	.200

Pitching	B-T	HT	WT	DOB	W	L	ERA	G	GS	CG	SV	IP	H	R	ER	HR	BB	SO	AVG	vLH	vRH	K/9	BB/9
Shaun Anderson	R-R	6-6	228	10-29-94	0	0	18.00	1	0	0	0	1	4	2	2	0	0	0	.667	.500	.750	0.00	0.00
Anthony Banda	L-L	6-2	220	8-10-93	0	1	4.26	7	1	0	0	6	7	3	3	1	3	7	.292	.250	.333	9.95	4.26
2-team total (2 New York Yankees)					0	1	7.71	9	1	0	0	7	9	6	6	1	8	8	.321	.231	.400	10.29	10.29
Anthony Bass	R-R	6-2	205	11-1-87	2	0	1.75	28	0	0	0	26	19	5	5	5	10	28	.207	.281	.167	9.82	3.51
Jeremy Beasley	R-R	6-2	235	11-20-95	0	0	4.80	9	0	0	0	15	14	9	8	4	5	19	.250	.182	.294	11.40	3.00
Jose Berrios	R-R	6-0	205	5-27-94	12	7	5.23	32	32	0	0	172	199	103	100	29	45	149	.288	.298	.276	7.80	2.35
Ryan Borucki	L-L	6-4	210	3-31-94	0	0	9.95	11	0	0	0	6	7	7	7	2	5	8	.269	.133	.455	11.37	7.11
2-team total (21 Seattle Mariners)					2	0	5.68	32	0	0	0	25	24	16	16	6	11	21	.247	.184	.313	7.46	3.91
Max Castillo	R-R	6-2	280	5-4-99	0	0	3.05	9	2	0	0	21	15	9	7	4	5	20	.197	.237	.158	8.71	2.18
2-team total (5 Kansas City Royals)					0	2	5.95	14	6	0	0	39	38	28	26	8	15	37	.252	.259	.242	8.47	3.43
Adam Cimber	R-R	6-3	195	8-15-90	10	6	2.80	77	0	0	4	71	66	28	22	6	13	58	.248	.214	.270	7.39	1.66
Bowden Francis	R-R	6-5	220	4-22-96	0	0	0.00	1	0	0	0	1	1	0	0	0	0	1	.333	.000	.500	13.50	0.00
Matt Gage	L-L	6-3	265	2-11-93	0	1	1.38	11	0	0	0	13	6	4	2	1	6	12	.146	.000	.188	8.31	4.15
Yimi Garcia	R-R	6-1	230	8-18-90	4	5	3.10	61	0	0	1	61	48	26	21	6	16	58	.215	.222	.211	8.56	2.36
Kevin Gausman	L-R	6-2	205	1-6-91	12	10	3.35	31	31	0	0	175	188	72	65	15	28	205	.272	.244	.292	10.56	1.44
Foster Griffin	R-L	6-3	225	7-27-95	0	0	0.00	1	0	0	0	2	1	0	0	0	1	2	.143	.000	.250	9.00	4.50
2-team total (5 Kansas City Royals)					0	0	8.53	6	0	0	0	6	7	7	6	0	5	4	.304	.125	.400	5.68	7.11
Thomas Hatch	R-R	6-1	195	9-29-94	0	1	19.29	1	1	0	0	5	12	10	10	3	2	4	.522	.333	.727	7.71	3.86
Anthony Kay	L-L	6-0	225	3-21-95	0	0	4.50	1	0	0	0	2	2	1	1	0	1	3	.286	.000	.333	13.50	4.50
Yusei Kikuchi	L-L	6-0	205	6-17-91	6	7	5.19	32	20	0	1	101	93	67	58	23	58	124	.243	.198	.256	11.09	5.19
Casey Lawrence	R-R	6-0	170	10-28-87	0	1	7.50	6	0	0	0	18	23	15	15	5	4	11	.315	.387	.262	5.50	2.00
Alek Manoah	R-R	6-6	285	1-9-98	16	7	2.24	31	31	0	0	197	144	55	49	16	51	180	.202	.237	.159	8.24	2.33
Tim Mayza	L-L	6-3	213	1-15-92	8	1	3.14	63	0	0	2	49	42	19	17	7	12	44	.237	.162	.291	8.14	2.22
Whit Merrifield	R-R	6-1	195	1-24-89	0	0	18.00	1	0	0	0	1	2	2	2	1	0	0	.400	.333	.500	0.00	0.00
Julian Merryweather	R-R	6-4	215	10-14-91	0	3	6.75	26	1	0	0	27	31	20	20	4	7	23	.292	.268	.308	7.76	2.36
David Phelps	R-R	6-2	200	10-9-86	0	2	2.83	65	1	0	1	64	52	22	20	2	31	64	.220	.225	.216	9.05	4.38
Zach Pop	R-R	6-4	220	9-20-96	2	0	1.89	17	0	0	0	19	18	4	4	1	2	11	.254	.281	.231	5.21	0.95
Trevor Richards	R-R	6-2	205	5-15-93	3	2	5.34	62	4	0	0	64	57	41	38	9	35	82	.238	.237	.238	11.53	4.92
Jordan Romano	R-R	6-5	210	4-21-93	5	4	2.11	63	0	0	36	64	44	18	15	4	21	73	.190	.202	.179	10.27	2.95

Sergio Romo	R-R	5-11	185	3-4-83	0	1	4.91	6	0	0	0	4	1	3	2	1	2	3	.083	.000	.111	7.36	4.91
2-team total (17 Seattle Mariners)					0	1	7.50	23	0	0	0	18	19	16	15	7	6	14	.268	.214	.302	7.00	3.00
Hyun Jin Ryu	R-L	6-3	250	3-25-87	2	0	5.67	6	6	0	0	27	32	17	17	5	4	16	.294	.222	.308	5.33	1.33
Tayler Saucedo	L-L	6-4	205	6-18-93	0	0	13.50	4	0	0	0	3	6	4	4	3	1	0	.429	.375	.500	0.00	3.38
Ross Stripling	R-R	6-1	215	11-23-89	10	4	3.01	32	24	0	1	134	117	49	45	12	20	111	.229	.215	.240	7.44	1.34
Trent Thornton	R-R	6-0	190	9-30-93	0	2	4.11	32	0	0	0	46	40	21	21	7	17	37	.237	.246	.231	7.24	3.33
Andrew Vasquez	L-L	6-6	235	9-14-93	0	0	8.10	9	0	0	0	7	6	6	6	1	3	6	.231	.273	.200	8.10	4.05
Mitch White	R-R	6-3	210	12-28-94	0	5	7.74	10	8	0	0	43	59	37	37	3	16	31	.321	.271	.364	6.49	3.35

Fielding

Catcher	PCT	G	PO	A	E	DP	PB
Collins	.986	11	64	6	1	0	0
Heineman	.982	9	50	4	1	0	0
Jansen	.987	63	501	18	7	3	1
Kirk	.996	78	655	31	3	7	1
Moreno	.986	19	134	12	2	1	0

First Base	PCT	G	PO	A	E	DP
Biggio	.992	33	221	13	2	20
Collins	1.000	1	3	0	0	0
Guerrero	.990	128	969	47	10	80
Gurriel Jr.	1.000	8	31	1	0	1
Katoh	1.000	3	17	0	0	1
Merrifield	1.000	2	4	0	0	0

Second Base	PCT	G	PO	A	E	DP
Biggio	.987	49	58	95	2	22
Capra	1.000	1	0	1	0	0
Espinal	.990	120	148	255	4	56
Katoh	1.000	2	1	3	0	1
Lopez	1.000	1	0	2	0	0
Merrifield	1.000	22	26	50	0	8
Moreno	.000	1	0	0	0	0

Third Base	PCT	G	PO	A	E	DP
Biggio	1.000	1	1	1	0	0
Chapman	.988	153	164	263	5	41
Espinal	.920	11	8	15	2	3
Guerrero	.000	1	0	0	0	0
Moreno	1.000	1	0	1	0	0

Shortstop	PCT	G	PO	A	E	DP
Bichette	.958	157	166	363	23	58
Espinal	1.000	11	6	15	0	2
Lopez	1.000	5	2	1	0	0

Outfield	PCT	G	PO	A	E	DP
Biggio	1.000	9	15	0	0	0
Bradley Jr.	.970	46	61	4	2	0
Capra	--	2	0	0	0	0
Gurriel Jr.	.985	105	185	7	3	2
Hernandez	.984	125	243	10	4	1
Lopez	--	1	0	0	0	0
Merrifield	1.000	24	34	0	0	0
Moreno	--	1	0	0	0	0
Springer	.995	112	191	6	1	2
Tapia	.987	134	217	4	3	0
Zimmer	.990	90	102	0	1	0

BUFFALO BISONS — *TRIPLE-A*

INTERNATIONAL LEAGUE

Batting	B-T	HT	WT	DOB	AVG	vLH	vRH	G	AB	R	H	2B	3B	HR	RBI	BB	HBP	SH	SF	SO	SB	CS	SLG	OBP
John Aiello	B-R	6-2	215	2-14-97	.235	.143	.259	10	34	5	8	1	0	0	3	4	3	0	1	10	0	0	.265	.357
Addison Barger	L-R	6-0	175	11-12-99	.355	.300	.381	8	31	8	11	1	0	3	9	5	0	0	0	5	0	1	.677	.444
Chris Bec	R-R	5-9	195	12-30-95	.185	.000	.238	11	27	4	5	1	0	0	0	8	0	0	0	8	1	0	.222	.371
Stevie Berman	R-R	6-2	225	11-28-94	.215	.203	.221	67	209	27	45	14	0	8	28	36	7	1	4	64	1	0	.397	.344
2-team total (1 St. Paul Saints)					.212	.203	.217	68	212	27	45	14	0	8	28	37	7	1	4	64	1	0	.392	.342
Cavan Biggio	L-R	6-2	200	4-11-95	.276	.571	.182	10	29	9	8	3	0	0	3	10	0	0	0	6	2	0	.379	.462
Vinny Capra	R-R	5-8	175	7-7-96	.283	.317	.267	52	191	31	54	6	1	5	28	29	1	0	1	29	5	2	.403	.378
Zack Collins	L-R	6-3	220	2-6-95	.195	.195	.195	36	118	15	23	7	1	5	28	32	1	0	4	40	3	0	.398	.361
2-team total (2 Indianapolis Indians)					.198	.195	.200	38	126	17	25	8	1	5	29	33	1	0	5	42	3	1	.397	.358
Luis De Los Santos	R-R	6-1	160	6-9-98	.067	.000	.077	5	15	0	1	1	0	0	0	1	0	0	0	3	1	0	.133	.125
Kellin Deglan	L-R	6-2	215	5-3-92	.111	.083	.116	25	81	3	9	3	0	0	4	7	0	0	0	26	2	1	.148	.182
Dexter Fowler	B-R	6-5	205	3-22-86	.417	.600	.286	3	12	5	5	0	0	0	3	2	0	0	1	2	0	0	.417	.467
Joshua Fuentes	R-R	6-2	209	2-19-93	.162	.267	.120	29	105	11	17	1	0	1	5	4	2	0	1	43	1	0	.200	.205
Juan Gonzalez	R-R	5-10	195	2-20-01	.000	--	.000	1	2	0	0	0	0	0	0	1	0	0	0	1	1	0	.000	.333
Jordan Groshans	R-R	6-3	200	11-10-99	.250	.254	.249	67	240	30	60	8	0	1	24	35	2	0	2	46	2	0	.296	.348
2-team total (31 Jacksonville Jumbo Shrimp)					.266	.278	.262	98	353	44	94	15	0	3	34	54	2	0	3	65	3	0	.334	.364
Tyler Heineman	B-R	5-10	190	6-19-91	.125	.500	.000	2	8	0	1	0	0	0	0	0	0	0	0	4	0	0	.125	.125
Spencer Horwitz	L-R	6-0	190	11-14-97	.246	.283	.229	44	171	31	42	14	0	2	12	30	1	0	0	41	4	1	.363	.361
Danny Jansen	R-R	6-2	215	4-15-95	.294	.400	.250	5	17	2	5	1	0	1	1	1	0	0	0	6	0	0	.529	.333
Gosuke Katoh	L-R	6-1	200	10-8-94	.000	.000	.000	1	5	0	0	0	0	0	2	0	0	0	0	1	0	0	.000	.000
2-team total (80 Syracuse Mets)					.219	.228	.215	81	292	42	64	15	2	9	34	32	4	1	0	73	7	1	.377	.305
Rafael Lantigua	R-R	5-8	153	4-28-98	.286	.286	.286	42	161	20	46	8	0	2	29	16	0	0	2	35	9	3	.373	.346
Cullen Large	B-R	6-1	175	1-22-96	.238	.304	.214	119	411	43	98	23	4	7	52	48	7	0	2	127	7	1	.365	.327
Otto Lopez	R-R	5-10	185	10-1-98	.297	.374	.266	91	340	53	101	19	6	3	34	41	5	2	3	61	14	5	.415	.378
Nathan Lukes	L-R	5-11	180	7-12-94	.285	.333	.268	111	428	62	122	25	1	11	61	47	7	0	2	89	20	3	.425	.364
Gabriel Moreno	R-R	5-11	195	2-14-00	.315	.380	.287	62	238	35	75	16	0	3	39	24	4	0	1	45	7	1	.420	.386
Tanner Morris	L-R	6-2	190	9-13-97	.173	.100	.192	31	98	8	17	0	0	0	7	25	2	1	0	25	0	2	.173	.352
Josh Palacios	L-R	6-1	200	7-30-95	.238	.167	.267	6	21	5	5	0	0	2	4	2	1	0	0	5	2	1	.524	.333
2-team total (76 Rochester Red Wings)					.294	.353	.270	82	296	48	87	12	2	9	48	35	6	2	1	55	21	8	.439	.379
Nick Podkul	R-R	6-1	200	4-11-97	.211	.283	.180	60	175	22	37	6	0	5	24	33	6	1	0	61	3	1	.331	.355
Jose Rivas	R-R	5-9	165	9-5-00	.000	.000	.000	3	4	0	0	0	0	0	0	0	0	0	0	2	0	0	.000	.000
Davis Schneider	R-R	5-10	190	1-26-99	.233	.214	.239	17	60	18	14	4	0	2	9	14	1	0	0	20	1	1	.400	.387
Trevor Schwecke	R-R	6-1	185	12-18-97	.206	.167	.216	19	63	10	13	2	1	3	11	6	0	0	1	19	0	2	.413	.271
Colton Shaver	R-R	6-1	249	9-18-95	.121	.286	.077	12	33	3	4	1	0	1	1	3	0	0	0	20	0	1	.242	.194
Mallex Smith	L-R	5-9	170	5-6-93	.195	.136	.218	25	77	15	15	1	0	0	5	13	1	0	0	23	11	2	.208	.319
Eric Stamets	R-R	6-0	183	9-25-91	.176	.185	.173	66	193	24	34	9	0	5	17	21	7	2	1	68	7	0	.301	.279
LJ Talley	L-R	6-2	203	5-7-97	.285	.219	.305	86	309	36	88	15	4	8	42	27	5	0	2	66	12	1	.437	.350
Samad Taylor	R-R	5-10	160	7-11-98	.258	.313	.237	70	244	41	63	10	2	9	45	28	3	1	4	62	23	5	.426	.337
Yoshi Tsutsugo	L-R	6-1	225	11-26-91	.265	.243	.279	29	98	15	26	4	0	5	18	19	0	0	1	38	0	1	.459	.381
2-team total (9 Indianapolis Indians)					.301	.267	.321	38	123	19	37	6	0	7	30	28	0	0	3	41	0	1	.520	.422
Logan Warmoth	R-R	6-0	195	9-6-95	.229	.253	.218	90	293	38	67	18	2	7	45	38	5	0	2	94	14	5	.375	.325
Chavez Young	B-R	6-0	200	7-8-97	.234	.212	.243	65	214	37	50	6	2	5	21	30	2	0	2	58	20	1	.350	.331

Pitching	B-T	HT	WT	DOB	W	L	ERA	G	GS	CG	SV	IP	H	R	ER	HR	BB	SO	AVG	vLH	vRH	K/9	BB/9
Nick Allgeyer	L-L	6-3	225	2-3-96	6	6	5.44	35	15	0	0	101	101	67	61	17	42	95	.255	.241	.265	8.47	3.74
Shaun Anderson	R-R	6-6	228	10-29-94	3	3	3.58	36	15	0	1	88	75	39	35	11	32	76	.225	.237	.213	7.77	3.27
Andrew Bash	R-R	6-0	190	8-1-96	0	2	5.85	7	3	0	0	20	18	14	13	3	10	13	.254	.184	.333	5.85	4.50
Jeremy Beasley	R-R	6-2	235	11-20-95	2	1	1.89	19	3	0	1	38	20	9	8	5	11	43	.153	.183	.127	10.18	2.61
2-team total (1 Indianapolis Indians)					2	1	2.61	20	3	0	1	38	22	12	11	5	12	43	.165	.197	.139	10.18	2.84
Joe Biagini	R-R	6-4	230	5-29-90	4	2	3.46	30	5	0	1	39	30	20	15	4	16	30	.210	.211	.208	6.92	3.69
Parker Caracci	R-R	6-0	205	9-13-96	0	0	0.00	4	0	0	0	3	0	0	0	0	2	2	.000	.000	.000	6.00	6.00
Max Castillo	R-R	6-2	280	5-4-99	2	0	0.66	5	3	0	0	27	10	2	2	2	10	29	.112	.053	.157	9.55	3.29
2-team total (7 Omaha Storm Chasers)					3	1	4.07	12	9	0	0	49	45	26	22	5	19	51	.239	.207	.264	9.43	3.51
Jose De Leon	R-R	6-0	220	8-7-92	0	0	4.35	8	5	0	0	10	10	8	5	2	7	15	.244	.318	.158	13.06	6.10
Brandon Eisert	L-L	6-2	205	1-18-98	4	3	3.41	45	5	0	0	61	54	29	23	8	15	77	.236	.222	.248	11.42	2.23
Mike Ellenbest	R-R	6-4	220	8-20-94	1	3	5.66	18	4	0	2	21	28	14	13	1	12	22	.318	.351	.294	9.58	5.23
Jake Elliott	R-R	6-7	230	3-22-95	1	1	6.00	14	1	0	0	18	25	13	12	5	6	15	.338	.400	.282	7.50	3.00
Bowden Francis	R-R	6-5	220	4-22-96	5	10	6.59	37	23	0	0	98	108	77	72	23	43	110	.278	.304	.255	10.07	3.94
Matt Gage	L-L	6-3	265	2-11-93	2	2	2.34	41	0	0	12	42	30	13	11	1	16	46	.197	.095	.295	9.78	3.40
Yimi Garcia	R-R	6-1	230	8-18-90	0	0	0.00	1	0	0	0	1	0	0	0	0	0	2	.000	.000	.000	18.00	0.00
Foster Griffin	R-L	6-3	225	7-27-95	2	0	2.31	18	0	0	1	23	21	6	6	1	9	25	.231	.214	.245	9.64	3.47
2-team total (20 Omaha Storm Chasers)					6	0	2.10	38	0	0	1	51	40	14	12	3	15	57	.208	.222	.198	9.99	2.63
Thomas Hatch	R-R	6-1	195	9-29-94	8	7	4.67	28	22	0	0	131	127	73	68	16	38	113	.253	.286	.221	7.76	2.61
Adrian Hernandez	R-R	5-8	190	1-22-00	3	0	4.96	31	0	0	7	33	25	22	18	6	16	44	.216	.222	.210	12.12	4.41
Derek Holland	B-L	6-2	223	10-9-86	0	1	5.53	20	6	0	3	28	30	19	17	6	13	25	.288	.190	.355	8.13	4.23
2-team total (10 Worcester Red Sox)					0	3	5.77	30	6	0	3	39	38	28	25	7	20	38	.262	.175	.318	8.77	4.62
Kyle Johnston	R-R	5-11	218	7-17-96	3	4	5.46	49	0	0	3	63	69	41	38	8	30	60	.279	.250	.304	8.62	4.31
Hayden Juenger	R-R	6-0	180	8-9-00	3	2	3.31	18	2	0	2	33	23	12	12	6	16	33	.195	.150	.241	9.09	4.41
Anthony Kay	L-L	6-0	225	3-21-95	1	3	8.36	8	1	0	0	14	18	14	13	4	11	15	.316	.318	.314	9.64	7.07
Yusei Kikuchi	L-L	6-0	205	6-17-91	1	0	0.00	1	1	0	0	5	2	0	0	0	3	4	.133	.167	.111	7.20	5.40
Casey Lawrence	R-R	6-0	170	10-28-87	9	5	2.79	23	23	2	0	126	95	41	39	18	17	106	.206	.199	.214	7.57	1.21
Tim Mayza	L-L	6-3	213	1-15-92	0	1	13.50	2	1	0	0	1	1	2	2	0	1	1	.200	--	.200	6.75	6.75
Julian Merryweather	R-R	6-4	215	10-14-91	2	0	0.00	13	0	0	0	14	5	1	0	0	6	18	.102	.091	.111	11.30	3.77
Andrew Moore	R-R	6-0	195	6-2-94	0	1	7.71	4	3	0	0	9	13	8	8	6	1	6	.333	.421	.250	5.79	0.96
Vinny Nittoli	R-R	6-1	210	11-11-90	0	0	2.79	10	0	0	2	10	6	3	3	0	1	15	.171	.143	.214	13.97	0.93
3-team total (5 L. V. IronPigs, 22 S./W.-B. RailRiders)					4	1	3.81	37	4	0	2	52	40	23	22	7	14	64	.213	.181	.238	11.08	2.42
Matt Peacock	R-R	6-1	185	2-27-94	1	2	4.02	14	0	0	0	16	17	9	7	3	4	15	.270	.167	.364	8.62	2.30
2-team total (8 Omaha Storm Chasers)					1	3	4.21	22	0	0	0	26	30	16	12	5	7	23	.280	.239	.311	8.06	2.45
Nate Pearson	R-R	6-6	255	8-20-96	2	1	3.55	11	0	0	0	13	7	5	5	2	7	18	.163	.167	.158	12.79	4.97
Gabriel Ponce	R-R	6-2	205	4-29-99	0	0	4.32	5	0	0	0	8	8	7	4	3	5	8	.242	.273	.227	8.64	5.40
Zach Pop	R-R	6-4	220	9-20-96	0	0	4.91	4	0	0	0	4	3	3	2	0	4	5	.200	.125	.286	12.27	9.82
2-team total (19 Jacksonville Jumbo Shrimp)					0	1	2.57	23	0	0	0	28	31	11	8	0	12	25	.284	.302	.268	8.04	3.86
Sean Rackoski	R-R	6-7	225	5-12-95	1	0	5.14	6	0	0	0	7	6	4	4	1	5	5	.222	.333	.133	6.43	6.43
Jackson Rees	R-R	6-4	210	7-30-94	0	1	5.79	9	0	0	0	9	15	7	6	0	3	10	.357	.421	.304	9.64	2.89
Marcus Reyes	L-L	5-11	180	3-10-95	0	0	9.00	1	0	0	0	1	2	1	1	0	1	3	.400	--	.400	27.00	9.00
Trevor Richards	R-R	6-2	205	5-15-93	0	1	27.00	1	0	0	0	1	3	3	3	2	0	1	.500	.333	.667	9.00	0.00
Hyun Jin Ryu	R-L	6-3	250	3-25-87	0	1	4.50	1	1	0	0	4	5	5	2	1	0	6	.278	.250	.300	13.50	0.00
Tayler Saucedo	L-L	6-4	205	6-18-93	1	0	2.37	20	0	0	1	19	14	5	5	1	10	28	.200	.130	.234	13.26	4.74
Colton Shaver	R-R	6-1	249	9-18-95	0	0	0.00	1	0	0	0	1	0	0	0	0	1	0	.000	.000	.000	0.00	9.00
Graham Spraker	R-R	6-2	187	3-19-95	1	4	4.82	29	3	0	0	37	28	24	20	6	25	44	.203	.213	.195	10.61	6.03
Eric Stamets	R-R	6-0	183	9-25-91	0	0	0.00	1	0	0	0	0	1	0	0	0	0	0	.500	--	.500	0.00	0.00
Ross Stripling	R-R	6-1	215	11-23-89	1	0	0.00	1	1	0	0	5	3	0	0	0	0	3	.176	.300	.000	5.40	0.00
Trent Thornton	R-R	6-0	190	9-30-93	2	2	2.89	21	0	0	3	28	26	11	9	1	12	30	.243	.241	.245	9.64	3.86
Andrew Vasquez	L-L	6-6	235	9-14-93	2	0	2.45	10	0	0	1	11	3	3	3	0	2	15	.083	.067	.095	12.27	1.64
2-team total (4 Lehigh Valley IronPigs)					2	0	2.40	14	0	0	1	15	6	5	4	0	3	18	.115	.087	.138	10.80	1.80
Mitch White	R-R	6-3	210	12-28-94	0	0	14.40	1	1	0	0	5	9	8	8	2	1	5	.409	.417	.400	9.00	1.80
Eric Yardley	R-R	6-0	170	8-18-90	3	2	4.13	32	0	0	0	33	31	18	15	3	17	31	.256	.386	.182	8.54	4.68
2-team total (5 Iowa Cubs)					3	2	5.79	37	0	0	0	37	43	28	24	4	20	33	.291	.431	.200	7.96	4.82
Yosver Zulueta	R-R	6-1	190	1-23-98	0	1	3.86	3	1	0	0	5	3	3	2	0	4	5	.200	.100	.400	9.64	7.71

Fielding

Catcher	PCT	G	PO	A	E	DP	PB
Bec	1.000	9	75	3	0	1	3
Berman	.985	54	452	23	7	3	3
Collins	.980	12	94	4	2	1	2
Deglan	.986	21	196	11	3	1	3
Gonzalez	1.000	1	6	0	0	0	0
Heineman	1.000	2	20	2	0	0	0
Jansen	1.000	3	33	1	0	0	0
Moreno	1.000	51	405	36	0	4	6
Shaver	1.000	3	18	0	0	0	0

First Base	PCT	G	PO	A	E	DP
Aiello	1.000	4	35	1	0	3
Biggio	.923	2	12	0	1	3
Collins	.967	14	112	6	4	7
Fuentes	.929	2	12	1	1	0
Groshans	.967	4	28	1	1	4
Horwitz	.996	29	232	16	1	18
Large	.989	36	235	26	3	18
Podkul	1.000	29	195	15	0	7
Schwecke	1.000	3	22	0	0	1
Shaver	1.000	5	41	0	0	5
Talley	1.000	24	156	20	0	15
Tsutsugo	1.000	1	8	0	0	0

Second Base	PCT	G	PO	A	E	DP
Biggio	1.000	1	1	3	0	0
De Los Santos	.818	4	3	6	2	1
Horwitz	1.000	1	1	1	0	0
Katoh	1.000	1	2	3	0	1
Lantigua	.976	11	17	23	1	6
Large	.939	11	9	22	2	0
Lopez	.947	36	54	88	8	18
Morris	1.000	8	6	6	0	0
Podkul	1.000	3	2	4	0	2
Rivas	1.000	2	2	5	0	0
Schneider	.958	7	10	13	1	4
Stamets	1.000	6	2	10	0	1
Talley	.974	18	29	46	2	13
Taylor	.987	39	66	90	2	17
Warmoth	.909	6	7	13	2	1

Third Base	PCT	G	PO	A	E	DP
Aiello	.917	4	5	6	1	0
Barger	1.000	3	1	5	0	0
Capra	.981	20	12	41	1	5
Fuentes	.973	16	20	16	1	2
Groshans	.935	14	5	24	2	0
Lantigua	.944	8	3	14	1	3
Large	1.000	8	8	14	0	3
Morris	.977	19	12	30	1	0

Podkul	.923	17	16	20	3	1
Stamets	.949	13	10	27	2	2
Talley	.962	29	24	51	3	6

Shortstop	PCT	G	PO	A	E	DP
Barger	.933	4	1	13	1	0
Capra	.947	20	26	45	4	12
De Los Santos	1.000	1	2	5	0	2
Fuentes	.970	9	16	16	1	3
Groshans	.947	39	39	86	7	16
Lantigua	.870	14	14	33	7	6
Lopez	.903	10	6	22	3	2

Schwecke	1.000	3	2	6	0	4
Stamets	.982	44	54	107	3	14
Taylor	.000	1	0	0	0	0
Warmoth	.920	7	11	12	2	2

Outfield	PCT	G	PO	A	E	DP
Biggio	1.000	4	7	0	0	0
Capra	1.000	7	13	1	0	0
Fowler	1.000	2	3	0	0	0
Groshans	1.000	4	3	0	0	0
Horwitz	.944	10	17	0	1	0
Lantigua	1.000	10	17	0	0	0
Large	.989	48	87	3	1	1
Lopez	.958	38	68	0	3	0
Lukes	.990	101	197	6	2	0
Palacios	1.000	5	3	0	0	0
Schneider	.941	8	15	1	1	0
Schwecke	.947	12	17	1	1	0
Smith	1.000	24	59	2	0	0
Taylor	1.000	25	50	1	0	0
Tsutsugo	1.000	20	31	1	0	0
Warmoth	.992	69	120	7	1	1
Young	.985	65	124	9	2	2

NEW HAMPSHIRE FISHER CATS — DOUBLE-A

EASTERN LEAGUE

Batting	B-T	HT	WT	DOB	AVG	vLH	vRH	G	AB	R	H	2B	3B	HR	RBI	BB	HBP	SH	SF	SO	SB	CS	SLG	OBP
John Aiello	B-R	6-2	215	2-14-97	.305	.343	.293	81	275	44	84	18	1	9	29	39	6	0	0	72	2	5	.476	.403
Addison Barger	L-R	6-0	175	11-12-99	.313	.273	.322	47	176	26	55	11	0	9	29	18	3	0	1	50	2	2	.528	.384
Chris Bec	R-R	5-9	195	12-30-95	.215	.154	.227	28	79	6	17	3	0	1	6	13	0	0	0	23	5	4	.291	.326
Steward Berroa	B-R	5-10	178	6-5-99	.182	.300	.156	21	55	6	10	0	1	1	5	5	0	0	0	17	7	0	.273	.250
Zach Britton	L-R	6-1	200	9-9-98	.234	.111	.255	19	64	14	15	5	0	3	8	12	0	0	0	17	0	0	.453	.355
Hugo Cardona	R-R	5-11	145	9-5-99	.139	.111	.148	14	36	7	5	0	0	1	2	5	1	1	0	12	4	3	.222	.262
Phil Clarke	L-R	5-11	190	3-24-98	.234	.196	.244	77	248	33	58	9	0	4	33	38	6	0	5	44	2	1	.319	.343
Zac Cook	L-R	6-1	195	4-29-98	.189	.234	.178	102	333	55	63	12	0	15	39	26	30	1	4	151	14	4	.360	.303
Luis De Los Santos	R-R	6-1	160	6-9-98	.264	.233	.272	112	406	47	107	19	2	10	57	34	3	0	6	99	7	4	.394	.321
Angel Del Rosario	R-R	6-0	160	1-11-03	.250	.000	.294	8	20	2	5	0	0	1	2	1	0	0	0	4	0	0	.400	.286
Cam Eden	R-R	6-1	181	3-31-98	.215	.224	.213	80	274	33	59	14	0	10	35	26	4	0	1	108	32	3	.376	.292
Karl Ellison	R-R	6-1	195	5-23-95	.179	.182	.176	9	28	3	5	3	1	1	1	1	0	1	0	12	0	0	.464	.207
Sebastian Espino	R-R	6-2	176	5-29-00	.181	.116	.196	106	354	39	64	19	2	14	38	22	3	0	1	166	4	2	.364	.234
Ryan Gold	L-R	5-11	215	10-10-97	.214	.143	.228	59	173	19	37	8	1	10	29	22	4	0	2	52	0	0	.445	.313
Spencer Horwitz	L-R	6-0	190	11-14-97	.297	.146	.330	70	232	46	69	19	1	10	39	43	4	0	2	54	3	1	.517	.413
Tyler Keenan	L-R	6-4	250	2-27-99	.045	.000	.050	7	22	2	1	0	0	0	0	3	0	0	0	11	0	0	.045	.160
Rafael Lantigua	R-R	5-8	153	4-28-98	.268	.274	.267	86	328	53	88	27	1	5	35	37	2	0	1	70	6	9	.402	.345
Orelvis Martinez	R-R	6-1	200	11-19-01	.203	.267	.187	118	433	57	88	15	0	30	76	40	12	0	4	140	6	3	.446	.286
Tanner Morris	L-R	6-2	190	9-13-97	.312	.400	.295	43	154	35	48	7	1	5	11	30	2	0	0	30	1	3	.468	.430
Robert Robertis	L-L	5-11	188	11-29-02	.294	.333	.250	5	17	4	5	1	0	2	5	0	0	0	0	5	0	0	.706	.294
Will Robertson	L-L	6-2	215	12-26-97	.215	.158	.228	90	307	39	66	21	0	12	41	27	6	0	0	96	1	4	.401	.291
Davis Schneider	R-R	5-10	190	1-26-99	.283	.154	.307	46	166	22	47	8	3	6	22	22	1	0	1	46	10	0	.476	.368
Trevor Schwecke	R-R	6-1	185	12-18-97	.238	.130	.258	39	143	19	34	6	2	3	14	13	2	0	1	55	1	1	.371	.308
LJ Talley	L-R	6-2	203	5-7-97	.188	.133	.200	25	85	11	16	2	0	4	13	13	1	0	2	22	0	0	.353	.297

Pitching	B-T	HT	WT	DOB	W	L	ERA	G	GS	CG	SV	IP	H	R	ER	HR	BB	SO	AVG	vLH	vRH	K/9	BB/9
John Aiello	B-R	6-2	215	2-14-97	0	0	40.50	1	0	0	0	1	3	3	3	0	1	1	.750	--	.750	13.50	13.50
Andrew Bash	R-R	6-0	190	8-1-96	10	4	3.81	27	2	0	1	76	62	34	32	1	27	59	.225	.210	.241	7.02	3.21
Ryan Boyer	R-R	6-2	225	5-4-97	0	0	5.06	4	0	0	0	5	5	3	3	1	1	7	.238	.200	.273	11.81	1.69
Jimmy Burnette	L-L	6-2	205	10-19-98	4	5	4.58	28	0	0	4	37	27	25	19	2	25	56	.199	.127	.247	13.50	6.03
Parker Caracci	R-R	6-0	205	9-13-96	2	4	4.31	39	0	0	6	48	47	25	23	4	31	56	.254	.324	.207	10.50	5.81
Max Castillo	R-R	6-2	280	5-4-99	3	1	3.10	6	6	0	0	29	21	10	10	3	14	35	.198	.152	.233	10.86	4.34
Jol Concepcion	R-R	6-5	195	9-17-98	1	2	5.59	6	0	0	0	10	10	7	6	1	7	10	.256	.333	.133	9.31	6.52
Trey Cumbie	L-L	6-2	200	7-12-96	1	0	10.80	12	1	0	1	13	17	16	16	4	12	18	.315	.429	.242	12.15	8.10
Hagen Danner	R-R	6-1	210	9-30-98	0	0	4.91	4	0	0	2	4	5	2	2	0	3	1	.313	.000	.385	2.45	7.36
Mike Ellenbest	R-R	6-4	220	8-20-94	1	0	2.16	7	0	0	1	8	5	4	2	0	3	7	.179	.211	.111	7.56	3.24
Jake Elliott	R-R	6-7	230	3-22-95	5	0	3.29	27	0	0	3	41	28	16	15	4	15	49	.190	.164	.209	10.76	3.29
Cre Finfrock	B-R	5-11	185	6-26-96	0	1	5.94	26	0	0	0	36	34	25	24	4	41	37	.260	.230	.286	9.17	10.16
Nick Fraze	R-R	6-3	180	10-24-97	2	4	4.85	13	11	0	0	59	55	33	32	7	9	54	.240	.235	.245	8.19	1.37
Ryan Gold	L-R	5-11	215	10-10-97	0	0	13.50	2	0	0	0	1	2	2	2	1	0	0	.333	.000	.500	0.00	0.00
Adrian Hernandez	R-R	5-8	190	1-22-00	1	0	2.25	3	0	0	1	4	2	1	1	0	3	6	.143	.000	.250	13.50	6.75
Hayden Juenger	R-R	6-0	180	8-9-00	0	5	4.02	20	17	0	0	56	40	25	25	12	21	67	.196	.149	.236	10.77	3.38
Adam Kloffenstein	R-R	6-5	243	8-25-00	2	5	6.07	19	18	0	0	86	98	61	58	12	45	88	.287	.281	.293	9.21	4.71
Brady Lail	R-R	6-2	200	8-9-93	1	2	7.31	13	2	0	0	32	45	26	26	6	10	35	.336	.276	.414	9.84	2.81
Elvis Luciano	R-R	6-3	210	2-15-00	0	2	21.00	2	2	0	0	3	8	8	7	1	3	2	.471	.667	.364	6.00	9.00
Alejandro Melean	R-R	6-0	175	10-11-00	0	4	5.10	8	8	0	0	30	26	18	17	5	17	24	.234	.245	.226	7.20	5.10
Sean Mellen	L-L	6-5	215	2-20-98	2	2	3.27	32	4	0	2	55	46	31	20	5	24	61	.225	.213	.234	9.98	3.93
Andrew Moore	R-R	6-0	195	6-2-94	1	1	4.76	6	3	0	0	23	34	12	12	7	4	23	.358	.400	.327	9.13	1.59
Joey Murray	L-R	6-2	195	9-23-96	1	1	7.84	5	4	0	0	21	16	18	18	4	13	23	.211	.233	.196	10.02	5.66
Juan Nunez	R-R	6-2	185	1-23-96	1	0	5.73	8	0	0	0	11	7	7	7	3	10	17	.175	.250	.100	13.91	8.18
Trent Palmer	R-R	6-1	230	4-2-99	1	1	3.69	7	7	0	0	32	22	13	13	3	15	33	.190	.177	.204	9.38	4.26
Gabriel Ponce	R-R	6-2	205	4-29-99	2	5	3.70	31	0	0	1	49	33	23	20	4	27	52	.192	.205	.179	9.62	4.99
Luis Quinones	R-R	6-0	205	7-2-97	0	7	5.45	19	16	0	1	71	55	48	43	7	50	91	.215	.158	.261	11.54	6.34
Sean Rackoski	R-R	6-7	225	5-12-95	5	1	6.69	32	0	0	3	38	46	29	28	4	17	43	.303	.231	.356	10.27	4.06
Marcus Reyes	L-L	5-11	180	3-10-95	1	3	8.41	24	1	0	0	35	46	34	33	5	24	27	.326	.377	.288	6.88	6.11
Sem Robberse	R-R	6-1	160	10-12-01	0	3	3.65	5	5	0	0	25	19	15	10	4	10	19	.211	.220	.204	6.93	3.65
Jimmy Robbins	L-L	6-3	190	12-22-97	1	2	1.52	5	5	0	0	24	20	7	4	2	6	26	.225	.200	.237	9.89	2.28
Thomas Ruwe	R-R	6-9	225	9-9-95	0	3	8.10	13	0	0	0	13	16	12	12	1	18	19	.302	.182	.387	12.83	12.15

Paxton Schultz	L-R	6-3	205	1-5-98	7	6	4.04	25	20	0	0	105	101	53	47	15	51	99	.252	.245	.258	8.51	4.39
Braden Scott	R-L	6-3	215	2-6-98	3	3	6.80	28	0	0	0	46	53	44	35	11	34	63	.277	.313	.258	12.24	6.60
Ricky Tiedemann	L-L	6-4	220	8-18-02	0	1	2.45	4	4	0	0	11	5	4	3	0	4	14	.147	.125	.154	11.45	3.27
Geison Urbaez	R-R	6-1	180	7-5-00	0	0	4.15	10	0	0	0	17	15	8	8	1	13	15	.234	.222	.243	7.79	6.75
Sean Wymer	R-R	6-1	205	3-19-97	0	0	9.00	1	0	0	0	1	1	1	1	1	1	0	.250	.333	.000	0.00	9.00
Yosver Zulueta	R-R	6-1	190	1-23-98	1	1	4.11	9	2	0	0	15	10	8	7	1	14	25	.179	.227	.147	14.67	8.22

Fielding

Catcher	PCT	G	PO	A	E	DP	PB
Bec	.989	21	175	6	2	0	4
Britton	1.000	5	55	2	0	1	0
Clarke	.993	59	531	32	4	2	8
Ellison	.988	7	76	3	1	1	0
Gold	.987	50	439	23	6	4	11

First Base	PCT	G	PO	A	E	DP
Aiello	.990	40	262	23	3	31
Cook	1.000	1	9	0	0	1
Ellison	1.000	1	2	0	0	1
Espino	.994	25	151	13	1	15
Gold	1.000	1	7	0	0	1
Horwitz	.997	44	288	26	1	21
Keenan	.920	5	21	2	2	2
Schwecke	1.000	19	134	10	0	14
Talley	1.000	11	68	6	0	4

Second Base	PCT	G	PO	A	E	DP
Cardona	.840	6	9	12	4	2
De Los Santos	.978	36	45	88	3	16
Del Rosario	1.000	6	7	5	0	0
Lantigua	.972	44	77	99	5	20
Morris	1.000	16	19	30	0	6
Schneider	1.000	28	34	71	0	17
Talley	1.000	8	17	27	0	7

Third Base	PCT	G	PO	A	E	DP
Aiello	1.000	22	19	22	0	1
Barger	.927	20	14	24	3	2
Cardona	1.000	5	1	6	0	1
De Los Santos	.935	25	15	43	4	4
Espino	.875	5	2	5	1	2
Lantigua	.750	3	1	2	1	1
Martinez	.948	43	31	61	5	6
Morris	.939	22	7	24	2	2
Schwecke	1.000	3	0	4	0	0
Talley	.333	1	0	1	2	0

Shortstop	PCT	G	PO	A	E	DP
Barger	.957	20	21	45	3	11
Cardona	.750	2	1	2	1	1
De Los Santos	.956	55	64	109	8	24
Lantigua	1.000	2	1	5	0	1
Martinez	.937	60	65	129	13	28
Schwecke	1.000	1	0	1	0	0

Outfield	PCT	G	PO	A	E	DP
Berroa	.976	21	39	1	1	1
Britton	.889	7	8	0	1	0
Cardona	1.000	1	3	0	0	0
Cook	.985	102	190	8	3	1
Eden	.989	80	182	5	2	1
Espino	.966	74	136	8	5	1
Horwitz	1.000	10	6	0	0	0
Lantigua	1.000	30	48	4	0	2
Robertis	1.000	4	7	0	0	0
Robertson	.980	88	141	6	3	1
Schneider	1.000	7	7	0	0	0
Schwecke	1.000	10	12	0	0	0

VANCOUVER CANADIANS — *HIGH CLASS A*

NORTHWEST LEAGUE

Batting	B-T	HT	WT	DOB	AVG	vLH	vRH	G	AB	R	H	2B	3B	HR	RBI	BB	HBP	SH	SF	SO	SB	CS	SLG	OBP
Addison Barger	L-R	6-0	175	11-12-99	.300	.295	.302	69	260	46	78	21	2	14	53	25	4	0	3	76	7	2	.558	.366
Steward Berroa	B-R	5-10	178	6-5-99	.219	.255	.208	60	215	46	47	11	6	6	22	33	4	1	2	67	40	7	.409	.331
Zach Britton	L-R	6-1	200	9-9-98	.239	.219	.244	57	188	34	45	15	1	7	25	41	6	0	1	70	10	2	.441	.390
Dasan Brown	R-R	6-0	185	9-25-01	.298	.406	.269	40	151	25	45	11	0	2	11	14	10	0	1	50	11	3	.411	.392
Hugo Cardona	R-R	5-11	145	9-5-99	.168	.095	.183	55	125	17	21	7	1	1	9	11	4	1	2	51	14	3	.264	.254
Alex De Jesus	R-R	6-2	170	3-22-02	.211	.353	.178	24	90	10	19	5	0	2	13	12	0	0	2	36	0	0	.333	.298
Cam Eden	R-R	6-1	181	3-31-98	.297	.333	.290	10	37	4	11	4	1	0	2	2	2	0	1	8	2	2	.459	.357
Francisco Fajardo	B-R	5-10	163	5-26-00	.250	.000	.333	2	4	1	1	0	0	0	0	0	0	0	0	1	1	0	.250	.250
Jommer Hernandez	R-R	5-11	181	10-20-00	.203	.105	.240	22	69	8	14	4	0	2	7	12	0	0	0	30	1	0	.348	.321
Miguel Hiraldo	R-R	5-11	197	9-5-00	.231	.265	.220	109	398	47	92	19	4	11	55	27	0	0	3	126	28	5	.382	.278
Leo Jimenez	R-R	5-11	215	5-17-01	.230	.177	.247	69	244	45	56	14	3	6	40	27	17	0	6	58	7	3	.385	.340
Tyler Keenan	L-R	6-4	250	2-27-99	.300	.385	.270	15	50	7	15	7	0	1	4	5	0	0	1	13	0	0	.500	.357
2-team total (25 Everett AquaSox)					.268	.226	.279	40	142	15	38	11	0	4	18	17	2	0	1	42	0	0	.430	.352
Gabriel Martinez	R-R	6-0	170	7-24-02	.324	.320	.325	28	102	11	33	8	0	3	13	9	1	0	1	17	0	0	.490	.381
Anthony Morales	B-R	6-0	175	11-13-98	.178	.167	.181	36	107	10	19	3	1	0	7	7	1	0	1	28	0	0	.224	.233
PK Morris	L-L	6-1	195	11-30-98	.241	.226	.245	95	311	33	75	19	2	13	61	42	1	0	7	103	2	0	.441	.327
MacKenzie Mueller	R-L	6-3	225	12-16-97	.175	.095	.205	52	154	13	27	2	3	3	23	23	2	0	0	57	4	2	.286	.291
Rainer Nunez	R-R	6-3	180	12-4-00	.321	.304	.325	27	106	15	34	6	0	4	19	10	0	0	0	27	0	0	.491	.379
Damiano Palmegiani	R-R	6-1	195	1-24-00	.224	.170	.240	62	228	44	51	11	0	13	46	31	9	0	4	60	3	0	.443	.335
Harrison Ray	R-R	6-0	200	1-11-98	.204	.184	.213	37	113	17	23	5	3	1	8	8	1	0	2	42	4	2	.327	.258
Glenn Santiago	R-R	6-0	165	12-14-00	.209	.161	.226	35	115	10	24	4	2	1	16	9	2	0	0	32	1	2	.304	.278
Davis Schneider	R-R	5-10	190	1-26-99	.229	.196	.243	50	157	26	36	10	1	8	25	29	2	0	1	50	6	1	.459	.354
Trevor Schwecke	R-R	6-1	185	12-18-97	.232	.286	.211	43	151	25	35	10	1	4	19	14	3	0	1	37	2	2	.391	.308
Andres Sosa	R-R	5-11	210	11-7-97	.226	.196	.236	73	208	42	47	20	1	5	27	45	16	1	3	60	6	0	.404	.397
Garrett Spain	L-R	5-11	178	9-21-00	.216	.179	.226	93	291	40	63	13	3	6	23	40	5	0	1	92	10	3	.344	.320
Riley Tirotta	R-R	6-3	195	8-21-98	.219	.200	.224	69	247	34	54	15	2	6	34	33	2	0	1	91	12	5	.368	.314
Michael Turconi	L-R	5-11	185	6-24-99	.281	.571	.200	11	32	6	9	0	0	0	1	7	0	0	0	6	1	2	.281	.410

Pitching	B-T	HT	WT	DOB	W	L	ERA	G	GS	CG	SV	IP	H	R	ER	HR	BB	SO	AVG	vLH	vRH	K/9	BB/9
Ryan Boyer	R-R	6-2	225	5-4-97	2	0	2.45	15	0	0	2	18	13	5	5	2	4	29	.194	.313	.086	14.24	1.96
T.J. Brock	R-R	6-1	200	8-10-99	1	0	5.56	9	0	0	1	11	13	7	7	1	6	20	.289	.238	.333	15.88	4.76
Jimmy Burnette	L-L	6-2	205	10-19-98	1	3	3.79	13	0	0	4	19	12	10	8	2	11	38	.174	.160	.182	18.00	5.21
Hugo Cardona	R-R	5-11	145	9-5-99	0	0	0.00	3	0	0	0	2	1	0	0	0	0	1	.125	.000	.200	3.86	0.00
Jol Concepcion	R-R	6-5	195	9-17-98	5	3	4.17	33	0	0	7	50	33	25	23	3	39	68	.192	.139	.237	12.32	7.07
Connor Cooke	R-R	6-1	203	11-2-99	0	2	6.75	11	0	0	8	11	9	10	8	2	3	12	.220	.292	.118	10.13	2.53
Chad Dallas	R-R	5-11	206	6-26-00	1	7	4.60	21	21	0	0	88	85	56	45	13	51	86	.245	.272	.219	8.80	5.22
Michael Dominguez	R-R	5-10	175	8-17-00	1	2	3.64	7	7	0	0	30	24	14	12	4	12	38	.220	.254	.180	11.53	3.64
Garrett Farmer	R-R	5-11	185	5-14-97	5	1	3.69	29	0	0	0	54	48	32	22	5	18	41	.225	.189	.252	6.88	3.02
Mason Fluharty	R-L	6-2	215	8-13-01	1	1	3.52	10	0	0	0	15	15	7	6	2	7	21	.268	.222	.310	12.33	4.11
Nick Frasso	R-R	6-5	200	10-18-98	0	0	0.82	3	3	0	0	11	3	2	1	1	2	15	.081	.063	.095	12.27	1.64
Hunter Gregory	R-R	6-3	215	11-16-98	1	4	7.24	10	6	0	0	32	37	26	26	3	11	40	.280	.234	.324	11.13	3.06
Devereaux Harrison	R-R	6-0	190	11-8-00	1	0	6.23	4	0	0	0	4	8	3	3	1	2	3	.400	.286	.667	6.23	4.15
Jommer Hernandez	R-R	5-11	181	10-20-00	0	0	18.00	1	0	0	0	1	1	2	2	0	2	1	.250	.250	--	9.00	18.00

Justin Kelly	R-R	6-1	195	12-2-98	9	2	4.69	23	0	0	2	40	46	30	21	6	15	33	.280	.254	.301	7.36	3.35
Adam Kloffenstein	R-R	6-5	243	8-25-00	0	2	3.81	6	6	0	0	26	28	13	11	4	10	30	.269	.241	.300	10.38	3.46
Conor Larkin	R-R	6-1	205	3-17-99	0	0	7.71	6	0	0	0	9	11	8	8	1	3	9	.306	.600	.095	8.68	2.89
Colton Laws	R-R	6-7	230	11-20-95	2	0	3.38	2	0	0	0	3	3	2	1	0	1	2	.333	.333	.333	6.75	3.38
Will McAffer	R-R	6-2	205	5-30-97	3	3	5.23	27	0	0	3	33	27	25	19	2	27	29	.221	.273	.179	7.99	7.44
Alejandro Melean	R-R	6-0	175	10-11-00	2	1	1.69	9	5	0	1	32	20	10	6	2	8	35	.174	.150	.200	9.84	2.25
Sean Mellen	L-L	6-5	215	2-20-98	1	1	1.64	5	0	0	0	11	7	2	2	1	5	19	.179	.143	.200	15.55	4.09
Abdiel Mendoza	R-R	5-10	160	9-19-98	6	2	2.78	29	8	0	1	81	65	33	25	5	39	64	.217	.287	.160	7.11	4.33
MacKenzie Mueller	R-L	6-3	225	12-16-97	0	1	1.93	5	0	0	1	5	1	2	1	0	3	6	.077	.000	.100	11.57	5.79
Alex Nolan	R-R	6-4	225	3-21-96	1	0	6.17	16	0	0	0	23	20	21	16	3	13	29	.220	.262	.184	11.19	5.01
Juan Nunez	R-R	6-2	185	1-23-96	4	0	2.70	12	0	0	1	17	10	7	5	2	12	22	.167	.050	.225	11.88	6.48
Trent Palmer	R-R	6-1	230	4-2-99	1	2	4.18	6	6	0	0	24	28	20	11	5	8	36	.277	.273	.286	13.69	3.04
Eric Pardinho	R-R	5-10	155	1-5-01	0	0	10.20	10	0	0	0	15	23	17	17	3	16	25	.354	.313	.394	15.00	9.60
Naswell Paulino	L-L	5-11	160	4-17-00	3	5	4.59	30	10	0	0	86	78	50	44	12	39	87	.239	.211	.255	9.07	4.07
Nathanael Perez Lopez	R-R	6-1	160	6-5-98	0	2	7.88	3	3	0	0	8	10	9	7	3	8	4	.294	.143	.400	4.50	9.00
Gabriel Ponce	R-R	6-2	205	4-29-99	0	0	0.00	2	0	0	1	4	0	0	0	0	5	7	.000	.000	.000	15.75	11.25
Sem Robberse	R-R	6-1	160	10-12-01	4	4	3.12	17	17	0	0	87	76	41	30	7	24	78	.231	.209	.251	8.10	2.49
Jimmy Robbins	L-L	6-3	190	12-22-97	0	2	3.82	10	9	0	0	35	30	16	15	4	17	46	.227	.224	.229	11.72	4.33
Thomas Ruwe	R-R	6-9	225	9-9-95	0	1	2.11	16	0	0	1	21	12	9	5	0	13	31	.162	.167	.156	13.08	5.48
Sam Ryan	R-R	6-3	205	9-22-98	1	0	13.50	7	0	0	0	7	11	15	11	4	10	4	.333	.500	.238	4.91	12.27
Dahian Santos	R-R	5-11	160	2-26-03	0	2	10.66	4	4	0	0	13	17	15	15	3	9	22	.333	.345	.318	15.63	6.39
Davis Schneider	R-R	5-10	190	1-26-99	0	0	45.00	1	0	0	0	1	6	5	5	0	0	0	.667	.667	.667	0.00	0.00
Braden Scott	R-L	6-3	215	2-6-98	0	0	0.00	1	0	0	0	1	0	0	0	0	0	3	.000	.000	.000	27.00	0.00
Mark Simon	R-R	6-0	185	8-4-95	0	0	8.84	19	0	0	0	18	33	21	18	3	9	15	.388	.368	.404	7.36	4.42
Matt Svanson	R-R	6-5	235	1-31-99	3	0	3.57	13	0	0	0	23	21	10	9	2	3	23	.244	.256	.234	9.13	1.19
Ricky Tiedemann	L-L	6-4	220	8-18-02	2	2	2.39	8	8	0	0	38	23	12	10	2	12	54	.176	.179	.175	12.90	2.87
Trenton Wallace	L-L	6-1	200	3-31-99	1	1	3.66	9	9	0	0	39	21	16	16	2	31	55	.156	.128	.167	12.58	7.09
Troy Watson	R-R	6-2	180	6-11-97	0	2	3.07	9	1	0	1	15	12	6	5	0	3	22	.218	.240	.200	13.50	1.84
Sean Wymer	R-R	6-1	205	3-19-97	4	1	3.96	14	0	0	0	25	17	12	11	2	13	25	.193	.189	.196	9.00	4.68
Yosver Zulueta	R-R	6-1	190	1-23-98	1	3	3.80	6	6	0	0	24	18	15	10	1	11	31	.209	.143	.255	11.79	4.18

Fielding

Catcher	PCT	G	PO	A	E	DP	PB
Britton	.997	32	303	7	1	0	4
Hernandez	.979	19	173	17	4	2	1
Morales	.983	33	328	27	6	4	5
Sosa	.984	52	455	42	8	4	15

First Base	PCT	G	PO	A	E	DP
Keenan	1.000	5	26	2	0	3
Morales	.000	1	0	0	0	0
Morris	.993	62	364	33	3	24
Nunez	.980	20	143	6	3	12
Palmegiani	.978	21	119	17	3	9
Santiago	1.000	1	11	2	0	1
Schwecke	.950	5	37	1	2	0
Sosa	.980	16	92	5	2	10
Tirotta	1.000	14	75	9	0	6

Second Base	PCT	G	PO	A	E	DP
Cardona	.947	7	6	12	1	2
Fajardo	1.000	2	2	4	0	1
Hiraldo	.931	101	127	212	25	42
Jimenez	1.000	3	5	3	0	0
Ray	1.000	3	2	1	0	0
Santiago	1.000	5	9	10	0	1
Schneider	.977	11	16	26	1	8
Schwecke	1.000	1	1	2	0	0
Tirotta	1.000	1	1	1	0	0

Third Base	PCT	G	PO	A	E	DP
Barger	.906	19	10	19	3	2
Cardona	.833	5	1	4	1	0
De Jesus	.889	5	6	10	2	1
Hiraldo	.833	4	3	2	1	0
Keenan	.923	7	5	7	1	0
Palmegiani	.919	32	21	47	6	4
Ray	.909	14	5	15	2	0
Santiago	1.000	1	2	2	0	1
Schneider	1.000	3	1	6	0	0
Schwecke	.914	13	15	17	3	6
Tirotta	.925	38	22	52	6	3

Shortstop	PCT	G	PO	A	E	DP
Barger	.946	36	39	66	6	17
Cardona	.891	17	18	39	7	4
De Jesus	.930	17	15	25	3	4
Jimenez	.940	47	55	102	10	17
Santiago	1.000	2	4	5	0	2
Schwecke	.941	7	6	10	1	3
Turconi	.906	9	15	14	3	4

Outfield	PCT	G	PO	A	E	DP
Berroa	.971	58	127	6	4	1
Britton	.895	12	16	1	2	0
Brown	.987	39	74	1	1	0
Cardona	.944	18	16	1	1	0
Eden	1.000	7	8	0	0	0
Martinez	.976	28	40	1	1	1
Morris	.912	20	30	1	3	0
Mueller	.918	51	84	6	8	0
Ray	.838	18	30	1	6	0
Santiago	.974	26	36	1	1	0
Schneider	.980	35	44	4	1	2
Schwecke	1.000	16	19	0	0	0
Spain	.990	95	180	10	2	3
Tirotta	.938	9	14	1	1	1

DUNEDIN BLUE JAYS — LOW CLASS A

FLORIDA STATE LEAGUE

Batting	B-T	HT	WT	DOB	AVG	vLH	vRH	G	AB	R	H	2B	3B	HR	RBI	BB	HBP	SH	SF	SO	SB	CS	SLG	OBP
Manuel Beltre	R-R	5-9	155	6-9-04	.381	.500	.333	5	21	3	8	1	0	1	3	1	0	0	0	3	0	0	.571	.409
Amell Brazoban	R-R	6-2	170	10-9-01	.205	.233	.194	47	151	15	31	8	0	3	15	15	2	0	1	42	3	1	.318	.284
Dasan Brown	R-R	6-0	185	9-25-01	.279	.323	.266	38	140	35	39	8	2	4	12	17	3	2	0	45	11	6	.450	.369
Devonte Brown	R-R	5-11	207	10-15-99	.308	.333	.300	27	78	20	24	3	1	2	15	24	3	0	2	21	4	1	.449	.477
Vinny Capra	R-R	5-8	175	7-7-96	.385	.333	.429	3	13	2	5	5	0	0	1	0	0	0	0	3	0	0	.769	.385
Hugo Cardona	R-R	5-11	145	9-5-99	.115	.000	.120	9	26	1	3	0	0	0	0	7	0	0	0	15	5	0	.115	.303
Rikelbin De Castro	R-R	6-0	150	1-23-03	.176	.275	.147	52	176	15	31	4	0	2	17	14	4	0	1	70	2	6	.233	.251
Marcos De La Rosa	B-R	5-11	160	1-28-02	.100	.250	.063	10	20	4	2	1	0	0	3	3	0	0	0	7	2	1	.150	.217
Angel Del Rosario	R-R	6-0	160	1-11-03	.211	.286	.186	56	194	22	41	6	0	1	13	13	7	2	0	61	32	5	.258	.285
Nicolas Deschamps	L-R	5-11	180	8-25-02	.148	.000	.182	11	27	5	4	1	0	0	0	10	1	0	0	11	0	1	.185	.395
Cade Doughty	R-R	6-1	195	3-26-01	.272	.231	.286	26	103	21	28	5	0	6	24	10	6	0	0	29	3	2	.495	.370
Cam Eden	R-R	6-1	181	3-31-98	.400	1.000	.357	4	15	4	6	1	0	2	4	1	2	0	0	4	2	0	.867	.500
Francisco Fajardo	B-R	5-10	163	5-26-00	.184	.059	.214	28	87	7	16	2	2	2	8	6	0	0	0	25	2	1	.322	.237
Jose Ferrer	R-R	5-11	175	3-1-99	.194	.167	.202	44	144	7	28	9	0	0	16	13	2	0	3	41	1	0	.257	.265
Juan Gonzalez	R-R	5-10	195	2-20-01	.202	.105	.231	29	84	8	17	3	0	1	8	9	7	0	3	27	0	1	.274	.320
Jordan Groshans	R-R	6-3	200	11-10-99	.211	.167	.231	5	19	2	4	1	0	0	0	1	0	0	0	5	0	0	.263	.250

Jommer Hernandez	R-R	5-11	181	10-20-00	.274	.278	.273	27	84	10	23	2	1	0	6	12	2	0	1	19	0	0	.321	.374
Teoscar Hernandez	R-R	6-2	215	10-15-92	.455	.250	.571	3	11	4	5	2	0	2	4	1	0	0	1	3	1	0	1.182	.462
Jerry Huntzinger	R-R	6-2	180	2-15-99	.100	1.000	.000	4	10	1	1	0	0	0	1	3	0	0	0	6	0	0	.100	.308
Danny Jansen	R-R	6-2	215	4-15-95	.300	--	.300	3	10	4	3	2	0	0	0	0	1	0	0	0	0	0	.500	.364
Josh Kasevich	R-R	6-2	200	1-17-01	.262	.115	.309	25	107	18	28	8	0	0	7	11	3	0	1	9	0	2	.336	.344
Otto Lopez	R-R	5-10	185	10-1-98	.050	.000	.059	5	20	0	1	0	0	0	2	2	0	0	0	4	0	0	.050	.136
Estiven Machado	B-R	5-10	170	10-4-02	.263	.146	.300	90	339	45	89	19	3	1	32	38	3	0	0	97	6	3	.345	.342
Gabriel Martinez	R-R	6-0	170	7-24-02	.288	.256	.294	65	240	46	69	14	0	11	46	22	1	0	1	15	3	1	.403	.340
J.C. Masson	L-R	6-3	193	8-22-02	.111	.000	.125	9	27	2	3	0	0	0	1	7	0	0	0	15	0	0	.111	.294
Ryan McCarty	R-R	5-10	182	4-22-99	.274	.118	.333	18	62	7	17	4	0	1	8	8	3	0	1	22	1	1	.387	.378
Victor Mesia	R-R	5-9	175	1-18-03	.152	.174	.146	32	112	10	17	2	0	1	12	10	0	1	0	37	0	0	.196	.221
Rainer Nunez	R-R	6-3	180	12-4-00	.299	.365	.282	93	361	50	108	19	1	15	63	14	4	0	5	82	0	0	.482	.328
Damiano Palmegiani	R-R	6-1	195	1-24-00	.256	.220	.266	56	195	30	50	14	1	11	37	23	7	0	3	47	2	0	.508	.351
Adrian Pinto	R-R	5-6	156	9-22-02	.242	.189	.258	47	157	36	38	5	4	2	10	24	10	2	1	32	18	7	.363	.375
Jose Rivas	R-R	5-9	165	9-5-00	.196	.211	.192	36	92	17	18	6	0	0	4	19	5	0	1	18	4	3	.261	.359
Robert Robertis	L-L	5-11	188	11-29-02	.150	.000	.214	5	20	1	3	0	0	0	2	0	0	0	0	5	0	0	.150	.150
Will Robertson	L-L	6-2	215	12-26-97	.615	.667	.571	3	13	2	8	0	1	2	3	1	0	0	0	1	0	0	1.231	.643
Dylan Rock	R-R	6-1	210	8-21-98	.213	.150	.236	21	75	13	16	5	1	1	7	10	4	0	0	22	1	1	.347	.337
Alan Roden	L-R	6-0	215	12-22-99	.233	.214	.242	25	90	17	21	4	0	1	9	17	5	0	3	13	5	1	.311	.374
Roque Salinas	L-L	5-7	180	11-8-02	.277	.292	.271	74	282	32	78	14	2	3	43	7	9	2	2	35	0	3	.372	.313
Emmanuel Sanchez	R-R	6-0	170	5-30-01	.163	.222	.150	15	49	4	8	0	0	0	6	4	0	0	1	7	0	0	.163	.222
Glenn Santiago	R-R	6-0	165	12-14-00	.268	.500	.230	23	71	13	19	5	0	2	13	7	0	0	1	22	3	1	.423	.329
Adriel Sotolongo	R-R	6-3	208	4-22-98	.237	.239	.237	79	274	21	65	18	1	3	28	30	3	0	2	81	1	1	.343	.317
Riley Tirotta	R-R	6-3	195	8-21-98	.182	.143	.250	3	11	1	2	0	0	1	3	2	0	0	0	6	0	0	.455	.308
Michael Turconi	L-R	5-11	185	6-24-99	.278	.417	.238	17	54	9	15	2	0	1	13	9	3	0	2	8	1	0	.370	.397
Peyton Williams	L-L	6-5	255	9-14-00	.242	.192	.260	28	99	11	24	3	0	2	13	21	2	0	1	33	0	0	.333	.382
Chavez Young	B-R	6-0	200	7-8-97	.278	.000	.294	5	18	4	5	0	0	1	1	1	1	0	0	5	1	0	.444	.350

Pitching	B-T	HT	WT	DOB	W	L	ERA	G	GS	CG	SV	IP	H	R	ER	HR	BB	SO	AVG	vLH	vRH	K/9	BB/9
Eliander Alcalde	R-R	5-9	171	8-9-03	0	0	0.00	1	0	0	0	3	4	0	0	0	0	2	.333	.200	.429	5.40	0.00
Wilgenis Alvarado	L-L	6-1	160	5-18-00	4	3	6.35	23	0	0	0	45	53	35	32	3	31	52	.291	.250	.301	10.32	6.15
Alex Amalfi	R-R	6-1	185	2-18-01	0	0	11.25	6	0	0	0	8	13	10	10	2	8	5	.361	.250	.450	5.63	9.00
Ben Baggett	R-R	5-10	195	2-28-96	3	1	0.96	17	1	0	2	19	12	4	2	2	0	20	.185	.194	.176	9.64	0.00
Cooper Benson	L-L	6-0	213	8-3-00	2	2	2.45	7	5	0	0	26	20	7	7	2	8	35	.220	.050	.268	12.27	2.81
Jonatan Bernal	R-R	6-1	194	6-29-02	1	5	5.47	14	7	0	0	53	54	35	32	5	22	47	.262	.182	.310	8.03	3.76
Ryan Boyer	R-R	6-2	225	5-4-97	1	0	5.68	5	0	0	0	6	6	6	4	1	3	9	.231	.286	.211	12.79	4.26
T.J. Brock	R-R	6-1	200	8-10-99	0	0	0.00	1	0	0	0	1	0	0	0	0	0	2	.000	.000	.000	18.00	0.00
Irv Carter	R-R	6-4	210	10-9-02	0	1	4.50	4	4	0	0	14	14	10	7	2	4	11	.259	.214	.308	7.07	2.57
Jiorgeny Casimiri	R-R	6-1	160	7-12-01	1	0	4.32	7	0	0	1	8	9	4	4	1	3	7	.273	.182	.318	7.56	3.24
Ryan Chasse	L-L	6-3	250	12-11-99	3	1	7.00	7	0	0	1	9	6	10	7	2	10	6	.182	.000	.250	6.00	10.00
Ian Churchill	L-L	6-2	190	2-28-99	1	1	0.75	8	0	0	0	12	6	2	1	0	5	18	.150	.333	.071	13.50	3.75
Connor Cooke	R-R	6-1	203	11-2-99	2	5	4.86	14	8	0	1	46	44	25	25	3	14	63	.253	.284	.234	12.24	2.72
Trey Cumbie	L-L	6-2	200	7-12-96	6	1	1.26	19	0	0	5	29	8	6	4	1	14	36	.088	.038	.108	11.30	4.40
Jose De Leon	R-R	6-0	220	8-7-92	0	0	4.50	2	0	0	0	2	1	1	1	0	1	3	.143	.000	.250	13.50	4.50
Michael Dominguez	R-R	5-10	175	8-17-00	0	4	5.82	13	11	0	0	51	59	38	33	7	19	66	.299	.417	.232	11.65	3.35
Mike Ellenbest	R-R	6-4	220	8-20-94	1	0	0.00	1	0	0	0	1	0	0	0	0	0	1	.000	.000	--	9.00	0.00
Lazaro Estrada	R-R	5-10	180	4-24-99	0	0	2.93	6	5	0	0	15	10	6	5	0	5	24	.182	.238	.147	14.09	2.93
Nick Frasso	R-R	6-5	200	10-18-98	0	0	0.70	7	7	0	0	26	13	2	2	0	8	42	.146	.073	.208	14.73	2.81
Edisson Gonzalez	R-R	5-10	160	10-2-99	0	0	3.09	4	3	0	0	12	9	4	4	2	1	11	.220	.300	.143	8.49	0.77
Devereaux Harrison	R-R	6-0	190	11-8-00	0	0	2.57	5	0	0	1	7	8	2	2	0	4	9	.296	.500	.133	11.57	5.14
Adrian Hernandez	R-R	5-8	190	1-22-00	0	0	0.00	2	0	0	0	3	2	0	0	0	0	7	.167	.333	.000	18.90	0.00
Ryan Jennings	R-R	6-0	190	6-23-99	1	0	2.16	5	0	0	0	8	7	3	2	1	6	8	.241	.200	.263	8.64	6.48
Anthony Kay	L-L	6-0	225	3-21-95	0	0	0.00	3	2	0	0	4	4	0	0	0	1	4	.235	.000	.364	8.31	2.08
Justin Kelly	R-R	6-1	195	12-2-98	0	4	5.40	16	0	0	2	30	29	20	18	7	11	29	.254	.216	.273	8.70	3.30
Brady Lail	R-R	6-2	200	8-9-93	0	1	6.00	2	1	0	0	3	2	3	2	0	2	2	.182	.000	.333	6.00	6.00
Conor Larkin	R-R	6-1	205	3-17-99	0	1	1.23	11	0	0	4	15	9	4	2	0	6	21	.173	.222	.147	12.89	3.68
Keiner Leon	R-R	5-11	190	10-29-03	0	0	3.86	1	0	0	0	2	3	1	1	0	1	1	.429	.333	.500	3.86	3.86
Soenni Martinez	L-L	6-0	180	5-26-01	0	0	4.73	24	0	0	3	32	26	19	17	7	17	42	.213	.222	.211	11.69	4.73
Julian Merryweather	R-R	6-4	215	10-14-91	1	0	0.00	1	0	0	0	1	0	0	0	0	0	2	.000	.000	.000	18.00	0.00
Juan Nunez	R-R	6-2	185	1-23-96	0	2	3.60	16	0	0	2	15	10	7	6	3	9	21	.204	.273	.148	12.60	5.40
Rafael Ohashi	R-R	6-1	185	10-8-02	3	2	2.96	11	8	0	0	46	41	19	15	6	15	54	.238	.160	.299	10.64	2.96
Eric Pardinho	R-R	5-10	155	1-5-01	3	0	0.75	6	0	0	0	12	6	1	1	1	2	13	.150	.091	.172	9.75	1.50
Nate Pearson	R-R	6-6	255	8-20-96	0	0	3.38	2	1	0	0	3	1	1	1	0	1	1	.125	.000	.167	3.38	3.38
Kelvin Perez	R-R	6-3	175	9-9-00	2	3	2.55	19	0	0	1	35	33	20	10	1	13	23	.246	.286	.224	5.86	3.31
Nathanael Perez Gonzalez	R-R	5-10	159	4-2-01	0	0	9.00	4	0	0	0	4	6	4	4	1	1	5	.353	.500	.308	11.25	2.25
Nathanael Perez Lopez	R-R	6-1	160	6-5-98	3	1	1.24	10	1	0	2	29	19	5	4	2	13	31	.196	.367	.119	9.62	4.03
Luis Quinones	R-R	6-0	205	7-2-97	1	0	2.70	2	1	0	0	7	2	2	2	0	4	14	.091	.071	.125	18.90	5.40
Jackson Rees	R-R	6-4	210	7-30-94	0	0	0.00	3	1	0	0	4	0	0	0	0	2	6	.000	.000	.000	13.50	4.50
Jimmy Robbins	L-L	6-3	190	12-22-97	0	0	1.56	6	1	0	0	17	10	3	3	0	9	26	.167	.200	.156	13.50	4.67
Kendry Rojas	L-L	6-2	190	11-26-02	2	2	4.08	12	10	0	0	40	36	23	18	1	19	43	.237	.243	.235	9.76	4.31
Yondrei Rojas	R-R	5-10	180	11-22-02	1	1	5.40	4	2	0	1	17	16	10	10	1	6	12	.258	.111	.318	6.48	3.24
Harry Rutkowski	R-L	6-2	230	4-22-99	1	1	4.64	13	0	0	1	21	21	13	11	3	9	21	.250	.526	.169	8.86	3.80
Sam Ryan	R-R	6-3	205	9-22-98	1	0	0.00	4	0	0	0	6	1	0	0	0	3	7	.050	.000	.063	9.95	4.26
Rafael Sanchez	R-R	6-1	215	8-22-99	0	1	4.50	2	1	0	0	8	7	4	4	1	3	8	.233	.250	.214	9.00	3.38
Dahian Santos	R-R	5-11	160	2-26-03	4	5	3.44	19	14	0	0	73	47	33	28	8	35	120	.181	.207	.169	14.73	4.30

Braden Scott	R-L	6-3	215	2-6-98	2	0	0.68	7	0	0	2	13	4	3	1	1	4	25	.089	.077	.094	16.88	2.70
Matt Svanson	R-R	6-5	235	1-31-99	5	5	4.37	15	9	0	0	60	61	35	29	8	20	60	.263	.256	.267	9.05	3.02
Ricky Tiedemann	L-L	6-4	220	8-18-02	3	1	1.80	6	6	0	0	30	11	6	6	1	13	49	.115	.091	.118	14.70	3.90
Anders Tolhurst	R-R	6-4	190	9-13-99	0	0	2.45	4	1	0	0	7	6	4	2	0	9	12	.214	.077	.333	14.73	11.05
Geison Urbaez	R-R	6-1	180	7-5-00	3	4	3.72	18	9	0	3	58	64	25	24	8	14	55	.281	.347	.233	8.53	2.17
Julian Valdez	R-R	6-2	192	12-13-98	3	4	7.88	21	0	0	1	40	47	37	35	10	28	43	.296	.163	.345	9.68	6.30
Trenton Wallace	L-L	6-1	200	3-31-99	2	1	1.11	11	5	0	1	41	19	6	5	1	13	55	.142	.094	.157	12.17	2.88
Kelsey Ward	L-L	6-2	200	1-7-01	0	0	6.35	4	0	0	0	6	3	4	4	1	6	6	.167	.125	.200	9.53	9.53
Troy Watson	R-R	6-2	180	6-11-97	0	0	3.86	3	2	0	0	7	6	3	3	0	1	11	.222	.000	.316	14.14	1.29
Sean Wymer	R-R	6-1	205	3-19-97	0	0	0.00	2	0	0	0	3	2	0	0	0	2	3	.182	.000	.250	9.00	6.00
Yosver Zulueta	R-R	6-1	190	1-23-98	0	0	3.00	3	3	0	0	12	9	5	4	0	3	23	.205	.235	.185	17.25	2.25

Fielding

Catcher	PCT	G	PO	A	E	DP	PB
Deschamps	1.000	11	82	5	0	0	0
Ferrer	.988	43	453	30	6	1	4
Gonzalez	.990	29	274	16	3	1	1
Hernandez	.986	18	192	19	3	2	2
Huntzinger	.958	4	21	2	1	0	1
Jansen	1.000	2	26	2	0	0	0
Mesia	.991	28	292	22	3	3	7

First Base	PCT	G	PO	A	E	DP
Hernandez	1.000	6	21	0	0	2
McCarty	1.000	3	12	3	0	1
Nunez	.989	73	516	40	6	43
Palmegiani	.923	2	10	2	1	2
Sotolongo	.992	20	116	12	1	10
Tirotta	1.000	1	7	0	0	0
Williams	.987	28	209	16	3	18

Second Base	PCT	G	PO	A	E	DP
Beltre	.923	3	5	7	1	2
De Castro	1.000	16	28	37	0	9
Del Rosario	.970	10	11	21	1	7
Doughty	.975	12	21	18	1	2
Fajardo	.967	10	14	15	1	4
Lopez	1.000	2	6	4	0	0
Machado	.970	37	48	81	4	17
Pinto	.980	12	27	21	1	3
Rivas	.987	23	31	43	1	9
Sanchez	.938	5	10	5	1	1
Turconi	1.000	3	7	8	0	3

Third Base	PCT	G	PO	A	E	DP
Capra	1.000	1	1	3	0	1
Cardona	.600	2	1	2	2	1
Del Rosario	.914	25	14	50	6	2
Doughty	.906	11	5	24	3	0
Fajardo	.789	6	3	12	4	2
Groshans	1.000	1	2	0	0	0
Kasevich	.900	10	6	12	2	0
McCarty	1.000	5	4	11	0	1
Palmegiani	.952	41	25	54	4	4
Rivas	.921	10	12	23	3	3
Sanchez	.955	10	5	16	1	2
Sotolongo	1.000	7	2	8	0	0
Tirotta	1.000	1	0	2	0	0
Turconi	.917	3	3	8	1	1

Shortstop	PCT	G	PO	A	E	DP
Beltre	1.000	3	2	2	0	0
Capra	1.000	2	2	2	0	1
De Castro	.953	36	47	76	6	14
Del Rosario	1.000	5	10	9	0	1
Groshans	1.000	2	0	4	0	0
Kasevich	.975	16	30	49	2	11
Lopez	1.000	1	1	2	0	1
Machado	.953	48	48	114	8	20
Pinto	.955	17	10	32	2	4
Turconi	1.000	3	3	7	0	1

Outfield	PCT	G	PO	A	E	DP
Brazoban	.945	47	62	7	4	0
Brown	.984	37	61	1	1	0
Brown	.979	24	45	2	1	0
Cardona	1.000	7	10	1	0	0
De La Rosa	1.000	7	14	1	0	0
Del Rosario	.926	17	24	1	2	0
Eden	1.000	3	6	0	0	0
Fajardo	1.000	5	4	0	0	0
Hernandez	1.000	2	4	0	0	0
Lopez	--	1	0	0	0	0
Martinez	.966	59	56	1	2	1
Masson	1.000	6	7	0	0	0
Pinto	1.000	7	12	0	0	0
Rivas	1.000	2	2	0	0	0
Robertis	1.000	6	9	0	0	0
Robertson	1.000	3	9	0	0	0
Rock	.963	20	25	1	1	0
Roden	1.000	25	44	3	0	1
Salinas	.992	74	118	7	1	1
Santiago	.969	22	28	3	1	0
Sotolongo	.927	32	36	2	3	1
Young	1.000	4	5	0	0	0

FCL BLUE JAYS — ROOKIE

FLORIDA COMPLEX LEAGUE

Batting	B-T	HT	WT	DOB	AVG	vLH	vRH	G	AB	R	H	2B	3B	HR	RBI	BB	HBP	SH	SF	SO	SB	CS	SLG	OBP
Yhoangel Aponte	R-R	5-11	190	2-12-04	.212	.300	.198	44	146	21	31	6	1	3	22	13	4	0	2	48	6	3	.329	.291
Jean Arnaez	R-R	5-10	160	8-22-02	.204	.125	.220	23	49	6	10	2	0	0	5	4	1	0	0	8	3	0	.245	.278
Manuel Beltre	R-R	5-9	155	6-9-04	.234	.192	.241	49	171	25	40	8	1	1	23	22	10	0	2	41	9	4	.310	.351
Amell Brazoban	R-R	6-2	170	10-9-01	.217	.000	.250	9	23	3	5	1	0	1	3	0	1	0	0	8	1	0	.391	.250
Peniel Brito	R-R	6-1	210	12-20-02	.132	.125	.133	20	38	3	5	0	0	0	3	10	1	0	1	20	1	1	.132	.320
Dasan Brown	R-R	6-0	185	9-25-01	.188	.000	.250	6	16	5	3	1	0	0	1	2	4	0	0	7	2	1	.250	.409
Leonel Callez	R-R	5-11	165	1-25-01	.154	.000	.200	5	13	0	2	0	1	0	0	1	0	0	0	4	0	1	.308	.214
2-team total (13 FCL Braves)					.140	.167	.132	18	50	4	7	1	1	0	0	4	1	0	0	16	0	1	.200	.218
Vinny Capra	R-R	5-8	175	7-7-96	.800	1.000	.750	3	5	2	4	4	0	0	0	2	1	0	0	0	0	0	1.600	.875
Rikelbin De Castro	R-R	6-0	150	1-23-03	.111	.000	.125	4	9	1	1	1	0	0	0	1	0	0	0	4	0	0	.222	.200
Alex De Jesus	R-R	6-2	170	3-22-02	.500	.000	.600	2	6	2	3	1	0	1	3	1	0	0	1	0	0	0	1.167	.500
Marcos De La Rosa	B-R	5-11	160	1-28-02	.207	.211	.207	43	111	23	23	5	2	6	17	17	5	2	1	45	21	3	.450	.336
Angel Del Rosario	R-R	6-0	160	1-11-03	.278	.250	.286	7	18	6	5	0	0	1	3	2	0	0	0	5	8	0	.444	.350
Nicolas Deschamps	L-R	5-11	180	8-25-02	.250	--	.250	13	24	9	6	2	1	1	3	11	2	0	1	7	0	0	.542	.500
Francisco Fajardo	B-R	5-10	163	5-26-00	.000	--	.000	2	6	0	0	0	0	0	1	2	1	0	0	0	0	2	.000	.333
Cristian Feliz	L-L	6-4	190	9-7-02	.167	.133	.171	38	120	13	20	6	1	4	14	16	5	0	0	51	2	0	.333	.291
Endri Garcia	R-R	6-0	163	11-9-02	.292	.300	.289	31	96	12	28	8	1	1	11	8	2	0	0	34	5	2	.427	.358
Luis Garcia	R-R	5-9	160	9-1-03	.201	.091	.222	43	139	21	28	5	3	1	12	18	2	0	3	41	11	1	.302	.296
Juan Gonzalez	R-R	5-10	195	2-20-01	.222	.200	.226	14	36	2	8	2	0	0	4	4	3	0	0	9	0	0	.278	.349
Sammy Hernandez	R-R	5-10	185	6-1-04	.067	.000	.071	7	15	2	1	0	0	0	0	1	0	0	0	2	0	0	.067	.125
Jerry Huntzinger	R-R	6-2	180	2-15-99	.100	.250	.000	5	10	2	1	0	0	0	0	4	0	0	0	4	0	0	.100	.357
Gabriel Martinez	R-R	6-0	170	7-24-02	.100	.000	.111	3	10	1	1	1	0	0	0	1	1	0	0	2	1	0	.200	.250
J.C. Masson	L-R	6-3	193	8-22-02	.288	.333	.278	23	66	11	19	5	2	0	7	13	4	0	2	23	0	1	.424	.424
Victor Mesia	R-R	5-9	175	1-18-03	.237	.250	.235	15	38	9	9	3	1	1	5	5	2	0	0	13	1	1	.447	.356
Albert Millan	R-R	5-10	160	1-31-05	.050	.000	.056	11	20	1	1	0	0	0	0	3	2	0	0	6	0	0	.050	.240
Yeuni Munoz	R-R	6-1	190	10-4-03	.318	.375	.286	9	22	2	7	0	1	1	6	6	0	0	0	7	1	0	.545	.464
Jonathan Peguero	L-R	5-11	165	7-23-04	.184	.267	.147	18	49	3	9	1	0	0	4	5	0	0	0	24	1	0	.204	.259
Juan Pizarro	L-L	5-11	150	1-18-02	.107	.000	.143	11	28	1	3	0	0	0	1	6	1	0	1	11	3	1	.107	.278
Robert Robertis	L-L	5-11	188	11-29-02	.290	.278	.292	34	107	18	31	6	3	0	11	11	0	0	1	24	3	1	.402	.353

Will Robertson	L-L	6-2	215	12-26-97	.100	.000	.125	3	10	1	1	0	0	1	2	0	0	0	0	5	0	0	.400	.100
Jaden Rudd	L-L	6-0	185	8-16-02	.203	.118	.216	46	128	24	26	5	2	2	16	28	4	1	0	31	8	4	.320	.363
Emmanuel Sanchez	R-R	6-0	170	5-30-01	.340	.333	.341	15	47	5	16	2	1	0	11	1	2	0	0	5	2	1	.426	.380
Glenn Santiago	R-R	6-0	165	12-14-00	.000	--	.000	1	3	0	0	0	0	0	0	0	0	0	0	0	0	0	.000	.000
Riley Tirotta	R-R	6-3	195	8-21-98	.250	--	.250	2	8	0	2	1	0	0	1	0	0	0	0	0	0	0	.375	.250
Tucker Toman	B-R	6-1	190	11-12-03	.289	.143	.323	11	38	4	11	3	0	0	5	7	0	0	1	12	0	0	.368	.391
Francisco Veracierto	R-R	5-11	160	1-29-02	.200	.000	.244	20	50	6	10	3	0	1	3	2	0	0	0	15	0	1	.320	.231

Pitching	B-T	HT	WT	DOB	W	L	ERA	G	GS	CG	SV	IP	H	R	ER	HR	BB	SO	AVG	vLH	vRH	K/9	BB/9
Eliander Alcalde	R-R	5-9	171	8-9-03	3	1	4.15	10	7	0	0	43	39	22	20	5	16	38	.238	.203	.257	7.89	3.32
Ben Baggett	R-R	5-10	195	2-28-96	0	0	0.00	1	0	0	1	1	0	0	0	0	0	2	.000	.000	.000	18.00	0.00
Cooper Benson	L-L	6-0	213	8-3-00	0	0	0.00	3	1	0	0	9	6	1	0	0	3	16	.171	.222	.154	15.43	2.89
Irv Carter	R-R	6-4	210	10-9-02	1	3	5.88	9	6	0	0	34	36	24	22	8	11	42	.275	.184	.312	11.23	2.94
Sergio Caruci	R-R	6-2	155	10-12-02	2	3	4.76	10	5	0	1	40	35	22	21	3	18	36	.238	.217	.248	8.17	4.08
Jiorgeny Casimiri	R-R	6-1	160	7-12-01	0	0	0.00	3	0	0	0	4	0	0	0	0	0	6	.000	.000	.000	13.50	0.00
Edgar Castro	R-R	6-1	165	2-7-02	3	2	2.81	15	0	0	3	26	13	9	8	2	17	30	.155	.194	.132	10.52	5.96
Fernando Chacon	R-R	5-10	160	11-16-01	0	0	0.00	1	1	0	0	1	1	0	0	0	0	1	.250	.000	.333	9.00	0.00
Marc Civit	L-L	6-0	150	6-23-02	2	2	5.50	15	0	0	1	18	22	14	11	1	13	24	.314	.188	.352	12.00	6.50
Darwin Cruz	R-R	6-0	190	9-11-01	0	1	9.69	10	0	0	1	13	16	14	14	3	7	16	.308	.235	.343	11.08	4.85
Jose De Leon	R-R	6-0	220	8-7-92	0	0	0.00	1	1	0	0	1	0	0	0	0	0	2	.000	.000	.000	18.00	0.00
Lazaro Estrada	R-R	5-10	180	4-24-99	0	0	7.36	3	1	0	0	4	2	3	3	0	2	8	.154	.167	.143	19.64	4.91
Edisson Gonzalez	R-R	5-10	160	10-2-99	0	0	0.00	3	2	0	0	5	1	0	0	0	0	4	.063	.167	.000	7.20	0.00
Adrian Hernandez	R-R	5-8	190	1-22-00	1	0	3.38	2	1	0	0	3	3	1	1	0	2	2	.375	.000	.600	6.75	6.75
Brahiam Jimenez	L-L	6-0	165	12-10-01	0	0	6.62	12	1	0	1	18	16	13	13	3	16	17	.246	.214	.255	8.66	8.15
Anthony Kay	L-L	6-0	225	3-21-95	0	0	0.00	2	1	0	0	3	1	0	0	0	0	4	.111	.000	.143	12.00	0.00
Brady Lail	R-R	6-2	200	8-9-93	0	0	0.00	1	1	0	0	1	1	0	0	0	0	1	.250	.000	.333	9.00	0.00
Keiner Leon	R-R	5-11	190	10-29-03	2	3	4.58	13	0	0	5	20	26	18	10	0	7	22	.321	.458	.263	10.07	3.20
Jean Lopez	R-R	6-0	170	10-18-02	2	0	4.50	12	0	0	0	18	19	11	9	0	15	13	.268	.296	.250	6.50	7.50
Frank Medina	R-R	5-11	164	10-28-00	2	0	9.42	11	0	0	0	14	15	16	15	4	12	13	.263	.304	.235	8.16	7.53
Julian Merryweather	R-R	6-4	215	10-14-91	0	0	0.00	1	1	0	0	1	0	0	0	0	0	2	.000	.000	.000	18.00	0.00
Eric Pardinho	R-R	5-10	155	1-5-01	0	0	3.00	2	0	0	0	3	4	1	1	0	0	4	.308	.250	.333	12.00	0.00
Kelvin Perez	R-R	6-3	175	9-9-00	0	0	0.00	1	0	0	0	3	0	0	0	0	0	1	.000	.000	.000	3.38	0.00
Nathanael Perez Gonzalez	R-R	5-10	159	4-2-01	1	1	6.64	11	0	0	1	20	24	20	15	6	11	20	.293	.250	.315	8.85	4.87
Nathanael Perez Lopez	R-R	6-1	160	6-5-98	0	0	3.00	2	1	0	0	3	4	1	1	0	1	4	.364	.000	.667	12.00	3.00
Jackson Rees	R-R	6-4	210	7-30-94	0	0	0.00	3	1	0	0	3	0	0	0	0	1	6	.000	.000	.000	18.00	3.00
Kendry Rojas	L-L	6-2	190	11-26-02	0	0	0.00	1	1	0	0	1	0	0	0	0	0	3	.000	--	.000	27.00	0.00
Yondrei Rojas	R-R	5-10	180	11-22-02	1	3	4.60	7	6	0	1	29	20	16	15	4	6	31	.190	.109	.254	9.51	1.84
Harry Rutkowski	R-L	6-2	230	4-22-99	2	0	0.00	2	0	0	0	3	2	1	0	0	0	3	.182	.667	.000	9.00	0.00
Sam Ryan	R-R	6-3	205	9-22-98	1	0	1.50	4	0	0	0	6	4	1	1	0	1	6	.190	.250	.154	9.00	1.50
Rafael Sanchez	R-R	6-1	215	8-22-99	0	1	3.00	3	3	0	0	12	14	4	4	0	2	12	.286	.261	.308	9.00	1.50
Angel Santana	R-R	6-2	155	5-17-02	0	0	4.97	12	0	0	1	13	12	9	7	2	8	7	.261	.294	.241	4.97	5.68
Tayler Saucedo	L-L	6-4	205	6-18-93	0	0	0.00	1	0	0	0	1	0	0	0	0	0	2	.000	.000	.000	18.00	0.00
Johan Simon	L-L	6-1	166	7-1-01	2	2	2.96	11	3	0	0	27	21	9	9	0	16	33	.216	.097	.273	10.87	5.27
Anders Tolhurst	R-R	6-4	190	9-13-99	0	2	5.40	3	2	0	0	5	6	3	3	0	1	8	.316	.200	.357	14.40	1.80
Stephen Vargas	R-R	5-10	168	2-12-02	0	2	5.87	9	5	0	1	31	37	21	20	4	9	22	.306	.268	.325	6.46	2.64
Andrew Vasquez	L-L	6-6	235	9-14-93	0	0	0.00	1	0	0	0	1	0	0	0	0	0	3	.000	.000	.000	27.00	0.00
Guillermo Villasmil	R-R	5-10	160	9-13-02	2	1	5.51	13	0	0	1	16	13	11	10	4	9	19	.220	.278	.195	10.47	4.96
Troy Watson	R-R	6-2	180	6-11-97	0	0	1.23	4	4	0	0	7	4	1	1	0	6	6	.148	.167	.143	7.36	7.36

Fielding

C: Arnaez 12, Callez 1, Deschamps 13, Gonzalez 14, Hernandez 3, Huntzinger 4, Mesia 13, Millan 5, Peguero 15. **1B:** Arnaez 14, Brito 4, Callez 4, De La Rosa 1, Feliz 35, Huntzinger 1, Sanchez 2, Veracierto 5. **2B:** Arnaez 1, Beltre 10, De Castro 3, De La Rosa 12, Del Rosario 6, Fajardo 2, Garcia 22, Veracierto 6. **3B:** Brito 1, Callez 1, De Jesus 1, De La Rosa 19, Del Rosario 1, Garcia 9, Sanchez 13, Tirotta 1, Toman 6, Veracierto 8. **SS:** Beltre 39, Capra 1, De Castro 1, De Jesus 1, De La Rosa 1, Garcia 11, Sanchez 1, Toman 4. **OF:** Aponte 34, Brazoban 8, Brito 7, Brown 4, De La Rosa 13, Del Rosario 1, Feliz 3, Garcia 26, Martinez 2, Masson 17, Munoz 6, Pizarro 8, Robertis 29, Robertson 2, Rudd 45, Santiago 1.

DSL BLUE JAYS — *ROOKIE*

DOMINICAN SUMMER LEAGUE

Batting	B-T	HT	WT	DOB	AVG	vLH	vRH	G	AB	R	H	2B	3B	HR	RBI	BB	HBP	SH	SF	SO	SB	CS	SLG	OBP
Victor Arias	L-L	5-11	150	8-24-03	.315	.556	.267	19	54	14	17	3	3	0	3	11	2	0	0	20	5	2	.481	.448
Jonathan Bautista	L-R	6-0	145	10-17-03	.111	.059	.125	30	81	9	9	1	2	2	14	15	2	0	1	51	0	0	.247	.263
Gregori Cano	L-R	6-1	180	7-18-04	.257	.231	.264	47	136	18	35	5	0	2	20	34	2	0	1	51	2	0	.338	.410
Kendry Chirinos	R-R	5-11	170	10-6-04	.180	.150	.186	48	133	18	24	10	0	1	13	35	7	0	2	48	0	0	.278	.373
Faruk De La Cruz	R-R	5-10	145	3-11-05	.212	.211	.213	39	113	16	24	3	2	0	7	19	2	0	0	22	1	2	.274	.336
Aneudi Escanio	B-R	5-9	150	11-27-04	.188	.231	.176	29	64	6	12	2	0	0	6	7	1	0	2	21	2	4	.219	.270
Jose Fernandez	L-R	6-0	150	3-23-05	.192	.294	.177	46	130	17	25	3	2	1	13	23	5	1	1	38	4	2	.269	.333
Martin Gimenez	R-R	6-1	155	2-15-04	.151	.115	.160	40	126	11	19	4	0	0	6	10	3	1	0	45	6	1	.183	.230
Jean Joseph	R-R	5-11	160	2-4-05	.204	.160	.212	48	157	16	32	2	0	0	12	22	4	1	1	28	6	6	.217	.315
Ali Lucena	L-R	5-10	145	2-12-05	.179	.273	.143	32	78	8	14	0	0	0	5	15	1	3	0	23	3	0	.179	.319
Luis Meza	R-R	5-10	150	9-23-04	.229	.182	.235	28	96	6	22	4	1	0	8	5	0	0	0	19	2	0	.292	.267
Maykel Minoso	R-R	5-10	170	7-3-05	.161	.000	.179	12	31	2	5	0	0	0	2	8	0	0	0	13	0	0	.161	.333
Julio Ozoria	R-R	6-3	180	11-6-02	.214	.056	.250	34	98	8	21	3	0	3	14	11	3	0	1	44	1	0	.337	.310
Omar Romero	R-R	5-7	155	8-25-05	.271	.235	.286	26	59	13	16	4	0	0	4	8	0	0	0	14	3	1	.339	.358
Railin Tejada	R-R	5-10	160	2-10-05	.127	.000	.152	20	55	6	7	0	0	2	4	13	2	0	0	29	3	3	.236	.314

Carlos Vasquez	L-R	5-8	150	6-4-05	.284	.316	.278	37	109	17	31	5	0	0	13	21	2	0	2	25	3	1	.330	.403

Pitching	**B-T**	**HT**	**WT**	**DOB**	**W**	**L**	**ERA**	**G**	**GS**	**CG**	**SV**	**IP**	**H**	**R**	**ER**	**HR**	**BB**	**SO**	**AVG**	**vLH**	**vRH**	**K/9**	**BB/9**
Felipe Bello	R-R	6-3	197	2-1-00	0	1	5.00	3	2	0	0	9	6	5	5	1	5	10	.188	.167	.200	10.00	5.00
Moises Brito	L-L	6-5	215	7-9-02	2	4	1.86	12	2	0	1	29	21	8	6	1	1	32	.198	.240	.185	9.93	0.31
2-team total (4 DSL LAD Mega)					3	4	1.79	16	3	0	1	40	27	11	8	2	1	45	.185	.258	.165	10.04	0.22
Robin De Jesus	R-R	6-0	160	9-28-02	2	2	7.23	15	1	0	1	19	22	19	15	2	20	26	.286	.321	.265	12.54	9.64
Eminen Flores	R-R	5-11	160	2-27-03	0	3	2.10	8	6	0	0	26	16	7	6	3	7	17	.182	.190	.174	5.96	2.45
Raudy Gomez	R-R	5-10	160	11-14-04	0	1	8.59	5	5	0	0	7	7	7	7	0	7	4	.292	.182	.385	4.91	8.59
Ivan Gonzalez	R-R	5-9	140	10-13-04	0	0	21.00	3	0	0	0	3	7	7	7	0	4	5	.438	.500	.400	15.00	12.00
Daniel Guerra	R-R	6-6	230	3-13-04	1	1	0.84	6	6	0	0	21	12	2	2	0	16	19	.162	.175	.147	8.02	6.75
Jorge Guerra	R-R	5-11	165	6-6-04	0	2	12.46	10	0	0	0	13	25	22	18	2	9	14	.397	.448	.353	9.69	6.23
Francisco Lucumi	R-R	6-2	170	6-14-02	2	2	6.43	12	0	0	0	28	36	27	20	1	10	34	.298	.359	.268	10.93	3.21
Yordi Martinez	R-R	6-2	180	6-3-03	0	5	7.94	14	0	0	0	17	23	19	15	2	9	20	.324	.235	.405	10.59	4.76
Carlos Meza	R-R	6-0	160	11-19-04	2	2	5.40	11	4	0	0	30	38	20	18	2	10	18	.317	.347	.296	5.40	3.00
Omar Munoz	R-R	5-10	160	9-8-04	2	3	6.04	14	0	0	0	28	32	23	19	1	12	16	.278	.195	.324	5.08	3.81
Pedro Munoz	L-L	5-9	150	7-29-04	0	0	9.90	7	0	0	1	10	17	14	11	1	6	7	.378	.250	.424	6.30	5.40
Neiyerbe Obeso	R-R	6-1	174	1-9-04	0	0	11.57	2	0	0	1	2	2	4	3	0	1	1	.222	.500	.000	3.86	3.86
Gabriel Ochoa	R-R	5-11	173	8-16-02	0	0	10.80	13	0	0	1	12	14	19	14	0	21	9	.298	.200	.370	6.94	16.20
Fernando Perez	R-R	6-3	170	2-12-04	1	4	4.53	12	12	0	0	44	50	32	22	4	5	48	.273	.273	.274	9.89	1.03
Julio Ramirez	R-R	6-0	180	7-29-01	2	0	6.63	13	0	0	2	19	17	18	14	2	15	12	.243	.273	.229	5.68	7.11
Rafael Sanchez	R-R	6-1	215	8-22-99	2	1	3.00	9	9	0	0	39	37	20	13	1	11	40	.242	.283	.220	9.23	2.54
Lluveres Severino	R-R	6-1	180	8-9-03	0	0	27.00	1	0	0	0	1	2	3	2	0	1	1	.400	.000	.667	13.50	13.50
Ramon Suarez	L-L	5-11	156	6-12-04	0	2	1.29	3	0	0	1	7	4	4	1	0	1	7	.167	.167	.167	9.00	1.29
Rodolfo Toledano	R-R	6-0	165	2-16-05	0	3	6.00	7	7	0	0	12	14	14	8	0	5	12	.280	.357	.250	9.00	3.75
Luis Torres	L-L	6-1	165	2-24-05	2	2	2.01	13	2	0	1	31	16	10	7	1	16	33	.150	.167	.145	9.48	4.60
Juanmi Vasquez	L-L	5-11	140	12-1-03	0	0	0.00	3	0	0	0	4	3	0	0	0	1	2	.250	.000	.273	4.91	2.45

Fielding

C: De La Cruz 18, Meza 24, Minoso 10, Vasquez 7. **1B:** Cano 24, Chirinos 15, De La Cruz 16, Vasquez 4. **2B:** Escanio 8, Fernandez 16, Romero 25, Vasquez 13. **3B:** Cano 23, Chirinos 31, Escanio 4, Gimenez 4. **SS:** Cano 1, Escanio 4, Fernandez 32, Gimenez 25, Romero 1. **OF:** Arias 7, Bautista 32, Escanio 12, Gimenez 12, Joseph 45, Lucena 33, Minoso 2, Ozoria 31, Vasquez 9.

Washington Nationals

SEASON IN A SENTENCE: No one expected the Nationals to be World Series contenders. In fact, no one expected them to be very good at all. However, they exceeded even the worst predictions. With 107 losses, it was the first time since 2009 that Washington owned the worst record in MLB. At the trade deadline, fans' worst fears were confirmed when a blockbuster trade sent Juan Soto and Josh Bell to the Padres in exchange for a package of top prospects.

HIGH POINT: While their roster still leaves much to be desired, you can point to the trade deadline as a clear investment in the Nationals future. Another fun story of the Nats season was the emergence of Joey Meneses. After 10 years in the minor leagues, the 30-year old rookie had his chance to shine in The Show.

LOW POINT: It's safe to say the Nationals season was full of more low points than high ones. Not only did they trade away the face of the franchise in Juan Soto, but the organization went on to lose a league-worst 107 games. To add salt to the wound, because of the new draft lottery, they are not even guaranteed the number one pick in the draft.

NOTABLE ROOKIES: After the trade deadline, the Nationals had their shortstop of the future. The organization had their first significant looks at shortstop CJ Abrams and Keibert Ruiz behind the plate. The young core in Washington is solid, but still has a lot to prove. In September, Cade Cavalli made his much anticipated debut, but ended the season sidelined with a shoulder injury.

KEY TRANSACTIONS: In the biggest trade in recent history, the Nationals traded superstar outfielder Juan Soto and first baseman Josh Bell to the Padres for a package that included veteran DH Luke Voit, LHP MacKenzie Gore, OF Robert Hassell III, SS C.J. Abrams, OF James Wood and RHP Jarlin Susana. Their farm system jumped from 26th overall to 14th. The organization also drafted Elijah Green at fifth overall in the 2022 draft.

ON THE FARM: Washington's affiliates ranked 22nd in overall win percentage, but this year marked a key point in the system's development. The Nationals' Low-A affiliate, the FredNats ended the year with the second-best record in the Carolina League. They fell short in a decisive game three in the 2022 Carolina League North Divisional Championship series.

OPENING DAY PAYROLL: $135,290,221 (17th)

PLAYERS OF THE YEAR

MAJOR LEAGUE

Lane Thomas
OF
.241/.301/.404
17 HR, 26 2B in 146 G
First full season in MLB

MINOR LEAGUE

Jeremy De La Rosa
OF
(LoA/HiA)
.280/.358/.436
11 HR, 39 SB in 101 G

ORGANIZATION LEADERS

Batting		*Minimum 250 AB
MAJORS		
* AVG	Josh Bell	.302
* OPS	Juan Soto	.894
HR	Juan Soto	21
RBI	Nelson Cruz	64
MINORS		
* AVG	Jake Alu, Harrisburg, Rochester	.299
* OBP	Josh Palacios, Rochester	.382
* SLG	Jake Alu, Harrisburg, Rochester	.506
* OPS	Jake Alu, Harrisburg, Rochester	.871
R	Jacob Young, Fredericksburg	118
H	Andrew Stevenson, Rochester	152
TB	Jake Alu, Harrisburg, Rochester	254
2B	Jake Alu, Harrisburg, Rochester	40
3B	Andrew Stevenson, Rochester	9
HR	Wilson Garcia, Harrisburg	24
RBI	Wilson Garcia, Harrisburg	81
	Jake Alu, Harrisburg, Rochester	
BB	Yasel Antuna, Wilmington, Harrisburg	89
SO	Omar Meregildo, Wilmington, Harrisburg	136
	Andrew Stevenson, Rochester	
SB	Jacob Young, Fredericksburg	52

Pitching		#Minimum 75 IP
MAJORS		
W	Josiah Gray	7
# ERA	Erasmo Ramirez	2.92
SO	Josiah Gray	154
SV	Tanner Rainey	12
MINORS		
W	Jose Atencio, FCL, Fredericksburg	9
L	Michael Cuevas, Wilmington	12
# ERA	Mitchell Parker, Wilmington	2.88
G	Alberto Baldonado, Rochester	56
GS	4 tied	24
SV	Jordan Weems, Rochester	16
IP	Ronald Herrera, Rochester	131
BB	Luis Reyes, Harrisburg, Rochester	69
SO	Alex Troop, Harrisburg, Rochester	130
# AVG	Logan Verrett, Rochester	.232

2022 PERFORMANCE

General Manager: Mike Rizzo. **Farm Director:** Ryan Thomas. **Scouting Director:** Eddie Longosz.

Class	Team	League	W	L	PCT	Finish	Manager
Majors	Washington Nationals	National	55	107	.340	15th (15)	Dave Martinez
Triple-A	Rochester Red Wings	International	67	81	.453	17th (20)	Matthew LeCroy
Double-A	Harrisburg Senators	Eastern	52	85	.380	12th (12)	Tripp Keister
High-A	Wilmington Blue Rocks	South Atlantic	65	65	.500	7th (12)	Mario Lisson
Low-A	Fredericksburg Nationals	Carolina	75	55	.577	2nd (12)	Jake Lowery
Rookie	FCL Nationals	Florida Complex	33	22	.600	5th (16)	Luis Ordaz
Overall 2022 Minor League Record			321	339	.486	20th (30)	

ORGANIZATION STATISTICS

WASHINGTON NATIONALS

NATIONAL LEAGUE

Batting	B-T	HT	WT	DOB	AVG	vLH	vRH	G	AB	R	H	2B	3B	HR	RBI	BB	HBP	SH	SF	SO	SB	CS	SLG	OBP
CJ Abrams	L-R	6-2	185	10-3-00	.258	.183	.303	44	159	17	41	7	2	0	10	1	3	0	0	23	6	2	.327	.276
2-team total (46 San Diego Padres)					.246	.157	.287	90	284	33	70	12	2	2	21	5	9	2	2	50	7	4	.324	.280
Riley Adams	R-R	6-4	249	6-26-96	.176	.138	.208	48	142	14	25	4	0	5	10	12	1	0	0	46	0	1	.310	.245
Ehire Adrianza	B-R	6-1	198	8-21-89	.179	.171	.184	31	84	5	15	2	0	0	7	8	1	0	1	22	1	0	.202	.255
2-team total (6 Atlanta Braves)					.175	.184	.169	37	97	8	17	3	0	0	7	11	1	0	1	25	1	0	.206	.264
Tres Barrera	R-R	6-0	215	9-15-94	.180	.088	.375	19	50	2	9	1	0	0	4	2	0	1	0	16	0	0	.200	.212
Josh Bell	B-R	6-4	261	8-14-92	.301	.285	.311	103	375	52	113	24	3	14	57	49	5	0	6	61	0	1	.493	.384
2-team total (53 San Diego Padres)					.266	.276	.261	156	552	78	147	29	3	17	71	81	5	0	6	102	0	1	.422	.362
Alex Call	R-R	5-11	188	9-27-94	.245	.188	.296	35	102	16	25	3	1	5	13	11	2	0	0	26	3	3	.441	.330
Nelson Cruz	R-R	6-2	230	7-1-80	.234	.248	.227	124	448	50	105	16	0	10	64	49	4	0	3	119	4	0	.337	.313
Alcides Escobar	R-R	6-1	205	12-16-86	.218	.209	.222	42	124	12	27	4	2	0	8	5	2	0	0	32	1	1	.282	.260
Lucius Fox	B-R	6-1	192	7-2-97	.080	.000	.100	10	25	2	2	0	0	0	2	1	0	2	0	9	1	0	.080	.115
Maikel Franco	R-R	6-1	225	8-26-92	.229	.241	.224	103	371	31	85	15	0	9	39	12	2	0	3	75	1	0	.342	.255
Luis Garcia	L-R	6-2	212	5-16-00	.275	.235	.290	93	360	29	99	23	2	7	45	11	1	1	4	84	3	4	.408	.295
Cesar Hernandez	B-R	5-10	183	5-23-90	.248	.282	.232	147	560	64	139	28	4	1	34	45	7	3	2	114	10	4	.318	.311
Yadiel Hernandez	L-R	5-10	197	10-9-87	.269	.264	.270	94	305	30	82	16	0	9	41	19	1	0	2	74	2	1	.410	.312
Joey Meneses	R-R	6-3	215	5-6-92	.324	.366	.305	56	222	33	72	14	0	13	34	15	1	0	2	52	1	0	.563	.367
Josh Palacios	L-R	6-1	200	7-30-95	.213	.400	.190	29	47	8	10	2	0	0	2	1	1	0	0	15	1	0	.255	.245
Israel Pineda	R-R	5-11	188	4-3-00	.077	.000	.091	4	13	1	1	0	0	0	0	1	0	0	0	7	0	0	.077	.143
Victor Robles	R-R	6-0	195	5-19-97	.224	.294	.188	132	366	42	82	10	2	6	33	17	9	11	4	104	15	4	.311	.273
Keibert Ruiz	B-R	6-0	225	7-20-98	.251	.237	.256	112	394	33	99	22	0	7	36	30	6	1	2	50	6	1	.360	.313
Juan Soto	L-L	6-2	224	10-25-98	.246	.223	.259	101	342	62	84	17	1	21	46	91	3	0	0	62	6	2	.485	.408
2-team total (52 San Diego Padres)					.242	.210	.261	153	524	93	127	25	2	27	62	135	4	0	0	96	6	2	.452	.401
Dee Strange-Gordon	L-R	5-11	166	4-22-88	.305	.500	.291	23	59	6	18	1	1	0	2	0	0	0	0	8	3	2	.356	.305
Lane Thomas	R-R	6-0	191	8-23-95	.241	.253	.234	146	498	62	120	26	2	17	52	41	4	0	5	132	8	4	.404	.301
Ildemaro Vargas	B-R	6-0	180	7-16-91	.280	.268	.287	53	186	15	52	13	0	3	19	5	3	1	1	21	3	1	.398	.308
2-team total (10 Chicago Cubs)					.263	.253	.269	63	209	19	55	13	1	4	23	8	3	1	1	23	3	1	.392	.299
Luke Voit	R-R	6-3	255	2-13-91	.228	.175	.248	53	202	17	46	4	0	9	21	16	4	0	2	69	0	0	.381	.295
2-team total (82 San Diego Padres)					.226	.174	.247	135	500	55	113	22	0	22	69	55	7	0	6	179	1	1	.402	.308

Pitching	B-T	HT	WT	DOB	W	L	ERA	G	GS	CG	SV	IP	H	R	ER	HR	BB	SO	AVG	vLH	vRH	K/9	BB/9
Cory Abbott	R-R	6-1	210	9-20-95	0	5	5.25	16	9	0	0	48	44	30	28	12	25	45	.239	.268	.207	8.44	4.69
Joan Adon	R-R	6-2	246	8-12-98	1	12	7.10	14	14	0	0	65	76	53	51	8	39	55	.290	.264	.312	7.65	5.43
Ehire Adrianza	B-R	6-1	198	8-21-89	0	0	0.00	1	0	0	0	1	0	0	0	0	1	1	.000	.000	.000	9.00	9.00
Victor Arano	R-R	6-2	228	2-7-95	1	1	4.50	43	0	0	1	42	47	30	21	5	12	44	.278	.333	.240	9.43	2.57
Cade Cavalli	R-R	6-4	240	8-14-98	0	1	14.54	1	1	0	0	4	6	7	7	0	2	6	.333	.200	.385	12.46	4.15
Steve Cishek	R-R	6-6	220	6-18-86	1	4	4.21	69	0	0	1	66	54	33	31	11	27	74	.223	.280	.194	10.04	3.66
Sam Clay	L-L	6-3	238	6-21-93	0	0	10.38	6	0	0	0	4	3	5	5	1	3	3	.200	.167	.222	6.23	6.23
2-team total (1 New York Mets)					0	0	8.44	7	0	0	0	5	4	6	5	1	4	5	.200	.125	.250	8.44	6.75
Tyler Clippard	R-R	6-3	200	2-14-85	0	0	7.20	4	0	0	0	5	6	4	4	1	4	4	.286	.000	.500	7.20	7.20
Patrick Corbin	L-L	6-4	222	7-19-89	6	19	6.31	31	31	1	0	153	210	119	107	27	49	128	.321	.321	.320	7.55	2.89
Sean Doolittle	L-L	6-2	227	9-26-86	0	0	0.00	6	0	0	0	5	1	0	0	0	0	6	.059	.111	.000	10.13	0.00
Carl Edwards Jr.	R-R	6-3	170	9-3-91	6	3	2.76	57	0	0	2	62	51	22	19	8	25	56	.224	.241	.208	8.13	3.63
Alcides Escobar	R-R	6-1	205	12-16-86	0	0	10.80	2	0	0	0	2	3	2	2	0	1	0	.375	.000	.750	0.00	5.40
Paolo Espino	R-R	5-10	211	1-10-87	0	9	4.84	42	19	1	0	113	131	64	61	24	24	92	.287	.306	.271	7.31	1.91
Erick Fedde	R-R	6-4	203	2-25-93	6	13	5.81	27	27	0	0	127	149	84	82	21	58	94	.293	.272	.313	6.66	4.11
Kyle Finnegan	R-R	6-2	197	9-4-91	6	4	3.51	66	0	0	11	67	54	28	26	9	22	70	.221	.163	.264	9.45	2.97
Reed Garrett	R-R	6-2	196	1-2-93	0	1	6.75	7	0	0	0	9	13	8	7	1	8	6	.325	.267	.360	5.79	7.71
Josiah Gray	R-R	6-1	199	12-21-97	7	10	5.02	28	28	0	0	149	136	84	83	38	66	154	.239	.265	.221	9.32	4.00
Hunter Harvey	R-R	6-2	225	12-9-94	2	1	2.52	38	0	0	0	39	33	12	11	1	12	45	.234	.179	.284	10.30	2.75
Evan Lee	L-L	6-1	210	6-18-97	0	1	4.15	4	1	0	0	9	9	5	4	1	7	7	.257	.182	.292	7.27	7.27
Andres Machado	R-R	6-0	235	4-22-93	2	0	3.34	51	0	0	0	59	55	32	22	7	26	46	.241	.305	.187	6.98	3.94

Jake McGee	L-L	6-4	229	8-6-86	0	1	6.30	12	0	0	0	10	7	7	7	2	5	10	.194	.364	.120	9.00	4.50
3-team total (6 Milwaukee Brewers, 24 San Francisco Giants)					1	3	6.81	42	0	0	3	37	41	29	28	6	12	25	.275	.306	.260	6.08	2.92
Patrick Murphy	R-R	6-5	211	6-10-95	0	0	6.35	6	0	0	0	6	8	6	4	0	8	4	.320	.182	.429	6.35	12.71
Francisco Perez	B-L	6-2	217	7-20-97	0	0	7.27	10	0	0	0	9	13	7	7	2	9	7	.333	.400	.292	7.27	9.35
Tanner Rainey	R-R	6-2	244	12-25-92	1	3	3.30	29	0	0	12	30	26	16	11	5	13	36	.228	.220	.234	10.80	3.90
Erasmo Ramirez	R-R	6-0	217	5-2-90	4	2	2.92	60	2	0	0	86	79	31	28	11	14	61	.245	.238	.249	6.36	1.46
Josh Rogers	L-L	6-3	211	7-10-94	2	2	5.13	16	3	0	0	26	24	15	15	6	11	12	.238	.079	.333	4.10	3.76
Tommy Romero	R-R	6-2	225	7-8-97	0	1	14.73	1	1	0	0	4	8	8	6	5	4	2	.421	.300	.556	4.91	9.82
Aaron Sanchez	R-R	6-4	212	7-1-92	3	3	8.33	7	7	0	0	31	47	30	29	6	8	16	.367	.268	.444	4.60	2.30
Anibal Sanchez	R-R	6-0	207	2-27-84	4	6	4.28	14	14	0	0	69	55	34	33	13	33	48	.217	.198	.232	6.23	4.28
Dee Strange-Gordon	L-R	5-11	166	4-22-88	0	0	27.00	1	0	0	0	1	2	3	3	1	3	0	.500	--	.500	0.00	27.00
Stephen Strasburg	R-R	6-5	239	7-20-88	0	1	13.50	1	1	0	0	5	8	7	7	1	2	5	.400	.667	.286	9.64	3.86
Jackson Tetreault	R-R	6-5	189	6-3-96	2	2	5.14	4	4	0	0	21	23	15	12	4	10	9	.274	.171	.347	3.86	4.29
Mason Thompson	R-R	6-6	236	2-20-98	1	1	2.92	24	0	0	1	25	19	8	8	2	9	15	.211	.250	.174	5.47	3.28
Ildemaro Vargas	B-R	6-0	180	7-16-91	0	0	0.00	1	0	0	0	1	0	0	0	0	0	0	.000	.000	.000	0.00	0.00
Austin Voth	R-R	6-2	215	6-26-92	0	0	10.13	19	0	0	0	19	34	22	21	4	6	18	.386	.358	.429	8.68	2.89
Jordan Weems	L-R	6-4	209	11-7-92	0	1	5.22	52	0	0	0	40	35	24	23	7	12	41	.230	.182	.267	9.30	2.72

Fielding

Catcher	PCT	G	PO	A	E	DP	PB
Adams	.994	44	319	15	2	1	1
Barrera	1.000	19	109	4	0	1	0
Pineda	1.000	4	26	3	0	0	2
Ruiz	.992	106	794	37	7	5	4

First Base	PCT	G	PO	A	E	DP
Adams	1.000	1	8	1	0	0
Bell	.989	103	751	73	9	69
Franco	1.000	4	13	2	0	1
Meneses	.996	40	259	13	1	24
Voit	.989	26	177	8	2	17

Second Base	PCT	G	PO	A	E	DP
Adrianza	1.000	4	7	6	0	1
Escobar	1.000	2	1	1	0	0
Garcia	.977	33	52	77	3	23
Hernandez	.992	126	191	284	4	70
Vargas	1.000	1	3	1	0	0

Third Base	PCT	G	PO	A	E	DP
Adrianza	.974	18	18	20	1	3
Fox	.857	4	3	3	1	0
Franco	.959	99	59	196	11	15
Hernandez	.957	9	8	14	1	2
Vargas	.971	43	33	99	4	9

Shortstop	PCT	G	PO	A	E	DP
Abrams	.941	43	55	120	11	26
Adrianza	1.000	2	0	3	0	1
Escobar	.965	37	48	90	5	15
Fox	.944	6	5	12	1	0
Garcia	.938	59	69	128	13	27
Strange-Gordon	.963	13	17	35	2	9
Vargas	1.000	9	9	22	0	4

Outfield	PCT	G	PO	A	E	DP
Adrianza	1.000	9	7	0	0	0
Call	1.000	32	44	0	0	0
Hernandez	.960	10	23	1	1	1
Hernandez	.993	80	132	4	1	1
Meneses	.945	25	51	1	3	1
Palacios	1.000	21	21	0	0	0
Robles	.983	128	340	7	6	3
Soto	.990	99	192	2	2	0
Strange-Gordon	.875	7	6	1	1	0
Thomas	.994	172	298	8	2	2

ROCHESTER RED WINGS — *TRIPLE-A*

INTERNATIONAL LEAGUE

Batting	B-T	HT	WT	DOB	AVG	vLH	vRH	G	AB	R	H	2B	3B	HR	RBI	BB	HBP	SH	SF	SO	SB	CS	SLG	OBP
CJ Abrams	L-R	6-2	185	10-3-00	.290	.400	.238	8	31	7	9	2	0	0	2	2	1	0	1	8	4	1	.355	.343
Riley Adams	R-R	6-4	249	6-26-96	.224	.235	.219	29	107	11	24	8	0	4	17	11	4	0	1	41	0	0	.411	.317
Ehire Adrianza	B-R	6-1	198	8-21-89	.294	.333	.273	5	17	3	5	1	0	1	4	1	1	1	0	4	1	0	.529	.368
2-team total (3 Gwinnett Stripers)					.286	.250	.300	8	28	4	8	1	0	1	4	2	1	1	0	7	1	0	.429	.355
Jake Alu	L-R	5-10	175	4-6-97	.323	.333	.318	59	217	37	70	15	1	11	45	19	1	0	5	44	6	2	.553	.372
Nick Banks	L-L	6-0	215	11-18-94	.265	.260	.266	79	272	36	72	12	3	11	36	25	5	0	0	89	3	0	.452	.338
Tres Barrera	R-R	6-0	215	9-15-94	.254	.368	.223	55	177	25	45	7	1	7	25	20	3	1	1	41	0	2	.424	.338
Alex Call	R-R	5-11	188	9-27-94	.444	.250	.500	5	18	6	8	2	0	2	6	2	1	0	1	5	3	1	.889	.500
2-team total (71 Columbus Clippers)					.292	.231	.307	76	257	62	75	18	1	13	52	51	12	1	6	55	9	1	.521	.423
Donovan Casey	R-R	6-2	220	2-23-96	.216	.238	.208	84	287	36	62	10	3	7	29	22	4	1	3	97	6	2	.345	.278
David Dahl	L-R	6-2	197	4-1-94	.224	.050	.298	18	67	10	15	5	0	1	10	8	1	0	3	22	1	0	.343	.304
2-team total (67 Nashville Sounds)					.279	.271	.283	85	319	54	89	20	1	10	51	34	1	0	5	84	4	0	.442	.345
Jack Dunn	R-R	6-2	185	9-5-96	.217	.071	.281	13	46	6	10	2	0	0	5	4	0	1	1	13	2	0	.261	.275
Alcides Escobar	R-R	6-1	205	12-16-86	.250	.400	.143	4	12	2	3	1	0	1	2	0	0	0	1	3	0	0	.583	.231
Jecksson Flores	R-R	5-11	145	10-28-93	.244	.323	.220	41	131	18	32	7	1	3	11	14	3	0	1	27	1	1	.382	.329
Lucius Fox	B-R	6-1	192	7-2-97	.228	.302	.203	55	206	28	47	7	2	4	25	22	1	2	0	61	12	4	.340	.306
Cole Freeman	R-R	5-9	175	9-27-94	.243	.244	.243	50	144	27	35	7	1	2	8	9	3	5	1	20	15	3	.347	.299
Luis Garcia	L-R	6-2	212	5-16-00	.308	.327	.300	45	185	39	57	7	4	8	32	18	0	0	2	36	3	0	.519	.366
Taylor Gushue	B-R	6-1	224	12-19-93	.201	.264	.174	57	174	17	35	8	0	4	21	32	0	1	1	65	0	0	.316	.324
Chris Herrmann	L-R	6-0	200	11-24-87	.173	.000	.224	28	75	8	13	1	0	0	8	10	0	0	1	25	0	0	.187	.267
Daniel Johnson	L-L	5-10	200	7-11-95	.189	.211	.183	26	90	8	17	1	1	1	8	11	0	0	1	24	1	1	.256	.275
3-team total (17 Columbus Clippers, 14 Syracuse Mets)					.187	.174	.191	57	203	18	38	4	1	5	25	12	1	0	3	71	2	2	.291	.233
Matt Lipka	R-R	6-1	215	4-15-92	.202	.133	.230	45	104	24	21	3	2	0	6	14	2	1	0	35	14	0	.269	.308
2-team total (32 Nashville Sounds)					.228	.196	.241	77	197	39	45	6	4	2	11	25	2	2	0	62	26	1	.330	.321
Junior Martina	R-R	6-0	190	12-12-97	.063	.111	.000	8	16	1	1	0	0	0	0	0	0	0	0	6	0	0	.063	.063
Joey Meneses	R-R	6-3	215	5-6-92	.286	.304	.279	96	374	51	107	14	1	20	64	32	2	0	6	89	1	0	.489	.341
John Nogowski	R-L	6-0	245	1-5-93	.290	.282	.293	47	162	28	47	12	0	2	24	33	3	0	5	24	6	2	.401	.409
2-team total (40 Gwinnett Stripers)					.266	.227	.280	87	286	42	76	17	0	4	38	51	6	0	8	53	12	3	.367	.379
Jake Noll	R-R	6-2	213	3-8-94	.256	.316	.232	103	390	48	100	26	3	10	53	20	10	0	3	77	6	0	.415	.307
Josh Palacios	L-R	6-1	200	7-30-95	.298	.367	.270	76	275	43	82	12	2	7	44	33	5	2	1	50	19	7	.433	.382
2-team total (6 Buffalo Bisons)					.294	.353	.270	82	296	48	87	12	2	9	48	35	6	2	1	55	21	8	.439	.379
Wilmer Perez	R-R	5-10	186	4-16-98	.296	.000	.364	11	27	5	8	2	1	1	6	1	0	2	0	5	0	0	.556	.321
DJ Peters	R-R	6-6	225	12-12-95	.174	.111	.214	13	46	2	8	1	1	0	4	3	0	0	2	21	0	1	.239	.216
Israel Pineda	R-R	5-11	188	4-3-00	.095	.000	.143	6	21	3	2	1	0	1	5	5	0	0	0	7	0	0	.286	.269
Alfredo Rodriguez	R-R	6-0	190	6-17-94	.226	.500	.095	10	31	2	7	3	0	0	2	1	0	1	0	8	0	0	.323	.250

Adrian Sanchez	R-R	6-0	197	8-16-90	.239	.200	.250	79	243	32	58	17	2	2	29	18	0	1	0	51	3	1	.350	.291
Andrew Stevenson	L-L	6-0	191	6-1-94	.279	.230	.297	135	545	81	152	31	9	16	67	46	10	0	3	136	39	7	.457	.344
Dee Strange-Gordon	L-R	5-11	166	4-22-88	.190	.125	.231	6	21	3	4	1	0	0	2	3	0	0	0	1	0	0	.238	.292
Richard Urena	B-R	6-0	195	2-26-96	.231	.250	.227	37	134	9	31	6	0	2	21	6	1	0	1	29	2	0	.321	.268
Ildemaro Vargas	B-R	6-0	180	7-16-91	.224	.259	.207	48	174	21	39	11	0	2	18	20	0	1	2	25	2	2	.322	.301
2-team total (25 Iowa Cubs)					.245	.270	.235	73	278	37	68	14	4	3	25	27	0	1	3	37	3	2	.356	.308
Onix Vega	R-R	5-10	200	9-7-98	.300	.000	.462	6	20	1	6	1	0	0	2	1	2	0	0	6	0	0	.350	.391
Andrew Young	R-R	6-0	196	5-10-94	.209	.105	.236	28	91	10	19	4	0	3	10	14	6	0	0	33	3	1	.352	.351

Pitching	B-T	HT	WT	DOB	W	L	ERA	G	GS	CG	SV	IP	H	R	ER	HR	BB	SO	AVG	vLH	vRH	K/9	BB/9
Cory Abbott	R-R	6-1	210	9-20-95	0	4	5.08	10	6	0	0	28	30	20	16	4	17	34	.265	.268	.264	10.80	5.40
2-team total (2 Iowa Cubs)					0	5	4.98	12	8	0	0	34	34	23	19	6	19	40	.254	.255	.253	10.49	4.98
Joan Adon	R-R	6-2	246	8-12-98	2	2	4.68	10	10	0	0	42	41	26	22	5	24	43	.258	.266	.250	9.14	5.10
Victor Arano	R-R	6-2	228	2-7-95	0	0	0.00	3	0	0	0	3	0	0	0	0	0	5	.000	.000	.000	15.00	0.00
Luis Avilan	L-L	6-2	235	7-19-89	1	1	5.19	27	0	0	0	26	26	16	15	6	11	29	.255	.186	.305	10.04	3.81
Alberto Baldonado	L-L	6-4	276	2-1-93	3	2	3.84	56	0	0	3	63	46	30	27	5	27	81	.201	.165	.230	11.51	3.84
Ben Braymer	L-L	6-2	212	4-28-94	2	1	6.75	11	1	0	0	19	20	15	14	1	20	19	.267	.222	.292	9.16	9.64
Matt Brill	R-R	6-2	190	10-25-94	2	0	5.70	26	0	0	0	30	29	23	19	1	27	31	.246	.283	.222	9.30	8.10
Zach Brzykcy	R-R	6-2	230	7-12-99	0	0	0.00	2	0	0	1	2	2	0	0	0	0	2	.286	.000	.333	10.80	0.00
Cade Cavalli	R-R	6-4	240	8-14-98	6	4	3.71	20	20	1	0	97	75	43	40	3	39	104	.215	.226	.204	9.65	3.62
Sam Clay	L-L	6-3	238	6-21-93	1	2	3.10	21	0	0	0	20	22	7	7	2	7	20	.265	.229	.292	8.85	3.10
2-team total (19 Syracuse Mets)					5	3	3.56	40	0	0	0	43	44	18	17	3	17	45	.265	.200	.302	9.42	3.56
Tyler Clippard	R-R	6-3	200	2-14-85	4	1	2.23	36	0	0	1	40	30	11	10	1	18	53	.200	.191	.207	11.83	4.02
Matt Cronin	L-L	6-2	197	9-20-97	3	1	3.53	34	0	0	0	36	30	16	14	3	15	34	.229	.236	.224	8.58	3.79
Carl Edwards Jr.	R-R	6-3	170	9-3-91	1	0	0.63	13	0	0	3	14	3	1	1	0	4	17	.068	.095	.043	10.67	2.51
Erick Fedde	R-R	6-4	203	2-25-93	0	0	0.00	1	1	0	0	4	3	0	0	0	1	4	.200	.143	.250	9.00	2.25
Jace Fry	L-L	6-1	209	7-9-93	3	0	3.77	15	0	0	0	14	14	6	6	1	8	20	.255	.286	.235	12.56	5.02
2-team total (18 Lehigh Valley IronPigs)					4	2	5.34	33	0	0	0	30	31	18	18	3	15	40	.270	.298	.250	11.87	4.45
Reed Garrett	R-R	6-2	196	1-2-93	4	4	3.04	42	0	0	3	47	40	20	16	5	18	53	.227	.257	.208	10.08	3.42
MacKenzie Gore	L-L	6-2	197	2-24-99	0	1	5.25	4	4	0	0	12	16	7	7	3	4	9	.320	.250	.342	6.75	3.00
Will Harris	R-R	6-4	234	8-28-84	0	1	10.38	6	1	0	0	4	8	5	5	2	1	4	.381	.583	.111	8.31	2.08
Hunter Harvey	R-R	6-2	225	12-9-94	0	0	0.00	4	0	0	0	4	3	0	0	0	2	4	.214	.333	.125	9.82	4.91
Cole Henry	R-R	6-4	215	7-15-99	1	0	4.50	2	2	0	0	8	9	4	4	1	2	6	.281	.357	.222	6.75	2.25
Ronald Herrera	R-R	5-11	185	5-3-95	0	0	22.50	1	0	0	0	2	4	5	5	2	2	3	.400	.500	.250	13.50	9.00
Franklyn Kilome	R-R	6-6	175	6-25-95	2	8	7.60	11	11	0	0	45	58	41	38	11	32	48	.312	.303	.320	9.60	6.40
Andrew Lee	L-R	6-5	225	12-2-93	0	0	27.00	1	0	0	0	0	1	1	1	1	0	0	.500	1.000	.000	0.00	0.00
Andres Machado	R-R	6-0	235	4-22-93	0	0	5.82	13	0	0	0	17	18	11	11	0	5	18	.273	.348	.233	9.53	2.65
Erik Manoah Jr.	R-R	6-2	190	12-22-95	1	0	6.75	3	0	0	0	3	3	2	2	0	3	2	.333	.200	.500	6.75	10.13
Juan Minaya	R-R	6-4	210	9-18-90	0	2	3.12	6	0	0	0	9	5	4	3	2	6	6	.172	.133	.214	6.23	6.23
2-team total (29 St. Paul Saints)					1	7	6.29	35	1	0	4	49	46	37	34	8	26	42	.250	.244	.255	7.77	4.81
Patrick Murphy	R-R	6-5	211	6-10-95	3	3	5.00	40	7	0	2	63	59	41	35	6	33	73	.243	.198	.277	10.43	4.71
Francisco Perez	B-L	6-2	217	7-20-97	1	3	4.82	45	0	0	1	47	34	29	25	3	32	61	.205	.147	.245	11.76	6.17
Daniel Ponce de Leon	R-R	6-3	200	1-16-92	1	3	5.65	7	7	0	0	29	29	19	18	3	12	36	.259	.182	.309	11.30	3.77
2-team total (3 Toledo Mud Hens)					4	3	4.23	10	10	0	0	45	38	22	21	3	17	51	.225	.179	.264	10.28	3.43
Erasmo Ramirez	R-R	6-0	217	5-2-90	0	0	0.00	5	0	0	0	7	4	0	0	0	1	12	.160	.222	.125	15.43	1.29
Luis Reyes	R-R	6-2	175	9-26-94	0	1	14.18	5	4	0	0	13	24	23	21	4	16	11	.393	.441	.333	7.43	10.80
Jefry Rodriguez	R-R	6-6	230	7-26-93	1	3	7.49	24	11	0	0	64	69	54	53	8	38	67	.271	.306	.243	9.47	5.37
Josh Rogers	L-L	6-3	211	7-10-94	0	3	10.95	3	3	0	0	12	18	16	15	7	3	7	.327	.294	.342	5.11	2.19
2-team total (9 Jacksonville Jumbo Shrimp)					4	7	6.03	12	12	0	0	60	65	42	40	13	24	39	.274	.329	.248	5.88	3.62
Tommy Romero	R-R	6-2	225	7-8-97	3	1	2.33	6	2	0	0	19	13	5	5	4	9	14	.188	.211	.161	6.52	4.19
2-team total (23 Durham Bulls)					9	6	3.24	29	15	0	1	86	70	34	31	16	34	72	.221	.245	.202	7.53	3.56
Connor Sadzeck	R-R	6-7	235	10-1-91	0	3	3.86	17	0	0	0	21	17	9	9	6	8	21	.221	.360	.154	9.00	3.43
2-team total (24 Nashville Sounds)					1	4	2.20	41	0	0	3	49	34	14	12	8	20	56	.193	.273	.131	10.29	3.67
Aaron Sanchez	R-R	6-4	212	7-1-92	1	0	3.60	3	3	0	0	15	17	6	6	2	5	10	.304	.185	.414	6.00	3.00
2-team total (10 St. Paul Saints)					4	2	3.75	13	13	0	0	62	60	30	26	9	20	43	.260	.234	.283	6.21	2.89
Anibal Sanchez	R-R	6-0	207	2-27-84	0	1	4.26	3	3	0	0	13	12	7	6	0	8	13	.240	.158	.290	9.24	5.68
Sterling Sharp	R-R	6-3	182	5-30-95	2	5	6.62	18	13	0	0	67	86	53	49	8	30	59	.319	.365	.278	7.97	4.05
Stephen Strasburg	R-R	6-5	239	7-20-88	0	0	0.00	1	1	0	0	6	1	0	0	0	1	4	.053	.167	.000	6.00	1.50
Curtis Taylor	R-R	6-6	235	7-25-95	1	1	4.08	27	0	0	0	35	25	16	16	6	15	41	.191	.226	.167	10.44	3.82
Carson Teel	L-L	6-0	160	12-17-95	2	2	6.70	20	4	0	0	43	51	35	32	4	17	41	.290	.300	.284	8.58	3.56
Jackson Tetreault	R-R	6-5	189	6-3-96	5	3	4.19	12	12	0	0	58	51	30	27	10	24	52	.231	.262	.203	8.07	3.72
Mason Thompson	R-R	6-6	236	2-20-98	0	4	3.52	11	1	0	0	15	15	9	6	0	5	19	.254	.333	.200	11.15	2.93
Alex Troop	L-L	6-5	210	7-19-96	0	0	0.00	1	0	0	0	1	1	0	0	0	1	0	.500	.500	--	0.00	13.50
Logan Verrett	R-R	6-2	190	6-19-90	8	9	3.80	24	21	0	0	126	111	57	53	14	28	102	.233	.228	.237	7.31	2.01
Jordan Weems	L-R	6-4	209	11-7-92	3	2	2.70	33	0	0	16	40	31	14	12	4	12	49	.215	.186	.238	11.03	2.70

Fielding

Catcher	PCT	G	PO	A	E	DP	PB
Adams	1.000	21	205	16	0	2	3
Barrera	.992	53	477	25	4	3	2
Gushue	.992	42	360	25	3	3	6
Herrmann	.995	25	198	8	1	1	1
Perez	1.000	7	47	3	0	1	0
Pineda	1.000	5	36	1	0	0	1
Vega	1.000	2	20	0	0	0	0

First Base	PCT	G	PO	A	E	DP
Adams	1.000	2	18	0	0	0
Gushue	1.000	3	11	0	0	0
Herrmann	1.000	1	10	2	0	0
Meneses	.992	64	426	52	4	37
Nogowski	.989	46	335	27	4	39
Noll	.996	39	232	22	1	23
Sanchez	1.000	2	15	1	0	2
Urena	1.000	2	1	0	0	0

Second Base	PCT	G	PO	A	E	DP
Alu	1.000	6	10	13	0	3
Flores	1.000	17	27	33	0	12
Fox	.980	14	20	29	1	7
Garcia	.920	11	17	29	4	6
Martina	.000	1	0	0	0	0

Noll	.975	47	69	84	4	23
Rodriguez	.947	4	6	12	1	1
Sanchez	.977	39	48	78	3	21
Strange-Gordon	1.000	1	0	3	0	2
Urena	.938	5	7	8	1	0
Vargas	1.000	7	13	17	0	3
Young	.917	7	9	13	2	1

Third Base	PCT	G	PO	A	E	DP
Adrianza	1.000	4	3	5	0	0
Alu	.977	50	37	89	3	10
Dunn	1.000	5	2	11	0	1
Flores	.923	8	3	21	2	1
Martina	1.000	6	1	8	0	0
Noll	.714	3	1	4	2	0
Sanchez	.983	26	20	39	1	4
Urena	.942	31	19	46	4	6
Vargas	.917	5	6	5	1	1
Young	1.000	19	13	27	0	0

Shortstop	PCT	G	PO	A	E	DP
Abrams	.926	8	7	18	2	4
Adrianza	1.000	1	1	2	0	2
Escobar	1.000	3	3	4	0	0
Flores	1.000	15	16	37	0	5
Fox	.969	39	53	104	5	27
Garcia	.931	35	43	65	8	14
Martina	1.000	1	0	1	0	1
Rodriguez	1.000	6	8	8	0	3
Sanchez	1.000	10	7	14	0	5
Strange-Gordon	1.000	5	6	9	0	3
Vargas	.965	38	46	93	5	12

Outfield	PCT	G	PO	A	E	DP
Banks	.982	60	102	8	2	0
Call	1.000	5	15	1	0	1
Casey	.968	72	146	3	5	0
Dahl	1.000	16	28	2	0	0
Dunn	1.000	9	15	0	0	0
Freeman	.974	43	73	2	2	0
Johnson	1.000	12	16	1	0	0
Lipka	.969	37	63	0	2	0
Meneses	1.000	2	2	0	0	0
Noll	1.000	5	5	0	0	0
Palacios	.982	62	107	4	2	1
Peters	1.000	11	25	1	0	1
Sanchez	.667	3	2	0	1	0
Stevenson	.981	128	254	3	5	0
Strange-Gordon	1.000	1	3	0	0	0
Young	--	1	0	0	0	0

HARRISBURG SENATORS — *DOUBLE-A*

EASTERN LEAGUE

Batting	B-T	HT	WT	DOB	AVG	vLH	vRH	G	AB	R	H	2B	3B	HR	RBI	BB	HBP	SH	SF	SO	SB	CS	SLG	OBP
Ehire Adrianza	B-R	6-1	198	8-21-89	.438	1.000	.357	6	16	3	7	1	0	1	1	3	1	0	0	3	0	0	.688	.550
Jake Alu	L-R	5-10	175	4-6-97	.281	.241	.291	73	285	44	80	25	1	9	36	32	5	0	3	59	9	1	.470	.360
Yasel Antuna	B-R	6-0	199	10-26-99	.143	.167	.139	26	91	9	13	4	0	1	4	17	0	0	0	33	1	2	.220	.278
Darren Baker	L-R	6-0	180	2-11-99	.290	.290	.290	43	169	23	49	9	0	1	14	18	0	3	1	30	5	2	.361	.356
Jackson Cluff	L-R	6-1	181	12-3-96	.194	.180	.197	111	356	40	69	21	1	6	28	35	7	5	3	128	9	3	.309	.277
Justin Connell	R-R	6-1	185	3-11-99	.230	.203	.237	96	318	60	73	18	1	11	38	48	9	2	2	111	8	5	.396	.345
Cole Daily	L-R	5-11	170	11-28-96	.250	.500	.167	4	16	3	4	1	1	0	2	0	0	0	0	4	0	1	.438	.250
Jack Dunn	R-R	6-2	185	9-5-96	.247	.239	.249	99	344	43	85	17	0	3	22	49	5	2	3	81	8	8	.323	.347
Jecksson Flores	R-R	5-11	145	10-28-93	.239	.255	.232	45	142	17	34	6	0	1	13	12	4	1	1	24	1	3	.303	.314
Wilson Garcia	B-R	5-11	227	1-11-94	.282	.283	.282	119	454	51	128	26	0	24	81	29	5	0	2	86	0	1	.498	.331
Taylor Gushue	B-R	6-1	224	12-19-93	.262	.125	.311	19	61	11	16	3	0	6	14	15	1	0	0	14	0	0	.607	.416
Trey Harris	R-R	5-11	220	1-15-96	.245	.269	.239	37	143	14	35	4	0	3	11	8	2	0	0	40	3	2	.336	.294
K.J. Harrison	R-R	6-0	208	8-11-96	.204	.295	.167	45	152	16	31	8	0	4	20	13	4	0	5	49	1	0	.336	.276
Robert Hassell III	L-L	6-2	195	8-15-01	.222	.100	.250	27	108	9	24	5	0	1	12	13	1	0	0	35	1	0	.296	.311
Dondrei Hubbard	R-R	6-0	220	5-5-95	.257	.276	.252	46	140	14	36	5	1	3	14	8	1	0	1	39	3	2	.371	.300
Daniel Johnson	L-L	5-10	200	7-11-95	.368	.400	.357	5	19	5	7	1	0	2	3	2	1	0	0	5	0	0	.737	.455
Gilbert Lara	R-R	6-4	198	10-30-97	.217	.158	.232	88	290	21	63	7	1	7	31	16	6	0	0	90	0	0	.321	.272
Brady Lindsly	L-R	6-1	221	3-3-98	.190	.125	.204	66	221	19	42	6	1	6	22	17	3	0	1	80	0	0	.308	.256
Mitch Longo	L-R	6-0	195	1-12-95	.221	.261	.213	39	131	22	29	6	0	5	11	8	1	0	0	33	1	3	.382	.271
Rudy Martin	L-L	5-8	155	1-31-96	.225	.111	.242	39	142	21	32	2	2	4	10	20	1	2	1	46	15	5	.352	.323
Omar Meregildo	R-R	6-1	185	8-18-97	.214	.273	.200	35	112	19	24	1	0	6	17	12	1	0	1	35	0	2	.384	.294
Drew Millas	B-R	6-2	202	1-15-98	.211	.216	.209	45	152	12	32	4	0	3	16	15	0	0	1	53	1	1	.296	.280
John Nogowski	R-L	6-0	245	1-5-93	.202	.143	.216	30	109	18	22	4	0	4	17	20	2	0	1	13	1	2	.349	.333
Wilmer Perez	R-R	5-10	186	4-16-98	.233	1.000	.179	9	30	3	7	0	0	0	1	2	0	0	1	4	0	0	.233	.273
Israel Pineda	R-R	5-11	188	4-3-00	.280	.125	.312	26	93	15	26	3	0	7	21	9	0	0	1	18	1	0	.538	.340
Jacob Rhinesmith	L-L	6-2	195	5-23-96	.172	.050	.209	25	87	7	15	1	0	0	4	8	3	0	0	24	2	0	.184	.265
Alfredo Rodriguez	R-R	6-0	190	6-17-94	.193	.217	.188	32	119	4	23	4	0	1	12	3	2	0	0	38	1	1	.252	.226
Andrew Young	R-R	6-0	196	5-10-94	.211	.325	.187	64	227	24	48	10	0	11	30	28	3	0	0	86	0	1	.401	.306

Pitching	B-T	HT	WT	DOB	W	L	ERA	G	GS	CG	SV	IP	H	R	ER	HR	BB	SO	AVG	vLH	vRH	K/9	BB/9
Garvin Alston	R-L	6-4	175	3-12-97	0	1	6.75	4	0	0	0	5	8	5	4	0	2	4	.381	.333	.417	6.75	3.38
Matt Brill	R-R	6-2	190	10-25-94	2	1	1.93	18	0	0	9	19	9	4	4	1	11	18	.145	.200	.119	8.68	5.30
Zach Brzykcy	R-R	6-2	230	7-12-99	2	1	1.89	32	0	0	9	38	21	12	8	3	19	54	.162	.170	.156	12.79	4.50
Gerardo Carrillo	R-R	5-11	163	9-13-98	1	1	11.32	10	0	0	0	10	14	13	13	1	8	17	.304	.429	.250	14.81	6.97
Tim Cate	L-L	6-0	185	9-30-97	2	5	6.16	11	11	0	0	57	62	41	39	9	22	51	.271	.297	.258	8.05	3.47
Dakody Clemmer	R-R	6-3	220	1-19-96	1	0	12.74	17	0	0	0	18	16	25	25	1	30	21	.246	.320	.200	10.70	15.28
Matt Cronin	L-L	6-2	197	9-20-97	1	0	0.00	14	0	0	0	16	5	1	0	0	7	22	.096	.158	.061	12.12	3.86
Danny Dopico	R-R	6-3	205	12-18-93	0	0	5.00	22	0	0	0	27	25	18	15	4	23	32	.253	.324	.215	10.67	7.67
Jose A. Ferrer	L-L	6-1	215	3-3-00	0	1	4.70	7	0	0	0	8	10	4	4	1	1	11	.323	.308	.333	12.91	1.17
Steven Fuentes	R-R	6-2	241	5-4-97	4	7	4.70	28	14	0	0	92	91	51	48	6	50	74	.265	.310	.233	7.24	4.89
Edgar Garcia	R-R	6-1	205	10-4-96	0	2	6.38	19	0	0	0	24	18	17	17	6	17	15	.214	.303	.157	5.63	6.38
Brian Gonzalez	R-L	6-3	230	10-25-95	1	3	3.40	37	0	0	0	42	37	18	16	2	26	42	.237	.274	.213	8.93	5.53
Richard Guasch	R-R	6-4	205	4-10-98	3	8	7.04	18	8	0	0	47	41	38	37	5	38	59	.224	.307	.167	11.22	7.23
Alberto Guerrero	R-R	6-4	267	12-13-97	2	3	6.97	27	0	0	0	41	51	35	32	8	17	43	.295	.315	.280	9.36	3.70
Cole Henry	R-R	6-4	215	7-15-99	0	0	0.76	7	7	0	0	24	5	2	2	1	9	28	.067	.111	.042	10.65	3.42
Ronald Herrera	R-R	5-11	185	5-3-95	5	9	4.40	24	24	1	0	129	120	71	63	16	34	114	.244	.237	.249	7.95	2.37
Dondrei Hubbard	R-R	6-0	220	5-5-95	0	0	0.00	1	0	0	0	1	0	0	0	0	0	0	.000	.000	.000	0.00	0.00
Jake Irvin	R-R	6-6	225	2-18-97	0	4	4.79	15	15	0	0	73	66	40	39	9	20	78	.240	.223	.250	9.57	2.45
Franklyn Kilome	R-R	6-6	175	6-25-95	3	3	3.56	9	8	0	0	48	36	20	19	3	11	51	.205	.141	.248	9.56	2.06
Andrew Lee	L-R	6-5	225	12-2-93	3	2	3.99	30	0	0	1	47	40	22	21	6	29	60	.223	.203	.238	11.41	5.51
Evan Lee	L-L	6-1	210	6-18-97	0	3	3.60	7	7	0	0	30	25	13	12	2	15	37	.229	.267	.215	11.10	4.50
Erik Manoah Jr.	R-R	6-2	190	12-22-95	0	0	13.50	3	0	0	0	4	6	6	6	2	2	5	.333	.286	.364	11.25	4.50
Francys Peguero	R-R	6-2	170	10-4-95	2	7	4.89	35	0	0	1	57	43	36	31	7	27	55	.205	.230	.191	8.68	4.26

Malvin Pena	R-R	6-2	180	6-24-97	0	0	3.00	14	0	0	0	18	13	7	6	3	4	18	.206	.211	.205	9.00	2.00
Luis Reyes	R-R	6-2	175	9-26-94	6	8	4.76	21	17	0	0	108	91	63	57	13	53	103	.233	.268	.210	8.61	4.43
Josh Rogers	L-L	6-3	211	7-10-94	1	1	9.64	2	2	0	0	9	15	10	10	4	4	7	.357	.167	.433	6.75	3.86
Seth Romero	L-L	6-3	213	4-19-96	0	1	3.95	5	5	0	0	14	10	6	6	4	11	25	.200	.250	.176	16.46	7.24
Joe Ross	R-R	6-4	232	5-21-93	0	0	0.00	1	1	0	0	3	2	0	0	0	0	4	.200	.250	.167	12.00	0.00
Ramon Santos	R-R	6-3	230	9-20-94	0	1	6.00	2	0	0	0	3	3	3	2	1	0	6	.250	.167	.333	18.00	0.00
Reid Schaller	R-R	6-3	210	4-2-97	4	7	5.70	38	0	0	3	43	48	30	27	4	21	47	.284	.224	.315	9.91	4.43
Ike Schlabach	R-L	6-5	185	12-27-96	0	0	0.00	2	0	0	0	2	1	0	0	0	2	2	.143	.000	.250	9.00	9.00
Curtis Taylor	R-R	6-6	235	7-25-95	1	0	0.00	3	0	0	0	6	4	0	0	0	1	6	.190	.125	.231	9.00	1.50
Carson Teel	L-L	6-0	160	12-17-95	1	1	3.98	13	1	0	0	20	27	11	9	4	5	17	.325	.297	.348	7.52	2.21
Alex Troop	L-L	6-5	210	7-19-96	7	5	4.81	28	17	0	0	112	114	64	60	21	31	130	.259	.247	.265	10.42	2.48

Fielding

Catcher	PCT	G	PO	A	E	DP	PB
Gushue	.984	14	119	8	2	0	2
Lindsly	.998	62	536	31	1	0	10
Millas	.991	35	313	20	3	2	3
Perez	.988	9	80	4	1	0	2
Pineda	1.000	22	203	18	0	0	4

First Base	PCT	G	PO	A	E	DP
Dunn	1.000	13	59	1	0	9
Garcia	.995	27	175	8	1	20
Harris	1.000	1	8	0	0	1
Harrison	.993	38	270	20	2	28
Hubbard	1.000	1	10	0	0	0
Lara	1.000	1	7	0	0	0
Lindsly	1.000	1	7	0	0	2
Meregildo	1.000	15	110	2	0	12
Nogowski	.996	30	221	21	1	22
Young	.993	18	142	9	1	9

Second Base	PCT	G	PO	A	E	DP
Adrianza	1.000	1	0	1	0	0
Alu	.889	3	3	5	1	1
Baker	.988	42	58	102	2	20
Cluff	1.000	29	45	67	0	15
Daily	1.000	1	5	2	0	2
Dunn	.982	15	24	30	1	10
Flores	.984	35	59	65	2	18
Rodriguez	1.000	23	42	56	0	15

Third Base	PCT	G	PO	A	E	DP
Adrianza	1.000	1	1	0	0	0
Alu	.959	64	34	129	7	17
Daily	1.000	2	1	2	0	0
Dunn	.975	15	10	29	1	2
Flores	1.000	1	0	1	0	0
Lara	.957	41	32	80	5	3
Meregildo	.886	16	11	20	4	2
Rodriguez	1.000	2	2	1	0	0
Young	1.000	2	3	2	0	2

Shortstop	PCT	G	PO	A	E	DP
Adrianza	.857	4	4	8	2	2
Cluff	.955	74	88	165	12	34
Dunn	1.000	4	2	17	0	2
Flores	.885	8	9	14	3	2
Lara	.938	47	65	86	10	18
Rodriguez	.947	8	12	24	2	9

Outfield	PCT	G	PO	A	E	DP
Alu	1.000	4	5	0	0	0
Antuna	.971	25	32	2	1	0
Cluff	.952	9	20	0	1	0
Connell	.985	95	191	5	3	1
Daily	1.000	1	1	1	0	0
Dunn	.992	56	113	4	1	1
Harris	.983	32	58	1	1	0
Harrison	1.000	3	6	0	0	0
Hassell III	.982	27	49	5	1	1
Hubbard	.985	39	66	1	1	1
Johnson	.900	4	8	1	1	0
Longo	1.000	34	51	2	0	0
Martin	.988	36	79	2	1	1
Rhinesmith	1.000	23	32	0	0	0
Young	.967	38	58	1	2	0

WASHINGTON NATIONALS

WILMINGTON BLUE ROCKS — *HIGH CLASS A*

SOUTH ATLANTIC LEAGUE

Batting	B-T	HT	WT	DOB	AVG	vLH	vRH	G	AB	R	H	2B	3B	HR	RBI	BB	HBP	SH	SF	SO	SB	CS	SLG	OBP
Yasel Antuna	B-R	6-0	199	10-26-99	.235	.259	.230	99	332	66	78	13	1	10	44	72	4	1	6	88	26	6	.370	.372
Darren Baker	L-R	6-0	180	2-11-99	.273	.262	.276	62	245	43	67	15	1	2	25	22	1	3	2	51	10	2	.367	.333
Nick Banks	L-L	6-0	215	11-18-94	.231	.222	.235	9	26	5	6	0	1	1	6	2	1	0	1	10	0	0	.423	.300
Jordy Barley	R-R	6-0	175	12-3-99	.203	.119	.217	85	295	37	60	11	4	2	21	22	0	0	2	100	34	4	.288	.257
Gage Canning	L-R	5-10	175	4-23-97	.135	.071	.147	31	89	9	12	0	1	2	7	4	1	0	1	38	0	1	.225	.179
Justin Connell	R-R	6-1	185	3-11-99	.254	.200	.262	20	71	10	18	4	0	3	5	7	2	1	0	19	2	1	.437	.338
Cole Daily	L-R	5-11	170	11-28-96	.222	.179	.227	78	239	33	53	8	1	1	24	39	1	1	2	74	18	0	.276	.331
Jeremy De La Rosa	L-L	5-11	160	1-16-02	.195	.158	.202	32	118	10	23	4	1	1	10	12	1	1	1	37	13	2	.271	.273
Winder Diaz	B-R	6-3	170	9-5-02	.000	.000	.000	2	4	0	0	0	0	0	0	1	0	0	0	3	0	0	.000	.200
Leandro Emiliani	L-L	6-1	180	3-22-00	.223	.250	.219	33	112	15	25	6	1	3	19	13	4	0	0	28	1	0	.375	.326
Jarrett Gonzales	R-R	5-11	185	3-27-98	.167	.333	.133	9	18	1	3	0	0	0	1	0	2	0	0	9	0	0	.167	.250
Robert Hassell III	L-L	6-2	195	8-15-01	.211	.375	.167	10	38	9	8	1	0	0	3	6	0	0	1	12	3	0	.237	.311
Rudy Martin	L-L	5-8	155	1-31-96	.333	.000	.364	4	12	8	4	0	0	0	2	7	0	0	0	3	2	0	.333	.579
Junior Martina	R-R	6-0	190	12-12-97	.263	.667	.188	8	19	2	5	0	0	0	3	0	0	0	1	5	0	0	.263	.250
Ricardo Mendez	L-L	5-10	185	1-24-00	.227	.271	.219	84	326	38	74	13	1	5	45	25	2	4	0	72	16	6	.319	.286
Drew Mendoza	L-R	6-5	225	10-10-97	.208	.263	.201	101	351	34	73	13	2	7	50	39	1	0	1	119	2	1	.316	.288
Omar Meregildo	R-R	6-1	185	8-18-97	.255	.213	.263	81	298	44	76	20	0	15	51	38	5	0	1	101	2	1	.473	.348
Drew Millas	B-R	6-2	202	1-15-98	.237	.143	.258	25	76	13	18	8	2	1	10	22	0	0	0	20	1	0	.434	.408
Viandel Pena	B-R	5-8	148	11-22-00	.227	.118	.250	26	97	8	22	5	3	0	11	12	0	2	0	31	4	4	.340	.312
Wilmer Perez	R-R	5-10	186	4-16-98	.500	--	.500	1	4	0	2	0	0	0	0	0	0	0	0	0	0	0	.500	.500
Israel Pineda	R-R	5-11	188	4-3-00	.264	.308	.256	67	246	31	65	16	2	8	45	22	1	0	2	70	2	2	.443	.325
Yoander Rivero	R-R	5-9	155	11-22-01	.178	.222	.167	14	45	2	8	2	0	0	0	6	1	0	0	19	2	3	.222	.288
Jose Sanchez	R-R	6-0	197	7-12-00	.231	.255	.227	112	398	39	92	17	1	5	40	45	5	1	3	84	4	1	.317	.315
Kevin Strohschein	R-R	6-1	215	7-25-97	.240	.283	.232	89	317	37	76	8	1	3	31	20	3	1	6	70	5	1	.300	.286
Onix Vega	R-R	5-10	200	9-7-98	.265	.394	.242	66	215	28	57	10	1	4	30	34	4	0	0	52	4	2	.377	.375
Cody Wilson	R-R	6-2	200	7-4-96	.271	.222	.276	25	85	17	23	4	1	2	11	8	2	1	1	35	16	0	.412	.344
Paul Witt	R-R	5-11	170	10-29-97	.276	.500	.240	10	29	5	8	2	0	1	4	1	1	0	0	8	0	0	.448	.323
Jeremy Ydens	R-R	6-2	200	7-3-97	.206	.174	.213	41	131	12	27	6	0	1	9	9	6	2	1	38	9	2	.275	.286

Pitching	B-T	HT	WT	DOB	W	L	ERA	G	GS	CG	SV	IP	H	R	ER	HR	BB	SO	AVG	vLH	vRH	K/9	BB/9
Garvin Alston	R-L	6-4	175	3-12-97	4	1	1.96	29	0	0	1	41	21	12	9	3	16	39	.147	.093	.170	8.49	3.48
Andrew Alvarez	L-L	6-3	215	6-13-99	0	2	5.90	13	3	0	1	29	34	23	19	1	11	31	.272	.250	.284	9.62	3.41
Luis Avilan	L-L	6-2	235	7-19-89	1	0	3.86	9	0	0	0	9	9	4	4	0	8	10	.265	.333	.227	9.64	7.71
Zach Brzykcy	R-R	6-2	230	7-12-99	6	1	1.66	17	0	0	4	22	10	5	4	2	10	39	.137	.200	.104	16.20	4.15
Zack Burdi	R-R	6-3	210	3-9-95	1	0	1.74	8	0	0	0	10	4	2	2	0	8	10	.125	.167	.100	8.71	6.97

A.J. Candelario	R-R	6-0	165	12-17-97	0	1	10.80	7	0	0	0	7	12	8	8	1	3	5	.375	.444	.348	6.75	4.05
Gerardo Carrillo	R-R	5-11	163	9-13-98	1	0	3.60	9	0	0	2	10	7	4	4	1	5	10	.189	.231	.167	9.00	4.50
Tim Cate	L-L	6-0	185	9-30-97	4	3	2.92	12	10	0	0	52	42	20	17	2	15	52	.216	.250	.201	8.94	2.58
Gilberto Chu	L-L	5-11	195	11-19-97	1	3	4.02	30	0	0	0	54	44	25	24	7	22	53	.229	.280	.211	8.89	3.69
Michael Cuevas	R-R	6-2	165	6-29-01	6	12	4.64	26	24	0	0	114	123	74	59	8	55	82	.278	.322	.246	6.45	4.33
Jose A. Ferrer	L-L	6-1	215	3-3-00	2	1	2.56	28	0	0	9	39	32	15	11	6	9	43	.225	.265	.204	10.01	2.09
Eris Filpo	R-R	6-3	170	5-3-98	0	0	27.00	1	0	0	0	2	6	5	5	2	0	2	.545	.500	.571	10.80	0.00
2-team total (3 Hickory Crawdads)					0	0	22.50	4	0	0	0	6	17	15	15	3	4	5	.500	.474	.533	7.50	6.00
Miguel Gomez	R-R	6-3	170	9-10-01	0	0	3.00	2	0	0	0	3	4	1	1	1	0	1	.333	.333	.333	3.00	0.00
Richard Guasch	R-R	6-4	205	4-10-98	1	1	3.24	11	0	0	1	17	11	6	6	0	6	23	.193	.130	.235	12.42	3.24
Jake Irvin	R-R	6-6	225	2-18-97	0	0	1.50	9	9	0	0	30	24	5	5	0	8	29	.222	.227	.219	8.70	2.40
Michael Kirian	R-L	6-6	260	2-1-99	1	0	9.19	13	0	0	0	16	19	16	16	5	6	16	.306	.333	.293	9.19	3.45
Lucas Knowles	L-L	6-2	185	3-14-98	8	1	3.19	28	13	0	0	93	75	35	33	9	24	88	.221	.239	.212	8.52	2.32
Evan Lee	L-L	6-1	210	6-18-97	0	1	4.50	3	3	0	0	6	5	3	3	0	6	6	.238	.125	.308	9.00	9.00
Matt Merrill	R-R	6-4	202	6-11-98	1	2	6.86	20	7	0	0	41	38	32	31	6	39	53	.252	.200	.291	11.73	8.63
Mitchell Parker	L-L	6-4	224	9-27-99	6	4	2.88	24	24	1	0	100	76	37	32	3	67	117	.208	.133	.238	10.53	6.03
Malvin Pena	R-R	6-2	180	6-24-97	2	2	3.00	21	0	0	1	33	19	13	11	2	12	41	.168	.256	.114	11.18	3.27
Orlando Ribalta	R-R	6-7	245	3-5-98	0	1	2.20	11	0	0	1	16	12	5	4	1	8	21	.203	.286	.158	11.57	4.41
Carlos Romero	R-R	6-6	179	7-15-99	5	4	3.36	34	1	0	1	72	44	29	27	6	41	97	.174	.208	.153	12.07	5.10
Dustin Saenz	L-L	5-11	197	6-2-99	2	7	7.07	10	10	0	0	42	56	33	33	8	13	30	.329	.388	.306	6.43	2.79
Ike Schlabach	R-L	6-5	185	12-27-96	0	1	1.99	19	0	0	0	23	18	9	5	0	9	22	.222	.148	.259	8.74	3.57
Seth Shuman	R-R	6-1	195	12-1-97	3	2	3.23	14	14	0	0	61	57	23	22	5	14	55	.238	.284	.203	8.07	2.05
Jack Sinclair	R-R	6-4	170	5-3-99	2	1	2.05	20	0	0	3	31	15	9	7	2	9	33	.152	.171	.138	9.68	2.64
Troy Stainbrook	L-L	6-7	250	10-31-96	2	3	4.75	27	0	0	1	30	22	22	16	2	32	34	.195	.152	.224	10.09	9.49
Curtis Taylor	R-R	6-6	235	7-25-95	0	1	7.71	4	0	0	0	5	4	4	4	2	2	5	.235	.333	.182	9.64	3.86
Rodney Theophile	R-R	6-5	230	9-16-99	1	7	5.03	15	12	0	0	54	52	39	30	3	33	48	.256	.291	.231	8.05	5.53
Amos Willingham	R-R	6-4	217	8-21-98	3	2	3.41	29	0	0	3	34	34	14	13	1	7	40	.260	.325	.231	10.49	1.83
Tyler Yankosky	L-R	6-6	225	5-28-98	2	1	1.78	21	0	0	3	30	28	9	6	1	1	29	.241	.317	.200	8.60	0.30

Fielding

Catcher	PCT	G	PO	A	E	DP	PB
Gonzales	1.000	9	39	2	0	0	1
Millas	1.000	19	153	14	0	2	1
Perez	1.000	1	11	0	0	0	0
Pineda	.992	55	487	42	4	7	4
Vega	.985	57	488	36	8	2	4

First Base	PCT	G	PO	A	E	DP
Emiliani	.990	29	201	6	2	25
Mendoza	.991	60	414	23	4	57
Meregildo	.981	41	285	17	6	31
Sanchez	1.000	4	5	1	0	0
Vega	1.000	1	6	1	0	0

Second Base	PCT	G	PO	A	E	DP
Baker	.975	60	114	157	7	42
Daily	.983	35	42	73	2	20
Martina	1.000	3	5	6	0	1
Pena	.974	26	51	63	3	19
Sanchez	1.000	15	20	33	0	7
Witt	1.000	1	3	5	0	3

Third Base	PCT	G	PO	A	E	DP
Daily	.920	12	10	13	2	2
Martina	.625	4	4	1	3	1
Mendoza	.682	9	8	7	7	3
Meregildo	1.000	12	5	16	0	1
Sanchez	.950	95	61	167	12	20
Witt	.889	6	6	10	2	1

Shortstop	PCT	G	PO	A	E	DP
Barley	.960	85	115	199	13	52
Daily	.950	36	37	78	6	20
Diaz	.857	2	3	3	1	1
Rivero	.939	14	17	29	3	5

Outfield	PCT	G	PO	A	E	DP
Antuna	.952	89	135	3	7	0
Banks	1.000	5	8	1	0	1
Canning	1.000	27	38	1	0	0
Connell	1.000	17	26	0	0	0
De La Rosa	.973	31	70	3	2	1
Hassell III	1.000	9	29	0	0	0
Martin	.750	3	3	0	1	0
Mendez	.975	85	151	3	4	1
Strohschein	.983	70	110	9	2	1
Wilson	1.000	26	72	5	0	2
Witt	1.000	3	3	0	0	0
Ydens	.990	41	99	3	1	2

FREDERICKSBURG NATIONALS — *LOW CLASS A*

CAROLINA LEAGUE

Batting	B-T	HT	WT	DOB	AVG	vLH	vRH	G	AB	R	H	2B	3B	HR	RBI	BB	HBP	SH	SF	SO	SB	CS	SLG	OBP
Andry Arias	L-L	6-3	180	6-19-00	.207	.174	.212	51	174	27	36	5	4	3	24	23	2	0	1	51	2	3	.333	.305
J.T. Arruda	B-R	5-10	180	10-20-97	.276	.217	.286	51	170	41	47	9	3	4	25	35	0	2	3	45	17	3	.435	.394
Allan Berrios	R-R	6-0	190	8-9-97	.209	.000	.214	31	86	10	18	3	0	1	6	9	8	1	0	29	0	1	.279	.340
Branden Boissiere	L-L	6-1	205	3-23-00	.247	.226	.251	100	361	57	89	14	2	5	64	66	4	0	4	109	3	0	.338	.366
Armando Cruz	R-R	5-10	160	1-16-04	.267	--	.267	3	15	3	4	1	0	0	2	2	0	0	0	2	0	0	.333	.353
Christopher De La Cruz	L-L	5-11	145	3-29-01	.225	1.000	.191	26	71	11	16	5	1	0	5	11	2	0	0	13	5	1	.324	.345
Jeremy De La Rosa	L-L	5-11	160	1-16-02	.315	.349	.309	69	279	56	88	19	2	10	57	36	0	0	0	78	26	5	.505	.394
Geraldi Diaz	L-R	6-0	205	7-8-00	.254	.231	.258	74	252	40	64	19	2	4	41	36	8	0	6	60	3	1	.393	.358
Leandro Emiliani	L-L	6-1	180	3-22-00	.231	.172	.240	59	225	31	52	14	1	10	47	22	2	0	2	70	0	0	.436	.303
Will Frizzell	L-R	6-5	225	2-21-99	.377	.174	.417	34	138	28	52	11	0	11	44	13	1	0	3	35	0	0	.696	.426
Brady House	R-R	6-4	215	6-4-03	.278	.381	.265	45	176	24	49	8	0	3	31	12	11	0	3	59	1	0	.375	.356
Sammy Infante	R-R	6-1	185	6-22-01	.210	.216	.209	100	367	59	77	19	1	17	56	40	8	0	2	127	15	4	.406	.300
Cortland Lawson	R-R	6-2	200	5-12-00	.167	.200	.162	12	42	6	7	0	0	2	9	5	0	0	0	20	2	0	.310	.255
Trey Lipscomb	R-R	6-1	200	6-14-00	.299	.538	.262	23	97	15	29	4	1	1	13	4	0	0	0	19	12	1	.392	.327
Junior Martina	R-R	6-0	190	12-12-97	.162	.250	.145	28	74	10	12	1	0	1	8	15	1	0	2	17	0	1	.216	.304
Jared McKenzie	L-L	6-0	180	5-16-01	.400	.375	.403	17	70	18	28	7	1	2	15	1	2	0	0	19	11	0	.614	.425
Drew Millas	B-R	6-2	202	1-15-98	.246	.143	.277	18	61	15	15	2	0	2	10	14	0	0	0	13	6	2	.377	.387
Viandel Pena	B-R	5-8	148	11-22-00	.230	.243	.228	82	296	60	68	11	5	6	41	48	0	5	3	95	30	3	.361	.334
Zion Pettigrew	R-R	6-1	175	12-20-98	.192	.333	.174	16	52	5	10	2	0	0	2	6	0	0	0	15	4	0	.231	.276
Yoander Rivero	R-R	5-9	155	11-22-01	.222	.194	.228	67	189	33	42	8	2	0	20	35	1	2	2	57	8	2	.286	.344
Maxwell Romero Jr.	L-R	6-1	218	4-29-01	.172	.000	.238	9	29	3	5	1	0	0	2	4	0	0	0	14	0	0	.207	.273
Murphy Stehly	R-R	5-10	205	9-27-98	.333	--	.333	1	3	1	1	0	0	0	0	0	0	0	0	1	0	0	.333	.333
Jake Sullivan	R-R	5-10	187	7-24-97	.208	.200	.209	20	48	7	10	1	0	0	3	7	0	2	0	12	0	0	.229	.309

T.J. White	B-R	6-2	210	7-23-03	.258	.286	.254	92	329	55	85	20	2	11	52	44	5	0	2	104	8	1	.432	.353
Steven Williams	L-R	6-3	216	2-18-99	.238	.133	.248	50	172	24	41	7	0	2	22	32	2	0	1	44	2	0	.314	.362
Paul Witt	R-R	5-11	170	10-29-97	.267	--	.267	6	15	3	4	2	0	1	3	3	2	0	0	5	0	0	.600	.450
James Wood	L-R	6-7	240	9-17-02	.293	.364	.282	21	82	14	24	8	0	2	17	10	0	0	1	26	4	0	.463	.366
Jacob Young	R-R	6-0	180	7-27-99	.262	.237	.267	115	465	118	122	10	8	2	46	59	14	1	3	82	52	7	.331	.360

Pitching	B-T	HT	WT	DOB	W	L	ERA	G	GS	CG	SV	IP	H	R	ER	HR	BB	SO	AVG	vLH	vRH	K/9	BB/9
Pablo Aldonis	L-L	6-1	160	3-21-02	2	0	2.77	3	3	0	0	13	11	4	4	2	6	16	.229	.250	.222	11.08	4.15
Andrew Alvarez	L-L	6-3	215	6-13-99	4	5	4.53	15	6	0	1	56	57	30	28	3	23	72	.254	.231	.264	11.64	3.72
Jose Atencio	R-R	5-11	165	9-18-01	5	2	3.58	8	8	0	0	38	34	17	15	3	14	29	.238	.239	.236	6.93	3.35
Bryan Caceres	R-R	6-1	170	2-19-00	5	8	5.92	23	22	0	0	117	125	82	77	14	47	100	.272	.286	.257	7.69	3.62
A.J. Candelario	R-R	6-0	165	12-17-97	0	0	0.00	2	0	0	0	3	0	0	0	0	4	5	.000	--	.000	16.88	13.50
Brendan Collins	R-R	6-4	215	9-10-99	4	2	3.69	30	8	0	1	68	58	31	28	5	26	88	.221	.198	.242	11.59	3.42
Marc Davis	R-R	6-3	195	11-11-99	2	1	3.97	9	0	0	1	23	11	10	10	3	11	26	.141	.133	.152	10.32	4.37
Mason Denaburg	R-R	6-4	195	8-8-99	0	1	4.15	13	13	0	0	39	33	19	18	3	24	38	.229	.229	.230	8.77	5.54
Jose A. Ferrer	L-L	6-1	215	3-3-00	1	0	1.42	13	0	0	2	19	12	4	3	1	1	24	.171	.095	.204	11.37	0.47
Reed Garrett	R-R	6-2	196	1-2-93	0	0	0.00	1	0	0	0	1	1	0	0	0	0	0	.250	.500	.000	0.00	0.00
Peyton Glavine	R-L	5-11	180	3-23-99	1	0	4.19	14	0	0	0	19	16	9	9	0	8	27	.219	.269	.191	12.57	3.72
Miguel Gomez	R-R	6-3	170	9-10-01	0	0	4.08	8	0	0	0	18	18	9	8	1	2	17	.257	.265	.250	8.66	1.02
Pedro Gonzalez	R-R	6-2	225	7-16-00	0	0	9.00	9	0	0	0	14	19	17	14	1	7	8	.311	.227	.359	5.14	4.50
Cody Greenhill	R-R	6-4	216	9-21-98	1	0	2.93	34	0	0	2	43	31	16	14	6	11	69	.194	.179	.204	14.44	2.30
Marquis Grissom Jr.	R-R	6-2	202	7-19-01	0	1	4.26	4	0	0	0	6	6	3	3	0	3	4	.231	.133	.364	5.68	4.26
Will Harris	R-R	6-4	234	8-28-84	0	0	0.00	1	0	0	0	1	1	0	0	0	0	1	.250	.000	.500	9.00	0.00
Chance Huff	R-R	6-4	220	4-19-00	2	0	0.00	4	0	0	1	6	3	0	0	0	0	4	.158	.333	.077	6.00	0.00
Michael Kirian	R-L	6-6	260	2-1-99	0	1	15.43	3	0	0	0	2	5	4	4	1	2	3	.417	.250	.500	11.57	7.71
Andry Lara	R-R	6-4	180	1-6-03	3	8	5.51	23	23	0	0	101	103	70	62	10	44	105	.258	.272	.247	9.33	3.91
Kyle Luckham	R-R	6-2	205	10-1-99	1	0	6.14	4	0	0	0	7	10	5	5	0	1	5	.323	.333	.313	6.14	1.23
Bryan Pena	L-L	6-1	210	1-10-00	6	2	5.74	28	0	0	0	53	49	35	34	7	28	69	.240	.200	.261	11.64	4.73
Marlon Perez	L-L	5-10	180	3-16-00	2	3	3.46	28	0	0	2	42	29	18	16	2	13	47	.192	.154	.212	10.15	2.81
Todd Peterson	R-R	6-5	230	1-22-98	0	2	5.09	14	0	0	2	18	19	12	10	4	4	21	.264	.324	.200	10.70	2.04
Holden Powell	R-R	6-0	190	9-9-99	0	1	5.68	10	0	0	0	13	14	9	8	0	7	9	.286	.290	.278	6.39	4.97
Orlando Ribalta	R-R	6-7	245	3-5-98	1	2	3.97	25	0	0	1	34	28	17	15	4	19	33	.230	.242	.217	8.74	5.03
Jackson Rutledge	R-R	6-8	243	4-1-99	8	6	4.90	20	20	0	0	97	106	58	53	7	29	99	.276	.309	.239	9.15	2.68
Dustin Saenz	L-L	5-11	197	6-2-99	4	1	2.95	11	11	0	0	55	49	18	18	3	16	55	.237	.250	.232	9.00	2.62
Tyler Schoff	R-R	6-4	220	12-6-98	6	3	4.89	35	0	0	1	53	55	33	29	5	21	61	.274	.259	.283	10.29	3.54
Karlo Seijas	R-R	6-1	215	9-6-00	1	1	9.38	8	2	0	1	24	37	29	25	5	11	14	.349	.400	.324	5.25	4.13
Jack Sinclair	R-R	6-4	170	5-3-99	4	1	1.21	18	0	0	2	22	15	3	3	0	6	28	.183	.152	.204	11.28	2.42
Stephen Strasburg	R-R	6-5	239	7-20-88	1	1	3.52	2	2	0	0	8	3	3	3	0	5	9	.115	.188	.000	10.57	5.87
Jarlin Susana	R-R	6-6	235	3-23-04	0	0	2.61	3	3	0	0	10	9	3	3	1	5	13	.231	.250	.211	11.32	4.35
Rodney Theophile	R-R	6-5	230	9-16-99	5	1	1.29	9	9	0	0	49	32	10	7	2	11	62	.182	.151	.204	11.47	2.03
Riggs Threadgill	R-R	6-4	220	9-14-99	6	2	3.35	38	0	0	9	46	42	23	17	4	22	46	.239	.239	.239	9.07	4.34
Jaren Zinn	R-R	6-4	205	8-5-98	0	0	0.00	1	0	0	0	1	2	0	0	0	0	2	.400	.667	.000	18.00	0.00

Fielding

Catcher	PCT	G	PO	A	E	DP	PB
Berrios	.996	31	243	22	1	1	2
Diaz	.986	72	641	39	10	4	6
Millas	.950	8	69	7	4	2	1
Romero Jr.	.987	9	73	2	1	0	1
Sullivan	1.000	20	141	9	0	0	1
Williams	1.000	2	22	3	0	0	1

First Base	PCT	G	PO	A	E	DP
Boissiere	.994	95	716	59	5	66
Emiliani	.981	35	236	27	5	20
Frizzell	.889	1	8	0	1	0
Williams	.917	2	9	2	1	1

Second Base	PCT	G	PO	A	E	DP
Arruda	.975	17	26	52	2	13
Infante	.917	11	12	21	3	5
Martina	.818	3	4	5	2	1
Pena	.968	77	104	201	10	36
Pettigrew	.956	14	14	29	2	4
Rivero	1.000	10	7	24	0	2
Stehly	1.000	1	4	1	0	0

Third Base	PCT	G	PO	A	E	DP
Arruda	1.000	6	6	10	0	2
Infante	.908	79	48	100	15	13
Lipscomb	.929	22	15	24	3	3
Martina	.950	22	7	31	2	5
Rivero	1.000	1	0	1	0	0
Witt	.882	6	0	15	2	1

Shortstop	PCT	G	PO	A	E	DP
Arruda	.950	25	51	62	6	14
Cruz	1.000	3	5	7	0	2
House	.893	36	33	75	13	10
Lawson	.941	12	17	31	3	9
Pena	.933	4	5	9	1	1
Rivero	.960	54	65	125	8	22

Outfield	PCT	G	PO	A	E	DP
Arias	.988	48	77	5	1	2
De La Cruz	.950	24	37	1	2	0
De La Rosa	.942	63	114	0	7	0
McKenzie	1.000	17	34	3	0	0
White	.935	86	127	3	9	1
Williams	.982	30	51	3	1	0
Wood	.936	18	44	0	3	0
Young	1.000	112	227	4	0	0

FCL NATIONALS — *ROOKIE*

FLORIDA COMPLEX LEAGUE

Batting	B-T	HT	WT	DOB	AVG	vLH	vRH	G	AB	R	H	2B	3B	HR	RBI	BB	HBP	SH	SF	SO	SB	CS	SLG	OBP
Jeisel Acosta	R-R	6-0	170	9-4-01	.220	.333	.213	17	50	3	11	0	0	1	5	6	2	0	0	15	0	2	.280	.328
Yeuri Amparo	R-R	6-2	170	9-25-01	.037	.000	.048	13	27	3	1	1	0	0	0	1	0	1	0	4	1	0	.074	.071
J.T. Arruda	B-R	5-10	180	10-20-97	.000	.000	.000	3	6	1	0	0	0	0	1	2	0	0	1	2	0	0	.000	.222
Tyler Baca	B-L	5-9	180	5-22-00	.250	.000	.333	5	4	1	1	0	0	0	1	2	0	0	0	0	0	0	.250	.500
Isan Castillo	R-R	6-1	160	12-3-01	.128	.273	.071	20	39	5	5	0	0	0	1	4	1	1	0	17	0	2	.128	.227
Jose Colmenares	R-R	5-10	165	8-23-02	.242	.250	.241	12	33	5	8	2	0	2	8	3	0	0	1	6	0	0	.485	.297
Everett Cooper III	B-R	6-1	184	7-31-03	.154	.000	.182	6	13	2	2	0	0	0	3	2	1	0	0	6	0	1	.154	.313
Jackson Coutts	L-R	6-3	230	9-1-98	.238	.154	.254	27	80	10	19	4	2	1	8	16	2	0	0	15	0	0	.375	.378
Brenner Cox	L-R	6-3	195	5-11-04	.286	.250	.296	10	35	4	10	1	0	1	5	5	0	0	1	14	2	0	.400	.366
Armando Cruz	R-R	5-10	160	1-16-04	.275	.395	.249	52	207	41	57	8	2	2	20	11	3	4	1	39	6	5	.362	.320

Christopher De La Cruz	L-L	5-11	145	3-29-01	.288	.333	.274	21	80	22	23	4	0	1	13	11	0	0	1	14	3	3	.375	.370
Landon Dieterich	R-R	6-5	225	5-5-98	.105	.000	.121	14	38	3	4	1	0	1	5	8	0	1	1	15	0	0	.211	.255
Caleb Farmer	R-R	6-2	205	9-8-99	.375	.333	.400	5	8	3	3	0	0	1	3	5	0	0	0	3	0	0	.750	.615
Jaden Fein	R-R	6-3	205	8-15-00	.209	.429	.167	16	43	6	9	2	0	1	4	5	1	0	0	12	0	1	.326	.306
Braian Fernandez	R-L	6-1	170	4-15-99	.238	.222	.242	17	42	7	10	1	0	1	5	7	0	0	0	10	1	0	.333	.347
Lucius Fox	B-R	6-1	192	7-2-97	.500	.750	.333	3	10	2	5	1	0	0	3	1	2	0	1	2	1	0	.600	.571
Will Frizzell	L-R	6-5	225	2-21-99	.438	.500	.423	11	32	7	14	4	0	0	14	6	1	0	0	6	0	0	.563	.538
Angel Geraldo	R-R	6-1	160	6-14-01	.282	.167	.314	35	110	16	31	5	0	1	23	10	3	0	2	25	1	1	.355	.352
Elijah Green	R-R	6-3	225	12-4-03	.302	.364	.281	12	43	9	13	4	0	2	9	6	2	0	1	21	1	0	.535	.404
Daniel Johnson	L-L	5-10	200	7-11-95	.200	.000	.250	3	10	0	2	1	0	0	0	0	0	0	0	1	0	0	.300	.200
Blake Klassen	L-L	6-2	205	9-26-00	.208	.167	.222	7	24	5	5	1	0	0	3	3	0	0	0	7	0	1	.250	.296
Daniel Marte	R-R	6-0	165	1-14-02	.200	.333	.188	13	35	3	7	1	0	1	6	6	0	0	1	10	1	0	.314	.310
Rudy Martin	L-L	5-8	155	1-31-96	.227	.143	.267	8	22	4	5	0	0	1	2	3	0	1	0	6	0	1	.364	.320
Junior Martina	R-R	6-0	190	12-12-97	.357	--	.357	4	14	3	5	2	0	0	2	5	0	0	0	2	1	1	.500	.526
Wilfrido Matos	R-R	5-11	160	9-28-00	.190	.400	.125	8	21	2	4	1	0	0	0	2	1	0	0	5	0	1	.238	.292
John McHenry	B-R	5-10	190	6-18-01	.154	.167	.150	9	26	4	4	0	0	0	1	4	1	0	0	5	1	0	.154	.290
Ivan Murzi	R-R	6-0	165	5-20-01	.192	.200	.190	9	26	3	5	1	1	0	3	2	1	0	0	12	0	0	.308	.276
Nathaniel Ochoa Leyva	R-R	6-4	215	10-15-03	.167	.167	.167	6	18	3	3	0	0	0	1	5	1	0	0	8	0	0	.167	.375
Roismar Quintana	R-R	6-1	175	2-6-03	.289	.344	.277	50	180	41	52	10	1	5	28	9	7	0	3	46	3	1	.439	.342
Eliesel Santana	R-R	6-2	185	10-2-02	.246	.500	.238	23	65	9	16	2	0	1	5	11	1	0	0	21	0	1	.323	.364
Dee Strange-Gordon	L-R	5-11	166	4-22-88	.200	--	.200	3	5	3	1	0	0	0	2	2	1	0	0	0	0	0	.200	.500
Matt Suggs	R-R	5-10	195	5-31-00	.250	.000	.333	3	4	2	1	0	0	0	3	4	2	0	0	1	0	0	.250	.700
Erick Tejeda	R-R	6-4	162	12-26-01	.236	.263	.231	32	110	18	26	6	1	2	13	18	2	0	0	31	0	0	.364	.354
Johnathon Thomas	R-R	5-7	175	3-1-00	.143	.000	.200	5	14	2	2	0	0	0	1	1	0	0	0	3	0	0	.143	.200
Quade Tomlin	L-R	6-1	185	2-11-02	.176	.214	.169	32	91	6	16	5	0	1	9	10	0	0	1	28	1	0	.264	.255
Ray Torres	B-R	5-11	190	4-9-00	.250	.182	.270	19	48	7	12	1	0	0	0	7	4	0	0	19	0	0	.271	.390
Cody Wilson	R-R	6-2	200	7-4-96	.231	.200	.235	13	39	5	9	2	0	0	1	1	1	0	0	13	2	1	.282	.268
Paul Witt	R-R	5-11	170	10-29-97	.295	.000	.340	21	61	9	18	4	1	1	10	9	3	2	0	14	0	0	.443	.411

Pitching	B-T	HT	WT	DOB	W	L	ERA	G	GS	CG	SV	IP	H	R	ER	HR	BB	SO	AVG	vLH	vRH	K/9	BB/9
Juan Abreu	R-R	6-2	190	6-12-00	2	1	4.91	15	0	0	0	22	19	21	12	4	16	33	.218	.133	.263	13.50	6.55
Gabriel Agostini	L-L	6-0	160	7-24-04	2	1	3.63	11	7	0	0	35	34	15	14	2	19	34	.254	.333	.221	8.83	4.93
Pablo Aldonis	L-L	6-1	160	3-21-02	1	2	4.39	6	3	0	0	27	26	13	13	2	5	33	.248	.238	.250	11.14	1.69
Victor Arano	R-R	6-2	228	2-7-95	0	0	13.50	2	2	0	0	2	3	3	3	1	0	1	.333	.000	.750	4.50	0.00
Jose Atencio	R-R	5-11	165	9-18-01	4	0	2.70	6	4	0	0	27	24	8	8	1	4	31	.242	.200	.266	10.46	1.35
Mirton Blanco	R-R	6-5	181	7-10-02	0	1	9.75	8	1	0	0	12	17	15	13	1	17	15	.347	.375	.333	11.25	12.75
Zack Burdi	R-R	6-3	210	3-9-95	0	0	0.00	2	2	0	0	3	2	0	0	0	2	2	.200	.143	.333	6.75	6.75
A.J. Candelario	R-R	6-0	165	12-17-97	3	0	1.86	8	0	0	1	10	8	3	2	0	2	10	.229	.231	.227	9.31	1.86
Gerardo Carrillo	R-R	5-11	163	9-13-98	0	0	3.00	2	1	0	0	3	5	1	1	0	0	1	.385	.500	.286	3.00	0.00
Jose Cedeno	R-R	6-3	170	10-5-01	3	0	3.26	12	1	0	0	30	17	11	11	2	13	35	.160	.097	.187	10.38	3.86
Christian Ciuffetelli	R-R	6-2	200	12-27-99	0	0	0.00	2	1	0	0	3	2	0	0	0	0	1	.200	.250	.167	3.00	0.00
Eris Filpo	R-R	6-3	170	5-3-98	0	2	4.76	10	0	0	0	11	7	11	6	2	5	14	.159	.429	.033	11.12	3.97
Peyton Glavine	R-L	5-11	180	3-23-99	0	0	0.00	2	0	0	0	3	1	0	0	0	1	4	.100	.000	.200	12.00	3.00
Miguel Gomez	R-R	6-3	170	9-10-01	2	1	0.00	7	0	0	2	12	5	2	0	0	2	14	.122	.250	.069	10.80	1.54
Pedro Gonzalez	R-R	6-2	225	7-16-00	1	1	2.49	12	0	0	3	22	26	8	6	1	4	15	.306	.387	.259	6.23	1.66
Marquis Grissom Jr.	R-R	6-2	202	7-19-01	0	0	2.45	3	0	0	0	4	4	2	1	0	2	2	.267	.143	.375	4.91	4.91
Bubba Hall	R-R	6-1	212	4-10-00	0	0	0.00	2	0	0	0	2	2	0	0	0	0	2	.250	.333	.200	9.00	0.00
Hunter Harvey	R-R	6-2	225	12-9-94	0	0	0.00	2	2	0	0	2	0	0	0	0	0	4	.000	.000	.000	18.00	0.00
Chance Huff	R-R	6-4	220	4-19-00	0	0	2.45	3	1	0	0	4	4	1	1	1	1	4	.267	.286	.250	9.82	2.45
Evan Lee	L-L	6-1	210	6-18-97	0	0	0.00	2	2	0	0	3	0	0	0	0	1	4	.000	.000	.000	12.00	3.00
Jefrem Leon	R-R	6-1	155	9-9-02	0	1	6.75	4	1	0	0	7	8	8	5	0	3	10	.286	.308	.267	13.50	4.05
Kyle Luckham	R-R	6-2	205	10-1-99	1	0	0.00	3	0	0	0	4	0	0	0	0	0	4	.000	.000	.000	9.00	0.00
Franklin Marquez	L-L	6-0	165	12-6-02	2	2	5.72	15	2	0	2	28	41	25	18	3	7	29	.333	.333	.333	9.21	2.22
Adrian Ogando	R-R	6-2	190	11-20-03	3	2	1.52	9	1	0	0	30	15	7	5	0	13	27	.153	.250	.114	8.19	3.94
Johan Otanez	R-R	6-1	168	2-19-02	4	2	5.50	11	3	0	0	38	38	28	23	4	30	35	.268	.182	.322	8.36	7.17
Nick Pogue	R-R	6-5	235	9-13-99	0	0	0.00	3	1	0	0	4	3	1	0	0	0	3	.214	.500	.100	6.75	0.00
Holden Powell	R-R	6-0	190	9-9-99	1	0	0.00	2	1	0	0	3	1	0	0	0	2	5	.111	.167	.000	15.00	6.00
Cole Quintanilla	R-R	6-5	225	5-13-99	1	0	0.00	7	1	0	0	8	7	3	0	0	1	10	.219	.231	.211	11.25	1.13
Kevin Rodriguez	R-R	6-1	145	8-13-00	0	1	1.31	15	0	0	4	21	22	5	3	0	5	26	.259	.241	.268	11.32	2.18
Josh Rogers	L-L	6-3	211	7-10-94	0	1	6.00	1	1	0	0	3	5	4	2	1	0	4	.357	1.000	.250	12.00	0.00
Brayan Romero	R-R	6-1	180	1-6-02	0	1	5.79	5	2	0	0	9	11	9	6	0	8	7	.268	.333	.231	6.75	7.71
Seth Romero	L-L	6-3	213	4-19-96	0	0	0.00	1	1	0	0	1	0	0	0	0	2	0	.000	--	.000	0.00	18.00
Anibal Sanchez	R-R	6-0	207	2-27-84	0	0	3.00	1	1	0	0	3	1	1	1	0	0	2	.111	.000	.200	6.00	0.00
Bryan Sanchez	R-R	6-1	175	8-12-02	0	2	3.79	9	8	0	0	19	22	11	8	0	7	21	.278	.250	.291	9.95	3.32
Camilo Sanchez	R-R	6-2	164	6-28-03	0	1	16.88	3	0	0	0	3	7	8	5	1	2	2	.467	.429	.500	6.75	6.75
Ike Schlabach	R-L	6-5	185	12-27-96	0	0	0.00	3	0	0	0	3	3	5	0	0	2	5	.231	.400	.125	16.88	6.75
Karlo Seijas	R-R	6-1	215	9-6-00	2	0	2.59	9	0	0	3	24	22	7	7	0	3	15	.253	.222	.275	5.55	1.11
Jarlin Susana	R-R	6-6	235	3-23-04	0	0	1.69	2	2	0	0	5	4	1	1	0	4	9	.200	.167	.214	15.19	6.75
Mason Thompson	R-R	6-6	236	2-20-98	0	0	3.38	3	3	0	0	3	2	2	1	0	0	7	.200	.000	.250	23.63	0.00
Jaren Zinn	R-R	6-4	205	8-5-98	1	0	19.29	3	0	0	0	2	2	5	5	0	5	3	.250	.500	.000	11.57	19.29

Fielding

C: Acosta 17, Colmenares 12, Farmer 5, Murzi 9, Suggs 3, Torres 19. **1B:** Coutts 8, Dieterich 14, Klassen 6, Tejeda 29. **2B:** Arruda 1, Cooper 6, Cruz 2, Martina 3, Matos 6, McHenry 2, Ochoa Leyva 1, Strange-Gordon 1, Tomlin 32, Witt 8. **3B:** Arruda 2, Geraldo 32, Martina 1, Matos 2, McHenry 6, Ochoa Leyva 3, Tejeda 3, Witt 13. **SS:** Cruz 51, Fox 3, Ochoa Leyva 1, Witt 2. **OF:** Amparo 8, Baca 1, Castillo 17, Cox 10, De La Cruz 25, Fein 13, Fernandez 15, Green 10, Johnson 2, Marte 13, Martin 7, Quintana 48, Santana 17, Thomas 5, Wilson 11.

DSL NATIONALS — *ROOKIE*

DOMINICAN SUMMER LEAGUE

Batting	B-T	HT	WT	DOB	AVG	vLH	vRH	G	AB	R	H	2B	3B	HR	RBI	BB	HBP	SH	SF	SO	SB	CS	SLG	OBP
Jeremy Bautista	R-R	6-0	175	10-20-04	.000	.000	.000	5	8	0	0	0	0	0	0	0	0	0	0	2	0	0	.000	.000
Albert Casado	L-R	5-11	145	9-17-04	.149	.111	.158	19	47	3	7	2	0	0	3	1	3	0	1	23	0	1	.191	.212
Sebastian Castro	R-R	6-1	168	12-25-02	.216	.250	.205	41	111	17	24	3	0	0	9	21	3	0	0	33	3	0	.243	.356
Jhoan Contreras	R-R	6-1	185	12-26-03	.283	.357	.265	48	145	29	41	11	2	2	21	19	7	0	2	38	2	0	.428	.387
Edward De La Cruz	R-R	5-11	165	8-27-02	.160	.067	.176	41	100	19	16	1	0	0	7	21	4	0	0	45	3	2	.170	.328
Winder Diaz	B-R	6-3	170	9-5-02	.252	.350	.236	52	147	27	37	9	3	1	20	36	3	0	2	39	7	4	.374	.404
Jean Estrada	R-R	5-11	147	2-13-04	.135	.000	.156	13	37	5	5	2	0	0	4	4	2	0	0	11	0	1	.189	.256
Jenier Fernandez	R-R	6-1	175	10-16-03	.159	.095	.174	41	113	9	18	3	1	0	7	8	1	1	0	34	2	1	.204	.221
Miguel Fernandez	L-L	6-2	200	8-26-04	.171	.000	.197	32	76	10	13	3	0	2	7	15	1	0	1	19	2	0	.289	.312
Juan Garcia	R-R	6-0	170	2-17-03	.188	.208	.184	45	138	18	26	6	1	4	18	19	2	0	0	48	3	1	.333	.296
Clarence Martina	R-R	6-2	195	12-16-04	.083	.000	.091	8	12	3	1	0	0	0	1	4	2	0	0	4	0	0	.083	.389
Dawry Martinez	B-R	5-10	160	10-12-02	.188	.136	.197	48	144	23	27	3	4	2	24	23	4	0	1	46	10	2	.306	.314
Misael Mojica	L-R	6-0	155	12-29-04	.233	.143	.255	56	172	29	40	7	3	3	29	34	9	0	3	60	2	3	.360	.381
Jorgelys Mota	R-R	6-3	170	6-3-05	.262	.143	.276	23	65	15	17	1	1	2	10	6	2	0	0	22	4	2	.400	.342
Enmanuel Ramirez	R-R	6-1	170	11-5-03	.231	.147	.254	50	156	21	36	7	5	1	18	16	1	1	2	31	5	1	.359	.303
Helder Rosario	R-R	6-1	165	1-26-05	.203	.273	.189	25	64	6	13	2	1	1	10	9	0	0	0	37	3	2	.313	.301
Cristhian Vaquero	B-R	6-3	180	9-13-04	.256	.250	.257	55	176	33	45	4	4	1	22	33	3	1	2	38	17	7	.341	.379

Pitching	B-T	HT	WT	DOB	W	L	ERA	G	GS	CG	SV	IP	H	R	ER	HR	BB	SO	AVG	vLH	vRH	K/9	BB/9
Luis Acevedo	L-L	6-1	170	3-3-04	0	0	13.50	5	0	0	0	4	4	6	6	0	7	6	.250	.167	.300	13.50	15.75
Josue Carmona	L-L	6-3	185	9-3-00	4	1	4.78	14	0	0	1	26	23	16	14	3	15	37	.235	.238	.234	12.65	5.13
Leodarlyn Colon	R-R	6-4	190	12-1-04	1	0	2.76	8	1	0	1	16	15	6	5	1	6	19	.238	.174	.275	10.47	3.31
Ramon Cuevas	R-R	6-3	170	8-3-03	3	1	7.84	13	0	0	0	21	30	19	18	2	8	18	.330	.192	.385	7.84	3.48
Marcos Fortunato	R-R	6-0	175	9-12-03	0	4	4.36	11	8	0	0	43	44	25	21	3	9	41	.256	.245	.260	8.52	1.87
Michael Francisco	R-R	6-1	163	5-13-01	4	2	6.26	17	0	0	2	23	26	17	16	1	12	28	.286	.263	.302	10.96	4.70
Randy Lara	R-R	6-3	190	10-30-01	1	3	3.20	11	10	0	0	45	39	20	16	2	24	50	.234	.125	.277	10.00	4.80
Jefrem Leon	R-R	6-1	155	9-9-02	2	0	2.00	7	7	0	0	36	32	9	8	0	8	38	.256	.298	.231	9.50	2.00
Andy Luis	L-R	6-0	150	1-14-03	0	1	5.40	9	0	0	0	7	3	5	4	0	8	5	.130	.111	.143	6.75	10.80
Ronni Montero	R-R	6-3	190	11-2-01	1	2	3.72	13	0	0	2	19	13	11	8	0	21	15	.191	.091	.239	6.98	9.78
Miguel Moreno	R-R	6-1	160	10-28-03	0	0	19.50	8	0	0	0	6	13	16	13	3	11	4	.433	.455	.421	6.00	16.50
Raynel Moron	R-R	6-3	190	3-17-01	2	4	4.99	9	9	0	0	40	36	22	22	3	20	35	.245	.265	.235	7.94	4.54
Adrian Ogando	R-R	6-2	190	11-20-03	1	0	0.00	1	1	0	0	5	2	0	0	0	0	6	.133	.000	.250	10.80	0.00
Wilfry Pena	R-R	6-2	170	4-20-05	0	1	1.93	4	0	0	0	5	2	1	1	0	2	8	.133	.250	.000	15.43	3.86
Doimil Perez	R-R	6-3	170	11-3-03	2	2	2.76	13	6	0	0	33	22	14	10	0	12	28	.188	.174	.197	7.71	3.31
Bryan Polanco	R-R	6-2	190	9-12-01	4	3	3.51	11	7	0	1	41	31	22	16	4	21	49	.204	.182	.216	10.76	4.61
Gustavo Rivas	R-R	6-2	165	11-21-03	0	6	7.91	10	9	0	0	33	51	43	29	5	13	39	.340	.407	.297	10.64	3.55
Angel Roman	L-L	5-11	162	9-24-03	2	1	2.96	14	0	0	0	27	19	11	9	1	12	35	.202	.154	.221	11.52	3.95
Brayan Romero	R-R	6-1	180	1-6-02	1	0	3.27	8	1	0	1	11	6	5	4	1	4	6	.154	.167	.148	4.91	3.27
Camilo Sanchez	R-R	6-2	164	6-28-03	1	0	2.53	11	1	0	2	21	17	6	6	0	3	18	.207	.200	.213	7.59	1.27
Genderson Zapata	R-R	6-3	170	6-26-04	0	0	4.50	2	0	0	0	2	2	3	1	0	3	2	.222	.250	.200	9.00	13.50

Fielding

C: Bautista 3, Casado 1, De La Cruz 40, Rosario 25. **1B:** Castro 5, Contreras 34, Garcia 24, Martinez 2. **2B:** Casado 1, Castro 14, Mojica 48. **3B:** Casado 10, Castro 18, Contreras 4, Garcia 17, Mota 16. **SS:** Diaz 50, Mojica 10, Mota 3. **OF:** Estrada 12, Fernandez 39, Fernandez 22, Martina 4, Martinez 40, Ramirez 47, Vaquero 26

MINOR LEAGUES

A New Kind Of Normal For Minor League Baseball

BY JOSH NORRIS

In 2022, the minor leagues were normal ... but not the same.

The season started in April and ended in September. There were little to no restrictions on attendance. Teams played throughout their league footprint rather than in more regionalized areas designed to limit the amount of travel.

Even the pre-pandemic league names returned. The Texas League, for example, which spent 2021 as the Double-A Central, was the Texas League once more. The only exceptions were at the lowest levels, where the former Arizona and Gulf Coast Leagues remained the Arizona and Florida Complex Leagues.

And although things mostly returned to the way they were, there were a few tweaks new to the 2022 season. From a tightly enforced pitch clock to bigger bases to shift restrictions to limits on pickoffs, the minor leagues served as a sprawling experiment for new rules.

Some of those rules were successful enough that they will be adopted for the 2023 season in the major leagues.

One of the more subtle changes involved a tweak to the automated ball-strike system (ABS), which was in play throughout the Florida State League in 2021. A year later, the ABS was still around and had expanded to select Triple-A parks as well.

This time, though, there was a twist: Human umpires would call the games as normal, but the ABS would be running. If a player decided he didn't like the umpire's call, he could ask the umpire to check with the ABS, which would either confirm or overrule the original call.

During those games, each team had three challenges to any ball-strike call. If the ABS ruled the home plate umpire was correct, the team lost that challenge. If the ABS overturned the call, the team kept the challenge.

The same challenge system was also used during the Arizona Fall League in games played at Salt River Fields.

Beyond the ABS, the pitch clock was the most influential change in the minor leagues. The clocks had been in play at Triple-A and Double-A and the AFL since 2018. Now, the clocks—15 seconds between pitches with nobody on base and 20 seconds with runners on—were implemented at all full-season levels.

For the first time, pitch clocks were in use in all full-season minor leagues in 2022.

BRIAN WESTERHOLT/FOUR SEAM IMAGES

Teams were given a grace period to adjust before umpires started enforcing the clock—a strike if a batter took too long to get in the box and a ball if a pitcher did the same—but once that time came, the effects were immediate and stark.

Year over year, game times dropped by more than 23 minutes throughout the minor leagues. With those results, MLB had seen enough. In September, the league announced the pitch clocks would come to the big leagues, starting in 2023.

The minor leagues also saw a ban on extreme shifting, which also received enough positive reviews to be enacted in the big leagues starting in 2023. The rules stipulated teams must position two infielders on either side of second base and with both feet in front of the infield grass.

The only level exempted from this was Triple-A, because extreme shifting was still in play in the big leagues and potential infielders needed to be able to practice those alignments in case they were called up.

Other rules changes included a limit of two pickoffs or step-offs per at-bat. If a third pickoff throw was made and was unsuccessful, the runner was allowed to take the additional base uncontested. The objective of the rules was more action on the basepaths, and the results showed they worked.

Year over year, full-season minor leaguers attempted 4,905 more stolen bases and were successful roughly 2.5% more often.

MiLB had one more change aimed at spurring more action on the bases: The bases themselves were increased from 15 inches square to 18 inches square.

While the conditions surrounding the minor leagues were largely back to pre-pandemic form, attendance was not. The drop in attendance was understandable, simply because there were fewer games and plenty of Covid-related restrictions were still in place throughout the country.

The 120 affiliated MiLB teams drew 30,916,465 fans during the 2022 season, as reported by the teams themselves. That's up significantly from 22,088,997 fans, as was reported in 2021. Compared to previous years, however, it's a major dip.

MiLB's reported attendance numbers for 2005-2019 topped 40 million fans each year, but those figures also included ticket-selling short-season and rookie ball teams, as well as the Mexican League, which was affiliated with MiLB. MLB's reduction of the minors in 2021 from 160 to 120 ticket-selling teams has likely assured that the all-time MiLB attendance record of 43,263,740 fans, set in 2007, will never be topped.

On a per game basis, minor league teams averaged 3,910 fans per game in 2022. That figure is up from the 3,205 fans per game who came through the gates in 2021, but in every season from 2005 to 2019, MiLB full-season teams averaged more than 4,150 fans per game.

Operators around the country said individual ticket sales had largely returned to normal, but corporate and group sales had yet to see the same rebound. Some clubs also pointed to sagging season-ticket sales.

The overall season attendance leader was Nashville, which welcomed 555,576 fans to First Horizon Park. On a per-game basis, the attendance champion was Dayton, which drew an average of 7,935 fans a night.

Perhaps the biggest win for minor leaguers came on Sept. 9, when Major League Baseball voluntarily recognized the Minor League Players Union. Previously, only players on MLB 40-man rosters could collectively bargain their rights. Now, all minor leaguers could join that club.

For years, minor leaguers had fought for better wages and overall working conditions. They had seen gains in recent years, including pay raises and housing furnished by the big league club, but the formation and acceptance of a union will allow the players to continue to bargain for future gains.

Earlier in the year, MLB settled the longstanding Senne lawsuit, a class-action lawsuit brought on behalf of a group of players arguing that they and their colleagues were owed back pay from years of not being paid during minor league spring training, extended spring training and instructional leagues. The court initially approved a settlement amount of $185 million.

NEW PLAYING RULES

In certain Low-A Florida State League games, the home plate umpire called balls and strikes, but both teams had three chances to appeal to the automated ball-strike (ABS) system if they believed the ump missed the call.

If ABS ruled that the home plate umpire was correct, the team lost that challenge. If ABS overturned the call, the team kept the challenge.

OTHER NEW EXPERIMENTAL RULES

■ The ABS system used in the FSL in 2021 was used in the Triple-A Pacific Coast League, starting on May 17, and all season at Triple-A Charlotte of the International League.

The computerized system uses the Hawk-Eye, multi-camera system to track the ball and where it crosses the plate.

■ Crowding one side of the infield—or shifting—for extreme pull hitters was prohibited at Double-A, High-A and Low-A. Teams were required to position four players on the infield dirt and two apiece on either side of second base and only as deep as the end of the dirt.

■ Pitch clocks of 15 seconds with nobody is on base and 20 seconds with runners on base were implemented in all minor league parks. Those standards had been in place at Triple-A and Double-A since 2018.

■ Pickoff throws were limited in all leagues. The pitcher may step off the rubber or attempt a pickoff three times per at-bat. If the third attempt fails, the runner advances one base.

■ The size of bases was increased from 15 to 18 inches square. This was aimed at increasing stolen base attempts and infield hits while reducing collisions around the bases.

On the field, the Orioles, who entered the season with the No. 1 farm system in the game, saw the fruits of their labor graduate to Baltimore. Catcher Adley Rutschman made his big league debut on May 21 and provided the enticing blend of offense and defense as had been predicted since his days at Oregon State.

Rutschman provided 5.2 wins above replacement, as measured by Baseball Reference. That mark placed him not only at the top of Baltimore's roster, but also ranked him behind only Philadelphia's J.T. Realmuto among big league catchers.

Later in the year, the Orioles got another glimpse at a potential cornerstone when it called up infielder Gunnar Henderson from Triple-A Norfolk. Henderson's stellar season spread across the upper levels earned him Baseball America's Minor League Player of the Year award.

The Alabama native was chosen one round after Rutschman in 2019, giving their draft class the look of a potential franchise-shifter.

After time against older competition in 2020 at Baltimore's alternate training site and a 2021 offseason spent adding some final coats of polish,

Henderson came out of the gates on fire. Before his callup, he hit .297/.416/.531 with 24 doubles, 19 home runs and 22 stolen bases between Double-A Bowie and Triple-A Norfolk.

Henderson added four more home runs in the big leagues, during Baltimore's quest for its first playoff appearance since 2016.

Elsewhere, Phillies righthander put together a season for the ages and took home BA's inaugural Minor League Pitcher of the Year award. In his first full pro season, Painter reached Double-A, a feat rarely achieved by a pitcher drafted in the first round out of high school. Since 2006, the only other prep arms to pull that off were Clayton Kershaw, Chad Billingsley, Forrest Whitley, Zack Greinke and Dylan Bundy.

Painter, who already breaks the mold by standing 6-foot-7, came about his success by pounding the strike zone with an impressive array of pitches, including a high-octane fastball and dastardly slider.

By season's end, Painter, who was drafted out of high school in Florida, had scaled from Low-A Clearwater to Double-A Reading—the latter of which plays in an extraordinarily hitter-friendly park—finished with the following line: 6-2, 1.56 with 155 strikeouts against just 25 walks over 103.2 innings. He allowed just 67 hits as well, putting his WHIP at an eye-popping 0.88.

Baseball America's Minor League Team of the Year went to the Charleston RiverDogs, who have won the Carolina League championship in each of their two seasons as the Rays' Low-A affiliate. This year's version won 88 games before sweeping Myrtle Beach in the divisional round and Lynchburg in the finals to keep the championship at Joseph P. Riley Park for another year.

The RiverDogs' roster featured plenty of prospects along the way, including standout shortstop Carson Williams, trade acquisition infielder Junior Caminero, 2022 first-rounder Brock Jones and a flotilla of pitching that at times included JJ Goss, Austin Vernon and Nick Bitsko.

The staggering of the season finales at different levels of the minor leagues also led to some of the game's youngest prospects getting upper-level cameos earlier than in previous seasons, when all leagues (except the Rookie-level Pioneer League) closed their seasons on a uniform date.

This led to a trio of talented prospects reaching Double-A at extremely youthful ages. Twenty-year-old Evan Carter (Rangers), 19-year-old Jasson Dominguez (Yankees) and 18-year-old Jackson Chourio (Brewers) all completed the feat, Carter and Dominguez helping Frisco and Somerset claim league championships.

Dominguez's time in the Eastern League playoffs was especially loud. He closed Somerset's season by homering from both sides of the plate in a 15-0 rout of Erie that featured a combined no-hitter from righties Randy Vasquez and Carson Coleman.

Chourio's season was arguably the biggest breakout in the minor leagues. The 18-year-old Venezuelan started the year in extended spring training back at Milwaukee's minor league complex in Maryvale, Ariz., before bashing his way to Low-A Carolina, High-A Wisconsin and Double-A Biloxi.

ORGANIZATION STANDINGS

Cumulative domestic minor league records for all 30 organizations, with annual winning percentages back to 2017. Beginning in 2021, most organizations have five affiliates.

		2022						
Rk	MLB Org	W	L	PCT	2021	2019	2018	2017
1.	Rays	361	237	.604	.623	.573	.591	.536
2.	Yankees	336	263	.561	.595	.518	.500	.602
3.	Guardians	331	268	.553	.521	.509	.529	.493
4.	Tigers	323	281	.535	.480	.468	.505	.502
5.	Dodgers	322	281	.534	.533	.562	.552	.546
6.	Brewers	347	303	.534	.497	.493	.502	.504
7.	Rockies	320	280	.533	.546	.472	.482	.496
8.	Twins	319	281	.532	.507	.539	.511	.581
9.	Rangers	316	287	.524	.534	.559	.466	.467
10.	Cubs	315	287	.523	.453	.476	.459	.504
11.	Giants	341	314	.521	.529	.516	.457	.446
12.	Angels	312	291	.517	.463	.411	.430	.492
13.	Padres	309	293	.513	.462	.534	.502	.505
14.	Marlins	304	289	.513	.505	.506	.465	.483
15.	Pirates	300	298	.502	.537	.529	.499	.499
16.	Red Sox	301	300	.501	.588	.459	.476	.497
17.	Blue Jays	296	303	.494	.525	.496	.523	.505
18.	Braves	294	304	.492	.513	.464	.471	.471
19.	Mariners	296	310	.488	.571	.487	.469	.487
20.	Mets	293	308	.488	.457	.493	.472	.456
21.	Nationals	292	308	.487	.415	.488	.481	.456
22.	Cardinals	289	313	.480	.398	.448	.534	.546
23.	Orioles	285	320	.471	.463	.526	.471	.482
24.	Reds	274	319	.462	.505	.449	.453	.456
25.	D-backs	301	355	.459	.443	.557	.541	.515
26.	Phillies	271	330	.451	.484	.494	.549	.528
27.	Astros	294	359	.450	.484	.527	.576	.521
28.	White Sox	261	345	.431	.404	.490	.515	.438
29.	Royals	260	344	.430	.509	.495	.492	.466
30.	Athletics	256	348	.424	.436	.477	.515	.494

POSTSEASON RESULTS

League (Lvl)	Champion	Runner-Up
International (AAA)	Durham (TB)*	Nashville (MIL)
Pacific Coast (AAA)	Reno (ARI)	El Paso (SD)
Eastern (AA)	Somerset (NYY)	Erie (DET)
Southern (AA)	Pensacola (MIA)	Tennessee (CHC)
Texas (AA)	Frisco (TEX)	Wichita (MIN)
Midwest (HiA)	South Bend (CHC)	Lake County (CLE)
Northwest (HiA)	Eugene (SF)*	Vancouver (TOR)
South Atlantic (HiA)	Bowling Green (TB)*	Aberdeen (BAL)
California (LoA)	Lake Elsinore (SD)	Fresno (COL)
Carolina (LoA)	Charleston (TB)*	Lynchburg (CLE)
Florida State (LoA)	St. Lucie (NYM)	Dunedin (TOR)
Arizona Complex (R)	Giants Black (SF)	Rockies (COL)
Florida Complex (R)	Yankees (NYY)	Rays (TB)

* Repeat champion from 2021

DANIEL SHIREY/GETTY IMAGES (HENDERSON)

MINOR LEAGUES

Gunnar Henderson Reigns Supreme

PLAYER OF THE YEAR

BY JOSH NORRIS

It's difficult to believe, but the summer of 2020 was a crucial step in Gunnar Henderson's education as a professional ballplayer.

After getting his feet wet in the Rookie-level Gulf Coast League the summer before, Henderson's natural progression likely would have taken him to Low-A.

Instead, the minor league season was canceled because of the Covid-19 pandemic, leaving thousands of prospects to train remotely until the fall, when instructional leagues were given the go-ahead.

Gunnar Henderson

Henderson was more fortunate. Drafted by the Orioles in the second round in 2019 out of high school in Selma, Ala., the shortstop was part of a group of prospects and veterans selected to head to the Orioles' alternate training site in Bowie, Md., home of the organization's Double-A affiliate.

Instead of facing pitchers more in line with his experience level, Henderson got at-bats against some of the more advanced arms in Baltimore's system.

Every day, he got to face pitchers like current big leaguers Kyle Bradish, D.L. Hall, Dean Kremer and Dillon Tate, as well as righthander Grayson Rodriguez, the Orioles' top pitching prospect and one of the best overall prospects in baseball.

When the minor leagues resumed as normal in 2021, he was ready. The numbers weren't eye-popping, but Henderson still zoomed from Low-A to Double-A in just 105 games.

But it was this year that Henderson truly began to hint at his potential. Neither Double-A Bowie nor Triple-A Norfolk provided much resistance, and the 21-year-old morphed from an upper-tier prospect into a truly elite talent who heads baseball's No. 1 farm system.

Henderson assumed the No. 1 spot on the Top 100 Prospects at midseason and earned his first big league callup on Aug. 31, with the Orioles in full pursuit of their first playoff berth since 2016.

At the two highest levels of minor league play, Henderson hit .297/.416/.531 with 19 homers and 22 stolen bases in 112 games.

Despite opening the year as the fourth-youngest player in the Eastern League and one of just nine players younger than 21 in all of Double-A, Henderson dominated. He overwhelmed the league with a 1.025 OPS in 47 games before earning a promotion to Triple-A.

Roughly a month later, Henderson was in Dodger Stadium, where he led off for the American League in the Futures Game. He walked once that day and scored twice in the AL's victory.

Back at Norfolk, Henderson was resplendent. The youngest player at Triple-A continued to hit for average and power while alternating with Jordan Westburg—another key piece of Baltimore's return to prominence—between shortstop and third base with a handful of games at the other two infield positions mixed in as well.

Being in the big leagues so early is tremendous enough on its own, but by bringing Henderson up in a moment steeped with opportunity, the Orioles have loudly signaled their confidence in Henderson to join Adley Rutschman as the potential faces of the franchise's next chapter.

For his outstanding season, Henderson is Baseball America's Minor League Player of the Year. ■

LAST 10 WINNERS

2011: Mike Trout, OF, Arkansas (Angels)
2012: Wil Myers, Northwest Arkansas/Omaha (Royals)
2013: Byron Buxton, Cedar Rapids/Fort Myers (Twins)
2014: Kris Bryant, Iowa (Cubs)
2015: Blake Snell, Charlotte/Montgomery/Durham (Rays)
2016: Yoan Moncada, Salem/Portland (Red Sox)
2017: Ronald Acuña Jr., Florida/Mississippi/Gwinnett (Braves)
2018: Vladimir Guerrero Jr., New Hampshire/Buffalo (Blue Jays)
2019: Gavin Lux, SS, Tulsa/Oklahoma City (Dodgers)
2021: Bobby Witt Jr., SS, NW Arkansas/Omaha (Royals)

Full list: search "Baseball America awards"

ROB TRINGALI/MLB PHOTOS VIA GETTY IMAGES

Reds prospect Elly De La Cruz had one of the great power-speed seasons ever.

MIKE JANES/FOUR SEAM IMAGES

In all, the talented teenager—whose brother Jaison is also a rising star in Cleveland's system—finished the year with a slash line of .288/.342/.538 with 30 doubles, 20 home runs and 16 stolen bases while playing the entire season at 18 years old. His numbers were met with similarly glowing reports from scouts, prompting a rise all the way to No. 2 on Baseball America's Top 100 by season's end.

In 2021, the title of biggest breakout went to Cincinnati's Elly De La Cruz, who went from backfield toolshed to full-season folk hero in a matter of months. A year later, he proved his breakout campaign was no fluke.

The lanky shortstop took a month or so to thaw out at High-A Dayton, but when he did he showed the same blend of pyrotechnics at the plate, on the bases and in the field that vaulted him up prospect boards in 2021. Between Dayton and Double-A Chattanooga, De La Cruz, still just 20 years old, hit 28 home runs and stole 47 bases while slashing .304/.359/.586 between the levels.

The D'backs' Corbin Carroll also put himself in the conversation for the best overall season in the minor leagues. Arizona showed its trust in Carroll on Opening Day by assigning him to Double-A Amarillo despite injuries and the pandemic limiting him to just 18 games outside of Rookie ball entering the year. His 2021 season ended after just seven games because of a shoulder injury that required surgery. Nevertheless, he immediately rewarded his believers with an outstanding turn at Double-A, where he produced a 1.073 OPS over 58 games before a promotion to Triple-A Reno. Carroll continued his dominance at the next level, tearing the cover off the ball for 33 games before earning his first big league callup. In 23 big league games, Carroll, still just 22 years old, hit four home runs and slugged his way to an OPS of .830.

On the pitching side, Eury Perez barely skipped a beat while repeating his dominance from 2021. The 6-foot-8 righthander who stymied Class A hitters in 2021, was given an aggressive assignment to Double-A Pensacola just a week before his 19th birthday. He took a few starts to get cooking, but after striking out a dozen in five one-hit innings on April 29, he never looked back.

The only thing that truly derailed Perez was a lat strain that cost him roughly a month between August and September. He kicked off the rust in time to strike out the first eight hitters he faced in Pensacola's Southern League championship-sealing win.

The Dodgers' pitching machine continued churning as well, with the latest product being righthander Gavin Stone, whose 1.48 ERA led the minor leagues. Stone, a Central Arkansas alum who was the Dodgers' fifth-round pick in the shortened 2020, jumped from High-A Great Lakes to Triple-A Oklahoma by season's end. Along the way, he struck out 168 and walked 44 over 121.2 innings. Stone, plus top pitching prospect Bobby Miller, have combined to give Los Angeles an enviable pitching haul in a six-player class from the 2020 draft.

The Rays have also done an excellent job in recent years of finding gem after gem to replenish their farm system. The newest addition was first baseman Kyle Manzardo, whose sublime approach and bat-to-ball skills led to a 1.043 OPS, the second-best mark in all the minor leagues. Manzardo, an alumnus of Washington State, slammed 22 home runs and racked up nearly as many walks (59) as strikeouts (65).

The Braves continued adding to their young core by graduating NL Rookie of the Year Michael Harris from Double-A to the big leagues and getting a historic year from righty Spencer Strider, who finished just behind Harris in the voting. Infielder Vaughn Grissom hinted at big things to come down the stretch as well.

The 2022 minor league season featured a few new twists sprinkled all season long. Above all, though, the biggest change it brought—after two long seasons—was a much-needed and welcomed return to normalcy. ■

Myrtle Beach's Kristin Call Does It All

BY CARROLL ROGERS WALTON

When people around the Myrtle Beach Pelicans say Kristin Call is a hands-on general manager, here's what they mean:

In the midst of a pop-up storm during a prom night promotion, Call once pulled tarp in a strapless bridesmaid's dress.

"We all got the radio call and I didn't have time to go put on shorts and a T-shirt," said Call, who had drawn the line at wearing heels. "There's a reason I work at the beach where you can wear flip-flops and tennis shoes."

Now in her 10th year in the Pelicans' front office, Call has built a reputation on work ethic, leadership and a keen eye for marketing. Just a year since her promotion to general manager, that reputation is only growing. Baseball America has named her Minor League Executive of the Year.

"She is such a dynamic leader," said Myrtle Beach team president Ryan Moore, whose promotion from GM created the opening. Call assumed the title of GM after the 2021 season.

"Not only in her strategy development but in her own personal efforts. She's one of the hardest workers and the smartest workers I've ever had the opportunity to work with, and it's a really motivating leadership style for the rest of the staff."

JOHN MUSE

Kristin Call

While most minor league operators have seen declines in both attendance and corporate sponsorships since the pandemic, Myrtle Beach has thrived.

Since 2019, only Myrtle Beach—the Low-A Carolina League affiliate of the Cubs—and other teams with new stadiums have gained ground.

Call is quick to share the credit with the entire Pelicans front office and said she's just maintaining momentum the team has set in recent years.

"Everybody's asking the same thing: 'What are the big changes?' " she said. "I don't have a big list of changes. We're doing really well. Let's keep doing what we do well, and relying on the knowledge of our staff that has been here for years."

EXECUTIVE OF THE YEAR

LAST 10 WINNERS

2013: Martie Cordaro, Omaha Storm Chasers (Pacific)
2014: Sam Bernabe, Iowa Cubs (Pacific Coast)
2015: Dave Oster, Lake Elsinore (California)
2016: Tom Kayser, President of the Texas League
2017: Ryan Keur, Daytona Tortugas (Florida State)
2018: Bob Murphy, Dayton Dragons (Midwest)
2019: Don Logan, Las Vegas Aviators (Pacific Coast)
2020: Adam Giardino, broadcaster
2021: K.L. Wombacher, president/GM, Hillsboro Hops (NW)
2022: Kristin Call, GM, Myrtle Beach (CAR)

For full list, search "Baseball America awards"

The Pelicans' 14 full-time staffers have a combined 186 years of experience in minor league baseball, 120 of them in Myrtle Beach. Moore said Call's leadership is part of the reason so many staffers stick around.

And Call, who arrived in 2013 as the team's director of marketing, helped set the club on this trajectory—and she's done it in a unique environment. Myrtle Beach has to build a fanbase from an audience that's constantly turning over in the South Carolina resort town.

While most teams draw their biggest attendance Friday and Saturday nights, that's when beach tourists are packing up and checking out of rental properties. If tourists are checking in, a ball game is probably the last thing on their minds. But dinner out is not.

The Pelicans partner with local restaurants and bars, offering tickets to incentivize employees to make sure at least one TV has the Pelicans game on.

The Pelicans market to local families on weekends instead. On Friday nights they host fireworks shows and offer a $25 family meal with four hot dogs, four sodas and popcorn.

"Everybody's pulled in 100 different directions during the week," Call said. "The Thirsty Thursday promotion was great in your 20s, but now you're older, you've got family obligations.

"We basically copied that promotion and put it on Saturdays, and I've seen that perform really well." ■

Velazquez Helps Reno Come Up Aces

BY NICK PIECORO

Minor league teams that cycle through 77 players during a season do not tend to end their season on a championship stage.

The Triple-A Reno Aces in 2022 were a different story. People connected to the team point to manager Gil Velazquez as a big reason why.

Velazquez's easygoing personality, open-door managerial style and ability to maintain stability despite a revolving clubhouse door helped the Aces pull off a sort of organizational double whammy. They not only developed players for the parent D-backs, but they also won the Pacific Coast League championship.

For his efforts, Velazquez is the Baseball America Minor League Manager of the Year.

"Of course, I'm honored," said Velazquez, 43. "For me, to get an honor like that, it comes down to having a good group of guys—players and coaches—and having a good atmosphere, a good clubhouse, with everyone wanting to come to the ballpark on a daily basis.

"That's kind of what we created as a team."

Velazquez wasn't even supposed to be in the position in the first place. As of mid January, he was slated to return as Arizona's minor league infield coordinator, a position he held the previous five seasons.

But when Chris Cron left to join manager Mark Kotsay's staff with the Athletics, the D-backs had a job to fill—and not much time to fill it.

EDDIE KELLY

Gil Velazquez

Arizona farm director Josh Barfield said the organization immediately thought of Velazquez. Not only did he have experience managing, but Barfield thought Velazquez had the sort of demeanor and ability to command a staff that would play well in the job.

Plus, he was already familiar with most of the players in the system and had relationships with many of them.

Velazquez, who had not managed since 2016 with Great Lakes in the Midwest League, made a seamless transition even though he had little time to prepare, Barfield said.

"He's almost like that father figure or brother-type presence with a lot of the guys," Barfield said. "He cares. I think that's what they ultimately know is that he cares a lot about them. That's how he's able to gain their trust and be able to help them so much."

The Aces hovered around .500 for most of the first half but took off in July. They went 46-27 over the final three months and defeated El Paso for the PCL title before falling to Durham in the one-game Triple-A National Championship. The Aces' 85 wins set a franchise record.

They did all that despite regularly having their roster plundered by the parent club. Aside from the challenges every Triple-A club has to deal with in managing a pitching staff, the Aces steadily graduated many of their most productive hitters, several of whom never returned.

At various points, Reno lost Corbin Carroll, Alek Thomas, Jake McCarthy and Stone Garrett, and the pitching staff lost starters Tommy Henry, Ryne Nelson and Drey Jameson over the final two months.

"We were losing players for the right reasons," Reno co-hitting coach Mark Reed said. "We were losing players because they were going to the big leagues.

"That is more important than us winning a PCL championship, but we were able to do both. Gil made everybody feel like the promotions didn't faze us." ■

MANAGER OF THE YEAR

LAST 10 WINNERS

2012: Dave Miley, Scranton/Wilkes-Barre (Yankees)
2013: Gary DiSarcina, Pawtucket (Red Sox)
2014: Mark Johnson, Kane County (Cubs)
2015: Tony DeFrancesco, Fresno (Astros)
2016: Dave Wallace, Akron (Indians)
2017: Stubby Clapp, Memphis (Cardinals)
2018: Drew Saylor, Rancho Cucamonga (Dodgers)
2019: Corey Ragsdale, Down East (Rangers)
2021: Chris Widger, Quad Cities (Royals)
2022: Gil Velazquez, Reno (D-backs)

For full list, search "Baseball America awards"

TRIPLE-A

Pos	Player, Team (Organization)	Age	AVG	OBP	SLG	AB	H	2B	3B	HR	RBI	BB	SO	SB
C	Shea Langeliers, Las Vegas (Athletics)	24	.283	.366	.510	353	100	19	2	19	56	43	88	5
1B	Vinnie Pasquantino, Omaha (Royals)	24	.277	.371	.561	264	73	17	2	18	70	40	39	3
2B	Jonathan Aranda, Durham (Rays)	24	.318	.394	.521	403	128	26	1	18	85	45	100	1
3B	Miguel Vargas, Oklahoma City (Dodgers)	22	.304	.404	.511	438	133	32	4	17	82	71	76	16
SS	Gunnar Henderson, Norfolk (Orioles)	21	.288	.390	.504	250	72	13	4	11	41	38	78	12
OF	Will Benson, Columbus (Guardians)	24	.278	.426	.522	316	88	20	3	17	45	75	91	16
OF	Alec Burleson, Memphis (Cardinals)	23	.331	.372	.532	432	143	25	1	20	87	29	67	4
OF	Bubba Thompson, Round Rock (Rangers)	24	.303	.355	.474	346	105	12	4	13	48	22	95	49
DH	David Villar, Sacramento (Giants)	25	.275	.404	.617	298	82	19	1	27	82	55	93	1

Pos	Pitcher, Team (Organization)	Age	W	L	ERA	G	GS	IP	H	BB	SO	HR	SO/9	WHIP
SP	Brayan Bello, Worcester (Red Sox)	23	6	2	2.76	11	10	59	46	24	81	3	12.4	1.19
SP	Hunter Brown, Sugar Land (Astros)	23	9	4	2.55	23	14	106	70	45	134	5	11.4	1.08
SP	Grayson Rodriguez, Norfolk (Orioles)	22	6	1	2.2	14	14	70	44	21	97	2	12.5	0.93
SP	Kyle Muller, Gwinnett (Braves)	24	6	8	3.41	23	23	135	119	40	159	14	10.6	1.18
SP	Ryan Pepiot, Oklahoma City (Dodgers)	24	9	1	2.56	19	17	91	62	36	114	10	11.2	1.07
RP	Greg Weissert, Scranton/Wilkes-Barre (Yankees)	27	2	1	1.69	42	0	48	24	19	70	3	13.1	0.90

DOUBLE-A

Pos	Player, Team (Organization)	Age	AVG	OBP	SLG	AB	H	2B	3B	HR	RBI	BB	SO	SB
C	Logan O'Hoppe, Reading/Rocket City (PHI/LAA)	22	.283	.416	.544	360	102	14	1	26	78	70	74	7
1B	Leandro Cedeño, Amarillo (D-backs)	23	.310	.374	.563	426	132	18	0	30	93	42	112	0
2B	Edouard Julien, Wichita (Twins)	23	.300	.441	.490	400	120	19	3	17	67	98	125	19
3B	Brett Baty, Binghamton (Mets)	22	.312	.406	.544	340	106	22	0	19	59	46	98	2
SS	Lenyn Sosa, Birmingham (White Sox)	22	.331	.384	.549	257	85	10	2	14	48	21	40	0
OF	Corbin Carroll, Amarillo (D-backs)	21	.313	.430	.643	227	71	11	8	16	39	41	68	20
OF	Justin Dirden, Corpus Christi (Astros)	24	.324	.411	.616	349	113	32	5	20	73	41	94	7
OF	Tyler Gentry, Northwest Arkansas (Royals)	23	.321	.417	.555	274	88	16	0	16	63	40	66	8
DH	Kerry Carpenter, Erie (Tigers)	24	.304	.359	.646	240	73	16	0	22	48	16	72	1

Pos	Pitcher, Team (Organization)	Age	W	L	ERA	G	GS	IP	H	BB	SO	HR	SO/9	WHIP
SP	Tanner Bibee, Akron (Guardians)	23	6	1	1.83	13	13	74	51	14	81	4	9.9	0.88
SP	Taj Bradley, Montgomery (Rays)	21	3	1	1.70	16	16	74	50	18	88	4	10.7	0.91
SP	Taylor Dollard, Arkansas (Mariners)	23	16	2	2.25	27	27	144	106	31	131	9	8.2	0.95
SP	Quinn Priester, Altoona (Pirates)	21	4	4	2.87	15	15	75	68	22	75	4	9.0	1.19
SP	Gavin Stone, Tulsa (Dodgers)	23	6	4	1.60	14	13	73	59	30	107	1	13.1	1.21
RP	Eric Torres, Rocket City (Angels)	22	2	2	1.59	42	0	51	25	23	81	3	14.3	0.94

DANIEL SHIREY/MLB PHOTOS VIA GETTY IMAGES

D-backs outfielder Corbin Carroll bashed his way from Double-A to the big leagues.

CLASSIFICATION ALL-STARS

HIGH-A

Pos	Player, Team (Organization)	Age	AVG	OBP	SLG	AB	H	2B	3B	HR	RBI	BB	SO	SB
C	Endy Rodriguez, Bradenton (Pirates)	22	.302	.392	.544	318	96	23	3	16	55	42	77	3
1B	Kyle Manzardo, Bowling Green (Rays)	21	.329	.436	.636	225	74	16	1	17	55	45	46	0
2B	Thomas Saggese, Hickory (Rangers)	20	.308	.359	.487	380	117	22	2	14	61	29	94	11
3B	Christian Encarnacion-Strand, Cedar Rapids (Twins)	22	.296	.370	.599	294	87	23	3	20	68	30	85	7
SS	Elly De La Cruz, Dayton (Reds)	20	.302	.359	.609	281	85	14	6	20	52	24	94	28
OF	Evan Carter, Hickory (Rangers)	19	.287	.388	.476	376	108	18	10	11	66	59	75	26
OF	Johnathan Rodriguez, Lake County (Guardians)	22	.292	.346	.573	295	86	16	2	21	59	22	92	2
OF	Aaron Zavala, Hickory (Rangers)	22	.278	.424	.441	299	83	10	3	11	41	68	79	10
DH	Addison Barger, Vancouver (Blue Jays)	22	.300	.366	.558	260	78	21	2	14	53	25	76	7

Pos	Pitcher, Team (Organization)	Age	W	L	ERA	G	GS	IP	H	BB	SO	HR	SO/9	WHIP
SP	Prelander Berroa, Eugene/Everett (Giants/Mariners)	22	2	2	2.06	17	17	66	34	38	97	2	13.3	1.10
SP	Joe Boyle, Dayton (Reds)	22	3	4	2.17	17	17	75	25	59	122	3	14.7	1.13
SP	DJ Herz, South Bend (Cubs)	21	2	2	2.26	17	17	64	33	37	99	3	14.0	1.10
SP	Andrew Hoffmann, Rome (Braves)	22	7	2	2.36	15	15	80	63	21	90	9	10.1	1.05
SP	Mason Montgomery, Bowling Green (Rays)	22	3	2	1.81	16	16	70	49	27	118	6	15.2	1.09
RP	Cam Robinson, Wisconsin (Brewers)	22	3	1	1.45	20	0	37	21	17	52	0	12.5	1.02

LOW-A

Pos	Player, Team (Organization)	Age	AVG	OBP	SLG	AB	H	2B	3B	HR	RBI	BB	SO	SB
C	Edgar Quero, Inland Empire (Angels)	19	.312	.435	.530	413	129	35	2	17	75	73	91	12
1B	Niko Kavadas, Salem (Red Sox)	23	.286	.453	.609	192	55	18	1	14	48	54	70	1
2B	Hao Yu Lee, Clearwater (Phillies)	19	.283	.384	.415	258	73	11	1	7	50	36	57	10
3B	Deyvison De Los Santos, Visalia (D-backs)	19	.329	.370	.513	316	104	18	2	12	67	22	84	4
SS	Edwin Arroyo, Modesto/Daytona (Mariners/Reds)	18	.297	.368	.486	461	137	25	10	14	83	44	121	25
OF	Vaun Brown, San Jose (Giants)	24	.346	.427	.636	228	79	14	5	14	41	25	67	23
OF	Jackson Chourio, Carolina (Brewers)	18	.324	.373	.600	250	81	23	5	12	47	19	76	10
OF	James Wood, Lake Elsinore/Fredericksburg (SD/WSH)	19	.324	.429	.560	275	89	27	1	12	62	47	68	19
DH	Hunter Goodman, Fresno (Rockies)	22	.291	.368	.592	282	82	17	1	22	68	26	78	4

Pos	Pitcher, Team (Organization)	Age	W	L	ERA	G	GS	IP	H	BB	SO	HR	SO/9	WHIP
SP	Edinson Batista, Fayetteville (Astros)	20	8	3	2.6	21	8	93	59	43	113	3	10.9	1.09
SP	Luis Devers, Myrtle Beach (Cubs)	22	9	3	2.58	15	14	66	57	14	75	3	10.2	1.07
SP	Will Dion, Lynchburg (Guardians)	22	8	4	2.26	23	23	115	88	31	142	8	11.1	1.03
SP	Tink Hence, Palm Beach (Cardinals)	19	0	1	1.38	16	16	52	31	15	81	1	13.9	0.88
SP	Inohan Paniagua, Palm Beach (Cardinals)	22	6	4	2.18	17	17	99	72	23	107	4	9.7	0.96
RP	Austin Vernon, Charleston (Rays)	23	9	1	1.69	15	1	59	32	23	91	6	14.0	0.94

ROOKIE COMPLEX

Pos	Player, Team (Organization)	Age	AVG	OBP	SLG	AB	H	2B	3B	HR	RBI	BB	SO	SB
C	Jorge Mendez, C, DSL Phillies	18	.400	.491	.522	90	36	8	0	1	19	6	9	9
1B	Bryant Betancourt, DSL Rockies	18	.355	.462	.674	138	49	11	0	11	36	27	21	0
2B	Pedro Ramirez, ACL Cubs	18	.329	.399	.541	146	48	9	5	4	14	17	26	11
3B	Gleider Figuereo, ACL Rangers	18	.280	.363	.616	125	35	5	5	9	31	15	33	7
SS	Michael Arroyo, DSL Mariners	17	.314	.457	.484	153	48	10	2	4	22	27	33	4
OF	Jace Avina, ACL Brewers	19	.294	.436	.630	119	35	8	1	10	29	15	51	2
OF	Gabriel Gonzalez, ACL Mariners	18	.357	.421	.548	126	45	9	0	5	17	8	21	5
OF	Hector Rodriguez FCL Mets/Reds	18	.359	.397	.580	131	47	8	6	3	20	9	10	15
DH	Yeison Morrobel, ACL Rangers	18	.329	.405	.487	152	50	13	1	3	21	17	34	5

Pos	Pitcher, Team (Organization)	Age	W	L	ERA	G	GS	IP	H	BB	SO	HR	SO/9	WHIP
SP	Maxwel Hernandez, DSL Phillies	19	3	2	0.72	11	11	50	24	16	51	1	9.2	0.81
SP	Nomar Medina, ACL Giants	19	6	0	2.22	14	12	65	58	16	70	1	9.7	1.14
SP	Emmanuel Reyes, DSL Royals	18	2	1	0.91	12	11	49	29	4	52	1	9.5	0.67
SP	Luis Serna, FCL Yankees	17	0	0	1.96	11	10	41	33	17	56	0	12.2	1.21
SP	Jarlin Susana, ACL Padres/FCL Nationals	18	0	0	2.34	10	9	35	19	15	53	1	13.8	0.98
RP	Luis Rodriguez, FCL Mets	19	3	2	1.41	16	0	32	20	14	37	2	10.4	1.06

MINOR LEAGUE ALL-STARS

The Rays' Kyle Manzardo ranked second in the minor leagues with a 1.043 OPS.

The Dodgers' Gavin Stone won the overall minor league ERA title at 1.48.

TRACY PROFFITT/FOUR SEAM IMAGES (MANZARDO), BILL MITCHELL (STONE)

FIRST TEAM

Pos	Player, Organization (Peak Level)	Age	AVG	OBP	SLG	AB	R	H	HR	RBI	BB	SO
C	Endy Rodriguez, Pirates (AAA)	22	.323	.407	.590	458	92	148	25	95	60	101
1B	Kyle Manzardo, Rays (AA)	21	.327	.426	.617	324	71	106	22	81	59	65
2B	Vaughn Grissom, Braves (AA)	21	.324	.405	.494	389	72	126	14	67	36	54
3B	Gunnar Henderson, Orioles (AAA)	21	.297	.416	.531	407	101	121	19	76	79	116
SS	Elly De La Cruz, Reds (AA)	20	.304	.359	.586	471	87	143	28	86	40	158
OF	Corbin Carroll, D-backs (AAA)	21	.307	.425	.610	362	89	111	24	62	67	107
OF	Moises Gomez, Cardinals (AAA)	23	.294	.371	.624	442	89	130	39	94	52	174
OF	Esteury Ruiz, Brewers/Padres (AAA)	23	.332	.447	.526	437	114	145	16	65	66	94
DH	Kerry Carpenter, Tigers (AAA)	24	.313	.380	.645	358	60	112	30	75	33	89

Pos	Pitcher, Organization (Peak Level)	Age	W	L	ERA	G	GS	IP	H	BB	SO	AVG
SP	Hunter Brown, Astros (AAA)	23	9	4	2.55	23	14	106	70	45	134	.186
SP	Andrew Painter, Phillies (AA)	19	6	2	1.56	22	22	104	67	25	155	.181
SP	Brandon Pfaadt, D-backs (AAA)	23	11	7	3.83	29	29	167	160	33	218	.251
SP	Gavin Stone, Dodgers (AAA)	23	9	6	1.48	26	25	122	92	44	168	.206
SP	Gavin Williams, Guardians (AA)	22	5	4	1.96	25	25	115	69	40	149	.173
RP	Cam Robinson, Brewers (AAA)	22	3	1	2.49	52	0	65	45	30	84	.197

SECOND TEAM

Pos	Player, Organization (Peak Level)	Age	AVG	OBP	SLG	AB	R	H	HR	RBI	BB	SO
C	Logan O'Hoppe, Phillies/Angels (AA)	22	.283	.416	.544	360	72	102	26	78	70	74
1B	Matt Mervis, Cubs (AAA)	24	.309	.379	.605	512	92	158	36	119	50	107
2B	Jonathan Aranda, Rays (AAA)	24	.318	.394	.521	403	71	128	18	85	45	100
3B	Brett Baty, Mets (AAA)	22	.315	.410	.533	362	76	114	19	60	49	104
SS	Jordan Lawlar, D-backs (AA)	19	.303	.401	.509	389	98	118	16	62	57	115
OF	Vaun Brown, Giants (AA)	24	.346	.437	.623	387	100	134	23	75	47	119
OF	Alec Burleson, Cardinals (AAA)	23	.331	.372	.532	432	68	143	20	87	29	67
OF	Tyler Gentry, Royals (AA)	23	.326	.422	.542	402	79	131	21	86	60	105
DH	Niko Kavadas, Red Sox (AA)	23	.280	.443	.547	393	71	110	26	86	102	152

Pos	Pitcher, Organization (Peak Level)	Age	W	L	ERA	G	GS	IP	H	BB	SO	AVG
SP	Tanner Bibee, Guardians (AA)	23	8	2	2.17	25	25	133	101	27	167	.211
SP	Brayan Bello, Red Sox (AAA)	23	10	4	2.34	18	17	96	64	36	129	.186
SP	Taylor Dollard, Mariners (AA)	23	16	2	2.25	27	27	144	106	31	131	.203
SP	Kyle Harrison, Giants (AA)	20	4	3	2.71	25	25	113	79	49	186	.196
SP	Mason Montgomery, Rays (AA)	22	6	3	2.10	27	27	124	89	43	171	.196
RP	Zach Brzykcy, Nationals (AAA)	22	8	2	1.76	51	0	61	33	29	95	.157

Rays bring winning ways to Charleston

TEAM OF THE YEAR

BY MARC TOPKIN

Being the best team in the minor leagues takes a team effort.

The Low-A Charleston RiverDogs were a prime example in 2022. The Rays affiliate won a franchise-record 88 games en route to a second consecutive Carolina League championship.

It added up to a nod as the Baseball America Minor League Team of the Year.

The 61 players who suited up for Charleston got the job done on the field. So, too, did the people behind the scenes, from the RiverDogs' coaches and manager Blake Butera to the Rays' player development and scouting staffs to the fans who created an environment conducive to winning at The Joe, as Joseph P. Riley, Jr. Park is known.

Carolina League champs

CHARLESTON RIVERDOGS

"Coming out of spring training, we felt really, really good about the way our roster was shaking out," Butera said. "We had a lot of young or recently drafted or recently acquired players who were kind of getting their first taste of affiliated baseball.

"We knew it was a young, highly talented group, and there was a lot of teaching. So obviously tons of credit goes to our staff in Charleston and our staff throughout the minor leagues, with the coordinators coming in and out as well.

"Just the sheer volume of teaching was just outstanding to see. And then you could really see, I think, month to month, just how much growth there was with each individual player."

It was business as usual for the parent Rays, whose affiliates had the best overall record in organization standings for a fourth year in a row. Tampa Bay's five domestic affiliates won 60% of their games in 2022 after establishing a modern minor league record with a .653 winning percentage in 2021.

Among Charleston's many contributors, outfielder Shane Sasaki stood out, hitting .324 with 27 doubles, nine home runs and 47 stolen bases, earning team MVP honors.

"We had so many players contribute that I feel like I'm going to miss somebody," Butera said. "But just going down the list, Shane Sasaki was outstanding. I think his second half of the season was one of the best second halves I've ever seen out of a player. In all facets—defensively, he got on base at a high clip and stole a ton of bases."

Rays top 2021 draft pick Carson Williams, a high school shortstop from San Diego who turned 19 halfway through the season, also played a big role. He hit .252 with 22 doubles, 10 triples, 19 homers and an .818 OPS. He won the organization's defensive player of the year award.

Third baseman Willy Vasquez was another key cog. As he had in 2021, he finished strong, hitting .256 with 10 homers, 73 RBIs and a .723 OPS.

Another measure of Charleston's team effort: RiverDogs players won three of the league's six monthly top position player awards and one pitcher award.

On the pitching side, 2019 supplemental first-round righthander JJ Goss played a key role, working his way back from injury and into top form. The 21-year-old went 4-1, 2.50 over his final 11 starts and led the postseason rotation. "He was our guy," Butera said.

As with the big league Rays, the RiverDogs dealt with a constantly changing roster. Several key players were promoted during the season to High-A Bowling Green, helping the Hot Rods win the South Atlantic League championship. ■

LAST 10 WINNERS

2011: Double-A Mobile BayBears/Southern (D-backs)
2012: Double-A Springfield Cardinals/Texas (Cardinals)
2013: High-A Daytona Cubs/Florida State (Cubs)
2014: Double-APortland Sea Dogs/Eastern (Red Sox)
2015: Double-A Biloxi Shuckers/Southern (Brewers)
2016: Low-A Rome Braves/South Atlantic (Braves)
2017: Double-A Midland RockHounds/Texas (Athletics)
2018: Low-A Bowling Green Hot Rods/Midwest (Rays)
2019: Double-A Amarillo/Texas (Padres)
2021: Triple-A Durham/International (Rays)

Full list: search "Baseball America awards"

2022 OVERALL MINOR LEAGUE DEPARTMENT LEADERS

FULL-SEASON TEAM LEADERS

WINS

Nashville Sounds (International)	91
Charleston RiverDogs (Carolina)	88
Toledo Mud Hens (International)	87
Durham Bulls (International)	86
Columbus Clippers (International)	85
El Paso Chihuahuas (Pacific Coast)	86
Reno Aces (Pacific Coast)	85

LONGEST WINNING STREAK

Toledo (International)	12
Myrtle Beach (South Atlantic)	12
Fresno (California)	11
San Jose (California)	11
Lehigh Valley (International)	10
South Bend (Midwest)	10

LOSSES

Charlotte Knights (International)	92
Louisville Bats (International)	90
Stockton Ports (California)	87
Visalia Rawhide (California)	87
Albuquerque Isotopes (Pacific Coast)	86

LONGEST LOSING STREAK

Rochester Red Wings	19
Montgomery Biscuits	12
Sacramento River Cats	11
Fayetteville Woodpeckers	11
St. Paul Saints	11

BATTING AVERAGE

El Paso Chihuahuas (Pacific Coast)	.284
Amarillo Sod Poodles (Texas)	.277
Fresno Grizzlies (California)	.276
Las Vegas Aviators (Pacific Coast)	.274
Reno Aces (Pacific Coast)	.273

RUNS

El Paso Chihuahuas (Pacific Coast)	974
Oklahoma City Dodgers (Pacific Coast)	949
Fresno Grizzlies (California)	911
Rancho Cucamonga Quakes (California)	906
Albuquerque Isotopes (Pacific Coast)	894

HOME RUNS

Albuquerque Isotopes (Pacific Coast)	240
El Paso Chihuahuas (Pacific Coast)	222
Tacoma Rainiers (Pacific Coast)	216
Sugar Land Space Cowboys (Pacific Coast)	214
Durham Bulls (International)	212

STOLEN BASES

Down East Wood Ducks (Carolina)	308
Lake Elsinore Storm (California)	259
Charleston RiverDogs (Carolina)	248
Hudson Valley Renegades (South Atlantic)	230
Fayetteville Woodpeckers (Carolina)	228

EARNED RUN AVERAGE

Eugene Emeralds (Norhwest)	3.42
Fort Myers Mighty Mussels (Florida State)	3.51
Somerset Patriots (Eastern)	3.60
Hudson Valley Renegades (South Atlantic)	3.62
Cedar Rapids Kernels (Midwest)	3.66

STRIKEOUTS

Round Rock Express (Pacific Coast)	1,535
Rancho Cucamonga Quakes (California)	1,481
Sacramento River Cats (Pacific Coast)	1,460
San Jose Giants (California)	1,443
Oklahoma City Dodgers (Pacific Coast)	1,439

INDIVIDUAL BATTING

BATTING AVERAGE*

Minimum 378 PA

Vaun Brown (San Jose, Eugene, Richmond)	.346
Jancarlos Cintron (Amarillo, Reno)	.338
Wynton Bernard (Albuquerque)	.333
Esteury Ruiz (San Antonio, El Paso, Nashville)	.332
Sal Frelick (Wisconsin, Biloxi, Nashville)	.331

RUNS

Michael Busch (Tulsa, Oklahoma City)	118
Jacob Young (Fredericksburg)	118
Colton Cowser (Aberdeen, Bowie, Norfolk)	114
Esteury Ruiz (San Antonio, El Paso, Nashville)	114
Wilyer Abreu (Corpus Christi, Portland)	106

Matt Mervis

DANNY PARKER/FOUR SEAM IMAGES

HITS

Will Brennan (Akron, Columbus)	166
Darius Hill (Tennessee, Iowa)	166
Dominic Fletcher (San Antonio, Reno)	163
Sal Frelick (Carolina, Biloxi, Nashville)	163
Jordan Diaz (Midland, Las Vegas)	160

TOP HITTING STREAKS

Dominic Fletcher (Amarillo, Reno)	30
Brandon Dixon (San Antonio, El Paso)	22
Alexfri Planez (Lake County)	22
Aaron Whitefield (Rocket City)	22
Roby Enriquez (Amarillo)	20

MOST HITS (ONE GAME)

Michael Guldberg (Midland)	6
91 others	5

TOTAL BASES

Matt Mervis (South Bend, Tenn, Iowa)	310
Hunter Goodman (Fresno, Spokane, Hartford)	299
Michael Busch (Tulsa, Oklahoma City)	285
Christian Encarnacion-Strand (C. Rapids, Wichita, Chatt.)	284
Josh Outman (Tulsa, Oklahoma City)	277

EXTRA-BASE HITS

Matt Mervis (South Bend, Tenn, Iowa)	78
Hunter Goodman (Fresno, Spokane, Hartford)	71
Michael Busch (Tulsa, Oklahoma City)	70
Josh Lester (Toledo)	70
Josh Outman (Tulsa, Oklahoma City)	69
Jordan Westburg (Bowie, Norfolk)	69
Justin Dirden (Corpus Christi, Sugar Land)	69

DOUBLES

Julio Carreras (Spokane, Hartford)	42
Jake Alu (Harrisburg, Rochester)	40
Will Brennan (Akron, Columbus)	40
Justin Dirden (Corpus Christi, Sugar Land)	40
Matt Mervis (South Bend, Tenn, Iowa)	40

TRIPLES

Mason Auer (Charleston, Bowling Green)	12
Drew Avans (Oklahoma City)	12
Jonatan Clase (Modesto)	11
11 others	10

HOME RUNS

Moises Gomez (Springfield, Memphis)	39
Alexander Canario (South Bend, Tenn, Iowa)	37
Hunter Goodman (Fresno, Spokane, Hartford)	36
Matt Mervis (South Bend, Tenn, Iowa)	36
Tristan Gray (Durham)	33

RUNS BATTED IN

Matt Mervis (South Bend, Tenn, Iowa)	119
Christian Encarnacion-Strand (C. Rapids, Wichita, Chatt.)	114
Roberto Perez Jr. (Modesto, Everett)	114
Yanquiel Fernandez (Fresno)	109
Michael Busch (Tulsa, Oklahoma City)	108

MOST RBIs(ONE GAME)

Chandler Redmond (Springfield)	11
Brandon Dixon (San Antonio)	9
Christian Encarnacion-Strand (Cedar Rapids)	9
9 others	8

WALKS

Jon Singleton (Nashville)	117
Wilyer Abreu (Corpus Christi, Portland)	114
Justin Farmer (Lake Elsinore, Fort Wayne)	106
Austin Gauthier (Rancho Cucamonga, Great Lake)	103
Niko Kavadas (Salem, Greenville, Portland)	102

INTENTIONAL WALKS

Matt Wallner (Wichita, St. Paul)	6
Drew Lugbauer (Mississippi)	5
4 tied	4

STRIKEOUTS

Craig Dedelow (Birmingham, Charlotte)	214
Drew Lugbauer (Mississippi)	212
Gage Workman (Erie)	206
Brewer Hicklen (Omaha)	202
Mason Martin (Indianapolis)	194

STOLEN BASES

Esteury Ruiz (San Antonio, El Paso, Nashville)	85
Luis Valdez (Delmarva, Aberdeen)	71
Omar De Los Santos (St. Lucie)	70
David Hamilton (Portland)	70
Nasim Nunez (Beloit, Pensacola)	70

CAUGHT STEALING

Pedro Leon (Sugar Land)	18
Alejandro Osuna (Down East, Hickory)	18
Maximo Acosta (Down East)	17
Nasim Nunez (Beloit, Pensacola)	16
Alex Ramirez (St. Lucie, Brooklyn)	16

ON-BASE PERCENTAGE*

Minimum 378 PA

Esteury Ruiz (San Antonio, El Paso, Nashville)	.447
Niko Kavadas (Salem, Greenville, Portland)	.443
Logan Porter (Northwest Arkansas, Omaha)	.442
Austin Gauthier (Rancho Cucamonga, Great Lakes)	.441
Edouard Julien (Wichita)	.441

SLUGGING PERCENTAGE*
Minimum 378 PA

Kerry Carpenter (Erie, Toledo)	.345
Moises Gomez (Springfield, Memphis)	.624
Vaun Brown (San Jose, Eugene, Richmond)	.623
Kyle Manzardo (Bowling Green, Montgomery)	.617
Matt Mervis (South Bend, Tenn., Iowa)	.605

ON-BASE PLUS SLUGGING (OPS)*
Minimum 378 PA

Vaun Brown (San Jose, Eugene, Richmond)	1.060
Kyle Manzardo (Bowling Green, Montgomery)	1.043
Corbin Carroll (Amarillo, Reno)	1.026
Kerry Carpenter (Erie, Toledo)	1.025
Endy Rodriguez (Greensboro, Altoona, Indianapolis)	.997

HIT BY PITCH

Braiden Ward (Fresno, Spokane)	33
Zac Cook (New Hampshire)	30
Esteury Ruiz (San Antonio, El Paso, Nashville)	27
Ripken Reyes (Fort Wayne, San Antonio)	26
Hudson Haskin (Bowie)	24
Ben Maigeri (West Michigan)	24
Darrien Miller (Wisconsin)	24

SACRIFICE BUNTS

Zac Cook (New Hampshire)	11
Ripken Reyes (Fort Wayne, San Antonio)	10
Julio Carreras (Spokane, Hartford)	9
Ramon Mendoza (Palm Beach, Peoria)	9
Tyler Reichenborn (Palm Beach, Peoria)	9

SACRIFICE FLIES

Blaine Crim (Frisco, Round Rock)	14
Brett Sullivan (El Paso)	13
David Calabrese (Inland Empire)	11
Trevor Hauver (Hickory, Frisco)	11
Roberto Perez Jr. (Modesto, Everett)	11

GROUNDED INTO DOUBLE PLAY

Leandro Cedeno (Amarillo, Reno)	23
Yainer Diaz (Corpus Christi, Sugar Land)	20
Jordan Dlaz (Midland, Las Vegas)	18
Jake Holton (West Michigan, Erie)	18
9 others	17

BATTING AVERAGE BY POSITION

CATCHERS

Endy Rodrigiuez (Greensboro, Altoona, Indianapolis)	.323
Edgar Quero (Inland Empire)	.312
J.C. Correa (Asheville)	.309
Yainer Diaz (Corpus Christi, Round Rock)	.306
Logan Porter (Northwest Arkansas, Omaha)	.301

FIRST BASEMEN

Kyle Manzardo (Bowling Green, Montgomery)	.327
Jordan Diaz (Midland, Las Vegas)	.326
Jonathan Aranda (Durham)	.318
Joey Loperfido (Fayetteville, Asheville)	.316
Matt Mervis (South Bend, Tenn, Iowa)	.309

SECOND BASEMEN

Jancarlos Cintron (Amarillo, Reno)	.338
Lenyn Sosa (Birmingham, Charlotte)	.315
Thomas Saggese (Hickory, Frisco)	.312
Edouard Julien (Wichita)	.300
Miles Mastrobuoni (Durham)	.300

THIRD BASEMEN

Connor Hollis (Amarillo, El Paso)	.329
Osleivis Basabe (Bowling Green, Montgomery)	.324
Brett Baty (Binghamton, Syracuse)	.315
Warning Bernabel (Fresno, Spokane)	.313
Addison Barger (Lansing, New Hampshire)	.308

SHORTSTOPS

Vaughn Grissom (Rome, Mississippi)	.324
Elly De La Cruz (Dayton, Chattanooga)	.304
Jordan Lawlar (Visalia, Hillsboro, Amarillo)	.303
Blaze Alexander (Amarillo, Reno)	.301
Jonathan Ornelas (Frisco)	.299

OUTFIELDERS

Vaun Brown (San Jose, Eugene, Richmond)	.346
Esteury Ruiz (San Antonio, El Paso, Nashville)	.332
Sal Frelick (Wisconsin, Biloxi, Nashville)	.331
Alec Burleson (Memphis)	.331
Tyler Gentry (Wilmington, Northwest Arkansas)	.326

INDIVIDUAL PITCHING

EARNED RUN AVERAGE*
Minimum 112 IP

Gavin Stone (Great Lakes, Tulsa, Oklahoma City)	1.48
Luis Devers (Myrtle Beach, South Bend)	1.91
Gavin Williams (Lake County, Akron)	1.96
Mason Montgomery (Bowling Green, Montgomery)	2.10
Will Dion (Lynchburg, Akron)	2.11

WORST ERA*

John Parke (Charlotte)	6.90
Alec Marsh (Northwest Arkansas, Omaha)	6.88
Edgar Escobar (Springfield)	6.73
Ryan Weathers (El Paso)	6.73
Cole Winn (Round Rock)	6.51

WINS

Taylor Dollard (Arkansas)	16
Anthony Molina (Charleston, Bowling Green)	14
Sean Boyle (Somerset, Scranton/Wilkes-Barre)	13
Luis Devers (Myrtle Beach, South Bend)	13
6 others	12

LOSSES

Alec Marsh (Northwest Arkansas, Omaha)	16
Tobias Myers (Sacramento, Columbus, Charlotte)	15
Drey Jameson (Amarillo, Reno)	13
Stephen Kolek (Arkansas)	13
Junior Santos (Brooklyn)	13

GAMES

Zach Lee (Albuquerque)	64
Andrew Perez (Charlotte)	59
Miguel Diaz (Toledo)	58
Julian Fernandez (Albuquerque)	58
Alberto Baldonado (Rochester)	56
Joey Marciano (Sacramento)	56
Zach McAllister (Memphis)	56

GAMES STARTED

Brandon Pfaadt (Amarillo, Reno)	29
10 others	28

COMPLETE GAMES

Cesar Valdez (Salt Lake)	3
Thomas Eshelman (San Antonio, El Paso)	2
Matt Harvey (Aberdeen, Bowie, Norfolk)	2
Casey Lawrence (Buffalo)	2
Victor Santos (Portland, Worcester)	2

SHUTOUTS

26 tied	1

GAMES FINISHED

Cam Robinson (Wisconsin, Biloxi, Nashville)	44
Zach Brzykcy (Harrisburg, Rochester)	43
Fernando Cruz (Louisville)	42
Kaleb Ort (Worcester)	39
Michael Tonkin (Gwinnett)	39
Cole Uvila (Norfolk)	39

HOLDS

Miguel Del Pozo (Toledo)	19
Julian Fernandez (Albuquerque)	14
Luis F. Castillo (Erie, Toledo)	13
Kolton Ingram (Rocket City)	13
Miguel Diaz (Toledo)	12
Zach Lee (Albuquerque)	12
Luke Murphy (Rocket City)	12
Braden Shipley (Arkansas)	12

SAVES

Cam Robinson (Wisconsin, Biloxi, Nashville)	25
Fernando Cruz (Louisville)	23
Eric Torres (Rocket City)	22
Carson Coleman (Hudson Valley, Somerset)	19
Brian Marconi (Lehigh Valley)	18

INNINGS PITCHED

Brandon Pfaadt (Amarillo, Reno)	167.0
Sean Boyle (Somerset, Scranton/Wilkes-Barre)	155.1
Darren McCaughan (Tacoma)	154.1
Peyton Battenfield (Columbus)	153.2
Chris Murphy (Portland, Columbus)	152.0

WALKS

Cole Winn (Round Rock)	87
Kai-Wei Teng (Richmond)	85
Joe Boyle (Dayton, Chattanooga)	84
Jason Bilous (Birmingham, Charlotte)	79
Karl Kauffman (Hartford, Albuquerque)	79
Doug Nikhazy (Lake County, Akron)	79

STRIKEOUTS

Brandon Pfaadt (Amarillo, Reno)	218
Kyle Harrison (Eugene, Richmond)	186
Logan T. Allen (Akron, Columbus)	177
Royber Salinas (Augusta, Rome)	175
Robert Gasser (Fort Wayne, Biloxi, Nashville)	172

HITS ALLOWED

John Parke (Charlotte)	180
Collin Wiles (Las Vegas)	175
Connor Thomas (Memphis)	172
Brian Van Belle (Greenville, Portland)	171
Matthew Kent (Jacksonville)	167

HOME RUNS ALLOWED

Parker Dunshee (Las Vegas)	38
Brian Van Belle (Greenville, Portland)	33
Ryan Weathers (El Paso)	31
Brandon Gold (Albuquerque)	30
Thomas Parsons (Memphis)	29
6 tied	28

STRIKEOUTS PER NINE (STARTERS)*
Minimum 100 IP

Kyle Harrison (Eugene, Richmond)	14.81
Royber Salinas (Augusta, Rome)	14.45
Nick Nastrini (Great Lakes, Tulsa)	13.04
Spencer Arrighetti (Asheville, Corpus Christi)	12.83
Landen Roupp (San Jose, Eugene, Richmond)	12.75

STRIKEOUTS PER NINE (RELIEVERS)*
Minimum 48 IP

Ronan Kopp (Rancho Cucamonga, Great Lakes)	15.59
Keegan Collett (Lake Elsinore, Fort Wayne)	15.58
Jack Neely (Tampa, Hudson Valley)	15.56
Gerson Moreno (Erie)	15.16
Clayton Beeter (Tulsa, Somerset)	15.08

OPPONENT AVERAGE (STARTERS)*
Minimum 100 IP

Joe Boyle (Dayton, Chattanooga)	.139
Prelander Berroa (Eugene, Richmond)	.157
Gavin Williams (Lake County, Akron)	.171
Edinson Batista (Asheville, Corpus Christi)	.177
Nick Nastrini (Great Lakes, Tulsa)	.178

OPPONENT AVERAGE (RELIEVERS)*
Minimum 48 IP

Jose Cruz (San Jose)	.119
Matt Minnick (Somerset, Scranton/Wilkes-Barre)	.131
Alaska Abney (Lake County)	.133
Eric Torres (Rocket City)	.142
Greg Weissert (Scranton/Wilkes-Barre)	.145

MOST STRIKEOUTS (ONE GAME)

Matt Sauer (Somerset)	17
Andrew Painter (Clearwater)	14
Inohan Paniagua (Palm Beach)	14
Shane Drohan (Greenville)	14
Tanner Gordon (Rome)	14
Robinson Pina (Tri-City)	14
Daniel Espino (Akron)	14
Bryce Miller (Arkansas)	14
Bobby Miller (Oklahoma City)	14
DL Hall (Norfolk)	14
Reid Detmers (Salt Lake)	14

WILD PITCHES

Jakob Brustoski (ACL Brewers, Carolina)	29
Josue Arias (DSL Miami)	25
Tyler Baum (ACL Athletics, Stockton)	25
Dielmon Urena (DSL Cleveland Red)	25
Luis Medina (Somerset, Midland)	24
Graeme Stinson (Bowling Green, Montgomery)	24

BALKS

John Rooney (Tulsa)	10
Freylin Garcia (Asheville, Fayetteville)	8
Alejandro Mendez (Delmarva)	8
Hancel Rincon (FCL Cardinals, Palm Beach)	7
Domingo Robles (Springfield)	7

HIT BATTERS

Wyatt Olds (Greenville, Portland)	28
Juan Carela (Tampa, Hudson Valley)	24
Joseph Hernandez (Modesto)	21
Graeme Stinson (Bowling Green, Montgomery)	21
2 tied	20

GROUNDBALL DOUBLE PLAYS

John Parke (Charlotte)	24
Matthew Kent (Jacksonville)	21
Michael McGreevy (Peoria, Springfield)	21
Bryan Hoeing (Pensacola, Jacksonville)	20
Will Stewart (Pensacola, Jacksonville)	20

INDIVIDUAL FIELDING

ERRORS

Capri Ortiz (DSL Angels)	26
Aeverson Arteaga (San Jose)	25
Miguel Hiraldo (Vancouver)	25
Ronny Mauricio (Binghamton)	25
Max Muncy (Stockton)	25
Roosbert Tapia (DSL Rays)	25

INTERNATIONAL LEAGUE TRIPLE-A

Awards selected by Major League Baseball

CHAMPION: Durham defeated Nashville in the International League championship game, 13-0, before moving on and winning the Triple-A Championship Game against Reno. Both games were played at Las Vegas Ballpark, the regular-season home of the Las Vegas Aviators. In-season acquisition Bligh Madris and 30-home run masher Tristan Gray led the way in the finale with a combined six hits, including a three-run home from Gray that helped break the game open.

MOST VALUABLE PLAYER: Jonathan Aranda bounced between first, second and third base for eventual-champion Durham, but he was most valuable in the box. In a year when he made his MLB debut, Aranda's .318 average placed him second in the IL behind only Memphis' Alec Burleson. Aranda added a league-best .915 OPS for good measure.

PITCHER OF THE YEAR: The league's top pitcher honors went to Scranton/Wilkes-Barre reliever Greg Weissert, who was a force for the RailRiders as they battled Durham down the stretch. The 27-year-old whiffed 70 in 48 innings and racked up 18 saves in 19 chances.

TOP MLB PROSPECT: After a standout turn at Double-A Bowie, shortstop Gunnar Henderson moved to Triple-A Norfolk and didn't miss a beat. The Minor League Player of the Year crushed much-older competition before earning his first big league callup for a Baltimore club hunting for its first playoff berth since 2016. In doing so, he ascended to No. 1 on the Top 100 Prospects.

Gunnar Henderson

BRIAN WESTERHOLT/FOUR SEAM IMAGES

MANAGER OF THE YEAR: Nashville's Rick Sweet helped the Sounds go 91-58 for the best record in the IL and the most wins in the minors.

INTERNATIONAL LEAGUE ALL-STARS

Pos	Player	Team	AVG	OPS	HR
C	Bo Naylor	Columbus	.257	.880	15
1B	Jonathan Aranda	Durham	.318	.915	18
2B	Miles Mastrobuoni	Durham	.300	.846	16
3B	Mark Vientos	Syracuse	.280	.877	24
SS	Gunnar Henderson	Norfolk	.288	.894	11
OF	Alec Burleson	Memphis	.331	.904	20
OF	Will Benson	Columbus	.278	.948	17
OF	Josh Lowe	Durham	.315	.958	14
DH	Mark Payton	Charlotte	.293	.908	25
Pos	**Pitcher**	**Team**	**G**	**ERA**	**SO**
RHP	Grayson Rodriguez	Norfolk	14	2.20	97
LHP	Kyle Muller	Gwinnett	23	3.41	159
RP	Greg Weissert	Scranton/WB	42	1.690	70

OVERALL STANDINGS

East Division	W	L	PCT	GB	Manager	Attendance	Avg	Last Penn
Durham Bulls (Rays)	86	64	.573	—	Brady Williams	472,090	6,295	2022
Scranton/Wilkes-Barre RailRiders (Yankees)	83	67	.553	3	Doug Davis	331,286	4,666	2016
Jacksonville Jumbo Shrimp (Marlins)	80	69	.537	5.5	Daren Brown	358,094	4,974	Never
Buffalo Bisons (Blue Jays)	76	72	.514	9	Casey Candaele	451,859	6,846	2004
Lehigh Valley IronPigs (Phillies)	76	72	.514	9	Anthony Contreras	544,220	7,665	Never
Worcester Red Sox (Red Sox)	75	73	.507	10	Chad Tracy	532,152	7,290	Never
Norfolk Tides (Orioles)	74	76	.493	12	Buck Britton	365,292	5,004	1999
Rochester Red Wings (Nationals)	67	81	.453	18	Matt LeCroy	432,580	6,180	1997
Syracuse Mets (Mets)	64	85	.430	21.5	Kevin Boles	335,490	4,793	1976
Charlotte Knights (White Sox)	58	92	.387	28	Wes Helms	531,465	7,280	1985

West Division	W	L	PCT	GB	Manager	Attendance	Avg	Last Penn
Nashville Sounds (Brewers)	91	58	.611	—	Rick Sweet	555,576	7,611	*2005
Toledo Mud Hens (Tigers)	87	63	.580	4.5	Lloyd McClendon	426,499	5,842	2006
Columbus Clippers (Guardians)	85	64	.570	6	Andy Tracy	534,393	7,634	2019
Indianapolis Indians (Pirates)	74	75	.497	17	Miguel Perez	534,610	7,425	2000
St. Paul Saints (Twins)	74	75	.497	17	Toby Gardenhire	473,911	6,582	Never
Memphis Redbirds (Cardinals)	73	77	.487	18.5	Ben Johnson	239,605	3,375	*2018
Omaha Storm Chasers (Royals)	71	78	.477	20	Scott Thorman	294,511	4,148	*2014
Gwinnett Stripers (Braves)	69	79	.466	21.5	Matt Tuiasosopo	216,177	2,961	2007
Iowa Cubs (Cubs)	68	81	.456	23	Marty Pevey	437,543	5,913	Never
Louisville Bats (Reds)	60	90	.400	31.5	Pat Kelly	424,035	5,730	2001

IL Championship Game: Durham 13, Nashville 0.

* Pacific Coast League title won prior to 2021 minor league realignment

CLUB BATTING

	AVG	G	AB	R	H	2B	3B	HR	RBI	BB	SO	SB	OBP	SLG
Nashville	.268	149	5029	809	1346	280	22	169	759	653	1288	192	.355	.433
Memphis	.263	150	5027	792	1322	233	22	197	733	584	1250	153	.345	.436
Durham	.261	150	5066	813	1320	281	25	212	765	580	1466	152	.342	.451
Charlotte	.258	150	5062	733	1307	236	20	177	685	478	1212	123	.328	.418
Columbus	.258	149	5020	855	1294	267	29	190	805	633	1145	107	.350	.436
Jacksonville	.257	149	5021	744	1291	249	27	183	691	514	1311	114	.333	.427
Indianapolis	.255	149	4949	749	1262	271	44	138	683	607	1393	157	.340	.411
Rochester	.254	148	4930	688	1251	248	38	133	651	480	1228	153	.326	.400
Iowa	.253	149	4999	696	1266	269	25	149	652	499	1312	119	.329	.406
Omaha	.250	149	4931	801	1234	276	25	194	752	586	1352	188	.338	.434
Scranton/Wilkes-Barre	.249	150	4871	689	1212	270	18	173	638	519	1277	172	.330	.418
Lehigh Valley	.248	148	4838	776	1201	275	20	136	666	633	1272	152	.342	.398
Louisville	.248	150	5043	643	1249	246	24	146	603	457	1319	94	.318	.393
St. Paul	.247	149	5015	812	1239	268	27	194	758	640	1405	136	.338	.427
Worcester	.246	148	4859	733	1197	276	22	181	687	595	1391	110	.336	.424
Buffalo	.246	148	4755	666	1169	228	24	104	614	640	1253	173	.342	.370
Norfolk	.244	150	4918	800	1200	254	31	175	748	663	1386	138	.344	.415
Toledo	.243	150	4946	729	1202	291	29	165	677	611	1389	130	.332	.414
Gwinnett	.239	148	4795	632	1147	233	16	132	591	516	1272	125	.316	.377
Syracuse	.239	149	4906	730	1172	225	13	170	677	549	1392	132	.326	.394

CLUB PITCHING

	ERA	G	CG	SHO	SV	IP	H	R	ER	HR	BB	SO	AVG
Scranton/Wilkes-Barre	3.89	150	0	11	40	1288	1114	634	556	152	544	1402	.231
Nashville	4.02	149	1	10	39	1305	1184	641	583	142	530	1265	.241
Buffalo	4.19	148	2	11	40	1264	1128	663	589	178	485	1272	.237
Jacksonville	4.19	149	0	12	38	1300	1184	680	606	153	524	1291	.242
Toledo	4.32	150	0	9	39	1312	1266	686	629	167	519	1281	.252
Gwinnett	4.37	148	1	8	35	1278	1197	675	620	160	476	1421	.246
Durham	4.38	150	0	10	38	1320	1289	722	642	198	470	1316	.254
Columbus	4.40	149	1	10	36	1310	1203	709	640	154	574	1365	.242
Worcester	4.40	148	3	9	32	1271	1169	697	621	117	543	1411	.243
Indianapolis	4.58	149	1	6	33	1288	1197	763	655	153	591	1256	.243
Memphis	4.66	150	1	8	32	1311	1328	746	679	178	535	1291	.262
Rochester	4.70	148	1	10	30	1284	1204	737	670	148	591	1341	.246
Iowa	4.78	149	0	7	32	1296	1217	758	688	164	672	1367	.246
Omaha	4.83	149	1	6	28	1287	1286	788	690	196	570	1216	.258
Lehigh Valley	4.85	148	1	4	32	1274	1236	741	687	138	679	1261	.255
St. Paul	4.94	149	0	4	31	1302	1257	798	715	187	566	1332	.253
Louisville	4.97	150	0	5	34	1314	1345	813	725	170	660	1307	.264
Norfolk	4.98	150	3	8	31	1293	1314	804	716	164	620	1380	.262
Syracuse	5.16	149	0	6	35	1284	1313	828	737	172	609	1266	.264
Charlotte	6.05	150	0	2	30	1301	1450	957	875	227	679	1272	.281

CLUB FIELDING

	PCT	PO	A	E	DP		PCT	PO	A	E	DP
Nashville	.985	3914	1326	78	126	Columbus	.979	3929	1304	110	122
Toledo	.984	3935	1307	87	114	Buffalo	.979	3792	1245	106	95
Memphis	.984	3934	1354	88	133	Louisville	.979	3942	1235	109	126
Lehigh Valley	.982	3823	1355	96	134	Charlotte	.979	3904	1376	114	141
Worcester	.981	3812	1222	95	117	St. Paul	.978	3906	1306	119	121
Gwinnett	.981	3835	1335	101	105	Durham	.977	3959	1252	120	136
Jacksonville	.981	3901	1354	103	149	Omaha	.977	3862	1383	122	123
Iowa	.980	3892	1261	105	119	Indianapolis	.976	3863	1355	127	124
Rochester	.980	3851	1261	105	114	Syracuse	.974	3853	1363	139	136
Scranton/Wilkes-Barre	.980	3864	1225	105	97	Norfolk	.973	3879	1187	140	120

INDIVIDUAL BATTING

Batter, Club	AVG	G	AB	R	H	2B	3B	HR	RBI	BB	SO	SB
Alec Burleson, Memphis	.331	109	432	68	143	25	1	20	87	29	67	4
Jonathan Aranda, Durham	.318	104	403	71	128	26	1	18	85	45	100	4
Will Brennan, Columbus	.316	93	393	53	124	28	3	9	68	33	53	15
Dairon Blanco, Omaha	.301	107	366	63	110	20	3	14	61	35	98	45
Miles Mastrobuoni, Durham	.300	129	507	92	152	32	3	16	64	63	95	23
Mark Payton, Charlotte	.293	119	471	85	138	31	5	25	95	54	76	15
Brian Miller, Jacksonville	.292	108	408	67	119	19	9	7	45	37	77	26
Ji Hwan Bae, Indianapolis	.289	108	419	81	121	23	6	8	53	48	80	30
Joey Meneses, Rochester	.286	96	374	51	107	14	1	20	64	32	89	1
Brice Turang, Nashville	.286	131	532	89	152	24	2	13	78	65	118	34

INDIVIDUAL PITCHING

Pitcher, Club	W	L	ERA	G	GS	CG	SV	IP	H	R	ER	BB	SO
Casey Lawrence, Buffalo	9	5	2.79	23	23	2	0	126	95	41	39	17	106
Caleb Boushley, Nashville	12	2	3.25	25	25	0	0	127	106	47	46	43	91
Kyle Muller, Gwinnett	6	8	3.41	23	23	1	0	135	119	53	51	40	159
Peyton Battenfield, Columbus	8	6	3.63	28	28	0	0	154	138	67	62	57	109
Logan Verrett, Rochester	8	9	3.80	24	21	0	0	126	111	57	53	28	102
Josh Lindblom, Nashville	9	7	4.05	26	24	0	0	133	120	62	60	47	133
Matt Krook, Scranton/Wilkes-Barre	10	7	4.09	29	22	0	0	139	120	71	63	73	155
Austin Cox, Omaha	7	7	4.21	29	24	1	1	147	161	80	69	50	105
Thomas Parsons, Memphis	12	4	4.31	38	17	0	0	136	102	68	65	57	110
Thomas Hatch, Buffalo	8	7	4.67	28	22	0	0	131	127	73	68	38	113

DEPARTMENT LEADERS

BATTING

OBP	Will Benson, Columbus	.426
SLG	Mark Payton, Charlotte	.539
OPS	Jonathan Aranda, Durham	.915
R	Miles Mastrobuoni, Durham	92
H	3 players	152
TB	Josh Lester, Toledo	267
XBH	Josh Lester, Toledo	70
2B	Josh Lester, Toledo	39
3B	Brian Miller, Jacksonville	9
3B	Andrew Stevenson, Rochester	9
HR	Tristan Gray, Durham	33
RBI	Josh Lester, Toledo	99
SAC	Xavier Edwards, Durham	7
BB	Jon Singleton, Nashville	117
HBP	Kramer Robertson, Memphis	20
SO	Brewer Hicklen, Omaha	202
SB	Dairon Blanco, Omaha	45
CS	Vidal Brujan, Durham	13

FIELDING

C	PCT	Carlos Pérez, Charlotte	.990
	PO	Carlos Pérez, Charlotte	715
	A	Carlos Pérez, Charlotte	46
	DP	2 tied	6
	E	Ford Proctor, Durham	12
	CS	Carlos Pérez, Charlotte	28
	SB	Carlos Pérez, Charlotte	75
	PB	Mario Feliciano, Nashville	14
1B	PCT	Josh Lester, Toledo	.996
	PO	Luken Baker, Memphis	894
	A	Jon Singleton, Nashville	89
	DP	Luken Baker, Memphis	93
	E	Mason Martin, Indianapolis	9
2B	PCT	Mitchell Tolman, Columbus	.988
	PO	Bryson Brigman, Jacksonville	121
	A	Bryson Brigman, Jacksonville	204
	DP	Bryson Brigman, Jacksonville	53
	E	2 tied	9
3B	PCT	Joe Dunand, Jacksonville/Gwinnett	.980
	PO	2 tied	56
	A	Joe Dunand, Jacksonville/Gwinnett	144
	DP	2 tied	22
	E	Rylan Bannon, Norfolk/Gwinnett	20
SS	PCT	Zack Short, Toledo	.978
	PO	Brice Turang, Nashville	139
	A	Brice Turang, Nashville	271
	DP	Zack Short, Toledo	57
	E	Oneil Cruz, Indianapolis	14
OF	PCT	David Dahl, Nashville/Rochester	1.000
	PO	2 tied	184
	A	Brewer Hicklen, Omaha	11
	DP	Peyton Burdick, Jacksonville	4
	E	Jerar Encarnacion, Jacksonville	7

PITCHING

G	Andrew Perez, Charlotte	59
GS	Peyton Battenfield, Columbus	28
GF	Fernando Cruz, Louisville	42
SV	Fernando Cruz, Louisville	23
W	Caleb Boushley, Nashville	12
W	Thomas Parsons, Memphis	12
L	Tobias Myers, Charlotte	15
IP	Peyton Battenfield, Columbus	154
H	John Parke, Charlotte	180
R	John Parke, Charlotte	105
ER	John Parke, Charlotte	103
HB	Osvaldo Bido, Indianapolis	13
BB	Matt Krook, Scranton/Wilkes-Barre	73
SO	Kyle Muller, Gwinnett	159
SO/9	Kyle Muller, Gwinnett	10.6
BB/9	Casey Lawrence, Buffalo	1.2
WP	Ethan Small, Nashville	14
BK	Seth Blair, Durham	4
BK	Ricardo Sanchez, Toledo	4
HRA	Thomas Parsons, Memphis	29
BAA	Thomas Parsons, Memphis	.204

PACIFIC COAST LEAGUE TRIPLE-A

Awards selected by Major League Baseball

CHAMPION: As part of the new Triple-A playoff format, the Reno Aces defeated the El Paso Chihuahuas in a one-game showdown. The Aces were led by righthander Brandon Pfaadt, who whiffed three over five two-run innings. Shortstop Jake Hager's three-run home run gave his team the margin it would need.

MOST VALUABLE PLAYER: After a breakout season with Double-A Richmond in 2021, David Villar moved to Triple-A Sacramento in 2022 and kept on hitting. The South Florida product bashed 27 home runs and produced a 1.021 OPS in 84 games with the RiverCats. He also slammed nine more homers in his big league debut.

PITCHER OF THE YEAR: There's never been a doubt about the filthiness of Hunter Brown's stuff, but plenty wondered whether the righthander would have enough command for it to matter. He proved the doubters wrong in 2022 by whiffing 134 in 106 innings with Sugar Land. That was enough to earn Brown a callup to the big leagues with eventual World Series champion Houston. He even made three postseason appearances. Brown's 134 strikeouts ranked third in the PCL.

TOP MLB PROSPECT: Dodgers third baseman Miguel Vargas has mashed at every stop in his professional career, and 2022 was no exception. The Cuban product posted a .915 OPS with Oklahoma City and racked up 32 doubles and 17 homers in the process. He matriculated to the big leagues, too, and clubbed his first MLB home run during the course of his 17-game stint with the Dodgers. His .304 average was second in the PCL, behind outfielder Wynton Bernard.

MANAGER OF THE YEAR: For his work with PCL champion Reno, Gil Velazquez takes home this honor. The Aces' skipper deftly navigated a season which included the gain and loss of several top prospects—including outfielders Corbin Carroll and Alek Thomas as well as starters Brandon Pfaadt, Drey Jameson and Ryne Nelson. Nevertheless, the wins came in bunches for the Aces for Velazquez, who also won BA Minor League Manger of the Year honors.

Miguel Vargas

EDDIE KELLY

PACIFIC COAST LEAGUE ALL-STARS

Pos	Player	Team	AVG	OPS	HR
C	Shea Langeliers	Las Vegas	.283	.876	19
1B	Matt Davidson	Reno/Las Vegas	.310	1.058	32
2B	Eguy Rosario	El Paso	.288	.876	22
3B	David Villar	Sacramento	.275	1.021	27
SS	David Hensley	Sugar Land	.298	.898	10
OF	Jason Martin	Oklahoma City	.285	.938	32
OF	Stone Garrett	Reno	.275	.900	28
OF	Wynton Bernard	Albuquerque	.333	.977	21
DH	Sean Bouchard	Albuquerque	.300	1.039	20
Pos	**Pitcher**	**Team**	**G**	**ERA**	**SO**
RHP	Hunter Brown	Sugar Land	23	2.55	134
LHP	Jake Kalish	Salt Lake	23	2.87	72
RP	Enoli Paredes	Sugar Land	50	2.63	81

OVERALL STANDINGS

East Division	W	L	PCT	GB	Manager	Attendance	Avg	Last Penn
El Paso Chihuahuas (Padres)	85	65	.567	—	Jared Sandberg	496,805	6,714	2016
Oklahoma City Dodgers (Dodgers)	84	66	.560	1	Travis Barbary	410,730	5,626	1965
Round Rock Express (Rangers)	79	71	.527	6	Matt Hagen	412,988	5,507	Never
Sugar Land Space Cowboys (Astros)	73	75	.493	11	Mickey Storey	285,827	3,970	Never
Albuquerque Isotopes (Rockies)	62	86	.419	22	Warren Schaeffer	515,498	7,062	1994
West Division	**W**	**L**	**PCT**	**GB**	**Manager**	**Attendance**	**Avg**	**Last Penn**
Reno Aces (D-backs)	85	63	.574	—	Gil Velazquez	336,079	4,801	2022
Tacoma Rainiers (Mariners)	72	78	.480	14	Tim Federowicz	366,469	5,020	2010
Las Vegas Aviators (Athletics)	71	79	.473	15	Fran Riordan	518,221	6,910	1998
Salt Lake Bees (Angels)	70	80	.467	16	Lou Marson	434,616	5,873	1979
Sacramento River Cats (Giants)	65	83	.439	20	Dave Brundage	372,769	4,970	2019

PCL Championship Game: Reno 6, El Paso 2.

CLUB BATTING

	AVG	G	AB	R	H	2B	3B	HR	RBI	BB	SO	SB	OBP	SLG
El Paso	.284	150	5252	974	1492	332	28	222	921	636	1247	122	.365	.485
Las Vegas	.274	150	5210	864	1426	288	38	189	810	618	1465	85	.359	.452
Reno	.273	148	5094	866	1391	293	40	178	817	565	1129	156	.352	.451
Albuquerque	.273	148	5138	894	1402	266	48	240	839	583	1345	109	.353	.483
Oklahoma City	.273	150	5082	949	1385	278	45	201	904	731	1379	109	.370	.464
Round Rock	.262	150	5155	852	1352	275	32	190	803	573	1334	135	.342	.439
Salt Lake	.260	150	5052	803	1313	264	47	162	743	578	1304	163	.342	.427
Sugar Land	.255	148	5089	860	1299	269	29	214	815	653	1427	157	.349	.446
Sacramento	.253	148	5042	782	1278	251	20	211	759	605	1357	100	.340	.437
Tacoma	.248	150	5061	789	1253	294	34	216	752	640	1511	205	.337	.447

CLUB PITCHING

	ERA	G	CG	SHO	SV	IP	H	R	ER	HR	BB	SO	AVG
Salt Lake	4.70	150	4	7	31	1311	1276	760	685	159	524	1269	.253
Sugar Land	4.86	148	0	6	27	1322	1252	814	714	175	679	1410	.247
Oklahoma City	4.87	150	2	5	29	1307	1245	793	707	165	700	1439	.248
Reno	4.96	148	0	3	34	1313	1307	775	724	209	562	1341	.258
Round Rock	4.97	150	0	8	37	1320	1271	817	729	192	700	1535	.251
Tacoma	5.28	150	0	9	34	1328	1397	848	779	191	542	1251	.270
El Paso	5.53	150	0	2	29	1330	1408	903	818	212	664	1413	.270
Sacramento	5.74	148	0	6	33	1302	1344	908	831	197	661	1460	.265
Las Vegas	6.11	150	2	3	30	1309	1504	964	888	265	557	1206	.288
Albuquerque	6.89	148	1	2	30	1283	1587	1051	982	258	593	1174	.303

CLUB FIELDING

	PCT	PO	A	E	DP
Tacoma	.986	3985	1363	78	130
Reno	.984	3940	1194	86	122
Albuquerque	.980	3849	1434	110	154
Salt Lake	.979	3935	1307	113	130
Sugar Land	.979	3966	1193	112	114
Las Vegas	.979	3927	1404	116	136
Sacramento	.979	3906	1225	112	111
El Paso	.979	3991	1290	116	128
Round Rock	.976	3961	1204	125	125
Oklahoma City	.976	3920	1195	126	117

INDIVIDUAL BATTING

Batter, Club	AVG	G	AB	R	H	2B	3B	HR	RBI	BB	SO	SB
Wynton Bernard, Albuquerque	.333	108	429	95	143	31	8	21	92	39	67	30
Miguel Vargas, Oklahoma City	.304	113	438	100	133	32	4	17	82	71	76	16
Dominic Fletcher, Reno	.301	101	396	70	119	29	8	5	38	42	88	5
David Hensley, Sugar Land	.298	104	379	80	113	30	4	10	57	80	103	20
Taylor Kohlwey, El Paso	.297	128	501	87	149	32	4	11	82	68	91	9
C.J. Hinojosa, El Paso	.291	122	461	69	134	33	2	17	83	45	86	8
Eguy Rosario, El Paso	.288	124	490	98	141	34	4	22	81	59	109	21
Jason Martin, Oklahoma City	.285	129	470	100	134	25	5	32	107	68	135	8
Brett Sullivan, El Paso	.285	113	421	73	120	28	6	9	81	38	58	3
Nate Mondou, Las Vegas	.283	108	385	59	109	30	3	7	64	46	83	1

INDIVIDUAL PITCHING

Pitcher, Club	W	L	ERA	G	GS	CG	SV	IP	H	R	ER	BB	SO
Cesar Valdez, Salt Lake	10	5	3.94	23	23	3	0	146	138	69	64	22	123
Darren McCaughan, Tacoma	8	9	4.55	28	28	0	0	154	140	82	78	42	141
Chad Donato, Sugar Land	4	8	5.34	29	18	0	2	125	122	83	74	60	101
Collin Wiles, Las Vegas	9	11	5.40	26	26	1	0	143	175	100	86	27	106
Ryne Nelson, Reno	10	5	5.43	26	26	0	0	136	142	88	82	47	128
Cole Winn, Round Rock	9	8	6.51	28	28	0	0	122	125	94	88	87	123
Ryan Weathers, El Paso	7	7	6.73	31	22	0	0	123	163	101	92	57	88

DEPARTMENT LEADERS

BATTING

OBP	David Hensley, Sugar Land	.420
SLG	Matt Davidson, Las Vegas	.644
OPS	Wynton Bernard, Albuquerque	0.977
R	3 tied	100
H	Taylor Kohlwey, El Paso	149
TB	Jason Martin, Oklahoma City	265
XBH	Jason Martin, Oklahoma City	62
2B	Eguy Rosario, El Paso	34
3B	Drew Avans, Oklahoma City	12
HR	Matt Davidson, Las Vegas	32
HR	Jason Martin, Oklahoma City	32
RBI	Jason Martin, Oklahoma City	107
SAC	Luis Liberato, El Paso	6
SAC	Matt Whatley, Round Rock	6
BB	Ryan Noda, Oklahoma City	92
HBP	Seth Beer, Reno	21
SO	Ryan Noda, Oklahoma City	162
SB	Forrest Wall, Tacoma	52
CS	Pedro Leon, Sugar Land	18

FIELDING

C	PCT	Korey Lee, Sugar Land	.994
	PO	Korey Lee, Sugar Land	678
	A	Shea Langeliers, Las Vegas	
	DP	2 tied	6
	E	Brett Sullivan, El Paso	10
	CS	Shea Langeliers, Las Vegas	24
	SB	Shea Langeliers, Las Vegas	69
	PB	Jhonny Pereda, Sacramento	17
1B	PCT	David MacKinnon, 2 teams	1.000
	PO	Ryan Noda, Oklahoma City	760
	A	Ryan Noda, Oklahoma City	37
	DP	Ryan Noda, Oklahoma City	75
	E	Dermis Garcia, Las Vegas	6
2B	PCT	Michael Stefanic, Salt Lake	.989
	PO	Michael Busch, Oklahoma City	138
	A	Michael Busch, Oklahoma City	200
	DP	Michael Busch, Oklahoma City	62
	E	Michael Busch, Oklahoma City	13
3B	PCT	Kean Wong, Salt Lake	.958
	PO	Miguel Vargas, Oklahoma City	46
	A	2 tied	124
	DP	Kean Wong, Salt Lake	16
	E	Miguel Vargas , Oklahoma City	15
SS	PCT	Mason McCoy, Tacoma	.986
	PO	Mason McCoy, Tacoma	127
	A	Mason McCoy, Tacoma	304
	DP	Mason McCoy, Tacoma	62
	E	Arquímedes Gamboa, Sacramento	13
OF	PCT	Wynton Bernard, Albuquerque	.995
	PO	Drew Avans, Oklahoma City	224
	A	Ryan Vilade, Albuquerque	8
	DP	3 tied	3
	E	3 tied	5

PITCHING

G	Zach Lee, Albuquerque	64
GS	Darren McCaughan, Tacoma	28
GF	Nick Ramirez, Tacoma	37
SV	Nick Ramirez, Tacoma	16
W	3 tied	10
L	Drey Jameson, Reno	12
IP	Darren McCaughan, Tacoma	154
H	Collin Wiles, Las Vegas	175
R	Parker Dunshee, Las Vegas	117
ER	Parker Dunshee, Las Vegas	114
HB	Parker Dunshee, Las Vegas	16
BB	Cole Winn, Round Rock	87
SO	Darren McCaughan, Tacoma	141
SO/9	Cole Winn, Round Rock	9.1
BB/9	Cesar Valdez, Salt Lake	1.4
WP	2 tied	12
BK	Andre Jackson, Oklahoma City	5
HRA	Parker Dunshee, Las Vegas	38
BAA	Darren McCaughan, Tacoma	.238

MINOR LEAGUES

EASTERN LEAGUE DOUBLE-A

Awards selected by Major League Baseball

CHAMPION: Somerset topped Erie for its first championship as an affiliated club—and the Patriots did so in emphatic fashion. Somerset sealed its championship with a 15-0 no-hitter over West Division-champion Erie. Righthanders Randy Vasquez and Carson Coleman did the honors on the mound, while teenaged outfielder Jasson Dominguez provided two home runs in the win.

MOST VALUABLE PLAYER: The 28-year-old Quincy Nieporte took home these honors after the first baseman slashed .270/.331/.536 with 25 doubles and 31 home runs. Originally a Phillies draft pick, Nieporte spent 2021 with the independent High Point Rockers before signing with the Tigers in March.

PITCHER OF THE YEAR: The Cleveland pitching factory continues unabated. The group's latest pop-up prospect was righthander Tanner Bibee, who went from an interesting arm at Cal State Fullerton to one of the system's top talents. With freshly amplified stuff and excellent command, Bibee went 6-1, 1.83 with Akron, including 81 strikeouts against just 14 walks over 73.2 innings.

TOP MLB PROSPECT: Heading into the 2022 season, Rockies shortstop Ezequiel Tovar was known as a standout defender whose glove would carry him to the big leagues. After an offseason spent first in the Arizona Fall League and then at the Rockies' minor league complex in Scottsdale, Ariz., the Venezuelan emerged stronger and lit the Eastern League on fire before an injury shelved him after just 66 games. He made his big league debut on Sept. 23 and hit his first MLB home run.

MANAGER OF THE YEAR: Dan Fiorito led Somerset to the league's best record at 83-53 and oversaw a club that featured many of the Yankees' best prospects, including shortstop Anthony Volpe, outfielder Jasson Dominguez, catcher Austin Wells and righthanders Randy Vasquez and Will Warren. The result was an EL title.

Ezequiel Tovar

BRIAN ROTHMULLER/ICON SPORTSWIRE VIA GETTY IMAGES

EASTERN LEAGUE ALL-STARS

Pos	Player	Team	AVG	OPS	HR
C	Francisco Alvarez	Binghamton	.277	.921	18
1B	Quincy Nieporte	Erie	.270	.867	31
2B	Connor Norby	Bowie	.298	.960	17
3B	Brett Baty	Binghamton	.312	.950	19
SS	Ezequiel Tovar	Hartford	.318	.932	15
OF	Parker Meadows	Erie	.275	.820	16
OF	Elijah Dunham	Somerset	.248	.796	17
OF	George Valera	Akron	.264	.837	15
DH	Andres Chaparro	Somerset	.289	.963	19
Pos	**Pitcher**	**Team**	**G**	**ERA**	**SO**
RHP	Tanner Bibee	Akron	13	1.83	81
LHP	Joey Cantillo	Akron	14	1.93	87
RP	Carson Coleman	Somerset	35	2.86	69

OVERALL STANDINGS

Northeast Division	W	L	PCT	GB	Manager	Attendance	Avg	Last Penn
Somerset Patriots (Yankees)	83	53	.610	—	Dan Fiorito	351,142	5,241	2022
Hartford Yard Goats (Rockies)	77	60	.562	6.5	Chris Denorfia	402,123	6,002	Never
Portland Sea Dogs (Red Sox)	75	63	.543	9	Chad Epperson	379,100	5,744	2006
Reading Fightin Phils (Phillies)	61	77	.442	23	Shawn Williams	368,068	5,577	2001
New Hampshire Fisher Cats (Blue Jays)	59	79	.428	25	Cesar Martin	282,514	4,346	2018
Binghamton Rumble Ponies (Mets)	53	83	.390	30	Reid Brignac	146,679	2,366	1994
Southwest Division	**W**	**L**	**PCT**	**GB**	**Manager**	**Attendance**	**Avg**	**Last Penn**
Erie SeaWolves (Tigers)	80	58	.580	—	Gabe Alvarez	175,810	2,664	Never
Akron RubberDucks (Guardians)	79	59	.572	1	Rouglas Odor	253,735	3,904	2021
Altoona Curve (Pirates)	71	66	.518	8.5	Kieran Mattison	285,777	4,330	2017
Bowie Baysox (Orioles)	68	70	.493	12	Kyle Moore	174,537	2,685	Never
Richmond Flying Squirrels (Giants)	66	71	.482	13.5	Dennis Pelfrey	406,560	6,160	2014
Harrisburg Senators (Nationals)	52	85	.380	27.5	Tripp Keister	244,433	3,595	1999

Northeast: Somerset def. Portland 2-0. **Southwest:** Erie def. Richmond 2-0. **Championship Series:** Somerset def. Erie 2-1.

CLUB BATTING

	AVG	G	AB	R	H	2B	3B	HR	RBI	BB	SO	SB	OBP	SLG
Altoona	.248	137	4559	681	1131	250	36	143	623	517	1254	162	.331	.413
Bowie	.248	138	4550	717	1127	250	18	163	670	558	1318	75	.342	.418
Hartford	.246	137	4513	676	1112	231	23	160	632	509	1298	177	.328	.414
Erie	.246	138	4556	663	1122	233	35	175	619	467	1279	132	.325	.428
Somerset	.244	136	4459	688	1086	237	23	205	655	538	1243	205	.334	.445
Portland	.238	138	4543	652	1083	228	36	136	605	533	1363	171	.326	.394
New Hampshire	.237	138	4408	622	1046	227	16	166	569	490	1356	107	.324	.409
Binghamton	.236	136	4500	627	1063	224	25	132	578	500	1305	87	.322	.385
Reading	.235	138	4481	598	1054	205	34	119	545	511	1242	110	.322	.376
Akron	.234	138	4476	641	1046	231	34	126	584	494	1205	127	.317	.385
Harrisburg	.233	137	4527	547	1054	202	9	130	505	460	1261	71	.311	.368
Richmond	.230	137	4474	641	1028	187	22	169	597	504	1507	100	.318	.395

CLUB PITCHING

	ERA	G	CG	SHO	SV	IP	H	R	ER	HR	BB	SO	AVG
Somerset	3.60	136	0	9	37	1194	961	563	478	129	437	1359	.218
Erie	3.79	138	1	12	39	1211	1031	577	510	148	413	1373	.227
Akron	3.92	138	1	8	46	1203	989	584	524	131	552	1408	.222
Altoona	3.97	137	0	5	32	1196	1080	613	528	129	472	1247	.240
Portland	4.00	138	2	9	36	1209	1038	611	538	158	482	1299	.231
Richmond	4.31	137	1	5	27	1196	1067	650	573	139	582	1367	.237
Bowie	4.42	138	1	8	32	1194	1114	644	587	172	433	1304	.245
Reading	4.59	138	0	11	31	1188	1157	684	606	154	545	1310	.255
Hartford	4.74	137	3	5	35	1189	1127	664	627	189	471	1216	.250
Harrisburg	4.75	137	1	4	23	1196	1077	686	632	147	550	1256	.239
New Hampshire	4.95	138	0	9	26	1171	1085	711	644	146	623	1262	.245
Binghamton	5.27	136	0	5	25	1176	1226	768	689	182	521	1230	.267

CLUB FIELDING

	PCT	PO	A	E	DP
Hartford	.985	3568	1069	71	110
Harrisburg	.983	3589	1176	83	109
Akron	.981	3610	999	90	95
Portland	.979	3627	1242	102	126
Erie	.979	3632	1119	101	78
Bowie	.979	3583	1111	100	82
Reading	.979	3564	1063	99	114
New Hampshire	.979	3513	1100	100	98
Altoona	.978	3588	1151	109	98
Richmond	.977	3589	1061	108	103
Somerset	.976	3581	1147	115	92
Binghamton	.972	3527	1007	130	94

INDIVIDUAL BATTING

Batter, Club	AVG	G	AB	R	H	2B	3B	HR	RBI	BB	SO	SB
Brett Baty, Binghamton	.312	89	340	73	106	22	0	19	59	46	98	2
Jared Triolo, Altoona	.282	112	425	66	120	21	5	9	39	63	87	24
Wilson Garcia, Harrisburg	.282	119	454	51	128	26	0	24	81	29	86	0
Blake Sabol, Altoona	.281	98	366	61	103	23	5	14	60	38	107	9
Parker Meadows, Erie	.275	113	425	64	117	21	6	16	51	52	90	17
Quincy Nieporte, Erie	.270	123	459	72	124	25	2	31	91	40	85	2
Joseph Ortiz, Bowie	.269	111	435	69	117	28	4	15	71	41	81	2
Dane Myers, Erie	.268	107	407	59	109	18	2	25	72	23	118	20
Hunter Stovall, Hartford	.267	108	393	48	105	27	3	9	55	34	91	10
Wendell Rijo, Reading	.266	94	342	57	91	23	1	12	53	41	85	24

INDIVIDUAL PITCHING

Pitcher, Club	W	L	ERA	G	GS	CG	SV	IP	H	R	ER	BB	SO
Chance Kirby, Erie	8	3	2.62	29	21	1	0	127	90	40	37	29	116
Randy Vasquez, Somerset	2	7	3.90	25	25	0	0	115	106	56	50	41	120
Reese Olson, Erie	8	6	4.14	26	25	0	0	120	109	65	55	38	168
Ronald Herrera, Harrisburg	5	9	4.40	24	24	1	0	129	120	71	63	34	114
Luis Ortiz, Altoona	5	9	4.64	24	23	0	0	114	100	63	59	34	126
Alex Troop, Harrisburg	7	5	4.81	28	17	0	0	112	114	64	60	31	130
Matt Frisbee, Richmond	6	10	5.16	27	26	1	0	140	149	85	80	38	132
Kai-Wei Teng, Richmond	6	12	5.22	28	28	0	0	136	122	87	79	85	169
Noah Davis, Hartford	8	8	5.54	26	26	1	0	133	133	86	82	60	152
Garrett Stallings, Bowie	6	10	6.28	26	22	1	0	119	140	90	83	29	124

DEPARTMENT LEADERS

BATTING

OBP	Brett Baty, Binghamton	.406
SLG	Brett Baty, Binghamton	.544
OPS	Brett Baty, Binghamton	.950
R	David Hamilton, Portland	81
H	Jose Tena, Akron	136
TB	Quincy Nieporte, Erie	246
XBH	Quincy Nieporte, Erie	58
2B	Aaron Schunk, Hartford	32
3B	David Hamilton, Portland	9
3B	Gage Workman, Erie	9
HR	Quincy Nieporte, Erie	31
RBI	Quincy Nieporte, Erie	91
SAC	Jonathan Guzman, Reading	8
BB	Andres Alvarez, Altoona	64
BB	Jeisson Rosario, Somerset	64
HBP	Zac Cook, New Hampshire	30
SO	Gage Workman, Erie	206
SB	David Hamilton, Portland	70
CS	Ronny Mauricio, Binghamton	11

FIELDING

C	PCT	Brady Lindsly, Harrisburg	.998
	PO	Willie MacIver, Hartford	856
	A	Cody Roberts, Bowie	48
	DP	Willie MacIver, Hartford	6
	E	Maverick Handley, Bowie	12
	CS	Willie MacIver, Hartford	36
	SB	Phil Clarke, New Hampshire	85
	PB	Brandon Martorano, Richmond	13
1B	PCT	Frankie Tostado, Richmond	.996
	PO	Michael Toglia, Hartford	647
	A	Micah Pries, Akron	48
	DP	Micah Pries, Akron	71
	E	Jeremy Vasquez, Binghamton	13
2B	PCT	Isaac Collins, Hartford	.989
	PO	Jesus Bastidas, Somerset	131
	A	Jesus Bastidas, Somerset	228
	DP	Jesus Bastidas, Somerset	54
	E	2 tied	10
3B	PCT	Daniel Schneemann, Akron	.986
	PO	Aaron Schunk, Hartford	89
	A	2 tied	165
	DP	Aaron Schunk, Hartford	18
	E	Brett Baty, Binghamton	14
SS	PCT	Jonathan Guzman, Reading	.978
	PO	Ronny Mauricio, Binghamton	151
	A	Jonathan Guzman, Reading	251
	DP	Jonathan Guzman, Reading	62
	E	Ronny Mauricio, Binghamton	25
OF	PCT	Matt Fraizer, Altoona	1.000
	PO	2 tied	244
	A	Carlos Cortes, Binghamton	12
	DP	Matt Fraizer, Altoona	4
	E	Jhailyn Ortiz, Reading	9

PITCHING

G	Yaya Chentouf, Erie	49
GS	Kai-Wei Teng, Richmond	28
GF	Gavin Hollowell, Hartford	37
SV	Brian Marconi, Reading	18
W	Andrew Bash, New Hampshire	10
L	Kai-Wei Teng, Richmond	12
IP	Matt Frisbee, Richmond	140
H	Matt Frisbee, Richmond	149
R	Garrett Stallings, Bowie	90
ER	Garrett Stallings, Bowie	83
HB	Kai-Wei Teng, Richmond	18
BB	Kai-Wei Teng, Richmond	85
SO	Kai-Wei Teng, Richmond	169
SO/9	Reese Olson, Erie	12.6
BB/9	Chance Kirby, Erie	2.06
WP	Kai-Wei Teng, Richmond	22
BK	3 tied	3
HRA	Garrett Stallings, Bowie	27
BAA	Chance Kirby, Erie	.197

SOUTHERN LEAGUE DOUBLE-A

Awards selected by Major League Baseball

CHAMPION: Pensacola defeated Tennessee in the winner-take-all Game 3 of the Southern League finals. The Blue Wahoos won the finale 7-1 behind lefthander Patrick Monteverde's five one-run innings and a seven-run, sixth-inning offensive outburst. It is Pensacola's first title since being named co-champion in 2017 when the finals were canceled by Hurricane Irma. It is the Marlins' first Southern League title since Jacksonville won in 2014.

MOST VALUABLE PLAYER: Biloxi catcher Jakson Reetz hit .281/.392/.636 and mashed 22 home runs in just 64 games prior to a promotion to Triple-A Nashville on July 12. The 26-year-old finished the season in the Royals organization after electing free agency in August. The Brewers had signed Reetz as a minor league free agent before the season to provide organizational catching depth. He was originally the Nationals' 2014 third-round pick out of high school in Nebraska.

PITCHER OF THE YEAR: Rays righthander Taj Bradley captured the overall minor league ERA title in 2021 and continued his high-level pitching in Double-A. He went 3-1, 1.70 in 16 starts for Montgomery and struck out 88, walked 18 and allowed four homers in 74.1 innings. Tampa Bay pushed Bradley to Triple-A Durham on July 24 and added him to the 40-man roster in November to make him ineligible for the Rule 5 draft.

TOP MLB PROSPECT: Taj Bradley entered the season ranked as the No. 58 prospect in baseball. The Georgia high school righthander was the Rays' fifth-round pick in 2018. The 21-year-old has made rapid progress in the past two seasons, working his way from Low-A to Triple-A while showcasing a lively mid-90s fastball that tops out at 98 mph and a cutter/slider hybrid that opposing batters struggle to barrel. While Bradley hit a bit of a speed bump at Triple-A, posing a 3.66 ERA in 12 starts, he finished the season ranked eighth in the minors with a 2.57 ERA in 133.1 innings, which is a testament to his Double-A dominance.

Taj Bradley

MANAGER OF THE YEAR: Andy Schatzley led Rocket City (Angels) to the league's best record at 81-57 (.587) before the Trash Pandas lost to Tennessee in the North Division playoffs. It was Schatzley's second year as a manager. He guided the Angels' High-A Tri-City affiliate in 2021.

SOUTHERN LEAGUE ALL-STARS

Pos	Player	Team	AVG	OPS	HR
C	Jakson Reetz	Biloxi	.281	1.028	22
1B	Troy Johnston	Pensacola	.292	.810	10
2B	Brett Wisely	Montgomery	.274	.831	15
3B	Jake Slaughter	Tennessee	.293	.923	20
SS	Lenyn Sosa	Birmingham	.331	.911	14
OF	Alexander Canario	Tennessee	.248	.881	24
OF	Yonathan Perlaza	Tennessee	.255	.849	23
OF	Kameron Misner	Montgomery	.251	.815	16
DH	Niko Hulsizer	Montgomery	.279	.924	18
Pos	**Pitcher**	**Team**	**G**	**ERA**	**SO**
RHP	Taj Bradley	Montgomery	16	1.70	88
LHP	Jared Shuster	Mississippi	17	2.78	106
RP	Eric Torres	Rocket City	42	1.59	81

OVERALL STANDINGS

North Division	W	L	PCT	GB	Manager	Attendance	Avg	Last Penn
Rocket City Trash Pandas (Angels)	81	57	.587	—	Andy Schatzley	327,007	5,031	Never
Tennessee Smokies (Cubs)	71	66	.518	9.5	Mike Ryan	294,334	4,328	2004
Chattanooga Lookouts (Reds)	61	75	.449	19	Jose Moreno	213,685	3,238	2017
Birmingham Barons (White Sox)	61	77	.442	20	Justin Jirschele	266,921	3,925	2013
South Division	**W**	**L**	**PCT**	**GB**	**Manager**	**Attendance**	**Avg**	**Last Penn**
Montgomery Biscuits (Rays)	70	61	.534	—	Morgan Ensberg	156,356	2,522	2007
Pensacola Blue Wahoos (Marlins)	68	63	.519	2	Kevin Randel	281,972	4,209	2022
Biloxi Shuckers (Brewers)	67	68	.496	5	Mike Guerrero	148,865	2,326	Never
Mississippi Braves (Braves)	62	74	.456	10.5	Bruce Crabbe	150,491	2,389	2021

North: Tennessee def. Rocket City 2-1. **South:** Pensacola def. Montgomery 2-1. **Championship Series:** Pensacola def. Tennessee 2-1.

RONALD MARTINEZ/GETTY IMAGES

MINOR LEAGUES

CLUB BATTING

	AVG	G	AB	R	H	2B	3B	HR	RBI	BB	SO	SB	OBP	SLG
Birmingham	.260	138	4706	730	1223	244	21	161	678	526	1287	197	.345	.423
Tennessee	.258	137	4550	752	1174	261	20	189	709	561	1266	143	.348	.449
Montgomery	.253	131	4374	681	1106	250	33	142	626	529	1357	203	.341	.422
Rocket City	.251	138	4473	683	1124	211	16	143	618	618	1355	170	.351	.402
Chattanooga	.248	136	4501	677	1117	232	33	158	617	540	1330	170	.339	.420
Biloxi	.248	135	4492	664	1112	234	13	154	623	544	1244	162	.337	.408
Mississippi	.247	136	4502	623	1112	216	19	116	572	546	1237	112	.335	.381
Pensacola	.243	131	4276	610	1038	210	15	119	557	481	1189	168	.331	.382

CLUB PITCHING

	ERA	G	CG	SHO	SV	IP	H	R	ER	HR	BB	SO	AVG
Montgomery	4.16	131	0	9	27	1140	1021	603	527	141	427	1178	.236
Mississippi	4.28	136	3	3	30	1179	1128	634	560	131	474	1344	.249
Rocket City	4.41	138	0	10	46	1188	1102	625	582	160	455	1270	.245
Pensacola	4.49	131	1	6	34	1138	1043	644	568	136	479	1272	.243
Biloxi	4.67	135	1	5	30	1173	1176	687	609	154	539	1235	.259
Tennessee	4.81	137	0	9	34	1191	1110	711	636	152	671	1316	.248
Chattanooga	5.01	136	1	3	36	1180	1168	734	657	148	670	1309	.258
Birmingham	5.25	138	0	3	20	1214	1258	782	708	160	630	1341	.267

CLUB FIELDING

	PCT	PO	A	E	DP
Mississippi	.979	3536	1066	101	87
Birmingham	.978	3642	1184	107	109
Rocket City	.978	3564	1184	107	124
Chattanooga	.977	3539	1037	109	108
Montgomery	.976	3421	1105	109	96
Pensacola	.976	3415	1071	110	104
Tennessee	.975	3570	1205	120	130
Biloxi	.974	3520	1147	123	99

INDIVIDUAL BATTING

Batter, Club	AVG	G	AB	R	H	2B	3B	HR	RBI	BB	SO	SB
Jake Slaughter, Tennessee	.293	86	328	60	96	17	1	20	68	37	83	28
Yonathan Perlaza, Tennessee	.292	85	329	42	96	20	1	10	49	32	71	3
Livan Soto, Rocket City	.281	119	456	69	128	17	1	6	57	71	102	18
Jose Rodriguez, Birmingham	.280	104	440	75	123	21	6	11	68	38	66	40
Brett Wisely, Montgomery	.274	112	430	84	118	23	6	15	56	62	104	31
Riley Delgado, Mississippi	.272	109	371	51	101	13	1	2	30	31	57	3
Bryce Ball, Tennessee	.265	131	486	77	129	31	2	11	76	69	121	1
Preston Palmeiro, Rocket City	.263	113	407	53	107	31	0	8	60	47	82	1
Kevin Maitan, Rocket City	.261	114	399	54	104	20	1	11	45	41	140	3
TJ Hopkins, Chattanooga	.260	101	373	57	97	21	2	17	66	40	117	6

INDIVIDUAL PITCHING

Pitcher, Club	W	L	ERA	G	GS	CG	SV	IP	H	R	ER	BB	SO
Nick Bennett, Biloxi	7	11	4.79	25	24	0	0	124	122	72	66	44	125
Coleman Crow, Rocket City	9	3	4.85	24	23	0	0	128	133	72	69	35	128
Scott Blewett, Birmingham	7	6	5.03	24	22	0	0	111	122	69	62	44	99
Eduardo Salazar, Chattanooga	6	10	5.16	27	27	0	0	126	130	78	72	64	111
Alan Rangel, Mississippi	5	8	5.26	26	26	0	0	115	122	74	67	50	139
Connor Curlis, Chattanooga	3	9	6.34	32	19	0	1	111	123	82	78	37	124

DEPARTMENT LEADERS

BATTING

OBP	Ryan Aguilar, Rocket City	0.415
SLG	Jake Slaughter, Tennessee	0.534
OPS	Jake Slaughter, Tennessee	0.923
R	Brett Wisely, Montgomery	84
H	Bryce Ball, Tennessee	129
TB	Yonathan Perlaza, Tennessee	231
XBH	Yonathan Perlaza, Tennessee	62
2B	Yonathan Perlaza, Tennessee	36
3B	Michael Siani, Chattanooga	7
HR	Drew Lugbauer, Mississippi	28
RBI	Drew Lugbauer, Mississippi	82
SAC	Livan Soto, Rocket City	5
BB	Kameron Misner, Montgomery	86
HBP	Yoelqui Cespedes, Birmingham	23
SO	Drew Lugbauer, Mississippi	212
SB	Michael Siani, Chattanooga	49
CS	2 tied	12

FIELDING

C	PCT	Roberto Alvarez, Montgomery	.996
	PO	Bryce Windham, Tennessee	747
	A	Zach Humphreys, Rocket City	48
	DP	2 tied	9
	E	Paul McIntosh, Pensacola	15
	CS	Bryce Windham, Tennessee	32
	SB	Bryce Windham, Tennessee	107
	PB	Blake Hunt, Montgomery	12
1B	PCT	Troy Johnston, Pensacola	.994
	PO	Drew Lugbauer, Mississippi	840
	A	Drew Lugbauer, Mississippi	58
	DP	Drew Lugbauer, Mississippi	69
	E	Thomas Dillard, Biloxi	14
2B	PCT	Felix Valerio, Biloxi	.977
	PO	Felix Valerio, Biloxi	118
	A	Felix Valerio, Biloxi	219
	DP	Chase Strumpf, Tennessee	42
	E	Ronny Simon, Montgomery	9
3B	PCT	Cobie Fletcher-Vance, Pensacola	.963
	PO	Cobie Fletcher-Vance, Pensacola	49
	A	Kevin Maitan, Rocket City	113
	DP	Cobie Fletcher-Vance, Pensacola	13
	E	CJ Alexander, 2 teams	11
SS	PCT	Luis Vazquez, Tennessee	.971
	PO	Luis Vazquez, Tennessee	129
	A	Luis Vazquez, Tennessee	235
	DP	Luis Vazquez, Tennessee	60
	E	Greg Jones, Montgomery	16
OF	PCT	Kameron Misner, Montgomery	.996
	PO	Bryce Teodosio, Rocket City	239
	A	Yoelqui Céspedes, Birmingham	13
	DP	Yoelqui Cespedes, Birmingham	4
	E	3 tied	4

PITCHING

G	Kolton Ingram, Rocket City	50
G	Justin Maese, Mississippi	50
GS	Eduardo Salazar, Chattanooga	27
GF	Justin Maese, Mississippi	29
GF	Eric Torres, Rocket City	29
SV	Eric Torres, Rocket City	22
W	Coleman Crow, Rocket City	9
W	Tanner Gordon, Mississippi	9
L	Nick Bennett, Biloxi	11
IP	Coleman Crow, Rocket City	128
H	Coleman Crow, Rocket City	133
R	Peyton Remy, Tennessee	83
ER	Connor Curlis, Chattanooga	78
HB	Peyton Remy, Tennessee	15
BB	Eduardo Salazar, Chattanooga	64
SO	Alan Rangel, Mississippi	139
SO/9	Alan Rangel, Mississippi	10.9
BB/9	Coleman Crow, Rocket City	2.5
WP	Scott Blewett, Birmingham	16
BK	Eduardo Salazar, Chattanooga	6
HRA	Connor Curlis, Chattanooga	25
BAA	Nick Bennett, Biloxi	.254

TEXAS LEAGUE DOUBLE-A

Awards selected by Major League Baseball

CHAMPION: The Frisco RoughRiders' roster was stocked with the Rangers' best prospects all season, and the result was a playoff sweep and a Texas League title. Frisco clinched the crown in extra innings of the second game of the finals against Wichita. Singles from Jonathan Ornelas and Evan Carter plated a pair in the top of the 10th, which proved crucial when Wichita struck for a lone run in the bottom half. Closer Nick Starr sealed the win four batters later.

MOST VALUABLE PLAYER: The Cardinals signed former Rays prospect Moises Gomez to a minor league deal and then watched the 24-year-old outfielder unleash his powerful swing. In total, Gomez hit a minor league-best 39 home runs. For his efforts, the Cardinals added him to the 40-man roster to keep him off the free agent market.

PITCHER OF THE YEAR: The Mariners have done an excellent job developing and graduating pitchers to the big leagues. Righthander Taylor Dollard might be the next in line. Dollard, whom Seattle selected out of Cal Poly in the five-round 2020 draft, led the TL with a 2.25 ERA and 16 wins. His 131 strikeouts were fifth on the circuit, behind leader Alec Marsh of the Royals system.

TOP MLB PROSPECT: Between Moises Gomez and Jordan Walker, the Springfield lineup had enough juice to keep Texas' power grid running all season long. Walker was the Cardinals' first-rounder in 2020 and has lit up opposing pitchers at every stop in his pro career. The hulking Walker hit .306/.388/.510 despite being the only teenager in the Texas League on Opening Day. Here's the scary part: Scouts believe there might even be more power coming for Walker as he learns to get the most out of his swing.

MANAGER OF THE YEAR: Jared Goedert led his Frisco squad to the TL crown, first downing San Antonio in the divisional round and then topping Wichita in two games in the championship series. He did so with a cast full of top prospects in tow all year long.

Jordan Walker

JOHN E. MOORE III/GETTY IMAGES

TEXAS LEAGUE ALL-STARS

Pos	Player	Team	AVG	OPS	HR
C	Juan Centeno	Amarillo	.302	.863	14
1B	Leandro Cedeno	Amarillo	.310	.937	30
2B	Edouard Julien	Wichita	.300	.931	17
3B	Jordan Walker	Springfield	.306	.898	19
SS	Blaze Alexander	Amarillo	.306	.927	17
OF	Justin Dirden	Corpus Christi	.324	1.027	20
OF	Corbin Carroll	Amarillo	.313	1.073	16
OF	Matt Wallner	Wichita	.299	1.033	21
DH	Moises Gomez	Springfield	.321	1.106	23
Pos	**Pitcher**	**Team**	**G**	**ERA**	**SO**
RHP	Taylor Dollard	Arkansas	27	2.25	131
LHP	Kody Funderburk	Wichita	32	2.94	103
RP	Cody Laweryson	Wichita	19	1.06	69

OVERALL STANDINGS

North Division	W	L	PCT	GB	Manager	Attendance	Avg	Last Penn
Wichita Wind Surge (Twins)	78	59	.569	—	Ramon Borrego	220,528	3,341	Never
Arkansas Travelers (Mariners)	73	65	.529	5.5	Collin Cowgill	300,042	4,478	2009
Tulsa Drillers (Dodgers)	69	67	.507	8.5	Scott Hennessey	357,200	5,495	2018
Springfield Cardinals (Cardinals)	68	70	.493	10.5	Jose Leger	259,044	3,754	2012
Northwest Arkansas Naturals (Royals)	58	79	.423	20	Chris Widger	240,615	3,538	2021
South Division	**W**	**L**	**PCT**	**GB**	**Manager**	**Attendance**	**Avg**	**Last Penn**
Frisco RoughRiders (Rangers)	74	63	.540	—	Jared Goedert	341,243	5,018	2022
San Antonio Missions (Padres)	68	68	.500	5.5	Phil Wellman	272,144	4,123	2013
Amarillo Sod Poodles (D-backs)	68	69	.496	6	Shawn Roof	379,029	5,493	2019
Midland RockHounds (Athletics)	66	71	.482	8	Bobby Crosby	226,249	3,428	2017
Corpus Christi Hooks (Astros)	63	74	.460	11	Gregorio Petit	257,991	3,909	2006

North: Wichita def. Tulsa 2-0. **South:** Frisco def. San Antonio 2-0. **Championship Series:** Frisco def. Wichita 2-0.

CLUB BATTING

	AVG	G	AB	R	H	2B	3B	HR	RBI	BB	SO	SB	OBP	SLG
Amarillo	.277	137	4735	832	1312	250	26	179	769	490	1166	147	.352	.454
San Antonio	.266	136	4593	723	1221	240	29	102	652	567	1129	165	.356	.397
Midland	.265	137	4636	710	1230	240	15	152	673	539	1271	78	.350	.422
Frisco	.265	137	4654	783	1234	259	23	168	725	547	1117	145	.350	.439
Wichita	.261	137	4543	729	1185	216	23	164	682	613	1265	170	.356	.427
NW Arkansas	.259	137	4644	782	1203	243	15	160	719	638	1289	179	.353	.421
Springfield	.258	138	4673	840	1207	243	17	178	766	687	1280	164	.360	.432
Arkansas	.251	138	4617	739	1160	209	25	125	675	646	1204	152	.349	.389
Corpus Christi	.247	137	4531	748	1119	237	25	174	705	640	1391	158	.351	.426
Tulsa	.246	136	4495	707	1107	214	23	196	664	534	1267	100	.334	.435

CLUB PITCHING

	ERA	G	CG	SHO	SV	IP	H	R	ER	HR	BB	SO	AVG
Wichita	4.13	137	1	8	32	1195	1131	627	549	127	559	1311	.247
Arkansas	4.27	138	1	11	27	12034	1022	631	571	129	540	1288	.229
Frisco	4.70	137	0	11	37	1207	1130	703	630	160	557	1272	.247
San Antonio	4.74	136	2	7	30	1197	1191	708	631	130	595	1159	.259
Midland	5.09	137	1	4	35	1195	1323	783	676	136	539	1103	.280
Tulsa	5.19	136	0	7	36	1172	1090	757	676	148	662	1324	.245
Corpus Christi	5.34	137	0	7	28	1187	1157	788	704	155	683	1293	.255
Springfield	5.50	138	1	4	30	1213	1262	813	741	186	547	1183	.268
Northwest Arkansas	5.95	137	1	6	21	1197	1297	891	791	165	702	1215	.275
Amarillo	6.09	137	1	5	29	1205	1375	892	816	262	517	1231	.288

CLUB FIELDING

	PCT	PO	A	E	DP
Arkansas	.980	3612	1139	96	98
Springfield	.980	3640	1198	101	118
Frisco	.979	3621	1156	103	111
Midland	.978	3585	1221	109	121
Wichita	.978	3587	1041	105	78

	PCT	PO	A	E	DP
Amarillo	.977	3616	1178	115	127
San Antonio	.976	3592	1282	119	119
Tulsa	.974	3516	1077	121	88
NW Arkansas	.974	3593	1179	127	119
Corpus Christi	.974	3562	1102	126	129

INDIVIDUAL BATTING

Batter, Club	AVG	G	AB	R	H	2B	3B	HR	RBI	BB	SO	SB
Connor Hollis, San Antonio	.333	103	403	82	134	22	3	9	59	62	93	19
Justin Dirden, Corpus Christi	.324	92	349	64	113	32	5	20	73	41	94	7
Jordan Diaz, Midland	.319	94	379	48	121	26	0	15	58	22	61	0
Chase Calabuig, Midland	.313	110	380	54	119	25	2	6	48	47	56	3
Leandro Cedeno, Amarillo	.310	109	426	86	132	18	0	30	93	42	112	0
Jordan Walker, Springfield	.306	119	461	100	141	31	3	19	68	58	116	22
Edouard Julien, Wichita	.300	113	400	77	120	19	3	17	67	98	125	19
Jonathan Ornelas, Frisco	.299	123	525	84	157	20	2	14	64	45	121	14
Blaine Crim, Frisco	.295	119	461	81	136	26	0	24	91	49	82	4
Tucker Bradley, Northwest Arkansas	.293	110	396	73	116	22	3	12	53	55	84	19

INDIVIDUAL PITCHING

Pitcher, Club	W	L	ERA	G	GS	CG	SV	IP	H	R	ER	BB	SO
Taylor Dollard, Arkansas	16	2	2.25	27	27	0	0	144	106	42	36	31	131
Jack Cushing, Midland	11	3	3.67	19	19	1	0	110	112	53	45	32	95
Slade Cecconi, Amarillo	7	6	4.37	26	25	0	0	130	139	76	63	32	127
Stephen Kolek, Arkansas	6	13	4.51	27	27	0	0	144	140	79	72	66	138
David Leal, Midland	4	6	4.84	20	19	0	0	115	138	66	62	14	77
Cody Bradford, Frisco	10	7	5.01	26	26	0	0	119	114	70	66	33	124
Kyle Leahy, Springfield	10	7	5.23	27	26	0	0	141	155	90	82	71	144
Colin Peluse, Midland	10	6	5.38	23	21	0	1	119	133	78	71	28	92
Anthony Veneziano, Northwest Arkansas	6	9	5.72	26	25	1	0	123	133	90	78	66	129
Edgar Escobar, Springfield	7	12	6.73	28	20	0	0	124	145	96	93	50	98

DEPARTMENT LEADERS

BATTING

OBP	Edouard Julien, Wichita	0.441
SLG	Justin Dirden, Corpus Christi	0.616
OPS	Justin Dirden, Corpus Christi	1.027
R	Jordan Walker, Springfield	100
H	Jonathan Ornelas, Frisco	157
TB	Leandro Cedeno, Amarillo	240
XBH	Andy Pages, Tulsa	58
2B	Jake Scheiner, Arkansas	34
3B	Corbin Carroll, Amarillo	8
HR	Leandro Cedeno, Amarillo	30
RBI	Jake Scheiner, Arkansas	105
SAC	Ripken Reyes, San Antonio	10
BB	Edouard Julien, Wichita	98
HBP	Austin Martin, Wichita	21
SO	Robbie Glendinning, Northwest Arkansas	168
SB	DaShawn Keirsey Jr., Wichita	42
CS	Connor Hollis, San Antonio	12

FIELDING

C	PCT	Juan Centeno, Amarillo	.997
	PO	Jake Anchia, Arkansas	734
	A	Chandler Seagle, San Antonio	49
	DP	Jake Anchia, Arkansas	6
	E	Luke Berryhill, Corpus Christi	12
	CS	Luke Berryhill, Corpus Christi	28
	SB	Carson Taylor, Tulsa	93
	PB	Jake Anchia, Arkansas	12
1B	PCT	Leandro Cedeño, Amarillo	.996
	PO	Blaine Crim, Frisco	712
	A	Jake Scheiner, Arkansas	58
	DP	Blaine Crim, Frisco	82
	E	Andy Yerzy, Amarillo	9
2B	PCT	Nick Dunn, Springfield	.981
	PO	Nick Dunn, Springfield	175
	A	Nick Dunn, Springfield	232
	DP	Nick Dunn, Springfield	72
	E	Edouard Julien, Wichita	9
3B	PCT	Brett Harris, Midland	.975
	PO	Jordan Walker, Springfield	60
	A	Joe Rizzo, Arkansas	142
	DP	Ti'Quan Forbes, Amarillo	16
	E	Jordan Walker, Springfield	18
SS	PCT	Masyn Winn, Springfield	.983
	PO	Logan Davidson, Midland	134
	A	Jonathan Ornelas, Frisco	236
	DP	Logan Davidson, Midland	57
	E	Leonel Valera, Tulsa	20
OF	PCT	DaShawn Keirsey Jr., Wichita	.996
	PO	Cade Marlowe, Arkansas	267
	A	Andy Pages, Tulsa	14
	DP	Andy Pages, Tulsa	5
	E	Cade Marlowe, Arkansas	7

PITCHING

G	Travis Kuhn, Arkansas	50
GS	Taylor Dollard, Arkansas	27
GS	Stephen Kolek, Arkansas	27
GF	Blake Rogers, Amarillo	33
SV	Michael Stryffeler, Arkansas	14
W	Taylor Dollard, Arkansas	16
L	Alec Marsh, Northwest Arkansas	15
IP	Taylor Dollard, Arkansas	144
H	Kyle Leahy, Springfield	155
R	Bryce Jarvis, Amarillo	104
ER	Bryce Jarvis, Amarillo	98
HB	Stephen Kolek, Arkansas	18
BB	Kyle Leahy, Springfield	71
SO	Alec Marsh, Northwest Arkansas	147
SO/9	Alec Marsh, Northwest Arkansas	11.6
BB/9	David LealMidland	1.1
WP	Jonathan Sprinkle, Corpus Christi	16
BK	John Rooney, Tulsa	10
HRA	Bryce Jarvis, Amarillo	27
HRA	Alec Marsh, Northwest Arkansas	27
BAA	Taylor Dollard, Arkansas	.203

MIDWEST LEAGUE HIGH-A

Awards selected by Major League Baseball

CHAMPION: After rolling through Cedar Rapids in the divisional round, South Bend slipped past Lake County in the finals to collect the Midwest League title. Owen Caissie, Pablo Aliendo and Luis Verdugo each homered in the clincher, and outfielder Pete Crow-Armstrong starred throughout the series.

MOST VALUABLE PLAYER: By the time Christian Encarnacion-Strand was named league MVP, he was not only out of the league, but he also had been traded out of the Twin organization. He was part of the package used to acquire righthander Tyler Mahle. Before the deal, the Oklahoma State product swatted 46 extra-base hits, including 20 home runs.

PITCHER OF THE YEAR: The Midwest League's top pitcher was Beloit righthander M.D. Johnson, who carved up the competition with 125 strikeouts against 28 walks in 112 innings. His 3.46 ERA was easily the best on the circuit.

TOP MLB PROSPECT: In the first month of the season, Elly De La Cruz struggled to get things going. But once the weather warmed up, the Reds' phenom looked like the version who took the sport by storm in 2021. From then on, De La Cruz put together one of the best overall seasons in the minor leagues, finishing two home runs shy of a 30-30 campaign. De La Cruz, 20, played 73 games with Dayton before getting the call to Double-A Chattanooga. At both stops, he showed an electric set of skills that jolted him to the top of the Reds' prospect list and into the upper echelon of the game as a whole.

Elly De La Cruz

PAUL R. GIERHART

MANAGER OF THE YEAR: The Great Lakes Loons, like most Dodgers affiliates, were stacked with talent, including Diego Cartaya, Eddys Leonard and Jose Ramos, along with pitchers like Ronan Kopp and Emmet Sheehan. Guiding the group was Austin Chubb, who led the Loons to 76 wins.

MIDWEST LEAGUE ALL-STARS

Pos	Player	Team	AVG	OPS	HR
C	Josh Crouch	West Michigan	.290	.811	10
1B	Tyler Soderstrom	Lansing	.260	.836	20
2B	Jorbit Vivas	Great Lakes	.269	.775	10
3B	C. Encarnacion-Strand	Cedar Rapids	.294	.969	20
SS	Elly De La Cruz	Dayton	.302	.968	20
OF	Johnathan Rodriguez	Lake County	.292	.919	21
OF	Robert Hassell III	Fort Wayne	.289	.813	10
OF	Pete Crow-Armstrong	South Bend	.287	.831	9
DH	Imanol Vargas	Great Lakes	.268	.871	18
Pos	**Pitcher**	**Team**	**G**	**ERA**	**SO**
RHP	M.D. Johnson	Beloit	20	3.46	125
LHP	DJ Herz	South Bend	17	2.26	99
RP	Cam Robinson	Wisconsin	28	1.45	52

OVERALL STANDINGS

East Division	W	L	PCT	GB	Manager	Attendance	Avg	Last Penn
Lake County Captains (Guardians)	76	53	.589	—	Greg DiCenzo	169,574	2,874	2010
Great Lakes Loons (Dodgers)	76	55	.580	1	Austin Chubb	174,050	2,807	2017
West Michigan Whitecaps (Tigers)	72	59	.550	5	Brayan Pena	337,167	5,527	2015
Dayton Dragons (Reds)	67	61	.523	8.5	Bryan LaHair	444,346	7,935	Never
Lansing Lugnuts (Athletics)	54	77	.412	23	Philip Pohl	288,840	4,659	2003
Fort Wayne TinCaps (Padres)	50	80	.385	26.5	Brian Esposito	303,680	5,061	2009

West Division	W	L	PCT	GB	Manager	Attendance	Avg	Last Penn
Cedar Rapids Kernels (Twins)	73	58	.557	—	Brian Dinkelman	136,360	2,164	1994
South Bend Cubs (Cubs)	73	58	.557	—	Lance Rymel	285,977	4,468	2022
Wisconsin Timber Rattlers (Brewers)	69	60	.535	3	Joe Ayrault	206,805	3,390	2012
Beloit Sky Carp (Marlins)	62	67	.481	10	Jorge Hernandez	102,794	1,632	1995
Peoria Chiefs (Cardinals)	56	76	.424	17.5	Patrick Anderson	135,784	2,089	2002
Quad Cities River Bandits (Royals)	54	78	.409	19.5	Brooks Conrad	170,731	2,668	2021

East: Lake County def. Great Lakes 2-1. **West:** South Bend def. Cedar Rapids 2-1. **Championship Series:** South Bend def. Lake County 2-1.

CLUB BATTING

	AVG	G	AB	R	H	2B	3B	HR	RBI	BB	SO	SB	OBP	SLG
South Bend	.252	131	4353	612	1095	229	28	119	571	442	1145	140	.329	.399
West Michigan	.248	131	4265	663	1059	218	35	101	595	585	1034	105	.348	.387
Lansing	.243	131	4285	579	1041	203	29	109	518	465	1220	133	.324	.380
Lake County	.238	129	4158	607	989	203	23	139	541	511	1202	102	.327	.398
Beloit	.237	129	4227	547	1003	174	28	85	501	432	1127	144	.318	.352
Peoria	.237	132	4323	579	1025	204	26	96	512	503	1169	180	.327	.363
Quad Cities	.235	132	4330	627	1019	192	41	136	579	540	1385	176	.329	.393
Cedar Rapids	.235	131	4302	680	1011	197	38	150	629	520	1366	143	.329	.403
Great Lakes	.234	131	4235	648	992	197	29	143	596	555	1245	65	.336	.396
Dayton	.231	128	4078	586	941	200	34	152	532	439	1437	175	.317	.408
Wisconsin	.230	129	4165	585	957	212	30	110	536	498	1209	135	.320	.374
Fort Wayne	.219	130	4122	535	904	175	32	90	470	578	1186	124	.325	.343

CLUB PITCHING

	ERA	G	CG	SHO	SV	IP	H	R	ER	HR	BB	SO	AVG
Cedar Rapids	3.66	131	0	9	26	1140	989	544	463	109	424	1250	.231
Lake County	3.70	129	2	13	34	1108	887	536	456	143	519	1268	.218
Beloit	3.79	129	0	6	27	1123	1008	553	473	101	382	1207	.238
Great Lakes	3.80	131	1	12	37	1133	909	564	478	103	628	1398	.216
South Bend	3.91	131	0	9	35	1138	931	566	494	97	532	1278	.222
Wisconsin	4.04	129	0	7	44	1120	962	568	503	110	503	1179	.229
West Michigan	4.07	131	1	13	34	1139	1021	590	515	112	477	1167	.238
Dayton	4.53	128	0	9	31	1086	918	615	547	117	582	1260	.228
Peoria	4.55	132	1	5	28	1155	1081	661	584	126	479	1236	.244
Fort Wayne	4.65	130	0	9	21	1102	1042	634	569	134	537	1255	.248
Lansing	5.10	131	2	7	27	1113	1132	705	631	143	482	1054	.261
Quad Cities	5.14	132	1	2	22	1136	1156	712	648	135	523	1173	.264

CLUB FIELDING

	PCT	PO	A	E	DP
Quad Cities	.980	3407	1211	92	101
West Michigan	.979	3418	1114	99	103
Fort Wayne	.978	3305	1058	98	112
Wisconsin	.978	3360	986	98	72
Peoria	.977	3465	1046	107	89
Dayton	.976	3259	1043	107	97
Lansing	.975	3338	1077	111	97
Lake County	.975	3324	974	112	96
South Bend	.974	3415	1107	121	104
Cedar Rapids	.973	3420	1073	124	74
Beloit	.972	3370	1100	131	98
Great Lakes	.971	3398	926	130	85

INDIVIDUAL BATING

Batter, Club	AVG	G	AB	R	H	2B	3B	HR	RBI	BB	SO	SB
Tristan Peters, Wisconsin	.306	90	330	61	101	22	8	7	51	45	61	13
Josh Crouch, West Michigan	.290	90	335	43	97	22	0	10	61	38	56	1
Diego Hernandez, Quad Cities	.279	83	330	55	92	17	4	7	29	27	72	27
Euribiel Angeles, Lansing	.278	97	363	29	101	19	1	2	32	17	58	8
Gabriel Rodriguez, Lake County	.272	94	320	45	87	15	2	9	38	34	72	4
Jorbit Vivas, Great Lakes	.269	128	479	73	129	19	7	10	66	63	58	2
Luis Verdugo, South Bend	.269	107	368	43	99	27	1	5	41	46	70	4
Imanol Vargas, Great Lakes	.268	116	381	65	102	20	1	18	63	80	145	5
Peyton Wilson, Quad Cities	.268	88	340	60	91	16	3	14	44	41	97	23
Jordan Nwogu, South Bend	.265	88	325	59	86	17	7	15	51	37	90	19

INDIVIDUAL PITCHING

Pitcher, Club	W	L	ERA	G	GS	CG	SV	IP	H	R	ER	BB	SO
M.D. Johnson, Beloit	9	9	3.46	20	20	0	0	112	89	46	43	28	125
Jackson Wolf, Fort Wayne	7	8	4.01	23	22	0	0	119	91	56	53	44	134
Justin Jarvis, Wisconsin	9	8	4.02	24	24	0	0	121	105	64	54	51	134
Carlos Guzman, West Michigan	9	6	4.16	25	23	1	0	106	90	56	49	34	89
Aaron Davenport, Lake County	7	6	4.21	23	23	1	0	107	89	52	50	52	118
Evan Fitterer, Beloit	4	7	4.28	22	22	0	0	107	102	56	51	46	80
Adrian Alcantara, Quad Cities	7	5	4.57	22	16	1	0	108	105	62	55	36	123
Dionys Rodriguez, Peoria	3	11	4.59	27	25	0	0	122	110	67	62	53	119
Wilfredo Pereira, Peoria	6	8	5.02	27	18	0	0	118	100	70	66	31	129
Austin Love, Peoria	7	12	5.73	26	25	0	0	126	139	80	80	52	151

DEPARTMENT LEADERS

BATTING

OBP	Imanol Vargas, Great Lakes	.404
SLG	Christian Encarnacion-Strand, Cedar Rapids	.599
OPS	Tristan Peters, Wisconsin	.871
OPS	Imanol Vargas, Great Lakes	.871
R	Eddys Leonard, Great Lakes	80
H	Eddys Leonard, Great Lakes	131
TB	Eddys Leonard, Great Lakes	216
XBH	Eddys Leonard, Great Lakes	51
2B	L.J. Jones, Peoria	33
3B	Tyler Tolbert, Quad Cities	10
HR	Johnathan Rodriguez, Lake County	21
RBI	Jose Ramos, Great Lakes	74
SAC	2 tied	8
BB	Joe Naranjo, Lake County	82
HBP	Ben Malgeri, West Michigan	24
HBP	Darrien Miller, Wisconsin	24
SO	Joe Gray Jr., Wisconsin	177
SB	Tyler Tolbert, Quad Cities	60
CS	2 tied	11

FIELDING

C PCT	Kekai Rios, Great Lakes	.997
PO	Pablo Aliendo, South Bend	898
A	2 tied	64
DP	Darrien Miller, Wisconsin	9
E	Bennett Hostetler, Beloit	11
CS	2 tied	29
SB	Darrien Miller, Wisconsin	129
PB	Bennett Hostetler, Beloit	14
1B PCT	Marcus Chiu, Beloit	.994
PO	Dillan Shrum, Quad Cities	726
A	Imanol Vargas, Great Lakes	57
DP	Joe Naranjo, Lake County	74
E	Imanol Vargas, Great Lakes	12
2B PCT	Jorbit Vivas, Great Lakes	.987
PO	Francisco Hernandez, Peoria	126
A	Francisco Hernandez, Peoria	192
DP	3 tied	35
E	2 tied	10
3B PCT	Gabriel Rodriguez, Lake County	.942
PO	Luis Verdugo, South Bend	63
A	Luis Verdugo, South Bend	157
DP	Luis Verdugo, South Bend	16
E	Christian Encarnacion-Strand, Cedar Rapids	21
SS PCT	Tyler Tolbert, Quad Cities	.967
PO	Tyler Tolbert, Quad Cities	157
A	Tyler Tolbert, Quad Cities	316
DP	Tyler Tolbert, Quad Cities	60
E	Jarryd Dale, Fort Wayne	19
OF PCT	2 tied	1.000
PO	Victor Mesa Jr., Beloit	240
A	Petey Halpin, Lake County	9
DP	2 tied	3
E	Joe Gray Jr., Wisconsin	6

PITCHING

G	Andrew Magno, West Michigan	47
GS	3 tied	25
GF	James Meeker, Wisconsin	31
SV	Cam Robinson, Wisconsin	19
W	Emilio Marquez, Quad Cities	10
L	Austin Love, Peoria	12
IP	Austin Love, Peoria	126
H	Austin Love, Peoria	139
R	Austin Love, Peoria	80
ER	Austin Love, Peoria	80
HB	2 tied	13
BB	Doug Nikhazy, Lake County	68
SO	Austin Love, Peoria	151
SO/9	Austin Love, Peoria	10.8
BB/9	M.D. Johnson, Beloit	2.3
WP	Evan Fitterer, Beloit	16
BK	Joe DeMers, Lansing	6
HRA	2 tied	19
BAA	Jackson Wolf, Fort Wayne	.209

NORTHWEST LEAGUE HIGH-A

Awards selected by Major League Baseball

CHAMPION: When the Eugene Emeralds won the Northwest League title in 2016, it was their first solo crown since 1975. Since then, they've added four more titles, including back-to-back championships in 2021 and 2022. This year's NWL finals featured a sweep of Vancouver, 3-0, with the deciding game sparked by a five-run rally in the sixth inning centered around a three-run blast by top Giants prospect Marco Luciano. Throughout their season, the Emeralds also got contributions from famous talents like Kyle Harrison, Luis Matos and Luciano, as well as breakout performers like outfielders Vaun Brown and Grant McCray and third baseman Casey Schmitt.

MOST VALUABLE PLAYER: In both of his turns at the lower levels in the last two seasons, Zac Veen has wowed fans, scouts and opposing managers alike with his blend of electric tools and aggressive style of play. The Spokane outfielder was unanimously voted the Most Exciting Player in the NWL in annual Best Tools survey.

PITCHER OF THE YEAR: The league's top arm talent pitched for two of the six NWL teams in 2022. Righthander Prelander Berroa, who was initially signed by the Twins and then dealt to the Giants, was traded once more—this time to the Mariners for utility infielder Donovan Walton. Berroa used one of the game's most electric fastballs to strike out 97 hitters over 65.2 innings between both Everett and Eugene.

TOP MLB PROSPECT: Zac Veen is the rare player to whom Major League Baseball bestowed both MVP and Top MLB Prospect honors. Before a promotion to Double-A Hartford, Veen, the Rockies' first-rounder in 2020 out of high school, produced an .807 OPS with 19 doubles, 11 home runs and 50 stolen bases in 54 attempts. He added 19 doubles and three triples, giving him a total of 33 extra-base hits in 400 plate appearances.

MANAGER OF THE YEAR: As the manager of league champion Eugene, Carlos Valderrama was charged with guiding a team full of prospect talent. His roster included some of the finest young players in the Giants' system, including lefthander Kyle Harrison, shortstop Marco Luciano and outfielder Luis Matos. None of that trio's tenures was lengthy, with both Matos and Luciano's seasons interrupted by injury and Harrison's over quickly because he had overpowered the league. Nonetheless, Valderrama kept the team afloat and led his group to 81 wins, the most in the NWL by a margin of 14 over second-place Vancouver.

Zac Veen

CHRIS BERNACCHI/DIAMOND IMAGES VIA GETTY IMAGES

NORTHWEST LEAGUE ALL-STARS

Pos	Player	Team	AVG	OPS	HR
C	Patrick Bailey	Eugene	.225	.761	12
1B	Colin Simpson	Spokane	.300	.900	17
2B	Eddy Diaz	Spokane	.261	.701	5
3B	Carter Aldrete	Eugene	.294	.914	15
SS	Julio Carreras	Spokane	.289	.825	11
OF	Zac Veen	Spokane	.269	.807	11
OF	Spencer Packard	Everett	.282	.887	12
OF	Jairo Pomares	Eugene	.254	.768	14
DH	Casey Schmitt	Eugene	.273	.837	17
Pos	**Pitcher**	**Team**	**G**	**ERA**	**SO**
RHP	Prelander Berroa	Eugene/Everett	17	2.06	97
LHP	Nick Swiney	Eugene	21	3.84	105
RP	Isaiah Campbell	Everett	19	0.82	35

OVERALL STANDINGS

Team	W	L	PCT	GB	Manager	Attendance	Avg	Last Penn
Eugene Emeralds (Giants)	81	48	.628	—	Carlos Valderrama	136,360	2,235	2022
Vancouver Canadians (Blue Jays)	67	62	.519	14	Brent Lavallee	313,256	5,135	2017
Spokane Indians (Rockies)	64	66	.492	17.5	Scott Little	231,081	3,668	2008
Hillsboro Hops (D-backs)	60	70	.462	21.5	Vince Harrison	150,792	2,356	2019
Everett AquaSox (Mariners)	59	72	.450	23	Eric Farris	128,836	1,982	2010
Tri-City Dust Devils (Angels)	58	71	.450	23	Jack Howell	108,136	1,744	Never

Championship Series: Eugene def. Vancouver 3-0.

CLUB BATTING

	AVG	G	AB	R	H	2B	3B	HR	RBI	BB	SO	SB	OBP	SLG
Spokane	.261	130	4346	660	1136	236	39	104	577	375	1141	214	.327	.405
Eugene	.239	129	4165	678	996	201	13	163	634	504	1321	102	.330	.411
Vancouver	.235	129	4153	616	974	244	37	119	563	516	1288	172	.329	.397
Hillsboro	.234	130	4270	586	999	216	21	103	530	452	1217	193	.318	.367
Everett	.232	131	4341	614	1006	211	25	147	560	595	1403	105	.332	.393
Tri-City	.224	129	4196	539	939	196	31	70	476	453	1354	155	.311	.335

CLUB PITCHING

	ERA	G	CG	SHO	SV	IP	H	R	ER	HR	BB	SO	AVG
Eugene	3.42	129	0	13	35	1103	906	513	419	97	440	1391	.220
Tri-City	3.87	129	1	12	30	1124	1058	571	484	107	385	1243	.247
Vancouver	4.22	129	0	7	34	1110	976	641	520	118	535	1259	.232
Hillsboro	4.43	130	1	3	21	1130	958	620	556	107	559	1318	.228
Spokane	4.49	130	2	8	27	1124	1085	633	561	150	444	1136	.253
Everett	4.91	131	1	6	31	1146	1067	715	626	127	532	1377	.245

CLUB FIELDING

	PCT	PO	A	E	DP
Hillsboro	.977	3389	1012	102	101
Spokane	.976	3372	1099	112	98
Tri-City	.975	3373	1104	113	93
Everett	.973	3439	1112	125	101
Eugene	.971	3310	1007	130	75
Vancouver	.965	3330	999	155	83

INDIVIDUAL BATTING

Batter, Club	AVG	G	AB	R	H	2B	3B	HR	RBI	BB	SO	SB
Colin Simpson, Spokane	.300	95	330	53	99	17	4	17	60	36	78	7
Julio Carreras, Spokane	.289	110	402	59	116	37	2	11	59	31	106	17
Bladimir Restituyo, Spokane	.280	105	396	55	111	16	5	8	44	11	87	22
Noelvi Marte, Everett	.275	85	342	62	94	19	0	15	55	42	84	13
A.J. Vukovich, Hillsboro	.274	106	424	55	116	26	2	15	69	18	105	35
Casey Schmitt, Eugene	.273	93	333	58	91	14	1	17	59	42	86	1
Zac Veen, Spokane	.269	92	342	72	92	19	3	11	60	50	90	50
Eddy Diaz, Spokane	.261	97	376	57	98	18	4	5	39	30	87	36
Alberto Rodriguez, Everett	.261	119	472	59	123	28	3	10	46	50	138	6
Osmy Gregorio, Tri-City	.255	113	444	58	113	18	6	2	44	32	125	22

INDIVIDUAL PITCHING

Pitcher, Club	W	L	ERA	G	GS	CG	SV	IP	H	R	ER	BB	SO
Scott Randall, Hillsboro	6	7	3.82	21	21	0	0	108	101	46	46	25	104
Joe Rock, Spokane	7	8	4.43	20	20	1	0	108	87	63	53	45	109
Juan Mercedes, Everett	7	8	4.51	22	21	1	0	108	99	59	54	30	124
Luke Albright, Hillsboro	6	10	5.49	26	26	0	0	123	125	80	75	56	130
Jimmy Joyce, Everett	7	11	5.75	23	23	0	0	113	106	80	72	47	133

DEPARTMENT LEADERS

BATTING

OBP	Andy Thomas, Eugene	.373
SLG	Colin Simpson, Spokane	.530
OPS	Colin Simpson, Spokane	.900
R	Zac Veen, Spokane	72
H	Alberto Rodriguez, Everett	123
TB	Dariel Gomez, Everett	193
XBH	Julio Carreras, Spokane	50
2B	Julio Carreras, Spokane	37
3B	Steward Berroa, Vancouver	6
3B	Osmy Gregorio, Tri-City	6
3B	Victor Labrada, Everett	6
HR	Dariel Gomez, Everett	26
RBI	A.J. Vukovich, Hillsboro	69
SAC	Eddy Diaz, Spokane	8
SAC	Bladimir Restituyo, Spokane	8
BB	Gabe Matthews, Tri-City	65
HBP	Leo Jimenez, Vancouver	17
HBP	Braiden Ward, Spokane	17
SO	Dariel Gomez, Everett	163
SB	Zac Veen, Spokane	50
CS	Eddy Diaz, Spokane	14

FIELDING

C	PCT	Andy Thomas, Everett/Eugene	.995
	PO	Andy Thomas, Everett/Eugene	769
	A	Andy Thomas, Everett/Eugene	64
	DP	Straton Podaras, Tri-City	6
	E	Straton Podaras, Tri-City	10
	CS	Andy Thomas, Everett/Eugene	30
	SB	Andy Thomas, Everett/Eugene	76
	PB	2 tied	15
1B	PCT	Grant Lavigne, Spokane	.993
	PO	Gabe Matthews, Tri-City	755
	A	Gabe Matthews, Tri-City	56
	DP	Gabe Matthews, Tri-City	68
	E	Luis Toribio, Eugene	12
2B	PCT	Eddy Diaz, Spokane	.974
	PO	Eddy Diaz, Spokane	146
	A	Eddy Diaz, Spokane	222
	DP	Eddy Diaz, Spokane	51
	E	Miguel Hiraldo, Vancouver	25
3B	PCT	A.J. Vukovich, Hillsboro	.903
	PO	A.J. Vukovich, Hillsboro	54
	A	A.J. Vukovich, Hillsboro	104
	DP	2 tied	9
	E	A.J. Vukovich, Hillsboro	17
SS	PCT	Ryan Bliss, Hillsboro	.962
	PO	Julio Carreras, Spokane	150
	A	Julio Carreras, Spokane	256
	DP	2 tied	47
	E	Noelvi Marte, Everett	24
OF	PCT	Luis Matos, Eugene	.988
	PO	Bladimir Restituyo, Spokane	225
	A	2 tied	8
	DP	Garrett Spain, Vancouver	3
	E	Alberto Rodriguez, Everett	7

PITCHING

G	Brooks Crawford, Eugene	43
GS	Luke Albright, Hillsboro	26
GF	Nick Avila, Eugene	27
SV	Nick Avila, Eugene	13
W	Abel Adames, Eugene	11
L	Jimmy Joyce, Everett	11
IP	Luke Albright, Hillsboro	123
H	Luke Albright, Hillsboro	125
R	Luke Albright, Hillsboro	80
R	Jimmy Joyce, Everett	80
ER	Luke Albright, Hillsboro	75
HB	Jimmy Joyce, Everett	20
BB	Luke Albright, Hillsboro	56
SO	Jimmy Joyce, Everett	133
SO/9	Jimmy Joyce, Everett	10.6
BB/9	Scott Randall, Hillsboro	2.1
WP	Marcos Tineo, Hillsboro	15
BK	Jol Concepcion, Vancouver	7
HRA	Will Ethridge, Spokane	18
BAA	Joe Rock, Spokane	.219

MINOR LEAGUES

SOUTH ATLANTIC LEAGUE HIGH-A

Awards selected by Major League Baseball

CHAMPION: The Rays typically have a high level of success in the minor leagues, and 2022 was no exception. Led by Manager of the Year Jeff Smith, Bowling Green was one of three full-season Tampa Bay affiliates to win its league's championship. In doing so, the Hot Rods took down Rome in the divisional round before besting Aberdeen for the title.

MOST VALUABLE PLAYER: The season of Endy Rodriguez stands as one of the biggest breakouts in the minor leagues. The switch-hitting catcher, whom the Pirates acquired from the Mets in a three-team trade that also sent righthander Joe Musgrove from Pittsburgh to San Diego, crushed his way from High-A Greensboro to Triple-A Indianapolis by season's end. Along the way, Rodriguez showed complete tool set, featuring power, contact, patience and standout defense. In 88 games with Greensboro he hit .302/.392/.544.

PITCHER OF THE YEAR: The Jersey Shore rotation featured a host of the Phillies' finest pitching prospects, headed by first-rounders Mick Abel and Andrew Painter. Righthander Ben Brown was less-heralded, but his stuff quickly caught the attention of scouts as he struck out 105 in 73 innings. Brown was flipped to the Cubs at the trade deadline in a deal that brought closer David Robertson to the eventual National League champions.

TOP MLB PROSPECT: When the season began, Endy Rodriguez and Henry Davis split time behind the plate at Greensboro. Once Davis was bumped to Altoona, Rodriguez had the chance to shine. Before he left, he produced league-best marks in slugging (.544) and OPS (.936) while adding 42 extra-base hits. Once he left Greensboro, his defense excelled further. At Double-A and Triple-A, he caught 43% of basestealers.

Endy Rodriguez

TONY FARLOW/FOUR SEAM IMAGES

MANAGER OF THE YEAR: Jeff Smith led league-champion Bowling Green to 78 wins, which tied for the best in the league. Smith also led the Hot Rods to the 2021 SAL title.

SOUTH ATLANTIC LEAGUE ALL-STARS

Pos	Player	Team	AVG	OPS	HR
C	Endy Rodriguez	Greensboro	.302	.936	16
1B	Kyle Manzardo	Bowling Green	.329	1.072	17
2B	Thomas Saggese	Hickory	.308	.864	14
3B	Tyler Hardman	Hudson Valley	.262	.808	22
SS	Vaughn Grissom	Rome	.312	.891	11
OF	Heriberto Hernandez	Bowling Green	.255	.867	24
OF	Cody Milligan	Rome	.329	.910	1
OF	Zach Daniels	Asheville	.282	.893	23
DH	Evan Carter	Hickory	.287	.864	11
Pos	**Pitcher**	**Team**	**G**	**ERA**	**SO**
RHP	Ben Brown	Jersey Shore	16	3.08	105
LHP	Nick Zwack	Brooklyn	20	2.52	108
RP	Xavier Moore	Aberdeen	30	1.36	58

OVERALL STANDINGS

North Division	W	L	PCT	GB	Manager	Attendance	Avg	Last Penn
Aberdeen IronBirds (Orioles)	78	54	.591	—	Roberto Mercado	121,916	1,966	Never
Hudson Valley Renegades (Yankees)	71	59	.546	6	Tyson Blaser	184,055	2,876	Never
Brooklyn Cyclones (Mets)	70	62	.530	8	Luis Rivera	167,846	2,707	Never
Wilmington Blue Rocks (Nationals)	65	65	.500	12	Mario Lisson	118,754	1,947	*2019
Greensboro Grasshoppers (Pirates)	58	70	.453	18	Callix Crabbe	265,943	4,221	2011
Jersey Shore BlueClaws (Phillies)	51	81	.386	27	Keith Werman	256,141	4,269	2010
South Division	**W**	**L**	**PCT**	**GB**	**Manager**	**Attendance**	**Avg**	**Last Penn**
Bowling Green Hot Rods (Rays)	78	52	.600	—	Jeff Smith	155,975	2,437	2022
Rome Braves (Braves)	74	54	.578	3	Kanekoa Texeira	89,176	1,415	2016
Hickory Crawdads (Rangers)	66	65	.504	12.5	Carlos Cardoza	105,378	1,700	2015
Asheville Tourists (Astros)	62	69	.473	16.5	Nate Shaver	172,726	2,742	2014
Winston-Salem Dash (White Sox)	58	74	.439	21	Lorenzo Bundy	287,529	4,493	*2003
Greenville Drive (Red Sox)	52	78	.400	26	Iggy Suarez	317,150	4,879	2017

* Carolina League title won prior to 2021 minor league realignment

North: Aberdeen def. Brooklyn 2-1. **South:** Bowling Green def. Rome 2-1. **Championship Series:** Bowling Green def. Aberdeen 2-1.

CLUB BATTING

	AVG	G	AB	R	H	2B	3B	HR	RBI	BB	SO	SB	OBP	SLG
Asheville	.270	131	4475	776	1210	229	29	161	716	514	1272	152	.355	.442
Hickory	.259	131	4309	731	1116	179	28	125	660	566	1117	168	.351	.401
Bowling Green	.255	130	4365	727	1113	209	31	157	661	525	1213	137	.343	.425
Rome	.251	128	4239	675	1065	195	20	129	615	579	1230	134	.352	.398
Greensboro	.246	128	4263	629	1047	187	25	158	589	424	1257	137	.325	.412
Winston-Salem	.244	132	4368	603	1064	189	18	115	543	498	1175	115	.330	.374
Hudson Valley	.241	130	4224	649	1017	190	30	129	592	597	1289	230	.341	.392
Aberdeen	.240	132	4304	634	1034	215	41	107	575	531	1272	172	.332	.384
Greenville	.240	130	4355	658	1044	201	33	165	597	534	1344	130	.330	.415
Brooklyn	.234	132	4191	555	981	208	40	86	508	497	1240	102	.329	.364
Wilmington	.232	130	4236	556	983	186	25	77	507	488	1196	176	.316	.342
Jersey Shore	.214	132	4160	485	892	173	26	88	421	429	1283	151	.297	.332

CLUB PITCHING

	ERA	G	CG	SHO	SV	IP	H	R	ER	HR	BB	SO	AVG
Hudson Valley	3.62	130	2	10	34	1128	917	524	454	84	518	1204	.223
Brooklyn	3.67	132	0	7	45	1123	941	510	458	76	471	1227	.226
Wilmington	3.77	130	1	8	31	1126	957	541	471	90	499	1164	.230
Bowling Green	3.97	130	0	12	40	1135	1071	580	501	133	388	1205	.248
Rome	3.97	128	2	10	36	1119	1022	576	494	115	491	1332	.239
Aberdeen	3.98	132	0	9	41	1150	976	585	509	116	514	1360	.228
Jersey Shore	4.11	132	2	11	27	1119	1000	615	511	86	507	1270	.236
Hickory	4.65	131	1	12	27	1128	1046	657	583	155	494	1266	.243
Winston-Salem	4.96	132	0	5	27	1144	1135	709	630	157	561	1121	.260
Greensboro	5.31	128	1	5	28	1120	1078	746	661	165	609	1193	.251
Greenville	5.42	130	0	3	27	1128	1225	769	679	164	497	1258	.274
Asheville	6.06	131	0	4	30	1134	1198	867	764	156	633	1288	.266

CLUB FIELDING

	PCT	PO	A	E	DP
Hudson Valley	.978	3385	1145	104	112
Bowling Green	.977	3405	1113	105	97
Brooklyn	.977	3370	1156	106	99
Winston-Salem	.977	3432	1176	108	121
Wilmington	.976	3377	1120	112	127
Rome	.975	3356	1055	111	93
Aberdeen	.975	3449	1045	116	88
Jersey Shore	.972	3358	1048	125	104
Greensboro	.972	3361	1140	129	106
Greenville	.972	3384	1045	129	87
Hickory	.971	3385	1065	131	92
Asheville	.970	3404	1054	139	90

INDIVIDUAL BATTING

Batter, Club	AVG	G	AB	R	H	2B	3B	HR	RBI	BB	SO	SB
Tyler Osik, Winston-Salem	.310	89	313	45	97	14	2	10	53	32	77	3
J.C. Correa, Asheville	.309	105	404	59	125	29	1	8	64	37	36	1
Thomas Saggese, Hickory	.308	98	380	56	117	22	2	14	61	29	94	11
Endy Rodriguez, Greensboro	.302	88	318	63	96	23	3	16	55	42	77	3
Luis Santana, Asheville	.297	97	343	58	102	23	2	11	62	38	69	11
Matthew Lugo, Greenville	.288	114	466	76	134	25	10	18	78	35	100	20
Evan Carter, Hickory	.287	100	376	78	108	18	10	11	66	59	75	26
Dariel Lopez, Greensboro	.286	102	391	58	112	15	1	19	58	21	107	6
Zach Daniels, Asheville	.282	95	358	76	101	15	1	23	64	48	127	22
Jacob Gonzalez, Greensboro	.281	88	334	41	94	13	1	9	45	27	49	2

INDIVIDUAL PITCHING

Pitcher, Club	W	L	ERA	G	GS	CG	SV	IP	H	R	ER	BB	SO
Luis De Avila, Rome	6	8	3.49	24	24	1	0	126	115	57	49	45	129
Blas Castano, Hudson Valley	5	8	3.49	21	20	1	0	106	99	48	41	33	101
Nick Garcia, Greensboro	4	4	3.66	25	23	1	0	113	90	48	46	46	109
Shane Drohan, Greenville	6	7	4.00	22	20	0	0	106	91	56	47	40	136
Chase Solesky, Winston-Salem	4	8	4.24	24	24	0	0	110	116	55	52	31	00
Junior Santos, Brooklyn	8	13	4.47	26	23	0	0	117	126	67	58	44	105
Jared Jones, Greensboro	5	7	4.62	26	26	0	0	123	115	68	63	51	142
Michael Cuevas, Wilmington	6	12	4.64	26	24	0	0	114	123	74	59	55	82
Aaron Brown, Asheville	4	9	5.28	25	14	0	2	109	129	73	64	34	95
Yusniel Padron-Artiles, Greenville	3	12	5.95	23	20	0	0	107	121	73	71	34	115

DEPARTMENT LEADERS

BATTING

OBP	Aaron Zavala, Hickory	.424
SLG	Endy Rodriguez, Greensboro	.544
OPS	Endy Rodriguez, Greensboro	.936
R	Michael Sandle, Asheville	79
H	Matthew Lugo, Greenville	134
TB	Matthew Lugo, Greenville	233
XBH	Heriberto Hernandez, Bowling Green	53
XBH	Matthew Lugo, Greenville	53
2B	Luis Mieses, Winston-Salem	34
3B	Evan Carter, Hickory	10
3B	Matthew Lugo, Greenville	10
HR	Nicholas Northcut, Greenville	26
RBI	Heriberto Hernandez, Bowling Green	89
SAC	Gilberto Jimenez, Greenville	5
BB	Yasel Antuna, Wilmington	72
HBP	Matt Rudick, Brooklyn	16
SO	Baron Radcliff, Jersey Shore	163
SB	Duke Ellis, Winston-Salem	50
CS	Yoyner Fajardo, Greensboro	13

FIELDING

C PCT	Tyler Tolve, Rome	.993
PO	Tyler Tolve, Rome	653
A	Adam Hackenberg, Winston-Salem	76
DP	Israel Pineda, Wilmington	7
E	Connor Pavolony, Aberdeen	11
CS	Adam Hackenberg, Winston-Salem	35
SB	Tyler Tolve, Rome	111
PB	J.C. Correa, Asheville	22
1B PCT	Bryson Horne, Rome	.995
PO	JT Schwartz, Brooklyn	769
A	JT Schwartz, Brooklyn	55
DP	Harvin Mendoza, Winston-Salem	81
E	Harvin Mendoza, Winston-Salem	10
2B PCT	Nick Yorke, Greenville	.997
PO	Nick Yorke, Greenville	130
A	Nick Yorke, Greenville	166
DP	Darren Baker, Wilmington	42
E	2 tied	8
3B PCT	Bryan Ramos, Winston-Salem	.954
PO	Bryan Ramos, Winston-Salem	73
A	Jose Sanchez, Wilmington	167
DP	Jose Sanchez, Wilmington	20
E	Dariel Lopez, Greensboro	15
SS PCT	Shervyen Newton, Brooklyn	.962
PO	Shervyen Newton, Brooklyn	118
A	Shervyen Newton, Brooklyn	232
DP	Jordy Barley, Wilmington	52
E	Matthew Lugo, Greenville	20
OF PCT	3 tied	1.000
PO	Luis Mieses, Winston-Salem	184
A	2 tied	9
DP	Jasson Dominguez, Hudson Valley	3
E	2 tied	6

PITCHING

G	Austin Smith, Rome	45
GS	Jared Jones, Greensboro	26
GF	Austin Smith, Rome	37
SV	Austin Smith, Rome	13
W	Anthony Molina, Bowling Green	13
L	Junior Santos, Brooklyn	13
IP	Luis De Avila, Rome	126
H	Aaron Brown, Asheville	129
R	Wyatt Olds, Greenville	80
ER	Wyatt Olds, Greenville	71
ER	Yusniel Padron-Artiles, Greenville	71
HB	Wyatt Olds, Greenville	27
BB	Mitchell Parker, Wilmington	67
SO	Jared Jones, Greensboro	142
SO/9	Shane Drohan, Greenville	11.6
BB/9	Chase Solesky, Winston-Salem	2.5
WP	Graeme Stinson, Bowling Green	21
BK	Blas Castano, Hudson Valley	5
BK	Davis Schwab, Rome	5
HRA	Chih-Jung Liu, Greenville	27
BAA	Nick Garcia, Greensboro	.219

MINOR LEAGUES

CALIFORNIA LEAGUE LOW-A

Awards selected by Major League Baseball

James Wood

CHAMPION: The Cal League was conquered by Lake Elsinore, whose roster was dotted with Padres prospects all season long, including toolsy titan James Wood early and rising star outfielder Samuel Zavala late in the year. The Storm swept through the playoffs, besting Inland Empire in the divisional round and Fresno in the finals.

MOST VALUABLE PLAYER: Inland Empire catcher Edgar Quero had one of quietest seasons of dominance in the minors. The 19-year-old hit .312/.435/.530 in a full season at Low-A and crushed 35 doubles and 17 home runs as well. He stole a dozen bases for good measure.

PITCHER OF THE YEAR: The Seattle pitching factory continues unabated. Righthander Joseph Hernandez took top honors in the Cal League, joining Taylor Dollard in the Texas League as Mariners who earned league Pitcher of the Year honors in a minor league. Hernandez, a 22-year-old from the Dominican Republic, was the only qualified pitcher in the hitter-friendly league to record an ERA under 4.00, and he allowed just 79 hits in 117 innings while striking out 143. He held the opposition to a average of just .193 as well.

TOP MLB PROSPECT: Before he was dealt to the Nationals as part of the package the Padres used to land superstar outfielder Juan Soto, 19-year-old James Wood had burned up the Cal League with a blend of high-end power, hitting ability and grace in the outfield. His ceiling is as high as any prospect in baseball. Despite missing time with a wrist injury, Wood, whom the Padres drafted in the second round in 2021, slammed 10 home runs and posted a 1.051 OPS in the Cal League before the deal. He performed well in Low-A Fredericksburg of the Carolina League after the trade, adding two more home runs to his season total of 12 in just 76 games. Despite his inexperience and massive size and levers, Wood struck out in just 21.5% of his plate appearances while working a walk rate of 14.3% across all three of his stops.

MANAGER OF THE YEAR: Lake Elsinore manager Eric Junge guided his youthful club, which spent most of the year without its two top talents—outfielder James Wood and shortstop Jackson Merrill—to the Cal League championship.

CALIFORNIA LEAGUE ALL-STARS

Pos	Player	Team	AVG	OPS	HR
C	Edgar Quero	Inland Empire	.312	.965	17
1B	Hunter Goodman	Fresno	.291	.960	22
2B	Juan Brito	Fresno	.286	.877	11
3B	Marcos Castanon	Lake Elsinore	.261	.882	23
SS	Adael Amador	Fresno	.292	.860	15
OF	Grant McCray	San Jose	.291	.908	21
OF	James Wood	Lake Elsinore	.337	1.054	10
OF	Damon Keith	Rancho Cucamonga	.299	.933	12
DH	Yanquiel Fernandez	Fresno	.284	.847	21
Pos	**Pitcher**	**Team**	**G**	**ERA**	**SO**
RHP	Joseph Hernandez	Modesto	24	3.39	143
LHP	Mason Green	Fresno	13	3.07	71
RP	Jose Cruz	San Jose	38	2.06	86

OVERALL STANDINGS

North Division	W	L	PCT	GB	Manager	Attendance	Avg	Last Penn
Fresno Grizzlies (Rockies)	83	49	.629	—	Robinson Cancel	261,652	4,025	Never
San Jose Giants (Giants)	74	58	.561	9	Lipso Nava	115,074	1,744	2021
Modesto Nuts (Mariners)	66	66	.500	17	Austin Knight	94,253	1,428	2017
Stockton Ports (Athletics)	45	87	.341	38	Franklin Font	114,480	1,735	2008

South Division	W	L	PCT	GB	Manager	Attendance	Avg	Last Penn
Lake Elsinore Storm (Padres)	77	55	.583	—	Eric Junge	102,950	1,584	2022
Inland Empire 66ers (Angels)	70	62	.530	7	Ever Magallanes	141,792	2,148	2013
Rancho Cucamonga Quakes (Dodgers)	68	64	.515	9	John Shoemaker	138,533	2,099	2018
Visalia Rawhide (D-backs)	45	87	.341	32	Jorge Cortes	121,006	1,833	2019

North: Fresno def. San Jose 2-0. **South:** Lake Elsinore def. Inland Empire 2-0. **Championship Series:** Lake Elsinore def. Fresno 2-0.

LARRY GOREN/FOUR SEAM IMAGES

CLUB BATTING

	AVG	G	AB	R	H	2B	3B	HR	RBI	BB	SO	SB	OBP	SLG
Fresno	.276	132	4575	911	1264	280	34	162	799	606	1064	183	.372	.459
Rancho Cucamonga	.268	132	4610	906	1236	255	36	143	810	729	1262	126	.379	.432
San Jose	.267	132	4626	770	1237	226	38	149	680	522	1323	141	.352	.429
Modesto	.257	132	4541	842	1166	251	39	124	748	607	1360	169	.358	.411
Lake Elsinore	.253	132	4434	871	1120	236	37	129	744	715	1280	259	.368	.410
Inland Empire	.247	132	4430	765	1093	232	38	82	649	660	1319	223	.355	.372
Stockton	.238	132	4491	609	1069	210	22	97	537	553	1432	112	.332	.359
Visalia	.238	132	4467	627	1062	213	31	97	561	488	1438	175	.323	.364

CLUB PITCHING

	ERA	G	CG	SHO	SV	IP	H	R	ER	HR	BB	SO	AVG
San Jose	4.11	132	0	6	33	1177	1015	639	537	92	585	1443	.230
Fresno	4.61	132	0	4	34	1166	1169	703	597	107	544	1202	.260
Modesto	4.66	132	0	9	23	1169	1122	711	606	99	522	1237	.250
Inland Empire	4.98	132	0	6	32	1167	1135	757	646	119	564	1291	.252
Lake Elsinore	5.08	132	0	5	34	1158	1180	759	653	109	574	1307	.262
Rancho Cucamonga	5.49	132	0	3	22	1166	1068	844	712	118	763	1481	.241
Visalia	5.97	132	0	0	26	1165	1182	945	772	135	781	1330	.260
Stockton	6.04	132	0	5	26	1169	1376	943	784	204	547	1187	.287

CLUB FIELDING

	PCT	PO	A	E	DP
Lake Elsinore	.969	3474	1225	149	107
Inland Empire	.968	3501	1137	151	108
Fresno	.968	3499	1237	155	111
Modesto	.967	3508	1192	159	108

	PCT	PO	A	E	DP
San Jose	.966	3530	1209	165	115
Rancho Cucamonga	.960	13499	1116	189	82
Stockton	.960	3506	1165	193	86
Visalia	.960	3494	1180	194	113

INDIVIDUAL BATTING

Batter, Club	AVG	G	AB	R	H	2B	3B	HR	RBI	BB	SO	SB
Deyvison De Los Santos, Visalia	.329	78	316	43	104	18	2	12	67	22	84	4
Edwin Arroyo, Modesto	.316	87	364	76	115	19	7	13	67	35	90	21
Edgar Quero, Inland Empire	.312	111	413	86	129	35	2	17	75	73	91	12
Yunior Garcia, Rancho Cucamonga	.305	87	334	58	102	28	1	13	74	33	75	2
Damon Keith, Rancho Cucamonga	.299	88	334	75	100	23	4	12	65	69	95	5
Yeiner Fernandez, R. Cucamonga	.292	89	363	76	106	16	2	10	68	46	55	3
Adael Amador, Fresno	.292	115	449	100	131	24	0	15	57	87	67	26
Grant McCray, San Jose	.291	106	436	92	127	21	9	21	69	58	148	35
Austin Gauthier, Rancho Cucamonga	.287	84	300	81	86	18	4	6	49	88	81	10
Juan Brito, Fresno	.286	107	402	91	115	29	6	11	72	78	71	17

INDIVIDUAL PITCHING

Pitcher, Club	W	L	ERA	G	GS	CG	SV	IP	H	R	ER	BB	SO
Joseph Hernandez, Modesto	9	5	3.39	24	22	0	0	117	79	47	44	54	143
Connor Van Scoyoc, Inland Empire	11	5	4.28	23	22	0	0	120	103	63	57	39	140
Mitch Myers, Stockton	4	10	5.50	23	22	0	0	124	143	83	76	38	98
Julio Goff, Inland Empire	7	9	5.51	25	17	0	2	111	121	83	68	44	115
Michael Morales, Modesto	5	7	5.91	26	26	0	0	120	143	96	79	50	125

DEPARTMENT LEADERS

BATTING

OBP	Austin Gauthier, Rancho Cucamonga	.461
SLG	Edgar Quero, Inland Empire	.530
OPS	Edgar Quero, Inland Empire	.965
R	Adael Amador, Fresno	100
H	Aeverson Arteaga, San Jose	136
TB	Yanquiel Fernandez, Fresno	241
XBH	Yanquiel Fernandez, Fresno	59
2B	Aeverson Arteaga, San Jose	35
2B	Edgar Quero, Inland Empire	35
3B	Jonatan Clase, Modesto	11
HR	Marcos Castanon, Lake Elsinore	23
RBI	Yanquiel Fernandez, Fresno	109
SAC	Danny Bautista, Stockton	7
BB	Justin Farmer, Lake Elsinore	95
HBP	Edgar Quero, Inland Empire	21
SO	Alexander Ramirez, Inland Empire	160
SB	Jonatan Clase, Modesto	55
CS	Adael Amador, Fresno	12

FIELDING

C	PCT	Braxton Fulford, Fresno	.997
	PO	Braxton Fulford, Fresno	778
	A	Braxton Fulford, Fresno	77
	DP	Braxton Fulford, Fresno	9
	E	Yeiner Fernandez, Rancho Cucamonga	19
	CS	Braxton Fulford, Fresno	32
	SB	Yeiner Fernandez, Rancho Cucamonga	131
	PB	Jared Alvarez-Lopez, Lake Elsinore	18
1B	PCT	Garrett Frechette, San Jose	.990
	PO	Garrett Frechette, San Jose	677
	A	Robert Perez Jr., Modesto	39
	DP	Garrett Frechette, San Jose	62
	E	Robert Perez Jr., Modesto	9
2B	PCT	2 tied	.972
	PO	Juan Brito, Fresno	198
	A	Juan Brito, Fresno	257
	DP	Juan Brito, Fresno	67
	E	Juan Brito, Fresno	13
3B	PCT	Marcos Castanon, Lake Elsinore	.954
	PO	Yorlis Rodriguez, San Jose	58
	A	Yorlis Rodriguez, San Jose	181
	DP	Warming Bernabel, Fresno	17
	E	Yorlis Rodriguez, San Jose	18
SS	PCT	Arol Vera, Inland Empire	.963
	PO	Aeverson Arteaga, San Jose	147
	A	Aeverson Arteaga, San Jose	302
	DP	Aeverson Arteaga, San Jose	69
	E	2 tied	25
OF	PCT	David Calabrese, Inland Empire	.983
	PO	David Calabrese, Inland Empire	224
	A	Walking Cabrera, Modesto	12
	DP	2 tied	3
	E	Yanquiel Fernandez, Fresno	10

PITCHING

G	Sergio Sanchez, Fresno	46
GS	Michael Morales, Modesto	26
GF	Hunter Breault, Stockton	29
GF	Madison Jeffrey, Rancho Cucamonga	29
SV	Jorge Benitez, Modesto	11
W	Connor Van Scoyoc, Inland Empire	11
L	Mitch Myers, Stockton	10
IP	Mitch Myers, Stockton	124.1
H	Michael Morales, Modesto	143
H	Mitch Myers, Stockton	143
R	Michael Morales, Modesto	96
ER	Michael Morales, Modesto	79
HB	Joseph Hernandez, Modesto	21
BB	Manuel Mercedes, San Jose	63
SO	Joseph Hernandez, Modesto	143
SO/9	Joseph Hernandez, Modesto	11
BB/9	Mitch Myers, Stockton	2.8
WP	Tyler Baum, Stockton	23
BK	Julio Goff, Inland Empire	6
BK	Fernando Guanare, Inland Empire	6
HRA	Mitch Myers, Stockton	26
BAA	Joseph Hernandez, Modesto	.193

CAROLINA LEAGUE LOW-A

Awards selected by Major League Baseball

CHAMPION: Like their siblings in the South Atlantic and International leagues, the Charleston RiverDogs were another Rays affiliate who not only won their championship, but also navigated the postseason without a loss. Charleston—the Baseball America Minor League Team of the Year—knocked off Myrtle Beach in the divisional round and then bounced Lynchburg in the finals.

MOST VALUABLE PLAYER: The Carolina League MVP was also the author of the biggest breakout in the minor leagues. Brewers outfielder Jackson Chourio started the year in extended spring training before bashing his way to Double-A by season's end while playing the whole season as an 18-year-old. Chourio arrived in Carolina in early May and hit .324/.373/.600 before earning a promotion to High-A Wisconsin. He also was voted into the annual Futures Game.

PITCHER OF THE YEAR: A Cleveland pitcher drafted out of college having success stands as the one of the most predictable Mad Libs in the minors. Former McNeese State lefthander Will Dion carved the competition in the Carolina League for 23 starts before being bumped to High-A Lake County. With Lynchburg, Dion whiffed 142 hitters in 115 innings and put forth a Carolina League-best 2.26 ERA.

TOP MLB PROSPECT: Chourio's outstanding turn at Low-A opened eyes, but he kept the momentum going at High-A and ultimately earned a late-season taste of the upper levels at Double-A Biloxi. He kept mashing in the Midwest League, where he hit eight home runs in 31 games despite missing time with a minor injury. In total, Chourio slugged 20 homers and added 30 doubles while batting .288/.342/.538 in 99 games to rise to No. 2 on the Top 100 Prospects ranking.

Jackson Chourio

BRIAN WESTERHOLT/FOUR SEAM IMAGES

MANAGER OF THE YEAR: Charleston manager Blake Butera piloted the RiverDogs' talented, youthful lineup to 88 wins and the championship.

CAROLINA LEAGUE ALL-STARS

Pos	Player	Team	AVG	OPS	HR
C	Carter Jensen	Columbia	.226	.745	11
1B	Niko Kavadas	Salem	.286	1.062	14
2B	Joey Loperfido	Fayetteville	.304	.872	9
3B	Eddinson Paulino	Salem	.266	.828	13
SS	Carson Williams	Charleston	.252	.818	19
OF	Jackson Chourio	Carolina	.324	.973	12
OF	Shane Sasaki	Charleston	.324	.907	9
OF	Jeremy De La Rosa	Fredericksburg	.315	.899	10
DH	Marcelo Mayer	Salem	.286	.910	9
Pos	**Pitcher**	**Team**	**G**	**ERA**	**SO**
RHP	J.J. Niekro	Augusta	15	2.09	77
LHP	Will Dion	Lynchburg	23	2.26	142
RP	Austin Vernon	Charleston	15	1.69	91

OVERALL STANDINGS

North Division	W	L	PCT	GB	Manager	Attendance	Avg	Last Penn
Fredericksburg Nationals (Nationals)	75	55	.577	—	Jake Lowery	260,546	4,071	Never
Carolina Mudcats (Brewers)	69	62	.527	6.5	Victor Estevez	138,579	2,165	2006
Down East Wood Ducks (Rangers)	65	66	.496	10.5	Steve Mintz	98,328	1,513	2017
Salem Red Sox (Red Sox)	64	66	.492	11	Luke Montz	181,287	2,878	2013
Lynchburg Hillcats (Guardians)	63	68	.481	12.5	Omir Santos	91,232	1,496	2017
Delmarva Shorebirds (Orioles)	49	81	.377	26	Felipe Alou Jr.	154,786	2,497	2001

South Division	W	L	PCT	GB	Manager	Attendance	Avg	Last Penn
Charleston RiverDogs (Rays)	88	44	.667	—	Blake Butera	251,491	3,992	2022
Myrtle Beach Pelicans (Cubs)	78	53	.595	9.5	Buddy Bailey	247,926	3,935	2016
Augusta GreenJackets (Braves)	69	62	.527	18.5	Nestor Perez	262,172	4,096	*2008
Kannapolis Cannon Ballers (White Sox)	58	74	.439	30	Guillermo Quiroz	192,161	2,912	*2005
Fayetteville Woodpeckers (Astros)	55	75	.423	32	Dickie Joe Thon	214,470	3,459	2018
Columbia Fireflies (Royals)	52	79	.397	35.5	Tony Peña Jr.	217,225	3,394	*2013

* South Atlantic League title won prior to 2021 minor league realignment

North: Lynchburg def. Fredericksburg 2-1. **South:** Charleston def. Myrtle Beach 2-0. **Championship Series:** Charleston def. Lynchburg 2-0.

CLUB BATTING

	AVG	G	AB	R	H	2B	3B	HR	RBI	BB	SO	SB	OBP	SLG
Charleston	.254	132	4436	744	1127	208	57	120	645	564	1339	248	.346	.408
Myrtle Beach	.253	131	4414	746	1115	209	38	113	661	538	1154	124	.342	.394
Fredericksburg	.252	130	4338	774	1095	211	35	100	665	592	1221	211	.349	.386
Salem	.249	130	4343	720	1081	254	42	98	616	645	1192	186	.352	.394
Augusta	.246	131	4353	757	1070	212	47	107	649	670	1255	201	.356	.390
Carolina	.239	131	4300	633	1027	197	24	101	571	515	1271	142	.328	.366
Delmarva	.238	130	4346	602	1036	197	31	68	520	564	1351	151	.335	.345
Lynchburg	.233	131	4237	624	989	202	36	50	531	638	1191	128	.342	.333
Kannapolis	.228	132	4339	580	989	187	28	111	512	526	1434	136	.322	.361
Down East	.226	131	4162	568	942	160	27	92	491	525	1294	308	.322	.344
Columbia	.220	131	4216	567	929	190	32	81	477	573	1213	220	.320	.338
Fayetteville	.220	130	4236	548	930	184	20	112	497	500	1408	228	.315	.352

CLUB PITCHING

	ERA	G	CG	SHO	SV	IP	H	R	ER	HR	BB	SO	AVG
Charleston	3.67	132	0	9	30	1158	954	570	472	85	598	1338	.222
Down East	3.84	131	0	12	30	1145	954	591	488	95	491	1330	.224
Myrtle Beach	3.93	131	0	11	34	1140	951	586	498	81	609	1393	.225
Lynchburg	4.26	131	1	3	29	1130	1063	616	535	91	469	1347	.245
Kannapolis	4.33	132	0	6	28	1150	1058	641	553	101	543	1200	.243
Fayetteville	4.33	130	0	9	22	1133	906	634	545	87	692	1376	.216
Fredericksburg	4.36	130	0	7	26	1119	1043	601	542	97	431	1209	.243
Carolina	4.43	131	0	6	34	1137	998	643	560	108	601	1302	.235
Augusta	4.54	131	0	4	29	1145	1071	666	578	105	509	1267	.244
Columbia	4.94	131	1	2	23	1143	1141	753	627	125	567	1178	.259
Salem	4.96	130	1	6	28	1127	1079	728	621	74	626	1207	.250
Delmarva	5.41	130	0	2	23	1130	1112	834	680	104	714	1176	.252

CLUB FIELDING

	PCT	PO	A	E	DP
Kannapolis	.972	3451	1187	136	107
Salem	.971	3384	1124	136	100
Down East	.971	3435	1093	137	90
Fredericksburg	.970	3357	1117	136	97
Fayetteville	.970	3399	1030	136	74
Charleston	.970	3474	1118	142	100
Carolina	.969	3412	1003	140	81
Lynchburg	.969	3390	1087	144	85
Myrtle Beach	.968	3419	1128	151	98
Augusta	.968	3434	1159	154	89
Columbia	.961	3430	1160	186	114
Delmarva	.956	3391	1019	203	75

INDIVIDUAL BATTING

Batter, Club	AVG	G	AB	R	H	2B	3B	HR	RBI	BB	SO	SB
Shane Sasaki, Charleston	.324	89	346	71	112	27	3	9	57	49	92	47
Ezequiel Pagan, Myrtle Beach	.292	104	384	59	112	15	5	11	68	40	57	13
Blaze Jordan, Salem	.286	95	370	48	106	29	3	8	57	37	67	4
Brandol Mezquita, Augusta	.281	87	331	57	93	14	4	3	46	41	101	14
Bobby Seymour, Charleston	.281	95	349	63	98	21	3	12	73	51	98	15
Jorge Burgos, Lynchburg	.278	105	396	54	110	18	3	6	66	56	85	6
Daniel Mateo, Down East	.274	98	376	59	103	9	5	11	51	21	99	42
Colby Smelley, Kannapolis	.274	87	307	48	84	20	1	4	35	45	86	0
Kevin Alcantara, Myrtle Beach	.273	112	428	76	117	19	6	15	85	55	123	14
James Triantos, Myrtle Beach	.272	113	456	74	124	19	6	7	50	39	81	20

INDIVIDUAL PITCHING

Pitcher, Club	W	L	ERA	G	GS	CG	SV	IP	H	R	ER	BB	SO
Will Dion, Lynchburg	8	4	2.26	23	23	0	0	115	88	39	29	31	142
Winston Santos, Down East	7	6	3.49	22	21	0	0	108	89	49	42	30	108
Antonio Jimenez, Charleston	11	5	3.74	26	19	0	0	108	96	50	45	51	123
Reid Johnston, Lynchburg	4	6	3.94	24	16	0	0	112	102	61	49	24	122
Luinder Avila, Columbia	6	10	4.54	26	26	1	0	115	102	66	58	49	97
Edwin Jimenez, Carolina	4	7	4.75	25	17	0	0	114	119	68	60	41	104
Noah Owen, Kannapolis	5	10	5.16	23	19	0	0	106	125	69	61	32	83
Bryan Caceres, Fredericksburg	5	8	5.92	23	22	0	0	117	125	82	77	47	100

DEPARTMENT LEADERS

BATTING

OBP	Shane Sasaki, Charleston	.410
SLG	Shane Sasaki, Charleston	.497
OPS	Shane Sasaki, Charleston	.907
R	Jacob Young, Fredericksburg	118
H	James Triantos, Myrtle Beach	124
TB	Eddinson Paulino, Salem	217
XBH	Eddinson Paulino, Salem	58
2B	Eddinson Paulino, Salem	35
3B	Eddinson Paulino, Salem	10
3B	Carson Williams, Charleston	10
HR	Yosy Galan, Down East	20
RBI	Kevin Alcantara, Myrtle Beach	85
SAC	Jean Ramirez, Columbia	11
BB	Isaiah Greene, Lynchburg	97
HBP	Colby Smelley, Kannapolis	15
SO	Tyler Whitaker, Fayetteville	180
SB	Luis Valdez, Delmarva	59
CS	Maximo Acosta, Down East	17

FIELDING

C PCT	Jose Sibrian, Carolina	.992
PO	Ethan Hearn, Myrtle Beach	859
A	Jose Sibrian, Carolina	63
DP	2 tied	6
E	Adam Zebrowski, Augusta	15
CS	Jose Sibrian, Carolina	40
SB	Ethan Hearn, Myrtle Beach	124
PB	Freddy Guilamo, Fayetteville	17
1B PCT	Branden Boissiere, Fredericksburg	.994
PO	Guillermo Quintana, Columbia	825
A	Branden Boissiere, Fredericksburg	59
DP	Guillermo Quintana, Columbia	80
E	Guillermo Quintana, Columbia	14
2B PCT	Juan Mora, Myrtle Beach	.980
PO	Viandel Pena, Fredericksburg	104
A	Viandel Pena, Fredericksburg	201
DP	Viandel Pena, Fredericksburg	36
E	Brainer Bonaci, Salem	11
3B PCT	Willy Vasquez, Charleston	.942
PO	Wes Kath, Kannapolis	73
A	Wes Kath, Kannapolis	159
DP	Wes Kath, Kannapolis	18
E	Wes Kath, Kannapolis	23
SS PCT	Carson Williams, Charleston	.968
PO	Carson Williams, Charleston	136
A	Carson Williams, Charleston	252
DP	Carson Williams, Charleston	59
E	Daniel Vazquez, Columbia	23
OF PCT	2 tied	1.000
PO	Erick Pena, Columbia	182
A	Jorge Burgos, Lynchburg	10
DP	David Hollie, Columbia	3
E	T.J. White, Fredericksburg	9

PITCHING

G	Aneudy Cortorreal, Charleston	39
G	Rob Griswold, Augusta	39
GS	Luinder Avila, Columbia	26
GF	Rob Griswold, Augusta	27
SV	5 tied	9
W	Over Galue, Charleston	12
L	Alex Santos II, Fayetteville	11
IP	Bryan Caceres, Fredericksburg	117
H	Bryan Caceres, Fredericksburg	125
H	Noah Owen, Kannapolis	125
R	Bryan Caceres, Fredericksburg	82
ER	Bryan Caceres, Fredericksburg	77
HB	Bryan Caceres, Fredericksburg	16
BB	Jayson Schroeder, Fayetteville	61
BB	Miguel Segura, Carolina	61
SO	Will Dion, Lynchburg	142
SO/9	Will Dion, Lynchburg	11.1
BB/9	Reid Johnston, Lynchburg	1.9
WP	Over Galue, Charleston	23
BK	Alejandro Mendez, Delmarva	8
HRA	Noah Owen, Kannapolis	20
BAA	Will Dion, Lynchburg	.207

FLORIDA STATE LEAGUE LOW-A

Awards selected by Major League Baseball

CHAMPION: The St. Lucie Mets defeated the Dunedin Blue Jays with a clean sweep through the playoffs. They knocked off Palm Beach in the divisional round before vanquishing Dunedin in two games for the title. St. Lucie received key contributions from two of the Mets' key 2022 draft picks. First-round catcher Kevin Parada went 6-for-15 with three runs and five RBIs in four playoff games, while second-round righthander Blade Tidwell tossed 9.2 scoreless innings with 13 strikeouts and two walks in his two starts.

MOST VALUABLE PLAYER: In a typically pitcher-friendly league, Mets outfielder Omar De Los Santos' .271 average and 16 home runs stood out as one of the best performances of the year. His 117 hits and 198 total bases were the best in the Florida State League, as were his 70 stolen bases.

PITCHER OF THE YEAR: Even with a workload of just 52.1 innings, Palm Beach righthander Tink Hence turned himself into one of the game's top pitching prospects. His electric arsenal and whippy, athletic delivery helped him strike out 81 hitters and walk just 15 in his 16 starts. He was impressive against more advanced competition after the season, when he went to the Arizona Fall League and worked out of the bullpen.

TOP MLB PROSPECT: Yankees outfield prospect Jasson Dominguez followed his professional debut in 2021 with a standout season in 2022 that saw him reach Double-A Somerset as a teenager. Before leaving the FSL, Dominguez hit .265/.373/.440 with nine homers in 75 games. The switch-hitter also showed off in his second straight berth in the Futures Game. On the big stage at Dodger Stadium, Dominguez launched a long home run to center field. The home run traveled 415 feet and left the bat at 107.5 mph. He closed his season in the Arizona Fall League, where he was one of the circuit's youngest players.

Jasson Dominguez

MANAGER OF THE YEAR: Fort Myers manager Brian Meyer guided his Mighty Mussels team to a West Division-best 69 wins and a playoff spot.

FLORIDA STATE LEAGUE ALL-STARS

Pos	Player	Team	AVG	OPS	HR
C	Noah Cardenas	Fort Myers	.261	.834	9
1B	Rainer Nunez	Dunedin	.299	.810	15
2B	Hao Yu Lee	Clearwater	.283	.799	7
3B	William Lugo	St. Lucie	.261	.774	10
SS	Tsung-Che Cheng	Bradenton	.270	.794	6
OF	Omar De Los Santos	St. Lucie	.271	.798	16
OF	Alex Ramirez	St. Lucie	.284	.802	6
OF	Gabriel Martinez	Dunedin	.288	.831	11
DH	Jasson Dominguez	Tampa	.265	.813	9
Pos	**Pitcher**	**Team**	**G**	**ERA**	**SO**
RHP	Tink Hence	Palm Beach	16	1.38	81
LHP	Jaylen Nowlin	Fort Myers	19	3.65	89
RP	Andrew Marrero	Palm Beach	32	1.27	55

OVERALL STANDINGS

East Division	W	L	PCT	GB	Manager	Attendance	Avg	Last Penn
St. Lucie Mets (Mets)	73	56	.566	—	Robbie Robinson	71,213	1,167	2022
Palm Beach Cardinals (Cardinals)	67	61	.523	5.5	Gary Kendall	36,880	605	2017
Jupiter Hammerheads (Marlins)	62	66	.484	10.5	Angel Espada	42,156	669	1991
Daytona Tortugas (Reds)	54	74	.422	18.5	Travis Dawkins	91,156	1,572	2011
West Division	**W**	**L**	**PCT**	**GB**	**Manager**	**Attendance**	**Avg**	**Last Penn**
Fort Myers Mighty Mussels (Twins)	69	59	.539	—	Brian Meyer	86,987	1,582	2018
Bradenton Marauders (Pirates)	67	62	.519	2.5	Jonathan Johnston	56,522	870	2021
Dunedin Blue Jays (Blue Jays)	66	63	.512	3.5	Donnie Murphy	24,402	381	2017
Lakeland Flying Tigers (Tigers)	66	64	.508	4	Andrew Graham	35,855	618	2012
Tampa Tarpons (Yankees)	61	67	.477	8	Rachel Balkovec	46,627	914	2010
Clearwater Threshers (Phillies)	57	71	.445	12	Marty Malloy	151,982	2,412	2007

East: St. Lucie def. Palm Beach 2-0. **West:** Dunedin def. Fort Myers 2-1. **Championship Series:** St. Lucie def. Dunedin 2-0.

MIKE JANES FOUR SEAM IMAGES

CLUB BATTING

	AVG	G	AB	R	H	2B	3B	HR	RBI	BB	SO	SB	OBP	SLG
Dunedin	.244	129	4181	579	1021	206	20	85	513	447	1083	114	.329	.364
Jupiter	.241	129	4169	543	1006	185	32	71	485	479	1229	98	.327	.352
St. Lucie	.239	129	4182	595	998	194	27	132	536	465	1355	145	.325	.393
Fort Myers	.236	128	3925	579	926	196	28	101	490	574	1243	179	.343	.377
Lakeland	.236	130	4032	570	950	207	24	87	501	487	1193	107	.330	.364
Bradenton	.234	129	4073	589	952	174	36	89	520	555	1335	208	.337	.360
Palm Beach	.231	128	4090	525	946	163	26	76	462	487	1231	80	.324	.340
Daytona	.225	128	3982	543	895	187	29	93	461	450	1294	146	.313	.356
Clearwater	.224	128	4067	493	911	156	31	81	439	421	1222	165	.311	.337
Tampa	.224	128	3912	557	875	166	19	114	497	548	1356	200	.328	.363

CLUB PITCHING

	ERA	G	CG	SHO	SV	IP	H	R	ER	HR	BB	SO	AVG
Fort Myers	3.51	128	0	13	34	1060	895	502	413	80	391	1188	.227
Dunedin	3.69	129	0	11	34	1106	919	530	454	106	461	1332	.226
Palm Beach	3.71	128	0	5	40	1103	1000	543	455	78	491	1221	.241
St. Lucie	3.92	129	1	6	37	1109	946	540	483	72	541	1345	.230
Tampa	3.96	128	1	7	23	1057	890	547	465	99	486	1295	.226
Clearwater	4.00	128	0	8	27	1091	981	579	485	102	494	1267	.241
Bradenton	4.04	129	0	10	32	1099	965	590	493	96	536	1176	.235
Jupiter	4.08	129	1	12	34	1097	943	581	497	88	502	1224	.230
Lakeland	4.11	130	1	8	41	1074	1002	600	490	108	460	1258	.243
Daytona	4.17	128	0	11	23	1069	939	561	495	100	551	1235	.235

CLUB FIELDING

	PCT	PO	A	E	DP
Palm Beach	.977	3309	1112	103	110
Daytona	.976	3208	1058	103	104
Dunedin	.975	3318	1082	113	86
Clearwater	.974	3272	1109	119	90
St. Lucie	.973	3326	1018	122	103
Fort Myers	.972	3180	1009	119	93
Jupiter	.971	3292	1135	134	102
Tampa	.970	3172	980	127	80
Bradenton	.969	3296	1118	139	105
Lakeland	.962	3222	1066	170	82

INDIVIDUAL BATTING

Batter, Club	AVG	G	AB	R	H	2B	3B	HR	RBI	BB	SO	SB
Rainer Nunez, Dunedin	.299	93	361	50	108	19	1	15	63	14	82	0
Jase Bowen, Bradenton	.278	98	367	60	102	17	2	14	66	38	110	20
Omar De Los Santos, St. Lucie	.271	111	431	75	117	23	5	16	62	35	151	70
Tsung-Che Cheng, Bradenton	.270	104	385	79	104	25	7	6	52	63	95	33
Izaac Pacheco, Lakeland	.267	88	330	54	88	21	2	8	39	38	80	12
Estiven Machado, Dunedin	.263	90	339	45	89	19	3	1	32	38	97	6
Noah Cardenas, Fort Myers	.261	99	310	42	81	18	1	9	43	73	70	11
William Lugo, St. Lucie	.261	84	314	47	82	18	2	10	45	37	90	0
Roberto Campos, Lakeland	.258	112	403	52	104	26	5	5	50	40	97	7
Justice Bigbie, Lakeland	.258	91	330	37	85	17	5	2	41	28	89	4

INDIVIDUAL PITCHING

Pitcher, Club	W	L	ERA	G	GS	CG	SV	IP	H	R	ER	BB	SO
Trent Baker, Palm Beach	9	7	3.14	25	25	0	0	123	114	53	43	48	138

DEPARTMENT LEADERS

BATTING

OBP	Noah Cardenas, Fort Myers	.421
SLG	Rainer Nunez, Dunedin	.482
OPS	Noah Cardenas, Fort Myers	.834
R	Tsung-Che Cheng, Bradenton	79
H	Omar De Los Santos, St. Lucie	117
TB	Omar De Los Santos, St. Lucie	198
XBH	Manuel Sequera, Lakeland	48
2B	Manuel Sequera, Lakeland	28
3B	Tsung-Che Cheng, Bradenton	7
HR	Carlos Dominguez, St. Lucie	20
RBI	Jase Bowen, Bradenton	66
SAC	Erick Brito, Clearwater	8
BB	Anthony Garcia, Tampa	83
HBP	Cristian Santana, Lakeland	18
SO	Carlos Dominguez, St. Lucie	173
SB	Omar De Los Santos, St. Lucie	70
CS	Omar De Los Santos, St. Lucie	15

FIELDING

C PCT	Wyatt Hendrie, Bradenton	.990
PO	Antonio Gomez, Tampa	670
A	Arturo De Freitas, Clearwater	78
DP	Hayden Jones, Daytona	6
E	Antonio Gomez, Tampa	13
CS	Arturo De Freitas, Clearwater	44
SB	Antonio Gomez, Tampa	93
PB	Wyatt Hendrie, Bradenton	13
1B PCT	Zach Zubia, Jupiter	.990
PO	Zach Zubia, Jupiter	568
A	Rainer Nunez, Dunedin	40
DP	Zach Zubia, Jupiter	53
E	Anthony Garcia, Tampa	16
2B PCT	Mikey Perez, Fort Myers	.970
PO	Javier Sanoja, Jupiter	87
A	Javier Sanoja, Jupiter	118
DP	Javier Sanoja, Jupiter	36
E	2 tied	9
3B PCT	Izaac Pacheco, Lakeland	.947
PO	Keoni Cavaco, Fort Myers	59
A	Marcos Cabrera, Tampa	140
DP	Marcos Cabrera, Tampa	18
E	Keoni Cavaco, Fort Myers	21
SS PCT	Noah Miller, Fort Myers	.980
PO	Jeremy Rivas, Palm Beach	151
A	Jeremy Rivas, Palm Beach	296
DP	Jeremy Rivas, Palm Beach	63
E	Alexander Vargas, Tampa	20
OF PCT	Brady Allen, Jupiter	1.000
PO	Carlos Dominguez, St. Lucie	147
A	Leandro Pineda, Clearwater	12
DP	Carlos Dominguez, St. Lucie	3
E	Kala'i Rosario, Fort Myers	7

PITCHING

G	Danny Watson, Tampa	38
GS	Trent Baker, Palm Beach	25
GF	Jack Neely, Tampa Tarpons	24
SV	Andrew Marrero, Palm Beach	11
W	Trent Baker, Palm Beach	9
L	4 tied	8
IP	Trent Baker, Palm Beach	123
H	Trent Baker, Palm Beach	114
R	Gabe Bierman, Jupiter	55
R	Tyrone Yulie, Tampa	55
ER	Gabe Bierman, Jupiter	51
HB	Juan Carela, Tampa	18
BB	Sandro Bargallo, Jupiter	70
SO	Trent Baker, Palm Beach	138
SO/9	Trent Baker, Palm Beach	10.1
BB/9	Trent Baker, Palm Beach	3.5
WP	Hunter Parks, Daytona	19
BK	4 tied	5
HRA	Richard Fitts, Tampa	13
HRA	Jose Franco, Daytona	13
BAA	Trent Baker, Palm Beach	.241

ARIZONA COMPLEX LEAGUE

CHAMPION: The Giants were one of a handful of organizations to field two Arizona Complex League teams. Their Giants Black squad was the hottest thing in the desert, winning a league-best 37 games and ultimately the championship. To claim the title, they topped the Rockies. The Giants dominated with an extremely excellent pitching staff, which worked to a league-best 2.82 ERA and tossed nine shutouts.

MOST VALUABLE PLAYER: Brewers outfielder Jace Avina crushed ACL competition before a promotion to Low-A Carolina. The 19-year-old was selected out of a Nevada high school in the 14th round of the 2021 draft but did not debut until 2022. Once the ACL season began in June, Avina showed a combination of power and speed with the ability to play center field as well. He left the league as its leader in slugging percentage (.630) and OPS (1.066) and was the only player in the league with 10 home runs.

PITCHER OF THE YEAR: Nomar Medina was part of the staff that fueled ACL Giants Black to the championship. The 19-year-old lefthander signed out of the Dominican Republic in September 2020 and has spent the past two seasons in the ACL. In 2022, he spun a league-best 65 innings and struck out 70 against just 16 walks. None of Medina's individual pitches jump off the page—his four-seamer averaged 88 mph and scraped 90—but his command was enough to overwhelm ACL hitters.

TOP MLB PROSPECT: The two best prospects in league, as gathered through conversations with scouts, were Guardians shortstop Angel Genao and Padres righthander Jarlin Susana, who was dealt to the Nationals as part of the blockbuster package used by San Diego to acquire Juan Soto.

Genao has the potential to provide value on both sides of the ball. He hit .322/.394/.416 before a late-season promotion to Low-A Lynchburg. Evaluators were enthused by the advanced barrel control and sneaky power shown by the switch-hitting Genao, who also has the quick feet, smooth actions and strong arm to stick at shortstop.

Susana's game is centered around a powerful arsenal that comes from a massive 6-foot-6 frame. His four-seam fastball that averaged around 98 mph and peaked at 103. He backed it up with a nasty slider and developing changeup, as well as body control that belies his size and youth.

MANAGER OF THE YEAR: Jose Montilla piloted the ACL Giants Black to the most wins in the league, and ultimately a championship win against the Rockies.

Jace Avina

BILL MITCHELL

ARIZONA COMPLEX LEAGUE ALL-STARS

Pos	Player	Team	AVG	OPS	HR
C	Thayron Liranzo	Dodgers	.236	.825	8
1B	Maick Collado	Guardians	.310	.854	2
2B	Pedro Ramirez	Cubs	.329	.940	9
3B	Gleider Figuereo	Rangers	.280	.979	9
SS	Jadher Areinamo	Brewers	.323	.889	1
OF	Jace Avina	Brewers	.294	1.067	10
OF	JoJo Blackmon	Rangers	.265	.920	8
OF	Jesus Bugarin	Rockies	.337	.896	4
DH	P.J. Hilson	Giants	.295	.944	9
Pos	**Pitcher**	**Team**	**G**	**ERA**	**SO**
RHP	Wardquelin Vasquez	Guardians	9	2.28	47
LHP	Nomar Medina	Giants	14	2.22	70
RP	Jenrry Gonzalez	Angels	15	0.89	32

OVERALL STANDINGS

Central Division	W	L	PCT	GB	Manager
ACL Reds	32	19	.627	—	Julio Morillo
ACL Brewers Gold	32	21	.604	1	David Tufo
ACL Guardians	28	24	.538	4.5	Jordan Smith
ACL Cubs	25	29	.463	8.5	Edgar Perez
ACL Athletics	20	34	.370	13.5	Adam Rosales
ACL Brewers Blue	19	34	.358	14	Rafael Neda

East Division	W	L	PCT	GB	Manager
ACL Giants Black	37	17	.685	—	Jose Montilla
ACL Rockies	34	19	.642	2.5	Fred Ocasio
ACL Angels	33	21	.611	4	Hector De La Cruz
ACL D-backs Black	23	32	.418	14.5	Rolando Arnedo
ACL D-backs Red	20	34	.370	17	Dee Garner
ACL Giants Orange	18	37	.327	19.5	Greg Tagert

West Division	W	L	PCT	GB	Manager
ACL Rangers	32	22	.593	—	Carlos Maldonado
ACL Padres	29	25	.537	3	Lukas Ray
ACL White Sox	26	28	.481	6	Patrick Leyland
ACL Mariners	26	29	.473	6.5	Luis Caballero
ACL Dodgers	25	29	.463	7	Jair Fernandez
ACL Royals	25	30	.455	7.5	Omar Ramirez

ACL Championship: ACL Giants Black def. ACL Rockies.

CLUB BATTING

	AVG	G	AB	R	H	2B	3B	HR	RBI	BB	SO	SB	OBP	SLG
ACL Rangers	.268	54	1822	335	488	102	21	47	276	215	596	96	.359	.424
ACL Angels	.265	54	1704	286	452	80	20	26	238	150	460	40	.333	.381
ACL Rockies	.254	53	1611	250	409	85	17	40	202	178	491	39	.341	.402
ACL Brewers Gold	.253	53	1594	292	404	80	13	22	237	227	459	78	.357	.361
ACL Reds	.252	51	1475	285	372	80	14	37	223	240	472	88	.373	.401
ACL D-backs Red	.252	54	1561	217	393	68	18	16	185	158	520	51	.333	.349
ACL Royals	.251	55	1739	258	437	99	23	43	213	183	552	78	.332	.409
ACL Padres	.250	54	1595	269	399	78	21	34	246	218	499	56	.350	.389
ACL Mariners	.248	55	1655	235	410	78	15	28	188	201	509	84	.342	.364
ACL Brewers Blue	.245	53	1601	276	392	81	10	39	229	218	511	62	.352	.381
ACL Cubs	.244	54	1623	262	396	66	17	29	210	217	485	72	.343	.359
ACL Guardians	.243	52	1653	277	402	55	15	29	217	258	475	78	.360	.347
ACL Giants Black	.243	54	1519	269	369	81	14	42	225	197	552	31	.342	.398
ACL D-backs Black	.236	55	1531	207	362	70	21	10	164	190	465	48	.326	.329
ACL White Sox	.236	54	1764	239	417	66	12	43	206	183	619	40	.316	.361
ACL Dodgers	.230	54	1760	267	405	95	9	47	236	196	560	57	.320	.374
ACL Athletics	.227	54	1566	245	355	67	17	24	192	203	539	45	.327	.337
ACL Giants Orange	.225	55	1510	181	340	55	11	22	149	150	519	30	.308	.320

CLUB PITCHING

	ERA	G	CG	SHO	SV	IP	H	R	ER	HR	BB	SO	AVG
ACL Giants Black	2.82	54	1	9	15	405	346	158	127	18	138	518	.230
ACL Rockies	3.24	53	0	5	16	428	393	188	154	19	110	521	.240
ACL Mariners	3.64	55	0	6	11	432	354	234	175	30	204	537	.221
ACL Angels	3.89	54	0	6	9	442	385	233	191	21	198	553	.230
ACL Giants Orange	3.95	55	0	2	9	397	407	229	174	29	147	512	.262
ACL Reds	4.19	51	0	1	10	396	365	240	184	26	184	501	.240
ACL Guardians	4.33	52	0	1	12	442	412	273	213	36	202	480	.240
ACL Dodgers	4.40	54	0	5	10	459	418	257	224	44	182	577	.240
ACL Royals	4.54	55	0	2	14	452	434	273	228	45	155	550	.243
ACL Rangers	4.60	54	0	2	16	472	488	289	241	39	208	611	.262
ACL White Sox	4.83	54	0	4	11	459	452	279	246	45	204	500	.258
ACL Cubs	5.07	54	0	2	6	419	318	273	236	23	333	547	.211
ACL Padres	5.07	54	0	3	9	419	376	281	236	46	236	519	.239
ACL Athletics	5.12	54	0	1	10	408	420	291	232	27	200	455	.263
ACL D-backs Red	5.21	54	0	1	4	399	409	273	231	29	205	478	.265
ACL Brewers Gold	5.23	53	0	3	12	413	386	294	240	36	254	480	.246
ACL D-backs Black	5.23	55	2	4	10	403	426	292	234	35	193	467	.271
ACL Brewers Blue	5.40	53	0	3	4	405	413	294	243	30	229	477	.262

CLUB FIELDING

	PCT	PO	A	E	DP
ACL Dodgers	.973	1376	452	51	36
ACL Giants Black	.970	1214	384	49	34
ACL Padres	.970	1256	420	52	32
ACL Rockies	.970	1284	448	54	27
ACL D-backs Red	.967	1196	411	54	49
ACL White Sox	.967	1376	475	63	40
ACL Angels	.967	1327	441	61	43
ACL Rangers	.964	1416	434	69	35
ACL Cubs	.962	1258	422	66	40
ACL D-backs Black	.959	1208	424	70	33
ACL Brewers Gold	.958	1239	421	72	45
ACL Giants Orange	.958	1190	396	69	34
ACL Guardians	.958	1327	427	77	22
ACL Mariners	.957	1297	402	77	34
ACL Athletics	.954	1223	453	80	37
ACL Royals	.954	1357	455	88	29
ACL Brewers Blue	.949	1216	414	87	45
ACL Reds	.946	1187	366	89	35

INDIVIDUAL BATTING

Batter, Club	AVG	G	AB	R	H	2B	3B	HR	RBI	BB	SO	SB
Jesus Bugarin, ACL Rockies	.337	51	184	34	62	9	5	4	24	15	50	7
Jorge Ruiz, ACL Angels	.335	53	203	36	68	12	2	0	23	12	20	8
Danyer Cueva, ACL Rangers	.330	44	176	39	58	10	1	5	31	10	40	3
Yeison Morrobel, ACL Rangers	.329	41	152	31	50	13	1	3	21	17	34	5
Pedro Ramirez, ACL Cubs	.329	43	146	26	48	9	5	4	14	17	26	11
Jadher Areinamo, ACL Brewers Gold	.323	34	127	31	41	10	3	1	21	19	19	4
Angel Genao, ACL Guardians	.322	38	149	22	48	6	1	2	18	16	40	6
Leonardo Balcazar, ACL Reds	.322	42	143	25	46	6	2	4	26	18	42	13
Dario Borrero, ACL White Sox	.313	46	166	12	52	8	1	0	13	7	29	1
Maick Collado, ACL Guardians	.310	35	126	20	39	9	0	2	15	24	24	2

INDIVIDUAL PITCHING

Pitcher, Club	W	L	ERA	G	GS	CG	SV	IP	H	R	ER	BB	SO
Nomar Medina, ACL Giants Black	6	0	2.22	14	12	1	1	65	58	20	16	16	70
Mauricio Veliz, ACL Royals	2	3	2.36	13	5	0	1	46	32	19	12	12	37
Ivan Oviedo, ACL Rangers	3	1	3.02	11	5	0	1	45	40	21	15	12	50
Alberto Pacheco, ACL Rockies	5	4	3.13	11	8	0	0	46	39	22	16	15	57
Jorge Marcheco, ACL Angels	5	2	3.20	11	8	0	0	51	42	21	18	12	76
Arielbi Gonzalez, ACL Brewers Blue	1	1	3.22	11	6	0	0	45	38	18	16	14	47
Miguel Mora, ACL Giants Black	4	4	3.29	13	12	0	0	55	43	25	20	26	78
Mikell Manzano, ACL Giants Orange	3	3	3.93	14	11	0	0	55	56	25	24	17	81
Gerson Calzadilla, ACL Brewers Gold	4	2	3.94	11	8	0	0	48	46	23	21	19	38
Dylan Burns, ACL White Sox	3	3	3.97	12	11	0	0	59	59	28	26	19	69

DEPARTMENT LEADERS

BATTING

OBP	Juan Alonso, ACL Dodgers	.477
SLG	Jace Avina, ACL Brewers Blue	.630
OPS	Jace Avina, ACL Brewers Blue	1.066
R	P.J. Hilson, ACL Giants Black	44
H	Jorge Ruiz, ACL Angels	68
TB	P.J. Hilson, ACL Giants Black	103
XBH	Rayne Doncon, ACL Dodgers	26
XBH	P.J. Hilson, ACL Giants Black	26
2B	Rayne Doncon, ACL Dodgers	16
3B	6 tied	5
HR	Jace Avina, ACL Brewers Blue	10
RBI	Rayne Doncon, ACL Dodgers	38
SAC	Johan Macias, ACL Angels	4
BB	Juan Alonso, ACL Dodgers	40
HBP	Angel Contreras, ACL Guardians	17
SO	Wilman Diaz, ACL Dodgers	80
SB	Carlos Jorge, ACL Reds	27
CS	2 tied	8

FIELDING

C PCT	Kenny Castillo, ACL D-Backs Red	.993
PO	Onil Perez, ACL Giants Black	426
A	Onil Perez, ACL Giants Black	39
DP	Kenny Castillo, ACL D-Backs Red	6
E	Jason Ollarve, 2 teams	9
CS	Blayberg Diaz, ACL Brewers Gold	20
SB	Luis Pineda, ACL White Sox	35
PB	Blayberg Diaz, ACL Brewers Gold	12
1B PCT	Jesus Parra, ACL Brewers Gold	.991
PO	Dario Borrero, ACL White Sox	288
A	3 tied	14
DP	Jesus Parra, ACL Brewers Gold	28
E	Wencer Inirio, ACL Reds	9
2B PCT	Dilan Rosario, ACL Giants Black	.954
PO	Carlos Jorge, ACL Reds	54
A	Ronny Polanco, ACL D-Backs Black	86
DP	Johan Macias, ACL Angels	17
E	2 tied	10
3B PCT	Derwin Laya, ACL Giants Orange	.943
PO	Derwin Laya, ACL Giants Orange	27
A	Victor Quezada, ACL White Sox	62
DP	Gavin Conticello, ACL D-Backs Red	11
E	2 tied	11
SS PCT	Diego Velasquez, ACL Giants Orange	.960
PO	Layant Tapia, ACL White Sox	63
A	Layant Tapia, ACL White Sox	109
DP	Layant Tapia, ACL White Sox	28
E	Layant Tapia, ACL White Sox	15
OF PCT	Alvaro Aguero, ACL White Sox	.985
PO	Jesus Bugarin, ACL Rockies	91
A	P.J. Hilson, ACL Giants Black	8
DP	Ariel Almonte, ACL Reds	3
E	2 tied	5

PITCHING

G	Samuel Dario, ACL Brewers Blue	22
GS	Nomar Medina, ACL Giants Black	12
GS	Miguel Mora, ACL Giants Black	12
GF	Osiris Santana, ACL Royals	17
SV	Francis Rivera, ACL Rockies	7
W	3 tied	6
L	Freddery Paulino, ACL Giants Orange	9
IP	Nomar Medina, ACL Giants Black	65
H	Freddery Paulino, ACL Giants Orange	68
R	Freddery Paulino, ACL Giants Orange	45
ER	Freddery Paulino, ACL Giants Orange	39
HB	3 tied	10
BB	Henrison Mota, ACL Brewers Gold	39
BB	Tommy Ventimiglia, ACL Guardians	39
SO	Mikell Manzano, ACL Giants Orange	81
SO/9	Jorge Marcheco, ACL Angels	13.5
BB/9	Jorge Marcheco, ACL Angels	2.1
WP	Sarlin Polanco, ACL D-backs Black	18
BK	5 tied	4
HRA	Javier Chacon, ACL Padres	7
HRA	Abdiel Medina, ACL Mariners	7
HRA	Riley Yeatman, ACL Padres	7
BAA	Mauricio Veliz, ACL Royals	.193

FLORIDA COMPLEX LEAGUE

CHAMPION: The Yankees claimed two minor league championships in 2022. The first came when their FCL club topped their Rays rivals in three games. Yankees starter Justin Lange gave up two runs in his 2.1 innings, but a quartet of relievers held the Rays to only one more run the rest of the way. The Baby Bombers' offense was provided in part by a pair of RBIs from third baseman Brenny Escanio and another RBI from center fielder Nelson Medina.

MOST VALUABLE PLAYER: Twins catcher Ricardo Olivar was one of the older players in the league at 20 years old, and he produced as such. Signed out of Venezuela in 2019, Olivar finished second on the circuit with a .349 average and led the FCL with a .442 on-base percentage and .605 slugging. Olivar got a three-game cameo with Low-A Fort Myers toward the end of the season and then stuck through the playoffs.

PITCHER OF THE YEAR: The FCL Mets had a number of intriguing prospects pass through Port St. Lucie during the season, but righthander Jawilme Ramirez stuck around long enough to rack up enough numbers to earn this honor. The 20-year-old, who signed out of the Dominican Republic in 2019, baffled hitters all summer long, finishing with a 1-0, 0.84 mark and 40 strikeouts against just six walks in 43 innings. He reached Low-A St. Lucie for a pair of appearances for the eventual FSL champions.

TOP MLB PROSPECT: Though there were plenty of quality players who made their way through the FCL, none shone brighter than Red Sox center fielder Miguel Bleis, who wowed scouts with the makings of a true five-tool set. The 18-year-old showed hitting ability, on-base skills and power while also hinting at a true plus defender in center field with a plus throwing arm as well. Behind Bleis were two pitchers. Pirates righthander Bubba Chandler has the raw ingredients to dominate, including a potentially special fastball, but will need the command and control to take a step forward. Yankees righthander Luis Serna showed uncommon pitchability and poise for an 18-year-old, and impressed scouts with a nasty changeup that could become at least plus.

MANAGER OF THE YEAR: Sergio Santos guided the FCL Yankees for most of the season but also was trusted enough to fill in at other affiliates when the need arose. His club was the FCL's best hitting group, finishing with league-best marks in batting average (.261) and home runs (59). The latter figure was 20 more than the second-place team.

Ricardo Olivar

MIKE JANES/FOUR SEAM IMAGES

FLORIDA COMPLEX LEAGUE ALL-STARS

Pos	Player	Team	AVG	OPS	HR
C	Ricardo Olivar	Twins	.349	1.047	5
1B	Jesus Rodriguez	Yankees	.348	1.010	4
2B	Jared Serna	Yankees	.302	.965	6
3B	Yiddi Cappe	Marlins	.305	.881	6
SS	Junior Caminero	Rays	.326	.895	5
OF	Miguel Bleis	Red Sox	.301	.895	5
OF	Roismar Quintana	Nationals	.289	.781	5
OF	Felix Negueis	Yankees	.287	.962	4
DH	Agustin Ramirez	Yankees	.304	.892	6
Pos	**Pitcher**	**Team**	**G**	**ERA**	**SO**
RHP	Jawilme Ramirez	Mets	11	0.84	40
LHP	Juan Rojas	Orioles	11	2.79	50
RP	Andri Tavarez	Rays	16	0.75	29

OVERALL STANDINGS

East Division	W	L	PCT	GB	Manager
FCL Mets	33	22	.600	—	Endy Chavez
FCL Nationals	33	22	.600	—	Luis Ordaz
FCL Marlins	31	24	.564	2	Luis Dorante
FCL Astros Orange	26	28	.481	6.5	Carlos Lugo
FCL Cardinals	25	29	.463	7.5	Roberto Espinoza
FCL Astros Blue	15	38	.283	17	Ricky Rivera
North Division	**W**	**L**	**PCT**	**GB**	**Manager**
FCL Yankees	38	17	.691	—	Sergio Santos
FCL Blue Jays	27	27	.500	10.5	Jose Mayorga
FCL Phillies	26	29	.473	12	Chris Adamson
FCL Tigers	18	37	.327	20	Mike Alvarez
South Division	**W**	**L**	**PCT**	**GB**	**Manager(s)**
FCL Rays	39	16	.709	—	Rafael Valenzuela
FCL Red Sox	35	20	.636	4	Jimmy Gonzalez/ Tom Kotchman
FCL Pirates	30	25	.545	9	Jose Mosquera
FCL Twins	25	30	.455	14	Seth Feldman
FCL Braves	20	35	.364	19	Cody Gabella
FCL Orioles	16	39	.291	23	Christian Frias/ Matt Packer

FCL Championship: FCL Yankees def. FCL Rays.

CLUB BATTING

	AVG	G	AB	R	H	2B	3B	HR	RBI	BB	SO	SB	OBP	SLG
FCL Yankees	.261	55	1731	367	452	107	16	59	318	301	474	104	.383	.444
FCL Rays	.257	55	1728	344	444	73	19	32	292	269	498	111	.367	.377
FCL Nationals	.245	55	1713	279	419	75	8	27	221	213	458	25	.340	.345
FCL Phillies	.244	55	1736	267	424	82	14	27	235	222	460	75	.343	.354
FCL Red Sox	.244	55	1754	291	428	111	20	18	247	271	497	95	.356	.361
FCL Astros Orange	.242	54	1593	276	386	66	13	29	224	202	511	117	.347	.355
FCL Marlins	.237	55	1774	269	420	94	19	31	229	216	482	66	.330	.364
FCL Tigers	.236	55	1749	251	412	92	11	36	212	220	510	55	.335	.362
FCL Pirates	.233	55	1664	282	387	73	17	26	224	260	457	59	.353	.344
FCL Astros Blue	.223	53	1508	193	337	58	8	18	146	214	405	68	.339	.308
FCL Blue Jays	.221	55	1675	244	370	82	21	26	197	227	516	89	.331	.341
FCL Orioles	.219	55	1659	236	364	74	6	25	200	284	502	62	.347	.316
FCL Twins	.219	55	1719	254	376	88	14	37	221	259	571	50	.334	.351
FCL Mets	.217	55	1680	260	365	70	21	39	213	239	511	76	.332	.354
FCL Braves	.211	55	1638	224	346	61	14	21	185	228	517	70	.322	.304
FCL Cardinals	.195	54	1637	213	320	64	15	26	170	215	604	66	.304	.301

CLUB PITCHING

	ERA	G	CG	SHO	SV	IP	H	R	ER	HR	BB	SO	AVG
FCL Mets	3.27	55	0	6	15	451	353	219	164	20	200	544	.213
FCL Rays	3.32	55	0	6	17	461	337	200	170	16	241	514	.204
FCL Nationals	3.58	55	0	3	15	452	420	244	180	26	188	483	.243
FCL Red Sox	3.72	55	0	7	18	472	376	226	195	30	215	531	.217
FCL Marlins	3.74	55	0	10	16	467	362	239	194	26	194	492	.211
FCL Cardinals	3.92	54	0	2	13	450	419	254	196	27	215	513	.243
FCL Yankees	3.92	55	0	5	14	462	406	247	201	28	210	580	.235
FCL Astros Orange	4.10	54	1	2	11	422	335	241	192	29	235	482	.216
FCL Twins	4.20	55	0	3	11	463	424	273	216	27	195	540	.237
FCL Pirates	4.30	55	0	6	11	452	366	261	216	21	313	519	.221
FCL Blue Jays	4.50	55	0	2	18	460	417	266	230	49	210	489	.243
FCL Phillies	4.60	55	0	3	13	456	402	264	233	28	237	461	.237
FCL Astros Blue	4.98	53	0	1	8	403	358	294	223	42	267	457	.235
FCL Braves	5.54	55	0	3	13	442	388	303	272	30	254	477	.236
FCL Tigers	6.01	55	0	2	11	461	433	352	308	43	313	430	.248
FCL Orioles	6.55	55	0	1	10	444	454	369	323	35	353	461	.270

CLUB FIELDING

	PCT	PO	A	E	DP
FCL Phillies	.974	1369	455	49	33
FCL Red Sox	.974	1417	481	51	47
FCL Rays	.972	1382	483	54	52
FCL Blue Jays	.970	1383	428	56	47
FCL Pirates	.968	1356	466	60	43
FCL Marlins	.967	1403	477	64	41
FCL Yankees	.964	1385	464	69	45
FCL Orioles	.964	1332	468	68	45
FCL Astros Orange	.963	1265	450	66	39
FCL Braves	.962	1325	443	70	26
FCL Mets	.960	1353	433	74	36
FCL Twins	.959	1390	401	77	28
FCL Nationals	.959	1356	455	78	32
FCL Tigers	.958	1383	504	83	53
FCL Astros Blue	.955	1209	376	75	32
FCL Cardinals	.950	1351	454	95	39

INDIVIDUAL BATTING

Batter, Club	AVG	G	AB	R	H	2B	3B	HR	RBI	BB	SO	SB
Jesus Castillo, FCL Pirates	.352	42	128	23	45	4	0	0	21	17	18	9
Ricardo Olivar, FCL Twins	.349	40	129	16	45	12	3	5	23	18	33	5
Jesus Rodriguez, FCL Yankees	.348	37	132	29	46	10	4	4	24	15	14	8
Junior Caminero, FCL Rays	.326	36	132	18	43	5	1	5	31	15	21	7
Agustin Ramirez, FCL Yankees	.304	44	168	34	51	14	1	6	51	23	31	13
Jared Serna, FCL Yankees	.302	37	129	40	39	9	1	6	28	25	24	16
Miguel Bleis, FCL Red Sox	.301	40	153	28	46	14	4	5	27	10	45	18
Roismar Quintana, FCL Nationals	.289	50	180	41	52	10	1	5	28	9	46	3
Jair Casanova, FCL Braves	.289	45	149	18	43	5	1	1	16	24	34	0
Samuel Basallo, FCL Orioles	.278	43	158	22	44	5	0	6	32	15	37	1

INDIVIDUAL PITCHING

Pitcher, Club	W	L	ERA	G	GS	CG	SV	IP	H	R	ER	BB	SO
Cristofer Mezquita, FCL Astros Orange	3	1	2.60	12	5	1	0	52	46	17	15	24	49

DEPARTMENT LEADERS

BATTING

OBP	Ricardo Olivar, FCL Twins	.442
SLG	Ricardo Olivar, FCL Twins	.605
OPS	Ricardo Olivar, FCL Twins	1.047
R	Armando Cruz, FCL Nationals	41
R	Roismar Quintana, FCL Nationals	41
H	Armando Cruz, FCL Nationals	57
TB	Agustin Ramirez, FCL Yankees	85
XBH	Miguel Bleis, FCL Red Sox	23
2B	Miguel Bleis, FCL Red Sox	14
2B	Agustin Ramirez, FCL Yankees	14
3B	Jordan McCants, FCL Marlins	5
HR	9 tied	6
RBI	Agustin Ramirez, FCL Yankees	51
SAC	Armando Cruz, FCL Nationals	4
BB	Daury Arias, FCL Yankees	34
HBP	Frank Perez, FCL Astros Orange	14
SO	Noah Williamson, FCL Marlins	71
SB	Rolando Espinosa, FCL Astros Orange	32
CS	2 tied	9

FIELDING

C PCT	2 tied	.996
PO	Agustin Ramirez, FCL Yankees	339
A	Antonio Barranca, FCL Braves	34
DP	2 tied	4
E	Agustin Ramirez, FCL Yankees	9
CS	Agustin Ramirez, FCL Yankees	21
SB	Ricardo Toro, FCL Astros Blue	50
PB	Antonio Barranca, FCL Braves	15
1B PCT	Ricardo Balogh, FCL Astros Orange	.995
PO	Daury Del Rosario, FCL Rays	234
A	Cristian Feliz, FCL Blue Jays	15
DP	Cristian Feliz, FCL Blue Jays	26
E	2 tied	5
2B PCT	Jared Serna, FCL Yankees	.981
PO	Jordan McCants, FCL Marlins	62
A	Jordan McCants, FCL Marlins	76
DP	3 tied	19
E	2 tied	8
3B PCT	Yohander Martinez, FCL Astros Blue	.955
PO	Anderson De Los Santos, FCL Braves	28
A	Angel Geraldo, FCL Nationals	56
DP	Anderson De Los Santos, FCL Orioles	7
E	2 tied	11
SS PCT	Luis Ravelo, FCL Red Sox	.975
PO	Armando Cruz, FCL Nationals	70
A	Armando Cruz, FCL Nationals	122
DP	Armando Cruz, FCL Nationals	20
E	Armando Cruz, FCL Nationals	16
OF PCT	2 tied	1.000
PO	Miguel Bleis, FCL Red Sox	92
A	Roilan Machandy, 2 teams	6
DP	Marcos De La Rosa, FCL Blue Jays	2
E	Adonis Giron, FCL Astros Blue	5

PITCHING

G	Edwin Nunez, FCL Cardinals	22
GS	Justin Lange, FCL Yankees	12
GF	Ian Foggo, FCL Astros Orange	18
SV	Ian Foggo, FCL Astros Orange	6
W	Francis Hernandez, FCL Red Sox	9
L	5 tied	5
IP	Jedixson Paez, FCL Red Sox	57
H	Rayner Castillo, FCL Tigers	56
R	Jhoniel Serrano, FCL Marlins	40
ER	Rayner Castillo, FCL Tigers	38
HB	Jose Ramirez, FCL Red Sox	16
BB	Jose Andujar, FCL Astros Orange	35
SO	Juan Nunez, FCL Orioles	56
SO	Luis Serna, FCL Yankees	56
SO/9	Reimy Beltre, FCL Astros Orange	10.8
BB/9	Jedixson Paez, FCL Red Sox	2.1
WP	3 tied	15
BK	Adam Shoemaker, FCL Braves	4
BK	Christopher Soriano, FCL Phillies	4
HRA	Luis Vega, FCL Astros Blue	10
BAA	Reimy Beltre, FCL Astros Orange	.172

ALL-STAR FUTURES GAME

BY GEOFF PONTES

With two teams made up of the best prospects in the American and National leagues, there were plenty of fireworks in the 23rd Futures Game.

We single out the prospects whose tools shined brightest in this year's Futures Game.

BEST PLAYER: Shea Langeliers, C

Acquired by Oakland in the Matt Olson trade last offseason, Langeliers had a standout game on both sides of the ball to earn MVP honors at this Futures Game. The 24-year-old threw out Corbin Carroll trying to steal third base and also homered off of a Jared Shuster changeup. The home run was 103 mph off the bat and traveled 392 feet.

BEST HITTER: Yainer Diaz, C

While Dustin Harris and Zac Veen also had two hits, both of Diaz's were struck at greater than 100 mph. The 23-year-old Astros prospect and Oscar Colas were the only two players to put two balls in play at greater than 100 mph.

BEST POWER: Matt Wallner, OF

Wallner takes this award in a landslide. His home run was hit 115.8 mph and traveled 380 feet. The 24-year-old Twins prospect had one of the most impressive BPs, parking eight balls into the seats at Dodger Stadium.

BEST ARM: Masyn Winn, SS

Winn has one of the strongest infield arms in professional baseball. The 20-year-old Cardinals prospect was also a prospect as a pitcher in high school, and it's easy to see why. Winn set the record for the hardest infield throw of the Statcast era, uncorking a ball at 100.5 mph for a 6-3 putout.

BEST PITCHER: Emerson Hancock, RHP

The 2020 first-rounder out of Georgia came on in the sixth inning and struck out the side on 17 pitches. The 23-year-old Mariners prospect topped out at 96 mph and missed bats with his sinker and changeup.

BEST FASTBALL: Mike Burrows, RHP

The 22-year-old righthander generated three whiffs on his fastball—more whiffs than all but two pitchers had in the game. Burrows topped out at 96 mph and was able to generate swings-and-misses with his elevated fastball.

BEST BREAKING BALL: Mike Burrows, RHP

The Pirates righthander's breaking ball averaged a spin rate of 2,850 rpm and peaked and 2,938 rpm, and used the pitch to get two swings and misses.

FUTURES GAME BOX SCORE

AMERICAN LEAGUE 6, NATIONAL LEAGUE 4
JULY 16 IN LOS ANGELES

NL	AB	R	H	RBI	AL	AB	R	H	RBI
Henderson, 3B	1	2	0	0	Carroll, CF	1	0	1	0
Colas, CF	2	0	1	0	Crow-Armstrong, CF	2	1	1	0
Dominguez, CF	2	1	1	2	Hassell, RF	2	0	1	1
Rafaela, SS	2	0	0	0	Wiemer, RF	1	0	0	1
Harris, 1B	3	1	2	1	Alvarez, DH	1	0	0	0
Volpe, SS	2	0	0	0	Chourio, DH	2	0	0	0
Steer, 2B	2	0	0	0	Walker, 3B	2	0	0	0
Wallner, RF	2	1	1	2	De La Cruz, 3B	1	0	0	0
Clarke, RF	1	0	0	0	Vargas, 2B	1	1	0	0
Diaz, DH	4	0	2	0	Baker, 2B	1	0	0	0
Valera, LF	2	0	0	0	Veen, LF	3	1	2	0
Noel, LF	1	0	0	0	Vientos, 1B	2	0	0	0
Mead, 3B	3	0	0	0	Winn, SS	2	0	0	0
Langeliers, C	2	1	1	1	Lawlar, SS	1	0	0	0
Dingler, C	1	0	0	0	Cartaya, C	2	1	0	0
					O'Hoppe, C	1	0	0	0
Totals	**30**	**6**	**8**	**6**	**Totals**	**25**	**4**	**5**	**2**

AMERICAN LEAGUE	**104**	**100**	**0**	**6**	**8**	**1**
NATIONAL LEAGUE	**030**	**000**	**1**	**4**	**5**	**1**

AL: HR: Domínguez (1, 3rd inning off Harrison, 1 on, 1 out); Wallner (1, 3rd inning off Harrison, 1 on, 2 out); Langeliers (1, 4th inning off Shuster, 0 on, 1 out). **RBI:** Domínguez 2 (2); Harris (1); Langeliers (1); Wallner 2 (2). **2-out RBI:** Wallner 2. **Team RISP:** 1-for-5. **Team LOB:** 6. **SB:** Harris (1, 2nd base off Abbott/O'Hoppe). **E:** Domínguez (1, fielding).

NL: 2B: Carroll (1, Bradley); Crow-Armstrong (1, Flores).**RBI:** Hassell (1); Wiemer (1). **2-out RBI:** Hassell. **SF:** Wiemer. **Team RISP:** 1-for-8. **Team LOB:** 5. **SB:** Veen 2 (2, 2nd base off Bush/Langeliers, 3rd base off Bush/Langeliers). **CS:** Carroll (1, 3rd base by Bradley/Langeliers). **E:** Winn (1, throw).

AL	IP	H	R	ER	BB	SO	NL	IP	H	R	ER	BB	SO
Bradley	1	1	0	0	1	0	Miller, B.	1	1	1	1	1	3
Brown	0.2	2	3	0	2	1	Perez	1	0	0	0	0	1
Zulueta	0.1	0	0	0	0	0	Harrison	0.2	2	4	1	1	2
Bush	1	1	0	0	1	1	Shuster	1.1	2	1	1	0	2
Leiter	1	0	0	0	0	0	Burrows	1	1	0	0	1	1
Tiedemann	1	0	0	0	0	0	Kelly	0.2	0	0	0	0	0
Hancock	1	0	0	0	0	3	Ferrer	0.1	1	0	0	0	1
Flores	0.2	1	1	1	0	0	Abbott	0.2	1	0	0	0	1
Waldichuk	0.1	0	0	0	0	0	Miller, E.	0.1	0	0	0	0	1
Totals	**7**	**5**	**4**	**1**	**4**	**5**	**Totals**	**7**	**8**	**6**	**3**	**3**	**12**

WP: Miller. **Balk:** Flores. **Pitches-strikes:** Bradley 21-10; Brown 25-12; Zulueta 1-1; Bush 15-9; Leiter 9-6; Tiedemann 9-6; Hancock 17-11; Flores 10-7; Waldichuk 3-3; Miller 23-14; Pérez 10-7; Harrison 27-13; Shuster 23-16; Burrows 18-11; Kelly 8-6; Ferrer 10-8; Abbott 11-9; Miller, E 5-3. Inherited runners-scored: Zulueta 2-0; Miller, E 1-0. T: 2:24.

BEST CHANGEUP: Kyle Harrison, LHP

Harrison served up two homers in the third inning but had one positive takeaway from his appearance. The 20-year-old Giants prospect used his changeup four times and threw all four for strikes, generating two whiffs. ■

MINOR LEAGUE BEST TOOLS

	INTERNATIONAL LEAGUE	PACIFIC COAST LEAGUE	EASTERN LEAGUE	SOUTHERN LEAGUE	TEXAS LEAGUE
Best Batting Prospect	Gunnar Henderson	Miguel Vargas	Ezequiel Tovar	Curtis Mead	Jordan Walker
Best Power Prospect	Vinnie Pasquantino	Stone Garrett	Francisco Alvarez	Alexander Canario	Moises Gomez
Best Strike-Zone Judgment	Gabriel Moreno	David Hensley	Gunnar Henderson	Ryan Aguilar	Edouard Julien
Best Baserunner	Samad Taylor	Bubba Thompson	Anthony Volpe	J.D. Orr	Austin Martin
Fastest Baserunner	Samad Taylor	Bubba Thompson	David Hamilton	Greg Jones	DaShawn Keirsey Jr.
Best Pitching Prospect	Brayan Bello	Hunter Brown	Kyle Harrison	Eury Perez	George Kirby
Best Fastball	Graham Ashcraft	Hunter Brown	Daniel Espino	Eury Perez	Bobby Miller
Best Breaking Pitch	Mike Burrows	Hunter Brown	Mike Burrows	Taj Bradley	Taylor Dollard
Best Changeup	Brayan Bello	Ryan Pepiot	Hunter Gaddis	Jared Shuster	Drew Parrish
Best Control	Easton McGee	Collin Wiles	Ryan Watson	Taj Bradley	Brandon Pfaadt
Best Reliever	Greg Weissert	Enoli Paredes	R.J. Dabovich	Eric Torres	Michael Stryffeler
Best Defensive C	Gabriel Moreno	Korey Lee	Dillon Dingler	Blake Hunt	Chandler Seagle
Best Defensive 1B	Triston Casas	Ryan Noda	Frankie Tostado	Bryce Ball	Robbie Glendinning
Best Defensive 2B	Oswaldo Cabrera	Eguy Rosario	Andres Alvarez	Chase Strumpf	Michael Massey
Best Defensive 3B	Gunnar Henderson	Miguel Vargas	Jared Triolo	CJ Alexander	Ti'Quan Forbes
Best Defensive SS	Gabriel Arias	Nick Allen	Ezequiel Tovar	Luis Vazquez	Maikel Garcia
Best Infield Arm	Oneil Cruz	Elehuris Montero	Tyler Fitzgerald	Cam Devanney	Masyn Winn
Best Defensive OF	Estevan Florial	Alek Thomas	Johan Rojas	Michael Harris II	DaShawn Keirsey Jr.
Best OF Arm	Kyle Stowers	Pedro Leon	Elijah Dunham	Michael Harris II	Seuly Matias
Most Exciting Player	Gunnar Henderson	Bubba Thompson	Ceddanne Rafaela	Michael Harris II	Corbin Carroll
Best Manager Prospect	Matt Tuiasosopo	Gil Velazquez	Gabe Alvarez	Michael Ryan	Jose Leger

	MIDWEST LEAGUE	NORTHWEST LEAGUE	SOUTH ATLANTIC LEAGUE	CALIFORNIA LEAGUE	CAROLINA LEAGUE	FLORIDA STATE LEAGUE
Best Batting Prospect	Elly De La Cruz	Zac Veen	Kyle Manzardo	Jordan Lawlar	Jackson Chourio	Hao Yu Lee
Best Power Prospect	Elly De La Cruz	Noelvi Marte	Nick Northcut	Hunter Goodman	Niko Kavadas	Emmanuel Rodriguez
Best Strike-Zone Judgment	Jorbit Vivas	Zac Veen	Colton Cowser	Austin Gauthier	Hendry Mendez	Emmanuel Rodriguez
Best Baserunner	Nasim Nuñez	Zac Veen	Duke Ellis	Max Ferguson	Shane Sasaki	Omar De Los Santos
Fastest Baserunner	Elly De La Cruz	Zac Veen	Duke Ellis	Wilderd Patino	Luis Valdez	Jay Allen
Best Pitching Prospect	Gavin Williams	Ricky Tiedemann	Andrew Painter	Ronan Kopp	Miguel Ullola	Andrew Painter
Best Fastball	Daniel Palencia	Ricky Tiedemann	Andrew Painter	Andrew Moore	Emiliano Teodo	Andrew Painter
Best Breaking Pitch	Antoine Kelly	Prelander Berroa	Andrew Painter	Landen Roupp	Will Dion	David Festa
Best Changeup	Tyler Mitzel	Nick Swiney	Edgar Barclay	Jose Cruz	Luis Devers	Ricky Tiedemann
Best Control	Tanner Bibee	Landon Marceaux	Owen White	Kyle Virbitsky	Will Dion	Luis Palacios
Best Reliever	Cam Robinson	Nick Avila	Edgar Barclay	Jose Cruz	Jose Ferrer	Tommy McCollum
Best Defensive C	Josh Crouch	Drew Romo	Endy Rodriguez	Braxton Fulford	Jeferson Quero	Arturo De Freitas
Best Defensive 1B	Joe Naranjo	Gabe Matthews	Harvin Mendoza	Robert Perez	Will Bartlett	Rainer Nuñez
Best Defensive 2B	Jorbit Vivas	Eddy Diaz	Ronny Simon	Juan Brito	Brainer Bonaci	Jose Salas
Best Defensive 3B	Nick Quintana	Casey Schmitt	Tyler Hardman	Warming Bernabel	Willy Vasquez	Keoni Cavaco
Best Defensive SS	Masyn Winn	Julio Carreras	Alika Williams	Aeverson Arteaga	Marcelo Mayer	Noah Miller
Best Infield Arm	Masyn Winn	Addison Barger	Bryan Ramos	Aeverson Arteaga	Carson Williams	Noah Miller
Best Defensive OF	Pete Crow-Armstrong	Garrett Spain	Evan Carter	Grant McCray	Pete Crow-Armstrong	Alex Ramirez
Best OF Arm	Alexfri Planez	Garrett Spain	Stanley Consuegra	Yanquiel Fernandez	Jeremy De La Rosa	Carlos Dominguez
Most Exciting Player	Elly De La Cruz	Zac Veen	Vaughn Grissom	Edwin Arroyo	Jackson Chourio	Emmanuel Rodriguez
Best Manager Prospect	Brayan Peña	Brent Lavallee	Callix Crabbe	Lipso Nava	Jake Lowery	Angel Espada

MINOR LEAGUES

DOMINICAN SUMMER LEAGUE

CHAMPION: The DSL Phillies White team battled the Rockies before prevailing in three games. Outfielder Raylin Heredia was the star of the finale, going 3-for-4 with two doubles and an RBI as his team clinched the title. Righthander Javier Fuenmayor struck out five over 5.1 shutout innings.

MOST VALUABLE PLAYER: Hulking Twins outfielder Jose Rodriguez ran away with this honor by crunching 13 home runs, the best mark in the league by one.

PITCHER OF THE YEAR: Red Sox righthander Wandy Abreu used a two-pitch mix of a low-90s fastball and a high-70s slider to take this award. He struck out 40 in 37 innings.

TOP MLB PROSPECT: Marlins outfielder Jose Gerardo showed impact potential, as did Rangers outfielder Anthony Gutierrez, who moved to the U.S. by year's end.

MANAGER OF THE YEAR: Ozzie Chavez's Red Sox Blue club won 44 games, tied for a DSL best.

DOMINICAN SUMMER LEAGUE ALL-STARS

Pos	Player	Team	AVG	OPS	HR
C	Bryant Betancourt	Rockies	.355	1.136	11
1B	Luis Torres	Angels	.345	.977	8
2B	Loidel Chapelli	White Sox	.344	1.084	8
3B	Marco Vargas	Marlins	.319	.877	2
SS	Keiner Delgado	Yankees	.310	1.010	3
OF	Jose Rodriguez	Twins	.289	.966	13
OF	Josue De Paula	Dodgers	.349	.970	5
OF	Luis Baez	Astros	.305	.903	9
DH	Samuel Munoz	Dodgers	.347	.920	1
Pos	**Pitcher**	**Team**	**G**	**ERA**	**SO**
RHP	Wandy Abreu	Red Sox	18	1.22	45
LHP	Victor Pena	Royals	13	0.99	42
RP	Dianye Florentino	Rangers	22	1.41	39

DSL CHAMPIONSHIP: DSL Phillies White def. DSL Rockies

BASEBALL CITY	W	L	PCT	GB
DSL D-backs Black	38	20	.655	—
DSL Padres	36	23	.610	2.5
DSL Reds	24	26	.480	10
DSL Orioles Orange	26	34	.433	13
DSL Orioles Black	23	34	.404	14.5
DSL D-backs Red	23	35	.397	15
DSL Blue Jays	18	38	.321	19

NORTHEAST	W	L	PCT	GB
DSL Pirates Gold	44	15	.746	—
DSL Mets 1	31	28	.525	13
DSL Yankees	30	28	.517	13.5
DSL Bombers	27	33	.450	17.5
DSL Pirates Black	26	33	.441	18
DSL Mets 2	24	33	.421	19
DSL Cubs Blue	23	37	.383	21.5
DSL Cubs Red	22	38	.367	22.5

SAN PEDRO	W	L	PCT	GB
DSL Phillies White	40	19	.678	—
DSL Rangers Blue	40	19	.678	—
DSL Phillies Red	36	23	.610	4
DSL Tigers 2	31	25	.554	7.5
DSL White Sox	32	26	.552	7.5
DSL Brewers 2	27	32	.458	13
DSL Brewers 1	22	37	.373	18
DSL Tigers 1	22	38	.367	18.5
DSL Rangers Red	21	39	.350	19.5

NORTH	W	L	PCT	GB
DSL Red Sox Blue	44	16	.733	—
DSL Astros Orange	36	23	.610	7.5
DSL Red Sox Red	36	23	.610	7.5
DSL Royals Glass	31	28	.525	12.5
DSL Guardians Blue	31	29	.517	13
DSL Astros Blue	23	37	.383	21
DSL Guardians Red	17	42	.288	26.5
DSL Royals Stewart	17	43	.283	27

NORTHWEST	W	L	PCT	GB
DSL Dodgers Mega	37	22	.627	—
DSL Braves	36	24	.600	1.5
DSL Dodgers Bautista	34	25	.576	3
DSL Marlins	31	26	.544	5
DSL Athletics	26	32	.448	10.5
DSL Tampa Bay	25	31	.446	10.5
DSL Rays	25	34	.424	12
DSL Miami	20	39	.339	17

SOUTH	W	L	PCT	GB
DSL Rockies	41	19	.683	—
DSL Angels	35	25	.583	6
DSL Colorado	34	26	.567	7
DSL Cardinals	33	26	.559	7.5
DSL Mariners	32	27	.542	8.5
DSL Twins	32	28	.533	9
DSL Nationals	29	31	.483	12
DSL Giants Orange	26	32	.448	14
DSL Giants Black	22	38	.367	19

INDIVIDUAL BATTING LEADERS

Player, Team	AVG	G	AB	R	H	2B	3B	HR	RBI	BB	SO	SB
Estanlin Cassiani, DSL Giants Orange	.375	50	176	40	66	3	2	0	10	14	21	15
Aron Estrada, DSL Orioles Black	.368	45	136	33	50	12	3	3	31	29	23	4
Bryant Betancourt, DSL Colorado	.355	44	138	34	49	11	0	11	36	27	21	0
Carlos Sanchez, DSL Reds	.355	46	138	42	49	4	1	2	26	40	28	14
Yasser Mercedes, DSL Twins	.355	41	155	34	55	13	3	4	20	18	35	30
Josue De Paula, DSL Dodgers Bautista	.349	53	186	42	65	13	2	5	30	32	31	16
Samuel Munoz, DSL Dodgers Mega	.347	47	173	39	60	12	5	1	42	26	34	4
Jansel Luis, DSL D-backs Black/DSL D-backs Red	.345	47	174	35	60	7	1	1	18	12	23	9
Luis Torres, DSL Angels	.345	59	203	47	70	20	1	8	41	17	35	8
Byron Chourio, DSL Marlins	.344	51	183	47	63	9	0	1	23	25	27	19

INDIVIDUAL PITCHING LEADERS

Player, Team	W	L	ERA	G	GS	CG	SV	IP	H	R	ER	BB	SO
Maxwel Hernandez, DSL Phillies White	3	2	0.72	11	11	0	0	49.2	24	9	4	16	51
Emmanuel Reyes, DSL KC Stewart	2	1	0.91	12	11	0	0	49.1	29	12	5	4	52
Miguel Olivares, DSL Twins	1	2	1.44	12	8	0	0	50	27	13	8	20	54
Eybersson Polanco, DSL BOS Red	2	1	1.78	12	12	0	0	50.2	31	10	10	17	50
Danyony Pulido, DSL Phillies White	2	2	1.82	11	11	0	0	49.1	32	13	10	28	34
Gerlin Rosario, DSL Tampa Bay	1	2	2.38	12	7	0	0	53	48	14	14	4	35
Ezequiel Ventura, DSL Phillies White	5	1	2.40	11	10	1	0	48.2	38	15	13	18	38
Wilkerman Munoz, DSL TEX Red	2	2	2.79	12	9	0	0	48.1	40	18	15	18	44
Jordarlin Mendoza, DSL NYY Yankees	1	1	2.95	13	12	0	0	55	44	23	18	19	77
Henry Lalane, DSL NYY Yankees	3	3	2.98	11	11	0	0	48.1	35	24	16	14	52

Excellence That Starts Off The Field

Triple-A

ST. PAUL (INTERNATIONAL)

Classic Saints.

When St. Paul decided on that as their slogan for the 2022 season, it was more to reinforce that, after nearly three decades as one of the gold standard franchises on the independent circuit, the parent Twins were letting them be . . . well, them.

But it could also certainly apply to yet another honor for an organization that has won more than a few of them. The St. Paul Saints are the Triple-A Freitas Award winners for 2022.

After thriving in the Northern League and then the American Association, the Saints continued to thrive in their second year as the Twins' International League affiliate. That's something that many in the organization credit to the fact that Minnesota did not want to change a unique brand that had been entertaining fans for nearly three decades.

"'Fun is good' is us, and we've stood on that rock for 30 seasons now, and it's what we'll continue to do," said Chris Schwab, the Saints' executive vice president of sales and operations.

Double-A

PORTLAND (EASTERN)

A little loyalty goes a long way.

The Portland Sea Dogs are the winners of the Double-A Freitas Award, thanks in large part to a big jump in attendance at Hadlock Field in 2022. The Red Sox affiliate averaged 5,744 fans a night and saw a 37% increase from the previous year.

It isn't hard to figure out why.

In the early stages of the pandemic in 2020, the Sea Dogs' ownership group of Bill Burke and Sally McNamara made the stunning commitment to pay their 19 full-time staff members and more than 200 game-day employees for any missed wages for games that weren't played. Ultimately, that ended up being the entire season.

It was something that Sea Dogs president and general manager Geoff Iacuessa says the team wasn't really looking to market at the time, but a gesture that they also weren't shying away from

That generosity didn't go unnoticed, and it has created genuine loyalty not only from the staff members who never missed a paycheck, but from fans in a smaller community who appreciated that the organization was going out of its way to do the right and honorable thing at a difficult time for everyone.

Class A

WISCONSIN (MIDWEST)

Sometimes, simple is best.

For the Wisconsin Timber Rattlers, the approach took them all the way to winning the Class A Freitas Award, capping off one of the more memorable years in the history of a storied franchise.

"If the customers like it, we continue to do it," said Rob Zerjav, the Timber Rattlers' president, CEO and managing partner. "If they say they don't like it, we figure out a way to change it."

Even on the heels of an announcement that more than $10 million is set to be invested to improve Neuroscience Group Field at Fox Cities Stadium, fans have shown there's little they want changed in an organization that prides itself in wanting to provide a family-friendly entertainment option at an affordable cost.

"That's our mission statement—pretty much in a nutshell—to create the best entertainment experience in Wisconsin, to make sure that every guest walks away with a smile on their face and a desire to return," Zerjav said.

"It's everybody's job to wow the fans at every game. What's it going to take for you to wow somebody today?"

LAST 10 WINNERS

TRIPLE-A	DOUBLE-A	CLASS A	SHORT-SEASON
2011: Colo. Springs (Pacific Coast)	**2011:** Harrisburg (Eastern)	**2011:** Fort Wayne (Midwest)	**2010:** Idaho Falls (Pioneer)
2012: Lehigh Valley (International)	**2012:** N-West Arkansas (Texas)	**2012:** Greenville (South Atlantic)	**2011:** Vancouver (Northwest)
2013: Indianapolis (International)	**2013:** Tulsa (Texas)	**2013:** Clearwater (Florida State)	**2012:** Billings (Pioneer)
2014: Charlotte (International)	**2014:** Montgomery (Southern)	**2014:** West Michigan (Midwest)	**2013:** State College (NY-Penn)
2015: Salt Lake (Pacific Coast)	**2015:** Richmond (Eastern)	**2015:** Myrtle Beach (Carolina)	**2014:** Brooklyn (NY-Penn)
2016: Round Rock (Pacific Coast)	**2016:** Pensacola (Southern)	**2016:** San Bernardino (California)	**2015:** Grand Junction (Pioneer)
2017: Fresno (Pacific Coast)	**2017:** Reading (Eastern)	**2017:** Charleston (South Atlantic)	**2016:** Pulaski (Appalachian)
2018: Oklahoma City (Pacific Coast)	**2018:** Tennessee (Southern)	**2018:** Winston-Salem (Carolina)	**2017:** Hillsboro (Northwest)
2019: Nashville (Pacific Coast)	**2019:** Tulsa (Texas)	**2019:** Lexington (South Atlantic)	**2018:** Spokane (Northwest)
2021: Las Vegas (Pacific Coast)	**2019:** Hartford (Eastern)	**2019:** Greensboro (South Atlantic)	**2019:** Hudson Valley (NY-Penn)

Surprise Wins AFL Crown

BY KYLE GLASER

For nearly four hours, Surprise and Glendale engaged in a taut, relentless battle for the Arizona Fall League championship. Every time one team managed to take the lead, the other quickly responded. Every time one team appeared to record the game-winning hit, the other made a spectacular defensive play. As the hours whittled on and the temperature dropped and the bullpens thinned, it appeared no one could strike the decisive blow to end the game.

No one, that is, except for Scott Schreiber.

Schreiber hit a walkoff RBI single in the bottom of the 11th inning to lift Surprise to a thrilling, 7-6 victory and the AFL championship.

The Astros' first base prospect drilled a 2-1 breaking ball into the left-center gap to score Astros teammate Will Wagner from second base with the winning run and complete Surprise's wire-to-wire run as the AFL's best team.

"It's exhausting, but it was also exhilarating," said Schreiber, a ninth-round pick from Nebraska in 2018. "I mean, our pitchers did a great job of keeping us in the game there at the end ... They were able to keep it at one run and then we were just able to produce to there to finish off the game."

Surprise came back from a deficit five times, including in the 11th. Glendale took a one-run lead on Austin Martin's RBI single in the top of the inning, but Surprise had one final comeback.

After Pirates prospect Nick Gonzales started the inning on second base, Wagner tied the score with an RBI single to left and advanced to second base on the throw to the plate. Schreiber summarily stepped up against Dodgers reliever Tanner Dodson, got ahead in the count and didn't miss a hanging breaking ball, pounding it into the gap and sending his teammates streaming from the dugout in celebration.

As soon as Schreiber rounded first base, his teammates mobbed him in a fit of joy.

Schreiber would not have been in position to win it for Surprise if not for some defensive heroics from his teammates.

With the score tied 4-4 in the eighth, Glendale loaded the bases with two outs and Reds slugger Noelvi Marte at the plate. Marte drilled a hard liner into right-center for what appeared to be at least a two-run double, but Phillies center fielder Carlos De La Cruz chased it down and used every inch of his 6-foot-8 frame to stretch out and make the catch at the last second to preserve the tie.

Surprise's defense came up big again in the ninth.

With one out and Glendale's Matt McLain on third as the go-ahead run, Martin hit a high chopper that should have been enough to score the speedy McLain. Instead, shortstop Luisangel Acuña (Rangers) leaped up to grab it, came down and fired a perfect throw to nail McLain at the plate, preserving the tie once again.

That set the stage for more drama in extras. Glendale took a 5-4 lead in the top of the 10th on Zavier Warren's flared RBI single to left, but Acuña tied it in the bottom of the inning when he ripped a single up the middle that deflected off Dodson's glove and into right field, scoring Blake Sabol from second with the tying run.

Surprise had a chance to win it in the 10th with runners on second and third and no outs, but Samad Taylor struck out and Jayce Easley grounded to second, where Glendale second baseman Edouard Julien stabbed it with his backhand, collected himself and fired a throw to the plate just in time to nail Acuña trying to score the winning run.

Dodson came back and struck out Gonzales to end the inning and escape with the score still 5-5. Just when it appeared Surprise had blown its best chance, Wagner pulled Schreiber aside.

"We were talking about it the inning before and I was like, 'You want me to walk it off or are you gonna walk it off?,' " Wagner said. "And I was like, 'I'll hit the double and here, you walk it off.' "

"I'd said it right in that inning right there, I go 'I'm tired of answering all game,' " Surprise manager Mickey Storey said. "Like, we keep answering, we keep answering. Knock. Them. Out. And Scotty knocked them out."

Prior to the game, Orioles outfielder Heston Kjerstad was named AFL MVP after leading the league in hits (35), doubles (nine), extra-base hits (15) and total bases (61). The No. 2 overall pick in the 2020 draft hit .357/.385/.622 with five home runs and 17 RBIs in 22 games for Scottsdale.The award marked a high point in Kjerstad's long road back to baseball. He was diagnosed with myocarditis, a viral inflammation of the heart, shortly after being drafted and missed 2020 instructional league and the entire 2021 season due to the condition. ■

STANDINGS

Team	W	L	PCT	GB
Surprise	19	10	.655	-
Glendale	15	13	.536	3.5
Peoria	14	14	.500	4.5
Mesa	13	15	.464	5.5
Scottsdale	13	16	.448	6
Salt River	12	18	.400	7.5

INDIVIDUAL BATTING LEADERS

(Minimum 2 Plate Appearances/League Games)

Player, Team	AVG	G	AB	R	H	HR	RBI
Julien, Edouard, GDD	.400	21	70	24	28	5	17
Rumfield, TJ, MSS	.400	17	55	14	22	1	10
Martin, Austin, GDD	.373	21	83	23	31	1	11
Kjerstad, Heston, SCO	.357	22	98	13	35	5	17
Wagner, Will, SUR	.346	14	52	10	18	3	15
Keith, Colt, SRR	.344	19	61	16	21	3	10
Yorke, Nick, SCO	.342	19	76	18	26	2	18
Veen, Zac, SRR	.333	21	81	15	27	1	10
Lavigne, Grant, SRR	.328	17	61	13	20	1	11
Simon, Ronny, MSS	.325	21	80	15	26	4	24

INDIVIDUAL PITCHING LEADERS

(Minimum .4 Innings Pitched/League Games)

Player, Team	W	L	ERA	IP	H	BB	SO
Wentz, Joey, SRR	2	0	0.00	12	2	4	14
Horn, Bailey, MSS	0	0	1.50	12	6	7	9
Myrick, Tyler, SCO	0	0	1.50	12	5	5	10
Peluse, Colin, MSS	0	0	1.50	18	13	4	14
Thomas, Connor, SRR	1	0	1.75	26	22	5	34
Shreve, Ryan, GDD	1	0	1.84	15	7	8	12
Benitez, Jorge, PEJ	0	0	2.08	13	9	8	11
Ginn, J.T., MSS	1	1	2.25	16	12	4	14
Contreras, Efrain, PEJ	1	1	2.45	18	10	7	16
Loutos, Ryan, SRR	0	1	2.57	14	10	4	13

GLENDALE DESERT DOGS

Name	AVG	AB	R	H	2B	3B	HR	RBI	BB	SO	SB
Black, Tyler	.279	61	14	17	3	0	1	10	10	18	4
Castillo, Moises	.347	49	11	17	5	0	1	13	6	8	2
Hackenberg, Adam	.160	50	7	8	0	0	1	11	7	16	0
Hinds, Rece	.226	84	15	19	5	1	3	11	6	35	5
Isola, Alex	.228	57	6	13	5	0	0	12	10	11	0
Julien, Edouard	.400	70	24	28	5	0	5	17	23	22	6
Marte, Noelvi	.211	71	10	15	1	0	2	10	12	14	1
Martin, Austin	.373	83	23	31	6	0	1	11	8	7	10
McLain, Matt	.190	79	11	15	2	1	2	11	14	31	6
Pages, Andy	.296	81	20	24	2	0	5	14	9	12	1
Quero, Jeferson	.222	45	8	10	3	1	0	3	7	13	2
Ramos, Jose	.275	80	14	22	4	1	3	16	5	20	0
Tatum, Terrell	.263	19	5	5	0	0	0	4	3	5	4
Vivas, Jorbit	.333	27	7	9	2	0	0	7	6	6	0
Ward, Je'Von	.231	39	8	9	3	0	1	9	11	15	4
Warren, Zavier	.278	72	11	20	1	1	1	15	22	16	2

Name	W	L	ERA	G	GS	SV	IP	H	BB	SO	AVG
Benschoter, Sam	1	2	4.73	6	4	0	13	15	7	11	.288
Bentley, Denny	1	0	3.18	8	0	0	11	7	14	9	.189
Choi, Hyun-il	1	0	5.40	9	0	0	13	11	8	8	.220
Contreras, Luis	0	0	12.00	6	0	0	6	9	6	7	.360
Cronin, Declan	0	0	4.50	9	0	0	10	15	0	7	.366
Dodson, Tanner	0	0	6.57	9	0	2	12	16	6	8	.296
Gozzo, Jake	0	1	8.71	9	0	0	10	15	10	10	.341
Harris, Ben	1	1	6.35	9	0	0	11	10	14	10	.250
Middendorf, Ryan	0	0	2.92	9	0	0	12	8	5	16	.182
Olsen, Jon	2	1	5.27	5	4	0	14	15	10	17	.288
Peguero, Francys	1	1	2.45	9	0	0	11	10	8	9	.227
Peralta, Sammy	1	0	3.21	9	0	0	14	14	4	14	.259
Ramsey, Lane	1	1	4.50	9	0	2	10	8	6	12	.229
Roa, Chrisitian	1	1	19.13	4	4	0	8	14	10	9	.368
Sheehan, Emmet	3	1	3.54	6	6	0	20	12	8	24	.169
Shreve, Ryan	1	0	1.84	9	0	0	15	7	8	12	.152
Smith, Russell	1	3	5.30	6	6	0	19	25	14	19	.313
Solesky, Chase	0	1	6.53	6	6	0	21	23	10	16	.284
Timpanelli, Vin	0	0	8.00	8	0	0	9	7	8	12	.226
Uribe, Abner	0	0	0.90	9	0	1	10	10	2	14	.256

MESA SOLAR SOX

Name	AVG	AB	R	H	2B	3B	HR	RBI	BB	SO	SB
Auer, Mason	.229	70	17	16	4	2	3	13	7	23	8
Barstad, Cameron	.231	13	2	3	0	0	0	0	2	8	0
Butler, Lawrence	.241	54	7	13	3	1	2	16	15	15	6
Caissie, Owen	.220	59	9	13	5	0	1	9	4	24	3
Clarke, Denzel	.275	40	6	11	5	0	1	4	4	16	3
Davis, Brennen	.278	18	7	5	1	0	2	4	2	1	1
Domínguez, Jasson	.159	69	9	11	4	0	0	3	8	17	5
Gelof, Zack	.228	79	11	18	3	0	3	7	7	20	4
Guldberg, Michael	.158	19	4	3	1	0	0	0	5	3	1
Hardman, Tyler	.325	77	21	25	6	1	6	15	6	22	1
Hunt, Blake	.265	49	9	13	1	1	1	8	6	14	0
Mack, Joe	.230	61	11	14	2	0	4	7	10	23	0
Mervis, Matt	.262	61	12	16	2	0	6	12	5	8	2
Mesa Jr., Victor	.207	58	11	12	1	3	2	9	8	14	0
Murray Jr., B.J.	.211	19	2	4	0	0	1	2	1	6	0
Murray, Tanner	.278	18	2	5	0	0	0	2	4	4	0
Rumfield, T.J.	.400	55	14	22	7	0	1	10	9	11	0
Salas, Jose	.224	58	5	13	3	1	0	7	8	12	4
Simon, Ronny	.325	80	15	26	4	1	4	24	10	20	3

Name	W	L	ERA	G	GS	SV	IP	H	BB	SO	AVG
Alvarez, Nelson	0	1	8.10	9	0	0	10	13	11	14	.325
Ayala Jr., Alex	1	1	11.57	7	3	0	12	20	9	15	.377
Calderon, Yorlin	0	2	8.53	6	0	0	13	16	4	17	.308
Cusick, Ryan	2	1	6.26	6	5	0	23	26	13	24	.280
Fall, Justin	2	1	14.11	5	4	0	15	24	16	7	.353
Gaston, Sandy	1	0	7.56	8	0	0	8	9	15	5	.290
Ginn, J.T.	1	1	2.25	5	5	0	16	12	4	14	.218
Horn, Bailey	0	0	1.50	8	0	1	12	6	7	9	.150
Jones, Holt	0	2	7.36	6	4	0	18	22	17	12	.306
Jozwiak, Chandler	0	1	3.86	9	0	2	12	7	7	18	.175
Leigh, Zac	1	0	4.91	6	0	1	7	7	4	6	.259
Martin, Riley	0	1	2.84	8	0	1	13	10	5	19	.196
McNeely, Shaine	0	0	13.50	1	0	0	2	2	0	2	.286
Mendez, Leam	1	2	3.95	9	0	0	14	11	7	6	.224
Menendez, Antonio	1	0	4.73	8	0	0	13	10	15	12	.208
Mercedes, Jorge	0	1	22.50	6	0	0	6	7	16	11	.259
Miller, Mason	1	1	3.24	6	6	0	17	9	4	20	.158
Peluse, Colin	0	0	1.50	6	3	0	18	13	4	14	.203
Reed, Sheldon	0	0	4.32	6	0	1	8	8	6	10	.258
Reifert, Evan	2	0	0.00	8	0	0	12	1	4	25	.028

PEORIA JAVELINAS

Name	AVG	AB	R	H	2B	3B	HR	RBI	BB	SO	SB
Antuna, Yasel	.225	40	5	9	3	0	0	9	8	8	0
Baker, Darren	.231	13	5	3	0	0	0	0	3	1	0
Caballero, Jose	.238	42	9	10	4	0	0	8	12	11	6
Cedeno, Nerwilian	.237	38	5	9	2	1	1	3	5	15	0
Consuegra, Stanley	.167	36	4	6	2	0	2	5	3	12	0
Frizzell, Will	.200	25	2	5	0	0	0	0	0	9	0
Fry, David	.286	42	4	12	3	0	1	8	4	11	0
Hassell III, Robert	.167	6	0	1	0	0	0	1	0	1	0
Kendall, Kevin	.208	77	16	16	3	0	1	5	13	22	4
Kokx, Connor	.283	60	10	17	3	1	0	6	9	15	1
Lindsly, Brady	.182	22	2	4	0	0	0	2	5	8	1
Martinez, Angel	.260	73	14	19	0	0	2	14	9	13	2
McIlwain, Brandon	.175	40	5	7	1	1	1	2	2	14	1
Merrill, Jackson	.261	88	16	23	1	2	1	10	8	21	2
Millas, Drew	.305	59	6	18	5	0	2	13	3	10	1
Ornelas, Tirso	.293	58	9	17	4	0	1	5	6	12	1
Packard, Spencer	.275	40	13	11	4	0	2	12	12	19	0
Perez Jr., Robert	.231	65	10	15	1	1	3	14	8	22	0
Ritter, Luke	.146	48	8	7	0	0	2	11	9	20	0
Rodriguez, Alberto	.243	37	8	9	1	0	1	6	6	11	2

Name	W	L	ERA	G	GS	SV	IP	H	BB	SO	AVG
Adcock, Ty	1	0	4.22	8	0	0	11	10	12	9	.250
Benitez, Jorge	0	0	2.08	9	0	0	13	9	8	11	.191
Cate, Tim	0	4	18.00	5	4	0	10	25	8	9	.472
Contreras, Efrain	1	1	2.45	5	4	0	18	10	7	16	.156
Guerrero, Jordan	0	0	63.00	2	0	0	1	5	3	0	.714
Hartwig, Grant	0	0	10.00	7	0	0	9	15	4	8	.375

MINOR LEAGUES

Hickman, Mason	1	0	4.66	8	0	0	10	12	6	15 .308
Jacob, Alek	1	0	3.55	9	0	0	13	10	5	17 .213
Knowles, Lucas	0	1	5.93	9	0	0	14	11	4	11 .224
Lincoln, Chris	1	1	11.57	4	0	0	2	4	2	3 .444
Lugo, Moises	1	0	3.60	8	0	1	10	7	2	10 .194
Macko, Adam	0	1	6.08	7	1	0	13	12	13	14 .240
Ribalta, Orlando	0	0	0.00	8	0	0	10	7	1	7 .194
Sanchez, Franklin	0	1	11.05	7	0	0	7	11	6	5 .355
Scott, Christian	0	2	10.38	4	4	0	13	27	3	10 .415
Smith, Cade	0	0	4.26	6	0	1	6	6	5	11 .240
Stanley, Hunter	2	2	4.43	6	6	0	20	16	7	24 .211
Then, Juan	0	0	2.25	8	0	2	8	6	4	11 .207
Torres, Lenny	0	0	7.27	7	0	0	9	18	7	11 .429
Vasil, Mike	3	0	2.93	6	5	0	15	10	9	18 .185
Walker, Josh	1	0	2.89	8	0	0	9	8	5	14 .222
Willingham, Amos	0	1	4.82	9	0	1	9	9	2	13 .257
Woo, Bryan	2	0	0.84	5	5	0	11	5	4	16 .122

SALT RIVER RAFTERS

Name	AVG	AB	R	H	2B	3B	HR	RBI	BB	SO	SB
Antico, Mike	.200	40	10	8	1	0	3	8	7	17	8
Barger, Addison	.189	53	9	10	1	0	2	7	8	10	2
Bernabel, Warming	.111	54	1	6	1	0	1	6	3	11	1
Britton, Zach	.404	47	7	19	3	1	1	13	7	7	0
De Los Santos, Deyvison	.219	64	5	14	5	1	0	9	5	22	0
Dingler, Dillon	.500	8	1	4	0	0	0	2	4	2	0
Duzenack, Camden	.212	33	5	7	0	0	1	4	3	11	1
Fulford, Braxton	.162	37	4	6	2	0	0	3	4	11	3
Hummel, Cooper	.471	17	4	8	1	0	1	6	5	1	1
Keith, Colt	.344	61	16	21	3	0	3	10	16	16	3
Lavigne, Grant	.328	61	13	20	7	2	1	11	8	17	3
Lawlar, Jordan	.278	36	9	10	1	1	2	7	11	14	4
Meadows, Parker	.224	67	13	15	3	1	3	7	7	16	2
Morris, Tanner	.279	43	11	12	1	0	1	3	15	9	0
O'Neill, Tyler	.333	3	1	1	0	0	0	0	0	2	0
Pages, Pedro	.279	43	2	12	4	0	1	7	4	9	0
Veen, Zac	.333	81	15	27	6	0	1	10	15	8	16
Walker, Jordan	.286	77	17	22	6	0	5	16	10	23	3
Winn, Masyn	.294	68	10	20	1	0	1	9	13	15	9
Workman, Gage	.193	57	7	11	1	2	2	9	3	24	2

Name	W	L	ERA	G	GS	SV	IP	H	BB	SO	AVG
Anderson, Jack	1	0	4.50	10	0	1	10	15	4	7	.385
Backhus, Kyle	0	0	2.08	4	0	1	4	3	3	5	.176
Bukauskas, J.B.	0	0	13.50	1	0	0	1	4	0	2	.444
Calvo, Blair	0	2	14.00	10	0	1	9	18	7	9	.429
Danner, Hagen	1	1	3.52	8	0	0	8	5	1	8	.185
Del Bonta-Smith, Fineas	2	2	6.48	9	2	0	17	17	7	18	.262
Goddard, Jackson	0	1	9.00	9	0	0	12	16	7	8	.320
Gregory, Hunter	1	2	12.00	7	3	0	12	14	14	9	.298
Hence, Tink	0	0	2.16	9	0	0	8	4	4	9	.154
Jones, Spencer	1	0	11.70	9	0	0	10	17	10	10	.370
Lambert, Peter	0	1	9.00	3	3	0	7	12	1	9	.375
Leahy, Kyle	0	0	10.67	9	0	0	14	19	10	21	.311
Loutos, Ryan	0	1	2.57	9	0	0	14	10	4	13	.200
Martinez, Justin	0	0	2.35	7	0	3	8	3	5	13	.115
Mattison, Tyler	1	0	3.18	10	0	1	11	7	8	19	.171
Patrick, Chad	0	2	10.57	5	5	0	15	23	9	7	.329
Robinson, Kobe	0	0	3.38	7	0	0	8	6	7	5	.222
Thomas, Connor	1	0	1.75	6	6	0	26	22	5	34	.224
Tolhurst, Anders	1	2	4.70	6	6	0	15	16	9	16	.267
Walker, Matt	0	1	8.22	4	2	0	8	10	3	6	.323
Watson, Troy	1	3	8.76	9	0	0	12	14	7	11	.292
Wentz, Joey	2	0	0.00	3	3	0	12	2	4	14	.053

SCOTTSDALE SCORPIONS

Name	AVG	AB	R	H	2B	3B	HR	RBI	BB	SO	SB
Abreu, Wilyer	.167	54	8	9	2	0	0	10	10	18	3
Blakely, Werner	.206	63	13	13	6	0	0	8	10	30	3
Bunnell, Cade	.167	36	8	6	0	0	0	4	9	21	0
Conley, Cal	.267	86	11	23	5	3	2	17	13	21	9
Kavadas, Niko	.239	46	7	11	3	0	2	6	13	24	0
Kjerstad, Heston	.357	98	13	35	9	1	5	17	5	31	0
Malloy, Justyn-Henry	.306	72	11	22	5	1	1	7	16	20	1
Matos, Luis	.233	86	12	20	3	1	2	13	5	20	1
Paris, Kyren	.218	55	13	12	0	0	0	7	13	24	2
Prieto, Cesar	.189	53	4	10	2	2	1	9	6	14	1
Scott, Stephen	.298	57	15	17	1	1	5	16	9	11	1
Sugastey, Adrian	.385	26	5	10	1	0	0	2	2	1	0
Teodosio, Bryce	.188	48	7	9	3	1	1	5	7	17	6
Thomas, Andy	.182	33	5	6	1	0	0	4	10	8	1
Trimble, Reed	.244	45	8	11	4	0	0	5	9	20	3
Wyatt, Logan	.306	49	12	15	2	0	0	6	17	7	0
Yorke, Nick	.342	76	18	26	8	0	2	18	12	16	1

Name	W	L	ERA	G	GS	SV	IP	H	BB	SO	AVG
Armstrong, Ivan	1	0	9.00	10	0	0	8	7	11	11	.219
Bednar, Will	0	0	16.20	2	2	0	3	5	2	3	.357
Bivens, Spencer	0	0	0.87	7	0	0	10	5	5	11	.143
Caceres, Kelvin	1	1	7.84	9	0	0	10	10	11	16	.250
Denoyer, Noah	3	1	4.50	6	5	0	20	17	11	21	.227
Dula, Hunter	0	0	4.82	9	0	0	9	10	6	10	.270
Hoffman, Nolan	0	0	3.65	10	0	0	12	11	2	17	.239
Kochanowicz, Jack	1	1	10.05	7	2	0	14	23	6	13	.397
Lucas, Easton	2	1	3.27	10	0	0	11	9	7	14	.237
Myrick, Tyler	0	0	1.50	10	0	3	12	5	5	10	.122
Perry, Aaron	0	0	12.46	10	0	0	9	15	10	4	.395
Richmond, Nick	1	1	13.00	9	0	0	9	14	8	9	.350
Segal, Alex	0	0	8.38	8	0	0	10	5	12	13	.152
Smith, Austin	0	0	3.38	10	0	0	11	9	6	14	.225
Van Scoyoc, Connor	1	4	7.62	7	7	0	26	33	13	17	.303
Ward, Thad	1	1	2.84	4	3	0	13	11	6	15	.234
Webb, Jacob	0	2	3.60	9	0	3	10	8	5	12	.222
Whisenhunt, Carson	0	1	2.84	3	3	0	6	7	3	11	.280
Winans, Allan	1	1	4.87	6	5	0	20	24	7	19	.289
Woods, William	1	1	8.53	9	2	0	13	19	4	13	.345
Zeferjahn, Ryan	0	1	4.80	9	1	0	15	11	8	18	.208

SURPRISE SAGUAROS

Name	AVG	AB	R	H	2B	3B	HR	RBI	BB	SO	SB
Acuña, Luisangel	.238	80	9	19	2	1	2	11	8	20	8
Correa, J.C.	.333	36	3	12	0	0	0	3	4	6	0
Daniels, Zach	.175	40	5	7	3	0	1	2	5	12	0
Davis, Henry	.260	50	11	13	6	0	1	6	10	11	4
De La Cruz, Carlos	.306	62	9	19	0	2	3	14	4	27	0
Easley, Jayce	.375	24	12	9	2	0	1	4	9	5	4
Freeman, Cody	.171	41	6	7	1	0	0	0	12	8	2
Gentry, Tyler	.139	36	7	5	1	0	2	3	5	8	0
Gonzales, Nick	.279	68	10	19	4	1	3	14	7	16	1
Gonzalez, Jacob	.212	33	5	7	2	0	1	5	2	9	0
Hauver, Trevor	.200	50	13	10	1	0	3	12	16	21	0
Ortiz, Jhailyn	.163	43	7	7	0	0	3	8	8	15	0
Rave, John	.217	69	8	15	3	1	2	10	6	22	2
Rojas, Johan	.310	42	10	13	4	1	0	7	8	8	13
Sabol, Blake	.234	47	7	11	2	0	1	7	7	15	1
Schreiber, Scott	.340	50	10	17	3	2	1	12	5	9	1
Taylor, Samad	.152	66	15	10	3	1	2	10	8	26	9
Wagner, Will	.346	52	10	18	6	2	3	15	7	12	1
Zavala, Aaron	.200	15	3	3	0	0	1	1	5	6	0

Name	W	L	ERA	G	GS	SV	IP	H	BB	SO	AVG
Chamberlain, Christian	1	0	3.48	8	0	1	10	7	5	12	.200
Cruz, Omar	1	1	5.25	9	0	0	12	13	10	11	.283
Dipoto, Jonah	0	0	1.93	9	0	1	9	8	1	14	.242
Gordon, Colton	3	1	6.38	5	5	0	18	21	3	19	.292
Hernandez, Cristian	2	0	0.82	8	1	0	11	9	1	11	.214
Kouba, Rhett	3	0	4.91	6	6	0	18	15	10	21	.224
Lehman, Taylor	0	2	6.17	8	0	0	12	10	8	16	.222
Morales, Francisco	1	0	0.00	9	0	2	11	4	7	17	.108
Murdock, Noah	0	0	2.25	3	0	0	4	3	2	3	.231
Pennington, Walter	0	0	5.79	8	2	1	9	7	4	10	.206
Priester, Quinn	1	2	6.26	6	6	0	23	26	10	22	.280
Robert, Daniel	0	2	9.64	8	0	1	9	11	3	17	.282
Rocker, Kumar	2	1	4.50	6	6	0	14	12	12	18	.231
Ruppenthal, Matthew	1	0	0.87	7	0	0	10	2	5	15	.061
Schulze, Brett	0	0	1.08	8	0	1	8	2	6	10	.077
Selby, Colin	0	0	2.00	9	0	1	9	8	4	9	.229
Sikkema, T.J.	2	0	2.45	3	3	0	11	8	6	9	.216
Sprinkle, Jonathan	0	0	9.53	5	0	0	6	5	9	7	.250
Starr, Nick	0	1	5.06	9	0	0	11	11	6	7	.256
Thomas, Tahnaj	0	0	9.64	9	0	0	9	7	9	11	.212
Webb, Nathan	1	0	0.00	6	0	0	6	4	2	6	.190
Wolfram, Grant	1	0	1.86	7	0	0	10	5	2	13	.147

INDEPENDENT LEAGUES

Partner Leagues Settle Into Stability

AL BELLO/GETTY IMAGES

Staten Island's Kelsie Whitmore became the Atlantic League's first female player.

BY J.J. COOPER

It would be too optimistic to call this a golden age of independent leagues and partner leagues baseball. But stability has somewhat returned to the main leagues once again, after a few years that were anything but stable.

There was the 2020 coronavirus pandemic. Indy ball teams actually in many cases figured out how to play games where affiliated leagues seasons were canceled, but it was anything but easy.

Then came the reorganization of the affiliated minor leagues which led to indy league stalwarts like St. Paul, Sugar Land and Somerset moving to affiliated ball. It also meant the arrival of some former affiliated teams, and in the case of the Pioneer League, an entire league, into the partner leagues.

All of that movement settled down in 2022, as teams were once again able to play a somewhat normal schedule without travel and roster restrictions. The games went back to normal, but more than that, the leagues have continued to innovate.

While there are a significant number of affiliated minor league teams who have yet to dip a toe into streaming video broadcasts of their games, streaming video has been a key part of the independent and now partner leagues for years, allowing fans of teams and friends and family of players to keep close tabs when a team is at home or on the road. In many ways it's easier to keep tabs on the partner league games than it is the affiliated minors.

The American Association and Pioneer Leagues even went into creating ancillary content around the games with weekly shows and specials.

It was also a year of milestones. Independent/ Partner Leagues Player of the Year Courtney Hawkins tied the independent leagues record for home runs in a single season with 48.

A few states over in New York, Kelsie Whitmore became the first female player in Atlantic League history. Whitmore pitched and played outfielder for the FerryHawks in their first season in the league.

Hawkins Crushes Home Run Record

PLAYER OF THE YEAR

Being released is never easy for a baseball player, but like many players before him, being let go has ended up being a key part of Courtney Hawkins' development as a player.

It provided the impetus for him to rework his swing. But maybe even more importantly, it provided a chance to revitalize his love of the game.

Courtney Hawkins

"When you first get released you're kind of lost. Going to indy ball brought the fun back to baseball. You get to put it out on the field. (Sugar Land manager) Pete Incaviglia started that for me. He's an old-school, hard-nosed dude I love and respect. He told me to let it rock," Hawkins said.

Playing for Incaviglia in Sugar Land and Brandon and PJ Phillips in Lexington, Hawkins, 29, did rework his swing, but more than anything he decided to swing for the fences. If he struck out, he struck out. But he went into at-bats with the focus of being an impact hitter.

The impacts have been loud, long and often. In the past two years, Hawkins has hit 80 home runs for Lexington in just 218 games. This year, he tied the Atlantic League and independent/partner leagues single-season home run record by hitting 48 homers for the Legends. That tied Ozzie Canseco's record, set in 2000. After hitting .298/.399/.655 with 72 extra-base hits, Hawkins is Baseball America's 2022 Independent/Partner Leagues Player of the Year.

Hawkins tied the home run record in dramatic fashion, as it came on his final at-bat of the season.

He had come into the final three-game series of the season sitting on 47 home runs. But in his first two plate appearances of that series, he was intentionally walked with the bases empty. He walked three times in a row in the second game of the series. He went 1-for-4 in the four at-bats where he did get to swing the bat in those first two games, but without homering. He struck out, popped out twice and then singled in his first four at-bats in the final game, but in the final inning of the Legends' season, he hit a 442-foot, no-doubt home run to tie the record.

"He should have hit 60 home runs. The last two weeks of the season, he was getting nothing to hit. He hit eight HRs in just a few days. After that, people weren't pitching to him," Lexington manager PJ Phillips said.

That sounds like hyperbole, but it's anchored in truth. Hawkins homered twice in both halves of a doubleheader on Aug. 28, giving him four home runs in one day. He homered again in the Legends' next game, homered twice the next day and once more the next day. In a five-game stretch, it was eight home runs that gave him 43 home runs with 18 games to go. He walked 17 times in the final 17 games of the season.

"Once he gets going, he hits them in bunches," Phillips said.

PREVIOUS WINNERS

1997: Mike Meggers, OF, Winnipeg/Duluth (Northern)
1998: Morgan Burkhart, 1B, Richmond (Frontier)
1999: Carmine Cappucio, OF, New Jersey (Northeast)
2000: Anthony Lewis, 1B, Duluth-Superior (Northern)
2001: Mike Warner, OF, Somerset (Atlantic)
2002: Bobby Madritsch, LHP, Winnipeg (Northern)
2003: Jason Shelley, RHP, Rockford (Frontier)
2004: Victor Rodriguez, SS, Somerset (Atlantic)
2005: Eddie Lantigua, 3B, Quebec (Can-Am)
2006: Ian Church, OF, Kalamazoo (Frontier)
2007: Darryl Brinkley, OF, Calgary (Northern)
2008: Patrick Breen, OF, Orange County (Golden)
2009: Greg Porter, OF, Wichita (American Association)
2010: Beau Torbert, OF, Sioux Falls (American Association)
2011: Chris Collabello, 1B, Worcester (Can-Am League)
2012: Blake Gailen, OF, Lancaster (Atlantic)
2013: C.J. Ziegler, 1B, Wichita (American Association)
2014: Balbino Fuenmayor, 1B, Quebec (Can-Am League)
2015: Joe Maloney, OF, Rocland (Can-Am League)
2016: Art Charles, 1B, New Jersey (Can-Am League)
2017: Alonzo Harris, OF, York (Atlantic League)
2018: Jordany Valdespin, INF, Long Island (Atlantic League)
2019: Keon Barnum, 1B, Chicago (American Association)
2021: Adam Brett Walker, OF, Milwaukee (American Association)

BRIAN WESTERHOLT/FOUR SEAM IMAGES

AMERICAN ASSOCIATION

Leobalda Pina's RBI single up the middle scored Christian Correa in the 10th inning of the deciding Game 7 to hand Fargo-Moorhead a 9-8 win over Milwaukee in the deciding Game 5 of the American Association Championship. The win was Fargo-Moorhead's first American Association title. The RedHawks had last won the Northern League title in 2010.

East Division	W	L	PCT	GB
Kane County Cougars	54	46	.540	0
Chicago Dogs	54	46	.540	0
Milwaukee Milkmen	53	47	.530	1
Cleburne Railroaders	50	50	.500	4
Gary SouthShore RailCats	42	58	.420	12
Lake Country DockHounds	34	66	.340	20

West Division	W	L	PCT	GB
Kansas City Monarchs	65	35	.650	0
Fargo-Moorhead RedHawks	64	36	.640	1
Winnipeg Goldeyes	53	47	.530	12
Lincoln Saltdogs	49	51	.490	16
Sioux City Explorers	49	51	.490	16
Sioux Falls Canaries	33	67	.330	32

PLAYOFFS—Quarterfinals: Milwaukee defeated Chicago 2-1, Cleburne defeated Kane County 2-1, Fargo-Moorhead defeated Winnipeg 2-1 and Kansas City defeated Lincoln 2-0 in best-of-3 series. **Semifinals:** Fargo-Moorhead defeated Kansas City 2-1 and Milwaukee defeated Cleburne 2-0 in best-of-3 series. **Finals:** Fargo-Moorhead defeated Milwaukee 3-2 in best-of-5 series..

Attendance: Kane County 248,354; Chicago 191,984; Winnipeg 163,893; Gary 152,894; Fargo-Moorhead 147,073; Lincoln 144,494; Kansas City 105,302; Lake Country 93,711; Milwaukee 86,028; Cleburne 65,062; Sioux Falls 59,425; Sioux City 52,121.

ALL-STAR TEAM: C: Ryan Lidge (CHI). **1B:** David Washington (WPG). **2B:** Grant Kay (CHI). **3B:** Leobaldo Piña (F-M). **SS:** Raul Navarro (WPG). **OF:** Jimmy Kerrigan (KCO); Max Murphy (WPG); Zach Nehrir (CLE). **DH:** Drew Ward (F-M). **UT:** Bryan Torres (MKE). **SP:** Matt Hall (KC). **RP:** Alex DuBord (F-M).

AWARDS—Player of the Year: Max Murphy, Winnipeg. **Defensive Player of the Year:** Zach Nehrir, Cleburne. **Manager of the Year:** Chris Coste, **Fargo:** Moorhead.

BATTING LEADERS

Player, Team	Team	AVG	AB	R	H	HR	RBI
Torres, Bryan	MKE	.374	372	73	139	3	56
Pina, Leobaldo	F-M	.346	373	66	129	8	67
Thompson, David	KC	.346	283	71	98	19	63
Ward, Drew	F-M	.345	296	64	102	17	48
Ulrich, Wyatt	SF	.338	269	52	91	4	24
Navarro, Raul	WPG	.335	370	75	124	6	51
Clemens, Kacy	CLE	.325	249	43	81	9	59
LaValley, Gavin	SF	.324	346	50	112	20	73
Lidge, Ryan	CHI	.322	335	60	108	12	80
Sweeney, Darnell	KC	.321	380	80	122	13	49

PITCHING LEADERS

Player, Team	Team	W	L	ERA	IP	H	BB	SO
Hall, Matt	KC	10	2	1.10	82	59	24	113
Minier, Greg	LIN	6	6	2.48	109	92	34	116
Kinley, Jeff	CHI	8	3	2.73	86	68	25	1119
Fox, Jack	KCO	11	3	3.04	92	93	44	73
Grauer, Tyler	F-M	10	5	3.51	126	120	32	103
McGovern, Kevin	F-M	10	3	3.70	127	119	37	141
Wigginton, Peyton	F-M	9	3	3.84	91	92	27	74
Kipper, Jordan	CHI	9	7	3.93	94	104	24	93
Erwin, Chris	GAR	3	5	4.01	83	83	40	86
McRae, Alex	LC	5	4	4.01	83	89	20	78

CHICAGO DOGS

Name	AVG	AB	R	H	HR	RBI	BB	SO	SB
Bauer, Trent	.200	130	15	26	4	26	19	38	1
Bohanek, Cody	.283	60	8	17	0	4	12	12	0
Grier, Anfernee	.238	252	35	60	4	28	22	65	10
Hobson, K.C.	.266	379	61	101	15	62	56	75	2
Kay, Grant	.296	371	67	110	21	67	42	89	11
Kopach, Connor	.249	337	60	84	14	47	36	120	20
Lidge, Ryan	.322	335	60	108	12	80	59	72	4
Mars, Danny	.288	205	35	59	9	50	22	79	9
Rivera, Eric	.241	29	4	7	0	2	7	3	0
Smith, Harrison	.191	241	31	46	8	32	17	87	2
Tilson, Charlie	.286	385	75	110	5	32	34	51	20
Wilkerson, Stevie	.264	212	26	56	8	35	15	40	2

Name	W	L	ERA	G	SV	IP	H	BB	SO
Barringer, Shane	7	7	5.81	24	0	93	114	40	79
Cavallaro, Joe	3	1	2.14	42	1	72	47	26	83
Clark, Ryan	2	0	2.12	38	0	51	34	21	65
Kipper, Jordan	9	7	3.93	17	0	94	104	24	93
Lane, Trevor	0	1	5.63	18	0	16	14	9	19
Lawson, Tanner	1	1	4.13	33	3	48	44	22	61
Marnon, Kevin	2	0	2.86	35	3	35	21	17	55
Murphy, Kyle	6	5	6.43	19	0	84	96	41	73
Reeves, James	1	1	3.42	22	0	26	20	15	35
Schlitter, Brian	4	1	3.29	32	7	38	46	9	26
Tripp, Johnathon	3	3	4.32	31	0	73	77	18	69

CLEBURNE RAILROADERS

Name	AVG	AB	R	H	HR	RBI	BB	SO	SB
DAlexander, Hill	.310	248	51	77	13	48	32	53	13
Arroyo, Edwin	.316	335	64	106	5	41	56	44	15
Bockelie, Jacob	.249	181	30	45	7	32	21	50	1
Clemens, Kacy	.325	249	43	81	9	59	35	54	7
Ghelfi, Mitch	.128	39	4	5	0	4	5	16	0
Hernandez, Eddie	.194	98	12	19	1	7	6	31	8
Nehrir, Zach	.314	379	81	119	17	72	48	84	35
Shumpert, Nick	.265	347	51	92	8	50	22	97	29
Simpson, Chase	.302	361	74	109	24	83	65	91	19
Taylor, Chuck	.307	303	64	93	8	40	33	64	15
Wolfe, Hunter	.256	211	40	54	7	35	40	55	19

Name	W	L	ERA	G	SV	IP	H	BB	SO
Alexander, Garrett	5	8	6.79	22	1	109	116	62	23
Bell, Brendan	3	2	5.72	40	1	46	52	19	45
Brickhouse, Bryan	0	0	4.05	8	0	13	9	12	15
Bullard, Kody	7	5	4.53	21	0	93	97	44	92
Cervenka, Hunter	5	0	1.27	26	1	28	17	8	39
Evans, Jalen	0	3	5.74	9	0	27	28	29	22
Fairchild, Austin	1	5	3.64	51	1	54	51	33	78
Gardewine, Nick	5	4	2.72	42	15	43	25	32	59
Hilton, Kevin	10	3	5.47	20	0	107	118	36	79
Lucas, Josh	2	2	3.62	17	0	55	50	30	53
Lucas, Josh	3	4	4.58	25	0	96	90	49	87
McCarthy, Kevin	3	2	4.80	45	2	60	57	24	50
Sanchez, Jesus	3	0	6.47	5	0	24	30	8	12

FARGO-MOORHEAD REDHAWKS

Name	AVG	AB	R	H	HR	RBI	BB	SO	SB
Alexander, Evan	.249	273	58	68	4	33	43	79	31
Boscan, Manuel	.292	370	59	108	16	68	22	63	12
Correa, Christian	.199	271	26	54	3	34	30	48	3
Dexter, Sam	.266	349	55	93	9	57	17	44	5
Livorsi, Ben	.340	103	20	35	2	16	18	24	0
Maris, Peter	.283	392	72	111	20	65	49	65	3
Novak, Nick	.257	202	43	52	3	13	21	64	9
Olund, Alec	.304	46	12	14	0	5	9	8	1
Pina, Leobaldo	.346	373	66	129	8	67	35	48	6
Silviano, John	.268	365	59	98	23	84	64	116	0
Ward, Drew	.345	296	64	102	17	48	63	68	1

Name	W	L	ERA	G	SV	IP	H	BB	SO
Allison, Ben	0	0	7.07	4	0	14	16	9	10
DuBord, Alex	2	2	2.83	37	23	41	42	13	50
Feldman, Davis	6	6	5.03	28	0	107	125	49	98
Grauer, Tyler	10	5	3.51	21	0	126	120	32	9
Jones, Joe	4	3	3.72	43	4	56	39	44	66
Lind, Luke	7	3	4.25	47	2	59	54	21	56

McGovern, Kevin	10	3	3.70	21	0	127	119	37	8
Riley, Tanner	4	3	2.84	31	0	38	34	31	41
Simms, Trevor	1	0	3.60	8	0	15	13	10	23
Stover, Brady	2	2	5.64	37	0	53	51	47	53
Wigginton, Peyton	9	3	3.84	15	1	91	92	27	74

GARY SOUTHSHORE RAILCATS

Name	AVG	AB	R	H	HR	RBI	BB	SO	SB
Abbott, Sam	.218	238	38	52	20	46	22	120	0
Castillo, LG	.318	192	31	61	7	37	14	42	3
Graves, Sherman	.255	55	4	14	2	14	5	18	0
Greely, Thomas	.237	76	9	18	0	2	10	21	1
Lingua, Daniel	.271	358	57	97	6	48	42	98	29
Madden, Lester	.157	51	4	8	1	4	1	18	0
Marriaga, Jesus	.307	280	54	86	6	61	29	75	21
Nova, Victor	.270	196	39	53	8	39	26	45	7
Scantlin, Nate	.275	131	23	36	1	8	14	45	16
Smith, Jackson	.239	159	22	38	3	15	3	36	2
Walraven, Thomas	.272	327	61	89	16	55	49	57	15
Woodworth, Michael	.294	401	75	118	5	43	31	59	23

Name	W	L	ERA	G	SV	IP	H	BB	SO
Campbell, Ryan	0	0	5.14	9	0	14	15	11	12
Cuello, Edward	3	6	8.94	11	0	46	70	12	43
Eisenbarger, Jack	2	7	5.29	35	6	65	55	43	88
Erwin, Chris	3	5	4.01	20	1	83	83	40	86
Francis, Harrison	5	8	5.29	20	0	95	110	48	95
Garcia, Nick	5	2	7.25	26	0	77	112	19	48
Heidenfelder, Adam	7	6	4.50	21	0	100	102	44	84
Medina, Yeison	1	2	5.06	26	4	32	32	25	21
Phillips, Aaron	3	3	4.14	36	3	63	57	38	51
Sheaks, John	5	8	4.64	18	0	99	109	30	74
Vivas, Julio	1	0	3.27	18	0	22	20	11	19

KANE COUNTY COUGARS

Name	AVG	AB	R	H	HR	RBI	BB	SO	SB
Anderson, Nick	.251	203	36	51	3	27	32	59	6
Busby, Dylan	.313	278	44	87	14	52	21	76	1
Cribbs, Galli	.259	320	38	83	1	43	21	79	9
De La Trinidad, Ernie	.305	357	69	109	7	49	55	62	2
Franklin, Nick	.260	77	17	20	5	19	14	24	1
Johnson, Sherman	.231	320	60	74	13	52	75	64	1
Kerrigan, Jimmy	.304	398	80	121	27	89	33	98	8
Lombardozzi, Steve	.301	153	19	46	2	18	14	26	3
Lopez, BJ	.238	261	28	62	5	30	27	61	0
Mangieri, Luke	.216	37	8	8	2	4	8	9	0
Nay, Mitch	.273	33	8	9	2	6	5	9	0
Pantoja, Alexis	.250	272	40	68	5	37	25	53	3
Randolph, Cornelius	.310	348	64	108	14	64	45	66	13
Rolette, Josh	.292	312	52	91	8	43	25	61	1
Williams, Donivan	.297	37	8	11	1	5	3	9	1

Name	W	L	ERA	G	SV	IP	H	BB	SO
Rogalla, Keith	0	0	1.50	5	6	2	1	3	9
Nissen, Logan	1	1	2.38	19	23	19	0	11	23
Stevenson, Jake	1	0	2.79	7	9	5	2	3	13
Fox, Jack	11	3	3.04	18	92	93	5	44	73
Carter, C.J.	1	4	3.48	39	52	36	4	36	64
Muir, Westin	7	0	3.77	17	60	58	8	30	34
Richardson, Ryan	4	2	4.05	41	58	54	7	18	53
Taggart, Danny	0	0	4.07	13	18	11	2	18	10
Anderson, Nick	0	0	4.15	4	4	5	2	1	0
Anderson, Jack	6	2	4.24	46	64	66	6	26	67
Fuentes, Jose	6	5	4.33	23	120	120	11	50	87
Tapani, Ryan	7	7	4.61	26	92	97	14	24	110
Worley, Vance	6	9	4.89	18	114	137	19	37	56
Morin, Michael	0	0	5.26	12	14	18	0	4	9
Bishop, Koby	0	4	6.35	26	57	66	9	41	46
Allison, Ben	3	7	7.05	20	80	92	19	38	39
Koch, Tyler	1	0	11.04	10	7	12	0	5	8
McMahan, Pearson	0	2	16.36	8	11	20	1	12	7

KANSAS CITY MONARCHS

Name	AVG	AB	R	H	HR	RBI	BB	SO	SB
Brusa, Gio	.226	62	6	14	1	7	10	16	0
Escarra, J.C.	.291	234	52	68	12	35	38	33	1
Gillaspie, Casey	.275	342	60	94	17	66	63	95	5
Grotjohn, Ryan	.298	84	24	25	5	25	24	18	4
Harris, Dylan	.333	24	7	8	0	2	5	3	0
Hernandez, Jan	.313	268	70	84	24	71	51	105	10
Olmeda, Alexis	.199	156	25	31	7	21	25	59	1
Robson, Jacob	.288	111	21	32	9	34	21	46	8
Santa, Kevin	.335	224	35	75	1	38	15	32	4
Thompson, David	.346	283	71	98	19	63	36	39	15

Name	W	L	ERA	G	SV	IP	H	BB	SO
Belzer, Nick	6	2	4.32	19	0	90	85	41	67
Gilliam, Brock	6	4	4.80	27	1	66	65	27	67
Glowicki, Brian	2	0	3.66	15	0	19.2	18	6	25
Hall, Matt	10	2	1.10	14	0	82	59	24	1
Harris, Jon	4	2	4.92	14	0	75	75	30	58
Hartman, Matt	7	5	4.71	24	1	99	86	60	10
Koch, Brandon	3	3	4.22	50	5	49	36	24	80
Martinson, Jordan	5	2	3.39	45	0	74	62	29	83
Miller, Jalen	2	0	1.13	3	0	16	9	11	20
Rubio, Frank	3	2	5.64	30	0	38	48	10	34
Thorpe, Lewis	8	2	4.96	16	0	82	88	24	75

LAKE COUNTRY DOCKHOUNDS

Name	AVG	AB	R	H	HR	RBI	BB	SO	SB
Bennett, T.J.	.275	378	65	104	17	56	43	117	11
Blanco, Manuel	.232	56	7	13	0	5	5	20	3
Briggs, Lamar	.223	287	43	64	10	46	25	80	7
Carranza, Tristen	.281	317	52	89	9	42	26	68	17
Dykstra, Casey	.186	102	20	19	6	16	17	46	1
Gimenez, Wilfredo	.234	269	32	63	8	42	23	54	1
Noriega, Gabriel	.269	402	51	108	9	56	20	93	1
Schaffer, Jordan	.280	161	22	45	0	20	6	29	4
Snider, Jake	.303	304	58	92	9	41	45	97	17
Yoh, Daikan	.260	285	43	74	9	35	42	79	7

Name	W	L	ERA	G	SV	IP	H	BB	SO
Gonzalez, Robert	2	2	6.13	26	0	40	51	17	30
Herold, Nick	1	1	2.23	9	0	32	18	21	47
Jimenez, Francisco	3	8	5.63	16	0	88	95	28	87
Kruczynski, Evan	6	6	5.45	19	0	102	111	53	15
McRae, Alex	5	4	4.01	14	0	83	89	20	78
Metoxen, Takoda	0	2	8.47	14	0	17	21	11	11
Murray, Shea	0	2	9.47	17	2	19	21	17	17
Remington, Jesse	3	5	6.44	23	0	73	89	47	50
Veliz, Greg	2	0	6.58	22	0	26	34	9	30
Ventura, Angel	2	5	5.06	11	0	64	70	22	52
Watson, Cyrillo	2	3	4.78	26	4	32	23	25	37

LINCOLN SALTDOGS

Name	AVG	AB	R	H	HR	RBI	BB	SO	SB
Altmann, Josh	.269	342	56	92	15	69	45	94	17
Ascanio, Rayder	.266	143	25	38	7	26	13	37	3
Devine, Drew	.269	93	11	25	1	7	10	20	6
Dotel, Welington	.277	285	42	79	5	24	19	91	5
Goodheart, Matt	.251	227	30	57	3	39	32	62	3
Long, Ryan	.288	288	56	83	10	44	59	51	11
Norris, Randy	.288	292	43	84	3	25	16	66	16
Rogers, Jason	.256	129	19	33	5	31	24	21	3
Roskam, Luke	.344	61	16	21	4	17	11	19	2
Weber, Skyler	.252	250	37	63	4	31	36	69	9

Name	W	L	ERA	G	SV	IP	H	BB	SO
Bezdicek, John	2	4	3.76	8	0	41	43	18	43
Cheshire, Jonathan	2	2	3.10	34	1	41	46	11	47
Cronin, Matt	3	3	1.99	26	3	41	23	15	43
Freure, R.J.	1	1	2.77	10	0	13	9	6	13
Hope, Carter	6	2	3.80	37	0	43	42	16	41
Lance, Carson	1	1	6.68	30	3	31	27	26	35
Moore, Steffon	0	4	4.32	39	11	42	30	33	49
St. Pierre, Zach	1	2	8.31	7	0	26	33	15	24
Zoz, David	3	2	4.14	38	0	41	46	20	47

MILWAUKEE MILKMEN

Name	AVG	AB	R	H	HR	RBI	BB	SO	SB

Name	AVG	AB	R	H	HR	RBI	BB	SO	SB
Barnum, Keon	.265	336	51	89	24	84	46	101	0
Burks, Jeremiah	.227	163	21	37	3	29	19	54	3
Chester, Carl	.230	87	9	20	3	14	10	19	2
Conley, Christ	.219	196	34	43	6	32	34	49	0
Davis, Mason	.295	227	35	67	5	28	20	42	19
Gomez, Miguel	.297	158	23	47	6	22	6	17	1
Hill, Aaron	.283	350	74	99	8	29	66	122	24
Kengor, Will	.264	360	62	95	14	59	50	100	10
Prime, Correlle	.257	292	47	75	11	52	28	82	5
Sanchez, Hector	.386	70	14	27	5	18	9	13	0
Torres, Bryan	.374	372	73	139	3	56	40	46	22

Name	W	L	ERA	G	SV	IP	H	BB	SO
Bartow, Frankie	2	1	3.70	24	0	24	21	8	22
Benoit, Rodrigo	4	0	1.63	32	8	39	21	19	61
Echevarria, Juan	2	3	5.72	39	0	50	53	31	43
Gray, Peyton	2	0	1.20	15	0	15	11	7	22
Holmes, Ben	4	0	6.03	11	1	37	48	18	27
Huckaby, Kyle	3	0	7.20	19	1	20	21	17	29
Jones, A.J.	5	6	7.01	22	0	86	126	24	56
Kowalczyk, Karch	1	2	3.38	27	10	27	24	9	25
Mahoney, Jack	1	1	5.40	28	0	37	35	15	46
Matthys, Jake	7	7	6.37	22	0	82	118	16	63
Schugel, A.J.	4	4	3.38	20	0	53	43	17	50
Smith, Myles	6	9	5.63	19	0	94	99	45	89
Young, Christian	3	3	5.09	25	0	76	67	24	95
Zimmerman, Ryan	4	5	4.46	20	0	99	95	49	11

SIOUX CITY EXPLORERS

Name	AVG	AB	R	H	HR	RBI	BB	SO	SB
Amaral, Danny	.295	322	67	95	8	26	35	79	48
Harris, Chase	.282	287	49	81	7	30	37	74	13
Kelly, Jack	.194	72	12	14	4	8	4	14	0
Kone, Zack	.212	156	15	33	2	14	10	35	0
Rifaela, Ademar	.315	216	30	68	9	43	22	58	0
Sierra, Miguel	.317	41	9	13	2	7	7	16	0
Snyder, Gabe	.259	290	55	75	18	54	37	72	7
Tiberi, Blake	.254	327	53	83	4	46	47	67	5

Name	W	L	ERA	G	SV	IP	H	BB	SO
Bates, Solomon	1	2	5.50	8	0	18	22	4	31
Brosher, Brandon	3	2	6.42	37	0	48	45	32	53
Gercken, Nate	2	1	3.38	25	0	24	18	26	26
Kuhns, Max	4	6	3.20	40	4	59	44	24	86
Ledet, Patrick	6	4	4.28	19	0	114	98	35	93
Lenik, Kevin	1	1	4.70	31	0	38	38	13	42
McIlraith, Thomas	5	5	4.14	40	19	46	43	20	69
Rodriguez, Nivaldo	3	1	1.50	5	0	30	16	9	40
Verburg, Mitchell	0	0	1.48	17	0	24	22	7	32

SIOUX FALLS CANARIES

Name	AVG	AB	R	H	HR	RBI	BB	SO	SB
Altavilla, Angelo	.249	281	32	70	2	20	28	55	5
Blair, Connor	.180	50	6	9	2	4	4	17	1
Christopher, Shamoy	.166	199	15	33	4	19	22	83	0
Gotta, Nick	.251	227	30	57	2	16	50	49	6
Gurwitz, Zane	.272	158	27	43	4	19	22	37	2
Henry, Jabari	.259	386	62	100	29	86	49	92	3
LaValley, Gavin	.324	346	50	112	20	73	33	72	0
Michalczewski, Trey	.243	334	45	81	13	45	46	125	0
Nester, John	.202	114	16	23	2	13	11	28	0
Quiggle, Kona	.237	329	44	78	8	40	29	109	2
Ulrich, Wyatt	.338	269	52	91	4	24	22	49	11

Name	W	L	ERA	G	SV	IP	H	BB	SO
Culbreth, Ty	7	6	5.18	18	0	108	118	27	82
Ferrell, Riley	1	3	1.73	27	11	26	12	16	36
Garkow, Nate	1	0	2.70	11	0	27	22	10	31
Garkow, Tyler	1	9	8.18	20	0	69	99	25	56
Hasty, Charlie	3	4	3.70	46	0	49	44	15	48
Johnson, Christian	1	1	7.34	27	0	61	85	35	46
Lang, Neil	2	5	4.96	20	0	98	105	38	68
Lanier, Tony	0	0	9.15	18	0	21	18	35	30
Ledesma, Stevie	6	4	4.64	32	1	52	52	17	60
Pimentel, Cesilio	1	6	7.77	11	0	44	58	24	34

Name	W	L	ERA	G	SV	IP	H	BB	SO
Walters, Mitchell	0	1	4.29	38	5	36	25	22	50
Wyatt, Colby	4	5	4.88	35	0	55	66	26	52

WINNIPEG GOLDEYES

Name	AVG	AB	R	H	HR	RBI	BB	SO	SB
Crouse, Michael	.148	27	4	4	0	2	8	14	0
Gonzalez, Hidekel	.188	191	33	36	9	28	22	58	1
Lachance, Kevin	.262	294	45	77	5	24	30	57	6
Murphy, Max	.308	403	76	124	31	97	27	103	6
Navarro, Raul	.335	370	75	124	6	51	31	65	18
Pruitt Jr., Reggie	.259	263	58	68	13	41	38	101	32
Rhinesmith, Jacob	.276	87	9	24	2	10	9	20	0
Sagdal, Ian	.317	372	70	118	6	69	53	73	5
Stafford Jr., Deon	.247	255	39	63	8	37	15	65	0

Name	W	L	ERA	G	SV	IP	H	BB	SO
Adames, Freisis	8	4	5.07	17	0	82	78	33	71
Blanton, Bryan	1	2	2.14	39	0	34	16	31	48
Bourassa, Landen	5	5	4.33	16	1	87	110	27	57
Hart, Alex	0	2	7.78	8	0	20	24	12	11
Manasa, Alex	4	6	6.20	19	0	90	127	32	64
Martinez, R.J.	8	5	4.84	21	0	84	94	32	71
McAffer, Will	1	0	1.54	12	1	12	4	5	16
Ramirez, Luis	10	7	4.51	21	0	126	133	33	16
Ryan, Zac	2	1	3.72	32	0	29	26	16	33
Seabrooke, Travis	3	2	4.76	60	0	53	68	23	49
Strobel, Tasker	2	3	3.42	53	21	55	53	21	58
Vargas, Jhon	5	3	4.78	36	0	58	52	36	59

ATLANTIC LEAGUE

The Lancaster Barnstormers won their first Atlantic League title since 2014 and their third all-time with a three-game sweep of the High Point Rockers. Oscar De La Cruz threw a complete-game four-hitter in the deciding 6-1 win in Game 3.

North	W	L	PCT	GB
**-Southern Maryland*	83	48	.634	—
#-Lancaster	73	58	.557	10
Long Island	64	68	.485	19.5
York	56	76	.424	27.5
Staten Island	48	84	.364	35.5
South	**W**	**L**	**PCT**	**GB**
*-Gastonia	88	44	.667	—
&-High Point	71	61	.538	17
Kentucky	67	65	.508	21
Lexington	56	76	.424	32
Charleston	53	79	.402	35

**First Half Winner. &-Wild Card. #Second-half division winner*

Playoffs—Semifinals: Lancaster defeated Southern Maryland 3-2 and High Point defeated Gastonia 3-2 in best-of-5 series. **Finals:** Lancaster swept High Point 3-0 in best-of-5 series.

ATTENDANCE: Long Island 285,888; Lancaster 222,167; Southern Maryland 174,293; York 172,519; Lexington 150,392; High Point 124,010; Charleston 119,598; Kentucky 102,502; Gastonia 101,471; Staten Island 76,759.'

Player of the Year: Courtney Hawkins, Lexington. **Pitcher of the Year:** Daryl Thompson, Southern Maryland. **Defensive Player of the Year:** Melvin Mercedes, Lancaster. **Manager of the Year:** Mauro Gozzo, Gastonia.

BATTING LEADERS

Player	Team	AVG	AB	R	H	HR	RBI
De Aza, Alejandro	LI	.343	376	77	129	10	68
Cordero, Andretty	LAN	.339	542	87	184	18	118
Castro, Carlos	3 Teams	.327	382	49	125	14	71
Harris, David	SMD	.322	351	71	113	16	86
Jarrett, Zach	GAS	.313	416	86	130	21	84
Travis, Sam	LI	.310	323	47	100	9	68
Rosa, Joseph	GAS	.308	458	88	141	21	92
Becker, Luke	WHG	.308	484	107	149	23	98
Lee, Braxton	SMD	.306	432	60	132	3	73
Downs, Jerry	HP	.303	403	80	122	22	83
Hawkins, Courtney	LEX	.298	473	110	141	48	125

PITCHING LEADERS

Player	Team	W	L	ERA	IP	H	BB	SO
Thompson, Daryl	SMD	15	4	3.43	186	183	22	119
Lambson, Mitch	SMD	8	9	3.60	163	155	42	145
Anderson, John	GAS	13	4	3.66	128	115	47	95
Sanabia, Alex	2 Teams	7	5	3.88	116	107	50	101
Merithew, Alex	SMD	8	3	3.91	106	110	24	73
Stem, Craig	HP	7	6	4.01	123	139	26	77
Ball, Nile	LAN	11	5	4.08	141	129	47	118
Solter, Matt	2 Teams	5	12	4.15	145	178	49	98
Adams, Derrick	CWV	7	9	4.21	120	124	43	101
De La Cruz, Oscar	LAN	9	3	4.26	125	114	46	135

CHARLESTON DIRTY BIRDS

Name	AVG	AB	R	H	HR	RBI	BB	SO	SB
Beltre, Engel	.293	297	46	87	8	45	17	42	11
Bird, Corey	.260	77	10	20	1	10	4	15	4
Blaum, Tyler	.238	239	22	57	2	21	16	63	4
Burcham, Scott	.246	349	39	86	6	39	25	86	8
Cannella, Cosimo	.246	65	6	16	0	2	5	19	2
Espinal, Edwin	.278	180	21	50	8	43	11	27	0
Garced, Angel	.193	176	31	34	3	12	30	70	10
Gonzalez, Alfredo	.281	267	46	75	17	49	27	61	17
Gonzalez, Yovan	.313	288	34	90	6	51	37	53	1
Goris, Diego	.251	295	34	74	2	30	15	66	7
Hart, Mike	.125	32	3	4	0	3	9	15	0
Heath, Nick	.238	261	49	62	4	33	47	73	42
Justus, Connor	.269	175	27	47	3	28	18	21	5
Kelly, Scott	.230	422	61	97	1	30	64	49	29
Kone, Zack	.175	40	3	7	0	3	2	10	1
Longhi, Nick	.294	201	34	59	10	41	23	40	0
Perez, Juan	.297	158	24	47	5	28	16	26	4
Rosario, Jose	.267	30	7	8	1	2	7	5	3
Scafariello, Liam	.042	24	4	1	0	0	4	18	1
Seymour, Anfernee	.253	297	50	75	6	36	27	70	24
Sullivan, Zach	.067	15	3	1	0	1	3	6	1
Torrence, Devon	.216	134	22	29	1	9	19	36	16
Williams, Miles	.156	192	19	30	8	24	13	94	3

Name	W	L	ERA	G	SV	IP	H	BB	SO
Adams, Derrick	7	9	4.21	24	0	120	124	43	101
Baez, Angelo	1	1	6.00	2	0	12	16	4	6
Carrillo, Francisco	0	3	5.47	24	0	25	29	12	23
Chamblee, Stephen	2	6	5.49	27	0	95	119	25	64
DeMasi, Dominic	1	1	3.60	2	0	10	15	2	4
Garcia, Ruben	0	1	5.51	11	0	16	15	16	19
Gomez, Ricardo	2	0	2.25	22	1	24	17	7	30
Gunn, Michael	1	5	6.75	12	0	49	58	28	28
Herget, Kevin	0	0	4.24	3	0	17	17	3	19
Hull, Denson	1	6	7.11	11	0	57	90	27	45
Kisena, Alec	0	5	8.36	9	0	42	67	18	33
Lawlor, Ryan	6	3	5.93	34	0	68	67	37	82
Mack, Courtney	0	1	9.31	6	0	10	15	8	6
Mesa, Jose	4	3	5.14	11	0	42	43	17	39
Osnowitz, Mitchell	1	1	6.35	21	0	23	29	13	17
Peden, Nate	3	1	5.81	19	1	26	31	13	27
Sanchez, Isaac	2	1	1.73	24	1	26	14	13	25
Scheetz, Kit	5	1	3.88	14	0	56	36	29	61
Sergey, Matt	1	1	8.87	9	0	22	29	16	20
Siegrist, Kevin	5	0	1.82	37	6	40	24	9	53
Stephens, Jordan	1	5	5.37	13	0	67	70	23	52
Tannenbaum, Max	2	6	6.42	42	0	55	51	33	48
Testa, Joe	2	5	5.24	37	0	67	91	15	58
Weickel, Walker	1	6	5.36	25	1	44	42	20	48
Weyman, Gavin	1	0	6.41	12	0	20	28	9	9
Wilson, Tyler	3	1	0.64	28	10	28	12	8	34

GASTONIA HONEY HUNTERS

Name	AVG	AB	R	H	HR	RBI	BB	SO	SB
Ascanio, Rayder	.246	183	28	45	3	29	20	29	9
Castro, Luis	.273	330	57	90	12	49	31	66	17
Davis, Johnny	.307	88	23	27	2	13	7	18	9
Freeman, Cole	.324	74	15	24	1	14	2	6	3
Hampton, Reece	.277	394	84	109	9	47	56	67	65
Holderbach, Alex	.253	178	29	45	3	34	26	45	1
Holmes, Tra	.321	28	7	9	0	3	4	10	5
Jarrett, Zach	.313	416	86	130	21	84	38	86	32
Jones, Eric	.172	29	4	5	0	3	3	8	0
Levy, Stuart	.227	260	47	59	5	39	49	66	1
Owings, Connor	.091	11	3	1	0	0	8	6	2
Reinheimer, Jack	.281	477	89	134	12	69	59	97	55
Rodriguez, Herlis	.272	268	34	73	8	29	20	42	19
Roman, Luis	.266	364	64	97	16	72	49	96	20
Rosa, Joseph	.308	458	88	141	21	92	70	118	16
Sandford, Darian	.231	65	8	15	1	8	4	7	6
Skole, Jake	.255	369	78	94	23	61	77	119	26
Smith, Jaylen	.250	80	15	20	2	16	11	20	10
Tapia, Emmanuel	.277	253	50	70	15	69	37	79	7
Trejo, Cesar	.353	17	3	6	2	5	3	2	2

Name	W	L	ERA	G	SV	IP	H	BB	SO
Anderson, John	13	4	3.66	23	0	128	115	47	95
Balaguer, Jesus	1	4	3.36	57	25	56	52	27	71
Bernal, Roger	2	1	7.43	3	0	13	12	7	9
Bordner, Sam	11	5	2.42	55	2	63	59	16	62
Chalmers, Dakota	1	2	6.87	11	0	38	37	30	51
Delgado, Randall	1	1	3.23	16	1	39	30	18	42
Farfan, Onas	3	3	3.57	46	1	68	63	34	59
Godley, Zack	4	1	4.64	15	0	54	52	15	64
Gunn, Michael	2	0	5.18	9	0	24	24	19	21
Hovis, Reilly	8	5	5.61	27	0	114	105	41	98
Keel, Jerry	6	3	3.50	14	0	72	79	27	52
Leyer, Euclides	4	3	3.05	42	0	44	40	21	37
Martinez, Henry	2	1	5.18	24	0	33	32	14	43
McGuire, Deck	5	0	1.91	6	0	38	23	7	41
McKinney, Ian	7	4	5.40	16	0	77	57	41	70
Naughton, Tim	1	1	4.09	21	0	22	21	11	35
Pérez, Luis	0	0	3.21	10	0	14	18	6	10
Sanabia, Alex	3	0	0.93	5	0	29	16	12	27
Sobotka, Chad	0	0	0.00	11	0	11	6	5	15
Solter, Matt	0	2	6.60	3	0	15	26	3	9
Torres-Costa, Quintin	4	2	2.76	47	3	49	38	22	66
Walden, Marcus	3	0	2.86	9	0	50	36	8	34
Zabaleta, Ezequiel	4	1	4.01	18	0	25	21	17	25

HIGH POINT ROCKERS

Name	AVG	AB	R	H	HR	RBI	BB	SO	SB
Aklinski, Ben	.268	448	93	120	19	74	73	89	20
Alfonzo, Giovanny	.285	344	49	98	3	46	35	81	4
Baldwin, Roldani	.264	72	10	19	6	19	3	23	0
DiSarcina, JR	.175	40	4	7	1	3	3	12	0
Downs, Jerry	.303	403	80	122	22	83	44	86	1
Field, Johnny	.229	192	29	44	6	25	30	54	10
Gonzalez, Jay	.277	300	39	83	3	34	42	81	14
Gulino, Mike	.221	208	30	46	2	24	25	53	1
Ladendorf, Tyler	.239	356	61	85	17	49	32	69	10
Latimore, Quincy	.259	375	68	97	21	79	58	92	8
Martinez, Michael	.304	250	44	76	5	35	26	37	6
Moore, Logan	.129	31	2	4	0	0	3	13	0
Morrison, Logan	.283	293	53	83	15	54	56	42	3
Mulcay, Dakota	.096	52	5	5	0	2	7	17	0
Okazaki, Yuta	.063	16	0	1	0	0	0	6	0
Proctor, Chris	.296	108	13	32	0	17	9	21	1
Russell, Michael	.292	394	76	115	9	53	44	54	18
Scafariello, Liam	.059	17	2	1	0	0	4	10	1
Taylor, Adam	.278	18	2	5	0	5	0	3	1
Trejo, Cesar	.172	29	1	5	0	4	2	12	1
Wiel, Zander	.260	384	83	100	32	98	45	111	11

Name	W	L	ERA	G	SV	IP	H	BB	SO
Atkins, Mitch	3	0	4.91	6	0	26	23	11	18
Bates, Nathan	1	0	6.1	17	0	21	26	11	25
Bradford, Chasen	2	3	6.51	28	7	28	39	8	20
Casad, Cooper	1	0	1.64	2	0	11	9	2	8
Castellanos, Gabriel	0	0	2.57	18	0	21	16	10	13
Choplick, Adam	3	3	3.42	25	1	24	21	12	31
Church, Andrew	3	0	3.27	6	0	33	29	7	20
Cotter, Cameron	1	0	1.65	17	0	16	12	6	14
Crawford, Jonathon	0	0	4.82	29	0	28	17	31	44

Dull, Ryan	7	1	3.88	50	13	51	41	10	72
Duncan, Tanner	0	0	3.38	10	1	11	5	4	6
Evangelista, Nick	1	3	8.15	4	0	18	23	6	7
Glorius, Austin	3	6	6.22	18	0	55	66	40	37
Hayes, John	3	1	4.08	23	0	29	25	11	20
Hensley, Bryce	2	2	3.9	51	0	67	62	24	48
Higgins, Tyler	2	1	1.72	15	4	16	13	3	19
Jannis, Mickey	2	2	2.72	11	0	40	23	20	44
Johnson, Joe	0	2	5.48	25	0	23	23	13	18
Lail, Brady	2	1	0.95	3	0	19	13	2	19
Manzueta, Jheyson	2	1	1.93	6	0	37	32	7	31
Mott, Kyle	2	1	6.03	21	0	31	19	29	38
Nicolino, Justin	4	1	2.06	6	0	35	26	6	29
O'Sullivan, Liam	4	6	7.98	13	0	62	79	25	37
Pineyro, Ivan	5	3	3.76	13	0	67	57	20	58
Rincon, Junior	2	3	2.33	29	0	39	32	25	44
Scolaro, Jonah	2	3	5.53	6	0	28	29	16	28
Stem, Craig	7	6	4.01	20	0	123	139	26	77
Uskali, Neil	5	5	5.38	16	0	84	100	28	54
Webb, Colt	1	2	10.05	4	0	14	22	7	7

LANCASTER BARNSTORMERS

Name	AVG	AB	R	H	HR	RBI	BB	SO	SB
Barfield, Jacob	.261	138	26	36	4	23	30	33	10
Boyd, BJ	.345	55	13	19	3	11	7	4	3
Carpenter, Joseph	.297	64	11	19	1	9	4	17	0
Clark, LeDarious	.279	247	52	69	13	38	25	69	24
Cordero, Andretty	.339	542	87	184	18	118	26	65	8
Dugan, Kelly	.326	236	58	77	23	69	32	50	7
Dunston, Shawon	.301	219	50	66	5	28	32	46	26
Feliz, Anderson	.244	356	41	87	7	56	40	84	9
Hill, Tyler	.273	22	5	6	0	0	3	8	0
Hoover, Jake	.254	331	46	84	4	39	20	79	17
Hubbard, Dondrei	.042	24	2	1	0	1	3	6	3
Lien, Connor	.323	31	4	10	0	4	0	12	0
Loehr, Trace	.238	344	58	82	2	34	58	73	22
Mercedes, Melvin	.294	479	105	141	12	72	83	68	15
Peroni, Anthony	.222	270	29	60	2	28	42	54	3
Proctor, Chris	.243	111	19	27	3	19	10	22	2
Reichenbach, Ed	.154	13	1	2	1	1	2	6	0
Robinson, Trayvon	.287	324	49	93	9	51	44	82	6
Sandoval, Ariel	.356	132	25	47	5	23	6	14	14
Shaver, Colton	.258	275	44	71	11	50	41	78	1
Torrence, Devon	.198	106	21	21	0	7	27	37	10
Zagunis, Mark	.203	59	10	12	1	5	11	16	2

Name	W	L	ERA	G	SV	IP	H	BB	SO
Aker, Cole	2	2	5.64	20	1	22	23	10	21
Ball, Nile	11	5	4.08	25	0	141	129	47	118
Booser, Cam	1	0	4.63	13	1	11.2	12	6	15
Cha, Erik	0	2	4.50	14	0	10	6	16	11
Clarke, Bret	3	2	3.91	34	1	69	63	25	66
De La Cruz, Oscar	9	3	4.26	28	0	125	114	46	135
DiSabatino, Dom	6	5	6.18	23	1	51	47	34	54
Fenter, Gray	2	1	2.95	9	2	21	18	6	32
Gann, Cameron	9	8	5.27	27	0	137	126	68	145
Goodson, Donald	1	0	5.36	39	1	47	44	31	53
Graham, Josh	1	1	1.72	48	7	52	41	12	59
Hall, Brooks	6	1	2.97	12	0	64	47	15	56
Johnson, Chase	2	7	4.40	46	2	59	51	37	59
Manoah, Erik	3	3	4.35	18	0	81	62	44	76
Shuman, Scott	1	1	0.90	10	4	10	8	2	9
Sittinger, Brandyn	1	2	3.44	13	0	18	11	8	21
Suellentrop, Tyler	2	2	3.15	39	0	40	30	29	55
Sylk, Augie	4	9	5.71	20	0	69	60	54	56
Teller, Brent	3	3	5.12	7	0	39	33	15	41
Tunnell, West	6	1	3.63	43	11	45	28	31	51

LEXINGTON LEGENDS

Name	AVG	AB	R	H	HR	RBI	BB	SO	SB
Bethancourt, Dom	.183	71	8	13	1	5	3	21	1
Briceno, Jose	.237	97	16	23	3	19	14	19	3
Cotto, Gabriel	.182	22	1	4	0	1	0	9	0
Cuevas, Cesar	.237	186	20	44	1	25	17	50	1
Ervin, Phil	.275	375	75	103	18	59	69	100	33
Estrada, Rusber	.368	68	15	25	9	19	8	23	0
Geraldo, Manuel	.260	389	47	101	7	44	27	95	21
Hawkins, Courtney	.298	473	110	141	48	125	74	102	6
Hunt, Trey	.171	35	6	6	1	7	1	13	1
Jackson, Ryan	.196	92	13	18	2	7	16	17	1
Koontz, T.K.	.200	70	8	14	1	9	7	29	3
Marshall, Montrell	.249	438	60	109	21	72	30	176	2
Martinez, Teodoro	.256	121	26	31	3	15	16	12	1
McDade, Jarel	.043	23	3	1	0	0	4	7	0
Mercado, Skylar	.400	55	18	22	6	12	8	16	3
Miller, Jalen	.235	34	4	8	0	0	5	7	0
Nelson, James	.250	156	22	39	4	18	11	23	4
Powell, Boog	.312	253	58	79	9	32	42	42	19
Pugh, Tillman	.258	356	53	92	18	59	43	107	13
Sandford, Darian	.244	78	14	19	0	5	5	21	10
Smith Jr., Dwight	.171	41	5	7	2	7	6	10	1
Swihart, Blake	.157	153	20	24	4	15	31	56	2
Tavarez, Jesus	.311	45	9	14	4	12	4	12	1
Tejeda, Isaias	.277	394	65	109	29	90	58	71	1
Thomas, Toro	.200	30	2	6	0	5	1	15	0
Thompson, Nate	.087	23	7	2	1	2	5	10	0
Valdespin, Jordany	.296	71	10	21	1	8	11	9	3
Yorgen, Pete	.274	175	29	48	0	14	20	41	1

Name	W	L	ERA	G	SV	IP	H	BB	SO
Adams, Austin	0	2	5.46	32	14	31	32	25	40
Albert, Wes	1	5	10.74	7	0	29	46	18	21
Cole, Mason	1	0	8.74	15	0	23	21	26	28
Corcino, Daniel	6	11	6.53	24	0	121	143	70	84
Dorminy, Thomas	5	7	5.52	18	0	88	91	47	75
Freese, Dakota	0	0	8.59	4	0	15	21	12	16
Gibson, Daniel	5	2	5.55	49	0	49	69	21	55
Hiraldo, Yaramil	0	1	5.83	50	1	54	49	31	78
Hoover, J.J.	2	6	6.34	11	0	61	72	27	50
Johnson, Jeff	1	3	5.21	39	1	38	47	17	45
Lavendier, Winston	3	5	3.92	35	0	44	48	20	43
Lebron, David	8	3	4.78	15	0	81	84	38	78
Lusk, Lance	0	0	1.80	13	1	15	13	4	24
Miller, Jalen	4	4	5.86	27	0	58	60	40	65
Owens, Henry	1	3	7.33	35	0	47	54	40	42
Ramos, Eury	2	1	3.86	16	2	16	16	10	17
Rosario, Aneuris	1	1	2.81	16	5	16	9	10	18
Sampson, Keyvius	3	2	3.41	7	0	37	34	11	50
Santamaria, Jose	3	1	3.89	11	0	35	30	15	32
Schneider, Brett	0	1	7.15	21	0	45	61	26	33
Suriel, Edison	3	2	4.08	12	0	18	15	10	22
Thompson, Jeff	3	6	8.18	24	0	69	88	48	64
Walda, Ean	2	3	6.81	7	0	37	44	19	30
Wright, Keegan	1	1	5.40	4	0	20	24	5	11

LONG ISLAND DUCKS

Name	AVG	AB	R	H	HR	RBI	BB	SO	SB
Achenbach, Trevor	.275	40	10	11	2	7	3	12	1
Bottari, Nick	.143	21	3	3	0	0	5	3	0
Castillo, Rusney	.278	216	20	60	3	24	16	20	3
Castro, Carlos	.342	202	29	69	8	38	10	46	7
Caulfield, Phil	.288	170	33	49	2	20	25	25	10
Chamberlain, Matt	.231	65	9	15	1	10	9	17	3
De Aza, Alejandro	.343	376	77	129	10	68	70	62	10
DeCarlo, Joe	.295	397	66	117	7	56	56	67	4
Fields, Daniel	.250	20	2	5	1	4	5	10	1
Ford, Lew	.270	126	21	34	5	18	5	22	0
Frias, Vladimir	.238	425	54	101	6	42	41	64	13
Lin, Tzu-Wei	.306	62	11	19	3	9	10	14	2
Marrero, Deven	.238	160	17	38	1	21	22	37	5
Marti, Johnny	.158	19	1	3	0	1	1	2	0
Mazzilli, L.J.	.263	369	76	97	11	46	64	55	21
McGowan, Jacson	.167	42	6	7	1	4	7	16	0
Racusin, Zach	.294	17	1	5	0	3	3	1	0
Rei, Austin	.142	106	11	15	2	9	10	31	0
Romero, Deibinson	.287	404	57	116	17	80	88	61	1

Sermo, Jose	.252	103	17	26	4	14	20	34	0
Seymour, Anfernee	.255	47	12	12	1	8	5	14	6
Travis, Sam	.310	323	47	100	9	68	29	53	0
Turbo, Johnni	.297	209	30	62	4	20	8	33	5
Whatley, Kevin	.171	82	11	14	2	8	11	32	3
Wielansky, Michael	.200	35	6	7	0	2	3	11	2
Woodcock, Dustin	.249	329	65	82	16	52	50	87	17
Zarrello, Jake	.156	45	3	7	0	2	6	21	0

Name	W	L	ERA	G	SV	IP	H	BB	SO
Baez, Sandy	3	3	3.15	39	5	46	39	33	38
Beckman, Cody	1	1	4.81	17	0	34	28	21	37
Carasiti, Matt	1	1	1.59	9	1	11	7	4	14
Caudelle, Hunter	1	1	10.80	6	0	12	21	13	8
Cepeda, Chris	5	2	4.30	32	0	59	67	20	39
Cywin, Chas	1	1	4.32	19	0	25	24	6	14
DeLeon, Anderson	3	4	5.45	27	1	79	80	34	73
Goody, Nick	0	2	4.20	15	5	15	16	6	24
Harkin, Scott	10	8	4.86	24	0	128	165	28	88
Hockin, Chad	2	2	2.76	30	1	29	21	19	28
Iorio, Joe	11	5	4.58	30	0	130	140	43	83
Jose, Jose	3	1	1.20	26	3	30	22	4	36
Kennedy, Brett	2	1	3.03	6	0	33	30	9	27
Lin, Kai-Wei	1	2	2.18	19	2	21	22	9	24
Meisinger, Ryan	3	3	7.06	22	0	43	54	31	48
Morris, Akeel	6	10	5.65	24	0	123	135	66	96
Parry, Bennett	0	2	6.57	7	0	25	29	15	24
Peiffer, Dylan	1	0	8.00	13	0	18	24	12	20
Pike, Chris	1	0	5.14	4	0	14	13	8	7
Pinto, Wladimir	1	0	1.17	13	0	15	9	11	14
Quinn, Patrick	1	1	6.55	9	0	11	10	6	6
Ramos, Edubray	0	2	9.20	16	1	15	24	7	13
Tarpley, Stephen	4	7	4.64	20	0	85	80	27	92
Varela, James	1	2	6.24	32	0	62	71	16	39
Webb, Tyler	2	5	2.93	53	15	55	58	13	68
Wright, Keegan	1	1	5.40	4	0	20	24	5	11

STATEN ISLAND FERRYHAWKS

Name	AVG	AB	R	H	HR	RBI	BB	SO	SB
Aguilar, Angel	.297	417	61	124	14	58	44	75	6
Alemais, Stephen	.320	25	4	8	0	1	3	6	7
Bautista, Mariel	.264	292	42	77	10	46	21	89	10
Bell, Brantley	.118	17	1	2	1	2	0	5	0
Betancourt, Javier	.226	358	36	81	5	34	35	54	3
Castillo, Rusney	.325	154	15	50	3	23	12	17	4
Céspedes, Cristopher	.231	134	17	31	2	21	11	22	2
Cespedes, Ricardo	.295	438	55	129	4	45	20	47	21
Clemens, Kacy	.222	117	9	26	3	10	6	27	0
De La Rosa, Darlin	.083	12	1	1	0	0	1	3	0
Duplantis, Antoine	.299	338	47	101	8	36	18	40	13
Gonzalez, Bryan	.214	103	3	22	0	7	7	31	0
Herrera, Dilson	.255	329	38	84	4	44	40	77	9
Krause, Kevin	.308	26	2	8	1	6	3	7	0
Liriano, Rymer	.157	70	8	11	1	10	15	27	3
Marinez, Eric	.318	22	2	7	0	4	1	4	0
Monge, Joseph	.223	260	46	58	2	25	36	66	26
Nester, John	.170	94	8	16	1	10	13	23	0
Noriega, Andres	.233	193	27	45	3	21	9	40	2
O'Conner, Justin	.270	74	7	20	2	16	6	30	0
Osuna, Ramon	.214	126	17	27	6	16	21	57	5
Racusin, Zach	.364	11	1	4	0	1	4	2	0
Reyes, Alfredo	.246	284	40	70	1	14	25	75	18
Reyes, Joseph	.118	34	1	4	1	4	3	21	1
Ruta, Ben	.192	125	17	24	4	13	22	28	7
Santana, Yunior	.128	47	2	6	0	1	3	24	1
Smith, Jaylen	.333	12	2	4	0	0	0	1	0
Susini, Norberto	.200	35	2	7	0	1	9	10	0
Wagner, Brandon	.198	126	14	25	2	6	18	36	2
Whitmore, Kelsie	.026	39	2	1	0	0	2	23	0

Name	W	L	ERA	G	SV	IP	H	BB	SO
Aiello, Vincenzo	2	3	7.77	18	0	22	31	19	18
Auletta, Anthony	1	0	5.56	7	0	11	9	9	9
Capellan, Victor	7	3	1.60	48	20	56	34	22	55
Capuano, Christian	1	0	4.50	2	0	12	14	2	14
Carrell, Nick	0	3	6.82	8	0	34	41	30	15
Carrillo, Francisco	1	3	6.47	18	0	49	64	24	33
Castaneda, Dylan	2	1	6.75	3	0	16	14	11	18
Freese, Dakota	1	7	4.09	13	0	73	57	48	59
Guance, Hector	4	7	6.72	17	0	82	75	65	73
Katz, Alex	1	1	4.50	23	0	24	15	22	31
Kuzia, Joe	3	4	3.96	52	1	75	69	42	72
Law, Connor	1	2	2.75	41	1	52	44	30	63
Marinez, Eric	1	5	6.60	37	0	59	66	47	53
Martinez, David	2	2	6.11	5	0	28	29	10	23
Nunn, Chris	0	3	3.00	15	3	18	11	13	37
Ramirez, Williams	0	1	1.23	11	1	15	6	10	25
Reynoso, Eddy	6	5	3.98	43	0	72	74	22	68
Rodriguez, Anthony	6	8	4.93	26	0	131	138	84	84
Simpson, Jordan	2	3	3.43	16	0	42	37	28	38
Solter, Matt	5	10	3.87	22	0	130	152	46	89
Sylk, Augie	1	2	7.11	7	0	32	26	41	30
Teheran, Julio	1	1	1.60	6	0	34	25	6	35
Velez, Jose	0	2	5.79	12	0	14	20	10	8
Whitmore, Kelsie	0	0	12.19	11	0	10	12	7	2

SOUTHERN MARYLAND BLUE CRABS

Name	AVG	AB	R	H	HR	RBI	BB	SO	SB
IBaca, Michael	.216	398	50	86	2	36	22	64	20
Chirino, Santiago	.368	19	3	7	0	1	1	1	0
Collier, Zach	.255	365	67	93	7	58	54	89	9
Crosby, Alex	.278	450	75	125	8	78	32	51	14
DeLuca, Joe	.261	272	36	71	10	36	31	74	5
Falsetti, Mike	.164	61	7	10	1	9	11	27	0
Harris, David	.322	351	71	113	16	86	33	76	2
Haug, Ryan	.266	199	32	53	2	36	23	49	6
Hibbert, Matt	.244	168	32	41	3	18	29	49	10
Howard, Jordan	.111	18	2	2	0	2	1	6	0
Lee, Braxton	.306	432	60	132	3	73	38	81	19
Lien, Connor	.364	11	3	4	1	6	1	6	1
Rei, Austin	.321	53	7	17	1	14	8	14	2
Shah, Raul	.229	170	27	39	4	21	16	43	0
Silva, Rubi	.313	64	12	20	1	18	1	10	4
Sundberg, Jack	.246	422	91	104	8	57	85	103	45
Walker, Jared	.236	416	75	98	17	64	82	127	15
Wielansky, Michael	.278	255	58	71	8	41	43	51	4
Yetsko, Ian	.255	184	28	47	5	21	11	65	4

Name	W	L	ERA	G	SV	IP	H	BB	SO
Baker, Patrick	5	2	2.28	40	0	51	31	28	51
Briceno, Endrys	5	0	0.76	46	10	48	20	19	73
Butler, Eddie	12	6	4.94	26	0	155	194	45	94
Cook, Adrian	1	2	7.92	7	0	31	37	29	23
Dykstra, James	0	2	0.00	10	1	11	5	4	20
Geekie, Dalton	1	3	4.57	33	0	43	51	15	42
Herrera, Alsis	1	5	3.03	8	1	33	36	6	22
Hull, Denson	2	5	4.97	13	0	63	67	30	50
Lambson, Mitchell	8	9	3.60	24	0	163	155	42	145
Latos, Mat	4	3	4.46	39	25	38	36	16	40
Merithew, Alex	8	3	3.91	28	0	106	110	24	73
Mills, McKenzie	9	1	2.99	12	0	72	63	23	56
Polanco, Dario	3	0	6.75	26	0	35	37	27	20
Roney, Bradley	4	0	3.58	28	0	33	19	15	47
Strayer, Cody	0	0	10.97	9	0	11	14	5	9
Thompson, Daryl	15	4	3.43	27	0	186	183	22	119
Wells, Nick	3	3	4.66	30	0	39	39	20	37

KENTUCKY WILD HEALTH GENOMES

Name	AVG	AB	R	H	HR	RBI	BB	SO	SB
Almadova, Breland	.120	25	0	3	0	1	1	7	0
Becker, Luke	.308	484	107	149	23	98	70	117	14
Castro, Carlos	.333	147	17	49	6	29	6	39	1
Cornett, Dalton	.231	26	7	6	0	2	2	1	1
Davis, Khris	.271	188	35	51	17	46	20	46	0
Decker, Will	.467	15	2	7	0	2	0	5	0
Dotel, Welington	.192	78	10	15	3	9	7	22	4
Duenez, Samir	.259	228	40	59	9	41	24	51	1
Herrera, Jhoendri	.583	12	3	7	1	1	1	4	1
Hopkins, Scrappy	.083	12	1	1	0	0	0	4	0

INDEPENDENT LEAGUES

Johns, Gavin	.320	225	38	72	1	31	5	42	18
Keefer, Andrew	.267	15	3	4	1	2	1	2	0
Kellerman, Robbie	.267	15	2	4	0	3	5	7	0
Mahan, Riley	.411	90	22	37	8	22	15	22	3
Martinez, Teodoro	.207	140	20	29	5	16	22	14	2
Mehlbauer, Clayton	.227	220	33	50	4	24	37	78	16
Miller, Anderson	.258	213	29	55	3	32	20	50	11
Moorer, Demetrius	.227	220	34	50	1	21	40	81	15
Paredes, Jimmy	.283	428	66	121	18	68	41	86	2
Perez, Eury	.400	60	12	24	0	6	3	7	1
Pie, Felix	.254	335	52	85	13	48	40	50	5
Rei, Austin	.299	127	24	38	6	24	17	28	1
Rondon, Cleuluis	.225	151	27	34	5	15	21	35	4
Rosario, Olmo	.286	42	9	12	0	4	7	8	1
Shaw, Chris	.264	416	77	110	17	72	93	142	0
Sierra, Moises	.288	267	52	77	8	47	42	64	11
Vallot, Chase	.209	201	36	42	15	37	38	99	0

Name	W	L	ERA	G	SV	IP	H	BB	SO
Almengo, Diogenes	0	0	6.23	18	6	17	14	9	14
Beggs, Dustin	9	5	5.90	23	0	122	144	58	102
Blair, Aaron	0	4	13.25	7	0	18	21	24	11
Bostick, Akeem	1	2	4.97	19	2	25	23	16	22
Candelario, Alexis	2	4	8.62	13	0	47	70	20	44
Chacin, Alejandro	2	1	3.03	31	0	30	22	20	38
Guzman, Luis	2	1	2.70	44	1	40	31	21	45
Harper, Ryne	1	1	6.94	20	2	23	31	7	31
Herrera, Jhoendri	1	0	5.83	22	0	29	29	16	28
Kellogg, Ryan	8	5	5.99	20	0	92	127	24	83
Kirwan, William	1	0	7.85	14	0	18	24	13	10
Martin, Josh	0	3	4.30	22	0	29	34	17	38
Moreno, Diego	2	0	1.40	19	6	19	16	5	23
Moya, Gabriel	0	2	10.34	16	0	16	22	6	18
Peden, Nate	1	3	5.91	23	0	53	65	29	44
Peterson, Tim	2	1	1.30	27	6	28	16	7	34
Povse, Max	6	10	5.98	25	0	129	155	57	129
Ramos, Edubray	2	0	5.71	16	0	17	22	6	15
Ross, Robbie	3	1	3.40	30	2	45	33	16	58
Scott, Robby	5	7	4.56	16	0	77	80	32	56
Villanueva, Elih	12	9	5.45	24	0	140	133	67	151
Weinberger, Jack	2	5	4.30	46	4	52	65	27	50

YORK REVOLUTION

Name	AVG	AB	R	H	HR	RBI	BB	SO	SB
Castro, Carlos	.212	33	3	7	0	4	3	13	0
Encarnación, JC	.287	394	71	113	14	60	27	117	12
Figuera, Edwin	.122	49	8	6	0	3	8	17	1
Franco, Carlos	.298	369	79	110	30	95	70	88	0
Herrera, Jhoendri	.240	304	38	73	10	52	29	95	0
Kenley, Jack	.260	246	30	64	2	26	29	64	1
Lien, Connor	.243	305	57	74	14	39	39	127	12
Mesa, Melky	.272	408	57	111	16	77	38	86	1
Mondesi, Paul	.244	41	2	10	0	6	3	9	0
Nash, Telvin	.270	152	28	41	10	26	38	48	0
Nunez, Jhon	.300	190	32	57	6	28	24	34	0
Ordonez Jr., Magglio	.174	23	2	4	0	2	0	6	0
Perez, Yefri	.276	398	54	110	7	31	29	108	30
Racusin, Zach	.167	30	4	5	0	0	0	5	0
Reyes, Elmer	.271	490	76	133	10	66	18	65	1
Rodriguez, Lenin	.238	210	32	50	7	28	33	47	3
Rodriguez, Nellie	.249	413	78	103	26	82	108	160	0
Stokes Jr., Troy	.274	435	84	119	19	62	55	104	3

Name	W	L	ERA	G	SV	IP	H	BB	SO
Almeida, Adrian	0	0	1.17	15	0	15	9	12	20
de Geus, Brett	2	2	6.43	33	0	35	45	17	31
Fuller, Jim	5	6	3.92	44	19	41	50	14	46
Gonzalez, Merandy	1	4	7.71	5	0	23	30	15	18
Green, Nick	0	3	5.70	24	0	24	27	14	13
Herrera, Jhoendri	1	1	3.26	25	0	30	31	17	21
Herrick, Ben	1	4	9.11	5	0	27	45	13	10
Howard, Nick	0	3	3.91	22	0	23	19	17	27
Julian, Deyvis	1	1	6.30	2	0	10	10	3	3
Mack, Courtney	2	1	6.47	8	0	32	34	24	18
Martin, Josh	1	1	8.69	29	1	29	40	10	28
Martínez, Jorge	9	5	3.48	18	0	103	94	26	121
Nicely, Austin	3	12	7.44	22	0	127	180	47	84
Norwood, Josh	0	1	14.81	6	0	10	19	10	8
Olcese, Doug	0	0	5.06	12	0	11	9	7	4
Parra, Robinson	2	2	5.31	19	0	20	19	16	17
Raudes, Roniel	0	0	1.82	28	0	30	18	6	35
Rivera, Eduardo	8	5	4.91	25	0	110	96	69	102
Rodriguez, Alberto	2	1	8.14	21	0	24	26	24	25
Sanabia, Alex	4	5	4.86	17	0	87	91	38	74
Sanchez, Isaac	0	1	6.66	21	0	26	27	20	20
Travieso, Nick	6	6	4.33	18	0	96	84	47	66
Tucker, Tuck	0	1	5.18	25	0	24	23	12	17
Van Gurp, Franklin	0	0	0.79	10	0	11	9	6	16
Ventura, Carlos	0	3	4.20	28	0	30	31	23	30
Von Schamann, Dalton	6	5	5.76	31	1	84	102	24	48
Zurak, Kyle	1	1	2.95	17	0	18	13	9	18

FRONTIER LEAGUE

The amalgamation of the former Can-Am League and Frontier League into the newer and larger Frontier League meant in 2022 that a long-time Can-Am stalwart is a new Frontier League champion. The Quebec Capitales rolled to a tie for the best record in the league in the regular season and then blitzed Ottawa and Schaumburg in the playoffs.

West Division	W	L	PCT	GB
Washington Wild Things	62	34	.646	-
Schaumburg Boomers	53	43	.552	9
Evansville Otters	52	43	.547	9.5
Joliet Slammers	49	47	.510	13
Lake Erie Crushers	49	47	.510	13
Gateway Grizzlies	47	49	.490	15
Florence Y'alls	39	56	.411	22.5
Windy City ThunderBolts	33	62	.347	28.5
East Division	**W**	**L**	**PCT**	**GB**
Quebec Capitales	62	34	.646	-
New York Boulders	57	38	.600	4.5
Ottawa Titans	56	39	.589	5.5
Sussex County Miners	54	41	.568	7.5
Tri-City ValleyCats	54	41	.568	7.5
New Jersey Jackals	45	49	.479	16
Trois-Rivieres Aigles	45	50	.474	16.5
Empire State Greys	6	90	.063	56

Division Champ. ^Wild Card

Playoffs—Wild Card: Schaumburg defeated Evansville and Ottawa defeated New York. **Semifinals:** Schaumburg defeated Washington 2-0 and Quebec defeated Ottawa 2-1 in best-of-3 series. **Finals:** Quebec defeated Schaumburg 3-1 in best-of-5 series.

"ALL-STAR TEAM C: Jeffry Parra, Quebec. **1B:**Dalton Combs, New Jersey. **2B:** Brantley Bell, Tri-City. **3B:** Brylie Ware, Joliet. **SS:** Nick Ward, Washington. **OF:** Josh Rehwaldt, New Jersey; David Vinsky, New York; L.P. Pelletier, Troi-Rivières. **DH:** Denis Phipps- Tri-City **SP:** Miguel Cienfuegos, Quebec. **RP:** Logan Sawyer, Evansville.

BATTING LEADERS

Player	Team	AVG	AB	R	H	HR	RBI
Bell, Brantley	TC	.368	375	92	138	24	81
Combs, Dalton	NJ	.354	364	78	129	14	77
Ward, Nick	Wash.	.349	292	71	102	19	61
Vinsky, David	NY	.349	387	98	135	20	84
Lagrange, Wagner	Wash.	.346	361	60	125	7	62
Pelletier, L.P.	T-R	.340	344	81	117	14	58
Martinez, Carlos	T-R	.336	247	55	83	16	62
McArthur, Liam	Emp.	.329	258	39	85	0	19
Ware, Brylie	Joliet	.327	315	50	103	10	61
Rehwaldt, Josh	NJ	.325	354	72	115	29	79
Phipps, Denis	T-C	.296	341	74	101	33	91

PITCHING LEADERS

Player	Team	W	L	ERA	IP	H	BB	SO
Cienfuegos, Miguel	Quebec	10	2	1.79	131	107	26	106
Marshall, Dwayne	Sussex	11	3	2.67	118	117	43	111
Baker, John	Sussex	12	2	2.67	104	98	19	122
Charpie, Trevor	Joliet	4	5	3.04	101	79	28	111

Paiva, Codie	Quebec	9	3	3.14	117	103	32	114
Cook, Cole	Joliet	11	7	3.22	117	105	28	109
Cabrera, Sandro	Wash.	8	4	3.42	103	97	35	91
Whalen, Rob	Wash.	12	2	3.50	100	93	22	79
Grills, Evan	Ottawa	4	6	3.53	99	112	19	110
Jandron, Tyler	Ottawa	7	4	3.56	111	108	27	113

EMPIRE STATE GREYS

Name	AVG	AB	R	H	HR	RBI	BB	SO	SB
Benevolent, John	.194	279	25	54	5	23	19	112	6
Carling, Robbie	.208	168	20	35	4	17	27	68	6
Cox, Khalyd	.237	80	6	19	1	7	11	35	0
Decker, Will	.264	121	10	32	0	10	8	18	1
Estevez, Marcos	.162	37	3	6	1	2	6	13	3
Estrada, Willie	.244	213	21	52	4	26	16	36	3
Garcia, Manny	.260	146	22	38	8	25	11	28	2
Garr, Jordan	.208	53	7	11	1	5	8	14	2
Hill, Tyler	.219	114	8	25	2	10	6	35	0
Holloman-Scott, Jordan	.225	306	30	69	4	35	36	94	6
Itakura, Hiroki	.234	124	10	29	1	11	6	49	0
Kendrick, Kolton	.125	24	0	3	0	2	1	9	0
Lantigua, John	.086	35	1	3	0	2	4	14	0
McArthur, Liam	.329	258	39	85	0	19	36	40	13
Mercado, Jose	.255	278	38	71	1	19	21	65	23
Molina, Miguel	.180	50	4	9	0	2	0	12	0
Mondesi, Paul	.165	158	12	26	3	11	5	35	0
Naccari, Christian	.223	103	11	23	3	9	7	24	0
Ordonez Jr., Magglio	.162	74	4	12	0	5	7	20	0
Sullivan, Zach	.158	38	3	6	1	3	3	20	0
Williams, Jaquez	.150	20	3	3	0	0	1	9	0
Williamson, Camden	.143	35	3	5	0	1	2	12	1
Woosley, Trey	.268	295	31	79	7	41	12	57	0

Name	W	L	ERA	G	SV	IP	H	BB	SO
Akatsuka, Mizuki	1	5	8.18	8	0	47	68	14	27
Arias, Johsson	2	9	7.04	17	0	63	75	44	47
Armsworthy, Kyle	0	0	8.49	9	0	12	21	4	8
Becerril, Marco	0	1	8.05	7	0	19	21	7	11
Bernhardt, Holden	1	1	1.62	14	0	17	11	3	32
Bernhardt, Locke	0	0	7.62	11	0	13	19	9	11
Derer, Thomas	0	7	7.99	23	0	60	82	28	52
Hernandez, Franklyn	1	4	9.50	20	0	42	57	32	32
Huizar, Ernesto	0	4	13.03	8	0	19	30	14	15
Luc, Nicholas	0	5	11.37	11	0	25	39	21	14
Maguire, Connor	0	6	7.13	24	0	64	92	29	36
Mieses, Jose	0	2	5.14	8	0	14	14	12	19
Pacheco, Luis	0	6	7.71	10	0	40	52	13	37
Palais, Jay	0	6	8.29	8	0	38	50	18	14
Pineda, Jason	1	5	8.41	19	0	20	28	12	19
Powell, Jordan	0	4	18.82	9	0	22	55	11	14
Rodriguez, Alberto	0	2	6.49	9	0	26	29	25	28
Rodriguez, Andres	0	8	8.94	14	0	53	78	35	39
Rosario, Jesus	0	3	12.52	22	0	23	30	27	27
Rotz, Jeff	0	1	4.73	11	0	13	13	12	7
Speranza, Donnie	0	2	11.03	10	0	24	29	25	6

EVANSVILLE OTTERS

Name	AVG	AB	R	H	HR	RBI	BB	SO	SB
Allen Jr., Ronnie	.250	20	1	5	0	4	1	7	0
Armstrong, Andy	.227	282	26	64	1	25	13	62	9
Baez, Jeffrey	.243	304	47	74	8	44	29	69	26
Biermann, Zach	.280	332	66	93	17	54	39	90	6
Callil, George	.218	257	39	56	6	25	17	100	1
Craig, Tanner	.176	34	2	6	2	4	1	15	0
Davis, J.R.	.276	333	44	92	6	56	37	50	5
Felix, Justin	.226	190	31	43	11	31	32	83	3
Gordon, Miles	.263	312	48	82	7	39	37	91	27
MacNamee, Elijah	.280	325	51	91	10	43	23	79	16
Mattis, Gary	.260	73	17	19	3	16	10	21	17
McKinley, Trevor	.238	21	1	5	0	2	1	10	1
Phillips, Dakota	.313	144	28	45	11	37	21	55	0
Rosario, Bryan	.288	111	19	32	0	9	13	26	7
Sensley, Steven	.263	228	44	60	14	45	37	60	4
Tanksley, Brody	.269	52	5	14	0	4	5	24	0
Torreullas, Anthony	.242	62	13	15	3	10	4	10	1

Name	W	L	ERA	G	SV	IP	H	BB	SO
Abernathy, Samson	2	1	6.63	17	0	19	26	15	14
Adcock, Brett	6	6	3.93	16	0	89	92	53	86
Bowles, Jacob	1	1	3.38	37	1	59	56	27	42
Brahms, Parker	5	1	2.55	9	0	60	39	21	63
Davis, Kevin	0	0	2.08	11	0	17	12	10	34
Gallardo, Augie	1	3	4.36	30	0	33	31	12	36
Gossmann, Austin	8	6	3.83	18	0	106	114	40	101
Holdgrafer, Tim	2	0	0.67	4	0	27	13	4	34
O'Reilly, Ryan	6	8	4.53	19	0	101	108	48	84
Polancic, Jake	5	3	2.66	39	0	47	21	20	71
Riley, Joe	3	1	1.64	12	1	11	6	4	19
Sawyer, Logan	2	1	0.00	30	22	29	11	3	39
Smith, Zach	2	2	3.86	8	0	28	22	14	23
Spring, Tyler	1	0	5.81	19	0	31	27	21	33
Stuteville, Brice	0	2	5.97	8	0	38	53	24	28
Watland, Justin	5	5	4.20	17	0	94	78	42	95

FLORENCE Y'ALLS

Name	AVG	AB	R	H	HR	RBI	BB	SO	SB
Almonte, Wady	.143	28	2	4	0	1	0	7	1
Bibiloni, Ian	.289	45	14	13	4	9	3	16	2
Brocato, Anthony	.307	254	53	78	22	66	27	85	3
Bumpass, A.J.	.280	50	12	14	3	10	6	20	0
Chavez, Alberti	.313	380	62	119	4	49	13	55	10
Combs, Casey	.288	66	17	19	3	8	5	22	1
Damon, Billy	.190	21	1	4	0	1	0	10	1
DiNicola, Harrison	.281	178	31	50	1	15	27	25	3
Edwards, Cooper	.133	98	14	13	1	5	13	44	0
Flete, Bryant	.198	177	20	35	6	31	25	57	3
Gomez, Justin	.094	32	2	3	0	2	7	10	0
Harper, Luke	.317	60	8	19	0	3	14	17	3
Johnson, Axel	.238	273	37	65	6	31	19	79	5
Leef, Bryan	.263	38	6	10	2	9	1	13	3
Lytle, Joe	.276	116	19	32	5	21	9	27	2
Massey, Craig	.299	197	34	59	3	26	22	22	8
Pintor, Luis	.291	55	12	16	0	5	9	12	0
Price, Brennan	.309	327	74	101	24	91	48	77	1
Rios, Andres	.250	32	2	8	0	6	3	7	1
Stern, Ethan	.279	233	38	65	6	38	17	54	8
Sthormes, Andres	.241	58	10	14	3	7	7	14	0
Tennie, Rodney	.371	124	20	46	0	18	6	26	5
Weaver, Lyndon	.182	22	3	4	1	3	2	11	2
Zuberer, Ray	.285	333	55	95	12	52	39	71	10

Name	W	L	ERA	G	SV	IP	H	BB	SO
Baker, Griffin	4	3	7.42	10	0	40	50	19	40
Brabrand, Evan	3	6	4.22	33	0	64	58	20	70
Cheek, Jared	1	3	6.00	8	0	36	45	7	31
Craigie, Karl	1	2	4.89	43	0	46	45	18	60
Damon, Billy	1	2	5.44	12	0	41	52	13	24
Dougherty, Joe	0	4	5.40	35	10	38	32	13	51
Flueck, Jared	1	0	4.50	2	0	10	12	3	4
Hockin, Grant	0	0	7.40	9	0	21	25	2	24
Hughes, Sean	2	0	2.45	13	0	11	9	7	11
Kylman, Kent	2	4	2.83	32	0	48	39	18	55
Martinez, Edgar	6	5	6.48	16	0	82	97	34	81
McMahill, Jake	1	1	2.92	5	0	25	18	10	26
Ovalle, Jeremy	1	6	5.63	10	0	54	65	21	44
Pferrer, Cameron	2	2	5.40	20	0	25	23	18	30
Ramos, Darwin	1	1	4.50	18	0	20	19	8	33
Ruibal, Evy	2	0	0.93	17	2	19	12	4	27
Santana, Yasel	2	4	3.38	9	0	43	36	20	43
Siemer, Tommy	0	0	3.65	5	0	12	13	6	5
Stiehl, David	0	1	8.16	6	0	14	24	2	10
Villalobos, Jonaiker	6	8	4.35	19	0	101	117	40	86
Wagner, Alex	1	1	5.91	6	0	21	29	7	23

GATEWAY GRIZZLIES

Name	AVG	AB	R	H	HR	RBI	BB	SO	SB
Achenbach, Trevor	.242	356	67	86	20	58	38	114	7
Almadova, Breland	.313	48	5	15	0	3	6	15	4
Benard, Isaac	.316	354	75	112	23	66	42	90	2

Name	AVG	AB	R	H	HR	RBI	BB	SO	SB
Bibiloni, Ian	.232	69	16	16	5	14	1	24	1
Diaz, Abdiel	.244	328	46	80	5	32	39	78	27
Freeman, Clint	.246	345	45	85	16	48	23	68	3
Hernandez, Alex	.186	102	9	19	1	10	14	43	0
Krause, Kevin	.338	148	27	50	10	36	22	31	2
Penner, Andrew	.279	369	68	103	9	38	36	87	6
Prather, Jay	.241	303	42	73	5	52	39	66	12
Pritchard, Jackson	.238	147	19	35	4	20	16	55	0
Racusin, Zach	.351	194	29	68	5	33	26	25	9
Rosario, Jose	.248	129	18	32	4	23	9	34	5
Touchette, Cam	.211	90	23	19	0	9	12	34	4
Trejo, Cesar	.206	63	5	13	2	8	5	23	7
Zimmermann, Peter	.235	153	25	36	9	25	21	54	4

Name	W	L	ERA	G	SV	IP	H	BB	SO
Cartier, Andrew	1	0	7.71	13	0	12	15	7	12
Cupo, Carson	0	2	5.33	25	1	27	29	16	28
DeLeon, Anderson	0	1	4.60	11	1	16	17	3	20
Easterwood, Colton	2	2	2.27	29	0	32	25	18	34
Feldmann, Brendan	7	8	4.18	19	0	116	99	28	116
Ferrell, Justin	1	2	7.43	8	0	23	21	18	15
Freeman, Clint	0	3	6.20	10	0	20	28	4	22
Gardner, Sam	6	2	4.72	32	4	69	56	19	97
Hayes, Carter	0	0	6.30	4	0	10	16	3	13
Hayes, Reed	1	2	2.74	19	6	23	13	9	28
Kennedy, Nick	1	1	6.21	25	0	29	46	9	22
LaRue, Carson	5	5	4.88	14	0	76	79	30	80
Milch, Jared	1	0	9.45	7	0	13	21	7	8
Mulhearn, Matt	2	1	7.71	7	0	19	22	7	21
Murphy, John	1	4	2.80	38	9	35	25	8	63
Ridings, Steven	5	2	5.34	12	0	61	62	23	60
Rodriguez, Manuel	1	2	5.79	9	0	42	42	17	38
Sugg, Taylor	4	2	6.10	26	0	41	37	34	40
Veinbergs, Lukas	6	1	3.12	17	0	58	51	15	51
Whaley, Alec	0	0	3.24	15	0	17	14	4	13
Williams, JP	3	7	5.67	17	0	79	96	28	70

JOLIET SLAMMERS

Name	AVG	AB	R	H	HR	RBI	BB	SO	SB
Baremore, Lane	.261	257	28	67	5	29	15	66	5
Burch, Matt	.285	291	43	83	7	29	22	51	2
Coutts, Jackson	.230	61	9	14	1	3	10	6	2
Depreta-Johnson, Tyler	.251	343	53	86	4	34	32	67	11
Feinstein, Matt	.286	91	18	26	4	14	22	28	0
Fullerton, JP	.233	163	24	38	4	21	33	69	2
Gomez, Justin	.162	68	7	11	0	2	9	20	0
Holzwasser, Scott	.276	225	45	62	9	37	24	60	11
Jacobsen, Kyle	.212	226	33	48	6	18	15	73	3
Mangieri, Luke	.202	168	25	34	8	26	28	45	6
Matthews, Dave	.149	67	13	10	2	7	10	21	1
Maxwell, Carson	.251	283	40	71	17	56	30	96	17
McGarry, Matt	.235	358	46	84	14	75	34	94	9
Schulefand, Jordan	.310	29	10	9	0	2	6	12	5
Steering, Phillip	.222	176	24	39	7	20	22	61	3
Wallace, Paxton	.343	67	11	23	4	11	5	9	0
Ware, Brylie	.327	315	50	103	10	61	25	45	0

Name	W	L	ERA	G	SV	IP	H	BB	SO
Aufderheide, Cameron	8	7	3.65	20	0	121	116	56	95
Brierley, Chandler	3	2	2.9	33	2	40	26	23	26
Charpie, Trevor	4	5	3.04	21	1	101	79	28	111
Cook, Cole	11	7	3.22	19	0	117	105	28	109
Feeney, Gage	1	0	5.40	4	0	13	14	7	12
Honea, Kaleb	0	2	10.32	14	2	11	18	7	11
Jay, Tyler	2	1	1.64	22	8	22	16	3	24
Johnston, Spencer	5	3	2.79	9	0	52	49	8	34
Kiest, Tanner	2	2	3.17	41	2	48	30	23	80
Larkins, Turner	2	2	3.94	6	0	32	30	5	23
Liebelt, Jared	1	1	6.85	21	2	22	21	10	27
Moyers, Steve	1	2	1.50	5	1	24	18	1	28
O'Brien, Caden	1	0	5.14	14	0	14	11	13	17
Ogg, Kenny	2	1	2.84	3	0	19	13	0	19
Roycroft, Chris	0	1	1.08	13	2	17	15	5	24
Schmitt, Logan	1	2	5.64	14	0	45	46	27	30
Stanton, Cole	2	1	8.27	29	2	33	35	27	45

Thomas, Alec	3	5	5.53	16	0	68	59	53	63

LAKE ERIE CRUSHERS

Name	AVG	AB	R	H	HR	RBI	BB	SO	SB
Cheely, Sean	.230	187	30	43	3	24	20	48	16
Cicci, Nick	.111	27	3	3	1	3	3	11	0
Combs, Casey	.228	79	7	18	0	9	6	23	1
De La Rosa, Bryan	.177	113	11	20	4	16	16	32	1
Escobar, Ermindo	.228	57	8	13	1	8	5	13	0
Figueiredo, Kokko	.254	276	37	70	4	30	48	58	11
Fisher, Devon	.150	20	1	3	0	2	3	5	0
Flete, Bryant	.219	137	18	30	4	12	22	28	2
Gaskins, Najee	.300	50	5	15	1	7	3	10	5
Gitter, Jake	.211	133	17	28	8	28	14	57	4
Green, London	.143	42	4	6	1	5	5	20	2
Harris, Jack	.377	53	12	20	5	16	6	18	0
Irizarry, Kenen	.287	362	64	104	11	54	50	77	10
Jones, Alonzo	.120	50	4	6	0	1	2	17	1
Mang, Jared	.288	73	10	21	1	11	8	15	7
McDermott, Matt	.171	41	6	7	0	0	3	11	2
Owings, Connor	.321	336	49	108	18	64	31	98	17
Perez, Danny	.232	95	12	22	1	8	11	19	0
Stewart, D.J.	.269	67	7	18	3	10	4	16	2
Tennie, Rodney	.317	41	5	13	0	1	4	8	8
Thomas-Rivera, Kemuel	.291	189	31	55	6	20	18	63	13
Valera, Jackson	.292	360	52	105	10	39	18	52	4
Watkins, Jarrod	.340	47	11	16	2	7	6	5	0
White, Austin	.279	262	43	73	1	22	26	46	23

Name	W	L	ERA	G	SV	IP	H	BB	SO
Alvarez, Jay	5	5	5.57	21	0	95	94	57	117
Begue, Brock	0	2	7.06	5	0	22	35	9	22
Carney, Elliot	1	1	3.51	20	0	41	33	18	59
Crouse, Marrick	1	1	5.52	7	1	15	18	7	15
Curtis, Sam	3	3	1.42	44	8	51	29	18	62
Gilliland, Jacob	0	1	11.32	8	0	10	21	7	11
Holcomb, Kevin	1	1	8.31	5	0	17	18	16	23
Holt, Nathan	2	0	3.48	11	0	21	22	6	16
Kasonovich, Paul	2	0	4.50	11	0	22	31	8	19
Kines, Gunnar	5	6	4.04	17	0	91	83	27	119
Kuncl, Trevor	2	0	3.62	28	1	37	30	23	33
Mulhearn, Matt	6	4	3.54	13	0	74	66	28	73
Pineda, Gleyvin	3	0	4.08	32	0	29	21	16	26
Rivero, Alexis	2	1	1.16	30	20	31	16	16	35
Schmidt, Kaleb	1	3	13.28	5	0	20	23	16	23
Seebach, Kyle	1	3	9.53	8	0	17	22	16	24
Sgambelluri, Joseph	10	6	3.75	20	0	113	96	46	114
Vivas, Julio	2	7	4.78	12	0	64	64	28	56
Walda, Ean	0	2	3.38	16	0	19	17	12	20
Wells, Kenny	1	0	6.91	15	0	14	11	20	19

NEW JERSEY JACKALS

Name	AVG	AB	R	H	HR	RBI	BB	SO	SB
Abrams, Trevor	.314	287	50	90	11	44	22	65	13
Agresti, Jason	.287	307	46	88	8	49	30	54	1
Bell Jr., George	.253	170	30	43	10	30	15	56	5
Chirino, Santiago	.300	327	65	98	4	37	35	33	0
Combs, Dalton	.354	364	78	129	14	77	48	49	9
Isaacs, Todd	.327	214	45	70	9	34	8	42	22
Markman, Austin	.234	111	14	26	2	11	4	28	2
Marte, Alfredo	.295	332	65	98	18	82	26	45	10
Rehwaldt, Josh	.325	354	72	115	29	79	38	101	3
Salcedo, Edward	.278	108	14	30	1	12	6	31	3
Simone, Joe	.216	176	30	38	1	19	23	49	6
Toni, Nicco	.143	21	1	3	0	0	3	7	0
Whalin, Zak	.240	96	12	23	0	12	6	23	1
Wylie, Justin	.306	337	75	103	20	77	49	74	12

Name	W	L	ERA	G	SV	IP	H	BB	SO
Baez, Angelo	7	5	3.89	28	1	86	92	18	81
Bruss, Thomas	1	0	6.27	12	0	19	23	12	17
DeSalvo, Nicholas	1	4	6.16	9	0	38	46	11	30
Gonzalez, Luis	0	0	9.80	8	0	11	14	14	16
Gregorio, Joan	1	1	3.94	4	0	16	15	5	13
Maarleveld, Max	0	0	4.15	7	2	13	14	6	9

Milch, Jared	0	2	15.88	3	0	11	24	8	8
Peiffer, Dylan	3	2	4.86	23	1	33	29	10	36
Perez, Juan	4	2	5.14	33	3	49	51	29	52
Pineda, Jason	0	1	2.95	9	1	18	19	6	18
Ramirez, Jose A.	4	3	3.00	21	6	27	25	13	48
Rodriguez, Hansel	3	1	2.05	35	1	44	25	22	64
Rodriguez, Leonardo	4	4	5.43	18	0	71	77	49	73
Rosati, Anthony	0	0	5.40	3	0	12	15	7	9
Salcedo, Adrian	0	2	9.88	3	0	14	23	8	10
Santana, Yasel	2	3	5.50	7	0	34	29	21	32
Shenefield, Hayden	0	5	11.40	8	0	30	54	16	29
Smart, Gage	0	1	6.14	11	0	15	18	13	11
Smith, Austin	3	0	5.08	19	2	34	29	22	34
Tavarez, Jorge	9	4	4.58	20	0	112	105	55	142
Tessitore, Christian	1	0	12.08	9	0	13	19	12	13
Valdez, Jefry	1	2	5.28	24	2	31	27	22	28

NEW YORK BOULDERS

Name	AVG	AB	R	H	HR	RBI	BB	SO	SB
Del Valle, Francisco	.299	244	41	73	7	42	29	33	4
Dennis, Austin	.314	264	57	83	6	58	36	43	16
Figueroa, Steven	.253	91	18	23	1	13	12	24	3
Garbella, Giovanni	.277	260	57	72	9	52	33	69	8
Garcia, Gabriel	.313	326	77	102	18	64	46	63	10
Hernandez, Ray	.278	115	25	32	4	26	19	27	3
Kwitzer, Chris	.301	382	68	115	20	96	26	104	13
MacKenzie, Jake	.302	374	92	113	14	65	46	64	35
Martellini, Gian	.216	245	39	53	9	33	24	78	0
Molina, Gerson	.190	58	5	11	2	7	1	24	1
Nathans, Tucker	.275	178	39	49	16	46	24	44	3
Reda, Alfonso	.203	79	15	16	1	8	13	29	0
Smith, Max	.288	319	71	92	20	48	52	91	2
Vinsky, David	.349	387	98	135	20	84	48	81	12

Name	W	L	ERA	G	SV	IP	H	BB	SO
Alintoff, Justin	0	0	6.65	5	0	23	35	4	13
Burton, Lucas	0	1	8.22	17	1	15	18	15	18
Dawson, Luke	0	1	6.23	9	0	13	16	10	8
Goggin, Dan	1	1	9.90	10	0	10	14	9	7
Hammond, Andrew	5	2	5.43	15	0	66	88	22	33
Kaplan, Austin	0	1	6.60	8	0	15	16	5	10
Leon, Matt	5	1	1.80	20	5	15	13	6	23
Loeschorn, Josh	0	2	6.49	5	0	26	31	10	18
Mack, Alex	8	4	5.03	19	0	91	94	40	74
Martinez, Algenis	0	1	3.95	3	0	14	13	8	5
Mott, Kyle	0	0	2.16	7	0	17	16	5	17
Munoz, Ryan	4	2	3.63	27	1	45	44	15	37
Pineda, Leudeny	3	2	6.68	30	7	32	34	20	40
Rios, Willie	0	2	8.57	6	0	21	34	13	12
Rowland, Robby	8	5	5.75	21	0	122	142	52	82
Schneider, Zach	4	4	3.23	34	4	53	51	15	46
Smith, Dylan	2	0	3.99	32	1	38	27	25	54
Sosa, July	7	2	3.57	12	0	58	46	15	49
Strahm, Ben	0	0	7.30	6	0	12	16	1	14
Vancena, Jayce	0	2	12.86	9	0	14	28	8	9
Wirchansky, Danny	5	4	2.80	20	3	87	69	27	103
Yakel, Ryder	4	0	5.88	18	0	26	26	6	21

OTTAWA TITANS

Name	AVG	AB	R	H	HR	RBI	BB	SO	SB
Dadson, Brendon	.261	218	38	57	9	33	32	54	3
Dicochea, Jason	.308	276	41	85	5	55	20	39	5
Feinstein, Matt	.333	60	10	20	2	11	8	18	3
Fisher, Clay	.261	272	37	71	8	45	22	53	9
Fukuda, Mitsuki	.194	72	8	14	0	10	14	28	1
Greene, Tyrus	.305	295	48	90	2	40	33	40	21
Maberry, David	.282	39	7	11	1	7	2	13	0
Martinez, Andrew	.292	24	7	7	1	4	3	7	1
McArthur, Liam	.306	49	13	15	0	4	8	8	0
Moody, Kai	.291	86	12	25	0	12	10	11	4
Navigato, Luke	.196	51	6	10	1	5	4	10	3
Orozco, Rodrigo	.288	309	44	89	7	41	43	48	14
Sanford, Jacob	.311	360	67	112	22	73	32	65	7
Talamante, Jacob	.241	133	20	32	0	19	24	42	7
Tofteland, Dane	.300	20	5	6	0	1	3	4	0
Urbaez, Jackie	.287	307	63	88	10	48	39	70	9
Wright, A.J.	.277	325	69	90	12	54	51	92	9
Wright, Taylor	.257	109	18	28	3	20	12	28	4
Zimmerman, Will	.280	132	35	37	2	17	25	32	13

Name	W	L	ERA	G	SV	IP	H	BB	SO
Alkire, Jack	1	3	8.81	13	0	32	45	22	25
Burica, Chris	9	6	4.51	20	0	112	126	37	84
Escorcia, Kevin	4	2	1.73	37	17	36	20	14	51
Gonzalez, Nelson	0	3	4.25	24	4	30	30	5	28
Grills, Evan	4	6	3.53	15	0	99	112	19	110
Jandron, Tyler	7	4	3.56	18	0	111	108	27	113
Larson, Grant	6	5	2.30	35	2	55	52	8	52
Schmidt, Kaleb	2	0	7.24	11	0	27	24	18	25
Serrano, Kyle	1	2	1.08	17	1	17	4	16	26
Sonnier, Gavin	4	0	2.64	37	0	44	30	20	30
Taveras, Jose	7	2	5.80	14	1	68	75	28	39
Terrones, Matt	0	0	6.04	17	0	22	29	11	14
Valin, Matt	0	0	3.46	12	0	13	7	10	26
Westcott, Zac	11	3	4.17	20	0	121	139	25	88
Williams, Kenny	0	1	8.47	12	0	17	18	10	16

WINDY CITY THUNDERBOLTS

Name	AVG	AB	R	H	HR	RBI	BB	SO	SB
Berry, Blake	.212	33	4	7	0	0	2	4	1
Castro, Ruben	.304	102	9	31	1	13	6	16	2
Crowl, Kyle	.306	350	56	107	9	57	42	71	4
Glaude, David	.325	351	78	114	16	60	36	51	26
Gonzalez, Pedro	.203	118	14	24	3	16	7	45	2
Guibert, Yoelkis	.225	89	13	20	0	9	6	9	5
Lacroix, Jonathan	.285	355	51	101	6	51	19	58	6
Lebreux, Marc-Antoine	.264	265	44	70	2	25	28	61	17
Little, Webb	.239	71	11	17	2	13	7	20	1
Manduley, Yordan	.251	175	20	44	3	21	12	16	15
McAdams, Josh	.228	224	35	51	7	27	20	78	4
Parra, Jeffry	.321	318	72	102	32	83	51	75	1
Pompey, Tristan	.215	144	28	31	4	13	33	43	2
Sears, Josh	.250	32	3	8	1	6	5	12	0
Takamatsu, Garrett	.291	127	16	37	2	23	11	27	3
White, T.J.	.296	351	69	104	26	75	26	95	1
Yeargain, Reece	.184	76	11	14	0	5	8	20	0

Name	W	L	ERA	G	SV	IP	H	BB	SO
Adames, Samuel	5	5	2.52	37	12	39	33	14	37
Austin, Michael	8	6	5.11	20	0	107	120	19	75
Cienfuegos, Miguel	10	2	1.79	21	0	131	107	26	106
Codina, Ian	2	0	3.43	34	1	39	35	17	23
Horvath, Nick	3	3	1.76	45	6	46	29	21	60
Huertas, Joel	1	2	4.99	23	0	49	46	18	50
Knapp, Stephen	1	1	8.71	10	0	10	14	1	11
Moscatiello, Frank	5	2	2.91	40	1	43	22	39	67
Omana, Henry	2	2	2.77	25	0	52	37	18	58
Paiva, Codie	9	3	3.14	20	0	117	103	32	114
Parra, Franklin	3	1	2.94	33	0	52	43	27	64
Richardson, David	1	1	5.40	7	0	10	10	3	13
Sano, Carlos	6	2	4.32	10	0	50	53	28	34
Shill, Marshall	0	0	8.14	25	0	21	25	11	16
Witkowski, John	4	2	3.88	14	0	49	56	13	49

SCHAUMBURG BOOMERS

Name	AVG	AB	R	H	HR	RBI	BB	SO	SB
Berry, Blake	.282	149	25	42	3	19	15	30	2
Bottcher, Matt	.383	149	28	57	7	28	17	31	6
Cannella, Cosimo	.174	46	3	8	1	5	4	12	0
Claycamp, Sam	.108	37	2	4	2	5	5	14	1
Craig, Alec	.267	348	72	93	8	44	92	73	30
Davidson, Braxton	.244	262	52	64	18	59	79	120	10
Dawson, Chase	.310	384	76	119	5	64	31	43	23
DeBonville, Thomas	.258	120	16	31	5	15	6	42	4
Grant-Parks, Blake	.271	155	13	42	2	25	10	38	0
Hardy, Clint	.288	337	56	97	8	55	23	62	7
Hart, Mike	.277	184	44	51	19	48	32	64	6
Milazzo, Brett	.292	260	37	76	2	36	37	63	20

Name	AVG	AB	R	H	HR	RBI	BB	SO	SB
Oddo, Nick	.181	216	22	39	3	17	21	69	1
Ruiz, Cris	.176	91	16	16	2	9	14	30	0
Salas, William	.245	326	53	80	6	42	36	60	13
Singh, Aaron	.222	27	6	6	1	3	3	8	0
Stapp, Wyatt	.333	39	4	13	0	4	11	8	0
Steinbach, Alex	.200	25	1	5	1	2	0	5	0
Wiley, Jordan	.191	47	7	9	2	10	3	18	0

Name	W	L	ERA	G	SV	IP	H	BB	SO
Akanuma, Jumpei	4	3	4.56	15	0	75	87	24	58
Arjona, Kyle	3	6	7.60	12	0	66	86	20	59
Glickstein, Aaron	7	6	4.37	28	0	93	94	17	99
Joyce, Jake	4	1	2.57	37	5	42	37	15	55
Martinez, Erik	3	3	3.03	8	0	33	31	6	32
Middendorf, Ryan	3	1	2.70	5	0	33	26	9	40
Nicoll, Thomas	0	2	4.22	27	1	32	31	14	41
Perez, Luis	1	0	6.92	13	0	26	34	18	19
Pichardo, Juan	2	1	6.32	25	0	31	36	21	40
Reyes, Miguel	0	1	4.76	7	0	17	17	8	16
Schlotman, Kobey	4	3	4.38	8	0	37	34	13	48
Scott, Kristian	5	2	2.23	43	0	44	30	18	48
Shears, Tanner	2	0	1.07	21	0	34	23	16	44
Stelzer, Blake	6	3	3.96	15	0	89	85	31	80
Thompson, Darrell	2	1	1.43	45	17	50	34	12	92
Yoshikawa, Shumpei	7	9	5.51	20	0	113	124	32	117

SUSSEX COUNTY MINERS

Name	AVG	AB	R	H	HR	RBI	BB	SO	SB
Anu, Oraj	.244	82	10	20	2	14	6	27	3
Culver, Cito	.196	153	20	30	2	18	34	39	0
Escala, Willie	.215	65	15	14	1	8	23	20	3
Figueroa, Martin	.305	325	70	99	11	68	66	52	24
Garland, Nick	.266	128	28	34	4	24	14	35	3
Harris, Jawuan	.250	256	52	64	12	51	52	96	34
Little, Webb	.250	68	9	17	1	6	7	16	1
Maberry, David	.297	219	34	65	9	41	18	51	0
Mateo, Edwin	.206	34	5	7	0	7	3	11	4
McCurdy, Carson	.233	116	18	27	4	17	13	41	2
Perez, Yanio	.340	106	18	36	3	14	8	20	0
Pritchard, Jackson	.136	22	2	3	0	0	4	12	0
Quiroz, Isaias	.176	165	19	29	4	16	19	61	0
Reynolds, Mikey	.298	265	41	79	3	41	36	45	21
Rijo, Nilo	.271	225	32	61	0	22	35	60	34
Robinson, Errol	.312	138	36	43	1	20	26	33	22
Rolon, Kevin	.177	175	29	31	2	18	21	65	11
Sandoval, Ariel	.261	111	21	29	1	20	7	18	8
Silverio, Juan	.347	147	26	51	2	29	16	32	5
Toral, Alex	.284	81	21	23	11	33	20	24	1
Washington, Justin	.196	46	11	9	1	4	8	16	14
Zimmerman, Will	.240	25	6	6	0	5	5	10	13

Name	W	L	ERA	G	SV	IP	H	BB	SO
Baker, John	12	2	2.67	25	3	104	98	19	122
Boyce, Jimmy	2	1	3.73	24	2	51	48	12	41
Dand, Conner	6	4	3.56	20	0	81	84	36	83
Klinchock, Robert	1	1	2.85	34	9	41	40	17	33
Layne Jr., Billy	1	0	7.63	11	0	15	22	5	15
Marshall, Dwayne	11	3	2.67	21	0	118	117	43	111
Matos, Darwin	0	1	8.38	8	0	10	12	10	12
Mazzaro, Vin	5	6	4.99	16	0	83	99	34	72
Mediavilla, Michael	5	6	4.27	20	1	118	125	33	105
Mulry, James	7	7	4.76	28	1	74	69	25	76
Pineyro, Ivan	0	2	9.82	3	0	11	18	3	7
Stull, Eston	1	0	5.06	15	1	16	12	16	23
Thornton, Tyler	1	3	1.74	15	4	21	11	4	18
Whitten, Cody	0	2	3.91	21	1	32	30	17	33

TRI-CITY VALLEY CATS

Name	AVG	AB	R	H	HR	RBI	BB	SO	SB
Angulo, Daniel	.260	50	7	13	1	6	4	11	1
Bell, Brantley	.368	375	92	138	24	81	35	65	32
Bernard, Austin	.283	46	10	13	0	5	7	10	0
Campagna, Joe	.266	128	22	34	4	20	16	24	1
Culver, Cito	.329	149	39	49	6	18	22	30	3
Elder, Austin	.283	53	10	15	3	12	14	11	0
Garcia, Willy	.305	131	23	40	6	24	9	32	0
Girand, Jonah	.154	104	15	16	5	12	8	46	0
Krabbe, Tyler	.300	20	2	6	0	2	2	4	0
Lujano, Jesus	.318	305	50	97	3	40	20	40	22
McCusker, Carson	.265	275	48	73	13	46	21	95	5
Mercer, Jace	.215	130	27	28	4	16	26	35	10
Parks, Pavin	.284	342	78	97	17	67	65	69	14
Phipps, Denis	.296	341	74	101	33	91	53	72	10
Piatnik, Mitch	.265	68	9	18	1	8	2	28	8
Santana, Juan	.290	138	21	40	5	22	6	7	2
Silverio, Juan	.263	205	37	54	9	35	20	31	4
Zunica, Brad	.283	304	50	86	26	69	30	66	1

Name	W	L	ERA	G	SV	IP	H	BB	SO
Abbatiello, Neil	2	2	4.22	22	1	21	23	10	21
Acosta, Aneudy	0	1	6.38	7	0	18	13	14	5
Arjona, Kyle	2	0	7.33	6	0	27	41	7	16
Cochran-Gill, Trey	6	2	1.76	44	14	51	47	20	36
Crawford, Leo	2	3	7.12	7	0	37	47	12	20
Cruz, Jose	2	7	6.67	20	0	57	66	21	44
Cruz, Troy	0	1	8.25	4	0	12	21	4	13
Dexter, Jake	2	1	6.52	31	0	48	69	12	37
Faith, Austin	3	3	6.31	12	0	46	52	20	40
Gonzalez, Joey	8	2	3.63	20	0	117	96	39	128
Guillen, Alexander	0	0	10.20	9	0	15	26	8	17
Hanewich, Brett	0	0	13.15	16	0	13	24	11	17
Hartman, Ryan	0	2	6.75	3	0	12	13	2	16
Hofacket, Adam	9	5	4.53	49	1	60	51	12	85
Nunez, Oddy	3	1	6.86	27	0	39	46	23	35
Parra, Olbis	4	3	6.31	21	0	83	88	37	69
Rocker, Kumar	1	0	1.35	5	0	20	11	4	32
Swift, Hunter	0	0	9.00	11	0	10	9	8	8
Warren, Brac	5	0	4.78	37	0	32	12	30	45
Williamson, Ryan	5	4	5.00	11	0	54	64	17	54

TROIS-RIVIERES AIGLES

Name	AVG	AB	R	H	HR	RBI	BB	SO	SB
Brown, Steve	.288	278	41	80	13	68	35	83	8
Campagna, Joe	.240	125	29	30	4	15	14	31	2
Curtis, Elliott	.234	171	21	40	3	23	16	41	0
Dagenais, Michel	.188	32	2	6	0	1	4	16	1
Desai, Vaibhav	.221	77	8	17	1	9	6	37	0
Ejoh, Canice	.284	183	38	52	5	29	18	49	9
Gauthier, David	.321	28	3	9	0	4	3	8	0
Gladu, Raphael	.307	339	63	104	8	60	25	67	6
Hunt, Ethan	.333	39	5	13	0	4	3	11	1
Kelly, Juan	.313	297	49	93	11	61	44	63	4
Lacasse, Marcel	.230	74	12	17	0	11	12	28	0
Macaluso, Dustyn	.130	46	5	6	0	3	6	21	2
Martinez, Carlos	.336	247	55	83	16	62	30	29	0
Martinez, Yareb	.175	57	6	10	0	6	5	27	0
Miller, Myles	.243	37	10	9	1	4	4	9	1
Panas, Connor	.254	287	67	73	15	53	44	53	20
Pelletier, L.P.	.340	344	81	117	14	58	23	68	23
Salcedo, Edward	.179	28	5	5	0	3	1	9	1
Sanchez, Ricardo	.250	232	55	58	9	40	32	65	1
Santana, Juan	.303	178	35	54	8	31	10	16	6
Toni, Nicco	.320	25	3	8	0	4	4	4	0

Name	W	L	ERA	G	SV	IP	H	BB	SO
Allegretti, Christian	3	2	6.64	31	2	39	51	21	29
Belisle-Springer, Sam	7	8	7.11	24	0	108	151	36	86
Bell, Kyle	0	1	11.81	4	0	11	11	12	14
Bradwell, James	2	3	4.95	32	3	36	40	24	29
Dozier, Mark	0	1	11.17	3	0	10	10	11	5
Gauthier, David	1	2	7.65	9	0	38	59	18	21
Gillespie, Scott	0	0	12.66	9	0	11	17	11	11
Graffeo, Carlo	1	1	9.98	8	0	15	18	14	11
Gutierrez, Osman	5	5	5.28	20	0	89	98	39	93
Henrich, Austin	0	3	11.12	7	0	17	28	14	9
Lepard, Taylor	2	2	8.61	12	0	23	26	24	23
Luneke, Tyler	2	3	6.23	32	3	43	54	19	36
McAlister, Mason	0	1	5.89	5	0	18	26	6	15
Perez, Kevin	4	2	5.94	11	0	47	55	33	39
Poliquin, Sam	5	7	5.19	20	0	87	94	39	45

Reitz, Matt	0	1	4.79	14	0	21	25	8	17
Smith, Josh	1	2	7.14	29	0	29	28	39	35
Smith, Tucker	3	1	2.23	9	1	32	25	6	27
Thomas, Kyle	4	1	3.29	19	8	38	45	9	41
Tindall, Mark	2	1	6.98	31	5	40	55	24	32
Vasquez, Jose	1	2	12.51	10	1	14	23	4	11

PIONEER LEAGUE

The Grand Junction Rockies will have a new name in 2023, but they sent their old moniker and owners out in style as the Rockies won their first Pioneer League title since 1981, when they were known as the Butte Copper Kings. The club was sold by Rockies owner Dick Monfort before the end of the season, but the handover was not going to take place until after the season. Grand Junction won the second-half South Division title and then rolled through the playoffs under manager Bobby Jenks.

North Division	W	L	PCT	GB
*@Missoula PaddleHeads	69	26	.726	-
#Billings Mustangs	53	41	.564	15.5
Great Falls Voyagers	48	47	.505	21
Idaho Falls Chukars	48	48	.500	21.5
Glacier Range Riders	39	56	.411	30
South Division	**W**	**L**	**PCT**	**GB**
@Grand Junction Rockies	62	33	.653	-
*Ogden Raptors	51	43	.543	10.5
Rocky Mountain Vibes	37	56	.398	24
Northern Colorado Owlz	35	56	.385	25
Boise Hawks	30	66	.313	32.5

**First-half Champion. @Second-half champion. #Wild Card*

Playoffs—Semifinals: Grand Junction defeated Ogden 2-1 and Missoula defeated Billings 2-1 in best-of-3 series. **Finals:** Grand Junction defeated Missoula 2-0 in best-of-3 series.

MVP: Jayson Newman, Missoula. **Pitcher of the Year:** Elijah Gill, Billings**. Manager of the Year:** Bobby Jenks, Grand Junction. **Rookie of the Year:** Nico Popa, Grand Junction.

BATTING LEADERS

Player	Team	AVG	AB	R	H	HR	RBI
Cruce, Jake	GJ	.430	86	26	37	8	30
Estrada, Calvin	IF	.428	208	62	89	13	66
Jepson, Riley	GF	.407	243	80	99	12	55
Popa, Nico	GJ	.406	392	88	159	6	85
Sparks, Lamar	Miss.	.399	346	108	138	18	85
Guadalupe, Adabel	NC	.398	128	35	51	6	28
Williams, Logan	Ogden	.394	71	15	28	2	8
Diaz, Gio	RM	.394	376	87	148	2	41
Broughton, Jack	Ogden	.381	365	112	139	14	71

PITCHING LEADERS

Player	Team	W	L	ERA	IP	H	BB	SO
Gill, Elijah	Bil.	3	1	3.26	86	85	29	80
Hamby, Rob	GR	4	3	4.11	81	80	26	59
Crowson, Austin	Miss.	7	0	4.23	87	93	46	59
Barros, Noah	GR	8	6	4.85	102	114	36	87
Pilot, Kelvan	Bill.	7	5	5.02	81	88	46	81
Buraconak, Will	NC	5	3	5.11	88	122	27	89
Day, Christian	Ogden	9	3	5.30	90	120	32	76
Orta, Ronny	Ogden	7	6	5.34	94	115	25	82
Rodriguez, Victor	IF	3	4	5.44	84	99	34	82

BILLINGS MUSTANGS

Name	AVG	AB	R	H	HR	RBI	BB	SO	SB
Teixeira, Juan	.393	56	15	22	2	11	9	6	1
Piatnik, Mitch	.329	76	19	25	1	11	10	23	2
Kline, Jacob	.327	223	45	73	9	39	15	69	7
Garcia, Jalen	.315	308	52	97	11	56	22	91	17
Raper, Jackson	.306	337	58	103	11	60	36	75	0
Wurtz, Gabe	.304	355	65	108	20	81	33	103	4
Mow, Abraham	.298	84	21	25	3	19	12	15	2
Barth, Jordan	.288	250	39	72	5	31	10	23	4
Fernandez, Andrew	.280	143	31	40	4	36	20	31	2
Taylor, Crews	.280	325	74	91	15	46	57	94	9
Pena, Christian	.277	47	8	13	0	8	7	12	1
Parreira, Brian	.277	249	46	69	8	46	36	56	0
Ultsch, Nick	.274	73	15	20	2	19	7	16	0
Hovey, Jordan	.264	212	37	56	8	41	34	73	6
Nagle, Adrian	.256	43	1	11	0	1	5	15	1
Jackson, Bryce	.206	160	14	33	4	21	31	46	0
Dixon, Burle	.203	64	17	13	1	10	8	18	6
Peterson, Tristan	.153	59	10	9	0	7	14	14	0

Name	W	L	ERA	G	SV	IP	H	BB	SO
Arevalo, Pablo	1	1	2.76	5	0	33	33	5	30
Bonvillain, Beaux	3	2	1.73	41	10	42	30	7	62
Correa, Jean	4	0	4.23	10	0	28	20	7	22
Cunningham, Jack	1	0	9.00	8	0	11	18	5	9
Dubbe, Logan	0	1	8.71	5	0	21	32	7	20
Gill, Elijah	3	1	3.26	16	0	86	85	29	80
Goonan, Jack	0	1	5.94	15	0	17	20	13	18
Harris, McLain	2	0	4.40	30	0	47	55	9	45
Kiley, Sean	3	1	5.01	12	0	41	40	19	29
Maybach, Pat	1	4	6.37	10	0	35	51	15	25
McRae, Ethan	3	1	4.22	6	0	32	35	10	17
Pace, Foster	8	3	3.13	37	1	55	66	11	47
Pesto, Al	1	5	4.30	27	6	23	25	6	27
Pilot, Kelvan	7	5	5.02	25	1	81	88	46	81
Ragins, Darrien	2	3	8.17	25	0	51	62	32	52
Serwa, Kenny	5	2	2.44	10	0	59	57	9	50

BOISE HAWKS

Name	AVG	AB	R	H	HR	RBI	BB	SO	SB
Bailey, Jayce	.128	47	6	6	1	3	5	17	2
Dudoit, Haloa	.281	302	51	85	2	42	31	45	2
Gil, Ray	.293	331	67	97	17	58	33	89	1
Gutierrez, Jorge	.128	39	5	5	0	6	10	15	0
Harris, Myles	.203	148	26	30	3	14	43	58	0
Jezioro, Frankie	.188	48	9	9	0	1	5	16	2
Jorgensen, Tyler	.289	401	70	116	4	56	36	69	10
Lebron, Charles	.372	43	9	16	0	14	4	13	0
Lopez, Kobe	.207	87	13	18	1	12	7	15	4
Minder, Trevor	.281	228	42	64	2	20	31	33	2
Poteet, D.J.	.219	64	11	14	1	12	10	26	1
Rathbone, Jordan	.224	125	21	28	6	22	13	38	0
Rojas, Freddy	.179	56	8	10	2	7	14	20	0
Romberg, Derek	.267	30	4	8	0	2	9	5	0
Schulefand, Jordan	.317	41	5	13	0	1	5	7	7
Sequera, Abraham	.355	197	44	70	2	38	26	28	1
Skelly, Sean	.220	191	29	42	7	25	37	50	0
Smyth, Jimmy	.198	106	22	21	1	10	13	23	5
Walstad, Ryan	.283	187	28	53	5	37	38	37	0
White, Greg	.243	37	3	9	1	4	0	9	0

Name	W	L	ERA	G	SV	IP	H	BB	SO
Baggs, Jay	0	0	5.93	6	0	14	10	13	17
C Costello	3	2	5.93	6	0	30	42	19	20
Dallas, Matt	2	3	7.24	30	0	55	56	32	56
Gabbert, Matt	5	6	6.62	19	0	87	111	26	95
Gorrell, Gavin	2	8	7.36	16	0	70	101	36	62
Johnson, Reid	1	1	7.36	4	0	15	21	7	12
Lines, Mitch	3	8	7.10	26	0	90	133	27	55
McBride, Noah	0	4	5.33	44	4	51	43	29	64
Nelson, Jordan	1	0	5.92	26	0	59	77	17	38
Peterson, Mike	1	3	6.27	14	1	33	46	7	26
Pindel, Kevin	4	7	5.81	19	1	53	66	10	63
Smith, Alexander	0	1	9.42	4	0	14	21	9	11
Spears, Brayden	2	3	7.11	13	0	49	67	21	46

GLACIER RANGE RIDERS

Name	AVG	AB	R	H	HR	RBI	BB	SO	SB
Bates, Austin	.185	54	6	10	0	1	7	11	2
Bologna, Vinny	.214	42	7	9	2	6	2	15	1
Broussard, Brandt	.277	321	63	89	3	38	55	51	11
Carr, Johnny	.333	27	6	9	1	8	4	5	0
Cash, Ryan	.326	331	68	108	3	56	47	41	24
Cole, Ryan	.246	138	13	34	3	14	12	29	9
Dinesen, Mason	.302	116	17	35	1	12	1	32	10

Enriquez, Ramon	.080	25	1	2	0	1	1	9	0
Howell, Gabe	.358	81	25	29	5	25	16	18	12
Jordan, Kevin	.226	31	2	7	0	3	1	14	0
Knell, Michael	.208	53	6	11	1	8	10	21	0
Kyriacou, David	.250	40	7	10	1	7	5	14	0
Linscott, Sam	.325	206	38	67	4	42	14	26	12
Mazzone, Justin	.266	79	12	21	3	11	12	14	0
McCabe, Eddie	.311	190	17	59	2	26	19	25	0
McConnell, Ben	.296	375	82	111	4	42	38	58	43
McNicholas, Austin	.212	33	7	7	1	4	3	6	0
Miller, Dean	.308	312	66	96	15	75	30	62	15
Morris, Livingston	.271	214	44	58	13	42	27	80	0
Sims, Drew	.258	93	13	24	2	15	12	22	0
Trammell, Brandon	.386	44	7	17	2	12	3	13	0
Wofford, Brody	.252	317	51	80	20	70	36	100	4

Name	W	L	ERA	G	SV	IP	H	BB	SO
Barros, Noah	8	6	4.85	19	0	102	114	36	87
Biasiello, Mike	0	0	4.85	7	0	13	17	3	16
Coleman, Justin	0	3	6.23	34	6	39	44	19	53
Day, Dawson	0	2	5.34	12	0	30	23	20	44
Edwards, Austin	0	5	8.60	8	0	38	52	18	28
Hamby, Rob	4	3	4.11	15	0	81	80	26	59
Henry, Isaiah	0	4	7.25	19	0	22	24	25	34
Holweger, Drew	1	1	4.03	14	0	22	24	14	18
Kyle, Kevin	2	4	6.45	14	0	53	66	38	47
Solomon, Tanner	4	6	6.25	26	0	86	102	41	69
Steinfort, Austin	3	1	4.93	34	4	35	33	21	30
Stout, Andrew	2	5	5.20	17	0	64	71	26	58
Thomas, Nate	2	0	2.29	21	3	20	11	10	25
Toplikar, Trenton	0	0	1.06	9	0	17	14	3	15
Tri, Andrew	0	1	8.76	5	1	12	21	6	16
Vanwey, Logan	2	2	6.64	9	0	39	47	21	46
Walters, Logan	0	0	7.82	6	0	13	21	7	10

GRAND JUNCTION ROCKIES

Name	AVG	AB	R	H	HR	RBI	BB	SO	SB
Cruce, Jake	.430	86	26	37	8	30	11	21	0
Elder, Austin	.362	116	19	42	0	15	19	9	1
Elvir, Josh	.312	308	79	96	19	83	34	89	11
Farmer, Caleb	.304	138	31	42	5	25	28	36	7
Fitzpatrick, Jordan	.344	160	38	55	7	35	13	35	2
Girand, Jonah	.260	77	21	20	5	16	9	23	0
Gordon, Colin	.279	68	21	19	3	18	14	28	4
Hubbard, Jaylen	.335	233	46	78	6	39	14	52	18
Johns, Gavin	.100	40	4	4	0	4	3	15	1
Johnson, Joe	.320	250	52	80	10	41	21	61	7
Middleton, Charles	.305	154	28	47	8	32	13	36	4
Monge, Alex	.160	25	6	4	0	4	4	4	1
Moore, Collin	.192	26	5	5	1	5	3	10	0
Nielsen, Alex	.332	250	47	83	2	28	21	31	5
Petersen, Casey	.360	264	66	95	14	75	46	79	8
Popa, Nico	.406	392	88	159	6	85	23	58	33
Ross, Shawn	.280	293	77	82	24	90	58	111	14
Sandoval, Tyler	.190	121	21	23	3	21	12	45	2
Scantlin, Nate	.354	113	32	40	0	13	15	17	8
Vazquez, Chris	.231	39	6	9	0	4	4	15	1
Wisner, Clay	.200	35	1	7	0	4	2	9	1

Name	W	L	ERA	G	SV	IP	H	BB	SO
Agnew, Josh	10	3	5.45	17	0	102	117	15	98
Baldenebro, Roberto	6	3	5.65	22	0	73	80	37	55
Bono, Michael	0	0	8.44	8	0	11	19	6	14
Dobrash, Jimmy	5	4	7.87	18	0	82	109	47	77
Fuentes, Izzy	8	5	6.37	18	0	89	114	34	85
Ibarra, Josh	2	0	2.38	20	0	34	29	16	40
Kahaloa, Ian	1	0	6.10	4	0	21	23	5	29
Kaufman, Ari	1	2	9.15	5	0	21	36	5	21
Morrill, Trey	0	0	6.48	8	0	17	21	5	22
Parisi, Jack	1	0	4.50	6	0	30	33	12	27
Patterson, Kyler	2	0	4.91	12	2	15	15	7	16
Price, Jared	1	1	8.44	12	0	16	22	11	19
Reynolds, Trevin	0	3	3.41	38	16	37	41	11	44
Schilperoort, Hunter	3	0	2.65	16	0	17	15	12	22
Smith, Alex	2	4	10.03	10	0	35	60	17	34

Townsend, Mike	2	2	7.85	34	0	37	53	8	39
Villa, Alfredo	7	1	3.13	20	0	63	57	24	81
Young, Gaylan	1	0	3.38	21	0	24	24	14	14

GREAT FALLS VOYAGERS

Name	AVG	AB	R	H	HR	RBI	BB	SO	SB
Aberouette, Felix	.259	27	3	7	0	4	6	11	3
Atwood, Andy	.337	92	24	31	3	20	11	14	8
Brunson, Tavis	.263	57	10	15	0	10	4	19	0
Daniel, Breydon	.320	338	83	108	12	56	59	81	29
Deeb, Michael	.260	331	54	86	3	60	43	57	4
DeGuzman, Cristopher	.271	192	36	52	5	26	30	57	15
Emanuel, Nick	.307	88	8	27	0	13	6	11	0
Jepson, Riley	.407	243	80	99	12	55	61	32	20
Kolbush, Derek	.308	266	51	82	5	50	32	71	4
Krabbe, Tyler	.296	54	9	16	2	13	4	12	0
Loera, Fernando	.333	42	11	14	0	4	4	10	1
Malec, Jake	.286	353	68	101	6	43	27	104	22
McKisic, Myles	.204	103	21	21	0	13	12	45	7
Monroe, Chris	.291	165	20	48	3	37	11	39	0
Olson, Will	.241	133	12	32	0	19	13	45	0
Oviedo, Adam	.236	157	28	37	2	31	24	53	3
Polanco, Lukas	.202	109	17	22	3	16	17	33	2
Runge, Collin	.307	336	67	103	11	60	48	64	18
Simmons, Aaron	.265	68	8	18	2	11	6	13	1
Zurbrugg, Zane	.185	27	4	5	0	3	3	11	1

Name	W	L	ERA	G	SV	IP	H	BB	SO
Becerra-Lopez, Anthony	5	3	5.45	34	2	71	76	50	81
Brown, Tanner	0	0	6.29	8	0	34	37	19	34
Castro, Alexander	2	2	10.13	7	0	19	30	12	14
Demco, Brad	4	3	5.58	34	1	40	31	36	64
Dollander, Hunter	2	0	1.35	2	0	13	6	1	12
Gainer, Josh	1	6	4.12	29	2	39	41	19	32
Garcia, Andrew	1	5	10.74	7	0	31	51	22	31
Gustafson, Shane	2	0	5.96	4	0	23	33	8	16
Jones, Quincy	6	5	6.31	18	0	87	113	28	58
Lorah, Brett	0	0	5.40	15	0	23	34	9	21
Naumann, Tyler	4	5	5.46	15	0	86	105	23	82
Pooler, Breonn	3	4	6.43	13	0	63	80	23	52
Quigley, Montana	4	0	4.15	40	13	48	48	12	44
Runge, Collin	1	0	0.64	7	0	14	11	3	7
Spear, Connor	0	2	10.13	20	2	37	55	21	26
Swanson, Ethan	1	0	5.48	19	0	23	30	24	30
Thomas, Matt	1	6	6.78	20	0	78	101	34	52

IDAHO FALLS CHUKARS

Name	AVG	AB	R	H	HR	RBI	BB	SO	SB
Barmakian, Steve	.335	391	97	131	4	72	53	63	12
Bermúdez, José	.291	55	14	16	0	7	4	14	6
Buendia, Aldo	.172	29	3	5	1	2	3	7	0
Callahan, Eric	.252	305	50	77	5	55	35	96	17
DeBonville, Thomas	.336	119	22	40	4	25	8	34	7
Don, Andrew	.362	69	12	25	0	13	5	15	2
Estrada, Calvin	.428	208	62	89	13	66	37	28	14
Feinstein, Matt	.350	120	45	42	7	23	26	31	7
Hisky, Hunter	.322	395	88	127	7	83	50	41	3
Hueth, Brendan	.319	254	60	81	2	33	33	32	18
Kelly, Tyler	.338	133	31	45	4	27	22	13	9
Little, Webb	.237	38	8	9	0	6	7	10	0
Phillips, Ricky	.311	74	24	23	0	14	10	22	2
Reyes, Jose	.363	281	51	102	6	56	24	39	3
Rosales, Eder	.207	29	5	6	0	1	1	5	1
Strong, Seth	.393	28	7	11	2	14	3	8	0
Stroup, Dusty	.368	394	76	145	24	108	27	97	14
Thomas, Damani	.178	45	12	8	0	7	4	17	1
Troyer, Sam	.362	116	31	42	0	21	8	26	12
West, Brady	.277	260	47	72	6	58	34	63	1
Wyatt, Tyler	.222	36	8	8	1	4	4	9	2

Name	W	L	ERA	G	SV	IP	H	BB	SO
Bender, Logan	1	0	5.88	29	0	34	37	25	38
Binder, Jake	4	7	7.38	16	0	61	87	39	53
Cartier, Andrew	0	0	5.26	24	0	38	48	17	27

Dicenso, Jack	5	6	6.34	18	0	88	111	33	77
Fishberg, Alex	4	1	7.08	34	1	61	64	34	71
Jenkins, Nate	5	1	4.56	42	7	53	69	16	64
Kornstad, Sam	3	3	8.33	8	0	36	55	17	19
Laurita, Luke	0	0	8.79	11	0	14	26	4	11
McGinnis, Keagan	3	2	4.47	44	0	56	51	33	74
Nunnally Jr., Jon	3	4	5.79	43	5	51	49	36	81
Rodriguez, Victor	3	4	5.44	28	1	84	99	34	82
Romano, Ramsey	3	2	4.87	10	0	44	50	13	37
Silva, Daniel	1	1	8.03	3	0	12	20	6	12
Slocum, Joe	4	1	5.18	5	0	24	24	12	13
Trabacchi, Nick	1	4	18.00	5	0	18	43	14	14
Walker, Tom	3	4	8.48	9	0	40	56	17	36
Wyatt, Tyler	1	1	8.91	17	0	32	46	28	43

MISSOULA PADDLEHEADS

Name	AVG	AB	R	H	HR	RBI	BB	SO	SB
Akins, Jared	.310	197	40	61	7	42	25	53	8
Chung, Patrick	.389	95	28	37	2	20	6	5	5
Cicci, Nick	.213	127	25	27	5	22	12	31	5
Davis, Brenton	.148	27	4	4	0	1	4	10	1
Gatewood, Nick	.337	403	74	136	14	96	20	67	1
Greenwalt, Keaton	.305	348	65	106	8	66	30	58	21
Newman, Jayson	.369	355	80	131	32	115	43	63	2
Noviello, Andrew	.378	37	7	14	0	9	4	5	0
O'Connor, McClain	.289	266	74	77	14	57	21	68	10
Perez, Henderson	.257	101	17	26	1	11	18	23	1
Riley, Brandon	.324	321	78	104	14	63	42	64	4
Sparks, Lamar	.399	346	108	138	18	85	49	60	16
Thompson, Cameron	.320	375	90	120	12	69	47	75	11
Whatley, Kevin	.296	125	25	37	2	17	10	34	6
Willman, Kamron	.322	258	62	83	6	43	34	64	6

Name	W	L	ERA	G	SV	IP	H	BB	SO
Alexander, Nathan	1	1	5.01	35	0	56	53	27	66
Boyle, Nate	3	0	4.54	18	0	36	40	18	29
Crowson, Austin	7	0	4.23	18	0	87	93	46	59
Elliott, Tyler	1	0	3.03	21	0	30	28	19	30
Hellinger, Sam	1	1	2.01	39	17	49	37	13	74
LaRossa, John	1	0	6.41	16	0	20	18	20	32
Merkel, Nick	5	1	2.79	7	0	39	36	13	33
Monsion, Rafael	3	1	7.07	8	0	28	43	13	22
Munsch, Jason	1	1	10.47	6	0	16	28	12	22
Newman, Jayson	1	0	4.30	15	6	15	18	4	14
Pena, Domingo	6	4	5.17	19	0	70	71	35	83
Schultz, Connor	2	1	8.33	8	0	27	39	7	25
Seidel, Austen	7	2	4.77	10	0	55	53	23	49
Simon, Mark	2	0	3.05	17	1	21	20	8	26
Smith, Zach	1	1	7.88	15	0	32	46	15	29
Sparks, Mitch	3	1	6.75	7	0	35	49	5	15
Swain, Dan	2	1	3.94	28	1	32	27	25	48
Thompson, Cody	7	1	3.35	37	0	46	46	14	43
Timmins, Mark	5	4	6.10	17	0	83	107	21	67
Wenzel, Palmer	3	1	5.95	5	0	20	23	11	15

NORTHERN COLORADO OWLZ

Name	AVG	AB	R	H	HR	RBI	BB	SO	SB
Allen, Ronnie	.196	51	8	10	2	7	14	21	1
Bottari, Nick	.188	32	3	6	2	9	2	10	1
Bouchard, Tim	.366	257	53	94	12	53	32	76	10
Crosby, Brandon	.302	295	60	89	11	62	28	91	15
Diaz, Euro	.251	199	29	50	1	25	20	53	6
Garr, Jordan	.246	61	9	15	1	9	9	6	2
Guadalupe, Abdel	.398	128	35	51	6	28	17	22	5
Higgins, Kevin	.352	335	61	118	3	57	13	62	4
Hudson, Hunter	.250	28	4	7	0	0	0	6	0
Jackson, Alex	.278	342	59	95	12	47	45	107	20
Kellerman, Robbie	.236	127	18	30	3	23	16	27	3
Phelts, Cam	.288	302	68	87	7	49	34	100	51
Popham, Dakota	.291	79	12	23	2	17	7	23	1
Rich, Marshall	.288	163	33	47	0	18	13	34	5
Scafariello, Liam	.133	30	2	4	1	2	7	16	4
Turner, Matt	.252	131	22	33	6	19	13	52	3
Vaughan, Slayton	.188	32	3	6	0	0	0	9	0

West, Zach	.236	106	16	25	0	10	13	27	6

Name	W	L	ERA	G	SV	IP	H	BB	SO
Adkins, Kyle	4	2	6.17	38	0	58	74	25	46
Benton, Chance	3	3	8.74	28	3	34	43	21	37
Buraconak, Will	5	3	5.11	18	0	88	122	27	89
De La Cruz, Kida	3	6	8.69	12	0	49	54	37	41
Dexter, Spenser	1	3	9.15	4	0	20	30	9	22
Diaz, LJ	0	1	7.66	13	0	25	30	21	25
Fischer, Tyler	0	0	7.59	6	0	11	15	6	14
Grant-DeBose, CJ	2	5	7.94	30	0	62	91	33	51
Griffin, Christian	2	2	5.34	29	9	32	35	18	38
Kirwan, William	1	1	7.04	12	0	15	19	10	15
Parsons, Noah	0	1	9.72	14	0	17	23	13	16
Ramos, Isaiah	2	1	6.88	18	0	17	28	13	23
Rivera, Jerryell	0	3	17.47	6	0	17	28	25	10
Schneider, Austin	2	7	7.61	27	1	73	92	44	66
Schoeninger, Tanner	2	5	9.78	11	0	42	71	17	31
Snavely, Preston	4	4	6.80	16	0	82	109	30	68
Wilkerson, Chase	0	2	9.88	31	0	37	45	47	49
Williams, Colton	1	4	6.84	12	0	50	80	15	34

OGDEN RAPTORS

Name	AVG	AB	R	H	HR	RBI	BB	SO	SB
Achecar, Freddy	.284	345	71	98	11	76	54	91	10
Adams, Pat	.326	316	81	103	5	60	62	68	24
Alexiades, Reese	.330	352	85	116	14	97	62	83	13
Bohning, Brandon	.327	156	39	51	1	21	21	33	4
Broughton, Josh	.381	365	112	139	14	71	39	56	29
Buhner, Gunnar	.400	25	7	10	0	2	3	5	1
Conners, Dakota	.312	324	74	101	6	62	46	61	10
Dansereau, Brian	.343	335	72	115	12	93	32	77	14
Elefante, Kevin	.250	68	12	17	0	11	11	30	0
Lancaster, Jackson	.148	27	3	4	0	1	0	14	0
Lewis, Ty	.291	247	42	72	5	41	26	75	3
Macaluso, Dustyn	.306	121	30	37	5	31	15	32	8
Michaels, Nick	.167	54	5	9	1	4	6	14	3
Ray, Anthony	.288	66	18	19	0	10	5	4	7
Rivero, Alejandro	.297	37	7	11	1	4	1	10	0
Ryan, Tyler	.077	26	5	2	1	7	6	13	0
Semones, Fox	.228	57	16	13	1	3	9	13	9
Ulliana, Sonny	.333	204	37	68	10	45	22	55	4
Valdez, Jesus	.369	379	83	140	21	109	33	55	10
Warkentin, Matt	.370	46	14	17	4	19	10	13	2
Williams, Logan	.394	71	15	28	2	8	8	25	3

Name	W	L	ERA	G	SV	IP	H	BB	SO
Burto, Samuel	3	0	6.05	4	0	19	21	12	12
Cirino, Miguel	0	1	7.41	34	0	34	47	13	36
Day, Christian	9	3	5.30	18	0	90	120	32	76
Duprey, Sidney	1	1	7.52	9	0	26	33	15	26
Gonzalez, Jorge	3	1	7.50	27	0	60	77	26	55
Groen, Gunnar	1	0	1.69	3	0	16	10	6	17
Lancaster, Jackson	2	1	1.13	26	12	24	11	16	43
McCabe, Brandon	3	3	6.48	27	0	33	32	26	45
Mulholland, Jake	3	0	1.88	33	0	24	23	9	26
Orta, Ronny	7	6	5.34	17	0	94	115	25	82
Ottesen, Riley	2	5	8.45	20	0	65	88	39	61
Parker, Evan	0	1	5.84	13	2	12	13	16	10
Pearce, Dylan	1	1	6.39	16	4	31	50	14	34
Portela, Polo	5	4	6.25	14	0	68	91	27	51
Stratton, Chase	5	2	4.22	36	0	49	47	22	53

ROCKY MOUNTAIN VIBES

Name	AVG	AB	R	H	HR	RBI	BB	SO	SB
Annone, Mike	.317	199	28	63	3	49	17	28	0
Binder, Dalys	.301	73	10	22	2	11	4	19	5
Cantu, Ulysses	.344	337	80	116	14	77	41	71	4
Carreno, Paul	.267	60	12	16	2	8	9	14	3
Diaz, Gio	.394	376	87	148	2	41	32	26	12
Encarnacion, Joe	.260	127	21	33	3	19	7	34	1
Esparza, Joshua	.286	56	9	16	2	7	2	18	0
Garcia, Alan	.339	62	15	21	0	14	7	13	3
Glenn, Josh	.272	92	23	25	2	18	19	37	1

Hanson, Andrew	.294	197	37	58	4	43	18	50	29
Hernandez, Domonique	.313	246	46	77	8	53	19	55	7
Lara, Julian	.366	41	11	15	0	4	4	16	1
Lopez, Cesar	.340	244	56	83	4	46	28	28	3
Lopez, Ethan	.336	259	56	87	10	48	22	50	8
Marquez, Caleb	.275	69	11	19	4	10	5	26	0
Michaels, Nick	.322	171	35	55	5	39	15	47	1
Navarro, Luis	.374	211	52	79	6	44	46	25	0
Nuñez, Ulises	.272	92	15	25	2	11	11	19	1
Perez, Brandon	.287	195	32	56	0	20	8	49	8
Rabago, Jesus	.250	44	11	11	0	10	4	14	0
Rosales, Eder	.175	40	5	7	0	3	2	14	0
Tejada, Miguel	.276	87	15	24	2	12	9	33	2

Name	W	L	ERA	G	SV	IP	H	BB	SO
Allen, Chris	0	1	8.60	14	0	38	47	14	33
Alvarez, Garrett	0	2	9.58	9	1	21	33	9	23
Baird, Dusty	4	2	7.16	9	0	33	46	11	30
Bayer, Pete	3	4	7.39	23	1	32	32	29	48
Caulfield, Tom	0	0	8.72	10	0	22	34	17	16
Davis, Seth	3	2	5.79	29	2	33	40	17	49
Draves, Nathan	3	0	5.46	23	0	30	48	14	39
Ellis, Damon	1	0	4.50	9	0	14	21	6	8
Erwin, Brett	1	4	11.88	6	0	25	49	11	20
Fletcher, Greyson	2	2	5.04	6	0	30	40	11	20
Harris, Joe	0	1	11.47	6	0	13	27	3	9
Knoten, Brock	0	4	8.64	7	0	33	59	14	21
Leo, Jorge	3	3	8.71	12	0	52	82	15	51
Mora, Jose	0	0	13.24	12	0	17	29	10	16
Morell, Johnny	0	2	12.08	8	0	13	18	13	14
Ochoa, Jassiel	0	3	12.60	5	0	15	21	11	7
Perez, Yohandry	4	4	7.92	22	0	86	116	58	87
Pozo, Miguel	0	1	3.97	31	10	34	42	11	47
Rios, Jesus	1	5	8.34	7	0	23	40	16	17
Rodriguez, Felipe	3	4	10.52	27	0	51	82	44	60
Valle, Armando	1	1	7.47	17	0	31	43	18	39
Viney, Gaylon	1	3	10.42	8	0	19	34	10	22
Wesselmann, Jacob	2	2	5.56	9	0	44	50	12	44

PECOS LEAGUE

The Roswell Invaders rolled to their fourth Pecos League title and first since 2015 by knocking off Tucson 4-1 in the best-of-7 Pecos League title series. Roswell had only finished fourth in the Mountain Division in the regular season, but the Invaders got hot at the right time, winning 8 of their 11 playoff games.

Pacific Division	W	L	PCT	GB
San Rafael Pacifics	41	9	.820	--
Tucson Saguaros	34	8	.809	4
Bakersfield Train Robbers	31	18	.632	9.5
Santa Rosa Scuba Divers	22	29	.431	19.5
Monterey AmberJacks	21	29	.420	20
Martinez Sturgeon	19	31	.380	22
Vallejo Seaweed	17	33	.340	24
Wasco Reserve	7	40	.148	32.5
Mountain Division	**W**	**L**	**PCT**	**GB**
Garden City Wind	36	10	.782	--
Alpine Cowboys	32	17	.653	5.5
Trinidad Triggers	25	18	.581	9.5
Roswell Invaders	27	22	.551	10.5
Santa Fe Fuego	21	25	.456	15
Austin Weirdos	19	31	.380	19
Weimar Hormigas	16	31	.340	20.5
Colorado Springs Snow Sox	14	31	.311	21.5

Playoffs—Quarterfinals: Roswell defeated Garden City 2-1, Trinidad defeated Alpine 2-1, San Rafael defeated Santa Rosa 2-0 and Tucson defeated Bakersfield 2-0 in best-of-3 series. **Semifinals:** Roswell defeated Trinidad 2-1 and Tucson defeated San Rafael 2-0 in best-of-three series. **Finals:** Roswell defeated Tucson 4-1 in best-of-7 series.

BATTING LEADERS

Player	Team	AVG	AB	R	H	HR	RBI
Koki Matsuda	GCK	.476	124	41	59	5	28
Mark Traylor	ALP	.465	172	57	80	7	57
Seth Strong	BAK	.451	153	45	69	7	61
Adam Purdy	TRI	.439	173	59	76	4	40
Jack Matero	ROS	.433	97	31	42	2	30
Parker DePasquale	SAF	.430	149	57	64	17	71
Beau Dorman	SRF	.429	196	74	84	13	80
Brock Ephan	TUC	.429	119	37	51	14	40
Manny Cachora	SAF	.424	172	46	73	11	51
David Arza	TRI	.414	152	50	63	8	42

PITCHING LEADERS

Player	Team	W	L	ERA	IP	H	BB	SO
Ethan McRae	MON	4	3	2.55	67	55	14	70
Keisy Portorreal	GCK	6	0	2.59	59	45	9	75
Luke Kelly	BAK	5	0	3.35	70	84	25	86
Mark Dozier	SRF	6	1	3.47	54	40	30	82
Nathan Lu	SRF	4	1	3.48	52	46	24	51
Chris Rodriguez	BAK	6	2	3.94	71	77	33	69
Jarod Sprinkle	ROS	4	3	4.21	53	66	11	55
Buzz Shirley	ALP	9	0	4.23	57	63	34	68
Manny Corpas	MAR	9	3	4.26	114	140	26	147
Spenser Dexter	CS	5	3	4.27	59	63	25	83

UNITED SHORES LEAGUE (USPBL)

Birmingham's Felix Aberouette hit three home runs and drove in five runs as Birmingham rallied from a four-run deficit to beat Utica 8-6 in the USPBL championship game.

East Division	W	L	PCT	GB
Utica Unicorns	28	16	.636	—
Eastside Diamond Hoppers	21	23	.477	7
West Division	**W**	**L**	**PCT**	**GB**
Birmingham Bloomfield Beaverss	22	22	.500	—
Westside Woolly Mammoth	17	27	.386	5

Playoffs—First Round: Westside defeated Eastside. **Semifinals:** Birmingham defeated Westside. **Finals:** Birmingham defeated Utica.

All-Star Team: C: Matt Parkinson, Unicorns. **1B:** Ari Sechopoulos, Unicorns. **2B**: Jon Hodo, Unicorns. **SS**: Alex Pup, Hoppers. **3B**: Houston Parker, Mammoths. **OF**: Drue Galassi, Unicorns; Marcos Castillo, Beavers; Noah Marcoux, Hoppers. **DH**: Noah Childress, Unicorns. UTIL: Dakota McFadden, Beavers; Elijah Brown, Mammoths.

SP: Derrick Edington, Hoppers; Collin Ledbetter, Mammoths; Trevor Jackson, Beavers. **P**: Keon Taylor, Unicorns; Perry Bewley, Unicorns; James Krick, Beavers.

Reserves: Luis Atiles, Unicorns; Kevin Lambert, Unicorns; Felix Aberouette, Beavers; Blake Porter, Hoppers; Nick Kreutzer, Hoppers; Nick Shaw, Beavers; Adam Riggleman, Unicorns; Zach Blankenship, Beavers; Harry Orth, Hoppers; Luke Drummond, Hoppers; Christian Dearman, Mammoths.

INTERNATIONAL

USA Wins Trio Of Baseball World Cups

BY J.J. COOPER

The world-wide coronavirus pandemic meant that international baseball tournaments unavoidable had to be paused for well over a year.

But as the world tried to return to normal in 2022, that meant that a backlog of international baseball tournaments meant it was a very busy year. And once again, as has become the norm, USA Baseball was standing on the top step at a number of medal ceremonies.

The World Baseball Softball Confederation held the 12U, 15U, 18U and 23U World Cups all in the same year. Team USA won three of the four. Japan won the 23-and-under World Cup, but the U.S. did not attend that tournament.

Of the three tournaments Team USA attended, its teams went a combined 24-2. Between Colin Anderson (12U Most Valuable Player), Coy James (15U Most Valuable Player) and Bryce Eldridge (18U Most Valuable Player), the U.S. also went 3-for-3 in winning the tournament MVPs as well.

As of mid-November, the WBSC had not updated its Men's Baseball World Rankings in 2022 (its last update was in December of 2021). Those rankings have Japan listed at No. 1 and the U.S. as fifth in the world. But by any rational measure, it's clear that the U.S. has climbed to the pinnacle of international baseball.

That wasn't the case for many years. For decades where Cuba dominated international men's baseball, and there was a stretch where Japan stood supreme. But now, it's USA Baseball that has become the dominant force in international baseball.

The U.S. has won four of the past five 12U World Cups. It has won the past two 15U World Cups and medaled in the previous two. It has won five of the past six 18U World Cups and finished second in 2019. The only major World Cup it has not won is the 23U World Cup. That was established in 2014 against the U.S. and other countries' objections, as they preferred the 21-and-under cutoff that was a better fit for college age players. The U.S. has never participated in the 23U World Cup.

The U.S. has also won the most recent World Baseball Classic and finished as a silver medalist at the Olympic Games in 2021. It is quite simply the best run of international success in USA Baseball history.

While the U.S. has climbed to the top, Cuba's struggles on the international stage have continued. Cuba did finish second in the 15U World Cup, but did not participate in the 12U and 18U and finished 10th in the 23U World Cup. Cuba at one point won nine Baseball World Cups in a row and 11 of 12. It has not won a major international competition this decade.

WBSC 15-U WORLD CUP

Team	W	L
United States	8	1
Cuba	6	2
Taiwan	6	2
Japan	5	3
Puerto Rico	4	4
Panama	2	5
Mexico	3	2
Venezuela	3	3
Colombia	1	4
Czech Republic	3	3
France	2	4
Guam	1	5
South Arica	0	6

Note: Standings reflect order of finish. Consolation games means some teams with better overall records finished behind other clubs that advanced . **Gold Medal Game:** USA defeated Cuba 4-3. **Bronze Medal Game:** Taiwan wins by forfeit over Japan. **15U All-World Team—C:** Yaider Ruiz (CUB); **1B:** Kanta Kanemoto (JPN); **2B:** Tien-Szu Huang (TPE); **3B:** Alejandro Cruz (CUB); **SS:** Ethan Holliday (USA); **OF:** Isaac Carrasquillo (PUR); Coy James (USA); Juan Caballero (PAN); **SP:** Yao-Yun Chang (TPE); **RP:** Daniel Reyes (PAN); **DH:** Andrew Costello (USA). **Most Valuable Player:** Coy James (USA)

18U WORLD CUP

Team	W	L
United States	8	1
Taiwan	7	2
Japan	6	3
South Korea	7	2
Netherlands	4	4
Mexico	3	5
Brazil	4	4
Panama	4	4
Australia	3	5
Italy	2	6
Canada	2	6
South Africa	0	8

Note: Standings reflect order of finish. Consolation games means some teams with better overall records finished behind other clubs that advanced . **Gold Medal Game:** USA defeated Taiwan 5-1. **Bronze Medal Game:** Japan defeated South Korea 6-2. **18U All-World Team—C:** Shion Matsuo (JPN); **1B:** Yael Romero (MEX); **2B:** Luis Escudero (); **3B:** Daeseon Jeong (KOR); **SS:** Rosman Verdugo (MEX); **OF:** Hsin Chiu (TPE); Junyoung Jeong (KOR); Aidan Miller (USA); **SP:** Shao-En Lin (TPE); **RP:** Shiki Kawahara (JPN); **DH:** Bryce Eldridge (USA). **Most Valuable Player:** Bryce Eldridge (USA)

INTERNATIONAL

Yucatan Claims Title As Run Scoring Soars

Offense is not a problem across the Mexican League. In fact, one could argue that there may right now be too much of a good thing.

Durango hit .340 as a team, but still finished 16 games under .500 because it also had an ERA of 7.83 as a team. That wasn't the worst ERA in the league. Leon posted an 8.62 ERA. Leon had three different games where it scored 10 or more runs and lost, including a 22-17 defeat.

As a whole, the league averaged over six runs per team per game. The league averaged 1.28 home runs per team per game as well.

That also has meant that Mexico has become the home of the four-hour game. Leon had seven games that took less than two and a half hours to play. Leon had 16 games that took four hours or longer, including one that took 6:19.

Yucatan had only the ninth-best record during the regular season, but they got hot at the right time. It took seven games to knock off Mexico City in the semifinals and needed seven games to knock off Monterrey as well.

The Mexican League remains a great landing spot for notable names as well. Nick Williams, Henry Urrutia, Keon Broxton, Addison Russell, Radhames Liz and Henderson Alvarez were just some of the notable names that are still plying their trade south of the border.

Pete O'Brien, the former D-Backs catcher, finished fourth in the league with 32 home runs. Urrutia was the batting leader (.420) and was one of four batting qualifiers to finish above .400.

Rainel Rosario led the league with a .792 slugging percentage, extra-base hits (65), runs (103) and RBIs (116).

Pedro Fernandez, the former Royals farmhand, led the league with 103 strikeouts.

STANDINGS

Northern Division	W	L	PCT	GB
Tijuana	62	28	.689	-
Dos Laredos	59	27	.686	1
Monclova	54	31	.635	5.5
Monterrey	51	39	.567	11
Laguna	48	40	.545	13
Aguascalientes	42	46	.477	19
Saltillo	38	52	.422	24
Durango	37	53	.411	25
Guadalajara	33	57	.367	29

Southern Division	W	L	PCT	GB
Mexico	50	34	.595	-
Tabasco	47	37	.560	3
Puebla	48	39	.552	3.5
Yucatan	46	43	.517	6.5
Quintana Roo	44	46	.489	9
Veracruz	41	48	.461	11.5
Oaxaca	34	53	.391	17.5
Campeche	29	58	.333	22.5
Leon	29	61	.322	24

Playoffs—Quarterfinals: Tijuana defeated Monclova 4-2; Yucatan defeated Quitana 4-1; Mexico defeated Puebla 4-0 and Monterrey defeated Laredo 4-1 in best-of-seven series. **Semifinals:** Yucatan defeated Mexico 4-3 and Monterrey defeated Tijuana 4-0 in best-of-7 series. **Finals:** Yucatan defeated Monterrey 4-3 in best-of-seven series.

BATTING LEADERS

Batter	Team	AVG	AB	R	H	HR	RBI	SB
Urrutia, Henry	SLT	.420	333	80	140	25	88	1
Martinez, Alberth	DUR	.416	344	74	143	14	96	4
Santos, Roel	TAB	.411	253	65	104	8	30	16
Lopez, Alfredo	DUR	.404	297	84	120	1	40	11
Tavárez, Aneury	DUR	.388	325	85	126	23	80	13
Rivera, Missael	SLT	.387	302	63	117	10	56	3
Elizalde, Sebastian	MTY	.385	299	70	115	12	62	20
Flores, Ramon	MEX	.382	288	58	110	10	67	2
Torres, Nick	LAG	.377	268	66	101	14	56	4
Rosario, Rainel	SLT	.372	341	103	127	38	116	7
Heras, Leo	2-T	.370	243	53	90	13	33	5
Williams, Nick	TIJ	.370	319	89	118	29	72	6
Hernandez, Ramon	TAB	.368	242	50	89	17	59	0
Otosaka, Tomo	2-T	.367	305	79	112	3	25	26
Mejia, Alex	MVA	.366	292	56	107	8	59	3
Robles, Edgar	LAG	.364	341	65	124	2	36	11
Gamboa, Juan Carlos	MEX	.363	248	66	90	16	54	0
Reyes, Angel	AGS	.361	219	58	79	16	58	8
Sardinas, Luis	2-T	.359	312	67	112	16	54	4
Reginatto, Leonardo	AGS	.356	312	71	111	11	65	5
Broxton, Keon	MVA	.356	253	64	90	20	48	12
Rodriguez, Henry	AGS	.354	308	69	109	20	61	9
Rios, Ramon	AGS	.349	275	52	96	7	34	7
Russell, Addison	MVA	.348	279	72	97	24	74	8
Jimenez, Luis	CAM	.347	340	58	118	17	78	8

PITCHING LEADERS

Pitcher	Team	W-L	ERA	IP	H	BB	SO
Méndez, Yohander	MTY	7-0	2.78	74	70	24	61
Yoanni Yera	TAB	8-2	3.01	87	82	34	88
Leal, Erick	AGS	7-6	3.50	90	86	31	100
Guerra, Junior	LAR	8-3	3.56	83	82	38	87
Liz, Radhames	YUC	3-5	3.96	73	77	19	69
Barreda, Manny	TIJ	7-3	4.28	88	62	41	102
Oramas, Juan Pablo	TAB	3-4	4.33	79	92	22	67
Fernandez, Pedro	TIG	8-4	4.42	96	93	25	103
Alvarez, Henderson	YUC	7-4	4.43	91	114	14	43
Rios, Wilmer	MVA	9-4	4.47	89	94	14	52
Reyes, David	VER	8-6	4.56	97	90	38	67
Heyer, Kurt	PUE	7-2	4.59	82	88	28	51
Flores, Jose	LAR	4-4	4.73	80	105	22	56
Huff, David	MEX	6-1	4.86	74	83	30	53
Flores, Manuel	CAM	4-8	5.30	90	119	18	58
Ynoa, Gabriel	PUE	7-6	5.34	86	95	18	54
Montes, Aldo	LAG	6-7	5.40	87	89	28	64
Carrillo, Raul	TIG	3-4	5.45	76	97	28	57
Struck, Nick	TIJ	8-4	5.50	82	113	35	64
Torres-Perez, Braulio	PUE	2-5	5.56	89	106	35	93
Haro, Francisco	2-T	4-6	5.59	93	117	20	76
Rogers, Esmil	MTY	3-5	5.60	72	101	19	46
Tellache, Nico	DUR	6-3	5.65	80	92	25	50
Vera, Eduardo	MVA	6-4	5.72	79	95	25	48
Tenuta, Matt	GDL	5-5	5.76	84	113	38	60

Murakami, Orix Star In 2022

Munetaka Murakami's 2022 season ended up falling short of a Japan Series title.

Munetaka Murakami

STR/JIJI PRESS/AFP VIA GETTY IMAGES

But that's about the only way that Murakami's season fell short in any way. Murakami became the first player to win the NPB Triple Crown since 2004. His 56 home runs were also the second-most in Japan leagues history. While he didn't match Wladimir Balentien's 60 home runs, he did break Sadaharu Oh's record for home runs by a Japanese-born player. Oh had hit 55 home runs in 1964.

Murakami's record-breaking 56th home run came in the final game of the season. He also edged Yohei Oshima for the Central League batting crown by two points.

Murakami is only 22 years old. He was also part of a energizing youth movement in Japanese baseball, as the league has seen an influx of impressive young talent.

In addition to Murakami's heroics, righthander Roki Sasaki threw a perfect game early in the season in which he struck out 19 batters. He touched 100 mph and carved up hitters with a devastating forkball. In his next start, Sasaki carried a perfect game through eight innings before being lifted.

As best as Baseball America's research can determine, no pitcher has ever thrown two perfect games in a career in any level of professional baseball. Sasaki came within three outs of doing it in back-to-back games.

Chiba Lotte limited Sasaki's innings over the course of the season in consideration to his youth. But even though he finished 13.2 innings short of qualifying for the ERA title, he still finished second in the league with 173 strikeouts. Overall he went 9-4, 2.20.

While Sasaki and Murakami's heroics were the stories of the regular season, the postseason was dominated by the Orix Buffaloes run to a title.

It had been 26 years since Orix had won the Japan Series. That last title came before the Orix BlueWave and Kintetsu Buffaloes merged in 2004.

Orix went into the final day of the regular season trailing the Fukuoka SoftBank Hawks by one game, but a win by them and a Hawks' loss left the two teams tied. Orix edged Fukuoka because they won the head-to-head matchup between the two teams. Orix had fallen back as many as 11 games in the early part of the season, but rallied with a strong second half.

In the Japan Series, Orix lost the first and third games of the series to Yakult and Game 2 was a tie, but after falling into another deep hole, the Buffaloes won four straight games to claim the title.

Jacob Waguespack was on the mound to close out the clinching 5-4 Game 7 win.

Orix ace Yoshinobu Yamamoto was named the Sawamura Award winner, Japan's equivalent of the Cy Young Award, for a second straight year. Yamamoto was exceptional, going 15-5, 1.68.

CENTRAL LEAGUE

Team	W	L	T	PCT	GB
Tokyo Yakult Swallows	80	59	4	.576	--
Yokohama DeNA Baystars	73	68	2	.518	8
Hanshin Tigers	68	71	4	.489	12
Yomiuri Giants	68	72	3	.486	12.5
Hiroshima Toyo Carp	66	74	3	.471	14.5
Chunichi Dragons	66	75	2	.468	15

Playoffs—First round: Hanshin defeated DeNa 2-1 in best-of-three series. **Climax Series:** Yakulti defeated Hanshin 3-0 in best-of-five series. **Japan Series:** Orix defeatued Yakult 4-2 in best-of-seven series.

CENTRAL LEAGUE BATTING LEADERS

Player, Team	AVG	AB	R	H	HR	RBI	SB
Murakami, Munetaka, Swal.	.318	487	114	155	56	134	12
Ohshima, Yohei, Drag.	.314	436	48	137	1	20	11
Sano, Keita, Bay.	.306	526	63	161	22	72	2
Miyazaki, Toshiro, Bay.	.300	434	51	130	16	50	0
Viciedo, Dayan, Drag.	.294	483	52	142	14	63	1
Chikamoto, Koji, Tigers	.293	525	71	154	3	34	30
Okabayashi, Yuki, Drag.	.291	553	58	161	0	32	24
Maki, Shugo, Bay.	.291	509	63	148	24	87	3
Sakakura, Shogo, Carp	.288	539	73	155	16	68	2
Yoshikawa, Naoki, Giants	.277	516	64	143	7	31	16
Nakano, Takumu, Tigers	.276	569	69	157	6	25	23
Shiomi, Yasutaka, Swal.	.276	508	83	140	16	54	24
Maru, Yoshihiro, Giants	.272	525	81	143	27	65	6
McBroom, Ryan, Carp	.272	448	57	122	17	74	0
Osuna, Jose, Swal.	.272	496	49	135	20	74	2
Abe, Toshiki, Drag.	.270	486	44	131	9	57	3
Ohyama, Yusuke, Tigers	.267	439	54	117	23	87	0
Kozono, Kaito, Carp	.266	473	57	126	7	38	2
Sato, Teruaki, Tigers	.264	541	70	143	20	84	11
Kikuchi, Ryosuke, Carp	.262	462	51	121	6	45	2
Kuwahara, Masayuki, Bay.	.257	475	61	122	4	39	13
Okamoto, Kazuma, Giants	.252	520	63	131	30	82	1
Itohara, Kento, Tigers	.247	445	31	110	3	36	2
Kinoshita, Takuya, Drag.	.246	419	24	103	6	48	2
Yamada, Tetsuto, Swal.	.243	469	69	114	23	65	10
Nagaoka, Hideki, Swal.	.241	511	44	123	9	48	2
Polanco, Gregory, Giants	.240	438	55	105	24	58	2

OTHER NOTABLE BATTERS

Player, Team	AVG	AB	R	H	HR	RBI	SB
Marte, Jefry, Giants	.256	90	8	23	1	11	0
Rojas Jr., Mel, Tigers	.224	183	19	41	9	27	0
Walker, Adam, Tigers	.271	406	58	110	23	52	5
Martinez, Ariel, Drag.	.276	254	29	70	8	24	1
Soto, Neftali, Bay.	.266	368	35	98	17	49	0
Kivlehan, Patrick, Swal.	.241	83	10	20	6	14	0

CENTRAL LEAGUE PITCHING LEADERS

Pitcher, Team	W	L	ERA	IP	H	HR	BB	SO
Aoyagi, Koyo, Tigers	13	4	2.05	162	126	7	32	132
Nishi, Yuki, Tigers	9	9	2.18	148	132	8	26	93
Imanaga, Shota, Bay.	11	4	2.26	144	106	14	29	132
Ohno, Yudai, Drag.	8	8	2.46	157	126	7	37	108
Togo, Shosei, Giants	12	8	2.62	172	146	11	51	154
Ogasawara, Shinnosuke, Drag.	10	8	2.76	147	127	9	39	142
Ogawa, Yasuhiro, Swal.	8	8	2.82	153	145	16	32	91
Sugano, Tomoyuki, Giants	10	7	3.12	147	138	15	26	104
Morishita, Masato, Carp	10	8	3.17	179	195	13	44	133
Yanagi, Yuya, Drag.	9	11	3.64	153	154	17	37	124

OTHER NOTABLE PITCHERS

Pitcher, Team	W	L	ERA	IP	H	HR	BB	SO
Martinez, Raidel, Drag.	4	3	0.97	56	30	2	12	62
Rodriguez, Yariel, Drag.	2	2	1.15	54	32	0	18	60
Ise, Hiromu, Bay.	3	3	1.72	68	52	1	17	69
De La Rosa, Rubby, Giants	0	0	2.30	27	18	2	10	24
McGough, Scott, Swal.	2	2	2.35	54	39	5	1	2
Escobar, Edwin, Bay.	4	2	2.42	63	48	4	29	51
Kriske, Brooks, Bay.	1	1	2.57	21	15	2	13	26
Gsellman, Robert, Bay.	1	1	2.66	20	15	1	2	0
Gunkel, Joe, Tigers	5	5	2.73	92	80	6	3	1
Cole, A.J., Swal.	2	0	2.75	145	36	25	3	1
Turley, Nik, Carp	2	4	3.11	38	26	7	2	2
Mercedes, Cristopher, Giants	5	7	3.18	110	107	7	3	1
Keller, Kyle, Tigers	3	2	3.31	33	25	2	5	46
Corniel, Robert, Carp	0	0	3.52	15	15	2	1	0
Sneed, Cy, Swal.	9	6	3.54	132	140	17	5	3
Anderson, Drew, Carp	3	4	3.60	70	61	9	3	0
Krol, Ian, Giants	1	1	3.86	21	17	1	10	15
Wilkerson, Aaron, Tigers	5	5	4.08	71	70	4	1	0
Alcantara, Raul, Tigers	1	3	4.70	38	38	5	8	29
Romero, Fernando, Bay.	6	8	4.87	92	100	8	9	5
Suarez, Andrew, Swal.	0	0	6.23	22	27	4	0	2
Vieira, Thyago, Giants	0	2	9.82	7	9	3	1	0
Peoples, Michael, Bay.	0	2	15.00	3	9	0	1	4

PACIFIC LEAGUE

Team	W	L	T	PCT	GB
Orix Buffaloes	76	65	2	.539	--
Fukuoka SoftBank Hawks	76	65	2	.539	--
Saitama Seibu Lions	72	68	3	.514	3.5
Tohoku Takuten Golden Eagles	69	71	3	.493	6.5
Chiba Lotte Marines	69	73	1	.486	7.5
Hokkaido Nippon-Ham Fighters	59	81	3	.421	16.5

Playoffs: First round: SoftBank defeated Seibu 2-0 in best-of-three series. **Climax Series:** Orix defeated SoftBank 3-1 in best-of-five series. **Japan Series:** Orix defeated Yakult 4-2 in best-of-seven series.

PACIFIC LEAGUE BATTING LEADERS

Player, Team	AVG	AB	R	H	HR	RBI	SB
Matsumoto, Go, Fight.	.347	395	48	137	3	44	21
Yoshida, Masataka, Buff.	.335	412	56	138	21	88	4
Shimauchi, Hiroaki, Eagles	.298	541	59	161	14	77	5
Imamiya, Kenta, Hawks	.296	450	56	133	7	47	3
Nakagawa, Keita, Buff.	.283	424	54	120	8	51	11
Yanagita, Yuki, Hawks	.275	437	63	120	24	79	2
Takabe, Akito, Marines	.274	541	66	148	3	38	44
Tatsumi, Ryosuke, Eagles	.271	409	60	111	11	35	12
Mune, Yuma, Buff.	.271	469	55	127	5	43	4
Fukuda, Shuhei, Buff.	.268	448	65	120	0	24	9
Kobukata, Hiroto, Eagles	.267	424	54	113	2	29	21
Genda, Sosuke, Lions	.266	414	39	110	2	17	12
Yamakawa, Hotaka, Lions	.266	448	62	119	41	90	0
Suzuki, Daichi, Eagles	.257	408	39	105	5	35	4
Nakamura, Shogo, Marines	.257	498	52	128	12	68	15
Asamura, Hideto, Eagles	.252	532	73	134	27	86	4
Kurebayashi, Kotaro, Buff.	.224	450	35	101	6	32	2
Kiyomiya, Kotaro, Fight.	.219	406	52	89	18	55	4
Nishikawa, Haruki, Eagles	.218	372	58	81	7	37	19
Tonosaki, Shuta, Lions	.215	478	54	103	12	47	10
O'Grady, Brian, Lions	.213	404	42	86	15	46	2

OTHER NOTABLE HITTERS

Player, Team	AVG	AB	R	H	HR	RBI	SB
Gracial, Yurisbel, Hawks	.271	347	24	94	7	30	1
Despaigne, Alfredo, Hawks	.269	297	29	80	14	40	0
Gittens, Chris, Eagles	.242	62	4	15	0	8	0
McCarthy, Joe, Buff.	.225	178	17	40	4	19	0
Hechavarria, Adeiny, Marines	.222	243	19	54	2	20	4
O'Grady, Brian, Lions	.213	404	42	86	15	46	2
Alcantara, Arismendy, Fight.	.209	263	27	55	14	28	4
Valera, Breyvic, Buff.	.205	112	7	23	1	6	0
Laird, Brandon, Marines	.189	365	24	69	15	48	0
Galvis, Freddy, Hawks	.171	111	11	19	2	11	0
Martin, Leonys, Marines	.163	221	22	36	9	25	5
Ravelo, Rangel, Buff.	.138	58	4	8	1	2	0

PACIFIC LEAGUE PITCHING LEADERS

Pitcher, Team	W	L	ERA	IP	H	HR	BB	SO
Yamamoto, Yoshinobu, Buff.	15	5	1.68	193	137	6	42	205
Senga, Koudai, Hawks	11	6	1.94	144	103	7	49	156
Katoh, Takayuki, Fight.	8	7	2.01	148	124	9	11	98
Takahashi, Kona, Lions	12	8	2.20	176	153	9	51	128
Itoh, Hiromi, Fight.	10	9	2.95	156	140	5	49	112
Ojima, Kazuya, Marines	3	11	3.14	143	140	10	43	89
Miyagi, Hiroya, Buff.	11	8	3.16	148	137	11	30	127
Tanaka, Masahiro, Eagles	9	12	3.31	163	160	16	30	126
Uwasawa, Naoyuki, Fight.	8	9	3.38	152	129	15	50	127

OTHER NOTABLE PITCHERS

Pitcher, Team	W	L	ERA	IP	H	HR	BB	SO
Osuna, Roberto, Marines	4	1	0.91	30	15	1	3	32
Moinelo, Livan, Hawks	1	1	1.03	53	22	2	20	87
Menez, Conner, Fight.	1	0	1.08	25	14	1	13	28
Taira, Kaima, Lions	1	3	1.56	58	36	2	18	75
Hirano, Yoshihisa, Buff.	3	2	1.57	46	25	3	12	42
Matsui, Yuki, Eagles	1	3	1.92	52	21	4	19	83
Rodriguez, Bryan, Fight.	3	2	2.20	16	14	0	3	13
Busenitz, Alan, Eagles	3	1	2.27	32	22	1	10	25
Masuda, Tatsushi, Lions	2	5	2.45	51	37	7	10	34
Sung, Chia-Hao, Eagles	4	2	2.61	52	45	5	15	38
Mori, Yuito, Hawks	2	4	2.62	34	30	4	12	27
Enns, Dietrich, Lions	10	7	2.94	122	103	14	45	92
Masuda, Naoya, Marines	1	2	3.29	52	46	6	19	47
Ponce, Cody, Fight.	3	5	3.35	83	69	10	23	66
Romero, Enny, Marines	8	9	3.36	115	107	7	38	77
Kitayama, Koki, Fight.	3	5	3.51	51	37	3	28	58
Guerrero, Tayron, Marines	3	3	3.52	46	34	2	20	63
Ishikawa, Naoya, Fight.	2	2	3.94	32	26	1	13	37
Rea, Colin, Hawks	5	6	3.96	100	82	13	32	80
Biddle, Jesse, Buff.	4	5	4.02	40	36	4	20	45
Vargas, Cesar, Buff.	0	1	6.59	14	18	1	8	11

KOREA

SSG Tops KBO

It took the SSG Landers six games to win the Korean Series, but the big blow landed in Game 5. With a win just an out away, Kiwoom saw the series shift dramatically when pinch-hitter Kim Kang-Min hit a walk-off three-run home run. SSG wrapped up the title in Game 6. The loss was a disappointing end for MVP Lee Jung Hoo, who led the league in batting average (.349) and RBIs (113).

STANDINGS & LEADERS

TEAM	W	L	T	PCT	GB
SSG Landers	88	52	4	.629	--
LG	87	55	2	.613	2
Kiwoom Heroes	80	62	2	.563	9
KT Wiz	80	62	2	.563	9
Kia	70	73	1	.490	19.5
NC	67	74	3	.475	21.5
Samsung	66	76	2	.465	23
Lotte	64	76	4	.457	24
Doosan Bears	60	82	2	.423	29
Hanwha	46	96	2	.324	43

Playoffs—Wild Card: KT defeated Kia. **First Round:** Kiwoom defeated KT 3-2 in best-of-five series. **Semifinals**: Kiwoom defeated LG 3-1 in best-of-five series. **Finals:** SSG defeated Kiwoom 4-2 in best-of-seven series.

BATTING LEADERS

Player, Team	AVG	AB	R	H	HR	RBI	SB
Lee Jung Hoo, Kiwoom	.349	553	85	193	23	113	5
Pirela Jose, Samsung	.342	561	102	192	28	109	15
Park Kun Woo, NC	.336	408	52	137	10	61	3
Lee Dae Ho, Lotte	.331	540	53	179	23	101	0
Na Sung Bum, Kia	.320	563	92	180	21	97	6
Kim Hye Seong, Kiwoom	.318	516	81	164	4	48	34
Moon Bo Gyeong, LG	.315	406	52	128	9	56	7
Brito Socrates, Kia	.311	514	83	160	17	77	12
Fernandez Jose, Doosan	.309	508	52	157	6	77	0
Cho Yong Ho, KT	.308	474	52	146	3	44	5
Han Dong Hui, Lotte	.307	456	43	140	14	65	0
Jeon Jun Woo, Lotte	.304	470	73	143	11	68	6
Choi Ji Hoon, SSG	.304	569	93	173	10	61	31
Park Seong Han, SSG	.298	494	68	147	2	56	12
Martini Nicholas, NC	.296	510	67	151	16	85	12
Chae Eun Seong, LG	.296	467	48	138	12	83	6
Park Hae Min, LG	.289	570	97	165	3	49	24
Heo Kyoung Min, Doosan	.289	432	59	125	8	60	10
Tauchman Michael, Hanwha	.289	575	88	166	12	43	19
Kim Sun Bin, Kia	.287	505	51	145	3	61	13

PITCHING LEADERS

Player, Team	W	L	ERA	IP	H	HR	BB	SO
An Woo Jin, Kiwoom	15	8	2.11	30	196	131	55	224
Kim Kwang Hyun, SSG	13	3	2.13	28	173	141	45	153
Plutko Adam, LG	15	5	2.39	28	162	125	38	149
Suarez Albert, Samsung	6	8	2.49	30	174	151	50	159
Kelly Casey, LG	16	4	2.54	27	166	144	35	153
Jokisch Eric, Kiwoom	10	8	2.57	30	185	169	33	154
Font Wilmer, SSG	13	6	2.69	28	184	141	34	170
Rucinski Drew, NC	10	12	2.97	31	194	184	34	194
Buchanan David, Samsung	11	8	3.04	26	160	176	39	117
So Hyeong Jun, KT	13	6	3.05	27	171	158	39	117
Ko Young Pyo, KT	13	8	3.26	28	182	191	23	156
Stock Robert, Doosan	9	10	3.60	29	165	162	83	138
Choi Won Joon, Doosan	8	13	3.60	30	165	183	37	113
Barnes Charlie, Lotte	12	12	3.62	31	186	176	47	160

TAIWAN

Brothers Wins Again

Over the last two season, not only as CTBC Brothers Elephant won back-to-back Taiwan Series titles, it's done so without ever losing a game.

For a second-consecutive year, Brothers swept its way to a title, this time routing the Rakuten Monkeys. This was Brothers' ninth CPBL title. Jose De Paula was once again Brothers' ace, as he went 13-4, 2.46 with a league-best 157 strikeouts.

Fubon righthander Mike Loree announced his retirement after spending 10 seasons in the CPNL. Loree has been in the league so long that he actually now qualifies as a domestic player, and would not require a foreign player slot.

The CPBL has announced that it will add a sixth expansion team for 2023, solving what has been a rather difficult scheduling problem with a five-team league with the addition of the TSG Hawks.

STANDINGS & LEADERS

Team	W	L	T	PCT	GB
*Rakuten Monkeys	70	46	4	.603	--
&Brothers Elephant	69	47	4	.595	1
Wei Chuan Dragons	57	58	5	.496	12.5
Uni-President Lions	48	69	3	.410	22.5
Fubon Guardians	33	85	2	.280	38

* First half champion &Second half champion
Finals: Brothers beat Rakuten 4-0 in best-of-seven series.

BATTING LEADERS

Player, Team	AVG	AB	R	H	HR	RBI	SB
Lin Li, Monkeys	.336	411	74	138	14	79	22
Chen Chen Wei, Monkeys	.324	367	64	119	2	31	38
Chiang Kun Yu, Brothers	.318	406	67	129	6	40	10
Cheng Chin, Monkeys	.317	357	50	113	1	36	23
Chen Chieh Hsien, U-Lions	.315	397	64	125	6	42	17
Wang Wei Chen, Brothers	.314	420	59	132	0	38	11
Kuo Tian Shin, Dragons	.304	451	59	137	2	32	25
Wang Sheng Wei, Guardians	.298	322	37	96	2	27	12
Chen Wun Jie, Brothers	.298	363	44	108	4	61	12
Fan Kuo Chen, Guardians	.296	442	45	131	9	51	2
Lin Chih Sheng, Dragons	.294	343	35	101	10	60	0
Liang Chia Jung, Monkeys	.289	311	39	90	3	25	2
Chen Tzu Hao, Brothers	.287	314	47	90	10	65	8
Hsu Chi Hung, Brothers	.287	349	52	100	6	49	11
Li Kai Wei, Dragons	.281	384	63	108	2	43	19

PITCHING LEADERS

Player, Team	W	L	ERA	IP	H	HR	BB	SO
Huang Tzu Peng, Monkeys	12	3	2.33	159	143	8	25	96
José De Paula, Brothers	13	4	2.46	157	140	3	21	157
Drew Gagnon, Dragons	12	6	2.68	174	141	5	50	150
Jake Brigham, Dragons	12	9	2.71	182	184	4	54	110
Hu Chih Wei, U-Lions	9	13	3.35	151	178	8	41	84
Dylan Covey, Monkeys	13	6	3.47	140	150	3	50	100
Joe Van Meter, Guardians	6	14	3.89	136	146	8	31	110
Ryan Bollinger, Monkeys	8	6	4.01	130	145	9	36	114
Chiang Shao Ching, Guardians	5	12	4.70	121	141	8	38	85

San Marino Wins Again

Serie A1 has reorganized its structure in recent years, ensuring that many more teams get a chance to compete at the highest level of Italian baseball.

But the same teams that have consistently dominated Italian baseball remain the best teams in Italy.

San Marino won its second consecutive Serie A1 title in truly thrilling fashion. In a deciding Game 7 of the Italy Series, Parma took a one-run lead in the top of the eighth on a Noel Gonzalez home run, but San Marino evened the score at 1-1 in the bottom of the eighth.

The game remained tied 1-1 until the bottom of the 12th when San Marino cleanup hitter Gabriel Lino walked-it off with a run-scoring single. It was the third consecutive year that Parma fell in the championship series.

Carlos Quevedo earned the win in relief.

STANDINGS

FIRST HALF

Group A	W	L	PCT	GB
Parmaclima	14	0	1.000	0
Torino	10	4	.714	4
Settimo	9	5	.643	5
Cagliari	7	7	.500	7
Ciemme Oltretorrente	7	7	.500	7
Poviglio	4	10	.286	10
Senago	3	11	.214	11
Brescia	2	12	.143	12

Group B	W	L	PCT	GB
Fortitudo Bologna	14	0	1.000	0
Camec Collecchio	11	3	.786	3
Ronchi Dei Legionari	7	7	.500	7
Rovigo	7	7	.500	7
Cervignano	6	8	.429	8
Padua	4	10	.286	10
Verona	4	10	.286	10
Venoto	3	11	.214	11

Group C	W	L	PCT	GB
San Marino	13	1	.929	0
Godo	11	3	.786	2
Modena	10	4	.714	3
Crocetta	9	5	.643	4
Longbridge Bologna	5	9	.357	8
New Rimini	5	9	.357	8
Torre Pedrera	3	11	.214	10
Sala Baganza	0	14	.000	13

Group D	W	L	PCT	GB
Grosseto	8	2	.800	0
Macerata	7	3	.700	1
Nettuno	7	3	.700	1
Grosseto	6	4	.600	2
Nettuno Academy	1	9	.100	7
Bologna Athletics	1	9	.100	7

SECOND HALF

Group A1	W	L	PCT	GB
San Marino	24	6	.800	0
ParmaClima	21	9	.700	3
Nettuno	10	20	.333	14
Camec Collecchio	7	23	.233	17

GROUP B1	W	L	PCT	GB
Fortitudo Bologna	26	4	.867	0
Grosseto	16	14	.533	10
Torino	11	19	.367	15
Godo	5	25	.167	21

GROUP D1	W	L	PCT	GB
Cagliari	18	2	.900	0
Settimo	11	9	.550	7
Verona	11	9	.550	7
Padova	9	11	.450	9
Ciemme Oltretorrente	7	13	.350	11
Veneto	4	16	.200	14

GROUP E1	W	L	PCT	GB
Rovigo	15	5	.750	0
Ronchi Dei Legionari	13	6	.684	2
Poviglio	12	8	.600	3
Senago	8	12	.400	7
Cervignano	7	13	.350	8
Brescia	4	15	.211	11

GROUP F1	W	L	PCT	GB
Modena	11	5	.688	0
Crocetta	11	5	.688	0
Bologna	9	7	.563	2
Baganza	5	11	.313	6
New Rimini	4	12	.250	7

GROUP G1	W	L	PCT	GB
Macerata	14	2	.875	0
Grosseto	11	5	.688	3
Nettuno Academy	7	9	.438	7
Longbridge Bologna	4	12	.250	10
Torre Pedrera	4	12	.250	10

Playoffs—**Semifinals:** San Marino defeated Grosseto 4-1 and Parma defeated Bologna 4-3 in a best-of-7 series. **Championship:** San Marino defeated Parmaclima 4-3 in a best-of-7 series.

INDVIDUAL BATTING LEADERS

Player, Team	AVG	OBP	SLG	AB	R	H	2B	3B	HR
Javier A. Lopez, MAC	.454	.611	.508	108	31	49	7	2	2
Dariel Rodriguez, CAG	.447	.576	.507	132	30	59	12	1	1
Raffaele Medoro, PAD	.429	.518	.522	56	10	24	3	1	0
Giovanni Garbella, NET	.429	.643	.556	14	2	6	1	1	0
Ramon A. Bonilla, VER	.419	.603	.497	136	33	57	17	1	2
José P. Cuesta, CAG	.419	.677	.513	124	42	52	9	4	5
Ricardo Segundo Paolini, BOL	.413	.545	.451	189	53	78	18	2	1
Giaconino Paolo Lasaracina, SET	.406	.574	.470	101	12	41	11	3	0
Danny Andres Turino, CAG	.403	.568	.488	139	35	56	12	4	1
Ericson Neptali Leonora, GRO	.402	.552	.490	87	26	35	7	0	2

INDIVIDUAL PITCHING LEADERS

Player	W	L	ERA	IP	H	R	ER	BB	SO
José Pablo Cuesta, CAG	2		00.41	22	7	1	1	2	35
Dimitrios Kourtis, RSM	2		10.68	26.1	11	3	2	12	47
Henry Centeno, RSM	2		10.79	22.2	11	2	2	11	33
Murilo Brolo, BOL	11		00.82	76.2	33	7	7	13	108
Frank Montieth, ATL	2		10.91	39.2	24	7	4	4	54
Frank Lopez, MAC	10		11.05	77	46	13	9	14	130
Eriel Carrillo, RIM	4		21.07	67	39	8	8	14	104
Antonio Noguera, BBC	7		31.12	64.1	56	14	8	8	64
Raul Rivero, BOL	10		31.19	75.2	41	14	10	9	100
Emailin Montilla, PAR	10		11.36	73	42	15	11	18	89

HCAW Sweeps Neptunus

For the first time this century, HCAW Bussman is the Holland Series champion. With the league's top ace Lars Huljer on the mound and a lineup led by Jeandro Tromp, HCAW swept Neptunus in the championship series after finishing one game behind them during the first stage of the season.

Huljer was unstoppable when he was on the mound. He led the league with a 0.79 ERA and won more than a third of HCAW's 36 wins. He also easily led the league in strikeouts (133).

This was HCAW's third-ever Holland Series title. It's previous two came in 1996 and 1998.

STANDINGS

Team	W	L	PCT	GB
Curaçao Neptunus	21	3	.875	0
HCAW	20	4	.833	1
L&D Amsterdam	17	6	.729	3.5
Twins Oosterhout	12	11	.521	8.5
DSS/Kinheim	11	13	.458	10
RCH Memorie Sieraden	10	14	.417	11
Hoofddorp Pioniers	7	16	.313	13.5
Quick Amersfoort	6	17	.271	14.5
Storks	2	22	.083	19

Follow-Up Round	W	L	PCT	GB
L&D Amsterdam	18	8	.685	0
Curaçao Neptunus	16	10	.611	2
HCAW	14	12	.537	4
Twins Oosterhout	4	22	.167	14

Playoffs—**Wild Card:** Neptunus defeated Amsterdam 2-1 in best-of-3 series**. Semifinals:** HCAW defeated L&D Amsterdam 3-1 and Neptunus defeated Twins Oosterhout 3-0 in best-of-3 series. **Holland Series:** HCAW defeated Neptunus 4-0 in best-of-7 series.

INDIVIDUAL BATTING LEADERS

Player, Team	AVG	OBP	SLG	AB	R	H	2B	3B	HR
Oliver Van Der Wijst, PIO	.371	.478	.664	143	39	53	16	1	8
Rogear Bernadina, NEP	.369	.463	.469	179	41	66	16	1	0
Ibrahin Redan, QUI	.364	.470	.500	110	20	40	9	0	2
Koen Halderman, DKI	.353	.430	.453	150	30	53	13	1	0
Delano Selassa, AMS	.348	.413	.414	198	28	69	5	1	2
Jochem Koedijk, DKI	.340	.460	.454	141	31	48	9	2	1
Jason Jakobus, DKI	.322	.416	.370	146	39	47	3	2	0
Jeandro Tromp, HCAW	.320	.409	.400	175	25	56	12	1	0
John Polonius, NEP	.319	.393	.433	210	47	67	10	1	4
Dwayne Kemp, NEP	.318	.376	.344	192	31	61	5	0	0
Stijn Van Der Meer, NEP	.317	.418	.381	189	32	60	6	3	0
Sheadion Jamanika, NEP	.313	.377	.424	144	21	45	11	1	1
Sicnarf Loopstok, AMS	.311	.407	.515	103	16	32	5	2	4
Roelie Henrique, AMS	.306	.402	.361	144	32	44	8	0	0
Denzel Richardson, AMS	.301	.376	.538	186	35	56	14	3	8
Alex Madera, QUI	.299	.364	.415	147	27	44	8	3	1
Jules Cremer, HCA	.298	.343	.344	131	16	39	4	1	0
Yurdion Martie, RCH	.297	.450	.314	118	15	35	2	0	0
Sem Kuijper, DKI	.293	.420	.463	147	40	43	10	3	3

INDIVIDUAL PITCHING LEADERS

Player	W	L	ERA	IP	H	R	ER	BB	SO
Lars Huijer, HCA	12	1	0.79	137	71	16	12	29	133
Scott Prins, AMS	5	2	0.96	75	49	12	8	12	45
Shairon Martis, AMS	7	2	1.44	94	54	17	15	16	90
Dennis Burgersdijk, HCA	11	2	1.52	124	81	24	21	21	83
Kevin Kelly, NEP	5	3	1.57	75	40	15	13	25	78
Misja Harcksen, NEP	5	2	2.11	43	42	20	10	18	23
Nelmerson Angela, AMS	6	2	2.45	92	70	32	25	42	69
Kaj Timmermans, NEP	8	3	2.66	101	96	39	30	23	54
Juancarlos Sulbaran, NEP	10	3	2.67	94	80	36	28	34	82
Aaron De Groot, NEP	4	2	2.79	58	43	20	18	30	51
Yassir Lachkar, PIO	3	3	2.90	59	55	27	19	16	27

LUIS GUTIERREZ/NORTE PHOTO/GETTY

Jeandro Tromp, 22, hit .320 for the HCAW, the Holland Series champions.

Granma Rolls Again

The coronavius pandemic couldn't derail the 60th season of Serie Nacional, but it definitely affected it.

Normally, Serie Nacional is divided into a first half and a second half, with teams drafting players from the eliminated teams to bulk up their rosters for the second half of the season. Because of the pandemic, a single 75-game season was adopted instead.

There was plenty of parity across the league, as 11 of the 16 teams finished with winning records, and Holguin failed to make the eight-team playoffs despite being only six games back of first-place Santi Spiritus. That parity was equally apparent in the playoffs. Las Tuna, which finished second in the regular season, was knocked out in the quarterfinals by seventh-seeded Matanzas.

Matanzas then made a run all the way to the championship series, and actually held a 3-2 lead in that series before Granma won back-to-back elimination games. Granma's 4-0 win in Game 7 clinched Gramna's fourth title in the past six years. Granma had not won a Serie Nacional title in the first 54 years of the league, now they are the power of the island.

STANDINGS

Team	W	L	PCT	GB
Santi Spiritus	45	30	.600	-
Las Tuna	43	32	.574	2
Granma	43	32	.574	2
Mayabeque	42	33	.560	3
Ciego de Avila	41	34	.547	4
Industriales	41	34	.547	4
Matanzas	40	35	.534	5
Pinar del Rio	40	35	.534	5
Holguin	39	36	.520	6
Villa Clara	38	37	.507	7
Santiago de Cuba	38	37	.507	7
Isla de la Juventud	37	38	.494	8
Camaguey	36	39	.480	9
Artemisa	27	46	.370	17
Guantanamo	27	48	.360	18
Cienfuegos	21	52	.288	23

PLAYOFFS — Quarterfinals: Matanzas defeated Las Tuna 4-1; Santi Spiritus defeated Pinar del Rio 4-3; Ciego de Avila defeated Mayabque 4-2 and Granma defeated Industriales 4-0 in best-of-7 series. **Semifinals:** Matanzas defeated Santi Spiritus 4-0 and Granma defeated Ciego de Avila 4-0 in best-of-7 series. **Finals**: Granma defeated Matanzas 4-3 in best-of-7 series.

BATTING LEADERS

Player, Team	AVG	AB	R	H	2B	3B	HR	RBI
Frederich Cepeda, SSP	.410	195	37	80	15	0	8	38
Yordan Manduley, HOL	.386	207	53	80	11	0	4	31
Carlos Benítez, GRA	.379	161	27	61	9	0	7	50
Eliseo Rojas, IJV	.371	213	55	79	13	3	0	16
Yadil Mujica, MTZ	.363	201	30	73	13	1	1	22
Yosvani Alarcón, LTU	.363	212	46	77	17	0	7	48
Javier Camero, MTZ	.360	200	32	72	12	0	4	35
Dasiel Sevila, SCU	.360	203	37	73	10	3	2	40
Leslie Anderson, CMG	.359	184	25	66	15	0	7	31
Adriel Labrada, SCU	.359	217	53	78	17	1	11	49
Abdel Civil, CAV	.358	176	40	63	15	0	3	31
Yordanis Alarcón, LTU	.357	224	37	80	16	0	7	40
Alexander Ayala, CMG	.356	247	35	88	11	0	13	45
Andrés De La Cruz, LTU	.354	175	30	62	16	0	1	20
Dayán García, ART	.354	212	41	75	18	1	5	37
Roidel Martínez, PRI	.352	179	40	63	11	4	1	21
Rodoleisi Moreno, SSP	.349	229	53	80	14	6	0	41
Juan Carlos Arencibia, PRI	.349	235	45	82	13	4	1	31
Richel López, CFG	.348	201	45	70	19	3	3	31
Jefferson Delgado, MTZ	.346	228	39	79	10	2	2	34
Osvaldo Abreu, GRA	.346	231	53	80	13	3	4	48
Juan Carlos López, VCL	.345	197	22	68	14	2	3	34
Pavel Quesada, CFG	.344	189	30	65	11	1	5	43
Yordanis Samón, CMG	.344	218	37	75	25	0	13	40
Alfredo Fadraga, CAV	.340	209	53	71	15	1	19	54
Yhosvani Peñalver, IND	.339	183	36	62	9	0	2	38
Leonel Moa, CMG	.335	200	33	67	10	4	5	35
Luis Angel Sánchez, GTM	.333	210	26	70	11	1	3	21
Yasiel Santoya, IND	.332	190	39	63	12	0	12	42
Yasmani Viera, IJV	.332	196	23	65	9	0	1	27
Dennis Laza, MAY	.325	194	48	63	9	1	13	48
Ariel Sánchez, MTZ	.325	212	42	69	18	1	2	30
Rubén Valdés, CAV	.324	222	33	72	7	3	5	53
Luis Felipe Rivera, IJV	.323	158	30	51	6	0	2	33
Alexquemer Sánchez, GRA	.323	201	32	65	9	2	5	34
Maikel Caceres, HOL	.322	202	35	65	16	1	4	36
Alberto Calderón, IND	.322	239	46	77	9	1	2	23
Andrés Hernández, IND	.321	184	43	59	15	2	8	52
Moisés Esquerres, SSP	.320	175	33	56	10	0	5	27
Rangel Ramos, MAY	.320	178	25	57	9	1	0	20

PITCHING LEADERS

Player, Team	W	L	ERA	G	IP	H	HR	BB	SO
Danny Betancourt, SCU	7	5	2.62	14	76	77	6	26	35
Hermes González, CFG	10	1	2.91	15	105	98	7	34	52
Pedro Angel Alvarez, IND	10	1	3.16	15	85	87	6	41	39
Vladimir Baños, PRI	6	3	3.18	14	79	85	4	29	34
Carlos Juan Viera, LTU	5	5	3.45	7	73	73	3	24	59
Geonel Gutiérrez, ART	7	4	3.46	15	83	81	6	34	68
Michel A. Cabrera, HOL	8	3	3.55	0	89	99	8	20	32
César García, GRA	4	4	3.57	15	91	111	3	29	31
Jonathan Carbo, IJV	6	4	3.61	15	90	87	5	32	53
Yosvani Torres, PRI	6	6	3.72	15	87	83	5	14	41
José Eduardo Santos, SSP	7	2	3.73	13	80	78	6	30	43
Enyer Fernández, GTM	5	8	3.89	15	86	88	4	41	33
Renner Rivero, MTZ	7	4	4.00	15	79	83	4	46	57
Alejandro Meneses, LTU	8	0	4.19	14	73	81	5	23	21
Dachel Duquesne, CAV	8	4	4.19	15	88	93	5	34	28
José Ramón Rodríguez, CMG	8	3	4.33	12	81	94	7	21	54
Frank Madan, CMG	3	8	4.38	12	74	70	6	31	55
Javier Mirabal, VCL	3	4	4.54	12	73	72	6	26	50
Yadián Martínez, MAY	7	5	4.54	14	85	101	7	30	37
Yander Guevara, CAV	7	4	4.60	12	78	100	6	21	26
Wilson Paredes, HOL	8	5	4.80	8	84	100	5	36	40
Yudier Rodríguez, LTU	3	3	5.10	15	90	118	9	29	44
Noelvis Entenza, MTZ	2	7	5.23	14	76	91	8	34	38
Alberto Bicet, SCU	4	7	5.27	13	80	105	8	24	28
Misael Villa, ART	4	7	6.33	12	81	120	9	25	41

Colombia celebrated a surprising Caribbean Series title.

ERIKA SANTELICES/AFP VIA GETTY IMAGES

In Just Third Try, Colombia Claims First Caribbean Series

For most of the long history of the Caribbean Series, Colombia was not a part of the biggest event of the winter ball season. It wasn't until Cuba dropped out of the 2020 event that it was even invited. But just two years, later Colombia has its first Caribbean Series title to celebrate.

After going 5-2 during the seven-game round robin series, Colombia cleanup hitter Reynaldo Rodriguez homered in an 8-1 semifinal win over Venezuela. In the championship game, Mauricio Ramos and Dilson Herrera hit back-to-back doubles and Bryan Vuelvas added a single as a three-run second-inning provided more than enough runs for Colombia's pitching staff.

Colombia's Elkin Alcala struck out seven and allowed one run in 5.2 innings to pick up the win. The Colombia bullpen threw 3.1 scoreless innings, with Rodrigo Benoit pitching the final 1.2 innings for the save in the 4-1 win.

CARIBBEAN SERIES

Team	W	L	PCT	GB
Colombia	5	2	.714	-
Dom. Rep.	5	2	.714	-
Mexico	3	3	.500	1.5
Venezuela	3	3	.500	1.5
Panama	1	4	.200	3
Puerto Rico	1	4	.200	3

Playoffs—Semifinals: Colombia defeated Venezuela 8-1 and the Dominican Republic defeated Mexico 2-1. **Championship Game:** Colombia defeated Dominican Republic 4-1.

INDIVIDUAL BATTING LEADERS

Player, Team	AVG	AB	R	H	2B	3B	HR	RBI	BB	SO	SB
Rodriguez, Reynaldo, Col.	.500	26	5	13	3	0	1	4	2	4	0
Urrutia, Henry, DR	.435	23	2	10	3	0	0	0	1	2	0
Canó, Robinson, DR	.417	24	3	10	1	1	0	8	7	1	0
Cardona, Jose, Mex.	.389	18	3	7	0	0	0	1	3	1	4
Deluca, Joe, Pan.	.368	19	1	7	0	0	0	0	1	1	0
Bethancourt, Christian, Pan.	.350	20	2	7	1	0	0	1	0	2	0
Hair, Trey, Pan.	.333	9	1	3	1	0	0	1	3	3	1
Ramírez, Harold, Col.	.333	30	2	10	2	0	0	3	0	4	0
Sandoval, Pablo, Ven.	.333	24	3	8	2	0	1	2	2	2	0
Thomas, Eduardo, Pan.	.333	15	2	5	0	0	0	1	5	1	0

INDIVIDUAL PITCHING LEADERS

Player, Team	W	L	ERA	G	SV	IP	H	BB	SO	AVG
Abreu, Albert, DR	0	0	0	1	0	4.2	6	2	4	.316
Bracho, Silvino, Ven.	0	0	0	3	0	4.1	3	1	4	.200
Delgado, Randall, Pan.	0	0	0	2	0	4.1	3	2	2	.214
García, Elneiry, Col.	1	0	0	1	0	6.2	1	4	3	.050
Méndez, Yohander, Ven.	1	0	0	1	0	5	1	2	5	.067
Minaya, Juan, DR	0	0	0	4	3	4	3	0	2	.214
Rios, Wilmer, Mex.	1	0	0	1	0	6.2	3	0	5	.125
Rodriguez, Nivaldo, PR	0	0	0	1	0	5	2	1	6	.111
Romero, Davis, Pan.	0	0	0	1	0	5.1	2	4	2	.118
Silva, Ernesto, Pan.	0	1	0	2	0	5.1	6	1	1	.300

DOMINICAN LEAGUE

Team	W	L	PCT	GB
Gigantes	23	17	.575	-
Estrellas	22	18	.550	1
Licey	21	19	.525	2
Aguilas	20	20	.500	3
Escogido	19	21	.475	4
Toros	15	25	.375	8

Playoffs—Round Robin: Gigantes and Estrellas advance out of round-robin play with 10 wins each in 16 games. **Finals:** Gigantes defeats Estrellas 4-1 in best-of-seven series.

INDIVIDUAL BATTING LEADERS

Player, Team	AVG	AB	R	H	2B	3B	HR	RBI	BB	SO	SB
Alberto, Hanser, GIG	.321	165	30	53	8	0	0	11	7	10	1
Taveras, Leody, AGU	.274	146	27	40	5	1	2	19	24	23	11
Urbaez, Francisco, ESC	.272	114	14	31	1	0	0	10	17	18	2

Lake, Junior, EST	.262	126	26	33	6	1	3	11	19	28	10
Brito, Socrates, EST	.260	150	13	39	7	2	2	14	15	27	6
Torres, Ramon, AGU	.260	127	18	33	6	1	0	13	14	15	4
Bonifácio, Emilio, LIC	.250	132	17	33	3	0	1	15	8	25	10
Almonte, Zolio, AGU	.244	123	5	30	5	0	3	17	11	28	1
Montero, Elehuris, EST	.221	140	12	31	4	1	2	15	16	35	1

INDIVIDUAL PITCHING LEADERS

Player, Team	W	L	ERA	G	SV	IP	H	BB	SO	AVG
Valdez, Cesar, LIC	5	1	1.77	8	0	45.2	36	6	46	.211
Otero, Andy, EST	3	0	1.79	8	0	40.1	37	7	33	.245
Maya, Yunesky, AGU	3	4	2.06	10	0	52.1	41	13	36	.218
Valdes, Raul, TOR	2	3	2.85	9	0	47.1	40	20	41	.229

MEXICAN PACIFIC LEAGUE

Team	W	L	PCT	GB
Navojoa	40	28	.588	-
Guasave	37	31	.544	3
Jalisco	36	31	.537	3.5
Mexicali	36	32	.529	4
Hermosillo	36	32	.529	4
Obregon	36	32	.529	4
Monterrey	33	34	.493	6.5
Culiacan	33	35	.485	7
Mazatlan	29	39	.426	11
Los Mochis	23	45	.338	17

Playoffs—Quarterfinals: Culiacan defeated Navojoa 4-0; Guasave defeated Obregon 4-1; Jalisco defeated Mexicali 4-2 and Monterrey defeated Hermosillo 4-3 in best-of-7 series. **Semifinals:** Culiacan defeated Guasave 4-2 and Jalisco defeated Monterrey 4-3 in best-of-seven series. **Finals:** Jalisco defeated Culiacan 4-2 in a best-of-seven series.

INDIVIDUAL BATTING LEADERS

Player, Team	AVG	AB	R	H	2B	3B	HR	RBI	BB	SO	SB
Ornelas, Tirso, NAV	.353	218	36	77	16	2	2	35	15	30	0
Mendoza, Victor, OBR	.352	196	24	69	11	0	10	37	14	25	3
Elizalde, Sebastian, CUL	.336	232	43	78	8	1	6	35	36	15	14
Rios, Ramon, MAZ	.336	262	33	88	10	1	2	29	9	12	16
Leyva, Samar, NAV	.315	165	19	52	10	4	5	17	5	17	3
Atondo, Jasson, HER	.312	202	18	63	10	0	0	18	19	16	5
Torres, Nick, HER	.311	228	35	71	10	1	9	37	27	80	5
Dean, Justin, 2 Teams	.307	176	28	54	10	1	6	25	17	40	16
Drake, Yadir, GSV	.305	223	39	68	12	1	5	32	30	33	4
Urena, Jhoan, GSV	.303	244	35	74	11	2	8	41	40	56	1

INDIVIDUAL PITCHING LEADERS

Player, Team	W	L	ERA	G	SV	IP	H	BB	SO	AVG
Leyva, Elian, HER	7	2	1.54	12	0	70	50	19	54	.205
Chavez, Manuel, MXC	2	4	2.04	18	0	57.1	47	28	57	.232
Holmberg, David, NAV	4	1	2.43	13	0	70.1	66	22	51	.255
Rios, Wilmer, HER	6	3	2.66	14	0	81.1	73	11	52	.243
Velázquez, Hector, OBR	5	1	2.68	11	0	57	45	14	38	.224
Bravo, Jose, CUL	2	2	2.70	12	0	56.2	51	15	37	.239
Acosta, Octavio, NAV	5	1	2.77	13	0	65	58	14	69	.236
Lopez, Arturo, OBR	3	2	2.84	12	0	66.2	75	17	56	.293
Verdugo, Ryan, HER	2	4	3.06	14	0	82.1	70	28	60	.229
Reyes, David, MXC	6	4	3.18	14	0	76.1	83	13	47	.281

PUERTO RICAN LEAGUE

Team	W	L	PCT	GB
Mayaguez	21	10	.677	-
Caguas	20	12	.625	1.5
Santurce	17	15	.531	4.5
Carolina	13	18	.419	8
RA12	8	24	.250	13.5

Playoffs—Semifinals: Mayaguez defeated Carolina 4-1 and Caguas defeated Santurce 4-2 in best-of-7 series. **Finals:** Caguas defeated Mayaguez 4-1 in a best-of-seven series.

INDIVIDUAL BATTING LEADERS

Player, Team	AVG	AB	R	H	2B	3B	HR	RBI	BB	SO	SB
Crim, Blaine, MAY	.406	101	14	41	8	1	3	25	7	11	0
Layer, Abdiel, RA12	.333	120	18	40	12	0	4	19	14	31	5
Rodriguez, Brett, MAY	.333	111	30	37	6	1	4	14	24	31	5
Fernández, Xavier, MAY	.302	96	12	29	5	0	1	18	8	6	0
Ortiz, Danny, MAY	.302	116	22	35	10	0	9	28	9	26	3
Morales, Roy, SAN	.299	87	9	26	0	0	0	14	19	8	0
Machín, Vimael, CAG	.287	108	17	31	8	0	2	18	12	9	1
Fargas, Johneshwy, CAG	.286	105	16	30	5	2	1	11	10	24	11
Grotjohn, Ryan, CAR	.270	100	10	27	7	2	1	17	10	24	1
De Jesús Jr., Ivan, SAN	.259	85	13	22	7	0	1	10	21	15	3

INDIVIDUAL PITCHING LEADERS

Player, Team	W	L	ERA	G	SV	IP	H	BB	SO	AVG
Stout, Eric, MAY	3	0	1.24	6	0	29	17	12	36	.173
Flores, Adalberto, SAN	3	1	1.30	5	0	27.2	20	8	19	.202
Williams, Ronnie, MAY	1	0	1.93	6	0	28	16	9	32	.158
Cruz, Jose, CAR	2	2	2.09	9	0	43	30	15	28	.201
Velez, Ricardo, RA12	1	3	2.73	10	0	33	18	13	30	.154
Webb, Braden, MAY	3	1	3.07	14	2	29.1	23	19	40	.219
Cruz, Luis, SAN	2	1	3.44	7	0	36.2	40	7	33	.272
Hernandez, Hector, SAN	1	2	3.44	7	0	34	36	8	23	.277
Espada, Jose, CAR	1	2	3.75	9	0	36	27	16	33	.209
Ramirez, Ruben, RA12	0	4	4.15	10	0	34.2	45	11	28	.315

VENEZUELAN LEAGUE

Team	W	L	PCT	GB
Magallanes	32	17	.653	-
Lara	28	21	.571	4
Caracas	26	23	.531	6
Aragua	26	24	.520	6.5
Caribes	25	24	.510	7
Margarita	25	25	.500	7.5
Zulia	20	29	.408	12
La Guaira	15	34	.306	17

Playoffs—Round Robin: Magallanes and Caribes advance. **Finals:** Magallanes defeated Caribes 4-3 in a best-of-seven series.

INDIVIDUAL BATTING LEADERS

Player, Team	AVG	AB	R	H	2B	3B	HR	RBI	BB	SO	SB
Flores, Ramon, MAR	.416	161	43	67	11	0	4	22	41	22	0
Romero, Niuman, ORI	.368	155	49	57	15	0	9	40	32	25	1
Tovar, Wilfredo, CAR	.364	184	32	67	7	0	4	22	21	9	3
Fuenmayor, Balbino, ORI	.361	191	31	69	15	0	11	53	15	25	0
Palacios, Jermaine, LAR	.351	131	35	46	11	2	4	16	15	31	7
Telis, Tomas, ORI	.343	172	35	59	16	0	4	35	20	15	0
Tocci, Carlos, ARA	.339	218	37	74	15	0	1	24	13	24	2
Noriega, Gabriel, MAG	.338	130	21	44	9	1	4	16	12	23	1
Gonzalez, Alberto, MAG	.337	166	36	56	11	1	1	23	11	14	6
Rincones, Diego, MAR	.335	161	30	54	8	0	4	30	13	10	0

INDIVIDUAL PITCHING LEADERS

Player, Team	W	L	ERA	G	SV	IP	H	BB	SO	AVG
Stephens, Jackson, LAR	6	3	1.82	14	0	49.1	51	10	44	.263
Camacho, Yoimer, CAR	6	1	3.40	13	0	45	48	16	31	.273
Leal, Erick, MAG	5	1	3.65	12	0	56.2	59	11	39	.266
Mujica, Jose, CAR	0	1	3.94	12	0	45.2	48	11	25	.273
Centeno, Henry, MAR	5	2	4.31	12	0	62.2	69	14	30	.283
Cavanerio, Jorgan, LAG	3	4	4.33	12	0	54	60	8	31	.283
Jimenez, Cesar, 2 Teams	2	6	4.72	10	0	47.2	50	17	40	.263
Guaipe, Mayckol, ORI	2	2	4.78	11	0	43.1	42	15	36	.249
Molina, Nestor, LAR	2	2	4.84	11	0	48.1	63	9	32	.318
Villanueva, Elih, ARA	3	3	4.97	11	0	50.2	57	28	45	.279

COLLEGE

C. MORGAN ENGEL NCAA PHOTOS VIA GETTY IMAGES

Mississippi's title in Omaha is the second NCAA championship in school history.

Ole Miss Completes Its Storybook Run

BY TEDDY CAHILL

OMAHA—One day, several years from now, Mississippi coach Mike Bianco will look around his pregame huddle and tell the story of the 2022 Rebels. Bianco is one of college baseball's best motivators and his pregame speeches take from history, from businessmen, from sports, from all walks of life. Anywhere he can find a motivational moment.

One day, Bianco will realize that the story his team needs to hear is the story of how Ole Miss won the 2022 national championship. It is a story of perseverance. It is a story of running with opportunity. It is the story of pushing through injury. It is the story of believing when no one else does. It is the story of turning a weakness into a strength. It is the story of turning into legends in real time.

Bianco might start the story at the end, which came when Ole Miss defeated Oklahoma, 4-2, to complete a sweep of the College World Series finals to win the first national championship in program history.

After a back-and-forth game, Ole Miss scored three times in the eighth inning to push into the lead and closer Brandon Johnson closed the win by striking out the side in the ninth inning. After the final whiff, when pinch hitter Diego Muniz swung through a breaking ball in the dirt, catcher Hayden Dunhurst leveled him with a bearhug. The rest of the Rebels soon joined in a dogpile on top of them.

The path to any national championship is full of twists and turns, turning points, elation, moments when Omaha feels unimaginable. But there's the typical ups and downs of a national championship team and then there's what Ole Miss did. Its journey had at least as many bends as the Missouri River, which flows through Omaha just past the parking lots for Charles Schwab Field.

Ole Miss lost four straight SEC series in April and was 7-14 in conference play on May 1, its margin for error all but exhausted. It lost its first-round game in the SEC Tournament, starting an anxious week ahead of Selection Monday. It was one of the last four teams selected to the NCAA Tournament. Given half a chance, the Rebels ran with it and never looked back.

Along the way, they picked up admirers around the country. They aren't a Cinderella—this is a program that plays in the mighty SEC, that was ranked No. 1 early this year, that has one of the largest fan bases in college baseball—but they captured hearts like a scrappy underdog. Their story was so compelling, and their players played so free

COACHING CAROUSEL

School	In (Previous Job)	Out
Akron	Greg Beals (former Ohio State coach)	Chris Sabo
Army	Chris Tracz (Marist coach)	Jim Foster
Austin Peay	Roland Fanning (Oklahoma State staff)	Travis Janssen
Baylor	Mitch Thompson (McLennan (Texas) JC coach)	Steve Rodriguez
Bellarmine	Chris Dominguez (Bellarmine assistant)	Larry Owens (retired)
Butler	Blake Beemer (Ball State assistant)	Dave Schrage (retired)
Brigham Young	Trent Pratt (BYU assistant)	Mike Littlewood
Cal State Northridge	Eddie Cornejo (CSUN assistant)	Dave Serrano (retired)
Clemson	Erik Bakich (Michigan coach)	Monte Lee
Delaware	Greg Mamula (Florida Atlantic assistant)	Jim Sherman
Fairleigh Dickinson	Manny Roman (FDU assistant)	Rob DiToma
Florida International	Rich Witten (Virginia Commonwealth assistant)	Mervyl Melendez
Florida State	Link Jarrett (Notre Dame coach)	Mike Martin Jr.
George Mason	Shawn Camp (interim)	Bill Brown (retired)
Grambling State	Davin Pierre (Grambling assistant)	James Cooper
Grand Canyon	Gregg Wallis (GCU assistant)	Andy Stankiewicz
Kansas	Dan Fitzgerald (Louisiana State assistant)	Ritch Price (retired)
Lafayette	AJ Miller (Navy assistant)	Tim Reilly
Manhattan	David Miller (PSU-Abington coach)	Mike Cole
Marist	Lance Ratchford (SUNY-Cobleskill coach)	Chris Tracz
Memphis	Kerrick Jackson (MLB Draft League president)	Daron Schoenrock (retired)
Middle Tennessee State	Jerry Meyers (interim)	Jim Toman
Michigan	Tracy Smith (former Arizona State coach)	Erik Bakich
Mississippi Valley State	Milton Barney	Stanley Stubbs
Nevada	Jake McKinley (Brewers staff)	TJ Bruce
Northwestern	Jim Foster (Army coach)	Spencer Allen
North Alabama	Jad Prachniak (Delaware assistant)	Mike Keehn (retired)
Northern Colorado	Mike Anderson (former Nebraska coach)	Carl Iwasaki (retired)
Notre Dame	Shawn Stiffler (Virginia Commonwealth coach)	Link Jarrett
Ohio State	Bill Mosiello (Texas Christian assistant)	Greg Beals
Radford	Alex Guerra (James Madison assistant)	Karl Kuhn
Sacred Heart	Pat Egan (Quinnipiac assistant)	Nick Restaino
Saint Peter's	Grant Neary (Saint Peter's assistant)	Lou Proietti
San Francisco	Rob DiToma (Fairleigh Dickinson coach)	Nino Giarratano
St. Bonaventure	Jason Rathburn (Herkimer (N.Y.) JC coach)	Larry Sudbrook (retired)
Southern California	Andy Stankiewicz (Grand Canyon coach)	Jason Gill
Texas-Arlington	Clay Van Hook (Oklahoma assistant)	Darin Thomas
Tulane	Jay Uhlman (Tulane assistant)	Travis Jewett
Virginia Commonwealth	Bradley LeCroy (Clemson assistant)	Shawn Stiffler
Virginia Military	Sam Roberts (VMI assistant)	Jonathan Hadra
Washington	Jason Kelly (Louisiana State assistant)	Lindsay Meggs (retired)
Western Carolina	Alan Beck (Georgia Southern assistant)	Bobby Moranda
Western Illinois	Tayler Sheriff (interim)	Andy Pascoe
Western Kentucky	Marc Rardin (Iowa Western JC coach)	John Pawlowski
Yale	Brian Hamm (Eastern Connecticut State coach)	John Stuper

and easy that the bandwagon quickly filled up.

"They had a lot of people rooting for them, and not just Ole Miss fans," Bianco said. "I can't—I've gotten so many texts over the last couple weeks from a lot of our rivals, a lot of the people that we compete against every single day that says they're pulling for us, that they've fallen in love with this story and these guys."

Among those that texted Bianco were Mississippi State coach Chris Lemonis and Jake Gautreau, his top assistant. There are few, if any, rivalries in college baseball that burn hotter than Ole Miss vs. Mississippi State. But such was the power of these Rebels.

First baseman and captain Tim Elko could have signed a professional contract after last season. But he opted to return to school for another shot at the national title. He was the face, the heartbeat and the leader of the Rebels and his legacy will live forever in Oxford.

"There's so much to be said about how much we overcame this year, how much we had to fight through, how much we had to pick each other up and never let ourselves get too down," Elko said. "This story of our season is going to be told for years and years and years to come.

"This is the best Ole Miss baseball team in history, and it feels so good, and it's an honor to be a part of it."

The story of the 2022 Rebels really starts in 2021. Those Rebels were led by the 1-2 punch of righthander Gunnar Hoglund and lefthander

Doug Nikhazy, or they were until Hoglund went down with an injury that required Tommy John surgery. Elko, meanwhile, suffered a torn ACL on April 5 but rather than undergoing season-ending surgery, he rehabbed the injury and played through it, limited to DH duties. Hobbled, but not broken, Ole Miss reached super regionals, falling one win shy of a CWS appearance at Arizona. Then, from home, the Rebels had to watch as Mississippi State won the national championship, its first in program history.

It was another disappointing end for Ole Miss, but it added more fuel to the fire for 2022. Elko, outfielder Kevin Graham and third baseman/center fielder Justin Bench opted to return for another season in Oxford, helping the Rebels build one of the best lineups in the country. They had to offset the loss of Hoglund, Nikhazy and closer Taylor Broadway to pro ball, but they still ranked No. 9 in the Preseason Top 25.

Ole Miss lived up to those lofty expectations early and ascended to No. 1 in the Top 25 in mid March. It was 16-4 going into a big early season series at Swayze Field against Tennessee. The Rebels were walloped by the Volunteers that weekend, swept at home by a combined score of 26-7. While Tennessee went on to prove it was a runaway freight train, easily winning the SEC and earning the No. 1 overall seed in the NCAA Tournament, it was a crushing blow at the time.

Ole Miss seemed to right the ship the next week with a series win at Kentucky, but it soon fell into a funk. Alabama swept a series at Swayze. The Rebels went to South Carolina and lost a series. They lost the rivalry series to Mississippi State in excruciating fashion, losing the rubber game in extra innings. The next week, they lost a series at Arkansas, falling in the rubber game when they left the bases loaded in the ninth inning.

As the skid deepened, the noise around the program grew to deafening levels. Expectations in Oxford are sky high and archrival Mississippi State had just won a national championship. The pressure had perhaps never been higher on Bianco and the Rebels.

Leaving Fayetteville, Ole Miss was 24-19 and

COLLEGE WORLD SERIES CHAMPIONS

Year	Champion	Coach	Record	Runner-Up	Most Outstanding Player
1948	Southern California	Sam Barry	40-12	Yale	None selected
1949	Texas*	Bibb Falk	23-7	Wake Forest	Charles Teague, 2B, Wake Forest
1950	Texas	Bibb Falk	27-6	Washington State	Ray VanCleef, OF, Rutgers
1951	Oklahoma*	Jack Baer	19-9	Tennessee	Sid Hatfield, 1B/P, Tennessee
1952	Holy Cross	Jack Barry	21-3	Missouri	Jim O'Neill, P, Holy Cross
1953	Michigan	Ray Fisher	21-9	Texas	J.L. Smith, P, Texas
1954	Missouri	Hi Simmons	22-4	Rollins	Tom Yewcic, C, Michigan State
1955	Wake Forest	Taylor Sanford	29-7	Western Michigan	Tom Borland, P, Oklahoma State
1956	Minnesota	Dick Siebert	33-9	Arizona	Jerry Thomas, P, Minnesota
1957	California*	George Wolfman	35-10	Penn State	Cal Emery, 1B/P, Penn State
1958	Southern California	Rod Dedeaux	35-7	Missouri	Bill Thom, P, Southern California
1959	Oklahoma State	Toby Greene	27-5	Arizona	Jim Dobson, 3B, Oklahoma State
1960	Minnesota	Dick Siebert	34-7	Southern California	John Erickson, 2B, Minnesota
1961	Southern California*	Rod Dedeaux	43-9	Oklahoma State	Littleton Fowler, P, Oklahoma State
1962	Michigan	Don Lund	31-13	Santa Clara	Bob Garibaldi, P, Santa Clara
1963	Southern California	Rod Dedeaux	37-16	Arizona	Bud Hollowell, C, Southern California
1964	Minnesota	Dick Siebert	31-12	Missouri	Joe Ferris, P, Maine
1965	Arizona State	Bobby Winkles	54-8	Ohio State	Sal Bando, 3B, Arizona State
1966	Ohio State	Marty Karow	27-6	Oklahoma State	Steve Arlin, P, Ohio State
1967	Arizona State	Bobby Winkles	53-12	Houston	Ron Davini, C, Arizona State
1968	Southern California*	Rod Dedeaux	45-14	Southern Illinois	Bill Seinsoth, 1B, Southern California
1969	Arizona State	Bobby Winkles	56-11	Tulsa	John Dolinsek, OF, Arizona State
1970	Southern California	Rod Dedeaux	51-13	Florida State	Gene Ammann, P, Florida State
1971	Southern California	Rod Dedeaux	53-13	Southern Illinois	Jerry Tabb, 1B, Tulsa
1972	Southern California	Rod Dedeaux	50-13	Arizona State	Russ McQueen, P, Southern California
1973	Southern California*	Rod Dedeaux	51-11	Arizona State	Dave Winfield, OF/P, Minnesota
1974	Southern California	Rod Dedeaux	50-20	Miami	George Milke, P, Southern California
1975	Texas	Cliff Gustafson	56-6	South Carolina	Mickey Reichenbach, 1B, Texas
1976	Arizona	Jerry Kindall	56-17	Eastern Michigan	Steve Powers, DH/P, Arizona
1977	Arizona State	Jim Brock	57-12	South Carolina	Bob Horner, 3B, Arizona State
1978	Southern California*	Rod Dedeaux	54-9	Arizona State	Rod Boxberger, P, Southern California
1979	Cal State Fullerton	Augie Garrido	60-14	Arkansas	Tony Hudson, P, Cal State Fullerton
1980	Arizona	Jerry Kindall	45-21	Hawaii	Terry Francona, OF, Arizona
1981	Arizona State	Jim Brock	55-13	Oklahoma State	Stan Holmes, OF, Arizona State
1982	Miami	Ron Fraser	57-18	Wichita State	Dan Smith, P, Miami
1983	Texas	Cliff Gustafson	66-14	Alabama	Calvin Schiraldi, P, Texas

7-14 in SEC play. With nine games left in conference play, a trip to the SEC Tournament hung in the balance, let alone an NCAA Tournament bid. And, then, the Rebs got hot.

Ole Miss swept Missouri. It won a midweek game at Southern Mississippi. It rolled into Baton Rouge and swept Louisiana State in Alex Box Stadium for the first time ever. Suddenly, the postseason no longer seemed farfetched. A series loss to Texas A&M on the final week of the regular season was a missed opportunity to remove all doubt, as was a 3-1 loss to Vanderbilt in the play-in round of the SEC Tournament.

The Rebels returned to Oxford after that loss hoping for just a chance to play together again. At the time, it seemed possible. But as conference tournament upsets shrunk the bubble, it started to seem likely that they would get left at home. But, in the end, the selection committee put them in the NCAA Tournament field, sending them to Coral Gables as the No. 3 seed.

Ole Miss arrived in Coral Gables along with a hurricane. The start of the regional was delayed a day by rain, but it didn't cool off the Rebels. They swept through the field, beating Arizona twice and host Miami once to advance to super regionals. Ole Miss faced a trip to Southern Miss, which had one of the best pitching staffs in the country. The Rebels outpitched them at Pete Taylor Park, shutting them out completely in a two-game sweep. Ole Miss, once left for dead, was going to Omaha for the first time since 2014.

In Omaha, Ole Miss just kept rolling. It beat Auburn, 5-1, and then Arkansas, 13-5. Its losing streak was finally snapped in the bracket final against the Razorbacks with a 3-2 loss that saw it again leave the bases loaded in the ninth inning against Arkansas. That loss might have been deflating, but Ole Miss bounced back the next day with a 2-0 win behind an all-time great Omaha performance from righthander Dylan Delucia, who threw a four-hit shutout. The Rebels were playing for the national title for the first time ever.

Oklahoma awaited in the CWS finals. But unlike Ole Miss, the Sooners had swept through the CWS, meaning their pitching staff was set up

Year	Champion	Coach	Record	Runner-Up	MOST OUTSTANDING PLAYER
1984	Cal State Fullerton	Augie Garrido	66-20	Texas	John Fishel, OF, Cal State Fullerton
1985	Miami*	Ron Fraser	64-16	Texas	Greg Ellena, DH, Miami
1986	Arizona	Jerry Kindall	49-19	Florida State	Mike Senne, OF, Arizona
1987	Stanford	Mark Marquess	53-17	Oklahoma State	Paul Carey, OF, Stanford
1988	Stanford	Mark Marquess	46-23	Arizona State	Lee Plemel, P, Stanford
1989	Wichita State	Gene Stephenson	68-16	Texas	Greg Brummett, P, Wichita State
1990	Georgia	Steve Webber	52-19	Oklahoma State	Mike Rebhan, P, Georgia
1991	Louisiana State*	Skip Bertman	55-18	Wichita State	Gary Hymel, C, Louisiana State
1992	Pepperdine*	Andy Lopez	48-11	Cal State Fullerton	Phil Nevin, 3B, Cal State Fullerton
1993	Louisiana State	Skip Bertman	53-17	Wichita State	Todd Walker, 2B, Louisiana State
1994	Oklahoma*	Larry Cochell	50-17	Georgia Tech	Chip Glass, OF, Oklahoma
1995	Cal State Fullerton*	Augie Garrido	57-9	Southern California	Mark Kotsay, OF/P, Cal State Fullerton
1996	Louisiana State*	Skip Bertman	52-15	Miami	Pat Burrell, 3B, Miami
1997	Louisiana State*	Skip Bertman	57-13	Alabama	Brandon Larson, SS, Louisiana State
1998	Southern California	Mike Gillespie	49-17	Arizona State	Wes Rachels, 2B, Southern California
1999	Miami*	Jim Morris	50-13	Florida State	Marshall McDougall, 2B, Florida State
2000	Louisiana State*	Skip Bertman	52-17	Stanford	Trey Hodges, P, Louisiana State
2001	Miami*	Jim Morris	53-12	Stanford	Charlton Jimerson, OF, Miami
2002	Texas*	Augie Garrido	57-15	South Carolina	Huston Street, P, Texas
2003	Rice	Wayne Graham	58-12	Stanford	John Hudgins, P, Stanford
2004	Cal State Fullerton	George Horton	47-22	Texas	Jason Windsor, P, Cal State Fullerton
2005	Texas*	Augie Garrido	56-16	Florida	David Maroul, 3B, Texas
2006	Oregon State	Pat Casey	50-16	North Carolina	Jonah Nickerson, P, Oregon State
2007	Oregon State*	Pat Casey	49-18	North Carolina	Jorge Reyes, P, Oregon State
2008	Fresno State	Mike Batesole	47-31	Georgia	Tommy Mendonca, 3B, Fresno State
2009	Louisiana State	Paul Mainieri	56-17	Texas	Jared Mitchell, OF, Louisiana State
2010	South Carolina	Ray Tanner	54-16	UCLA	Jackie Bradley Jr., OF, South Carolina
2011	South Carolina*	Ray Tanner	55-14	Florida	Scott Wingo, 2B, South Carolina
2012	Arizona*	Andy Lopez	48-17	South Carolina	Robert Refsnyder, OF, Arizona
2013	UCLA*	John Savage	49-17	Mississippi State	Adam Plutko, P, UCLA
2014	Vanderbilt	Tim Corbin	51-21	Virginia	Dansby Swanson, 2B, Vanderbilt
2015	Virginia	Brian O'Connor	44-24	Vanderbilt	Josh Sborz, P, Virginia
2016	Coastal Carolina	Gary Gilmore	55-18	Arizona	Andrew Beckwith, P, Coastal Carolina
2017	Florida	Kevin O'Sullivan	52-19	Louisiana State	Alex Faedo, P, Florida
2018	Oregon State	Pat Casey	55-12-1	Arkansas	Adley Rutschman, C, Oregon State
2019	Vanderbilt	Tim Corbin	59-12	Michigan	Kumar Rocker, RHP, Vanderbilt
2020	Canceled due to pandemic				
2021	Mississippi State	Chris Lemonis	50-18	Vanderbilt	Will Bednar, RHP, Mississippi State
2022	Ole Miss	Mike Bianco	42-23	Oklahoma	Dylan DeLucia, RHP, Ole Miss

perfectly for the best-of-three finals. Ole Miss had needed to throw DeLucia to reach the finals and he wouldn't be able to pitch again until game 3—and even then, he would be on short rest. Freshman lefthander Hunter Elliott, the team's No. 2 starter, would be on short rest for the first time in his career if he threw game 1, so Ole Miss held him for Game 2 and instead turned to righthander Jack Dougherty, who hadn't started a game in months.

Like Ole Miss, Dougherty took his postseason opportunity and ran with it. He started the game by retiring the first 15 batters he faced, and the Rebels went on to a 10-3 victory.

That win set the stage for a wild, back-and-forth game Sunday. Elliott and Oklahoma righthander Cade Horton locked in a pitcher's duel that was scoreless for five innings. Ole Miss avoided disaster in the top of the sixth inning when an interference call on a squeeze bunt took a run off the board for Oklahoma. Jacob Gonzalez gave the Rebels the lead in the bottom of the inning with a solo home run. The Sooners came back with two runs of their own in the top of the seventh and with closer Trevin Michael fully rested, they were in a strong position at the stretch.

But Ole Miss had been down and out plenty of times this season. It wasn't fazed, and T.J. McCants chased Horton with a one-out single in the eighth inning. Bench and Gonzalez greeted Michael with back-to-back singles to tie the game. Then, two wild pitches allowed them to come home and all of a sudden, Ole Miss held a 4-2 lead going into the ninth inning.

Johnson, who got plenty of rest during the postseason because Ole Miss almost never played a game close enough to insert its closer into, came in and blew three Sooners away. The Rebels' journey was complete. They had gone from the last team in the tournament to the last team standing.

"They've fallen down, where not a lot of people believed that they were any good anymore, and a lot of people may have been disappointed in them," Bianco said. "And I get that. It's sports, and that's part of it. But they didn't let that affect them. They continued to believe in one another. They continued to push.

"I think that's why you had 20,000-plus fans show up here, because this is a special group. They knew it was a special group. It wasn't just a national championship. I honestly believe that."

This Ole Miss team wasn't some plucky underdog. It has legitimate college baseball stars like Elko, who may one day have a statue outside Swayze Field—though he said he'd prefer to see one of the whole team holding the trophy aloft. It has premium draft prospects like Gonzalez, who is a potential top-five pick in the 2023 draft. DeLucia was named CWS Most Outstanding Player, completing his own improbable journey from junior college transfer who wasn't in the Opening Weekend rotation to ace and, now, Ole Miss legend. Elliott was a prominent recruit who has made good on his potential. Catcher Hayden Dunhurst was one of the best defenders in the

RPI RANKINGS

The Ratings Percentage Index is an important tool used by the NCAA in selecting at-large teams for the 64-team Division I tournament. These were the top 100 finishers for 2022. A team's rank in the final Baseball America Top 25 is indicated in parentheses, and College World Series teams are bolded.

Rank School	Record	Rank School	Record
1. Tennessee (8)	57-9	51. UC Santa Barbara	44-14
2. Oregon State (11)	48-16	52. Kennesaw State	36-28
3. Stanford (7)	45-18	53. VCU	42-20
4. Virginia Tech (10)	45-13	54. La.-Lafayette	37-23
5. North Carolina (13)	42-22	55. Pennsylvania	33-15
6. Notre Dame (5)	40-17	56. Missouri	28-23
7. Auburn (6)	42-22	57. Michigan	34-28
8. Texas A&M (3)	43-20	58. Campbell	41-19
9. Mississippi (1)	42-23	59. Grand Canyon	40-22
10. Oklahoma (2)	44-24	60. Mercer	40-18
11. Vanderbilt	39-23	61. Iowa	35-18
12. Maryland (18)	48-14	62. Xavier	33-27
13. Texas (9)	47-21	63. Belmont	39-20
14. Florida (22)	42-24	64. Ball State	40-19
15. Oklahoma St. (19)	42-22	65. Southern Illinois	44-16
16. Wake Forest	41-19-1	66. Middle Tenn.	29-26
17. East Carolina (17)	45-21	67. College of Charleston	37-20
18. Louisville (12)	42-20-1	68. South Carolina	27-28
19. So. Mississippi (16)	47-19	69. Central Michigan	42-19
20. Arkansas (4)	46-21	70. SE Missouri	37-22
21. Louisiana St. (24)	40-22	71. Pittsburgh	29-27
22. Ga. Southern	41-20	72. Davidson	43-13
23. Texas State (21)	47-14	73. South Alabama	31-23
24. Georgia	36-23	74. Washington State	26-26
25. Georgia Tech	36-24	75. Charlotte	36-22
26. Miami (14)	40-20	76. Fla. Gulf Coast	35-23
27. Virginia	39-19	77. Illinois	30-22
28. Connecticut (15)	50-15	78. California	29-27
29. Coastal Carolina	39-20-1	79. Houston	37-24
30. Gonzaga	37-19	80. Baylor	26-28
31. Dallas Baptist	34-24-1	81. Evansville	32-24
32. Oregon	36-25	82. Central Florida	35-25
33. Florida State	34-25	83. Nevada	29-26
34. North Carolina St.	36-21	84. William & Mary	26-23
35. Wofford	42-16-1	85. Tulane	33-26-1
36. Clemson	35-23	86. Florida Atlantic	35-23
37. Louisiana Tech	43-21	87. Creighton	31-18
38. Texas Christian (20)	38-22	88. Ala.-Birmingham	30-25
39. Texas-San Antonio	38-20	89. Missouri State	31-29
40. Liberty	37-23	90. Portland	32-23
41. Arizona	39-25	91. UNC Wilmington	31-24
42. Texas Tech (25)	39-22	92. Washington	30-26
43. Rutgers	44-15	93. UC Irvine	32-24
44. Columbia	32-18	94. UNC Greensboro	34-30
45. Alabama	31-27	95. Cal St.Northridge	32-22
46. Old Dominion	41-17	96. Air Force	32-29
47. Kentucky	33-26	97. Kansas State	29-29
48. West Virginia	32-22	98. Georgia State	29-27
49. UCLA (23)	40-24	99. Oral Roberts	38-20
50. San Diego	37-20	100. Troy	32-24

COLLEGE ALL-AMERICA TEAM

FIRST TEAM

Pos.	Name	AVG	OBP	SLG	AB	R	H	HR	RBI	BB	SO	SB
C	Kevin Parada, Georgia Tech	.360	.453	.715	253	78	91	26	88	30	31	11
1B	Ivan Melendez, Texas	.387	.508	.863	248	75	96	32	94	52	51	1
2B	Jace Jung, Texas Tech	.335	.481	.612	224	68	75	14	57	59	42	5
3B	Max Wagner, Clemson	.369	.496	.852	203	66	75	27	76	45	51	2
SS	Peyton Graham, Oklahoma	.335	.417	.640	278	75	93	20	71	28	69	34
OF	Chris Alleyne, Maryland	.331	.422	.673	263	73	87	24	79	33	41	24
OF	Dylan Crews, Louisiana State	.349	.463	.691	249	73	87	22	72	42	56	5
OF	Jacob Melton, Oregon State	.360	.424	.670	261	66	94	17	83	26	51	21
DH	Sonny DiChiara, Auburn	.383	.549	.777	206	59	79	22	59	68	55	0
UTL	Paul Skenes, Air Force	.314	.412	.634	153	39	48	13	38	21	40	0

Pos.	Name	W	L	ERA	G	CG	SV	IP	H	BB	SO	AVG
SP	Tanner Hall, Southern Mississippi	9	3	2.81	19	0	0	109	98	14	146	.233
SP	Cooper Hjerpe, Oregon State	11	2	2.53	18	0	1	103	67	23	161	.180
SP	Rhett Lowder, Wake Forest	11	3	3.08	16	1	0	99	91	26	105	.239
SP	Drew Thorpe, Cal Poly	10	1	2.32	15	1	0	105	65	25	149	.175
RP	Andrew Walters, Miami	0	1	1.65	24	0	14	33	13	6	62	.116
RP	Tyler Guilfoil, Kentucky	3	1	1.59	21	0	6	51	27	17	80	.156
UTL	Paul Skenes, Air Force	10	3	2.73	15	0	0	86	70	30	96	.224

SECOND TEAM

Pos.	Name	AVG	OBP	SLG	AB	R	H	HR	RBI	BB	SO	SB
C	Daniel Susac, Arizona	.366	.429	.582	273	50	100	12	61	23	52	0
1B	Carter Graham, Stanford	.331	.399	.642	260	64	86	22	79	27	55	1
2B	Chandler Simpson, Georgia Tech	.433	.506	.517	203	64	88	1	25	31	16	27
3B	Trey Lipscomb, Tennessee	.355	.428	.717	251	68	89	22	84	26	37	4
SS	Brooks Lee, Cal Poly	.357	.462	.664	235	56	84	15	55	46	28	3
OF	Drew Gilbert, Tennessee	.362	.455	.673	199	60	72	11	70	33	32	4
OF	Wyatt Langford, Florida	.355	.447	.719	256	73	91	26	63	36	44	7
OF	Murphy Stehly, Texas	.367	.424	.662	278	65	102	19	61	17	43	8
DH	Tommy White, North Carolina State	.362	.425	.757	235	54	85	27	74	23	50	1
UTL	Zach Agnos, East Carolina	.330	.405	.479	267	56	88	7	42	34	66	9

Pos.	Name	W	L	ERA	G	CG	SV	IP	H	BB	SO	AVG
SP	John Michael Bertrand, Notre Dame	10	3	2.81	18	0	0	109	97	21	111	.234
SP	Chase Dollander, Tennessee	10	0	2.39	16	0	0	79	50	13	108	.175
SP	Gabriel Hughes, Gonzaga	8	3	3.21	15	0	0	98	75	37	138	.209
SP	Parker Messick, Florida State	7	5	3.38	16	0	0	99	78	18	144	.215
RP	Jacob Palisch, Stanford	6	3	2.39	29	0	5	60	53	12	73	.230
RP	Triston Stivors, Texas State	7	1	2.21	32	0	18	61	47	19	86	.210
UTL	Zach Agnos, East Carolina	3	0	2.31	21	0	3	23	11	7	19	.151

THIRD TEAM

Pos.	Name	AVG	OBP	SLG	AB	R	H	HR	RBI	BB	SO	SB
C	Michael Carico, Davidson	.406	.559	.843	197	71	80	21	57	46	35	3
1B	Tyler Locklear, Virginia Commonwealth	.402	.542	.799	224	77	90	20	78	47	25	6
2B	Hogan Windish, UNC Greensboro	.370	.485	.681	216	54	80	16	60	40	42	9
3B	Jake Gelof, Virginia	.377	.477	.764	212	65	80	21	81	41	49	3
SS	Zach Neto, Campbell	.407	.514	.769	199	65	81	15	50	39	19	19
OF	Enrique Bradfield, Vamderbilt	.317	.415	.498	243	69	77	8	36	41	40	46
OF	Vance Honeycutt, North Carolina	.296	.409	.672	247	66	73	25	57	41	90	29
OF	Brock Jones, Stanford	.324	.451	.664	253	78	82	21	57	55	78	16
DH	Tanner Schobel, Virginia Tech	.362	.445	.689	235	68	85	19	74	35	40	7
UTL	Shermar Page, Grambling State	.351	.457	.614	114	31	40	3	28	21	19	1

Pos.	Name	W	L	ERA	G	CG	SV	IP	H	BB	SO	AVG
SP	Jake Bennett, Oklahoma	10	4	3.69	20	0	1	117	106	22	133	.236
SP	Dylan DeLucia, Mississippi	8	2	3.68	21	2	1	95	87	26	105	.238
SP	Thomas Harrington, Campbell	12	2	2.53	15	0	0	93	69	18	111	.204
SP	Jason Savacool, Maryland	8	3	2.93	17	0	0	108	84	28	123	.213
RP	Ben Ferrer, Oregon State	4	0	1.82	23	0	2	59	36	14	75	.176
RP	William Privette, College of Charleston	3	1	0.91	25	0	12	59	31	15	80	.148
UTL	Shermar Page, Grambling State	8	5	2.60	15	5	0	104	72	34	142	.193

country. Second baseman Peyton Chatagnier was one of the best sparkplugs.

The Ole Miss fan base and many college baseball fans around the country fell in love with them because of the way they played and the way, when given half a chance by the selection committee, they capitalized on the opportunity.

It's a story Bianco can tell forever. And he won't be the only one. Omaha has a way of turning the fantastical into reality. The 2022 Rebels are the latest storybook to find a fitting conclusion in Middle America.

Transfers Are Now A Big Deal

Everywhere you looked through during the CWS, there were transfers coming through in big spots.

Oklahoma closer Trevin Michael, who arrived in Norman from Lamar in the offseason, threw a combined 6.2 scoreless innings in three Sooners wins. Notre Dame lefthander John Michael Bertrand, who began his career at Furman, tossed a gem in the team's opening win against Texas.

Chris Lanzilli, originally from Wake Forest, and Michael Turner, who began his career at Kent State, combined for six hits in Arkansas' blowout win over Stanford, and Lanzilli had three home runs in Arkansas' first four games in Omaha. Lefthander Tommy Sheehan, who came over from Notre Dame, got important outs for Auburn in a win against Stanford, and the Tigers also had the most prominent transfer in the field in first baseman Sonny DiChiara, who came from Samford.

All eight teams in Omaha have at least one transfer playing a role, and most of the teams here count transfers among the most important players on the roster.

Some of these teams used the transfer portal in a pretty traditional way, to add a finishing piece or to fill an immediate need.

With the departure of third baseman Cam Williams via the draft after last season, Texas had a need at the position and was able to fill it with Skyler Messinger from Kansas. At Oklahoma, Jason Ruffcorn and Luke Taggart, two top relievers, had to be replaced, so the Sooners went out and got Michael.

"With Michael Turner, we did a lot of evaluating of his catching to see if he could catch first. And it was all done with the computer, just watching pitches. How did he catch? We graded him out really high," said Arkansas coach Dave Van Horn. "(We) made a few phone calls and did a couple Zoom calls with him and his parents. And he told me basically, I remember, he told me 'you just give me a chance,' because people weren't beating his door down to take him. And that was a pretty good move by us taking him."

Texas A&M, however, shopped the entire store in the transfer portal in a way that few teams did.

Recall that in 2021, Texas A&M didn't just miss the NCAA Tournament but also missed the SEC Tournament. To be better in 2022, it needed a quick infusion of talent and upon coming over from Texas Christian, coach Jim Schlossnagle wasted little time looking toward the portal to get it.

As a result, the Aggies arrived in Omaha with four starting position players—first baseman Jack Moss, left fielder Dylan Rock, catcher Troy Claunch and shortstop Kole Kaler—from the transfer portal, plus the team leader in strikeouts on the mound, Micah Dallas, and their most trusted reliever, Jacob Palisch.

COLLEGE WORLD SERIES

STANDINGS

Bracket One	W	L
Oklahoma	3	0
Texas A&M	2	2
Notre Dame	1	2
Texas	0	2

Bracket Two	W	L
Mississippi	3	1
Arkansas	3	2
Auburn	1	2
Stanford	0	2

CWS FINALS (BEST OF THREE)

June 25: Mississippi 10, Oklahoma 3
June 26: Mississippi 4, Oklahoma 2

ALL-TOURNAMENT TEAM

C: Michael Turner, Arkansas. **1B:** Tim Elko, Mississippi. **2B**: Jared Miller, Notre Dame. **3B**: Justin Bench, Mississippi. **SS**: Peyton Graham, Oklahoma. **OF**: Kevin Graham, Mississippi; Tanner Tredaway, Oklahoma; Calvin Harris, Mississippi. DH: Kemp Alderman, Mississippi. **P**: *Dylan DeLucia, Mississippi; Cade Horton, Oklahoma.

*Named Most Outstanding Player.

BATTING

(Minimum 2.5 PA per team game)

Player	AVG	R	H	2B	3B	HR	RBI	SB
Adam Crampton-STAN	.667	0	4	2	0	0	1	0
Michael Turner-ARK	.455	2	10	2	0	0	5	0
Jared Miller-ND	.455	1	5	2	0	1	1	0
Calvin Harris-OM	.400	5	8	2	0	2	6	1
Jordan Thompson-TAMU	.400	5	4	1	0	1	5	2
Carter Putz-ND	.385	2	5	0	0	1	2	0
Austin Bost-TAMU	.375	1	6	3	0	1	2	0
Chris Lanzilli-ARK	.364	5	8	0	0	3	7	0
Peyton Stovall-ARK	.360	5	9	1	0	1	10	0
Kevin Graham-OM	.360	4	9	2	0	1	5	1

PITCHING

(Minimum 1 IP per team game)

Pitcher	W-L	ERA	G	SV	IP	H	BB	SO
Drew Dowd-STAN	0-0	0.00	1	0	4	3	1	6
Will Mercer-ND	0-0	0.00	1	0	4	1	1	4
Luke Harrison-UT	0-0	0.00	1	0	2	1	2	0
Dylan DeLucia-OM	2-0	0.54	2	0	17	8	0	17
Jacob Palisch-TAMU	0-0	1.08	2	0	8	4	3	13
Will McEntire-ARK	1-0	1.29	1	0	7	3	1	9
Hagen Smith-ARK	1-0	1.80	1	0	5	2	4	8
Micah Dallas-TAMU	1-0	1.80	1	0	5	6	2	3
Tristan Stevens-UT	0-0	1.93	1	0	5	2	1	2
Hunter Elliott-OM	1-0	2.08	2	0	13	9	4	10

REGIONALS

JUNE 3-JUNE 6

64 teams, 16 four-team, double-elimination tournaments. Winners advance to super regionals.

KNOXVILLE

Host: Tennessee (No. 1 national seed).
Participants: No. 1 Tennessee (52-7), No. 2 Georgia Tech (34-22), No. 3 Campbell (40-17), No. 4 Alabama State (34-23).
Champion: Tennessee (3-0).
Runner-up: Georgia Tech (2-2).
Outstanding player: Jorel Ortega, DH, Tennessee.

STANFORD, CALIF.

Host: Stanford (No. 2 national seed).
Participants: No. 1 Stanford (41-14), No. 2 Texas State (45-12), No. 3 UC Santa Barbara (43-12), No. 4 Binghamton (22-28).
Champion: Stanford (4-1).
Runner-up: Texas State (2-2).
Outstanding player: Eddie Park, OF, Stanford.

CORVALLIS, ORE.

Host: Oregon State (No. 3 national seed).
Participants: No. 1 Oregon State (44-15), No. 2 Vanderbilt (36-21), No. 3 San Diego (36-18), No. 4 New Mexico State (24-32).
Champion: Oregon State (3-1).
Runner-up: Vanderbilt (3-2).
Outstanding player: Spencer Jones, OF, Vanderbilt.

BLACKSBURG, VA.

Host: Virginia Tech (No. 4 national seed).
Participants: No. 1 Virginia Tech (41-12), No. 2 Gonzaga (36-17), No. 3 Columbia (30-16), No. 4 Wright State (30-25).
Champion: Virginia Tech (3-0).
Runner-up: Columbia (2-2).
Outstanding player: Gavin Cross, OF, Virginia Tech.

COLLEGE STATION, TEXAS

Host: Texas A&M (No. 5 national seed).
Participants: No. 1 Texas A&M (37-18), No. 2 Texas Christian (36-20), No. 3 Louisiana-Lafayette (36-21), No. 4 Oral Roberts (38-18).
Champion: Texas A&M (3-0).
Runner-up: TCU (2-2).
Outstanding player: Jack Moss, 1B, Texas A&M.

CORAL GABLES, FLA.

Host: Miami (No. 6 national seed).
Participants: No. 1 Miami (39-18), No. 2 Arizona (37-23), No. 3 Mississippi (32-22), No. 4 Canisius (29-23).
Champion: Ole Miss (3-0).
Runner-up: Arizona (2-2).
Outstanding player: Tim Elko, 1B, Ole Miss.

STILLWATER, OKLA.

Host: Oklahoma State (No. 7 national seed).
Participants: No. 1 Oklahoma State 39-20), No. 2 Arkansas (38-18), No. 3 Grand Canyon (41-19), No. 4 Missouri State (30-27).
Champion: Arkansas (3-1).
Runner-up: Oklahoma State (3-2).
Outstanding player: Michael Turner, C, Arkansas.

GREENVILLE, N.C.

Host: East Carolina (No. 8 national seed).
Participants: No. 1 East Carolina (42-18), No. 2 Virginia (38-17), No. 3 Coastal Carolina (36-18-1), No. 4 Coppin State (24-28).
Champion: East Carolina (3-1).
Runner-up: Coastal Carolina (3-2).
Outstanding player: Bryson Worrell, OF, East Carolina.

AUSTIN

Host: Texas (No. 9 national seed).
Participants: No. 1 Texas (42-19), No. 2 Louisiana Tech (42-19), No. 3 Dallas Baptist (34-22-1), No. 4 Air Force (30-27).
Champion: Texas (3-0).
Runner-up: Air Force (2-2).
Outstanding player: Skyler Messenger, 3B, Texas.

CHAPEL HILL, N.C.

Host: North Carolina (No. 10 national seed).
Participants: No. 1 North Carolina (38-19), No. 2 Georgia (35-21), No. 3 Virginia Commonwealth (40-18), No. 4 Hofstra (30-21).
Champion: North Carolina (4-1).
Runner-up: VCU (2-2).
Outstanding player: Mikey Madej, OF, North Carolina.

HATTIESBURG, MISS.

Host: Southern Mississippi (No. 11 national seed).
Participants: No. 1 Southern Miss (43-16), No. 2 Louisiana State (38-20), No. 3 Kennesaw State (35-26), No. 4 Army (31-23).
Champion: Southern Miss (4-1).
Runner-up: LSU (2-2).
Outstanding player: Christopher Sargent, 1B, Southern Miss.

LOUISVILLE

Host: Louisville (No. 12 national seed).
Participants: No. 1 Louisville (38-18-1), No. 2 Oregon (35-23), No. 3 Michigan (32-26), No. 4 Southeast Missouri State (37-20).
Champion: Louisville (4-1).
Runner-up: Michigan (2-2).
Outstanding player: Cam Masterman, OF, Louisville.

GAINESVILLE, FLA.

Host: Florida (No. 13 national seed).
Participants: No. 1 Florida (39-22), No. 2 Oklahoma (37-20), No. 3 Liberty (37-21), No. 4 Central Michigan (42-17).
Champion: Oklahoma (3-1).
Runner-up: Florida (3-2).
Outstanding player: Kendall Pettis, OF, Oklahoma.

AUBURN, ALA.

Host: Auburn (No. 14 national seed).
Participants: No. 1 Auburn (37-19), No. 2 UCLA (38-22), No. 3 Florida State (33-23), No. 4 Southeastern Louisiana (30-29).
Champion: Auburn (3-0).
Runner-up: UCLA (2-2).
Outstanding player: Sonny DiChiara, 1B, Auburn.

COLLEGE PARK, MD.

Host: Maryland (No. 15 national seed).
Participants: No. 1 Maryland (45-12), No. 2 Wake Forest (40-17-1), No. 3 Connecticut (46-13), No. 4 Long Island (37-19).
Champion: UConn (3-1).
Runner-up: Maryland (3-2).
Outstanding player: Matt Donlan, C, UConn.

STATESBORO, GA.

Host: Georgia Southern (No. 16 national seed).
Participants: No. 1 Georgia Southern (40-18), No. 2 Notre Dame (35-14), No. 3 Texas Tech (37-20), No. 4 UNC Greensboro (34-28).
Champion: Notre Dame (3-0).
Runner-up: Texas Tech (2-2).
Outstanding player: John Michael Bertrand, SP, Notre Dame.

SUPER REGIONALS

JUNE 10-12

16 teams, best-of-three series.
Winners advance to College World Series.

NOTRE DAME AT TENNESSEE

Site: Knoxville, Tenn.
Notre Dame wins, 2-1, advances to CWS.

CONNECTICUT AT STANFORD

Site: Stanford, Calif.
Stanford wins, 2-1, advances to CWS.

AUBURN AT OREGON STATE

Site: Corvallis, Ore.
Auburn wins, 2-1, advances to CWS.

OKLAHOMA AT VIRGINIA TECH

Site: Blacksburg, Va.
Oklahoma wins, 2-1, advances to CWS.

LOUISVILLE AT TEXAS A&M

Site: College Station, Texas.
Texas A&M wins, 2-0, advances to CWS.

MISSISSIPPI AT SOUTHERN MISSISSIPPI

Site: Hattiesburg, Miss.
Ole Miss wins, 2-0, advances to CWS.

ARKANSAS AT NORTH CAROLINA

Site: Chapel Hill, N.C.
Arkansas wins, 2-0, advances to CWS.

TEXAS AT EAST CAROLINA

Site: Greenville, N.C.
Texas wins, 2-1, advances to CWS.

Ivan The Tremendous

PLAYER OF THE YEAR

BY JOE HEALY

There are myriad reasons why Texas first baseman Ivan Melendez's 2022 season shouldn't have happened the way it did, beginning with the fact that it's unreasonable to expect any player, no matter how talented, to do what he did.

It certainly wasn't the expectation upon his arrival in Austin.

"I can just look back and see him hanging out in our dugout, a little insecure and just hoping that he fits into the program and that he can be a contributor," Texas coach David Pierce said. "I never saw this coming."

EDDIE KELLY

Ivan Melendez

This, as it turns out, is arguably the best offensive season any player has had since college baseball switched to the current BBCOR bats for the 2011 season.

Melendez hit .387/.508/.863 with 32 home runs and 94 RBIs. The 6-foot-3, 225-pound righthanded hitter won the triple crown in the Big 12 Conference and was the runaway leader in homers and RBIs nationally.

He is also our pick for College Player of the Year.

When you start to talk about the early indications Melendez showed that he could be a special player, the conversation begins with his game-changing power.

"You started seeing signs of it once we got into (his first) spring. And his power is different," Pierce said. "You have guys who have 5 o'clock power (in batting practice) and the game starts at 6:30. He's not a five o'clock guy. He's a gamer.

"And there's guys who have that power that doesn't equate in the game—and he has game power. He has the knack of staying through the baseball as well as anybody (we've) had."

Melendez's numbers are eye-popping, but so is his consistency. After a 3-for-5 game against Texas State on March 9, his average jumped from .298 to .327 and it never again dipped below .300. In fact, his average was actually above .400 from April 24 until June 11. For much of that time, it looked like he might challenge for the national triple crown.

Melendez had a really nice year in 2021, hitting .319/.438/.603 with 13 homers and 51 RBIs, but this season was something on an entirely different level.

Maybe he was a pretty straightforward power hitter in his first season in Austin in 2021. But this season, the 22-year-old redshirt junior showed he was a complete hitter.

He hit near .400. After having nearly twice as many strikeouts as walks last season, he had more walks (52) than strikeouts (48) this time around. He hits the ball to all fields with authority, and he's willing to put in the work to be someone who's not just bullying balls over the fence.

PREVIOUS WINNERS

1982: Jeff Ledbetter, OF/LHP Florida St.
1983: Dave Magadan, 1B, Alabama
1984: Oddibe McDowell, OF, Arizona St.
1985: Pete Incaviglia, OF, Oklahoma State
1986: Casey Close, OF, Michigan
1987: Robin Ventura, 3B, Oklahoma State
1988: John Olerund, 1B/LHP, Washington St.
1989: Ben McDonald, RHP, Louisiana State
1990: Mike Kelly, OF, Arizona State
1991: David McCarthy, 1B, Stanford
1992: Phil Nevin, 3B, Cal State Fullerton
1993: Brooks Kieschnick, DH/RHP, Texas
1994: Jason Varitek, C, Georgia Tech
1995: Todd Helton, 1B/LHP, Tennessee
1996: Kris Benson, RHP, Clemson
1997: J.D. Drew, OF, Florida State
1998: Jeff Austin, RHP, Stanford
1999: Jason Jennings, RHP, Baylor
2000: Mark Teixeira, 3B, Georgia Tech
2001: Mark Prior, RHP, S. California
2002: Khalil Greene, SS, Clemson
2003: Rickie Weeks, 2B, Southern
2004: Jered Weaver, RHP, Long Beach St.
2005: Alex Gordon, 3B, Nebraska
2006: Andrew Miller, LHP, North Carolina
2007: David Price, LHP, Vanderbilt
2008: Buster Posey, C/RHP, Florida State
2009: Stephen Strasburg, RHP, San Diego St.
2010: Anthony Rendon, 3B, Rice
2011: Trevor Bauer, RHP, UCLA
2012: Mike Zunino, C, Florida
2013: Kris Bryant, 3B, San Diego
2014: A.J. Reed, 1B/LHP, Kentucky
2015: Andrew Benintendi, OF, Arkansas
2016: Klye Lewis, OF, Mercer
2017: Brendan McKay, LHP/1B, Louisville
2018: Brady Singer, RHP, Florida
2019: Adley Rutschman, C, Oregon State
2021: Kumar Rocker, RHP, Vanderbilt

Mike Bianco Reaches The Mountaintop

COACH OF THE YEAR

BY TEDDY CAHILL

Mike Bianco has been a coach for 32 years and a head coach for 25 years, the last 22 at Mississippi. Over more than three decades, Bianco had seen just about everything the game has to offer. But then the 2022 season delivered a whole new challenge for him and the Rebels.

SAMUEL LEWIS/ICON SPORTSWIRE VIA GETTY IMAGES
Mike Bianco

Ole Miss ranked No. 9 in the Preseason Top 25. It returned what was expected to be one of the best lineups in the country and got off to a hot start, ascending to the top of the rankings in mid-March. A top-10 showdown against Tennessee in Swayze Field awaited and it was with that series that the season changed.

Tennessee swept Ole Miss in Oxford, outscoring the Rebels 26-7 on the weekend. It was the Rebels' first series loss of the season and by the end of April, they had lost five of their last six SEC series and four straight. They were 7-14 in conference play, had long since dropped out of the Top 25 and had all but used up their margin for error for an at-large bid in the NCAA Tournament.

Ole Miss didn't give in. It swept Missouri and then Louisiana State. Still, the Rebels were on the bubble of the NCAA Tournament on Selection Monday and waited anxiously to learn their fate. The selection committee listed Ole Miss as one of the last four teams in the field, giving the Rebels an opening. It was all they needed. They swept through regionals and super regionals to advance to the College World Series for the first time since 2014.

In Omaha, they continued to roll. Ole Miss beat Auburn and Arkansas to advance to the finals, where it met Oklahoma. As they had with every other team they met in the postseason, the Rebels summarily beat the Sooners. They swept the best-of-three series, giving Ole Miss its first national championship.

Fittingly, the 2022 team required one of Bianco's best coaching efforts yet. These Rebels had a little bit of everything. They had elite players like shortstop Jacob Gonzalez, a likely top-10 pick next year, and program greats like first baseman Tim Elko and outfielder Kevin Graham. They had in-season development, as the pitching staff rounded into form in the second half behind the 1-2 punch of Dylan DeLucia and Hunter Elliott, both members of last year's recruiting class who did not start the season in the rotation. They required the know-how to keep the team together through the difficult times, the motivation to help them dig out of the slump and the in-game tactics to help them through the NCAA Tournament. For all of his efforts this season, Bianco is the Baseball America 2022 Coach of the Year.

PREVIOUS WINNERS

1982: Gene Stephenson, Wichita State
1983: Barry Shollenberger, Alabama
1984: Augie Garrido, Cal State Fullerton
1985: Ron Polk, Mississippi State
1986: Skip Bertman, LSU/Dave Snow, LMU
1987: Mark Marquess, Stanford
1988: Jim Brock, Arizona State
1989: Dave Snow, Long Beach State
1990: Steve Webber, Georgia
1991: Jim Hendry, Creighton
1992: Andy Lopez, Pepperdine
1993: Gene Stephenson, Wichita State
1994: Jim Morris, Miami
1995: Pat Murphy, Arizona State
1996: Skip Bertman, Louisiana State
1997: Jim Wells, Alabama
1998: Pat Murphy, Arizona State
1999: Wayne Graham, Rice
2000: Ray Tanner, South Carolina
2001: Dave Van Horn, Nebraska
2002: Augie Garrido, Texas
2003: George Horton, Cal State Fullerton
2004: David Perno, Georgia
2005: Rick Jones, Tulane
2006: Pat Casey, Oregon State
2007: Dave Serrano, UC Irvine
2008: Mike Fox, North Carolina
2009: Paul Mainieri, Louisiana State
2010: Ray Tanner, South Carolina
2011: Kevin O'Sullivan, Florida
2012: Mike Martin, Florida State
2013: John Savage, UCLA
2014: Tim Corbin, Vanderbilt
2015: Brian O'Connor, Virginia
2016: Jim Schlossnagle, Texas Christian
2017: Dan McDonnell, Louisville
2018: David Pierce, Texas
2019: Mike Martin, Florida State
2021: Chris Lemonis, Mississippi State

White Sets Homer Record

FRESHMAN OF THE YEAR

BY J.J. COOPER

The legend of Tommy White didn't take long to sweep the nation.

In his first game at North Carolina State, White hit three home runs, including a grand slam.

That's great, kid. Now what can you do for an encore?

In the next game he homered again. And in Sunday's third game of the Wolfpack season, he homered again.

BRIAN WESTERHOLT/FOUR SEAM IMAGES

Tommy White

Three games, five home runs. And before he'd even played his first midweek game, Tommy White was know as "Tommy Tanks."

So it was an impressive first weekend. But many freshman have had enjoyed one great weekend. The next weekend White homered on Friday, Saturday and Sunday again. Well, he didn't just homer on Friday night. He hit two. So eight games into the season, he had nine home runs.

In the first two weeks of the season, he hit more home runs than UC Riverside did all year.

White did slow down after that. After all, no one can keep up that pace, but he continued to be one of the nation's best power hitters all season.

White finished the year with 27 home runs, breaking the NCAA Division I freshman record. He topped the 26 that Georgia Southern's Todd Greene hit in 1990. He finished tied for third most home runs in the country in 2022.

White wasn't just a slugger. He also hit .362, second best on the Wolfpack team. His 178 total bases were also among the top 10 in the nation for Division I hitters. He showed he could hit for average and power, and that he could get as hot as any hitter can be.

PREVIOUS

1992: Todd Walker, 2B, Louisiana State
1993: Brett Laxton, RHP, Louisiana State
1994: R.A. Dickey, RHP, Tennessee
1995: Kyle Peterson, RHP, Stanford
1996: Pat Burrell, 3B, Miami
1997: Brian Roberts, SS, North Carolina
1998: Xavier Nady, 2B, California
1999: James Jurries, 2B, Tulane
2000: Kevin Howard, 3B, Miami
2001: Michael Aubrey, OF/LHP, Texas
2002: Stephen Drew, SS, Florida State
2003: Ryan Braun, SS, Miami
2004: Wade LeBlanc, LHP, Alabama
2005: Joe Savery, LHP, Rice
2006: Pedro Alvarez, 3B, Vanderbilt
2007: Dustin Ackley, 1B, North Carolina
2008: Chris Hernandez, LHP, Miami
2009: Anthony Rendon, 3B, Rice
2010: Matt Purke, LHP, Texas Christian
2011: Colin Moran, 3B, North Carolina
2012: Carlos Rodon, LHP, N.C. State
2013: Alex Bregman, SS, Louisiana State
2014: Zack Collins, C, Miami
2015: Brendan McKay, LHP/1B, Louisville
2016: Seth Beer, OF, Clemson
2017: Matt Wallner, OF/RHP, Southern Miss
2018: Kevin Abel, RHP, Oregon State
2019: Kumar Rocker, RHP, Vanderbilt
2021: Jack Leiter, RHP, Vanderbilt
Full list of winners can be found at BaseballAmerica.com/Stories/Baseball-America-Awards

FRESHMAN ALL-AMERICA TEAMS

FIRST TEAM

Pos.		AVG	OBP	SLG	HR	RBI	SB
C	Ryan Stafford, Cal Poly	.321	.384	.431	3	33	3
1B	Nick Kurtz, Wake Forest	.338	.471	.637	15	56	2
2B	Travis Bazzana, Oregon State	.306	.425	.478	6	44	14
3B	Carson DeMartini, Virginia Tech	.341	.452	.659	15	50	5
SS	Cody Schrier, UCLA	.298	.383	.492	9	42	11
OF	Keaton Anthony, Iowa	.361	.455	.678	14	55	0
OF	Vance Honeycutt, North Carolina	.296	.409	.672	25	57	29
OF	Casey Sauce, Virginia	.360	.438	.591	7	46	6
DH	Tommy White, NC State	.362	.425	.757	27	74	1
UT	Cade Horton, Oklahoma	.234	.323	.324	1	14	8

		W	L	ERA	SV	IP	SO
SP	Drew Beam, Tennessee	8	1	2.72	0	76	62
SP	Chase Burns, Tennessee	8	2	2.91	0	80	103
SP	Hunter Elliott, Mississippi	5	3	2.70	0	80	102
SP	Carter Holton, Vanderbilt	8	4	3.14	0	80	97
SP	Jack Findlay, Notre Dame	6	2	2.17	4	50	54
RP	Alonzo Tredwell, UCLA	4	1	2.11	6	47	62
RP	Cade Horton, Oklahoma	5	2	4.86	0	54	64

SECOND TEAM

C: Owen Carapoletti, Georgetown. **1B:** Donovan Cash, Kennesaw State. **2B:** Roc Riggio, Oklahoma State. **3B:** Cade McGee, Gonzaga. **SS:** Griff O'Ferrall, Virginia. **OF:** Cam Fisher, Charlotte; Tommy Hawke, Wake Forest; Kennedy Jones, UNC Greensboro. **DH:** Hunter Hines, Mississippi State. **UT:** Braden Montgomery, Stanford. **SP:** Ryan Feczko, Davidson; Drue Hackenburg, Virginia Tech; Blake Morgan, Old Dominion; Juaron Watts-Brown, Long Beach State. **RP:** AJ Causey, Jacksonville State; Jay Woolfolk, Virginia. **UT:** Braden Montgomery, Stanford.

NCAA DIVISION I LEADERS

HITTING (MINIMUM 140 AT-BATS)

BATTING AVERAGE

Rk.	Player, Team	Class	AVG	OBP	SLG	AB	H	2B	3B	HR	RBI	BB	SO	SB
1.	Chandler Simpson, Georgia Tech	So	.433	.517	.506	203	88	8	3	1	25	31	16	27
2.	Drew Cowley, Oregon	Jr	.424	.616	.506	151	64	16	2	3	29	21	30	2
3.	Sam Kulasingam, Air Force	So	.411	.683	.487	265	109	26	5	12	64	32	33	6
4.	Brayden Johnson, Prairie View	Jr	.410	.602	.476	161	66	12	2	5	33	15	20	4
5.	John Garcia, Grambling	So	.409	.679	.515	193	79	18	2	10	67	26	47	4
6.	Dom Toso, Richmond	Sr	.408	.624	.462	218	89	22	2	7	62	16	22	0
7.	Zach Neto, Campbell	So	.407	.769	.514	199	81	23	2	15	50	39	19	19
8.	Trey Paige, Delaware St.	So	.407	.756	.507	172	70	15	3	13	49	36	35	7
9.	Guy Lipscomb, Belmont	So	.406	.548	.484	217	88	13	3	4	42	29	18	42
10.	Michael Carico, Davidson	So	.406	.843	.559	197	80	21	1	21	57	46	35	3
11.	Ethan Groff, Tulane	So	.404	.709	.503	151	61	15	2	9	35	24	26	7
12.	Tyler Locklear, VCU	So	.402	.799	.542	224	90	25	2	20	78	47	25	6
13.	Tyler Cox, Dartmouth	So	.402	.484	.452	184	74	10	1	1	40	17	12	11
14.	Carlos Contreras, Sam Houston	Jr	.400	.713	.468	230	92	18	6	14	89	27	28	2
15.	Jeremy Gaines, Texas Southern	Sr	.400	.611	.502	175	70	16	3	5	45	27	17	27
16.	Max Grant, Canisius	So	.398	.646	.489	226	90	14	6	10	53	30	39	7
17.	Ivan Melendez, Texas	Jr	.396	.887	.516	240	95	18	2	32	94	52	48	1
18.	Henry Zeisler, UNLV	Sr	.396	.693	.494	225	89	17	4	14	73	33	57	1
19.	Maui Ahuna, Kansas	So	.396	.634	.479	202	80	16	4	8	48	28	49	13
20.	David Martin, California Baptist	So	.395	.542	.506	190	75	10	0	6	43	32	22	4
21.	Ryan Ignoffo, Eastern Ill.	Jr	.395	.708	.436	185	73	16	0	14	58	16	22	7
22.	Jackson Feltner, Morehead St.	So	.393	.706	.478	214	84	17	1	16	51	26	42	1
23.	Alejandro Figueredo, FGCU	Jr	.392	.659	.476	232	91	21	1	13	62	36	36	0
24.	Sonny DiChiara, Auburn	Sr	.392	.809	.560	194	76	15	0	22	59	68	51	0
25.	Connor O'Brien, Bradley	Jr	.392	.624	.456	189	74	14	0	10	44	22	48	3
26.	Josh Hatcher, Kennesaw St.	Sr	.391	.667	.452	279	109	26	3	15	59	24	39	11
27.	Jack Moss, Texas A&M	So	.391	.538	.448	253	99	17	1	6	47	27	41	8
28.	Sam Ruta, Army West Point	So	.390	.626	.493	187	73	15	4	7	36	38	44	6
29.	Cole Carrigg, San Diego St.	So	.388	.509	.426	214	83	15	1	3	40	12	28	19
30.	Ty Hill, Jackson St.	Jr	.388	.568	.498	206	80	20	4	3	41	31	32	6
31.	Alan Roden, Creighton	So	.387	.598	.492	194	75	25	2	4	46	29	8	9
32.	Myles Nicholson, UMBC	Sr	.387	.538	.470	186	72	11	4	3	29	19	16	29
33.	Chad Castillo, California Baptist	Jr	.386	.635	.442	233	90	23	1	11	69	19	56	13
34.	David McCabe, Charlotte	So	.386	.784	.513	153	59	13	0	16	52	40	28	4
35.	Nick Cimillo, Rutgers	Jr	.385	.707	.492	205	79	18	0	16	52	39	36	1
36.	Matt Woods, Bryant	Sr	.384	.635	.458	219	84	17	7	8	45	21	43	9
37.	Miles Simington, South Alabama	Sr	.383	.579	.452	214	82	15	3	7	53	20	21	5
38.	Brett Callahan, Saint Joseph's	So	.383	.587	.482	206	79	12	3	8	34	30	37	23
39.	Wyatt Henseler, Penn	So	.383	.697	.487	188	72	17	0	14	53	23	39	0
40.	Rylan Charles, UNLV	So	.382	.529	.452	259	99	16	2	6	46	26	31	7
41.	Canyon McWilliams, Little Rock	Sr	.382	.634	.445	191	73	14	2	10	50	18	29	5
42.	Andrew Jenkins, Georgia Tech	So	.381	.679	.440	252	96	22	1	17	70	21	64	5
43.	Zach Morgan, Fresno St.	Jr	.381	.592	.454	218	83	20	1	8	41	25	17	2
44.	David Bermudez, Manhattan	Sr	.380	.668	.449	208	79	18	0	14	52	22	21	6
45.	Colin Kasperbauer, Ohio	Sr	.380	.572	.465	187	71	19	4	3	48	20	32	4
46.	Tommy Hawke, Wake Forest	Fr	.380	.465	.502	187	71	8	1	2	20	43	38	8
47.	Brian Ellis, FGCU	Jr	.379	.562	.505	235	89	25	0	6	44	40	43	1
48.	Lawson Hill, Wofford	Sr	.379	.496	.456	224	85	18	1	2	39	30	13	12
49.	Juan Colato, Grand Canyon	Sr	.379	.589	.417	219	83	16	3	8	51	13	25	6
50.	Matt Wood, Penn St.	Jr	.379	.667	.480	198	75	15	3	12	53	36	26	5
51.	Luke Harper, North Ala.	Sr	.379	.497	.511	177	67	16	1	1	22	46	25	15
52.	Robert Hamchuk, San Jose St.	So	.378	.582	.437	249	94	17	2	10	39	22	47	2
53.	Dalton Shuffield, Texas St.	Sr	.378	.668	.444	238	90	20	5	13	48	28	32	16
54.	Payton Harden, McNeese	Jr	.378	.502	.444	225	85	14	4	2	40	27	54	26
55.	Brandon Pimentel, UTRGV	Jr	.377	.619	.427	236	89	17	2	12	47	16	34	2
56.	Jake Gelof, Virginia	So	.377	.764	.477	212	80	15	2	21	81	41	49	3
57.	Matt Coutney, Old Dominion	Sr	.376	.808	.473	229	86	18	0	27	70	38	54	3
58.	Mario Camilletti, Central Mich.	Sr	.376	.563	.498	229	86	20	1	7	51	54	26	4
59.	Murphy Stehly, Texas	Sr	.375	.680	.434	269	101	23	1	19	61	17	40	8
60.	Jack Hurley, Virginia Tech	So	.375	.664	.452	232	87	23	1	14	55	32	51	10
61.	Carson Roccaforte, Louisiana	So	.374	.671	.435	219	82	11	3	16	68	26	34	25
62.	Cameron Jones, Georgia St.	So	.374	.512	.429	211	79	14	0	5	31	15	31	12
63.	Tanner Treadaway, Oklahoma	Sr	.373	.567	.416	263	98	18	3	9	61	17	27	23
64.	Justin Boyd, Oregon St.	So	.373	.577	.490	241	90	14	4	9	53	52	58	24
65.	Caleb Ricketts, San Diego	Jr	.373	.658	.423	228	85	13	2	16	55	14	29	0
66.	Brad Burckel, McNeese	Jr	.373	.618	.459	217	81	17	3	10	44	27	50	18

67. Skyler Messinger, Texas	Sr	.372	.574	.422	242	90	14	1	11	59	18	56	1
68. Jason Hinchman, Tennessee Tech	Sr	.372	.758	.470	231	86	11	0	26	73	41	62	1
69. Brendan Hueth, Saint Joseph's	Sr	.372	.581	.440	215	80	24	3	5	54	27	25	13
70. Tyrese Clayborne, Texas Southern	Sr	.372	.589	.449	180	67	12	6	5	36	18	30	34
71. Nate Furman, Charlotte	So	.371	.474	.502	232	86	14	2	2	23	49	26	21
72. Dominic Keegan, Vanderbilt	Sr	.371	.646	.458	229	85	17	2	14	67	39	51	2
73. Josh Johnson, Kent St.	Jr	.371	.629	.446	159	59	10	2	9	43	18	30	14
74. Spencer Jones, Vanderbilt	Jr	.370	.643	.460	230	85	21	3	12	60	32	64	14
75. Hogan Windish, UNC Greensboro	Jr	.370	.681	.485	216	80	19	0	16	60	40	42	8
76. Amani Larry, New Orleans	So	.370	.578	.477	211	78	13	2	9	56	32	29	16
77. Jacob Berry, LSU	So	.370	.630	.464	208	77	9	0	15	48	27	22	0
78. Brett Cain, UTRGV	Sr	.370	.614	.450	189	70	16	3	8	41	21	30	4
79. Christian Hall, UAB	Jr	.370	.614	.443	189	70	9	2	11	48	26	37	0
80. Nolan Schanuel, Fla. Atlantic	So	.369	.658	.477	225	83	17	0	16	56	39	22	11
81. Justin Wishkoski, Sam Houston	Jr	.369	.514	.455	222	82	17	3	3	49	24	20	3
82. Max Wagner, Clemson	So	.369	.852	.496	203	75	15	1	27	76	45	51	2
83. Tommy Barth, ETSU	Fr	.369	.585	.434	195	72	16	4	6	38	24	26	1
84. Nick Wang, Holy Cross	Fr	.369	.574	.468	141	52	18	1	3	21	25	29	6
85. Danny DiGeorgio, Rutgers	Sr	.368	.561	.471	228	84	17	3	7	59	36	37	18
86. Alex Haba, Merrimack	Jr	.368	.558	.462	190	70	17	2	5	15	19	22	6
87. Ed Johnson, Tennessee Tech	Jr	.367	.591	.420	259	95	14	1	14	55	19	31	6
88. Kennedy Jones, UNC Greensboro	Fr	.367	.594	.420	251	92	16	4	11	73	20	42	5
89. Pierce Bennett, Wake Forest	So	.367	.533	.456	210	77	14	0	7	49	28	20	6
90. Daniel Susac, Arizona	So	.366	.582	.429	273	100	19	2	12	61	23	52	0
91. CJ Kayfus, Miami (FL)	So	.366	.525	.460	238	87	12	1	8	51	38	36	16
92. Alex Tappen, Virginia	Sr	.366	.612	.421	227	83	15	1	13	71	19	40	3
93. Mitch Moralez, Utah Valley	Sr	.366	.527	.406	224	82	14	2	6	27	10	40	6
94. Matt Higgins, Bellarmine	Sr	.366	.770	.469	213	78	20	0	22	61	34	41	15
95. Ryan Wilson, Davidson	So	.366	.571	.502	205	75	18	0	8	56	43	31	18
96. Casey Rother, Lehigh	Sr	.366	.604	.424	202	74	19	1	9	50	20	25	5
97. Sean Ross, Indiana St.	Sr	.366	.634	.429	142	52	16	2	6	34	9	31	2
98. Danny Serretti, North Carolina	Jr	.365	.567	.437	263	96	17	3	10	54	32	38	2
99. Harrison Spohn, California Baptist	Sr	.365	.546	.422	249	91	28	1	5	38	22	31	14
100. Evin Sullivan, Binghamton	Fr	.365	.562	.424	192	70	15	1	7	42	18	30	1

ON-BASE PERCENTAGE

Rank	Player, Pos., Team	OBP
1.	Michael Carico, Davidson	.559
2.	Sonny DiChiara, Auburn	.549
3.	Tyler Locklear, VCU	.542
4.	John Garcia, Grambling	.515
5.	Zach Neto, Campbell	.514
6.	Ivan Melendez, Texas	.508
7.	Trey Paige, Delaware St.	.507
8.	Taylor Young, Louisiana Tech	.506
9.	Chandler Simpson, Ga. Tech	.506
10.	Brian Ellis, FGCU	.505

SLUGGING PERCENTAGE

Rank	Player, Pos., Team	SLG
1.	Ivan Melendez, Texas	.863
2.	Max Wagner, Clemson	.852
3.	Michael Carico, Davidson	.843
4.	Luke Franzoni, Xavier	.821
5.	Matt Coutney, Old Dominion	.808
6.	Tyler Locklear, VCU	.799
7.	Sonny DiChiara, Auburn	.777
8.	Zach Neto, Campbell	.769
9.	Brett Johnson, SIUE	.765
10.	Jake Gelof, Virginia	.764

RUNS BATTED IN

Rank	Player, Pos., Team	RBI
1.	Ivan Melendez, Texas	94
2.	Carlos Contreras, Sam Houston	89
3.	Kevin Parada, Georgia Tech	88
4.	Trey Lipscomb, Tennessee	84
5.	Jacob Melton, Oregon St.	83
6.	Jake Gelof, Virginia	81
7.	Andy Garriola, Old Dominion	80
8.	Chris Alleyne, Maryland	79
-	Carter Graham, Stanford	79
10.	Luke Franzoni, Xavier	78
-	Tyler Locklear, VCU	78

HOME RUNS

Rank	Player, Pos., Team	HR
1.	Ivan Melendez, Texas	32
2.	Luke Franzoni, Xavier	29
3.	Matt Coutney, Old Dominion	27
-	Max Wagner, Clemson	27
-	Tommy White, NC State	27
6.	Jason Hinchman, Tenn. Tech	26
-	Wyatt Langford, Florida	26
-	Kevin Parada, Georgia Tech	26
9.	Andy Garriola, Old Dominion	25
-	Vance Honeycutt, North Carolina	25

DOUBLES

Rank	Player, Pos., Team	2B
1.	Josh Hatcher, Kennesaw St.	26
-	Douglas Hodo, Texas	26
-	Sam Kulasingam, Air Force	26
-	Joey Walls, UNLV	26
5.	Brian Ellis, FGCU	25
-	Matt Kirk, Eastern Mich.	25
-	Brooks Lee, Cal Poly	25
-	Tyler Locklear, VCU	25
-	Steven Rivera-Chijin, A&M-Corpus Christi	25
-	Alan Roden, Creighton	25
-	Erik Stock, UConn	25

TRIPLES

Rank	Player, Pos., Team	3B
1.	Zach Cole, Ball St.	9
2.	Gavin Cross, Virginia Tech	8
-	Gabe Vasquez, Texas Southern	8
4.	Kevin Bermudez, Lamar	7
-	Mac Bingham, Arizona	7
-	Casey Mayes, Michigan St.	7
-	Jake Slunder, Murray St.	7
-	Matt Woods, Bryant	7
-	Amir Wright, Ball St.	7
10.	14 tied	6

STOLEN BASES

Rank	Player, Pos., Team	SB
1.	Johnathon Thomas, Texas Southern	62
2.	Enrique Bradfield Jr., Vanderbilt	46
-	Jacob Humphrey, UMass Lowell	46
4.	Jason Bottari, UAlbany	44
5.	Guy Lipscomb, Belmont	42
6.	Victor Scott, West Virginia	38
7.	Robert Gallagher, UMass Lowell	37
8.	Levi Usher, Louisville	36
9.	Jack Renwick, Wofford	35
-	Justin Sierra, Fairleigh Dickinson	35

RUNS

Rank	Player, Pos., Team	R
1.	Taylor Young, Louisiana Tech	89
2.	Ryan Lasko, Rutgers	81
-	Wade Meckler, Oregon St.	81
4.	Kevin Parada, Georgia Tech	79
-	Luke Shliger, Maryland	79
6.	Brock Jones, Stanford	78
-	Dalton Shuffield, Texas St.	78
8.	Tyler Locklear, VCU	77
9.	Peyton Graham, Oklahoma	75
-	Ivan Melendez, Texas	75

HITS

Rank	Player, Pos., Team	H
1.	Josh Hatcher, Kennesaw St.	109
-	Sam Kulasingam, Air Force	109
3.	Tanner Treadaway, Oklahoma	105
4.	Jack Moss, Texas A&M	103
5.	Murphy Stehly, Texas	102
6.	Daniel Susac, Arizona	100
-	Angel Zarate, North Carolina	100
8.	Rylan Charles, UNLV	99

Rank Player, Pos., Team	
- Erik Stock, UConn	99
10. Andrew Jenkins, Georgia Tech	96
- Ivan Melendez, Texas	96

TOTAL BASES

Rank Player, Pos., Team	TB
1. Ivan Melendez, Texas	214
2. Josh Hatcher, Kennesaw St.	186
3. Matt Coutney, Old Dominion	185
4. Wyatt Langford, Florida	184
- Murphy Stehly, Texas	184
6. Kevin Parada, Georgia Tech	183
7. Sam Kulasingam, Air Force	181
8. Trey Lipscomb, Tennessee	180
9. Tyler Locklear, VCU	179
10. Peyton Graham, Oklahoma	178
- Tommy White, NC State	178

WALKS

Rank Player, Pos., Team	BB
1 Sonny DiChiara, Auburn	68
- Blake Robertson, Oklahoma	68
3 Garret Forrester, Oregon St.	64
4 Jud Fabian, Florida	62
5 Ryan Cupit, ULM	59
- Jace Jung, Texas Tech	59
- Luc Lipcius, Tennessee	59
8 Elijah Nunez, TCU	58
- Taylor Young, Louisiana Tech	58
10 Brock Jones, Stanford	55
- Jake Reinisch, Wake Forest	55

TOUGHEST TO STRIKE OUT

Rank Player, Pos., Team	AB/SO
1. Jacob Wilson, Grand Canyon	35.1
2. Alan Roden, Creighton	24.2
3. Ryan Morash, Hofstra	18.5
4. Lawson Hill, Wofford	17.2
5. David Hogarth, William & Mary	17.0
6. Nick Mistone, Saint Mary's (CA)	16.9
7. Danny Hosley, George Mason	16.4
8. Amir Wright, Ball St.	16.1
9. Tyler Cox, Dartmouth	15.3
10. Josh Kasevich, Oregon	15.3

HIT BY PITCH

Rank Player, Pos., Team	HBP
1. Rhett Rosevear, Southeastern La.	37
2. Justin McIntyre, Western Mich.	29
3. Easton Murrell, Texas Tech	27
- Cam Thompson, Purdue	27
5. Michael Carico, Davidson	26
6. Tim Borden, Georgia Tech	25
- Robert Gallagher, UMass Lowell	25
8. 7 tied,	23

SACRIFICE BUNTS

Rank Player, Pos., Team	SAC
1. Justin Simpson, Central Mich.	20
2. Tilo Skole, The Citadel	19
3. Cooper Benzin, VCU	15
- Taishi Nakawake, UC Irvine	15
- Devonta" Rhodes, Jackson St.	15
- Cameron Tissue, South Alabama	15
7. Jacob Marcos, Gardner-Webb	14
8. Christian Avant, Ga. Southern	13
- Adam Crampton, Stanford	13
- Spencer Myers, Notre Dame	13

SACRIFICE FLYS

Rank Player, Pos., Team	SF
1. Casey Dana, UConn	12
- Steven Moretto, Sacramento St.	12
3. Anthony Herron Jr., New Orleans	10
4. Josh Hood, NC State	9
- Gabe Vasquez, Texas Southern	9
6. Bryson Bloomer, Murray St.	8
- Zach Bushling, UConn	8
- Pat Caulfield, Nevada	8
- Matt Clayton, Nevada	8
- Connor Denning, Campbell	8
- Andrew Jenkins, Georgia Tech	8
- Kyle Karros, UCLA	8
- Kenny Levari, Old Dominion	8
- Leo Markotic, A&M-Corpus Christi	8
- Dylan Minghini, Lafayette	8

PITCHING (MINIMUM 40 INNINGS PITCHED)

Rk.	Pitcher, Team	Class	W	L	ERA	GS	SV	IP	H	R	ER	HR	BB	SO
1.	Cade Denton, Oral Roberts	So	4	0	0.41	0	6	44	23	4	2	1	11	55
2.	William Privette, Col. of Charleston	So	3	1	0.91	0	12	59	31	14	6	3	15	80
3.	Luke Garofalo, Central Conn. St.	So	5	1	1.26	0	3	43	25	6	6	2	14	57
4.	Jackson Kelley, Mercer	Jr	7	0	1.35	0	6	60	32	9	9	4	18	82
5.	Jonathan Brand, Miami (OH)	Sr	8	2	1.40	13	0	77	59	20	12	3	29	86
6.	Caleb Riedel, Omaha	So	4	2	1.49	13	0	60	50	12	10	4	21	65
7.	Tyler Guilfoil, Kentucky	Jr	3	1	1.59	0	6	51	27	9	9	5	17	80
8.	Tommy Steier, Creighton	Jr	4	1	1.62	1	8	56	42	11	10	3	22	48
9.	Quinn Flanagan, Arizona	Jr	5	1	1.63	1	2	50	45	16	9	2	13	49
10.	Zander Sechrist, Tennessee	So	4	0	1.67	11	0	43	27	8	8	4	7	46
11.	Blake Morgan, Old Dominion	Fr	8	0	1.69	13	0	69	57	23	13	4	8	66
12.	Ben Ferrer, Oregon St.	Jr	4	0	1.72	1	3	63	38	15	12	4	14	78
13.	Justin Honeycutt, UNC Asheville	So	4	2	1.73	2	2	52	40	17	10	2	16	36
14.	Gordon Ingebritson, UC Irvine	Sr	6	0	1.75	0	3	67	50	15	13	3	5	62
15.	Cameron Foster, McNeese	Sr	4	2	1.86	0	12	63	35	17	13	2	20	84
16.	Connor Staine, UCF	So	4	1	1.87	12	0	43	31	15	9	1	21	51
17.	Shea Sprague, Elon	Fr	6	3	1.89	10	0	62	50	19	13	6	13	41
18.	Garrett Horn, Liberty	Fr	6	1	1.93	7	0	51	30	17	11	6	24	80
19.	Jack Dallas, Lamar University	Sr	4	1	1.94	0	14	42	36	16	9	0	14	55
20.	Lance Lusk, Sam Houston	Sr	5	0	1.94	0	8	42	37	13	9	1	15	49
21.	Sam Garcia, High Point	So	5	4	1.94	8	1	60	45	20	13	2	14	58
22.	Matt Fields, Long Beach St.	Sr	3	2	1.99	0	4	41	29	11	9	1	8	39
23.	Jack Findlay, Notre Dame	Fr	6	2	1.99	8	3	45	29	12	10	4	15	51
24.	Zach Franklin, Western Caro.	Jr	5	1	2.06	6	3	57	41	15	13	2	19	70
25.	Troy Melton, San Diego St.	Jr	5	2	2.07	11	0	65	57	20	15	2	15	67
26.	Burrell Jones, McNeese	Jr	4	0	2.11	1	0	43	44	16	10	3	19	36
27.	Alonzo Tredwell, UCLA	Fr	4	1	2.11	0	6	47	33	13	11	3	6	62
28.	Wyatt Crowell, Florida St.	So	6	1	2.12	0	2	51	39	18	12	4	17	72
29.	Ryan Bourassa, South Dakota St.	Jr	2	3	2.13	0	5	42	20	17	10	3	26	64
30.	Ryan Brown, Ball St.	So	4	2	2.14	0	0	46	24	19	11	8	38	65
31.	Jordy Allard, Northeastern	Sr	4	3	2.16	2	2	50	42	13	12	4	9	58
32.	Jack Collins, Binghamton	Jr	3	2	2.17	0	5	46	28	13	11	4	12	58
33.	Camden Minacci, Wake Forest	So	2	4	2.18	0	6	45	34	17	11	6	18	59
34.	Tristan Stivors, Texas St.	Sr	7	1	2.21	1	18	61	47	18	15	6	19	86
35.	Brett Gillis, Portland	Jr	9	2	2.24	14	0	84	61	30	21	2	32	115
36.	Jacob Edwards, UNC Asheville	Sr	8	3	2.24	14	0	88	77	33	22	4	26	82
37.	Zach Maxey, Miami (OH)	So	4	3	2.27	13	0	71	65	31	18	4	24	62
38.	Fynn Chester, Cal St. Fullerton	Jr	3	1	2.30	6	0	63	59	20	16	2	12	32

COLLEGE

39.	Drew Thorpe, Cal Poly	So	10	1	2.32	15	0	105	65	31	27	5	25	149
40.	Kyle Crigger, Louisiana Tech	Sr	6	3	2.35	0	9	69	60	23	18	5	17	79
41.	Adam Mrakitsch, Central Mich.	Fr	7	1	2.37	5	1	49	48	15	13	3	18	42
42.	Chase Dollander, Tennessee	So	10	0	2.39	14	0	79	50	25	21	7	13	108
43.	Matt McShane, Saint Joseph's	Fr	5	0	2.40	1	2	45	45	22	12	5	16	51
44.	Luke Rettig, Lehigh	Sr	8	2	2.40	13	0	71	60	26	19	0	34	71
45.	Nolan DeVos, Davidson	Jr	9	2	2.40	15	0	79	63	23	21	5	31	106
46.	Tyler Thomas, Baylor	Sr	4	4	2.45	9	0	51	40	16	14	7	9	51
47.	Jared Hart, Illinois St.	Sr	2	3	2.45	6	2	55	49	22	15	4	16	50
48.	Eric Yost, Northeastern	So	4	3	2.48	10	1	62	51	18	17	5	17	58
49.	Luke Stephens, Wofford	Jr	2	1	2.50	0	1	40	31	14	11	1	8	44
50.	Hunter Barco, Florida	Jr	5	2	2.50	9	0	50	34	14	14	6	11	69
51.	Reed Parris, Col. of Charleston	Sr	6	0	2.50	2	0	50	41	19	14	1	9	47
52.	Ledgend Smith, Oral Roberts	Jr	7	5	2.50	14	0	83	70	30	23	9	22	98
53.	Joe Adametz III, Liberty	Jr	6	3	2.51	16	0	86	94	34	24	6	25	84
54.	Camden Sewell, Tennessee	Sr	7	1	2.52	1	1	50	40	17	14	3	8	42
55.	Matthew Marchal, Wofford	So	7	2	2.52	17	0	86	75	32	24	7	12	93
56.	Ivran Romero, San Diego	So	4	4	2.53	3	3	46	47	14	13	2	16	44
57.	Thomas Harrington, Campbell	So	12	2	2.53	15	0	93	69	32	26	1	18	111
58.	Cooper Hjerpe, Oregon St.	So	11	2	2.53	17	1	103	67	31	29	3	23	161
59.	Jack Masloff, VCU	So	4	1	2.56	2	5	56	43	19	16	1	14	65
60.	Isaiah Magwood, Jacksonville St.	Jr	7	2	2.58	10	0	70	58	25	20	6	33	78
61.	Ty Fisher, Ga. Southern	So	6	2	2.58	14	0	87	81	30	25	7	23	60
62.	Hunter Riggins, Southern Miss.	Sr	8	4	2.59	16	0	97	85	36	28	4	21	85
63.	Jacob Palisch, Texas A&M	Sr	6	3	2.60	0	5	52	49	17	15	1	9	60
64.	Shemar Page, Grambling	Sr	8	5	2.60	15	0	104	72	38	30	5	34	143
65.	Logan Mercado, Oregon	So	6	2	2.61	0	0	41	38	14	12	4	12	41
66.	AJ Causey, Jacksonville St.	Fr	4	4	2.61	1	9	48	37	16	14	1	10	58
67.	Sean Harney, Kentucky	Sr	5	4	2.62	5	2	65	55	19	19	2	17	65
68.	Quinn Mathews, Stanford	Jr	9	1	2.62	9	9	96	71	31	28	4	47	110
69.	Will Mabrey, Tennessee	Jr	2	0	2.63	0	0	41	34	13	12	5	5	52
70.	Tyler Schweitzer, Ball St.	So	11	2	2.65	16	0	92	69	29	27	5	30	112
71.	Matt Brosky, Youngstown St.	Jr	6	7	2.65	15	0	99	86	49	29	6	22	102
72.	Jack Lynch, Xavier	Jr	9	0	2.66	0	1	64	47	24	19	4	21	77
73.	Kevin Stevens, UTRGV	Sr	9	2	2.66	14	0	81	69	26	24	2	29	100
74.	Adam Wheaton, Lamar University	Sr	10	2	2.66	14	0	91	83	35	27	9	29	69
75.	Luke Malone, UTSA	Jr	9	3	2.67	11	2	88	81	35	26	12	14	62
76.	Eli Ankeney, Grand Canyon	Jr	3	3	2.68	0	0	40	28	13	12	3	13	61
77.	Owen Hackman, LMU (CA)	So	3	2	2.68	0	5	44	32	17	13	4	12	51
78.	Lucas Gordon, Texas	So	7	1	2.68	15	0	84	67	32	25	2	25	76
79.	Duncan Howard, Presbyterian	So	7	4	2.69	14	1	84	87	36	25	2	25	67
80.	John Michael Bertrand, Notre Dame	Sr	9	3	2.69	17	0	104	91	36	31	8	20	107
81.	Jonah Hurney, Virginia Tech	Jr	6	1	2.70	0	1	43	34	15	13	5	14	54
82.	Ricky Gerik Jr., UTRGV	Sr	5	3	2.70	0	7	53	53	25	16	1	15	56
83.	Dylan Tebrake, Creighton	Jr	8	2	2.71	17	0	93	73	34	28	9	33	115
84.	Luke Savage, TCU	So	1	1	2.72	0	2	40	34	14	12	1	17	35
85.	Drew Beam, Tennessee	Fr	8	1	2.72	15	0	76	50	26	23	8	21	62
86.	Paul Skenes, Air Force	So	10	3	2.73	15	0	86	70	30	26	4	30	96
87.	Nate Dahle, BYU	So	2	4	2.74	4	2	43	40	16	13	2	11	61
88.	Brandon Birdsell, Texas Tech	Jr	9	3	2.75	15	0	85	67	29	26	7	29	106
89.	Mike Biasiello, Delaware	Sr	2	2	2.76	1	6	49	31	16	15	4	23	62
90.	Peter Allegro, Portland	Jr	4	2	2.76	1	13	49	33	17	15	3	23	49
91.	Davis Palermo, North Carolina	So	2	2	2.78	0	5	58	40	20	18	7	24	74
92.	Collin Lowe, Bryant	Sr	5	4	2.79	14	0	81	70	33	25	7	16	79
93.	Owen Coady, Penn	Jr	7	1	2.80	2	2	55	41	20	17	2	22	74
94.	Payton Harris, Alabama St.	Sr	3	2	2.80	0	4	55	43	23	17	4	32	48
95.	Ryan Chasse, Campbell	Jr	3	2	2.81	3	6	42	32	25	13	1	26	60
96.	Will McEntire, Arkansas	Jr	1	2	2.81	7	1	42	31	14	13	3	22	40
97.	Tommy Hopfe, Fresno St.	So	2	1	2.81	1	1	42	43	17	13	5	13	30
98.	Nick Sando, Santa Clara	Jr	4	4	2.81	5	4	51	40	25	16	2	23	79
99.	Tanner Hall, Southern Miss.	So	9	3	2.81	17	0	109	98	46	34	7	14	146
100.	Caden Favors, Wichita St.	Fr	2	1	2.82	6	0	51	45	20	16	6	12	47

WINS

Rank	Pitcher, Team	W
1.	Thomas Harrington, Campbell	12
2.	Ryan Ramsey, Maryland	11
	Cooper Hjerpe, Oregon St.	11
	Tyler Schweitzer, Ball St.	11
	Pat Gallagher, UConn	11
	Pete Hansen, Texas	11
	Josh Loeschorn, LIU	11
	Rhett Lowder, Wake Forest	11
	Austin Peterson, UConn	11
10.	13 tied	10

SAVES

Rank	Pitcher, Team	SV
1.	Tristan Stivors, Texas St.	18
2.	Blake Burkhalter, Auburn	16
3.	Justin Willis, UConn	15
	Will Brian, Eastern Ky.	15
5.	Andrew Walters, Miami (FL)	14
	Jack Dallas, Lamar University	14
	Kyle Brennan, Belmont	14
	Vince Reilly, Grand Canyon	14
9.	Peter Allegro, Portland	13
	7 tied	12

STRIKEOUTS

Rank	Pitcher, Team	SO
1.	Cooper Hjerpe, Oregon St.	161
2.	Drew Thorpe, Cal Poly	149
3.	Austin Peterson, UConn	147
4.	Tanner Hall, Southern Miss.	146
5.	Parker Messick, Florida St.	144
6.	Shemar Page, Grambling	143
7.	Justin Campbell, Oklahoma St.	141
8.	Hurston Waldrep, Southern Miss.	140
9.	Gabriel Hughes, Gonzaga	138
10.	Jake Bennett, Oklahoma	133

STRIKEOUTS PER NINE

Rank	Pitcher, Team	SO/9
1.	Pat Pridgen, FIU	14.07
2.	Cooper Hjerpe, Oregon St.	14.02
3.	Hurston Waldrep, Southern Miss.	14.00
4.	Isaiah Coupet, Ohio St.	13.64
5.	Juaron Watts-Brown, Long Beach St.	13.62
6.	Andrew Taylor, Central Mich.	13.50
-	Jaren Zinn, Harvard	13.50
8.	Colin Fields, Valparaiso	13.44
9.	Preston Johnson, Mississippi St.	13.33
10.	Alex Theis, Wright St.	13.27

FEWEST HITS PER NINE

Rank	Pitcher, Team	H/9
1.	William Privette, Col. of Charleston	4.70
2.	Jackson Kelley, Mercer	4.80
3.	Cameron Foster, McNeese	5.00
4.	Carter Lovasz, William & Mary	5.54
5.	Drew Thorpe, Cal Poly	5.59
6.	Landon Gartman, Memphis	5.65
7.	Chase Dollander, Tennessee	5.70
8.	Adam Mazur, Iowa	5.77
9.	Cooper Hjerpe, Oregon St.	5.84
10.	Ben Cruikshank, Kent St.	5.87

FEWEST WALKS PER NINE

Rank	Pitcher, Team	BB/9
1.	Nate Mitchell, Navy	0.37
2.	Gordon Ingebritson, UC Irvine	0.68
3.	Matt Jachec, Indiana St.	0.84
4.	Billy Corcoran, Pittsburgh	0.84
5.	Wyatt Scotti, Northeastern	0.89
6.	Joseph Battaglia III, Southern U.	0.95
7.	Jonathan Fincher, Louisiana Tech	1.02
8.	Matt Gilbertson, Pittsburgh	1.03
9.	Blake Morgan, Old Dominion	1.04
10.	Ben Sears, Houston	1.08

TEAM LEADERS

SCORING

Rank	Team	G	R	R/G
1.	Rutgers	59	565	9.6
2.	Texas Southern	53	503	9.5
3.	Georgia Tech	60	564	9.4
4.	Tennessee	66	613	9.3
5.	Maryland	62	572	9.2
6.	Wake Forest	61	561	9.2
7.	UNLV	58	530	9.1
8.	Grambling	57	514	9
9.	Campbell	60	523	8.7
10.	Virginia Tech	59	513	8.7
11.	Davidson	56	483	8.6
12.	Louisville	64	551	8.6
13.	Virginia	58	499	8.6
14.	Old Dominion	58	491	8.5
15.	Charlotte	58	489	8.4
16.	Air Force	61	507	8.3
17.	FGCU	58	482	8.3
18.	Marist	46	382	8.3
19.	Texas Tech	61	506	8.3
20.	Mercer	58	480	8.3
21.	Wofford	59	485	8.2
22.	Nevada	55	450	8.2
23.	LSU	62	503	8.1
24.	Columbia	50	403	8.1
25.	UTSA	58	467	8.1
26.	UConn	66	528	8
27.	Wright St.	57	455	8
28.	Michigan	62	492	7.9
29.	Tennessee Tech	57	452	7.9
30.	NC State	57	450	7.9
31.	Richmond	56	440	7.9
32.	Texas	69	541	7.8
33.	Saint Joseph's	54	423	7.8
34.	SIUE	55	430	7.8
35.	Coastal Carolina	60	468	7.8
36.	Central Mich.	62	480	7.7
37.	Missouri St.	60	464	7.7
38.	Texas St.	61	471	7.7
39.	McNeese	57	440	7.7
40.	Oklahoma St.	64	492	7.7
41.	Jackson St.	56	429	7.7
42.	Southern Ill.	60	459	7.7
43.	Oklahoma	68	518	7.6
44.	Miami (FL)	60	457	7.6
45.	Oral Roberts	58	441	7.6
46.	Clemson	58	440	7.6
47.	Alabama St.	59	445	7.5
48.	Penn	48	362	7.5
49.	New Orleans	53	399	7.5
50.	Abilene Christian	59	444	7.5

BATTING AVERAGE

Rank	Team	AVG
1.	Georgia Tech	.327
2.	UNLV	.326
3.	Rutgers	.320
4.	Wake Forest	.319
5.	Texas Southern	.318
6.	Wofford	.315
7.	Texas	.314
8.	Grambling	.314
9.	Air Force	.312
10.	Oregon	.310

HOME RUNS

Rank	Team	HR
1.	Tennessee	158
2.	Maryland	137
3.	Old Dominion	128
-	Texas	128
5.	Virginia Tech	126
6.	Wake Forest	122
7.	Florida	121
8.	Campbell	118
-	Stanford	118
10.	Georgia Tech	115

DOUBLES

Rank	Team	2B
1.	UConn	165
2.	Texas	157
3.	Tennessee	156
4.	Air Force	148
5.	Rutgers	147
6.	Davidson	144
-	UNLV	144
8.	Maryland	143
9.	Texas Tech	142
10.	Oregon St.	141

TRIPLES

Rank	Team	3B
1.	Texas Southern	29
2.	Ball St.	28
-	Grambling	28
-	Louisiana	28
5.	Arizona	26
6.	A&M-Corpus Christi	24
-	Coppin St.	24
-	Dartmouth	24
-	McNeese	24
-	UConn	24

ON-BASE PERCENTAGE

Rank	Team	OBP
1.	Texas Southern	.436
2.	Davidson	.425
3.	Wake Forest	.425
4.	Grambling	.420
5.	Tennessee	.419
6.	Georgia Tech	.419
7.	Wofford	.419
8.	Maryland	.418
9.	Rutgers	.417
10.	Central Mich.	.417

SLUGGING PERCENTAGE

Rank	Team	SLG
1.	Tennessee	.604
2.	Virginia Tech	.574
3.	Maryland	.563
4.	Old Dominion	.552
5.	Georgia Tech	.551
6.	Texas	.550
7.	Campbell	.548
8.	Wake Forest	.548
9.	Stanford	.536
10.	Rutgers	.535

STOLEN BASES

Rank	Team	SB
1.	Texas Southern	37
2.	West Virginia	43
3.	Wofford	37
4.	Oklahoma	43
5.	McNeese	25
6.	Louisiana	42
7.	UMass Lowell	31
8.	Campbell	34
9.	Coppin St.	26
10.	Purdue	19

WALKS

Rank	Team	BB
1.	Oregon St.	389
2.	Tennessee	388
3.	Oklahoma	374
4.	Charlotte	371
5.	Wake Forest	364
6.	Central Mich.	355
7.	Texas A&M	351
8.	Louisville	342
9.	TCU	341
10.	Maryland	337

PITCHING

EARNED RUN AVERAGE

Rank	Team	ERA
1.	Tennessee	2.51
2.	Southern Miss.	3.29
3.	Northeastern	3.61
4.	Iowa	3.72
5.	BYU	3.76
6.	UConn	3.78
7.	Long Beach St.	3.83
8.	Davidson	3.86
9.	VCU	3.91
10.	Notre Dame	3.91
11.	CSUN	3.94
12.	Vanderbilt	3.95
13.	UC Santa Barbara	3.99
14.	Virginia	3.99
15.	UCLA	3.99
16.	Arkansas	4.07
17.	Oral Roberts	4.07
18.	Elon	4.09
19.	Penn	4.11
20.	Col. of Charleston	4.12
21.	North Carolina	4.16
22.	Oregon St.	4.19
23.	Rutgers	4.22
24.	Florida	4.22
25.	Louisiana	4.23
26.	Stanford	4.23
27.	Florida St.	4.23
28.	Ole Miss	4.25
29.	Louisiana Tech	4.25
30.	UCF	4.25
31.	East Carolina	4.26
32.	Texas	4.28
33.	Liberty	4.29
34.	Portland	4.30
35.	Gonzaga	4.32
36.	LSU	4.32
37.	Creighton	4.33
38.	William & Mary	4.34
39.	Texas St.	4.35
40.	UC Irvine	4.35
41.	McNeese	4.39
42.	Virginia Tech	4.41
43.	Lamar University	4.41
44.	LIU	4.48
45.	Pepperdine	4.49
46.	Cal Poly	4.49
47.	Auburn	4.49
48.	Wake Forest	4.50
49.	Miami (FL)	4.52
50.	Grand Canyon	4.57

STRIKEOUTS PER NINE

Rank	Team	SO/9
1.	Florida St.	11.8
2.	Southern Miss.	11.3
3.	Iowa	11.2
4.	Mississippi St.	10.9
5.	Ole Miss	10.9
6.	Miami (FL)	10.8
7.	Oklahoma St.	10.7
8.	Notre Dame	10.7
9.	Gonzaga	10.6
10.	Duke	10.6

FEWEST WALKS PER NINE

Rank	Team	BB/9
1.	Tennessee	2.48
2.	Elon	2.54
3.	Southern Miss.	2.73
4.	Wofford	2.79
5.	Oregon St.	2.85
6.	UConn	2.90
7.	Cal Poly	3.01
8.	UCLA	3.01
9.	Louisiana Tech	3.08
10.	VCU	3.12

FIELDING

FIELDING PERCENTAGE

Rank	Team	PCT
1.	Texas	.985
2.	Houston	.984
3.	East Carolina	.984
4.	Belmont	.983
5.	Mississippi St.	.983
6.	Arkansas	.982
7.	Oregon St.	.982
8.	Ga. Southern	.982
9.	Florida	.981
10.	Auburn	.981
11.	Alabama	.981
12.	Rutgers	.980
13.	San Diego	.980
14.	Notre Dame	.980
15.	Virginia Tech	.980
16.	Tennessee	.980
17.	Oregon	.979
18.	Gonzaga	.979
19.	Oklahoma St.	.978
20.	Georgia	.978
21.	TCU	.978
22.	Sacramento St.	.978
23.	Southeastern La.	.978
24.	Southern Miss.	.977
25.	Oral Roberts	.977
26.	Old Dominion	.977
27.	Kentucky	.977
28.	Vanderbilt	.977
29.	Charlotte	.977
30.	Texas Tech	.976
31.	Abilene Christian	.976
32.	Missouri	.976
33.	Rider	.976
34.	Illinois	.976
35.	Stanford	.976
36.	Evansville	.976
37.	Long Beach St.	.975
38.	Bowling Green	.975
39.	Eastern Ky.	.975
40.	UAlbany	.975
41.	Illinois St.	.975
42.	Fla. Atlantic	.975
43.	Navy	.975
44.	Washington	.975
45.	Seton Hall	.975
46.	Memphis	.975
47.	DBU	.975
48.	Eastern Ill.	.975
49.	Bucknell	.975
50.	Purdue	.975

DOUBLE PLAYS

Rank	Team	DP
1.	Baylor	64
2.	Arkansas	60
3.	North Carolina	59
4.	Arizona	57
5.	New Mexico	56
-	New Orleans	56
7.	BYU	55
-	Kennesaw St.	55
-	TCU	55
10.	4-tied	54

1. MISSISSIPPI

Coach: Mike Bianco. **Record:** 42-23

Player, Pos., Year	AVG	OBP	SLG	AB	R	2B	3B	HR	RBI	SB
Alderman, Kemp, OF/INF/C,So.	.286	.388	.522	203	41	15	0	11	45	2
Bench, Justin, 3B, RSr.	.316	.409	.438	256	62	17	1	4	42	4
Burford, Reagan, 3B, So.	.260	.322	.423	104	24	8	0	3	19	2
Chatagnier, Peyton, 2B, Jr.	.248	.317	.461	230	47	12	2	11	45	6
Dunhurst, Hayden, C, Jr.	.231	.370	.385	169	30	8	0	6	30	0
Elko, Tim, 1B, Sr.	.300	.407	.642	240	63	10	0	24	75	2
Gonzalez, Jacob, SS, So.	.273	.405	.558	242	67	9	3	18	52	4
Graham, Kevin, LF, RSr.	.335	.371	.562	194	32	11	0	11	51	1
Harris, Calvin, C, So.	.336	.417	.500	110	26	7	1	3	21	2
Kramer, John, OF, Fr.	.214	.389	.643	14	3	0	0	2	2	0
Leatherwood, Hayden, RF, Sr.	.250	.317	.432	132	24	7	1	5	17	0
Loposer, Knox, C, RSr.	.222	.417	.333	9	3	1	0	0	4	0
Malone, Tywone, INF, Fr.	.444	.500	1.111	9	3	0	0	2	4	0
McCants, TJ, CF, So.	.236	.324	.410	178	34	5	1	8	31	10
Sapp, Hudson, OF, RFr.	.200	.385	.300	10	3	1	0	0	2	0
Tolley, Banks, OF, Jr.	.267	.353	.400	15	5	2	0	0	3	1
Van Cleve, Ben, INF, Sr.	.302	.415	.419	43	10	5	0	0	4	0
Wood, Garrett, 3B,R,Sr.	.152	.349	.212	33	5	2	0	0	1	0T

Pitcher, Year	W	L	ERA	G	GS	SV	IP	H	BB	SO
Baker, Cole, Jr.	1	0	0.00	2	0	0	1.1	0	1	2
Burton, Wes, Jr.	0	0	15.43	5	0	0	2.1	1	8	5
Cioffi, Max, Sr.	0	0	10.13	4	0	0	2.2	3	3	4
DeLucia, Dylan, Jr.	8	2	3.68	21	12	1	95.1	87	26	105
Diamond, Derek, Jr.	4	4	6.89	16	14	0	65.1	81	13	57
Dougherty, Jack, So.	4	3	4.91	17	4	2	44	48	16	61
Elliott, Hunter, Fr.	5	3	2.70	20	12	0	80	57	34	102
Gaddis, John, Sr.	4	2	4.20	17	7	1	49.1	50	19	49
Johnson, Brandon, RSr.	1	3	4.32	24	0	12	41.2	31	21	71
Kimbrell, Jackson, Jr.	1	0	4.00	8	0	0	9	3	4	12
Maddox, Riley, Fr.	2	1	5.24	14	0	0	22.1	26	9	16
Mallitz, Josh, So.	1	0	1.45	17	0	2	31	19	12	48
McDaniel, Drew, Jr.	5	3	6.06	15	7	0	32.2	32	23	45
Murrell, Mitch, Jr.	0	0	3.52	9	0	0	7.2	8	5	11
Nichols, Mason, Fr.	1	0	2.84	21	0	0	31.2	22	12	41
Parenteau, Matt, Jr.	0	0	4.77	8	0	0	5.2	7	4	7
Savell, Logan, Jr.	0	0	9.00	2	0	0	2	2	1	4
Washburn, Jack, Jr.	5	2	3.35	15	9	0	40.1	33	23	42

2. OKLAHOMA

Coach: Skip Johnson. **Record:** 45-24

Player, Pos., Year	AVG	OBP	SLG	AB	R	2B	3B	HR	RBI	SB
Brown, Trent, RF, RSo.	.200	.284	.367	60	8	4	0	2	12	2
Clark, Wallace, 3B, Fr.	.257	.397	.296	152	31	6	0	0	27	2
Crooks, Jimmy, C, RSo.	.305	.430	.506	249	49	21	1	9	51	10
Graham, Peyton, SS, RSo.	.335	.417	.640	278	75	17	4	20	71	34
Horton, Cade, 3B, RFr.	.234	.323	.324	145	28	6	2	1	17	8
McGwire, Max, INF, Fr.	.189	.295	.302	53	8	0	0	2	6	0
Muniz, Diego, LF, RJr.	.259	.410	.330	112	18	8	0	0	24	4
Nicklaus, Jackson, 2B, Fr.	.288	.397	.495	212	48	11	0	11	36	6
Orduno, Sebastian, RF, RSo.	.240	.408	.281	96	10	4	0	0	13	1
Pettis, Kendall, LF, RSo.	.259	.449	.400	135	45	4	0	5	27	22
Polk, Hudson, C, So.	.313	.522	.563	16	5	2	1	0	5	1
Robertson, Blake,1B, RSo.	.300	.453	.467	257	62	24	2	5	52	12
Spikerman, John, RF, Fr.	,317	.434	.450	120	30	8	1	2	15	12
Squires, Brett, INF/OF, RJr.	.310	.432	.516	126	34	5	0	7	33	7
Tredaway, Tanner, CF, RSr.	.370	.414	.549	284	63	18	3	9	66	24

Pitcher, Year	W	L	ERA	G	GS	SV	IP	H	BB	SO
Abram, Ben, RJr.	1	0	9.41	22	0	0	22	38	5	15
Allen, Keegan, Fr.	0	0	9.00	9	0	0	7	9	5	8
Atwood, Carson, So.	2	4	5.65	26	1	0	28.2	32	11	24
Bennett, Jake, RSo.	10	4	3.69	20	19	1	117	106	22	133
Calhoun, Aaron, Fr.	0	1	6.00	12	1	0	12	11	7	9
Campbell, Carter, So.	3	0	5.22	31	0	0	29.1	39	9	17
Carmichael, Braden, RJr.	3	2	9.00	13	8	0	29	40	20	29
Godman, Jaret, RJr.	1	0	6.98	20	0	3	19.1	30	7	17
Horton, Cade, RFr.	5	2	4.86	14	11	0	53.2	55	15	64
Lodes, Jett, So.	0	0	9.64	5	0	0	4.2	9	6	3
Martinez, Chazz, RSo.	4	3	5.32	22	8	1	64.1	66	32	67
Michael, Trevin, Gr.	4	2	2.89	32	2	10	71.2	55	20	95
Miller, Griffin, RJr.	0	1	8.68	10	0	0	9.1	8	6	10
Ramos, Javier, RSo.	1	1	5.16	15	1	0	22.2	22	15	24
Sandlin, David, RSo.	9	4	5.59	19	18	0	95	100	31	102
Sundloff, Colton, Fr.	2	0	6.86	18	0	0	21	33	11	16

3. TEXAS A&M

Coach: Jim Schlossnagle. **Record:** 44-20

Player, Pos., Year	AVG	OBP	SLG	AB	R	2B	3B	HR	RBI	SB
Barker, Rody,OF/C,Gr.	.200	.500	.400	5	1	1	0	0	0	0
Bost, Austin, OF/INF, Jr.	.360	.451	.572	236	52	14	3	10	45	6
Britt, Logan, CF, So.	.197	.262	.432	132	24	7	0	8	24	3
Claunch, Troy, C, Gr.	.292	.371	.392	240	46	15	0	3	49	4
Harrison, Kalae, SS, So.	.162	.295	.216	37	4	2	0	0	4	0
Hodge, Ty, 2B, Fr.	.056	.105	.056	18	1	0	0	0	1	0
Kaler, Kole, SS, Gr.	.237	.376	.324	241	54	8	2	3	30	10
Minnich, Brett, RF, Jr.	.306	.409	.453	245	52	15	0	7	51	9
Moss, Jack, 1B, So.	.380	.437	.520	271	50	18	1	6	49	8
Rock, Dylan, LF, Gr.	.318	.468	.641	223	67	13	1	19	65	16
Scarnardo, Chanden, C, Fr.	.071	.316	.071	14	2	0	0	0	0	0
Smith, Taylor, C, Jr.	.179	.313	.254	67	12	5	0	0	7	2
Stracener, Austin, 3B, Fr.	.250	.250	.375	8	1	1	0	0	0	0
Targac, Ryan, 2B, So.	.294	.430	.569	211	46	9	2	15	58	12
Thompson, Jordan, CF, Jr.	.258	.400	.475	120	35	8	0	6	31	8
Werner, Trevor, 3B, So.	.256	.357	.489	133	27	8	1	7	29	3

Pitcher, Year	W	L	ERA	G	GS	SV	IP	H	BB	SO
Cortez, Chris, Fr.	6	3	4.91	25	1	0	44	47	13	32
Curtis, Khristian, RFr.	2	0	1.42	5	5	0	19	17	8	15
Dallas, Micah, Jr.	7	3	5.18	18	16	0	81.2	100	22	86
Dettmer, Nathan, So.	6	3	4.99	19	19	0	92	98	25	82
Hamilton, Jack, Fr.	0	0	3.18	5	0	0	5.2	4	4	5
Hector, Rawley, Fr.	1	0	7.98	9	0	0	14.2	18	2	7
Hogan, Robert, Fr.	3	1	4.91	18	0	2	18.1	13	12	17
Johnston, Will, So.	3	1	3.25	23	2	4	36	33	18	49
Lovett, Xavier, RSo.	0	0	12.00	7	0	0	6	5	5	6
Magers, Alex, So.	0	0	5.59	8	0	0	9.2	15	5	9
Menefee, Joseph, Jr.	6	2	5.60	28	0	2	53	46	42	87
Palisch, Jacob, Gr.	6	3	2.39	29	0	5	60.1	53	12	73
Prager, Ryan, Fr.	1	4	5.16	18	16	0	59.1	61	25	53
Rudis, Brad, Fr.	3	0	5.22	26	2	3	39.2	42	13	36
Tucker, Wyatt, So.	0	0	4.79	10	2	0	20.2	19	12	26
Zander, Walker, So.	0	0	5.79	5	1	0	4.2	11	0	4

4. ARKANSAS

Coach: Dave Van Horn. **Record:** 46-21

Player, Pos., Year	AVG	OBP	SLG	AB	R	2B	3B	HR	RBI	SB
Battles, Jalen, SS, Sr.	.289	.364	.480	246	51	15	1	10	45	2
Bohrofen, Jace, LF, So.	.228	.333	.435	92	17	8	1	3	17	0
Diggs, Kendall, DH, Fr.	.197	.367	.361	61	14	1	0	3	14	1
Gregory, Zack, LF, RJr.	.212	.414	.363	146	42	7	0	5	18	6
Lanzilli, Chris, RF, Gr.	.326	.424	.513	224	39	9	0	11	40	3
Leach, Dylan, C, So.	.224	.297	.517	58	16	3	1	4	16	4
Moore, Robert, 2B, Jr.	.232	.374	.427	241	48	19	2	8	44	5
Slavens, Brady, DH, Sr.	.255	.332	.523	239	35	10	3	16	58	2
Soliz, Jr., Max, DH, Fr.	.222	.300	.333	9	2	1	0	0	1	0
Stovall, Peyton, 1B, Fr.	.295	.373	.425	200	40	8	0	6	31	1
Turner, Michael, C, Gr.	.323	.388	.502	257	40	17	1	9	53	1
Varnado, Drake, LF, Fr.	.235	.391	.294	17	6	1	0	0	4	1
Wallace, Cayden, 3B, So.	.298	.387	.553	275	62	20	1	16	60	12
Webb, Braydon, CF, Gr.	.283	.418	.542	212	60	8	1	15	42	11

Pitcher, Year	W	L	ERA	G	GS	SV	IP	H	BB	SO
Adamiak, Mark, RSo.	2	0	3.95	9	3	0	13.2	14	8	18
Bracken, Isaac, Gr.	0	0	1.59	5	0	0	5.2	3	3	7

Faherty, Jake, Fr.	0	0	0.00	1	0	0	0.1	0	1	1
Gray, Evan, RSo.	0	0	0.00	3	0	0	1.2	0	1	3
Griffin, Nick, RFr.	0	0	2.70	7	0	0	6.2	4	11	11
Ledbetter, Austin, Fr.	0	0	2.84	7	2	0	12.2	10	1	12
McEntire, Will, RSo.	2	2	2.59	12	8	1	48.2	34	23	49
Morris, Zack, Jr.	6	1	2.31	22	2	1	35	29	19	26
Noland, Connor, Sr.	8	6	3.65	20	19	0	116	109	34	113
Pleimann, Miller, RJr.	0	0	7.71	6	1	0	7	12	1	12
Ramage, Kole, RSr.	3	2	4.80	31	2	3	50.2	44	19	61
Smith,Hagen, Fr.	7	2	4.66	20	15	2	77.1	66	46	90
Starks, Gabriel, So.	0	0	4.63	12	0	0	11.2	9	10	18
Taylor, Evan, Sr.	5	0	3.65	33	0	2	44.1	28	16	54
Tole, Heston, So.	2	0	3.77	10	0	1	14.1	20	3	20
Trest, Elijah, Sr.	0	1	3.77	13	0	0	14.1	6	12	17
Tygart, Brady, Fr.	3	4	3.82	24	0	8	37.2	28	21	51
Vermillion, Zebulon, RSr.	2	0	2.39	24	0	2	26.1	22	10	28
Wiggins, Jaxon, So.	6	3	6.55	17	15	0	66	65	43	82

5. NOTRE DAME

Coach: Link Jarrett. **Record:** 41-17

Player, Pos., Year	AVG	OBP	SLG	AB	R	2B	3B	HR	RBI	SB
Brannigan, Jack, 3B, Jr.	.291	.360	.540	213	47	15	1	12	46	10
Coetzee, Brooks, RF, Sr.	.267	.354	.466	221	42	8	0	12	43	6
Cole, Ryan, LF, Gr.	.295	.422	.481	210	47	10	1	9	33	22
DeMarco, Nick, 3B, Fr.	.333	.400	.667	9	4	0	0	1	1	0
Gumpf, Brady, OF, So.	.375	.444	1.000	8	3	2	0	1	5	0
Jefferson, DM, OF, Fr.	.220	.273	.220	41	7	0	0	0	8	2
Juaire, Nick, C/OF, RSo.	.344	.377	.500	64	11	5	1	1	10	1
Kmet, Casey, 3B, Jr.	.200	.200	.400	5	1	1	0	0	1	0
LaManna, David, C, Gr.	.346	.409	.464	153	35	9	0	3	28	4
Lindwedel, Tony, C, So.	.500	.600	.750	4	3	1	0	0	1	0
Miller, Jared, 2B, Gr.	.283	.393	.428	152	32	7	0	5	24	9
Myers, Spencer, CF, Gr.	.229	.333	.286	140	20	3	1	1	22	7
Neri, Danny, C, So.	.266	.333	.438	64	10	3	1	2	11	1
Penney, Jack, 2B, Fr.	.288	.407	.589	73	16	6	2	4	19	4
Prajzner, Zack, SS, Sr.	.282	.349	.408	206	44	8	0	6	35	2
Putz, Carter, 1B, Sr.	.339	.392	.519	239	55	13	3	8	48	2
Spence, Joey, Fr., Fr.	.231	.313	.462	13	1	3	0	0	3	0
Williams, TJ, CF, So.	.254	.289	.394	71	16	3	2	1	10	2
Zyska, Jack, OF, Sr.	.294	.381	.627	153	34	12	0	13	38	7

Pitcher, Year	W	L	ERA	G	GS	SV	IP	H	BB	SO
Aoki, Caden, Fr.	0	2	3.86	4	0	0	9.1	7	2	10
Bedford, Matt, So.	1	0	6.10	10	0	0	10.1	15	4	13
Bertrand, John Michael, Gr.	10	3	2.81	18	18	0	109	97	21	111
Birkholz, Radek, Fr.	1	0	4.99	21	1	0	21.2	24	14	29
Brannigan, Jack, Jr.	2	2	7.36	11	1	2	14.2	16	8	28
Cooper, Sammy, So.	0	0	6.75	6	0	0	5.1	4	4	5
Dennies, Jackson, So.	1	1	6.35	20	0	0	17	18	11	20
Findlay, Jack, Fr.	6	2	2.17	20	8	4	49.2	34	16	54
Kimball, Roman, Fr.	4	0	5.76	17	0	0	25	19	14	32
Lazzaro, Matt, Gr.	0	0	3.00	8	0	0	9	7	5	10
McLinskey, Ryan, Gr.	0	1	2.42	14	0	3	26	19	8	39
Mercer, Will, Sr.	2	1	4.18	13	3	1	23.2	22	9	24
Rao, Alex, Sr.	3	1	3.83	25	0	3	47	32	28	57
Simon, Liam, Jr.	2	1	4.99	16	7	0	30.2	21	28	56
Temple, Austin, Gr.	4	1	3.51	18	15	2	69.1	49	37	87
Tyrell, Aidan, Sr.	5	2	3.75	26	5	2	48	55	15	37

6. AUBURN

Coach: Butch Thompson. **Record:** 43-22

Player, Pos., Year	AVG	OBP	SLG	AB	R	2B	3B	HR	RBI	SB
Bello, Mike, LF, Fr.	.253	.350	.323	99	18	4	0	1	12	1
Brown, Brayton, LF, Jr.	.167	.375	.167	12	2	0	0	0	3	0
Burk, Luke, PH, Jr.	.125	.125	.125	8	1	0	0	0	0	0
Carlson, Brooks, INF, Gr.	.297	.379	.454	185	36	11	0	6	31	0
DiChiara, Sonny, 1B, Sr.	.383	.549	.777	206	59	15	0	22	59	0
Dyal, Ryan, C, RSo.	.217	.368	.391	92	23	4	0	4	26	0
Farquhar, Garrett, 2B, RSr.	.236	.337	.375	72	17	4	0	2	12	0
Foster, Cole, 2B, So.	.267	.395	.488	172	40	11	0	9	47	2
Hall, Josh, LF, RJr.	.269	.387	.308	26	5	1	0	0	2	1
Hill, Cam, INF, So.	.278	.358	.370	108	16	7	0	1	19	0
Howell, Kason, CF, Sr.	.287	.385	.402	251	50	19	2	2	35	11
Land, Mason, LF, Jr.	.244	.320	.267	45	4	1	0	0	3	0
LaRue, Nate, C, Jr.	.211	.272	.382	152	19	8	0	6	34	2
Moore, Brody, SS, Sr.	.291	.351	.406	254	46	12	1	5	38	6
Moss, Brody, INF, Fr.	.333	.250	.333	3	0	0	0	0	1	0
Peirce, Bobby, RF, RJr.	.284	.350	.562	162	33	7	4	10	31	5
Rambusch, Blake, 3B, RJr.	.327	.415	.429	266	55	13	1	4	37	16
Schorr, Ben, C, RFr.	.000	.000	.000	1	0	0	0	0	0	0
Ware, Bryson, RF, Jr.	.234	.336	.394	94	23	8	2	1	21	4
Wyandt, Jake, C, Gr.	.233	.320	.326	43	8	1	0	1	12	1

Pitcher, Year	W	L	ERA	G	GS	SV	IP	H	BB	SO
Allsup, Chase, Fr.	1	0	3.38	23	0	2	29.1	24	17	36
Armstrong, John, Fr.	1	0	4.26	19	0	0	19	20	11	21
Armstrong, Jordan, Sr.	3	1	5.93	14	6	1	30.1	36	15	40
Barnett, Mason, Jr.	3	3	4.38	19	14	0	63.2	63	32	83
Bosse, Ben, Fr.	0	0	3.86	7	0	0	4.2	4	2	6
Bright, Trace, Jr.	5	4	5.13	18	17	0	80.2	78	38	94
Burkhalter, Blake, Jr.	4	2	3.69	30	0	16	46.1	35	7	71
Carlson, Parker, Fr.	1	1	8.59	5	0	0	7.1	8	3	10
Copeland, Konner, So.	3	0	4.20	9	2	0	15	20	8	19
Drabick, Tyler, Gr.	1	0	9.82	8	0	0	7.1	10	5	13
Fuller, Brooks, Sr.	0	0	8.10	9	0	0	6.2	9	7	7
Gonzalez, Joseph, So.	7	4	3.22	15	14	0	78.1	83	15	54
Granzow, Cade, Fr.	0	0	4.91	7	0	0	7.1	9	4	4
Isbell, Chase, Jr.	1	1	4.82	14	0	0	18.2	17	14	23
LaRue, Nate, Jr.	0	0	1.69	5	0	0	5.1	7	3	4
Mullins, Hayden, Jr.	2	1	3.64	11	8	0	34.2	23	25	43
Sheehan, Tommy, Gr.	2	0	4.28	16	3	1	33.2	25	22	29
Skipper, Carson, Sr.	6	3	4.45	27	1	0	58.2	56	14	70
Swilling, Carson, So.	3	2	5.72	21	0	0	28.1	29	14	35

7. STANFORD

Coach: Dave Esquer. **Record:** 47-18

Player, Pos., Year	AVG	OBP	SLG	AB	R	2B	3B	HR	RBI	SB
Haskins, Trevor, INF, Fr.	.357	.333	.643	14	3	1	0	1	6	0
Barrera, Brett, 2B, Jr.	.351	.394	.575	259	50	19	3	11	53	0
Troy, Tommy, INF/OF, So.	.339	.371	.568	183	34	15	3	7	23	5
Graham, Carter, 1B, So.	.331	.399	.642	260	64	13	1	22	79	1
Jones, Brock, CF, Jr.	.324	.451	.664	253	78	13	5	21	57	16
Park,Eddie, LF, So.	.318	.412	.368	220	47	9	1	0	15	8
Crampton, Adam, SS, Jr.	.316	.395	.392	212	34	9	2	1	40	11
Huff, Kody, C, Jr.	.315	.411	.567	238	52	21	0	13	51	2
Montgomery, Braden, RF, Fr.	.294	.361	.596	245	50	16	2	18	57	6
Bowder, Drew, 3B, So.	.293	.350	.573	239	50	11	1	18	50	0
Burton, Grant, OF, Sr.	.286	.375	.429	7	1	1	0	0	1	0
Lomuscio, Joe, LF, Gr.	.237	.268	.368	38	6	2	0	1	7	1
Martinez, Vincent, C, Sr.	.203	.309	.464	69	11	3	0	5	11	0
Cobb, Owen, RF, Jr.	.190	.227	.238	21	5	1	0	0	3	0
Kretzschmar, Austin, 2B, Sr.	.167	.359	.233	30	3	2	0	0	1	0
Charlie Saum, C, Fr.	.143	.143	.214	14	1	1	0	0	1	0

Pitcher, Year	W	L	ERA	G	GS	SV	IP	H	BB	SO
Bruno, Ryan, So.	6	1	2.72	30	0	1	39.2	12	35	71
Dixon, Joey, So.	6	3	3.96	27	7	1	63.2	28	19	44
Dowd, Drew, So.	6	0	4.54	22	15	0	75.1	38	34	77
Fleischli, Nathan, Jr.	0	0	9.53	10	0	0	11.1	12	7	10
Jensen, Cody, RJr.	1	0	7.77	21	1	0	22	19	9	15
Mathews, Quinn, Jr.	9	2	3.08	27	9	9	99.1	34	49	111
Meier, Max, Jr.	1	0	7.31	12	0	0	16	13	4	16
Montgomery, Braden, Fr.	0	2	5.79	62	3	2	18.2	12	21	28
Moore, Justin, RJr.	0	0	7.84	8	0	0	10.1	9	1	10
O'Rourke, Tommy, So.	3	5	4.41	30	2	0	32.2	16	16	35
Pancer, Brandt, So.	3	0	3.18	25	0	2	39.2	14	11	32
Uber, Ty, Fr.	4	1	4.99	18	10	0	48.2	27	26	49
Williams, Alex, Sr.	8	4	3.20	18	18	0	101.1	36	25	96

8. TENNESSEE

Coach: Tony Vitello. **Record:** 57-9

Player, Pos., Year	AVG	OBP	SLG	AB	R	2B	3B	HR	RBI	SB
Beck, Jordan, RF, Jr.	.298	.391	.595	252	70	15	3	18	61	6
Booker, Kyle, OF, So.	.222	.364	.356	45	12	3	0	1	10	1
Burke, Blake, 1B/OF, Fr.	.326	.467	.821	95	30	3	1	14	32	2
Chambers, Logan, UTL, Jr.	.200	.371	.200	25	6	0	0	0	4	0

Dickey, Jared, LF, RFr.	.380	.484	.690	100	29	8	1	7	19	3
Ensley, Hunter, OF, RFr.	.188	.350	.313	16	5	2	0	0	0	0
Gilbert, Drew, CF, Jr.	.362	.455	.673	199	60	21	4	11	70	4
Lawson, Cortland, SS, Jr.	.269	.402	.512	201	42	9	2	12	45	2
Lipcius, Luc, 1B, Gr.	.313	.466	.667	198	70	11	1	19	44	14
Lipscomb, Trey, 3B, Sr.	.355	.428	.717	251	68	19	3	22	84	4
Moore, Christian, INF, Fr.	.305	.443	.619	118	30	3	2	10	36	1
Ortega, Jorel, 2B, RSo.	.323	.398	.672	235	57	20	4	18	61	3
Payne, Ethan, INF/OF, Jr.	.286	.500	.643	14	7	2	0	1	3	0
Russell, Evan, C, Gr.	.289	.390	.587	201	40	16	1	14	45	7
Scott, Christian, LF, Sr.	.200	.380	.400	70	24	2	0	4	14	8
Steenstra, Logan, SS, Jr.	.295	.426	.591	44	11	4	0	3	15	1
Stephenson, Seth, LF, Jr.	.339	.408	.508	183	46	17	1	4	28	25
Taylor, Charlie, C, RFr.	.056	.306	.083	36	6	1	0	0	3	3

Pitcher, Year	W	L	ERA	G	GS	SV	IP	H	BB	SO
Beam, Drew, Fr.	8	1	2.72	16	15	0	76	50	21	62
Brasosky, Gavin, Fr.	1	0	0.00	5	0	0	4.1	2	3	6
Burns, Chase, Fr.	8	2	2.91	17	14	0	80.1	65	25	103
Cherry, Grant, Fr.	0	0	5.40	5	0	0	3.1	1	9	5
Connell, Kirby, Jr.	4	0	1.66	30	0	0	38	27	6	36
Dollander, Chase, So.	10	0	2.39	16	14	0	79	50	13	108
Evans, Wyatt, Fr.	0	0	2.25	19	0	0	16	12	3	22
Fanning, Hollis, So.	0	0	2.70	5	0	0	3.1	7	1	3
Fitzgibbons, Jake, So.	0	0	3.86	6	1	0	7	2	9	10
Joyce, Ben, RJr.	2	1	2.23	27	1	0	32.1	18	14	53
Mabrey, Will, Jr.	2	0	2.63	29	0	0	41	34	5	52
McCracken, JD, Fr.	1	0	8.10	3	0	0	3.1	5	1	2
McLaughlin, Mark, Jr.	2	1	2.01	27	0	1	31.1	22	12	45
Patterson, Drew, RFr.	0	0	2.08	6	0	0	4.1	3	0	6
Sechrist, Zander, So.	4	0	1.67	17	11	0	43	27	7	46
Sewell, Camden, Sr.	7	1	2.52	26	1	1	50	40	8	42
Smith, Ethan, Sr.	1	0	7.36	6	0	0	3.2	6	6	3
Tidwell, Blade, So.	3	2	3.00	13	9	0	39	31	11	51
Walsh, Redmond, Gr.	4	1	2.52	27	0	7	39.1	26	10	40
Witt, Tanner, So.	2	0	1.64	2	2	0	11	9	3	14

9. TEXAS

Coach: David Pierce. **Record:** 47-22

Player, Pos., Year	AVG	OBP	SLG	AB	R	2B	3B	HR	RBI	SB
Ardoin, Silas, C, RSo.	.271	.391	.513	240	48	20	1	12	50	1
Campbell, Dylan, LF, So.	.267	.370	.494	176	40	8	1	10	29	14
Constantine, Cam, LF, RFr.	.000	.111	.000	7	0	0	0	0	1	0
Daly, Mitchell, 2B, So.	.237	.351	.367	207	34	13	1	4	37	4
Dayton, Cameron, 1B, Jr.	.000	.000	.000	2	0	0	0	0	0	0
Faltine, Trey, SS, RSo.	.282	.393	.552	241	60	18	1	15	56	6
Hodo, Douglas, CF, RSo.	.319	.418	.532	282	73	26	2	10	47	9
Kash, Gavin, INF, Fr.	.174	.269	.217	23	1	1	0	0	0	0
Kennedy, Eric, LF, RJr.	.300	.386	.471	170	42	6	1	7	29	10
Melendez, Ivan, 1B, RJr.	.387	.508	.863	248	75	18	2	32	94	1
Messinger, Skyler, 3B, RSr.	.364	.414	.560	250	46	14	1	11	59	1
O'Dowd, Jack, INF, So.	.231	.348	.308	39	8	0	0	1	5	0
Powell, Peyton, UTL, RSo.	.250	.333	.250	8	0	0	0	0	0	0
Schuessler, Kimble, C, So.	.350	.435	.500	20	3	0	0	1	4	0
Stehly, Murphy, RF, RSr.	.367	.424	.662	278	65	23	1	19	61	8
Todd, Austin, OF, RSr.	.332	.407	.481	187	38	8	1	6	31	1
Whitehead, Ace, LF, Fr.	.556	.619	.667	18	8	2	0	0	2	0

Pitcher, Year	W	L	ERA	G	GS	SV	IP	H	BB	SO
Blair, Daniel, RJr.	2	1	7.47	12	0	0	15.2	18	13	17
Cobb, Coy, RJr.	2	1	4.60	15	0	0	15.2	14	2	10
Duplantier II, Andre, RFr.	3	1	5.93	17	6	0	30.1	28	17	25
Eckhardt, Justin, RSo.	1	1	8.17	11	5	0	25.1	30	12	23
Gordon, Lucas, So.	7	2	3.05	18	16	0	85.2	71	26	77
Hansen, Pete, RSo.	11	3	3.76	17	17	0	107.2	94	19	120
Harrison, Luke, Fr.	0	0	3.06	32	1	2	35.1	34	16	32
Johnson, Jr., Lebarron, RFr.	0	1	3.18	18	0	0	17	12	11	21
Morehouse, Zane, RSo.	3	1	6.00	20	6	0	39	39	16	43
Nixon, Aaron, So.	1	3	5.04	26	0	5	30.1	24	25	38
Olivarez, Marcus, RSr.	1	0	0.69	19	0	0	26	16	13	21
Southard, Jared, RSo.	4	1	2.76	25	0	0	29.1	15	19	46
Stevens, Tristan, RSr.	7	6	4.73	26	12	3	85.2	90	24	72
Stewart, Joshua, Fr.	0	0	4.63	10	1	0	11.2	13	8	13
Sthele, Travis, RFr.	3	1	6.03	21	3	0	34.1	34	19	32
Whitehead, Ace, Fr.	0	0	13.50	1	0	0	0.2	3	0	0

10. VIRGINIA TECH

Coach: John Szcef. **Record:** 45-14

Player, Pos., Year	AVG	OBP	SLG	AB	R	2B	3B	HR	RBI	SB
Biddison, Nick, RF, Jr.	.351	.434	.598	251	65	14	3	14	47	21
Cross, Gavin, CF, So.	.328	.411	.660	244	70	14	8	17	50	12
DeMartini, Carson, 3B, Fr.	.341	.452	.659	205	54	14	3	15	50	5
Donlon, Lucas, 1B, So.	.217	.341	.304	69	17	3	0	1	11	0
Ebel, Gehrig, C, So.	.167	.318	.333	18	5	0	0	1	3	0
Hartigan, Conor, OF, Sr.	.232	.310	.384	164	22	11	1	4	32	3
Hatfield, Dylan, C, Fr.	.000	.100	.000	0	2	0	0	0	0	0
Holesa, Nick, 1B, RJr.	.209	.306	.349	86	14	9	0	1	9	0
Hunter, Cade, C, So.	.330	.440	.637	212	46	14	0	17	66	11
Hurley, Jack, LF, So.	.375	.452	.664	232	59	23	1	14	55	10
Jones, Carson, RF, So.	.327	.439	.800	55	19	2	0	8	23	0
Malinowski, Eduardo, 2B, Gr.	.252	.341	.514	210	47	13	3	12	48	6
Martin, Christian, 2B, Fr.	.261	.424	.435	46	8	5	0	1	3	1
Reback, Brennan, CF, Sr.	.333	.500	.333	6	4	0	0	0	0	0
Schobel, Tanner, SS, So.	.362	.445	.689	235	68	18	1	19	74	7
Seagears, Jonah, OF, Jr.	.143	.143	.143	7	0	0	0	0	0	0
Swisher, Cade, OF, So.	.095	.259	.238	21	3	0	0	1	3	0
Tackett, Sam, INF, RFr.	.237	.456	.316	38	9	0	0	1	5	0

Pitcher, Year	W	L	ERA	G	GS	SV	IP	H	BB	SO
Dean, Tyler, Fr.	0	0	13.50	6	0	0	4	5	9	7
Firoved, Graham, Jr.	5	0	4.77	27	0	2	51	44	28	72
Fisher, Sean, Gr.	0	0	3.86	10	0	0	7	0	13	10
Geber, Jordan, Gr.	1	2	5.40	16	7	0	35	39	9	40
Green, Griffin, So.	7	3	4.83	16	16	0	72.2	83	26	61
Hackenberg, Drue, Fr.	10	2	3.30	17	16	0	92.2	95	19	87
Higgins, Kiernan, Gr.	3	0	1.99	21	0	5	31.2	22	14	38
Hurney, Jonah, Jr.	6	1	2.70	25	0	1	43.1	34	14	54
Johnson, Noah, So.	0	0	13.50	2	0	0	1.1	2	3	0
Kennedy, Ryan, Sr.	1	3	6.85	11	4	0	22.1	40	10	23
Kirtner, Brady, RFr.	1	0	7.31	18	0	0	16	13	9	21
Metz, Ryan, Sr.	2	0	3.64	18	4	1	34.2	33	9	28
Okuda, Ryan, Sr.	2	1	3.66	13	8	0	32	27	17	24
Ritchey, Jackson, So.	0	1	9.53	6	2	0	5.2	6	3	8
Sakellaris, Peter ,So.	0	0	11.57	5	0	0	4.2	7	5	1
Umberger, Grant, So.	0	0	5.06	8	0	0	5.1	5	5	9
Weycker, Henry, So.	6	1	4.38	25	1	1	49.1	52	19	39
Worley, Christian, So.	1	0	5.06	14	0	1	21.1	17	8	34

11. OREGON STATE

Coach: Mitch Canham. **Record:** 48-18

Player, Pos., Year	AVG	OBP	SLG	AB	R	2B	3B	HR	RBI	SB
Bazzana, Travis, 2B, Fr.	.306	.425	.478	245	58	16	4	6	44	14
Boyd, Justin, RF, So.	.373	.490	.577	241	72	14	4	9	53	24
Dernedde, Kyle, SS, So.	.216	.319	.271	199	35	6	1	1	15	5
Dukart, Jake, 3B, Jr.	.262	.368	.418	122	18	5	4	2	20	1
Forrester, Garret, 1B, So.	.332	.480	.498	229	50	11	0	9	60	1
Fuchs, Greg, OF, Jr.	.231	.379	.291	134	23	6	1	0	24	1
Gretler, Matthew, 3B, Jr.	.193	.306	.377	114	15	6	0	5	21	0
Guerra, Mason, 3B, Fr.	.333	.412	.489	45	8	7	0	0	7	0
Kasper, Brady, RF, So.	.206	.282	.353	34	5	2	0	1	5	0
Logan, Gavin, C, Jr.	.281	.370	.431	167	28	12	2	3	36	1
McDowell, Micah, CF, So.	.147	.256	.176	34	5	1	0	0	3	1
Meckler, Wade, LF, Jr.	.347	.456	.478	268	81	23	3	2	32	12
Melton, Jacob, CF, Jr.	.360	.424	.670	261	66	22	4	17	83	21
Myro IV, Paul, SS, RFr.	.200	.385	.200	10	4	0	0	0	1	0
Smith, Tanner, C, Fr.	.232	.327	.411	95	11	8	0	3	13	0
Trosky, Jabin, SS, Fr.	.288	.386	.305	59	5	1	0	0	11	0
Wheeler, TJ, C/INF, Jr.	.244	.417	.333	45	5	1	0	1	17	0

Pithcer, Year	W	L	ERA	G	GS	SV	IP	H	BB	SO
Boisvert, Braden, Jr.	0	0	8.59	10	0	0	7.1	10	5	7
Brown, Ryan, RFr.	5	1	4.91	28	0	9	33	28	12	40
Carpenter, DJ, Jr.	2	3	7.77	22	0	1	24.1	33	8	31
Ferrer, Ben, Jr.	4	0	1.72	24	1	3	62.2	38	14	78
Grewe, David, Fr.	0	0	18.00	4	0	0	4	10	2	2
Hibbard, Jayson, So.	0	0	8.03	12	0	0	12.1	20	4	7
Hjerpe, Cooper, So.	11	2	2.53	18	17	1	103.1	67	23	161

Pitcher, Year	W	L	ERA	G	GS	SV	IP	H	BB	SO
Hunter, Jaren, So.	2	2	3.97	14	12	0	56.2	52	11	47
Kmatz, Jacob, Fr.	8	2	4.19	16	15	0	77.1	73	20	65
Lattery, AJ, So.	0	1	2.57	13	5	0	28	21	8	24
Lawson, Ian, So.	3	0	6.41	14	0	0	19.2	29	12	19
Pfennigs, Jake, Jr.	4	1	3.96	11	11	0	36.1	35	27	30
Sebby, Reid, Sr.	2	2	3.46	26	0	3	41.2	36	15	39
Thorsteinson, Justin, So.	0	0	6.75	9	0	0	8	8	4	4
Townsend, Brock, Jr.	2	1	4.40	19	4	1	43	54	7	36
Verburg, Mitchell, RSr.	5	3	5.61	25	1	1	33.2	34	14	37

12. LOUISVILLE

Coach: Dan McDonnell. **Record:** 42-21-1

Player, Pos., Year	AVG	OBP	SLG	AB	R	2B	3B	HR	RBI	SB
Anderson, Brandon, 3B, Fr.	.316	.422	.316	38	7	0	0	0	5	0
Beard, Logan, 2B, So.	.310	.410	.431	216	40	12	1	4	54	2
Benson, JT, LF, So.	.224	.308	.403	67	9	3	3	1	10	1
Bianco, Ben, 1B, Sr.	.267	.337	.475	221	41	7	3	11	52	6
Bode, Austin, C, Fr.	.294	.409	.412	17	5	2	0	0	5	0
Hawkins, Tyeler, RF, Jr.	.313	.421	.500	16	8	1	1	0	5	3
Humphrey, Isaac, RF, So.	.328	.458	.490	198	44	15	1	5	38	11
Knapczyk, Christian, SS, So.	.346	.480	.465	217	72	12	4	2	27	17
Masterman, Cameron, LF, Sr.	.305	.399	.597	233	51	14	0	18	61	1
Metzinger, Ben, 3B, Sr.	.312	.427	.591	269	66	14	2	19	69	11
Payton, Jack, C, So.	.350	.429	.504	254	58	23	2	4	54	5
Rushing, Dalton, C, Jr.	.310	.470	.686	226	68	16	0	23	62	4
Seng, Chris, OF, Sr.	.385	.636	.615	13	15	3	0	0	3	5
Smith, Noah, SS, Fr.	.318	.340	.386	44	12	1	1	0	4	1
Usher, Levi, CF, Sr.	.285	.362	.455	246	53	15	3	7	49	36
Westcott, Drake, 1B, So.	.158	.190	.368	19	2	1	0	1	6	0

Pitcher, Year	W	L	ERA	G	GS	SV	IP	H	BB	SO
Barrett, Seamus, So.	0	0	11.68	6	3	0	12.1	17	9	19
Corbett, Kaleb, So.	2	1	8.10	20	2	1	23.1	32	10	24
Dowler, Adam, Fr.	0	0	4.91	14	0	0	14.2	20	8	18
Ferris, Jacob, Jr.	0	1	6.00	11	1	0	15	19	17	18
Galvan, Alex, So.	0	0	6.35	16	0	0	17	19	6	20
Grundy, Kade, Fr.	1	1	6.48	15	2	0	16.2	17	12	11
Hawks, Ryan, Jr.	5	3	4.96	27	1	1	49	54	16	65
Koger, Will, Fr.	0	1	12.27	11	2	0	14.2	24	12	10
Kuehner, Tate, Jr.	7	3	3.57	25	8	4	70.2	61	32	70
Langworthy, JR, Sr.	0	0	0.00	3	0	0	0.2	0	1	0
Liggett, Carson, Fr.	3	0	4.68	18	4	0	25	18	15	21
Lohman, Carter, Sr.	1	2	6.04	15	4	0	25.1	21	26	24
Phillips, Riley, So.	5	1	4.35	15	13	0	58	57	17	69
Poland, Jared, Sr.	5	5	3.46	17	15	0	83.1	79	32	103
Prosecky, Michael, Jr.	2	1	3.38	26	0	11	37.1	31	22	44
Robinson, Cameron, Sr.	1	0	9.00	12	0	0	16	21	8	22
Schmeltz, Garrett, Sr.	2	0	3.99	20	3	0	29.1	21	14	40
Seed, Luke, Sr.	1	1	9.28	5	3	0	10.2	7	10	17
Walter, Kyle, Fr.	2	0	8.25	17	1	0	12	14	14	11
Webster, Evan, Jr.	2	1	4.40	21	0	1	30.2	31	6	31
Wiegman, Ben, So.	3	0	5.93	13	2	0	13.2	13	11	9

13. NORTH CAROLINA

Coach: Scott Forbes. **Record:** 42-22

Player, Pos., Year	AVG	OBP	SLG	AB	R	2B	3B	HR	RBI	SB
Alvarez, Patrick, 2B, So.	.147	.256	.235	34	11	0	0	1	6	0
Castagnozzi, Johnny, 2B, So.	.257	.363	.447	206	36	9	0	10	30	1
Causey, Tyler, LF, So.	.167	.167	.167	6	0	0	0	0	2	0
Cook, Casey, LF, Fr.	.000	.111	.000	8	0	0	0	0	1	0
Frick, Tomas, C, So.	.260	.348	.372	215	22	15	0	3	33	0
Grintz, Eric, C, So.	.310	.432	.448	29	6	1	0	1	9	0
Holbrook, Reece, LF, Fr.	.160	.192	.280	25	9	1	1	0	3	2
Honeycutt, Vance, CF, Fr.	.296	.409	.672	247	66	10	4	25	57	29
Horvath, Mac, 3B, So.	.268	.390	.557	246	64	15	1	18	53	19
Inclan, Clemente, 3B, Sr.	.000	.167	.000	5	0	0	0	0	0	0
Jaconski, Joe, RF, Fr.	.174	.269	.174	23	1	0	0	0	0	0
Madej, Mikey, LF, Sr.	.325	.410	.456	160	27	5	2	4	25	2
Osuna, Alberto, 1B, So.	.265	.360	.551	234	40	7	0	20	57	1
Riemer, Max, C, RJr.	.185	.353	.222	27	1	1	0	0	3	0
Serretti, Danny, SS, Jr.	.365	.437	.567	263	56	17	3	10	54	2
Stewart, Will, RF, So.	.091	.222	.182	22	4	2	0	0	1	0
Stokely, Hunter, 1B, So.	.285	.387	.376	186	20	9	1	2	25	2
Wilkerson, Colby, 2B, So.	.222	.355	.270	63	14	1	1	0	4	0
Zarate, Angel, RF, RJr.	.352	.425	.500	284	58	19	1	7	40	4

Pitcher, Year	W	L	ERA	G	GS	SV	IP	H	BB	SO
Bovair, Connor, So.	5	4	5.50	23	9	1	54	53	32	49
Carlson, Max, So.	4	3	3.71	18	18	0	77.2	70	38	88
Cozart, Caleb, RSo.	0	0	1.08	8	0	0	8.1	7	4	7
Gillian, Gage, Sr.	3	3	4.13	33	1	0	52.1	55	16	40
Mott, Kyle, Jr.	6	3	6.03	24	1	1	40.1	44	17	55
O'Brien, Caden, Sr.	3	1	3.86	25	0	5	28	24	15	35
Ollio, Connor, Jr.	1	1	6.75	21	3	0	24	37	8	21
Palermo, Davis, So.	2	1	2.78	37	0	5	58.1	40	24	74
Peavyhouse, Shaddon, Gr.	3	3	4.97	18	6	0	29	29	19	23
Pry, Nik, Jr.	3	0	4.54	32	0	0	37.2	44	18	43
Rapp, Shawn, So.	4	0	3.80	42	2	1	45	42	22	59
Sandy, Will, So.	1	0	2.59	12	6	0	24.1	18	18	14
Schaeffer, Brandon, Jr.	7	3	3.75	21	18	1	96	110	24	71

14. MIAMI

Coach: Gino DiMare. **Record:** 40-20

Player, Pos., Year	AVG	OBP	SLG	AB	R	2B	3B	HR	RBI	SB
Burke, Jacob, CF, So.	.347	.425	.599	222	59	13	2	13	58	10
Carrier, Lorenzo, RF, Fr.	.250	.413	.528	36	10	2	1	2	9	0
Garcia, Ariel, INF, Fr.	.306	.389	.548	62	12	0	0	5	14	0
Gonzalez, Jr., Dorian, 2B, Fr.	.263	.354	.346	156	32	7	0	2	21	1
Gonzalez, Renzo, RF, Fr.	.241	.353	.414	58	12	2	1	2	7	1
Gutierrez, Gaby, RF, Fr.	.247	.379	.424	85	18	3	0	4	15	0
Jones, JD, C, Fr.	.294	.400	.294	17	6	0	0	0	1	0
Kayfus, CJ, 1B, So.	.366	.460	.525	238	64	12	1	8	51	16
Levenson, Zach, OF, So.	.300	.420	.531	130	28	5	2	7	28	0
Long, Jacoby, CF, So.	.250	.315	.333	48	12	1	0	1	5	6
Morales, Yohandy, 3B, So.	.329	.411	.650	240	65	17	3	18	59	6
Perez, Carlos, C, So.	.191	.298	.319	47	3	3	0	1	5	0
Pitelli, Dominic, SS, So.	.249	.335	.403	221	39	10	0	8	45	9
Romero, Jr., Maxwell, C, Jr.	.272	.378	.507	217	41	15	0	12	54	0
Rosario, Mike, RF, Jr.	.222	.357	.272	81	14	2	1	0	4	1
Villegas, Edgardo, LF, Fr.	.262	.405	.445	164	37	12	0	6	30	3
Wallen, Henry, 2B, So.	.217	.415	.326	46	5	2	0	1	7	0

Pitcher, Year	W	L	ERA	G	GS	SV	IP	H	BB	SO
Arguelles, Anthony, Jr.	2	0	4.82	18	0	0	18.2	20	11	28
Dubberly, Jordan, RJr.	2	0	5.74	20	1	0	26.2	28	12	31
Gallo, Ronaldo, So.	3	0	3.47	26	0	0	36.1	27	17	42
Garland, Jake, So.	6	2	4.00	14	12	1	65.1	72	11	54
Gates, JP, Jr.	1	0	6.75	14	0	0	9.1	9	7	6
Ligon, Karson, Fr.	6	6	4.90	16	15	0	75.1	82	32	67
McFarlane, Alex, So.	3	2	4.00	27	4	0	45	41	20	68
Palmquist, Carson, So.	9	4	2.89	16	16	0	84	70	32	118
Raudelunas, Matt, RJr.	0	0	8.22	10	0	0	7.2	6	10	10
Rosario, Alejandro, So.	2	3	7.05	15	12	0	60	83	25	52
Schlesinger, Rafe, RFr.	1	0	3.38	19	0	0	10.2	10	9	8
Torres, Alejandro, Fr.	3	0	7.13	25	0	0	24	19	11	38
Walters, Andrew, So.	0	1	1.65	24	0	14	32.2	13	6	62
Ziehl, Gage, Fr.	2	2	4.04	30	0	1	35.2	28	16	52

15. CONNECTICUT

Coach: Jim Penders. **Record:** 50-16

Player, Pos. Year	AVG	OBP	SLG	AB	R	2B	3B	HR	RBI	SB
Brown, Chris, 3B, So.	.179	.226	.321	56	9	3	1	1	7	0
Bushling, Zach, 3B, Sr.	.270	.357	.435	248	51	16	2	7	47	9
Dana, Casey, RF, Gr.	.313	.381	.546	262	57	21	2	12	61	4
Donlan, Matt, C, RJr.	.260	.375	.489	219	47	14	0	12	60	3
Fedko, Christian, INF, Sr.	.169	.354	.220	59	9	3	0	0	10	0
Ferrer, Kevin, OF, RSo.	.264	.344	.396	53	12	4	0	1	10	0
Garbowski, Matt, C, Fr.	.294	.368	.412	51	8	3	0	1	12	0
Huber, Ben, 1B, Gr.	.327	.431	.546	260	69	20	2	11	66	7
Morton, Korey, DH, So.	.411	.451	.661	124	26	11	1	6	28	9
Padilla, Bryan, SS, RFr.	.278	.383	.467	227	51	15	2	8	37	4
Simmons, TC, CF, RJr.	.278	.437	.466	223	55	19	4	5	42	6
Smith, David, 2B, RSo.	.307	.405	.496	254	64	11	5	9	48	23
Stephenson, Zach, PH, Fr.	.071	.133	.214	14	5	0	1	0	0	1
Stock, Erik, LF, Sr.	.364	.435	.596	272	65	25	4	10	55	6

Pitcher, Year	W	L	ERA	G	GS	SV	IP	H	BB	SO

Afthim, Brady, Fr.	0	0	3.60	22	0	0	20	18	9	27
Alejandro, Hector, RFr.	1	1	8.62	12	2	0	15.2	23	9	17
Chudoba, Cole, Gr.	3	1	2.89	16	6	0	43.2	48	12	32
Coe, Garrett, So.	2	2	3.79	23	0	2	38	34	21	38
Cooke, Ian, Fr.	7	1	3.64	20	6	1	54.1	52	17	54
Favieri, Sam, So.	0	0	6.35	7	0	0	5.2	2	7	8
Gallagher, Pat, So.	11	3	3.41	17	17	0	103	97	29	110
Kirby, Devin, Sr.	2	1	4.60	20	0	0	31.1	35	8	36
McBride, Bobby, So.	0	0	6.00	5	0	0	3	4	5	5
O'Donnell, Brendan, So.	3	1	3.00	31	0	1	15	21	7	19
Peterson, Austin, Sr.	11	3	3.83	18	17	0	110.1	100	25	147
Quinn, Braden, Fr.	1	0	5.28	11	2	1	15.1	19	7	13
Stefanoni, Enzo, Gr.	6	1	3.51	17	16	0	84.2	80	16	61
Sullivan, Jack, Fr.	1	1	0.79	21	0	0	22.2	15	7	26
Wang, Jimmy, RJr.	0	0	3.38	2	0	0	2.2	2	1	3
Willis, Justin, Sr.	2	1	5.54	24	0	15	26	24	11	44

16. SOUTHERN MISSISSIPPI

Coach: Scott Berry. **Record:** 47-19

Player, Pos., Year	AVG	OBP	SLG	AB	R	2B	3B	HR	RBI	SB
Dickerson, Dustin, SS, So.	.320	.397	.409	269	44	24	0	0	32	6
Ewing, Reece, LF, Jr.	.260	.430	.480	200	43	10	2	10	34	2
Faust, Brady, CF, So.	.176	.282	.176	34	8	0	0	0	1	3
Fischer, Charlie, DH, Jr.	.167	.310	.271	48	5	3	1	0	4	0
Johnson, Blake, C, Jr.	.269	.381	.419	93	16	5	0	3	23	1
Lynch, Danny, 3B, Jr.	.286	.375	.408	245	42	15	0	5	30	0
McGillis, Will, 2B, Jr.	.265	.394	.543	230	53	12	2	16	51	6
Montenegro, Gabe, CF, Sr.	.277	.342	.336	256	33	8	2	1	34	2
Montenegro, Rodrigo, C, So.	.307	.447	.378	127	21	9	0	0	16	0
Paetow, Carson, RF, RFr.	.271	.383	.546	229	46	15	0	16	48	4
Sargent, Christopher, 1B, Jr.	.269	.312	.545	275	56	9	2	21	58	2
Wilks, Slade, OF, So.	.288	.394	.511	219	41	17	1	10	37	4

Pitcher, Year	W	L	ERA	G	GS	SV	IP	H	BB	SO
Adams, Matthew, So.	2	2	6.56	9	5	0	23.1	23	6	32
Best, Chandler, So.	0	1	4.91	14	0	0	18.1	18	8	26
Boyd, Drew, Jr.	1	0	3.38	11	1	0	10.2	16	6	14
Ethridge, Ben, So.	1	3	4.15	12	5	0	34.2	33	7	39
Gillentine, Aubrey, Jr.	2	0	1.93	6	0	0	9.1	8	5	8
Hall, Tanner, So.	9	3	2.81	19	17	0	109	98	14	146
Harper, Landon, So.	2	2	3.30	31	0	12	43.2	36	9	50
Mazza, Niko, Fr.	0	0	5.06	5	0	0	5.1	3	3	6
Ramsey, Garrett, Jr.	5	1	2.61	21	0	4	31	32	11	45
Rhodes, Isaiah, So.	3	0	4.15	21	0	1	30.1	24	16	38
Riggins, Hunter, Gr.	8	4	2.59	16	16	0	97.1	85	21	85
Rogers, Dalton, So.	1	1	1.95	23	0	6	37	16	23	57
Storm, Justin, So.	3	0	4.30	13	0	0	14.2	10	5	20
Stuart, Tyler, So.	4	0	3.38	22	4	1	40	34	13	38
Waldrep, Hurston, So.	6	2	3.20	17	17	0	90	71	33	140
Wehunt, Blake, So.	0	0	16.20	1	1	0	1.2	5	1	2

17. EAST CAROLINA

Coach: Cliff Godwin Record: 46-21

Player, Pos., Year	AVG	OBP	SLG	AB	R	2B	3B	HR	RBI	SB
Alec Makarewicz, 3B, So.	.270	.346	.464	248	52	15	0	11	45	2
Ben Newton, C, Sr.	.276	.378	.353	156	28	9	0	1	19	2
Bryson Worrell, CF, Sr.	.335	.401	.631	263	61	12	3	20	62	10
Cam Clonch, OF/1B, So.	.283	.311	.478	113	21	4	0	6	21	0
Carter Cunningham, RF, So.	.227	.317	.386	88	13	3	1	3	16	4
CJ Boyd, 1B/OF, So.	.125	.200	.125	32	3	0	0	0	0	0
Garrett Saylor, P, Jr.	1.000	1.000	1.000	1	1	0	0	0	0	0
Jacob Jenkins-Cowart, RF, Fr.	.330	.367	.549	233	44	10	1	13	65	6
Jacob Starling, 2B, So.	.243	.383	.403	144	34	5	0	6	31	2
Joey Berini, INF, So.	.240	.316	.260	50	10	1	0	0	7	0
Joey Rezek, OF/C, So.	.250	.333	.375	8	6	1	0	0	3	0
Josh Moylan, 1B, So.	.221	.355	.416	190	31	11	4	6	27	2
Justin Wilcoxen, C, So.	.276	.327	.398	98	9	6	0	2	9	0
Lane Hoover, LF, Jr.	.341	.423	.416	255	55	15	2	0	33	12
Ryan McCrystal, C, Fr.	.148	.294	.259	27	2	0	0	1	5	0
Ryder Giles, SS, Jr.	.176	.288	.235	68	10	1	0	1	7	2
Ryley Johnson, RF, So.	.105	.227	.105	19	1	0	0	0	0	0
Zach Agnos, SS, So.	.330	.405	.479	267	56	15	2	7	42	9

Pitcher, Year	W	L	ERA	G	GS	SV	IP	H	BB	SO
Agnos, Zach, So.	3	0	2.31	21	0	3	23.1	11	7	19
Beal, Danny, So.	5	2	4.97	30	2	1	38	33	21	40
Beeker, Merritt, Fr.	0	0	2.70	12	3	0	13.1	11	12	13
Brooks, Skylar, So.	0	1	4.50	14	0	2	12	14	9	14
Giles, Ryder, Jr.	4	1	3.27	15	9	1	44	45	8	35
Grosz, Jake, So.	4	5	5.65	25	11	0	57.1	62	19	61
Hunter, Jake, Fr.	1	2	5.18	18	12	0	41.2	42	7	43
Kuchmaner, Jake, Sr.	4	3	3.83	13	10	0	44.2	50	16	39
Logusch, Nick, Sr.	0	2	7.36	9	3	1	11	17	9	15
Lunsford-Shenkman, Wyatt, Fr.	1	1	3.09	12	0	0	11.2	14	7	9
Mayhue, CJ, So.	6	1	3.36	31	12	1	72.1	53	17	75
Saylor, Garrett, Jr.	6	3	5.01	39	2	5	79	69	23	108
Spivey, Carter, Jr.	8	0	2.83	35	2	5	76.1	70	19	76
Terwilliger, Ben, Jr.	2	0	3.86	27	0	5	35	25	13	46
Wilson, Bradley, RFr.	0	0	7.04	7	0	1	7.2	8	8	8
Yesavage, Trey, Fr.	1	0	4.50	34	0	2	26	26	19	45

18. MARYLAND

Coach: Rob Vaughn. **Record:** 48-14

Player, Pos., Year	AVG	OBP	SLG	AB	R	2B	3B	HR	RBI	SB
Shliger, Luke, C, So.	.353	.495	.602	249	79	22	2	12	58	14
Schreffler, Jr., Troy, RF, Jr.	.340	.421	.557	253	67	23	1	10	57	14
Heffley, James, C, RSo.	.333	.333	1.333	3	1	0	0	1	1	0
Alleyne, Chris, CF, RSr.	.331	.422	.673	263	73	16	1	24	79	24
Petrutz, Ian, OF, Fr.	.324	.444	.639	108	28	7	0	9	35	0
Lorusso, Nick, 3B, Jr.	.322	.409	.562	258	62	17	0	15	70	0
Keister, Kevin, 2B, So.	.317	.420	.582	189	53	15	1	11	44	4
Costes, Maxwell, 1B, Sr.	.296	.441	.575	226	57	15	0	16	52	0
Zmarzlak, Bobby, LF, Jr.	.291	.403	.526	234	64	8	1	15	43	6
Shaw, Matt, SS, So.	.290	.381	.604	245	50	11	0	22	67	12
Orr, Jacob, 2B, Fr.	.250	.292	.341	44	8	4	0	0	12	0
Martin, Zach, OF, Fr.	.207	.368	.345	29	6	1	0	1	2	0
Lane, Sean, INF, Fr.	.200	.360	.300	40	7	1	0	1	7	0
Langerman, Riley, C, Jr.	.194	.390	.226	31	9	1	0	0	3	0
Grace, Drew, 2B, Jr.	.143	.219	.214	28	5	2	0	0	3	0
Bouma, Michael, INF, Jr.	.133	.350	.133	15	3	0	0	0	1	0

Pitcher, Year	W	L	ERA	G	GS	SV	IP	H	BB	SO
Belgrave, Nigel, RFr.	2	0	7.50	16	0	3	18	14	22	25
Dean, Nick, Jr.	6	2	4.57	15	15	0	82.2	84	27	80
Falco, Jr., David, RSo.	7	1	2.84	19	0	2	31.2	26	7	31
Glock, Will, RJr.	1	0	5.40	20	0	1	18.1	21	12	15
Heine, Sean, Sr.	2	1	8.67	30	0	3	27	30	24	32
Johnson, Andrew, Fr.	2	1	4.12	17	4	0	19.2	13	19	18
Lorusso, Nick, Jr.	1	1	6.52	8	0	0	9.2	11	4	8
Mrotek, Noah, Fr.	3	1	5.40	14	0	0	18.1	20	11	19
Orlando, Matt, Jr.	1	0	5.56	12	0	0	11.1	16	9	11
Ott, Logan, So.	2	0	5.86	14	8	1	50.2	54	11	25
Ramsey, Ryan, Jr.	11	1	3.22	16	15	0	92.1	63	41	90
Robinson, Nick, Gr.	0	1	6.28	17	2	0	28.2	28	9	23
Savacool, Jason, So.	8	3	2.93	17	16	0	107.2	84	28	123
Stellpflug, Gavin, So.	0	0	11.70	10	0	0	10	16	6	9
Van Buren, Ryan, Fr.	2	1	9.97	16	2	1	21.2	31	8	15
Walsh, Michael, Fr.	0	1	14.73	8	0	0	7.1	7	10	10

19. OKLAHOMA STATE

Coach: Josh Holliday. **Record:** 42-22

Player, Pos., Year	AVG	OBP	SLG	AB	R	2B	3B	HR	RBI	SB
Adkison, Chase, C, So.	.240	.316	.370	146	30	7	0	4	25	1
Bay, John, RF, RFr.	.324	.415	.500	34	8	3	0	1	4	0
Brown, Brett, INF/OF, Jr.	.313	.436	.563	32	9	2	0	2	13	1
Brown, Marcus, SS, So.	.316	.378	.441	247	44	15	2	4	31	5
Brumbaugh, Cayden, 2B, Fr.	.318	.348	.409	22	1	0	1	0	1	0
Crull, Jaxson, RF, So.	.262	.347	.333	42	18	3	0	0	8	6
Daugherty, Ian, C, Fr.	.309	.402	.412	68	11	4	0	1	12	1
Doersching, Griffin, 1B, Gr.	.296	.407	.673	159	29	13	1	15	58	1
Ehrhard, Zach, RF, Fr.	.332	.429	.409	220	60	8	0	3	31	18
Martin, Garrett, INF/OF, Jr.	.250	.345	.458	48	6	2	1	2	9	0
McLean, Nolan, 3B, So.	.285	.397	.595	242	55	16	1	19	47	2
Mendham, David, 1B, Jr.	.276	.385	.498	221	46	16	0	11	45	0
Meola, Aidan, 3B, Fr.	.286	.333	.457	35	7	4	1	0	8	0
Miller-Green, Lyle, INF/OF, So.	.059	.238	.059	17	2	0	0	0	2	0

Player, Pos., Year	AVG	OBP	SLG	AB	R	2B	3B	HR	RBI	SB
Morrill, Hueston, SS, Jr.	.242	.398	.303	66	16	4	0	0	6	7
Riggio, Roc, 2B, Fr.	.295	.413	.519	210	54	14	0	11	47	2
Thompson, Jake, LF, Gr.	.350	.453	.610	254	52	20	2	14	67	3
Trenkle, Caeden, CF, So.	.302	.429	.467	182	44	8	2	6	41	11

Pitcher, Year	W	L	ERA	G	GS	SV	IP	H	BB	SO
Bogusz, Ryan, So.	3	1	3.86	20	3	1	37.1	32	16	34
Bowman, Colton, So.	0	0	10.80	4	0	0	1.2	1	3	1
Campbell, Justin, So.	9	2	3.82	17	16	0	101.1	83	25	141
Davis, Kale, So.	1	1	4.25	26	2	0	42.1	32	20	56
Kyle, Landry, So.	1	0	0.00	4	0	0	2.2	0	2	5
Marsh, Dillon, Jr.	1	0	4.62	14	4	0	25.1	30	15	25
Martin, Trevor, So.	4	3	4.75	30	5	9	47.1	40	22	79
McLean, Nolan, So.	2	1	4.97	23	0	5	25.1	20	13	39
Mederos, Victor, So.	4	4	5.59	14	13	0	66	69	21	62
Morrill, Hueston ,Jr.	1	3	5.87	14	1	1	23	25	9	26
Osmond, Bryce, So.	4	2	4.75	12	12	0	60.2	52	31	77
Phansalkar, Roman, Jr.	6	3	3.46	29	0	0	54.2	45	22	45
Ramsey, Jimmy, Gr.	1	0	1.80	6	0	0	5	1	5	5
Root, Bayden, Jr.	3	1	7.96	21	0	0	26	25	13	30
Stone, Mitchell, Jr.	2	0	6.10	15	8	0	41.1	58	13	39
Ure, Ryan, Fr.	0	1	7.36	13	0	0	11	10	11	15

20. TEXAS CHRISTIAN

Coach: Kirk Saarloos. **Record:** 38-22

Player, Pos., Year	AVG	OBP	SLG	AB	R	2B	3B	HR	RBI	SB
Berkley, Garrison, LF, RFr.	.189	.304	.216	37	5	1	0	0	2	3
Bishop, David, 1B, Fr.	.261	.345	.399	218	40	8	2	6	47	3
Blackledge, Owen, INF, Fr.	.083	.350	.167	12	2	1	0	0	2	0
Boyers, Luke, RF, So.	.250	.345	.397	224	46	11	2	6	37	11
Brown, Porter, LF, RSo.	.276	.385	.480	98	24	5	0	5	23	8
Byrne, Kurtis, C, So.	.291	.361	.447	206	33	15	1	5	44	2
Goodloe, Bobby, UTL, Jr.	.252	.354	.364	107	18	9	0	1	18	1
Green, Brody, 3B, Fr.	.143	.333	.571	7	2	0	0	1	1	0
Maxwell, Logan, LF, Fr.	.194	.372	.250	72	11	4	0	0	12	5
Nunez, Elijah, CF, So.	.287	.435	.368	223	61	7	4	1	31	31
Petrie, Michael, C, Gr.	.083	.368	.167	12	4	1	0	0	2	0
Rodgers, Gray, 2B, Sr.	.255	.357	.382	212	47	13	1	4	40	6
Sacco, Tommy, SS, Sr.	.355	.443	.645	231	58	23	1	14	58	18
Speaker, Mason, C/INF, So.	.143	.250	.214	14	0	1	0	0	5	0
Spenrath, Reed, INF, So.	.209	.318	.374	91	12	3	0	4	13	1
Taylor, Brayden, 3B, So.	.314	.454	.576	210	55	14	1	13	50	10
Teplanszky, Hunter, 2B, Fr.	.167	.286	.222	18	1	1	0	0	2	0
Thompson, Sam, LF, So.	.154	.333	.423	26	9	1	0	2	7	2

Pitcher, Year	W	L	ERA	G	GS	SV	IP	H	BB	SO
Banta, Trip, Fr.	0	0	0.00	3	0	0	2.1	1	1	2
Bolden, Caleb, Gr.	5	2	6.23	23	1	1	39	37	19	46
Brown, Cam, So.	5	2	4.42	13	9	0	53	45	31	49
Cornelio, Riley, So.	4	5	4.68	15	15	0	75	63	35	77
Feser, Cohen, Fr.	1	0	3.86	9	0	0	16.1	21	0	11
Hierholzer, Storm, So.	0	0	12.79	7	0	0	6.1	10	5	6
Hill, Drew, Sr.	1	0	6.91	13	0	0	14.1	19	10	15
Krob, Austin, Jr.	2	0	5.12	13	6	0	31.2	31	15	45
Mihlbauer, Augie, Sr.	3	0	3.00	26	0	0	21	16	11	25
Oliver, Connor, Jr.	0	1	9.82	9	1	0	11	19	9	14
Parker, Caedmon, Fr.	2	2	5.19	9	7	0	26	24	20	22
Pearson, Braxton, So.	0	0	4.50	4	0	0	4	5	3	3
Perez, Marcelo, Jr.	6	3	3.23	17	9	1	61.1	48	27	52
Ridings, River, So.	2	3	6.96	21	1	10	22	29	17	22
Savage, Luke, So.	1	1	2.72	25	0	2	39.2	34	17	35
Thomas, Gray, Fr.	0	1	4.50	7	0	0	4	5	5	5
Vail, Tommy, Gr.	1	0	3.65	13	0	0	12.1	9	6	15
Walker, Brett, Gr.	5	2	4.75	15	11	0	66.1	80	16	52
Wright, Garrett, So.	0	0	2.89	20	0	5	18.2	12	16	27

21. TEXAS STATE

Coach: Steven Trout. **Record:** 47-14

Player, Pos., Year	AVG	OBP	SLG	AB	R	2B	3B	HR	RBI	SB
Atkinson, Kyle, OF, Fr.	.333	.556	.333	6	7	0	0	0	2	0
Faison Wesley, INF, Sr.	.255	.391	.495	188	45	12	0	11	46	0
Gibbons, Cameron, 2B, Sr.	.277	.342	.328	195	31	10	0	0	28	3
Gonzalez, Jose, LF, Jr.	.298	.413	.553	208	42	14	0	13	60	9
Keithley, Carson, LF, RFr.	.667	.667	1.000	3	0	1	0	0	4	0
Kerbow, Dylan, INF, Fr.	.500	.333	.500	2	1	0	0	0	1	0
Leary, Ryan, 2B, Fr.	.182	.364	.303	33	7	1	0	1	5	0
Lewis, Peyton, C, Jr.	.291	.411	.439	148	24	3	2	5	26	1
Manning, Cade, INF, So.	.071	.133	.286	14	2	0	0	1	4	0
McClain, Ben, CF, RJr.	.281	.418	.503	167	42	10	3	7	35	5
Ortega-Jones Isaiah, CF, Sr.	.287	.443	.454	108	25	8	2	2	17	11
Pena, Daylan, 1B, Fr.	.270	.368	.409	215	44	9	0	7	44	4
Ramirez, August, C, RSo.	.312	.426	.571	77	19	6	1	4	16	1
Shuffield, Dalton, SS, Sr.	.378	.444	.668	238	78	20	5	13	48	16
Thompson, Justin, 3B, Sr.	.323	.425	.500	232	53	14	0	9	44	10
Wuthrich, John, RF, Sr.	.267	.360	.494	243	51	13	0	14	44	6

Pitcher, Year	W	L	ERA	G	GS	SV	IP	H	BB	SO
Bush, Cameron, RSo.	2	2	7.25	17	5	0	36	35	26	35
Dixon, Triston, Jr.	8	0	2.93	27	1	0	58.1	50	14	56
Gann, McCray, Fr.	0	0	15.43	3	0	0	2.1	6	2	3
Keithley, Carson, RFr.	2	0	6.50	16	0	0	18	20	10	15
Loa, Victor, Fr.	0	0	10.13	6	0	0	8	15	3	6
Martinez, Jonathan, So.	0	0	3.78	14	0	1	16.2	17	7	13
Moore, Nick ,Fr.	0	0	1.69	5	0	0	5.1	2	3	7
Nicholas, Matthew, RJr.	2	1	2.65	24	0	0	17	10	9	17
Robie, Tony, So.	4	1	5.05	19	11	0	57	68	28	48
Smith, Austin, RJr.	2	0	2.91	19	0	1	21.2	21	5	24
Stivors, Tristan, Sr.	7	1	2.21	32	1	18	61	47	19	86
Sundren, Trevis, Sr.	2	4	7.32	13	8	0	35.2	46	9	22
Wells, Levi, So.	8	3	3.07	18	16	0	91	79	32	86
Wofford, Otto, So.	3	0	8.49	13	2	0	11.2	18	4	14
Wood, Zeke, Jr.	7	1	3.78	17	16	0	88	59	51	103
Zabel, Peyton, RSo.	0	1	8.31	8	1	0	8.2	14	10	4

22. FLORIDA

Coach: Kevin O'Sullivan. **Record:** 42-24

PLAYER, POS., YEAR	AVG	OBP	SLG	AB	R	2B	3B	HR	RBI	SB
Armstrong, Kris, INF, Jr.	.230	.322	.360	100	15	5	1	2	10	0
Caglianone, Jac, 1B, Fr.	.288	.339	.548	104	19	6	0	7	27	0
Calilao, Kendrick, 1B, Jr.	.209	.289	.316	158	17	8	0	3	22	0
De Goti, Jorge, 3B, Fr.	.286	.375	.429	7	1	1	0	0	0	0
Evans, Ty, RF, Fr.	.242	.301	.465	99	13	5	1	5	16	3
Fabian, Jud, CF, Jr.	.239	.414	.598	234	63	10	1	24	55	9
Fabien, Deric, 3B, Fr.	.218	.323	.331	142	25	4	0	4	22	4
Guscette, Mac, C, So.	.238	.296	.419	105	15	4	0	5	18	1
Halter, Colby, 2B, So.	.240	.338	.380	250	44	11	0	8	27	7
Langford, Wyatt, LF, So.	.355	.447	.719	256	73	9	3	26	63	7
Lastres, Rene, C, Fr.	.333	.333	.533	15	3	0	0	1	4	0
Prevesk, Matt, OF, Fr.	.200	.381	.333	15	1	0	1	0	1	1
Riopelle, BT, C, Jr.	.304	.371	.551	227	38	9	1	15	55	6
Rivera, Josh, SS, So.	.254	.351	.429	224	41	8	2	9	32	5
Robinson, Corey, OF, Fr.	.133	.278	.333	15	9	0	0	1	3	2
Talbott, Tucker, RF, RFr.	.316	.316	.368	19	1	1	0	0	3	0
Thompson, Sterlin, RF, So.	.354	.443	.563	254	59	16	2	11	51	10

Pitcher, Year	W	L	ERA	G	GS	SV	IP	H	BB	SO
Abner, Philip, Fr.	1	1	8.06	26	1	0	22.1	20	21	24
Barco, Hunter, So.	5	2	2.50	9	9	0	50.1	34	11	69
Coppola, Pierce, Fr.	0	0	4.15	1	1	0	4.1	5	2	7
Ficarrotta, Nick, RFr.	4	0	3.90	28	1	3	60	54	15	63
Finnvold, Carsten, Fr.	2	1	5.00	6	1	0	18	15	9	13
Hartman, Karl, Fr.	0	0	9.00	12	1	1	15	19	10	16
Jameson, Fisher, Fr.	1	0	3.72	10	0	1	19.1	13	7	16
Manning, Timmy, So.	1	0	4.77	10	7	0	22.2	27	14	26
Milchin, Garrett, Gr.	1	0	3.14	8	3	0	14.1	18	4	6
Neely, Brandon, Fr.	3	3	3.76	21	10	1	69.1	53	20	74
Nesbitt, Tyler, RFr.	2	3	4.59	20	2	0	33.1	29	14	29
Pogue, Nick, RSo.	4	3	4.81	11	10	0	39.1	34	12	37
Purnell, Blake, RFr.	3	3	2.86	36	0	4	50.1	50	15	39
Slater, Ryan, RFr.	6	4	5.34	26	3	6	57.1	53	25	48
Sproat, Brandon, So.	9	4	3.41	17	16	0	89.2	84	33	82
Ursitti, Anthony, Fr.	0	0	5.06	15	1	0	21.1	19	8	26

23. UCLA

Coach: John Savage. **Record:** 40-24

Player, Pos., Year	AVG	OBP	SLG	AB	R	2B	3B	HR	RBI	SB

Player, Pos., Year	AVG	OBP	SLG	AB	R	2B	3B	HR	RBI	SB
Beres, Tommy, C, RSo.	.200	.381	.307	75	19	5	0	1	13	0
Curialle, Michael, RF, Jr.	.319	.395	.479	238	49	17	3	5	41	9
Dean, Emanuel, OF, RSo.	.000	.250	.000	9	1	0	0	0	1	0
Gourson, Ethan, 2B, Fr.	.294	.439	.455	231	48	23	1	4	44	7
Hahn, Josh, OF, Jr.	.186	.319	.322	59	12	2	0	2	13	1
Holman, Jack, C, Fr.	.263	.417	.474	19	4	1	0	1	6	0
Karros, Kyle, 3B, So.	.308	.365	.473	169	28	8	1	6	42	0
Knight, Malakhi, CF, Fr.	.250	.330	.354	96	11	5	1	1	15	6
Moberg, Jake, 3B, Sr.	.188	.264	.208	48	3	1	0	0	1	1
Oyama, Kenny, LF, Gr.	.284	.403	.337	208	48	5	0	2	27	20
Palmer, Jake, 1B, Gr.	.296	.430	.371	240	43	10	1	2	40	5
Paton, Eli, INF, RFr.	.000	.111	.000	8	1	0	0	0	0	0
Perry, Darius, C, Jr.	.286	.388	.376	133	17	6	0	2	24	2
Reyes, Daylen, INF, So.	.287	.404	.357	157	30	6	1	1	21	4
Schrier, Cody, SS, Fr.	.298	.383	.492	258	41	21	1	9	42	11
Vaughns, JonJon, RF, So.	.192	.408	.346	104	17	5	1	3	17	1
Yates, Carson, CF, So.	.288	.346	.512	170	34	10	2	8	33	4

Pitcher, Year	W	L	ERA	G	GS	SV	IP	H	BB	SO
Aldrich, Chris, RFr.	1	1	8.27	16	0	1	16.1	28	7	11
Austin, Kelly, RSo.	4	3	4.07	25	16	1	77.1	79	16	74
Brooks, Jake, So.	5	4	3.96	10	10	0	63.2	55	10	57
Colwell, Daniel, Sr.	2	2	4.73	28	3	0	40	40	12	25
Filby, Jack, Sr.	0	0	18.69	6	0	0	4.1	5	9	3
Flanagan, Ethan, Fr.	3	0	3.28	25	7	2	60.1	49	28	76
Hahn, Josh, Jr.	0	0	12.00	9	1	0	6	10	4	3
Harrison, Charles, Jr.	2	4	4.31	31	0	0	39.2	32	16	38
Hepp, James, Fr.	1	2	10.50	6	2	0	6	10	4	4
Hurd, Thatcher, Fr.	2	0	1.06	9	6	0	34	16	10	48
Jewett, Luke, Fr.	3	1	3.68	35	0	1	44	47	13	28
Jump, Gage, Fr.	1	1	3.86	7	3	2	16.1	10	11	22
Kottinger, Caedon, So.	0	0	18.00	2	1	0	2	5	2	0
Leibold, Nate, Fr.	0	0	16.20	5	0	0	3.1	11	2	2
Rajcic, Max, So.	8	5	3.28	15	15	0	85	73	20	92
Saum, Jake, Jr.	4	0	4.11	26	0	0	30.2	28	21	33
Tredwell, Alonzo, Fr.	4	1	2.11	25	0	6	47	33	6	62

24. LOUISIANA STATE

Coach: Jay Johnson. **Record:** 40-22

Player, Pos., Year	AVG	OBP	SLG	AB	R	2B	3B	HR	RBI	SB
Berry, Jacob, 3B, So.	.370	.464	.630	208	47	9	0	15	48	0
Bianco, Drew, LF, RJr.	.128	.306	.154	39	12	1	0	0	4	3
Cranford, Collier, 3B, RSo.	.133	.328	.222	45	15	2	1	0	6	0
DiGiacomo, Giovanni, RF, RJr.	.206	.329	.382	68	11	3	0	3	13	2
Doughty, Cade, 2B, RSo.	.298	.393	.567	238	56	19	0	15	57	4
Drews, Dylan, CF, So.	.349	.463	.691	249	73	11	4	22	72	5
Dugas, Gavin, LF, RJr.	.306	.479	.519	108	26	8	0	5	25	3
Jobert, Brayden, DH, RSo.	.246	.354	.578	199	46	10	1	18	58	1
Leto, Luke, 1B, Fr.	.100	.308	.100	10	2	0	0	0	1	0
McManus, Tyler, C, Gr.	.283	.387	.586	145	33	6	4	10	32	0
Merrifield, Jack, 3B, RJr.	.238	.358	.310	42	9	3	0	0	10	1
Milazzo, Alex, C, RSo.	.227	.346	.227	22	5	0	0	0	4	0
Morgan, Tre', 1B, So.	.324	.414	.462	253	50	18	1	5	54	0
Pearson, Josh, RF, Fr.	.299	.432	.524	147	34	9	0	8	35	0
Stevenson, Josh, LF, Fr.	.200	.379	.308	65	17	4	0	1	9	0
Thompson, Jordan, SS, So.	.286	.395	.432	220	54	14	0	6	36	3
Travinski, Hayden, C, RSo.	.242	.356	.581	62	13	3	0	6	13	0

Pitcher, Year	W	L	ERA	G	GS	SV	IP	H	BB	SO
Coleman, Javen, So.	1	0	4.50	3	0	0	6	1	2	6
Collins, Bryce, RSo.	3	1	3.62	20	2	0	32.1	24	20	37
Cooper, Riley, So.	4	3	4.21	30	1	1	40.2	49	8	35
Dutton, Samuel, Fr.	1	1	5.12	18	11	0	38.2	42	12	26
Edwards, Garrett, So.	0	0	6.75	9	1	0	8	10	5	9
Floyd, Ty, So.	5	4	3.77	16	10	0	59.2	43	23	70
Fontenot, Devin, Gr.	3	2	4.71	23	2	1	28.2	28	14	35
Fowler, Michael, So.	0	0	13.50	3	0	0	2.2	3	3	7
Gervase, Paul, RJr.	4	1	1.85	29	0	6	39	22	15	52
Hasty, Jacob, RSo.	2	1	3.55	13	1	0	25.1	14	15	28
Hellmers, Will, So.	2	0	6.55	6	4	0	11	17	5	13
Hilliard, Ma'Khail, RSr.	7	1	4.56	16	16	0	77	90	20	73
Lansville, Cale, Fr.	0	0	7.50	5	0	0	6	9	1	6
Money, Blake, So.	2	4	5.31	16	12	0	61	64	20	60
Reyzelman, Eric, RSo.	1	3	4.04	29	0	3	42.1	32	18	66

Pitcher, Year	W	L	ERA	G	GS	SV	IP	H	BB	SO
Shaffer, Trey, Gr.	0	0	7.00	11	0	0	9	7	9	11
Taylor, Grant, Fr.	4	1	5.81	17	2	0	31	32	21	39
Vietmeier, Trent, Gr.	1	0	2.28	20	0	0	27.2	17	9	37

25. TEXAS TECH

Coach: Tim Tadlock. **Record:** 39-22

Player, Pos., Year	AVG	OBP	SLG	AB	R	2B	3B	HR	RBI	SB
ABrome, Ryan, RF, Fr.	.286	.423	.429	21	5	3	0	0	5	0
Brooks, Lauden, SS, Fr.	.188	.263	.188	16	5	0	0	0	1	1
Carter, Dillon, CF, So.	.199	.339	.322	146	36	5	2	3	21	4
Coleman, Ty, INF/OF, Jr.	.318	.374	.489	223	38	14	0	8	59	0
Conley, Trevor, C, Fr.	.071	.235	.071	14	5	0	0	0	2	0
Hunt, Sam, CF, RFr.	.348	.475	.457	46	12	5	0	0	13	1
Jung, Jace, 2B, So.	.335	.481	.612	224	68	18	1	14	57	5
Kelly, Parker, 3B, Sr.	.284	.387	.528	218	45	19	2	10	48	6
Masters, Cody, OF, Sr.	.200	.333	.533	15	9	2	0	1	5	1
Murrell, Easton, LF, Sr.	.313	.495	.578	147	44	10	1	9	23	1
Porter, Dalton, LF, So.	.241	.324	.370	54	5	4	0	1	14	2
Reynolds, Drew, C, Fr.	.571	.700	.714	7	6	1	0	0	3	0
Stilwell, Cole, 1B, Jr.	.313	.405	.504	246	61	16	2	9	49	1
Swanson, Cooper, LF, Sr.	.118	.318	.176	17	3	1	0	0	2	2
Vooletich, Zac, LF, Jr.	.279	.405	.441	68	20	8	0	1	18	0
Washburn, Owen, RF, Fr.	.277	.369	.433	224	41	10	2	7	48	2
White, Hudson, C, Fr.	.260	.369	.395	215	42	11	0	6	40	4
Wilson, Kurt, SS, Sr.	.313	.393	.588	243	60	15	5	14	64	4

Pitcher, Year	W	L	ERA	G	GS	SV	IP	H	BB	SO
Beckel, Brandon, So.	0	1	5.32	18	0	0	23.2	22	12	29
Becker, Austin, RSo.	2	1	4.29	13	3	2	21	28	15	30
Birdsell, Brandon, Jr.	9	3	2.75	15	15	0	85	67	29	106
Blessie, Bo, Jr.	0	0	8.22	7	0	0	7.2	8	6	9
Bridges, Derek, So.	1	0	3.27	27	0	1	22	20	9	24
Clark, Colin, Sr.	0	1	6.23	14	0	1	21.2	25	8	19
Crowley, Garrett, Jr.	0	0	27.00	4	0	0	1.1	2	5	4
Devine, Andrew, So.	2	1	4.30	16	4	1	23	20	15	26
Girton, Brendan, So.	3	0	4.08	9	0	0	17.2	10	7	18
Hampton, Chase, So.	5	4	4.29	15	11	0	56.2	51	28	72
Hartis, Shay, So.	1	0	6.06	13	0	0	16.1	19	2	14
Hitt, Jamie, RFr.	1	2	7.40	17	3	0	24.1	25	13	21
Lopez, Jase, So.	1	0	14.14	8	0	0	7	15	3	6
Molina, Mason, Fr.	2	5	3.90	20	9	1	57.2	44	29	71
Morris, Andrew, Jr.	8	2	4.59	16	15	0	88.1	80	28	91
Parish, Trendan, Fr.	2	2	8.26	20	1	6	28.1	38	8	33
Robinson, Kyle, Fr.	1	0	4.63	12	0	0	11.2	15	5	9
Sanders, Josh, So.	1	0	7.20	18	0	1	25	36	9	26

CONFERENCE STANDINGS & LEADERS

NCAA regional teams in bold. Conference category leaders in bold.
*Team won conference's automatic regional bid. #Category leader who did not qualify for batting or pitching title.

AMERICA EAST CONFERENCE

	Conference		Overall	
Divison A	W	L	W	L
Maine	21	9	27	22
UMass-Lowell	15	15	28	30
Hartford	11	19	13	37
Albany	11	19	22	25
Division B				
Stony Brook	21	9	27	25
*Binghamton	15	15	22	30
NJIT	15	15	26	27
Maryland-Baltimore County	11	19	23	32

ALL-CONFERENCE TEAM: C: Shane Paradine, Jr., Stony Brook **1B:** Joe Bramanti, Gr., Maine **2B:** Quinn McDaniel, So., Maine **3B:** Evan Giordano, Sr., Stony Brook **SS:** Tremayne Cobb, Jr., Jr., Hartford **OF:** Matt Brown-Eiring, So., Stony Brook; Albert Choi, Jr., NJIT; Gerry Siracusa, Sr., UMass-Lowell DH: Evin Sullivan, Fr., Binghamton **UTL:** Jordan Schulefand, Gr., Maine SP:Joshua Becker, Sr., UMass-Lowell; Ryan Fischer, Jr., NJIT; Luke Johnson, So., Maryland-Baltimore County; Trevor LaBonte, Gr., Maine **RP:** Jack Collins, Jr., Binghamton **Player of the Year:** Evan Giordano, Stony Brook **Pitcher of the Year:** Ryan Fischer, NJIT **Coach of the Year:** Nick Derba, Maine **Rookie of the Year:** Evin Sullivan, Binghamton.

INDIVIDUAL BATTING LEADERS

(Minimum 140 at-bats)

	AVG	OBP	SLG	AB	2B	3B	HR	RBI	SB
Evin Sullivan, Binghamton	.365	.424	.563	192	15	1	7	42	1
Jordan Schulefand, Maine	.350	.457	.520	177	13	1	5	28	25
Will Binder, Albany	.350	.410	.489	180	13	0	4	42	0
David Marcano, NJIT	.344	.413	.518	224	13	1	8	38	24
Brad Malm, Albany	.340	.403	.655	200	14	2	15	49	2
Jacob Humphrey, UMass-Lowell	.337	.456	.426	202	6	3	2	23	46
Evan Giordano, Stony Brook	.333	.442	.628	183	13	1	13	49	8
Gerry Siracusa, UMass-Lowell	.331	.391	.537	242	16	2	10	65	15
Quinn McDaniel, Maine	.330	.414	.569	197	11	3	10	46	22
Derek Tenney, Hartford	.323	.368	.574	195	13	3	10	31	15
Evan Fox, Stony Brook	.322	.430	.546	174	14	5	5	27	31
Robert Gallagher, UMass-Lowell	.312	.472	.524	189	15	2	7	40	37
Tremayne Cobb Jr., Hartford	.311	.382	.563	183	14	1	10	47	15
Logan Haskell, Binghamton	.310	.409	.386	145	5	0	2	19	9
Johnny Marti, Albany	.310	.390	.478	184	19	0	4	36	5
Justin Taylor, Maryland-Baltimore County	.309	.438	.463	188	11	0	6	34	8
Shane Paradine, Stony Brook	.308	.368	.455	198	15	1	4	33	4
Nick Roselli, Binghamton	.307	.405	.536	140	8	0	8	22	4
Tony Krueger, Maryland-Baltimore County	.303	.407	.393	145	7	0	2	24	4
Jason Bottari, Albany	.302	.418	.391	169	7	1	2	27	44
Jake Marquez, Maine	.300	.358	.406	180	13	0	2	23	2
Ian Diaz, Maryland-Baltimore County	.297	.437	.441	202	11	3	4	33	7
Jeff Mejia, Maine	.297	.411	.361	155	5	1	1	22	2
John Daly, Albany	.297	.387	.497	175	14	3	5	32	10
Nick Hussey, NJIT	.295	.397	.463	190	12	1	6	28	3
Matt Brown-Eiring, Stony Brook	.294	.368	.552	194	16	2	10	50	4
Cavan Tully, Binghamton	.292	.400	.432	185	13	2	3	27	7
Luke Trythall, Maryland-Baltimore County	.290	.373	.392	176	12	0	2	27	1
Fritz Genther, UMass-Lowell	.290	.388	.516	221	15	1	11	44	17
Julio Marcano, NJIT	.288	.411	.509	212	23	0	8	34	12

INDIVIDUAL PITCHING LEADERS

(Minimum 40 innings pitched)

	W	L	ERA	G	SV	IP	H	BB	SO
Luke Johnson, Maryland-Baltimore County	3	2	3.93	14	0	73.1	66	34	69
Ryan Fischer, NJIT	7	3	3.97	15	0	95.1	93	23	90
Josh O'Neill, Stony Brook	7	3	3.97	16	3	59	53	33	42
Jayden Shertel, Maryland-Baltimore County	4	3	4.41	15	0	69.1	70	34	48
Brett Erwin, Maine	2	6	4.52	14	0	71.2	82	19	74
Ben Fero, Stony Brook	4	4	4.54	15	0	69.1	72	17	57
Caleb Leys, Maine	3	3	4.64	15	0	66	64	47	68
LJ Keevan, UMass-Lowell	5	5	4.71	14	0	80.1	94	21	60
Cregg Scherrer, Albany	2	5	4.73	16	0	64.2	54	41	75
Connor Eisenmann, Albany	6	2	4.90	17	0	60.2	51	36	51
Gabe Driscoll, Binghamton	3	1	5.01	15	0	55.2	60	22	56
Brandon Lashley, Stony Brook	2	3	5.07	14	0	60.1	66	21	34
Trevor LaBonte, Maine	5	4	5.16	15	1	73.1	83	37	60
Grant Vurpillat, NJIT	6	4	5.23	21	2	62	63	28	66
Joshua Becker, UMass-Lowell	6	5	5.32	20	2	94.2	119	25	75
Anthony Germinerio, Albany	3	4	5.62	11	0	49.2	50	22	51
Ryan Bryggman, Binghamton	5	6	5.71	16	0	75.2	86	40	52
Thomas Babalis, Binghamton	4	7	6.04	16	0	85	95	31	86
Ryan Towle, UMass-Lowell	3	6	6.10	19	2	79.2	80	44	88
Ray Weber, Albany	4	8	6.12	14	0	75	87	28	57
Tim Blaisdell, Hartford	3	7	6.25	14	0	72	101	19	46
Edwin Almanzar Jr., Hartford	3	5	6.68	17	0	63.1	67	35	40
Jake Rappaport, NJIT	3	7	7.86	21	2	63	89	33	25
John Lumpinski, Binghamton	3	6	7.91	17	2	52.1	68	25	49

AMERICAN ATHLETIC CONFERENCE

	Conference		Overall	
	W	L	W	L
*East Carolina	20	4	46	21
Central Florida	14	10	35	25
Houston	13	11	37	24
Cincinnati	12	12	24	31
Tulane	11	13	33	26
Wichita State	9	15	21	36
Memphis	9	15	26	29
South Florida	8	16	28	29

ALL-CONFERENCE TEAM: C: Anthony Tulimero, RSo., Houston **1B:** Ryan Hernandez, Sr., Houston **2B:** Brock Rodden, So., Wichita State **3B:** Carmine Lane, RSo., South Florida **SS:** Zach Agnos, So., East Carolina **OF:** Griffin Merritt, RJr., Cincinnati; Lane Hoover, Jr., East Carolina; Chuck Ingram, So., Wichita State **DH:** Jacob Compton, So., Memphis **UTL:** Ryder Giles, Jr., East Carolina **P:** Connor Staine, RSo., Central Florida; Ben Vespi, So., Central Florida; Landon Gartman, Fr., Memphis; Dylan Carmouche, So., Tulane; Cameron Bye, So., Wichita State **RP:** Carter Spivey, Jr., **East** Carolina **Player of the Year:** Griffin Merritt, Cincinnati **Pitcher of the Year:** Carter Spivey, East Carolina **Coach of the Year:** Cliff Godwin, East Carolina **Newcomer Position Player of the Year:** Brock Rodden, Wichita State **Newcomer Pitcher of the Year:** Landon Gartman, Memphis.

INDIVIDUAL BATTING LEADERS

(Minimum 140 at-bats)

	AVG	OBP	SLG	AB	2B	3B	HR	RBI	SB
Lane Hoover, East Carolina	.341	.423	.416	255	15	2	0	33	12
Gephry Pena, Central Florida	.339	.413	.492	242	8	4	7	40	25
Brock Rodden, Wichita State	.338	.441	.653	216	13	2	17	48	3
Bryson Worrell, East Carolina	.335	.401	.631	263	12	3	20	62	10
Carmine Lane, South Florida	.332	.390	.523	235	13	1	10	54	2
Jacob Jenkins-Cowart, East Carolina	.330	.367	.549	233	10	1	13	65	6
Lex Boedicker, Central Florida	.330	.414	.426	188	8	2	2	28	2
Zach Agnos, East Carolina	.330	.405	.479	267	15	2	7	42	9
Anthony Tulimero, Houston	.326	.396	.455	233	15	0	5	39	11
Noah Orlando, Central Florida	.322	.427	.531	177	7	3	8	26	20
Ian Bibiloni, Memphis	.319	.449	.509	163	10	0	7	28	8
Paul Komistek, Cincinnati	.319	.426	.491	216	11	1	8	28	9
Griffin Merritt, Cincinnati	.315	.382	.695	200	17	1	19	53	7
Cole Harting, Cincinnati	.313	.380	.500	214	9	2	9	47	14
Chuck Ingram, Wichita State	.310	.362	.582	232	13	4	14	53	5
Luis Aviles, Tulane	.306	.417	.596	193	11	3	13	45	8
Wyatt Stapp, Cincinnati	.305	.391	.344	154	6	0	0	27	6
Ben Brooks, Memphis	.304	.405	.387	217	7	1	3	35	4
Ryan Hernandez, Houston	.304	.402	.565	214	14	0	14	56	3

	AVG	OBP	SLG	AB	2B	3B	HR	RBI	SB
Alex Lopez, Houston	.302	.387	.465	215	17	0	6	33	3
Ian McMillan, Houston	.302	.375	.514	212	11	2	10	40	8
Drew Brutcher, South Florida	.299	.447	.610	154	9	0	13	40	1
Ben McCabe, Central Florida	.298	.369	.544	215	11	0	14	54	12
Jacob Compton, Memphis	.291	.365	.540	213	18	1	11	55	0
Kerrington Cross, Cincinnati	.291	.386	.526	196	9	5	9	30	17
Tom Josten, Central Florida	.286	.417	.500	168	11	2	7	42	5
Brandon Uhse, Houston	.286	.349	.472	231	16	0	9	47	8
Zach Arnold, Houston	.283	.348	.452	230	9	0	10	45	9
Logan Kohler, Memphis	.282	.374	.436	195	12	0	6	35	4
Brandon Burckel, Houston	.282	.383	.372	156	9	1	1	12	13

INDIVIDUAL PITCHING LEADERS

(Minimum 40 innings pitched)

	W	L	ERA	G	SV	IP	H	BB	SO
Carter Spivey, East Carolina	8	0	2.83	35	5	76.1	70	19	76
Ben Sears, Houston	6	3	3.11	33	12	66.2	59	8	48
C.J. Mayhue, East Carolina	6	1	3.36	31	1	72.1	53	17	75
Landon Gartman, Memphis	7	1	3.56	15	1	86	54	29	94
Ben Vespi, Central Florida	6	4	3.56	25	2	65.2	60	17	66
Cameron Bye, Wichita State	5	2	3.76	17	0	67	57	35	62
Payton Tolle, Wichita State	4	6	4.48	13	0	66.1	79	22	49
Dylan Carmouche, Tulane	5	5	4.48	16	0	90.1	88	31	87
Beau Keathley, Cincinnati	5	3	4.87	16	0	85	89	31	87
Garrett Saylor, East Carolina	6	3	5.01	39	5	79	69	23	108
Michael Massey, Tulane	3	4	5.03	15	1	68	79	16	52
Nathan Medrano, Houston	6	4	5.18	21	1	80	83	32	74
Jaycob Deese, Houston	5	3	5.19	17	1	85	95	33	62
Brad Lord, South Florida	3	7	5.25	14	0	61.2	75	22	60
David Litchfield, Central Florida	4	2	5.34	21	0	64	76	11	41
Jace Kaminska, Wichita State	3	9	5.49	15	0	78.2	80	29	86
Orion Kerkering, South Florida	5	7	5.72	19	3	67.2	75	19	91
Dalton Fowler, Memphis	3	3	6.25	14	0	63.1	66	54	67
Tristan Weaver, Cincinnati	5	7	6.34	14	0	55.1	64	29	45

ATLANTIC COAST CONFERENCE

	Conference		Overall	
Atlantic Division	**W**	**L**	**W**	**L**
*Louisville	18	11	42	21
*Notre Dame	16	11	41	17
*Wake Forest	15	14	41	19
*Florida State	15	15	34	25
North Carolina State	14	15	36	21
Clemson	13	16	35	23
Boston College	5	25	19	34

	Conference		Overall	
Coastal Division	**W**	**L**	**W**	**L**
*Virginia Tech	19	9	45	14
*Miami	20	10	40	19
*Virginia	17	13	39	19
*North Carolina	15	15	42	22
*Georgia Tech	15	15	36	24
Pittsburgh	13	16	29	27
Duke	10	20	22	32

ALL-CONFERENCE TEAM: C: Kevin Parada, So., Georgia Tech **1B:** Andrew Jenkins, So., Georgia Tech **2B:** Chandler Simpson, So., Georgia Tech **3B:** Max Wagner, So., Clemson; Jake Gelof, So., Virginia **SS:** Tanner Schobel, So., Virginia Tech **OF:** Alex Tappen, Gr., Virginia; Gavin Cross, So., Virginia Tech; Jack Hurley, So., Virginia Tech **DH:** Tommy White, Fr., North Carolina State **SP:** Parker Messick, So., Florida State; Carson Palmquist, So., Miami; John Michael Bertrand, Gr., Notre Dame; Drue Hackenberg, Fr., Virginia Tech; Rhett Lowder, So., Wake Forest **RP:** Andrew Walters, So., Miami **Player of the Year:** Max Wagner, Clemson **Pitcher of the Year:** Rhett Lowder, Wake Forest **Coach of the Year:** John Szefc, Virginia Tech **Freshman of the Year:** Tommy White, North Carolina State **Defensive Player of the Year:** Levi Usher, Louisville.

INDIVIDUAL BATTING LEADERS

(Minimum 140 at-bats)

	AVG	OBP	SLG	AB	2B	3B	HR	RBI	SB
Chandler Simpson, Georgia Tech	.433	.506	.517	203	8	3	1	25	27
Andrew Jenkins, Georgia Tech	.381	.440	.679	252	22	1	17	70	5
Tommy Hawke, Wake Forest	.380	.502	.465	187	8	1	2	20	8
Jake Gelof, Virginia	.377	.477	.764	212	15	2	21	81	3
Jack Hurley, Virginia Tech	.375	.452	.664	232	23	1	14	55	10
Max Wagner, Clemson	.369	.496	.852	203	15	1	27	76	2
Pierce Bennett, Wake Forest	.367	.456	.533	210	14	0	7	49	6
CJ Kayfus, Miami	.366	.460	.525	238	12	1	8	51	16
Alex Tappen, Virginia	.366	.421	.612	227	15	1	13	71	3
Danny Serretti, North Carolina	.365	.437	.567	263	17	3	10	54	2
LuJames Groover III, North Carolina State	.364	.440	.568	236	16	1	10	47	4
Tanner Schobel, Virginia Tech	.362	.445	.689	235	18	1	19	74	7
Tommy White, North Carolina State	.362	.425	.757	235	12	0	27	74	1
Kevin Parada, Georgia Tech	.360	.452	.709	258	10	1	26	88	11
Casey Saucke, Virginia	.360	.438	.591	186	16	3	7	46	6
Brendan Tinsman, Wake Forest	.355	.397	.710	245	15	0	24	69	1
Angel Zarate, North Carolina	.352	.425	.500	284	19	1	7	40	4
Nick Biddison, Virginia Tech	.351	.434	.598	251	14	3	14	47	21
Cooper Ingle, Clemson	.351	.449	.526	211	13	0	8	44	1
Jack Payton, Louisville	.350	.429	.504	254	23	2	4	54	5
Blake Wright, Clemson	.349	.397	.602	166	9	0	11	40	0
Jacob Burke, Miami	.347	.425	.599	222	13	2	13	58	10
Christian Knapczyk, Louisville	.346	.480	.465	217	12	4	2	27	17
Carson DeMartini, Virginia Tech	.341	.452	.659	205	14	3	15	50	5
Carter Putz, Notre Dame	.339	.392	.519	239	13	3	8	48	2
Tres Gonzalez, Georgia Tech	.339	.458	.474	230	14	1	5	57	6
Nick Kurtz, Wake Forest	.338	.471	.637	204	14	1	15	56	2
Tim Borden II, Georgia Tech	.335	.466	.689	206	13	0	20	63	2
Stephen Reid, Georgia Tech	.333	.388	.593	216	8	0	16	63	1
Cade Hunter, Virginia Tech	.330	.440	.637	212	14	0	17	66	11

INDIVIDUAL PITCHING LEADERS

(Minimum 40 innings pitched)

	W	L	ERA	G	SV	IP	H	BB	SO
John Michael Bertrand, Notre Dame	10	3	2.81	18	0	109	97	21	111
Carson Palmquist, Miami	9	4	2.89	16	0	84	70	32	118
Rhett Lowder, Wake Forest	11	3	3.08	16	0	99.1	91	26	105
Canaan Silver, North Carolina State	8	1	3.21	21	1	70	69	15	65
Drue Hackenberg, Virginia Tech	10	2	3.30	17	0	92.2	95	19	87
Bryce Hubbart, Florida State	8	3	3.32	15	0	76	67	21	96
Parker Messick, Florida State	7	5	3.38	16	0	98.2	78	18	144
Jared Poland, Louisville	5	5	3.46	17	0	83.1	79	32	103
Austin Temple, Notre Dame	4	1	3.51	18	2	69.1	49	37	87
Tate Kuehner, Louisville	7	3	3.57	25	4	70.2	61	32	70
Nate Savino, Virginia	6	6	3.69	15	0	78	78	32	79
Max Carlson, North Carolina	4	3	3.71	18	0	77.2	70	38	88
Matt Gilbertson, Pittsburgh	9	3	3.74	15	0	96.1	102	11	88
Brandon Schaeffer, North Carolina	7	3	3.75	21	1	96	110	24	71
Brian Gursky, Virginia	7	3	3.97	14	0	70.1	69	32	84
Jake Garland, Miami	6	2	4.00	14	1	65.1	72	11	54
Teddy McGraw, Wake Forest	5	2	4.08	15	0	70.2	53	38	67
Matt Willadsen, North Carolina State	5	4	4.19	16	0	88	81	45	95
Billy Corcoran, Pittsburgh	7	5	4.43	14	0	85.1	93	8	69
Mack Anglin, Clemson	6	6	4.48	15	0	76.1	63	52	78
Joe Mancini, Boston College	4	4	4.70	13	0	76.2	74	24	63
Logan Whitaker, North Carolina State	2	4	4.73	17	0	66.2	62	32	62
Griffin Green, Virginia Tech	7	3	4.83	16	0	72.2	83	26	61
Karson Ligon, Miami	6	6	4.90	16	0	75.1	82	32	67
Josh Hartle, Wake Forest	7	6	5.30	14	0	69.2	81	24	54
Marcus Johnson, Duke	1	8	5.61	13	0	69	80	25	76
Marquis Grissom Jr., Georgia Tech	4	5	5.75	18	0	61	60	42	57
Chance Huff, Georgia Tech	5	4	6.98	16	0	68.1	81	24	74
Alejandro Rosario, Miami	2	3	7.05	15	0	60	83	25	52
Logan Evans, Pittsburgh	4	8	7.43	14	0	66.2	90	17	52

ATLANTIC SUN CONFERENCE

	Conference		Overall	
EAST	**W**	**L**	**W**	**L**
*Liberty	19	11	37	23
*Kennesaw State	19	11	36	28
Florida Gulf Coast	17	13	35	23
Jacksonville	13	16	27	28
North Florida	11	18	22	33
Stetson	10	20	26	29

EAST	Conference W	Conference L	Overall W	Overall L
Eastern Kentucky	20	10	38	20
Lipscomb	20	10	35	23
Jacksonville State	19	11	27	28
Central Arkansas	18	12	24	29
Bellarmine	8	22	11	43
North Alabama	5	25	12	41

ALL-CONFERENCE TEAM: C: Will King, So., Eastern Kentucky **1B:** Joe Kinker, Jr., Florida Gulf Coast **2B:** Cole Frederick, Sr., Jacksonville State **3B:** Alejandro Figueredo, Jr., Florida Gulf Coast **SS:** Isaiah Byars, Sr., North Florida **OF:** Matt Higgins, Sr., Bellarmine; Kendal Ewell, So., Eastern Kentucky; Josh Hatcher, Sr., Kennesaw State **DH:** Brady Gulakowski, Sr., Liberty **SP:** Tyler Cleveland, So., Central Arkansas; Joe Adametz III, Jr., Liberty; Isaiah Magwood, Jr., Jacksonville State **RP:** Will Brian, Jr., Eastern Kentucky **Player of the Year:** Matt Higgins, Bellarmine **Pitcher of the Year:** Tyler Cleveland, Central Arkansas **Coach of the Year:** Jeff Forehand, Lipscomb **Freshman of the Year:** Donovan Cash, Kennesaw State **Defensive Player of the Year:** Caleb Ketchup, Lipscomb.

INDIVIDUAL BATTING LEADERS

(Minimum 140 at-bats)

	AVG	OBP	SLG	AB	2B	3B	HR	RBI	SB
Alejandro Figueredo, Florida Gulf Coast	.392	.476	.659	232	21	1	13	62	0
Josh Hatcher, Kennesaw State	.391	.452	.667	279	26	3	15	59	11
Luke Harper, North Alabama	.379	.511	.497	177	16	1	1	22	15
Brian Ellis, Florida Gulf Coast	.379	.505	.562	235	25	0	6	44	1
Matt Higgins, Bellarmine	.366	.469	.770	213	20	0	22	61	15
Malik Williams, Lipscomb	.362	.427	.585	229	7	1	14	66	4
Kendal Ewell, Eastern Kentucky	.361	.482	.607	219	10	1	14	51	11
Donovan Cash, Kennesaw State	.357	.417	.560	252	21	0	10	60	0
Austin Thrasher, North Alabama	.348	.498	.482	164	8	1	4	37	6
Mason Maners, Jacksonville	.335	.431	.506	164	12	2	4	31	5
Isaiah Byars, North Florida	.330	.387	.478	209	12	2	5	28	16
Rudy Maxwell, Lipscomb	.330	.365	.569	218	16	3	10	54	3
Aidan Sweatt, North Florida	.329	.387	.408	213	8	0	3	38	8
Hunter Hicks, Central Arkansas	.326	.418	.616	172	17	0	11	53	3
Brock Edge, North Florida	.324	.406	.510	210	15	3	6	28	6
Alejandro Rodriguez, Florida Gulf Coast	.323	.401	.471	223	6	0	9	54	0
Ian Farrow, Florida Gulf Coast	.322	.410	.624	245	9	1	21	75	5
Tyler Simon, Kennesaw State	.319	.380	.490	263	13	4	8	50	13
T.J. Reeves, Jacksonville State	.317	.426	.512	205	14	1	8	30	8
Brennen Norton, Jacksonville State	.315	.386	.517	149	8	2	6	21	0
Will King, Eastern Kentucky	.313	.393	.553	217	19	0	11	60	0
Cameron Hill, Stetson	.311	.414	.484	219	11	6	5	30	24
Cade Westbrook, North Florida	.311	.380	.368	190	11	0	0	23	8
Spencer Hanson, Kennesaw State	.311	.381	.461	167	11	1	4	41	4
Aaron Anderson, Liberty	.310	.423	.479	242	17	0	8	44	0
Cole Frederick, Jacksonville State	.309	.368	.487	230	18	1	7	30	7
Three Hillier, Liberty	.309	.414	.478	207	14	0	7	43	2
Abraham Sequera, North Florida	.307	.352	.522	228	14	1	11	53	5
Devne Daniel, North Alabama	.307	.404	.408	179	9	0	3	35	1
Zac Corbin, Kennesaw State	.304	.393	.438	224	10	1	6	37	8

INDIVIDUAL PITCHING LEADERS

(Minimum 40 innings pitched)

	W	L	ERA	G	SV	IP	H	BB	SO
Joe Adametz III, Liberty	6	3	2.51	16	0	86	94	25	84
Isaiah Magwood, Jacksonville State	7	2	2.58	14	0	69.2	58	33	78
Tyler Cleveland, Central Arkansas	7	2	2.93	14	0	95.1	84	16	101
Peter Holden, North Florida	4	3	3.41	17	0	68.2	56	28	58
Michael Dunkelberger, Lipscomb	7	2	3.45	15	0	78.1	81	18	64
Rese Brown, Eastern Kentucky	6	3	3.76	14	0	76.2	59	30	82
John Bezdicek, Kennesaw State	5	1	3.76	18	0	81.1	61	35	86
Ike Buxton, Lipscomb	7	3	3.86	15	0	74.2	74	39	66
Jason Woodward, Florida Gulf Coast	6	4	4.11	15	0	76.2	72	34	82
Michael Schuler, Eastern Kentucky	5	2	4.11	16	1	61.1	58	27	51
Michael Darrell-Hicks, Jacksonville	5	5	4.13	15	0	72	69	33	82
Trent Gregson, Central Arkansas	6	4	4.30	22	4	60.2	54	18	80
Tyler Shuck, Florida Gulf Coast	5	5	4.36	14	0	74.1	82	17	58
Christian Graham, Jacksonville	2	5	4.37	14	0	57.2	39	38	48
Cole Stallings, Stetson	5	5	4.41	14	0	65.1	65	21	56
Reid Fagerstrom, Jacksonville State	4	3	4.45	17	0	64.2	67	38	74
Jack Myers, Kennesaw State	5	3	4.47	18	0	90.2	88	32	72
Jason Gonzalez, North Florida	6	3	4.62	21	0	64.1	61	19	57
Mason Adams, Jacksonville	5	5	4.80	15	0	90	84	31	108
Andrew Shoultz, Central Arkansas	3	6	4.87	20	4	61	60	25	68
Smith Pinson, Kennesaw State	6	6	4.99	24	3	65	62	13	80
Dylan Cumming, Liberty	5	5	5.05	19	0	76.2	90	27	64
Nolan Pender, Bellarmine	3	9	5.13	16	0	86	101	29	62
Jesse Barker, Central Arkansas	2	7	5.27	16	2	68.1	76	18	55
Jonathan Gonzalez, Stetson	4	6	5.34	17	1	64	71	21	58
Max McKinley, North Florida	3	6	5.56	18	2	69.2	75	15	66
Tony Roca, North Florida	0	6	5.91	15	0	64	75	38	60
Gavin Braunecker, Bellarmine	3	7	5.99	15	0	79.2	88	26	61
Jacob James, North Alabama	3	6	6.66	20	0	71.2	73	42	66
Drew Buhr, Bellarmine	0	6	6.97	15	0	62	75	31	53

ATLANTIC 10 CONFERENCE

	Conference W	Conference L	Overall W	Overall L
Davidson	20	4	43	13
*Virginia Commonwealth	19	5	45	25
Saint Louis	14	9	29	24
Rhode Island	14	10	20	35
George Mason	13	11	23	33
Saint Joseph's	12	11	29	25
Richmond	11	13	30	26
Dayton	10	14	23	27
George Washington	10	14	22	30
Fordham	9	15	16	36
Massachusetts	8	16	22	26
St. Bonaventure	3	21	5	39

ALL-CONFERENCE TEAM: C: Michael Carico, So., Davidson **1B:** Tyler Locklear, RSo., Virginia Commonwealth **2B:** Ben Nippolt, RSo., Virginia Commonwealth **3B:** Dominic Toso, RSr., Richmond **SS:** Addison Kopack, RSo., Rhode Island **OF:** Trevor Candelaria, Sr., Davidson; Parker Nolan, Sr., Davidson; Cade Fergus, Sr., George Washington **DH:** Cam Redding, Jr., Saint Louis **SP:** Nolan DeVos, Jr., Davidson; Blake Hely, Sr., Davidson **RP:** Bennett Flynn, Jr., Davidson **Player of the Year:** Michael Carico, Davidson **Pitcher of the Year:** Blake Hely, Davidson **Coach of the Year:** Rucker Taylor, Davidson **Rookie of the Year:** Ryan Feczko, Davidson.

INDIVIDUAL BATTING LEADERS

(Minimum 140 at-bats)

	AVG	OBP	SLG	AB	2B	3B	HR	RBI	SB
Dominic Toso, Richmond	.408	.462	.624	218	22	2	7	62	0
Michael Carico, Davidson	.406	.559	.843	197	21	1	21	57	3
Tyler Locklear, Virginia Commonwealth	.402	.542	.799	224	25	2	20	78	6
Brett Callahan, Saint Joseph's	.383	.482	.587	206	12	3	8	34	23
Brendan Hueth, Saint Joseph's	.374	.442	.584	214	24	3	5	54	13
Ryan Wilson, Davidson	.366	.502	.571	205	18	0	8	56	18
Addison Kopack, Rhode Island	.364	.461	.713	195	13	2	17	60	7
Cam Redding, Saint Louis	.360	.435	.495	200	12	0	5	37	2
Cole Hebble, Massachusetts	.354	.419	.538	195	20	2	4	25	5
Alden Mathes, Richmond	.344	.398	.567	247	13	6	10	59	7
Matt Turino, Saint Louis	.343	.447	.509	175	11	3	4	30	9
Trevor Candelaria, Davidson	.342	.452	.607	234	19	2	13	62	12
Jacob Hinderleider, Davidson	.336	.445	.611	211	16	3	12	56	6
Steve DiTomaso, George Washington	.332	.403	.491	220	11	3	6	35	8
Brett Ahalt, George Mason	.329	.411	.453	161	12	1	2	32	15
Johnny Hipsman, Richmond	.329	.372	.507	219	16	1	7	41	2
South Trimble, George Mason	.327	.437	.424	165	9	2	1	23	25
Andrew Cossetti, Saint Joseph's	.327	.454	.714	199	16	2	19	65	0
Will Carlone, VIrginia Commonwealth	.326	.412	.522	178	11	0	8	47	4
Jake Elbeery, Richmond	.323	.391	.412	226	5	0	5	44	1
Will MacLean, Massachusetts	.321	.447	.530	134	8	1	6	39	5
Cade Fergus, George Washington	.315	.405	.601	213	20	1	13	37	11
Garrett Boldt, St. Bonaventure	.314	.408	.463	121	6	3	2	14	2
Christian Beal, Richmond	.314	.413	.376	242	9	0	2	32	4
Henry Strmecki, Dayton	.313	.406	.589	163	12	3	9	30	8
Henry Koehler, Davidson	.313	.389	.445	211	13	0	5	43	8
Derek Ripp, George Washington	.311	.403	.409	193	14	1	1	28	1
Parker Nolan, Davidson	.310	.442	.663	187	11	5	15	50	12

	AVG	OBP	SLG	AB	2B	3B	HR	RBI	SB
Kyle Fitzgerald, Saint Louis	.308	.424	.514	185	7	2	9	43	3
Ben Nippolt, Virginia Commonwealth	.308	.430	.407	172	9	1	2	31	4

INDIVIDUAL PITCHING LEADERS

(Minimum 40 innings pitched)

	W	L	ERA	G	SV	IP	H	BB	SO
Nolan DeVos, Davidson	9	2	2.40	15	0	78.2	63	31	106
Logan Schmitt, Saint Louis	8	2	3.18	15	0	76.1	72	16	60
Ryan Feczko, Davidson	10	0	3.21	15	0	73	61	20	60
Campbell Ellis, Virginia Commonwealth	5	4	3.27	21	0	74.1	70	21	62
Chase Hungate, Virginia Commonwealth	6	4	3.57	21	0	63	62	14	46
Mark Manfredi, Dayton	1	2	3.66	13	0	59	45	15	62
Trevor Harris, Saint Louis	7	6	3.77	15	0	76.1	91	16	58
Blake Hely, Davidson	9	2	3.80	15	0	85.1	65	40	97
Harrison Cohen, George Washington	7	7	3.92	14	0	87.1	82	28	93
Ryan Peterson, George Mason	4	3	3.93	16	0	73.1	74	39	45
Chad Gartland, George Mason	3	2	3.99	16	3	67.2	72	20	65
Sean Sposato, Rhode Island	1	4	4.35	17	2	58	64	29	37
Trystan Levesque, Rhode Island	5	6	4.37	14	0	78.1	84	22	69
Ryan Steinhauer, Dayton	3	4	4.39	11	0	53.1	42	25	63
Logan Koester, George Washington	3	2	4.73	14	0	53.1	61	13	22
Justin Solt, George Washington	3	4	5.25	14	0	58.1	65	33	50
Brock Weirather, Richmond	6	5	5.54	16	0	89.1	113	25	68
Connor Harris, George Washington	2	7	5.57	15	0	72.2	98	21	48
Ian McCole, Saint Joseph's	3	6	5.59	15	0	77.1	86	22	48
Jeremy Neff, Richmond	3	5	5.63	16	0	78.1	82	49	87
Kenny Serwa, Dayton	4	6	5.68	13	0	57	82	8	56
Jared Lyons, George Mason	6	5	5.69	18	1	80.2	76	40	65
Luke Smith, Saint Joseph's	4	5	6.12	14	0	60.1	91	17	41
Liam Devine, St. Bonaventure	0	6	6.32	14	2	68.1	83	27	55
Scott Youngbrandt, Saint Louis	6	4	6.68	15	0	62	74	21	52
Luke Roggenburk, St. Bonaventure	1	5	6.89	22	0	47	59	28	29
Brooks Ey, Fordham	4	7	6.90	15	0	75.2	99	25	65
Kevin Dow, Massachusetts	6	5	7.71	12	0	58.1	102	18	49
Tripp Breen, St. Bonaventure	1	7	8.57	13	0	48.1	59	42	47
Domenic Picone, Rhode Island	4	5	8.62	14	0	62.2	70	32	76

BIG EAST CONFERENCE

	Conference W	Conference L	Overall W	Overall L
*Connecticut	16	5	50	16
Creighton	15	5	31	18
Xavier	13	8	33	27
Georgetown	11	10	32	24
Villanova	8	12	19	29
St. John's	7	12	22	32
Seton Hall	7	13	18	35
Butler	4	16	20	35

ALL-CONFERENCE TEAM: C: Matt Donlon, RJr., Connecticut **1B:** Luke Franzoni, Sr., Xavier **2B:** Ethan Stern, Gr., Georgetown **3B:** Jared Cushing, Jr., Xavier **SS:** Kevin Michaels, RSo., St. John's **OF:** Erik Stock, Sr., Connecticut; Jared Wegner, Jr., Creighton; Chris Rotondo, Sr., Villanova **DH:** Korey Morton, So., Connecticut **SP:** Austin Peterson, RJr., Connecticut; Dylan Tebrake, Jr., Creighton; Nolan McCarthy, Gr., Georgetown; Pat Gallagher, RSo., Connecticut **RP:** Jack Lynch, Jr., Xavier **Co-Players of the Year:** Luke Franzoni, Xavier; Alan Roden, Creighton **Pitcher of the Year:** Dylan Tebrake, Creighton **Coaching Staff of the Year:** Georgetown **Freshman of the Year:** Owen Carapellotti, Georgetown.

INDIVIDUAL BATTING LEADERS

(Minimum 140 at-bats)

	AVG	OBP	SLG	AB	2B	3B	HR	RBI	SB
Alan Roden, Creighton	.387	.492	.598	194	25	2	4	46	9
Erik Stock, Connecticut	.364	.435	.596	272	25	4	10	55	6
Chris Rotondo, Villanova	.359	.475	.656	192	15	3	12	37	14
Luke Franzoni, Xavier	.358	.489	.825	212	12	0	29	78	1
Jake Hyde, Georgetown	.354	.442	.679	237	18	1	19	57	9
Jared Wegner, Creighton	.343	.459	.635	181	14	3	11	53	11
Tate Ballestero, St. John's	.333	.427	.483	207	18	2	3	35	2
Andrew Walker, Xavier	.332	.437	.505	208	15	3	5	41	15
Kevin Michaels, St. John's	.330	.389	.543	188	15	2	7	46	1
Ben Huber, Connecticut	.327	.431	.546	260	20	2	11	66	7
Andrew Meggs, Creighton	.324	.412	.443	210	14	1	3	27	2
Joey Castellanos, Villanova	.323	.398	.429	198	7	1	4	33	0
Garrett Schultz, Xavier	.322	.396	.400	205	13	0	1	33	3
Casey Dana, Connecticut	.313	.381	.546	262	21	2	12	61	4
Jack Housinger, Xavier	.311	.445	.588	228	13	1	16	58	12
Travis Holt, Butler	.309	.377	.430	230	13	0	5	21	30
Tyler DeMartino, Xavier	.309	.384	.564	204	14	1	12	47	3
David Smith, Connecticut	.307	.405	.496	254	11	5	9	48	23
Ethan Stern, Georgetown	.303	.436	.555	211	11	0	14	51	20
Andrew Ciufo, Georgetown	.297	.382	.474	192	5	1	9	37	11
David Glancy, St. John's	.294	.389	.505	214	10	1	11	43	3
Jared Cushing, Xavier	.290	.333	.493	207	8	2	10	31	10
Jackson Tucker, St. John's	.283	.396	.364	187	5	2	2	23	17
Owen Carapellotti, Georgetown	.282	.396	.552	163	18	1	8	38	0
Jerry Huntzinger, Xavier	.280	.384	.483	236	7	1	13	38	20
Bryan Padilla, Connecticut	.278	.383	.467	227	15	2	8	37	4
T.C. Simmons, Connecticut	.278	.437	.466	223	19	4	5	42	6
Aaron Steinhart, Butler	.277	.379	.475	202	10	0	10	38	5
Zach Bushling, Connecticut	.270	.357	.435	248	16	2	7	47	9
Devin Hack, Seton Hall	.268	.363	.376	205	11	4	1	25	14

INDIVIDUAL PITCHING LEADERS

(Minimum 40 innings pitched)

	W	L	ERA	G	SV	IP	H	BB	SO
Tommy Steier, Creighton	4	1	1.62	25	8	55.2	42	22	48
Dylan Tebrake, Creighton	8	2	2.71	17	0	93	73	33	115
Jack Lynch, Xavier	9	0	2.8	28	1	64.1	48	21	77
Pat Gallagher, Connecticut	11	3	3.41	17	0	103	97	29	110
Enzo Stefanoni, Connecticut	6	1	3.51	17	0	84.2	80	16	61
Austin Peterson, Connecticut	11	3	3.83	18	0	110.1	100	25	147
Cole Patten, Villanova	3	7	3.98	14	0	86	82	30	77
Carter Bosch, Georgetown	6	4	4.50	18	0	64	68	25	64
Nolan McCarthy, Georgetown	6	2	4.77	14	0	79.1	82	21	86
Dominic Cancellieri, Creighton	5	3	4.84	13	0	61.1	56	31	52
Tyler Arella, Villanova	5	3	5.07	14	0	60.1	74	23	39
Chic DeGaetano, Villanova	4	0	5.79	17	0	51.1	45	25	47
Joe Joe Rodriguez, St. John's	2	6	5.94	15	1	63.2	66	44	53
Cade Lommel, Creighton	1	5	6.40	14	0	52	64	29	54
Matthew Sapienza, Georgetown	2	4	6.45	17	0	60	69	19	42
Cory Bosecker, Butler	0	7	6.75	14	0	68	78	25	69

BIG SOUTH CONFERENCE

	Conference W	Conference L	Overall W	Overall L
Campbell	20	3	41	19
USC Upstate	17	6	35	22
UNC-Asheville	14	9	21	29
High Point	14	10	23	33
Charleston Southern	13	11	24	30
Gardner-Webb	11	13	24	36
Winthrop	11	13	18	34
Longwood	10	14	20	33
Presbyterian	9	15	22	32
Radford	8	15	15	33
North Carolina A&T	3	21	15	38

ALL-CONFERENCE TEAM: C: Ty Babin, RSr., Campbell **INF:** Zach Neto, RSo., Campbell **INF:** Drake Pierson, RJr., Campbell **INF:** Jarrod Belbin, RJr., Campbell **INF:** Eric Toth, Sr., Presbyterian **INF:** Hunter Gilliam, RJr., Longwood **OF:** Noah Myers, RSr., USC Upstate; Tyler Halstead, RJr., Campbell; Noah Rabon, So., USC Upstate **DH:** Connor Denning, RSr., Campbell **UTL:** Dominic Freeberger, Sr. UNC-Asheville **SP:** Thomas Harrington, So., Campbell; Jacob Edwards, Sr., UNC-Asheville; Sam Garcia, So., High Point **RP:** Ryan Chasse, RJr., Campbell; Justin Honeycutt, So., UNC-Asheville **Player of the Year:** Zach Neto, Campbell **Pitcher of the Year:** Thomas Harrington, Campbell **Coach of the Year:** Justin Haire, Campbell **Freshman of the Year:** Noah Sullivan, USC Upstate.

INDIVIDUAL BATTING LEADERS

(Minimum 140 at-bats)

	AVG	OBP	SLG	AB	2B	3B	HR	RBI	SB
Zach Neto, Campbell	.407	.514	.769	199	23	2	15	50	19

DANNY PARKER/FOUR SEAM IMAGES

Campbell's Thomas Harrington posted a 2.53 ERA and won 12 games in 2022.

Eric Toth, Presbyterian	.351	.422	.474	211	9	1	5	34	16
Dominic Freeberger, UNC-Asheville	.338	.432	.428	201	14	2	0	28	1
Anthony Hennings, N.C. A&T	.335	.374	.425	212	14	1	1	24	6
Drake Pierson, Campbell	.333	.449	.703	219	16	4	19	63	18
Devin Buckner, USC Upstate	.332	.472	.523	220	14	2	8	51	5
Peyton Carr, High Point	.327	.436	.457	199	11	0	5	33	0
Connor Carter, Charleston Southern	.326	.427	.440	175	11	0	3	21	8
Robbie Burnett, UNC-Asheville	.322	.416	.481	183	8	3	5	33	6
Ty Babin, Campbell	.319	.417	.644	163	7	2	14	50	3
Michael Peterson, Longwood	.319	.409	.431	160	8	2	2	27	24
Noah Myers, USC Upstate	.317	.423	.509	230	13	2	9	38	21
Javon Fields, High Point	.316	.406	.418	177	10	1	2	26	11
Hayden Harris, Charleston So.	.315	.421	.491	165	11	0	6	31	5
Ty Dooley, Radford	.315	.385	.397	184	10	1	1	28	12
Connor Denning, Campbell	.311	.400	.557	219	16	1	12	56	9
Alec Burns, Gardner-Webb	.311	.438	.647	167	9	1	15	47	1
Ryan Waldschmidt, Charleston So.	.310	.485	.559	145	5	2	9	43	18
Ajay Sczepkowski, Charleston So.	.310	.415	.582	158	16	0	9	35	7
Noah Rabon, USC Upstate	.307	.360	.493	225	12	3	8	56	17
David Bryant, Radford	.307	.431	.436	140	12	0	2	29	5
Tyrell Brewer, Charleston So.	.305	.408	.442	154	12	0	3	23	4
Noah Sullivan, USC Upstate	.303	.410	.394	221	9	1	3	42	5
Jay Wetherington, Presbyterian	.302	.370	.401	192	8	1	3	22	17
Cameron Pittman, Radford	.301	.423	.367	166	6	1	1	20	11
Brody Fahr, Presbyterian	.301	.392	.368	193	6	2	1	24	3
Julian Rojas, Radford	.300	.413	.457	140	8	1	4	30	3
Dillon Morton, Winthrop	.299	.398	.592	174	7	1	14	45	0
Troy Hamilton, USC Upstate	.298	.341	.468	188	14	3	4	25	7
Jack Schnell, Longwood	.298	.386	.497	181	13	1	7	37	2

INDIVIDUAL PITCHING LEADERS

(Minimum 40 innings pitched)

	W	L	ERA	G	SV	IP	H	BB	SO
Justin Honeycutt, UNC-Asheville	4	2	1.73	16	2	52	40	16	36
Sam Garcia, High Point	5	4	1.94	16	1	60.1	45	14	58
Jacob Edwards, UNC-Asheville	8	3	2.24	15	0	88.1	77	26	82
Thomas Harrington, Campbell	12	2	2.53	15	0	92.2	69	18	111
Duncan Howard, Presbyterian	7	4	2.69	15	1	83.2	87	25	67
Sean Duffy, High Point	4	3	3.45	23	2	60	53	31	55
Joe Simeone, Gardner-Webb	9	6	3.59	15	0	105.1	78	31	116
Cade Kuehler, Campbell	4	6	4.07	16	0	84	57	38	111
Tyler Switalski, Gardner-Webb	5	5	4.13	16	0	72	70	28	48
Evan Truitt, Charleston Southern	4	4	4.28	16	0	54.2	55	23	60
Peyton Reesman, Radford	4	2	4.41	13	0	49	43	28	51
Carter Sheppard, High Point	6	5	4.66	14	0	77.1	79	31	62
Jacob Curry, USC Upstate	5	4	5.31	14	0	78	94	16	47
Ryan Douglas, UNC-Asheville	2	6	5.31	14	0	59.1	61	29	55
Andrew Potojecki, Longwood	6	6	5.45	13	0	67.2	84	21	41
Charlie McDaniel, Presbyterian	7	4	5.54	14	0	79.2	105	21	63
Austin Morgan, USC Upstate	5	2	5.57	18	5	63	64	31	59
Carter Sutton, Winthrop	2	4	5.83	17	0	58.2	77	32	52
Peyton Winebarger, N.C. A&T	3	7	6.00	15	0	72	75	48	72
Kaleb Hill, Charleston Southern	6	5	6.09	15	0	68	95	26	64
Teddy Merritt, High Point	3	6	6.39	16	1	69	82	37	62
Kevin Warunek, Longwood	4	4	6.41	14	0	53.1	67	20	26
Daniel Carter, North Carolina A&T	2	7	6.42	12	0	54.2	67	23	50
Jerry Couch, Charleston Southern	3	3	6.55	17	2	56.1	82	19	55
Garrett Gainey, Winthrop	5	6	6.62	15	0	70.2	93	17	55
Zach Davidson, Radford	1	5	6.75	13	0	48	50	28	45
Jaheim Brown, North Carolina A&T	1	6	7.57	17	1	69	99	27	51

BIG 10 CONFERENCE

	Conference		Overall	
	W	L	W	L
*Maryland	18	5	47	14
Rutgers	17	7	44	15
Iowa	17	7	36	19
Illinois	17	7	31	22
*Michigan	12	12	34	26
Penn State	11	13	26	29
Purdue	9	12	29	21
Northwestern	10	14	24	27
Indiana	10	14	27	32
Nebraska	10	14	23	30
Ohio State	8	14	21	30
Michigan State	8	16	24	30
Minnesota	6	18	16	36

ALL-CONFERENCE TEAM: C: Matt Wood, Jr., Penn State **1B:** Peyton Williams, RJr., Iowa **2B:** Kevin Keister, So., Maryland **3B:** Nick Lorusso, Jr., Maryland **SS:** Danny DiGeorgio, Gr., Rutgers **OF:** Chris Alleyne, RSr., Maryland; Clark Elliott, Jr., Michigan; Ryan Lasko, So., Rutgers **DH:** CJ Valdez, Jr., Purdue **At-Large:** Matt Shaw, So., Maryland **SP:** Adam Mazur, RJr., Iowa; Ryan Ramsey, Jr., Maryland; Jason Savacool, So., Maryland **RP:** Dale Stanavich, RJr., Rutgers **Player of the Year:** Chris Alleyne, Maryland **Pitcher of the Year:** Adam Mazur, Iowa **Coach of the Year:** Rob Vaughn, Maryland **Freshman of the Year:** Keaton Anthony, Iowa.

INDIVIDUAL BATTING LEADERS

(Minimum 2.5 at-bats per team game)

	AVG	OBP	SLG	AB	2B	3B	HR	RBI	SB
Nick Cimillo, Rutgers	.390	.498	.720	200	18	0	16	52	1
Matt Wood, Penn State	.379	.480	.667	198	15	3	12	53	5
Danny DiGeorgio, Rutgers	.373	.475	.570	228	18	3	7	59	18
Evan Albrecht, Purdue	.365	.452	.470	181	14	1	1	34	22
Cam McDonald, Illinois	.363	.413	.561	212	17	2	7	59	2
Keaton Anthony, Iowa	.361	.455	.678	202	22	0	14	55	0
Mitch Jebb, Michigan State	.356	.448	.511	219	10	3	6	46	20
Hunter Jessee, Indiana	.355	.467	.494	172	7	1	5	28	8
Luke Shliger, Maryland	.353	.495	.602	249	22	2	12	58	14
Joe Stewart, Michigan	.349	.409	.572	269	17	2	13	56	23
Phillip Glasser, Indiana	.346	.442	.479	188	12	2	3	25	6
Ryan Lasko, Rutgers	.346	.430	.642	257	24	2	16	51	13
Justin Janas, Illinois	.343	.489	.531	175	11	2	6	37	0
Troy Schreffler Jr., Maryland	.340	.421	.557	253	23	1	10	57	14
Danny Doligale, Illinois	.340	.438	.467	212	14	2	3	22	18
Marcus Ernst, Ohio State	.337	.441	.452	199	7	2	4	24	1
Clark Elliott, Michigan	.337	.460	.630	243	17	3	16	69	19
Jay Beshears, Northwestern	.335	.387	.608	194	17	3	10	46	2

	AVG	OBP	SLG	AB	2B	3B	HR	RBI	SB
Peyton Williams, Iowa	.335	.464	.622	209	17	2	13	41	4
Jay Harry, Penn State	.333	.414	.469	213	10	2	5	26	4
Chris Alleyne, Maryland	.331	.422	.673	263	16	1	24	79	24
Richie Schiekofer, Rutgers	.330	.414	.462	182	10	1	4	44	2
Josh Pyne, Indiana	.327	.386	.504	226	20	1	6	57	1
Anthony Calarco, Northwestern	.325	.432	.619	194	18	0	13	54	1
Jack Kelly, Minnesota	.324	.421	.592	179	18	3	8	45	4
CJ Valdez, Purdue	.324	.432	.472	176	14	0	4	43	2
Branden Comia, Illinois	.323	.419	.523	220	19	2	7	50	4
Nick Lorusso, Maryland	.322	.409	.562	258	17	0	15	70	0
Matt Frey, Michigan	.322	.446	.541	233	15	0	12	57	2
Troy Viola, Purdue	.321	.409	.541	196	19	0	8	42	8

INDIVIDUAL PITCHING LEADERS

(Minimum 40 innings pitched)

	W	L	ERA	G	SV	IP	H	BB	SO
Jackson Smeltz, Purdue	6	1	2.83	10	0	57.1	40	22	79
Emmett Olson, Nebraska	3	3	2.86	19	1	66	61	16	65
Jason Savacool, Maryland	8	3	2.93	17	0	107.2	84	28	123
Adam Mazur, Iowa	7	3	3.08	15	0	93.2	60	30	98
Ryan Ramsey, Maryland	11	1	3.22	16	0	92.1	63	41	90
Nathan Florence, Rutgers	6	2	3.36	15	0	67	48	31	90
Cole Kirschsieper, Illinois	7	2	3.40	15	0	87.1	75	29	88
Dylan Nedved, Iowa	6	2	3.47	20	3	72.2	51	28	75
Ty Langenberg, Iowa	7	2	3.71	14	0	63	60	23	74
Koty Frank, Nebraska	5	0	3.81	14	0	59	54	19	70
Aidan Maldonado, Minnesota	2	3	3.91	14	0	73.2	63	35	90
Chase Allen, Michigan	7	2	4.01	27	3	76.1	70	29	57
Jared Kollar, Rutgers	9	2	4.07	16	0	79.2	73	24	89
Michael Farinelli, Northwestern	6	5	4.43	14	0	87.1	96	25	61
Conner Tomasic, Michigan State	4	4	4.43	17	0	65	64	26	41
Shay Schanaman, Nebraska	2	8	4.44	15	0	77	75	29	76
Sean Sullivan, Northwestern	5	2	4.45	13	0	64.2	66	25	78
Travis Luensmann, Penn State	2	3	4.52	15	2	67.2	68	34	78
Wyatt Loncar, Ohio State	2	4	4.56	13	0	51.1	43	30	73
Nick Dean, Maryland	6	2	4.57	15	0	82.2	84	27	80
Cameron Weston, Michigan	5	4	4.74	20	4	81.2	92	38	92
Riley Gowens, Illinois	5	4	4.86	13	0	66.2	52	27	68
Jack Perkins, Indiana	3	4	5.10	16	0	83	77	47	91
Sam Ireland, Minnesota	4	5	5.27	14	0	71.2	74	38	80
Bradley Brehmer, Indiana	5	4	5.30	17	0	74.2	74	33	77
Troy Wansing, Purdue	4	4	5.44	15	0	51.1	51	33	61
Connor O'Halloran, Michigan	5	4	5.44	19	0	92.2	97	40	104
Jaden Henline, Penn State	2	3	5.64	17	3	59	74	16	56
Isaiah Coupet, Ohio State	5	5	5.71	13	0	64.2	49	41	98
Wyatt Wendell, Purdue	5	3	5.88	14	0	56.2	70	18	56

BIG 12 CONFERENCE

	Conference W	Conference L	Overall W	Overall L
*Texas Christian	16	8	38	22
*Texas Tech	15	9	39	22
*Oklahoma	15	9	45	24
*Oklahoma State	15	9	42	22
*Texas	14	10	47	22
West Virginia	14	10	33	22
Kansas State	8	16	29	29
Baylor	7	17	26	28
Kansas	4	20	20	35

ALL-CONFERENCE TEAM: C: Silas Ardoin, RSo., Texas **INF:** Ivan Melendez, RJr., Texas **INF:** Maui Ahuna, So., Kansas **INF:** Peyton Graham, RSo., Oklahoma **INF:** Tommy Sacco, Sr., Texas Christian **INF:** Jace Jung, So., Texas Tech **OF:** Jake Thompson, Gr., Oklahoma State; Murphy Stehly, RSr., Texas; Austin Davis, Sr., West Virginia **DH:** Griffin Doersching, Gr., Oklahoma State **UTL:** Nolan McLean, So., Oklahoma State **SP:** Pete Hansen, RSo., Texas; Jake Bennett, RSo., Oklahoma; Brandon Birdsell, Jr., Texas Tech; Justin Campbell, So., Oklahoma State **RP:** Luke Savage, So., Texas Christian; Roman Phansalkar, Jr., Oklahoma State; Trey Braithwaite, RSr., West Virginia **Player of the Year:** Ivan Melendez, Texas **Pitcher of the Year:** Brandon Birdsell, Texas Tech **Coach of the Year:** Kirk Saarloos, Texas Christian **Newcomer of the Year:** Blake Robertson, Oklahoma **Freshman of the Year:** Hudson White, Texas Tech.

INDIVIDUAL BATTING LEADERS

(Minimum 140 at-bats)

	AVG	OBP	SLG	AB	2B	3B	HR	RBI	SB
Maui Ahuna, Kansas	.396	.479	.634	202	16	4	8	48	13
Ivan Melendez, Texas	.387	.508	.863	248	18	2	32	94	1
Tanner Tredaway, Oklahoma	.370	.414	.549	284	18	3	9	66	24
Murphy Stehly, Texas	.367	.424	.662	278	23	1	19	61	8
Skyler Messinger, Texas	.364	.414	.560	250	14	1	11	59	1
Tommy Sacco, Texas Christian	.355	.443	.645	231	23	1	14	58	18
Jake Thompson, Oklahoma State	.350	.453	.610	254	20	2	14	67	3
Dominic Johnson, Kansas State	.345	.419	.593	226	20	0	12	42	12
Jace Jung, Texas Tech	.335	.481	.612	224	18	1	14	57	5
Peyton Graham, Oklahoma	.335	.417	.640	278	17	4	20	71	34
Zach Ehrhard, Oklahoma State	.332	.429	.409	220	8	0	3	31	18
Austin Davis, West Virginia	.330	.402	.442	224	11	1	4	26	29
McGwire Holbrook, West Virginia	.327	.401	.509	171	13	0	6	43	5
Douglas Hodo III, Texas	.319	.418	.532	282	26	2	10	47	9
Ty Coleman, Texas Tech	.318	.374	.489	223	14	0	8	59	0
Marcus Brown, Oklahoma State	.316	.378	.441	247	15	2	4	31	5
Nolan Metcalf, Kansas	.315	.377	.538	197	16	2	8	49	0
Brayden Taylor, Texas Christian	.314	.454	.576	210	14	1	13	50	10
Cole Stiwell, Texas Tech	.313	.405	.504	246	16	2	9	49	1
Easton Murrell, Texas Tech	.313	.495	.578	147	10	1	9	23	1
Kurt Wilson, Texas Tech	.313	.393	.588	243	15	5	14	64	4
J.J. Wetherholt, West Virginia	.308	.411	.471	208	17	1	5	39	15
Justin Mitchell, Kansas State	.308	.392	.481	156	12	0	5	22	0
Jimmy Crooks, Oklahoma	.305	.430	.506	249	21	1	9	51	10
Kyle Nevin, Baylor	.304	.361	.514	214	15	3	8	49	6
Caeden Trenkle, Oklahoma State	.302	.429	.467	182	8	2	6	41	11
Blake Robertson, Oklahoma	.300	.453	.467	257	24	2	5	52	12
Jack Pineda, Baylor	.300	.391	.502	227	15	5	7	35	10
Tre Richardson, Baylor	.297	.398	.434	212	15	1	4	35	9
Roc Riggio, Oklahoma State	.295	.413	.519	210	14	0	11	47	2

INDIVIDUAL PITCHING LEADERS

(Minimum 40 innings pitched)

	W	L	ERA	G	SV	IP	H	BB	SO
Brandon Birdsell, Texas Tech	9	3	2.75	15	0	85	67	29	106
Trevin Michael, Oklahoma	4	2	2.89	32	10	71.2	55	20	95
Lucas Gordon, Texas	7	2	3.05	18	0	85.2	71	26	77
Marcelo Perez, Texas Christian	6	3	3.23	17	1	61.1	48	27	52
Jake Bennett, Oklahoma	10	4	3.69	20	1	117	106	22	133
Pete Hansen, Texas	11	3	3.76	17	0	107.2	94	19	120
Justin Campbell, Oklahoma State	9	2	3.82	17	0	101.1	83	25	141
Andrew Morris, Texas Tech	8	2	4.59	16	0	88.1	80	28	91
Ben Hampton, West Virginia	8	5	4.66	15	0	83	81	27	90
Riley Cornelio, Texas Christian	4	5	4.68	15	0	75	63	35	77
Tristan Stevens, Texas	7	6	4.73	26	3	85.2	90	24	72
Brett Walker, Texas Christian	5	2	4.75	15	0	66.1	80	16	52
Blake Adams, Kansas State	6	6	5.07	17	0	87	90	34	90
Connor McCullough, Kansas State	3	4	5.25	15	1	73.2	77	30	66
Daniel Hegarty, Kansas	6	6	5.33	18	0	72.2	88	20	32
David Sandlin, Oklahoma	9	4	5.59	19	0	95	100	31	102
Victor Mederos, Oklahoma State	4	4	5.59	14	0	66	69	21	62
Jacob Watters, West Virginia	3	7	6.22	18	1	59.1	64	41	75
Griffin Hassall, Kansas State	4	7	6.24	18	0	66.1	73	25	49
Ryan Vanderhei, Kansas	5	6	6.46	14	0	78	79	43	83
Cole Larsen, Kansas	1	9	8.47	15	0	79.2	120	31	42
Jake Jackson, Baylor	4	5	8.48	16	1	57.1	90	19	40

BIG WEST CONFERENCE

	Conference W	Conference L	Overall W	Overall L
*UC Santa Barbara	27	3	44	14
Cal Poly	22	8	37	21
Hawaii	19	11	28	24
Cal State Northridge	17	13	32	22
Long Beach State	17	13	29	27
UC Irvine	16	14	32	24
Cal State Fullerton	14	16	22	33
UC San Diego	13	17	24	32
Cal State Bakersfield	11	19	18	34

UC Davis	5	25	6	35
UC Riverside	4	26	8	45

ALL-CONFERENCE TEAM: C: Ryan Stafford, Fr., Cal Poly **1B:** Joe Yorke, So., Cal Poly **2B:** Kai Moody, RSr., Cal State Northridge **3B:** Bryce Willits, RJr., UC Santa Barbara **SS:** Brooks Lee, So., Cal Poly **OF:** Caden Kendle, So., UC Irvine; Christian Kirtley, Jr., UC Santa Barbara; Andrew Sojka, Jr., Cal State Northridge; Mark Wolbert, Fr., UC Davis **DH:** Blake Klassen, So., UC Santa Barbara; Austin Schell, Sr., Cal State Fullerton **UTL:** Justin Torres, RJr., UC Irvine **SP:** Cory Lewis, So., UC Santa Barbara; Blaze Koali'i Pontes, Jr., Hawaii; Drew Thorpe, So., Cal Poly; Blaine Traxel, Sr., Cal State Northridge **RP:** Gordon Ingebritson, Gr., UC Irvine **CL:** Jason Franks, Sr., Cal Poly **Field Player of the Year:** Brooks Lee, Cal Poly **Pitcher of the Year:** Drew Thorpe, Cal Poly **Coach of the Year:** Andrew Checketts, UC Santa Barbara Freshman **Field Player of the Year:** Mark Wolbert, UC Davis **Freshman Pitcher of the Year:** Ryan Gallagher, UC Santa Barbara **Defensive Player of the Year:** Connor Burns, Long Beach State.

INDIVIDUAL BATTING LEADERS

(Minimum 140 at-bats)

	AVG	OBP	SLG	AB	2B	3B	HR	RBI	SB
Brooks Lee, Cal Poly	.357	.462	.664	235	25	1	15	55	3
Mark Wolbert, UC Davis	.351	.428	.497	151	10	3	2	15	3
Joe Yorke, Cal Poly	.348	.436	.455	224	12	0	4	51	0
Bart West, Cal State Northridge	.338	.363	.528	195	11	1	8	39	7
Andrew Sojka, Cal State Northridge	.335	.420	.488	209	18	1	4	25	9
Jackson Lyon, Cal State Fullerton	.328	.399	.519	189	11	2	7	29	2
Caden Connor, Cal State Fullerton	.327	.414	.460	226	14	2	4	37	2
Rocco Peppi, Long Beach State	.321	.408	.443	212	11	0	5	30	2
Ryan Stafford, Cal Poly	.321	.384	.431	246	16	1	3	33	3
Zach Lew, Cal State Fullerton	.317	.427	.377	199	9	0	1	29	0
Nick Vogt, UC Santa Barbara	.316	.405	.539	206	15	5	7	49	10
Emiliano Gonzalez, UC San Diego	.312	.404	.414	157	13	0	1	18	0
Chase Luttrell, Long Beach State	.312	.365	.520	221	17	1	9	46	2
Jonathon Long, Long Beach State	.311	.411	.454	183	8	0	6	37	2
Nathan Church, UC Irvine	.309	.387	.438	217	9	2	5	38	6
Nick Marinconz, Cal Poly	.309	.397	.382	178	10	0	1	16	1
Jalen Smith, UC San Diego	.305	.404	.517	203	16	3	7	34	7
Bryce Willits, UC Santa Barbara	.302	.410	.517	172	18	2	5	33	5
Jason Brandow, Cal State Fullerton	.301	.394	.479	146	3	1	7	23	4
Christian Kirtley, UC Santa Barbara	.300	.412	.526	213	11	2	11	45	7
James Bell, Cal State Bakersfield	.300	.379	.483	180	13	1	6	34	2
Matt Wong, Hawaii	.298	.367	.434	198	12	0	5	41	1
Jordan Donahue, Hawaii	.298	.383	.354	161	7	1	0	20	9
James Williams III, UC Davis	.295	.404	.438	112	8	1	2	16	0
A.J. Miller, Cal State Bakersfield	.294	.371	.552	201	16	0	12	38	1
Eddie Saldivar, Long Beach State	.293	.376	.378	188	9	2	1	25	8
Dallas Duarte, Hawaii	.293	.379	.401	147	10	0	2	26	7
Jashia Morrissey, Cal State Bakersfield	.292	.376	.458	168	13	3	3	20	3
Cole Cabrera, Hawaii	.292	.410	.406	192	10	0	4	34	14
Stone Miyao, Hawaii	.292	.371	.405	168	8	1	3	35	3

INDIVIDUAL PITCHING LEADERS

(Minimum 40 innings pitched)

	W	L	ERA	G	SV	IP	H	BB	SO
Gordon Ingebritson, UC Irvine	6	0	1.76	32	3	66.2	50	5	62
Fynn Chester, Cal State Fullerton	3	1	2.3	23	0	62.2	59	12	32
Drew Thorpe, Cal Poly	10	1	2.32	15	0	104.2	65	25	149
Lucas Braun, Cal State Northridge	7	4	2.91	20	0	74.1	62	17	77
Blaze Koali'i Pontes, Hawaii	5	1	2.94	20	1	70.1	68	26	88
Blaine Traxel, Cal State Northridge	7	4	3.00	19	1	105	112	23	86
Mike Gutierrez, UC Santa Barbara	9	1	3.20	16	0	87.1	80	38	86
Nick Pinto, UC Irvine	2	6	3.23	15	0	86.1	87	31	82
Ryan Gallagher, UC Santa Barbara	8	0	3.25	16	0	83	90	28	67
Jack Noble, Long Beach State	6	4	3.36	17	0	64.1	60	20	61
Tyler Stultz, Cal State Fullerton	5	5	3.36	15	0	88.1	84	24	86
Cory Lewis, UC Santa Barbara	9	1	3.57	16	0	88.1	61	42	107
Juaron Watts-Brown, Long Beach State	4	4	3.68	15	0	73.1	50	29	111
Kellen O'Connor, Cal State Bakersfield	4	4	3.79	12	0	54.2	65	14	56
Travis Weston, Cal Poly	7	3	3.91	16	0	94.1	106	15	76
Benji Caggianelli, Cal State Bakersfield	2	3	4.53	14	0	53.2	37	39	71
Cade Halemanu, Hawaii	4	5	4.69	15	0	71	76	41	71
Jaykob Acosta, Cal State Bakersfield	3	7	4.73	16	0	72.1	75	32	46
Andy Archer, Hawaii	2	5	5.04	19	1	60.2	73	18	47
Michael Frias, UC Irvine	5	2	5.19	11	0	59	62	21	60
Jeremiah Priddy, UC Riverside	0	3	5.23	16	0	53.1	62	26	42
Bryan Green, UC Davis	2	6	5.45	15	0	71	78	28	52
Adrian Santa Cruz, Cal State Bakersfield	1	4	5.52	15	0	58.2	88	16	46
Blake Sodersten, Cal State Northridge	5	6	5.67	19	1	81	103	28	75
Kaden Riccomini, UC Davis	2	5	5.93	12	0	57.2	75	18	34
Noah Conlon, UC San Diego	4	9	6.35	16	0	66.2	75	43	64
Nate Freeman, UC Davis	1	1	6.41	14	0	71.2	84	34	43
Tucker Juline, UC Riverside	2	7	7.49	19	0	57.2	76	25	29
Tyler Frazier, UC Riverside	0	8	7.93	14	0	53.1	73	37	34
Eric Marrujo, UC Riverside	2	7	8.52	15	0	56	74	28	30

COLONIAL ATHLETIC ASSOCIATION

	Conference		Overall	
	W	L	W	L
College of Charleston	19	5	37	20
*Hofstra	15	9	30	23
UNC-Wilmington	15	9	31	24
William & Mary	14	10	26	23
James Madison	12	11	27	26
Northeastern	10	14	31	29
Elon	9	14	27	28
Delaware	8	15	25	26
Towson	4	19	14	39

ALL-CONFERENCE TEAM: C: JT Marr, Jr., College of Charleston **INF:** Brooks Baldwin, Jr., UNC-Wilmington **INF:** Joey Loynd, So., Delaware **INF:** Taber Mongero, Jr., UNC-Wilmington **INF:** Cole Ragone, Sr., William & Mary **INF:** Ben Williamson, Jr., William & Mary **OF:** Ethan Baucom, Gr., UNC-Wilmington; Alex Iadisernia, So., Elon; Brian Morrell, Sr., Hofstra; Matt Thomas, Sr., William & Mary **DH:** Ryan Dooley, Fr., James Madison **UTL:** Travis Reifsnider, Jr., James Madison **SP:** Brad Camarda, Sr., Hofstra; Ty Good, Jr., College of Charleston; RJ Sales, Fr., UNC-Wilmington; Shea Sprague, Fr., Elon

RP: Michael O'Hanlon, So., Hofstra; William Privette, So., College of Charleston **Player of the Year:** Brooks Baldwin, UNC-Wilmington **Pitcher of the Year:** William Privette, College of Charleston **Coach of the Year:** Chad Holbrook, College of Charleston **Co-Rookies of the Year:** Tyler Sorrentino, College of Charleston; Shea Sprague, Elon **Defensive Player of the Year:** Ben Williamson, William & Mary.

INDIVIDUAL BATTING LEADERS

(Minimum 140 at-bats)

	AVG	OBP	SLG	AB	2B	3B	HR	RBI	SB
Brooks Baldwin, UNC-Wilmington	.347	.406	.621	190	13	3	11	39	16
Brian Morrell, Hofstra	.346	.412	.546	205	13	2	8	39	1
Matt Thomas, William & Mary	.318	.416	.502	201	12	2	7	34	10
Bryce Greenly, Delaware	.316	.387	.440	193	8	5	2	21	16
Jake Dunion, Delaware	.313	.389	.407	182	7	2	2	23	3
Joe Delossantos, William & Mary	.313	.398	.556	160	12	0	9	38	13
Joseph Carpenter, Delaware	.310	.376	.552	203	19	3	8	41	2
Jack McLaughlin, Towson	.309	.404	.507	152	6	0	8	22	3
Trotter Harlan, College of Charleston	.305	.419	.505	200	16	0	8	46	17
Travis Reifsnider, James Madison	.303	.369	.632	152	9	1	13	37	11
Trevon Dabney, James Madison	.303	.459	.543	175	14	2	8	38	10
Taber Mongero, UNC-Wilmington	.301	.368	.464	209	12	2	6	23	2
JT Marr, College of Charleston	.298	.348	.465	228	9	4	7	42	13
Cam Dean, College of Charleston	.298	.389	.393	178	12	1	1	28	2
Joey Loynd, Delaware	.298	.383	.508	181	12	1	8	45	6
Ben Williamson, William & Mary	.296	.397	.436	179	11	1	4	16	9
Sam Cochrane, College of Charleston	.295	.395	.434	173	10	4	2	37	10
Kevin Bruggeman, Hofstra	.293	.360	.467	184	7	2	7	33	2
Jake Liberatore, Hofstra	.292	.408	.422	161	9	0	4	22	2
Kyle Novak, James Madison	.292	.370	.434	219	14	1	5	49	6
Ryan Morash, Hofstra	.289	.324	.397	204	11	1	3	29	12
Cole Ragone, William & Mary	.287	.349	.543	164	12	0	10	47	5
Joseph Mershon, College of Charleston	.286	.451	.410	161	4	2	4	26	12
Charlie Granatell, Elon	.286	.379	.455	189	13	2	5	27	10
Tyler Sorrentino, College of Charleston	.284	.384	.372	218	8	4	1	32	15
Nick Zona, James Madison	.282	.360	.295	156	2	0	0	12	9
Mark Trotta, William & Mary	.278	.389	.377	151	7	1	2	27	7

Mason Dunaway, James Madison	.277	.361	.387	173	8	1	3	26	15
David Hogarth, William & Mary	.276	.369	.329	170	4	1	1	21	4
Fenwick Trimble, James Madison	.276	.382	.442	199	12	0	7	39	2

INDIVIDUAL PITCHING LEADERS

(Minimum 40 innings pitched)

	W	L	ERA	G	SV	IP	H	BB	SO
William Privette, College of Charleston	3	1	0.91	25	12	59.1	31	15	80
Shea Sprague, Elon	6	3	1.89	19	0	62	50	13	41
Eric Yost, Northeastern	4	3	2.48	20	1	61.2	51	17	58
Liam McDonnell, James Madison	6	1	2.83	16	0	63.2	50	23	52
Wyatt Scotti, Northeastern	8	3	2.88	14	0	81.1	70	8	65
Carter Lovasz, William & Mary	2	1	2.94	16	5	52	32	12	41
Cam Schlittler, Northeastern	5	8	3.44	15	0	91.2	77	32	85
RJ Sales, UNC-Wilmington	6	1	3.52	15	0	76.2	76	37	59
Brian Edgington, Elon	6	4	3.56	15	0	86	82	27	86
Ty Good, College of Charleston	10	5	3.61	17	0	82.1	58	38	88
Ryan Murphy, James Madison	4	2	3.86	14	0	65.1	64	12	43
Brad Camarda, Hofstra	8	2	3.87	16	0	95.1	85	31	76
Trey Pooser, College of Charleston	5	2	3.92	18	0	62	67	24	51
Zane Taylor, UNC-Wilmington	4	1	4.03	13	0	60.1	59	11	42
Chris Ludman, Delaware	4	4	4.17	11	0	69	81	14	58
Cyle Phelan, UNC-Wilmington	2	3	4.55	15	0	59.1	42	36	51
Joey Silan, Delaware	3	5	4.63	14	1	70	67	35	56
Zach Tsakounis, William & Mary	5	3	4.82	17	0	56	59	26	43
Joe Savino, Elon	2	5	5.01	16	1	55.2	68	10	51
Zach Klapak, Delaware	6	4	5.09	19	0	53	44	31	52
Justin Showalter, James Madison	4	8	5.10	14	0	72.1	89	13	67
Mark Faello, Hofstra	7	4	5.15	14	0	80.1	75	40	62
Sebastian Keane, Northeastern	5	5	5.99	15	0	70.2	86	26	50

CONFERENCE USA

	Conference		Overall	
	W	L	W	L
*Southern Mississippi	23	7	47	19
*Louisiana Tech	20	10	43	21
Old Dominion	19	11	41	17
Florida Atlantic	19	11	35	23
Texas-San Antonio	19	11	38	20
Middle Tennessee State	17	13	29	26
Charlotte	17	13	36	22
Alabama-Birmingham	13	17	31	25
Rice	9	21	17	39
Marshall	9	21	20	34
Florida International	8	22	16	34
Western Kentucky	7	23	18	36

ALL-CONFERENCE TEAM: C: Brock Gagliardi, Sr., Old Dominion **INF:** Matt Coutney, Sr., Old Dominion **INF:** Nolan Schanuel, So., Florida Atlantic **INF:** Taylor Young, Sr., Louisiana Tech **INF:** Jack Dragum, Jr., Charlotte **OF:** Andy Garriola, Sr., Old Dominion; Cole McConnell, So., Louisiana Tech; Gabriel Rincones, So., Florida Atlantic **DH:** David McCabe, So., **Charlotte UTL:** Luke Edwards, Jr., Marshall **P:** Tanner Hall, So., Southern Mississippi; Blake Morgan, Fr., Old Dominion; Hurston Waldrep, So., Southern Mississippi; Luke Malone, RJr., Texas-San Antonio **RP:** Kyle Crigger, Sr., Louisiana Tech; Landon Harper, So., Southern Mississippi **Player of the Year:** Matt Coutney, Old Dominion **Pitcher of the Year:** Tanner Hall, Southern Mississippi **Coach of the Year:** Scott Berry, Southern Mississippi **Freshman of the Year:** Blake Morgan, Old Dominion **Newcomer of the Year:** Gabriel Rincones, Florida Atlantic **Defensive Player of the Year:** Logan McLeod, Louisiana Tech **Assistant Coach of the Year:** Christian Ostrander, Southern Mississippi.

INDIVIDUAL BATTING LEADERS

(Minimum 140 at-bats)

	AVG	OBP	SLG	AB	2B	3B	HR	RBI	SB
Matt Coutney, Old Dominion	.376	.473	.808	229	18	0	27	70	3
Nate Furman, Charlotte	.371	.502	.474	232	14	2	2	23	21
Christian Hall, Alabama-Birmingham	.370	.443	.614	189	9	2	11	48	0
Nolan Schanuel, Florida Atlantic	.369	.477	.658	225	17	0	16	56	11
Luke Edwards, Marshall	.364	.405	.593	231	14	0	13	53	10
Taylor Young, Louisiana Tech	.364	.506	.644	239	23	4	12	51	28
Jack Dragum, Charlotte	.352	.440	.541	233	11	0	11	54	5
Gabriel Rincones Jr., Florida Atlantic	.346	.451	.658	237	17	0	19	69	2
Leyton Barry, Texas-San Antonio	.343	.405	.474	230	14	2	4	38	7
Jackson Galloway, Middle Tennessee State	.341	.381	.559	170	10	3	7	32	4
Cole McConnell, Louisiana Tech	.336	.417	.535	256	24	0	9	76	6
Dylan Goldstein, Florida Atlantic	.333	.473	.662	198	9	1	18	63	4
Chase Keng, Texas-San Antonio	.324	.390	.545	222	18	2	9	57	4
Andy Garriola, Old Dominion	.322	.384	.715	242	18	1	25	80	2
Ryan Flores, Texas-San Antonio	.322	.434	.541	205	4	1	13	53	0
Shane Sirdashney, Texas-San Antonio	.321	.429	.482	168	10	1	5	36	4
Dustin Dickerson, Southern Mississippi	.320	.397	.409	269	24	0	0	32	6
John Marc Mullins, Alabama-Birmingham	.318	.422	.439	223	13	1	4	21	13
Sammy Diaz, Texas-San Antonio	.315	.423	.463	149	8	1	4	29	1
Steele Netterville, Louisiana Tech	.313	.398	.547	256	15	0	15	67	2
Robbie Petracci, Old Dominion	.312	.375	.608	186	19	0	12	36	1
Nathan Becker	.310	.397	.421	171	11	1	2	26	0
Brock Gagliardi	.310	.420	.585	171	8	0	13	40	0
Jonathan Tapia, Texas-San Antonio	.309	.412	.478	230	21	0	6	50	3
Ryan Leitch, Marshall	.307	.368	.563	215	17	1	12	43	1
Jake Cunningham, Charlotte	.304	.410	.595	227	12	3	16	52	16
Ian Bailey, Texas-San Antonio	.302	.389	.603	232	16	3	16	51	3
Travis Sankovich, Marshall	.301	.410	.373	209	11	2	0	25	1
Darryl Buggs, Alabama-Birmingham	.301	.380	.422	166	9	1	3	31	6
Fausto Lopez, Middle Tennessee State	.300	.388	.478	203	12	0	8	23	10

INDIVIDUAL PITCHING LEADERS

(Minimum 40 innings pitched)

	W	L	ERA	G	SV	IP	H	BB	SO
Blake Morgan, Old Dominion	8	0	1.69	16	0	69.1	57	8	66
Kyle Crigger, Louisiana Tech	6	3	2.35	37	9	69	60	17	79
Hunter Riggins, Southern Mississippi	8	4	2.59	16	0	97.1	85	21	85
Luke Malone, Texas-San Antonio	9	3	2.67	19	2	87.2	81	14	62
Tanner Hall, Southern Mississippi	9	3	2.81	19	0	109	98	14	146
Hurston Waldrep, Southern Mississippi	6	2	3.20	17	0	90	71	33	140
Jaden Hamm, Middle Tennessee State	4	2	3.34	16	2	59.1	46	29	65
Jonathan Fincher, Louisiana Tech	8	2	3.52	19	0	79.1	88	9	73
Ryan Jennings, Louisiana Tech	6	1	3.59	21	0	90.1	68	37	95
Spencer Giesting, Charlotte	7	4	3.72	21	0	75	59	42	105
Jackson Reynolds, Alabama-Birmingham	2	6	3.92	15	0	80.1	85	21	71
Trent Seibert, Middle Tennessee State	4	5	4.04	21	1	62.1	61	24	66
Nick Pantos, Old Dominion	6	2	4.36	17	0	76.1	83	31	76
Peyton Wigginton, Middle Tennessee State	6	5	4.44	19	1	77	85	16	66
Hunter Cooley, Florida Atlantic	8	4	4.67	15	0	104	106	17	79
Brooks Walton, Alabama-Birmingham	6	5	4.68	14	0	65.1	75	15	33
Patrick Pridgen, Florida International	2	7	4.77	14	0	71.2	69	44	112
Cade Gibson, Louisiana Tech	6	5	4.87	19	1	85	83	19	93
Cooper Chandler, Rice	2	7	5.09	14	0	63.2	71	22	71
Carlos Lequerica, Florida International	2	5	5.16	16	1	52.1	51	21	51
Devyn Terbrak, Western Kentucky	7	4	5.36	14	0	89	104	14	79
Jeffrey Purnell, Marshall	5	6	5.40	14	0	80	82	28	75
Sam Armstrong, Old Dominion	3	2	5.40	15	0	63.1	70	27	53
Jake Kates, Western Kentucky	4	5	5.56	18	0	55	57	18	55
Zach Keenan, Middle Tennessee State	4	3	5.61	15	0	78.2	88	27	59
Will Lancaster, Charlotte	4	2	5.68	15	0	65	62	29	41
Patrick Copen, Marshall	3	3	5.83	14	0	63.1	59	35	65
Jacob Josey, Florida Atlantic	4	5	5.85	16	1	60	70	28	42
Zac Addkison, Marshall	1	3	5.97	14	0	63.1	72	28	70
Jarret Whorff, Louisiana Tech	5	7	6.26	20	0	64.2	69	34	68

HORIZON LEAGUE

	Conference		Overall	
	W	L	W	L
Wright State	20	9	30	25
Oakland	18	11	30	25
Illinois-Chicago	14	11	22	25
Purdue Fort Wayne	13	15	18	36
Youngstown State	12	16	20	36
Northern Kentucky	11	17	19	35
Wisconsin-Milwaukee	9	17	20	29

ALL-CONFERENCE TEAM: C: Cole Conn, So., Illinois-Chicago **1B:** Gehrig Anglin, RJr., Wright State **2B:** Braeden O'Shaughnessy, Jr., Youngstown State **3B:** Manny Vorhees, Jr., Northern Kentucky **SS:** Brad Goulet, Gr.,

Oakland **OF:** Bryan Rosario, RSr., Illinois-Chicago; Julian Greenwell, So., Wright State; Alec Sayre, So., Wright State **DH:** Brandon Nigh, Fr., Oakland **SP:** Tyler Ingram, Jr., Illinois-Chicago; Nate Peterson, RSo., Illinois-Chicago; Matt Brosky, Jr., Youngstown State **RP:** AJ Blubaugh, So., Wisconsin-Milwaukee **Player of the Year:** Alec Sayre, Wright State **Pitcher of the Year:** Matt Brosky, Youngstown State **Coach of the Year:** Jordon Banfield, Oakland **Freshman of the Year:** Brandon Nigh, Oakland **Relief Pitcher of the Year:** AJ Blubaugh, Wisconsin-Milwaukee.

INDIVIDUAL BATTING LEADERS

(Minimum 140 at-bats)

	AVG	OBP	SLG	AB	2B	3B	HR	RBI	SB
Alec Sayre, Wright State	.358	.446	.576	229	18	1	10	54	9
Braeden O'Shaughnessy, Youngstown State	.357	.434	.543	221	16	2	7	41	7
Breck Nowik, Illinois-Chicago	.335	.421	.581	167	14	0	9	42	2
Rayth Petersen, Illinois-Chicago	.330	.417	.466	176	8	2	4	34	10
Justin Riemer, Wright State	.329	.454	.459	146	13	0	2	27	7
Cade Fitzpatrick, Purdue Fort Wayne	.321	.372	.543	162	6	3	8	33	0
Bryan Rosario, Illinois-Chicago	.320	.437	.433	178	10	2	2	27	12
Julian Greenwell, Wright State	.314	.422	.560	207	17	5	8	50	5
Manny Vorhees, Northern Kentucky	.309	.403	.543	223	18	2	10	58	3
Zane Harris, Wright State	.308	.389	.529	208	15	2	9	67	2
Luke Seidel, Wisconsin-Milwaukee	.305	.399	.383	167	8	1	1	19	15
Jack Lang, Purdue Fort Wayne	.303	.391	.540	198	13	2	10	30	13
Liam McFadden-Ackman, Northern Kentucky	.300	.386	.424	170	4	1	5	27	4
Jared Miller, Oakland	.299	.435	.486	144	7	1	6	30	4
Jay Luikart, Wright State	.299	.409	.544	204	14	3	10	31	5
Brenton Phillips, Oakland	.298	.364	.451	215	11	2	6	32	10
Gehrig Anglin, Wright State	.297	.424	.598	209	15	0	16	49	11
Aaron Chapman, Wisconsin-Milwaukee	.297	.358	.427	192	11	1	4	35	14
Brennan Gick, Northern Kentucky	.296	.375	.571	189	13	0	13	35	3
Alex Evenson, Purdue Fort Wayne	.293	.374	.335	164	7	0	0	15	4
Cole Conn, Illinois-Chicago	.290	.368	.506	176	14	0	8	42	9
Treyvin Moss, Northern Kentucky	.288	.344	.407	226	16	1	3	35	10
Dylan Swarmer, Youngstown State	.284	.385	.414	169	8	1	4	16	2
Ben Higgins, Purdue Fort Wayne	.283	.381	.487	187	6	1	10	28	1
Sammy Sass, Wright State	.281	.376	.452	217	6	2	9	52	6
Ryan Lin-Peistrup, Illinois-Chicago	.281	.387	.453	139	12	0	4	23	8
Noah Fisher, Northern Kentucky	.280	.366	.500	168	11	1	8	32	1
Ryan Nagelbach, Illinois-Chicago	.280	.360	.526	175	15	2	8	33	4
Brandon Heidal, Oakland	.278	.369	.305	187	5	0	0	24	4
Steven D'Eusanio, Youngstown State	.277	.349	.435	191	7	1	7	28	2

INDIVIDUAL PITCHING LEADERS

(Minimum 40 innings pitched)

	W	L	ERA	G	SV	IP	H	BB	SO
Matt Brosky, Youngstown State	6	7	2.65	15	0	98.2	86	22	102
AJ Blubaugh, Wisconsin-Milwaukee	3	3	3.25	16	6	52.2	40	16	51
Alex Theis, Wright State	6	1	3.36	18	0	59	59	35	87
Tyler Ingram, Illinois-Chicago	4	4	3.79	13	0	71.1	72	35	58
Nate Peterson, Illinois-Chicago	4	5	3.89	14	0	88	85	21	102
Riley Frey, Wisconsin-Milwaukee	5	5	4.10	14	1	79	81	31	85
JD Deany, Purdue Fort Wayne	5	3	5.20	19	0	71	85	27	57
Ben Gerl, Northern Kentucky	4	6	5.24	19	1	89.1	105	47	67
Chad Coles, Youngstown State	4	5	5.26	26	1	77	69	42	70
Jake Shirk, Wright State	6	6	5.55	16	0	86	94	23	65
Cristian Lopez, Illinois-Chicago	5	4	5.86	16	1	50.2	66	21	64
Jacob Wosinski, Oakland	2	5	5.86	14	1	58.1	79	25	45
Sebastian Gongora, Wright State	5	1	5.88	16	0	82.2	85	31	81
Travis Perry, Youngstown State	4	3	6.26	15	0	64.2	73	32	49
Kaden Echeman, Northern Kentucky	2	9	6.28	18	0	61.2	75	38	48
Travis Densmore, Oakland	5	3	6.32	15	0	62.2	81	22	58
Mitchell Spencer, Purdue Fort Wayne	2	5	6.39	15	0	62	77	25	53
Brett Hagen, Oakland	4	3	6.79	16	0	65	74	20	44
Kyle Klingenbeck, Northern Kentucky	3	8	9.51	15	0	64.1	73	49	81

IVY LEAGUE

	Conference		Overall	
	W	L	W	L
Pennsylvania	17	4	33	15
*Columbia	17	4	32	18
Dartmouth	14	7	24	19
Yale	10	11	20	18
Harvard	10	11	19	22
Brown	8	13	13	23
Cornell	5	16	11	25
Princeton	3	18	7	33

ALL-CONFERENCE TEAM: C: Weston Eberly, Jr., Columbia **1B:** Ben Miller, Jr., Pennsylvania **2B:** Cole Palis, Jr., Pennsylvania **3B:** Wyatt Henseler, Jr., Pennsylvania **SS:** Tyler Cox, So., Dartmouth **OF:** Hayden Schott, Jr., Columbia; Cole Hage, So., Columbia; Kade Kretzschmar, Sr., Dartmouth **DH:** Andrew Hernandez, Sr., Pennsylvania **UTL:** Justin Murray, Sr., Dartmouth **SP:** Kevin Eaise, Sr., Pennsylvania; Joe Miller, Sr., Pennsylvania; Tobey McDonough, Jr., Brown **RP:** Jay Driver, So., Harvard **Player of the Year:** Kade Kretzschmar, Dartmouth **Pitcher of the Year:** Kevin Eaise, Pennsylvania **Coach of the Year:** Brett Boretti, Columbia **Rookie of the Year:** Tyler Cox, Dartmouth.

INDIVIDUAL BATTING LEADERS

(Minimum 140 at-bats)

	AVG	OBP	SLG	AB	2B	3B	HR	RBI	SB
Tyler Cox, Dartmouth	.402	.452	.484	184	10	1	1	40	11
Wyatt Henseler, Pennsylvania	.383	.487	.697	188	17	0	14	53	0
Brendan Cumming, Princeton	.361	.405	.552	183	12	1	7	29	5
Logan Bravo, Harvard	.355	.423	.618	152	16	0	8	44	3
Kade Kretzschmar, Dartmouth	.353	.406	.635	167	16	5	7	46	2
Justin Murray, Dartmouth	.352	.416	.586	145	20	1	4	32	3
Jackson Appel, Pennsylvania	.346	.420	.525	179	9	1	7	29	6
Max Jensen, Cornell	.338	.403	.554	130	15	2	3	26	4
Cole Hage, Columbia	.335	.454	.520	179	15	0	6	37	8
Reece Rappoli, Brown	.333	.404	.403	129	9	0	0	19	2
Tyler MacGregor, Columbia	.332	.413	.508	187	18	3	3	39	16
Connor Bertsch, Dartmouth	.331	.386	.513	154	13	0	5	35	2
Ben Miller, Pennsylvania	.330	.420	.537	188	18	0	7	42	0
Nadir Lewis, Princeton	.329	.428	.613	155	12	1	10	36	9
Will Jacobsen, Harvard	.327	.353	.442	147	6	1	3	19	4
Chris Snopek, Harvard	.323	.418	.406	155	6	2	1	22	0
Hayden Schott, Columbia	.320	.349	.594	197	18	0	12	55	2
Anton Lazits, Columbia	.314	.409	.438	169	11	2	2	26	6
Nathan Waugh, Cornell	.310	.403	.570	100	5	3	5	18	0
Weston Eberly, Columbia	.306	.429	.563	160	10	5	7	41	2
Ryan Marra, Brown	.304	.402	.558	138	5	0	10	27	9
Andy Blake, Columbia	.304	.379	.580	181	12	4	10	42	5
Jimmy Chatfield, Yale	.303	.472	.523	132	5	0	8	30	10
Nathan Cmeyla, Dartmouth	.301	.342	.515	136	9	4	4	19	0
Tommy Courtney, Pennsylvania	.299	.352	.381	197	5	1	3	25	9
Austin Mowrey, Columbia	.297	.370	.391	138	5	1	2	15	7
Kolton Freeman, Dartmouth	.292	.409	.539	154	8	3	8	33	5
Craig Larsen, Pennsylvania	.289	.339	.398	201	7	0	5	42	2
Ben Rounds, Harvard	.288	.407	.387	111	11	0	0	18	4
Matt Scannell, Princeton	.287	.381	.476	143	6	0	7	44	9

INDIVIDUAL PITCHING LEADERS

(Minimum 40 innings pitched)

	W	L	ERA	G	SV	IP	H	BB	SO
Owen Coady, Pennsylvania	7	1	2.80	14	2	54.2	40	22	74
Paxton Meyers, Brown	4	2	3.16	19	1	37	31	15	39
Tobey McDonough, Brown	3	3	3.17	11	0	65.1	57	16	52
Joe Miller, Pennsylvania	6	4	3.63	13	0	74.1	64	36	91
Kevin Eaise, Pennsylvania	7	1	4.03	13	0	67	66	28	79
Jackson Emus, Princeton	2	6	4.77	12	0	68	66	23	69
Trystan Sarcone, Dartmouth	6	4	4.85	12	0	59.1	67	13	49
Sean Matson, Harvard	3	3	5.32	13	0	42.1	45	17	49
Sean Higgins, Columbia	6	3	5.34	14	0	62.1	74	15	59
Santhosh Gottam, Brown	4	5	5.52	14	0	44	55	10	35
Luke Yacinich, Cornell	4	4	5.67	13	0	73	67	35	56
Mike Walsh, Yale	4	2	5.68	11	0	65	58	31	80
Bobby Olsen, Brown	0	4	5.83	13	0	58.2	68	19	48
Joe Sheets, Columbia	2	2	6.04	13	0	53.2	76	24	41
Tim Williamson, Harvard	3	3	6.14	13	0	44	41	37	42
Nathan Skinner, Dartmouth	5	4	6.25	11	0	63.1	78	14	49
Zach Fogell, Brown	0	4	6.46	12	0	39	50	23	46
Grant Kipp, Yale	4	3	6.79	12	0	65	84	19	56
Colton Shaw, Yale	2	5	7.21	11	0	53.2	64	28	39
Jaren Zinn, Harvard	3	3	7.50	11	0	42	44	44	63

	W	L	ERA	G	SV	IP	H	BB	SO
Justin Murray, Dartmouth	4	3	7.57	11	0	52.1	65	23	43
Andrew D'Alessio, Princeton	1	6	7.63	11	0	61.1	74	40	26
Chris Ellison, Cornell	0	1	8.06	18	0	41.1	59	24	26
Spencer Edwards, Cornell	2	8	8.46	13	0	55.1	56	36	45
Tom Chmielewski, Princeton	2	7	8.61	12	0	54.1	91	17	45

METRO ATLANTIC ATHLETIC CONFERENCE

	Conference		Overall	
	W	L	W	L
Fairfield	18	5	31	20
Marist	18	6	30	17
*Canisius	15	9	29	25
Rider	12	10	28	26
Monmouth	12	10	24	25
Niagara	13	11	22	32
Manhattan	12	12	24	26
Quinnipiac	8	15	15	33
Siena	8	15	11	37
Saint Peter's	6	17	9	41
Iona	6	18	6	41

ALL-CONFERENCE TEAM: C: Gene Napolitano, Gr., Marist **1B:** Gavin Noriega, RFr., Marist **2B:** Max Grant, So., Canisius **3B:** Charlie Pagliarini, Jr., Fairfield **SS:** David Bermudez, Gr., Manhattan **OF:** Brian Hart, Sr., Marist; Mike DeStefano, Jr. Canisius; Pete Durocher, Jr., Manhattan **DH:** Mike Steffan, Gr., Canisius **UTL:** Danny Melnick, Jr., Quinnipiac **P:** Erubiel Candelario, Sr., Marist; Trey Dombroski, Jr., Monmouth; Mike Duffy, So., Canisius **Player of the Year:** Max Grant, Canisius **Pitcher of the Year:** Trey Dombroski, Monmouth **Coach of the Year:** Chris Tracz, Marist **Rookie of the Year:** Peyton Consigli, Canisius **Relief Pitcher of the Year:** Peyton Consigli, Canisius.

INDIVIDUAL BATTING LEADERS

(Minimum 140 at-bats)

	AVG	OBP	SLG	AB	2B	3B	HR	RBI	SB
Max Grant, Canisius	.398	.489	.646	226	14	6	10	53	7
David Bermudez, Manhattan	.380	.449	.668	208	18	0	14	52	7
Mike DeStefano, Canisius	.363	.427	.527	237	7	4	8	46	22
Gene Napolitano, Marist	.359	.459	.484	184	12	1	3	41	6
Jack Lynch, Manhattan	.354	.448	.530	164	11	3	4	39	7
Gavin Noriega, Marist	.350	.411	.525	183	14	3	4	51	3
Pete Durocher, Manhattan	.350	.414	.530	183	13	1	6	50	15
Danny Melnick, Quinnipiac	.344	.422	.656	160	17	0	11	33	4
Anthony Donofrio, Quinnipiac	.343	.392	.545	178	11	2	7	25	15
Mike Steffan, Canisius	.342	.431	.545	202	12	1	9	59	3
Matt Padre, Manhattan	.339	.504	.460	174	12	0	3	33	1
Robbie Armitage, Marist	.331	.388	.579	178	19	2	7	58	4
Jake Field, Iona	.319	.380	.506	166	13	6	2	22	3
Benny Serrano, Niagara	.319	.437	.541	135	17	2	3	20	11
Matt Venuto, Fairfield	.318	.403	.541	157	9	1	8	33	0
Dylan Vincent, Canisius	.312	.406	.365	189	8	1	0	20	21
Dawson Bailey, Niagara	.309	.402	.552	223	14	2	12	41	9
Jared Zimbardo, Quinnipiac	.307	.380	.509	163	11	2	6	24	7
Alex Milone, Siena	.305	.436	.450	151	8	1	4	27	1
Cole O'Connor, Niagara	.303	.364	.404	218	14	1	2	35	9
Brian Hart, Marist	.302	.360	.503	179	15	6	3	37	14
Mike Becchetti, Fairfield	.301	.398	.524	206	18	2	8	32	2
Nick Forney, Iona	.298	.333	.388	178	8	4	0	18	8
Harrison Treble, Manhattan	.297	.395	.385	195	14	0	1	30	7
Cole Tucker, Niagara	.296	.390	.394	203	14	0	2	26	3
Matt Zaffino, Fairfield	.295	.351	.542	190	15	1	10	55	5
Socrates Bardatsos, Rider	.294	.432	.437	197	10	0	6	41	6
Dylan Hoy, Marist	.292	.446	.403	154	12	1	1	32	4
Matt Livingston, Siena	.290	.354	.421	145	10	0	3	29	1
Collin Jensen, Saint Peter's	.290	.361	.393	183	10	0	3	23	0

INDIVIDUAL PITCHING LEADERS

(Minimum 40 innings pitched)

	W	L	ERA	G	SV	IP	H	BB	SO
Trey Dombroski, Monmouth	6	2	3.13	15	0	95	80	14	120
Matt Duffy, Canisius	8	2	3.81	17	0	104	86	26	124
Tom Peltier, Canisius	3	3	3.83	22	2	54	55	30	61
Rob Hensey, Monmouth	3	7	3.87	14	0	81.1	81	13	102
Alex Pansini, Marist	8	4	4.21	14	0	77	78	21	90
Erubiel Candelario, Marist	8	3	4.25	14	0	76.1	74	36	88
Kyle Lesler, Manhattan	4	2	4.26	15	2	61.1	60	26	69
Ben Seiler, Siena	4	6	4.35	13	0	80.2	89	28	86
Marcus Cashman, Niagara	2	5	4.39	17	0	69.2	51	31	66
Michael Sansone, Fairfield	5	2	4.48	11	0	68.1	49	12	78
Chris Pouliot, Canisius	8	3	4.70	14	0	59.1	62	32	57
Vincent Vitacco, Rider	3	2	4.79	17	1	62	75	23	45
Dan Klepchick, Monmouth	3	4	4.87	15	0	61	72	11	50
Bryson Cafaro, Fairfield	6	2	5.19	13	0	52	48	18	52
Will Hesslink, Manhattan	5	7	5.36	14	0	82.1	108	29	71
Frank Doelling, Rider	4	7	5.40	16	0	66.2	78	31	63
Jordan Warecke, Manhattan	4	6	5.49	14	0	78.2	101	35	56
Jake Noviello, Fairfield	3	2	5.80	13	0	59	61	36	40
Blake Helmstetter, Iona	2	7	5.98	12	0	55.2	74	20	53
Kevin Seitter, Quinnipiac	3	10	6.13	15	0	76.1	118	31	64
Drew Helmstetter, Iona	2	2	6.19	10	0	48	58	20	26
Arlo Marynczak, Siena	2	6	6.37	17	1	65	86	16	81
Joe Papeo, Rider	6	5	6.57	17	0	75.1	93	27	67
Gabriel Romano, Quinnipiac	3	1	6.61	18	1	62.2	98	16	54
Brandyn Garcia, Quinnipiac	4	7	7.15	13	0	61.2	60	43	74
Evan Wilde, Niagara	2	8	8.00	15	0	72	95	41	67
Kyle Mahady, Saint Peter's	3	8	8.81	15	0	80.2	130	34	37
Matthew Dubois, Saint Peter's	2	8	9.00	14	0	79	121	37	40
Jack Gannon, Saint Peter's	1	8	11.09	24	0	56	94	27	37

MID-AMERICAN CONFERENCE

	Conference		Overall	
	W	L	W	L
Ball State	32	7	39	17
*Central Michigan	30	7	39	16
Toledo	23	16	32	24
Ohio	21	15	29	22
Kent State	19	19	24	29
Miami	18	22	23	33
Eastern Michigan	16	24	22	34
Western Michigan	15	24	18	36
Bowling Green	14	24	18	34
Northern Illinois	13	25	14	40
Akron	11	29	15	41

ALL-CONFERENCE TEAM: C: Connor Charping, Sr., Western Michigan **1B:** Trenton Quartermaine, RSr., Ball State **2B:** Mario Camilletti, Sr., Central Michigan **3B:** Colin Kasperbauer, Sr., Ohio **SS:** Justin Simpson, Jr., Central Michigan **OF:** Zach Cole, Jr., Ball State; Matt Kirk, Jr., Eastern Michigan; Justin Kirby, Sr., Kent State **DH:** David Novak, Fr., Miami **SP:** Tyler Schweitzer, Jr., Ball State; Andrew Taylor, So., Central Michigan; Jonathan Brand, Sr., Miami; Kyle Jones, Jr., Toledo **RP:** Sam Klein, So., Ball State At-Large Jakob Marsee, So., Central Michigan **Player of the Year:** Matt Kirk, Eastern Michigan **Pitcher of the Year:** Tyler Schweitzer, Ball State **Coach of the Year:** Rich Maloney, Ball State **Freshman of the Year:** Dylan Nevar, Western Michigan **Freshman Pitcher of the Year:** Ryan Brown, Ball State **Defensive Player of the Year:** Ryan Peltier, Ball State.

INDIVIDUAL BATTING LEADERS

(Minimum 140 at-bats)

	AVG	OBP	SLG	AB	2B	3B	HR	RBI	SB
Colin Kasperbauer, Ohio	.380	.465	.572	187	19	4	3	48	4
Mario Camilletti, Central Michigan	.376	.498	.563	229	20	1	7	51	4
Josh Johnson, Kent State	.371	.446	.629	159	10	2	9	43	14
Zach Cole, Ball State	.361	.449	.727	183	10	9	13	47	8
Matt Kirk, Eastern Michigan	.356	.408	.693	225	25	0	17	49	6
Amir Wright, Ball State	.350	.462	.482	226	10	7	2	33	9
Connor Charping, Western Michigan	.348	.440	.483	207	17	1	3	23	26
Jakob Marsee, Central Michigan	.345	.467	.550	229	14	6	7	66	18
Aaron Dolney, Eastern Michigan	.344	.446	.597	154	12	3	7	27	0
Garret Pike, Toledo	.344	.391	.514	183	11	1	6	29	13
Gavin Doyle, Western Michigan	.343	.459	.497	175	18	0	3	45	0
Benji Brokemond, Miami	.342	.438	.493	152	10	5	1	25	8
Isaiah Peterson, Ohio	.337	.457	.535	202	10	3	8	39	6

	AVG	OBP	SLG	AB	2B	3B	HR	RBI	SB
Kyle Gurney, Bowling Green	.330	.424	.542	179	11	0	9	37	9
Jeron Williams, Toledo	.329	.385	.429	231	6	4	3	30	23
Adam Fallon, Bowling Green	.325	.392	.403	154	3	3	1	22	21
Dylan Nevar, Western Michigan	.325	.406	.614	197	20	2	11	49	2
AJ Rausch, Ohio	.323	.392	.530	198	13	2	8	36	8
Justin Kirby, Kent State	.323	.420	.646	198	17	1	15	45	14
Nathan Rose, Bowling Green	.322	.382	.439	171	12	1	2	27	2
Nick Powell, Ball State	.322	.402	.458	227	15	2	4	42	2
Aidan Shepardson, Central Michigan	.319	.428	.399	188	15	0	0	37	5
Collin Mathews, Kent State	.319	.419	.544	182	9	1	10	40	15
Danny Wuestenfeld, Central Michigan	.317	.410	.520	221	16	1	9	68	3
Nathan Archer, Bowling Green	.317	.395	.567	180	11	5	8	34	20
Mack Timbrook, Kent State	.317	.395	.457	164	12	1	3	35	1
Mason Sykes, Toledo	.317	.393	.596	208	10	0	16	52	9
Cade Sullivan, Western Michigan	.315	.398	.548	197	16	0	10	52	1
Jimmy Allen, Western Michigan	.315	.417	.475	200	11	3	5	31	3
Carlos Aranda, Northern Illinois	.313	.452	.507	150	8	0	7	21	6

INDIVIDUAL PITCHING LEADERS

(Minimum 40 innings pitched)

	W	L	ERA	G	SV	IP	H	BB	SO
Jonathan Brand, Miami	8	2	1.40	13	0	77.1	59	29	86
Zach Maxey, Miami	4	3	2.27	13	0	71.1	65	24	62
Tyler Schweitzer, Ball State	11	2	2.65	17	0	91.2	69	30	112
Andrew Taylor, Central Michigan	8	4	3.21	17	1	84	61	27	126
Kyle Jones, Toledo	7	3	4.24	17	1	91.1	86	25	114
Connor Brandon, Toledo	7	5	4.76	17	1	75.2	73	42	88
Jordan Patty, Central Michigan	6	5	4.83	16	0	82	75	38	82
Benjamin Cruikshank, Kent State	3	3	4.86	13	0	53.2	35	43	53
Brenden Roder, Ohio	4	3	4.94	14	0	54.2	68	10	29
Adam Falinski, Eastern Michigan	4	5	5.12	12	0	58	59	31	61
Edward Kutt IV, Ohio	5	4	5.15	15	1	85.2	102	25	82
Garrett Navarra, Central Michigan	10	3	5.15	18	1	80.1	96	27	85
Jordan Power, Toledo	6	3	5.33	15	1	74.1	81	25	53
Ty Johnson, Ball State	7	3	5.47	16	0	75.2	66	25	76
Collin Romel, Kent State	5	4	5.48	14	0	65.2	73	25	59
Trennor O'Donnell, Ball State	6	2	5.48	14	0	65.2	67	27	74
Eric Chalus, Kent State	3	2	5.56	12	0	56.2	62	12	54
Gage Schenk, Bowling Green	3	6	5.63	14	0	64	57	38	59
Hayden Berg, Western Michigan	4	4	6.27	17	2	56	69	27	60
Thomas House, Eastern Michigan	1	7	6.31	14	0	65.2	64	47	64
Dane Armbrustmacher, Western Michigan	4	6	6.47	16	1	65.1	85	29	73
Nick Crandell, Western Michigan	2	6	7.19	15	0	61.1	94	18	33
Kyle Seebach, Northern Illinois	2	7	7.30	14	0	74	82	44	64
Zach Fruit, Eastern Michigan	4	5	7.71	14	0	67.2	91	34	65
Taed Heydinger, Akron	2	10	8.42	14	0	72.2	110	30	51
Andrew Abrahamowicz, Bowling Green	2	5	8.45	15	0	59.2	75	35	60
Anthony Fett, Akron	0	10	8.71	13	0	61	86	23	35
Brenden Lovell, Western Michigan	2	3	9.05	19	1	55.2	80	29	48

MID-EASTERN ATHLETIC CONFERENCE

	Conference		Overall	
Northern Division	**W**	**L**	**W**	**L**
Delaware State	19	14	25	23
*Coppin State	17	13	24	30
Maryland Eastern Shore	15	18	17	37
Norfolk State	12	18	15	32

ALL-CONFERENCE TEAM: C: Mike Dorcean, RSo., Coppin State **1B:** Sebastien Sarabia, So., Coppin State **2B:** Corey Miley, RJr., Coppin State **3B:** Brian Nicolas, RJr., Coppin State **SS:** Trey Paige, So., Delaware State **OF:** Marcos Castillo, Sr., Coppin State; Wellington Balsley, RJr., Coppin State; Dionte Brown, RJr., Norfolk State **UTL:** Jordan Hamberg, So., Coppin State **SP:** Jordan Hamberg, So., Coppin State; Peter Carreca, So., Delaware State **RP:** Justin Johnson, Fr., Coppin State **Player of the Year:** Trey Paige, Delaware State **Pitcher of the Year:** Jordan Hamberg, Coppin State **Coach of the Year:** JP Blandin, Delaware State **Rookie of the Year:** Josh Hankins, Coppin State.

INDIVIDUAL BATTING LEADERS

(Minimum 140 at-bats)

	AVG	OBP	SLG	AB	2B	3B	HR	RBI	SB
Trey Paige, Delaware State	.409	.510	.762	164	15	2	13	46	7
Jordan Hamberg, Coppin State	.347	.463	.611	144	10	2	8	34	11
Jacob Council, Norfolk State	.346	.411	.497	159	10	1	4	33	6
Sebastien Sarabia, Coppin State	.320	.406	.426	169	8	2	2	37	3
Corey Miley, Coppin State	.319	.478	.428	138	11	2	0	27	3
Marcos Castillo, Coppin State	.316	.409	.490	196	13	3	5	40	18
Dionte Brown, Norfolk State	.314	.371	.456	169	8	5	2	40	18
Raphy Rodriguez, Norfolk State	.309	.390	.430	165	7	2	3	19	12
Krew Bouldin, Delaware State	.298	.434	.483	151	10	0	6	36	1
Ryan Howe, Maryland Eastern Shore	.297	.350	.427	185	9	0	5	40	2
Miguel Rivera, Delaware State	.293	.403	.419	167	9	3	2	29	11
Wellington Balsley, Coppin State	.291	.409	.364	206	5	5	0	32	27
Brian Nicolas, Coppin State	.286	.398	.476	168	6	4	6	39	17
Alan Alonso, Delaware State	.286	.461	.550	140	11	4	6	33	11
Brantley Cutler, Maryland Eastern Shore	.262	.359	.427	164	13	1	4	24	1
Josh Hankins, Coppin State	.261	.349	.332	184	10	0	1	27	13
Tommy Woods, Norfolk State	.260	.340	.402	127	5	2	3	18	3
Mike Worthington, Delaware State	.256	.343	.301	156	7	0	0	17	13
Dillon Oxyer, Maryland Eastern Shore	.256	.359	.333	168	11	1	0	19	5
Alec Rodriguez, Delaware State	.255	.344	.383	141	9	0	3	27	5
Brian Cordell, Maryland Eastern Shore	.255	.397	.331	157	5	2	1	16	7
Steven Shaffer, Norfolk State	.240	.340	.357	129	8	2	1	24	13
Brandon Cleveland, Norfolk State	.229	.356	.313	131	8	0	1	14	4

INDIVIDUAL PITCHING LEADERS

(Minimum 40 innings pitched)

	W	L	ERA	G	SV	IP	H	BB	SO
Evan Nibblett, Maryland Eastern Shore	2	2	3.43	11	0	57.2	59	9	40
Noah Covington, Maryland Eastern Shore	6	5	4.23	12	0	72.1	82	10	51
Jordan Hamberg, Coppin State	6	3	5.15	13	0	64.2	63	40	87
James Deloatch, Norfolk State	4	5	5.26	13	0	65	66	45	63
Cameron Bratton, Maryland Eastern Shore	3	6	5.28	13	0	76.2	74	29	59
Tyler Nichol, Coppin State	2	3	5.55	14	0	71.1	76	47	72
Dalton Barham, Norfolk State	2	6	5.79	11	0	51.1	56	33	50
Justin Walton, Norfolk State	2	4	5.81	16	1	52.2	58	33	41
Zac Capps, Norfolk State	2	5	6.75	13	1	50.2	51	48	56
Jordan Haddaway, Delaware State	5	3	6.8	12	0	50.1	61	29	45

MISSOURI VALLEY CONFERENCE

	Conference		Overall	
	W	**L**	**W**	**L**
Southern Illinois	16	5	44	16
Evansville	14	6	32	24
*Dallas Baptist	11	9	34	22
Bradley	11	10	20	29
Indiana State	10	10	26	22
*Missouri State	8	13	31	29
Illinois State	7	14	20	31
Valparaiso	5	15	16	32

ALL-CONFERENCE TEAM: C: Ryan Wrobleski, RSo., Dallas Baptist **1B:** Cole Moore, Jr., Dallas Baptist **1B:** Connor O'Brien, Jr., Bradley **2B:** Nolan Tucker, RSo., Valparaiso **3B:** Brent Widder, Sr., Evansville **SS:** Jordan Schaeffer, RSr., Indiana State **SS:** Kaeber Rog, Jr., Southern Illinois **OF:** Mark Shallenberger, Sr., Evansville; JT Weber, Sr., Southern Illinois; Ryan Cermak, So., Illinois State **SP:** Shane Gray, Gr., Evansville; Nick Smith, Jr., Evansville; Matt Jachec, RSo., Indiana State **RP:** Chandler Arnold, Jr., Dallas Baptist; Matthew Steidl, Jr., Southern Illinois **Player of the Year:** Kaeber Rog, Southern Illinois **Pitcher of the Year:** Nick Smith, Evansville **Coach of the Year:** Wes Carroll, Evansville **Newcomer of the Year:** Kaeber Rog, Southern Illinois **Freshman of the Year:** Luke Heefner, Dallas Baptist **Defensive Player of the Year:** Ryan Cermak, Illinois State.

INDIVIDUAL BATTING LEADERS

(Minimum 140 at-bats)

	AVG	OBP	SLG	AB	2B	3B	HR	RBI	SB
Connor O'Brien, Bradley	.392	.456	.624	189	14	0	10	44	3
Sean Ross, Indiana State	.366	.429	.634	142	16	2	6	34	2
Nolan Tucker, Valparaiso	.365	.431	.516	126	14	1	1	17	3

	AVG	OBP	SLG	AB	2B	3B	HR	RBI	SB
Kaeber Rog, Southern Illinois	.362	.429	.618	246	21	0	14	56	7
J.T. Weber, Southern Illinois	.355	.441	.649	245	15	0	19	56	6
Cole Moore, Dallas Baptist	.352	.466	.606	216	22	0	11	47	5
Spencer Nivens, Missouri State	.346	.443	.542	240	12	1	11	52	4
Drake Baldwin, Missouri State	.341	.448	.647	232	14	0	19	70	1
Ryan Cermak, Illinois State	.340	.441	.696	194	12	0	19	43	8
Mark Shallenberger, Evansville	.336	.444	.573	220	17	1	11	54	1
Seth Gergely, Indiana State	.326	.418	.468	141	14	3	0	22	3
Pier-Olivier Boucher, Southern Illinois	.325	.426	.533	169	11	0	8	33	10
Josue Urdaneta, Indiana State	.321	.380	.469	209	10	3	5	37	5
Jordan Schaffer, Indiana State	.320	.420	.448	194	11	1	4	23	5
Nathan Bandy, Southern Illinois	.318	.386	.400	195	8	1	2	34	14
Grant Wood, Missouri State	.315	.429	.498	219	14	1	8	49	2
Ryan Vogel, Bradley	.312	.406	.473	186	11	2	5	21	7
Mason Greer, Missouri State	.312	.377	.541	231	21	1	10	53	1
Jace Grady, Dallas Baptist	.310	.419	.509	232	12	2	10	37	25
Keaton Rice, Bradley	.310	.396	.536	168	21	1	5	37	0
Ryan Rodriguez, Southern Illinois	.308	.379	.426	195	11	0	4	38	2
Tanner Craig, Evansville	.305	.382	.636	236	24	0	18	61	0
Randall Diaz, Indiana State	.304	.361	.525	181	17	1	7	37	2
Brent Widder, Evansville	.303	.393	.443	228	11	0	7	42	5
Alex Thurston, Valparaiso	.301	.357	.409	186	11	3	1	19	0
Jake McCaw, Illinois State	.296	.372	.505	206	7	0	12	42	8
Luke Heefner, Dallas Baptist	.294	.373	.467	197	11	1	7	29	12
Simon Scherry, Evansville	.293	.333	.430	249	16	0	6	48	6
Kyle Schmack, Valparaiso	.292	.382	.470	185	10	1	7	27	8
Blayne Jones, Dallas Baptist	.289	.348	.526	228	16	1	12	45	6

INDIVIDUAL PITCHING LEADERS

(Minimum 40 innings pitched)

	W	L	ERA	G	SV	IP	H	BB	SO
Jared Hart, Illinois State	2	3	2.46	23	2	55	49	16	50
Matt Jachec, Indiana State	9	2	2.88	14	0	97	96	9	80
Matthew Steidl, Southern Illinois	7	4	3.45	30	6	75.2	77	31	91
Nick King, Bradley	5	3	3.48	20	0	77.2	59	46	81
Trey McDaniel, Southern Illinois	8	1	3.53	26	5	63.2	71	15	55
Colin Wyman, Illinois State	3	2	3.69	18	3	53.2	51	11	39
Noah Farmer, Southern Illinois	7	2	3.87	17	0	86	101	26	54
Derek Salata, Illinois State	4	6	4.11	13	0	65.2	62	13	63
Nick Smith, Evansville	6	4	4.35	15	0	78.2	79	25	75
Shane Gray, Evansville	8	3	4.39	15	0	98.1	100	25	95
Luke Eldred, Dallas Baptist	5	2	4.63	16	0	70	80	16	55
Adam Link, Missouri State	6	5	4.80	18	0	90	114	22	70
Jacob Kisting, Bradley	6	4	4.88	15	0	83	76	33	79
Luke Patzner, Indiana State	3	4	4.99	14	1	61.1	64	12	59
Taylor Catton, Bradley	3	5	5.02	23	4	66.1	67	37	65
Sean Sinisko, Illinois State	2	5	5.03	13	0	53.2	69	16	32
Jacob Meador, Dallas Baptist	7	3	5.24	15	0	68.2	61	44	91
Forrest Barnes, Missouri State	6	6	5.25	19	0	85.2	83	33	65
Colin Fields, Valparaiso	4	7	5.38	15	0	73.2	71	46	110
Jake Miller, Valparaiso	6	2	5.58	12	1	61.1	71	17	75
Trey Ziegenbein, Missouri State	5	5	5.95	33	2	62	73	20	58
Jack Parisi, Indiana State	4	3	6.31	19	1	51.1	55	29	74

MOUNTAIN WEST CONFERENCE

	Conference		Overall	
	W	L	W	L
Nevada-Las Vegas	21	9	36	22
Nevada	18	12	29	26
San Jose State	16	14	30	29
*Air Force	15	15	32	29
Fresno State	15	15	27	28
New Mexico	10	20	21	33
San Diego State	10	20	18	38

ALL-CONFERENCE TEAM: C: Zach Morgan, Jr., Fresno State **INF:** Sam Kulasingam, So., Air Force **INF:** Jay Thompson, So., Air Force **INF:** Joshua Zamora, Sr., Nevada **INF:** Cole Carrigg, So., San Diego State **INF:** Hank Zeisler, Sr., Nevada-Las Vegas **OF:** Robert Hamchuk, So., San Jose State; Rylan Charles, So., Nevada-Las Vegas; Austin Kryszczuk, So., Nevada-Las Vegas **UTL:** Charles McAdoo, So., San Jose State **P:** Paul Skenes, So., Air Force; Ixan Henderson, So., Fresno State; Troy Melton, Jr., San Diego State; Darren Jansen, Jr., San Jose State **Player of the Year:** Sam Kulasingam, Air Force **Co-Pitchers of the Year:** Paul Skenes, Air Force; Troy Melton, San Diego State **Coach of the Year:** Stan Stolte, Nevada-Las Vegas **Co-Freshman of the Year:** Irvin Weems, San Diego State; Santino Panaro, Nevada-Las Vegas.

INDIVIDUAL BATTING LEADERS

(Minimum 140 at-bats)

	AVG	OBP	SLG	AB	2B	3B	HR	RBI	SB
Sam Kulasingam, Air Force	.411	.487	.683	265	26	5	12	64	6
Henry Zeisler, Nevada-Las Vegas	.396	.494	.693	225	17	4	14	73	1
Cole Carrigg, San Diego State	.388	.426	.509	214	15	1	3	40	19
Rylan Charles, Nevada-Las Vegas	.382	.452	.529	259	16	2	6	46	7
Zach Morgan, Fresno State	.381	.454	.592	218	20	1	8	41	2
Robert Hamchuk, San Jose State	.378	.437	.582	249	17	2	10	39	2
Joshua Zamora, Nevada	.362	.470	.674	218	18	1	16	69	4
Gabriel Garcia, Air Force	.353	.431	.635	255	21	3	15	65	1
Joey Walls, Nevada-Las Vegas	.350	.444	.614	197	26	1	8	48	6
Ivan Luna, Fresno State	.348	.415	.580	224	19	0	11	54	3
Jay Thomason, Air Force	.348	.417	.611	244	14	1	16	53	10
Santino Panaro, Nevada-Las Vegas	.346	.410	.396	159	6	1	0	27	2
Charles McAdoo, San Jose State	.345	.406	.629	229	23	3	12	63	6
Ryan Jackson, Nevada	.344	.456	.448	163	9	1	2	24	0
Diego Alarcon, Nevada-Las Vegas	.343	.420	.544	248	18	1	10	53	2
Austin Kryszczuk, Nevada-Las Vegas	.342	.461	.611	234	21	3	12	58	4
Lenny Junior Ashby, New Mexico	.342	.406	.667	219	18	1	17	59	3
Dario Gomez, Nevada	.316	.362	.532	237	18	6	7	51	10
Jeffrey David, New Mexico	.316	.384	.478	209	14	4	4	37	5
Jake Greiving, Air Force	.315	.391	.522	203	15	0	11	53	0
Edarian Williams, Nevada-Las Vegas	.313	.414	.554	233	11	6	11	67	6
Jacob Stinson, Nevada	.313	.428	.396	182	10	1	1	27	11
Landon Wallace, Nevada	.313	.459	.469	160	8	1	5	34	7
Kamron Willman, New Mexico	.310	.372	.490	155	7	3	5	22	2
Willie Cano, New Mexico	.310	.369	.465	155	12	3	2	24	2
Poncho Ruiz, San Diego State	.309	.413	.459	207	14	1	5	33	4
Patrick Caulfield, Nevada	.308	.384	.440	234	13	3	4	50	28
Ben Newton, Fresno State	.307	.402	.356	163	6	1	0	17	3
Vinny Bologna, Fresno State	.304	.366	.509	161	10	1	7	37	2
Payton Allen, Fresno State	.303	.368	.432	185	13	1	3	28	2

INDIVIDUAL PITCHING LEADERS

(Minimum 40 innings pitched)

	W	L	ERA	G	SV	IP	H	BB	SO
Troy Melton, San Diego State	5	2	2.07	11	0	65.1	57	15	67
Paul Skenes, Air Force	10	3	2.73	15	0	85.2	70	30	96
Kade Morris, Nevada	7	5	4.32	18	3	66.2	68	22	53
Doyle Gehring, Air Force	4	3	4.36	23	6	64	67	23	66
Jake Dixon, Fresno State	1	5	4.56	16	1	79	88	23	84
TJ Fondtain, San Diego State	3	7	4.58	14	0	72.2	66	31	60
Darren Jansen, San Jose State	9	2	4.67	31	3	61.2	63	31	57
Ixan Henderson, Fresno State	7	4	4.69	14	0	78.2	74	37	98
Roman Angelo, Fresno State	4	3	4.82	18	3	61.2	60	22	50
Cam Walty, Nevada	5	7	5.14	15	0	91	108	37	66
Jonathan Clark, San Jose State	2	4	5.27	15	0	68.1	65	33	60
Josh Ibarra, Nevada-Las Vegas	6	2	5.73	14	0	70.2	83	29	63
Noah Beal, Nevada-Las Vegas	8	1	5.75	18	1	61	69	27	55
Josh Sharman, Nevada-Las Vegas	4	4	6.30	17	0	74.1	111	14	59
Peyton Stumbo, Nevada	5	2	6.49	16	0	69.1	85	22	55
Aaron Eden, San Jose State	6	3	6.55	17	0	67.1	89	28	32
Noah Mattera, Nevada-Las Vegas	5	1	6.63	14	0	58.1	75	21	58
Riley Egloff, New Mexico	6	5	6.90	15	0	61.1	92	18	52
Ethan Ross, San Jose State	1	5	7.81	21	0	65.2	70	65	63
Brett Russell, New Mexico	1	6	8.70	15	0	59	107	29	46
Matt Haley, New Mexico	2	5	8.85	15	0	59	90	21	40

NORTHEAST CONFERENCE

	Conference		Overall	
	W	L	W	L
*Long Island	18	9	37	21
Bryant	17	10	30	27
Central Connecticut State	17	10	29	18
Fairleigh Dickinson	16	11	24	30
Merrimack	12	15	17	31

Wagner	12	15	17	34
Sacred Heart	9	18	12	41
Mount St. Mary's	7	20	14	34

ALL-CONFERENCE TEAM: C: George Rosales, Sr., Fairleigh Dickinson **1B:** Noah Martinez, Jr., Central Connecticut State **2B:** Dan Covino, Jr., Central Connecticut State **3B:** Hunter D'Amato, So., Fairleigh Dickinson **SS:** Alex Haba, Jr., Merrimack OF: Michael Edelman, Gr., Long Island; Dante Faicchio, Sr., Wagner; Matt Woods, Sr., Bryant **DH:** Alex Lane, Jr., Bryant **SP:** Joshua Loeschorn, Sr., Long Island; Collin Lowe, Gr., Bryant; Anthony Mozzicato, So., Central Connecticut State **RP:** Luke Garofalo, So., Central Connecticut **State Player of the Year:** Matt Woods, Bryant **Pitcher of the Year:** Joshua Loeschorn, Long Island **Coach of the Year:** Dan Pirillo, Long Island **Rookie of the Year:** Vincent Spizzoucco, Central Connecticut State.

INDIVIDUAL BATTING LEADERS

(Minimum 140 at-bats)

	AVG	OBP	SLG	AB	2B	3B	HR	RBI	SB
Matt Woods, Bryant	.384	.458	.635	219	17	7	8	45	9
Alex Haba, Merrimack	.368	.462	.558	190	17	2	5	15	6
Justin Jordan, Sacred Heart	.358	.399	.458	190	12	2	1	14	9
Hunter Pasqualini, C.Conn. St.	.338	.429	.471	204	9	3	4	32	8
Justin Sierra, Fairleigh Dickinson	.332	.406	.469	196	11	2	4	31	35
Ryan Donnelly, Sacred Heart	.331	.422	.410	178	12	1	0	21	19
Tom Ruscitti, Fairleigh Dickinson	.330	.429	.528	197	15	0	8	41	10
George Rosales, Fairleigh Dickinson	.329	.468	.506	158	10	0	6	25	8
Dan Covino, C.Conn. St.	.328	.441	.579	183	19	0	9	59	4
Joan Sosa, Fairleigh Dickinson	.326	.434	.463	190	6	1	6	26	7
Maimu Kobayashi, Wagner	.321	.430	.408	184	10	0	2	22	8
Michael Edelman, Long Island	.319	.415	.483	238	12	3	7	34	27
Scott Elliott, Merrimack	.316	.433	.477	155	7	3	4	28	5
Tristan McAlister, Mount St. Mary's	.316	.405	.374	174	7	0	1	32	26
Noah Martinez, C.Conn. St.	.313	.411	.620	179	8	1	15	62	0
Tyler Long, Mount St. Mary's	.308	.406	.414	169	12	0	2	27	8
Thomas Bramley, Mount St. Mary's	.307	.444	.540	176	4	2	11	38	4
Giovanni Ciaccio, Long Island	.305	.429	.467	210	11	4	5	45	20
Sam Mongelli, Sacred Heart	.304	.386	.471	138	6	1	5	20	2
Jay Devito, C.Conn. St.	.304	.443	.332	184	5	0	0	18	4
Seth Surrett, Long Island	.301	.449	.408	196	11	2	2	35	15
Sam Loda, C.Conn. St.	.297	.434	.465	155	10	2	4	28	0
Hunter D'Amato, Fairleigh Dickinson	.293	.365	.439	205	14	2	4	40	16
Alex Lane, Bryant	.292	.363	.552	192	14	0	12	48	0
Dante Faicchio, Wagner	.285	.367	.549	193	15	0	12	52	8
Christopher Wasson, Long Island	.284	.406	.394	208	9	1	4	32	16
Robert Farruggio, Sacred Heart	.284	.323	.408	169	9	0	4	33	1
John Tuccillo, Bryant	.282	.388	.425	174	14	1	3	34	8
Michael Golankiewicz, Merrimack	.282	.368	.547	181	14	2	10	42	1
George Sutherland, Sacred Heart	.282	.357	.339	174	5	1	1	26	8

INDIVIDUAL PITCHING LEADERS

(Minimum 40 innings pitched)

	W	L	ERA	G	SV	IP	H	BB	SO
Collin Lowe, Bryant	5	4	2.80	14	0	80.1	70	16	79
Joshua Loeschorn, Long Island	11	3	3.06	17	1	97	87	29	104
Anthony Mozzicato, C.Conn. St.	7	4	3.25	13	0	69.1	66	36	39
Dominic Niman, C.Conn. St.	4	4	3.62	13	0	77	86	22	63
Nick DeSalvo, Long Island	5	1	3.67	23	1	61.1	69	18	81
Vincent Spizzoucco, C.Conn. St.	6	2	3.77	15	3	57.1	58	21	61
Logan Frasier, Bryant	5	3	4.45	14	0	58.2	75	20	58
Nick Evangelista, Fairleigh Dickinson	2	3	5.55	15	0	71.1	93	18	50
Joey Kosowsky, Fairleigh Dickinson	5	4	5.67	17	0	81	81	30	75
Frankie Wright, Wagner	6	4	6.05	14	0	67	85	32	49
Jalen Wade, Long Island	4	5	6.36	16	0	69.1	79	41	50
Cedric Gillette, Merrimack	4	6	6.92	14	0	67.2	86	24	29
Wyatt Villella, Merrimack	2	5	6.98	12	0	68.1	79	35	50
Cooper Adams, Mount St. Mary's	3	6	7.30	13	0	65.1	80	22	59
Luke Pryor, Mount St. Mary's	1	5	7.90	11	0	54.2	73	37	38
Jake Babuschak, Sacred Heart	2	8	8.59	15	0	58.2	79	29	31
Bryant Shives, Mount St. Mary's	1	3	9.74	14	0	49	69	34	36

OHIO VALLEY CONFERENCE

	Conference		Overall	
	W	L	W	L
Belmont	18	6	39	20
*Southeast Missouri State	16	8	37	22
Morehead State	14	10	27	27
Eastern Illinois	12	12	33	20
Southern Illinois-Edwardsville	12	12	27	28
Tennessee Tech	11	13	30	27
Murray State	11	13	30	25
Austin Peay	10	14	19	37
Tennessee-Martin	4	20	11	34

ALL-CONFERENCE TEAM: C: Jack Alexander, Sr., Austin Peay **1B:** Jackson Feltner, So., Morehead State **2B:** Nick Gooden, So., Morehead State **3B:** Bryson Bloomer, RSr., Murray State **SS:** Tyler Wilber, Sr., Southeast Missouri State **OF:** Guy Lipscomb, So., Belmont; Jason Hinchman, Sr., Tennessee Tech; Brett Johnson, Jr., Southern Illinois-Edwardsville **DH:** Brady Bunten, Jr., Southern Illinois-Edwardsville **UTL:** Ryan Ignoffo, Jr., Eastern Illinois **SP:** Andy Bean, So., Belmont; Hayden Wynja, RJr., Murray State; Kaid Karnes, Sr., Southern Illinois-Edwardsville **RP:** Hayden Birdsong, So., Eastern Illinois **Player of the Year:** Guy Lipscomb, Belmont **Pitcher of the Year:** Andy Bean, Belmont **Coach of the Year:** Dave Jarvis, Belmont **Freshman of the Year:** Chris Worcester, Eastern Illinois.

INDIVIDUAL BATTING LEADERS

(Minimum 140 at-bats)

	AVG	OBP	SLG	AB	2B	3B	HR	RBI	SB
Guy Lipscomb, Belmont	.406	.484	.548	217	13	3	4	42	42
Ryan Ignoffo, Eastern Illinois	.395	.436	.708	185	16	0	14	58	7
Jackson Feltner, Morehead State	.393	.478	.706	214	17	1	16	51	1
Jason Hinchman, Tennessee Tech	.372	.470	.758	231	11	0	26	73	1
Ed Johnson, Tennessee Tech	.367	.420	.591	259	14	1	14	55	6
Alex Jacobs, Morehead State	.363	.457	.532	201	13	3	5	38	12
Brennan Orf, Southern Illinois-Edwardsville	.357	.492	.713	143	10	1	13	46	2
Brett Johnson, Southern Illinois-Edwardsville	.350	.452	.765	217	13	4	23	63	6
Jack Alexander, Austin Peay	.346	.425	.649	208	19	1	14	55	1
Ryan Guardino, Tennessee Tech	.339	.408	.661	186	12	0	16	45	3
Nick Gooden, Morehead State	.332	.406	.458	190	12	0	4	33	5
Jake Slunder, Murray State	.332	.393	.478	232	8	7	4	31	25
Tyler Wilber, Southeast Missouri State	.331	.403	.619	236	14	0	18	74	0
Gabe Lacy, Tennessee Tech	.329	.401	.540	237	14	0	12	63	3
Andrew Keck, Southeast Missouri State	.326	.403	.638	224	15	2	17	68	11
Brodey Heaton, Belmont	.325	.376	.597	243	19	4	13	62	9
Nathan Aide, Eastern Illinois	.321	.388	.560	218	10	6	10	52	9
Brett Graber, Southeast Missouri State	.321	.431	.560	218	16	3	10	46	13
Lucas DiLuca, Eastern Illinois	.320	.440	.424	203	13	1	2	35	9
Chris Worcester, Eastern Illinois	.320	.375	.425	153	8	1	2	29	10
Connor Kiffer, Southern Illinois-Edwardsville	.318	.411	.488	211	16	1	6	37	12
Jevon Mason, Southeast Missouri State	.317	.438	.587	230	14	3	14	44	16
Richie Well, Southern Illinois-Edwardsville	.316	.351	.604	212	19	0	14	58	3
Carson Shacklett, Belmont	.316	.426	.448	174	11	0	4	25	5
Casey Harford, Tennessee-Martin	.315	.355	.589	168	14	1	10	36	1
Josh Ohl, Southern Illinois-Edwardsville	.314	.378	.529	204	13	2	9	39	5
Logan Eickhoff, Eastern Illinois	.313	.369	.406	192	4	1	4	34	15
Hayden Gilliland, Tennessee Tech	.313	.440	.456	147	6	0	5	31	0
Brady Bunten, Southern Illinois-Edwardsville	.308	.365	.548	208	9	1	13	42	4
Harrison Brown, Austin Peay	.306	.370	.490	157	11	0	6	26	1

INDIVIDUAL PITCHING LEADERS

(Minimum 40 innings pitched)

	W	L	ERA	G	SV	IP	H	BB	SO
Kaid Karnes, Southern Illinois-Edwardsville	6	4	2.83	16	1	76.1	85	21	71
Jalen Borders, Belmont	5	2	3.04	15	0	80	70	42	61
Hayden Wynja, Murray State	7	4	3.67	15	0	73.2	67	24	86
John Bakke, Morehead State	4	3	4.05	26	8	60	59	24	70
Jason Rackers, Southeast Missouri State	6	4	4.62	17	0	89.2	89	31	79
Andy Bean, Belmont	9	1	4.64	15	0	85.1	73	36	75
Trevor Nicholson, Eastern Illinois	5	2	4.71	15	2	72.2	71	30	96
Peyton Calitri, Tennessee Tech	6	5	5.04	15	0	85.2	87	22	61
Joshua South, Belmont	8	2	5.11	15	0	88	88	28	82
Brant Glidewell, Southern Illinois-Edwardsville	5	2	5.25	14	0	82.1	88	24	67
Cameron Doherty, Eastern Illinois	4	5	5.43	14	0	68	96	13	63

Luke Helton, Morehead State	3	6	5.65	14	0	73.1	98	22	60
Connor Adams, Tennessee Tech	4	3	5.86	16	0	58.1	71	28	48
Blake Malatestinic, Eastern Illinois	4	4	6.09	16	0	54.2	65	21	51
Harley Gollert, Austin Peay	2	7	6.10	15	0	82.2	90	38	87
Tyler Delong, Austin Peay	4	4	6.29	19	0	58.2	66	33	57
Brock Myers, Tennessee Tech	5	2	6.60	22	2	58.2	79	23	57
Seth Petry, Tennessee-Martin	2	9	7.43	15	0	59.1	77	25	32
Drew McIllwain, Austin Peay	4	6	8.66	15	0	62.1	74	35	61

PACIFIC-12 CONFERENCE

	Conference		Overall	
	W	L	W	L
*Stanford	21	9	47	18
*Oregon State	20	10	48	18
*UCLA	19	11	40	24
*Oregon	18	12	36	25
*Arizona	16	14	39	25
Washington	14	16	30	26
California	14	16	29	27
Arizona State	13	17	26	32
Washington State	12	18	27	26
Utah	10	20	26	27
Southern California	8	22	25	28

ALL-CONFERENCE TEAM: C: Kody Huff, Jr., Stanford; Gavin Logan, Jr., Oregon State; Darius Perry, Jr., UCLA; Daniel Susac, So., Arizona; Johnny Tincher, RSo., Washington **1B:** Garret Forrester, So., Oregon State; Carter Graham, So., Stanford; Nathan Martorella, Jr., California; Jake Palmer, Gr., UCLA; Will Simpson, RSo., Washington **INF:** Nate Baez, RSo., Arizona State; Brett Barrera, Jr., Stanford; Travis Bazzana, Fr., Oregon State; Josh Kasevich, So., Oregon; Cody Shrier, Fr., UCLA; Tyresse Turner, RSo., Southern California **OF:** Dylan Beavers, Jr., California; Brock Jones, Jr., Stanford; Wade Meckler, Jr., Oregon State; Jacob Melton, Jr., Oregon State; Tanner O'Tremba, Jr., Arizona; **DH:** Caleb Lomavita, Fr., California; Jacob McKeon, Jr., Washington State; Brennan Milone, So., Oregon; Jacob Tobias, Fr., Arizona State **P:** Ryan Brown, RFr., Oregon State; Ben Ferrer, Jr., Oregon State; Quinn Flanagan, Jr., Arizona; Ethan Flanagan, Fr., UCLA; Cooper Hjerpe, So., Oregon State; Stefan Raeth, RJr., Washington; Max Rajcic, So., UCLA; Kolby Somers, Sr., Oregon; Alonzo Tredwell, Fr., UCLA; Alex Williams, Sr., Stanford **Player of the Year:** Jacob Melton, Oregon State **Pitcher of the Year:** Alex Williams, Stanford **Coach of the Year:** David Esquer, Stanford **Freshman of the Year:** Braden Montgomery, Stanford **Defensive Player of the Year:** Adam Crampton, Stanforda.

INDIVIDUAL BATTING LEADERS

(Minimum 140 at-bats)

	AVG	OBP	SLG	AB	2B	3B	HR	RBI	SB
Justin Boyd, Oregon State	.373	.490	.577	241	14	4	9	53	24
Daniel Susac, Arizona	.366	.429	.582	273	19	2	12	61	0
Rhylan Thomas, Southern California	.363	.422	.444	223	10	1	2	23	8
Jacob Melton, Oregon State	.360	.424	.670	261	22	4	17	83	21
Jack Smith, Washington State	.358	.422	.461	193	17	0	1	36	2
Ryan Campos, Arizona State	.357	.430	.439	171	8	0	2	30	4
Tanner O'Tremba, Arizona	.351	.446	.591	259	21	4	11	56	9
Brett Barrera, Stanford	.351	.394	.575	259	19	3	11	53	0
Jacob McKeon, Washington State	.348	.446	.584	161	15	1	7	32	1
Wade Meckler, Oregon State	.347	.456	.478	268	23	3	2	32	12
Joe Lampe, Arizona State	.340	.394	.590	256	22	3	12	41	17
Tommy Troy, Stanford	.339	.371	.568	183	15	3	7	23	5
Brennan Milone, Oregon	.337	.405	.545	246	15	0	12	55	2
Nathan Martorella, California	.333	.424	.553	228	15	1	11	46	1
Sean McLain, Arizona State	.333	.430	.458	225	13	3	3	34	3
Anthony Hall, Oregon	.333	.402	.640	225	17	5	14	56	4
Garret Forrester, Oregon State	.332	.480	.498	229	11	0	9	60	1
Carter Graham, Stanford	.331	.399	.642	260	13	1	22	79	1
Landon Frei, Utah	.330	.407	.421	209	10	0	3	33	4
Tyresse Turner, Southern California	.330	.419	.524	191	15	2	6	33	15
Brock Jones, Stanford	.324	.451	.664	253	13	5	21	57	16
Nate Baez, Arizona State	.319	.403	.562	210	21	0	10	48	2
Michael Curialle, UCLA	.319	.395	.479	238	17	3	5	41	9
Eddie Park, Stanford	.318	.412	.368	220	9	1	0	15	8
Tanner Smith, Oregon	.317	.370	.489	268	13	0	11	38	12
Adam Crampton, Stanford	.316	.395	.392	212	9	2	1	40	11
Jayden Kiernan, Utah	.316	.392	.412	187	15	0	1	37	0
Keshawn Ogans, California	.315	.378	.420	219	12	1	3	30	4
Kody Huff, Stanford	.315	.411	.567	238	21	0	13	51	2
McKay Barney, Washington	.315	.372	.388	232	10	2	1	23	15

INDIVIDUAL PITCHING LEADERS

(Minimum 40 innings pitched)

	W	L	ERA	G	SV	IP	H	BB	SO
Cooper Hjerpe, Oregon State	11	2	2.53	18	1	103.1	67	23	161
Quinn Mathews, Stanford	9	2	3.08	27	9	99.1	77	49	111
Alex Williams, Stanford	8	4	3.20	18	0	101.1	87	25	96
Max Rajcic, UCLA	8	5	3.28	15	0	85	73	20	92
Garrett Irvin, Arizona	5	4	3.38	16	0	96	85	29	71
Stefan Raeth, Washington	5	4	3.39	30	4	66.1	57	19	89
Carson Lambert, Southern California	6	3	3.46	27	1	54.2	46	11	58
Joseph King, California	5	3	3.72	15	0	72.2	80	15	60
Kelly Austin, UCLA	4	3	4.07	25	1	77.1	79	16	74
Steven Zobac, California	4	4	4.09	20	0	61.2	55	20	72
Jared Engman, Washington	4	5	4.15	15	0	73.2	82	26	59
Tyler Stromsborg, Southern California	1	5	4.18	12	0	60.1	70	18	39
Jacob Kmatz, Oregon State	8	2	4.19	16	0	77.1	73	20	65
Charlie Hurley, Southern California	6	2	4.19	16	0	73	68	32	45
Jaden Agassi, Southern California	3	2	4.34	15	0	64.1	81	19	38
Kyle Luckham, Arizona State	7	3	4.36	15	0	86.2	98	23	72
Drew Dowd, Stanford	6	0	4.54	22	0	75.1	77	34	77
Grant Taylor, Washington State	4	5	4.67	14	0	71.1	75	28	71
Josh White, California	2	6	5.05	16	2	67.2	70	42	91
Cole McMillan, Washington State	5	5	5.45	14	0	76	81	34	71
Calvin Kirchoff, Washington	3	3	5.46	19	0	64.1	69	30	43
TJ Nichols, Arizona	6	4	5.50	16	0	88.1	98	38	84
Matthew Sox, Utah	4	5	5.51	14	0	83.1	89	26	68
Sam Stoutenborough, California	2	4	5.58	17	0	59.2	73	8	38
RJ Gordon, Oregon	4	3	5.64	20	1	68.2	75	34	48
Isaac Ayon, Oregon	4	4	5.77	17	0	87.1	109	29	80
Cam Day, Utah	1	6	7.22	14	0	62.1	87	24	36
Adam Tulloch, Arizona State	2	4	8.42	18	0	67.1	89	38	85

PATRIOT LEAGUE

	Conference		Overall	
	W	L	W	L
Army	18	7	31	25
Bucknell	14	11	22	25
Lehigh	12	13	26	24
Holy Cross	11	14	17	37
Lafayette	10	15	15	35
Navy	10	15	19	26

ALL-CONFERENCE TEAM: C: Adam Retzbach, Jr., Lehigh **1B:** Ross Friedrick, Jr., Army **2B:** Derek Berg, So., Army **3B:** Sam Ruta, So., Army **SS:** Kevin Dubrule, Jr., Army **OF:** Nick Manesis, Sr., Army; Chris Cannizzaro, Sr., Bucknell; Casey Rother, Sr., Lehigh At-Large: Christian Policelli, Sr., Navy **SP:** Connelly Early, So., Navy; Jake Bloss, Jr., Lafayette; Luke Rettig, Sr., Lehigh RP: Tanner Gresham, So., Army **Player of the Year:** Casey Rother, Lehigh **Pitcher of the Year:** Connelly Early, Navy **Coach of the Year:** Jim Foster, Army **Rookie of the Year:** NIck Wang, Holy Cross **Defensive Player of the Year:** Eduardo Diaz, Navy.

INDIVIDUAL BATTING LEADERS

(Minimum 140 at-bats)

	AVG	OBP	SLG	AB	2B	3B	HR	RBI	SB
Sam Ruta, Army	.390	.493	.626	187	15	4	7	36	6
Casey Rother, Lehigh	.366	.424	.604	202	19	1	9	50	5
Tyler Young, Lehigh	.348	.439	.451	164	10	2	1	31	10
Ross Friedrick, Army	.340	.398	.484	215	13	0	6	49	0
Pete Ciuffreda, Lafayette	.330	.438	.494	176	12	1	5	42	22
Chris Cannizzaro, Bucknell	.329	.396	.524	170	13	1	6	37	4
Christian Policelli, Navy	.328	.405	.466	174	11	2	3	33	11
Jacob Corson, Bucknell	.325	.439	.448	163	12	1	2	32	1
Kevin Dubrule, Army	.321	.363	.413	240	17	1	1	47	4
Kyle Lyons, Bucknell	.321	.379	.365	159	5	1	0	22	10
Grant Voytovich, Bucknell	.320	.384	.418	194	13	0	2	37	6
Jake Whitlinger, Lehigh	.313	.447	.394	160	10	0	1	18	15

Colin Smith, Navy	.309	.367	.428	152	9	0	3	32	5
Nick Manesis, Army	.308	.402	.438	208	4	1	7	49	10
Derek Berg, Army	.307	.377	.409	176	10	1	2	31	10
Tyler Dunn, Bucknell	.300	.389	.381	160	4	3	1	27	3
Carter Macias, Army	.298	.412	.340	188	5	0	1	19	21
Alex Smith, Navy	.298	.359	.424	151	6	2	3	30	1
Riley Davis, Lehigh	.298	.392	.437	151	13	1	2	22	1
Sean Scanlon, Holy Cross	.297	.401	.405	148	10	0	2	19	3
Adam Retzbach, Lehigh	.293	.397	.560	184	12	2	11	46	5
Dylan Minghini, Lafayette	.288	.364	.507	146	9	1	7	33	0
Brendan Lowery, Bucknell	.284	.395	.465	155	14	1	4	29	3
Sam Kirkpatrick, Holy Cross	.283	.332	.340	191	9	1	0	10	5
Hunter Meade, Army	.282	.390	.332	202	10	0	0	23	32
Carter Dorighi, Lafayette	.282	.355	.345	177	8	0	1	15	5
Anthony Sherwin, Bucknell	.268	.413	.344	183	10	2	0	20	5
Eduardo Diaz, Navy	.262	.353	.421	164	12	1	4	23	1
Justin Grech, Lafayette	.254	.347	.321	193	8	1	1	14	16
Brendan Jones, Holy Cross	.253	.372	.319	166	5	3	0	11	6

INDIVIDUAL PITCHING LEADERS

(Minimum 40 innings pitched)

	W	L	ERA	G	SV	IP	H	BB	SO
Luke Rettig, Lehigh	8	2	2.40	13	0	71.1	60	34	71
Connelly Early, Army	7	4	3.26	16	0	85.2	69	38	88
Jake Bloss, Lafayette	6	3	3.57	11	0	58	61	28	68
Tyler O'Neill, Bucknell	3	4	3.81	14	0	54.1	52	25	40
Austin Odell, Bucknell	8	2	3.82	12	0	73	71	27	45
Will Greer, Bucknell	5	3	4.39	13	0	82	78	25	50
Luke Benneche, Lafayette	1	10	4.50	12	0	66	58	32	73
Nolan Morr, Lafayette	2	5	5.26	14	1	51.1	73	9	41
Liam Golden, Navy	3	7	5.40	11	0	45	50	11	28
Matthew Shirah, Navy	3	2	5.51	11	0	49	59	16	34
Matt Stamford, Lehigh	3	6	5.68	13	0	63.1	82	22	45
Jack DiLauro, Holy Cross	1	7	5.95	12	0	59	61	29	65
Nate Mitchell, Navy	2	3	6.43	10	0	49	76	2	31
Ben Magovern, Bucknell	2	5	6.53	12	0	51	62	22	36

SOUTHEASTERN CONFERENCE

	Conference		Overall	
East Division	**W**	**L**	**W**	**L**
*Tennessee	25	5	57	9
*Georgia	15	15	36	23
*Florida	15	15	42	24
*Vanderbilt	14	16	39	23
South Carolina	13	17	27	28
Kentucky	12	18	33	26
Missouri	10	20	28	23

	Conference		Overall	
West Division	**W**	**L**	**W**	**L**
*Texas A&M	19	11	44	20
*Arkansas	18	12	46	21
*Louisiana State	17	13	40	22
*Auburn	16	13	43	22
*Mississippi	14	16	42	23
Alabama	12	17	31	27
Mississippi State	9	21	26	30

ALL-CONFERENCE TEAM: C: BT Riopelle, Jr., Florida **1B:** Sonny DiChiara, Sr., Auburn **2B:** RJ Yeager, Gr., Mississippi State **3B:** Trey Lipscomb, Sr., Tennessee **SS:** Jacob Gonzalez, So., Mississippi **OF:** Enrique Bradfield, Jr., So., Vanderbilt; Dylan Crews, So., Louisiana State; Drew Gilbert, Jr., Tennessee **DH:** Dominic Keegan, Sr., Vanderbilt **SP:** Chase Dollander, So., Tennessee; Jonathan Cannon, Jr., Georgia **RP:** Tyler Guilfoil, Jr., Kentucky **Co-Player of the Year:** Dylan Crews, Louisiana State; Sonny DiChiara, Auburn **Pitcher of the Year:** Chase Dollander, Tennessee **Coach of the Year:** Tony Vitello, Tennessee **Freshman of the Year:** Drew Beam, Tennessee.

INDIVIDUAL BATTING LEADERS

(Minimum 140 at-bats)

	AVG	OBP	SLG	AB	2B	3B	HR	RBI	SB
Sonny DiChiara, Auburn	.383	.549	.777	206	15	0	22	59	0
Jack Moss, Texas A&M	.380	.437	.520	271	18	1	6	49	8
Dominic Keegan, Vanderbilt	.371	.458	.646	229	17	2	14	67	2
Spencer Jones, Vanderbilt	.370	.460	.643	230	21	3	12	60	14
Jacob Berry, Louisiana State	.370	.464	.630	208	9	0	15	48	0
Torin Montgomery, Missouri	.365	.462	.547	181	12	0	7	49	4
Drew Gilbert, Tennessee	.362	.455	.673	199	21	4	11	70	4
Austin Bost, Texas A&M	.360	.451	.572	236	14	3	10	45	6
Trey Lipscomb, Tennessee	.355	.428	.717	251	19	3	22	84	4
Wyatt Langford, Florida	.355	.447	.719	256	9	3	26	63	7
Sterlin Thompson, Florida	.354	.443	.563	254	16	2	11	51	10
Dylan Crews, Louisiana State	.349	.463	.691	249	11	4	22	72	5
Connor Tate, Georgia	.345	.436	.614	223	19	1	13	58	3
Brandt Belk, South Carolina	.340	.420	.500	188	10	1	6	38	11
Joshua Day, Missouri	.340	.435	.508	197	10	1	7	29	9
Seth Stephenson, Tennessee	.339	.408	.508	183	17	1	4	28	25
Blake Rambusch, Auburn	.327	.415	.429	266	13	1	4	37	16
Chris Lanzilli, Arkansas	.326	.424	.513	224	9	0	11	40	3
Tre' Morgan, Louisiana State	.324	.414	.462	253	18	1	5	54	0
Jorel Ortega, Tennessee	.323	.398	.672	235	20	4	18	61	3
Michael Turner, Arkansas	.323	.388	.502	257	17	1	9	53	1
Dylan Rock, Texas A&M	.318	.468	.641	223	13	1	19	65	16
Andrew Eyster, South Carolina	.318	.399	.520	198	10	0	10	53	1
Enrique Bradfield Jr., Vanderbilt	.317	.415	.498	243	10	5	8	36	46
RJ Yeager, Mississippi State	.317	.389	.668	202	15	1	18	56	3
Justin Bench, Mississippi	.316	.409	.438	256	17	1	4	42	4
Luc Lipcius, Tennessee	.313	.466	.667	198	11	1	19	44	14
Braylen Wimmer, South Carolina	.312	.361	.466	221	13	0	7	35	13
Daniel Harris IV, Kentucky	.310	.394	.409	203	10	2	2	28	16
Parks Harber, Georgia	.307	.365	.528	218	5	2	13	53	0

INDIVIDUAL PITCHING LEADERS

(Minimum 40 innings pitched)

	W	L	ERA	G	SV	IP	H	BB	SO
Chase Dollander, Tennessee	10	0	2.39	16	0	79	50	13	108
Sean Harney, Kentucky	5	4	2.62	16	2	65.1	55	17	65
Hunter Elliott, Mississippi	5	3	2.70	20	0	80	57	34	102
Drew Beam, Tennessee	8	1	2.72	16	0	76	50	21	62
Chase Burns, Tennessee	8	2	2.91	17	0	80.1	65	25	103
Carter Holton, Vanderbilt	8	4	3.14	15	0	80.1	56	29	97
Joseph Gonzalez, Auburn	7	4	3.22	15	0	78.1	83	15	54
Devin Futrell, Vanderbilt	9	3	3.41	14	0	63.1	53	13	64
Brandon Sproat, Florida	9	4	3.41	17	0	89.2	84	33	82
Will Sanders, South Carolina	7	3	3.43	15	0	89.1	84	31	91
Connor Noland, Arkansas	8	6	3.65	20	0	116	109	34	113
Dylan DeLucia, Mississippi	8	2	3.68	21	1	95.1	87	26	105
Brandon Neely, Florida	3	3	3.76	21	1	69.1	53	20	74
Cade Smith, Mississippi State	4	4	3.86	14	0	72.1	61	36	66
Jonathan Cannon, Georgia	9	4	4.02	13	0	78.1	67	12	68
Chris McElvain, Vanderbilt	6	5	4.27	16	0	86.1	68	44	100
Garrett McMillan, Alabama	4	5	4.29	16	0	86	79	26	83
Noah Hall, South Carolina	3	5	4.34	15	0	76.2	75	31	78
Ma'Khail Hilliard, Louisiana State	7	1	4.56	16	0	77	90	20	73
Jacob McNairy, Alabama	6	2	4.63	16	0	72	78	18	65
Hagen Smith, Arkansas	7	2	4.66	20	2	77.1	66	46	90
Carter Rustad, Missouri	3	2	4.73	16	1	51.1	50	15	42
Nathan Dettmer, Texas A&M	6	3	4.99	19	0	92	98	25	82
Trace Bright, Auburn	5	4	5.13	18	0	80.2	78	38	94
Micah Dallas, Texas A&M	7	3	5.18	18	0	81.2	100	22	86
Grayson Hitt, Alabama	4	3	5.34	14	0	60.2	66	30	68
Preston Johnson, Mississippi State	3	4	5.47	14	0	79	73	38	117
Tony Neubeck, Missouri	3	3	5.63	15	0	54.1	52	29	60
Brandon Smith, Mississippi State	3	5	5.88	19	0	64.1	76	17	58
Spencer Miles, Missouri	5	5	6.20	13	0	69.2	90	23	67

SOUTHERN CONFERENCE

	Conference W	Conference L	Overall W	Overall L
Wofford	16	4	42	16
Mercer	12	9	40	18
*UNC-Greensboro	12	9	34	30
Samford	12	9	28	29
East Tennessee State	11	10	30	21
Western Carolina	9	11	26	31
VMI	6	15	16	40
The Citadel	5	16	26	31

ALL-CONFERENCE TEAM: C: Lawson Hill, RSr., Wofford **1B:** John Dempsey, Sr., Wofford **2B:** Hogan Windish, Jr., UNC-Greensboro **3B:** Ryan Galanie, Jr., Wofford **SS:** Pascanel Ferreras, So., Western Carolina **OF:** Tommy Barth, Fr., East Tennessee State; Bill Knight, Jr., Mercer; Colby Thomas, So., Mercer **DH:** Brennen Dorighi, Sr., Wofford **SP:** Zach Franklin, RJr., Western Carolina; Matthew Marchal, Jr., Wofford **RP:** Alex Hoppe, Sr., UNC-Greensboro **Player of the Year:** Hogan Windish, UNC-Greensboro **Pitcher of the Year:** Alex Hoppe, UNC-Greensboro **Coach of the Year:** Todd Interdonato, Wofford **Freshman of the Year:** Tommy Barth, East Tennessee State.

INDIVIDUAL BATTING LEADERS

(Minimum 140 at-bats)

	AVG	OBP	SLG	AB	2B	3B	HR	RBI	SB
Lawson Hill, Wofford	.379	.456	.496	224	18	1	2	39	12
Hogan Windish, UNC-Greensboro	.370	.485	.681	216	19	0	16	60	8
Tommy Barth, East Tennessee State	.369	.434	.585	195	16	4	6	38	1
Kennedy Jones, UNC-Greensboro	.367	.420	.594	251	16	4	11	73	5
Pascanel Ferreras, Western Carolina	.362	.443	.672	235	22	3	15	60	5
John Dempsey, Wofford	.356	.458	.597	216	16	0	12	50	7
Pres Cavenaugh, UNC-Greensboro	.340	.403	.507	268	13	4	8	56	15
Brennen Dorighi, Wofford	.339	.399	.552	192	12	1	9	53	9
Bill Knight, Mercer	.337	.415	.642	243	19	2	17	64	10
Greg Hardison, UNC-Greensboro	.336	.423	.390	241	11	1	0	41	4
Cam Norgren, East Tennessee State	.333	.412	.586	198	16	2	10	32	0
Will Prater, Western Carolina	.332	.409	.454	238	17	3	2	45	13
Zac Morris, VMI	.332	.416	.558	208	11	3	10	41	13
Brice Martinez, Wofford	.331	.416	.420	157	6	1	2	41	11
Stephen Klein, Samford	.331	.452	.473	169	9	0	5	35	2
Ryan Galanie, Wofford	.329	.437	.653	219	10	5	17	59	13
Mitchell Smith, UNC-Greensboro	.324	.412	.475	238	23	2	3	45	4
Tilo Skole, The Citadel	.322	.397	.370	211	10	0	0	28	4
Nolen Hester, Wofford	.321	.442	.402	209	11	0	2	42	8
Bryce Hodge, East Tennessee State	.318	.378	.616	198	17	0	14	43	2
Colton Ledbetter, Samford	.318	.407	.640	211	16	2	16	57	14
Treyson Hughes, Mercer	.317	.403	.576	224	12	2	14	53	5
Collin Price, Mercer	.315	.460	.626	203	7	1	18	58	3
Immanuel Wilder, Western Carolina	.314	.431	.497	153	13	0	5	30	2
Noah Webb, East Tennessee State	.313	.395	.590	166	11	1	11	49	1

INDIVIDUAL PITCHING LEADERS

(Minimum 40 innings pitched)

	W	L	ERA	G	SV	IP	H	BB	SO
Jackson Kelley, Mercer	7	0	1.35	25	6	60	32	18	82
Matthew Marchal, Wofford	7	2	2.52	18	0	85.2	75	12	93
Alex Hoppe, UNC-Greensboro	8	2	2.97	26	3	66.2	49	30	84
Devin Beckley, The Citadel	4	4	3.18	19	2	82	65	38	81
Zach Kirby, East Tennessee State	3	4	3.38	14	0	74.2	72	20	57
Zebby Matthews, Western Carolina	4	6	3.67	22	4	95.2	94	21	122
Dalton Rhadans, Wofford	7	4	3.72	34	10	72.2	75	13	71
Michael Ross, Samford	7	1	3.77	15	0	76.1	63	21	66
Cameron Reeves, The Citadel	4	7	3.84	14	0	89	88	25	81
Hunter Loyd, East Tennessee State	4	4	3.89	13	0	71.2	62	36	74
Austin Parsley, UNC-Greensboro	10	5	4.02	21	1	114.1	125	16	95
Jacob Cravey, Samford	5	3	4.03	15	0	82.2	80	35	71
Ben Hutchins, The Citadel	4	4	4.15	16	0	69.1	68	33	50
Jared Mathewson, UNC-Greensboro	5	7	4.44	18	0	97.1	100	31	70
Ryan Lobus, Mercer	5	5	4.54	16	0	69.1	79	25	67

SOUTHLAND CONFERENCE

	Conference W	Conference L	Overall W	Overall L
McNeese State	15	9	34	23
*Southeastern Louisiana	14	10	30	31
New Orleans	13	11	30	23
Nicholls	12	12	26	25
Northwestern State	12	12	25	29
Houston Baptist	11	13	18	36
Texas A&M-Corpus Christi	10	14	27	28
Incarnate Word	9	15	21	31

ALL-CONFERENCE TEAM: C: Bo Willis, So., Northwestern State **1B:** Preston Faulkner, Gr., Southeastern Louisiana **2B:** Amani Larry, So., New Orleans **3B:** Josh Leslie, RJr., McNeese State **SS:** Grant Smith, Jr., Incarnate Word **OF:** Payton Harden, RJr., McNeese State; Pearce Howard, Sr., New Orleans; Brendan Ryan, Jr., Texas A&M-Corpus Christi **DH:** Tre Jones, So., Texas A&M-Corpus Christi **SP:** Johnathan Harmon, So., Northwestern State; Grant Rogers, RSo., McNeese State; Tyler Theriot, Jr., Nicholls **RP:** Cameron Foster, RSr., McNeese State **UTL:** Alec Carr, Jr., Incarnate Word **Player of the Year:** Payton Harden, McNeese State **Pitcher of the Year:** Grant Rogers, McNeese State **Hitter of the Year:** Pearce Howard, New Orleans **Relief Pitcher of the Year:** Cameron Foster, McNeese State **Coach of the Year:** Justin Hill, McNeese State **Freshman of the Year:** Zach Garcia, Texas A&M-Corpus Christi **Newcomer of the Year:** Amani Larry, New Orleans.

INDIVIDUAL BATTING LEADERS

(Minimum 140 at-bats)

	AVG	OBP	SLG	AB	2B	3B	HR	RBI	SB
Payton Harden, McNeese State	.378	.444	.502	225	14	4	2	40	26
Brad Burckel, McNeese State	.373	.459	.618	217	17	3	10	44	18
Amani Larry, New Orleans	.370	.477	.578	211	13	2	9	56	16
Pearce Howard, New Orleans	.356	.421	.521	219	10	1	8	69	0
Tre Jones, Texas A&M-Corpus Christi	.354	.441	.743	144	15	4	11	37	6
Preston Faulkner, Southeastern Louisiana	.338	.457	.667	222	18	2	17	70	15
Brennen Bales, Houston Baptist	.333	.410	.494	156	11	1	4	28	3
Braden Duhon, McNeese State	.329	.382	.391	207	7	3	0	37	13
Roberto Gonzalez, Incarnate Word	.327	.372	.495	214	13	4	5	37	4
Brendan Ryan, Texas A&M-Corpus Christi	.327	.433	.528	159	13	2	5	26	25
Kasten Furr, New Orleans	.317	.405	.396	227	7	1	3	26	1
Max Puls, Texas A&M-Corpus Christi	.314	.349	.436	220	14	2	3	38	3
Steven Rivera-Chijin, Texas A&M-Corpus Christi	.314	.414	.507	207	25	3	3	32	8
Garrett Felix, Nicholls	.303	.413	.507	152	8	4	5	25	8
Leo Markotic, Texas A&M-Corpus Christi	.300	.359	.437	190	14	0	4	38	1
Nixon Brannan, Incarnate Word	.299	.356	.435	154	9	0	4	23	0
Alec Carr, Incarnate Word	.298	.362	.490	198	8	3	8	27	13
Xane Washington, Nicholls	.298	.416	.508	181	11	0	9	30	12
Tyler Bischke, New Orleans	.294	.370	.387	163	10	1	1	13	7
Jaden Collura, Nicholls	.293	.385	.331	133	0	1	1	20	1
Alec Paz, Nicholls	.293	.435	.520	150	7	0	9	31	1
Larson Fontenot, Northwestern State	.292	.407	.416	178	5	1	5	31	12
Edgar Alvarez, Nicholls	.290	.399	.495	186	11	0	9	49	0
Grant Smith, Incarnate Word	.289	.401	.493	201	13	2	8	34	5
Parker Coddou, Nicholls	.289	.355	.387	173	5	3	2	16	9

INDIVIDUAL PITCHING LEADERS

(Minimum 40 innings pitched)

	W	L	ERA	G	SV	IP	H	BB	SO
Cameron Foster, McNeese State	4	2	1.86	29	12	63	35	20	84
Johnathan Harmon, Northwestern State	5	6	3.52	13	0	79.1	77	23	49
Will Kinzeler, Southeastern Louisiana	4	2	3.60	14	0	80	80	31	60
Tyler Theriot, Nicholls	7	5	3.72	13	0	87	71	28	58
Zach Garcia, Texas A&M-Corpus Christi	6	3	3.86	18	2	67.2	65	19	65
Grant Rogers, McNeese State	7	4	4.26	15	0	82.1	72	22	72
Kyle Khachadourian, New Orleans	5	2	4.42	16	0	57	54	21	41
Drayton Brown, Northwestern State	5	6	4.43	13	0	67	52	29	63
Cal Carver, Northwestern State	4	5	4.71	14	0	84	104	21	76
Chase Gearing, Nicholls	5	3	4.75	23	4	60.2	60	19	43
Devin Desandro, Nicholls	3	4	4.92	16	1	60.1	62	30	47
Nico Saltaformaggio, Nicholls	3	1	5.01	18	0	55.2	64	24	46
Tyler LeBlanc, New Orleans	7	1	5.09	14	0	70.2	64	33	74
Chandler David, Incarnate Word	3	2	5.17	22	5	55.2	53	29	59
Jared Burch, Houston Baptist	1	5	5.30	14	0	71.1	69	33	65

SOUTHWESTERN ATHLETIC CONFERENCE

East Division	Conference W	Conference L	Overall W	Overall L
*Alabama State	21	8	34	24
Bethune-Cookman	20	11	28	32
Florida A&M	19	11	29	30
Jackson State	16	14	29	27
Alabama A&M	11	19	15	34
Mississippi Valley State	4	24	10	30

West Division	Conference W	Conference L	Overall W	Overall L
Southern	21	9	25	29
Grambling	20	10	26	31
Texas Southern	19	11	28	25
Prairie View A&M	19	11	30	27
Arkansas-Pine Bluff	9	21	13	36
Alcorn State	2	28	2	39

ALL-CONFERENCE TEAM: C: John Garcia, So., Grambling **1B:** Grant Rowell, Sr., Florida A&M **2B:** Jarficur Parker, Gr., Grambling **3B:** Jeremy Almaguer, Gr., Texas Southern **SS:** Cameron Bufford, RSo., Grambling **OF:** Tyrese Clayborn, Sr., Texas Southern; Jaylen Armstrong, Jr., Southern; Brayden Johnson, Jr., Prairie View A&M **DH:** Corey King, So., Alabama State **SP:** Shemar Page, Gr., Grambling; Joseph Battaglia, Sr., Southern **RP:** Brenton Fisher, So., Bethune-Cookman **Player of the Year:** Corey King, Alabama State **Pitcher of the Year:** Shemar Page, Grambling **Hitter of the Year:** Corey King, Alabama State **Relief Pitcher of the Year:** Brenton Fisher, Bethune-Cookman Coach of the Year: Jose Vazquez, Alabama State Freshman of the Year: Terry Burrell III, Grambling **Newcomer of the Year:** Corey King, Alabama State.

INDIVIDUAL BATTING LEADERS

(Minimum 140 at-bats)

	AVG	OBP	SLG	AB	2B	3B	HR	RBI	SB
Brayden Johnson, Prairie View A&M	.410	.476	.602	161	12	2	5	33	4
John Garcia, Grambling	.409	.515	.679	193	18	2	10	67	4
Jeremy Gaines, Texas Southern	.400	.502	.611	175	16	3	5	45	27
Ty Hill, Jackson State	.388	.498	.568	206	20	4	3	41	6
Tyrese Clayborne, Texas Southern	.372	.449	.589	180	12	6	5	36	34
Gabe Vasquez, Texas Southern	.363	.474	.709	179	19	8	9	67	21
Corey King, Alabama State	.355	.438	.616	245	16	3	14	64	0
Johnathon Thomas, Texas Southern	.345	.442	.610	200	16	5	9	42	62
Christopher Patterson, Bethune-Cookman	.344	.427	.411	192	13	0	0	27	24
Zachary Trevino, Prairie View A&M	.341	.462	.418	170	9	2	0	36	4
Julian Murphy, Grambling	.339	.420	.466	189	8	5	2	40	3
Devontae Rhodes, Jackson State	.339	.442	.427	171	10	1	1	33	4
Grant Rowell, Florida A&M	.336	.407	.463	214	15	0	4	42	3
Terry Burrell III, Grambling	.335	.432	.411	209	7	3	1	41	11
CJ Castillo, Texas Southern	.333	.480	.473	150	12	3	1	31	9
Davon Mims, Mississippi Valley State	.331	.375	.449	118	2	3	2	20	10
Benjamin Ybarra, Prairie View A&M	.328	.419	.394	180	8	2	0	42	2
Demarie Smith, Prairie View A&M	.326	.469	.411	190	9	2	1	21	19
Kacy Higgins, Arkansas-Pine Bluff	.325	.370	.464	166	14	3	1	33	21
Cameron Bufford, Grambling	.324	.421	.567	210	9	3	12	54	6

INDIVIDUAL PITCHING LEADERS

(Minimum 40 innings pitched)

	W	L	ERA	G	SV	IP	H	BB	SO
Shemar Page, Grambling	8	5	2.60	15	0	104	72	34	142
Hunter Viets, Florida A&M	8	4	2.98	15	0	90.2	84	27	93
Breon Pooler, Alabama State	10	3	3.33	17	0	89.1	79	44	88
Roberto Maldonado, Prairie View A&M	7	4	3.50	15	0	100.1	87	44	100
Hector Vazquez, Bethune-Cookman	7	5	3.79	16	1	80.2	91	14	80
Louis Lipthratt, Bethune-Cookman	6	4	3.91	14	0	80.2	69	32	68
Nikelle Galatas, Jackson State	6	2	3.94	15	0	82.1	81	31	77
Joseph Battaglia, Southern	8	4	3.98	16	0	104	110	11	59
Nolan Santos, Bethune-Cookman	6	3	4.38	15	0	90.1	79	33	113
Juan Marulanda, Jackson State	7	8	4.79	21	0	82.2	75	34	85
Kelyn Fox, Florida A&M	4	4	4.83	14	0	72.2	99	15	55
Joan Gonzalez, Bethune-Cookman	3	5	4.95	15	2	60	65	24	73
Erik Gonzales, Jackson State	6	5	4.97	19	0	92.1	79	47	101
DJ Wilkinson, Florida A&M	5	6	5.69	15	0	74.1	85	33	83
Austin King, Alabama State	6	3	5.72	16	0	67.2	81	38	63
Kyler McIntosh, Alabama State	4	4	5.78	17	1	67	79	17	64
Jordan Martinez, Texas Southern	6	5	5.91	15	0	70	80	33	65
Josue Torres, Alabama A&M	3	5	6.02	15	0	83.2	105	18	44
Brian Williams, Texas Southern	4	2	6.15	13	0	60	76	26	47
Matthew Krall, Prairie View A&M	5	6	6.20	15	0	69.2	89	38	52
Calvin McClendon, Mississippi Valley State	2	7	6.69	18	0	75.1	86	65	57
Noah Whitted, Alabama A&M	2	5	7.14	11	0	51.2	72	17	23
Jacorey Boudreaux, Grambling	7	4	7.29	17	0	70.1	72	54	67
Hunter Stallings, Mississippi Valley State	2	4	7.67	13	1	51.2	54	33	57
Brandon Little, Arkansas-Pine Bluff	1	4	7.73	17	1	64	82	58	57

SUMMIT LEAGUE

	Conference W	Conference L	Overall W	Overall L
North Dakota State	17	5	31	19
*Oral Roberts	17	7	38	20
South Dakota State	13	9	22	23
Nebraska-Omaha	12	12	26	31
St. Thomas	10	14	16	29
Northern Colorado	8	16	12	39
Western Illinois	5	19	8	44

ALL-CONFERENCE TEAM: C: Derek Hackman, Sr., South Dakota State **1B:** Jake McMurray, Jr., Oral Roberts **2B:** Shaydon Kubo, So., Northern Colorado **3B:** Mike Boeve, So., Nebraska-Omaha **SS:** Jackson Loftin, RJr., Oral Roberts **OF:** Caleb Denny, RSo., Oral Roberts; Joshua Cox, Sr., Oral Roberts; Calen Schwabe, Sr., North Dakota State **DH:** Logan Williams, Sr., North Dakota State **UTL:** AJ Archambo, Sr., Oral Roberts **SP:** Ledgend Smith, RSr., Oral Roberts; Isaac Coffey, Jr., Oral Roberts; Caleb Riedel, So., Nebraska-Omaha **RP:** Ryan Bourassa, Jr., South Dakota State **Player of the Year:** Mike Boeve, Nebraska-Omaha **Pitcher of the Year:** Ledgend Smith, Oral Roberts **Coach of the Year:** Tyler Oakes, North Dakota State **Newcomer of the Year:** Caleb Riedel, Nebraska-Omaha.

INDIVIDUAL BATTING LEADERS

(Minimum 140 at-bats)

	AVG	OBP	SLG	AB	2B	3B	HR	RBI	SB
Mike Boeve, Nebraska-Omaha	.364	.491	.584	214	23	0	8	33	12
Jackson Loftin, Oral Roberts	.349	.447	.572	215	14	2	10	54	25
Calen Schwabe, North Dakota St.	.343	.441	.403	134	3	1	1	20	12
Nick Mitchell, Western Illinois	.342	.384	.408	184	5	2	1	26	30
Druw Sackett, North Dakota St.	.338	.458	.567	157	13	1	7	28	9
Holden Breeze, Oral Roberts	.337	.400	.490	208	19	2	3	42	2
Joshua Cox, Oral Roberts	.332	.393	.481	187	11	1	5	35	10
Caleb Denny, Oral Roberts	.331	.389	.565	239	19	2	11	57	9
Ryan McDonald, South Dakota State	.329	.446	.630	146	12	1	10	34	2
Mac McCroskey, Oral Roberts	.322	.416	.445	236	8	3	5	40	6
Shaydon Kubo, Northern Colorado	.318	.371	.512	201	13	1	8	37	0
Charlie Bartholomew, St. Thomas	.308	.361	.371	143	6	0	1	19	0
Kory Olsen, Western Illinois	.302	.375	.380	192	10	1	1	27	17
Jake McMurray, Oral Roberts	.299	.390	.410	244	13	1	4	36	1
Hayden Heinze, Northern Colorado	.298	.351	.354	161	5	2	0	11	9
Jack Lombardi, Nebraska-Omaha	.297	.339	.411	202	13	2	2	30	8
Logan Williams, North Dakota St.	.294	.392	.556	160	6	0	12	41	8
Henry George, South Dakota St.	.294	.394	.447	170	10	2	4	17	13
Derek Hackman, South Dakota St.	.291	.393	.525	158	10	0	9	37	0
Cadyn Schwabe, North Dakota St.	.290	.374	.343	169	5	2	0	20	18
Luke Ira, South Dakota State	.290	.362	.508	183	10	0	10	32	6
Ben Vujovich, St. Thomas	.287	.365	.496	129	6	3	5	23	5
Jake King, Northern Colorado	.285	.397	.402	179	9	0	4	19	2
Derek Botaletto, Western Illinois	.284	.350	.328	183	5	0	1	18	9
Eddie Satisky, Nebraska-Omaha	.278	.413	.328	180	6	0	1	17	0

INDIVIDUAL PITCHING LEADERS

(Minimum 40 innings pitched)

	W	L	ERA	G	SV	IP	H	BB	SO
Caleb Riedel, Nebraska-Omaha	4	2	1.49	13	0	60.1	50	21	65
Ledgend Smith, Oral Roberts	7	5	2.50	15	0	82.2	70	22	98
Joey Machado, Nebraska-Omaha	4	6	2.96	21	4	73	78	27	82
Mark Timmins, Nebraska-Omaha	2	3	3.31	15	0	81.2	82	15	58

	W	L	ERA	G	SV	IP	H	BB	SO
Cody Carlson, South Dakota State	7	5	3.66	13	0	64	62	16	34
Evan Sankey, North Dakota State	5	4	3.69	14	0	68.1	84	15	49
Isaac Coffey, Oral Roberts	7	6	3.77	15	0	88.1	69	16	78
Charlie Bell, Nebraska-Omaha	5	5	3.82	14	0	70.2	69	25	69
Owen Bishop, South Dakota State	4	5	4.19	11	0	58	54	15	50
Cade Feeney, North Dakota State	7	3	4.54	14	0	79.1	102	15	62
Graham Laubscher, St. Thomas	4	6	5.47	14	1	79	79	42	98
Evan Esch, St. Thomas	1	5	5.55	14	0	48.2	49	17	46
Nic McCay, South Dakota State	4	4	5.80	14	0	68.1	85	29	68

SUN BELT CONFERENCE

	Conference		Overall	
	W	L	W	L
*Texas State	26	4	44	11
*Georgia Southern	23	7	38	17
*Coastal Carolina	21	8	34	17
*Louisiana	19	11	33	21
South Alabama	17	13	31	22
Troy	15	15	31	23
Georgia State	15	15	30	26
Arkansas-Little Rock	11	18	24	26
Appalachian State	10	20	19	32
Louisiana-Monroe	9	20	19	34
Texas-Arlington	7	23	15	39
Arkansas State	5	24	11	38

ALL-CONFERENCE TEAM: C: Julian Brock, So., Louisiana **1B:** Carson Roccaforte, So., Louisiana **2B:** Jesse Sherrill, Jr., Georgia Southern **3B:** Justin Thompson, Sr., Texas State **SS:** Dalton Shuffield, Sr., Texas State **OF:** Max Ryerson, Jr., Georgia State; Mason Holt, Sr., Louisiana-Monroe; Miles Simington, Sr., Purdue **DH:** Noah Ledford, RJr., Georgia Southern **UTL:** Cameron Jones, So., Georgia State **SP:** Reid VanScoter, RSr., Coastal Carolina; Levi Wells, So., Texas State; Zeke Wood, Jr., Texas State **RP:** Tristan Stivors, Sr., Texas State **Player of the Year:** Dalton Shuffield, Texas State **Pitcher of the Year:** Reid VanScoter, Coastal Carolina **Coach of the Year:** Steven Trout, Texas State **Freshman of the Year:** Austin St. Laurent, Appalachian State **Newcomer of the Year:** Max Ryerson, Georgia State.

INDIVIDUAL BATTING LEADERS

(Minimum 140 at-bats)

	AVG	OBP	SLG	AB	2B	3B	HR	RBI	SB
Miles Simington, South Alabama	.383	.452	.579	214	15	3	7	53	5
Canyon McWilliams, Arkansas-Little Rock	.382	.445	.634	191	14	2	10	50	5
Dalton Shuffield, Texas State	.378	.444	.668	238	20	5	13	48	16
Carson Roccaforte, Louisiana	.374	.435	.671	219	11	3	16	68	25
Cameron Jones, Georgia State	.374	.429	.512	211	14	0	5	31	12
Jesse Sherrill, Georgia Southern	.361	.480	.452	219	13	2	1	23	13
Tyler Johnson, Coastal Carolina	.357	.467	.754	171	11	0	19	61	2
Noah Dickerson, Arkansas-Little Rock	.354	.429	.657	175	18	1	11	46	1
Griffin Cheney, Georgia State	.350	.445	.640	197	9	0	16	38	12
Noah Ledford, Georgia Southern	.348	.444	.665	227	19	1	17	70	0
Erick Orbeta, South Alabama	.340	.444	.395	200	9	1	0	30	1
Heath Hood, Louisiana	.337	.396	.536	196	15	6	4	39	19
Max Ryerson, Georgia State	.335	.414	.705	224	17	0	22	62	1
Luke Boynton, Georgia State	.333	.408	.605	162	8	0	12	37	3
Eric Brown, Coastal Carolina	.330	.460	.544	206	19	2	7	40	12
Jesse Hall, Troy	.326	.424	.439	221	19	0	2	44	8
Justin Thompson, Texas State	.323	.425	.500	232	14	0	9	44	10
Connor Kimple, Louisiana	.319	.384	.549	204	10	5	9	36	9
Mason Holt, Louisiana-Monroe	.317	.413	.621	227	15	3	16	39	14
Hunter Stokes, South Alabama	.314	.382	.475	223	16	1	6	32	3
Tyler Robertson, Louisiana	.314	.407	.467	210	13	2	5	33	21
Jason Swan, Georgia Southern	.314	.409	.426	242	18	0	3	43	11
Hayden Cross, Appalachian State	.305	.399	.429	177	16	0	2	33	2
Austin St. Laurent, Appalachian State	.305	.380	.462	197	13	3	4	25	6
Jarrett Brown, Georgia Southern	.305	.387	.433	210	9	3	4	37	5

INDIVIDUAL PITCHING LEADERS

(Minimum 40 innings pitched)

	W	L	ERA	G	SV	IP	H	BB	SO
Tristan Stivors, Texas State	7	1	2.21	32	18	61	47	19	86
Ty Fisher, Georgia Southern	6	2	2.58	14	0	87.1	81	23	60
Garrett Gainous, Troy	5	4	2.98	12	0	57.1	54	25	69
Levi Wells, Texas State	8	3	3.07	18	0	91	79	32	86
Hayden Arnold, Arkansas-Little Rock	5	6	3.14	15	0	94.2	82	15	86
Michael Knorr, Coastal Carolina	5	0	3.39	13	0	69	60	13	86
Reid VanScoter, Coastal Carolina	9	4	3.65	16	0	88.2	84	24	85
Brandon Talley, Louisiana	3	3	3.74	21	2	74.2	77	26	67
Zeke Wood, Texas State	7	1	3.78	17	0	88	59	51	103
Jay Thompson, Georgia Southern	7	4	3.91	37	6	76	71	23	63
Jacob Schultz, Louisiana	4	3	4.05	22	3	82.1	85	23	79
David Moffat, Texas-Arlington	2	8	4.10	23	2	63.2	81	14	51
Tanner King, Texas-Arlington	2	6	4.35	17	2	80.2	74	14	67
Nick Parker, Coastal Carolina	6	3	4.45	15	0	85	83	23	81
Sawyer Smallwood, Arkansas-Little Rock	5	6	4.73	29	5	51.1	50	16	49
Michael Wong, Texas-Arlington	1	7	4.78	14	0	75.1	92	22	53
Jeff Wilson, Louisiana	4	4	4.81	17	0	76.2	89	23	57
Matt Boswell, South Alabama	6	5	4.82	15	0	84	79	19	92
Trey Tujetsch, Appalachian State	4	5	4.98	12	0	56	64	25	50
Cam Barlow, Louisiana-Monroe	2	7	5.14	15	0	77	82	31	69
Tyler Lehrmann, South Alabama	3	2	5.22	18	0	60.1	66	32	45
Jaylen Paden, Georgia Southern	6	2	5.30	16	0	71.1	54	51	64
Justin Medlin, Arkansas State	1	7	5.37	15	0	70.1	81	33	65
JoJo Booker, South Alabama	4	2	5.40	14	0	63.1	55	22	42
Cade Winquest, Texas-Arlington	2	4	5.40	15	0	58.1	56	23	57

WEST COAST CONFERENCE

	Conference		Overall	
	W	L	W	L
*Grand Canyon	25	5	41	21
Cal Baptist	18	12	36	20
Sacramento State	17	13	32	26
Dixie State	14	16	22	33
Seattle	11	19	16	34
*New Mexico State	10	20	24	34
Utah Valley	10	20	18	37

ALL-CONFERENCE TEAM: C: David Martin, So., California Baptist **1B:** Logan Gallina, So., New Mexico State **2B:** Harrison Spohn, Sr., California Baptist **3B:** Juan Colato, RSr., Grand Canyon **SS:** Jacob Wilson, So., Grand Canyon **OF:** Tayler Aguilar, Jr., Grand Canyon; Chad Castillo, Jr., California Baptist; Carlos Contreras, Jr., Sam Houston State **UTL/DH:** Parker Schmidt, So., Dixie State **At-Large:** Tyler Wilson, So., Grand Canyon **SP:** Daniel Avitia, Fr., Grand Canyon; Kevin Stevens, RSr., Texas-Rio Grande Valley **RP:** Jack Dallas, Sr., Lamar **At-Large:** Vince Reilly, Jr., Grand Canyon **Player of the Year:** Carlos Contreras, Sam Houston State **Pitcher of the Year:** Daniel Avitia, Grand Canyon **Coach of the Year:** Andy Stankiewicz, Grand Canyon **Freshman of the Year:** Daniel Avitia, Grand Canyon **Defensive Player of the Year:** Harrison Spohn, California Baptist.

INDIVIDUAL BATTING LEADERS

(Minimum 140 at-bats)

	AVG	OBP	SLG	AB	2B	3B	HR	RBI	SB
Carlos Contreras, Sam Houston State	.400	.468	.713	230	18	6	14	89	2
David Martin, California Baptist	.395	.506	.542	190	10	0	6	43	4
Chad Castillo, California Baptist	.386	.442	.635	233	23	1	11	69	13
Juan Colato, Grand Canyon	.379	.417	.589	219	16	3	8	51	6
Brandon Pimentel, Texas-Rio Grande Valley	.377	.427	.619	236	17	2	12	47	2
Brett Cain, Texas-Rio Grande Valley	.370	.450	.614	189	16	3	8	41	4
Justin Wishkoski, Sam Houston State	.369	.455	.514	222	17	3	3	49	3
Mitch Moralez, Utah Valley	.366	.406	.527	224	14	2	6	27	6
Harrison Spohn, California Baptist	.365	.422	.546	249	28	1	5	38	14
Michael Carpentier, California Baptist	.363	.451	.497	157	9	0	4	20	1
Matthew McDonald, Lamar	.361	.424	.558	208	18	1	7	42	3
Jacob Wilson, Grand Canyon	.358	.418	.585	246	18	1	12	65	0
Kemuel Thomas-Rivera, Tarleton State	.357	.442	.577	168	6	2	9	37	9
Matt Boissoneault, Seattle	.354	.420	.601	178	16	2	8	45	3
Cal Villareal, New Mexico State	.352	.394	.543	162	13	3	4	30	3
Shane Taylor, Dixie State	.350	.452	.498	203	13	1	5	40	7
Josh Blankenship, Lamar	.340	.439	.505	188	15	2	4	53	0
Elijah Buries, Grand Canyon	.335	.390	.454	260	13	0	6	36	6
Mitchell Dickson, Abilene Christian	.335	.436	.428	236	8	1	4	26	13
Clayton Chadwick, Sam Houston State	.332	.460	.460	211	14	2	3	35	6

Kaden Hollow, Dixie State	.327	.418	.525	202	11	1	9	39	1
Derek Gellos, Seattle	.326	.379	.406	187	5	2	2	22	0
Tayler Aguilar, Grand Canyon	.326	.397	.719	224	13	3	23	75	2
Logan Gallina, New Mexico State	.326	.393	.660	215	7	1	21	62	5
Jake Skipworth, California Baptist	.324	.418	.574	204	15	0	12	53	1
Bash Randle, Abilene Christian	.324	.405	.507	213	13	1	8	43	13
Kevin Jimenez, New Mexico State	.324	.424	.502	219	23	2	4	31	7
Dawsen Bacho, Sacramento State	.324	.405	.535	170	15	0	7	27	0
Tyler Wilson, Grand Canyon	.321	.383	.487	187	11	1	6	32	3
Tanner Tweedt, Abilene Christian	.320	.390	.518	197	17	2	6	49	2

INDIVIDUAL PITCHING LEADERS

(Minimum 40 innings pitched)

	W	L	ERA	G	SV	IP	H	BB	SO
Kevin Stevens, Texas-Rio Grande Valley	9	2	2.66	14	0	81.1	69	29	100
Adam Wheaton, Lamar	10	2	2.66	15	0	91.1	83	29	69
CJ Culpepper, California Baptist	5	3	3.26	16	1	69	55	24	76
Drew Necochea, California Baptist	8	3	3.42	16	0	68.1	68	21	36
Braxton Douthit, Lamar	6	2	3.65	15	0	81.1	79	20	76
Eli Saul, Sacramento State	6	1	3.71	15	0	87.1	77	42	66
Nick Hull, Grand Canyon	7	1	3.72	16	0	96.2	90	28	102
Daniel Avitia, Grand Canyon	8	5	4.06	15	0	84.1	70	19	111
Steven Beard, Sam Houston State	6	4	4.28	16	0	82	95	20	70
Ian Mejia, New Mexico State	6	4	4.29	16	0	100.2	116	32	102
Colin Hunter, Sacramento State	5	4	4.75	15	0	72	81	19	62
Peter Chronowski, Seattle	4	7	4.75	15	0	77.2	93	17	59
Tyler Morgan, Abilene Christian	6	5	4.92	16	0	75	86	30	82
Matt Dillard, Sam Houston State	5	6	4.93	15	0	80.1	92	27	80
Brandon Downer, California Baptist	5	2	5.05	15	0	57	66	19	50
Genner Cervantes, Abilene Christian	6	4	5.19	15	0	59	71	21	71
Joe Richter, Stephen F. Austin	3	4	5.21	11	0	55.1	59	15	34
Ryan Hardman, Dixie State	4	2	5.31	20	4	59.1	75	21	54
Jesus Aldaz, Texas-Rio Grande Valley	5	6	5.35	15	1	67.1	73	22	74
Connor Markl, Grand Canyon	6	3	5.43	16	0	69.2	85	17	75
Colten Davis, Texas-Rio Grande Valley	4	4	5.74	15	0	64.1	85	20	50
Mason Gray, Utah Valley	3	5	6.31	14	0	61.1	75	34	39
Brady Liddle, Seattle	2	5	6.40	14	0	57.2	80	12	38
Devin Smith, Utah Valley	1	4	6.60	14	0	60	74	42	47
Brett Porthan, Dixie State	7	4	6.75	16	0	74.2	96	24	61
Dillon Holliday, Dixie State	3	8	6.79	18	0	55.2	78	37	43
Pablo Cortes, New Mexico State	4	5	6.85	16	1	68.1	92	15	53
Nestor German, Seattle	2	4	6.99	14	0	56.2	71	31	35
Joe Todd, Stephen F. Austin	1	7	7.18	13	0	67.2	81	31	46
Bryce Hackett, Tarleton State	2	7	7.44	15	0	61.2	85	27	51

WESTERN ATHLETIC CONFERENCE

	Conference		Overall	
	W	L	W	L
*Gonzaga	20	7	37	19
*San Diego	17	10	37	20
Portland	17	10	32	23
Brigham Young	16	11	33	20
San Francisco	14	13	28	28
Loyola Marymount	14	13	20	33
Pepperdine	12	15	24	26
Santa Clara	11	16	24	29
Saint Mary's	9	18	25	30
Pacific	5	22	14	38

ALL-CONFERENCE TEAM: C: David Martin, So., California Baptist. **1B**: Logan Gallina, So., New Mexico State. **2B**: Harrison Spohn, Sr., California Baptist. **3B**: Juan Colato, RSr., Grand Canyon. **SS**: Jacob Wilson, So., Grand Canyon. **OF**: Tayler Aguilar, Jr., Grand Canyon; Chad Castillo, Jr., California Baptist; Carlos Contreras, Jr., Sam Houston State. **UTL/DH**: Parker Schmidt, So., Dixie State. **At-Large**: Tyler Wilson, So., Grand Canyon. **SP**: Daniel Avitia, Fr., Grand Canyon; Kevin Stevens, RSr., Texas-Rio Grande Valley. **RP**: Jack Dallas, Sr., Lamar. **At-Large**: Vince Reilly, Jr., Grand Canyon . **Player of the Year:** Carlos Contreras, Sam Houston State. **Pitcher of the Year:** Daniel Avitia, Grand Canyon**. Coach of the Year:** Andy Stankiewicz**,** Grand Canyon**. Freshman of the Year: Daniel Avitia,** Grand Canyon**. Defensive Player of the Year:** Harrison Spohn, California Baptist.

INDIVIDUAL BATTING LEADERS

(Minimum 140 at-bats)

	AVG	OBP	SLG	AB	2B	3B	HR	RBI	SB
Caleb Ricketts, San Diego	.373	.423	.658	228	13	2	16	55	0
John Peck, Pepperdine	.361	.417	.578	166	11	2	7	33	7
Jake Holcroft, Portland	.343	.420	.473	207	15	0	4	26	9
Chase Meidroth, San Diego	.329	.440	.544	228	19	0	10	47	6
Dylan Dennis, Loyola Marymount	.325	.403	.478	203	11	1	6	32	3
Diego Baqueiro, Loyola Marymount	.320	.373	.553	228	20	0	11	58	0
Tyler Rando, Gonzaga	.315	.400	.532	203	16	2	8	37	5
Brandon Motheral, Pacific	.313	.378	.494	166	9	0	7	27	0
Charles Masino, Pepperdine	.313	.375	.386	166	4	1	2	18	1
Jack Costello, San Diego	.307	.369	.487	238	15	2	8	42	2
Luke Keaschall, San Francisco	.305	.445	.502	213	18	0	8	34	30
Gavin Napier, Saint Mary's	.301	.386	.422	173	9	3	2	25	3
Cade McGee, Gonzaga	.298	.393	.514	208	15	0	10	31	2
Savier Pinales, Gonzaga	.297	.360	.423	182	7	2	4	24	15
Austin Deming, Brigham Young	.295	.371	.456	193	14	1	5	28	0
Eamonn Lance, Santa Clara	.295	.415	.482	139	11	0	5	24	1
Brock Watkins, Brigham Young	.294	.356	.472	214	8	3	8	33	4
Kevin Sim, San Diego	.292	.387	.527	226	13	2	12	57	8
Coleman Brigman, Santa Clara	.292	.361	.476	212	16	4	5	34	11
Dustin Allen, San Diego	.292	.424	.400	185	8	3	2	37	15
Ben Patacsil, Portland	.290	.403	.355	155	7	0	1	21	2
Ozzie Pratt, Brigham Young	.289	.368	.390	159	8	1	2	19	5
Chaz Myers, Pacific	.287	.408	.414	181	15	1	2	24	2
Chris Santiago, Saint Mary's	.287	.363	.525	181	9	2	10	31	1
Grant Weiss, Loyola Marymount	.287	.374	.451	195	12	1	6	28	3
Grayson Sterling, Gonzaga	.285	.355	.395	200	16	0	2	36	1
Ryan Sepede, Brigham Young	.283	.347	.466	191	16	2	5	45	2
Harris Williams III, San Francisco	.281	.360	.416	221	10	1	6	45	21
Enzo Apodaca, Gonzaga	.279	.358	.413	240	19	2	3	45	8
Benny Casillas, Loyola Marymount	.276	.313	.362	185	8	1	2	25	2

INDIVIDUAL PITCHING LEADERS

(Minimum 40 innings pitched)

	W	L	ERA	G	SV	IP	H	BB	SO
Brett Gillis, Portland	9	2	2.24	14	0	84.1	61	32	115
Diego Barrera, Loyola Marymount	4	3	2.85	12	0	72.2	65	15	59
Owen Wild, Gonzaga	9	1	3.03	16	1	74.1	70	24	83
Jack Sterner, Brigham Young	4	4	3.18	14	0	73.2	78	22	68
Gabriel Hughes, Gonzaga	8	3	3.21	15	0	98	75	37	138
Ryan Brady, Brigham Young	4	3	3.73	14	0	60.1	57	17	44
Conner Roberts, Saint Mary's	3	3	3.74	14	0	65	58	25	68
Trevor Hinkel, Pepperdine	5	4	3.81	14	0	73.1	69	25	52
Brycen Mautz, San Diego	10	2	3.87	16	0	90.2	90	22	129
Eli Morse, Portland	8	2	3.91	16	0	89.2	91	26	96
Bryce Robison, Brigham Young	7	1	4.01	19	1	60.2	67	16	51
Garrett Rennie, San Diego	2	4	4.01	15	0	67.1	75	25	50
Brandon Llewellyn, Pepperdine	3	7	4.14	13	0	71.2	78	20	44
Cole Kitchen, Santa Clara	4	4	4.36	15	1	72.1	68	32	101
Owen Stevenson, San Francisco	2	4	4.57	19	1	69	77	22	49
Brock Gillis, Portland	4	4	4.61	18	0	66.1	59	30	59
Jared Feikes, Santa Clara	5	6	4.81	18	1	67.1	70	26	43
Caleb Franzen, Portland	2	5	4.85	18	1	59.1	60	21	69
Trystan Vrieling, Gonzaga	4	4	4.91	15	0	80.2	75	46	107
Skylar Hales, Santa Clara	3	3	4.91	15	0	69.2	71	36	75
Ryan Wiltse, Saint Mary's	4	2	5.04	18	1	60.2	59	23	59
Ryan Taurek, Saint Mary's	4	3	5.53	15	0	55.1	59	23	53
Quinn Lavelle, Loyola Marymount	1	5	6.02	16	0	58.1	79	22	36
Jesse Barron, San Francisco	4	4	6.12	17	0	60.1	71	22	64
Hunter Hayes, Pacific	2	9	6.82	14	0	64.2	106	25	55
Alex Reelfs, Santa Clara	4	7	6.86	23	2	59	75	29	54
Zach Patterson, Pacific	1	7	6.96	14	0	63.1	67	29	35
Matt McClure, Loyola Marymount	3	6	8.03	17	0	61.2	87	32	36
Jimmy Galicia, Loyola Marymount	1	7	8.32	17	0	66	87	23	53

SMALL COLLEGES

NCAA DIVISION II

North Greenville (S.C.) went 4-0 in the Division II baseball championship, capped off with a 5-3 win over Point Loma Nazarene (Calif.) in the national championship game, to win the program's first-ever title. Righthander Reece Fields gave up one run in five innings for NGU on the mound, helping him earn tournament MVP honors.

DIVISION II WORLD SERIES

Site: Cary, N.C.
Participants: 1. North Greenville (S.C.); 2. Point Loma Nazarena (Calif.); 3. Southern Arkansas; 4. Southern New Hampshire; 5. Angelo State (Texas); 6. Rollins (Fla.); 7. Illinois-Springfield; 8. West Chester (Pa.)
Champion: North Greenville (S.C.)
Runner-up: Point Loma Nazarene (Calif.).

LEADERS: BATTING AVERAGE
(Minimum 140 at bats)

Rk. Player, Pos., Team	Class	AVG	OBP	SLG
1. Haydn McGeary, C, Colorado Mesa	Jr.	.481	.579	1.061
2. Bradon O'Connor, OF, Benedict (S.C.)	Sr.	.454	.551	.579
3. Micah Morgan, UTL, Spring Hill (Ala.)	So.	.446	.560	.819
4. Joseph Smith, OF, Savannah State (Ga.)	Jr.	.441	.528	.776
5. Connor Evans, UTL, Chestnut Hill (Pa.)	Fr.	.440	.455	.580
6. Roger Riley, C, Regis (Colo.)	Sr.	.439	.498	.673
7. EJ Taylor, INF, Southern Nazarene (Okla.)	Sr.	.438	.536	.846
8. Kit Wigington, UTL, Colorado-Colorado Springs	Fr.	.437	.477	.845
9. Aidan Brewer, INF, Hillsdale (Mich.)	Jr.	.435	.500	.726
10. Marc Cisco, 2B, Queens (N.Y.)	So.	.435	.526	.747

EARNED RUN AVERAGE
(Minimum 40 innings pitched)

Rk. Pitcher, Team	Class	W	L	ERA
1. Noah Takac, North Greenville (S.C.)	Jr.	7	0	1.60
2. Braydon Nelson, Tampa	Jr.	6	1	1.79
3. Jared Marshman, Bloomsburg (Pa.)	Jr.	9	1	1.81
4. Jared Donalson, Georgia Southwestern	Sr.	10	3	1.81
5. Jaylyn Whitehead, Rollins (Fla.)	Sr.	11	3	1.81
6. Jake Osowski, Minnesota-Crookston	So.	5	0	1.94
7. Michael Boswell, Tiffin (Ohio)	Sr.	8	3	1.96
8. Jem Sisco, Thomas Jefferson (Pa.)	So.	4	2	1.96
9. Dawson Lane, Florida Southern	Sr.	5	1	2.07
10. Kyle Roche, Franklin Pierce (N.H.)	So.	6	2	2.07

CATEGORY LEADERS: BATTING
*Minimum 140 at bats

Dept.	Player, Pos., Team	Class	G	Total
OBP*	Josh Elvir, OF, Angelo State (Texas)	Jr.	55	.584
OBP*	Haydn McGeary, C, Colorado Mesa	Jr.	57	.579
SLG*	Haydn McGeary, C, Colorado Mesa	Jr.	57	1.061
R	Caleb Farmer, INF, Colorado Mesa	Sr.	60	95
H	Haydn McGeary, C, Colorado Mesa	Jr.	57	103
2B	Luke Folsom, UTL, Colorado School of Mines	So.	52	29
3B	Nolan Anspaugh, OF, Davenport (Mich.)	Sr.	59	14
HR	Haydn McGeary, C, Colorado Mesa	Jr.	57	35
RBI	Zion Pettigrew, INF, Illinois-Springfield	Sr.	59	95
SB	Bradon O'Connor, OF, Benedict (S.C.)	Sr.	43	97
SB	Brandon O'Connor, OF, Benedict (S.C.)	So.	34	47

CATEGORY LEADERS: PITCHING
*Minimum 40 innings

Dept.	Pitcher, Team	Class	Total
W	Jeremy Adorno, Southern Arkansas	Fr.	15
SV	Cole Hillier, Point Loma Nazarene (Calif.)	So.	17
G	Austin Long, Rollins (Fla.)	Sr.	34
IP	Jaylyn Whitehead, Rollins (Fla.)	Sr.	124
SO	Jeremy Adorno, Southern Arkansas	Fr.	136
SO/9*	Jack Choate, Assumption (Mass.)	Jr.	16.25
BB/9*	McLain Harris, Young Harris (Ga.)	Sr.	0.73
WHIP*	Noah Takac, North Greenville (S.C.)	Jr.	0.84

NCAA Division III

Eastern Connecticut State won the program's fifth national title by defeating Salisbury (Md.) by scores of 11-6 and 3-2 in the championship series of the Division III baseball championship, stopping defending champion Salisbury's bid for back-to-back titles. The championship was a fitting end to an outstanding season that saw the Warriors finish with a 49-3 record.

DIVISION III WORLD SERIES

Site: Cedar Rapids, Iowa
Participants: Marietta (Ohio); Eastern Connecticut State; LaGrange (Ga.); Salisbury (Md.); Wisconsin-Stevens Point; Trinity (Texas); Baldwin Wallace (Ohio); Catholic (Washington, D.C.)
Champion: Eastern Connecticut State
Runner-up: Salisbury (Md.).

LEADERS: BATTING AVERAGE
(Minimum 120 at bats)

RK. Player, Pos., Team	Class	AVG	OBP	SLG
1. Ryan McCarty, INF, Penn State-Abington	Sr.	.529	.591	1.164
2. Jake Blinstrub, OF, Mount Saint Vincent (N.Y.)	Sr.	.494	.563	.659
3. Jack Hanson, 3B, Gustavus Adolphus (Minn.)	Sr.	.491	.544	.856
4. Mac McCain, 2B, Grinnell (Iowa)	Fr.	.472	.514	.683
5. Miles Reid, OF, Tufts (Mass.)	Sr.	.469	.541	.594
6. Derek Holmes, C, Moravian (Pa.)	Jr.	.467	.529	.653
7. Alex Madera, INF, Arcadia (Pa.)	Jr.	.464	.554	.559
8. Jackson Hornung, C, Skidmore (N.Y.)	Jr.	.460	.539	.760
9. Mark Kirkland, 1B, Redlands (Calif.)	Sr.	.454	.497	.632
10. Ryan Decoursey, INF, St. Joseph's (N.Y.)	Jr.	.453	.503	.741

EARNED RUN AVERAGE
(Minimum 30 innings pitched)

Rk. Pitcher, Team	Class	W	L	ERA
1. Ben Smith, Worcester State (Mass.)	Jr.	3	1	0.90
2. Dominic Perachi, Salve Regina (R.I.)	Jr.	9	1	1.00
3. Sam Mathews, Marietta (Ohio)	Sr.	5	1	1.40
4. Owen Boerema, Northwestern (Minn.)	Jr.	9	2	1.42
5. Kenny Lippman, Denison (Ohio)	Sr.	7	1	1.56
6. Tyler Herrera, Centenary (La.)	Fr.	7	1	1.59
7. Shayne Audet, New England (N.H.)	So.	3	2	1.61
8. Tate Ostrowski, Grove City (Pa.)	Sr.	8	1	1.63
9. Stephen Clancy, Farmingdale State (N.Y.)	Jr.	1	1	1.64
10. Kiefer Lord, Carleton (Minn.)	So.	4	1	1.65

CATEGORY LEADERS: BATTING
*Minimum 120 at bats

Dept.	Player, Pos., Team	Class	G	Total
OBP*	Jack Thomson, INF, Lewis & Clark (Ore.)	Sr.	37	.614
SLG*	Ryan McCarty, INF, Penn State-Abington	Sr.	44	1.164
R	McKinley Erves, OF, LaGrange (Ga.)	Sr.	53	91
H	Joe Ruth, INF, LaGrange (Ga.)	Jr.	53	109
2B	Damian Yenzi, 3B, Marietta (Ohio)	Sr.	51	31
3B	Shane Daly, OF, McDaniel (Md.)	Fr.	40	11
HR	Ryan McCarty, INF, Penn State-Abington	Sr.	44	29
RBI	Ryan McCarty, INF, Penn State-Abington	Sr.	44	91
SB	Seth Betts, SS, Crown (Minn.)	Sr.	45	42

CATEGORY LEADERS: PITCHING

*Minimum 30 innings

Dept.	Pitcher, Team	Class	Total
W	Trent Valentine, Marietta (Ohio)	Jr.	14
SV	Ethan Peters, Loras (Iowa)	Sr.	13
	Grayson Thurman, Lynchburg (Va.)	Sr.	13
	Sam Mathews, Marietta (Ohio)	Sr.	13
IP	Grant Manning, Chapman (Calif.)	Jr.	106.2
SO	Owen Boerema, Northwestern (Minn.)	Jr.	139
SO/9*	Alex Amalfi, Massachusetts-Boston	Jr.	16.04
BB/9*	Mason Newman, Brandeis (Mass.)	Sr.	0.34
WHIP*	Kiefer Lord, Carleton (Minn.)	So.	0.69

NAIA

Southeastern (Fla.) defeated historical NAIA powerhouse Lewis-Clark State (Idaho) by an 11-5 score in the NAIA World Series championship game to win its second national championship in five years.

NAIA WORLD SERIES

Site: Lewiston, Idaho
Participants: Southeastern (Fla.); Tennessee Wesleyan; Lewis-Clark State (Idaho); Louisiana State-Shreveport; Bellevue (Neb.); Westmont (Calif.); Faulkner (Ala.); Georgia Gwinnett; MidAmerica Nazarena (Kan.); Webber International (Fla.)
Champion: Southeastern (Fla.)
Runner-up: Lewis-Clark State (Idaho).

LEADERS: BATTING AVERAGE

(Minimum 140 at bats)

RK.	Player, Pos., Team	Class	AVG	OBP	SLG
1.	Cross Factor, OF, Oklahoma City	Sr.	.525	.591	1.155
2.	Keelyn Johnson, INF, Louisiana Christian	RSr.	.481	.625	.778
3.	Koki Matsuda, OF, Central Christian (Kan.)	Sr.	.465	.510	.799
4.	Nolan Machibroda, 1B, Cumberland (Tenn.)	Sr.	.460	.558	.893
5.	Peyton Crispin, OF, Oklahoma City	Sr.	.456	.526	.887

EARNED RUN AVERAGE

(Minimum 40 innings pitched)

Rk.	Pitcher, Team	Class	W	L	ERA
1.	Kobe Foster, Tennessee Wesleyan	Sr.	13	1	1.42
2.	Eli Davis, Oklahoma City	Jr.	10	1	1.45
3.	Kobey Schlotman, Mount Mercy (Iowa)	Sr.	9	1	1.64
4.	July Sosa, Faulkner (Ala.)	Sr.	12	1	1.72
5.	Zack Simon, Corban (Ore.)	Jr.	5	5	1.85

CATEGORY LEADERS: BATTING

*Minimum 140 at bats

Dept.	Player, Pos., Team	Class	G	Total
OBP*	Keelyn Johnson, INF, Louisiana Christian	RSr.	45	.625
SLG*	Cross Factor, OF, Oklahoma City	Sr.	53	1.155
HR	Livan Reinoso, INF, Tennessee Wesleyan	Sr.	64	32
RBI	Livan Reinoso, INF, Tennessee Wesleyan	Sr.	64	95
SB	Jay French, OF, Central Baptist (Ark.)	Sr.	55	61
SB	Collin Baber, OF, Freed-Hardeman (Tenn.)	Jr.	52	47

CATEGORY LEADERS: PITCHING

Dept.	Pitcher, Team	Class	Total
W	Robb Adams, Southeastern (Fla.)	Jr.	14
	Trent Sellers, Lewis-Clark State (Idaho)	Jr.	14
SV	Cruz McFadden, Mount Vernon Nazarene	So.	15
IP	Robb Adams, Southeastern (Fla.)	Jr.	113.2
SO	Kevin Miranda, Louisiana State-Shreveport	Sr.	156

NJCAA Division I

In its third straight appearance in the NJCAA Division I Baseball World Series, Central Arizona defeated Cowley (Kan.) 4-2 in the championship game for its second national title in three years. The Vaqueros' Kiko Romero won tournament MVP honors.

NJCAA DIVISION I WORLD SERIES

Site: Grand Junction, Colo.
Participants: Walters State (Tenn.); Wabash Valley (Ill.); McLennan (Texas); Central Florida; Crowder (Mo.); Central Arizona; Cowley (Kan.); San Jacinto (Texas); Snead State (Ala.); Harford (Md.)
Champion: Central Arizona
Runner-up: Cowley (Kan.).

LEADERS: BATTING AVERAGE

Minimum 140 at bats)

RK.	Player, Pos., Team	Class	AVG	OBP	SLG
1.	Zach Johnson, C, Southeast (Neb.)	Fr.	.474	.528	.912
2.	Jonathan Hogart, OF, Wabash Valley (Ill.)	So.	.463	.544	.710
3.	Cade Zalewski, INF, Frank Phillips (Texas)	Fr.	.452	.500	.751
4.	Bradke Lohry, INF, Wabash Valley (Ill.)	Fr.	.452	.541	.675
5.	Dariyan Pendergrass, OF, Spartanburg Methodist (S.C.)	Fr.	.452	.546	.597

EARNED RUN AVERAGE

(Minimum 40 innings pitched)

Rk.	Pitcher, Team	Class	W	L	ERA
1.	Derik Eaquinto, Salt Lake (Utah)	Fr.	13	1	1.48
2.	Jacob Bimbi, Wabash Valley (Ill.)	So.	11	1	1.49
3.	Ernesto Lugo-Canchola, Salt Lake (Utah)	Fr.	8	1	1.66
4.	Daxton Purser, Salt Lake (Utah)	So.	11	0	1.70
5.	Alex Cook, Colby (Kan.)	Fr.	9	1	1.71

CATEGORY LEADERS: BATTING

*Minimum 140 at bats

Dept.	Player, Pos., Team	Class	G	Total
OBP*	Alex Rodgers, Barton (Kan.)	Fr.	59	.560
SLG*	Matt Goetzmann, Southeast (Neb.)	So.	54	.925
HR	Caleb McNeely, Walters State (Tenn.)	RSo.	68	26
RBI	Brian Kalmer, Wabash Valley (Ill.)	RSo.	68	109
SB	Alex Rodgers, Barton (Kan.)	Fr.	59	61

CATEGORY LEADERS: PITCHING

Dept.	Pitcher, Team	Class	Total
W	Kohl Drake, Walters State (Tenn.)	RSo.	14
	Jake Knapp, Walters State (Tenn.)	RSo.	14
	Treyjen Meza, Cochise (Ariz.)	So.	14
	Shane Spencer, Central Arizona	RSo.	14
SV	Marco Ozuna, Cochise (Ariz.)	So.	15
IP	Shane Spencer, Central Arizona	RSo.	98
SO	Kohl Drake, Walters State (Tenn.)	RSo.	160

NJCAA Division II

Pearl River (Miss.) won its first-ever national title after taking two of three games against Madison (Wis.) in the championship series of the NJCAA Division II World Series. After losing the opening game 11-4, Pearl River won the final two games of the series by 19-1 and 7-2 scores. In the clinching win, starting pitcher Cole Tolbert gave up two runs on five hits with one walk and 11 strikeouts over seven innings.

NJCAA DIVISION II WORLD SERIES

Site: Enid, Okla.
Participants: Pearl River (Miss.); Madison (Wis.); Heartland (Ill.); Frederick (Md.); Lansing (Mich.); Kirkwood (Iowa); Murray State (Okla.);

Florida State Jacksonville; Phoenix; Mercer County (N.J.)
Champion: Pearl River (Miss.)
Runner-up: Madison (Wis.).

LEADERS: BATTING AVERAGE
(Minimum 120 at bats)

RK.	Player, Pos., Team	Class	AVG	OBP	SLG
1.	Domonic Prevesk, INF, Bryant & Stratton (Ohio)	So.	.512	.584	.904
2.	Kyle Leapaldt, INF, Bismarck State (N.D.)	So.	.487	.524	.940
3.	Houston Koon, OF, Pitt (N.C.),	RSo.	.478	.580	.767
4.	Sam Antonacci, INF,OF,Heartland (Ill.)	So.	.471	.554	.827
5.	Josearmando Diaz, C, 1B,Mercer County (N.J.)	RSo.	.470	.581	.705

EARNED RUN AVERAGE
(Minimum 40 innings pitched)

Rk.	Pitcher, Team	Class	W	L	ERA
1.	Grady Gorgen, McHenry County (Ill.)	Fr.	7	2	1.09
2.	Jonah Giblin, Phoenix	Fr.	4	0	1.17
3.	Randy Pritchard, Jackson (Mich.)	So.	5	2	1.36
4.	Hunter Rossi, Sussex County (N.J.)	So.	5	3	1.37
5.	Reese Dutton, Heartland (Ill.)	So.	10	0	1.51

CATEGORY LEADERS: BATTING
*Minimum 120 at bats

Dept.	Player, Pos., Team	Class	G	Total
OBP*	Jace Dew, Bismarck State (N.D.)	So.	44	.593
SLG*	Mike Hallquist, Bismarck State (N.D.)	So.	42	.946
HR	Ethan Moore, Murray State (Okla.)	Fr.	61	24
RBI	Bobby Atkinson, Heartland (Ill.)	Fr.	56	81
SB	Kole Myers, Louisiana State-Eunice	So.	55	58
	Angelo Ramirez, Baltimore County-Catonsville	Fr.	51	58
SB	Gary Mattis, INF, GateWay (Ariz.)	So.	58	64

CATEGORY LEADERS: PITCHING

Dept.	Pitcher, Team	Class	Total
W	Brendan Beaver, Lansing (Mich.)	So.	11
	Brett Sears, Iowa Central	RSo.	11
	Trent Spoon, Kankakee (Ill.)	So.	11
	Patrick Vienne, Louisiana State-Eunice	Fr.	11
SV	Bryce Schares, Kirkwood (Iowa)	Fr.	12
IP	Daniel Gaviria, Florida State Jacksonville	RSo.	93.1
	Ryan Turbeville, Murray State (Okla.)	Fr.	93.1
SO	Grant Dittmer, Lansing (Mich.)	So.	118

NJCAA Division III

Herkimer (N.Y.) became the first New York-based team to win the NJCAA Division III World Series with a 9-3 win over Dallas-Eastfield (Texas), capping off a 4-0 run for the Generals through the event in their ninth overall appearance.

NJCAA DIVISION III WORLD SERIES

Site: Greeneville, Tenn.
Participants: Caldwell Tech (N.C.); Rowan Gloucester (N.J.); Northern Essex (Mass.); Niagara County (N.Y.); Dallas-Eastfield (Texas); Herkimer (N.Y.); Oakton (Ill.); St. Cloud Tech (Minn.)
Champion: Herkimer (N.Y.)
Runner-up: Dallas-Eastfield (Texas).

LEADERS: BATTING AVERAGE
(Minimum 120 at bats)

RK.	Player, Pos., Team	Class	AVG	OBP	SLG
1.	Hazel Martinez, 1B, Cayuga (N.Y.)	Fr.	.543	.589	1.000
2.	Adam Rankie, OF, Erie (N.Y.)	So.	.493	.570	.781
3.	Jeffrey Sabater, OF, Northampton (Pa.)	Fr.	.490	.580	.629
4.	Sam Witt, 1B, Owens (Ohio)	So.	.489	.544	.626
5.	Nicholas White, 1B, Northern Essex (Mass.)	So.	.476	.556	.796

EARNED RUN AVERAGE
(Minimum 40 innings pitched)

Rk.	Pitcher, Team	Class	W	L	ERA
1.	Todd Tringale, Northern Essex (Mass.)	So.	10	0	1.11
2.	Ryan Packard, Herkimer (N.Y.)	RSo.	10	0	1.32
3.	Ryan Gordon, Northampton (Pa.)	Fr.	5	2	1.54
4.	Greg Farone, Herkimer (N.Y.)	So.	7	0	1.65
5.	Ethan Shaub, Rowan Gloucester	Fr.	8	0	1.67

CATEGORY LEADERS: BATTING
*Minimum 120 at bats

Dept.	Player, Pos., Team	Class	G	Total
OBP*	Hazel Martinez, Cayuga (N.Y.)	Fr.	38	.589
SLG*	Hazel Martinez, Cayuga (N.Y.)	Fr.	38	1
HR	Angel Rodriguez, Dallas-Eastfield (Texas)	So.	44	20
RBI	Greg Hare, Erie (N.Y.)	RSo.	54	83
SB	Christian Petrillo, Middlesex (N.J.)	So.	56	63

CATEGORY LEADERS: PITCHING

Dept.	Pitcher, Team	Class	Total
W	Seth Willis, Caldwell Tech (N.C.)	RSo.	13
SV	Pablo Veras, Virginia Peninsula	So.	7
IP	Seth Willis, Caldwell Tech (N.C.)	RSo.	92.1
SO	Greg Farone, Herkimer (N.Y.)	So.	139
SO	Grant Dittmer, Lansing (Mich.)	So.	118

California Junior Colleges

In the first full season of California junior college baseball since 2019, Riverside City College won its first state championship in 15 years with a 10-8 victory over Folsom Lake.

CALIFORNIA CC ATHLETIC ASSOCIATION

Champion: Riverside City College.

LEADERS: BATTING AVERAGE
(Minimum 120 at bats)

RK.	Player, Pos., Team	Class	AVG	OBP	SLG
1.	Jack Sanders, OF, Palomar	Fr.	.456	.510	.687
2.	Jeter Ybarra, 3B, Ohlone	Fr.	.444	.494	.618
3.	Matthew Bardowell, OF, Riverside	So.	.436	.537	.756
4.	Taylor Steig, 1B, Redwoods	RSo.	.434	.497	.721
5.	Phoenix Sommay, INF, Mt. San Jacinto	Fr.	.433	.505	.720

EARNED RUN AVERAGE
(Minimum 40 innings pitched)

Rk.	Pitcher, Team	Class	W	L	ERA
1.	Noah Galvan, Fresno	RFr.	9	2	1.38
2.	Garrett Edy, Santa Rosa	Fr.	3	0	2.05
3.	Andrew Gauna, San Diego Mesa	Fr.	2	4	2.14
4.	Gio Armas, Southwestern	Fr.	1	0	2.20
5.	Sergio Gutierrez, Butte	Fr.	4	0	2.23

CATEGORY LEADERS: BATTING
*Minimum 120 at bats

Dept.	Player, Pos., Team	Class	G	Total
OBP*	Jerry Thomas, Feather River	RSo.	47	.549
SLG*	Matthew Bardowell, Riverside	So.	46	.756
HR	Tafton Hensley, Canyons	Fr.	40	15
	Devlin Lindeman, Palomar	RFr.	49	15
RBI	Jeter Ybarra, Ohlone	Fr.	51	71
SB	Damian Stone, Ohlone	So.	49	54

CATEGORY LEADERS: PITCHING

Dept.	Pitcher, Team	Class	Total
W	Sky Wells, Folsom Lake	So.	12
SV	Cesar Avila, Merced	So.	12
	Austin Schroeder, Palomar	RFr.	12
IP	Thomas Bainton, El Camino	Fr.	102.2
SO	TJ Czyz, Cosumnes River	Fr.	117

COLLEGE SUMMER BASEBALL

For the first time since 2019, USA Baseball's Collegiate National Team returned to foreign competition. After two summers that were disrupted by the pandemic—the team did not play in 2020 and in 2021 played an expanded intrasquad schedule and the USA Olympic Team—it was back to normal for the CNT.

After a short series stateside to set the roster, Team USA traveled to Haarlem, Netherlands to play in Honkbalweek Haarlem under the direction of coach Mike Bianco (Mississippi). It was the CNT's first appearance in the tournament since 2014.

Team USA shined on the mound in the Netherlands, holding its opponents to 16 runs - five earned - in seven games. At one point, the USA Baseball pitching staff had a 22-inning scoreless streak.

The CNT's bats didn't find the same level of success, however, leading to a lot of close games in the tournament. Team USA lost back-to-back games to Curacao by 3-2 scores, which cost it an opportunity to play for the gold medal.

In the semifinal, the game went to extra-inning rules after the seventh inning. Both teams scored in the eighth and both teams failed to score in the ninth. In the top of the 10th, the U.S. failed to bring in either of the runners placed on base as Wyatt Langford grounded into a fielder's choice where Tre Morgan was out at home and Maui Ahuna stuck out for the third out. In the bottom of the 10th, Curacao scored the winning run without ever having to swing the bat. After runners were placed on first and second to begin the inning. Curacao scored on back-to-back hit-by-pitches.

The U.S. bounced back to defeat Japan, 5-1, in the bronze medal game to finish with a 4-3 record.

"I could not be prouder of this team and what it accomplished," Bianco said. "Although the medal isn't the color we were hoping for, this team played its heart out, battled every day, and represented their families, universities, and our country with distinction."

Infielder Yohandy Morales (Miami) led the team in batting in the tournament, going 8-for-20 and he was one of only three players in the event to homer. Infielder Jacob Wilson (Grand Canyon) also impressed and led the team in on-base percentage. Outfielder Wyatt Langford (Florida) was the other member of the team to hit over .300.

On the mound, lefthander Hunter Elliott (Ole Miss) started the bronze medal game, making for a memorable summer for the sophomore. Just a month before, he started the title-clinching game for Ole Miss at the College World Series.

COLLEGIATE NATIONAL TEAM STATS

Year indicates 2022-23 class standing

Player, Pos.	Year	School	AVG	OBP	SLG	G	AB	R	H	2B	3B	HR	RBI	BB	SO	SB
Yohandy Morales, INF	Jr.	Miami	.400	.400	.600	7	20	3	8	1	0	1	4	0	8	1
Jacob Wilson, INF	Jr.	Grand Canyon	.364	.461	.455	6	11	3	4	1	0	0	2	2	1	1
Wyatt Langford, OF	Jr.	Florida	.333	.385	.381	6	21	4	7	1	0	0	3	3	4	2
Jacob Gonzalez, INF	Jr.	Mississippi	.261	.333	.304	7	23	3	6	1	0	1	4	2	3	0
Jack Hurley, OF	Jr.	Virginia Tech	.200	.200	.200	6	5	2	1	0	0	0	1	0	1	1
Enrique Bradfield, OF	Jr.	Vanderbilt	.190	.370	.381	7	21	4	4	2	1	0	3	5	2	2
Maui Ahuna, INF	Jr.	Tennessee	.182	.357	.182	6	11	1	2	0	0	0	1	3	6	1
Kyle Teel, C	Jr.	Virginia	.176	.263	.235	6	17	2	3	1	0	0	3	1	3	0
Jack Payton, C	Jr.	Louisville	.143	.333	.286	4	7	1	1	1	0	0	0	1	2	1
Tre' Morgan, 1B	Jr.	Louisiana State	.133	.278	.133	6	15	2	2	0	0	0	1	3	5	1
Brayden Taylor, INF	Jr.	Texas Christian	.111	.364	.111	6	9	1	1	0	0	0	0	2	1	1
Dylan Crews, OF	Jr.	Louisiana State	.100	.308	.100	7	20	4	2	0	0	0	1	6	8	1
Zach Agnos, INF	Sr.	East Carolina	.000	.000	.000	1	1	0	0	0	0	0	0	0	0	0

Pitcher, Pos.	Year	School	W	L	ERA	G	SV	IP	H	R	ER	BB	SO	AVG
Joseph Gonzalez	Jr.	Auburn	1	0	0.00	2	0	8	5	1	0	0	8	.208
Tanner Hall	Jr.	Southern Mississippi	1	0	0.00	1	0	4	4	0	0	2	7	.200
Paul Skeenes	Jr.	Louisiana State	1	0	0.00	1	0	4	2	0	0	1	4	.143
Ross Dunn	Jr.	Arizona State	0	0	0.00	1	0	3	0	0	0	2	6	.000
Carter Holton	So.	Vanderbilt	0	0	0.00	2	0	5	1	0	0	2	6	.125
Teddy McGraw	Jr.	Wake Forest	0	0	0.00	1	1	3	1	0	0	0	4	.091
Cade Kuehler	Jr.	Campbell	0	2	0.00	2	0	2	1	2	0	2	1	.200
Wyatt Crowell	Jr.	Florida State	0	0	0.00	2	0	1	1	1	0	1	3	.200
Zach Agnos	Sr.	East Carolina	0	0	0.00	2	0	1	1	1	0	0	2	.200
Carson Montgomery	Jr.	Florida State	0	0	0.00	2	0	3	2	1	0	0	4	.333
Ryan Bruno	Jr.	Stanford	0	0	0.00	1	0	1	0	0	0	2	1	.000
Rhett Lowder	Jr.	Wake Forest	0	0	1.11	2	0	6	5	5	1	2	5	.217
Hunter Elliott	So.	Mississippi	0	0	1.59	2	0	6	3	1	1	5	9	.222
Hurston Waldrep	Jr.	Florida	0	1	9.00	1	0	2	4	4	3	1	2	.364

For players who played for multiple teams: 1: Stats with first team. 2: Stats with second team. 3: Stats with third team. T: combined stats.

COURTESY ALYSA RUBIN

Cam Collier played for Cotuit before being a first-round pick in the 2022 MLB draft.

CAPE COD LEAGUE

East Division	W	L	T	PTS
Brewster Whitecaps	19	17	8	46
Yarmouth-Dennis Red Sox	19	17	8	46
Orleans Firebirds	18	22	4	40
Harwich Mariners	17	21	6	40
Chatham Anglers	15	20	9	39
West Division	**W**	**L**	**T**	**PTS**
Bourne Braves	23	14	7	53
Cotuit Kettleers	23	16	5	51
Hyannis Harbor Hawks	22	16	6	50
Falmouth Commodores	19	21	4	42
Wareham Gatemen	13	24	7	331

CHAMPIONSHIP: Bourne Braves defeated Brewster Whitecaps, 2-0, in best-of-three championship series.

TOP 50 PROSPECTS:

1. Matt Shaw, Bourne, 2B (Maryland, 2023 Eligible).
2. Tommy Troy, Cotuit, SS (Stanford, 2023 Eligible).
3. Mitch Jebb, Hyannis, 3B (Michigan State, 2023 Eligible).
4. Cole Carrigg, Yarmouth-Dennis, SS/OF/P (San Diego State, 2023 Eligible).
5. Marcus Brown, Chatham, SS (Oklahoma State, 2023 Eligible).
6. Grant Taylor, Brewster, RHP (LSU, 2023 Eligible).
7. Bryce Warrecker, Orleans, RHP (Cal Poly, 2023 Draft Eligible).
8. Travis Honeyman, Orleans, OF (Boston College, 2023 Eligible).
9. Braden Montgomery, Yarmouth-Dennis, OF/P (Stanford, 2024 Eligible).
10. Juaron Watts-Brown, Falmouth, RHP (Okla. State, 2023 Eligible).
11. Carson DeMartini, Brewster, SS (Virginia Tech, 2024 Eligible).
12. Luke Keaschall, Orleans, OF (Arizona State, 2023 Eligible).
13. Mike Sirota, Hyannis, OF (Northeastern, 2024 Eligible).
14. Jackson Baumeister, Hyannis, RHP (Florida State, 2023 Eligible).
15. Gage Ziehl, Harwich, RHP (Miami, 2024 Eligible).
16. Roman Kimball, Chatham, RHP (South Carolina, 2024 Eligible).
17. Nick Goodwin, Harwich, SS (Kansas State, 2023 Eligible).
18. Kade Morris, Cotuit, RHP (Nevada, 2023 Eligible).
19. Magdiel Cotto, Hyannis, LHP (Kentucky, 2023 Eligible).
20. Brock Wilken, Harwich, 3B (Wake Forest, 2023 Eligible).
21. Jonathan Santucci, Harwich, RHP (Duke, 2024 Eligible).
22. Ben Hampton, Chatham, LHP (West Virginia, 2023 Eligible).
23. Liam Sullivan, Harwich, LHP (Georgia, 2023 Eligible).
24. Alex Mooney, Falmouth, SS (Duke, 2023 Eligible).
25. Luke Shliger, Yarmouth-Dennis, C (Maryland, 2023 Eligible).
26. Teddy McGraw, Brewster, RHP (Wake Forest, 2023 Eligible).
27. Jay Driver, Hyannis, RHP (Harvard, 2023 Eligible).
28. Ryan Lasko, Brewster, OF (Rutgers, 2023 Eligible).
29. Nolan Schanuel, Hyannis, 1B (Florida Atlantic, 2023 Eligible).
30. Ben Hess, Falmouth, RHP (Alabama, 2024 Eligible).
31. Levi Wells, Falmouth, RHP (Texas State, 2023 Eligible)
32. Alejandro Rosario, Hyannis, RHP (Miami, 2023 Eligible).
33. Homer Bush Jr., Yarmouth-Dennis, OF (Grand Canyon, 2023 Eligible).
34. Sean Sullivan, Harwich, LHP (Wake Forest, 2024 Eligible).
35. Kevin Sim, Orleans, 3B (San Diego, 2023 Eligible).
36. Peyton Stovall, Falmouth, 2B (Arkansas, 2024 Eligible).
37. Ty Langenberg, Hyannis, RHP (Iowa, 2023 Eligible).
38. C.J. Kayfus, Cotuit, 1B (Miami, 2023 Eligible).
39. Ethan O'Donnell, Harwich, OF (Virginia, 2023 Eligible).
40. Cooper Ingle, Chatham, C (Clemson, 2023 Eligible).
41. Carter Trice, Cotuit, OF (North Carolina State, 2023 Eligible).
42. Caleb Lomavita, Cotuit, C (California, 2024 Eligible).
43. Luke Jewett, Yarmouth-Dennis, RHP (UCLA, 2023 Eligible).
44. Owen Diodati, Wareham, OF (Oregon, 2023 Eligible).
45. Max Anderson, Wareham, 3B (Nebraska, 2023 Eligible).
46. Colby Halter, Falmouth, 3B (Florida, 2023 Eligible).
47. Mike Boeve, Yarmouth-Dennis, 3B (Omaha-Nebraska, 2023 Eligible).
48. Ty Cummings, Bourne, RHP (Campbell, 2023 Eligible).
49. Dominic Pitelli, Hyannis, SS (Miami, 2023 Eligible).
50. Rikuu Nishida, Hyannis, 2B (Oregon, 2023 Eligible).

INDIVIDUAL BATTING LEADERS

	AVG	AB	R	H	2B	3B	HR	RBI	SB
Matt Shaw, Braves	.360	136	28	49	10	2	5	19	21
Mitch Jebb, Harbor Hawks	.356	149	40	53	8	3	2	22	26
Cole Carrigg, Red Sox	.329	143	20	47	5	1	1	19	15
Matt Anderson, Gatemen	.312	173	17	54	7	0	2	17	1
Tommy Troy, Kettleers	.310	113	19	35	6	2	5	20	5
Colby Halter, Commodores	.307	140	22	43	7	0	7	19	12
Evan Sleight, Braves	.306	111	17	34	5	0	2	13	1
Rikuu Nishida, Harbor Hawks	.291	117	25	34	3	0	0	11	28
Connor Brito, Braves	.286	140	21	40	14	0	5	22	4
Michael Boeve, Red Sox	.275	102	18	28	6	0	0	7	3

INDIVIDUAL PITCHING LEADERS

Player, Team	W	L	ERA	G	SV	IP	H	BB	SO
Brennan Oxford, Whitecaps	2	0	0.44	13	1	20	12	9	23
Cam Schuelke, Kettleers	5	0	0.81	11	3	22	16	7	19
Cam Weston, Gatemen	4	0	0.84	7	2	21	14	5	21
Roman Kimball, Anglers	2	0	0.90	5	0	20	7	14	28
Chase Jeter, Commodores	0	1	1.05	8	1	26	24	5	19
Zachary Voelker, Harbor Hawks	1	2	1.42	9	0	25	20	6	16
Ryan Ure, Whitecaps	1	1	1.50	8	0	24	16	4	18
Jason Savino, Mariners	3	0	1.59	10	1	28	19	9	38
Jared Lyons, Red Sox	3	1	1.84	6	0	29	16	13	33
Seth Keener, Braves	2	0	1.88	7	0	24	18	8	21

BOURNE

Batting	AVG	AB	R	H	2B	3B	HR	RBI	SB
Conor Brito	.286	140	21	40	14	0	5	22	4
Brendan Cumming	.125	16	1	2	0	0	1	3	0
Jack Duffy	.324	68	9	22	3	0	1	7	3
Bryce Eblin	.238	105	12	25	1	0	0	6	9
Ryan Enos	.333	33	6	11	2	0	1	4	4
Alan Espinal	.193	57	3	11	1	0	1	5	1
Lane Forsythe	.111	9	3	1	0	0	0	0	3
Tomas Frick	.128	47	3	6	0	1	0	1	1
Dakota Harris	.234	47	3	11	1	1	0	2	2
Wyatt Henseler	.209	91	10	19	1	1	0	8	0
Mac Horvath	.250	72	13	18	1	0	6	15	8
Jack Hurley	.286	21	1	6	2	0	0	2	1
Carson Jones	.184	49	6	9	2	1	1	9	5
Joshua Kuroda-Grauer	.286	7	2	2	0	0	0	1	0
Ryan Leitch	.074	27	1	2	1	0	0	0	0
Nadir Lewis	.000	9	0	0	0	0	0	1	0
Brennan Milone	.174	23	5	4	0	0	0	3	0
Joshua Moylan	.159	82	7	13	1	0	3	11	0
Elijhah Nunez	.143	21	4	3	0	0	0	2	2
John Peck	.195	123	13	24	4	2	0	11	8
Ryan Proto	.250	12	1	3	0	0	0	3	1
Carson Roccaforte	.182	77	5	14	2	1	0	3	7
Matt Shaw	.360	136	28	49	10	2	5	19	21
Evan Sleight	.306	111	17	34	5	0	2	13	1
Jared Sprague-Lott	.400	10	1	4	0	0	0	0	0
Nelson Taylor	.188	16	2	3	0	0	1	4	0

Pitching	W	L	ERA	G	SV	IP	H	BB	SO
Robb Adams	1	0	2.40	5	0	15	13	6	11
Anthony Arguelles	0	1	1.76	4	0	15	7	9	19
Nigel Belgrave	3	0	3.14	11	3	14	11	7	10
Sam Bello	0	0	4.26	3	0	6	5	3	4
Nelson Berkwich	1	0	1.96	5	0	18	11	4	18
Cade Boxrucker	1	0	2.00	7	0	27	19	16	20
Cameron Bye	0	0	1.42	10	0	19	18	7	16
Ty Cummings	1	0	0.53	10	4	17	15	5	16
Bryce Cunningham	0	3	4.56	6	0	26	18	12	25
Matt Duffy	1	0	0.00	4	2	8	1	1	8
Garrett Edwards	2	0	2.13	3	0	13	12	3	9
Ryan Fischer	1	2	3.58	8	0	28	25	13	32
Hunter Furtado	0	1	5.06	5	0	21	22	5	19
Kade Grundy	3	1	2.16	9	0	25	20	9	25
Seth Keener	2	0	1.88	7	0	24	18	8	21
Hunter Loyd	0	2	4.50	3	0	12	14	2	5
Mason Pelio	2	0	3.97	6	0	11	12	7	13
Will Sandy	2	1	4.34	7	0	19	18	7	13
Cregg Scherrer	0	0	2.25	4	0	8	7	6	7
Reese Sharp	0	0	7.56	5	0	8	7	8	11
Adam Tulloch	0	1	4.86	4	0	17	15	12	18
Tyler Vogel	2	0	0.84	6	0	11	4	5	9
Justin Willis	0	1	7.27	6	1	9	6	5	7

BREWSTER

Batting	AVG	AB	R	H	2B	3B	HR	RBI	SB
Chase Adkison	.229	48	5	11	2	1	0	3	1
Dixon Black	.130	23	2	3	2	0	0	1	1
Logan Bravo	.222	90	13	20	6	0	0	7	2
Kurtis Byrne	.255	94	9	24	8	0	3	21	0
Carson DeMartini	.248	109	22	27	5	1	2	15	15
Davis Diaz	.217	83	14	18	0	0	3	8	3
Cameron Fisher	.227	66	13	15	4	1	4	11	2
Alex Freeland	.256	90	15	23	4	0	5	12	6
Fritz Genther	.056	18	0	1	0	0	0	0	0
Dylan Goldstein	.375	16	2	6	2	0	0	4	1
Parks Harber	.221	95	4	21	3	0	0	6	0
Kevin Keister	.206	34	3	7	1	0	1	4	0
Ryan Lasko	.239	113	16	27	0	2	0	5	13
Cameron Leary	.105	19	2	2	0	0	0	1	1
Nick Lorusso	.379	29	5	11	4	0	0	6	0
David Mendham	.212	99	10	21	3	0	0	10	1
Brennan Milone	.233	43	7	10	1	0	1	4	3
Joaquin Monque	.167	6	0	1	0	0	0	1	0
Caleb Pendelton	.111	9	0	1	0	0	0	0	0
Savier Pinales	.100	10	1	1	0	0	0	0	0
Dylan Rogers	.100	10	0	1	0	0	0	0	0
Michael Sirota	.250	24	3	6	1	0	0	1	1
Grayson Tatrow	.230	122	11	28	7	1	0	18	8
Javier Vaz	.273	55	4	15	3	0	0	6	7
Trevor Werner	.304	23	3	7	0	0	0	3	2

Pitching	W	L	ERA	G	SV	IP	H	BB	SO
Matthew Bedford	0	1	5.79	5	0	9	11	3	7
Ryan Chasse	0	1	1.23	9	3	15	5	12	27
Joe Cinnella	0	0	0.00	1	0	2	1	0	2
Patrick Copen	0	1	5.79	7	2	9	12	6	11
Brian Fitzpatrick	2	0	0.00	4	0	19	11	2	19
Paul Gervase	1	0	1.59	7	0	11	5	9	18
Will Greer	0	0	6.00	3	0	6	4	2	9
Grant Kipp	0	0	1.35	3	0	7	4	1	10
Cade Kuehler	0	0	0.00	2	0	7	4	3	7
Henry Leake	1	1	3.65	3	0	12	14	4	15
Carson Liggett	0	1	4.12	7	0	20	14	9	19
Ryan Lobus	1	0	2.84	4	0	6	7	5	5
Joseph Mancini	1	0	4.15	4	0	17	14	4	20
Teddy McGraw	1	1	3.27	2	0	11	9	4	12
Zane Morehouse	1	2	5.25	5	0	24	28	9	23
Jackson Nezuh	2	2	6.20	8	0	20	17	12	25
Hunter Owen	1	1	3.24	5	0	8	7	5	7
Brennan Oxford	2	0	0.44	13	1	20	12	9	23
Ryan Packard	0	0	2.16	6	0	8	10	5	9
Braxton Pearson	0	0	2.50	13	1	18	17	3	23
Liam Simon	1	0	4.05	3	0	13	13	6	11
Colton Sundloff	0	0	8.59	7	1	7	6	8	8
Grant Taylor	1	1	2.14	5	0	21	15	2	30
Heston Tole	0	0	3.09	4	0	12	16	8	5
Ryan Ure	1	1	1.50	8	0	24	16	4	18
Najer Victor	0	2	11.81	3	0	5	6	5	4
George Welch	1	1	3.52	4	0	8	8	1	8
John West	1	0	2.00	4	0	9	9	1	4

CHATHAM

Batting	AVG	AB	R	H	2B	3B	HR	RBI	SB
Marcus Brown	.236	144	20	34	7	1	0	13	9

Will Butcher	.267	15	2	4	1	0	1	1	0
Johnny Castagnozzi	.164	55	6	9	1	0	1	2	2
Thomas Caufield	.154	26	0	4	0	0	0	2	0
Mitchell Daly	.185	27	5	5	1	0	0	5	0
Jake DeLeo	.248	121	16	30	5	1	4	14	9
Guy Garibay Jr.	.212	99	13	21	5	0	5	19	5
Caden Grice	.213	127	14	27	7	0	4	11	0
Adonys Herrera	.192	26	1	5	0	0	0	1	0
Matthew Hogan	.220	41	9	9	2	0	0	1	8
Kaden Hopson	.056	18	0	1	1	0	0	0	0
Cooper Ingle	.252	119	18	30	5	0	1	8	3
Chuck Ingram	.113	71	6	8	2	0	0	6	0
Noah Ledford	.163	43	2	7	1	0	2	5	1
Aidan Meola	.100	10	0	1	0	0	0	0	0
Lyle Miller-Green	.196	46	10	9	0	0	3	7	1
Nate Nankil	.269	26	0	7	1	0	0	0	2
Anthony Nunez	.190	42	5	8	1	0	1	5	0
Roc Riggio	.200	115	16	23	3	2	3	19	6
Nelson Rivera	.188	16	4	3	0	0	1	1	0
Jack Rubensteub	.241	29	4	7	2	0	1	5	0
Dominic Tamez	.163	43	4	7	2	0	0	3	0
Hayden Travinski	.162	37	3	6	2	0	1	3	0
Alex Ulloa	.077	13	3	1	0	0	0	1	0
Paul Winland Jr.	.077	13	0	1	0	0	0	1	1

Pitching	W	L	ERA	G	SV	IP	H	BB	SO
Connor Bovair	0	0	2.25	5	0	8	8	3	8
Cam Brown	0	2	7.00	4	0	9	12	9	11
William Carsten	0	1	4.70	2	0	8	7	3	2
Cade Citelli	0	0	4.26	2	0	6	6	0	6
Hayden Durke	0	1	20.25	1	0	1	4	1	2
Magnus Ellerts	1	0	2.84	4	1	13	9	8	21
Wyatt Evans	1	3	5.89	6	0	18	19	10	20
Caden Grice	0	0	0.00	4	0	11	3	5	13
Ben Hampton	0	2	2.32	11	2	43	32	4	49
Brian Hendry	0	0	2.70	3	0	3	1	2	6
Brian Holiday	1	0	2.28	13	2	24	17	11	31
Labarron Johnson	1	1	14.73	6	0	7	12	6	9
Roman Kimball	2	0	0.90	5	0	20	7	14	28
PJ Labriola	1	0	1.93	2	0	5	3	3	4
Trevor Martin	0	1	5.63	3	0	8	8	5	12
Alex McFarlane	1	0	0.71	5	0	13	7	5	16
Joe Miller	1	2	3.77	4	1	14	12	4	17
Tommy Molsky	1	0	5.40	5	0	10	10	4	13
Cy Nielson	2	0	1.98	4	0	14	8	7	17
Ben Peterson	0	0	5.52	5	0	15	22	2	17
Nicholas Regalado	0	1	4.18	6	0	24	16	18	28
Carlos Rey	0	2	5.57	10	2	21	17	18	25
Owen Stevenson	2	0	3.10	4	0	20	17	3	12
Chris Villaman	0	1	2.94	4	0	15	10	9	12
Jacob Watters	0	0	3.00	2	0	6	1	6	9
Carson Whisenhunt	1	3	7.88	4	0	16	16	6	21
Ricky Williams	0	0	2.84	4	0	6	4	6	8

COTUIT

Batting	AVG	AB	R	H	2B	3B	HR	RBI	SB
Brooks Baldwin	.361	97	8	35	5	2	1	14	11
Enrique Bradfield	.194	36	5	7	0	0	0	3	4
Zachary Cole	.161	56	8	9	1	1	1	6	0
Cameron Collier	.217	23	2	5	0	0	0	1	0
Trotter Harlan	.283	53	11	15	3	0	1	11	2
Calvin Harris	.269	52	5	14	1	0	1	2	0
Tyler Johnson	.265	98	12	26	7	0	7	19	1
Kyle Karros	.157	51	5	8	0	0	0	2	0
CJ Kayfus	.302	96	7	29	2	0	1	14	1
Kade Kern	.146	41	7	6	1	0	0	3	4
Caleb Ketchup	.125	32	1	4	0	0	0	1	2
Caleb Lomavita	.316	76	13	24	5	0	1	5	1
Justin Miknis	.163	49	4	8	1	0	2	7	0
Eddie Park	.284	81	13	23	2	0	0	7	5
Graham Pauley	.192	26	4	5	1	0	0	1	4
Josh Pearson	.182	55	6	10	2	0	1	5	1
Ryan Ritter	.262	65	9	17	6	0	3	11	1
Sam Ruta	.250	24	3	6	2	0	0	5	0
Cody Schrier	.143	7	0	1	0	0	0	0	0
Victor Scott II	.173	52	11	9	2	1	1	4	11
Chandler Simpson	.455	44	11	20	3	0	0	1	8
Carter Trice	.237	114	23	27	6	0	5	15	1
Tommy Troy	.310	113	19	35	6	2	5	20	5
Colby Wilkerson	.222	27	3	6	2	0	0	3	0
Peyton Williams	.100	10	1	1	0	0	1	3	0

Pitching	W	L	ERA	G	SV	IP	H	BB	SO
Tyler Bosma	0	0	1.69	4	0	16	13	9	14
Adam Boucher	0	1	6.46	7	0	15	11	18	16
TJ Brock	0	1	2.16	8	4	8	3	2	15
Daniel Brooks	0	1	3.13	9	0	23	14	15	25
Ryan Bruno	0	0	0.00	4	2	3	3	0	7
Zach Chappell	0	1	5.56	8	0	11	12	8	5
Ethan Chenault	1	0	0.00	3	0	8	2	1	6
Harrison Cohen	3	3	2.78	9	0	36	33	11	25
Isaiah Coupet	2	0	0.87	4	0	10	5	2	8
Joseph Gieg	1	1	3.00	9	1	18	12	6	14
Kenya Huggins	1	0	1.50	2	0	6	4	4	8
Will Jacobsen	2	0	2.86	11	0	22	17	8	20
Ben Johnson	0	1	2.11	9	0	21	18	13	18
Ty Johnson	0	3	4.99	9	0	22	15	15	19
Matt Joyce	0	1	7.20	2	0	5	8	1	7
Jackson Kelley	2	0	0.56	5	1	16	11	2	25
Christian Little	1	1	6.94	5	0	12	13	5	13
Mark McLaughlin	0	0	6.23	4	0	4	4	5	5
Cole McNamee	1	0	8.44	3	0	5	7	5	7
Max Meier	0	0	11.57	8	0	9	17	6	7
Ethan Mishra	0	0	6.00	1	0	3	4	2	2
Kade Morris	1	0	1.08	3	0	17	11	6	9
Jaylen Paden	0	0	5.40	6	0	7	4	10	4
William Privette	2	0	1.74	6	0	10	7	5	13
Dalton Rogers	0	0	5.68	2	0	6	1	3	8
Cam Schuelke	5	0	0.81	11	3	22	16	7	19
Noah Short	0	1	32.40	3	0	2	5	3	1
Chris Stuart	1	0	6.75	2	0	1	1	1	2
Carson Swilling	0	1	8.03	6	0	12	12	10	6
Cameron Wagoner	0	0	7.20	7	0	10	13	4	13
Joseph Whitman	0	0	1.59	2	0	6	4	2	5

FALMOUTH

Batting	AVG	AB	R	H	2B	3B	HR	RBI	SB
Maui Ahuna	.167	24	0	4	0	0	0	2	0
Jace Bohrofen	.281	57	10	16	5	2	2	9	5
Luke Boyers	.111	45	4	5	1	0	0	0	0
Drew Brutcher	.264	125	17	33	8	0	3	15	3
Travis Chestnut	.276	29	10	8	1	0	0	1	6
Corey Collins	.165	79	1	13	6	0	1	4	0
Jacob Cozart	.135	52	6	7	1	0	0	2	1
Josiah Cromwick	.183	60	3	11	1	0	0	5	0
Angelo D'Ancunto	.077	13	0	1	1	0	0	0	0
Cross Factor	.129	31	3	4	2	0	0	1	1
Colby Halter	.307	140	22	43	7	0	7	19	12
Tafton Hensley	.143	7	1	1	0	0	0	1	0
Justin Jordan	.400	5	1	2	0	0	0	1	1
Kodie Kolden	.400	5	0	2	0	0	0	0	0
Anthony MacKenzie	.241	79	8	19	4	0	1	8	3
Alex Mooney	.261	176	24	46	7	1	5	19	14
Daniel Neri	.154	26	2	4	0	0	0	3	0
Jackson Nicklaus	.042	24	2	1	0	0	0	2	0
Jack Payton	.250	20	2	5	0	1	0	4	0
Andrew Pinckney	.240	121	24	29	5	2	4	16	11
Patrick Roche	.000	5	2	0	0	0	0	0	0
Kyle Russell	.000	10	0	0	0	0	0	1	0
Eddie Saldivar	.133	15	0	2	0	0	0	0	0
Peyton Stovall	.250	76	12	19	2	0	2	11	1
Brayden Taylor	.242	33	8	8	1	0	3	6	1
Jacob Walsh	.203	143	13	29	5	0	5	16	0

Pitching	W	L	ERA	G	SV	IP	H	BB	SO
Philip Abner	3	0	1.93	8	0	28	22	13	20
George Arias	0	0	4.50	2	0	2	2	1	2
Matthew Bohnert	0	0	0.00	1	0	2	0	4	2
Ike Buxton	0	0	7.20	2	0	5	9	5	5
AJ Causey	0	0	0.00	4	0	4	3	0	5
Garrett Coe	1	0	3.93	11	0	18	23	9	15
Kaleb Corbett	0	1	9.64	12	0	14	21	10	18
Cole Cressend	0	0	10.80	2	0	2	4	2	1
Anthony DeFabbia	0	1	0.00	2	0	5	2	3	5
Evan Harmon	0	0	8.31	4	0	4	6	9	0
Josh Hartle	1	1	2.65	4	0	17	18	0	13
Ben Hess	0	0	1.64	3	0	11	7	5	15
Grayson Hitt	0	1	4.36	6	0	21	21	10	25
Antoine Jean	0	1	10.80	1	0	3	5	1	1
Chase Jeter	0	1	1.05	8	1	26	24	5	19
Will Johnston	0	1	5.65	5	0	14	11	9	14
Luke Malone	2	2	14.00	6	0	9	17	3	4
Brayden Matthews	2	0	3.00	5	0	9	9	2	7
Jakob Meyer	0	0	4.15	2	0	4	3	2	7
Camden Minacci	0	0	4.70	5	0	8	5	0	11
Carson Montgomery	0	0	0.00	1	0	4	3	1	4
Nolan Morr	2	0	3.12	5	0	9	6	3	8
Tyler Mudd	0	0	0.00	1	0	1	0	0	0
Jake Peppers	0	2	5.87	5	0	8	5	8	8
Joshua Roberge	0	4	7.00	5	0	18	18	11	22
Cole Roland	0	0	3.60	1	0	5	4	3	3
Joey Ryan	0	0	1.69	13	3	16	14	3	19
Ryan SLater	1	0	2.35	8	0	15	15	3	16
Drew Sommers	1	0	0.00	6	0	16	10	3	20
Josh Stewart	1	0	0.55	11	2	16	8	3	20
Mikey Tepper	0	1	4.85	9	0	13	14	6	15
Juaron Watts-Brown	3	3	3.71	8	0	34	26	15	45
Levi Wills	2	2	2.08	10	3	17	10	8	22

HARWICH

Batting	AVG	AB	R	H	2B	3B	HR	RBI	SB
Bryan Arendt	.172	29	6	5	1	0	0	6	0
Pres Cavenaugh	.170	47	4	8	3	0	0	2	2
Danny Corona	.214	14	1	3	1	0	0	1	0
Chase Engelhard	.222	18	4	4	0	1	1	4	1
Jake Gelof	.087	23	1	2	0	0	0	0	0
Nick Goodwin	.268	149	29	40	10	1	6	22	4
Gino Groover	.222	27	2	6	0	0	0	0	0
Mac Guscette	.153	59	6	9	2	0	0	4	0
William Hamiter	.274	62	9	17	4	0	0	5	0
Kalae Harrison	.278	54	9	15	0	0	0	4	2
Cole Harting	.130	69	9	9	0	0	1	4	1
Kenny Levari	.204	49	3	10	2	0	1	5	0
Tatem Levins	.167	30	2	5	1	0	0	3	0
Ryan McCarty	.200	25	3	5	0	0	1	3	1
Bradley Mutz	.000	4	0	0	0	0	0	0	0
Chris Newell	.289	45	8	13	1	1	3	6	4
Ethan O'Donnell	.314	51	10	16	4	0	0	7	2
Hunter Pasqualini	.000	3	0	0	0	0	0	0	0
Graham Pauley	.333	21	2	7	0	0	0	2	1
Jonathan Santucci	.188	32	4	6	2	0	1	3	0
Tommy Seidl	.230	135	20	31	6	2	4	17	13
David Smith	.200	70	9	14	0	0	0	3	5
Hunter Stokely	.187	75	12	14	5	0	2	17	0
Kyle Teel	.125	24	3	3	1	0	0	1	0
Joe Vetrano	.243	140	19	34	4	0	5	30	1
Brock Wilken	.229	109	17	25	5	0	5	15	0

Pitching	W	L	ERA	G	SV	IP	H	BB	SO
Luke Benneche	1	0	4.50	5	0	14	13	9	15
Drew Conover	0	0	1.50	12	3	18	10	5	18
Jacob Edwards	2	1	4.50	5	0	12	17	3	13
German Fajardo	0	2	12.46	2	0	4.1	6	4	4
Sean Hard	0	0	9.00	1	0	1	2	1	2
Garrett Harker	0	0	4.36	8	0	10.1	10	5	14
Karl Hartman	0	1	5.40	4	0	8.1	8	12	15
Hunter Hodges	0	1	2.25	10	3	12	5	10	21
Cameron Mayer	2	1	3.74	8	0	21.2	27	10	23
Jake Neuman	0	0	0.00	2	0	3.2	4	2	2
Jack Pawloski	1	0	0.00	2	0	4.1	4	0	3
Gerry Peacock	0	0	9.00	1	0	1	1	0	0
Zane Probst	1	0	3.09	9	1	23.1	23	11	20
Blake Purnell	1	1	4.38	9	0	12.1	15	5	12
Carlson Reed	1	3	9.39	7	0	23	23	24	31
Eric Reyzelman	1	1	1.69	2	0	10.2	5	5	11
Andrew Ronne	0	0	8.68	4	0	9.1	13	6	10
Jonathan Santucci	0	2	3.65	6	0	24.2	20	10	28
Joe Savino	3	0	1.59	11	1	28.1	19	9	38
Wyatt Scotti	0	2	23.40	3	0	5	14	3	3
Billy Seidl	0	1	3.86	4	0	16.1	10	12	16
Teddy Sharkey	0	0	6.00	7	0	9	11	2	5
Liam Sullivan	2	1	2.17	8	1	29	26	8	45
Sean Sullivan	1	1	3.86	7	0	28	22	9	29
Danny Wilkinson	0	0	0.00	3	0	6.1	0	1	15
Jaden Woods	0	1	8.44	3	1	5.1	7	1	6
Griffin Young	0	1	0.00	1	0	2.2	1	1	3
Gage Ziehl	1	0	2.35	7	0	23	15	6	31

HYANNIS

Batting	AVG	AB	R	H	2B	3B	HR	RBI	SB
Jacob Cambell	.233	60	6	14	3	0	0	4	1
Jorge Corona	.128	39	3	5	0	0	0	2	0
Brendan Cumming	.167	12	3	2	1	0	0	4	0
Drew Ehrhard	.292	24	2	7	0	0	0	2	1
Tito Flores	.227	110	17	25	4	0	2	9	2
AJ Guerrero	.000	10	0	0	0	0	0	1	0
Alex Haba	.143	7	1	1	0	0	0	0	0
Justin Janas	.307	88	12	27	5	1	0	10	0
Mitch Jebb	.356	149	40	53	8	3	2	22	26
Philip Matulia	.174	69	15	12	1	0	2	8	4
Cole McConnell	.264	144	15	38	5	0	3	22	11
Christian Moore	.176	74	6	13	2	1	0	8	1
Rikuu Nishida	.291	117	25	34	3	0	0	11	28
Rocco Peppi	.194	72	7	14	1	1	3	13	2
Dominic Pitelli	.252	119	16	30	5	0	3	12	11
Jackson Ross	.250	4	1	1	0	0	0	0	0
Ildefonso Ruiz	.191	89	10	17	3	0	1	7	0
Nolan Schanuel	.200	125	16	25	4	1	1	11	4
Caleb Shpur	.273	11	2	3	0	0	0	0	0
Michael Sirota	.339	62	12	21	2	2	2	14	4
Tyler Wulfert	.125	8	0	1	1	0	0	1	0

Pitching	W	L	ERA	G	SV	IP	H	BB	SO
Jordy Allard	4	0	0.49	12	2	18	6	4	21
Austin Amaral	0	1	6.53	8	0	21	27	7	15
Thomas Balboni	0	1	18.00	2	0	2	5	0	0
Jackson Baumiester	0	1	4.29	6	0	21	17	10	30
Jonathan Bautista	0	0	2.25	2	0	4	1	2	3
Jake Berry	3	0	2.66	7	0	24	15	9	20
Wes Burton	1	0	5.87	8	0	8	7	13	8
Chase Centala	0	0	4.00	5	2	9	11	3	9
Magdiel Cotto	2	1	2.67	9	0	27	24	12	29
Jay Driver	2	3	4.56	11	1	24	21	9	39
Jackson Emus	0	0	0.53	13	0	17	11	7	21
Jonathan Fincher	0	1	4.97	3	0	13	17	1	9
Ty Good	1	0	2.03	3	0	13	6	7	14
Ethan Hammerberg	2	0	1.93	9	0	14	10	7	9
Ty Langenberg	1	2	3.38	12	4	21	23	4	33
Brandon Llewellyn	0	0	9.82	2	0	4	6	2	2
Brody McCullough	0	0	2.70	5	0	20	10	8	30
Brandon Neeck	0	0	5.40	5	0	5	3	6	4
Connor O'Halloran	1	0	7.82	7	0	13	10	9	17
Tommy O'Rourke	0	2	6.91	7	0	14	21	9	14
Isaiah Rhodes	0	0	1.86	7	0	10	14	4	15
Alejandro Rosario	1	0	1.74	3	0	10	8	1	13

Ryan Steinhauer	1	0	7.36	2	0	4	3	2	2
Austin Strickland	2	2	4.05	10	0	27	26	9	31
Holland Townes	0	0	0.00	2	0	4	2	2	3
Zachary Voelker	1	2	1.42	9	0	25	20	6	16

ORLEANS

Batting	AVG	AB	R	H	2B	3B	HR	RBI	SB
Diego Baqueiro	.067	15	1	1	0	0	0	0	0
Logan Beard	.138	58	6	8	2	1	0	2	1
Jack Bulger	.250	88	13	22	3	0	0	7	10
Connor Burns	.204	54	5	11	0	0	3	7	0
Jake Cunningham	.174	23	2	4	1	0	0	2	0
Nate Furman	.306	98	8	30	4	1	0	8	2
Garret Guillemette	.188	80	7	15	4	0	2	12	0
Travis Honeyman	.289	83	14	24	8	0	4	10	4
Tommy Hopfe	.005	20	1	1	0	0	0	1	0
Isaac Humphrey	.265	113	14	30	3	0	1	10	3
Cam Jones	.341	82	9	28	4	0	0	8	1
Luke Keaschall	.267	165	17	44	6	0	5	20	5
Austin Knight	.172	58	5	10	1	0	0	3	0
Bennett Lee	.219	32	4	7	1	1	1	3	0
Nik McClaughry	.133	75	8	10	1	0	0	6	1
Drew Metzdorf	.419	31	3	13	1	0	0	7	2
Garrett Pennington	.111	18	0	2	0	0	0	0	0
Brock Rodden	.133	15	0	2	0	0	0	1	1
Kevin Sim	.239	92	9	22	2	0	5	9	1
Jacob Stinson	.169	89	11	15	2	0	0	8	1
JD Urso	.193	57	3	11	2	0	0	3	0
Jacob Wilson	.278	36	4	10	1	0	1	4	0

Pitching	W	L	ERA	G	SV	IP	H	BB	SO
Josh Allen	2	1	4.87	12	0	20	21	11	17
Alex Amalfi	0	1	4.24	5	0	17	17	7	19
AJ Blubaugh	0	0	0.00	8	4	9	2	0	13
Ryan Bourassa	1	0	2.25	8	2	8	4	3	16
Kyle Carr	1	2	3.57	7	0	23	21	9	21
Chris Clark	0	3	5.40	14	3	22	22	10	24
Sam Conte	0	1	4.50	6	0	10	8	3	11
Donye Evans	1	2	2.82	6	0	22	12	9	23
Gray Harrison	0	1	2.31	4	0	12	7	3	7
Tommy Hopfe	3	1	3.42	14	1	24	25	6	23
Cam Jones	1	0	2.20	8	0	16	15	5	14
Collin Kramer	2	0	0.00	3	0	7	2	1	6
Wyatt Loncar	0	2	6.30	5	0	10	16	7	11
Cooper McKeehan	0	0	0.00	5	0	10	2	1	13
Patrick Reilly	0	3	4.26	6	0	25	18	19	20
Cole Reynolds	0	0	6.56	12	0	23	26	11	24
Ryan Rissas	0	0	3.48	8	0	10	6	9	5
Ben Shields	3	1	2.73	9	1	30	18	13	29
Cole Stallings	0	1	3.68	10	0	15	17	11	16
Shane Telfer	0	2	5.40	9	0	13	13	5	14
Cam Walty	0	0	3.86	6	0	7	9	2	9
Bryce Warrecker	4	1	2.08	10	0	39	26	8	35

WAREHAM

Batting	AVG	AB	R	H	2B	3B	HR	RBI	SB
Max Anderson	.312	173	17	54	7	0	2	17	1
Devin Burkes	.258	31	2	8	0	0	0	3	0
Peter Burns	.205	39	9	8	0	0	0	4	0
Ryan Campos	.242	128	17	31	4	0	2	11	3
Cameron Chick	.120	25	3	3	1	0	0	0	1
Kellum Clark	.264	72	10	19	5	0	0	6	2
Termayne Cobb Jr.	.143	7	1	1	0	0	0	0	0
Chase Davis	.212	52	11	11	2	0	0	2	0
Owen Diodati	.344	61	10	21	2	1	3	12	0
Cole Elvis	.400	10	2	4	1	0	0	2	0
Ty Evans	.273	22	4	6	0	0	1	4	1
Deric Fabian	.211	90	11	19	2	0	1	7	5
Ian Farrow	.143	28	1	4	1	0	0	3	0
Carter Graham	.200	75	6	15	1	0	2	5	0
Jack Housinger	.209	91	7	19	4	0	0	7	2
Cam Meyer	.188	16	0	3	0	1	0	4	0
Torin Montgomery	.280	25	3	7	1	0	1	4	0
Brian Morrell	.292	24	0	7	0	0	0	2	0
Connor O'Brien	.105	19	1	2	0	0	0	0	0
Bryan Padilla	.138	65	7	9	0	0	1	4	0
Michael Robertson	.063	16	2	1	1	0	0	1	2
Alan Roden	.212	66	5	14	5	0	0	6	1
William Rogers	.182	33	5	6	2	0	1	6	0
Caden Rose	.067	15	3	1	0	0	0	0	0
Hogan Windish	.265	113	18	30	9	0	3	20	0
Blake Wright	.206	107	13	22	3	0	1	13	1

Pitching	W	L	ERA	G	SV	IP	H	BB	SO
Bobby Alcock	1	2	7.36	6	0	11	9	10	7
Luke Benneche	2	1	7.00	4	0	9	13	2	10
Jonathan Brand	1	1	2.57	5	0	21	17	2	21
Jacob Cravey	0	3	3.08	7	0	26	28	10	26
Jackson Fristoe	0	0	11.12	4	0	6	5	8	3
Alex Galvan	0	1	6.40	10	2	13	22	1	7
Ryan Hagenow	0	0	15.00	2	0	3	4	6	4
Patrick Harrington	0	0	6.23	4	0	4	3	1	6
Nick Hoffman	2	0	3.60	3	0	10	10	0	4
Jack Housinger	0	0	3.86	3	0	2	2	1	0
Wyatt Hudepohl	0	2	6.11	9	0	18	21	11	11
Matt Jachec	0	2	5.06	5	0	21	28	4	19
Will Koger III	0	1	4.21	9	0	26	23	12	25
Timmy Manning	0	1	27.00	1	0	2	7	1	2
Nikolas Mazza	1	1	5.28	10	0	15	17	6	12
Grayson Moore	0	0	0.47	6	0	19	12	6	25
Will Rogers	0	0	2.25	2	0	4	1	2	6
Michael Sansone	0	2	3.94	6	0	30	26	1	34
Jack Sokol	0	1	9.72	3	0	8	10	7	6
Travis Sthele	0	1	9.00	6	0	12	18	7	14
Jack Sullivan	1	0	2.89	9	0	19	15	4	15
Eriq Swan	0	0	0.00	3	0	8	4	1	11
Cameron Wagoner	0	1	4.50	3	1	4	5	1	5
Michael Walsh	1	0	2.38	8	2	11	12	5	23
Cameron Weston	4	0	0.84	7	2	21	14	5	21
Joseph White	0	0	2.08	1	0	4	3	2	1
Jason Woodward	0	1	8.10	7	0	23	33	8	24
Brian Young	0	1	4.50	2	0	4	5	1	6

YARMOUTH-DENNIS

Batting	AVG	AB	R	H	2B	3B	HR	RBI	SB
Gunner Antillon	.231	26	1	6	1	0	0	1	0
Michael Boeve	.275	102	18	28	6	0	0	7	3
Drew Bowser	.136	22	0	3	0	0	0	1	0
Robbie Burnett	.182	11	0	2	0	0	0	0	0
Homer Bush Jr.	.284	102	19	29	2	0	0	9	10
Cole Carrigg	.329	143	20	47	5	1	1	19	15
Caden Connor	.257	140	20	36	8	2	0	11	1
Jack Costello	.270	37	4	10	0	0	1	4	0
Pascanel Ferrera	.111	45	5	5	2	0	2	6	0
Luke Franzoni	.216	37	5	8	2	0	2	8	1
Dominc Freeberger	.167	12	2	2	0	0	0	2	0
Fernando Gonzalez	.197	71	9	14	1	1	0	3	0
Gunner Gouldsmith	.240	25	1	6	0	0	0	2	0
Hunter Haas	.211	95	10	20	4	0	1	4	2
Woody Hadeen	.286	14	2	4	1	0	0	1	1
William Hamiter	.136	22	1	3	0	0	0	2	0
Kodie Kolden	.143	7	1	1	1	0	0	0	0
Zach Lew	.132	38	4	5	0	0	0	0	1
Jonathon Long	.210	105	12	22	3	0	5	21	1
Chase Meidroth	.286	63	9	18	3	0	1	7	3
Braden Montgomery	.250	60	12	15	1	1	4	19	0
Ryan Proto	.000	6	0	0	0	0	0	0	0
Simon Reid	.222	9	0	2	0	0	0	0	0
Cole Roberts	.000	5	0	0	0	0	0	0	1
Hayden Schott	.263	38	2	10	1	0	1	5	0

Luke Shliger	.273	77	15	21	2	0	0	7	4
Jordan Thompson	.173	52	5	9	1	0	1	10	1
Carson Wells	.250	4	0	1	0	0	0	0	0

Pitching	W	L	ERA	G	SV	IP	H	BB	SO
Kristofer Bow	0	0	2.12	7	0	17	15	8	19
Sam Brodersen	0	0	10.13	2	0	3	4	6	4
Aaron Calhoun	2	0	3.97	6	0	11	7	7	16
Bryce Collins	0	1	10.80	5	0	7	5	9	10
Drew Dowd	0	1	2.70	4	0	13	13	5	18
Dominic Freeberger	0	0	7.11	5	0	6	4	4	3
Garrett Gainous	0	1	9.00	2	0	7	10	5	11
Shaun Gamelin	1	1	3.46	11	2	13	5	8	20
Owen Hackman	1	0	2.35	5	1	8	7	3	13
Luke Jewett	2	0	2.37	10	2	19	18	8	24
Matthew Kavanaugh	0	1	4.79	8	0	21	17	10	19
Sam Klein	0	0	6.00	6	1	9	9	8	6
Jared Lyons	3	1	1.84	6	0	29	16	13	33
Connor Markl	1	1	2.39	6	0	26	13	15	26
Dylan Ray	0	0	1.64	6	1	11	8	2	17
Bryce Robison	1	1	2.84	7	0	32	31	6	23
Ivran Romero	2	1	2.20	6	0	16	13	7	19
Will Rudy	0	0	5.40	1	0	5	4	1	3
Grant Taylor	1	1	2.57	7	0	28	21	16	42
Conner Thurman	0	0	0.00	6	2	9	3	4	11
Zach Veen	2	0	1.35	7	0	13	11	2	14
Eric Yost	2	5	3.58	7	0	33	30	10	24

ALASKA LEAGUE

	W	L	PCT	GB
Anchorage Glacier Pilots †	27	9	.750	-
Mat Su Miners †	27	12	.692	1.5
Anchorage Bucs †	17	18	.486	9.5
Peninsula Oilers †	15	23	.395	13
Chugiak Chinooks	6	30	.167	21

CHAMPIONSHIP: Anchorage Glacier Pilots defeated the Mat Su Miners.

ALL-STAR TEAM: C: Steven Lancia, Miners. **1B:** Ryan Mathiesen, Chinooks. **2B:** Shunsuke Sakaino, Oilers. **3B:** Casey Sunseri, Miners. **SS:** Josh Paino, Miners. **OF:** Ben Weaver, Chinooks; Alex Vergara, Miners; Grayson Sterling, Pilots; Michael Diaz, Bucs. **UTIL:** James Shimashita, Oilers. **DH:** Blake Avila, Miners.

SP: Owen Wild, Bucs; Casron Seeman, Oilers; Zach Filos, Chinooks; Xavier Martinez, Pilots; Nico Zeglin, Pilots; Josh Hansell, Bucs; Brad Mullin, Bucs. **RP:** Keaton Fuller, Pilots; Blake Hammond, Bucs. Closer: Jacob King, Pilots.

Player of the Year: Alex Vergara, Miners. **Top Prospect:** Alex Vergara, Miners. **Gold Glove:** Ali Camarillo, Pilots. **Coach of the Year:** Dave Serrano, Miners.

ATLANTIC COLLEGIATE LEAGUE

Kaiser Division	W	L	PCT	GB
New York Phenoms	27	12	.692	-
Atlantic Whitecaps	25	11	.689	0.5
Nassau Collegians	22	18	.550	5.5
LIB Neptunes	23	13	.639	2.5
New York Valor	16	16	.500	7.5
Hitters Club Hawkeyes	12	23	.343	13
East Coast Sandhogs	10	24	.294	14.5
New York Crush	6	25	.212	17
Wolff Division	**W**	**L**	**PCT**	**GB**
Quakertown Blazers	32	11	.739	-
Bergen Metros	29	16	.644	4
South Jersey Kings	24	16	.598	6.5
Trenton Generals	21	20	.512	10
New Brunswick MATRIX	14	23	.378	15
Jersey Pilots	11	25	.306	17.5
Ocean Ospreys	9	28	.243	20

CHAMPIONSHIP: Bergen Metros defeated the New York Phenoms.

CAL RIPKEN COLLEGIATE LEAGUE

	W	L	PCT	GB
Alexandria Aces	26	10	.722	0
Bethesda Big Train	26	10	.722	0
Gaithersburg Giants	17	19	.472	9
Cropdusters Baseball	16	20	.444	10
South County Braves	15	21	.417	11
D.C. Grays	15	21	.417	11
SS-T T Bolts	11	25	.306	15

CHAMPIONSHIP: Alexandria Aces defeated Bethesda Big Train 2-0 in best-of-3 championship series.

ALL-LEAGUE TEAM: 1B: Dane Camphausen, DC Grays (Wooster College). **2B**: Brandon Harrity, Alexandria Aces (Western Michigan). **SS:** Emile Pitre, Bethesda Big Train (Kentucky). **3B**: Joseph Mershon, Cropdusters Baseball (College of Charleston). C: Nathan Waugh, Silver Spring-Takoma Thunderbolts (Cornell). **OF**: Eddie Hacopian, Alexandria Aces (Maryland College Park). **OF**: Joseph Quelch, Gaithersburg Giants (Georgia Gwinnet College). **OF:** Dylan Koontz, Alexandria Aces (Campbell). **OF:** Luke Nowak, Bethesda Big Train (East Carolina). **OF**: Cameron Hyder, Cropdusters Baseball (Salisbury). **UTL:** Henry Zipay, DC Grays (Nebraska: Omaha). **DH**: Adam Tellier, Alexandria Aces (Ball State).

P: Kristian Ashbury, South County Braves (Troy). **P**: Caleb Guisewite, Gaithersburg Giants (Belmont). **P:** Nick Del Prado, Bethesda Big Train (Florida Atlantic). **P:** Ryan Sanders, Bethesda Big Train (St. Mary's College of California). **P:** Ethan Mishra, Silver Spring-Takoma Thunderbolts (Virginia Commonwealth). **RP**: Jake Whittington, South County Braves (Wilson College). **RP**: Matt Delano, Alexandria Aces (Mississippi Gulf Coast JC). **RP**: Ryan Brown, Alexandria Aces (Ball State). **Closer**: Jordan Little, Bethesda Big Train (East Carolina).

CALIFORNIA COLLEGIATE LEAGUE

California Collegiate League South	W	L	PCT	GB
Santa Barbara Foresters	22	11	.662	-
Conejo Oaks	20	14	.588	2.5
Orange County Riptide	17	17	.500	5.5
Arroyo Seco Saints	15	18	.456	7
San Luis Obispo Blues	14	20	.412	8.5
Academy Barons	13	21	.382	9.5
California Collegiate League North	**W**	**L**	**PCT**	**GB**
Healdsburg Prune Packers	25	9	.735	-
Walnut Creek Crawdads	18	16	.529	7
Lincoln Potters	16	18	.471	9
Solano Mudcats	15	19	.441	10
Sonoma Stompers	11	23	.324	14.5

CHAMPIONSHIP: Healdsburg defeated Conejo 14-1in championship game.

COASTAL PLAIN LEAGUE

EAST	W	L	PCT	GB
Morehead City Marlins	37	10	.787	--
Wilson Tobs	26	21	.553	11
Holly Springs Salamanders	25	23	.521	12.5
Wilmington Sharks	23	24	.489	14
Peninsula Pilots	22	24	.478	14.5
Tri-City Chili Peppers	22	24	.478	14.5
Florence Flamingos	14	31	.311	22
WESST	**W**	**L**	**PCT**	**GB**
Savannah Bananas	34	14	.708	--
Macon Bacon	24	24	.500	10
High Point-Thomasville HiToms	24	24	.500	10
Forest City Owls	22	25	.468	11.5
Lexington County Blowfish	22	26	.458	12
Martinsville Mustangs	21	27	.438	13
Asheboro Zookeepers	14	33	.298	19.5

CHAMPIONSHIP: Savannah Bananas defeated Wilson Tobs 2-0 in best-of-3 series.

ALL-LEAGUE TEAM: C: Indy Stanley, Savannah (Columbia). **1B**: Brock Vradenburg, Lexington County (Michigan State). **2B**: McGwire Tuffy, Morehead City (Quinnipiac). **3B**: Eli Weisner, High Point-Thomasville (Louisburg College). **SS**: Andrew Ciufo, Wilmington (Georgetown). **DH/UTL**: Trent Youngblood, Asheboro (Transylvania). **DH/UTL**: Will Butcher, Forest City (Charlotte). **DH/UTL**: Trey Morgan, Peninsula (Virginia Military Institute). **DH/UTL**: Eric Grintz, High Point-Thomasville (North

Carolina). **DH/UTL**: Brandon Eike, Tri-City (North Carolina). **OF**: Ben Watson, Morehead City (Elizabethtown College). **OF**: Cameron Pittman, Martinsville (Radford). **OF**: Sean Johnson, Morehead City (Belmont Abbey). **OF**: Armando Becerra, Savannah (Erskine). **OF**: Mason Sykes, Wilson (Toledo). **OF**: Drew Yniesta, Savannah (Lenoir-Rhyne). **OF**: Nate Carriere, Holly Springs (Lamar).

LHP: Dalton Pence, Forest City (North Carolina). **RHP**: Tyler Wehrle, Morehead City (Tiffin). **RHP**: Jared Donalson, Savannah (Georgia Southwestern). **LHP**: Jay Cassady, Peninsula (Christopher Newport). **RHP**: Jared Kollar, Morehead City (Rutgers). **RHP**: Cade Carlson, Martinsville (East Tennessee State). **RHP**: Matt Hickey, Morehead City (Tarleton State). **LHP**: Logan Garza, Morehead City (Texas A&M: Kingsville). **RHP**: Reece Wissinger, Morehead City (Southeastern). **LHP**: Michael Foltz, Holly Springs (Duke). **LHP**: Brendan Bean, Morehead City (Pennsylvania).

FLORIDA COLLEGIATE SUMMER LEAGUE

	W	L	PCT	GB
Winter Park Diamond Dawgs	23	10	.697	-
Leesburg Lightning	23	11	.676	0.5
Sanford River Rats	16	14	.533	5.5
Seminole County Snappers	13	18	.419	9
Winter Garden Squeeze	13	19	.406	9.5
DeLand Suns	8	24	.250	14.5

CHAMPIONSHIP: Winter Park defeated Leesburg 2-1 in best-of-three championship series.

ALL-LEAGUE TEAM: C: Travis Stapleton, Leesburg (Polk State). **1B**: Jeff Liquori, Sanford (Florida Southern). **2B**: Robbie Scott, Sanford (King). **SS**: Dale Thomas, Winter Park (Florida). **3B**: Michael Ballard, Winter Park (Eckerd). **OF**: Noah Dickerson, Winter Garden (Little Rock); Brandon Fields, Sanford (Texas); Kyle Mock, Winter Park (Troy). **DH**: Edgar Alvarez, Winter Park (Nicholls State); Jakob Runnels, Leesburg (North Florida); Sean Sparling, DeLand (Daytona State). **UTIL**: Noah Best, Leesburg (Birmingham Southern).
SP: Garrett Brewer, Winter Garden (Seminole State); Jacob Burr, Winter Park (Webber); Chase Costello, Sanford (St. Thomas); Michael Laudando, Winter Park (Southeast Missouri); Dylan Simmons, Winter Park (Pittsburgh). **RP**: Connor Glesson, Leesburg (Gardner-Webb); Zach Holcomb, Sanford (Illinois State); Andrew Lewis, Winter Garden (East Mississippi); Jaxon Mills, Winter Park (Rollins); Ty Van Dyke, Leesburg (Seminole State). **Two-Way**: Braden Calise, Winter Park (Louisville).

FUTURES COLLEGIATE LEAGUE

	W	L	PCT	GB
Vermont Lake Monsters †	44	19	.698	-
New Britain Bees †	37	26	.587	7
Nashua Silver Knights †	33	29	.532	10.5
Westfield Starfires	30	33	.476	14
Norwich Sea Unicorns	30	33	.476	14
Pittsfield Suns	27	36	.429	17
Worcester Bravehearts	26	36	.419	17.5
Brockton Rox	24	39	.381	20

CHAMPIONSHIP: Nashua defeated Vermont 2-1 in best-of-three championship series.

ALL-LEAGUE TEAM: P: Sean Matson, Vermont Lake Monsters, Harvard). **P**: Izaiya Mestre, Pittsfield (New Haven). **P**: Tim Noone, Vermont (Babson College). **P**: Jonah Wachter, Nashua (Tulane). **P**: Michael Quigley, Brockton (Connecticut). **RP**: George Goldstein, Vermont (Middlebury College). **RP**: Wyatt Cameron, Vermont (New England College).

C: Jackson Hornung, Westfield (Skidmore College). **1B**: Gavin Noriega, Worcester (Bryant). **2B**: D'Angelo Ortiz, Brockton (Miami Dade College). **SS**: Noah Campanelli, Westfield (St. John Fisher College). **SS:** Cooper Kelly, Vermont (Kansas). **3B**: Drew Metzdorf, Pittsfield (UMass Boston). **OF**: Jimmy Evans, Vermont (Tufts). **OF**: Joel Lara, New Britain (Franklin Pierce). **OF**: Andy Martin, Brockton (Dyersburg State JC). **OF**: Caleb Shpur, Pittsfield (Endicott College). **DH/Utility**: Marco Ali, Pittsfield (Marist College). **DH/Utility**: CJ Brito-Trinidad, New Britain (Bowdoin College).

GREAT LAKES LEAGUE

North Division	W	L	PCT	GB
Michigan Monarchs * †	23	15	.605	--
Lima Locos	21	17	.553	2
Sandusky Ice Haulers	19	19	.500	4
Jet Box Baseball Club	19	19	.500	4
Royal Oak Leprechauns	17	21	.447	6
Muskegon Clippers	17	21	.447	6
South Division	**W**	**L**	**PCT**	
Licking County Settlers	22	16	.579	--
Hamilton Joes †	21	17	.553	1
Cincinnati Steam	21	17	.553	1
Xenia Scouts	18	20	.474	4
Richmond Jazz	17	21	.447	5
Grand Lake Mariners	17	21	.447	5
S Ohio Copperheads	15	23	.395	7

CHAMPIONSHIP: Hamilton defeated Lima 2-1 in best-of-three championship series.

North Division Player and Prospect of the Year: Reece Longstaff, Nichigan (Arizona Western College); **South Division Player and Prospect of the Year**: Kyle Ratliff, Southern Ohio (SIU Edwardsville). **North Division Pitcher and Prospect of the Year:** Carter Doorn, Lima (Purdue). **South Division Pitcher of the Year:** Garrett DeClue, Xenia(University of the Cumberlands). **Top South Division Pitching Prospect:** Chase Hopewell, Hamilton (Cincinnati). **Manager of the Year:** Ben Komonosky, Michigan.

HAMPTONS COLLEGIATE LEAGUE

	W	L	T	PTS
South Shore Clippers †	21	13	2	44
Sag Harbor Whalers †	18	15	3	39
Southampton Breakers †	17	14	5	39
Westhampton Aviators †	17	16	3	37
North Fork Ospreys	15	17	4	34
Shelter Island Bucks	15	18	3	33
Riverhead Tomcats	13	23	0	26

CHAMPIONSHIP: Sag Harbor defeated Westhampton 2-1 in best-of-three championship series.
ALL-LEAGUE TEAM: C: Jason Shockley, Riverhead (Rutgers). **1B**: Blake Salamon, Shelter Island (Northwood). **2B**: Jack Halloran, Westhampton (Emory). **SS**: Ryan McIntyre, South Shore (Amherst). **3B**: Aidan Larkin, South Shore (Hofstra). **OF**: Conor Kiely, Shelter Island (Stonehill); Asher Bradd, Riverhead (Illinois Springfield); CJ Dean, Sag Harbor (Cincinnati). **DH**: Nic Adamo, North Fork (Pennsylvania). UTIL: Esai Santos, Southampton (Holy Names). **SP**: Liam Pulsipher, South Shore (Queens). **SP**: Teo Torrado, Westhampton (Gettysburg). **SP**: John Rizzo, South Shore (Adelphi). **SP**: Zach Karson, Southampton (Florida Southern). **RP**: Danny Gargano, South Shore (Queens). **RP**: Jacob Young, Southampton (Brown). **RP**: Max Brulport, Shelter Island (Stonehill). **UTIL P**: Cole Hansen, Riverhead (Seton Hall). **Two-Way:** AJ Anzai, North Fork (Chapman).

MINK LEAGUE

North Division	W	L	PCT
St. Joseph Mustangs	37	15	.712
Clarinda A's	31	15	.674
Des Moines Peak Prospects	18	22	.450
Carroll Merchants	19	24	.442
Chillicothe Mudcats	17	25	.405

South	W	L	PCT
Joplin Outlaws	25	23	.521
Sedalia Bombers	22	22	.500
Jefferson City Renegades	19	25	.432
Nevada Griffons	16	27	.372

CHAMPIONSHIP: St. Joseph defeated Joplin, 2-1, in best-of-three championship series.

MINK Player of the Year: Will Walsh, Clarinda. **MINK Pitcher of the Year:** Brian Kraft, Clarinda. **Manager of the Year:** Craig McAndrews, Sedalia.

NEW ENGLAND COLLEGIATE LEAGUE

Coastal Division	W	L	PCT	GB
Newport Gulls	30	14	.682	-
Martha's Vineyard Sharks	29	15	.659	1
Mystic Schooners	23	21	.523	7
Ocean State Waves	21	23	.477	9
North Shore Navigators	13	31	.295	17
North Division	**W**	**L**	**PCT**	**GB**
Vermont Mountaineers	32	12	.727	-
Sanford Mainers	22	22	.500	10
Winnipesaukee Muskrats	19	23	.452	12
Upper Valley Nighthawks	19	23	.452	12
Keene Swamp Bats	17	27	.386	15
West Division	**W**	**L**	**PCT**	**GB**
Bristol Blues	32	12	.727	-
Danbury Westerners	22	22	.500	10
Valley Blue Sox	16	28	.364	16

CHAMPIONSHIP: Martha's Vineyard defeated Vermont, 2-0, in best-of-three championship series.

ALL-LEAGUE TEAM: C: Thomas Bramley, Martha's Vineyard (Penn St.). **1B**: Noah Martinez, Newport (Central Connecticut St.). **2B**: Quinn McDaniel, Sanford (UMaine). **SS**: Chaz Myers, Bristol (Pacific). **3B**: Ryan Ignoffo, Upper Valley (Eastern Illinois). **OF**: Colton Ledbetter, Newport (Mississippi St); Logan Chambers, Martha's Vineyard (Tennessee); Kevin Ferrer, Mystic (Connecticut).

SP: Bryce Afthim, Sanford (Southern Maine); Tyler Mudd, Ocean State, (Holy Cross); **RP**: Alejandro Torres, Martha's Vineyard, (Miami); Brooks Ey, Ocean State, (Virginia Commonwealth). **Closer**: Camron Hill, Martha's Vineyard, (Georgia Tech).

NORTHWOODS LEAGUE

Great Lakes East	W	L	PCT	GB
Traverse City Pit Spitters	45	27	.625	-
Rockford Rivets	37	35	.514	8
Kalamazoo Growlers	36	35	.507	8.5
Battle Creek Battle Jacks	35	37	.486	10
Kenosha Kingfish	33	38	.465	11.5
Kokomo Jackrabbits	19	52	.268	25.5
Great Lakes West	**W**	**L**	**PCT**	**GB**
Wisconsin Rapids Rafters	57	15	.792	-
Wausau Woodchucks	38	33	.535	18.5
Fond du Lac Dock Spiders	36	35	.507	20.5
Lakeshore Chinooks	36	36	.500	21
Green Bay Rockers	30	42	.417	27
Madison Mallards	26	46	.361	31
Great Plains East	**W**	**L**	**PCT**	**GB**
Eau Claire Express	42	26	.618	-
Duluth Huskies	34	33	.507	7.5
La Crosse Loggers	31	37	.456	11
Waterloo Bucks	16	52	.235	26
Minnesota Mud Puppies	7	29	.194	19
Great Plains West	**W**	**L**	**PCT**	**GB**
St. Cloud Rox	50	18	.735	-
Willmar Stingers	48	20	.706	2
Mankato MoonDogs	40	28	.588	10
Rochester Honkers	32	36	.471	18
Bismarck Larks	23	45	.338	27

CHAMPIONSHIP: Kalamazoo defeated Duluth 2-0 in best-of-3 series.
ALL-LEAGUE TEAM: C: Drey Dirksen, Willmar (Augustana); Matt DePrey, Lakeshore (Xavier). **1B**: Charlie Condon, St. Cloud (Georgia); Brendan Bobo, Wisconsin (Cal State Fullerton). **2B**: Aidan Sweatt, La Crosse (North Florida); Tristin Garcia, Green Bay (Western Kentucky). **3B**: Aidan Byrne, Willmar (Minnesota State Mankato); Parker Noland, Fond du Lac (Vanderbilt); **SS**: Kristian Campbell, Duluth (Georgia Tech); Ben Ross, Wisconsin (Notre Dame). **OF**: Joey Walls, Willmar (Long Beach State); Sean Ross, Mankato (Indiana State); John Nett, St. Cloud (St. Cloud State); Nick Mitchell, Fond du Lac Dock (Western Illinois); Patrick Mills, Battle Creek (Utah Valley); Chase Hug, Wausau (Evansville). DH: Ethan Mann, St. Cloud (Dallas Baptist); Kemp Alderman, Fond du Lac (Mississippi).
P: Jack Habeck, Willmar (St. Cloud State); Hunter Day, St. Cloud (Tarleton State); Chase Grillo, St. Cloud (Washington State); Matt Helwig, Eau Claire (Lewis University); Tucker Novotny, Willmar (Minnesota); Carter Rost, Bismarck (Wichita State); Nolan Lebamoff, Duluth (Valparaiso); Jacob Mrosko, Minnesota (St. Thomas); Josh Howitt, Wisconsin (California State Fullerton); Dylan Carter, Green Bay (Arkansas); Ty Rybarcyzk, Rockford (Illinois); Grayson Thurman, Kenosha (Lynchburg); Mitch Mueller, Lakeshore (Parkland College); Aren Gustafson, Traverse City (Olivet Nazarene).
Most Valuable Player: Sean Ross, OF, Mankato (Indiana State).
Pitcher of the Year: Jack Habeck, LHP, Willmar (St. Cloud State).
Manager of the Year: Kirk Shrider, Wisconsin. **Coach of the Year:** John Halama, Wisconsin.

PERFECT GAME COLLEGIATE LEAGUE

East Division	W	L	PCT	GB
Amsterdam Mohawks	39	6	.859	--
Mohawk Valley DiamondDawgs	28	18	.609	11.5
Saugerties Stallions	27	19	.583	12.5
Oneonta Outlaws	23	23	.500	16.5
Albany Dutchmen	22	24	.478	17.5
Watertown Rapids	21	24	.467	18
Boonville Baseball Club	14	29	.326	24
Glens Falls Dragons	6	37	.140	32
West Division	**W**	**L**	**PCT**	**GB**
Batavia Muckdogs	30	15	.667	--
Utica Blue Sox	27	19	.585	3.5
Auburn DoubleDays	25	21	.543	5.5
Elmira Pioneers	24	21	.533	6
Geneva Red Wings	21	21	.500	7.5
Jamestown Tarp Skunks	21	24	.467	9
Niagara Power	16	28	.364	13.5
Newark Pilots	15	30	.333	15

CHAMPIONSHIP: Amsterdam defeated Batavia 2-1 in best-of-three championship series.
ALL-LEAGUE TEAM: C: Shane Dux, Geneva. **1B**: Dewey Roden, Utica. **2B**: Gage Miller, Amsterdam. **3B**: Tyree Bradley, Watertown. **SS**: Brett Coker, Amsterdam. **Infield Utility**: Devin Boone, Oneonta. **OF**: Aaron Whitley, Newark. **OF**: Dan Tauken, Boonville. **OF**: Pete Durocher, Mohawk Valley. **DH**: Scott Seeker, Boonville. **Utility**: Nick Serce, Geneva. **SP**: Nolan Sparks, Batavia. **SP**: Ryan Bailey, Auburn. **SP**: Aidan Kidd, Amsterdam. **SP**: Alex Canino, Utica. **SP**: Cade Citelli, Amsterdam. **RP**: Santhosh Gottam, Amsterdam. **RP**: Jack Sylvia, Amsterdam

PROSPECT LEAGUE

Ohio River Valley Division	W	L	PCT	
Chillicothe Paints	38	22	.633	--
Johnstown Mill Rats	29	31	.483	9
Champion City Kings	23	34	.404	13.5
West Virginia Miners	20	37	.351	16.5
Wabash River Division	**W**	**L**	**PCT**	
Danville Dans	40	17	.702	--
REX Baseball	37	23	.617	4.5
Illinois Valley Pistol Shrimp	38	21	.644	3
Lafayette Aviators	25	34	.424	16
Great River Division	**W**	**L**	**PCT**	
Normal CornBelters	31	28	.525	--
Quincy Gems	31	29	.517	0.5
Clinton LumberKings	28	32	.467	3.5
Burlington Bees	20	39	.339	11
Prairie Land Division	**W**	**L**	**PCT**	
Alton River Dragons	32	28	.533	--
O'Fallon Hoots	28	32	.467	4
Cape Catfish	26	33	.441	5.5
Springfield Lucky Horseshoes	27	33	.450	5

CHAMPIONSHIP: Chillicothe defeated Alton River in championship game.
EAST DIVISION ALL-STARS: 1B: Tucker Bougie, Illinois Valley Pistol Shrimp (California). **2B**: Carlos Vasquez, Danville (Missouri State). **3B**: Keenan Taylor, Danville (Parkland College). **SS**: Drake DiGiorno, Danville (Folsom Lake College). **OF**: Alec Brunson, REX Baseball (St. Francis). **OF**: Zach Lane, Illinois Valley (Ball State). **OF**: Aaron Beck, REX Baseball (Indiana State). **C**: Mike Sprockett, Chillicothe (Akron). **DH**: Tim Orr, Chillicothe (Tiffin).

SP: Josh Leerssen, Danville (Birmingham Southern College). **SP**: Parker Carlson, Danville (Auburn). **SP**: Gyeongju Kim, Lafayette (Dordt). **RP**: Landon Tomkins, Danville (Louisiana Tech). **RP**: Harrison Bodendorf, Illinois Valley (Hawaii at Manoa). **RP**: Nick Lallathin, Chillicothe (Walsh).
WEST DIVISION ALL-STARS: 1B: Zach Stewart, Quincy (Missouri State). **2B**: Danny Sperling, Cape (Southeast Missouri State). **3B**: Kolton Poorman, Cape (Three Rivers JC). **SS**: Jackson Chatterton, Normal (Bradley). **OF**: Eddie King, Jr., Alton (Louisville). **OF**: Blake Burris, Alton (Lewis & Clark JC). **OF**: Patrick Clohisy, O'Fallon (Saint Louis). **C**: Cade Moss, Clinton (Iowa). **DH**: Kevin Santiago, Burlington (Texas Wesleyan). **SP**: Jake Curtis, Springfield (Lincoln Land JC). **SP**: Jackson Kent, Clinton (Arizona). **SP**: Adam Stilts, Alton (Lewis & Clark JC). **RP**: Colin Bryant, Cape (West Virginia State). **RP**: Noah Bush, Alton (Iowa Western JC). **RP**: Austin Brock, Cape (Arkansas State).

SOUTH FLORIDA COLLEGIATE LEAGUE

NORTH	W	L	PCT	GB
Delray Beach Lightning	32	12	.727	--
Boynton Beach Buccaneers	25	19	.567	7
Palm Beach Diamond Ducks	18	19	.486	10.5
Phipps Park Barracudas	12	24	.338	16
Boca Raton Blazers	10	29	.256	19.5
SOUTH	**W**	**L**	**PCT**	**GB**
Palm Beach Xtreme	30	13	.698	--
West Boca Snappers	22	16	.579	5.5
West Palm Beach Knights	22	17	.564	6
Pompano Beach Clippers	23	21	.523	7.5
Florida Pokers	5	29	.147	20.5

CHAMPIONSHIP: Delray Beach defeated Palm Beach 2-0 in best-of-three championship series.

SUNBELT LEAGUE

Central	W	L	PCT	GB
Atlanta Crackers	19	14	.576	-
Atlanta Blues	14	15	.483	3
Brookhaven Bucks	13	16	.448	4
East	**W**	**L**	**PCT**	**GB**
Gainesville GolDiggers	25	7	.781	-
Waleska Wild Things	17	14	.548	7.5
Alpharetta Aviators	7	20	.259	15.5
West	**W**	**L**	**PCT**	**GB**
Columbus Chatt-a-Hoots	17	13	.567	-
Choccolocco Monsters	11	17	.393	5
Gwinnett Astros	10	17	.370	5.5

CHAMPIONSHIP: Gainesville defeated Atlanta Crackers 2-0 in best-of-three championship series.

SUNFLOWER COLLEGIATE LEAGUE

	W	L	PCT	GB
Cheney Diamond Dawgs	26	6	.813	--
Hutchinson Monarchs	25	7	.781	1
Great Bend Bat Cats	22	10	.688	4
Derby Twins	20	12	.625	6
Newton Sluggin Rebels	17	15	.531	9
Haysville Aviators	14	16	.468	11
Kingman Islanders	14	18	.438	12
316 Elite 18U	0	26	.019	23
Mulvane Patriots	0	28	.000	24

CHAMPIONSHIP: Cheney Diamond Dawgs defeated Hutchinson in championship game.

VALLEY LEAGUE

NORTH	W	L	PCT	GB
Woodstock River Bandits	27	15	.643	0
Strasburg Express	22	20	.524	5
Purcellville Cannons	19	21	.475	7
New Market Rebels	19	22	.463	7.5
Front Royal Cardinals	16	26	.381	11
Winchester Royals	14	27	.341	12.5
SOUTH	**W**	**L**	**PCT**	**GB**
Charlottesville TomSox	26	16	.619	0
Waynesboro Generals	26	16	.619	0
Harrisonburg Turks	25	17	.595	1
Covington Lumberjacks	19	23	.452	7
Staunton Braves	16	26	.381	10

CHAMPIONSHIP: Charlottesville defeated Woodstock 2-0 in best-of-three championship series.
North Division Awards. Most Valuable Player: Seaver King, Harrisonburg (Wingate). **Pitcher of the Year:** Kelsey Ward, Waynesboro (Embry-Riddle).
South Division Awards. Most Valuable Player: Ryne Guida, Purcellville (Florida International). **Pitcher of the Year:** Kelan Hoover, Woodstock (Garrett College). Coach of the Year: Mike Bocock, Woodstock

WEST COAST LEAGUE

North Division	W	L	PCT	GB
Bellingham Bells	33	20	.623	-
Wenatchee AppleSox	27	27	.500	6.5
Kamloops NorthPaws	26	27	.491	7
Victoria HarbourCats	26	28	.481	7.5
Edmonton Riverhawks	25	28	.472	8
Nanaimo NightOwls	22	32	.407	11.5
Kelowna Falcons	20	33	.377	13
Port Angeles Lefties	20	34	.370	13.5
South Division	**W**	**L**	**PCT**	**GB**
Corvallis Knights	39	15	.722	-
Portland Pickles	36	16	.692	2
Ridgefield Raptors	32	21	.604	6.5
Yakima Valley Pippins	29	25	.537	10
Bend Elks	28	26	.519	11
Cowlitz Black Bears	25	28	.472	13.5
Walla Walla Sweets	23	31	.426	16
Springfield Drifters	17	37	.315	22

CHAMPIONSHIP: Corvallis defeated Bellingham in championship game.
ALL-LEAGUE TEAM: C: Beau Sylvester (Oklahoma State), Bend Elks. **1B**: Evan Scavotto (Portland), Bend Elks. **2B**: Joichiro Oyama (UC Irvine), Wenatchee AppleSox. **3B**: Tim Holyk (Cumberland), Nanaimo NightOwls. **SS**: Elijah Jackson (Chico State), Bend Elks. OF: Jacob Sharp (UNLV), Ridgefield Raptors. **OF**: Calyn Halvorson (Utah Valley), Cowlitz Black Bears. **OF**: Clay Loranger (Stephen F. Austin), Edmonton Riverhawks. **UTL**: Travis Welker (Fresno State), Ridgefield Raptors. . **SP**: Trevin Hope (Lewis-Clark State), Bellingham Bells. **SP**: Tyler Frieders (MidAmerica Nazarene), Yakima Valley Pippins. **SP**: Ryan Beitel (British Columbia), Bellingham Bells. **SP**: Kaden Segel (Linn-Benton CC), Corvallis Knights. **SP**: Jon Mocherman (Riverside CC), Cowlitz Black Bears. **RP**: Sean Wiese (Hawaii), Corvallis Knights. RP: Nathan Shinn (San Francisco State), Portland Pickles. **RP**: Evan Tomlinson (Cal Poly), Portland Pickles.
MOST VALUABLE PLAYERS: Joichiro Oyama (UC Irvine) Wenatchee; Jacob Sharp (UNLV) Ridgefield.
PITCHER OF THE YEAR: Trevin Hope (Lewis-Clark State) Bellinghan.
WCL TOP PROSPECT: Beau Sylvester (Oklahoma State) Bend

HIGH SCHOOL

Stoneman Douglas Keeps Racking Up Titles

COURTESY USA BASEBALL

Stoneman Douglas High of Parkland has won back-to-back Florida 7A state titles.

BY SAVANNAH McCANN

Stoneman Douglas High is building a dynasty in South Florida.

Located in Parkland—about 25 miles north of Fort Lauderdale and 45 miles north of Miami—the program captured back-to-back Florida 7A state championships this season.

Earlier in 2022, Stoneman Douglas became the second non-California program to win USA Baseball's National High School Invitational, which has operated since 2012.

On its way to complete domination this season, the team won a school-record of 30 games, ending the season on a 22-game win streak. Hopefully, the Eagles have room on their trophy shelf for one last accolade: BA High School Team of the Year.

Stoneman Douglas won the TOY award previously in 2016, giving it two nods in the past seven seasons.

Coach Todd Fitz-Gerald has coached Stoneman Douglas for 11 seasons but knew this year's team was something special from the start.

"It's really the best group of guys I've ever coached as a collective unit," Fitz-Gerald said. "There are so many talented guys in our program and they rally around each other. They're so close, not just on the field, but off the field. It was a really fun group to coach and I couldn't be happier for them."

Of the 10 seniors graduating from the program, eight were expected to play college baseball next season, with another turning pro.

Senior outfielder Roman Anthony was drafted by the Red Sox in the second round and reached the Low-A Carolina League for 10 games.

Anthony joined distinguished Stoneman Douglas alums Anthony Rizzo (class of 2007), Jesus Luzardo (2016) and Coby Mayo (2020) as players drafted out of the program.

"He is one of the top players I've ever had the privilege of coaching," Fitz-Gerald said. "I put him right there with Eric Hosmer."

Fitz-Gerald coached Hosmer while at American Heritage in Plantation, Fla., before he became the third overall pick in the 2008 draft.

Anthony is a quiet leader. His coach describes him as a lead-by-example type of player. The Gatorade Florida player of the year came into his own during his senior season. He led Stoneman Douglas in almost every offensive category, including RBIs, OPS and home runs.

Anthony also created a team motto: "Who's second?" The team had a few sayings it would turn to, but each night before a game the players would ask each other "who's second," and the goal was for it not to be them.

"Win the last game"—or WTLG—was another saying commonly heard around the clubhouse.

The team had one other saying it turned to during its record-breaking season: INAM. This four-letter acronym is inscribed on its state championship ring:

"It's not about me."

"We didn't have one ego on the team," Fitz-Gerald said. "We didn't have one guy who thought that he was better than everybody else. It was just a total team effort."

Jake Clemente took the mound for the semifinal game. The righthander tossed a complete game to bring the Eagles back to the championship stage.

For the finale, Stoneman Douglas gave lefthander Chris Arroyo the ball. On the mound, he was locating very well. After smacking a three-run homer, Arroyo ended Palm Beach Gardens' night via the 10-run mercy rule.

Despite losing 10 seniors, including Anthony, plus both Clemente and Arroyo, both to Florida—Fitz-Gerald is confident in the future of his team.

Fitz-Gerald's son Devin, who was sidelined with an injury for part of the season, will make up one part of the nucleus of the future roster. Devin is committed to North Carolina State as a member of the class of 2024, while his older brother Hunter transferred to Old Dominion after two juco seasons.

Alongside coach Fitz-Gerald, righthander Christian Rodriguez and lefty Jacob Gomberg will head the Stoneman Douglas rotation and continue to push the dynasty forward for years to come.

California Run At NHSI Halted

For just the second time in the history of the National High School Invitational, it was a Florida team standing above the rest.

In fact, for the first time in NHSI history, no team from California was involved in the championship game. Instead, it was two Florida high schools. Stoneman Douglas of Parkland took down St. Johns Country Day of Orange Park, 5-3.

Stoneman Douglas entered the championship game as the most dominant club in the tournament. They led the NHSI field of 16 teams with a collective .500 batting average and 0.44 ERA.

Stoneman Douglas blitzed through their first three opponents, defeating host Conley High of Greenville, N.C., 15-0 in the first round, then beating Yucaipa (Calif.) High 12-1 in the second and then taking down three-time defending NHSI champion Orange (Calif.) Lutheran 11-0 in five innings to reach the championship.

The championship game was a scrappier affair. The Eagles took a quick 3-0 lead in the bottom of the first inning thanks to a few walks and hit batters, plus a two-run single from DH Chris Arroyo.

In the top of the third, St. Johns would claw back and score three runs, with Stoneman Douglas helping with three errors in the field.

Tournament MVP Arroyo, who had previously tossed 3.2 shutout innings in round one, entered the game with two St. Johns runners on base and a 5-3 Stoneman Douglas lead. He promptly walked the bases loaded and then spiked a pitch that got past catcher Santiago Ordonez. The wild pitch caromed fortuitously back to Ordonez, who threw to Arroyo for the out at the plate.

"Whenever you play for a championship in any tournament, you always want to be the one to come out on top," Stoneman Douglas coach Todd Fitz-Gerald said. "To do it here at the NHSI with 16 of the top teams in the country—and for us to run through it like we did was pretty impressive.

"I couldn't be happier for them or my coaching staff." ■

HIGH SCHOOL TOP 50

Rk	School	Record
1.	Stoneman Douglas HS, Parkland, Fla.	30-2
2.	Sumrall (Miss.) HS	35-1
3.	St. Mary Prep, Orchard Lake, Mich.	39-0
4.	North Oconee HS, Bogart, Ga.	39-1
5.	Northwest Rankin HS, Brandon, Miss.	32-2
6.	Providence HS, Charlotte, N.C.	33-0
7.	Hamilton HS, Chandler, Ariz.	29-4
8.	Reagan HS, San Antonio	31-6
9.	De La Salle HS, Concord, Calif.	27-7
10.	Bishop Gorman HS, Las Vegas	36-7
11.	St. Frances HS, Mountain View, Calif.	31-5
12.	Doral (Fla.) Academy	26-4
13.	Rockwall-Heath HS, Rockwall, Texas	35-6
14.	Stinton (Texas) HS	34-1
15.	Reno (Nev.) HS	31-6
16.	Olympia (Wash.) HS	26-3
17.	Pope HS, Marietta, Ga.	33-7
18.	Calvary Christian HS, Clearwater, Fla.	26-2
19.	Hanover HS, Mechanicsville, Va.	21-2
20.	Blue Valley Southwest HS, Overland Park, Kan.	20-2
21.	Jackson (Miss) Prep	31-7
22.	Southlake (Texas) Carroll HS	32-8
23.	Huntington Beach (Calif.) HS	25-9
24.	Austin Prep, Reading, Mass.	20-0
25.	Mason (Ohio) HS	26-4
26.	Villa Park (Calif.) HS	27-5
27.	Legacy HS, Broomfield, Colo.	27-4
28.	JSerra Catholic HS, San Juan Capistrano, Calif.	22-11
29.	Jesuit HS, Tampa	24-8
30.	Colgan HS, Manassas, Va.	22-1
31.	Georgetown (Texas) HS	32-7
32.	Millard West HS, Omaha, Neb.	31-6
33.	Madison-Ridgeland Academy, Madison, Miss.	35-4
34.	Brother Rice HS, Chicago	34-5
35.	North Broward Prep, Coconut Creek, Fla.	23-9
36.	Orange (Calif.) Lutheran HS	25-5
37.	Barbe HS, Lake Charles, La.	36-4
38.	St. Augustine Prep, Richland, N.J.	25-1
39.	Ray HS, Corpus Christi, Texas	35-4
40.	Stockdale HS, Bakersfield, Calif.	26-4
41.	Lake Travis HS, Austin	34-7
42.	Edwardsville (Ill.) HS	29-4
43.	Basic HS, Henderson, Nev.	31-10
44.	Andrean HS, Merrillville, Ind.	29-4
45.	Liberty (Mo.) North HS	33-9
46.	American Heritage Academy, Plantation, Fla.	25-2
47.	Archbishop Spalding HS, Severn, Md.	25-4
48.	Fort Mill (S.C.) HS	25-7
49.	St. Paul Catholic HS, Bristol, Conn.	21-0
50.	Notre Dame HS, Sherman Oaks, Calif.	25-9

JOSHUA BESSEX/GETTY IMAGES

Hawaii defeated Curacao 13-3 in the championship game to win the Little League World Series.

AMATEUR/YOUTH CHAMPIONS 2022

ALL-AMERICAN AMATEUR BASEBALL ASSOCIATION (AAABA)

Event	Site	Champion	Runner-up
World Series (21U)	Johnstown, Pa.	New Orleans Boosters	Johnstown Paul Carpenter Capital Advisors

AMERICAN LEGION BASEBALL

Event	Site	Champion	Runner-up
World Series (19U)	Shelby, N.C.	Troy, Ala.	Idaho Falls, Idaho

BABE RUTH BASEBALL

Event	Site	Champion	Runner-up
Cal Ripken (10U)	Phenix City, Ala.	Marlton, N.J.	—
Cal Ripken 12-year-old (60 feet)	Branson, Mo.	Andy Valley, Maine	—
13-year-old	Demopolis, Ala.	Kado, Hawai	—
13-15-year-olds	Bismarck, N.D.	Greenville, N.C.	—
16-18-year-olds	Mobile, Ala.	Mobile, Ala.	—

LITTLE LEAGUE BASEBALL

Event	Site	Champion	Runner-up
Little League (11-12)	South Williamsport, Pa.	Hawaii	Curacao
Junior League (12-14)	Taylor, Mich.	Taiwan	Corpus Christi, Texas
Senior League (13-16)	Easley, S.C.	Puerto Rico	Norfolk, Va.
Intermediate (50-70)	Livermore, Calif.	Danville, Calif.	South Korea

NATIONAL AMATEUR BASEBALL FEDERATION (NBAF)

Event	Site	Champion	Runner-up
Sophomore (14U)	Struthers, Ohio	Fielder's Choice	Astro Falcons
Junior (16U)	Struthers, Ohio	Youngstown Astro Falcons	FTB Mid-Atlantic
High School (17U)	Jackson, Miss.	Jackson 96ers Blue, Miss.	Knoxville Tribe, Tenn.
Senior (18U)	Struthers, Ohio	Ohio Longhorns	Knightline
College (22U)	Sandusky, Ohio	Stark County Terriers	Grand Rapids Brewers
Major	Battle Creek, Mich.	Buffalo Battistoni Diesel	Lombard Orioles

PERFECT GAME/BCS FINALS

Event	Site	Champion	Runner-up
12U	Sanford, Fla.	TBT Ballers 12U National	Blue Collar Dawgs - 12U
13U	Fort Myers, Fla.	ZT Elite Florida 13U	Canes SC 13U Reames
14U	Fort Myers, Fla.	TBT Ballers AS4	CBU United 2026 Red
15U	Fort Myers, Fla.	CBU 2025 Scout Team	X Team 2025
16U	Fort Myers, Fla.	Original Florida Pokers 2024	X Team 2024
17U	Fort Myers, Fla.	Scorpions/Giants Scout Team 2023	Resmondo FTB Baseball
18U	Fort Myers, Fla.	Nelson Baseball School	Okotoks Dawgs 18U Black

PERFECT GAME/WORLD WOOD BAT ASSOCIATION SUMMER CHAMPIONSHIPS

Event	Site	Champion	Runner-up
14U	Hoover Ala.	Wo Factor National 14U	Canes National 14U
15U	Marietta, Ga.	Canes National 15U	Artillery Baseball 2025 Scout Team
16U	Marietta, Ga.	Power Baseball 2024 Marucci	East Cobb AStros 16U
17U	Marietta, Ga..	Ostingers Baseball Academy 2023	Georgia Bombers 17U Marucci
18U	Marietta, Ga.	643 DP Cougars 18U Pagan	Chi Town Cream

PONY BASEBALL .....

Event	Site	Champion	Runner-up
Mustang 9U	Modesto, Calif.	Placentia, Calif.	—
Mustang 10U	Youngsville, La.	Orange, Calif.	—
Bronco 11U	Chesterfield, Va.	San Diego	—
Bronco 12U	Laredo, Texas	Placentia, Calif.	—
Pony 13U	Modesto, Calif.	Alton, Texas	—
Pony 14U	Washington, Pa.	Brownsville, Texas	—
Colt 16U	Marion, Ill.	Marion, Ill.	—
Palomino 18U	Laredo, Texas	Taoyuan City, Taiwan	—

REVIVING BASEBALL IN INNER CITIES (RBI)

Event	Site	Champion	Runner-up
Junior (13-15)	Vero Beach, Fla.	Chicago White Sox RBI	Atlanta Braves RBI
Senior (16-18)	Vero Beach, Fla.	Chicago White Sox RBI	Cleveland Gaurdians RBI

U.S. SPECIALTY SPORTS ASSOCIATION (USSSA)

Event	Site	Champion	Runner-up
8U/Majors Elite	Brevard County, Fla.	MVP Hustle 8U Casillas	Team Florida JSM Elite
10U/Majors Elite	Brevard County, Fla.	Canes SC - 864	Turn 2 Baseball 10U Alpha
11U/Majors Elite	Brevard County, Fla.	MVP Hustle - Hooks 11U Garcia	Prime Baseball Lujan
13U/Majors Elite	Brevard County, Fla.	Fieldhouse Thunder	Louisville Legends - Graeter

USA Baseball

Event	Site	Champion	Runner-up
14 U West	Phoenix, Ariz.	TB SoCal Evo	Lamorinda Arsenal
14U East	Cary, N.C.	Canes National	Burn Atlantic Navy
15U West	Phoenix, Ariz.	OC Elite Baseball	NorCal U 2025 Black
15U East	Cary, N.C.	Alpha Prime	Texas Twelve
16U West	Phoenix, Ariz.	Alpha Power 2024	Easton Prime Red

JOSHJA BESSEX/GETTY IMAGES

Kama Angell of the Hawaii team celebrates after hitting a Little League World Series home run.

Holliday Sets National Hit Record

BY JASON ELMQUIST

Jackson Holliday was destined to be a star baseball player in high school, and a veteran starter for one of the top high school baseball programs in Oklahoma knew it would happen before Holliday was even in high school.

Holliday spent time playing with Stillwater High over the summer as a rising ninth grader. That was when his family lived in Florida while they were figuring out the future in the closing months of his father's MLB career.

Seven-time all-star Matt Holliday was putting a cap on his 15-year career in a 2018 playoff run with the same Rockies organization that had drafted him in the seventh round in 1998 out of Stillwater High.

"(Jackson) was always about whatever was best for the family, and we just felt like getting back closer to home," said Matt Holliday, who hit .299 with 316 home runs and was the left fielder for the World Series-champion 2011 Cardinals.

"He just handled it all really well. Even at that age, his humility and just his wanting to fit in and to play and be part of the team. I think that's sort of how it all went down."

Without any hesitation, Stillwater High's starting shortstop at the time, senior Jackson Ford, told head coach Jimmy Harris that he would make way for the oldest son of the program's most famous alum to assume the role as a freshman.

It was a moment of the many layers that created the foundation that earned Holliday the honor of Baseball America High School Player of the Year.

"I definitely thought I could have a chance after having a great high school season, but it's really exciting to reach a goal," Holliday said of the honor. "Obviously, you want to be the best, and it's very exciting."

The son of an MLB all-star, nephew of Oklahoma State baseball coach Josh Holliday and grandson of longtime baseball coach Tom Holliday notched 89 hits in 2022, setting a new national record.

The record Holliday eclipsed for hits in a season was previously held by Oklahoma prep J.T. Realmuto of Albert High in Midwest City.

In 40 games, Holliday hit .685 with an on-base percentage of .749, thanks to drawing 33 walks on the season against just seven strikeouts. But the biggest leap in his game came from an increase in power.

With the guidance of his father, he built on his frame by gaining about 10 pounds prior to his senior year. Coupling that with a small tweaking of his swing, he saw his home run numbers leap threefold from the year before.

The solo shot against Owasso in the regional tournament was his 17th of a campaign in which he had one week when he hit five over a four-game stretch, including three in an important district game against Tulsa Union.

"Being able to play on the (showcase) circuit last summer, being able to play against the best kids in the country, the game kind of just slowed down for me," Holliday said. "(I was) looking for pitches that I can do damage with throughout each at-bat, and not missing was important for me—getting my pitch, and being able to put a good swing on it." ■

PLAYER OF THE YEAR

PREVIOUS WINNERS

1992: Preston Wilson, OF/RHP, Bamberg-Ehrhardt (S.C.) HS
1993: Trot Nixon, OF/LHP, New Hanover HS, Wilmington, N.C.
1994: Doug Million, LHP, Sarasota (Fla.) HS
1995: Ben Davis, C, Malvern (Pa.) Prep
1996: Matt White, RHP, Waynesboro Area (Pa.) HS
1997: Darnell McDonald, OF, Cherry Creek HS, Englewood, Colo.
1998: Drew Henson, 3B/RHP, Brighton (Mich.) HS
1999: Josh Hamilton, OF/LHP, Athens Drive HS, Raleigh, N.C.
2000: Matt Harrington, RHP, Palmdale (Calif.) HS
2001: Joe Mauer, C, Cretin-Derham Hall HS, St. Paul, Minn.
2002: Scott Kazmir, LHP, Cypress Falls HS, Houston
2003: Jeff Allison, RHP, Veterans Memorial HS, Peabody, Mass.
2004: Homer Bailey, RHP, LaGrange (Texas) HS
2005: Justin Upton, SS, Great Bridge HS, Chesapeake, Va.
2006: Adrian Cardenas, SS/2B, Mons. Pace HS, Opa Locka, Fla.
2007: Mike Moustakas, SS, Chatsworth (Calif.) HS
2008: Ethan Martin, RHP/3B, Stephens County HS, Toccoa, Ga.
2009: Bryce Harper, C, Las Vegas HS
2010: Kaleb Cowart, RHP/3B, Cook HS, Adel, Ga.
2011: Dylan Bundy, RHP, Owasso (Okla.) HS
2012: Byron Buxton, OF, Appling County HS, Baxley, Ga.
2013: Clint Frazier, OF, Loganville (Ga.) HS
2014: Alex Jackson, OF, Rancho Bernardo (Calif.) HS
2015: Kyle Tucker, OF, Plant HS, Tampa
2016: Mickey Moniak, OF, La Costa Canyon HS, Carlsbad, Calif.
2017: MacKenzie Gore, LHP, Whiteville (N.C.) HS
2018: Cole Winn, RHP, Orange (Calif.) Lutheran HS
2019: Bobby Witt Jr., SS, Colleyville (Texas) Heritage HS
2020: No award given in truncated season
2021: Jackson Jobe, RHP/SS, Heritage Hall HS, Oklahoma City

2022 HIGH SCHOOL ALL-AMERICA TEAM

Jackson Holliday

BRIAN WESTERHOLT/FOUR SEAM IMAGES

Druw Jones

BRIAN WESTERHOLT/FOUR SEAM IMAGES

FIRST TEAM

Pos.	Player, School	YR.	AVG	AB	R	H	2B	3B	HR	RBI	SB	Drafted
C	Malcolm Moore, McClatchy HS, Sacramento	Sr.	.523	86	47	45	14	2	13	50	6	Not drafted
INF	Tucker Toman, Hammond HS, Columbia, S.C.	Sr.	.486	70	30	34	10	0	7	27	—	Blue Jays (2s)
INF	Sal Stewart, Westminster Christian HS, Miami	Sr.	.506	77	46	39	13	1	9	23	9	Reds (1)
INF	Jackson Holliday, Stillwater (Okla.) HS	Sr.	.685	130	74	89	29	6	17	79	30	Orioles (1)
INF	Termarr Johnson, Mays HS, Atlanta	Sr.	Statistics not available									Pirates (1)
OF	Druw Jones, Wesleyan HS, Norcross, Ga.	Sr.	.570	114	72	65	7	3	13	39	39	D-backs (1)
OF	Elijah Green, IMG Academy, Bradenton, Fla.	Sr.	.461	102	48	47	12	2	11	40	16	Nationals (1)
OF	Justin Crawford, Bishop Gorman HS, Las Vegas	Sr.	.503	153	60	77	17	8	5	52	20	Phillies (1)
DH	Xavier Isaac, East Forsyth HS, Kernersville, N.C.	Sr.	.580	69	38	40	7	2	13	29	11	Rays (1)

Pos.	Player, School	YR.	W	L	ERA	IP	H	R	ER	BB	SO	Drafted
P	Brock Porter, St. Mary Prep, Orchard Lake, Mich.	Sr.	6	0	0.43	42	3	—	2	17	87	Rangers (4)
P	Robby Snelling, McQueen HS, Reno, Nev.	Sr.	8	0	0.72	62	—	—	5	6	145	Padres (2)
P	Jackson Cox, Toutle Lake HS, Toutle, Wash.	Sr.	6	0	0.00	42	13	—	0	3	95	Rockies (2)
P	Brandon Barriera, American Heritage HS, Plantation, Fla.	Sr.	5	—	2.92	37	27	—	12	11	68	Blue Jays (1)
P	Jackson Ferris, IMG Academy, Bradenton, Fla.	Sr.	10	0	1.27	64	34	—	9	19	118	Cubs (2)

SECOND TEAM

Pos.	Player, School	YR.	AVG	AB	R	H	2B	3B	HR	RBI	SB	Drafted
C	Brooks Brannon, Randleman (N.C.) HS	Sr.	—	—	—	70	17	3	20	91	—	Red Sox (9)
INF	Jacob Reimer, Yucaipa (Calif.) HS	Sr.	.398	83	32	33	9	0	8	28	—	Mets (4)
INF	Jayson Jones, Braswell HS, Little Elm, Texas	Sr.	.397	68	25	27	8	2	1	15	18	Not drafted
INF	Paxton Kling, Central HS, Martinsburg, Pa.	Sr.	.596	57	41	34	6	3	4	29	31	Not drafted
INF	Cole Young, North Allegheny HS, Wexford, Pa.	Sr.	.456	57	21	26	8	4	2	15	8	Mariners (1)
OF	Henry Bolte, Palo Alto (Calif.) HS	Sr.	.467	92	57	43	6	2	13	41	48	Athletics (2)
OF	Roman Anthony, Stoneman Douglas HS, Parkland, Fla.	Sr.	.520	100	36	52	14	1	10	40	21	Red Sox (2s)
OF	Max Clark, Franklin (Ind.) Community HS	Jr.	.577	71	41	41	8	2	9	32	22	Class of 2023
DH	Chandler Pollard, Woodward Academy, College Park, Ga.	Sr.	.520	98	56	51	13	4	11	36	59	Rangers (5)

Pos.	Player, School	YR.	W	L	ERA	IP	H	R	ER	BB	SO	Drafted
P	Dylan Lesko, Buford (Ga.) HS	Sr.	—	—	—	—	—	—	—	—	—	Padres (1)
P	Eli Jerzembeck, Providence HS, Charlotte, N.C.	Sr.	14	0	0.41	87	28	—	4	10	200	Not drafted
P	Owen Murphy, Riverside-Brookfield HS, Riverside, Ill.	Sr.	8	0	0.18	51	9	—	1	3	122	Braves (1)
P	Walter Ford, Pace (Fla.) HS	Sr.	10	2	1.15	70	39	—	9	25	126	Mariners (2s)
P	Thomas White, Phillips Academy, Andover, Mass.	Jr.	4	1	0.26	27	6	3	1	13	58	Class of 2023

DRAFT

Orioles Opt To Take A Holliday

BY CARLOS COLLAZO, KYLE GLASER AND J.J. COOPER

LOS ANGELES—For the second time in the last four drafts, the Orioles held the No. 1 overall pick. The first time around, in 2019, there was a clear-cut top prospect in Oregon State catcher Adley Rutschman.

The dynamic was very different this year. The Orioles considered five players for the No. 1 overall pick, and it came down until very late in the process before they made their selection.

After much deliberation, they got the player they wanted.

The Orioles drafted Stillwater (Okla.) High shortstop Jackson Holliday with the first overall pick in the 2022 draft on Sunday. Holliday, the son of seven-time all-star outfielder Matt Holliday, was the 2022 Baseball America High School Player of the Year and finished No. 3 on the final BA 500 draft rankings.

"It was a very difficult decision in a good way," Orioles executive vice president and general manager Mike Elias said. "I liken it to deciding what to order at a five-star restaurant. This was a very good class. We boiled it down to five players. We had advocates and rationale for taking any one of the five players. But ultimately, you're only allowed to come home with one of them, and we picked our favorite one."

DANIEL SHIREY/MLB PHOTOS VIA GETTY

With one of their pair of first-round picks, the Mets landed catcher Kevin Parada.

Holliday, 18, blossomed his senior year into one

FIRST-ROUND BONUS PROGRESSION

After several years of fairly consistent growth of first round bonuses, the money has reached a bit of a plateau in the three years since the covid, five-round draft. In part that stemmed from bonus values remaining static, though the 2022 draft saw slot values increase once again, while being tied to increased revenues around the league.

Still, first round bonus averages have mostly hovered around $4 million in each of the last three drafts and the 2022 average failed to top the 2020 mark as the highest average of all time.

After the first draft in 1965, first-round bonuses rose by an average of just 0.6 percent annually for the rest of the 1960s and 5.2 percent per year in the 1970s. Bonus inflation picked up in the 1980s, averaging 10.2 percent annually, and soared to 26.9 percent per year in the 1990s.

Below are the annual averages for first-round bonuses since the draft started in 1965. The 1996 total does not include four players who became free agents through a loophole in the draft rules.

Year	Average	Change	Year	Average	Change	Year	Average	Change	Year	Average	Change
1965	$42,516	—	1980	$74,025	8.70%	1995	$918,019	16.10%	2010	$2,220,966	-8.80%
1966	$44,430	4.50%	1981	$78,573	6.10%	1996*	$944,404	2.90%	2011	$2,653,375	19.50%
1967	$42,898	-3.40%	1982	$82,615	5.10%	1997	$1,325,536	40.40%	2012	$2,475,167	-6.70%
1968	$43,850	2.20%	1983	$87,236	5.60%	1998	$1,637,667	23.10%	2013	$2,641,538	6.70%
1969	$43,504	-0.80%	1984	$105,391	20.80%	1999	$1,809,767	10.50%	2014	$2,612,109	-1.10%
1970	$45,230	3.90%	1985	$118,115	12.10%	2000	$1,872,586	3.50%	2015	$2,774,945	6.23%
1971	$45,197	-0.10%	1986	$116,300	-1.60%	2001	$2,154,280	15.00%	2016	$2,897,557	4.42%
1972	$44,952	-0.50%	1987	$128,480	10.50%	2002	$2,106,793	-2.20%	2017	$3,880,723	25.4%
1973	$48,832	8.60%	1988	$142,540	10.90%	2003	$1,765,667	-16.20%	2018	$3,754,123	-3.37%
1974	$53,333	9.20%	1989	$176,008	23.50%	2004	$1,958,448	10.90%	2019	$3,791,729	1.01%
1975	$49.33	-7.50%	1990	$252,577	43.50%	2005	$2,018,000	3.00%	2020	$4,080,307	7.61%
1976	$49,631	0.60%	1991	$365,396	44.70%	2006	$1,933,333	-4.20%	2021	$4,009,424	-1.74%
1977	$48,813	-1.60%	1992	$481,893	31.90%	2007	$2,098,083	8.50%	2022	$4,074,268	1.62%
1978	$67,892	39.10%	1993	$613,037	27.20%	2008	$2,458,714	17.20%			
1979	$68,094	0.20%	1994	$790,357	28.90%	2009	$2,434,800	-1.00%			

of the top players in the draft class. He stood out as a talented but hardly elite prospect on the summer showcase circuit and into the fall, but he came out bigger, stronger and faster in the spring and rapidly rose up draft boards. He hit .685 with 17 home runs, 79 RBIs and 30 stolen bases in 40 games for Stillwater and led the Pioneers to the Oklahoma 6A regional playoffs.

Orioles scouts Ken Guthrie and Jim Richardson, who both live in Oklahoma, identified Holliday's improvements early in the spring and alerted the front office. Elias spent multiple days personally scouting Holliday, including seeing three games and a workout, and the O's put him in their mix for No. 1 by late March.

"He was not viewed as a top couple pick sort of guy in the fall and the summer last year and was not somebody that we focused on in our winter meetings for this pick, but we liked him and were planning on following him for the draft," Elias said. "And then the physical gains that he made over the winter enabled his swing to just come together in a more postured and balanced way. His performance shot through the roof and the speed and power ticked up. When the local scouts in the Midwest in the early part of the spring to see him, it was like there was a fire alarm in the scouting industry, and we certainly poured in there very heavily from that point forward."

Elias identified, by description but not by name, Wesleyan (Suwanee, Ga.) High outfielder Druw Jones, IMG Academy (Bradenton, Fla.) outfielder Elijah Green and Cal Poly shortstop Brooks Lee as three of the other players the club considered with the No. 1 overall pick. He did not identify the fifth player in consideration.

Elias said the decision to take Holliday wasn't unanimous in the draft room, but there was a strong consensus for him to be the pick.

"We had arguments for any of these five guys, but this was a player we were all happy with," Elias said. "He was a 'yes,' so to speak, for anybody involved in this process. Ultimately, he was our favorite choice, and this is the way we went tonight."

BONUS SPENDING BY TEAM

Teams combined to spend $313.8 million on draft bonuses in 2022, which is the first time teams have eclipsed the $300 million mark since the 2019 draft, which is still the year teams spent the most on bonuses at $316.5 million.

Spending fell significantly during 2020 and 2021 thanks to the covid pandemic, which limited the 2020 draft to just five rounds, and also saw the 2021 draft class slot values remain stagnant. While the 2022 draft remained 20 rounds (and is expected to remain at 20 rounds moving forward), increased slot values led to increased bonuses overall.

The CBA that went into effect in 2012 curtailed spending by instituting harsh penalties for teams that exceeded their bonus pools by more than five percent. It also ended the practice of awarding major league contracts to draftees. But as revenues within the game have increased, so too have the bonus pools MLB allocated to teams for the first 10 rounds. No team has yet been willing to exceed the five percent mark.

The Orioles spent more than any other club in 2022, thanks to owning the first overall pick, as well as five selections among the top 100—in addition to SS Jackson Holliday's $8.19 million bonus as the No. 1 pick, which was also the top signing bonus of the 2022 draft, while Baltimore also handed out four more bonuses worth more than a million: OF Dylan Beavers ($2.2), 3B Max Wagner ($1.9), SS Carter Young ($1.3) and OF Jud Fabian ($1.0).

TEAM	2022	2021	2020
Angels	$8,352,250	$10,722,500	$6,454,200
Astros	$7,972,630	$3,427,500	$2,283,000
Athletics	$9,448,700	$7,196,500	$5,447,400
Blue Jays	$9,536,100	$6,884,200	$10,202,325
Braves	$11,886,600	$7,590,000	$3,991,800
Brewers	$7,572,500	$10,623,400	$5,417,900
Cardinals	$7,744,300	$9,445,000	$8,290,000
Cubs	$11,583,000	$7,748,300	$6,866,800
Diamondbacks	$15,470,200	$11,946,900	$7,184,900
Dodgers	$5,559,990	$5,754,000	$6,224,000
Giants	$6,886,220	$9,213,200	$9,457,500
Guardians	$11,635,000	$8,468,400	$7,390,000
Mariners	$8,421,500	$9,359,600	$9,961,100
Marlins	$11,300,900	$11,257,290	$12,004,700
Mets	$14,716,560	$4,342,900	$7,499,000
Nationals	$12,688,200	$10,106,600	$6,647,000
Orioles	$17,735,600	$12,514,700	$13,672,300
Padres	$11,647,800	$7,763,300	$11,180,004
Phillies	$7,417,100	$9,530,600	$5,700,000
Pirates	$14,543,800	$15,938,700	$11,067,400
Rangers	$10,700,500	$13,362,000	$7,275,000
Rays	$8,511,700	$8,694,800	$7,474,200
Red Sox	$9,204,750	$10,761,900	$5,250,000
Reds	$12,225,800	$13,638,300	$8,546,000
Rockies	$14,338,300	$11,372,200	$10,332,800
Royals	$11,042,000	$12,557,300	$12,520,000
Tigers	$9,221,900	$16,165,700	$13,978,600
Twins	$10,971,500	$8,845,900	$4,330,000
White Sox	$7,557,900	$8,087,000	$7,757,500
Yankees	$7,969,500	$8,089,800	$3,687,400

Texas Rocks The Baseball World

All we had been saying leading up to this draft was how hitter heavy it was at the top and how it could take some time before the first pitcher was drafted.

Texas had other plans, and made the most surprising move of day one when it selected former Vanderbilt righthander Kumar Rocker—and reunited him with Vandy teammate Jack Leiter—with the third overall pick.

We regularly mentioned that Rocker was one of the bigger wild cards in the class given his exceptional talent and the risk associated with him given his medical situation. Around the 10th pick in the draft was the earliest we anticipated him coming off the board, and No. 3 was downright shocking, especially considering Texas wouldn't pick again until the 109th pick (fourth round).

It was a risky gambit, particularly with a number of highly regarded hitters on the board, but one that could pay off if Rocker simply stays on the mound and logs his innings. There's a case to be made that he was still the most talented pitcher in the class and the stuff he showed with Tri-City in the Frontier League was essentially equal to what made him a top-five prospect in the 2021 draft a year ago with the Commodores.

Mets Snag High-Quality Bats

It's becoming almost commonplace in the draft for one of the top players on our draft board to slide down further than we expect, but to a team with multiple picks and plenty of bonus pool money to make that slide worthwhile.

This year, it was Georgia Tech catcher Kevin Parada—who we expected to be in play as high as the No. 3 pick in the draft—who fell outside of his expected range and landed with the Mets and their third-highest bonus pool.

There was a case to be made that Parada was the best pure hitter in the draft (he was in the running with Termarr Johnson and Brooks Lee) and the fact that he hit 26 home runs and plays the most premium position on the field is simply icing on the cake.

The Mets continued to target standout pure hitters with their subsequent picks, taking Texas high school shortstop Jett Williams with their second first-round pick at No. 14, and then nabbing pop-up Washington D.C. prep infielder Nick Morabito—who was drafted as an outfielder and has more than enough speed to play center—with the No. 75 pick in the second supplemental round.

In between Morabito and Williams, the Mets drafted flame-throwing Tennessee righthander Blade Tidwell, who entered the year as a potential middle-of-the-first round talent.

Having extra picks and pool money always helps and it's easy to come away from night one excited about what's happening in New York.

MIKE JANES/FOUR SEAM IMAGES

Termarr Johnson received a $7.2 million bonus as the No. 4 overall pick.

HIGHEST BONUSES EVER

Four of the top-five picks in the 2022 draft joined the list for the highest bonuses in draft history: Jackson Holliday, Druw Jones, Termarr Johnson and Elijah Green. No player topped the all-time bonus record that Spencer Torkelson set in 2020, when the Tigers signed him for $8,416,300 as the No. 1 overall pick.

Player, Pos.	Team, Year (Pick)	Bonus
Spencer Torkelson, 1B	Tigers, 2020 (No. 1)	$8,416,300
Jackson Holliday, SS	Orioles, 2022 (No. 1)	$8,190,000
Druw Jones, OF	D-backs, 2022 (No. 2)	$8,189,400
Adley Rutschman, C	Orioles, 2019 (No. 1)	$8,100,000
Gerrit Cole, RHP	Pirates, 2011 (No. 1)	$8,000,000
Jack Leiter, RHP	Rangers, 2021 (No. 2)	$7,922,000
Bobby Witt Jr., SS	Royals, 2019 (No. 2)	$7,787,400
Stephen Strasburg, RHP	Nationals, 2009 (No. 1)	*$7,500,000
Bubba Starling, OF	Royals, 2011 (No. 5)	+$7,500,000
Casey Mize, RHP	Tigers, 2018 (No. 1)	$7,500,000
Hunter Greene, RHP/SS	Reds, 2017 (No. 2)	$7,230,000
Andrew Vaughn, 1B	White Sox, 2019 (No. 3)	$7,221,200
Termarr Johnson, SS	Pirates, 2022 (No. 4)	$7,219,000
Joey Bart, C	Giants, 2018 (No. 2)	$7,025,000
Brendan McKay, 1B/LHP	Rays, 2017 (No. 4)	$7,005,000
Austin Martin, SS	Blue Jays, 2020 (No. 5)	$7,000,825
Kyle Wright, RHP	Braves, 2017 (No. 5)	$7,000,000
Jackson Jobe, RHP	Tigers, 2021 (No. 3)	$6,900,000
Royce Lewis, SS	Twins, 2017 (No. 1)	$6,725,000
Jordan Lawlar, SS	D-backs, 2021 (No. 6)	$6,713,300
Kris Bryant, 3B	Cubs, 2013 (No. 2)	$6,708,400
MacKenzie Gore, LHP	Padres, 2017 (No. 3)	$6,700,000
Max Meyer, RHP	Marlins, 2020 (No. 3)	$6,700,000
JJ Bleday, OF	Marlins, 2019 (No. 4)	$6,670,000
Marcelo Mayer, SS	Red Sox, 2021 (No. 4)	$6,664,000
Asa Lacy, LHP	Royals, 2020 (No. 4)	$6,670,000
Carlos Rodon, LHP	White Sox, 2014 (No. 3)	$6,582,000
Elijah Green, OF	Nationals, 2022 (No. 5)	$6,500,000
Jameson Taillon, RHP	Pirates, 2010 (No. 2)	$6,500,000
Dansby Swanson, SS	D-backs, 2015 (No. 1)	$6,500,000

**Part of major league contract. +Bonus spread over multiple years under MLB two-sport provisions*

An All-Time Draft For Georgia?

There's a good chance the scouting directors and high-end decision-makers with teams picking at the top of the draft this year got heavily acquainted with baseball fields in Georgia.

The Peach State is annually one of the better talent-producers in the country. Georgia falls behind only behind California, Florida and Texas on the volume of pro players produced, and the 2022 class has a chance to be one of the strongest years ever for the state.

High school center fielder Druw Jones, the consensus top player in the class, hails from Georgia. So does shortstop Termarr Johnson, the No. 4 prospect, who is one of the most impressive amateur hitters scouts have seen in years.

The duo represented the best pairing of Georgia high school prospects since the 2013 class produced top 10 overall draft picks Clint Frazier and Austin Meadows, both outfielders.

Georgia Tech catcher Kevin Parada (No. 6) was one of college baseball's best hitters this spring and is the best college prospect to come out of the state since fellow Yellow Jackets catcher Joey Bart in 2018.

NO. 1 OVERALL PICKS

Year	Team: Player, Pos., School	Bonus
1965	**Athletics:** Rick Monday, OF, Arizona State	$100,000
1966	**Mets:** Steve Chilcott, C, Antelope Valley HS, Lancaster, Calif.	$75,000
1967	**Yankees:** Ron Blomberg, 1B, Druid Hills HS, Atlanta	$65,000
1968	**Mets:** Tim Foli, SS, Notre Dame HS, Sherman Oaks, Calif.	$74,000
1969	**Senators:** Jeff Burroughs, OF, Centennial HS, Long Beach	$88,000
1970	**Padres:** Mike Ivie, C, Walker HS, Atlanta	$75,000
1971	**White Sox:** Danny Goodwin, C, Peoria (Ill.) HS	Did Not Sign
1972	**Padres:** Dave Roberts, 3B, Oregon	$70,000
1973	**Rangers:** David Clyde, LHP, Westchester HS, Texas	*$65,000
1974	**Padres:** Bill Almon, SS, Brown	*$90,000
1975	**Angels:** Danny Goodwin, C, Southern	*$125,000
1976	**Astros:** Floyd Bannister, LHP, Arizona State	$100,000
1977	**White Sox:** Harold Baines, OF, St. Michaels (Md.) HS	$32,000
1978	**Braves:** Bob Horner, 3B, Arizona State	*$162,000
1979	**Mariners:** Al Chambers, 1B, Harris HS, Harrisburg, Pa.	$60,000
1980	**Mets:** Darryl Strawberry, OF, Crenshaw HS, Los Angeles	$152,500
1981	**Mariners:** Mike Moore, RHP, Oral Roberts	$100,000
1982	**Cubs:** Shawon Dunston, SS, Jefferson HS, New York	$135,000
1983	**Twins:** Tim Belcher, RHP, Mount Vernon Nazarene (Ohio)	Did Not Sign
1984	**Mets:** Shawn Abner, OF, Mechanicsburg (Pa.) HS	$150,500
1985	**Brewers:** B.J. Surhoff, C, North Carolina	$150,000
1986	**Pirates:** Jeff King, 3B, Arkansas	$180,000
1987	**Mariners:** Ken Griffey Jr., OF, Moeller HS, Cincinnati	$160,000
1988	**Padres:** Andy Benes, RHP, Evansville	$235,000
1989	**Orioles:** Ben McDonald, RHP, Louisiana State	*$350,000
1990	**Braves:** Chipper Jones, SS, The Bolles School, Jacksonville	$275,000
1991	**Yankees:** Brien Taylor, LHP, East Carteret HS, Beaufort, N.C.	$1,550,000
1992	**Astros:** Phil Nevin, 3B, Cal State Fullerton	$700,000
1993	**Mariners:** Alex Rodriguez, SS, Westminster Christian HS, Miami	*$1,000,000
1994	**Mets:** Paul Wilson, RHP, Florida State	$1,550,000
1995	**Angels:** Darin Erstad, OF, Nebraska	$1,575,000
1996	**Pirates:** Kris Benson, RHP, Clemson	$2,000,000
1997	**Tigers:** Matt Anderson, RHP, Tigers	$2,505,000
1998	**Phillies:** Pat Burrell, 3B, Miami	*$3,150,000
1999	**Devil Rays:** Josh Hamilton, OF, Athens Drive HS, Raleigh	$3,960,000
2000	**Marlins:** Adrian Gonzalez, 1B, Eastlake HS, Chula Vista, Calif.	$3,000,000
2001	**Twins:** Joe Mauer, C, Cretin-Derham Hall, St. Paul	$5,150,000
2002	**Pirates:** Bryan Bullington, RHP, Ball State	$4,000,000
2003	**Devil Rays:** Delmon Young, OF, Camarillo (Calif.) HS	*$3,700,000
2004	**Padres:** Matt Bush, SS, Mission Bay HS, San Diego	$3,150,000
2005	**D-backs:** Justin Upton, SS, Great Bridge HS, Chesapeake, Va.	$6,100,000
2006	**Royals:** Luke Hochevar, RHP, Fort Worth (American Assoc.)	*$3,500,000
2007	**Devil Rays:** David Price, LHP, Vanderbilt	*$5,600,000
2008	**Rays:** Tim Beckham, SS, Griffin (Ga.) HS	$6,150,000
2009	**Nationals:** Stephen Strasburg, RHP, San Diego State	*$7,500,000
2010	**Nationals:** Bryce Harper, OF, JC of Southern Nevada	*$6,250,000
2011	**Pirates:** Gerrit Cole, RHP, UCLA	$8,000,000
2012	**Astros:** Carlos Correa, SS, Puerto Rico Baseball Acad., Gurabo, P.R.	$4,800,000
2013	**Astros:** Mark Appel, RHP, Stanford	$6,350,000
2014	**Astros:** Brady Aiken, LHP, Cathedral Catholic, San Diego	Did Not Sign
2015	**D-backs:** Dansby Swanson, SS, Vanderbilt	$6,500,000
2016	**Phillies:** Mickey Moniak, OF, La Costa Canyon HS, Carlsbad, Calif.	$6,100,000
2017	**Twins:** Royce Lewis, SS, JSerra Catholic HS, San Juan Capistrano, Calif.	$6,750,000
2018	**Tigers:** Casey Mize, RHP, Auburn	$7,500,000
2019	**Orioles:** Adley Rutschman, C, Oregon State	$8,100,000
2020	**Tigers:** Spencer Torkelson, 3B, Arizona State	$8,416,300
2019	**Pirates:** Henry Davis, C, Louisville	$6,500,000
2022	**Orioles:** Jackson Holliday, SS, Stillwater (Okla.) HS	$8,190,000

**Part of major league contract.*

The high-end talent didn't stop there. Buford High righthander Dylan Lesko was the clear top pitching prospect in the class when healthy. If not for Tommy John surgery, he would also rank among the class' top prospects.

Each of the players mentioned were drafted in the first round, and while that group of four doesn't surpass a 2010 class that had six Georgia players selected in the first round, the 2022 group far and away sets the record for total signing bonus from the state among first round draftees, with more than $24 million in total.

A Lack Of Pitching

Speaking of injured pitchers, the 2022 class was decimated by injuries to top-end pitching talents, particularly on the college side.

The wave of injuries hit so hard that this class had a chance to be the worst college pitching crop the industry had seen—and that's coming just a few years after a 2019 class was criticized in a similar manner.

Seven college pitchers ranked among the top 30 on our preseason top 200 draft prospects list. Of those, five dealt with injuries and the other two—Kumar Rocker and Carson Whisenhunt—didn't throw a single pitch in college baseball this spring. The former was showcasing for scouts in the independent Frontier League, the latter in the Cape Cod League in the lead-up to the draft.

Tennessee righthander Blade Tidwell suffered shoulder soreness and missed time early in the season. Arkansas righty Peyton Pallette had Tommy John surgery before the season began. Mississippi State righty Landon Sims made just three starts before TJ ended his season. Alabama lefthander Connor Prielipp had TJ in 2021 and didn't pitch at all this spring.

Florida lefthander Hunter Barco was well on his way to a strong season—he had a 2.50 ERA through 50.1—before his own Tommy John surgery.

If a team was looking for a polished, fast-moving pitcher at the top of the 2022 draft, then it was out of luck.

Bloodlines Abound

If the 2022 draft isn't remembered for its lack of college arms or its impressive depth of bats, it very well could be remembered as the "bloodlines draft."

Each year, there are notable prospects who are the sons, brothers or nephews of prominent former players or coaches. The 2022 class stands out for both the quantity and quality of those prospects.

Six of the top 10 prospects come from notable athletic families:

- Druw Jones is the son of Andruw Jones, one of the best defensive center fielders in MLB history
- Brooks Lee's father is Larry Lee, who has coached the Cal Poly baseball team for two decades
- Jackson Holliday is the son of seven-time all-star Matt Holliday
- Elijah Green is the son of Eric Green, who was a 10-year tight end in the NFL
- Jace Jung is the younger brother of Rangers 2019 first-rounder Josh Jung
- Cam Collier is the son of eight-year big leaguer Lou Collier.

Beyond the top 10, notable bloodlines players include Daniel Susac (brother of former MLB catcher Andrew Susac), Justin Crawford (son of four-time all-star Carl Crawford), Cade Hunter (son of Mariners scouting director Scott Hunter) and Robert Moore (son of Royals president of baseball operations Dayton Moore).

THE BONUS RECORD

Rick Monday, the No. 1 overall pick in baseball's first draft in 1965, signed with the Athletics for $100,000—a figure that no draftee bettered for a decade. The record has been broken many times since, including in 2019, when Adley Rutschman signed with the Orioles as the No. 1 overall pick for $8,100,000. Spencer Torkelson broke the record immediately, signing for $8,416,300 as the No. 1 pick in the 2020 draft with the Tigers and holds it still today.

The longest bonus record stretch dates back to Todd Demeter, whose $208,000 bonus in 1979 held the mark for nine years until 1988 when Andy Benes topped him with a $235,000 bonus.

The list below represents only cash bonuses and doesn't include guaranteed money from major league deals, college scholarship plans or incentives. It also considers only players who signed with the clubs that drafted them and doesn't include draft picks who signed after being granted free agency.

Year	Player, Pos., Club (Round)	Bonus
1965	Rick Monday, OF, Athletics (1)	$100,000
1975	Danny Goodwin, C, Angels (1)	$125,000
1978	Kirk Gibson, OF, Tigers (1)	$150,000
	*Bob Horner, 3B, Braves (1)	$162,000
1979	Todd Demeter, 1B, Yankees (2)	$208,000
1988	Andy Benes, RHP, Padres (1)	$235,000
1989	Tyler Houston, C, Braves (1)	$241,500
	*Ben McDonald, RHP, Orioles (1)	$350,000
	*John Olerud, 1B, Blue Jays (3)	$575,000
1991	Mike Kelly, OF, Braves (1)	$575,000
	Brien Taylor, LHP, Yankees (1)	$1,550,000
1994	Paul Wilson, RHP, Mets (1)	$1,550,000
	Josh Booty, 3B, Marlins (1)	$1,600,000
1996	Kris Benson, RHP, Pirates (1)	$2,000,000
1997	Rick Ankiel, LHP, Cardinals (2)	$2,500,000
	Matt Anderson, RHP, Tigers (1)	$2,505,000
1998	*J.D. Drew, OF, Cardinals (1)	$3,000,000
	*Pat Burrell, 3B, Phillies (1)	$3,150,000
	Mark Mulder, LHP, Athletics (1)	$3,200,000
	Corey Patterson, OF, Cubs (1)	$3,700,000
1999	Josh Hamilton, OF, Devil Rays (1)	$3,960,000
2000	Joe Borchard, OF, White Sox (1)	$5,300,000
2005	Justin Upton, SS, D-backs (1)	$6,100,000
2008	Tim Beckham, SS, Rays (1)	$6,150,000
	Buster Posey, C, Giants (1)	$6,200,000
2009	Donavan Tate, OF, Padres (1)	$6,250,000
	*Stephen Strasburg, RHP, Nationals (1)	$7,500,000
2011	Gerrit Cole, RHP, Pirates (1)	$8,000,000
2019	Adley Rutschman, C, Orioles (1)	$8,100,000
2020	Spencer Torkelson, 3B, Tigers (1)	$8,416,300

Other Draft Tidbits

Baseball America teamed up with Pramana to use the company's SHIFT tool. SHIFT helps companies find instant answers to a wide variety of questions by using natural language search and free text to turn data into content and insights. Pramana used the SHIFT tool to find a variety of insights and nuggets about each of the first-round picks in the 2022 draft.

1. With the top pick the Orioles selected Jackson Holliday. This is the second time ever a player from the state of Oklahoma has been selected No. 1 overall. Oral Roberts RHP Mike Moore (Mariners, 1981) was the only other Oklahoman picked with the top pick.

2. Jackson Holliday is the 10th high school shortstop to be picked first overall. The others are Royce Lewis (2017), Carlos Correa (2012), Tim Beckham (2008), Justin Upton (2005), Matt Bush (2004), Alex Rodriguez (1993), Chipper Jones (1990), Shawon Dunston (1982) and Tim Foli (1968).

3. Before selecting Holliday with the No. 1 pick, the last time the Orioles selected a high school shortstop in the first round was Ryan Mountcastle in 2015. They've drafted four prep shortstops all-time in the first round.

4. Druw Jones was the fifth high school outfielder picked second overall, joining Byron Buxton—Twins (2012), Ben Grieve—Athletics (1994), Tony Clark—Tigers (1990) and Mark Merchant—Pirates (1987).

5. The Rangers selecting Kumar Rocker at pick

DRAFT

BONUSES VS. PICK VALUES

After the 2020 and 2021 drafts saw frozen slot values due to the covid pandemic, 2022 slot values increased by more than 5% and will continue to increase at the same level as MLB revenues moving forward. Slot value for the No. 1 overall pick was more than $8.8 million, which would have represented a new all-time signing bonus record if a player signed for that amount.

No. 1 pick Jackson Holliday signed a significantly under slot deal, but still managed a bigger bonus than every other player in the 2022 draft class.

The top-50 bonuses added up to $173,268,495 compared to slot values of $168,455,700 for those picks. RHP Brock Porter was responsible for the biggest over-slot deal in the draft in 2022. The second overall pick for the Rangers, Porter signed for mid-first round money ($3.7 million) while the slot value for his pick selection was just $560,200.

Player, Pos., Team (Round/Overall Pick)	Bonus	Pick Value
1. Jackson Holliday, SS, Stillwater (Okla.) HS (1st round/No. 1)	$8,190,000	$8,846,900
2. Druw Jones, OF, Wesleyan HS, Norcross, Ga. (1st round/No. 2)	$8,189,400	$8,189,400
3. Termarr Johnson, SS, Mays HS, Atlanta (1st round/No. 4)	$7,219,000	$7,005,800
4. Elijah Green, OF, IMG Academy, Bradenton, Fla. (1st round/No. 5)	$6,500,000	$6,497,700
5. Jacob Berry, 3B, Louisiana State (1st round/No. 6)	$6,000,000	$6,037,500
6. Brooks Lee, SS, Cal Poly (1st round/No. 8)	$5,675,000	$5,442,400
7. Gavin Cross, OF, Virginia Tech (1st round/No. 9)	$5,200,400	$5,202,900
8. Kumar Rocker, RHP, Tri-City (Frontier) (1st round/No. 3)	$5,200,000	$7,591,600
9. Kevin Parada, C, Georgia Tech (1st round/No. 11)	$5,019,735	$4,780,700
10. Cam Collier, 3B, Chipola (Fla.) JC (1st round/No. 18	$5,000,000	$3,659,800
11. Jace Jung, 2B, Texas Tech (1st round/No. 12)	$4,590,300	$4,590,300
12. Cade Horton, RHP, Oklahoma (1st round/No. 7)	$4,450,000	$5,711,000
13. Gabriel Hughes, RHP, Gonzaga (1st round/No. 10)	$4,000,000	$4,983,000
14. Jett Williams, SS, Rockwall-Heath HS, Rockwall, Texas (1st round/No. 14)	$3,900,000	$4,243,800
15. Dylan Lesko, RHP, Buford (Ga.) HS (1st round/No. 15)	$3,900,000	$4,085,000
16. Justin Crawford, OF, Bishop Gorman HS, Las Vegas (1st round/No. 17)	$3,894,000	$3,794,800
17. Chase DeLauter, OF, James Madison (1st round/No. 16)	$3,750,000	$3,937,600
18. Brock Porter, RHP, St. Mary's Prep, Orchard Lake, Mich. (4th round/No. 109)	$3,700,000	$560,200
19. Brandon Barriera, LHP, American Heritage HS, Plantation, Fla. (1st round/No. 23)	$3,597,500	$3,076,900
20. Daniel Susac, C, Arizona (1st round/No. 19)	$3,531,200	$3,531,200
21. Zach Neto, SS, Campbell (1st round/No. 13)	$3,500,000	$4,412,500
22. Cole Young, SS, North Allegheny HS, Wexford, Pa. (1st round/No. 21)	$3,300,000	$3,292,900
23. Cooper Hjerpe, LHP, Oregon State (1st round/No. 22)	$3,182,200	$3,182,200
24. Jackson Ferris, LHP, IMG Academy, Bradenton, Fla. (2nd round/No. 47)	$3,005,000	$1,661,200
25. Robby Snelling, LHP, McQueen HS, Reno, Nev. (supp. 1st round/No. 39)	$3,000,000	$2,004,500
26. Spencer Jones, OF, Vanderbilt (1st round/No. 25)	$2,880,800	$2,880,800
27. Noah Schultz, LHP, Oswego (Ill.) East HS (1st round/No. 26)	$2,800,000	$2,789,400
28. Owen Murphy, RHP, Riverside-Brookfield HS, Riverside, Ill. (1st round/No. 20)	$2,556,900	$3,409,200
29. Xavier Isaac, 1B, East Forsyth HS, Kernersville, N.C. (1st round/No. 29)	$2,548,900	$2,548,900
30. Roman Anthony, OF, Stoneman Douglas HS, Parkland, Fla. (supp. 2nd round/No. 79)	$2,500,000	$820,400
31. Drew Gilbert, OF, Tennessee (1st round/No. 28)	$2,497,500	$2,621,700
32. Sterlin Thompson, OF, Florida (1st round/No. 31)	$2,430,500	$2,430,500
33. JR Ritchie, RHP, Bainbridge HS, Bainbridge Island, Wash. (supp. 1st round/No. 35)	$2,397,500	$2,203,200
34. Jacob Misiorowski, RHP, Crowder (Mo.) JC (2nd round/No. 63)	$2,350,000	$1,131,500
35. Landon Sims, RHP, Mississippi State (supp. 1st round/No. 34)	$2,347,050	$2,258,300
36. Mikey Romero, SS, Orange Lutheran HS, Orange, Calif. (1st round/No. 24)	$2,300,000	$2,976,400
37. Reggie Crawford, LHP, Connecticut (1st round/No. 30)	$2,297,500	$2,486,800
38. Dylan Beavers, OF, California (supp. 1st round/No. 33)	$2,200,000	$2,315,100
39. Jordan Beck, OF, Tennessee (supp. 1st round/No. 38)	$2,200,000	$2,052,300
40. Sal Stewart, 3B, Westminster Christian HS, Miami (1st round/No. 32)	$2,100,000	$2,373,000
41. Eric Brown, SS, Coastal Carolina (1st round/No. 27)	$2,050,000	$2,701,900
42. Thomas Harrington, RHP, Campbell (supp. 1st round/No. 36)	$2,047,500	$2,150,300
43. Henry Bolte, OF, Palo Alto (Calif.) HS (2nd round/No. 56)	$2,000,000	$1,341,900
44. Tucker Toman, SS, Hammond HS, Columbia, S.C. (supp. 2nd round/No. 77)	$2,000,000	$846,900
45. Dalton Rushing, C, Louisville (2nd round/No. 40)	$1,956,890	$1,951,900
46. Max Wagner, 3B, Clemson (2nd round/No. 42)	$1,900,000	$1,861,900
47. Carson Whisenhunt, LHP, East Carolina (2nd round/No. 66)	$1,866,220	$1,054,700
48. Jackson Cox, RHP, Toutle Lake HS, Toutle, Wash. (2nd round/No. 50)	$1,850,000	$1,545,300
49. Blade Tidwell, RHP, Tennessee (2nd round/No. 52)	$1,850,000	$1,475,100
50. Cutter Coffey, SS, Liberty HS, Bakersfield, Calif. (2nd round/No. 41)	$1,847,500	$1,906,500
Total	**$173,268,495**	**$168,455,700**

No 3 marks the third time in franchise history they selected a four-year collegian in the first round in consecutive years. The other years were Bobby Witt (1985) and Kevin Brown (1986), Jonathan Johnson (1995) and R.A. Dickey (1996).

6. The Pirates selected Termarr Johnson at pick No. 4. The last time the Pirates selected a first-round high school shortstop was Cole Tucker in 2014.

7. The selections of Druw Jones and Termarr Johnson at picks No. 2 and No. 4 were the first time two players from the state of Georgia have been selected in the first four picks in MLB Draft history.

TOP 100 PICKS

Team, Player, Pos., School	Bonus
1. BAL. Jackson Holliday, SS, Stillwater (Okla.) HS	$8,190,000
2. ARI. Druw Jones, OF, Wesleyan HS, Norcross, Ga.	$8,189,400
3. TEX. Kumar Rocker, RHP, Tri-City (Frontier)	$5,200,000
4. PIT. Termarr Johnson, SS, Mays HS, Atlanta	$7,219,000
5. WAS. Elijah Green, OF, IMG Academy, Bradenton, Fla	$6,500,000
6. MIA. Jacob Berry, 3B, Louisiana State	$6,000,000
7. CHC. Cade Horton, RHP, Oklahoma	$4,450,000
8. MIN. Brooks Lee, SS, Cal Poly	$5,675,000
9. KCR. Gavin Cross, OF, Virginia Tech	$5,200,400
10. COL. Gabriel Hughes, RHP, Gonzaga	$4,000,000
11. NYM. Kevin Parada, C, Georgia Tech	$5,019,735
12. DET. Jace Jung, 2B, Texas Tech	$4,590,300
13. LAA. Zach Neto, SS, Campbell	$3,500,000
14. NYM. Jett Williams, SS, Rockwall-Heath HS, Rockwall, Texas	$,3900,000
15. SDP. Dylan Lesko, RHP, Buford (Ga.) HS	$3,900,000
16. CLE. Chase DeLauter, OF, James Madison	$3,750,000
17. PHI. Justin Crawford, OF, Bishop Gorman HS, Las Vegas	$3,894,000
18. CIN. Cam Collier, 3B, Chipola (Fla.) JC	$5,000,000
19. OAK. Daniel Susac, C, Arizona	$3,531,200
20. ATL. Owen Murphy, RHP, Riverside-Brookfield HS, Riverside, Ill	$2,556,900
21. SEA. Cole Young, SS, North Allegheny HS, Wexford, Pa	$3,300,000
22. STL. Cooper Hjerpe, LHP, Oregon State	$3,182,200
23. TOR. Brandon Barriera, LHP, American Heritage HS, Plantation, Fla.	$3,597,500
24. BOS. Mikey Romero, SS, Arkansas	$2,300,000
25. NYY. Spencer Jones, OF, Vanderbilt	$2,880,800
26. CWS. Noah Schultz, LHP, Oswego (Ill.) East HS	$2,800,000
27. MIL. Eric Brown, SS, Coastal Carolina	$2,050,000
28. HOU. Drew Gilbert, OF, Tennessee	$2,497,500
29. TBR. Xavier Isaac, 1B, East Forsyth HS, Kernersville, N.C	$2,548,900
30. SFG. Reggie Crawford, LHP, Connecticut	$2,297,500
31. COL. Sterlin Thompson, OF, Florida	$2,430,500
32. CIN. Sal Stewart, 3B, Westminster Christian HS, Miami	$2,100,000
33. BAL. Dylan Beavers, OF, California	$2,200,000
34. ARI. Landon Sims, RHP, Mississippi State	$2,347,050
35. ATL. JR Ritchie, RHP, Bainbridge HS, Bainbridge Island, Wash .	$2,397,500
36. PIT. Thomas Harrington, RHP, Campbell	$2,047,500
37. CLE. Justin Campbell, RHP, Oklahoma State	$1,700,000
38. COL. Jordan Beck, OF, Tennessee	$2,200,000
39. SDP. Robby Snelling, LHP, McQueen HS, Reno, Nev	$3,000,000
40. LAD. Dalton Rushing, C, Louisville	$1,956,890
41. BOS. Cutter Coffey, SS, Liberty HS, Bakersfield, Calif	$1,847,500
42. BAL. Max Wagner, 3B, Clemson	$1,900,000
43. ARI. Ivan Melendez, 1B, Texas	$1,400,000
44. PIT. Hunter Barco, LHP, Florida	$1,525,000
45. WAS. Jake Bennett, LHP, Oklahoma	$1,734,800
46. MIA. Jacob Miller, RHP, Liberty Union HS, Baltimore, Ohio	$1,697,900
47. CHC. Jackson Ferris, LHP, IMG Academy, Bradenton, Fla	$3,005,000
48. MIN. Connor Prielipp, LHP, Alabama	$1,825,000
49. KCR. Cayden Wallace, 3B, Orange (Calif.) Lutheran HS	$1,697,500
50. COL. Jackson Cox, RHP, Toutle Lake HS, Toutle, Wash	$1,850,000
51. DET. Peyton Graham, SS, Oklahoma	$1,800,000
52. NYM. Blade Tidwell, RHP, Tennessee	$1,850,000
53. SDP. Adam Mazur, RHP, Iowa	$1,250,000
54. CLE. Parker Messick, LHP, Florida State	$1,300,000
55. CIN. Logan Tanner, C, Mississippi State	$1,030,500
56. OAK. Henry Bolte, OF, Palo Alto (Calif.) HS	$2,000,000
57. ATL. Cole Phillips, RHP, Boerne (Texas) HS	$1,497,500
58. SEA. Tyler Locklear, 3B, Virginia Commonwealth	$1,276,500
59. STL. Brycen Mautz, LHP, San Diego	$1,100,000
60. TOR. Josh Kasevich, SS, Oregon	$997,500
61. NYY. Drew Thorpe, RHP, Cal Poly	$1,187,600
62. CWS. Peyton Pallette, RHP, Arkansas	$1,500,000
63. MIL. Jacob Misiorowski, RHP, Crowder (Mo.) JC	$2,350,000
64. HOU. Jacob Melton, OF, Oregon State	$1,000,000
65. TBR. Brock Jones, OF, Stanford	$1,077,600
66. SFG. Carson Whisenhunt, LHP, East Carolina	$1,866,220

MIKE JANES/FOUR SEAM IMAGES

Jackson Holliday's bonus was $600 more than No. 2 pick Druw Jones received.

Team, Player, Pos., School	Bonus
67. BAL. Jud Fabian, OF, Florida	$1,026,800
68. MIN. Tanner Schobel, SS, Virginia Tech	$1,002,000
69. OAK. Clark Elliott, OF, Michigan	$900,000
70. TBR. Chandler Simpson, SS, Georgia Tech	$747,500
71. TBR. Ryan Cermak, SS, Illinois State	$747,500
72. MIL. Robert Moore, SS, Arkansas	$800,000
73. CIN. Justin Boyd, OF, Oregon State	$847,500
74. SEA. Walter Ford, RHP, Pace (Fla.) HS	$1,250,000
75. NYM. Nick Morabito, OF, Gonzaga HS, Washington D.C	$1,000,000
76. ATL. Blake Burkhalter, RHP, Auburn	$647,500
77. TOR. Tucker Toman, SS, Hammond HS, Columbia, S.C	$2,000,000
78. TOR. Cade Doughty, 2B, Louisiana State	$831,100
79. BOS. Roman Anthony, OF, Stoneman Douglas HS, Parkland, Fla	$2,500,000
80. HOU. Andrew Taylor, RHP, Central Michigan	$804,700
81. BAL. Nolan McLean, 3B, Oklahoma State	Did not sign
82. ARI. Nate Savino, LHP, Virginia	$700,000
83. PIT. Jack Brannigan, RHP, Notre Dame	$770,700
84. WAS. Trey Lipscomb, 3B, Tennessee	$758,900
85. MIA. Karson Milbrandt, RHP, Liberty (Mo.) HS	$1,497,500
86. CHC. Christopher Paciolla, SS, Temecula (Calif.) Valley HS	$900,000
87. KCR. Mason Barnett, RHP, Auburn	$697,500
88. COL. Carson Palmquist, LHP, Miami	$775,000
89. LAA. Ben Joyce, RHP, Tennessee	$997,500
90. NYM. Brandon Sproat, RHP, Florida	Did not sign
91. SDP. Henry Williams, RHP, Duke	$800,000
92. CLE. Joe Lampe, OF, Arizona State	$800,000
93. PHI. Gabriel Rincones, OF, Florida Atlantic	$627,500
94. CIN. Bryce Hubbart, LHP, Florida State	$522,500
95. OAK. Colby Thomas, OF, Mercer	$750,000
96. ATL. Drake Baldwin, C, Missouri State	$633,300
97. STL. Pete Hansen, LHP, Texas	$629,800
98. TOR. Alan Roden, OF, Creighton	$497,500
99. BOS. Dalton Rogers, LHP, Southern Mississippi	$44,7500
100. NYY. Trystan Vrieling, RHP, Gonzaga	$608,900

2022 CLUB-BY-CLUB SELECTIONS

Order Of Selection In Parentheses | Players Signed In Bold

DRAFT

ARIZONA DIAMONDBACKS (2)

1. Druw Jones, OF, Wesleyan HS, Norcross, Ga.
1s. Landon Sims, RHP, Mississippi State
2. Ivan Melendez, 1B, Texas
3. Nate Savino, LHP, Virginia
4. Dylan Ray, RHP, Alabama
5. Andrew Pintar, SS, Brigham Young
6. Will Mabrey, LHP, Tennessee
7. Demetrio Crisantes, SS, Nogales (Ariz.) HS
8. Adrian Rodriguez, SS, International Baseball Academy
9. Gavin Logan, C, Oregon State
10. Brett Johnson, OF, Southern Illinois University Edwardsville
11. Spencer Giesting, LHP, Charlotte
12. Malachi Witherspoon, RHP, Fletcher HS, Neptune Beach, Fla.
13. Eli Saul, RHP, Sacramento State
14. Kevin Graham, OF, Mississippi
15. Josh Day, SS, Missouri
16. David Martin, C, California Baptist
17. Logan Clayton, RHP, Houston
18. Aiva Arquette, SS, Saint Louis HS, Honolulu
19. Gavin Turley, OF, Hamilton HS, Chandler, Ariz.
20. Riley Kelly, RHP, Tustin (Calif.) HS

ATLANTA BRAVES (20)

1. Owen Murphy, RHP, Riverside-Brookfield HS, Riverside, Ill.
1s. JR Ritchie, RHP, Bainbridge HS, Bainbridge Island, Wash.
2. Cole Phillips, RHP, Boerne (Texas) HS
2s. Blake Burkhalter, RHP, Auburn
3. Drake Baldwin, C, Missouri State
4. David McCabe, 3B, Charlotte
5. Ignacio Alvarez, 3B, Riverside (Calif.) JC
6. Seth Keller, RHP, Hanover (Va.) HS
7. Adam Maier, RHP, Oregon
8. Jason Franks, RHP, Cal Poly
9. Cory Acton, 2B, Georgia
10. Andrew Keck, C, Southeast Missouri St U
11. Ian Mejia, RHP, New Mexico State
12. Justin Janas, 1B, Illinois
13. Cedric De Grandpre, RHP, Chipola (Fla.) JC
14. Landon Harper, RHP, Southern Mississippi
15. William Silva, RHP, Miami Dade (Fla.) JC
16. E.J. Exposito, SS, Long Island University
17. Kevin Kilpatrick, OF, Central Florida JC
18. Noah Williams, OF, Redondo Union HS
19. Christian Jackson, OF, Dutchtown HS
20. Keshawn Ogans, SS, California

BALTIMORE ORIOLES (1)

1. Jackson Holliday, SS, Stillwater (Okla.) HS
1s. Dylan Beavers, OF, California
2. Max Wagner, 3B, Clemson
2s. Jud Fabian, OF, Florida
3. Nolan McLean, 3B, Oklahoma State
4. Silas Ardoin, C, Texas
5. Trace Bright, RHP, Auburn
6. Douglas Hodo, OF, Texas
7. Preston Johnson, RHP, Mississippi State
8. Cameron Weston, RHP, Michigan
9. Adam Crampton, SS, Stanford
10. Wyatt Cheney, P, McLennan (Texas) CC
11. Zack Showalter, RHP, Wesley Chapel (Fla.) HS
12. Bradley Brehmer, RHP, Indiana
13. Jared Beck, LHP, Saint Leo (Fla.)
14. Adam Retzbach, C, Lehigh U
15. James Hicks, RHP, U South Carolina
16. Graham Firoved, RHP, Virginia Tech
17. Carter Young, SS, Vanderbilt
18. Andrew Walters, RHP, Miami
19. Alden Mathes, OF, U Richmond
20. Reese Sharp, RHP, Indiana

BOSTON RED SOX (24)

1. Mikey Romero, SS, Arkansas
2. Cutter Coffey, SS, Liberty HS, Bakersfield, Calif.
2s. Roman Anthony, OF, Stoneman Douglas HS, Parkland, Fla.
3. Dalton Rogers, LHP, Southern Mississippi
4. Chase Meidroth, SS, San Diego
5. Noah Dean, LHP, Old Dominion
6. Alex Hoppe, RHP, UNC Greensboro
7. Caleb Bolden, RHP, TCU
8. Jonathan Brand, RHP, Miami University
9. Brooks Brannon, C, Randleman (N.C.) HS
10. Isaac Coffey, RHP, Oral Roberts U
11. Marques Johnson, RHP, Long Beach State
12. Hayden Mullins, LHP, Auburn
13. Gavin Kilen, SS, Milton (Wisc.) HS
14. Travis Sanders, SS, Copperas Cove HS
15. Nathan Landry, LHP, U Missouri
16. Garrett Ramsey, RHP, Southern Mississippi
17. Deundre Jones, 1B, Lutheran South Academy
18. Austin Ehrlicher, RHP, Santa Rosa (Calif.) JC
19. Jaret Godman, RHP, Oklahoma
20. Connor Butler, LHP, Biola (Calif.)

CHICAGO CUBS (7)

1. Cade Horton, RHP, Oklahoma
2. Jackson Ferris, LHP, IMG Academy, Bradenton, Fla.
3. Christopher Paciolla, SS, Temecula (Calif.) Valley HS
4. Nazier Mule, SS, Passaic County Tech HS, Wayne, N.J.
5. Brandon Birdsell, RHP, Texas Tech
6. Will Frisch, RHP, Oregon State
7. Nick Hull, RHP, Grand Canyon University
8. Mason McGwire, RHP, Capistrano Valley HS, Mission Viejo, Calif.
9. Connor Noland, RHP, Arkansas
10. Brody McCullough, RHP, Wingate
11. Branden Noriega, LHP, No School
12. Mathew Peters, RHP, Indiana Institute of Tech
13. Luis Rujano, RHP, Sunshine State Elite Academy
14. Shane Marshall, RHP, U Georgia
15. Haydn McGeary, C, Colorado Mesa University
16. JP Wheat, RHP, Next Level Academy
17. Andy Garriola, OF, Old Dominion
18. Garrett Brown, RHP, Georgia
19. Brock Blatter, RHP, Billings (Mon.) Central Catholic HS
20. Ke'Shun Collier, OF, Meridian (Miss.) JC

CHICAGO WHITE SOX (26)

1. Noah Schultz, LHP, Oswego (Ill.) East HS
2. Peyton Pallette, RHP, Arkansas
3. Jonathan Cannon, RHP, Georgia
4. Jordan Sprinkle, SS, UC Santa Barbara
5. Tyler Schweitzer, LHP, Ball State
6. Eric Adler, RHP, Wake Forest
7. Mark McLaughlin, RHP, Tennessee
8. Mario Camilletti, 2B, Central Michigan
9. Michael Turner, C, Arkansas
10. Tim Elko, 1B, Ole Miss
11. Jacob Burke, OF, Miami
12. Brooks Baldwin, SS, UNC-Wilmington
13. Mason Adams, RHP, Jacksonville
14. Shane Murphy, LHP, Chandler Gilbert (Ariz.) JC

15. Billy Seidl, RHP, Duke
16. Tristan Stivors, RHP, Texas State
17. Nick Altermatt, RHP, Minnesota State - Mankato
18. Bryce Willits, 3B, UC Santa Barbara
19. Drake Logan, 3B, Shelton State (Ala.) JC
20. Ethan Hammerberg, RHP, Ohio State

CINCINNATI REDS (18)

1. Cam Collier, 3B, Chipola (Fla.) JC
1. Sal Stewart, 3B, Westminster Christian HS, Miami
2. Logan Tanner, C, Mississippi State
2s. Justin Boyd, OF, Oregon State
3. Bryce Hubbart, LHP, Florida State
4. Kenya Huggins, RHP, Chipola (Fla.) JC
5. Cade Hunter, C, Virginia Tech
6. Zach Maxwell, RHP, Georgia Tech
7. Trey Faltine, SS, Texas
8. Chris McElvain, RHP, Vanderbilt
9. Rob Hensey, LHP, Monmouth
10. Brody Jessee, RHP, Gonzaga
11. Ben Brutti, RHP, South Kingstown HS, Wakefield, R.I.
12. Mason Pelio, RHP, Boston College
13. Johnathan Harmon, RHP, Northwestern State
14. Jared Lyons, RHP, George Mason
15. Adam Serwinowski, LHP, Eastside HS
16. Trey Braithwaite, RHP, West Virginia
17. Easton Sikorski, RHP, Western Michigan
18. Mason Neville, OF, Basic HS, Las Vegas
19. Tyler Chadwick, RHP, Iowa Western JC
20. Joseph Menefee, LHP, Texas A&M

CLEVELAND GUARDIANS (16)

1. Chase DeLauter, OF, James Madison
1s. Justin Campbell, RHP, Oklahoma State
2. Parker Messick, LHP, Florida State
3. Joe Lampe, OF, Arizona State
4. Nate Furman, 2B, UNC Charlotte
5. Guy Lipscomb, OF, Belmont
6. Dylan DeLucia, RHP, Mississippi
7. Javier Santos, RHP, Georgia Premier Academy, Statesboro, Ga.
8. Jackson Humphries, LHP, Fuquay-Varina (N.C.) HS
9. Austin Peterson, RHP, Connecticut
10. Jacob Zibin, RHP, TNXL Academy, Altamonte Springs, Fla.
11. Magnus Ellerts, RHP, Florida Southwestern JC
12. Jack Jasiak, RHP, South Florida
13. Tyresse Turner, SS, Southern California
14. Pres Cavenaugh, OF, UNC Greensboro
15. Adam Tulloch, LHP, Arizona State
16. Logun Clark, C, Taft HS, Woodlands Hills, Calif.
17. Angel Zarate, OF, North Carolina
18. Zach Jacobs, RHP, UC Riverside
19. Geo Rivera, RHP, Walters State (Tenn.) JC
20. Shawn Rapp, LHP, North Carolina

COLORADO ROCKIES (10)

1. Gabriel Hughes, RHP, Gonzaga
1. Sterlin Thompson, OF, Florida
1s. Jordan Beck, OF, Tennessee
2. Jackson Cox, RHP, Toutle Lake HS, Toutle, Wash.
3. Carson Palmquist, LHP, Miami
4. Ryan Ritter, SS, Kentucky
5. Connor Staine, RHP, Central Florida
6. Michael Prosecky, LHP, Louisville
7. Kody Huff, C, Stanford
8. Davis Palermo, RHP, North Carolina
9. Brad Cumbest, OF, Mississippi State
10. Zach Agnos, 3B, East Carolina
11. Carson Skipper, LHP, Auburn
12. Caleb Franzen, LHP, Portland
13. Blake Adams, RHP, Kansas State
14. Braxton Hyde, RHP, Butler (Kan.) JC
15. Brady Hill, RHP, San Jose State
16. Austin Becker, RHP, Texas Tech
17. Tyler Hoffman, RHP, Tulane
18. Javier Ramos, RHP, Oklahoma
19. Skyler Messinger, 3B, Texas
20. Carlos Torres, RHP, Lehigh

DETROIT TIGERS (12)

1. Jace Jung, 2B, Texas Tech
2. Peyton Graham, SS, Oklahoma
4. Troy Melton, RHP, San Diego State
5. Luke Gold, 2B, Boston College
6. Danny Serretti, SS, North Carolina
7. Seth Stephenson, SS, Tennessee
8. Jake Miller, LHP, Valparaiso
9. Andrew Jenkins, 1B, Georgia Tech
10. Trevin Michael, RHP, Oklahoma
11. Joe Miller, LHP, Pennsylvania
12. Cole Stupp, RHP, Kentucky
13. Dominic Johnson, OF, Kansas State
14. Joe Adametz, LHP, Liberty
15. Patrick Pridgen, RHP, Florida International
16. Quinn Gudaitis, RHP, University of Illinois Springfield
17. Cole Patten, RHP, Villanova
18. Chris Williams, OF, William Carey University
19. Albert Oliva, RHP, New Mexico Military JC
20. Drew Conover, RHP, Seton Hall

HOUSTON ASTROS (28)

1. Drew Gilbert, OF, Tennessee
2. Jacob Melton, OF, Oregon State
2s. Andrew Taylor, RHP, Central Michigan
3. Michael Knorr, RHP, Coastal Carolina
4. Trey Dombroski, LHP, Monmouth
5. Nolan DeVos, RHP, Davidson
6. Collin Price, C, Mercer
7. A.J. Blubaugh, RHP, Wisconsin-Milwaukee
8. Tyler Guilfoil, RHP, Kentucky
9. Brett Gillis, RHP, University of Portland
10. Zach Cole, OF, Ball State
11. Ryan Clifford, OF, Pro5 Baseball Academy, Apex, N.C.
12. Zach Dezenzo, SS, Ohio State
13. Jackson Loftin, SS, Oral Roberts
14. Tommy Sacco, SS, TCU
15. Joey Mancini, RHP, Boston Col
16. Tim Borden, SS, Georgia Tech
17. Garrett McGowan, 1B, Pittsburg State University
18. Isaiah Jackson, OF, Cienega HS, Vail, Ariz.
19. John Garcia, C, Grambling State
20. Ryan Wrobleski, C, Dallas Baptist

KANSAS CITY ROYALS (9)

1. Gavin Cross, OF, Virginia Tech
2. Cayden Wallace, 3B, Orange (Calif.) Lutheran HS
3. Mason Barnett, RHP, Auburn
4. Steven Zobac, RHP, California
5. Hunter Patteson, LHP, Central Florida
6. Hayden Dunhurst, C, Mississippi
7. Mack Anglin, RHP, Clemson
8. Wesley Scott, RHP, Walters State (Tenn.) JC
9. Brandon Johnson, RHP, Ole Miss
10. Levi Usher, OF, Louisville
11. David Sandlin, RHP, Oklahoma
12. Jack Pineda, SS, Baylor
13. Ryan Ramsey, LHP, Maryland
14. Ben Sears, RHP, Houston
15. Javier Vaz, SS, Vanderbilt
16. Cooper McKeehan, LHP, Brigham Young
17. Chazz Martinez, LHP, Oklahoma
18. Milo Rushford, OF, Sahuarita HS

DRAFT

19. Tommy Szczepanski, RHP, Garber HS, Essexville, Mich.
20. Austin Charles, SS, Stockdale HS, Bakersfield, Calif.

LOS ANGELES ANGELS (13)

1. Zach Neto, SS, Campbell
3. Ben Joyce, RHP, Tennessee
4. Jake Madden, RHP, Northwest Florida JC
5. Sonny DiChiara, 1B, Auburn
6. Victor Mederos, RHP, Oklahoma State
7. Roman Phansalkar, RHP, Oklahoma State
8. Dylan Phillips, OF, Kansas State
9. Joe Stewart, OF, Michigan
10. Matt Coutney, 1B, Old Dominion
11. Caden Dana, RHP, Don Bosco Prep HS, Ramsey, N.J.
12. Jared Southard, RHP, Texas
13. Tucker Flint, 1B, Chipola (Fla.) JC
14. Sabin Ceballos, SS, San Jacinto (Texas) JC
15. Bryce Osmond, RHP, Oklahoma State
16. Casey Dana, OF, Connecticut
17. Sammy Natera, LHP, New Mexico State
18. Max Gieg, RHP, Boston College
19. Luke Franzoni, OF, Xavier
20. Brendan Tinsman, C, Wake Forest

DRAFT

LOS ANGELES DODGERS (40)

2. Dalton Rushing, C, Louisville
3. Alex Freeland, SS, Central Florida
4. Nick Biddison, 2B, Virginia Tech
5. Sean McLain, SS, Arizona State
6. Logan Wagner, SS, P27 Academy, Lexington, S.C.
7. Christopher Campos, SS, St. Mary's
8. Taylor Young, 2B, Louisiana Tech
9. Brandon Neeck, LHP, Virginia
10. Simon Reid, C, Westmont (Calif.)
11. Kyle Nevin, OF, Baylor
12. Jacob Meador, RHP, Dallas Baptist
13. Chris Newell, OF, Virginia
14. Jose Izarra, SS, Florida Southwestern JC
15. Nicolas Perez, SS, B-You Prospects Academy, Caguas, P.R.
16. Jared Karros, RHP, UCLA
17. Payton Martin, RHP, West Forsyth HS
18. Cameron Decker, SS, Evansville North HS
19. Chris Alleyne, OF, Maryland
20. Carter McCulley, SS, Pensacola Catholic HS

MIAMI MARLINS (6)

1. Jacob Berry, 3B, Louisiana State
2. Jacob Miller, RHP, Liberty Union HS, Baltimore, Ohio
3. Karson Milbrandt, RHP, Liberty (Mo.) HS
4. Marcus Johnson, RHP, Duke
5. Josh White, RHP, California
6. Jared Poland, RHP, Louisville
7. Kyle Crigger, RHP, Louisiana Tech
8. Dale Stanavich, LHP, Rutgers
9. Evan Taylor, LHP, Arkansas
10. Cade Gibson, LHP, Louisiana Tech
11. Alex Williams, RHP, Stanford
12. Cole Kirschsieper, LHP, Illinois
13. Chase Luttrell, OF, Long Beach State
14. Torin Montgomery, 1B, Missouri
15. Ike Buxton, RHP, Lipscomb University
16. Brett Roberts, 2B, Florida State
17. Evan Chrest, RHP, Wharton HS, Tampa, Fla.
18. Spencer Bramwell, C, Colorado Mesa University
19. Carmine Lane, 3B, South Florida
20. Jack Gowen, RHP, Georgia

MILWAUKEE BREWERS (27)

1. Eric Brown, SS, Coastal Carolina
2. Jacob Misiorowski, RHP, Crowder (Mo.) JC
2s. Robert Moore, SS, Arkansas
3. Dylan O'Rae, SS, Northern Collegiate
4. Matthew Wood, C, Penn State
5. Will Rudy, RHP, Cal Poly Pomona
6. Tyler Woessner, RHP, Central Arizona JC
7. Ben Metzinger, 3B, Louisville
8. Nate Peterson, LHP, Illinois-Chicago
9. Tayden Hall, C, Manatee (Fla.) JC
10. Brian Fitzpatrick, LHP, Rutgers
11. Cameron Wagoner, RHP, Eastern Michigan
12. Luke Adams, 3B, Hinsdale Central HS
13. Zane Petty, RHP, Corsicana HS
14. Aidan Maldonado, RHP, Minnesota
15. Satchell Norman, C, Florida Southwestern JC
16. Ethan Lege, 3B, Delgado (La.) JC
17. Brady Neal, C, IMG Academy, Bradenton, Fla.
18. Jurrangelo Cijntje, SHP, Champagnat Catholic HS, Hialeah, Fla.
19. Jaden Noot, RHP, Sierra Canyon HS, Chatsworth, Calif.
20. Noah Hall, RHP, South Carolina

MINNESOTA TWINS (8)

1. Brooks Lee, SS, Cal Poly
2. Connor Prielipp, LHP, Alabama
2s. Tanner Schobel, SS, Virginia Tech
4. Andrew Morris, RHP, Texas Tech
5. Ben Ross, SS, Notre Dame Col
6. Jorel Ortega, SS, Tennessee
7. Kyle Jones, RHP, Toledo
8. Zebby Matthews, RHP, Western Carolina
9. Cory Lewis, RHP, UC Santa Barbara
10. Dalton Shuffield, SS, Texas State
11. Andrew Cossetti, C, Saint Joseph's
12. Nate Baez, C, Arizona State
13. C.J. Culpepper, RHP, California Baptist
14. Omari Daniel, SS, Walker HS, Marrietta, Ga.
15. Ben Ethridge, RHP, Southern Mississippi
16. Jankel Ortiz, SS, Academia Presbiteriana HS
17. Alec Sayre, OF, Wright State
18. Zachary Veen, LHP, Point Loma (Calif.) Nazarene
19. Garrett McMillan, RHP, Alabama
20. Korbyn Dickerson, OF, Trinity HS, Louisville

NEW YORK METS (11)

1. Kevin Parada, C, Georgia Tech
1. Jett Williams, SS, Rockwall-Heath HS, Rockwall, Texas
2. Blade Tidwell, RHP, Tennessee
2s. Nick Morabito, OF, Gonzaga HS, Washington D.C.
3. Brandon Sproat, RHP, Florida
4. Jacob Reimer, 3B, Yucaipa (Calif.) HS
5. D'Andre Smith, 2B, Southern California
6. Tyler Stuart, RHP, Southern Mississippi
7. Jonah Tong, RHP, Bill Crothers SS
8. Dylan Tebrake, RHP, Creighton
9. Chase Estep, 2B, Kentucky
10. Zebulon Vermillion, RHP, Arkansas
11. Rhylan Thomas, OF, Southern California
12. Paul Gervase, RHP, Louisiana State
13. Dylan Ross, RHP, Georgia
14. Cameron Foster, RHP, McNeese State
15. Jackson Jaha, 3B, Clackamas HS
16. Jimmy Loper, RHP, Duke
17. Connor Brandon, RHP, Toledo
18. Chris Santiago, RHP, St. Mary's
19. Jackson Lovich, SS, Blue Valley West HS, Stilwell, Kan.
20. Eli Ankeney, LHP, Grand Canyon University

NEW YORK YANKEES (25)

1. Spencer Jones, OF, Vanderbilt
2. Drew Thorpe, RHP, Cal Poly
3. Trystan Vrieling, RHP, Gonzaga
4. Anthony Hall, OF, Oregon
5. Eric Reyzelman, RHP, Louisiana State

6. Chase Hampton, RHP, Texas Tech
7. Cam Schlittler, RHP, Northeastern
8. Brett Barrera, SS, Stanford
9. Matt Keating, RHP, Southern California
10. Will Brian, LHP, Eastern Kentucky
11. Ryan Harvey, RHP, UC Santa Barbara
12. Jackson Fristoe, RHP, Mississippi State
13. Geoffrey Gilbert, LHP, Clemson
14. Kris Bow, RHP, Southern Nevada JC
15. Tayler Aguilar, OF, Grand Canyon University
16. Shane Gray, RHP, Evansville
17. Hayden Merda, RHP, Azusa (Calif.) Pacific
18. Sebastian Keane, RHP, Northeastern
19. Beau Brewer, 3B, Paris (Texas) JC
20. Trevor Kirk, RHP, Elon University

OAKLAND ATHLETICS (19)

1. Daniel Susac, C, Arizona
2. Henry Bolte, OF, Palo Alto (Calif.) HS
2s. Clark Elliott, OF, Michigan
3. Colby Thomas, OF, Mercer
4. Jacob Watters, RHP, West Virginia
5. Jack Perkins, RHP, Indiana
6. Brennan Milone, SS, Oregon
7. Yeniel Laboy, SS, Carlos Beltran Baseball Academy
8. Micah Dallas, RHP, Texas A&M
9. Caeden Trenkle, OF, Oklahoma State
10. Brock Rodden, 2B, Wichita State
11. Christian Oppor, LHP, Columbus (Wisc.) HS
12. T.J. Czyz, RHP, Consumes River (Calif.) JC
13. Jake Pfennigs, RHP, Oregon State
14. Jamaliel Rosado, SS, Leadership Christian Academy
15. Mark Adamiak, RHP, Arkansas
16. Blaze Pontes, RHP, U Hawaii
17. Jake Garland, RHP, Miami
18. Vince Reilly, RHP, Grand Canyon
19. Tommy Stevenson, 1B, Missouri Southern St Col
20. Derek True, RHP, Cal Poly

PHILADELPHIA PHILLIES (17)

1. Justin Crawford, OF, Bishop Gorman HS, Las Vegas
3. Gabriel Rincones, OF, Florida Atlantic
4. Alex McFarlane, RHP, Miami
5. Orion Kerkering, RHP, South Florida
6. Mavis Graves, LHP, Eastside HS, Taylors, S.C.
7. Caleb Ricketts, C, San Diego
8. Alex Rao, RHP, Notre Dame
9. Chad Castillo, OF, California Baptist
10. Gustavo Sosa, C, South Mountain (Ariz.) JC
11. Emaarion Boyd, OF, South Panola HS, Batesville, Miss.
12. Jordan Dissin, C, Saddleback (Calif.) JC
13. Cade Fergus, OF, George Washington
14. Bryan Rincon, SS, Shaler Area HS
15. Troy Schreffler, OF, Maryland
16. Josh Bortka, RHP, U Central Missouri
17. Daniel Harper, RHP, Kentucky
18. Braylen Wimmer, 2B, South Carolina
19. Drew Garrett, RHP, Missouri
20. Nathan Karaffa, RHP, Ohio State

PITTSBURGH PIRATES (4)

1. Termarr Johnson, SS, Mays HS, Atlanta
1s. Thomas Harrington, RHP, Campbell
2. Hunter Barco, LHP, Florida
3. Jack Brannigan, RHP, Notre Dame
4. Michael Kennedy, LHP, Troy (N.Y.) HS
5. Tres Gonzalez, OF, Georgia Tech
6. Derek Diamond, RHP, Mississippi
7. J.P. Massey, RHP, Minnesota
8. Cy Nielson, LHP, Brigham Young
9. Mike Walsh, RHP, Yale
10. Tanner Tredaway, OF, Oklahoma
11. Dominic Perachi, LHP, Salve Regina U
12. K.C. Hunt, RHP, Mississippi State
13. Miguel Fulgencio, LHP, Cowley (Kan.) JC
14. Julian Bosnic, LHP, South Carolina
15. Josiah Sightler, LHP, South Carolina
16. Nick Cimillo, C, Rutgers
17. Jaycob Deese, RHP, Houston
18. Elijah Birdsong, RHP, Pacific
19. Yoel Tejeda, RHP, North Broward Prep, Coconut Creek, Fla.
20. Joshua Loeschorn, RHP, Long Island University

SAN DIEGO PADRES (15)

1. Dylan Lesko, RHP, Buford (Ga.) HS
1s. Robby Snelling, LHP, McQueen HS, Reno, Nev.
2. Adam Mazur, RHP, Iowa
3. Henry Williams, RHP, Duke
4. Lamar King, C, Calvert Hall HS, Baltimore
5. Nathan Martorella, 1B, California
6. Jakob Marsee, OF, Central Michigan
7. Nick Vogt, OF, UC Santa Barbara
8. Griffin Doersching, 1B, Oklahoma State
9. Dylan Nedved, RHP, Iowa
10. Jackson Smeltz, LHP, Purdue
11. Isaiah Lowe, RHP, Combine Academy
12. Austin Krob, LHP, Texas Christian
13. Graham Pauley, 3B, Duke
14. Tyler Robertson, OF, University of Louisiana at Lafayette
15. Thomas Balboni, RHP, Northeastern
16. Henry Martinez, RHP, Miami Christian School
17. Hugh Pinkney, C, Silverthorn Collegiate Inst
18. Romeo Sanabria, C, Indian River (Fla.) JC
19. Spence Coffman, SS, Tishomingo Co HS
20. Andrew Vail, LHP, Rowan University

SAN FRANCISCO GIANTS (30)

1. Reggie Crawford, LHP, Connecticut
2. Carson Whisenhunt, LHP, East Carolina
3. William Kempner, RHP, Gonzaga
4. Spencer Miles, RHP, Missouri
5. Liam Simon, RHP, Notre Dame
6. Hayden Birdsong, RHP, Eastern Illinois U
7. Zach Morgan, C, Fresno State
8. Wade Meckler, OF, Oregon State
9. Jack Choate, LHP, Assumption (Mass.)
10. John Bertrand, LHP, Notre Dame
11. Sam Bower, RHP, Saint Mary's
12. Tyler Vogel, RHP, Jacksonville University
13. Thomas Gavello, SS, Pacific
14. Nomar Diaz, C, Carlos Beltran Baseball Academy
15. Tanner O'Tremba, OF, Arizona
16. Andrew Kachel, 3B, Fresno State
17. Justin Bench, 3B, Ole Miss
18. Tanner Thach, 1B, Perquimans HS
19. Cade Perkins, LHP, Manhattan HS
20. Ethan Long, 1B, Arizona State

SEATTLE MARINERS (21)

1. Cole Young, SS, North Allegheny HS, Wexford, Pa.
2. Tyler Locklear, 3B, Virginia Commonwealth
2s. Walter Ford, RHP, Pace (Fla.) HS
4. Ashton Izzi, RHP, Oswego (Ill.) East HS
5. Reid VanScoter, LHP, Coastal Carolina
6. Josh Hood, SS, North Carolina State
7. Hogan Windish, 2B, UNC Greensboro
8. Tatem Levins, C, Pittsburgh
9. Tyler Gough, RHP, JSerra Catholic HS, San Juan Capistrano, Calif.
10. Bill Knight, OF, Mercer
11. Marcelo Perez, RHP, TCU
12. Troy Taylor, RHP, UC Irvine

13. Darren Bowen, RHP, UNC Pembroke
14. Tyler Cleveland, RHP, Central Arkansas
15. Blake Rambusch, SS, Auburn
16. Jacob McNairy, RHP, Alabama
17. Stefan Raeth, RHP, U Washington
18. Brandon Schaeffer, LHP, North Carolina
19. Curtis Washington, OF, Purdue
20. Nick Zona, 2B, James Madison U

ST. LOUIS CARDINALS (22)

1. Cooper Hjerpe, LHP, Oregon State
2. Brycen Mautz, LHP, San Diego
3. Pete Hansen, LHP, Texas
4. Jimmy Crooks, C, Oklahoma
5. Victor Scott, OF, West Virginia
6. Max Rajcic, RHP, UCLA
7. Alex Iadisernia, OF, Elon
8. Cade Winquest, RHP, University of Texas - Arlington
9. Joseph King, RHP, California
10. Tanner Jacobson, RHP, Queens University of Charlotte
11. Nathan Church, OF, UC Irvine
12. Michael Curialle, SS, UCLA
13. Chandler Arnold, RHP, Dallas Baptist
14. D.J. Carpenter, RHP, Oregon State
15. Matt Hickey, RHP, Tarleton St U
16. Hunter Hayes, RHP, Pacific
17. Brody Moore, SS, Auburn
18. John Lynch, P, Xavier U
19. Chris Rotondo, OF, Villanova U
20. Gavin Van Kempen, RHP, Maple Hill HS, Castleton-on-Hudson, N.Y.

TAMPA BAY RAYS (29)

1. Xavier Isaac, 1B, East Forsyth HS, Kernersville, N.C.
2. Brock Jones, OF, Stanford
2s. Chandler Simpson, SS, Georgia Tech
2s. Ryan Cermak, SS, Illinois State
3. Trevor Martin, RHP, Oklahoma State
4. Dominic Keegan, C, Vanderbilt
5. Jalen Battles, SS, Arkansas
6. Gary Gill Hill, RHP, Kennedy Catholic HS, Somers, N.Y.
7. Blake Robertson, 1B, Oklahoma
8. Sean Harney, RHP, Kentucky
9. Chris Villaman, LHP, North Carolina State
10. Cade Halemanu, RHP, Hawaii
11. Drew Sommers, LHP, Central Arizona JC
12. Alex Cook, RHP, Colby (Kan.) JC
13. Nate Dahle, RHP, BYU
14. Roel Garcia, RHP, Rice
15. Jake Christianson, RHP, Feather River (Calif.) JC
16. Kamren James, 3B, Mississippi State
17. Levi Huesman, LHP, Hanover (Va.) HS
18. Duncan Davitt, RHP, Iowa
19. Quinn Mathews, LHP, Stanford
20. Matt Wyatt, RHP, Virginia

TEXAS RANGERS (3)

1. Kumar Rocker, RHP, Tri-City (Frontier)
4. Brock Porter, RHP, St. Mary's Prep, Orchard Lake, Mich.
5. Chandler Pollard, OF, Woodward Academy, College Park, Ga.
6. Tommy Specht, OF, Wahlert HS, Dubuque, Iowa
7. Luis Ramirez, RHP, Long Beach State
8. Matt Brosky, RHP, Youngstown State
9. Griffin Cheney, SS, Georgia State
10. Josh Hatcher, OF, Kennesaw State
11. Kohl Drake, LHP, Walters State (Tenn.) JC
12. Jackson Kelley, RHP, Mercer
13. Caden Marcum, RHP, Paola (Kan.) HS
14. Andrew Owen, RHP, Grossmont (Calif.) JC
15. Jack Goodman, SS, Medfield HS
16. Nick Bautista, RHP, Cypress (Calif.) JC
17. Carson Dorsey, LHP, Gulf Coast (Fla.) JC
18. Justin Sanchez, LHP, Msgr McClancy Memorial HS
19. Grayson Saunier, RHP, Collierville (Tenn.) HS
20. Matt Scott, RHP, Joel Barlow HS, Redding, Conn.

TORONTO BLUE JAYS (23)

1. Brandon Barriera, LHP, American Heritage HS, Plantation, Fla.
2. Josh Kasevich, SS, Oregon
2s. Tucker Toman, SS, Hammond HS, Columbia, S.C.
2s. Cade Doughty, 2B, Louisiana State
3. Alan Roden, OF, Creighton
4. Ryan Jennings, RHP, Louisiana Tech
5. Mason Fluharty, LHP, Liberty
6. T.J. Brock, RHP, Ohio State
7. Peyton Williams, 1B, Iowa
8. Dylan Rock, OF, Texas A&M
9. Devereaux Harrison, RHP, Long Beach State
10. Ian Churchill, LHP, San Diego
11. Pat Gallagher, RHP, Connecticut
12. Nolan Perry, RHP, Carlsbad HS
13. Bo Bonds, RHP, University of Louisiana at Lafayette
14. Sammy Hernandez, C, Lakeland Senior HS
15. Michael Turconi, SS, Wake Forest
16. Kale Davis, RHP, Oklahoma State
17. Ryan Chasse, LHP, Campbell University
18. Jeremy Pilon, LHP, Ecole Secondaire De Montagne
19. Gage Stanifer, RHP, Westfield HS
20. Gregory Pace, OF, Edison Academy, Detroit

WASHINGTON NATIONALS (5)

1. Elijah Green, OF, IMG Academy, Bradenton, Fla.
2. Jake Bennett, LHP, Oklahoma
3. Trey Lipscomb, 3B, Tennessee
4. Brenner Cox, OF, Prosper HS
5. Jared McKenzie, OF, Baylor
6. Nathaniel Ochoa Leyva, 3B, Notre Dame Catholic SS
7. Riley Cornelio, RHP, Texas Christian
8. Chance Huff, RHP, Georgia Tech
9. Maxwell Romero, C, Miami
10. Murphy Stehly, 3B, Texas
11. Luke Young, RHP, Midland (Texas) JC
12. Nick Peoples, OF, Northview HS, Covina, Calif.
13. Marquis Grissom, RHP, Georgia Tech
14. Cortland Lawson, SS, Tennessee
15. Kyle Luckham, RHP, Arizona State
16. Everett Cooper, SS, Pro5 Baseball Academy
17. Blake Klassen, 1B, UC Santa Barbara
18. Brad Lord, RHP, South Florida
19. Johnathon Thomas, OF, Texas Southern U
20. JeanPierre Ortiz, SS, IMG Academy, Bradenton, Fla.

CHRIS BERNACCHI/DIAMOND IMAGES VIA GETTY IMAGES

Kumar Rocker was a first-round pick for a second consecutive season.

DRAFT

APPENDIX

OBITUARIES

APPENDIX

TOMMY BOGGS, a pitcher for the Rangers and Braves in the 1970s and 1980s, died Oct. 5, 2022. He was 66. After his playing career, Boggs was Concordia (Texas) head coach from 2009-2022. With 339 wins, Boggs was the winningest coach in the school's history.

PETE BURNSIDE, a lefthander who spent eight years in the majors with four organizations, died Aug. 26. He was 92. Burnside was 19-36, 4.81 for his career.

CHUCK CARR was one of the stars of the Marlins' first year as an expansion team in 1993 Carr led the National League with 58 steals in 1993. He also led the league with 22 caught stealing attempts. Carr spent two more seasons as a regular for the Marlins. Carr died on Nov. 15, 2022. He was 55.

GENE CLINES, an outfielder who was part of the Pirates 1971 World Series champs, died Jan. 27, 2022. He was 75. Clines hit .308 for those 1971 Pirates. He played in the majors from 1970-1979.

DON COLLINS, a lefthander who logged 76 innings with the Braves and Indians, died May 22. He was 69. He was a second-round pick in 1972.

JIM CORSI, a righthander who pitched for five MLB teams from 1988-1999, died Jan. 4, 2022. He was 60. Corsi went 4-2, 1.43 in 44 innings with the Athletics in 1992 in his best season.

JULIO CRUZ, a long-time Seattle Mariner second baseman, died on Feb. 22. He was 67. Cruz made his MLB debut on July 4, 1977. Traded to the White Sox in 1983, where he made his lone postseason appearance, Cruz played with the White Sox until 1986.

STEVE DAVIS, a lefthander who threw 57 innings in the majors between 1985-1989, died Sept. 28. He was 61.

A multi-sport star growing up in Brooklyn, **TOMMY DAVIS** could always hit. Davis never batted under .300 in any of his five minor league stops, earning him a spot in the Dodgers' lineup by the time he was 21. e found nearly instant success. By 1962, he won the first of back-to-back batting titles with a .346/.374/.535 season. He also led the league with 230 hits and 153 RBIs. He hit .326 the next year, snaring a batting title while helping the Dodgers win the World Series. Davis died on April 3, 2022. He was 83.

IKE DELOCK, a long-time Red Sox starter/reliever in the 1950s-1960s, died on Feb. 28, 2022. He was 92. Delock earned a spot in the Red Sox bullpen and eventually pitched his way into the Red Sox rotation. In his best year he went 11-6, 2.95 in 1959 in 134 innings.

JOHN ELLIS signed with the Yankees in 1966, just at the point where New York was heading into a decline phase. The catcher was traded to Cleveland in 1972 in a deal that sent Graig Nettles to the Yankees. He played 883 games and hit .262/.312/.392 for his career. Ellis died April 6, 2022. He was 73.

DICK ELLSWORTH, a lefthander who was a fixture in the Cubs rotation for seven seasons, died Oct. 10, 2022. He was 82. Ellsworth was an all-star in 1964 when he went 14-18, 3.75. He led the league in losses in 1966, but he was durable. He threw over 2,000 career innings, finishing his career with two seasons with the Brewers in 1970-1971.

KEN FRAILING, a reliever for the Cubs and White Sox in the 1970s, died Aug. 25. He was 74. Frailing went 6-9, 3.88 in 125 innings with the Cubs in 1976 in his best season.

JEREMY GIAMBI, an outfielder for four MLB teams, died on Feb. 9. He was 47. Giambi, the younger brother of 2000 American League MVP Jason Giambi, was a sixth round pick of the Royals in 1996 coming out of Cal State Fullerton. He last played in the majors in 2003 with the Red Sox.

DAVID GREEN, an outfielder who spent five seasons with the Cardinals in the 1980s, died Jan. 25, 2022. He was 61. Green stole 34 bases in 1983.

CALVIN JONES, a first round pick in the 1984 secondary phase of the MLB draft, died on Feb. 12. He was 58.

JOE HORLEN, a righthander who spent 12 years in the majors from 1961-1972, died April 10, 2022. He was 84. Horlen led the American League in ERA in 1967 as he went 19-7, 2.06 for the White Sox. He was 116-117, 3.11 for his career.

FRED LASHER, a righthander who spent six

seasons in the American League, died on Feb. 27. He was 80.

MARK LITTELL, a reliever with the Cardinals and Royals, died Sept. 5, 2022. He was 69. Littell finished with 56 saves.

BOB LOCKER, a righthander who spent 10 years in the majors, mainly with the White Sox and Athletics, died Aug. 15, 2022. He was 84. Locker went 57-39, 2.75 for his career.

HECTOR LOPEZ, a second baseman/third baseman who spent 12 years in the majors with the Kansas City Athletics and New York Yankees, died Sept. 29, 2022. He was 93.

CARLTON "CORKY" PALMER, Southern Mississippi's head coach from 1998 to 2009 died Aug. 10, 2022. He was 68.

ODALIS PEREZ, a lefthander who made an all-star appearance with the Dodgers in 2002, died March 10, 2022. He was 43. Perez came up through the Braves system, but his biggest MLB success came with the Dodgers. He pitched in the majros from 1998 to 2008, going 73-81, 4.46.

COREY PHELAN was supposed to get his first chance at full-season baseball in 2022, but this April he was diagnosed with non-Hodgkins lymphoma. He died on Oct. 13, 2022 at age 20.

RAY RIPPLEMEYER, the pitching coach for the Phillies from 1970-78, died Sept. 9. He was 89. He managed and coached in the minors from 1965-69 before being promoted to the majors.

DICK SCHOFIELD, a shortstop who played for seven MLB teams from 1953-1971, died July 11, 2022. He was 87. Schofield was known as a glove-first infielder. He was the father of MLB shortstop DIck Schofield Jr. and the grandfather of MLB outfielder Jayson Werth.

JOHN STEARNS was an excellent catcher for some bad Mets teams in the late 1970s and early 1980s. Stearns served as the team's main catcher for 10 seasons. After he retired, Stearns spent the better part of three decades working as a scout, major league coach and minor league manager. Stearns died on Sept. 15, 2022. He was 71.

BRUCE SUTTER finished in the top 10 in the Cy Young Award and MVP voting for the Cubs. Five times in six years, Sutter led the majors in saves. Sutter was elected to the Hall of Fame in 2006. Sutter died Oct. 13, 2022. He was 69.

BILL TEED, a scout for the Giants, Orioles and Phillies, died Sept. 6. He was 91. Teed was the signing scout for Mike Remlinger.

RALPH TERRY, a righthander who was an all-star in 1962 with the Yankees, died March 16, 2022. He was 86. Terry led the league in wins (23) and innings (298.2) in 1962 in his best season. He was the World Series MVP that year as well.

In 1993, **LEE THOMAS**, the general manager of the 1993 World Series champion Phillies, died on Aug. 31, 2022 in St. Louis. He was 86. Thomas had also been the farm director for the Cardinals in the 1980s. Before he moved into the front office, Thomas had an eight-year MLB career as a power-hitting outfielder/first baseman.

THOMAS ANTHONY VARVARO left major league baseball to serve as an officer for the New York Port Authority. He was killed in a car accident on his way to serve at a 9/11 remembrance event on Sept. 11, 2022. He was 37. Varvaro spent the majority of his MLB career with Atlanta.

STEVE WEBBER, head coach of the 1990 national championship Georgia team, died on Nov. 12, 2022. He was 74. Webber served as Georgia's head coach from 1981-1996. His 1987 team also went to Omaha, and he remains Georgia's all-time winningest coach with 500 wins.

DAVE WICKERSHAM, a righthander who pitched for the Tigers and Athletics in the 1960s, died June 18, 2022. He was 86. He went 68-57, 3.66.

Dodgers shortstop **MAURY WILLS** led the NL in steals for six consecutive seasons from 1960 to 1965. In 1962, Wills stole 104 bases to break Ty Cobb's MLB record. Wills died on Sept. 19, 2022. He was 89. He was a seven-time all-star and the 1962 NL MVP.

JOHN WOCKENFUSS, a catcher/first baseman who spent the majority of his 12-year MLB career with the Tigers, died Aug. 19, 2022. He was 73. He hit .262/.349/.432 in 795 career games.

APPENDIX

STATISTICS INDEX

APPENDIX